678

Robert O Beirn
087 9758245

Compani

1963-2012

Student Edition

Companies Acts

1963-2012

Student Edition

General editors

Lyndon MacCann
BA (Mod), M Litt, SC

Dr Thomas B. Courtney
Partner, Arthur Cox
Chairman of CLRG

Bloomsbury Professional

Published by
Bloomsbury Professional
Maxwelton House
41–43 Boltro Road
Haywards Heath
West Sussex
RH16 1BJ

Bloomsbury Professional
The Fitzwilliam Business Centre
26 Upper Pembroke Street
Dublin 2

ISBN 978 184766 873 8

Bloomsbury Professional, an imprint of Bloomsbury Publishing Plc

British Library Cataloguing-in-Publication Data
A catalogue record for this book is available from the British Library

Typeset by Marlex Editorial Services Ltd, Dublin, Ireland
Printed and bound in Great Britain by
CPI Group (UK) Ltd, Croydon, CR0 4YY

Contents

Division A: Primary Legislation

Division B: Secondary Legislation

Division C: European Legislation

List of Abbreviations

Primary Legislation

CA 1963	Companies Act 1963
CA 1990	Companies Act 1990
C(AA)A 2003	Companies (Auditing and Accounting) Act 2003
C(A)(No 1)A 1999	Companies (Amendment) (No 1) Act 1999
C(A)(No 2)A 1999	Companies (Amendment) (No 2) Act 1999
C(A)A 1977	Companies (Amendment) Act 1977
C(A)A 1982	Companies (Amendment) Act 1982
C(A)A 1983	Companies (Amendment) Act 1983
C(A)A 1986	Companies (Amendment) Act 1986
C(A)A 1990	Companies (Amendment) Act 1990
C(A)A 1999	Companies (Amendment) Act 1999
C(A)A 2009	Companies (Amendment) Act 2009
C(A)A 2012	Companies (Amendment) Act 2012
C(MP)A 2009	Companies (Miscellaneous Provisions) Act 2009
CBFSAIA 2003	Central Bank and Financial Services Authority of Ireland Act 2003
CBFSAIA 2004	Central Bank and Financial Services Authority of Ireland Act 2004
CLEA 2001	Company Law Enforcement Act 2001
FA	Finance Act
IA 2005	Interpretation Act 2005
IFCMPA 2005	Investment Funds, Companies and Miscellaneous Provisions Act 2005
IFCMPA 2006	Investment Funds, Companies and Miscellaneous Provisions Act 2006
NAMA Act 2009	National Asset Management Agency Act 2009
RBNA 1963	Registration of Business Names Act 1963
SDCA 1999	Stamp Duties Consolidation Act 1999
STA 1963	Stock Transfer Act 1963

Secondary Legislation

CA 1963 (A8S) O 2009 SI 302/2009	Companies Act 1963 (Alterations of Eighth Schedule) Order 2009
CA 1963(Sch 9)R 2010 SI 484/2010	Companies Act 1963 (Ninth Schedule) Regulations 2010

C(Fees)O 2010 SI 430/2010	Companies (Fees) Order 2010
EC(A)R 1993 SI 396/1993	European Communities (Accounts) Regulations 1993
EC(C)(A)R 2007 SI 49/2007	European Communities (Companies) (Amendment) Regulations 2007
EC(C)R 1973 SI 163/1973	European Communities (Companies) Regulations 1973
EC(CBM)R 2008 SI 157/2008	European Communities (Cross-Border Mergers) Regulations 2008
EC(CGA)R 1992 SI 201/1992	European Communities (Companies: Group Accounts) Regulations 1992
EC(CI)(FVA)R 2004 SI 720/2004	European Communities (Credit Institutions) (Fair Value Accounting) Regulations 2004
EC(CI)R 2002 SI 333/2002	European Communities (Corporate Insolvency) Regulations 2002
EC(CIA)R 1992 SI 294/1992	European Communities (Credit Institutions: Accounts) Regulations 1992
EC(Dir)(A)R 2010 83/2010	European Communities (Directive 2006/46/EC) (Amendment) Regulations 2010
EC(EEIG)R 1989 SI 191/1989	European Communities (European Economic Interest Groupings) Regulations 1989
EC(EPLLC)R 2007 SI 21/2007	European Communities (European Public Limited Liability Company) Regulations 2007
EC(EPLLC)(F)R 2007 SI 22/2007	European Communities (European Public Limited Liability Company) (Forms) Regulations 2007
EC(FVA)R 2004 SI 765/2004	European Communities (Fair Value Accounting) Regulations 2004
EC(GA)R 2010 SI 606/2010	European Communities (Group Accounts) Regulations 2010
EC(IFRSMA)R 2005 SI 116/2005	European Communities (International Financial Reporting Standards and Miscellaneous Amendments) Regulations 2005
EC(IUA)R 1996 SI 23/1996	European Communities (Insurance Undertakings: Accounts) Regulations 1996
EC(MDC)(A)R 2008 SI 572/2008	European Communities (Mergers and Division of Companies) (Amendment) Regulations 2008
EC(MDC)(A)R 2011 SI 306/2011	European Communities (Mergers and Divisions of Companies) (Amendment) Regulations 2011
EC(MDC)R 1987 SI 137/1987	European Communities (Mergers and Division of Companies) Regulations 1987
EC(PLC)R 2008 SI 89/2008	European Communities (Public Limited Companies — Directive 2006/68/EC) Regulations 2008
EC(SA)(Dir)R 2010 SI 220/2010	European Communities (Statutory Audits) (Directive 2006/43/EC) Regulations 2010
EC(SA)R 2011 SI 685/2011	European Communities (Statutory Audits) (Directive 2006/43/EC) Regulations 2011

EC(SE)R 1984 SI 282/1984	European Communities (Stock Exchange) Regulations 1984
P(Dir)(A)R 2012 SI 239/2012	Prospectus (Directive 2003/71/EC) (Amendment) Regulations 2012
P(Dir)(A)R (No 2) 2012 SI 317/2012	Prospectus (Directive 2003/71/EC) (Amendment) (No 2) Regulations 2012
T(Dir)(A)R 2010 SI 102/2010	Transparency (Directive 2004/109/EC) (Amendment) Regulations
Shareholders' Rights Regulations SI 316/2009	Shareholders' Rights (Directive 2007/36/EC) Regulations 2009

Other

AGM	annual general meeting
ASB	Accounting Standards Board
CLRG	Company Law Review Group
CRO	Companies Registration Office
DPP	Director of Public Prosecutions
IFRS	International Financial Reporting Standards
ODCE	Office of the Director of Corporate Enforcement
NAMA	National Asset Management Agency
plc	public limited company
RSC	Rules of the Superior Court

Division A: Primary Legislation

Registration of Business Names Act 1963

No 30/1963

ARRANGEMENT OF SECTIONS

An Act to Provide for the Registration of Persons carrying on Business under Business Names and for Purposes Connected therewith. [11th December, 1963.]

Be it Enacted by the Oireachtas as Follows:

1 Commencement

This Act shall come into operation on such day as the Minister appoints by order.

2 Interpretation

(1) In this Act—

'business' includes profession;

'business name' means the name or style under which any business is carried on, and, in relation to a newspaper, includes the title of the newspaper;

'Christian name' includes any forename;

'director', in relation to a body corporate, includes a member of the managing body thereof;

'firm' means an unincorporated body of two or more individuals, or one or more individuals and one or more bodies corporate, or two or more bodies corporate, who have entered into partnership with one another with a view to publishing a newspaper or to carrying on business for profit;

'initials' includes any recognised abbreviation of a Christian name;

'the Minister' means the Minister for Industry and Commerce;

'newspaper' means any paper containing public news or observations thereon, or consisting wholly or mainly of advertisements, which is printed for sale and is published in the State either periodically or in parts or numbers at intervals not exceeding thirty-six days;

'prescribed' means prescribed by regulations made in pursuance of this Act;

'the repealed enactment' means the Registration of Business Names Act, 1916, repealed by this Act;

'surname', in the case of a person usually known by a title different from his surname, means that title.

(2) References in this Act to a former Christian name or surname do not include—

(a) in the case of a person usually known by a title different from his surname, the name by which he was known previous to the adoption of or succession to the title; or

(b) in the case of any person, a former Christian name or surname where that name or surname was changed or disused before the person bearing the name attained the age of 18 years or has been changed or disused for a period of not less than 20 years; or

(c) in the case of a married woman, the name or surname by which she was known previous to the marriage.

3 Persons to be registered

(1) Subject to the provisions of this Act—

(a) every firm having a place of business in the State and carrying on business under a business name which does not consist of the true surnames of all partners who are individuals and the corporate names of all partners which are bodies corporate without any addition other than the true Christian names of individual partners or initials of such Christian names;

(b) every individual having a place of business in the State and carrying on business under a business name which does not consist of his true surname without any addition other than his true Christian names or the initials thereof;

(c) every individual or firm having a place of business in the State, who, or a member of which, has either before or after the passing of this Act changed his name, except in the case of a woman in consequence of marriage;

(d) every body corporate having a place of business in the State and carrying on business under a business name which does not consist of its corporate name without any addition;

(e) without prejudice to the generality of the foregoing, every person having a place of business in the State and carrying on the business of publishing a newspaper,

shall be registered in the manner directed by this Act.

(2) Where the addition merely indicates that the business is carried on in succession to a former owner of the business, that addition shall not of itself render registration necessary.

(3) Where two or more individual partners have the same surname, the use of the plural form of that surname shall not of itself render registration necessary.

(4) The use by a body corporate of a recognised abbreviation for 'Company' or 'Limited' or for any analogous expression forming part of its corporate name shall not of itself render registration necessary.

(5) Where the business is carried on by an assignee or trustee in bankruptcy, a trustee of the estate of an arranging debtor, or a receiver or manager appointed by any court, registration shall not be necessary under paragraph (a), (b) or (d) of subsection (1).

(6) An individual or firm shall not require to be registered by reason only of a change of his name or of the name of a partner in the firm, if the change has taken place before the person who has changed his name has attained the age of eighteen years or if not less than twenty years have elapsed since it took place, or by reason only of the adoption by an individual of a title to which he has succeeded.

4 Manner and particulars of registration

(1) Every person required under this Act to be registered shall furnish by sending by post or delivery to the registrar a statement in writing in the prescribed form containing the following particulars:

- (a) the business name, including, in the case of the proprietor of a newspaper, the title of the newspaper;
- (b) the general nature of the business;
- (c) the principal place of the business;
- (d) where the registration to be effected is that of a firm, the present Christian name and surname, any former Christian name or surname, the nationality, if not Irish, the usual residence, and the other business occupation (if any) of each of the individuals who are partners, and the corporate name and registered or principal office in the State of every body corporate which is a partner;
- (e) where the registration to be effected is that of an individual, the present Christian name and surname, any former Christian name or surname, the nationality, if not Irish, the usual residence, and the other business occupation (if any) of such individual;
- (f) where the registration to be effected is that of a body corporate, its corporate name and registered or principal office in the State;
- (g) the date of the adoption of the business name by that person.

(2) Where a business is carried on under two or more business names, each of those business names must be stated.

5 Statement to be signed by persons registering

(1) The statement required for the purpose of registration must be signed—

- (a) in the case of an individual—by him, and
- (b) in the case of a body corporate—by a director or secretary thereof, and
- (c) in the case of a firm, either—

(i) by all the individuals who are partners, and by a director or the secretary of all bodies corporate who are partners, or

(ii) by some individual who is a partner, or a director or the secretary of some body corporate which is a partner,

and in a case to which paragraph (c)(ii) applies must be verified by a statutory declaration made by the signatory.

(2) A statutory declaration stating that any person other than the declarant is a partner, or omitting to state that any person other than the declarant is a partner, shall not be evidence for or against any such other person in respect of his liability or non liability as a partner.

(3) The High Court may on application of any person alleged or claiming to be a partner direct the rectification of the register and decide any question arising under this section.

6 Time for registration

(1) The particulars required to be furnished under this Act by any person shall be furnished within one month after his adoption of the business name.

(2) If the person has adopted the business name before the commencement of this Act, the particulars shall, if not already furnished under the repealed enactment, be furnished within one month from the commencement of this Act.

(3) This section shall apply, where registration is required in consequence of a change of name, as if for references to the date of adoption of the business name there were substituted references to the date of such change.

7 Registration of changes

Whenever a change is made or occurs in any of the particulars registered in respect of any person, that person shall, within one month after the change or, if such change occurred before the commencement of this Act, within one month after such commencement, furnish by sending by post or delivering to the registrar a statement in writing in the prescribed form specifying the nature and date of the change signed, and where necessary verified, in like manner as the statement required on registration.

8 Certificate of registration

(1) On receiving a statement under section 4, or a statement under section 7 specifying a change in the business name, the registrar shall send by post or deliver a certificate of the registration thereof to the person registering.

(2) A certificate of registration shall be kept exhibited in a conspicuous position at, in the case of a firm or individual, the principal place of business and, in the case of a body corporate, its registered or principal office in the State and, in every case, in every branch office or place where the business is normally carried on, and if not kept so exhibited, the person registered or, in the case of a firm, every partner in the firm shall be liable on summary conviction to a [class C fine].[a]

Amendments

a £100 converted to €127.90 by Council Regulations (EC) No 1103/97, No 974/98 and No 2866/98 and the Economic and Monetary Union Act 1998, s 6; the above being implicitly substituted, by Fines Act 2010, s 6, for a fine not exceeding the aforesaid amount. A class C fine currently means a fine not exceeding €2,500.

---

9 Duty to furnish particulars

(1) The Minister may require any person to furnish to him within such time as the Minister may require a statement of such particulars as appear necessary to the Minister for the purpose of ascertaining whether or not that person or the firm of which he is partner should be registered under this Act, or an alteration made in the registered particulars.

(2) If from any information so furnished it appears to the Minister that any person ought to be registered under this Act, or an alteration ought to be made in the registered particulars, the Minister may require that person to furnish to the registrar the required particulars within such time as may be allowed by the Minister but, where any default under this Act has been discovered from the information acquired under this section, no proceedings under this Act shall be taken against any person in respect of such default prior to the expiration of the time within which that person is so required to furnish particulars to the registrar.

10 Penalty for default in furnishing statements

If any person required under this Act to furnish a statement of particulars or of any change in particulars makes default without reasonable excuse in so doing, the person so in default or, in the case of a firm, every partner in the firm shall be liable on summary conviction to a [class C fine][a].

Amendments

a £100 converted to €127.90 by Council Regulations (EC) No 1103/97, No 974/98 and No 2866/98 and the Economic and Monetary Union Act 1998, s 6; the above being implicitly substituted, by Fines Act 2010, s 6, for a fine not exceeding the aforesaid amount. A class C fine currently means a fine not exceeding €2,500.

---

11 Penalty for false statements

If any statement furnished under this Act contains any matter which is false in any material particular to the knowledge of any person signing it, that person shall, on summary conviction, be liable to imprisonment for a term not exceeding six months or to a [class C fine][a], or to both.

Amendments

a £100 converted to €127.90 by Council Regulations (EC) No 1103/97, No 974/98 and No 2866/98 and the Economic and Monetary Union Act 1998, s 6; the above being implicitly substituted, by Fines Act 2010 s 6, for a fine not exceeding the aforesaid amount. A class C fine currently means a fine not exceeding €2,500.

---

12 Removal of names from register

(1) If a person registered under this Act in respect of a business name ceases to carry on business under that name, it shall be the duty of that person or, in the case of an individual who dies, of his personal representative or, in the case of a firm, of every person who was a partner in the firm at the time when it ceased to carry on business under that name, and also, in the case of a body corporate, of any liquidator, within three months thereafter to send by post or deliver to the registrar a statement in the prescribed form to that effect, and if he makes default in doing so he shall be liable on summary conviction to a [class C fine][a].

(2) On receipt of such statement the registrar may delete from the register the particulars relating to that business name.

(3) Where, by virtue of subsection (6) of section 3, a person registered under this Act no longer requires to be so registered—

- (a) the registrar, if so requested by that person, shall remove that person from the register, and
- (b) section 8 shall no longer require that person to keep exhibited the certificate of registration,

and where the particulars registered under this Act in respect of any person include a former name or surname which, by virtue of subsection (2) of section 2, no longer requires to be included among those particulars, the registrar, if so requested by that person, shall amend the particulars by deleting that name or surname.

(4) Where the registrar has reasonable cause to believe that any person registered under this Act in respect of a business name is not carrying on business under that name, he may send to that person by registered post a notice that, unless an answer is received to such notice within one month from the date thereof, the particulars relating to that business name may be deleted from the register.

(5) If the registrar either receives an answer to the effect that the person is not carrying on business under that business name or does not within one month after sending the notice receive an answer, he may delete the particulars relating to that name from the register.

Amendments

a £100 converted to €127.90 by Council Regulations (EC) No 1103/97, No 974/98 and No 2866/98 and the Economic and Monetary Union Act 1998, s 6; the above being implicitly substituted, by Fines Act 2010, s 6, for a fine not exceeding the aforesaid amount. A class C fine currently means a fine not exceeding €2,500.

---

13 Index of business names

The registrar shall keep an index of all business names registered under this Act.

14 Undesirable business names

(1) The Minister may refuse to permit the registration under this Act of any name which in his opinion is undesirable but an appeal shall lie to the High Court against such refusal.

(2) Where registration of a business name is refused under this section any person or, in the case of a firm, every partner in the firm, carrying on business under that name in such circumstances as to require registration under this Act, shall be liable on summary conviction to a [class C fine][a].

(3) The registration of a business name under this Act shall not be construed as authorising the use of that name if apart from such registration the use thereof could be prohibited.

Amendments

a £100 converted to €127.90 by Council Regulations (EC) No 1103/97, No 974/98 and No 2866/98 and the Economic and Monetary Union Act 1998, s 6; the above being implicitly substituted, by Fines Act 2010, s 6, for a fine not exceeding the aforesaid amount. A class C fine currently means a fine not exceeding €2,500.

---

15 Registrar, assistant registrars and offices

(1) The registrar of companies or such other person as the Minister may determine shall be the registrar for the purposes of this Act.

(2) Such persons as the Minister may determine shall be assistant registrars for the purposes of this Act.

(3) For the purposes of the registration of persons under this Act, the Minister shall maintain and administer an office or offices in the State at such places as the Minister thinks fit.

16 Inspection, production and evidence of registered documents

(1) Any person may—

(a) inspect the documents kept by the registrar, on payment of such fee as may be prescribed;

(b) require a certificate of the registration of any person or a copy of or extract from any other document or any part of any other document, to be certified by the registrar, an assistant registrar or other officer authorised by the Minister, on payment for the certificate, certified copy or extract of such fees as may be prescribed.

(2) No process for compelling the production of any document kept by the registrar shall issue from any court except with the leave of that court, and any such process if issued shall bear thereon a statement that it is issued with the leave of the court.

(3) A certificate of registration or a copy of, or extract from, any document kept by the registrar, certified under the hand of the registrar, an assistant registrar or other officer authorised by the Minister (whose official position or authority it shall not be necessary to prove), shall in all legal proceedings be admissible in evidence.

17 Regulations

(1) The Minister may make regulations concerning any of the following matters—

(a) the fees to be paid to the registrar under this Act;

(b) the forms to be used under this Act;

(c) generally the conduct and regulation of registration under this Act, and any matters incidental thereto.

(2) All fees payable in pursuance of this Act shall be paid into or disposed of for the benefit of the Exchequer in such manner as the Minister for Finance shall direct.

(3) Regulations made under this Act shall be laid before each House of the Oireachtas as soon as may be after they are made and, if a resolution annulling the regulations is passed by either House within the next twenty-one days on which that House has sat after the regulations are laid before it, the regulations shall be annulled accordingly but without prejudice to the validity of anything previously done thereunder.

18 Publication of true names, etc

(1) A person required by this Act to be registered shall, in all business letters, circulars and catalogues on or in which the business name appears and which are sent by that person to any person, state in legible characters—

(a) in the case of an individual, his present Christian name, or the initials thereof, and present surname, any former Christian names and surnames, and his nationality, if not Irish;

(b) in the case of a firm, the present Christian names, or the initials thereof, and present surnames, any former Christian names and surnames, and the nationality, if not Irish, of all the partners in the firm or, in the case of a body corporate being a partner, the corporate name;

(c) in the case of a body corporate (not being a company to which section 196 of the Companies Act, 1963, applies), its corporate name, and the present Christian name, or the initials thereof, the present surname, any former Christian names and surnames, and the nationality, if not Irish, of every director or, in the case of a body corporate being a director, the corporate name.

(2) If default is made in compliance with this section the person or, in the case of a firm, every partner in the firm shall be liable on summary conviction for each offence to a [class D fine][a].

Amendments

a £25 converted to €31.74 by Council Regulations (EC) No 1103/97, No 974/98 and No 2866/98 and the Economic and Monetary Union Act 1998, s 6; the above being implicitly substituted, by Fines Act 2010, s 7, for a fine not exceeding the aforesaid amount. A class D fine currently means a fine not exceeding €1,000.

---

19 Offences by bodies corporate

Where a body corporate is guilty of an offence under this Act every director, secretary and officer of the body corporate who is knowingly a party to the default shall be guilty of a like offence and liable to a like penalty.

20 Summary proceedings

(1) Summary proceedings in relation to an offence under this Act may be brought and prosecuted by the Minister.

(2) Notwithstanding subsection (4) of section 10 of the Petty Sessions (Ireland) Act, 1851, summary proceedings for an offence under this Act may be instituted within three years from the date of the offence.

21 Repeals and consequential provisions

(1) The Registration of Business Names Act, 1916, is hereby repealed.

(2) The Defamation Act, 1961, is hereby amended—

(a) by the deletion, in the definition of 'newspaper' in section 2, of 'except in section 27',

(b) by the repeal of section 27.

(3) The register kept under the repealed enactment shall be deemed part of the register for the purposes of this Act.

(4) All statements and particulars furnished, statutory declarations made, notices, certificates, certified copies and extracts given and things done under the repealed enactment shall have effect as if furnished, made, given or done under this Act.

22 Expenses

The expenses incurred by the Minister in the administration of this Act shall to such extent as may be sanctioned by the Minister for Finance be paid out of moneys, provided by the Oireachtas.

23 Short title

This Act may be cited as the Registration of Business Names Act, 1963.

Companies Act 1963

(Number 33 of 1963)

Arrangement of Sections

Part I
Preliminary

Part II
Incorporation of Companies and Matters incidental thereto

Memorandum of Association

Articles of Association

Form of Memorandum and Articles

Registration

Provisions relating to Names of Companies

REDUCTION OF SHARE CAPITAL

VARIATION OF SHAREHOLDER'S RIGHTS

NUMBERING AND TRANSFER OF AND EVIDENCE OF TITLE TO SHARES AND DEBENTURES

SPECIAL PROVISIONS AS TO DEBENTURES

PART IV
REGISTRATION OF CHARGES

REGISTRATION OF CHARGES WITH REGISTRAR OF COMPANIES

MEETINGS AND PROCEEDINGS

ACCOUNTS AND AUDIT

Offences Antecedent to or in the Course of Winding Up

Supplementary Provisions as to Winding Up

Provisions as to Dissolution

Rules of Court

Disposal of Documents filed with Registrar

PART VII
RECEIVERS

PART XIV
MISCELLANEOUS PROVISIONS RELATING TO BANKING COMPANIES, PARTNERSHIPS AND UNREGISTERED COMPANIES

PROVISIONS RELATING TO BANKING COMPANIES

PROHIBITION OF PARTNERSHIPS WITH MORE THAN TWENTY MEMBERS

APPLICATION OF CERTAIN PROVISIONS OF THIS ACT TO UNREGISTERED COMPANIES

PART XV
GENERAL

FORM OF REGISTERS

SERVICE OF DOCUMENTS

OFFENCES

LEGAL PROCEEDINGS

GENERAL PROVISIONS AS TO THE MINISTER

SUPPLEMENTAL

SCHEDULES

FIRST SCHEDULE

SECOND SCHEDULE

THIRD SCHEDULE

FOURTH SCHEDULE

FIFTH SCHEDULE

SIXTH SCHEDULE

SEVENTH SCHEDULE

EIGHTH SCHEDULE

NINTH SCHEDULE

TENTH SCHEDULE

PROVISIONS REFERRED TO IN SECTION 380

ELEVENTH SCHEDULE

AMENDMENTS OF OTHER ACTS

TWELFTH SCHEDULE

ENACTMENTS REPEALED

THIRTEENTH SCHEDULE

ENACTMENT SAVED

Companies Act 1963

(Number 33 of 1963)

An Act to consolidate with amendments certain enactments relating to companies and for purposes connected with that matter. [23rd December, 1963]
Be It Enacted by the Oireachtas as Follows:

PART I
PRELIMINARY

1 Short title and commencement

(1) This Act may be cited as the Companies Act, 1963.

(2) This Act shall come into operation on such day as the Minister appoints by order.

2 General provisions as to interpretation

(1) In this Act unless the context otherwise requires:

['annual accounts' or 'accounts' means—

(a) individual accounts required by section 148, and

(b) group accounts required by section 150;

'Act of 1986' means the Companies (Amendment) Act 1986;

'Act of 1990' means the Companies Act 1990;

'Act of 2003' means the Companies (Auditing and Accounting) Act 2003;] [a]

'agent' does not include a person's counsel acting as such;

['annual return' means the return required to be made under section 125;

'annual return date' means the date in each year not later than that to which the annual return shall be made up, the calculation of which is provided for in section 127;] [b]

'articles' means the articles of association of a company, as originally framed or as altered by [a resolution of the company], [c] including, so far as they apply to the company, the regulations contained (as the case may be) in Table B in the Schedule annexed to the Joint Stock Companies Act, 1856, or in Table A in the First Schedule to the Companies Act, 1862, or in that Table as altered in pursuance of section 71 of the last mentioned Act, or in Table A in the First Schedule to the Companies (Consolidation) Act, 1908;

['auditor' means a statutory auditor or statutory audit firm within the meaning of the European Communities (Statutory Audits) (Directive 2006/43/EC) Regulations 2010;] [d]

'bank holiday' means a day which is a bank holiday under the Public Holidays Acts, 1871 to 1924;

'the Bankruptcy Acts' means the Irish Bankrupt and Insolvent Act, 1857, the Bankruptcy (Ireland) Amendment Act, 1872, the Debtors Act (Ireland) 1872 and the Local Bankruptcy (Ireland) Act, 1888;

'book and paper' and 'book or paper' include accounts, deeds, writings and documents;

['Companies Act accounts' means Companies Act individual accounts (within the meaning of section 148) or Companies Act group accounts (within the meaning of section 150);

'Companies Act group accounts' shall be read in accordance with section 150;

'Companies Act individual accounts' shall be read in accordance with section 148;] [e]

'company' means a company formed and registered under this Act, or an existing company;

'company limited by guarantee' and 'company limited by shares' have the meanings assigned to them respectively by subsection (2) of section 5;

['company traded on a regulated market' means a company whose registered office is in the State and whose shares are admitted to trading on a regulated market situated or operating within a Member State and does not include—

(a) collective investment undertakings within the meaning of Article 1(2) of Council Directive 85/611/EEC of 20 December 1985 on the coordination of laws, regulations and administrative provisions relating to undertakings for collective investment in transferable securities (UCITS) (OJ L 375, 31.12.1985, p 3), or

(b) undertakings the sole object of which is the collective investment of capital provided by the public within the meaning of Article 1(3)(b) of Directive 2007/36/EC of the European Parliament and of the Council of 11 July 2007 on the exercise of certain rights of shareholders in listed companies (OJ L 184, 14.07.2007, p 17);] [f]

'contributory' has the meaning assigned to it by section 208;

['the court' unless the context otherwise requires 'the court' used in any provision of the Companies Acts in relation to a company means:

(a) the High Court, or

(b) where another court is prescribed for the purposes of that provision, that court;] [g]

['1993 Regulations' means the European Communities (Accounts) Regulations 1993 (S.I. No. 396 of 1993);

'Credit Institutions Regulations' means the European Communities (Credit Institutions: Accounts) Regulations 1992 (S.I. No. 294 of 1992);] [h]

'creditors' voluntary winding up' has the meaning assigned to it by subsection (7) of section 256;

'debenture' includes debenture stock, bonds and any other securities of a company whether constituting a charge on the assets of the company or not;

'director' includes any person occupying the position of director by whatever name called;

['Directive 2004/25/EC' means Directive 2004/25/EC of the European Parliament and of the Council of 21 April 2004, on takeover bids (OJ L 142, 30.4.2004, p 1);] [i]

'document' includes summons, notice, order and other legal process, and registers;

['EEA state' means a state, including the State, which is a Contracting Party to the EEA Agreement;

'EEA Agreement' means the Agreement on the European Economic Area signed at Oporto on 2 May 1992, as adjusted by the Protocol signed at Brussels on 17 March 1993;][j]

['electronic means' are means of electronic equipment for the processing (including digital compression), storage and transmission of data, employing wires, radio, optical technologies, or any other electromagnetic means;][k]

'existing company' means a company formed and registered in a register kept in the State under the Joint Stock Companies Acts, the Companies Act, 1862, or the Companies (Consolidation) Act, 1908;

'extended notice' has the meaning assigned to it by section 142;

'financial year' means, [subject to subsection (1A)][l], in relation to any body corporate, the period in respect of which any profit and loss account of the body corporate laid before it in general meeting is made up, whether that period is a year or not;

has the meaning assigned to it by subsection (1) of section 150;

['Group Accounts Regulations' means the European Communities (Companies: Group Accounts) Regulations 1992 (S.I. No. 201 of 1992);

'IAS Regulation' means Regulation (EC) No. 1606/2002 of the European Parliament and of the Council of 19 July 2002;

'income statement' means a financial statement prepared in accordance with international financial reporting standards and is equivalent to a profit and loss account;

'individual accounts' shall be read in accordance with section 148;

'IFRS accounts' means IFRS individual accounts (within the meaning of section 148) or IFRS group accounts (within the meaning of section 150);

'IFRS group accounts' shall be read in accordance with section 150;

'IFRS individual accounts' shall be read in accordance with section 148;][m]

'holding company' means a holding company as defined by section 155;

['insolvency proceedings' means insolvency proceedings opened under Article 3 of the Insolvency Regulation in a member state of the European Communities other than the State and Denmark where the proceedings relate to a body corporate;

'Insolvency Regulation' means Council Regulation (EC) No. 1346/2000 of 29 May 2000 on insolvency proceedings;][n]

['Insurance Undertakings Regulations' means the European Communities (Insurance Undertakings: Accounts) Regulations 1996 (S.I. No. 23 of 1996);

'international financial reporting standards' means the international financial reporting standards, within the meaning of the IAS Regulation, adopted from time to time by the European Commission in accordance with the IAS Regulation;][o]

'issued generally' means, in relation to a prospectus, issued to persons who are not existing members or debenture holders of the company;

as well as to articles coming into force thereafter, and shall apply also in relation to a company's memorandum as it applies in relation to its articles.

(5) References in this Act to any enactment shall, unless the context otherwise requires, be construed as references to that enactment as amended or extended by any subsequent enactment including this Act.

(6) In this Act, a reference to a Part, section or schedule is to a Part, section or schedule of this Act, unless it is indicated that reference to some other enactment is intended.

(7) In this Act, a reference to a subsection, paragraph, subparagraph or other division is to the subsection, paragraph, subparagraph or other division of the provision in which the reference occurs, unless it is indicated that reference to some other provision is intended.

Amendments

a Definition of 'annual accounts' or 'accounts' substituted for the definition of 'accounts' and definitions of C(A)A 1986, CA 1990 and C(AA)A 2003 inserted by European Communities (International Financial Reporting Standards and Miscellaneous Amendments) Regulations 2005 (SI 116/2005), Sch 1, Pt 1, Item No. 1, (a)(i) with effect from 24 February 2005.

b Definition of 'annual return' substituted and definition of 'annual return date' inserted by CLEA 2001, s 84(a) with effect from 1 March 2002.[1]

c Definition of 'articles' amended by substitution of the words 'a resolution of the company' for 'special resolution' by C(A)A 1983, Sch 1, para 1 with effect from 13 October 1983.[2]

d Definition of 'auditor' inserted by EC(SA)(Dir)R 2010, reg 4(1)(a).

e Definition of 'Companies Act accounts', 'Companies Act group accounts' and 'Companies Act individual accounts' inserted by European Communities (International Financial Reporting Standards and Miscellaneous Amendments) Regulations 2005 (SI 116/2005), Sch 1, Pt 1, Item No. 1, (a)(ii) with effect from 24 February 2005.

f Definition of 'company traded on a regulated market' inserted by Shareholders' Rights Regulations 2009, reg 3(a).

g Definition of 'the court' substituted by CA 1990, s 235 with effect from 27 December 1990.[3]

h Definition of '1993 Regulations' and 'Credit Institutions Regulations' inserted by European Communities (International Financial Reporting Standards and Miscellaneous Amendments) Regulations 2005 (SI 116/2005), Sch 1, Pt 1, Item No. 1, (a)(iii) with effect from 24 February 2005.

i Definition of 'Directive 2004/25/EC' inserted by Shareholders' Rights Regulations 2009, reg 3(a).

j Definition of 'EEA state' and 'EEA Agreement' inserted by European Communities (International Financial Reporting Standards and Miscellaneous Amendments) Regulations 2005 (SI 116/2005), Sch 1, Pt 1, Item No. 1, (a)(iv) with effect from 24 February 2005.

k Definition of 'electronic means' inserted by Shareholders' Rights Regulations 2009, reg 3(a).

l Definition of 'financial year' amended by inserting 'subject to sub-section (1A)' after 'means' by European Communities (International 116/2005), Sch 1, Pt 1, Item No. 1, (a)(viii) with effect from 24 February 2005.

m Definition of 'Group Accounts Regulations', 'IAS Regulation', 'income statement', 'individual accounts', 'IFRS accounts', 'IFRS group accounts' and 'IFRS individual accounts' inserted by European Communities (International Financial Reporting Standards and Miscellaneous Amendments) Regulations 2005 (SI 116/2005), Sch 1, Pt 1, Item No. 1, (a)(v) with effect from 24 February 2005.

n Definition of 'insolvency proceedings' and 'Insolvency Regulation' inserted by European Communities (Corporate Insolvency) Regulations 2002 (SI 333/2002), r 3(a) with effect from 31 May 2002.

o Definition of 'Insurance Undertakings Regulations' and 'international financial reporting standards' inserted by European Communities (International Financial Reporting Standards and Miscellaneous Amendments) Regulations 2005 (SI 116/2005), Sch 1, Pt 1, Item No. 1, (a)(vi) with effect from 24 February 2005.

p Definition of 'parent company' or 'parent undertaking' inserted by European Communities (International Financial Reporting Standards and Miscellaneous Amendments) Regulations 2005 (SI 116/2005), Sch 1, Pt 1, Item No. 1, (a)(ix) with effect from 24 February 2005.

q Definition of 'profit and loss account' inserted by European Communities (International Financial Reporting Standards and Miscellaneous Amendments) Regulations 2005 (SI 116/2005), Sch 1, Pt 1, Item No. 1, (a)(vii) with effect from 24 February 2005.

r Definition of 'property' inserted by European Communities (Corporate Insolvency) Regulations 2002 (SI 333/2002), r 3(a) with effect from 31 May 2002.

s Definition of 'recognised stock exchange' substituted by CA 1990, s 3(2) with effect from 27 December 1990.[4]

t Definition of 'regulated market' substituted by Shareholders' Rights Regulations 2009, reg 3(b).

u Definitions of 'statutory meetings' and 'statutory reports' repealed by C(A)A 1983, Sch 3, Pt I.

v Definition of 'Supervisory Authority' inserted by EC(SA)(Dir)R 2010, reg 4(1)(b).

w Definition of 'undertaking' inserted by European Communities (International Financial Reporting Standards and Miscellaneous Amendments) Regulations 2005 (SI 116/2005), Sch 1, Pt 1, Item No. 1, (a)(xi) with effect from 24 February 2005.

x Definition of 'undischarged bankrupt' inserted by CLEA 2001, s 84(b) with effect from 1 March 2002.[5]

y CA 1963, s 2(1A) and (1B) inserted by European Communities (International Financial Reporting Standards and Miscellaneous Amendments) Regulations 2005 (SI 116/2005), Sch 1, Pt 1, Item No. 1, (b) with effect from 24 February 2005.

1 Company Law Enforcement Act, 2001 (Commencement) (No 2) Order 2001 (SI 438/2001).

2 Companies (Amendment) Act, 1983 (Commencement) Order 1983 (SI 288/1983).

3 Companies Act, 1990 (Commencement) Order 1990 (SI 336/1990).

4 Companies Act, 1990 (Commencement) Order 1990 (SI 336/1990).

5 Company Law Enforcement Act, 2001 (Commencement) (No 2) Order 2001 (SI 438/2001).

---

3 Repeal and savings

(1) The enactments mentioned in the Twelfth Schedule are hereby repealed to the extent specified in the third column of that Schedule.

(2) Nothing in this Act shall affect any Order in Council, order, rule, regulation, appointment, conveyance, mortgage, deed or agreement made, resolution passed, direction given, proceeding taken, instrument issued or thing done under any former enactment relating to companies, but any such Order in Council, order, rule, regulation, appointment, conveyance, mortgage, deed, agreement, resolution, direction, proceeding, instrument or thing shall, if in force immediately before the operative date continue in

force, and so far as it could have been made, passed, given, taken, issued or done under this Act shall have effect as if made, passed, given, taken, issued or done under this Act.

(3) Nothing in this Act shall affect the operation of sections 109 and 110 of the Companies (Consolidation) Act, 1908, as regards inspectors appointed before, or the continuance of an inspection began by inspectors appointed before, the operative date, and section 172 shall apply to a report of inspectors appointed under the said sections as it applies to a report of inspectors appointed under sections 165 and 166.

(4) Nothing in this Act shall affect:

(a) the provisions of section 5 of the Trade Union Act, 1871 (which avoids the registration of a trade union under the enactments relating to companies);

(b) the enactment set out in the Thirteenth Schedule, being an enactment continued in force by section 205 of the Companies Act, 1862,

or be construed as repealing any provision of the Insurance Acts, 1909 to 1961.

(5) Subject to the provisions of subsection (4), any document referring to any former enactment relating to companies shall be construed as referring to the corresponding enactment of this Act.

(6) Any person, appointed to any office under or by virtue of any former enactment relating to companies, who is in office immediately before the operative date shall be deemed to have been appointed to that office under or by virtue of this Act.

(7) Any register kept under any former enactment relating to companies shall be deemed part of the register to be kept under the corresponding provisions of this Act.

(8) All funds and accounts constituted under this Act shall be deemed to be in continuation of the corresponding funds and accounts constituted under the former enactments relating to companies.

(9) The repeal by this Act of any enactment shall not affect:

(a) the incorporation of any company registered under any enactment hereby repealed;

(b) Table B in the Schedule annexed to the Joint Stock Companies Act, 1856, or any part thereof, so far as the same applies to any company existing on the operative date;

(c) Table A in the First Schedule annexed to the Companies Act, 1862, or any part thereof, either as originally contained in that Schedule or as altered in pursuance of section 71 of that Act, so far as the same applies to any company existing on the operative date;

(d) Table A of the First Schedule to the Companies (Consolidation) Act, 1908, or any part thereof, so far as the same applies to any company existing on the operative date.

(10) Where any offence, being an offence for the continuance of which a penalty was provided, has been committed under any former enactment relating to companies, proceedings may be taken under this Act in respect of the continuance of the offence after the operative date, in the same manner as if the offence had been committed under the corresponding provisions of this Act.

(11) In this section 'former enactment relating to companies' means any enactment repealed by this Act and any enactment repealed by the Companies (Consolidation) Act, 1908.

4 Construction of references in other Acts to companies registered under the Companies (Consolidation) Act, 1908

Notwithstanding subsection (1) of section 20 of the Interpretation Act, 1937, (which provides that where an Act repeals and re-enacts, with or without modification, any provisions of a former Act, references in any other Act to the provisions so repealed shall, unless the contrary intention appears, be construed as references to the provisions so re-enacted) references in any Act other than this Act to a company formed and registered, or registered, under the Companies (Consolidation) Act, 1908, shall, unless the contrary intention appears, be construed as references to a company formed and registered, or registered, under that Act or this Act.

PART II
INCORPORATION OF COMPANIES AND MATTERS INCIDENTAL THERETO

Memorandum of Association

5 Way of forming incorporated company

(1) Any seven or more persons or, where the company to be formed will be a private company [or an investment company (within the meaning of Part XIII of the Companies Act, 1990)],[a] any two or more persons, associated for any lawful purpose may, by subscribing their names to a memorandum of association and otherwise complying with the requirements of this Act relating to registration, form an incorporated company, with or without limited liability.

(2) Such a company may be either:

(a) a company having the liability of its members limited by the memorandum to the amount, if any, unpaid on the shares respectively held by them (in this Act termed 'a company limited by shares'); or

(b) a company having the liability of its members limited by the memorandum to such amount as the members may respectively thereby undertake to contribute to the assets of the company in the event of its being wound up (in this Act termed 'a company limited by guarantee'); or

(c) a company not having any limit on the liability of its members (in this Act termed 'an unlimited company').

Amendments

a Words inserted by CA 1990, s 260 (as substituted by C(A)(No 2)A 1999, s 54(3)).

---

6 Requirements in relation to memorandum

[(1) The memorandum of every company must state—

(a) in the case of a public limited company, the name of the company, with 'public limited company' or 'cuideachta phoiblí theoranta' as the last words of the name;

(b) in the case of a company (other than a public limited company) which is limited by shares or by guarantee, the name of the company, with 'limited' or 'teoranta' as the last word of the name;

(c) the objects of the company.][a]

(2) The memorandum of a company limited by shares or by guarantee must also state that the liability of its members is limited.

(3) The memorandum of a company limited by guarantee must also state that each member undertakes to contribute to the assets of the company in the event of its being wound up while he is a member, or within one year after he ceases to be a member, for payment of the debts and liabilities of the company contracted before he ceases to be a member, and of the costs, charges and expenses of winding up, and for adjustment of the rights of the contributories among themselves, such amount as may be required, not exceeding a specified amount.

(4) In the case of a company having a share capital—

(a) the memorandum must also, unless the company is an unlimited company, state the amount of share capital with which the company proposes to be registered, and the division thereof into shares of a fixed amount;

(b) no subscriber of the memorandum may take less than one share;

(c) each subscriber must write opposite to his name the number of shares he takes.

Amendments

a CA 1963, s 6(1) substituted by C(A)A 1983, Sch 1, para 2.

7 Printing, stamp and signature of memorandum

The memorandum must be printed [in an entire format or in a form pursuant to section 80 of the Company Law Enforcement Act, 2001][a] [...][b] and must be signed by each subscriber in the presence of at least one witness who must attest the signature.

Amendments

a The words 'in an entire format or in a form pursuant to section 80 of the Company Law Enforcement Act 2001' inserted by CLEA 2001, s 81.

b The words ', must bear the same stamp as if it were a deed,' deleted by FA 1996, s 112(1)(a).

8 Modification of the *ultra vires* rule

(1) Any act or thing done by a company which if the company had been empowered to do the same would have been lawfully and effectively done, shall, notwithstanding that the company had no power to do such act or thing, be effective in favour of any person relying on such act or thing who is not shown to have been actually aware, at the time when he so relied thereon, that such act or thing was not within the powers of the company, but any director or officer of the company who was responsible for the doing by the company of such act or thing shall be liable to the company for any loss or damage suffered by the company in consequence thereof.

(2) The court may, on the application of any member or holder of debentures of a company, restrain such company from doing any act or thing which the company has no power to do.

9 Restriction on alteration of memorandum

A company may not alter the provisions contained in its memorandum except in the cases, in the mode and to the extent for which express provision is made in this Act.

10 Way in which and extent to which objects of company may be altered

(1) Subject to subsection (2), a company may, by special resolution, alter the provisions of its memorandum by abandoning, restricting or amending any existing object or by adopting a new object and any alteration so made shall be as valid as if originally contained therein, and be subject to alteration in like manner.

(2) If an application is made to the court in accordance with this section for the alteration to be cancelled, it shall not have effect except in so far as it is confirmed by the court.

(3) Subject to subsection (4), an application under this section may be made—

(a) by the holders of not less in the aggregate than 15% in nominal value of the company's issued share capital or any class thereof or, if the company is not limited by shares, not less than 15% of the company's members; or

(b) by the holders of not less than 15% of the company's debentures, entitling the holders to object to alterations of its objects.

(4) An application shall not be made under this section by any person who has consented to or voted in favour of the alteration.

(5) An application under this section must be made within 21 days after the date on which the resolution altering the company's objects was passed, and may be made on behalf of the persons entitled to make the application by such one or more of their number as they may appoint in writing for the purpose.

(6) On an application under this section, the court may make an order cancelling the alteration or confirming the alteration either wholly or in part and on such terms and conditions as it thinks fit, and may, if it thinks fit, adjourn the proceedings in order that an arrangement may be made to the satisfaction of the court for the purchase of the interests of dissentient members, and may give such directions and make such orders as it may think expedient for facilitating or carrying into effect any such arrangement[...].[a]

[(6A) An order under this section may, if the court thinks fit, provide for the purchase by the company of the shares of any members of the company and for the reduction accordingly of the company's capital and may make such alterations in the memorandum and articles of the company as may be required in consequence of that provision.

(6B) Where an order under this section requires the company not to make any, or any specified, alteration in its memorandum or articles, then, notwithstanding anything in the Companies Acts, 1963 to 1983 the company shall not have power without the leave of the court to make any such alteration in breach of that requirement.

(6C) Any alteration in the memorandum or articles of a company made by virtue of an order under this section, other than one made by resolution of the company, shall be of the same effect as if duly made by resolution of the company, and the provisions of the

Companies Acts, 1963 to 1983, shall apply to the memorandum or articles as so altered accordingly.][b]

(7) The debentures entitling the holders to object to alterations of a company's objects shall be any debentures secured by a floating charge which were issued or first issued before the operative date or form part of the same series as any debentures so issued, and a special resolution altering a company's objects shall require the same notice to the holders of any such debentures as to members of the company, so however that not less than 10 days' notice shall be given to the holders of any such debentures.

In default of any provisions regulating the giving of notice to any such debenture holders, the provisions of the company's articles regulating the giving of notice to members shall apply.

(8) In the case of a company which is, by virtue of a licence from the Minister, exempt from the obligation to use the word 'limited' or 'teoranta' as part of its name, a resolution altering the company's objects shall also require the same notice to the [registrar of companies][c] as to holders of debentures.

(9) Where a company passes a resolution altering its objects—

(a) if no application is made with respect thereto under this section, it shall, within 15 days from the end of the period for making such an application, deliver to the registrar of companies a printed copy of its memorandum as altered; and

(b) if such an application is made, it shall—

(i) forthwith give notice of that fact to the registrar; and

(ii) within 15 days from the date of any order cancelling or confirming the alteration, deliver to the registrar an office copy of the order and, in the case of an order confirming the alteration, a printed copy of the memorandum as altered.

The court may by order at any time extend the time for delivery of documents to the registrar under paragraph (b) for such period as the court may think proper.

(10) If a company makes default in giving notice or delivering any document to the registrar as required by subsection (9), the company and every officer of the company who is in default [shall be guilty of an offence and liable to a [class C fine][d].][e]

(11) In relation to a resolution for altering the provisions of a company's memorandum relating to the objects of the company passed before the operative date, this section shall have effect as if, in lieu of subsections (2) to (10), there had been enacted subsections (2) to (7) of section 9 of the Companies (Consolidation) Act, 1908.

Amendments

a Words 'so, however, that no part of the capital of the company shall be expanded in any such purchase', deleted by C(A)A 1983, Sch 1, para 3(a).

b CA 1963, s 10(6A),(6C) and (6B) inserted by C(A)A 1983, Sch 1, para 3(b).

c 'registrar of companies' substituted for 'Minister' by CLEA 2001, s 85.

d '£250' substituted for '£50' by C(A)A 1982, Sch 1, increased to £1,500 by CA 1990, s 240(7) as inserted by CLEA 2001, s 104(c) and converted to €1,904.61 by Council Regulations (EC) No 1103/97, No 974/98 and No 2866/98 and the Economic and Monetary Union Act 1998,

s 6; the above being implicitly substituted, by Fines Act 2010, s 6, for a fine not exceeding the aforesaid amount. A class C fine currently means a fine not exceeding €2,500.

e CA 1963, s 10(10) words 'shall be guilty of an offence and liable to a fine' substituted for 'shall be liable to a fine' by C(A&A)A 2003, Sch 2, Item No 1.

Articles of Association

11 Articles prescribing regulations for companies

[There may, in the case of a company limited by shares and in the case of a company limited by guarantee and not having a share capital, and there shall, in the case of a company limited by guarantee and having share capital or unlimited, be registered with the memorandum articles of association signed by the subscribers to the memorandum and prescribing regulations for the company.][a]

Amendments

a CA 1963, s 11, substituted by C(A)A 1982, s 2.

12 Regulations required in the case of an unlimited company or company limited by guarantee

(1) In the case of an unlimited company, the articles must state the number of members with which the company proposes to be registered and, if the company has a share capital, the amount of share capital with which the company proposes to be registered.

(2) In the case of a company limited by guarantee, the articles must state the number of members with which the company proposes to be registered.

(3) Where an unlimited company or a company limited by guarantee has increased the number of its members beyond the registered number, it shall, within 15 days after the increase was resolved on or took place, give to the registrar notice of the increase, and he shall record the increase.

If default is made in complying with this subsection, the company and every officer of the company who is in default [shall be guilty of an offence and liable to a [class C fine][a]].[b]

Amendments

a '£250' substituted for '£50' by C(A)A 1982, Sch 1, increased to £1,500 by CA 1990, s 240(7) as inserted by CLEA 2001, s 104(c), and converted to €1,904.61 by Council Regulations (EC) No 1103/97, No 974/98 and No 2866/98 and the Economic and Monetary Union Act 1998, s 6; the above being implicitly substituted, by Fines Act 2010, s 6, for a fine not exceeding the aforesaid amount. A class C fine currently means a fine not exceeding €2,500.

b CA 1963, s 12(3) words 'shall be guilty of an offence and liable to a fine' substituted for 'shall be liable to a fine' by C(AA)A 2003, Sch 2, Item No 1.

13 Adoption and application of Table A or Tábla A

(1) Articles of association may adopt all or any of the regulations contained in Table A, or of the equivalent regulations in the Irish language contained in Tábla A.

(2) In the case of a company limited by shares and registered after the operative date, if articles are not registered or, if articles are registered, in so far as the articles do not exclude or modify the regulations contained in Table A, those regulations shall, so far as applicable, be the regulations of the company in the same manner and to the same extent as if they were contained in duly registered articles.

(3) If the memorandum of the company is in the Irish language, the references in subsection (2) to Table A shall be construed as references to Tábla A.

[13A Adoption and application of Table C

(1) In the case of a company limited by guarantee and not having a share capital articles of association may adopt all or any of the regulations contained in Table C or all or any of the regulations contained in the version in the Irish language of Table C set out in the First Schedule to the Principal Act.

(2) In the case of a company limited by guarantee and not having a share capital and registered after the commencement of the Companies (Amendment) Act, 1982, if articles are not registered or, if articles are registered, in so far as the articles do not exclude or modify the regulations contained in Table C, those regulations shall, so far as applicable, be the regulations of the company in the same manner and to the same extent as if they were contained in duly registered articles.

(3) If the memorandum of the company is in the Irish language, the references in subsection (2) to Table C shall be construed as references to the regulations contained in the version in the Irish language of Table C set out in the First Schedule to the Principal Act.][a]

Amendments

a CA 1963, s 13A inserted by C(A)A 1982, s 14.

14 Printing, stamp and signature of articles

Articles must—

(a) be printed [in an entire format or in a form pursuant to section 80 of the Company Law Enforcement Act, 2001];[a]

(b) be divided into paragraphs numbered consecutively;

(c) [...] [b]

(d) be signed by each subscriber of the memorandum in the presence of at least one witness who must attest the signature.

Amendments

a The words 'in an entire format or in a form pursuant to section 80 of the Company Law Enforcement Act, 2001' inserted by CLEA 2001, s 82.[1]

b CA 1963, s 14(c) deleted by FA 1996, s 112.[2]

1 With effect from 1 October 2001; Company Law Enforcement Act 2001 (Commencement) (No 2) Order 2001 (SI 438/2001).

2 With effect from 15 May 1996.

15 Alteration of articles by special resolution

(1) Subject to the provisions of this Act and to the conditions contained in its memorandum, a company may by special resolution alter or add to its articles.

(2) Any alteration or addition so made in the articles shall, subject to the provisions of this Act, be as valid as if originally contained therein, and be subject in like manner to alteration by special resolution.

Form of Memorandum and Articles

16 Statutory forms of memorandum and articles

The form of—

(a) the memorandum of a company limited by shares;

(b) the memorandum [...][a] of a company limited by guarantee and not having a share capital;

(c) the memorandum and articles of a company limited by guarantee and having a share capital;

(d) the memorandum and articles of an unlimited company having a share capital;

shall be respectively in accordance with the forms set out in Tables B, C, D and E in the First Schedule or as near thereto as circumstances admit.

Amendments

a The words 'and articles' deleted by C(A)A 1982, s 17 with effect from 3 August 1982.[1]

1 Companies (Amendment) Act, 1982 (Commencement) Order 1982 (SI 225/1982).

Registration

17 Registration of memorandum and articles

The memorandum and the articles, if any, shall be delivered to the registrar of companies [in an entire format or in a form pursuant to section 80 of the Company Law Enforcement Act, 2001],[a] and he shall retain and register them.

Amendments

a The words 'in an entire format or in a form pursuant to section 80 of the Company Law Enforcement Act, 2001' inserted by CLEA 2001, s 83 with effect from 1 October 2001.[1]

1 Company Law Enforcement Act, 2001 (Commencement) (No 2) Order, 2001 (SI 438/2001).

---

18 Effect of registration

(1) On the registration of the memorandum of a company the registrar shall certify under his hand that the company is incorporated and, in the case of a limited company, that the company is limited.

(2) From the date of incorporation mentioned in the certificate of incorporation, the subscribers of the memorandum, together with such other persons as may from time to time become members of the company, shall be a body corporate with the name contained in the memorandum, capable forthwith of exercising all the functions of an incorporated company, and having perpetual succession and a common seal, but with

such liability on the part of the members to contribute to the assets of the company in the event of its being wound up as is mentioned in this Act.

19 Conclusiveness of certificate of incorporation

[...][a]

Amendments

a CA 1963, s 19 repealed by C(A)A 1983, Sch 3.

20 Registration of unlimited company as limited

(1) Subject to the provisions of this section, a company registered as unlimited may register under this Act as limited, or a company already registered as a limited company may re-register under this Act, but the registration of an unlimited company as a limited company shall not affect the rights or liabilities of the company in respect of any debt or obligation incurred, or any contract entered into by, to, with or on behalf of the company before the registration, and those rights or liabilities may be enforced in manner provided by Part IX of this Act in the case of a company registered in pursuance of that Part.

(2) On registration in pursuance of this section, the registrar shall close the former registration of the company, and may dispense with the delivery to him of copies of any documents with copies of which he was furnished on the occasion of the original registration of the company, but, save as aforesaid, the registration shall take place in the same manner and have effect as if it were the first registration of the company under this Act, and as if the provisions of the Acts under which the company was previously registered and regulated had been contained in different Acts from those under which the company is registered as a limited company.

Provisions relating to Names of Companies

21 Prohibition of registration of companies by undesirable names

No company shall be registered by a name which, in the opinion of the [registrar of companies][a], is undesirable but an appeal shall lie to the court against a refusal to register.

Amendments

a The words 'registrar of companies' substituted for 'Minister' by CLEA 2001, s 86.

[1] With effect from 1 October 2001; Company Law Enforcement Act 2001 (Commencement) (No 2) Order 2001 (SI 438/2001).

22 Registration of business name

(1) Every company carrying on business under a name other than its corporate name shall register in the manner directed by law for the registration of business names.

[(2) The use of the abbreviation 'Ltd.' for 'Limited' or 'Teo.' for 'Teoranta' or 'p.l.c.' for 'public limited company' or 'c.p.t.' for 'cuideachta phoiblí theoranta' shall not of itself render such registration necessary.][a]

Amendments

a CA 1963, s 22(2) substituted by C(A)A 1983, Sch 1, para 4. With effect from 13 October 1983; Companies (Amendment) Act 1983 (Commencement) Order 1983 (SI 288/1983).

23 Change of name

(1) A company may, by special resolution and with the approval of the [registrar of companies][a] signified in writing, change its name.

(2) If, through inadvertence or otherwise, a company on its first registration, or on its registration by a new name, is registered by a name which, in the opinion of the [registrar of companies],[a] is too like the name by which a company in existence is already registered, the first mentioned company may change its name with the sanction of the [registrar of companies][a] and, if he so directs within 6 months of its being registered by that name, shall change it within a period of 6 weeks from the date of the direction or such longer period as the [registrar of companies][a] may think fit to allow.

If a company makes default in complying with a direction under this subsection, it shall be liable to a [class C fine].[b]

(3) Where a company changes its name under this section, the registrar shall enter the new name in the register in place of the former name, and shall issue a certificate of incorporation altered to meet the circumstances of the case.

(4) A change of name by a company under this section shall not affect any rights or obligations of the company, or render defective any legal proceedings by or against the company, and any legal proceedings which might have been continued or commenced against it by its former name may be continued or commenced against it by its new name.

(5) A company which was registered by a name specified by statute, may, notwithstanding anything contained in that statute, change its name in accordance with subsection (1), [but if the registrar of companies is of opinion that any Minister][c] is concerned in the administration of the statute which specified the name of the company he shall not approve of the change of name save after consultation with [that Minister].[c]

(6) Where the winding up of a company commences within one year after the company has changed its name, the former name as well as the existing name of the company shall appear on all notices and advertisements in relation to the winding up.

[(7) Summary proceedings in relation to an offence under subsection (2) may be brought and prosecuted by the registrar of companies.][d]

Amendments

a In CA 1963, s 23(1) and (2) 'registrar of companies' substituted for 'Minister' wherever occurring by CLEA 2001, s 87(a).

b '£500' substituted for '£100' by C(A)A 1982, Sch 1, increased to £1,500 by CA 1990, s 240(7), as inserted by CLEA 2001, s 104(c), and converted to €1,904.61 by Council Regulations (EC) No 1103/97, No 974/98 and No 2866/98 and the Economic and Monetary Union Act 1998, s 6; the above being implicitly substituted, by Fines Act 2010, s 6, for a fine not exceeding the aforesaid amount. A class C fine currently means a fine not exceeding €2,500.

c In CA 1963, s 23(5); 'but if the registrar of companies is of opinion that any Minister' and 'that Minister' substituted for 'but if the Minister is of opinion that any other Minister' and 'that other Minister' respectively by CLEA 2001, s 87(b).

d CA 1963, s 23(7) inserted by CLEA 2001, s 87(c).

---

24 Power to dispense with 'limited' or 'teoranta' in name of charitable and other companies

[(1) A company shall, notwithstanding its registration as a company with limited liability, be exempt from the provisions of this Act relating to the use of the word 'limited' or 'teoranta' as part of its name and the publishing of its name, but shall enjoy all the privileges and shall (subject to this section) be subject to all the obligations of limited companies, where—

(a) its objects are the promotion of commerce, art, science, education, religion, charity or any other prescribed object, and

(b) its memorandum or articles of association—

(i) require its profits (if any) or other income to be applied to the promotion of its objects,

(ii) prohibit the payment of dividends to its members, and

(iii) require all the assets which would otherwise be available to its members to be transferred on its winding up to another company whose objects comply with paragraph (a) and which meets the requirements of this paragraph, and

(c) a director or secretary of the company (or, in the case of an association about to be formed as a limited company, one of the persons who are to be the first directors or the person who is to be the first secretary of the company) has delivered to the registrar of companies a statutory declaration in the prescribed form that the company complies or, where applicable, will comply with the requirements of paragraphs (a) and (b).

(2) The registrar shall refuse to register as a limited company any association about to be formed as a limited company by a name which does not include the word 'limited' or 'teoranta' unless a declaration as provided for under subsection (1)(c) has been delivered to the registrar.

(3) An application by a company registered as a limited company for a change of name including or consisting of the omission of the word 'limited' or 'teoranta' shall be made in accordance with section 23 and the registrar shall refuse to grant the application unless a declaration as provided for under subsection (1)(c) has been delivered to the registrar.

(4) A company which is exempt under subsection (1) and whose name does not include the word 'limited' or 'teoranta' shall not alter its memorandum or articles of association so that it ceases to comply with the requirements of that subsection.

(5) If it appears to the registrar that a company which is registered under a name not including the word 'limited' or 'teoranta'—

(a) has carried on any business other than the promotion of any of the objects mentioned in subsection (1)(a),

(b) has applied any of its profits or other income otherwise than in promoting such objects, or

(c) has paid a dividend to any of its members,

the registrar may, in writing, direct the company to change its name within such period as may be specified in the direction so that its name ends with the word 'limited' or 'teoranta', and the change of name shall be made in accordance with section 23.

(6) A company which has received a direction under subsection (5) shall not thereafter be registered by a name which does not include the word 'limited' or 'teoranta' without the approval of the registrar.

(7) A person who—

(a) provides incorrect, false or misleading information in a statutory declaration under subsection (1)(c),

(b) alters its memorandum or articles of association in contravention of subsection (4), or

(c) fails to comply with a direction from the registrar under subsection (5),

shall be guilty of an offence.

(8) Summary proceedings in relation to an offence under subsection (7) may be brought and prosecuted by the registrar of companies.][a].

Amendments

a CA 1963, s 24 has been repealed and substituted by CLEA 2001, s 88 with effect from 1 March 2002.[1]

[1] Company Law Enforcement Act 2001 (Commencement) (No 3) Order 2001 (SI 523/2001).

General provisions relating to memorandum and articles

25 Effect of memorandum and articles

(1) Subject to the provisions of this Act, the memorandum and articles shall, when registered, bind the company and the members thereof to the same extent as if they respectively had been signed and sealed by each member, and contained covenants by each member to observe all the provisions of the memorandum and of the articles.

(2) All money payable by any member to the company under the memorandum or articles shall be a debt due from him to the company.

(3) An action to recover a debt created by this section shall not be brought after the expiration of 12 years from the date on which the cause of action accrued.

26 Provisions as to memorandum and articles of company limited by guarantee

(1) In the case of a company limited by guarantee and not having a share capital, and registered on or after the 1st day of January, 1901, every provision in the memorandum or articles, or in any resolution of the company, purporting to give any person a right to

participate in the divisible profits of the company, otherwise than as a member, shall be void.

(2) For the purpose of the provisions of this Act relating to the memorandum of a company limited by guarantee and of this section, every provision in the memorandum or articles, or in any resolution, of a company limited by guarantee and registered on or after the date aforesaid, purporting to divide the undertaking of the company into shares or interests, shall be treated as a provision for a share capital, notwithstanding that the nominal amount or number of the shares or interests is not specified thereby.

27 Alterations in memorandum or articles increasing liability to contribute to share capital not to bind existing members without consent

(1) Subject to subsection (2), and notwithstanding anything in the memorandum or articles of a company, no member of the company shall be bound by an alteration made in the memorandum or articles after the date on which he became a member, if and so far as the alteration requires him to take or subscribe for more shares than the number held by him at the date on which the alteration is made, or in any way increases his liability as at that date to contribute to the share capital of, or otherwise to pay money to, the company.

(2) Subsection (1) shall not apply in any case where the member agrees in writing, either before or after the alteration is made, to be bound thereby.

28 Power to alter provisions in memorandum which could have been contained in articles

(1) Subject to subsection (2) and sections 27 and 205, any provision contained in a company's memorandum which could lawfully have been contained in articles of association instead of in the memorandum may, subject to the provisions of this section, be altered by the company by special resolution.

(2) If an application is made to the court for the alteration to be cancelled, it shall not have effect except in so far as it is confirmed by the court.

(3) This section shall not apply where the memorandum itself provides for or prohibits the alteration of all or any of the said provisions, and shall not authorise any variation or abrogation of the special rights of any class of members.

(4) Subsections (3), (4), (5), (6), [(6A), (6B), (6C),][a] (9) and (10) of section 10 (except paragraph (b) of the said subsection (3)) shall apply in relation to any alteration and to any application made under this section as they apply in relation to alterations and to applications made under that section.

(5) This section shall apply to a company's memorandum whether registered before, on or after the operative date.

Amendments

a The figures '(6A), (6B), (6C)', inserted into CA 1963, s 28 (4) by C(A)A 1983, Sch 1, para 5 with effect from 13 October 1983.[1]

[1] Companies (Amendment) Act 1983 (Commencement) Order 1983 (SI 288/1983).

29 Copies of memorandum and articles to be given to members

(1) A company shall, on being so required by any member, send to him a copy of the memorandum and of the articles, if any, and a copy of any Act of the Oireachtas which alters the memorandum, subject to payment in the case of a copy of the memorandum and of the articles, of [76 cents][a] or such less sum as the company may prescribe, and, in the case of a copy of such Act, of such sum not exceeding the published price thereof as the company may require.

(2) If a company makes default in complying with this section, the company and every officer of the company who is in default shall be liable for each offence to a [class C fine].[b]

Amendments

a 5s converted to 60p and converted again to 76 cents by Council Regulation (EC) No 1103/97, No 974/98 and No 2866/98 and the Economic Monetary Union Act 1998, s 6.

b '£25' substituted for '£5' by C(A)A 1982, Sch 1 increased to £1,500 by CA 1990, s 240(7) as inserted by CLEA 2001, s 104(c), and converted to €1,904.61 by Council Regulation (EC) No 1103/97, No 974/98 and No 2866/98 and the Economic Monetary Union Act 1998, s 6) with effect from 1 October 2001: Company Law Enforcement Act 2001 (Commencement) (No 2) Order 2001 (SI 438/2001)); the above being implicitly substituted, by Fines Act 2010, s 6, for a fine not exceeding the aforesaid amount. A class C fine currently means a fine not exceeding €2,500.

---

30 Issued copies of memorandum to embody alterations

(1) Where an alteration is made in the memorandum of a company, every copy of the memorandum issued after the date of the alteration shall be in accordance with the alteration.

(2) If, where any such alteration has been made, the company at any time after the date of the alteration issues to any person any copy of the memorandum which is not in accordance with the alteration, it shall be liable to a [class C fine],[a] and every officer of the company who is in default shall be liable to the like penalty.

Amendments

a '£125' substituted for '£25' by C(A)A 1982, Sch 1, increased to £1,500 by CA 1990, s 240(7) as inserted by CLEA 2001, s 104(c) and converted to €1,904.61 by Council Regulations (EC) No 1103/97, No 974/98 and No 2866/98 and the Economic and Monetary Union Act 1998, s 6 with effect from 1 October 2001: Company Law Enforcement Act 2001 (Commencement) (No 2) Order 2001 (SI 438/2001); the above being implicitly substituted, by Fines Act 2010, s 6, for a fine not exceeding the aforesaid amount. A class C fine currently means a fine not exceeding €2,500.

Membership of company

31 Definition of member

(1) The subscribers of the memorandum of a company shall be deemed to have agreed to become members of the company, and, on its registration, shall be entered as members in its register of members.

(2) Every other person who agrees to become a member of a company, and whose name is entered in its register of members, shall be a member of the company.

32 Membership of holding company

(1) Subject to the provisions of this section, a body corporate cannot be a member of a company which is its holding company, and any allotment or transfer of shares in a company to its subsidiary shall be void.

(2) Nothing in this section shall apply where the subsidiary is concerned as personal representative, or where it is concerned as trustee, unless the holding company or a subsidiary thereof is beneficially interested under the trust and is not so interested only by way of security for the purposes of a transaction entered into by it in the ordinary course of a business which includes the lending of money.

(3) This section shall not prevent a subsidiary which on the 5th day of May, 1959, was a member of its holding company, from continuing to be a member.

(4) This section shall not prevent a company which at the date on which it becomes a subsidiary of another company is a member of that other company, from continuing to be a member.

(5) This section shall not prevent a subsidiary which is a member of its holding company from accepting and holding further shares in the capital of its holding company if such further shares are allotted to it in consequence of a capitalisation by such holding company and if the terms of such capitalisation are such that the subsidiary is not thereby involved in any obligation to make any payment or to give other consideration for such further shares.

(6) Subject to subsection (2), a subsidiary which is a member of its holding company shall have no right to vote at meetings of the holding company or any class of members thereof.

(7) Subject to subsection (2), this section shall apply in relation to a nominee for a body corporate which is a subsidiary, as if references therein to such a body corporate included references to a nominee for it.

(8) Where a holding company makes an offer of shares to its members it may sell, on behalf of a subsidiary, any such shares which the subsidiary could, but for this section, have taken by virtue of shares already held by it in the holding company, and pay the proceeds of sale to the subsidiary.

(9) In relation to a company limited by guarantee, or unlimited, which is a holding company, the reference in this section to shares, whether or not it has a share capital, shall be construed as including a reference to the interests of its members as such, whatever the form of that interest.

Private companies

33 Meaning of 'private company'

[(1) For the purposes of this Act, 'private company' means a company which has a share capital and which, by its articles—

(a) restricts the right to transfer its shares, and

(b) limits the number of its members to 99 or fewer persons, not including persons who are in the employment of the company and persons who, having been formerly in the employment of the company, were, while in that employment, and have continued after the determination of that employment to be, members of the company, and

(c) prohibits any invitation or offer to the public to subscribe for any shares, debentures or other securities of the company.

(2) A provision of a company's articles that prohibits any invitation to the public to subscribe for any shares or debentures of the company shall be construed as a prohibition on any invitation or offer being made to the public to subscribe for any shares, debentures or other securities of the company.

(3) Where two or more persons hold one or more shares in a company jointly, they shall, for the purposes of this section, be treated as a single member.

(4) Subsections (5) and (6) shall apply for the purposes of—

(a) subsection (1)(c), and

(b) unless a contrary intention appears in the company's articles, any provision of a company's articles which—

(i) corresponds in its terms to those of subsection (1)(c),

(ii) incorporates by reference the terms of subsection (1)(c), or

(iii) has the same legal effect as subsection (1)(c) even though its terms are not identical to those of sub section (1)(c) (and the cases to which this subparagraph applies include the case where subsection (2) applies to the interpretation of the provision).

(5) Each of the following offers of debentures by a company (wheresoever made) shall not be regarded as falling within subsection (1)(c) or the provision of a company's articles referred to in subsection (4)(b), namely—

(a) an offer of debentures addressed solely to qualified investors,

(b) an offer of debentures addressed to fewer than 100 persons, other than qualified investors,

(c) an offer of debentures addressed to investors where the minimum consideration payable pursuant to the offer is at least €50,000 per investor, for each separate offer,

(d) an offer of debentures whose denomination per unit amounts to at least €50,000,

(e) an offer of debentures where the offer expressly limits the amount of the total consideration for the offer to less than €100,000,

(f) an offer of those classes of instruments which are normally dealt in on the money market (such as treasury bills, certificates of deposit and commercial papers) having a maturity of less than 12 months.

(6) The following offer of shares by a company (of any amount or wheresoever made) shall not be regarded as falling within subsection (1)(c) or the provision of a company's articles referred to in subsection (4)(b), namely an offer of shares addressed to—

(a) qualified investors, or

(b) 99 or fewer persons, or

(c) both qualified investors and 99 or fewer other persons.

(7) A word or expression that is used in this section and is also used in the Prospectus (Directive 2003/71/EC) Regulations 2005 (S.I. No. 324 of 2005) shall have in this section the same meaning as it has in those Regulations.

(8) For the purposes of subsection (7), the Regulations referred to in that subsection, shall have effect as if Regulation 8 were omitted therefrom.][a]

Amendments

a This section was substituted by IFCMPA 2006, s 7 with effect from 1 July 2005.[1]

1 IFCMPA 2006, s 2(3): CA 1963, s 33, as amended by IFCMPA 2006, s 7, is deemed to come into effect on 1 July 2005. This is the date on which Directive 2003/71/EC was implemented in Ireland by virtue of the Prospectus (Directive 2003/71/EC) Regulations 2005 (SI 324/2005) and IFCMPA 2005.

---

34 Consequences of default in complying with conditions constituting a company a private company

(1) Subject to subsection (2), where the articles of a company include the provisions which, under section 33, are required to be included in the articles of a company in order to constitute it a private company, but default is made in complying with any of those provisions, the company shall cease to be entitled to the privileges and exemptions conferred on private companies under section 36, paragraph (a) of subsection (4) of section 128, paragraph (d) of section 213, and subparagraph (i) of paragraph (a) of section 215, and thereupon, sections 36, 128, 213 and 215, shall apply to the company as if it were not a private company.

(2) The court, on being satisfied that the failure to comply with the conditions was accidental or due to inadvertence or to some other sufficient cause, or that, on other grounds, it is just and equitable to grant relief, may, on the application of the company, or any other person interested, and on such terms and conditions as seem to the court just and expedient, order that the company be relieved from the consequences referred to in subsection (1).

35 [Statement in lieu of prospectus to be delivered to registrar by company on ceasing to be a private company

(1) Subject to subsection (2), if a company, being a private company, alters its articles in such a manner that they no longer include the provisions which, under section 33, are required to be included in the articles of a company in order to constitute it a private company, the company shall cease to be a private company.

(2) The alteration referred to in subsection (1) shall not take effect unless the company has been re-registered as a public limited company in accordance with section 9 of the Companies (Amendment) Act, 1983 or as an unlimited public company in accordance with section 52 of that Act.

(3) Where an application is made to re-register a private company as an unlimited public company, there shall be delivered with the application for re-registration a statement in lieu of prospectus in the form and containing the particulars set out in Part I of the Second Schedule, and, in the cases mentioned in Part II of that Schedule, setting out the reports specified therein, and the said Parts I and II shall have effect subject to the provision contained in Part III of that Schedule.

(4) A statement in lieu of prospectus need not be delivered under subsection (3) if a prospectus relating to the company which complies, or is deemed by virtue of a certificate of exemption under section 45 to comply, with the Third Schedule, is issued and is delivered to the registrar of companies as required by section 47.

(5) Every statement in lieu of prospectus delivered under subsection (3) shall, where the persons making any such report as referred to in that subsection have made therein or have, without giving the reasons, indicated therein any such adjustments as are mentioned in paragraph 5 of Part III of the Second Schedule, have endorsed thereon or attached thereto a written statement signed by those persons, setting out the adjustments and giving the reasons therefor.

(6) If default is made in complying with subsection (2), (3) or (5), the company and every officer of the company who is in default shall be guilty of an offence and shall be liable on summary conviction to a [class C fine].[b]

(7) Where a statement in lieu of prospectus, delivered to the registrar under subsection (3) includes any untrue statement, any person who authorised the delivery of the statement in lieu of prospectus for registration shall be guilty of an offence and shall be liable—

(a) on conviction on indictment, to imprisonment for a term not exceeding 2 years or a fine not exceeding [€6,348.70],[c] or both, or

(b) on summary conviction, to imprisonment for a term not exceeding 6 months or a [class C fine][b] or both;

unless he proves either that the untrue statement was immaterial or that he had reasonable ground to believe and did, up to the time of the delivery for registration of the statement in lieu of prospectus, believe that the untrue statement was true.

(8) For the purposes of this section—

(a) a statement included in a statement in lieu of prospectus shall be deemed to be untrue if it is misleading in the form and context in which it is included, and

(b) a statement shall be deemed to be included in a statement in lieu of prospectus if it is contained therein or in any report or memorandum appearing on the face thereof, or by reference incorporated therein.][a]

Amendments

a CA 1963, s 35 substituted by C(A)A 1983, Sch 1, para 6.

b Fines increased from £500 to £1,500 by CA 1990, s 240(7) as inserted by CLEA 2001, s 104(c) and converted to €1,904.61 by Council Regulations (EC) No 1103/97, No 974/98 and No 2866/98 and the Economic and Monetary Union Act 1998, s 6; the above being implicitly substituted, by Fines Act 2010, s 6, for a fine not exceeding the aforesaid amount. A class C fine currently means a fine not exceeding €2,500.

c £2,500 converted to €3,174.35 by Council Regulations (EC) No 1103/97, No 974/98 and No 2866/98 and the Economic and Monetary Union Act 1998, s 6, and multiplied by a multiplier of 2 pursuant to Fines Act 2010, s 9.

Reduction of Number of Members below Legal Minimum

36 Members severally liable for debts where business carried on with fewer than seven, or in case of private company [or an investment company (within the meaning of Part XIII of the Companies Act, 1990)][a], two members

If at any time the number of members of a company is reduced, in the case of a private company [or an investment company (within the meaning of Part XIII of the Companies Act, 1990)][a], below two, or, in the case of any other company, below seven, and it carries on business for more than 6 months while the number is so reduced, every person who is a member of the company during the time that it so carries on business after those 6 months and knows that it is carrying on business with fewer than two members, or seven members, as the case may be, shall be severally liable for the payment of the whole debts of the company contracted during that time, and may be severally sued therefor.

Amendments

a 'or an investment company (within the meaning of Part XIII of the Companies Act, 1990)' inserted by CA 1990, s 260(1) which was substituted by C(A)(No 2) 1999, s 54 with effect from 21 December 1999.[1]

[1] Companies (Amendment) (No 2) Act 1999 (Commencement) Order 1999 (SI 406/1999).

Contracts, Deeds and Powers of Attorney

37 Pre-incorporation contracts

(1) Any contract or other transaction purporting to be entered into by a company prior to its formation or by any person on behalf of the company prior to its formation may be ratified by the company after its formation and thereupon the company shall become bound by it and entitled to the benefit thereof as if it had been in existence at the date of such contract or other transaction and had been a party thereto.

(2) Prior to ratification by the company the person or persons who purported to act in the name or on behalf of the company shall in the absence of express agreement to the contrary be personally bound by the contract or other transaction and entitled to the benefit thereof.

(3) This section shall not apply to a company incorporated before the operative date.

38 Form of contracts

(1) Contracts on behalf of a company may be made as follows:

(a) a contract which if made between private persons would be by law required to be in writing and to be under seal, may be made on behalf of the company in writing under the common seal of the company;

(b) a contract which if made between private persons would be by law required to be in writing, signed by the parties to be charged therewith, may be made on behalf of the company in writing, signed by any person acting under its authority, express or implied;

(c) a contract which if made between private persons would by law be valid although made by parol only, and not reduced into writing may be made by parol on behalf of the company by any person acting under its authority, express or implied.

(2) A contract made according to this section shall bind the company and its successors and all other parties thereto.

(3) A contract made according to this section may be varied or discharged in the same manner in which it is authorised by this section to be made.

39 Bills of exchange and promissory notes

A bill of exchange or promissory note shall be deemed to have been made, accepted or endorsed on behalf of a company, if made, accepted or endorsed in the name of or by or on behalf or on account of, the company by any person acting under its authority.

40 Execution of deeds outside the State

(1) A company may, by writing under its common seal, empower any person, either generally or in respect of any specified matters, as its attorney, to execute deeds on its behalf in any place outside the State.

(2) A deed signed by such attorney on behalf of the company and under his seal shall bind the company and have the same effect as if it were under its common seal.

41 Power for company to have official seal for use abroad

(1) A company whose objects require or comprise the transaction of business outside the State may, if authorised by its articles, have for use in any territory, district or place not situate in the State, an official seal which shall be a facsimile of the common seal of the company with the addition on its face of the name of every territory, district or place where it is to be used.

(2) A deed or other document to which an official seal is duly affixed shall bind the company as if it had been sealed with the common seal of the company.

(3) A company having an official seal for use in any such territory, district or place, may, by writing under its common seal, authorise any person appointed for the purpose in that territory, district or place to affix the official seal to any deed or other document to which the company is party in that territory, district or place.

(4) The authority of any such agent shall, as between the company and any person dealing with the agent, continue during the period, if any, mentioned in the instrument conferring the authority, or, if no period is there mentioned, then until the notice of

revocation or determination of the agent's authority has been given to the person dealing with him.

(5) The person affixing any such official seal shall, by writing under his hand, certify on the deed or other instrument to which the seal is affixed the date on which and the place at which it is affixed.

Authentication of Documents

42 Authentication of documents

A document or proceeding requiring authentication by a company may be signed by a director, secretary or other authorised officer of the company, and need not be under its common seal.

PART III

SHARE CAPITAL AND DEBENTURES

Prospectus

43 Dating of prospectus

[...][a]

Amendments

a Section repealed by IFCMPA 2005, s 40(1)(a).

44 Matters to be stated and reports to be set out in prospectus

[...][a]

Amendments

a Section repealed by IFCMPA 2005, s 40(1)(a).

45 Exclusion of section 44 and relaxation of Third Schedule in case of certain prospectuses

[...][a]

Amendments

a Section repealed by IFCMPA 2005, s 40(1)(a).

46 Expert's consent to issue of prospectus containing statement by him

[...][a]

Amendments

a Section repealed by IFCMPA 2005, s 40(1)(a).

47 Registration of prospectus

[...][a]

Amendments

a Section repealed by IFCMPA 2005, s 40(1)(a).

48 Restriction on alteration of terms mentioned in prospectus or statement in lieu of prospectus

[...][a]

Amendments

a CA 1963, s 48 repealed by C(A)A 1983 Sch 3.

49 Civil liability for mis-statements in prospectus

[...][a]

Amendments

a Section repealed by IFCMPA 2005, s 40(1)(a).

50 Criminal liability for mis-statements in prospectus

[...][a]

Amendments

a Section repealed by IFCMPA 2005, s 40(1)(a).

51 Document containing offer of shares or debentures for sale deemed to be a prospectus

[...][a]

Amendments

a Section repealed by IFCMPA 2005, s 40(1)(a).

52 Interpretation of provisions relating to prospectuses

[...][a]

Amendments

a Section repealed by IFCMPA 2005, s 40(1)(a).

Allotment

53 Minimum subscription and amount payable on application

[(1) Where a prospectus states the minimum amount which, in the opinion of the directors, must be raised from an issue of shares and that no allotment shall be made of any of those shares unless that minimum amount has been subscribed and the sum payable on application for the amount so stated has been paid up, then no such allotment shall be made unless that minimum amount has been subscribed and the said sum so payable has been paid up.][a]

(2) The amount so stated in the prospectus shall be reckoned exclusively of any amount payable otherwise than in cash and is in this Act referred to as 'the minimum subscription'.

(3) [Except in the case of a public limited company the amount payable][b] on application on each share shall not be less than 5 per cent. of the nominal amount of the share.

(4) If the conditions aforesaid have not been complied with on the expiration of 40 days after the first issue of the prospectus, all money received from applicants for shares shall be forthwith repaid to them without interest, and, if any such money is not so repaid within 48 days after the issue of the prospectus, the directors of the company shall be jointly and severally liable to repay that money with interest at the rate of 5 per cent. per annum from the expiration of the forty-eighth day, so however that a director shall not be liable if he proves that the default in the repayment of the money was not due to any misconduct or negligence on his part.

(5) Any condition requiring or binding any applicant for shares to waive compliance with any requirement of this section shall be void.

(6) This section, except subsection (3) thereof, shall not apply to any allotment of shares subsequent to the first allotment of shares offered to the public for subscription.

Amendments

a Sub-s (1) substituted by IFCMPA 2005, s 53.

b Words substituted by C(A)A 1983, Sch 1, para 7.

---

54 Prohibition of allotment in certain cases unless statement in lieu of prospectus delivered to registrar

[...][a]

Amendments

a Section repealed by IFCMPA 2005, s 40(1)(a).

---

55 Effect of irregular allotment

[(1) An allotment made by a company to an applicant in contravention of sections 53 [...][b], shall be voidable at the instance of the applicant within one month after the date of the allotment, and not later, and shall be so voidable notwithstanding that the company is in the course of being wound up.][a]

(2) Where an allotment is avoided under this section the company shall within one month thereafter deliver to the registrar of companies for registration a notice to that effect, and subsections (3) and (4) of section 58, shall apply in relation to this subsection as they apply in relation to that section.

(3) If any director of a company knowingly contravenes, or permits or authorises the contravention of, any of the provisions of [section 53][b] with respect to allotment, he shall be liable to compensate the company and the allottee respectively for any loss, damages or costs which the company or allottee may have sustained or incurred thereby, so however that proceedings to recover any such loss, damages or costs shall not be commenced after the expiration of 2 years from the date of the allotment.

Amendments

a CA 1963, s 55(1) substituted by C(A)A 1983, Sch 1, para 9.

b Reference to section 54 removed by IFCMPA 2005, s 54.

---

56 Applications for, and allotment of, shares and debentures

[...][a]

Amendments

a Section repealed by IFCMPA 2005, s 40(1)(a).

---

57 Allotment of shares and debentures to be dealt in on stock exchange

(1) Where a prospectus, whether issued generally or not, states that application has been or will be made for permission for the [securities][a] offered thereby to be dealt in on any stock exchange [or regulated market],[b] any allotment made on an application in pursuance of the prospectus shall, whenever made, be void if the permission has not been applied for before the third day after the first issue of the prospectus or if the permission has not been granted within 6 weeks from the date of the closing of the subscription lists.

(2) Where the permission has not been applied for as aforesaid or has not been granted, the company shall forthwith repay without interest all money received from applicants in pursuance of the prospectus, and, if any such money is not repaid within 8 days after the company becomes liable to repay it, the directors of the company shall be jointly and severally liable to repay that money with interest at the rate of 5 per cent. per annum from the expiration of the eighth day, so however that a director shall not be liable if he proves that the default in the repayment of the money was not due to any misconduct or negligence on his part.

(3) All money received as aforesaid shall be kept in a separate bank account so long as the company may become liable to repay it under subsection (2); and, if default is made in complying with this subsection, the company and every officer of the company who is in default shall be [guilty of an offence and liable to a [class C fine][c]].[d]

(4) Any condition requiring or binding any applicant for [securities][a] to waive compliance with any requirement of this section shall be void.

(5) This section shall have effect—

(a) in relation to any [securities][a] agreed to be taken by a person underwriting an offer thereof by a prospectus as if he had applied therefor in pursuance of the prospectus, and

(b) in relation to a prospectus offering [securities][a] for sale with the following modifications,—

(i) references to sale shall be substituted for references to allotment,

(ii) the persons by whom the offer is made, and not the company, shall be liable under subsection (2) to repay money received from applicants, and references to the company's liability under that subsection shall be construed accordingly, and

(iii) for the reference in subsection (3) to the company and every officer of the company who is in default there shall be substituted a reference to any person by or through whom the offer is made and who knowingly and wilfully authorises or permits the default.

(6) In reckoning for the purposes of this section the third day after another day, any intervening day which is a Saturday or Sunday or which is a bank holiday shall be disregarded and if the third day (as so reckoned) is itself a Saturday or Sunday or such a bank holiday there shall for the said purposes be substituted the first day thereafter which is none of them.

[(7) The provisions of this section shall not apply in relation to an allotment of non-equity securities.][e]

Amendments

a Substitution of 'securities' for 'shares or debentures': IFCMPA 2005, s 55(a).

b Insertion of reference to 'regulated market': IFCMPA 2005, s 55(b).

c '£500' substituted for '£100' by C(A)A 1982, Sch 1 and increased to £1,500 by CA 1990, s 240(7) as inserted by CLEA 2001, s 104(c) and converted to €1,904.61 by Council Regulations (EC) No 1103/97, No 974/98 and No 2866/98 and the Economic and Monetary Union Act 1998, s 6; the above being implicitly substituted, by Fines Act 2010, s 6, for a fine not exceeding the aforesaid amount. A class C fine currently means a fine not exceeding €2,500.

d CA 1963, s 57(3) words 'shall be guilty of an offence and liable to a fine' substituted for 'shall be liable to a fine' by C(A&A)A 2003, Sch 2, Item No 1.

e Sub-s (7) inserted by IFCMPA 2005, s 55(c).

---

58 Return as to allotments

(1) Whenever a company limited by shares or a company limited by guarantee and having a share capital makes any allotment of its shares, the company shall within one month thereafter deliver to the registrar of companies for registration—

(a) a return of the allotments, stating the number and nominal amount of the shares comprised in the allotment, the names, addresses [...][a] of the allottees and the amount, if any, paid or due and payable on each share; and

(b) in the case of shares allotted as fully or partly paid up otherwise than in cash, a contract in writing constituting the title of the allottee to the allotment together with any contract of sale, or for services or other consideration in respect of which that allotment was made, such contracts being duly stamped, and a return stating the number and nominal amount of shares so allotted, the extent to which they are to be treated as paid up, and the consideration for which they have been allotted,

provided that, where shares are allotted to the members of a company on a capitalisation or provisionally allotted on a rights issue, it shall not be necessary to make a return of the particular allottees, notwithstanding that in either case there may be a right of renunciation.

(2) Where such a contract as above mentioned is not reduced to writing, the company shall within one month after the allotment deliver to the registrar of companies for registration the prescribed particulars of the contract stamped with the same stamp duty as would have been payable if the contract had been reduced to writing, and those particulars shall be deemed to be an instrument within the meaning of the Stamp Act, 1891, and the registrar may, as a condition of filing the particulars, require that the duty payable thereon be adjudicated under section 12 of that Act.

(3) If default is made in complying with this section, every officer of the company who is in default [shall be guilty of an offence and liable to a [class C fine][b]].[c]

(4) In case of default in delivering to the registrar of companies within one month after the allotment any document required to be delivered by this section, the company, or any officer liable for the default, may apply to the court for relief, and the court, if satisfied that the omission to deliver the document was accidental or due to inadvertence or that it is just and equitable to grant relief, may make an order extending the time for the delivery of the document for such period as the court may think proper.

Amendments

a Words 'and occupations' deleted by C(A)A 1963, s 19.

b CA 1963, s 58(3) words 'shall be guilty of an offence and liable to a fine' substituted for 'shall be liable to a fine' by C(A&A)A 2003, Sch 2, Item No 1.

c '£500' substituted for '£100' by C(A)A 1982, Sch 1, increased to £1,500 by CA 1990, s 240(7) as inserted by CLEA 2001, s 104(c) and converted to €1,904.61 by Council Regulations (EC) No 1103/97, No 974/98 and No 2866/98 and the Economic and Monetary Union Act 1998, s 6; the above being implicitly substituted, by Fines Act 2010, s 6, for a fine not exceeding the aforesaid amount. A class C fine currently means a fine not exceeding €2,500.

Commissions and Discounts and Financial Assistance for Purchase of Shares

59 Power to pay certain commissions, and prohibition of payment of all other commissions and discounts

[...][a]

Amendments

a Section repealed by IFCMPA 2005, s 40(1)(a).

60 Giving of financial assistance by a company for the purchase of its shares

(1) Subject to subsections (2), (12) and (13), it shall not be lawful for a company to give, whether directly or indirectly, and whether by means of a loan, guarantee, the provision of security or otherwise, any financial assistance for the purpose of or in connection with a purchase or subscription made or to be made by any person of or for any shares in the company, or, where the company is a subsidiary company, in its holding company.

(2) Subsection (1) shall not apply to the giving of financial assistance by a company if—

(a) such financial assistance is given under the authority of a special resolution of the company passed not more than 12 months previously; and

(b) [the company has forwarded with each notice of the meeting at which the special resolution is to be considered, or, if the procedure referred to in subsection (6) is followed, the company has appended to the resolution, a copy of a statutory declaration which complies with subsections (3) and (4) and also delivers, within 21 days after the date on which the financial assistance was given, a copy of the declaration to the registrar of companies for registration.][a]

(3) The statutory declaration shall be made at a meeting of the directors held not more than 24 days before the said meeting and shall be made by the directors or, in the case of a company having more than two directors, by a majority of the directors.

(4) The statutory declaration shall state—

(a) the form which such assistance is to take;

(b) the persons to whom such assistance is to be given;

(c) the purpose for which the company intends those persons to use such assistance;

(d) that the declarants have made a full inquiry into the affairs of the company and that, having done so, they have formed the opinion that the company, having carried out the transaction whereby such assistance is to be given, will be able to pay its debts in full as they become due.

(5) Any director of a company making the statutory declaration without having reasonable grounds for the opinion that the company having carried out the transaction whereby such assistance is to be given will be able to pay its debts in full as they become due, [shall be guilty of an offence and liable to imprisonment for a period not exceeding 6 months or to a class C fine][b] or to both; and if the company is wound up within the period of 12 months after the making of the statutory declaration and its debts are not paid or provided for in full within the period of 12 months after the commencement of the winding up, it shall be presumed until the contrary is shown that the director did not have reasonable grounds for his opinion.

(6) [The special resolution referred to in subsection (1)(a) may be passed in accordance with section 141(8).][c]

(7) Unless all of the members of the company entitled to vote at general meetings of the company vote in favour of the special resolution, the transaction whereby such assistance is to be given shall not be carried out before the expiry of 30 days after such special resolution has been passed or, if an application under subsection (8) is made, until such application has been disposed of by the court.

(8) If application is made to the court in accordance with this section for the cancellation of the special resolution, such special resolution shall not have effect except to the extent to which it is confirmed by the court.

(9) Subject to subsection (10), an application under subsection (8) may be made by the holders of not less in the aggregate than 10 per cent. in nominal value of the company's issued share capital or any class thereof.

(10) An application shall not be made under subsection (8) by any person who has consented to or voted in favour of the special resolution.

(11) An application under subsection (8) must be made within 28 days after the date on which the special resolution was passed and may be made on behalf of the persons entitled to make the application by such one or more of their number as they may appoint in writing for the purpose.

[(12) Nothing in this section shall be taken to prohibit—

(a) the payment by a company of a dividend or making by it of any distribution out of profits of the company available for distribution;

(b) the discharge by a company of a liability lawfully incurred by it;

(c) the provision of finance or delivery of security to discharge, or effect what is commonly known as refinancing of, an existing loan or other liability or security in relation to that existing loan where the incurring of the existing loan or liability or the delivery of the existing security had occurred under the authority of a special resolution of the company passed in accordance with subsection (2);

(d) subject to subsection (13), where the lending of money is part of the ordinary business of the company, the lending of money by a company in the ordinary course of its business;

(e) subject to subsection (13), the provision by a company, in accordance with any scheme for the time being in force, of money for the purchase of, or subscription for, fully paid shares in the company or its holding company, being a purchase or subscription of or for shares to be held by or for the benefit of employees or former employees of the company or of any subsidiary of the company including any person who is or was a director holding a salaried employment or office in the company or any subsidiary of the company;

(f) subject to subsection (13), the making by a company of loans to persons, other than directors, bona fide in the employment of the company or any subsidiary of the company with a view to enabling those persons to purchase or subscribe for fully paid shares in the company or its holding company to be held by themselves as beneficial owners thereof;

(g) the making or giving by a company of one or more representations, warranties or indemnities to a person who has purchased or subscribed for, or proposes to purchase or subscribe for, shares in the company or its holding company for the purpose of or in connection with that purchase or subscription;

(h) the payment by a company of fees and expenses of the advisers of any subscriber for shares in the company or its holding company that are incurred in connection with that subscription;

(i) the incurring of expenses (including professional fees and expenses) by a company either or both—

(i) in the preparation and publication of a prospectus concerning any shares in the company or its holding company,

(ii) for the purpose of facilitating the admission of any shares in the company or its holding company to, or the continuance of a facility afforded to the company or its holding company for the trading of such shares on, a regulated market;

(j) the incurring of expenses by a company for the purpose of facilitating the admission of any shares in the company or its holding company to, or the continuance of a facility afforded to the company or its holding company for the trading of such shares on, a regulated market or other securities market (including the expense of preparation and publication of any documents required for that purpose by the laws of the jurisdiction in which that market is established);

(k) the incurring of any expenses by a company in order to ensure compliance by the company or its holding company with the Irish Takeover Panel Act 1997 or an instrument thereunder or any measures for the time being adopted by the State to implement Directive 2004/25/EC of the European Parliament and of the Council of 21 April 2004 on takeover bids (OJ L142, 30.4.2004, p. 12);

(l) the reimbursement by a company which is an offeree (within the meaning of the Irish Takeover Panel Act 1997) or by a subsidiary of such an offeree of expenses of an offeror (within the meaning of that Act) pursuant to an agreement approved by, or on terms approved by, the Irish Takeover Panel;

(m) in connection with an allotment of shares by a company or its holding company, the payment by the company of commissions not exceeding 10 per cent of the money received in respect of such allotment to intermediaries, and the payment by the company of professional fees;

(n) to the extent that provision of this kind is not authorised by paragraph (e) or (f), the provision of financial assistance by a holding company or a subsidiary of it in connection with the holding company or subsidiary purchasing or subscribing for shares in the holding company on behalf of—

(i) the present or former employees of the holding company or any subsidiary of it,

(ii) an employees' share scheme within the meaning of the Companies (Amendment) Act 1983, or

(iii) an employee share ownership trust referred to in section 519 of the Taxes Consolidation Act 1997.

(13) (a) A public limited company may, in accordance with paragraph (d), (e) or (f) of subsection (12), give financial assistance to any person only if the company's

net assets are not thereby reduced or, to the extent that those assets are thereby reduced, if the financial assistance is provided out of profits which are available for dividend.

(b) In this section 'net assets' means the aggregate of the company's assets less the aggregate of its liabilities; and 'liabilities' includes any provision (within the meaning of the Schedule to the Companies (Amendment) Act 1986) except to the extent that provision is taken into account in calculating the value of any asset to the company.][d]

(14) Any transaction in breach of this section shall be voidable at the instance of the company against any person (whether a party to the transaction or not) who had notice of the facts which constitute such breach.

(15) If a company acts in contravention of this section every officer of the company who is in default shall be liable;

(a) on conviction on indictment, to imprisonment for a term not exceeding [5][e] years or to a fine not exceeding [€6,348.70][f] or to both, or

(b) on summary conviction, to imprisonment for a term not exceeding 6 months or to a [class C fine][g] or to both.

[(15A) Subsections (2) to (11) shall not apply to a public limited company originally incorporated as such or to a company registered or re-registered as a public limited company under the Companies (Amendment) Act, 1983 unless a special resolution as provided under subsection (2) was passed before the company's application for registration or re-registration.][h]

[....][i]

[....][j]

(16) Nothing in this section shall prejudice the provisions of section 72.

Amendments

a CA 1963, s 60(2)(b) substituted by CLEA 2001, s 89(a).

b Words substituted by C(AA)A 2003, s 57 and Sch 2 with effect from 8 April 2004 (SI 132/2004); the above being implicitly substituted, by Fines Act 2010, s 6, for a fine not exceeding the aforesaid amount. A class C fine currently means a fine not exceeding €2,500.

c CA 1963, s 60(6) substituted by CLEA 2001, s 89(b).

d Sub-s (12) and (13) substituted by IFCMPA 2005, s 56(1).

e '5' substituted for '2' by CA 1990, s 240(8) as inserted by CLEA 2001, s 104(c).

f '£2,500' substituted for '£500' by C(A)A 1982, Sch 1 and converted to €3,174.35 by Council Regulations (EC) No 1103/97, No 974/98 and No 2866/98 and the Economic and Monetary Union Act 1998, s 6, and multiplied by a multiplier of 2 pursuant to Fines Act 2010, s 9.

g £100 increased to £1,500 by CA 1990, s 240(7) as inserted by CLEA 2001, s 104(c) and converted to €1,904.61 by Council Regulations (EC) No 1103/97, No 974/98 and No 2866/98 and the Economic and Monetary Union Act 1998, s 6; the above being implicitly substituted, by Fines Act 2010, s 6, for a fine not exceeding the aforesaid amount. A class C fine currently means a fine not exceeding €2,500.

h Sub-s (15A) inserted by C(A)A 1983, s 3 and commenced 13 October 1983 (SI 288/1983).

i Sub-s (15B) which was inserted by C(A)A 1983, s 3 was repealed by IFCMPA 2005, s 40 with effect from 1 July 2005.

j Sub-s (15C) which was inserted by C(A)A 1983, s 3 with effect from 13 October 1983 (SI 288/1983) was substituted by EC(IFRSMA)R 2005 with effect from 1 January 2005 but subsequently repealed by IFCMPA 2005, s 40 with effect from 1 July 2005 (SI 393/2005).

Construction of References to Offering Shares or Debentures to the Public

61 Construction of references to offering shares or debentures to the public

[...][a]

Amendments

a Section repealed by IFCMPA 2005, s 40(1)(a).

Issues of Shares at Premium and Discount and Redeemable Preference Shares

62 Application of premiums received on issue of shares

(1) Where a company issues shares at a premium, whether for cash or otherwise, a sum equal to the aggregate amount or value of the premiums on those shares shall be transferred to an account, to be called 'the share premium account', and the provisions of this Act relating to the reduction of the share capital of a company shall, except as provided in this section [and section 207(2) of the Companies Act, 1990],[a] apply as if the share premium account were paid up share capital of the company.

(2) The share premium account may, notwithstanding anything in subsection (1) be applied by the company in paying up unissued shares of the company (other than redeemable [...][b] shares) [to be allotted][c] to members of the company as fully paid bonus shares, in writing off

(a) the preliminary expenses of the company, or

(b) the expenses of, or the commission paid or discount allowed on, any issue of shares or debentures of the company;

or in providing for the premium payable on redemption of any redeemable preference shares [in pursuance of section 220 of the Companies Act, 1990],[d] or of any debentures of the company.

(3) Where a company has before the operative date issued any shares at a premium, this section shall apply as if the shares had been issued after the operative date, so however that any part of the premiums which has been so applied that it does not at the operative date form an identifiable part of the company's reserves within the meaning of the Sixth Schedule shall be disregarded in determining the sum to be included in the share premium account.

Amendments

a Words inserted by CA 1990, s 231, with effect from 1 July 1991 (SI 117/1991).

b Word deleted by CA 1990, s 231, with effect from 1 July 1991 (SI 117/1991).

c Words substituted by C(A)A 1983, s 3, with effect from 13 October 1983 (SI 288/1983).

d Words inserted by CA 1990, s 231, with effect from 1 July 1991 (SI 117/1991).

63 Power to issue shares at a discount

[...][a]

Amendments

a CA 1963, s 63 repealed by C(A)A 1983, Sch 3.

64 Power to issue redeemable preference shares

[(1) Subject to the provisions of this section, a company limited by shares may, if so authorised by its articles, issue preference shares which are, or at the option of the company are to be liable, to be redeemed, so, however, that—

(a) no such shares shall be redeemed except out of profits of the company which would otherwise be available for dividend or out of the proceeds of a fresh issue of shares made for the purposes of the redemption;

(b) no such shares shall be redeemed unless they are fully paid;

[(c) the premium, if any, payable on redemption must have been provided for out of the profits of the company which would otherwise be available for dividend or out of the company's share premium account before the shares are redeemed;][b]

(d) where any such shares are redeemed otherwise than out of the proceeds of a fresh issue, there shall out of profits which would otherwise have been available for dividend be transferred to a reserve fund to be called 'the capital redemption reserve fund', a sum equal to the nominal amount of the shares redeemed and the provisions of this Act relating to the reduction of the share capital of a company shall, except as provided in this section, apply as if the capital redemption reserve fund were paid up share capital of the company.

(2) Subject to the provisions of this section, the redemption of preference shares thereunder may be effected on such terms and in such manner as may be provided by the articles of the company.

(3) The redemption of preference shares under this section by a company shall not be taken as reducing the amount of the company's authorised share capital.

(4) Subject to subsection (5), where in pursuance of this section a company has redeemed or is about to redeem any preference shares, it shall have power to issue shares up to the nominal amount of the shares redeemed or to be redeemed as if those shares had never been issued, [and, accordingly, for the purposes of section 68 of the Finance Act, 1973, shares issued by a company in place of shares redeemed under this section shall constitute a chargeable transaction if, but only if, the actual value of the shares so issued exceeds the actual value of the preference shares redeemed at the date of their redemption and, where the issue of the shares does constitute a chargeable transaction for those purposes, the amount on which stamp duty on the relevant statement relating to that transaction is chargeable under section 69 of the Finance Act, 1973, shall be the difference between—

(a) the amount on which the duty would be so chargeable if the shares had not been issued in place of shares redeemed under this section, and

(b) the value of the shares redeemed at the date of their redemption.][c]

(5) Where new shares are issued before the redemption of the old shares, the new shares shall not, so far as relates to stamp duty, be deemed to have been issued in pursuance of subsection (4) unless the old shares are redeemed within one month after issue of the new shares.

(6) The capital redemption reserve fund may, notwithstanding anything in this section, be applied by the company in paying up unissued shares of the company (other than redeemable preference shares) [to be allotted][d] to members of the company as fully paid bonus shares.][a]

Amendments

a Repealed by CA 1990, s 220 but has some application to preference shares issued prior to commencement of CA 1990, Pt XI.

b CA 1963, s 64(1)(c) substituted by C(A)A 1983, Sch 1 para 12(a).

c Words substituted by FA 1990, s 119.

d CA 1963, s 64(6) substituted by C(A)A 1983, Sch 1 para 12(b).

---

65 Power to redeem preference shares issued before 5th May, 1959

(1) Subject to the provisions of this section, a company limited by shares may, if so authorised by its articles, redeem any preference shares issued by it before the 5th day of May, 1959, so, however, that—

(a) no such shares shall be redeemed unless they are fully paid;

(b) no such shares shall be redeemed except out of profits of the company which would otherwise be available for dividend or out of the proceeds of a fresh issue of shares made for the purposes of the redemption;

(c) no such shares shall be redeemed at a sum greater than the issue price of such shares;

(d) the redemption of such shares and the terms and the manner thereof must have been authorised by a special resolution of the company;

(e) notice of the meeting at which the special resolution referred to in paragraph (d) is to be proposed and a copy of the said resolution must be published in [the Companies Registration Office Gazette][a] and in at least one daily newspaper circulating in the district in which the registered office of the company is situated not less than 14 days and not more than 30 days before the date of the meeting;

(f) no holder of such shares shall be obliged to accept redemption thereof;

(g) in the case of a private company the redemption must have been sanctioned by the court.

(2) The powers conferred by this section may be availed of only by means of an offer made to all the holders of the preference shares concerned.

(3) Where any such shares are redeemed otherwise than out of the proceeds of a fresh issue, there shall out of profits which would otherwise have been available for dividend be transferred to a reserve fund to be called 'the capital redemption reserve fund' a sum equal to the nominal amount of the shares redeemed, and the provisions of this Act relating to the reduction of the share capital of a company shall, except as provided in this section, apply as if the capital redemption reserve fund were paid up share capital of the company.

(4) Subject to the provisions of this section, the redemption of preference shares under this section may be effected on such terms and in such manner as may be provided by the special resolution referred to in paragraph (d) of subsection (1).

(5) The redemption of preference shares under this section by a company shall not be taken as reducing the amount of the company's authorised share capital.

(6) Subject to subsection (7), where in pursuance of this section a company has redeemed or is about to redeem any preference shares, it shall have power to issue shares up to the nominal amount of the shares redeemed or to be redeemed as if those shares had never been issued, and accordingly the share capital of the company shall not for the purposes of any enactments relating to stamp duty be deemed to be increased by the issue of shares in pursuance of this subsection.

(7) Where new shares are issued before the redemption of the old shares, the new shares shall not, so far as relates to stamp duty, be deemed to have been issued in pursuance of subsection (6) unless the old shares are redeemed within one month after the issue of the new shares.

(8) The capital redemption reserve fund may, notwithstanding anything in this section, be applied by the company in paying up unissued shares of the company (other than redeemable preference shares) to be issued to members of the company as fully paid bonus shares.

Amendments

a 'the Companies Registration Office Gazette' substituted for '*Iris Oifigiúil*' by IFCMPA 2005, s 72.

Miscellaneous Provisions as to Share Capital

66 Power of company to arrange for different amounts being paid on shares

A company, if so authorised by it articles, may do any one or more of the following things—

(a) make arrangements on the issue of shares for a difference between the shareholders in the amounts and times of payment of calls on their shares;

(b) accept from any member the whole or a part of the amount remaining unpaid on any shares held by him, although no part of that amount has been called up;

(c) pay a dividend in proportion to the amount paid up on each share where a larger amount is paid up on some shares than on others.

67 Reserve liability of limited company

A limited company may be special resolution determine that any portion of its share capital which has not been already called up shall not be capable of being called up except in the event and for the purposes of the company being wound up, and thereupon that portion of its share capital shall not be capable of being called up except in the event and for the purposes aforesaid.

68 Power of company to alter its share capital

(1) A company limited by shares or a company limited by guarantee and having a share capital, if so authorised by its articles, may in general meeting alter the conditions of its memorandum as follows, that is, it may—

(a) increase its share capital by new shares of such amount as it thinks expedient;

(b) consolidate and divide all or any of its share capital into shares of larger amount than its existing shares;

(c) convert all or any of its paid up shares into stock, and re-convert that stock into paid up shares of any denominations;

(d) subdivide its shares, or any of them, into shares of smaller amount than is fixed by the memorandum, so however, that in the subdivision the proportion between the amount paid and the amount, if any, unpaid on each reduced share shall be the same as it was in the case of the share from which the reduced share is derived;

(e) cancel shares which, at the date of the passing of the resolution in that behalf, have not been taken or agreed to be taken by any person, and diminish the amount of its share capital by the amount of the shares so cancelled.

(2) A cancellation of shares in pursuance of this section shall not be deemed to be a reduction of share capital within the meaning of this Act.

69 Notice to registrar of certain alterations in share capital

(1) If a company having a share capital has—

(a) consolidated and divided its share capital into shares of larger amount than its existing shares; or

(b) converted any shares into stock; or

(c) reconverted stock into shares; or

(d) subdivided its shares or any of them; or

(e) redeemed any redeemable preference shares; or

(f) redeemed any preference shares; or

(g) cancelled any shares, otherwise than in connection with a reduction of share capital under section 72:

it shall, within one month after so doing, give notice thereof to the registrar of companies, specifying, as the case may be, the shares consolidated, divided, converted, subdivided, redeemed or cancelled, or the stock reconverted.

(2) If default is made in complying with this section, the company and every officer of the company who is in default [shall be guilty of an offence and liable to a [class C fine][a]].[b]

Amendments

a '£250' substituted for '£50' by C(A)A 1982, Sch 1, increased to £1,500 by CA 1990, s 240(7) as inserted by CLEA 2001, s 104(c) and converted to €1,904.61 by Council Regulations (EC) No 1103/97, No 974/98 and No 2866/98 and the Economic and Monetary Union Act 1998, s 6; the above being implicitly substituted, by Fines Act 2010, s 6, for a fine not exceeding the aforesaid amount. A class C fine currently means a fine not exceeding €2,500.

b CA 1963, s 69(2) words 'shall be guilty of an offence and liable to a fine' substituted for 'shall be liable to a fine' by C(AA)A 2003, Sch 2, Item No 1.

70 Notice of increase of share capital

(1) Where a company, having a share capital, whether its shares have or have not been converted into stock, has increased its share capital above the registered capital, it shall, within 15 days after the passing of the resolution increasing its share capital, give to the registrar of companies notice of the increase, and the registrar shall record the increase.

(2) The notice to be given as aforesaid shall include such particulars as may be prescribed with respect to the classes of shares affected, and the conditions subject to which the new shares have been or are to be issued.

(3) If default is made in complying with this section, the company and every officer of the company who is in default [shall be guilty of an offence and liable to a [class C fine][a]].[b]

Amendments

a '£250' substituted for '£50' by C(A)A 1982, Sch 11, increased to £1,500 by CA 1990, s 240(7) as inserted by CLEA 2001, s 104(c) and converted to €1,904.61 by Council Regulations (EC) No 1103/97, No 974/98 and No 2866/98 and the Economic and Monetary Union Act 1998, s 6; the above being implicitly substituted, by Fines Act 2010, s 6, for a fine not exceeding the aforesaid amount. A class C fine currently means a fine not exceeding €2,500.

b CA 1963, s 70(3) words 'shall be guilty of an offence and liable to a fine' substituted for 'shall be liable to a fine by C(AA)A 2003, Sch 2, Item No 1.

71 Power of unlimited company to provide for reserve share capital on re-registration

An unlimited company having a share capital may, by its resolution for registration as a limited company in pursuance of this Act, do either or both of the following things:

(a) increase the nominal amount of its share capital by increasing the nominal amount of each of its shares, but subject to the condition that no part of the increased capital shall be capable of being called up, except in the event and for the purposes of the company being wound up;

(b) provide that a specified portion of its uncalled share capital shall not be capable of being called up except in the event and for the purposes of the company being wound up.

Reduction of share capital

72 Power of company to reduce its share capital

(1) Except in so far as this Act expressly permits, it shall not be lawful for a company limited by shares or a company limited by guarantee and having a share capital [...][a] to reduce its share capital in any way.

(2) Subject to confirmation by the court, a company limited by shares or a company limited by guarantee and having a share capital, may, if so authorised by its articles, by special resolution reduce its share capital in any way and, in particular, without prejudice to the generality of the foregoing power, may—

(a) extinguish or reduce the liability on any of its shares in respect of share capital not paid up; or

(b) either with or without extinguishing or reducing liability on any of its shares, cancel any paid up share capital which is lost or unrepresented by available assets; or

(c) either with or without extinguishing or reducing liability on any of its shares, pay off any paid up share capital which is in excess of the wants of the company;

and may, if and so far as is necessary, alter its memorandum by reducing the amount of its share capital and of its shares accordingly.

(3) A special resolution under this section is, in this Act, referred to as 'a resolution for reducing share capital'.

Amendments

a Words deleted by CA 1990, s 231.

---

73 Application to court for confirming order, objections by creditors and settlement of list of objecting creditors

(1) Where a company has passed a resolution for reducing share capital, it may apply to the court for an order confirming the reduction.

(2) Where the proposed reduction of share capital involves either diminution of liability in respect of unpaid share capital, or the payment to any shareholder of any paid up share capital, and in any other case if the court so directs, the following provisions shall have effect, subject nevertheless to subsection (3);

[(a) in the case of a public limited company—

(i) every creditor of the company who—

(I) at the date fixed by the court, is entitled to a debt or claim that, if that date were the commencement of the winding up of the company, would be admissible in proof against the company, and

(II) can credibly demonstrate that the proposed reduction in the share capital would be likely to put the satisfaction of that debt or claim at risk, and that no adequate safe-guards have been obtained from the company, is entitled to object to the reduction, and

(ii) the court shall settle a list of creditors entitled to object, and for that purpose may publish notices fixing a day or days within which creditors are to claim to be entered on the list or are to be excluded from the right of objecting to the reduction of capital;

(b) in the case of any other company—

(i) every creditor of the company who, at the date fixed by the court, is entitled to any debt or claim that, if that date were the commencement of the winding up of the company, would be admissible in proof against the company is entitled to object to the reduction;

(ii) the court shall settle a list of creditors so entitled to object, and for that purpose shall ascertain, as far as possible without requiring an application from any creditor, the names of those creditors and the nature and amount of their debts or claims, and may publish notices fixing a day or days within which creditors not entered on the list are to claim to be so entered or are to be excluded from the right of objecting to the reduction;][a]

(c) [in either case][b] where a creditor entered on the list whose debt or claim is not discharged or has not determined does not consent to the reduction, the court may, if it thinks fit, dispense with the consent of that creditor, on the company securing payment of his debt or claim by appropriating, as the court may direct, the following amount:–

(i) if the company admits the full amount of the debt or claim, or, though not admitting it, is willing to provide for it, then the full amount of the debt or claim;

(ii) if the company does not admit and is not willing to provide for the full amount of the debt or claim, or, if the amount is contingent or not ascertained, then an amount fixed by the court after the like inquiry and adjudication as if the company were being wound up by the court.

(3) Where a proposed reduction of share capital involve either the diminution of any liability in respect of unpaid share capital or the payment to any shareholder of any paid up share capital, the court may, if, having regard to any special circumstances of the case, it thinks proper so to do, direct that subsection (2) shall not apply as regards any class or any classes of creditors.

Amendments

a CA 1963, s 73(2)(a) and (b) inserted by EC(PLC)R 2008, reg 3(a)(i).

b Words 'in either case' inserted by EC(PLC)R 2008, reg 3(a)(ii).

---

74 Order confirming reduction and powers of court on making such order

(1) The court, if satisfied in relation to every creditor of the company who, under section 73, is entitled to object to the reduction, that either his consent to the reduction has been obtained or that his debt or claim has been discharged or has determined, or has been secured, may make an order confirming the reduction on such terms and conditions as it thinks fit.

(2) Where the court makes any such order, it may—

(a) if for any special reason it thinks proper so to do, make an order directing that the company shall, during such period, commencing on or at any time after the date of the order, as is specified in the order, add to its name as the last words thereof the words 'and reduced' or where the word 'teoranta' is part of such name, the words 'agus laghdaithe',

(b) make an order requiring the company to publish as the court directs the reasons for reduction or such other information in regard thereto as the court may think expedient, with a view to giving proper information to the public, and, if the court thinks fit, the causes which led to the reduction.

(3) Where a company is ordered to add to its name the words 'and reduced', or the words 'agus laghdaithe' those words shall, until the expiration of the period specified in the order, be deemed to be part of the name of the company.

75 Registration of order and minute of reduction

(1) The registrar of companies, on production to him of an order of the court confirming the reduction of the share capital of a company, and the delivery to him of a copy of the order and of a minute approved by the court showing, with respect to the share capital of the company as altered by the order, the amount of the share capital, the number of shares into which it is to be divided, and the amount of each share, and the amount, if any, at the date of the registration deemed to be paid up on each share, shall register the order and minute.

(2) On the registration of the order and minute, and not before, the resolution for reducing share capital as confirmed by the order so registered shall take effect.

(3) Notice of the registration shall be published in such manner as the court may direct.

(4) The registrar shall certify under his hand the registration of the order and minute, and his certificate shall be conclusive evidence that all the requirements of this Act relating to reduction of share capital have been complied with, and that the share capital of the company is such as is stated in the minute.

(5) The minute when registered shall be deemed to be substituted for the corresponding part of the memorandum, and shall be valid and alterable as if it had been originally contained therein.

(6) The substitution of any such minute as aforesaid for part of the memorandum of the company shall be deemed to be an alteration of the memorandum within the meaning of section 30.

76 Liability of members in respect of reduced shares

(1) Subject to subsection (2), in the case of a reduction of share capital, a member of the company, past or present, shall not be liable in respect of any share to any call or contribution exceeding in amount the difference, if any, between the amount of the share as fixed by the minute and the amount paid, or the reduced amount, if any, which is to be deemed to have been paid, on the share, as the case may be.

(2) If any creditor entitled in respect of any debt or claim to object to the reduction of the share capital, is, by reason of his ignorance of the proceedings for reduction, or of their nature and effect with respect to his debt or claim, not entered on the list of creditors, and, after the reduction, the company is unable within the meaning of the provisions of

this Act relating to winding up by the court, to pay the amount of his debt or claim, then—

(a) every person who was a member of the company at the date of the registration of the order for reduction and minute, shall be liable to contribute for the payment of that debt or claim an amount not exceeding the amount which he would have been liable to contribute if the company had commenced to be wound up on the day before the said date, and

(b) if the company is wound up, the court, on the application of any such creditor and proof of his ignorance as aforesaid, may, if it thinks fit, settle accordingly a list of persons so liable to contribute, and make and enforce calls and orders on the contributories settled on the list, as if they were ordinary contributories in a winding up.

(3) Nothing in this section shall affect the rights of the contributories among themselves.

77 Penalty for concealment of certain matters in proceedings for reduction

If any officer of [a company (other than a public limited company) the subject of an application under section 73][a]—

(a) wilfully conceals the name of any creditor entitled to object to the reduction; or

(b) wilfully misrepresents the nature or amount of the debt or claim of any creditor,

he shall be liable on summary conviction to a [class C fine][b].

Amendments

a Words 'the company' substituted by 'a company (other than a public limited company) the subject of an application under section 73' by EC(PLC)R 2008, reg 3(b).

b '£500' substituted for '£100' by C(A)A 1982, Sch 1, increased to £1,500 by CA 1990, s 240(7) as inserted by CLEA 2001, s 104(c) and converted to €1,904.61 by Council Regulations (EC) No 1103/97, No 974/98 and No 2866/98 and the Economic and Monetary Union Act 1998, s 6; the above being implicitly substituted, by Fines Act 2010, s 6, for a fine not exceeding the aforesaid amount. A class C fine currently means a fine not exceeding €2,500.

Variation of Shareholders' Rights

78 Rights of holders of special classes of shares

(1) If, in the case of a company the share capital of which is divided into different classes of shares, provision is made by the memorandum or articles for authorising the variation of the rights attached to any class of shares in the company, subject to the consent of any specified proportion of the holders of the issued shares of that class or the sanction of a resolution passed at a separate meeting of the holders of those shares, and in pursuance of the said provision the rights attached to any such class of shares are at any time varied, the holders of not less in the aggregate than 10 per cent of the issued shares of that class, being persons who did not consent to or vote in favour of the resolution for the variation, may apply to the court to have the variation cancelled and, where any such application is made, the variation shall not have effect unless and until it is confirmed by the court.

(2) An application under this section must be made within 28 days (or such longer period as the court, on application made to it by any shareholder before the expiry of the said 28 days, may allow) after the date on which the consent was given or the resolution was passed, as the case may be, and may be made on behalf of the shareholders entitled to make the application by such one or more of their number as they may appoint in writing for the purpose.

(3) On any such application the court, after hearing the applicant and any other persons who apply to the court to be heard and appear to the court to be interested in the application, may, if it is satisfied having regard to all the circumstances of the case that the variation would unfairly prejudice the shareholders of the class represented by the applicant, disallow the variation and shall, if not so satisfied, confirm the variation.

(4) The decision of the court on any such application shall be final but an appeal shall lie to the Supreme Court from the determination of the court on a question of law.

(5) The company shall, within 21 days after the making of an order by the court on any such application, forward a copy of the order to the registrar of companies and, if default is made in complying with this provision, the company and every officer of the company who is in default, [shall be guilty of an offence and liable to a [class C fine][a]].[b]

(6) In this section 'variation' includes abrogation, and 'varied' shall be construed accordingly.

Amendments

a '£250' substituted for '£50' by C(A)A 1982, Sch 1, increased to £1,500 by CA 1990, s 240(7) as inserted by CLEA 2001, s 104(c) and converted to €1,904.61 by Council Regulations (EC) No 1103/97, No 974/98 and No 2866/98 and the Economic and Monetary Union Act 1998, s 6; the above being implicitly substituted, by Fines Act 2010, s 6, for a fine not exceeding the aforesaid amount. A class C fine currently means a fine not exceeding €2,500.

b CA 1963, s 78(5) words 'shall be guilty of an offence and liable to a fine' substituted for 'shall be liable to a fine' by C(AA)A 2003, Sch 2, Item No 1.

Numbering and Transfer of and Evidence of Title to Shares and Debentures

79 Nature of shares

The shares or other interest of any member in a company shall be personal estate, transferable in manner provided by the articles of the company, and shall not be of the nature of real estate.

80 Numbering of shares

(1) Subject to subsections (2) and (3), each share in a company having a share capital shall be distinguished by its appropriate number.

(2) If at any time all the issued shares in a company, or all the issued shares therein of a particular class, are fully paid up and rank *pari passu* for all purposes, none of those shares need thereafter have a distinguishing number, so long as it remains fully paid up and ranks *pari passu* for all purposes with all shares of the same class for the time being issued and fully paid up.

(3) Where new shares are issued by a company on the terms that, within a period not exceeding 12 months, they will rank *pari passu* for all purposes with all the existing

shares, or all the existing shares of a particular class, in the company, neither the new shares nor the corresponding existing shares need have distinguishing numbers so long as all of them are fully paid up and rank *pari passu* but the share certificates of the new shares shall, if not numbered, be appropriately worded or enfaced.

81 Transfer not to be registered unless instrument of transfer delivered to the company

(1) Subject to subsection (2), and notwithstanding anything in the articles of a company, it shall not be lawful for the company to register a transfer of shares in or debentures of the company unless a proper instrument of transfer has been delivered to the company.

(2) Nothing in subsection (1) shall prejudice any power of the company to register as shareholder or debenture holder any person to whom the right to any shares in, or debentures of the company, has been transmitted by operation of law.

82 Transfer by personal representative

A transfer of the share or other interest of a deceased member of a company made by his personal representative shall, although the personal representative is not himself a member of the company, be as valid as if he had been such a member at the time of the execution of the instrument of transfer.

83 Registration of transfer at request of transferor

On application of the transferor of any share or interest in a company, the company shall enter in its register of members the name of the transferee in the same manner and subject to the same conditions as if the application for the entry were made by the transferee.

84 Notice of refusal to register transfer

(1) If the company refuses to register a transfer of any shares or debentures, the company shall, within 2 months after the date on which the transfer was lodged with the company, send to the transferee notice of the refusal.

(2) If default is made in complying with this section, the company and every officer of the company who is in default [shall be guilty of an offence and liable to a class C fine][a].[b]

Amendments

a '£250' substituted for '£50' by C(A)A 1982, Sch 1, increased to £1,500 by CA 1990, s 240(7) as inserted by CLEA 2001, s 104(c) and converted by €1,904.61 by Council Regulations (EC) No 1103/97, No 974/98 and No 2866/98 and the Economic and Monetary Union Act 1998, s 6; the above being implicitly substituted, by Fines Act 2010, s 6, for a fine not exceeding the aforesaid amount. A class C fine currently means a fine not exceeding €2,500.

b CA 1963, s 84(2) words 'shall be guilty of an offence and liable to a fine' substituted for 'shall be liable to a fine' by C(AA)A 2003, Sch 2, Item No 1.

---

85 Certification of transfers

(1) The certification by a company of any instrument of transfer of shares in or debentures of the company shall be taken as a representation by the company to any person acting on the faith of the certification that there have been produced to the

company such documents as on the face of them show a *prima facie* title to the shares or debentures in the transferor named in the instrument of transfer, but not as a representation that the transferor has any title to the shares or debentures.

(2) Where any person acts on the faith of a false certification by a company made negligently, the company shall be under the same liability to him as if the certification had been made fraudulently.

(3) For the purposes of this section—

(a) an instrument of transfer shall be deemed to be certificated if it bears the words, 'certificate lodged' or words to the like effect;

(b) the certification of an instrument of transfer shall be deemed to be made by a company if—

(i) the person issuing the instrument is a person authorised to issue certificated instruments of transfer on the company's behalf, and

(ii) the certification is signed by a person authorised to certificate transfers on the company's behalf or by any officer or servant either of the company or of a body corporate so authorised;

(c) a certification shall be deemed to be signed by any person if—

(i) it purports to be authenticated by his signature or initials (whether hand written or not), and

(ii) it is not shown that the signature or initials was or were placed there neither by himself nor by any person authorised to use the signature or initials for the purpose of certificating transfers on the company's behalf.

86 Duties of company in relation to the issue of certificates

(1) Every company shall, within 2 months after the allotment of any of its shares, debentures or debenture stock, and within 2 months after the date on which a transfer of any such shares, debentures or debenture stock is lodged with the company, complete and have ready for delivery the certificates of all shares, the debentures, and the certificates of all debenture stock allotted or transferred, unless the conditions of issue of the shares, debentures or debenture stock otherwise provide.

The expression 'transfer' for the purpose of this subsection means a transfer duly stamped and otherwise valid, and does not include such a transfer as the company is, for any reason, entitled to refuse to register and does not register.

(2) If default is made in complying with this section, the company and every officer of the company who is in default [shall be guilty of an offence and liable to a [class C fine][a]].[b]

(3) If any company on which a notice has been served requiring the company to make good any default in complying with the provisions of subsection (1) fails to make good the default within 10 days after the service of the notice, the court may, on the application of the person entitled to have the certificates or the debentures delivered to him, make an order directing the company and any officer of the company to make good the default within such time as may be specified in the order, and any such order may provide that all costs of and incidental to the application shall be borne by the company or by any officer of the company responsible for the default.

Amendments

a '£100' substituted for '£20' by C(A)A 1982, Sch 1, increased to £1,500 by CA 1990, s 240(7) as inserted by CLEA 2001, s 104(c) and converted to e1,904.61 by Council Regulations (EC) No 1103/97, No 974/98 and No 2866/98 and the Economic and Monetary Union Act 1998, s 6; the above being implicitly substituted, by Fines Act 2010, s 6, for a fine not exceeding the aforesaid amount. A class C fine currently means a fine not exceeding €2,500.

b CA 1963, s 86(2) words 'shall be guilty of an offence and liable to a fine' substituted for 'shall be liable to a fine' by C(AA)A 2003, Sch 2, Item No 1.

87 Evidence of title, probate and letters of administration

[(1) A certificate under the common seal of the company or the seal kept by the company (not being a private company) by virtue of section 3 of the Companies (Amendment) Act, 1977, specifying any shares held by any member shall be *prima facie* evidence of the title of the member to the shares.][a]

(2) The production to a company of any document which is by law sufficient evidence of probate of the will or letters of administration of the estate of a deceased person having been granted to some person shall be accepted by the company, notwithstanding anything in its articles, as sufficient evidence of the grant.

Amendments

a CA 1963, s 87(1) substituted by C(A)A 1977, s 5.

88 Issue and effect of share warrants to bearer

(1) A company limited by shares if so authorised by its articles, may, in relation to any fully paid up shares, issue under its common seal a warrant stating that the bearer of the warrant is entitled to the shares therein specified, and may provide by coupons or otherwise for the payment of the future dividends on the shares included in the warrant.

(2) Such a warrant as aforesaid is in this Act referred to as 'a share warrant'.

(3) A share warrant shall entitle the bearer thereof to the shares therein specified, and the shares may be transferred by delivery of the warrant.

89 Validation of invalid issue, redemption or purchase of shares

[(1) If a company has created or issued shares in its capital, or acquired any of its shares by a redemption or purchase in purported compliance with Part XI of the Companies Act, 1990, and if there is reason to apprehend that such shares were invalidly created, issued or acquired as aforesaid, the court may, on the application of the company, any holder or former holder of such shares or any member or former member or creditor, or the liquidator, of the company, declare that such creation, issue or acquisition shall be valid for all purposes if the court is satisfied that it would be just and equitable to do so and thereupon such shares shall from the creation, issue or acquisition thereof, as the case may be, be deemed to have been validly created, issued or acquired.

(2) Where shares have been redeemed or purchased in contravention of paragraph (d), (e) or (f) of section 207 (2) or section 207 (3) of the Companies Act, 1990, then the court shall not make a declaration under subsection (1) above in respect of those shares.

(3) The grant of relief by the court under this section shall, if the court so directs, not have the effect of relieving the company or its officers of any liability incurred under section 41 (3) of the Companies (Amendment) Act, 1983.][a]

Amendments

a CA 1963, s 89 substituted by CA 1990, s 227.

90 Penalty for personation of shareholder

If any person falsely and deceitfully personates any owner of any share or interest in any company, or of any share warrant or coupon, issued in pursuance of this Act, and thereby obtains or endeavours to obtain any such share or interest or share warrant or coupon, or receives or endeavours to receive any money due to any such owner, or votes at any meeting, as if the offender were the true and lawful owner, he shall be liable, on conviction on indictment, to imprisonment for a term not exceeding [5][a] years or to a fine not exceeding [€6,348.70][b] or to both, or, on summary conviction to imprisonment for a term not exceeding 6 months or to a [class C fine][c] or to both.

Amendments

a '5' substituted for '2' by CA 1990, s 240(8) as inserted by CLEA 2001, s 104(c).

b '£2,500' substituted for '£500' by C(A)A 1982, Sch 1 and converted to €3,174.35 by Council Regulations (EC) No 1103/97, No 974/98 and No 2866/98 and the Economic and Monetary Union Act 1998, s 6, and multiplied by a multiplier of 2 pursuant to Fines Act 2010, s 9.

c '£500' substituted for '£100' by C(A)A 1982, Sch 1, increased to £1,500 by CA 1990, s 240(7) as inserted by CLEA 2001, s 104(c) and converted to €1,904.61 by Council Regulations (EC) No 1103/97. No 974/98 and No 2866/98 and the Economic and Monetary Union Act 1998, s 6; the above being implicitly substituted, by Fines Act 2010, s 6, for a fine not exceeding the aforesaid amount. A class C fine currently means a fine not exceeding €2,500.

Special Provisions as to Debentures

91 Provisions as to register of debenture holders

(1) Every company shall keep a register of holders of debentures of the company and enter therein the names and addresses of the debenture holders and the amount of debentures currently held by each.

For the purposes of this subsection, debentures do not include any debenture which does not form part of a series ranking *pari passu* nor any debenture which is transferable by delivery.

(2) A company shall keep such register at the registered office of the company, any other office of the company at which the work of making it up is done, or if the company arranges with some other person for the making up of the register to be undertaken on

behalf of the company by that other person, at the office of that other person at which the work is done.

(3) Subject to subsection (4), every company shall send notice to the registrar of companies of the place where the register is kept, and of any change in that place.

(4) A company shall not be bound to send notice under subsection (3) where the register has, at all times since it came into existence, or, in the case of a company which came into existence after the operative date, at all times since then, been kept at the registered office of the company.

(5) Where a company makes default in complying with subsection (1) or (2) or makes default for 14 days in complying with subsection (3), the company and every officer of the company who is in default [shall be guilty of an offence and liable to a [class C fine][a]].[b]

Amendments

a ‘£250’ substituted for ‘£50’ by C(A)A 1982, Sch 1, increased to £1,500 by CA 1990, s 240(7) as inserted by CLEA 2001, s 104(c) and converted to €1,904.61 by Council Regulations (EC) No 1103/97, No 974/98 and No 2866/98 and the Economic and Monetary Union Act 1998, s 6; the above being implicitly substituted, by Fines Act 2010, s 6, for a fine not exceeding the aforesaid amount. A class C fine currently means a fine not exceeding €2,500.

b CA 1963, s 91(5) words ‘shall be guilty of an offence and liable to a fine’ substituted for ‘shall be liable to a fine’ by C(AA)A 2003, Sch 2, Item No 1.

---

92 Rights of inspection of register of debenture holders and to copies of register and trust deed

(1) Every register of holders of debentures of a company shall, except when duly closed (but subject to such reasonable restrictions as the company in general meeting may impose, so that not less than 2 hours in each day shall be allowed for inspection), be open to the inspection of the registered holder of any such debentures or any holder of shares in the company without fee, and of any other person on payment of a fee of [6 cent][a] or such less sum as may be prescribed by the company.

(2) Any such registered holder of debentures or holder of shares as aforesaid or any other person may require a copy of the register of the holders of debentures of the company or any part thereof, on payment of [4 cent][b] for every 100 words required to be copied.

(3) A copy of any trust deed for securing any issue of debentures shall be forwarded to every holder of any such debentures at his request on payment in the case of a printed trust deed of the sum of [32 cent][c] or such less sum as may be prescribed by the company, or, where the trust deed has not been printed, on payment of [4 cent][b] for every 100 words required to be copied.

(4) If inspection is refused, or a copy is refused or not forwarded, the company and every officer of the company who is in default [shall be guilty of an offence and liable to a [class C fine][d]].[e]

(5) Where a company is in default as aforesaid, the court may by order compel an immediate inspection of the register or direct that the copies required shall be sent to the person requiring them.

(6) For the purposes of this section, a register shall be deemed to be duly closed if closed in accordance with provisions contained in the articles or in the debentures or, in the case of debenture stock, in the stock certificates, or in the trust deed or other document securing the debentures or debenture stock, during such period or periods, not exceeding in the whole 30 days in any year, as may be therein specified.

Amendments

a One shilling (5 pence) converted to 6 cent by Council Regulations (EC) No 1103/97, No 974/98 and No 2866/98 and the Economic and Monetary Union Act 1998, s 6.

b Sixpence to be read as 'three new pence' pursuant to the Decimal Currency Act 1970, s 9, and converted to 4 cent by Council Regulations (EC) No 1103/97, No 974/98 and No 2866/98 and the Economic and Monetary Union Act 1998, s 6.

c Five shillings (25p) converted to 32 cent by Council Regulations (EC) No 1103/97, No 974/98 and No 2866/98 and the Economic and Monetary Union Act 1998, s 6.

d '£125' substituted for '£25' by C(A)A 1982, Sch 1, increased to £1,500 by CA 1990, s 240(7) as inserted by CLEA 2001, s 104(c) and converted to €1,904.61 by Council Regulations (EC) No 1103/97, No 974/98 and No 2866/98 and the Economic and Monetary Union Act 1998, s 6; the above being implicitly substituted, by Fines Act 2010, s 6, for a fine not exceeding the aforesaid amount. A class C fine currently means a fine not exceeding €2,500.

e CA 1963, s 92(4) words 'shall be guilty of an offence and liable to a fine' substituted for 'shall be liable to a fine' by C(AA)A 2003, Sch 2, Item No 1.

---

93 Liability of trustees for debenture holders

(1) Subject to subsections (2) to (4), any provision contained in a trust deed for securing an issue of debentures, or in any contract with the holders of debentures secured by a trust deed, shall be void in so far as it would have the effect of exempting a trustee thereof from or indemnifying him against liability for breach of trust where he fails to show the degree of care and diligence required of him as trustee, having regard to the provisions of the trust deed conferring on him any powers, authorities or discretions.

(2) Subsection (1) shall not invalidate—

(a) any release otherwise validly given in respect of anything done or omitted to be done by a trustee before the giving of the release; or

(b) any provision enabling such a release to be given—

(i) on the agreement thereto of a majority of not less than three-fourths in value of the debenture holders present and voting in person or, where proxies are permitted, by proxy at a meeting summoned for the purpose, and

(ii) either with respect to specific acts or omissions or on the trustee dying or ceasing to act.

(3) Subsection (1) shall not operate—

(a) to invalidate any provision in force on the operative date so long as any person then entitled to the benefit of that provision or afterwards given the benefit thereof under subsection (4) remains a trustee of the deed in question; or

(b) to deprive any person of any exemption or right to be indemnified in respect of anything done or omitted to be done by him while any such provision was in force.

(4) While any trustee of a trust deed remains entitled to the benefit of a provision saved by subsection (3), the benefit of that provision may be given either—

(a) to all trustees of the deed, present and future; or

(b) to any named trustee or proposed trustees thereof;

by a resolution passed by a majority of not less than three-fourths in value of the debenture holders present in person or, where proxies are permitted, by proxy at a meeting summoned for the purpose in accordance with the provisions of the deed or, if the deed makes no provision for summoning meetings, a meeting summoned for the purpose in any manner approved by the court.

94 Perpetual debentures

A condition contained in any debentures or in any deed for securing any debentures, whether issued or executed before or after the operative date, shall not be invalid by reason only that the debentures are thereby made irredeemable or redeemable only on the happening of a contingency, however remote, or on the expiration of a period, however long, notwithstanding any rule of law to the contrary.

95 Power to re-issue redeemed debentures

(1) Where either before, on or after the operative date, a company has redeemed any debentures, then—

(a) unless any provision to the contrary, whether express or implied, is contained in the articles or in any contract entered into by the company; or

(b) unless the company has, by passing a resolution to that effect or by some other act, shown its intention that the debentures shall be cancelled;

the company shall have, and shall be deemed always to have had, power to re-issue the debentures, either by re-issuing the same debentures or by issuing other debentures in their place.

(2) Subject to section 96, on a re-issue of redeemed debentures, the person entitled to the debentures shall have, and shall be deemed always to have had, the same priorities as if the debentures had never been redeemed.

(3) Where a company has, either before, on or after the operative date deposited any of its debentures to secure advances from time to time on current account or otherwise, the debentures shall not be deemed to have been redeemed by reason only of the account of the company having ceased to be in debit whilst the debentures remained so deposited.

(4) Subject to subsection (5), the re-issue of a debenture or the issue of another debenture in its place under the power by this section given to, or deemed to have been possessed by, a company, whether the re-issue or issue was made before, on or after the operative date, shall be treated as the issue of a new debenture for the purposes of stamp

duty, but it shall not be so treated for the purposes of any provision limiting the amount or number of debentures to be issued.

(5) Any person lending money on the security of a debenture re-issued under this section, which appears to be duly stamped, may give the debenture in evidence in any proceedings for enforcing his security without payment of the stamp duty or any penalty in respect thereof, unless he had notice or, but for his negligence, might have discovered that the debenture was not duly stamped, but in any such case the company shall be liable to pay the proper stamp duty and penalty.

96 Saving of rights of certain mortgagees in case of re-issued debentures

Where any debentures which have been redeemed before the operative date are re-issued on or subsequently to that date, the re-issue of the debentures shall not prejudice and shall be deemed never to have prejudiced any right or priority which any person would have had under or by virtue of any mortgage or charge created before the operative date, if section 104 of the Companies (Consolidation) Act, 1908, had been enacted in this Act instead of section 95.

97 Specific performance of contracts to subscribe for debentures

A contract with a company to take up and pay for any debentures of the company may be enforced by an order for specific performance.

98 Preferential payments when receiver is appointed under floating charge

(1) Where either a receiver is appointed on behalf of the holders of any debentures of a company secured by a floating charge, or possession is taken by or on behalf of those debenture holders of any property comprised in or subject to the charge, then, if the company is not at the time in course of being wound up, the debts which in every winding up are, under the provisions of Part VI relating to preferential payments to be paid in priority to all other debts, shall be paid out of any assets coming to the hands of the receiver or other person taking possession as aforesaid in priority to any claim for principal or interest in respect of the debentures.

(2) In the application of the said provisions section 285 of this Act shall be construed as if the provision for payment of accrued holiday remuneration becoming payable on the termination of employment before or by the effect of the winding up order or resolution, were a provision for payment of such remuneration becoming payable on the termination of employment before or by the effect of the appointment of the receiver or possession being taken as aforesaid.

(3) The periods of time mentioned in the said provisions of Part VI shall be reckoned from the date of the appointment of the receiver or of possession being taken as aforesaid, as the case may be.

(4) Where the date referred to in subsection (3) occurred before the operative date, subsections (1) and (3) shall have effect with the substitution for references to the said provisions of Part VI of references to the provisions which, by virtue of subsection (12) of the said section 285 are deemed to remain in force in the case therein mentioned, and subsection (2) of this section shall not apply.

(5) Any payments made under this section shall be recouped so far as may be out of the assets of the company available for payment of general creditors.

PART IV
REGISTRATION OF CHARGES

Registration of Charges with Registrar of Companies

99 Registration of charges created by companies

(1) Subject to the provisions of this Part, every charge created after the fixed date by a company, and being a charge to which this section applies, shall, so far as any security on the company's property or undertaking is conferred thereby, be void against the liquidator and any creditor of the company, unless the prescribed particulars of the charge, verified in the prescribed manner, are delivered to or received by the registrar of companies for registration in manner required by this Act within 21 days after the date of its creation, but without prejudice to any contract or obligation for repayment of the money thereby secured, and when a charge becomes void under this section, the money secured thereby shall immediately become payable.

(2) This section applies to the following charges—

(a) a charge for the purpose of securing any issue of debentures;

(b) a charge on uncalled share capital of the company;

(c) a charge created or evidenced by an instrument which, if executed by an individual, would require registration as a bill of sale;

(d) a charge on land, wherever situate, or any interest therein, but not including a charge for any rent or other periodical sum issuing out of land;

(e) a charge on book debts of the company;

(f) a floating charge on the undertaking or property of the company;

(g) a charge on calls made but not paid;

[(h) a charge on a ship or aircraft or any share in a ship or aircraft;][a]

(i) a charge on goodwill, on a patent or a licence under a patent, on a trade mark or on a copyright or a licence under a copyright.

[(2A) The Minister may by regulations amend subsection (2) so as to add any description of charge to, or remove any description of charge from, the charges requiring registration under this section.

(2B) The power of the Minister under subsection (2A) shall include a power to amend by regulations the description of any charge referred to in subsection (2).

(2C) Every regulation made by the Minister under this section shall be laid before each House of the Oireachtas as soon as may be after it is made and, if a resolution annulling the regulation is passed by either House within the next 21 days on which that House has sat after the regulation is laid before it, the regulation shall be annulled accordingly, but without prejudice to the validity of anything previously done thereunder.][b]

(3) In the case of a charge created out of the State comprising property situate outside the State, 21 days after the date on which the prescribed particulars could, in due course of post, and if despatched with due diligence, have been received in the State shall be substituted for 21 days after the date of the creation of the charge as the time within which the particulars are to be delivered to the registrar.

(4) Where a charge is created in the State but comprises property outside the State, the prescribed particulars may be sent for registration under this section, notwithstanding

that further proceedings may be necessary to make the charge valid or effectual according to the law of the country in which the property is situate.

(5) Where a charge comprises property situate outside the State and registration in the country where the property is situate is necessary to make the charge valid or effectual according to the law of that country, a certificate in the prescribed form stating that the charge was presented for registration in the country where the property is situate on the date on which it was so presented shall be delivered to the registrar of companies for registration.

(6) Where a negotiable instrument has been given to secure the payment of any book debts of a company, the deposit of the instrument for the purpose of securing an advance to the company shall not, for the purposes of this section, be treated as a charge on those book debts.

(7) The holding of debentures entitling the holder to a charge on land shall not, for the purposes of this section, be deemed to be an interest in land.

(8) Where a series of debentures containing, or giving by reference to any other instrument, any charge to the benefit of which the debenture holders of that series are entitled *pari passu* is created by a company, it shall, for the purposes of this section, be sufficient if there are delivered to or received by the registrar, within 21 days after the execution of the deed containing the charge, or, if there is no such deed, after the execution of any debentures of the series, the following particulars—

(a) the total amount secured by the whole series; and

(b) the dates of the resolutions authorising the issue of the series, and the date of the covering deed, if any, by which the security is created or defined; and

(c) a general description of the property charged; and

(d) the names of the trustees, if any, for the debenture holders;

so, however, that where more than one issue is made of debentures in the series, there shall be sent to the registrar for entry in the register particulars of the amount and date of each issue, but an omission to do this shall not affect the validity of the debentures issued.

(9) Where any commission, allowance or discount has been paid or made either directly or indirectly by a company to any person in consideration of his subscribing or agreeing to subscribe, whether absolutely or conditionally, for any debentures of the company, or procuring or agreeing to procure subscriptions, whether absolute or conditional, for any such debentures, the particulars required to be sent for registration under this section shall include particulars as to the amount and rate per cent of the commission, discount or allowance so paid or made, but omission to do this shall not affect the validity of the debentures issued, so, however, that the deposit of any debentures as security for any debt of the company shall not, for the purposes of this subsection, be treated as the issue of the debentures at a discount.

(10) In this Part—

(a) 'charge' includes mortgage;

(b) 'the fixed date' means, in relation to the charges specified in paragraphs (a) to (f), of subsection (2), the 1st July, 1908, and in relation to the charges specified in paragraphs (g) to (i), the operative date.

Amendments

a CA 1963, s 99(h) substituted by CA 1990, s 122.

b CA 1963, s 99(2A), (2B), (2C) inserted by CA 1990, s 122.

100 Duty of company to register charges created by company

(1) It shall be the duty of a company to send to the registrar of companies for registration within the time required by section 99 the particulars of every charge created by the company, and of the issues of debentures of a series requiring registration under section 99, together with any documents required by that section, but registration of any such charge may be effected on the application of any person interested therein.

(2) Where registration is effected on the application of some person other that the company, that person shall be entitled to recover from the company the amount of any fees properly paid by him to the registrar on the registration.

(3) If any company makes default in sending to the registrar for registration the particulars of any charge created by the company or of the issues of debentures of a series requiring registration under section 99 or any documents required by that section then, unless registration has been effected on the application of some other person, the company and every officer of the company who is in default [shall be guilty of an offence and liable to a [class C fine][a]][b].

(4) Proceedings in relation to an offence under this section may be brought and prosecuted by the registrar of companies.

Amendments

a '£500' substituted for '£100' by C(A)A 1982, Sch 1 and increased to £1,500 by CA 1990, s 240(7) as inserted by CLEA 2001, s 104(c); £1,500 converted to €1,904.61 by Council Regulations (EC) No 1103/97, No 974/98 and No 2866/98 and the Economic and Monetary Union Act, 1988, s 6; the above being implicitly substituted, by Fines Act 2010, s 6, for a fine not exceeding the aforesaid amount. A class C fine currently means a fine not exceeding €2,500.

b Words substituted by C(AA)A 2003, s 57 and Sch 2, para 1.

101 Duty of company to register charges existing on property acquired

(1) Where a company acquires any property which is subject to a charge of any such kind as would, if it had been created after the acquisition of the property, have been required to be registered under this Part, the company shall cause the prescribed particulars of the charge, verified in the prescribed manner, to be delivered to the registrar of companies for registration in manner required by this Act within 21 days after the date on which the acquisition is completed so, however, that if the property is situated outside the State, 21 days after the date on which the prescribed particulars could, in due course of post and if despatched with due diligence, have been received in the State, shall be substituted for 21 days after the completion of the acquisition as the time within which the particulars are to be delivered to the registrar.

(2) If default is made in complying with this section, the company and every officer of the company who is in default [shall be guilty of an offence and liable to a [class C fine][a]][b]

Amendments

a '£500' substituted for '£100' by C(A)A 1982, Sch 1 and increased to £1,500 by CA 1990, s 240(7) as inserted by CLEA 2001, s 104(c); £1,500 converted to €1,904.61 by Council Regulations (EC) No 1103/97, No 974/98 and No 2866/98 and the Economic and Monetary Union Act, 1988, s 6; the above being implicitly substituted, by Fines Act 2010, s 6, for a fine not exceeding the aforesaid amount. A class C fine currently means a fine not exceeding €2,500.

b Words substituted by C(AA)A 2003, s 57 and Sch 2, para 1.

---

102 Registration of judgment mortgages

(1) When judgment is recovered against a company and such judgment is subsequently converted into a judgment mortgage affecting any property of the company, the judgment creditor shall cause 2 copies (certified by the Land Registry or the Registry of Deeds, as the case may be, to be correct copies) of the affidavit required for the purpose of registering the judgment as a mortgage to be delivered to the company within 21 days after the date of such registration, and the company shall within 3 days of receipt of such copies deliver one of such copies to the registrar of companies for registration in manner required by this Act. By way of further precaution, the Land Registry, or Registry of Deeds, shall as soon as may be deliver a copy of the said affidavit to the registrar of companies.

[(2) If a judgment creditor makes default in complying with subsection (1) he shall be guilty of an offence and liable to a [class C fine],[a] and if a company makes default in complying with that subsection, the company and every officer who is in default shall be guilty of an offence and liable to a [class C fine].[b]

(3) This section shall not apply to any judgment mortgage created before the operative date.

Amendments

a As implicitly substituted for 'fine not exceeding €1,904.61' by Fines Act 2010, s 6. A class C fine currently means a fine not exceeding €2,500."

b CA 1963, s 102(2) substituted by C(AA)A 2003, s 57 and Sch 2, para 3.

---

103 Register of charges to be kept by registrar of companies

(1) The registrar of companies shall keep, in relation to each company, a register in the prescribed form of all the charges requiring registration under this Part, and shall, on payment of such fee as may be prescribed, enter in the register, in relation to such charges, the following particulars:

(a) in the case of a charge to the benefit of which the holders of a series of debentures are entitled, such particulars as are specified in subsection (8) of section 99;

(b) in the case of any other charge—

(i) if the charge is a charge created by the company, the date of its creation;

(ii) if the charge was a charge existing on property acquired by the company, the date of the acquisition of the property;

(iii) if the charge was a judgment mortgage, the date of the creation of such judgment mortgage;

[(iiia) if the charge is a floating one, granted by a company to the Central Bank and Financial Services Authority of Ireland for the purposes either of providing or securing collateral, particulars of any provision of the charge that has the effect of prohibiting or restricting the company from issuing further securities that rank equally with that charge or modifying the ranking of that charge in relation to securities previously issued by the company;] [a]

(iv) the amount secured by the charge;

(v) short particulars of the property charged;

(vi) the persons entitled to the charge.

(2) The register kept in pursuance of this section shall be open to inspection by any person on payment of such fee as may be prescribed.

Amendments

a CBFSAIA 2004, s 33 and Sch 3, Pt 2 inserted sub-para (iiia) after s 103(1)(b)(iii).

---

104 Certificate of registration

The registrar shall give a certificate under his hand of the registration of any charge registered in pursuance of this Part, stating the amount thereby secured, and the certificate shall be conclusive evidence that the requirements of this Part as to registration have been complied with.

105 Entries of satisfaction and release of property from charge

The registrar of companies, on evidence being given to his satisfaction with respect to any registered charge

(a) that the debt in relation to which the charge was created has been paid or satisfied in whole or in part; or

(b) that part of the property or undertaking charged has been released from the charge or has ceased to form part of the company's property or undertaking;

and after giving notice to the person to whom such charge was originally given or to the judgment creditor, as the case may be, may enter on the register a memorandum of satisfaction in whole or in part, or of the fact that part of the property or undertaking has been released from the charge or has ceased to form part of the company's property or undertaking, as the case may be, and where he enters a memorandum of satisfaction in whole he shall, if required, furnish the company with a copy thereof.

106 Extension of time for registration of charges

(1) The court, on being satisfied that the omission to register a charge within the time required by this Act or that the omission or mis-statement of any particular with respect

to any such charge or in a memorandum of satisfaction was accidental, or due to inadvertence or to some other sufficient cause, or is not of a nature to prejudice the position of creditors or shareholders of the company, or that on other grounds it is just and equitable to grant relief, may, on the application of the company or any person interested, and on such terms and conditions as seem to the court just and expedient, order that the time for registration shall be extended, or, as the case may be, that the omission or mis-statement shall be rectified.

(2) The grant of relief by the court under this section shall, if the court so directs, not have the effect of relieving the company or its officers of any liability already incurred under section 100.

107 Notice to registrar of appointment of receiver, and of receiver ceasing to act

(1) If any person obtains an order for the appointment of a receiver of the property of a company or appoints such a receiver under any powers contained in any instrument, he shall, within 7 days after the date of the order or of the appointment, publish in [the Companies Registration Office Gazette][a] and in at least one daily newspaper circulating in the district where the registered office of the company is situated, and deliver to the registrar of companies, a notice in the form prescribed.

(2) When any person appointed receiver of the property of a company ceases to act as such receiver, he shall, on so ceasing, deliver to the registrar of companies a notice in the form prescribed.

(3) If any person makes default in complying with the requirements of this section, he [shall be guilty of an offence and liable to a [class C fine][b]].[c]

Amendments

a 'the Companies Registration Office Gazette' substituted for '*Iris Oifigiúil*' by IFCMPA 2005, s 72.

b '£500' substituted for '£100' by C(A)A 1982, Sch 1 and increased to £1,500 by CA 1990, s 240(7) as inserted by CLEA 2001, s 104(c); £1,500 converted to €1,904.61 by Council Regulations (EC) No 1103/97, No 974/98 and No 2866/98 and the Economic and Monetary Union Act, 1988, s 6; the above being implicitly substituted, by Fines Act 2010, s 6, for a fine not exceeding the aforesaid amount. A class C fine currently means a fine not exceeding €2,500.

c Words inserted by C(AA)A 2003, s 57 and Sch 2, para 1.

108 Effect of provisions of former Companies Acts as to registration of charges on land

Paragraph (d) of subsection (1) of section 10 of the Companies Act, 1907, and paragraph (d) of subsection (1) of section 93 of the Companies (Consolidation) Act, 1908 (by virtue whereof charges created on land by a company required registration under those Acts respectively), shall be deemed never to have applied to a charge for any rent or other periodical sum issuing out of the land.

Provisions as to copies of Instruments creating Charges

109 Copies of instruments creating charges to be kept at registered office

Every company shall cause a copy of every instrument creating any charge requiring registration under this Part, including every affidavit a copy of which has been delivered to the company under section 102, to be kept at the registered office of the company so, however, that, in the case of a series of uniform debentures, a copy of one debenture of the series shall be sufficient.

110 Right to inspect copies of instruments creating charges

(1) The copies of instruments referred to in section 109 may be inspected during business hours (but subject to such reasonable restrictions as the company in general meeting may impose, so that not less than 2 hours in each day shall be allowed for inspection) by any creditor or member of the company without fee.

(2) If inspection is refused, every officer of the company who is in default [shall be guilty of an offence and liable to a [class C fine][a]].[b]

(3) In the event of any such refusal, the court may by order compel an immediate inspection.

Amendments

a ‘£500’ substituted for ‘£100’ by C(A)A 1982, Sch 1 and increased to £1,500 by CA 1990, s 240(7) as inserted by CLEA 2001, s 104(c); £1,500 converted to €1,904.61 by Council Regulations (EC) No 1103/97, No 974/98 and No 2866/98 and the Economic and Monetary Union Act, 1988, s 6; the above being implicitly substituted, by Fines Act 2010, s 6, for a fine not exceeding the aforesaid amount. A class C fine currently means a fine not exceeding €2,500.

b Words substituted by C(AA)A 2003, s 57 and Sch 2, para 1.

Application of this part to companies incorporated outside the State

111 Application of this Part to companies incorporated outside the State

The provisions of this Part shall extend to charges on property in the State which are created on or after the operative date, and to charges on property in the State which is acquired on or after the operative date, by a company incorporated outside the State which has an established place of business in the State, and to judgment mortgages created on or after the operative date and affecting property in the State of such a company and to receivers, appointed on or after the operative date, of property in the State of such a company, and for the purposes of those provisions, the principal place of business of such a company in the State shall be deemed to be its registered office.

Registration of charges existing before application of this Act

112 Registration of charges existing before application of this Act

(1) It shall be the duty of a company within 6 months after the operative date to send to the registrar of companies for registration the prescribed particulars of

(a) any charge created by the company before the operative date and remaining unsatisfied at that date which would have been required to be registered under paragraphs (g), (h) and (i) of subsection (2) of section 99 or under section 111, if the charge has been created after the operative date;

(b) any charge to which any property acquired by the company before the operative date is subject and which would have been required to be registered under section 101 or under section 111 if the property had been acquired after the operative date;

(c) any charge created before the operative date to which any property of the company is subject and which would have required registration under section 102 or under section 111 if created after the operative date.

(2) The registrar on payment of the prescribed fee shall enter the said particulars on the register kept by him in pursuance of this Part.

(3) If a company fails to comply with this section, the company and every officer of the company or other person who is knowingly a party to the default shall be liable to a [class C fine].[a]

(4) The failure of the company to send to the registrar the prescribed particulars of any charge mentioned in paragraphs (a), (b) and (c) of subsection (1) shall not prejudice any rights which any person in whose favour the charge was made may have thereunder.

(5) For the purposes of this section, 'company' includes a company incorporated outside the State which has an established place of business in the State.

(6) In relation to a company incorporated outside the State which, on or after the operative date, establishes a place of business in the State, this section shall have effect as if—

(a) for the references to the operative date there were substituted references to the date of such establishment, and

(b) for the references to charges created or property acquired before the operative date there were substituted references to charges created or property acquired before such establishment, whether before the operative date or not.

Amendments

a '£500' substituted for '£100' by C(A)A 1982, Sch 1, increased to £1,500 by CA 1990, s 240(7) as inserted by CLEA 2001, s 104(c) and converted to €1,904.61 by Council Regulations (EC) No 1103/97, No 974/98 and No 2866/98 and the Economic and Monetary Union Act, 1988, s 6; the above being implicitly substituted, by Fines Act 2010, s 6, for a fine not exceeding the aforesaid amount. A class C fine currently means a fine not exceeding €2,500.

PART V

MANAGEMENT AND ADMINISTRATION

Registered Office and Name

113 [Registered office of company

(1) A company shall, at all times, have a registered office in the State to which all communications and notices may be addressed.

(2) Particulars of the situation of the company's registered office shall be specified in the statement delivered pursuant to section 3 of the Companies (Amendment) Act, 1982, prior to the incorporation of the company.

(3) Notice of any change in the situation of the registered office of a company shall be given within fourteen days after the date of the change to the registrar who shall record the same. The inclusion in the annual return of a company of a statement as to the address of its registered office shall not be taken to satisfy the obligation imposed by this subsection.

(4) Where the memorandum of a company has been delivered to the registrar for registration under section 17 of the Principal Act prior to the commencement of the Companies (Amendment) Act, 1982, that company shall—

(a) as from the date on which it begins to carry on business, or as from the fourteenth day after the date of its incorporation, whichever is the earlier, have a registered office in the State to which all communications and notices may be addressed, and

(b) give notice of the situation of the registered office, and of any change therein within 14 days after the date of the incorporation of the company, or of the change as the case may be, to the registrar who shall record the same.

The inclusion in the annual return of a company of a statement as to the address of its registered office shall not be taken to satisfy the obligation imposed by this subsection.

(5) If default is made in complying with this section, the company and every officer of the company who is in default [shall be guilty of an offence and liable to a [class C fine][b]][c].

(6) Proceedings in relation to an offence under this section may be brought and prosecuted by the registrar of companies.][a]

Amendments

a CA 1963, s 113 substituted by C(A)A 1982, s 4.

b Penalty of £100 increased to £1,500 by CA 1990, 240(7) as inserted by CLEA 2001, s 104(c) and converted to €1,904.61 by Council Regulations (EC) No 1103/97, No 974/98 and No 2866/98 and the Economic and Monetary Union Act 1998, s 6; the above being implicitly substituted, by Fines Act 2010, s 6, for a fine not exceeding the aforesaid amount. A class C fine currently means a fine not exceeding €2,500.

c Words 'shall be guilty of an offence and liable to a fine' substituted for 'shall be liable for a fine' by C(AA)A 2003, s 57 and Sch 2, Item No. 1.

---

114 Publication of name by company

(1) Every company—

(a) shall paint or affix, and keep painted or affixed, its name on the outside of every office or place in which its business is carried on, in a conspicuous position, in letters easily legible;

(b) shall have its name engraven in legible characters on its seal;

(c) shall have it name mentioned in legible characters in all business letters of the company and in all notices and other official publications of the company, and in all bills of exchange, promissory notes, endorsements, cheques and orders for money or goods purporting to be signed by or on behalf of the company and in all invoices, receipts and letters of credit of the company.

(2) If a company does not paint or affix its name in manner directed by this Act, the company and every officer of the company who is in default [shall be guilty of an offence and liable to a [class C fine][a]][b], and if a company does not keep its name painted or affixed in manner so directed, the company and every officer of the company who is in default [shall be guilty of an offence and liable to a [class C fine][a]][b].

(3) If a company fails to comply with paragraph (b) or paragraph (c) of subsection (1), the company [shall be guilty of an offence and liable to a fine][c]][d].

(4) If an officer of a company or any person on its behalf—

(a) uses or authorises the use of any seal purporting to be a seal of the company whereon its name is not so engraven as aforesaid, or

(b) issues or authorises the issue of any business letter of the company or any notice or other official publication of the company, or signs or authorises to be signed on behalf of the company any bill of exchange, promissory note, endorsement, cheque or order for money or goods wherein its name is not mentioned in manner aforesaid, or

(c) issues or authorises the issue of any invoice, receipt or letter of credit of the company wherein its name is not mentioned in manner aforesaid;

he [shall be guilty of an offence and liable to a [class C fine][c]] [d], and shall further be personally liable to the holder of the bill of exchange, promissory note, cheque or order for money or goods for the amount thereof unless it is duly paid by the company.

[(5) The use of the abbreviation 'Ltd.' for 'Limited' or 'Teo.' for 'Teoranta' or 'p.l.c.' for 'public limited company' or 'c.p.t.' for 'cuideachta phoiblí theoranta' shall not be a breach of the provisions of this section.][e]

Amendments

a '£125' substituted for '£25' by C(A)A 1982, Sch 1, increased to £1,500 by CA 1990, s 240(7) as inserted by CLEA 2001, s 104(c) and converted to €1,904.61 by Council Regulations No 1103/97, No 974/98 and No 2866/98 and the Economic and Monetary Union Act 1998, s 6; the above being implicitly substituted, by Fines Act 2010, s 6, for a fine not exceeding the aforesaid amount. A class C fine currently means a fine not exceeding €2,500.

b Words 'shall be guilty of an offence and liable to a fine' in CA 1963, s 114(2) substituted for 'shall be liable for a fine' by C(AA)A 2003, s 57 and Sch 2, Item No. 4.

c '£250' substituted for '£50' by C(A)A 1982, Sch 1, increased to £1,500 by CA 1990, s 240(7) as inserted by CLEA 2001, s 104(c) and converted to €1,904.61 by Council Regulations No 1103/97, No 974/98 and No 2866/98 and the Economic and Monetary Union Act 1998, s 6; the above being implicitly substituted, by Fines Act 2010, s 6, for a fine not exceeding the aforesaid amount. A class C fine currently means a fine not exceeding €2,500.

d Words 'shall be guilty of an offence and liable to a fine' in CA 1963, s 114(3) and (4) substituted for 'shall be liable for a fine' by C(AA)A 2003, s 57 and Sch 2, Item No. 1.

e CA 1963, s 114(5) substituted by C(A)A 1983, Sch 1, para 13.

Restrictions on Commencement of Business

115 Restrictions on commencement of business

(1) Where a company having a share capital has issued a prospectus inviting the public to subscribe for its shares, the company shall not commence any business or exercise any borrowing powers unless—

(a) shares held subject to the payment of the whole amount thereof in cash have been allotted to an amount not less in the whole than the minimum subscription; and

(b) every director of the company has paid to the company on each of the shares taken or contracted to be taken by him and for which he is liable to pay in cash, a proportion equal to the proportion payable on application and allotment on the shares offered for public subscription; and

(c) no money is or may become liable to be repaid to applicants for any shares or debentures which have been offered for public subscription by reason of any failure to apply for or to obtain permission for the shares or debentures to be dealt in on any stock exchange; and

(d) there has been delivered to the registrar of companies for registration a statutory declaration by the secretary or one of the directors, in the prescribed form, that the aforesaid conditions have been complied with.

(2) Where a company having a share capital has not issued a prospectus inviting the public to subscribe for its shares, the company shall not commence any business or exercise any borrowing powers unless—

(a) there has been delivered to the registrar of companies for registration a statement in lieu of prospectus; and

(b) every director of the company has paid to the company, on each of the shares taken or contracted to be taken by him and for which he is liable to pay in cash, a proportion equal to the proportion payable on application and allotment on the shares payable in cash; and

(c) there has been delivered to the registrar of companies for registration a statutory declaration by the secretary or one of the directors, in the prescribed form, that paragraph (b) of this subsection has been complied with.

(3) The registrar of companies shall, on the delivery to him of the said statutory declaration, and, in the case of a company which is required by this section to deliver a statement in lieu of prospectus, of such a statement, certify that the company is entitled to commence business, and that certificate shall be conclusive evidence that the company is so entitled.

(4) Any contract made or ratified by a company before the date at which it is entitled to commence business shall be provisional only, and shall not be binding on the company until that date, and on that date it shall become binding.

(5) Nothing in this section shall prevent the simultaneous offer for subscription or allotment of any shares and debentures or the receipt of any money payable on application for debentures.

[(6)If any company commences business or exercises borrowing powers in contravention of this section, every person who is responsible for the contravention shall, without prejudice to any other liability, be guilty of an offence and liable to a [class C fine][a]].[b]

(7) Nothing in this section shall apply to—

(a) a private company, or

(b) a company registered before the 1st day of January, 1901, or

(c) a company registered before the 1st day of July, 1908, which has not issued a prospectus inviting the public to subscribe for its shares.

[(d) a public limited company registered as such on its original incorporation under the Companies (Amendment) Act, 1983.][c]

Amendments

a As implicitly substituted for "fine not exceeding €1,904.61" by Fines Act 2010, s 6. A class C fine currently means a fine not exceeding €2,500.

b CA 1963, s 115(6) substituted by IFCMPA 2005, s 73.

c CA 1963, s 115(7)(d) inserted by C(A)A 1983, Sch 1, para 14.

Register of Members

116 Register of members

(1) Subject to subsection (4), every company shall keep a register of its members and enter therein the following particulars—

(a) the names, addresses [...][a] of the members, and, in the case of a company having a share capital, a statement of the shares held by each member, distinguishing each share by its number so long as the share has a number, and of the amount paid or agreed to be considered as paid on the shares of each member;

(b) the date at which each person was entered in the register as a member;

(c) the date at which any person ceased to be a member.

(2) The entries required under paragraphs (a) and (b) of subsection (1) shall be made within 28 days after the conclusion of the agreement with the company to become a member or, in the case of a subscriber of the memorandum, within 28 days after the registration of the company.

(3) The entry required under paragraph (c) of the subsection (1) shall be made within 28 days after the date when the person concerned ceased to be a member, or, if he ceased to be a member otherwise than as a result of action by the company, within 28 days of production to the company of evidence satisfactory to the company of the occurrence of the event whereby he ceased to be a member.

(4) Where the company has converted any of its shares into stock and given notice of the conversion to the registrar of companies, the register shall show the amount of stock held by each member instead of the amount of shares and the particulars relating to shares specified in paragraph (a) of subsection (1).

(5) Subject to subsection (6), the register of members shall, except when it is closed under the provisions of this Act, be kept at the registered office of the company, so, however, that—

(a) if the work of making it up is done at another office of the company, it may be kept at that other office; and

(b) if the company arranges with some other person for the making up of the register to be undertaken on behalf of the company by that other person, it may be kept at the office of that other person at which the work is done.

(6) The register of members shall not be kept at a place outside the State.

(7) Subject to subsection (8), every company shall send notice to the registrar of companies of the place where its register of members is kept and of any change in that place.

(8) A company shall not be bound to send notice under subsection (7) where the register has, at all times since it came into existence or, in the case of a register in existence on the operative date, at all times since then, been kept at the registered office of the company.

(9) Where a company makes default in complying with any of the requirements of subsections (1) to (6) or makes default for 14 days in complying with subsection (7), the company and every officer of the company who is in default [shall be guilty of an offence and liable to a [class C fine][b].[c]

Amendments

a Words 'and occupations' deleted by C(A)A 1982, s 20.

b '£500' substituted for '£100' by C(A)A 1982 Sch 1, increased to £1,500 by CA 1990, s 240(7) as inserted by CLEA 2001, s 104(c) and converted to €1,904.61 by Council Regulations (EC) No 1103/97, No 974/98 and No 2866/98 and the Economic and Monetary Union Act 1998, s 6; the above being implicitly substituted, by Fines Act 2010, s 6, for a fine not exceeding the aforesaid amount. A class C fine currently means a fine not exceeding €2,500.

c Words substituted by C(AA)A 2003, s 57 and Sch 2, Item No 1.

---

117 Index of members

(1) Every company having more than fifty members shall, unless the register of members is in such a form as to constitute in itself an index, keep an index of the names of the members of the company and shall, within 14 days after the date on which any alteration is made in the register of members, make any necessary alteration in the index.

(2) The index shall in respect of each member contain a sufficient indication to enable the account of that member in the register to be readily found.

(3) The index shall be at all times kept at the same place as the register of members.

(4) If default is made in complying with this section, the company and every officer of the company who is in default [shall be guilty of an offence and liable to a [class C fine][a]][b].

Amendments

a '£250' substituted for '£50' by C(A)A 1982 Sch 1, increased to £1,500 by CA 1990, s 240(7) as inserted by CLEA 2001, s 104(c) and converted to €1,904.61 by Council Regulations (EC) No 1103/97, No 974/98 and No 2866/98 and the Economic and Monetary Union Act 1998,

s 6; the above being implicitly substituted, by Fines Act 2010, s 6, for a fine not exceeding the aforesaid amount. A class C fine currently means a fine not exceeding €2,500.

b Words substituted by C(AA)A 2003, s 57 and Sch 2, Item No 1.

118 Provisions as to entries in register in relation to share warrants

(1) On the issue of a share warrant the company shall strike out of its register of members the name of the member then entered therein as holding the shares specified in the warrant as if he had ceased to be a member and shall enter in the register the following particulars:

(a) the fact of the issue of the warrant; and

(b) a statement of the shares included in the warrant, distinguishing each share by its number so long as the share has a number; and

(c) the date of the issue of the warrant.

(2) The bearer of a share warrant shall, subject to the articles of the company, be entitled on surrendering it for cancellation to have his name entered as a member in the register of members.

(3) The company shall be responsible for any loss incurred by any person by reason of the company entering in the register the name of a bearer of a share warrant in respect of the shares therein specified without the warrant being surrendered and cancelled.

(4) Until the warrant is surrendered, the particulars specified in subsection (1) shall be deemed to be the particulars required by this Act to be entered in the register of members, and, on surrender, the date of the surrender must be entered.

(5) Subject to the provisions of this Act, the bearer of a share warrant may, if the articles of the company so provide, be deemed to be a member of the company within the meaning of this Act, either to the full extent or for any purposes defined in the articles.

119 Inspection of register and index

(1) Except when the register of members is closed under the provisions of this Act, the register, and index of the names, of the members of a company shall during business hours (subject to such reasonable restrictions as the company in general meeting may impose, so that not less than 2 hours in each day be allowed for inspection) be open to the inspection of any member without charge, and of any other person on payment of [6 cent][a], or such less sum as the company may prescribe, for each inspection.

(2) Any member or other person may require a copy of the register, or of any part thereof, on payment of [4 cent][b], or such less sum as the company may prescribe, for every 100 words or fractional part thereof required to be copied.

The company shall cause any copy so required by any person to be sent to that person within a period of 10 days commencing on the day next after the day on which the requirement is received by the company.

(3) If any inspection required under this section is refused or if any copy required under this section is not sent within the proper period, the company and every officer of the company who is in default shall be liable in respect of each offence to a [class C fine][c].

(4) In the case of any such refusal or default, the court may by order compel an immediate inspection of the register and index or direct that the copies required shall be sent to the persons requiring them.

Amendments

a 'One shilling' to be read as 'five new pence' pursuant to the Decimal Currency Act 1970, s 9, and converted to 6 cent by Council Regulations (EC) No 1103/97, No 974/98 and No 2866/98 and the Economic and Monetary Union Act 1998, s 6.

b 'Sixpence' to be read as 'three new pence' pursuant to the Decimal Currency Act 1970, s 9, and converted to 4 cent by Council Regulations (EC) No 1103/97, No 974/98 and No 2866/98 and the Economic and Monetary Union Act 1998, s 6.

c '£250' substituted for '£50' by C(A)A 1982, Sch 1, increased to £1,500 by CA 1990, s 240(7) as inserted by CLEA 2001, s 104(c) and converted to €1,904.61 by Council Regulations (EC) No 1103/97, No 974/98 and No 2866/98 and the Economic and Monetary Union Act 1998, s 6; the above being implicitly substituted, by Fines Act 2010, s 6, for a fine not exceeding the aforesaid amount. A class C fine currently means a fine not exceeding €2,500.

120 Consequences of failure to comply with requirements as to register owing to agent's default

Where, by virtue of paragraph (b) of subsection (5) of section 116, the register of members is kept at the office of some person other than the company, and by reason of any default of his the company fails to comply with subsection (7) of that section or subsection (3) of section 117 or section 119, or with any requirements of this Act as to the production of the register, that other person shall be liable to the same penalties as if he were an officer of the company who is in default, and the power of the court under subsection (4) of section 119, shall extend to the making of orders against that other person and his officers or servants.

121 Power to close register

A company may, on giving notice by advertisement in some newspaper circulating in the district in which the registered office of the company is situate, close the register of members for any time or times not exceeding in the whole 30 days in each year.

122 Rectification of register

(1) If—

(a) the name of any person is, without sufficient cause, entered in the register of members or omitted therefrom in contravention of subsections (1) and (2) of section 116; or

(b) default is made in entering on the register within the period fixed by subsection (3) of section 116 the fact of any person having ceased to be a member;

the person aggrieved, or any member of the company, or the company, may apply to the court for rectification of the register.

(2) Where an application is made under this section, the court may either refuse the application or may order rectification of the register and payment by the company of compensation for any loss sustained by any party aggrieved.

(3) On an application under this section the court may decide any question relating to the title of any person who is a party to the application to have his name entered in or omitted from the register, whether the question arises between members or alleged members, or between members or alleged members on the one hand and the company on

the other hand, and generally may decide any question necessary or expedient to be decided for rectification of the register.

(4) In the case of a company required by this Act to send a list of its members to the registrar of companies, the court when making an order for rectification of the register shall by its order direct notice of the rectification to be given to the registrar.

(5) A company may, without application to the court, at any time rectify any error or omission (whether occurring before, on or after the operative date) in the register but such a rectification shall not adversely affect any person unless he agrees to the rectification made. The company shall, within 21 days, give notice of the rectification to the registrar of companies if the error or omission also occurs in any document forwarded by the company to him.

123 Trusts not to be entered on register

No notice of any trust, express, implied or constructive, shall be entered on the register or be receivable by the registrar.

124 Register to be evidence

The register of members shall be *prima facie* evidence of any matters by this Act directed or authorised to be inserted therein.

Annual return

125 [Annual Return

(1) Every company shall, once at least in every year, subject to section 127, make a return to the registrar of companies, being its annual return, in the prescribed form.

(2) If a company fails to comply with this section, the company and—

(a) every officer of the company who is in default, and

(b) any person in accordance with whose directions or instructions the directors of the company are accustomed to act and to whose directions or omissions the default is attributable,

shall be guilty of an offence.

(3) Proceedings in relation to an offence under this section may be brought and prosecuted by the registrar of companies.][a]

Amendments

a CA 1963, s 125 repealed and substituted by CLEA 2001, s 59.

---

126 Annual return to be made by company not having a share capital

[...][a]

Amendments

a CA 1963, s 126 repealed by CLEA 2001, s 59.

---

127 [Annual return date

[(1) The annual return of a company shall be made up to a date that is not later than its annual return date, except that the first annual return of a company incorporated after the commencement of section 46 of the Companies (Auditing and Accounting) Act 2003, shall be made up to the date that is its first annual return date.][b]

(2) Subject to subsection (3), the annual return shall be delivered to the registrar of companies—

(a) in the case of the first annual return following the commencement date of a company incorporated before the commencement date — not later than 28 days after the annual return date or 3 months after the commencement date, whichever is the later, and

(b) in any other case — not later than 28 days after the annual return date, unless it is made up to an earlier date in which case it shall be delivered to the registrar not later than 28 days after that earlier date.

(3) The court, on an application made (on notice to the registrar of companies) by a company, may, if it is satisfied that it would be just to do so, make an order extending the time for the purposes of paragraph (a) or (b) of subsection (2) in which the annual return of the company in relation to a particular year may be delivered to the registrar of companies.

(4) As soon as practicable after the making of an order under subsection (3), the company to whom the order relates shall deliver an office copy of the order to the registrar of companies and, if the company fails to do so, the company and every officer of the company who is in default shall be guilty of an offence.

(5) For companies incorporated before the commencement date, the annual return date is[, subject to subsection (8),][c] each anniversary of the date to which the then most recent annual return delivered to the registrar by the company was made up, but if no annual return had been delivered by the company to the registrar, the first annual return date is[, subject to subsection (8),][c] the first day after the commencement date that is 6 months after the date on which the anniversary of incorporation of the company falls and, subject to subsection (8), subsequent annual return dates fall on each anniversary of that first annual return date.

(6) For companies incorporated on or after the commencement date, the first annual return date is the day 6 months after the date of incorporation of the company and, subject to subsection (8), subsequent annual return dates fall on each anniversary of the first annual return date.

(7) Notwithstanding anything to the contrary in the Companies Acts, companies incorporated on or after the commencement date shall not be required to annex accounts to the first annual return delivered to the registrar after the commencement date in compliance with the Companies Acts.

[(8) Where the annual return of a company is made up to a date earlier than its annual return date, the annual return date shall thereafter be each anniversary of the date to which that annual return is made up, unless the company elects in the annual return to retain its existing annual return date or establishes a new annual return date pursuant to subsection (9).][d]

(9) A company may establish a new annual return date by—

(a) delivering an annual return to the registrar not later than 28 days after the annual return date to which, notwithstanding any provision to the contrary in the Companies Acts, it is by virtue of this subsection not required to annex accounts, and

(b) nominating to the registrar, on the prescribed form, the new annual return date, which date shall be no later than 6 months after the existing annual return date.

(10) Where a company has established a new annual return date pursuant to subsection (9), it shall not again establish a new annual return date pursuant to that subsection until at least 5 years have elapsed since the establishment of the first-mentioned new annual return date.

(11)(a) Notwithstanding subsection (5), a company incorporated before the commencement date may establish a new annual return date by—

(i) delivering an annual return to the registrar not later than 28 days after the first annual return date after the commencement date to which, notwithstanding anything to the contrary in the Companies Acts, it is by virtue of this subsection not required to annex accounts, and

(ii) nominating to the registrar, on the prescribed form, the new annual return date, which date shall be no later than 6 months after the existing annual return date.

(b) Where a company has nominated a new annual return date pursuant to paragraph (a), it may not establish a new annual return date pursuant to subsection (9) before such time as it has delivered to the registrar an annual return made up to the new annual return date nominated pursuant to paragraph (a)(ii).

(12) If a company fails to comply with this section, the company and—

(a) every officer of the company who is in default, and

(b) any person in accordance with whose directions or instructions the directors of the company are accustomed to act, and on whose directions or omissions the default is attributable,

shall be guilty of an offence.

(13) Proceedings in relation to an offence under this section may be brought and prosecuted by the registrar of companies.

(14) In this section, 'commencement date' means the date of commencement of section 60 of the Company Law Enforcement Act, 2001.][a]

Amendments

a CA 1963, s 127 substituted by CLEA 2001, s 60.

b CA 1963, s 127(1) substituted by C(AA)A 2003, s 46(a).

c Words ', subject to subsection (8),' inserted in CA 1963, s 127(5) by C(AA)A 2003, s 46(b).

d CA 1963, s 128(8) substituted by C(AA)A 2003, s 46(c).

128 Documents to be annexed to annual return

(1) Subject to the provisions of this Act, there shall be annexed to the annual return—

(a) a written copy certified both by a director and by the secretary of the company to be a true copy of every balance sheet laid before the annual general meeting of the company held during the period to which the return relates (including every document required by law to be annexed to the balance sheet); and

(b) a copy certified as aforesaid of the report of the auditors on, and of the report of the directors accompanying, each such balance sheet; and

(c) where any such balance sheet or document required by law to be annexed thereto is in any language other than the English or Irish language, there shall be annexed to that balance sheet a translation in English or Irish of the balance sheet or document certified in the prescribed manner to be a correct translation.

(2) If any such balance sheet as aforesaid or document required by law to be annexed thereto did not comply with the requirements of the law as in force at the date of the audit with respect to the form of balance sheets or documents aforesaid, as the case may be, there shall be made such additions to and corrections in the copy as would have been required to be made in the balance sheet or document in order to make it comply with the said requirements, and the fact that the copy has been so amended shall be stated thereon.

(3) If a company fails to comply with this section, the company and every officer of the company who is in default [shall be guilty of an offence and liable to a [class C fine][a]].[b]

For the purposes of this subsection, 'officer' shall include any person in accordance with whose directions or instructions the directors of the company are accustomed to act.

(4) This section shall not apply to—

(a) a private company; or

(b) [...][c]

(c) a company, not having a share capital, which is formed for an object that is charitable and is under the control of a religion recognised by the State under Article 44 of the Constitution, and which exercises its functions in accordance with the laws, canons and ordinances of the religion concerned.

(5) (a) The Commissioners of Charitable Donations and Bequests for Ireland may, if they think fit, by order exempt, either altogether or for a limited period, from the application of this section a specified company, formed for charitable purposes, not having a share capital.

(b) The Commissioners may by order revoke an order under paragraph (*a*).

(c) A sealed copy of every order of the Commissioners under this subsection shall be delivered by the company to the registrar of companies for registration within fourteen days of the making of the order.

[(6) Nothing in this section requires the balance sheet of a private company or any document or report relating to the balance sheet, other than the report prepared in accordance with subsection (6B), to be annexed to the annual return.

(6A) Nothing in subsection (4) or in section 2(1) of the Companies (Amendment) Act 1986 exempts any of the following companies from the requirement to annex to its annual return the report prepared in accordance with subsection (6B):

(a) a private company not trading for the acquisition of gain by the members;

(b) a company to which subsection (4)(c) applies;

(c) a company in respect of which an order under subsection (5) is in force.

(6B) The auditors of a company referred to in subsection (6) or (6A) shall prepare a separate report to the directors which—

(a) confirms that they audited the accounts for the relevant year, and

(b) includes within it the report made to the members of the company pursuant to section 193 [of the Act of 1990].[d]

(6C) A copy of the report prepared in accordance with subsection (6B) shall be certified by a director and by the secretary of the company to be a true copy of that report and shall be attached to the company's annual return.][e]

(7) Proceedings in relation to an offence under this section may be brought and prosecuted by the registrar of companies.

Amendments

a '£1,000' substituted for '£500' by CA 1990, s 244, increased to £1,500 by CA 1990, s 240(7) as inserted by CLEA 2001, s 104(c) and converted to €1,904.61 by Council Regulations (EC) No 1103/97, No 974/98 and No 2866/98 and the Economic and Monetary Union Act 1998, s 6; the above being implicitly substituted, by Fines Act 2010, s 6, for a fine not exceeding the aforesaid amount. A class C fine currently means a fine not exceeding €2,500.

b Words in CA 1963, s 128(3) substituted by C(AA)A 2003, s 57 and Sch 2, Item No 1.

c CA 1963, s 128(4)(b) repealed by EC(IUA)R 1996, reg 20(1).

d Words inserted by IFCMPA 2005, s 61.

e CA 1963, s 128(6) substituted and CA 1963, s 128(6A)–(6C) inserted by C(AA)A 2003, s 47.

---

129 Certificates to be sent by private company with annual return

A private company shall send with the annual return required by section 125 a certificate signed both by a director and by the secretary of the company that the company has not, since the date of the last return or, in the case of a first return, since the date of the incorporation of the company, issued any invitation to the public to subscribe for any shares or debentures of the company, and, where the annual return discloses the fact that the number of members of the company exceeds fifty, also a certificate so signed that the excess consists wholly of persons who, under paragraph (b) of subsection (1) of section 33 are not to be included in reckoning the number of fifty.

Meetings and Proceedings

130 Statutory meeting and statutory report

[...][a]

Amendments

a CA 1963, s 130 repealed by C(A)A 1983, Sch 3, Pt 1.

---

131 Annual general meeting

(1) Subject to subsection (2), every company shall in each year hold a general meeting as its annual general meeting in addition to any other meetings in that year and shall specify the meeting as such in the notices calling it and not more than 15 months shall elapse between the date of one annual general meeting of a company and that of the next.

(2) So long as a company holds its first annual general meeting within 18 months of its incorporation, it need not hold it in the year of its incorporation or in the following year.

(3) If default is made in holding a meeting of the company in accordance with subsection (1), the [Director][a] may, on the application of any member of the company, call or direct the calling of a general meeting of the company and give such ancillary or consequential directions as the [Director][a] thinks expedient, including directions modifying or supplementing in relation to the calling, holding and conducting of the meeting, the operation of the company's articles, and it is hereby declared that the directions which may be given under this subsection include a direction that one member of the company present in person or by proxy shall be deemed to constitute a meeting.

(4) A general meeting held in pursuance of subsection (3) shall, subject to any directions of the [Director][a], be deemed to be an annual general meeting of the company but, where a meeting so held is not held in the year in which the default in holding the company's annual general meeting occurred, the meeting so held shall not be treated as the annual general meeting for the year in which it is held unless at that meeting the company resolves that it shall be so treated.

(5) Where a company resolves that a meeting shall be so treated, a copy of the resolution shall, within 15 days after the passing thereof, be forwarded to the registrar of companies and recorded by him.

(6) If default is made in holding a meeting of the company in accordance with subsection (1), or in complying with any direction of the [Director] [a] under subsection (3), the company and every officer of the company who is in default [shall be guilty of an offence and liable to a [class C fine][b]][c], and if default is made in complying with subsection (5), the company and every officer of the company who is in default [shall be guilty of an offence and liable to a [class C fine][d]][c].

Amendments

a 'Director' substituted for 'Minister' by CLEA 2001, s 14.

b '£500' substituted for '£100' by C(A)A 1982, Sch 1, increased to £1,500 by CA 1990, s 240(7) as inserted by CLEA 2001, s 104(c) and converted to €1,904.61 by Council Regulations (EC) No 1103/97, No 974/98 and No 2866/98 and the Economic and Monetary Union Act 1998, s 6; the above being implicitly substituted, by Fines Act 2010, s 6, for a fine not exceeding the aforesaid amount. A class C fine currently means a fine not exceeding €2,500.

c Words 'shall be guilty of an offence and liable to a fine' substituted for 'shall be liable for a fine' in CA 1963, s 131(6) substituted by C(AA)A 2003, s 57 and Sch 2, Item No 4.

d '£100' substituted for '£20' by C(A)A 1982, Sch 1, increased to £1,500 by CA 1990, s 240(7) as inserted by CLEA 2001, s 104(c) and converted to €1,904.61 by Council Regulations (EC)

No 1103/97, No 974/98 and No 2866/98 and the Economic and Monetary Union Act 1998, s 6; the above being implicitly substituted, by Fines Act 2010, s 6, for a fine not exceeding the aforesaid amount. A class C fine currently means a fine not exceeding €2,500.

132 Convening of extraordinary general meeting on requisition

(1) The directors of a company, notwithstanding anything in its articles, shall, on the requisition of members of the company holding at the date of the deposit of the requisition not less than one-tenth of such of the paid up capital of the company as at the date of the deposit carries the right of voting at general meetings of the company, or, in the case of a company not having a share capital, members of the company representing not less than one-tenth of the total voting rights of all the members having at the said date a right to vote at general meetings of the company, forthwith proceed duly to convene an extraordinary general meeting of the company.

[(1A) Notwithstanding subsection (1) or anything in its articles, the directors of a company traded on a regulated market, shall, on the requisition of members of the company holding at the date of the deposit of the requisition not less than 5 per cent of such of the paid up capital of the company as at the date of the deposit carries the right of voting at general meetings of the company, forthwith proceed duly to convene an extraordinary general meeting of the company.][a]

(2) The requisition must state the objects of the meeting and must be signed by the requisitionists and deposited at the registered office of the company and may consist of several documents in like form each signed by one or more requisitionists.

(3) If the directors do not within 21 days from the date of the deposit of the requisition proceed duly to convene a meeting to be held within 2 months from the said date, the requisitionists, or any of them representing more than one half of the total voting rights of all of them, may themselves convene a meeting, but any meeting so convened shall not be held after the expiration of 3 months from the said date.

(4) A meeting convened under this section by the requisitionists shall be convened in the same manner as nearly as possible as that in which meetings are to be convened by directors.

(5) Any reasonable expenses incurred by the requisitionists by reason of the failure of the directors duly to convene a meeting shall be repaid to the requisitionists by the company and any sum so repaid shall be retained by the company out of any sums due or to become due from the company by way of fees or other remuneration in respect of their services to such of the directors as were in default.

(6) For the purposes of this section, the directors shall, in the case of a meeting at which a resolution is to be proposed as a special resolution, be deemed not to have duly convened the meeting if they do not give such notice thereof as is required by section 141.

Amendments

a CA 1963, s 132(1A) inserted by Shareholders' Rights Regulations 2009, reg 4.

[132A Equal treatment of members

A company traded on a regulated market shall ensure equal treatment for all members who are in the same position with regard to the exercise of voting rights and participation in a general meeting.][a]

Amendments

a CA 1963, s 132A inserted by Shareholders' Rights Regulations 2009, reg 5.

133 Length of notice for calling meetings

(1) Any provision of a company's articles shall be void in so far as it provides for the calling of a meeting of the company (other than an adjourned meeting) by a shorter notice than—

(a) in the case of the annual general meeting, 21 days' notice in writing; and

(b) in the case of a meeting (other than an annual general meeting or a meeting for the passing of a special resolution) 14 days' notice in writing where the company is neither a private company nor an unlimited company and 7 days' notice in writing where it is a private company [or an unlimited company, and][a]

[(c) in the case of a company traded on a regulated market, without prejudice to Articles 9(4) and 11(4) of Directive 2004/25/EC—

(i) in the case of an annual general meeting, 21 days' notice in writing, and

(ii) in the case of a general meeting (other than an annual general meeting or a meeting for the passing of a special resolution) 14 days' notice in writing where—

(I) the company offers the facility for members to vote by electronic means accessible to all members who hold shares that carry rights to vote at general meetings, and

(II) a special resolution reducing the period of notice to 14 days has been passed at the immediately preceding annual general meeting, or at a general meeting held since that meeting.][b]

(2) Save in so far as the articles of a company make other provision in that behalf (not being a provision avoided by sub-section (1)) a meeting of the company (other than an adjourned meeting) may be called—

(a) in the case of the annual general meeting by 21 days' notice in writing; and

(b) in the case of a meeting (other than an annual general meeting or a meeting for the passing of a special resolution), by 14 days' notice in writing where the company is neither a private company nor an unlimited company and by 7 days' notice in writing where it is a private company [or an unlimited company, and][c]

[(c) in the case of a company traded on a regulated market, without prejudice to Articles 9(4) and 11(4) of Directive 2004/25/EC—

(i) in the case of an annual general meeting, 21 days' notice in writing, and

(ii) in the case of a general meeting (other than an annual general meeting or a meeting for the passing of a special resolution) 14 days' notice in writing where—

(I) the company offers the facility for members to vote by electronic means accessible to all members who hold shares that carry rights to vote at general meetings, and

(II) a special resolution reducing the period of notice to 14 days has been passed at the immediately preceding annual general meeting, or at a general meeting held since that meeting.][d]

(3) A meeting of a company[, other than a company traded on a regulated market,][e] shall, notwithstanding that it is called by shorter notice than that specified in subsection (2) or in the company's articles, as the case may be, be deemed to have been duly called if it is so agreed by the auditors of the company and by all the members entitled to attend and vote thereat.

Amendments

a Words 'or an unlimited company, and' substituted for 'or an unlimited company.' by Shareholders' Rights Regulations 2009, reg 6(a).

b CA 1963, s 133(1)(c) inserted by Shareholders' Rights Regulations 2009, reg 6(b).

c Words 'or an unlimited company, and' substituted for 'or an unlimited company.' by inserted by Shareholders' Rights Regulations 2009, reg 6(c).

d CA 1963, s 133(2)(c) inserted by Shareholders' Rights Regulations 2009, reg 6(d).

e Words ', other than a company traded on a regulated market,' inserted by Shareholders' Rights Regulations 2009, reg 6(e).

[133A Further provisions on notice

(1) Notwithstanding section 13 or anything contained in its articles, this section applies to a company traded on a regulated market.

(2) Notice of a general meeting shall be issued, free of charge, in a manner ensuring fast access to the notice on a non-discriminatory basis, using such media as may reasonably be relied upon for the effective dissemination of information to the public throughout Member States.

(3) Notice of a general meeting under subsections (1)(c) and (2)(c) of section 133 shall set out:

(a) when and where the meeting is to take place and the proposed agenda for the meeting;

(b) a clear and precise statement of any procedures a member must comply with in order to participate and vote in the meeting, including—

(i) the right of a member to put items on the agenda of a general meeting and to table draft resolutions pursuant to section 133B and to ask questions relating to items on the agenda pursuant to section 134C, and the time limits applicable to the exercise of any of those rights,

(ii) the right of a member entitled to attend, speak, ask questions and vote, to appoint a proxy pursuant to section 136 (including a proxy who is not a member) by electronic means or otherwise or, where allowed, one or more proxies, to attend, speak, ask questions and vote instead of the member,

(iii) the procedure for voting by proxy pursuant to section 136, including the forms to be used and the means by which the company is prepared to accept electronic notification of the appointment of a proxy, and

(iv) the procedure (where applicable) to be followed pursuant to sections 134B and 138 for voting electronically or by correspondence respectively;

(c) the record date for eligibility for voting as defined in section 134A and state that only members registered on the record date shall have the right to participate and vote in the general meeting;

(d) where and how the full, unabridged text of the documents and draft resolutions referred to in subsection 4(c) and (d) may be obtained, and

(e) the internet site at which the information contained in subsection (4) shall be made available.

(4) A company shall make available to its members on its internet site, for a continuous period beginning not later than 21 days before a general meeting (inclusive of the day of the meeting), the following—

(a) a notice under section 133A(2),

(b) the total number of shares and voting rights at the date of the giving of the notice (including separate totals for each class of shares where the company's capital is divided into 2 or more classes of shares),

(c) the documents to be submitted to the meeting,

(d) a copy of any draft resolution or, where no such resolution is proposed to be adopted, a comment from the board of directors on each item of the proposed agenda of the meeting,

(e) a copy of forms to be used to vote by proxy and to vote by correspondence unless these forms are sent directly to each member.

(5) The company shall make available, on its internet site as soon as possible following their receipt, draft resolutions tabled by members.

(6) Where the forms referred to in subsection (4)(e) cannot be made available on the company's internet site for technical reasons, the company shall indicate on its internet site how the forms may be obtained in hard copy form and the company shall send the forms by post, free of charge, to every member who requests them.

(7) Where notice of a general meeting is issued later than on the twenty first day before the meeting pursuant to section 133(1)(c)(ii) or 133(2)(c)(ii) or Articles 9(4) or 11(4) of Directive 2004/25/EC, the period specified in subsection (4) shall be reduced accordingly.][a]

Amendments

a CA 1963, s 133A inserted by Shareholders' Rights Regulations 2009, reg 7.

[133B Right to put items on the agenda of the general meeting and to table draft resolutions

(1) A member of a company traded on a regulated market, shall have the right, by electronic or postal means, at an address specified by the company, to—

(a) put an item on the agenda of an annual general meeting, provided that each such item is accompanied by stated grounds justifying its inclusion or a draft resolution to be adopted at the general meeting, and

(b) table a draft resolution for an item on the agenda of a general meeting,

subject to the member or members concerned holding 3 per cent of the issued share capital, representing at least 3 per cent of the total voting rights of all the members who have a right to vote at the meeting to which the request for inclusion of the item relates.

(2) A request by a member to put an item on the agenda or to table a draft resolution under subsection (1)(a) shall be received by the company in hardcopy form or in electronic form at least 42 days before the meeting to which it relates.

(3) Where the exercise of the right conferred by subsection (1)(a) involves a modification of the agenda for the annual general meeting, in situations where the agenda has already been communicated to the members, and only in such situations, the company shall make available a revised agenda in the same manner as the previous agenda in advance of the applicable record date (as defined in section 134A) of share-ownership for purposes of entitlement to vote, or, if no such record date applies, sufficiently in advance of the date of the annual general meeting so as to enable other members to appoint a proxy or, where applicable, to vote by correspondence.

(4) In order to facilitate a member to avail of subsection (1)(a), the company shall ensure that the date of the next annual general meeting is placed on its internet site by—

(a) the end of the previous financial year, or

(b) not later than 70 days prior to the annual general meeting,

whichever is the earlier.][a]

Amendments

a CA 1963, s 133B inserted by Shareholders' Rights Regulations 2009, reg 7.

134 General Provisions as to meetings and votes

The following provisions shall have effects in so far as the articles of the company do not make other provision in that behalf—

(a) notice of the meeting of a company shall be served on every member of the company in the manner in which notices are required to be served by Table A and for the purpose of this paragraph 'Table A' means that Table as for the time being in force;

(b) two or more members holding not less than one-tenth of the issued share capital or, if the company has not a share capital, not less than 5 per cent in number of all the members of the company may call a meeting;

(c) in the case of a private company two members, and in the case of any other company three members, personally present shall be a quorum;

(d) any member elected by the members present at a meeting may be chairman thereof;

(e) in the case of a company originally having a share capital, every member shall have one vote in respect of each share or each [€12.69][a] of stock held by him, and in any other case, every member shall have one vote.

Amendments

a £10 converted to €12.69 by Council Regulations (EC) No 1103/97, No 974/98 and No 2866/98 and the Economic and Monetary Union Act 1998, s 6.

[134A Requirements for participation and voting in general meeting

(1) This section applies to a company traded on a regulated market.

(2) In this section—

'record date' means a date not more than 48 hours before the general meeting to which it relates;

'register of securities' has the same meaning as it has in Regulation 3 of the Companies Act 1990 (Uncertificated Securities) Regulations 1996 (S.I. No. 68 of 1996).

(3) A person shall be entered on the relevant register of securities by the record date in order to exercise the right of a member to participate and vote at a general meeting and any change to an entry on the relevant register of securities after the record date shall be disregarded in determining the right of any person to attend and vote at the meeting.

(4) The right of a member to participate in a general meeting and to vote in respect of his shares shall not be subject to any requirement that the shares be deposited with, or transferred to, or registered in the name of another person before the general meeting.

(5) A member is free to sell or otherwise transfer shares in a company at any time between the record date and the general meeting to which it applies if the right to sell would not otherwise be subject to such a restriction.

(6) Proof of qualification as a member may be made subject only to such requirements as are necessary to ensure the identification of the member and only to the extent that such requirements are proportionate to the achievement of that objective.][a]

Amendments

a CA 1963, s 134A inserted by Shareholders' Rights Regulations 2009, reg 8.

[134B Participation in general meeting by electronic means

(1) A company traded on a regulated market may provide for participation in a general meeting by electronic means including—

(a) a mechanism for casting votes, whether before or during the meeting, and the mechanism adopted shall not require the member to be physically present at the meeting or require the member to appoint a proxy who is physically present at the meeting,

(b) real time transmission of the meeting,

(c) real time two way communication enabling members to address the meeting from a remote location.

(2) (a) The use of electronic means pursuant to subsection (1) may be made subject only to such requirements and restrictions as are necessary to ensure the identification of those taking part and the security of the electronic communication, to the extent that such requirements and restrictions are proportionate to the achievement of those objectives.

(b) Members shall be informed of any requirements or restrictions which a company puts in place pursuant to paragraph (a).

(c) A company that provides electronic means for participation at a general meeting by a member shall ensure, as far as practicable, such means—

(i) guarantee the security of any electronic communication by the member,

(ii) minimise the risk of data corruption and unauthorised access,

(iii) provide certainty as to the source of the electronic communication, and

(iv) are remedied as soon as practicable, in the case of any failure or disruption.][a]

Amendments

a CA 1963, s 134B inserted by Shareholders' Rights Regulations 2009, reg 8.

[134C Right to ask questions

(1) A member of a company traded on a regulated market has the right to ask questions related to items on the agenda of a general meeting and to have such questions answered by the company subject to any reasonable measures the company may take to ensure the identification of the member.

(2) An answer to a question asked pursuant to subsection (1) is not required where—

(a) to give an answer would interfere unduly with the preparation for the meeting or the confidentiality and business interests of the company,

(b) the answer has already been given on the company's internet site in a question and answer forum, or

(c) it appears to the Chairman of the meeting that it is undesirable in the interests of good order of the meeting that the question be answered.][a]

Amendments

a CA 1963, s 134C inserted by Shareholders' Rights Regulations 2009, reg 8.

135 Power of court to order a meeting

(1) If for any reason it is impracticable to call a meeting of a company in any manner in which meetings of that company may be called, or to conduct the meeting of the company in manner prescribed by the articles or this Act, the court may, either of its own motion or on the application of any director of the company or of any member of the

company who would be entitled to vote at the meeting, order a meeting of the company to be called, held and conducted in such manner as the court thinks fit, and where any such order is made may give such ancillary or consequential directions as it thinks expedient; and it is hereby declared that the directions that may be given under this subsection include a direction that one member of the company present in person or by proxy shall be deemed to constitute a meeting.

(2) Any meeting called, held and conducted in accordance with an order under subsection (1) shall for all purposes be deemed to be a meeting of the company duly called, held and conducted.

136 Proxies

(1) Subject to subsection (2), any member of a company entitled to attend and vote at a meeting of the company shall be entitled to appoint another person (whether a member or not) as his proxy to attend and vote instead of him, and a proxy so appointed shall have the same right as the member to speak at the meeting and to vote on a show of hands and on a poll.

[(1A)(a) This subsection applies to a company traded on a regulated market.

(b) A proxy appointed may be any natural or legal person (whether a member or not) and shall act in accordance with any instructions given by the member by whom the proxy is appointed.

(c) A proxy shall be appointed by written notification to a company or by electronic means.

(d) A member shall be entitled to—

(i) appoint a proxy by electronic means, to an address specified by the company,

(ii) have the electronic notification of such appointment accepted by the company, and

(iii) have at least one effective method of notification of a proxy by electronic means offered to it by a company.

(e) The appointment and notification of appointment of a proxy to a company and the issuing of voting instructions to a proxy may be subject only to such formal requirements as are necessary to ensure identification of a member, or the proxy, or the possibility of verifying the content of voting instructions, if any, and only to the extent that those requirements are proportionate to achieving those objectives.

(1B) Subsection (1A) shall apply mutatis mutandis to the revocation of the appointment of a proxy.][a]

(2) Unless the articles otherwise provide—

(a) subsection (1) shall not apply in the case of a company not having a share capital; and

(b) a member of a company shall not be entitled to appoint more than one proxy to attend on the same occasion.

[(2A) Notwithstanding subsection (2) or anything in its articles, in the case of a company traded on a regulated market—

(a) no limitation may be placed on the right of a member to appoint more than one proxy to attend and vote at a general meeting in respect of shares held in different securities accounts, and

(b) subject to paragraph (a), a member shall not be entitled to appoint more than one proxy to attend and vote on the same occasion, provided however that a member (being a natural or legal person) acting as an intermediary on behalf of a client, shall not be prohibited from granting a proxy to each of his clients or to any third party designated by a client. Such intermediary shall be permitted to cast votes attaching to some of the shares differently from others.][b]

(3) In every notice calling a meeting of a company having a share capital there shall appear with reasonable prominence a statement that a member entitled to attend and vote is entitled to appoint a proxy or, where that is allowed, one or more proxies, to attend, speak and vote instead of him, and that a proxy need not be a member; and if default is made in complying with this subsection in relation to any meeting, every officer of the company who is in default [shall be guilty of an offence and liable to a [class C fine][c]][d].

(4) Any provision contained in a company's articles shall be void in so far as it would have the effect of requiring the instrument appointing a proxy, or any other document necessary to show the validity of or otherwise relating to the appointment of a proxy, to be received by the company or any other person more than 48 hours before a meeting or adjourned meeting in order that the appointment may be effective thereat.

[(4A) Any provision contained in the articles of a company traded on a regulated market (other than a requirement that a person appointed as a proxy shall possess legal capacity) shall be void in so far as it would have the effect of restricting the eligibility of a person to be appointed as a proxy.][e]

(5) Subject to subsection (6), if for the purpose of any meeting of a company invitations to appoint as proxy a person or one of a number of persons specified in the invitations are issued at the company's expense to some only of the members entitled to be sent a notice of the meeting and to vote thereat by proxy, every officer of the company who knowingly and wilfully authorises or permits their issue as aforesaid [shall be guilty of an offence and liable to a [class C fine][f]][g].

(6) An officer shall not be liable under subsection (5) by reason only of the issue to a member at his request in writing of a form of appointment naming the proxy or of a list of persons willing to act as proxy if the form or list is available on request in writing to every member entitled to vote at the meeting by proxy.

(7) This section shall apply to meetings of any class of members of a company as it applies to general meetings of the company.

Amendments

a CA 1963, s 136(1A) and (1B) inserted by Shareholders' Rights Regulations 2009, reg 9(a).

b CA 1963, s 136(2A) inserted by Shareholders' Rights Regulations 2009, reg 9(b).

c '£250' substituted for '£50' by C(A)A 1982, Sch 1, increased to £1,500 by CA 1990, s 240(7) as inserted by CLEA 2001, s 104(c) and converted to €1,904.61 by Council Regulations (EC) No 1103/97, No 974/98 and No 2866/98 and the Economic and Monetary Union Act 1998,

s 6; the above being implicitly substituted, by Fines Act 2010, s 6, for a fine not exceeding the aforesaid amount. A class C fine currently means a fine not exceeding €2,500.

d Words 'shall be guilty of an offence and liable to a fine' substituted for 'shall be liable to a fine' in CA 1963, s 136(3) by C(AA)A 2003, s 57 and Sch 2, Item No 1.

e CA 1963, s 136(4A) inserted by Shareholders' Rights Regulations 2009, reg 9(c).

f '£500' substituted for '£100' by C(A)A 1982, Sch 1, increased to £1,500 by CA 1990, s 240(7) as inserted by CLEA 2001, s 104(c) and converted to €1,904.61 by Council Regulations (EC) No 1103/97, No 974/98 and No 2866/98 and the Economic and Monetary Union Act 1998, s 6; the above being implicitly substituted, by Fines Act 2010, s 6, for a fine not exceeding the aforesaid amount. A class C fine currently means a fine not exceeding €2,500.

g Words 'shall be guilty of an offence and liable to a fine' substituted for 'shall be liable to a fine' in CA 1963, s 136(5) by C(AA)A 2003, s 57 and Sch 2, Item No 1.

---

137 Right to demand a poll

(1) Any provision contained in a company's articles shall be void in so far as it would have the effect either—

- (a) of excluding the right to demand a poll at a general meeting on any question other than the election of the chairman of the meeting or the adjournment of the meeting, or
- (b) of making ineffective a demand for a poll on any such question which is made—
  - (i) by not less than five members having the right to vote at the meeting, or
  - (ii) by a member or members representing not less than one-tenth of the total voting rights of all the members having the right to vote at the meeting, or
  - (iii) by a member or members holding shares in the company conferring a right to vote at the meeting, being shares on which an aggregate sum has been paid up equal to not less than one-tenth of the total sum paid up on all the shares conferring that right.

(2) The instrument appointing a proxy to vote at a meeting of a company shall be deemed also to confer authority to demand or join in demanding a poll, and for the purposes of subsection (1), a demand by a person as proxy for a member shall be the same as a demand by the member.

[138 Voting on a poll

(1) On a poll taken at a meeting of a company or a meeting of any class of members of a company, a member, whether present in person or by proxy, entitled to more than one vote need not, if he votes, use all his votes or cast all the votes he uses in the same way.

(2) A company traded on a regulated market, may provide for a vote exercised under subsection (1) to include a vote cast in advance by correspondence, subject only to such requirements and restrictions as are necessary to ensure the identification of the person voting, and as are proportionate to the achievement of that objective.

(3) A company traded on a regulated market shall only be required to count votes cast in advance by correspondence pursuant to subsection (2), where such votes are received before the date and time specified by the company, provided the date and time is no more than 24 hours before the time at which the vote is to be concluded.][a]

Amendments

a CA 1963, s 138 substituted by Shareholders' Rights Regulations 2009, reg 10.

139 Representation of bodies corporate at meetings of companies and of creditors

(1) A body corporate may—

(a) if it is a member of a company, by resolution of its directors or other governing body authorise such person as it thinks fit to act as its representative at any meeting of the company or at any meeting of any class of members of the company [....][a]

(b) if it is a creditor (including a holder of debentures) of a company, by resolution of its directors or other governing body authorise such person as it thinks fit to act as its representative at any meeting of any creditors of the company held in pursuance of this Act or of any rules made thereunder or in pursuance of the provisions contained in any debenture or trust deed, as the case [may be, and][b].

[(c) if it has been appointed as the proxy to attend and vote at a general meeting of a company traded on a regulated market on behalf of a member of the company, by resolution of its directors or other governing body authorise such person as it thinks fit to act as its representative at any meeting of the company or at any meeting of any class of members of the company for the purpose of such appointment.][c]

(2) A person authorised as aforesaid shall be entitled to exercise the same powers on behalf of the body corporate which he represents as that body corporate could exercise if it were an individual member, creditor or holder of debentures of the company.

Amendments

a Word 'and' deleted by Shareholders' Rights Regulations 2009, reg 11(a).

b Words 'may be, and' substituted for 'may be.' by Shareholders' Rights Regulations 2009, reg 11(b).

c CA 1963, s 139(1)(c) inserted by Shareholders' Rights Regulations 2009, reg 11(c).

140 Annual general meeting to be held in the State

(1) Subject to subsection (2), the annual general meeting of a company shall be held in the State and any business transacted at a meeting held in breach of this requirement shall be void unless—

(a) either all the members entitled to attend and vote at such meeting consent in writing to its being held elsewhere or a resolution providing that it be held elsewhere has been passed at the preceding annual general meeting, and

(b) the articles do not provide that the annual general meeting shall be held in the State.

(2) Subsection (1) shall not apply to the first annual general meeting of a company held on or after the operative date.

141 Resolutions

(1) A resolution shall be a special resolution when it has been passed by not less than three-fourths of the votes cast by such members as, being entitled so to do, vote in person or, where proxies are allowed, by proxy at a general meeting of which not less than 21 days' notice, specifying the intention to propose the resolution as a special resolution, has been duly given.

(2) A resolution may be proposed and passed as a special resolution at a meeting of which less than 21 days' notice has been given if it is so agreed by a majority in number of the members having the right to attend and vote at any such meeting, being a majority together holding not less than ninety per cent. in nominal value of the shares giving that right or, in the case of a company not having a share capital, together representing not less than ninety per cent. of the total voting rights at that meeting of all the members.

(3) At any meeting at which a special resolution is submitted to be passed, a declaration of the chairman that the resolution is carried shall, unless a poll is demanded, be conclusive evidence of the fact without proof of the number or proportion of the votes recorded in favour of or against the resolution.

(4) For the purposes of this section, notice of a meeting shall be deemed to be duly given and the meeting to be duly held when the notice is given and the meeting held in manner provided by this Act or the articles.

(5) The terms of any resolution (whether special or otherwise) before a general meeting may be amended by ordinary resolution moved at the meeting provided that the terms of the resolution as amended will still be such that adequate notice of the intention to pass the same can be deemed to have been given.

(6) Any reference to an extraordinary resolution contained in any statute which was passed or document which existed before the operative date shall, in relation to a resolution passed or to be passed on or after the operative date, be deemed to be a reference to a special resolution.

(7) Where before the operative date a meeting has been convened for the purpose of passing an extraordinary resolution as defined in the Companies Acts, 1908 to 1959, and at that meeting that resolution has after the operative date been passed in the manner required by those Acts for the passing of an extraordinary resolution and such resolution would under the Companies Acts, 1908 to 1959, have been effective for its purpose, such resolution shall be as effective as if it had been a special resolution.

(8) (a) Notwithstanding anything to the contrary in this Act, in any case in which a company is so authorised by its articles, a resolution in writing signed by all the members for the time being entitled to attend and vote on such resolution at a general meeting (or being bodies corporate by their duly appointed representatives) shall be as valid and effective for all purposes as if the resolution had been passed at a general meeting of the company duly convened and held, and if described as a special resolution shall be deemed to be a special resolution within the meaning of this Act.

(b) Any such resolution shall be deemed to have been passed at a meeting held on the date on which it was signed by the last member to sign, and where the resolution states a date as being the date of his signature thereof by any member the statement shall be *prima facie* evidence that it was signed by him on that date.

(c) This section does not apply to a resolution for any of the purposes of section 160 or 182.

142 Extended notice

(1) Subject to subsection (2), where by any provision hereafter contained in this Act extended notice is required of a resolution, the resolution shall not be effective unless (except when the directors of the company have resolved to submit it) notice of the intention to move it has been given to the company not less than 28 days before the meeting at which it is moved, and the company shall give its members notice of any such resolution at the same time and in the same manner as it gives notice of the meeting or, if that is not practicable, shall give them notice thereof, either by advertisement in a daily newspaper circulating in the district in which the registered office of the company is situate or in any other mode allowed by the articles, not less than 21 days before the meeting.

(2) If, after notice of the intention to move such a resolution has been given to the company, a meeting is called for a date 28 days or less after the notice has been given, the notice though not given within the time required by subsection (1) shall be deemed to have been properly given for the purposes of that subsection.

143 Registration of, and obligation of company to supply copies of certain resolutions and agreements

(1) A printed copy of every resolution or agreement to which this section applies shall, within 15 days after the passing or making thereof, be forwarded to the registrar of companies and recorded by him.

(2) Where articles have been registered, a copy of every such resolution or agreement for the time being in force shall be embodied in or annexed to every copy of the articles issued after the passing of the resolution or the making of the agreement.

(3) A copy of every such resolution or agreement shall be forwarded to any member at his request on payment of [6 cent][a] or such less sum as the company may direct.

(4) This section shall apply to:

(a) special resolutions;

(b) resolutions which have been agreed to by all the members of a company, but which, if not so agreed to, would not have been effective for their purpose unless they had been passed as special resolutions;

(c) resolutions or agreements which have been agreed to by all the members of some class of shareholders but which, if not so agreed to, would not have been effective for their purpose unless they had been passed by some particular majority or otherwise in some particular manner, and all resolutions or agreements which effectively bind all the members of any class of shareholders though not agreed to by all those members;

(d) resolutions increasing the share capital of a company;

(e) resolutions that a company be wound up voluntarily passed under paragraph (*a*) or paragraph (c) of subsection (1) of section 251.

[(f) resolutions attaching rights or restrictions to any share;

(g) resolutions varying any such rights or restrictions;

(h) resolutions classifying any unclassified share;

(i) resolutions converting shares of one class into shares of another class;][b]

[(j) resolutions of the directors of a company passed by virtue of sections 12(3)(a) and 43(3) of the Companies (Amendment) Act, 1983.][c]

(5) If a company fails to comply with subsection (1), the company and every officer of the company who is in default [shall be guilty of an offence and liable to a [class C fine][d]].[e]

(6) If a company fails to comply with subsection (2) or subsection (3), the company and every officer of the company who is in default [shall be guilty of an offence and liable to a [class C fine][f]][g] for each copy in respect of which default is made.

(7) For the purposes of subsections (5) and (6), a liquidator of a company shall be deemed to be an officer of the company.

Amendments

a ‘One shilling’ to be read as ‘five new pence’ pursuant to the Decimal Currency Act 1970, s 9, and converted to 6 cent by Council Regulations (EC) No 1103/97, No 974/98 and No 2866/98 and the Economic and Monetary Union Act 1998, s 6.

b CA 1963, s 143(4)(f)–(i) inserted by C(A)A 1982, s 5.

c CA 1963, s 143(4)(j) inserted by C(A)A 1983, Sch1, para 15.

d ‘£250’ substituted for ‘£50’ by C(A)A 1982, Sch 1, increased to £1,500 by CA 1990, s 240(7) as inserted by CLEA 2001, s 104(c) and converted to €1,904.61 by Council Regulations (EC) No 1103/97, No 974/98 and No 2866/98 and the Economic and Monetary Union Act 1998, s 6; the above being implicitly substituted, by Fines Act 2010, s 6, for a fine not exceeding the aforesaid amount. A class C fine currently means a fine not exceeding €2,500.

e Words ‘shall be guilty of an offence and liable to a fine’ substituted for ‘shall be liable to a fine’ in CA 1963, s 143(5) by C(AA)A 2003, s 57 and Sch 2, Item No 1.

f ‘£5’ substituted for ‘£1’ by C(A)A 1982, Sch 1, increased to £1,500 by CA 1990, s 240(7) as inserted by CLEA 2001, s 104(c) and converted to €1,904.61 by Council Regulations (EC) No 1103/97, No 974/98 and No 2866/98 and the Economic and Monetary Union Act 1998, s 6; the above being implicitly substituted, by Fines Act 2010, s 6, for a fine not exceeding the aforesaid amount. A class C fine currently means a fine not exceeding €2,500.

g Words ‘shall be guilty of an offence and liable to a fine’ substituted for ‘shall be liable to a fine’ in CA 1963, s 143(6) by C(AA)A 2003, s 57 and Sch 2, Item No 1.

---

144 Resolutions passed at adjourned meetings

Where a resolution is passed at an adjourned meeting of—

(a) a company;

(b) the holders of any class of shares in a company;

(c) the directors of a company;

the resolution shall for all purposes be treated as having been passed on the date on which it was in fact passed and shall not be deemed to have been passed on any earlier date.

145 Minutes of proceedings of meetings of company and directors

(1) Every company shall as soon as may be cause minutes of all proceedings of general meetings and all proceedings at meetings of its directors or committees of directors to be entered in books kept for that purpose.

(2) Any such minute if purporting to be signed by the chairman of the meeting at which the proceedings were had, or by the chairman of the next succeeding meeting, shall be evidence of the proceedings.

(3) Where minutes have been made in accordance with this section of the proceedings at any general meeting of the company or meeting of directors or committee of directors, then, until the contrary is proved, the meeting shall be deemed to have been duly held and convened, and all proceedings had thereat to have been duly had, and all appointments of directors or liquidators shall be deemed to be valid.

[(3A) A company shall, if required by the Director, produce to the Director for inspection the book or books kept in accordance with subsection (1) and shall give to the Director such facilities for inspecting and taking copies of the contents of the book or books as the Director may require.][a]

(4) If a company fails to comply with subsection (1) [or 3A][b], the company and every officer of the company who is in default [shall be guilty of an offence and liable to a [class C fine][c]][d].

Amendments

a CA 1963, s 145(3A) inserted by CLEA 2001, s 19(a).

b The words 'or (3A)' in CA 1963, s 145(4) inserted by CLEA 2001, s 19(b)

c '£500' substituted for '£100' by C(A)A 1982, Sch 1, increased to £1,500 by CA 1990, s 240(7) as inserted by CLEA 2001, s 104(c) and converted to €1,904.61 by Council Regulations (EC) No 1103/97, No 974/98 and No 2866/98 and the Economic and Monetary Union Act 1998, s 6; the above being implicitly substituted, by Fines Act 2010, s 6, for a fine not exceeding the aforesaid amount. A class C fine currently means a fine not exceeding €2,500.

d The words 'shall be guilty of an offence and liable to a fine' in CA 1963, s 145(4) substituted by C(AA)A 2003, s 57 and Sch 2, Item No. 1.

[145A Voting Results

(1) This section applies to a company traded on a regulated market.

(2) Where a member requests a full account of a vote before or on the declaration of the result of a vote at a general meeting, then with respect to each resolution proposed at a general meeting the company shall establish—

(a) the number of shares for which votes have been validly cast,

(b) the proportion of the company's issued share capital at close of business on the day before the meeting represented by those votes,

(c) the total number of votes validly cast, and

(d) the number of votes cast in favour of and against each resolution and, if counted, the number of abstentions.

(3) Where no member requests a full account of the voting before or on the declaration of the result of a vote at a general meeting, it shall be sufficient for the company to establish the voting results only to the extent necessary to ensure that the required majority is reached for each resolution.

(4) A company shall ensure that a voting result established in accordance with this section is published on its internet site not later than the end of the fifteenth day after the date of the meeting at which the voting result was obtained.][a]

Amendments

a CA 1963, s 145A inserted by Shareholders' Rights Regulations 2009, reg 12.

---

146 Inspection of minute books

(1) The books containing the minutes of proceedings of any general meeting of a company held after the operative date shall be kept at the registered office of the company, and shall during business hours (subject to such reasonable restrictions as the company may by its articles or in general meeting impose, so that not less than 2 hours in each day be allowed for inspection) be open to the inspection of any member without charge.

(2) Any member shall be entitled to be furnished within 7 days after he has made a request in that behalf to the company with a copy of any such minutes as aforesaid at a charge not exceeding [6 cent][a] for every 100 words.

(3) If any inspection required under this section is refused or if any copy required under this section is not sent within the proper time, the company and every officer of the company who is in default shall be liable in respect of each offence to a [class C fine][b].

(4) In the case of any such refusal or default, the court may by order compel an inspection of the books in respect of all proceedings of general meetings or direct that the copies required shall be sent to the persons requiring them.

Amendments

a 'One shilling' to be read as 'five new pence' pursuant to the Decimal Currency Act 1970, s 9, and converted to 6 cent by Council Regulations (EC) No 1103/97, No 974/98 and No 2866/98 and the Economic and Monetary Union Act 1998, s 6.

b '£125' substituted for '£25' by C(A)A 1982, Sch 1, increased to £1,500 by CA 1990, s 240(7) as inserted by CLEA 2001, s 104(c) and converted to €1,904.61 by Council Regulations (EC) No 1103/97, No 974/98 and No 2866/98 and the Economic and Monetary Union Act 1998, s 6; the above being implicitly substituted, by Fines Act 2010, s 6, for a fine not exceeding the aforesaid amount. A class C fine currently means a fine not exceeding €2,500.

Accounts and Audit

147 Keeping of books of account

[...][a]

Amendments

a CA 1963, s 147 repealed by CA 1990, s 6.

[148 Duty to prepare individual accounts

(1) The directors of every company shall on a date not later than 18 months after the incorporation of the company and subsequently once at least in every calendar year prepare accounts for the company for each financial year (to be known and in this Act referred to as 'individual accounts').

(2) Subject to subsections (3) to (11), a company's individual accounts shall be prepared—

(a) in accordance with section 149 (to be known and in this Act referred to as 'Companies Act individual accounts'), or

(b) in accordance with international financial reporting standards and section 149A (to be known and in this Act referred to as 'IFRS individual accounts').

(3) Companies Act individual accounts shall be prepared by a company—

(a) not trading for the acquisition of gain by the members, or

(b) to which section 128(4)(c) applies, or

(c) in respect of which an order under section 128(5) is in force.

(4) After the first financial year in which the directors of a company prepare IFRS individual accounts (in this section referred to as 'the first IFRS year'), all subsequent individual accounts of the company shall be prepared in accordance with international financial reporting standards unless there is a relevant change of circumstances as referred to in subsection (5).

(5) There is a relevant change of circumstances where at any time during or after the first IFRS year—

(a) the company becomes a subsidiary undertaking of another undertaking that does not prepare IFRS individual accounts,

(b) the company ceases to be a company with securities admitted to trading on a regulated market, or

(c) a parent undertaking of the company ceases to be an undertaking with securities admitted to trading on a regulated market.

(6) Where, following a relevant change of circumstances, Companies Act individual accounts are prepared, the directors may subsequently prepare IFRS individual accounts for the company and subsections (4) and (5) apply as if that financial year for which such IFRS individual accounts are subsequently prepared was the first IFRS year.

(7) The directors of the company shall lay the individual accounts before the annual general meeting of the company within 9 months of the balance sheet date.

(8) Subsection (7) shall not apply to the profit and loss account or income statement of a company where—

(a) the company is a parent company,

(b) the company prepares group accounts in accordance with section 150, and

(c) the notes to the company's individual balance sheet show the company's profit or loss for the financial year determined in accordance with section 149 or 149A, as appropriate.

(9) Where, in the case of a company, advantage is taken of subsection (8), that fact shall be disclosed—

(a) in the notes on the company's individual accounts, and

(b) in the notes on the group accounts referred to in subsection (8)(b).

(10) For the purposes of this Act unless the contrary intention appears—

(a) a reference to a balance sheet or profit and loss account or income statement shall include any notes thereon or document annexed thereto giving information required by this Act and allowed by this Act to be so given, and

(b) a reference to a profit and loss account shall be read, in the case of a company not trading for profit, as referring to its income and expenditure account, and references to profit or to loss and, if the company has subsidiaries, references to a consolidated profit and loss account shall be read accordingly.

(11) Where any person being a director of a company fails to take all reasonable steps to comply with this section, the person is, in respect of each offence, liable on summary conviction to imprisonment for a term not exceeding 6 months or to a [class D fine][b] or to both, so, however that—

(a) in any proceedings against a person in respect of an offence under this section, it shall be a defence to prove that the person had reasonable ground to believe and did believe that a competent and reliable person was charged with the duty of seeing that this section was complied with and was in a position to discharge that duty, and

(b) a person shall not be sentenced to imprisonment for such an offence unless, in the opinion of the court dealing with the case, the offence was committed wilfully.][a]

Amendments

a CA 1963, s 148 was repealed and replaced by reg 4 of EC(IFRSMA)R 2005.

b As implicitly substituted for "fine not exceeding €635" by Fines Act 2010, s 7. A class D fine currently means a fine not exceeding €1,000.

[149 Companies Act individual accounts

(1) Companies Act individual accounts shall comprise—

(a) a balance sheet as at the last day of the financial year, and

(b) a profit and loss account.

(2) The balance sheet shall give a true and fair view of the state of affairs of the company as at the end of the financial year and the profit and loss account shall give a true and fair view of the profit or loss of the company for the financial year.

(3) Companies Act individual accounts shall—

(a) in the case of an undertaking to which the Act of 1986 applies, comply with that Act,

(b) in the case of an undertaking to which the 1993 Regulations apply, comply with those Regulations and the Act of 1986,

(c) in the case of an undertaking to which the Credit Institutions Regulations apply, comply with those Regulations,

(d) in the case of an undertaking to which the Insurance Undertakings Regulations apply, comply with those Regulations, and

(e) in all other cases comply with the provisions of the Sixth Schedule in so far as that Schedule applies to Companies Act individual accounts.

(4) Save as expressly provided in subsections (5) and (6) or in Part III of the Sixth Schedule, the requirements of subsection (3)(e) and of the Sixth Schedule shall be without prejudice either to the general requirements of subsection (2) or to any other requirements of this Act.

(5) The profits or losses attributable to any shares in a subsidiary for the time being held by a holding company or any other of its subsidiaries shall not, for any purpose, be treated in the holding company's accounts as revenue profits or losses so far as they are profits or losses for the period before the date on or as from which the shares were acquired by the company or any of its subsidiaries, and for the purpose of determining whether any profits or losses are to be treated as profits or losses for the said period the profit or loss for any financial year of the subsidiary may, if it is not practicable to apportion it with reasonable accuracy by reference to the facts, be treated as accruing from day to day during that year and be apportioned accordingly. Provided however that where the directors and the auditors are satisfied and so certify that it would be fair and reasonable and would not prejudice the rights and interests of any person, the profits or losses attributable to any shares in a subsidiary may be treated in a manner otherwise than in accordance with this subsection.

(6) Where, in relation to any accounts laid before the annual general meeting of a company, any person being a director of a company fails to take all reasonable steps to secure compliance with this section and with the other requirements of this Act as to the matters to be stated in accounts, the person is, in respect of each offence, liable on summary conviction to imprisonment for a term not exceeding 6 months or to a [class D fine][b] or to both, so, however, that—

(a) in any proceedings against a person in respect of an offence under this section, it shall be a defence to prove that the person had reasonable ground to believe and did believe that a competent and reliable person was charged with the duty of seeing that this section or those other requirements, as the case may be, were complied with and was in a position to discharge that duty, and

(b) a person shall not be sentenced to imprisonment for any such offence unless, in the opinion of the court dealing with the case, the offence was committed wilfully.][a]

Amendments

a CA 1963, s 149 was repealed and replaced by reg 4 of EC(IFRSMA)R 2005.

b As implicitly substituted for "fine not exceeding €635" by Fines Act 2010, s 7. A class D fine currently means a fine not exceeding €1,000.

[149A IFRS individual accounts

(1) Where the directors of a company prepare IFRS individual accounts—

(a) they shall state in the notes to those accounts that the accounts have been prepared in accordance with international financial reporting standards, and

(b) shall ensure that those notes contain the information required by—

(i) section 191 and paragraph 39(6) of the Schedule to the Act of 1986 (details of directors' remuneration),

(ii) sections 41 to 45 of the Act of 1990 to be disclosed in individual accounts (transactions with directors),

(iii) section 63 of the Act of 1990 unless it is disclosed in the directors' report (interests in shares and debentures),

(iv) sections 16 and 16A (inserted by Regulation 23 of the 1993 Regulations) of the Act of 1986 (details on group undertakings),

(v) paragraphs 26 to 28 of the Schedule to the Act of 1986 (details of share capital and debentures),

(vi) paragraph 32A (inserted by section 233 of the Act of 1990) of the Schedule to the Act of 1986 (restriction on distributability of profits),

(vii) paragraph 36 of the Schedule to the Act of 1986 (guarantees and other financial commitments),

(viii) paragraph 37(2) of the Schedule to the Act of 1986 (financial assistance for the purchase of own shares),

(ix) paragraph 42 of the Schedule to the Act of 1986 (details of staff numbers and remuneration),

(x) paragraph 46 of the Schedule to the Act of 1986 (shares and debentures held by subsidiary undertakings), [...][b]

(xi) [...][c] section 205D (inserted by section 44 of the Act of 2003) of the Act of 1990 [(remuneration of auditors), and][d]][a]

[(xii) where appropriate, paragraph 36A of the Schedule to the Act of 1986.][e]

Amendments

a Section 149A was inserted by reg 4 of EC(IFRSMA)R 2005.

b Word 'and' deleted by European Communities (Directive 2006/46/EC) Regulations 2009, reg 11(a).

c Words 'paragraph 39(5) of the Schedule to the Act of 1986 and' deleted by EC(SA)(Dir)R 2010, reg 4(2).

d Section 149A(1)(b)(xi) amended by European Communities (Directive 2006/46/EC) Regulations 2009, reg 11(b).

e Subparagraph (xii) inserted by European Communities (Directive 2006/46/EC) Regulations 2009, reg 11(c).

[150 Duty to prepare group accounts

(1) Where at the end of its financial year a company is a parent company, the directors, as well as preparing individual accounts for the year, shall prepare consolidated accounts (to be known and in this Act referred to as 'group accounts') for the group for that year.

[(1A)(a) The requirement to prepare group accounts pursuant to subsection (1) shall not apply to a parent company whose subsidiary undertakings taken together are not material for the purpose of giving a true and fair view of the state of affairs as at the end of the financial year and the profit or loss for the financial year of that parent company and those subsidiary undertakings taken as whole.

(b) In this subsection 'parent company' does not include a parent company—

(i) to which subsection (4) applies, or

(ii) that is an unlimited company, other than an unlimited company to which Part III of the European Communities Accounts Regulations 1993 (S. I. No. 396 of 1993) applies.][a]

(2) (a) Subject to paragraph (b), companies are obliged for financial years commencing on or after 1 January 2005 to prepare their group accounts in accordance with international financial reporting standards (to be known and in this Act referred to as 'IFRS group accounts') if, at their balance sheet date their securities are admitted to trading on a regulated market of any EEA State.

(b) The requirements referred to in paragraph (a) shall only apply for each financial year starting on or after 1 January 2007 to those companies whose debt securities only have been admitted to trading on a regulated market of any EEA State.

(3) Subject to subsections (4) to (11), other companies which are required to prepare group accounts shall prepare—

(a) group accounts in accordance with section 150A (to be known and in this Act referred to as 'Companies Act group accounts'), or

(b) IFRS group accounts.

(4) Companies Act group accounts shall be prepared by a parent company—

(a) not trading for the acquisition of gain by the members, or

(b) to which section 128(4)(c) applies, or

(c) in respect of which an order under section 128(5) is in force.

(5) After the first financial year in which the directors of a parent company prepare IFRS group accounts (in this section referred to as 'the first IFRS year'), all subsequent group accounts of the company shall be prepared in accordance with international financial reporting standards unless there is a relevant change of circumstances as referred to in subsection (6).

(6) There is a relevant change of circumstances where at any time during or after the first IFRS year—

(a) the company becomes a subsidiary undertaking of another undertaking that does not prepare IFRS group accounts,

(b) the company ceases to be a company with securities admitted to trading on a regulated market, or

(c) a parent undertaking of the company ceases to be an undertaking with securities admitted to trading on a regulated market.

(7) Where, following a relevant change of circumstances, Companies Act group accounts are prepared, the directors may subsequently prepare IFRS group accounts for the company and subsections (5) and (6) apply as if that financial year for which such IFRS group accounts are subsequently prepared was the first IFRS year.

(8) In the case of a company to which the Group Accounts Regulations, the Credit Institutions Regulations or the Insurance Undertakings Regulations apply, this section is subject to the exemptions from the preparation of group accounts provided by those Regulations as applicable to the company concerned and set out in—

(a) Regulations 7, 8, 8A and 9 of the Group Accounts Regulations,

(b) Regulations 7, 8, 8A and 9 of the Credit Institutions Regulations, and

(c) Regulations 10, 12 and 12A of the Insurance Undertakings Regulations.

(9) The directors of the company shall lay any group accounts prepared in accordance with subsection (1) before the annual general meeting of the company when the individual accounts are so laid.

(10)[(a) Where—

(i) the group accounts do not deal with a subsidiary of the company, or

(ii) a parent company is exempt pursuant to subsection (1A) from the requirement to prepare group accounts,

any member of the company shall be entitled to be furnished without charge within 14 days after the member has made a request in that behalf to the company with a copy of the latest balance sheet of that subsidiary which has been sent to the members of the subsidiary together with a copy of every document required by law to be annexed thereto and a copy of the directors' and auditors' reports.][b]

(b) Where any copy required under paragraph (a) is not sent within the period specified in that paragraph, the company and every officer of the company who is in default is liable, in respect of each offence, to a [class D fine][a] unless it is proved that the member has already made a demand for and been furnished with a copy and in the case of any default under this subsection the court may direct that the copies required shall be sent to the member requiring them.

(11) Where, in relation to a company, any person being a director of a company fails to take all reasonable steps to secure compliance with this section the person is, in respect of each offence, liable on summary conviction to imprisonment for a term not exceeding 6 months or to a [class D fine][c] or to both, so, however, that—

(a) in any proceedings against a person in respect of an offence under this section, it shall be a defence to prove that the person had reasonable ground to believe and did believe that a competent and reliable person was charged with the duty of seeing that the requirements of this section were complied with and was in a position to discharge that duty, and

(b) a person shall not be sentenced to imprisonment for an offence under this section unless, in the opinion of the court dealing with the case, the offence was committed wilfully.][d]

Amendments

a Subsection (1A) inserted by EC(GA)R 2010, reg 4(a).

b Paragraph (a) of sub-s (10) substituted by EC(GA)R 2010, reg 4(b).

c As implicitly substituted for "fine not exceeding €635" by Fines Act 2010, s 7. A class D fine currently means a fine not exceeding €1,000.

d CA 1963, s 150 was repealed and replaced by reg 4 of EC(IFRSMA)R 2005.

[150A Companies Act group accounts

(1) Without prejudice to section 151, Companies Act group accounts shall comprise—

(a) a consolidated balance sheet dealing with the state of affairs of the parent company and its subsidiary undertakings (including those in liquidation), and

(b) a consolidated profit and loss account dealing with the profit or loss of the parent company and its subsidiary undertakings (including those in liquidation).

(2) The Companies Act group accounts shall give a true and fair view of the state of affairs as at the end of the financial year, and the profit or loss for the financial year, of the undertakings included in the consolidation as a whole, so far as concerns members of the company.

(3) Companies Act group accounts shall—

(a) in the case of an undertaking to which the Group Accounts Regulations apply, comply with those Regulations,

(b) in the case of an undertaking to which the 1993 Regulations apply, comply with those Regulations and the Group Accounts Regulations,

(c) in the case of an undertaking to which the Credit Institutions Regulations apply, comply with those Regulations,

(d) in the case of an undertaking to which the Insurance Undertakings Regulations apply, comply with those Regulations, and

(e) in all other cases comply with this section and sections 151 to 155.][a]

Amendments

a CA 1963, s 150A was inserted by reg 4 of EC(IFRSMA)R 2005.

[150B IFRS group accounts

(1) Where the directors of a parent company prepare IFRS group accounts, they shall state in the notes to those accounts that the accounts have been prepared in accordance with international financial reporting standards.

(2) Where the directors of a parent company prepare IFRS group accounts in compliance with section 150(2)(a) or under section 150(3)(b), they shall ensure that the notes to those group accounts include the information required by—

(a) section 191 and paragraph 16 of the Schedule to the Group Accounts Regulations (details of directors' remuneration),

(b) sections 41 to 45 of the Act of 1990 to be disclosed in group accounts by virtue of paragraph 17 of the Schedule to the Group Accounts Regulations (transactions with directors),

(c) section 63 of the Act of 1990 unless it is disclosed in the directors' report (interests in shares and debentures),

(d) subject to Regulation 36 of the Group Accounts Regulations, paragraphs 18 to 22 of the Schedule to those Regulations (details of group undertakings),

(e) paragraph 15 of the Schedule to the Group Accounts Regulations (details of staff numbers and remuneration),

(f) paragraphs 26 to 28 of the Schedule to the Act of 1986 (details of share capital and debentures),

(g) paragraph 32A of the Schedule to the Act of 1986 (restriction on distributability of profits),

(h) paragraph 36 of the Schedule to the Act of 1986 (guarantees and other financial commitments),

(i) paragraph 37(2) of the Schedule to the Act of 1986 (financial assistance for the purchase of own shares),

(j) paragraph 46 of the Schedule to the Act of 1986 (shares and debentures held by subsidiary undertakings), [...][b]

(k) [...][c] section 205D of the Act of 1990 [(remuneration of auditors), and][d]][a]

[(l) where appropriate, Regulation 7(1)(a) of the European Communities (Directive 2006/46/EC) Regulations 2009.][e]

Amendments

a CA 1063, s 150B was inserted by reg 4 of EC(IFRSMA)R 2005.

b Word 'and' deleted by European Communities (Directive 2006/46/EC) Regulations 2009, reg 12(a).

c Words 'paragraph 39(5) of the Schedule to the Act of 1986 and' deleted by EC(SA)(Dir)R 2010, reg 4(3).

d Words '(remuneration of auditors).' substituted by '(remuneration of auditors), and' by European Communities (Directive 2006/46/EC) Regulations 2009, reg 12(b).

e Subparagraph (l) inserted by European Communities (Directive 2006/46/EC) Regulations 2009, reg 12(c).

[150C Consistency of accounts

(1) The directors of a parent company shall ensure that the individual accounts of—

(a) the parent company, and

(b) each of the subsidiary undertakings of the parent company,

are all prepared using the same financial reporting framework, except to the extent that in their opinion there are good reasons for not doing so, and those reasons are disclosed in the individual accounts of the parent company.

(2) Subsection (1) only applies to accounts of subsidiary undertakings that are required to be prepared under this Act.

(3) Subsection (1) does not apply:

(a) where the directors do not prepare group accounts for the parent company;

(b) to the accounts of undertakings to which section 148(3) applies.

(4) Subsection (1)(a) does not apply where the directors of a parent company prepare IFRS group accounts and IFRS individual accounts for the parent.][a]

Amendments

a CA 1963, s 150C was inserted by reg 4 of EC(IFRSMA)R 2005.

[151 Form of group accounts

(1) Subject to subsections (2) and (3), Companies Act group accounts prepared in accordance with sections 151 to 155 shall be group accounts comprising—

(a) a consolidated balance sheet dealing with the state of affairs of the parent company and all the subsidiaries to be dealt with in group accounts, and

(b) a consolidated profit and loss account dealing with the profit or loss of the parent company and those subsidiaries.

(2) Notwithstanding anything in section 150 or 150A, Companies Act group accounts prepared in accordance with this section—

(a) shall not be required where the company is, at the end of its financial year, the wholly owned subsidiary of another body corporate incorporated in the State, and

(b) need not deal with a subsidiary of the company where the company's directors are of the opinion that—

(i) it is impracticable, or would be of no real value to members of the company, in view of the insignificant amounts involved, or would involve expenses or delay out of proportion to the value to members of the company, or

(ii) the result would be misleading,

and if the directors are of such an opinion about each of the company's subsidiaries, group accounts shall not be required.

(3) If the company's directors are of the opinion that it is better for the purpose—

(a) of presenting the same or equivalent information about the state of affairs and profit or loss of the company and those subsidiaries, and

(b) and of so presenting that information that it may be readily appreciated by the company's members, the group accounts may be prepared in a form other than that required by subsection (1) and, in particular, may consist of—

(i) more than one set of consolidated accounts dealing respectively with the company and one group of subsidiaries and with other groups of subsidiaries, or

(ii) individual accounts dealing with each of the subsidiaries, or

(iii) statements expanding the information about the subsidiaries in the company's own accounts, or

(iv) any combination of those forms.

(4) The group accounts may be wholly or partly incorporated in the company's own balance sheet and profit and loss account.

(5) For the purposes of this section, a body corporate shall be deemed to be the wholly owned subsidiary of another if it has no members except that other and that other's wholly owned subsidiaries and its or their nominees.][a]

Amendments

a CA 1963, s 151 was repealed and replaced by reg 4 of the EC(IFRSMA)R 2005.

152 Contents of group accounts

(1) [Companies Act group accounts prepared in accordance with sections 151 to 155 of this Act][a] laid before the annual general meeting of a company shall give a true and fair view of the state of affairs and profit or loss of the company and the subsidiaries dealt with thereby as a whole, so far as concerns members of the company.

(2) Where the financial year of a subsidiary does not coincide with that of the holding company, [the group accounts referred to in subsection (1)][b] shall deal with the subsidiary's state of affairs as at the end of its financial year ending with or last before that of the holding company and with the subsidiary's profit or loss for the financial year.

(3) Without prejudice to subsection (1), [the group accounts referred to in subsection (1)][b], if prepared as consolidated accounts, shall comply with the requirements of the Sixth Schedule so far as applicable thereto, and if not so prepared shall give the same or equivalent information.

Amendments

a Words substituted by EC(IFRSMA)R 2005, reg 9, Sch 1, Pt 1, Item No 3(a).

b Words substituted by EC(IFRSMA)R 2005, reg 9, Sch 1, Pt 1, Item No 3(b).

153 Financial year and annual return date of holding company and subsidiary

(1) A holding company's directors shall secure that except where there are good reasons against it, the financial year of each of its subsidiaries shall coincide with the company's own financial year.

(2) [Where it appears to the Minister desirable for a holding company or a holding company's subsidiary to extend its financial year so that the subsidiary's financial year may end with that of the holding company, and for that purpose to postpone the submission of the relevant accounts to an annual general meeting from one calendar year to the next, or for a holding company or a holding company's subsidiary to extend its annual return date so that the subsidiary's annual return date may correspond with that of the holding company, the Minister may—

(a) on the application or with the consent of the directors of the company whose financial year is to be extended, direct that in the case of that company, the submission of accounts to an annual general meeting or the holding of an annual general meeting shall not be required in the earlier of the calendar years, or

(b) on the application or with the consent of the directors of the company whose annual return date is to be extended, direct that an extension is to be permitted in the case of that company.][a]

(3) If any person being a director of a company fails to take all reasonable steps to secure compliance by the company with the provisions of this section, he shall in respect of each offence be liable on summary conviction to a [class C fine].[b]

(4) No proceedings shall be instituted under this section except by, or with the consent of, the Minister.

(5) This section shall not apply to a private company which is a holding company and which takes advantage of subsection (1) of section 154.

Amendments

a CA 1963, s 153(2) substituted by CLEA 2001, s 61.

b '£250' substituted for '£50' by C(A)A 1982 Sch 1, increased to £1,500 by CA 1990, s 240(7) as inserted by CLEA 2001, s 104(c) and converted to €1,904.61 by Council Regulations (EC) No 1103/97, No 974/98 and No 2866/98, and the Economic and Monetary Union Act 1998, s 6; the above being implicitly substituted, by Fines Act 2010, s 6, for a fine not exceeding the aforesaid amount. A class C fine currently means a fine not exceeding €2,500.

---

154 Right of member of private company to get balance sheet of subsidiary

(1) Notwithstanding section 150, a private company which is a holding company need not prepare group accounts but if it does not do so the subsequent provisions of this section shall apply.

(2) Any member of the company shall be entitled to be furnished without charge within 14 days after he has made a request in that behalf to the company with a copy of the latest balance sheet of each of its subsidiaries which has been sent to the members of that subsidiary together with a copy of every document required by law to be annexed thereto and a copy of the directors' and auditors' reports.

(3) Without prejudice to subsection (2), any member of the company shall be entitled to be furnished within 14 days after he has made a request in that behalf to the company with a copy of any balance sheet (including every document required by law to be annexed thereto and a copy of the directors' and auditors' reports) of any subsidiary of the company laid before any annual general meeting of such subsidiary held since the operative date, at a charge not exceeding [13 cent][a] for each balance sheet so furnished so, however, that a member shall not be entitled to be furnished with a copy of any balance sheet laid before an annual general meeting held more than 10 years before the date on which such request is made.

(4) Copies of balance sheets need not be sent to any member of a private company if, on the application either of the company or of any person who claims to be aggrieved, the court is satisfied that the rights conferred by this section are being abused, and the court may order the company's costs on an application under this subsection to be paid in whole or in part by the member who has made the request for such copies.

(5) Subject to subsection (4), if any copy required under this section is not sent within the proper time, the company and every officer of the company who is in default shall be liable, in respect of each offence, to a [class C fine][b] unless it is proved that the member has already made a demand for and been furnished with a copy.

(6) In the case of any default under this section, the court may direct that the copies required shall be sent to the member requiring them.

Amendments

a '2 shillings' converted to 13 cent by Council Regulations (EC) No 1103/97, No 974/98 and No 2866/98 and the Economic and Monetary Union Act 1998, s 6.

b '£500' substituted for '£100' by C(A)A 1982, Sch 1, increased to £1,500 by CA 1990, s 240(7) as inserted by CLEA 2001, s 104(c) and converted to €1,904.61 by Council Regulations (EC) No 1103/97, No 974/98 and No 2866/98 and the Economic and Monetary Union Act 1998, s 6; the above being implicitly substituted, by Fines Act 2010, s 6, for a fine not exceeding the aforesaid amount. A class C fine currently means a fine not exceeding €2,500.

---

155 Meaning of 'holding company' and 'subsidiary'

(1) For the purposes of this Act, a company shall, subject to subsection (3), be deemed to be a subsidiary of another if, but only if—

- (a) that other—
  - (i) is a member of it and controls the composition of its board of directors, or
  - (ii) holds more than half in nominal value of its equity share capital, or
  - (iii) holds more than half in nominal value of its shares carrying voting rights (other than voting rights which arise only in specified circumstances); or
- (b) the first-mentioned company is a subsidiary of any company which is that other's subsidiary.

(2) For the purposes of subsection (1), the composition of a company's board of directors shall be deemed to be controlled by another company if, but only if, that other company by the exercise of some power exercisable by it without the consent or concurrence of any other person can appoint or remove the holders of all or a majority of the directorships; but for the purposes of this provision that other company shall be deemed to have power to appoint to a directorship in relation to which any of the following conditions is satisfied—

- (a) that a person cannot be appointed thereto without the exercise in his favour by that other company of such a power as aforesaid; or
- (b) that a person's appointment thereto follows necessarily from his appointment as director of that other company.

(3) In determining whether one company is a subsidiary of another—

- (a) any shares held or power exercisable by that other in a fiduciary capacity shall be treated as not held or exercisable by it;
- (b) subject to paragraphs (c) and (d), any shares held or power exercisable—

(i) by any person as a nominee for that other (except where that other is concerned only in a fiduciary capacity); or

(ii) by, or by a nominee for, a subsidiary of that other, not being a subsidiary which is concerned only in a fiduciary capacity;

shall be treated as held or exercisable by that other;

(c) any shares held or power exercisable by any person by virtue of the provisions of any debentures of the first-mentioned company or of a trust deed for securing any issue of such debentures shall be disregarded;

(d) any shares held or power exercisable by, or by a nominee for, that other or its subsidiary (not being held or exercisable as mentioned in paragraph (*c*)) shall be treated as not held or exercisable by that other if the ordinary business of that other or its subsidiary, as the case may be, includes the lending of money and the shares are held or power is exercisable as aforesaid by way of security only for the purposes of a transaction entered into in the ordinary course of that business.

(4) For the purposes of this Act, a company shall be deemed to be another's holding company if, but only if, that other is its subsidiary.

(5) In this section 'company' includes any body corporate and 'equity share capital' means, in relation to a company, its issued share capital excluding any part thereof which, neither as respects dividends nor as respects capital, carries any right to participate beyond a specified amount in a distribution.

156 Signing of balance sheet and profit and loss account

[(1) (a) Where the directors of a company prepare Companies Act individual accounts, every balance sheet and profit and loss account of the company shall be signed on behalf of the directors by 2 of the directors of the company.

(b) Where the directors of a company prepare IFRS individual accounts, every balance sheet and income statement of a company shall be signed on behalf of the directors by 2 of the directors of the company.

(2) In the case of a banking company registered after 15 August 1879, the balance sheet and profit and loss account, or, where the directors of a company prepare IFRS accounts, the income statement, must be signed by the secretary and where there are more than 3 directors of the company by at least 3 of those directors, and where there are not more than 3 directors by all the directors.][a]

(3) If any copy of a balance sheet or profit and loss account which has not been signed as required by this section is issued, circulated or published, the company and every officer of the company who is in default [shall be guilty of an offence and liable to a [class C fine][b]].[c]

(4) Subsection (3) shall not prohibit the issue, circulation or publication of—

(a) a fair and accurate summary of any profit and loss account and balance sheet and the auditors' report thereon after such profit and loss account and balance sheet shall have been signed on behalf of the directors;

(b) a fair and accurate summary of the profit or loss figures for part of the company's financial year.

Amendments

a CA 1963, s 156(1) and (2) substituted by EC(IFRSMA)R 2005, Sch 1, Pt 1, Item No 4.

b '£500' substituted for '£100' by C(A)A 1982, Sch 1, increased to £1,500 by CA 1990, s 240(7) as inserted by CLEA 2001, s 104(c) and converted to €1,904.61 by Council Regulations (EC) No 1103/97, No 974/98 and No 2866/98 and the Economic and Monetary Union Act 1998, s 6; the above being implicitly substituted, by Fines Act 2010, s 6, for a fine not exceeding the aforesaid amount. A class C fine currently means a fine not exceeding €2,500.

c Words in CA 1963, s 156(3) substituted by C(AA)A 2003, s 57 and Sch 2, para 1.

157 Documents to be attached and annexed to balance sheet

(1) The profit and loss account and, so far as not incorporated in the balance sheet or profit and loss account, any group accounts laid before the annual general meeting of a company shall be annexed to the balance sheet and the auditors' report shall be attached thereto and any accounts so annexed shall be approved by the board of directors before the balance sheet and profit and loss account are signed on their behalf.

(2) If any copy of a balance sheet is issued, circulated or published without compliance with subsection (1), the company and every officer of the company who is in default [shall be guilty of an offence and liable to a [class C fine][a]][b].

Amendments

a '£500' substituted for '£100' by C(A)A 1982, Sch 1, increased to £1,500 by CA 1990, s 240(7) as inserted by CLEA 2001, s 104(c) and converted to €1,904.61 by Council Regulations (EC) No 1103/97, No 974/98 and No 2866/98 and the Economic and Monetary Union Act 1998, s 6; the above being implicitly substituted, by Fines Act 2010, s 6, for a fine not exceeding the aforesaid amount. A class C fine currently means a fine not exceeding €2,500.

b Words in CA 1963, s 157(2) substituted by C(AA)A 2003, s 57 and Sch 2, para 1.

158 Directors' report to be attached to balance sheet and contents of such report

(1) There shall be attached to every balance sheet laid before the annual general meeting of a company a report by the directors on the state of the company's affairs and, if the company is a holding company, on the state of affairs of the company and its subsidiaries as a group, the amount, if any, which they recommend should be paid by way of dividend and the amount, if any, which they propose to carry to reserves within the meaning of the Sixth Schedule.

(2) The said report shall be signed on behalf of the directors by two of the directors of the company.

(3) The said report shall deal, so far as is material for the appreciation of the state of the company's affairs, with any change during the financial year in the nature of the business of the company or of the company's subsidiaries, or in the classes of business in

which the company has an interest whether as a member of another company or otherwise.

(4) The said report shall contain a list of bodies corporate in relation to which either of the following conditions is fulfilled at the end of the company's financial year—

(a) the body corporate is a subsidiary of the company;

(b) although the body corporate is not a subsidiary of the company, the company is beneficially entitled to more than 20 per cent in nominal value of its shares carrying voting rights (other than voting rights which arise only in specified circumstances).

(5) The list referred to in subsection (4) shall distinguish between bodies corporate falling within paragraph (a) and paragraph (b) thereof and shall state in relation to each such body corporate—

(a) its name;

(b) where it is incorporated; and

(c) the nature of the business carried on by it.

(6) Subsections (4) and (5) shall not apply to a company which is principally engaged in the acquisition and underwriting of shares or other securities of companies carrying on a trade or industry in the State and which holds a certificate of exemption issued by the Minister from the requirements of those subsections.

[(6A) The report referred to in subsection (1) shall contain a statement of the measures taken by the directors to secure compliance with the requirements of section 202 of the Companies Act, 1990, with regard to the keeping of proper books of account and the exact location of those books.][a]

[(6B) The report referred to in subsection (1) shall contain a copy of any Disclosure Issue Notice issued under section 33AK (inserted by the Central Bank and Financial Services Authority of Ireland Act 2003) during the financial year ending with the relevant balance sheet date.][b]

[(6C) Subject to subsection (6E), a company whose securities are admitted to trading on a regulated market shall include a corporate governance statement in respect of the financial year in the report by the directors referred to in subsection (1).

(6D) The corporate governance statement referred to in subsection (6C) shall be included as a specific section of the report of the directors referred to in subsection (1), and shall include, at least, all of the following information:

(a) a reference to—

  (i) the corporate governance code—

    (I) to which the company is subject and where the relevant text is publicly available, or

    (II) which the company has voluntarily decided to apply and where the relevant text is publicly available, and

  (ii) all relevant information concerning corporate governance practices applied in respect of the company which are additional to any statutory requirement, and where the information on such corporate governance practices is available for inspection by the public;

(b) where the company departs, in accordance with any statutory provision, from a corporate governance code referred to in clause (I) or (II) of paragraph (a)(i)—

(i) an explanation by the company as to which parts of the corporate governance code it departs from in accordance with the statutory provision and the extent to which it departs from such code and

(ii) the reasons for such departure,

and where the company has decided not to apply any provisions of a corporate governance code referred to in clause (I) or (II) of paragraph (a)(i), the company shall explain its reasons for doing so;

(c) a description of the main features of the internal control and risk management systems of the company in relation to the financial reporting process;

(d) the information required under subparagraphs (c), (d), (f), (h) and (i) of paragraph (2) of Regulation 21 of the European Communities (Takeover Bids (Directive 2004/25/EC)) Regulations 2006 (S.I. 255 of 2006), where the company is subject to those Regulations;

(e) a description of the operation of the shareholder meeting, the key powers of the shareholder meeting, shareholders' rights and the exercise of such rights;

(f) the composition and operation of the board of directors and the committees of the board of directors with administrative, management and supervisory functions.

(6E) The information required under subsection (6D) may be set out in a separate report published in conjunction with the annual report in accordance with subsections (6F) or (6G), or provided by a reference in the annual report to where the separate report is publicly available on the website of the company, and where a separate report is provided, the corporate governance statement may contain a reference to the annual report where the information referred to in subsection (6D)(d) is provided.

(6F) Where a company produces a corporate governance statement in the form of a separate report, such report shall be attached to every balance sheet, referred to in subsection (1), laid before the annual general meeting of the company and shall be signed on behalf of the directors by 2 of the directors of the company.

(6G) Where a company produces a corporate governance statement in the form of a separate report—

(a) a copy of such report shall be published on the website of the company, and a statement that a copy of the report has been so published together with the address of the website of the company, shall be included in the report of the directors of the company, or

(b) be annexed to the annual return, under section 7 of the Act of 1986, of the company and shall be certified both by a director and the secretary of the company to be a true copy of such corporate governance statement laid or to be laid before the annual general meeting of the company.

[(6H) Where a company, in accordance with subsection (6E), produces a corporate governance statement in a separate report in respect of a financial year—

(a) the auditors of the company, in their report under section 193 of the Act of 1990, shall state whether, in their opinion, the information in the corporate governance statement, required by paragraph (c) of subsection (6D) is consistent with the annual accounts for that financial year,

(b) the auditors of the company, in their report under section 193 of the Act of 1990, shall state whether, in their opinion, the information in the corporate governance statement, required by paragraph (d) of subsection (6D) is consistent with the annual accounts for that financial year, and

(c) the auditors of the company, when preparing their report under section 193 of the Act of 1990 in respect of the annual accounts for that year, shall ascertain that a separate corporate governance statement has, in accordance with subsection (6E), been produced and contains the information required by paragraphs (a), (b), (e) and (f) of subsection (6D).][c]

(6I) Paragraphs (a), (b), (e) and (f) of subsection (6D) shall not apply to companies which have only issued securities other than shares admitted to trading on a regulated market, unless such companies have issued shares which are traded in a multilateral trading facility.

(6J) In subsection (6I), 'multilateral trading facility' has the meaning assigned to it by Article 4(1), point (15) of Directive 2004/39/EC6.][d]

(7) If any person, being a director of a company, fails to take all reasonable steps to comply with the requirements of this section he shall in respect of each offence be liable on summary conviction to imprisonment for a term not exceeding 6 months or to a [class C fine][e] or to both so, however, that—

(a) in any proceedings against a person in respect of an offence under this section it shall be a defence to prove that he had reasonable ground to believe and did believe that a competent and reliable person was charged with the duty of seeing that the provisions of this section were complied with and was in a position to discharge that duty; and

(b) a person shall not be liable to be sentenced to imprisonment for such an offence unless, in the opinion of the court dealing with the case, the offence was committed wilfully.

Amendments

a CA 1963, s 158(6A) inserted by CLEA 2001, s 90.

b Subsection (6B) inserted by CBFSAIA 2003, s 35(1) and Sch 1, Pt 4.

c Subsection (6H) substituted by EC(Dir)(A)R 2010, reg 5.

d Subsections (6C)–(6J) inserted by European Communities (Directive 2006/46/EC) Regulations 2009, reg 13.

e '£500' substituted for '£100' by C(A)A 1982, Sch 1, increased to £1,500 by CA 1990, s 240(7) as inserted by CLEA 2001, s 104(c) and converted to €1,904.61 by Council Regulations (EC) No 1103/97, No 974/98 and No 2866/98 and the Economic and Monetary Union Act 1998, s 6; the above being implicitly substituted, by Fines Act 2010, s 6, for a fine not exceeding the aforesaid amount. A class C fine currently means a fine not exceeding €2,500.

159 Obligation of company to send copies of balance sheets and directors' and auditors' reports

(1) Subject to subsections (2) and (3), a copy of every balance sheet including every document required by law to be annexed thereto, which is to be laid before the annual general meeting of a company together with a copy of the directors' and auditors' reports shall, not less than 21 days before the date of the meeting, be sent to every member of the company (whether he is or is not entitled to receive notices of general meetings of the company), every holder of debentures of the company (whether he is or is not so entitled) and all persons other than members or holders of debentures of the company who are so entitled.

(2) In the case of a company not having a share capital, subsection (1) shall not require a copy of the documents referred to in that subsection to be sent to a member of the company who is not entitled to receive notices of general meetings of the company or to a holder of debentures of the company who is not so entitled.

(3) If the copies of the documents referred to in subsection (1) are sent less than 21 days before the date of the meeting, they shall, notwithstanding that fact, be deemed to have been duly sent if it is so agreed by all the members entitled to attend and vote at the meeting.

(4) Any member of a company, whether he is or is not entitled to have sent to him copies of the company's balance sheets, and any holder of debentures of the company, whether he is or is not so entitled, shall be entitled to be furnished on demand without charge with a copy of the last balance sheet of the company, including every document required by law to be annexed thereto, together with copies of the directors' and auditors' reports.

(5) If default is made in complying with subsection (1), the company and every officer of the company who is in default [shall be guilty of an offence and liable to a [class C fine][a]][b], and if, when any person makes a demand for any document with which he is by virtue of subsection (4) entitled to be furnished, default is made in complying with the demand within 7 days after the making thereof, the company and every officer of the company who is in default [shall be guilty of an offence and liable to a [class C fine][a]][b] unless it is proved that that person has already made a demand for and been furnished with a copy of the document.

(6) Subsection (4) shall not apply to a balance sheet of a private company laid before it before the operative date and the right of any person to be furnished with a copy of any such balance sheet and the liability of the company in respect of a failure to satisfy that obligation shall be the same as they would have been if this Act had not been passed.

Amendments

a '£250' substituted for '£50' by C(A)A 1982, Sch 1, increased to £1,500 by CA 1990, s 240(7) as inserted by CLEA 2001, s 104(c) and converted to €1,904.61 by Council Regulations (EC) No 1103/97, No 974/98 and No 2866/98 and the Economic and Monetary Union Act 1998, s 6; the above being implicitly substituted, by Fines Act 2010, s 6, for a fine not exceeding the aforesaid amount. A class C fine currently means a fine not exceeding €2,500.

b Words in CA 1963, s 156(3) substituted by C(AA)A 2003, s 57 and Sch 2 and 4.

---

160 Appointment and remuneration of auditors

(1) Subject to subsection (2), every company shall at each annual general meeting appoint an auditor or auditors to hold office from the conclusion of that until the conclusion of the next annual general meeting.

(2) Subject to subsection (3), at any annual general meeting a retiring auditor, however appointed, shall be re-appointed without any resolution being passed unless—

(a) he is not qualified for re-appointment; or

(b) a resolution has been passed at that meeting appointing somebody instead of him or providing expressly that he shall not be re-appointed; or

(c) he has given the company notice in writing of his unwillingness to be re-appointed.

(3) Where notice is given of an intended resolution to appoint some other person or persons in place of a retiring auditor, and by reason of the death, incapacity or disqualification of that person or of all those persons, as the case may be, the resolution cannot be proceeded with, the retiring auditor shall not be automatically re-appointed by virtue of subsection (2).

(4) Where, at an annual general meeting, no auditors are appointed or re-appointed, the Minister may appoint a person to fill the vacancy.

[(5) Without prejudice to any rights of the auditor in relation to his removal under this subsection [and subject to section 161C][a], a company may, by ordinary resolution at a general meeting, remove an auditor other than an auditor who is the first auditor or one of the first auditors of the company and appoint in his place any other person who has been nominated for appointment by any member of the company, who is qualified under the Companies Acts to be an auditor of a company and of whose nomination notice has been given to its members.

[(5A)(a) A company shall—

(i) within one week of the Minister's power under subsection (4) becoming exercisable, give the Minister notice of that fact, and

(ii) where a resolution removing an auditor is passed, give notice of that fact in the prescribed form to the registrar of companies within 14 days of the meeting at which the resolution removing the auditor was passed.

(b) If a company fails to give notice as required by paragraph (a) of this subsection, the company and every officer of the company who is in default shall be guilty of an offence and liable, on summary conviction, to a [class C fine][b].][c]

(6) Subject as hereinafter provided, the first auditors of a company may be appointed by the directors at any time before the first annual general meeting, and auditors so appointed shall hold office until the conclusion of that meeting, so, however, that—

(a) the company may at a general meeting remove any such auditors and appoint in their place any other persons who have been nominated for appointment by any member of the company, and of whose nomination notice has been given to the members of the company not less than 14 days before the date of the meeting; and

(b) if the directors fail to exercise their powers under this subsection, the company in general meeting may appoint the first auditors, and thereupon the said powers of the directors shall cease.

[(7) The directors of a company or the company in general meeting may fill any casual vacancy in the office of auditor, but while any such vacancy continues, the surviving or continuing auditor or auditors, if any, may act.][d]

(8) The remuneration of the auditors of a company—

(a) in the case of an auditor appointed by the directors or by the Minister, may be fixed by the directors or by the Minister, as the case may be;

(b) Subject to paragraph (a), shall be fixed by the company at the annual general meeting or in such manner as the company at the annual general meeting may determine.

For the purposes of this subsection, any sums paid by the company in respect of the auditors' expenses shall be deemed to be included in the term 'remuneration'.

(9) The appointment of a firm [(not being a body corporate)][e] by its firm name to be the auditors of a company shall be deemed to be an appointment of those persons who shall from time to time during the currency of the appointment be the partners in that firm as from time to time constituted and who are qualified to be auditors of that company.

Amendments

a Words 'and subject to section 161C' inserted by EC(SA)(Dir)R 2010, reg 62(a).

b '£1,000' increased to '£1,500' by CA 1990, s 240(7) as inserted by CLEA 2001, s 104(c) and converted to €1,904.61 by Council Regulations (EC) No 1103/97, No 974/98 and No 2866/98 and the Economic and Monetary Union Act 1998, s 6; the above being implicitly substituted, by Fines Act 2010, s 6, for a fine not exceeding the aforesaid amount. A class C fine currently means a fine not exceeding €2,500.

c CA 1963, s 160(5) substituted and subs (5A) inserted by CA 1990, s 183.

d CA 1963, s 160(7) substituted by CA 1990, s 183.

e Words '(not being a body corporate)' inserted by EC(SA)(Dir)R 2010, reg 4(4).

---

161 Provisions as to resolutions relating to appointment and removal of auditors

[(1) Extended notice within the meaning of section 142 shall be required for—

(a) a resolution at an annual general meeting of a company appointing as auditor a person other than a retiring auditor or providing expressly that a retiring auditor shall not be re-appointed,

(b) a resolution at a general meeting of a company removing an auditor before the expiration of his term of office, and

(c) a resolution at a general meeting of a company filling a casual vacancy in the office of auditor.

(2) On receipt of notice of such an intended resolution as is mentioned in subsection (1), the company shall forthwith—

(a) if the resolution is a resolution mentioned in paragraph (a) of the said subsection (1), send a copy thereof to the retiring auditor (if any),

(b) if the resolution is a resolution mentioned in paragraph (b) of the said subsection (1), send a copy thereof to the auditor proposed to be removed, and

(c) if the resolution is a resolution mentioned in paragraph (*c*) of the said subsection (1), send a copy thereof to the person (if any) whose ceasing to hold the office of auditor of the company occasioned the casual vacancy.

(2A) An auditor of a company who has been removed shall be entitled to attend—

(a) the annual general meeting of the company at which, but for his removal, his term of office as auditor of the company would have expired, and

(b) the general meeting of the company at which it is proposed to fill the vacancy occasioned by his removal, and

to receive all notices of, and other communications relating to, any such meeting which a member of the company is entitled to receive and to be heard at any general meeting that such a member attends on any part of the business of the meeting which concerns him as former auditor of the company.][a]

(3) Subject to subsection (4), where notice is given of such an intended resolution as aforesaid, and the retiring auditor makes in relation to the intended resolution representations in writing to the company (not exceeding a reasonable length) and requests their notification to members of the company, the company shall, unless the representations are received by it too late for it to do so—

(a) in any notice of the resolution given to members of the company, state the fact of the representations having been made; and

(b) send a copy of the representations to every member of the company to who notice of the meeting is sent (whether before or after receipt of the representations by the company);

and if a copy of the representations is not sent as aforesaid because received too late or because of the company's default, the auditor may (without prejudice to his right to be heard orally) require that the representations shall be read out at the meeting.

(4) Copies of the representations need not be sent out as aforesaid and the representations need not be read out at the meeting as aforesaid if, on the application either of the company or of any other person who claims to be aggrieved, the court is satisfied that the rights conferred by this section are being abused to secure needless publicity for defamatory matter and the court may order the company's costs on an application under this section to be paid in whole or in part by the auditor, notwithstanding that he is not a party to the application.

(5) Subsections (3) and (4) shall apply to a resolution to remove the first auditors by virtue of subsection (6) of section 160 as they apply in relation to a resolution that a retiring auditor shall not be re-appointed.

Amendments

a CA 1963, s 161(1), (2) substituted and (2A) inserted by CA 1990, s 184.

[161A Duty of auditor to notify Supervisory Authority regarding cessation of office

(1) Where, for any reason, during the period between the conclusion of the last annual general meeting and the conclusion of the next annual general meeting of a company, an auditor ceases to hold office either by virtue of section 160, or section 185 of the Act of 1990, the auditor shall—

(a) in such form and manner as the Supervisory Authority specifies, and

(b) within 1 month after the date of that cessation.

notify the Supervisory Authority that the auditor has ceased to hold office.

(2) That notification shall be accompanied by:

(a) in the case of resignation of the auditor, the notice served under section 185(1) of the Act of 1990, or

(b) in the case of removal of the auditor at a general meeting pursuant to section 160(5), a copy of any representations in writing made to the company, pursuant to section 161(3), in relation to the intended resolution except where such representations were not sent out to the members of the company in consequence of an application to the court under section 161(4).

(3) Where, in the case of resignation, the notice served under section 185(1) of the Act of 1990 is to the effect that there are no circumstances connected with the resignation to which it relates that the auditor concerned considers should be brought to the notice of members or creditors of the company, the notification under subsection (1) shall also be accompanied by a statement of the reasons for the auditor's resignation.

(4) In this section—

(a) 'resignation' includes an indication of unwillingness to bere-appointed at an annual general meeting; and

(b) a reference to a notice served under section 185(1) of the Act of 1990 includes a reference to a notice given by the auditor under section 160(2)(c).][a]

Amendments

a Section 161A inserted by EC(SA)(Dir)R 2010, reg 62(b).

[161B Duty of company to notify Supervisory Authority of auditor's cessation of office

(1) Where, for any reason, during the period between the conclusion of the last annual general meeting and the conclusion of the next annual general meeting, an auditor ceases to hold office either by virtue of section 160, or section 185 of the Act of 1990, the company shall—

(a) in such form and manner as the Supervisory Authority specifies, and

(b) within 1 month after the date of that cessation,

notify the Supervisory Authority that the auditor has ceased to hold office.

(2) That notification shall be accompanied by:

(a) in the case of resignation of the auditor, the notice served by the auditor under section 185(1) of the Act of 1990, or

(b) in the case of removal of the auditor at a general meeting pursuant to section 160(5)—

(i) a copy of the resolution removing the auditor, and

(ii) a copy of any representations in writing made to the company, pursuant to section 161(3), by the outgoing auditor in relation to the intended resolution except where such representations were not sent out to the members of the company in consequence of an application to the court under section 161(4).

(3) In this section—

(a) 'resignation' includes an indication of unwillingness to be re-appointed at an annual general meeting; and

(b) a reference to a notice served under section 185(1) of the Act of 1990 includes a reference to a notice given by the auditor under section 160(2)(c).][a]

Amendments

a Section 161B inserted by EC(SA)(Dir)R 2010, reg 62(b).

[161C Restrictions on removal of auditor

(1) The passing of a resolution to which this section applies shall not be effective with respect to the matter it provides for unless—

(a) in case the resolution provides for the auditor's removal from office, there are good and substantial grounds for the removal related to the conduct of the auditor with regard to the performance of his duties as auditor of the company or otherwise; or

(b) in the case of any other resolution to which this section applies, the passing of the resolution is, in the company's opinion, in the best interests of the company,

but—

(i) for the foregoing purposes, diverging opinions on accounting treatments or audit procedures cannot constitute the basis for the passing of any such resolution, and

(ii) in paragraph (b) 'best interests of the company' does not include any illegal or improper motive with regard to avoiding disclosures or detection of any failure by the company to comply with the Companies Acts.

(2) This section applies to—

(a) a resolution removing an auditor from office,

(b) a resolution at an annual general meeting appointing somebody other than the retiring auditor as auditor,

(c) a resolution providing expressly that the retiring auditor shall not be re-appointed.][a]

Amendments

a Section 161C inserted by EC(SA)(Dir)R 2010, reg 62(b).

[161D Disclosure of remuneration for audit, audit-related and non-audit work

(1) In this section—

'group auditor' means the auditor carrying out the audit of group accounts;

'relevant undertaking' means—

(a) a company, or

(b) an undertaking referred to in Regulation 6 of the 1993 Regulations;

'remuneration' includes benefits in kind and payments in cash.

(2) Subject to subsection (5), a relevant undertaking shall disclose in the notes to its annual accounts relating to each financial year the following information:

(a) the remuneration for all work in each category specified in subsection (3) that was carried out—

(i) for the relevant undertaking;

(ii) in respect of that financial year,

by the auditor of the relevant undertaking;

(b) the remuneration for all work in each category specified in subsection (3) that was carried out—

(i) for the relevant undertaking;

(ii) in respect of the preceding financial year,

by the auditor of the relevant undertaking;

(c) where all or part of the remuneration referred to in paragraph (a) or (b) is in the form of a benefit in kind, the nature and estimated monetary value of the benefit.

(3) Remuneration shall be disclosed under subsection (2) for each of the following categories of work:

(a) the audit of individual accounts;

(b) other assurance services;

(c) tax advisory services;

(d) other non-audit services.

(4) Where the auditor of a relevant undertaking is a statutory audit firm, any work carried out by a partner in the firm or a statutory auditor on its behalf is considered for the purposes of this section to have been carried out by the audit firm.

(5) A company need not make the disclosure required by subsection (2) where:

(a) the company is to be treated as a small company in accordance with section 8(1) of the Act of 1986, or

(b) the company is to be treated as a medium-sized company in accordance with section 8(1) of the Act of 1986, or

(c) the company is a subsidiary undertaking, the parent of which is required to prepare and does prepare group accounts in accordance with any Regulations mentioned in subsection (7), provided that:

   (i) the subsidiary undertaking is included in the group accounts, and

   (ii) the information specified in subsection (3) is disclosed in the notes to the group accounts.

(6) Where a company that is to be treated as a medium-sized company in accordance with section 8(1) of the Act of 1986 does not make the disclosure of information required by subsection (2) it shall provide such information to the Supervisory Authority when requested so to do.

(7) A parent undertaking preparing group accounts in accordance with:

(a) the Group Accounts Regulations,

(b) the European Communities (Credit Institutions: Accounts) Regulations, 1992 (S.I. No. 294 of 1992), or

(c) the European Communities (Insurance Undertakings: Accounts) Regulations 1996 (S.I. No. 23 of 1996),

shall disclose in the notes to its consolidated accounts relating to each financial year the following information:

(i) the remuneration for all work in each category specified in subsection (8) that was carried out in respect of that financial year by the group auditor;

(ii) the remuneration for all work in each category specified in subsection (8) that was carried out in respect of the preceding financial year by the group auditor;

(iii) where all or part of the remuneration referred to in paragraph (*a*) or (*b*) is in the form of a benefit in kind, the nature and estimated monetary value of the benefit.

(8) Remuneration shall be disclosed under subsection (7) for each of the following categories of work:

(a) the audit of the group accounts;

(b) other assurance services;

(c) tax advisory services;

(d) other non-audit services.

(9) Where more than one auditor (whether a statutory auditor or a statutory audit firm) has been appointed as the auditor of a relevant undertaking in a single financial year, separate disclosure in respect of the remuneration of each of them must be provided in the notes to the company's individual accounts.

(10) Where a relevant undertaking fails to comply with subsection (2), (3) or (9), each company or other entity that forms all or part of that undertaking shall be guilty of an offence.

(11) For the purpose of applying this section to a partnership that is referred to in Regulation 6 of the 1993 Regulations and that is a relevant undertaking, the partnership is to be treated as though it were a company formed and registered under the Companies Acts.][a]

Amendments

a Section 161D inserted by EC(SA)(Dir)R 2010, reg 120(1).

162 Qualifications for appointment as auditor

[...][a]

Amendments

a CA 1963, s 162 repealed by CA 1990, s 6.

163 Auditors' report and right of access to books and to attend and be heard at general meetings

[...][a]

Amendments

a CA 1963, s 163 repealed by CA 1990, s 6.

164 Construction of references to documents annexed to accounts

(1) Subject to subsection (2), references in this Act to a document annexed or required to be annexed to a company's accounts or any of them shall not include the directors' report or the auditors' report.

(2) Any information which is required by this Act to be given in accounts, and is thereby allowed to be given in a statement annexed, may be given in the directors' report instead of in the accounts and, if any such information is so given, the report shall be annexed to the accounts, and this Act shall apply in relation thereto accordingly, except that the auditors shall report thereon only so far as it gives the said information.

165 Investigation of company's affairs on application of members

[...][a]

Amendments

a CA 1963, s 165 repealed by CA 1990, s 6.

166 Investigation of company's affairs in other cases

[...][a]

Amendments

a CA 1963, s 166 repealed by CA 1990, s 6.

167 Power of inspectors to extend investigation into affairs of related companies

[...][a]

Amendments

a CA 1963, s 167 repealed by CA 1990, s 6.

168 Production of documents, and evidence, on investigation

[...][a]

Amendments

a CA 1963, s 168 repealed by CA 1990, s 6.

169 Inspectors' report

[...][a]

Amendments

a CA 1963, s 169 repealed by CA 1990, s 6.

170 Proceedings on inspectors' report

[...][a]

Amendments

a CA 1963, s 170 repealed by CA 1990, s 6.

171 Expenses of investigation of company's affairs

[...][a]

Amendments

a CA 1963, s 171 repealed by CA 1990, s 6.

172 Inspectors' report to be evidence

[...][a]

Amendments

a CA 1963, s 172 repealed by CA 1990, s 6.

173 Saving for solicitors and bankers

[...][a]

Amendments

a CA 1963, s 173 repealed by CA 1990, s 6.

Directors and Other Officers

174 Directors

Every company shall have at least two directors.

175 Secretary

(1) Every company shall have a secretary, who may be one of the directors.

(2) Anything required or authorised to be done by or to the secretary may, if the office is vacant or there is for any other reason no secretary capable of acting, be done by or to any assistant or deputy secretary or, if there is no assistant or deputy secretary capable of acting, by or to any officer of the company authorised generally or specially in that behalf by the directors.

176 Prohibition of body corporate being director

(1) A company shall not, after the expiration of 3 months from the operative date, have as director of the company a body corporate.

(2) A body corporate which, on the operative date is a director of a company shall within a period of 3 months from that date vacate its office as director of the company, and all acts or things purporting to be made or done after the expiration of that period, by a body corporate as director of any company shall be null and void.

177 Avoidance of acts done by person in dual capacity as director and secretary

A provision requiring or authorising a thing to be done by or to a director and the secretary shall not be satisfied by its being done by or to the same person acting both as director and as, or in place of, the secretary.

178 Validity of acts of directors

The acts of a director shall be valid notwithstanding any defect which may afterwards be discovered in his appointment or qualification.

179 Restrictions on appointment or advertisement of director

(1) A person shall not be capable of being appointed a director of a company by the articles, and shall not be named as a director or proposed director of a company in a prospectus issued by or on behalf of the company, or as proposed director of an intended company in a prospectus issued in relation to that intended company, or in a statement in lieu of prospectus delivered to the registrar by or on behalf of a company unless, before the registration of the articles or the publication of the prospectus or the delivery of the statement in lieu of prospectus, as the case may be, he has by himself or by his agent authorised in writing—

(a) signed and delivered to the registrar of companies for registration a consent in writing to act as such director; and

(b) either—

(i) signed the memorandum for a number of shares not less than his qualification, if any; or

(ii) taken from the company and paid or agreed to pay for his qualification shares, if any; or

(iii) signed and delivered to the registrar for registration an undertaking in writing to take from the company and pay for his qualification shares, if any; or

(iv) made and delivered to the registrar for registration a statutory declaration to the effect that a number of shares, not less than his qualification, if any, are registered in his name.

(2) Where a person has signed and delivered as aforesaid an undertaking to take and pay for his qualification shares, he shall, as regards those shares, be in the same position as if he had signed the memorandum for that number of shares.

(3) References in this section to a share qualification of a director or proposed director shall be construed as including only a share qualification required on appointment or within a period determined by reference to the time of appointment, and references therein to qualification shares shall be construed accordingly.

(4) On the application for registration of the memorandum and articles of a company, the applicant shall deliver to the registrar a list of the persons who have consented to be directors of the company and, if this list contains the name of any person who has not so consented, the applicant [shall be guilty of an offence and liable to a [class C fine][a]][b].

(5) This section shall not apply to—

(a) a company not having a share capital; or

(b) a private company; or

(c) a company which was a private company before becoming a public company; or

(d) a prospectus issued by or on behalf of a company after the expiration of one year from the date on which the company was entitled to commence business.

Amendments

a '£250' substituted for '£50' by C(A)A 1982, Sch 1, increased to £1,500 by CA 1990, s 240(7) as inserted by CLEA 2001, s 104(c) and converted to €1,904.61 by Council Regulations (EC) No 1103/97, No 974/98 and No 2866/98 and the Economic and Monetary Union Act 1998, s 6; the above being implicitly substituted, by Fines Act 2010, s 6, for a fine not exceeding the aforesaid amount. A class C fine currently means a fine not exceeding €2,500.

b Words 'shall be guilty of an offence and liable to a fine' substituted for 'shall be liable to a fine' in CA 1963, s 179(4) by C(AA)A 2003, Sch 2, Item No 1.

---

180 Share qualifications of directors

(1) Without prejudice to the restrictions imposed by section 179, it shall be the duty of every director who is by the articles of the company required to hold a specified share qualification, and who is not already qualified, to obtain his qualification within 2 months after his appointment, or such shorter time as may be fixed by the articles.

(2) For the purpose of any provision in the articles requiring a director to hold a specified share qualification, the bearer of a share warrant shall not be deemed to be the holder of the shares specified in the warrant.

(3) The office of director of a company shall be vacated if the director does not within 2 months from the date of his appointment or within such shorter time as may be fixed by the articles, obtain his qualification, or if after the expiration of the said period or shorter time, he ceases at any time to hold his qualification.

(4) A person vacating office under this section shall be incapable of being re-appointed director of the company until he has obtained his qualification.

(5) If after the expiration of the said period or shorter time any unqualified person acts as a director of the company, he [shall be guilty of an offence and liable to a [class C fine][a]][b].

Amendments

a '£500' substituted for '£100' by C(A)A 1982, Sch 1, and increased to £1,500 by CA 1990, s 240(7) as inserted by CLEA 2001, s 104(c) and converted to €1,904.61 by Council Regulations (EC) No 1103/97, No 974/98 and No 2866/98 and the Economic and Monetary Union Act 1998, s 6; the above being implicitly substituted, by Fines Act 2010, s 6, for a fine not exceeding the aforesaid amount. A class C fine currently means a fine not exceeding €2,500.

b Words 'shall be guilty of an offence and liable to a fine' substituted for 'shall be liable to a fine' in CA 1963, s 180(5) by C(AA)A 2003, Sch 2.

---

181 Appointment of directors to be voted on individually

(1) At a general meeting of a company, a motion for the appointment of two or more persons as directors of the company by a single resolution shall not be made, unless a resolution that it shall be so made has first been agreed to by the meeting without any vote being given against it.

(2) Subject to subsections (3) and (4), a resolution moved in contravention of this section shall be void, whether or not its being so moved was objected to at the time.

(3) Subsection (2) shall not be taken as excluding the operation of section 178.

(4) Where a resolution moved in contravention of this section is passed, no provision for the automatic re-appointment of retiring directors in default of another appointment shall apply.

(5) For the purposes of this section, a motion for approving a person's appointment or for nominating a person for appointment shall be treated as a motion for his appointment.

(6) Nothing in this section shall apply to a resolution altering the company's articles.

182 Removal of directors

(1) A company may by ordinary resolution remove a director before the expiration of his period of office notwithstanding anything in its articles or in any agreement between it and him so, however, that this subsection shall not, in the case of a private company, authorise the removal of a director holding office for life.

(2) Extended notice within the meaning of section 142 shall be required of any resolution to remove a director under this section or to appoint somebody instead of the director so removed at the meeting at which he is removed, and on receipt of notice of an intended resolution to remove a director under this section, the company shall forthwith send a copy thereof to the director concerned, and the director (whether or not he is a member of the company) shall be entitled to be heard on the resolution at the meeting.

(3) Subject to subsection (4), where notice is given of an intended resolution to remove a director under this section and the director concerned makes in relation thereto representations in writing to the company (not exceeding a reasonable length) and requests their notification to the members of the company, the company shall, unless the representations are received by it too late for it to do so—

(a) in any notice of the resolution given to members of the company, state the fact of the representations having been made; and

(b) send a copy of the representations to every member of the company to whom notice of the meeting is sent (whether before or after receipt of the representations by the company);

and if a copy of the representations is not sent as aforesaid because received too late or because of the company's default, the director may (without prejudice to his right to be heard orally) require that the representations shall be read out at the meeting.

(4) Copies of the representations need not be sent out as aforesaid, and the representations need not be read out at the meeting as aforesaid if, on the application either of the company or of any other person who claims to be aggrieved, the court is satisfied that the rights conferred by this section are being abused to secure needless publicity for defamatory matter, and the court may order the company's costs on an application under this section to be paid in whole or in part by the director concerned, notwithstanding that he is not a party to the application.

(5) A vacancy created by the removal of a director under this section may be filled at the meeting at which he is removed and, if not so filled, may be filled as a casual vacancy.

(6) A person appointed director in place of a person removed under this section shall be treated, for the purpose of determining the time at which he or any other director is to retire, as if he had become director on the day on which the person in whose place he is appointed was last appointed director.

(7) Nothing in this section shall be taken as depriving a person removed thereunder of compensation or damages payable to him in respect of the determination of his appointment as director or compensation or damages payable to him in respect of the determination of any appointment terminating with that as director or as derogating from any power to remove a director which may exist apart from this section.

183 [Prohibition of undischarged bankrupts acting as directors and other officers of companies

(1) Subject to subsection (2), if any person being an undischarged bankrupt acts as officer, auditor, liquidator or examiner of, or directly or indirectly takes part or is concerned in the promotion, formation or management of, any company except with the leave of the court, he shall be guilty of an offence.

(2) Where a person is convicted of an offence under subsection (1) he shall be deemed to be subject to a disqualification order from the date of such conviction if he was not, or was not deemed to be, subject to such an order on that date.

(3) In this section 'company' includes a company incorporated outside the State which has an established place of business within the State.][a]

Amendments

a CA 1963, s 183 substituted by CA 1990, s 169.

[183A Examination as to solvency status

Where the Director has reason to believe that a director of a company is an undischarged bankrupt, the Director may require the director of the company to produce by a specified date a sworn statement of all relevant facts pertaining to the company director's financial position, both within the State and elsewhere, and, in particular, to any matter pertaining to bankruptcy as at a particular date.

The court may, on the application of the Director, require a director of a company who has made a statement under subsection (1) to appear before it and answer on oath any question pertaining to the content of the statement.

The court may, on the application of the Director, make a disqualification order (as defined in section 159 of the Companies Act, 1990) against a director of a company on the grounds that he is an undischarged bankrupt.

A director of a company who fails to comply with a requirement under subsection (1) shall be guilty of an offence.][a]

Amendments

a CA 1963, s 183A inserted by CLEA 2001, s 40.

---

184 Power of court to restrain certain persons from acting as directors of or managing companies

[...][a]

Amendments

a CA 1963, s 184 repealed by CA 1990, s 6.

---

185 Prohibition of tax-free payments to directors

(1) It shall not be lawful for a company to pay a director remuneration (whether as director or otherwise) free of income tax or of income tax and sur-tax or of sur-tax, or otherwise calculated by reference to or varying with the amount of his income tax or his income tax and sur-tax or his sur-tax, or to or with the rate of income tax or sur-tax except under a contract which was in force on the 31st day of March, 1962, and provides expressly, and not by reference to the articles, for payment of remuneration as aforesaid.

(2) Any provision contained in a company's articles or in any contract other than such a contract as aforesaid, or in any resolution of a company or a company's directors, for payment to a director of remuneration as aforesaid shall have effect as if it provided for payment, as a gross sum subject to income tax and sur-tax, of the net sum for which it actually provides.

(3) This section shall not apply to remuneration due before the operative date or in respect of a period before the operative date.

186 Approval of company necessary for payment by it to director for loss of office

It shall not be lawful for a company to make to any director of the company any payment by way of compensation for loss of office, or as consideration for or in connection with his retirement from office, without particulars relating to the proposed payment (including the amount thereof) being disclosed to the members of the company and the proposal being approved by the company in general meeting.

187 Approval of company necessary for payment to director of compensation in connection with transfer of property

(1) It is hereby declared that it is not lawful in connection with the transfer of the whole or any part of the undertaking or property of a company for any payment to be made to any director of the company by way of compensation for loss of office or as consideration for or in connection with his retirement from office, unless particulars relating to the proposed payment (including the amount thereof) have been disclosed to the members of the company and the proposal approved by the company in general meeting.

(2) Where a payment which is hereby declared to be illegal is made to a director of the company, the amount received shall be deemed to have been received by him in trust for the company.

188 Duty of director to disclose to company payments to be made to him in connection with transfer of shares in a company

(1) Where, in connection with the transfer to any persons of all or any of the shares in a company being a transfer resulting from—

- (a) an offer made to the general body of shareholders; or
- (b) an offer made by or on behalf of some other body corporate, with a view to the company becoming its subsidiary or a subsidiary of its holding company; or
- (c) an offer made by or on behalf of an individual with a view to his obtaining the right to exercise or control the exercise of not less than one-third of the voting power at any general meeting of the company; or
- (d) any other offer which is conditional on acceptance to a given extent;

a payment is to be made to a director of the company by way of compensation for loss of office, or as a consideration for or in connection with his retirement from office, it shall be the duty of that director to take all reasonable steps to secure that particulars of the proposed payment (including the amount thereof) shall be included in or sent with any notice of the offer made for their shares which is given to any shareholders.

(2) If—

(a) any such director fails to take reasonable steps as aforesaid; or

(b) any person who has been properly required by any such director to include the said particulars in or send them with any such notice as aforesaid fails so to do,

he [shall be guilty of an offence and liable to a [class C fine][a]][b].

(3) Unless—

(a) the requirements of subsection (1) are complied with in relation to any such payment as is therein mentioned; and

(b) the making of the proposed payment is, before the transfer of any shares in pursuance of the offer, approved by a meeting summoned for the purpose of the holders of the shares to which the offer relates and of other holders of shares of the same class as any of the said shares,

any sum received by the director on account of the payment shall be deemed to have been received by him in trust for any persons who have sold their shares as a result of the offer made, and the expenses incurred by him in distributing that sum amongst those persons shall be borne by him and not retained out of that sum.

(4) Where the shareholders referred to in paragraph (*b*) of subsection (3) are not all the members of the company and no provision is made by the articles for summoning or regulating such a meeting as is mentioned in that paragraph, the provisions of this Act and of the company's articles relating to general meetings of the company shall, for that purpose, apply to the meeting either without modification or with such modifications as the Minister on the application of any person concerned may direct for the purpose of adapting them to the circumstances of the meeting.

(5) If at a meeting summoned for the purpose of approving any payment as required by paragraph (b) of subsection (3), a quorum is not present and, after the meeting has been adjourned to a later date, a quorum is again not present, the payment shall be deemed, for the purposes of that subsection, to have been approved.

Amendments

a '£125' substituted for '£25' by C(A)A 1982, Sch 1, increased to £1,500 by CA 1990, s 240(7) as inserted by CLEA 2001, s 104(c) and converted to €1,904.61 by Council Regulations (EC) No 1103/97, No 974/98 and No 2866/98 and the Economic and Monetary Union Act 1998, s 6; the above being implicitly substituted, by Fines Act 2010, s 6, for a fine not exceeding the aforesaid amount. A class C fine currently means a fine not exceeding €2,500.

b Words 'shall be guilty of an offence and liable to a fine' substituted for 'shall be liable to a fine' in CA 1963, s 188(2) by C(AA)A 2003, Sch 2, Item No. 1.

---

189 Provisions supplementary to sections 186, 187 and 188

(1) Where in proceedings for the recovery of any payment as having, by virtue of subsections (1) and (2) of section 187 or subsections (1) and (3) of section 188, been received by any person in trust, it is shown that—

(a) the payment was made in pursuance of any arrangement entered into as part of the agreement for the transfer in question, or within one year before or 2 years after that agreement or the offer leading thereto; and

(b) the company or any person to whom the transfer was made was privy to that arrangement;

the payment shall be deemed, except in so far as the contrary is shown, to be one to which the subsections apply.

(2) If in connection with any such transfer as is mentioned in section 187 or section 188—

(a) the price to be paid to a director of the company for any shares in the company held by him is in excess of the price which could at the time have been obtained by other holders of the like shares; or

(b) any valuable consideration is given to any such director,

the excess or the money value of the consideration, as the case may be, shall, for the purposes of that section, be deemed to have been a payment made to him by way of compensation for loss of office or as consideration for or in connection with his retirement from office.

(3) It is hereby declared that references in sections 186, 187 and 188 to payments to any director of a company by way of compensation for loss of office, or as consideration for or in connection with his retirement from office, include payments to him by way of compensation for loss of office as director of the company or for the loss, while director of the company, or on or in connection with his ceasing to be a director of the company, of any other office in connection with the management of the company's affairs or of any office as director or otherwise in connection with the management of the affairs of any subsidiary company but do not include any *bona fide* payment by way of damages for breach of contract or by way of pension in respect of past services, and for the purposes of this subsection 'pension' includes any superannuation allowance, superannuation gratuity or similar payment.

(4) Nothing in sections 187 and 188 shall be taken to prejudice the operation of any rule of law requiring disclosure to be made with respect to any such payments as are therein mentioned or with respect to any other like payments made or to be made to the directors of a company or to prejudice the operation of any rule of law in relation to the accountability (if any) of any director for any such payment received by him.

(5) References in sections 186, 187, 188 and this section to a director include references to a past-director.

190 Register of directors' shareholdings

(1) Every company shall keep a register showing, in relation to each director and secretary of the company, the number, description and amount of any shares in or debentures of the company or any other body corporate, being the company's subsidiary or holding company, or a subsidiary of the company's holding company, which are held by, or in trust for, him or his spouse or any child of his or of which he or they have any right to become the holder (whether on payment or not), so however, that the register need not include shares in any body corporate which is the wholly-owned subsidiary of another body corporate, and for this purpose a body corporate shall be deemed to be the wholly-owned subsidiary of another if it has no members but that other and that other's wholly-owned subsidiaries and its or their nominees.

(2) Subject to subsection (3), where any shares or debentures have to be, or cease to be, recorded in the said register in relation to any director or secretary by reason of a transaction entered into after the operative date and while he is a director or secretary the register shall also show the date of, and price or other consideration for, the transaction.

(3) Where there is an interval between the agreement for any such transaction as aforesaid and the completion thereof, the date shall be that of the agreement.

(4) The nature and extent of the interest or right in or over any shares or debentures recorded in relation to a director or secretary in the said register shall, if he so requires, be indicated in the register.

(5) The company shall not, by virtue of anything done for the purposes of this section, be affected with notice of, or put upon inquiry as to, the rights of any person in relation to any shares or debentures.

(6) Subject to subsection (7), the said register shall be kept at the same office as the register of members is kept, and shall be open to inspection during business hours (subject to such reasonable restrictions as the company may by its articles or in general meeting impose, so that not less than 2 hours in each day be allowed for inspection) by any member or holder of debentures of the company.

(7) The said register shall also be produced at the commencement of the company's annual general meeting and shall remain open and accessible during the continuance of the meeting to any person attending the meeting.

(8) Any member or holder of debentures of the company may require a copy of the register, or of any part thereof, on payment of [6 cent][a], or such less sum as the company may prescribe, for every 100 words or fractional part thereof required to be copied. The company shall cause any copy so required by any person to be sent to that person within a period of 10 days commencing on the day next after the day on which the requirement is received by the company.

(9) If default is made in complying with subsection (7), the company and every officer of the company who is in default [shall be guilty of an offence and liable to a [class C fine][b]][c]; and if default is made in complying with subsection (1) or subsection (2), or if any inspection required under this section is refused or if any copy required under this section if not sent within the proper period, the company and every officer of the company who is in default [shall be guilty of an offence and liable to a [class C fine][d]][c].

(10) To ensure compliance with the provisions of this section the court may by order compel an inspection of the register or direct that the copies required shall be sent to the persons requiring them.

(11) For the purposes of this section—

(a) any person in accordance with whose directions or instructions the directors of a company are accustomed to act shall be deemed to be a director of the company; and

(b) a person shall be deemed to hold, or to have an interest in or right over, any shares or debentures in which he has an interest jointly or in common with any other person or a limited, reversionary or contingent interest or an interest as the object of a discretionary trust; and

(c) a person shall be deemed to hold, or to have an interest or right in or over any shares or debentures if a body corporate other than the company holds them or has that interest or right in or over them, and either—

(i) that body corporate or its directors are accustomed to act in accordance with his directions or instructions; or

(ii) he is entitled to exercise or control the exercise of one-third or more of the voting power at any general meeting of that body corporate.

(12) This section shall not apply to a private company if and so long as all the members of such private company are directors thereof.

Amendments

a 'One shilling' to be read as 'five new pence' pursuant to the Decimal Currency Act 1970, s 9, and converted to 6 cent by Council Regulations (EC) No 1103/97, No 974/98 and No 2866/98 and the Economic and Monetary Union Act 1998, s 6.

b '£250' substituted for '£50' by C(A)A 1982, Sch 1, increased to £1,500 by CA 1990, s 240(7) as inserted by CLEA 2001, s 104(c) and converted to €1,904.61 by Council Regulations (EC) No 1103/97, No 974/98 and No 2866/98 and the Economic and Monetary Union Act 1998, s 6; the above being implicitly substituted, by Fines Act 2010, s 6, for a fine not exceeding the aforesaid amount. A class C fine currently means a fine not exceeding €2,500.

c Words 'shall be guilty of an offence and liable to a fine' substituted for 'shall be liable to a fine' in both instances where it occurs in CA 1963, s 190(9) by C(AA)A 2003, Sch 2, Item No 4. Notwithstanding the fact that CA 1963, s 190 ceased to have effect on 1 August 1991 (the operative date of CA 1990, s 53), it was amended by C(AA)A 2003.

d '£500' substituted for '£100' by C(A)A 1982, Sch 1, increased to £1,500 by CA 1990, s 240(7) as inserted by CLEA 2001, s 104(c) and converted to €1,904.61 by Council Regulations (EC) No 1103/97, No 974/98 and No 2866/98 and the Economic and Monetary Union Act 1998, s 6; the above being implicitly substituted, by Fines Act 2010, s 6, for a fine not exceeding the aforesaid amount. A class C fine currently means a fine not exceeding €2,500.

---

191 Particulars of directors' salaries and payments to be given in accounts

(1) In any accounts of a company laid before the annual general meeting or in a statement annexed thereto, there shall, subject to and in accordance with the provisions of this section, be shown so far as the information is contained in the company's books and papers or the company has the right to obtain it from the persons concerned—

(a) the aggregate amount of the directors' emoluments;

(b) the aggregate amount of directors' or past-directors' pensions; and

(c) the aggregate amount of any compensation to directors or past-directors in respect of loss of office.

(2) The amount to be shown under paragraph (a) of subsection (1)—

(a) shall include any emoluments paid to or receivable by any person in respect of his services as director of the company or in respect of his services, while director of the company, as director of any subsidiary thereof or otherwise in connection with the management of the affairs of the company or any subsidiary thereof; and

(b) shall distinguish between emoluments in respect of services as director, whether of the company or of its subsidiary, and other emoluments;

and, for the purposes of this section, 'emoluments' in relation to a director, includes fees and percentages, any sums paid by way of expenses allowance in so far as those sums are charged to income tax, any contribution paid in respect of him under any pension scheme, and the estimated money value of any other benefits received by him otherwise than in cash in so far as the same are charged to income tax.

(3) The amount to be shown under paragraph (b) of subsection (1) —

(a) shall not include any pension paid or receivable under a pension scheme if the scheme is such that the contributions thereunder are substantially adequate for the maintenance of the scheme, but save as aforesaid, shall include any pension paid or receivable in respect of any such services of a director or past-director of the company as are mentioned in subsection (2), whether to or by him or, on his nomination or by virtue of dependence on or other connection with him, to or by any other person; and

(b) shall distinguish between pensions in respect of services as director, whether of the company or its subsidiary, and other pensions;

and, for the purposes of this section, 'pension' includes any superannuation allowance, superannuation gratuity or similar payment, and 'pension scheme' means a scheme for the provision of pensions in respect of services as director or otherwise which is maintained in whole or in part by means of contributions, and 'contribution' in relation to a pension scheme means any payment (including an insurance premium) paid for the purposes of the scheme by or in respect of persons rendering services in respect of which pensions will or may become payable under the scheme, except that it does not include any payment in respect of two or more persons if the amount paid in respect of each of them is not ascertainable.

(4) The amount to be shown under paragraph (*c*) of subsection (1) —

(a) shall include any sums paid to or receivable by a director or past-director by way of compensation for loss of office as director of the company or for the loss, while director of the company, or on or in connection with his ceasing to be a director of the company, of any other office in connection with the management of the company's affairs or of any office as director or otherwise in connection with the management of the affairs of any subsidiary thereof; and

(b) shall distinguish between compensation in respect of the office of director, whether of the company or of its subsidiary, and compensation in respect of other offices;

and, for the purposes of this section, references to compensation for loss of office shall include sums paid as consideration for or in connection with a person's retirement from office.

(5) The amounts to be shown under each paragraph of subsection (1)—

(a) shall include all relevant sums paid by or receivable from—

(i) the company; and

(ii) the company's subsidiaries; and

(iii) any other person;

except sums to be accounted for to the company or any of its subsidiaries or, by virtue of section 188, to past or present members of the company or any of its subsidiaries or any class of those members; and

(b) shall distinguish, in the case of the amount to be shown under paragraph (*c*) of subsection (1), between the sums respectively paid by or receivable from the company, the company's subsidiaries and persons other than the company and its subsidiaries.

(6) The amounts to be shown under this section for any financial year shall be the sums receivable in respect of that year, whenever paid, or, in the case of sums not receivable in respect of a period, the sums paid during that year, so, however, that where—

(a) any sums are not shown in the accounts for the relevant financial year on the ground that the person receiving them is liable to account therefor as mentioned in paragraph (a) of subsection (5), but the liability is thereafter wholly or partly released or is not enforced within a period of 2 years; or

(b) any sums paid by way of expenses allowances are charged to income tax after the end of the relevant financial year;

those sums shall, to the extent to which the liability is released or not enforced or they are charged as aforesaid, as the case may be, be shown in the first accounts in which it is practicable to show them, or in a statement annexed thereto, and shall be distinguished from the amounts to be shown therein apart from this provision.

(7) Where it is necessary so to do for the purpose of making any distinction required by this section in any amount to be shown thereunder, the directors may apportion any payments between the matters in respect of which they have been paid or are receivable in such manner as they think appropriate.

(8) If in the case of any accounts the requirements of this section are not complied with, it shall be the duty of the auditors of the company by whom the accounts are examined to include in the report thereon, so far as they are reasonably able to do so, a statement giving the required particulars.

(9) In this section, any reference to a company's subsidiary—

(a) in relation to a person who is or was, while a director of the company, a director also, by virtue of the company's nomination, direct or indirect, of any other body corporate, shall, subject to the following paragraph, include that body corporate, whether or not it is or was in fact the company's subsidiary; and

(b) shall, for the purposes of subsections (2) and (3), be taken as referring to a subsidiary at the time the services were rendered, and, for the purposes of subsection (4), be taken as referring to a subsidiary immediately before the loss of office as director of the company.

192 Particulars of loans to directors to be given in accounts

(1) The accounts which, in pursuance of this Act, are to be laid before the annual general meeting of every company shall, subject to the provisions of this section, contain particulars showing—

(a) the amount of any loans made during the company's financial year to—

(i) any director of the company;

(ii) any person who, after the making of the loan, became during that year a director of the company; and

(iii) any body corporate in which the directors of the company (or any of them) are beneficially entitled to more than 20 per cent in nominal value of the shares of such body corporate which carry voting rights other than voting rights which arise only in specified circumstances;

by the company or a subsidiary thereof or by any other person under a guarantee from or on a security provided by the company or a subsidiary thereof (including any such loans which were repaid during that year); and

(b) the amount of any loans made in manner aforesaid to any such director, person or body corporate as aforesaid at any time before the company's financial year and outstanding at the expiration thereof.

(2) Subsection (1) shall not require the inclusion in accounts of particulars of—

(a) a loan made in the ordinary course of its business by the company or a subsidiary thereof, where the ordinary business of the company, or, as the case may be, the subsidiary, includes the lending of money; or

(b) a loan made by the company or a subsidiary thereof to an employee of the company or subsidiary, as the case may be, if the loan does not exceed [€2,539.48][a] and is certified by the directors of the company or subsidiary, as the case may be, to have been made in accordance with any practice adopted or about to be adopted by the company or subsidiary relating to loans to its employees;

not being, in either case, a loan made by the company under a guarantee from or on a security provided by a subsidiary thereof or a loan made by a subsidiary of the company under a guarantee from or on a security provided by the company or any other subsidiary thereof.

(3) If in the case of any such accounts as aforesaid, the requirements of this section are not complied with, it shall be the duty of the auditors of the company by whom the accounts are examined to include in their report on the balance sheet of the company, so far as they are reasonably able to do so, a statement giving the required particulars.

(4) References in this section to a subsidiary shall be taken as referring to a subsidiary at the end of the company's financial year (whether or not a subsidiary at the date of the loan).

Amendments

a £2,000 converted to €2,539.48 by Council Regulations (EC) No 1103/97, No 974/98 and No 2866/98 and the Economic and Monetary Union Act 1998, s 6.

---

193 General duty to make disclosure for the purposes of sections 190, 191 and 192

(1) It shall be the duty of every director and secretary of a company to give notice in writing to the company as soon as may be of such matters relating to [himself or herself and to his or her spouse or civil partner within the meaning of the Civil Partnership and Certain Rights and Obligations of Cohabitants Act 2010][a] and children as may be necessary for the purposes of section 190.

(2) It shall be the duty of every director of a company to give notice in writing to the company of such matters relating to himself as may be necessary for the purposes of sections 191 and 192 except in so far as the latter section relates to loans made by the company or by any other person under a guarantee from or on a security provided by the company to a director thereof.

(3) If any such notice is not given at a meeting of directors, the director or secretary, as the case may be, giving it shall take reasonable steps to secure that it is brought up and read at the next meeting of the directors after it is given.

(4) Any person who fails to comply with this section [shall be guilty of an offence and liable to a not [class C fine][b]][c].

Amendments

a Words 'himself or herself and to his or her spouse or civil partner within the meaning of the Civil Partnership and Certain Rights and Obligations of Cohabitants Act 2010' substituted for 'himself and to his spouse' by Civil Partnership and Certain Rights and Obligations of Cohabitants Act 2010, Sch, Pt 1, Item No. 1.

b Words 'shall be guilty of an offence and liable to a fine' substituted for 'shall be liable to a fine' in CA 1963, s 193(4) by C(AA)A 2003, Sch 2, Item No. 1.

c '£500' substituted for '£100' by C(A)A 1982, Sch 1, increased to £1,500 by CA 1990, s 240(7) as inserted by CLEA 2001, s 104(c) and converted to €1,904.61 by Council Regulations (EC) No 1103/97, No 974/98 and No 2866/98 and the Economic and Monetary Union Act 1998, s 6; the above being implicitly substituted, by Fines Act 2010, s 6, for a fine not exceeding the aforesaid amount. A class C fine currently means a fine not exceeding €2,500.

---

194 Duty of director to disclose his interest in contracts made by the company

(1) It shall be the duty of a director of a company who is in any way, whether directly or indirectly, interested in a contract or proposed contract with the company to declare the nature of his interest at a meeting of the directors of the company.

(2) In the case of a proposed contract the declaration required by this section to be made by a director shall be made at the meeting of the directors at which the question of entering into the contract is first taken into consideration, or if the director was not at the date of that meeting interested in the proposed contract, at the next meeting of the directors held after he became so interested, and in a case where the director becomes interested in a contract after it is made, the said declaration shall be made at the first meeting of the directors held after the director becomes so interested.

[(3) Subject to subsection (4), for the purposes of this section, a general notice given to the directors of a company by a director to the effect that—

(a) he is a member of a specified company or firm and is to be regarded as interested in any contract which may, after the date of the notice, be made with that company or firm; or

(b) he is to be regarded as interested in any contract which may after the date of the notice be made with a specified person who is connected with him (within the meaning of section 26 of the Companies Act, 1990), shall be deemed to be a sufficient declaration of interest in relation to any such contract.][a]

(4) No such notice as aforesaid shall be of effect unless either it is given at a meeting of the directors or the director takes reasonable steps to secure that it is brought up and read at the next meeting of the directors after it is given.

(5) (a) A copy of every declaration made and notice given in pursuance of this section shall, within 3 days after the making or giving thereof, be entered in a book kept for this purpose. Such book shall be open for inspection without charge by any director, secretary, auditor or member of the company at the registered office of the company and shall be produced at every general meeting of the company, and at any meeting of the directors if any director so requests in sufficient time to enable the book to be available at the meeting.

(b) If a company [fails to comply with this subsection or subsection (5A)][b] the company and every officer of the company who is in default [shall be guilty of an offence and liable to a [class C fine][c]][d] and if any inspection or production required thereunder is refused, the court may by order compel an immediate inspection or production.

[(5A) A company shall, if required by the Director, produce to the Director for inspection the book kept by it in accordance with subsection (5)(a) and shall give the Director such facilities for inspecting and taking copies of the contents of the book as the Director may require.][e]

(6) Any director who fails to comply with this section [shall be guilty of an offence and liable to a [class C fine][c]][f].

(7) Nothing in this section shall be taken to prejudice the operation of any rule of law restricting directors of a company from having any interest in contracts with the company.

Amendments

a CA 1963, s 194(3) substituted by CA 1990, s 47(3).

b Words 'fails to comply with this subsection or subsection (5A)' substituted for 'fails to comply with this subsection' in CA 1963, s 194(5)(b) by C(A)A 2009, s 2(a).

c '£500' substituted for '£100' by C(A)A 1982, Sch 1, increased to £1,500 by CA 1990, s 240(7) as inserted by CLEA 2001, s 104(c) and converted to €1,904.61 by Council Regulations (EC) No 1103/97, No 974/98 and No 2866/98 and the Economic and Monetary Union Act 1998, s 6; the above being implicitly substituted, by Fines Act 2010, s 6, for a fine not exceeding the aforesaid amount. A class C fine currently means a fine not exceeding €2,500.

d Words 'shall be guilty of an offence and liable to a fine' substituted for 'shall be liable to a fine' in CA 1963, s 194(5)(b) and (6) by C(AA)A 2003, Sch 2, Item No. 1.

e CA 1963, s 194(5A) inserted by C(A)A 2009, s 2(b).

f Words 'shall be guilty of an offence and liable to a fine' substituted for 'shall be liable to a fine' in CA 1963, s 194(6) and (6) by C(AA)A 2003, Sch 2, Item No. 1.

[195 Register of directors and secretaries

(1) Every company shall keep at its registered office a register of its directors and secretaries.

(2) Subject to subsection (3), the said register shall contain the following particulars relating to each director—

(a) his present forename and surname and any former fore-name and surname; and

(b) his date of birth; and

(c) his usual residential address; and

(d) his nationality; and

(e) his business occupation, if any; and

(f) particulars of any other directorships of bodies corporate, whether incorporated in the State or elsewhere, held by him or which have been held by him.

(3) It shall not be necessary for the said register to contain on any day particulars of any directorship—

(a) which has not been held by a director at any time during the ten years preceding that day;

(b) which is held or was held by a director in bodies corporate of which the company is or was the wholly owned subsidiary or which are or were the wholly owned subsidiaries either of the company or of another body corporate of which the company is or was the wholly owned subsidiary;

and for the purposes of this subsection a body corporate shall be deemed to be the wholly owned subsidiary of another if it has no members except that other and that other's wholly owned subsidiaries and its or their nominees.

(4) Subject to subsection (5), the said register shall contain the following particulars relating to the secretary or, where there are joint secretaries, in relation to each of them—

(a) in the case of an individual, his present forename and surname, any former forename and surname and his usual residential address; and

(b) in the case of a body corporate, the corporate name and registered office.

(5) Where all partners in a firm are joint secretaries of a company, the name and principal office of the firm may be stated instead of the said particulars.

(6) The company shall, within the period of 14 days from the happening of—

(a) any change among its directors or in its secretary, or

(b) any change in any of the particulars contained in the register,

send to the registrar of companies a notification in the prescribed form of the change and of the date on which it occurred.

[(6A) In the case of a person who is a director of more than one company (the 'relevant companies') the following provisions apply—

(a) the person may send a notification in the prescribed form to the registrar of companies of a change in his or her usual residential address or of a change in his or her name and (in each case) of the date on which the change occurred,

(b) if such a notification is sent to the registrar and the relevant companies are listed in the notification as being companies of which the person is a director—

(i) each of the relevant companies shall be relieved, as respects, and only as respects, that particular change or, as the case may be, those particular changes, of the obligation under subsection (6) to send a notification of it or them to the registrar,

and

(ii) the registrar may proceed to record the relevant change or changes concerning the person in relation to each of the relevant companies.][b]

(7) A notification sent to the registrar of companies pursuant to subsection (6) of the appointment of a person as a director, secretary or joint secretary of a company shall be accompanied by a consent signed by that person to act as director, secretary or joint secretary, as the case may be.

[(8) Without prejudice to subsection (7), if the notification to be sent to the registrar of companies pursuant to subsection (6) is a notification of the appointment of a person as a director of a company and that person is a person who is disqualified under the law of another state (whether pursuant to an order of a judge or a tribunal or otherwise) from being appointed or acting as a director or secretary of a body corporate or an undertaking, that person shall ensure that the notification is accompanied by (but as a separate document from the notification) a statement in the prescribed form signed by him specifying—

(a) the jurisdiction in which he is so disqualified,

(b) the date on which he became so disqualified, and

(c) the period for which he is so disqualified.][c]

(9) Subsection (6) shall not apply to any change in the particulars contained in a company's register of directors and secretaries made solely by reason of the coming into force of section 51 of the Companies Act, 1990 but if after any such change has occurred and before the company makes its next annual return, any other change in those particulars occurs, the company shall send to the registrar of companies a notification in the prescribed form of any such earlier changes and the date on which they occurred at the same time as it notifies the registrar of the later changes in accordance with this section.

(10) The register to be kept under this section shall, during business hours (subject to such reasonable restrictions as the company may by its articles or in general meeting impose, so that not less than 2 hours in each day be allowed for inspection) be open to the inspection of any member of the company without charge, and of any other person, on payment of one pound or such less sum as the company may prescribe, for each inspection.

[(10A) Any member of a company or other person may require the company to supply to him a copy of the register required to be kept under this section, or any part of the register, on payment of [19c][d], or such less sum as the company may prescribe, for every hundred words or fractional part thereof required to be copied. The company shall cause a copy so required by a person to be sent to the person within 10 days of the receipt by the company of the request, and if it fails to do so it shall be guilty of an offence.][e]

(11) It shall be the duty of each director and secretary of a company to give information in writing to the company as soon as may be of such matters as may be necessary to enable the company to comply with this section.

[(11A) If a company fails to send, in accordance with subsection (6), a notification, in the prescribed form, to the registrar of companies of the fact of a person's having ceased, for whatever reason, to be a director or secretary of the company and of the date on which that event occurred that person may serve on the company a notice—

(a) requesting it to send forthwith the notification of that matter, in the prescribed form, to the registrar, and

(b) stating that if the company fails to comply with that request within 21 days of the service of the notice on it, he will forward to the registrar of companies and to every person who, to his knowledge, is an officer of the company a copy of any notice of resignation by him as a director or secretary of the company or any other documentary proof of his having ceased to be such a director or secretary together with—

(i) in the case of the registrar of companies, such additional information as may be prescribed (which may include a statutory declaration made by the person stating the names of the persons who, to his knowledge, are officers of the company), and

(ii) in the case of every other person as aforesaid, a written request of the person that he take such steps as will ensure that the failure of the company to comply with the notice continues no further.

(11B) If a company fails to comply with a request made of it under a notice referred to in subsection (11A) the person who served the notice may forward to the registrar of companies and to every person who, to his knowledge, is an officer of the company a copy of the notice of resignation or other documentary proof referred to in subsection (11A) if, but only if, there is forwarded together with that notice or proof, in the case of the registrar, the additional information referred to in that subsection and, in the case of every other person as aforesaid, the written request referred to in that subsection.

(11C) No notice of resignation or other documentary proof of a person's having ceased to be a director or secretary of a company which is forwarded to the registrar of companies by that person (other than such a notice or other proof which is forwarded by him under and in accordance with subsections (11A) and (11B), or section 43(9) of the Companies (Amendment) (No. 2) Act, 1999) shall be considered by the registrar.

(11D) No additional information referred to in subsection (11A)(b)(i) that is included in a notice of resignation or other documentary proof referred to in this section which is forwarded, under and in accordance with the foregoing provisions, to the registrar of companies shall, of itself, be regarded as constituting defamatory matter.

(11E) Any person may give notice (accompanied by such proof of the matter concerned as may be prescribed) to the registrar of companies of the fact that a person holding the office of director or secretary of a particular company has died.][f]

(12) If an inspection required under this section is refused or if default is made in complying with subsections (1), (2), (4), (6) or (7), the company and every officer of the company who is in default [shall be guilty of an offence and liable to a [class C fine][g]][h] and, for continued contravention, to a daily default [class E fine][i].

(13) In the case of any such refusal, the court may by order compel an immediate inspection of the register.

(14) A person who fails to comply with subsection (11) shall be guilty of an offence and liable to a fine.

(15) For the purposes of this section—

- (a) in the case of a person usually known by a title different from his surname, the expression 'surname' means that title;
- (b) references to a 'former forename' or 'surname' do not include—
  - (i) in the case of a person usually known by a title different from his surname, the name by which he was known previous to the adoption of or succession to the title; or
  - (ii) in the case of any person, a former forename or surname where that name or surname was changed or disused before the person bearing the name attained the age of 18 years or has been changed or disused for a period of not less than 20 years; or
  - (iii) in the case of a married woman, the name or surname by which she was known previous to the marriage.][a]

Amendments

a CA 1963, s 195 substituted by CA 1990, s 51.

b CA 1963, s 195(6A) inserted by IFCMPA 2005, s 62. This provision has not yet been commenced.

c CA 1963, s 195(8) substituted by C(A)A 1982, s 8; deleted by C(A)(No 2)A 1999 s 47; inserted by CLEA 2001, s 91. CA 1963, s 195(8) is not yet operative.

d 15p converted to 19c by Council Regulations (EC) No 1103/97, No 974/98 and No 2866/98 and the Economic and Monetary Union Act 1998, s 6.

e CA 1963, s 10A inserted by CLEA 2001, s 91.

f CA 1963, ss (11A) – (11E) inserted by CLEA C(A)(No 2)A 1999, s 47.

g £1,000 increased to £1,500 by CA 1990, s 240(7) as inserted by CLEA 2001, s 104(c) and converted to €1,904.61 by Council Regulations (EC) No 1103/97, No 974/98 and No 2866/98 and the Economic and Monetary Union Act 1998, s 6; the above being implicitly substituted, by Fines Act 2010, s 6, for a fine not exceeding the aforesaid amount. A class C fine currently means a fine not exceeding €2,500.

h Words 'shall be guilty of an offence and liable to a fine' substituted for 'shall be liable to a fine' in CA 1963, s 195(12) by C(AA)A 2003, Sch 2.

i £50 converted to €63.49 by Council Regulations (EC) No 1103/97, No 974/98 and No 2866/98 and the Economic and Monetary Union Act 1998, s 6; as implicitly substituted, by Fines Act 2010, s 8, for a fine not exceeding the aforesaid amount. A class E fine currently means a fine not exceeding €500.

---

196 Particulars relating to directors to be shown on all business letters of the company

(1) Subject to subsection (2), every company to which this section applies shall, in all business letters on or in which the company's name appears and which are sent by the company to any person, state in legible characters in relation to every director the following particulars:

(a) his present Christian name, or the initials thereof, and present surname; and

(b) any former Christian names and surnames; and

(c) his nationality, if not Irish.

(2) If special circumstances exist which render it in the opinion of the Minister expedient that such an exemption should be granted, the Minister may, subject to such conditions as he may think fit, grant exemption from the obligations imposed by this section.

(3) This section shall apply to—

(a) every company registered under this Act or under the Companies (Consolidation) Act, 1908, unless it was registered before the 23rd day of November, 1916, and

(b) every company incorporated outside the State which has an established place of business within the State, unless it had established such a place of business before the said date; and

(c) every company licensed under the Moneylenders Act, 1933, whenever it was registered or whenever it established a place of business.

(4) Subject to subsection (5), if a company makes default in complying with this section, every officer of the company who is in default shall be liable on summary conviction for each offence to a [class C fine],[a] and, for the purpose of this subsection, where a body corporate is an officer of the company, any officer of the body corporate shall be deemed to be an officer of the company.

(5) No proceedings shall be instituted under this section except by, or with the consent of, the Minister.

(6) For the purposes of this section—

(a) 'director' includes any person in accordance with whose directions or instructions the directors of the company are accustomed to act, and 'officer' shall be construed accordingly; and

(b) 'initials' includes a recognised abbreviation of a Christian name; and paragraphs (b), (c) and (d) of subsection (12) of section 195 shall apply as they apply for the purposes of that section.

Amendments

a '£125' substituted for '£25' by C(A)A 1982, Sch 1, increased to £1,500 by CA 1990, s 240(7) as inserted by CLEA 2001, s 104(c) and converted to €1,904.61 by Council Regulations (EC) No 1103/97, No 974/98 and No 2866/98 and the Economic and Monetary Union Act 1998, s 6; the above being implicitly substituted, by Fines Act 2010, s 6, for a fine not exceeding the aforesaid amount. A class C fine currently means a fine not exceeding €2,500.

---

197 Limited company may have directors with unlimited liability

(1) In a limited company the liability of the directors, or of the managing director, may, if so provided by the memorandum, be unlimited.

(2) In a limited company in which the liability of a director is unlimited, the directors of the company and the member who proposes a person for election or appointment to the

office of director, shall add to that proposal a statement that the liability of the person holding that office will be unlimited, and before the person accepts the office or acts therein, notice in writing that his liability will be unlimited shall be given to him by the following or one of the following persons, namely, the promoters of the company, the directors of the company, and the secretary of the company.

(3) If any director or proposer makes default in adding such a statement, or if any promoter or director or secretary makes default in giving such a notice, he [shall be guilty of an offence and liable to a [class C fine][a]][b] and shall also be liable for any damage which the person so elected or appointed may sustain from the default, but the liability of the person elected or appointed shall not be affected by the default.

Amendments

a '£500' substituted for '£100' by C(A)A 1982, Sch 1, increased to £1,500 by CA 1990, s 240(7) as inserted by CLEA 2001, s 104(c) and converted to €1,904.61 by Council Regulations (EC) No 1103/97, No 974/98 and No 2866/98 and the Economic and Monetary Union Act 1998, s 6; the above being implicitly substituted, by Fines Act 2010, s 6, for a fine not exceeding the aforesaid amount. A class C fine currently means a fine not exceeding €2,500.

b Words 'shall be guilty of an offence and liable to a fine' substituted for 'shall be liable to a fine' in CA 1963, s 197(3) by C(AA)A 2003, Sch 2, Item No. 1.

---

198 Power of limited company to make liability of directors unlimited

(1) A limited company, if so authorised by its articles, may, by special resolution, alter its memorandum so as to render unlimited the liability of its directors or of any managing director.

(2) Upon the passing of any such special resolution, the provisions thereof shall be as valid as if they had been originally contained in the memorandum.

199 Provisions as to assignment of office by directors

If in the case of any company provision is made by the articles or by any agreement entered into between any person and the company for empowering a director of the company to assign his office as such to another person, any assignment of office made in pursuance of the said provision shall, notwithstanding anything to the contrary contained in the said provision, be of no effect unless and until it is approved by a special resolution of the company.

Avoidance of Provisions in Articles or Contracts relieving Officers from Liability

200 Avoidance of provisions exempting officers and auditors of company from liability

[(1)][a] Subject as hereinafter provided, any provision whether contained in the articles of a company or in any contract with a company or otherwise for exempting any officer of the company or any person employed by the company as auditor from, or indemnifying him against, any liability which by virtue of any rule of law would otherwise attach to him in respect of any negligence, default, breach of duty or breach of trust of which he may be guilty in relation to the company shall be void, so, however, that—

(a) nothing in this section shall operate to deprive any person of any exemption or right to be indemnified in respect of anything done or omitted to be done by him while any such provision was in force; and

(b) notwithstanding anything in this section, a company may, in pursuance of any such provision as aforesaid, indemnify any such officer or auditor against any liability incurred by him in defending proceedings, whether civil or criminal, in which judgment is given in his favour or in which he is acquitted, or in connection with any application under section 391 [or section 42 of the Companies (Amendment) Act, 1983][b] in which relief is granted to him by the court.

[(2) Notwithstanding subsection (1), a company may purchase and maintain for any of its officers or auditors insurance in respect of any liability referred to in that subsection.

(3) Notwithstanding any provision contained in an enactment, the articles of a company or otherwise, a director may be counted in the quorum and may vote on any resolution to purchase or maintain any insurance under which the director might benefit.

(4) Any directors' and officers' insurance purchased or maintained by a company before the date on which the amendments made to this section by the Companies (Auditing and Accounting) Act 2003 came into operation is as valid and effective as it would have been if those amendments had been in operation when that insurance was purchased or maintained.

(5) In this section a reference to an officer or auditor includes any former or current officer or auditor of the company, as the case may be.][c]

Amendments

a CA 1963, s 200 renumbered as s 200(1) by C(AA)A 2003, s 56.[1]

b Words 'or section 42 of the Companies (Amendment) Act, 1983' inserted by C(A)A 1983, Sch 1, para 16.

c CA 1963, s 200(2)–(5) inserted by C(AA)A 2003, s 56.

1 Amendments to CA 1963, s 200 were introduced to the Companies (Auditing and Accounting) Bill 2003 by way of amendment at the Select Committee on Enterprise and Small Business, 4 December 2003.

Arrangements and Reconstructions

201 Compromise between company and its member or creditors

(1) Where a compromise or arrangement is proposed between a company and its creditors or any class of them or between the company and its members or any class of them, the court may, on the application of the company or of any creditor or member of the company, or, in the case of a company being wound up, of the liquidator, order a meeting of the creditors or class of creditors, or of the members of the company or class of members, as the case may be, to be summoned in such manner as the court directs.

(2) Whenever such an application as is mentioned in subsection (1) is made, the court may on such terms as seem just, stay all proceedings or restrain further proceedings against the company for such period as to the court seems fit.

(3) If a majority in number representing three-fourths in value of the creditors or class of creditors or members or class of members, as the case may be, present and voting either in person or by proxy at the meeting, vote in favour of a resolution agreeing to any compromise or arrangement, the compromise or arrangement shall, if sanctioned by the court, be binding on all the creditors or the class of creditors, or on the members or class of members, as the case may be, and also on the company or, in the case of a company in the course of being wound up, on the liquidator and contributories of the company.

(4) Section 144 shall apply to any such resolution as is mentioned in subsection (3) which is passed at any adjourned meeting held under this section.

(5) An order made under subsection (3) shall have no effect until an office copy of the order has been delivered to the registrar of companies for registration, and a copy of every such order shall be annexed to every copy of the memorandum of the company issued after the order has been made, or, in the case of a company not having a memorandum, of every copy so issued of the instrument constituting or defining the constitution of the company.

(6) If a company fails to comply with subsection (5), the company and every officer of the company who is in default [shall be guilty of an offence and liable to a [class C fine][a]][b].

[(6A) For the avoidance of doubt, nothing in this section or sections 202 to 204 prejudices the jurisdiction of the Irish Takeover Panel under the Irish Takeover Panel Act, 1997, with respect to a compromise or scheme of arrangement that is proposed between a relevant company (within the meaning of that Act) and its members or any class of them and which constitutes a takeover within the meaning of that Act and, accordingly, the said Panel has, and shall be deemed always to have had, power to make rules under section 8 of the said Act in relation to a takeover of the kind aforesaid, to the same extent and subject to the like conditions, as it has power to make rules under that section in relation to any other kind of takeover.

(6B) The Irish Takeover Panel, in exercising its powers under the Irish Takeover Panel Act, 1997, and the High Court, in exercising its powers under this section and sections 203 and 204, shall each have due regard to the other's exercise of powers under the said Act or those sections, as the case may be.][c]

(7) In this section and in section 202, 'company' means any company liable to be wound up under this Act, and 'arrangement' includes a reorganisation of the share capital of the company by the consolidation of shares of different classes or by the division of shares into shares of different classes or by both those methods.

Amendments

a '£100' substituted for '£20' by C(A)A 1982, Sch 1, increased to £1,500 by CA 1990, s 240(7) as inserted by CLEA 2001, s 104(c) and converted to €1,904.61 by Council Regulations (EC) No 1103/97, No 974/98 and No 2866/98 and the Economic and Monetary Union Act 1998, s 6; the above being implicitly substituted, by Fines Act 2010, s 6, for a fine not exceeding the aforesaid amount. A class C fine currently means a fine not exceeding €2,500.

b Words 'shall be guilty of an offence and liable to a fine' substituted for 'shall be liable to a fine' in CA 1963, s 201(6) by C(AA)A 2003, Sch 2, Item No. 1.

c CA 1963, s 201(6A) and (6B) inserted by CLEA 2001, s 92.

---

202 Information as to compromises with members and creditors

(1) Where a meeting of creditors or any class of creditors or members or any class of members is summoned under section 201 there shall—

(a) with every notice summoning the meeting which is sent to a creditor or member, be sent also a statement explaining the effect of the compromise or arrangement and in particular stating any material interests of the directors of the company, whether as directors or as members or as creditors of the company or otherwise, and the effect thereon of the compromise or arrangement, in so far as it is different from the effect on the like interests of other persons; and

(b) in every notice summoning the meeting which is given by advertisement, be included either such a statement as aforesaid or a notification of the place at which and the manner in which creditors or members entitled to attend the meeting may obtain copies of such a statement as aforesaid.

(2) Where the compromise or arrangement affects the rights of debenture holders of a company, the said statement shall give the like explanation in relation to the trustees of any deed for securing the issue of the debentures as it is required to give in relation to the company's directors.

(3) Where a notice given by advertisement includes a notification that copies of a statement explaining the effect of a compromise or arrangement proposed can be obtained by creditors or members entitled to attend the meeting, every such creditor or member shall, on making application in the manner indicated by the notice, be furnished by the company free of charge with a copy of the statement.

(4) Subject to subsection (5), where a company fails to comply with any requirement of this section, the company and every officer of the company who is in default [shall be guilty of an offence and liable to a [class C fine][a]][b], and for the purpose of this subsection any liquidator of the company and any trustee of a deed for securing the issue of debentures of the company shall be deemed to be an officer of the company.

(5) A person shall not be liable under subsection (4) if that person shows that the default was due to the refusal of any other person, being a director or trustee for debenture holders, to supply the necessary particulars as to his interests.

(6) It shall be the duty of any director of the company and of any trustee for debenture holders of the company to give notice to the company of such matters relating to himself as may be necessary for the purposes of this section, and any person who makes default in complying with this subsection [shall be guilty of an offence and liable to a [class C fine][a]][c].

Amendments

a '£500' substituted for '£100' by C(A)A 1982, Sch 1, increased to £1,500 by CA 1990, s 240(7) as inserted by CLEA 2001, s 104(c) and converted to €1,904.61 by Council

Regulations (EC) No 1103/97, No 974/98 and No 2866/98 and the Economic and Monetary Union Act 1998, s 6; the above being implicitly substituted, by Fines Act 2010, s 6, for a fine not exceeding the aforesaid amount. A class C fine currently means a fine not exceeding €2,500.

b Words 'shall be guilty of an offence and liable to a fine' substituted for 'shall be liable to a fine' in CA 1963, s 202(4) and (6) by C(AA)A 2003, Sch 2, Item 1.

c '£250' substituted for '£50' by C(A)A 1982, Sch 1, increased to £1,500 by CA 1990, s 240(7) as inserted by CLEA 2001, s 104(c) and converted to €1,904.61 by Council Regulations (EC) No 1103/97, No 974/98 and No 2866/98 and the Economic and Monetary Union Act 1998, s 6.

---

203 Provisions to facilitate reconstruction and amalgamation of companies

(1) Where an application is made to the court under section 201 for the sanctioning of a compromise or arrangement proposed between a company and any such persons as are mentioned in that section, and it is shown to the court that the compromise or arrangement has been proposed for the purposes of or in connection with a scheme for the reconstruction of any company or companies or the amalgamation of any two or more companies, and that under the scheme the whole or any part of the undertaking or the property of any company concerned in the scheme (in this section referred to as 'a transferor company') is to be transferred to another company (in this section referred to as 'the transferee company'), the court may, either by the order sanctioning the compromise or arrangement or by any subsequent order make provision for all or any of the following matters—

(a) the transfer to the transferee company of the whole or any part of the undertaking and of the property or liabilities of any transferor company;

(b) the allotting or appropriation by the transferee company of any shares, debentures, policies or other like interests in that company which under the compromise or arrangement are to be allotted or appropriated by that company to or for any person;

(c) the continuation by or against the transferee company of any legal proceedings pending by or against any transferor company;

(d) the dissolution, without winding up, of any transferor company;

(e) the provision to be made for any persons who, within such time and in such manner as the court directs, dissent from the compromise or arrangement;

(f) such incidental, consequential and supplemental matters as are necessary to secure that the reconstruction or amalgamation shall be fully and effectively carried out.

(2) Where an order under this section provides for the transfer of property or liabilities, that property shall, by virtue of the order, be transferred to and vest in, and those liabilities shall, by virtue of the order, be transferred to and become the liabilities of the transferee company, and in the case of any property, if the order so directs, freed from any charge which is, by virtue of the compromise or arrangement, to cease to have effect.

(3) Where an order is made under this section, every company in relation to which the order is made shall cause an office copy thereof to be delivered to the registrar of

companies for registration within 21 days after the making of the order, and if default is made in complying with this subsection, the company and every officer of the company who is in default [shall be guilty of an offence and liable to a [class C fine][a]] [b].

(4) In this section, 'property' includes property, rights and powers of every description, and 'liabilities' includes duties.

(5) Notwithstanding subsection (7) of section 201, 'company' in this section does not include any company other than a company within the meaning of this Act.

Amendments

a '£125' substituted for '£25' by C(A)A 1982, Sch 1, increased to £1,500 by CA 1990, s 240(7) as inserted by CLEA 2001, s 104(c) and converted to €1,904.61 by Council Regulations (EC) No 1103/97, No 974/98 and No 2866/98 and the Economic and Monetary Union Act 1998, s 6; the above being implicitly substituted, by Fines Act 2010, s 6, for a fine not exceeding the aforesaid amount. A class C fine currently means a fine not exceeding €2,500.

b Words 'shall be guilty of an offence and liable to a fine' substituted for 'shall be liable to a fine' in CA 1963, s 203(3) by C(AA)A 2003, Sch 2, Item No. 1.

---

204 Power to acquire shares of shareholders dissenting from scheme or contract which has been approved by majority

(1) Subject to subsection (2), where a scheme, contract or offer involving the acquisition by one company, whether a company within the meaning of this Act or not (in this section referred to as 'the transferee company') of the beneficial ownership of all the shares (other than shares already in the beneficial ownership of the transferee company) in the capital of another company, being a company within the meaning of this Act (in this section referred to as 'the transferor company') has become binding or been approved or accepted in respect of not less than four-fifths in value of the shares affected not later than the date 4 months after publication generally to the holders of the shares affected of the terms of such scheme, contract or offer, the transferee company may at any time before the expiration of the period of 6 months next following such publication give notice in the prescribed manner to any dissenting shareholder that it desires to acquire the beneficial ownership of his shares, and when such notice is given the transferee company shall, unless on an application made by the dissenting shareholder within one month from the date on which the notice was given, the court thinks fit to order otherwise, be entitled and bound to acquire the beneficial ownership of those shares on the terms on which under the scheme, contract or offer, the beneficial ownership of the shares in respect of which the scheme, contract or offer has become binding or been approved or accepted is to be acquired by the transferee company.

(2) Where shares in the transferor company are, at the date of such publication, already in the beneficial ownership of the transferee company to a value greater than one-fifth of the aggregate value of those shares and the shares affected, subsection (1) shall not apply unless the assenting shareholders besides holding not less than four-fifths in value of the shares affected are not less than three-fourths in number of the holders of those shares.

(3) For the purpose of this section, shares in the transferor company in the beneficial ownership of a subsidiary of the transferee company shall be deemed to be in the

beneficial ownership of the transferee company, the acquisition of the beneficial ownership of shares in the transferor company by a subsidiary of the transferee company shall be deemed to be the acquisition of such beneficial ownership by the transferee company and shares shall not be treated as not being in the beneficial ownership of the transferee company merely by reason of the fact that those shares are or may become subject to a charge in favour of another person.

(4) Where, in consequence of any such scheme, contract or offer, the beneficial interest in shares in the transferor company is acquired by the transferee company and as a result of such acquisition the transferee company has become the beneficial owner of four-fifths in value of all the shares in the transferor company then—

(a) the transferee company shall, within one month of the date of such acquisition, give notice of that fact in the prescribed manner to all holders of shares in the transferor company not in the beneficial ownership of the transferee company; and

(b) any such holder may, within 3 months from the giving of the notice to him, require the transferee company to acquire his shares;

and, where a shareholder gives notice under paragraph (*b*) in relation to any shares, the transferee company shall be entitled and bound to acquire the beneficial ownership of those shares on the terms on which under the scheme, contract or offer the beneficial ownership of the shares of the assenting shareholders was acquired by it, or on such other terms as may be agreed or as the court on the application either of the transferee company or of a shareholder thinks fit to order, and subsections (5), (6) and (7) shall be applicable *mutatis mutandis* as if any reference therein to a notice given under subsection (1) were a reference to a notice given under paragraph (*b*).

(5) Where a notice has been given by the transferee company under subsection (1) and the court has not, on application made by the dissenting shareholder, ordered to the contrary, the transferee company shall, on the expiration of one month from the date on which the notice was given, or, if an application to the court by the dissenting shareholder is then pending, after that application has been disposed of, transmit to the transferor company a copy of the notice together with an instrument of transfer of the shares of the dissenting shareholder executed on behalf of the dissenting shareholder as transferor by any person appointed by the transferee company and by the transferee (being either the transferee company or a subsidiary of the transferee company or a nominee of the transferee company or of such a subsidiary) and pay to or vest in the transferor company the amount or other consideration representing the price payable by the transferee company for the shares the beneficial ownership of which by virtue of this section the transferee company is entitled to acquire, and the transferor company shall thereupon register as the holder of those shares the person who executed such instrument as the transferee, so however, that an instrument of transfer shall not be so required for any share for which a share warrant is for the time being outstanding.

(6) Any sums received by the transferor company under this section shall be paid into a separate bank account and any such sums and any other consideration so received shall be held by that company on trust for the several persons entitled to the shares in respect of which the said sums or other consideration were respectively received.

(7) The transferor company or a nominee of the transferor company shall not be entitled to exercise any right of voting conferred by any shares in the transferee company issued to it or to its nominee as aforesaid except by and in accordance with instructions given by the shareholder in respect of whom those shares were so issued or his successor in title.

(8) In this section, 'the shares affected' means the shares the acquisition of the beneficial ownership of which by the transferee company is involved in the scheme, contract or offer, 'assenting shareholder' means a holder of any of the shares affected in respect of which the scheme, contract or offer has become binding or been approved or accepted and 'dissenting shareholder' means a holder of any of the shares affected in respect of which the scheme, contract or offer has not become binding or been approved or accepted or who has failed or refused to transfer his shares in accordance with the scheme, contract or offer.

(9) Where the scheme, contract or offer becomes binding on or is approved or accepted by a person in respect of a part only of the shares held by him, he shall be treated as an assenting shareholder as regards that part of his holding and as a dissenting shareholder as regards the remainder of his holding.

(10) Where the scheme, contract or offer provides that an assenting shareholder may elect between 2 or more sets of terms for the acquisition by the transferee company of the beneficial ownership of the shares affected, the notice given by the transferee company under subsection (1) shall be accompanied by or embody a notice stating the alternative sets of terms between which assenting shareholders are entitled to elect and specifying which of those sets of terms shall be applicable to the dissenting shareholder if he does not before the expiration of 14 days from the date of the giving of the notice notify to the transferee company in writing his election as between such alternative sets of terms, and the terms upon which the transferee company shall under this section be entitled and bound to acquire the beneficial ownership of the shares of the dissenting shareholder shall be the set of terms which the dissenting shareholder shall so notify or, in default of such notification, the set of terms so specified as applicable.

(11) In the application of this section to a transferor company the share capital of which consists of two or more classes of shares, references to the shares in the capital of the transferor company shall be construed as references to the shares in its capital of a particular class.

(12) Subject to subsection (13), this section shall not apply to a scheme, contract or offer the terms of which were published generally to the holders of the shares affected before the operative date and section 8 of the Companies Act, 1959, shall continue to apply to any such scheme, contract or offer and for the purposes of any such scheme, contract or offer, the said section shall be deemed to remain in full force.

(13) Where any such scheme, contract or offer as is mentioned in subsection (1) was approved or accepted in the manner described in that subsection at any time before the passing of the Companies Act, 1959, the court may by order on an application made to it by the transferee company within 6 months after the operative date authorise notice to be given under this section within such time after the making of the order as the court shall direct, and this section shall apply accordingly, except that the terms on which the shares

of the dissenting shareholder are to be acquired shall be such terms as the court may by the order direct, instead of the terms provided by the scheme, contract or offer.

Minorities

205 Remedy in cases of oppression

(1) Any member of a company who complains that the affairs of the company are being conducted or that the powers of the directors of the company are being exercised in a manner oppressive to him or any of the members (including himself), or in disregard of his or their interests as members, may apply to the court for an order under this section.

(2) In a case falling within subsection (3) of section 170, the Minister may apply for an order under this section.

(3) If, on any application under subsection (1) or subsection (2) the court is of opinion that the company's affairs are being conducted or the directors' powers are being exercised as aforesaid, the court may, with a view to bringing to an end the matters complained of, make such order as it thinks fit, whether directing or prohibiting any act or cancelling or varying any transaction or for regulating the conduct of the company's affairs in future, or for the purchase of the shares of any members of the company by other members of the company or by the company and in the case of a purchase by the company, for the reduction accordingly of the company's capital, or otherwise.

(4) Where an order under this section makes any alteration in or addition to any company's memorandum or articles, then, notwithstanding anything in any other provision of this Act but subject to the provisions of the order, the company concerned shall not have power without the leave of the court to make any further alteration in or addition to the memorandum or articles inconsistent with the provisions of the order; but, subject to the foregoing provisions of this subsection, the alterations or additions made by the order shall be of the same effect as if duly made by resolution of the company, and the provisions of this Act shall apply to the memorandum or articles as so altered or added to accordingly.

(5) An office copy of any order under this section altering or adding to or giving leave to alter or add to a company's memorandum or articles shall, within 21 days after the making thereof, be delivered by the company to the registrar of companies for registration; and if a company fails to comply with this subsection, the company and every officer of the company who is in default [shall be guilty of an offence and liable to a [class C fine] [a]].[b]

(6) The personal representative of a person who, at the date of his death was a member of a company, or any trustee of, or person beneficially interested in, the shares of a company by virtue of the will or intestacy of any such person, may apply to the court under subsection (1) for an order under this section and, accordingly, any reference in that subsection to a member of a company shall be construed as including a reference to any such personal representative, trustee or person beneficially interested as aforesaid or to all of them.

(7) If, in the opinion of the court, the hearing of proceedings under this section would involve the disclosure of information the publication of which would be seriously prejudicial to the legitimate interests of the company, the court may order that the hearing of the proceedings or any part thereof shall be *in camera*.

Amendments

a '£125' substituted for '£25' by C(A)A 1982, Sch 1, increased to £1,500 by CA 1990, s 240(7) as inserted by CLEA 2001, s 104(c) and converted to €1,904.61 by Council Regulations (EC) No 1103/97, No 974/98 and No 2866/98 and the Economic and Monetary Union Act 1998, s 6; the above being implicitly substituted, by Fines Act 2010, s 6, for a fine not exceeding the aforesaid amount. A class C fine currently means a fine not exceeding €2,500.

b Words 'shall be guilty of an offence and liable to a fine' substituted for 'shall be liable to a fine' in CA 1963, s 203(3) by C(AA)A 2003, Sch 2, Item No. 1.

PART VI
WINDING UP

(I) PRELIMINARY

Modes of Winding Up

[205A Restriction of this Part

This Part is subject to Chapters I (general provisions) and III (secondary insolvency proceedings) of the Insolvency Regulation.][a]

Amendments

a CA 1963, s 205A inserted by EC(CI)R 2002, reg 3(b).

206 Modes of winding up

(1) The winding up of a company may be—

(a) by the court; or

(b) voluntary.

(2) The provisions of this Act relating to winding up apply, unless the contrary appears, to the winding up of a company in either of those modes.

Contributories

207 Liability as contributories of past and present members

(1) In the event of a company being wound up, every present and past member shall be liable to contribute to the assets of the company to an amount sufficient for payment of its debts and liabilities, and the costs, charges and expenses of the winding up, and for the adjustment of the rights of the contributories among themselves, subject to subsection (2) and the following qualifications—

(a) a past member shall not be liable to contribute if he has ceased to be a member for one year or more before the commencement of the winding up;

(b) a past member shall not be liable to contribute in respect of any debt or liability of the company contracted after he ceased to be a member;

(c) a past member shall not be liable to contribute unless it appears to the court that the existing members are unable to satisfy the contributions required to be made by them in pursuance of this Act;

(d) in the case of a company limited by shares, no contribution shall be required from any member exceeding the amount, if any, unpaid on the shares in respect of which he is liable as a present or past member;

(e) in the case of a company limited by guarantee, no contribution shall, subject to subsection (3), be required from any member exceeding the amount undertaken to be contributed by him to the assets of the company in the event of its being wound up;

(f) nothing in this Act shall invalidate any provision contained in any policy of insurance or other contract whereby the liability of individual members on the policy or contract is restricted, or whereby the funds of the company are alone made liable in respect of the policy or contract;

(g) a sum due to any member of the company, in his character of a member, by way of dividends, profits or otherwise, shall not be deemed to be a debt of the company, payable to that member in a case of competition between himself and any other creditor not a member of the company, but any such sum may be taken into account for the purpose of the final adjustment of the rights of the contributories among themselves.

(2) In the winding up of a limited company, any director, whether past or present, whose liability is, under this Act, unlimited, shall, in addition to his liability (if any) to contribute as an ordinary member, be liable to made a further contribution as if he were at the commencement of the winding up a member of an unlimited company, so, however, that—

(a) a past director shall not be liable to make such further contribution if he has ceased to hold office for a year or more before the commencement of the winding up;

(b) a past director shall not be liable to make such further contribution in respect of any debt or liability of the company contracted after he ceased to hold office;

(c) subject to the articles of the company, a director shall not be liable to make such further contribution unless the court deems it necessary to require that contribution in order to satisfy the debts and liabilities of the company and the costs, charges and expenses of the winding up.

(3) In the winding up of a company limited by guarantee which has a share capital, every member of the company shall be liable, in addition to the amount undertaken to be contributed by him to the assets of the company in the event of its being wound up, to contribute to the extent of any sums unpaid on any shares held by him.

208 Definition of 'contributory'

The term 'contributory' means every person liable to contribute to the assets of a company in the event of its being wound up, and for the purposes of all proceedings for determining, and all proceedings prior to the final determination of, the persons who are to be deemed contributories, includes any person alleged to be a contributory.

209 Liability of contributory

(1) The liability of a contributory shall create a debt accruing due from him at the time when his liability commenced, but payable at the times when calls are made for enforcing the liability.

(2) An action to recover a debt created by this section shall not be brought after the expiration of 12 years from the date on which the cause of action accrued.

210 Contributories in case of death of member

(1) If a contributory dies, either before or after he has been placed on the list of contributories, his personal representatives shall be liable in due course of administration to contribute to the assets of the company in discharge of his liability and shall be contributories accordingly.

(2) If the personal representatives make default in paying any money ordered to be paid by them, proceedings may be taken for the administration of the estate of the deceased contributory or otherwise for compelling payment thereout of the money due.

211 Contributories in case of bankruptcy of member

If a contributory becomes bankrupt, either before or after he has been placed on the list of contributories—

(a) the Official Assignee shall represent him for all the purposes of the winding up, and shall be a contributory accordingly, and may be called on to admit to proof against the estate of the bankrupt or otherwise to allow to be paid out of his assets in due course of law any money due from the bankrupt in respect of his liability to contribute to the assets of the company; and

(b) there may be proved against the estate of the bankrupt the estimated value of his liability to future calls as well as calls already made.

(II) WINDING UP BY THE COURT

Jurisdiction

212 Jurisdiction to wind up companies

The High Court shall have jurisdiction to wind up any company.

Cases in which Company may be wound up by the Court

213 Circumstances in which company may be wound up by the court

A company may be wound up by the court if—

(a) the company has by special resolution resolved that the company be wound up by the court;

(b) [...];[a]

(c) the company does not commence its business within a year from its incorporation or suspends its business for a whole year;

(d) the number of members is reduced, in the case of a private company, [or an investment company (within the meaning of Part XIII of the Companies Act, 1990],[b] below two, or, in the case of any other company, below seven;

(e) the company is unable to pay its debts;

[(ea) the company is an SE, within the meaning of the European Communities (European Public Limited – Liability Company) Regulations 2007, that no longer complies with the requirements specified in Article 7 of Council Regulation (EC) No 2157/2001 on the Statute for a European company;][c]

(f) the court is of opinion that it is just and equitable that the company [other than an investment company within the meaning of Part XIII of the Companies Act,

1990, or the European Communities (Undertakings for Collective Investment in Transferable Securities) Regulations, 1989 (SI No 78 of 1989,][d] should be wound up;

[(fa) the court is of opinion that it is just and equitable that the company, being an investment company within the meaning aforesaid, should be wound up and the following conditions are complied with—

(i) in the case of an investment company within the meaning of Part XIII of the Companies Act, 1990—

(I) the petition for such winding-up has been presented by the trustee of the company, that is to say, the person nominated by the Central Bank of Ireland under section 257(4)(c) of the Companies Act, 1990, in respect of that company;

(II) the said trustee has notified the investment company of its intention to resign as such trustee and six or more months have elapsed since the giving of that notification without a trustee having been appointed to replace it;

(III) the court, in considering the said petition, has regard to—

(A) any conditions imposed under section 257 of the Companies Act, 1990, in relation to the resignation from office of such a trustee and the replacement of it by another trustee; and

(B) whether a winding-up would best serve the interests of shareholders in the company; and

(IV) the petition for such winding-up has been served on the company (if any) discharging, in relation to the first-mentioned company, functions of a company referred to in conditions imposed under section 257 of the Companies Act, 1990, as a 'management company'; and

(ii) in the case of an investment company within the meaning of the European Communities (Undertakings for Collective Investment in Transferable Securities) Regulations, 1989, such conditions as the Minister may prescribe by regulations.][e]

(g) the court is satisfied that the company's affairs are being conducted, or the powers of the directors are being exercised, in a manner oppressive to any member or in disregard of his interests as a member and that, despite the existence of an alternative remedy, winding up would be justified in the general circumstances of the case so, however, that the court may dismiss a petition to wind up under this paragraph if it is of opinion that proceedings under section 205 would, in all the circumstances, be more appropriate.

[(h) after the end of the general transitional period, within the meaning the of the Companies (Amendment) Act, 1983, the company is an old public limited company within the meaning of that Act;

(i) after the end of the transitional period for share capital, within the meaning of the Companies (Amendment) Act, 1983, the company has not complied with the conditions specified in section 12 (9) of that Act.][f]

Amendments

a CA 1963, s 213(b) repealed by C(A)A 1983, Sch 3.

b CA 1963, s 213(d) amended by CA 1990, s 260(1) as substituted by C(A)(No 2)A 1999, s 54(3).

c CA 1963, s 213(ea) inserted by EC(EPLLC)R 2007, reg 25(4).

d CA 1963, s 213(f) amended by CLEA 2001, s 93(a) by the insertion after 'company' of ', other than an investment company within the meaning of Part XIII of the Companies Act, 1990, or the European Communities (Undertakings for Collective Investment in Transferable Securities) Regulations 1989 (SI 78 of 1989),'.

e CA 1963, s 213(fa) inserted by CLEA 2001, s 93(b). The provisions of para (fa)(ii) have yet to be brought into force.

f CA 1963, s 213(h) and (i) inserted by C(A)A 1983, Sch 1 para 17.

214 Circumstances in which company deemed to be unable to pay its debts

A company shall be deemed to be unable to pay its debts—

(a) if a creditor, by assignment or otherwise, to whom the company is indebted in a sum exceeding [€1,269.74][a] then due, has served on the company, by leaving it at the registered office of the company, a demand in writing requiring the company to pay the sum so due, and the company has for 3 weeks thereafter neglected to pay the sum or to secure or compound for it to the reasonable satisfaction of the creditor; or

(b) if execution or other process issued on a judgment, decree or order of any court in favour of a creditor of the company is returned unsatisfied in whole or in part; or

(c) if it is proved to the satisfaction of the court that the company is unable to pay its debts, and in determining whether a company is unable to pay its debts, the court shall take into account the contingent and prospective liabilities of the company.

Amendments

a '£1,000' substituted for '£50' by CA 1990, s 213. £1,000 converted to €1,269.74 by Council Regulation (EC) 1103/97, No 974/98 and No 2866/98 and the Economic and Monetary Union Act, s 6.

Petition for Winding Up and Effects thereof

215 Provisions as to applications for winding up

An application to the court for the winding up of a company shall be by petition presented, subject to the provisions of this section, either by the company or by any creditor or creditors (including any contingent or prospective creditor or creditors), contributory or contributories, or by all or any of those parties, together or separately, so, however, that—

(a) a contributory shall not be entitled to present a winding up petition unless—

(i) either the number of members is reduced, in the case of a private company [or an investment company (within the meaning of Part XIII of the Companies Act, 1990][a], below two, or in the case of any other company, below seven; or

(ii) the shares in respect of which he is a contributory, or some of them, either were originally allotted to him or have been held by him, and registered in his name, for at least 6 months during the 18 months before the commencement of the winding up, or have devolved on him through the death of a former holder; and

(b) [...],[b]

(c) the court shall not give a hearing to a winding-up petition presented by a contingent or prospective creditor until such security for costs has been given as the court thinks reasonable, and until a prima facie case for winding up has been established to the satisfaction of the court; and

(d) in a case falling within subsection (3) of section 170 a winding-up petition may be presented by the Minister; and

(e) a petition for winding up on the grounds mentioned in paragraph (g) of section 213 may be presented by any person entitled to bring proceedings for an order under section 205.

[(f) a petition for winding up on the grounds mentioned in section 213 (h) or (i), may be presented by the registrar of companies;][c] [...][d]

[(g) a petition presented for winding-up on the grounds mentioned in paragraph (fa) of section 213 shall be presented by the person referred to in subparagraph (i) of that paragraph or, as the case may be, the person specified in that behalf by regulations under subparagraph (ii) of that [paragraph; and[e]][f]

[(h) a petition for winding-up on the grounds mentioned in paragraph (ea) of section 213 may be presented by the Director.][g]

Amendments

a Words inserted by CA 1990, s 260 which was substituted by C(A)(No 2)A 1999, s 54.

b CA 1963, s 215(b) repealed by C(A)A 1983, Sch 3.

c CA 1963, s 215(f) inserted by C(A)A 1983, Sch 1 para 18 and amended by CLEA 2001, s 94.

d 'and' deleted by EC(EPLLC)R 2007, reg 25(5)(a).

e 'paragraph; and' substituted for 'paragraph' by EC(EPLLC)R 2007, reg 25(5)(b).

f CA 1963, s 215(g) inserted by CLEA 2001, s 94.

g CA 1963, s 215(h) inserted by EC(EPLLC)R 2007, reg 25(5)(c).

---

216 Powers of court on hearing petition

(1) On hearing a winding-up petition, the court may dismiss it, or adjourn the hearing conditionally or unconditionally, or make any interim order, or any other order that it thinks fit, but the court shall not refuse to make a winding-up order on the ground only

that the assets of the company have been mortgaged to an amount equal to or in excess of those assets, or that the company has no assets.

[(2) The court shall not make an order for the winding up of a company unless—

(a) the court is satisfied that the company has no obligations in relation to a bank asset that has been transferred to the National Asset Management Agency or a NAMA group entity, or

(b) if the company has any such obligation—

(i) a copy of the petition has been served on that Agency, and

(ii) the court has heard that Agency in relation to the making of the order.

(3) In subsection (2) 'bank asset' and 'NAMA group entity' have the same respective meanings as in the National Asset Management Agency Act 2009.][a]

Amendments

a CA 1963, s 216(2) repealed by C(A)A 1983, Sch 3. New subsections (2) and (3) inserted by NAMA Act 2009, s 233.

217 Power to stay or restrain proceedings against company

At any time after the presentation of a winding-up petition, and before a winding-up order has been made, the company or any creditor or contributory may—

(a) where any action or proceeding against the company is pending in the High Court or on appeal in the Supreme Court apply to the court in which the action or proceeding is pending for a stay of proceedings therein; and

(b) where any other action or proceeding is pending against the company, apply to the High Court to restrain further proceedings in the action or proceeding;

and the court to which application is so made may, as the case may be, stay or restrain the proceedings accordingly on such terms and for such period as it thinks fit.

218 Avoidance of dispositions of property and transfer of shares after commencement of winding up

In a winding up by the court, any disposition of the property of the company, including things in action, and any transfer of shares or alteration in the status of the members of the company, made after the commencement of the winding up, shall, unless the court otherwise orders, be void.

219 Avoidance of executions against property of company

Where any company is being wound up by the court, any attachment, sequestration, distress or execution put in force against the property or effects of the company after the commencement of the winding up shall be void to all intents.

Commencement of Winding Up

220 Commencement of winding up by the court

(1) Where, before the presentation of a petition for the winding up of a company by the court, a resolution has been passed by the company for voluntary winding up, the winding up of the company shall be deemed to have commenced at the time of the passing of the resolution, and unless the court, on proof of fraud or mistake, thinks fit to

direct otherwise, all proceedings taken in the voluntary winding up shall be deemed to have been validly taken.

(2) In any other case, the winding up of a company by the court shall be deemed to commence at the time of the presentation of the petition for the winding up.

221 Copy of order for winding up to be forwarded to registrar

(1) On the making of a winding-up order, an office copy of the order must forthwith be delivered by the company, or by such person as the court may direct, to the registrar of companies for registration.

(2) If a company makes default in complying with subsection (1), the company and every officer of the company who is in default [shall be guilty of an offence and liable to a [class C fine][a]][b] and if any other person makes default in complying with subsection (1) such person [shall be guilty of an offence and liable to a [class C fine][a]].[b]

Amendments

a '£125' increased to '£1,500' by CA 1990, s 240(7) as inserted by CLEA 2001, s 104(c) and converted to €1,904.61 by Council Regulation (EC) 1103/97, No 974/98 and No 2866/98 and the Economic and Monetary Union Act 1998, s 6; the above being implicitly substituted, by Fines Act 2010, s 6, for a fine not exceeding the aforesaid amount. A class C fine currently means a fine not exceeding €2,500.

b Words in CA 1963, s 221(2) substituted by C(AA)A 2003, s 57 and Sch 2, para 4.

---

222 Actions against company stayed on winding-up order

When a winding-up order has been made or a provisional liquidator has been appointed, no action or proceeding shall be proceeded with or commenced against the company except by leave of the court and subject to such terms as the court may impose.

223 Effect of winding-up order

An order for winding up a company shall operate in favour of all the creditors and of all the contributories of the company, as if made on the joint petition of a creditor and of a contributory.

224 Statement of company's affairs to be filed in court

(1) Where the court has made a winding-up order or appointed a provisional liquidator, there shall, unless the court thinks fit to order otherwise and so orders, be made out and filed in the court a statement as to the affairs of the company in the prescribed form, verified by affidavit, and showing the particulars of its assets, debts and liabilities, the names, residences and occupations of its creditors, the securities held by them respectively, the dates when the securities were respectively given, and such further or other information as may be prescribed or as the court may require.

(2) The statement shall be filed and verified by one or more of the persons who are at the relevant date the directors and by the person who is at that date the secretary of the company or by such of the persons hereinafter mentioned in this subsection as the court may require to file and verify the statement, that is, persons—

(a) who are or have been officers of the company;

(b) who have taken part in the formation of the company at any time within one year before the relevant date;

(c) who are in the employment of the company, or have been in the employment of the company within the said year, and are in the opinion of the court, capable of giving the information required;

(d) who are or have been within the said year officers of or in the employment of a company which is, or within the said year was, an officer of the company to which the statement relates.

(3) The statement shall be filed within 21 days from the relevant date or within such extended time as the court may for special reasons appoint.

(4) Any person making or concurring in making the statement and affidavit required by this section shall be allowed, and shall be paid out of the assets of the company, such costs and expenses incurred in and about the preparation and making of the statement and affidavit as the court may allow.

(5) If any person, without reasonable excuse, makes default in complying with the requirements of this section, he [shall be guilty of an offence and liable to a [class C fine][a]].[b]

(6) Any person who states in writing that he is a creditor or contributory of the company shall be entitled by himself or by his agent at all reasonable times, on payment of the prescribed fee, to inspect the statement filed in pursuance of this section, and to a copy thereof or extract therefrom.

(7) Any person untruthfully so stating himself to be a creditor or contributory shall be guilty of a contempt of court and shall, on the application of the liquidator, be punishable accordingly.

(8) In this section, 'the relevant date' means, in a case where a provisional liquidator is appointed, the date of his appointment, and, in a case where no such appointment is made, the date of the winding-up order.

Amendments

a '£500' increased to £1,500 by CA 1990, s 240(7) as inserted by CLEA 2001, s 104(c). £1,500 converted to €1,904.61 by Council Regulation (EC) 1103/97, No 974/98 and No 2866/98 and the Economic and Monetary Union Act 1998, s 6; the above being implicitly substituted, by Fines Act 2010, s 6, for a fine not exceeding the aforesaid amount. A class C fine currently means a fine not exceeding €2,500.

b Words in CA 1963, s 224(5) substituted by C(AA)A 2003, s 57 and Sch 2, para 1.

Liquidators

225 Appointment of liquidator

For the purpose of conducting the proceedings in winding up a company and performing such duties in reference thereto as the court may impose, the court may appoint a liquidator or liquidators.

226 Appointment and powers of provisional liquidator

(1) Subject to subsection (2), the court may appoint a liquidator provisionally at any time after the presentation of a winding-up petition and before the first appointment of liquidators.

(2) Where a liquidator is provisionally appointed by the court, the court may limit and restrict his powers by the order appointing him.

227 Publication by liquidator of his appointment

(1) In a winding up by the court, the liquidator shall within 21 days after his appointment, publish in [the Companies Registration Office Gazette][a] a notice of his appointment and deliver to the registrar of companies an office copy of the court order appointing him.

(2) If the liquidator fails to comply with subsection (1), he [shall be guilty of an offence and liable to a [class C fine][b]].[c]

Amendments

a 'the Companies Registration Office Gazette' substituted for '*Iris Oifigiúil*' by IFCMPA 2005, s 72.

b '£250' increased to '£1,500' by CA 1990, s 240(7) as inserted by CLEA 2001, s 104(c). £1,500 converted to €1,904.61 by Council Regulation (EC) 1103/97, No 974/98 and No 2866/98 and the Economic and Monetary Union Act 1998, s 6; the above being implicitly substituted, by Fines Act 2010, s 6, for a fine not exceeding the aforesaid amount. A class C fine currently means a fine not exceeding €2,500.

c Words in CA 1963, s 227(2) substituted by C(AA)A 2003, s 57 and Sch 2 para 1.

[227A Registration of Judgements given in insolvency proceedings

(1) Without prejudice to Article 16(1) of the Insolvency Regulation, a liquidator appointed in insolvency proceedings who intends—

(a) to request under Article 21 of the Regulation that notice of the judgment opening the proceedings and, where appropriate, the decision appointing him or her be published in the State, or

(b) to take any other action in the State under the Regulation,

shall deliver to the Registrar of Companies for registration a duly certified copy of the judgment and, where appropriate, of the decision appointing the liquidator.

(2) Registration under subsection (1) may also be effected by the Registrar of Companies on application by a liquidator who does not intend to take any action in the State under the Insolvency Regulation.

(3) The certified copy or copies mentioned in subsection (1) shall be accompanied by—

(a) if the judgment or decision is not expressed in Irish or English, a translation, certified to be correct by a person competent to do so, into either of those languages,

(b) the prescribed form, and

(c) the fee payable under the Eighth Schedule, as altered by order of the Minister under section 395(2).

(4) The Registrar shall issue a certificate of the registration to the liquidator.

(5) In any proceedings a document purporting to be—

(a) a duly certified copy of a judgment opening insolvency proceedings or a decision appointing a liquidator in such proceedings, or

(b) a translation of such a document which is certified as correct by a person competent to do so,

shall, without further proof, be admissible as evidence of the judgment, the liquidator's appointment or the translation, unless the contrary is shown.][a]

Amendments

a Section inserted by EC(CI)R 2002, reg 31.

[227B Publication in relation to insolvency proceedings

(1) In this section 'publication' means publication of—

(a) notice of the judgment opening the insolvency proceedings concerned,

(b) where appropriate, the decision appointing the liquidator in those proceedings,

(c) the name and business address of the liquidator, and

(d) the provision (either paragraph 1 or paragraph 2) of Article 3 of the Insolvency Regulation giving jurisdiction to open the proceedings,

in [the Companies Registration Office Gazette][b] and once at least in two daily morning newspapers circulating in the State.

(2) Without prejudice to section 227A(1), publication shall be effected by the liquidator concerned.

(3) Where the debtor company has an establishment (within the meaning of Article 2(h) of the Insolvency Regulation) in the State, the liquidator or any authority mentioned in Article 21(2) of the Regulation shall ensure that publication takes place as soon as practicable after the opening of the insolvency proceedings.][a]

Amendments

a Section inserted by EC(CI)R 2002, reg 3.

b Words inserted by reg 9 of the European Communities (Companies) Regulations 2004 (SI 839/2004).

228 General provisions as to liquidators

The following provisions relating to liquidators shall have effect on a winding-up order being made—

(a) the court may determine whether any and what security is to be given by a liquidator on his appointment;

(b) a liquidator shall be described by the style of 'the official liquidator' of the particular company in respect of which he is appointed and not by his individual name;

(c) a liquidator appointed by the court may resign or, on cause shown, be removed by the court;

(d) a person appointed liquidator shall receive such salary or remuneration by way of percentage or otherwise as the court may direct, and if more such persons than on are appointed liquidators, their remuneration shall be distributed among them in such proportions as the court directs;

(e) a vacancy in the office of a liquidator appointed by the court shall be filled by the court;

(f) if more than one liquidator is appointed by the court, the court shall declare whether any act by this Act required or authorised to be done by the liquidator is to be done by all or any one or more of the persons appointed;

(g) subject to section 300, the acts of a liquidator shall be valid notwithstanding any defects that may afterwards be discovered in his appointment or qualification.

229 Custody of company's property

(1) Where a winding-up order has been made or where a provisional liquidator has been appointed, the liquidator or the provisional liquidator, as the case may be, shall take into his custody or under his control all the property and things in action to which the company is or appears to be entitled.

(2) If and so long as there is no liquidator, all the property of the company shall be deemed to be in the custody of the court.

230 Vesting of property of company in liquidator

Where a company is being wound up by the court, the court may, on the application of the liquidator, by order direct that all or any part of the property of whatsoever description belonging to the company or held by trustees on its behalf shall vest in the liquidator by his official name, and thereupon the property to which the order relates shall vest accordingly, and the liquidator may, after giving such indemnity, if any, as the court may direct, bring or defend in his official name any action or other legal proceeding which relates to that property or which it is necessary to bring or defend for the purpose of effectually winding up the company and recovering its property.

231 Powers of liquidator

(1) The liquidator in a winding up by the court shall have power, with the sanction of the court or of the committee of inspection—

(a) to bring or defend any action or other legal proceeding in the name and on behalf of the company;

(b) to carry on the business of the company so far as may be necessary for the beneficial winding up thereof;

(c) to appoint a solicitor to assist him in the performance of his duties;

(d) to pay any classes of creditors in full;

(e) to make any compromise or arrangement with creditors or persons claiming to be creditors, or having or alleging themselves to have any claim present or future, certain or contingent, ascertained or sounding only in damages against the company, or whereby the company may be rendered liable;

(f) to compromise all calls and liabilities to calls, debts and liabilities capable of resulting in debts, and all claims, present or future, certain or contingent, ascertained or sounding only in damages, subsisting or supposed to subsist between the company and a contributory or alleged contributory or other debtor or person apprehending liability to the company, and all questions in any way relating to or affecting the assets or winding up of the company, on such terms as may be agreed, and take any security for the discharge of any such call, debt, liability or claim, and give a complete discharge in respect thereof.

[(1A)(a) The liquidator of a company shall not sell by private contract a non-cash asset of the requisite value to a person who is, or who, within three years prior to the date of commencement of the winding-up, has been, an officer of the company unless the liquidator has given at least 14 days notice of his intention to do so to all creditors of the company who are known to him or who have been intimated to him.

(b) In this subsection—

(i) 'non-cash asset' and 'requisite value' have the meanings assigned to them by section 29 of the Companies Act, 1990, and

(ii) 'officer' includes a person connected, within the meaning of section 26 of the Companies Act, 1990, with a director, and a shadow director.][a]

(2) The liquidator in a winding up by the court shall have power—

(a) to sell the real and personal property and things in action of the company by public auction or private contract, with power to transfer the whole thereof to any person or company or to sell the same in lots and for the purpose of selling the company's land or any part thereof to carry out such sales by fee farm grant, sub fee farm grant, lease, sub-lease or otherwise, and to sell any rent reserved on any such grant or any reversion expectant upon the determination of any such lease;

(b) to do all acts and to execute, in the name and on behalf of the company, all deeds, receipts and other documents, and for that purpose to use, when necessary, the company's seal;

(c) where any contributory has been adjudged bankrupt or has presented a petition for arrangement with his creditors in pursuance of the Bankruptcy Acts, to prove, rank and claim in the bankruptcy or arrangement for any balance against his estate, and to receive dividends in the bankruptcy or arrangement in respect of that balance, as a separate debt due from the bankrupt or arranging debtor, and rateably with the other separate creditors;

(d) to draw, accept, make and endorse any bill of exchange or promissory note in the name and on behalf of the company, with the same effect with respect to the liability of the company as if the bill or note had been drawn, accepted, made or endorsed by or on behalf of the company in the course of its business;

(e) to raise on the security of the assets of the company any money requisite;

(f) to take out in his official name letters of administration to any deceased contributory and to do in his official name any other act necessary for obtaining payment of any money due from a contributory or his estate which cannot be conveniently done in the name of the company, and in all such cases the money due shall, for the purpose of enabling the liquidator to take out the letters of administration or recover the money, be deemed to be due to the liquidator himself;

(g) to give security for costs in any proceedings commenced by the company or by him in the name of the company;

(h) to appoint an agent to do any business which the liquidator is unable to do himself;

(i) to do all such other things as may be necessary for winding up the affairs of the company and distributing its assets.

(3) The exercise by the liquidator in a winding up by the court of the powers conferred by this section shall be subject to the control of the court, and any creditor or contributory may apply to the court in relation to any exercise or proposed exercise of any of those powers.

(4) The court may provide by any order that the liquidator may, where there is no committee of inspection, exercise any of the powers mentioned in paragraph (a) or paragraph (b) of subsection (1) without the sanction or intervention of the court.

Amendments

a CA 1963, s 231(1A) inserted by CA 1990, s 124.

Committees of Inspection

232 Meetings of creditors and contributories to determine whether committee of inspection should be appointed

(1) When a winding-up order has been made by the court, the liquidator shall if the court by order so directs summon a meeting of the creditors of the company or separate meetings of the creditors and contributories of the company for the purpose of determining whether or not an application is to be made to the court for the appointment of a committee of inspection to act with the liquidator and who are to be the members of the committee if appointed.

(2) The court may make any appointment and order required to give effect to any such determination, and if there is a difference between the determinations of the meetings of the creditors and contributories in respect of the matters aforesaid, the court shall decide the difference and make such order thereon as the court may think fit.

233 Constitution and proceedings of committee of inspection

(1) A committee of inspection appointed in pursuance of this Act shall consist of creditors and contributories of the company or persons holding general powers of attorney from creditors or contributories in such proportions as may be agreed on by the meetings of creditors and contributories or as, in case of difference, may be determined by the court.

(2) The committee shall meet at such times as they from time to time appoint, and the liquidator or any member of the committee may also call a meeting of the committee as and when he thinks necessary.

(3) The committee may act by a majority of their members present at a meeting but shall not act unless a majority of the committee are present.

(4) A member of the committee may resign by notice in writing signed by him and delivered to the liquidator.

(5) If a member of the committee becomes bankrupt or compounds or arranges with his creditors or is absent from 5 consecutive meetings of the committee without the leave of those members who, together with himself, represent the creditors or contributories, as the case may be, his office shall thereupon become vacant.

(6) A member of the committee may be removed by an ordinary resolution at a meeting of creditors, if he represents creditors, or of contributories, if he represents contributories, of which 7 days' notice has been given, stating the object of the meeting.

(7) Subject to subsection (8), on a vacancy occurring in the committee the liquidator shall forthwith summon a meeting of creditors or of contributories, as the case may require, to fill the vacancy, and the meeting may, by resolution, reappoint the same or appoint another person, qualified under subsection (1) to be a member of the committee, to fill the vacancy.

(8) If the liquidator, having regard to the position in the winding up, is of opinion that it is unnecessary for a vacancy occurring in the committee to be filled, he may apply to the court and the court may make an order that the vacancy shall not be filled or shall not filled except in such circumstances as may be specified in the order.

(9) The continuing members of the committee, if not less than two, may act notwithstanding any vacancy in the committee.

General Powers of Court in case of Winding Up by the Court

234 Power to annul order for winding up or to stay winding up

(1) The court may at any time after an order for winding up, on the application of the liquidator or any creditor or contributory and on proof to the satisfaction of the court that the order for winding up ought to be annulled, make an order annulling the order for winding up on such terms and conditions as the court thinks fit.

(2) The court may at any time after an order for winding up, on the application of the liquidator or any creditor or contributory, and on proof to the satisfaction of the court that all proceedings in relation to the winding up ought to be stayed, make an order staying the proceedings, either altogether or for a limited time, on such terms and conditions as the court thinks fit.

(3) On any application under this section the court may, before making an order, require the liquidator to furnish to the court a report relating to any facts or matters which are in his opinion relevant to the application.

(4) An office copy of every order made under this section shall forthwith be forwarded by the company, or by such person as the court may direct, to the registrar of companies for registration.

(5) If a company makes default in complying with subsection (4), the company and every officer of the company who is in default [shall be guilty of an offence and liable to a [class C fine][a]][b] and if any other person makes default in complying with subsection (4) such person [shall be guilty of an offence and liable to a [class C fine][a]].[b]

Amendments

a '£125' substituted for '£25' by C(A)A 1982, Sch 1 and increased to '£1,500' by CA 1990, s 240(7) as inserted by CLEA 2001, s 104(c). £1,500 converted to €1,904.61 by Council Regulation (EC) 1103/97, No 974/98 and No 2866/98 and the Economic and Monetary Union

Act 1998, s 6; the above being implicitly substituted, by Fines Act 2010, s 6, for a fine not exceeding the aforesaid amount. A class C fine currently means a fine not exceeding €2,500.

b Words in CA 1963, s 234(5) substituted by C(AA)A 2003, s 57 and Sch 2 para 4.

---

235 Settlement of list of contributories and application of assets

(1) Subject to subsection (2), as soon as may be after making a winding-up order, the court shall settle a list of contributories, with power to rectify the register of members in all cases where rectification is required in pursuance of this Act, and shall cause the assets of the company to collected and applied in discharge of its liabilities.

(2) Where it appears to the court that it will not be necessary to make calls on or adjust the rights of contributories, the court may dispense with the settlement of a list of contributories.

(3) In settling the list of contributories, the court shall distinguish between persons who are contributories in their own right and persons who are contributories as being representatives of or liable for the debts of others.

236 Delivery of property of company to liquidator

The court may, at any time after making a winding-up order, require any contributory for the time being on the list of contributories and any trustee, receiver, banker, agent or officer of the company to pay, deliver, convey, surrender or transfer forthwith, or within such time as the court directs, to the liquidator any money, property or books and papers in his hands to which the company is prima facie entitled.

237 Payment of debts due by contributory to the company and extent to which set-off allowed

(1) The court may, at any time after making a winding up order, make an order on any contributory for the time being on the list of contributories, to pay in manner directed by the order, any money due from him or from the estate of the person whom he represents to the company, exclusive of any money payable by him or the estate by virtue of any call in pursuance of this Act.

(2) The court in making such an order may—

(a) in the case of an unlimited company, allow to the contributory by way of set-off any money due to him or to the estate which he represents from the company on any independent dealing or contract with the company, but not any money due to him as a member of the company in respect of any dividend or profit; and

(b) in the case of a limited company, make to any director whose liability is unlimited or to his estate a like allowance.

(3) In the case of any company, whether limited or unlimited, when all the creditors are paid in full, any money due on any account whatever to a contributory from the company may be allowed to him by way of set-off against any subsequent call.

238 Power of court to make calls

(1) The court may, at any time after making a winding up order, and either before or after it has ascertained the sufficiency of the assets of the company, make calls on all or any of the contributories for the time being on the list of contributories to the extent of

their liability, for payment of any money which the court considers necessary to satisfy the debts and liabilities of the company, and the costs, charges and expenses of winding up, and for the adjustment of the rights of the contributories among themselves, and make an order for payment of any calls so made.

(2) In making a call, the court may take into consideration that some of the contributories may partly or wholly fail to pay the call.

239 Payment into bank of moneys due to company

(1) The court may order any contributory, purchaser or other person from whom money is due to the company to pay the amount due into such bank as the court may appoint to the account of the liquidator instead of to the liquidator, and any such order may be enforced in like manner as if it had directed payment to the liquidator.

(2) All moneys and securities paid or delivered into any such bank as aforesaid in the event of a winding up by the court shall be subject in all respects to the orders of the court.

240 Order on contributory to be conclusive evidence

(1) An order made by the court on a contributory shall, subject to any right of appeal, be conclusive evidence that the money, if any, thereby appearing to be due or ordered to be paid is due.

(2) All other relevant matters stated in the order shall be taken to be truly stated as against all persons and in all proceedings.

241 Power to exclude creditors not proving in time

The court may fix a time or times within which creditors are to prove their debts or claims or to be excluded from the benefit of any distribution made before those debts are proved.

242 Adjustment of rights of contributories

The court shall adjust the rights of the contributories among themselves and distribute any surplus among the persons entitled thereto.

243 Inspection of books by creditors, contributories and director

(1) The court may, at any time after making a winding up order, make such order for inspection of the books and papers of the company by creditors and contributories as the court thinks just, and any books and papers in the possession of the company may be inspected by creditors or contributories accordingly, but not further or otherwise.

[(1A) The court may, on the application of the Director, make an order for the inspection by the Director of any books and papers in the possession of a company the subject of a winding-up order and the company, every officer of the company and the liquidator shall give to the Director such access to and facilities as are necessary for inspecting and taking copies of those books and papers as the Director may require.][a]

(2) Nothing in this section shall be taken as excluding or restricting any statutory rights of a Minister of the Government or a person acting under the authority of a Minister of the Government.

Amendments

a CA 1963, s 243(1A) inserted by CLEA 2001, s 43.

244 Power to order costs of winding up to be paid out of assets

The court may, in the event of the assets being insufficient to satisfy the liabilities, make an order as to the payment out of the assets of the costs, charges and expenses incurred in the winding up in such order of priority as the court thinks just.

[244A No lien over company's books, records, etc

Where the court has appointed a provisional liquidator or a company is being wound up by the court or by means of a creditors' voluntary winding up, no person shall be entitled as against the liquidator or provisional liquidator to withhold possession of any deed, instrument, or other document belonging to the company, or the books of account, receipts, bills, invoices, or other papers of a like nature relating to the accounts or trade, dealings or business of the company, or to claim any lien thereon provided that—

(a) where a mortgage, charge or pledge has been created by the deposit of any such document or paper with a person, the production of the document or paper to the liquidator or provisional liquidator by the person shall be without prejudice to the person's rights under the mortgage, charge or pledge (other than any right to possession of the document or paper),

(b) where by virtue of this section a liquidator or provisional liquidator has possession of any document or papers of a receiver or that receiver is entitled to examine, the liquidator or provisional liquidator shall, unless the court otherwise orders, make the document or papers available for inspection by the receiver at all reasonable times.][a]

Amendments

a CA 1963, s 244A inserted by CA 1990, s 125.

245 Power of court to summon persons for examination

[(1) The court may, [of its own motion or on the application of the Director,][b] at any time after the appointment of a provisional liquidator or the making of a winding-up order, summon before it any officer of the company or person known or suspected to have in his possession any property of the company or supposed to be indebted to the company, or any person whom the court deems capable of giving information relating to the promotion, formation, trade, dealings, affairs or property of the company.

(2) The court may examine such person on oath concerning the matters aforesaid, either by word of mouth or on written interrogatories, and may reduce his answers to writing and require him to sign them.

(3) The court may require such person to produce any accounting records, deed, instrument, or other document or paper relating to the company that are in his custody or power.

(4) The court may, before the examination takes place, require such person to place before it a statement, in such form as the court may direct, of any transactions between him and the company of a type or class which the court may specify.

(5) If, in the opinion of the court, it is just and equitable to do so, it may direct that the costs of the examination be paid by the person examined.

[(6) A person who is examined under this section shall not be entitled to refuse to answer any question put to him on the ground that his answer might incriminate him and any answer by him to such a question may be used in evidence against him in any proceedings whatsoever (save proceedings for an offence (other than perjury in respect of such an answer)).][c]

(7) If a person without reasonable excuse fails at any time to attend his examination under this section, he shall be guilty of contempt of court and liable to be punished accordingly.

(8) In a case where a person without reasonable excuse fails at any time to attend his examination under this section or there are reasonable grounds for believing that a person has absconded, or is about to abscond, with a view to avoiding or delaying his examination under this section, the court may cause that person to be arrested and his books and documents and moveable personal property to be seized and him and them to be detained until such time as the court may order.][a]

Amendments

a CA 1963, s 245, substituted by CA 1990, s 126.

b The words 'of its own motion or on the application of the Director' inserted in CA 1963, s 245(1) by CLEA 2001, s 44(a).

c Subsection (6) substituted by CLEA 2001, s 44(b).

[245A Order for payment or delivery of property against person examined under section 245 of Principal Act

[(1) If in the course of an examination][b] under section 245 it appears to the court that any person being examined—

(a) is indebted to the company, or

(b) has in his possession or control any money, property or books and papers of the company,

[the court may, of its own motion or on the application of the Director, order such person][c]—

(i) to pay to the liquidator the amount of the debt or any part thereof, or

(ii) to pay, deliver, convey, surrender or transfer to the liquidator such money, property or books and papers or any part thereof, as the case may be, at such time and in such manner and on such terms as the court may direct.

[(2) Where the court has made an order under subsection (1), it may, on the application of the Director or the liquidator, make a further order permitting the applicant, accompanied by such persons as the applicant thinks appropriate, to enter at any time or times within one month from the date of issue of the order, any premises (including a dwelling) owned or occupied by the person the subject of the order under subsection (1) (using such force as is reasonably necessary for the purpose), to search the premises and to seize any money, property or books and papers of the company found on the premises.

(3) Where the court has made an order under subsection (2), the applicant shall report to it as soon as may be on the outcome of any action on foot of the court's order and the court shall direct the applicant as to the disposition of anything seized on foot of the order.

(4) A direction under subsection (3) shall not be made in favour of the Director except in respect of the Director's costs and reasonable expenses.

(5) A person who obstructs the exercise of a right of entry, search and seizure conferred by virtue of an order made under subsection (2) or who obstructs the exercise of a right so conferred to take possession of anything referred to in that subsection, shall be guilty of an offence.

(6) Proceedings on foot of an offence under subsection (5) shall not prejudice the power of the court to issue proceedings for contempt of court for failure by a person to comply with an order under this section.][d]][a]

Amendments

a CA 1963, s 245A inserted by CA 1990, s 127.

b '(1) If in the course of an examination' substituted for 'If in the course of an examination' by CLEA 2001, s 45(a).

c 'the court may, of its own motion or on the application of the Director, order such person' substituted for 'the court may order such person' by CLEA 2001, s 45(b).

d CA 1963, s 245A(2)–(6) inserted by CLEA 2001, s 45(c).

---

246 Attendance of officers of company at meetings

In the case of a winding up by the court, the court shall have power to require the attendance of any officer of the company at any meeting of creditors or of contributories or of a committee of inspection for the purpose of giving information as to the trade, dealings, affairs or property of the company.

247 Power to arrest absconding contributory or officer of company

[The court, at any time either before or after making a winding-up order, on proof of probable cause for believing that a contributory, director, shadow director, secretary or other officer is about to quit the State or otherwise to abscond or to remove or conceal any of his property for the purpose of evading payment of calls or of avoiding examination about the affairs of the company, may, of its own motion or on the application of the Director, a creditor of the company or any other interested person, cause the contributory, director, shadow director, secretary or other officer to be arrested, and his books and papers and movable personal property to be seized and him and them to be detained until such time as the court may order.][a]

Amendments

a CA 1963, s 247, substituted by CLEA 2001, s 46.

248 Powers of court cumulative

Any powers by this Act conferred on the court shall be in addition to and not in restriction of any existing powers of instituting proceedings against any contributory or debtor of the company or the estate of any contributory or debtor, for the recovery of any call or other sums.

249 Dissolution of company

(1) When the affairs of a company have been completely wound up, the court, if the liquidator makes an application in that behalf, shall make an order that the company be dissolved from the date of the order, and the company shall be dissolved accordingly.

(2) An office copy of the order shall within 21 days from the date thereof be forwarded by the liquidator to the registrar of companies for registration.

(3) If the liquidator makes default in complying with the requirements of this section, he [shall be guilty of an offence and liable to a [class C fine][a]].[b]

Amendments

a '£250' substituted for '£50' by C(A)A 1982, Sch 1, increased to '£1,500' by CA 1990, s 240(7) as inserted by CLEA 2001, s 104(c) and converted to €1,904.61 by Council Regulation (EC) 1103/97, No 974/98 and No 2866/98 and the Economic and Monetary Union Act 1998, s 6; the above being implicitly substituted, by Fines Act 2010, s 6, for a fine not exceeding the aforesaid amount. A class C fine currently means a fine not exceeding €2,500.

b Words in CA 1963, s 249(3) substituted by C(AA)A 2003, s 57 and Sch 2, para 1.

Enforcement of Orders made in Winding Up by Courts outside the State

250 Enforcement of orders made in winding up by courts outside the State

(1) Any order made by a court of any country recognised for the purposes of this section and made for or in the course of winding up a company may be enforced by the High Court in the same manner in all respects as if the order had been made by the High Court.

(2) When an application is made to the High Court under this section, an office copy of any order sought to be enforced shall be sufficient evidence of the order.

(3) In this section, 'company' means a body corporate incorporated outside the State, and 'recognised' means recognised by order made by the Minister.

[(4) This section does not apply in relation to an order made by a court of a member state of the European Communities other than the State and Denmark.][a]

Amendments

a CA 1963, s 250(4) inserted by EC(CI)R 2002, reg 3.

(III) VOLUNTARY WINDING UP

Resolutions for and Commencement of Voluntary Winding Up

251 Circumstances in which company may be wound up voluntarily

(1) A company may be wound up voluntarily—

(a) when the period, if any, fixed for the duration of the company by the articles expires, or the event, if any, occurs, on the occurrence of which the articles provide that the company is to be dissolved, and the company in general meeting has passed a resolution that the company be wound up voluntarily;

(b) if the company resolves by special resolution that the company be wound up voluntarily;

(c) if the company in general meeting resolves that it cannot by reason of its liabilities continue its business, and that it be wound up voluntarily.

(2) In this Act, 'a resolution for voluntary winding up' means a resolution passed under any paragraph of subsection (1).

252 Publication of resolution to wind up voluntarily

(1) When a company has passed a resolution for voluntary winding up, it shall, within 14 days after the passing of the resolution, give notice of the resolution by advertisement in [the Companies Registration Office Gazette].[a]

(2) If default is made in complying with this section, the company and every officer of the company who is in default [shall be guilty of an offence and liable to a [class C fine][b]][c] and for the purposes of this subsection, the liquidator of the company shall be deemed to be an officer of the company.

Amendments

a 'the Companies Registration Office Gazette' substituted for '*Iris Oifigiúil*' by IFCMPA 2005, s 72.

b '£125' substituted for '£25' by C(A)A 1982 Sch 1, increased to £1,500 by CA 1990, s 240(7) as inserted by CLEA 2001, s104 and converted to €1,904.61 by Council Regulations (EC) No 1103/97, No 974/98 and No 2866/98 and the Economic and Monetary Union Act 1998, s 6; the above being implicitly substituted, by Fines Act 2010, s 6, for a fine not exceeding the aforesaid amount. A class C fine currently means a fine not exceeding €2,500.

c Words substituted by C(AA)A 2003, s 57 and Sch 2.

---

253 Commencement of voluntary winding up

A voluntary winding up shall be deemed to commence at the time of the passing of the resolution for voluntary winding up.

Consequences of Voluntary Winding up

254 Effect of voluntary winding up on business and status of company

In case of a voluntary winding up, the company shall, from the commencement of the winding up, cease to carry on its business, except so far as may be required for the beneficial winding up thereof, so, however, that the corporate state and corporate powers of the company shall, notwithstanding anything to the contrary in its articles, continue until it is dissolved.

255 Avoidance of transfers of shares after commencement of voluntary winding up

Any transfer of shares, not being a transfer made to or with the sanction of the liquidator, and any alteration in the status of the members of the company, made after the commencement of a voluntary winding up, shall be void.

Declaration of Solvency

256 [Statutory declaration of solvency in case of proposal to wind up voluntarily

(1) Where it is proposed to wind up a company voluntarily, the directors of the company or, in the case of a company having more than two directors, the majority of the directors may, at a meeting of the directors, make a statutory declaration to the effect that they have made a full inquiry into the affairs of the company, and that having done so, they have formed the opinion that the company will be able to pay its debts in full within such period not exceeding 12 months from the commencement of the winding up as may be specified in the declaration.

(2) A declaration made as aforesaid shall have no effect for the purposes of this Act unless—

(a) it is made within the 28 days immediately preceding the date of the passing of the resolution for winding up the company and delivered to the registrar of companies not later than the date of the delivery to the registrar, in accordance with the provisions of section 143, of a copy of the resolution for winding up the company;

(b) it embodies a statement of the company's assets and liabilities as at the latest practicable date before the making of the declaration and in any event at a date not more than three months before the making of the declaration;

(c) a report made by an independent person in accordance with the provisions of this section is attached thereto;

(d) it embodies a statement by the independent person referred to in paragraph (c) that he has given and has not withdrawn his written consent to the issue of the declaration with the report attached thereto; and

(e) a copy of the declaration is attached to the notice issued by the company of the general meeting at which it is intended to propose a resolution for voluntary winding up under paragraph (a) or (b) of section 251(1).

(3) The report referred to in paragraph (c) of subsection (2) shall be made by an independent person, that is to say, a person qualified at the time of the report to be appointed, or to continue to be, auditor of the company.

(4) The report shall state whether, in his opinion and to the best of his information and according to the explanations given to him—

(a) the opinion of the directors referred to in subsection (1), and

(b) the statement of the company's assets and liabilities embodied in the said declaration,

are reasonable.

(5) If within 28 days after the resolution for voluntary winding up has been advertised under subsection (1) of section 252, a creditor applies to the court for an order under this subsection, and the court is satisfied that such creditor together with any creditors supporting him in his application represents one-fifth at least in number or value of the creditors of the company, and the court is of opinion that it is unlikely that the company will be able to pay its debts within the period specified in the declaration, the court may order that all the provisions of this Act relating to a creditors' voluntary winding up, shall apply to the winding up.

(6) If the court orders that all the provisions of this Act in relation to a creditors' voluntary winding up shall apply to the winding up, the person who held the office of liquidator immediately prior to the making of the order or, if no liquidator is acting, the company shall within 21 days after the making of the order, deliver an office copy of such order to the registrar of companies.

(7) If default is made in complying with subsection (6), any person who is in default [shall be guilty of an offence and liable to a [class C fine][b]].[c]

(8) Where a statutory declaration is made under this section and it is subsequently proved to the satisfaction of the court that the company is unable to pay its debts, the court on the application of the liquidator or any creditor or contributory of the company may, if it thinks it proper to do so, declare that any director who was a party to the declaration without having reasonable grounds for the opinion that the company would be able to pay its debts in full within the period specified in the declaration shall be personally responsible, without any limitation of liability, for all or any of the debts or other liabilities of the company as the court may direct.

(9) Where a company's debts are not paid or provided for in full within the period stated in the declaration of solvency, it shall for the purposes of subsection (8) be presumed, until the contrary is shown, that the director did not have reasonable grounds for his opinion.

(10) Where the court makes a declaration under subsection (8), it may give such further directions as it thinks proper for the purpose of giving effect to that declaration.

(11) A winding up in the case of which a declaration has been made and delivered in accordance with this section is in this Act referred to as 'a members' voluntary winding up' and a voluntary winding up in the case of which a declaration has not been made and delivered as aforesaid or in the case of which an order is made under subsection (5) or in the case to which section 261(3) applies is in this Act referred to as 'a creditors' voluntary winding up'.][a]

Amendments

a CA 1963, s 256 substituted by CA 1990, s 128.

b £1,000 increased to £1,500 by CA 1990, s 240(7) as inserted by CLEA 2001, s 104 and converted to €1,904.61 by Council Regulations (EC) No 1103/97, No 974/98 and No 2866/98 and the Economic and Monetary Union Act 1998, s 6; the above being implicitly substituted, by Fines Act 2010, s 6, for a fine not exceeding the aforesaid amount. A class C fine currently means a fine not exceeding €2,500.

c Words substituted by C(AA)A 2003, s 57 and Sch 2.

Provisions applicable to a Members' Voluntary Winding Up

257 Provisions applicable to a members' voluntary winding up

Sections 258 to 264 shall, subject to the last-mentioned section, apply to a members' voluntary winding up.

258 Power of company to appoint and fix remuneration of liquidators

(1) The company in general meeting shall appoint one or more liquidators for the purpose of winding up the affairs and distributing the assets of the company, and may fix the remuneration to be paid to him or them.

(2) On the appointment of a liquidator all the powers of the directors shall cease, except so far as the company in general meeting or the liquidator sanctions the continuance thereof.

259 Power to fill vacancy in office of liquidator

(1) If a vacancy occurs by death, resignation or otherwise in the office of liquidator appointed by the company, the company in general meeting may fill the vacancy.

(2) For that purpose a general meeting may be convened by any contributory or, if there are more liquidators than one, by the continuing liquidators.

(3) The meeting shall be held in manner provided by this Act or by the articles or in such manner as may, on application by any contributory or by the continuing liquidators, be determined by the court.

260 Power of liquidator to accept shares as consideration for sale of property of company

(1) Where a company is proposed to be, or is in course of being, wound up voluntarily, and the whole or part of its business or property is proposed to be transferred or sold to another company, whether a company within the meaning of this Act or not (in this section referred to as 'the transferee company'), the liquidator of the first-mentioned company (in this section referred to as 'the transferor company') may, with the sanction of a special resolution of that company, conferring either a general authority on the liquidator or an authority in respect of any particular arrangement, receive in compensation or part compensation for the transfer or sale, shares, policies or other like interests in the transferee company for distribution among the members of the transferor company, or may enter into any other arrangement whereby the members of the transferor company may, in lieu of receiving cash, shares, policies or other like interests, or in addition thereto, participate in the profits of or receive any other benefit from the transferee company.

(2) Any sale or arrangement in pursuance of this section shall be binding on the members of the transferor company.

(3) If the voting rights conferred by any shares in the company were not cast in favour of the special resolution and the holder of those shares expresses his dissent from the special resolution in writing addressed to the liquidator and left at the registered office of the company within 7 days after the passing of the special resolution, he may require the liquidator either to abstain from carrying the resolution into effect or to purchase that part of his interest which those shares represent at a price to be determined by agreement or by arbitration in manner provided by this section.

(4) If the liquidator elects to purchase the member's interest, the purchase money must be paid before the company is dissolved and, unless otherwise provided for, shall be deemed to be and shall be paid as part of the costs, charges and expenses of the winding up.

(5) A special resolution shall not be invalid for the purposes of this section by reason that it is passed before or concurrently with a resolution for voluntary winding up or for appointing liquidators, but, if an order is made within a year for winding up the company by the court, the special resolution shall not be valid unless sanctioned by the court.

(6) For the purposes of an arbitration under this section, the provisions of the Companies Clauses Consolidation Act, 1845, relating to the settlement of disputes by arbitration, shall be incorporated with this Act, and in the construction of those provisions this Act shall be deemed to be the special Act, and 'the company' shall mean the transferor company, and any appointment by the said incorporated provisions directed to be made under the hand of the secretary or any two of the directors may be made under the hand of the liquidator, or, if there is more than one liquidator, then of any two or more of the liquidators.

261 [Duty of liquidator to call creditors' meeting if he is of opinion that company unable to pay its debts

(1) If the liquidator is at any time of the opinion that the company will not be able to pay its debts in full within the period stated in the declaration under section 256 he shall—

(a) summon a meeting of creditors for a day not later than the fourteenth day after the day on which he formed that opinion;

(b) send notices of the creditors' meeting to the creditors by post not less than seven days before the day on which that meeting is to be held;

(c) cause notice of the creditors' meeting to be advertised, at least ten days before the date of the meeting, once in [the Companies Registration Office Gazette][b] and once at least in two daily newspapers circulating in the locality in which the company's principal place of business in the State was situated during the relevant period; and

(d) during the period before the day on which the creditors' meeting is to be held, furnish creditors free of charge with such information concerning the affairs of the company as they may reasonably require;

and the notice of the creditors' meeting shall state the duty imposed by paragraph (d).

(2) The liquidator shall also—

(a) make out a statement in the prescribed form as to the affairs of the company, including a statement of the company's assets and liabilities, a list of the outstanding creditors and the estimated amount of their claims;

(b) lay that statement before the creditors' meeting; and

(c) attend and preside at that meeting.

(3) As from the day on which the creditors' meeting is held under this section, the Companies Acts shall have effect as if—

(a) without prejudice to the powers of the court under section 256, the directors' declaration under that section had not been made; and

(b) the creditors' meeting and the company meetings at which it was resolved that the company be wound up voluntarily were the meetings mentioned in section 266;

and, accordingly, the winding up shall become a creditors' voluntary winding up and any appointment made or committee established by the creditors' meeting shall be deemed to have been made or established by the creditors' meeting so mentioned.

(4) The appointment of a liquidator at a meeting called under this section shall not, subject to subsection (5), affect the validity of any action previously taken by the liquidator appointed by the members of the company.

(5) Where the creditors appoint a liquidator at a meeting called under this section and there is a dispute as to any or all of the costs, charges or expenses incurred by, including the remuneration of, the liquidator appointed by the members of the company, the liquidator appointed by the creditors, or any creditor, may apply to the court to determine the dispute and the court may, on such application, make such order as it deems fit.

(6) Nothing in this section shall be deemed to take away any right in this Act of any person to present a petition to the court for the winding up of a company.

(7) If the liquidator fails to comply with subsection (1) he [shall be guilty of an offence and liable to a fine].[c]][a]

Amendments

a CA 1963, s 261 substituted by CA 1990, s 129.

b 'the Companies Registration Office Gazette' substituted for '*Iris Oifigiúil*' by IFCMPA 2005, s 72.

c Words substituted by C(AA)A 2003, s 57 and Sch 2.

---

262 Duty of liquidator to call general meeting at end of each year

(1) Subject to section 264, in the event of the winding up continuing for more than one year, the liquidator shall summon a general meeting of the company at the end of the first year from the commencement of the winding up, and of each succeeding year, or at the first convenient date within 3 months from the end of the year and shall lay before the meeting an account of his acts and dealings and of the conduct of the winding up during the preceding year and shall within 7 days after such meeting send a copy of that account to the registrar.

(2) If the liquidator fails to comply with this section, he [shall be guilty of an offence and liable to a [class C fine][a]].[b]

Amendments

a '£250' substituted for '£50' by C(A)A 1982, Sch 1. '£250' increased to '£1,000' by CA 1990, s 145 and further increased to £1,500 by CA 1990, s 240(7) as inserted by CLEA 2001, s104. £1,500 converted to €1,904.61 by Council Regulations (EC) No 1103/97, No 974/98 and No

2866/98 and the Economic and Monetary Union Act 1998, s 6; the above being implicitly substituted, by Fines Act 2010, s 6, for a fine not exceeding the aforesaid amount. A class C fine currently means a fine not exceeding €2,500. See also CA 1990, s 145(2).

b Words substituted by C(AA)A 2003, s 57 and Sch 2.

263 Final meeting and dissolution

(1) Subject to section 264, as soon as the affairs of the company are fully wound up, the liquidator shall make up an account of the winding up showing how the winding up has been conducted and the property of the company has been disposed of, and thereupon shall call a general meeting of the company for the purpose of laying before it the account and giving any explanation thereof.

(2) The meeting shall be called by advertisement in 2 daily newspapers circulating in the district where the registered office of the company is situate, specifying the time, place and object thereof, and published 28 days at least before the meeting.

(3) Within one week after the meeting, the liquidator shall send to the registrar of companies a copy of the account, and shall make a return to him of the holding of the meeting and of its date, and if the copy is not sent or the return is not made in accordance with this subsection, the liquidator [shall be guilty of an offence and liable to a [class C fine][a],[b] so, however, that if a quorum is not present at the meeting, the liquidator shall, in lieu of the return hereinbefore mentioned, make a return that the meeting was duly summoned and that no quorum was present thereat, and upon such a return being made, the provisions of this subsection as to the making of the return shall be deemed to have been complied with.

(4) Subject to subsection (5), the registrar on receiving the account and either of the returns hereinbefore mentioned shall forthwith register them, and on the expiration of 3 months from the registration of the return the company shall be deemed to be dissolved.

(5) The court may, on the application of the liquidator or of any other person who appears to the court to be interested, make an order deferring the date at which the dissolution of the company is to take effect for such time as the court thinks fit.

(6) It shall be the duty of the person on whose application an order of the court under this section is made, within 14 days after the making of the order, to deliver to the registrar an office copy of the order for registration, and if that person fails so to do he [shall be guilty of an offence and liable to a [class C fine][a]].[c]

(7) If the liquidator fails to call a general meeting of the company as required by this section, he [shall be guilty of an offence and liable to a [class C fine][a]].[d]

Amendments

a '£500' substituted for '£100' by C(A)A 1982, Sch 1 and increased to £1,500 by CA 1990, s 240(7) as inserted by CLEA 2001, s 104. £1,500 converted to €1,904.61 by Council Regulations (EC) No 1103/97, No 974/98 and No 2866/98 and the Economic and Monetary Union Act 1998, s 6; the above being implicitly substituted, by Fines Act 2010, s 6, for a fine not exceeding the aforesaid amount. A class C fine currently means a fine not exceeding €2,500.

b Words substituted by C(AA)A 2003, s 57 and Sch 2.

c '£25' substituted for '£5' by C(A)A 1982, Sch 1 and increased to £1,500 by CA 1990, s 240(7) as inserted by CLEA 2001, s 104. £1,500 converted to €1,904.61 by Council Regulations (EC) No 1103/97, No 974/98 and No 2866/98 and the Economic and Monetary Union Act 1998, s 6; the above being implicitly substituted, by Fines Act 2010, s 6, for a fine not exceeding the aforesaid amount. A class C fine currently means a fine not exceeding €2,500.

d '£250' substituted for '£25' by C(A)A 1982, Sch 1 and increased to £1,500 by CA 1990, s 240(7) as inserted by CLEA 2001, s 104. £1,500 converted to €1,904.61 by Council Regulations (EC) No 1103/97, No 974/98 and No 2866/98 and the Economic and Monetary Union Act 1998, s 6; the above being implicitly substituted, by Fines Act 2010, s 6, for a fine not exceeding the aforesaid amount. A class C fine currently means a fine not exceeding €2,500.

---

264 Alternative provisions as to annual and final meetings if liquidator is of opinion that company unable to pay its debts

(1) Subject to subsection (2), where section 261 has effect, sections 272 and 273 shall apply to the winding up to the exclusion of sections 262 and 263, as if the winding up were a creditors' voluntary winding up and not a members' voluntary winding up.

(2) The liquidator shall not be required to summon a meeting of creditors under section 272 at the end of the first year from the commencement of the winding up, unless the meeting held under section 261 is held more than 3 months before the end of that year.

Provisions applicable to a Creditors' Voluntary Winding Up

265 Provisions applicable to a creditors' voluntary winding up

Sections 266 to 273, shall apply in relation to a creditors' voluntary winding up.

266 Meeting of creditors

(1) The company shall cause a meeting of the creditors of the company to be summoned for the day, or the day next following the day, on which there is to be held the meeting at which the resolution for voluntary winding up is to be proposed, and shall cause the notices of the said meeting of creditors to be sent by post to the creditors at least 10 days before the date of the said meeting of the company.

(2) The company shall cause notice of the meeting of the creditors to be advertised [, at least ten days before the date of the meeting,][a] once at least in 2 daily newspapers circulating in the district where the registered office or principal place of business of the company is situate.

(3) The directors of the company shall—

(a) cause a full statement of the position of the company's affairs, together with a list of the creditors of the company and the estimated amount of their claims to be laid before the meeting of the creditors to be held as aforesaid; and

(b) appoint one of their number to preside at the said meeting.

(4) It shall be the duty of the director appointed to preside at the meeting of creditors to attend the meeting and preside thereat.

(5) If the meeting of the company at which the resolution for voluntary winding up is to be proposed is adjourned and the resolution is passed at an adjourned meeting, any resolution passed at the meeting of the creditors held in pursuance of subsection (1)

shall have effect as if it had been passed immediately after the passing of the resolution for winding up the company.

[(6) If default is made—

(a) by the company in complying with subsections (1) and (2);

(b) by the directors of the company in complying with subsection (3);

(c) by any director of the company in complying with subsection (4);

the company, directors or director, as the case may be, shall be guilty of an offence and liable to a [class C fine][b], and in case of default by the company, every officer of the company who is in default shall be guilty of an offence and liable to a [class C fine][b].][c]

Amendments

a Words inserted by CA 1990, s 130.

b As implicitly substituted for 'fine not exceeding €1,904.61' by Fines Act 2010, s 6. A class C fine currently means a fine not exceeding €2,500.

c Subsection (6) substituted by C(AA)A 2003, s 57 and Sch 2.

---

267 Appointment of liquidator

(1) Subject to subsection (2), the creditors and the company at their respective meetings mentioned in section 266 may nominate a person to be liquidator for the purpose of winding up the affairs and distributing the assets of the company, and if the creditors and the company nominate different persons, the person nominated by the creditors shall be liquidator, and if no person is nominated by the creditors, the person, if any, nominated by the company shall be liquidator.

(2) Where different persons are nominated as liquidator, any director, member or creditor of the company may, within 14 days after the date on which the nomination was made by the creditors, apply to the court for an order either directing that the person nominated as liquidator by the company shall be liquidator instead of or jointly with the person nominated by the creditors, or appointing some other person to be liquidator instead of the person appointed by the creditors.

[(3) If at a meeting of creditors mentioned in section 266(1) a resolution as to the creditors' nominee as liquidator is proposed, it shall be deemed to be passed when a majority, in value only, of the creditors present personally or by proxy and voting on the resolution have voted in favour of the resolution.][a]

Amendments

a Subsection (3) inserted by CLEA 2001, s 47.

[267A Confirmation of creditors' voluntary winding up

(1) Where—

(a) a liquidator is appointed in a creditors' voluntary winding up of a company in pursuance of section 267, and

(b) the centre of the company's main interests is situated in the State, the Master of the High Court may, on application by the liquidator in the prescribed form and payment of the prescribed fee, confirm the creditors' voluntary winding up for the purposes of the Insolvency Regulation and shall so certify.][a]

Amendments

a Inserted by EC(CI)R 2002, reg 3.

268 Appointment of committee of inspection

(1) Subject to subsection (2), the creditors at the meeting to be held in pursuance of section 266 or at any subsequent meeting may, if they think fit, appoint a committee of inspection consisting of not more than five persons, and, if such committee is appointed the company may, either at the meeting at which the resolution for voluntary winding up is passed or at any time subsequently in general meeting, appoint three persons to act as members of the committee, provided that the number of members of the committee shall not at any time exceed eight.

(2) The creditors may, if they think fit, resolve that all or any of the persons so appointed by the company ought not to be members of the committee of inspection, and if the creditors so resolve, the persons mentioned in the resolution shall not, unless the court otherwise directs, be qualified to act as members of the committee, and on any application to the court under this subsection the court may, if it thinks fit, appoint other persons to act as such members in place of the persons mentioned in the resolution.

(3) Subject to subsections (1) and (2), and to rules of court, section 233 (except subsection (1)) shall apply to a committee of inspection appointed under this section as it applies to a committee of inspection appointed in a winding up by the court.

269 Fixing of liquidators' remuneration and cesser of directors' powers

(1) The committee of inspection, or if there is no such committee, the creditors, may fix the remuneration to be paid to the liquidator or liquidators.

(2) Within 28 days after the remuneration to be paid to the liquidator or liquidators has been fixed by the committee of inspection or by the creditors, any creditor or contributory who alleges that such remuneration is excessive may apply to the court to fix the remuneration to be paid to the liquidator or liquidators.

(3) On the appointment of a liquidator, all the powers of the directors shall cease, except so far as the committee of inspection or, if there is no such committee, the creditors, sanction the continuance thereof.

270 Power to fill vacancy in office of liquidator

If a vacancy occurs by death, resignation or otherwise in the office of a liquidator, other than a liquidator appointed by, or by the direction of, the court, the creditors may fill the vacancy.

271 Application of section 260 to a creditors' voluntary winding up

Section 260 shall apply in the case of a creditors' voluntary winding up as in the case of a members' voluntary winding up, with the modification that the powers of the liquidator under that section shall not be exercised except with the sanction either of the court or of the committee of inspection.

272 Duty of liquidator to call meetings of company and of creditors at end of each year

(1) In the event of the winding up continuing for more than one year, the liquidator shall summon a general meeting of the company and a meeting of the creditors at the end of the first year from the commencement of the winding up, and of each succeeding year, or at the first convenient date within 3 months from the end of the year, and shall lay before the meetings an account of his acts and dealings and of the conduct of the winding up during the preceding year and shall within 7 days after the later of such meetings send a copy of that account to the registrar.

(2) If the liquidator fails to comply with this section, he [shall be guilty of an offence and liable to a [class C fine][a]].[b]

Amendments

a '£1000' substitute for '£250' by CA 1990, s 145 and increased to £1,500 by CA 1990, s 240(7) as inserted by CLEA 2001, s 104. £1,500 converted to €1,904.61 by Council Regulations (EC) No 1103/97, No 974/98 and No 2866/98 and the Economic and Monetary Union Act 1998, s 6; the above being implicitly substituted, by Fines Act 2010, s 6, for a fine not exceeding the aforesaid amount. A class C fine currently means a fine not exceeding €2,500. See also CA 1990, s 145(2).

b Words substituted by C(AA)A 2003, s 57 and Sch 2.

---

273 Final meeting and dissolution

(1) As soon as the affairs of the company are fully wound up, the liquidator shall make up an account of the winding up, showing how the winding up has been conducted and the property of the company has been disposed of, and thereupon shall call a general meeting of the company and a meeting of the creditors for the purpose of laying the account before the meetings and giving any explanation thereof.

(2) Each such meeting shall be called by advertisement in 2 daily newspapers circulating in the district where the registered office of the company is situate, specifying the time, place and object thereof, and published 28 days at least before the meeting.

(3) Within one week after the date of the meetings, or if the meetings are not held on the same date, after the date of the later meeting, the liquidator shall send to the registrar of companies a copy of the account, and shall make a return to him of the holding of the meetings and of their dates, and if the copy is not sent or the return is not made in accordance with this subsection, the liquidator [shall be guilty of an offence and liable to a [class C fine][a]],[b] so, however, that if a quorum is not present at either such meeting, the liquidator shall, in lieu of the return hereinbefore mentioned, make a return that the meeting was duly summoned and that no quorum was present thereat, and upon such a return being made, the provisions of this subsection as to the making of the return shall, in respect of that meeting, be deemed to have been complied with.

(4) Subject to subsection (5), the registrar on receiving the account and, in respect of each such meeting, either of the returns hereinbefore mentioned, shall forthwith register them, and on the expiration of 3 months from the registration thereof the company shall be deemed to be dissolved.

(5) The court may, on the application of the liquidator or of any other person who appears to the court to be interested, make an order deferring the date at which the dissolution of the company is to take effect for such time as the court thinks fit.

(6) It shall be the duty of the person on whose application an order of the court under this section is made, within 14 days after the making of the order, to deliver to the registrar an office copy of the order for registration, and if that person fails so to do, he [shall be guilty of an offence and liable to a [class C fine][a]].[b]

(7) If the liquidator fails to call a general meeting of the company or a meeting of the creditors as required by this section, he [shall be guilty of an offence and liable for a [class C fine][a]].[b]

Amendments

a '£250' substituted for '£50' by C(A)A 1982, Sch 1, increased to £1,500 by CA 1990, s 240(7) as inserted by CLEA 2001, s104 and converted to €1,904.61 by Council Regulations (EC) No 1103/97, No 974/98 and No 2866/98 and the Economic and Monetary Union Act 1998, s 6; the above being implicitly substituted, by Fines Act 2010, s 6, for a fine not exceeding the aforesaid amount. A class C fine currently means a fine not exceeding €2,500. See also CA 1990, s 145(2).

b Words substituted by C(AA)A 2003, s 57 and Sch 2.

Provisions applicable to every Voluntary Winding Up

274 Provisions applicable to every voluntary winding up

Sections 275 to 282 shall apply to every voluntary winding up whether a members' or a creditors' winding up.

275 [Distribution of property of company

(1) Subject to the provisions of this Act as to preferential payments, the property of a company on its winding up—

(a) shall, subject to subsection (2), be applied in satisfaction of its liabilities *pari passu*, and

(b) shall, subject to such application, and unless the articles otherwise provide, be distributed among the members according to their rights and interests in the company.

(2) Nothing in paragraph (a) of subsection (1) shall in any way affect any rights or obligations of the company or any other person arising as a result of any agreement entered into (whether before or after the commencement of section 132 of the Companies Act, 1990) by any person under which any particular liability of the company to any general creditor is postponed in favour of or subordinated to the rights or claims of any other person to whom the company may be in any way liable.

(3) In subsection (2)—

'liability' includes a contingent liability; and

'person' includes a class of persons.][a]

Amendments

CA 1963, s 275 substituted by CA 1990, s 132.

276 Powers and duties of liquidator in voluntary winding up

(1) The liquidator may—

(a) in the case of a members' voluntary winding up, with the sanction of a special resolution of the company, and, in the case of a creditors' voluntary winding up, with the sanction of the court or the committee of inspection or (if there is no such committee) a meeting of the creditors, exercise any of the powers given by paragraphs (d), (e) and (f) of subsection (1) of section 231 to a liquidator in a winding up by the court;

(b) without sanction, exercise any of the other powers by this Act given to the liquidator in a winding up by the court;

(c) exercise the power of the court under this Act of settling a list of contributories, and the list of contributories shall be *prima facie* evidence of the liability of persons named therein to be contributories;

(d) exercise the power of the court of making calls;

(e) summon general meetings of the company for the purpose of obtaining the sanction of the company by resolution or for any other purpose he may think fit.

(2) The liquidator shall pay the debts of the company and shall adjust the rights of the contributories among themselves.

(3) When several liquidators are appointed, any power given by this Act may be exercised by such one or more of them as may be determined at the time of their appointment, or, in default of such determination, by any number not less than two.

[276A Consent to appointment as liquidator and notification of appointment

(1) The appointment of a liquidator shall be of no effect unless the person nominated has, prior to his appointment, signified his written consent to the appointment.

(2) The chairman of any meeting at which a liquidator is appointed shall, within 7 days of the meeting, notify the liquidator in writing of his appointment, unless the liquidator or his duly authorised representative is present at the meeting where the appointment is made.

(3) A person who fails to comply with subsection (2) [shall be guilty of an offence and liable to a [class C fine][a]][b].][c]

Amendments

a £1,000 to increased to £1,500 by CA 1990, s 240(7) as inserted by CLEA 2001, s 104. £1,500 converted to €1,904.61 by Council Regulations (EC) No 1103/97, No 974/98 and No 2866/98 and the Economic and Monetary Union Act 1998, s 6; the above being implicitly substituted, by Fines Act 2010, s 6, for a fine not exceeding the aforesaid amount. A class C fine currently means a fine not exceeding €2,500.

b Words substituted by C(AA)A 2003, s 57 and Sch 2.

c CA 1963, s 276A substituted by CA 1990, s 133.

---

277 Power of court to appoint and remove liquidator in a voluntary winding up

(1) If from any cause whatever there is no liquidator acting, the court may appoint a liquidator.

(2) The court may, on cause shown, remove a liquidator and appoint another liquidator.

278 Notice by liquidator of his appointment

(1) The liquidator shall, within 14 days after his appointment, deliver to the registrar of companies for registration a notice of his appointment [and the registrar shall forward a copy to the Director][a].

(2) If the liquidator fails to comply with the requirements of this section, he [shall be guilty of an offence and liable to a [class C fine][b]].[c]

Amendments

a Words inserted by CLEA 2001, s 48.

b '£250' substituted for '£50' by C(A)A 1982, Sch 1, increased to £1,500 by CA 1990, s 240(7) as inserted by CLEA 2001, s 104 and converted to €1,904.61 by Council Regulations (EC) No 1103/97, No 974/98 and No 2866/98 and the Economic and Monetary Union Act 1998, s 6; the above being implicitly substituted, by Fines Act 2010, s 6, for a fine not exceeding the aforesaid amount. A class C fine currently means a fine not exceeding €2,500.

c Words substituted by C(AA)A 2003, s 57 and Sch 2.

---

279 Provisions as to arrangement binding creditors

(1) Any arrangement entered into between a company about to be, or in the course of being, wound up and its creditors shall, subject to the right of appeal under this section, be binding on the company if sanctioned by a special resolution and on the creditors if acceded to by three-fourths in number and value of the creditors.

(2) Any creditor or contributory may, within 3 weeks from the completion of the arrangement, appeal to the court against it, and the court may thereupon, as it thinks just, amend, vary or confirm the arrangement.

280 Power to apply to court to have questions determined or powers exercised

(1) The liquidator or any contributory or creditor may apply to the court to determine any question arising in the winding up of a company, or to exercise in relation to the enforcing of calls or any other matter, all or any of the powers which the court might exercise if the company were being wound up by the court.

(2) The court, if satisfied that the determination of the question or the required exercise of power will be just and beneficial, may accede wholly or partially to the application on such terms and conditions as it thinks fit or may make such other order on the application as it thinks just.

(3) An office copy of an order made by virtue of this section annulling the resolution to wind up or staying the proceedings in the winding up shall forthwith be forwarded by the company to the registrar of companies for registration.

(4) If a company fails to comply with subsection (3), the company and every officer of the company who is in default [shall be guilty of an offence and liable to a [class C fine][a]].[b]

Amendments

a '£125' substituted for '£25' by C(A)A 1982, Sch 1, increased to £1,500 by CA 1990, s 240(7) as inserted by CLEA 2001, s 104 and converted to €1,904.61 by Council Regulations (EC) No 1103/97, No 974/98 and No 2866/98 and the Economic and Monetary Union Act 1998, s 6; the above being implicitly substituted, by Fines Act 2010, s 6, for a fine not exceeding the aforesaid amount. A class C fine currently means a fine not exceeding €2,500.

b Words substituted by C(AA)A 2003, s 57 and Sch 2.

281 Costs of voluntary winding up

All costs, charges and expenses properly incurred in the winding up, including the remuneration of the liquidator, shall be payable out of the assets of the company in priority to all other claims.

282 Savings for rights of creditors and contributories

The winding up of a company shall not bar the right of any creditor or contributory to have it wound up by the court, but in the case of an application by a contributory the court must be satisfied that the rights of the contributories will be prejudiced by a voluntary winding up.

[282A Inspection of books in voluntary winding-up

(1) The court may, on the application of the Director, make an order for the inspection by the Director of any books and papers in the possession of a company which is in voluntary liquidation and the company, every officer of the company and the liquidator shall give to the Director such access and facilities as are necessary for inspecting and taking copies of those books and papers as the Director may require.

(2) Nothing in this section shall be taken as excluding or restricting any statutory rights of a Minister of the Government or a person acting under the authority of a Minister of the Government.][a]

Amendments

a Section inserted by CLEA 2001, s 49.

[282B Power of court to summon persons for examination in voluntary winding up

(1) The court may, of its own motion or on the application of the Director, at any time where a company is in voluntary liquidation, summon before it any officer of the company or person known or suspected to have in his possession any property of the company or supposed to be indebted to the company, or any person whom the court deems capable of giving information relating to the promotion, formation, trade, dealings, affairs or property of the company.

(2) The court may examine such person on oath concerning the matters aforesaid, either by word of mouth or on written interrogatories, and may reduce his answers to writing and require him to sign them.

(3) The court may require such person to produce any accounting records, deed, instrument, or other document or paper relating to the company that are in his custody or power.

(4) The court may, before the examination takes place, require such person to place before it a statement, in such form as the court may direct, of any transactions between him and the company of a type or class which the court may specify.

(5) If, in the opinion of the court, it is just and equitable so to do, it may direct that the costs of the examination be paid by the person examined.

(6) A person who is examined under this section is not entitled to refuse to answer any question put to him on the ground that his answer might incriminate him and any answer by him to such a question may be used in evidence against him in any proceedings whatsoever (save proceedings for an offence (other than perjury in respect of such an answer)).

(7) If a person without reasonable excuse fails at any time to attend his examination under this section, he shall be guilty of contempt of court and liable to be punished accordingly.

(8) In a case where a person without reasonable excuse fails at any time to attend his examination under this section or there are reasonable grounds for believing that a person has absconded, or is about to abscond, with a view to avoiding or delaying his examination under this section, the court may cause the person to be arrested and his books and documents and moveable personal property to be seized and him and them to be detained until such time as the court may order.][a]

Amendments

a Section inserted by CLEA 2001, s 49.

[282C Order for payment or delivery of property against person examined under section 282B

(1) If in the course of an examination under section 282B it appears to the court that any person being examined—

(a) is indebted to the company, or

(b) has in his possession or control any money, property or books and papers of the company,

the court may, of its own motion or on the application of the Director, order the person—

(i) to pay to the liquidator the amount of the debt or any part thereof, or

(ii) to pay, deliver, convey, surrender or transfer to the liquidator such money, property or books and papers or any part thereof,

as the case may be, at such time and in such manner and on such terms as the court may direct.

(2) Where the court has made an order under subsection (1), it may, on the application of the Director or the liquidator, make a further order permitting the applicant, accompanied by such persons as the applicant thinks appropriate, to enter at any time or times within one month from the date of issue of the order any premises (including a dwelling) owned or occupied by the person the subject of the order under subsection (1) (using such force as is reasonably necessary for the purpose), to search the premises and to seize any money, property or books and papers of the company found on the premises.

(3) Where the court has made an order under subsection (2), the applicant shall report to it as soon as may be on the outcome of any action on foot of the court's order and the court shall direct the applicant as to the disposition of anything seized on foot of the order.

(4) A direction under subsection (3) shall not be made in favour of the Director except in respect of the Director's costs and reasonable expenses.

(5) A person who obstructs the exercise of a right of entry, search and seizure conferred by virtue of an order made under subsection (2) or who obstructs the exercise of a right so conferred to take possession of anything referred to in that subsection, shall be guilty of an offence.

(6) Proceedings on foot of an offence under subsection (5) shall not prejudice the power of the court to issue proceedings for contempt of court for failure by a person to comply with an order under this section.][a]

Amendments

a Section inserted by CLEA 2001, s 49.

[282D Power to arrest absconding contributory or officer of company in voluntary winding-up

The court, at any time in respect of a voluntary winding-up, on proof of probable cause for believing that a contributory, director, shadow director, secretary or other officer is about to quit the State or otherwise to abscond or to remove or conceal any of his property for the purpose of evading payment of calls or of avoiding examination about the affairs of the company, may, of its own motion or on the application of the Director, a creditor of the company or any other interested person, cause the contributory, director, shadow director, secretary or other officer to be arrested, and his books and papers and movable personal property to be seized and him and them to be detained until such time as the court may order.][a]

Amendments

a Section inserted by CLEA 2001, s 49.

(IV) Provisions Applicable to Every Mode of Winding Up

Proof and Ranking of Claims

283 Debts which may be proved

(1) Subject to subsection (2), in every winding up (subject, in the case of insolvent companies, to the application in accordance with the provisions of this Act of the law of bankruptcy) all debts payable on a contingency, and all claims against the company, present or future, certain or contingent, ascertained or sounding only in damages, shall be admissible to proof against the company, a just estimate being made, so far as possible, of the value of such debts or claims which may be subject to any contingency or which sound only in damages, or for some other reason do not bear a certain value.

(2) Where a company is being wound up, dividends declared by the company more than 6 years preceding the commencement of the winding up which have not been claimed within the said 6 years shall not be a claim admissible to proof against the company for the purposes of the winding up, unless the articles of the company or the conditions of issue provide otherwise.

284 Application of bankruptcy rules in winding up of insolvent companies

(1) In the winding up of an insolvent company the same rules shall prevail and be observed relating to the respective rights of secured and unsecured creditors and to debts provable and to the valuation of annuities and future and contingent liabilities as are in force for the time being under the law of bankruptcy relating to the estates of persons adjudged bankrupt, and all persons who in any such case would be entitled to prove for and receive dividends out of the assets of the company may come in under the winding up and make such claims against the company as they respectively are entitled to by virtue of this section.

(2) [Section 51 of the Bankruptcy Act, 1988,][a] shall apply in the winding up of an insolvent company and accordingly the reference in that section to the filing of the petition shall be read as a reference to the presentation of a petition for the winding up of the company by the court or the passing of a resolution for voluntary winding up, as the case may be, and where, before the presentation of a petition for the winding up of the company by the court, a resolution has been passed by the company for voluntary winding up, shall be read as a reference to the passing of the resolution.

(3) Subsection (2) shall not apply to a judgment mortgage created before the operative date.

Amendments

a CA 1963, s 284 amended by the Bankruptcy Act 1988, s 51(2).

---

285 Preferential payments in a winding up

(1) In this section 'the relevant date' means—

(i) where the company is ordered to be wound up compulsorily, the date of the appointment (or first appointment) of a provisional liquidator or, if no such appointment was made, the date of the winding-up order, unless in either case the company had commenced to be wound up voluntarily before that date; and

(ii) where subparagraph (i) does not apply, the date of the passing of the resolution for the winding up of the company.

(2) In a winding up there shall be paid in priority to all other debts—

(a) the following rates and taxes,—

(i) all local rates due from the company at the relevant date and having become due and payable within 12 months next before that date;

(ii) all assessed taxes, including income tax and corporation profits tax, assessed on the company up to the 5th day of April next before the relevant date and not exceeding in the whole one year's assessment;

(iii) any amount due at the relevant date in respect of sums which an employer is liable under the Finance (No. 2) Act, 1959, and any regulations thereunder to deduct from emoluments to which Part II of that Act applies paid by him during the period of 12 months next before the relevant date reduced by any amount which he was under that Act and any regulation thereunder liable to repay during the said period, with the addition of interest payable under section 8 of that Act;

(b) all wages or salary (whether or not earned wholly or in part by way of commission) of any clerk or servant in respect of services rendered to the company during the 4 months next before the relevant date;

(c) all wages (whether payable for time or for piece work) of any workman or labourer in respect of services rendered to the company during the 4 months next before the relevant date;

(d) all accrued holiday remuneration becoming payable to any clerk, servant, workman or labourer (or in the case of his death to any other person in his right) on the termination of his employment before or by the effect of the winding-up order or resolution;

[(e) unless the company is being wound up voluntarily merely for the purposes of reconstruction or of amalgamation with another company—

(i) all amounts due in respect of contributions which are payable during the 12 months next before the relevant date by the company as the employer of any persons under the Social Welfare Acts, and

(ii) all amounts due in respect of contributions which would have been payable under the provisions of section 10(1)(b) of the Social Welfare (Consolidation) Act, 1981, by the company as the employer of any persons in respect of any remuneration in respect of any period of employment during the 12 months next before the relevant date even if such remuneration is paid after the relevant date;][a]

(f) unless the company is being wound up voluntarily merely for the purposes of reconstruction or of amalgamation with another company, all amounts (including costs) due in respect of compensation or liability for compensation under the Workmen's Compensation Acts, 1934 to 1955 (being amounts which have accrued before the relevant date), to the extent that the company is not effectively indemnified by insurers against liability for such compensation;

(g) unless the company is being wound up voluntarily merely for the purposes of reconstruction or of amalgamation with another company, all amounts due from the company in respect of damages and costs or liability for damages and costs, payable to a person employed by it in connection with an accident occurring before the relevant date and in the course of his employment with the company, to the extent that the company is not effectively indemnified by insurers against such damages and costs;

[(h) all sums due to any employee pursuant to any scheme or arrangement for the provision of payments to the employee while he is absent from employment due to ill health;

(i) any payments due by the company pursuant to any scheme or arrangement for the provision of superannuation benefits to or in respect of employees of the company whether such payments are due in respect of the company's contribution to that scheme or under that arrangement or in respect of such contributions payable by the employees to the company under any such scheme or arrangement which have been deducted from the wages or salaries of employees.][b]

(3) Subject to subsection (4), and notwithstanding anything in paragraphs (b) and (c) of subsection (2) the sum to which priority is to be given under those paragraphs respectively shall not, in the case of any one claimant, exceed [€3,174.35].[c]

(4) Where a claimant under paragraph (c) of subsection (2) is a farm labourer who has entered into a contract for payment of a portion of his wages in a lump sum at the end of the year of hiring, he shall have priority in respect of the whole of such sum, or such part thereof as the court may decide to be due under the contract, proportionate to the time of service up to the relevant date.

(5) Where any compensation under the Workmen's Compensation Acts, 1934 and 1955 is a weekly payment, the amount due in respect thereof shall, for the purposes of paragraph (f) of subsection (2) be taken to be the amount of the lump sum for which the weekly payment could be redeemed if the employer made an application for that purpose under the said Acts.

(6) Where any payment has been made—

(a) to any clerk, servant, workman or labourer in the employment of a company, on account of wages or salary; or

(b) to any such clerk, servant, workman or labourer or, in the case of his death, to any other person in his right, on account of accrued holiday remuneration;

[or

(c) to any such clerk, servant, workman or labourer while he is absent from employment due to ill health or pursuant to any scheme or arrangement for the provision of superannuation benefit to or in respect of him;][d]

out of money advanced by some person for that purpose, the person by whom the money was advanced shall, in a winding up, have a right of priority in respect of the money so advanced and paid up to the amount by which the sum, in respect of which the clerk, servant, workman or labourer or other person in his right, would have been entitled to priority in the winding up has been diminished by reason of the payment having been made.

(7) The foregoing debts shall—

(a) rank equally among themselves and be paid in full, unless the assets are insufficient to meet them, in which case they shall abate in equal proportions; and

(b) so far as the assets of the company available for payment of general creditors are insufficient to meet them, have priority over the claims of holders of debentures under any floating charge created by the company, and be paid accordingly out of any property comprised in or subject to that charge.

(8) Subject to the retention of such sums as may be necessary for the costs and expenses of the winding up, the foregoing debts shall be discharged forthwith so far as the assets are sufficient to meet them, and in the case of debts to which priority is given by paragraph (e) of subsection (2), formal proof thereof shall not be required except in so far as is otherwise provided by rules of court.

(9) Subject to subsection (10), in the event of a landlord or other person distraining or having distrained on any goods or effects of the company within 3 months next before the relevant date, the debts to which priority is given by this section shall be a first charge on the goods or effects so distrained on, or the proceeds of the sale thereof.

(10) In respect of any money paid under any such charge as is referred to in subsection (9), the landlord or other person shall have the same rights or priority as the person to whom the payment is made.

(11) Any remuneration in respect of a period of holiday [or absence from work through][e] good cause shall be deemed to be wages in respect of services rendered to the company during that period.

(12) This section shall not apply in the case of a winding up where the relevant date occurred before the operative date, and in such a case, the provisions relating to preferential payments which would have applied if this Act had not been passed shall be deemed to remain in full force.

[(13) The Minister may by order made under this subsection vary the sum of money specified in subsection (3) of this section.][f]

[(14) The priority conferred by subsection (2) shall apply only to those debts which, within the period of six months after advertisement by the liquidator for claims in at least two daily newspapers circulating in the district where the registered office of the company is situated, either—

(a) have been notified to him; or

(b) have become known to him.][g]

Amendments

a Subsection (e) substituted by the Social Welfare Act 1991, s 37.

b CA 1963, s 285(2)(h)–(i) inserted by C(A)A 1982, s 10.

c '£2,500' substituted for '£300' by C(A)A 1982, s 10 and converted to €3,174.35 by Council Regulations (EC) No 1103/97, No 974/98 and No 2866/98 and the Economic and Monetary Union Act 1998, s 6.

d CA 1963, s 285(6)(c) inserted by C(A)A 1982, s 10.

e Words substituted by C(A)A 1982, s 10.

f CA 1963, s 285(13) inserted by C(A)A 1982, s 10.

g CA 1963, s 285(14) inserted by CA 1990, s 134.

Effect of Winding Up on Antecedent and other Transactions

286 [Fraudulent preference

(1) Subject to the provisions of this section, any conveyance, mortgage, delivery of goods, payment, execution or other act relating to property made or done by or against a company which is unable to pay its debts as they become due in favour of any creditor, or of any person on trust for any creditor, with a view to giving such creditor, or any surety or guarantor for the debt due to such creditor, a preference over the other creditors, shall, if a winding-up of the company commences within 6 months of the making or doing the same and the company is at the time of the commencement of the winding-up unable to pay its debts (taking into account the contingent and prospective liabilities), be deemed a fraudulent preference of its creditors and be invalid accordingly.

(2) Any conveyance or assignment by a company of all its property to trustees for the benefit of all its creditors shall be void to all intents.

(3) A transaction to which subsection (1) applies in favour of a connected person which was made within two years before the commencement of the winding up of the company shall, unless the contrary is shown, be deemed in the event of the company being wound up—

(a) to have been made with a view to giving such person a preference over the other creditors, and

(b) to be a fraudulent preference,

and be invalid accordingly.

(4) Subsections (1) and (3) shall not affect the rights of any person making title in good faith and for valuable consideration through or under a creditor of the company.

(5) In this section, 'a connected person' means a person who, at the time the transaction was made, was—

(a) a director of the company;

(b) a shadow director of the company;

(c) a person connected, within the meaning of section 26 (1)(a) of the Companies Act, 1990, with a director;

(d) a related company, within the meaning of section 140 of the said Act, or

(e) any trustee of, or surety or guarantor for the debt due to, any person described in paragraph (a), (b), (c) or (d).][a]

Amendments

a CA 1963, s 286 substituted by CA 1990, s 135.

287 Liabilities and rights of certain persons who have been fraudulently preferred

(1) Where—

(a) a company is being wound up; and

(b) anything made or done on or after the operative date is void under section 286 as a fraudulent preference of a person interested in property mortgaged or charged to secure the company's debt;

then (without prejudice to any rights or liabilities arising apart from this section) the person preferred shall be subject to the same liabilities and shall have the same rights as if he had undertaken to be personally liable as surety for the debt to the extent of the charge on the property or the value of his interest, whichever is the less.

(2) The value of the said person's interest shall be determined as at the date of the transaction constituting the fraudulent preference, and shall be determined as if the interest were free of all encumbrances other than those to which the charge for the company's debt was then subject.

(3) On any application made to the court in relation to any payment on the ground that the payment was a fraudulent preference of a surety or guarantor, the court shall have jurisdiction to determine any questions relating to the payment arising between the person to whom the payment was made and the surety or guarantor, and to grant relief in respect thereof notwithstanding that it is not necessary so to do for the purposes of the winding up, and for that purpose may give leave to bring in the surety or guarantor as a third party as in the case of an action for the recovery of the sum paid.

(4) Subsection (3) shall apply, with the necessary modifications, in relation to transactions other than the payment of money as it applies to payments.

288 [Circumstances in which floating charge is invalid

(1) Where a company is being wound up, a floating charge on the undertaking or property of the company created within 12 months before the commencement of the winding up shall, unless it is proved that the company immediately after the creation of the charge was solvent, be invalid, except as to money actually advanced or paid, or the actual price or value of goods or services sold or supplied, to the company at the time of or subsequently to the creation of, and in consideration for, the charge, together with interest on that amount at the rate of 5 per cent per annum.

(2) For the purposes of subsection (1) the value of any goods or services sold or supplied by way of consideration for a floating charge is the amount in money which at the time they were sold or supplied could reasonably have been expected to be obtained for the goods or services in the ordinary course of business and on the same terms (apart from the consideration) as those on which they were sold or supplied to the company.

(3) Where a floating charge on the undertaking or property of a company is created in favour of a connected person, subsection (1) shall apply to such a charge as if the period of 12 months mentioned in that subsection were a period of 2 years.

(4) In this section 'a connected person' means a person who, at the time the transaction was made, was—

(a) a director of the company;

(b) a shadow director of the company;

(c) a person connected, within the meaning of section 26 (1) (a) of the Companies Act, 1990, with a director;

(d) a related company, within the meaning of section 140 of the said Act; or

(e) any trustee of, or any surety or guarantor for the debt due to, any person described in paragraph (a), (b), (c) or (d).][a]

Amendments

a CA 1963, s 288 substituted by CA 1990, s 136.

289 Other circumstances in which floating charge is invalid

(1) Subject to subsection (2), where—

(a) a company is being wound up; and

(b) the company was within 12 months before the commencement of the winding up indebted to any officer of the company; and

(c) such indebtedness was discharged whether wholly or partly by the company or by any other person; and

(d) the company created a floating charge on any of its assets or property within 12 months before the commencement of the winding up in favour of the officer to whom such company was indebted;

then (without prejudice to any rights or liabilities arising apart from this section) such charge shall be invalid to the extent of the repayment referred to in paragraph (c) unless it is proved that the company immediately after the creation of the charge was solvent.

(2) Subsection (1) shall not apply if the charge referred to in paragraph (d) was created before the operative date.

(3) In this section, 'officer' includes the spouse [or civil partner within the meaning of the Civil Partnership and Certain Rights and Obligations of Cohabitants Act 2010][a], child or nominee of an officer.

Amendments

a Words 'or civil partner within the meaning of the Civil Partnership and Certain Rights and Obligations of Cohabitants Act 2010' inserted by Civil Partnership and Certain Rights and Obligations of Cohabitants Act 2010, Sch, Pt 3, Item No. 4.

290 Disclaimer of onerous property in case of company being wound up

(1) Subject to subsections (2) and (5), where any part of the property of a company which is being wound up consists of land of any tenure burdened with onerous covenants, of shares or stock in companies, of unprofitable contracts, or of any other property which is unsaleable or not readily saleable by reason of its binding the possessor thereof to the performance of any onerous act or to the payment of any sum of money, the liquidator of the company, notwithstanding that he has endeavoured to sell or has taken possession of the property or exercised any act of ownership in relation thereto, may, with the leave of the court and subject to the provisions of this section, by writing signed by him, at any time within 12 months after the commencement of the

winding up or such extended period as may be allowed by the court, disclaim the property.

(2) Where any such property as aforesaid has not come to the knowledge of the liquidator within one month after the commencement of the winding up, the power under this section of disclaiming the property may be exercised at any time within 12 months after he has become aware thereof or such extended period as may be allowed by the court.

(3) The disclaimer shall operate to determine, as from the date of disclaimer, the rights, interests and liabilities of the company, and the property of the company, in or in respect of the property disclaimed, but shall not, except so far as is necessary for the purpose of releasing the company and the property of the company from liability, affect the rights or liabilities of any other person.

(4) The court, before or on granting leave to disclaim, may require such notices to be given to persons interested and impose such terms as a condition of granting leave, and make such other order in the matter as the court thinks just.

(5) The liquidator shall not be entitled to disclaim any property under this section in any case where an application in writing has been made to him by any persons interested in the property requiring him to decide whether he will or will not disclaim, and the liquidator has not, within a period of 28 days after the receipt of the application or such further period as may be allowed by the court, given notice to the applicant that he intends to apply to the court for leave to disclaim.

(6) The court may, on the application of any person who is, as against the liquidator, entitled to the benefit or subject to the burden of a contract made with the company, make an order rescinding the contract on such terms as to payment by or to either party of damages for the non-performance of the contract, or otherwise as the court thinks just, and any damages payable under the order to any such person shall be deemed to be a debt proved and admitted in the winding up.

(7) Subject to subsection (8), the court may, on an application by any person who either claims any interest in any disclaimed property or is under any liability not discharged by this Act in respect of any disclaimed property and on hearing any such persons as it thinks fit, make an order for the vesting of the property in or the delivery of the property to any person entitled thereto, or to whom it may seem just that the property should be delivered by way of compensation for such liability as aforesaid, or a trustee for him, and on such terms as the court may think just, and on any such vesting order being made, the property comprised therein shall vest accordingly in the person therein named in that behalf without any conveyance or assignment for the purpose.

(8) Where the property disclaimed is of a leasehold nature, the court shall not make a vesting order in favour of any person claiming under the company, whether as under-lessee or as mortgagee by demise, except upon the terms of making that person—

(a) subject to the same liabilities and obligations as those to which the company was subject under the lease in respect of the property at the commencement of the winding up; or

(b) if the court thinks fit, subject only to the same liabilities and obligations as if the lease had been assigned to that person at that date;

and in either event (if the case so requires), as if the lease had comprised only the property comprised in the vesting order, and any mortgagee or under-lessee declining to accept a vesting order upon such terms shall be excluded from all interest in and security upon the property, and, if there is no person claiming under the company who is willing to accept an order upon such terms, the court shall have power to vest the estate and interest of the company in the property in any person liable either personally or in a representative character, and either alone or jointly with the company, to perform the lessee's covenants in the lease, freed and discharged from all estates, encumbrances and interests created therein by the company.

(9) Any person damaged by the operation of a disclaimer under this section shall be deemed to be a creditor of the company to the amount of the damages, and may accordingly prove the amount as a debt in the winding up.

291 Restriction of rights of creditor as to execution or attachment in case of company being wound up

(1) Subject to subsections (2) to (4), where a creditor has issued execution against the goods or lands of a company or has attached any debt due to the company, and the company is subsequently wound up, he shall not be entitled to retain the benefit of the execution or attachment against the liquidator in the winding up of the company unless he has completed the execution or attachment before the commencement of the winding up.

(2) Where any creditor has had notice of a meeting having been called at which a resolution for voluntary winding up is to be proposed, the date on which the creditor so had notice shall, for the purposes of subsection (1), be substituted for the date of the commencement of the winding up.

(3) A person who purchases in good faith under a sale by the sheriff any goods of a company on which an execution has been levied shall in all cases acquire a good title to them against the liquidator.

(4) The rights conferred by subsection (1) on the liquidator may be set aside by the court in favour of the creditor to such extent and subject to such terms as the court thinks fit.

(5) For the purposes of this section, an execution against goods shall be taken to be completed by seizure and sale, and an attachment of a debt shall be deemed to be completed by receipt of the debt, and an execution against land shall be deemed to be completed by seizure and, in the case of an equitable interest, by the appointment of a receiver.

(6) Nothing in this section shall give any validity to any payment constituting a fraudulent preference.

(7) In this section, 'goods' includes all chattels personal and 'sheriff' includes any officer charged with the execution of a writ or other process.

292 Duties of sheriff as to goods taken in execution

(1) Subject to subsection (3), where any goods of a company are taken in execution, and, before the sale thereof or the completion of the execution by the receipt or recovery of the full amount of the levy, notice is served on the sheriff that a provisional liquidator has been appointed or that a winding-up order has been made or that a resolution for voluntary winding up has been passed, the sheriff shall, on being so required, deliver the

goods and any money seized or received in part satisfaction of the execution to the liquidator, but the costs of the execution shall be a first charge on the goods or the money so delivered, and the liquidator may sell the goods or a sufficient part thereof for the purpose of satisfying that charge.

(2) Subject to subsection (3), where under an execution in respect of a judgment for a sum exceeding [€25.39][a] the goods of a company are sold or money is paid in order to avoid sale, the sheriff shall deduct the costs of the execution from the proceeds of the sale or the money paid and retain the balance for 14 days, and if within that time notice is served on him of a petition for the winding up of the company having been presented or of a meeting having been called at which there is to be proposed a resolution for the voluntary winding up of the company and an order is made or a resolution is passed, as the case may be, for the winding up of the company, the sheriff shall pay the balance to the liquidator who shall be entitled to retain it as against the execution creditor.

(3) The rights conferred by this section on the liquidator may be set aside by the court in favour of the creditor to such extent and subject to such terms as the court thinks fit.

(4) In this section, 'goods' includes all chattels personal and 'sheriff' includes any officer charged with the execution of a writ or other process.

Amendments

a £20 converted to €25.39 by Council Regulations (EC) No 1103/97, No 974/98 and No 2866/98 and the Economic and Monetary Union Act 1998, s 6.

Offences antecedent to or in the course of Winding Up

293 Offences by officers of companies in liquidation

(1) Subject to subsection (2), if any person, being a past or present officer of a company which at the time of the commission of the alleged offence is being wound up, whether by the court or voluntarily, or is subsequently ordered to be wound up by the court or subsequently passes a resolution for voluntary winding up—

(a) does not to the best of his knowledge and belief fully and truly disclose to the liquidator when he requests such disclosure all the property, real and personal, of the company and how and to whom and for what consideration and when the company disposed of any part thereof, except such part as has been disposed of in the ordinary way of the business of the company; or

(b) does not deliver up to the liquidator, or as he directs, all such part of the real and personal property of the company as is in his custody or under his control, and which he is required by law to deliver up; or

(c) does not deliver up to the liquidator, or as he directs, all books and papers in his custody or under his control belonging to the company and which he is required by law to deliver up; or

(d) within 12 months next before the commencement of the winding up or at any time thereafter conceals any part of the property of the company to the value of [€12.70][a] or upwards, or conceals any debt due to or from the company; or

(e) within 12 months next before the commencement of the winding up or at any time thereafter fraudulently removes any part of the property of the company to the value of [€12.70][a] or upwards; or

(f) makes any material omission in any statement relating to the affairs of the company; or

(g) knowing or believing that a false debt has been proved by any person under the winding up, fails for the period of a month to inform the liquidator thereof; or

(h) after the commencement of the winding up prevents the production of any book or paper affecting or relating to the property or affairs of the company; or

(i) within 12 months next before the commencement of the winding up or at any time thereafter conceals, destroys, mutilates or falsifies or is privy to the concealment, destruction, mutilation or falsification of any book or paper affecting or relating to the property or affairs of the company; or

(j) within 12 months next before the commencement of the winding up or at any time thereafter makes or is privy to the making of any false entry in any book or paper affecting or relating to the property or affairs of the company; or

(k) within 12 months next before the commencement of the winding up or at any time thereafter fraudulently parts with, alters or makes any omission in, or is privy to the fraudulent parting with, altering or making any omission in, any document affecting or relating to the property or affairs of the company; or

(l) after the commencement of the winding up or at any meeting of the creditors of the company within 12 months next before the commencement of the winding up attempts to account for any part of the property of the company by fictitious losses or expenses; or

(m) has within 12 months next before the commencement of the winding up or at any time thereafter, by any false representation or other fraud, obtained any property for or on behalf of the company on credit which the company does not subsequently pay for; or

(n) within 12 months next before the commencement of the winding up or at any time thereafter, under the false pretence that the company is carrying on its business, obtains on credit for or on behalf of the company, any property which the company does not subsequently pay for; or

(o) within 12 months next before the commencement of the winding up or at any time thereafter pawns, pledges or disposes of any property of the company which has been obtained on credit and has not been paid for, unless such pawning, pledging or disposing is in the ordinary way of business of the company; or

(p) is guilty of any false representation or other fraud for the purpose of obtaining the consent of the creditors of the company or any of them to an agreement with reference to the affairs of the company or to the winding up;

he shall in the case of an offence mentioned in paragraph (m), (n) or (o), be liable, on conviction on indictment, to penal servitude for a term not exceeding 5 years or to imprisonment for a term not exceeding [5][b] years or to a fine not exceeding [€12,697.38][d] or to both such penal servitude or imprisonment and such fine and, in the case of an offence mentioned in any other paragraph, be liable, on conviction on indictment, to imprisonment for a term not exceeding [5][b] years or to a fine not exceeding [€6,348.70][c] or to both, or, in the case of any offence under this subsection, be liable, on summary conviction, to imprisonment for a term not exceeding 6 months or to a [class C fine][e] or to both.

(2) It shall be a good defence to a charge under any of paragraphs (a), (b), (c), (d), (f), (n) and (o) of subsection (1), if the accused proves that he had no intent to defraud and to a charge under any of paragraphs (h), (i) and (j) of subsection (1), if he proves that he had no intent to conceal the state of affairs of the company or to defeat the law.

(3) Where any person pawns, pledges or disposes of any property in circumstances which amount to an offence under paragraph (o) of subsection (1), every person who takes in pawn or pledge or otherwise receives the property knowing it to be pawned, pledged or disposed of in such circumstances as aforesaid shall be guilty of an offence and shall be liable to be punished in the same way as if he had been guilty of an offence under the said paragraph (o).

(4) For the purposes of this section, 'officer' shall include any person in accordance with whose directions or instructions the directors of a company have been accustomed to act.

Amendments

a £10 converted to €12.70 by Council Regulations (EC) No 1103/97, No 974/98 and No 2866/98 and the Economic and Monetary Union Act 1998, s 6.

b '2 years' increased to '5 years' by CA 1990, s 240(8) as inserted by CLEA 2001, s 104.

c '£5,000' substituted for '£1,000' by C(A)A 1982, Sch 1 and converted to €6,348.69 by Council Regulations (EC) No 1103/97, No 974/98 and No 2866/98 and the Economic and Monetary Union Act 1998, s 6, and multiplied by a multiplier of 2 pursuant to Fines Act 2010, s 9.

d '£2,500' substituted for '£500' by C(A)A 1982, Sch 1 and converted to €3,174.35 by Council Regulations (EC) No 1103/97, No 974/98 and No 2866/98 and the Economic and Monetary Union Act 1998, s 6, and multiplied by a multiplier of 2 pursuant to Fines Act 2010, s 9.

e '£500' substituted for '£100' by C(A)A 1982, Sch 1 and converted to €634.87 by Council Regulations (EC) No 1103/97, No 974/98 and No 2866/98 and the Economic and Monetary Union Act 1998, s 6; the above being implicitly substituted, by Fines Act 2010, s 6, for a fine not exceeding the aforesaid amount. A class C fine currently means a fine not exceeding €2,500.

---

294 Alteration or falsification of books

[...][a]

Amendments

a Repealed by CA 1990, s 6. See instead CA 1990, s 243.

---

295 Frauds by officers of companies which have gone into liquidation

If any person, being at the time of the commission of the alleged offence an officer of a company which is subsequently ordered to be wound up by the court or subsequently passes a resolution for voluntary winding up—

(a) has by false pretences or by means of any other fraud induced any person to give credit to the company;

(b) with intent to defraud creditors of the company, has made or caused to be made any gift or transfer of or charge on, or has caused or connived at the levying of any execution against, the property of the company;

(c) with intent to defraud creditors of the company, has concealed or removed any part of the property of the company since or within 2 months before the date of any unsatisfied judgment or order for payment of money obtained against the company;

he shall be liable, on conviction on indictment, to imprisonment for a term not exceeding [5][a] years or to a fine not exceeding [€6,348.70][b] or to both or, on summary conviction, to imprisonment for a term not exceeding 6 months or to a [class C fine][c] or to both.

Amendments

a '2 years' increased to '5 years' by CA 1990, s 240(8) as inserted by CLEA 2001, s 104.

b '£2,500' substituted for '£500' by C(A)A 1982, Sch 1 and converted to €3,174.35 by Council Regulations (EC) No 1103/97, No 974/98 and No 2866/98 and the Economic and Monetary Union Act 1998, s 6, and multiplied by a multiplier of 2 pursuant to Fines Act 2010, s 9.

c '£500' substituted for '£100' by C(A)A 1982, Sch 1 and increased to £1,500 by CA 1990, s 240(7) as inserted by CLEA 2001, s 104 and converted to €1,904.61 by Council Regulations (EC) No 1103/97, No 974/98 and No 2866/98 and the Economic and Monetary Union Act 1998, s 6; the above being implicitly substituted, by Fines Act 2010, s 6, for a fine not exceeding the aforesaid amount. A class C fine currently means a fine not exceeding €2,500.

---

296 Liability where proper books of account not kept

[…][a]

Amendments

a CA 1963, s 296 repealed by CA 1990, s 6.

---

297 [Criminal liability of persons concerned for fraudulent trading of company

(1) If any person is knowingly a party to the carrying on of the business of a company with intent to defraud creditors of the company or creditors of any other person or for any fraudulent purpose, that person shall be guilty of an offence.

(2) Any person who is convicted of an offence under this section shall be liable–

(a) on summary conviction to imprisonment for a term not exceeding 12 months or to a [class C fine][b] or to both, or

(b) on conviction on indictment, to imprisonment for a term not exceeding 7 years or to a fine not exceeding [€111,102.08][c] or to both.][a]

Amendments

a CA 1963, s 297 substituted by CA 1990, s 137.

b £1,000 increased to £1,500 by CA 1990, s 240(7) as inserted by CLEA 2001, s 104 and increased to €1,904.61 by Council Regulations (EC) No 1103/97, No 974/98 and No 2866/98 and the Economic and Monetary Union Act 1998, s 6; the above being implicitly substituted, by Fines Act 2010, s 6, for a fine not exceeding the aforesaid amount. A class C fine currently means a fine not exceeding €2,500.

c £50,000 converted to €63,486.90 by Council Regulations (EC) No 1103/97, No 974/98 and No 2866/98 and the Economic and Monetary Union Act 1998, s 6, and multiplied by a multiplier of 1.75 pursuant to Fines Act 2010, s 9.

[297A Civil liability of persons concerned for fraudulent or reckless trading of company

(1) If in the course of winding up of a company or in the course of proceedings under the Companies (Amendment) Act, 1990, it appears that—

(a) any person was, while an officer of the company, knowingly a party to the carrying on of any business of the company in a reckless manner; or

(b) any person was knowingly a party to the carrying on of any business of the company with intent to defraud creditors of the company, or creditors of any other person or for any fraudulent purpose;

the court, on the application of the receiver, examiner, liquidator or any creditor or contributory of the company, may, if it thinks it proper to do so, declare that such person shall be personally responsible, without any limitation of liability, for all or any part of the debts or other liabilities of the company as the court may direct.

(2) Without prejudice to the generality of subsection (1) (a), an officer of a company shall be deemed to have been knowingly a party to the carrying on of any business of the company in a reckless manner if—

(a) he was a party to the carrying on of such business and, having regard to the general knowledge, skill and experience that may reasonably be expected of a person in his position, he ought to have known that his actions or those of the company would cause loss to the creditors of the company, or any of them, or

(b) he was a party to the contracting of a debt by the company and did not honestly believe on reasonable grounds that the company would be able to pay the debt when it fell due for payment as well as all its other debts (taking into account the contingent and prospective liabilities).

(3) Notwithstanding anything contained in subsection (1) the court may grant a declaration on the grounds set out in paragraph (a) of that subsection only if—

(a) paragraph (a), (b) or (c) of section 214 applies to the company concerned, and

(b) an applicant for such a declaration, being a creditor or contributory of the company, or any person on whose behalf such application is made, suffered loss or damage as a consequence of any behaviour mentioned in subsection (1).

(4) In deciding whether it is proper to make an order on the ground set out in subsection (2) (b), the court shall have regard to whether the creditor in question was, at the time the debt was incurred, aware of the company's financial state of affairs and, notwithstanding such awareness, nevertheless assented to the incurring of the debt.

(5) On the hearing of an application under this section, the applicant may himself give evidence or call witnesses.

(6) Where it appears to the court that any person in respect of whom a declaration has been sought under subsection (1) (a), has acted honestly and responsibly in relation to the conduct of the affairs of the company or any matter or matters on the ground of which such declaration is sought to be made, the court may, having regard to all the circumstances of the case, relieve him either wholly or in part, from personal liability on such terms as it may think fit.

(7) Where the court makes any such declaration, it may—

(a) give such further directions as it thinks proper for the purpose of giving effect to that declaration and in particular may make provision for making the liability of any such person under the declaration a charge on any debt or obligation due from the company to him, or on any mortgage or charge or any interest in any mortgage or charge on any assets of the company held by or vested in him or any company or person on his behalf, or any person claiming as assignee from or through the person liable or any company or person acting on his behalf, and may from time to time make such further order as may be necessary for the purpose of enforcing any charge imposed under this subsection;

(b) provide that sums recovered under this section shall be paid to such person or classes of persons, for such purposes, in such amounts or proportions at such time or times and in such respective priorities among themselves as such declaration may specify.

(8) Subsection (1) (a) shall not apply in relation to the carrying on of the business of a company during a period when the company is under the protection of the court.

(9) This section shall have effect notwithstanding that—

(a) the person in respect of whom the declaration has been sought under subsection (1) may be criminally liable in respect of the matters on the ground of which such declaration is to be made; or

(b) any matter or matters on the ground of which the declaration under subsection (1) is to be made have occurred outside the State.

(10) For the purposes of this section—

'assignee' includes any person to whom or in whose favour, by the directions of the person liable, the debt, obligation, mortgage or charge was created, issued or transferred or the interest created, but does not include an assignee for valuable consideration (not including consideration by way of marriage) given in good faith and without notice of any of the matters on the ground of which the declaration is made;

'company' includes any body which may be wound up under the Companies Acts; and

'officer' includes any auditor, liquidator, receiver, or shadow director.][a]

Amendments

a CA 1963, s 297A inserted by CA 1990, s 138.

298 Power of court to assess damages against directors

[(1) Subsection (2) applies if in the course of winding up a company it appears that any person who has taken part in the formation or promotion of the company, or any past or present officer, liquidator, receiver or examiner of the company, has misapplied or retained or become liable or accountable for any money or property of the company, or has been guilty of any misfeasance or other breach of duty or trust in relation to the company.

(2) The court may, on the application of the liquidator, or any creditor or contributory, examine the conduct of the promoter, officer, liquidator, receiver, or examiner and compel him—

(a) to repay or restore the money or property or any part thereof respectively with interest at such rate as the court thinks just, or

(b) to contribute such sum to the assets of the company by way of compensation in respect of the misapplication, retainer, misfeasance or other breach of duty as the court thinks just.

(3) This section has effect notwithstanding that the offence is one for which the offender may be criminally liable.][a]

Amendments

a CA 1963, s 298 substituted by CA 1990, s 142.

299 Prosecution of criminal offences committed by officers and members of company

[(1) If it appears to the court in the course of a winding-up by the court that any past or present officer, or any member, of the company has been guilty of an offence in relation to the company for which he is criminally liable, the court may either on the application of any person interested in the winding-up or of its own motion direct the liquidator to refer the matter to the Director of Public Prosecutions and in such a case the liquidator shall furnish to the Director of Public Prosecutions such information and give to him such access to and facilities for inspecting and taking any copies of any documents, being information or documents in the possession or under the control of the liquidator and relating to the matter in question, as the Director of Public Prosecutions may require.][a]

[(1A) Where the court directs a liquidator, in accordance with subsection (1), to refer a matter to the Director of Public Prosecutions, it shall also direct the liquidator to refer the matter to the Director and, in such a case, the liquidator shall furnish to the Director such information, and give to the Director such access to and facilities for inspecting and taking copies of any documents, being information or documents in the possession or under the control of the liquidator and relating to the matter in question, as the Director may require.][b]

(2) If it appears to the liquidator in the course of a voluntary winding up that any past or present officer, or any member, of the company has been guilty of any offence in relation to the company for which he is criminally liable, he shall forthwith report the matter to the [Director of Public Prosecutions][b] and shall furnish to the [Director of Public Prosecutions][b] such information and give to him such access to and facilities for inspecting and taking copies of any documents, being information or documents in the possession or under the control of the liquidator and relating to the matter in question, as the [Director of Public Prosecutions][b] may require.

[(2A) Where a liquidator, in accordance with subsection (2), reports a matter to the Director of Public Prosecutions, the liquidator shall also refer the matter to the Director and, in such a case, the liquidator shall furnish to the Director such information and give to the Director such access to and facilities for inspecting and taking copies of any documents, being information or documents in the possession or under the control of the liquidator and relating to the matter in question, as the Director may require.][b]

(3) If it appears to the court in the course of a voluntary winding up that any past or present officer, or any member, of the company has been guilty as aforesaid, and that no report relating to the matter has been made by the liquidator to [the Director of Public Prosecutions under subsection (2), or to the Director under subsection (2A)][b], the court may, on the application of any person interested in the winding up or of its own motion, direct the liquidator to make such a report, and on a report being made accordingly, this section shall have effect as though the report had been made [in pursuance of subsection (2) or subsection (2A), as the case may be][b].

(4) If, where any matter is reported or referred to the [Director of Public Prosecutions and the Director under this section, either the Director of Public Prosecutions or the Director considers][b] that the case is one in which a prosecution ought to be instituted and institutes proceedings accordingly, it shall be the duty of the liquidator and of every officer and agent of the company past and present (other than the defendant in the proceedings) to give all assistance in connection with the prosecution which he is reasonably able to give.

For the purposes of this subsection, 'agent' in relation to a company shall be deemed to include any banker or solicitor of the company and any person employed by the company as auditor, whether that person is or is not an officer of the company.

(5) If any person fails or neglects to give assistance in the manner required by subsection (4), the court may, on the application [of the Director of Public Prosecutions or of the Director][b], direct that person to comply with the requirements of that subsection, and where any such application is made in relation to a liquidator the court may, unless it appears that the failure or neglect to comply was due to the liquidator not having in his hands sufficient assets of the company to enable him so to do, direct that the costs of the application shall be borne by the liquidator personally.

Amendments

a CA 1963, s 299(1) substituted by CA 1990, s 143.

b Sub-ss (1A) and (2A) inserted and words substituted by CLEA 2001, s 51.

Supplementary Provisions as to Winding Up

300 Disqualification for appointment as liquidator

A body corporate shall not be qualified for appointment as liquidator of a company whether in a winding up by the court or in a voluntary winding up and—

(a) any appointment made in contravention of this provision shall be void; and

(b) any body corporate which acts as liquidator of a company [shall be guilty of an offence and liable to a [class C fine][a]][b].

Amendments

a '£500' substituted for '£100' by C(A)A 1982, Sch 1, increased to '£1,500' by CA 1990, s 240(7) as inserted by CLEA 2001, s 104(c) and £1,500 converted to €1,904.61 by Council Regulations (EC) No 1103/97, No 974/98 and No 2866/98 and the Economic and Monetary Union Act 1998, s 6; the above being implicitly substituted, by Fines Act 2010, s 6, for a fine not exceeding the aforesaid amount. A class C fine currently means a fine not exceeding €2,500.

b Words in CA 1963, s 300(b) substituted by C(AA)A 2003, s 57 and Sch 2, para 1.

[300A Disqualification for appointment as liquidator

(1) None of the following persons shall be qualified for appointment as liquidator of a company—

(a) a person who is, or who has within 12 months of the commencement of the winding up been, an officer or servant of the company;

(b) except with the leave of the court, a parent, spouse [or civil partner within the meaning of the Civil Partnership and Certain Rights and Obligations of Cohabitants Act 2010][b], brother, sister or child of an officer of the company;

(c) a person who is a partner or in the employment of an officer or servant of the company;

(d) a person who is not qualified by virtue of this subsection for appointment as liquidator of any other body corporate which is that company's subsidiary or holding company or a subsidiary of that company's holding company, or would be so disqualified if the body corporate were a company.

References in this subsection to an officer or servant of the company include references to an auditor.

(2) An application for leave under subsection (1)(b) shall be supported by such evidence as the court may require.

(3) If a liquidator becomes disqualified by virtue of this section he shall thereupon vacate his office and give notice in writing within 14 days to—

(a) the court in a court winding up,

(b) the company in a members' voluntary winding up,

(c) the company and the creditors in a creditors' voluntary winding up,

that he has vacated it by reason of such disqualification.

(4) Any person who acts as a liquidator when disqualified by this section from so doing or who fails to comply with subsection (3), if that subsection applies to him, shall be guilty of an offence and shall be liable—

(a) on summary conviction, to a [class C fine][c] and, for continued contravention, a daily default [class E fine][d];

(b) on conviction on indictment, to a fine of [€22,220.42][e] and, for continued contravention, a daily default fine not exceeding [€555.50][f].

(5) This section shall not apply to a winding-up commenced before the commencement of section 146 of the Companies Act, 1990].[a]

Amendments

a CA 1963, s 300A inserted by CA 1990, s 146.

b Words 'or civil partner within the meaning of the Civil Partnership and Certain Rights and Obligations of Cohabitants Act 2010' inserted by Civil Partnership and Certain Rights and Obligations of Cohabitants Act 2010, Sch, Pt 3, Item No. 5.

c '£1,000' increased to '£1,500' by CA 1990, s 240(7) as inserted by CLEA 2001, s 104(c) and converted to €1,904.61 by Council Regulations (EC) No 1103/97, No 974/98 and No 2866/98 and the Economic and Monetary Union Act 1998, s 6; the above being implicitly substituted, by Fines Act 2010, s 6, for a fine not exceeding the aforesaid amount. A class C fine currently means a fine not exceeding €2,500.

d £50 converted to €63.49 by Council Regulations (EC) No 1103/97, No 974/98 and No 2866/98 and the Economic and Monetary Union Act 1998, s 6; as implicitly substituted, by Fines Act 2010, s 8, for a fine not exceeding the aforesaid amount. A class E fine currently means a fine not exceeding €500.

e £10,000 converted to €12,697.38 by Council Regulations (EC) No 1103/97, No 974/98 and No 2866/98 and the Economic and Monetary Union Act 1998, s 6, and multiplied by a multiplier of 1.75 pursuant to Fines Act 2010, s 9.

f £250 converted to €317.43 by Council Regulations (EC) No 1103/97, No 974/98 and No 2866/98 and the Economic and Monetary Union Act 1998, s 6, and multiplied by a multiplier of 1.75 pursuant to Fines Act 2010, s 9.

---

301 Corrupt inducement affecting appointment as liquidator

Any person who gives or agrees or offers to give to any member or creditor of a company any valuable consideration with a view to securing his own appointment or nomination or to securing or preventing the appointment or nomination of some person other than himself as the company's liquidator [shall be guilty of an offence and liable to a [class C fine][a]].[b]

Amendments

a '£500' substituted for '£100' by C(A)A 1982, Sch 1, increased to '£1,500' by CA 1990, s 240(7) as inserted by CLEA 2001, s 104(c) and converted to €1,904.61 by Council Regulations (EC) No 1103/97, No 974/98 and No 2866/98 and the Economic and Monetary Union Act 1998, s 6; the above being implicitly substituted, by Fines Act 2010, s 6, for a fine not exceeding the aforesaid amount. A class C fine currently means a fine not exceeding €2,500.

b Words substituted by C(AA)A 2003, s 57 and Sch 2.

[301A Disclosure of interest by creditors, etc. at creditors' meeting

(1) Where, at a meeting of creditors, a resolution is proposed for the appointment of a liquidator, any creditor who has a connection with the proposed liquidator shall, before the resolution is put, make such connection known to the chairman of the meeting who shall disclose that fact to the meeting, together with details thereof.

(2) Subsection (1) shall also apply to any person at the meeting, being a representative of a creditor and entitled to vote on the resolution on his behalf.

(3) Where the chairman of a meeting of creditors has any such connection as is mentioned in subsection (1), he shall disclose that fact to the meeting, together with details thereof.

(4) For the purposes of this section, a person has a connection with a proposed liquidator if he is—

(a) a parent, spouse[, civil partner within the meaning of the Civil Partnership and Certain Rights and Obligations of Cohabitants Act 2010][b], brother, sister or child of, or

(b) employed by, or a partner of,

the proposed liquidator.

(5) A person who fails to comply with this section [shall be guilty of an offence and liable to a [class C fine][c]].[d]

(6) In exercising its jurisdiction under sections 267 (2) or 272 (2) (which relate to the appointment or removal of a liquidator) the court may have regard to any failure to comply with this section.][a]

Amendments

a CA 1963, s 301A inserted by CA 1990, s 147.

b Words ', civil partner within the meaning of the Civil Partnership and Certain Rights and Obligations of Cohabitants Act 2010' inserted by Civil Partnership and Certain Rights and Obligations of Cohabitants Act 2010, Sch, Pt 1, Item No. 2.

c '£1,000' increased to '£1,500' by CA 1990, s 240(7) as inserted by CLEA 2001, s 104(c). £1,500 converted to €1,904.61 by Council Regulations (EC) No 1103/97, No 974/98 and No 2866/98 and the Economic and Monetary Union Act 1998, s 6; the above being implicitly substituted, by Fines Act 2010, s 6, for a fine not exceeding the aforesaid amount. A class C fine currently means a fine not exceeding €2,500.

d Words in CA 1963, s 301A(5) substituted by C(AA)A 2003, s 57 and Sch 2, para 1.

302 Enforcement of duty of liquidator to make returns

(1) If any liquidator who has made any default in filing, delivering or making any return, account or other document, or in giving any notice which he is by law required to file, deliver, make or give, fails to make good the default within 14 days after the service on him of a notice requiring him to do so, [or such greater period as may be specified in the notice],[a] the court may, on an application made to the court by any contributory or creditor of the company or by the registrar of companies, make an order directing the liquidator to make good the default within such time as may be specified in the order.

(2) Any such order may provide that all costs of and incidental to the application shall be borne by the liquidator.

(3) Nothing in this section shall be taken to prejudice the operation of any enactment imposing penalties on a liquidator in respect of any such default as aforesaid.

Amendments

a Words inserted by IFCMPA 2005, s 63.

---

303 Notification that a company is in liquidation

(1) Where a company is being wound up, whether by the court or voluntarily, every invoice, order for goods or business letter issued by or on behalf of the company or a liquidator of the company, or a receiver of the property of the company, being a document on or in which the name of the company appears, shall contain a statement that the company is being wound up.

(2) If default is made in complying with this section, the company and any of the following persons who knowingly and wilfully authorises or permits the default, namely, any officer of the company, any liquidator of the company and any receiver, [shall be guilty of an offence and liable to a [class C fine][a]].[b]

Amendments

a '£250' substituted for '£50' by C(A)A 1982, Sch 1, increased to '£1,500' by CA 1990, s 240(7) as inserted by CLEA 2001, s 104(c) and converted to €1,904.61 by Council Regulations (EC) No 1103/97, No 974/98 and No 2866/98 and the Economic and Monetary Union Act 1998, s 6; the above being implicitly substituted, by Fines Act 2010, s 6, for a fine not exceeding the aforesaid amount. A class C fine currently means a fine not exceeding €2,500.

b Words in CA 1963, s 303(2) substituted by C(AA)A 2003, s 57 and Sch 2, para 1.

---

304 Books of company to be evidence

When a company is being wound up, all books and papers of the company and of the liquidators shall, as between the contributories of the company, be *prima facie* evidence of the truth of all matters purporting to be recorded therein.

305 Disposal of books and papers of company in winding up

(1) When a company has been wound up and is about to be dissolved, the books and papers of the company and of the liquidator may be disposed of as follows—

(a) in the case of a winding up by the court, in such way as the court directs;

(b) in the case of a members' voluntary winding up, in such way as the company by special resolution directs, and in the case of a creditors' voluntary winding up, in such way as the committee of inspection or, if there is no such committee, as the creditors of the company, may direct, so, however, that such books and papers shall be retained by the liquidator for a period of 3 years from the date of the dissolution of the company and, in the absence of any direction as to their disposal, he may then dispose of them as he thinks fit.

(2) If a liquidator fails to comply with the requirements of this section he [shall be guilty of an offence and liable to a [class C fine][a]].[b]

Amendments

a '£500' substituted for '£100' by C(A)A 1982, Sch 1, increased to '£1,500' by CA 1990, s 240(7) as inserted by CLEA 2001, s 104(c) and converted to €1,904.61 by Council Regulations (EC) No 1103/97, No 974/98 and No 2866/98 and the Economic and Monetary Union Act 1998, s 6; the above being implicitly substituted, by Fines Act 2010, s 6, for a fine not exceeding the aforesaid amount. A class C fine currently means a fine not exceeding €2,500.

b Words in CA 1963, s 305(2) substituted by C(AA)A 2003, s 57 and Sch 2, para 1.

---

306 Information about progress of liquidation

(1) If, where a company is being wound up, the winding up is not concluded within 2 years after its commencement, the liquidator shall, at such intervals as may be prescribed, until the winding up is concluded, send to the registrar of companies a statement in the prescribed form and containing the prescribed particulars about the proceedings in and position of the liquidation.

(2) If a liquidator fails to comply with this section, he [shall be guilty of an offence and liable to a [class C fine][a]].[b]

(3) An offence under this section may be prosecuted by the registrar of companies.

Amendments

a '£1,000' substituted for '£500' by CA 1990, s 145 and increased to '£1,500' by CA 1990, s 240(7) as inserted by CLEA 2001, s 104(c). £1,500 converted to €1,904.61 by Council Regulations (EC) No 1103/97, No 974/98 and No 2866/98 and the Economic and Monetary Union Act 1998, s 6; the above being implicitly substituted, by Fines Act 2010, s 6, for a fine not exceeding the aforesaid amount. A class C fine currently means a fine not exceeding €2,500.

b Words in CA 1963, s 306(2) substituted by C(AA)A 2003, s 57 and Sch 2, para 1.

---

307 Unclaimed dividends and balances to be paid into Companies Liquidation Account

(1) Where a company has been wound up voluntarily and is about to be dissolved, the liquidator shall lodge to an account to be known as The Companies Liquidation Account

in the Bank of Ireland in such manner as may be prescribed by rules of court the whole unclaimed dividends admissible to proof and unapplied or undistributable balances.

(2) The Companies Liquidation Account shall be under the control of the court.

(3) Any application by a person claiming to be entitled to any dividend or payment out of a lodgment made in pursuance of subsection (1), and any payment out of such lodgment in satisfaction of such claim, shall be made in manner prescribed by rules of court.

(4) At the expiration of 7 years from the date of any lodgment made in pursuance of subsection (1), the amount of the lodgment remaining unclaimed shall be paid into the Exchequer, but where the court is satisfied that any person claiming is entitled to any dividend or payment out of the moneys paid into the Exchequer, it may order payment of the same and the Minister for Finance shall issue such sum as may be necessary to provide for that payment.

308 Resolutions passed at adjourned meetings of creditors and contributories

Where a resolution is passed at an adjourned meeting of any creditors or contributories of a company, the resolution shall, for all purposes, be treated as having been passed on the date on which it was in fact passed and shall not be deemed to have been passed on any earlier date.

309 Meetings to ascertain wishes of creditors and contributories

(1) The court may, as to all matters relating to the winding up of a company, have regard to the wishes of the creditors or contributories of the company, as proved to it by any sufficient evidence, and may, if it thinks fit, for the purpose of ascertaining those wishes, direct meetings of the creditors or contributories to be called, held and conducted in such manner as the court directs, and may appoint a person to act as chairman of any such meeting and report the result thereof to the court.

(2) In the case of creditors, regard shall be had to the value of each creditor's debt.

(3) In the case of contributories, regard shall be had to the number of votes conferred on each contributory by this Act or the articles.

Provisions as to Dissolution

310 Power of court to declare dissolution of company void

(1) Where a company has been dissolved, the court may at any time within 2 years of the date of the dissolution, on an application being made for the purpose by the liquidator of the company or by any other person who appears to the court to be interested, make an order, upon such terms as the court thinks fit, declaring the dissolution to have been void, and thereupon such proceedings may be taken as might have been taken if the company had not been dissolved.

(2) It shall be the duty of the person on whose application the order was made, within 14 days after the making of the order, or such further time as the court may allow, to deliver to the registrar of companies for registration an office copy of the order, and if that person fails to do so, he [shall be guilty of an offence and liable to a [class C fine][a]].[b]

Amendments

a '£25' substituted for '£5' by C(A)A 1982, Sch 1, increased to £1,500 by CA 1990, s 240(7) as inserted by CLEA 2001, s 104 (c) and converted to €1,904.61 by Council Regulations (EC) No 1103\97, No 974\98 and No 2866\98 and the Economic and Monetary Union Act 1998, s 6; the above being implicitly substituted, by Fines Act 2010, s 6, for a fine not exceeding the aforesaid amount. A class C fine currently means a fine not exceeding €2,500.

b 'shall be guilty of an offence and liable to a fine' substituted for 'shall be liable to a fine' by CA(A)A 2003, s 57 and Sch 2.

311 Power of registrar to strike defunct company off register

[(1) Where the registrar of companies has reasonable cause to believe that a company is not carrying on business, he may send to the company by post a registered letter inquiring whether the company is carrying on business and stating that, if an answer is not received within one month from the date of that letter, a notice will be published in [the Companies Registration Office Gazette][a] with a view to striking the name of the company off the register.

(2) If the registrar either receives an answer to the effect that the company is not carrying on business or does not within one month after sending the letter receive any answer, he may publish in [the Companies Registration Office Gazette][a] and send to the company by registered post a notice that at the expiration of one month from the date of that notice, the name of the company mentioned therein will, unless cause is shown to the contrary, be struck off the register, and the company will be dissolved.

(3) If in any case where a company is being wound up the registrar has reasonable cause to believe either that no liquidator is acting, or that the affairs of the company are fully wound up, and the returns required to be made by the liquidator have not been made for a period of 6 consecutive months, the registrar shall publish in [the Companies Registration Office Gazette][a] and send to the company or the liquidator, if any, a like notice as is provided in subsection (2).

(4) ...][b]

(5) Subject to subsections (6) and (7), at the expiration of the time mentioned in the notice, the registrar may, unless cause to the contrary is previously shown by the company, strike its name off the register, and shall publish notice thereof in [the Companies Registration Office Gazette][a] and on the publication in [the Companies Registration Office Gazette][a] of this notice, the company shall be dissolved.

(6) The liability, if any, of every director, officer and member of the company shall continue and may be enforced as if the company had not been dissolved.

(7) Nothing in subsection (5) or (6) shall affect the power of the court to wind up a company the name of which has been struck off the register.

(8) If a company or any member or creditor thereof feels aggrieved by the company having been struck off the register, the court, on an application made (on notice to the registrar) by the company or member or creditor before the expiration of 20 years from the publication in [the Companies Registration Office Gazette][a] of the notice aforesaid, may, if satisfied that the company was at the time of the striking off carrying on business

or otherwise that it is just that the company be restored to the register, order that the name of the company be restored to the register, and upon an office copy of the order being delivered to the registrar for registration, the company shall be deemed to have continued in existence as if its name had not been struck off; and the court may by the order give such directions and make such provisions as seem just for placing the company and all other persons in the same position as nearly as may be [as if the name of the company had not been struck off or make such other order as seems just (and such other order is referred to in subsection (8A) as an 'alternative order').][c]

[(8A) An alternative order may, if the court considers it appropriate that it should do so, include a provision that, as respects a debt or liability incurred by, or on behalf of, the company during the period when it stood struck off the register, the officers of the company or such one or more of them as is or are specified in the order shall be liable for the whole or part (as the court thinks just) of the debt or liability.][d]

(9) A notice to be sent under this section to a liquidator may be addressed to the liquidator at his last known place of business, and a letter or notice to be sent under this section to a company may be addressed to the company at its registered office, or, if no office has been registered, to the care of some officer of the company, or, if there is no officer of the company whose name and address are known to the registrar of companies, may be sent to each of the persons who subscribed the memorandum, addressed to him at the address mentioned in the memorandum.

Amendments

a 'the Companies Registration Office Gazette' substituted for '*Iris Oifigiúil*' by IFCMPA 2005, s 72.

b CA 1963, s 311(1), (2), (3) substituted and sub-s (4) deleted by C(A)A 1982, s 11.

c The words 'as if the name of the company had not been struck off or make such other order as seems just (and such other order is referred to in subsection (8A) as an 'alternative order')' substituted for 'as if the name of the company had not been struck off' in CA 1963, s 311(8) by C(A)(No 2)A 1999, s 49, para (a).

d CA 1963, s 311(8A) inserted by C(A)(No 2)A 1999, s 49, para (b).

[311A Restoration to register of company struck off

[(1) Without prejudice to the provisions of section 311 (8) of this Act or subsection or (7) of section 12B or subsection 1 of section 12C of the Companies (Amendment) Act, 1982][b], if a company feels aggrieved by having been struck off the register, the registrar of companies, on an application made in the prescribed form by the company before the expiration of twelve months after the publication in [the Companies Registration Office Gazette][c] of the notice striking the company name from the register, and provided he has received all annual returns outstanding, if any, from the company, may restore the name of the company to the register.

(2) Upon the registration of an application under subsection (1) and on payment of such fees as may be prescribed, the company shall be deemed to have continued in existence as if its name had not been struck off.

(3) Subject to any order made by the court in the matter, the restoration of the name of a company to the register under this section shall not affect the rights or liabilities of the

company in respect of any debt or obligation incurred, or any contract entered into by, to, with or on behalf of, the company between the date of its dissolution and the date of such restoration.][a]

Amendments

a CA 1963, s 311A inserted by CA 1990, s 246.

b The words 'Without prejudice to the provisions of section 311(8) of this Act or subsection (3) or (7) of section 12B, or subsection (1) of section 12C, of the Companies (Amendment) Act 1982,' substituted for 'Without prejudice to the provisions of section 311(8) of this Act and section 12(6) of the Companies (Amendment) Act, 1982,' in CA 1963, s 311A by C(A)(No 2)A 1999, s 50.

c 'the Companies Registration Office Gazette' substituted for '*Iris Oifigiúil*' by IFCMPA 2005, s 72.

Rules of Court

312 Rules of Court for winding up

Section 68 of the Courts of Justice Act, 1936 (which confers power on a rule-making authority to make rules regulating the practice and procedure of the court in certain cases) shall extend to the making of rules in respect of the winding up of companies 3 whether by the court or voluntarily.

Disposal of Documents filed with Registrar

313 Disposal of documents filed with registrar

The registrar of companies, shall, after the expiration of 20 years from the dissolution of a company, send all the documents filed in connection with such company to the Public Record Office.

[313A Provision of certain documents to liquidator or examiner

On—

(a) the making of—

(i) a winding up order, or

(ii) an order under section 2 of the Companies (Amendment) Act 1990 appointing an examiner to a company, or

(b) the issue of a certificate by the Master of the High Court under section 267A (inserted by the European Communities (Corporate Insolvency) Regulations 2002 (S.I. No 333 of 200)) of this Act in relation to the confirmation by the Master of a creditors' voluntary winding up,

the proper officer of the Central Office of the High Court shall, on request and payment of the prescribed fee and subject to any conditions that may be specified in rules of court, give to the liquidator or examiner concerned—

(i) a copy of the order or certificate, certified by the officer to be a true copy, and

(ii) any other prescribed particulars.][a]

Amendments

a CA 1963, s 313A inserted by EC(CI)R 2002, reg 3(f).

PART VII
RECEIVERS

314 Disqualification of body corporate for appointment as receiver

A body corporate shall not be qualified for appointment as receiver of the property of a company, and any body corporate which acts as such a receiver [shall be guilty of an offence and liable to a [class C fine][a]][b].

Amendments

a '£500' substituted for '£100' by C(A)A 1982, Sch 1, increased to £1,500 by CA 1990, s 240(7) as inserted by CLEA 2001, s 104 and converted to €1,904.61 by Council Regulations (EC) No 1103/97, No 974/98 and No 2866/98 and the Economic and Monetary Union Act 1998, s 6; the above being implicitly substituted, by Fines Act 2010, s 6, for a fine not exceeding the aforesaid amount. A class C fine currently means a fine not exceeding €2,500.

b Section 314 amended an offence created by C(AA)A 2003, s 57 and Sch 2 with effect from 6 April 2004.

---

315 [Disqualification for appointment as receiver

(1) None of the following persons shall be qualified for appointment as receiver of the property of a company—

(a) an undischarged bankrupt;

(b) a person who is, or who has within 12 months of the commencement of the receivership been, an officer or servant of the company;

(c) a parent, spouse[, civil partner within the meaning of the Civil Partnership and Certain Rights and Obligations of Cohabitants Act 2010][b], brother, sister or child of an officer of the company;

(d) a person who is a partner of or in the employment of an officer or servant of the company;

(e) a person who is not qualified by virtue of this subsection for appointment as receiver of the property of any other body corporate which is that company's subsidiary or holding company or a subsidiary of that company's holding company, or would be so disqualified if the body corporate were a company.

References in this subsection to an officer or servant of the company include references to an auditor.

(2) If a receiver of the property of a company becomes disqualified by virtue of this section, he shall thereupon vacate his office and give notice in writing within 14 days to—

(a) the company;

(b) the registrar of companies;

(c) (i) the debenture-holder, if the receiver was appointed by a debenture-holder, or

(ii) the court, if the receiver was appointed by the court,

that he has vacated it by reason of such disqualification.

(3) Subsection (2) is without prejudice to sections 107, 319 (2) and 321.

(4) Nothing in this section shall require a receiver appointed before the commencement of section 170 of the Companies Act, 1990, to vacate the office to which he was so appointed.

(5) Any person who acts as a receiver when disqualified by this section from so doing or who fails to comply with subsection (2), if that subsection applies to him, shall be guilty of an offence and shall be liable—

(a) on summary conviction, to a [class C fine][c] and, for continued contravention, to a daily default [class E fine][d];

(b) on conviction on indictment, to a fine not exceeding [€11,110.21][e] and, for continued contravention, to a daily default fine not exceeding [€555.50][f].][a]

Amendments

a CA 1963, s 315 substituted by CA 1990, s 170.

b Words ', civil partner within the meaning of the Civil Partnership and Certain Rights and Obligations of Cohabitants Act 2010' inserted by Civil Partnership and Certain Rights and Obligations of Cohabitants Act 2010, Sch, Pt 1, Item No. 3.

c '£1,000' in sub-s (5)(a) increased to £1,500 by CA 1990, s 240(7) as inserted by CLEA 2001, s 104 and converted to €1,904.61 by Council Regulations (EC) No 1103/97, No 974/98 and No 2866/98 and the Economic and Monetary Union Act 1998, s 6; the above being implicitly substituted, by Fines Act 2010, s 6, for a fine not exceeding the aforesaid amount. A class C fine currently means a fine not exceeding €2,500.

d £50 converted to €63.49 by Council Regulations (EC) No 1103/97, No 974/98 and No 2866/98 and the Economic and Monetary Union Act 1998, s 6; as implicitly substituted, by Fines Act 2010, s 8, for a fine not exceeding the aforesaid amount. A class E fine currently means a fine not exceeding €500.

e £5,000 converted to €6,348.69 by Council Regulations (EC) No 1103/97, No 974/98 and No 2866/98 and the Economic and Monetary Union Act 1998, s 6, and multiplied by a multiplier of 1.75 pursuant to Fines Act 2010, s 9.

f £250 converted to €317.43 by Council Regulations (EC) No 1103/97, No 974/98 and No 2866/98 and the Economic and Monetary Union Act 1998, s 6, and multiplied by a multiplier of 1.75 pursuant to Fines Act 2010, s 9.

---

316 Power of receiver to apply to the court for directions and his liability on contracts

[(1) Where a receiver of the property of a company is appointed under the powers contained in any instrument, any of the following persons may apply to the court for directions in relation to any matter in connection with the performances or otherwise by the receiver of his functions, that is to say—

(a) (i) the receiver;

(ii) an officer of the company;

(iii) a member of the company;

(iv) employees of the company comprising at least half in number of the persons employed in a full-time capacity by the company;

(v) a creditor of the company; and

(b) (i) a liquidator;

(ii) a contributory;

and on any such application, the court may give such directions, or make such order declaring the rights of persons before the court or otherwise, as the court thinks just.

(1A) An application to the court under subsection (1), except an application under paragraph (a) (i) of that subsection, shall be supported by such evidence that the applicant is being unfairly prejudiced by any actual or proposed action or omission of the receiver as the court may require.

(1B) For the purposes of subsection (1), 'creditor' means one or more creditors to whom the company is indebted by more, in aggregate, than [€12,697.38][b].][a]

(2) A receiver of the property of a company shall be personally liable on any contract entered into by him in the performance of his functions (whether such contract is entered into by him in the name of such company or in his own name as receiver or otherwise) unless the contract provides that he is not to be personally liable on such contract, and he shall be entitled in respect of that liability to indemnity out of the assets; but nothing in this subsection shall be taken as limiting any right to indemnity which he would have apart from this subsection, or as limiting his liability on contracts entered into without authority or as conferring any right to indemnity in respect of that liability.

(3) Where a receiver of the property of a company has been appointed or purported to be appointed and it is subsequently discovered that the charge or purported charge in respect of which he was so appointed or purported to be appointed was not effective as a charge on such property or on some part of such property, the court may, if it thinks fit, on the application of such receiver, order that he be relieved wholly or to such extent as the court shall think fit from personal liability in respect of anything done or omitted by him in relation to any property purporting to be comprised in the charge by virtue of which he was appointed or purported to be appointed which if such property had been effectively included in such charge or purported charge would have been properly done or omitted by him and he shall be relieved from personal liability accordingly, but in that event the person by whom such receiver was appointed or purported to be appointed shall be personally liable for everything for which, but for such order, such receiver would have been liable.

(4) This section shall apply whether the receiver was appointed before, on, or after the operative date, but subsection (2) shall not apply to contracts entered into before the operative date.

Amendments

a CA 1963, s 316(1) substituted and CA 1963, s 316(1A) and (1B) inserted by CA 1990, s 171.

b £10,000 converted to €12,697.38 by Council Regulations (EC) No 1103/97, No 974/98 and No 2866/98 and the Economic and Monetary Union Act 1998, s 6.

[316A Duty of receiver selling property to get best possible price reasonably obtainable

(1) A receiver, in selling property of a company, shall exercise all reasonable care to obtain the best price reasonably obtainable for the property as at the time of sale.

(2) Notwithstanding the provisions of any instrument—

(a) it shall not be a defence to any action or proceeding brought against a receiver in respect of a breach of his duty under subsection (1) that the receiver was acting as the agent of the company or under a power of attorney given by the company; and

(b) notwithstanding anything in section 316(2), a receiver shall not be entitled to be compensated or indemnified by the company for any liability he may incur as a result of a breach of his duty under this section.

(3) (a) A receiver shall not sell by private contract a non-cash asset of the requisite value to a person who is, or who, within three years prior to the date of appointment of the receiver, has been, an officer of the company unless he has given at least 14 days' notice of his intention to do so to all creditors of the company who are known to him or who have been intimated to him.

(b) In this subsection—

(i) 'non-cash asset' and 'requisite value' have the meanings assigned to them by section 29 of the Companies Act, 1990, and

(ii) 'officer' includes a person connected, within the meaning of section 26 of the Companies Act, 1990, with a director, and a shadow director.][a]

Amendments

a CA 1963, s 316A inserted by CA 1990, s 172.

---

317 Notification that receiver appointed

(1) Where a receiver of the property of a company has been appointed, every invoice, order for goods or business letter issued by or on behalf of the company or the receiver or the liquidator of the company, being a document on or in which the name of the company appears, shall contain a statement that a receiver has been appointed.

(2) If default is made in complying with the requirements of this section, the company and any of the following persons who knowingly and wilfully authorises or permits the default, namely, any officer of the company, any liquidator of the company and any receiver, [shall be guilty of an offence and liable to a [class C fine][a]][b].

Amendments

a '£100' substituted for '£20' by C(A)A 1982, Sch 1. £100 increased to £1,500 by CA 1990, s 240(7) as inserted by CLEA 2001, s 104, and converted to €1,904.61 by Council Regulations (EC) No 1103/97, No 974/98 and No 2866/98 and the Economic and Monetary Union Act 1998, s 6; the above being implicitly substituted, by Fines Act 2010, s 6, for a fine not exceeding the aforesaid amount. A class C fine currently means a fine not exceeding €2,500.

b Offence created by C(AA)A 2003, s 57 and Sch 2 with effect from 6 April 2004.

318 Power of court to fix remuneration of receiver

(1) The Court may, on an application made to it by the liquidator of a company or by any creditor or member of the company, by order fix the amount to be paid by way of remuneration to any person who, under the powers contained in any instrument, has been appointed as receiver of the property of the company notwithstanding that the remuneration of such receiver has been fixed by or under that instrument.

(2) Subject to subsection (3), the power of the court under subsection (1) shall, where no previous order has been made in relation thereto under that subsection—

- (a) extend to fixing the remuneration for any period before the making of the order or the application therefor; and
- (b) be exercisable notwithstanding that the receiver has died or ceased to act before the making of the order or the application therefor; and
- (c) where the receiver has been paid or has retained for his remuneration for any period before the making of the order any amount in excess of that fixed by the court for that period, extend to requiring him or his personal representatives to account for the excess or such part thereof as may be specified in the order.

(3) The power conferred by paragraph (c) of subsection (2) shall not be exercised in relation to any period before the making of the application for the order unless in the opinion of the court there are special circumstances making it proper for the power to be so exercised.

(4) The court may from time to time on an application made by the liquidator or by any creditor or member of the company or by the receiver, vary or amend an order made under subsection (1).

(5) This section shall apply whether the receiver was appointed before, on, or after the operative date and to periods before, as well as to periods after, the operative date.

319 Information to be given when receiver is appointed

(1) Where a receiver of the whole or substantially the whole of the property of a company (hereinafter in this section and in section 320 referred to as 'the receiver') is appointed on behalf of the holders of any debentures of the company secured by a floating charge, then subject to the provisions of this section and section 320—

- (a) the receiver shall forthwith send notice to the company of his appointment; and
- (b) there shall, within 14 days after receipt of the notice, or such longer period as may be allowed by the court or by the receiver, be made out and submitted to the receiver in accordance with section 320 a statement in the prescribed form as to the affairs of the company; and
- (c) the receiver shall within 2 months after receipt of the said statement send to the registrar of companies, to the court, to the company, to any trustees for the debenture holders on whose behalf he was appointed and, so far as he is aware of their addresses, to all such debenture holders, a copy of the statement and of any comments he sees fit to make thereon.

(2) The receiver shall within one month after the expiration of the period of 6 months from the date of his appointment and of every subsequent period of 6 months, and within one month after he ceases to act as receiver of the property of the company, send to the registrar of companies an abstract in the prescribed form showing the assets of the company of which he has taken possession since his appointment, their estimated value, the proceeds of sale of any such assets since his appointment, his receipts and payments during that period of 6 months or, where he ceases to act as aforesaid, during the period from the end of the period to which the last preceding abstract related up to the date of his so ceasing, and the aggregate amounts of his receipts and of his payments during all preceding periods since his appointment.

[(2A) Where a receiver ceases to act as receiver of the property of the company, the abstract under subsection (2) shall be accompanied by a statement from the receiver of his opinion as to whether or not the company is solvent and the registrar shall, on receiving the statement, forward a copy of it to the Director.][a]

(3) Where a receiver is appointed under the powers contained in any instrument, this section shall have effect with the omission of the references to the court in subsection (1), and in any other case, references to the court shall be taken as referring to the court by which the receiver was appointed.

(4) Subsection (1) shall not apply in relation to the appointment of a receiver to act with an existing receiver or in place of a receiver dying or ceasing to act, except that, where that subsection applies to a receiver who dies or ceases to act before it has been fully complied with, the references in paragraphs (b) and (c) thereof to the receiver shall (subject to subsection (5)) include references to his successor and to any continuing receiver.

Nothing in this subsection shall be taken as limiting the meaning of 'the receiver' where used in or in relation to subsection (2).

(5) This section and section 320, where the company is being wound up, shall apply notwithstanding that the receiver and the liquidator are the same person, but with any necessary modifications arising from that fact.

(6) Nothing in subsection (2) shall be taken to prejudice the duty of the receiver to render proper accounts of his receipts and payments to the persons to whom, and at the times at which, he may be required to do so apart from that subsection.

[(7) Where the registrar of companies becomes aware of the appointment of a receiver under this section, he shall forthwith inform the Director of the appointment.

(8) If the receiver makes default in complying with this section, he shall be guilty of an offence.][a]

Amendments

a CA 1963, s 319(2A), (7) and (8) were inserted by CLEA 2001, s 52.

---

320 Contents of statement to be submitted to receiver

(1) The statement as to the affairs of a company required by section 319 to be submitted to the receiver (or his successor) shall show as at the date of the receiver's appointment

particulars of the company's assets, debts and liabilities, the names and residences of its creditors, the securities held by them respectively, the dates when the securities were respectively given and such further or other information as may be prescribed.

(2) The said statement shall be submitted by, and be verified by affidavit of, one or more of the persons who are, at the date of the receiver's appointment, the directors and by the person who is at that date the secretary of the company, or by such of the persons hereafter in this subsection mentioned as the receiver (or his successor), may require to submit and verify the statement, that is, persons—

(a) who are or have been officers of the company;

(b) who have taken part in the formation of the company at any time within one year before the date of the receiver's appointment;

(c) who are in the employment of the company or have been in the employment of the company within the said year, and are in the opinion of the receiver capable of giving the information required;

(d) who are or have been within the said year officers of or in the employment of a company which is, or within the said year was, an officer of the company to which the statement relates.

(3) Any person making the statement and affidavit shall be allowed, and shall be paid by the receiver (or his successor) out of his receipts, such costs and expenses incurred in and about the preparation and making of the statement and affidavit as the receiver (or his successor) may consider reasonable, subject to an appeal to the court.

(4) Where the receiver is appointed under the powers contained in any instrument, this section shall have effect with the substitution for references to an affidavit of references to a statutory declaration; and in any other case references to the court shall be taken to refer to the court by which the receiver was appointed.

[(5) If any person to whom subsection (2) applies makes default in complying with the requirements of this section, he shall, unless he can prove to the satisfaction of the court that it was not possible for him to comply with the requirements of the section, be liable—

(a) on summary conviction, to imprisonment for a term not exceeding six months or to a [class C fine][a] or to both; or

(b) on conviction on indictment, to imprisonment for a term not exceeding three years or to a fine not exceeding [€11,110.21][b] or to both.][c]

(6) References in this section to the receiver's successor shall include a continuing receiver.

Amendments

a £1,000 increased to £1,500 by CA 1990, s 240(7) and converted to €1,904.61 by Council Regulations (EC) No 1103/97, No 974/98 and No 2866/98 and the Economic and Monetary Union Act 1998, s 6; the above being implicitly substituted, by Fines Act 2010, s 6, for a fine not exceeding the aforesaid amount. A class C fine currently means a fine not exceeding €2,500.

b £5,000 converted to €6,348.69 by Council Regulations (EC) No 1103/97, No 974/98 and No 2866/98 and the Economic and Monetary Union Act 1998, s 6, and multiplied by a multiplier of 1.75 pursuant to Fines Act 2010, s 9.

c CA 1963, s 320(5) substituted by CA 1990, s 173.

[320A Consequences of contravention of section 319 or 320

Where, in contravention of section 319 (1) (b) and section 320, a statement of affairs is not submitted to the receiver as required by those provisions, the court may, on the application of the receiver or any creditor of the company, and notwithstanding the provisions of section 320 (5) (inserted by section 173 of the Companies Act, 1990), makes whatever order it thinks fit, including an order compelling compliance with section 319 and section 320.][a]

Amendments

a CA 1963, s 320A inserted by CA 1990, s 174.

321 Delivery to registrar of accounts of receivers

(1) Except where subsection (2) of section 319 applies, every receiver of the property of a company shall, within one month after the expiration of the period of 6 months from the date of his appointment and of every subsequent period of 6 months, and within one month after he ceases to act as receiver, deliver to the registrar of companies for registration an abstract in the prescribed form showing the assets of the company of which he has taken possession since his appointment, their estimated value, the proceeds of sale of any such assets since his appointment, his receipts and his payments during that period of 6 months or, where he ceases to act as aforesaid, during the period from the end of the period to which the last preceding abstract related up to the date of his so ceasing, and the aggregate amounts of his receipts and of his payments during all the preceding periods since his appointment.

(2) Every receiver who makes default in complying with this section [shall be guilty of an offence and liable to a [class C fine][a]].[b]

Amendments

a '£1000' substituted for '£500' by CA 1990, s 145, increased to £1,500 by CA 1990, 240(7) as inserted by CLEA 2001, s 104 and converted to €1,904.61 by Council Regulations (EC) No 1103/97, No 974/98 and No 2866/98 and the Economic and Monetary Union Act 1998, s 6; the above being implicitly substituted, by Fines Act 2010, s 6, for a fine not exceeding the aforesaid amount. A class C fine currently means a fine not exceeding €2,500.

b Words substituted by C(AA)A 2003, s 57 and Sch 2.

322 Enforcement of duty of receiver to make returns

(1) If any receiver of the property of a company—

(a) having made default in filing, delivering or making any return, account or other document, or in giving any notice, which a receiver is by law required to file, deliver, make or give, fails to make good the default within 14 days after the service on him of a notice requiring him to do so; or

(b) having been appointed under the powers contained in any instrument, has, after being required at any time by the liquidator of the company to do so, failed to render proper accounts of his receipts and payments and to vouch the same and to pay over to the liquidator the amount properly payable to him;

the court may, on an application made for the purpose, make an order directing the receiver to make good the default within such time as may be specified in the order.

(2) In the case of any such default as is mentioned in paragraph (a) of subsection (1), an application for the purposes of this section may be made by any member or creditor of the company or by the registrar of companies, and in the case of any such default as is mentioned in paragraph (b) of that subsection, the application shall be made by the liquidator, and in either case the order may provide that all costs of and incidental to the application shall be borne by the receiver.

(3) Nothing in this section shall be taken to prejudice the operation of any enactments imposing penalties on receivers in respect of any such default as is mentioned in subsection (1).

[322A Removal of receiver

(1) The court may, on cause shown, remove a receiver and appoint another receiver.

(2) Notice of such proceedings shall be served on the receiver and on the person who appointed him not less than 7 days before the hearing of such proceedings and, in any such proceedings, the receiver and the person who appointed him may appear and be heard.][a]

Amendments

a CA 1963, s 322A inserted by CA 1990, s 175.

[322B Court may determine or limit receivership on application of liquidator

(1) On the application of the liquidator of a company that is being wound up (other than by means of a members' voluntary winding up) and in respect of which a receiver has been appointed (whether before or after the commencement of the winding up), the court may—

(a) order that the receiver shall cease to act as such from a date specified by the court, and prohibit the appointment of any other receiver; or

(b) order that the receiver shall, from a date specified by the court, act as such only in respect of certain assets specified by the court.

An order under this subsection may be made on such terms and conditions as the court thinks fit.

(2) The court may from time to time, on an application made either by the liquidator or by the receiver, rescind or amend an order made under subsection (1).

(3) A copy of an application made under this section shall be served on the receiver and on the person who appointed him not less than 7 days before the hearing of the

application, and the receiver and any such party may appear before and be heard by the court in respect of the application.

(4) Except as provided in subsection (1), no order make under this section shall affect any security or charge over the undertaking or property of the company.][a]

Amendments

a CA 1963, s 322B inserted by CA 1990, s 176.

[322C Resignation of receiver

(1) A receiver of the property of a company appointed under the powers contained in any instrument may resign, provided he has given one month's notice thereof to—

(a) the holders of floating charges over all or any part of the property of the company;

(b) the company or its liquidator; and

(c) the holders of any fixed charge over all or any part of the property of the company.

(2) A receiver appointed by the court may resign only with the authority of the court and on such terms and conditions, if any, as may be laid down by the court.

(3) If any person makes default in complying with the requirements of this section, he [shall be guilty of an offence and liable to a [class C fine][a]][b]][c].

Amendments

a £1,000 increased to £1,500 by CA 1990, s 240(7) as inserted by CLEA 2001, s 104 and converted to €1,904.61 by Council Regulations (EC) No 1103/97, No 974/98 and No 2866/98 and the Economic and Monetary Union Act 1998, s 6; the above being implicitly substituted, by Fines Act 2010, s 6, for a fine not exceeding the aforesaid amount. A class C fine currently means a fine not exceeding €2,500.

b Words substituted by C(AA)A 2003, s 57 and Sch 2 with effect from 6 April 2004.

c CA 1963, s 322C inserted by CA 1990, s 177.

323 Construction of references to receiver

It is hereby declared that, unless the contrary intention appears—

(a) any reference in this Act to a receiver of the property of a company includes a reference to a receiver and manager of the property of a company and to a manager of the property of a company and includes a reference to a receiver or to a receiver and manager or to a manager, of part only of that property, and to a receiver only of the income arising from that property or from part thereof; and

(b) any reference in this Act to the appointment of a receiver under powers contained in any instrument includes a reference to an appointment made under powers which, by virtue of any enactment, are implied in and have effect as if contained in an instrument.

[323A Director may request production of receiver's books

(1) The Director may, where he considers it necessary or appropriate, request (specifying the reason why the request is being made) the production of a receiver's books for examination, either in regard to a particular receivership or to all receiverships undertaken by the receiver.

(2) Where the Director has requested the production of a receiver's books for examination under subsection (1), the receiver to whom the request is made shall furnish the books to the Director and answer any questions concerning the content of the books and the conduct of a particular receivership or receiverships, and give to the Director all assistance in the matter as the receiver is reasonably able to give.

(3) A request under subsection (1) may not be made in respect of books relating to a receivership that has concluded more than 6 years prior to the request.

(4) If the receiver makes default in complying with this section, he shall be guilty of an offence.][a]

Amendments

a CA 1963, s 323A inserted by CLEA 2001, s 53.

PART VIII

APPLICATION OF ACT TO COMPANIES FORMED OR REGISTERED UNDER FORMER ACTS

324 Application of Act to companies formed and registered under former Companies Acts

(1) Subject to subsection (2), in the application of this Act to existing companies, it shall apply in the same manner—

(a) in the case of a limited company other than a company limited by guarantee, as if the company had been formed and registered under this Act as a company limited by shares;

(b) in the case of a company limited by guarantee, as if the company had been formed and registered under this Act as a company limited by guarantee; and

(c) in the case of a company other than a limited company, as if the company had been formed and registered under this Act as an unlimited company.

(2) Reference, express or implied, to the date of registration shall be construed as a reference to the date at which the company was registered under the Joint Stock Companies Acts, the Companies Act, 1862, or the Companies (Consolidation) Act, 1908, as the case may be.

325 Application of Act to companies registered but not formed under former Companies Acts

(1) Subject to subsection (2), this Act shall apply to every company registered (in a register kept in the State) but not formed under the Joint Stock Companies Acts, the Companies Act, 1862, or the Companies (Consolidation) Act, 1908, in the same manner as it is in Part IX declared to apply to companies registered but not formed under this Act.

(2) Reference, express or implied, to the date of registration shall be construed as a reference to the date at which the company was registered under the Joint Stock Companies Acts, the Companies Act, 1862, or the Companies (Consolidation) Act, 1908, as the case may be.

326 Application of Act to unlimited companies re-registered as limited companies under former Companies Acts

(1) Subject to subsection (2), this Act shall apply to every unlimited company registered (in a register kept in the State) as a limited company in pursuance of the Companies Act, 1879, or section 57 of the Companies (Consolidation) Act, 1908, in the same manner as it applies to an unlimited company registered in pursuance of this Act as a limited company.

(2) Reference, express or implied, to the date of registration shall be construed as a reference to the date at which the company was registered as a limited company under the said Act of 1879 or the said section 57, as the case may be.

327 Provisions as to companies registered under Joint Stock Companies Acts

(1) A company registered under the Joint Stock Companies Acts may cause its shares to be transferred in manner hitherto in use, or in such other manner as the company may direct.

(2) The power of altering articles under section 15 shall, in the case of an unlimited company formed and registered under the Joint Stock Companies Acts, extend to altering any regulations relating to the amount of capital or to its distribution into shares, notwithstanding that those regulations are contained in the memorandum.

PART IX

COMPANIES NOT FORMED UNDER THIS ACT AUTHORISED TO REGISTER UNDER THIS ACT

328 Companies capable of being registered

(1) With the exceptions and subject to the provisions contained in this section—

- (a) any company consisting of seven or more members, which was in existence on the 2nd day of November, 1862, including any company registered under the Joint Stock Companies Acts; and
- (b) any company formed after the date aforesaid, whether before or after the operative date, in pursuance of any statute other than this Act, or of letters patent, or being otherwise duly constituted according to law, and consisting of seven or more members;

may at any time register under this Act as an unlimited company, or as a company limited by shares, or as a company limited by guarantee; and the registration shall not be invalid by reason that it has taken place with a view to the company's being wound up.

(2) This section shall not apply to a company registered under the Companies Act, 1862, or the Companies (Consolidation) Act, 1908, or to a company which has not its registered office or principal place of business in the State.

(3) A company having the liability of its members limited by statute or letters patent, and not being a joint stock company as hereinafter defined, shall not register in pursuance of this section.

(4) A company, having the liability of its members limited by statute or letters patent, shall not register in pursuance of this section as an unlimited company or as a company limited by guarantee.

(5) A company that is not a joint stock company as hereinafter defined shall not register in pursuance of this section as a company limited by shares.

(6) A company shall not register in pursuance of this section without the assent of a majority of such of its members as are present in person or by proxy at a general meeting summoned for the purpose.

(7) Where a company, not having the liability of its members limited by statute or letters patent, is about to register as a limited company, the majority required to assent as aforesaid shall consist of not less than three-fourths of the members present in person or by proxy at the meeting.

(8) Where a company is about to register as a company limited by guarantee, the assent to its being so registered shall be accompanied by a resolution declaring that each member undertakes to contribute to the assets of the company, in the event of its being wound up while he is a member, or within one year after he ceases to be a member, for payment of the debts and liabilities of the company contracted before he ceased to be a member, and of the costs and expenses of winding up and for the adjustment of the rights of the contributories among themselves, such amount as may be required, not exceeding a specified amount.

(9) In computing any majority under this section when a poll is demanded, regard shall be had to the number of votes to which each member is entitled according to the regulations of the company.

329 Definition of joint stock company

For the purposes of this Part, as far as relates to registration of companies as companies limited by shares, a joint stock company means a company having a permanent paid up or nominal share capital of fixed amount divided into shares, also of fixed amount, or held and transferable as stock, or divided and held partly in one way and partly in the other, and formed on the principle of having for its members the holders of those shares or that stock, and no other persons, and such a company when registered with limited liability under this Act shall be deemed to be a company limited by shares.

330 Requirements for registration of joint stock companies

Before the registration in pursuance of this Part of a joint stock company, there shall be delivered to the registrar the following documents—

(a) a list showing the names, addresses and occupations of all persons who, on a day named in the list, not being more than 6 clear days before the day of registration, were members of the company, with the addition of the shares or stock held by them respectively, distinguishing, in cases where the shares are numbered, each share by its number;

(b) a copy of any statute, charter, letters patent, deed of settlement, contract of co-partnery or other instrument constituting or regulating the company; and

(c) if the company is intended to be registered as a limited company, a statement specifying the following particulars—

(i) the nominal share capital of the company and the number of shares into which it is divided, or the amount of stock of which it consists;

(ii) the number of shares taken and the amount paid on each share;

[(iii) the name of the company with the addition of the word 'limited' or 'teoranta' as the last word thereof or, in the case of a public limited company, with the addition of the words 'public limited company' or 'cuideachta phoiblí theoranta' as the last words thereof; and][a]

(iv) in the case of a company intended to be registered as a company limited by guarantee, the resolution declaring the amount of the guarantee.

Amendments

a Subparagraph (c)(iii) substituted by C(A)A 1963, Sch 1, para 19.

331 Requirements for registration of company not being a joint stock company

Before the registration in pursuance of this Part of any company not being a joint stock company, there shall be delivered to the registrar—

(a) a list showing the names, addresses and occupations of the directors of the company; and

(b) a copy of any statute, letters patent, deed of settlement, contract of co-partnery or other instrument constituting or regulating the company; and

(c) in the case of a company intended to be registered as a company limited by guarantee, a copy of the resolution declaring the amount of the guarantee.

332 Verification of lists of members and directors of company for purposes of registration

The lists of members and directors and any other particulars relating to the company required to be delivered to the registrar shall be verified by a statutory declaration of any two or more directors or other principal officers of the company.

333 Registrar may require evidence as to nature of company

The registrar may require such evidence as he thinks necessary for the purpose of satisfying himself whether any company proposing to be registered is or is not a joint stock company as hereinbefore defined.

334 Change of name for purposes of registration

(1) Subject to subsection (2), where the name of a company seeking registration under this Part is one by which it may not be so registered by reason of the name being, in the opinion of the [registrar of companies][a], undesirable, it may, with the approval of the [registrar of companies][a] signified in writing, change its name with effect from its registration as aforesaid.

(2) The like assent of the members of the company shall be required to the change of name as is by section 328 required to the registration under this Act.

Amendments

a Words substituted by CLEA 2001, s 95, with effect from 1 October 2001.

335 Addition of 'limited' or 'teoranta' to name

[(1) Subject to subsection (2), when a company registers in pursuance of this Part with limited liability, the word 'limited' or 'teoranta' or in the case of a public limited company the words 'public limited company' or 'cuideachta phoiblí theoranta' shall form and be part of its name.][a]

(2) Subsection (1) shall not be taken as excluding the operation of section 24.

Amendments

a Substituted by C(A)A 1983, Sch 1 para 20.

---

336 Certificate of registration of existing companies

[(1)][a] On compliance with the requirements of this Part relating to registration, and on payment of such fees, if any, as are payable under the following provisions of this Act, the registrar shall certify under his hand that the company applying for registration is incorporated as a company under this Act, and in the case of a limited company that it is limited and thereupon the company shall be so incorporated.

[(2) A certificate given under this section in respect of a company shall be conclusive evidence that the requirements of this Part in respect of registration and of matters precedent and incidental thereto have been complied with.][b]

Amendments

a Renumbered by C(A)A 1983, Sch 1 para 21.

b Inserted by C(A)A 1983, Sch 1 para 21.

---

337 Vesting of property on registration

(1) All property, real and personal (including things in action) belonging to or vested in a company at the date of its registration in pursuance of this Part, shall on registration pass to and vest in the company as incorporated under this Act for all the estate and interest of the company therein.

[(2) ...][a]

Amendments

a Deleted by FA 1998, Sch 8 with effect from 27 March 1998.

---

338 Saving for existing liabilities

Registration of a company in pursuance of this Part shall not affect the rights or liabilities of the company in respect of any debt or obligation incurred, or any contract entered into by, to, with or on behalf of, the company before registration.

339 Continuation of existing actions

(1) Subject to subsection (2), all actions and other legal proceedings which at the time of the registration of a company in pursuance of this Part are pending by or against the

company, or the public officer or any member thereof, may be continued in the same manner as if the registration had not taken place.

(2) Execution shall not issue against the effects of any individual member of the company on any judgment, decree or order obtained in any such action or proceeding, but, in the event of the property and effects of the company being insufficient to satisfy the judgment, decree or order, an order may be obtained for winding up the company.

340 Effect of registration under this Part

(1) When a company is registered in pursuance of this Part, subsections (2) to (7) shall have effect.

(2) All provisions contained in any statute or instrument constituting or regulating the company, including, in the case of a company registered as a company limited by guarantee, the resolution declaring the amount of the guarantee [and including any statement under section 330 (c)][a], shall be deemed to be conditions and regulations of the company, in the same manner and with the same incidents as if so much thereof as would, if the company had been formed under this Act, have been required to be inserted in the memorandum, were contained in a registered memorandum, and the residue thereof were contained in registered articles.

(3) All the provisions of this Act shall apply to the company and the members, contributories and creditors thereof, in the same manner in all respects as if it had been formed under this Act, subject as follows—

(a) Table A or Tábla A shall not apply unless adopted by special resolution;

(b) the provisions of this Act relating to the numbering of shares shall not apply to any joint stock company whose shares are not numbered;

(c) subject to the provisions of this section, the company shall not have power to alter any provision contained in any statute relating to the company;

(d) subject to the provisions of this section, the company shall not have power without the sanction of the Minister, to alter any provision contained in any letters patent relating to the company;

(e) the company shall not have power to alter any provision contained in a charter or letters patent relating to the objects of the company;

(f) in the event of the company being wound up, every person shall be a contributory, in respect of the debts and liabilities of the company contracted before registration, who is liable to pay or contribute to the payment of any debt or liability of the company contracted before registration or to pay or contribute to the payment of any sum for the adjustment of the rights of the members among themselves in respect of any such debt or liability, or to pay or contribute to the payment of the costs and expenses of winding up the company, so far as relates to such debts or liabilities as aforesaid;

(g) in the event of the company being wound up, every contributory shall be liable to contribute to the assets of the company, in the course of the winding up, all sums due from him in respect of any such liability as aforesaid, and, in the event of the death or bankruptcy of any contributory, the provisions of this Act relating to the personal representatives of deceased contributories and to the assignees of bankrupt contributories shall apply.

(4) The provisions of this Act relating to—

(a) the registration of an unlimited company as limited;

(b) the powers of an unlimited company on registration as a limited company to increase the nominal amount of its share capital and to provide that a portion of its share capital shall not be capable of being called up except in the event of winding up;

(c) the power of a limited company to determine that a portion of its share capital shall not be capable of being called up except in the event of winding up;

shall apply notwithstanding any provisions contained in any statute, charter or other instrument constituting or regulating the company.

(5) Nothing in this section shall authorise the company to alter any such provisions contained in any instrument constituting or regulating the company, as would, if the company had originally been formed under this Act, have been required to be contained in the memorandum and are not authorised to be altered by this Act.

(6) None of the provisions of this Act (apart from those of subsection (4) of section 205) shall derogate from any power of altering its constitution or regulations which may, by virtue of any statute or other instrument constituting or regulating the company, be vested in the company.

(7) In this section, 'instrument' includes deed of settlement, contract of co-partnery and letters patent.

Amendments

a Words inserted by C(A)A 1983, Sch 1 para 22.

---

341 Power to substitute memorandum and articles for deed of settlement

(1) Subject to subsections (2) to (4), a company registered in pursuance of this Part may by special resolution alter the form of its constitution by substituting a memorandum and articles for a deed of settlement.

(2) The provisions of section 10 relating to applications to the court for cancellation of alterations of the objects of a company and matters consequential on the passing of resolutions for such alterations shall, so far as applicable, apply to an alteration under this section with the following modifications—

(a) there shall be substituted for the printed copy of the altered memorandum required to be delivered to the registrar of companies a printed copy of the substituted memorandum and articles; and

(b) on the delivery to the registrar of a printed copy of the substituted memorandum and articles or on the date when the alteration is no longer liable to be cancelled by order of the court, whichever last occurs, the substituted memorandum and articles shall apply to the company in the same manner as if it were a company registered under this Act with that memorandum and those articles, and the company's deed of settlement shall cease to apply to the company.

(3) An alteration under this section may be made either with or without any alteration of the objects of the company under this Act.

(4) In this section, 'deed of settlement' includes any contract of co-partnery or other instrument constituting or regulating the company, not being a statute, charter or letter patent.

342 Power of court to stay or restrain proceedings

The provisions of this Act relating to staying and restraining actions and proceedings against a company at any time after the presentation of a petition for winding up and before the making of a winding-up order shall, in the case of a company registered in pursuance of this Part, where the application to stay or restrain is by a creditor, extend to actions and proceedings against any contributory of the company.

343 Actions stayed on winding-up order

Where an order has been made for winding up a company registered in pursuance of this Part, no action or proceeding shall be commenced or proceeded with against the company or any contributory of the company in respect of any debt of the company, except by leave of the court, and subject to such terms as the court may impose.

PART X

WINDING UP OF UNREGISTERED COMPANIES

[343A Restriction of this Part

This Part is subject to Chapters I (general provisions) and III (secondary insolvency proceedings) of the Insolvency Regulation.][a]

Amendments

a Inserted by EC(CI)R 2002, reg 3, with effect from 1 July 2002.

---

344 Meaning of unregistered company

For the purposes of this Part, 'unregistered company' shall include any trustee savings bank certified under the Trustee Savings Banks Acts, 1863 to 1958, any partnership, whether limited or not, any association and any company with the following exceptions—

(a) a company as defined by section 2;

(b) a partnership, association or company which consists of less than eight members and is not formed outside the State.

345 Winding up of unregistered companies

(1) Subject to the provisions of this Part, any unregistered company may be wound up under this Act, and all the provisions of this Act relating to winding up shall apply to an unregistered company, with the exceptions and additions mentioned in this section.

(2) The principal place of business in the State of an unregistered company shall, for all the purposes of the winding up, be deemed to be the registered office of the company.

(3) No unregistered company shall be wound up under this Act voluntarily.

(4) The circumstances in which an unregistered company may be wound up are as follows—

(a) if the company is dissolved, or has ceased to carry on business, or is carrying on business only for the purpose of winding up its affairs;

(b) if the company is unable to pay its debts;

(c) if the court is of opinion that it is just and equitable that the company should be wound up.

(5) An unregistered company shall, for the purposes of this Act, be deemed to be unable to pay its debts—

(a) if a creditor, by assignment or otherwise, to whom the company is indebted in a sum exceeding [€1,269.74][a] then due, has served on the company, by leaving at its principal place of business in the State, or by delivering to the secretary or some director or principal officer of the company, or by serving otherwise in such manner as the court may approve or direct, a demand in writing requiring the company to pay the sum so due, and the company has, for 3 weeks after the service of the demand, neglected to pay the sum or to secure or compound for it to the satisfaction of the creditor;

(b) if any action or other proceeding has been instituted against any member for any debt or demand due or claimed to be due, from the company, or from him in his character of member, and notice in writing of the institution of the action or proceeding having been served on the company by leaving the same at its principal place of business in the State, or by delivering it to the secretary, or some director or principal officer of the company, or by otherwise serving the same in such manner as the court may approve or direct, the company has not within 10 days after service of the notice paid, secured or compounded for the debt or demand, or procured the action or proceeding to be stayed, or indemnified the defendant to his reasonable satisfaction against the action or proceeding, and against all costs, damages and expenses to be incurred by him by reason of the same;

(c) if in the State or in any country recognised by the Minister for the purposes of section 250, execution or other process issued on a judgment, decree or order obtained in any court in favour of a creditor against the company, or any member thereof as such, or any person authorised to be sued as nominal defendant on behalf of the company, is returned unsatisfied;

(d) if it is otherwise proved to the satisfaction of the court that the company is unable to pay its debts.

(6) A petition for winding up a trustee savings bank may be presented by the Minister for Finance as well as by any person authorised under the other provisions of this Act to present a petition for winding up a company.

(7) Where a company incorporated outside the State which has been carrying on business in the State ceases to carry on business in the State, it may be wound up as an unregistered company under this Part, notwithstanding that it has been dissolved or otherwise ceased to exist as a company under or by virtue of the laws of the country under which it was incorporated.

(8) [...][b]

Amendments

a '£1,000' substituted for '£50' by CA 1990, s 213 and increased to £1,500 by CA 1990, s 240(7) as inserted by CLEA 2001, s 104. £1,500 converted to €1,904.61 by Council Regulations (EC) No 1103/97, No 974/98 and No 2866/98 and the Economic and Monetary Union Act 1998, s 6.

b Subsection (8) was repealed by the Bankruptcy Act 1988, Sch 2.

346 Contributories in winding up of unregistered company

(1) In the event of an unregistered company being wound up, every person shall be deemed to be a contributory who is liable to pay or contribute to the payment of any debt or liability of the company, or to pay or contribute to the payment of any sum for the adjustment of the rights of the members among themselves, or to pay or contribute to the payment of the costs and expenses of winding up the company, and every contributory shall be liable to contribute to the assets of the company all sums due from him in respect of any such liability as aforesaid.

(2) In the event of the death or bankruptcy of any contributory, the provisions of this Act relating to the personal representatives of deceased contributories and to the assignees of bankrupt contributories respectively shall apply.

347 Power of court to stay or restrain proceedings

The provisions of this Act relating to staying and restraining actions and proceedings against a company at any time after the presentation of a petition for winding up and before the making of a winding-up order shall, in the case of an unregistered company, where the application to stay or restrain is by a creditor, extend to actions and proceedings against any contributory of the company.

348 Actions stayed on winding-up order

Where an order has been made for winding up an unregistered company, no action or proceeding shall be proceeded with or commenced against any contributory of the company in respect of any debt of the company, except by leave of the court, and subject to such terms as the court may impose.

349 Provisions of this Part to be cumulative

The provisions of this Part relating to unregistered companies shall be in addition to and not in restriction of any provisions hereinbefore contained in this Act relating to winding up companies by the court, and the court or liquidator may exercise any powers or do any act in the case of unregistered companies which might be exercised or done by it or him in winding up companies formed and registered under this Act.

350 Saving for enactments providing for winding up under former Companies Acts

Nothing in this Part shall affect the operation of any enactment which provides for any partnership, association or company being wound up, or being wound up as a company or as an unregistered company under the Companies (Consolidation) Act, 1908 or any enactment repealed by that Act.

PART XI
COMPANIES INCORPORATED OUTSIDE THE STATE ESTABLISHING A PLACE OF BUSINESS WITHIN THE STATE

351 Application of this Part

This Part shall apply to all companies incorporated outside the State which, after the operative date, establish a place of business within the State, and to companies incorporated outside the State which have, before the operative date, established a place of business within the State and continue to have an established place of business within the State on the operative date.

352 Documents to be delivered to registrar by certain companies incorporated outside the State

(1) Companies incorporated outside the State, which, after the operative date, establish a place of business within the State, shall, within one month of the establishment of the place of business, deliver to the registrar of companies for registration—

(a) a certified copy of the charter, statutes or memorandum and articles of the company, or other instrument constituting or defining the constitution of the company, and, if the instrument is not written in the English or Irish language, a certified translation thereof;

(b) a list of the directors and secretary of the company containing the particulars mentioned in subsection (2);

(c) the names and addresses of some one or more persons resident in the State authorised to accept on behalf of the company service of process and any notices required to be served on the company and also the address of the company's principal place of business in the State.

(2) Subject to subsection (3), the list referred to in paragraph (b) of subsection (1) shall contain the following particulars—

(a) in relation to each director—

(i) in the case of an individual, his present Christian name and surname, and any former Christian name or surname, his usual residential address, his nationality (if not Irish) and his business occupation (if any), and particulars of any other directorships of bodies corporate incorporated in the State held by him; and

(ii) in the case of a body corporate, its corporate name and registered or principal office:

(b) in relation to the secretary or, where there are joint secretaries, in relation to each of them—

(i) in the case of an individual, his present Christian name and surname, any former Christian name and surname and his usual residential address; and

(ii) in the case of a body corporate, its corporate name and registered or principal office.

Paragraphs (b), (c) and (d) of subsection (12) of section 195 shall apply for the purpose of the construction of references in this subsection to present and former Christian names and surnames as they apply for the purpose of the construction of such references in that section.

(3) Where all the partners in a firm are joint secretaries of the company, the name and principal office of the firm may be stated instead of the particulars mentioned in paragraph (b) of subsection (2).

(4) Companies to which this Part applies, other than those mentioned in subsection (1), shall, if on the operative date they have not delivered to the registrar the documents and particulars specified in subsection (1) of section 274 of the Companies (Consolidation) Act, 1908, deliver the documents and particulars mentioned in subsection (1) of this section within 2 months after the operative date.

353 Return to be delivered to registrar where documents altered

If, in the case of any company to which this Part applies, any alteration is made in—

(a) the charter, statutes or memorandum and articles of the company, or other instrument constituting or defining the constitution of the company; or

(b) the directors or secretary of the company or the particulars contained in the list of the directors and secretaries; or

(c) the names or addresses of the persons authorised to accept service on behalf of the company or the address of its principal place of business in the State;

the company shall, within the prescribed time, deliver to the registrar of companies for registration a return containing the prescribed particulars of the alteration.

354 Accounts of company to which this Part applies to be delivered to registrar

(1) Every company to which this Part applies shall, in every calendar year, make out a balance sheet and profit and loss account and, if the company is a holding company, group accounts, in such form and containing such particulars and including such documents, as under the provisions of this Act it would, if it had been a company within the meaning of this Act, have been required to make out and lay before the company in general meeting, and deliver copies of those documents to the registrar of companies.

(2) If any such document as is mentioned in subsection (1) is not written in the English or Irish language, there shall be annexed to it a certified translation thereof.

(3) The Minister may grant to any company or to any class of companies exemption from the obligation imposed by subsection (1) subject to such conditions as he may think fit.

(4) Subsection (1) shall not apply to any company having provisions in its constitution that would entitle it to rank as a private company if it had been registered in the State.

355 Obligation to state name of company to which this Part applies, whether limited and country where incorporated

Every company to which this Part applies shall—

(a) in every prospectus inviting subscriptions for its shares or debentures in the State state the country in which the company is incorporated; and

(b) exhibit conspicuously on every place where it carries on business in the State the name of the company and the country in which the company is incorporated; and

(c) cause the name of the company and of the country in which the company is incorporated to be stated in legible characters on all billheads and letter-paper, and in all notices and other official publications of the company; and

(d) if the liability of the members of the company is limited, cause notice of that fact to be stated in legible characters in every such prospectus as aforesaid and in all billheads, letter-paper, notices and other official publications of the company in the State, and to be affixed on every place where it carries on its business.

356 Service of documents on company to which this Part applies

(1) Subject to subsection (2), any process or notice required to be served on a company to which this Part applies shall be sufficiently served if addressed to any person whose name has been delivered to the registrar of companies under the foregoing provisions of this Part and left at or sent by post to the address which has been so delivered.

(2) A document may be served on any such company by leaving it at or sending it by post to any place of business established by the company in the State—

(a) where the company makes default in delivering to the registrar the name and address of a person resident in the State who is authorised to accept on behalf of the company service of process or notices; or

(b) if at any time all the persons whose names and addresses have been so delivered are dead or have ceased so to reside, or refuse to accept service on behalf of the company, or for any reason cannot be served.

(3) This section shall cease to apply to a company on the expiration of two years after it has given the notice referred to in section 357.

357 Notice to be given when company to which this Part applies ceases to carry on business in the State

If any company to which this Part applies ceases to have a place of business in the State, it shall forthwith give notice of the fact to the registrar of companies, and as from the date on which notice is so given, the obligation of the company to deliver any document to the registrar shall cease.

358 Penalties for non-compliance with this Part

If any company to which this Part applies fails to comply with any of the foregoing provisions of this Part, the company and every officer or agent of the company who knowingly and wilfully authorises or permits the default [shall be guilty of an offence and liable to a [class C fine][a]].[b]

Amendments

a '£500' substituted for '£100' by C(A)A 1982, Sch 1 and increased to £1,500 by CA 1990, s 240(7) as inserted by CLEA 2001, s 104. £1,500 converted to €1,904.61 by Council Regulations (EC) No 1103/97, No 974/98 and No 2866/98 and the Economic and Monetary Union Act 1998, s 6; the above being implicitly substituted, by Fines Act 2010, s 6, for a fine not exceeding the aforesaid amount. A class C fine currently means a fine not exceeding €2,500.

b Words substituted by C(AA)A 2003, s 57 and Sch 2 with effect from 6 April 2004.

---

359 Construction of section 275 of Companies (Consolidation) Act, 1908

In its application to the State, section 275 of the Companies (Consolidation) Act, 1908, shall be deemed to have always applied as if—

(a) the words 'in Northern Ireland or in Great Britain or in a British possession' were substituted for the words 'in a British possession', and

(b) the words 'the State' were substituted for the words 'the United Kingdom'.

360 Interpretation of this Part

For the purposes of this Part—

'certified' means certified in the prescribed manner to be a true copy or a correct translation;

'director' in relation to a company includes any person in accordance with whose directions and instructions the directors of the company are accustomed to act;

'place of business' includes a share transfer or share registration office;

'prospectus' has the same meaning as when used in relation to a company incorporated under this Act;

'secretary' includes any person occupying the position of secretary by whatever name called.

PART XII
RESTRICTIONS ON SALE OF SHARES AND OFFERS OF SHARES FOR SALE

361 Prospectuses relating to companies incorporated outside the State

[...][a]

Amendments

a Section 361 repealed by IFCMPA 2005, s 40(1)(a).

---

362 Exclusion of section 361 and relaxation of Third Schedule in case of certain prospectuses

[...][a]

Amendments

a Section 362 repealed by IFCMPA 2005, s 40(1)(a).

---

363 Provisions as to expert's consent and allotment

[...][a]

Amendments

a Section 363 repealed by IFCMPA 2005, s 40(1)(a).

---

364 Registration of prospectus

[...][a]

Amendments

a Section 364 repealed by IFCMPA 2005, s 40(1)(a).

365 Penalty for contravention of section 361 to 364

[…][a]

Amendments

a Section 365 repealed by IFCMPA 2005, s 40(1)(a).

366 Civil liability for mis-statements in prospectus

[…][a]

Amendments

a Section 366 repealed by IFCMPA 2005, s 40(1)(a).

367 Interpretation of provisions as to prospectuses

[…][a]

Amendments

a Section 367 repealed by IFCMPA 2005, s 40(1)(a).

PART XIII
GENERAL PROVISIONS AS TO REGISTRATION

368 Registration office

(1) For the purposes of the registration of companies under this Act, the Minister shall maintain and administer an office or offices in the State at such places as the Minister thinks fit.

(2) The Minister may appoint such registrars and assistant registrars as he thinks necessary for the registration of companies under this Act, and may make regulations with respect to their duties and may remove any persons so appointed.

(3) The Minister may direct a seal or seals to be prepared for the authentication of documents required for or connected with the registration of companies.

(4) Whenever any act is by this Act or by any statute directed to be done to or by the registrar of companies, it shall, until the Minister otherwise directs, be done to or by the existing registrar of joint stock companies or, in his absence, to or by such person as the Minister may for the time being authorise.

369 Fees

(1) Subject to subsection (2), in respect of the several matters mentioned in the first column of the table set out in Part I of the Eight Schedule, there shall, subject to the limitations imposed by Part II of that Schedule, be paid to the registrar the several fees specified in the second column of that table.

(2) No fees shall be charged in respect of the registration in pursuance of Part IX of a company if it is not registered as a limited company, or if before its registration as a limited company, the liability of the shareholders was limited by statute or letters patent.

(3) All fees paid to the registrar in pursuance of this Act shall be paid into or disposed of for the benefit of the Exchequer in such manner as the Minister for Finance may direct.

370 Inspection, production and evidence of documents kept by registrar

(1) Any person may—

- (a) inspect the documents kept by the registrar of companies, on payment of such fee as may be fixed by the Minister;
- (b) require a certificate of the incorporation of any company, or a copy or extract of any other document or any part of any other document, to be certified by the registrar, on payment for the certificate, certified copy or extract of such fees as the Minister may fix.

(2) No process for compelling the production of any document kept by the registrar shall issue from any court except with the leave of that court, and any such process if issued shall bear thereon a statement that it is issued with the leave of the court.

(3) A copy of, or extract from, any document kept and registered at the office for the registration of companies, certified to be a true copy under the hand of the registrar, assistant registrar or other officer authorised by the Minister (whose official position it shall not be necessary to prove), shall in all legal proceedings by admissible in evidence as of equal validity with the original document.

[(4) A certificate in writing made by the registrar of companies as to-

- (a) the contents of a register kept by the registrar,
- (b) the date on which a document was filed or registered with or delivered to the registrar,
- (c) the date on which a document was received by the registrar, or
- (d) the most recent date (if any) on which a requirement under the Companies Acts was complied with by or in relation to a company,

shall in all legal proceedings be admissible without further proof, until the contrary is shown, as evidence of the facts stated in the certificate.][a]

Amendments

a CA 1963, s 370(4) inserted by CLEA 2001, s 62 with effect from 1 October 2001: Company Law Enforcement Act 2001 (Commencement) (No 2) Order 2001 (SI 438/2001).

---

371 Enforcement of duty to comply with Act

(1) If a company or any officer of a company having made default in complying with any provision of this Act fails to make good the default within 14 days after the service of a notice on the company or officer requiring it or him to do so, [or such greater period as may be specified in the notice],[a] the court may, on an application made to the court by any member or creditor of the company [, by the Director][b] or by the registrar of companies, make an order directing the company and any officer thereof to make good the default within such time as may be specified in the order.

(2) Any such order may provide that all cost of and incidental to the application shall be borne by the company or by any officers of the company responsible for the default.

(3) Nothing in this section shall be taken to prejudice the operation of any enactment imposing penalties [(including restriction under section 150, or disqualification under section 160, of the Companies Act, 1990)][c] on a company or its officers in respect of any such default as aforesaid.

[(4) In this section, 'officer of a company' and cognate words include a director, a shadow director, an officer, a promoter, a receiver, a liquidator or an auditor of a company.][d]

Amendments

a Words 'or such greater period as may be specified in the notice' inserted in CA 1963, s 371(1) by IFCMPA 2005, s 64 with effect from 30 June 2005.[1]

b Words ', by the Director' inserted in CA 1963, s 371(1) by CLEA 2001, s 96 with effect from 28 November 2001.[2]

c Words '(including restriction under section 150, or disqualification under section 160, of the Companies Act, 1990)' inserted in CA 1963, s 371(3) by CLEA 2001, s 96 with effect from 28 November 2001.[3]

d CA 1963, s 371(4) inserted by CLEA 2001, s 96 with effect from 28 November 2001.[4]

1 Investment Funds, Companies and Miscellaneous Provisions Act 2005 (Commencement) Order 2005 (SI 323/2005).

2 Company Law Enforcement Act 2001 (Commencement) (No 3) Order, 2001 (SI 523/2001).

3 Company Law Enforcement Act 2001 (Commencement) (No 3) Order, 2001 (SI 523/2001).

4 Company Law Enforcement Act 2001 (Commencement) (No 3) Order, 2001 (SI 523/2001).

[371A Power to compel compliance with requirement made under section 19(3)(b) of Act of 1990

(1) If a person having made default in complying with a requirement made of him under [section 19(3)(c)][b] of the Companies Act, 1990, fails to make good the default within 14 days after the service of a notice on him requiring him to do so, the court may, on an application made to the court by the Director, make an order directing the person to make good the default within such time as may be specified in the order.

(2) Any such order may provide that all costs of and incidental to the application shall be borne by the person who has made the default concerned.

(3) Nothing in this section shall be taken to prejudice the operation of section 19(6) of the Companies Act, 1990.][a]

Amendments

a CA 1963, s 371A inserted by CLEA 2001, s 97 with effect from 28 November 2001.[1]

[1] Company Law Enforcement Act 2001 (Commencement) (No 3) Order 2001 (SI 523/2001).

b Words 'section 19(3)(c)' substituted for 'section 19(3)(b)' by C(A)A 2009, s 3.

PART XIV
MISCELLANEOUS PROVISIONS RELATING TO BANKING COMPANIES, PARTNERSHIPS AND UNREGISTERED COMPANIES

Provisions relating to Banking Companies

372 Prohibition of banking partnerships with more than ten members

No company, association or partnership consisting of more than ten persons shall be formed for the purpose of carrying on the business of banking, unless it is registered as a company under this Act, or is formed in pursuance of some other statute.

373 Notice to be given to customers on registration of banking company with limited liability

(1) Where a banking company which was in existence on the 7th day of August, 1862, proposes to register as a limited company under this Act, it shall, at least 30 days before so registering, give notice of its intention so to register to every person who has a banking account with the company, either by delivery of the notice to him, or by posting it to him at, or by delivering it at, his last known address.

(2) If the company omits to give the notice required by this section then, as between the company and the person for the time being interested in the account in respect of which the notice ought to have been given, and so far as respects the account down to the time at which notice is given, but not further or otherwise, the certificate of registration with limited liability shall have no operation.

374 Liability of bank of issue unlimited in respect of notes

[...][a]

Amendments

a CA 1963, s 374 was repealed by the CBA 1989, s 4 and Sch with effect from 12 July 1989.[1]

[1] Central Bank Act 1989 (Commencement) Order 1989 (SI 176/1989).

375 Privileges of banks making annual return

(1) Where a company carrying on the business of bankers has duly forwarded to the registrar of companies the annual return required by section 125 and has added thereto a statement of the names of the several places where it carries on business, the company shall not be required to furnish any returns under the Bankers (Ireland) Act, 1825, or section 22 of the Bankers (Ireland) Act, 1845.

(2) The fact of the said annual return and statement having been duly forwarded may be proved in any legal proceedings by the certificate of the registrar.

Prohibition of Partnerships with more than twenty Members

376 Prohibition of partnerships with more than twenty members

No company, association or partnership consisting of more than twenty persons shall be formed for the purpose of carrying on any business (other than the business of banking), that has for its object the acquisition of gain by the company, association or partnership, or by the individual members thereof, unless it is registered as a company under this Act or is formed in pursuance of some other statute.

Application of certain Provisions of this Act to Unregistered Companies

377 Application of certain provisions of this Act to unregistered companies

[(1) The provisions specified in the Ninth Schedule shall apply to all bodies corporate incorporated in and having a principal place of business in the State, other than those mentioned in subsection (2), as if they were companies registered under this Act and subject to such adaptations and modifications (if any) as may be prescribed.][a]

(2) The said provisions shall not apply by virtue of this section to any of the following bodies—

(a) any body corporate incorporated by or registered under any public general statute; and

(b) any body corporate not formed for the purpose of carrying on a business which has for its object the acquisition of gain by the body or by the individual members thereof; and

(c) any body corporate which is prohibited by statute or otherwise from making any distribution of its income or property among its members while it is a going concern or when it is in liquidation; and

(d) any body corporate for the time being exempted by direction of the Minister.

(3) The said provisions shall apply also in like manner in relation to any unincorporated body of persons entitled by virtue of letters patent to any of the privileges conferred by the Chartered Companies Act, 1837, and not registered under any other public general statute, but subject to the like exceptions as are provided for in the case of bodies corporate by paragraphs (b), (c) and (d) of subsection (2).

(4) This section shall not repeal or revoke in whole or in part any enactment, charter or other instrument constituting or regulating any body in relation to which the said provisions are applied by virtue of this section, or restrict the power of the Government to grant a charter in lieu of or supplementary to any such charter as aforesaid; but in relation to any such body, the operation of any such enactment, charter or instrument shall be suspended in so far as it is inconsistent with any of the said provisions as they apply for the time being to that body.

(5) Every body to which this section applies and which was in existence before the operative date shall within six months after the operative date deliver to the registrar of companies for registration a certified copy of the charter, statutes, memorandum and articles, or other instrument constituting or defining the constitution of the body.

(6) Every body to which this section applies and which comes into existence on or after the operative date shall within three months after coming into existence deliver to the registrar of companies for registration a certified copy of the charter, statutes,

memorandum and articles or other instrument constituting or defining the constitution of the body.

(7) If default is made in complying with subsection (5) or (6), the body and every officer of the body who is in default [shall be guilty of an offence and liable to a [class C fine][b]][c].

Amendments

a CA 1963, s 377(1) substituted by CA 1990, s 250(1)(a) with effect from 1 August 1991.[1]

b '£500' substituted for '£100' by C(A)A 1982, Sch 1, increased to £1,500 by CA 1990, s 240(7) as inserted by CLEA 2001, s 104(c) and converted to €1,904.61 by Council Regulations (EC) No 1103/97, No 974/98 and No 2866/98 and the Economic and Monetary Union Act 1998, s 6; the above being implicitly substituted, by Fines Act 2010, s 6, for a fine not exceeding the aforesaid amount. A class C fine currently means a fine not exceeding €2,500.

c Words 'shall be guilty of an offence and liable to a fine' substituted for 'shall be liable to a fine' in CA 1963, s 180(5) by C(AA)A 2003, Sch 2 with effect from 6 April 2004.[2]

1 Companies Act, 1990 (Commencement) (No 2) Order, 1991 (SI 117/1991).

2 Companies (Auditing and Accounting) Act, 2003 (Commencement) Order, 2004 (SI 132/2004).

PART XV
GENERAL

Form of Registers

378 Form of registers, minute books and books of account

(1) Any register, index, minute book or book of account required by this Act to be kept by a company or by the registrar of companies may be kept either by making entries in bound books or by recording the matters in question in any other manner.

(2) Where any register, index, minute book or book of account to be kept by a company is not kept by making entries in a bound book but by some other means, adequate precautions shall be taken for guarding against falsification and facilitating its discovery, and where default is made in complying with this subsection, the company and every officer of the company with this subsection, the company and every officer of the company who is in default [shall be guilty of an offence and liable to a [class C fine][a]].[b]

Amendments

a '£250' substituted for '£50' by C(A)A 1982, Sch 1, increased to £1,500 by CA 1990, s 240(7) as inserted by CLEA 2001, s 104(c) and converted to €1,904.61 by Council Regulations (EC) No 1103/97, No 974/98 and No 2866/98 and the Economic and Monetary Union Act 1998, s 6; the above being implicitly substituted, by Fines Act 2010, s 6, for a fine not exceeding the aforesaid amount. A class C fine currently means a fine not exceeding €2,500.

b Words 'shall be guilty of an offence and liable to a fine' substituted for 'shall be liable to a fine' by C(AA)A 2003, Sch 2.

Service of Documents

379 Service of documents on a company

(1) A document may be served on a company by leaving it at or sending it by post to the registered office of the company or, if the company has not given notice to the registrar of companies of the situation of its registered office, by registering it at the office for the registration of companies.

(2) For the purposes of this section, any document left at or sent by post to the place for the time being recorded by the registrar of companies as the situation of the registered office of a company shall be deemed to have been left at or sent by post to the registered office of the company notwithstanding that the situation of its registered office may have been changed.

Offences

380 Penalty for false statements

[...][a]

Amendments

a Repealed by CA 1990, s 6 and replaced by CA 1990, s 242.

---

381 Improper use of 'limited' or 'teoranta'

[(1) If any person or persons trade or carry on business under a name or title of which 'limited' or 'teoranta', or any contraction or imitation of either word, is the last word, that person or those persons shall be, unless duly incorporated with limited liability, guilty of an offence.

(2) If any person or persons, having committed an offence under subsection (1), fails within 14 days after the service of a notice on him or them to do so, to cease to so trade or carry on business, in breach of that subsection, the court may, on the application of the registrar of companies or the Director, make an order directing the person or persons to so cease within such time as may be specified in the order and the person or persons shall comply with the order.

(3) An order under subsection (2) may provide that all costs of and incidental to the application shall be borne by the person or persons against whom it is made.][a]

Amendments

a CA 1963, s 381 repealed and substituted by CLEA 2001, s 98.

---

382 Prosecution of companies on indictment

(1) Where a company is charged either alone or jointly with some other person with an indictable offence the subsequent provisions of this section shall have effect.

(2) The company may appear at all stages of the proceedings by a representative and the answer to any question to be put to a person charged with an indictable offence may be made on behalf of the company by that representative but if the company does not so

appear it shall not be necessary to put the questions and the District Court may, notwithstanding its absence, take depositions and send forward the company for trial.

(3) Any right of objection or election conferred upon the accused person by any enactment may be exercised on behalf of the company by its representative.

(4) Any plea which may be entered or signed by an accused person, whether before the District Court or before the trial judge, may be entered in writing on behalf of the company by its representative, and, if the company does not appear by its representative or, though it does so appear, fails to enter any such plea, the trial shall proceed as though the company had duly entered a plea of not guilty.

(5) In this section, 'representative' in relation to a company means a person duly appointed by the company to represent it for the purpose of doing any act or thing which the representative of a company is by this section authorised to do, but a person so appointed shall not, by virtue only of being so appointed, be qualified to act on behalf of the company before any court for any other purpose.

(6) A representative for the purpose of this section need not be appointed under the seal of the company and a statement in writing purporting to be signed by a managing director of the company or by some other person (by whatever name called) having, or being one of the persons having, the management of the affairs of the company, to the effect that the person named in the statement has been appointed as the representative of the company for the purposes of this section shall be admissible without further proof as evidence that that person has been so appointed.

(7) In this section, 'company' includes a company incorporated outside the State which has an established place of business in the State.

383 Meaning of 'officer in default'

[(1) For the purpose of any provision of the Companies Acts which provides that an officer of a company who is in default shall be liable to a fine or penalty, an officer who is in default is any officer who authorises or who, in breach of his duty as such officer, permits, the default mentioned in the provision.

(2) For the purposes of this section, an officer shall be presumed to have permitted a default by the company unless the officer can establish that he took all reasonable steps to prevent it or that, by reason of circumstances beyond his control, was unable to do so.

(3) It is the duty of each director and secretary of a company to ensure that the requirements of the Companies Acts are complied with by the company.

(4) In this section 'default' includes a refusal or contravention.][a]

Amendments

a CA 1963, s 383 repealed and substituted by CLEA 2001, s 100.

---

384 Production and inspection of books when offence suspected

(1) If on an application to a Judge of the High Court by the Attorney General, the [Director][a] or a Superintendent of the Garda Síochána, there is shown to be reasonable cause to believe that any person has, while an officer of a company, committed an offence in connection with the management of the company's affairs and that evidence

of the commission of the offence is to be found in any books or papers of or under the control of the company, an order may be made—

(a) authorising any person named therein to inspect the said books or papers or any of them for the purpose of investigating and obtaining evidence of the offence; or

(b) requiring the secretary of the company or such other officer thereof as may be named in the order to produce the said books or any of them to a person named in the order at a place so named.

(2) Subsection (1) shall apply also in relation to any books or papers of a person carrying on the business of banking so far as they relate to the company's affairs, as it applies to any books or papers of or under the control of the company, except that no such order as is referred to in paragraph (b) thereof shall be made by virtue of this subsection.

(3) The decision of a Judge of the High Court on an application under this section shall be final subject to an appeal to the Supreme Court on a question of law.

(4) In this section, 'company' includes a company incorporated outside the State which has an established place of business in the State.

Amendments

a CA 1963, s 384 word 'Director' substituted for 'Minister' by CLEA 2001, s 14.

---

385 Summary proceedings

[...][a]

Amendments

a Repealed by CA 1990, s 6.

---

386 Minimum fine for second or subsequent offences

Where a person is convicted of an offence under this Act and is subsequently convicted of another offence under this Act, the fine to be imposed by the court in respect of such second or subsequent offence shall not be less than [€1,904.61][a] unless the court, having regard to all the circumstances of the case, otherwise decides.

Amendments

a '£250' substituted for '£50' by C(A)A 1982 Sch 1, increased to £1,500 by CA 1990, s 240(7) as inserted by CLEA 2001, s 104(c) and converted to €1,904.61 by Council Regulations (EC) No 1103/97, No 974/98 and No 2866/98 and the Economic and Monetary Union Act 1998, s 6.

---

387 Saving for privileged communications

Where proceedings are instituted under this Act against any person, nothing in sections 170 or 299 shall be taken to require any person who has acted as solicitor for the company to disclose any privileged communication made to him otherwise than as such solicitor.

388 Proof of incorporation of companies incorporated outside the State

A copy of any Act by which a corporation is incorporated, purporting to be published by the Government publishers of any country prescribed by the Minister for the purposes of this section, shall without further proof be *prima facie* evidence of the incorporation of that corporation.

389 Proof of certificates as to incorporation

A certificate signed by any person purporting to hold the office of registrar of companies or assistant registrar of companies or any office similar thereto in any country prescribed by the Minister for the purposes of this section, certifying that a company named in such certificate has been incorporated in that country, shall be *prima facie* evidence of such incorporation without proof of the signature of the person signing such certificate and without proof that the person signing such certificate holds that office.

Legal Proceedings

390 Security for costs by company

Where a limited company is plaintiff in any action or other legal proceeding, any judge having jurisdiction in the matter, may, if it appears by credible testimony that there is reason to believe that the company will be unable to pay the costs of the defendant if successful in his defence, require sufficient security to be given for those costs and may stay all proceedings until the security is given.

391 Power of court to grant relief to officers of company

(1) If in any proceeding for negligence, default, breach of duty or breach of trust against an officer of a company or a person employed by a company as auditor, it appears to the court hearing the case that that officer or person is or may be liable in respect of the negligence, default, breach of duty or breach of trust, but that he has acted honestly and reasonably, and that, having regard to all the circumstances of the case, including those connected with his appointment, he ought fairly to be excused for the negligence, default, breach of duty or breach of trust, that court may relieve him, either wholly or partly from his liability on such terms as the court may think fit.

(2) Where any such officer or person as aforesaid has reason to apprehend that any claim will or might be made against him in respect of any negligence, default, breach of duty or breach of trust, he may apply to the court for relief, and the court on any such application shall have the same power to relieve him as under this section it would have had if it had been a court before which proceedings against that person for negligence, default, breach of duty or breach of trust had been brought.

(3) Where any case to which subsection (1) applies is being tried by a judge with a jury, the judge, after hearing the evidence, may, if he is satisfied that the defendant ought in pursuance of that subsection to be relieved, either in whole or in part, from the liability sought to be enforced against him, withdraw the case in whole on in part from the jury, and direct judgment to be entered for the defendant on such terms as to costs or otherwise as the judge may think proper.

General Provisions as to the Minister

392 Annual report by the Minister

The Minister shall cause a general annual report of matters within this Act to be prepared and laid before both Houses of the Oireachtas [not later than 7 months after the end of the calendar year to which the report relates] [a].

Amendments

a Words 'not later than 7 months after the end of the calendar year to which the report relates' inserted after 'Houses of the Oireachtas' in CA 1963, s 392 by CLEA 2001, s 99.

393 Expenses

The expenses incurred by the Minister in the administration of this Act shall to such extent as may be sanctioned by the Minister for Finance be paid out of moneys provided by the Oireachtas.

394 Authentication of documents issued by the Minister

Any approval, sanction, direction or licence or revocation of licence which under this Act may be given or made by the Minister may be under the hand of any person authorised in that behalf by the Minister.

395 Power to alter Tables and Forms

(1) The Minister shall have power by order to alter or add to the requirements of this Act as to the matters to be stated in a company's balance sheet, profit and loss account and group accounts, and in particular of those of the Sixth Schedule; and any reference in this Act to the Sixth Schedule shall be construed as a reference to that Schedule with any alterations of additions made by orders for the time being in force under this subsection.

[(2) The Minister may by order—

(a) alter Table A, Tábla A and the Third, Seventh and Eighth Schedules;

(b) alter or add to Tables B, C, D and E in the First Schedule[...][a]; and

(c) alter the forms set out in the Second Schedule to the Companies (Amendment) Act, 1983;

but no alteration made by the Minister in Table A or in Tábla A shall affect any company registered before the alteration, or repeal in relation to that company any portion of Table A or Tábla A.][b]

[(3) To avoid doubt, an alteration to the Eighth Schedule under subsection (2)(a) may provide for different fees to be charged for the registration of documents depending on whether they are delivered to the registrar of companies within a specified time or at various times after a specified time.] [c]

Amendments

a Words 'and the form in Part II of the Fifth Schedule' deleted from CA 1963, s 395(2)(b) by CLEA 2001, s 63(1)(a).[1]

b CA 1963, s 385(2) substituted by C(A)A 1983, Sch 1, para 23.

c CA 1963, s 395(3) inserted by CLEA 2001, s 63(1)(b).[2]

1 With effect from 1 March 2002; the Company Law Enforcement Act 2001 (Commencement) (No 2) Order 2001 (SI 438/2001), reg 5.

2 With effect from 26 October 2001; the Company Law Enforcement Act 2001 (Commencement) (No 2) Order 2001 (SI 438/2001), reg 4.

396 Laying of orders before Houses of Oireachtas and power to revoke or amend orders and to prescribe forms

(1) Every order made under this Act shall be laid before each House of the Oireachtas as soon as may be after it is made and if a resolution annulling the order is passed by either House within the next 21 days on which that House has sat after the order is laid before it, the order shall be annulled accordingly but without prejudice to the validity of anything previously done thereunder.

(2) The Minister may by order revoke or amend an order (other than an order made under subsection (2) of section 1) made under this Act.

(3) The Minister may by order prescribe forms to be used in connection with any of the provisions of this Act other than those relating to the winding up of companies.

Supplemental

397 Restriction of section 58 of Solicitors Act, 1954

Notwithstanding section 58 of the Solicitors Act, 1954, a person to whom paragraph (a) or (b) of subsection (1) of section 162 applies may draw or prepare any document for the purpose of this Act other than a deed or a memorandum or articles of association.

398 Provisions as to winding-up proceedings commenced before the operative date

(1) The provisions of this Act relating to winding up (other than subsections (2) and (3)) shall not apply to any company of which the winding up commenced before the operative date but every such company shall be wound up in the same manner and with the same incidents as if this Act (apart from the enactments aforesaid) had not been passed, and for the purposes of the winding up, the Act or Acts under which the winding up commenced shall be deemed to remain in full force.

(2) An office copy of every order staying the proceedings in a winding up commenced as aforesaid shall forthwith be forwarded by the company or by such person as the court may direct, to the registrar of companies for registration.

(3) If a company fails to comply with subsection (2), the company and every officer of the company who is in default [shall be guilty of an offence and liable to a [class C fine][a]],[b] and if any other person fails to comply with subsection (2) such person [shall be guilty of an offence and liable to a [class C fine][a]].[b]

Amendments

a '£125' substituted for '£25' by C(A)A 1982, Sch 1, increased to £1,500 by CA 1990, s 240(7) as inserted by CLEA 2001, s 104(c) and converted to €1,904.61 by Council Regulations (EC) No 1103/97, No 974/98 and No 2866/98 and the Economic and Monetary Union Act 1998, s 6; the above being implicitly substituted, by Fines Act 2010, s 6, for a fine not exceeding the aforesaid amount. A class C fine currently means a fine not exceeding €2,500.

b Words 'shall be guilty of an offence and liable to a fine' substituted for 'shall be liable to a fine' in both instances where they occur in CA 1963, s 398 by C(AA)A 2003, Sch 2, para 4.

399 Amendments of other Acts

The enactments set out in the Eleventh Schedule shall have effect subject to the amendments specified in that Schedule.

SCHEDULES

FIRST SCHEDULE

TABLE A [...][a] AND TABLES B, C, D AND E

TABLE A

PART I

REGULATIONS FOR MANAGEMENT OF A COMPANY LIMITED BY SHARES NOT BEING A PRIVATE COMPANY

Interpretation

1. In these regulations:

'the Act' means the Companies Act, 1963 (No. 33 of 1963);

'the directors' means the directors for the time being of the company or the directors present at a meeting of the board of directors and includes any person occupying the position of director by whatever name called;

'the register' means the register of members to be kept as required by section 116 of the Act;

'secretary' means any person appointed to perform the duties of the secretary of the company;

'the office' means the registered office for the time being of the company;

'the seal' means the common seal of the company.

Expressions referring to writing shall, unless the contrary intention appears, be construed as including references to printing, lithography, photography, and any other modes of representing or reproducing words in a visible form.

Unless the contrary intention appears, words or expressions contained in these regulations shall bear the same meaning as in the Act or in any statutory modification thereof in force at the date at which these regulations become binding on the company.

Amendments

a The Irish language version of Table A is omitted from this book.

Share Capital and Variation of Rights

2. Without prejudice to any special rights previously conferred on the holders of any existing shares or class of shares, any share in the company may be issued with such preferred, deferred or other special rights or such restrictions, whether in regard to dividend, voting, return of capital or otherwise, as the company may from time to time by ordinary resolution determine.

[**3**. If at any time the share capital is divided into different classes of shares, the rights attached to any class may, whether or not the company is being wound up, be varied or abrogated with the consent in writing of the holders of three-fourths of the issued shares of that class, or with the sanction of a special resolution passed at a separate general meeting of the holders of the shares of the class.][a]

Amendments

a Substituted by C(A)A 1983, Sch 1 para 24.

4. The rights conferred upon the holders of the shares of any class issued with preferred or other rights shall not, unless otherwise expressly provided by the terms of issue of the shares of that class, be deemed to be varied by the creation or issue of further shares ranking *pari passu* therewith.

[**5**. Subject to the provisions of these regulations relating to new shares, the shares shall be at the disposal of the directors, and they may (subject to the provisions of the Companies Acts, 1963 to 1983) allot, grant options over or otherwise dispose of them to such persons, on such terms and conditions and at such times as they may consider to be in the best interests of the company and its shareholders, but so that no share shall be issued at a discount and so that, in the case of shares offered to the public for subscription by a public limited company, the amount payable on application on each share shall not be less than one-quarter of the nominal amount of the share and the whole of any premium thereon.] [a]

Amendments

a Substituted by C(A)A 1983, Sch 1 para 24.

6. The company may exercise the powers of paying commissions conferred by section 59 of the Act, provided that the rate per cent. and the amount of the commission paid or agreed to be paid shall be disclosed in the manner required by that section, and the rate of the commission shall not exceed the rate of 10 per cent. of the price at which the shares in respect whereof the same is paid are issued or an amount equal to 10 per cent. of such price (as the case may be). Such commission may be satisfied by the payment of cash or the allotment of fully or partly paid shares or partly in one way and partly in the other. The company may also, on any issue of shares, pay such brokerage as may be lawful.

7. Except as required by law, no person shall be recognised by the company as holding any share upon any trust, and the company shall not be bound by or be compelled in any way to recognise (even when having notice thereof) any equitable, contingent, future or partial interest in any share or any interest in any fractional part of a share or (except only as by these regulations or by law otherwise provided) any other rights in respect of any share except an absolute right to the entirety thereof in the registered holder: this shall not preclude the company from requiring the members or a transferee of shares to furnish the company with information as to the beneficial ownership of any share when such information is reasonably required by the company.

[**8**. Every person whose name is entered as a member in the register shall be entitled without payment to receive within 2 months after allotment or lodgement of a transfer (or within such other period as the conditions of issue shall provide) one certificate for all his shares or several certificates each for one or more of his shares upon payment of [16 cent][b] for every certificate after the first or such less sum as the directors shall from time to time determine, so, however, that in respect of a share or shares held jointly by several persons the company shall not be bound to issue more than one certificate, and delivery of a certificate for a share to one of several joint holders shall be sufficient delivery to all such holders. Every certificate shall be under the seal or under the official seal kept by the company by virtue of section 3 of the Companies (Amendment) Act, 1977, and shall specify the shares to which it relates and the amount paid up thereon.][a]

Amendments

a Reg 8 substituted by C(A)A 1977, s 5.

b '12½ new pence' converted to 16 cent by Council Regulations (EC) No 1103/97, No 974/98 and No 2866/98 and the Economic and Monetary Union Act 1998, s 6.

---

9. If a share certificate be defaced, lost or destroyed, it may be renewed on payment of [17 cent][a] or such less sum and on such terms (if any) as to evidence and indemnity and the payment of out-of-pocket expenses of the company of investigating evidence as the directors think fit.

Amendment

a '2s. 6d.' to be read as 'thirteen new pence' pursuant to the Decimal Currency Act 1970, s 9, and converted to 17 cent by Council Regulations (EC) No 1103/97, No 974/98 and No 2866/98 and the Economic and Monetary Union Act 1998, s 6.

---

10. The company shall not give, whether directly or indirectly, and whether by means of a loan, guarantee, the provision of security or otherwise, any financial assistance for the purpose of or in connection with a purchase or subscription made or to be made by any person of or for any shares in the company or in its holding company, but this regulation shall not prohibit any transaction permitted by section 60 of the Act.

Lien

11. The company shall have a first and paramount lien on every share (not being a fully paid share) called or payable at a fixed time in respect of that share [...][a] but the directors may at any time declare any share to be wholly or in part exempt from the provisions of this regulation. The company's lien on a share shall extend to all dividends payable thereon.

Amendments

a Words deleted by C(A)A 1983, Sch 3.

---

12. The company may sell, in such manner as the directors think fit, any shares on which the company has a lien, but no sale shall be made unless a sum in respect of which the lien exists is immediately payable, nor until the expiration of 14 days after a notice in writing, stating and demanding payment of such part of the amount in respect of which the lien exists as is immediately payable, has been given to the registered holder for the time being of the share, or the person entitled thereto by reason of his death or bankruptcy.

13. To give effect to any such sale, the directors may authorise some person to transfer the shares sold to the purchaser thereof. The purchaser shall be registered as the holder of the shares comprised in any such transfer, and he shall not be bound to see to the application of the purchase money, nor shall his title to the shares be affected by any irregularity or invalidity in the proceedings in reference to the sale.

14. The proceeds of the sale shall be received by the company and applied in payment of such part of the amount in respect of which the lien exists as is immediately payable, and the residue, if any, shall (subject to a like lien for sums not immediately payable as existed upon the shares before the sale) be paid to the person entitled to the shares at the date of the sale.

Calls on Shares

15. The directors may from time to time make calls upon the members in respect of any moneys unpaid on their shares (whether on account of the nominal value of the shares or by way of premium) and not by the conditions of allotment thereof made payable at fixed times, provided that no call shall exceed one-fourth of the nominal value of the share or be payable at less than one month from the date fixed for the payment of the last preceding call, and each member shall (subject to receiving at least 14 days' notice specifying the time or times and place of payment) pay to the company at the time or times and place so specified the amount called on his shares. A call may be revoked or postponed as the directors may determine.

16. A call shall be deemed to have been made at the time when the resolution of the directors authorising the call was passed and may be required to be paid by instalments.

17. The joint holders of a share shall be jointly and severally liable to pay all calls in respect thereof.

18. If a sum called in respect of a share is not paid before or on the day appointed for payment thereof, the person from whom the sum is due shall pay interest on the sum from the day appointed for payment thereof to the time of actual payment at such rate, not exceeding 5 per cent. per annum, as the directors may determine, but the directors shall be at liberty to waive payment of such interest wholly or in part.

19. Any sum which by the terms of issue of a share becomes payable on allotment or at any fixed date, whether on account of the nominal value of the share or by way of premium, shall, for the purposes of these regulations, be deemed to be a call duly made and payable on the date on which, by the terms of issue, the same becomes payable, and in case of non-payment all the relevant provisions of these regulations as to payment of interest and expenses, forfeiture or otherwise, shall apply as if such sum had become payable by virtue of a call duly made and notified.

20. The directors may, on the issue of shares, differentiate between the holders as to the amount of calls to be paid and the time of payment.

21. The directors may, if they think fit, receive from any member willing to advance the same, all or any part of the moneys uncalled and unpaid upon any shares held by him, and upon all or any of the moneys so advanced may (until the same would, but for such advance, become payable) pay interest at such rate not exceeding (unless the company in general meeting otherwise directs) 5 per cent. per annum, as may be agreed upon between the directors and the member paying such sum in advance.

Transfer of Shares

22. The instrument of transfer of any share shall be executed by or on behalf of the transferor and transferee, and the transferor shall be deemed to remain the holder of the share until the name of the transferee is entered in the register in respect thereof.

23. Subject to such of the restrictions of these regulations as may be applicable, any member may transfer all or any of his shares by instrument in writing in any usual or common form or any other form which the directors may approve.

24. The directors may decline to register the transfer of a share (not being a fully paid share) to a person of whom they do not approve, and they may also decline to register the transfer of a share on which the company has a lien. The directors may also decline to register any transfer of a share which, in their opinion, may imperil or prejudicially affect the status of the company in the State or which may imperil any tax concession or rebate to which the members of the company are entitled or which may involve the company in the payment of any additional stamp or other duties on any conveyance of any property made or to be made to the company.

25. The directors may also decline to recognise any instrument of transfer unless—

(a) a fee of 2s. 6d. or such lesser sum as the directors may from time to time require, is paid to the company in respect thereof; and

(b) the instrument of transfer is accompanied by the certificate of the shares to which it relates, and such other evidence as the directors may reasonably require to show the right of the transferor to make the transfer; and

(c) the instrument of transfer is in respect of one class of share only.

26. If the directors refuse to register a transfer they shall, within 2 months after the date on which the transfer was lodged with the company, send to the transferee notice of the refusal.

27. The registration of transfers may be suspended at such times and for such periods, not exceeding in the whole 30 days in each year, as the directors may from time to time determine.

28. The company shall be entitled to charge a fee not exceeding [17 cent][a] on the registration of every probate, letters of administration, certificate of death or marriage, power of attorney, notice as to stock or other instrument.

Amendments

a '2s.6d' to be read as 'thirteen new pence' pursuant to the Decimal Currency Act 1970, s 9, and converted to 17 cent by Council Regulations (EC) No 1103/97, No 974/98 and No 2866/ 98 and the Economic and Monetary Union Act 1998, s 6.

Transmission of Shares

29. In the case of the death of a member, the survivor or survivors where the deceased was a joint holder, and the personal representatives of the deceased where he was a sole holder, shall be the only persons recognised by the company as having any title to his interest in the shares; but nothing herein contained shall release the estate of a deceased joint holder from any liability in respect of any share which had been jointly held by him with other persons.

...on becoming entitled to a share in consequence of the death or bankruptcy of a member may, upon such evidence being produced as may from time to time properly be required by the directors and subject as hereinafter provided, elect either to be registered himself as holder of the share or to have some person nominated by him registered as the transferee thereof, but the directors shall, in either case, have the same right to decline or suspend registration as they would have had in the case of a transfer of the share by that member before his death or bankruptcy, as the case may be.

31. If the person so becoming entitled elects to be registered himself, he shall deliver or send to the company a notice in writing signed by him stating that he so elects. If he elects to have another person registered, he shall testify his election by executing to that person a transfer of the share. All the limitations, restrictions and provisions of these regulations relating to the right to transfer and the registration of transfers of shares shall be applicable to any such notice or transfer as aforesaid as if the death or bankruptcy of the member had not occurred and the notice or transfer were a transfer signed by that member.

32. A person becoming entitled to a share by reason of the death or bankruptcy of the holder shall be entitled to the same dividends and other advantages to which he would be entitled if he were the registered holder of the share, except that he shall not, before being registered as a member in respect of the share, be entitled in respect of it to exercise any right conferred by membership in relation to meetings of the company, so, however, that the directors may at any time give notice requiring any such person to elect either to be registered himself or to transfer the share, and if the notice is not complied with within 90 days, the directors may thereupon withhold payment of all dividends, bonuses or other moneys payable in respect of the share until the requirements of the notice have been complied with.

Forfeiture of Shares

33. If a member fails to pay and call or instalment of a call on the day appointed for payment thereof, the directors may, at any time thereafter during such time as any part of the call or instalment remains unpaid, serve a notice on him requiring payment of so much of the call or instalment as is unpaid together with any interest which may have accrued.

34. The notice shall name a further day (not earlier than the expiration of 14 days from the date of service of the notice) on or before which the payment required by the notice is to be made, and shall state that in the event of non-payment at or before the time appointed the shares in respect of which the call was made will be liable to be forfeited.

35. If the requirements of any such notice as aforesaid are not complied with, any share in respect of which the notice has been given may at any time thereafter, before the payment required by the notice has been made, be forfeited by a resolution of the directors to that effect.

36. A forfeited share may be sold or otherwise disposed of on such terms and in such manner as the directors think fit, and at any time before a sale or disposition the forfeiture may be cancelled on such terms as the directors think fit.

37. A person whose shares have been forfeited shall cease to be a member in respect of the forfeited shares, but shall, notwithstanding, remain liable to pay to the company all moneys which, at the date of forfeiture, were payable by him to the company in respect of the shares, but his liability shall cease if and when the company shall have received payment in full of all such moneys in respect of the shares.

38. A statutory declaration that the declarant is a director or the secretary of the company, and that a share in the company has been duly forfeited on a date stated in the declaration, shall be conclusive evidence of the facts therein stated as against all persons claiming to be entitled to the share. The company may receive the consideration, if any, given for the share on any sale or disposition thereof and may execute a transfer of the share in favour of the person to whom the share is sold of disposed of and he shall thereupon be registered as the holder of the share, and shall not be bound to see to the application of the purchase money, if any, nor shall his title to the share be affected by any irregularity or invalidity in the proceedings in reference to the forfeiture, sale or disposal of the shares.

39. The provisions of these regulations as to forfeiture shall apply in the case of non-payment of any sum which, by the terms of issue of a share, becomes payable at a fixed time, whether on account of the nominal value of the share or by way of premium, as if the same had been payable by virtue of a call duly made and notified.

Conversion of Shares into Stock

40. The company may by ordinary resolution convert any paid up shares into stock, and reconvert any stock into paid up shares of any denomination.

41. The holders of stock may transfer the same, or any part thereof, in the same manner, and subject to the same regulations, as and subject to which the shares from which the stock arose might previously to conversion have been transferred, or as near thereto as circumstances admit; and the directors may from time to time fix the minimum amount of stock transferable but so that such minimum shall not exceed the nominal amount of each share from which the stock arose.

42. The holders of stock shall, according to the amount of stock held by them, have the same rights, privileges and advantages in relation to dividends, voting at meetings of the company and other matters as if they held the shares from which the stock arose, but no such right, privilege or advantage (except participation in the dividends and profits of the company and in the assets on winding up) shall be conferred by an amount of stock which would not, if existing in shares, have conferred that right, privilege or advantage.

43. Such of the regulations of the company as are applicable to paid up shares shall apply to stock, and the words 'share' and 'shareholder' therein shall include 'stock' and 'stockholder'.

Alteration of Capital

44. The company may from time to time by ordinary resolution increase the share capital by such sum, to be divided into shares of such amount, as the resolution shall prescribe.

45. The company may by ordinary resolution—

(a) consolidate and divide all or any of its share capital into shares of larger amount than its existing shares;

(b) subdivide its existing shares, or any of them, into shares of smaller amount than is fixed by the memorandum of association subject, nevertheless, to section 68(1)(d) of the Act;

(c) cancel any shares which, at the date of the passing of the resolution, have not been taken or agreed to be taken by any person.

46. The company may by special resolution reduce its share capital, any capital redemption reserve fund or any share premium account in any manner and with and subject to any incident authorised, and consent required, by law.

General Meetings

47. All general meetings of the company shall be held in the State.

48. (1) Subject to paragraph (2) of this regulation, the company shall in each year hold a general meeting as its annual general meeting in addition to any other meeting in that year, and shall specify the meeting as such in the notices calling it; and not more than 15 months shall elapse between the date of one annual general meeting of the company and that of the next.

(2) So long as the company holds its first annual general meeting within 18 months of its incorporation, it need not hold it in the year of its incorporation or in the year following. Subject to regulation 47, the annual general meeting shall be held at such time and place as the directors shall appoint.

49. All general meetings other than annual general meetings shall be called extraordinary general meetings.

50. The directors may, whenever they think fit, convene an extraordinary general meeting, and extraordinary general meetings shall also be convened on such requisition, or in default, may be convened by such requisitionists, as provided by section 132 of the Act. If at any time there are not within the State sufficient directors capable of acting to form a quorum, any director or any 2 members of the company may convene an extraordinary general meeting in the same manner as nearly as possible as that in which meetings may be convened by the directors.

Notice of General Meetings

51. Subject to sections 133 and 141 of the Act, an annual general meeting and a meeting called for the passing of a special resolution shall be called by 21 days' notice in writing at the least, and a meeting of the company (other than an annual general meeting or a meeting for the passing of a special resolution) shall be called by 14 days' notice in writing at the least. The notice shall be exclusive of the day on which it is served or deemed to be served and of the day for which it is given, and shall specify the place, the day and the hour of the meeting, and in the case of special business, the general nature of that business, and shall be given, in manner hereinafter mentioned, to such persons as are, under the regulations of the company, entitled to receive such notices from the company.

52. The accidental omission to give notice of a meeting to, or the non-receipt of notice of a meeting by, any person entitled to receive notice shall not invalidate the proceedings at the meeting.

Proceedings at General Meetings

53. All business shall be deemed special that is transacted at an extraordinary general meeting, and also all that is transacted at an annual general meeting, with the exception of declaring a dividend, the consideration of the accounts, balance sheets and the reports of the directors and auditors, the election of directors in the place of those retiring, the re-appointment of the retiring auditors and the fixing of the remuneration of the auditors.

54. No business shall be transacted at any general meeting unless a quorum of members is present at the time when the meeting proceeds to business; save as herein otherwise provided, three members present in person shall be a quorum.

55. If within half an hour from the time appointed for the meeting a quorum is not present, the meeting, if convened upon the requisition of members, shall be dissolved; in any other case it shall stand adjourned to the same day in the next week, at the same time and place or to such other day and at such other time and place as the directors may determine, and if at the adjourned meeting a quorum is not present within half an hour from the time appointed for the meeting, the members present shall be a quorum.

56. The chairman, if any, of the board of directors shall preside as chairman at every general meeting of the company, or if there is no such chairman, or if he is not present within 15 minutes after the time appointed for the holding of the meeting or is unwilling to act, the directors present shall elect one of their number to be chairman of the meeting.

57. If at any meeting no director is willing to act as chairman or if no director is present within 15 minutes after the time appointed for holding the meeting, the members present shall choose one of their number to be chairman of the meeting.

58. The chairman may, with the consent of any meeting at which a quorum is present, and shall if so directed by the meeting, adjourn the meeting from time to time and from place to place, but no business shall be transacted at any adjourned meeting other than the business left unfinished at the meeting from which the adjournment took place. When a meeting is adjourned for 30 days or more, notice of the adjourned meeting shall be given as in the case of an original meeting. Save as aforesaid it shall not be necessary to give any notice of an adjournment or of the business to be transacted at an adjourned meeting.

59. At any general meeting a resolution put to the vote of the meeting shall be decided on a show of hands unless a poll is (before or on the declaration of the result of the show of hands) demanded—

(a) by the chairman; or

(b) by at least three members present in person or by proxy; or

(c) by any member or members present in person or by proxy and representing not less than one-tenth of the total voting rights of all the members having the right to vote at the meetings; or

(d) by a member or members holding shares in the company conferring the right to vote at the meeting being shares on which an aggregate sum has been paid up equal to not less than one-tenth of the total sum paid up on all the shares conferring that right.

Unless a poll is so demanded, a declaration by the chairman that a resolution has, on a show of hands, been carried or carried unanimously, or by a particular majority, or lost, and an entry to that effect in the book containing the minutes of the proceedings of the company shall be conclusive evidence of the fact without proof of the number or proportion of the votes recorded in favour of or against such resolution.

The demand for a poll may be withdrawn.

60. Except as provided in regulation 62, if a poll is duly demanded it shall be taken in such manner as the chairman directs, and the result of the poll shall be deemed to be the resolution of the meeting at which the poll was demanded.

61. Where there is an equality of votes, whether on a show of hands or on a poll, the chairman of the meeting at which the show of hands takes place or at which the poll is demanded, shall be entitled to a second or casting vote.

62. A poll demanded on the election of a chairman or on a question of adjournment shall be taken forthwith. A poll demanded on any other question shall be taken at such time as the chairman of the meeting directs, and any business other than that on which a poll is demanded may be proceeded with pending the taking of the poll.

Votes of Members

63. Subject to any rights or restrictions for the time being attached to any class or classes of shares, on a show of hands every member present in person and every proxy shall have one vote, so, however, that no individual shall have more than one vote, and on a poll every member shall have one vote for each share of which he is the holder.

64. Where there are joint holders, the vote of the senior who tenders a vote, whether in person or by proxy, shall be accepted to the exclusion of the votes of the other joint holders; and for this purpose, seniority shall be determined by the order in which the names stand in the register.

65. A member of unsound mind, or in respect of whom an order has been made by any court having jurisdiction in lunacy, may vote, whether on a show of hands or on a poll, by his committee, receiver, guardian or other person appointed by that court, and any such committee, receiver, guardian or other person may vote by proxy on a show of hands or on a poll.

66. No member shall be entitled to vote at any general meeting unless all calls or other sums immediately payable by him in respect of shares in the company have been paid.

67. No objection shall be raised to the qualification of any voter except at the meeting or adjourned meeting at which the vote objected to is given or tendered, and every vote not disallowed at such meeting shall be valid for all purposes. Any such objection made in due time shall be referred to the chairman of the meeting, whose decision shall be final and conclusive.

68. Votes may be given either personally or by proxy.

69. The instrument appointing a proxy shall be in writing under the hand of the appointer or of his attorney duly authorised in writing, or, if the appointer is a body corporate, either under seal or under the hand of an officer or attorney duly authorised. A proxy need not be a member of the company.

70. The instrument appointing a proxy and the power of attorney or other authority, if any, under which it is signed, or a notarially certified copy of that power or authority shall be deposited at the office or at such other place within the State as is specified for that purpose in the notice convening the meeting, not less than 48 hours before the time for holding the meeting or adjourned meeting at which the person named in the instrument proposes to vote, or, in the case of a poll, not less than 48 hours before the time appointed for the taking of the poll, and, in default, the instrument of proxy shall not be treated as valid.

71. An instrument appointing a proxy shall be in the following form or a form as near thereto as circumstances permit—

'Limited.

I/We of ....

in the Country of..., being a member/members of the above-named company hereby appoint ....

of..

or failing him, ...

of..

as my/our proxy to vote for me/us on my/our behalf at the (annual or extraordinary, as the case may be) general meeting of the company to be held on the .... day of ...., 19.............. and at any adjournment thereof.

Signed this.................day of............................., 19......

This form is to be used *in favour/against the resolution.

Unless otherwise instructed the proxy will vote as he thinks fit.

*Strike out whichever is not desired.'

72. The instrument appointing a proxy shall be deemed to confer authority to demand or join in demanding a poll.

73. A vote given in accordance with the terms of an instrument of proxy shall be valid notwithstanding the previous death or insanity of the principal or revocation of the proxy or of the authority under which the proxy was executed or the transfer of the share in respect of which the proxy is given, if not intimation in writing of such death, insanity, revocation or transfer as aforesaid is received by the company at the office before the commencement of the meeting or adjourned meeting at which the proxy is used.

Bodies Corporate acting by Representatives at Meetings

74. Any body corporate which is a member of the company may, by resolution of its directors or other governing body, authorise such person as it thinks fit to act as its representative at any meeting of the company or of any class of members of the company, and the person so authorised shall be entitled to exercise the same powers on behalf of the body corporate which he represents as that body corporate could exercise if it were an individual member of the company.

Directors

75. The number of the directors and the names of the first directors shall be determined in writing by the subscribers of the memorandum of association or a majority of them.

76. The remuneration of the directors shall from time to time be determined by the company in general meeting. Such remuneration shall be deemed to accrue from day to day. The directors may also be paid all travelling, hotel and other expenses properly incurred by them in attending and returning from meetings of the directors or any committee of the directors or general meetings of the company or in connection with the business of the company.

77. The shareholding qualification for directors may be fixed by the company in general meeting and unless and until so fixed, no qualification shall be required.

78. A director of the company may be or become a director or other officer of, or otherwise interested in, any company promoted by the company or in which the company may be interested as shareholder or otherwise, and no such director shall be accountable to the company for any remuneration or other benefits received by him as a director or officer of, or from his interest in, such other company unless the company otherwise directs.

Borrowing Powers

79. The directors may exercise all powers of the company to borrow money, and to mortgage or charge its undertaking, property and uncalled capital, or any part thereof, and [subject to section 20 of the Companies (Amendment) Act, 1983][a] to issue debentures, debenture stock and other securities, whether outright or as security for any debt, liability or obligation of the company or of any third party, so, however, that the amount for the time being remaining undischarged of moneys borrowed or secured by the directors as aforesaid (apart from temporary loans obtained from the company's bankers in the ordinary course of business) shall not at any time, without the previous sanction of the company in general meeting, exceed the nominal amount of the share capital of the company for the time being issued, but nevertheless no lender or other person dealing with the company shall be concerned to see or inquire whether this limit is observed. No debt incurred or security given in excess of such limit shall be invalid or ineffectual except in the case of express notice to the lender or the recipient of the security at the time when the debt was incurred or security given that the limit hereby imposed had been or was thereby exceeded.

Amendments

a Inserted by C(A)A 1983, Sch 1 para 24.

Powers and Duties of Directors

80. The business of the company shall be managed by the directors, who may pay all expenses incurred in promoting and registering the company and may exercise all such powers of the company as are not, by [the Companies Acts, 1963 to 1983][a] or by these regulations, required to be exercised by the company in general meeting, subject, nevertheless, to any of these regulations, to the provisions of the Act and to such directions, being not inconsistent with the aforesaid regulations or provisions, as may be given by the company in general meeting; but no direction given by the company in general meeting shall invalidate any prior act of the directors which would have been valid if that direction had not been given.

Amendments

a Substituted by C(A)A 1983, Sch 1 para 24.

---

81. The directors may from time to time and at any time by power of attorney appoint any company, firm or person or body of persons, whether nominated directly or indirectly by the directors, to be the attorney or attorneys of the company for such purposes and with such powers, authorities and discretions (not exceeding those vested in or exercisable by the directors under these regulations) and for such period and subject to such conditions as they may think fit, and any such power of attorney may contain such provisions for the protection of persons dealing with any such attorney as the directors may think fit, and may also authorise any such attorney to delegate all or any of the powers, authorities and discretions vested in him.

82. The company may exercise the powers conferred by section 41 of the Act with regard to having an official seal for use abroad, and such powers shall be vested in the directors.

83. A director who is in any way, whether directly or indirectly, interested in a contract or proposed contract with the company shall declare the nature of his interest at a meeting of the directors in accordance with section 194 of the Act.

84. A director shall not vote in respect of any contract or arrangement in which he is so interested, and if he shall so vote, his vote shall not be counted, nor shall he be counted in the quorum present at the meeting but neither of these prohibitions shall apply to—

(a) any arrangement for giving any director any security or indemnity in respect of money lent by him to or obligations undertaken by him for the benefit of the company; or

(b) any arrangement for the giving by the company of any security to a third party in respect of a debt or obligation of the company for which the director himself has assumed responsibility in whole or in part under a guarantee or indemnity or by the deposit of security; or

(c) any contract by a director to subscribe for or underwrite shares or debenture of the company; or

(d) any contract or arrangement with any other company in which he is interested only as an officer of such other company or as a holder of shares or other securities in such other company;

and these prohibitions may at any time be suspended or relaxed to any extent and either generally or in respect of any particular contract, arrangement or transaction by the company in general meeting.

85. A director may hold any other office or place of profit under the company (other than the office of auditor) in conjunction with his office of director for such period and on such terms as to remuneration and otherwise as the directors may determine, and no director or intending director shall be disqualified by his office from contracting with the company either with regard to his tenure of any such other office or place of profit or as vendor, purchaser or otherwise, nor shall any such contract or any contract or arrangement entered into by or on behalf of the company in which any director is in any way interested, be liable to be avoided, nor shall any director so contracting or being so interested be liable to account to the company for any profit realised by any such contract or arrangement by reason of such director holding that office or of the fiduciary relation thereby established.

86. A director, notwithstanding his interest, may be counted in the quorum present at any meeting whereat he or any other director is appointed to hold any such office or place of profit under the company or whereat the terms of any such appointment are arranged, and he may vote on any such appointment or arrangement other than his own appointment or the arrangement of the terms thereof.

87. Any director may act by himself or his firm in a professional capacity for the company, and he or his firm shall be entitled to remuneration for professional services as if he were not a director; but nothing herein contained shall authorise a director or his firm to act as auditor to the company.

88. All cheques, promissory notes, drafts, bills of exchange and other negotiable instruments and all receipts for moneys paid to the company shall be signed, drawn, accepted, endorsed or otherwise executed, as the case may be, by such person or persons and in such manner as the directors shall from time to time by resolution determine.

89. The directors shall cause minutes to be made in books provided for the purpose—

(a) of all appointment of officers made by the directors;

(b) of the names of the directors present at each meeting of the directors and of any committee of the directors;

(c) of all resolutions and proceedings at all meetings of the company and of the directors and of committees of directors.

90. The directors on behalf of the company may pay a gratuity or pension or allowance on retirement to any director who has held any other salaried office or place of profit with the company or to [his or her surviving spouse or surviving civil partner, within the meaning of the Civil Partnership and Certain Rights and Obligations of Cohabitants Act 2010, or dependants][a], and may make contributions to any fund any pay premiums for the purchase or provision of any such gratuity, pension or allowance.

Amendments

a Words 'his or her surviving spouse or surviving civil partner, within the meaning of the Civil Partnership and Certain Rights and Obligations of Cohabitants Act 2010, or dependants' substituted for 'his widow or dependants' by Civil Partnership and Certain Rights and Obligations of Cohabitants Act 2010, Sch, Pt 2, Item No. 17.

Disqualification of Directors

91. The office of director shall be vacated if the director—

(a) ceases to be a director by virtue of section 180 of the Act; or

(b) is adjudged bankrupt in the State or in Northern Ireland or Great Britain or makes any arrangement or composition with his creditors generally; of

(c) becomes prohibited from being a director by reason of any order made under section 184 of the Act; or

(d) becomes of unsound mind; or

(e) resigns his office by notice in writing to the company; or

(f) is convicted of an indictable offence unless the directors otherwise determine; or

(g) is for more than 6 months absent without permission of the directors from meetings of the directors held during that period.

Rotation of Directors

92. At the first annual general meeting of the company all the directors shall retire from office, and at the annual general meeting in every subsequent year, one-third of the directors for the time being, or, if their number is not three or a multiple of three, then the number nearest one-third shall retire from office.

93. The directors to retire in every year shall be those who have been longest in office since their last election but as between persons who became directors on the same day, those to retire shall (unless they otherwise agree among themselves) be determined by lot.

94. A retiring director shall be eligible for re-election.

95. The company, at the meeting at which a director retires in manner aforesaid, may fill the vacated office by electing a person thereto, and in default the retiring director shall, if offering himself for re-election, be deemed to have been re-elected, unless at such meeting it is expressly resolved not to fill such vacated office, or unless a resolution for the re-election of such director has been put to the meeting and lost.

96. No person other than a director retiring at the meeting shall, unless recommended by the directors, be eligible for election to the office of director at any general meeting unless not less than 3 nor more than 21 days before the day appointed for the meeting there shall have been left at the office notice in writing signed by a member duly qualified to attend and vote at the meeting for which such notice is given, of his intention to propose such person for election and also notice in writing signed by that person of his willingness to be elected.

97. The company may from time to time by ordinary resolution increase or reduce the number of directors and may also determine in what rotation the increased or reduced number is to go out of office.

98. The directors shall have power at any time and from time to time to appoint any person to be a director, either to fill a casual vacancy or as an addition to the existing directors, but so that the total number of directors shall not at any time exceed the number fixed in accordance with these regulations. Any director so appointed shall hold office only until the next following annual general meeting, and shall then be eligible for re-election but shall not be taken into account in determining the directors who are to retire by rotation at such meeting.

99. The company may, by ordinary resolution, of which extended notice has been given in accordance with section 142 of the Act, remove any director before the expiration of his period of office notwithstanding anything in these regulations or in any agreement between the company and such director. Such removal shall be without prejudice to any claim such director may have for damages for breach of any contract of service between him and the company.

100. The company may, by ordinary resolution, appoint another person in place of a director removed from office under regulation 99 and without prejudice to the powers of the directors under regulation 98 the company in general meeting may appoint any person to be a director either to fill a casual vacancy or as an additional director. A person appointed in place of a director so removed or to fill such a vacancy shall be subject to retirement at the same time as if he had become a director on the day on which the director in whose place he is appointed was last elected a director.

Proceedings of Directors

101. The directors may meet together for the despatch of business, adjourn and otherwise regulate their meetings as they think fit. Questions arising at any meeting shall be decided by a majority of votes. Where there is an equality of votes, the chairman shall have a second or casting vote. A director may, and the secretary on the requisition of a director shall, at any time summon a meeting of the directors. If the directors so resolve, it shall not be necessary to give notice of a meeting of directors to any director who, being resident in the State, is for the time being absent from the State.

102. The quorum necessary for the transaction of the business of the directors may be fixed by the directors, and unless so fixed shall be two.

103. The continuing directors may act notwithstanding any vacancy in their number but, if and so long as their number is reduced below the number fixed by or pursuant to the regulations of the company as the necessary quorum of directors, the continuing directors or director may act for the purpose of increasing the number of directors to that number or of summoning a general meeting of the company but for no other purpose.

104. The directors may elect a chairman of their meeting and determine the period for which he is to hold office, but if no such chairman is elected, or, if at any meeting the chairman is not present within 5 minutes after the time appointed for holding the same, the directors present may choose one of their number to be chairman of the meeting.

105. The directors may delegate any of their powers to committees consisting of such member or members of the board as they think fit; any committee so formed shall, in the exercise of the powers so delegated, conform to any regulations that may be imposed on it by the directors.

106. A committee may elect a chairman of its meetings; if no such chairman is elected, or if at any meeting the chairman is not present within 5 minutes after the time appointed for holding the same, the members present may choose one of their number to be chairman of the meeting.

107. A committee may meet and adjourn as it thinks proper. Questions arising at any meeting shall be determined by a majority of votes of the members present, and where there is an equality of votes, the chairman shall have a second or casting vote.

108. All acts done by any meeting of the directors or of a committee of directors or by any person acting as a director shall, notwithstanding that it be afterwards discovered that there was same defect in the appointment of any such director or person acting as aforesaid, or that they or any of them were disqualified, be as valid as if every such person had been duly appointed and was qualified to be a director.

109. A resolution in writing signed by all the directors for the time being entitled to receive notice of a meeting of the directors shall be as valid as if it had been passed at a meeting of the directors duly convened and held.

Managing Director

110. The directors may from time to time appoint one or more of themselves to the office of managing director for such period and on such terms as to remuneration and otherwise as they think fit, and subject to the terms of any agreement entered into in any particular case, may revoke such appointment. A director so appointed shall not, whilst holding that office, be subject to retirement by rotation or be taken into account in determining the rotation of retirement of directors but (without prejudice to any claim he may have for damages for breach of any contract of service between him and the company), his appointment shall be automatically determined if he ceases from any cause to be a director.

111. A managing director shall receive such remuneration whether by way of salary, commission or participation in the profits, or partly in one way and partly in another, as the directors may determine.

112. The directors may entrust to and confer upon a managing director any of the powers exercisable by them upon such terms and conditions and with such restrictions as they may think fit, and either collaterally with or to the exclusion of their own powers, and may from time to time revoke, withdraw, alter or vary all or any of such powers.

Secretary

113. [Subject to section 3 of the Companies (Amendment) Act, 1982,][a] the secretary shall be appointed by the directors for such term, at such remuneration and upon such conditions as they may think fit; and any secretary so appointed may be removed by them.

Amendments

a Words inserted by C(A)A 1982, s 21.

---

114. A provision of the Act or these regulations requiring or authorising a thing to be done by or to a director and the secretary shall not be satisfied by its being done by or to the same person acting both as director and as, or in place of, the secretary.

The Seal

115. The seal shall be used only by the authority of the directors or of a committee of directors authorised by the directors in that behalf, and every instrument to which the seal shall be affixed shall be signed by a director and shall be countersigned by the secretary or by a second director or by some other person appointed by the directors for the purpose.

Dividends and Reserve

116. The company in general meeting may declare dividends, but no dividend shall exceed the amount recommended by the directors.

117. The directors may from time to time pay to the members such interim dividends as appear to the directors to be justified by the profits of the company.

[**118**. No dividend or interim dividend shall be paid otherwise than in accordance with the provisions of Part IV of the Companies (Amendment) Act, 1983 which apply to the company.][a]

Amendments

a Substituted by C(A)A 1983, Sch 1 para 24.

---

119. The directors may, before recommending any dividend, set aside out of the profits of the company such sums as they thinks proper as a reserve or reserves which shall, at the discretion of the directors, be applicable for any purpose to which the profits of the company may be properly applied, and pending such application may, at the like discretion, either be employed in the business of the company or be invested in such investments as the directors may lawfully determine. The directors may also, without placing the same to reserve, carry forward any profits which they may think it prudent not to divide.

120. Subject to the rights of persons, if any, entitled to shares with special rights as to dividend, all dividends shall be declared and paid according to the amounts paid or credited as paid on the shares in respect whereof the dividend is paid, but no amount paid or credited as paid on a share in advance of calls shall be treated for the purposes of this regulation as paid on the share. All dividends shall be apportioned and paid proportionately to the amounts paid or credited as paid on the shares during any portion or portions of the period in respect of which the dividend is paid; but if any share is issued on terms providing that it shall rank for dividend as from a particular date, such share shall rank for dividend accordingly.

121. The directors may deduct from any dividend payable to any member all sums of money (if any) immediately payable by him to the company on account of calls or otherwise in relation to the shares of the company.

122. Any general meeting declaring a dividend or bonus may direct payment of such dividend or bonus wholly or partly by the distribution of specific assets and in particular of paid up shares, debentures or debenture stock of any other company or in any one or more of such ways, and the directors shall give effect to such resolution, and where any difficulty arises in regard to such distribution, the directors may settle the same as they think expedient, and in particular may issue fractional certificates and fix the value for distribution of such specific assets or any part thereof and may determine that cash payment shall be made to any members upon the footing of the value so fixed, in order to adjust the rights of all the parties, and may vest any such specific assets in trustees as may seem expedient to the directors.

123. Any dividend, interest or other moneys payable in cash in respect of any shares may be paid by cheque or warrant sent through the post directed to the registered address of the holder, or, where there are joint holders, to the registered address of that one of the joint holders who is first named on the register or to such person and to such address as the holder or joint holders may in writing direct. Every such cheque or warrant shall be made payable to the order of the person to whom it is sent. Any one of two or more joint holders may give effectual receipts for any dividends, bonuses or other moneys payable in respect of the shares held by them as joint holders.

124. No dividend shall bear interest against the company.

Accounts

125. The directors shall cause proper books of account to be kept relating to—

(a) all sums of money received and expended by the company and the matters in respect of which the receipt and expenditure takes place; and

(b) all sales and purchases of goods by the company; and

(c) the assets and liabilities of the company.

Proper books shall not be deemed to be kept if there are not kept such books of account as are necessary to give a true and fair view of the state of the company's affairs and to explain its transactions.

126. The books of account shall be kept at the office or, subject to section 147 of the Act, at such other place as the directors think fit, and shall at all reasonable times be open to the inspiration of the directors.

127. The directors shall time to time determine whether and to what extent and at what times and places and under what conditions or regulations the accounts and books of the company or any of them shall be open to the inspection of members, not being directors, and no member (not being a director) shall have any right of inspection any account or book or document of the company except as conferred by statute or authorised by the directors or by the company in general meeting.

128. The directors shall from time to time, in accordance with sections 148, 150, 157 and 158 of the Act cause to be prepared and to be laid before the annual general meeting of the company such profit and loss accounts, balance sheets, group accounts and reports as are required by those sections to be prepared and laid before the annual general meeting of the company.

129. A copy of every balance sheet (including every document required by law to be annexed thereto) which is to be laid before the annual general meeting of the company together with a copy of the directors' report and auditors' report shall, not less than 21 days before the date of the annual general meeting be sent to every person entitled under the provisions of the Act to receive them.

Capitalisation of Profits

130. The company in general meeting may upon the recommendation of the directors resolve that any sum for the time being standing to the credit of any of the company's reserves (including any capital redemption reserve fund or share premium account) or to the credit of profit and loss account be capitalised and applied on behalf of the members who would have been entitled to receive the same if the same had been distributed by way of dividend and in the same proportions either in or towards paying up amounts for the time being unpaid on any shares held by them respectively or in paying up in full unissued shares or debentures of the company of a nominal amount equal to the sum capitalised (such shares or debentures to be allotted and distributed credited as fully paid up to and amongst such holders in the proportions aforesaid) or partly in one way and partly in another, so however, that the only purpose for which sums standing to the credit of the capital redemption reserve fund or the share premium account shall be applied shall be those permitted by sections 62 and 64 of the Act.

[130A. The company in general meeting may on the recommendation of the directors resolve that it is desirable to capitalise any part of the amount for the time being standing to the credit of any of the company's reserve accounts or to the credit of the profit and loss account which is not available for distribution by applying such sum in paying up in full unissued shares to be allotted as fully paid bonus shares to those members of the company who would have been entitled to that sum if it were distributed by way of dividend (and in the same proportions), and the directors shall give effect to such resolution.][a]

Amendments

a Inserted by C(A)A 1983, Sch 1 para 24.

131. [Whenever a resolution is passed in pursuance of regulation 130 or 130A] [a], the directors shall make all appropriations and applications of the undivided profits resolved to be capitalised thereby and all allotments and issues of fully paid shares or debentures, if any, and generally shall do all acts and things required to give effect thereto with full power to the directors to make such provision as they shall think fit for the case of shares or debentures becoming distributable in fractions (and, in particular, without prejudice to the generality of the foregoing, to sell the shares or debentures represented by such fractions and distribute the net proceeds of such sale amongst the members otherwise entitled to such fractions in due proportions) and also to authorise any person to enter on behalf of all the members concerned into an agreement with the company providing for the allotment to them respectively credited as fully paid up of any further shares or debentures to which they may become entitled on such capitalisation or, as the case may require, for the payment up by the application thereto of their respective proportions of the profits resolved to be capitalised of the amounts remaining unpaid on their existing shares and any agreement made under such authority shall be effective and binding on all such members.

Amendments

a Words substituted by C(A)A 1983, Sch 1 para 24.

Audit

132. Auditors shall be appointed and their duties regulated in accordance with sections 160 to 163 of the Act.

Notices

133. A notice may be given by the company to any member either personally or by sending it by post to him to his registered address. Where a notice is sent by post, service of the notice shall be deemed to be effected by properly addressing, prepaying and posting a letter containing the notice, and to have been effected in the case of the notice of a meeting at the expiration of 24 hours after the letter containing the same is posted, and in any other case at the time at which the letter would be delivered in the ordinary course of post.

134. A notice may be given by the company to the joint holders of a share by giving the notice to the joint holder first named in the register in respect of the share.

135. A notice may be given by the company to the persons entitled to a share in consequence of the death or bankruptcy of a member by sending it through the post in a prepaid letter addressed to them by name or by the title of representatives of the deceased of Official Assignee in bankruptcy or by any like description at the address supplied for the purpose by the persons claiming to be so entitled, or (until such an address has been so supplied) by giving the notice in any manner in which the same might have been given if the death or bankruptcy had not occurred.

136. Notice of every general meeting shall be given in any manner hereinbefore authorised to—

(a) every member; and

(b) every person upon whom the ownership of a share devolves by reason of his being a personal representative or the Official Assignee in bankruptcy of a member, where the member but for his death or bankruptcy would be entitled to receive notice of the meeting; and

(c) the auditor for the time being of the company.

No other person shall be entitled to receive notices of general meetings.

Winding Up

137. If the company is wound up, the liquidator may, with the sanction of a special resolution of the company and any other sanction required by the Act, divide among the members in specie or kind the whole or any part of the assets of the company (whether they shall consist of property of the same kind or not) and may, for such purpose, set such value as he deems fair upon any property to divided as aforesaid any may determine how such division shall be carried out as between the members or different classes of members. The liquidator may, with the like sanction, vest the whole or any part of such assets in trustees upon such trusts for the benefit of the contributories as the liquidator, with the like sanction, shall think fit, but so that no member shall be compelled to accept any shares or other securities whereon there is any liability.

Indemnity

138. Every director, managing director, agent, auditor, secretary and other officer for the time being of the company shall be indemnified out of the assets of the company against any liability incurred by him in defending any proceedings, whether civil or criminal, in relation to his acts while acting in such office, in which judgment is given in his favour or in which he is acquitted or in connection with any application under section 391 of the Act in which relief is granted to him by the court.

PART II

REGULATIONS FOR THE MANAGEMENT OF A PRIVATE COMPANY LIMITED BY SHARES

1. The regulations contained in Part I of Table A [(with the exception of regulations 8, 24, 51, 54, 84 and 86)][a] shall apply.

Amendments

a Words substituted by C(A)A 1977, s 5.

---

2. The company is a private company and accordingly—

(a) the right to transfer shares is restricted in the manner hereinafter prescribed;

(b) the number of members of the company (exclusive of persons who are in the employment of the company and of persons who, having been formerly in the employment of the company, were while in such employment, and have continued after the determination of such employment to be, members of the company) is limited to fifty, so, however, that where two or more persons hold one or more shares in the company jointly, they shall, for the purpose of this regulation, be treated as a single member;

(c) any invitation to the public to subscribe for any shares or debentures of the company is prohibited;

(d) the company shall not have power to issue share warrants to bearer.

3. The directors may, in their absolute discretion, and without assigning any reason therefor, decline to register any transfer of any share, whether or not it is a fully paid share.

4. Subject to section 133 and 141 of the Act, an annual general meeting and a meeting called for the passing of a special resolution shall be called by 21 days' notice in writing at the least and a meeting of the company (other than an annual general meeting or a meeting for the passing of a special resolution) shall be called by 7 days' notice in writing at the least. The notice shall be exclusive of the day on which it is served or deemed to be served and of the day for which it is given and shall specify the day, the place and the hour of the meeting and, in the case of special business, the general nature of that business and shall be given in manner authorised by these regulations to such persons as are under the regulations of the company entitled to receive such notices from the company.

5. No business shall be transacted at any general meeting unless a quorum of members is present at the time when the meeting proceeds to business; save as herein otherwise provided, two member present in person or by proxy shall be a quorum.

6. Subject to section 141 of the Act, a resolution in writing signed by all the members for the time being entitled to attend and vote on such resolution at a general meeting (or being bodies corporate by their duly authorised representatives) shall be as valid and effective for all purposes as if the resolution had been passed at a general meeting of the company duly convened and held, and if described as a special resolution shall be deemed to be a special resolution within the meaning of the Act.

7. A director may vote in respect of any contract, appointment or arrangement in which he is interested, and he shall be counted in the quorum present at the meeting.

8. The directors may exercise the voting powers conferred by the shares of any other company held or owned by the company in such manner in all respects as they think fit and in particular they may exercise the voting powers in favour of any resolution appointing the directors or any of them as directors or officers of such other company or providing for the payment of remuneration or pensions to the directors or officers of such other company. Any director of the company may vote in favour of the exercise of such voting rights, notwithstanding that he may be or may be about to become a director or officer of such other company, and as such or in any other manner is or may be interested in the exercise of such voting rights in manner aforesaid.

9. Any director may from time to time appoint any person who is approved by the majority of the directors to be an alternate or substitute director. The appointee, while he holds office as an alternate director, shall be entitled to notice of meetings of the directors and to attend and vote thereat as a director and shall not be entitled to be remunerated otherwise than out of the remuneration of the director appointing him. Any appointment under this regulation shall be effected by notice in writing given by the appointer to the secretary. Any appointment so made may be revoked at any time by the appointer or by a majority of the other directors or by the company in general meeting.

Revocation by an appointer shall be effected by notice in writing given by the appointer to the secretary.

[**10**. Every person whose name is entered as a member in the register shall be entitled without payment to receive within 2 months after allotment or lodgment of a transfer (or within such other period as the conditions of issue shall provide) one certificate for all his shares or several certificates each for one or more of his shares upon payment of 12½ new pence for every certificate after the first or such less sum as the directors shall from time to time determine, so, however, that in respect of a share or shares held jointly by several persons the company shall not be bound to issue more than one certificate, and delivery of a certificate for a share to one of several joint holders shall be sufficient delivery to all such holders. Every certificate shall be under the seal and shall specify the shares to which it relates and the amount paid up thereon.] [a]

Amendments

a Reg 10 inserted by C(A)A 1977, s 5.

[Note: Regulations 3, 4, 5 and 10 of this Part are alternative to regulations 24, 51, 54 and 8 respectively of Part 1. Regulations 7 and 8 of this Part are alternative to regulations 84 and 86 of Part I.] [a]

Amendments

a Note substituted by C(A)A 1977, s 5.

TABLE B

FORM OF MEMORANDUM OF ASSOCIATION OF A COMPANY LIMITED BY SHARES

1. The name of the company is 'The Western Mining Company, Limited'.

2. The objects for which the company is established are the mining of minerals of all kinds and the doing of all such other things as are incidental or conducive to the attainment of the above object.

3. The liability of the members is limited.

4. The share capital of the company is £200,000, divided into 200,000 shares of £1 each.

We, the several persons whose names and addresses are subscribed, wish to be formed into a company in pursuance of this memorandum of association, and we agree to take the number of shares in the capital of the company set opposite our respective names.

Names, Addresses and Descriptions of Subscribers	Number of Shares taken by Each Subscriber
1. James Walsh of..................................... in the County of....................................... Solicitor.	50
2. John Murphy of.................................... in the County of....................................... Engineer.	2,700

3. Patrick Ryan of.................................... in the County of..................................... Geologist.	1,250
4. Thomas O'Connell of........................... in the County of..................................... Engineer.	500
5. Daniel Clarke of.................................. in the County of..................................... Geologist.	50
6. Patrick Byrne of.................................. in the County of..................................... Accountant.	300
7. John Collins of.................................... in the County of..................................... Solicitor.	150
Total Shares taken	5,000

Dated the.............................day of......................................, 19......................

Witness to the above Signatures: ....

Name:...

Address: ....

TABLE C

FORM OF MEMORANDUM AND ARTICLES OF ASSOCIATION OF A COMPANY LIMITED BY GUARANTEE AND NOT HAVING A SHARE CAPITAL

Memorandum of Association

1. The name of the company is 'The Scientific Research Association, Limited.'

2. The objects for which the company is established are the promotion of research into matters of a scientific nature and the doing of all such other things as are incidental or conducive to the attainment of the above object.

3. The liability of the members is limited.

4. Every member of the company undertakes to contribute to the assets of the company in the event of its being wound up while he is a member, or within one year afterwards, for payment of the debts and liabilities of the company contracted before he ceases to be a member, and the costs, charges and expenses of winding up, and for the adjustment of the rights of the contributories among themselves, such amount as may be required not exceeding £1.

We, the several persons whose names and addresses are subscribed, wish to be formed into a company in pursuance of this memorandum of association.

Names, Addresses and Descriptions of Subscribers

1. Charles O'Brien of...........in the County of...........University Professor.

2. Francis Power of..............in the County of...........Research Chemist.

3. James O'Connor of...........in the County of...........Biologist.

4. Thomas Daly of................in the County of............Science Teacher.

5. Richard O'Donnell of........in the County of...........Librarian.

6. Joseph Murray of.............in the County of..................Physicist.

7. Michael Nolan of....... ....in the County of...................Statistician.

Dated the............................day of...................................., 19..........................

Witness to the above signatures:..

Name: ....

Address: ....

ARTICLES OF ASSOCIATION TO ACCOMPANY PRECEDING MEMORANDUM OF ASSOCIATION

Interpretation

1. In these articles—

'the Act' means the Companies Act, 1963 (No. 33 of 1963);

'the directors' means the directors for the time being of the company or the directors present at a meeting of the board of directors and includes any person occupying the position of director by whatever name called;

'secretary' means any person appointed to perform the duties of the secretary of the company;

'the seal' means the common seal of the company;

'the office' means the registered office for the time being of the company.

Expressions referring to writing shall, unless the contrary intention appears, be construed as including references to printing, lithography, photography and any other modes of representing or reproducing words in a visible form.

Unless the contrary intention appears, words or expressions contained in these articles shall bear the same meaning as in the Act or any statutory modification thereof in force at the date at which these articles become binding on the company.

Members

2. The number of members with which the company proposes to be registered is 500, but the directors may from time to time register an increase of members.

3. The subscribers to the memorandum of association and such other persons as the directors shall admit to membership shall be members of the company.

General Meetings

4. All general meetings of the company shall be held in the State.

5. (1) Subject to paragraph (2), the company shall in each year hold a general meeting as its annual general meeting in addition to any other meetings in that year and shall specify the meeting as such in the notices calling it; and not more than 15 months shall elapse between the date of one annual general meeting of the company and that of the next.

(2) So long as the company holds its first annual general meeting within 18 months of its incorporation, it need not hold it in the year of its incorporation or in the following year. Subject to article 4, the annual general meeting shall be held at such time and at such place in the State as the directors shall appoint.

6. All general meetings other than annual general meetings shall be called extraordinary general meetings.

7. The directors may, whenever they think fit, convene an extraordinary general meeting and extraordinary general meetings shall also be convened on such requisition, or, in default, may be convened by such requisitionists, as provided by section 132 of the Act. If at any time there are not within the State sufficient directors capable of acting to form a quorum, any director or any two members of the company may convene an extraordinary general meeting in the same manner as nearly as possible as that in which meeting may be convened by the directors.

Notice of General Meetings.

8. Subject to sections 133 and 141 of the Act, an annual general meeting and a meeting called for the passing of a special resolution shall be called by 21 days' notice in writing at the least, and a meeting of the company (other than an annual general meeting or a meeting for the passing of a special resolution) shall be called by 14 days' notice in writing at the least. The notice shall be exclusive of the day on which it is served or deemed to be served and of the day for which it is given and shall specify the place, the day and the hour of meeting and, in the case of special business, the general nature of that business and shall be given, in manner hereinafter mentioned, to such persons as are, under the articles of the company, entitled to receive such notices from the company.

9. The accidental omission to give notice of a meeting to, or the non-receipt of notice of a meeting by, any person entitled to receive notice shall not invalidate the proceedings at that meeting.

Proceedings at General Meetings

10. All business shall be deemed special that is transacted at an extraordinary general meeting, and also all that is transacted at an annual general meeting with the exception of declaring a dividend, the consideration of the accounts, balance sheets and the reports of the directors and auditors, the election of directors in the place of those retiring, the re-appointment of the retiring auditors, and the fixing of the remuneration of the auditors.

11. No business shall be transacted at any general meeting unless a quorum of members is present at the time when the meeting proceeds to business; save as herein otherwise provided, three members present in person shall be a quorum.

12. If within half an hour from the time appointed for the meeting a quorum is not present, the meeting, if convened upon the requisition of members, shall be dissolved; in any other case it shall stand adjourned to the same day in the next week at the same time and place, or to such other day and at such other time and place as the directors may determine, and if at the adjourned meeting a quorum is not present within half an hour from the time appointed for the meeting, the members present shall be a quorum.

13. The chairman, if any, of the board of directors shall preside as chairman at every general meeting of the company, or if there is no such chairman, or if he is not present within 15 minutes after the time appointed for the holding of the meeting or is unwilling to act, the directors present shall elect one of their number to be chairman of the meeting.

14. If at any meeting no director is willing to act as chairman or if no director is present within 15 minutes after the time appointed for holding the meeting, the members present shall choose one of their number to be chairman of the meeting.

15. The chairman may with the consent of any meeting at which a quorum is present (and shall, if so directed by the meeting), adjourn the meeting from time to time and from place to place, but no business shall be transacted at any adjourned meeting other than the business left unfinished at the meeting from which the adjournment took place. When a meeting is adjourned for 30 days or more, notice of the adjourned meeting shall be given as in the case of an original meeting. Save as aforesaid, it shall not be necessary to give any notice of an adjournment or of the business to be transacted at an adjourned meeting.

16. At any general meeting a resolution put to the vote of the meeting shall be decided on a show of hands unless a poll is (before or on the declaration of the result of the show of hands) demanded—

(a) by the chairman; or

(b) by at least three members present in person or by proxy; or

(c) by any member or members present in person or by proxy and representing not less than one-tenth of the total voting rights of all the members having the right to vote at the meeting.

Unless a poll is so demanded, a declaration by the chairman that a resolution has, on a show of hands, been carried or carried unanimously or by a particular majority or lost, and an entry to that effect in the book containing the minutes of proceedings of the company shall be conclusive evidence of the fact without proof of the number or proportion of the votes recorded in favour of or against such resolution.

The demand for a poll may be withdrawn.

17. Except as provided in article 19, if a poll is duly demanded it shall be taken in such manner as the chairman directs and the result of the poll shall be deemed to be the resolution of the meeting at which the poll was demanded.

18. Where there is an equality of votes, whether on a show of hands or on a poll, the chairman of the meeting at which the show of hands takes place or at which the poll is demanded, shall be entitled to a second or casting vote.

19. A poll demanded on the election of a chairman, or on a question of adjournment shall be taken forthwith. A poll demanded on any other question shall be taken at such time as the chairman of the meeting directs, and any business other than that upon which a poll has been demanded may be proceeded with pending the taking of the poll.

20. Subject to section 141 of the Act, a resolution in writing signed by all the members for the time being entitled to attend and vote on such resolution at a general meeting (or being bodies corporate by their duly authorised representatives) shall be as valid and effective for all purposes as if the resolution had been passed at a general meeting of the company duly convened and held, and if described as a special resolution shall be deemed to be a special resolution within the meaning of the Act.

Votes of Members

21. Every member shall have one vote.

22. A member of unsound mind, or in respect of whom an order has been made by any court having jurisdiction in lunacy, may vote, whether on a show of hands or on a poll, by his committee, receiver, guardian, or other person appointed by that court, and any such committee, receiver, guardian, or other person may vote by proxy on a show of hands or on a poll.

23. No member shall be entitled to vote at any general meeting unless all moneys immediately payable by him to the company have been paid.

24. No objection shall be raised to the qualification of any voter except at the meeting or adjourned meeting at which the vote objected to is given or tendered, and every vote not disallowed at such meeting shall be valid for all purposes. Any such objection made in due time shall be referred to the chairman of the meeting whose decision shall be final and conclusive.

25. Votes may be given either personally or by proxy.

26. The instrument appointing a proxy shall be in writing under the hand of the appointer or of his attorney duly authorised in writing, or, if the appointer is a body corporate, either under seal or under the hand of an officer or attorney duly authorised. A proxy need not be a member of the company.

27. The instrument appointing a proxy and the power of attorney or other authority, if any, under which it is signed or a notarially certified copy of that power or authority shall be deposited at the office or at such other place within the State as is specified for that purpose in the notice convening the meeting not less than 48 hours before the time for holding the meeting or adjourned meeting at which the person named in the instrument purposes to vote, or, in the case of a poll, not less than 48 hours before the time appointed for the taking of the poll, and in default the instrument of proxy shall not be treated as valid.

28. An instrument appointing a proxy shall be in the following form or a form as near thereto as circumstances permit—

' Limited.

I/We,..

of..

in the County of.., being a member/members of the above-named company, hereby appoint..

of..

or failing him, ...

of..

as may/our proxy to vote for me/us on my/our behalf at the (annual or extra-ordinary, as the case may be) general meeting of the company to be held on the .... day of ...., 19........... and at any adjournment thereof.

Signed this..............................day of.., 19..................

This form is to be used *in favour of/against the resolution. Unless otherwise instructed, the proxy will vote as he thinks fit.'

*Strike out whichever is not desired.

29. The instrument appointing a proxy shall be deemed to confer authority to demand or join in demanding a poll.

30. A vote given in accordance with the terms of an instrument of proxy shall be valid notwithstanding the previous death or insanity of the principal or revocation of the proxy or of the authority under which the proxy was executed, if no intimation in writing of such death, insanity or revocation as aforesaid is received by the company at the office before the commencement of the meeting or adjourned meeting at which the proxy is used.

Bodies Corporate acting by Representatives at Meetings

31. Any body corporate which is a member of the company may by resolution of its directors or other governing body authorise such person as it thinks fit to act as its representative at any meeting of the company, and the person so authorised shall be entitled to exercise the same powers on behalf of the body corporate which he represents as that body corporate could exercise if it were an individual member of the company.

Directors

32. The number of the directors and the names of the first directors shall be determined in writing by the subscribers of the memorandum of association or a majority of them.

33. The remuneration of the directors shall from time to time be determined by the company in general meeting. Such remuneration shall be deemed to accrue from day to day. The directors may also be paid all travelling, hotel and other expenses properly incurred by them in attending and returning from meetings of the directors or any committee of the directors or general meetings of the company or in connection with the business of the company.

Borrowing Powers

34. The directors may exercise all the powers of the company to borrow money and to mortgage or charge its undertaking and property or any part thereof, and to issue debentures, debenture stock and other securities, whether outright or as security for any debt, liability or obligation of the company or of any third part.

Powers and Duties of Directors

35. The business of the company shall be managed by the directors, who may pay all expenses incurred in promoting and registering the company, and may exercise all such powers of the company as are not by the Act or by these articles required to be exercised by the company in general meeting, subject nevertheless to the provisions of the Act and of these articles and to such directions, being not inconsistent with the aforesaid provisions, as may be given by the company in general meeting: but no direction given by the company in general meeting shall invalidate any prior act of the directors which would have been valid if that direction had not been given.

36. The directors may from time to time and at any time by power of attorney appoint any company, firm or person or body of persons, whether nominated directly or indirectly by the directors, to be the attorney or attorneys of the company for such purposes and with such powers, authorities and discretions (not exceeding those vested in or exercisable by the directors under these articles) and for such period and subject to such conditions as they may think fit, and any such powers of attorney may contain such provisions for the protection and convenience of persons dealing with any such attorney as the directors may think fit, and may also authorise any such attorney to delegate all or any of the powers, authorities and discretions vested in him.

37. All cheques, promissory notes, drafts, bills of exchange and other negotiable instruments, and all receipts for moneys paid to the company, shall be signed, drawn, accepted, endorsed or otherwise executed, as the case may be, by such person or persons and in such manner as the directors shall from time to time by resolution determine.

38. The directors shall cause minutes to be made in books provided for the purpose-

- (a) of all appointment of officers made by the directors;
- (b) of the names of the directors present at each meeting of the directors and of any committee of the directors;
- (c) of all resolutions and proceedings at all meetings of the company, and of the directors and of committees of directors.

Disqualification of Directors

39. The office of director shall be vacated if the director—

- (a) without the consent of the company in general meeting holds any other office or place of profit under the company; or
- (b) is adjudged bankrupt in the State or in Northern Ireland or Great Britain or makes any arrangement or composition with his creditors generally; or
- (c) becomes prohibited from being a director by reason of any order made under section 184 of the Act; or
- (d) becomes of unsound mind; or
- (e) resigns his office by notice in writing to the company; or

(f) is convicted of an indictable offence unless the directors otherwise determine; or

(g) is directly or indirectly interested in any contract with the company and fails to declare the nature of his interest in manner required by section 194 of the Act.

Voting on Contracts

40. A director may vote in respect of any contract in which he is interested or any matter arising thereout.

Rotation of Directors

41. At the first annual general meeting of the company, all the directors shall retire from office and at the annual general meeting in every subsequent year one-third of the directors for the time being, or, if their number is not three or a multiple of three, then the number nearest one-third, shall retire from office.

42. The directors to retire in every year shall be those who have been longest in office since the last election, but as between persons who became directors on the same day, those to retire shall (unless they otherwise agree amongst themselves) be determined by lot.

43. A retiring director shall be eligible for re-election.

44. The company, at the meeting at which a director retires in manner aforesaid, may fill the vacated office electing a person thereto, and in default the retiring director shall, if offering himself for re-election, be deemed to have been re-elected, unless at such meeting it is expressly resolved not to fill such vacated office or unless a resolution for the re-election of such director has been put to the meeting and lost.

45. No person other than a director retiring at the meeting shall, unless recommended by the directors, be eligible for election to the office of director at any general meeting unless, not less than 3 nor more than 21 days before the date appointed for the meeting, there has been left at the office notice in writing, signed by a member duly qualified to attend and vote at the meeting for which such notice is given, of his intention to propose such a person for election, and also notice in writing signed by that person of his willingness to be elected.

46. The company may from time to time by ordinary resolution increase or reduce the number of directors, and may also determine in what rotation the increased or reduced number is to go out of office.

47. The directors shall have power at any time, and from time to time, to appoint any person to be a director, either to fill a casual vacancy or as an addition to the existing directors, but so that the total number of directors shall not at any time exceed the number fixed in accordance with these articles. Any director so appointed shall hold office only until the next annual general meeting, and shall then be eligible for re-election, but shall not be taken into account in determining the directors who are to retire by rotation at such meeting.

48. The company may by ordinary resolution of which extended notice has been given in accordance with section 142 of the Act remove any director before the expiration of his period of office, notwithstanding anything in these articles or in any agreement between the company and such director. Such removal shall be without prejudice to any claim such director may have for damages for breach of any contract of service between him and the company.

49. The company may by ordinary resolution appoint another person in place of a director removed from office under article 48. Without prejudice to the powers of the directors under article 47, the company in general meeting may appoint any person to be a director, either to fill a casual vacancy or as an additional director. A person appointed in place of a director so removed or to fill such a vacancy shall be subject to retirement at the same time as if he had become a director on the day on which the director in whose place he is appointed was last elected a director.

Proceedings of Directors

50. The directors may meet together for the despatch of business, adjourn and otherwise regulate their meetings as the think fit. Questions arising at any meeting shall be decided by a majority of votes. Where there is an equality of votes, the chairman shall have a second or casting vote. A director may, and the secretary on the requisition of a director shall, at any time summon a meeting of the directors. If the directors so resolve it shall not be necessary to give notice of a meeting of directors to any director who being resident in the State is for the time being absent from the State.

51. The quorum necessary for the transaction of the business of the directors may be fixed by the directors, and unless so fixed shall be two.

52. The continuing directors may act notwithstanding any vacancy in their number but, if and so long as their number is reduced below the number fixed by or pursuant to the articles of the company as the necessary quorum of directors, the continuing directors or director may act for the purpose of increasing the number of directors to that number or of summoning a general meeting of the company, but for no other purpose.

53. The directors may elect a chairman of their meetings and determine the period for which he is to hold office; but, if no such chairman is elected, or if at any meeting the chairman is not present within 5 minutes after the time appointed for holding the same, the directors present may choose one of their number to be chairman of the meeting.

54. The directors may delegate any of their powers to committees consisting of such member or members of the board as they think fit; any committee so formed shall, in the exercise of the powers so delegated, conform to any regulations that may be imposed on it by the directors.

55. A committee may elect a chairman of its meetings; if no such chairman is elected, or if at any meeting the chairman is not present within 5 minutes after the time appointed for holding the same, the members present may choose one of their number to be chairman of the meeting.

56. A committee may meet and adjourn as it thinks proper. Questions arising at any meeting shall be determined by a majority of votes of the members present, and when there is an equality of votes, the chairman shall have a second or casting vote.

57. All acts done by any meeting of the directors or of a committee of directors or by an person acting as a director shall, notwithstanding that it is afterwards discovered that there was some defect in the appointment of any such director or person acting as aforesaid, or that they or any of them were disqualified, be as valid as if every such person had been duly appointed and was qualified to be a director.

58. A resolution in writing, signed by all the directors for the time being entitled to receive notice of a meeting of the directors, shall be as valid as if it had been passed at a meeting of the directors duly convened and held.

Secretary

59. [Subject to section 3 of the Companies (Amendment) Act, 1982,] [a] the secretary shall be appointed by the directors for such term and at such remuneration and upon such conditions as they may think fit; and any secretary so appointed may be removed by them.

Amendments

a Words inserted by C(A)A 1982, s 21.

---

60. A provision of the Act or these articles requiring or authorising a thing to be done by or to a director and the secretary shall not be satisfied by its being done by or to the same person acting both as director and as, or in place of, the secretary.

The Seal

61. The seal shall be used only by the authority of the directors or of a committee of directors authorised by the directors in that behalf, and every instrument to which the seal shall be affixed shall be signed by a director and shall be countersigned by the secretary or by a second director or by some other person appointed by the directors for the purpose.

Accounts

62. The directors shall cause proper books of account to be kept relation to—

(a) all sums of money received and expended by the company and the matters in respect of which the receipt and expenditure takes place.

(b) all sales and purchases of goods by the company; and

(c) the assets and liabilities of the company.

Proper books shall not be deemed to be kept if there are not kept such books of account as are necessary to give a true and fair view of the state of the company's affairs and to explain its transactions.

63. The books of account shall be kept at the office or, subject to section 147 of the Act, at such other place as the directors think fit, and shall at all reasonable times be open to the inspection of the directors.

64. The directors shall from time to time determine whether and to what extent and at what times and places and under what conditions or regulations the accounts and books of the company or any of them shall be open to the inspection of members not being directors, and no member (not being a director) shall have any right of inspecting any account or book or document of the company except as conferred by statute or authorised by the director or by the company in general meeting.

65. The directors shall from time to time in accordance with sections 148,150, 157 and 158 of the Act cause to be prepared and to be laid before the annual general meeting of the company such profit and loss accounts, balance sheets, group accounts and reports as are required by those sections to be prepared and laid before the annual general meeting of the company.

66. A copy of every balance sheet (including every document required by law to be annexed thereto) which is to be laid before the annual general meeting of the company together with a copy of the directors' report and auditors' report shall, not less than 21 days before the date of the annual general meeting, be sent to every person entitled under the provisions of the Act to receive them.

Audit

67. Auditors shall be appointed an their duties regulated in accordance with sections 160 to 163 of the Act.

Notices

68. A notice may be given by the company to any member either personally or by sending it by post to him to his registered address. Where a notice is sent by post, service of the notice shall be deemed to be effected by properly addressing, prepaying and posting a letter containing the notice, and to have been effected in the case of a notice of a meeting at the expiration of 24 hours after the letter containing the same is posted and in any other case at the time at which the letter would be delivered in the ordinary course of post.

69. Notice of every general meeting shall be given in any manner hereinbefore authorised to—

(a) every member;

(b) every person being a personal representative or the Official Assignee in bankruptcy or a member where the member but for his death or bankruptcy would be entitled to receive notice of the meeting; and

(c) the auditor for the time being of the company.

No other person shall be entitled to receive notices of general meetings.

Names, Addresses and Descriptions of Subscribers

1. Charles O'Brien of..................in the County of...................University Professor.
2. Francis Power of...................in the County of...................Research Chemist.
3. James O'Connor of................in the County of...................Biologist.
4. Thomas Daly of....................in the County of..................Science Teacher.
5. Richard O'Donnell of.............in the County of..................Librarian.
6. Joseph Murray of..................in the County of..................Physicist.
7. Michael Nolan of..................in the County of..................Statistician.

Dated the......................... day of....................................., 19.........................

Witness to the above signatures: ....

Name:..

Address: ....

TABLE D

PART I

FORM OF MEMORANDUM AND ARTICLES OF ASSOCIATION OF A COMPANY LIMITED BY GUARANTEE AND HAVING A SHARE CAPITAL

Memorandum of Association

1. The name of the company is 'The Western Counties Tourist Development Company, Limited.'

2. Objects for which the company is established are the promotion of tourism in the western counties of Ireland by providing facilities for tourists, and the doing of all such other things as are incidental or conducive to the attainment of the above object.

3. The liability of the members is limited.

4. Every member of the company undertakes to contribute to the assets of the company in the event of its being wound up while he is a member, or within one year afterwards, for payment of the debts and liabilities of the company contracted before he ceases to be a member, and the costs, charges and expenses of winding up, and for the adjustment of the rights of the contributories among themselves, such amount as may be required, not exceeding £5.

5. The share capital of the company is £100,000 divided into 10,000 shares of £1 each.

We, the several persons whose names and addresses are subscribed, wish to be formed into a company in pursuance of this memorandum of association, and we agree to take the number of shares in the capital of the company set opposite our respective names.

Names, Addresses and Descriptions of Subscribers	*Number of shares taken by each subscriber*
1. Patrick Walsh of..................in the County of..................Solicitor	100
2. Thomas Murphy of.................in the County of.................Hotel Proprietor	500
3. James Ryan of................in the County of................Engineer	45
4. Francis O'Brien of................in the County of................Travel Agent	100
5. Thomas Duffy of...............in the County of...............Farmer	100
6. Joseph Moran of...............in the County of...............Architect	150
7. Martin O'Reilly of...............in the County of...............Clerk	5

Total shares taken...............1,000

Dated the........................day of..., 19...................

Witness to the above signatures:...

Name:..

Address:..

PART II

ARTICLES OF ASSOCIATION TO ACCOMPANY PRECEDING MEMORANDUM OF ASSOCIATION WHERE THE COMPANY IS NOT A PRIVATE COMPANY

[...][a]

Amendments

a Repealed by C(A)A 1983, Sch 3.

PART III

ARTICLES OF ASSOCIATION TO ACCOMPANY PRECEDING MEMORANDUM OF ASSOCIATION WHERE THE COMPANY IS A PRIVATE COMPANY

1. The number of members with which the company proposes to be registered is 40 but the directors may from time to time, subject to Article 2, register an increase of members.

2. The regulations of Table A, Part II, set out in the First Schedule to the Companies Act, 1963, shall be deemed to be incorporated with these articles and shall apply to the company.

Names, Addresses and Descriptions of Subscribers

1. Patrick Walsh of........................in the County of................Solicitor.
2. Thomas Murphy of.....................in the County of................Hotel Proprietor.
3. James Ryan of...........................in the County of.................Engineer.
4. Francis O'Brien of....................in the County of.................Travel Agent.
5. Thomas Duffy of.......................in the County of..................Farmer.
6. Joseph Moran of........................in the County of..................Architect.
7. Martin O'Reilly of....................in the County of..................Clerk.

Dated the..............................day of.., 19.....................

Witness to the above signatures:...

Name..

Address: ....

TABLE E

PART I

FORM OF MEMORANDUM AND ARTICLES OF ASSOCIATION OF AN UNLIMITED COMPANY HAVING A SHARE CAPITAL

Memorandum of Association

1. The name of the company is 'The Turf Harvester Company'.

2. The object for which the company is established are the development of improved methods of cutting and harvesting turf and the doing of all such things as are incidental or conducive to the attainment of the above object.

We, the several persons whose names and addresses are subscribed, wish to be formed into a company in pursuance of this memorandum of association, and we agree to take the number of shares in the capital of the company set opposite our respective names.

Names, Addresses and Descriptions of Subscribers			*Number of shares taken by each subscriber*
1. Patrick O'Connor of	in the County of	Merchant	100
2. Joseph O'Brien of	in the County of	, Solicitor	500
3. Thomas Ryan of	in the County of	, Engineer	50
4. James Murphy of	in the County of	, Engineer	500
5. Patrick Nolan of	in the County of	, Farmer	350
6. James Byrne of	in the County of	, Metal Worker	50
7. James Duffy of	in the County of	, Farmer	50
Total shares taken			1,600

Dated the.................................day of.................................., 19.................

Witness to the above signatures:...

Name: ....

Address: ....

PART II

ARTICLES OF ASSOCIATION TO ACCOMPANY PRECEDING MEMORANDUM OF ASSOCIATION WHERE THE COMPANY IS NOT A PRIVATE COMPANY

1. The number of members with which the company proposes to be registered is 100 but the directors may from time to time register an increase of members.

2. The share capital of the company is £10,000 divided into 10,000 shares of £1 each.

3. The company may by special resolution—

(a) increase the share capital by such to be divided into shares of such amount as the resolution may prescribe;

(b) consolidate its shares into shares of a larger amount than its existing shares;

(c) subdivide its shares into shares of a smaller amount than its existing shares;

(d) cancel any shares which at the date of the passing of the resolution have not been taken or agreed to be taken by an person;

(e) reduce its share capital in any way.

4. Subject to sections 133 and 141 of the Act, an annual general meeting and a meeting called for the passing of a special resolution shall be called by 21 days' notice in writing at the least, and a meeting of the company other than—

(a) an annual general meeting, or

(b) a meeting for the passing of a special resolution;

shall be called by 7 days' notice in writing at the least. The notice shall be exclusive of the day on which it is served or deemed to be served and of the day for which it is given, and shall specify the place, the day and the hour of the meeting, and, in the case of special business, the general nature of that business, and shall be given in manner authorised by these articles to such persons as are, under the articles of the company, entitled to receive such notices from the company.

5. The regulations of Table A, Part I, set out in the First Schedule to the Companies Act, 1963 (other than regulations 40 to 46 (inclusive) and 51) shall be deemed to be incorporated with these articles and shall apply to the company.

Names, Addresses and Descriptions of Subscribers

1. Patrick O'Connor of....................in the County of...................., Merchant.
2. Joseph O'Brien of.......................in the County of...................., Solicitor.
3. Thomas Ryan of..........................in the County of...................., Engineer.
4. James Murphy of.........................in the County of...................., Engineer.
5. Patrick Nolan of..........................in the County of...................., Farmer.
6. James Byrne of...........................in the County of...................., Metal Worker.
7. James Duffy of...........................in the County of......................, Farmer.

Dated the...................................day of..................................., 19................

Witness to the above signatures:..

Name:..

Address: ....

PART III

ARTICLES OF ASSOCIATION TO ACCOMPANY PRECEDING MEMORANDUM OF ASSOCIATION WHERE THE COMPANY IS A PRIVATE COMPANY

1. The number of members with which the company proposes to be registered is 40 but the directors may from time to time, subject to Article 4, register an increase of members.

2. The share capital of the company is £10,000 divided into 10,000 shares of £1 each.

3. The company may by special resolution—

(a) increase the share capital by such sum to be divided into shares of such amount as the resolution may prescribe;

(b) consolidate its shares into shares of a larger amount than its existing shares;

(c) subdivide its shares into shares of a smaller amount than its existing shares;

(d) cancel any shares which at the date of the passing of the resolution have not been taken or agreed to be taken by any person;

(e) reduce its share capital in any way.

4. The regulations of Table A, Part II set out in the First Schedule to the Companies Act, 1963, (with the exception of regulations 40 to 46 (inclusive) of Part I of that Table), shall be deemed to be incorporated with these articles and shall apply to the company.

Names, Addresses and Descriptions of Subscribers

1. Patrick O'Connor of....................in the County of...................., Merchant.
2. Joseph O'Brien of.......................in the County of...................., Solicitor.
3. Thomas Ryan of..........................in the County of...................., Engineer.
4. James Murphy of.........................in the County of...................., Engineer.
5. Patrick Nolan of..........................in the County of...................., Farmer.

6. James Byrne of............................in the County of......................, Metal Worker.

7. James Duffy of............................in the County of......................, Farmer.

Dated the....................................day of...................................., 19.................

Witness to the above signatures:...

Name: ....

Address: ....

SECOND SCHEDULE

FORM OF STATEMENT IN LIEU OF PROSPECTUS TO BE DELIVERED TO REGISTRAR BY A PRIVATE COMPANY ON BECOMING [AN UNLIMITED PUBLIC COMPANY][a] AND REPORTS TO BE SET OUT THEREIN

Amendments

a Words substituted by C(A)A 1983, Sch 1 para 26.

Part I

Form of Statement and Particulars to be contained therein

The Companies Act, 1963

Statement in lieu of prospectus delivered for registration by

(Insert the name of the company)

Pursuant to section 35 of the Companies Act, 1963

Delivered for registration by

1.	The nominal share capital of the company	1.	£
2.	Divided into	2.	Shares of £ each Shares of £ each
3	Amount, if any, of above capital which consists of redeemable preference shares.	3.	Shares of £ each
4.	The earliest date on which the company has power to redeem these shares.	4.	
5.	Names, descriptions and addresses of directors or proposed directors.	5.	
6.	Number of shares issued and amounts paid up thereon.	6.	Shares of £ each on which £ paid up shares of £ paid up on which £ paid up
7.	Amount of commissions paid or payable in connection with the issue of any shares or debentures.	7.	£

8	Amount of discount, if any, allowed on the issue of any shares, or so much thereof as has not been written off at the date of the statement.	8. £
9.	Unless more than 2 years have elapsed since the date on which the company was entitled to commence business:—	9.
	(a) Amount of preliminary expenses.	(a) £
	(b) By whom these expenses have been paid or are payable.	(b)
	(c) Amount paid to any promoter.	(c) Name of promotor
	(d) Consideration for the payment.	(d) Consideration
	(e) Any other benefit given to any promoter.	(e) Name of promoter: Nature and value of benefit
	(f) Consideration for giving of benefit.	(f) Consideration
10.	If the share capital of the company is divided into different classes of shares, the right of voting at meetings of the company conferred by and the rights in respect of capital and dividends attached to the several classes of shares respectively.	10.
11.	Number and amount of shares and debentures issued within the 2 years preceding the date of this statement as fully or partly paid up otherwise than for cash or agreed to be so issued at the date of this statement.	11. (a) shares of £ fully paid (b) shares upon which £ per share credited as paid (c) debentures £
	Consideration for the issue of those shares or debentures.	(d) Consideration
12.(a)	Number, description and amount of any shares or debentures which any person has or is entitled to be given an option to subscribe for, or to acquire from a person to whom they have been allotted or agreed to be allotted with a view to his offering them for sale.	12. (a) shares of £ and debentures of £
	(b) Period during which option is exercisable.	(b) Until
	(c) Price to be paid for shares or debentures subscribed for or acquired under option.	(c)
	(d) Consideration for option or right to option.	(d) Consideration:

(e) Persons to whom option or right to option was given or, if given to existing shareholders or debenture holders as such, the relevant shares or debentures.	(e) Names and addresses
13.(a) Names and addresses of vendors of property (1) purchased or acquired by the company within the 2 years preceding the date of this statement or (2) agreed or proposed to be purchased or acquired by the company, except where the contract for its purchase or acquisition was entered into in the ordinary course of business and there is no connection between the contract and the company ceasing to be a private company or where the amount of the purchase money is not material.	13. (a)
(b) Amount (in cash, shares or debentures) paid or payable to each separate vendor.	(b)
(c) Amount paid or payable in cash, shares or debentures for any such property, specifying the amount paid or payable for goodwill.	(c) Total purchase £ ___ Cash £ Shares £ Debentures £ ___ Goodwill £ ___
14. Short particulars of any transaction relating to any such property which was completed within the 2 preceding years and in which any vendor to the company or any person who is, or was at the time thereof, a promoter, director or proposed director of the company, had any interest direct or indirect.	14.
15. Dates of parties to, and general nature of every material (other than contracts entered into in the ordinary course of business carried on by the company or entered into more than 2 years before the delivery of this statement.	15.

16. Time and place at which the contracts or copies thereof may be inspected or (1) in the case of a contract not reduced into writing, a memorandum giving full particulars thereof, and (2) in the case of a contract wholly or partly in a language other than English or Irish, a copy of a translation thereof in English or Irish or embodying a translation in English or Irish of the parts not in English or Irish, as the case may be, being a translation certified in the prescribed manner to be a correct translation. 16.

17. Names and addresses of the auditors of the company. 17.

18. Full particulars of the nature and extent of the interest of every director in any property purchased or acquired by the company within the 2 years preceding the date of this statement or proposed to be purchased or acquired by the company or, where the interest of such a director consists in being a partner in a firm, the nature and extent of the interest of the firm, with a statement of all sums paid or agreed to be paid to him or to the firm in cash or shares or otherwise by any person either to induce him to become, or to qualify him as, a director, or otherwise for services rendered or to be rendered to the company by him or by the firm. 18.

19. Rates of the dividends, if any, paid by the company in respect of each class of shares in the company in each of the 5 financial years immediately preceding the date of this statement or since the incorporation of the company whichever period is the shorter. 19.

20. Particulars of the cases in which no dividends have been paid in respect of any class of shares in any of these years. 20.

(Signatures of the persons above-named as directors or proposed director or of their agents authorised in writing).

Date ....

....

PART II
REPORTS TO BE SET OUT

1. If unissued shares or debentures of the company are to be applied in the purchase of a business, a report made by accountants (who shall be named in the statement) upon—

(a) the profits or losses of the business in respect of each of the 5 financial years immediately preceding the delivery of the statement to the registrar; and

(b) the assets and liabilities of the business at the last date to which the accounts of the business were made up.

2. (1) If unissued shares or debentures of the company are to be applied directly or indirectly in any manner resulting in the acquisition of shares in a body corporate which by reason of the acquisition or anything to be done in consequence thereof or in connection therewith will become a subsidiary of the company, a report made by accountants (who shall be named in the statement) upon the profits and losses and assets and liabilities of the other body corporate in accordance with subparagraph (2) or (3), as the case requires, indicating how the profits or losses of the other body corporate dealt with by the report would, in respect of the shares to be acquired, have concerned members of the company, and what allowance would have had to be made, in relation to assets and liabilities so dealt with, for holders of other shares, if the company had at all material times held the shares to be acquired.

(2) If the other body corporate has no subsidiaries, the report referred to in subparagraph (1) shall—

(a) so far as regards profits and losses, deal with the profits or losses of the body corporate in respect of each of the 5 financial years immediately preceding the delivery of the statement to the registrar; and

(b) so far as regards assets and liabilities, deal with the assets and liabilities of the body corporate at the last date to which the accounts of the body corporate were made up.

(3) If the other body corporate has subsidiaries, the report referred to in subparagraph (1) shall—

(a) so far as regards profits and losses, deal separately with the other body corporate's profits or losses as provided by subparagraph (2), and in addition deal either—

(i) as a whole with the combined profits or losses of its subsidiaries, so far as they concern members of the other body corporate; or

(ii) separately with the profits or losses of each subsidiary, so far as they concern members of the other body corporate;

or, instead of dealing separately with the other body corporate's profits or losses, deal as a whole with the profits or losses of the other body corporate and, so far as they concern members of the other body corporate, with the combined profits or losses of its subsidiaries; and

(b) so far as regards assets and liabilities, deal separately with the other body corporate's assets and liabilities as provided by subparagraph (2) and in addition, deal either—

(i) as a whole with the combined assets and liabilities of its subsidiaries, with or without the other body corporate's assets and liabilities; or

(ii) separately with the assets and liabilities of each subsidiary;

and shall indicate in relation to the assets and liabilities of the subsidiaries, the allowance to be made for persons other than members of the company.

PART III
PROVISIONS APPLYING TO PARTS I AND II

3. In this Schedule, 'vendor' includes a vendor as defined in Part III of the Third Schedule and 'financial year' has the meaning assigned to it in that Part of that Schedule.

4. If in the case of a business which has been carried on, or of a body corporate which has been carrying on business, for less than 5 years, the accounts of the business or body corporate have been made up only in respect of 4 years, 3 years, 2 years or one year, Part II shall have effect as if references to 4 years, 3 years, 2 years or one year, as the case may be, were substituted for references to 5 years.

5. Any report required by Part II shall either indicated by way of note any adjustments relating to the figures of any profits or losses or assets and liabilities dealt with by the report which appear to the persons making the report necessary or shall make those adjustments and indicate that adjustments have been made.

6. Any report by accountants required by Part II shall be made by accountants qualified under this Act for appointment as auditors of the company.

THIRD SCHEDULE
MATTERS TO BE SPECIFIED IN PROSPECTUS AND REPORTS TO BE SENT OUT THEREIN

[...][a]

Amendments

a Repealed by IFCMPA 2005, s 40.

FOURTH SCHEDULE
FORM OF STATEMENT IN LIEU OF PROSPECTUS TO BE DELIVERED TO REGISTRAR BY A COMPANY WHICH DOES NOT ISSUE A PROSPECTUS OR WHICH DOES NOT MAKE AN ALLOTMENT ON A PROSPECTUS ISSUED, AND REPORTS TO BE SET OUT THEREIN

[...][a]

Amendments

a Repealed by IFCMPA 2005, s 40.

FIFTH SCHEDULE

SECTIONS 125, 395

CONTENTS AND FORM OF ANNUAL RETURN OF A COMPANY HAVING A SHARE CAPITAL

[...][a]

Amendments

a Repealed by CLEA 2001, s 63(2) with effect from 1 March 2002.[1]

[1] Company Law Enforcement Act 2001 (Commencement) (No. 2) Order 2001 (SI 438/2001).

SIXTH SCHEDULE

ACCOUNTS

Preliminary

1. Paragraphs 2 to 11 apply to the balance sheet and 12 to 14 to the profit and loss account and are subject to the exceptions and modifications provided for by Parts II and III of this Schedule; and this Schedule has effect in addition to sections 191 and 192.

PART I

GENERAL PROVISIONS AS TO BALANCE SHEET AND PROFIT AND LOSS

Account

BALANCE SHEET

2. The authorised share capital, issued share capital, liabilities and assets shall be summarised, with such particulars as are necessary to disclose the general nature of the assets and liabilities, and there shall be specified—

(a) any part of the issued capital that consists of redeemable preference shares, the amount of the premium (if any) payable on redemption, the earliest and latest dates on which the company has power to redeem those shares and whether redemption is at the option of the company or obligatory;

(b) any part of the issued capital that consists of preference shares which are redeemable in accordance with a resolution passed under section 65, the amount of the premium (if any) payable on redemption, the earliest and latest dates on which the company has power to redeem those shares and whether redemption is at the option of the company or obligatory;

(c) the amount of the share premium account;

(d) particulars of any redeemed debentures which the company has power to re-issue.

3. There shall be stated under separate headings, so far as they are not written off—

(a) the preliminary expenses;

(b) any expenses incurred in connection with any issue of share capital or debentures;

(c) any sums paid by way of commission in respect of any shares or debentures;

(d) any sums allowed by way of discount in respect of any debentures; and

(e) the amount of the discount allowed on any issue of shares at a discount.

4. (1) Subject to subparagraphs (2) and (3), the reserves, provisions, liabilities and fixed and current assets shall be classified under headings appropriate to the company's business. Amounts set aside to meet future tax liabilities or for tax equalisation purposes shall be treated as provisions but separately indicated.

(2) Where the amount of any class is not material, it may be included under the same heading as some other class.

(3) Where any assets of one class are not separable from assets of another class, those assets may be included under the same heading.

(4) Fixed assets shall also be distinguished from current assets.

(5) The method or methods used to arrive at the amount of the fixed assets under each heading shall be stated.

5. (1) The method of arriving at the amount of any fixed asset shall, subject to subparagraph (2), be to take the difference between—

(a) its cost or, if it stands in the company's books at a valuation, the amount of the valuation; and

(b) the aggregate amount provided or written off since the date of acquisition or valuation, as the case may be, for depreciation or diminution in value;

and for the purposes of this paragraph the net amount at which any assets stand in the company's books on the operative date (after deduction of the amounts previously provided or written off for depreciation or diminution in value) shall, if the figures relating to the period before the operative date cannot be obtained without unreasonable expense or delay, be treated as if it were the amount of a valuation of those assets made on the operative date and, where any of those assets are sold, the said net amount less the amount of the sales shall be treated as if it were the amount of the valuation so made of the remaining assets.

(2) Subparagraph (1) shall not apply—

(a) to assets for which the figures relating to the period beginning with the operative date cannot be obtained without unreasonable expense or delay; or

(b) to assets the replacement of which is provided for wholly or partly—

(i) by making provision for renewals and charging the cost of replacement against the provision so made; or

(ii) by charging the cost of replacement direct to revenue; or

(c) to any investments of which the market value (or, in the case of investments not having a market value, their value as estimated by the directors) is shown either as the amount of the investments or by way of note; or

(d) to goodwill, patents or trademarks.

(3) For the assets under each heading whose amount is arrived in accordance with subparagraph (1), there shall be shown—

(a) the aggregate of the amounts referred to in head (a) of that subparagraph; and

(b) the aggregate of the amounts referred to in head (b) thereof.

(4) As respects the assets under each heading whose amount is not arrived at in accordance with subparagraph (1) because their placement is provided for as mentioned in subparagraph (2)(b), there shall be stated—

(a) the means by which their replacement is provided for; and

(b) the aggregate amount of the provision (if any) made for renewals and not used.

6.(1) Subject to subparagraph (2), the aggregate amounts respectively of capital reserves, revenue reserves and provisions (other than provisions for depreciation, renewals or diminution in value of assets) shall be stated under separate headings.

(2) Subparagraph (1) shall not require a separate statement of any of the 3 amounts referred to in that subparagraph which is not material.

7. (1) There shall also be shown (unless it is shown in the profit and loss account or a statement or report annexed thereto or the amount involved is not material)—

(a) where the amount of the capital reserves, of the revenue reserves or of the provisions (other than provisions for depreciation, renewals or diminution in value of assets) shows an increase as compared with the amount at the end of the immediately preceding financial year, the source from which the amount of the increase has been derived; and

(b) where—

(i) the amount of the capital reserves or of the revenue reserves shows a decrease as compared with the amount at the end of the immediately preceding financial year; or

(ii) the amount at the end of the immediately preceding financial year of the provisions (other than provisions for depreciation, renewals or diminution in value of assets) exceeded the aggregate of the sums since applied and amounts still retained for the purposes thereof;

the application of the amounts derived from the difference.

(2) Where the heading showing any of the reserves or provisions aforesaid is divided into subheadings, this paragraph shall apply to each of the separate amounts shown in the subheadings instead of applying to the aggregate amount thereof.

8. There shall be shown under separate headings—

(a) the aggregate amounts respectively of the company's quoted investments and unquoted investments;

(b) the amount of the goodwill so far as ascertainable from the books of the company or from any contracts or documents relating to the purchase or sale of property and so far as not written off;

(c) the amount of the patents and trademarks so far as ascertainable and so far as not written off;

(d) the aggregate amount of any outstanding loans permitted by section 60 (other than loans to which paragraph (a) of subsection (13) refers) indicating separately loans permitted by paragraphs (b) and (c) of subsection (13);

(e) the aggregate amount of bank loans and overdrafts;

(f) the net aggregate amount (after deduction of income tax) which is recommended for distribution by way of dividend.

9. Where any liability of the company is secured otherwise than by operation of law on any assets of the company, the fact that that liability is so secured shall be stated but it shall not be necessary to specify the assets on which the liability is secured.

10. Where any of the company's debentures are held by a nominee of or a trustee for the company, the nominal amount of the debentures and the amount paid for such debentures by the company shall be stated.

11. (1) The matters referred to in subparagraphs (2) to (10) shall be stated by way of note, or in statement or report annexed, if not otherwise shown.

(2) The amount of any arrears of fixed cumulative dividends on the company's shares and the period for which the dividends or, if there is more than one class, each class of them are in arrear the amount to be stated before deduction of income tax, except that, in the case of tax free dividends, the amount shall be shown free of tax and the fact that it is so shown shall also be stated.

[(2A) Where shares in a public limited company, other than an old public limited company within the meaning of the Companies (Amendment) Act, 1983 are acquired by the company by forfeiture or surrender in lieu of forfeiture, or in pursuance of section 41 of that Act, or are acquired by another person in circumstances where paragraph (c) or (d) of section 43 (1) of that Act applies or are made subject to a lien or charge taken (whether expressly or otherwise) by the company and permitted by section 44 (2) (a), (c) or (d) of that Act—

(a) the number and nominal value of the shares so acquired by the company, acquired by another person in such circumstances and so charged respectively during the financial year;

(b) the maximum number and nominal value of shares which, having been so acquired by the company, acquired by another person in such circumstances or so charged (whether or not during the financial year) are held at any time by the company or that other person during that year;

(c) the number and nominal value of the shares so acquired by the company, acquired by another person in such circumstances or so charged (whether or not during that year) which are disposed of by the company or that other person or cancelled by the company during that year;

(d) where the number and nominal value of the shares of any particular description are stated in pursuance of any of the preceding paragraphs, the percentage of the called-up share capital which shares of that description represent;

(e) where any of the shares have been so charged, the amount of the charge in each case; and

(f) where any of the shares have been disposed of by the company or the person who acquired them in such circumstances for money or money's worth, the amount or value of the consideration in each case.

(2B) Any distribution by an investment company within the meaning of Part IV of the Companies (Amendment) Act, 1983, which reduces the amount of its net assets to less than the aggregate of its called-up share capital and undistributable reserves. In this subparagraph 'net assets' and 'called up share capital' have the same meanings as in section 2 of the Companies (Amendment) Act, 1983 and 'undistributable reserves' has the same meaning as in section 46(2) of that Act.][a]

(3) Particulars of any charge on the assets of the company to secure the liabilities of any other person, including, where practicable, the amount secured.

(4) The general nature of any other contingent liabilities not provided for and, where practicable, the aggregate amount or estimated amount of those liabilities, if it is material.

(5) The aggregate amount or estimated amount, if it is material, of contracts for capital expenditure, so far as not provided for.

(6) If in the opinion of the directors any of the current assets have not a value, on realisation in the ordinary course of the company's business, at least equal to the amount at which they are stated, the fact that the directors are of that opinion.

(7) The aggregate market value of the company's quoted investments where it differs from the amount of the investments as stated, and the stock exchange value of any investments of which the market value is shown (whether separately or not) and is taken as being higher than their stock exchange value.

(8) The basis on which foreign currencies have been converted into Irish currency where the amount of the assets or liabilities affected is material.

(9) The basis on which the amount, if any, set aside for taxation on profits is computed.

(10) Except in the case of the first balance sheet laid before the company after the operative date, the corresponding amounts at the end of the immediately preceding financial year for all items shown in the balance sheet.

Amendments

a Sub-paragraphs (2A) and (2B) inserted by C(A)A 1983, Sch 1, para 27.

Profit and Loss Account

12. There shall be shown—

(a) the amount charged to revenue by way of provision for depreciation, renewals or diminution in value of fixed assets;

(b) the amount of the interest on the company's debentures and other fixed loans;

(c) the amount of the charge for income tax and other taxation on profits including income tax and other taxation payable outside the State on profits and distinguishing where practicable between income tax and other taxation;

[(d) the amounts respectively provided for purchase of the company's share capital, for redemption of share capital and for redemption of loans;][a]

(e) the amount set aside or proposed to be set aside to, or withdrawn from reserves, excluding amounts which would not, in accordance with good accountancy practice, normally pass through the profit and loss account;

(f) the amount set aside to provisions other than provisions for depreciation, renewals or diminution in value of assets or, as the case may be, the amount, if material, withdrawn from such provisions and not applied for the purposes thereof, excluding amounts which would not, in accordance with good accountancy practice, normally pass through the profit and loss account;

(g) the amount of income from investments;

(h) the aggregate amount of the dividends paid;

(i) the aggregate amount of the dividends proposed.

Amendments

a Sub–paragraph (d) substituted by CA 1990, s 231.

---

13. The amount of remuneration of the auditors shall be shown under a separate heading, and for the purposes of this paragraph, any sums paid by the company for the auditors' expenses shall be deemed to be included in the expression 'remuneration'.

14. (1) The matters referred to in subparagraphs (2) to (7) shall be stated by way of note, if not otherwise shown.

(2) If depreciation or replacement of fixed assets is provided for by some method other than a depreciation charge or provision for renewals, or is not provided for, the method by which it is provided for or the fact that it is not provided for, as the case may be, but this subparagraph shall not apply to freehold land.

(3) The basis on which the charge for income tax and other taxation on profits (whether payable in or outside the State) is computed.

(4) Whether or not the amount stated for dividends paid is for dividends subject to deduction of income tax.

(5) Whether or not the amount stated for dividends proposed is for dividends subject to deduction of income tax.

(6) Except in the case of the first profit and loss account laid before the company after the operative date, the corresponding amounts for the immediately preceding financial year for all items shown in the profit and loss account.

(7) Any material respects in which any items shown in the profit and loss account are affected—

(a) by transactions of a sort not usually undertaken by the company or otherwise by circumstances of an exceptional or non-recurrent nature; or

(b) by any change in the basis of accounting.

PART II

SPECIAL PROVISIONS WHERE THE COMPANY IS A HOLDING COMPANY OR A SUBSIDIARY COMPANY

Modifications of and Additions to Requirements as to Company's own Accounts

15. (1) This paragraph shall apply where the company is a holding company, whether or not it is itself a subsidiary of another body corporate but subparagraphs (4), (5) and (6) shall not apply to a private company taking advantage of subsection (1) of section 154 nor to a company which is at the end of its financial year the wholly owned subsidiary of another body corporate incorporated in the State.

(2) The aggregate amount of assets consisting of shares in, or amounts owing (whether on account of a loan or otherwise) from, the company's subsidiaries, distinguishing shares from indebtedness, shall be set out in the balance sheet separately from all the other assets of the company, and the aggregate amount of its indebtedness (whether on account of a loan or otherwise) to the company's subsidiaries shall be so set out separately from all its other liabilities, and—

(a) the references in Part I to the company's investments shall not include investments in its subsidiaries required by this paragraph to be separately set out; and

(b) paragraph 5, subparagraph (a) of paragraph 12, and subparagraph (2) of paragraph 14 shall not apply in relation to fixed assets consisting of interests in the company's subsidiaries.

(3) There shall be shown by way of note on the balance sheet or in a statement or report annexed thereto the number, description and amount of the shares in and debentures of the company held by its subsidiaries or their nominees, but excluding any of those shares or debentures in the case of which the subsidiary is concerned as personal representative or in the case of which it is concerned as trustee and neither the company nor any subsidiary thereof is beneficially interested under the trust, otherwise than by way of security only for the purposes of a transaction entered into by it in the ordinary course of a business which includes the lending of money.

(4) Where group accounts are not submitted, there shall, subject to subparagraph (5), be annexed to the balance sheet a statement showing—

(a) the reasons why subsidiaries are not dealt with in group accounts;

(b) the net aggregate amount (so far as it concerns members of the holding company) of the subsidiaries' profits after deducting the subsidiaries' losses, or vice versa, for the respective financial years of the subsidiaries ending with or during the financial year of the company—

(i) so far as dealt with in the company's accounts for that year; and

(ii) so far as not so dealt with;

(c) the net aggregate amount, so far as concerns members of the holding company, of the subsidiaries' profits after deducting the subsidiaries' losses, or vice versa, for their previous financial years since they respectively became subsidiaries of the holding company—

(i) so far as dealt with in the company's accounts for the year referred to in head (b)(i); and

(ii) so far as not dealt with in the company's accounts for that or previous years;

(d) any qualifications contained in the report of the auditors of the subsidiaries on their accounts for their respective financial years ending as aforesaid, and any note or saving contained in those accounts to call attention to a matter which, apart from the note or saving, would properly have been referred to in such a qualification, in so far as the matter which is the subject of the qualification or note is not covered by the company's own accounts and is material from the point of view of its members;

or, in so far as the information required by this subparagraph is not obtainable, a statement that it is not obtainable.

(5) Heads (b) and (c) of subparagraph (4) shall apply only to profits and losses of a subsidiary which may properly be treated in the holding company's accounts as revenue profits or losses.

(6) Where group accounts are not submitted, there shall be annexed to the balance sheet a statement showing, in relation to the subsidiaries, if any, whose financial years did not end with that of the company—

(a) the reasons why the company's directors consider the subsidiaries' financial years should not end with that of the company; and

(b) the dates on which the subsidiaries' financial years ending last before that of the company respectively ended or the earliest and latest of those dates.

16. (1) The balance sheet of a company which is a subsidiary of another body corporate, whether or not it is itself a holding company, shall show the aggregate amount of its indebtedness to all bodies corporate of which it is a subsidiary or a fellow subsidiary and the aggregate amount of the indebtedness of all such bodies corporate to it, distinguishing in each case between indebtedness in respect of debentures and otherwise.

(2) For the purposes of this paragraph a company shall be deemed to be a fellow subsidiary of another body corporate if both are subsidiaries of the same body corporate but neither is the other's.

Consolidated Accounts of Holding Company and Subsidiaries

17. Subject to paragraphs 18 to 22, the consolidated balance sheet and profit and loss account shall combine the information contained in the separate balance sheets and profit and loss accounts of the holding company and of the subsidiaries dealt with by the consolidated accounts, but with such adjustments, if any, as the directors of the holding company think necessary.

18. Subject as aforesaid and to Part III, the consolidated accounts shall, in giving the said information, comply, so far as practicable, with the requirements of this Act as if they were the accounts of an actual company.

19. Sections 191 and 192 shall not, by virtue of paragraphs 17 and 18 apply for the purpose of the consolidated accounts.

20. Paragraph 7 shall not apply for the purpose of any consolidated accounts laid before a company with the first balance sheet so laid after the operative date.

21. In relation to any subsidiaries of the holding company not dealt with by the consolidated accounts—

(a) subparagraphs (2) and (3) of paragraph 15 shall apply for the purpose of those accounts as if those accounts were the accounts of an actual company of which they were subsidiaries; and

(b) there shall be annexed the like statement as is required by subparagraph (4) of that paragraph where there are no group accounts, but as if references therein to the holding company's accounts were references to the consolidated accounts.

22. In relation to any subsidiaries (whether or not dealt with by the consolidated accounts), whose financial years did not end with that of the company, there shall be annexed the like statement as is required by subparagraph (6) of paragraph 15 where there are no group accounts.

PART III
EXCEPTIONS FOR SPECIAL CLASSES OF COMPANY

23. (1) A banking or discount company shall not be subject to the requirements of Part I other than—

(a) in relation to its balance sheet, those of paragraphs 2 and 3, paragraph 4 (so far as it relates to fixed and current assets), paragraph 8 (except subparagraph (e)), paragraphs 9 and 10 and paragraph 11 (except subparagraph (7)); and

(b) in relation to its profit and loss account, those of subparagraphs (h) and (i) of paragraph 12, paragraph 13 and subparagraphs (1), (4), (5) and (6) of paragraph 14;

but where in its balance sheet capital reserves, revenue reserves or provisions (other than provisions for depreciation, renewals or diminution in value of assets) are not stated separately, and heading stating an amount arrived at after taking into account such a reserve or provision shall be so framed or marked as to indicate that fact, and its profit and loss account shall indicate by appropriate words the manner in which the amount stated for the company's profit or loss has been arrived at.

(2) The accounts of a banking or discount company shall not be deemed, by reason only of the fact that they do not comply with any requirements of Part I from which the company is exempt by virtue of this paragraph, not to give the true and fair view required by this Act.

(3) In this paragraph, 'banking or discount company' means any company which satisfies the Minister that it ought to be treated for the purposes of this Schedule as a banking company or as a discount company.

24. In relation to an assurance company within the meaning of the Insurance Acts, 1909 to 1961, which is subject to and complies with the requirements of those Acts relating to the preparation and deposit with the Minister of a balance sheet and profit and loss account, paragraph 23 shall apply as it applies in relation to a banking or a discount company, and such an assurance company shall also not be subject to the requirements of subparagraph (a) of paragraph 8 and subparagraph (3), (4), (6) and (9) of paragraph 11.

25. (1) A company to which this paragraph applies shall not be subject to the following requirements of this Schedule:

(a) in relation to its balance sheet, those of paragraph 4 (except so far as that paragraph relates to fixed and current assets) and paragraphs 5, 6 and 7; and

(b) in relation to its profit and loss account, those of subparagraph (a), (e) and (f) of paragraph 12;

but a company taking advantage of this paragraph shall be subject, instead of the said requirements, to any prescribed conditions in relation to matters to be stated in its accounts or by way of note thereto and in relation to information to be furnished to the Minister or a person authorised by the Minister to require it.

(2) The accounts of a company shall not be deemed, by reason only of the fact that they do not comply with any of the requirements of Part I from which the company is exempt by virtue of this paragraph, not to give the true and fair view required by this Act.

(3) Subject to subparagraph (4), this paragraph applies to companies of any class prescribed for the purposes thereof, and a class of companies may be so prescribed if it appears to the Minister desirable in the public interest.

(4) If the Minister is of opinion that any of the conditions prescribed for the purposes of this paragraph have not been complied with in the case of any company, the Minister may direct that so long as the direction continues in force this paragraph shall not apply to the company.

26. Where a company entitled to the benefit of any provision contained in this Part is a holding company, the references in Part II to consolidated accounts complying with the requirements of this Act shall, in relation to consolidated accounts of that company, be construed as referring to those requirements in so far only as they apply to the separate accounts of that company.

PART IV

INTERPRETATION OF SCHEDULE

27. (1) For the purposes of this Schedule—

(a) 'provision' shall, subject to subparagraph (2), mean any amount written off or retained by way of providing for depreciation, renewals or diminution in value of assets or retained by way of providing for any known liability of which the amount cannot be determined with substantial accuracy;

(b) 'reserve' shall not, subject as aforesaid, include any amount written off or retained by way of providing for depreciation, renewals or diminution in value of assets or retained by way of providing for any known liability;

(c) 'capital reserve' shall not include any amount regarded as free for distribution through the profit and loss account, and 'revenue reserve' shall mean any reserve other than a capital reserve;

and in this paragraph 'liability' shall include all liabilities in respect of expenditure contracted for and all disputed or contingent liabilities.

(2) Where—

(a) any amount written off or retained by way of providing for depreciation, renewals or diminution in value of assets, not being an amount written off in relation to fixed assets before the operative date; or

(b) any amount retained by way of providing for any known liability;

is in excess of that which in the opinion of the directors is reasonably necessary for the purpose, the excess shall be treated for the purposes of this Schedule as a reserve and not as a provision.

28. For the purposes aforesaid 'quoted investment' means an investment for which there has been granted a quotation or permission to deal on a recognised stock exchange within the State or on any stock exchange of repute outside the State, and 'unquoted investment' shall be construed accordingly.

SEVENTH SCHEDULE

MATTERS TO BE EXPRESSLY STATED IN AUDITORS' REPORT

[...][a]

Amendments

a Repealed by CA 1990, s 6 and replaced by CA 1990, s 193.

EIGHTH SCHEDULE

FEES TO BE PAID TO THE REGISTRAR OF COMPANIES

[PART I

'electronic form' means in relation to the doing of any act specified in the first column to the table set out in this Part the doing of that act by means of—

(a) the electronic form filing system in use by the registrar of companies, or

(b) the Companies Registration Office disk electronic filing system where the act is also effected in paper form;

'paper form' means, in relation a matter specified in the first column to the table set out in this Part—

(a) the filing of documents or an application in paper form, or

(b) the inspection of documents or an application submitted in paper form, or

(c) the submission of documents in paper form;

'Societas Europaea' or European Public Limited Liability Company shall be construed in accordance with the European Communities (European Public Limited Liability Company) Regulations 2007 (S.I. No. 21 of 2007).

TABLE OF FEES

Matter in respect of which Fee is payable	*Amount of Fee*
Provision of an electronic certified copy certificate of incorporation for public sector use pursuant to section 370(1)(b)	Paper form — not applicable Electronic form — nil
Provision of a certified copy of any matter entered in the register kept by the registrar of companies for the registration of companies (including the register referred to in section 103) pursuant to section 370(1)(b)	Paper form — €12 Electronic form — not applicable
Each inspection of any register kept in the office for the registration of companies (including the register referred to in section 103) pursuant to section 370(1)(a)	Paper form — €3.50 Electronic form — €3.50
Provision of an uncertified copy of any matter entered in the register aforesaid pursuant to section 370(1)(b)	Paper form —€2.50 Electronic form — €2.50

Matter in respect of which Fee is payable	*Amount of Fee*
Registration of any company (other than a Societas Europaea) under the Companies Acts	Paper form — €100 Electronic form — €50
Registration of a company to which section 328(1) applies	Paper form — €100 Electronic form — €50
Application for a certificate pursuant to section 6 of the Companies (Amendment) Act 1983 (No. 13 of 1983)	Paper form — €300 Electronic form — not applicable
Delivery, pursuant to section 352, for registration of documents referred to in that section by a company incorporated outside the State	Paper form — €60 Electronic form — not applicable
Registration of a company to which Part II or III of the European Communities (Branch Disclosures) Regulations 1993 (S.I. No. 395 of 1993) applies	Paper form — €60 Electronic form — not applicable
Re-registration of a company in any of the ways provided for under the Companies Acts	Paper form — €60 Electronic form — not applicable
Registration of an annual return made up to a date prior to 1 March 2002	Paper form — €1,240 Electronic form — €1,220
Delivery of annual return within the period referred to in section 127(2) (amended by section 60 of the Company Law Enforcement Act 2001 (No. 28 of 2001))	Paper form — €40 Electronic form — €20
Delivery of an annual return later than the period referred to in section 127(2) (amended by section 60 of the Company Law Enforcement Act 2001 (No. 28 of 2001))	Paper form — €140 plus €3.00 in respect of each day on which the failure to file the return continues after the statutory filing period, subject to a maximum fee of €1,240 for each return Electronic form — €120 plus €3.00 in respect of each day on which the failure to file the return continues after the statutory filing period, subject to a maximum fee of €1,220 for each return
Entry of new name in the register in place of the former name pursuant to section 23(3)	Paper form — €100 Electronic form — €50
Registration of particulars of a series of debentures required to be registered pursuant to section 99(8)	Paper form — €40 Electronic form — not applicable

Matter in respect of which Fee is payable	*Amount of Fee*
Giving of notice of a change in the situation of the registered office of the company pursuant to subsection (3) of section 113 (inserted by section 4 of the Companies (Amendment) Act 1982 (No. 10 of 1982))	Paper form — €15 Electronic form — nil
Sending of notification of a change of director or secretary, or of any particulars contained in the register, pursuant to subsection (6) of section 195 (inserted by section 51 of the Companies Act 1990 (No. 33 of 1990))	Paper form — €15 Electronic form — nil
Sending of a notice of the place where the register of members of a company is kept or of any change in that place, pursuant to section 116(7)	Paper form — €15 Electronic form — nil
Sending of a notice of the place where the register of debenture holders of a company is kept or of a change in that place, pursuant to section 91(3)	Paper form — €15 Electronic form — nil
Sending of a notice of the place where copies and memoranda required by section 50(1) of the Companies Act 1990 (No. 33 of 1990) are kept or of any change in that place, pursuant to section 50(4) of that Act	Paper form — €15 Electronic form — nil
Delivery of a notice referred to in Regulation 4(3)(c), 7(3)(c), 4(3)(d) or 7(3)(d), of the European Communities (Branch Disclosures) Regulations 1993 (S.I. No. 395 of1993)	Paper form — €15 Electronic form — nil
Delivery pursuant to section 353 of a return containing prescribed particulars of an alteration made in respect of persons referred to in paragraph (c) of that section	Paper form — €15 Electronic form — nil
Forwarding of an ordinary resolution or agreement, or a special resolution or agreement (other than a special resolution or agreement relating to a change of name of a company pursuant to section 23) pursuant to section 143 (amended by section 5 of the Companies (Amendment) Act 1982 (No. 6 of 1982) and paragraph 15 of the First Schedule to the Companies (Amendment) Act 1983 (No. 13 of 1983)) and any document lodged in connection with such resolution	Paper form — €15 Electronic form — nil

Matter in respect of which Fee is payable	*Amount of Fee*
Notification of a company becoming a single-member company and identity of its sole member pursuant to Regulation 5 of the European Communities (Single-Member Private Limited Companies) Regulations 1994 (S.I. No. 275 of 1994)	Paper form — €15 Electronic form — nil
Notification that a company has ceased to be a single- member company, pursuant to Regulation 6 of the European Communities (Single-Member Private Limited Companies) Regulations 1994 (S.I. No. 275 of 1994)	Paper form — €15 Electronic form — nil
Sending, pursuant to section 34(3)(a) of the Companies (Amendment) (No.2) Act 1999 (No. 30 of 1999), of a copy of a notice under subsection (1)(i) of that section)	Paper form — nil Electronic form — not applicable
Filing a document to which section 80(1) of the Company Law Enforcement Act 2001 (No. 28 of 2001) applies, for the purposes of registration	Paper form — €100 Electronic form — not applicable
Application for a grant of a certificate pursuant to section 44(2) of the Companies (Amendment) (No. 2) Act 1999 (No. 30 of 1999)	Paper form — €40 Electronic form — not applicable
Delivering a notice and statutory declaration, pursuant to subsections (3)(b)(i) and (5) respectively, of section 45 of the Companies (Amendment) (No. 2) Act 1999 (No. 30 of1999)	Paper form — €40 Electronic form — not applicable
Delivery of nomination of a new annual return date, pursuant to subsection (9) of section 127 (inserted by section 60 of the Company Law Enforcement Act 2001 (No. 28 of 2001))	Paper form — €15 Electronic form — nil
Application for the formation by merger of a Societas Europaea pursuant to Regulation 4(1)(a) of the European Communities (European Public Limited Liability Company) Regulations 2007 (S.I. No. 21 of 2007)	Paper form — €100 Electronic form — not applicable
Application for the formation of a holding Societas Europaea pursuant to Regulation 4(1)(b) of the European Communities (European Public Limited Liability Company) Regulations 2007 (S.I. No. 21 of 2007)	Paper form — €100 Electronic form — not applicable

Matter in respect of which Fee is payable	*Amount of Fee*
Application for the formation of a subsidiary Societas Europaea pursuant to Regulation 4(1)(c) of the European Communities (European Public Liability Company) Regulations 2007 (S.I. No. 21 of 2007)	Paper form — €100 Electronic form — not applicable
Application for the conversion of a public limited company to a Societas Europaea pursuant to Regulation 4(1)(d) of the European Communities (European Public Limited Liability) Regulations 2007 (S.I. No. 21 of 2007)	Paper form — €100 Electronic form — not applicable
Application for the formation of a subsidiary Societas Europaea of a Societas Europaea pursuant to Regulation 4(1)(e) of the European Communities (European Public Limited Liability) Regulations 2007 (S.I. No. 21 of 2007)	Paper form — €60 Electronic form — not applicable
Application to transfer a Societas Europaea's registered office to the State pursuant to Regulation 5 of the European Communities (European Communities (European Public Limited Liability Company) Regulations 2007 (S.I. No. 21 of 2007)	Paper form — €100 Electronic form — not applicable
Application to register the transfer of an Societas Europaea's registered office from the State pursuant to Regulation 7 of the European Communities (European Public Limited Liability Company) Regulations 2007 (S.I. No. 21 of 2007)	Paper form — €100 Electronic form — not applicable
Registration of any notice and accompanying copy common draft terms of merger delivered to the registrar of companies by an Irish merging company pursuant to Regulation 8(1) of the European Communities (Cross-Border Merger) Regulations 2008 (S.I. No. 157 of 2008)	Paper form — €100 Electronic form — not applicable
Delivery to the registrar of companies of draft terms of conversion of a Societas Europaea into a public limited company for publication by the registrar of companies pursuant to Article 66(4) of Council Regulation No. 2157/2001/EC of 8 October 2001 (O.J. L.294 of 10.11.2001)	Paper form — €100 Electronic form — not applicable

Matter in respect of which Fee is payable	*Amount of Fee*
Re-registration of a Societas Europaea as a public limited company following approval by the general meeting of the Societas Europaea of the draft terms of conversion pursuant to Article 66(6) of Council Regulation No. 2157/2001/EC of 8 October 2001	Paper form — €100 Electronic form — not applicable
Delivery for registration, pursuant to Regulation 11(1)(a) of the European Communities (Mergers and Division of Companies) Regulations 1987 (S.I. No. 137 of 1987), to the registrar of companies of a copy of the draft terms of merger, signed and dated, required by Regulation 6 of those Regulations and delivery to the registrar of companies, pursuant to Regulation 4(1) of the European Communities (European Public Limited-Liability Company) Regulations 2007 (S.I. No. 21 of 2007), of particulars for publication set out in Article 21 of Council Regulation No. 2157/2001 of 8 October 2001, in respect of the formation of an Societas Europaea by means of a merger where the Societas Europaea will be registered outside the state.	Paper form — €100 Electronic form — not applicable
Subject to this Schedule, registration or application for registration of, or delivery or giving of, any document to the registrar of companies, pursuant to the Companies Acts.	Paper form — €15 Electronic form (where applicable) — nil][a]
[For dealing with an application made under section 256F(2) of the Companies Act 1990, inserted by section 3(j) of the Companies (Miscellaneous Provisions) Act 2009 for registration as a company in the State by means of continuation from a relevant jurisdiction.	€445 N/A
For dealing with an application made under section 256G(2) of the Companies Act 1990, inserted by section 3(j) of the Companies (Miscellaneous Provisions) Act 2009 for de-registration as a company in the State on continuance in a relevant jurisdiction.	€445 N/A][b]

Amendments

a CA 1963, Sch 8 substituted by Companies Act 1963 (Alteration of Eighth Schedule) Order 2009 (SI 302/2009), reg 2 and Sch.

b Text inserted by C(Fees)O 2010, reg 2 and Sch.

[PART II

LIMITATIONS ON OPERATION OF PART I

Where the registrar directs, pursuant to section 23(2), that a company shall change its name, any fee that would, but for this Part, be required to be paid under Part I of this Schedule in respect of the registration of that change shall not be charged, levied or paid.][a]

Amendments

a CA 1963, Sch 8, Pt II substituted by Companies (Fees)(No 3) Order 2005 (SI 2005/517) Sch, Pt I.

NINTH SCHEDULE

[PROVISIONS APPLIED TO UNREGISTERED COMPANIES

Principal Act

Subject matter	*Provisions applied*
Acts done by company (ultra vires rule).	Section 8.
Pre-incorporation contracts.	Section 37(1) and (2).
Prospectus and allotments.	Sections 43 to 52, 56, 57, 61 and the Third Schedule.
[Share premium account.][a]	[Section 62.][b]
[Reduction of Share Capital.][c]	[Sections 72 to 77.][d]
[Validation of invalid issue, redemption or purchase of shares.	Section 89.][e]
Registered office.	Section 113 (inserted by the Companies (Amendment) Act, 1982).
Annual Return	Sections 125 to 129 and the Fifth Schedule
Accounts and Audit	Sections 148 to 153, 155 to 161, 191 and the Sixth Schedule (except subparagraphs (a) to (d) of paragraph 2, subparagraphs (c) to (e) of paragraph 3 and subparagraph (d) of paragraph 8), as amended by the Companies (Amendment) Act, 1986.
Validity of acts of directors.	Section 178.
Register of directors and secretaries. Particulars relating to directors to be shown on all business letters of the company	Sections 195 (inserted by the Companies Act, 1990) and 196.

Subject matter	*Provisions applied*
Registration of documents, enforcement and other supplemental matters.	Sections 2, 193, 369 to 371, 378, 379, 383, 384, 386, 387, 395(1) and the Eighth Schedule.
Liability of officers and others for negligence etc.	Sections 200 and 391.

Companies (Amendment) Act, 1977

Subject matter	*Provisions applied*
Share certificates	Sections 2 and 3.
Company records	Section 4.

Companies (Amendment) Act, 1983

Subject matter	*Provisions applied*
Maintenance of capital. Restrictions on distribution of profits and assets.	Sections 40 to 42, 45, 45A (inserted by the Companies (Amendment) Act, 1986, and 49 to 51. Sections 43, [43A,][f] 44, 46 and 47, with the modification that those sections shall apply to all bodies corporate to which section 377(1) of the Principal Act applies other than those which, if they were registered, would be private companies.

European Communities (Stock Exchange) Regulations, 1984 (SI No 282 of 1984)

Provisions applied

All of the Regulations

Companies (Amendment) Act, 1986

Subject matter	*Provisions applied*
Power to alter form of accounts.	Section 24.

European Communities (Mergers And Divisions of Companies) Regulations, 1987 (SI No. 137 of 1987)

Provisions applied

All of the Regulations

COMPANIES (AMENDMENT) ACT, 1990

Provisions applied

The whole Act.

COMPANIES ACT, 1990

Provisions applied

Parts I to III.

Part IV, with the modification that Chapter 2 of that Part shall apply to all bodies corporate to which section 377 (1) of the Principal Act applies other than those which, if they were registered, would be private companies and Chapter 3 of that Part shall apply to all such bodies corporate which, if they were registered, would be private companies.

Part V.

Part VI, except sections 122, 128 to 131 and 133.

Parts VII,IX,X,[XI,][g] and XII.][h]

[European Communities (Public Limited Companies Subsidiaries) Regulations, 1997 (SI No 67 of 1997)

Provisions applied

All of the Regulations][i]

Amendments

a Words 'Share premium account' inserted by CA1963(Sch 9)R 2010, reg 2(a)(i).

b Words 'Section 62' inserted by CA1963(Sch 9)R 2010, reg 2(b)(i).

c Words 'Reduction of Share Capital' inserted by CA1963(Sch 9)R 2010, reg 2(a)(ii).

d Words 'Sections 72 to 77' inserted by CA1963(Sch 9)R 2010, reg 2(b)(ii).

e Words 'Validation of invalid issue, redemption or purchase of shares' and 'Section 89' inserted in the first and second column respectively, under the title 'Principal Act', by Companies Act 1963 (Ninth Schedule) Regulations 1999 (SI 63/1999), reg 3(a) with effect from 1 April 1999.

f Words '43A,' inserted in the second column, under the title 'Companies (Amendment) Act, 1983' by Companies Act 1963 (Ninth Schedule) Regulations 1999 (SI 63/1999), reg 3(b) with effect from 1 April 1999.

g Words ',XI' inserted in the second column, under the title 'Companies Act, 1990' by Companies Act 1963 (Ninth Schedule) Regulations 1999 (SI 63/1999), reg 3(c) with effect from 1 April 1999.

h CA 1963, Sch 9 substituted by CA 1990, s 250 and Sch.

i Additional table inserted by Companies Act 1963 (Ninth Schedule) Regulations 1999 (SI 63/1999), reg 3(d) with effect from 1 April 1999.

TENTH SCHEDULE

PROVISIONS REFERRED TO IN SECTION 380

[...][a]

Amendments

a CA 1963, Sch 10 repealed by CA 1990, s 6 with effect from 1 July 1991.[1]

[1] Companies Act 1990 (Commencement) (No 2) Order 1991 (SI 117/1991).

ELEVENTH SCHEDULE

AMENDMENTS OF OTHER ACTS

THE BANKRUPTCY ACTS

1.(1) The Bankruptcy Acts shall have effect as if for section 53 of the Bankruptcy (Ireland) Amendment Act, 1872 (which relates to the avoidance of fraudulent preferences) there were substituted the following section:

'53. Every conveyance or transfer of property or charge thereon made, every obligation incurred and every judicial proceeding taken or suffered by any person unable to pay his debts as they become due from his own moneys, in favour of any creditor or of any person in trust for any creditor, with a view to giving such creditor, or any surety or guarantor for the debt due to such creditor, a preference over the other creditors, shall, if the person making, taking, paying or suffering the same is adjudged bankrupt on a bankruptcy petition or a petition for arrangement, presented within 6 months after the date of making, taking, paying or suffering the same, be deemed fraudulent and void against the assignees or trustees of such bankrupt; but this section shall not affect the rights of any person making title in good faith and for valuable consideration through or under a creditor of the bankrupt.'

(2) Subparagraph (1) shall not apply in relation to things made or done before the operative date and section 53 of the Bankruptcy (Ireland) Amendment Act, 1872, as originally enacted shall continue to apply to things made or done before the operative date as if this Act had not been passed.

2. Section 287 shall apply also in relation to the said Act of 1872 (with the necessary modification of any reference to a company and to winding up) as if a reference to section 53 of the said Act of 1872 were substituted in section 287 for the reference to section 286.

The Insurance Acts, 1909 to 1961

3. The Insurance Acts, 1909 to 1961, shall have effect as if for subsection (5) of section 46 of the Insurance Act, 1936, there were substituted the following subsection:

'(5) Sections 167 and 168 of the Companies Act, 1963, shall apply in relation to an inspector appointed under this section in like manner as they apply to an inspector appointed under section 165 of that Act, and any such refusal as under subsection (3) of the said section 168 is, or might be, made the ground of the punishment of an officer or agent of the company or other body corporate whose affairs are investigated by virtue of the said section 167, shall also be a ground on which the Minister may present a petition for the winding up of such company and upon which the High Court may, on the hearing of any such petition, make an order for the winding up of such company under and in accordance with the Companies Act, 1963.'

TWELFTH SCHEDULE

ENACTMENTS REPEALED

Session and Chapter or Number & Year	*Short title*	*Extent of Repeal*
3 & 4 Will. 4 c. 31.	The Sunday Observance Act, 1833	The whole Act
45 & 46 Vict., c 72	The Revenue Friendly Societies and National Debt Act, 1882	Subsection (1) of Section 11 and in the First Schedule the words '6 Geo. 4, c. 42, 8 & 9 Vic., c. 37, s. 22

Session and Chapter or Number & Year	*Short title*	*Extent of Repeal*
8 Edw 7, c.69	The Companies (Consolidation) Act, 1908	The whole Act.
3 & 4 Geo.5, c. 25	The Companies Act, 1913	The whole Act.
7 & 8 Geo. 5 c. 28	The Companies (Particulars as to Directors) Act, 1917.	The whole Act.
No 9 of 1934	The Workmen's Compensation Act, 1934.	Subsections (3) and (4) of section 20.
No. 7 of 1942	The Insurance (Intermittent Unemployment) Act, 1942.	Subsections (1) and (2) of section 27.
No. 11 of 1952	The Social Welfare Act, 1952.	Subsections (1) and (2) of section 58.
No. 7 of 1959	The Companies Act, 1959.	The whole Act.
No. 42 of 1959	The Finance (No. 2) Act, 1959.	Subsections (2) and (3) of section 12.

THIRTEENTH SCHEDULE

ENACTMENT SAVED

THE JOINT STOCK BANKING COMPANIES ACT, 1857, PART OF SECTION 12

Notwithstanding anything contained in any Act passed in the session holden in the seventh and eighth years of Queen Victoria, chapter one hundred and thirteen, and intituled 'An Act to regulate Joint Stock Banks in England', or in any other Act, it shall be lawful for any number of persons, not exceeding ten, to carry on in partnership the business of banking, in the same manner and upon the same conditions in all respects as any company of not more than six persons could before the passing of the Joint Stock Banking Companies Act, 1857, have carried on such business.

Stock Transfer Act 1963

Number 34 of 1963

ARRANGEMENT OF SECTIONS

An Act to amend the Law with Respect to the Transfer of Securities. [24th December, 1963.]

Be It Enacted by the Oireachtas as follows:—

1 Interpretation

(1) In this Act—

'the Minister' means the Minister for Finance;

'registered securities' means securities the holders of which are entered in a register;

'securities' includes shares, stock, debentures, debenture stock, loan stock and bonds;

'stock exchange transaction' means a sale and purchase of securities in which each of the parties is a member of a stock exchange acting in the ordinary course of his business as such or is acting through the agency of such a member;

'stock exchange' means the Cork Stock Exchange, the Dublin Stock Exchange and any other stock exchange which is declared by the Minister by regulations to be a recognised stock exchange for the purposes of this Act.

[(2) References in this Act to 'a stock transfer' shall, in addition to applying to an instrument under hand in a form set out in the First Schedule to this Act, be construed, where the context so allows, as including a transfer to which section 139 of the Central Bank Act, 1989, applies as if it were a transfer in a form so set out and in respect of which no brokers transfer is necessary.] [a]

Amendments

a Central Bank Act 1989, s 139(3) inserted STA 1963, s 1(2) with effect from 12 July 1989.[1]

[1] Central Bank Act 1989 (Commencement) Order 1989 (SI 176/1989).

2 Simplified transfer of securities

(1) Registered securities to which this section applies may be transferred by means of an instrument under hand in [the form][a] set out in the First Schedule to this Act (in this Act referred to as a stock transfer), executed by the transferor only and specifying (in addition to the particulars of the consideration, of the description and number or amount of the securities, and of the person by whom the transfer is made) the full name and address of the transferee.

[Provided that—

(a) in the case of an instrument in the form set out in Part I of the Schedule to the Stock Transfer (Forms) Regulations 1980, and inserted in the said First Schedule, by Regulation 4 of those Regulations, the instrument need not specify—

(i) particulars of the consideration, or

(ii) the address of the transferee, and

(b) in the case of an instrument in the form set out in Part II of the Schedule to the said Regulations and inserted in the said First Schedule by the said Regulation 4, if the transferor is a body corporate, the instrument need not be executed under hand but shall be sufficiently executed by or on behalf of such transferor if it bears a facsimile of the corporate seal of the transferor, authenticated by the signature (whether actual or facsimile) of a director or the secretary of the transferor.] [b]

[(c) in the case of an instrument in the forms set out in Parts I and II of the Schedule to the Stock Transfer (Forms) Regulations 1987, and inserted in the First Schedule, or, as the case may be, the Second Schedule, to this Act, by Regulation 4 of those Regulations, the instrument shall not specify particulars of the consideration.] [c]

[(d) designated stock may be transferred by means of—

(i) [an instrument in a form set out in the First Schedule to this Act, or an instrument in the form set out in Part II of the Second Schedule of this Act, that—][d]

(I) is produced by fax in the [Central Bank of Ireland Securities Settlements Office][e] by, or by a person acting on behalf of, a person authorised to transfer designated stock (referred to subsequently in this subsection as 'a member of the [Central Bank of Ireland Securities Settlements Office]'.

(II) bears a representation purporting to be of—

(A) the signature of the member of the [Central Bank of Ireland Securities Settlements][e] entitled to transfer the stock concerned, or

(B) the signature or signatures of a person or persons authorised to sign, on behalf of the member aforesaid, the document of which the instrument is a facsimile,

and

(III) specifies (in addition to the particulars of the consideration and of the description and the number or amount of the securities) the full name of the transferee or, if abbreviation thereof has been specified by the [Central Bank of Ireland Securities Settlements Office][e], the abbreviation.

or

(ii) an instrument of which the instrument specified in subparagraph (i) of this paragraph is a facsimile and which is received in the [Central Bank of Ireland Securities Settlements Office][e], from a member of that Office,

(e) designated stock may be transferred by means of an instrument in the form set out in Part III of the said Second Schedule that—

(i) is produced by telex in the [Central Bank of Ireland Securities Settlements Office][e] by a member of that Office,

(ii) bears the name of the member of the [Central Bank of Ireland Securities Settlements Office][e] entitled to transfer the stock concerned together with the tested code number allocated to the member for the purpose, pursuant to an agreement between the Bank and the member of the [Central Bank of Ireland Securities Settlements Office] [e], and

(iii) specifies (in addition to the particulars of the consideration and of the description and number or amount of the securities) the full name of the transferee or, if an abbreviation thereof has been specified by the [Central Bank of Ireland Securities Settlements Office][e], the abbreviation.] [f]

[(f) Exchequer Notes held by any company or other body corporate (whether incorporated in Ireland or elsewhere) may be transferred by means of an instrument in writing in the form set out in Part IV of the Second Schedule to this Act and signed by a person duly authorised in that behalf by such company or such other body corporate.] [g]

[(g) designated stock held by any company or other body corporate (whether incorporated in the State or elsewhere) may be transferred by means of an instrument in the form set out in the First Schedule to this Act, which—

(i) is or has been produced by fax in the Bank by or on behalf of such company or body corporate, and

(ii) bears a representation purporting to be the signature of a person authorised by such company or body corporate to sign, on its behalf the instrument.][h]

(2) The execution of a stock transfer need not be attested; and where such a transfer has been executed for the purpose of a stock exchange transaction, the particulars of the consideration and of the transferee may either be inserted in that transfer or, as the case may require, be supplied by means of separate instruments in the form set out in the Second Schedule to this Act (in this Act referred to as brokers transfers), identifying the stock transfer and specifying the securities to which each such instrument relates and the consideration paid for those securities.

(3) Nothing in this section shall be construed as affecting the validity of any instrument which would be effective to transfer securities apart from this section; and any instrument purporting to be made in any form which was common or usual before the commencement of this Act, or in any other form authorised or required for that purpose apart from this section, shall be sufficient, whether or not it is completed in accordance with the form, if it complies with the requirements as to execution and contents which apply to a stock transfer.

(4) This section applies to fully paid up transferable registered securities of any description, except securities of a company limited by guarantee or an unlimited company.

[(5) In this section and in the Second Schedule to this Act

'the Bank' means the Central Bank of Ireland;

['company' means—

(a) a company within the meaning of the Companies Acts 1963 to 1999, or

(b) a body established under the laws of a state other than the State and corresponding to a body referred to in paragraph (a) of this definition;][i]

'designated stock' means—

(a) such registered securities created by the Minister as for the time being stand specified by the Bank in relation to the [Central Bank of Ireland Securities Settlements Office][e] [or for the purpose of paragraph (g) of the proviso to subsection (1) of this section][j], and

(b) such other registered securities (if any) as for the time stand specified by the Minister in relation to the [Central Bank of Ireland Securities Settlements Office][e] and as respect which the specification has been communicated in writing to the Bank;

'fax' means the system whereby a facsimile of a document is produced at a place other than that at which the document is located;

'[Central Bank of Ireland Securities Settlements Office]' [e] means the office managed by the Bank that provides a settlement service in designated stock for its members].[k]

[(6) In this section and in the Second Schedule to this Act,

Exchequer Notes means:

(a) such securities as may be issued from time to time by Ireland acting through the National Treasury Management Agency under Ireland's Exchequer Notes Programme.][l]

Amendments

a Stock Transfer (Forms) Regulations 1980 (SI 139/1980), r 4(a) substituted 'a form' for 'the form' with effect from 16 May 1980.

b Stock Transfer (Forms) Regulations 1980 (SI 139/1980), r 4(b) inserted STA 1963, sub-ss 2(1)(a) and 2(1)(b) with effect from 16 May 1980.

c Stock Transfer (Forms) Regulations 1987 (SI 117/1987), r 3 inserted STA 1963, sub-s 2(1)(c) with effect from 30 April 1987.

d Stock Transfer (Forms) Regulations 1998 (SI 546/1998), r 3 substituted the words 'an instrument in a form set out in the First Schedule to this Act, or an instrument in the form set out in Part II of the Second Schedule of this Act, that—' for 'an instrument in the form set out in Part II of the Second Schedule to this Act that—', with effect from 1 January 1998.

e Central Bank Act 1997, s 83 substituted 'Central Bank of Ireland Securities Settlements Office' for 'Gilts Settlement Office' with effect from 9 April 1997[1].

f Stock Transfer (Forms) Regulations 1991 (SI 77/1991), r 4(a) inserted STA 1963, sub-ss 2(1)(d) and 2(1)(e) with effect from 31 March 1991.

g Stock Transfer (Forms) Regulations 1994 (SI 173/1994), r 4(a) inserted sub-s 2(1)(f), with effect from 30 June 1994.

h Stock Transfer (Forms) Regulations 2000 (SI 206/2000), r 2(a) inserted sub-s 2(1)(g), with effect from 29 June 2000.

i Stock Transfer (Forms) Regulations 2000 (SI 206/2000), r 2(b)(i) inserted the definition of 'company' in STA 1963, sub-s 2(5), with effect from 29 June 2000.

j Stock Transfer (Forms) Regulations 2000 (SI 206/2000), r 2(b)(ii) inserted in STA 1963, sub-s 2(5) 'or for the purpose of the proviso to subsection (1) of this section' in para (a) of the definition of 'designated stock', with effect from 29 June 2000.

k Stock Transfer (Forms) Regulations 1991 (SI 77/1991), r 4(b) inserted STA 1963, sub-s 2(5) with effect from 31 March 1991.

l Stock Transfer (Forms) Regulations 1994 (SI 173/1994), r 4(a) inserted STA 1963, sub-s 2(6), with effect from 30 June 1994.

1 Central Bank Act 1997 Commencement Order 1997 (SI 150/1997).

3 Supplementary provisions as to simplified transfer

(1) Section 2 of this Act shall have effect in relation to the transfer of any securities to which that section applies notwithstanding anything to the contrary in any enactment (including the Companies Act, 1963) or instrument relating to the transfer of those securities; but nothing in that section affects—

(a) any right to refuse to register a person as the holder of any securities on any ground other than the form in which those securities purport to be transferred to him; or

(b) any enactment or rule of law regulating the execution of documents by companies or other bodies corporate, or any articles of association or other instrument regulating the execution of documents by any particular company or body corporate.

(2) Subject to the provisions of this section, any enactment or instrument relating to the transfer of securities to which section 2 of this Act applies shall, with any necessary modifications, apply in relation to an instrument of transfer authorised by that section as it applies in relation to an instrument of transfer to which it applies apart from this subsection.

(3) In relation to the transfer of securities by means of a stock transfer and a brokers transfer—

(a) any reference in any enactment or instrument to the delivery or lodging of an instrument (or proper instrument) of transfer shall be construed as a reference to the delivery or lodging of the stock transfer and the brokers transfer;

(b) any such reference to the date on which an instrument of transfer is delivered or lodged shall be construed as a reference to the date by which the later of those transfers to be delivered or lodged has been delivered or lodged; and

(c) subject to paragraphs (a) and (b) of this subsection, the brokers transfer (and not the stock transfer) shall be deemed to be the conveyance or transfer for the purposes of the enactments relating to stamp duty.

4 Prohibition of circulation of blank transfers

(1) Where a transfer in blank relating to registered securities has been delivered, pursuant to a sale of those securities, to or to the order of the purchaser or any person acting on his behalf, any person who in the State parts with possession of that transfer, or who removes it or causes or permits it to be removed from the State, before it has been duly completed shall, as well as being liable for the stamp duty chargeable in respect of that transfer, be liable to [a class D fine][a], and the penalty shall be recoverable in the same manner as if it were part of the duty.

(2) For the purposes of this section 'transfer in blank' means a transfer in which the name of the transferee has not been inserted, and a transfer shall be treated as duly completed if, and only if, the name of the transferee is inserted therein, being the name of—

(a) the purchaser of the securities under the sale;

(b) a person entitled to a charge upon the securities for money lent to that purchaser;

(c) a nominee holding as a bare trustee for that purchaser or for any such person as is mentioned in paragraph (b) of this subsection; or

(d) a person acting as the agent of that purchaser for the purposes of the sale.

(3) The foregoing provisions of this section shall apply in relation to a transfer delivered by way of or pursuant to a voluntary disposition *inter vivos*, being a transfer to which [section 30 of the Stamp Duties (Consolidation) Act, 1999][b], applies, as they apply in relation to a transfer delivered pursuant to a sale, and as if for any reference to the purchaser there were substituted a reference to the person (in this section referred to as the donee) to whom the disposition is made.

(4) References in this section to the purchaser or donee of any registered securities include references to any person to whom the rights of the purchaser or donee are transmitted by operation of law; and in relation to a transfer chargeable with duty in accordance with [subsection (1) or (2) of section 46 of the Stamp Duties (Consolidation) Act, 1999][c], references in this section to the purchaser and a sale shall be construed as references to the sub-purchaser and a sub-sale.

Amendments

a FA 1991, s 107, substituted the words and figures 'a penalty of €634.87'[1] in STA 1963, s 4 for 'a penalty of one hundred pounds' with effect from 29 May 1991; the above being implicitly substituted, by Fines Act 2010, s 7, for a fine not exceeding the aforesaid amount. A class D fine currently means a fine not exceeding €1,000.

b SDCA 1999, Sch 4 substituted the words and figures 'section 30 of the Stamp Duties (Consolidation) Act 1999' for 'section 74 of the Finance (1909–10) Act 1910' in STA 1963, s 4(3) with effect from 15 December 1999 (the date on which SDCA 1999 came in to force).

c SDCA 1999, Sch 4 substituted the words and figures 'subsection (1) or (2) of section 46 of the Stamp Duties (Consolidation) Act 1999' for 'subsection (4) or subsection (5) of section 58 of the Stamp Act, 1891' in STA 1963, s 4(4) with effect from 15 December 1999 (the date on which SDCA 1999 came in to force).

1 £500 converted to €634.87 by Council Regulations (EC) No 1103/97, No 974/98 and No 2866/98 and the Economic and Monetary Union Act 1998, s 6.

5 Additional provisions as to transfer forms

(1) References in this Act to the forms set out in the First and Second Schedules to this Act include references to forms substantially corresponding to those forms respectively.

(2) The Minister may by regulations amend the said Schedules either by altering the forms set out therein or by substituting different forms for those forms or by the addition of forms for use as alternatives to those forms; and references in this Act to the forms set out in those Schedules (including references in this section) shall be construed accordingly.

(3) Any regulations under subsection (2) of this section which substitute a different form for a form set out in the First Schedule to this Act may direct that subsection (3) of section 2 of this Act shall apply with any necessary modifications, in relation to the form for which that form is substituted as it applies to any form which was common or usual before the commencement of this Act.

[(4) Any regulations under subsection (2) of this section may—

(a) provide for forms on which some of the particulars mentioned in subsection (1) of section 2 of this Act are not required to be specified;

(b) provide for that section to have effect, in relation to such forms as are mentioned in paragraph (a) of this subsection or other forms specified in the regulations, subject to such amendments as are so specified (which may include an amendment of the reference in subsection (1) of section 2 of this Act to an instrument under hand);

(c) provide for all or any of the provisions of the regulations to have effect in such cases only as are specified in the regulations.] [a]

[(5) The Minister, having consulted with the Bank, may by regulation provide for the substitution for the references in that section of that name, or references to another name.] [b]

Amendments

a C(A)A 1977, s 8 inserted STA 1963, s 5(4) with effect from 1 April 1978.[1]

b Central Bank Act 1997, s 83 inserted STA 1963, s 5(5) with effect from 9 April 1997.[2]

1 Companies (Amendment) Act 1977 Commencement Order 1978 (SI 95/1978).

2 Central Bank Act 1997 Commencement Order 1997 (SI 150/1997).

6 Laying of regulations before Houses of Oireachtas

Every regulation made under this Act shall be laid before each House of the Oireachtas as soon as may be after it is made and, if a resolution annulling the regulations is passed by either such House within the next twenty-one days upon which that House has sat after the regulation is laid before it, the regulation shall be annulled accordingly, but without prejudice to the validity of anything previously done thereunder.

7 Short title and commencement

(1) This Act may be cited as the Stock Transfer Act, 1963.

(2) This Act shall come into operation on such day as the Minister appoints by order.

FIRST SCHEDULE

FORM (STOCK TRANSFER)

(Above this line for Registrars only)

STOCK TRANSFER FORM[a]

<table>
<tr><td>Consideration Money €......[b]</td><td colspan="2">Certificate lodged with the Registrar

(For completion by the Registrar/ Stock Exchange)</td></tr>
<tr><td>Full Name of Undertaking</td><td colspan="2"></td></tr>
<tr><td>Full Description of Security</td><td colspan="2"></td></tr>
<tr><td>Number or amount of Shares, Stock or other security and, in figures column only, number and denomination of units, if any.</td><td>Words</td><td>Figures
(units of)</td></tr>
<tr><td>Name(s) of registered holder(s) should be given in full; the address should be given where there is only one holder.
If the transfer is not made by the registered holder(s) insert also the name(s) and capacity (e.g., Executor (s)) of the person(s) making the transfer.</td><td colspan="2">In the name(s) of</td></tr>
<tr><td>I/We hereby transfer the above security out of the name(s) aforesaid to the person(s) named below or to the several persons named in Parts 2 of Brokers Transfer Forms relating to the above security:

Delete words in italics except for stock exchange transactions.
Signature(s) of transferor(s)
1..................................
2..................................
3..................................
4..................................
A body corporate should execute this transfer under its common seal or otherwise in accordance with applicable statutory requirements.</td><td colspan="2">Stamp of Selling Broker(s) or, for transactions which are not stock exchange transactions, of Agent(s), if any acting for the Transferor(s).

Date…......................................</td></tr>
</table>

Full name(s) and full postal address(es) (including County or, if applicable, Postal District number) of the person(s) to whom the security is transferred.	
Please state title, if any, or whether Mr., Mrs. or Miss. Please complete in type or in Block Capitals.	
I/ We request that such entries be made in the register as are necessary to give effect to this transfer.	
Stamp of Buying Broker(s) (if any)	Stamp or name and address of person lodging this form (if other than the Buying Broker(s))
Reference to the Registrar in this form means the registrar or registration agent of the undertaking, not the Registrar of Companies.	
(Endorsement for use only in stock exchange transactions) The security represented by the transfer overleaf has been sold as follows:—	
..........Shares/Stock ....Shares/Stock ....Shares/Stock ....Shares/Stock ....Shares/Stock ....Shares/Stock ....Shares/Stock ....Shares/Stock ....Shares/Stock ....Shares/Stock	..........Shares/Stock ....Shares/Stock ....Shares/Stock ....Shares/Stock ....Shares/Stock ....Shares/Stock ....Shares/Stock ....Shares/Stock ....Shares/Stock ....Shares/Stock
	______
	....
Balance (if any) due to Selling Broker(s)	______
Amount of Certificate(s)	______
	Brokers Transfer Forms for above amounts certified
Stamp of certifying Stock Exchange	Stamp of Selling Broker(s)

Amendments

a Stock Transfer (Forms) Regulations 1996 (SI 263/1996), r 3(1) substituted the first form set out in STA 1963, Sch 1 with effect from 9 September 1996.

b '£' may be converted to '€' pursuant to the Economic and Monetary Union Act 1998, s 21.

[TALISMAN SOLD TRANSFER][a]

Amendments

a Stock Transfer (Forms) Regulations 1980 (SI 139/1980), r 5(a) inserted the Talisman Sold Transfer in 1963, Sch 1 with effect from 16 May 1980.

[TALISMAN BOUGHT TRANSFER][a]

Amendments

a Stock Transfer (Forms) Regulations 1980 (SI 139/1980), r 5(b) inserted the Talisman Bought Transfer in 1963, Sch 1 with effect from 16 May 1980.

(Above this line for Registrar's use)

TRANSFER[a]	Counter Location Stamp	Barcode or reference *RN*
	Above this line for completion by the depositing system-user only.	
	Consideration Money €......[b]	Certificate(s) lodged with Registrar (To be completed by Registrar)
Name of Undertaking		
Description of Security		
Please complete in type or in block capitals.	Amount of shares or other security in words	Figures
Name(s) of registered holder(s) should be given in full; the address should be given where there is only one holder.	In the name(s) of	Designation (if any)
If the transfer is not made by the registered holder(s) insert also the name(s) and capacity (e.g. executor(s)) of the person(s) making the transfer.		Balance certificate(s) required
	I/We hereby transfer the above security out of the name(s) aforesaid into the name(s) of the system-member set out below and request that the necessary entries be made in the undertaking's own register of members.	Stamp of depositing system-user

Please Sign Here	1	
	2	
	3	
	4	
	A body corporate should execute this transfer under its common seal or otherwise in accordance with applicable statutory requirements.	Date
Full name(s) of the person(s) to whom the security is transferred.		Participant ID
Such person(s) must be a system-member.		Member Account ID
References to the Registrar in this form means the registrar or registration agent of the undertaking, *not* the Registrar of Companies.	is delivering this transfer at the direction and on behalf of the depositing system-user whose stamp appears herein and does not in any manner or to any extent warrant or represent the validity, genuineness or correctness of the transfer instructions contained herein or the genuineness of the signature(s) of the transferor(s). The depositing system-user by delivering this transfer to authorises to deliver this transfer for registration and agrees to be deemed for all purposes to be the person(s) actually so delivering this transfer for registration.	

Amendments

a Stock Transfer (Forms) Regulations 1996 (SI 263/1996), r 4(1) inserted the second form in STA 1963, Sch 1 with effect from 9 September 1996.[1]

b '£' may be converted to '€' pursuant to the Economic and Monetary Union Act 1998, s 21.

1 Stock Transfer (Forms) Regulations 1996 (SI 263/1996).

[STOCK TRANSFER FORM][a]

(Above this line for Registrars only)

Certificate lodged with the Registrar		
(For completion by the Registrar/Stock Exchange)		
Full name of Undertaking		
Full description of Security		
Amount of security and, in figures column only, number and denomination of units, if any.	Words	Figures (units of)

<table>
<tr><td>Name(s) of registered holder(s) should be given in full; the address should be given where there is only one holder.
If the transfer is not made by the registered holder(s) insert also the name(s) and capacity (e.g., Executor(s)) of the person(s) making the transfer.</td><td colspan="2">In the name(s) of</td><td></td></tr>
<tr><td colspan="2">I/We hereby transfer the above security out of the name(s) aforesaid to the person(s) named below or to the several persons named in Parts 2 of Brokers Transfer Forms relating to the above security:

Delete words in italics except for stock exchange transactions.
Signature(s) of transferor(s)
1...
2...
3...
4...
Bodies corporate should execute under their common seal</td><td colspan="2">Stamp of Selling Broker(s) for transactions which are stock exchange transactions Agent(s), if any, acting for the transferor(s).

Date...............................</td></tr>
<tr><td>Full name(s) and full postal address(es) (including County or, if a applicable, Postal District number) of the person(s) to whom the security is transferred.

Please state title, if any, or whether Mr., Mrs. or Miss.
Please complete in type-writing or in Block Capitals.</td><td colspan="3"></td></tr>
<tr><td colspan="4">I/ We request that such entries be made in the register as are necessary to give effect to this transfer.</td></tr>
<tr><td>Stamp of Buying Broker(s) (if any)</td><td colspan="3">Stamp or name and address of person lodging this form (if other than the Buying Broker(s))</td></tr>
<tr><td colspan="4">The security represented by the transfer overleaf has been sold as follows:-</td></tr>
</table>

....Stock	....Stock
....Stock	....Stock
....Stock	....Stock
....Stock	....Stock
....Stock	....Stock
....Stock	....Stock
....Stock	....Stock
....Stock	....Stock
....Stock	....Stock
....Stock	....Stock
Balance (if any) due to Selling Broker(s)	
Amount of Certificate(s)	
Brokers Transfer Forms for above amounts certified Stamp of certifying Stock Exchange	Stamp of Selling Broker(s)

Amendments

a Stock Transfer (Forms) Regulations 1987 (SI 117/1987), r 4(1) inserted STA 1963, Sch 1, Stock Transfer Form, with effect from 30 April 1987.

[STOCK TRANSFER FORM II][a]

(Above this line for Registrars only)

Certificate lodged with the Registrar (For completion by the Registrar/Stock Exchange)			
Full name of Undertaking	GOVERNMENT SECURITIES (IRELAND)		
Full description of Security			
Amount of security and, in figures column only, number and denomination of units, if any.	Words		Figures (units of)
Name(s) of registered holder(s) should be given in full: the address should be given where there is only one holder.			
If the transfer is not made by the registered holder(s) insert also the name(s) and capacity (e.g., Executor (s)) of the person(s) making the transfer.			
I/We hereby transfer the above security out of the name(s) aforesaid to he person(s) named below *or to the several persons named in Parts 2 of Brokers Transfer Forms relating to the above security*: Delete words in italics except for stock exchange transactions. Signature(s) of transferor(s)			Stamp of Selling Broker(s) or, for transactions which are not stock exchange transactions of Agent(s), if any, acting for the Transferor(s):

<table>
<tr><td colspan="2">1..
2..
3..
4..
Bodies corporate should execute under their common seal</td><td>Date
.............................</td></tr>
<tr><td colspan="3">Full name(s) and full postal address(es) (including County or, if applicable, Postal District number of the person(s) to whom the security is transferred.
Please state title, if any, or whether Mr., Mrs. or Miss.
Please complete in typewriting or in Block Capitals.</td></tr>
<tr><td colspan="3">I/We request that such entries be made in the register as are necessary to give effect to this transfer.</td></tr>
<tr><td>Stamp of Buying Broker(s) (if any)</td><td colspan="2">Stamp or name and address of person lodging this form (if other than the Buying Broker(s))</td></tr>
<tr><td colspan="3">SCHEDULE
The security represented by the transfer overleaf has been sold as follows:-</td></tr>
<tr><td>..Stock
....Stock
....Stock
....Stock
....Stock
....Stock
....Stock
....Stock
....Stock
....Stock</td><td colspan="2">..Stock
....Stock
....Stock
....Stock
....Stock
....Stock
....Stock
....Stock
....Stock
....Stock</td></tr>
<tr><td>Balance (if any) due to Selling Broker(s)
Amount of Certificate(s)
Brokers Transfer Forms for above amounts certified
Stamp of certifying Stock Exchange</td><td colspan="2">...

Stamp of Selling Broker(s)</td></tr>
</table>

Amendments

a Stock Transfer (Forms) Regulations 1998 (SI 546/1998), r 4 inserted STA 1963, Sch 1, Stock Transfer Form II, with effect from 1 January 1999.

SECOND SCHEDULE

FORM (BROKER'S TRANSFER)

BROKERS TRANSFER FORM

(Above this line for Registrars only)

<table>
<tr><td>Consideration Money € ...[a]</td><td colspan="2">Certificate lodged with the Registrar

(For completion by the Registrar/ Stock Exchange)</td></tr>
<tr><td>PART 1
[Name of Undertaking] [b]</td><td colspan="2"></td></tr>
<tr><td>[Description of Security] [b]</td><td colspan="2"></td></tr>
<tr><td>Number or amount of Shares, Stock or other security and, in figures column only, number and denomination of units, if any.</td><td>Words</td><td>Figures
(units of)</td></tr>
<tr><td>Name(s) of registered holder(s) should be given in full; the address should be given where there is only one holder.
If the transfer is not made by the registered holder(s) insert also the name(s) and capacity (e.g., Executor(s)) of the person(s) making the transfer.</td><td>In the name(s) of</td><td></td></tr>
<tr><td colspan="3">I/We confirm that the Stock Transfer Form relating to the security set out above has been lodged with the Registrar, and that the said security has been sold by me/us by a stock exchange transaction within the meaning of the Stock Transfer Act 1963.

Date and Stamp of Selling Brokers(s)</td></tr>
<tr><td>Part 2
Full name(s) and full postal address(es) (including County or, if applicable, Postal District number) of the person(s) to whom the security is transferred.
Please state title, if any, or whether Mr, Mrs. or Miss. Please complete in typewriting or in Block Capitals.</td><td colspan="2"></td></tr>
<tr><td colspan="3">I/We confirm that the security set out in Part I above has been purchased by a stock exchange transaction within the meaning of the Stock Transfer Act, 1963 and I/we request that such entries be made in the register as are necessary to give effect to this transfer.</td></tr>
<tr><td>Stamp of Buying Broker(s)</td><td colspan="2">Stamp of Lodging Agent (if other than the Buying Broker(s)</td></tr>
</table>

Amendments

a £' may be converted to '€' pursuant to the Economic and Monetary Union Act 1998, s 21.

b Stock Transfer Act, 1963 (Amendment of Forms) Regulations 1975 (SI 117/1987), r 4 substituted the words 'Full name of Undertaking' and 'Full description of Security' with 'Name of Undertaking' and 'Description of Security'.

[STOCK TRANSFER FORM][a]

(Above this line for Registrars only)

Certificate lodged with the Registrar		
(For completion by the Registrar/Stock Exchange)		
PART 1 Name of Undertaking		
Full description of Security		
Amount of security and, in figures column only, number and denomination of units, if any.	Words	Figures (units of)
Name(s) of registered holder(s) should be given in full; the address should be given where there is only one holder. If the transfer is not made by the registered holder(s) insert also the name(s) and capacity (e.g., Executor(s)) of the person(s) making the transfer.	In the name(s) of	
I/We confirm that the Stock Transfer Form relating to the security set out above has been lodged with the Registrar, and that the said security has been sold by me/us by a stock exchange transaction within the meaning of the Stock Transfer Act, 1963. Date and Stamp of Selling Brokers(s)		
PART 2 Full name(s) and full postal address(es) (including County or, if applicable, Postal District number) of the person(s) to whom the security is transferred. Please state title, if any, or whether Mr., Mrs. or Miss. Please complete in typewriting or in Block Capitals.		
I/We confirm that the security set out in Part I above has been purchased by a stock exchange transaction within the meaning of the Stock Transfer Act, 1963, and I/we request that such entries be made in the register as are necessary to give effect to this transfer.		
Stamp of Buying Broker(s)	Stamp of Lodging Agent (if other than the Buying Broker(s))	

Amendments

a Stock Transfer (Forms) Regulations 1987 (SI 117/1987), r 4(2) inserted STA 1963, Sch 2, Form (Brokers Transfer), with effect from 30 April 1987.

[PART II

FORM FOR DESIGNATED STOCK TRANSFER (FAX)][a]

Amendments

a Stock Transfer (Forms) Regulations 1991(SI 77/1991), r 5 inserted STA 1963, Sch 2, Pt II, with effect from 31 March 1991.

[PART III

FORM FOR DESIGNATED STOCK TRANSFER (TELEX)

(FOR USE ONLY BY MEMBERS OF GILTS SETTLEMENT OFFICE)][a]

Amendments

a Stock Transfer (Forms) Regulations 1991 (SI 77/1991), r 5 inserted STA 1963, Sch 2, Pt III, with effect from 31 March 1991.

[PART IV

FORM OF TRANSFER FOR EXCHEQUER NOTES

NATIONAL TREASURY MANAGEMENT AGENCY][a]

A	For Completion by the National Treasury Management Agency		
	Full Name of Undertaking	Government Securities (Ireland)	
	Full Description of Security	Exchequer Note: (Number)	
	Amount of Security and, in figures column only, number and denomination of units, if any.	Words	Figures (units of)
	Name(s) of registered holder(s) should be given in full; the address should be given where there is only one holder. If the transfer is not made by the registered holder(s) insert also the name(s) and capacity (e.g. Executor(s)) of the person(s) making the transfer).	In the name(s) of	
B	I/We, being an authorised signatory or signatories, hereby transfer the above security out of the name(s) aforesaid to the person(s) named in Section C below: 1.__________ 2.__________ 3.__________ 4.__________	Stamp of Selling Broker(s) or, for transactions which are not stock exchange transactions of Agent(s) if any acting for the Transferor(s). Date: __________	

C	Full name(s) and full postal address(es), including Country or, if applicable, Postal District number, of the person(s) to whom the security is transferred. Bank account, name, address for payment on maturity. Please complete in typewriting or in Block Capitals.
I/We request that such entries be made in the register as are necessary to give effect to this transfer.	
Stamp of Buying Broker(s) (if any)	Stamp or name and address of person lodging this form (if other than the Buying Broker(s))

Amendments

a Stock Transfer (Forms) Regulations 1994 (SI 173/1994), r 5 inserted STA 1963, Sch 2, Pt IV, with effect from 30 June 1994.

Companies (Amendment) Act 1977

(Number 31 of 1977)

ARRANGEMENT OF SECTIONS

SECTION

An Act to Provide for the Simplification of Certain Activities connected with the Periodic Completion of Bargains made on the Stock Exchange, for that Purpose to amend and extend the Companies Act, 1963, and to provide for other Connected Matters. [12th December, 1977]

Be it Enacted by the Oireachtas as follows:

1 Interpretation

(1) In this Act—

'the Act of 1963' means the Companies Act, 1963;

'the Minister' means the Minister for Industry, Commerce and Energy;

'stock exchange nominee' means a person designated, by regulations made by the Minister, as a nominee of a recognised stock exchange for the purposes of this Act.

(2) In this Act any word or expression to which a meaning is assigned by the Act of 1963 has that meaning except where the context requires otherwise.

2 Modification of obligation to prepare share certificates etc

A company of which shares or debentures are allotted or debenture stock is allotted to a stock exchange nominee, or with which a transfer is lodged for transferring any shares, debentures or debenture stock of the company to a stock exchange nominee, shall not be required in consequence of the allotment or the lodging of the transfer to complete and have ready for delivery in pursuance of section 86(1) of the Act of 1963 the certificates of the shares or the debentures or the certificates of the debenture stock, as the case may be.

3 Official seals for sealing share certificates etc

(1) A company other than a private company may have, for use for sealing securities issued by the company and for sealing documents creating or evidencing securities so issued, an official seal which is a facsimile of the common seal of the company with the addition on its face of the word 'Securities' or the word 'Urrúis'.

(2) A company which was incorporated before the commencement of this Act and which has such an official seal as is mentioned in subsection (1) of this section may use the seal for sealing such securities and documents as are mentioned in that subsection notwithstanding anything in any instrument constituting or regulating the company or in any instrument made before such commencement which relates to any securities issued by the company, and any provision of such an instrument which requires any such securities or documents to be signed shall not apply to the securities or documents if they are sealed with that seal.

4 Use of computers etc for certain company records

(1) It is hereby declared that the power conferred on a company by section 378(1) of the Act of 1963 to keep a register or other record by recording the matters in question otherwise than by making entries in bound books includes power to keep the register or other record other than minute books kept pursuant to section 145 of the Act of 1963 by recording the matters in question otherwise than in a legible form so long as the recording is capable of being reproduced in a legible form.

(2) Any provision of an instrument made by a company before the commencement of this Act which requires a register of holders of debentures of the company to be kept in a legible form shall be construed as requiring the register to be kept in a legible or non-legible form, provided, however, that a register kept in non-legible form shall be capable of being reproduced in legible form.

(3) If any such register or other record of a company as is mentioned in section 378(1) of the Act of 1963 is kept by the company by recording the matters in question otherwise than in a legible form, any duty imposed on the company by virtue of that Act to allow inspection of, or to furnish a copy of, the register or other record or any part of it shall be treated as a duty to allow inspection of, or to furnish, a reproduction of the recording or of the relevant part of it in a legible form.

(4) The Minister may by regulations make such provision in addition to subsection (3) of this section as he considers appropriate in connection with such registers or other records as are mentioned in that subsection and are kept as there mentioned, and the regulations may make modifications of provisions of the Act of 1963 relating to such registers or other records as are mentioned in that subsection.

5 Consequential amendments of Act of 1963

(1) [...][a]

(2) [...][b]

(3) [...][c]

(4) [...][d]

(5) [...][e]

(6) [...][f]

(7) [...][g]

(8) [...][h]

(9) [...][i]

Amendments

a CA 1977, s 5(1) substituted CA 1963, s 87(1).

b CA 1977, s 5(2) substituted CA 1963, Sch 1, Table A, Part 1, reg 8.

c CA 1977, s 5(3) substituted CA 1963, Sch 1, Table A, Part 1, reg 8.

d CA 1977, s 5(4) substituted 'with the exception of regulations 8, 24, 51, 54, 84 and 86' in CA 1963, Sch 1, Table A, Part II, reg 1 and deleted 'with the exception of regulations 24, 51, 54, 84, 86'.

e CA 1977, s 5(5) inserted CA 1963, Sch 1, Table A, Part II, reg 10.

f CA 1977, s 5(6) substituted CA 1963, Sch 1, Table A, Part II, Note.

g CA 1977, s 5(7) substituted the Irish translation of substitution by sub-s (4).

h CA 1977, s 5(8) substituted the Irish translation of the substitution by sub-s (5).

i CA 1977, s 5(9) substituted the Irish translation of substitution by sub-s (6).

6 Application of *sections 2 to 4* to unregistered companies

[...][a]

Amendments

a CA 1977, s 6 repealed by CA 1990, s 6(2).

7 Acquisition and disposal of securities by trustees and personal representatives

A trustee or personal representative shall not be chargeable with breach of trust or, as the case may be, with default in administering the estate by reason only of the fact that—

(a) he has, for the purpose of acquiring securities which he has power to acquire in connection with the trust or estate, paid for the securities under arrangements which provide for them to be transferred to him from a stock exchange nominee but not to be so transferred until after payment of the price; or

(b) he has, for the purpose of disposing of securities which he has power to dispose of in connection with the trust or estate, transferred the securities to a stock exchange nominee under arrangements which provide that the price is not to be paid to him until after the transfer is made.

8 Forms for transfer of securities

[...][a]

Amendments

a CA 1977, s 8 inserted sub-s (4) of the STA 1963.

9 Laying of regulations before Houses of Oireachtas

Every regulation under this Act shall be laid before each House of the Oireachtas as soon as may be after it is made and, if a resolution annulling the regulation is passed by either House within the next 21 days on which that House has sat after the regulation is laid before it, the regulation shall be annulled accordingly, but without prejudice to the validity of anything previously done thereunder.

10 Expenses

The expenses incurred in the administration of this Act shall, to such extent as may be sanctioned by the Minister for Finance, be paid out of moneys provided by the Oireachtas.

11 Short title, collective citation and commencement

(1) This Act may be cited as the Companies (Amendment) Act, 1977.

(2) This Act and the Act of 1963 may be cited together as the Companies Acts, 1963 to 1977.

(3) This Act shall come into operation on such date as the Minister may appoint by order.

Companies (Amendment) Act 1982

(Number 10 of 1982)

ARRANGEMENT OF SECTIONS

Section

Companies (Amendment) Act 1982

(Number 10 of 1982)

An Act To Amend And Extend The Companies Act, 1963, and to Provide for Other Connected Matters. [15th June, 1982]

Be It Enacted by the Oireachtas as Follows:

1 Interpretation

In this Act 'the Principal Act' means the Companies Act, 1963.

2 Articles prescribing regulations for companies

[...][a]

Amendments

a C(A)A 1982, s 2 substituted CA 1963, s 11.

---

3 Particulars to be delivered with memorandum

(1) There shall be delivered to the registrar together with every memorandum of a company delivered to him pursuant to section 17 of the Principal Act a statement in the prescribed form containing the name and the particulars specified in subsection (2) of this section in relation to—

(a) the persons who are to be the first directors of the company,

(b) the person who is, or the persons who are, to be the first secretary or joint secretaries of the company, and

(c) the situation of the company's registered office.

(2) The particulars referred to in subsection (1) of this section are—

(a) in relation to a person named as director of the company concerned all particulars which are, in relation to a director, required pursuant to section 195(2) of the Principal Act to be contained in the register kept under that section,

(b) in relation to a person named as secretary, or as one of the joint secretaries, all particulars which are, in relation to the secretary or to each joint secretary, required pursuant to section 195(4) of the Principal Act to be contained in the register kept under that section, and

(c) in relation to the registered office of the company, the particulars which are required to be given to the registrar pursuant to section 113 of the Principal Act.

(3) The statement required to be delivered pursuant to this section shall be signed by or on behalf of the subscribers and shall be accompanied by a consent signed by each of the persons named in it as a director, secretary or joint secretary to act in that capacity.

(4) Where the memorandum is delivered to the registrar pursuant to section 17 of the Principal Act by a person as agent for the subscribers to the memorandum the statement required to be delivered to the registrar pursuant to this section shall so specify and shall specify the name and address of the person by whom the memorandum is delivered.

(5) The persons who are specified in the statement required to be delivered to the registrar pursuant to this section as the directors, secretary or joint secretaries of the company to which the statement refers shall, on the incorporation of the company, be deemed to have been appointed as the first directors, secretary or joint secretaries, as the case may be, of the company, and any indication in any articles delivered to the registrar with the memorandum specifying a person as a director or secretary of a company shall be void unless such person is specified as a director or as secretary in the said statement.

(6) [...][a]

Amendments

a C(A)A 1982, s 3(6) repealed by C(A)A 1983, Sch 3, Pt II.

[3A Additional statement to be delivered to the registrar

(1) If any of the persons named in the statement to be delivered pursuant to section 3 of this Act as directors of the company concerned is a person who is disqualified under the law of another state (whether pursuant to an order of a judge or a tribunal or otherwise) from being appointed or acting as a director or secretary of a body corporate or an undertaking, that person shall ensure that that statement is accompanied by (but as a separate document from that statement) a statement in the prescribed form signed by him specifying—

- (a) the jurisdiction in which he is so disqualified,
- (b) the date on which he became so disqualified, and
- (c) the period for which he is so disqualified.

(2) This section is without prejudice to section 3(3) of this Act or the requirements of any other enactment with regard to the registration of companies.][a]

Amendments

a C(A)A 1982, s 3A was inserted by CLEA 2001, s 101.

4 Registered office of company

[...][a]

Amendments

a C(A)A 1982, s 4 substituted CA 1963, s 113.

5 Amendment of section 143 of Principal Act

(1) [...][a]

(2) Every company shall, within three months after the commencement of this section, forward to the registrar of companies a return containing particulars not previously forwarded to him or any right or restriction attaching to shares in the share capital of the company existing upon such commencement and the particulars shall be recorded by him.

Amendments

a C(A)A 1982, s 5(1) inserted CA 1963, s 143(4)(f)–(i).

6 Qualification for appointment as auditor

[...][a]

Amendments

a C(A)A 1982, s 6 substituted CA 1963, s 162.[1]

[1] CA 1963, s 162 repealed by CA 1990, s 6 with effect from 21 September 1992.

7 Amendment of section 168 of Principal Act

[...][a]

Amendments

a C(A)A 1982, s 7 substituted CA 1963, s 168(3).[1]

[1] CA 1963, s 168 repealed by CA 1990, s 6 with effect from 1 July 1991.

8 Register of directors and secretaries

[...][a]

Amendments

a C(A)A 1982, s 8(1) substituted CA 1963, s 195, sub-ss (6), (7) and (8); C(A)A 1982, s 8(2) substituted '(6), (7) or (8)' for 'or (6)'; and '€634.87'[1] for '€126.97'[2] in CA 1963, s 195(1).

[1] £500 converted to €634.87 by Council Regulations (EC) No 1103/97, No 974/98 and No 2866/98 and the Economic and Monetary Union Act 1998, s 6.

[2] £100 converted to €126.97 by Council Regulations (EC) No 1103/97, No 974/98 and No 2866/98 and the Economic and Monetary Union Act 1998, s 6.

9 Amendment of section 256 of Principal Act

[...][a]

Amendments

a C(A)A 1982, s 9 substituted CA 1963, s 256(2).[1]

[1] CA 1990, s 128 substituted CA 1963, s 256. C(AA)A 2003, s 57 amended CA 1963, s 256 (7) by substitution of 'shall be guilty of an offence and liable to a fine' for 'shall be liable to a fine'.

10 Preferential payments in a winding up

[...][a]

Amendments

a C(A)A 1982, s 10(a) inserted CA 1963, s 285(2)(h)-(i); C(A)A 1982, s 10(b) substituted '€3,174.35[1]' for '€380.922'[2] in CA 1963, s 285(3); C(A)A 1982, s 10(c) inserted CA 1963, s 285(6)(c); C(A)A 1982, s 10(d) substituted 'or absence from work through' for ', absence from work through sickness or other' in CA 1963, s 285(11); C(A)A 1982, s 10(e) inserted CA 1963, s 285(13).

1 £2,500 converted to €3,174.35 by Council Regulations (EC) No 1103/97, No 974/98 and No 2866/98 and the Economic and Monetary Union Act 1998, s 6.

2 £300 converted to €380.92 by Council Regulations (EC) No 1103/97, No 974/98 and No 2866/98 and the Economic and Monetary Union Act 1998, s 6.

11 Power of registrar to strike defunct company off register

[...][a]

Amendments

a C(A)A 1982, s 11 substituted CA 1963, s 311(1)–(3) and deleted s 311(4).

12 Power of registrar to strike off register companies who fail to make returns[a]

[(1) Without prejudice to the generality of section 311 of the Principal Act, where a company does not, for one or more years, make an annual return required by section 125 or 126 of the Principal Act, the registrar of companies may send to the company by post a registered letter stating that, unless all annual returns which are outstanding are delivered to him within 1 month of the date of the letter, a notice will be published in [the Companies Registration Office Gazette][b] with a view to striking the name of the company off the register.

(2) If the registrar of companies either receives an answer to the effect that the company is not carrying on business, or does not within 1 month after sending the letter receive all annual returns which are outstanding, he may publish in [the Companies Registration Office Gazette][b] a notice stating that, at the expiration of 1 month from the date of that notice, the name of the company mentioned therein will, unless all outstanding returns are delivered to the registrar, be struck off the register, and the company will be dissolved.

(3) Subject to subsections (1) and (2) of section 12B of this Act, at the expiration of the time mentioned in the notice, the registrar of companies may, unless cause to the contrary is previously shown by the company, strike its name off the register, and shall publish notice thereof in [the Companies Registration Office Gazette][b] and on the publication in [the Companies Registration Office Gazette][b] of this notice, the company shall be dissolved.][a]

Amendments

a C(A)A 1982, s 12 substituted by C(A)(No 2)A 1999, s 46.

b 'the Companies Registration Office Gazette' substituted for '*Iris Oifigiúil*' by IFCMPA 2005, s 72.

[12A

(1) Where the Revenue Commissioners give a notice in writing under subsection (3) of section 882 (inserted by the Finance Act, 1999) of the Taxes Consolidation Act, 1997,

to the registrar of companies stating that a company has failed to deliver a statement which it is required to deliver under that section, then, without prejudice to section 311 of the Principal Act or section 12 of this Act, the registrar may send to the company by post a registered letter stating that, unless the company delivers to the Revenue Commissioners the said statement within 1 month of the date of the letter, a notice will be published in [the Companies Registration Office Gazette][b] with a view to striking the name of the company off the register.

(2) If the statement referred to in subsection (1) of this section is not delivered by the company concerned to the Revenue Commissioners within 1 month after the sending of the letter referred to in that subsection, the registrar of companies may publish in [the Companies Registration Office Gazette][b] a notice stating that, at the expiration of 1 month from the date of that notice, the name of the company mentioned therein will, unless the said statement is delivered to the Revenue Commissioners, be struck off the register, and the company will be dissolved.

(3) Subject to subsections (1) and (2) of section 12B of this Act, at the expiration of the time mentioned in the notice, the registrar of companies may, unless cause to the contrary is previously shown by the company, strike its name off the register, and shall publish notice thereof in [the Companies Registration Office Gazette][b] and on the publication in [the Companies Registration Office Gazette][b] of this notice, the company shall be dissolved.][a]

Amendments

a C(A)A 1982, s 12A inserted by C(A)(No 2)A 1999, s 46.

b 'the Companies Registration Office Gazette' substituted for '*Iris Oifigiúil*' by IFCMPA 2005, s 72.

[12B

(1) The liability, if any, of every director, officer and member of a company the name of which has been struck off the register under section 12(3) or 12A(3) of this Act shall continue and may be enforced as if the company had not been dissolved.

(2) Nothing in subsection (1) of this section or section 12(3) or 12A(3) of this Act shall affect the power of the court to wind up a company the name of which has been struck off the register.

(3) If any member, officer or creditor of a company is aggrieved by the fact of the company's having been struck off the register under section 12(3) or 12A(3) of this Act, the court, on an application made (on notice to the registrar of companies, the Revenue Commissioners and the Minister for Finance) by the member, officer or creditor, before the expiration of 20 years from the publication in [the Companies Registration Office Gazette][b] of the notice referred to in section 12(3) or, as the case may be, 12A(3) of this Act, may, if satisfied that it is just that the company be restored to the register, order that the name of the company be restored to the register, and, subject to subsection (4) of this section, upon an office copy of the order being delivered to the registrar for registration, the company shall be deemed to have continued in existence as if its name had not been struck off; and the court may by the order give such directions and make such provisions as seem just for placing the company and all other persons in the same position as nearly

as may be as if the name of the company had not been struck off or make such other order as seems just (and such other order is referred to in subsection (4) of this section as an 'alternative order').

(4) An alternative order may, if the court considers it appropriate that it should do so, include a provision that, as respects a debt or liability incurred by, or on behalf of, the company during the period when it stood struck off the register, the officers of the company or such one or more of them as is or are specified in the order shall be liable for the whole or a part (as the court thinks just) of the debt or liability.

(5) The court shall, unless cause is shown to the contrary, include in an order under subsection (3) of this section, being an order made on the application of a member or officer of the company, a provision that the order shall not have effect unless, within 1 month from the date of the court's order—

(a) if the order relates to a company that has been struck off the register under section 12(3) of this Act, all outstanding annual returns required by section 125 or 126 of the Principal Act are delivered to the registrar of companies,

(b) if the order relates to a company that has been struck off the register under section 12A(3) of this Act, all outstanding statements required by section 882 of the Taxes Consolidation Act, 1997, are delivered to the Revenue Commissioners.

(6) The court shall, in making an order under subsection (3) of this section, being an order that is made on the application of a creditor of the company, direct that one or more specified members or officers of the company shall, within a specified period—

(a) if the order relates to a company that has been struck off the register under section 12(3) of this Act, deliver all outstanding annual returns required by section 125 or 126 of the Principal Act to the registrar of companies,

(b) if the order relates to a company that has been struck off the register under section 12A(3) of this Act, deliver all outstanding statements required by section 882 of the Taxes Consolidation Act, 1997, to the Revenue Commissioners.

(7) The court, on an application made by the registrar of companies (on notice to each person who, to his knowledge, is an officer of the company) before the expiration of 20 years from the publication in [the Companies Registration Office Gazette][b] of the notice referred to in section 12(3) or, as the case may be, 12A(3) of this Act, may, if satisfied that it is just that the company be restored to the register, order that the name of a company which has been struck off the register under the said section 12(3) or 12A(3) be restored to the register and, upon the making of the order by the court, the company shall be deemed to have continued in existence as if its name had not been struck off; and the court may by the order give such directions and make such provisions as seem just for placing the company and all other persons in the same position as nearly as may be as if the name of the company had not been struck off or make such other order as seems just (and such other order may, if the court considers it appropriate that it should do so, include a provision of the kind referred to in subsection (4) of this section).

(8) A letter or notice to be sent under this section to a company may be addressed to the company at its registered office, or, if no office has been registered, to the care of some officer of the company, or, if there is no officer of the company whose name and address

are known to the registrar of companies, may be sent to each of the persons who subscribed to the memorandum, addressed to him at the address mentioned in the memorandum.

[(8A) For the purposes of subsection (1) of section 12 of this Act where—

(a) a company does not, for 20 or more consecutive years, make an annual return required by section 125 of the Principal Act, and

(b) no notice of the situation of the registered office of the company has been given to the registrar of companies as required by section 113 of the Principal Act,

the registrar of companies may, instead of sending, in accordance with the said subsection (1), a registered letter to the company stating that he proposes to take the course of action mentioned in that subsection in relation to the company, publish a notice in the Companies Registration Office Gazette stating that he proposes to take that course of action in relation to the company, and where the registrar publishes such a notice the reference in subsection (2) of section 12 of this Act to the sending of a letter of the foregoing kind shall be construed as a reference to the publishing of that notice.][c]

(9) Without prejudice to section 2(1) of the Principal Act where such an application is made by any other person, in the case of an application under this section that is made by a creditor of the company or the registrar of companies, 'the court', for the purposes of this section, means the Circuit Court.

(10) An application under this Act to the Circuit Court by a creditor of the company concerned shall be made to the judge of the Circuit Court for the circuit in which the registered office of the company was, immediately before it was struck off the register, situated or, if no office was registered at that time, for the circuit in which the creditor resides or, in case the creditor resides outside the State, for the Dublin Circuit.

(11) An application under this section to the Circuit Court by the registrar of companies shall be made to the judge of the Circuit Court for the Dublin Circuit.][a]

Amendments

a C(A)A 1982, s 12B inserted by C(A)(No 2)A 1999, s 46.

b 'the Companies Registration Office Gazette' substituted for '*Iris Oifigiúil*' by IFCMPA 2005, s 72.

c C(A)A 1982, s 12B(8A) inserted by IFCMPA 2005, s 65 with effect from 30 June 2005.[1]

1 Investment Funds, Companies and Miscellaneous Provisions Act 2005 (Commencement) Order 2005 (SI 323/2005).

[12C

(1) Without prejudice to the provisions of section 311(8) or 311A(1) of the Principal Act or subsection (3) or (7) of section 12B of this Act, if a member or officer of a company is aggrieved by the fact of the company's having been struck off the register under section 12A(3) of this Act, the registrar of companies, on an application made in the prescribed form by the member or officer before the expiration of 12 months from the publication in [the Companies Registration Office Gazette][b] of the notice striking the company name from the register, and provided he has received confirmation from the Revenue Commissioners that all outstanding, if any, statements required by section 882

of the Taxes Consolidation Act, 1997, have been delivered to the Revenue Commissioners, may restore the name of the company to the register.

(2) Upon the registration of an application under subsection (1) of this section and on payment of such fees as may be prescribed, the company shall be deemed to have continued in existence as if its name had not been struck off.

(3) Subject to any order made by the court in the matter, the restoration of the name of a company to the register under this section shall not affect the rights or liabilities of the company in respect of any debt or obligation incurred, or any contract entered into by, to, with or on behalf of, the company between the date of its dissolution and the date of such restoration.][a]

Amendments

a C(A)A 1982, s 12C inserted by C(A)(No 2)A 1999, s 46.

b 'the Companies Registration Office Gazette' substituted for '*Iris Oifigiúil*' by IFCMPA 2005, s 72.

[12D

If the question of whether a statement which a company has failed to deliver to the Revenue Commissioners in accordance with section 882(3) of the Taxes Consolidation Act, 1997, has or has not been subsequently delivered to them falls to be determined for the purpose of the exercise by the registrar of companies of any of the powers under sections 12A to 12C of this Act, the Revenue Commissioners may, notwithstanding any obligations as to secrecy or other restriction upon disclosure of information imposed by or under statute or otherwise, disclose to the registrar any information in their possession required by him for the purpose of that determination.][a]

Amendments

a C(A)A 1982, s 12D inserted by C(A)(No 2)A 1999, s 46.

---

13 Non-application of section 376 of Principal Act to certain partnerships

(1) The provisions of section 376 of the Principal Act shall not apply to the formation of a partnership—

(a) for the purpose of carrying on practice as accountants in a case where each partner is a person who is qualified under section 162(1)(a) or (b) of the Principal Act, as amended by this Act, or

(b) for the purpose of carrying on practice as solicitors in a case where each partner is a solicitor.

[(2) The Minister may by an order made under this section declare that the provisions of section 376 of the Principal Act shall not apply to a partnership that is of a description, and that has been or is formed for a purpose, specified in the order.][a]

(3) Every order made under subsection (2) of this section shall be laid before each House of the Oireachtas as soon as may be after it is made and, if a resolution annulling the order is passed by either House within the next 21 days on which that House has sat

after the order is laid before it, the order shall be annulled accordingly, but without prejudice to the validity of anything previously done thereunder.

(4) The Minister may revoke or amend an order made under this section, including this subsection.

(5) The provisions of section 4(2) of the Limited Partnerships Act, 1907 shall not apply to a partnership specified in subsection (1) of this section nor to a partnership specified in an order made pursuant to subsection (2) of this section.

Amendments

a C(AA)A 2003, s 55 substitutes C(A)A 1982, s 13(2).

---

14 Adoption and application of Table C

[...][a]

Amendments

a C(A)A 1982, s 14 inserted CA 1963, s 13A.

---

15 Increase of penalties

A person convicted of an offence for which a penalty is provided in any section of the Principal Act specified in column (2) of the First Schedule at any reference number shall, in lieu of the penalty provided in any such section and specified in column (3) of that Schedule, be liable to the penalty specified in column (4) of that Schedule at that reference number, and that section shall be construed and have effect accordingly.

16 Prosecution of certain offences

Proceedings in relation to offences under sections 227, 234, 249, 252, 262, 263, 272, 273, 278, 280, 319, 320 and 321 of the Principal Act may be brought and prosecuted by the registrar of companies.

17 Amendment of section 16 of Principal Act

[...][a]

Amendments

a C(A)A 1982, s 17 deleted 'and articles' from CA 1963, s 16(a).

---

18 Amendment of section 19 of Principal Act

[...][a]

Amendments

a C(A)A 1982, s 18 substituted 'a person named as director or secretary of the company in the statement delivered pursuant to section 3 of the Companies (Amendment) Act, 1982' for 'a person named in the articles as a director or secretary of the company' in CA 1963, s 19(2).

---

19 Amendment of section 58 of Principal Act

[...][a]

Amendments

a C(A)A 1982, s 19 deleted 'and occupations' from CA 1963, s 58(1)(b).

---

20 Amendment of section 116 of Principal Act

[...][a]

Amendments

a C(A)A 1982, s 20 deleted 'and occupations' from CA 1963, s 116(1)(a).

---

21 Amendment of First Schedule to Principal Act

[...][a]

Amendments

a C(A)A 1982, s 21(a) inserted 'Subject to section 3 of the Companies (Amendment) Act, 1982,' before 'The secretary' in CA 1963, Sch 1, Table A, Pt I, Reg 113; C(A)A 1982, s 21(c) inserted 'Subject to section 3 of the Companies (Amendment) Act, 1982,' before 'The secretary' in CA 1963, Sch 1, Table C, Reg 59.

---

22 Amendment of Fifth Schedule to Principal Act

[...][a]

Amendments

a C(A)A 1982, s 22(a) deleted 'and occupations' in CA 1963, Sch 5, Pt I, para 5(a); C(A)A 1982, s 22(b) deleted 'and occupations' in CA 1963, Sch 5, Pt II, para 5, Col 2.

---

23 Repeals

Sections 29 and 30 of the Industrial Research and Standards Act, 1961, are hereby repealed.

24 Short title, collective citation, construction and commencement

(1) This Act may be cited as the Companies (Amendment) Act, 1982.

(2) This Act and the Companies Acts, 1963 to 1977, shall be construed together as one Act and may be cited together as the Companies Acts, 1963 to 1982.

(3) This Act shall come into operation on such day or days as may be fixed therefor by order or orders of the Minister, either generally or with reference to a particular purpose or provision, and different days may be so fixed for different purposes and different provisions of this Act.

FIRST SCHEDULE[a]

INCREASE OF PENALTIES

Amendments

a This Schedule increased the penalties in CA 1963 as follows: '€6,348.69[1]' substituted for '£1,000' in s 293(1); '€3,174.35'[2] substituted for '£500' in ss 35(5)(a), 50(1)(a), 54(5)(a), 60(15)(a), 90, 183(1), 184(5), 293(1), 294, 295, 296(1), 297(3), 365(a), 380(a); '€634.87'[3] substituted for '£100' in ss 23(2), 24(8), 35(4), 35(5)(b), 44(8), 46(2), 47(4), 50(1)(b), 54(4), 54(5)(b), 56(3), 57(3), 58(3), 59(5), 60(5), 60(15)(b), 63(5), 77, 90, 100(3), 101(2), 102(2), 107(3), 110(2), 112(3), 115(6), 116(9), 125(2); 126(4), 127(2), 128(3), 130(10), 131(6), 136(5), 145(4), 147(6), 148(3), 149(7), 150(3), 150(4), 154(5), 156(3), 157(2), 158(7), 180(5); 183(1), 184(5), 190(9), 193(4), 194(5)(b), 194(6), 197(3), 202(4), 224(5), 256(6), 263(3), 266(6), 293(1), 294, 295, 296(1), 297(3), 300, 301, 305(2), 306(2), 314, 315(1), 319(7), 320(5), 321(2), 358, 365(b), 377(7), 380(b), 381, 385; '€317.43'[4] substituted for '£50' in ss 10(10), 12(3), 69(2), 70(3), 78(5), 84(2), 91(5), 114(3), 114(4), 117(4), 119(3), 136(3), 143(5), 153(3), 159(5), 160(5), 165(2), 179(4), 190(9), 202(6), 227(2), 249(3), 261(2), 262(2), 263(7), 272(3), 273(5), 273(6), 273(7); 278(2); 303(2), 378(2), 386; '€158.72'[5] substituted for '£25' in ss 30(2), 92(4), 114(2), 146(3), 188(2), 196(4), 203(3), 205(5), 221(2), 234(5), 252(2), 256(5), 280(4), 398(3); '€126.97'[6] substituted for '£20' in 86(2), 131(6), 201(6); 317(2); '€31.74'[7] substituted for '£5' in ss 29(2), 263(6), 310(2); '€6.35'[8] substituted for '£1' in s 143(6).

1 £5,000 converted to €6,348.69 by Council Regulations (EC) No 1103/97, No 974/98 and No 2866/98 and the Economic and Monetary Union Act 1998, s 6.

2 £2,500 converted to €3,174.35 by Council Regulations (EC) No 1103/97, No 974/98 and No 2866/98 and the Economic and Monetary Union Act 1998, s 6.

3 £500 converted to €634.87 by Council Regulations (EC) No 1103/97, No 974/98 and No 2866/98 and the Economic and Monetary Union Act 1998, s 6.

4 £250 converted to €317.43 by Council Regulations (EC) No 1103/97, No 974/98 and No 2866/98 and the Economic and Monetary Union Act 1998, s 6.

5 £125 converted to €158.72 by Council Regulations (EC) No 1103/97, No 974/98 and No 2866/98 and the Economic and Monetary Union Act 1998, s 6.

6 £100 converted to €126.97 by Council Regulations (EC) No 1103/97, No 974/98 and No 2866/98 and the Economic and Monetary Union Act 1998, s 6.

7 £25 converted to €31.74 by Council Regulations (EC) No 1103/97, No 974/98 and No 2866/98 and the Economic and Monetary Union Act 1998, s 6.

8 £5 converted to €6.35 by Council Regulations (EC) No 1103/97, No 974/98 and No 2866/98 and the Economic and Monetary Union Act 1998, s 6.

Companies (Amendment) Act 1983

(Number 13 of 1983)

ARRANGEMENT OF SECTIONS

PART 1
PRELIMINARY

Section

PART II
NAME OF PUBLIC LIMITED COMPANY, REGISTRATION AND RE-REGISTRATION OF COMPANIES

PART III
THE CAPITAL OF A COMPANY

Authorised share capital and the issue of share capital

Pre-emption rights

An Act to amend the Law Relating to Companies. [5th June, 1983]

Be It Enacted By The Oireachtas as Follows:

PART 1
PRELIMINARY

1 Short title, collective citation and commencement

(1) This Act may be cited as the Companies (Amendment) Act, 1983.

(2) The collective citation 'the Companies Acts, 1963 to 1983' shall include this Act.

(3) This Act shall come into operation on such day as the Minister may appoint by order.

2 Interpretation

(1) In this Act unless the context otherwise requires—

'the appointed day' means the day appointed by the Minister under section 1(3) for the coming into operation of this Act;

'the appropriate rate', in relation to interest, means five per cent. per annum or such other rate as may be specified by order made by the Minister under subsection (7);

'the authorised minimum' has the meaning assigned to it by section 19;

'balance sheet date', in relation to a balance sheet, means the date as at which the balance sheet was prepared;

'called-up share capital', in relation to a company, means so much of its share capital as equals the aggregate amount of the calls made on its shares, whether or not those calls have been paid, together with any share capital paid up without being called and any share capital to be paid on a specified future date under the articles, the terms of allotment of the relevant shares or any other arrangements for payment of those shares, and 'uncalled share capital' shall be construed accordingly;

'the Companies Acts' means the Acts which by virtue of subsection (5) shall be construed as one Act;

'employees' share scheme' means any scheme for the time being in force, in accordance with which a company encourages or facilitates the holding of shares or debentures in the company or its holding company by or for the benefit of employees or former employees of the company or of any subsidiary of the company including any person who is or was a director holding a salaried employment or office in the company or any subsidiary of the company;

'equity security' has the meaning assigned to it by section 23(13);

'the general transitional period' means the period of 18 months commencing on the appointed day;

'hire-purchase agreement' has the same meaning as in the Hire-Purchase Act, 1946;

'the Minister' means the Minister for Trade, Commerce and Tourism;

'non-cash asset' means any property or interest in property other than cash (including foreign currency);

'old public limited company' has the meaning assigned to it by section 12 (1);

'the Principal Act' means the Companies Act, 1963;

'public company' means a company which is not a private company;

'public limited company' means a public company limited by shares or a public company limited by guarantee and having a share capital, being a company—

(a) the memorandum of which states that the company is to be a public limited company; and

(b) in relation to which the provisions of the Companies Acts as to the registration or re-registration of a company as a public limited company have been complied with on or after the appointed day;

['Regulations of 1987' means the European Communities (Mergers and Divisions of Companies) Regulations 1987 (S.I. No. 137 of 1987);

'Regulations of 2008' means the European Communities (Cross-Border Mergers) Regulations 2008 (S.I. No. 157 of 2008);][a]

'the re-registration period' has the meaning assigned to it by section 13(1);

'the transitional period for share capital' means the period of 3 years commencing on the appointed day.

(2) In relation to an allotment of shares in a company, the shares shall be taken for the purposes of the Companies Acts to be allotted when a person acquires the unconditional right to be included in the company's register of members in respect of those shares.

(3) For the purposes of the Companies Acts—

(a) a share in a company shall be taken to have been paid up (as to its nominal value or any premium on it) in cash or allotted for cash if the consideration for the allotment or the payment up is cash received by the company or is a cheque received by the company in good faith which the directors have no reason for suspecting will not be paid or is the release of a liability of the company for a liquidated sum or is an undertaking to pay cash to the company at a future date; and

(b) in relation to the allotment or payment up of any shares in a company, references in the Companies Acts, except in section 23, to consideration other than cash and to the payment up of shares and premiums on shares otherwise than in cash include references to the payment of, or an undertaking to pay, cash to any person other than the company;

and for the purposes of determining whether a share is or is to be allotted for cash or paid up in cash, 'cash' includes foreign currency.

(4) For the purposes of this Act—

(a) any reference to a balance sheet or to a profit and loss account shall include a reference to any notes thereon or document annexed thereto giving information which is required by the Companies Acts [or by international financial reporting standards][b] and is thereby allowed to be so given;

(b) any reference to the transfer or acquisition of a non-cash asset includes a reference to the creation or extinction of an estate or interest in, or a right over, any property and also a reference to the discharge of any person's liability, other than a liability for a liquidated sum; and

[(c) the net assets of a company are the aggregate of its assets less the aggregate of its liabilities;

and in paragraph (c) 'liabilities' includes—

(i) any provision (within the meaning of the Sixth Schedule to the Principal Act) that is made in Companies Act individual accounts except to the extent that that provision is taken into account in calculating the value of any asset to the company,

(ii) any provision for liabilities within the meaning of paragraph 70 of the Schedule to the Companies (Amendment) Act 1986 that is made in Companies Act individual accounts, and

(iii) any provision that is made in IFRS individual accounts.][c]

(5) The Companies Act, 1963, the Companies (Amendment) Act, 1977, the Companies (Amendment) Act, 1982, and this Act shall be construed together as one Act.

(6) In this Act—

(a) a reference to a Part, section or Schedule is to a Part, section or Schedule of this Act unless it is indicated that a reference to some other enactment is intended;

(b) a reference to a subsection, paragraph or subparagraph is to the subsection, paragraph or subparagraph of the provision in which the reference occurs, unless it is indicated that reference to some other provision is intended; and

(c) a reference to any other enactment shall, unless the context otherwise requires, be construed as a reference to that enactment as amended by or under any other enactment, including this Act.

(7) The Minister may by order specify that the appropriate rate of interest for the purposes of this Act shall be a rate other than five per cent. per annum.

Amendments

a Definitions of 'Regulations of 1987' and 'Regulations of 2008' inserted by EC(MDC)(A)R 2011, reg 3.

b Words inserted by EC(IFRSMA)R 2005 (SI 116/2005), reg 9, Part 2 of Schedule 1, Item No 1.

c Paragraph (c) substituted by EC(IFRSMA)R 2005 (SI 116/2005), reg 9, Part 2 of Schedule 1, Item No 1.

---

3 Amendments, repeals and savings

(1) The provisions of the Principal Act specified in the First Schedule are hereby amended to the extent specified in that Schedule.

(2) The provisions of the Principal Act and the Companies (Amendment) Act, 1982, specified in the first column of the Third Schedule are hereby repealed to the extent specified in the second column of that Schedule.

(3) Paragraphs 24 and 25 of the First Schedule (which amend Table A and Tábla A respectively in the First Schedule to the Principal Act) and any repeal specified in the Third Schedule of anything contained in the said Table A and the said Tábla A shall not affect any company registered before the appointed day.

(4) In the Principal Act, a reference to a company registered under any specified enactment shall continue to have effect as a reference to a company registered under that enactment, notwithstanding that it has subsequently been re-registered under this Act.

PART II

NAME OF PUBLIC LIMITED COMPANY, REGISTRATION AND RE-REGISTRATION OF COMPANIES

4 Name of a public limited company

(1) The name of a public limited company must end with the words 'public limited company' or 'cuideachta phoiblí theoranta' which may be abbreviated to 'p.l.c.' or 'c.p.t.' respectively and those words or abbreviations may not be preceded by the word 'limited' or its abbreviation 'ltd.' or 'teoranta' or its abbreviation 'teo.'.

(2) Subject to subsection (1), a resolution in accordance with section 12 that a company be re-registered as a public limited company may change the name of the company by deleting—

(a) the word 'company' or the words 'and company'; or

(b) the word 'cuideachta' or the words 'agus cuideachta',

including any abbreviation of them, and no fee shall be payable in respect of any change of name mentioned in this subsection.

(3) The memorandum of a public limited company which is limited by shares shall be in the form set out in Part I of the Second Schedule or, if it is a company limited by guarantee and having a share capital, in the form set out in Part II of that Schedule or, in either case, as near thereto as circumstances admit; and those forms supersede in the case of a public limited company the forms of memorandum set out respectively in Tables B and D in the First Schedule to the Principal Act.

5 Registration of companies

(1) Where any memorandum is delivered for registration under section 17 of the Principal Act, the registrar shall not register the memorandum unless he is satisfied that all the requirements of the Companies Acts in respect of registration and of matters precedent and incidental thereto have been complied with.

(2) Where a memorandum which is so delivered states that the association to be registered is to be a public limited company, the amount of the share capital stated in the memorandum to be that with which the company proposes to be registered must not be less than the authorised minimum.

(3) Where the registrar registers an association's memorandum which states that the association is to be a public limited company, the certificate of incorporation given in respect of that association under section 18 of the Principal Act shall contain a statement that the company is a public limited company.

(4) A certificate of incorporation given under that section in respect of any association shall be conclusive evidence—

(a) that the requirements mentioned in subsection (1) have been complied with, and that the association is a company authorised to be registered and is duly registered under the Principal Act; and

(b) if the certificate contains a statement that the company is a public limited company, that the company is such a company.

(5) A statutory declaration in the prescribed form by a solicitor engaged in the formation of a company, or by a person named as a director or secretary of the company in the statement delivered under section 3 of the Companies (Amendment) Act, 1982 that the requirements mentioned in subsection (1) have been complied with shall be delivered to the registrar, and the registrar may accept such a declaration as sufficient evidence of compliance.

6 Restriction on commencement of business by a public limited company

(1) A company registered as a public limited company on its original incorporation shall not do business or exercise any borrowing powers unless the registrar of companies has issued it with a certificate under this section or the company is re-registered as another form of company.

(2) The registrar shall issue a public limited company with a certificate under this section if, on an application made to him in the prescribed form by the company, he is satisfied that the nominal value of the company's allotted share capital is not less than the authorised minimum, and there is delivered to him a statutory declaration complying with subsection (3).

(3) The statutory declaration shall be in the prescribed form and signed by a director or secretary of the company and shall state—

(a) that the nominal value of the company's allotted share capital is not less than the authorised minimum;

(b) the amount paid up, at the time of the application, on the allotted share capital of the company;

(c) the amount, or estimated amount, of the preliminary expenses of the company and the persons by whom any of those expenses have been paid or are payable; and

(d) any amount or benefit paid or given or intended to be paid or given to any promoter of the company, and the consideration for the payment or benefit.

(4) For the purposes of subsection (2), a share allotted in pursuance of an employees' share scheme may not be taken into account in determining the nominal value of the

company's allotted share capital unless it is paid up at least as to one-quarter of the nominal value of the share and the whole of any premium on the share.

(5) The registrar may accept a statutory declaration delivered to him under subsection (2) as sufficient evidence of the matters stated therein.

(6) A certificate under this section in respect of any public limited company be conclusive evidence that the company is entitled to do business and exercise any borrowing powers.

(7) If a public limited company does business or exercises borrowing powers in contravention of this section, the company and any officer of the company who is in default shall be guilty of an offence and shall be liable on summary conviction to a [class C fine][a].

(8) The provisions of this section are without prejudice to the validity of any transaction entered into by a public limited company; but if a public limited company enters into a transaction in contravention of those provisions and fails to comply with its obligations in connection therewith within 21 days from being called upon to do so, the directors of the company shall be jointly and severally liable to indemnify the other party to the transaction in respect of any loss or damage suffered by him by reason of the failure of the company to comply with those obligations.

Amendments

a £500 increased to £1,500 by CA 1990, s 240(7) as inserted by CLEA 2001, s 104(c), and converted to €1,904.61 by Council Regulations (EC) No 1103/97, No 974/98 and No 2866/98 and the Economic and Monetary Union Act 1998, s 6; the above being implicitly substituted, by Fines Act 2010, s 6, for a fine not exceeding the aforesaid amount. A class C fine currently means a fine not exceeding €2,500.

---

7 Prohibition on formation of public company limited by guarantee and having a share capital

On or after the appointed day, no company shall be formed as, or become, a public company limited by guarantee and having a share capital.

8 Power of registrar to strike public limited company off register

(1) Where a public limited company registered as such on its original incorporation has not been issued with a certificate under section 6 within one year from the date on which it was registered, the registrar may send to the company, by registered post, a letter stating that a notice will be published in [the Companies Registration Office Gazette][a] with a view to striking the name of that public limited company off the register unless such a certificate has been issued to the company within on month from the date of that letter.

(2) Where a certificate referred to in section 6 has not been issued within one month from the date of the letter referred to in subsection (1), the registrar may publish such notice and may proceed to strike the name of the public limited company off the register in accordance with section 311 (5) of the Principal Act.

(3) Section 311 (6), [(7), (8) and (8A)][b] of the Principal Act shall apply to a public limited company the name of which has been struck off the register in accordance with subsection (2) as those subsections apply for the purposes of the said section 311.

Amendments

a 'the Companies Registration Office Gazette' substituted for '*Iris Oifigiúil*' by IFCMPA 2005, s 72.

b '(7), (8) and (8A)' substituted for '(7) and (8)' by C(A)(No 2)A 1999, s 51.

---

9 Re-registration of private company as public limited company

(1) Subject to section 11, a private company may be re-registered as a public limited company if—

(a) a special resolution, complying with subsection (2) that it should be so re-registered is passed; and

(b) an application for the purpose, in the prescribed form and signed by a director or secretary of the company, is delivered to the registrar together with the documents mentioned in subsection (3); and

(c) the conditions specified in subsection (5)(a) and (b) (where applicable) and section 10(1)(a) to (d) are satisfied in relation to the company.

(2) The special resolution must—

(a) alter the company's memorandum so that it states that the company is to be a public limited company;

(b) make such other alterations in the memorandum as are necessary to bring it in substance and in form into conformity with the requirements of this Act with respect to the memorandum of a public limited company; and

(c) make such alterations in the company's articles as are requisite in the circumstances.

(3) The documents referred to in subsection (1) are—

(a) a printed copy of the memorandum and articles as altered in pursuance of the resolution;

(b) a copy of a written statement by the auditors of the company that in their opinion the relevant balance sheet shows that at the balance sheet date the amount of the company's net assets was not less than the aggregate of its called-up share capital and undistributable reserves;

(c) a copy of the relevant balance sheet, together with a copy of an unqualified report by the company's auditors in relation to that balance sheet;

(d) a copy of any report prepared under subsection (5)(b); and

(e) a statutory declaration in the prescribed form by a director or secretary of the company—

(i) that the special resolution mentioned in subsection (1)(a) has been passed and that the conditions specified in subsection (1)(c) have been satisfied; and

(ii) that, between the balance sheet date and the application of the company for re-registration, there has been no change in the financial position of the company that has resulted in the amount of the company's net assets becoming less than the aggregate of its called-up share capital and undistributable reserves.

(4) The registrar may accept a statutory declaration under subsection (3)(e) as sufficient evidence that the special resolution has been passed and the said conditions have been satisfied.

(5) Where shares are allotted by the company between the balance sheet date and the passing of the special resolution as fully or partly paid up as to their nominal value or any premium on them otherwise than in cash, the company shall not make an application for re-registration under this section unless before the making of the application—

(a) the consideration for that allotment has been valued in accordance with the provisions of section 30 applied by this subsection and section 31; and

(b) a report with respect to its value has been made to the company in accordance with those provisions during the six months immediately preceding the allotment of the shares;

and subsections (2) to (8) and (12) to (14) of section 30 shall apply for the purposes of this subsection as they apply for the purposes of that section and as if the references to subsection (1) of section 30 were references to this subsection.

(6) If the registrar is satisfied on an application made under subsection (1) that a company may be re-registered under this section as a public limited company, he shall—

(a) retain the application and other documents delivered to him under that subsection; and

(b) issue the company with a certificate of incorporation stating that the company is a public limited company.

(7) The registrar shall not issue a certificate of incorporation under subsection (6) if it appears to him that the court has made an order confirming a reduction of the company's capital which has the effect of bringing the nominal value of the company's allotted share capital below the authorised minimum.

(8) Upon the issue to a company of a certificate of incorporation under subsection (6)—

(a) the company shall by virtue of the issue of that certificate become a public limited company; and

(b) any alterations in the memorandum and articles set out in the resolution shall take effect accordingly.

(9) A certificate of incorporation issued to a company under sub-section (6) shall be conclusive evidence—

(a) that the requirements of this Act in respect of re-registration and of matters precedent and incidental thereto have been complied with; and

(b) that the company is a public limited company.

(10) The re-registration of a private company as a public limited company pursuant to this Act shall not affect any rights or obligations of the company or render defective any legal proceedings by or against the company, and any legal proceedings which might

have been continued or commenced against it in its former status may be continued or commenced against it in its new status.

(11) A qualification shall be treated for the purposes of the definition of an unqualified report in subsection (13) as being not material in relation to any balance sheet if, but only if, the person making the report states in writing that the thing giving rise to the qualification is not material for the purposes of determining, by reference to that balance sheet, whether at the balance sheet date the amount of the company's net assets was not less than the aggregate of its called-up share capital and undistributable reserves.

(12) For the purposes of the making, in relation to the balance sheet of a company, of a report falling within the definition in subsection (13) of an unqualified report, section 149 of the Sixth Schedule to the Principal Act shall be deemed to have effect in relation to that balance sheet with such modifications as are necessary by reason of the fact that that balance sheet is prepared otherwise than in respect of a financial year.

(13) In this section—

'undistributable reserves' has the same meaning as in section 46(2);

'relevant balance sheet' means, in relation to a company, a balance sheet prepared as at a date not more than seven months before the company's application for re-registration under this section; and

'unqualified report' means, in relation to the balance sheet of a company, a report stating without material qualification—

[(a) that in the opinion of the person making the report, the balance sheet complies with the requirements of section 148 and either section 149 or 149A of the Principal Act, where applicable and with section 156 of the Principal Act;][a]

(b) without prejudice to paragraph (a) that, except where the company is entitled to avail itself, and has availed itself, of the benefit of any of the provisions of Part III of the Sixth Schedule to the Principal Act, in the opinion of that person, the balance sheet gives a true and fair view of the state of the company's affairs as at the balance sheet date.

Amendments

a Paragraph 13(a) substituted by EC(IFRSMA)R 2005 (SI 116/2005), reg 9, Part 2 of Schedule 1, Item No 2.

---

10 Requirements as to share capital of private company applying to re-register as public limited company

(1) Subject to subsection (2), a private company shall not be re-registered under section 9 as a public limited company unless, at the time the special resolution referred to in that section is passed—

(a) the nominal value of the company's allotted share capital is not less than the authorised minimum;

(b) each of its allotted shares is paid up at least as to one-quarter of the nominal value of that share and the whole of any premium on it;

(c) where any share in the company or any premium payable on it has been fully or partly paid up by an undertaking given by any person that he or another should do work or perform services for the company or another, the undertaking has been performed or otherwise discharged; and

(d) where shares have been allotted as fully or partly paid up as to their nominal value or any premium payable on them otherwise than in cash and the consideration for the allotment consists of or includes an undertaking (other than one to which paragraph (c) applies) to the company, either—

(i) that undertaking has been performed or otherwise discharged; or

(ii) there is a contract between the company and any person pursuant to which that undertaking must be performed within five years from that time.

(2) Subject to subsection (3), any share allotted by the company—

(a) which was allotted before the end of the general transitional period; or

(b) which was allotted in pursuance of an employees' share scheme and by reason of which the company would, but for this subsection, be precluded under subsection (1)(b), but not otherwise, from being re-registered as a public limited company,

may be disregarded for the purpose of determining whether subsection (1)(b) to (d) is complied with in relation to the company, and a share so disregarded shall be treated for the purposes of subsection (1)(a) as if it were not part of the allotted share capital of the company.

(3) A share shall not be disregarded by virtue of subsection (2)(a) if the aggregate in nominal value of that share and the other shares which it is proposed so to disregard is more than one-tenth of the nominal value of the company's allotted share capital (not including any share disregarded by virtue of subsection (2)(b)).

11 Re-registration of unlimited company as public limited company

(1) An unlimited company may be re-registered as a public limited company and for the purposes of such a re-registration sections 9 and 53(6) and (7) shall have effect subject to the modifications contained in this section.

(2) The special resolution required by section 9(1) must, in addition to the matters mentioned in section 9(2)—

(a) state that the liability of the members is to be limited by shares and what the share capital of the company is to be; and

(b) make such alterations in the company's memorandum as are necessary to bring it in substance and in form into conformity with the requirements of the Companies Acts with respect to the memorandum of a company limited by shares.

(3) The certificate of incorporation issued under section 9(6) shall, in addition to containing the statement required by paragraph (b) of that subsection, state that the company has been incorporated as a company limited by shares and—

(a) the company shall by virtue of the issue of that certificate become a public limited company so limited; and

(b) the certificate shall be conclusive evidence of the fact that it is such limited company.

(4) Section 53(6) and (7) shall have effect as if any reference to the re-registration of a company in pursuance of that section included a reference to the re-registration of an unlimited company as a public limited company in accordance with subsection (1), but except as aforesaid the said section 53 shall not apply in relation to the re-registration of an unlimited company as a public limited company.

12 Old public limited companies

(1) In this Act 'old public limited company' means a public company limited by shares or a public company limited by guarantee and having a share capital in respect of which the following conditions are satisfied, that is to say—

(a) the company either existed on the appointed day or was incorporated after that day pursuant to an application made before that day; and

(b) the company has not since the appointed day or the day of the company's incorporation, as the case may be, either been re-registered as a public limited company or become another form of company.

(2) The references in the Principal Act to a company other than a private company and, after the end of the general transitional period, in this Act other than this Part to a public limited company shall, unless the context otherwise requires, include references to an old public limited company.

(3) An old public limited company may (either before or after the end of the general transitional period) be re-registered as a public limited company if—

(a) the directors pass a resolution, complying with subsection (4), that it should be so re-registered; and

(b) an application for the purpose in the prescribed form and signed by a director or secretary of the company is delivered to the registrar, together with the documents mentioned in subsection (5); and

(c) at the time of the resolution, the conditions specified in subsection (9) are satisfied.

(4) The resolution referred to in subsection (3) must alter the company's memorandum so that it states that the company is to be a public limited company and make such other alterations in it as are necessary to bring it in substance and in form into conformity with the requirements of this Act with respect to the memorandum of a public limited company.

(5) The documents referred to in subsection (3) are—

(a) a printed copy of the memorandum as altered in pursuance of the resolution; and

(b) a statutory declaration in the prescribed form by a director or secretary of the company that the resolution mentioned in subsection (3)(a) has been passed and that the conditions specified in subsection (9) were satisfied at the time of the resolution.

(6) The registrar may accept a declaration under subsection (5)(b) as sufficient evidence that the said resolution has been passed and that the said conditions were so satisfied.

(7) Subsections (6) to (9) of section 9, shall apply on an application for re-registration under this section as they apply on an application for re-registration under that section and as if the reference to subsection (1) of that section were a reference to subsection (3) of this section.

(8) If an old public limited company applies for re-registration as a public limited company in accordance with subsection (3) and at the time of making that application delivers to the registrar a statutory declaration in the prescribed form by a director or secretary of the company that the company does not at the time of the declaration satisfy the conditions specified in subsection (9), the registrar shall re-register the company as a public limited company but shall notify it that if, within the transitional period for share capital, it has not satisfied the aforesaid conditions it must re-register as another form of company or wind up voluntarily under section 251 of the Principal Act. Failure so to re-register or wind up shall constitute grounds for a winding-up by the court under section 213(i) of the Principal Act.

(9) The conditions referred to in subsections (3)(c) and (8) are that, at the time of the resolution, the nominal value of the company's allotted share capital is not less than the authorised minimum and that in the case of all the shares of the company or all those of its shares which are comprised in a portion of that capital which satisfies that condition—

- (a) each share is paid up at least as to one-quarter of the nominal value of that share and the whole of any premium on it;
- (b) where any of the shares in question or any premium payable on them has been fully or partly paid up by an undertaking given by any person that he or another should do work or perform services for the company or another, the undertaking has been performed or otherwise discharged; and
- (c) where any of the shares in question has been allotted as fully or partly paid up as to its nominal value or any premium payable on it otherwise than in cash and the consideration for the allotment consists of or includes an undertaking (other than one to which paragraph (b) applies) to the company, either—
  - (i) that undertaking has been performed or otherwise discharged; or
  - (ii) there is a contract between the company and any person pursuant to which that undertaking must be performed within five years from the time of the resolution.

(10) The re-registration of an old public limited company as a public limited company pursuant to this Act shall not affect any rights or obligations of the company or render defective any legal proceedings by or against the company, and any legal proceedings which might have been continued or commenced against it in its former status may be continued or commenced against it in its new status.

13 Failure by an old public limited company to re-register as public limited company

(1) If, at any time after the end of the period of fifteen months from the appointed day (in this Act referred to as 'the re-registration period'), a company which is an old public limited company has not re-registered as a public limited company under section 12, the

company and any officer of the company who is in default shall be guilty of an offence unless at that time the company—

(a) has applied to be re-registered under section 12 and the application has not been refused or withdrawn;

(b) has applied to be re-registered as another form of company.

(2) A person guilty of an offence under subsection (1) shall be liable on summary conviction to a [class C fine][a] together with, in the case of a continuing offence, a fine not exceeding [class E fine][b] for every day on which the offence continues, but not exceeding [€1,904.61][c] in total.

Amendments

a £250 increased to £1,500 by CA 1990, s 240(7) as inserted by CLEA 2001, s 104(c), and converted to €1,904.61 by Council Regulations (EC) No 1103/97, No 974/98 and No 2866/98 and the Economic and Monetary Union Act 1998, s 6; the above being implicitly substituted, by Fines Act 2010, s 6, for a fine not exceeding the aforesaid amount. A class C fine currently means a fine not exceeding €2,500.

b £25 converted to €31.74 by Council Regulations (EC) No 1103/97, No 974/98 and No 2866/98 and the Economic and Monetary Union Act 1998, s 6; as implicitly substituted, by Fines Act 2010, s 8, for a fine not exceeding the aforesaid amount. A class E fine currently means a fine not exceeding €500.

c £500 increased to £1,500 by CA 1990, s 240(7) as inserted by CLEA 2001, s 104(c) and converted to €1,904.61 by Council Regulations (EC) No 1103/97, No 974/98 and No 2866/98 and the Economic and Monetary Union Act 1998, s 6. Note the effect of the retention of the €1,904.61 limit is to significantly restrict the amount of the fines that might otherwise have been imposed, and in particular limit the deterrent effect of the daily default fine.

---

14 Re-registration of public limited company as private company

(1) A public limited company may be re-registered as a private company if—

(a) a special resolution complying with subsection (2) that it should be so re-registered is passed and has not been cancelled by the court under section 15(6);

(b) an application for the purpose in the prescribed form and signed by a director or secretary of the company is delivered to the registrar, together with a printed copy of the memorandum and articles of the company as altered by the resolution; and

(c) the period during which an application for the cancellation of the resolution under section 15 (2) may be made has expired without any such application having been made; or

(d) where such an application has been made, the application has been withdrawn or an order has been made under section 15 (6) confirming the resolution and a copy of that order has been delivered to the registrar.

(2) The resolution must—

(a) alter the company's memorandum so that it no longer states that the company is to be a public limited company and must make such other alterations in the company's memorandum as are requisite in the circumstances; and

(b) make such alterations in the company's articles as are requisite in the circumstances and in such a manner that they include the provisions which, under section 33 of the Principal Act, are required to be included in the articles of a company in order to constitute it a private company.

(3) If the registrar is satisfied that a public limited company may be re-registered under subsection (1), he shall—

(a) retain the application and other documents delivered to him under that subsection; and

(b) issue the company with a certificate of incorporation appropriate to a private company.

(4) Upon the issue of a certificate of incorporation under subsection (3)—

(a) the company shall by virtue of the issue of that certificate become a private company; and

(b) the alterations in the memorandum and articles set out in the resolution shall take effect accordingly.

(5) A certificate of incorporation issued to a company under subsection (3) shall be conclusive evidence—

(a) that the requirements of this section in respect of re-registration and of matters precedent and incidental thereto have been complied with; and

(b) that the company is a private company.

(6) The re-registration of a public limited company as a private company pursuant to this Act shall not affect any rights or obligations of the company or render defective any legal proceedings by or against the company, and any legal proceedings which might have been continued or commenced against it in its former status may be continued or commenced against it in its new status.

15 Provisions supplementary to section 14

(1) This section applies to a special resolution by a public limited company to be re-registered under section 14 as a private company.

(2) Where a special resolution to which this section applies has been passed, an application may be made to the court for the cancellation of that resolution.

(3) An application under subsection (2) may be made—

(a) by the holders of not less in the aggregate than five per cent. in nominal value of the company's issued share capital or any class thereof;

(b) if the company is not limited by shares, by not less than five per cent. of the company's members; or

(c) by not less than 50 of the company's members;

but any such application shall not be made by any person who has consented to or voted in favour of the resolution.

(4) Any such application must be made within 28 days after the passing of the resolution and may be made on behalf of the persons entitled to make the application by such one or more of their number as they may appoint in writing for the purpose.

(5) If an application is made under subsection (2), the company—

(a) shall forthwith give notice of that fact to the registrar; and

(b) where on the hearing of that application an order cancelling or confirming the resolution is made under subsection (6), shall, within 15 days from the making of that order, or within such longer period as the court may at any time by order direct, deliver an office copy of the order to the registrar.

(6) On the hearing of an application under subsection (2) the court shall make an order either cancelling or confirming the resolution and—

(a) may make that order on such terms and conditions as it thinks fit, and may, if it thinks fit, adjourn the proceedings in order that an arrangement may be made to the satisfaction of the court for the purchase of the interests of dissentient members; and

(b) may give such directions and make such orders as it thinks expedient for facilitating or carrying into effect any such arrangement.

(7) An order under this section may, if the court thinks fit, provide for the purchase by the company of the shares of any members of the company and for the reduction accordingly of the company's capital and may make such alterations in the memorandum and articles of the company as may be required in consequence of that provision.

(8) Where an order under this section requires the company not to make any, or any specified, alteration in its memorandum or articles, then, notwithstanding anything in the Companies Acts, the company shall not have power without the leave of the court to make any such alteration in breach of that requirement.

(9) Any alteration in the memorandum or articles of the company made by virtue of an order under this section, other than one made by resolution of the company, shall be of the same effect as if duly made by resolution of the company, and the provisions of the Companies Acts shall apply to the memorandum or articles as so altered accordingly.

(10) A company which fails to comply with subsection (5) and any officer of the company who is in default shall be guilty of an offence and shall be liable on summary conviction to a [class C fine][a] together with, in the case of a continuing offence, a [class E fine][b] for every day on which the offence continues, but not exceeding [€1,904.61][c] in total.

Amendments

a £250 increased to £1,500 by CA 1990, s 240(7) as inserted by CLEA 2001, s 104(c), and converted to €1,904.61 by Council Regulations (EC) No 1103/97, No 974/98 and No 2866/98 and the Economic and Monetary Union Act 1998, s 6; the above being implicitly substituted, by Fines Act 2010, s 6, for a fine not exceeding the aforesaid amount. A class C fine currently means a fine not exceeding €2,500.

b £25 converted to €31.74 by Council Regulations (EC) No 1103/97, No 974/98 and No 2866/98 and the Economic and Monetary Union Act 1998, s 6; as implicitly substituted, by Fines Act 2010, s 8, for a fine not exceeding the aforesaid amount. A class E fine currently means a fine not exceeding €500.

c £500 increased to £1,500 by CA 1990, s 240(7) as inserted by CLEA 2001, s 104(c) and converted to €1,904.61 by Council Regulations (EC) No 1103/97, No 974/98 and No 2866/98 and the Economic and Monetary Union Act 1998, s 6. Note that the effect of the retention of the €1,904.61 limit is to significantly restrict the amount of the fines that might otherwise have been imposed, and in particular to limit the deterrent effect of the daily default fine.

---

16 Failure by old public limited company to re-register as another form of company

(1) Where an old public limited company has within the re-registration period applied for re-registration as a form of company other than a public limited company, and the registrar has notified the company that it has failed to fulfil the requirements for such re-registration, the company and any officer of the company who is in default shall be guilty of an offence unless within a period of 12 months from the end of the re-registration period—

(a) those requirements have been fulfilled and the re-registration has taken place; or

(b) the company has been re-registered in a form other than that for which application was made; or

(c) the company has been wound up voluntarily under section 251 of the Principal Act.

(2) A person guilty of an offence under subsection (1) shall be liable on summary conviction to a [class C fine][a] together with, in the case of a continuing offence, a [class E fine][b] for every day on which the offence continues, but not exceeding [€1904.61][c] in total.

Amendments

a £250 increased to £1,500 by CA 1990, s 240(7) as inserted by CLEA 2001, s 104(c), and converted to €1,904.61 by Council Regulations (EC) No 1103/97, No 974/98 and No 2866/98 and the Economic and Monetary Union Act 1998, s 6; the above being implicitly substituted, by Fines Act 2010, s 6, for a fine not exceeding the aforesaid amount. A class C fine currently means a fine not exceeding €2,500.

b £25 converted to €31.74 by Council Regulations (EC) No 1103/97, No 974/98 and No 2866/98 and the Economic and Monetary Union Act 1998, s 6; as implicitly substituted, by Fines Act 2010, s 8, for a fine not exceeding the aforesaid amount. A class E fine currently means a fine not exceeding €500.

c £500 increased to £1,500 by CA 1990, s 240(7) as inserted by CLEA 2001, s 104(c) and converted to €1,904.61 by Council Regulations (EC) No 1103/97, No 974/98 and No 2866/98 and the Economic and Monetary Union Act 1998, s 6. Note that the effect of the retention of the €1,904.61 limit is to significantly restrict the amount of the fines that might otherwise have been imposed, and in particular to limit the deterrent effect of the daily default fine.

---

17 Limitation on reduction by a public limited company of its allotted share capital

(1) Subject to subsections (2) and (3), a public limited company may not reduce its allotted share capital below the authorised minimum and section 72(1) of the Principal Act shall be construed accordingly.

(2) Subsection (1) shall not apply to an old public limited company which has been re-registered as a public limited company until expiry of the transitional period for share capital.

(3) Where the court makes an order confirming a reduction of the capital of a public limited company which has the effect of bringing the nominal value of the company's allotted share capital below the authorised minimum, the registrar shall not register the order under section 75(1) of the Principal Act unless the court otherwise directs or the company is first re-registered as another form of company.

(4) A court making any such order in respect of a public limited company may authorise the company to be re-registered as another form of company without its having passed a special resolution and, where the court so authorises a public limited company, the court shall specify in the order the alterations in the company's memorandum and articles to be made in connection with that re-registration.

(5) In its application to a public limited company that applies to be re-registered as a private company in pursuance of an authority given under subsection (4), section 14, shall have effect with the following modifications—

(a) references to the special resolution of the company shall have effect as references to the order of the court under the said subsection (4);

(b) section 14 (1)(a), (c) and (d) and (2) shall not apply; and

(c) section 14 (3) shall be read as if the words— 'If the registrar is satisfied that a public limited company may be re-registered under subsection (1) he shall' were deleted and the following words substituted therefor 'On receipt of an application for re-registration under this section made in pursuance of an order of the court under section 17, the registrar shall'.

18 Registration of joint stock companies

(1) A joint stock company (within the meaning of section 329 of the Principal Act) applying to be registered in pursuance of Part IX of that Act as a company limited by shares may, subject to satisfying the conditions specified in section 9(5)(a) and (b) (where applicable) and section 10(1)(a) to (d), as applied by this section, and to complying with the requirements of subsection (4), apply to be so registered as a public limited company.

(2) The said sections 9(5) and 10 shall apply to a joint stock company applying to register under the said Part IX as they apply to a private company applying to be re-registered under section 9, but as if any reference to the special resolution referred to in section 9 were a reference to the resolution referred to in subsection (4)(a).

(3) In the following provisions of this section an application by a company made in pursuance of the said Part IX to register as a public company limited by shares is referred to as a relevant application.

(4) A relevant application shall be made in the prescribed form and shall be delivered to the registrar together with the following documents (as well as with the documents referred to in section 330 of the Principal Act), namely—

(a) a copy of the resolution that the company be a public limited company;

(b) a copy of a written statement by a person, who would be qualified under section 162 of the Principal Act for appointment as auditor of the company if it were a company registered under that Act, that in his opinion a relevant balance sheet shows that at the balance sheet date the amount of the company's net assets was not less than the aggregate of the called-up share capital of the company and its undistributable reserves;

(c) a copy of the relevant balance sheet together with a copy of an unqualified report by such a person in relation to that balance sheet;

(d) a copy of any report prepared under section 9(5)(b) as applied by this section; and

(e) a statutory declaration in the prescribed form by a director or secretary of the company—

(i) that the conditions specified in section 9(5)(a) and (b) (where applicable) and section 10(1)(a) to (d) have been satisfied; and

(ii) that, between the balance sheet date referred to in paragraph (b) and the date of the relevant application, there has been no change in the financial position of the company that has resulted in the amount of the company's net assets becoming less than the aggregate of its called-up share capital and undistributable reserves.

(5) The registrar may accept a declaration under subsection (4)(e) as sufficient evidence that the conditions referred to in subparagraph (i) of that paragraph have been satisfied.

(6) Where on a relevant application the registrar is satisfied that the company may be registered as a public company limited by shares, the certificate of incorporation given by him under section 336 of the Principal Act shall state that the company is a public limited company; and such a statement shall be conclusive evidence that the requirements of this section have been complied with and that the company is a public company so limited.

(7) The registration of a joint stock company as a public limited company shall not affect any rights or obligations of the company or render defective any legal proceedings by or against the company, and any legal proceedings which might have been continued or commenced against it in its former status may be continued or commenced against it in its new status.

(8) In this section—

'relevant balance sheet' means, in relation to a company, a balance sheet prepared as at a date not more than seven months before the relevant application;

'undistributable reserves' has the same meaning as in section 46(2); and

'unqualified report' has the same meaning as in section 9(13);

and section 9(11) applies to the making in pursuance of this section of an unqualified report such as is mentioned in that subsection as it applies to the making of such a report in pursuance of the said section 9.

PART III
THE CAPITAL OF A COMPANY

Authorised share capital and the issue of share capital

19 Meaning of 'authorised minimum'

(1) In this Act 'the authorised minimum' means [€38,092.41][a] or such greater sum as may be specified by order made by the Minister under sub-section (2).

(2) The Minister may by order specify that the authorised minimum for the purposes of this Act shall be an amount other than [€38,092.41][a] and such and order may—

(a) require any public limited company having an allotted share capital of which the nominal value is less than the amount specified in the order as the authorised minimum to increase that value to not less than that amount or make an application to be re-registered as another form of company;

(b) make, in connection with any such requirement, provision for any of the matters for which provision is made by any enactment in the Companies Acts relating to a company's registration, re-registration or change of name, to payment for any share comprised in a company's capital and to offers of shares in or debentures of a company to the public, including provision as to the consequences (whether in criminal law or otherwise) of a failure to comply with any requirement of the order; and

(c) contain such supplemental and transitional provision as the Minister thinks appropriate, make different provision for different cases and, in particular, provide for any provision of the order to come into operation on different days for different purposes.

Amendments

a £30,000 converted to €38,092.14 by Council Regulations (EC) No 1103/97, No 974/98 and No 2866/98 and the Economic and Monetary Union Act 1998, s 6.

---

20 Authority of company required for allotment of certain securities by directors

(1) The directors of a company shall not exercise any power of the company to allot relevant securities, unless the directors are, in accordance with this section, authorised to do so by—

(a) the company in general meeting; or

(b) the articles of the company.

(2) Authority for the purposes of this section may be given for a particular exercise of that power or for the exercise of that power generally, and may be unconditional or subject to conditions.

(3) Any such authority shall state the maximum amount of relevant securities that may be allotted thereunder and the date on which the authority will expire, which shall be not more than five years from whichever is relevant of the following dates—

(a) in the case of an authority contained at the time of the original incorporation of the company in the articles of the company, the date of that incorporation; and

(b) in any other case, the date on which the resolution is passed by virtue of which that authority is given;

but any such authority (including an authority contained in the articles of the company) may be previously revoked or varied by the company in general meeting.

(4) Any such authority (whether or not it has been previously renewed under this subsection) may be renewed by the company in general meeting for a further period not exceeding five years; but the resolution must state (or restate) the amount of relevant securities which may be allotted under the authority or, as the case may be, the amount remaining to be allotted thereunder, and must specify the date on which the renewed authority will expire.

(5) The directors may allot relevant securities, notwithstanding that any authority for the purposes of this section has expired, if the relevant securities are allotted in pursuance of an offer or agreement made by the company before the authority expired and the authority allowed it to make an offer or agreement which would or might require relevant securities to be allotted after the authority expired.

(6) A resolution of a company to give, vary, revoke or renew such an authority may, notwithstanding that it alters the articles of the company, be an ordinary resolution but section 143 of the Principal Act shall apply to it.

(7) Any director who knowingly and wilfully contravenes, or permits or authorises a contravention of, this section shall be guilty of an offence.

(8) Nothing in this section shall affect the validity of any allotment of relevant securities.

(9) This section does not apply to any allotment of relevant securities by a company, other than a public limited company registered as such on its original incorporation, if it is made in pursuance of an offer or agreement made before the date on which the earlier of the following events occurs, that is to say, the holding of the first general meeting of the company after its re-registration or registration as a public limited company and the end of the general transitional period; but any resolution to give, vary or revoke an authority for the purposes of this section shall have effect for those purposes if it is passed at any time after the passing of this Act.

(10) In this section 'relevant securities' means, in relation to a company,—

(a) shares in the company other than shares shown in the memorandum to have been taken by the subscribers thereto or shares allotted in pursuance of an employees' share scheme; and

(b) any right to subscribe for, or to convert any security into, shares in the company other than shares so allotted; and any reference to the allotment of relevant securities shall include a reference to the grant of such a right but shall not include any reference to the allotment of shares pursuant to such a right.

21 Shares and debentures of private company not to be offered to public

[(1) A private company and any officer of the company who is in default shall be guilty of an offence if the company—

(a) offers to the public (whether for cash or otherwise) any shares in or debentures of the company, or

(b) allots, or agrees to allot, (whether for cash or otherwise) any shares in or debentures of the company with a view to all or any of those shares or debentures being offered for sale to the public.

(2) Subsection (1) does not apply to the following offers or allotments (wheresoever made):

(a) an offer of debentures addressed or allotment made solely to qualified investors,

(b) an offer of debentures addressed to fewer than 100 persons, other than qualified investors,

(c) an offer of debentures addressed to investors where the minimum consideration payable pursuant to the offer is at least €50,000 per investor, for each separate offer,

(d) an offer of debentures whose denomination per unit amounts to at least €50,000,

(e) an offer of debentures where the offer expressly limits the amount of the total consideration for the offer to less than €100,000, or

(f) an offer of those classes of instruments which are normally dealt in on the money market (such as treasury bills, certificates of deposit and commercial papers) having a maturity of less than 12 months,

(g) an offer of shares addressed to—

(i) qualified investors, or

(ii) 99 or fewer persons, or

(iii) both qualified investors and 99 or fewer other persons,

(h) an allotment of shares or debentures, an agreement to make such an allotment, with a view to those shares or debentures being the subject of any one or more of the offers referred to in paragraphs (a) to (g).

(3) A word or expression that is used in this section and is also used in the Prospectus (Directive 2003/71/EC) Regulations 2005 (S.I. No.324 of 2005) shall have in this section the same meaning as it has in those Regulations.

(4) Nothing in this section shall affect the validity of any allotment or sale of shares or debentures or of any agreement to allot or sell shares or debentures.

(5) A person guilty of an offence under subsection (1) shall be liable on summary conviction to a [class C fine][a].][b]

Amendments

a As implicitly substituted for "fine not exceeding €1,904.61" by Fines Act 2010, s 6. A class C fine currently means a fine not exceeding €2,500.

b This section was substituted by IFCMPA 2006, s 8 with effect from 1 July 2005.[1]

[1] IFCMPA 2006, s 2(3): C(A)A 1983, s 21, as amended by IFCMPA 2006, s 8, is deemed to come into effect on 1 July 2005. This is the date on which Directive 2003/71/EC was implemented in Ireland by virtue of the Prospectus (Directive 2003/71/EC) Regulations 2005 (SI 324/2005) and IFCMPA 2005.

22 Document containing offer to state whether shares will be allotted where issue not fully subscribed

(1) Without prejudice to section 53 of the Principal Act no allotment shall be made of any share capital of a public limited company offered for subscription unless—

(a) that capital is subscribed for in full; or

(b) the offer states that, even if the capital is not subscribed for in full, the amount of that capital subscribed for may be allotted in any event or in the event of the conditions specified in the offer being satisfied.

and, where conditions are so specified, no allotment of the capital shall be made by virtue of paragraph (b) unless those conditions are satisfied.

(2) Section 53 (4) and section 55 of the Principal Act shall apply where shares are prohibited from being allotted by subsection (1) as they apply where the conditions mentioned in subsection (1) of the said section 53 are not complied with; and subsection (5) of the said section 53 shall apply to this section as it applies to that section.

(3) The provisions of this section shall apply in the case of shares offered as wholly or partly payable otherwise than in cash as they apply in the case of shares offered for subscription and—

(a) in subsection (1), the word 'subscribed' shall be construed accordingly; and

(b) in the said section 53 (4), as it applies by virtue of subsection (2) to the former case, references to the repayment of money received from applicants for shares shall include references to the return of any other consideration so received (including, if the case so requires, the release of the applicant from any undertaking) or, if it is not reasonably practicable to return the consideration, the payment of money equal to the value of the consideration at the time it was so received, and references to interest shall have effect accordingly.

Pre-emption rights

23 Pre-emption rights

(1) Subject to the following provisions of this section and sections 24 and 25, a company proposing to allot any equity securities—

(a) shall not allot any of those securities on any terms to any person unless it has made an offer to each person who holds relevant shares or relevant employee shares to allot to him on the same or more favourable terms a proportion of those securities which is as nearly as practicable equal to the proportion in nominal value held by him of the aggregate of relevant shares and relevant employee shares;

and

(b) shall not allot any of those securities to any person unless the period during which any such offer may be accepted has expired or the company has received notice of the acceptance or refusal of every offer so made.

(2) Subsection (3) applies to any provision of the memorandum or articles of a company which requires the company, when proposing to allot equity securities consisting of relevant shares of any particular class, not to allot those securities on any terms unless it has complied with the condition that it makes such an offer as is described in subsection (1) to each person who holds relevant shares or relevant employee shares of that class.

(3) If, in accordance with a provision to which this subsection applies—

(a) a company makes an offer to allot any securities to such a holder; and

(b) he or anyone in whose favour he has renounced his right to their allotment accepts the offer.

subsection (1) shall not apply to the allotment of those securities and the company may allot them accordingly; but this subsection is without prejudice to the application of subsection (1) in any other case.

(4) Subsection (1) shall not apply in relation to a particular allotment of equity securities if the securities are, or are to be, wholly or partly paid up otherwise than in cash.

(5) Securities which a company has offered to allot to a holder of relevant shares or relevant employee shares may be allotted to him or anyone in whose favour he has renounced his right to their allotment without contravening subsection (1)(b).

(6) Subsection (1) shall not apply in relation to the allotment or any securities which would apart from a renunciation or assignment of the right to their allotment be held under an employees' share scheme.

(7) An offer which is required by subsection (1) or by any provision to which subsection (3) applies to be made to any person shall be made by serving it on him in the manner in which notices are authorised to be given by regulations 133, 134 and 135 of Table A; but where he is the holder of a share warrant the offer may instead be made by causing the offer, or a notice specifying where a copy of the offer can be obtained or inspected, to be published in [the Companies Registration Office Gazette][a].

(8) Any such offer as is mentioned in subsection (7) must state a period of not less than 21 days during which the offer may be accepted; and the offer shall not be withdrawn before the end of that period.

(9) Subsections (7) and (8) shall not invalidate a provision to which subsection (3) applies by reason that that provision requires or authorises an offer thereunder to be made in contravention of one or both of those subsections, but, to the extent that the provision requires or authorises such an offer to be so made, it shall be of no effect.

(10) Subsection (1), (7) or (8) may, in its application in relation to allotments by a private company of equity securities or to such allotments of a particular description, be excluded by a provision contained in the memorandum or articles of that company; and a requirement or authority contained in the memorandum or articles of a private company shall, if it is inconsistent with any of those subsections, have effect as a provision excluding that subsection, but a provision to which subsection (3) applies shall not be treated as being inconsistent with subsection (1).

(11) Where there is a contravention of subsections (1), (7) or (8) or of a provision to which subsection (3) applies, the company, and every officer of the company who knowingly authorised or permitted the contravention, shall be jointly and severally liable to compensate any person to whom an offer should have been made under the subsection or provision contravened for any loss, damage, costs or expenses which that person has sustained or incurred by reason of the contravention; but no proceedings to recover any such loss, damage, costs or expenses shall be commenced after the expiration of two years from the delivery to the registrar of companies of the return of allotments in

question or, where equity securities other than shares are granted, from the date of the grant.

(12) In relation to any offer to allot any securities required by subsection (1) or by any provision to which subsection (3) applies, references in this section (however expressed) to the holder of shares of any descriptions shall be read as including references to any person who held shares of that description on any day within the period of twenty-eight days ending with the day immediately preceding the date of the offer.

(13) In this section and sections 24 and 25—

> 'equity security', in relation to a company, means a relevant share in the company (other than a share shown in the memorandum to have been taken by a subscriber thereto or a bonus share) or a right to subscribe for, or to convert any securities into, relevant shares in the company, and references to the allotment of equity securities or of equity securities consisting of relevant shares of a particular class shall include references to the grant of a right to subscribe for, or to convert any securities into, relevant shares in the company or, as the case may be, relevant shares of a particular class, but shall not include references to the allotment of any relevant shares pursuant to such a right;
>
> 'relevant employee shares', in relation to a company, means shares of the company which would be relevant shares in the company but for the fact that they are held by a person who acquired them in pursuance of an employees' share scheme; and
>
> 'relevant shares' in relation to a company, means shares in the company other than—
>
> (a) shares which as respects dividends and capital carry a right to participate only up to a specified amount in a distribution; and
>
> (b) shares which are held by a person who acquired them in pursuance of an employees' share scheme, or, in the case of shares which have not been allotted, are to be allotted in pursuance of such a scheme;

and any reference to a class of shares shall be construed as a reference to shares to which the same rights are attached as to voting and as to participation, both as respects dividends and as respects capital, in a distribution.

Amendments

a 'the Companies Registration Office Gazette' substituted for '*Iris Oifigiúil*' by IFCMPA 2005, s 72.

---

24 Further provisions relating to pre-emption rights

(1) Where the directors of a company are generally authorised for the purposes of section 20, they may be given power by the articles or by a special resolution of the company to allot equity securities pursuant to that authority as if—

(a) section 23(1) did not apply to the allotment; or

(b) that subsection applied to the allotment with such modifications as the directors may determine;

and where the directors make an allotment under this subsection, the said section 23, shall have effect accordingly.

(2) Where the directors of a company are authorised for the purposes of section 20 (whether generally or otherwise), the company may by special resolution resolve either—

- (a) that section 23(1) shall not apply to a specified allotment of equity securities to be made pursuant to that authority; or
- (b) that that subsection shall apply to the allotment with such modifications as may be specified in the resolution;

and where such a resolution is passed the said section 23 shall have effect accordingly.

(3) A power conferred by virtue of subsection (1) or a special resolution under subsection (2) shall cease to have effect when the authority to which it relates is revoked or would, if not renewed, expire, but if that authority is renewed, the power or, as the case may be, the resolution may also be renewed, for a period not longer than that for which the authority is renewed, by a special resolution of the company.

(4) Notwithstanding that any such power or resolution has expired, the directors may allot equity securities in pursuance of an offer or agreement previously made by the company, if the power or resolution enabled the company to make an offer or agreement which would or might require equity securities to be allotted after it expired.

(5) A special resolution under subsection (2), or a special resolution to renew such a resolution, shall not be proposed unless it is recommended by the directors and there has been circulated, with the notice of the meeting at which the resolution is proposed, to the members entitled to have that notice a written statement by the directors setting out—

- (a) their reasons for making the recommendation;
- (b) the amount to be paid to the company in respect of the equity securities to be allotted; and
- (c) the directors' justification of that amount.

(6) A person who knowingly or recklessly authorises or permits the inclusion in a statement circulated under subsection (5) of any matter which is misleading, false or deceptive in a material particular shall be guilty of an offence.

25 Transitional provisions relating to pre-emption rights

(1) Sections 23 and 24, shall not apply—

- (a) to any allotment of equity securities made by a company, other than a public limited company registered as such on its original incorporation, before the date on which the earlier of the following events occurs, that is to say, the holding of the first general meeting of the company after its re-registration or registration as a public limited company and the end of the general transitional period; or
- (b) where subsection (2) applies, to an allotment of the equity securities which are subject to the requirement mentioned in that subsection.

(2) This subsection applies where any company which is re-registered or registered as a public limited company is or, but for the provisions of this Act, would be subject at the time of re-registration or, as the case may be, registration to a requirement imposed

(whether by the company's memorandum or articles or otherwise) before the relevant time by virtue of which it must, when making an allotment of equity securities, make an offer to allot those securities or some of them in a manner which (otherwise than by virtue of its involving a contravention of section 23(7) or (8)) is inconsistent with section 23.

(3) Any requirement which—

(a) is imposed on a private company before the relevant time otherwise than by the company's memorandum or articles;
and

(b) if contained in the memorandum or articles of the company, would have effect by virtue of section 23(10) to the exclusion of any provision of that section,

shall have effect, so long as the company remains a private company, as if it were contained in the memorandum or articles of the company.

(4) If at the relevant time a company, other than a public limited company registered as such on its original incorporation, is subject to a requirement such as is mentioned in section 23(2) and which was imposed otherwise than by the company's memorandum or articles, the requirement shall be treated for the purposes of that section as if it were contained in the company's memorandum or articles.

(5) In this section 'the relevant time' means—

(a) except in a case falling within paragraph (b), the end of the general transitional period;
and

(b) in the case of a company which is re-registered or registered as a public limited company in pursuance of an application made before the end of that period, the time at which the application is made.

Payment for share capital

26 Subscription of share capital

(1) Subject to the following provisions of this Part, shares allotted by a company and any premium payable on them may be paid up in money or money's worth (including goodwill and expertise).

(2) A public limited company shall not accept at any time in payment up of its shares or any premium on them, an undertaking given by any person that he or another should do work or perform services for the company or any other person.

(3) Where a public limited company accepts such an undertaking as payment up of its shares or any premium payable on them, the holder of the shares when they or the premium are treated as paid up, in whole or in part, by the undertaking—

(a) shall be liable to pay the company in respect of those shares an amount equal to their nominal value, together with the whole of any premium or, if the case so requires, such proportion of that amount as is treated as paid up by the undertaking; and

(b) shall be liable to pay interest at the appropriate rate on the amount payable under paragraph (a).

(4) Where any person becomes a holder of any shares in respect of which—

(a) there has been a contravention of this section; and

(b) by virtue of that contravention, another is liable to pay any amount under this section,

that person also shall be liable to pay that amount (jointly and severally with any other person so liable) unless either he is a purchaser for value and, at the time of the purchase, he did not have actual notice of the contravention or he derived title to the shares (directly or indirectly) from a person who became a holder of them after the contravention and was not so liable.

(5) Subsection (1) shall not prevent a company from allotting bonus shares in the company to its members or from paying up, with sums available for the purpose, any amounts for the time being unpaid on any of its shares (whether on account of the nominal value of the shares or by way of premium).

(6) References in this section to a holder, in relation to any shares in a company, include references to any person who has an unconditional right to be included in the company's register of members in respect of those shares or to have an instrument of transfer of the shares executed in his favour.

27 Prohibition on allotment of shares at a discount

(1) Subject to subsection (4) the shares of a company shall not be allotted at a discount.

(2) Where shares are allotted in contravention of subsection (1), the allottee shall be liable to pay the company an amount equal to the amount of the discount and shall be liable to pay interest thereon at the appropriate rate.

(3) Section 26(4) shall apply for the purposes of this section as it applies for the purposes of that section.

(4) The repeal of section 63 of the Principal Act effected by section 3(2) shall not affect an application for an order sanctioning the issue of shares at a discount which has been made to the court under that section and which has not been withdrawn or disposed of before the appointed day, or an order made on or after that day in pursuance of any such application, and—

(a) any such application may be proceeded with and any such order, if not made before the appointed day, may be made as if that section had not been repealed; and

(b) shares may be allotted at a discount in accordance with any such order (whether made, before, on or after the appointed day) accordingly.

28 Payment for allotted shares

(1) Subject to subsection (4), a public limited company shall not allot a share except as paid up at least as to one-quarter of the nominal value of the share and the whole of any premium on it.

(2) Where a public limited company allots a share in contravention of subsection (1), the share shall be treated as if one-quarter of its nominal value together with the whole of any premium had been received, but the allottee shall be liable to pay the company the minimum amount which should have been received in respect of the share under that subsection less the value of any consideration actually applied in payment up (to any

extent) of the share and any premium on it, and interest at the appropriate rate on the amount payable under this subsection.

(3) Subsection (2) shall not apply in relation to the allotment of a bonus share in contravention of subsection (1) unless the allottee knew or ought to have known the share was so allotted.

(4) Subsections (1) to (3) shall not apply to shares allotted in pursuance of an employees' share scheme.

(5) Section 26 (4) shall apply for the purposes of this section as it applies for the purposes of that section.

29 Payment of non-cash consideration

(1) A public limited company shall not allot shares as fully or partly paid up (as to their nominal value or any premium payable on them) otherwise than in cash if the consideration for the allotment is or includes an undertaking which is to be or may be performed more than five years after the date of the allotment.

(2) Where a public limited company allots shares in contravention of subsection (1), the allottee of the shares shall be liable to pay the company an amount equal to their nominal value, together with the whole of any premium, or, if the case so requires, such proportion of that amount as is treated as paid up by the undertaking and shall be liable to pay interest at the appropriate rate on the amount payable under this subsection.

(3) Where a contract for the allotment of shares does not contravene subsection (1), any variation of the contract which has the effect that the contract would have contravened that subsection if the terms of the contract as varied had been its original terms shall be void.

(4) Subsection (3) shall apply to the variation by a public limited company of the terms of a contract entered into before the company was registered or re-registered as a public limited company.

(5) Where a public limited company allots shares for a consideration which consists of or includes (in accordance with subsection (1)) an undertaking which is to be performed within five years of the allotment but that undertaking is not performed within the period allowed by the contract for the allotment of the shares, the allottee of the shares in question shall be liable to pay the company at the end of that period an amount equal to the nominal value of the shares, together with the whole of any premium, or, if the case so requires, such proportion of that amount as is treated as paid up by the undertaking, together with interest at the appropriate rate on the amount payable under this subsection.

(6) Section 26 (4) shall apply in relation to a contravention of this section and to a failure to carry out a term of a contract as mentioned in subsection (5) as it applies in relation to a contravention of that section.

(7) Any reference in this section to a contract for the allotment of shares includes a reference to an ancillary contract relating to payment in respect of those shares.

30 Experts' reports on non-cash consideration before allotment of shares

(1) Subject to subsection (2), a public limited company shall not allot shares as fully or partly paid up (as to their nominal value or any premium payable on them) otherwise than in cash unless—

(a) the consideration for the allotment has been valued in accordance with the following provisions of this section;

(b) a report with respect to its value has been made to the company by a person appointed by the company in accordance with those provisions during the six months immediately preceding the allotments of the shares; and

(c) a copy of the report has been sent to the proposed allottee of the shares.

(2) Subject to subsection (3), subsection (1) shall not apply to the allotment of shares by a company in connection with—

(a) an arrangement providing for the allotment of shares in that company on terms that the whole or part of the consideration for the shares allotted is to be provided by the transfer to that company or the cancellation of all or some of the shares, or of all or some of the shares of a particular class, in another company (with or without the issue to that company of shares, or of shares of any particular class, in that other company); or

(b) [...][a]

(3) Subsection (2)(a) does not exclude the application of subsection (1) to the allotment of shares by a company in connection with any such arrangement as is there mentioned unless it is open to all the holders of the shares in the other company in question or, where the arrangement applies only to shares of a particular class, to all the holders of shares in that other company of that class, to take part in the arrangement. In determining whether that is the case, shares held by or by a nominee of the company proposing to allot the shares in connection with the arrangement, or by or by a nominee of a company which is that company's holding company or subsidiary or a company which is a subsidiary of its holding company, shall be disregarded.

(4) For the purposes of subsection [(5A)][b] there is a proposed merger of two companies when one of them proposes to acquire all the assets and liabilities of the other in exchange for the issue of shares or other securities in that one to shareholders of the other, with or without any cash payment to those shareholders.

(5) [Subject to subsection (5A), the valuation and report required by subsection (1)][c] shall be made by an independent person, that is to say, a person qualified at the time of the report to be appointed or to continue to be auditor of the company, except that where it appears to him to be reasonable for the valuation of the consideration, or a valuation of part of the consideration, to be made, or to accept such a valuation made, by any person who—

(a) appears to him to have the requisite knowledge and experience to value the consideration or that part of the consideration; and

(b) is not an officer or servant of the company or any other body corporate which is that company's subsidiary or holding company or a subsidiary of that company's holding company or a partner or employee of such an officer or servant,

that independent person may arrange for or accept such a valuation, together with a report which will enable him to make his own report under that subsection and provide a note in accordance with subsection (8).

[(5A) Where the allotment of shares by a company is in connection with—

(a) a proposed merger, where that company was formed as an acquiring company for the purpose of the proposed merger, the merger being a 'merger by formation of a new company' within the meaning of Part II of the Regulations of 1987 or the Regulations of 2008,

(b) a proposed merger of that company with another company, or

(c) a proposed division of that company,

the valuation and report required by subsection (1) may be made by the person appointed pursuant to Regulation 8 or 28 of the Regulations of 1987 or an "expert" within the meaning of Regulation 7 of the Regulations of 2008 in which case the person so appointed shall be deemed to be an independent person for the purposes of subsection (5).][d]

(6) The independent person's report under subsection (1) shall state—

(a) the nominal value of the shares to be wholly or partly paid for by the consideration in question;

(b) the amount of any premium payable on those shares;

(c) the description of the consideration and, as respects so much of the consideration as he himself has valued, a description of that part of the consideration, the method used to value it and the date of the valuation; and

(d) the extent to which the nominal value of the shares and any premium are to be treated as paid up—

(i) by the consideration;

(ii) in cash.

(7) Where any consideration is valued under this section by a person other than the independent person, the latter's report under subsection (1) shall state that fact and shall also—

(a) state the former's name and what knowledge and experience he has to carry out the valuation; and

(b) describe so much of the consideration as was valued by that other person, the method used to value it and state the date of valuation.

(8) The report of the independent person made under subsection (1) shall contain or be accompanied by a note by him—

(a) in the case of a valuation made by another person, that it appeared to the independent person reasonable to arrange for it to be so made, or to accept a valuation so made;

(b) whoever made the valuation, that the method of valuation was reasonable in all the circumstances;

(c) that it appears to the independent person that there has been no material change in the value of the consideration in question since the valuation; and

(d) that on the basis of the valuation the value of the consideration, together with any cash by which the nominal value of the shares or any premium payable on them is to be paid up, is not less than so much of the aggregate of the nominal value and the whole of any such premium as is treated as paid up by the consideration and any such cash.

(9) Subsection (10) applies where a public limited company allots any share in contravention of subsection (1) and either—

(a) the allottee has not received a report under this section; or

(b) there has been some other contravention of this section and the allottee knew or ought to have known that it amounted to a contravention.

(10) Where this subsection applies, the allottee shall be liable to pay the company an amount equal to the nominal value of the shares, together with the whole of any premium or, if the case so requires, such proportion of that amount as is treated as paid up by the consideration, and shall be liable to pay interest at the appropriate rate on the amount payable under this subsection.

(11) Section 26(4) shall apply for the purposes of this section as it applies for the purposes of that section.

(12) Where the consideration is accepted partly in payment up of the nominal value of the shares and any premium and partly for some other consideration given by the company, the provisions of this section shall apply as if references to the consideration accepted by the company included references to the proportion of that consideration which is properly attributable to the payment up of that value and any premium; and

(a) the independent person shall carry out or arrange for such other valuations as will enable him to determine that proportion; and

(b) his report under subsection (1) shall state what valuations have been made by virtue of this subsection and also the reason for and method and date of any such valuations and any other matters which may be relevant to that determination.

(13) It is hereby declared for the avoidance of doubt that subsection (1) does not apply by reference to the application of an amount for the time being standing to the credit of any of the company's reserve accounts or to the credit of its profit and loss account in paying up (to any extent) any shares allotted to members of the company or any premiums on any shares so allotted; and in relation to any such allotment references in this section to the consideration for the allotment do not include any such amount so applied.

(14) In this section—

(a) 'arrangement' means any agreement, scheme or arrangement (including an arrangement sanctioned in accordance with section 201 or 260 of the Principal Act);

(b) any reference to a company, except where it is or is to be construed as a reference to a public limited company, includes a reference to any body corporate and any body to which letters patent have been issued under the Chartered Companies Act, 1837; and

(c) any reference to an officer or servant shall not include a reference to an auditor.

Amendments

a Subsection (2)(b) deleted by EC(MDC)(A)R 2011, reg 4(a).

b '(5A)' substituted for '(2)(b)' by EC(MDC)(A)R 2011, reg 4(b).

c Words 'Subject to subsection (5A), the valuation and report required by subsection (1)' substituted for 'The valuation and report required by subsection (1)' by EC(MDC)(A)R 2011, reg 4(c).

d Subsection (5A) inserted by EC(MDC)(A)R 2011, reg 4(d).

31 Experts' reports: supplementary

(1) Any person carrying out a valuation or making a report under section 30 with respect to any consideration proposed to be accepted or given by a company shall be entitled to require from the officers of the company such information and explanation as he thinks necessary to enable him to carry out the valuation or to make the report and provide a note, under that section.

(2) A company to which such a report is made as to the value of any consideration for which, or partly for which, it proposes to allot shares shall deliver a copy of the report to the registrar of companies for registration at the same time that it files the return of the allotments of those shares under section 58 of the Principal Act, and subsections (3) and (4) of that section shall apply to a default in complying with this subsection as they apply to a default in complying with that section.

(3) Any person who knowingly or recklessly makes a statement which—

(a) is misleading, false or deceptive in a material particular, and

(b) is a statement to which this subsection applies,

shall be guilty of an offence.

(4) Subsection (3) applies to any statement made (whether orally or in writing) to any person carrying out a valuation or making a report under section 30, being a statement which conveys or purports to convey any information or explanation which that person requires, or is entitled to require, under subsection (1).

32 Experts' reports on non-cash assets acquired from subscribers, etc.

(1) A public limited company, other than a company re-registered under section 12, shall not, unless the conditions mentioned in subsection (3) have been complied with, enter into an agreement with a relevant person for the transfer by him during the initial period of one or more non-cash assets to the company or another for a consideration to be given by the company equal in value at the time of the agreement to at least one-tenth of the nominal value of the company's share capital issued at that time.

(2) In this section—

(a) in relation to a company formed as a public limited company, 'relevant person' means any subscriber to the memorandum of the company and 'initial period' means the period of two years beginning with the date on which the company is issued with a certificate under section 6 that it is entitled to do business;

(b) in relation to a company re-registered, or registered in accordance with section 18, as a public limited company, 'relevant person' means any person who was a member of the company on the date of the re-registration or registration and 'initial period' means the period of two years beginning with that date.

(3) The conditions referred to in subsection (1) are that—

(a) the consideration to be received by the company (that is to say, the asset to be transferred to the company or the advantage to the company of its transfer to another person) and any consideration other than cash to be given by the company have been valued under the following provisions of this section (without prejudice to any requirement to value any consideration under section 30);

(b) a report with respect to the consideration to be so received and given has been made to the company in accordance with those provisions during the six months immediately preceding the date of the agreement;

(c) the terms of the agreement have been approved by an ordinary resolution of the company; and

(d) not later than the giving of the notice of the meeting at which the resolution is proposed, copies of the resolution and report have been circulated to the members of the company entitled to receive that notice and, if the relevant person is not then such a member, to that person.

(4) Subsection (1) shall not apply to the following agreements for the transfer of an asset for a consideration to be given by the company, that is to say—

(a) where it is part of the ordinary business of the company to acquire or arrange for other persons to acquire assets of a particular description, an agreement entered into by the company in the ordinary course of its business for the transfer of an asset of that description to it or such a person, as the case may be; or

(b) an agreement entered into by the company under the supervision of the court or an officer authorised by the court for the purpose, for the transfer of an asset to the company or to another.

(5) Section 30 (5) and (7) shall apply to a valuation and report of any consideration under this section as those subsections apply to a valuation of and report on any consideration under subsection (1) of that section.

(6) The report of the independent person under this section shall—

(a) state the consideration to be received by the company, describing the asset in question, specifying the amount to be received in cash, and the consideration to be given by the company, specifying the amount to be given in cash;

(b) state the method and date of valuation;

(c) contain or be accompanied by a note as to the matters mentioned in section 30 (8)(a) to (c); and

(d) contain or be accompanied by a note that on the basis of the valuation the value of the consideration to be received by the company is not less than the value of the consideration to be given by it.

(7) If a public limited company enters into an agreement with any relevant person in contravention of subsection (1) and either he has not received a report under this section or there has been some other contravention of this section or section 30 (5) or (7) which

he knew or ought to have known amounted to a contravention, then, subject to subsection (8)—

(a) the company shall be entitled to recover from the relevant person any consideration given by the company under the agreement or an amount equivalent to its value at the time of the agreement; and

(b) the agreement, so far as not carried out, shall be void.

(8) Where a company enters into an agreement in contravention of subsection (1) and that agreement is or includes an agreement for the allotment of shares in that company, then, whether or not the agreement also contravenes section 30—

(a) subsection (7) shall not apply to the agreement insofar as it is an agreement for the allotment of shares; and

(b) section 26 (4) and section 30 (10) shall apply in relation to the shares as if they had been allotted in contravention of section 30.

33 Provisions supplementary to section 32

(1) Any person carrying out a valuation or making a report under section 32, shall be entitled to require from the officers of the company such information and explanation as he thinks necessary to enable him to carry out the valuation or make the report and provide the note required by that section; and section 31(3) shall apply in relation to any such valuation and report as it applies in relation to a valuation and report under section 30(1) with the substitution of a reference to this subsection for the reference in section 31(4) to section 31(1).

(2) A company which has passed a resolution under section 32 with respect to the transfer of an asset shall, within 15 days of the passing of the resolution, deliver to the registrar of companies a copy of the resolution together with the report required by that section and, if it fails to do so, the company and every officer of the company who is in default shall be liable on summary conviction to a [class C fine][a] together with, in the case of a continuing offence, a [class E fine][b] for every day on which the offence continues, but not exceeding [€1,904.61][c] in total.

(3) Any reference in section 32 or this section to consideration given for the transfer of an asset includes a reference to consideration given partly for its transfer but—

(a) the value of any consideration partly so given shall be taken to be the proportion of that consideration properly attributable to its transfer;

(b) the independent person shall carry out or arrange for such valuations of anything else as will enable him to determine that proportion; and

(c) his report under that section shall state what valuation has been made by virtue of this paragraph and also the reason for and method and date of any such valuation and any other matters which may be relevant to that determination.

Amendments

a £250 increased to £1,500 by CA 1990, s 240(7) as inserted by CLEA 2001, s 104(c), and converted to €1,904.61 by Council Regulations (EC) No 1103/97, No 974/98 and No 2866/98 and the Economic and Monetary Union Act 1998, s 6; the above being implicitly substituted, by Fines Act 2010, s 6, for a fine not exceeding the aforesaid amount. A class C fine currently means a fine not exceeding €2,500.

b £25 converted to €31.74 by Council Regulations (EC) No 1103/97, No 974/98 and No 2866/98 and the Economic and Monetary Union Act 1998, s 6; as implicitly substituted, by Fines Act 2010, s 8, for a fine not exceeding the aforesaid amount. A class E fine currently means a fine not exceeding €500.

c £500 increased to £1,500 by CA 1990, s 240(7) as inserted by CLEA 2001, s 104(c) and converted to €1,904.61 by Council Regulations (EC) No 1103/97, No 974/98 and No 2866/98 and the Economic and Monetary Union Act 1998, s 6. Note that the effect of the retention of the €1,904.61 limit is to significantly restrict the amount of the fines that might otherwise have been imposed, and in particular to limit the deterrent effect of the daily default fine.

---

34 Relief

(1) Where any person is liable to a company under section 26, 29, 30 or 32 in relation to payment in respect of any shares in the company or is liable by virtue of any undertaking given to the company in, or in connection with, payment for any such shares, the person so liable may make an application to the court under this subsection to be exempted in whole or in part from that liability.

(2) Where the liability mentioned in subsection (1) arises under any of those sections in relation to payment in respect of any shares, the court may, on an application under that subsection, exempt the applicant from that liability only—

(a) if and to the extent that it appears to the court just and equitable to do so having regard to the following, namely—

(i) whether the applicant has paid, or is liable to pay, any amount in respect of any other liability arising in relation to those shares under any of those sections or of any liability arising by virtue of any undertaking given in or in connection with payment for those shares;

(ii) whether any person other than the applicant has paid or is likely to pay (whether in pursuance of an order of the court or otherwise) any such amount; and

(iii) whether the applicant or any other person has performed, in whole or in part, or is likely so to perform any such undertaking or has done or is likely to do any other thing in payment or part payment in respect of those shares;

(b) if and to the extent that it appears to the court just and equitable to do so in respect of any interest which he is liable to pay to the company under any of those sections.

(3) Where the liability mentioned in subsection (1) arises by virtue of an undertaking given to the company in, or in connection with, payment for any shares in the company, the court may, on an application under that subsection, exempt the applicant from that liability only if and to the extent that it appears to the court just and equitable to do so having regard to the following, namely—

(a) whether the applicant has paid or is liable to pay any amount in respect of any liability arising in relation to those shares under sections 26, 29, 30 or 32; and

(b) whether any person other than the applicant has paid or is likely to pay (whether in pursuance of an order of the court or otherwise) any such amount.

(4) In determining in pursuance of an application under subsection (1) whether it should exempt the applicant in whole or in part from any liability, the court shall have regard to the following overriding principles, namely—

(a) that a company which has allotted shares should receive money or money's worth at least equal in value to the aggregate of the nominal value of those shares and the whole of any premium or, if the case so requires, so much of that aggregate as is treated as paid up; and

(b) subject to paragraph (a), that where such a company would, if the court did not grant that exemption, have more than one remedy against a particular person, it should be for the company to decide which remedy it should remain entitled to pursue.

(5) Where a person brings any proceedings against another ('the contributor') for a contribution in respect of any liability to a company arising under any of sections 26 to 30 and 32 and it appears to the court that the contributor is liable to make such a contribution, the court may, if and to the extent that it appears to the court, having regard to the respective culpability in respect of the liability to the company of the contributor and the person bringing the proceedings, that it is just and equitable to do so—

(a) exempt the contributor in whole or in part from his liability to make such a contribution; or

(b) order the contributor to make a larger contribution than, but for this subsection, he would be liable to make.

(6) Where a person is liable to a company by virtue of section 32(7)(a), the court may, on an application under this subsection, exempt that person in whole or in part from that liability if and to the extent that it appears to the court just and equitable to do so having regard to any benefit accruing to the company by virtue of anything done by that person towards the carrying out of the agreement mentioned in that subsection.

35 Special provisions as to issue of shares to subscribers

Any shares taken by a subscriber to the memorandum of a public limited company in pursuance of an undertaking of his in the memorandum and any premium on the shares shall be paid up in cash.

36 Contravention of sections 26 to 35

(1) Where a company contravenes any of the provisions of sections 26 to 30, 32 and 35, the company and any officer of the company who is in default shall be guilty of an offence.

(2) Subject to section 34, an undertaking given by any person in or in connection with payment for shares in a company to do work or perform services or to do any other thing shall, if it is enforceable by the company apart from this Act, be so enforceable notwithstanding that there has been a contravention in relation thereto of sections 26, 29 or 30 and where such an undertaking is given in contravention of section 32 in respect of the allotment of any shares it shall be so enforceable notwithstanding that contravention.

37 Application of sections 26 to 36 in special cases

(1) Subject to subsection (2), sections 26, 28 to 31 and 34 to 36, shall apply—

(a) to a company which has passed and not revoked a special resolution to be re-registered under section 9 or section 11;

(b) to a company whose directors have passed and not revoked a resolution to be re-registered under section 12; and

(c) to a joint stock company (within the meaning of section 329 of the Principal Act) which has passed and not revoked a resolution that the company be a public limited company;

as those sections apply to a public limited company.

(2) Section 26 and sections 28 to 31, shall not apply to the allotment of shares by a company, other than a public limited company registered as such on its original incorporation, where the contract for their allotment was entered into—

(a) except in a case falling within paragraph (b), before the end of the general transitional period;

(b) in the case of a company re-registered or registered as a public limited company in pursuance of a resolution of any description mentioned in subsection (1) that is passed before the end of that period, before the date on which that resolution is passed.

Class rights

38 Variation of rights attached to special classes of shares

(1) This section shall have effect with respect to the variation of the rights attached to any class of shares in a company whose share capital is divided into shares of different classes.

(2) Where the rights are attached to a class of shares in the company otherwise than by the memorandum, and the articles of the company do not contain provisions with respect to the variation of the rights, those rights may be varied if, but only if—

(a) the holders of three-quarters in nominal value of the issued shares of that class consent in writing to the variation; or

(b) a special resolution passed at a separate general meeting of the holders of that class sanctions the variation;

and any requirement (howsoever imposed) in relation to the variation of those rights is complied with to the extent that it is not comprised in paragraphs (a) and (b).

(3) Where—

(a) the rights are attached to a class of shares in the company by the memorandum or otherwise;

(b) the memorandum or articles contain provision for the variation of those rights; and

(c) the variation of those rights is connected with the giving, variation, revocation or renewal of an authority for the purposes of section 20 or with a reduction of the company's share capital under section 72 of the Principal Act,

those rights shall not be varied unless—

(i) the condition mentioned in subsection (2)(a) or (b) is satisfied; and

(ii) any requirement of the memorandum or articles in relation to the variation of rights of that class is complied with to the extent that it is not comprised in the condition in subparagraph (i).

(4) Where the rights are attached to a class of shares in the company by the memorandum or otherwise and—

(a) where they are so attached by the memorandum, the articles contain provision with respect to their variation which had been included in the articles at the time of the company's original incorporation; or

(b) where they are so attached otherwise, the articles contain such provision (whenever first so included);

and in either case the variation is not connected as mentioned in subsection (3)(c), those rights may only be varied in accordance with that provision of the articles.

(5) Where the rights are attached to a class of shares in the company by the memorandum and the memorandum and articles do not contain provision with respect to the variation of the rights, those rights may be varied if all the members of the company agree to the variation.

(6) The provision of sections 133 and 134 of the Principal Act and the provisions of the articles relating to general meetings shall, so far as applicable, apply in relation to any meeting of shareholders required by this section or otherwise to take place in connection with the variation of the rights attached to a class of shares, and shall so apply with the necessary modifications and subject to the following provisions, namely—

(a) the necessary quorum at any such meeting other than an adjourned meeting shall be two persons holding or representing by proxy at least one-third in nominal value of the issued shares of the class in question and at an adjourned meeting one person holding shares of the class in question or his proxy;

(b) any holder of shares of the class in question present in person or by proxy may demand a poll.

(7) Any alteration of a provision contained in the articles of a company for the variation of the rights attached to a class of shares or the insertion of any such provision into the company's articles shall itself be treated as a variation of those rights.

(8) Section 78 of the Principal Act shall apply in relation to subsection (2) as it applies in relation to a provision of the memorandum or articles of a company to the like effect.

(9) In this section and, except where the context otherwise requires, in any provision for the variation of the rights attached to a class of shares contained in the company's memorandum or articles references to the variation of those rights shall include references to their abrogation.

(10) Nothing in subsections (2) to (5) shall be construed as derogating from the powers of the court under section 15 or any of the following sections of the Principal Act, that is to say, sections 10, 201, 203 and 205.

(11) This section shall not apply in relation to any variation made by a company, other than a public limited company registered as such on its original incorporation, before the date on which the earlier of the following events occurs, that is to say, the re-registration or registration of the company as a public limited company and the end of the general transitional period.

39 Registration of particulars of special rights

(1) Where a company allots shares with rights which are not stated in its memorandum or articles or in any resolution or agreement to which section 143 of the Principal Act

applies, the company shall, unless the shares are in all respects uniform with shares previously allotted, deliver to the registrar of companies within one month from allotting the shares a statement in the prescribed form containing particulars of those rights.

(2) Shares allotted with such rights shall not be treated for the purposes of subsection (1) as different from shares previously allotted by reason only of the fact that the former do not carry the same rights to dividends as the latter during the twelve months immediately following the former's allotment.

(3) Where the rights attached to any shares of a company are varied otherwise than by an amendment of the company's memorandum or articles or by resolution or agreement to which the said section 143 applies, the company shall within one month from the date on which the variation is made deliver to the registrar of companies a statement in the prescribed form containing particulars of the variation.

(4) Where a company (otherwise than by any such amendment, resolution or agreement as is mentioned in subsection (3)) assigns a name or other designation, or a new name or other designation, to any class of its shares it shall within one month from doing so deliver to the registrar of companies a notice in the prescribed form giving particulars thereof.

(5) If a company fails to comply with this section, the company and every officer of the company who is in default shall be guilty of an offence and shall be liable on summary conviction to a [class C fine][a] together with, in the case of a continuing offence, a [class E fine][b] for every day on which the offence continues but not exceeding [€1,904.61][c] in total.

Amendments

a £250 increased to £1,500 by CA 1990, s 240(7) as inserted by CLEA 2001, s 104(c), and converted to €1,904.61 by Council Regulations (EC) No 1103/97, No 974/98 and No 2866/98 and the Economic and Monetary Union Act 1998, s 6; the above being implicitly substituted, by Fines Act 2010, s 6, for a fine not exceeding the aforesaid amount. A class C fine currently means a fine not exceeding €2,500.

b £25 converted to €31.74 by Council Regulations (EC) No 1103/97, No 974/98 and No 2866/98 and the Economic and Monetary Union Act 1998, s 6; as implicitly substituted, by Fines Act 2010, s 8, for a fine not exceeding the aforesaid amount. A class E fine currently means a fine not exceeding €500.

c £500 increased to £1,500 by CA 1990, s 240(7) as inserted by CLEA 2001, s 104(c) and converted to €1,904.61 by Council Regulations (EC) No 1103/97, No 974/98 and No 2866/98 and the Economic and Monetary Union Act 1998, s 6. Note that the effect of the retention of the €1,904.61 limit is to significantly restrict the amount of the fines that might otherwise have been imposed, and in particular to limit the deterrent effect of the daily default fine.

Maintenance of capital

40 Obligation to convene extraordinary general meeting in event of serious loss of capital

(1) Subject to subsection (4), where the net assets of a company are half or less of the amount of the company's called-up share capital, the directors of the company shall, not later than 28 days from the earliest day on which that fact is known to a director of the

company, duly convene an extraordinary general meeting of the company for a date not later than 56 days from that day for the purpose of considering whether any, and if so what, measures should be taken to deal with the situation.

(2) If there is a failure to convene an extraordinary general meeting of a company as required by subsection (1), each of the directors of the company who—

(a) knowingly and wilfully authorises or permits that failure; or

(b) after the expiry of the period during which that meeting should have been convened, knowingly and wilfully authorises or permits that failure to continue,

shall be guilty of an offence.

(3) Nothing in this section shall be taken as authorising the consideration, at a meeting convened in pursuance of subsection (1), of any matter which could not have been considered at that meeting apart from this section.

(4) This section shall not apply where the day mentioned in subsection (1) is before the appointed day.

41 Restriction on company acquiring its own shares

(1) Subject to the following provisions of this section, no company limited by shares or limited by guarantee and having a share capital shall acquire its own shares (whether by purchase, subscription or otherwise).

(2) A company limited by shares may acquire any of its own fully paid shares otherwise than for valuable consideration.

(3) If a company purports to act in contravention of this section the company and every officer of the company who is in default shall be guilty of an offence and the purported acquisition shall be void.

(4) Subsection (1) shall not apply in relation to—

[(a) the redemption of preference shares in pursuance of section 65 of the Principal Act or the redemption or purchase of shares in pursuance of Part XI of the Companies Act, 1990];[a]

(b) the acquisition of any shares in a reduction of capital duly made;

(c) the purchase of any shares in pursuance of an order of the court under section 15 or under section 10 or section 205 of the Principal Act; or

(d) the forfeiture of any shares, or the acceptance of any shares surrendered in lieu, in pursuance of the articles for failure to pay any sum payable in respect of those shares.

Amendments

a C(A)A 1983, s 41(a) substituted by CA 1990, s 232.

---

42 Acquisition of shares in a company by company's nominee

(1) Subject to subsections (5) and (6), where shares are issued to a nominee of a company referred to in section 41(1) or are acquired by a nominee of such a company from a third party as partly paid up, then, for all purposes the shares shall be treated as

held by the nominee on his own account and the company shall be regarded as having no beneficial interest in them.

(2) Subject to subsection (6), if a person is called on to pay any amount for the purpose of paying up, or paying any premium on, any shares in any such company which were issued to him, or which he otherwise acquired, as the nominee of the company and he fails to pay that amount within 21 days from being called on to do so, then—

(a) if the shares were issued to him as a subscriber to the memorandum by virtue of an undertaking of his in the memorandum, the other subscribers to the memorandum; or

(b) if the shares were otherwise issued to or acquired by him, the directors of the company at the time of the issue or acquisition,

shall be jointly and severally liable with him to pay that amount.

(3) If in proceedings for the recovery of any such amount from any such subscriber or director under this section it appears to the court that he is or may be liable to pay that amount, but that he has acted honestly and reasonably and that, having regard to all the circumstances of the case, he ought fairly to be excused from liability, the court may relieve him, either wholly or partly, from his liability on such terms as the court thinks fit.

(4) Where any such subscriber or director has reason to apprehend that a claim will or might be made for the recovery of any such amount from him, he may apply to the court for relief and on the application the court shall have the same power to relieve him as it would have had in proceedings for the recovery of that amount.

(5) Subsection (1) shall not apply to shares acquired otherwise than by subscription by a nominee of a public limited company in a case falling within section 43(1)(d).

(6) Subsections (1) and (2) shall not apply—

(a) to shares acquired by a nominee of a company where the company has no beneficial interest in those shares (disregarding any right which the company itself may have as trustee, whether as personal representative or otherwise, to recover its expenses or be remunerated out of the trust property); or

(b) to shares issued in consequence of an application made before the appointed day or transferred in pursuance of an agreement to acquire them made before that day.

43 Treatment of shares held by or on behalf of a public limited company

(1) Subject to subsections (12) and (15), this section applies to a public limited company—

(a) where shares in the company are forfeited, or are surrendered to the company in lieu, in pursuance of the articles for failure to pay any sum payable in respect of those shares;

(b) where shares in the company are acquired by the company otherwise that by any of the methods mentioned in section 41(4) and the company has a beneficial interest in those shares;

(c) where the nominee of the company acquires shares in the company from a third person without financial assistance being given directly or indirectly by the company and the company has a beneficial interest in those shares; or

(d) where any person acquires shares in the company with financial assistance given to him directly or indirectly by the company for the purpose of or in connection with the acquisition and the company has a beneficial interest in those shares.

(2) In determining for the purposes of subsection (1)(b) and (c) whether a company has a beneficial interest in any shares, there shall be disregarded, in any case where the company is a trustee (whether as personal representative or otherwise), any right of the company (as trustee) to recover its expenses or be remunerated out of the trust property.

(3) Unless the shares or any interest of the company in them are previously disposed of, the company must not later than the end of the relevant period from their forfeiture or surrender or, in a case to which subsection (1)(b), (c) or (d) applies, their acquisition—

(a) cancel them and reduce the amount of the share capital by the nominal value of the shares; and

(b) where the effect of cancelling the shares will be that the nominal value of the company's allotted share capital is brought below the authorised minimum, apply for re-registration as another form of company, stating the effect of the cancellation,

and the directors may take such steps as are requisite to enable the company to carry out its obligations under this subsection without complying with sections 72 and 73 of the Principal Act, including passing a resolution in accordance with subsection (5).

(4) The company and, in a case falling within subsection (1)(c) or (d), the company's nominee or, as the case may be, the other shareholder must not exercise any voting rights in respect of the shares and any purported exercise of those rights shall be void.

(5) The resolution authorised by subsection (3) may alter the company's memorandum so that it no longer states that the company is to be a public limited company and may make such other alterations in the memorandum and articles as are requisite in the circumstances.

(6) The application for re-registration required by subsection (3)(b) must be in the prescribed form and signed by a director or secretary of the company and must be delivered to the registrar together with a printed copy of the memorandum and articles of the company as altered by the resolution.

(7) If a public limited company required to apply to be re-registered as another form of company under this section fails to do so before the end of the relevant period, section 21 shall apply to it as if it were a private company such as is mentioned in that section, but, except as aforesaid, the company shall continue to be treated for the purposes of the Companies Acts as a public limited company until it is re-registered as another form of company.

(8) If a company when required to do so by subsection (3) fails to cancel any shares in accordance with paragraph (a) of that subsection or to make an application for re-registration in accordance with paragraph (b) of that subsection, the company and every officer of the company who is in default shall be guilty of an offence and shall be liable on summary conviction to a [class C fine][a] together with, in the case of a continuing offence, a [class E fine][b] for every day on which the offence continues, but not exceeding [€1,904.61][c] in total.

(9) If the registrar is satisfied that a company may be re-registered in accordance with this section he shall—

(a) retain the application and other documents delivered to him under subsection (6); and

(b) issue the company with an appropriate certificate of incorporation.

(10) Upon the issue of a certificate of incorporation under subsection (9)—

(a) the company shall by virtue of the issue of that certificate become the form of company stated in the certificate; and

(b) the alterations in the memorandum and articles set out in the resolution shall take effect accordingly.

(11) A certificate of incorporation issued to a company under subsection (9) shall be conclusive evidence—

(a) that the requirements of this section in respect of re-registration and of matters precedent and incidental thereto have been complied with; and

(b) that the company is the form of company stated in the certificate.

(12) Where, after shares in a company—

(a) are forfeited in pursuance of the articles of the company or are surrendered to the company in lieu of forfeiture or are otherwise acquired by the company;

(b) are acquired by a nominee of the company in the circumstances mentioned in subsection (1)(c); or

(c) are acquired by any person in the circumstances mentioned in subsection (1)(d),

the company is re-registered as a public limited company, the foregoing provisions of this section shall apply to the company as if it had been a public limited company at the time of the forfeiture, surrender or acquisition and as if for any reference to the relevant period from the forfeiture, surrender or acquisition there were substituted a reference to the relevant period from the re-registration of the company as a public limited company.

(13) [...][d]

(14) In this section 'relevant period', in relation to any shares, means—

(a) in the case of shares forfeited or surrendered to the company in lieu of forfeiture or acquired as mentioned in subsection (1)(b) or (c), three years;

(b) in the case of shares acquired as mentioned in subsection (1)(d), one year.

(15) Notwithstanding anything in section 12(2), a reference in this section to a public limited company does not include a reference to an old public limited company.

Amendments

a £250 increased to £1,500 by CA 1990, s 240(7) as inserted by CLEA 2001, s 104(c), and converted to €1,904.61 by Council Regulations (EC) No 1103/97, No 974/98 and No 2866/98 and the Economic and Monetary Union Act 1998, s 6; the above being implicitly substituted, by Fines Act 2010, s 6, for a fine not exceeding the aforesaid amount. A class C fine currently means a fine not exceeding €2,500.

b £25 converted to €31.74 by Council Regulations (EC) No 1103/97, No 974/98 and No 2866/98 and the Economic and Monetary Union Act 1998, s 6; as implicitly substituted, by Fines

Act 2010, s 8, for a fine not exceeding the aforesaid amount. A class E fine currently means a fine not exceeding €500.

c £500 converted to €1,904.61 by Council Regulations (EC) No 1103/97, No 974/98 and No 2866/98 and the Economic and Monetary Union Act 1998, s 6. Note that the effect of the retention of the €1,904.61 limit is to significantly restrict the amount of the fines that might otherwise have been imposed, and in particular to limit the deterrent effect of the daily default fine.

d C(A)A 1983, s 43(13) repealed by CA 1990, s 232.

[43A Accounting for own shares

Where a company or a nominee of a company holds shares in the company or an interest in such shares, such shares shall not be shown in the balance sheet of the company as an asset, but—

(a) the deduction of the cost of the acquired shares from the profits available for distribution, and

(b) the nominal value of such shares,

shall be disclosed in the notes to the accounts and the profits available for distribution shall accordingly be restricted by the amount of such deduction.][a]

Amendments

a C(A)A 1983, s 43A inserted by CA 1990, s 232.

---

44 Charges taken by public limited companies on own shares

(1) A lien or other charge of a public limited company on its own shares (whether taken expressly or otherwise), except a charge permitted by subsection (2), is void.

(2) The following are permitted charges, that is to say—

(a) in the case of every description of company, a charge on its own shares (not being fully paid) for any amount payable in respect of the shares;

(b) in the case of a public limited company whose ordinary business includes the lending of money or consists of the provision of credit or the bailment or hiring of goods under a hire-purchase agreement, or both, a charge of the company on its own shares (whether fully paid or not) which arises in connection with a transaction entered into by the company in the ordinary course of its business;

(c) in the case of a company (other than a company in relation to which paragraph (d) applies) which is re-registered or is registered under section 18 as a public limited company, a charge on its own shares which was in existence immediately before its application for re-registration or, as the case may be, registration;

(d) in the case of any company which after the end of the re-registration period remains or remained an old public limited company and did not before the end of that period apply to be re-registered under section 12 as a public limited company, any charge on its own shares which was in existence immediately before the end of that period.

PART IV
RESTRICTIONS ON DISTRIBUTION OF PROFITS AND ASSETS

45 Profits available for distribution

(1) A company shall not make a distribution (as defined by section 51) except out of profits available for the purpose.

(2) For the purposes of this Part, but subject to section 47(1), a company's profits available for distribution are its accumulated, realised profits, so far as not previously utilised by distribution or capitalisation, less its accumulated, realised losses, so far as not previously written off in a reduction or reorganisation of capital duly made.

(3) A company shall not apply an unrealised profit in paying up debentures or any amounts unpaid on any of its issued shares.

[(4)For the purposes of subsections (2) and (3)—

(a) where the company prepares Companies Act individual accounts, any provision (within the meaning of the Sixth Schedule to the Principal Act or paragraph 70 of the Schedule to the Companies (Amendment) Act 1986), other than one in respect of any diminution in value of a fixed asset appearing on a revaluation of all the fixed assets or of all the fixed assets other than goodwill of the company, shall be treated as a realised loss, and

(b) where the company prepares IFRS individual accounts, a provision of any kind shall be treated as a realized loss.][a]

(5) Subject to section 49(8), any consideration by the directors of a company of the value at any particular time of any fixed asset of the company shall be treated as a revaluation of that asset for the purposes of determining whether any such revaluation of the company's fixed assets as is required for the purposes of the exception from subsection (4) has taken place at that time; but where any such assets which have not actually been revalued are treated as revalued for those purposes by virtue of this subsection that exception shall only apply if the directors are satisfied that their aggregate value at the time in question is not less than the aggregate amount at which they are for the time being stated in the company's accounts.

(6) If, on the revaluation of a fixed asset, an unrealised profit is shown to have been made and, on or after the revaluation, a sum is written off or retained for depreciation of that asset over a period, then, an amount equal to the amount by which that sum exceeds the sum which would have been so written off or retained for depreciation of that asset over that period, if that profit had not been made, shall be treated for the purposes of subsections (2) and (3) as a realised profit made over that period.

(7) Where there is no record of the original cost of an asset of a company (whether acquired before, on or after the appointed day) or any such record cannot be obtained without unreasonable expense or delay, then, for the purposes of determining whether the company has made a profit or loss in respect of that asset, the cost of the asset shall be taken to be the value ascribed to it in the earliest available record of its value made on or after its acquisition by the company.

(8) Where the directors of a company are, after making all reasonable enquiries, unable to determine whether a particular profit made before the appointed day is realised or unrealised they may treat the profit as realised, and where after making such enquiries

they are unable to determine whether a particular loss so made is realised or unrealised, they may treat the loss as unrealised.

(9) In this section 'fixed asset' includes any other asset which is not a current asset.

Amendments

a Sub-s (4) substituted by EC(IFRSMA)R 2005, reg 9, Part 2 of Schedule 1, Item No 3.

[45A Development costs shown as an asset of a company to be set off against company's distributable profits

(1) Subject to the following provisions of this section, where development costs are shown as an asset in a company's accounts, any amount shown in respect of those costs shall be treated—

(a) for the purposes of section 45, as a realised loss and

(b) for the purposes of section 47, as a realised revenue loss.

(2) Subsection (1) shall not apply to any part of the amount aforesaid representing an unrealised profit made on revaluation of those costs.

(3) Subsection (1) shall not apply if—

(a) there are special circumstances justifying the directors of the company concerned in deciding that the amount mentioned in respect thereof in the company's accounts shall not be treated as required by that subsection, and

[(b) it is stated—

(i) where the company prepares Companies Act individual accounts, in the note to the accounts required by paragraph 8(2) of the Schedule to the Companies (Amendment) Act 1986, or

(ii) where the company prepares IFRS individual accounts, in any note to the accounts, that that amount is not to be so treated, and the note explains the circumstances relied upon to justify the decision of the directors to that effect']^{b}.]^{a}

Amendments

a Section 45A inserted by C(A)A 1986, s 20.

b Sub-s (3)(b) substituted by EC(IFRSMA)R 2005, reg 9, Part 2 of Schedule 1, Item No 4.

46 Restriction on distribution of assets

(1) Subject to section 47, a public limited company may only make a distribution at any time—

(a) if at that time the amount of its net assets is not less than the aggregate of the company's called-up share capital and its undistributable reserves; and

(b) if, and to the extent that, the distribution does not reduce the amount of those assets to less than that aggregate.

(2) For the purposes of this section the undistributable reserves of a public limited company are—

(a) the share premium account;

(b) the capital redemption reserve fund;

(c) the amount by which the company's accumulated, unrealised profits, so far as not previously utilised by any capitalisation, exceed its accumulated, unrealised losses, so far as not previously written off in a reduction or reorganisation of capital duly made; and

(d) any other reserve which the company is prohibited from distributing by any enactment, other than one contained in this Part, or by its memorandum or articles.

(3) Subsections (4) to (8) of section 45, shall apply for the purposes of this section as they apply for the purposes of that section.

(4) A public limited company shall not include any uncalled share capital as an asset in any account relevant for the purposes of this section.

47 Other distributions of investment companies

(1) Subject to the following provisions of this section, an investment company may also make a distribution at any time out of its accumulated, realised revenue profits, so far as not previously utilised by distribution or capitalisation, less its accumulated revenue losses (whether realised or unrealised), so far as not previously written off in a reduction or reorganisation of capital duly made—

(a) if at that time the amount of its assets is at least equal to one and a half times the aggregate of its liabilities [to creditors][a]; and

(b) if, and to the extent that, the distribution does not reduce that amount to less than one and a half times that aggregate.

[(2) In subsection (1) ['liabilities to creditors'][b] includes—

(a) any provision [for liabilities to creditors][c] (within the meaning of the Sixth Schedule to the Principal Act) that is made in Companies Act individual accounts except to the extent that that provision is taken into account in calculating the value of any asset to the company,

(b) any provision [for liabilities to creditors][c] within the meaning of paragraph 70 of the Schedule to the Companies (Amendment) Act 1986 that is made in Companies Act individual accounts, and

(c) any provision [for liabilities to creditors][c] that is made in IFRS individual accounts, and subsection (4) of section 46 shall apply for those purposes as it applies for the purposes of that section.][d]

(3) In this Part 'investment company' means a public limited company which has given notice in writing (which has not been revoked) to the registrar of its intention to carry on business as an investment company (the 'requisite notice') and has since the date of that notice complied with the requirements set out in subsection (4).

(4) The requirements referred to in subsection (3) are—

(a) that the business of the company consists of investing its funds mainly in securities, with the aim of spreading investment risk and giving members of the company the benefit of the results of the management of its funds;

(b) that none of the company's holdings in companies other than companies which are for the time being investment companies represents more than 15 per cent. by value of the investing company's investment;

(c) that distribution of the company's capital profits is prohibited by its memorandum or articles of association;

(d) that the company has not retained, otherwise than in compliance with this Part in respect of any financial year more than 15 per cent. of the income it derives from securities.

(5) An investment company may not make a distribution by virtue of subsection (1) unless its shares are listed on a recognised stock exchange and, during the period beginning with the first day of the financial year immediately preceding the financial year in which the proposed distribution is to be made or, where the distribution is proposed to be made during the company's first financial year, the first day of that financial year and ending with the date of the distribution (whether or not any part of those financial years falls before the appointed day), it has not—

(a) distributed any of its capital profits; or

(b) applied any unrealised profits or any capital profits (realised or unrealised) in paying up debentures or any amounts unpaid on any of its issued shares.

(6) An investment company may not make a distribution by virtue of subsection (1) unless the company gave the requisite notice—

(a) before the beginning of the appropriate period referred to in subsection (5); or

(b) where that period began before the appointed day, as soon as may be reasonably practicable after the appointed day;
or

(c) where the company was incorporated on or after the appointed day, as soon as may be reasonably practicable after the date of its incorporation.

(7) A notice by a company to the registrar under subsection (3) may be revoked at any time by the company on giving notice to the registrar that it no longer wishes to be an investment company within the meaning of this section and, on giving such notice, the company shall cease to be such an investment company.

(8) In determining capital and revenue profits and losses for the purposes of this section an asset which is not a fixed asset or a current asset shall be treated as a fixed asset.

(9) An investment company shall include the expression 'investment company' on its letters and order forms.

(10) Where a company fails to comply with subsection (9), the company and every officer of the company who is in default shall be guilty of an offence and shall be liable on summary conviction to a [class C fine].[e]

(11) Proceedings in relation to an offence under this section may be brought and prosecuted by the registrar of companies.

(12) For the purposes of paragraph (b) of subsection (4)—

(a) 'holding' means the shares or securities (whether of one class or more than one class) held in any one company;

(b) holdings in companies which are members of a group (whether or not including the investing company) and are not excluded from the said paragraph (b) shall be treated as holdings in a single company;

(c) where the investing company is a member of a group, money owed to it by another member of the group shall be treated as a security of the latter held by the investing company and accordingly as, or as part of, the holding of the investing company in the company owing the money,

and for the purposes of this subsection 'group' means a company and all companies which are its subsidiaries within the meaning of section 155 of the Principal Act.

Amendments

a Words inserted by SI 840/2005, reg 8(a).

b Words substituted by SI 840/2005, reg 8(b)(i).

c Words inserted by SI 840/2005, reg 8(b)(ii).

d Sub-s (2) was substituted by EC(IFRSMA)R 2005, reg 9, Part 2 of Schedule 1, Item No 5.

e '£250' increased to £1,500 by CA 1990, s 240(7) as inserted by CLEA 2001, s 104(c), and converted to €1,904.61 by Council Regulations (EC) No 1103/97, No 974/98 and No 2866/98 and the Economic and Monetary Union Act 1998, s 6; the above being implicitly substituted, by Fines Act 2010, s 6, for a fine not exceeding the aforesaid amount. A class C fine currently means a fine not exceeding €2,500.

---

48 Realised profits of assurance companies

(1) In the case of an assurance company carrying on life assurance business, or industrial assurance business or both, any amount properly transferred to the profit and loss account of the company from a surplus in the fund or funds maintained by it in respect of that business and any deficit in that fund or those funds shall be respectively treated for the purposes of this Part as a realised profit and a realised loss, and, subject to the foregoing, any profit or loss arising on the fund or funds maintained by it in respect of that business shall be left out of account for those purposes.

(2) In subsection (1)—

(a) the reference to a surplus in any fund or funds of an assurance company is a reference to an excess of the assets representing that fund or those funds over the liabilities of the company attributable to its life assurance or industrial assurance business, as shown by an actuarial investigation; and

(b) the reference to a deficit in any such fund or funds is a reference to the excess of those liabilities over those assets, as so shown.

(3) In this section—

'actuarial investigation' means an investigation to which section 5 of the Assurance Companies Act, 1909 applies;

'life assurance business' and 'industrial assurance business' have the same meanings as in section 3 of the Insurance Act, 1936.

49 The relevant accounts

(1) Subject to the following provisions of this section, the question whether a distribution may be made by a company without contravening section 45, 46 or 47 (the relevant section) and the amount of any distribution which may be so made shall be determined by reference to the relevant items as stated in the relevant accounts, and the relevant section shall be treated as contravened in the case of a distribution unless the requirements of this section about those accounts are complied with in the case of that distribution.

(2) The relevant accounts for any company in the case of any particular distribution are—

- (a) except in a case falling within paragraph (b) or (c), the last annual accounts that is to say, the accounts prepared in accordance with the requirements of the Principal Act [(and, where applicable, in accordance with the requirements of Article 4 of the IAS Regulation)][a] which were laid in respect of the last preceding financial year in respect of which accounts so prepared were laid;
- (b) if that distribution would be found to contravene the relevant section if reference were made only to the last annual accounts, such accounts (interim accounts) as are necessary to enable a reasonable judgment to be made as to the amounts of any of the relevant items;
- (c) if that distribution is proposed to be declared during the company's first financial year or before any accounts are laid in respect of that financial year, such accounts (initial accounts) as are necessary as aforesaid.

(3) The following requirements apply where the last annual accounts of a company constitute the only relevant accounts in the case of any distribution, that is to say—

- (a) those accounts must have been properly prepared or have been so prepared subject only to matters which are not material for the purpose of determining, by reference to the relevant items as stated in those accounts, whether that distribution would be in contravention of the relevant section;
- (b) the auditors of the company must have made a report under section 163 of the Principal Act in respect of those accounts;
- (c) if, by virtue of anything referred to in that report, the report is not an unqualified report, the auditors must also have stated in writing (either at the time the report was made or subsequently) whether, in their opinion, that thing is material for the purpose of determining, by reference to the relevant items as stated in those accounts, whether that distribution would be in contravention of the relevant section; and
- (d) a copy of any such statement must have been laid before the company in general meeting.

(4) A statement under subsection (3)(c) suffices for the purposes of a particular distribution not only if it relates to a distribution which has been proposed but also if it relates to distributions of any description which include that particular distribution, notwithstanding that at the time of the statement it has not been proposed.

(5) The following requirements apply to interim accounts prepared for a proposed distribution by a public limited company, that is to say—

(a) the accounts must have been properly prepared or have been so prepared subject only to matters which are not material for the purpose of determining, by reference to the relevant items as stated in those accounts, whether that distribution would be in contravention of the relevant section;

(b) a copy of those accounts must have been delivered to the registrar of companies;

(c) if the accounts are in a language other than the English or Irish language, a translation into English or Irish of the accounts which has been certified in the prescribed manner to be a correct translation must also have been delivered to the registrar.

(6) The following requirements apply to initial accounts prepared for a proposed distribution by a public limited company, that is to say—

(a) those accounts must have been properly prepared or have been so prepared subject only to matters which are not material for the purpose of determining, by reference to the relevant items as stated in those accounts, whether that distribution would be in contravention of the relevant section;

(b) the auditors of the company must have made a report stating whether in their opinion the accounts have been properly prepared;

(c) if, by virtue of anything referred to in that report, the report is not an unqualified report, the auditors must also have stated writing whether, in their opinion, that thing is material for the purpose of determining, by reference to the relevant items as stated in those accounts, whether that distribution would be in contravention of the relevant section;

(d) a copy of those accounts, of the report made under paragraph (b) and of any such statement must have been delivered to the registrar of companies; and

(e) if the accounts are, or that report or statement is, in a language other than the English or Irish language, a translation into English or Irish of the accounts, the report or statement, as the case may be, which has been certified in the prescribed manner to be a correct translation, must also have been delivered to the registrar.

(7) For the purpose of determining by reference to particular accounts whether a proposed distribution may be made by a company, this section shall have effect, in any case where one or more distributions have already been made in pursuance of determinations made by reference to those same accounts, as if the amount of the proposed distribution was increased by the amount of the distributions so made.

(8) Where subsection (3)(a), (5)(a) or (6)(a) applies to the relevant accounts, section 45(5) shall not apply for the purposes of determining whether any revaluation of the company's fixed assets affecting the amount of the relevant items as stated in those accounts has taken place, unless it is stated in a note to those accounts—

(a) that the directors have considered the value at any time of any fixed assets of the company without actually revaluing those assets;

(b) that there are satisfied that the aggregate value of those assets at the time in question is or was not less than the aggregate amount at which they are or were for the time being stated in the company's accounts; and

(c) that the relevant items affected are accordingly stated in the relevant accounts on the basis that a revaluation of the company's fixed assets which by virtue of section 45(5) included the assets in question took place at that time.

(9) In this section—

'properly prepared' means, in relation to any accounts of a company, that the following conditions are satisfied in relation to those accounts, that is to say—

[(a) in the case of annual individual accounts, that they have been properly prepared in accordance with the Principal Act,

(b) in the case of interim or initial accounts that they comply with the requirements of section 148 and either section 149 or 149A (inserted by the European Communities (International Financial Reporting Standards and Miscellaneous Amendments) Regulations 2005) of the Principal Act, where applicable, and any balance sheet comprised in those accounts has been signed in accordance with section 156 of the Principal Act; and][b]

(c) in either case, without prejudice to the foregoing, that, except where the company is entitled to avail itself, and has availed itself, of any of the provisions of Part III of the Sixth Schedule to the Principal Act—

(i) so much of the accounts as consists of a balance sheet gives a true and fair view of the state of the company's affairs as at the balance sheet date; and

(ii) so much of those accounts as consists of a profit and loss account gives a true and fair view of the company's profit or loss for the period in respect of which the accounts were prepared;

['relevant item' means the following amounts as dealt with in the company's relevant accounts—

(a) profits, losses, assets and liabilities,

(b) where the company prepares Companies Act individual accounts, any provisions mentioned in the Companies (Amendment) Act 1986 or any provisions mentioned in the Sixth Schedule to the Principal Act (depreciation, diminution in value of assets, retention to meet liabilities, etc,),

(c) where the company prepares IFRS individual accounts, provisions of any kind, and

(d) share capital and reserves;][c]

'reserves' includes undistributable reserves within the meaning of section 46(2);

'unqualified report' in relation to any accounts of a company, means a report, without qualification, to the effect that in the opinion of the person making the report the accounts have been properly prepared; and for the purposes of this section, accounts are laid if section 148 of the Principal Act has been complied with in relation to those accounts.

(10) For the purpose of paragraph (b) of the definition of 'properly prepared' in subsection (9), [section 148 and either section 149 or 149A of the Principal Act, where applicable, of,][d] and the Sixth Schedule to the Principal Act shall be deemed to have effect in relation to interim and initial accounts with such modifications as are necessary

by reason of the fact that the accounts are prepared otherwise than in respect of a financial year.

Amendments

a Words inserted by EC(IFRSMA)R 2005 (SI 116/2005), reg 9, Part 2 of Schedule 1, Item No 6.

b Sub-s (9)(a) and (b) in definition of 'properly prepared', substituted by EC(IFRSMA)R 2005 (SI 116/2005), reg 9, Part 2 of Schedule 1, Item No 6.

c Definition of 'relevant item' substituted by EC(IFRSMA)R 2005 (SI 116/2005), reg 9, Part 2 of Schedule 1, Item No 6.

d Words inserted by EC(IFRSMA)R 2005 (SI 116/2005), reg 9, Part 2 of Schedule 1, Item No 6.

---

50 Consequences of making unlawful distribution

(1) Where a distribution, or part of one, made by a company to one of its members is made in contravention of the provisions of this Part and, at the time of the distribution, he knows or has reasonable grounds for believing that it is so made, he shall be liable to repay it or that part, as the case may be, to the company or (in the case of a distribution made otherwise than in cash) to pay the company a sum equal to the value of the distribution or part at that time.

(2) The provisions of this section are without prejudice to any obligation imposed apart from this section on a member of a company to repay a distribution unlawfully made to him.

51 Ancillary provisions

(1) Where immediately before the appointed day a company is authorised by any provision of its articles to apply its unrealised profits in paying up in full or in part unissued shares to be allotted to members of the company as fully or partly paid bonus shares, that provision shall, subject to any subsequent alteration of the articles, continue to be construed as authorising those profits to be so applied after the appointed day.

(2) In this Part 'distribution' means every description or distribution of a company's assets to members of the company, whether in cash or otherwise, except distributions made by way of—

(a) an issue of shares as fully or partly paid bonus shares;

[(b) the redemption of preference shares pursuant to section 65 of the Principal Act out of the proceeds of a fresh issue of shares made for the purposes of redemption;][a]

[(bb) the redemption of or purchase of shares pursuant to Part XI of the Companies Act, 1990 out of the proceeds of a fresh issue of shares made for the purposes of the redemption or purchase and the payment of any premium out of the company's share premium account on a redemption pursuant to section 220 in the said Part;][b]

(c) the reduction of share capital by extinguishing or reducing the liability of any of the members on any of its shares in respect of share capital not paid up or by paying off paid up share capital; and

(d) a distribution of assets to members of the company on its winding up.

(3) In this Part 'capitalisation', in relation to any profits of a company, means any of the following operations, whether carried out before, on or after the appointed day, that is to say, applying the profits in wholly or partly paying up unissued shares in the company to be allotted to members of the company as fully or partly paid bonus shares or transferring the profits to the capital redemption reserve fund.

(4) In this Part reference to profits and losses of any description are references respectively to profits and losses of that description made at any time, whether before, on, or after the appointed day and, except where the context otherwise requires, are references respectively to revenue and capital profits and revenue and capital losses.

(5) The provisions of this Part are without prejudice to any enactment or rule of law or any provision of a company's memorandum or articles restricting the sums out of which, or the cases in which, a distribution may be made.

(6) The provision of this Part shall not apply to any distribution made by a company, other than a public limited company registered as such on its original incorporation, before the date on which the earlier of the following events occurs, that is to say, the re-registration or registration of the company as a public limited company and the end of the general transitional period.

Amendments

a Section 51(2)(b) substituted by CA 1990, s 232(d).

b Section 51(2)(bb) substituted by CA 1990, s 232(e).

PART V
CHANGE OF STATUS OF CERTAIN COMPANIES

52 Re-registration of limited company as unlimited

(1) A company which, on the appointed day, is registered as limited or thereafter is so registered (otherwise than in pursuance of section 53) may be re-registered under the Principal Act as unlimited in pursuance of an application in that behalf complying with the requirements of subsection (2), made in the prescribed form and signed by a director or by the secretary of the company and delivered to the registrar together with the documents mentioned in subsection (3).

(2) The requirements referred to in subsection (1) are that the application must—

(a) set out alterations in the company's memorandum as—

(i) if it is to have a share capital, are requisite to bring it, both in substance and in form into conformity with the requirements imposed by the Principal Act with respect to the memorandum of a company to be formed under that Act as an unlimited company having a share capital; or

(ii) if it is not to have a share capital, are requisite in the circumstances; and

(b) if articles have been registered, set out such alterations therein and additions thereto as—

(i) if it is to have a share capital, are requisite to bring them, both in substance and in form, into conformity with the requirements imposed by the Principal Act with respect to the articles of a company to be formed under that Act as an unlimited company having a share capital; or

(ii) if it is not to have a share capital, are requisite in the circumstances; and

(c) if articles have not been registered—

(i) have annexed thereto, and request the registration of, printed articles, bearing the same stamp as if they were contained in a deed, being, if the company is to have a share capital, articles complying with the said requirements; or

(ii) if it is not to have a share capital, articles appropriate to the circumstances.

(3) The documents referred to in subsection (1) are—

(a) the prescribed form of assent to the company's being registered as unlimited subscribed by or on behalf of all members of the company.

(b) a statutory declaration made by the directors of the company that the persons by whom or on whose behalf the form of assent is subscribed constitute the whole membership of the company, and, if any of the members have not subscribed that form themselves, that the directors have taken all reasonable steps to satisfy themselves that each person who subscribed it on behalf of a member was lawfully empowered so to do;

(c) a printed copy of the memorandum incorporating the alterations therein set out in the application; and

(d) if articles have been registered, a printed copy thereof incorporating the alterations therein and additions thereto set out in the application.

(4) The registrar shall retain the application and other documents delivered to him under subsection (1), shall, if articles are annexed to the application, register them and shall issue to the company a certificate of incorporation appropriate to the status to be assumed by the company by virtue of this section, and upon the issue of the certificate—

(a) the status of the company shall, by virtue of the issue, be changed from limited to unlimited; and

(b) the alterations in the memorandum set out in the application and (if articles have been previously registered) any alterations and additions to the articles so set out shall, notwithstanding anything in the Principal Act, take effect as if duly made by resolution of the company and the provisions of the Principal Act shall apply to the memorandum and articles as altered or added to by virtue of this section accordingly.

(5) A certificate of incorporation issued by virtue of this section shall be conclusive evidence that the requirements of this section with respect to re-registration and of matters precedent and incidental thereto have been complied with, and that the company was authorised to be re-registered under the Principal Act in pursuance of this section and was duly so re-registered.

(6) Where a company is re-registered in pursuance of this section a person who, at the time when the application for it to be re-registered was delivered to the registrar, was a past member of the company and did not thereafter again become a member thereof shall not, in the event of the company's being wound up, be liable to contribute to the assets of the company more than he would have been liable to contribute thereto had it not been so re-registered.

(7) The re-registration of a limited company as an unlimited company pursuant to this Act shall not affect any rights or obligations of the company, or render defective any legal proceedings by or against the company, and any legal proceedings which might have been continued or commenced against it in its former status may be continued or commenced against it in its new status.

(8) For the purposes of this section—

(a) subscription to a form of assent by the legal personal representative of a deceased member of a company shall be deemed to be subscription by him;

(b) a trustee in bankruptcy of a person who is a member of a company shall, to the exclusion of that person, be deemed to be a member of the company.

53 Re-registration of unlimited company as limited

(1) A company which, on the appointed day, is registered as unlimited or thereafter is so registered (otherwise than by virtue of section 52) may be re-registered under the Principal Act as limited if a special resolution that it should be so re-registered (complying with the requirements of subsection (2)) is passed and an application in that behalf, made in the prescribed form and signed by a director or by the secretary of the company, is delivered to the registrar, together with the documents mentioned in subsection (3) not earlier than the day on which the copy of the resolution forwarded to him in pursuance of section 143 of the Principal Act is received by him.

(2) The said requirements are that the resolution must state whether the company is to be limited by shares or by guarantee and—

(a) if it is to be limited by shares, must state what the share capital is to be and provide for the making of such alterations in the memorandum as are necessary to bring it, both in substance and in form, into conformity with the requirements of the Companies Acts with respect to the memorandum of a company so limited, and such alterations in the articles as are requisite in the circumstances;

(b) if it is to be limited by guarantee, must provide for the making of such alterations in its memorandum and articles as are necessary to bring them, both in substance and in form, into conformity with the requirements of the Principal Act with respect to the memorandum and articles of a company so limited.

(3) The documents referred to in subsection (1) are a printed copy of the memorandum as altered in pursuance of the resolution and a printed copy of the articles as so altered.

(4) The registrar shall retain the application and other documents delivered to him under subsection (1) and shall issue to the company a certificate of incorporation appropriate to the status to be assumed by the company by virtue of this section; and upon the issue of the certificate—

(a) the status of the company shall, by virtue of the issue, be changed from unlimited to limited; and

(b) the alterations in the memorandum specified in the resolution and the alterations in, and additions to, the articles so specified shall, notwithstanding anything in the Principal Act, take effect.

(5) A certificate of incorporation issued by virtue of this section shall be conclusive evidence that the requirements of this section with respect to re-registration and of matters precedent and incidental thereto have been complied with, and that the company was authorised to be re-registered under the Principal Act in pursuance of this section and was duly so re-registered.

(6) Section 71 of the Principal Act shall have effect as if, for the reference to its resolution for registration as a limited company in pursuance of that Act, there were substituted a reference to its resolution for registration as a limited company in pursuance of that Act or re-registration as a limited company in pursuance of this section.

(7) In the event of the winding-up of a company re-registered in pursuance of this section, the following provisions shall have effect—

(a) notwithstanding paragraph (a) of subsection (1) of section 207 of the Principal Act, a past member of the company who was a member thereof at the time of re-registration shall, if the winding-up commences within the period of three years beginning with the day on which the company is re-registered, be liable to contribute to the assets of the company in respect of its debts and liabilities contracted before that time;

(b) where no persons who were members of the company at that time are existing members of the company, a person who, at that time, was a present or past member thereof shall, subject to paragraph (a) of the said subsection (1) and to paragraph (a) of this subsection, but notwithstanding paragraph (c) of the said subsection (1), be liable to contribute as aforesaid notwithstanding that the existing members have satisfied the contributions required to be made by them in pursuance of the Principal Act;

(c) notwithstanding paragraphs (d) and (e) of the said subsection (1), there shall be no limit on the amount which a person who, at that time, was a past or present member of the company is liable to contribute as aforesaid.

(8) The re-registration of an unlimited company as a limited company pursuant to this Act shall not affect any rights or obligations of the company, or render defective any legal proceedings by or against the company, and any legal proceedings which might have been continued or commenced against it in its former status may be continued or commenced against it in its new status.

54 Cesser of section 20 of Principal Act

No company shall register or re-register in pursuance of section 20 (1) of the Principal Act after the appointed day except upon an application in that behalf made before that day.

PART VI
MISCELLANEOUS

55 Public limited company to publish certain matters in [the Companies Registration Office Gazette][a]

(1) A public limited company shall publish in [the Companies Registration Office Gazette][a] notice of the delivery to the registrar of companies of the following documents—

(a) a statutory declaration under section 6(2);

(b) a copy of a resolution which gives, varies, revokes or renews an authority for the purposes of section 20;

(c) a copy of a special resolution under section 24(1), (2) or (3);

(d) any expert's valuation report on a non-cash consideration under section 31(2);

(e) any expert's valuation report on a non-cash asset acquired from a subscriber under section 33(2);

(f) any statement or notice under section 39(1), (3) or (4);

(g) any return of allotments under section 58(1) of the Principal Act;

(h) any notification of the redemption of preference shares under section 69(1) of the Principal Act;

(i) a copy of a special resolution to reduce its share capital under section 72(2) of the Principal Act;

(j) a copy of any resolution or agreement to which section 143 of the Principal Act applies and which—

(i) states the rights attached to any shares in the company, other than shares which are, in all respects, uniform (for the purposes of section 39(1)) with shares previously allotted;

(ii) varies rights attached to any shares in the company; or

(iii) assigns a name or other designation, or a new name or other designation, to any class of shares in the company.

(2) The notice mentioned in subsection (1) shall be published within six weeks of the relevant delivery.

(3) Where a company fails to comply with this section, the company and every officer of the company who is in default shall be guilty of an offence and shall be liable on summary conviction to a [class C fine].[b]

(4) Proceedings in relation to an offence under this section may be brought and prosecuted by the registrar of companies.

Amendments

a 'the Companies Registration Office Gazette' substituted for '*Iris Oifigiúil*' by IFCMPA 2005, s 72.

b '£250' increased to £1,500 by CA 1990, s 240(7) as inserted by CLEA 2001, s 104(c), and converted to €1,904.61 by Council Regulations (EC) No 1103/97, No 974/98 and No 2866/98 and the Economic and Monetary Union Act 1998, s 6; the above being implicitly substituted,

by Fines Act 2010, s 6, for a fine not exceeding the aforesaid amount. A class C fine currently means a fine not exceeding €2,500.

56 Trading under misleading name

(1) A person who is not a public limited company or (after the end of the general transitional period) is an old public limited company shall be guilty of an offence if he carries on any trade, profession or business under a name which includes, as its last part, the words 'public limited company', or 'cuideachta phoiblí theoranta' or abbreviations of those words.

(2) A public limited company other than an old public limited company shall be guilty of an offence if, in circumstances in which the fact that it is a public limited company is likely to be material to any person, it uses a name which may reasonably be expected to give the impression that it is a company other than a public limited company.

(3) Where, within the re-registration period, an old public limited company applies to be re-registered under section 12 as a public limited company, then—

(a) during the twelve months following the re-registration, any provision of section 114(1)(b) or (c) of the Principal Act; and

(b) during the three years following the re-registration, section 114(1)(a) of the Principal Act or any provision of any other Act or statutory instrument requiring or authorising the name of the company to be shown on any document or other object.

shall apply as if any reference in that provision to the name of the company were a reference to a name which either is its name or was its name before re-registration.

(4) Subsection (1) shall not apply to any company—

(a) to which Part XI of the Principal Act applies; and

(b) which has provisions in its constitution that would entitle it to rank as a public limited company if its had been registered in the State.

(5) A person guilty of an offence under subsection (1) or (2) and, if that person is a company, any officer of the company who is in default shall be liable on summary conviction to a [class C fine][a] together with, in the case of a continuing offence, a [class E fine][b] for every day on which the offence continues, but not exceeding [€1,904.61][c] in total.

Amendments

a '£500' increased to £1,500 by CA 1990, s 240(7) as inserted by CLEA 2001, s 104(c), and converted to €1,904.61 by Council Regulations (EC) No 1103/97, No 974/98 and No 2866/98 and the Economic and Monetary Union Act 1998, s 6; the above being implicitly substituted, by Fines Act 2010, s 6, for a fine not exceeding the aforesaid amount. A class C fine currently means a fine not exceeding €2,500.

b £50 converted to €31.74 by Council Regulations (EC) No 1103/97, No 974/98 and No 2866/98 and the Economic and Monetary Union Act 1998, s 6; as implicitly substituted, by Fines Act 2010, s 8, for a fine not exceeding the aforesaid amount. A class E fine currently means a fine not exceeding €500.

c £1,000 increased to £1,500 by CA 1990, s 240(7) as inserted by CLEA 2001, s 104(c) and converted to €1,904.61 by Council Regulations (EC) No 1103/97, No 974/98 and No 2866/98 and the Economic and Monetary Union Act 1998, s 6. Note that the effect of the retention of the €1,904.61 limit is to significantly restrict the amount of the fines that might otherwise have been imposed, and in particular to limit the deterrent effect of the daily default fine.

---

57 Penalties

(1) A company or other person guilty of an offence under section 20 or 36, shall be liable, on conviction on indictment, to a fine not exceeding [€6,348.70].[a]

(2) A company or other person guilty of an offence under section 24, 40 or 41 shall be liable, on conviction on indictment—

(a) in the case of a company, to a fine not exceeding [€6,348.70];[a]

(b) in the case of a person other than a company, to a fine not exceeding [€6,348.70][a] or, at the discretion of the court, to imprisonment for a term not exceeding [5][b] years or to both the fine and the imprisonment.

(3) Any person guilty of an offence under section 31, shall be liable on conviction on indictment to a fine not exceeding [€12,697.38][c] or, at the discretion of the court, to imprisonment for a term not exceeding [5][d] years or to both the fine and the imprisonment.

(4) A Justice of the District Court shall have jurisdiction to try summarily an offence under sections 20, 24, 31, 36, 40 and 41 if—

(a) the Justice is of the opinion that the facts proved or alleged against the defendant charged with any such offence constitute a minor offence fit to be tried summarily;

(b) the Director of Public Prosecutions consents; and

(c) the defendant (on being informed by the Justice of his right to be tried by a jury) does not object to being tried summarily,

and, upon conviction under this subsection the said defendant shall be liable—

(i) in the case where the defendant is guilty of an offence under section 20 or 36, to a [class C fine];[e]

(ii) in the case where the defendant is guilty of an offence under section 24, 31, 40 or 41—

(I) in the case of a company, to a [class C fine];[e]

(II) in the case of a person other than a company, to a [class C fine][e] or, at the discretion of the Court, to imprisonment for a term not exceeding 6 months or to both the fine and the imprisonment.

(5) Section 13 of the Criminal Procedure Act, 1967, shall apply in relation to an offence under the said section 20, 24, 31, 36, 40 and 41 as if, in lieu of the penalties specified in subsection (3) of the said section 13, there were specified therein the penalty provided for by subsection (4) of this section, and the reference in subsection 2 (a) of the said section 13 to the penalties provided for in subsection (3) of the said section 13, shall be construed and have effect accordingly.

Amendments

a £2,500 converted to €3,174.35 by Council Regulations (EC) No 1103/97, No 974/98 and No 2866/98 and the Economic and Monetary Union Act 1998, s 6, and multiplied by a multiplier of 2 pursuant to Fines Act 2010, s 9.

b 2 years increased to 5 years by CA 1990, s 240(8).

c £5,000 converted to €6,348.69 by Council Regulations (EC) No 1103/97, No 974/98 and No 2866/98 and the Economic and Monetary Union Act 1998, s 6, and multiplied by a multiplier of 2 pursuant to Fines Act 2010, s 9.

d 3 years increased to 5 years by CA 1990, s 240(8).

e £500 increased to £1,500 by CA 1990, s 240(7) and converted to €1,904.61 by Council Regulations (EC) No 1103/97, No 974/98 and No 2866/98 and the Economic and Monetary Union Act 1998, s 6; the above being implicitly substituted, by Fines Act 2010, s 6, for a fine not exceeding the aforesaid amount. A class C fine currently means a fine not exceeding €2,500.

58 Revocation of power under section 24 of Principal Act to dispense with 'limited' in name of public limited companies

(1) No licence under section 24 of the Principal Act shall be granted in respect of a public limited company or an association about to be formed into a public limited company or have effect in respect of such a company.

(2) Any such licence already granted to a company shall cease to have effect if, after the appointed day, the company is registered or re-registered as a public limited company.

59 Power by order to prescribe forms and to revoke and amend orders

(1) The Minister may by order prescribe forms to be used in connection with any of the provisions of this Act.

(2) The Minister may by order revoke or amend an order (other than an order made under section 1(3)) made under this Act.

60 Laying of orders before Houses of Oireachtas

Every order made under this Act shall be laid before each House of the Oireachtas as soon as may be after it is made and if a resolution annulling the order is passed by either House within the next 21 days on which that House has sat after the order is laid before it, the order shall be annulled accordingly but without prejudice to the validity of anything previously done thereunder.

61 Expenses

The expenses incurred in the administration of this Act shall, to such extent as may be sanctioned by the Minister for Finance, be paid out of moneys provided by the Oireachtas.

FIRST SCHEDULE

MINOR AND CONSEQUENTIAL AMENDMENTS TO THE COMPANIES ACT, 1963

Section 3

1. [...][a]

Amendments

This para substituted 'a resolution of the company' for 'special resolution' in the definition of 'articles' in CA 1963, s 2(1).

2. [...][a]

Amendments

C(A)A 1983, Sch 1, para 2, substituted CA 1963, s 6(1).

3. [...][a]

Amendments

This para deleted 'so, however, that no part of the capital of the company shall be expended in any such purchase' in CA 1963, s 10(6); para (b) inserted CA 1963, s 10(6A),(6B),(6C).

4. [...][a]

Amendments

CA 1963, s 22(2) substituted by this para.

5. [...][a]

Amendments

This para substituted '(6A), (6B), (6C),' in CA 1963, s 28(4).

6. [...][a]

Amendments

a C(A)A 1983, Sch 1, para 6, substituted CA 1963, s 35.

7. [...][a]

Amendments

a C(A)A 1983, Sch 1, para 7, substituted 'Except in the case of a public limited company the amount payable' for 'The amount payable' in CA 1963, s 53.

8. [...][a]

Amendments

a C(A)A 1983, Sch 1, para 8, substituted CA 1963, s 54(3).

9. [...][a]

Amendments

a C(A)A 1983, Sch 1, para 9, substituted CA 1963, s 55(1).

10. [...][a]

Amendments

a C(A)A 1983, Sch 1, para 10 inserted CA 1963, s 60(15A), (15B).

11. [...][a]

Amendments

a C(A)A 1983, Sch 1, para 11, substituted 'to be allotted' for 'to be issued' in CA 1963, s 62(2).

12. [...][a]

Amendments

a C(A)A 1983, Sch 1, para 12, substituted CA 1963, s 64(1)(c).

13. [...][a]

Amendments

a C(A)A 1983, Sch 1, para 12, substituted CA 1963, s 114(5).

14. [...][a]

Amendments

a C(A)A 1983, Sch 1, para 14 inserted CA 1963, s 115(7)(d).

15. [...][a]

Amendments

a C(A)A 1983, Sch 1, para 15 inserted CA 1963, s 143(4)(j).

16. [...][a]

Amendments

a C(A)A 1983, Sch 1, para 16 inserted 'or section 42 of the Companies (Amendment) Act, 1983' after 'section 391' in CA 1963, s 200(b).

17. [...][a]

Amendments

a C(A)A 1983, Sch 1, para 17 inserted CA 1963, s 213(h)–(i).

18. [...][a]

Amendments

a C(A)A 1983, Sch 1, para 18 inserted CA 1963, s 215(f).

19. [...][a]

Amendments

a C(A)A 1983, Sch 1, para 19, substituted CA 1963, s 330(c)(iii).

20. [...][a]

Amendments

a C(A)A 1983, Sch 1, para 20 substituted CA 1963, s 335(1).

21. [...][a]

Amendments

a C(A)A 1983, Sch 1, para 21 renumbered CA 1963, s 336 and inserted sub-s (2).

22. [...][a]

Amendments

a C(A)A 1983, Sch 1, para 22 inserted 'and including any statement under section 330 (c)' after 'the amount of the guarantee' in CA 1963, s 340.

23. [...][a]

Amendments

a C(A)A 1983, Sch 1, para 23, substituted CA 1963, s 395(2).

24. [...][a]

Amendments

a C(A)A 1983, Sch 1, para 24(a) substituted CA 1963, Sch 1, Table A, Pt I, reg 3; C(A)A 1983, Sch 1, para 24(b) substituted CA 1963, Sch I, Table A, Pt I, reg 5; C(A)A 1983, Sch 1, para 24(c) inserted 'the following ', subject to section 20 of the Companies (Amendment) Act, 1983' after 'or any part thereof,' in CA 1963, Sch 1, Table A, Pt I, reg 79; C(A)A 1983, Sch 1, para 24(d) substituted the 'Companies Acts, 1963 to 1983' for 'the Act' in CA 1963, Sch 1, Table A, Pt I, reg 80; C(A)A 1983, Sch 1, para 24(e) substituted CA 1963, Sch 1, Table A, Pt I, reg 118; C(A)A 1983, Sch 1, para 24(f) inserted CA 1963, Sch 1, Table A, Pt I, reg 130A; C(A)A 1983, Sch 1, para 24(g) substituted 'Whenever a resolution is passed in pursuance of regulation 130 or 130A' for 'Whenever such a resolution as aforesaid shall have been passed' in CA 1963, Sch 1, Table A, Pt I, reg 131.

25. [...][a]

Amendments

a C(A)A 1983, Sch 1, para 25, substituted CA 1963, Sch 1, Table A, Pt 1; regs 3, 5, 79, 80, 118, 130, 131.

26. [...][a]

Amendments

a C(A)A 1983, Sch 1, para 26, substituted 'AN UNLIMITED PUBLIC COMPANY' for 'A PUBLIC COMPANY' in the heading of CA 1963, Sch 2.

27. [...][a]

Amendments

a C(A)A 1983, Sch 1, para 27 inserted CA 1963, Sch 6 para 11(2A) and (2B).

28. [...][a]

Amendments

a C(A)A 1983, Sch 1, para 28 inserted CA 1963, Sch 7 para 5.

29. [...][a]

Amendments

a C(A)A 1983, Sch 1, para 29 inserted 'Particulars relating to directors to be shown on all business letters of the company' after 'Register of directors and secretaries' in CA 1963 Sch 9.

30. [...][a]

Amendments

a C(A)A 1983, Sch 1, para 30 deleted '130 Statutory meeting and statutory report' from CA 1963, Sch 10.

SECOND SCHEDULE

FORM OF MEMORANDUM OF ASSOCIATION OF A PUBLIC LIMITED COMPANY

Section 4

PART 1
A PUBLIC COMPANY LIMITED BY SHARES

1. The name of the company is 'The Northern Mining, public limited company'.

2. The company is to be a public limited company.

3. The objects for which the company is established are the mining of minerals of all kinds and the doing of all such other things as are incidental or conducive to the attainment of the above object.

4. The liability of the member is limited.

5. The share capital of the company is £30,000, divided into 30,000 shares of £1 each.

We, the several persons whose names and addresses are subscribed, wish to be formed into a company in pursuance of this memorandum of association, and we agree to take the number of shares in the capital of the company set opposite our respective names.

Names, Addresses and Descriptions of Subscribers	*Number of Shares taken by each Subscriber*
1. James Maher of .... in the County of .... Solicitor	5
2. John O'Brien of .... in the County of .... Engineer	375
3. Michael Nolan of .... in the County of .... Solicitor	225
4. Patrick Hayes of .... in the County of .... Geologist	55
5. Paul McCarthy of .... in the County of .... Geologist	10
6. Thomas Kennedy of .... in the County of .... Accountant	30
7. Joseph O'Meara of .... in the County of .... Solicitor	15
Total shares taken	715

Dated the .... day of ...., 19..........

Witness to the above signatures:

Name:

Address:

PART II

A PUBLIC COMPANY LIMITED BY GUARANTEE AND HAVING A SHARE CAPITAL

1. The name of the company is 'The Southern Counties Tourist Development,

2. The company is to be a public limited company.

3. The objects for which the company is established are the promotion of tourism in the southern counties of Ireland by providing facilities for tourists, and the doing of all such other things as are incidental or conducive to the attainment of the above object.

4. The liability of the member is limited.

5. Every member of the company undertakes to contribute to the assets of the company in the event of its being wound up while he is a member, or within one year afterwards, for payment of the debts and liabilities of the company contracted before he ceases to be a member, and the costs, charges and expenses of winding up, and for the adjustment of the rights of the contributories among themselves, such amount as may be required, not exceeding £25.

6. The share capital of the company shall consist of £30,000 divided into 30,000 shares of £1 each.

We, the several persons whose names and addresses are subscribed, wish to be formed into a company in pursuance of this memorandum of association, and we agree to take the number of shares in the capital of the company set opposite our respective names.

Names, Addresses and Descriptions of Subscribers	*Number of Shares taken by each Subscriber*
1. John Boland of	
in the County of	
Solicitor	5
2. Martin Cullen of	
in the County of	
Hotel Proprietor	375
3. Sean Keogh of	
in the County of	
Engineer	225
4. James Mangan of	
in the County of	
Travel Agent	55
5. Paul Roche of	
in the County of	
Farmer	10
6. Kevin O'Sullivan of	
in the County of	
Architect	30

Names, Addresses and Descriptions of Subscribers	*Number of Shares taken by each Subscriber*
7. Teresa O'Connell of .... in the County of .... Housewife	15
Total shares taken	715

Dated the .... day of ...., 19...........

Witness to the above signatures:

Name:

Address:

THIRD SCHEDULE
REPEALS

Companies (Amendment) Act 1986

(Number 25 of 1986)

Section

PART V

[SPECIAL PROVISIONS WHERE A COMPANY IS A PARENT UNDERTAKING OR SUBSIDIARY UNDERTAKING]

PART VI

SPECIAL PROVISIONS WHERE A COMPANY IS AN INVESTMENT COMPANY

PART VII

INTERPRETATION OF SCHEDULE

An Act to amend the Law Relating To Companies. [12th July, 1986]

Be it Enacted by the Oireachtas as Follows:

1 Interpretation

(1) In this Act, except where the context otherwise requires—

'the Act of 1983' means the Companies (Amendment) Act, 1983;

['abridged accounts' has the meaning given to it by section 19 of the Principal Act;][a]

'company' does not include an unlimited company;

'private company' does not include an unlimited company;

'public company' means a company other than a private company;

'the Principal Act' means the Companies Act, 1963.

(2) In this Act, except where the context otherwise requires, a reference to a balance sheet or profit and loss account shall include a reference to any notes to or documents annexed to the accounts in question giving information which is required by any provision of the Companies Acts, 1963 to 1986, and required or allowed by any such provision to be given in a note to or a document annexed to a company's accounts.

[(3) In this Act, except where the context otherwise requires, a reference to a subsidiary is to a subsidiary undertaking as defined in Regulation 4 of the European Communities (Companies: Group Accounts) Regulations, 1992, and a reference to a holding company shall be construed accordingly.][b]

Amendments

a Definition inserted by the Schedule to EC(IFRSMA)R 2005. However, the reference to the 'Principal Act' appears to be an error. The correct reference should be to s 19 of C(A)A 1986.

b C(A)A 1986, s 1(3) inserted by EC(CGA)R 1992, reg 42.

---

2 Scope of Act

(1) This Act does not apply to—

(a) a company not trading for the acquisition of gain by the members,

(b) a company to which subsection (4)(c) of section 128 of the Principal Act applies,

(c) a company in respect of which there is in force an order under subsection (5) of that section.

(2) Sections 3 to 6, 8 to 12, 17 to 19, and 24 of this Act do not apply in relation to—

(a) a company that is the holder of a licence under the Central Bank Act, 1971,

(b) a company that is a trustee savings bank certified under the Trustee Savings Banks Acts, 1863 to 1965,

(c) a company engaged solely in the making of hire-purchase agreements (within the meaning of the Hire-Purchase Act, 1946) and credit-sale agreements (within the meaning of that Act), in respect of goods owned by the company,

(d) a company engaged in the business of accepting deposits or other repayable funds or granting credit for its own account,

(e) [...],[a]

(f) Fóir Teoranta, or

(g) [...].[b]

[(3) Sections 3 to 6, 8, 12, 17, 18 and 24 of this Act do not apply in relation to undertakings to which the European Communities (Insurance Undertakings: Accounts) Regulations 1996 (No 23 of 1991) apply by virtue of regulation 3 of those Regulations).][c]

Amendments

a C(A)A 1986, s 2(2)(e) repealed by ACC Bank Act 2001, s 12(1).

b C(A)A 1986, s 2(2)(g) repealed by ICC Bank Act 2000, s 7(1).

c C(A)A 1986, s 2(3) substituted by EC(IUA)R 1996, reg 20(2)(a).

3 General provisions in relation to accounts

[(1)Companies Act individual accounts, including a balance sheet and profit and loss account, prepared in accordance with section 149 of the Principal Act shall comply with the following requirements]:[a]

(a) every such balance sheet and profit and loss account shall comply with the provisions of sections 4 and 5 of, and the Schedule to, this Act,

(b) every such balance sheet of a company shall give a true and fair view of the state of affairs of the company as at the end of its financial year and every such profit and loss account of a company shall give a true and fair view of the profit or loss of the company for the financial year,

(c) where a balance sheet or profit and loss account drawn up in accordance with paragraph (a) of this subsection would not provide sufficient information to comply with paragraph (b) of this subsection, any necessary additional information shall be provided in that balance sheet or profit and loss account or in a note to the accounts,

(d) where, owing to special circumstances, the preparation of accounts of a company in compliance with the said paragraph (a) would prevent those accounts from complying with paragraph (b) (even if additional information were provided under paragraph (c) of this subsection), the directors of the company shall depart from the requirements of the Schedule to this Act in preparing those accounts insofar as is necessary in order to comply with that paragraph,

(e) where the directors of a company depart from the requirements of this section, they shall attach a note to the accounts of the company giving details of the particular departures made, the reasons therefor and the effect of those departures on the accounts, and, accordingly, in the Companies Acts, 1963 to 1982, and the Companies (Amendment) Act, 1983, in relation to a company to which this Act applies—

(i) references to the said section 149, shall be construed as references to subsection (5) and, insofar as it relates to the said subsection (5), subsection (7) of the said section 149 and to the provisions of this Act corresponding to the other provisions of the said section 149, and

(ii) references to the Sixth Schedule shall be construed as references to the corresponding provisions of this Act.

(2) [...][b]

(3) [...][b]

(4) Subsection (1)(b) of this section overrides the requirements of sections 4 and 5 of, and the Schedule to, this Act and all other requirements of the Companies Acts, 1963 to 1986, as to the matters to be included in the accounts of a company or in notes to those accounts; and, accordingly, where a balance sheet or profit and loss account of a company drawn up in accordance with those requirements would not provide sufficient information to comply with the said subsection (1)(b), any necessary additional information shall be provided in that balance sheet or profit and loss account or in a note to the accounts.

Amendments

a Amended by EC(IFRSMA)R 2005, reg 5(a)(i).

b C(A)A 1986, s 3(2) and (3) deleted by EC(IFRSMA)R 2005, reg 5(a)(ii).

4 Format of accounts

(1) [Where the directors of a company prepare Companies Act individual accounts and subject to this section,][a] every balance sheet of a company shall show the items listed in either of the balance sheets formats set out in the Schedule to this Act and every profit and loss account of a company shall show the items listed in any one of the profit and loss accounts formats so set out in either case in the order and under the headings and sub-headings given in the format adopted.

(2) Subsection (1) of this section shall not be construed as requiring the heading or sub-heading for any item in the balance sheet, or profit and loss account, of a company to be distinguished by any letter or number assigned to that item in the formats set out in the Schedule to this Act.

(3) Where the balance sheet, or profit and loss account, of a company has been prepared by reference to one of the formats set out in the Schedule to this Act, the directors of the company shall adopt the same format in preparing the accounts for subsequent financial years unless, in their opinion, there are special reasons for a change.

(4) Where any change is made in accordance with subsection (3) of this section in the format adopted in preparing a balance sheet, or profit and loss account, of a company,

the reasons for the change, together with full particulars of the change, shall be given in a note to the accounts in which the new format is first adopted.

(5) Any item required in accordance with the Schedule to this Act to be shown in the balance sheet, or profit and loss account, of a company, may be shown in greater detail than that required by the format adopted.

(6) Any items to which an Arabic number is assigned in any of the formats set out in the Schedule to this Act may be combined in the accounts of a company—

(a) in any case where the individual amounts of such items are not material to assessing the state of affairs or profit or loss of the company for the financial year concerned, or

(b) in any case where the combination of such items facilitates that assessment.

(7) Where items are combined in a company's accounts pursuant to subsection (6)(b) of this section, the individual amounts of any items so combined shall be disclosed in a note to the accounts.

[(8) In respect of every item shown in the balance sheet, or profit and loss account, of a company, the corresponding amount for the financial year immediately preceding that to which the balance sheet or profit and loss account refers shall also be shown. Where that corresponding amount is not comparable with the amount to be shown for the item in question in respect of the financial year to which the balance sheet or profit and loss account relates, the former amount may be adjusted, and, if the former amount is adjusted, particulars as regards the respect or respects in which the foregoing amounts are not comparable and of the adjustment shall be given in a note to the accounts.][b]

(9) Subject to subsection (10) of this section, a heading or sub-heading corresponding to an item listed in the format adopted in preparing the balance sheet, or profit and loss account, of a company, shall not be included in the balance sheet or profit and loss account, as the case may be, if there is no amount to be shown for that item in respect of the financial year to which the balance sheet or profit and loss account relates.

(10) Subsection (9) of this section shall not apply in any case where an amount can be shown for the item in question in respect of the financial year immediately preceding that to which the balance sheet or profit and loss account relates, and that amount shall be shown under the heading or sub-heading required by the format adopted as aforesaid.

(11) Amounts in respect of items representing assets or income may not be set off in the accounts of a company against amounts in respect of items representing liabilities or expenditure, as the case may be, or vice versa.

(12) The balance sheet, or profit and loss account, of a company may include an item representing or covering the amount of any asset or liability or income or expenditure not otherwise covered by any of the items listed in the format adopted but the following shall not be treated as assets in the balance sheet of a company—

(a) preliminary expenses,

(b) expenses of, and commission on, any issue of shares or debentures, and

(c) costs of research.

(13) In preparing the balance sheet, or profit and loss account, of a company, the directors of the company shall adapt the arrangement and headings and sub-headings otherwise required by subsection (1) of this section in respect of items to which an

arabic number is assigned in the format adopted, in any case where the special nature of the company's business requires such adaptation.

(14) Every profit and loss account of a company shall show the amount of the profit or loss of the company on ordinary activities before taxation.

[(15) The notes to the profit and loss account of a company shall show—

(a) dividends paid (other than dividends for which a liability existed at the immediately preceding balance sheet date) or which the company is liable to pay,

(b) separately, any transfers between the profit and loss account and other reserves,

(c) any increase or reduction in the balance on the profit and loss account since the immediately preceding financial year,

(d) the profit or loss brought forward at the beginning of the financial year, and

(e) the profit or loss carried forward at the end of the financial year.

(16) There shall be shown in the notes to the accounts the aggregate amount of any dividends proposed before the date of approval of the accounts which have not been shown in the notes to the profit and loss account in accordance with subsection (15) of this section.][c]

Amendments

a Amended by EC(IFRSMA)R 2005, reg 5(b)(i).

b Substituted by SI 840/2005, reg 4.

c Amended by EC(IFRSMA)R 2005, reg 5(b)(ii).

5 Accounting principles

Subject to section 6 of this Act, the amount to be included in the accounts of a company in respect of the items shown shall be determined in accordance with the following principles:

(a) the company shall be presumed to be carrying on business as a going concern,

(b) accounting policies shall be applied consistently from one financial year to the next,

(c) the amount of any item in the accounts shall be determined on a prudent basis and in particular—

(i) only profits realised at the balance sheet date shall be included in the profit and loss account, and

(ii) [all liabilities which have arisen][a] in respect of the financial year to which the accounts relate, or a previous financial year, shall be taken into account, including those liabilities and losses which only become apparent between the balance sheet date and the date on which the accounts are signed in pursuance of section 156 of the Principal Act,

(d) all income and charges relating to the financial year to which the accounts relate shall be taken into account without regard to the date of receipt or [payment][b]

(e) in determining the aggregate amount of any item the amount of each individual asset or liability that fails to be taken into account shall be determined [separately, and][c]

[(f) in determining how amounts are presented within items in the profit and loss account and balance sheet, the directors of a company shall have regard to the substance of the reported transaction or arrangement, in accordance with generally accepted accounting principles or practice.][d]

Amendments

a Amended by EC(IFRSMA)R 2005, reg 5(c)(i).

b Amended by EC(IFRSMA)R 2005, reg 5(c)(ii).

c Amended by EC(IFRSMA)R 2005, reg 5(c)(iii).

d Amended by EC(IFRSMA)R 2005, reg 5(c)(iv).

6 Departure from the accounting principles

If it appears to the directors of a company that there are special reasons for departing from any of the principles specified in section 5 of this Act, they may so depart, but particulars of the departure, the reasons for it and its effect on the balance sheet and profit and loss account of the company shall be stated in a note to the accounts, for the financial year concerned, of the company.

7 Documents to be annexed to annual return

(1) Subject to the provisions of this Act, there shall be annexed to the annual return—

(a) [(i) in the case of a company other than a company to which section 2(2) or (3) of this Act applies, a copy of the company's individual accounts which shall be either IFRS individual accounts or Companies Act individual accounts prepared in accordance with sections 3, 4 and 5 of, and the Schedule to, this Act,

(ii) in the case of a company to which section 2(2) of this Act applies, a copy of the company's individual accounts which shall be either IFRS individual accounts or Companies Act individual accounts prepared in accordance with the Credit Institutions Regulations,

(iii) in the case of an undertaking to which section 2(3) of this Act applies, a copy of the undertaking's individual accounts which shall be either IFRS individual accounts or Companies Act individual accounts prepared in accordance with the Insurance Undertakings Regulations,

and a copy of the report of the auditors on, and the report of the directors accompanying, each such individual accounts, and each such copy shall be certified both by a director, and the secretary of the company, to be a true copy of such individual accounts, or report, as the case may be, laid or to be laid before the annual general meeting of the company for that year, and][a]

(b) where a document, being a balance sheet, profit and loss account, report, or statement, annexed to the annual return, is in a language other than the English language or the Irish language, there shall be annexed to each such document a translation in the English language or the Irish language certified in the prescribed manner to be a correct translation.

[(1A) Subsection (1) of this section shall not apply to the profit and loss account or income statement of a company where—

(a) the company is a parent undertaking,

(b) the company prepares group accounts in accordance with section 150 of the Principal Act, and

(c) the notes to the company's individual balance sheet show the company's profit or loss for the financial year determined in accordance with this Act or section 149A of the Principal Act, as appropriate.

(1B) Where, in the case of a company, advantage is taken of subsection (1A) of this section, that fact shall be disclosed—

(a) in the notes on the company's individual accounts, and

(b) in the notes on the group accounts referred to in subsection (1A)(b) of this section.] [b]

[[(1C)] Every document, being a balance sheet, profit and loss account, report or statement, annexed to the annual return in accordance with paragraph (a) of subsection (1) shall cover the period—

(a) in the case of the first annual return to which such documents are annexed – since the incorporation of the company, and

(b) in any other case – since the end of the period covered by the balance sheet, profit and loss account, report or statement, as the case may be, annexed to the preceding annual return,

made up to a date not earlier by more than 9 months than the date to which the annual return is made up.][c]

(2) If a document required by this section to be annexed to the annual return referred to in subsection (1) of this section does not comply with the provisions of the law in force at the date of the relevant audit with respect to the form and the contents of the document, there shall be made by the company concerned such amendments in the copy as are necessary in order to bring it into compliance with those provisions, and the fact that the copy has been so amended shall be stated therein.

(3) Section 128 of the Principal Act shall not apply to a company to which this section applies.

Amendments

a C(A)A 1986, s 7(a)(i)–(iii) amended by EC(IFRSMA)R 2005, reg 5(d)(i).

b C(A)A 1986, s 7(1A) and (1B) inserted by EC(IFRSMA)R 2005, reg 5(d)(ii)

c C(A)A 1986, s 7(1A) inserted by CLEA 2001, s 64(b) and renumbered as s 7(1C) by EC(IFRSMA)R 2005, reg 5(d)(ii).

---

8 Small companies and medium-sized companies

(1) Subject to section 9 of this Act—

(a) a private company[, subject to subsection (1A)][a] shall qualify to be treated as a small company for the purposes of this Act in respect of any financial year of the company if, in respect of that year and the financial year of the company immediately preceding that year, the company satisfies at least two of the conditions specified in subsection (2) of this section, and

(b) a private company[, subject to subsection (1B)][b] shall qualify to be treated as a medium-sized company for the purposes of this Act in respect of any financial year of the company if, in respect of that year and the financial year of the company immediately preceding that year, the company satisfies at least two of the conditions specified in subsection (3) of this section.

[(1A) Subsection (1)(a) shall not apply to a private company whose securities are admitted to trading on a regulated market.

(1B) Subsection (1)(b) shall not apply to a private company whose securities are admitted to trading on a regulated market.][c]

(2) The qualifying conditions for a company to be treated as a small company in respect of any financial year are as follows:

(a) its balance sheet total for that year shall not exceed [€4.4 million],[d]

(b) the amount of its turnover for that year shall not exceed [€8.8 million],[e] and

(c) the average number of persons employed by the company in that year shall not exceed 50.

(3) The qualifying conditions for a company to be treated as a medium-sized company in respect of any financial year are as follows:

(a) its balance sheet total for that year shall not exceed [€7,618,428],[f]

(b) the amount of its turnover for that year shall not exceed [€15,236,857],[g] and

(c) the average number of persons employed by the company in that year shall not exceed 250.

(4) In this section 'balance sheet total', in relation to any financial year of a company, means—

(a) where Format 1 of the balance sheet formats set out in the Schedule to this Act is adopted by the company, the aggregate of the amounts shown in the company's balance sheet for that year under headings corresponding to items A and B in that Format, [...][h]

(b) where Format 2 of those formats is adopted by the company, the aggregate of the amounts so shown [under 'Assets', and][i]

[(c) where the company prepares IFRS individual accounts, the aggregate of the amounts shown as assets in the balance sheet.][j]

(5) In this section 'amount of turnover', in relation to any financial year of a company, means the amounts of the turnover shown in the profit and loss account of the company under headings corresponding to the relevant items in any of the Formats of profit and loss accounts set out in the Schedule to this Act.

(6) In the application of this section to any period which is a financial year of a company, but is not in fact a year, the amounts specified in subsections (2)(b) and (3)(b) of this section shall be proportionately adjusted.

(7) A private company which is incorporated on or after the commencement of this section shall qualify to be treated as a small company or, as the case may be, as a medium-sized company, in respect of its first financial year if it satisfies at least two of

the relevant qualifying conditions specified in subsection (2) or (3), as may be appropriate, of this section in respect of that financial year.

(8) A private company which was incorporated before such commencement shall qualify to be treated under subsection (1) of this section as a small company or, as the case may be, as a medium-sized company, in respect of the first financial year of the company in which accounts of the company are required to be prepared in accordance with section 3 of this Act if it satisfies at least two of the relevant qualifying conditions specified in subsection (2) or (3), as may be appropriate, of this section in respect of either that first financial year or the financial year immediately preceding that year.

(9) For the purposes of subsection (2)(c) and (3)(c) of this section, the average number of persons employed by a company shall be determined by applying the method of calculation prescribed by paragraph 42(4) of the Schedule to this Act for determining the number required by subparagraph (1) of that paragraph to be stated in a note to the accounts of a company.

(10) In determining for the purposes of subsection (8) of this section whether a company satisfies at least two of the relevant conditions specified in subsection (2) or (3), as may be appropriate, of this section in respect of a financial year in a case where the accounts of the company in respect of that year prepared under the Companies Acts, 1963 to 1983 are not prepared in accordance with this Act, subsection (4) of this section shall be construed as referring to the aggregate of any amounts included in the balance sheet of the company for that year which correspond to the amounts mentioned in paragraph (a) or (b), as may be appropriate, of that subsection.

(11) The Minister may by order substitute different amounts, totals and numbers, respectively, for the amounts, totals and number specified for the time being in subsections (2) and (3) of this section and those subsections shall have effect in accordance with any order for the time being in force under this section.

(12) An order under this section shall be laid before each House of the Oireachtas as soon as may be after it is made and, if a resolution annulling the order is passed by either such House within the next twenty-one days on which that House has sat after the order is laid before it, the order shall be annulled accordingly but without prejudice to the validity of anything previously done thereunder.

[(13) In subsections (1A) and (1B), 'regulated market' has the meaning assigned to it by Article 4(1), point (14) of Directive 2004/39/EC (OJ L 145, 30.4.2004, p 1).][k]

Amendments

a Words inserted by European Communities (Directive 2006/46/EC) Regulations 2009, reg 4(a).

b Words inserted by European Communities (Directive 2006/46/EC) Regulations 2009, reg 4(b).

c Subsections (1A) and (1B) inserted by European Communities (Directive 2006/46/EC) Regulations 2009, reg 4(c).

d '£1,500,000' substituted for '£1,250,000' by EC(A)R 1993, reg 4 and converted to €1,904,607 by Council Regulation (EC) No 1103/97, No 974/98, No 2866/98 and the European and Monetary Act 1998, s 6; '€4.4 million' substituted for this amount by EU(A)R 2012 (SI 304/2012) reg 2(a).

e ‘£3,000,000’ substituted for ‘£2,500,000’ by EC(A)R 1993, reg 4 and converted to €3,809,214 by Council Regulation (EC) No 1103/97, No 974/98, No 2866/98 and the European and Monetary Act 1998, s 6; ‘€8.8 million’ substituted for this amount by EU(A)R 2012 (SI 304/2012) reg 2(b).

f ‘£6,000,000’ substituted for ‘£5,000,000’ by EC(A)R 1993, reg 4 and converted to €7,618,428 by Council Regulation (EC) No 1103/97, No 974/98, No 2866/98 and the European and Monetary Act 1998, s 6.

g ‘£12,000,000’ substituted for ‘£10,000,000’ by EC(A)R 1993, reg 4 and converted to €15,236,957 by Council Regulation (EC) No 1103/97, No 974/98, No 2866/98 and the European and Monetary Act 1998, s 6.

h Amended by EC(IFRSMA)R 2005, reg 5(e)(i).

i Amended by EC(IFRSMA)R 2005, reg 5(e)(ii).

j Amended by EC(IFRSMA)R 2005, reg 5(e)(iii).

k Subsection (13) inserted by European Communities (Directive 2006/46/EC) Regulations 2009, reg 4(d).

---

9 Reclassification of small companies and medium-sized companies

(1) Where a private company has qualified to be treated as a small company under subsection (1) of section 8 of this Act, it shall continue to be so qualified, unless, in the latest financial year of the company and the financial year of the company immediately preceding that year, it does not satisfy at least two of the conditions set out in subsection (2) of the said section 8 and if, during each of those two years, it does not satisfy at least two of those conditions, it shall, in respect of its latest financial year, cease to be so qualified.

(2) Where a private company has qualified to be treated as a medium-sized company under subsection (1) of section 8 of this Act, it shall continue to be so qualified unless, in the latest financial year of the company and the financial year of the company immediately preceding that year, it does not satisfy at least two of the conditions set out in subsection (3) of the said section 8 for treatment as a medium-sized company and, if during each of those two years, it does not satisfy at least two of those conditions, it shall, in respect of its latest financial year, cease to be so qualified.

(3) A company which qualified to be treated as a medium-sized company under subsection (2) of this section in the financial year immediately preceding its latest financial year shall qualify to be treated as a small company for the purposes of this Act in respect of its latest financial year if, in those two years, it satisfies at least two of the conditions set out in section 8(2) of this Act.

(4) Where a private company ceases to be qualified as specified in subsection (1) or (2) of this section, section 8 of this Act shall apply in respect of the company as if it had never previously qualified to be treated as a small company or a medium-sized company under that section.

10 Exemption for small companies from certain provision of sections 3 and 7

[(1) A company treated as a small company pursuant to section 8(1) of this Act may, in lieu of complying with the requirements in that behalf in section 7 of this Act, annex to the annual return in relation to the company referred to in the said section 7 a copy of the abridged balance sheet of the company drawn up in accordance with subsection (2) of this section in respect of the period to which the return refers and, notwithstanding section 7 of this Act, the company shall not be required to annex to the return a copy of the profit and loss account of the company or the report of the directors accompanying the balance sheet of the company.

(2) (a) Where the directors of a company prepare IFRS individual accounts and the company is to be treated as a small company pursuant to section (8)(1) of this Act, the abridged balance sheet referred to in subsection (1) of this section shall comprise the full balance sheet included in the IFRS individual accounts.

(b) Where the directors of a company prepare Companies Act individual accounts and the company is to be treated as a small company pursuant to section (8)(1) of this Act, the directors may extract from the balance sheet of the company prepared in accordance with section 3(1) of this Act an abridged balance sheet showing only those items preceded by letters or roman numerals in Formats 1 and 2 of the balance sheet formats set out in the Schedule to this Act but the total amounts falling due within one year and after one year shall be shown separately for item B. II in Format 1 and items B. II under 'Assets' and C under 'Liabilities' in Format 2 of the balance sheet formats in relation to debtors and creditors.][a]

Amendments

a C(A)A 1986, s 10 substituted by EC(IFRSMA)R 2005, reg 5(f).

11 Exemption for medium-sized companies from certain provisions of sections 3 and 7

[(1) A company treated as a medium-sized company pursuant to section 8(1) of this Act may, in lieu of complying with the requirements in that behalf in section 7 of this Act, annex to the annual return in relation to the company referred to in the said section 7 a copy of the abridged balance sheet of the company drawn up in accordance with subsection (2) of this section and an abridged profit and loss account or abridged income statement of the company drawn up in accordance with subsection (3) of this section in respect of the period to which the return refers.

(2) (a) Where the directors of a company prepare IFRS individual accounts and the company is to be treated as a medium-sized company pursuant to section 8(1) of this Act, the abridged balance sheet referred to in subsection (1) of this section shall comprise the full balance sheet included in the IFRS individual accounts.

(b) (i) Subject to subparagraph (ii) of this paragraph, where the directors of a company prepare Companies Act individual accounts and the company is to be treated as a medium-sized company pursuant to section 8(1) of this Act, the directors may extract from the balance sheet of the company prepared in accordance with section 3(1) of this Act an abridged balance sheet showing only those items preceded by letters or roman numerals in Formats 1 and 2 of the balance sheet formats set out in the Schedule to this Act but the amounts in respect of the following items shall be disclosed separately either in the balance sheet of the company or in the notes to the accounts of the company-

(I) in Format 1 of the balance sheet formats, items A. I. 3, A. II. 1, 2, 3 and 4, A. III. 1, 2, 3, 4 and 7, B. II. 2, 3 and 6, B. III. 1 and 2, C. 1, 2, 6, 7, 8 and 9 and F. 1, 2, 6, 7, 8 and 9, and

(II) in Format 2 of the balance sheet formats, under 'Assets', items A. I. 3, A. II. 1, 2, 3 and 4, A. III. 1, 2, 3, 4 and 7, B. II. 2, 3 and 6 and B. III. 1 and 2 and under 'Liabilities', items C. 1, 2, 6, 7, 8 and 9.

(ii) The balance sheet of the company shall show separately—

(I) the amounts falling due within one year and after one year in respect of items B. II in the said Format 1 in total and in respect, individually, of items B. II. 2 and 3 in the said Format 1, and

(II) the amounts falling due in a similar manner in respect of the total of the amounts in respect of the following items, that is to say, in the said Format 2 under 'Assets' item B. II and under 'Liabilities' item C and in respect, individually, of the following items, that is to say, in the said Format 2 under 'Assets' items B. II. 2 and 3 and under 'Liabilities' items C. 1, 2, 6 and 7.

(3) (a) Where the directors of a company prepare IFRS individual accounts and the company is to be treated as a medium-sized company pursuant to section 8(1) of this Act, the directors may extract from the income statement, prepared in accordance with international financial reporting standards and section 149A (inserted by the European Communities (International Financial Reporting Standards and Miscellaneous Amendments) Regulations 2005) of the Principal Act, an abridged income statement which combines as one item the company's revenue and certain expenses for the period.

(b) The expenses that may be combined as one item with the revenue of the company are—

(i) where expenses are classified by function, only those expenses classified as 'cost of sales' may be so combined, and

(ii) where expenses are classified by nature, only changes in finished goods and work-in-progress and raw materials and consumables used may be so combined.

(c) Where the directors of a company prepare Companies Act individual accounts and the company is to be treated as a medium-sized company pursuant to section 8(1) of this Act, the directors may extract from the profit and loss account of the company prepared in accordance with section 3(1) of this Act an abridged profit and loss account which combines as one item under the heading 'gross profit or loss' the following items:

(i) items 1, 2, 3 and 6 in Format 1 of the profit and loss account formats set out in the Schedule to this Act;

(ii) items 1 to 5 in Format 2 of the said profit and loss account formats;

(iii) items A.1, B.1 and B.2 in Format 3 of the said profit and loss account formats;

(iv) items A.1, A.2 and B.1 to B.4 in Format 4 of the said profit and loss account formats.][a]

Amendments

a C(A)A 1986, s 11 was replaced by EC(IFRSMA)R 2005, reg 5(f).

12 Exemptions in relation to notes to accounts for small companies and medium-sized companies

[(1) (a) Where the directors of a company prepare IFRS individual accounts and the company is to be treated as a small company in accordance with section 8(1) of this Act, the following notes shall be extracted from those accounts and included with the abridged balance sheet annexed to the annual return pursuant to section 10(1) of this Act:

(i) accounting policies applied in the preparation of the accounts;

(ii) information in relation to the maturity of non-current liabilities and any security given in respect of those liabilities;

(iii) disclosures made in accordance with section 149A(2)(a) to (k) of the Principal Act.

(b) Where the directors of a company prepare Companies Act individual accounts and the company is to be treated as a small company in accordance with section 8(1) of this Act, any notes resulting from the provisions of the Schedule to this Act (other than paragraphs 24, 26, 27, 31B, 31C, 33, 34 and 44) may be excluded from the abridged balance sheet annexed to the annual return pursuant to section 11(1) of this Act;

(2) (a) Where the directors of a company prepare IFRS individual accounts and the company is to be treated as a medium-sized company in accordance with section 8(1) of this Act, all notes forming part of those accounts shall be included with the abridged balance sheet and abridged income statement annexed to the annual return pursuant to section 11(1) of this Act, except that items that are combined on the face of the income statement need not be separately identified in the notes.

(b) Where the directors of a company prepare Companies Act individual accounts and the company is to be treated as a medium-sized company in accordance with section 8(1) of this Act, all notes forming part of those accounts shall be included with the abridged balance sheet and abridged profit and loss account annexed to the annual return pursuant to section 11(1) of this Act, except that the information required by paragraph 41 of the Schedule to this Act need not be given.][a]

Amendments

a C(A)A, 1986, s 12 replaced by EC(IFRSMA)R 2005, reg 5(f).

13 Information to be included in directors' report

[(1)][a] The report of the directors of a company under section 158 of the Principal Act shall contain, in addition to the information specified in that section, the following information:

[(a) a fair review of the development and performance of the company's business and of its position and, in relation to its subsidiary undertakings, if any, of the development and performance of their business and of their position, during the financial year ending with the relevant balance sheet date together with a description of the principal risks and uncertainties that they face, which review—

(i) shall be a balanced and comprehensive analysis of the development and performance of the company's business and of its position and, in relation to its subsidiary undertakings, if any, of the development and performance of their business and of their position, consistent with the size and complexity of the business, and

(ii) to the extent necessary for an understanding of the company's development, performance or position, and that of its subsidiary undertakings, if any, shall include an analysis of financial, and, where appropriate, non-financial key performance indicators relevant to the particular business, including information relevant to environmental and employee matters,

and, where appropriate, the report shall include additional explanations of amounts included in the annual accounts;][b]

(b) particulars of any important events affecting the company or any of its subsidiaries, if any, which have occurred since the end of that year;

[(c) an indication of likely future developments in the business of the company and of its subsidiaries, if any;

(d) an indication of the activities, if any, of the company and its subsidiaries, if any, in the field of research and development;

(e) an indication of the existence of branches (within the meaning of Council Directive 89/666/EEC[1]) of the company outside the State and the country in which each such branch is located, and] [c]

[(f) in relation to the use by the company and its subsidiaries, if any, of financial instruments and where material for the assessment of the assets, liabilities, financial position and profit or loss of the company and, as the case may be, the group—

(i) the financial risk management objectives and policies of the company and the group, including the policy for hedging each major type of forecasted transaction for which hedge accounting is used, and

(ii) the exposure of the company and the group to price risk, credit risk, liquidity risk and cash flow risk.][d]

[(2) Where a company is to be treated as a small or medium sized company pursuant to section 8(1) of this Act, the directors shall be exempt from the requirement to include in the report of the directors the information required by subsection (1)(a)(ii) and (f) of this section.][e]

Amendments

a C(A)A 1986, s 13 renumbered by EC(IFRSMA)R 2005, reg 5(g)(ii).

b C(A) A 1986 s 13 (1)(a) substituted by EC(IFRSMA)R 2005, reg 5(g)(i).

c C(A)A 1986, s 13(1)(c), (d) and (e) inserted by EC(FVA)R 2004, reg 3.

d C(A)A 1986, s 13(1) (f) inserted by EC(FVA)R 2004, reg 5.

e C(A)A 1986, s 13(2) inserted by EC(IFRSMA)R 2005, reg 5(g)(ii).

14 Information to be included in directors' report regarding acquisition by company of own shares

Where, in any financial year of a company, shares in the company—

(a) are acquired by the company by forfeiture or surrender in lieu of forfeiture, or

(b) are acquired by the company in pursuance of section 41 of the Act of 1983, or

(c) are required by another person in the circumstances specified in paragraph (c) or (d) of section 43(1) of that Act, or

(d) are made subject to a lien or other charge that is taken (whether expressly or otherwise) by the company and is permitted by paragraph (a), (c) or (d) of section 44(2) of that Act,

the directors' report with respect to that financial year of the company shall state—

(i) the number and nominal value of any shares of the company acquired as aforesaid by the company, the number and nominal value of any shares of the company acquired as aforesaid by another person, and the number and nominal value of any shares charged as aforesaid, respectively,

(ii) the maximum number and nominal value of any shares which, having been acquired as aforesaid (whether or not during that year) by the company or by another person or charged as aforesaid (whether or not during that year) are held at any time by the company or that other person during that year,

(iii) the number and nominal value of any shares acquired as aforesaid (whether or not during that year) by the company or another person or charged as aforesaid (whether or not during that year) which are disposed of by the company or that other person or cancelled by the company during that year,

(iv) where the number and nominal value of the shares of any particular description are stated in pursuance of any of the preceding paragraphs, the percentage of the called-up share capital of the company which shares of that description represent.

(v) in the case of a charge as aforesaid, the amount of the charge in each case, and

(vi) in the case of an [acquisition or disposal][a] as aforesaid for money or money's worth, the amount or value of the consideration in each case.

[(vii) the reasons for the acquisition, lien or charge, as the case may be].[b]

Amendments

a Words substituted by CA 1990, s 233.

b C(A)A 1986, s 14(vii) inserted by CA 1990, s 233.

---

15 Consideration by auditors of consistency of directors' report with company's accounts

It shall be the duty of the auditors of a company, in preparing the report in relation to the company required by [section 193 of the Companies Act 1990],[a] to consider whether the information given in the report of the directors of the company relating to the financial year concerned is consistent with the accounts prepared by the company for that year and they shall state in the report whether, in their opinion, such information is consistent with those accounts.

Amendments

a C(A)A 1986, s 15 amended by EC(IFRSMA)R 2005, reg 5(h).

---

16 Publication of information regarding subsidiary and associated companies

(1) Subject to the provisions of this section, where at the end of the financial year of a company, the company—

(a) has a subsidiary, or

[(b) holds a qualifying capital interest equal to 20 per cent or more of all such interests in an undertaking that is not its subsidiary undertaking (in this section referred to as 'an undertaking of substantial interest');][a]

[(c) for the purposes of subparagraph (b), interests held by persons acting in their own name but on behalf of the company shall be deemed to be held by the company,

(d) in this section, 'qualifying capital interest' shall have the meaning assigned to it in Regulation 35(2) of the European Communities (Companies: Group Accounts) Regulations, 1992,

(e) paragraph (4) of Regulation 35 of the European Communities (Companies: Group Accounts) Regulations, 1992, shall apply in determining the percentage of qualifying capital interests held by a company in an undertaking with share capital, for the purposes of this section];[b]

a note shall be included in the accounts of the company for that year annexed to the annual return distinguishing between the subsidiaries and the [undertaking of substantial interest][c] and giving the following information in relation to them—

(i) the name and registered office of each subsidiary or [undertaking of substantial interest][c] and the nature of the business carried on by it,

(ii) the identity of each class of shares held by the company in each subsidiary or [undertaking of substantial interest][c] and the proportion of the nominal value of the allotted shares in the subsidiary or [undertaking of substantial interest][c] of each such class represented by the shares of that class held by the company,

(iii) the aggregate amount of the capital and reserves of each subsidiary or [undertaking of substantial interest][c] as at the end of the financial year of the subsidiary or [undertaking of substantial interest][c] ending with or last before the end of the financial year of the company to which the accounts relate, and

(iv) the profit or loss of the subsidiary or [undertaking of substantial interest][c] for the financial year thereof mentioned in paragraph (iii) of this subsection.

[(2) Paragraphs (iii) and (iv) of subsection (l) of this section shall not apply—

[(a) in respect of a subsidiary undertaking of a company, if the company prepares Companies Acts group accounts in accordance with section 150 of the Principal Act, and either—

(i) the subsidiary undertaking is dealt with in the group accounts prepared by the company or where the company avails of the exemption in Regulation 8, 9 or 9A of the Group Accounts Regulations, the group accounts referred to in Regulation 8(3)(a) or 9A(2)(a) of those Regulations, or

(ii) the qualifying capital interest of the company in the subsidiary undertaking is included in or in a note to the company's accounts by way of the equity method of valuation,

or

(aa) in respect of a subsidiary undertaking of a company, where the company prepares IFRS group accounts in accordance with section 150 of the Principal Act, and either—

(i) the subsidiary undertaking is dealt with in the IFRS group accounts prepared by the company, or

(ii) where the company is exempt from preparing IFRS group accounts, the subsidiary undertaking is dealt with in IFRS group accounts prepared by a parent undertaking of the company,] [d]

(b) in respect of an undertaking of substantial interest of a company if the qualifying capital interest in the undertaking of substantial interest is included in or in a note to the company's accounts by way of the equity method of valuation,

or

(c) if—

(i) the subsidiary undertaking or the undertaking of substantial interest is not required to publish its accounts, and

(ii) the qualifying capital interest held in the subsidiary undertaking or the undertaking of substantial interest do not amount to at least 50 per cent of all such interests,

(d) if the information specified in subsection (l) of this section is not material.];[e]

(3) (a) Subject to paragraph (b) of this subsection, the information specified in subsection (1) of this section may, in lieu of being stated in a note to the

accounts of the company concerned for any particular financial year of the company, be given in a statement in writing signed by a director, and the secretary, of the company and annexed to the first annual return made by the company next after its accounts for that year are laid before the annual general meeting of the company if, in the opinion of the directors of the company, compliance with subsection (1) of this section would require a note to the accounts of the company of excessive length.

(b) Paragraph (a) of this subsection shall not apply in relation to information concerning a subsidiary or associated company of a company (referred to subsequently in this paragraph as the 'second-mentioned company') if the financial state of the subsidiary or associated company, as disclosed by its accounts, has, in the opinion of the directors of the second-mentioned company, a substantial effect on the profit or loss, or the amount of the assets, of the second-mentioned company and its subsidiaries.

(c) A copy of a statement annexed, pursuant to paragraph (a) of this subsection, to the annual return referred to in that subsection made by a company shall be certified both by a director, and the secretary, of the company to be a true copy of such statement.

(4) [...][f]

(5) Subsection (4) and (5) of section 158 of the Principal Act shall not apply to a company to which this section applies.

(6) [...][f]

Amendments

a C(A)A 1986, s 16(1)(b) substituted by EC(CGA)R 1992, reg 44(a).

b C(A)A 1986, s 16(1)(c)–(e) inserted by EC(CGA)R 1992, reg 44(b).

c 'undertaking of substantial interest' substituted for 'associated company' by EC(CGA)R 1992, reg 44(c).

d C(A)A 1986, s 16(2)(a)–(aa) substituted by EC(IFRSMA)R 2005, reg 5(i).

e C(A)A 1986, s 16(2) substituted by EC(CGA)R 1992, reg 44(d).

f C(A)A 1986, s 16(4) and (6) deleted by EC(CGA)R 1992, reg 44(e).

[16A

(1) A note shall be included in the accounts of the company annexed to the annual return stating the name, the head or registered office and the legal form of each of the undertakings of which the company is a member having unlimited liability, unless such information is of negligible importance only for the purpose of section 3(1)(b).

(2) Subsection 3 of section 16, shall apply to the information referred to in subsection (1) of this section.][a]

Amendments

a C(A)A 1986, s 16A inserted by EC(A)R 1993, reg 23.

17 Exemption for subsidiaries from section 7

[(1) Where a private company is a subsidiary undertaking of a parent undertaking established under the laws of a member state, the company shall, as respects any particular financial year of the company, stand exempted from the provisions of section 7 (other than subsection (1)(b)) of this Act if, but only if, the following conditions are fulfilled:

(a) every person who is a shareholder of the company on the date of the holding of the next annual general meeting of the company after the end of that financial year [or on the next annual return date of the company after the end of that financial year, which ever is the earlier],[b] shall declare his consent to the exemption,

[(b) there is in force in respect of the whole of that financial year an irrevocable guarantee by the parent undertaking of—

(i) the liabilities of the company referred to in section 5(c) of this Act in respect of that financial year, in a case where the company prepares Companies Act individual accounts, or

(ii) all liabilities in respect of that financial year, in a case where the company prepares IFRS individual accounts,

and the company has notified in writing every person referred to in paragraph (a) of this subsection of the guarantee,],[c]

(c) the annual accounts of the company for that financial year are consolidated in the group accounts prepared by the parent undertaking and the exemption of the company under this section is disclosed in a note to the group accounts,

(d) a notice stating that the company has availed of the exemption under this section in respect of that financial year and a copy of the guarantee and notification referred to in paragraph (b) of this subsection, together with a declaration by the company in writing that paragraph (a) of this subsection has been complied with in relation to the exemption, is annexed to the annual return for the financial year made by the company under the Principal Act to the registrar of companies,

[(e) the group accounts of the parent undertaking are drawn up in accordance with the requirements of the Seventh Council Directive 83/349/EEC of 13 June 1983 or in accordance with international financial reporting standards, and][d]

(f) the group accounts of the parent undertaking are annexed to the annual return aforesaid and are audited in accordance with Article 37 of the said Seventh Council Directive.

(2) The Minister may make such orders (if any) as may be necessary for the purpose of enabling this section to have full effect.][a]

Amendments

a C(A)A 1986, s 17, substituted by EC(CGA)R 1992, reg 45.

b Words inserted by CLEA 2001, s 65.

c C(A)A 1986, s 17(1)(b) substituted by EC(IFRSMA)R 2005, reg 5(j)(i).

d C(A)A 1986, s 17(1)(e) substituted by EC(IFRSMA)R 2005, reg 5(j)(ii).

---

18 Provisions in relation to documents delivered to registrar of companies

[(1) Abridged accounts (within the meaning of section 19 of this Act) annexed to the annual return required by the Principal Act to be made by the company to the registrar of companies shall be signed as required by section 156 of the Principal Act and the abridged balance sheet so annexed shall contain the statement required by subsection (2) of this section in a position immediately above the signatures appended pursuant to the said section 156 and shall be accompanied by a copy of the report of the auditors of the company in relation to the abridged accounts of the company under subsection (3) of this section.][a]

(2) [An abridged balance sheet][b] of a company prepared pursuant to any of the provisions of sections 10 to 12 of this Act and annexed to the said annual return shall contain a statement by the directors that—

(a) they have relied on specified exemptions contained in the said sections 10 to 12, and

(b) they have done so on the ground that the company is entitled to the benefit of those exemptions as a small company or (as the case may be) as a medium-sized company.

[(3) Abridged accounts delivered to the registrar of companies need not be accompanied by the report of the auditors under section 193 of the Companies Act 1990 on the company's individual accounts, but shall be accompanied by a special report of the auditors containing—

(a) a copy of the report made by the auditors of the company under subsection (4) of this section on those abridged accounts, and

(b) a copy of the report of the auditors under section 193 of the Companies Act 1990 on the company's individual accounts.][c]

(4) Where the directors of a company propose to annex to the annual return [abridged accounts][d] for any accounting period prepared pursuant to any of the provisions of sections 10 to 12 of this Act and the auditors of the company are satisfied that the directors of the company are entitled, for that purpose, to rely on exemptions specified in sections 10 to 12 of this Act and that the [abridged accounts][d] have been properly prepared pursuant to those provisions, it shall be the duty of the auditors of the company to provide the directors of the company with a report in writing stating that, in the opinion of the auditors of the company, the directors of the company are entitled to annex those [abridged accounts][d] to the annual return and that the [abridged accounts][d] so annexed are properly prepared as aforesaid.

(5) A copy of the report of the auditors of a company under subsection (3) of this section furnished to the registrar of companies pursuant to this section shall be certified both by a director, and the secretary, of the company to be a true copy of such report.

Amendments

a C(A)A 1986, s 18(1) substituted by EC(IFRSMA)R 2005, reg 5(k)(i).

b C(A)A 1986, s 18(2) amended by EC(IFRSMA)R 2005, reg 5(k)(ii).

c C(A)A 1986, s 18(3) substituted by EC(IFRSMA)R 2005, reg 5(k)(iiii).

d C(A)A 1986, s 18(4) amended by EC(IFRSMA)R 2005, reg 5(k)(iv).

19 Publication of full or abbreviated accounts

[(1) Where a company publishes its full individual accounts, it shall also publish with those accounts any report of the auditors made in accordance with section 193 of the Companies Act 1990.

(1A) Where a company publishes its abridged accounts, it shall also publish with those accounts any report in relation to those accounts specified in subsection (3) of section 18 of this Act and, if the auditors of the company have refused to provide the directors of the company with a report under subsection (4) of that section, an indication of the refusal.][a]

(2) Where a company publishes abbreviated accounts relating to any financial year, it shall also publish a statement indicating—

(a) that the accounts are not the accounts copies of which are required by this Act to be annexed to the annual return,

(b) whether the copies of the accounts so required to be so annexed have in fact been so annexed,

(c) whether the auditors of the company have made a report under section 163 of the Principal Act in respect of the accounts of the company which relate to any financial year with which the abbreviated accounts purport to deal,

[(d) whether any matters referred to in the auditors' report were qualified or unqualified, or whether the auditors' report included a reference to any matters to which the auditors drew attention by way of emphasis without qualifying the report.][b]

(3) Where a company published abbreviated accounts, it shall not publish with those accounts any such report of the auditors as is mentioned in subsection (2)(c) of this section.

[(3A) Where a company publishes its full individual accounts for a financial year it shall indicate if group accounts have been prepared and, if so, where those group accounts can be obtained.][c]

(4) In this section—

'abbreviated accounts', in relation to a company, means any balance sheet or profit and loss account, or summary or abstract of a balance sheet or profit and loss account, relating to a financial year of the company which is published by the company otherwise than as part of the full accounts of the company for that financial year and, in relation to a holding company, includes an account in any form purporting to be a balance sheet or profit and loss account, or a summary or abstract of a balance sheet or profit and loss account, of the group consisting of the holding company and its subsidiaries;

['abridged accounts', in relation to a company, means accounts of the company prepared in accordance with sections 10 to 12 of this Act and, except in the case of a company which is exempt by virtue of section 10 of this Act from annexing a copy of such a report to the annual return, the report of the directors of the company specified in section 158(1) of the Principal Act;][d]

['full individual accounts', in relation to a company, means the accounts of the company prepared in accordance with section 148 of the Principal Act;][e]

'publish', in relation to a document, includes issue, circulate or otherwise make it available for public inspection in a manner calculated to invite the public generally, or any class of members of the public, to read the document, and cognate words shall be construed accordingly.

Amendments

a C(A)A 1986, s 19(1) and (1A) substituted by EC(IFRSMA)R 2005, reg 5(l)(i).

b C(A)A 1986, s 19(2)(d) substituted by EC(IFRSMA)R 2005, reg 5(l)(ii).

c C(A)A 1986, s 19(3A) inserted by EC(CGA)R 1992, reg 46.

d Definition of 'abridged accounts' in C(A)A 1986, s 19(4) inserted by EC(IFRSMA)R 2005, reg 5(l)(iii)(I).

e Definition of 'full individual accounts' in C(A)A 1986, s 19(4) amended by EC(IFRSMA)R 2005, reg 5(l)(iii)(II).

---

20 Amendment of Act of 1983

[...][a]

Amendments

a C(A)A 1986, s 20 inserted CA 1963, s 45A.

---

21 Power to apply Act to unregistered companies

[...][a]

Amendments

a C(A)A 1986, s 21 repealed by CA 1990, s 6(2)(c).

---

22 Offences and penalties

(1) (a) If a company fails to comply with a provision of section 5, 6, 7, 10, 11, 16, 18 or 19 of this Act, the company and every officer of the company who is in default [shall be guilty of an offence][a].

(b) [Summary proceedings][b] for an offence under this subsection, in relation to sections 7, 10, 11, 16 or 18 of this Act, may be brought and prosecuted by the registrar of companies.

(2) If any person, being a director of a company, fails to take all reasonable steps to secure compliance with the requirements of section 3 or section 4 (other than subsections (3) and (13)) of this Act or to comply with the provisions of subsections (3) or (13) of section 4 or section 13 or 14 of this Act, he shall – [in respect of each such failure be guilty of an offence, but—][c]

(a) in any proceedings against a person in respect of an offence under this subsection, it shall be a defence to prove that he had reasonable grounds to believe and did believe that a competent and reliable person was charged with he duty of ensuring that the provisions of the said section 3 or section 4 (other than subsections (3) and (13)), as may be appropriate, were complied with and that the latter person was in a position to discharge that duty, and

(b) a person shall not be liable to be sentenced to imprisonment for such an offence unless, in the opinion of the court, the offence was committed wilfully.

(3) If any person in any return, report, certificate, balance sheet or other documents required by or for the purposes of any of the provisions of this Act wilfully makes a statement false in any material particular, knowing it to be false, he shall be liable –

(a) on conviction on indictment, to imprisonment for a term not exceeding three years or a fine not exceeding [€6,348.70][d] or both, or

(b) on summary conviction, to imprisonment for a term not exceeding six months or a [class C fine][e] or both.

(4) Section 385 of the Principal Act shall have effect as if for the sum mentioned in subsection (1) there were substituted [€1,269.74][f].

(5) In this section 'director' and 'officer' includes any person in accordance with whose directions or instructions the directors of the company are accustomed to act.

Amendments

a C(A)A 1986, s 22(1)(a) amended by IFCMPA 2005, s 66.

b C(A)A 1986, s 22(1)(b) amended by IFCMPA 2005, s 66.

c C(A)A 1986, s 22(2) amended by IFCMPA 2005, s 66.

d '£2,500' converted to €3,174.35 by Council Regulation (EC) No 1103/97, No 974/98, No 2866/98 and the European and Monetary Act 1998, s 6, and multiplied by a multiplier of 2 pursuant to Fines Act 2010, s 9.

e '£1,000' increased to £1,500 by CA 1990, s 240(7) as inserted by CLEA 2001, s 104(c), and converted to €1,904.61 by Council Regulations (EC) No 1103/97, No 974/98 and No 2866/98 and the Economic and Monetary Union Act 1998, s 6; the above being implicitly substituted, by Fines Act 2010, s 6, for a fine not exceeding the aforesaid amount. A class C fine currently means a fine not exceeding €2,500.

f '£1,000' converted to €1,269.74 by Council Regulation (EC) No 1103/97, No 974/98, No 2866/98 and the European and Monetary Act 1998, s 6.

23 Restriction of section 222 of Principal Act

Section 222 of the Principal Act shall not apply to proceedings before the Employment Appeals Tribunal.

24 Power of Minister to modify Act in certain respects

(1) The Minister may by order alter or add to the provisions of this Act, in so far as it relates to the balance sheet and profit and loss account of a company and the notes to and documents to be attached to such a balance sheet or profit and loss account, either generally or in relation to a specified class or classes of company.

(2) An order under this section shall be laid before each House of the Oireachtas as soon as may be after it is made and, if a resolution annulling the order is passed by either such House within the next 21 days on which that House has sat after the order is laid before it, the order shall be annulled accordingly but without prejudice to the validity of anything previously done thereunder.

25 Short title, collective citation, construction and commencement

(1) This Act may be cited as the Companies (Amendment) Act, 1986.

(2) The Companies Acts, 1963 to 1982, the Companies (Amendment) Act, 1983, section 6 of the Designated Investment Funds Act, 1985, and this Act may be cited together as the Companies Acts, 1963 to 1986.

(3) The Companies Acts, 1963 to 1982, the Companies (Amendment) Act, 1983, section 6 of the Designated Investment Funds Act, 1985, and this Act shall be construed together as one.

(4) Save as is otherwise specifically provided thereby, this Act shall come into operation on such day or days as, by order or orders made by the Minister under this section, may be fixed therefor either generally or with reference to any particular purpose or provision and different days may be so fixed for different purposes and different provisions.

(5) (a) Subject to paragraph (b) of this subsection, each provision of this Act shall apply as respects the accounts of a company, and the report by the directors of a company specified in section 158 of the Principal Act, for each financial year of the company beginning or ending, as may be specified by the Minister by order, after such date after the commencement of the provision as may be specified by the Minister by order.

(b) Paragraph (a) of this subsection does not apply in relation to subsection (7) or (8) of section 8 of this Act.

SCHEDULE

FORM AND CONTENTS OF ACCOUNTS

PART I

THE REQUIRED FORMATS FOR ACCOUNTS

Preliminary

1. References in this Part of this Schedule to the items listed in any of the formats set out in this Part are references to those items read together with any notes following the formats which apply to any of those items.

2. A number in brackets following any item in, or any heading to, any of the formats set out in this Part is a reference to the note of that number in the notes following the formats.

3. In the notes following the formats—

(a) the heading of each note gives the required heading or subheading for the item to which it applies and a reference to any letters and numbers assigned to that item in the formats set out in this Part; and

(b) references to a numbered format are references to the balance sheet format or (as the case may require) to the profit and loss account format of that number set out in this Part.

BALANCE SHEET FORMATS

Format 1

A. Fixed Assets

I. Intangible assets

1. Development costs
2. Concessions, patents, licences, trade marks and similar rights and assets (1)
3. Goodwill (2)
4. Payments on account

II. Tangible assets

1. Land and buildings
2. Plant and machinery
3. Fixtures, fittings, tools and equipment
4. Payments on account and assets in course of construction

III. Financial assets

1. Shares in [group undertakings][a]
2. Loans to [group undertakings][a]
3. [Participating interests][b]
4. Loans to [undertakings in which a participating interest is held][c]
5. Other investments other than loans
6. Other loans
7. [...][d]

B. Current Assets

I. Stocks

1. Raw materials and consumables
2. Work in progress
3. Finished goods and goods for resale
4. Payments on account

II. Debtors (4)

1. Trade debtors
2. Amounts owed by [group undertakings][a]

3. Amounts owed by [undertakings in which a participating interest is held][c]
4. Other debtors
5. Called up share capital not paid
6. Prepayments and accrued income

III. Investments

1. Shares in [group undertakings][a]
2. [...][d]
3. Other investments

IV. Cash at bank and in hand

C. Creditors: amounts falling due within one year

1. Debenture loans (5)
2. Bank loans and overdrafts
3. Payments received on account (6)
4. Trade creditors
5. Bills of exchange payable
6. Amounts owed to [group undertakings][a]
7. Amounts owed to [undertakings in which a participating interest is held][c]
8. Other creditors including tax and social welfare (7)
9. Accruals and deferred income (8)

D. Net current assets (liabilities)

E. Total assets less current liabilities

F. Creditors: Amounts falling due after more than one year

1. Debenture loans (5)
2. Bank loans and overdrafts
3. Payments received on account (6)
4. Trade creditors
5. Bills of exchange payable
6. Amounts owed to [group undertakings][a]
7. Amounts owed to [undertakings in which a participating interest is held][c]
8. Other creditors including tax and social welfare (7)
9. Accruals and deferred income (8)

G. [Provisions for liabilities][e]

1. Pensions and similar obligations
2. Taxation, including deferred taxation
3. Other provisions

H. Capital and reserves

I. Called up share capital (9)

II. Share premium account

III. Revaluation reserve

IV. Other reserves

1. The capital redemption reserve fund
2. [...][d]
3. Reserves provided for by the articles of association
4. Other reserves

V. Profit and loss account

[Minority Interest][f]

Amendments

a 'group undertakings' substituted for 'group companies' by EC(CGA)R 1992, Sch, Pt I para 1.

b 'participating interests' substituted for 'shares in related companies' by EC(CGA)R 1992, Sch, Pt 1 para 2.

c 'undertakings in which a participating interest is held' substituted for 'related companies' by EC(CGA)R 1992, Sch, Pt 1 para 3.

d Item deleted by CA 1990, s 233(2)(a).

e 'Provisions for liabilities' substituted for 'Provisions for liabilities and charges' by EC(IFRSMA)R 2005, reg 5(m)(i)(I).

f Inserted by EC(CGA)R 1992, Sch, Pt 1 para 8(1)(a).

BALANCE SHEET FORMATS

Format 2

ASSETS

A. Fixed Assets

I. Intangible assets

1. Development costs
2. Concessions, patents, licences, trade marks and similar rights and assets (1)
3. Goodwill (2)
4. Payments on account

II. Tangible assets

1. Land and buildings
2. Plant and machinery
3. Fixtures, fittings, tools and equipment
4. Payments on account and assets in course of construction

III. Financial assets

1. Shares in [group undertakings][a]
2. Loans to [group undertakings][a]
3. [Participating interests][b]
4. Loans to [undertakings in which a participating interest is held][c]
5. Other investments other than loans
6. Other loans

7. [...][d]

B. Current Assets

I. Stocks

1. Raw materials and consumables
2. Work in progress
3. Finished goods and goods for resale
4. Payments on account

II. Debtors (4)

1. Trade debtors
2. Amounts owed by [group undertakings][a]
3. Amounts owed by [undertakings in which a participating interest is held][c]
4. Other debtors
5. Called up share capital not paid
6. Prepayments and accrued income

III. Investments

1. Shares in [group undertakings][a]
2. [...][d]
3. Other investments

IV. Cash at bank and in hand

LIABILITIES

A. Capital and reserves

I. Called up share capital (9)

II. Share premium account

III. Revaluation reserve

IV. Other reserves

1. The capital redemption reserve fund

[...][d]

3. Reserves provided for by the articles of association
4. Other reserves

V. Profit and loss account

[Minority Interest][e]

B. [Provisions for liabilities][f]

1. Pensions and similar obligations
2. Taxation, including deferred taxation
3. Other provisions

C. Creditors (10)

1. Debenture loans (5)
2. Bank loans and overdrafts
3. Payments received on account (6)
4. Trade creditors

5. Bills of exchange payable
6. Amounts owed to [group undertakings][a]
7. Amounts owed to [undertakings in which a participating interest is held][c]
8. Other creditors including tax and social welfare (7)
9. Accruals and deferred income (8)

Amendments

a 'group undertakings' substituted for 'group companies' by EC(CGA)R 1992, Sch, Pt 1 para 1.

b 'participating interests' substituted for 'shares in related companies' by EC(CGA)R 1992, Sch, Pt 1 para 2.

c 'undertakings in which a participating interest is held' substituted for 'related companies' by EC(CGA)R 1992, Sch, Pt 1 para 3.

d Item deleted by CA 1990, s 233(2)(b).

e Inserted by EC(CGA)R 1992, Sch, Pt 1 para 8(b).

f 'Provisions for liabilities' substituted for 'Provisions for liabilities and charges' by EC(IFRSMA)R 2005, reg 5(m)(i)(II).

NOTES ON THE BALANCE SHEET FORMATS

(1) *Concessions, patents, licences, trade marks and similar rights and assets*

(Formats 1 and 2, items A. I. 2)

Amounts in respect of assets shall only be included in a company's balance sheet under this item if either—

(a) the assets were acquired for valuable consideration and are not required to be shown under goodwill, or

(b) the assets in question were created by the company itself.

(2) *Goodwill*

(Formats 1 and 2, items A. I. 3)

Amounts representing goodwill shall only be included to the extent that the goodwill was acquired for valuable consideration.

(3) [...][a]

(4) *Debtors*

(Formats 1 and 2, items B. II. 1 to 6)

The amount failing due after more than one year shall be shown separately for each item included under debtors.

(5) *Debenture loans*

(Format 1, item C.1 and F.1 and Format 2, item C.1)

The amount of any convertible loans shall be shown separately.

(6) *Payments received on account*

(Format 1, items C.3 and F.3 and Format 2, item C.3)

Payments received on account of orders shall be shown for each of these items insofar as they are not shown as deductions from stocks.

(7) *Other creditors including tax and social welfare*

(Format 1, items C.8 and F.8 and Format 2, item C.8)

The amount for creditors in respect of taxation and social welfare shall be shown separately from the amount for other creditors and in respect of taxation there shall be stated separately the amounts included in respect of income tax payable on emoluments to which Chapter IV of Part V of the Income Tax Act, 1967, applies, any other income tax, corporation tax, capital gains tax, value-added tax and any other tax.

(8) *Accruals and deferred income*

(Format 1, items C. 9 and F. 9 and Format 2, item C. 9)

The amount in respect of Government grants, that is to say, grants made by or on behalf of the Government, included in this item shall be shown separately in a note to the accounts unless it is shown separately in the balance sheet.

(9) *Called up share capital*

(Format 1, item H. I and Format 2, item A. I)

The amount of allotted share capital and the amount of called up share capital which has been paid up shall be shown separately.

(10) *Creditors*

(Format 2, items C.1 to 9)

Amounts falling due within one year and after one year shall be shown separately for each of these items and their aggregate shall be shown separately for all of these items.

Amendments

a Deleted by CA 1990, s 233(c).

PROFIT AND LOSS ACCOUNT FORMATS

Format 1 (14)

1. Turnover
2. Cost of Sales (11)
3. Gross Profit or Loss
4. Distribution costs (11)
5. Administrative expenses (11)
6. Other operating income
7. Income from shares in [group undertakings][a]
8. Income from [participating interests][b]
9. Income from other financial assets (12)
10. Other interest receivable and similar income (12)
11. Amounts written off financial assets and investments held as current assets
12. Interest payable and similar charges (13)
13. Tax on profit or loss on ordinary activities
14. Profit or loss on ordinary activities after taxation

[Minority Interest][c]

15. Extraordinary income
16. Extraordinary charges
17. Extraordinary profit or loss
18. Tax on extraordinary profit or loss
    [Minority Interest][d]
19. Other taxes not shown under the above items
20. Profit or loss for the financial year

Amendments

a 'group undertakings' substituted for 'group companies' by EC(CGA)R 1992, Sch, Pt I para 1.

b 'participating interests' substituted for 'shares in related companies' by EC(CGA)R 1992, Sch, Pt 1 para 2.

c Inserted by EC(CGA)R 1992, Sch, Pt 1 para 9(1)(a).

d Inserted by EC(CGA)R 1992, Sch, Pt 1 para 9(3)(a).

PROFIT AND LOSS ACCOUNT FORMATS

Format 2

1. Turnover
2. Variation in stocks of finished goods and in work in progress
3. Own work capitalised
4. Other operating income
5. (a) Raw materials and consumables
   (b) Other external charges
6. Staff costs:
   (a) Wages and salaries
   (b) Social welfare costs
   (c) Other pension costs
7. (a) Depreciation and other amounts written off tangible and intangible fixed assets
   (b) Exceptional amounts written off current assets
8. Other operating charges
9. Income from shares in [group undertakings][a]
10. Income from [participating interests][b]
11. Income from other financial assets (12)
12. Other interest receivable and similar income (12)
13. Amounts written off financial assets and investments held as current assets
14. Interest payable and similar charges (13)
15. Tax on profit or loss on ordinary activities
16. Profit or loss on ordinary activities after taxation

[Minority Interest][c]

17. Extraordinary income
18. Extraordinary charges
19. Extraordinary profit or loss
20. Tax on extraordinary profit or loss

    [Minority Interest][d]

21. Other taxes not shown under the above items
22. Profit or loss for the financial year

Amendments

a 'group undertakings' substituted for 'group companies' by EC(CGA)R 1992, Sch, Pt I para 1.

b 'participating interests' substituted for 'shares in related companies' by EC(CGA)R 1992, Sch, Pt 1 para 2.

c Inserted by EC(CGA)R 1992, Sch, Pt 1 para 9(1)(b).

d Inserted by EC(CGA)R 1992, Sch, Pt 1 para 9(3)(b).

PROFIT AND LOSS ACCOUNT FORMATS

Format 3 (14)

A. Charges

1. Cost of sales (11)
2. Distribution costs (11)
3. Administrative expenses (11)
4. Amounts written off financial assets and investments held as current assets
5. Interest payable and similar charges (13)
6. Tax on profit or loss on ordinary activities
7. Profit or loss on ordinary activities after taxation

   [Minority Interest][a]

8. Extraordinary charges
9. Tax on extraordinary profit or loss

   [Minority Interest][b]

10. Other taxes not shown under the above items
11. Profit or loss for the financial year

B. Income

1. Turnover
2. Other operating income
3. Income from shares in [group undertakings][c]
4. Income from [participating interests][d]
5. Income from other financial assets (12)
6. Other interest receivable and similar income (12)
7. Profit or loss on ordinary activities after taxation

[Minority Interest][a]

8. Extraordinary income

[Minority Interest][b]

9. Profit or loss for the financial year

Amendments

a Inserted by EC(CGA)R 1992, Sch, Pt 1 para 9(1)(c).

b Inserted by EC(CGA)R 1992, Sch, Pt 1 para 9(3)(c).

c 'group undertakings' substituted for 'group companies' by EC(CGA)R 1992, Sch, Pt I para 1.

d 'participating interests' substituted for 'shares in related companies' by EC(CGA)R 1992, Sch, Pt 1 para 2.

PROFIT AND LOSS ACCOUNT FORMATS

Format 4

A. Charges

1. Reduction in stocks of finished goods and in work in progress
2. (a) Raw materials and consumables
   (b) Other external charges
3. Staff costs:
   (a) Wages and salaries
   (b) Social welfare costs
   (c) Other pension costs
4. (a) Depreciation and other amounts written off tangible and intangible fixed assets
   (b) Exceptional amounts written off current assets
5. Other operating charges
6. Amounts written off financial assets and investments held as current assets
7. Interest payable and similar charges (13)
8. Tax on profit or loss on ordinary activities
9. Profit or loss on ordinary activities after taxation
   [Minority Interest][a]
10. Extraordinary charges
11. Tax on extraordinary profit or loss
    [Minority Interest][b]
12. Other taxes not shown under the above items
13. Profit or loss for the financial year

B. Income

1. Turnover
2. Increase in stocks of finished goods and in work in progress
3. Own work capitalised

4. Other operating income
5. Income from shares in [group undertakings][c]
6. Income from [participating interests][d]
7. Income from other financial assets (12)
8. Other interest receivable and similar income (12)
9. Profit or loss on ordinary activities after taxation
   [Minority Interest][a]
10. Extraordinary income
    [Minority Interest][b]
11. Profit or loss for the financial year

Amendments

a Inserted by EC(CGA)R 1992, Sch, Pt 1 para 9(1)(d).

b Inserted by EC(CGA)R 1992, Sch, Pt 1 para 9(3)(d).

c 'group undertakings' substituted for 'group companies' by EC(CGA)R 1992, Sch, Pt I para 1.

d 'participating interests' substituted for 'shares in related companies' by EC(CGA)R 1992, Sch, Pt 1 para 2.

NOTES ON THE PROFIT AND LOSS ACCOUNT FORMATS

(11) *Cost of sales: Distribution costs: Administrative expenses*

(Format 1, items 2, 4 and 5 and Format 3, items A. 1, 2 and 3)

These items shall be stated after taking into account any necessary provisions for depreciation or diminution in value of assets.

(12) *Income from other financial assets: other interest receivable and similar income*

(Format 1, items 9 and 10; Format 2, items 11 and 12; Format 3, items B. 5 and 6; Format 4, items B. 7 and 8)

Income and interest derived from [group undertakings][a] shall be shown separately from income and interest derived from other sources.

(13) *Interest payable and similar charges*

(Format 1, item 12; Format 2, item 14; Format 3, item A. 5; Format 4, item A. 7)

The amount payable to [group undertakings][a] shall be shown separately.

(14) *Formats 1 and 3*

The amounts of any provisions for depreciation and diminution in value of tangible and intangible fixed assets falling to be shown under items 7 (a) and A. 4 (a), respectively, in Formats 2 and 4 shall be disclosed in a note to the accounts in any case where the profit and loss account is prepared by reference to Format 1 or Format 3.

Amendments

a 'group undertakings' substituted for 'group companies' by EC(CGA)R 1992, Sch, Pt I para 1.

PART II

HISTORICAL COST RULES IN RELATION TO THE DRAWING UP OF ACCOUNTS

Preliminary

4. Subject to [Parts III and IIIA][a] of this Schedule, the amounts to be included in respect of all items shown in a company's accounts shall be determined in accordance with the rules set out in the following paragraphs of this Part.

Amendments

a 'Parts III and IIIA' substituted for 'Part III' by EC(FVA)R 2004, reg 3(c)(i).

FIXED ASSETS

General rules

5. Subject to any provision for depreciation or diminution in value made in accordance with paragraph 6 or 7 of this Schedule the amount to be included in respect of any fixed asset shall be its purchase price or production cost.

6. In the case of any fixed asset which has a limited useful economic life, the amount of—

(a) its purchase price or production cost, or

(b) where it is estimated that any such asset will have a residual value at the end of the period of its useful economic life, its purchase price or production cost less that estimated residual value,

shall be reduced by provisions for depreciation calculated to write off that amount systematically over the period of the asset's useful economic life.

7. (1) Where a financial asset of a description falling to be included under item A. III of either of the balance sheet formats set out in Part I of this Schedule has diminished in value, provisions for diminution in value may be made in respect of it and the amount to be included in respect of it may be reduced accordingly; and any such provisions which are not shown separately in the profit and loss account shall be disclosed (either separately or in aggregate) in a note to the accounts.

(2) Provisions for diminution in value shall be made in respect of any fixed asset which has diminished in value if the reduction in its value is expected to be permanent (whether its useful economic life is limited or not) and the amount to be included in respect of it shall be reduced accordingly; and any such provisions which are not shown separately in the profit and loss account shall be disclosed (either separately or in aggregate) in a note to the accounts.

(3) Where the reasons for which any provision was made in accordance with subparagraph (1) or (2) of this paragraph have ceased to apply to any extent, that provision shall be written back to the extent that it is no longer necessary; and any amounts written back in accordance with this subparagraph which are not shown in the profit and loss account shall be disclosed (either separately or in aggregate) in a note to the accounts.

Rules for determining particular fixed asset items

8. (1) Notwithstanding that an item in respect of 'development costs' is included under 'fixed assets' in the balance sheet formats set out in Part I of this Schedule, an amount may only be included in a company's balance sheet in respect of that item in special circumstances.

(2) If an amount is included in a company's balance sheet in respect of development costs, the following information shall be given in a note to the accounts—

(a) the period over which the amount of those costs originally capitalised is being or is to be written off, and

(b) the reasons for capitalising the costs in question.

9. (1) The application of paragraphs 5 to 7 of this Schedule in relation to goodwill (in any case where goodwill is treated as an asset) is subject to the following provisions of this paragraph.

(2) Subject to subparagraph (3) of this paragraph, the amount of the consideration for any goodwill acquired by a company shall be reduced by provisions for depreciation calculated to write off that amount systematically over a period chosen by the directors of the company.

(3) The period chosen shall not exceed the useful economic life of the goodwill in question.

(4) In any case where any goodwill acquired by a company is shown or included as an asset in the company's balance sheet, the period chosen for writing off the consideration for that goodwill and the reasons for choosing that period shall be disclosed in a note to the accounts.

CURRENT ASSETS

10. Subject to paragraph 11 of this Schedule the amount to be included in respect of any current asset shall be its purchase price or production cost.

11. (1) If the net realisable value of any current asset is lower than its purchase price or production cost, the amount to be included in respect of that asset shall be the net realisable value.

(2) Where the reasons for which any provision for diminution in value was made under subparagraph (1) of this paragraph have ceased to apply to any extent, that provision shall be written back to the extent that it is no longer necessary.

MISCELLANEOUS

Excess of money owed over value received as an asset item

12. (1) Where the amount repayable on any debt owed by a company is greater than the value of the consideration received in the transaction giving rise to the debt, the amount of the difference may be treated as an asset.

(2) Where any such amount exists—

(a) it shall be written off by reasonable amounts each year and shall be completely written off before repayment of the debt; and

(b) if the amount not written off is not shown as a separate item in the company's balance sheet, it shall be disclosed in a note to the accounts.

ASSETS INCLUDED AT A FIXED AMOUNT

13. (1) Subject to subparagraph (2) of this paragraph, assets which fall to be included—

(a) amongst the fixed assets of a company under the item 'tangible assets', or

(b) amongst the current assets of a company under the item 'raw materials and consumables',

may be included at a fixed quantity and value.

(2) Subparagraph (1) of this paragraph applies to assets of a kind which are constantly being replaced, where—

(a) their overall value is not material to assessing the company's state of affairs, and

(b) their quantity, value and composition are not subject to material variation.

DETERMINATION OF PURCHASE PRICE OR PRODUCTION COST

14. (1) The purchase price of an asset shall be determined by adding to the actual price paid any expenses incidental to its acquisition.

(2) The production cost of an asset shall be determined by adding to the purchase price of the raw materials and consumables used the amount of the costs incurred by the company which are directly attributable to the production of that asset.

(3) In addition there may be included in the production cost of an asset—

(a) a reasonable proportion of the costs incurred by the company which are only indirectly attributable to the production of that asset, but only to the extent that they relate to the period of production, and

(b) interest on capital borrowed to finance the production of that asset, to the extent that it accrues in respect of the period of production:

Provided, however, in a case within clause (b) of this subparagraph that the inclusion of the interest in determining the cost of that asset is disclosed in a note to the accounts.

(4) In the case of current assets, distribution costs may not be included in production costs.

15. (1) Subject to the qualification mentioned in this subparagraph, the purchase price or production cost of—

(a) any assets which fall to be included under any item shown in a company's balance sheet under the general item 'stocks', and

(b) any assets which are fungible assets (including investments),

may be determined by the application of any of the methods mentioned in subparagraph (2) of this paragraph in relation to any such assets of the same class.

The method chosen must be one which appears to the directors to be appropriate in the circumstances of the company.

(2) Those methods are:

(a) the method known as 'first in, first out' (FIFO),

(b) a weighted average price, and

(c) any other method similar to any of the methods mentioned above.

(3) Where, in the case of any company—

(a) the purchase price or production cost of assets falling to be included under any item shown in the company's balance sheet has been determined by the application of any method permitted by this paragraph, and

(b) the amount shown in respect of that item differs materially from the relevant alternative amount given below in this paragraph,

the amount of that difference shall be disclosed in a note to the accounts.

(4) Subject to subparagraph (5) of this paragraph, for the purposes of subparagraph (3)(b) of this paragraph, the relevant alternative amount, in relation to any item shown in a company's balance sheet, is the amount which would have been shown in respect of that item if assets of any class included under that item at an amount determined by any method permitted by this paragraph had instead been included at their replacement cost as at the balance sheet date.

(5) The relevant alternative amount may be determined by reference to the most recent actual purchase price or production cost before the balance sheet date of assets of any class included under the item in question instead of by reference to their replacement cost as at that date, but only if the former appears to the directors of the company to constitute the more appropriate approach in the case of assets of that class.

(6) For the purpose of this paragraph, assets of any description shall be regarded as fungible if assets of that description are substantially indistinguishable one from another.

Substitution of original stated amount where price or cost unknown

16. Where there is no record of the purchase price or production cost of any asset of a company or of any price, expense or costs relevant for determining its purchase price or production cost in accordance with paragraph 14 of this Schedule or any such record cannot be obtained without unreasonable expense or delay, its purchase price or production cost shall be taken for the purposes of paragraphs 5 to 11 of this Schedule to be the value ascribed to it in the earliest available record of its value made on or after its acquisition or production by the company.

Part III

Alternative Rules in Relation to the Drawing Up of Accounts

Preliminary

17. (1) The rules set out in Part II of this Schedule are referred to subsequently in this Schedule as the historical cost accounting rules.

(2) Those rules, with the omission of paragraphs 4, 9 and 13 to 16, are referred to subsequently in this Part of this Schedule as the depreciation rules; and references subsequently in this Schedule to the historical cost accounting rules do not include the depreciation rules as they apply by virtue of paragraph 20 of this Schedule.

18. Subject to paragraphs 20 to 22 of this Schedule, the amounts to be included in respect of assets of any description mentioned in paragraph 19 of this Schedule may be determined on any basis so mentioned.

Alternative accounting rules

19.(1) Intangible fixed assets, other than goodwill, may be included at their current cost.

(2) Tangible fixed assets may be included at a market value determined as at the date of their last valuation or at their current cost.

(3) Financial fixed assets may be included either—

(a) at a market value determined as at the date of their last valuation; or

(b) at a value determined on any basis which appears to the directors to be appropriate in the circumstances of the company,

but in the latter case particulars of the method of valuation adopted and of the reasons for adopting it shall be disclosed in a note to the accounts.

(4) Investments of any description falling to be included under item B. III of either of the balance sheet formats set out in Part I of this Schedule may be included at their current cost.

(5) Stocks may be included at their current cost.

Application of the depreciation rules

20. (1) Where the value of any asset of a company is determined on any basis mentioned in paragraph 19 of this Schedule, that value shall be, or (as the case may require) be the starting point for determining, the amount to be included in respect of that asset in the company's accounts, instead of its purchase price or production cost or any value previously so determined for that asset; and the depreciation rules shall apply accordingly in relation to any such asset with the substitution for any reference to its purchase price or production cost of a reference to the value most recently determined for that asset on any basis mentioned in the said paragraph 19.

(2) The amount of any provision for depreciation required in the case of any fixed asset by paragraph 6 or 7 of this Schedule as it applies by virtue of subparagraph (1) of this paragraph is referred to below in this paragraph as the adjusted amount; and the amount of any provision which would be required by that paragraph in the case of that asset according to the historical cost accounting rules is referred to as the historical cost amount.

(3) Where subparagraph (1) of this paragraph applies in the case of any fixed asset. the amount of any provision for depreciation in respect of that asset—

(a) included in any item shown in the profit and loss account in respect of amounts written off assets of the description in question; or

(b) taken into account in stating any item so shown which is required by note (11) of the notes on the profit and loss account formats set out in Part I of this Schedule to be stated after taking into account any necessary provisions for depreciation or diminution in value of assets included under it,

may be the historical cost amount instead of the adjusted amount:

Provided that, if the amount of the provision for depreciation is the historical cost amount, the amount of any difference between the two shall be shown separately in the profit and loss account or in a note to the accounts.

Additional information in case of departure from historical cost rules

21. (1) This paragraph applies where the amounts to be included in respect of assets covered by any items shown in a company's accounts have been determined on any basis mentioned in paragraph 19 of this Schedule.

(2) The items affected and the basis of valuation adopted in determining the amounts of the assets in question in the case of each such item shall be disclosed in a note to the accounts.

(3) In the case of each balance sheet item affected (except stocks) either—

(a) the comparable amounts determined according to the historical cost accounting rules, or

(b) the differences between those amounts and the corresponding amounts actually shown in the balance sheet in respect of that item,

shall be shown separately in the balance sheet or in a note to the accounts.

(4) In subparagraph (3) of this paragraph, references in relation to any item to the comparable amounts determined as there mentioned are references to—

(a) the aggregate amount which would be required to be shown in respect of that item if the amounts to be included in respect of all the assets covered by that item were determined according to the historical cost accounting rules, and

(b) the aggregate amount of the cumulative provisions for depreciation or diminution in value which would be permitted or required in determining those amounts according to those rules.

Revaluation reserve

22. (1) With respect to any determination of the value of an asset of a company on any basis mentioned in paragraph 19 of this Schedule, the amount of any profit or loss arising from that determination (after allowing, where appropriate, for any provisions for depreciation or diminution in value made otherwise than by reference to the value so determined and any adjustments of any such provisions made in the light of that determination) shall be credited or (as the case may be) debited to a separate reserve (referred to in this paragraph as 'the revaluation reserve').

(2) Subparagraph (1) of this paragraph applies in relation to any determination of the value of an asset of a company which takes place before the commencement of this paragraph as it applies to any such determination taking place on or after such commencement.

(3) The amount of the revaluation reserve shall be shown in the company's balance sheet under a separate sub-heading in the position given for the item 'revaluation reserve' in Format 1 or 2 of the balance sheet formats set out in Part I of this Schedule.

(4) The revaluation reserve shall be reduced to the extent that the amounts standing to the credit of the reserve are, in the opinion of the directors of the company, no longer necessary for the purpose of the accounting policies adopted by the company; but an amount may only be transferred from the reserve to the profit and loss account if either—

(a) the amount in question was previously charged to that account, or

(b) it represents realised profit.

(5) The treatment for taxation purposes of amounts credited or debited to the revaluation reserve shall be disclosed in a note to the accounts.

[Part IIIA Valuation At Fair Value

Inclusion of financial instruments at fair value

22A. (1) Subject to subparagraphs (2) to (4) of this paragraph [and paragraph 22AA][b], financial instruments, including derivative financial instruments, may be accounted for by companies at fair value.

(2) Subparagraph (1) of this paragraph does not apply to financial instruments which constitute liabilities unless—

- (a) they are held as part of a trading portfolio, or
- (b) they are derivative financial instruments.

(3) Subparagraph (1) of this paragraph does not apply to—

- (a) non-derivative financial instruments held to maturity,
- (b) loans and receivables originated by the company and not held for trading purposes,
- (c) interests in subsidiary undertakings, associated undertakings and joint ventures,
- (d) equity instruments issued by the company,
- (e) contracts for contingent consideration in a business combination, and
- (f) other financial instruments with such special characteristics that the instruments, according to what is generally accepted, should be accounted for differently from other financial instruments.

(4) In this paragraph—

'Regulations of 1992' means the European Communities (Companies: Group Accounts) Regulations 1992 (S.I. No. 201 of 1992);

'associated undertaking' has the same meaning as in Regulation 34 of the Regulations of 1992;

'joint venture' has the same meaning as in Regulation 32 of the Regulations of 1992;

'subsidiary undertaking' has the same meaning as in Regulation 4 of the Regulations of 1992.][a]

Amendments

a Paragraph 22A inserted by EC(FVA)R 2004, reg 3(c)(ii).

b Inserted by the European Communities (Directive 2006/46/EC) Regulations 2009, reg 3(a).

[22AA. (1) Financial instruments which constitute liabilities other than such instruments referred to in subparagraphs (2)(a) and (2)(b) of paragraph 22A may be accounted for by companies at fair value if—

- (a) they are accounted for in accordance with international accounting standards as adopted by the Commission Regulation on or before 5 September 2006, and

(b) the associated disclosure requirements, provided for in international financial reporting standards adopted in accordance with the IAS Regulation, are made.

(2) Financial instruments referred to in subparagraph (3) of paragraph 22A may be accounted for by companies at fair value if—

(a) they are accounted for in accordance with international accounting standards as adopted by the Commission Regulation, on or before 5 September 2006, and

(b) the associated disclosure requirements, provided for in international financial reporting standards adopted in accordance with the IAS Regulation, are made.

(3) In this paragraph—

'Commission Regulation' means Commission Regulation (EC) No. 1725/2003 (OJ L 261, 13.10.2003, p.1) of 29 September 2003;

'IAS Regulation' has the meaning assigned to by the Principal Act;

'international financial reporting standards' has the meaning assigned to it by section 2 of the Principal Act.][a]

Amendments

a Paragraph 22AA inserted by European Communities (Directive 2006/46/EC) Regulations 2009, reg 3(b).

[Methods for determining fair value

22B. (1) The fair value of a financial instrument is its value determined in accordance with this paragraph.

(2) Where a reliable market can readily be identified for a financial instrument its fair value is to be determined by reference to its market value.

(3) Where a reliable market value cannot readily be identified for a financial instrument but can be identified for its components or for a similar instrument, its fair value is to be determined by reference to the market value of its components or of the similar instrument.

(4) Where neither subparagraph (2) nor (3) of this paragraph apply, the fair value of the financial instrument is to be a value resulting from generally accepted valuation models and techniques.

(5) Valuation models and techniques used for the purposes of subparagraph (4) of this paragraph shall ensure a reasonable approximation of the market value.

(6) Financial instruments that cannot be measured reliably by any of the methods described in paragraphs (1) to (5) of this paragraph shall be measured in accordance with Part II or III of this Schedule.][a]

Amendments

a Paragraph 22B inserted by EC(FVA)R 2004, reg 3(c)(ii).

[Hedged items

22C. A company may, in respect of any assets and liabilities which qualify as hedged items under a fair value hedge accounting system, or identified portions of those assets and liabilities, value those assets and liabilities at the amount required under that system.][a]

Amendments

a Paragraph 22C inserted by EC(FVA)R 2004, reg 3(c)(ii).

[Other assets that may be included at fair value

22CA. (1) This paragraph applies to—

(a) investment property, and

(b) living animals and plants,

that, under relevant international financial reporting standards, may be included in accounts at fair value.

(2) Investment property and living animals and plants may be included at fair value, provided that all such investment property or, as the case may be, all such living animals and plants are so included where their fair value can reliably be determined.

(3) In this paragraph, 'fair value' means fair value determined in accordance with relevant international financial reporting standards.][a]

Amendments

a Paragraph 22CA inserted by EC(IFRSMA)R 2005, reg 5(m)(ii).

[Accounting for changes in fair value of financial instruments

22D. (1) This paragraph applies where the fair value at which a financial instrument is included in accordance with paragraph 22A or 22C of this Schedule [or where the fair value at which an asset is included in accordance with paragraph 22CA of this Schedule][b] is different from the value at which it was last included in accordance with that paragraph.

(2) Notwithstanding section 5(c) of this Act, and subject to subparagraphs (3) and (4) of this paragraph, the amount of the difference in value [of the financial instrument or of the investment property or living animals or plants][c] shall be included in the profit and loss account.

(3) Where—

(a) the financial instrument accounted for is a hedging instrument under a system of hedge accounting that allows some or all of the difference in value not to be shown in the profit and loss account, or

(b) the difference in value relates to an exchange difference arising on a monetary item that forms part of a company's net investment in a foreign entity,

the difference in value shall be credited to (or debited from as the case may be) a separate reserve to be known as the 'fair value reserve'.

(4) Where the instrument accounted for—

(a) is an available for sale financial asset, and

(b) is not a derivative financial instrument,

the difference in value may be credited to (or debited from as the case may be) the fair value reserve.][a]

Amendments

a Paragraph 22D inserted by EC(FVA)R 2004, reg 3(c)(ii).

b Words inserted by EC(IFRSMA)R 2005, reg 5(m)(ii)(I).

c Words inserted by EC(IFRSMA)R 2005, reg 5(m)(ii)(II).

[The fair value reserve

22E. (1) An amount may be transferred—

(a) from the fair value reserve to the profit and loss account if the amount represents realised profit, or

(b) to or from the fair value reserve any amount credited or debited to the reserve.

(2) The fair value reserve shall be adjusted when amounts therein are no longer necessary for the purposes of paragraph 22D (3) or (4) of this Schedule.

(3) The fair value reserve shall not be reduced except as provided for in this paragraph.

(4) The treatment for taxation purposes of amounts credited or debited to the fair value reserve shall be disclosed in a note to the accounts.][a]

Amendments

a Paragraph 22E inserted by EC(FVA)R 2004, reg 3(c)(ii).

PART IV

INFORMATION REQUIRED BY WAY OF NOTES TO ACCOUNTS

Preliminary

23. (1) Any information required in the case of any company by the following provisions of this Part shall (if not given in the company's accounts) be given by way of a note to those accounts.

(2) Notes to a company's accounts may be contained in the accounts or in a separate document annexed to the accounts.

24. The accounting policies adopted by the company in determining the amounts to be included in respect of items shown in the balance sheet and in determining the profit or loss of the company shall be stated (including such policies with respect to the depreciation and diminution in value of assets).

Information supplementing the balance sheet

25. Paragraphs 26 to 37 of this Schedule require information which either supplements the information given with respect to any particular items shown in the balance sheet or

is otherwise relevant to assessing the company's state of affairs in the light of the information so given.

Share capital and debentures

26. (1) The following information shall be given with respect to the company's share capital—

(a) the authorised share capital, and

(b) where shares of more than one class have been allotted, the number and aggregate nominal value of shares of each class allotted.

(2) In the case of any part of the allotted share capital that consists of redeemable shares, the following information shall be given—

(a) the earliest and latest dates on which the company has power to redeem those shares,

(b) whether those shares must be redeemed in any event or are liable to be redeemed at the option of the company, and

(c) whether any (and, if so, what) premium is payable on redemption.

27. If the company has allotted any shares during the financial year to which the accounts relate, the following information shall be given—

(a) the reason for making the allotment,

(b) the classes of shares allotted, and

(c) in respect of each class of shares, the number allotted, their aggregate nominal value and the consideration received by the company for the allotment.

28. (1) If the company has issued any debentures during the financial year to which the accounts relate, the following information shall be given—

(a) the reason for making the issue,

(b) the classes of debentures issued, and

(c) in respect of each class of debentures, the amount issued and the consideration received by the company for the issue.

(2) Particulars of any redeemed debentures which the company has power to re-issue shall also be given.

(3) Where any of the company's debentures are held by a nominee of or trustee for the company, the nominal amount of the debentures and the amount at which they are stated in the accounting records kept by the company in accordance with section 147 of the Principal Act shall be stated.

FIXED ASSETS

29. (1) In respect of each item which is or would, but for section 4 (6) (b) of this Act, be shown under the general item 'fixed assets' in the company's balance sheet, the following information shall be given—

(a) the appropriate amounts in respect of that item as at the date of the beginning of the financial year and as at the balance sheet date respectively,

(b) the effect on any amount shown in the balance sheet in respect of that item of—

(i) any revision of the amount in respect of any assets included under that item made during that year on any basis mentioned in paragraph 19 of this Schedule,

(ii) acquisitions during that year of any assets,

(iii) disposals during that year of any assets, and

(iv) any transfers of assets of the company to and from that item during that year.

(2) The reference in subparagraph (1) (a) of this paragraph to the appropriate amounts in respect of any item as at any date there mentioned is a reference to amounts representing the aggregate amounts determined, as at that date, in respect of assets falling to be included under that item either—

(a) on the basis of purchase price or production cost (determined in accordance with paragraphs 14 and 15 of this Schedule,) or

(b) on any basis mentioned in paragraph 19 of this Schedule

(leaving out of account in either case any provisions for depreciation or diminution in value).

(3) In respect of each item within subparagraph (1) of this paragraph—

(a) the cumulative amount of provisions for depreciation or diminution in value of assets included under that item as at each date mentioned in subparagraph (1) (a) of this paragraph,

(b) the amount of any such provisions made in respect of the financial year concerned,

(c) the amount of any adjustments made in respect of any such provisions during that year in consequence of the disposal of any assets, and

(d) the amount of any other adjustments made in respect of any such provisions during that year,

shall be also stated.

30. Where any fixed assets of the company (other than listed investments) are included under any item shown in the company's balance sheet at an amount determined on any basis mentioned in paragraph 19 of this Schedule, the following information shall be given—

(a) the years (so far as they are known to the directors) in which the assets were severally valued and the several values, and

(b) in the case of assets that have been valued during the financial year, the names of the persons who valued them or particulars of their qualifications for doing so and (in either case) the bases of valuation used.

Financial assets and investments held as current assets

31. (1) In respect of the amount of each item which is or would, but for section 4 (6) (b) of this Act, be shown in the company's balance sheet under the general items 'financial assets' or 'investments held as current assets' there shall be stated—

(a) how much of that amount is ascribable to listed investments, and

(b) how much of any amount so ascribable is ascribable to investments as respects which there has been granted a listing on a recognised stock exchange and how much to other listed investments.

(2) Where the amount of any listed investments is stated for any item in accordance with subparagraph (1) (a) of this paragraph, the following amounts shall also be stated—

(a) the aggregate market value of those investments where it differs from the amount so stated, and

(b) both the market value and stock exchange value of any investments of which the former value is, for the purposes of the accounts, taken as being higher than the latter.

[Information about fair valuation of assets and liabilities

31A. (1) This paragraph applies where financial instruments have been included at fair value pursuant to paragraph 22A or 22C of this Schedule.

(2) There shall be disclosed—

(a) the significant assumptions underlying the valuation models and techniques where fair values have been determined in accordance with paragraph 22B(4) of this Schedule,

(b) for each category of financial instrument, the fair value of the financial instruments in that category and the amounts—

(i) included in the profit and loss account, and

(ii) credited to or debited from the fair value reserve, in respect of instruments in that category,

(c) for each class of derivative financial instrument, the extent and nature of the instruments including significant terms and conditions that may affect the amount, timing and certainty of future cash flows, and

(d) a table showing movements in the fair value reserve during the financial year.][a]

Amendments

a Paragraph 31A inserted by EC(FVA)R 2004, reg 3(c)(iii).

[31B. Where valuation of financial instruments at fair value has not been applied, for each class of derivative financial instrument there shall be stated—

(a) the fair value of the instruments in that class, if such a value can be determined in accordance with paragraph 22B of this Schedule,
and

(b) the extent and nature of the instruments.][a]

Amendments

a Paragraph 31B inserted by EC(FVA)R 2004, reg 3(c)(iii).

[31C. (1) Subparagraph (2) of this paragraph applies where—

(a) the company has financial fixed assets that could be included at fair value by virtue of paragraph 22A of this Schedule,

(b) the amount at which those assets are included under any item in the company's accounts is in excess of their fair value, and

(c) the company has not made provision for the diminution in value of those assets in accordance with paragraph 7(1) of this Schedule.

(2) There shall be stated—

(a) the amount at which either the individual assets or appropriate groupings of those assets is stated in the company's accounts,

(b) the fair value of those assets or groupings, and

(c) the reasons for not making a provision for diminution in value of those assets, including the nature of the evidence that provides the basis for the belief that the book value will be recovered.][a]

Amendments

a Paragraph 31C inserted by EC(FVA)R 2004, reg 3(c)(iii) but substituted by EC(IFRSMA)R 2005, reg 5(m)(iv).

[Information where investment property and living animals and plants included at fair value

31D. (1) This paragraph applies where the amounts to be included in a company's accounts in respect of investment property or living animals and plants have been determined in accordance with paragraph 22CA of this Schedule.

(2) The balance sheet items affected and the basis of valuation adopted in determining the amounts of the assets concerned in the case of each such item shall be disclosed in a note to the accounts.

(3) In the case of investment property, for each balance sheet item affected there shall be shown, either separately in the balance sheet or in a note to the accounts—

(a) the comparable amounts determined according to the historical cost accounting rules, or

(b) the differences between those amounts and the corresponding amounts actually shown in the balance sheet in respect of that item.

(4) In subparagraph (3) of this paragraph, references in relation to any item to the comparable amounts determined in accordance with that subparagraph are references to—

(a) the aggregate amount which would be required to be shown in respect of that item if the amounts to be included in respect of all the assets covered by that item were determined according to the historical cost accounting rules, and

(b) the aggregate amount of the cumulative provisions for depreciation or diminution in value which would be permitted or required in determining those amounts according to those rules][a].

Amendments

a Paragraph 31D inserted by EC(IFRSMA)R 2005, reg 5(m)(v).

Reserves and provisions

32. (1) Where any amount is transferred—

(a) to or from any reserves, or

(b) to any provisions for [provisions for liabilities][a], or

(c) from any [provisions for liabilities][b] otherwise than for the purpose for which the provision was established,

and the reserves or provisions are or would, but for section 4 (6) (b) of this Act, be shown as separate items in the company's balance sheet, the information mentioned in subparagraph (2) of this paragraph shall be given in respect of the aggregate of reserves or provisions included in the same item.

(2) That information is—

(a) the amount of the reserves or provisions as at the date of the beginning of the financial year and as at the balance sheet date respectively,

(b) any amount transferred to or from the reserves or provisions during that year, and

(c) the source and application respectively of any amounts so transferred.

(3) Particulars shall be given of each provision included in the item 'other provisions' in the company's balance sheet in any case where the amount of that provision is material.

Amendments

a Words inserted by EC(IFRSMA)R 2005, reg 5(m)(vi)(I).

b Words inserted by EC(IFRSMA)R 2005, reg 5(m)(vi)(II).

[32A. Particulars of any restriction on profits available for distribution by virtue of section 224(2)(b)(i) of the Companies Act, 1990, must also be stated.][a]

Amendments

a Paragraph 32A inserted by CA 1990, s 233(3)(a).

Provision for taxation

33. The amount of any provision for taxation other than deferred taxation shall be stated.

Details of indebtedness

34. (1) In respect of each item shown under 'creditors' in the company's balance sheet there shall be stated—

(a) the aggregate amount of any debts included under that item which are payable or repayable otherwise than by instalments and fall due for payment or repayment after the end of the period of five years beginning with the day next following the end of the financial year,

(b) the aggregate amount of any debts so included which are payable or repayable by instalments any of which fall due for payment after the end of that period,

(c) the aggregate amount of any debts included under that item in respect of which any security has been given, and

(d) an indication of the nature of the securities so given,

and, in the case of debts within clause (b) of this subparagraph, the aggregate amount of instalments falling due after the end of that period shall also be disclosed for each such item.

(2) References in subparagraph (1) of this paragraph to an item shown under 'creditors' in the company's balance sheet include references, where amounts failing due to creditors within one year and after more than one year are distinguished in the balance sheet—

(a) in a case within subparagraph (1) (a) of this paragraph, to an item shown under the latter of those categories, and

(b) in a case within subparagraph (1) (d) of this paragraph, to an item shown under either of those categories,

and references to items shown under 'creditors' include references to items which would, but for section 4(6)(b) of this Act, be shown under that heading.

35. If any fixed cumulative dividends on the company's shares are in arrears, there shall be stated—

(a) the amount of the arrears, and

(b) the period for which the dividends or, if there is more than one class, each class of them are in arrears.

Guarantees and other financial commitments

36. (1) Particulars shall be given of any charge on the assets of the company to secure the liabilities of any other person, including, where practicable, the amount secured.

(2) The following information shall be given with respect to any other contingent liability not provided for—

(a) the amount or estimated amount of that liability,

(b) its legal nature, and

(c) whether any valuable security has been provided by the company in connection with that liability and, if so, what.

(3) There shall be stated, where practicable—

(a) the aggregate amount or estimated amount of contracts for capital expenditure, so far as not provided for, and

(b) the aggregate amount or estimated amount of capital expenditure authorised by the directors which has not been contracted for.

(4) Particulars shall be given of:

(a) any pension commitments included under any provision shown in the company's balance sheet, and

(b) any such commitments for which no provision has been made,

and, where any such commitment relates wholly or partly to pensions payable to past directors of the company, separate particulars shall be given of that commitment so far as it relates to such pensions.

(5) The following information shall also be given:

(a) the nature of every pension scheme operated by or on behalf of the company including information as to whether or not each scheme is a defined benefit scheme or a defined contribution scheme,

(b) whether each such scheme is externally funded or internally financed,

(c) whether any pension costs and liabilities are assessed in accordance with the advice of a professionally qualified actuary and, if so, the date of the most recent relevant actuarial valuation,

(d) whether and, if so, where any such actuarial valuation is available for public inspection.

(6) Particulars shall also be given of any other financial commitments which—

(a) have not been provided for, and

(b) are relevant to assessing the company's state of affairs.

(7) [...][a]

Amendments

a Paragraph 36(7) deleted by EC(CGA)R 1992, Sch, Pt 1 para 4(6)(a).

[Information on arrangements not included in balance sheet

36A. The nature and business purpose of the arrangements of the company that are not included in its balance sheet and the financial impact on the company of those arrangements shall be provided in the notes to the accounts of the company if the risks or benefits arising from such arrangements are material and in so far as the disclosure of such risks or benefits is necessary for assessing the financial position of the company.][a]

Amendments

a Paragraph 36A inserted by European Communities (Directive 2006/46/EC) Regulations 2009, reg 6.

[Related party transactions

[36B][a]. (1) Particulars shall be given in the notes to the accounts of the company of transactions which have been entered into with related parties by the company if such transactions are material and have not been concluded under normal market conditions and the particulars shall include the amount of such transactions, the nature of the related party relationship and other information about the transactions which is necessary for an understanding of the financial position of the company.

(2) [The provision of particulars][b] and other information about individual transactions may be aggregated according to their nature, except where separate information is necessary for an understanding of the effects of related party transactions on the financial position of the company.

(3) Subparagraph (1) shall not apply to transactions which are entered into between 2 or more members of a group if any subsidiary undertaking which is party to the transaction is wholly owned by such a member.

[...][c]

(5) A word or expression used in subparagraphs (1) to (3) has the same meaning as it has in Directive 2006/46/EC.][a]

Amendments

a Paragraph 36 inserted by European Communities (Directive 2006/46/EC) Regulations 2009, reg 66 and renumbered to para 36B by European Communities (Directive 2006/46/EC) (Amendment) Regulations 2010, reg 6(a).

b Words 'The provision of particulars' substituted for 'Subject to subparagraph (4), the provision of particulars' by European Communities (Directive 2006/46/EC) (Amendment) Regulations 2010, reg 6(b).

c Subparagraph (4) deleted by European Communities (Directive 2006/46/EC) (Amendment) Regulations 2010, reg 6(c).

Miscellaneous matters

37. (1) Particulars shall be given of any case where the purchase price or production cost of any asset is for the first time determined under paragraph 16 of this Schedule.

(2) The aggregate amount of any outstanding loans permitted by section 60 of the Principal Act, as amended by the Act of 1983 (other than loans to which subsection (13) (a) of that section refers), shall be shown, indicating separately loans permitted by paragraphs (b) and (c) of the said subsection (13).

(3) The aggregate amount which is recommended for distribution by way of dividend shall be stated.

Information supplementing the profit and loss account

38. Paragraphs 39 to 43 of this Part require information which either supplements the information given with respect to any particular items shown in the profit and loss account or otherwise provides particulars of income or expenditure of the company or of circumstances affecting the items shown in the profit and loss account.

Separate statement of certain items of income and expenditure

39. (1) Subject to the following provisions of this paragraph, each of the amounts mentioned in subparagraphs (2) to (6) of this paragraph shall be stated.

(2) The amount of interest on or any similar charges in respect of—

- (a) bank loans and overdrafts, and loans made to the company (other than bank loans and overdrafts) which—
  - (i) are repayable otherwise than by instalments and fall due for repayment before the end of the period of five years beginning with the day next following the end of the financial year of the company, or
  - (ii) are repayable by instalments the last of which falls due for payment before the end of that period, and
- (b) loans of any other kind made to the company.

This subparagraph does not apply to interest or charges on loans to the company from [group undertakings][a], but, with that exception, it applies to interest or charges on all loans, whether made on the security of debentures or not.

[(3) The amounts respectively provided for the purchase of the company's share capital, for redemption of share capital and for redemption of loans.][b]

(4) The amount of income from listed and unlisted investments.

[...][c]

(6) The aggregate amounts of the emoluments of, and compensation in respect of loss of office to, directors and compensation in respect of loss of office to past-directors.

Amendments

a 'group undertakings' substituted for 'group companies' by EC(CGA)R 1992, Sch, Pt I para 1.

b Para 39(3) substituted by CA 1990, s 233(3)(b).

c Subparagraph (5) deleted by EC(SA)(Dir)R 2010, reg 5(1).

Particulars of tax

40. (1) The basis on which the charge for corporation tax, income tax and other taxation on profits (whether payable in or outside the State) is computed shall be stated.

(2) Particulars shall be given of any special circumstances which affect liability in respect of taxation on profits, income or capital gains for the financial year concerned or liability in respect of taxation of profits, income or capital gains for succeeding financial years.

(3) The amount of the charge for corporation tax, income tax and other taxation on profits or capital gains, so far as charged to revenue, including taxation payable outside the State on profits (distinguishing where practicable between corporation tax and other taxation) shall be stated.

These amounts shall be stated separately in respect of each of the amounts which is or would, but for section 4 (6) (b) of this Act, be shown under the following items in the profit and loss account, that is to say, 'tax on profit or loss on ordinary activities' and 'tax on extraordinary profit or loss'.

Particulars of turnover

41. (1) If in the course of the financial year, the company has carried on business of two or more classes which, in the opinion of the directors, differ substantially from each other, there shall be stated in respect of each class (describing it) the amount of the turnover attributable to that class.

(2) If, in the course of the financial year, the company has supplied markets which, in the opinion of the directors, differ substantially from each other, the amount of the turnover attributable to each such market shall also be stated.

In this subparagraph 'market' means a market delimited in a geographical manner.

(3) In analysing for the purposes of this paragraph the source (in terms of business or in terms of market) of turnover, the directors of the company shall have regard to the manner in which the company's activities are organised.

(4) For the purpose of this paragraph—

(a) classes of business which, in the opinion of the directors, do not differ substantially from each other shall be treated as one class, and

(b) markets which, in the opinion of the directors, do not differ substantially from each other shall be treated as one market,

and any amounts properly attributable to one class of business or (as the case may be) to one market which are not material may be included in the amount stated in respect of another.

(5) Where in the opinion of the directors the disclosure of any information required by this paragraph would be seriously prejudicial to the interests of the company, that information need not be disclosed, but the fact that any such information has not been disclosed must be stated.

Particulars of staff

42. (1) The following information shall be given with respect to the employees of the company—

(a) the average number of persons employed by the company in the financial year, and

(b) the average number of persons employed within each category of persons employed by the company.

(2) In respect of all persons employed by the company during the financial year who are taken into account in determining the relevant annual number for the purposes of subparagraph (1) (a) of this paragraph, there shall also be stated the aggregate amounts respectively of—

(a) wages and salaries paid or payable in respect of that year to those persons,

(b) social welfare costs incurred by the company on their behalf, and

(c) other pension costs so incurred,

save insofar as these amounts or any of them are stated in the profit and loss account.

(3) The categories of persons employed by the company by reference to which the number required to be disclosed by subparagraph (1) (b) of this paragraph is to be determined shall be such as the directors may select, having regard to the manner in which the company's activities are organised.

(4) (a) For the purposes of clauses (a) and (b) of subparagraph (1) of this paragraph, the average number of persons employed by a company shall be determined by dividing the relevant annual number by the number of weeks in the financial year of the company.

(b) For the purposes of this subparagraph, the relevant annual number shall be determined by ascertaining for each week in the financial year of the company concerned—

(i) in the case of the said clause (a), the number of persons employed under contracts of service by the company in that week (whether throughout the week or not), and

(ii) in the case of the said clause (b), the number of persons in the category in question of persons so employed, and, in either case, adding together all the weekly numbers.

Miscellaneous matters

43. (1) Where any amount relating to any preceding financial year is included in any item in the profit and loss account, the effect shall be stated.

(2) Particulars shall be given of any extraordinary income or charges arising in the financial year.

(3) The effect shall be stated of any transactions that are exceptional by virtue of size or incidence notwithstanding the fact that they fall within the ordinary activities of the company.

(4) Any amount expended on research and development in the financial year, and any amount committed in respect of research and development in subsequent years, shall be stated.

(5) Where, in the opinion of the directors, the disclosure of any information required by subparagraph (4) of this paragraph would be prejudicial to the interests of the company, that information need not be disclosed, but the fact that any such information has not been disclosed shall be stated.

General

44. (1) Where sums originally denominated in foreign currencies have been brought into account under any items shown in the balance sheet or profit and loss account, the basis on which those sums have been translated into Irish currency shall be stated.

[(2) In respect of every balance sheet or profit and loss account item which would, but for its inclusion in a note to the accounts, be shown in the balance sheet, or profit and loss account format set out in Part I of this Schedule and chosen pursuant to section 4 of this Act, there shall also be shown in a note to the accounts the corresponding amount for the financial year immediately preceding that to which the accounts relate. Where that corresponding amount is not comparable with the amount to be shown for the item in question in respect of the financial year to which the accounts relate, the former amount may be adjusted, and, if the former amount is adjusted, particulars as regards the respect or respects in which the foregoing amounts are not comparable and of the adjustment shall be given in a note to the accounts.][a]

(3) Subparagraph (2) of this paragraph does not apply in relation to any amount stated by virtue of paragraphs 29 and 32 of this Schedule.

Amendments

a Subparagraph 44(2) substituted by EC(ANAADCIC)R 2005, reg 5.

PART V

[SPECIAL PROVISIONS WHERE A COMPANY IS A PARENT UNDERTAKING OR SUBSIDIARY UNDERTAKING][A]

Amendments

a Heading of Part V substituted by EC(CGA)R 1992, Sch, Pt I para 4(1).

Company's own accounts

[45. (1) This Part applies where the company is a parent undertaking, whether or not it is itself a subsidiary undertaking.

(2) Where a company is a parent undertaking or a subsidiary undertaking and any item required by Part I of this Schedule to be shown in the company's balance sheet, in relation to group undertakings, includes—

(a) amounts attributable to dealings with or interests in any parent undertaking or fellow subsidiary undertaking, or

(b) amounts attributable to dealings with or interests in any subsidiary undertaking of the company,

the aggregate amounts within paragraph (a) and (b) respectively shall be shown as separate items, either by way of subdivision of the relevant item in the balance sheet or in a note to the company's accounts.][a]

Amendments

a Paragraph 45 substituted by EC(CGA)R 1992, Sch, Pt 1 para 4(2).

Guarantees and other financial commitments in favour of group undertakings

[45A. Commitments within any of subparagraphs (1) to (6) of paragraph 36 (guarantees and other financial commitments) which are undertaken on behalf of or for the benefit of—

(a) any parent undertaking or fellow subsidiary undertaking, or

(b) any subsidiary undertaking of the company,

shall be stated separately from the other commitments within that subparagraph, and commitments within paragraph (a) shall also be stated separately from those within paragraph (b).][a]

Amendments

a Paragraph 45A inserted by EC(CGA)R 1992, Sch, Pt 1 para 4(3).

[46. (1) Subject to subparagraph (2) of this paragraph, where the company is a parent undertaking, the number, description and amount of the shares in, and debentures of the company held by its subsidiary undertakings or their nominees shall be disclosed in a note to the company's accounts.

(2) Subparagraph (1) of this paragraph does not apply in relation to any shares or debentures—

(a) in the case of which the subsidiary undertaking is concerned as personal representative, or

(b) in the case of which it is concerned as trustee:

Provided that in the latter case neither the company nor a subsidiary undertaking of the company is beneficially interested under the trust, otherwise than by way of security only for the purposes of a transaction entered into by it in the ordinary course of a business which includes the lending of money.][a]

Amendments

a Paragraph 46 substituted by EC(CGA)R 1992, Sch, Pt 1 para 4(4).

[46A. (1) Where a company is a subsidiary undertaking, the following information shall be stated with respect to the parent undertaking of—

(a) the largest group of undertakings for which group accounts are drawn up and of which the company is a member, and

(b) the smallest such group of undertakings.

(2) The name of the parent undertaking shall be stated.

(3) There shall be stated—

(a) if the undertaking is incorporated, the country in which it is incorporated;

(b) if it is unincorporated, the address of its principal place of business.

(4) If copies of the group accounts referred to in subparagraph (1) are available to the public, there shall also be stated the addresses from which copies of the accounts can be obtained.][a]

Amendments

a Paragraph 46A inserted by EC(CGA)R 1992, Sch, Pt 1 para 4(5).

Consolidated accounts of holding company and subsidiaries

47. [...][a]

Amendments

a Paragraph 47 deleted by EC(CGA)R 1992, Sch, Pt 1 para 4(6)(b).

48. [...][a]

Amendments

a Paragraph 48 deleted by EC(CGA)R 1992, Sch, Pt 1 para 4(6)(b).

49. [...][a]

Amendments

a Paragraph 49 deleted by EC(CGA)R 1992, Sch, Pt 1 para 4(6)(b).

50. […][a]

Amendments

a Paragraph 50 deleted by EC(CGA)R 1992, Sch, Pt 1 para 4(6)(b).

---

51. […][a]

Amendments

a Paragraph 51 deleted by EC(CGA)R 1992, Sch, Pt 1 para 4(6)(b).

---

52. […][a]

Amendments

a Paragraph 52 deleted by EC(CGA)R 1992, Sch, Pt 1 para 4(6)(b).

Group accounts not prepared as consolidated accounts

53. […][a]

Amendments

a Paragraph 53 deleted by EC(CGA)R 1992, Sch, Pt 1 para 4(6)(b).

Provisions of general application

54. (1) This paragraph applies where a company is a holding company and either—

(a) does not prepare group accounts, or

(b) prepares group accounts which do not deal with one or more of its subsidiaries,

and references in this paragraph to subsidiaries shall be read in a case within clause (b) of this subparagraph as references to such of the subsidiaries of the company concerned as are excluded from the group accounts.

(2) Subject to the following provisions of this paragraph—

(a) the reasons why subsidiaries are not dealt with in group accounts, and

(b) a statement showing any qualifications contained in the reports of the auditors of the subsidiaries on their accounts for their respective financial years ending with or during the financial year of the company, and any note or saving contained in those accounts to call attention to a matter which, apart from the note or saving, would properly have been referred to in such a qualification, insofar as the matter which is the subject of the qualification or note is not covered by the company's own accounts and is material from the point of view of its members, shall be given in a note to the company's accounts.

(3) Subject to the following provisions of this paragraph, the aggregate amount of the total investment of the holding company in the shares of the subsidiaries shall be stated in a note to the company's accounts by way of the equity method of valuation.

(4) Insofar as information required by any of the preceding provisions of this paragraph to be stated in a note to the company's accounts is not obtainable, a statement to that effect shall be given instead in a note to those accounts.

(5) Where in any case within subparagraph (1)(b) of this paragraph the group accounts are consolidated accounts, references in the preceding subparagraphs of this paragraph to the company's accounts shall be read as references to the consolidated accounts.

55. Where a company has subsidiaries whose financial years did not end with that of the company, the following information shall be given in relation to each such subsidiary (whether or not dealt with in any group accounts prepared by the company) by way of a note to the company's accounts or (where group accounts are prepared) to the group accounts, that is to say—

- (a) the reasons why the company's directors consider that the subsidiaries' financial years should not end with that of the company, and
- (b) the dates on which the subsidiaries' financial years ending last before that of the company respectively ended or the earliest and latest of those dates.

PART VI

SPECIAL PROVISIONS WHERE A COMPANY IS AN INVESTMENT COMPANY

56. (1) Paragraph 22 of this Schedule shall not apply to the amount of any profit or loss arising from a determination of the value of any investments of an investment company on any basis mentioned in paragraph 19 (3) of this Schedule.

(2) Any provisions made by virtue of subparagraph (1) or (2) of paragraph 7 of this Schedule in the case of an investment company in respect of any fixed asset investments need not be charged to the company's profit and loss account if they are either—

- (a) charged against any reserve account to which any amount excluded by subparagraph (1) of this paragraph from the requirements of the said paragraph 22 has been credited, or
- (b) shown as a separate item in the company's balance sheet under the sub-heading 'other reserves'.

(3) For the purposes of this paragraph as it applies in relation to any company, 'fixed asset investment' means any asset falling to be included under any item shown in the company's balance sheet under the subdivision 'financial assets' under the general item 'fixed assets'.

57. [(1)][a] Any distribution made by an investment company which reduces the amount of its net assets to less than the aggregate of its called-up share capital and undistributable reserves shall be disclosed in a note to the company's accounts.

[(2) In this paragraph 'net assets' means the aggregate of the company's assets less the aggregate of its liabilities, and 'liabilities' includes—

- (a) any provision for liabilities within the meaning of paragraph 70 of this Schedule that is made in Companies Act individual accounts, and
- (b) any provision that is made in IFRS individual accounts.][b]

Amendments

a Renumbered by EC(IFRSMA)R 2005, reg 5(m)(vii).

b Subparagraph (2) inserted by EC(IFRSMA)R 2005, reg 5(m)(vii).

58. A company shall be treated as an investment company for the purposes of this Part in relation to any financial year of the company if—

(a) during the whole of that year, it was an investment company within the meaning of Part IV of the Act of 1983,

(b) it was not at any time during that year prohibited by section 47 of that Act from making a distribution.

59. [...][a]

Amendments

a Paragraph 59 deleted by EC(CGA)R 1992, Sch, Pt 1 para 4(6)(b).

PART VII

INTERPRETATION OF SCHEDULE

Assets: fixed or current

60. For the purposes of this Schedule, assets of a company shall be taken to be fixed assets if they are intended for use on a continuing basis in the company's activities, and any assets not intended for such use shall be taken to be current assets.

Balance sheet date

61. For the purposes of this Schedule, 'balance sheet date', in relation to a balance sheet, means the date as at which the balance sheet was prepared.

Capitalisation

62. References in this Schedule to capitalising any work or costs are references to treating that work or those costs as a fixed asset.

Fellow subsidiary

[63. References in this Schedule to 'fellow subsidiary undertakings' are to undertakings which are subsidiary undertakings of the same parent undertaking but are not parent undertakings or subsidiary undertakings of each other.][a]

Amendments

a Paragraph 63 substituted by EC(CGA)R 1992, Sch, Pt 1 para 5.

[Group undertakings

64. (1) For the purposes of this Schedule, 'group undertaking' in relation to any undertaking, means any undertaking which is—

(a) a parent undertaking or subsidiary undertaking of that undertaking, or

(b) a subsidiary undertaking of any parent undertaking of that undertaking.

(2) For the purposes of this paragraph, 'undertaking' shall have the meaning assigned to it by Regulation 3 of the European Communities (Companies: Group Accounts) Regulations, 1992.][a]

Amendments

a Paragraph 64 substituted by EC(CGA)R 1992, Sch, Pt 1 para 6.

Historical cost accounting rules

65. References in this Schedule to the historical cost accounting rules shall be read in accordance with paragraph 17 of this Schedule.

[Investment property

65A. In this Schedule 'investment property' means land or buildings (or both) held to earn rentals or for capital appreciation (or both).][a]

Amendments

a Paragraph 65A inserted by EC(IFRSMA)R 2005, reg 5(m)(viii).

Listed investments

66. In this Schedule, 'listed investments' means an investment as respects which there has been granted a listing on a recognised stock exchange within the State or on any stock exchange of repute outside the State.

Loans

67. For the purposes of this Schedule, a loan shall be treated as falling due for payment, and an instalment of a loan shall be treated as falling due for payment, on the earliest date on which the lender could require repayment or (as the case may be) payment, if he exercised all options and rights available to him.

Materiality

68. Amounts which in the particular context of any provision of this Schedule are not material may be disregarded for the purposes of that provision.

Provisions

69. (1) References in this Schedule to provisions for depreciation or diminution in value of assets are references to any amount written off by way of providing for depreciation or diminution in value of assets.

(2) Any reference in the profit and loss account formats set out in Part I of this Schedule to the depreciation of, or amounts written off, assets of any description is a reference to any provision for depreciation or diminution in value of assets of that description.

70. References in this Schedule to provisions for liabilities [...][a] are references to any amount retained as reasonably necessary for the purpose of providing for any [liability the nature of which is clearly defined and][b] which is either likely to be incurred, or certain to be incurred but uncertain as to amount or as to the date on which it will arise.

Amendments

a 'or changes' deleted by EC(IFRSMA)R 2005, reg 5(m)(ix)(I).

b Words substituted by EC(IFRSMA)R 2005, reg 5(m)(ix)(II).

Purchase price

71. References in this Schedule (however expressed) to the purchase price of an asset of a company or of any raw materials or consumables used in the production of any such asset shall be read as including references to any consideration (whether in cash or otherwise) given by the company in respect of that asset or in respect of those materials or consumables (as the case may require).

Realised profits

72. Without prejudice to—

(a) the construction of any other expression by reference (where appropriate) to accepted accounting principles or practice, or

(b) any specific provision for the treatment of profits of any description as realised,

it is hereby declared for the avoidance of doubt that references in this Schedule to realised profits, in relation to a company's accounts, are references to such profits of the company as fall to be treated as realised profits for the purposes of those accounts in accordance with principles generally accepted with respect to the determination for accounting purposes of realised profits at the time when those accounts are prepared.

Related companies

[73. For the purposes of this Schedule, 'participating interest' shall have the meaning assigned to it in Regulation 35 of the European Communities (Companies: Group Accounts) Regulations, 1992.][a]

Amendments

a Paragraph 73 substituted by EC(CGA)R 1992, Sch, Pt 1 para 7.

Staff costs

74. In this Schedule—

'social welfare costs' means any contribution by a company to any state social welfare, social security or pension scheme, fund or arrangement, being a fund or arrangement connected with such a scheme, and 'social welfare' means any such scheme fund or arrangement;

'pension costs' include any other contributions by a company for the purposes of any pension scheme established for the purpose of providing pensions for persons employed by the company, any sums set aside for that purpose and any amounts paid by the company in respect of pensions without first being so set aside;

and any amount stated in respect of either of the above items or in respect of the item 'wages and salaries' in a company's profit and loss account shall be determined by reference to payments made or costs incurred in respect of all persons employed by the company during the financial year concerned who are taken into account in determining the relevant annual number for the purposes of paragraph 42(1)(a) of this Schedule.

Turnover

75. For the purposes of this Schedule, 'turnover', in relation to any company, means the amounts derived from the provision of goods and services falling within the company's ordinary activities, after deduction of—

(a) trade discounts,

(b) value-added tax, and

(c) any other taxes based on the amounts so derived.

Wholly-owned Subsidiaries

76. A body corporate shall be deemed for the purposes of this Schedule to be a wholly-owned subsidiary of another if it would be so deemed for the purposes of section 150 of the Principal Act.

[Financial instruments

77. References to 'derivative financial instruments' are deemed to include commodity-based contracts that give either contracting party the right to settle in cash or some other financial instrument except where those contracts—

(a) were entered into and continue to meet the company's expected purchase, sale or usage requirements,

(b) were designed for that purpose at their inception, and

(c) are expected to be settled by delivery of the commodity.][a]

Amendments

a Paragraph 77 inserted by EC(FVA)R 2004, reg 3(iv).

[78. The words and expressions set out in the Table to this paragraph have the same meaning in this Schedule as they have in Council Directive 78/660/EEC of 25 July 1978 (OJ L222, 14/08/1978 p 11), as amended by Council Directive 2001/65/EEC of the European Parliament and of the Council of 27 September 2001 (OJ No. L283, 27.10.01, p 28).][a]

TABLE

available for sale financial asset

business combination

commodity-based contracts

equity instrument

exchange difference

fair value hedge accounting system

financial fixed asset

financial instrument

foreign entity

hedge accounting

hedge accounting system

hedged items

hedging instrument

held to maturity

held for trading purposes

monetary item

receivables

reliable market

trading portfolio

Amendments

a Paragraph 78 inserted by EC(FVA)R 2004, reg 3(iv).

Companies (Amendment) Act 1990

Number 27 of 1990

Arrangement of Sections

Section

An Act to Amend the Law Relating to Companies and to Provide for Related Matters. [29th August, 1990]

Be It Enacted By The Oireachtas As Follows:

1 Definitions

In this Act, unless the context otherwise required—

['Central Bank' means the Central Bank and Financial Services Authority of Ireland;][a]

'the Companies Acts' means the Principal Act, and every enactment (including this Act) which is to be construed as one with that Act;

'examiner' means an examiner appointed under section 2;

'interested party', in relation to a company to which section 2(1) relates, means—

(a) a creditor of the company,

(b) a member of the company;

'the Minister' means the Minister for Industry and Commerce;

'the Principal Act' means the Companies Act, 1963.

Amendments

a C(A)A 1990, s 1 inserted by the Central Bank and Financial Services Authority Act 2003, Sch 1, part 12, with effect from 1 May 2003.

[1A Restriction of this Act

This Act is subject to Chapters I (general provisions) and III (secondary insolvency proceedings) of Council Regulation (EC) No 1346/2000 of 29 May 2000 (OJ L160 of 30.6.2000.) on insolvency proceedings.][a]

Amendments

a C(A)A 1990, s 1A inserted by European Communities (Corporate Insolvency) Regulations 2002 (SI 333/2002) reg 4.

---

2 Power of court to appoint examiner

(1) [Subject to subsection (2), where it appears to the court that][a]—

(a) a company is or is likely to be unable to pay its debts, and

[(b) no resolution subsists for the winding-up of the company, and][b]

(c) no order has been made for the winding-up of the company,

it may, on application by petition presented, appoint an examiner to the company for the purpose of examining the state of the company's affairs and performing such duties in relation to the company as may be imposed by or under this Act.

[(2) The court shall not make an order under this section unless it is satisfied that there is a reasonable prospect of the survival of the company and the whole or any part of its undertaking as a going concern.][c]

(3) For the purposes of this section, a company is unable to pay its debts if—

(a) it is unable to pay its debts as they fall due,

(b) the value of its assets is less than the amount of its liabilities, taking into account its contingent and prospective liabilities, or

(c) section 214 (a) or (b) of the Principal Act applies to the company.

(4) In deciding whether to make an order under this section the court may also have regard to whether the company has sought from its creditors significant extensions of time for the payment of its debts, from which it could reasonably be inferred that the company was likely to be unable to pay its debts.

[(5) The court shall not make an order under this section unless –

(a) the court is satisfied that the company has no obligations in relation to a bank asset that has been transferred to the National Asset Management Agency or a NAMA group entity, or

(b) if the company has any such obligation –

(i) if a copy of the petition has been served on that Agency, and

(ii) the court has heard that Agency in relation to the making of the order.

(6) In subsection (5) 'bank asset' and 'NAMA group entity' have the same respective meanings as in the National Asset Management Agency Act 2009.][d]

Amendments

a C(A)A 1990, s 2(1) amended by C(A) (No 2) 1999, s 5(a).

b C(A)A 1990, s 2(1)(b) substituted by CA 1990, s 181.

c C(A)A 1990, s 2(2) substituted by C(A) (No 2) 1999, s 5(b).

d C(A)A 1990, s 2(5) and s 2(6) inserted by NAMA Act 2009, s 234.

---

3 Petition for protection of the court

(1) Subject to subsection (2), a petition under section 2 may be presented by—

(a) the company, or

(b) the directors of the company, or

(c) a creditor, or contingent or prospective creditor (including an employee), of the company, or

(d) members of the company holding at the date of the presentation of a petition under that section not less than one-tenth of such of the paid-up capital of the company as carries at that date the right of voting at general meetings of the company,

or by all or any of those parties, together or separately.

(2) (a) Where the company referred to in section 2 is an insurer, a petition under that section may be presented only by the Minister, and subsection (1) of this section shall not apply to the company.

[(b) Where the company referred to in section 2 is—

(i) the holder of a licence under section 9 of the Central Bank Act, 1971,

(ii) a company which a building society has converted itself into under Part XI of the Building Societies Act, 1989,

(iii) a company which one or more trustee savings banks have been reorganised into pursuant to an order under section 57 of the Trustee Savings Banks Act, 1989,

a petition under section 2 may be presented only by the Central Bank, and subsection (1) of this section shall not apply to the company.][a]

[(c) Where the company referred to in section 2 is a company referred to in the Second Schedule to the Companies (Amendment) (No. 2) Act, 1999, (not being a company referred to in paragraph 18, 19 or 20 of that Schedule or to which paragraph (b) applies) the following provisions shall apply—

(i) a petition under section 2 may be presented by—

(I) any of the persons referred to in paragraph (a), (b), (c) or (d) of subsection (1) of this section (including by one or more of such persons acting together),

(II) the Central Bank, or

(III) one or more of such persons and the Central Bank acting together,

(ii) if the Central Bank does not present such a petition—

(I) the petitioner shall, before he presents the petition at the office of the court, cause to be received by the Central Bank a notice in writing of his intention to present the petition, and shall serve a copy of the petition on the Central Bank as soon as may be after the presentation of it at the said office,

(II) the Central Bank shall be entitled to appear and be heard at any hearing relating to the petition.][a]

(3) A petition presented under section 2 shall—

(a) nominate a person to be appointed as examiner, and

[...][b]

[(3A) In addition to the matters specified in subsection (4), a petition presented under section 2 shall be accompanied by a report in relation to the company prepared by a person (in this Act referred to as 'the independent accountant') who is either the auditor of the company or a person who is qualified to be appointed as an examiner of the company.

(3B) The report of the independent accountant shall comprise the following:

(a) the names and permanent addresses of the officers of the company and, in so far as the independent accountant can establish, any person in accordance with whose directions or instructions the directors of the company are accustomed to act,

(b) the names of any other bodies corporate of which the directors of the company are also directors,

(c) a statement as to the affairs of the company, showing in so far as it is reasonably possible to do so, particulars of the company's assets and liabilities (including contingent and prospective liabilities) as at the latest practicable date, the names and addresses of its creditors, the securities held by them respectively and the dates when the securities were respectively given,

(d) whether in the opinion of the independent accountant any deficiency between the assets and liabilities of the company has been satisfactorily accounted for or, if not, whether there is evidence of a substantial disappearance of property that is not adequately accounted for,

(e) his opinion as to whether the company, and the whole or any part of its undertaking, would have a reasonable prospect of survival as a going concern and a statement of the conditions which he considers are essential to ensure such survival, whether as regards the internal management and controls of the company or otherwise,

(f) his opinion as to whether the formulation, acceptance and confirmation of proposals for a compromise or scheme of arrangement would offer a reasonable prospect of the survival of the company, and the whole or any part of its undertaking, as a going concern,

(g) his opinion as to whether an attempt to continue the whole or any part of the undertaking would be likely to be more advantageous to the members as a whole and the creditors as a whole than a winding-up of the company,

(h) recommendations as to the course he thinks should be taken in relation to the company including, if warranted, draft proposals for a compromise or scheme of arrangement,

(i) his opinion as to whether the facts disclosed would warrant further inquiries with a view to proceedings under section 297 or 297A of the Principal Act,

(j) details of the extent of the funding required to enable the company to continue trading during the period of protection and the sources of that funding,

(k) his recommendations as to which liabilities incurred before the presentation of the petition should be paid,

(l) his opinion as to whether the work of the examiner would be assisted by a direction of the court in relation to the role or membership of any creditor's committee referred to in section 21, and

(m) such other matters as he thinks relevant.][c]

(4) A petition presented under section 2, shall be accompanied—

(a) by a consent signed by the person nominated to be examiner, and

(b) if proposals for a compromise or scheme of arrangement in relation to the company's affairs have been prepared for submission to interested parties for their approval, by a copy of the proposals.

(5) The court shall not give a hearing to a petition under section 2 presented by a contingent or prospective creditor until such security for costs has been given as the court thinks reasonable [...][d]

(6) The court shall not give a hearing to a petition under section 2 if a receiver stands appointed to the company the subject of the petition and such receiver has stood so appointed for a continuous period of at least [3 days][e] prior the presentation of the petition.

(7) On hearing a petition under this section, the court may dismiss it, or adjourn the hearing conditionally or unconditionally, or make any interim order, or any other order it thinks fit.

(8) Without prejudice to the generality of subsection (7), an interim order under that subsection may restrict the exercise of any powers of the directors or of the company (whether by reference to the consent of the court or otherwise).

(9) (a) Where it appears to the court that the total liabilities of the company (taking into account its contingent and prospective liabilities) do not exceed [€317,434.52][f] the court may, after making such interim or other orders as it thinks fit, order that the matter be remitted to the judge of the Circuit Court in whose circuit the company has its registered office or principal place of business.

(b) Where an order is made by the court under this subsection the Circuit Court shall have full jurisdiction to exercise all the powers of the court conferred by this Act in relation to the company and every reference to the court in this Act shall be construed accordingly.

(c) Where, in any proceedings under this Act which have been remitted to the Circuit Court by virtue of this subsection, it appears to the Circuit Court that the total liabilities of the company exceed [€317,434.52][f], it shall make, after making such interim orders as it thinks fit, an order transferring the matter to the court.

Amendments

a C(A)A 1990, s 3(2)(b) and (c) substituted by C(A)(No 2)A 1999, s 6. Subsection 2(b) was further substituted with effect from 28 February 2002 by ACC Bank Act 2001, s 11.

b C(A)A 1990, s 3(3)(b) and (c) repealed by C(A)(No 2)A 1999, s 30.

c C(A)A 1990, s 3(3A) and (3B) inserted by C(A)(No 2)A 1999, s 7.

d C(A)A 1990, s 3(5) amended by C(A)(No 2)A 1999, s 8.

e Words '3 days' substituted for '14 days' by CA 1990, s 180.

f £250,000 converted to €317,434.52 by Council Regulations (EC) No 1103/97, No 974/98 and No 2866/98 and the Economic and Monetary Union Act 1998, s 6.

[3A Interim protection pending report

(1) If a petition presented under section 2 shows, and the court is satisfied—

(a) that, by reason of exceptional circumstances outside the control of the petitioner, the report of the independent accountant is not available in time to accompany the petition, and

(b) that the petitioner could not reasonably have anticipated the circumstances referred to in paragraph (a), and, accordingly, the court is unable to consider the making of an order under that section, the court may make an order under this section placing the company concerned under the protection of the court for such period as the court thinks appropriate in order to allow for the submission of the independent accountant's report.

(2) That period shall be a period that expires not later than the 10th day after the date of making of the order concerned or, if the 10th day after that date would fall on a Saturday, Sunday or public holiday, the first following day that is not a Saturday, Sunday or public holiday.

(3) For the avoidance of doubt, the fact that a receiver stands appointed to the whole or any part of the property or undertaking of the company at the time of the presentation of a petition under section 2 in relation to the company shall not, in itself, constitute, for the purposes of subsection (1), exceptional circumstances outside the control of the petitioner.

(4) If the petition concerned has been presented by any of the persons referred to in paragraph (c) or (d) of section 3(1) and an order under subsection (1) is made in relation to the company concerned, the directors of the company shall cooperate in the preparation of the report of the independent accountant, particularly in relation to the matters specified in paragraphs (a), (b) and (c) of section 3(3B).

(5) If the directors of the company concerned fail to comply with subsection (4), the person who has presented the petition concerned or the independent accountant may apply to the court for an order requiring the directors to do specified things by way of compliance with subsection (4) and the court may, as it thinks fit, grant such an order accordingly.

(6) If the report of the independent accountant is submitted to the court before the expiry of the period of protection specified in an order under subsection (1), the court shall proceed to consider the petition together with the report as if they were presented in accordance with section 2.

(7) If the report of the independent accountant is not submitted to the court before the expiry of the period of protection specified in an order under subsection (1), then, at the expiry of that period, the company concerned shall cease to be under the protection of the court, but without prejudice to the presentation of a further petition under section 2.

(8) Any liabilities incurred by the company concerned during the period of protection specified in an order under subsection (1) may not be the subject of a certificate under section 10(2).][a]

Amendments

a C(A)A 1990, s 3A was inserted by C(A)(No 2)A 1999, s 9.

[3B Creditors to be heard

(1) The court shall not make an order dismissing a petition presented under section 2 or an order appointing an examiner to a company without having afforded each creditor of the company who has indicated to the court his desire to be heard in the matter an opportunity to be so heard.

(2) Nothing in this section shall affect the power of the court under section 3(7) to make an interim order in the matter.][a]

Amendments

a C(A)A 1990, s 3B was inserted by C(A)(No 2)A 1999, s 10.

[3C Availability of independent accountant's report

(1) The independent accountant shall supply a copy of the report prepared by him under section 3(3A) to the company concerned or any interested party on written application being made to him in that behalf.

(2) If the court, on application to it in that behalf, directs that that supply may be the subject of such omission, there may be omitted from any copy of the report supplied to the company or an interested party such parts of it as are specified in the direction of the court.

(3) The court may, in particular, on such an application, direct that there may be omitted from such a supply of a copy of the report any information the inclusion of which in such a copy would be likely to prejudice the survival of the company or the whole or any part of its undertaking as a going concern.

(4) If the company concerned is a company referred to in section 3(2)(c) and the Central Bank does not propose to present, or has not presented, (whether alone or acting together with other persons) a petition under section 2 in relation to the company, the independent accountant shall, as soon as may be after it is prepared, supply a copy of the report prepared by him under section 3(3A) to the Central Bank and subsections (2) and (3) shall not apply to such a copy.][a]

Amendments

a C(A)A 1990, s 3C was inserted by C(A)(No 2)A 1999, s 11.

4 Related companies

(1) [Subject to subsection (2), where the court appoints an examiner to a company][a], it may, at the same or any time thereafter, make an order—

(a) appointing the examiner to be examiner for the purposes of this Act to a related company, or

(b) conferring on the examiner, in relation to such company, all or any of the powers or duties conferred on him in relation to the first-mentioned company.

(2) In deciding whether to make an order under subsection (1), the court shall have regard to whether the making of the order would be likely to facilitate the survival of the company, or of the related company, or both, and the whole or any part of its or their undertaking, as a going concern [and shall not, in any case, make such an order unless it is satisfied that there is a reasonable prospect of the survival of the related company, and the whole or any part of its undertaking, as a going concern'.][b]

(3) A related company to which an examiner is appointed shall be deemed to be under the protection of the court for the period beginning on the date of the making of an order under this section and continuing for the period during which the company to which it is related is under such protection.

(4) Where an examiner stands appointed to two or more related companies, he shall have the same powers and duties in relation to each company, taken separately, unless the court otherwise directs.

(5) For the purposes of this Act, a company is related to another company if—

(a) that other company is its holding company or subsidiary; or

(b) more than half in nominal value of its equity share capital (as defined in section 155(5) of the Principal Act) is held by the other company and companies related to that other company (whether directly or indirectly, but other than in a fiduciary capacity); or

(c) more than half in nominal value of the equity share capital (as defined in section 155(5) of the Principal Act) of each of them is held by members of the other (whether directly or indirectly, but other than in a fiduciary capacity); or

(d) that other company or a company or companies related to that other company or that other company together with a company or companies related to it are entitled to exercise or control the exercise of more than one half of the voting power at any general meeting of the company; or

(e) the businesses of the companies have been so carried on that the separate business of each company, or a substantial part thereof, is not readily identifiable; or

(f) there is another [body corporate][c] to which both companies are related;

and 'related company' has a corresponding meaning.

(6) For the purposes of this section 'company' includes any body which is liable to be wound up under the Companies Acts.

[(7) The court shall not make an order under this section unless—

(a) the court is satisfied that the related company has no obligations in relation to a bank asset that has been transferred to the National Asset Management Agency or a NAMA group entity, or

(b) if the related company has any such obligation—

(i) a copy of the petition has been served on that Agency, and

(ii) the court has heard that Agency in relation to the making of the order.

(8) In subsection (7) 'bank asset' and 'NAMA group entity' have the same respective meanings as in the National Asset Management Agency Act 2009.][d]

Amendments

a C(A)A 1990, s 4(1) amended by C(A)(No 2)A 1999, s 12(a).

b C(A)A 1990, s 4(2) amended by C(A)(No 2)A 1999, s 12(b).

c Words 'body corporate' substituted for 'company' by CA 1990, s 181.

d C(A)A 1990, s 4(7) and (8) inserted by NAMA Act 2009, s 234.

[4A Duty to act in good faith

The court may decline to hear a petition presented under section 2 or, as the case may be, may decline to continue hearing such a petition if it appears to the court that, in the preparation or presentation of the petition or in the preparation of the report of the independent accountant, the petitioner or independent accountant—

(a) has failed to disclose any information available to him which is material to the exercise by the court of its powers under this Act, or

(b) has in any other way failed to exercise utmost good faith.][a]

Amendments

a C(A)A 1990, s 4A inserted by C(A)(No 2)A 1999, s 13.

5 Effect of petition to appoint examiner on creditors and others

[(1) Subject to section 3A, during the period beginning with the date of the presentation of a petition under section 2 and (subject to subsections (3) and (4) of section 18) ending on the expiry of 70 days from that date or on the withdrawal or refusal of the petition, whichever first happens, the company shall be deemed to be under the protection of the court.][a]

(2) For so long as a company is under the protection of the court in a case under this Act, the following provisions shall have effect—

(a) no proceedings for the winding-up of the company may be commenced or resolution for winding-up passed in relation to that company and any resolution so passed shall be of no effect;

(b) no receiver over any part of the property or undertaking of the company shall be appointed, or, if so appointed before the presentation of a petition under section 2, shall, subject to section 6, be able to act;

(c) no attachment, sequestration, distress or execution shall be put into force against the property or effects of the company, except with the consent of the examiner;

[(d) where any claim against the company is secured by a mortgage, charge, lien or other encumbrance or a pledge of, on or affecting the whole or any part of the property, effects or income of the company, no action may be taken to realize the whole or any part of that security, except with the consent of the examiner;][b]

(e) no steps may be taken to repossess goods in the company's possession under any hire-purchase agreement (within the meaning of section 11(8)), except with the consent of the examiner;

(f) where, under any enactment, rule of law or otherwise, any person other than the company is liable to pay all or any part of the debts of the company—

(i) no attachment, sequestration, distress or execution shall be put into force against the property or effects of such person in respect of the debts of the company, and

(ii) no proceedings of any sort may be commenced against such person in respect of the debts of the company;

[(g) no order for relief shall be made under section 205 of the Principal Act against the company in respect of complaints as to the conduct of the affairs of the company or the exercise of the powers of the directors prior to the presentation of the petition];[c]

[(h) ...][d]

(3) Subject to subsection (2), no other proceedings in relation to the company may be commenced except by leave of the court and subject to such terms as the court may impose and the court may on the application of the examiner make such order as it thinks proper in relation to any existing proceedings including an order to stay such proceedings.

(4) Complaints concerning the conduct of the affairs of the company while it is under the protection of the court shall not constitute a basis for the making of an order for relief under section 205 of the Principal Act.

Amendments

a C(A)A 1990, s 5(1) substituted by C(A)(No 2)A 1999, s 14(a).

b C(A)A 1990, s 2(2)(d) substituted by C(A)(No 2)A 1999, s 14(b)(i).

c C(A)A 1990, s 5(g) inserted by CA 1990, s 180.

d C(A)A 1990, s 5(h) inserted by CA 1990, s 181 and subsequently deleted by C(A)(No 2)A 1999, s 14(b)(ii).

[5A Restriction on payment of pre-petition debts

(1) Subject to subsection (2), no payment may be made by a company, during the period it is under the protection of the court, by way of satisfaction or discharge of the whole or a part of a liability incurred by the company before the date of the presentation under section 2 of the petition in relation to it unless the report of the independent accountant contains a recommendation that the whole or, as the case may be, the part of that liability should be discharged or satisfied.

(2) Notwithstanding subsection (1), the court may, on application being made to it in that behalf by the examiner or any interested party, authorise the discharge or satisfaction, in whole or in part, by the company concerned of a liability referred to in subsection (1) if it is satisfied that a failure to discharge or satisfy, in whole or in part,

that liability would considerably reduce the prospects of the company or the whole or any part of its undertaking surviving as a going concern.][a]

Amendments

a C(A)A 1990, s 5A was inserted by C(A)(No 2)A 1999, s 15.

6 Effect on receiver or provisional liquidator of order appointing examiner

(1) [Where, at the date of the presentation of a petition under section 2 in relation to a company,][a] a receiver stands appointed to the whole or any part of the property or undertaking of that company the court may make such order as it thinks fit including an order as to any or all of the following matters—

(a) that the receiver shall cease to act as such from a date specified by the court,

(b) that the receiver shall, from a date specified by the court, act as such only in respect of certain assets specified by the court,

(c) directing the receiver to deliver all books, papers and other records, which relate to the property or undertaking of the company (or any part thereof) and are in his possession or control, to the examiner within a period to be specified by the court,

(d) directing the receiver to give the examiner full particulars of all his dealings with the property or undertaking of the company.

(2) [Where, at the date of the presentation of a petition under section 2 in relation to a company,][b] a provisional liquidator stands appointed to that company, the court may make such order as it thinks fit including an order as to any or all of the following matters—

(a) that the provisional liquidator be appointed as examiner of the company,

(b) appointing some other person as examiner of the company,

(c) that the provisional liquidator shall cease to act as such from the date specified by the court,

(d) directing the provisional liquidator to deliver all books, papers and other records, which relate to the property or undertaking of the company or any part thereof and are in his possession or control, to the examiner within a period to be specified by the court,

(e) directing the provisional liquidator to give the examiner full particulars of all his dealings with the property or undertaking of the company.

[(3) The court shall not make an order under paragraph (a) or (b) of subsection (1) or paragraph (c) of subsection (2) unless the court is satisfied that there is a reasonable prospect of the survival of the company, and the whole or any part of its undertaking, as a going concern.][c]

(4) Where the court makes an order under subsection (1) or (2), it may, for the purpose of giving full effect to the order, include such conditions in the order and make such ancillary or other orders as it deems fit.

(5) Where a petition is presented under section 2 in respect of a company at a date subsequent to the presentation of a petition for the winding-up of that company, but

before a provisional liquidator has been appointed or an order made for its winding-up, both petitions shall be heard together.

Amendments

a C(A)A 1990, s 6(1) amended by C(A)(No 2) 1999, s 16(a).

b C(A)A 1990, s 6(2) amended by C(A)(No 2) 1999, s 16(b).

c C(A)A 1990, s 6(3) amended by C(A)(No 2) 1999, s 16(c).

[6A Disapplication of section 98 of Principal Act to receivers in certain circumstances

(1) Without prejudice to the generality of section 6(1), the court, on application being made in that behalf, may, in relation to a receiver who stands appointed to the whole or any part of the property or undertaking of a company, make an order providing that section 98 of the Principal Act shall not apply as respects payments made by the receiver out of assets coming into his hands as such receiver if—

(a) (i) an examiner has been appointed to the company, or

(ii) an examiner has not been appointed to the company but, in the opinion of the court, such an appointment may yet be made, and

(b) the making of the order would, in the opinion of the court, be likely to facilitate the survival of the company, and the whole or any part of its undertaking, as a going concern.

(2) An order under subsection (1) shall not be made without each creditor of the company of the following class being afforded an opportunity to be heard, namely a creditor any of the debts owed to whom by the company are debts which in a winding-up are, by virtue of the provisions of Part VI of the Principal Act relating to preferential payments, required to be paid in priority to all other debts.][a]

Amendments

a C(A)A 1990, s 6A inserted by C(A)(No 2)A 1999, s 17.

---

7 Powers of an examiner

(1) Any provision of the Companies Acts relating to the rights and powers of an auditor of a company and the supplying of information to and co-operation with such auditor shall, with the necessary modifications, apply to an examiner.

(2) Notwithstanding any provision of the Companies Acts relating to notice of general meetings, and examiner shall have power to convene, set the agenda for, and preside at meetings of the board of directors and general meetings of the company to which he is appointed and to propose motions or resolutions and to give reports to such meetings.

(3) An examiner shall be entitled to reasonable notice of, to attend and be heard at, all meetings of the board of directors of a company and all general meetings of the company to which he is appointed.

(4) For the purpose of subsection (3) 'reasonable notice' shall be deemed to include a description of the business to be transacted at any such meeting.

(5) Where an examiner becomes aware of any actual or proposed act, omission, course of conduct, decision or contract, by or on behalf of the company to which he has been appointed, its officers, employees, members or creditors or by any other person in relation to the income, assets or liabilities of that company which, in his opinion, is or is likely to be to the detriment of that company, or any interested party, he shall, subject to the rights of parties acquiring an interest in good faith and for value in such income, assets or liabilities, have full power to take whatever steps are necessary to halt, prevent or rectify the effects of such act, omission, course of conduct, decision or contract.

[(5A) Without prejudice to subsection (5B), nothing in this section shall enable an examiner to repudiate a contract that has been entered into by the company prior to the period during which the company is under the protection of the court.

(5B) A provision referred to in subsection (5C) shall not be binding on the company at any time after the service of the notice under this subsection and before the expiration of the period during which the company concerned is under the protection of the court if the examiner is of the opinion that the provision, were it to be enforced, would be likely to prejudice the survival of the company or the whole or any part of its undertaking as a going concern and he serves a notice on the other party or parties to the agreement in which the provision is contained informing him or them of that opinion.

(5C) The provision referred to in subsection (5B) is a provision of an agreement entered into by the company concerned and any other person or persons at any time (including a time that is prior to the period during which the company is under the protection of the court) that provides that the company shall not, or shall not otherwise than in specified circumstances—

(a) borrow moneys or otherwise obtain credit from any person other than the said person or persons, or

(b) create or permit to subsist any mortgage, charge, lien or other encumbrance or any pledge over the whole or any part of the property or undertaking of the company.][a]

(6) The examiner may apply to the court to determine any question arising in the course of his office, or for the exercise in relation to the company of all or any of the powers which the court may exercise under this Act, upon the application to it of any member, contributory, creditor or director of a company.

(7) The examiner shall, if so directed by the court, have power to ascertain and agree claims against the company to which he has been appointed.

Amendments

a C(A)A 1990, s 7(5A), (5B) and (5C) inserted by C(A)(No 2)A 1999, s 18.

---

8 Production of documents and evidence

(1) It shall be the duty of all officers and agents of the company or a related company to produce to the examiner all books and documents of or relating to any such company which are in their custody or power, to attend before him when required so to do and otherwise to give to him all assistance in connection with his functions which they are reasonably able to give.

(2) If the examiner considers that a person other than an officer or agent of any such company is or may be in possession of any information concerning its affairs, he may require that person to produce to him any books or documents in his custody or power relating to the company, to attend before him and otherwise to give him all assistance in connection with his functions which he is reasonably able to give; and it shall be the duty of that person to comply with the requirement.

(3) If the examiner has reasonable grounds for believing that a director [...][a] of any such company maintains or has maintained a bank account of any description, whether alone or jointly with another person and whether in the State or elsewhere, into or out of which there has been paid—

(a) any money which has resulted from or been used in the financing of any transaction, arrangement or agreement particulars of which have not been disclosed in the accounts of any company for any financial year as required by law; or

(b) any money which has been in any way connected with any act or omission, or series of acts or omissions, which on the part of that director constituted misconduct (whether fraudulent or not) towards that company or its members;

the examiner may require the director to produce to him all documents in the director's possession, or under his control, relating to that bank account; and in this subsection 'bank account' includes an account with any person exempt by virtue of section 7(4) of the Central Bank Act, 1971, from the requirement of holding a licence under section 9 of that Act [and 'director' includes any present or past director or any person connected, within the meaning of section 26 of the Companies Act, 1990, with such director, and any present or past shadow director][b].

(4) An examiner may examine on oath, either by word of mouth or on written interrogatories, the officers and agents of such company or other person as is mentioned in subsection (1) or (2) in relation to its affairs and may—

(a) administer an oath accordingly,

(b) reduce the answers of such person to writing and require him to sign them.

[(5) If any officer or agent of such company or other person—

(a) refuses to produce to the examiner any book or document which it is his duty under this section to produce, or

(b) refuses to attend before the examiner when requested to do so, or

(c) refuses to answer any question which is put to him by the examiner with respect to the affairs of the company, the examiner may certify the refusal under his hand to the court, and the court may thereupon enquire into the case and, after hearing any witnesses who may be produced against or on behalf of the said officer, agent or other person or any statement which may be offered in defence, make any order or direction it thinks fit.][c]

(5A) Without prejudice to the generality of subsection (5), the court may, after a hearing under that subsection, make a direction—

(a) to the person concerned to attend or re-attend before the examiner or produce particular books or documents or answer particular questions put to him by the examiner, or

(b) that the person concerned need not produce a particular book or document or answer a particular question put to him by the examiner.][d]

[(5B) Section 23(1) of the Companies Act, 1990, shall apply for the purposes of this section.][e]

(6) In this section, any reference to officers or to agents shall include past, as well as present, officers or agents, as the case may be, and 'agents', in relation to a company, shall include the bankers and solicitors of the company and any persons employed by the company as auditors, whether those persons are or are not officers of the company.

Amendments

a Words deleted by CA 1990, s 180.

b Words inserted by CA 1990, s 180.

c C(A)A 1990, s 8(5) substituted by C(A)(No 2)A 1999, s 19.

d C(A)A 1990, s 8(5A), inserted by CA 1990, s 180 and substituted by C(A)(No2)A 1999, s 19.

e C(A)A 1990, s 8(5B) inserted by CA 1990, s 180.

9 Further powers of court

(1) Where it appears to the court, on the application of the examiner, that, having regard to the matters referred to in subsection (2), it is just and equitable to do so, it may make an order that all or any of the functions or powers which are vested in or exercisable by the directors (whether by virtue of the memorandum or articles of association of the company or by law or otherwise) shall be performable or exercisable only by the examiner.

(2) The matters to which the court is to have regard for the purpose of subsection (1) are—

(a) that the affairs of the company are being conducted, or are likely to be conducted, in a manner which is calculated or likely to prejudice the interests of the company or of its employees or of its creditors as a whole, or

(b) that it is expedient, for the purpose of preserving the assets of the company or of safeguarding the interests of the company or of its employees or of its creditors as a whole, that the carrying on of the business of the company by, or the exercise of the powers of, its directors or management should be curtailed or regulated in any particular respect, or

(c) that the company, or its directors, have resolved that such an order should be sought, or

(d) any other matter in relation to the company the court thinks relevant.

(3) Where the court makes an order under subsection (1), it may, for the purpose of giving full effect to the order, include such conditions in the order and make such ancillary or other orders as it sees fit.

(4) Without prejudice to the generality of subsections (1) and (3), an order under this section may provide that the examiner shall have all or any of the powers that he would have if he were a liquidator appointed by the court in respect of the company and, where such order so provides, the court shall have all the powers that it would have if it had made a winding-up order and appointed a liquidator in respect of the company concerned.

10 Incurring of certain liabilities by examiner

(1) [Any][a] liabilities incurred by the company during the protection period which are referred to in subsection (2) shall be treated as expenses properly incurred, for the purpose of section 29, by the examiner.

(2) The liabilities referred to in subsection (1) are those certified by the examiner at the time they are incurred, in circumstances where, in the opinion of the examiner, the survival of the company as a going concern during the protection period would otherwise be seriously prejudiced.

(3) In this section, 'protection period' means the period, beginning with the appointment of an examiner, during which the company is under the protection of the court.

Amendments

a Substituted by CA 1990, s 180.

---

11 Power to deal with charged property, etc

(1) Where, on an application by the examiner, the court is satisfied that the disposal (with or without other assets) of any property of the company which is subject to a security which, as created, was a floating charge or the exercise by the examiner of his powers in relation to such property would be likely to facilitate the survival of the whole or any part of the company as a going concern, the court may by order authorise the examiner to dispose of the property, or exercise his powers in relation to it, as the case may be, as if it were not subject to the security.

(2) Where, on an application by the examiner, the court is satisfied that the disposal (with or without other assets) of—

(a) any property of the company subject to a security other than a security to which subsection (1) applies, or

(b) any goods in the possession of the company under a hire-purchase agreement,

would be likely to facilitate the survival of the whole or any part of the company as a going concern, the court may by order authorise the examiner to dispose of the property as if it were not subject to the security or to dispose of the goods as if all rights of the owner under the hire-purchase agreement were vested in the company.

(3) Where property is disposed of under subsection (1), the holder of the security shall have the same priority in respect of any property of the company directly or indirectly representing the property disposed of as he would have had in respect of the property subject to the security.

(4) It shall be a condition of an order under subsection (2) that—

(a) the net proceeds of the disposal, and

(b) where those proceeds are less than such amount as may be determined by the court to be the net amount which would be realised on a sale of the property or goods in the open market by a willing vendor, such sums as may be required to make good the deficiency,

shall be applied towards discharging the sums secured by the security or payable under the hire-purchase agreement.

(5) Where a condition imposed in pursuance of subsection (4) relates to two or more securities, that condition requires the net proceeds of the disposal and, where paragraph (b) of that subsection applies, the sums mentioned in that paragraph to be applied towards [discharging][a] the sums secured by those securities in the order of their priorities.

(6) An office copy of an order under subsection (1) or (2) in relation to a security shall, within 7 days after the making of the order, be delivered by the examiner to the registrar of companies.

(7) If the examiner without reasonable excuse fails to comply with subsection (6), he [shall be guilty of an offence and liable to a class C fine][b]][c].

(8) References in this section to a hire-purchase agreement include a conditional sale agreement, a retention of title agreement and an agreement for the bailment of goods which is capable of subsisting for more than 3 months.

Amendments

a Word inserted by CA 1990, s 181.

b £1,000 increased to £1,500 by CA 1990, s 140(7) as inserted by CLEA 2001, s 104. £1,500 converted to €1,904.61 by Council Regulations (EC) No 1103/97, No 974/98 and No 2866/98 and the Economic and Monetary Union Act, 1998, s 6; the above being implicitly substituted, by Fines Act 2010, s 6, for a fine not exceeding the aforesaid amount. A class C fine currently means a fine not exceeding €2,500.

c Words inserted by C(AA)A 2003, Sch 2.

---

12 Notification of appointment of examiner

(1) Where a petition is presented under section 2, notice of the petition in the prescribed form shall, within 3 days after its presentation, be delivered by the petitioner to the registrar of companies.

(2) [(a) An examiner shall, within the time limits specified in paragraph (b), cause to be published in [the Companies Registration Office Gazette][a] and in at least two daily newspapers circulating in the district in which the registered office or principal place of business of the company is situate a notice of his appointment and the date thereof.][b]

(b) The time limits referred to in paragraph (a) are—

(i) twenty-one days after his appointment in the case of [the Companies Registration Office Gazette],[a] and

(ii) three days after his appointment in the other case referred to in that paragraph.

(3) An examiner shall, within three days after his appointment, deliver to the registrar of companies a copy of the order appointing him.

[(4) Where a company is, by virtue of section 5, deemed to be under the protection of the court, every invoice, order for goods or business letter issued by or on behalf of the company, being a document on or in which the name of the company appears, shall immediately after the mention of that name, include the words 'in examination (under the Companies (Amendment) Act, 1990).][c]

(5) A person who fails to comply with the provisions of this section shall be guilty of an offence and shall be liable, on summary conviction, to a class C fine][d] and, on conviction on indictment, to a fine not exceeding [€22,220.42].[e]

Amendments

a 'the Companies Registration Office Gazette' substituted for '*Iris Oifigiúil*' by IFCMPA 2005, s 72.

b C(A)A 1990, s 12(2)(a) substituted by C(A)(No 2)A 1999, s 20(1).

c C(A)A 1990, s 12(4) substituted by C(A)(No 2)A 1999, s 20(2).

d £1,000 increased to £1500 by CA 1990, s 240(7) as inserted by CLEA 2001, s 104. £1,500 converted to €1,904.61 by Council Regulations (EC) No 1103/97, No 974/98 and No 2866/98 and the Economic and Monetary Union Act, 1998, s 6; the above being implicitly substituted, by Fines Act 2010, s 6, for a fine not exceeding the aforesaid amount. A class C fine currently means a fine not exceeding €2,500.

e £10,000 converted to €12,697.38 by Council Regulations (EC) No 1103/97, No 974/98 and No 2866/98 and the Economic and Monetary Union Act 1998, s 6, and multiplied by a multiplier of 1.75 pursuant to Fines Act 2010, s 9.

13 General provisions as to examiners

(1) An examiner may resign or, on cause shown, be removed by the court.

(2) If for any reason a vacancy occurs in the office of examiner, the court may by order fill the vacancy.

(3) An application for an order under subsection (2) may be made by—

(a) any committee of creditors established under section 21, or

(b) the company or any interested party.

(4) An examiner shall be described by the style of 'the examiner' of the particular company in respect of which he is appointed and not by his individual name.

(5) The acts of an examiner shall be valid notwithstanding any defects that may afterwards be discovered in his appointment or qualification.

(6) An examiner shall be personally liable on any contract entered into by him in the performance of his functions (whether such contract is entered into by him in the name of the company or in his own name as examiner or otherwise) unless the contract provides that he is not to be personally liable on such contract, and he shall be entitled in respect of that liability to indemnity out of the assets; but nothing in this subsection shall

be taken as limiting any right to indemnity which he would have apart from this subsection, or as limiting his liability on contracts entered into without authority or as conferring any right to indemnity in respect of that liability.

(7) A company to which an examiner has been appointed or an interested party may apply to the court for the determination of any question arising out of the performance or otherwise by the examiner of his functions.

[13A Hearing regarding irregularities

(1) Where, arising out of the presentation to it of the report of the independent accountant or otherwise, it appears to the court that there is evidence of a substantial disappearance of property of the company concerned that is not adequately accounted for, or of other serious irregularities in relation to the company's affairs having occurred, the court shall, as soon as it is practicable, hold a hearing to consider that evidence.

(2) If, before the hearing referred to in subsection (1) is held, the court directs the examiner to do so, the examiner shall prepare a report setting out any matters which he considers will assist the court in considering the evidence concerned on that hearing.

(3) The examiner shall supply a copy of a report prepared by him under subsection (2) to the company concerned on the same day as he causes the report to be delivered to the office of the court.

(4) The examiner shall also supply a copy of a report prepared by him under subsection (2) to each person who is mentioned in the report and any interested party on written application being made to him in that behalf.

(5) If the court, on application to it in that behalf, directs that that supply may be the subject of such omission, there may be omitted from any copy of the report supplied to a person referred to in subsection (4) or an interested party such parts of it as are specified in the direction of the court.

(6) The court may, in particular, on such an application, direct that there may be omitted from such a supply of a copy of the report any information the inclusion of which in such a copy would be likely to prejudice the survival of the company or the whole or any part of its undertaking as a going concern.

(7) The examiner shall, as soon as may be after it is prepared, supply a copy of the report prepared by him under subsection (2) to—

- (a) if the company concerned is a company referred to in paragraph (a) of section 3(2), the Minister, or
- (b) if the company concerned is a company referred to in paragraph (b) or (c) of section 3(2), the Central Bank, and subsections (5) and (6) shall not apply to such a copy.

(8) The following persons shall be entitled to appear and be heard at a hearing under this section—

- (a) the examiner,
- (b) if the court decided to hold a hearing under this section because of matters contained in the report of the independent accountant, the independent accountant,

(c) the company concerned,

(d) any interested party,

(e) any person who is referred to in the report of the independent accountant or the report prepared under subsection (2),

(f) if the company concerned is a company referred to in paragraph (a) of section 3 (2), the Minister,

(g) if the company concerned is a company referred to in paragraph (b) or (c) of section 3(2), the Central Bank.

(9) The court may, on a hearing under this section, make such order or orders as it deems fit (including, where appropriate, an order for the trial of any issue relating to the matter concerned).

(10) The court may, if it considers it appropriate to do so, direct that an office copy of an order under subsection (9) shall be delivered to the registrar of companies by the examiner or such other person as it may specify.][a]

Amendments

a C(A)A 1990, s 13A was inserted by C(A)(No 2)A 1999, s 21.

---

14 Information to be given when examiner appointed

[...][a]

Amendments

a C(A)A 1990, s 14 was repealed by C(A)(No 2)A 1999, s 30.

---

15 Examination of affairs of company

[...][a]

Amendments

a C(A)A 1990, s 15 was repealed by C(A)(No 2)A 1999, s 30.

---

16 Examiner's report

[...][a]

Amendments

a C(A)A 1990, s 16 was repealed by C(A)(No 2)A 1999, s 30.

---

17 Hearing of matters arising from examiner's report

[...][a]

Amendments

a C(A)A 1990, s 17 was repealed by C(A)(No 2)A 1999, s 30.

18 Further report by examiner

[(1) An examiner shall—

(a) as soon as practicable after he is appointed, formulate proposals for a compromise or scheme of arrangement in relation to the company concerned,

(b) without prejudice to any other provision of this Act, carry out such other duties as the court may direct him to carry out.][a]

(2) Notwithstanding any provision of the Companies Acts relating to notice of general meetings, (but subject to notice of not less than three days in any case) the examiner shall convene and preside at such meetings of members and creditors as he thinks proper, [for the purpose of section 23 and shall report on those proposals to the court, within 35 days of his appointment or such longer period as the court may allow, in accordance with section 19.][b].

(3) Where, on the application of the examiner, the court is satisfied that the examiner would be unable to report to the court within the period of [70 days][c] referred to in section 5(1) but that he would be able to make a report if that period were extended, the court may by order extend that period by not more than 30 days to enable him to do so.

(4) Where the examiner has submitted a report under this section to the court and, but for this subsection, the period mentioned in section 5(1) (and any extended period allowed under subsection (3) of this section) would expire, the court may, of its own motion or on the application of the examiner, extend the period concerned by such period as the court considers necessary to enable it to take a decision under section 24.

[(5) The examiner shall supply a copy of his report under this section—

(a) to the company concerned on the same day as he causes the report to be delivered to the office of the court, and

(b) to any interested party on written application being made to him in that behalf.

(6) The examiner shall, as soon as may be after it is prepared, supply a copy of his report under this section to—

(a) if the company concerned is a company referred to in paragraph (a) of section 3(2), the Minister, or

(b) if the company concerned is a company referred to in paragraph (b) or (c) of section 3(2), the Central Bank.

(7) If the court, on application to it in that behalf, directs that that supply may be the subject of such omission, there may be omitted from any copy of the report supplied under subsection (5)(b) to an interested party such parts of it as are specified in the direction of the court.

(8) The court may, in particular, on such an application, direct that there may be omitted from such a supply of a copy of the report any information the inclusion of which in such a copy would be likely to prejudice the survival of the company or the whole or any part of its undertaking as a going concern.

(9) If the examiner is not able to enter into an agreement with the interested parties and any other persons concerned in the matter or formulate proposals for a compromise or scheme of arrangement in relation to the company concerned, he may apply to the court for the grant of directions in the matter and the court may, on such application, give such directions or make such order as it deems fit, including, if it considers it just and equitable to do so, an order for the winding-up of the company.][d]

Amendments

a C(A)A 1990, s 18(1) substituted by C(A)(No 2)A 1999, s 22(a).

b C(A)A 1990, s 18(2) amended by C(A)(No 2)A 1999, s 22(b).

c C(A)A 1990, s 18(3) amended by C(A)(No 2)A 1999, s 22(c).

d C(A)A 1990, s 18(5) and (6) substituted and subsections (7) to (9) inserted by C(A)(No 2)A 1999, s 22(d).

---

19 Examiner's report under section 18

An Examiner's report under section 18 shall include—

(a) the proposals placed before the required meetings,

(b) any modification of those proposals adopted at any of those meetings,

(c) the outcome of each of the required meetings,

(d) the recommendation of the committee of creditors, if any,

(e) a statement of the assets and liabilities (including contingent and prospective liabilities) of the company as at the date of his report,

(f) a list of the creditors of the company, the amount owing to each such creditor, the nature and value of any security held by any such creditor, and the priority status of any such creditor under section 285 of the Principal Act or any other statutory provision or rule of law,

(g) a list of the officers of the company,

(h) his recommendations,

(i) such other matters as the examiner deems appropriate or the court directs.

20 Repudiation of certain contracts

(1) Where proposals for a compromise or scheme of arrangement are to be formulated in relation to a company, the company may, subject to the approval of the court, affirm or repudiate any contract under which some element of performance other than payment remains to be rendered both by the company and the other contracting party or parties.

(2) Any person who suffers loss or damage as a result of such repudiation shall stand as an unsecured creditor for the amount of such loss or damage.

(3) In order to facilitate the formulation, consideration or confirmation of a compromise or scheme of arrangement, the court may hold a hearing and make an order determining the amount of any such loss or damage and the amount so determined shall be due by the company to the creditor as a judgement debt.

(4) Where the examiner is not a party to an application to the court for the purposes of subsection (1), the company shall serve notice of such application on the examiner and the examiner may appear and be heard on the hearing of any such application.

(5) Where the court approves the affirmation or repudiation of a contract under this section, it may in giving such approval make such orders as it thinks fit for the purposes of giving full effect to its approval including orders as to notice to, or declaring the rights of, any party affected by such affirmation or repudiation.

21 Appointment of creditors' committee

(1) An examiner may, and if so directed by the court shall, appoint a committee of creditors to assist him in the performance of his functions.

(2) Save as otherwise directed by the court, a committee appointed under subsection (1) shall consist of not more than five members and shall include the holders of the three largest unsecured claims who are willing to serve.

(3) The examiner shall provide the committee with a copy of any proposals for a compromise or scheme of arrangement and the committee may express an opinion on the proposals on its own behalf or on behalf of the creditors or classes of creditors represented thereon.

(4) As soon as practicable after the appointment of a committee under subsection (1) the examiner shall meet with the committee to transact such business as may be necessary.

22 Contents of proposals

(1) Proposals for a compromise or scheme of arrangement shall—

(a) specify each class of members and creditors of the company,

(b) specify any class of members and creditors whose interests or claims will not be impaired by the proposals,

(c) specify any class of members and creditors whose interests or claims will be impaired by the proposals,

(d) provide equal treatment for each claim or interest of a particular class unless the holder of a particular claim or interest agrees to less favourable treatment,

(e) provide for the implementation of the proposals,

(f) if the examiner considers it necessary or desirable to do so to facilitate the survival of the company, and the whole or any part of its undertaking, as a going concern, specify whatever changes should be made in relation to the management or direction of the company,

(g) if the examiner considers it necessary or desirable as aforesaid, specify any changes he considers should be made in the memorandum or articles of the company, whether as regards the management or direction of the company or otherwise,

(h) include such other matters as the examiner deems appropriate.

(2) A statement of the assets and liabilities (including contingent and prospective liabilities) of the company as at the date of the proposals shall be attached to each copy of the proposals to be submitted to meetings of members and creditors under section 23.

(3) There shall also be attached to each such copy of the proposals a description of the estimated financial outcome of a winding-up of the company for each class of members and creditors.

(4) The court may direct that the proposals include whatever other provisions it deems fit.

(5) For the purpose of this section and sections 24 and 25, a creditor's claim against a company is impaired if he receives less in payment of his claim than the full amount due in respect of the claim at the date of presentation of the petition for the appointment of the examiner.

(6) For the purposes of this section and sections 24 and 25, the interest of a member of a company in a company is impaired if—

- (a) the nominal value of his shareholding in the company is reduced,
- (b) where he is entitled to a fixed dividend in respect of his shareholding in the company, the amount of that dividend is reduced,
- (c) he is deprived of all or any part of the rights accruing to him by virtue of his shareholding in the company,
- (d) his percentage interest in the total issued share capital of the company is reduced, or
- (e) he is deprived of his shareholding in the company.

23 Consideration by members and creditors of proposals

(1) This section applies to a meeting of members or creditors or any class of members or creditors summoned to consider proposals for a [compromise or scheme of arrangement; save where expressly provided otherwise in this section, this section shall not authorise, at such a meeting, anything to be done in relation to such proposals by any member or creditor.][a]

(2) At a meeting to which this section applies a modification of the proposals may be put to the meeting but may only be accepted with the consent of the examiner.

(3) [...][b].

(4) Proposals shall be deemed to have been accepted by a meeting of creditors or of a class of creditors when a majority in number representing a majority in value of the claims represented at that meeting have voted, either in person or by proxy, in favour of the resolution for the proposals.

[(4A) Nothing in subsection (4) shall, in the case of a creditor who abstains from voting, or otherwise fails to cast a vote, in respect of the proposals, be construed as permitting such an abstention or failure to be regarded as a casting by that person of a vote against the proposals.][c]

(5) (a) Where a State authority is a creditor of the company, such authority shall be entitled to accept proposals under this section notwithstanding—

- (i) that any claim of such authority as a creditor would be impaired under the proposals, or
- (ii) any other enactment.

(b) In this subsection, 'State authority' means the State, a Minister of the Government[, a local authority][d] or the Revenue Commissioners.

(6) Section 144 of the Principal Act shall apply to any resolution to which subsection [...][e] (4) relates which is passed at any adjourned meeting.

(7) Section 202, subsections (2) to (6), of the Principal Act shall, with the necessary modifications, apply to meetings held under this section.

(8) With every notice summoning a meeting to which this section applies which is sent to a creditor or member, there shall be sent also a statement explaining the effect of the compromise or scheme of arrangement and in particular stating any material interests of the directors of the company, whether as directors or as members or as creditors of the company or otherwise and the effect thereon of the compromise or arrangement, insofar as it is different from the effect on the like interest of other persons.

[(9) Without prejudice to subsections (1) to (8), in the case of a company referred to in paragraph (b) or (c) of section 3(2), the examiner shall also afford the Central Bank an opportunity to consider the proposals for a compromise or scheme of arrangement and for this purpose shall furnish to the Central Bank a statement containing the like information to that referred to in subsection (8).][f]

Amendments

a C(A)A 1990, s 23(1) amended by C(A)(No 2)A 1999, s 23(a).

b C(A)A 1990, s 23(3) deleted by C(A)(No 2)A 1999, s 23(b).

c C(A)A 1990, s 23(4A) inserted by C(A)(No 2)A 1999, s 23(c).

d Words inserted by CA 1990, s 180.

e C(A)A 1990, s 23(6) amended by C(A)(No 2)A 1999, s 23(d).

f C(A)A 1990, s 23(9) inserted by C(A)(No 2)A 1999, s 23(e).

24 Confirmation of proposals

(1) The report of the examiner under section 18 shall be set down for consideration by the court as soon as may be after receipt of the report by the court.

(2) The following persons may appear and be heard at a hearing under subsection (1)—

(a) the company,

(b) the examiner,

(c) any creditor or member whose claim or interest would be impaired if the proposals were implemented,

[(d) in case the company is a company referred to in paragraph (b) or (c) of section 3(2), the Central Bank.][a]

(3) At a hearing under subsection (1) the court may, as it thinks proper, subject to the provisions of this section and section 25, confirm, confirm subject to modifications, or refuse to confirm the proposals.

(4) The court shall not confirm any proposals—

[(a) unless at least one class of creditors whose interests or claims would be impaired by implementation of the proposals has accepted the proposals, or][b]

(b) if the sole or primary purpose of the proposals is the avoidance of payment of tax due, or

(c) unless the court is satisfied that—

(i) the proposals are fair and equitable in relation to any class of members or creditors that has not accepted the proposals and whose interests or claims would be impaired by implementation, and

(ii) the proposals are not unfairly prejudicial to the interests of any interested party.

[(4A) Without prejudice to subsection (4), the court shall not confirm any proposals in respect of a company to which an examiner has been appointed under section 4 if the proposals would have the effect of impairing the interests of the creditors of the company in such a manner as to favour the interests of the creditors or members of any company to which it is related, being a company to which that examiner has been appointed examiner under section 2 or, as the case may be, 4.][c]

(5) Where the court confirms proposals (with or without modification), the proposals shall be binding on all the members or class or classes of members, as the case may be, affected by the proposal and also on the company.

(6) Where the court confirms proposals (with or without modification), the proposals shall, notwithstanding any other enactment, be binding on all the creditors or the class or classes of creditors, as the case may be, affected by the proposals in respect of any claim or claims against the company and any person other than the company who, under any statute, enactment, rule of law or otherwise, is liable for all or any part of the debts of the company.

(7) Any alterations in, additions to or deletions from the memorandum and articles of the company which are specified in the proposals shall, after confirmation of the proposals by the court and notwithstanding any other provisions of the Companies Acts, take effect from a date fixed by the court.

(8) Where the court confirms proposals under this section it may make such orders for the implementation of its decision as it deems fit.

(9) A compromise or scheme of arrangement, proposals for which have been confirmed under this section shall come into effect from a date fixed by the court, which date shall be not later than 21 days from the date of their confirmation.

(10) On the confirmation of proposals a copy of any order made by the court under this section shall be delivered by the examiner, or by such person as the court may direct, to the registrar of companies for registration.

(11) Where—

(a) the court refuses to confirm proposals under this section, or

(b) the report of an examiner under section 18 concludes that, following the required meetings of [...][d] creditors of a company under this Act, it has not been possible to reach agreement on a compromise or scheme of arrangement,

the court may, if it considers it just and equitable to do so, make an order for the winding-up of the company, or any other order as it deems fit.

[(12) Notwithstanding subsection (4), or any other provision of this Act, nothing in this Act shall prevent the examiner from including in a report under section 18 proposals which will not involve the impairment of the interests of members or creditors of the company, nor the court from confirming any such proposals',][e]

Amendments

a C(A)A 1990, s 24(2)(d) inserted by C(A)(No 2)A 1999, s 24(a).

b C(A)A 1990, s 24(4)(a) substituted by C(A)(No 2)A 1999, s 24(b).

c C(A)A 1990, s 24(4A) inserted by C(A)(No 2)A 1999, s 24(c).

d C(A)A 1990, s 24(11) amended by C(A)(No 2)A 1999, s 24(d).

e C(A)A 1990, s 24(12) inserted by CA 1990, s 180 and substituted by C(A)(No 2)A 1999, s 24(e).

25 Objection to confirmation by court of proposals

(1) At a hearing under section 24 in relation to proposals a member or creditor whose interest or claim would be impaired by the proposals may object in particular to their confirmation by the court on any of the following grounds—

(a) that there was some material irregularity at or in relation to a meeting to which section 23 applies,

(b) that acceptance of the proposals by the meeting was obtained by improper means,

(c) that the proposals were put forward for an improper purpose,

(d) that the proposals unfairly prejudice the interests of the objector.

(2) Any person who voted to accept the proposals may not object to their confirmation by the court except on the grounds—

(a) that such acceptance was obtained by improper means, or

(b) that after voting to accept the proposals he became aware that the proposals were put forward for an improper purpose.

(3) Where the court upholds an objection under this section, the court may make such order as it deems fit, including an order that the decision of any meeting be set aside and an order that any meeting be reconvened.

[25A Provisions with respect to guarantees

(1) The following provisions shall have effect in relation to the liability of any person ('the third person') whether under a guarantee or otherwise, in respect of a debt ('the debt') of a company to which an examiner has been appointed:

(a) subject to paragraph (b) and save where the contrary is provided in an agreement entered into by the third person and the person to whom he is liable in respect of the debt ('the creditor'), the liability shall, notwithstanding section 24(6), not be affected by the fact that the debt is the subject of a compromise or scheme of arrangement that has taken effect under section 24(9),

(b) neither paragraph (a) nor any of the subsequent provisions of this subsection shall apply if the third person is a company to which an examiner has been appointed,

(c) if the creditor proposes to enforce by legal proceedings or otherwise the obligation of the third person in respect of the liability, then—

(i) he shall—

(I) if 14 days' or more notice is given of such meeting, at least 14 days before the day on which the meeting concerned under section 23 to consider the proposals is held, or

(II) if less than 14 days' notice is given of such meeting, not more than 48 hours after he has received notice of such meeting,

serve a notice on the third person containing an offer in writing by the creditor to transfer to the third person (which the creditor is hereby empowered to do) any rights, so far as they relate to the debt, he may have under section 23 to vote in respect of proposals for a compromise or scheme of arrangement in relation to the company,

(ii) if the said offer is accepted by the third person, that offer shall, if the third person furnishes to the examiner at the meeting concerned a copy of the offer and informs the examiner of his having accepted it, operate, without the necessity for any assignment or the execution of any other instrument, to entitle the third person to exercise the said rights, but neither the said transfer nor any vote cast by the third person on foot of the transfer shall operate to prejudice the right of the creditor to object to the proposals under section 25,

(iii) if the creditor fails to make the said offer in accordance with subparagraph (ii), then, subject to subparagraph (iv), the creditor may not enforce by legal proceedings or otherwise the obligation of the third person in respect of the liability,

(iv) subparagraph (iii) shall not apply if a compromise or scheme of arrangement in relation to the company is not entered into or does not take effect under section 24(9) and the creditor has obtained the leave of the court to enforce the obligation of the third person in respect of the liability,

(d) if the third person makes a payment to the creditor in respect of the liability after the period of protection has expired, then any amount that would, but for that payment, be payable to the creditor in respect of the debt under a compromise or scheme of arrangement that has taken effect under section 24(9) in relation to the company shall become and be payable to the third person upon and subject to the same terms and conditions as the compromise or scheme of arrangement provided that it was to be payable to the creditor.

(2) Nothing in subsection (1) shall affect the operation of—

(a) section 5(2)(f), or

(b) any rule of law whereby any act done by the creditor referred to in that subsection results in the third person referred to therein being released from his obligation in respect of the liability concerned.][a]

Amendments

a Inserted by C(A)A (No2) 1999, s 25.

[25B Provisions with respect to leases

(1) Subject to subsection (3), proposals for a compromise or scheme of arrangement shall not contain, nor shall any modification by the court under section 24 of such proposals result in their containing, a provision providing for either or both—

(a) a reduction in the amount of any rent or other periodical payment reserved under a lease of land that falls to be paid after the compromise or scheme of arrangement would take effect under section 24(9) or the complete extinguishment of the right of the lessor to any such payments,

(b) as respects a failure—

(i) to pay an amount of rent or make any periodical payment reserved under a lease of land, or

(ii) to comply with any other covenant or obligation of such a lease,

that falls to be paid or complied with after the date referred to in paragraph (a), a requirement that the lessor under such a lease shall not exercise, or shall only exercise in specified circumstances, any right, whether under the lease or otherwise, to recover possession of the land concerned, effect a forfeiture of the lease or otherwise enter on the land or to recover the amount of such rent or other payment or to claim damages or other relief in respect of the failure to comply with such a covenant or obligation.

(2) Subject to subsection (3), proposals for a compromise or scheme of arrangement in relation to a company shall not be held by the court to satisfy the condition specified in paragraph (c)(ii) of section 24(4) if the proposals contain a provision relating to a lease of, or any hiring agreement in relation to, property other than land and, in the opinion of the court—

(a) the value of that property is substantial, and

(b) the said provision is of like effect to a provision referred to in paragraph (a) or (b) of subsection (1).

(3) Subsection (1) or (2) shall not apply if the lessor or owner of the property concerned has consented in writing to the inclusion of the provision referred to in subsection (1) or (2) in the proposals for the compromise or scheme of arrangement.

(4) In deciding, for the purposes of subsection (2), whether the value of the property concerned is substantial the matters to which the court shall have regard shall include the length of the unexpired form of the lease or hiring agreement concerned.][a]

Amendments

a Inserted by C(A)(No2)A 1999, s 26.

26 Cessation of protection of company and termination of appointment of examiner

(1) Subject to section 5, the protection deemed to be granted to a company under that section shall cease—

(a) on the coming into effect of a compromise or scheme of arrangement under this Act, or

(b) on such earlier date as the court may direct.

(2) Where a company ceases to be under the protection of the court, the appointment of the examiner shall terminate on the date of such cessation.

27 Revocation

[(1)][a] The company or any interested party may, within 180 days after the confirmation of the proposals by the court, apply to the court for revocation of that confirmation on the grounds that it was procured by fraud and the court, if satisfied that such was the case, may revoke that confirmation on such terms and conditions, particularly with regard to the protection of the rights of parties acquiring interests or property in good faith and for value in reliance on that confirmation, as it deems fit.

[(2) As soon as practicable after the revocation under this section of such a confirmation, a copy of the order made by the court shall be delivered to—

(a) the registrar of companies,

(b) in case the company to which the order relates is a company referred to in paragraph (a) of section 3(2), the Minister, and

(c) in case the company to which the order relates is a company referred to in paragraph (b) or (c) of section 3(2), the Central Bank,

by such person as the court may direct.][a]

Amendments

a '(1)' and subsection (2) inserted by C(A)(No2)A 1999, s 27.

---

28 Disqualification of examiners

(1) A person shall not be qualified to be appointed or act as an examiner of a company if he would not be qualified to act as its liquidator.

(2) A person who acts as examiner of a company while disqualified under this section shall be guilty of an offence, and shall be liable, on summary conviction, to a [class C fine][a] and, on conviction on indictment, to a fine not exceeding [€22,220.42].[b]

Amendments

a £1,000 increased to £1,500 by CA 1990, s 240(7) as inserted by CLEA 2001, s 104. £1,500 converted to €1,904.61 by Council Regulations (EC) No 1103/97, No 974/98 and No 2866/98 and the Economic and Monetary Union Act, 1998, s 6; the above being implicitly substituted, by Fines Act 2010, s 6, for a fine not exceeding the aforesaid amount. A class C fine currently means a fine not exceeding €2,500.

b '£10,000' converted to €12,697.38 by Council Regulations (EC) No 1103/97, No 974/98 and No 2866/98 and the Economic and Monetary Union Act, 1998, s 6, and multiplied by a multiplier of 1.75 pursuant to Fines Act 2010, s 9.

---

29 Costs and remuneration of examiners

(1) The court may from time to time make such orders as it thinks proper for payment of the remuneration and costs of, and reasonable expenses properly incurred by, an examiner.

(2) Unless the court otherwise orders, the remuneration, costs and expenses of an examiner shall be paid and the examiner shall be entitled to be indemnified in respect thereof out of the revenue of the business of the company to which he has been appointed, or the proceeds of realisation of the assets (including investments).

[(3) The remuneration, costs and expenses of an examiner which have been sanctioned by order of the court (other than the expenses referred to in subsection (3A)) shall be paid in full and shall be paid before any other claim, secured or unsecured, under any compromise or scheme of arrangement or in any receivership or winding-up of the company to which he has been appointed.

(3A) Liabilities incurred by the company to which an examiner has been appointed that, by virtue of section 10(1), are treated as expenses properly incurred by the examiner shall be paid in full and shall be paid before any other claim (including a claim secured by a floating charge), but after any claim secured by a mortgage, charge, lien or other encumbrance of a fixed nature or a pledge, under any compromise or scheme of arrangement or in any receivership or winding-up of the company to which he has been appointed.

(3B) In subsections (3) and (3A) references to a claim shall be deemed to include references to any payment in a winding-up of the company in respect of costs, charges and expenses of that winding-up (including the remuneration of any liquidator).][a]

(4) The functions of an examiner may be performed by him with the assistance of persons appointed or employed by him for that purpose provided that an examiner shall, insofar as is reasonably possible, make use of the services of the staff and facilities of the company to which he has been appointed to assist him in the performance of his functions.

(5) In considering any matter relating to the costs, expenses and remuneration of an examiner the court shall have particular regard to the proviso to subsection (4).

Amendments

a Sub-s (3) substituted and sub-ss (3A) & (3B) inserted by C(A)(No2)A 1999, s 28.

---

30 Publicity

(1) An examiner or, where appropriate, such other person as the court may direct, shall, within 14 days after the delivery to the registrar of companies of every order made under [section 13A, 24 or 27][a], cause to be published in [the Companies Registration Office Gazette][b] notice of such delivery.

(2) Where a person fails to comply with this section, that person, and where that person is a company, the company and every officer of the company who is in default, shall be guilty of an offence and shall be liable to a [class C fine].[c]

(3) [...][d]

Amendments

a Words amended by C(A)(No2)A 1999, s 30.

b 'the Companies Registration Office Gazette' substituted for '*Iris Oifigiúil*' by IFCMPA 2005, s 72.

c £1,000 increased to £1,500 by CA 1990, s 240(7) as inserted by CLEA 2001, s 104. £1,500 converted to €1,904.61 by Council Regulations (EC) No 1103/97, No 974/98 and No 2866/98 and the Economic and Monetary Union Act, 1998, s 6; the above being implicitly substituted, by Fines Act 2010, s 6, for a fine not exceeding the aforesaid amount. A class C fine currently means a fine not exceeding €2,500.

d C(A)A 1990, s 30(3) repealed by CA 1990, s 181.

31 Hearing of proceedings otherwise than in public

The whole or part of any proceedings under this Act may be heard otherwise than in public if the court, in the interests of justice, considers that the interests of the company concerned or of its creditors as a whole so require.

32 No lien over company's books, records etc

[...][a]

Amendments

a C(A)A 1990, s 32 repealed by CA 1990, s 180.

Replaced by CA 1963, s 244A (as inserted by CA 1990, s 125) and applied to companies under the protection of the court, by CA 1990, s 180(2).

33 Civil liability of persons concerned for fraudulent trading of company

[...][a]

Amendments

a C(A)A 1990, s 33 repealed by CA 1990, s 180.

34 Criminal liability of persons concerned for fraudulent trading of company

[...][a]

Amendments

a C(A)A 1990, s 34 repealed by CA 1990, s 180.

35 Power of court to order the return of assets which have been improperly transferred

[...][a]

Amendments

a C(A)A 1990, s 35 repealed by CA 1990, s 180.

C(A)A 1990, s 35 replaced by CA 1990, s 139 as applied to companies under the protection of the court by CA 1990, s 180(2).

36 Enforcement of reconstruction orders made by courts outside the State

(1) Any order made by a court of any country recognised for the purposes of this section and made for or in the course of the reorganisation or reconstruction of a company may be enforced by the High Court in all respects as if the order had been made by the High Court.

(2) When an application is made to the High Court under this section, an office copy of any order sought to be enforced shall be sufficient evidence of the order.

(3) In this section, 'company' means a body corporate incorporated outside the State, and 'recognised' means recognised by order made by the Minister.

[36A Proceedings by registrar

Proceedings in relation to an offence under section 11(6), 12 or 30 may be brought and prosecuted by the registrar of companies.][a]

Amendments

a C(A)A 1990, s 36A inserted by CA 1990, s 181.

37 Short title, collective citation and construction

(1) This Act may be cited as the Companies (Amendment) Act, 1990.

(2) This Act and the Companies Acts, 1963 to 1986, may be cited together as the Companies Acts, 1963 to 1990.

(3) The Companies Acts, 1963 to 1986, and this Act shall be construed together as one Act.

Companies Act 1990

Number 33 of 1990

ARRANGEMENT OF SECTIONS

PART I
PRELIMINARY

PART II
INVESTIGATIONS

PART III
TRANSACTIONS INVOLVING DIRECTORS

PRELIMINARY

CHAPTER 2

INDIVIDUAL AND GROUP ACQUISITIONS

CHAPTER 3

DISCLOSURE ORDERS: COMPANIES OTHER THAN PUBLIC LIMITED COMPANIES

Chapter 3
Enforcement

Part VIII
Receivers

Part IX
Companies under Court Protection

Part X
Accounts and Audit

Part XI
Acquisition of Own Shares and Shares in Holding Company

PART XII
GENERAL

PART XIII
INVESTMENT COMPANIES

An Act to Amend the Law Relating to Companies and to Provide for Related Matters. [22nd December, 1990]

Be it Enacted by the Oireachtas as Follows:

PART I
PRELIMINARY

1 Short title, collective citation and construction

(1) This Act may be cited as the Companies Act, 1990.

(2) This Act and the Companies Acts, 1963 to 1986, may be cited together as the Companies Acts, 1963 to 1990.

(3) The Companies Acts, 1963 to 1986, and this Act shall be construed together as one Act.

2 Commencement

This Act shall come into operation on such day or days as may be fixed therefor by order or orders of the Minister, either generally or with reference to a particular purpose or provision, and different days may be so fixed for different purposes and different provisions of this Act.

[3 Interpretation

(1) In this Act, unless the context otherwise requires—

'books and documents' and 'books or documents' include accounts, deeds, writings and records made in any other manner;

'child' includes a step-child and an adopted child and 'son', 'daughter' and 'parent' shall be construed accordingly;

['Central Bank' means the Central Bank and Financial Services Authority of Ireland;][a]

'the Companies Acts' means the Companies Act, 1963, and every enactment (including this Act) which is to be construed as one with that Act;

'connected person' has the meaning assigned to it by section 26;

'contravention' includes failure to comply;

'daily default fine' has the meaning assigned to it by section 240(6);

'the Minister' means the Minister for Industry and Commerce;

'prescribe' means prescribe by regulations;

'the Principal Act' means the Companies Act, 1963;

'recognised stock exchange' has the meaning assigned to it by subsection (2);

'related company' has the meaning assigned to it by section 140;

'shadow director' has the meaning assigned to it by section 27.

(2) (a) [A recognised stock exchange for the purposes of any provision of the Companies Acts is an exchange or a market, whether within or outside the State, prescribed by the Minister for the purposes of that provision.][b]

(b) The definition of 'recognised stock exchange' in paragraph (a) is in substitution for the definition in section 2(1) of the Principal Act.

(3) The Minister may make regulations in relation to any matter referred to in this Act as prescribed or to be prescribed.

(4) In this Act—

(a) a reference to a Part or section is to a Part or section of this Act unless it is indicated that a reference to some other enactment is intended;

(b) a reference to a subsection, paragraph or subparagraph is to the subsection, paragraph or subparagraph of the provision in which the reference occurs, unless it is indicated that reference to some other provision is intended; and

(c) a reference to any other enactment shall, unless the context otherwise requires, be construed as a reference to that enactment as amended by or under any other enactment, including this Act.][a]

Amendments

a CA 1990, s 3 inserted by CBFSAIA 2003, Sch 1.

b CA 1990, s 3(2)(a) substituted by C(MP)A 2009, s 3(a).

---

4 Periods of time

(1) Where the time limited by any provision of this Act for the doing of anything expires on a Saturday, Sunday or public holiday, the time so limited shall extend to and the thing may be done on the first following day that is not a Saturday, Sunday or public holiday.

(2) Where in this Act anything is required or allowed to be done within a number of days not exceeding six a day that is a Saturday, Sunday or public holiday shall not be reckoned in computing that number.

5 Orders

The Minister may by order revoke or amend an order made by him under any provision of this Act, other than section 2.

6 Repeals

(1) The following provisions of the Principal Act are hereby repealed – sections 147, 162 (inserted by section 6 of the Companies (Amendment) Act, 1982), 163, 165 to 173, 184, 294, 296, 380 and 385, and the Seventh and Tenth Schedules.

(2) The following provisions are also hereby repealed—

(a) Regulation 8 of the European Communities (Companies) Regulations, 1973,

(b) section 6 of the Companies (Amendment) Act, 1977, and

(c) section 21 of the Companies (Amendment) Act, 1986.

PART II
INVESTIGATIONS

7 Investigation of company's affairs

(1) The court may appoint one or more competent inspectors to investigate the affairs of a company in order to enquire into matters specified by the court and to report thereon in such manner as the court directs—

(a) in the case of a company having a share capital, on the application either of not less than 100 members or of a member or members holding not less than one-tenth of the paid up share capital of the company;

(b) in the case of a company not having a share capital, on the application of not less than one-fifth in number of the persons on the company's register of members;

(c) in any case, on the application of the company;

(d) in any case, on the application of a director of the company;

(e) in any case, on the application of a creditor of the company.

(2) The application shall be supported by such evidence as the court may require, including such evidence as may be prescribed.

(3) Where an application is made under this section, the court may require the applicant or applicants to give security [...][a] for payment of the costs of the investigation.

(4) Where the court appoints an inspector under this section or section 8, it may, from time to time, give such directions as it thinks fit, whether to the inspector or otherwise, with a view to ensuring that the investigation is carried out as quickly and as inexpensively as possible.

Amendments

a Words deleted by C(MP)A 2009, s 3(b).

---

8 Investigation of company's affairs on application of [Director]

(1) Without prejudice to its powers under section 7, the court may [on the application of the Director appoint one or more competent inspectors (who may be or include an officer of officers of the Director][a] to investigate the affairs of a company and to report thereon in such manner as the court shall direct, if the court is satisfied that there are circumstances suggesting—

(a) that its affairs are being or have been conducted with intent to defraud its creditors or the creditors of any other person or otherwise for a fraudulent or unlawful purpose or in an unlawful manner or in a manner which is unfairly prejudicial to some part of its members, or that any actual or proposed act or omission of the company (including an act or omission on its behalf) is or would be so prejudicial, or that it was formed for any fraudulent or unlawful purpose; or

(b) that persons connected with its formation or the management of its affairs have in connection therewith been guilty of fraud, misfeasance or other misconduct towards it or towards its members; or

(c) that its members have not been given all the information relating to its affairs which they might reasonably expect.

(2) (a) The power conferred by section 7 or this section shall be exercisable with respect to a body corporate not withstanding that it is in course of being wound up.

(b) The reference in subsection (1)(a) to the members of a company shall have effect as if it included a reference to any person who is not a member but to whom shares in the company have been transferred or transmitted by operation of law.

Amendments

a Subsection (1) amended by the substitution for 'on the application of the Minister appoint one or more competent inspectors' of 'on the application of the Director appoint one or more competent inspectors (who may be or include an officer or officers of the Director)' by CLEA 2001, s 21.

---

9 Power of inspectors to extend investigation into affairs of related companies

[(1) If an inspector][a] appointed under section 7 or 8 to investigate the affairs of a company thinks it necessary for the purposes of his investigation to investigate also the affairs of any other body corporate which is related to such company, he shall, with the approval of the court, have power so to do, and shall report on the affairs of the other body corporate so far as he thinks the results of his investigation thereof are relevant to the investigation of the affairs of the first-mentioned company.

[(2) For the purposes of this section, a body corporate which is related to a company includes a body corporate with which the company has a commercial relationship, and a commercial relationship exists where goods or services are sold or given by one party to another.][b]

Amendments

a '(1) If an inspector' substituted for 'If an inspector' by CLEA 2001, s 22(a).

b Subsection (2) inserted by CLEA 2001, s 22(b).

---

10 Production of documents and evidence on investigation

(1) It shall be the duty of all officers and agents of the company and of all officers and agents of any other body corporate whose affairs are investigated by virtue of section 9 to produce to the inspectors all books and documents of or relating to the company, or, as the case may be, the other body corporate which are in their custody or power, to attend before the inspectors when required so to do and otherwise to give to the inspectors all assistance in connection with the investigation which they are reasonably able to give [; but where any such person claims a lien on books or documents produced by the person, the production shall be without prejudice to the lien.][a]

(2) If the inspectors consider that a person other than an officer or agent of the company or other body corporate is or may be in possession of any information concerning its affairs, they may require that person to produce to them any books or documents in his custody or power relating to the company or other body corporate, to attend before them and otherwise to give them all assistance in connection with the investigation which he is reasonably able to give; and it shall be the duty of that person to comply with the requirement [; but where any such person claims a lien on books or documents produced by the person, the production shall be without prejudice to the lien.][b]

(3) If an inspector has reasonable grounds for believing that a director of the company or other body corporate whose affairs the inspector is investigating maintains or has maintained a bank account of any description, whether alone or jointly with another person and whether in the State or elsewhere, into or out of which there has been paid—

- (a) any money which has resulted from or been used in the financing of any transaction, arrangement or agreement—
  - (i) particulars of which have not been disclosed in a note to the accounts of any company for any financial year as required by section 41; or
  - (ii) in respect of which any amount outstanding was not included in the aggregate amounts outstanding in respect of certain transactions, arrangements or agreements as required by section 43 to be disclosed in a note to the accounts of any company for any financial year; or
  - (iii) particulars of which were not included in any register of certain transactions, arrangements and agreements as required by section 44; or
- (b) any money which has been in any way connected with any act or omission, or series of acts or omissions, which on the part of that director constituted misconduct (whether fraudulent or not) towards that company or body corporate or its members;

the inspector may require the director to produce to him all documents in the director's possession, or under his control, relating to that bank account; and in this subsection 'bank account' includes an account with any person exempt by virtue of section 7 (4) of the Central Bank Act, 1971, from the requirement of holding a licence under section 9 of that Act, and 'director' includes any present or past director or any person connected, within the meaning of section 26, with such director, and any present or past shadow director.

(4) An inspector may examine on oath, either by word of mouth or on written interrogatories, the officers and agents of the company or other body corporate and such person as is mentioned in subsection (2) in relation to its affairs and may—

(a) administer an oath accordingly,

(b) reduce the answers of such person to writing and require him to sign them.

[(5) If an officer or agent of the company or other body corporate, or any such person as is mentioned in subsection (2), refuses or fails within a reasonable time to—

(a) produce to the inspectors any book or document which it is his duty under this section so to produce,

(b) attend before the inspectors when required so to do, or

(c) answer a question put to him by the inspectors with respect to the affairs of the company or other body corporate as the case may be,

the inspectors may certify the refusal or failure under their hand to the court, and the court may thereupon enquire into the case and, after hearing any witnesses who may be produced against or on behalf of the person alleged to have so refused or failed and any statement which may be offered in defence, make any order or direction it thinks fit.

(6) Without prejudice to the generality of subsection (5), the court may, after a hearing under that subsection, direct—

(a) the person concerned to attend or re-attend before the inspectors or produce particular books or documents or answer particular questions put to him by the inspectors, or

(b) that the person concerned need not produce a particular book or document or answer a particular question put to him by the inspectors.][c]

(7) In this section, any reference to officers or to agents shall include past, as well as present, officers or agents, as the case may be, and 'agents', in relation to a company or other body corporate, shall include the bankers and solicitors of the company or other body corporate and any persons employed by the company or other body corporate as auditors, [accountants, book-keepers or taxation advisers,][d] whether those persons are or are not officers of the company or other body corporate.

Amendments

a Words in sub-s (1) inserted by CLEA 2001, s 23(a).

b Words in sub-s (2) inserted by CLEA 2001, s 23(b).

c Subsections (5) and (6) inserted by CLEA 2001, s 23(c).

d Words in sub-s (7) inserted by CLEA 2001, s 23(d).

---

11 Inspectors' reports

(1) Inspectors appointed under section 7 or 8 may, and if so directed by the court shall, make interim reports to the court and on the conclusion of the investigation, shall make a final report to the court.

(2) Notwithstanding anything contained in subsection (1), an inspector appointed under section 7 or 8 may at any time in the course of his investigation, without the necessity of making an interim report, inform the court of matters coming to his knowledge as a result of the investigation tending to show that an offence has been committed.

(3) Where inspectors were appointed under section 7 or 8, the court shall furnish a copy of every report of theirs to the [Director][a] and the court may, if it thinks fit—

(a) forward a copy of any report made by the inspectors to the company's registered office,

(b) furnish a copy on request and payment of the prescribed fee to—

(i) any member of the company or other body corporate which is the subject of the report;

(ii) any person whose conduct is referred to in the report;

(iii) the auditors of that company or body corporate;

(iv) the applicants for the investigation;

(v) any other person (including an employee) whose financial interests appear to the court to be affected by the matters dealt with in the report whether as a creditor of the company or body corporate or otherwise;

(vi) the Central Bank, in any case in which the report of the inspectors relates, wholly or partly, to the affairs of the holder of a licence under section 9 of the Central Bank Act, 1971;[...][b]

[(ba) furnish a copy to—

(i) an appropriate authority in relation to any of the matters referred to in section 21(1)(a) to (fb); or

(ii) a competent authority as defined in section 21(3)(a) to (i); and][c]

(c) cause any such report to be printed and published.

(4) Where the court so thinks proper it may direct that a particular part of a report made by virtue of this section be omitted from a copy forwarded or furnished under [subsection (3)(a), (b) or (ba)][d] or from the report as printed and published under subsection (3)(c).

Amendments

a 'Director' substituted for 'Minister' by CLEA 2001, s 14.

b CLEA 2001, s 24(1)(a) amends CA 1990, s 11(3)(b)(vi) by the deletion of 'and' from the end thereof.

c CLEA 2001, s 24(1) inserts CA 1990, s 11(3)(ba).

d CLEA 2001, s 24(2) amends CA 1990, s 11(4) by the substitution for 'subsection (3)(a) or (b)' of 'subsection (3)(a), (b) or (ba)'.

---

12 Proceedings on inspectors' report

(1) Having considered a report made under section 11, the court may make such order as it deems fit in relation to matters arising from that report including—

(a) an order of its own motion for the winding up of a body corporate, or

(b) an order for the purpose of remedying any disability suffered by any person whose interests were adversely affected by the conduct of the affairs of the company, provided that, in making any such order, the court shall have regard to the interests of any other person who may be adversely affected by the order.

(2) If, in the case of any body corporate liable to be wound up under the Companies Acts, it appears to the [Director][a] from—

(a) any report made under section 11 as a result of an application by the [Director][a] under section 8, or

(b) any report made by inspectors appointed by the [Director][a] under this Act, or

(c) any information or document obtained by the [Director][a] under this Part,

that a petition should be presented for the winding up of the body, the [Director][a] may, unless the body is already being wound up by the court, present a petition for it to be so wound up if the court thinks it just and equitable for it to be so wound up.

Amendments

a 'Director' substituted for 'Minister' by CLEA 2001, s 14.

---

13 Expenses of investigation of company's affairs

(1) The expenses of and incidental to an investigation by an inspector appointed by the court under the foregoing provisions of this Act shall be defrayed in the first instance by the [relevant Minister][a] but the court may direct that any person being—

(a) a body corporate dealt with in the report, or

(b) the applicant or applicants for the investigation,

shall be liable, to such extent as the court may direct, to repay the [relevant Minister.][b]

(2) Without prejudice to subsection (1), any person who is—

(a) convicted on indictment of an offence on a prosecution instituted as a result of an investigation,

(b) ordered to pay damages or restore any property in proceedings brought as a result of an investigation, or

(c) awarded damages or to whom property is restored in proceedings brought as a result of an investigation,

may, in the same proceedings, be ordered to repay all or part of the expenses referred to in subsection (1) to the [relevant Minister][a] or to any person on whom liability has been imposed by the court under that subsection, provided that, in the case of a person to whom paragraph (c) relates, the court shall not order payment in excess of one-tenth of the amount of the damages awarded or of the value of the property restored, as the case may be, and any such order shall not be executed until the person concerned has received his damages or the property has been restored, as the case may be.

(3) The report of an inspector may, if he thinks fit, and shall, if the court so directs, include a recommendation as to the directions (if any) which he thinks appropriate, in the light of his investigation, to be given under subsection (1).

[(3A) In this section 'relevant Minister' means—

(a) in case the inspector or inspectors concerned was or were appointed under section 7, the Minister for Justice, Equality and Law Reform, and

(b) in case the inspector or inspectors concerned was or were appointed under section 8, the Minister.][c]

Amendments

a 'relevant Minister' substituted for 'Minister for Justice' by CLEA 2001, s 25.

b Words substituted by C(MP)A 2009, s 3(c).

c Subsection (3A) inserted by CLEA 2001, s 25.

14 Appointment and powers of inspectors to investigate ownership of company

(1) The [Director][a] may, subject to subsection (2), appoint one or more competent inspectors to investigate and report on the membership of any company and otherwise with respect to the company for the purpose of determining the true persons who are or have been financially interested in the success or failure (real or apparent) of the company or able to control or materially to influence the policy of the company.

(2) An appointment may be made by the [Director][a] if he is of the opinion that there are circumstances suggesting that it is necessary—

(a) for the effective administration of the law relating to companies;

(b) for the effective discharge by the [Director][a] of his functions under any enactment; or

(c) in the public interest.

(3) The appointment of an inspector under this section may define the scope of his investigation, whether as respects the matters or the period to which it is to extend or otherwise, and in particular may limit the investigation to matters connected with particular shares or debentures.

(4) Subject to the terms of an inspector's appointment his powers shall extend to the investigation of any circumstances suggesting the existence of an arrangement or understanding which, though not legally binding, is or was observed or likely to be observed in practice and which is relevant to the purposes of his investigation.

(5) For the purposes of any investigation under this section, sections 9 to 11, except section 10 (3), shall apply with the necessary modifications of references to the affairs of the company or to those of any other body corporate, so, however, that—

(a) the said sections shall apply in relation to all persons who are or have been, or whom the inspector has reasonable cause to believe to be or have been, financially interested in the success or failure or the apparent success or failure of the company or any other body corporate whose membership is investigated with that of the company, or able to control or materially to influence the policy thereof, including persons concerned only on behalf of others and to any other person whom the inspector has reasonable cause to believe possesses information relevant to the investigation, as they apply in relation to officers and agents of the company or of the other body corporate, as the case may be;

(b) if the [Director][a] is of opinion that there is good reason for not divulging any part of a report made by virtue of this section he may disclose the report with the omission of that part; and may cause to be kept by the registrar of companies a copy of the report with that part omitted or, in the case of any other such report, a copy of the whole report; and

(c) for references to the court (except in section 10(5) and (6)), there shall be substituted references to the [Director].[a]

[(6) The court may, on the application of the Director, direct that a company the subject of an investigation under this section shall be liable, to such extent as the court may direct, to repay the Director the expenses of and incidental to the investigation.

(7) Without prejudice to subsection (6) but subject to subsection (8), a person—

(a) convicted on indictment of an offence on a prosecution instituted,

(b) ordered to pay damages or restore any property in proceedings brought, or

(c) awarded damages or to whom property is restored in proceedings brought,

as a result of an investigation under this section may, in the same proceedings, be ordered to repay the Director all or part of the expenses referred to in subsection (6).

(8) The court shall not order a person to whom subsection (7)(c) relates to make payment in excess of one-tenth of the amount of the damages awarded or of the value of the property restored, as the case may be, and any such order shall not be executed until the person concerned has received his damages or the property has been restored.][b]

Amendments

a 'Director' substituted for 'Minister' by CLEA 2001, s 14.

b Subsections (6) to (8) inserted by CLEA 2001, s 26.

---

15 Power to require information as to persons interested in shares or debentures

(1) Where it appears to the [Director][a] that it is necessary—

(a) for the effective administration of the law relating to companies;

(b) for the effective discharge by the [Director][a] of his functions under any enactment; or

(c) in the public interest;

to investigate the ownership of any shares in or debentures of a company and that it is unnecessary to appoint an inspector for the purpose, he may require any person whom he has reasonable cause to believe to have or to be able to obtain any information as to the present and past interests in those shares or debentures and the names and addresses of the persons interested and of any persons who act or have acted on their behalf in relation to the shares or debentures to give any such information to the [Director][a].

(2) For the purposes of this section a person shall be deemed to have an interest in a share or debenture if he has any right to acquire or dispose of the share or debenture or any interest therein or to vote in respect thereof or if his consent is necessary for the exercise of any of the rights of other persons interested therein or if the other persons interested therein can be required or are accustomed to exercise their rights in accordance with his instructions.

(3) Any person who fails to give any information required of him under this section or who in giving any such information makes any statement which he knows to be false in a material particular, or recklessly makes any statement which is false in a material particular, shall be guilty of an offence.

Amendments

a 'Director' substituted for 'Minister' by CLEA 2001, s 14.

16 Power to impose restrictions on shares or debentures

(1) Where in connection with an investigation or enquiry under section 14 or 15 it appears to the [Director][a] that there is difficulty in finding out the relevant facts about any shares (whether issued or to be issued), the [Director][a] may by notice in writing direct that the shares shall until further notice be subject to the restrictions imposed by this section.

(2) So long as a direction under subsection (1) in respect of any shares is in force—

- (a) any transfer of those shares, or in the case of unissued shares any transfer of the right to be issued therewith and any issue thereof, shall be void;
- (b) no voting rights shall be exercisable in respect of those shares;
- (c) no further shares shall be issued in right of those shares or in pursuance of any offer made to the holder thereof; and
- (d) [...][b] no payment shall be made of any sums due from the company on those shares, whether in respect of capital or otherwise.

(3) Where shares are subject to the restrictions imposed by subsection (2)(a) any agreement to transfer the shares or in the case of unissued shares the right to be issued with the shares shall be void except an agreement to sell the shares pursuant to subsection (6)(b).

(4) Where shares are subject to the restrictions imposed by subsection (2)(c) or (2)(d) any agreement to transfer any right to be issued with other shares in right of those shares or to receive any payment on those shares [...][c] shall be void except an agreement to transfer any such right on the sale of the shares pursuant to subsection (6)(b).

(5) Where the [Director][a] directs that shares shall be subject to the said restrictions, or refuses to direct that shares shall cease to be subject thereto, any person aggrieved thereby may apply to the court for an order that the shares shall cease to be subject thereto.

(6) Subject to subsections (7) and (13), an order of the court or a direction of the Minister that shares shall cease to be subject to the restrictions imposed by this section may be made only if—

- [(a) in the case of an order by the court, the court is satisfied that the relevant facts about the shares have been disclosed to the company or, as the case requires, to the Director, or that it is otherwise equitable to lift the restrictions;
- (b) in the case of a direction of the Director, the Director is satisfied that the relevant facts about the shares have been disclosed to him; or
- (c) the shares are to be sold and the court or the Director approves the sale.][d]

(7) Where any shares in a company are subject to the restrictions imposed by this section, the court may on the application of the [Director][a] or the company [, having given notice to the Director][e] order the shares to be sold, subject to the approval of the

court as to the sale, and may also direct that the shares shall cease to be subject to those restrictions.

(8) Where an order has been made under subsection (7) then, on application of the [Director],[a] the company, the person appointed by or in pursuance of the order to effect the sale or any person interested in the shares, the court may make such further order relating to the sale or to the transfer of the shares as it thinks fit.

(9) Where any shares are sold in pursuance of an order made under subsection (7), the proceeds of sale, less the costs of the sale, shall be paid into court for the benefit of the persons who are beneficially interested in the shares; and any such person may apply to the court for the whole or part of those proceeds to be paid to him.

(10) On an application under subsection (9) the court shall, subject to subsection (11), order the payment to the applicant of the whole of the proceeds of sale together with any interest thereon or, if any other person had a beneficial interest in the shares at the time of their sale, such proportion of those proceeds and interest as is equal to the proportion which the value of the applicant's interest in the shares bears to the total value of the shares.

(11) On granting an application for an order under subsection (7) or (8), the court may order that the costs of the applicant shall be paid out of the proceeds of sale; and, where an order under this subsection is made, the applicant shall be entitled to payment of his costs out of the proceeds of sale before any person interested in the shares in question receives any part of those proceeds.

(12) Any order or direction that shares shall cease to be subject to the said restrictions which is expressed to be made or given with a view to permitting a transfer of those shares or which is made under subsection (7) may continue the restrictions mentioned in subsection (2)(c) and (2)(d) in whole or in part, so far as they relate to any right acquired or offer made before the transfer.

(13) Subsection (6) shall not apply in relation to any order of the court or of the [Director][a] directing that shares shall cease to be subject to any restrictions which have been continued in force in relation to those shares by virtue of subsection (12).

(14) Any person who—

- (a) exercises or purports to exercise any right to dispose of any shares which, to his knowledge, are for the time being subject to the said restrictions or of any right to be issued with any such shares; or
- (b) votes in respect of any such shares, whether as holder or proxy, or appoints a proxy to vote in respect thereof; or
- (c) being the holder of any such shares, fails to notify of their being subject to the said restrictions any person whom he does not know to be aware of that fact but does know to be entitled, apart from the said restrictions, to vote in respect of those shares whether as holder or proxy; or
- (d) being the holder of any such shares, or being entitled to any such right as is mentioned in subsection (4) enters into an agreement which is void by virtue of subsection (3) or (4);

shall be guilty of an offence.

(15) Where shares in any company are issued in contravention of the said restrictions, the company and every officer of the company who is in default shall be guilty of an offence.

(16) Summary proceedings shall not be instituted under this section except by or with the consent of the [Director].[a]

(17) This section shall apply in relation to debentures as it applies in relation to shares.

(18) The [Director][a] shall cause notice of any direction given by him under this section—

(a) to be sent to the company concerned at its registered office, and

(b) to be delivered to the registrar of companies,

(c) to be published in [the Companies Registration Office Gazette][f] and in at least two daily newspapers,

as soon as may be after the direction is given.

Amendments

a 'Director' substituted for 'Minister' by CLEA 2001, s 14.

b 'except in a liquidation' deleted from sub-s (2)(d) by CLEA 2001, s 27(a).

c '(otherwise than in a liquidation)' deleted from sub-s (4) by CLEA 2001, s 27(b).

d Paras (a) to (c) substituted by CLEA 2001, s 27(c).

e ', having given notice to the Director,' inserted by CLEA 2001, s 27(d).

f 'the Companies Registration Office Gazette' substituted for '*Iris Oifigiúil*' by IFCMPA 2005, s 72.

---

17 Extension of powers of investigation to certain bodies incorporated outside the State

Sections 8 to 11, 13, 18 and 22 shall apply to all bodies corporate incorporated outside the State which are carrying on business in the State or have at any time carried on business therein as if they were companies registered under the Principal Act, subject to any necessary modifications.

18 Admissibility in evidence of certain matters

[(1) An answer given by an individual][a] to a question put to him in exercise of powers conferred by—

(a) section 10;

(b) section 10 as applied by sections 14 and 17; or

(c) rules made in respect of the winding-up of companies whether by the court or voluntarily under section 68 of the Courts of Justice Act, 1936, as extended by section 312 of the Principal Act;

may be used in evidence against him [in any proceedings whatsoever (save proceedings for an offence (other than perjury in respect of such an answer)).][b]

[(2) A statement required by section 224 of the Principal Act may, in any proceedings whatsoever (save proceedings for an offence (other than perjury in respect of any matter contained in the statement)), be used in evidence against any individual making or concurring in making it.][c]

Amendments

a Words substituted by CLEA 2001, s 28(a).

b Words substituted by CLEA 2001, s 28(b).

c Subsection (2) inserted by CLEA 2001, s 28(c).

---

19 [Power of Director to require production of documents

(1) The Director may, subject to subsection (2), give directions to any body being—

(a) a company formed and registered under the Companies Acts;

(b) an existing company within the meaning of those Acts;

(c) a company to which the Principal Act applies by virtue of section 325 thereof or which is registered under that Act by virtue of Part IX thereof;

(d) a body corporate incorporated in, and having a principal place of business in, the State, being a body to which any of the provisions of the said Act with respect to prospectuses and allotments apply by virtue of section 377 of that Act;

(e) a body corporate incorporated outside the State which is carrying on business in the State or has at any time carried on business therein;

(f) any other body, whether incorporated or not, which is, or appears to the Director to be, an insurance undertaking to which the Insurance Acts, 1909 to 2000, or regulations on insurance made under the European Communities Act, 1972, would apply, requiring the body, at such time and place as may be specified in the directions, to produce such books or documents as may be so specified.

(2) Directions may be given by the Director if he is of the opinion that there are circumstances suggesting that—

(a) it is necessary to examine the books and documents of the body with a view to determining whether an inspector should be appointed to conduct an investigation of the body under the Companies Acts;

(b) the affairs of the body are being or have been conducted with intent to defraud—

(i) its creditors,

(ii) the creditors of any other person, or

(iii) its members;

(c) the affairs of the body are being or have been conducted for a fraudulent purpose other than described in paragraph (b);

(d) the affairs of the body are being or have been conducted in a manner which is unfairly prejudicial to some part of its members;

[(da) the affairs of the body are being or have been conducted in a manner which is unfairly prejudicial to some or all of its creditors;][b]

(e) any actual or proposed act or omission or series of acts or omissions of the body or on behalf of the body [have been, are or would][c] be unfairly prejudicial to some part of its members;

(f) any actual or proposed act or omission or series of acts or omissions of the body or on behalf of the body or by an officer of the body acting in his capacity as such officer [have been, or are likely][d] to be unlawful;

(g) the body was formed for any fraudulent purpose;

(h) the body was formed for any unlawful purpose; or

(i) the body may be in possession of books or documents containing information relating to the books or documents of a body which comes within the terms of one or more of paragraphs (a) to (h).

[(3) Where by virtue of subsection (1) the Director has power to require the production of any books or documents from any body, the Director shall have power to require the production of—

(a) those books or documents from any person who appears to the Director to be in possession of them,

(b) copies of any books or documents of the body from any person who appears to the Director to be in possession of them, and

(c) subject to subsection (4), other books or documents (whether the originals of them or otherwise) which may relate to any books or documents of the body from any person who appears to the Director to be in possession of such other books or documents,

but where any such person claims a lien on books or documents produced by him, the production shall be without prejudice to the lien.][e]

[(3A) Any requirement under subsection (3) shall be made by the giving by the Director of a direction to the person of whom the requirement is being made that specifies—

(a) the books or documents to be produced by the person, and

(b) the time and place at which they are to be produced.][f]

(4) The power under [subsection (3)(c)][g] shall not be exercised unless—

(a) in the opinion of the Director, there are reasonable grounds for believing the first and second-mentioned books or documents in [subsection (3)(c)][g] are related to one another (and those grounds may include grounds related to the relationship between the body and the person of whom the requirement under [subsection (3)(c)][g] is proposed to be made, a common origin of some or all of the information contained in the said books or documents or similar considerations), and

(b) save where the Director is of opinion that compliance with this paragraph could result in the concealment, falsification, destruction or the disposal otherwise of the books or documents concerned, the Director notifies the person of whom the requirement under [subsection (3)(c)][g] is proposed to be made ('the third party') that the Director proposes to make that requirement and states in that notification the grounds for his opinion under paragraph (a) and that the third party may (if such is his contention) make submissions to the Director, within 21 days from the date of the making of the notification, as to why he believes the said opinion of the Director to be erroneous (and the Director shall have regard to any such submissions so made before finally deciding whether to make the said requirement or not),

but in no case shall the third party be obliged to comply with such a requirement in relation to a particular book or document concerned if he would be entitled, by virtue of any rule of law or enactment, to refuse to produce, in any proceedings, the book or document on the ground of any privilege (whether the privilege to which section 23 applies or not).

(5) Any power conferred by or by virtue of this section to require a body or other person to produce books or documents shall include power—

(a) if the books or documents are produced—

(i) to take copies of them or extracts from them, and

(ii) to require that person, or any other person who is a present or past officer of, or is or was at any time employed (including in a professional, consultancy or similar capacity) by, the body in question, to provide, insofar as the person may be reasonably able so to do, an explanation of any of them, including an explanation of any apparent omissions from them or any omission of any book or document, and

(b) if the books or documents are not produced, to require the person who was required to produce them to state, to the best of his knowledge and belief, where they are,

and in either event to give all assistance to the Director as the body or person is reasonably able to give in connection with an examination or proposed examination of books or documents under this section.

(6) If a requirement to produce books or documents or provide an explanation or make a statement which is imposed by virtue of this section is not complied with, the body or other person on whom the requirement was so imposed shall be guilty of an offence; but where a person is charged with an offence under this subsection in respect of a requirement to produce any books or documents, it shall be a defence to prove that they were not in his possession or under his control and that it was not reasonably practicable for him to comply with the requirement.

(7) A statement made or an explanation provided by an individual in compliance with a requirement imposed by virtue of this section may be used in evidence against him in any proceedings whatsoever (save proceedings for an offence (other than an offence under subsection (6) or (8))).

(8) A person who provides an explanation or makes a statement required under this section which is false or misleading in a material respect, knowing it to be so false or misleading, shall be guilty of an offence.

(9) Notwithstanding section 202(9), it shall be an offence for a person or body with notice of [a direction under subsection (1) or (3A)][h] (whether given or coming to the notice of the person or body before or after the commencement of section 29 of the Company Law Enforcement Act, 2001) to destroy, mutilate, falsify or conceal any book or document the subject of a direction.

(10) The court may, on the application of the Director, direct that a body the subject of a direction under subsection (1) shall be liable, to such extent as the court may direct, to repay the Director the expenses of and incidental to the examination.

(11) Without prejudice to subsection (10) but subject to subsection (12), a person—

(a) convicted on indictment of an offence on a prosecution instituted,

(b) ordered to pay damages or restore any property in proceedings brought, or

(c) awarded damages or to whom property is restored in proceedings brought,

as a result of a direction under subsection (1) may, in the same proceedings, be ordered to repay the Director all or part of the expenses referred to in subsection (10).

(12) The court shall not order a person to whom subsection (11)(c) relates to make payment in excess of one-tenth of the amount of the damages awarded or of the value of the property restored, as the case may be, and any such order shall not be executed until the person concerned has received his damages or the property has been restored.][a]

Amendments

a Section 19 substituted by CLEA 2001, s 29.

b Subsection (2)(da) inserted by IFCMPA 2005, s 67(a).

c Words substituted by IFCMPA 2005, s 67(b).

d Words substituted by IFCMPA 2005, s 67(c).

e CA 1990, s 19(3) substituted by C(A)A 2009, s 4(1)(a).

f CA 1990, s 19(3A) inserted by C(A)A 2009, s 4(1)(a).

g Words 'subsection 3(c)' substituted for 'subsection 3(b)' by C(A)A 2009, s 4(1)(b).

h Words 'a direction under subsection (1) or (3A)' substituted for 'a direction under subsection (1)' by C(A)A 2009, s 4(1)(c).

[19A Concealing facts disclosed by documents

(1) A person who—

(a) knows or suspects that an investigation by the Director into an offence under the Companies Acts is being or is likely to be carried out, and

(b) falsifies, conceals, destroys or otherwise disposes of a document or record which he knows or suspects is or would be relevant to the investigation or causes or permits its falsification, concealment, destruction or disposal,

shall be guilty of an offence.

(2) Where a person—

(a) falsifies, conceals, destroys or otherwise disposes of a document or record, or

(b) causes or permits its falsification, concealment, destruction or disposal,

in such circumstances that it is reasonable to conclude that the person knew or suspected—

(i) that an investigation by the Director into an offence under the Companies Acts was being or was likely to be carried out, and

(ii) that the document or record was or would be relevant to the investigation, the person shall be taken for the purposes of this section to have so known or suspected, unless the court or the jury, as the case may be, is satisfied having regard to all the evidence that there is reasonable doubt as to whether the person so knew or suspected.][a]

Amendments

a Section was inserted by CLEA 2001, s 29.

20 Entry and search of premises

[(1) If a judge of the District Court is satisfied by information on oath laid by a designated officer that there are reasonable grounds for suspecting that any material information is to be found on any premises (including a dwelling), the judge may issue a search warrant under this section.

(2) A search warrant issued under this section shall be expressed and operate to authorise a named designated officer ('the officer'), accompanied by such other persons as the officer thinks necessary, [at any time or times within the period of validity of the warrant][b], on production if so requested of the warrant, to—

- (a) enter the premises named in the warrant, if necessary by force,
- (b) search the premises,
- (c) require any person found on the premises—
  - (i) to give to the officer his name, home address and occupation, and
  - (ii) to produce to the officer any material information which is in the custody or possession of that person,
- (d) seize and retain any material information found on the premises or in the custody or possession of any person found on the premises, and
- (e) take any other steps which appear to the officer to be necessary for preserving or preventing interference with material information.

[(2A) Without prejudice to subsection (2B), where—

- (a) the officer finds anything at, or in the custody or possession of any person found on, the premises named in the warrant that the officer has reasonable grounds for believing may be or may contain material information, and
- (b) it is not reasonably practicable for a determination to be made on the premises—
  - (i) whether what he has found is something that he is entitled to seize under the warrant (whether as mentioned in subsection (2)(d) or subsection (2B)), or
  - (ii) the extent to which what he has found contains something that he is entitled to seize under the warrant in either of those cases,

the officer's powers of seizure under the warrant shall include power to seize so much of what he has found as it is necessary to remove from the premises to enable that to be determined (in subsections (2D) to (2G) referred to as an 'extended power of seizure').

(2B) Where—

(a) the officer finds anything at, or in the custody or possession of any person found on, the premises named in the warrant being a book, document or other thing constituting material information ('seizable information') which he would be entitled to seize but for its being comprised in something else that he has (apart from this subsection) no power to seize, and

(b) it is not reasonably practicable for the seizable information to be separated, on those premises, from that in which it is comprised,

the officer's powers of seizure shall include power to seize both the seizable information and that from which it is not reasonably practicable to separate it (in subsections (2D) to (2G) also referred to as an 'extended power of seizure').

(2C) Where, for the purposes of subsection (2A) or (2B), an issue arises as to either of the following matters, namely—

(a) whether or not it is reasonably practicable on particular premises for something to be determined, or

(b) whether or not it is reasonably practicable on particular premises for something to be separated from something else,

the issue shall be decided by reference solely to the following matters:

(i) how long it would take to carry out the determination or separation on those premises;

(ii) the number of persons that would be required to carry out that determination or separation on those premises within a reasonable period;

(iii) whether the determination or separation would (or would if carried out on those premises) involve damage to property;

(iv) the apparatus or equipment that it would be necessary or appropriate to use for the carrying out of the determination or separation;

(v) the costs of carrying out the determination or separation on those premises as against the costs of carrying out the determination or separation in another place (being a place in which the Director can show it would be appropriate to do the thing concerned and in which the Director intends to arrange, or does arrange, for the thing to be done), and

(vi) in the case of separation, whether the separation—

(I) would be likely, or

(II) if carried out by the only means that are reasonably practicable on those premises, would be likely,

to prejudice the use of some or all of the separated seizable information for a purpose for which something seized under the warrant is capable of being used.

(2D) Save where the officer is of opinion that compliance with this subsection could result in the concealment, falsification, destruction or the disposal otherwise of material information, an extended power of seizure shall not be exercised unless the officer has first made the following arrangements in relation to the thing or things, the subject of the proposed exercise of that power, namely reasonable arrangements—

(a) providing for the appropriate storage of that thing or those things,

(b) allowing reasonable access, from time to time, to that thing or those things by the owner, lawful custodian or possessor thereof (including, in the case of documents or information in non-legible form, by the making of copies or the transmission of matter by electronic means), and

(c) providing for confidentiality to be maintained as regards any confidential matter comprised in that thing or those things,

being arrangements to apply pending the making of the foregoing determination or the carrying out of the foregoing separation and the consequent return of anything to the owner, lawful custodian or possessor that is not material information; in deciding what the terms of those arrangements shall be, the officer shall have regard to any representations reasonably made on the matter by the owner, lawful custodian or possessor of the thing or things and endeavour, where practicable, to secure the agreement of that person to those terms.

(2E) Where—

(a) by reason of the officer being of the opinion referred to in subsection (2D), the arrangements referred to in paragraphs (a) to (c) of that subsection are not made in relation to the thing or things the subject of the proposed exercise of the extended power of seizure, or

(b) circumstances arise subsequent to the exercise of the extended power of seizure that make it appropriate to vary the arrangements made under that subsection,

the officer shall, as the case may be—

(i) make, as soon as practicable after the exercise of that power of seizure, the arrangements referred to in subsection (2D)(a) to (c) in relation to the thing or things concerned, or

(ii) vary the arrangements made under that subsection in a manner he considers appropriate,

and, in deciding what shall be the terms of those arrangements or that variation, the officer shall have regard to any representations on the matter reasonably made by the owner, lawful custodian or possessor of the thing or things concerned and endeavour, where practicable, to secure the agreement of that person to those terms.

(2F) Where an extended power of seizure is exercised, it shall be the duty of the officer—

(a) to carry out the determination or separation concerned as soon as practicable, and, in any event, subject to subsection (2G), within the prescribed period, after its exercise, and

(b) as respects anything seized in exercise of the power found not to be material information or, as the case may be, anything separated from another thing in the exercise of the power that is not material information, to return, as soon as practicable, and, in any event, subject to subsection (2G), within the prescribed period, after that finding or separation, the thing to its owner or the person appearing to the officer to be lawfully entitled to the custody or possession of it.

(2G) On application to the court by the Director or any person affected by the exercise of an extended power of seizure, the court may, if it thinks fit and having had regard, in particular, to any submissions made on behalf of the Director with regard to the progress of any investigation being carried on by the Director for the purpose of which the powers under this section had been exercised, give one or more of the following:

(a) a direction that the doing of an act referred to in subsection (2F)(a) or (b) shall be done within such lesser or greater period of time than that specified in that provision as the court determines,

(b) a direction with respect to the making, variation or operation of arrangements referred to in subsection (2D)(a) to (c) in relation to a thing concerned or a direction that such arrangements as the court provides for in the direction shall have effect in place of any such arrangements that have been or were proposed to be made,

(c) a direction of any other kind that the court considers it just to give for the purpose of further securing the rights of any person affected by the exercise of an extended power of seizure, including, if the exceptional circumstances of the case warrant doing so, a direction that a thing seized be returned to its owner or the person appearing to the court to be lawfully entitled to the custody or possession of it, not-withstanding that the determination or separation concerned has not occurred,

and any such direction may—

(i) relate to some or all of the things the subject of the exercise of the extended power of seizure,

(ii) be expressed to operate subject to such terms and conditions as the court specifies, including,

in the case of a direction under paragraph (c), a condition that an officer of the Director be permitted, during a specified subsequent period, to re-take and retain possession of the thing returned for the purpose of carrying out the determination or separation concerned (and, retain after the expiry of that period, that which is found to be material information or is material information).

(2H) An application under subsection (2G) shall be by motion and may, if the court directs, be heard otherwise than in public.

(2I) In subsection (2F) 'prescribed period' means—

(a) in the case of paragraph (a) of it—

(i) unless subparagraph (ii) applies, 3 months, or

(ii) such other period as the Minister prescribes in consequence of a review that may, from time to time, be carried out by or on behalf of the Minister of the operation and implementation of the amendments effected by section 5 of the Companies (Amendment) Act 2009,

(b) in the case of paragraph (b) of it—

(i) unless subparagraph (ii) applies, 7 days, or

(ii) such other period as the Minister prescribes in consequence of such a review that may, from time to time, be carried out by or on behalf of the Minister, but no regulations made to prescribe such a period shall be read as operating to affect any direction given by the court under subsection (2G)(a) in force on the commencement of those regulations.

(2J) The Minister may make regulations providing for such supplementary, consequential and incidental matters to or in respect of subsections (2A) to (2F) as he considers necessary or expedient.][c]

(3) [...][d]

(4) The officer may—

(a) operate any computer at the place which is being searched or cause any such computer to be operated by a person accompanying the officer, and

(b) require any person at that place who appears to the officer to be in a position to facilitate access to the information held in any such computer or which can be accessed by the use of that computer—

(i) to give to the officer any password necessary to operate it,

(ii) otherwise to enable the officer to examine the information accessible by the computer in a form in which the information is visible and legible, or

(iii) to produce the information in a form in which it can be removed and in which it is, or can be made, visible and legible.

(5) The power to issue a warrant under this section is in addition to and not in substitution for any other power to issue a warrant for the search of any place or person.

(6) A person who—

(a) obstructs the exercise of a right of entry or search conferred by virtue of a search warrant issued under this section,

(b) obstructs the exercise of a right so conferred to seize and retain material information,

(c) fails to comply with a requirement under subsection (2)(c) or gives a name, address or occupation which is false or misleading, or

(d) fails to comply with a requirement under subsection (4)(b),

shall be guilty of an offence.

(7) In this section—

'computer' includes a personal organiser or any other electronic means of information storage or retrieval;

'computer at the place which is being searched' includes any other computer, whether at that place or at any other place, which is lawfully accessible by means of that computer;

'designated officer' means the Director or an officer of the Director authorised in that behalf by the Director; and

'material information' means—

(a) any books or documents of which production has been required under or by virtue of section 14, 15 or 19 and which have not been produced in compliance with that requirement, or

(b) any books or documents or other things (including a computer) which the officer has reasonable grounds for believing may provide evidence of or relating to the commission of an offence under the Companies Acts.][a]

[(8) The period of validity of a warrant shall be 1 month from its date of issue but that period of validity may be extended in accordance with subsections (9) and (10).

(9) The officer may, during the period of validity of a warrant (including such period as previously extended under subsection (10)), apply to a judge of the District Court for an order extending the period of validity of the warrant and such an application shall be grounded upon information on oath laid by the officer stating, by reference to the purpose or purposes for which the warrant was issued, the reasons why he considers the extension to be necessary.

(10) If the judge of the District Court is satisfied that there are reasonable grounds for believing, having regard to that information so laid, that further time is needed so that the purpose or purposes for which the warrant was issued can be fulfilled, the judge may make an order extending the period of validity of the warrant by such period as, in the opinion of the judge, is appropriate and just; where such an order is made, the judge shall cause the warrant to be suitably endorsed to indicate its extended period of validity.

(11) Nothing in the preceding subsections prevents a judge of the District Court from issuing, on foot of a fresh application made under subsection (1), a further search warrant under this section in relation to the same premises.][e]

Amendments

a Section substituted by CLEA 2001, s 30.

b Words 'at any time or times within the period of validity of the warrant' substituted for 'at any time or times within 1 month from the date of issue of the warrant' by C(A)A 2009, s 5(a).

c CA 1990, s 20(2A)–(2J) inserted by C(A)A 2009, s 5(b).

d Subsection (3) repealed by IFCMPA, s 68(2).

e CA 1990, s 20(8)–(11) inserted by C(A)A 2009, s 5(c).

---

21 Provision for security of information

[(1) No information, book or document relating to a body which has been obtained under section 19 or 20, shall, without the previous consent in writing of that body, be published or disclosed, except to a competent authority, unless the publication or disclosure is, in the opinion of the [Director][b], required—

(a) with a view to the investigation or prosecution of any offence, being an offence—

(i) under

(I) the Companies Acts;

(II) the Central Bank Acts, 1942 to 1998;

(III) the Exchange Control Acts, 1954 to 1986;

(IV) the Insurance Acts, 1909 to 1990;

[(V) the Taxes Consolidation Act, 1997, or an offence under an enactment referred to in section 1078(1) of that Act;][c]

(VI) regulations relating to insurance made under the European Communities Act, 1972; or

(ii) entailing misconduct in connection with the management of the body's affairs or misapplication or wrongful retainer of its property;

(b) for the purpose of assessing the liability of a person in respect of a tax or duty or other payment owed or payable to the State, a local authority (within the meaning of the Local Government Act, 1941) or a health board or for the purpose of collecting an amount due in respect of such a tax or duty or other payment;

(c) for the purpose of the performance by a tribunal (to which the Tribunals of Inquiry (Evidence) Acts, 1921 to 1998, apply) of any of its functions;

(d) for the purpose of assisting or facilitating the performance by any Minister of the Government of any of his functions;

(e) for the purpose of assisting or facilitating any accountancy or other professional organisation in the performance of its disciplinary functions with respect to any of its members;

(f) for the purpose of the performance by the Irish Takeover Panel or any stock exchange established in the State of any of its functions in relation to the body or any other person who, in its opinion, is connected with the body;

[(fa) for the purpose of the performance by the Competition Authority of any of its functions;

(fb) for the purpose of the performance by a committee (being a committee within the meaning of the Committees of the Houses of the Oireachtas (Compellability, Privileges and Immunities of Witnesses) Act, 1997, to which sections 3 to 14 and 16 of that Act apply) of any of its functions;][d]

(g) for the purposes of complying with the requirements of procedural fairness, to be made to—

(i) any company in relation to which an inspector has been appointed under section 14 or any person required by the [Director][b] to give any information under section 15, or

[(ii) any body to which the Director has given a direction under section 19 or any person named in a report relating to an examination under that section;][e]

(h) for the purpose of complying with any requirement, or exercising any power, imposed or conferred by this Part with respect to reports made by inspectors appointed thereunder by the court or the [Director][b];

(i) with a view to the institution by the [Director][b] of proceedings for the winding-up under the Principal Act of the body or otherwise for the purposes of proceedings instituted by him for that purpose;

(j) for the purposes of proceedings under section 20 or 160].[a]

(2) A person who publishes or discloses any information, book or document in contravention of this section shall be guilty of an offence.

(3) For the purposes of this section 'competent authority' includes—

(a) the Minister,

(b) a person authorised by the Minister,

(c) an inspector appointed under this Act,

(d) the Minister for Finance,

(e) an officer authorised by the Minister for Finance,

[(ea) the Irish Auditing and Accounting Supervisory Authority,][f]

(f) any court of competent jurisdiction,

(g) a supervisory authority within the meaning of regulations relating to insurance made under the European Communities Act, 1972, [...][g]

[(h) the Central Bank, and

(i) any authority established outside the State in which there are vested—

(i) functions of investigating or prosecuting an offence similar to an offence referred to in paragraph (a) of subsection (1),

(ii) functions of assessing the liability of a person in respect of a tax or duty or other payment owed or payable to the state in which it is established or any other authority established in that state or of collecting an amount due in respect of such a tax or duty or other payment, or

(iii) functions which are similar to the functions referred to in paragraph (c), (d), (e) or (f) of subsection (1).][h]

Amendments

a C(A)(No 2)A 1999, s 53(2) substitutes CA 1990, s 21(1).

b CLEA 2001, s 31(a) amends CA 1990, s 21(1) by the substitution for 'Minister' where ever occurring, except in para (d) of 'Director'.

c CLEA 2001, s 31(b) substitutes CA 1990, s 21(1)(a)(i)(V).

d CLEA 2001, s 31(c) inserts CA 1990, s 21(1)(fa) and (fb).

e CLEA 2001, s 31(d) substitutes CA 1990, s 21(1)(g)(ii).

f Subsection (3)(ea) inserted by IFCMPA 2005, s 69.

g C(A)(No 2)A 1999, s 53(3)(a) amends CA 1990, s 21(3)(g) by the deletion of 'and'.

h C(A)(No 2)A 1999, s 53 (3)(b) substitutes CA 1990, s 21(3)(h) and inserts CA 1990, s 21(3)(i).

---

22 Inspectors' reports to be evidence

A document purporting to be a copy of a report of an inspector appointed under the provisions of this Part shall be admissible in any civil proceedings as evidence—

(a) of the facts set out therein without further proof unless the contrary is shown, and

(b) of the opinion of the inspector in relation to any matter contained in the report.

23 Saving for privileged information

[(1) In this section—

'computer' has the same meaning as it has in section 20;

'information' means information contained in a document, a computer or otherwise;

'privileged legal material' means information which, in the opinion of the court, a person is entitled to refuse to produce on the grounds of legal professional privilege.

(1A) Subject to subsection (1B), nothing in this Part shall compel the disclosure by any person of privileged legal material or authorise the taking of privileged legal material.

(1B) The disclosure of information may be compelled, or possession of it taken, pursuant to the powers in this Part, not-withstanding that it is apprehended that the information is privileged legal material provided the compelling of its disclosure or the taking of its possession is done by means whereby the confidentiality of the information can be maintained (as against the person compelling such disclosure or taking such possession) pending the determination by the court of the issue as to whether the information is privileged legal material.

(1C) Without prejudice to subsection (1D), where, in the circumstances referred to in subsection (1B), information has been disclosed or taken possession of pursuant to the powers in this Part, the person—

(a) to whom such information has been so disclosed, or

(b) who has taken possession of it,

shall (unless the person has, within the period subsequently mentioned in this subsection, been served with notice of an application under subsection (1D) in relation to the matter concerned) apply to the court for a determination as to whether the information is privileged legal material and an application under this subsection shall be made within 7 days after the disclosure or the taking of possession.

(1D) A person who, in the circumstances referred to in sub-section (1B), is compelled to disclose information, or from whose possession information is taken, pursuant to the powers in this Part, may apply to the court for a determination as to whether the information is privileged legal material.

(1E) Pending the making of a final determination of an application under subsection (1C) or (1D), the court may give such interim or interlocutory directions as the court considers appropriate including, without prejudice to the generality of the fore-going, directions as to—

(a) the preservation of the information, in whole or in part, in a safe and secure place in any manner specified by the court,

(b) the appointment of a person with suitable legal qualifications possessing the level of experience, and the independence from any interest falling to be determined between the parties concerned, that the court considers to be appropriate for the purpose of—

(i) examining the information, and

(ii) preparing a report for the court with a view to assisting or facilitating the court in the making by the court of its determination as to whether the information is privileged legal material.

(1F) An application under subsection (1C), (1D) or (1E) shall be by motion and may, if the court directs, be heard other-wise than in public.][a]

[(2) The Director shall not, under section 19, require the production by a person carrying on the business of banking of a document relating to the affairs of a customer, or relating to the affairs of any other person, unless either it appears to the Director that it is necessary to do so for the purposes of investigating the affairs of the person carrying on the business of banking, or the customer or other person is a person on whom a requirement has been imposed by virtue of that section.][b]

(3) The publication, in pursuance of any provision of this Part, of any report, information, book or document shall be privileged.

[(4) In this section, 'customer', in relation to a person carrying on the business of banking, includes a person who has in the past availed of one or more services of the person, as defined in section 149(12) of the Consumer Credit Act, 1995.][c]

Amendments

a C(A)A 2009, s 6 substitutes CA 1990, s 23(1) and inserts CA 1990, s 23(1A)–(1F).

b CLEA 2001, s 32(a) substitutes CA 1990, s 23(2).

c CLEA 2001, s 32(b) inserts CA 1990, s 23(4).

23A Assistance to overseas company law authorities

[(1) The powers conferred on the Director by this Part are also exercisable by the Director on foot of a request from a company law authority for assistance in connection with inquiries being carried out by it or on its behalf where the Director is satisfied that such assistance is for the purpose of the discharge by the authority of its supervisory or regulatory functions.

(2) The Director may decline to accede to a request referred to in subsection (1) if, in the opinion of the Director, it is not appropriate to so accede or where the company law authority making the request does not undertake to make such contribution to the costs attendant on the request as the Director considers appropriate.

(3) In this section, 'company law authority' means an authority outside the State which performs functions of a supervisory or regulatory nature in relation to bodies corporate or undertakings or their officers, or a person acting on behalf of such an authority.][a]

Amendments

a CLEA 2001, s 33 inserts CA 1990, s 23A.

---

24 Power to make supplementary regulations

(1) If, in any respect, any difficulty arises in bringing any provision of this Part into operation or in relation to the operation of any such provision, the Minister may by regulations do anything which appears to him to be necessary or expedient for removing that difficulty, for bringing the provision into operation, or for securing or facilitating its operation, and any such regulations may modify any provision of this Part so far as may be necessary or expedient for carrying such provision into effect for the purposes aforesaid.

(2) Every regulation made by the Minister under this section shall be laid before each House of the Oireachtas as soon as may be after it is made and, if a resolution annulling the regulation is passed by either House within the next 21 days on which that House has

sat after the regulation is laid before it, the regulation shall be annulled accordingly, but without prejudice to the validity of anything previously done thereunder.

PART III

TRANSACTIONS INVOLVING DIRECTORS

Preliminary

25 Interpretation of Part III

(1) In this Part, unless the context otherwise requires—

'credit transactions' has the meaning assigned to it by *subsection (3)*;

'guarantee' includes indemnity;

'quasi-loan' has the meaning assigned to it by *subsection (2)*;

'licensed bank' means the holder of a licence under section 9 of the Central Bank Act, 1971.

(2) For the purposes of this Part—

(a) a quasi-loan is a transaction under which one party ('the creditor') agrees to pay, or pays otherwise than in pursuance of an agreement, a sum for another ('the borrower') or agrees to reimburse, or reimburses otherwise than in pursuance of an agreement, expenditure incurred by another party for another ('the borrower')—

(i) on terms that the borrower (or a person on his behalf) will reimburse the creditor; or

(ii) in circumstances giving rise to a liability on the borrower to reimburse the creditor;

(b) any reference to the person to whom a quasi-loan is made is a reference to the borrower; and

(c) the liabilities of a borrower under a quasi-loan include the liabilities of any person who has agreed to reimburse the creditor on behalf of the borrower.

(3) For the purposes of this Part a credit transaction is a transaction under which one party ('the creditor')—

(a) supplies any goods or sells any land under a hire-purchase agreement or conditional sale agreement;

(b) leases or licenses the use of land or hires goods in return for periodical payments;

(c) otherwise disposes of land or supplies goods or services on the understanding that payment (whether in a lump-sum or instalments or by way of periodical payments or otherwise) is to be deferred.

[(3A) For the purposes of this Part, a lease of land which reserves a nominal annual rent of not more than [€12.70] [b] is not a credit transaction where a company grants the lease in return for a premium or capital payment which represents the open market value of the land thereby disposed of by the company.] [a]

(4) For the purposes of this Part the value of a transaction or arrangement is—

(a) in the case of a loan, the principal of the loan;

(b) in the case of a quasi-loan, the amount, or maximum amount, which the person to whom the quasi-loan is made is liable to reimburse the creditor;

(c) in the case of a transaction or arrangement, other than a loan or quasi-loan or a transaction or arrangement within paragraph (d) or (e), the price which it is reasonable to expect could be obtained for the goods, land or services to which the transaction or arrangement relates if they had been supplied at the time the transaction or arrangement is entered into in the ordinary course of business and on the same terms (apart from price) as they have been supplied or are to be supplied under the transaction or arrangement in question;

(d) in the case of a guarantee or security, the amount guaranteed or secured;

(e) in the case of an arrangement to which section 31(2) or 31(3) applies the value of the transaction to which the arrangement relates less any amount by which the liabilities under the arrangement or transaction of the person for whom the transaction was made have been reduced.

(5) For the purposes of subsection (4), the value of a transaction or arrangement which is not capable of being expressed as a specific sum of money (because the amount of any liability arising under the transaction is unascertainable, or for any other reason) shall, whether or not any liability under the transaction has been reduced, be deemed to exceed [€63,486.90].[c]

(6) For the purposes of this Part, a transaction or arrangement is made for a person if—

(a) in the case of a loan or quasi-loan, it is made to him;

(b) in the case of a credit transaction, he is the person to whom goods or services are supplied, or land is sold or otherwise disposed of, under the transaction;

(c) in the case of a guarantee or security, it is entered into or provided in connection with a loan or quasi-loan made to him or a credit transaction made for him;

(d) in the case of an arrangement to which section 31(2) or 31(3) applies, the transaction to which the arrangement relates was made for him; and

(e) in the case of any other transaction or arrangement for the supply or transfer of goods, land or services (or any interest therein), he is the person to whom the goods, land or services (or the interest) are supplied or transferred.

(7) This Part, except sections 41, 43 and 44, does not apply to arrangements or transactions entered into before the commencement of this section but, for the purposes of determining whether an arrangement is one to which section 31(2) or 31(3) applies the transaction to which the arrangement relates shall, if it was entered into before the said commencement, be deemed to have been entered into thereafter.

(8) This Part shall have effect in relation to an arrangement or transaction whether governed by the law of the State or of another country.

Amendments

a CLEA 2001, s 75 inserts CA 1990, s 25(3A).

b £10 converted to €12.70 by Council Regulations (EC) No 1103/97, No 974/98 and No 2866/98 and the Economic and Monetary Union Act 1998, s 6.

c £50,000 converted to €63,486.90 by Council Regulations (EC) No 1103/97, No 974/98 and No 2866/98 and the Economic and Monetary Union Act 1988, s 6.

---

26 Connected persons

[(1) For the purposes of this Part, a person is connected with a director of a company if, but only if, the person (not being himself a director of the company) is—

(a) that director's spouse[, civil partner within the meaning of the Civil Partnership and Certain Rights and Obligations of Cohabitants Act 2010][b], parent, brother, sister or child;

(b) a person acting in his capacity as the trustee of any trust, the principal beneficiaries of which are the director, his spouse[, civil partner within the meaning of the Civil Partnership and Certain Rights and Obligations of Cohabitants Act 2010][b] or any of his children or any body corporate which he controls; or

(c) in partnership, within the meaning of section 1(1) of the Partnership Act, 1890, with that director.][a]

(2) A body corporate shall also be deemed to be connected with a director of a company if it is controlled by that director.

[(3) For the purposes of this section, a director of a company shall be deemed to control a body corporate if, but only if, he is, alone or together with any other director or directors of the company, or any person connected with the director or such other director or directors, interested in one-half or more of the equity share capital of that body or entitled to exercise or control the exercise of one-half or more of the voting power at any general meeting of that body.][c]

(4) In subsection (3) —

(a) 'equity share capital' has the same meaning as in section 155 of the Principal Act; and

(b) references to voting power exercised by a director shall include references to voting power exercised by another body corporate which that director controls.

(5) The provisions of section 54, shall have effect for the purposes of subsection (3) with the substitution of the words 'more than half' for the words 'one-third or more' in subsections (5) and (6) of that section.

[(6) It shall be presumed for the purposes of this Part, until the contrary is shown, that the sole member of a single-member private limited company within the meaning of the European Communities (Single-Member Private Limited Companies) Regulations, 1994 (S.I. No. 275 of 1994) is a person connected with a director of that company.][d]

Amendments

a CLEA 2001, s 76(a) substitutes CA 1990, s 26(1).

b Words ', civil partner within the meaning of the Civil Partnership and Certain Rights and Obligations of Cohabitants Act 2010' inserted by Civil Partnership and Certain Rights and Obligations of Cohabitants Act 2010, Sch, Pt 3, Item No. 18.

c CLEA 2001, s 76(b) substitutes CA 1990, s 26(3).

d CLEA 2001, s 76(c) inserts CA 1990, s 26(6). Regulation 12 of the European Communities (Single-Member Private Limited Companies) Regulations, 1994 (SI No 275 of 1994) was deleted following the commencement on 1 October 2001 of s 26(6) (which was inserted by

CLEA 2001, s 76(c)): see the European Communities (Single-Member Private Limited Companies) Regulations, 1994 (Amendment) Regulations, 2001 (SI No 437 of 2001).

---

27 Shadow directors

(1) Subject to subsection (2), a person in accordance with whose directions or instructions the directors of a company are accustomed to act (in this Act referred to as 'a shadow director') shall be treated for the purposes of this Part as a director of the company unless the directors are accustomed so to act by reason only that they do so on advice given by him in a professional capacity.

(2) A shadow director shall not be guilty of an offence under section 44(8) by virtue only of subsection (1).

(3) Section 194 of the Principal Act shall apply in relation to a shadow director of a company as it applies in relation to a director of a company, except that the shadow director shall declare his interest, not at a meeting of the directors, but by a notice in writing to the directors which is either—

(a) a specific notice given before the date of the meeting at which, if he had been a director, the declaration would be required by subsection (2) of that section to be made; or

(b) a notice which under subsection (3) of that section falls to be treated as a sufficient declaration of that interest or would fall to be so treated apart from the proviso;

and section 145 of that Act shall have effect as if the declaration had been made at the meeting in question and had accordingly formed part of the proceedings at that meeting.

Particular transactions involving conflict of interest

28 Contracts of employment of directors

(1) Subject to subsection (6), a company shall not incorporate in any agreement a term to which this section applies unless the term is first approved by a resolution of the company in general meeting and, in the case of a director of a holding company, by a resolution of that company in general meeting.

(2) This section applies to any term by which a director's employment with the company of which he is the director or, where he is the director of a holding company, his employment within the group is to continue, or may be continued, otherwise than at the instance of the company (whether under the original agreement or under a new agreement entered into in pursuance of the original agreement), for a period exceeding five years during which the employment—

(a) cannot be terminated by the company by notice; or

(b) can be so terminated only in specified circumstances.

(3) In any case where—

(a) a person is or is to be employed with a company under an agreement which cannot be terminated by the company by notice or can be so terminated only in specified circumstances; and

(b) more than six months before the expiration of the period for which he is or is to be so employed, the company enters into a further agreement (otherwise than in pursuance of a right conferred by or by virtue of the original agreement on the other party thereto) under which he is to be employed with the company or, where he is a director of a holding company, within the group,

subsection (2) shall apply as if to the period for which he is to be employed under that further agreement there were added a further period equal to the unexpired period of the original agreement.

(4) A resolution of a company approving a term to which this section applies shall not be passed at a general meeting of the company unless a written memorandum setting out the proposed agreement incorporating the term is available for inspection by members of the company both—

(a) at the registered office of the company for not less than the period of 15 days ending with the date of the meeting; and

(b) at the meeting itself.

(5) A term incorporated in an agreement in contravention of this section shall to the extent that it contravenes this section be void; and that agreement and, in a case where subsection (3) applies, the original agreement shall be deemed to contain a term entitling the company to terminate it at any time by the giving of reasonable notice.

(6) No approval is required to be given under this section by any body corporate unless it is a company within the meaning of the Principal Act or registered under Part IX of that Act, or if it is, for the purposes of section 150 of that Act, a wholly owned subsidiary of any body corporate, wherever incorporated.

(7) In this section—

(a) 'employment' includes employment under a contract for services; and

(b) 'group', in relation to a director of a holding company, means the group which consists of that company and its subsidiaries.

29 Substantial property transactions involving directors, etc.

(1) Subject to subsections (6), (7) and (8), a company shall not enter into an arrangement—

(a) whereby a director of the company or its holding company or a person connected with such a director acquires or is to acquire one or more non-cash assets of the requisite value from the company; or

(b) whereby the company acquires or is to acquire one or more non-cash assets of the requisite value from such a director or a person so connected;

unless the arrangement is first approved by a resolution of the company in general meeting and, if the director or connected person is a director of its holding company or a person connected with such a director, by a resolution in general meeting of the holding company.

(2) For the purposes of this section a non-cash asset is of the requisite value if at the time the arrangement in question is entered into its value is not less than [€1,269.74] [a] but, subject to that, exceeds [€63,486.90] [b] or ten per cent of the amount of the company's relevant assets, and for those purposes the amount of a company's relevant assets is—

(a) except in a case falling within paragraph (b), the value of its net assets determined by reference to the accounts prepared and laid in accordance with the requirements of section 148 of the Principal Act in respect of the last preceding financial year in respect of which such accounts were so laid;

(b) where no accounts have been prepared and laid under that section before that time, the amount of its called-up share capital.

(3) An arrangement entered into by a company in contravention of this section and any transaction entered into in pursuance of the arrangement (whether by the company or any other person) shall be voidable at the instance of the company unless—

(a) restitution of any money or any other asset which is the subject-matter of the arrangement or transaction is no longer possible or the company has been indemnified in pursuance of subsection (4)(b) by any other person for the loss or damage suffered by it; or

(b) any rights acquired bona fide for value and without actual notice of the contravention by any person who is not a party to the arrangement or transaction would be affected by its avoidance; or

(c) the arrangement is, within a reasonable period, affirmed by the company in general meeting and, if it is an arrangement for the transfer of an asset to or by a director of its holding company or a person who is connected with such a director, is so affirmed with the approval of the holding company given by a resolution in general meeting.

(4) Without prejudice to any liability imposed otherwise than by this subsection, but subject to subsection (5), where an arrangement is entered into with a company by a director of the company or its holding company or a person connected with him in contravention of this section, that director and the person so connected, and any other director of the company who authorised the arrangement or any transaction entered into in pursuance of such an arrangement, shall (whether or not it has been avoided in pursuance of subsection (3)) be liable—

(a) to account to the company for any gain which he had made directly or indirectly by the arrangement or transaction; and

(b) (jointly and severally with any other person liable under this subsection) to indemnify the company for any loss or damage resulting from the arrangement or transaction.

(5) Where an arrangement is entered into by a company and a person connected with a director of the company or its holding company in contravention of this section, that director shall not be liable under subsection (4) if he shows that he took all reasonable steps to secure the company's compliance with this section and, in any case, a person so connected and any such other director as is mentioned in that subsection shall not be so liable if he shows that, at the time the arrangement was entered into, he did not know the relevant circumstances constituting the contravention.

(6) No approval is required to be given under this section by any body corporate unless it is a company within the meaning of the Principal Act or registered under Part IX of that Act or, if it is, for the purposes of section 150 of that Act, a wholly owned subsidiary of any body corporate, wherever incorporated.

(7) Subsection (1) shall not apply in relation to any arrangement for the acquisition of a non-cash asset—

(a) if the non-cash asset in question is or is to be acquired by a holding company from any of its wholly owned subsidiaries or from a holding company by any of its wholly owned subsidiaries or by one wholly owned subsidiary of a holding company from another wholly owned subsidiary of that same holding company; or

(b) if the arrangement is entered into by a company which is being wound up unless the winding up is a members' voluntary winding up.

(8) Subsection (1)(a) shall not apply in relation to any arrangement whereby a person acquires or is to acquire an asset from a company of which he is a member if the arrangement is made with that person in his character as such member.

(9) In this section—

(a) 'non-cash asset' means any property or interest in property other than cash, and for this purpose 'cash' includes foreign currency;

(b) any reference to the acquisition of a non-cash asset includes a reference to the creation or extinction of an estate or interest in, or a right over, any property and also a reference to the discharge of any person's liability other than a liability for a liquidated sum; and

[(c) 'net assets', in relation to a company, means the aggregate of the company's assets less the aggregate of its liabilities, and for this purpose 'liabilities' includes—

(i) any provision (within the meaning of the Sixth Schedule to the Principal Act) that is made in Companies Act individual accounts except to the extent that that provision is taken into account in calculating the value of any asset to the company,

(ii) any provision for liabilities within the meaning of paragraph 70 of the Schedule to the Companies (Amendment) Act 1986 that is made in Companies Act individual accounts, and

(iii) any provision that is made in IFRS individual accounts.][c]

Amendments

a £1,000 converted to €1,269.74 by Council Regulations (EC) No 1103/97, No 974/98 and No 2866/98 and the Economic and Monetary Union Act 1988, s 6.

b £50,000 converted to €63,486.90 by Council Regulations (EC) No 1103/97, No 974/98 and No 2866/98 and the Economic and Monetary Union Act 1988, s 6.

c EC(IFRSMA)R 2005, reg 9, Sch 1, Pt 4, item 1 substitutes s 29(9)(c).

30 Penalisation of dealing by director of a company in options to buy or sell certain shares in, or debentures of, the company or associated companies

(1) A director of a company who buys—

(a) a right to call for delivery at a specified price and within a specified time of a specified number of relevant shares or a specified amount of relevant debentures; or

(b) a right to make delivery at a specified price and within a specified time of a specified number of relevant shares or a specified amount of relevant debentures; or

(c) a right (as he may elect) to call for delivery at a specified price and within a specified time or to make delivery at a specified price and within a specified time of a specified number of relevant shares or a specified amount of relevant debentures;

shall be guilty of an offence.

(2) In subsection (1) —

(a) 'relevant shares', in relation to a director of a company, means shares in the company or in any other body corporate, being the company's subsidiary or holding company or a subsidiary of the company's holding company, being shares for which dealing facilities are provided by a stock exchange (whether within the State or elsewhere); and

(b) 'relevant debentures', in relation to a director of a company, means debentures of the company or of any other body corporate, being the company's subsidiary or holding company or a subsidiary of the company's holding company, being debentures as respects which there has been granted such dealing facilities as aforesaid.

(3) Nothing in this section shall be taken to penalise a person who buys a right to subscribe for shares in, or debentures of, a body corporate or buys debentures of a body corporate that confer upon the holder thereof a right to subscribe for, or to convert the debentures (in whole or in part) into, shares of the body.

[(3A) Nothing in this section shall prevent a person from acquiring a right to shares in a company pursuant to a scheme approved by the Revenue Commissioners for the purposes of the Tax Acts and the Capital Gains Tax Acts, and in respect of which approval has not been withdrawn at the time the right is obtained.][a]

(4) For the purposes of this section any reference, however expressed, to any price paid, given or received in respect of any interest in shares or debentures shall be construed as including a reference to any consideration other than money given or received in respect of any such interest, and any reference to a specified price includes a reference to a specified price range.

(5) This section shall also apply to any person (not being a director of the company) who—

(a) buys a right referred to in subsection (1), and

(b) does so on behalf or at the instigation of a director of the company.

Amendments

a CLEA 2001, s 102 inserts CA 1990, s 30(3A).

31 Prohibition of loans, etc. to directors and connected persons

(1) Except as provided by sections 32 to 37, a company shall not—

(a) make a loan or a quasi-loan to a director of the company or of its holding company or to a person connected with such a director;

(b) enter into a credit transaction as creditor for such a director or a person so connected;

(c) enter into a guarantee or provide any security in connection with a loan, quasi-loan or credit transaction made by any other person for such a director or a person so connected.

(2) A company shall not arrange for the assignment to it or the assumption by it of any rights, obligations or liabilities under a transaction which, if it had been entered into by the company, would have contravened *subsection (1)*; but for the purposes of this Part the transaction shall be treated as having been entered into on the date of the arrangement.

(3) A company shall not take part in any arrangement whereby—

(a) another person enters into a transaction which, if it had been entered into by the company, would have contravened subsection (1) or (2); and

(b) that other person, in pursuance of the arrangement, has obtained or is to obtain any benefit from the company or its holding company or a subsidiary of the company or its holding company.

32 Arrangements of certain value

(1) Section 31, shall not prohibit a company from entering into an arrangement with a director or a person connected with a director if—

(a) the value of the arrangement, and

(b) the total amount outstanding under any other arrangements entered into by the company with any director of the company, or any person connected with a director,

together, is less than ten per cent of the company's relevant assets.

(2) For the purposes of this section—

(a) a company enters an arrangement with a person if it makes a loan or quasi-loan to, or enters into a credit transaction as creditor for, that person, and

(b) the amount of a company's relevant assets shall be determined in accordance with section 29(2).

33 Reduction in amount of company's relevant assets

(1) This section applies to a company in respect of which the total amount outstanding under any arrangements referred to in section 32 comes to exceed 10 per cent of the company's relevant assets for any reason, but in particular because the value of those assets has fallen.

(2) Where the directors of a company become aware, or ought reasonably to become aware, that there exists a situation referred to in subsection (1), it shall be the duty of the company, its directors and any persons for whom the arrangements referred to in that subsection were made, to amend, within two months, the terms of the arrangements concerned so that the total amount outstanding under the arrangements again falls within the percentage limit referred to in that subsection.

[(3) Where the terms of the arrangements referred to in subsection (2) are not amended within the period specified in that subsection, the arrangements shall be voidable at the instance of the company unless section 38(1)(a) or (b) applies.][a]

Amendments

a CLEA 2001, s 77 inserts CA 1990, s 33(3).

34 [Exceptions to section 31 in certain circumstances

(1) Section 31 does not prohibit a company from entering into a guarantee or providing any security in connection with a loan, quasi-loan or credit transaction made by any other person for a director of the company or of its holding company, or for a person connected with such a director, if—

(a) the entering into the guarantee is, or the provision of the security is given, under the authority of a special resolution of the company passed not more than 12 months previously; and

(b) the company has forwarded with each notice of the meeting at which the special resolution is to be considered or, if the procedure detailed in subsection (6) is followed, the company has appended to the resolution, a copy of a statutory declaration which complies with subsections (2) and (3) and also delivers, within 21 days after the date on which the guarantee was entered into or the date on which the security was provided, as the case may be, a copy of the declaration to the registrar of companies for registration.

(2) The statutory declaration shall be made at a meeting of the directors held not earlier than 24 days before the meeting referred to in subsection (1)(b) or, if the special resolution is passed in accordance with subsection (6), not earlier than 24 days before the signing of the special resolution, and shall be made by the directors or, in the case of a company having more than 2 directors, by a majority of the directors.

(3) The statutory declaration shall state—

(a) the circumstances in which the guarantee is to be entered into or the security is to be provided;

(b) the nature of the guarantee or security;

(c) the person or persons to or for whom the loan, quasi-loan or credit transaction (in connection with which the guarantee is to be entered into or the security is to be provided) is to be made;

(d) the purpose for which the company is entering into the guarantee or is providing the security;

(e) the benefit which will accrue to the company directly or indirectly from entering into the guarantee or providing the security; and

(f) that the declarants have made a full inquiry into the affairs of the company and that, having done so, they have formed the opinion that the company, having entered into the guarantee or provided the security, will be able to pay its debts in full as they become due.

(4) A statutory declaration under subsection (3) has no effect for the purposes of this Act unless it is accompanied by a report—

(a) drawn up in the prescribed form, by an independent person who is qualified at the time of the report to be appointed, or to continue to be, the auditor of the company; and

(b) which shall state whether, in the opinion of the independent person, the statutory declaration is reasonable.

(5) Where a director of a company makes the statutory declaration without having reasonable grounds for the opinion that the company having entered into the guarantee or provided the security will be able to pay its debts in full as they become due—

(a) the court, on the application of a liquidator, creditor, member or contributory of the company, may declare that the director shall be personally responsible, without any limitation of liability, for all or any of the debts or other liabilities of the company; and

(b) if the company is wound up within 12 months after the making of the statutory declaration and its debts are not paid or provided for in full within 12 months after the commencement of the winding-up, it shall be presumed, until the contrary is shown, that the director did not have reasonable grounds for his opinion.

(6) The special resolution referred to in subsection (1)(a) may be passed in accordance with section 141(8) of the Principal Act.

(7) Unless all of the members of the company entitled to vote at general meetings of the company vote in favour of the special resolution, the company shall not enter into the guarantee or provide the security before the expiry of 30 days after the special resolution has been passed or, if an application referred to in subsection (8) is made, until the application has been disposed of by the court.

(8) If application is made to the court in accordance with this section for the cancellation of the special resolution, the special resolution shall not have effect except to the extent to which it is confirmed by the court.

(9) Subject to subsection (10), an application referred to in subsection (8) may be made by the holders of not less in the aggregate than 10 per cent in nominal value of the company's issued share capital or any class thereof.

(10) An application shall not be made under subsection (8) by a person who has consented to, signed or voted in favour of the special resolution.

(11) An application referred to in subsection (8) must be made within 28 days after the date on which the special resolution was passed and may be made on behalf of the persons entitled to make the application by such one or more of their number as they may appoint in writing for the purpose.][a]

Amendments

a CLEA 2001, s 78 substitutes CA 1990, s 34.

35 Transactions with holding company

Section 31, shall not prohibit a company from—

(a) making a loan or quasi-loan to [any company which is its holding company, subsidiary or a subsidiary of its holding company][a] or entering into a guarantee or providing any security in connection with a loan or quasi-loan made by any person to [any company which is its holding company, subsidiary or a subsidiary of its holding company][a];

(b) entering into a credit transaction as creditor for [any company which is its holding company, subsidiary or a subsidiary of its holding company][a] or entering into a guarantee or providing any security in connection with any credit transaction made by any other person for [any company which is its holding company, subsidiary or a subsidiary of its holding company][a].

Amendments

a CLEA 2001, s 79 amends CA 1990, s 35 by the substitution for 'its holding company' wherever occurring, of 'any company which is its holding company, subsidiary or a subsidiary of its holding company'.

36 Directors' expenses

(1) Section 31 shall not prohibit a company from doing anything to provide any of its directors with funds to meet vouched expenditure properly incurred or to be incurred by him for the purposes of the company or the purpose of enabling him properly to perform his duties as an officer of the company or doing anything to enable any of its directors to avoid incurring such expenditure.

(2) Where a company enters into any transaction pursuant to subsection (1), any liability falling on any person arising from any such transaction shall be discharged by him within six months from the date on which it was incurred.

(3) A person who contravenes subsection (2) shall be guilty of an offence.

37 Business transactions

Section 31, shall not prohibit a company from making any loan or quasi-loan or entering into any credit transaction as creditor for any person if—

(a) the company enters into the transaction concerned in the ordinary course of its business; and

(b) the value of the transaction is not greater, and the terms on which it is entered into are no more favourable, in respect of the person for whom the transaction is made, than that or those which—

  (i) the company ordinarily offers, or

  (ii) it is reasonable to expect the company to have offered, to or in respect of a person of the same financial standing as that person but unconnected with the company.

38 Civil remedies for breach of section 31

(1) Where a company enters into a transaction or arrangement in contravention of section 31 the transaction or arrangement shall be voidable at the instance of the company unless—

(a) restitution of any money or any other asset which is the subject matter of the arrangement or transaction is no longer possible, or the company has been indemnified in pursuance of subsection (2)(b) for the loss or damage suffered by it; or

(b) any rights acquired *bona fide* for value and without actual notice of the contravention by any person other than the person for whom the transaction or arrangement was made would be affected by its avoidance.

(2) Without prejudice to any liability imposed otherwise than by this subsection but subject to subsection (3), where an arrangement or transaction is made by a company for a director of the company or its holding company or person connected with such a director in contravention of section 31, that director and the person so connected and any other director of the company who authorised the transaction or arrangement shall (whether or not it has been avoided in pursuance of subsection (1)) be liable—

(a) to account to the company for any gain which he has made directly or indirectly by the arrangement or transaction; and

(b) (jointly and severally with any other person liable under this subsection) to indemnify the company for any loss or damage resulting from the arrangement or transaction.

(3) Where an arrangement or transaction is entered into by a company and a person connected with a director of the company or its holding company in contravention of section 31 that director shall not be liable under subsection (2) if he shows that he took all reasonable steps to secure the company's compliance with that section and, in any case, a person so connected and any such other director as is mentioned in the said subsection (2) shall not be so liable if he shows that, at the time the arrangement or transaction was entered into, he did not know the relevant circumstances constituting the contravention.

39 Personal liability for company debts in certain cases

(1) If a company is being wound up and is unable to pay its debts, and the court considers that any arrangement of a kind described in section 32 has contributed materially to the company's inability to pay its debts or has substantially impeded the orderly winding up thereof, the court, on the application of the liquidator or any creditor or contributory of the company, may, if it thinks it proper to do so, declare that any person for whose benefit the arrangement was made shall be personally liable, without any limitation of liability, for all, or such part as may be specified by the court, of the debts and other liabilities of the company.

(2) In deciding whether to make a declaration under subsection (1), the court shall have particular regard to whether, and to what extent, any outstanding liabilities arising under any arrangement referred to in that subsection were discharged before the commencement of the winding up.

(3) In deciding the extent of any personal liability under this section, the court shall have particular regard to the extent to which the arrangement in question contributed materially to the company's inability to pay its debts or substantially impeded the orderly winding up of the company.

40 Criminal penalties for breach of section 31

[If a company enters into a transaction or arrangement that contravenes section 31, every officer of the company who is in default shall be guilty of an offence.][a]

Amendments

a C(A)A 2009, s 7 substitutes CA 1990, s 40.

Disclosure of transactions involving directors and others

41 Substantial contracts, etc., with directors and others to be disclosed in accounts

(1) Subject to subsections (5) and (6) and to section 45, group accounts prepared by a holding company in accordance with the requirements of section 150 of the Principal Act in respect of the relevant period shall contain the particulars specified in section 42 of—

(a) any transaction or arrangement of a kind described in section 31 entered into by the company or by a subsidiary of the company for a person who at any time during the relevant period was a director of the company or its holding company or was connected with such a director;

(b) any agreement by the company or by a subsidiary of the company to enter into any such transaction or arrangement for a person who at any time during the relevant period was a director of the company or its holding company or was connected with such a director;

(c) any other transaction or arrangement with the company or with a subsidiary of the company in which a person who at any time during the relevant period was a director of the company or its holding company had, directly or indirectly, a material interest.

(2) Subject as aforesaid, accounts prepared by any company other than a holding company in respect of the relevant period shall contain the particulars specified in section 42 of—

(a) any transaction or arrangement of a kind described in section 31 entered into by the company for a person who at any time during the relevant period was a director of the company or of its holding company or was connected with such a director;

(b) any agreement by the company to enter into any such transaction or arrangement for a person who at any time during the relevant period was a director of the company or of its holding company or was connected with such a director;

(c) any other transaction or arrangement with the company in which a person who at any time during the relevant period was a director of the company or of its holding company had, directly or indirectly, a material interest.

(3) Particulars which are required by subsection (1) or (2) to be contained in any accounts shall be given by way of notes to those accounts.

(4) Where by virtue of [sections 151(2) and 154][a] of the Principal Act a company does not produce group accounts in relation to any financial year, subsection (1) shall have effect in relation to the company and that financial year as if the word 'group' were omitted.

(5) For the purposes of subsections (1)(c) and (2)(c)—

(a) a transaction or arrangement between a company and a director of the company or of its holding company or a person connected with such a director shall (if it would not otherwise be so treated) be treated as a transaction, arrangement or agreement in which that director is interested; and

(b) an interest in such a transaction or arrangement is not material if in the opinion of the majority of the directors (other than that director) of the company which is preparing the accounts in question it is not material (but without prejudice to the question whether or not such an interest is material in any case where those directors have not considered the matter).

[(6) Subsections (1) and (2) do not apply for the purposes of any accounts prepared by any company which is a licensed bank, or the holding company of a licensed bank, in relation to—

(a) a transaction or arrangement of a kind described in section 31 entered into for a person who at any time during the relevant period was connected with a director of that company or that holding company; or

(b) an agreement to enter into such a transaction or arrangement for a person so connected, to which the licensed bank is a party.][b]

(7) Subsections (1) and (2) do not apply in relation to the following transactions, arrangements and agreements—

(a) a transaction, arrangement or agreement between one company and another in which a director of the first company or of its subsidiary or holding company is interested only by virtue of his being a director of the other;

(b) a contract of service between a company and one of its directors or a director of its holding company or between a director of a company and any of that company's subsidiaries;

(c) a transaction, arrangement or agreement which was not entered into during the relevant period for the accounts in question and which did not subsist at any time during that period; and

(d) a transaction, arrangement or agreement which was made before the commencement of this section and which does not subsist thereafter.

(8) Subsections (1) and (2) apply whether or not—

(a) the transaction or arrangement was prohibited by section 31;

(b) the person for whom it was made was a director of the company or was connected with a director of the company at the time it was made;

(c) in the case of a transaction or arrangement made by a company which at any time during a relevant period is a subsidiary of another company, it was a subsidiary of that other company at the time the transaction or arrangement was made.

(9) In this section and in sections 43 and 45, 'relevant period', in relation to a company, means a financial year of the company ending not earlier than 6 months after the commencement of the section concerned.

[(10) Nothing in this section or sections 42 to 45 prejudices the operation of any—

(a) rule or other instrument; or

(b) direction or requirement,

made, issued, granted or otherwise created under the Central Bank Acts 1942 to 1998, the Central Bank and Financial Services Authority of Ireland Acts 2003 and 2004 or any other enactment requiring a licensed bank, or a holding company of a licensed bank, to disclose particulars, whether in accounts prepared by it or otherwise, of transactions, arrangements or agreements (whether of the kind described in section 31 or not) entered into by the licensed bank.

(11) Where a company makes default in complying with this section, the company and every person who at the time of that default is a director of the company shall be guilty of an offence.

(12) It shall be a defence in proceedings for an offence under subsection (11) for the defendant to prove that he took all reasonable steps for securing compliance with the requirements of this section.][c]

Amendments

a EC(IFRSMA)R 2005, reg 9 and Sch 1, Pt 4, Item 2 substitutes 'sections 151(2) and 154' for 'sections 150(2) and 154' in s 41(4).

b C(A)A 2009, s 8(1)(a) substitutes CA 1990, s 41(6).

c C(A)A 2009, s 8(1)(b) inserts CA 1990, s 41(10)–(12).

---

42 Particulars required to be included in accounts by section 41

The particulars of a transaction, arrangement or agreement which are required by section 41 to be included in the annual accounts prepared by a company are particulars of the principal terms of the transaction, arrangement or agreement and (without prejudice to the generality of the foregoing provision)—

(a) a statement of the fact either that the transaction, arrangement or agreement was made or subsisted, as the case may be, during the financial year in respect of which those accounts are made up;

(b) the name of the person for whom it was made, and, where that person is or was connected with a director of the company or of its holding company, the name of that director;

(c) in any case where subsection (1)(c) or (2)(c) of section 41 applies, the name of the director with the material interest and the nature of that interest;

(d) in the case of a loan or an agreement for a loan or an arrangement within section 31(2) or 31(3) relating to a loan—
   (i) the amount of the liability of the person to whom the loan was or was agreed to be made, in respect of principal and interest, at the beginning and at the end of that period;
   (ii) the maximum amount of that liability during that period;
   (iii) the amount of any interest which, having fallen due, has not been paid; and
   (iv) the amount of any provision (within the meaning of the Sixth Schedule to the Principal Act or the Companies (Amendment) Act, 1986) made in respect of any failure or anticipated failure by the borrower to repay the whole or part of the loan or to pay the whole or part of any interest thereon;

(e) in the case of a guarantee or security or an arrangement within *section 31 (2)* relating to a guarantee or security—
   (i) the amount for which the company (or its subsidiary) was liable under the guarantee or in respect of the security both at the beginning and at the end of the financial year in question;
   (ii) the maximum amount for which the company (or its subsidiary) may become so liable; and
   (iii) any amount paid and any liability incurred by the company (or its subsidiary) for the purpose of fulfilling the guarantee or discharging the security (including any loss incurred by reason of the enforcement of the guarantee or security); and

(f) in the case of any transaction, arrangement or agreement, other than those mentioned in paragraphs (d) and (e) the value of the transaction or arrangement or, as the case may be, the value of the transaction or arrangement to which the agreement relates; and

(g) in the case of arrangements to which section 32 relates, the aggregate value of such arrangements at the end of the financial year concerned, in relation to any persons specified in that section, expressed as a percentage of the company's relevant assets at that time; and

(h) any amendment of the terms of any such arrangement in accordance with section 33.

43 Particulars of amounts outstanding to be included in accounts

(1) This section applies in relation to the following classes of transactions, arrangements and agreements—

(a) loans, guarantees and securities relating to loans, arrangements of a kind described in section 31(2) or 31(3) relating to loans, and agreements to enter into any of the foregoing transactions and arrangements;

(b) quasi-loans, guarantees and securities relating to quasi-loans, arrangements of a kind described in those subsections relating to quasi-loans and agreements to enter into any of the foregoing transactions and arrangements;

(c) credit transactions, guarantees and securities relating to credit transactions and arrangements of a kind described in those subsections relating to credit transactions and agreements to enter into any of the foregoing transactions and arrangements.

(2) The group accounts of a holding company prepared in accordance with the requirements of section 150 of the Principal Act and the accounts of any other company prepared in accordance with the requirements of section 148 of the Principal Act in respect of the relevant period shall contain a statement in relation to transactions, arrangements and agreements made by the company and, in the case of a holding company, by a subsidiary of the company for persons who at any time during the relevant period were officers of the company (but not directors) of the aggregate amounts outstanding at the end of the relevant period under transactions, arrangements and agreements within any paragraph of subsection (1) and the number of officers for whom the transactions, arrangements and agreements falling within each of those paragraphs were made.

(3) Subsection (2) shall not apply, in relation to the accounts prepared by any company in respect of any relevant period, to transactions, arrangements and agreements made by the company or any of its subsidiaries for any officer of the company if the aggregate amount outstanding at the end of that period under the transactions, arrangements and agreements so made for that officer does not exceed [€3,174.35].[a]

(4) Subsection (2) shall not apply in relation to any transaction, arrangement or agreement made by a licensed bank for any of its officers or for any of the officers of its holding company.

[(5) The following, namely—

(a) the group accounts of a company which is, or is the holding company of, a licensed bank prepared in accordance with the requirements of section 150 of the Principal Act; and

(b) the accounts of any other company which is a licensed bank prepared in accordance with the requirements of section 148 of the Principal Act,

in respect of the relevant period shall contain a statement in relation to transactions, arrangements and agreements made by—

(i) the company preparing the accounts, if it is a licensed bank; and

(ii) in the case of a holding company, by any of its subsidiaries which is a licensed bank,

for persons who at any time during the relevant period were connected with a director of the company of—

(I) the aggregate amounts outstanding at the end of the relevant period under transactions, arrangements and agreements coming within any paragraph of sub-section (1) (which transactions, arrangements and agreements, coming within any particular such paragraph, are referred to subsequently in this section as 'relevant transactions, arrangements and agreements');

(II) the aggregate maximum amounts outstanding during the relevant period under relevant transactions, arrangements and agreements made for persons so connected;

(III) the number of persons so connected for whom relevant transactions, arrangements and agreements that subsisted at the end of the relevant period were made; and

(IV) the maximum number of persons so connected for whom relevant transactions, arrangements and agreements that subsisted at any time during the relevant period were made.

(6) A transaction, arrangement or agreement to which sub-section (5) applies need not be included in the statement referred to in that subsection if—

(a) it is entered into by the company concerned in the ordinary course of its business, and

(b) its value is not greater, and its terms no more favour-able, in respect of the person for whom it is made, than that or those which—

(i) the company ordinarily offers, or

(ii) it is reasonable to expect the company to have offered,

to or in respect of a person of the same financial standing but unconnected with the company.

(6A) In reckoning the aggregate maximum amounts or the maximum number of persons referred to in subsection (5)(II) or (IV), as appropriate, there shall not be counted, as the case may be—

(a) relevant transactions, arrangements and agreements made by the company, or a subsidiary of it, referred to in subsection (5) and which is a licensed bank for any person connected as mentioned in that subsection if the aggregate maximum amount outstanding during the relevant period under relevant transactions, arrangements and agreements made for that person does not exceed €3,174.35; or

(b) a person so connected for whom the aggregate maximum amount outstanding as mentioned in paragraph (a) does not exceed the amount there mentioned.][b]

(7) Particulars which are required by [subsection (2) or (5)][c] to be contained in any accounts shall be given by way of notes to those accounts.

(8) Where by virtue of [sections 151(2) and 154][d] of the Principal Act, a company does not produce group accounts in relation to any financial year, [subsections (2) and (5)][e] shall have effect in relation to the company and that financial year as if the word 'group' were omitted.

[...][f]

(10) For the purposes of this section, 'amount outstanding' means the amount of the outstanding liabilities of the person for whom the transaction, arrangement or agreement in question was made, or, in the case of a guarantee or security, the amount guaranteed or secured.

[(11) Where a company makes default in complying with this section, the company and every person who at the time of that default is a director of the company shall be guilty of an offence.

(12) It shall be a defence in proceedings for an offence under subsection (11) for the defendant to prove that he took all reasonable steps for securing compliance with the requirements of this section.][g]

Amendments

a £2,500 converted to €3,174.35 by Council Regulations (EC) No 1103/97, No 974/98 and No 2866/98 and the Economic and Monetary Union Act 1988, s 6.

b C(A)A 2009, s 8(2) substituted CA 1990, s 43(5) and (6) and inserted s 43(6A).

c Words 'subsection (2) or (5)' substituted for 'subsection (2), (5) or (6)' by C(A)A 2009, s 8(3)(a).

d EC(IFRSMA)R 2005, reg 9 and Sch 1, Pt 4, Item 3 substitutes 'sections 151(2) and 154' for 'sections 150(2) and 154' in s 43(8).

e Words 'subsection (2) and (5)' substituted for 'subsection (2), (5) or (6)' by C(A)A 2009, s 8(3)(c).

f C(A)A 2009, s 8(d) deletes CA 1990, s 43(9).

g C(A)A 2009, s 8(3)(d) inserts CA 1990, s 43(11) and (12).

44 Further provisions relating to licensed banks

(1) Subject to section 45, a company which is, or is the holding company of, a licensed bank, shall maintain a register containing a copy of every transaction, arrangement or agreement of which particulars [are required by subsection (1) or (2) of section 41 or would, but for section 41(6), be required by subsection (1) or (2) of that section][a] to be disclosed in the company's accounts or group accounts for the current financial year and for each of the preceding ten financial years (but excluding any financial year ending prior to the passing of this Act) or, if such a transaction, arrangement or agreement is not in writing, a written memorandum setting out its terms.

(2) Subsection (1) shall not require a company to keep in its register a copy of any transaction, arrangement or agreement made for a connected person if—

(a) it is entered into in the ordinary course of the company's business, and

(b) its value is not greater, and its terms no more favourable, in respect of the person for whom it is made, than that or those which—

(i) the company ordinarily offers, or

(ii) it is reasonable to expect the company to have offered,

to or in respect of a person of the same financial standing but unconnected with the company.

(3) Subject to section 45, a company which is, or is the holding company of, a licensed bank shall before its annual general meeting make available, at the registered office of the company for not less than the period of 15 days ending with the date of the meeting, for inspection by members of the company a statement containing the particulars of transactions, arrangements and agreements which the company would, but for section 41 (6), be required by subsection (1) or (2) of that section to disclose in its accounts or group accounts for the last complete financial year preceding that meeting and such a statement shall also be made available for inspection by the members at the annual general meeting.

(4) Subsection (3) shall not require the inclusion in the statement of particulars of any transaction, arrangement or agreement if—

(a) it is entered into in the ordinary course of the company's business, and

(b) its value is not greater, and its terms no more favourable, in respect of the person for whom it is made, than that or those which—

(i) the company ordinarily offers, or

(ii) it is reasonable to expect the company to have offered,

to or in respect of a person of the same financial standing but unconnected with the company.

[(4A) Subsection (3) shall not require the inclusion in the statement of particulars of any transaction, arrangement or agreement if, by reason of—

(a) the company's not taking advantage of section 41(6); or

(b) the company's being required by a rule, instrument, direction or requirement referred to in section 41(10) to disclose such information in the following manner,

the company has included in the group accounts or accounts referred to in section 41(1) or (2), as the case may be, for the last complete financial year mentioned in subsection (3) particulars of the transaction, arrangement or agreement which, but for either of those reasons, it would not have disclosed in those accounts by virtue of section 41(6).

(4B) Where subsection (1) falls to be applied to a company which is the holding company of a licensed bank, each of the references in subsection (2) to the company, other than the first such reference, shall be deemed to be a reference to the licensed bank.

(4C) A company shall, if required by the Director, produce to the Director for inspection the register kept by it in accordance with subsection (1) and shall give the Director such facilities for inspecting and taking copies of the contents of the register as the Director may require.][b]

(5) It shall be the duty of the auditors of the company to examine any such statement before it is made available to the members of the company in accordance with subsection (3) and to make a report to the members on that statement; and the report shall be annexed to the statement before it is made so available.

(6) A report under subsection (5) shall state whether in the opinion of the auditors the statement contains the particulars required by subsection (3) and, where their opinion is that it does not, they shall include in the report, so far as they are reasonably able to do so, a statement giving the required particulars.

(7) Subsection (3) shall not apply in relation to a licensed bank which is for the purposes of section 150 of the Principal Act the wholly owned subsidiary of a company incorporated in the State.

(8) Where a company fails to comply with [subsection (1), (3) or (4C)][c], the company and every person who at the time of that failure is a director of the company shall be guilty of an offence and liable to a fine.

[(9) It shall be a defence in proceedings for an offence under subsection (8) (being an offence consisting of a failure to comply with subsection (1) or (3)) for the defendant to prove that he took all reasonable steps for securing compliance with subsection (1) or (3), as the case may be.][d]

Amendments

a Words 'are required by subsection (1) or (2) of section 41 or would, but for section 41(6), be required by subsection (1) or (2) of that section' substituted for 'would, but for section 41 (6), be required by subsection (1) or (2) of that section' by C(A)A 2009, s 9(a).

b C(A)A 2009, s 9(b) inserts CA 1990, s 44(4A)–(4C).

c Words 'subsection (1), (3) or (4C)' substituted for 'subsection (1) or (3)' by C(A)A 2009, s 9(c).

d C(A)A 2009, s 9(d) substitutes CA 1990, s 44(9).

---

45 Arrangements excluded from sections 41 and 44

(1) Section 41(1) and (2) and section 44 do not apply to arrangements of the kind mentioned in section 32(2) entered into by a company or by a subsidiary of the company for a person who at any time during the relevant period was a director of the company or of its holding company or was connected with such a director, if the aggregate of the values of each arrangement so made for that director or any person connected with him, less the amount (if any) by which the liabilities of the person for whom the arrangement was made has been reduced, did not at any time during the relevant period exceed [€3,174.35].[a]

(2) Subsections (1)(c) and (2)(c) of section 41 do not apply, in relation to any accounts prepared by a company in respect of any relevant period, to any transaction or arrangement with a company or any of its subsidiaries in which a director of the company or of its holding company had, directly or indirectly, a material interest if—

- (a) the value of each transaction or arrangement within subsection (1)(c) or (2)(c), as the case may be, in which that director had, directly or indirectly, a material interest and which was made after the commencement of that relevant period with the company or any of its subsidiaries; and
- (b) the value of each such transaction or arrangement which was made before the commencement of that period less the amount (if any) by which the liabilities of the person for whom the transaction or arrangement was made have been reduced;

did not at any time during the relevant period exceed in the aggregate [€1,269.74][b] or, if more, did not exceed [€6,348.69][c] or one per cent of the value of the net assets of the company preparing the accounts in question as at the end of the relevant period for those accounts, whichever is the less and for this purpose, 'net assets' has the same meaning as in section 29 (9).

Amendments

a £2,500 converted to €3,174.35 by Council Regulations (EC) No 1103/97, No 974/98 and No 2866/98 and the Economic and Monetary Union Act 1988, s 6.

b £1,000 converted to €1,269.74 by Council Regulations (EC) No 1103/97, No 974/98 and No 2866/98 and the Economic and Monetary Union Act 1988, s 6.

c £5,000 converted to €6,348.69 by Council Regulations (EC) No 1103/97, No 974/98 and No 2866/98 and the Economic and Monetary Union Act 1988, s 6.

---

46 Duty of auditors of company in breach of section 41 or 43

If in the case of any group or other accounts of a company the requirements of section 41 or 43 are not complied with, it shall be the duty of the auditors of the company by whom the accounts are examined to include in their report on the balance sheet of the company, so far as they are reasonably able to do so, a statement giving the required particulars.

47 Disclosure by directors of interests in contracts, etc.

(1) Any reference in section 194 of the Principal Act to a contract shall be construed as including a reference to any transaction or arrangement (whether or not constituting a contract) made or entered into on or after the commencement of this section.

(2) For the purposes of the said section 194, a transaction or arrangement of a kind described in section 31 made by a company for a director of the company or a person connected with such a director shall, if it would not otherwise be so treated (and whether or not prohibited by that section), be treated as a transaction or arrangement in which that director is interested.

(3) [...][a]

Amendments

a Subsection (3) substituted CA 1963, s 194(3).

Supplemental

48 Power to alter financial limits under Part III

(1) The Minister may, by order, alter any of the financial limits specified in this Part.

(2) Every order made under this section shall be laid before each House of the Oireachtas as soon as may be after it is made and if a resolution annulling the order is passed by either House within the next 21 days on which that House has sat after the order is laid before it, the order shall be annulled accordingly but without prejudice to the validity of anything previously done thereunder.

49 Cessation of section 192 of Principal Act

Section 192 of the Principal Act shall cease to have effect except—

(a) in relation to accounts and directors' reports prepared in respect of any financial year ending before the commencement of this section; and

(b) in relation to accounts and directors' reports prepared in respect of the first financial year ending after the commencement of this section but only in relation to loans and contracts entered into before the commencement of this section which do not subsist on or after that day.

50 Inspection of director's service contracts

(1) Subject to the provisions of this section every company shall keep at an appropriate place—

(a) in the case of each director whose contract of service with the company is in writing, a copy of that contract;

(b) in the case of each director whose contract of service with the company is not in writing, a written memorandum setting out the terms of that contract;

(c) in the case of each director who is employed under a contract of service with a subsidiary of the company, a copy of that contract or, if it is not in writing, a written memorandum setting out the terms of that contract;

(d) a copy or written memorandum, as the case may be, of any variation of any contract of service referred to in paragraph (a), (b) or (c);

and all copies and memoranda kept by a company in pursuance of this subsection shall be kept at the same place.

(2) Where a contract of service is only partially in writing, paragraphs (a), (b), (c) and (d), as appropriate, of subsection (1), and subsections (4) and (5), shall also apply to such a contract.

(3) The following shall, as regards a company, be appropriate places for the purposes of subsection (1), namely—

(a) its registered office;

(b) the place where its register of members is kept if other than its registered office;

(c) its principal place of business.

(4) Every company shall send notice in the prescribed form to the registrar of companies of the place where copies and memoranda required by subsection (1) to be kept by it are kept and of any change in that place, save in a case in which they have at all times been kept at its registered office.

(5) Subsection (1) shall not apply in relation to a director's contract of service with the company or with a subsidiary of the company if that contract required him to work wholly or mainly outside the State, but the company shall keep a memorandum—

(a) in the case of a contract of service with the company, setting out the name of the director and the provisions of the contract relating to its duration;

(b) in the case of a contract of service with a subsidiary of the company setting out the name of the director, the name and place of incorporation of the subsidiary and the provisions of the contract relating to its duration,

at the same place as copies and the memoranda are kept by the company in pursuance of subsection (1).

(6) Every copy and memorandum required to be kept by subsections (1) and (5) shall, during business hours (subject to such reasonable restrictions as the company may in general meeting impose, so that not less than two hours in each day be allowed for inspection), be open to the inspection of any member of the company without charge.

[(7) If default is made in complying with subsection (1) or (5) or if an inspection required under subsection (6) is refused, the company and every officer of the company who is in default shall be guilty of an offence and liable on summary conviction to a [class C fine][b] and, for continued contravention, to a daily default [class E fine][c] and, if default is made for 14 days in complying with subsection (4), the company and every officer of the company who is in default shall be guilty of an offence and liable to a [class C fine][b] and, for continued contravention, to a daily default [class E fine][c]][a].

(8) In the case of a refusal of an inspection required under subsection (6) of a copy or memorandum the court may by order compel an immediate inspection thereof.

(9) This section shall not require to be kept a copy of, or memorandum setting out the terms of, a contract or a copy of, or memorandum setting out the terms of a variation of, a contract at a time at which the unexpired portion of the term for which the contract is to be in force is less than three years or at a time at which the contract can, within the next ensuing three years, be terminated by the company without payment of compensation.

Amendments

a C(AA)A 2003, s 57 and Sch 2 substitutes CA 1990, s 50(7).

b As implicitly substituted for "fine not exceeding €1,904.61" by Fines Act 2010, s 6. A class C fine currently means a fine not exceeding €2,500.

c As implicitly substituted for "fine not exceeding €63.49" by Fines Act 2010, s 8. A class E fine currently means a fine not exceeding €500.

---

51 Register of directors and secretaries

[...][a]

Amendments

a This section substituted CA 1963, s 195.

---

52 Directors to have regard to interests of employees

(1) The matters to which the directors of a company are to have regard in the performance of their functions shall include the interests of the company's employees in general, as well as the interests of its members.

(2) Accordingly, the duty imposed by this section on the directors shall be owed by them to the company (and the company alone) and shall be enforceable in the same way as any other fiduciary duty owed to a company by its directors.

PART IV
DISCLOSURE OF INTERESTS IN SHARES

Chapter 1
Share dealings by directors, secretaries and their families

53 Obligation of director or secretary to notify interests in shares or debentures of company

(1) Subject to the provisions of this section a person who, at the commencement of this section is a director or secretary of a company and is then interested in shares in, or debentures of, the company or any other body corporate, being the company's subsidiary or holding company or a subsidiary of the company's holding company or thereafter becomes a director or secretary of a company and, at the time when he becomes a

director or secretary of a company, is so interested, shall notify the company in writing—

(a) of the subsistence of his interests at that time, and

(b) of the number of shares of each class in, and the amount of debentures of each class of, the company or any such other body corporate as aforesaid in which each interest of his subsists at that time.

(2) A director or secretary of a company shall notify the company in writing of the occurrence, while he is a director or secretary, of any of the following events and the date on which it occurred—

(a) any event in consequence of whose occurrence he becomes, or ceases to be, interested in shares in, or debentures of, the company or any other body corporate, being the company's subsidiary or holding company or a subsidiary of the company's holding company;

(b) the entering into by him of a contract to sell any such shares or debentures;

(c) the assignment by him of a right granted to him by the company to subscribe for shares in, or debentures of, the company; and

(d) the grant to him by another body corporate, being the company's subsidiary or holding company or a subsidiary of the company's holding company, of a right to subscribe for shares in, or debentures of, that other body corporate, the exercise of such a right granted to him and the assignment by him of such a right so granted;

stating the number or amount, and class, of shares or debentures involved.

(3) The provisions of section 54 shall have effect for the interpretation of, and otherwise in relation to, subsections (1) and (2).

(4) Section 56 shall have effect with respect to the periods within which obligations imposed by subsections (1) and (2) on persons must be fulfilled by them.

(5) Section 57 shall have effect with respect to certain circumstances in which obligations imposed by subsections (1) and (2) are to be treated as not discharged.

(6) In the case of a person who is a director or secretary of a company at the time when this section comes into operation subsection (2) shall not require the notification by him of the occurrence of an event before that time; and that subsection shall not require the notification by a person of the occurrence of an event whose occurrence comes to his knowledge after he has ceased to be a director or secretary.

(7) A person who fails to fulfil, within the proper period, an obligation to which he is subject by virtue of subsection (1) or (2) shall be guilty of an offence.

(8) An obligation imposed by this section shall be treated as not being fulfilled unless the notice by means of which it purports to be fulfilled is expressed to be given in fulfilment of that obligation.

(9) This section applies to shadow directors as to directors, but the making of a notification by a person under this section shall not, in itself, be proof that the person making the notification is a shadow director.

(10) Nothing in this section shall operate so as to impose an obligation with respect to shares in a body corporate which is the wholly owned subsidiary of another body corporate; and for this purpose a body corporate shall be deemed to be the wholly

owned subsidiary of another if it has no members but that other and that other's wholly owned subsidiaries and its or their nominees.

(11) This section and sections 54, 56, 57 and 59 shall have effect in place of section 190 of the Principal Act and of so much of section 193 of that Act as relates to section 190, and that section and so much of section 193 as relates thereto shall, accordingly, cease to have effect.

54 Nature of an interest within section 53

(1) The provisions of this section shall apply in determining for the purposes of section 53 whether a person has an interest in shares or debentures.

(2) Any reference to an interest in shares or debentures shall be read as including a reference to any interest of any kind whatsoever in shares or debentures; and accordingly there shall be disregarded any restraints or restrictions to which the exercise of any right attached to the interest is or may be subject.

(3) Where any property is held on trust and any interest in shares or debentures is comprised in that property, any beneficiary of that trust who, apart from this subsection, does not have an interest in the shares or debentures shall be taken to have such an interest; but this subsection is without prejudice to the following provisions of this section.

(4) A person shall be taken to have an interest in shares or debentures if—

(a) he enters into a contract for their purchase by him (whether for cash or other consideration); or

(b) not being the registered holder, he is entitled to exercise any right conferred by the holding of those shares or debentures or is entitled to control the exercise of any such right.

(5) A person shall be taken to be interested in shares or debentures if a body corporate is interested in them and—

(a) that body corporate or its directors are accustomed to act in accordance with his directions or instructions; or

(b) he is entitled to exercise or control the exercise of one-third or more of the voting power at general meetings of that body corporate.

(6) Where a person is entitled to exercise or control the exercise of one-third or more of the voting power at general meetings of a body corporate and that body corporate is entitled to exercise or control the exercise of any of the voting power at general meetings of another body corporate (the 'relevant voting power'), then, for the purposes of subsection (5)(b), the relevant voting power shall be taken to be exercisable by that person.

(7) A person shall be taken to have an interest in shares or debentures if, otherwise than by virtue of having an interest under a trust—

(a) he has a right to call for delivery of the shares or debentures to himself or to his order; or

(b) he has a right to acquire an interest in shares or debentures or is under an obligation to take an interest in shares or debentures;

whether in any case the right or obligation is conditional or absolute.

(8) For the purposes of subsection (4)(b) a person shall be taken to be entitled to exercise or control the exercise of any right conferred by the holding of shares or debentures if he has a right (whether subject to conditions or not) the exercise of which would make him so entitled or is under an obligation (whether so subject or not) the fulfilment of which would make him so entitled.

(9) A person shall not by virtue of subsection (4)(b) be taken to be interested in any shares or debentures by reason only that he has been appointed a proxy to vote at a specified meeting of a company or of any class of its members and at any adjournment of that meeting or has been appointed by a body corporate to act as its representative at any meeting of a company or of any class of its members.

(10) Without prejudice to subsection (2), rights or obligations to subscribe for any shares or debentures shall not be taken for the purposes of subsection (7) to be rights to acquire, or obligations to take, any interest in shares or debentures.

(11) Where persons have a joint interest each of them shall be deemed to have that interest.

(12) It is immaterial that shares or debentures in which a person has an interest are unidentifiable.

(13) Delivery to a person's order of shares or debentures in fulfilment of a contract for the purchase thereof by him or in satisfaction of a right of his to call for delivery thereof, or failure to deliver shares or debentures in accordance with the terms of such a contract or on which such a right falls to be satisfied, shall be deemed to constitute an event in consequence of the occurrence of which he ceases to be interested in them, and so shall the lapse of a person's right to call for delivery of shares or debentures.

55 Interests to be disregarded

(1) The following interests shall be disregarded for the purposes of section 54 and sections 56 to 58—

(a) where property is held on trust and an interest in shares or debentures is comprised in that property, an interest in reversion or remainder or of a bare trustee and any discretionary interest;

(b) an interest of a person subsisting by virtue of—

(i) his holding units in—

(I) a registered unit trust scheme within the meaning of section 3 of the Unit Trusts Act, 1972;

(II) a unit trust to which section 31 of the Capital Gains Tax Act, 1975, as amended by section 34 of the Finance Act, 1977 relates;

(III) an undertaking for collective investment in transferable securities, within the meaning of the European Communities (Undertakings for Collective Investment in Transferable Securities) Regulations, 1989 (S.I. No 78 of 1989);

(ii) a scheme made under section 46 of the Charities Act, 1961;

(c) an interest for the life of himself or another of a person under a settlement in the case of which the property comprised in the settlement consists of or includes shares or debentures, and the conditions mentioned in subsection (3) are satisfied;

(d) an interest in shares or debentures held by a member of a recognised stock exchange carrying on business as a stock broker which is held by way of security only for the purposes of a transaction entered into by the person or body concerned in the ordinary course of business of such person or body;

(e) such interests, or interests of such a class, as may be prescribed for the purposes of this paragraph by regulations made by the Minister.

(2) A person shall not by virtue of section 54(4)(b) be taken to be interested in shares or debentures by reason only that he has been appointed a proxy to vote at a specified meeting of a company or of any class of its members and at any adjournment of that meeting, or has been appointed by a body corporate to act as its representative at any meeting of a company or of any class of its members.

(3) The conditions referred to in subsection (1)(c) are, in relation to a settlement—

(a) that it is irrevocable, and

(b) that the settlor (within the meaning of section 96 of the Income Tax Act, 1967) has no interest in any income arising under, or property comprised in, the settlement.

56 Periods within which obligations under section 53 must be discharged

(1) An obligation imposed on a person by section 53(1) to notify an interest must, if he knows of the existence of the interest on the relevant day (that is to say, in a case in which he is a director or secretary at the beginning of the day on which that section comes into operation, the last previous day, and, in a case in which he thereafter becomes a director or secretary, the day on which he becomes it), be fulfilled before the expiration of the period of five days beginning with the day next following the relevant day; otherwise it must be fulfilled before the expiration of the period of five days beginning with the day next following that on which the existence of the interest comes to his knowledge.

(2) An obligation imposed on a person by section 53(2) to notify the occurrence of an event must, if at the time at which the event occurs he knows of its occurrence, be fulfilled before the expiration of the period of five days beginning with the day next following that on which it occurs; otherwise, it must be fulfilled before the expiration of the period of five days beginning with the day next following that on which the occurrence of the event comes to his knowledge.

57 Circumstances in which obligation under section 53 is not discharged

(1) Where an event of whose occurrence a director or secretary is, by virtue of section 53(2)(a), under obligation to notify a company consists of his entering into a contract for the purchase by him of shares or debentures, the obligation shall be taken not to be discharged in the absence of inclusion in the notice of a statement of the price to be paid by him under the contract, and an obligation imposed on a director or secretary by virtue of section 53(2)(b) shall be taken not to be discharged in the absence of inclusion in the notice of the price to be received by him under the contract.

(2) An obligation imposed on a director or secretary by virtue of section 53(2)(c) to notify a company shall be taken not to be discharged in the absence of inclusion in the notice of a statement of the consideration for the assignment (or, if it be the case that there is no consideration, that fact), and where an event of whose occurrence a director

is, by virtue of section 53(2)(d), under obligation to notify) a company consists in his assigning a right, the obligation shall be taken not to be discharged in the absence of inclusion in the notice of a similar statement.

(3) Where an event of whose occurrence a director or secretary is, by virtue of section 53 (2)(d), under obligation to notify a company consists in the grant to him of a right to subscribe for shares or debentures, the obligation shall not be taken to be discharged in the absence of inclusion in the notice of a statement of—

(a) the date on which the right was granted,

(b) the period during which or time at which the right is exercisable,

(c) the consideration for the grant (or, if it be the case that there is no consideration, that fact), and

(d) the price to be paid for the shares or debentures.

(4) Where an event of whose occurrence a director or secretary is, by virtue of section 53 (2)(d), under obligation to notify a company consists in the exercise of a right granted to him to subscribe for shares or debentures, the obligation shall be taken not to be discharged in the absence of inclusion in the notice of a statement of—

(a) the number of shares or amount of debentures in respect of which the right was exercised, and

(b) if it be the case that they were registered in his name, that fact, and, if not, the name or names of the person or persons in whose name or names they were registered,

together (if they were registered in the names of two persons or more) with the number or amount thereof registered in the name of each of them.

(5) For the purposes of this section any reference, however expressed, to any price paid, given or received in respect of any interest in shares or debentures shall be construed as including a reference to any consideration other than money given or received in respect of any such interest.

58 Other provisions relating to notification

(1) Where a person authorises any other person ('the agent') to acquire or dispose of, on his behalf, interests in shares in, or debentures of, a company, he shall secure that the agent notifies him immediately of acquisitions or disposals of interests in such shares or debentures effected by the agent which will or may give rise to any obligation on his part to make a notification under this Chapter with respect to his interest in those shares or debentures.

(2) An obligation to make any notification imposed on any person by this Chapter shall be treated as not being fulfilled unless the notice by means of which it purports to be fulfilled identifies him and gives his address.

(3) Where a person fails to fulfil, within the proper period, an obligation to which he is subject by virtue of section 53, no right or interest of any kind whatsoever in respect of the shares or debentures concerned shall be enforceable by him, whether directly or indirectly, by action or legal proceeding.

(4) Where any right or interest is restricted under subsection (3), any person in default under that subsection or any other person affected by such restriction may apply to the court for relief against a disability imposed by or arising out of subsection (3) and the

court on being satisfied that the default was accidental, or due to inadvertence, or some other sufficient cause, or that on other grounds it is just and equitable to grant relief, may grant such relief either generally, or as respects any particular right or interest on such terms and conditions as it sees fit.

(5) Where an applicant for relief under subsection (4) is a person referred to in subsection (3), the court may not grant such relief if it appears that the default has arisen as a result of any deliberate act or omission on the part of the applicant.

(6) Subsection (3) shall not apply to an obligation relating to a person ceasing to be interested in shares in, or debentures of, a company.

(7) A person who fails without reasonable excuse to comply with subsection (1) shall be guilty of an offence.

59 Register of interests

(1) Every company shall keep a register for the purposes of section 53.

(2) Whenever the company receives information from a director or secretary in consequence of the fulfilment of an obligation imposed on him by that section, the company shall enter in the register, against the name of that person, that information and the date of the entry.

(3) Every company shall, whenever it grants to a director or secretary a right to subscribe for shares in, or debentures of, the company, enter in the register against his name—

(a) the date on which the right is granted,

(b) the period during which or time at which it is exercisable,

(c) the consideration for the grant (or, if it be the case that there is no consideration, that fact), and

(d) the description of shares or debentures involved and the number or amount thereof, and the price to be paid therefor.

(4) Whenever such a right as is mentioned in subsection (3) is exercised by a director or secretary, the company shall enter in the said register against his name that fact (identifying the right), the number or amount of shares or debentures in respect of which it is exercised and, if it be the case that they were registered in his name, that fact, and, if not, the name or names of the person or persons in whose name or names they were registered, together (if they were registered in the names of two persons or more) with the number or amount thereof registered in the name of each of them.

(5) This section applies to shadow directors as to directors.

60 Provisions relating to register

(1) The register to be kept under section 59 shall be so made up that the entries therein against the several names inscribed therein appear in chronological order.

(2) An obligation imposed by section 59(2) to (4) shall be fulfilled before the expiration of the period of 3 days beginning with the day next following that on which it arises.

(3) The nature and extent of an interest recorded in the said register of a director or secretary in any shares or debentures shall, if he so requires, be recorded in the said register.

(4) The company shall not, by virtue of anything done for the purposes of this section, be affected with notice of, or put upon inquiry as to, the rights of any person in relation to any shares or debentures.

(5) The said register shall—

(a) if the company's register of members is kept at its registered office, be kept there;

(b) if the company's register of members is not so kept, be kept at the company's registered office or at the place where its register of members is kept;

and shall during business hours (subject to such reasonable restrictions as the company in general meeting may impose, so that not less than two hours in each day be allowed for inspection) be open to the inspection of any member of the company without charge and of any other person on payment of [38 cents][a] or such less sum as the company may prescribe for each inspection.

(6) The company shall send notice to the registrar of companies of the place where the said register is kept and of any change in that place, save in a case in which it has at all times been kept at its registered office.

(7) Unless the said register is in such a form as to constitute in itself an index, the company shall keep an index of the names entered therein which shall—

(a) in respect of each name, contain a sufficient indication to enable the information inscribed against it to be readily found; and

(b) be kept at the same place as the said register;

and the company shall, within 14 days after the date on which a name is entered in the said register, make any necessary alteration in the index.

(8) Any member of the company or other person may require a copy of the said register, or of any part thereof, on payment of [19 cents][b] or such less sum as the company may prescribe, for every hundred words or fractional part thereof required to be copied.

The company shall cause any copy so required by any person to be sent to that person within the period of 10 days beginning with the day next following that on which the requirement is received by the company.

(9) The said register shall also be and remain open and accessible to any person attending the company's annual general meeting at least one quarter hour before the appointed time for the commencement of the meeting and during the continuance of the meeting.

[(10) If default is made in compliance with subsection (9), the company and every officer of the company who is in default shall be guilty of an offence and liable to a [class C fine][c] and if default is made for 14 days in complying with subsection (6) the company and every officer of the company who is in default shall be guilty of an offence and liable to a [class C fine][c]; and if default is made in complying with section 59 or with subsection (1), (2) or (7) of this section or if an inspection required under this section is refused or any copy required thereunder is not sent within the proper period the company and every officer of the company who is in default shall be guilty of an offence and liable to a [class C fine][c]][d].

(11) In the case of a refusal of an inspection required under this section of the said register, the court may by order compel an immediate inspection thereof; and in the case

of a failure to send within the proper period a copy required under this section, the court may by order direct that the copy required shall be sent to the person requiring it.

Amendments

a ‘30p’ converted to 38 cents by Council Regulations (EC) No 1103/97, No 974/98 and No 2866/98 and the European and Monetary Union Act 1998, s 6.

b ‘15p’ converted to 19 cents by Council Regulations (EC) No 1103/97, No 974/98 and No 2866/98 and the European and Monetary Union Act 1998, s 6.

c As implicitly substituted for “fine not exceeding €1,904.61” by Fines Act 2010, s 6. A class C fine currently means a fine not exceeding €2,500.

d Substituted by IFCMPA 2005, s 73(2)(a).

61 Removal of entries from register

(1) A company may remove an entry against a person’s name from the register of interests in shares and debentures kept under section 59 if more than 6 years has elapsed since the date of the entry being made, and either—

(a) that entry recorded the fact that the person in question has ceased to have an interest notifiable under this Chapter in shares in, or debentures of, the company, or

(b) it has been superseded by a later entry made under the said section 59 against the same person’s name;

and in a case within paragraph (a) the company may also remove that person’s name from the register.

(2) Where a name is removed from a company’s register of interests in shares or debentures in pursuance of subsection (1), the company shall within 14 days of the date of that removal make any necessary alterations in any associated index.

(3) If default is made in complying with subsection (2), the company and every officer of it who is in default shall be guilty of an offence and liable to a fine.

62 Entries, when not to be removed

(1) Entries in a company’s register of interests in shares and debentures under this Chapter shall not be deleted except in accordance with section 61.

(2) If an entry is deleted from a company’s register of interests in shares in contravention of subsection (1), the company shall restore that entry to the register as soon as is reasonable and practicable.

(3) If default is made in complying with subsection (1) or (2), the company and every officer of it who is in default shall be guilty of an offence and liable to a fine.

63 Disclosure of interests in directors’ report

(1) Subject to subsection (2), the directors’ report or the notes to the company’s accounts in respect of a financial year shall, as respects each person who, at the end of that year, was a director of the company, state—

(a) whether or not he was, at the end of that year, interested in shares in, or debentures of, the company or any other body corporate being the company’s subsidiary or holding company or a subsidiary of the company's holding company;

(b) if he was so interested—

(i) the number and amount of shares in, and debentures of, each body (specifying it) in which he was then interested,

(ii) whether or not he was, at the beginning of that year (or, if he was not then a director, when he became a director), interested in shares in, or debentures of, the company or any other such body corporate, and,

(iii) if he was, the number and amount of shares in, and debentures of, each body (specifying it) in which he was interested at the beginning of that year or, as the case may be, when he became a director.

(2) The reference in subsection (1) to the directors' report and the notes to the company's accounts are references to the report and notes respectively which are required by virtue of the Companies (Amendment) Act, 1986 to be annexed to the Annual Return and where a company does not annex the report of the directors, as permitted by section 10(2) of the aforementioned Act, the information required in subsection (1) shall be contained in the notes to the company's accounts.

(3) The references in subsection (1) to the time when a person became a director shall, in the case of a person who became a director on more than one occasion, be construed as referring to the time when he first became a director.

(4) For the purposes of this section 'the directors' report' means the report by the directors of a company which, by section 158(1) of the Principal Act, is required to be attached to every balance sheet of the company.

(5) The information required by subsection (1) to be given in respect of the directors of the company shall also be given in respect of the person who was the secretary of the company at the end of the financial year concerned.

64 Extension of section 53 to spouses and children

(1) For the purposes of section 53—

(a) an interest of the spouse [or civil partner within the meaning of the Civil Partnership and Certain Rights and Obligations of Cohabitants Act 2010][a] of a director or secretary of a company (not being himself or herself a director or secretary thereof) in shares or debentures shall be treated as being the director's or secretary's interest, and

(b) the same applies to an interest of a minor child of a director or secretary of a company (not being himself or herself a director or secretary thereof) in shares or debentures.

(2) For those purposes—

(a) a contract, assignment or right of subscription entered into, exercised or made by, or grant made to, the spouse [or civil partner within the meaning of the Civil Partnership and Certain Rights and Obligations of Cohabitants Act 2010][a] of a director or secretary of a company (not being himself or herself a director or secretary thereof) shall be treated as having been entered into, exercised or made by, or, as the case may be, as having been made to, the director or secretary, and

(b) the same applies to a contract, assignment or right of subscription entered into, exercised or made by, or grant made to, a minor child of a director or secretary of a company (not being himself or herself a director or secretary thereof).

(3) A director or secretary of a company shall be under obligation to notify the company in writing of the occurrence, while he or she is director or secretary, of either of the following events, namely—

(a) the grant to his or her spouse [or civil partner within the meaning of the Civil Partnership and Certain Rights and Obligations of Cohabitants Act 2010][a] or minor child by the company, of a right to subscribe for shares in, or debentures of, the company; and

(b) the exercise by the spouse [or civil partner within the meaning of the Civil Partnership and Certain Rights and Obligations of Cohabitants Act 2010][a] or minor child of such a right as aforesaid granted by the company to the spouse [or civil partner within the meaning of the Civil Partnership and Certain Rights and Obligations of Cohabitants Act 2010][a] or child.

(4) In a notice given to the company under subsection (3) there shall be stated—

(a) in the case of the grant of a right, the like information as is required by section 53 to be stated by the director or secretary on the grant to him by another body corporate of a right to subscribe for shares in, or debentures of, that other body corporate, and

(b) in the case of the exercise of a right, the like information as is required by that section to be stated by the director or secretary on the exercise of a right granted to him by another body corporate to subscribe for shares in, or debentures of, that other body corporate.

(5) An obligation imposed by subsection (3) on a director or secretary must be fulfilled by him before the expiration of the period of 5 days beginning with the day next following that on which the occurrence of the event that gives rise to it comes to his knowledge.

(6) A person who fails to fulfil, within the proper period, an obligation to which he is subject under subsection (3) shall be guilty of an offence.

(7) The provisions set out in sections 54 and 55, shall have effect for the interpretation of, and otherwise in relation to, subsections (1) and (2), and subsections (8) and (9) of section 53, shall, with any requisite modification, have effect for the purposes of this section as they have effect for the purposes of that section.

(8) For the purposes of section 59 an obligation imposed on a director or secretary by this section shall be treated as if imposed by section 53.

Amendments

a Words 'or civil partner within the meaning of the Civil Partnership and Certain Rights and Obligations of Cohabitants Act 2010' inserted by Civil Partnership and Certain Rights and Obligations of Cohabitants Act 2010, Sch, Pt 3, Item No. 19.

---

65 Duty of company to notify stock exchange

(1) Whenever a company in the case of whose shares or debentures dealing facilities are provided by a recognised stock exchange is notified of any matter by a director or secretary in consequence of the fulfilment of an obligation imposed on him by section 53 or 64, and that matter relates to shares or debentures for which such dealing facilities are provided, the company shall be under an obligation to notify that stock exchange of that matter; and the stock exchange may publish, in such manner as it may determine, any information received by it under this subsection.

(2) An obligation imposed by subsection (1) must be fulfilled before the end of the day next following that on which it arises.

(3) If default is made in complying with this section, the company and every officer of the company who is in default shall be guilty of an offence.

66 Investigation of share dealing

(1) If it appears to the [Director][a] that there are circumstances suggesting that contraventions may have occurred, in relation to shares in, or debentures of, a company, of section 30, 53 or 64(3) to (5) he may appoint one or more competent inspectors to carry out such investigations as are requisite to establish whether or not contraventions have occurred as aforesaid and to report the result of their investigations to the [Director].[a]

(2) The appointment under this section of an inspector may limit the period to which his investigation is to extend or confine it to shares or debentures of a particular class or both.

(3) For the purposes of any investigation under this section, section 10 shall apply—

- (a) with the substitution, for references to any other body corporate whose affairs are investigated by virtue of section 9, of a reference to any other body corporate which is, or has at any relevant time been, the company's subsidiary or holding company, and
- (b) with the necessary modification of the reference, in section 10(5), to the affairs of the company or other body corporate, so, however, that it shall apply to members of a recognised stock exchange who are individuals and to officers (past as well as present) of members of such an exchange who are bodies corporate as it applies to officers of the company or of the other body corporate.

(4) The inspectors may, and, if so directed by the [Director],[a] shall, make interim reports to the [Director],[a] and, on the conclusion of the investigation, shall make a final report to the [Director][a].

(5) Any such report shall be written or printed, as the [Director][a] may direct, and the [Director][a] may cause it to be published.

(6) Sections 9, 16 to 18, 22, 23(1) and 23(3) shall, with any necessary modifications, apply for the purposes of this section.

(7) The expenses of an investigation under this section shall be defrayed by the Minister.

(8) Where a person is convicted of an offence on a prosecution instituted as a result of the investigation the High Court may, on the application of the [Director],[a] order that person to pay the said expenses to such extent as the court may direct.

Amendments

a 'Director' substituted for 'Minister' by CLEA 2001, s 14 as enacted by the Company Law Enforcement Act 2001 (Commencement) (No 3) Order 2001 (SI 523/2001) on 28 November 2001.

Chapter 2
Individual and Group Acquisitions

67 Obligation of disclosure and the cases in which it may arise

(1) Where a person either—

(a) to his knowledge acquires an interest in shares comprised in a public limited company's relevant share capital, or ceases to be interested in shares so comprised (whether or not retaining an interest in other shares so comprised), or

(b) becomes aware that he has acquired an interest in shares so comprised or that he has ceased to be interested in shares so comprised in which he was previously interested,

then, subject to the provisions of sections 68 to 79, he shall be under an obligation ('the obligation of disclosure') to make notification to the company of the interests which he has, or had, in its shares.

(2) In relation to a public limited company, 'relevant share capital' means the company's issued share capital of a class carrying rights to vote in all circumstances at general meetings of the company and it is hereby declared for the avoidance of doubt that—

(a) where a company's relevant share capital is divided into different classes of shares, references in this Chapter to a percentage of the nominal value of its relevant share capital are to a percentage of the nominal value of the issued shares comprised in each of the classes taken separately, and

(b) the temporary suspension of voting rights in respect of shares comprised in issued share capital of a company of any such class does not affect the application of this Chapter in relation to interests in those or any other shares comprised in that class.

(3) Where, otherwise than in circumstances within subsection (1), a person—

(a) is aware at the time when it occurs of any change of circumstances affecting facts relevant to the application of the next following section to an existing interest of his in shares comprised in a company's share capital of any description, or

(b) otherwise becomes aware of any such facts (whether or not arising from any such change of circumstances),

then, subject to the provisions of sections 68 to 79, he shall be under the obligation of disclosure.

(4) The acquisition by any person of an interest in shares or debentures of a company registered in the State shall be deemed to be a consent by that person to the disclosure by him, his agents or intermediaries of any information required to be disclosed in relation to shares or debentures by the Companies Acts.

68 Interests to be disclosed

(1) For the purposes of the obligation of disclosure, the interests to be taken into account are those in relevant share capital of the company concerned.

(2) A person has a notifiable interest at any time when he is interested in shares comprised in that share capital of an aggregate nominal value equal to or more than the percentage of the nominal value of that share capital which is for the time being the notifiable percentage.

(3) All facts relevant to determining whether a person has a notifiable interest at any time (or the percentage level of his interest) are taken to be what he knows the facts to be at that time.

(4) The obligation of disclosure arises under section 67(1) or (3) where the person has a notifiable interest immediately after the relevant time, but did not have such an interest immediately before that time.

(5) The obligation also arises under section 67(1) where—

(a) the person had a notifiable interest immediately before the relevant time, but does not have such an interest immediately after it, or

(b) he had a notifiable interest immediately before that time, and has such an interest immediately after it, but the percentage levels of his interest immediately before and immediately after that time are not the same.

(6) For the purposes of this section, 'the relevant time' means—

(a) in a case within section 67(1)(a) or (3)(a), the time of the event or change of circumstances there mentioned, and

(b) in a case within section 67(1)(b) or (3)(b), the time at which the person became aware of the facts in question.

69 'Percentage level' in relation to notifiable interests

(1) Subject to the qualification mentioned below, 'percentage level', in section 68 (5)(b), means the percentage figure found by expressing the aggregate nominal value of all the shares comprised in the share capital concerned in which the person is interested immediately before or (as the case may be) immediately after the relevant time as a percentage of the nominal value of that share capital and rounding that figure down, if it is not a whole number, to the next whole number.

(2) Where the nominal value of the share capital is greater immediately after the relevant time than it was immediately before, the percentage level of the person's interest immediately before (as well as immediately after) that time is determined by reference to the larger amount.

70 The notifiable percentage

(1) The reference in section 68(2) to the notifiable percentage. is to 5 per cent, or such other percentage as may be prescribed by the Minister under this section.

(2) The Minister may prescribe the percentage to apply in determining whether a person's interest in a company's shares is notifiable under section 67; and different percentages may be prescribed in relation to companies of different classes or descriptions.

(3) Where in consequence of a reduction prescribed under this section in the percentage made by such order a person's interest in a company's shares becomes notifiable, he shall then come under the obligation of disclosure in respect of it; and the obligation must be performed within the period of 10 days next following the day on which it arises.

71 Particulars to be contained in notification

(1) Subject to section 70(3) a person's obligation to make a notification under section 67 must be performed within the period of 5 days next following the day on which the obligation arises; and the notification must be in writing to the company.

(2) The notification must specify the share capital to which it relates, and must also—

(a) state the number of shares comprised in that share capital in which the person making the notification knows he was interested immediately after the time when the obligation arose, or

(b) in a case where the person no longer has a notifiable interest in shares comprised in that share capital, state that he no longer has that interest.

(3) A notification with respect to a person's interest in a company's relevant share capital (other than one stating that he no longer has a notifiable interest in shares comprised in that share capital) shall include particulars of—

(a) the identity of each registered holder of shares to which the notification relates, and

(b) the number of those shares held by each such registered holder,

so far as known to the person making the notification at the date when the notification is made.

(4) A person who has an interest in shares comprised in a company's relevant share capital, that interest being notifiable, is under obligation to notify the company in writing—

(a) of any particulars in relation to those shares which are specified in subsection (3), and

(b) of any change in those particulars,

of which in either case he becomes aware at any time after any interest notification date and before the first occasion following that date on which he comes under any further obligation of disclosure with respect to his interest in shares comprised in that share capital.

An obligation arising under this section must be performed within the period of 5 days next following the day on which it arises.

(5) The reference in subsection (4) to an interest notification date, in relation to a person's interest in shares comprised in a public limited company's relevant share capital, is to either of the following—

(a) the date of any notification made by him with respect to his interest under this Part, and

(b) where he has failed to make a notification, the date on which the period allowed for making it came to an end.

(6) A person who at any time has an interest in shares which is notifiable is to be regarded under subsection (4) as continuing to have a notifiable interest in them unless and until he comes under obligation to make a notification stating that he no longer has such an interest in those shares.

72 Notification of [...][a] interests

(1) For the purposes of sections 67 to 71 a person is taken to be interested in any shares in which [his or her spouse or civil partner within the meaning of the Civil Partnership and Certain Rights and Obligations of Cohabitants Act 2010][b] or any minor child of his is interested.

(2) For those purposes, a person is taken to be interested in shares if a body corporate is interested in them and—

(a) that body or its directors are accustomed to act in accordance with his directions or instructions, or

(b) he is entitled to exercise or control the exercise of one-third or more of the voting power at general meetings of that body corporate.

(3) Where a person is entitled to exercise or control the exercise of one-third or more of the voting power at general meetings of a body corporate and that body corporate is entitled to exercise or control the exercise of any of the voting power at general meetings of another body corporate ('the effective voting power') then, for the purposes of subsection (2)(b), the effective voting power is taken as exercisable by that person.

(4) For the purposes of subsections (2) and (3) a person is entitled to exercise or control the exercise of voting power if—

(a) he has a right (whether subject to conditions or not) the exercise of which would make him so entitled, or

(b) he is under an obligation (whether or not so subject) the fulfilment of which would make him so entitled.

Amendments

a Words 'family and corporate' deleted by Civil Partnership and Certain Rights and Obligations of Cohabitants Act 2010, Sch, Pt 1, Item No. 9(a).

b Words 'his or her spouse or civil partner within the meaning of the Civil Partnership and Certain Rights and Obligations of Cohabitants Act 2010' substituted for 'his spouse' by Civil Partnership and Certain Rights and Obligations of Cohabitants Act 2010, Sch, Pt 1, Item No. 9(b).

---

73 Agreement to acquire interests in a public limited company

(1) Subject to the following provisions of this section an agreement between two or more persons which includes provision for the acquisition by any one or more of the parties to the agreement of interests in shares comprised in relevant share capital of a

particular public limited company ('the target company') is an agreement to which this section applies if—

(a) it also includes provisions imposing obligations or restrictions on any one or more of the parties to the agreement with respect to their use, retention or disposal of interests in that company's shares acquired in pursuance of the agreement (whether or not together with any other interests of theirs in that company's shares to which the agreement relates); and

(b) any interest in the company's shares is in fact acquired by any of the parties in pursuance of the agreement;

and in relation to such an agreement references in this section, and in sections 74 and 75, to the target company are to the company which is the target company for that agreement in accordance with this section.

(2) The reference in subsection (1)(a) to the use of interests in shares in the target company is to the exercise of any rights or of any control or influence arising from those interests (including the right to enter into any agreement for the exercise, or for control of the exercise, of any of those rights by another person).

(3) Once any interest in shares in the target company has been acquired in pursuance of such an agreement as is mentioned above, this section continues to apply to that agreement irrespective of—

(a) whether or not any further acquisitions of interests in the company's shares take place in pursuance of the agreement, and

(b) any change in the persons who are for the time being parties to it, and

(c) any variation of the agreement, so long as the agreement continues to include provisions of any description mentioned in subsection (1)(a).

References in this subsection to the agreement include any agreement having effect (whether directly or indirectly) in substitution for the original agreement.

(4) In this section, and also in references elsewhere in this Part to an agreement to which this section applies, 'agreement' includes any agreement or arrangement; and references in this section to provisions of an agreement—

(a) accordingly include undertakings, expectations or understandings operative under any arrangement, and

(b) (without prejudice to the above) also include any provisions, whether express or implied and whether absolute or not.

(5) This section does not apply to an agreement which is not legally binding unless it involves mutuality in the undertakings, expectations or understandings of the parties to it; nor does the section apply to an agreement to underwrite or sub-underwrite any offer of shares in a company, provided the agreement is confined to that purpose and any matters incidental to it.

74 Obligation of disclosure arising under section 73

(1) In the case of an agreement to which section 73 applies, each party to the agreement shall be taken (for purposes of the obligation of disclosure) to be interested in all shares in the target company in which any other party to it is interested apart from the agreement (whether or not the interest of the other party in question was acquired, or includes any interest which was acquired, in pursuance of the agreement).

(2) For those purposes, and also for those of section 75, an interest of a party to such an agreement in shares in the target company is an interest apart from the agreement if he is interested in those shares otherwise than by virtue of the application of section 73 and this section in relation to the agreement.

(3) Accordingly, any such interest of the person (apart from the agreement) includes for those purposes any interest treated as his under section 72 or by the application of section 73 and this section in relation to any other agreement with respect to shares in the target company to which he is a party.

(4) A notification with respect to his interest in shares in the target company made to that company under this Part by a person who is for the time being a party to an agreement to which section 73 applies shall—

(a) state that the person making the notification is a party to such an agreement,

(b) include the names and (so far as known to him) the addresses of the other parties to the agreement, identifying them as such, and

(c) state whether or not any of the shares to which the notification relates are shares in which he is interested by virtue of section 73 and this section and, if so, the number of those shares.

(5) Where a person makes a notification to a company under this Part in consequence of ceasing to be interested in any shares of that company by virtue of the fact that he or any other person has ceased to be a party to an agreement to which section 73 applies, the notification shall include a statement that he or that other person has ceased to be a party to the agreement (as the case may require) and also (in the latter case) the name and (if known to him) the address of that other.

75 Obligation of persons acting together to keep each other informed

(1) A person who is a party to an agreement to which section 73 applies shall be subject to the requirements of this section at any other time when—

(a) the target company is a public limited company, and he knows it to be so, and

(b) the shares in that company to which the agreement relates consist of or include shares comprised in relevant share capital of the company, and he knows that to be the case, and

(c) he knows the facts which make the agreement one to which section 73 applies.

(2) Such a person shall be under obligation to notify every other party to the agreement, in writing, of the relevant particulars of his interest (if any) apart from the agreement in shares comprised in relevant share capital of the target company—

(a) on his first becoming subject to the requirements of this section, and

(b) on each occurrence after that time while he is still subject to those requirements of any event or circumstances within section 67(1) (as it applies to his case otherwise than by reference to interests treated as his under section 74 as applying to that agreement).

(3) The relevant particulars to be notified under subsection (2) are—

(a) the number of shares (if any) comprised in the target company's relevant share capital in which the person giving the notice would be required to state his interest if he were under the obligation of disclosure with respect to that interest (apart from the agreement) immediately after the time when the obligation to give notice under subsection (2) arose, and

(b) the relevant particulars with respect to the registered ownership of those shares, so far as known to him at the date of the notice.

(4) A person who is for the time being subject to the requirements of this section shall be under obligation to notify every other party to the agreement, in writing—

(a) of any relevant particulars with respect to the registered ownership of any shares comprised in relevant share capital of the target company in which he is interested apart from the agreement, and

(b) of any change in those particulars, of which in either case he becomes aware at any time after any interest notification date and before the first occasion following that date on which he becomes subject to any further obligation to give notice under subsection (2) with respect to his interest in shares comprised in that share capital.

(5) The reference in subsection (4) to an interest notification date, in relation to a person's interest in shares comprised in the target company's relevant share capital, is to either of the following—

(a) the date of any notice given by him with respect to his interest under subsection (2), and

(b) where he has failed to give that notice, the date on which the period allowed by this section for giving the notice came to an end.

(6) A person who is a party to an agreement to which section 73 applies shall be under an obligation to notify each other party to the agreement, in writing, of his current address—

(a) on his first becoming subject to the requirements of this section, and

(b) on any change in his address occurring after that time and while he is still subject to those requirements.

(7) A reference to the relevant particulars with respect to the registered ownership of shares is to such particulars in relation to those shares as are mentioned in section 71 (3)(a) or (b).

(8) A person's obligation to give any notice required by this section to any other person must be performed within the period of 5 days next following the day on which that obligation arose.

76 Interest in shares by attribution

(1) Where section 67 or 68 refers to a person acquiring an interest in shares or ceasing to be interested in shares, that reference in certain cases includes his becoming or ceasing to be interested in those shares by virtue of another person's interest.

(2) This section applies where he becomes or ceases to be interested by virtue of section 72 or (as the case may be) section 74 whether—

(a) by virtue of the fact that the person who is interested in the shares becomes or ceases to be a person whose interests (if any) fall by virtue of either section to be treated as his, or

(b) in consequence of the fact that such a person has become or ceased to be interested in the shares, or

(c) in consequence of the fact that he himself becomes or ceases to be a party to an agreement to which section 73 applies to which the person interested in the shares is for the time being a party, or

(d) in consequence of the fact that an agreement to which both he and that person are parties becomes or ceases to be one to which the said section 73 applies.

(3) The person shall be treated under section 67 as knowing he has acquired an interest in the shares or (as the case may be) that he has ceased to be interested in them, if and when he knows both—

(a) the relevant facts with respect to the other person's interest in the shares, and

(b) the relevant facts by virtue of which he himself has become or ceased to be interested in them in accordance with section 72 or 74.

(4) He shall be deemed to know the relevant facts referred to in subsection (3)(a) if he knows (whether contemporaneously or not) either of the subsistence of the other person's interest at any material time or of the fact that the other has become or ceased to be interested in the shares at any such time; and 'material time' is any time at which the other's interests (if any) fall or fell to be treated as his under section 72 or 74.

(5) A person is to be regarded as knowing of the subsistence of another's interest in shares or (as the case may be) that another has become or ceased to be interested in shares if he has been notified under section 75 of facts with respect to the other's interest which indicate that he is or has become or ceased to be interested in the shares (whether on his own account or by virtue of a third party's interest in them).

77 Interests in shares which are to be notified

(1) This section applies, subject to section 78, in determining for purposes of sections 67 to 71 whether a person has a notifiable interest in shares.

(2) A reference to an interest in shares is to be read as including an interest of any kind whatsoever in the shares. Accordingly there are to be disregarded any restraints or restrictions to which the exercise of any right attached to the interest is or may be subject.

(3) Where property is held on trust and an interest in shares is comprised in the property, a beneficiary of the trust who apart from this subsection does not have an interest in the shares is to be taken as having such an interest; but this subsection is without prejudice to the following provisions of this section.

(4) A person is taken to have an interest in shares if—

(a) he enters into a contract for their purchase by him (whether for cash or other consideration), or

(b) not being the registered holder, he is entitled to exercise any right conferred by the holding of the shares or is entitled to control the exercise of any such right.

(5) For the purposes of subsection (4)(b), a person is entitled to exercise or control the exercise of any right conferred by the holding of shares if he—

(a) has a right (whether subject to conditions or not) the exercise of which would make him so entitled, or

(b) is under an obligation (whether so subject or not) the fulfilment of which would make him so entitled.

(6) A person is taken to have an interest in shares if, otherwise than by virtue of having an interest under a trust—

(a) he has a right to call for delivery of the shares to himself or to his order, or

(b) he has a right to acquire an interest in shares or is under an obligation to take an interest in shares,

whether in any case the right or obligation is conditional or absolute.

(7) Without prejudice to subsection (2), rights or obligations to subscribe for any shares shall not be taken for the purposes of subsection (6) to be rights to acquire, or obligations to take, any interest in shares.

(8) Where persons have a joint interest each of them shall be taken to have that interest.

(9) It is immaterial that shares in which a person has an interest are unidentifiable.

(10) Delivery to a person's order of shares in fulfilment of a contract for the purchase thereof by him or in satisfaction of a right of his to call for delivery thereof, or failure to deliver shares in accordance with the terms of such a contract or on which such a right falls to be satisfied, shall be deemed to constitute an event in consequence of the occurrence of which he ceases to be interested in them, and so shall the lapse of a person's right to call for delivery of shares.

78 Interests to be disregarded

(1) The following interests in shares shall be disregarded for the purposes of sections 67 to 71—

(a) where property is held on trust and an interest in shares is comprised in that property, an interest in reversion or remainder or of a bare trustee and any discretionary interest;

(b) an interest of a person subsisting by virtue of—

(i) his holding units in—

(I) a registered unit trust scheme within the meaning of section 3 of the Unit Trusts Act, 1972;

(II) a unit trust to which section 31 of the Capital Gains Tax Act, 1975, as amended by section 34 of the Finance Act, 1977, relates;

(III) an undertaking for collective investment in transferable securities, within the meaning of the European Communities (Undertakings for Collective Investment in Transferable Securities) Regulations, 1989 (S.I. No 78 of 1989); or

(ii) a scheme made under section 46 of the Charities Act, 1961;

(c) an interest for the life of himself or another of a person under a settlement in the case of which the property comprised in the settlement consists of or includes shares, and the conditions mentioned in subsection (3) are satisfied;

(d) an exempt security interest;

(e) an interest of the President of the High Court subsisting by virtue of section 13 of the Succession Act, 1965;

(f) an interest of the Accountant of the High Court in shares held by him in accordance with rules of court;

(g) such interests, or interests of such a class, as may be prescribed for purposes of this paragraph by regulations made by the Minister.

(2) A person shall not by virtue of section 77(4)(b) be taken to be interested in shares by reason only that he has been appointed a proxy to vote at a specified meeting of a company or of any class of its members and at any adjournment of that meeting, or has been appointed by a body corporate to act as its representative at any meeting of a company or of any class of its members.

(3) The conditions referred to in subsection (1)(c) are, in relation to a settlement—

(a) that it is irrevocable, and

(b) that the settlor (within the meaning of section 96 of the Income Tax Act, 1967) has no interest in any income arising under, or property comprised in, the settlement.

(4) An interest in shares is an exempt security interest for purposes of subsection (1)(d) if—

(a) it is held by—

(i) the holder of a licence under section 9 of the Central Bank Act, 1971, or an insurance company within the meaning of the Insurance Acts, 1909 to 1990,

(ii) a trustee savings bank (within the meaning of the Trustee Savings Banks Acts, 1863 to 1979) or a Post Office Savings Bank within the meaning of the Post Office Savings Bank Acts, 1861 to 1958,

(iii) [...][a] [...][b]

(iv) a member of a recognised stock exchange carrying on business as a stockbroker, and

(b) it is held by way of security only for the purposes of a transaction entered into by the person or body concerned in the ordinary course of business of such person or body.

Amendments

a Section 73(4)(a)(iii) repealed by ACC Bank Act 2001, s 12(1) and Pt 1 of the Schedule.

b The words 'or Industrial Credit Corporation plc' deleted by ICC Bank Act 2000, s 7(1) and Pt 1 of the Schedule.

---

79 Other provisions relating to notification

(1) Where a person authorises any other person ('the agent') to acquire or dispose of, on his behalf, interests in shares comprised in relevant share capital of a public limited company, he shall secure that the agent notifies him immediately of acquisitions or disposals of interests in shares so comprised effected by the agent which will or may give rise to any obligation on his part to make a notification under this Chapter with respect to his interest in that share capital.

(2) An obligation to make any notification imposed on any person by this Chapter shall be treated as not being fulfilled unless the notice by means of which it purports to be

fulfilled identifies him and gives his address, and in a case where he is a director or secretary of the company, is expressed to be given in fulfilment of that obligation.

(3) Where a person—

(a) fails to fulfil, within the proper period, an obligation to make any notification required by this Chapter; or

(b) in purported fulfilment of any such obligation makes to a company a statement which he knows to be false or recklessly makes to a company a statement which is false; or

(c) fails to fulfil, within the proper period, an obligation to give any other person any notice required by section 75,

no right or interest of any kind whatsoever in respect of any shares in the company concerned, held by him, shall be enforceable by him, whether directly or indirectly, by action or legal proceeding.

(4) Where any right or interest is restricted under subsection (3), any person in default under that subsection or any other person affected by such restriction may apply to the court for relief against a disability imposed by or arising out of subsection (3) and the court on being satisfied that the default was accidental, or due to inadvertence, or some other sufficient cause, or that on other grounds it is just and equitable to grant relief, may grant such relief either generally, or as respects any particular right or interest on such terms and conditions as it sees fit.

(5) Where an applicant for relief under subsection (4) is a person referred to in subsection (3), the court may not grant such relief if it appears that the default has arisen as a result of any deliberate act or omission on the part of the applicant.

(6) Subsection (3) shall not apply to an obligation relating to a person ceasing to be interested in shares in any company.

(7) A person who—

(a) fails to fulfil, within the proper period, an obligation of disclosure imposed on him by this Chapter, or

(b) fails to fulfil, within the proper period, an obligation to give any other person a notice required by section 75, or

[(bb) fails to fulfil, within the period of 5 days next following the day on which he becomes aware of the matters referred to in section 91(2), the obligation to give the Exchange (within the meaning of that section) a notice required by that section, or][a]

(c) fails without reasonable excuse to comply with subsection (1),

shall be guilty of an offence.

(8) It shall be a defence for a person charged with an offence under subsection (7)(b) to prove that it was not possible for him to give the notice to that other person required by section 75 within the proper period, and either—

(a) that it has not since become possible for him to give the notice so required; or

(b) that he gave that notice as soon after the end of that period as it became possible for him to do so.

Amendments

a CLEA 2001, s 35 inserts CA 1990, s 79(7)(bb).

80 Register of interests in shares

(1) Every public limited company shall keep a register for purposes of sections 67 to 71 and whenever the company receives information from a person in consequence of the fulfilment of an obligation imposed on him by any of those sections, it is under obligation to inscribe in the register, against that person's name, that information and the date of the inscription.

(2) Without prejudice to subsection (1), where a company receives a notification under this Part which includes a statement that the person making the notification, or any other person, has ceased to be a party to an agreement to which section 73 applies, the company shall be under obligation to record that information against the name of that person in every place where his name appears in the register as a party to that agreement (including any entry relating to him made against another person's name).

(3) An obligation imposed by subsection (1) or (2) must be fulfilled within the period of 3 days next following the day on which it arises.

(4) The nature and extent of an interest recorded in the said register of a person in any shares shall, if he so requires, be recorded in the said register.

(5) The company shall not, by virtue of anything done for the purposes of this section, be affected with notice of, or put upon enquiry as to, the rights of any person in relation to any shares.

(6) The register must be so made up that the entries against the several names entered in it appear in chronological order.

(7) Unless the register is in such form as to constitute in itself an index, the company shall keep an index of the names entered in the register which shall in respect of each name contain a sufficient indication to enable the information entered against it to be readily found; and the company shall, within 10 days after the date on which a name is entered in the register, make any necessary alteration in the index.

(8) If the company ceases to be a public limited company it shall continue to keep the register and any associated index until the end of the period of 6 years beginning with the day next following that on which it ceases to be such a company.

(9) The register and any associated index—

(a) shall be kept at the place at which the register required to be kept by the company by section 59 (register of directors' and secretaries' interests) is kept, and

(b) shall be available for inspection in accordance with section 88.

(10) If default is made in complying with any of the provisions of this section, the company and every officer of it who is in default [shall be guilty of an offence and liable to a [class C fine][a]][b] and for continued contravention, to a daily default [class E fine].[c]

Amendments

a £1,000 increased to £1,500 by CA 1990, s 240(7) (as inserted by CLEA 2001, s 104) and converted to €1,904.61 by Council Regulations (EC) No 1103/97, No 974/98 and No 2866/98 and the Economic and Monetary Union Act 1998, s 6; the above being implicitly substituted, by Fines Act 2010, s 6, for a fine not exceeding the aforesaid amount. A class C fine currently means a fine not exceeding €2,500.

b Words inserted by C(AA)A 2003, Sch 2.

c £50 converted to €63.49 by Council Regulations (EC) No 1103/97, No 974/98 and No 2866/98 and the Economic and Monetary Union Act 1998, s 6; as implicitly substituted, by Fines Act 2010, s 8, for a fine not exceeding the aforesaid amount. A class E fine currently means a fine not exceeding €500.

81 Company investigations

(1) A public limited company may by notice in writing require a person whom the company knows or has reasonable cause to believe to be or, at any time during the 3 years immediately preceding the date on which the notice is issued (but excluding any time before the commencement of this section), to have been interested in shares comprised in the company's relevant share capital—

(a) to confirm that fact or (as the case may be) to indicate whether or not it is the case, and

(b) where he holds or has during that time held an interest in shares so comprised, to give such further information as may be required in accordance with the following subsection.

(2) A notice under this section may require the person to whom it is addressed—

(a) to give particulars of his own past or present interest in shares comprised in relevant share capital of the company (held by him at any time during the 3 year period mentioned in subsection (1)),

(b) where the interest is a present interest and any other interest in shares subsists or, in any case, where another interest in the shares subsisted during that 3 year period at any time when his own interest subsisted, to give (so far as lies within his knowledge) such particulars with respect to that other interest as may be required by the notice,

(c) where his interest is a past interest, to give (so far as lies within his knowledge) particulars of the identity of the person who held that interest immediately upon his ceasing to hold it.

(3) The particulars referred to in subsection (2)(a) and (2)(b) include particulars of the identity of persons interested in the shares in question and of whether persons interested in the same shares are or were parties to any agreement to which section 73 applies or to any agreement or arrangement relating to the exercise of any rights conferred by the holding of the shares.

(4) A notice under this section shall require any information given in response to the notice to be given in writing within such reasonable time as may be specified in the notice.

(5) Sections 72 to 74 and 77 apply for the purpose of construing references in this section to persons interested in shares and to interests in shares respectively, as they apply in relation to sections 67 to 70 (but with the omission of any reference to section 78).

(6) This section applies in relation to a person who has or previously had, or is or was entitled to acquire, a right to subscribe for shares in a public limited company which would on issue be comprised in relevant share capital of that company as it applies in relation to a person who is or was interested in shares so comprised; and references in this section to an interest in shares so comprised and to shares so comprised are to be read accordingly in any such case as including respectively any such right and shares which would on issue be so comprised.

82 Registration of interests disclosed under section 81

(1) Whenever in pursuance of a requirement imposed on a person under section 81 a company receives information to which this section applies relating to shares comprised in its relevant share capital, it is under obligation to enter against the name of the registered holder of those shares, in a separate part of its register of interests in shares—

- (a) the fact that the requirement was imposed and the date on which it was imposed, and
- (b) any information to which this section applies received in pursuance of the requirement.

(2) This section applies to any information received in pursuance of a requirement imposed by section 81 which relates to the present interests held by any persons in shares comprised in relevant share capital of the company in question.

(3) Subsections (3) to (10) of section 80 apply in relation to any part of the register maintained in accordance with subsection (1) of this section, reading references to subsection (1) of that section to include subsection (1) of this section.

83 Company investigations on requisition by members

(1) A company may be required to exercise its powers under section 81 on the requisition of members of the company holding at the date of the deposit of the requisition not less than one-tenth of such of the paid-up capital of the company as carries at that date the right of voting at general meetings of the company.

(2) The requisition must—

- (a) state that the requisitionists are requiring the company to exercise its powers under section 81,
- (b) specify the manner in which they require those powers to be exercised, and
- (c) give reasonable grounds for requiring the company to exercise those powers in the manner specified,

and must be signed by the requisitionists and deposited at the company's registered office.

(3) The requisition may consist of several documents in like form each signed by one or more requisitionists.

(4) On the deposit of a requisition complying with this section the company shall exercise its powers under section 81 in the manner specified in the requisition.

(5) If default is made in complying with subsection (4), the court may, on the application of the requisitionists, or any of them, and on being satisfied that it is reasonable to do so, require the company to exercise its powers under section 81 in a manner specified in the order.

84 Company report to members

(1) On the conclusion of an investigation carried out by a company in pursuance of a requisition under section 83 it is the company's duty to cause a report of the information received in pursuance of that investigation to be prepared, and the report shall be made available at the company's registered office within a reasonable period after the conclusion of that investigation.

(2) Where—

(a) a company undertakes an investigation in pursuance of a requisition under section 83, and

(b) the investigation is not concluded before the end of 3 months beginning with the date immediately following the date of the deposit of the requisition,

the company shall cause to be prepared, in respect of that period and each successive period of 3 months ending before the conclusion of the investigation, an interim report of the information received during that period in pursuance of the investigation. Each such report shall be made available at the company's registered office within a reasonable period after the end of the period to which it relates.

(3) The period for making any report prepared under this section available as required by subsection (1) or (2) shall not exceed 15 days.

(4) The company shall, within 3 days of making any report prepared under this section available at its registered office, notify the requisitionists that the report is so available.

(5) An investigation carried out by a company in pursuance of a requisition under section 83 shall be regarded for the purposes of this section as concluded when the company has made all such inquiries as are necessary or expedient for the purposes of the requisition and in the case of each such inquiry, either a response has been received by the company or the time allowed for a response has elapsed.

(6) A report prepared under this section—

(a) shall be kept at the company's registered office from the day on which it is first available there in accordance with subsection (1) or (2) until the expiration of 6 years beginning with the day next following that day, and

(b) shall be available for inspection in accordance with section 88 so long as it is so kept.

(7) If default is made in complying with subsection (1), (2), (3), (4) or (6)(a), the company and every officer of the company who is in default shall be guilty of an offence and be liable to a fine.

85 Penalty for failure to provide information

(1) Where notice is served by a company under section 81 on a person who is or was interested in shares of the company and that person fails to give the company any information required by the notice within the time specified in it, the company may

apply to the court for an order directing that the shares in question be subject to restrictions under section 16.

(2) Such an order may be made by the court notwithstanding any power contained in the applicant company's memorandum or articles enabling the company itself to impose similar restrictions on the shares in question.

(3) Subject to the following subsections, a person who fails to comply with a notice under section 81 shall be guilty of an offence.

(4) A person shall not be guilty of an offence by virtue of failing to comply with a notice under section 81 if he proves that the requirement to give the information was frivolous or vexatious.

(5) Where an order is made under this section directing that shares shall be subject to restrictions under section 16, the company or any person aggrieved by the order may apply to the court for an order directing that the shares shall cease to be subject thereto.

(6) Subsections (6) to (16) of section 16 shall apply in relation to any shares subject to the restrictions imposed by that section by virtue of an order under this section but with the omission in subsections (6) to (15) of any reference to the [Director][a].

Amendments

a 'Director' substituted for 'Minister' by CLEA 2001, s 14 as enacted by the Company Law Enforcement Act 2001 (Commencement) (No 3) Order 2001 (SI 523/2001) on 28 November 2001.

---

86 Removal of entries from register

(1) A company may remove an entry against a person's name from its register of interests in shares if more than 6 years have elapsed since the date of the entry being made, and either—

- (a) that entry recorded the fact that the person in question had ceased to have an interest notifiable under this Chapter in relevant share capital of the company, or
- (b) it has been superseded by a later entry made under section 80 against the same person's name;

and in a case within paragraph (a) the company may also remove that person's name from the register.

(2) If a person in pursuance of an obligation imposed on him by any provision of this Chapter gives to a company the name and address of another person as being interested in shares in the company, the company shall, within 15 days of the date on which it was given that information, notify the other person that he has been so named and shall include in that notification—

- (a) particulars of any entry relating to him made, in consequence of its being given that information, by the company in its register of interests in shares, and
- (b) a statement informing him of his right to apply to have the entry removed in accordance with the following provisions of this section.

(3) A person who has been notified by a company in pursuance of subsection (2) that an entry relating to him has been made in the company's register of interests in shares may apply in writing to the company for the removal of that entry from the register; and the company shall remove the entry if satisfied that the information in pursuance of which the entry was made was incorrect.

(4) If a person who is identified in a company's register of interests in shares as being a party to an agreement to which section 73 applies (whether by an entry against his own name or by an entry relating to him made against another person's name as mentioned in subsection (2)(a)) ceases to be a party to that agreement, he may apply in writing to the company for the inclusion of that information in the register; and if the company is satisfied that he has ceased to be a party to the agreement, it shall record that information (if not already recorded) in every place where his name appears as a party to that agreement in the register.

(5) If an application under subsection (3) or (4) is refused (in a case within subsection (4), otherwise than on the ground that the information has already been recorded) the applicant may apply to the court for an order directing the company to remove the entry in question from the register or (as the case may be) to include the information in question in the register; and the court may, if it thinks fit, make such an order.

(6) Where a name is removed from a company's register of interests in shares in pursuance of subsection (1) or (3) or an order under subsection (5), the company shall within 14 days of the date of that removal make any necessary alteration in any associated index.

(7) If default is made in complying with subsection (2) or (6), the company and every officer of it who is in default shall be guilty of an offence and liable to a fine.

87 Entries, when not to be removed

(1) Entries in a company's register of interests in shares under this Chapter shall not be deleted except in accordance with section 86.

(2) If an entry is deleted from a company's register of interests in shares in contravention of subsection (1), the company shall restore that entry to the register as soon as is reasonably practicable.

(3) If default is made in complying with subsection (1) or (2), the company and every officer of it who is in default shall be guilty of an offence and liable to a fine.

88 Inspection of register and reports

(1) Any register of interests in shares and any report which is required by section 84 (6) to be available for inspection in accordance with this section shall, during business hours (subject to such reasonable restrictions as the company may in general meeting impose, but so that not less than 2 hours in each day are allowed for inspection) be open to the inspection of any member of the company or of any other person without charge.

(2) The register referred to in subsection (1) shall also be and remain open and accessible to any person attending the company's annual general meeting at least one quarter hour before the appointed time for the commencement of the meeting and during the continuance of the meeting.

(3) Any such member or other person may require a copy of any such register or report, or any part of it, on payment of [19 cents][a] or such less sum as the company may

prescribe, for every 100 words or fractional part of 100 words required to be copied; and the company shall cause any copy so required by a person to be sent to him before the expiration of the period of 10 days beginning with the day next following that on which the requirement is received by the company.

(4) If an inspection required under this section is refused or a copy so required is not sent within the proper period, the company and every officer of it who is in default shall be guilty of an offence and liable to a fine.

(5) In the case of a refusal of an inspection required under this section of any register or report, the court may by order compel an immediate inspection of it; and in the case of failure to send a copy required under this section, the court may by order direct that the copy required shall be sent to the person requiring it.

Amendments

a ‘15p’ converted to 19 cents by Council Regulations (EC) No 1103/97, No 974/98 and No 2866/98 and the European and Monetary Union Act 1998, s 6.

---

89 The 1988 Directive

[...][a]

Amendments

a Section 89 repealed by the European Communities (Admissions to Listing and Miscellaneous Provisions) Regulations 2007 (SI 286/2007), reg 13.

---

90 Provisions as to interpretation

[...][a]

Amendments

a Section 90 repealed by the European Communities (Admissions to Listing and Miscellaneous Provisions) Regulations 2007 (SI 286/2007), reg 13.

---

91 Obligation to notify certain interests to the Exchange

[...][a]

Amendments

a Section 91 repealed by the European Communities (Admissions to Listing and Miscellaneous Provisions) Regulations 2007 (SI 286/2007), reg 13.

---

92 Duty of relevant authority to report to Director

[...][a]

Amendments

a Section 92 repealed by the European Communities (Admissions to Listing and Miscellaneous Provisions) Regulations 2007 (SI 286/2007), reg 13.

93 Application and amendment of the 1984 Regulations

[...][a]

Amendments

a Section 93 repealed by the European Communities (Admissions to Listing and Miscellaneous Provisions) Regulations 2007 (SI 286/2007), reg 13.

94 Obligation of professional secrecy

[...][a]

Amendments

a Section 94 repealed by the European Communities (Admissions to Listing and Miscellaneous Provisions) Regulations 2007 (SI 286/2007), reg 13.

95 Immunity from suit

[...][a]

Amendments

a Section 95 repealed by the European Communities (Admissions to Listing and Miscellaneous Provisions) Regulations 2007 (SI 286/2007), reg 13.

96 Co-operation between authorities in Member States

[...][a]

Amendments

a Section 96 repealed by the European Communities (Admissions to Listing and Miscellaneous Provisions) Regulations 2007 (SI 286/2007), reg 13.

Chapter 3
Disclosure Orders: Companies other than Public Limited Companies

97 Application of Chapter 3

(1) The provisions of this Chapter shall apply to all bodies corporate incorporated in the State other than—

(a) a public limited company;

(b) a society registered under the Industrial and Provident Societies Acts, 1893 to 1978;

(c) a society registered under the Building Societies Act, 1989; and

(d) any body corporate which is prohibited by statute or otherwise from making any distribution of its income or property among its members while it is a going concern or when it is in liquidation.

(2) Any reference in this Chapter to a company shall be deemed to be a reference to any body corporate to which, by virtue of subsection (1), this Chapter applies.

(3) Any reference in this Chapter to share capital or relevant share capital shall, in relation to a company, be deemed to be a reference to the issued share capital of a class carrying rights to vote in all circumstances at general meetings of the company, and references to shares shall be construed accordingly.

98 Disclosure order

(1) For the purposes of this Chapter, 'disclosure order' means an order of the court which obliges—

(a) any person whom the court believes to have or to be able to obtain any information as to—

(i) persons interested at present, or at any time during a period specified in the order, in the shares or debentures of a company,

(ii) the names and addresses of any of those persons,

(iii) the name and address of any person who acts or has acted on behalf of any of those persons in relation to the shares or debentures,

to give such information to the court; or

(b) any person whom the court believes to be, or at any time during a period specified in the order to have been, interested in shares or debentures of a company to confirm that fact or (as the case may be) to indicate whether or not it is the case and, where he holds or has during that period held any interest in such shares or debentures, to give such further information as the court may require; or

(c) any person interested in shares or debentures of a company specified in the order to disclose to the court the information required under subparagraphs (i) and (ii) and (iii) of paragraph (a) and such further information as the court may require.

(2) Any person who has a financial interest in a company may apply to the court for a disclosure order in respect of all or any of the shares of or debentures in the company.

(3) An application under subsection (2) shall be supported by such evidence as the court may require.

(4) The court may, before hearing an application under subsection (2), require the applicant to give security for payment of the costs of hearing the application or any consequential proceedings.

(5) The court may make a disclosure order only if—

(a) it deems it just and equitable to do so; and

(b) it is of the opinion that the financial interest of the applicant is or will be prejudiced by the non-disclosure of any interest in the shares or debentures of the company.

(6) For the purposes of subsection (2) 'financial interest' includes any interest as member, contributory, creditor, employee, co-adventurer, examiner, lessor, lessee, licensor, licensee, liquidator or receiver either in relation to the company in respect of whose shares or debentures a disclosure order is sought or a related company.

(7) Where a person authorises any other person ('the agent') to acquire or dispose of, on his behalf, interests in shares comprised in relevant share capital of a company or in debentures of the company in respect of which a disclosure order is made, he shall, for the duration of that order, ensure that the agent notifies him immediately of acquisitions or disposals of interests in shares or debentures so comprised effected by the agent which will or may give rise to any obligation on his part to provide information in accordance with the terms of the order with respect to his interest in that share capital or those debentures.

99 Procedure on application for disclosure order

(1) A person intending to apply for the making of a disclosure order shall give not less than 10 days' notice of his intention to the company in respect of whose shares or debentures the order is sought and to the person to whom the order is intended to be directed.

(2) The applicant shall also serve on any person specified by the court such notice of the application as the court may direct.

(3) On the hearing of the application every person notified under subsection (1) or (2) may appear and adduce evidence.

100 Scope of disclosure order

(1) A disclosure order may require the person to whom it is addressed—

(a) to give particulars of his own past or present interest in shares comprised in relevant share capital of the company or in debentures of the company held by him at any time during the period mentioned in the order;

(b) where the interest is a present interest and any other interest in the shares or debentures subsists or, in any case, where another interest in the shares or debentures subsisted during that period at any time when his own interest subsisted, to give so far as lies within his knowledge such particulars with respect to that other interest as may be required by the order;

(c) where his interest is a past interest, to give so far as lies within his knowledge particulars of the identity of the person who held that interest immediately upon his ceasing to hold it.

(2) A disclosure order shall specify the information to be supplied to the court under the order in respect of any person, shares or debentures to which it refers and any such information shall be given in writing.

(3) Sections 68 to 79 shall apply as appropriate for the purposes of construing references in this Chapter to persons interested in shares and debentures and to interests in shares

and debentures respectively as they apply in relation to section 67 (disregarding section 78) and any reference in those sections to a 'percentage level' shall be disregarded.

(4) For the purposes of this section any reference in sections 67 to 79 to 'shares' shall, where appropriate and unless the contrary is stated, be deemed to include a reference to debentures.

(5) This section shall apply in relation to a person who has or previously had or is or was entitled to acquire a right to subscribe for shares in or debentures of a company which would on issue be comprised in relevant share capital of that company as it applies in relation to a person who is or was interested in shares so comprised or in debentures of the company; and references in the preceding provisions of this section to an interest in shares so comprised or an interest in debentures and to shares so comprised or debentures shall be read accordingly in any such case as including references respectively to any such right and to shares which would on issue be so comprised.

101 Powers of court

(1) The court may, on cause shown, rescind or vary a disclosure order.

(2) A disclosure order may specify a person, group or class of persons to which the order applies.

(3) The court may, if it considers—

(a) that it would be just and equitable to do so, and

(b) that the financial interest of the applicant would not be prejudiced thereby,

exempt in whole or in part from the requirements of a disclosure order—

(i) any person or class of persons,

(ii) any interest or class of interest in shares or debentures,

(iii) any share, group or class of shares,

(iv) any debenture, group or class of debentures.

(4) When the court makes a disclosure order it may impose, for a specific period of time, such conditions or restrictions on the rights or obligations attaching to the shares or debentures in respect of which the order is made as it deems fit.

(5) Any person whose interests are affected by any conditions or restrictions imposed on shares or debentures under subsection (4) may apply to the court for relief from all or any of those conditions and the court may, if it considers it just and equitable to do so, grant such relief in whole or in part and on such terms and conditions as it sees fit.

102 Notice of disclosure order

(1) The applicant shall cause notice in the prescribed form of the making of a disclosure order together with a copy of the order to be sent by registered post within 7 days of the making of the order to—

(a) the company (at its registered office) in respect of whose shares or debentures the order has been made,

(b) the registrar of companies,

(c) the registered holder of any shares or debentures in respect of which the disclosure order has been made where it appears to the court that—

(i) such holder is not at the date of the making of the order resident in the State, and

(ii) such holder should be notified,

(d) such other person as the court sees fit.

(2) The applicant shall cause notice of the making of a disclosure order to be published, within 7 days of the making of the order, in at least 2 daily newspapers which circulate in the district in which the registered office of the company, in respect of whose shares or debentures the order has been made, is situate.

(3) For the purposes of subsection (1)(a)—

(a) the address of the registered office of the company at the date of the making of the disclosure order shall be deemed to be the address of that office which was last delivered to the registrar of companies or otherwise published, as such case may be (in accordance with and in the manner required by the law relating to the company) prior to the date of making the order; and

(b) if no address of the registered office has ever been duly delivered to the registrar of companies or if the location of the last delivered address has been destroyed, the requirements of subsection (1)(a) shall be deemed to have been complied with by sending the required notice of the order together with a copy thereof to the registrar of companies.

(4) For the purposes of subsection (1)(c)—

(a) the address of a non-resident registered holder of shares or debentures shall be deemed to be the address of that holder which was last delivered to the registrar of companies or otherwise published, as the case may be (in accordance with and in the manner required by the law relating to the company) prior to the date of making of the order; and

(b) if no address of the non-resident registered holder has ever been duly delivered to the registrar of companies the requirements of subsection (1)(c) shall be deemed to have been complied with by sending the required notice of the order together with a copy thereof to the registrar of companies.

(5) Any reference in this section to the registered office of a company shall, in the case of a company not registered under the Companies Acts, be construed as a reference to the principal office of the company.

103 Information disclosed under order

(1) An obligation to provide any information imposed on any person by a disclosure order shall be treated as not being fulfilled unless the notice by means of which it purports to be fulfilled identifies him and gives his current address.

(2) Where information is given to the court in compliance with the terms of a disclosure order, a prescribed officer of the court shall, unless the court otherwise directs, cause such information to be furnished (in whole or in part as the court may direct) to the applicant and to the company in respect of whose shares or debentures the order was made.

(3) In reaching its decision under subsection (2), the court shall have regard to whether the requirements of section 102 have been complied with.

(4) Where any information is furnished to the applicant or the company in pursuance of subsection (2), the court may impose such restrictions as it sees fit as to the publication of the information by the person to whom it has been furnished.

104 Civil Consequences of Contravention of Disclosure Order

(1) Where a person—

(a) fails to fulfil, within the proper period, an obligation to provide information required by a disclosure order, or

(b) in purported fulfilment of any such obligation makes to the court a statement which he knows to be false or recklessly makes to the court a statement which is false,

no right or interest of any kind whatsoever in respect of any shares in or debentures of the company concerned held by him shall be enforceable by him whether directly or indirectly, by action or legal proceeding.

(2) Where any right or interest is restricted under subsection (1), any person in default under that subsection or any other person affected by such restriction may apply to the court for relief against a disability imposed by or arising out of subsection (1) and the court on being satisfied that the default was accidental, or due to inadvertence, or some other sufficient cause, or that on other grounds it is just and equitable to grant relief, may grant such relief either generally, or as respects any particular right or interest on such terms and conditions as it sees fit.

(3) Where an applicant for relief under subsection (2) is a person referred to in subsection (1), the court may not grant such relief if it appears that the default has arisen as a result of any deliberate act or omission on the part of the applicant.

(4) The acquisition by any person of an interest in shares or debentures of a company registered in the State shall be deemed to be a consent by that person to the disclosure by him, his agents or intermediaries of any information required to be disclosed in relation to shares or debentures by the Companies Acts.

Chapter 4
General Provisions about Share Registers etc.

105 Power to alter maximum inspection etc charges

(1) The Minister may, by order, alter any of the charges referred to in—

(a) section 60(5) of this Act or section 92(1), 119(1) or 195(10) (inserted by section 51 of this Act) of the Principal Act, or

(b) section 60(8) or 88(3) of this Act, or section 92(2), 92(3), 119(2) or 146(2) of the Principal Act.

(2) The Minister may also, by order, alter the basis of any of the charges referred to in the provisions specified in subsection (1)(b) from the basis referred to in those provisions to some other basis.

(3) In making any order under this section, the Minister shall take into account the general costs incurred by a company in facilitating the inspection, or providing copies, of the registers or other documents referred to in subsection (1).

(4) Every order made under this section shall be laid before each House of the Oireachtas as soon as may be after it is made and if a resolution annulling the order is

passed by either House within the next 21 days on which that House has sat after the order is laid before it, the order shall be annulled accordingly but without prejudice to the validity of anything previously done thereunder.

106 Transitional provisions

(1) Where on the commencement of this section a person has an interest which, if it was acquired after such commencement, would be subject to a notification requirement under Chapter 1 or 2 he shall be under an obligation to make to the company the notification with respect to his interest required by the Chapter concerned.

(2) For the purposes of subsection (1), sections 56 and 71(1) shall apply as if, for the period of 5 days mentioned in each of those provisions, there were substituted a period of 14 days.

(3) Section 73 shall apply in relation to an agreement not withstanding that it was made before the commencement of this section or that any such acquisition of shares as is mentioned in subsection (1)(b) of that section took place before such commencement.

PART V
INSIDER DEALING

Amendments

This Part has been repealed by IFCMPA 2005, s 31. However, the Investment Funds, Companies and Miscellaneous Provisions Act 2005 (Commencement) Order 2005 (SI 323/2005), art 5 provides: 'The 6th day of July 2005 is appointed as the day on which the following provisions of the Act come into operation, namely – (a) section 31 (but only for the purpose of repealing the enactments specified in that section in so far as they relate to a regulated market (within the meaning of Directive 2003/71/EC of the European Parliament and of the Council of 4 November 2003) operated by a recognised stock exchange within the meaning Part V of the Companies Act 1990 (No 33/1990)).'

Therefore, the repeal is only in so far as the securities concerned are admitted to trading on a 'regulated market', ie on the official list. Therefore this Part applies to securities admitted to trading on a 'recognised stock exchange', of which there is only one, the Irish Stock Exchange: Companies (Stock Exchange) Regulations 1995 (SI 310/1995).

Part V is anomalous in one key aspect, and that is because it was enacted in the first place in order to transpose the 1989 Insider Trading Directive (Council Directive 89/592/EEC of 13 November 1989 coordinating regulations on insider dealing OJ L 334, 18/11/1989). Now that the 1989 Directive has been repealed, it is submitted that Part V must be read on its own terms, rather than with a view to apply the principles of a now-repealed Directive.

---

107 Interpretation

In this Part, except where the context otherwise requires

> 'dealing', in relation to securities, means (whether as principal or agent) acquiring, disposing of, subscribing for or underwriting the securities, or making or offering to make, or inducing or attempting to induce a person to make or to offer to make, an agreement—
>
> (a) for or relating to acquiring, disposing of, subscribing for or underwriting the securities; or

(b) the purpose or purported purpose of which is to secure a profit or gain to a person who acquires, disposes of, subscribes for or underwrites the securities or to any of the parties to the agreement in relation to the securities;

'director' includes a shadow director within the meaning of section 27;

'officer', in relation to a company, includes—

(a) a director, secretary or employee;

(b) a liquidator;

(c) any person administering a compromise or arrangement made between the company and its creditors;

(d) an examiner;

(e) an auditor; and

(f) a receiver;

'public office' means an office or employment which is remunerated out of the Central Fund or out of moneys provided by the Oireachtas or money raised by local taxation or charges, or an appointment to or employment under any commission, committee, tribunal, board or body established by the Government or any Minister of the Government or by or under any statutory authority;

'recognised stock exchange' includes, in particular, any exchange prescribed by the Minister which provides facilities for the buying and selling of rights or obligations to acquire stock;

'related company', in relation to a company, means any body corporate which is the company's subsidiary or holding company, or a subsidiary of the company's holding company;

'relevant authority', in relation to a recognised stock exchange, means—

(i) its board of directors, committee of management or other management body, or

(ii) its manager, however described;

'securities' means—

(a) shares, debentures or other debt securities issued or proposed to be issued, whether in the State or otherwise, and for which dealing facilities are, or are to be, provided by a recognised stock exchange;

(b) any right, option or obligation in respect of any such shares, debentures or other debt securities referred to in paragraph (a);

(c) any right, option or obligation in respect of any index relating to any such shares, debentures or other debt securities referred to in paragraph (a); or

(d) such interests as may be prescribed;

'underwrite' includes sub-underwrite.

Amendments

Section repealed in the limited manner noted in IFCMPA 2005, s 31 with effect from 6 July 2005. See IFCMPA 2005, s 31 and notes thereto.

The Companies (Stock Exchange) Regulations, 1995 (SI 310/1995), reg 3(c) obliquely amends this section, stating: 'the Irish Stock Exchange is hereby prescribed as a recognised stock exchange for the purposes of the following provisions of the Companies Acts— ... sections ... 90 to 96, 107 of the Companies Act, 1990'. It provides that 'recognised stock exchange' means 'The Irish Stock Exchange Limited'.

---

108 Unlawful dealings in securities by insiders

(1) It shall not be lawful for a person who is, or at any time in the preceding 6 months has been, connected with a company to deal in any securities of that company if by reason of his so being, or having been, connected with that company he is in possession of information that is not generally available, but, if it were, would be likely materially to affect the price of those securities.

(2) It shall not be lawful for a person who is, or at any time in the preceding 6 months has been, connected with a company to deal in any securities of any other company if by reason of his so being, or having been, connected with the first-mentioned company he is in possession of information that—

(a) is not generally available but, if it were, would be likely materially to affect the price of those securities, and

(b) relates to any transaction (actual or contemplated) involving both those companies or involving one of them and securities of the other, or to the fact that any such transaction is no longer contemplated.

(3) Where a person is in possession of any such information as is mentioned in subsection (1) or (2) that if generally available would be likely materially to affect the price of securities but is not precluded by either of those subsections from dealing in those securities, it shall not be lawful for him to deal in those securities if he has received the information, directly or indirectly, from another person and is aware, or ought reasonably to be aware, of facts or circumstances by virtue of which that other person is then himself precluded by subsection (1) or (2) from dealing in those securities.

(4) It shall not be lawful for a person at any time when he is precluded by subsection (1), (2) or (3) from dealing in any securities, to cause or procure any other person to deal in those securities.

(5) It shall not be lawful for a person, at any time when he is precluded by subsection (1), (2) or (3) from dealing in any securities by reason of his being in possession of any information, to communicate that information to any other person if he knows, or ought reasonably to know, that the other person will make use of the information for the purpose of dealing, or causing or procuring another person to deal, in those securities.

(6) Without prejudice to subsection (3), but subject to subsections (7) and (8), it shall not be lawful for a company to deal in any securities at a time when any officer of that company is precluded by subsection (1), (2) or (3) from dealing in those securities.

(7) Subsection (6) does not preclude a company from entering into a transaction at any time by reason only of information in the possession of an officer of that company if—

(a) the decision to enter into the transaction was taken on its behalf by a person other than the officer;

(b) it had in operation at that time written arrangements to ensure that the information was not communicated to that person and that no advice relating to the transaction was given to him by a person in possession of the information; and

(c) the information was not so communicated and such advice was not so given.

(8) Subsection (6) does not preclude a company from dealing in securities of another company at any time by reason only of information in the possession of an officer of the first-mentioned company, being information that was received by the officer in the course of the performance of his duties as an officer of the first-mentioned company and that consists only of the fact that the first-mentioned company proposes to deal in securities of that other company.

(9) This section does not preclude a person from dealing in securities, or rights or interests in securities, of a company if—

(a) he enters into the transaction concerned as agent for another person pursuant to a specified instruction of that other person to effect that transaction; and

(b) he has not given any advice to the other person in relation to dealing in securities, or rights or interests in securities, of that company that are included in the same class as the first-mentioned securities.

(10) This section does not preclude a person from dealing in securities if, while not otherwise taking advantage of his possession of information referred to in subsection (1) —

(a) he gives at least 21 days' notice to a relevant authority of the relevant stock exchange of his intention to deal, within the period referred to in paragraph (b), in the securities of the company concerned, and

(b) the dealing takes place within a period beginning 7 days after the publication of the company's interim or final results, as the case may be and ending 14 days after such publication, and

(c) the notice referred to in paragraph (a) is published by the exchange concerned immediately on its receipt.

(11) For the purposes of this section, a person is connected with a company if, being a natural person—

(a) he is an officer of that company or of a related company;

(b) he is a shareholder in that company or in a related company; or

(c) he occupies a position (including a public office) that may reasonably be expected to give him access to information of a kind to which subsections (1) and (2) apply by virtue of—

  (i) any professional, business or other relationship existing between himself (or his employer or a company of which he is an officer) and that company or a related company; or

  (ii) his being an officer of a substantial shareholder in that company or in a related company.

(12) For the purposes of subsection (11) 'substantial shareholder' means a person who holds shares in a company, the number of which is above the notifiable percentage for the time being in force under section 70.

(13) The prohibitions in subsections (1), (3), (4) and (5) shall extend to dealings in securities issued by the State as if the references in subsections (1), (9) and (11)(other than paragraphs (a) and (b) of the last mentioned subsection) to a company were references to the State.

Amendments

Section repealed in the limited manner noted in IFCMPA 2005, s 31 with effect from 6 July 2005. See IFCMPA 2005, s 31 and notes thereto.

C(A)A 1999, s 2 provides: 'Section 108 of the Act of 1990, shall not be regarded as having been contravened by reason of—

(a) anything done in the State for the purpose of stabilising or maintaining the market price of securities if it is done in conformity with the Stabilisation Rules, or

(b) any action taken during the stabilising period by a person in any jurisdiction other than the State for the purpose of stabilising or maintaining the market price of securities, but only if the action taken is, in all material respects, permitted by or is otherwise in accordance with all relevant requirements applicable to such actions in the jurisdiction where such action is effected, including, if those securities are also listed on a stock exchange in that jurisdiction, the rules or other regulatory requirements governing that stock exchange.'

---

109 Civil liability for unlawful dealing

(1) Where a person deals in or causes or procures another person to deal in securities in a manner declared unlawful by section 108 or communicates information in any such manner, that person shall, without prejudice to any other cause of action which may lie against him, be liable—

(a) to compensate any other party to the transaction who was not in possession of the relevant information for any loss sustained by that party by reason of any difference between the price at which the securities were dealt in that transaction and the price at which they would have been likely to have been dealt in such a transaction at the time when the first-mentioned transaction took place if that information had been generally available; and

(b) to account to the company that issued or made available those securities for any profit accruing to the first-mentioned person from dealing in those securities.

(2) The amount of compensation for which a person is liable under subsection (1) or the amount of the profit for which a person is liable to account under that subsection is—

(a) subject to paragraph (b), the amount of the loss sustained by the person claiming the compensation or the amount of the profit referred to in subsection (1)(b), as the case may be; or

(b) if the person so liable has been found by a court to be liable to pay an amount or amounts to any other person or persons by reason of the same act or transaction, the amount of that loss or profit less the amount or the sum of the amounts for which that person has been found to be liable.

(3) For the purposes of subsection (2), the onus of proving that the liability of a person to pay an amount to another person arose from the same act or transaction from which another liability arose lies on the person liable to pay the amount.

(4) An action under this section for recovery of a loss or profit shall not be commenced after the expiration of 2 years after the date of completion of the transaction in which the loss or profit occurred.

Amendments

Section repealed in the limited manner noted in IFCMPA 2005, s 31 with effect from 6 July 2005. See IFCMPA 2005, s 31 and notes thereto.

110 Exempt transactions

(1) Nothing in section 108, shall prevent a person from—

- (a) acquiring securities under a will or on the intestacy of another person; or
- (b) acquiring securities in a company pursuant to an employee profit sharing scheme—
  - (i) approved by the Revenue Commissioners for the purposes of the Finance Acts, and
  - (ii) the terms of which were approved by the company in general meeting, and
  - (iii) under which all permanent employees of the company are offered the opportunity to participate on equal terms relative to specified objective criteria;
- [(ba) acquiring a right to shares in a company pursuant to a scheme approved by the Revenue Commissioners for the purposes of the Tax Acts and the Capital Gains Tax Acts.][a]
- (c) entering in good faith into a transaction to which subsection (2) applies.

(2) This subsection applies to the following kinds of transactions—

- (a) the obtaining by a director of a share qualification under section 180 of the Principal Act;
- (b) a transaction entered into by a person in accordance with his obligations under an underwriting agreement;
- (c) a transaction entered into by a personal representative of a deceased person, a trustee, or liquidator, receiver or examiner in the performance of the functions of his office; or
- (d) a transaction by way of, or arising out of, a mortgage of or charge on securities or a mortgage, charge, pledge or lien on documents of title to securities.

[(2A) A person shall be regarded as having entered in good faith into a transaction to which subsection (2)(b) relates, if such person enters in good faith into—

- (a) negotiations with a view to entering an agreement to which paragraph (b) or (c) would relate, or
- (b) an agreement to underwrite securities, or
- (c) an agreement, in advance of dealing facilities being provided by a recognised stock exchange for securities, to acquire or subscribe for a specified number of those securities, or

(d) a transaction in accordance with such person's obligations under an agreement to which paragraph (b) or (c) relates.][b]

(3) This Part shall not apply to transactions entered into in pursuit of monetary, exchange rate, national debt management or foreign exchange reserve policies by any Minister of the Government or the Central Bank, or by any person on their behalf.

Amendments

Section repealed in the limited manner noted in IFCMPA 2005, s 31 with effect from 6 July 2005. See IFCMPA 2005, s 31 and notes thereto.

a CLEA 2001, s 103 inserts CA 1990, s 110(1)(ba).

b C(A)A 1999, s 4 inserts CA 1990, s 110(2A).

---

111 Criminal liability for unlawful dealing

A person who deals in securities in a manner declared unlawful by section 108 shall be guilty of an offence.

Amendments

Section repealed in the limited manner noted in IFCMPA 2005, s 31 with effect from 6 July 2005. See IFCMPA 2005, s 31 and notes thereto.

---

112 Restriction on dealing

(1) Subject to subsection (2), a person convicted of an offence under section 111 or this section shall not deal within the period of 12 months from the date of the conviction.

(2) Where a person convicted of an offence under subsection (1) has, before the date of his conviction, initiated a transaction under which some element of performance remains to be rendered, subsection (1) shall not prohibit him from completing the transaction where a relevant authority of a recognised stock exchange has indicated in writing, to the parties to the transaction, its satisfaction that—

(a) the transaction was initiated but not completed before the date of the conviction, and

(b) if the transaction were not concluded, the rights of an innocent third party would be prejudiced, and

(c) the transaction would not be unlawful under any other provision of this Part.

(3) A person who contravenes this section shall be guilty of an offence.

Amendments

Section repealed in the limited manner noted in IFCMPA 2005, s 31 with effect from 6 July 2005. See IFCMPA 2005, s 31 and notes thereto.

---

113 Duty of agents in relation to unlawful dealing

(1) A person shall not deal on behalf of another person if he has reasonable cause to believe or ought to conclude that the deal would be unlawful, within the meaning of section 108.

(2) A person who contravenes this section shall be guilty of an offence.

Amendments

Section repealed in the limited manner noted in IFCMPA 2005, s 31 with effect from 6 July 2005. See IFCMPA 2005, s 31 and notes thereto.

---

114 Penalties for offences under this Part

A person who commits an offence under this Part shall be liable—

(a) on summary conviction to imprisonment for a term not exceeding 12 months or to a [class C fine][a] or to both, or

(b) on conviction on indictment, to imprisonment for a term not exceeding 10 years or to a fine not exceeding [€444,408.32][b] or to both.

Amendments

Section repealed in the limited manner noted in IFCMPA 2005, s 31 with effect from 6 July 2005. See IFCMPA 2005, s 31 and notes thereto.

a '£1,000' increased to £1,500 by CA 1990, s 240(7) as inserted by CLEA 2001, s 104(c), and converted to €1,904.61 by Council Regulations (EC) No 1103/97, No 974/98 and No 2866/98 and the Economic and Monetary Union Act 1998, s 6; the above being implicitly substituted, by Fines Act 2010, s 6, for a fine not exceeding the aforesaid amount. A class C fine currently means a fine not exceeding €2,500.

b '£200,000' converted to €253,947.61 by Council Regulations (EC) No 1103/97, No 974/98 and No 2866/98 and the Economic and Monetary Union Act 1998, s 6, and multiplied by a multiplier of 1.75 pursuant to Fines Act 2010, s 9.

---

115 Duty of recognised stock exchange in relation of unlawful dealing

(1) If it appears to a relevant authority of a recognised stock exchange that any person has committed an offence under this Part, such authority shall forthwith report the matter to the [Director][a] and shall furnish to the [Director][a] such information and give to him such access to and facilities for inspecting and taking copies of any documents, being information or documents in the possession or under the control of such authority and relating to the matter in question, as the [Director][a] may require.

(2) Where it appears to a member of a recognised stock exchange that any person has committed an offence under this Part, he shall report the matter forthwith to a relevant authority of the recognised stock exchange concerned, who shall thereupon come under the duty referred to in subsection (1).

(3) If it appears to a court in any proceedings that any person has committed an offence as aforesaid, and that no report relating to the matter has been made to the [Director][a] under subsection (1), that court may, on the application of any person interested in the

proceedings concerned or of its own motion, direct a relevant authority of the recognised stock exchange concerned to make such a report, and on a report being made accordingly, this section shall have effect as though the report had been made in pursuance of subsection (1).

[(4) If, where any matter is reported or referred to the Director under this section, he has reasonable grounds for believing that an offence under this Part has been committed and—

(a) institutes proceedings in respect of the offence, or

(b) refers the matter to the Director of Public Prosecutions and the Director of Public Prosecutions institutes proceedings in respect of the offence,

it shall be the duty of a relevant authority of the recognised stock exchange concerned, and of every officer of the company whose securities are concerned, and of any other person who appears to the Director or to the Director of Public Prosecutions, as the case may be, to have relevant information (other than any defendant in the proceedings) to give all assistance in connection with the proceedings which he or they are reasonably able to give.][b]

(5) If it appears to the [Director][c], arising from a complaint to a relevant authority of a recognised stock exchange concerning an alleged offence under this Part, that there are circumstances suggesting that—

(a) the relevant authority ought to use its powers under this Part but has not done so, or

(b) that a report ought to be made to the [Director][a] under subsection (1), but that the relevant authority concerned has not so reported,

he may direct the relevant authority to use such powers or make such a report, and on a report being made accordingly, this section shall have effect as though the report had been made in pursuance of subsection (1).

[…][d].

(7) A relevant authority of a recognised stock exchange shall not be liable in damages in respect of anything done or omitted to be done by the authority in connection with the exercise by it of its functions under this Part unless the act or omission complained of was done or omitted to be done in bad faith.

Amendments

Section repealed in the limited manner noted in IFCMPA 2005, s 31 with effect from 6 July 2005. See IFCMPA 2005, s 31 and notes thereto.

a CLEA 2001, s 37(a) amends CA 1990, s 115 by the substitution for 'Director of Public Prosecutions' wherever occurring, except in subsection (4) of 'Director'.

b CLEA 2001, s 37(b) substitutes CA 1990, s 115(4).

c CLEA 2001, s 37(c) amends CA 1990, s 115(5) by the substitution for 'Minister' of 'Director'.

d CLEA 2001, s 37(d) deletes CA 1990, s 115(6).

116 Co-operation with other authorities outside the State

(1) This section applies where a relevant authority of a recognised stock exchange receives a request for information from a similar authority in another Member State of the European Communities in relation to the exercise by the second-named authority of its functions under any enactment of the European Communities relating to unlawful dealing within the meaning of this Part, whether in the State or elsewhere.

(2) The relevant authority concerned shall, in so far as it is reasonably able to do so, and making use of its powers under this Part where appropriate, obtain the information requested and shall, subject to the following provisions of this section, provide such information accordingly.

(3) Where a relevant authority of a recognised stock exchange receives a request under subsection (1), it shall advise the [Director][a] who, on being satisfied as to any of the matters referred to in subsection (4), may direct the authority to refuse to provide all or part of the information requested.

(4) The matters referred to in subsection (3) are that—

- (a) communication of the information requested might adversely affect the sovereignty, security or public policy of the State;
- (b) civil or criminal proceedings in the State have already been commenced against a person in respect of any acts in relation to which a request for information has been received under subsection (1);
- (c) any person has been convicted in the State of a criminal offence in respect of any such acts.

Amendments

Section repealed in the limited manner noted in IFCMPA 2005, s 31 with effect from 6 July 2005. See IFCMPA 2005, s 31 and notes thereto.

a 'Director' substituted for 'Minister' by CLEA 2001, s 14 as enacted by the Company Law Enforcement Act 2001 (Commencement) (No 3) Order 2001 (SI 523/2001) on November 2001.

---

117 Authorised persons

(1) In this section and sections 118 and 121, 'authorised person' means a person approved by the [Director][a] to be an authorised person for the purposes of this Part being—

- (a) the manager, however described, of a recognised stock exchange, or
- (b) a person nominated by a relevant authority of a recognised stock exchange.

(2) Where an alleged offence under this Part is investigated by an authorised person, the relevant authorities of the recognised stock exchange concerned shall be under a general duty to ensure that potential conflicts of interest are avoided, as far as possible, on the part of any such authorised person.

(3) For the purpose of obtaining any information necessary for the exercise by a relevant authority of such exchange of the function referred to in section 115, an authorised person may, on production of his authorisation if so required, require any person whom

he or such relevant authority has reasonable cause to believe to have dealt in securities, or to have any information about such dealings, to give the authorised person any information which he may reasonably require in regard to—

(a) the securities concerned,

(b) the company which issued the securities,

(c) his dealings in such securities, or

(d) any other information the authorised person reasonably requires in relation to such securities or such dealings,

and give him such access to and facilities for inspecting and taking copies of any documents relating to the matter as he reasonably requires.

(4) Every document purporting to be a warrant or authorisation and to be signed or authenticated by or on behalf of a relevant authority shall be received in evidence and shall be deemed to be such warrant or authorisation without further proof until the contrary is shown.

(5) An authorised person, or any person on whom he has made a requirement under this section, may apply to the court for a declaration under this section.

(6) The court, having heard such evidence as may be adduced and any representations that may be made by the authorised person and a person referred to in subsection (5), may at its discretion declare—

(a) that the exigencies of the common good do not warrant the exercise by the authorised person of the powers conferred on him by this section, or

(b) that the exigencies of the common good do so warrant.

(7) Where the court makes a declaration under subsection (6)(a), the authorised person shall, as soon as may be, withdraw the relevant requirement under this section.

(8) Where the court makes a declaration under subsection (6)(b), the person on whom the requirement was imposed shall, as soon as may be, furnish the required information to the authorised person.

(9) Where, in contravention of subsection (8), a person refuses, or fails within a reasonable time, to comply with a requirement of an authorised person, the authorised person may certify the refusal under his hand to the court, and the court may, after hearing any statement which may be offered in defence, punish the offender in like manner as if he had been guilty of contempt of court.

Amendments

Section repealed in the limited manner noted in IFCMPA 2005, s 31 with effect from 6 July 2005. See IFCMPA 2005, s 31 and notes thereto.

a 'Director' substituted for 'Minister' by CLEA 2001, 14 as enacted by the Company Law Enforcement Act 2001 (Commencement) (No 3) Order 2001 (SI 523/2001) on November 2001.

---

118 Obligation of professional secrecy

(1) Information obtained by any of the following persons by virtue of the exercise by a recognised stock exchange of its functions under this Part shall not be disclosed except in accordance with law, namely—

(a) a relevant authority of the exchange,

(b) an authorised person, or

(c) any person employed or formerly employed by the exchange.

(2) Subsection (1) shall not prevent a relevant authority of a recognised stock exchange from disclosing any information to the [Director],[a] whether pursuant to a request under section 115 (5) or otherwise, or to a similar authority in another Member State of the European Communities.

[(2A) Subsection (1) shall not prevent a member, authorised person, relevant authority or employee or former employee of a recognised stock exchange from disclosing information concerning suspected breaches of the Companies Acts to the Director and it is the duty of each such person to so report any such suspected breach to the Director.][b]

(3) Any person who contravenes subsection (1) shall be guilty of an offence.

Amendments

Section repealed in the limited manner noted in IFCMPA 2005, s 31 with effect from 6 July 2005. See IFCMPA 2005, s 31 and notes thereto.

a 'Director' substituted for 'Minister' by CLEA 2001, 14 as enacted by the Company Law Enforcement Act 2001 (Commencement) (No 3) Order 2001 (SI 523/2001) on November 2001.

b CLEA 2001, s 38 inserts CA 1990, s 118(2A).

---

119 Extension of Council Directive 79/279/EEC

The provisions of Schedule C.5 (a) of Council Directive 79/279/EEC of 5 March 1979 co-ordinating the conditions for the admission of securities to official stock exchange listing, as given effect by the European Communities (Stock Exchange) Regulations, 1984 (S.I. No 282 of 1984), shall also apply to securities within the meaning of section 107.

Amendments

Section repealed in the limited manner noted in IFCMPA 2005, s 31 with effect from 6 July 2005. See IFCMPA 2005, s 31 and notes thereto.

---

120 Annual report of recognised stock exchange

(1) An annual report shall be presented to the Minister on behalf of every recognised stock exchange on the exercise of the functions of the relevant authorities of the exchange concerned under this Part and, in particular, the report shall include—

(a) the number of written complaints received concerning possible contraventions of this Part,

(b) the number of reports made to the Director of Public Prosecutions under this Part,

(c) the number of instances in which, following the exercise of powers by authorised persons under this Part, reports were not made to the Director of Public Prosecutions, and

(d) such other information as may be prescribed.

(2) A copy of the report referred to in subsection (1) shall, subject to subsection (3), be laid before each House of the Oireachtas.

(3) If the Minister, after consultation with a relevant authority of the recognised stock exchange concerned, is of the opinion that the disclosure of any information contained in the report referred to in subsection (1) would materially injure or unfairly prejudice the legitimate interests of any person, or that otherwise there is good reason for not divulging any part of such a report, he may lay the report under subsection (2) with that information or that part omitted.

Amendments

Section repealed in the limited manner noted in IFCMPA 2005, s 31 with effect from 6 July 2005. See IFCMPA 2005, s 31 and notes thereto.

---

121 Power of Minister to make supplementary regulations

(1) If, in any respect, any difficulty arises in bringing any provision of this Part into operation or in relation to the operation of any such provision, the Minister may by regulations do anything which appears to him to be necessary or expedient for removing that difficulty, for bringing the provision into operation, or for securing or facilitating its operation, and any such regulations may modify any provision of this Part so far as may be necessary or expedient for carrying such provision into effect for the purposes aforesaid.

(2) Without prejudice to the generality of subsection (1), where the Minister considers it necessary or expedient to do so for the proper and effective administration of sections 115 and 117, he may make such regulations as he thinks appropriate in relation to—

(a) the powers of authorised persons, or

(b) the matters in respect of which, or the persons from whom, authorised persons may require information under this Part.

(3) Every regulation made by the Minister under this section shall be laid before each House of the Oireachtas as soon as may be after it is made and, if a resolution annulling the regulation is passed by either House within the next 21 days on which that House has sat after the regulation is laid before it, the regulation shall be annulled accordingly, but without prejudice to the validity of anything previously done thereunder.

Amendments

Section repealed in the limited manner noted in IFCMPA 2005, s 31 with effect from 6 July 2005. See IFCMPA 2005, s 31 and notes thereto.

PART VI
WINDING UP AND RELATED MATTERS

Registration of charges

122 Amendment of section 99 of the Principal Act

[...][a]

[...][b]

Amendments

a This sub-s substitutes CA 1963, s 99(2)(h).

b This sub-s inserts CA 1963, s 99(2A), (2B) & (2C).

Winding up by the court

123 Amendment of sections 214 and 345 of Principal Act

[...][a]

Amendments

a This section substitutes '£1,000' for '£50' in CA 1963, s 214(a) & s 345(a).

124 Amendment of section 231 of the Principal Act

[...][a]

Amendments

a This section inserts CA 1963, s 231(1A).

125 No lien over company's books, records etc

[...][a]

Amendments

a This section inserts CA 1963, s 244A.

126 Power of court to summon persons for examination

[...][a]

Amendments

a This section substitutes CA 1963, s 245.

127 Order for payment or delivery of property against person examined under section 245 of Principal Act

[...][a]

Amendments

a This section inserts CA 1963, s 245A.

Declaration of solvency

128 Statutory declaration of solvency in case of proposal to wind up voluntarily

[...][a]

Amendments

a This section substitutes CA 1963, s 256.

Provisions applicable to a members' voluntary winding up

129 Duty of liquidator to call creditors' meeting if he is of opinion that company is unable to pay its debts

[...][a]

Amendments

a This section substitutes CA 1963, s 261.

Provisions applicable to a Creditors' Voluntary Winding Up

130 Amendment of section 266 of the Principal Act

[...][a]

Amendments

a This section inserts ', at least ten days before the date of the meeting,' after 'advertised' in CA 1963, s 266(2).

---

131 Creditors' voluntary winding up

(1) This section applies where, in the case of a creditors' voluntary winding up, a liquidator has been nominated by the company.

(2) The powers conferred on the liquidator by section 276 of the Principal Act shall not be exercised, except with sanction of the court, during the period before the holding of the creditors' meeting under section 266 of that Act.

(3) Subsection (2) does not apply in relation to the power of the liquidator—

(a) to take into his custody or under his control all the property to which the company is or appears to be entitled;

(b) to dispose of perishable goods and other goods the value of which is likely to diminish if they are not immediately disposed of;

(c) to do all such other things as may be necessary for the protection of the company's assets.

(4) The liquidator shall attend the creditors' meeting held under section 266 of the Principal Act and shall report to the meeting on any exercise by him of his powers (whether or not under this section or under section 276 or 280 of that Act).

(5) If default is made—

(a) by the company in complying with subsection (1) or (2) of section 266 of the Principal Act, or

(b) by the directors in complying with subsection (3) of the said section,

the liquidator shall, within 7 days of the relevant day, apply to the court for directions as to the manner in which that default is to be remedied.

(6) 'The relevant day' means the day on which the liquidator was nominated by the company or the day on which he first became aware of the default, whichever is the later.

(7) If a liquidator without reasonable excuse fails to comply with this section, he shall be guilty of an offence.

Provisions applicable to every voluntary winding up

132 Amendment of section 275 of the Principal Act

[...][a]

Amendments

a This section substitutes CA 1963, s 275.

---

133 Consent to appointment as liquidator and notification of appointment

[...][a]

Amendments

a This section inserts CA 1963, s 276A.

Provisions applicable to every winding up

134 Preferential payments in a winding up

[...][a]

Amendments

a This section inserts CA 1963, s 285(14).

---

135 Fraudulent preference

[...][a]

Amendments

a This section substitutes CA 1963, s 286.

136 Circumstances in which floating charge is invalid

[...][a]

Amendments

a This section substitutes CA 1963, s 288.

137 Criminal liability of persons concerned for fraudulent trading of company

[...][a]

Amendments

a This section substitutes CA 1963, s 297.

138 Civil liability of persons concerned for fraudulent or reckless trading of company

[...][a]

Amendments

a This section inserts CA 1963, s 297A.

139 Power of the court to order the return of assets which have been improperly transferred

(1) Where, on the application of a liquidator, creditor or contributory of a company which is being wound up, it can be shown to the satisfaction of the court that—

(a) any property of the company of any kind whatsoever was disposed of either by way of conveyance, transfer, mortgage, security, loan, or in any way whatsoever whether by act or omission, direct or indirect, and

(b) the effect of such disposal was to perpetrate a fraud on the company, its creditors or members,

the court may, if it deems it just and equitable to do so, order any person who appears to have the use, control or possession of such property or the proceeds of the sale or development thereof to deliver it or pay a sum in respect of it to the liquidator on such terms or conditions as the court sees fit.

(2) Subsection (1) shall not apply to any conveyance, mortgage, delivery of goods, payment, execution or other act relating to property made or done by or against a company to which section 286 (1) of the Principal Act applies.

(3) In deciding whether it is just and equitable to make an order under this section, the court shall have regard to the rights of persons who have bona fide and for value acquired an interest in the property the subject of the application.

140 Company may be required to contribute to debts of related companies

(1) On the application of the liquidator or any creditor or contributory of any company that is being wound up, the court, if it is satisfied that it is just and equitable to do so, may order that any company that is or has been related to the company being wound up shall pay to the liquidator of that company an amount equivalent to the whole or part of all or any of the debts provable in that winding up. Any order under this section may be made on such terms and conditions as the court thinks fit.

(2) In deciding whether it is just and equitable to make an order under subsection (1) the court shall have regard to the following matters—

(a) the extent to which the related company took part in the management of the company being wound up;

(b) the conduct of the related company towards the creditors of the company being wound up;

(c) the effect which such order would be likely to have on the creditors of the related company concerned.

(3) No order shall be made under subsection (1) unless the court is satisfied that the circumstances that gave rise to the winding up of the company are attributable to the actions or omissions of the related company.

(4) Notwithstanding any other provision, it shall not be just and equitable to make an order under subsection (1) if the only ground for making the order is—

(a) the fact that a company is related to another company, or

(b) that creditors of the company being wound up have relied on the fact that another company is or has been related to the first mentioned company.

(5) For the purposes of this Act, a company is related to another company if—

(a) that other company is its holding company or subsidiary; or

(b) more than half in nominal value of its equity share capital (as defined in section 155(5) of the Principal Act) is held by the other company and companies related to that other company (whether directly or indirectly, but other than in a fiduciary capacity); or

(c) more than half in nominal value of the equity share capital (as defined in section 155(5) of the Principal Act) of each of them is held by members of the other (whether directly or indirectly, but other than in a fiduciary capacity); or

(d) that other company or a company or companies related to that other company or that other company together with a company or companies related to it are entitled to exercise or control the exercise of more than one half of the voting power at any general meeting of the company; or

(e) the businesses of the companies have been so carried on that the separate business of each company, or a substantial part thereof, is not readily identifiable; or

(f) there is another company to which both companies are related;

and 'related company' has a corresponding meaning.

(6) For the purposes of this section 'company' includes any body which is liable to be wound up under the Companies Acts and 'creditor' means one or more creditors to whom the company being wound up is indebted by more, in aggregate, than [€12,697.38].[a]

(7) Where an application for an order under subsection (1) seeks to require a licensed bank, within the meaning of section 25, to contribute to the debts of a related company, a copy of every such application shall be sent by the applicant to the Central Bank who shall be entitled to be heard by the court before an order is made.

Amendments

a £10,000 converted to €12,697.38 by Council Regulations (EC) No 1103/97, No 974/98 and No 2866/98 and the Economic and Monetary Union Act 1998, s 6.

---

141 Pooling of assets of related companies

(1) Where two or more related companies are being wound up and the court, on the application of the liquidator of any of the companies, is satisfied that it is just and equitable to make an order under this section, the court may order that, subject to such terms and conditions as the court may impose and to the extent that the court orders, the companies shall be wound up together as if they were one company, and, subject to the provisions of this section, the order shall have effect and all the provisions of this Part and Part VI of the Principal Act shall apply accordingly.

(2) In deciding the terms and conditions of an order under this section the court shall have particular regard to the interests of those persons who are members of some, but not all, of the companies.

(3) Where the court makes an order under subsection (1) —

(a) the court may remove any liquidator of any of the companies, and appoint any person to act as liquidator of any one or more of the companies;

(b) the court may give such directions as it thinks fit for the purpose of giving effect to the order;

(c) nothing in this section or the order shall affect the rights of any secured creditor of any of the companies;

(d) debts of a company that are to be paid in priority to all other debts of the company pursuant to section 285 of the Principal Act shall, to the extent that they are not paid out of the assets of that company, be subject to the claims of holders of debentures under any floating charge (as defined in that section) created by any of the other companies;

(e) unless the court otherwise orders, the claims of all unsecured creditors of the companies shall rank equally among themselves.

(4) In deciding whether it is just and equitable to make an order under subsection (1) the court shall have regard to the following matters—

(a) the extent to which any of the companies took part in the management of any of the other companies;

(b) the conduct of any of the companies towards the creditors of any of the other companies;

(c) the extent to which the circumstances that gave rise to the winding up of any of the companies are attributable to the actions or omissions of any of the other companies;

(d) the extent to which the businesses of the companies have been intermingled.

(5) Notwithstanding any other provision, it shall not be just and equitable to make an order under subsection (1) if the only ground for making the order is—

(a) the fact that a company is related to another company, or

(b) that creditors of a company being wound up have relied on the fact that another company is or has been related to the first mentioned company.

(6) Notice of an application to the court for the purposes of this section shall be served on every company specified in the application, and on such other persons as the court may direct, not later than the end of the eighth day before the day the application is heard.

142 Amendment of section 298 of the Principal Act

[...][a]

Amendments

a This section substitutes CA 1963, s 298.

---

143 Amendment of section 299 of the Principal Act

[...][a]

Amendments

a This section substitutes CA 1963, s 299(1).

---

144 Duty of liquidators and receivers to include certain information in returns etc

(1) Where a receiver or liquidator of a company is obliged by the Companies Acts to make a periodic account, abstract, statement or return in relation to his activities as receiver or liquidator he shall incorporate in such account, abstract, statement or return a report as to whether, at the date of such account, abstract, statement or return any past or present director or other officer, or any member, of the company is a person—

(a) in respect of whom a declaration has been made under any provision of the Companies Acts that he should be personally liable for all or any part of the debts of a company,

(b) who is, or is deemed to be, subject to a disqualification order under Part VII.

(2) A receiver or liquidator who contravenes subsection (1) shall be guilty of an offence and liable to a fine.

145 Penalty for default of receiver or liquidator in making certain accounts and returns

(1) Where a receiver or liquidator is in default in relation to the making or filing of a periodic account, abstract, statement or return in pursuance of any provision of the Companies Acts he shall be guilty of an offence and liable—

(a) on summary conviction to a [class C fine][a] and, for continued contravention, to a daily default [class E fine][b];

(b) on conviction on indictment to a fine not exceeding [€22,220.42][c] and, for continued contravention, to a daily default fine not exceeding [€555.50].[d]

(2) A person convicted of an offence under any of the following provisions, namely section 262, 272, 306, 319 (2) or 321 of the Principal Act, shall, in lieu of the penalty provided in any such section (as increased by section 15 of the Companies (Amendment) Act, 1982), be liable to the penalties specified in subsection (1).

Amendments

a ‘£1,000’ in subsection (1)(a) increased to ‘£1,500’ by CA 1990, s 240(7) as inserted by CLEA 2001, s 104 and converted to €1,904.61 by Council Regulations (EC) No 1103/97, No 974/98 and No 2866/98 and the Economic and Monetary Union Act 1998, s 6; the above being implicitly substituted, by Fines Act 2010, s 6, for a fine not exceeding the aforesaid amount. A class C fine currently means a fine not exceeding €2,500.

b ‘£50’ in subsection (1)(a) converted to €63.49 by Council Regulations (EC) No 1103/97, No 974/98 and No 2866/98 and the Economic and Monetary Union Act 1998, s 6; as implicitly substituted, by Fines Act 2010, s 8, for a fine not exceeding the aforesaid amount. A class E fine currently means a fine not exceeding €500.

c ‘£10,000’ in subsection (1)(b) converted to €12,697.38 by Council Regulations (EC) No 1103/97, No 974/98 and No 2866/98 and the Economic and Monetary Union Act 1998, s 6, and multiplied by a multiplier of 1.75 pursuant to Fines Act 2010, s 9.

d ‘£250’ in subsection (1)(b) converted to €317.44 by Council Regulations (EC) No 1103/97, No 974/98 and No 2866/98 and the Economic and Monetary Union Act 1998, s 6, and multiplied by a multiplier of 1.75 pursuant to Fines Act 2010, s 9.

Supplementary provisions

146 Disqualification for appointment as liquidator

[...][a]

Amendments

a This section inserts CA 1963, s 300A.

147 Disclosure of interest by creditors etc. at creditors’ meetings

[...][a]

Amendments

a This section inserts CA 1963, s 301A.

148 Extension of power of court to assess damages against directors

(1) Subsection (2) applies if in the course of winding up a company which is a subsidiary of another company, it appears that any director of the subsidiary's holding company has misapplied or retained or become liable or accountable for any money or property of the subsidiary, or has been guilty of any misfeasance or other breach of duty or trust in relation to the subsidiary.

(2) The court may, on the application of the liquidator, any creditor or contributory of the subsidiary, examine into the conduct of the director concerned and compel him—

(a) to repay or restore the money or property or any part thereof respectively with interest at such rate as the court thinks just, or

(b) to contribute such sum to the assets of the subsidiary by way of compensation in respect of the misapplication, retainer, misfeasance or other breach of duty or trust as the court thinks just.

PART VII
DISQUALIFICATIONS AND RESTRICTIONS: DIRECTORS AND OTHER OFFICERS

Chapter 1
Restriction on Directors of Insolvent Companies

149 Application of Chapter I

(1) This Chapter applies to any company if—

(a) at the date of the commencement of its winding-up it is proved to the court, or

(b) at any time during the course of its winding-up the liquidator of the company certifies, or it is otherwise proved, to the court,

that it is unable to pay its debts (within the meaning of section 214 of the Principal Act).

(2) This Chapter applies to any person who was a director of a company to which this section applies at the date of, or within 12 months prior to, the commencement of its winding-up.

(3) This Chapter shall not apply to a company which commences to be wound up before the commencement of this section.

(4) In this Chapter 'company' includes a company to which section 351 of the Principal Act applies.

(5) This Chapter applies to shadow directors as it applies to directors.

150 Restriction

(1) The court shall, unless it is satisfied as to any of the matters specified in subsection (2), declare that a person to whom this Chapter applies shall not, for a period of five years, be appointed or act in any way, whether directly or indirectly, as a director or secretary or be concerned or take part in the promotion or formation of any company unless it meets the requirements set out in subsection (3); and, in subsequent provisions

of this Part, the expression 'a person to whom section 150 applies' shall be construed as a reference to a person in respect of whom such a declaration has been made.

(2) The matters referred to in subsection (1) are—

- (a) that the person concerned has acted honestly and responsibly in relation to the conduct of the affairs of the company and that there is no other reason why it would be just and equitable that he should be subject to the restrictions imposed by this section, or
- (b) subject to paragraph (a), that the person concerned was a director of the company solely by reason of his nomination as such by a financial institution in connection with the giving of credit facilities to the company by such institution, provided that the institution in question has not obtained from any director of the company a personal or individual guarantee of repayment to it of the loans or other forms of credit advanced to the company, or
- (c) subject to paragraph (a), that the person concerned was a director of the company solely by reason of his nomination as such by a venture capital company in connection with the purchase of, or subscription for, shares by it in the first-mentioned company.

(3) The requirements specified in subsection (1) are that—

- (a) the nominal value of the allotted share capital of the company shall—
  - (i) in the case of a public limited company, be at least [€317,434.52],[a]
  - (ii) in the case of any other company, be at least [€63,486.90],[b]
- (b) each allotted share to an aggregate amount not less than the amount referred to in subparagraph (i) or (ii) of paragraph (a), as the case may be, shall be fully paid up, including the whole of any premium thereon, and
- (c) each such allotted share and the whole of any premium thereon shall be paid for in cash.

(4) Where a court makes a declaration under subsection (1), a prescribed officer of the court shall cause the registrar of companies to be furnished with prescribed particulars of the declaration in such form and manner as may be prescribed.

[(4A) An application for a declaration under subsection (1) may be made to the court by the Director, a liquidator or a receiver.][c]

[(4B) The court, on the hearing of an application for a declaration under subsection (1) by the Director, a liquidator or a receiver (in this subsection referred to as 'the applicant'), may order that the directors against whom the declaration is made shall bear—

- (a) the costs of the application, and
- (b) the whole (or such portion of them as the court specifies) of the costs and expenses incurred by the applicant—
  - (i) in investigating the matters the subject of the application, and
  - (ii) in so far as they do not fall within paragraph (a), in collecting evidence in respect of those matters,

  including so much of the remuneration and expenses of the applicant as are attributable to such investigation and collection.][d]

(5) In this section—

'financial institution' means—

(a) a licensed bank, within the meaning of section 25, or

(b) a company the ordinary business of which includes the making of loans or the giving of guarantees in connection with loans, and

'venture capital company' means a company prescribed by the Minister the principal ordinary business of which is the making of share investments.

Amendments

a CLEA 2001, s 41(1)(a) amends CA 1990, s 150(3)(a)(i) by the substitution for '£100,000' of '£250,000'. £250,000 was converted to €317,434.52 by Council Regulations (EC) No 1103/97, No 974/98 and No 2866/98 and the Economic and Monetary Union Act 1998, s 6.

b CLEA 2001, s 41(1)(b) amends CA 1990, s 150(3)(a)(ii) by the substitution for '£20,000' of '£50,000'. £50,000 was converted to €63,486.90 by Council Regulations (EC) No 1103/97, No 974/98 and No 2866/98 and the Economic and Monetary Union Act 1998, s 6.

c CLEA 2001, s 41(1)(c) inserts CA 1990, s 150(4A).

d CLEA 2001, s 41(c) inserts sub-s (4B) which was substituted with effect from 29 January 2007 by IFCMPA 2006, s 11(1).

---

151 Duty of liquidator under this Chapter

(1) Where it appears to the liquidator of a company to which under this Chapter applies that the interests of any other company or its creditors may be placed in jeopardy by the relevant matters referred to in subsection (2) the liquidator shall inform the court of his opinion forthwith and the court may, on receipt of such report, make whatever order it sees fit.

(2) The relevant matters are that a person to whom section 150 applies is appointed or is acting in any way, whether directly or indirectly, as a director or is concerned or is taking part in the promotion or formation of such other company as is referred to in subsection (1).

(3) Any liquidator who contravenes subsection (1) shall be guilty of an offence and shall be liable—

(a) on summary conviction, to a [class C fine][a] and, for continued contravention, to a daily default [class E fine][b], or

(b) on conviction on indictment, to a fine not exceeding [€22,220.42][c] and, for continued contravention, to a daily default fine not exceeding [€555.50][d].

Amendments

a '£1,000' in subsection (3)(a) increased to '£1,500' by CA 1990, s 240(7) as inserted by CLEA 2001, s 104 and converted to €1,904.61 by Council Regulations (EC) No 1103/97, No 974/98 and No 2866/98 and the Economic and Monetary Union Act 1998, s 6; the above being implicitly substituted, by Fines Act 2010, s 6, for a fine not exceeding the aforesaid amount. A class C fine currently means a fine not exceeding €2,500.

b '£50' in subsection (3)(a) converted to €63.49 by Council Regulations (EC) No 1103/97, No 974/98 and No 2866/98 and the Economic and Monetary Union Act 1998, s 6; as implicitly substituted, by Fines Act 2010, s 8, for a fine not exceeding the aforesaid amount. A class E fine currently means a fine not exceeding €500.

c '£10,000' in subsection (3)(b) converted to €12,697.38 by Council Regulations (EC) No 1103/97, No 974/98 and No 2866/98 and the Economic and Monetary Union Act 1998, s 6, and multiplied by a multiplier of 1.75 pursuant to Fines Act 2010, s 9.

d '£250' in subsection 3(b) converted to €317.44 by Council Regulations (EC) No 1103/97, No 974/98 and No 2866/98 and the Economic and Monetary Union Act 1998, s 6, and multiplied by a multiplier of 1.75 pursuant to Fines Act 2010, s 9.

---

152 Relief

(1) A person to whom section 150 applies may, within not more than one year after a declaration has been made in respect of him under that section, apply to the court for relief, either in whole or in part, from the restrictions referred to in that section or from any order made in relation to him under section 151 and the court may, if it deems it just and equitable to do so, grant such relief on whatever terms and conditions it sees fit.

(2) Where it is intended to make an application for relief under subsection (1) the applicant shall give not less than 14 days' notice of his intention to the liquidator (if any) of the company the insolvency of which caused him to be subject to this Chapter.

(3) On receipt of a notice under subsection (2), the liquidator shall forthwith notify such creditors and contributories of the company as have been notified to him or become known to him, that he has received such notice.

(4) On the hearing of an application under this section the liquidator or any creditor or contributory of the company, the insolvency of which caused the applicant to be subject to this Chapter may appear and give evidence.

(5) Any liquidator who contravenes subsection (3) shall be guilty of an offence and liable to a fine.

153 Register of restricted persons

(1) The registrar shall, subject to the provisions of this section, keep a register of the particulars which have been notified to him under section 150, and the following provisions of this section shall apply to the keeping of such a register.

(2) Where the court grants partial relief to a person under section 152 a prescribed officer of the court shall cause the registrar to be furnished with prescribed particulars of the relief, and the registrar shall, as soon as may be, enter the particulars on the register referred to in subsection (1).

(3) Where the court grants full relief to a person under section 152 a prescribed officer of the court shall cause the registrar to be so notified, and the registrar shall, as soon as may be, remove the particulars of any such person from the register referred to in subsection (1).

(4) The registrar shall also remove from the register any particulars in relation to a person on the expiry of five years from the date of the declaration to which the original notification under section 150 relates.

(5) Nothing in this section shall prevent the registrar from keeping the register required by this section as part of any other system of classification, whether pursuant to section 247 or otherwise.

154 Application of this Chapter to receivers

Where a receiver of the property of a company is appointed, the provisions of this Chapter shall, with the necessary modifications, apply as if the references therein to the liquidator and to winding up were construed as references to the receiver and to receivership.

155 Restrictions on company to which section 150 (3) applies

(1) This section applies to any company in relation to which a person who is the subject of a declaration under section 150 is appointed or acts in any way, whether directly or indirectly, as a director or secretary or is concerned in or takes part in the promotion or formation of that company.

(2) Subsections (2) to (11) of section 60 of the Principal Act shall not apply to any company to which this section applies.

(3) Sections 32 to 36 of the Companies (Amendment) Act, 1983, shall, with the necessary modifications, apply to any company to which this section applies as if the company were a public limited company so, however, that for the purposes of this subsection those sections shall apply as if—

- (a) in subsection (1) of section 32 the words 'during the initial period' were deleted;
- (b) any other reference in any of those sections to 'initial period' were deleted; and
- (c) in subsection (2) of section 32 the words 'relevant person' were defined to mean 'any subscriber to the memorandum, any director or any person involved in the promotion or formation of the company'.

(4) Without prejudice to section 39, sections 32 and 37 shall not apply to any company to which subsection (1) applies.

(5) From the date of a declaration under section 150 a person in respect of whom the declaration was made shall not accept appointment to a position or act in any manner mentioned in subsection (1) of this section in relation to a company unless he has, within the 14 days immediately preceding such appointment or so acting, sent to the registered office of the company a notification that he is a person to whom section 150 applies.

156 Requirements as to share allotted by a company to which section 155 applies

(1) Where a company to which section 155 applies allots a share which is not fully paid up as required by section 150(3)(b) the share shall be treated as if its nominal value together with the whole of any premium had been received, but the allottee shall be liable to pay the company in cash the full amount which should have been received in respect of the share under that subsection less the value of any consideration actually applied in payment up (to any extent) of the share and any premium on it, and interest at the appropriate rate on the amount payable under this subsection.

(2) Where a company to which section 155 applies allots a share which is not fully paid for in cash as required by section 150(3)(c) the allottee of the share shall be liable to pay the company in cash an amount equal to its nominal value, together with the whole of any premium, and shall be liable to pay interest at the appropriate rate on the amount payable under this subsection.

(3) Subsection (1) shall not apply in relation to the allotment of a bonus share which is not fully paid up as required by section 150(3)(b) unless the allottee knew or ought to have known that the share was so allotted.

(4) Subsection (1) does not apply to shares allotted in pursuance of an employees' share scheme within the meaning of section 2 of the Companies (Amendment) Act, 1983.

(5) In this section, 'appropriate rate' has the meaning assigned to it by section 2 of the Companies (Amendment) Act, 1983.

(6) Section 26(4) of the Companies (Amendment) Act, 1983, shall apply for the purposes of this section as it applies for the purposes of that section.

157 Relief for a company in respect of prohibited transactions

(1) The court may, if it deems it just and equitable to do so, grant relief to a company to which section 155 applies in respect of any act or omission which, by virtue of that section, contravened a provision of the Companies Acts or to any person adversely affected thereby, on whatever terms and conditions the court sees fit, including exemption from any such provision.

(2) Relief shall not be granted to the company where the person referred to in section 155 (1) complied with subsection (5) of that section.

158 Power to vary amounts mentioned in section 150(3)

The Minister may, by order, vary the amounts mentioned in section 150 (3)(a) and the order may—

(a) require any company to which that section applies having an allotted share capital of which the nominal value is less than the amount specified in the order to increase the value to not less than that amount;

(b) make, in connection with any such requirement provision for any of the matters for which provision is made in the Companies Acts in relation to a company's registration, Re-registration, change of name, winding-up or dissolution, payment for any share comprised in a company's capital and offers of shares in or debentures of a company to the public, including provision as to the consequences (whether in criminal law or otherwise) of a failure to comply with any requirement of the order, and

(c) contain such supplemental and transitional provisions as the Minister thinks appropriate, specify different amounts in relation to companies of different classes or descriptions and, in particular, provide for any provision of the order to come into operation on different days for different purposes.

Chapter 2
Disqualification generally

159 Interpretation of Chapters 2 and 3

In this Chapter and Chapter 3, except where the context otherwise requires—

'company' includes every company and every body, whether corporate or unincorporated, which may be wound up under Part X of the Principal Act and, without prejudice to the generality of the foregoing, includes a friendly society within the meaning of the Friendly Societies Acts, 1896 to 1977;

'the court' means the High Court except in relation to a disqualification order made by a court of its own motion under section 160(2), paragraph (a), (b), (c), (d) or (f), in which case it includes any court;

'default order' means an order made against any person under section 371 of the Principal Act by virtue of any contravention of or failure to comply with any relevant requirement (whether on his own part or on the part of any company);

'disqualification order' means—

(a) an order under this Part that the person against whom the order is made shall not be appointed or act as an auditor, director or other officer, receiver, liquidator or examiner or be in any way, whether directly or indirectly, concerned or take part in the promotion, formation or management of any company, or any society registered under the Industrial and Provident Societies Acts, 1893 to 1978, or

(b) an order under section 184 of the Principal Act;

'officer' in relation to any company, includes any director, shadow director or secretary of the company;

'relevant requirement' means any provision of the Companies Acts (including a provision repealed by this Act) which requires or required any return, account or other document to be filed with, delivered or sent to, or notice of any matter to be given to, the registrar of companies.

160 Disqualification of certain persons from acting as directors or auditors of or managing companies

(1) Where a person is convicted on indictment of any indictable offence in relation to a company, or involving fraud or dishonesty, then during the period of five years from the date of conviction or such other period as the court, on the application of the prosecutor and having regard to all the circumstances of the case, may order—

(a) he shall not be appointed or act as an auditor, director or other officer, receiver, liquidator or examiner or be in any way, whether directly or indirectly, concerned or take part in the promotion, formation or management of any company or any society registered under the Industrial and Provident Societies Acts, 1893 to 1978;

(b) he shall be deemed, for the purposes of this Act, to be subject to a disqualification order for that period.

[(1A) Without prejudice to subsection (1), a person who—

(a) fails to comply with section 3A(1) of the Companies (Amendment) Act, 1982, or section 195(8) of the Principal Act, or

(b) in purported compliance with the said section 3A(1) or 195(8), permits the first-mentioned statement in the said section 3A(1) or, as the case may be, the first-mentioned notification in the said section 195(8) to be accompanied by a statement signed by him which is false or misleading in a material respect,

shall, upon the delivery to the registrar of companies of the said first-mentioned statement or notification or, as the case may be, the said statement or notification accompanied by a statement as aforesaid, be deemed, for the purposes of this Act, to be subject to a disqualification order for the period referred to in subsection (1B).

(1B) The period mentioned in subsection (1A) is—

(a) so much as remains unexpired, at the date of the delivery mentioned in that subsection, of the period for which the person concerned is disqualified under the law of the other state referred to in section 3A(1) of the Companies (Amendment) Act, 1982, or section 195(8) of the Principal Act from being appointed or acting in the manner described therein, or

(b) if the person concerned is so disqualified under the law of more than one other such state and the portions of the respective periods for which he is so disqualified that remain unexpired at the date of that delivery are not equal, whichever of those unexpired portions is the greatest.][a]

(2) Where the court is satisfied in any proceedings or as a result of an application under this section that—

(a) a person has been guilty, while a promoter, officer, auditor, receiver, liquidator or examiner of a company, of any fraud in relation to the company, its members or creditors; or

(b) a person has been guilty, while a promoter, officer, auditor, receiver, liquidator or examiner of a company, of any breach of his duty as such promoter, officer, auditor, receiver, liquidator or examiner; or

(c) a declaration has been granted under section 297A of the Principal Act (inserted by section 138 of this Act) in respect of a person; or

(d) the conduct of any person as promoter, officer, auditor, receiver, liquidator or examiner of a company, makes him unfit to be concerned in the management of a company; or

(e) in consequence of a report of inspectors appointed by the court or the [Director][b] under the Companies Acts, the conduct of any person makes him unfit to be concerned in the management of a company; or

(f) a person has been persistently in default in relation to the relevant [requirements; or][c]

[(g) a person has been guilty of 2 or more offences under section 202(10); or

(h) a person was a director of a company at the time of the sending, after the commencement of section 42 of the Company Law Enforcement Act, 2001, of a letter under subsection (1) of section 12 of the Companies (Amendment) Act, 1982, to the company and the name of which, following the taking of the other steps under that section consequent on the sending of that letter, was struck off the register under subsection (3) of that section;

[(hh) a person has contravened section 4 or 5 of the Competition Act 2002 or Article 101 or 102 of the Treaty on the Functioning of the European Union; or][d]

(i) a person is disqualified under the law of another state (whether pursuant to an order of a judge or a tribunal or otherwise) from being appointed or acting as a director or secretary of a body corporate or an undertaking and the court is satisfied that, if the conduct of the person or the circumstances otherwise affecting him that gave rise to the said order being made against him had occurred or arisen in the State, it would have been proper to make a disqualification order otherwise under this subsection against him;][e]

the court may, of its own motion, or as a result of the application, make a disqualification order against such a person for such period as it sees fit.

(3) (a) For the purposes of subsection (2)(f) the fact that a person has been persistently in default in relation to the relevant requirements may (without prejudice to its proof in any other manner) be conclusively proved by showing that in the five years ending with the date of the application he has been adjudged guilty (whether or not on the same occasion) of three or more defaults in relation to those requirements.

(b) A person shall be treated as being adjudged guilty of a default in relation to a relevant requirement for the purposes of this subsection if he is convicted of any offence consisting of a contravention of a relevant requirement or a default order is made against him.

[(3A) The court shall not make a disqualification order under paragraph (h) of subsection (2) against a person who shows to the court that the company referred to in that paragraph had no liabilities (whether actual, contingent or prospective) at the time its name was struck off the register or that any such liabilities that existed at that time were discharged before the date of the making of the application for the disqualification order.

(3B) A disqualification order under paragraph (i) of subsection (2) may be made against a person notwithstanding that, at the time of the making of the order, the person is deemed, by virtue of subsection (1A), to be subject to a disqualification order for the purposes of this Act, and where a disqualification order under the said paragraph (i) is made, the period of disqualification specified in it shall be expressed to begin on the expiry of the period of disqualification referred to in subsection (1B) to which the person, by virtue of subsection (1A), is subject or the said period of disqualification as varied, if such be the case, under subsection (8).][f]

(4) An application under paragraph (a), (b), (c) or (d) of subsection (2) may be made by—

(a) the Director of Public Prosecutions; or

(b) any member, contributory, officer, employee, receiver, liquidator, examiner or creditor of any company in relation to which the person who is the subject of the application—

(i) has been or is acting or is proposing to or being proposed to act as officer, auditor, receiver, liquidator or examiner, or

(ii) has been or is concerned or taking part, or is proposing to be concerned or take part, in the promotion, formation or management of any company,

and where the application is made by a member, contributory, employee or creditor of the company, the court may require security for all or some of the costs of the application.

(5) An application under [paragraph (e) or g][g] of subsection (2) may be made by the Director of Public Prosecutions.

(6) An application under paragraph (f) of subsection (2) may be made by—

(a) the Director of Public Prosecutions; or

(b) the registrar of companies.

[(6A) In addition to the persons who in pursuance of subsections (4), (5) and (6) may make such an application, an application under subsection (2)(a), (b), (c), (d), (e), (f), (g), (h) or (i) may be made by the Director.][h]

[(6B) An application to which paragraph (hh) of subsection (2) applies may be made by the competent authority (within the meaning of the Competition Act 2002).][i]

(7) Where it is intended to make an application under subsection (2) in respect of any person, the applicant shall give not less than ten days' notice of his intention to that person.

(8) Any person who is subject or deemed subject to a disqualification order by virtue of this Part may apply to the court for relief, either in whole or in part, from that disqualification and the court may, if it deems it just and equitable to do so, grant such relief on whatever terms and conditions it sees fit.

(9) A disqualification order may be made on grounds which are or include matters other than criminal convictions notwithstanding that the person in respect of whom the order is to be made may be criminally liable in respect of those matters.

[(9A) In considering the penalty to be imposed under this section, the court may as an alternative, where it adjudges that disqualification is not justified, make a declaration under section 150.][j]

[(9B) The court, on the hearing of an application for a disqualification order under subsection (2), may order that the persons disqualified or against whom a declaration under section 150 is made as a result of the application shall bear—

(a) the costs of the application, and

(b) in the case of an application by the Director, the Director of Public Prosecutions, a liquidator, a receiver or an examiner (in this paragraph referred to as 'the applicant'), in addition to the costs referred to in paragraph (a), the whole (or such portion of them as the court specifies) of the costs and expenses incurred by the applicant—

(i) in investigating the matters the subject of the application, and

(ii) in so far as they do not fall within paragraph (a), in collecting evidence in respect of those matters,

including so much of the remuneration and expenses of the applicant as are attributable to such investigation and collection.][k]

(10) A reference in any other enactment to section 184 of the Principal Act shall be construed as including a reference to this section.

Amendments

a CLEA 2001, s 42(a) inserts CA 1990, s 160(1A) and (1B).

b 'Director' substituted for 'Minister' by CLEA 2001, s 14.

c CLEA 2001, s 42(b)(i) amends CA 1990, s 160(2)(f) by the substitution for 'requirements' of 'requirements; or'.

d C(A)A 2012, s 9(a) inserts CA 1990, s 160(2)(hh).

e CLEA 2001, s 42(b)(ii) inserts CA 1990, s 160(2)(g), (h) and (i).

f CLEA 2001, s 42(c) inserts CA 1990, s 160(3A) and (3B).

g CLEA 2001, s 42(d) amends CA 1990, s 160(5) by the substitution for 'paragraph (e)' of 'paragraph (e) or (g)'.

h CLEA 2001, s 42(e) inserts CA 1990, s 160(6A).

i C(A)A 2012, s 9(b) inserts CA 1990, s 160(6B).

j CLEA 2001, s 42(f) inserts CA 1990, s 160(9A).

k CLEA 2001, s 42(f) inserts CA 1990, s 160(9B) which was substituted with effect from 29 January 2007 by IFCMPA 2005, s 11(2).

---

161 Penalty for acting contrary to the provisions of Chapter 1 or 2

(1) Any person who, in relation to any company, acts in a manner or capacity which, by virtue of being a person to whom section 150 applies or being subject or deemed to be subject to a disqualification order, he is prohibited from doing shall be guilty of an offence.

(2) Where a person is convicted of an offence under subsection (1) he shall be deemed to be subject to a disqualification order from the date of such conviction if he was not, or was not deemed to be, subject to such an order on that date.

(3) Where a person convicted of an offence under subsection (1) was subject, or deemed to be subject, to a disqualification order immediately prior to the date of such conviction, the period for which he was disqualified shall be extended for a further period of ten years from such date, or such other further period as the court, on the application of the prosecutor and having regard to all the circumstances of the case, may order.

(4) Section 160 (8) shall not apply to a person convicted of an offence under subsection (1) of this section.

(5) Where—

(a) a person who is a person to whom section 150 applies is or becomes a director of a company which commences to be wound up within the period of 5 years after the date of commencement of the winding-up of the company whose insolvency caused that section to apply to him; and

(b) it appears to the liquidator of the first-mentioned company that that company is, at the date of commencement of its winding-up or at any time during the course of its winding up, unable to pay its debts;

the liquidator shall report those matters to the court and the court, on receiving the report and if it considers it proper to do so, may make a disqualification order against that person for such period as it thinks fit.

(6) If the liquidator fails to comply with subsection (5) he shall [be guilty of an offence and liable to a [class C fine][a]][b].

Amendments

a £1,000 increased to £1,500 by CA 1990, s 240(7) as inserted by CLEA 2001, s 104 and converted to €1,904.61 by Council Regulations (EC) No 1103/97, No 974/98 and No 2866/98 and the Economic and Monetary Union Act 1998, s 6; the above being implicitly substituted,

by Fines Act 2010, s 6, for a fine not exceeding the aforesaid amount. A class C fine currently means a fine not exceeding €2,500.

b Words inserted by C(AA)A 2003, Sch 2.

---

162 Period of disqualification order to which person is deemed to be subject

Where a person is, as a consequence of his conviction of an offence under this Chapter, deemed to be subject to a disqualification order, he shall be deemed to be so subject for a period of five years from the date of such conviction or such other period as the court, on the application of the prosecutor and having regard to all the circumstances of the case, may order.

163 Civil consequences of acting contrary to the provisions of Chapter 1 or 2

(1) Subsections (2) and (3) apply to any person who acts, in relation to a company, in a manner or capacity which, by virtue of being a person to whom section 150 applies or being subject or deemed to be subject to a disqualification order, he is prohibited from doing.

(2) Where any consideration is given by or on behalf of a company for an act done or service performed by a person referred to in subsection (1) while he was acting in a manner or capacity described in that subsection, the company shall be entitled to recover from him, as a simple contract debt in any court of competent jurisdiction, the consideration or an amount representing its value.

(3) Where—

(a) a person referred to in subsection (1) acts, in relation to a company, in a manner or capacity described in that subsection, and

(b) the company concerned commences to be wound up—

(i) while he is acting in such a manner or capacity, or

(ii) within 12 months of his so acting, and

(c) the company is unable to pay its debts, within the meaning of section 214 of the Principal Act,

the court may, on the application of the liquidator or any creditor of the company, declare that such person shall be personally liable, without any limitation of liability, for all or any part of the debts or other liabilities of the company incurred in the period during which he was acting in such a manner or capacity.

(4) Where a company which has received a notification under section 155 (5) and which carries on business following such notification without the requirements of section 150 (3) being fulfilled within a reasonable period—

(a) is subsequently wound up, and

(b) is at the time of the commencement of the winding-up unable to pay its debts (taking into account the contingent and prospective liabilities),

the court may, on the application of the liquidator or any creditor or contributory of the company, declare that any person who was an officer of the company while the company so carried on business and who knew or ought to have known that the company had been so notified shall be personally responsible, without any limitation of liability, for all or any part of the debts or other liabilities of the company as the court may direct.

(5) In any proceedings brought against a person by virtue of this section the court may if, having regard to the circumstances of the case, it considers it just and equitable to do so, grant relief in whole or in part from the liability to which he would otherwise be subject thereunder and the court may attach to its order such conditions as it sees fit.

164 Penalty for acting under directions of disqualified person

(1) If any person while a director or other officer or a member of a committee of management or trustee of any company acts in accordance with the directions or instructions of another person knowing that such other person is disqualified or that, in giving the directions or instructions, he is acting in contravention of any provision of this Part he shall be guilty of an offence.

(2) Where a person is convicted of an offence under subsection (1) he shall be deemed to be subject to a disqualification order from the date of such conviction if he was not, or was not deemed to be, subject to such an order on that date.

165 Civil consequences of acting under directions of disqualified person

(1) A person who is convicted of an offence under section 164 for acting in accordance with the directions or instructions of a disqualified person shall, subject to subsection (2), be personally liable for the debts of the company concerned incurred in the period during which he was so acting.

(2) In any proceedings brought against a person for the recovery of any such debt the court may if, having regard to the circumstances of the case, it considers it just and equitable to do so, grant relief in whole or in part from the liability to which he would otherwise be subject under subsection (1) and the court may attach to its order such conditions as it sees fit.

166 Information to be given by directors to the court

[(1) Where—

(a) a director of a company is charged with an offence or civil proceedings are instituted against such a director, and

(b) the charge or proceedings relate to the company or involve alleged fraud or dishonesty,

the court before which the proceedings consequent on that charge or those civil proceedings are pending may (either of its own motion or at the request of any of the parties to the proceedings), if satisfied that it is appropriate to do so, require the director to lodge with the office of the court a notice in writing—

(i) giving the names of all companies of which he is a director at the date of the notice,

(ii) giving the names of all companies of which he was a director within a period commencing not earlier than 12 months prior to his being charged with the offence or the commencement of the civil proceedings and ending at the date of the notice,

(iii) stating whether he is at the date of the notice or ever was subject or deemed to be subject to a disqualification order, and

(iv) giving the dates and duration of each period in respect of which he is or was disqualified.][a]

(2) This section applies to shadow directors as it applies to directors.

(3) [...][b]

Amendments

a CA 1990, s 166(1) substituted by IFCMPA 2005, s 70(a) with effect from 30 June 2005.

b Subsection (3) repealed by IFCMPA 2005, s 70(b).

167 Information to be supplied to registrar of companies

Where a court—

(a) makes a disqualification order;

(b) grants or varies relief under section 160(8); or

(c) convicts a person of an offence—

  (i) which has the effect of his being deemed to be subject to a disqualification order, or

  (ii) under section 161(1) or 164,

a prescribed officer of the court shall cause the registrar of companies to be furnished with prescribed particulars of the order, relief or conviction at such time and in such form and manner as may be prescribed.

168 Register of persons subject to disqualification orders

(1) The registrar shall, subject to the provisions of this section, keep a register of the particulars which have been notified to him under section 167, and the following provisions of this section shall apply to the keeping of such a register.

(2) Where the particulars referred to in section 167(b) comprise the grant of full relief under section 160 (8), the registrar shall not enter such particulars on the register referred to in subsection (1), but shall, as soon as may be, remove any existing particulars in respect of the person concerned from the register.

(3) The registrar shall also remove from the register any particulars in relation to a person on the expiry of five years from the date of the original notification under section 167, or such other period in respect of which the person concerned is deemed to be subject to a disqualification order, unless the registrar has received a further notification in respect of that person under this section.

(4) Nothing in this section shall prevent the registrar from keeping the register required by this section as part of any other system of classification, whether pursuant to section 247 or otherwise.

169 Prohibition of undischarged bankrupts acting as directors or other officers of companies

[...][a]

Amendments

a This section substitutes CA 1963, s 183.

PART VIII
RECEIVERS

170 Disqualification for appointment as receiver

[...][a]

Amendments

a This section substitutes CA 1963, s 315.

171 Amendment of section 316 of the Principal Act

[...][a]

Amendments

a This section substitutes CA 1963, s 316(1) and inserts CA 1963, s 316(1A) & (1B).

172 Duty of receiver selling property to get best price reasonably obtainable

[...][a]

Amendments

a This section inserts CA 1963, s 316A.

173 Amendment of section 320 of the Principal Act

[...][a]

Amendments

a This section substitutes CA 1963, s 320(5).

174 Consequences of contravention of section 319 or 320 of the Principal Act

[...][a]

Amendments

a This section inserts CA 1963, s 320A.

175 Removal of receiver

[...][a]

Amendments

a This section inserts CA 1963, s 322A.

176 Court may determine or limit receivership on application of liquidator

[...][a]

Amendments

a This section inserts CA 1963, s 322B.

177 Resignation of receiver

[...][a]

Amendments

a This section inserts CA 1963, s 322C.

178 Application of section 139 to receivers

The provisions of section 139, shall, with the necessary modifications, apply to a company in receivership as if the references therein to the liquidator and to winding up were construed as references to the receiver and to receivership.

179 Application of section 299(2), (4) and (5) of the Principal Act to receivers

Section 299 (2), (4) and (5) of the Principal Act shall apply, with the necessary modifications, to receivers as it applies to liquidators.

PART IX

COMPANIES COURT PROTECTION

180 Amendments to the Companies (Amendment) Act, 1990

(1) The Companies (Amendment) Act, 1990, is hereby amended as follows:

(a) […][a]

(b) […][b]

(c) […][c]

(d) […][d]

(e) […][e]

(f) […][f]

(g) […][g]

(h) […][h]

(i) […][i]

(2) Section 244A of the Principal Act (inserted by section 125 of the Companies Act, 1990) and section 139 of the Companies Act, 1990, shall apply to a company under the protection of the court as they apply to a company being wound up, and any references in those sections to a liquidator or provisional liquidator shall be construed for the purposes of this subsection as a reference to an examiner.

(3) […][j]

Amendments

a Subsection (1)(a) substitutes '3 days' for '14 days' in C(A)A 1990, s 3(6).

b Subsection (1)(b) inserts C(A)A 1990, s 5(2)(g).

c Subsection (1)(c) deletes ', or past director,' in C(A)A 1990, s 8(3).

d Subsection (1)(d) inserts 'and "director" includes any present or past director or any person connected, within the meaning of CA 1990, s 26, with such director, and any present or past shadow director' after 'Act' where it secondly occurs in C(A)A 1990, s 8(3).

e Subsection (1)(e) inserts C(A)A 1990, s 8(5A), (5B).

f Subsection (1)(f) substitutes 'Any' for 'Where an order is made under this Act for the winding-up of the company or a receiver is appointed, any' in C(A)A 1990, s 10(1).

g Subsection (1)(g) substitutes s 16(i).

h Subsection (1)(h) inserts ', a local authority' after 'Government' in s 23(5)(b).

i Subsection (1)(i) inserts C(A)A 1990, s 24(12).

j Subsection (3) repeals C(A)A 1990, ss 32 to 35.

181 Further amendments to the Companies (Amendment) Act, 1990

(1) The Companies (Amendment) Act, 1990, is hereby further amended as follows:

(a) [...][a]

(b) [...][b]

(c) [...][c]

(d) [...][d]

(e) [...][e]

(2) [...][f]

Amendments

a Subsection (1)(a) substitutes C(A)A 1990, s 2(1)(b).

b Subsection (1)(b) substitutes 'body corporate' for 'company' in C(A)A 1990, s 4(5)(f).

c Subsection (1)(c) inserts C(A)A 1990, s 5(2)(h).

d Subsection (1)(d) inserts 'discharging' after 'towards' in C(A)A 1990, s 11(5).

e Subsection (1)(e) inserts C(A)A 1990, s 36A.

f Subsection (2) repeals C(A)A 1990, s 30(3).

PART X
ACCOUNTS AND AUDIT

182 Interpretation of Part X

[(1)][a] In this Part—

'the Council Directive' means Council Directive No 84/253/EEC of 10 April, 1984 (OJ No L126, 12.5.1984, p 20) on the approval of persons responsible for carrying out the statutory audits of accounting documents;

'friendly society' means a society registered under the Friendly Societies Acts, 1896 to 1977;

'practising certificate' means a certificate awarded to a person by a body of accountants entitling that person to practise as auditor of a company or as a public auditor;

'public auditor' means a public auditor for the purposes of the Industrial and Provident Societies Acts, 1893 to 1978, and the Friendly Societies Acts, [1896 to 1993].[b]

['the Act of 2003' means the Companies (Auditing and Accounting) Act 2003;

'the 1993 Regulations' means the European Communities (Accounts) Regulations 1993 (S.I. No. 396 of 1993);

'the 1992 Regulations' means the European Communities (Companies: Group Accounts) Regulations 1992 (S.I. No. 201 of 1992)';][c]

[(2) For the purposes of sections 205B and 205D, each of the following is considered to be an affiliate of an auditor in a financial year:

(a) if the auditor is a firm—

(i) any other firm where, at any time during the financial year, both firms were under common ownership and control,

(ii) any body corporate in which the auditor, any firm mentioned in subparagraph (i) or (iv) or any body corporate mentioned in subparagraph (iii) or (iv) was, at any time in the financial year, entitled to exercise or control the exercise of 20 per cent or more of the voting rights at a general meeting,

(iii) any body corporate that was, at any time in the financial year, in the same group as a body corporate mentioned in subparagraph (ii),

(iv) any other firm, or body corporate, that because of the use of a common name or corporate identity or the sharing of common professional services could reasonably be considered to be associated with the auditor,

(b) if the auditor is an individual—

(i) any partnership in which the auditor was, at any time in the financial year, a partner,

(ii) any body corporate in which the auditor, any partnership mentioned in subparagraph (i) or any body corporate mentioned in subparagraph (iii) was, at any time in the financial year, entitled to exercise or control the exercise of 20 per cent or more of the voting rights at a general meeting,

(iii) any body corporate that was, at any time in the financial year, in the same group as a body corporate mentioned in subparagraph (ii).

(3) A reference in this Part to group accounts is to be construed as follows:

(a) in accordance with the 1992 Regulations, in the case of an undertaking to which those Regulations apply;

(b) in accordance with the Principal Act, in the case of any other undertaking.][a]

Amendments

a C(AA)A 2003, s 34(c) renumbers CA 1990, s 182 as CA 1990, s 182 (1) and inserts CA 1990, s 182 (2) and (3).

b C(AA)A 2003, s 34(a) amends the definition of public auditor in CA 1990, s 182 by substituting '1896 to 1993' for '1896 to 1977'.

c C(AA)A 2003, s 34(b) inserts definitions of 'the Act of 2003', 'the 1993 Regulations' and 'the 1992 Regulations' after the definition of 'public auditor' in CA 1990, s 182.

183 Appointment and removal of auditors

(a) [...][a]

(b) [...][b]

Amendments

a Subsection (a) substitutes sub-ss (5), (5A) for CA 1963, s 160(5).

b Subsection (b) substitutes CA 1963, s 160(7).

184 Resolutions relating to appointment and removal of auditors and rights of auditors who have been removed

(1) [...][a]

(2) The reference in subsection (5) of the said section 161 to a resolution to remove the first auditors by virtue of subsection (6) of section 160 of the Principal Act shall be construed as including a reference to a resolution to remove an auditor other than the first auditors before the expiration of his term of office.

Amendments

a Sub-s (1) substitutes CA 1963, s 160(1), (2).

185 Resignation of auditors

(1) An auditor of a company may, by a notice in writing that complies with subsection (2) served on the company and stating his intention to do so, resign from the office of auditor to the company; and the resignation shall take effect on the date on which the notice is so served or on such later date as may be specified in the notice.

(2) A notice under subsection (1) shall contain either—

(a) a statement to the effect that there are no circumstances connected with the resignation to which it relates that the auditor concerned considers should be brought to the notice of the members or creditors of the company, or

(b) a statement of any such circumstances as aforesaid.

(3) Where a notice under subsection (1) is served on a company—

(a) the auditor concerned shall, within 14 days after the date of such service, send a copy of the notice to the registrar of companies, and

(b) subject to subsection (4), the company shall, if the notice contains a statement referred to in subsection (2)(b), not later than 14 days after the date of such service send a copy of the notice to every person who is entitled under section 159 (1) of the Principal Act to be sent copies of the documents referred to in the said section 159(1).

(4) Copies of a notice served on a company under subsection (1) need not be sent to the persons specified in subsection (3)(b) if, on the application of the company concerned or any other person who claims to be aggrieved, the court is satisfied that the notice contains material which has been included to secure needless publicity for defamatory matter and the court may order the company's costs on an application under this section to be paid in whole or in part by the auditor concerned notwithstanding that he is not a party to the application.

(5) This section shall also apply to a notice given by an auditor under section 160(2)(c) of the Principal Act, indicating his unwillingness to be Re-appointed.

(6) A person who fails to comply with subsection (2) or (3)(a) shall be guilty of an offence.

(7) If default is made in complying with subsection (3)(b), the company concerned, and every officer of such company who is in default, shall be guilty of an offence.

186 Requisitioning of general meeting of company by resigning auditor

(1) A notice served on a company under section 185 which contains a statement in accordance with subsection (2)(b) of that section may also requisition the convening by the directors of the company of a general meeting of the company for the purpose of receiving and considering such account and explanation of the circumstances connected with his resignation from the office of auditor to the company as he may wish to give to the meeting.

(2) Where an auditor makes a requisition under subsection (1), the directors of the company shall, within 14 days of the service on the company of the said notice, proceed duly to convene a general meeting of the company for a day not more than 28 days after such service.

(3) Subject to subsection (4), where—

- (a) a notice served on a company under section 185 contains a statement in accordance with subsection (2)(b) of that section, and
- (b) the auditor concerned requests the company to circulate to its members—
  - (i) before the general meeting at which, apart from the notice, his term of office would expire, or
  - (ii) before any general meeting at which it is proposed to fill the vacancy caused by his resignation or convened pursuant to a requisition under subsection (1),

  a further statement in writing prepared by the auditor of circumstances connected with the resignation that the auditor considers should be brought to the notice of the members,

the company shall—

- (i) in any notice of the meeting given to members of the company state the fact of the statement having been made, and
- (ii) send a copy of the statement to the registrar of companies and to every person who is entitled under section 159(1) of the Principal Act to be sent copies of the documents referred to in the said section 159(1).

(4) Subsection (3) need not be complied with by the company concerned if, on the application either of the company or any other person who claims to be aggrieved, the

court is satisfied that the rights conferred by this section are being abused to secure needless publicity for defamatory matter and the court may order the company's costs on an application under this section to be paid in whole or in part by the auditor concerned notwithstanding that he is not a party to the application.

(5) An auditor of a company who has resigned from the office of auditor shall be permitted by the company to attend—

(a) the annual general meeting at which, but for his resignation, his term of office would have expired, and

(b) any general meeting at which it is proposed to fill the vacancy caused by his resignation or convened pursuant to a requisition of his under subsection (1),

and the company shall send him all notices of, and other communications relating to, any such meeting that a member of the company is entitled to receive and the company shall permit him to be heard at any such meeting which he attends on any part of the business of the meeting which concerns him as a former auditor of the company.

(6) If default is made in complying with subsection (2), (3) or (5), the company concerned, and every officer of the company who is in default, shall be guilty of an offence.

187 Qualification for appointment as auditor

(1) Subject to section 190, a person shall not be qualified for appointment [...][a] as a public auditor unless—

(a) (i) he is a member of a body of accountants for the time being recognised by the [Supervisory Authority][b] for the purposes of this section and holds a valid practising certificate from such a body, or

(ii) he holds an accountancy qualification that is, in the opinion of the [Supervisory Authority][b], of a standard which is not less than that required for such membership as aforesaid and which would entitle him to be granted a practising certificate by that body if he were a member of it, and is for the time being authorised by the [Supervisory Authority][b] to be so appointed, or

(iii) he was, on the 31st day of December, 1990, a member of a body of accountants for the time being recognised under section 162(1)(a) of the Principal Act [and holds a valid practising certificate from such a body][c], or

[(iv) he was authorised by the Minister before the 3rd day of February, 1983, and is for the time being authorised by the Supervisory Authority to be so appointed, or][d]

(v) he is a person to whom section 188 applies, or

(vi) he is a person to whom section 189 applies, and is for the time being authorised by the [Supervisory Authority][b] to be so appointed, and

(b) the particulars required by sections 199 and 200 in respect of such a person have been forwarded to the registrar of companies.

[(1A) A firm shall be qualified for appointment as auditor of a company or as a public auditor if—

(a) at least one member of the firm is entitled to hold a practising certificate from a body referred to in subparagraph (i), (ii) or (iii) of subsection (1)(a) and is otherwise qualified under the applicable subparagraph for appointment as auditor of a company or as a public auditor, and

(b) the particulars required by sections 199 and 200 in respect of such a member have been forwarded to the registrar of companies.

(1B) A body referred to in subsection (1A) may grant a practising certificate to a firm that satisfies the conditions in that subsection, and, if a practising certificate is granted—

(a) each member of the firm who from time to time during the currency of the certificate is qualified for appointment as auditor of a company or as a public auditor is deemed to hold the certificate, and

(b) the name of such a member is deemed to be entered in the register of auditors.][e]

(2)[f]

(3) None of the following persons shall be qualified for appointment as a public auditor of a society—

(a) an officer or servant of the society,

(b) a person who has been an officer or servant of the society within a period in respect of which accounts would fall to be audited by him if he were appointed auditor of the society,

(c) a parent, spouse[, civil partner within the meaning of the Civil Partnership and Certain Rights and Obligations of Cohabitants Act 2010][g], brother, sister or child of an officer of the society,

(d) a person who is a partner of or in the employment of an officer of the society,

(e) a person who is disqualified under this subsection for appointment as a public auditor of any other society that is a subsidiary or holding company of the society or a subsidiary of the society's holding company,

[(f) a person who is disqualified under Regulation 71 of the European Communities (Statutory Audits) (Directive 2006/43/EC) Regulations 2010 for appointment as auditor of a company that is a subsidiary or holding company of the society,][h]

(g) a body corporate.

(4) None of the following persons shall be qualified for appointment as a public auditor of a friendly society—

(a) an officer or servant of the friendly society,

(b) a person who has been an officer or servant of the friendly society within a period in respect of which accounts would fall to be audited by him if he were appointed auditor of the friendly society,

(c) a parent, spouse[, civil partner within the meaning of the Civil Partnership and Certain Rights and Obligations of Cohabitants Act 2010][g], brother, sister or child of an officer of the friendly society,

(d) a person who is a partner of or in the employment of an officer of the friendly society,

(e) a body corporate.

(5) A person shall not, by virtue of subsection (3) or (4), be disqualified for appointment as public auditor of a society or a friendly society at any time during the period of 2 years from the commencement of this section if on such commencement he stands duly appointed as public auditor of the society or friendly society, as the case may be.

(6) Subject to subsection (5), a person shall not act [...][i] as a public auditor at a time when he is disqualified under this section for appointment to that office.

(7) If, during his term of office as [...][j] public auditor, a person becomes disqualified under the Companies Acts for appointment to that office, he shall thereupon vacate his office and give notice in writing to the company, society or friendly society that he has vacated his office by reason of such disqualification.

(8) This section shall not apply to the Comptroller and Auditor General.

(9) A person who contravenes subsection (6) or (7) shall be guilty of an offence and liable—

(a) on summary conviction, to a [class C fine],[k] and, for continued contravention, to a daily default [class E fine],[l] or

(b) on conviction on indictment, to a fine not exceeding [€11,110.21][m] and, for continued contravention, to a daily default fine not exceeding [€222.20].[n]

(10)(a) In this section 'society' means a society registered under the Industrial and Provident Societies Acts, 1893 to 1978.

(b) References in this section to an officer or servant do not include references to an auditor or a public auditor.

(11) A recognition or authorisation by the Minister under section 162 of the Principal Act shall, notwithstanding the repeal of that section by this Act, continue in force as if given under this section—

(a) in the case of a recognition, until the time limit provided expires, or the Minister's decision is communicated to the body concerned, under section 191, whichever is the earlier, and

(b) in the case of an authorisation, until the time limit for the person to make the notification required by section 199(3) expires.

[(12)(a) The Director may demand of a person acting [...][p] as a public auditor, or purporting to be qualified to so act, the production of evidence of his qualifications under subsection (1) in respect of any time or period during which he so acted or purported to be qualified to so act, and if the person refuses or fails to produce the evidence within 30 days of the demand, or such longer period as the Director may allow, he shall be guilty of an offence.

(b) In a prosecution for an offence under this subsection, it shall be presumed, until the contrary is shown by the defendant, that the defendant did not, within 30 days, or any longer period allowed, after the day on which the production was demanded, produce evidence in accordance with paragraph (a).

(13)(a) Where a person is the subject of a prosecution under subsection (9) for a contravention of subsection (6) or (7), it shall be sufficient evidence, until the contrary is shown by the person, of non-membership of a body of accountants for the time being recognised by the Minister for the purposes of this section for any or all such bodies to certify in writing to the court such non-membership, provided that the first-mentioned person is provided by the prosecutor with a copy of the certificate or certificates, served by registered post, not later than 21 days before any such certificate is presented in evidence to the court.

(b) Where a person the subject of a prosecution proposes to contest the certification of non-membership contained in a certificate provided for by paragraph (a), he shall give written notice thereof, served by registered post, to the prosecutor within 21 days, or such longer period as the court may allow, of receipt of the certificate from the prosecutor.][o]

[(14) An authorisation granted to a person under subsection (1)(a)(iv) ceases to have effect on the expiry of 3 years after the commencement of this subsection unless, within that 3 year period, the person becomes a member of, or becomes subject to the regulations of, a body of accountants recognised for the purposes of section 187.

(15) On an authorisation ceasing to have effect under subsection (14), the person to whom it was granted ceases to be qualified for appointment as auditor of a company or as a public auditor.][q]

Amendments

a EC(SA)(Dir)R 2010, reg 6(a) deletes 'either as auditor of a company or'.

b C(AA)A 2003, Sch 1, Pt 1, substitutes 'Supervisory Authority' for 'Minister'.

c CLEA 2001, s 72(a) amends CA 1990, s 187(1)(a)(iii) by the insertion after 'Principal Act' of 'and holds a valid practising certificate from such a body'.

d C(AA)A 2003, Sch 1, Pt 1, substitutes CA 1990, s 187(1)(a)(iv).

e C(AA)A 2003, s 35(a) inserts CA 1990, s 187(1A) and (1B).

f EC(SA)(Dir)R 2010, reg 6(b) deletes sub-s (2).

g Words ', civil partner within the meaning of the Civil Partnership and Certain Rights and Obligations of Cohabitants Act 2010' inserted by Civil Partnership and Certain Rights and Obligations of Cohabitants Act 2010, Sch, Pt 1, Item No. 10.

h EC(SA)(Dir)R 2010, reg 6(c) substitutes sub-s (3)(f).

i Words 'as auditor of a company or' deleted by EC(SA)(Dir)R 2010, reg 6(d).

j Words 'auditor of a company or' deleted by EC(SA)(Dir)R 2010, reg 6(e).

k £1,000 increased to £1,500 by CA 1990, s 240(7) as inserted by CLEA 2001, s 104(c), and converted to €1,904.61 by Council Regulations (EC) No 1103/97, No 974/98 and No 2866/98 and the Economic and Monetary Union Act 1998, s 6; the above being implicitly substituted, by Fines Act 2010, s 6, for a fine not exceeding the aforesaid amount. A class C fine currently means a fine not exceeding €2,500.

l £50 converted to €63.49 by Council Regulations (EC) No 1103/97, No 974/98 and No 2866/98 and the Economic and Monetary Union Act 1998, s 6; as implicitly substituted, by Fines Act 2010, s 8, for a fine not exceeding the aforesaid amount. A class E fine currently means a fine not exceeding €500.

m £5,000 converted to €6,348.69 by Council Regulations (EC) No 1103/97, No 974/98 and No 2866/98 and the Economic and Monetary Union Act 1998, s 6, and multiplied by a multiplier of 1.75 pursuant to Fines Act 2010, s 9.

n £100 converted to €126.97 by Council Regulations (EC) No 1103/97, No 974/98 and No 2866/98 and the Economic and Monetary Union Act 1998, s 6, and multiplied by a multiplier of 1.75 pursuant to Fines Act 2010, s 9.

o CLEA 2001, s 72(b) inserts CA 1990, s 187(12) and (13).

p Words 'as an auditor of a company or' deleted by EC(SA)(Dir)R 2010, reg 6(f).

q C(AA)A 2003, s 35(c) inserts CA 1990, s 187(14) and (15).

188 Persons undergoing training on 1 January, 1990

(1) Without prejudice to section 187, a person to whom this section applies shall also be qualified for appointment as [...][a] a public auditor.

(2) This section applies to a person—

(a) who on the 1st day of January, 1990, was a person to whom Article 18 of the Council Directive applies, and

(b) who, following his admission, before the 1st day of January, 1996, to the membership of a body of accountants recognised under section 191, was subsequently awarded a practising certificate by that body, and

(c) in respect of whom such certificate remains valid.

Amendments

a Words 'auditor of a company or' deleted by EC(SA)(Dir)R 2010, reg 7.

189 Approval of qualifications obtained outside the State

(1) Without prejudice to section 187, the [Supervisory Authority][a] may declare that, subject to subsection (2), persons who hold—

(a) a qualification entitling them to audit accounts under the law of a specified country outside the State, or

(b) a specified accountancy qualification recognised under the law of a country outside the State,

shall be regarded as qualified for appointment as [...][b] a public auditor.

(2) Before making a declaration under subsection (1), the [Supervisory Authority][a]—

(a) must be satisfied that the qualification concerned is of a standard not less than is required by the Companies Acts to qualify a person for appointment as [...][c] a public auditor, and

(b) may direct that such a person shall not be treated as qualified for the purposes of subsection (1) unless he holds such additional educational qualifications as the Minister may specify for the purpose of ensuring that such persons have an adequate knowledge of the law and practice in the State relevant to the audit of accounts, and

(c) may have regard to the extent to which persons qualified under the Companies Acts for appointment as [...][c] a public auditor are recognised by the law of the country in question as qualified to audit accounts there.

(3) Different directions may be given under subsection (2)(b) in relation to different qualifications.

(4) The [Supervisory Authority][a] may, if he thinks fit, revoke or suspend for a specified period, in such manner and on such conditions as he may think appropriate, any declaration previously made under subsection (1).

Amendments

a C(AA)A 2003, Sch 1, Pt 1, substitutes 'Supervisory Authority' for 'Minister'.

b Words 'auditor of a company or' deleted by EC(SA)(Dir)R 2010, reg 8(a).

c Words 'auditor of a company or' deleted by EC(SA)(Dir)R 2010, reg 8(b).

190 [Consultation by Supervisory Authority regarding standards and qualifications

(1) Before granting, renewing, withdrawing, revoking, suspending or refusing a recognition of a body of accountants under or for the purposes of—

(a) the Companies Acts; or

(b) the European Communities (Statutory Audits) (Directive 2006/43/EC) Regulations 2010 (the 'Regulations of 2010'),

the Supervisory Authority may consult with any body of persons or other person as to the conditions or standards required by the body of accountants concerned in connection with membership of that body or, as the case may be, the awarding to persons of practising certificates or the approval of persons as auditors.

(2) Without prejudice to any obligations in that behalf in connection with the performance of the foregoing functions as they relate to the Regulations of 2010, the Supervisory Authority may also consult with any body of persons or other person before forming any opinion or making any declaration in relation to the qualifications held by any person or class of persons as respects qualification for appointment as a public auditor.][a]

Amendments

a EC(SA)(Dir)R 2010, reg 9 substitutes CA 1990, s 190.

191 [Recognition of body of accountants

(1) The Supervisory Authority may grant recognition to a body of accountants under or for the purposes of section 187 or the European Communities (Statutory Audits) (Directive 2006/43/EC) Regulations 2010 but may only grant such recognition if satisfied—

(a) in the case of a grant of recognition—

(i) to a body of accountants under or for the purposes of section 187, that the standards relating to training, qualifications and repute required by that body for the awarding of a practising certificate to a person are not less than those that were specified in Articles 3 to 6, 8 and 19 of the Council Directive before the repeal thereof by Directive No. 2006/43/EC of the European Parliament and of the Council of 17 May 2006; and

(ii) to a body of accountants under or for the purposes of the European Communities (Statutory Audits) (Directive 2006/43/EC) Regulations 2010, that the standards relating to training, qualifications and repute required by that body for the approval of a person as an auditor are not less than those specified in Articles 4, 6 to 8 and 10 of Directive No. 2006/43/EC of the European Parliament and of the Council of 17 May 2006;

and

(b) in either of those 2 cases, as to the standards that body applies to its members in the area of ethics, codes of conduct and practice, independence, professional integrity, auditing and accounting standards and investigation and disciplinary procedures.

(2) In subsection (3) 'relevant amendment' means the amendment of this section by Regulation 10 of the European Communities (Statutory Audits) (Directive 2006/43/EC) Regulations 2010.

(3) Each of the following—

(a) the Association of Chartered Certified Accountants;

(b) the Institute of Chartered Accountants in Ireland;

(c) the Institute of Chartered Accountants in England and Wales;

(d) the Institute of Chartered Accountants of Scotland;

(e) the Institute of Certified Public Accountants in Ireland;

(f) the Institute of Incorporated Public Accountants,

being a body of accountants that stood recognised under or for the purposes of section 187 immediately before the relevant amendment, continues to stand recognised under or for the purposes of section 187 (and such recognition shall be deemed to have been granted by the Supervisory Authority).

(4) Each of the bodies of accountants referred to in subsection (3) shall be deemed to have been granted recognition by the Supervisory Authority under or for the purposes of the European Communities (Statutory Audits) (Directive 2006/43/EC) Regulations 2010.][a]

Amendments

a EC(SA)(Dir)R 2010, reg 10 substitutes CA 1990, s 191.

---

192 Provisions in relation to recognitions and authorisations by Supervisory Authority under section 187

(1) The [Supervisory Authority][a] may, at the time it is granted or at any time during the currency of a recognition or authorisation [under or for the purposes of section 187][a] [or the European Communities (Statutory Audits) (Directive 2006/43/EC) Regulations 2010][b] by notice in writing given to the body of accountants or individual concerned, attach to the recognition or authorisation, as the case may be, such terms and conditions as he thinks necessary or expedient and specified in the notice.

(2) The [Supervisory Authority][a] may, at any time during the currency of a recognition or authorisation [under or for the purposes of section 187][a] [or the European Communities (Statutory Audits) (Directive 2006/43/EC) Regulations 2010][b], by notice in writing given to the body of accountants or individual concerned, amend its terms or conditions or insert into it or delete from it other terms or conditions.

(3) The [Supervisory Authority][c] may, at any time during its currency, by notice in writing given to the body of accountants or individual concerned, revoke, or suspend for a specified period, a recognition or authorisation [under or for the purposes of section 187][c] [or the European Communities (Statutory Audits) (Directive 2006/43/EC) Regulations 2010][b].

(4) (a) The [Supervisory Authority][d] may require a body of accountants recognised for the purposes of the said section 187 [or the Regulations referred to in the preceding subsections][e] to prepare and, within such period as may be specified in the requirement, to submit to the [Supervisory Authority][d] for his approval a code prescribing standards of professional conduct for its members and providing for sanctions for breaches of the code, and the body of accountants shall comply with the requirement.

(b) A body of accountants may, at any time, prepare and submit to the [Supervisory Authority][d] a code amending or revoking a code prepared by it under this subsection.

(c) The [Supervisory Authority][d] may approve of a code submitted to him under this subsection.

(d) A code approved of by the [Supervisory Authority][d] under this section shall be brought into operation and enforced by the body of accountants concerned in accordance with its terms.

[...][f]

(5) References in this section to recognitions under section 187 include references to recognitions under section 162 (inserted by the Companies (Amendment) Act, 1982) of the Principal Act and references in this section to an authorisation under section 187 include references to authorisations under the said section 162.

[(6) Where a disciplinary committee or tribunal (however called) of a body of accountants recognised for the purposes of section 187 [or the European Communities (Statutory Audits) (Directive 2006/43/EC) Regulations 2010][g] has reasonable grounds for believing that an indictable offence under the Companies Acts may have been committed by a person while the person was a member of the body, the body shall, as soon as possible, provide a report to the Director giving details of the alleged offence and shall furnish the Director with such further information in relation to the matter as the Director may require.

(7) Where a body referred to in subsection (6) fails to comply with that subsection or a requirement of the Director under that subsection, it, and every officer of the body to whom the failure is attributable, shall be guilty of an offence.][h]

Amendments

- a C(AA)A 2003, Sch 1, Pt 1, Item No 5(a) substitutes 'Supervisory Authority' for 'Minister' and substitutes 'under or for the purposes of section 187' for 'under section 187' in sub-ss (1)–(2).
- b EC(SA)(Dir)R 2010, reg 11(a) inserts 'or the European Communities (Statutory Audits) (Directive 2006/43/EC) Regulations 2010' in sub-ss (1)–(3).
- c C(AA)A 2003, Sch 1, Pt 1, Item No 5(b) substitutes 'Supervisory Authority' for 'Minister' and substitutes 'under or for the purposes of section 187' for 'under the said section 187'.
- d C(AA)A 2003, Sch 1, Pt 1, Item No 5(c) substitutes 'Supervisory Authority' for 'Minister'.
- e EC(SA)(Dir)R 2010, reg 11(b) inserts 'or the Regulations referred to in the preceding subsections' in sub-s (4)(a).
- f C(AA)A 2003, Sch 1, Pt 1, Item No 5(d) repeals CA 1990, s 192(4)(e), (f) and (g).
- g EC(SA)(Dir)R 2010, reg 11(c) inserts 'or the European Communities (Statutory Audits) (Directive 2006/43/EC) Regulations 2010' in sub-s (6).
- h CLEA 2001, s 73 inserts CA 1990, s 192(6) and (7).

[192A Statutory backing for disciplinary procedures of prescribed accountancy bodies

(1) In this section—

'client' includes an individual, a body corporate, an unincorporated body of persons and a partnership;

'disciplinary committee' means any disciplinary committee or tribunal (however called) of a prescribed accountancy body;

'member', in relation to a prescribed accountancy body, means—

(a) a person, or

(b) a firm,

that is, or was at the relevant time, subject to the investigation and disciplinary procedures approved by the Supervisory Authority under section 9(2)(c) of the Act of 2003 for that body;

'prescribed accountancy body' has the meaning given by section 4 of the Act of 2003;

'refusal' includes failure and 'refuses' includes fails;

'relevant person', in relation to an investigation of a member of a prescribed accountancy body, means—

(a) a member of the prescribed accountancy body,

(b) a client or former client of such a member,

(c) if the client or former client is a body corporate, a person who is or was an officer, employee or agent of the client or former client, or

(d) any person whom the prescribed accountancy body reasonably believes has information or documents relating to the investigation other than information or documents the disclosure of which is prohibited or restricted by law;

'standards', in relation to a prescribed accountancy body, means the rules, regulations and standards that body applies to its members and to which, by virtue of their membership, they are obliged to adhere.

(2) For the purposes of an investigation of a possible breach of a prescribed accountancy body's standards by a member, a disciplinary committee may require a relevant person to do one or more of the following:

(a) produce to the committee all books or documents relating to the investigation that are in the relevant person's possession or control;

(b) attend before the committee;

(c) give the committee any other assistance in connection with the investigation that the relevant person is reasonably able to give.

(3) For the purposes of an investigation referred to in subsection (2), the disciplinary committee may—

(a) examine on oath, either by word of mouth or on written interrogatories, a relevant person,

(b) administer oaths for the purpose of that examination, and

(c) record, in writing, the answers of a person so examined and require that person to sign them.

(4) The disciplinary committee may certify the refusal to the High Court if a relevant person refuses to do one or more of the following:

(a) produce to the committee any book or document that it is the person's duty under this section to produce;

(b) attend before the committee when required to do so under this section;

(c) answer a question put to the person by the committee with respect to the matter under investigation.

(5) On receiving a certificate of refusal concerning a relevant person, the Court may enquire into the case and, after hearing any evidence that may be adduced, may do one or more of the following:

(a) direct that the relevant person attend or Re-attend before the disciplinary committee or produce particular books or documents or answer particular questions put to him or her by that committee;

(b) direct that the relevant person need not produce a particular book or document or answer a particular question put to him or her by that committee;

(c) make any other ancillary or consequential order or give any other direction that the Court thinks fit.

(6) The production of any books or documents under this section by a person who claims a lien on them does not prejudice the lien.

(7) Any information produced or answer given by a member of a prescribed accountancy body in compliance with a requirement under this section may be used in evidence against the member in any proceedings whatsoever, save proceedings for an offence (other than perjury in respect of such an answer).][a]

Amendments

a C(AA)A 2003, s 36 inserted CA 1990, s 192A.

193 Auditors' report and right of access to books and of attendance and audience at general meetings

[(1) The auditors of a company shall make a report to the members on the individual accounts examined by them, and on every balance sheet and profit and loss account or income statement, and all group accounts, laid before the company in general meeting during their tenure of office.][a]

(2) The auditors' report shall be read at the annual general meeting of the company and shall be open to inspection by any member.

(3) Every auditor of a company shall have a right of access at all reasonable times to the books, accounts and vouchers of the company and shall be entitled to require from the officers (within the meaning of section 197(5)) of the company such information and explanations that are within their knowledge or can be procured by them as he thinks necessary for the performance of the duties of the auditors.

[(4) The auditors' report shall include—

(a) an introduction identifying the individual accounts, and where appropriate, the group accounts, that are the subject of the audit and the financial reporting framework that has been applied in their preparation, and

(b) a description of the scope of the audit identifying the auditing standards in accordance with which the audit was conducted.

(4A)(a) Except in the case of a company that has taken advantage of any of the provisions of Part III of the Sixth Schedule to the Principal Act, the auditors' report shall state clearly whether in the auditors' opinion the annual accounts have been properly prepared in accordance with the requirements of the Companies Acts (and, where applicable, Article 4 of the IAS Regulation).

(b) In the case of a company that has taken advantage of any of the provisions of Part III of the Sixth Schedule to the Principal Act, the auditors' report shall state whether, in their opinion, the annual accounts and, where it is a holding company submitting group accounts, the group accounts have been properly prepared in accordance with the Companies Acts (and, where applicable, Article 4 of the IAS Regulation) and give a true and fair view of the matters referred to in subsection (4B)(e)(i) and (ii) and, where appropriate, subsection (4B)(e)(iii) subject to the non-disclosure of any matters (to be indicated in the report) which by virtue of the said Part III are not required to be disclosed.

(4B) The auditors' report shall also state—

(a) whether they have obtained all the information and explanations which, to the best of their knowledge and belief, are necessary for the purposes of their audit,

(b) whether, in their opinion, proper books of account have been kept by the company,

(c) whether, in their opinion, proper returns adequate for their audit have been received from branches of the company not visited by them, and

(d) whether the company's balance sheet and (unless it is framed as a consolidated profit and loss account) profit and loss account are in agreement with the books of account and returns.

(4C) The auditors' report shall state, in particular—

(i) whether the annual accounts give a true and fair view in accordance with the relevant financial reporting framework–

(I) in the case of an individual balance sheet, of the state of affairs of the company as at the end of the financial year,

(II) in the case of an individual profit and loss account, of the profit or loss of the company for the financial year,

(III) in the case of group accounts, of the state of affairs as at the end of the financial year and of the profit or loss for the financial year of the undertakings included in the consolidation as a whole, so far as concerns members of the company,

and

(ii) whether, in their opinion, there existed at the balance sheet date a financial situation which under section 40(1) of the Companies (Amendment) Act 1983 would require the convening of an extraordinary general meeting of the company.

(4D) The auditors' report—

(a) [...][b]

(b) shall, in relation to each matter referred to in subsections (4A), (4B) and (4C) contain a statement or opinion, as the case may be, which shall be either—

(i) unqualified, or

(ii) qualified, and

(c) shall include a reference to any matters to which the auditors wish to draw attention by way of emphasis without qualifying the report.

(4E) For the purposes of subsection (4D)(b)(ii), a statement or opinion may be qualified, including to the extent of an adverse opinion or a disclaimer of opinion, where there is a disagreement or limitation in scope of work.

(4F) Where the individual accounts of a parent undertaking are attached to the group accounts, the auditors' report on the group accounts may be combined with the report on the individual accounts.'][c]

[(4G)(a) The auditors' report shall state the name of the auditor and be signed, as provided for in paragraph (b), and dated.

(b) Where the auditor is—

(i) a statutory auditor (within the meaning of the European Communities (Statutory Audits) (Directive 2006/43/EC) Regulations 2010, the report shall be signed by that person, or

(ii) a statutory audit firm (within the meaning of the foregoing Regulations), the report shall be signed by—

(I) the statutory auditor (or, where more than one, each statutory auditor) designated by the statutory audit firm for the particular audit engagement as being primarily responsible for carrying out the statutory audit on behalf of the audit firm, or

(II) in the case of a group audit, at least the statutory auditor (or, where more than one, each statutory auditor) designated by the statutory audit firm as being primarily responsible for carrying out the statutory audit at the level of the group,

in his or her own name, for and on behalf of, the audit firm.][d]

(5) The auditors of a company shall be entitled to attend any general meeting of the company and to receive all notices of, and other communications relating to, any general meeting which any member of the company is entitled to receive and to be heard at any general meeting which they attend on any part of the business of the meeting which concerns them as auditors.

(6) A person who is appointed as auditor of a company or as a public auditor shall be under a general duty to carry out such audit with professional integrity.

(7) Any reference in the Principal Act to section 163 of or the Seventh Schedule to that Act shall be construed as references to this section.

Amendments

a Subsection (1) substituted by EC(IFRSMA)R 2005, reg 9.

b Subparagraph (4D)(a) deleted by EC(SA)(Dir)R 2010, reg 57(a).

c Subsection (4) substituted and sub-ss (4A)–(4F) were added by EC(IFRSMA)R 2005, reg 8.

d Subsection (4G) inserted by EC(SA)(Dir)R 2010, reg 57(b).

---

194 Duty of auditors if proper books of account not being kept

(1) If, at any time, the auditors of a company form the opinion that the company is contravening, or has contravened, section 202 by failing to cause to be kept proper books of account (within the meaning of that section) in relation to the matters specified in subsection (1) and (2) of that section, the auditors shall—

[(a) as soon as may be, by recorded delivery, serve a notice in writing on the company stating their opinion, and][a]

(b) not later than 7 days after the service of such notice on the company, notify the registrar of companies in the prescribed form of the notice [and the registrar shall forthwith forward a copy of the notice to the Director][b].

(2) Where the auditors form the opinion that the company has contravened section 202 but that, following such contravention, the directors of the company have taken the necessary steps to ensure that proper books of account are kept as required by that section, subsection (1)(b) shall not apply.

(3) This section shall not require the auditors to make the notifications referred to in subsection (1) if they are of opinion that the contraventions concerned are minor or otherwise immaterial in nature.

[(3A) Where the auditors of a company file a notice pursuant to subsection (1)(b), they shall, if requested by the Director—

(a) furnish to the Director such information, including an explanation of the reasons for their opinion that the company had contravened section 202, and

(b) give to the Director such [access to books and documents][c], including facilities for inspecting and taking copies,

[being information, books or documents][d] in their possession or control and relating to the matter the subject of the notice, as the Director may require.

(3B) Any written information given in response to a request of the Director under subsection (3A) shall in all legal proceedings be admissible without further proof, until the contrary is shown, as evidence of the facts stated therein.][e]

(4) A person who contravenes [subsection (1), (3A), (5) or (5A)][f] shall be guilty of an offence.

[(5) Where, in the course of, and by virtue of, their carrying out an audit of the accounts of the company, information comes into the possession of the auditors of a company that leads them to form the opinion that there are reasonable grounds for believing that the company or an officer or agent of it has committed an indictable offence under the Companies Acts [...][g] [(other than an indictable offence under section 125(2) or 127(12) of the Principal Act)][h] the auditors shall, forthwith after having formed it, notify that opinion to the Director and provide the Director with details of the grounds on which they have formed that opinion.][i]

[(5A) Where the auditors of a company notify the Director of any matter pursuant to subsection (5), they shall, in addition to performing their obligations under that subsection, if requested by the Director—

(a) furnish the Director with such further information in their possession or control relating to the matter as the Director may require, including further information relating to the details of the grounds on which they formed the opinion referred to in that subsection,

(b) give the Director such access to books and documents in their possession or control relating to the matter as the Director may require, and

(c) give the Director such access to facilities for the taking of copies of or extracts from those books and documents as the Director may require.

(5B) Nothing in this section compels the disclosure by any person of any information that the person would be entitled to refuse to produce on the grounds of legal professional privilege or authorises the inspection or copying of any document containing such information that is in the person's possession.][j]

[(6) No professional or legal duty to which an auditor is subject by virtue of his appointment as an auditor of a company shall be regarded as contravened by, and no liability to the company, its shareholders, creditors or other interested parties shall attach to, an auditor, by reason of his compliance with an obligation imposed on him by or under this section.][i]

Amendments

a CLEA 2001, s 74(a) substitutes CA 1990, s 194(1)(a).

b CLEA 2001, s 74(b) amends CA 1990, s 194(1)(b) by the insertion after 'form of the notice' of 'and the registrar shall forthwith forward a copy of the notice to the Director'.

c C(AA)A 2003, s 37(a) amends CA 1990, s 194(3A)(b) by substituting 'access to books and documents' for 'access to documents'.

d C(AA)A 2003, s 37(b) amends CA 1990, s 194(3A) by substituting 'being information, books or documents' for 'being information or documents'.

e CLEA 2001, s 74(c) inserts CA 1990, s 194(3A) and (3B).

f C(AA)A 2003, s 37(c) amends CA 1990, s 194(4) by substituting 'subsection (1), (3A), (5) or (5A)' for 'subsection (1), (3A) or (5)'; which had been substituted for 'subsection (1) by CLEA 2001, s 74(d).

g C(AA)A 2003, s 37(d) amends CA 1990, s 194(5) by inserting '(other than an indictable offence under section 125(1) or 127(12) of the Principal Act)' after 'an indictable offence under the Companies Acts'; this was repealed by IFCMPA 2005, s 73(3).

h Words inserted by IFCMPA 2005, s 73(2)(d).

i CLEA 2001, s 74(e) inserts CA 1990, s 194(5) and (6), which took effect from 28 November 2001.[1]

j C(AA)A 2003, s 37(e) inserted CA 1990, s 194(5A) and (5B), which took effect from 1 March 2007.[2]

1 Company Law Enforcement Act, 2001 (Commencement) (No 3) Order 2001 (523/2001).

2 Companies (Auditing and Accounting) Act 2003 (Commencement) Order 2007 (SI 61/2007).

---

195 Prohibition on acting in relation to audit while disqualification order in force

(1) If a person who is subject or deemed to be subject to a disqualification order—

(a) becomes, or remains after 28 days from the date of the making of the order, a partner in a firm of auditors.

(b) gives directions or instructions in relation to the conduct of any part of the audit of the accounts of a company, or

(c) works in any capacity in the conduct of an audit of the accounts of a company,

he shall be guilty of an offence.

(2) Where a person is convicted of an offence under subsection (1), the period for which he was disqualified shall be extended for a further period of ten years from such date, or such other further period as the court, on the application of the prosecutor and having regard to all the circumstances of the case, may order.

(3) In this section—

(a) 'company' has meaning assigned to it by section 159, and also includes any society registered under the Industrial and Provident Societies Acts, 1893 to 1978.

(b) 'disqualification order' has the meaning assigned to it by section 159.

196 Powers of auditors in relation to subsidiaries

(1) Where a company (referred to in this section as 'the holding company') has a subsidiary, then—

(a) in case the subsidiary is a body corporate incorporated in the State, it shall be the duty of the subsidiary and its auditors to give to the auditors of the holding company such information and explanations as those auditors may reasonably require for the purposes of their duties as auditors of the holding company,

(b) in any other case, it shall be the duty of the holding company, if required by its auditors to do so, to take all such steps as are reasonably open to it to obtain from the subsidiary such information and explanations as aforesaid.

(2) If a company or an auditor fails to comply with subsection (1) within five days of the making of the relevant requirement under that subsection, the company and every officer thereof who is in default, or the auditor, as the case may be, shall be guilty of an offence.

(3) In a prosecution for an offence under this section, it shall be a defence for the defendant to show that it was not reasonably possible for him to comply with the requirement under subsection (1) to which the offence relates within the time specified in subsection (2) but that he complied therewith as soon as was reasonably possible after the expiration of such time.

(4) A person guilty of an offence under this section shall be liable to a fine.

197 Penalty for false statements to auditors

(1) An officer of a company who knowingly or recklessly makes a statement to which this section applies that is misleading, false or deceptive in a material particular shall be guilty of an offence.

(2) This section applies to any statement made to the auditors of a company (whether orally or in writing) which conveys, or purports to convey, any information or explanation which they require under the Companies Acts, or are entitled so to require, as auditors of the company.

(3) An officer of a company who fails to provide to the auditors of the company or of the holding company of the company, within two days of the making of the relevant requirement, any information or explanations that the auditors require as auditors of the company or of the holding company of the company and that is within the knowledge of or can be procured by the officer shall be guilty of an offence.

(4) In a prosecution for an offence under this section, it shall be a defence for the defendant to show that it was not reasonably possible for him to comply with the requirement under subsection (3) to which the offence relates within the time specified in that subsection but that he complied therewith as soon as was reasonably possible after the expiration of such time.

(5) In this section 'officer', in relation to a company, includes any employee of the company.

[198 Register of auditors

(1) The registrar of companies shall maintain a register [('the register of public auditors')][b] containing the names of persons or firms that have been notified to him as qualified for appointment [...][c] as public auditor.

(2) A person shall not—

(a) act [...][d] as a public auditor,

(b) describe himself [...][d] as a public auditor, or

(c) so hold himself out as to indicate, or be reasonably understood to indicate, that he is, or is registered as, [...][e] a public auditor, unless—

(i) his name is entered, or is deemed under subsection (3) to be entered, in the [register of public auditors][f] and he holds a valid practising certificate, or

(ii) he is a member of a firm that holds a valid practising certificate under section 187(1B) and he is deemed under that section to hold a practising certificate.

(3) In the following circumstances, the name of a person is deemed to be entered in the [register of public auditors][g]:

(a) if the person becomes qualified for appointment as [a public auditor][h] or is granted an authorisation by the Supervisory Authority under section 187(1) and if the time allowed under section 200(1), (2) or (3) for forwarding that person's particulars to the registrar of companies has not yet expired;

(b) if the person is entitled to have his name entered in the [register of public auditors][i] and his particulars have been forwarded to the registrar of companies in accordance with section 200(1), (2) or (3) but his name has not yet been entered in that register

(4) This section does not apply to the Comptroller and Auditor-General.

(5) A person who contravenes subsection (2) is guilty of an offence and is liable—

(a) on summary conviction, to a [class C fine][j] and, for continued contravention, a daily default [class E fine][k], and

(b) on conviction on indictment, to a fine not exceeding €12,500 and, for continued contravention, a daily default fine not exceeding €300.

(6) In this section and sections 199 and 200, 'address' in relation to a person means—

(a) the person's usual business address, and

(b) if the person is a partner or employee of a firm, the name of the firm and the address of its head office.][a]

Amendments

a C(AA)A 2003, s 38 substitutes CA 1990, s 198.

b Words '('the register of public auditors')' inserted by EC(SA)(Dir)R 2010, reg 12(1)(a)(i).

c Words 'as auditor of a company or' deleted by EC(SA)(Dir)R 2010, reg 12(1)(a)(ii).

d Words 'as an auditor of a company or' deleted by EC(SA)(Dir)R 2010, reg 12(1)(b)(i).

e Words 'an auditor of a company or' deleted by EC(SA)(Dir)R 2010, reg 12(1)(b)(ii).

f Words 'register of public auditors' substituted for 'register of auditors' by EC(SA)(Dir)R 2010, reg 12(1)(b)(iii).

g Words 'register of public auditors' substituted for 'register of auditors' by EC(SA)(Dir)R 2010, reg 12(1)(c)(i).

h Words 'a public auditor' substituted for 'an auditor' by EC(SA)(Dir)R 2010, reg 12(1)(c)(ii).

i Words 'register of public auditors' substituted for 'register of auditors' by EC(SA)(Dir)R 2010, reg 12(1)(c)(iii).

j As implicitly substituted for "fine not exceeding €2,000" by Fines Act 2010, s 6. A class C fine currently means a fine not exceeding €2,500.

k As implicitly substituted for "fine not exceeding €60" by Fines Act 2010, s 8. A class E fine currently means a fine not exceeding €500.

199 Transitional provisions concerning register

[(1) Subject to subsection (2), a body of accountants which has been recognised by the Supervisory Authority under section 191, shall, within one month after such recognition, deliver to the registrar of companies, the name and address of each of its members who is qualified for appointment under the Companies Acts as [...][b] public auditor.][a]

(2) Without prejudice to the generality of subsection (1), a body of accountants based outside the State, [whose recognition is continued under section 32(2) of the Act of 2003][c] or granted as aforesaid, shall notify details of those of its members who wish to practise in the State [as public auditors][d].

[(2A) A body of accountants referred to in subsection (1) or (2) shall, as soon as possible but not later than 6 months after the event, notify the registrar of companies of any change in the particulars previously provided to him under the applicable subsection.][e]

(3) Every person who, immediately before the commencement of this section, holds an authorisation from the Minister under the Companies Acts to act [...][f] as a public auditor (otherwise than by virtue of membership of a recognised body of accountants) shall, within one month after such commencement, deliver his name and address to the registrar of companies.

[(3A) A person referred to in subsection (3) or in section 32(6) of the Act of 2003, shall notify the registrar of companies—

(a) at least once in each year during the currency of the authorisation referred to in that subsection or section, as the case may be, of the fact that the person holds the authorisation,

(b) as soon as possible but not later than one month after the event, of any change in the particulars provided by the person to the registrar, and

(c) as soon as possible but not later than one month after ceasing to hold the authorisation, of the occurrence of that event.][g]

[(4) If default is made in complying with subsection (1) or (2A), the body of accountants concerned shall be guilty of an offence.][h]

[(5) Information required to be delivered to the registrar of companies under this section shall be delivered in such form and manner as that registrar may specify.][i]

Amendments

a C(AA)A 2003, s 39(a) substitutes CA 1990, s 199(1).

b EC(SA)(Dir)R 2010, reg 13(1)(a) deletes 'auditor of a company or'.

c C(AA)A 2003, s 39(b) amends CA 1990, s 199(2) by substituting 'whose recognition is continued under section 32(2) of the Act of 2003' for 'whose recognition is renewed'.

d EC(SA)(Dir)R 2010, reg 13(1)(b) inserts 'as public auditors'.

e C(AA)A 2003, s 39(c) inserts CA 1990, s 199(2A).

f EC(SA)(Dir)R 2010, reg 13(1)(c) deletes 'as auditor of a company or'.

g C(AA)A 2003, s 39(d) inserts CA 1990, s 199(3A).

h C(AA)A 2003, s 39(e) substitutes CA 1990, s 199(4).

i C(AA)A 2003, s 39(f) inserts CA 1990, s 199(5).

200 Duty to keep registrar informed

(1) Subject to subsection (2), where, by virtue of his becoming a member of a body of accountants, a person (other than a person referred to in section 199 (1)) becomes qualified for appointment [...][a] as a public auditor, the body concerned shall, within one month of his becoming so qualified, deliver his name and address to the registrar of companies for inclusion in the register referred to in section 198.

(2) Without prejudice to the generality of subsection (1), a recognised body of accountants based outside the State shall notify details of those of its members who wish to practise in the State [as public auditors][b].

[(2A) A body of accountants referred to in subsection (1) or a recognised body of accountants referred to in subsection (2) shall, as soon as possible but not later than 6 months after the event, notify the registrar of companies of any change in the particulars previously provided to him under the applicable subsection.][c]

(3) Every person who, after the commencement of this section, is granted an authorisation by the Minister under the Companies Acts to act [...][d] as a public auditor (otherwise than by virtue of membership of a recognised body of accountants) shall, within one month after such grant, deliver his name and address to the registrar of companies.

[(3A) A person referred to in subsection (3) shall notify the registrar of companies—

(a) at least once in each year during the currency of the authorisation referred to in that subsection, of the fact that the person holds the authorisation,

(b) as soon as possible but not later than one month after the event, of any change in the particulars provided by the person to the registrar, and

(c) as soon as possible but not later than one month after ceasing to hold the authorisation, of the occurrence of that event.][e]

[(4) If default is made in complying with subsection (1) or (2A), the body of accountants concerned, or the recognised body of accountants concerned, shall be guilty of an offence.][f]

[(5) Information required to be delivered to the registrar of companies under this section shall be delivered in such form and manner as that registrar may specify.][g]

Amendments

a EC(SA)(Dir)R 2010, reg 13(2)(a) deletes 'as auditor of a company or'.

b EC(SA)(Dir)R 2010, reg 13(2)(b) inserts 'as public auditors'.

c C(AA)A 2003, s 40(a) inserts CA 1990, s 200(2A).

d EC(SA)(Dir)R 2010, reg 13(2)(c) deletes 'as auditor of a company or'.

e C(AA)A 2003, s 40(b) inserts CA 1990, s 200(3A).

f C(AA)A 2003, s 40(c) substitutes CA 1990, s 200(4).

g C(AA)A 2003, s 40(d) inserts CA 1990, s 200(5).

201 Power to make supplementary regulations

(1) The Minister may make such supplementary regulations as he considers necessary for the proper and effective implementation of the Council Directive.

(2) Without prejudice to the generality of subsection (1), if, in any respect, any difficulty arises in regard to the implementation of the Directive, the Minister may by regulations do anything which appears to him to be necessary or expedient for removing that difficulty, and any such regulations may modify any provision of this Part so far as may be necessary or expedient to implement the Directive but no regulations shall be made under this subsection in relation to any provision of this Part after the expiration of 3 years commencing on the day on which the relevant provision of this Part came into operation.

(3) Every regulation made by the Minister under this section shall be laid before each House of the Oireachtas as soon as may be after it is made and, if a resolution annulling the regulation is passed by either House within the next 21 days on which that House has sat after the regulation is laid before it, the regulation shall be annulled accordingly, but without prejudice to the validity of anything previously done thereunder.

202 Keeping of books of account

(1) Every company shall cause to be kept proper books of account, whether in the form of documents or otherwise, that—

(a) correctly record and explain the transactions of the company,

(b) will at any time enable the financial position of the company to be determined with reasonable accuracy,

[(c) will enable the directors to ensure that any annual accounts of the company comply with the requirements of the Companies Acts and, where applicable, Article 4 of the IAS Regulations, and] [a]

(d) will enable the [annual accounts][a] of the company to be readily and properly audited.

(2) The books of account of a company shall be kept on a continuous and consistent basis, that is to say, the entries therein shall be made in a timely manner and be consistent from one year to the next.

(3) Without prejudice to the generality of subsections (1) and (2), books of account kept pursuant to those subsections shall contain—

(a) entries from day to day of all sums of money received and expended by the company and the matters in respect of which the receipt and expenditure takes place,

(b) a record of the assets and liabilities of the company,

(c) if the company's business involves dealing in goods—

(i) a record of all goods purchased, and of all goods sold (except those sold for cash by way of ordinary retail trade), showing the goods and the sellers and buyers in sufficient detail to enable the goods and the sellers and buyers to be identified and a record of all the invoices relating to such purchases and sales,

(ii) statements of stock held by the company at the end of each financial year and all records of stocktakings from which any such statement of stock has been, or is to be, prepared, and

(d) if the company's business involves the provision of services, a record of the services provided and of all the invoices relating thereto.

(4) For the purposes of subsections (1), (2) and (3), proper books of account shall be deemed to be kept if they comply with those subsections and give a true and fair view of the state of affairs of the company and explain its transactions.

(5) Subject to subsection (6), the books of account shall be kept at the registered office of the company or at such other place as the directors think fit.

(6) If books of account are kept at a place outside the State, there shall be sent to and kept at a place in the State and be at all reasonable times open to inspection by the directors such accounts and returns relating to the business dealt with in the books of account so kept as will disclose with reasonable accuracy the financial position of that business at intervals not exceeding 6 months and will enable to be prepared in accordance with the Companies Acts [(and, where applicable, Article 4 of the IAS Regulation) the company's accounts and any document annexed to those accounts][b] giving information which is required by the said Acts and is thereby allowed to be so given.

(7) Books of account required by this section to be kept, and accounts and returns referred to in subsection (6), shall be kept either in written form in an official language of the State or so as to enable the books of account and the accounts and returns to be readily accessible and readily convertible into written form in an official language of the State.

(8) A company shall make its books of account, and any accounts and returns referred to in subsection (6), available in written form in an official language of the State at all reasonable times for inspection without charge by the officers of the company and by other persons entitled pursuant to the Companies Acts to inspect the books of account of the company.

(9) A record, being a book of account required by this section to be kept or an account or return referred to in subsection (6), shall be preserved by the company concerned for a period of at least 6 years after the latest date to which it relates.

(10) A company that contravenes this section and a person who, being a director of a company, fails to take all reasonable steps to secure compliance by the company with the requirements of this section, or has by his own wilful act been the cause of any default by the company thereunder, shall be guilty of an offence:

Provided, however, that—

(a) in any proceedings against a person in respect of an offence under this section consisting of a failure to take reasonable steps to secure compliance by a company with the requirements of this section, it shall be a defence to prove that he had reasonable grounds for believing and did believe that a competent and reliable person was charged with the duty of ensuring that those requirements were complied with and was in a position to discharge that duty, and

(b) a person shall not be sentenced to imprisonment for such an offence unless, in the opinion of the court, the offence was committed wilfully.

Amendments

a Section 202(1)(c) substituted and (d) amended by EC(IFRSMA)R 2005, reg 9, Sch 1, Pt 4, Item No 6(a).

b Words substituted by EC(IFRSMA)R 2005, reg 9, Sch 1, Pt 4, Item No 6(b).

203 Liability of officers of company to penalty where proper books of account not kept

(1) If—

(a) a company that is being wound up and that is unable to pay all of its debts, has contravened section 202, and

(b) the court considers that such contravention has contributed to the company's inability to pay all of its debts or has resulted in substantial uncertainty as to the assets and liabilities of the company or has substantially impeded the orderly winding up thereof,

every officer of the company who is in default shall be guilty of an offence and liable—

(i) on summary conviction, to a [class C fine][a] or to imprisonment for a term not exceeding 6 months or to both, or

(ii) on conviction on indictment, to a fine not exceeding [€22,220.42][b] or to imprisonment for a term not exceeding 5 years or to both.

(2) In a prosecution for an offence under this section it shall be a defence for the person charged with the offence to show that—

(a) he took all reasonable steps to secure compliance by the company with section 202, or

(b) he had reasonable grounds for believing and did believe that a competent and reliable person, acting under the supervision or control of a director of the company who has been formally allocated such responsibility, was charged with the duty of ensuring that that section was complied with and was in a position to discharge that duty.

Amendments

a £1,000 increased to £1,500 by CA 1990, s 240(7) as inserted by CLEA 2001, s 104(c), and converted to €1,904.61 by Council Regulations (EC) No 1103/97, No 974/98 and No 2866/98 and the Economic and Monetary Union Act 1998, s 6; the above being implicitly substituted, by Fines Act 2010, s 6, for a fine not exceeding the aforesaid amount. A class C fine currently means a fine not exceeding €2,500.

b £10,000 converted to €12,697.38 by Council Regulations (EC) No 1103/97, No 974/98 and No 2866/98 and the Economic and Monetary Union Act 1998, s 6, and multiplied by a multiplier of 1.75 pursuant to Fines Act 2010, s 9.

204 Personal liability of officers of company where proper books of account not kept

(1) Subject to subsection (2), if—

(a) a company that is being wound up and that is unable to pay all of its debts has contravened section 202, and

(b) the court considers that such contravention has contributed to the company's inability to pay all of its debts or has resulted in substantial uncertainty as to the assets and liabilities of the company or has substantially impeded the orderly winding up thereof,

the court, on the application of the liquidator or any creditor or contributory of the company, may, if it thinks it proper to do so, declare that any one or more of the officers and former officers of the company who is or are in default shall be personally liable, without any limitation of liability, for all, or such part as may be specified by the court, of the debts and other liabilities of the company.

(2) On the hearing of an application under this subsection, the person bringing the application may himself give evidence or call witnesses.

(3) (a) Where the court makes a declaration under subsection (1), it may give such directions as it thinks proper for the purpose of giving effect to the declaration and in particular may make provision for making the liability of any such person under the declaration a charge on any debt or obligation due from the company to him, or on any mortgage or charge or any interest in any mortgage or charge on any assets of the company held by or vested in him or any company or other person on his behalf, or any person claiming as assignee from or through the person liable under the declaration or any company or person acting on his behalf, and may from time to time make such further order as may be necessary for the purpose of enforcing any charge imposed under this subsection.

(b) In paragraph (a) 'assignee' includes any person to whom or in whose favour, by the directions of the person liable, the debt, obligation, mortgage or charge was created, issued or transferred or the interest created, but does not include an assignee for valuable consideration (not including consideration by way of marriage) given in good faith and without notice of any of the matters on the ground of which the declaration is made.

(4) The court shall not make a declaration under subsection (1) in respect of a person if it considers that—

(a) he took all reasonable steps to secure compliance by the company with section 202, or

(b) he had reasonable grounds for believing and did believe that a competent and reliable person, acting under the supervision or control of a director of the company who has been formally allocated such responsibility, was charged with the duty of ensuring that that section was complied with and was in a position to discharge that duty.

(5) This section shall have effect notwithstanding that the person concerned may be criminally liable in respect of the matters on the ground of which the declaration is to be made.

(6) In this section 'officer', in relation to a company, includes a person who has been convicted of an offence under section 194, 197 or 242 in relation to a statement concerning the keeping of proper books of account by the company.

205 Commencement of Part X

Each of the following provisions, that is to say sections 202 to 204, shall apply as respects the accounts of a company for each financial year of the company beginning or ending after such date after the commencement of the provision as may be specified by the Minister by order.

[205A Accounting standards

(1) In this section—

'accounting standards' means—

(a) statements of accounting standards, and

(b) any written interpretation of those standards,

issued by any body or bodies prescribed by regulation;

'relevant undertaking' means—

(a) a company, or

(b) an undertaking referred to in Regulation 6 of the 1993 Regulations,

but does not include a company or an undertaking of a class exempt under section 48(1)(j) of the Act of 2003 from this section.

(2) Each relevant undertaking shall ensure—

(a) that its [individual accounts][b] and, where relevant, its group accounts include a statement as to whether they have been prepared in accordance with applicable accounting standards, and

(b) that any material departure from applicable accounting standards, the effect of the departure and the reasons for it are noted in the [individual accounts][b] and, where relevant, in the group accounts.

(3) Accounting standards are applicable to a relevant undertaking's [individual accounts][b] and, where relevant, to its group accounts, if those standards are, in accordance with their terms, relevant to its circumstances and those accounts.

(4) Where a relevant undertaking fails to comply with subsection (2), each company or other entity that forms all or part of that undertaking is guilty of an offence.][a]

Amendments

a C(AA)A 2003, s 41 inserts CA 1990, s 205A.

b 'Individual accounts' substituted for 'annual account' by EC(IFRSMA)R 2005, reg 9, Sch 1, Pt 4, Item No 7.

[205B Audit committee

(1) In this section—

'affiliate' in relation to an auditor, means a firm, body corporate or partnership considered under section 182(2) to be an affiliate of the auditor at the relevant time;

'amount of turnover' and 'balance sheet total' have the same meanings as in section 8 of the Companies (Amendment) Act 1986;

'internal audit' means an examination of the internal control system of a public limited company, a large private company or a relevant undertaking that is conducted within the public limited company, large private company or undertaking or otherwise at the request of its audit committee, directors or other officers;

'internal auditor' means a person who conducts an internal audit;

'large private company' means either of the following:

(a) a private company limited by shares that, in both the most recent financial year of the company and the immediately preceding financial year, meets the following criteria:

   (i) the balance sheet total of that company exceeds for the year—

      (A) €25,000,000, or

      (B) if an amount is prescribed under section 48(1)(l) of the Act of 2003 for the purpose of this provision, the prescribed amount;

   (ii) the amount of turnover of that company exceeds for the year—

      (A) €50,000,000, or

      (B) if an amount is prescribed under section 48(1)(l) of the Act of 2003 for the purpose of this provision, the prescribed amount;

(b) a private company limited by shares if the company and all its subsidiary undertakings together, in both the most recent financial year of that company and the immediately preceding financial year, meet the criteria in paragraph (a);

'parent undertaking' and 'subsidiary undertaking' have the same meaning as in the 1992 Regulations;

'relevant undertaking' means either of the following:

(a) an undertaking referred to in Regulation 6 of the 1993 Regulations that, in both the most recent financial year and the immediately preceding financial year of the undertaking, meets the following criteria:

   (i) the balance sheet total of that undertaking exceeds for the year—

      (A) €25,000,000, or

      (B) if an amount is prescribed under section 48(1)(l) of the Act of 2003 for the purpose of this provision, the prescribed amount;

   (ii) the amount of turnover of that undertaking exceeds for the year—

      (A) €50,000,000, or

      (B) if an amount is prescribed under section 48(1)(l) of the Act of 2003 for the purpose of this provision, the prescribed amount;

(b) an undertaking referred to in Regulation 6 of the 1993 Regulations if that undertaking and all of its subsidiary undertakings together, in both the most recent financial year and the immediately preceding financial year of the parent undertaking, meet the criteria in paragraph (a).

(2) Subject to subsection (16), the board of directors of a public limited company (whether listed or unlisted) shall establish and adequately resource a committee of directors, to be known as the audit committee, with the following responsibilities:

(a) reviewing, before they are presented to the board of directors for approval—

(i) the company's [individual accounts],[b] and

(ii) if the company is a parent undertaking, the group accounts of the group of undertakings of which the company is the parent undertaking;

(b) determining whether the [individual accounts][b] so reviewed comply with section 205A(2) and whether, in the committee's opinion, they give at the end of the financial year a true and fair view of—

(i) the state of affairs of the company, and

[(ii) the profit or loss of the company, even if, by virtue of section 7(1A) of the Companies (Amendment) Act 1986 or section 148(8) of the Act of 1963, it is not laid before the members in annual general meeting;][c]

(c) determining whether the group accounts so reviewed comply with section 205A(2) and whether, in the committee's opinion, they give at the end of the financial year a true and fair view of—

(i) the state of affairs of the group of undertakings of which the company is the parent undertaking, and

(ii) the profit or loss of that group;

(d) recommending to the board of directors whether or not to approve the [individual accounts][b] and group accounts so reviewed;

(e) determining, at least annually, whether in the committee's opinion, the company has kept proper books of account in accordance with section 202;

(f) reviewing, before its approval by the board of directors, the statement required to be made under section 205E(5) and (6);

(g) determining whether, in the committee's opinion, the statement so reviewed—

(i) complies with section 205E(5) and (6), and

(ii) is fair and reasonable and is based on due and careful enquiry;

(h) recommending to the board of directors whether or not to approve a statement reviewed under paragraph (f);

(i) advising the board of directors as to the recommendation to be made by the board to the shareholders concerning the appointment of the company's auditor;

(j) monitoring the performance and quality of the auditor's work and the auditor's independence from the company;

(k) obtaining from the auditor up to date information to enable the committee to monitor the company's relationship with the auditor, including, but not limited to, information relating to the auditor's affiliates;

(l) recommending whether or not to award contracts to the auditor or an affiliate of the auditor for non-audit work;

(m) satisfying itself that the arrangements made and the resources available for internal audits are in the committee's opinion suitable;

(n) reporting, as part of the report under section 158 of the Principal Act, on the committee's activities for the year, including, but not limited to, the discharge of its responsibilities under paragraph (j);

(o) performing any additional functions prescribed by regulation under section 48(1)(m) of the Act of 2003;

(p) performing any other functions relating to the company's audit and financial management that are delegated to it by the board of directors.

(3) Subject to subsection (16), the board of directors of each large private company and of each relevant undertaking shall either—

(a) establish an audit committee that—

(i) has all or some of the responsibilities specified in subsection (2), and

(ii) subject to subsection (8), otherwise meets the requirements of this section, or

(b) decide not to establish an audit committee.

(4) The board of directors of each large private company and of each relevant undertaking to which subsection (3) applies shall state in their report under section 158 of the Principal Act—

(a) whether the company or undertaking, as the case may be, has established an audit committee or decided not to do so,

(b) if the company or undertaking, as the case may be, has established an audit committee, whether it has only some of the responsibilities specified in subsection (2), and

(c) if the company or undertaking, as the case may be, has decided not to establish an audit committee, the reasons for that decision.

(5) For the purpose of applying subsection (2) to a large private company or relevant undertaking that decides under subsection (3)(a) to establish an audit committee with some or all of the responsibilities specified in subsection (2)—

(a) a reference in any applicable paragraph of subsection (2) to a public limited company or the company is to be construed as a reference to the large private company or relevant undertaking, as the case may be, and

(b) subsection (2) applies to the extent specified by the large private company or the relevant undertaking with any other modifications necessary for that purpose.

(6) The audit committee is to consist of such directors as the board of directors concerned thinks fit, provided, subject to subsection (8), both of the following requirements are met:

(a) the committee consists of not fewer than 2 members;

(b) all those appointed to the committee qualify under subsection (7).

(7) A director qualifies for appointment to the audit committee unless he or she—

(a) is, or was at any time during the 3 years preceding appointment to the committee—

(i) an employee of the company or undertaking concerned, or

(ii) an employee of any subsidiary of the company concerned or of a subsidiary undertaking of the undertaking concerned, or

(b) is the chairperson of the board of directors.

(8) The requirements specified in paragraphs (a) and (b) of subsection (6) do not apply if—

(a) only one director on the board of directors of the company or undertaking concerned qualifies under subsection (7),

(b) that director—

(i) is appointed as the sole member of the audit committee, or

(ii) is appointed as the chairperson of an audit committee consisting of not more than 2 members (including the chairperson) and has, in the case of an equal division of votes, a second or casting vote,

(c) any conditions prescribed under section 48(1)(m) of the Act of 2003 are met, and

(d) the directors of the company or undertaking concerned state in their report under section 158 of the Principal Act the reasons for the company's or undertaking's exemption from those requirements.

(9) Written terms of reference concerning the audit committee's role in the audit and financial management of the company or relevant undertaking concerned shall—

(a) be prepared and approved by the board of directors,

(b) be submitted for the information of the shareholders of the company or undertaking concerned at its annual general meeting, and

(c) be reviewed each year by the board of directors.

(10) Without limiting the matters that may be included under subsection (9), the terms of reference must—

(a) specify how the audit committee will discharge its responsibilities, and

(b) provide for a programme of separate and joint meetings with the management, auditor and internal auditor of the company or undertaking concerned.

(11) Subsection (9) applies also in relation to any amendments of the audit committee's terms of reference.

(12) Where the board of directors of a public limited company to which subsection (2) applies fails to establish an audit committee that is constituted in accordance with this section, each director to whom the failure is attributable is guilty of an offence.

(13) Where a director of a large private company or relevant undertaking to which subsection (3) applies fails to take all reasonable steps to comply with the requirements of subsection (4), the director is guilty of an offence.

(14) A reference in this section to the directors of a relevant undertaking is to be construed in the case of an undertaking that does not have a board of directors as a reference to the corresponding persons appropriate to that undertaking.

(15) For the purpose of applying this section to a partnership that is referred to in Regulation 6 of the 1993 Regulations and that is a relevant undertaking—

(a) the partnership is to be treated as though it were a company formed and registered under the Companies Acts,

(b) a reference in this section to a report under section 158 of the Principal Act is to be construed as a reference to a report under Regulation 14 of the 1993 Regulations, and

(c) this section applies with any other modifications necessary for that purpose.

(16) This section does not apply to—

(a) a public limited company that is a wholly owned subsidiary undertaking of another public limited company, or

(b) any company or undertaking of a class exempted under section 48(1)(j) of the Act of 2003 from the application of this section.][a]

Amendments

a C(AA)A 2003, s 42 inserts CA 1990, s 205B.

b 'Individual accounts' substituted for 'annual accounts' by EC(IFRSMA)R 2005, reg 9, Sch 1, Pt 4, Item No 8(a).

c Subsection (2)(b)(ii) substituted by EC(IFRSMA)R 2005, reg 9, Sch 1, Pt 4, Item No 8(b).

[205C Disclosure of accounting policies

(1) In this section 'relevant undertaking' means—

(a) a company, or

(b) an undertaking referred to in Regulation 6 of the 1993 Regulations,

but does not include a company or an undertaking of a class exempted under section 48(1)(j) of the Act of 2003 from this section;

(2) A relevant undertaking shall disclose in the notes to its annual accounts the accounting policies adopted by the undertaking in determining—

(a) the items and amounts to be included in its balance sheet, and

(b) the amounts in its profit and loss account.

(3) The accounting policies that a relevant undertaking is required to disclose under this section include, but are not limited to, those relating to the depreciation and diminution in the value of its assets.

(4) Where a relevant undertaking fails to comply with subsection (2), each company or other entity that forms all or part of that undertaking is guilty of an offence.][a]

Amendments

a C(AA)A 2003, s 43 inserts CA 1990, s 205C.

[205D Disclosure of remuneration for audit, audit-related and non-audit work

(1) In this section—

'affiliate' in relation to an auditor, means a firm, body corporate or partnership considered under section 182(2) to be an affiliate of the auditor;

'audit committee' means the committee established under section 205B;

'audit-related work' means work required by any relevant undertaking, body or person to be done by an auditor of the relevant undertaking by virtue of his or her position as auditor of that undertaking, but does not include audit work;

'audit work' means—

(a) in relation to a relevant undertaking other than a partnership referred to in Regulation 6 of the 1993 Regulations, work required to fulfil the duties imposed under section 193 of this Act on an auditor of a company, and

(b) in relation to a partnership referred to in Regulation 6 of the 1993 Regulations, work required to fulfil the duties imposed under Regulation 22 of those Regulations on an auditor appointed by the partners;

'connected undertaking', in relation to a relevant undertaking, means an undertaking that under the 1992 Regulations, or under those Regulations as applied by Regulation 9 of the 1993 Regulations, is—

(a) a subsidiary undertaking of the relevant undertaking,

(b) a joint venture of the relevant undertaking proportionally consolidated in accordance with Regulation 32 of the 1992 Regulations, or

(c) an associated undertaking of the relevant undertaking;

'firm' means a firm that qualifies for appointment as auditor of a company or as a public auditor under section 187(1A);

'non-audit work' means work other than audit work or audit-related work;

'relevant undertaking' means—

(a) a company, or

(b) an undertaking referred to in Regulation 6 of the 1993 Regulations, but does not include a company or an undertaking of a class exempted under section 48(1)(j) of the Act of 2003 from this section;

'remuneration' includes benefits in kind and payments in cash.

(2) Subject to subsection (5), a relevant undertaking shall disclose in the notes to its annual accounts relating to each financial year beginning on or after the commencement of this section the following information:

(a) the remuneration for all work in each category specified in subsection (3) that was carried out for the relevant undertaking or a connected undertaking of the relevant undertaking, during that financial year—

(i) by an auditor of the relevant undertaking, and

(ii) by any firm or individual that, at any time during the financial year, was an affiliate of the auditor;

(b) the remuneration for all work in each category specified in subsection (3) that was carried out for the relevant undertaking or a connected undertaking of the relevant undertaking, during the preceding financial year—

(i) by an auditor of the relevant undertaking, and

(ii) by any firm or individual that, at any time during the financial year, was an affiliate of the auditor;

(c) where the remuneration referred to in paragraph (a) or (b) is for non-audit work, the nature of the work;

(d) where all or part of the remuneration referred to in paragraph (a) or (b) is in the form of a benefit in kind, the nature and estimated monetary value of the benefit.

(3) Remuneration must be disclosed under subsection (2) for each of the following categories of work carried out as described in that subsection:

(a) audit work;

(b) audit-related work;

(c) non-audit work.

(4) Where the auditor of a relevant undertaking is a firm, any work carried out by a partner in the firm is considered for the purposes of this section to have been carried out by the auditor.

(5) The disclosure requirements of this section apply in relation to a financial year of the relevant undertaking only if—

(a) the aggregate of the remuneration for all work in each specified category that was carried out as described in subsection (2)(a) in that financial year exceeds €1,000, and

(b) the aggregate of the remuneration for all work in each specified category that was carried out as described in subsection (2)(b) in the preceding financial year exceeds €1,000.

(6) Where the remuneration required to be disclosed by a relevant undertaking in respect of a financial year for non-audit work exceeds the aggregate of the remuneration required to be disclosed in respect of that year for audit work and audit-related work, the audit committee shall state in its report for that year under section 205B(2)(m)—

(a) whether it has satisfied itself that the carrying out of the non-audit work by the auditor or an affiliate of the auditor has not affected the auditor's independence from the relevant undertaking, and

(b) if it has satisfied itself to that effect, the reasons for the decision to have the non-audit work carried out by the auditor or an affiliate of the auditor.

(7) Subsection (6) applies also where the relevant undertaking has no audit committee, but in that case the required statement shall be made by the directors in their report under section 158 of the Principal Act.

(8) Where more than one firm or individual has been appointed as the auditor of a relevant undertaking in a single financial year, separate disclosure in respect of the remuneration of each of them and of their affiliates must be provided in the notes to the company's annual accounts.

(9) The auditor of a relevant undertaking shall provide the directors of that undertaking with the information necessary to enable the auditor's affiliates to be identified for the purposes of this section.

(10) Where a relevant undertaking fails to comply with subsection (2), (3) or (8), each company or other entity that forms all or part of that undertaking is guilty of an offence.

(11) Where the audit committee of a relevant undertaking fails to comply with subsection (6) or the directors of a relevant undertaking fail to comply with that subsection as applied by subsection (7), each member of the committee or each director of the undertaking, as the case may be, to whom the failure is attributable is guilty of an offence.

(12) Where an auditor fails to comply with subsection (9), the auditor is guilty of an offence.

(13) Section 205B(14) applies in relation to any reference in this section to the directors of a relevant undertaking and section 205B(15) applies for the purpose of applying this section to a partnership.][a]

Amendments

a C(AA)A 2003, s 44 inserts CA 1990, s 205D.

[205E Directors' compliance statement and related statement

(1) In this section—

'amount of turnover' and 'balance sheet total' have the same meanings as in section 8 of the Companies (Amendment) Act 1986; 'relevant obligations', in relation to a company, means the company's obligations under—

(a) the Companies Acts,

(b) tax law, and

(c) any other enactments that provide a legal framework within which the company operates and that may materially affect the company's financial statements;

'tax law' means—

(a) the Customs Acts,

(b) the statutes relating to the duties of excise and to the management of those duties,

(c) the Tax Acts,

(d) the Capital Gains Tax Acts,

(e) the Value-Added Tax Act 1972 and the enactments amending or extending that Act,

(f) the Capital Acquisitions Tax Act 1976 and the enactments amending or extending that Act,

(g) the statutes relating to stamp duty and to the management of that duty, and

(h) any instruments made under an enactment referred to in any of paragraphs (a) to (g) or made under any other enactment and relating to tax.

(2) This section applies to—

(a) a public limited company (whether listed or unlisted), and

(b) a private company limited by shares, but it does not apply to a company referred to in paragraph (a) or (b) that is of a class exempted under section 48(1)(j) of the Act of 2003 from this section or to a company referred to in paragraph (b) while that company qualifies for an exemption under subsection (9).

(3) The directors of a company to which this section applies shall, as soon as possible after the commencement of this section or after this section becomes applicable to the company, prepare or cause to be prepared a directors' compliance statement containing the following information concerning the company:

(a) its policies respecting compliance with its relevant obligations;

(b) its internal financial and other procedures for securing compliance with its relevant obligations;

(c) its arrangements for implementing and reviewing the effectiveness of the policies and procedures referred to in paragraphs (a) and (b).

(4) The directors' compliance statement (including any revisions) must—

(a) be in writing,

(b) be submitted for approval by the board of directors,

(c) at least once in every 3 year period following its approval by the board, be reviewed and, if necessary, revised by the directors, and

(d) be included in the directors' report under section 158 of the Principal Act.

(5) The directors of a company to which this section applies shall also include in their report under section 158 of the Principal Act a statement—

(a) acknowledging that they are responsible for securing the company's compliance with its relevant obligations,

(b) confirming that the company has internal financial and other procedures in place that are designed to secure compliance with its relevant obligations, and, if this is not the case, specifying the reasons, and

(c) confirming that the directors have reviewed the effectiveness of the procedures referred to in paragraph (b) during the financial year to which the report relates, and, if this is not the case, specifying the reasons.

(6) In addition, the directors of a company to which this section applies shall in the statement required under subsection (5)—

(a) specify whether, based on the procedures referred to in that subsection and their review of those procedures, they are of the opinion that they used all reasonable endeavours to secure the company's compliance with its relevant obligations in the financial year to which the annual report relates, and

(b) if they are not of that opinion, specify the reasons.

(7) For the purposes of this section, a company's internal financial and other procedures are considered to be designed to secure compliance with its relevant obligations and to be effective for that purpose if they provide a reasonable assurance of compliance in all material respects with those obligations.

(8) Where the directors of a company to which this section applies fail—

(a) to prepare, or to cause to be prepared, a directors' compliance statement as required by subsections (3) and (4)(a) to (c),

(b) to include a directors' compliance statement in the directors' report as required by subsection (4)(d), or

(c) to comply with subsections (5) and (6), each director to whom the failure is attributable is guilty of an offence.

(9) A private company limited by shares qualifies for an exemption from this section in respect of any financial year of the company if—

(a) its balance sheet total for the year does not exceed—

(i) €7,618,428, or

(ii) if an amount is prescribed under section 48(1)(l) of the Act of 2003 for the purpose of this provision, the prescribed amount, and

(b) the amount of its turnover for the year does not exceed—

(i) €15,236,856, or

(ii) if an amount is prescribed under section 48(1)(l) of the Act of 2003 for the purpose of this provision, the prescribed amount.][a]

Amendments

a C(AA)A 2003, s 45 inserts CA 1990, s 205E.

[205F Auditor's review of compliance statements and related statements

(1) The auditor of a company to which section 205E applies shall undertake an annual review of—

(a) the directors' compliance statement under subsections (3) and (4) of that section, and

(b) the directors' statement under subsections (5) and (6) of that section, to determine whether, in the auditor's opinion, each statement is fair and reasonable having regard to information obtained by the auditor, or by an affiliate of the auditor within the meaning of section 205D, in the course of and by virtue of having carried out audit work, audit-related work or non-audit work for the company.

(2) The auditor shall—

(a) include in the auditor's report appended to the company's annual accounts a report on, and the conclusions of, the review undertaken under subsection (1), and

(b) where any statement reviewed under subsection (1) is not, in the auditor's opinion, fair and reasonable—

(i) make a report to that effect to the directors, and

(ii) include that report in the auditor's report appended to the annual accounts.

(3) Where, in the auditor's opinion, the directors have failed—

(a) to prepare, or to cause to be prepared, a directors' compliance statement as required by section 205E(3) and (4)(a) to (c),

(b) to include a directors' compliance statement in the directors' report as required by section 205E(4)(d), or

(c) to comply with section 205E(5) and (6), the auditor shall report that opinion and the reasons for forming that opinion to the Director of Corporate Enforcement.

(4) Section 194(6) applies, with the necessary modifications, in relation to an auditor's compliance with an obligation imposed on him by or under this section as it applies in relation to an obligation imposed by or under section 194.

(5) A person who contravenes this section is guilty of an offence.][a]

Amendments

a C(AA)A 2003, s 45 inserts CA 1990, s 205F.

PART XI
ACQUISITION OF OWN SHARES AND SHARES IN HOLDING COMPANY

206 Interpretation

In this Part—

'the Act of 1983' means the Companies (Amendment) Act, 1983;

'company' means a company to which section 207 relates;

'distribution' has the meaning assigned to it by section 51(2) of the Act of 1983 (as amended by section 232 (d) and (e) of this Act);

'redeemable shares' includes shares which are liable at the option of the company or the shareholder to be redeemed.

207 Power to issue redeemable shares

(1) Subject to the provisions of this Part, a company limited by shares or limited by guarantee and having a share capital may, if so authorised by its articles, issue redeemable shares and redeem them accordingly.

(2) The issue and redemption of shares by a company pursuant to subsection (1) shall be subject to the following conditions—

(a) No redeemable shares shall be issued or redeemed at any time when the nominal value of the issued share capital which is not redeemable is less than one tenth of the nominal value of the total issued share capital of the company.

(b) No such shares shall be redeemed unless they are fully paid.

(c) The terms of redemption must provide for payment on redemption.

(d) [(i) Subject to subparagraph (ii), no such shares shall be redeemed otherwise than—

(I) out of profits available for distribution, and

(II) if the company is a public limited company, in accordance with the restriction on the distribution of assets specified in section 46 of the Companies (Amendment) Act 1983.][a]

(ii) Where the company proposes to cancel shares on redemption pursuant to section 208, such shares may also be redeemed out of the proceeds of a fresh issue of shares made for the purposes of redemption.

(e) The premium, if any, payable on redemption, must, subject to paragraph (f), have been provided for out of the said profits of the company.

(f) Where the shares were issued at a premium, any premium payable on their redemption (being a redemption to which paragraph (d)(ii) applies) may be paid out of the proceeds of a fresh issue of shares made for the purposes of the redemption, up to an amount equal to—

(i) the aggregate of the premiums received by the company on the issue of the shares redeemed, or

(ii) the current amount of the company's share premium account (including any sum transferred to that account in respect of premiums on the new shares),

whichever is the less, and in any such case the amount of the company's share premium account shall, not withstanding anything in section 62(1) of the Principal Act, be reduced by a sum corresponding (or by sums in the aggregate corresponding) to the amount of any payment made by virtue of this paragraph out of the proceeds of the issue of the new shares.

(3) Subject to the provisions of this Part, the redemption of shares may be effected on such terms and in such manner as may be provided by the articles of the company.

Amendments

a CA 1990, s 207(d)(i) substituted by EC(PLC)R 2008, reg 4(a).

---

208 Cancellation of shares on redemption

Shares redeemed pursuant to this Part may be cancelled on redemption, in which case the following provisions shall apply as respects those shares:

(a) The amount of the company's issued share capital shall be reduced by the nominal value of the shares redeemed but no such cancellation shall be taken as reducing the amount of the company's authorised share capital.

(b) Where the shares are—

(i) redeemed wholly out of the profits available for distribution, or

(ii) redeemed wholly or partly out of the proceeds of a fresh issue and the aggregate amount of those proceeds (disregarding any part of those proceeds used to pay any premium on redemption) is less than the aggregate nominal value of the shares redeemed ('the aggregable difference'),

then a sum equal to, in the case of subparagraph (i), the nominal amount of the shares redeemed and, in the case of subparagraph (ii), the aggregable difference shall be transferred to a reserve fund ('the capital redemption reserve fund') and the provisions of the Principal Act relating to the reduction of the share capital of a company shall, except as provided in this section, apply as if the capital redemption reserve fund were paid-up share capital of the company.

(c) Where a company—

(i) has redeemed and cancelled shares, or

(ii) is about to redeem shares and cancel them upon redemption,

it shall have the power to issue shares up to the nominal amount of the shares redeemed or to be redeemed as if those shares had never been issued and for the purposes of [section 116 of the Stamp Duties Consolidation Act, 1999],[a] shares issued by a company in place of shares redeemed under this Part shall constitute a chargeable transaction if, but only if, the actual value of the shares so issued exceeds the actual value of the shares redeemed at the date of their redemption and, where the issue of shares does constitute a chargeable transaction for those purposes, the amount on which stamp duty on the relevant statement relating to that transaction is chargeable under [section 117 of the Stamp Duties Consolidation Act, 1999],[a] shall be the difference between—

(I) the amount on which the duty would be so chargeable if the shares had not been issued in place of shares redeemed under this section, and

(II) the value of the shares redeemed at the date of their redemption.

(d) Where new shares are issued before the redemption of the old shares, the new shares shall not, so far as relates to stamp duty, be deemed to have been issued in pursuance of paragraph (c) unless the old shares are redeemed within one month after the issue of the new shares.

(e) The capital redemption reserve fund may, notwithstanding anything in this section, be applied by the company in paying up unissued shares of the company (other than redeemable shares) to be allotted to members of the company as fully paid bonus shares.

Amendments

a Amended by SDCA 1999, s 162 which came into effect on 15 December 1999.

---

209 Treasury shares

(1) Subject to the provisions of this section, a company may instead of cancelling shares upon their redemption hold them (as 'treasury shares') and shares so held may be dealt with by the company in the manner provided for in subsection (4) but not otherwise.

(2) (a) The nominal value of treasury shares held by a company may not, at any one time, exceed ten per cent of the nominal value of the issued share capital of the company.

(b) For the purposes of paragraph (a), the following shall also be deemed to be shares held by the company—

(i) shares held in the company by any subsidiary in pursuance of section 224, and

(ii) shares held in the company by any subsidiary in pursuance of section 9 of the Insurance Act, 1990, and

(iii) shares held in the company by any person acting in his own name but on the company's behalf.

(3) For so long as the company holds shares as treasury shares—

(a) the company shall not exercise any voting rights in respect of those shares and any purported exercise of those rights shall be void; and

(b) no dividend or other payment (including any payment in a winding up of the company) shall be payable to the company in respect of those shares.

(4) Treasury shares may either be—

(a) cancelled by the company in which case the provisions of section 208 shall apply as if the shares had been cancelled on redemption, or

(b) subject to subsections (5) and (6), may be re-issued as shares of any class or classes.

(5) A re-issue of shares under this section shall be deemed for all the purposes of the Companies Acts to be an issue of shares but the issued share capital of the company shall not be regarded for any purpose (including the purposes of any enactments relating to stamp duties) as having been increased by the re-issue of the shares.

(6) (a) The maximum and minimum prices at which treasury shares may be re-issued off-market ('the re-issue price range') shall be determined in advance by the company in general meeting in accordance with paragraphs (b), (c) and (d) and such determination may fix different maximum and minimum prices for different shares.

(b) Where the treasury shares to be re-issued are derived in whole or in part from shares purchased by the company in accordance with the provisions of this Part the re-issue price range of the whole or such part (as the case may be) of those shares shall be determined by special resolution of the company passed at the meeting at which the resolution authorising the said purchase has been passed and such determination shall, for the purposes of this subsection, remain effective with respect to those shares for the requisite period.

(c) Where the treasury shares to be re-issued are derived in whole or in part from shares redeemed by the company in accordance with the provisions of this Part the re-issue price range of the whole or such part (as the case may be) of those shares shall be determined by special resolution of the company passed before any contract for the re-issue of those shares is entered into and such determination shall, for the purposes of this subsection, remain effective with respect to those shares for the requisite period.

(d) The company may from time to time by special resolution vary or renew a determination of re-issue price range under paragraph (b) or (c) with respect to particular treasury shares before any contract for re-issue of those shares is entered into and any such variation or renewal shall, for the purposes of this subsection, remain effective as a determination of the re-issue price range of those shares for the requisite period.

(e) (i) For the purposes of determining in this subsection whether treasury shares are re-issued off-market, the provisions of section 212 (off-market and market purchases) shall have effect with the substitution of the words 're-issue', 'off-market re-issue' and 'reissued' respectively for the words 'purchase', 'off market purchase' and 'purchased' in subsection (1)(a) of that section.

(ii) In this subsection, 'the requisite period' means the period of eighteen months from the date of the passing of the resolution determining the re-issue price range or varying or renewing (as the case may be) such determination or such lesser period of time as the resolution may specify.

(7) A re-issue by a company of treasury shares in contravention of any of the provisions of subsection (6) shall be unlawful.

210 Power to convert shares into redeemable shares

(1) Subject to subsections (2), (3), (4) and (5) and the provisions of the Companies Acts governing the variation of rights attached to classes of shares and the alteration of a company's memorandum or articles, a company may convert any of its shares into redeemable shares.

(2) A conversion of shares under subsection (1) shall not have effect with respect to any shares, the holder of which notifies the company, before the date of conversion, of his unwillingness to have his shares converted but, subject to that and the other provisions of this section, the conversion shall have effect according to its terms.

(3) Subsection (2) shall not, where a shareholder objects to a conversion, prejudice any right he may have under the Companies Acts or otherwise to invoke the jurisdiction of the court to set aside the conversion or otherwise provide relief in respect thereof.

(4) No shares shall be converted into redeemable shares if as a result of the conversion the nominal value of the issued share capital which is not redeemable would be less than one tenth of the nominal value of the total issued share capital of the company.

(5) The provisions of sections 207, 208 and 209, shall apply to shares which have been converted into redeemable shares under this section.

211 Power of company to purchase own shares

(1) Subject to [subsection (4) and][a] the following provisions of this Part, a company may, if so authorised by its articles, purchase its own shares (including any redeemable shares).

(2) Sections 207 (2), 208 and 209 shall apply in relation to the purchase by a company under this section of any of its own shares as those sections apply in relation to the redemption of shares by a company under section 207.

(3) A company shall not purchase any of its shares under this section if as a result of such purchase the nominal value of the issued share capital which is not redeemable would be less than one tenth of the nominal value of the total issued share capital of the company.

[(4) This section has effect without prejudice to—

(a) the principle of equal treatment of all shareholders who are in the same position,

(b) the Market Abuse (Directive 2003/6/EC) Regulations 2005 (S.I. No. 342 of 2005), and

(c) Part 4 of the Investment Funds, Companies and Miscellaneous Provisions Act 2005.][b]

Amendments

a Words inserted by EC(PLC)R 2008, reg 4(b)(i).

b CA 1990, s 211(4) inserted by EC(PLC)R 2008, reg 4(b)(ii).

---

212 Off-market and market purchases

(1) For the purposes of sections 213 and 215, a purchase by a company of its own shares is—

(a) an 'off-market purchase' if the shares are purchased either—

(i) otherwise than on a recognised stock exchange, or

(ii) on a recognised stock exchange but are not subject to a marketing arrangement on that stock exchange,

(b) a 'market purchase' if the shares are purchased on a recognised stock exchange [within the State][a] and are subject to a marketing arrangement.

[(1A) For the purposes of sections 215, 226, 226A and 229, a purchase by a company that issues shares, or by a subsidiary of that company, of the first-mentioned company's shares, is an 'overseas market purchase' if the shares are purchased on a recognised stock exchange outside the State and are subject to a marketing arrangement.][b]

(2) For the purposes of [subsections (1) and (1A)][c], a company's shares are subject to a marketing arrangement on a recognised stock exchange if either—

(a) they are listed on that stock exchange, or

(b) the company has been afforded facilities for dealings in those shares to take place on that stock exchange without prior permission for individual transactions from the authority governing that stock exchange and without limit as to the time during which those facilities are to be available.

Amendments

a Words 'within the State' inserted by C(MP)A 2009, s 3(d)(i).

b Subsection (1A) inserted by C(MP)A 2009, s 3(d)(ii).

c Words 'subsections (1) and (1A)' substituted for 'subsection (1)' by C(MP)A 2009, s 3(d)(iii).

---

213 Authority for off-market purchase

(1) A company shall not make an off-market purchase of its own shares otherwise than in pursuance of a contract authorised in advance in accordance with this section.

(2) The terms of the proposed contract of purchase shall be authorised by special resolution before the contract is entered into and any such authority may be varied, revoked or from time to time renewed by special resolution.

(3) A special resolution under subsection (2) shall not be effective for the purposes of this section if any member of the company holding shares to which the resolution relates exercises the voting rights carried by any of those shares in voting on the resolution and the resolution would not have been passed if he had not done so.

(4) Notwithstanding anything contained in section 137 of the Principal Act or in a company's articles, any member of the company may demand a poll on a special resolution under subsection (2).

(5) A special resolution under subsection (2) shall not be effective unless a copy of the proposed contract of purchase or, if the contract is not in writing, a written memorandum of its terms is available for inspection by members of the company both—

(a) at the registered office of the company for not less than the period of 21 days ending with the date of the meeting at which the resolution is passed, and

(b) at the meeting itself.

(6) Any memorandum of the terms of the contract of purchase made available for the purposes of this section must include the names of any members holding shares to which the contract relates, and any copy of the contract made available for those purposes must have annexed to it a written memorandum specifying any such names which do not appear in the contract itself.

(7) A company may agree to a variation of an existing contract of purchase approved under this section only if the variation is authorised by special resolution of the company before it is agreed to, and subsections (2) to (5) shall apply in relation to that authority save that a copy or memorandum (as the case may require) of the existing contract must also be available for inspection in accordance with subsection (5).

214 Contingent purchase contract

(1) In this section 'contingent purchase contract' means a contract entered into by a company and relating to any of its shares which does not amount to a contract to purchase those shares but under which the company may become entitled or obliged to purchase those shares.

(2) A company shall only make a purchase of its own shares in pursuance of a contingent purchase contract if the terms of the contract have been authorised by a special resolution of the company before the contract is entered into and subsections (2) to (7) of section 213 shall apply to such contract and resolution.

215 Authority for market purchase

(1) A company shall not make a market purchase [or overseas market purchase][a] of its own shares unless the purchase has first been authorised by the company in general meeting and any such authority may be varied, revoked or from time to time renewed by the company in general meeting. This subsection shall not be construed as requiring any particular contract for the market purchase [or overseas market purchase][a] of shares to be authorised by the company in general meeting and for the purposes of this Part where a market purchase [or overseas market purchase][a] of shares has been authorised in accordance with this section any contract entered into pursuant to that authority in respect of such a purchase shall be deemed also to be so authorised.

(2) Section 143 of the Principal Act shall apply to a resolution under subsection (1).

(3) In the case of a public limited company, any authority granted under subsection (1) shall—

- (a) specify the maximum number of shares authorised to be acquired; and
- (b) determine both the maximum and minimum prices which may be paid for the shares.

(4) A resolution to which subsection (3) applies may determine either or both the prices mentioned in paragraph (b) of that subsection by—

- (a) specifying a particular sum; or
- (b) providing a basis or formula for calculating the amount of the price in question without reference to any person's discretion or opinion.

Amendments

a Words 'or overseas market purchase' inserted by C(MP)A 2009, s 3(e).

---

216 Duration of authority granted by public limited companies to purchase own shares

(1) Without prejudice to the generality of sections 213, 214 and 215, in the case of a public limited company, any authority granted under those sections shall specify the date on which the authority is to expire which shall not be later than 18 months after the date on which the special resolution or ordinary resolution, as the case may be, granting the authority is passed.

(2) A public limited company may make a purchase after the expiry of any time limit imposed by virtue of subsection (1) in any case where the contract of purchase was concluded before the authority expired and the terms of the authority permit the company to make a contract of purchase which would or might be executed wholly or partly after the authority expired.

217 Assignment or release of company's right to purchase own shares

(1) Any purported assignment of the rights of a company under any contract authorised under section 213, 214 or 215 shall be void.

(2) Nothing in subsection (1) shall prevent a company from releasing its right under any contract authorised under section 213, 214 or 215 provided that, in the case of a contract authorised under section 213 or 214, the release has been authorised by special resolution of the company before the release is entered into, and any such purported release by a company which has not been authorised as aforesaid shall be void.

(3) Subsections (2) to (7) of section 213, shall apply to a resolution under subsection (2).

218 Incidental payments with respect to purchase of own shares

(1) Any payment made by a company in consideration of—

- (a) acquiring any right with respect to the purchase of its own shares in pursuance of a contract authorised under section 214, or
- (b) the variation of a contract authorised under section 213 or 214, or
- (c) the release of any of the company's obligations with respect to the purchase of any of its own shares under a contract authorised under section 213, 214 or 215,

shall be unlawful if any such payment is made otherwise than out of distributable profits of the company.

(2) If the requirements of subsection (1) are not satisfied in relation to a contract—

(a) in a case to which paragraph (a) of that subsection applies, no purchase by the company of its own shares in pursuance of that contract shall be lawful under this Part;

(b) in a case to which paragraph (b) of that subsection applies, no such purchase following the variation shall be lawful under this Part; and

(c) in a case to which paragraph (c) of that subsection applies, the purported release shall be void.

219 Effect of company's failure to redeem or purchase

(1) This section applies to—

(a) redeemable shares issued after the coming into operation of this Part;

(b) shares which have been converted into redeemable shares pursuant to section 210; and

(c) shares which a company has agreed to purchase pursuant to section 213, 214 or 215.

(2) Without prejudice to any other right of the holder of any shares to which this section applies a company shall not be liable in damages in respect of any failure on its part to redeem or purchase any such shares.

(3) The court shall not grant an order for specific performance of the terms of redemption or purchase of the shares to which this section applies if the company shows that it is unable to meet the cost of redeeming or purchasing the shares out of profits available for distribution.

(4) Where at the commencement of the winding up of a company any shares to which this section applies have not been redeemed or purchased then, subject to subsections (5), (6) and (7), the terms of redemption or purchase may be enforced against the company and the shares when so redeemed or purchased under this subsection shall be treated as cancelled.

(5) Subsection (4) shall not apply if—

(a) the terms of redemption or purchase provided for the redemption or purchase to take place at a date later than that of the commencement of the winding-up, or

(b) during the period beginning with the date on which the redemption or purchase was to have taken place and ending with the commencement of the winding-up the company could not at any time have lawfully made a distribution equal in value to the price at which the shares were to have been redeemed or purchased.

(6) There shall be paid in priority to any amount for which the company is liable by virtue of subsection (4) to pay in respect of any shares—

(a) all other debts and liabilities of the company other than any due to members in their character as such, and

(b) if other shares carry rights, whether as to capital or to income, which are preferred to the rights as to capital attaching to the first mentioned shares, any amount due in satisfaction of those preferred rights, but subject as aforesaid, any such amount shall be paid in priority to any amounts due to members in satisfaction of their rights (whether as to capital or income) as members.

(7) Where by virtue of the application by section 284 of the Principal Act of the rules of bankruptcy in the winding-up of insolvent companies a creditor of a company is entitled to payment of any interest only after payment of all other debts of the company, the company's debts and liabilities shall for the purposes of subsection (6) include the liability to pay that interest.

220 Redemption of existing redeemable preference shares

Section 64 of the Principal Act is hereby repealed but any redeemable preference shares issued by a company limited by shares before the coming into operation of this Part which could but for the repeal of section 64 have been redeemed under that section shall be subject to redemption in accordance with the provisions of this Part save that any premium payable on redemption may, notwithstanding section 207(2)(e) and (f), be paid out of the share premium account instead of out of profits or may be paid partly out of that account and partly out of profits available for distribution.

221 Construction of references to redeemable preference shares

A reference to redeemable preference shares in—

(a) section 69(1)(e) of, and the Second, Third, Fourth and Sixth Schedules to, the Principal Act, and

(b) section 55(1)(h) of the Act of 1983,

shall be construed as a reference to redeemable shares.

222 Retention and inspection of documents

(1) Every company which enters into a contract under section 213, 214 or 215 shall, until the expiration of ten years after the contract has been fully performed, keep at its registered office a copy of that contract or, if it is not in writing, a memorandum of its terms.

(2) Every document required to be kept under subsection (1) shall during business hours (subject to such reasonable restrictions as the company in general meeting may impose, so that not less than 2 hours in each day be allowed for inspection) be open to the inspection of any member and, if the company is a public limited company, of any other person.

(3) If a company fails to comply with this section, the company and every officer of the company who is in default shall be guilty of an offence.

(4) In the case of a refusal of an inspection of a document required under subsection (2), the court may, on the application of a person who has requested an inspection and has been refused, by order require the company to allow the inspection of that document.

223 Application of section 108(6) to dealings by company in its own securities

Subsection (6) of section 108, in its application to dealings by a company in its own securities, shall not preclude a company from dealing in its own shares at any time by reason only of information in the possession of an officer of that company if—

(a) the decision to enter into the transaction was taken on its behalf by a person other than the officer, and

(b) the information was not communicated to that person and no advice relating to the transaction was given to him by a person in possession of the information.

224 Holding by subsidiary of shares in its holding company

(1) Notwithstanding sections 32 and 60 of the Principal Act a company may, subject to the provisions of this section, acquire and hold shares in a company which is its holding company.

(2) The acquisition and holding by a subsidiary under subsection (1) of shares in its holding company shall be subject to the following conditions:

(a) The consideration for the acquisition of such shares shall be provided for out of the profits of the subsidiary available for distribution

(b) Upon the acquisition of such shares and for so long as the shares are held by the subsidiary—

(i) the profits of the subsidiary available for distribution shall for all purposes be restricted by a sum equal to the total cost of the shares acquired;

(ii) the shares shall, for the purposes of the consolidated accounts prepared by the holding company in accordance with sections 150 to 152 of The Principal Act, be treated in the same manner as is required in respect of shares held as treasury shares under section 43A of the Act of 1983 (inserted by section 232(c) of this Act); and.

(iii) the subsidiary shall not exercise any voting rights in respect of the shares and any purported exercise of those rights shall be void.

(3) A contract for the acquisition (whether by allotment or transfer) by a subsidiary of shares in its holding company shall not be entered into without being authorised in advance both by the subsidiary and its holding company and the provisions of sections 212 to 217 shall apply, with the necessary modifications, to the granting, variation, revocation and release of such authority.

(4) For the purposes of this section, a subsidiary's profits available for distribution shall not include the profits attributable to any shares in the subsidiary for the time being held by the subsidiary's holding company so far as they are profits for the period before the date on or from which the shares were acquired by the holding company.

(5) This section shall not apply to shares held by a subsidiary in its holding company in the circumstances permitted by section 32 of the Principal Act.

(6) This section, except subsection (2)(b)(iii), shall not apply to shares subscribed for, purchased or held by a subsidiary in its holding company pursuant to section 9(1) of the Insurance Act, 1990.

225 Civil liability for improper purchase in holding company

(1) Where the winding-up of a company which has acquired shares in its holding company in accordance with section 224 commences within six months after such acquisition and the company is at the time of the commencement of the winding-up unable to pay its debts (taking into account the contingent and prospective liabilities), the court, on the application of a liquidator, creditor, employee or contributory of the company, may subject to subsection (2), declare that the directors of the company shall

be jointly and severally liable to repay to the company the total amount paid by the company for the shares.

(2) Where it appears to the court that any person in respect of whom a declaration has been sought under subsection (1) believed on reasonable grounds that the said purchase was in the best interests of the company, the court may relieve him, either wholly or in part, from personal liability on such terms as it may think fit.

226 Return to be made to registrar

(1) Every company which has purchased shares pursuant to this Part shall, within 28 days [or, in the case of an overseas market purchase, within 3 working days,][a] after delivery to the company of those shares, deliver to the registrar for registration a return in the prescribed form stating with respect to shares of each class purchased the number and nominal value of those shares and the date on which they were delivered to the company.

(2) In the case of a public limited company, the return shall also state—

(a) the aggregate amount paid by the company for the shares, and

(b) the maximum and minimum prices paid in respect of each class purchased.

(3) Particulars of shares delivered to the company on different dates and under different contracts may be included in a single return to the registrar, and in such a case the amount required to be stated under subsection (2)(a) shall be the aggregate amount paid by the company for all the shares to which the return relates.

(4) If a company fails to comply with the requirements of this section, the company and every officer who is in default shall be guilty of an offence.

(5) Summary proceedings in relation to an offence under this section may be brought and prosecuted by the registrar of companies.

Amendments

a Words 'or, in the case of an overseas market purchase, within 3 working days,' inserted by C(MP)A 2009, s 3(e).

[226A Duty of company to publish particulars of overseas market purchase

(1) Whenever shares for which dealing facilities are provided on a recognised stock exchange are the subject of an overseas market purchase either by the company which issued the shares or by a company which is that company's subsidiary, the company which issued the shares shall publish, on its website for a continuous period of not less than 28 days beginning on the day that next follows the overseas market purchase concerned and is a day on which the recognised stock exchange concerned is open for business, or in any other prescribed manner, the following information for total purchases on the recognised stock market concerned on each such day:

(a) the date, in the place outside the State where the recognised stock market concerned is located, of the overseas market purchase;

(b) the purchase price at which the shares were purchased, or the highest such price and lowest such price paid by that company or subsidiary;

(c) the number of shares which were purchased;

(d) the recognised stock exchange on which the shares were purchased.

(2) If default is made in complying with this section, the company and every officer of the company who is in default shall be guilty of an offence.][a]

Amendments

a CA 1990, s 226A inserted by C(MP)A 2009, s 3(g).

---

227 Amendment of section 89 of the Principal Act

[...][a]

Amendments

a This section substitutes CA 1963, s 89.

---

228 Regulations as to purchase of shares

(1) The Minister may make regulations governing the purchase by companies of their own shares or of shares in their holding company and the sale by companies of their own shares held as treasury shares and such regulations may relate to companies in general or to a particular category or class of company.

(2) Without prejudice to the generality of subsection (1), regulations under this section may provide for in particular—

(a) the class or description of shares which may (or may not) be purchased or sold,

(b) the price at which they may be purchased or sold,

(c) the timing of such purchases or sales,

(d) the method by which the shares may be purchased or sold, and

(e) the volume of trading in the shares which may be carried out by companies.

(3) If a company fails to comply with the provisions of regulations made under this section, the company and every officer who is in default shall be guilty of an offence.

229 Duty of company to notify stock exchange

(1) Whenever shares for which dealing facilities are provided on a recognised stock exchange have been purchased either by the company which issued the shares or by a company which is that company's subsidiary[, other than when the purchase was an overseas market purchase,][a] the company whose shares have been purchased shall be under an obligation to notify that stock exchange of that matter; and the stock exchange may publish, in such manner as it may determine, any information received by it under this subsection.

(2) An obligation imposed by subsection (1) shall be fulfilled before the end of the day next following that on which it arises.

(3) If default is made in complying with this section, the company and every officer of the company who is in default shall be guilty of an offence.

Amendments

a Words ', other than when the purchase was an overseas market purchase,' inserted by C(MP)A 2009, s 3(h).

230 Duty of stock exchange in relation to unlawful purchases

(1) If it appears to a relevant authority of a recognised stock exchange that a company in the case of whose shares dealing facilities have been provided on that stock exchange has committed an offence under section 228 or 229, such authority shall forthwith report the matter to the [Director][a] and shall furnish to the [Director][a] such information and give to him such access to and facilities for inspecting and taking copies of any documents, being information or documents in the possession or under the control of such authority and relating to the matter in question, as the [Director][a] may require.

(2) Where it appears to a member of a recognised stock exchange that any person has committed an offence under section 228 or 229 he shall report the matter forthwith to a relevant authority of the recognised stock exchange concerned, who shall thereupon come under the duty referred to in subsection (1).

(3) If it appears to a court in any proceedings that any person has committed an offence as aforesaid, and that no report relating to the matter has been made to the [Director][a] under subsection (1), that court may, on the application of any person interested in the proceedings concerned or of its own motion, direct the relevant authority of the recognised stock exchange concerned to make such a report, and on a report being made accordingly, this section shall have effect as though the report had been made in pursuance of subsection (1).

[(4) If, where any matter is reported or referred to the Director under this section, he has reasonable grounds for believing that an offence under section 228 or 229 has been committed and—

(a) institutes proceedings in respect of the offence, or

(b) refers the matter to the Director of Public Prosecutions and the Director of Public Prosecutions institutes proceedings in respect of the offence,

it shall be the duty of a relevant authority of the recognised stock exchange concerned, and of every officer of the company whose shares are concerned, and of any other person who appears to the Director or to the Director of Public Prosecutions, as the case may be, to have relevant information (other than any defendant in the proceedings) to give all assistance in connection with the proceedings which he or they are reasonably able to give.][b]

(5) If it appears to the [Director],[c] arising from a complaint to a relevant authority of a recognised stock exchange concerning an alleged offence under section 228 or 229, that there are circumstances suggesting that—

(a) the relevant authority ought to use its powers under this section but has not done so, or

(b) that a report ought to be made to the [Director][a] under subsection (1), but that the relevant authority concerned has not so reported, he may request the relevant authority to use such powers or make such a report, and on a report being made accordingly, this section shall have effect as though the report had been made in pursuance of subsection (1).

[…][d]

(7) A relevant authority of a recognised stock exchange shall not be liable in damages in respect of anything done or omitted to be done by the authority in connection with the exercise by it of its functions under this section unless the act or omission complained of was done or omitted to be done in bad faith.

(8) For the purposes of this section each of the following shall be a 'relevant authority' in relation to a recognised stock exchange—

(i) its board of directors, committee of management or other management body,

(ii) its manager, however described.

(9) A relevant authority shall have the same powers and duties for the purposes of this section as it has under sections 117 and 120.

(10) Where the Minister considers it necessary or expedient to do so for the proper and effective administration of this section, he may make such regulations 4d as he thinks appropriate in relation to—

(a) the powers of authorised persons, or

(b) the matters in respect of which, or the persons from whom, authorised persons may require information under section 117, as applied by subsection (9).

Amendments

a CLEA 2001, s 39(a) amends CA 1990, s 230 by the substitution for 'Director of Public Prosecutions' wherever occurring, except in subsection (4) of 'Director'.

b CLEA 2001, s 39(b) substitutes CA 1990, s 230(4).

c CLEA 2001, s 39(c) amends CA 1990, s 230(5) by the substitution for 'Minister' of 'Director'.

d CLEA 2001, s 39(d) deletes CA 1990, s 230(6).

---

231 Amendments to the Principal Act in respect of share capital

(1) The Principal Act is hereby amended—

(a) [...][a];

(b) [...][b]; and

(c) [...][c].

(2) [...][d]

Amendments

a Subsection (1)(a) amends CA 1963, s 62(1) by the insertion after 'except as provided in this section' of 'and section 207(2) of the Companies Act, 1990'.

b Subsection (1)(b) amends CA 1963, s 62(2).

c Subsection (1)(c) amends CA 1963, s 72(1) by the deletion of 'to purchase any of its shares or'.

d Subsection (2) substitutes CA 1963, Sch 6, para 12(d).

---

232 Amendments to the Act of 1983

The Act of 1983 is hereby amended—

(a) [...][a];

(b) [...][b];

(c) [...][c];

(d) [...][d]; and

(e) [...][e].

Amendments

a Subsection (a) substitutes C(A)A 1983, s 41(4)(a).

b Subsection (b) deletes C(A)A 1983, s 43(13).

c Subsection (c) inserts C(A)A 1983, s 43A.

d Subsection (d) substitutes C(A)A 1983, s 51(2)(b).

e Subsection (e) inserts C(A)A 1983, s 51(2)(bb).

---

233 Amendments to the Companies (Amendment) Act, 1986

(1) Section 14 of the Companies (Amendment) Act, 1986, is hereby amended—

(a) in paragraph (vi) by the substitution of 'acquisition or disposal' for 'disposal'; and

(b) [...][a].

(2) Part I of the Schedule to the Companies (Amendment) Act, 1986, is hereby amended—

(a) by the deletion in Format 1 of the balance sheet formats of items A.III.7, B.III.2 and H.IV.2;

(b) by the deletion in Format 2 of the balance sheet formats—

(i) under 'Assets', of items A.III.7 and B.III.2 (Assets), and

(ii) under 'liabilities', of item A.IV.2; and

(c) by the deletion of note (3) in the notes on the balance sheet formats following the aforesaid formats.

(3) Part IV of the Schedule to the Companies (Amendment) Act, 1986, is hereby amended—

(a) [...][b]; and

(b) [...][c].

Amendments

a Subsection (1)(b) inserts C(A)A 1986, s 14(vii).

b Subsection (3)(a) inserts C(A)A 1986, Sch, Pt IV para 32A.

c Subsection (3)(c) substitutes C(A)A 1986, Sch, Pt IV para 39(3).

234 Offences under this Part

(1) A company which contravenes any of the following provisions shall be guilty of an offence, namely sections 207 to 211, 218 and 222 to 224.

(2) Section 241 shall apply to an offence under this Part.

PART XII
GENERAL

235 Amendment of section 2 of the Principal Act

(1) Unless the context otherwise requires, 'the court', used in any provision of the Companies Acts in relation to a company, means—

(a) the High Court, or

(b) where another court is prescribed for the purposes of that provision, that court.

(2) The definition of 'the court' in subsection (1) is in substitution for the definition in section 2 (1) of the Principal Act.

236 Qualifications of secretary of public limited company

It shall be the duty of the directors of a public limited company to take all reasonable steps to secure that the secretary (or each joint secretary) of the company is a person who appears to them to have the requisite knowledge and experience to discharge the functions of secretary of the company and who—

(a) on the commencement of this section held the office of secretary of the company; or

(b) for at least three years of the five years immediately preceding his appointment as secretary held the office of secretary of a company; or

(c) is a member of a body for the time being recognised for the purposes of this section by the Minister; or

(d) is a person who, by virtue of his holding or having held any other position or his being a member of any other body, appears to the directors to be capable of discharging those functions.

237 Qualifications of liquidators and receivers

(1) The Minister may, if he considers it necessary or expedient to do so in the interests of the orderly and proper regulation of the winding-up of companies generally, by regulations add to the list of persons in section 300A of the Principal Act (inserted by section 146) who shall not be qualified for appointment as liquidator of a company.

(2) The Minister may, if he considers it necessary or expedient to do so in the interests of the orderly and proper regulation of receiverships generally, by regulations add to the list of persons in section 315 of the Principal Act (inserted by section 170) who shall not be qualified for appointment as receiver of the property of a company.

(3) Every regulation made by the Minister under this section shall be laid before each House of the Oireachtas as soon as may be after it is made and, if a resolution annulling the regulation is passed by either House within the next 21 days on which that House has sat after the regulation is laid before it, the regulation shall be annulled accordingly, but without prejudice to the validity of anything previously done thereunder.

238 Amendment of section 61 of the Principal Act

[...][a]

Amendments

a This section inserts CA 1963, s 61(3).

---

239 Power to make regulations for transfer of securities

(1) The Minister may make provision by regulations for enabling title to securities to be evidenced and transferred without a written instrument.

[(1A) Subject to any exceptions that may be specified in the regulations, the regulations may, in respect of—

(a) securities of companies admitted to trading on a regulated market,

(b) securities of companies admitted to trading on a market other than a regulated market, or

(c) securities of public limited companies of a specified class,

provide that the means provided by the regulations for evidencing and transferring title to such securities shall constitute the sole and exclusive means for doing so (and, accordingly, that any purported transfer of such securities otherwise than by those means shall be void).][a]

(2) In this section—

(a) 'securities' means shares, stock, debentures, debenture stock, loan stock, bonds, units in undertakings for collective investments in transferable securities within the meaning of the European Communities (Undertakings for Collective Investment in Transferable Securities) Regulations, 1989 (S.I. No 78 of 1989), and other securities of any description;

(b) references to title to securities include any legal or equitable interest in securities; and

(c) references to a transfer of title include a transfer by way of security.

(3) The regulations may make provision—

(a) for procedures for recording and transferring title to securities, and

(b) for the regulation of those procedures and the persons responsible for or involved in their operation, and

(c) for dispensing with the obligations of a company under section 86 of the Principal Act to issue certificates and providing for alternative procedures.

(4) The regulations shall contain such safeguards as appear to the Minister appropriate for the protection of investors and for ensuring that competition is not restricted, distorted or prevented.

(5) (a) The regulations may for the purpose of enabling or facilitating the operation of the new procedures make provision with respect to the rights and obligations of persons in relation to securities dealt with under the procedures.

(b) The regulations shall be framed so as to secure that the rights and obligations in relation to securities dealt with under the new procedures correspond, so far as practicable, with those which would arise apart from any regulations under this section.

[(c) The regulations may—

(i) require the provision of statements by a company to holders of securities (at specified intervals or on specified occasions) of the securities held in their name;

(ii) make provision removing any requirement for the holders of securities to surrender existing share certificates to issuers; and

(iii) make provision that the requirements of the regulations supersede any existing requirements in the articles of association of a company which would be incompatible with the requirements of the regulations.][b]

[(5A) Without prejudice to the generality of subsections (4) and (5), the regulations shall not contain provisions that would result in a person who, but for the regulations, would be entitled—

(a) to have his or her name entered in the register of members of a company, or

(b) to give instructions in respect of any securities,

ceasing to be so entitled.][c]

(6) (a) The regulations may include such supplementary, incidental and transitional provisions as appear to the Minister to be necessary or expedient.

(b) In particular, provision may be made for the purpose of giving effect to—

(i) the transmission of title of securities by operation of law;

(ii) any restriction on the transfer of title to securities arising by virtue of the provisions of any enactment or instrument, court order or agreement;

(iii) any power conferred by any such provision on a person to deal with securities on behalf of the person entitled.

(7) The regulations may for the purposes mentioned in this section make provision with respect to the persons who are to be responsible for the operation of the new procedures and for those purposes may empower the Minister to delegate to any person willing and able to discharge them any functions of his under the regulations.

(8) The regulations may make different provision for different cases.

(9) Every regulation made under this section shall be laid before each House of the Oireachtas as soon as may be after it is made and if a resolution annulling the regulation is passed by either such House within the next twenty-one days on which that House has sat after the regulation is laid before it, the regulation shall be annulled accordingly, but without prejudice to the validity of anything previously done thereunder.

Amendments

a Subsection (1A) inserted by IFCMPA 2006, s 12(a).

b Subsection (5)(c) inserted by IFCMPA 2006, s 12(b).

c Subsection (5A) inserted by IFCMPA 2006, s 12(c).

240 Offences

(1) A person guilty under any provision of the Companies Acts of an offence for which no punishment is specifically provided shall be liable—

(a) on summary conviction, to a [class C fine][a] or, at the discretion of the court, to imprisonment for a term not exceeding 12 months or to both, or

(b) on conviction on indictment, to a fine not exceeding [€22,220.42][b] or, at the discretion of the court, to imprisonment for a term not exceeding [5 years][c] or to both.

(2) A person guilty under any provision of the Companies Acts of an offence made punishable by a fine of an unspecified amount shall be liable—

(a) on summary conviction to a [class C fine],[a] or

(b) on conviction on indictment, to a fine not exceeding [€22,220.42].[b]

(3) Every offence under the Companies Acts made punishable by a [class C fine][a] or by imprisonment for a term not exceeding 12 months, or by both, may be prosecuted summarily.

(4) Summary proceedings in relation to an offence under the Companies Acts may be brought and prosecuted by the Director of Public Prosecutions or the [Director].[d]

[(5) Notwithstanding section 10(4) of the Petty Sessions (Ireland) Act, 1851, summary proceedings in relation to an offence under the Companies Acts may be commenced—

(a) at any time within 3 years from the date on which the offence was committed, or

(b) if, at the expiry of that period, the person against whom the proceedings are to be brought is outside the State, within 6 months from the date on which he next enters the State, or

(c) at any time within 3 years from the date on which evidence that, in the opinion of the person by whom the proceedings are brought, is sufficient to justify the bringing of the proceedings comes to that person's knowledge,

whichever is the later.][e]

[(5A) For the purpose of subsection (5)(c), a certificate signed by or on behalf of the person bringing the proceedings as to the date on which the evidence referred to in that provision relating to the offence concerned came to his knowledge shall be prima facie evidence thereof and in any legal proceedings a document purporting to be a certificate issued for the purpose of this subsection and to be so signed shall be deemed to be so signed and shall be admitted as evidence without proof of the signature of the person purporting to sign the certificate.][f]

(6) Where, in relation to a contravention of any provision of the Companies Acts, it is provided that for continued contravention a person shall be liable to a daily default fine,

he shall be guilty of contravening the provision on every day on which the contravention continues after conviction of the original contravention and for each such offence he shall be liable to a fine not exceeding the amount specified in the provision, instead of the penalty specified for the original contravention.

[(7) In any provision of the Companies Acts for which a fine of any amount of less than [€1,904.61][h] is provided in respect of a summary conviction, the maximum amount of that fine shall be taken to be [€1,904.61].[h]

(8) In any provision of the Companies Acts for which a term of imprisonment of less than 5 years is provided in respect of a conviction on indictment, the maximum term of imprisonment shall be taken to be 5 years.][g]

Amendments

- a CLEA 2001, s 104(a) amends CA 1990, s 240 by the substitution for '£1,000' wherever occurring of '£1,500'. '£1,500' converted to '€1,904.61' by Council Regulations (EC) No 1103/97, No 974/98 and No 2866/98 and the Economic and Monetary Union Act 1998, s 6; the above being implicitly substituted, by Fines Act 2010, s 6, for a fine not exceeding the aforesaid amount. A class C fine currently means a fine not exceeding €2,500.
- b '£10,000' converted to '€12,697.38' by Council Regulations (EC) No 1103/97, No 974/98 and No 2866/98 and the Economic and Monetary Union Act, 1998, s 6, and multiplied by a multiplier of 1.75 pursuant to Fines Act 2010, s 9.
- c CLEA 2001, s 104(b) amends CA 1990, s 240(1)(b) by the substitution for '3 years' of '5 years'.
- d 'Director' substituted for 'Minister' by CLEA 2001, s 14(4).
- e C(A)(No 2)A 1999, s 41 substitutes CA 1990, s 240(5).
- f C(A)(No 2)A 1999, s 41 inserts CA 1990, s 240(5A).
- g CLEA 2001, s 104(c) inserts CA 1990, s 240(7) and (8).
- h £1,000 increased to £1,500 by CA 1990, s 240(7) and converted to €1,904.61 by Council Regulations (EC) No 1103/97, No 974/98 and No 2866/98 and the Economic and Monetary Union Act 1998, s 6.

[240A Court in which proceedings for certain offences may be brought

For the purposes of any provision of the Companies Acts which provides that the company and every officer of the company is guilty of an offence, summary proceedings against the company or an officer of the company may be brought, heard and determined either—

(a) in the court area in which the offence charged or, if more than one offence is stated to have been committed, any one of the offences charged, is stated to have been committed,

(b) in the court area in which the accused has been arrested,

(c) in the court area in which the accused resides,

(d) in the court area specified by order made pursuant to section 15 of the Courts Act, 1971, or

(e) in the court area in which the registered office of the company is situated.][a]

Amendments

a CLEA 2001, s 105 inserts CA 1990, s 240A.

241 Offences by certain bodies

(1) Where an offence under section 19, 21, 79 or 242 which is committed by a body to which any such section applies is proved to have been committed with the consent or connivance of or to be attributable to any neglect on the part of any person being a director, manager, secretary or other officer of the body, or any person who was purporting to act in any such capacity, that person shall also be guilty of an offence under that section.

(2) Where the affairs of a body are managed by its members, subsection (1) shall apply in relation to the acts and defaults of a member in connection with his functions of management as if he were a director or manager of the body.

242 Furnishing false information

(1) A person who, in purported compliance with any provision of the Companies Acts, answers a question, provides an explanation, makes a statement or produces, lodges or delivers any return, report, certificate, balance sheet or other document false in a material particular, knowing it to be false, or recklessly answers a question, provides an explanation, makes a statement or [completes, signs,][a] produces, lodges or delivers any such document false in a material particular shall be guilty of an offence.

[(1A) A person who knowingly or recklessly furnishes false information to an electronic filing agent that is subsequently transmitted in a return made, on the person's behalf, to the registrar of companies shall be guilty of an offence.][b]

(2) [Where a person is convicted on indictment][c] of an offence under subsection (1) [or (1A)][d] and the court is of opinion that any act, omission or conduct which constituted that offence has—

- (a) substantially contributed to a company being unable to pay its debts;
- (b) prevented or seriously impeded the orderly winding-up of the company; or
- (c) substantially facilitated the defrauding of the creditors of the company or creditors of any other person,

that person shall be liable [...][e] to imprisonment for a term not exceeding 7 years or to a fine not exceeding [€22,220.42][f] or to both.

Amendments

a 'completes, signs,' inserted in sub-s (1) by IFCMPA 2005, s 71.

b Sub-s (1A) inserted by IFCMPA 2005, s 71.

c CLEA 2001, s 106(a) amends CA 1990, s 242(2) by the substitution for 'Where a person is guilty' of 'Where a person is convicted on indictment'.

d 'or (1A)' inserted in sub-s (2) by IFCMPA 2005, s 71.

e CLEA 2001, s 106(b) amends CA 1990, s 242(2) by the deletion of 'on conviction on indictment.'

f £10,000 converted to €12,697.38 by Council Regulations (EC) No 1103/97, No 974/98 and No 2866/98 and the Economic and Monetary Union Act 1998, s 6, and multiplied by a multiplier of 1.75 pursuant to Fines Act 2010, s 9.

---

243 Penalisation of destruction, mutilation or falsification of documents

(1) A person, being an officer of any such body as is mentioned in paragraphs (a) to (e) of section 19(1) who destroys, mutilates or falsifies, or is privy to the destruction, mutilation or falsification of any book or document affecting or relating to the property or affairs of the body, or makes or is privy to the making of a false entry therein, shall, unless he proves that he had no intention to defeat the law, be guilty of an offence.

(2) Any such person who fraudulently either parts with, alters or makes an omission in any such book or document, or who is privy to fraudulent parting with, fraudulent altering or fraudulent making of an omission in, any such book or document, shall be guilty of an offence.

244 Increase of penalties

Sections 125(2), 126(4), 127(2) and 128(3) of the Principal Act shall have effect as if for the sums mentioned therein there were substituted '[€1,269.74]'[a] in each case.

Amendments

a £1,000 converted to €1,269.74 by Council Regulations (EC) No 1103/97, No 974/98 and No 2866/98 and the Economic and Monetary Union Act 1998, s 6.

---

245 Amendment of section 12 of Companies (Amendment) Act, 1982

[...][a]

Amendments

a This section substitutes 'two consecutive years' for 'three consecutive years' in C(A)A 1982, s 12(1).

---

246 Restoration to register of company struck off

[...][a]

Amendments

a This section inserts CA 1963, s 311A, which was in turn amended by C(A)(No 2)A 1999, s 50.

---

247 System of classification of information

(1) Where, under the Companies Acts, any information relating to any person is required to be delivered to the registrar of companies and is so received by him, the registrar may apply such system of classification as he considers appropriate to such information and

may assign symbols of identification to persons or classes of persons to whom any such information relates.

(2) The Minister may make regulations requiring that the symbol assigned under subsection (1) to any person or persons of any class shall be entered on all documents which, under any provision of the Companies Acts, are required to contain the name of that person.

(3) Regulations under subsection (2) may, in particular, specify particular persons whose duty it shall be to comply or ensure compliance with the regulations.

(4) A person who makes default in complying with regulations under subsection (2) shall be guilty of an offence and liable to a fine.

248 Delivery to the registrar of documents in legible form

(1) This section applies to the delivery to the registrar under any provision of the Companies Acts of documents in legible form.

(2) The document must—

(a) state in a prominent position the registered number of the company to which it relates,

(b) satisfy any requirements prescribed for the purposes of this section as to the form and content of the document, and

(c) conform to such requirements as may be prescribed for the purpose of enabling the registrar to copy the document.

[...][a]

(6) Regulations made for the purposes of this section may make different provision as to the form and content of the document with respect to different descriptions of document.

(7) Every regulation made under this section shall be laid before each House of the Oireachtas as soon as may be after it is made and if a resolution annulling the regulation is passed by either such House within the next twenty-one days on which that House has sat after the regulation is laid before it, the regulation shall be annulled accordingly, but without prejudice to the validity of anything previously done thereunder.

(8) In this section, 'document' includes any periodic account, abstract, statement or return required to be delivered to the registrar.

Amendments

a CLEA 2001, s 107(2) deletes CA 1990, s 248(3), (4) and (5).

---

249 Delivery to the registrar of documents otherwise than in legible form

(1) This section applies to the delivery to the registrar under any provision of the Companies Acts of documents otherwise than in legible form (whether by electronic means or otherwise).

(2) Any requirement to deliver a document to the registrar, or to deliver a document in the prescribed form, shall be satisfied by the communication to the registrar of the requisite information in any non-legible form prescribed for the purposes of this section.

(3) Where any document is required to be signed or sealed, it shall instead be authenticated in such manner as may be prescribed for the purposes of this section.

(4) The document must—

(a) contain in a prominent position the registered number of the company to which it relates,

(b) satisfy any requirements prescribed for the purposes of this section, and

(c) be furnished in such manner and conform to such requirements as may be prescribed for the purposes of enabling the registrar to read and copy the document.

[...][a]

(8) The Minister may by regulations make further provision with respect to the application of this section in relation to instantaneous forms of communication.

(9) Regulations made for the purpose of this section may make different provision with respect to different descriptions of documents and different forms of communication.

(10) Every regulation made under this section shall be laid before each House of the Oireachtas as soon as may be after it is made and if a resolution annulling the regulation is passed by either such House within the next twenty-one days on which that House has sat after the regulation is laid before it, the regulation shall be annulled accordingly, but without prejudice to the validity of anything previously done thereunder.

(11) In this section, 'document' includes any periodic account, abstract, statement or return required to be delivered to the registrar.

Amendments

a CLEA 2001, s 107(2) deletes CA 1990, s 249(5), (6) and (7).

[249A Power to reject documents sent for registration and amendments consequential on that section's insertion

(1) If a document is delivered to the registrar which does not comply with—

(a) the requirements of section 248 or 249,

(b) any other requirement of the Companies Acts (and in particular the provisions of the section or sections under which a requirement to deliver the document concerned to the registrar arises), or

(c) any requirements imposed by or under any other enactment relating to the completion of a document and its delivery to the registrar,

the registrar may serve on the person by whom the document was delivered (or, if there are two or more such persons, on any of them) a notice indicating the respect in which the document does not comply.

(2) Where the registrar serves such a notice, then, unless a replacement document—

(a) is delivered to him within 14 days after the service of the notice, and

(b) complies with the requirements referred to in subsection (1) or is not rejected by him for failure to comply with those requirements,

the original document shall be deemed not to have been delivered to him.

(3) For the purposes of any provision which—

(a) imposes a penalty for failure to deliver a document, so far as it imposes a penalty for continued contravention, or

(b) provides for the payment of a fee in respect of the registration of a document being a fee of a greater amount than the amount provided under the provision in respect of the registration of such a document that has been delivered to the registrar within the period specified for its delivery to him,

no account shall be taken of the period between the delivery of the original document and the end of the period of 14 days after the service of the notice under subsection (1)(but only if, before the end of the latter period, a replacement document that complies with the requirements referred to in subsection (1) is delivered to the registrar).

(4) Nothing in this section shall have the effect of making valid any matter which a provision of the Companies Acts or of any other enactment provides is to be void or of no effect in circumstances where a document in relation to it is not delivered to the registrar within the period specified for the document's delivery to him.][a]

Amendments

a CLEA 2001, s 107(1) inserts CA 1990, s 249A.

---

250 Amendment of section 377 of, and Ninth Schedule to, the Principal Act

(1) [...][a]

(2) The Minister may, if he considers it necessary to do so in the interests of the orderly and proper regulation of the business of unregistered companies, make regulations adding to, or subtracting from, the list of the provisions of the Companies Acts specified in the Ninth Schedule to The Principal Act.

(3) Every regulation made by the Minister under this section shall be laid before each House of the Oireachtas as soon as may be after it is made and, if a resolution annulling the regulation is passed by either House within the next 21 days on which that House has sat after the regulation is laid before it, the regulation shall be annulled accordingly, but without prejudice to the validity of anything previously done thereunder.

Amendments

a Sub-s (1)(a) substitutes CA 1963, s 377(1) and sub-s (1)(b) substitutes CA 1963, Sch 9.

---

251 Application of certain provisions to companies not in liquidation

(1) This section applies in relation to a company that is not being wound up where—

(a) execution or other process issued on a judgment, decree or order of any court in favour of a creditor of the company is returned unsatisfied in whole or in part; or

(b) it is proved to the satisfaction of the court that the company is unable to pay its debts, taking into account the contingent and prospective liabilities of the company, and it appears to the court that the reason or the principal reason for its not being wound up is the insufficiency of its assets.

(2) The following sections, with the necessary modifications, shall apply to a company to which this section applies, notwithstanding that it is not being wound up—

(a) [sections 139, 140, 148, 149 or 149A, 203 and 204, and][a]

(b) the provisions of the Principal Act mentioned in the Table to this section.

[(2A) The Director may apply to the court pursuant to this section for an order or judgement, as the case may be, under any of the sections which apply to a company to which this section applies.][b]

(3) References in the sections mentioned in subsection (2) to the commencement of the winding-up of a company, the appointment of a provisional liquidator or the making of a winding up order and to the 'relevant date' shall, for the purposes of this section, be construed as references to the date—

(a) of the judgment, decree or order mentioned in subsection (1)(a); or

(b) on which the court determines that the company is unable to pay its debts.

[(4) (a) Where, by virtue of this section, proceedings are instituted under section 139, 140 or 204 of this Act or section 245A, 297A or 298 of the Principal Act, section 297A(7)(b) of the Principal Act shall apply in relation to any order made as a result of those proceedings except that an order made as a result of an application by the Director pursuant to subsection (2A) shall not be made in favour of the Director, otherwise than as to his costs and expenses.

(b) A person having a claim against the company may apply for an enforcement order for a share of any sums or assets recovered or available following a successful action by the Director pursuant to subsection (2A), provided that the order is sought within a period of one month from the date of judgement on behalf of the Director.][c]

(5) Where section 295 of the Principal Act is applied by virtue of this section, it shall apply as if the words 'which is subsequently ordered to be wound up or subsequently passes a resolution for voluntary winding-up' were deleted therefrom.

TABLE

SECTIONS OF PRINCIPAL ACT TO WHICH THIS SECTION APPLIES

Section	*Subject*	*Comment*
243	Inspection of books by creditors and contributories	
245	Power of court to summon persons for examination	Inserted by section 126 of this Act
245A	Order for payment or delivery of property against person examined under section 245	Inserted by section 127 of this Act
247	Power to arrest absconding contributory	
295	Frauds by officers of companies which have gone into liquidation	

Section	*Subject*	*Comment*
297	Criminal liability for fraudulent trading	Inserted by section 137 of this Act
297A	Civil liability for fraudulent trading	Inserted by section 138 of this Act
298	Power of court to assess damages against directors	Amended by section 142 of this Act

Amendments

a Sub-s (2)(a) amended by CLEA 2001, s 54 and substituted by reg 9 of and the Schedule to the EC(IFRSMA)R 2005.

b CLEA 2001, s 54(b) inserts CA 1990, s 251(2A).

c CLEA 2001, s 54(c) substitutes CA 1990, s 251(4).

PART XIII
INVESTMENT COMPANIES

252 Interpretation of this Part

(1) In this Part—

[…][a]

'investment company' means a company to which this Part applies and 'company' shall be construed accordingly;

['management company' means a company designated by an investment company to undertake the management of the investment company;] [b]

'property' means real or personal property of whatever kind (including securities);

['sub-fund' means a separate portfolio of assets maintained by an investment company in accordance with its articles;] [c]

'the UCITS Regulations' means the European Communities (Undertakings for Collective Investment in Transferable Securities) Regulations, 1989 (S.I. No 78 of 1989).

['umbrella fund' means an investment company which has one or more sub-funds and which is authorised by the Central Bank pursuant to section 256.][d]

(2) For the purposes of the application by this Part of certain provisions of the UCITS Regulations to investment companies, the said provisions shall be construed as one with the Companies Acts.

Amendments

a Deleted by the CBFSAA 2003, Sch 1.

b Added by IFCMPA 2005, s 22.

c Added by IFCMPA 2005, s 22.

d Added by IFCMPA 2005, s 22.

253 Share capital of investment companies

(1) Notwithstanding anything in the Companies Acts, the memorandum of a company to which this Part applies may in respect of the share capital of the company state in lieu of the matters specified in paragraph (a) of section 6 (4) of the Principal Act—

(a) that the share capital of the company shall be equal to the value for the time being of the issued share capital of the company,[...][a]

(b) the division of that share capital into a specified number of shares without assigning any nominal value thereto, [and][b]

[(c) that the issued share capital of the company for the time being shall not be less than a minimum amount nor more than a maximum amount specified in the memorandum,][c]

and the form of memorandum set out in Table B of the First Schedule to the Principal Act or Part I of the Second Schedule to the Companies (Amendment) Act, 1983, as may be appropriate, s hall have effect with respect to such company with the necessary modifications.

(2) This Part applies to a company limited by shares (not being a company to which the UCITS Regulations apply)—

(a) the sole object of which is stated in its memorandum to be the collective investment of its funds in property with the aim of spreading investment risk and giving members of the company the benefit of the results of the management of its funds; and

(b) the articles or memorandum of which provide—

(i) that the actual value of the paid up share capital of the company shall be at all times equal to the value of the assets of any kind of the company after the deduction of its liabilities, and

(ii) that the shares of the company shall, at the request of any of the holders thereof, be purchased by the company directly or indirectly out of the company's assets.

[(2A)(a) Notwithstanding subsection (2)(b)(ii), this Part shall also apply to a company to which subsection (2) otherwise applies, the articles or memorandum of which do not provide that the shares of the company shall, at the request of any holders thereof, be purchased in the manner therein provided, to the extent as may be approved and subject to such conditions as may be applied by the [Central Bank][d].][e,]

(b) [...],[f]

(3) For the purposes of subsection (2)(b)(ii), action taken by a company to ensure that the stock exchange value of its shares does not deviate from its net asset value by more than a percentage specified in its articles (which deviation shall not be so specified as greater than 5 per cent) shall be regarded as the equivalent of purchase of its shares by the company.

(4) The memorandum or articles of a company shall be regarded as providing for the matters referred to in paragraphs (a) and (b) of subsection (2) notwithstanding the inclusion in the memorandum or articles with respect thereto of incidental or supplementary provisions.

(5) In the Companies Acts—

(a) a reference to a company limited by shares shall be construed as including an investment company within the meaning of this Part and a reference to a share in, or the share capital of, a company limited by shares shall be construed accordingly, and

(b) a reference to the nominal value of an issued or allotted share in, or of the issued or allotted share capital of, a company limited by shares shall be construed, in the case of an investment company, as a reference to the value of the consideration for which the share or share capital (as the case may be) has been issued or allotted.

Amendments

a CA 1990, s 253(1)(a) amended by C(A)(No 2)1999, s 54(1)(a)(i) by the deletion of the word 'and'.

b CA 1990, s 253(1)(b) amended by C(A)(No 2)1999, s 54(1)(a)(ii) by the insertion after 'nominal value thereto' of 'and'.

c CA 1990, s 253(1)(c) inserted by C(A)(No 2)1999, s 54(1)(a)(iii).

d CA 1990, s 253(2A)(a) amended by the CBFSA Act 2003 Part 9, s ch 3 by the insertion of the word 'Central' in before the word 'Bank'.

e CA 1990, s 253(2A) inserted by Investment Intermediaries Act 1995, s 80.

f CA 1990, s 253(2A)(b) deleted by C(A)(No 2)1999, s 54(1)(b).

---

254 Power of company to purchase own shares

(1) Subject to subsection (2), the purchase by an investment company of its own shares shall be on such terms and in such manner as may be provided by its articles.

[(2) An investment company shall not purchase its own shares, for the purposes referred to in section 253(2)(*b*)(ii), unless they are fully paid, but nothing in this subsection shall prevent a purchase being made in accordance with section 255(3).][a]

(3) For the avoidance of doubt, nothing in the Companies Acts shall require an investment company to create any reserve account.

Amendments

a Section 254(2) substituted by CA 2005, s 23. The old provision read provided that 'An investment company shall not purchase its own shares unless they are fully paid.'

---

255 Treatment of purchased shares

(1) Shares of an investment company which have been purchased by the company shall be cancelled and the amount of the company's issued share capital shall be reduced by the amount of the consideration paid by the company for the purchase of the shares.

(2) (a) Where a company has purchased or is about to purchase any of its own shares, it shall have the power to issue an equal number of shares in place of those purchased and for the purposes of section 68 of the Finance Act, 1973, the issue of those replacement shares shall constitute a chargeable transaction if,

but only if, the actual value of the shares so issued exceeds the actual value of the shares purchased at the date of their purchase and, where the issue of shares does constitute a chargeable transaction for those purposes, the amount on which stamp duty on the relevant statement relating to that transaction is chargeable under section 69 of the Finance Act, 1973, shall be the difference between—

(i) the amount on which the duty would be so chargeable if the shares had not been issued in place of shares purchased under this section, and

(ii) the value of the shares purchased at the date of their purchase.

(b) Where new shares are issued before the purchase of the old shares, the new shares shall not, s o far as relates to stamp duty, be deemed to have been issued in pursuance of paragraph (a) unless the old shares are purchased within one month after the issue of the new shares.

[(3)Notwithstanding subsection (1), an umbrella fund may, for the account of any of its sub-funds, and in accordance with conditions imposed by the Central Bank pursuant to section 257, acquire by subscription or transfer for consideration, shares of any class or classes, howsoever described, representing other sub-funds of the same umbrella fund provided that the acquisition is for a purpose otherwise than that provided for in section 253(2)(*b*)(ii).][a]

Amendments

a Subsection (3) inserted by IFCMPA 2005, s 24.

---

256 Authorisation by Bank

(1) An investment company shall not carry on business in the State unless it has been authorised to do so by the [Central Bank][a] on the basis of criteria approved by the Minister.

(2) A person shall not carry on business on behalf of an investment company, insofar as relates to the purchase or sale of the shares of the investment company, unless the investment company has been authorised in the manner referred to in subsection (1).

(3) The [Central Bank][a] shall not authorise an investment company to carry on business in the State unless the company has paid up share capital which, in the opinion of the [Central Bank][a], will be sufficient to enable it to conduct its business effectively and meet its liabilities.

(4) An application by an investment company for the authorisation referred to in subsection (1) shall be made in writing to the [Central Bank][a] and contain such information as the [Central Bank][a] may specify for the purpose of determining the application (including such additional information as the [Central Bank][a] may specify in the course of determining the application).

(5) Where the [Central Bank][a] proposes to grant an authorisation to an investment company under this section and the [Central Bank][a] is satisfied that the company will raise capital [by providing facilities for the direct or indirect participation by the public in the profits and income of the company][b], the [Central Bank][a] shall, in granting the authorisation, designate the company as an investment company which may raise capital

in that manner, and 'designated company' in this section and section 257, shall be construed accordingly.

(6) In the event that a designated company does not [provide facilities for the direct or indirect participation by the public in the profits and income of the company][c] within a period, not greater than six months, which shall be specified in the authorisation under this section, the company shall, on the expiry of the period so specified, be deemed to have ceased to be a designated company.

(7) An investment company which is not a designated company shall not raise capital [by providing facilities for the direct or indirect participation by the public in the profits and income of the company].[b]

(8) A company incorporated outside the State which, if it were incorporated in the State, would be a company to which this Part applies[, other than a company to which section 256F applies,][d] shall not advertise or market its shares in any way in the State without the approval of the [Central Bank][a], which approval may be subject to such conditions as the [Central Bank][a] considers appropriate and prudent for the purposes of the orderly and proper regulation of so much of the business of companies of that type as is conducted in the State.

(9) [...][e]

Amendments

a Words inserted by CBFSAIA 2003, Sch 1.

b CA 1990, s 256(5) and (7) amended by C(A)(No 2)A 1999, s 54(2)(a) by the substitution for 'by promoting the sale of its shares to the public', in each place where it occurs, of 'by providing facilities for the direct or indirect participation by the public in the profits and income of the company'.

c CA 1990, s 256(6) amended by C(A)(No 2) A 1999, s 54(2)(b) by the substitution for 'promote the sale of its s hares to the public' of 'provide facilities for the direct or indirect participation by the public in the profits and income of the company'.

d Words ', other than a company to which section 256F applies,' inserted by C(MP)A 2009, s 3(i).

e Subsection (9) deleted by C(A)(No2)A 1999, s 54.

[256A Segregated liability of investment company sub-funds

(1) Notwithstanding any statutory provision or rule of law to the contrary, but subject to subsection (2), any liability incurred on behalf of or attributable to any sub-fund of an umbrella fund shall be discharged solely out of the assets of that sub-fund, and no umbrella fund nor any director, receiver, examiner, liquidator, provisional liquidator or other person shall apply, nor be obliged to apply, the assets of any such sub-fund in satisfaction of any liability incurred on behalf of or attributable to any other sub-fund of the same umbrella fund, whether such liability was incurred before, on or after the date this section commences.

(2) Subsection (1) shall not apply to an umbrella fund which was authorised and commenced trading prior to the date this section commences unless—

(a) the members of the umbrella fund shall have resolved by special resolution that the provisions of subsection (1) should apply to that umbrella fund, and

(b) the special resolution has taken effect in accordance with subsection (4).

(3) For the purposes of subsection (2), an umbrella fund shall be deemed to have commenced to trade prior to the date this section commences if—

(a) shares, other than the subscriber shares issued for the purposes of incorporation of the umbrella fund, were issued in any sub-fund of that umbrella fund prior to that commencement date and one or more of those shares remains in issue on that commencement date, or

(b) the umbrella fund, or any person acting on its behalf, entered into an agreement with a third party prior to that commencement date, which remains in force on that commencement date and pursuant to which the assets of any sub-fund may be applied in satisfaction of any liability incurred on behalf of or attributable to any other sub-fund of the same umbrella fund.

(4) If—

(a) no application to the court is made pursuant to section 256C, a special resolution passed pursuant to subsection (2) shall take effect on the date on which such resolution is passed or the 31st day following the date of service of notice on creditors issued pursuant to subsection (5)(b), whichever is the later, or

(b) an application is or applications are made to the court pursuant to section 256C, a special resolution pursuant to subsection (2) shall not take effect until—

(i) in the event that all applications made are withdrawn, the day on which such resolution is passed or the day next following the withdrawal of the last outstanding application, whichever is the later, subject to this day being no earlier than the 31st day following the date of service of notice on creditors; and

(ii) in the event that all applications made are not withdrawn, whichever of the following is the later, that is to say, the later of the day on which such resolution is passed, and:

(I) where an order is granted by the court pursuant to section 256C or on appeal pursuant to section 256D, the date specified in that order or, if no such date is specified, the day next following the date on which the period for which the order is specified to remain in force expires or, as appropriate, following the day on which it otherwise ceases to be in force; or

(II) where no appeal against any decision of the court is lodged pursuant to section 256D, the day next following the date on which the time period for such an appeal in relation to the last such determination of the court shall have elapsed; or

(III) where an appeal is lodged against any decision of the court pursuant to section 256D, the day next following the date on which the last outstanding such appeal is disposed of or withdrawn,

unless a court has otherwise ordered under section 256C or 256D.

(5) Any notice of a meeting to consider a special resolution of the type referred to in subsection (2) shall be—

(a) accompanied by audited accounts for the umbrella fund which include a statement of the assets and liabilities of each sub-fund of the umbrella fund and which are prepared as at a date which is not more than four months before the date on which the notice convening the meeting is served (hereafter referred to in this section and section 256B as 'statement of assets and liabilities');

(b) given to all creditors of the umbrella fund accompanied by a copy of the statement of assets and liabilities, in accordance with the provisions of section 256B; and

(c) delivered to the registrar of companies, accompanied by the statement of assets and liabilities, no later than the third day after the date on which the notice is first sent to members of the umbrella fund.][a]

Amendments

a Section 256A inserted by IFCMPA 2005, s 25.

[256B Notice to creditors of special resolution under section 256A

(1) The requirement in section 256A to give all creditors of the umbrella fund notice of a meeting to consider a special resolution shall be met if—

(a) a notice in writing, accompanied by the statement of assets and liabilities, is sent to each relevant creditor of a sub-fund, and

(b) a notice is published in at least one national newspaper in accordance with the terms of the prospectus for the umbrella fund, stating that the umbrella fund intends to avail of section 256A(1) and that an application may be made in accordance with section 256C, for an order pursuant to that section.

(2) For the purpose of this section, a relevant creditor of a sub-fund is any creditor for whom provision was made, in accordance with the articles of association, in the net asset value of the sub-fund calculated—

(a) in the case of a sub-fund in respect of which the net asset value is not calculated on a daily basis, as at the last valuation point for that sub-fund prior to the date of service of the notice pursuant to section 256A(5)(b); and

(b) in the case of a sub-fund in respect of which the net asset value is calculated on a daily basis, as at the second last valuation point for that sub-fund.][a]

Amendments

a Section 256B inserted by IFCMPA 2005, s 25.

[256C Application to court opposing special resolution under section 256A

(1) An application may be made to the court in accordance with this section for an order preventing any resolution passed or proposed to be passed pursuant to section 256A(2) from taking effect in relation to any umbrella fund to which that section applies.

(2) An order under this section may be granted only if the court considers that it would be just and equitable to do so.

(3) Each order granted pursuant to this section shall specify the period in respect of which the order shall remain in force and, without prejudice to the powers of the court to specify such period, may specify that the order shall cease to be in force on the date on which the applicant ceases to be a creditor of the umbrella fund or the date on which the applicant consents to the application of section 256A(1) to that umbrella fund, whichever is the later.

(4) An application under this section may only be made by a relevant creditor or relevant creditors constituting not less than 1 per cent in number of the creditors of any sub-fund, or whose debts account for not less than 1 per cent in value of the debts owed by any sub-fund, in each case as provided for in the net asset value of that sub-fund referred to in section 256B.

(5) Any application pursuant to this section must be made by a relevant creditor within 28 days after the date of service of the notice referred to in section 256A(5)(b), and may be made on behalf of the creditors entitled to make the application by one or more of their number as they may appoint in writing for such purpose.

(6) Notice of an application to the court for the purposes of this section shall be sent by the relevant creditor or relevant creditors to the umbrella fund and to the Central Bank within two days after the date on which the application is made, and the umbrella fund and the Central Bank shall each be entitled to make representations to the court before an order is made.

(7) In considering whether it is just and equitable to make an order pursuant to this section, the court shall have regard to the following matters:

(a) the terms of any agreement or arrangement between the creditor or creditors and the umbrella fund or its delegates;

(b) the course of dealings between the creditor or creditors and the umbrella fund or its delegates;

(c) the conduct of the umbrella fund or its delegates towards the creditor or creditors;

(d) the extent to which the umbrella fund or its delegates represented to the creditor or creditors that it would have recourse to the assets of any other sub-fund to discharge the liabilities owed to the creditor or creditors;

(e) the extent to which it was reasonable for the relevant creditor or relevant creditors to expect to have recourse to the assets of any other sub-fund; and

(f) any other matters which the court shall deem relevant.][a]

Amendments

a Section 256C inserted by IFCMPA 2005, s 25.

[256D Appeal from court order under section 256C

(1) Any creditor who has made an application pursuant to section 256C, or the umbrella fund in respect of which the application is made, may appeal to the Supreme Court against any decision of the court in respect of that application.

(2) Notice of any such appeal must be lodged within five days after the date on which the order is perfected by the court.

(3) Notice of any appeal lodged by the umbrella fund shall be sent to the Central Bank and to the relevant creditor or relevant creditors who made the application pursuant to section 256C within two days after the date on which the appeal is made.

(4) Notice of any appeal by the party which made the application pursuant to section 256C shall be sent to the Central Bank and to the umbrella fund within two days after the date on which the appeal is made.][a]

Amendments

a Section 256D inserted by IFCMPA 2005, s 25.

[256E Requirements to be complied with by, and other matters respecting, an umbrella fund to which section 256A applies

(1) Every umbrella fund to which section 256A applies shall be required to include the words 'An umbrella fund with segregated liability between sub-funds' in all its letterheads and in any agreement entered into in writing with a third party, and shall be obliged to disclose that it is a segregated liability umbrella fund to any third party with which it enters into an oral contract.

(2) There shall be implied in every contract, agreement, arrangement or transaction entered into by an umbrella fund to which section 256A applies the following terms, that—

(a) the party or parties contracting with the umbrella fund shall not seek, whether in any proceedings or by any other means whatsoever or wheresoever, to have recourse to any assets of any sub-fund of the umbrella fund in the discharge of all or any part of a liability which was not incurred on behalf of that sub-fund,

(b) if any party contracting with the umbrella fund shall succeed by any means whatsoever or wheresoever in having recourse to any assets of any sub-fund of the umbrella fund in the discharge of all or any part of a liability which was not incurred on behalf of that sub-fund, that party shall be liable to the umbrella fund to pay a sum equal to the value of the benefit thereby obtained by it, and

(c) if any party contracting with the umbrella fund shall succeed in seizing or attaching by any means, or otherwise levying execution against, any assets of a sub-fund of an umbrella fund in respect of a liability which was not incurred on behalf of that sub-fund, that party shall hold those assets or the direct or indirect proceeds of the sale of such assets on trust for the umbrella fund and shall keep those assets or proceeds separate and identifiable as such trust property.

(3) All sums recovered by an umbrella fund as a result of any such trust as is described in subsection (2)(c) shall be credited against any concurrent liability pursuant to the implied term set out in subsection (2)(b).

(4) Any asset or sum recovered by an umbrella fund pursuant to the implied term set out in subsection (2)(b) or (c) or by any other means whatsoever or wheresoever in the

events referred to in those paragraphs shall, after the deduction or payment of any costs of recovery, be applied so as to compensate the sub-fund affected.

(5) In the event that assets attributable to a sub-fund to which section 256A applies are taken in execution of a liability not attributable to that sub-fund, and in so far as such assets or compensation in respect thereof cannot otherwise be restored to that sub-fund affected, the directors of the umbrella fund, with the consent of the custodian, s hall certify or cause to be certified, the value of the assets lost to the sub-fund affected and transfer or pay from the assets of the sub-fund or sub-funds to which the liability was attributable, in priority to all other claims against such sub-fund or sub-funds, assets or sums sufficient to restore to the sub-fund affected, the value of the assets or sums lost to it.

(6) Without prejudice to the other provisions of sections 256A to 256D and this section, a sub-fund of an umbrella fund is not a legal person separate from that umbrella fund, but an umbrella fund may sue and be sued in respect of a particular sub-fund and may exercise the same rights of set-off, if any, as between its sub-funds as apply at law in respect of companies and the property of a sub-fund is subject to orders of the court as it would have been if the sub-fund were a separate legal person.

(7) Nothing in sections 256A to 256D and this section shall prevent the application of any enactment or rule of law which would require the application of the assets of any sub-fund in discharge of some or all of the liabilities of any other sub-fund on the grounds of fraud or misrepresentation and, in particular, by reason of the application of—

(a) section 286 of the Principal Act; and

(b) section 139 of this Act.

(8) A sub-fund may be wound up in accordance with the provisions of section 213(e) and section 251(1)(c) of the Principal Act as if the sub-fund were a separate company, provided always that the appointment of the liquidator or any provisional liquidator and the powers, rights, duties and responsibilities of the liquidator or any provisional liquidator shall be confined to the sub-fund or sub-funds which is or are being wound up.

(9) For the purposes of subsection (8), all references made in sections 213(e) and 251(1)(c) of the Principal Act and all relevant provisions of the Companies Acts relating to the winding up of a company pursuant to sections 213(e) and 251(1)(c) of the Principal Act to one of the following words shall be construed as follows—

(a) 'company' shall be read as referring to the sub-fund or sub-funds which is or are being wound up;

(b) a 'member' or 'members' shall be read as referring to the holders of the shares in that sub-fund or sub-funds; and

(c) 'creditors' shall be read as referring to the creditors of that sub-fund or sub-funds.][a]

Amendments

a Section 256E inserted by IFCMPA 2005, s 25.

[256F Continuation of foreign investment companies

(1) In this section—

'migrating company' means a body corporate which is established and registered under the laws of a relevant jurisdiction and which is a collective investment undertaking;

'registration documents', in relation to a migrating company, means the following documents and, when the original registration documents are not written in the Irish language or the English language, means a translation into the Irish language or the English language certified as being a correct translation thereof by a person who is competent to so certify:

(a) a copy, certified and authenticated in the prescribed manner, of the certificate of registration or equivalent certificate or document issued with respect to the migrating company under the laws of the relevant jurisdiction;

(b) a copy, certified and authenticated in the prescribed manner, of the memorandum and articles of association of the migrating company or equivalent constitutive document of the migrating company;

(c) a list setting out particulars in relation to the directors and secretary of the migrating company in accordance with the provisions of section 195 of the Principal Act;

(d) a statutory declaration of a director of the migrating company made not more than 28 days prior to the date on which the application is made to the registrar to the effect that—

(i) the migrating company is, as of the date of the declaration, established and registered in the relevant jurisdiction, no petition or other similar proceeding to wind up or liquidate the migrating company has been notified to it and remains outstanding in any place, and no order has been notified to the migrating company or resolution adopted to wind up or liquidate the migrating company in any place,

(ii) the appointment of a receiver, liquidator, examiner or other similar person has not been notified to the migrating company and, at the date of the declaration, no such person is acting in that capacity in any place with respect to the migrating company or its property or any part thereof,

(iii) the migrating company is not, at the date of the declaration, operating or carrying on business under any scheme, order, compromise or other similar arrangement entered into or made by the migrating company with creditors in any place,

(iv) at the date of the declaration the migrating company has served notice of the proposed registration on the creditors of the migrating company,

(v) any consent or approval to the proposed registration in the State required by any contract entered into or undertaking given by the migrating company has been obtained or waived, as the case may be, and

(vi) the registration is permitted by and has been approved in accordance with the memorandum and articles of association or equivalent constitutive document of the migrating company;

(e) a declaration of solvency prepared in accordance with section 256H;

(f) a schedule of the charges or security interests created or granted by the migrating company that would, if such charges created or granted by a company incorporated under the Companies Acts, have been registrable under Part IV of the Principal Act and such particulars of those security interests and charges as are specified in section 103 of the Principal Act;

(g) notification of the proposed name of the migrating company if different from its existing name; and

(h) a copy of the memorandum and articles of association of the migrating company which the migrating company has resolved to adopt, which shall be in the Irish language or the English language, which shall take effect on registration under this section and which the migrating company undertakes not to amend before registration without the prior authorisation of the registrar;

'relevant jurisdiction' means the prescribed place outside the State where the migrating company is established and registered at the time of its application under this section.

(2) A migrating company may apply to the registrar to be registered as a company in the State by way of continuation.

(3) Where an application is made under subsection (2), the registrar shall not register the migrating company as a company in the State unless he or she is satisfied that all of the requirements of the Companies Acts in respect of the registration and of matters precedent and incidental thereto have been complied with and, in particular, but without prejudice to the generality of the foregoing, he or she is satisfied that—

(a) the migrating company has delivered to the registrar an application for the purpose, in the prescribed form and signed by a director of the migrating company, together with the registration documents,

(b) the name or, if relevant, the proposed new name of the migrating company has not been determined to be undesirable pursuant to section 21 of the Principal Act,

(c) the migrating company has paid to the registrar such fee as may be specified from time to time pursuant to section 369 of the Principal Act,

(d) the migrating company has filed with the registrar notice of the address of its proposed registered office in the State,

(e) the migrating company has applied to the Central Bank to be authorised to carry on business as a company under section 256(1) and the Central Bank has notified the migrating company and the registrar that it proposes to authorise the migrating company to so carry on business.

(4) An application under this section shall be accompanied by a statutory declaration in the prescribed form made by a solicitor engaged for this purpose by the migrating company, or by a director of the migrating company, and stating that the requirements

mentioned in subsection (3) have been complied with. The registrar may accept such a declaration as sufficient evidence of compliance.

(5) The registrar shall, as soon as is practicable after receipt of the application for registration, publish notice of it in the Companies Registration Office Gazette.

(6) Where the registrar receives a notification under subsection (3)(e), the registrar—

(a) may issue a certificate of registration of the migrating company by way of continuation of the migrating company as a body corporate under the laws of the State, and

(b) if he or she issues such a certificate, shall enter in the register maintained for the purpose of section 103 of the Principal Act, in relation to charges and security interests of the migrating company specified in paragraph (f) of the definition of 'registration documents' in subsection (1), the particulars prescribed by section 103 of the Principal Act which have been supplied by the migrating company.

(7) The migrating company shall, as soon as may be after being registered under subsection (6), apply to be de-registered in the relevant jurisdiction.

(8) The registrar shall enter in the register of companies the date of registration of the migrating company and shall forthwith publish notice in the Companies Registration Office Gazette of the following matters:

(a) the date of the registration of the migrating company under this section;

(b) the relevant jurisdiction; and

(c) the previous name of the migrating company if different from the name under which it is being registered.

(9) From the date of registration, the migrating company shall be deemed to be a company formed and registered under this Act and shall continue for all purposes under this Act, and the provisions of this Part shall apply to the migrating company, provided always that this section shall not operate—

(a) to create a new legal entity,

(b) to prejudice or affect the identity or continuity of the migrating company as previously established and registered under the laws of the relevant jurisdiction for the period that the migrating company was established and registered in the relevant jurisdiction,

(c) to affect any contract made, resolution passed or any other act or thing done in relation to the migrating company during the period that the migrating company was so established and registered,

(d) to affect the rights, powers, authorities, functions and liabilities or obligations of the migrating company or any other person, or

(e) to render defective any legal proceedings by or against the migrating company.

(10) Without prejudice to the generality of subsection (9)—

(a) the failure of a migrating company to send to the registrar the particulars of a charge or security interest created prior to the date of registration shall not prejudice any rights which any person in whose favour the charge was made or security interest created may have thereunder, and

(b) any legal proceedings that could have been continued or commenced by or against the migrating company before its registration under this section may, notwithstanding the registration, be continued or commenced by or against the migrating company after registration.

(11) The migrating company shall notify the registrar in the prescribed form, and notify the Central Bank, within 3 days of its de-registration in the relevant jurisdiction, of that de-registration.

(12) On registration of the migrating company under subsection (6), the Central Bank shall forthwith authorise the migrating company to carry on business under this Part.

(13) If there is any material change in any of the information contained in the statutory declaration mentioned in paragraph (d) of the definition of 'registration documents' in subsection (1) after the date of the declaration and before the date of the registration under this section, the director who made that statutory declaration, and any other director who becomes aware of that material change shall forth with deliver a new statutory declaration to the registrar relating to the change.

(14) If the migrating company fails to comply with any provision of this section, the registrar may send to the company by post a registered letter stating that, unless the migrating company rectifies the failure within 1 month of the date of the letter and confirms that it has rectified the failure, a notice may be published in the Companies Registration Office Gazette with a view to striking the name of the migrating company off the register.

(15) If the failure mentioned in subsection (14) is not rectified within 1 month after the sending of the letter referred to in that subsection, the registrar may publish in the Companies Registration Office Gazette a notice stating that, at the expiration of 1 month from the date of that notice, the name of the migrating company mentioned therein will, unless the matter is resolved, be struck off the register, and the migrating company will be dissolved.

(16) At the expiration of the time mentioned in the notice, the registrar may, unless cause to the contrary is previously shown by the migrating company, strike its name off the register, and shall publish notice thereof in the Companies Registration Office Gazette, and on that publication, the migrating company shall be dissolved.

(17) The Minister may make regulations prescribing places as relevant jurisdictions for the purposes of this section, where he or she is satisfied that the law of the place concerned makes provision for migrating companies to continue under the laws of the State or for companies to continue under the laws of that place in a substantially similar manner to continuations under this section.

(18) Every regulation made by the Minister under subsection (17) shall be laid before each House of the Oireachtas as soon as may be after it is made and, if a resolution annulling the regulation is passed by either House within the next 21 days on which that House has sat after the regulation is laid before it, the regulation shall be annulled accordingly, but without prejudice to the validity of anything previously done thereunder.][a]

Amendments

a CA 1990, s 256F inserted by C(MP)A 2009, s 3(j).

[256G De-registration of companies when continued under the law of place outside the State

(1) In this section—

'applicant' means a company that applies to be de-registered under this section;

'relevant jurisdiction' means the prescribed place outside the State in which the company proposes to be registered;

'transfer documents', in relation to an applicant, means the following documents:

(a) a statutory declaration of a director of the applicant made not more than 28 days prior to the date on which the application is made to the registrar to the effect that—

(i) the applicant will, upon registration, continue as a body corporate under the laws of the relevant jurisdiction,

(ii) no petition or other similar proceeding to wind up or liquidate the applicant has been notified to the applicant and remains outstanding in any place, and no order has been notified to the applicant or resolution adopted to wind up or liquidate the applicant in any place,

(iii) the appointment of a receiver, liquidator, examiner or other similar person has not been notified to the applicant and, at the date of the declaration, no such person is acting in that capacity in any place with respect to the applicant or its property or any part thereof,

(iv) the applicant is not, at the date of the declaration, operating or carrying on business under any scheme, order, compromise or other similar arrangement entered into or made by the applicant with creditors in any place,

(v) the application for de-registration is not intended to defraud persons who are, at the date of the declaration, creditors of the applicant,

(vi) any consent or approval to the proposed de-registration required by any contract entered into or undertaking given by the applicant has been obtained or waived, as the case may be, and

(vii) the de-registration is permitted by the memorandum and articles of association of the applicant;

(b) a declaration of solvency prepared in accordance with the provisions of section 256H; and

(c) a copy of a special resolution of the applicant that approves the proposed de-registration and the transfer of the applicant to the relevant jurisdiction.

(2) An applicant which proposes to be registered in a relevant jurisdiction by way of continuation as a body corporate may apply to the registrar to be de-registered in the State.

(3) Where an application is made under subsection (2), the registrar shall not deregister the applicant as a company in the State unless he or she is satisfied that all of the requirements of the Companies Acts in respect of the de-registration and of matters precedent and incidental thereto have been complied with and, in particular, but without prejudice to the generality of the foregoing, he or she is satisfied that—

(a) the applicant has delivered to the registrar an application for the purpose, in the prescribed form and signed by a director of the applicant, together with the transfer documents,

(b) the applicant has paid to the registrar such fee as may be specified from time to time pursuant to section 369 of the Principal Act,

(c) the applicant has informed the Central Bank of its intention to be de-registered and the Central Bank has notified the registrar that it has no objection to the de-registration, so long as the applicant complies with any conditions that the Central Bank may impose on the applicant, and

(d) the applicant has filed with the registrar notice of any proposed change in its name and of its proposed registered office or agent for service of process in the relevant jurisdiction.

(4) An application under this section shall be accompanied by a statutory declaration in the prescribed form made by a solicitor engaged for this purpose by the applicant, or by a director of the applicant, and stating that the requirements mentioned in subsection (3) have been complied with. The registrar may accept such a declaration as sufficient evidence of compliance.

(5) The registrar shall, as soon as is practicable after receipt of the application for de-registration, publish notice of it in the Companies Registration Office Gazette.

(6) (a) Where an application is made under subsection (2), a person mentioned in paragraph (b) may apply to the High Court, on notice to the applicant, the Central Bank, the registrar and all creditors of the applicant, not later than 60 days after the publication of the notice under subsection (5), for an order preventing the proposal or passage of a resolution specified in paragraph (c) of the definition of 'transfer documents' in subsection (1) from taking effect in relation to the application.

(b) The following persons may apply for an order under this subsection:

(i) the holders of not less than 5 per cent of the issued share capital of the applicant and who have not voted in favour of the resolution, or

(ii) any creditor of the applicant.

(c) Notice of an application for an order under this subsection may be given to the creditors concerned by publication in at least one national newspaper in the State.

(d) The Central Bank and the applicant concerned shall be entitled to make representations to the High Court before an order under this subsection is made.

(7) The High Court may make an order mentioned in subsection (6) only if it is satisfied that—

(a) the proposed de-registration of the applicant would contravene the terms of an agreement or arrangement between the applicant and any shareholder or creditor of the applicant; or

(b) the proposed de-registration would be materially prejudicial to any shareholder or creditor of the applicant and the interests of shareholders and creditors or both taken as a whole would be materially prejudiced.

(8) An order made under subsection (7) shall specify the period in respect of which it shall remain in force.

(9) An order of the High Court under subsection (7) is final and conclusive.

(10) Unless the High Court orders otherwise, when one or more than one application is made under subsection (6), a resolution specified in paragraph (c) of the definition of 'transfer documents' in subsection (1) in relation to a company shall not take effect until—

(a) where the application or all the applications to the High Court are withdrawn—

(i) the day on which the resolution is passed,

(ii) the day next following the day on which the last outstanding application is withdrawn, or

(iii) the 31st day following the publication of the notice on the creditors under subsection (4),

whichever is the latest, and

(b) where all applications to the High Court are not withdrawn—

(i) the day on which the resolution is passed,

(ii) the day specified in the order or, if no date is specified in the order, the day next following the day on which the period for which the order is specified to remain in force expires or otherwise ceases to be in force, or

(iii) the day next following the decision of the High Court,

whichever is the latest.

(11) When the applicant is registered as a company under the laws of the relevant jurisdiction, it shall give notice to the registrar of that fact within 3 working days of becoming so registered, including its new name, if any, and, as soon as practicable after receiving that notice, the registrar shall issue a certificate of de-registration of the applicant.

(12) The registrar shall enter in the register of companies the date of the deregistration of the applicant and shall, within 7 days of the issuance of the certificate under subsection (11), publish in the Companies Registration Office Gazette notice of the following matters:

(a) the date of the de-registration of the applicant under this section;

(b) the relevant jurisdiction; and

(c) the new name of the applicant if different from the name under which it was registered.

(13) From the date of registration of the applicant in the relevant jurisdiction, it shall cease to be a company for all purposes of the Companies Acts and shall continue for all purposes as a body corporate under the laws of the relevant jurisdiction, provided always that this section shall not operate—

(a) to create a new legal entity,

(b) to prejudice or affect the identity or continuity of the applicant as previously constituted under the laws of the State for the period that the applicant was so constituted,

(c) to affect any contract made, resolution passed or any other act or thing done in relation to the applicant during the period that the applicant was constituted under the laws of the State,

(d) to affect the rights, powers, authorities, functions and liabilities or obligations of the applicant or any other person, or

(e) to render defective any legal proceedings by or against the applicant.

(14) Without prejudice to the generality of subsection (13), any legal proceedings that could have been continued or commenced by or against the applicant before its de-registration under this section may, notwithstanding the de-registration, be continued or commenced by or against the applicant after registration.

(15) The Minister may make regulations prescribing places as relevant jurisdictions for the purposes of this section, where he or she is satisfied that the law of the place concerned makes provision for bodies corporate that are substantially similar to applicants under this section to continue under the laws of the State in a substantially similar manner to continuations under section 256F or for companies to continue under the laws of that place.

(16) Every regulation made by the Minister under subsection (15) shall be laid before each House of the Oireachtas as soon as may be after it is made and, if a resolution annulling the regulation is passed by either House within the next 21 days on which that House has sat after the regulation is laid before it, the regulation shall be annulled accordingly, but without prejudice to the validity of anything previously done thereunder.][a]

Amendments

a CA 1990, s 256G inserted by C(MP)A 2009, s 3(j).

[256H Statutory declarations

(1) Where an application is made under section 256F or 256G, a director of the migrating company or applicant, as the case may be, making the application shall make a statutory declaration stating that he or she has made a full inquiry into its affairs and has formed the opinion that it is able to pay its debts as they fall due.

(2) A declaration under subsection (1) shall have no effect for the purposes of this section unless—

(a) it is made not more than 28 days prior to the date on which the application is made to the registrar,

(b) it contains a statement of the migrating company's or applicant's assets and liabilities as at the latest practicable date before the making of the declaration, and, in any case as at a date that is not more than 3 months before the making of the declaration, and

(c) a report made by an independent person under subsection (3) is attached to the declaration, along with a statement by the independent person that he or she has given and has not withdrawn consent to the making of the declaration with the report attached to it.

(3) The report mentioned in subsection (2)(c) shall state whether, in the independent person's opinion, based on the information and explanations given to him or her, the opinion of the director mentioned in subsection (1) and the statement of the migrating company's or applicant's assets and liabilities referred to in subsection (2)(b), are reasonable.

(4) For the purposes of subsection (3), the independent person shall be a person who, at the time the report is made, is qualified to be the auditor of the company or applicant, or of bodies corporate—

(a) in the case of an application under section 256F, under the laws of the relevant jurisdiction, and

(b) in the case of an application under section 256G, under the laws of the State.

(5) A director who makes a declaration under this section without having reasonable grounds for the opinion that the migrating company or applicant is able to pay its debts as they fall due commits an offence and is liable—

(a) on summary conviction to a [class A fine][b], or imprisonment for a term not exceeding 12 months, or to both, or

(b) on conviction on indictment to a fine not exceeding €50,000, or imprisonment for a term not exceeding 5 years, or to both.

(6) Where the migrating company or applicant is wound up within 1 year of the date on which the application is made to the registrar and its debts are not paid or provided for in full within that year, it shall be presumed, unless the contrary is shown, that the director did not have reasonable grounds for his or her opinion.][a]

Amendments

a CA 1990, s 256H inserted by C(MP)A 2009, s 3(j).

b As implicitly substituted for "fine not exceeding €5,000" by Fines Act 2010, s 4. A class A fine currently means a fine not exceeding €5,000.

---

257 Powers of [Central Bank][a]

(1) Notwithstanding any other powers which may be available to the [Central Bank][a] under any other enactment, order or regulation, the [Central Bank][a] may impose such conditions for the granting of an authorisation to a company under section 256 as it considers appropriate and prudent for the purposes of the orderly and proper regulation of the business of investment companies.

(2) Conditions imposed under subsection (1) may be imposed generally, or by reference to particular classes of company or business (including, but not limited to, whether or not an investment company is a designated company), or by reference to any other

matter the [Central Bank][a] considers appropriate and prudent for the purposes of the orderly and proper regulation of the business of investment companies.

(3) The power to impose conditions referred to in subsection (1) shall include a power to impose such further conditions from time to time as the [Central Bank][a] considers appropriate and prudent for the purposes of the orderly and proper regulation of the business of investment companies.

(4) Without prejudice to the generality of subsections (1), (2) and (3), conditions imposed by the [Central Bank][a] on an investment company may make provision for any or all of the following matters—

(a) the prudential requirements of the investment policies of the company,

(b) prospectuses and other information disseminated by the company,

(c) the vesting of the assets or specified assets of the company in a person nominated by the [Central Bank][a] with such of the powers or duties of a trustee with regard to the company as are specified by the [Central Bank],[a]

(d) such other supervisory and reporting requirements and conditions relating to its business as the [Central Bank][a] considers appropriate and prudent to impose on the company from time to time for the purposes referred to in the aforesaid subsections [,][b]

[(e) supervisory and reporting requirements and conditions relating to the business of a management company as the Central Bank considers appropriate or prudent to impose on the management company from time to time.][c]

(5) A company shall comply with any conditions relating to its authorisation or business imposed by the [Central Bank][a].

Amendments

a 'Central Bank' substituted for 'Bank' by CBFSAIA 2003, Sch 1.

b 'subsections,' substituted for 'subsections.' by IFCMPA 2005, s 26(a).

c Para (e) of sub-s(4) inserted by IFCMPA 2005, s 26(b).

---

258 Adaptation of certain provisions of UCITS Regulations

Regulations 14, 30, 63, [72(3)][a], 83(2) to (7), and 99 to 105 of the UCITS Regulations shall apply to an investment company [or, in the case of the said Regulation 72(3), such a company other than one to which section 253(2A)(a) applies][b] as they apply to the bodies to which those Regulations relate subject to the following modifications—

(a) a reference in those Regulations to a term or expression specified in the second column of the Table to this section at any reference number shall be construed, where the context admits, as a reference to the term or expression specified in the third column of the said Table at that reference number, and

(b) references to cognate terms or expressions in those Regulations shall be construed accordingly.

TABLE

Ref. No (1)	*Term or expression referred to in UCITS Regulations* (2)	*Construction of term or expression for purposes of this section* (3)
1.	'repurchase'	'purchase'
2.	'these Regulations'	'Part XIII of the Companies Act, 1990'
3.	'UCITS'	'investment company'
4.	'unit'	'share'
5.	'unit-holder'	'shareholder'

Amendments

a CLEA 2001, s 108(a) amends CA 1990, s 258 by the insertion after '63,' of '72(3),'.

b CLEA 2001, s 108(b) amends CA 1990, s 258 by the insertion after 'investment company' of 'or, in the case of the said Regulation 72(3), such a company other than one to which section 253(2A)(a) applies,'.

259 Default of investment company or failure in performance of its investments

An authorisation by the [Central Bank][a] under section 256 of an investment company shall not constitute a warranty by the [Central Bank][a] as to the creditworthiness or financial standing of that company and the [Central Bank][a] shall not be liable by virtue of that authorisation or by reason of its exercise of the functions conferred on it by this Part (or any regulations made under this Part) in relation to investment companies for any default of the company unless the [Central Bank][a] acted in bad faith in exercising such functions.

Amendments

a 'Central Bank' substituted for 'Bank' by CBFSIA 2003, Sch 1.

[260 Amendment and restriction of certain provisions of Companies Acts

(1) The following provisions of the Principal Act, namely sections 5(1), 36, 213(d) and 215(a)(i), are hereby amended by the insertion after 'private company', in each place where it occurs in those provisions, of 'or an investment company (within the meaning of Part XIII of the Companies Act, 1990)'.

(2) None of the following provisions of the Principal Act shall apply to an investment company, namely sections 53, 56, 58, 60, 69, 70, 72, 119 and 125.

(3) None of the following provisions of the Companies (Amendment) Act, 1983, shall apply to an investment company, namely sections 5(2), 6 and 19, subsections (3) and (4) of section 20, sections 22, 23 to 25, 30 to 33, 40, 41, [43, 43A][b] and Part IV.

(4) Section 14 of the Companies (Amendment) Act, 1986, shall not apply to an investment company.

(5) None of the following provisions of this Act shall apply to an investment company, namely, Chapters 2 to 4 of Part IV, section 140 (whether as regards a case in which the

investment company is being wound up or a case in which it is a related company (within the meaning of that section)) and Part XI.][a]

Amendments

a CA 1990, s 260 substituted by C(A)(No 2)A 1999, s 54(3).

b '43, 43A' inserted by IFCMPA 2005, s 27.

[260A Application of section 148 of Principal Act

(1) Notwithstanding section 148(2) of the Principal Act (inserted by the European Communities (International Financial Reporting Standards and Miscellaneous Amendments) Regulations 2005 (S.I. No. 116 of 2005)) an investment company may, in respect of its individual accounts, opt to prepare those accounts in accordance with both of the following, namely—

(a) an alternative body of accounting standards, and

(b) section 149A of the Principal Act,

as if the references in that section 149A to international financial reporting standards were references to that alternative body of accounting standards.

(2) In the application of subsections (4), (5) and (6) of section 148 of the Principal Act to an investment company which has opted under subsection (1) to prepare its accounts in accordance with an alternative body of accounting standards—

(a) the reference in that subsection (4) to international financial reporting standards shall be read as a reference to that alternative body of accounting standards, and

(b) there shall be substituted for 'IFRS', in each place where it occurs in those subsections (4), (5) and (6), 'ABAS' (which shall be read as referring to that alternative body of accounting standards).

(3) For the purposes of this section, accounts shall not be regarded as having been prepared in accordance with an alternative body of accounting standards unless the accounts concerned would, were they to have been prepared by a company or undertaking registered in the relevant jurisdiction, be regarded as having been prepared in accordance with those standards.

(4) In this section—

'alternative body of accounting standards' means standards that accounts of companies or undertakings must comply with that are laid down by such body or bodies having authority to lay down standards of that kind in—

(a) United States of America,

(b) Canada,

(c) Japan, or

(d) any other prescribed state or territory,

as may be prescribed;

'relevant jurisdiction' means the state or territory in which the alternative body of accounting standards concerned have effect.

(5) Before making regulations for the purposes of subsection (4), the Minister—

(a) shall consult with the Central Bank, and

(b) may consult with any other persons whom the Minister considers should be consulted.

(6) If particular regulations for the purposes of subsection (4) are proposed to be made at a time subsequent to the commencement of Part 2 of the Companies (Auditing and Accounting) Act 2003, then, before making those regulations, the Minister shall also consult with the Irish Auditing and Accounting Supervisory Authority.][a]

Amendments

a This section was added by IFCMPA 2005, s 28.

261 Power to make supplementary regulations

The Minister may make such regulations as he considers necessary for the purposes of giving full effect to the provisions of this Part.

262 Offences

Where a company contravenes—

(a) any of the provisions of this Part, or

(b) any regulations made in relation thereto (whether under this Part or under any other enactment), or

(c) any condition in relation to its authorisation or business imposed by the [Central Bank][a] under section 257,

the company and every officer thereof who is in default shall be guilty of an offence.

Amendments

a 'Central Bank' substituted for 'Bank' by CBFSAIA 2003, Sch 1.

SCHEDULE

PROVISIONS SUBSTITUTED FOR NINTH SCHEDULE TO PRINCIPAL ACT

[...][a]

Amendments

a Schedule inserts new Ninth Sch of CA 1963.

COMPANIES (AMENDMENT) ACT, 1977

Subject matter	*Provisions applied*
Share certificates	Sections 2 and 3.
Company records	Section 4.

COMPANIES (AMENDMENT) ACT, 1983

Subject matter	*Provisions applied*
Maintenance of capital. Restrictions on distribution of profits and assets	Sections 40 to 42, 45, 45A (inserted by the Companies (Amendment) Act, 1986) and 49 to 51. Sections 43, 44, 46 and 47, with the modification that those sections shall apply to all bodies corporate to which section 377(1) of the Principal Act applies other than those which, if they were registered, would be private companies.

EUROPEAN COMMUNITIES (STOCK EXCHANGE) REGULATIONS, 1984
(S.I. NO 282 OF 1984)

Provisions applied

All of the Regulations.	

COMPANIES (AMENDMENT) ACT, 1986

Subject matter	Provisions applied
Power to alter form of accounts	Section 24.

EUROPEAN COMMUNITIES (MERGERS AND DIVISIONS OF COMPANIES) REGULATIONS, 1987
(S.I. NO 137 OF 1987)

Provisions applied

All of the Regulations.	

COMPANIES (AMENDMENT) ACT, 1990

Provisions applied

The whole Act.

COMPANIES ACT, 1990

Provisions applied

Parts I to III.
Part IV, with the modification that Chapter 2 of that Part shall apply to all bodies corporate to which section 377 (1) of the Principal Act applies other than those which, if they were registered, would be private companies and Chapter 3 of that Part shall apply to all such bodies corporate which, if they were registered, would be private companies.
Part V.
Part VI, except sections 122, 128 to 131 and 133.
Parts VII, IX, X and XII.

Companies (Amendment) Act 1999

Number 8 of 1999

ARRANGEMENT OF SECTIONS

An Act to amend and extend Parts IV and V of the Companies Act, 1990, to permit stabilising activity in relation to the issue or sale of securities and to provide for connected matters. [19th May, 1999]

Be It Enacted by the Oireachtas as Follows:

1 Interpretation

(1) In this Act—

'the Act of 1990' means the Companies Act, 1990;

'closing date' has the meaning assigned by the Stabilisation Rules;

'the Principal Act' means the Companies Act, 1963;

'stabilising period' has, in relation to anything done in the State pursuant to the Stabilisation Rules, the meaning assigned by the Stabilisation Rules and, in relation to anything done in a jurisdiction outside the State for the purpose of stabilising or maintaining the market price of securities, means the period beginning on—

(a) in the case of an issue or offer for sale of securities (not being an issue of debentures or other debt securities), the date on which the earliest public announcement of such issue or offer is made which states the issue price or the offer price, as the case may be, for those securities, or

(b) in the case of an issue of debentures or other debt securities, the date on which the earliest public announcement of such issue is made, whether or not that announcement states the issue price, and ending on the expiration of—

(i) the day which is 30 days after the closing date, or

(ii) the day which a manager appointed by the issuer or, as the case may be, the offeror to conduct stabilising activity shall have notified a stock exchange on which stabilising activity was being conducted as the day on which it determined that it would take no further action to stabilise or maintain the market price of the securities concerned, whichever first occurs;

'Stabilisation Rules' means the rules referred to by that name which are set out in the Schedule.

(2) In this Act—

(a) a reference to a Part, section or Schedule is a reference to a Part or section of, or a Schedule to, this Act, unless it is indicated that reference to some other enactment is intended,

(b) a reference to a subsection, paragraph, subparagraph, clause or subclause is a reference to the subsection, paragraph, subparagraph, clause or subclause of the provision in which the reference occurs unless it is indicated that reference to some other provision is intended, and

(c) a reference to any enactment is a reference to that enactment as amended, extended or adapted by or under any subsequent enactment including this Act.

Amendments

Section repealed in limited manner as per IFCMPA 2005, s 31 as enacted by SI 323/2005. See IFCMPA 2005, s 31 and notes thereto.

---

2 Restriction of section 108 of Act of 1990

Section 108 of the Act of 1990 shall not be regarded as having been contravened by reason of—

(a) anything done in the State for the purpose of stabilising or maintaining the market price of securities if it is done in conformity with the Stabilisation Rules, or

(b) any action taken during the stabilising period by a person in any jurisdiction other than the State for the purpose of stabilising or maintaining the market price of securities, but only if the action taken is, in all material respects, permitted by or is otherwise in accordance with all relevant requirements applicable to such actions in the jurisdiction where such action is effected, including, if those securities are also listed on a stock exchange in that jurisdiction, the rules or other regulatory requirements governing that stock exchange.

Amendments

Section repealed in limited manner as per IFCMPA 2005, s 31 as enacted by SI 323/2005. See IFCMPA 2005, s 31 and notes thereto.

---

3 Disclosure of interests in relevant share capital

(1) The acquisition or disposal of interests in relevant share capital by a person during the stabilising period concerned, which—

(a) is done for the purpose of stabilising or maintaining the market price of securities, and

(b) is so done either in conformity with the Stabilisation Rules or is an acquisition or disposal to which section 2(b) relates,

shall be disregarded during the stabilising period for the purposes of sections 67 to 79 of the Act of 1990.

(2) Any interest in relevant share capital which—

(a) was acquired by a person during the stabilising period for the purpose of stabilising or maintaining the market price of securities,

(b) was so acquired in accordance with this Act, and

(c) continues to be held by such person at the end of the stabilizing period,

shall be treated, for the purposes of sections 67 to 79 of the Act of 1990, as having been acquired by such person on the first day following the end of the stabilising period that is not a Saturday, Sunday or public holiday.

(3) Notwithstanding subsection (1), subsection (4) of section 91 of the Act of 1990 shall operate to determine the interests which are to be notified to the Irish Stock Exchange Limited, and the manner in which they are to be so notified, under subsection (2) of that section.

(4) In this section 'relevant share capital' has the meaning assigned by section 67(2) of the Act of 1990.

Amendments

Section repealed in limited manner as per IFCMPA 2005, s 31 as enacted by SI 323/2005. See IFCMPA 2005, s 31 and notes thereto.

---

4 Amendment of section 110 of Act of 1990

[...][a]

Amendments

a C(A)A 1999, s 4 inserts CA 1990, s 110(2A) which in essence incorporates the provisions of the Companies Act, 1990 (Insider Dealing) Regulations, 1991[1] which have now been repealed by C(A)A 1999, s 6. See the amended Act.

[1] SI 151/1991.

---

5 Removal of difficulties

(1) Where, in any respect, any difficulty arises in the operation of any provision of the Stabilisation Rules, the Minister for Enterprise, Trade and Employment may by regulations amend the Stabilisation Rules to do anything which appears to him or her to be necessary or expedient for removing that difficulty, and any such regulations may modify any provision of the Stabilisation Rules or add thereto so far as may be necessary or expedient for carrying the Schedule into effect.

(2) Every regulation made under this section shall be laid before each House of the Oireachtas as soon as may be after it is made and if a resolution annulling the regulation is passed by either such House within the next 21 days on which that House has sat after

the regulation is laid before it, the regulation shall be annulled accordingly, but without prejudice to the validity of anything previously done thereunder.

6 Revocations

The Companies Act, 1990 (Insider Dealing) Regulations, 1991 (SI No 151 of 1991), and the Companies Act, 1990 (Insider Dealing) Regulations, 1992 (SI No 131 of 1992), are hereby revoked.

Amendments

Section repealed in limited manner as per IFCMPA 2005, s 31 as enacted by SI 323/2005. See IFCMPA 2005, s 31 and notes thereto.

---

7 Short title, collective citation, construction and commencement

(1) This Act may be cited as the Companies (Amendment) Act, 1999.

(2) This Act and the Companies Acts, 1963 to 1990, may be cited together as the Companies Acts, 1963 to 1999, and shall be construed together as one.

(3) This Act shall come into operation on such day or days as may be appointed by order or orders made by the Minister for Enterprise, Trade and Employment, either generally or with reference to any particular purpose or provision, and different days may be so appointed for different purposes and different provisions of this Act.

Amendments

Section repealed in the limited manner as per IFCMPA 2005, s 31 as enacted by SI 323/2005.

SCHEDULE

STABILISATION RULES

Section 1(1).

1 Definitions

In these Rules—

'associated securities' means securities—

(a) which are in all respects uniform with the relevant securities,

or

(b) for which the relevant securities may be exchanged or into which they may be converted, or

(c) which the holders of the relevant securities have, by virtue of their holdings of those securities, rights to acquire or to subscribe for, or

(d) which are depository receipts which represent or confer property rights in respect of relevant securities or securities to which paragraph (a), (b), (c) or (f) relates or which represent or confer a contractual right (other than an option) to acquire such securities otherwise than by subscription;

or

(e) which represent or confer any right, option or obligation in respect of an index relating to relevant securities or to securities to which paragraph (a), (b), (c) or (d) relates,

or

(f) which represent or confer a right to acquire a particular amount of relevant securities or of any securities to which paragraph (a), (b), (c), (d) or (e) relates at a future date at a particular price ('associated call options') or which otherwise represent or confer any right, option or obligation in respect of such securities;

'closing date' means—

(a) in the case of an issue of securities, the date on which the issuer of the securities receives the proceeds of the issue or, where the issuer receives those proceeds in instalments, the date on which it receives the first instalment; and

(b) in the case of an offer for sale of securities, the date on which the offeror or, as the case may be, the offerors receive the proceeds of the offer for sale, or where the offeror or, as the case may be, the offerors receive those proceeds in instalments, the date on which the offeror or, where there is more than one offeror, one or more of the offerors receives the first instalment;

'introductory period' means the period starting at the time of the first public announcement from which it could reasonably be deducted that the issue was intended to take place in some form and at some time, and ending with the beginning of the stabilising period;

'issue', except in the definitions of 'closing date' and 'stabilising period' and in Rule 2, includes offer for sale and 'issued' shall be construed accordingly;

'issue price' means the specified price at which the relevant securities are issued without deducting any selling concession or commission;

'issuer', except in the definition of 'closing date', includes offeror;

'manager' means the person instructed by the issuer of the securities to manage the issue;

'public announcement' means any communication made by or on behalf of the issuer or the manager, being a communication made in circumstances in which it is likely that members of the public will become aware of the communication;

'recognised stock exchange' has the meaning assigned by section 107 of the Companies Act, 1990;

'the Register' has the meaning assigned by Rule 5(1)(d);

'relevant day' means—

(a) the 30th day after the closing date or,

(b) where before the 30th day after the closing date the stabilising manager has determined that he or she would take no further action to stabilise or maintain the market price of the relevant securities and has notified the

Irish Stock Exchange Limited accordingly pursuant to Rule 8; the day he or she so determined;

'relevant securities' has the meaning given by Rule 2;

'securities' has the meaning assigned by section 107 of the Companies Act, 1990;

'stabilising action' means a purchase of, or agreement to purchase or offer to purchase relevant securities or associated securities permitted to be made by Rule 3;

'stabilising manager' means the person who is manager or, if there be more than one manager, such one of the managers as shall have been agreed between them to be the one to conduct stabilising action in the State in relation to the issue of the relevant securities;

'stabilising period' means the period beginning with the date on which the earliest public announcement of the issue or offer for sale which states the issue price or offer price, as the case may be, is made and ending with the relevant day, save that, in relation to an issue of relevant securities which are debentures or other debt securities, the stabilising period means the period beginning with the date on which the earliest public announcement of the issue is made (whether or not that announcement states the issue price) and ending with the relevant day;

'takeover offer' means an offer made generally to holders of shares in a company to acquire those shares or a specified proportion of them, or to holders of a particular class of those shares to acquire the shares of that class or a specified proportion of them.

2 Application

These Rules apply to—

(a) an issue of securities for cash,

(b) an offer of securities for cash for which securities dealing facilities are not already provided by a recognised stock exchange, and

(c) an offer of securities for cash for which securities dealing facilities are already provided by a recognised stock exchange, if the total cost of the securities which are the subject of the offer is at least [€19,046,071.18][a] (or the equivalent in the currency or unit of account in which the price of the securities is stated),

and which is made other than in connection with a takeover offer and at a specified price and which securities may be dealt in on a recognised stock exchange without a formal application, or in respect of which application has been made to a recognised stock exchange for the securities to be dealt in on that exchange, and such securities are in these Rules referred to as 'relevant securities'.

Amendments

a £15,000,000 converted to €19,046,071.18 by Council Regulation (EC) No 1103/97, No 974/98 and No 2866/98 and the Economic and Monetary Union Act 1998, s 6.

3 Permitted stabilising action

(1) Subject to paragraph (2) and Rules 6 and 7, the stabilising manager may during the stabilising period do any or all of the following, with a view to stabilising or maintaining the market price of the relevant securities:

(a) purchase, agree to purchase or offer to purchase any of the relevant securities, and

(b) purchase, agree to purchase or offer to purchase any associated securities.

(2) A stabilising manager may effect a stabilising action pursuant to paragraph (1) only if the stabilising manager reasonably believes that the conditions specified in Rule 5 have been fulfilled.

(3) A stabilising manager who effects a stabilising action pursuant to paragraph (1) shall comply with Rule 9.

4 Permitted action ancillary to stabilising action

(1) Subject to paragraph (2) and Rule 6, the stabilising manager may—

(a) with a view to effecting stabilising actions, either or both—

(i) make allocations of a greater number of relevant securities than will be issued, and

(ii) sell, offer to sell, or agree to sell a greater number of relevant securities or associated securities than the stabilising manager has available for sale,

(b) sell, offer to sell, or agree to sell relevant securities or associated securities in order to close out or liquidate any position established by stabilising actions whether or not those actions were in accordance with Rule 3, and

(c) purchase, offer to purchase or agree to purchase relevant securities or associated securities in order to close out or liquidate any position established pursuant to clause (i) or (ii) of subparagraph (a).

(2) A stabilising manager may act pursuant to paragraph (1) only if he or she reasonably believes that the conditions specified in Rule 5 have been fulfilled.

(3) A stabilising manager who acts pursuant to paragraph (1) shall comply with Rule 9.

(4) A transaction of the type described in paragraph (1)(c) may be effected without regard to the requirements as to purchasing price limits set out in Rule 7.

5 Preliminary steps before stabilising action, etc

(1) The following are the conditions which have, in the reasonable belief of the stabilising manager, to have been fulfilled before any stabilising action or action pursuant to Rule 4(1) may be taken in accordance with these Rules:

(a) from the beginning of the introductory period—

(i) any electronic screen-based statement, including any screen facility provided by the stabilising manager through which persons are informed of the sale or purchase price of securities, or

(ii) any announcement intended for publication in any newspaper and any other announcement of a public nature, or

(iii) any invitation telex or equivalent document;

which refers to the issue concerned and is made or published by or on behalf of the issuer or the stabilising manager shall during the introductory period, include a reference to the future prospectus or to the prospectus or include the word 'Stabilisation',

(b) from the beginning of the introductory period, any preliminary offering circular, preliminary offering prospectus, final offering circular or final offering prospectus relating to the issue of the securities concerned shall include the following statement or a statement to the like effect:

'In connection with this issue [name of stabilizing manager] may over-allot or effect transactions which stabilise or maintain the market price of [description of relevant securities and of any associated securities] at a level which might not otherwise prevail. Such stabilising, if commenced, may be discontinued at any time',

and references in these Rules to a 'disclosure statement' shall be to such statement or such statement to like effect,

(c) if there are associated securities in existence the market price of which was, at the time the issue price of the relevant securities was determined, at a level higher than it otherwise would have been because of any act performed by, or any course of conduct engaged in by, any person which the stabilising manager knows or ought reasonably to know created a false or misleading impression in the market in or the price or value of that security which may induce, or may have induced, another person—

(i) to enter into, or refrain from entering into any bargain or other transaction relative to such security, or

(ii) to exercise or refrain from exercising any rights conferred by that security,

the stabilising manager is satisfied that the issue price of the relevant securities is no higher than it would have been had that act not been performed or that course of conduct not been engaged in,

and

(d) the stabilising manager has established a register (in these Rules referred to as 'the Register') to record in relation to each transaction effected in the relevant securities or associated securities the matters required to be recorded by Rule 9.

(2) (a) Any disclosure required by paragraph (1)(a) to be included in a document or communication, or any disclosure statement required by paragraph (1)(b) to be included in a circular or prospectus, shall be set out prominently and in a legible form in the document or communication concerned.

(b) The disclosure statement may be adapted or omitted to comply with the requirements of any other jurisdiction in which transactions to stabilise or maintain the market price of securities may be conducted in connection with the issue and so as not to require any person duly appointed to conduct stabilising activity in respect of a jurisdiction other than the State to commit any breach of any legal rule or requirement in respect of any communication or announcement made or advertisement or document issued in that jurisdiction.

(3) (a) Except where provided for by subparagraphs (a) and (b) of paragraph (1), this Rule shall not apply to any communication, advertisement or document.

(b) Without prejudice to the generality of subparagraph (a), a disclosure or a disclosure statement need not be set out in any—

(i) allotment telex or similar document,

(ii) pricing telex or similar document,

(iii) contract note, or

(iv) short form or image advertisement, including any newspaper, radio or television advertisement designed to generate interest in the issue of the securities concerned and any marketing brochure as long as it does not constitute a preliminary offering circular or preliminary offering prospectus.

6 Restriction on stabilising action in associated securities

No stabilising action shall be taken in any associated securities of those relevant securities which are debentures or other debt securities and which associated securities are associated securities because—

(a) the relevant securities may be exchanged for or converted into the associated securities, or

(b) the holders of the relevant securities have a right to subscribe for or to acquire the associated securities,

unless the terms on which the relevant securities may be exchanged for or converted into the associated securities, or the rights of holders of the relevant securities to subscribe for or to acquire the associated securities, have been finally settled and been made the subject of a public announcement.

7 Limits on prices

(1) No stabilising action shall be effected by the stabilising manager at a price higher than any relevant price determined in accordance with this Rule.

(2) The limits on prices at which stabilising action may be effected shall be as follows:

(a) in the case of relevant securities and associated securities which are in all respects uniform with the relevant securities (not being debentures or other debt securities)—

(i) for the initial stabilising action, the issue price,

(ii) for subsequent actions—

(I) where there has been a deal at a price above the price at which the initial stabilising action took place (the 'initial stabilising price') on the relevant exchange which has not been done by or on the instructions of the stabilising manager, the issue price, or the price at which that deal was done, whichever is the lower, or

(II) where there has been no deal of the type described in subclause (I), the issue price, or the initial stabilising price, whichever is the lower,

(b) in the case of associated securities (not being debentures or other debt securities, associated securities which are in all respects uniform with the relevant securities, or associated call options)—

(i) for the initial stabilising action, the market bid price of the associated securities at the beginning of the stabilising period,

(ii) for subsequent actions—

(I) where there has been a deal at a price above the price at which the initial stabilising action took place (the 'initial stabilising price') on the relevant exchange which has not been done by or on the instructions of the stabilising manager, the market bid price in clause (i) or the price at which that deal in the associated securities was done, whichever is the lower, or

(II) where there has been no deal of the type described in subclause (I), the market bid price as in clause (i), or the initial stabilising price for the associated securities, whichever is the lower,

and

(c) in the case of associated call options—

(i) for the initial stabilising action, the market price of the associated call option at the beginning of the stabilising period,

(ii) for subsequent actions—

(I) where there has been a deal at a price above the price at which the initial stabilising action took place (the 'initial stabilising price') on the relevant exchange which has not been done by or on the instructions of the stabilising manager, the market price in clause (i) or the price at which that deal in the associated call option was done, whichever is the lower, or

(II) where there has been no deal of the type described in subclause (I), the market price as in clause (i), or the initial stabilising price for the associated call option, whichever is the lower.

(3) (a) In this Rule 'relevant exchange' means the stock exchange which the stabilising manager reasonably believes to be the principal stock exchange on which those securities, or as the case may be, options, are dealt in at the time of the transaction.

(b) For the purposes of this Rule—

(i) where the price of any relevant securities or associated securities on the relevant exchange is in a currency other than the currency of the price of the securities to be stabilised, stabilising actions may be made at a price that reflects any movement in the relevant rate of exchange, but this shall not permit stabilising action under paragraph (2)(a) at a price above the equivalent, in the other currency, of the issue price in the currency on the relevant exchange,

(ii) any convertible bond which is both a debenture or other debt security and an associated call option shall be treated as a debenture only,

(iii) where no market bid price is quoted in respect of the associated security concerned at the beginning of the stabilising period, the relevant price shall be the closing quotation price in respect of such securities on the previous business day as published in the relevant stock exchange list.

8 Notification of termination of stabilising action

Where the stabilising manager determines, before the 30th day after the closing date that he or she will take no further action to stabilise or maintain the market price of the relevant securities, he or she shall notify the Irish Stock Exchange Limited without delay of that determination and the Irish Stock Exchange Limited shall publish that information in such form as it sees fit.

9 Recording of stabilisation transactions

(1) The stabilising manager shall record in the Register the matters specified in subparagraph (2) in relation to transactions effected pursuant to Rules 3 and 4 and that record shall be made before the opening of business on the day that is not a Saturday, Sunday or public holiday which next follows the day the transaction was effected and a copy of that record shall be communicated to the Irish Stock Exchange Limited before the end of that day.

(2) The following matters shall be recorded in the Register:

(a) the names of the persons to whom the relevant securities were allocated or issued and, in relation to each person, the amount allocated or issued to him or her;

(b) the description of the security which is the subject of the transaction;

(c) the price (excluding any commission payable) of each security which is the subject of the transaction;

(d) the number of securities which are the subject of the transaction;

(e) the date and time of the transaction; and

(f) the identity of the counterparty to the transaction.

(3) A stabilising manager who offers or effects a stabilising action at a price determined in accordance with subparagraph (a)(ii)(I), (b)(ii)(I) or (c)(ii)(I) of Rule 7(2) shall record in the Register details of the transaction which affects the maximum price of the stabilising action.

Companies (Amendment) (No 2) Act 1999

Number 30 of 1999

ARRANGEMENT OF SECTIONS

PART I
PRELIMINARY AND GENERAL

PART II
EXAMINERSHIPS

PART III
EXEMPTION FROM REQUIREMENT TO HAVE ACCOUNTS AUDITED

PART IV
MISCELLANEOUS

FIRST SCHEDULE

SECOND SCHEDULE

Companies (Amendment) (No 2) Act 1999

Number 30 of 1999

An Act to amend the Companies (Amendment) Act, 1990, to provide for an exemption from the requirement that the accounts of companies and certain partnerships be audited, to prohibit the formation of a company unless it appears to the registrar of companies that the company will carry on an activity in the state, to require, save in certain circumstances, one of the directors of a company to be a person resident in the state, to otherwise amend the law relating to companies and certain partnerships and to provide for related matters. [15th December, 1999]

Be it Enacted by the Oireachtas as Follows:

PART I

PRELIMINARY AND GENERAL

1 Short Title, collective citation, construction and commencement

(1) This Act may be cited as the Companies (Amendment) (No 2) Act, 1999.

(2) The Companies Acts, 1963 to 1986, the Companies (Amendment) Act, 1990, the Companies Act, 1990, the Companies (Amendment) Act, 1999, and this Act (other than section 40) may be cited together as the Companies Acts, 1963 to 1999.

(3) The enactments referred to in subsection (2) shall be construed together as one.

(4) This Act shall come into operation on such day or days as the Minister may appoint by order or orders either generally or with reference to any particular purpose or provision and different days may be so appointed for different purposes or different provisions.

(5) The power under subsection (4) shall be so exercised that—

(a) the one day is appointed on which every provision of Part III (other than subsections (2), (3) and (7) of section 33), the First Schedule and the Second Schedule (in so far as it relates to the said Part) shall come into operation, and

(b) the day appointed on which subsections (2), (3) and (7) of section 33 shall come into operation is the day that is 2 months earlier than the said day.

2 Interpretation generally

(1) In this Act—

'the Central Bank' means the Central Bank of Ireland;

'the Principal Act' means the Companies Act, 1963.

(2) In this Act—

(a) a reference to a Part, section or Schedule is a reference to a Part or section of, or a Schedule to, this Act unless it is indicated that reference to some other enactment is intended,

(b) a reference to a subsection, paragraph or subparagraph is a reference to the subsection, paragraph or subparagraph of the provision in which the reference occurs unless it is indicated that reference to some other provision is intended,

(c) a reference to any enactment is a reference to that enactment as amended, extended or adapted by or under any subsequent enactment (including this Act).

3 Orders

(1) The Minister may by order prescribe any matter or thing which is referred to in this Act as prescribed or to be prescribed.

(2) The Minister may by order amend or revoke an order under this Act (other than an order under section 1(4) but including an order under this subsection).

(3) Every order under this Act (other than an order under section 1(4)) shall be laid before each House of the Oireachtas as soon as may be after it is made and, if a resolution annulling the order is passed by either such House within the next 21 days on which that House has sat after the order is laid before it, the order shall be annulled accordingly but without prejudice to the validity of anything previously done thereunder.

PART II
EXAMINERSHIPS

4 Definition

In this Part 'the Act of 1990' means the Companies (Amendment) Act, 1990.

5 Amendment of section 2 of Act of 1990

[...][a]

Amendments

a C(A)(No 2)A 1999, s 5(a) amended C(A)A 1990, s 2(1) by the substitution for 'Where it appears to the court that' of 'Subject to subsection (2), where it appears to the court that'. C(A)(No 2)A 1999, s 5(b) substituted C(A)A 1990, s 2(2).

---

6 Amendment of section 3 of Act of 1990

[...][a]

Amendments

a C(A)(No 2)A 1999, s 6 substituted C(A)A 1990, s 3(2)(b) and inserted C(A)A 1990, s 3(2)(c).

---

7 Pre-petition report in relation to company

[...][a]

Amendments

a C(A)(No 2)A 1999, s 7 inserted C(A)A 1990, s 3(3A) and (3B).

---

8 Amendment of section 3(5) of Act of 1990

[...][a]

Amendments

a C(A)(No 2)A 1999, s 8 deleted ', and until a prima facie case for protection has been established to the satisfaction of the court' in C(A)A 1990, s 3(5).

9 Interim protection pending report

[...][a]

Amendments

a C(A)(No 2)A 1999, s 9 inserted C(A)A 1990, s 3A.

10 Creditors to be heard

[...][a]

Amendments

a C(A)(No 2)A 1999, s 10 inserted C(A)A 1990, s 3B.

11 Availability of independent accountant's report

[...][a]

Amendments

a C(A)(No 2)A 1999, s 11 inserted C(A)A 1990, s 3C.

12 Amendment of section 4 of Act of 1990

[...][a]

Amendments

a C(A)(No 2)A 1999, s 12(a) substituted 'Subject to subsection (2), where the court appoints an examiner to a company' for 'Where the court appoints an examiner to a company' in C(A)A 1990, s 4(1). C(A)(No 2)A 1999, s 12(b) substituted C(A)A 1990, s 4(2).

13 Duty to act in good faith

[...][a]

Amendments

a C(A)(No 2)A 1999, s 13 inserted C(A)A 1990, s 4A.

14 Amendment of section 5 of Act of 1990

[...][a]

Amendments

a C(A)(No 2)A 1999, s 14(a) substituted C(A)A 1990, s 5(1). C(A)(No 2)A 1999, s 14(b) substituted C(A)A 1990, s 5(2)(d) and deleted C(A)A 1990, s 5(2)(h).

15 Restriction of payment of pre-petition debts

[...][a]

Amendments

a C(A)(No 2)A 1999, s 15 inserted C(A)A 1990, s 5A.

16 Amendment of section 6 of Act of 1990

[...][a]

Amendments

a C(A)(No 2)A 1999, s 16(a) amended C(A)A 1990, s 6(1) by the substitution for 'Where the court appoints an examiner to a company and' of 'Where, at the date of the presentation of a petition under section 2 in relation to a company'. C(A)(No 2)A 1999, s 16(b) amended C(A)A 1990, s 6(2) by the substitution for 'Where the court appoints an examiner to a company and' of 'Where, at the date of the presentation of a petition under section 2 in relation to a company'. C(A)(No 2)A 1999, s 16(c) substitutes C(A)A 1990, s 6(3).

17 Disapplication of section 98 of Principal Act to receivers in certain circumstances

[...][a]

Amendments

a C(A)(No 2)A 1999, s 17 inserts C(A)A 1990, s 6A.

18 Repudiation of contracts

[...][a]

Amendments

a C(A)(No 2)A 1999, s 18 inserts C(A)A 1990, s 7(5A), (5B) and (5C).

19 Amendment of section 8 of Act of 1990

[...][a]

Amendments

a C(A)(No 2)A 1999, s 19 substitutes C(A)A 1990, s 8(5) and (5A).

20 Amendment of section 12 of Act of 1990

[...][a]

Amendments

a C(A)(No 2)A 1999, s 20(1) substitutes C(A)A 1990, s 12(2)(a). C(A)(No 2)A 1999, s 20(2) substitutes C(A)A 1990, s 12(4).

21 Hearing regarding irregularities

[...][a]

Amendments

a C(A)(No 2)A 1999, s 21 inserts C(A)A 1990, s 13A.

22 Amendment of section 18 of Act of 1990

[...][a]

Amendments

a C(A)(No 2)A 1999, s 22(a) substitutes C(A)A 1990, s 18(1). C(A)(No 2)A 1999, s 22(b) amends C(A)A 1990, s 18(2) by the deletion of all the words from 'to consider such proposals' to the end of that subsection and the substitution of 'for the purpose of section 23 and shall report on those proposals to the court, within 35 days of his appointment or such longer period as the court may allow, in accordance with section 19.' C(A)(No 2)A 1999, s 22(c) amends C(A)A 1990, s 18(3) by the substitution of '70 days' for 'three months'. C(A)(No 2)A 1999, s 22(d) substitutes C(A)A 1990, s 18(5) and (6) and inserts C(A)A 1990, s 18(7), (8) and (9).

23 Amendment of section 23 of Act of 1990

[...][a]

Amendments

a C(A)(No 2)A 1999, s 23(a) amends C(A)A 1990, s 23(1) by the substitution for 'compromise or scheme of arrangement' of 'compromise or scheme of arrangement; save where expressly provided otherwise in this section, this section shall not authorise, at such a meeting, anything to be done in relation to such proposals by any member or creditor.' C(A)(No 2)A 1999, s 23(b) deletes C(A)A 1990, s 23(3). C(A)(No 2)A 1999, s 23(c) inserts C(A)A 1990, s 23(4A). C(A)(No 2)A 1999, s 23(d) amends C(A)A 1990, s 23(6) by the deletion of '(3) or'. C(A)(No 2)A 1999, s 23(e) inserts C(A)A 1990, s 23(9).

24 Amendment of section 24 of Act of 1990

[...][a]

Amendments

a C(A)(No 2)A 1999, s 24(a) inserts C(A)A 1990, s 24(2)(d). C(A)(No 2)A 1999, s 24(b) substitutes C(A)A 1990, s 24(4)(a). C(A)(No 2)A 1999, s 24(c) inserts C(A)A 1990, s 24(4A). C(A)(No 2)A 1999, s 24(d) amends C(A)A 1990, s 24(11)(b) by the deletion of 'members and'. C(A)(No 2)A 1999, s 24(e) substitutes C(A)A 1990, s 24(12).

25 Provisions with respect to guarantees

[...][a]

Amendments

a C(A)(No 2)A 1999, s 25 inserts C(A)A 1990, s 25A.

26 Provisions with respect to leases

[...][a]

Amendments

a C(A)(No 2)A 1999, s 26 inserts C(A)A 1990, s 25B.

27 Amendment of section 27 of Act of 1990

[...][a]

Amendments

a C(A)(No 2)A 1999, s 27(a) amends C(A)A 1990, s 27 by the insertion of '(1) before 'The company or any interested party'. C(A)(No 2)A 1999, s 27(b) inserts C(A)A 1990, s 27(2).

28 Priority of costs, remuneration and expenses of examiner

[...][a]

Amendments

a C(A)(No 2)A 1999, s 28 substitutes C(A)A 1990, s 29(3) and inserts C(A)A 1990, s 29(3A) and (3B).

29 Amendment of section 30 of Act of 1990

[...][a]

Amendments

a C(A)(No 2)A 1999, s 29 amends C(A)A 1990, s 30(1) by the substitution of 'section 13A, 24 or 27' for 'section 17 or 24'.

30 Repeals

[...][a]

Amendments

a C(A)(No 2)A 1999, s 30 repeals C(A)A 1990, s 3(3)(b) and (c) and ss 14, 15, 16 and 17.

PART III

EXEMPTION FROM REQUIREMENT TO HAVE ACCOUNTS AUDITED

31 Definitions

In this Part—

'the Act of 1986' means the Companies (Amendment) Act, 1986;

'the exemption' means the non-application, by virtue of section 32, of section 160 of the Principal Act and the provisions referred to in subsection (2) of section 32;

'financial year' means the financial year of the company concerned;

'private company' does not include an unlimited company other than such a company (being a private company) to which Part III of the 1993 Regulations applies;

'the 1993 Regulations' means the European Communities (Accounts) Regulations, 1993 (S.I. No. 396 of 1993).

32 Exemption from requirement to have accounts audited

(1) [Subject to sections 32A and [32B]][a], if—

(a) the directors of a private company are of opinion that the company will satisfy the conditions specified in subsection (3) in respect of a financial year and decide that the company should avail itself of the exemption in that year (and they record that decision in the minutes of the meeting concerned), and

(b) unless that financial year is the first financial year of the company, the company satisfied the said conditions in respect of the preceding financial year, then—

(i) without prejudice to section 35, section 160 of the Principal Act (which requires the appointment of an auditor to a company) shall not apply to the said company in respect of that financial year, and

(ii) [unless and until –

(I) circumstances, if any, arise in that financial year which result in one or more of the said conditions not being satisfied in respect of that year, or

(II) circumstances otherwise arise by reason of which the said company is not entitled to the exemption in respect of that financial year,

the provisions mentioned in subsection (2) shall not apply to the said company in respect of that year.][b]

(2) The provisions mentioned in subsection (1) are those provisions of the Companies Acts, 1963 to 1999, (other than this Part) the 1993 Regulations and the European Communities (Single-Member Private Limited Companies) Regulations, 1994 (S.I. No. 275 of 1994), that apply to the company, being provisions that—

(a) confer any powers on an auditor or require anything to be done by or to or as respects an auditor,

(b) make provision on the basis of a report of an auditor having been prepared in relation to the accounts of the company in a financial year, and, without prejudice to the generality of the foregoing, include the provisions specified in the First Schedule.

(3) The conditions mentioned in subsection (1) are that—

(a) in respect of the year concerned—

(i) the company is a company to which the Act of 1986 applies,

(ii) the amount of the turnover of the company does not exceed [€8.8 million][c],

(iii) the balance sheet total of the company does not exceed [€4.4 million][c],

(iv) the average number of persons employed by the company does not exceed 50,

(v) the company is not—

(I) a parent undertaking or a subsidiary undertaking (within the meaning of the European Communities (Companies: Group Accounts) Regulations, 1992 (S.I. No. 201 of 1992)),

(II) a holder of a licence under section 9 of the Central Bank Act, 1971, or a company that is exempt from the requirement under that Act to hold such a licence,

(III) a company to which the European Communities (Insurance Undertakings: Accounts) Regulations, 1996 (S.I. No. 23 of 1996) apply, [...][d]

(IV) a company referred to in the Second Schedule [(other than paragraph 18 thereof, or)][e]

[(V) a company whose securities are admitted to trading on a regulated market.][f]

[...][g]

(4) In this section 'amount of turnover' and 'balance sheet total' have the same meaning as they have in section 8 of the Act of 1986.

(5) For the purpose of subsection (3)(a)(iv), the average number of persons employed by a company shall be determined by applying the method of calculation prescribed by paragraph 42(4) of the Schedule to the Act of 1986 for determining the number required by subparagraph (1) of that paragraph to be stated in a note to the accounts of a company.

(6) In the application of this section to any period which is a financial year of a company, but is not in fact a year, the amount specified in subsection (3)(a)(ii) shall be proportionally adjusted.

(7) Each occasion of an amendment of the kind referred to in subsection (8) being effected shall operate to enable the Minister to amend, by order, subparagraphs (ii) and (iii) of subsection (3)(a) by substituting for the amount and the total, respectively, specified in those provisions a greater amount and total (not being an amount or total that is greater than the amount or total it replaces by 25 per cent.).

(8) The amendment referred to in subsection (7) is an amendment of the total and the amount specified in paragraphs (a) and (b), respectively, of section 8(2) of the Act of 1986, being an amendment made for the purpose of giving effect to an act adopted by an institution of the European Communities.

[(9) In subsection (3), 'regulated market' has the meaning assigned to it by Article 4(1), point (14) of Directive 2004/39/EC.][h]

Amendments

a C(AA)A 2003, s 53(a) amends C(A)(No 2)A 1999, s 32(1) by substituting 'Subject to sections 32A and 33(1)' for 'Subject to section 33(1)'. The IFCMPA 2006 further amends this section by substituting '32B' for 33(1).

b The IFCMPA 2006 substitutes this wording in s 32(1)(b)(2).

c C(AA)A 2003, s 53(b) amended C(A)(No 2)A 1999, s 32(3)(a)(ii) by substituting '€1,500,000' for '£250,000'. Subsequently, the IFCMPA 2006 amended C(A)(No 2)A 1999, s 32(3)(a)(ii) by substituting €7.3 million for €1,500,000 and s 32(3)(a)(iii) by substituting €3.65 million for €1,904,607.10; €8.8 million was substituted for €7.3 million and €4.4 million for €3.65 million by the Companies (Amendment) (No 2) Act 1999 (Section 32) Order 2012 (SI 308/2012), reg 2.

d European Communities (Directive 2006/46/EC) Regulations 2009, reg 5(a) amends C(A)(No 2)A 1999, s 32(3)(a)(v)(III) by deleting word 'or'.

e C(AA)A 2003, s 53(c) amends C(A)(No 2)A 1999, s 32(3)(a)(v)(IV) by substituting '(other than paragraph 18 thereof).' for '(other than paragraph 18 thereof),' and is further amended by European Communities (Directive 2006/46/EC) Regulations 2009, reg 5(b) by the substitution of 'paragraph 18 thereof, or for 'paragraph 18 thereof' .

f European Communities (Directive 2006/46/EC) Regulations 2009, reg 5(c) inserts C(A)(No 2)A 1999, s 32(3)(a)(v)(V).

g C(AA)A 2003, s 53(d) amends C(A)(No 2)A 1999, s 32(3) by deleting 'and' where it occurs after paragraph (a)(v)(IV) and by repealing paragraph (b).

h European Communities (Directive 2006/46/EC) Regulations 2009, reg 5(d) inserts C(A)(No 2)A 1999, s 32(9).

[32A Exemption conditional on timely filing of annual return

Notwithstanding that the conditions specified in section 32(3) are satisfied, a company is not entitled to the exemption in a financial year unless—

(a) the company's annual return to which the accounts for that financial year are annexed is delivered to the registrar of companies in compliance with section 127 of the Principal Act, and

(b) if the annual return referred to in paragraph (a) is not the company's first annual return, its annual return to which the accounts for its preceding financial year were annexed was also delivered to the registrar of companies in compliance with section 127 of the Principal Act.'][a]

Amendments

a C(A)(No 2)A 1999, s 32A inserted by C(AA)A 2003, s 53(e).

[32B Exemption conditional on notice under section 33(1) not being served

Notwithstanding that the conditions specified in section 32(3) are satisfied, a company is not entitled to the exemption in a financial year if a notice, with respect to that year, is served, under and in accordance with section 33(1) and (2), on the company.][a]

Amendments

a Section 32B inserted by the IFCMPA 2006, s 9(1)(c).

33 Section 32: supplemental provisions

[(1) Any member or members of a company holding shares in the company that confer, in aggregate, not less than one-tenth of the total voting rights in the company may serve a notice in writing on the company stating that that member or those members do not wish the exemption to be available to the company in a financial year specified in the notice.

(2) A notice under subsection (1) may be served on the company either –

(a) during the financial year immediately preceding the financial year to which the notice relates, or

(b) during the financial year to which the notice relates (but not later than 1 month before the end of that year).][a]

(3) [...][b]

(4) If a company avails itself of the exemption in a financial year, the balance sheet prepared by the company in respect of that year shall contain a statement by the directors of the company that, in respect of that year—

(a) the company is availing itself of the exemption (and the exemption shall be expressed to be 'the exemption provided for by Part III of the Companies (Amendment) (No 2) Act, 1999)',

(b) the company is availing itself of the exemption on the grounds that it satisfies the conditions specified in section 32,

(c) [no notice under subsection (1) has, in accordance with subsection (2), been served on the company, and,][c]

(d) the directors acknowledge the obligations of the company, under the Companies Acts, 1963 to 1999, to keep proper books of account and prepare accounts which give a true and fair view of the state of affairs of the company at the end of its financial year and of its profit or loss for such a year and to otherwise comply with the provisions of those Acts relating to accounts so far as they are applicable to the company.

(5) The statement required by subsection (4) shall appear in the balance sheet in a position immediately above the signatures of the directors required by section 156 of the Principal Act or, as the case may be, the statement required by section 18(2) of the Act of 1986.

(6) If subsection (4) or (5) is not complied with, the company and every officer of the company who is in default shall be guilty of an offence and be liable to a fine.

(7) The reference in subsection (1) to a voting right in a company shall be construed as a reference to a right exercisable for the time being to cast, or to control the casting of, a vote at general meetings of members of the company, not being such a right that is exercisable only in special circumstances.

Amendments

a Section 33(1) and (2) were substituted by s 9(1)(d)(i) of the IFCMPA 2006.

b Section 33(3) was deleted by s 9(1)(d)(ii) of the IFCMPA 2006.

c Section 33(4)(c) was substituted by s 9(1)(d)(iii) of the IFCMPA 2006.

---

34 Removal of auditor consequent on exemption being availed of

(1) If a company—

(a) decides that the appointment of a person as auditor to the company should not be continued during the whole or part of a financial year in which the exemption is being availed of in relation to the company, and

(b) decides, accordingly, to terminate the appointment of that person as auditor to the company,

then—

(i) that person shall, within the period of 21 days beginning on the date of his or her being notified by the company of that decision, serve a notice on the company containing the statement referred to in subsection (2),

(ii) unless and until that person serves such a notice, any purported termination of his or her appointment as auditor to the company shall not have effect.

(2) The statement to be contained in a notice under subsection (1)(i) shall be whichever of the following is appropriate, namely—

(a) a statement to the effect that there are no circumstances connected with the decision of the company referred to in subsection (1) that he or she considers should be brought to the notice of the members or creditors of the company, or

(b) a statement of any such circumstances as aforesaid.

(3) Where a notice under subsection (1)(i) is served on a company—

(a) the auditor concerned shall, within 14 days after the date of such service, send a copy of the notice to the registrar of companies, and

(b) subject to subsection (4), the company shall, if the notice contains a statement referred to in subsection (2)(b), within 14 days after the date of such service, send a copy of the notice to every person who is entitled under section 159(1) of the Principal Act to be sent copies of the documents referred to in the said section 159(1).

(4) Copies of a notice served on a company under subsection (1) need not be sent to the persons specified in subsection (3)(b), if, on the application of the company concerned or any other person who claims to be aggrieved, the court is satisfied that the notice contains material which has been included to secure needless publicity for defamatory matter and the court may order the company's costs on an application under this subsection to be paid in whole or in part by the auditor concerned notwithstanding that he or she is not a party to the application.

(5) Subsection (2A) (inserted by the Companies Act, 1990) of section 161 of the Principal Act shall not apply to an auditor as respects his or her removal from office in the circumstances referred to in subsection (1).

35 Appointment of auditor consequent on exemption ceasing to have effect

[(1) Whenever by reason of—

(a) circumstances referred to in section 32(1)(ii) arising in the financial year concerned the exemption ceases to have effect in relation to a company in respect of that year, or

(b) circumstances otherwise arising a company is not entitled to the exemption in respect of the financial year concerned,

it shall be the duty of the directors of the company to appoint an auditor of the company as soon as may be after those circumstances arise and such an appointment may be made by the directors notwithstanding the provisions of section 160 of the Principal Act.][a]

(2) An auditor appointed pursuant to subsection (1) shall hold office until the conclusion of the next meeting of the company held after his or her appointment at which accounts are required to be laid.

(3) If the directors of the company fail to carry out their duty under subsection (1), the company in general meeting may appoint an auditor to the company and subsection (2) shall apply to an auditor appointed by it.

Amendments

a Subsection 35(1) substituted by s 9(1)(e) of the IFCMPA 2006.

---

36 Application of Part

This Part shall apply to a company as respects a financial year that commences on or after the commencement of this Part.

37 False statements in returns, balance sheets, etc

(1) If a person in any return, statement, balance sheet or other document required by or for the purposes of any provision of this Part wilfully makes a statement, false in any material particular, knowing it to be so false, he or she shall be guilty of an offence.

(2) A person guilty of an offence under this section shall be liable—

(a) on summary conviction, to a [class C fine][a] or imprisonment for a term not exceeding 12 months or both, or

(b) on conviction on indictment, to a fine not exceeding [€12,697.38][b] or imprisonment for a term not exceeding [5 years][c] or both.

Amendments

a '£1,000 increased to £1,500 by CA 1990, s 240(7) as inserted by CLEA 2001, s 104(c), and converted to €1,904.61 by Council Regulations (EC) No 1103/97, No 974/98 and No 2866/98 and the Economic and Monetary Union Act 1998, s 6; the above being implicitly substituted, by Fines Act 2010, s 6, for a fine not exceeding the aforesaid amount. A class C fine currently means a fine not exceeding €2,500.

b '£10,000 converted to €12,697.38 by Council Regulations (EC) No 1103/97, No 974/98 and No 2866/98 and the Economic and Monetary Union Act 1998, s 6.

c 3 years increased to 5 years by CA 1990, s 240(8).

---

38 Application of Part to partnerships to which Part III of the 1993 Regulations applies

This Part shall apply to a partnership to which Part III of the 1993 Regulations applies as this Part applies to a private company with the following modifications—

(a) the substitution in this Part for references to section 160 of the Principal Act of references to Regulation 22 of the 1993 Regulations,

(b) the substitution in this Part for references to other provisions of the Companies Acts, 1963 to 1999, of references to so much of those provisions as are applied to partnerships by the 1993 Regulations,

(c) the substitution in this Part for references to directors of a company of references to partners of a partnership, and any other necessary modifications (including any modifications necessary to take account of the fact that such partnerships are unincorporated).

39 Saving

Nothing in this Part shall authorise the removal of an auditor from office which, apart from this Part, would not be lawful.

PART IV
MISCELLANEOUS

40 Amendment of section 16 of Investment Limited Partnerships Act, 1994

Section 16 of the Investment Limited Partnerships Act, 1994, is hereby amended by the substitution of the following subsection for subsection (10):

[...][a]

Amendments

a C(A)(No 2)A 1999, s 40 substituted s 16(10) of the Investment Limited Partnerships Act 1994.

---

41 Amendment of section 240 of Companies Act, 1990

[...][a]

Amendments

a C(A)(No 2)A 1999, s 41 substituted CA 1990, s 240(5) and inserted CA 1990, s 240(5A).

---

42 Additional requirement to be complied with before company may be formed

(1) A company shall not be formed and registered under the Companies Acts, 1963 to 1999, after the commencement of this section, unless it appears to the registrar of companies that the company, when registered, will carry on an activity in the State, being an activity that is mentioned in its memorandum.

(2) The registrar of companies may accept as sufficient evidence that a company, when registered, will carry on an activity in the State a statutory declaration, in the prescribed form, that the purpose or one of the purposes for which the company is being formed is the carrying on by it of an activity in the State and which declaration includes the following particulars—

- (a) if it appears to the person making the declaration that the activity belongs to a division, group and class appearing in the relevant classification system—
  - (i) the general nature of the activity, and
  - (ii) the division, group and class in that system to which the activity belongs,
- (b) if it appears to the said person that the activity does not belong to any such division, group and class, a precise description of the activity,
- (c) the place or places in the State where it is proposed to carry on the activity,
- (d) the place, whether in the State or not, where the central administration of the company will normally be carried on.

(3) For the purposes of subsection (2), if the purpose or one of the purposes for which the company is being formed is the carrying on of 2 or more activities in the State, the particulars in respect of the matters referred to in paragraphs (a) to (c) of that subsection to be given in the statutory declaration shall be the particulars that relate to whichever of those activities the person making the declaration considers to be the principal activity for which the company is being formed to carry on in the State.

(4) The statutory declaration referred to in subsection (2) shall be made by—

- (a) one of the persons named in the statement delivered under section 3 of the Companies (Amendment) Act, 1982, in relation to the company as directors of the company,
- (b) the person or, as the case may be, one of the persons named in the said statement as secretary or joint secretaries of the company, or

(c) the solicitor, if any, engaged in the formation of the company.

(5) The form prescribed for the purposes of the statutory declaration referred to in subsection (2) may enable the declarant to include therein a declaration as to the matters referred to in section 5(5) of the Companies (Amendment) Act, 1983, and such a declaration that is so included shall suffice for the purposes of that section 5(5) as if it had been separately made and delivered to the registrar of companies.

(6) Without prejudice to its construction for the purposes of any other provision of that section, the expression 'the requirements mentioned in subsection (1)' in subsection (5) of section 5 of the Companies (Amendment) Act, 1983, shall not be construed as including the requirements of this section.

(7) In this section—

'activity' means any activity that a company may be lawfully formed to carry on and includes the holding, acquisition or disposal of property of whatsoever kind;

'relevant classification system' means NACE Rev 1, that is to say, the common basis for statistical classifications of economic activities within the European Community set out in the Annex to Council Regulation (EEC) No 3037/90 of 9 October 1990 (OJ No L293/1, 24 October 1990) on the statistical classification of economic activities in the European Community, as amended for the time being.

43 Company to have director resident in the State

(1) Subject to subsection (3) and section 44, one, at least, of the directors for the time being of a company, not being a company referred to in subsection (2), shall, on and from the commencement of this section, be a person who is resident in [a Member State of the EEA].[a]

(2) Subject to subsection (3) and section 44, one, at least, of the directors for the time being of a company, being—

(a) a company the memorandum of which was delivered to the registrar of companies for registration under section 17 of the Principal Act before the commencement of this section, or

(b) an existing company (within the meaning of the Principal Act),

shall, on and from the date that is 12 months after the commencement of this section, be a person who is resident in [a Member State of the EEA].[a]

(3) Subsection (1) or (2), as the case may be, shall not apply in relation to a company if the company for the time being holds a bond, in the prescribed form, in force to the value of [€25,394.76][b] and which provides that, in the event of a failure by the company to pay the whole or part of—

(a) a fine, if any, imposed on the company in respect of an offence under the Companies Acts, 1963 to 1999, committed by it, being an offence which is prosecutable by the registrar of companies, and

(b) (i) a fine, if any, imposed on the company in respect of an offence under section 1078 of the Taxes Consolidation Act, 1997, committed by it, being an offence that consists of a failure by the company to deliver a statement which it is required to deliver under section 882 of that Act or to comply with a notice served on it under section 884 of that Act, and

(ii) a penalty, if any, which it has been held liable to pay under section 1071 or 1073 of the Taxes Consolidation Act, 1997,

there shall become payable under the bond to a person nominated for the purpose ('the nominated person') by the registrar of companies or the Revenue Commissioners, as appropriate, (or jointly by the registrar and the Commissioners in the case of both a fine referred to in paragraph (a) and a fine or penalty, or a fine and penalty, referred to in paragraph (b)), a sum of money for the purposes of that sum being applied by the nominated person in discharging the whole or part, as the case may be, of the company's liability in respect of any such fine or penalty, and any sum that becomes so payable shall be applied by the nominated person accordingly.

(4) The bond referred to in subsection (3) may be entered into and shall have effect according to its terms notwithstanding any rule of law whereby any agreement to insure or indemnify a person in respect of any punishment or liability imposed on him or her in relation to any offence or unlawful act committed by him or her is void or unenforceable.

(5) The bond referred to in subsection (3) shall also provide that, in addition to the sum referred to in that subsection, there shall become payable under the bond to the nominated person, on demand being made, with the consent of the Revenue Commissioners, by him or her in that behalf, a sum of money, not exceeding such sum as the Revenue Commissioners and the Minister may sanction, for the purpose of defraying such expenses as may have been reasonably incurred by that person in carrying out his or her duties under subsection (3).

(6) The nominated person shall keep all proper and usual accounts, including an income and expenditure account and a balance sheet, of all moneys received by him or her on foot of the bond referred to in subsection (3) and of all disbursements made by him or her from any such moneys.

(7) The Minister, after consultation with the Minister for Finance, the Revenue Commissioners and any other person whom, in the opinion of the Minister, might be concerned with or interested in the matter, may prescribe—

(a) that arrangements in relation to the bond referred to in subsection (3) shall only be entered into with persons of a prescribed class or classes,

(b) the form of that bond and the minimum period to be specified in the bond as being the period for which it shall be valid.

(8) A copy of the bond referred to in subsection (3) held by a company shall be appended—

(a) in case none of the directors of the company is resident in [a Member State of the EEA][a] the State on its incorporation, to the statement required by section 3 of the Companies (Amendment) Act, 1982, to be delivered to the registrar of companies in relation to the company,

(b) in case a notification is made under subsection (9) to the registrar of companies in relation to the company, to that notification,

(c) in case during the period to which an annual return concerning the company relates none of the directors of the company is resident in [a Member State of the EEA],[a] to that annual return (unless such a copy has been appended to a notification under subsection (9) made to the registrar of companies in that period).

(9) Without prejudice to anything in section 195 (as amended by this Act) of the Principal Act, if a person ceases to be a director of a company and, at the time of that cessation—

(a) he or she is resident in [a Member State of the EEA],[a] and

(b) to his or her knowledge, no other director of the company is resident in [a Member State of the EEA],[a] that person shall, within 14 days after that cessation, notify, in writing, the registrar of companies of that cessation and the matter referred to in paragraph (b).

(10) A notification in writing to the registrar of companies of the matter referred to in subsection (9)(b) shall not, of itself, be regarded as constituting defamatory matter.

(11) If a person fails to comply with subsection (9), he or she shall be jointly and severally liable with the company of which he or she has ceased to be a director for any fine or penalty referred to in subsection (3) imposed on the company or which it is held liable to pay after that cessation, and any such fine or penalty for which that person is so liable may be recovered by the registrar of companies or the Revenue Commissioners, as appropriate, from him or her as a simple contract debt in any court of competent jurisdiction.

[...][c]

(13) If subsection (1) or, as the case may be, subsection (2) is not complied with, the company concerned and every officer of the company who is in default shall be guilty of an offence.

(14) Summary proceedings in relation to an offence under subsection (13) may be brought and prosecuted by the registrar of companies.

(15) The provisions of section 311 of the Principal Act shall apply for the purposes of this section as they apply for the purposes of that section 311, subject to the following modifications—

(a) for subsections (1) and (2) thereof (inserted by the Companies (Amendment) Act, 1982) there shall be substituted the following subsections:

> "(1) Where the registrar of companies has reasonable cause to believe that subsection (1) or, as the case may be, subsection (2) of section 43 of the Companies (Amendment) (No. 2) Act, 1999, is not being complied with in relation to a company, he may send to the company by post a registered letter requesting the company to furnish to him evidence that the provision concerned is being complied with and stating that, if that request is not complied with within 1 month from the date of that letter, a notice will be published in [the Companies Registration Office Gazette][d] with a view to striking the name of the company off the register.
>
> (2) If the registrar does not, within 1 month after sending the letter, receive evidence from the company that satisfies him that subsection (1)

or, as the case may be, subsection (2) of section 43 of the Companies (Amendment) (No. 2) Act, 1999, is being complied with in relation to the company, he may publish in [the Companies Registration Office Gazette][d] and send to the company by registered post a notice that, at the expiration of 1 month from the date of that notice, the name of the company mentioned therein will, unless cause is shown to the contrary, be struck off the register, and the company will be dissolved.".

and

(b) in subsection (8), there shall be substituted for "if satisfied that the company was at the time of the striking off carrying on business", "if satisfied that subsection (1) or, as the case may be, subsection (2) of section 43 of the Companies (Amendment) (No. 2) Act, 1999, was at the time of the striking off being complied with in relation to the company".][d]

[(16) In this section—

'director' does not include an alternate director;

'Member State of the EEA' means a state that is a contracting party to the Agreement on the European Economic Area signed at Oporto on 2 May 1992, as amended for the time being.][e]

Amendments

a Words 'a Member State of the EEA' substituted for 'the State' by C(A)A 2009, s 10(1)(a).

b £20,000 converted to €25,394.76 by Council Regulation (EC) No 1103/97, No 974/98 and No 2866/98 and the Economic and Monetary Union Act 1998, s 6.

c C(A)A 2009, s 10(1)(b) repeals C(A)(No 2)A 1999, s 43(12).

d 'the Companies Registration Office Gazette' substituted for 'Iris Oifigiúil' by IFCMPA 2005, s 72.

e C(AA)A 2003, s 54 inserted C(A)(No 2)A 1999, s 43(16), which was substituted by C(A)A 2009, s 10(1)(c).

---

44 Section 43: supplemental provisions

(1) Subsection (1) or, as the case may be, subsection (2) of section 43 shall not apply in relation to a company in respect of which there is in force a certificate under this section.

(2) The registrar of companies may grant to a company, on application in the prescribed form being made by it in that behalf, a certificate stating that the company has a real and continuous link with one or more economic activities that are being carried on in the State.

(3) The registrar of companies shall not grant such a certificate unless the company concerned tenders proof to him or her that it has such a link.

(4) A statement referred to in subsection (5) that is tendered by the applicant shall be deemed to be proof, for the purposes of subsection (3), that the applicant has such a link.

(5) The statement mentioned in subsection (4) is a statement in writing that has been given to the company concerned by the Revenue Commissioners within the period of 2 months ending on the date on which an application is made under subsection (2) by the company and which states that the Revenue Commissioners have reasonable grounds to

believe that the company has a real and continuous link with one or more economic activities being carried on in the State.

(6) If, in consequence of information that has come into the possession of the registrar, the registrar of companies is of opinion that a company in respect of which a certificate under subsection (2) has been granted has ceased to have a real and continuous link with any economic activity being carried on in the State, he or she shall revoke that certificate.

(7) If, in consequence of information that has come into their possession, the Revenue Commissioners are of opinion that a company in respect of which a certificate under subsection (2) has been granted has ceased to have a real and continuous link with any economic activity being carried on in the State, then notwithstanding any obligations as to secrecy or other restrictions upon disclosure of information imposed by or under statute or otherwise, they may give a notice in writing to the registrar of companies stating that they are of that opinion and such a notice that is received by the registrar shall constitute information in his or her possession for the purposes of subsection (6).

(8) [So far as it is the person's residence in the State that falls to be determined for the purposes of that section, for the purposes of section 43][a], a person is resident in the State at a particular time ('the relevant time') if—

(a) he or she is present in the State at—

(i) any one time or several times in the period of 12 months preceding the relevant time ('the immediate 12 month period') for a period in the aggregate amounting to 183 days or more, or

(ii) any one time or several times—

(I) in the immediate 12 month period, and

(II) in the period of 12 months preceding the immediate 12 month period ('the previous 12 month period'), for a period (being a period comprising in the aggregate the number of days on which the person is present in the State in the immediate 12 month period and the number of days on which the person was present in the State in the previous 12 month period) in the aggregate amounting to 280 days or more, or

(b) that time is in a year of assessment (within the meaning of the Taxes Consolidation Act, 1997) in respect of which the person has made an election under section 819(3) of that Act.

(9) Notwithstanding subsection (8)(a)(ii), where in the immediate 12 month period concerned a person is present in the State at any one time or several times for a period in the aggregate amounting to not more than 30 days—

(a) the person shall not be resident in the State, for the purposes of section 43, at the relevant time concerned, and

(b) no account shall be taken of the period for the purposes of the aggregate mentioned, in subsection (8)(a)(ii).

(10) For the purposes of subsections (8) and (9)—

(a) references in this section to a person's being present in the State are references to the person's being personally present in the State, and

(b) a person shall be deemed to be present in the State for a day if the person is present in the State at the end of the day.

(11) An application under subsection (2) may be made, and a certificate under that subsection may be granted, before the commencement of subsection (1) or (2) of section 43.

[(12) For the purposes of this section a company has a real and continuous link with an economic activity that is being carried on in the State if one or more of the following conditions are satisfied by it:

(a) the affairs of the company are managed by one or more persons from a place of business established in the State and that person or those per-sons is or are authorised by the company to act on its behalf;

(b) the company carries on a trade in the State;

(c) the company is a subsidiary or a holding company of a company or another body corporate that satisfies either or both of the conditions specified in paragraphs (a) and (b);

(d) the company is a subsidiary of a company, another subsidiary of which satisfies either or both of the conditions specified in paragraphs (a) and (b).][b]

Amendments

a Words 'So far as it is the person's residence in the State that falls to be determined for the purposes of that section, for the purposes of section 43' substituted for 'For the purposes of section 43' by C(A)A 2009, s 10(2)(a).

b C(A)A 2009, s 10(2)(b) inserts C(A)(No 2)A 1999, s 44(12).

45 Limitation on number of directorships

(1) A person shall not, at a particular time, be a director of more than 25 companies.

(2) In subsection (1), (but not any other subsection of this section) 'director' includes a shadow director (within the meaning of the Companies Act, 1990).

(3) In reckoning, for the purposes of subsection (1), the number of companies of which the person concerned is a director at a particular time the following provisions shall apply—

(a) without prejudice to paragraph (b) or subsection (4), there shall not be included any of the following companies of which he or she is a director at that time, namely—

(i) a public limited company,

(ii) a public company (within the meaning of the Companies (Amendment) Act, 1983),

(iii) a company in respect of which a certificate under section 44(2) is in force,

(b) there shall not be included any company of which he or she is a director at that time (not being a time that is before the date of the giving of the certificate or direction referred to hereafter in this paragraph) if—

(i) he or she, or the company, delivers to the registrar of companies a notice, in the prescribed form, stating that the company is a company falling within one or more of the categories of company specified in the Table to this section, and

(ii) either—

(I) the registrar of companies, having considered the said notice and having made such enquiries as he or she thinks fit, certifies in writing, or as the case may be the Minister under subsection (6) so certifies, that the company is a company falling within one or more of the categories aforesaid, or

(II) the Minister directs, under subsection (6), that the company is not to be included amongst the companies that shall be reckoned for the purposes aforesaid,

(c) there shall be counted as the one company of which he or she is a director at that time, 2 or more companies of which he or she is a director at that time if one of those companies is the holding company of the other or others.

(4) Without prejudice to subsection (3), in reckoning, for the purposes of subsection (1), the number of companies of which the person concerned is a director at a particular time, being a time that is before the expiration of the period of 12 months from the commencement of this section, there shall not be included any company of which the person is a director at that time if he or she was such a director immediately before such commencement.

(5) For the purposes of subsection (3)(b)(ii), the registrar of companies may accept as sufficient evidence that the company concerned falls within a category of company specified in the Table to this section a statutory declaration, in the prescribed form, to that effect made by an officer of the company or the other person referred to in subsection (3)(b)(i).

(6) If the registrar of companies refuses to certify that the company to which a notice under subsection (3)(b) relates is a company falling within a category of company specified in the Table to this section, the company or the person referred to in that subsection may appeal to the Minister against such a refusal and the Minister may, having considered the matter and made such enquiries as he or she thinks fit, do one of the following—

(a) confirm the decision of the registrar of companies,

(b) certify in writing that the company is a company falling within a category aforesaid, or

(c) notwithstanding that he or she confirms the decision of the registrar of companies, if—

(i) the person concerned was a director of the company before the commencement of this section, and

(ii) in the opinion of the Minister the inclusion of the company amongst the companies that shall be reckoned for the purposes of subsection (1), in so far as that subsection applies to the person concerned, would result in serious injustice or hardship to that person, and

(iii) the giving of a direction under this subsection would not operate against the common good, direct that the company is not to be included amongst the companies that shall be reckoned for the purposes of subsection (1) in so far as that subsection applies to the person concerned.

(7) A notice referred to in subsection (3)(b)(i) may, for the purposes of that provision, be delivered to the registrar of companies before the person concerned becomes a director of the company to which the notice relates.

(8) If a person, in contravention of subsection (1), becomes or remains a director or shadow director of one or more companies he or she shall be guilty of an offence.

(9) An appointment of a person as a director of a company made after the commencement of this section shall, if it contravenes subsection (1), be void.

(10) An appointment of a person as a director of a company made before the commencement of this section, being an appointment which, but for this section, would subsist on or after the expiration of the period of 12 months from that commencement, shall, if its subsistence at any time on or after the expiration of that period contravenes subsection (1), cease to have effect upon that contravention occurring.

(11) For the avoidance of doubt—

(a) each appointment, in excess of the limit (reckoned in accordance with subsections (3) and (4)) that is provided for by subsection (1), of a person as a director of a company shall constitute a separate contravention of that subsection,

(b) an appointment, not in excess of the said limit, of a person as a director of a company shall not, by virtue of this section, become unlawful, be rendered void or cease to have effect by reason of a subsequent appointment, in excess of that limit, of the person as a director of a company,

(c) in determining whether one particular appointment referred to in subsection (10), as distinct from another such appointment, has ceased to have effect by virtue of that subsection or whether a person's remaining in office under one such appointment, as distinct from another such appointment, constitutes an offence under subsection (8), the provisions of this section (other than subsections (3)(b), (5), (6), (7) and (8)) shall be deemed to have been in operation at the time of the making of that appointment.

(12) If—

(a) the appointments of a person as a director of 2 or more companies are made at the same time, or

(b) the times at which the appointments of a person as a director of 2 or more companies were made are not capable of being distinguished from one another,

then those appointments shall, for the purposes of this section, be deemed to have been made at different times on the day concerned and in the same order as the order in which the companies to which the appointments relate were registered under the Companies Acts, 1963 to 1999.

(13) Summary proceedings in relation to an offence under subsection (8) may be brought and prosecuted by the registrar of companies.

TABLE

1. A company that is the holder of a licence under section 9 of the Central Bank Act, 1971, or is exempt from the requirement under that Act to hold such a licence.

2. A company referred to in the Second Schedule.

46 Power of registrar to strike company off register for failure to make annual return

[...][a]

Amendments

a C(A)(No 2)A 1999, s 46 substitutes C(A)A 1982, s 12 and inserts C(A)A 1982, ss 12A–12D.

---

47 Amendment of section 195 of Principal Act

[...][a]

[...][b]

Amendments

a C(A)(No 2)A 1999, s 47(a) deletes CA 1963, s 195(8) (as inserted by CA 1990, s 51).

b C(A)(No 2)A 1999, s 47(b) inserts CA 1963, ss 195(11A)–(11E).

---

48 Exercise of power to strike company off register where it is not carrying on business

The fact that, for the time being, in consequence of the forwarding to the registrar, under and in accordance with subsections (11A) and (11B) of section 195 of the Principal Act, of a copy of a notice of resignation or other documentary proof of a person's having ceased to be a director of the company concerned, there are no persons recorded in the office of the registrar of companies as being directors of a particular company shall, for the purposes of section 311 of the Principal Act, afford the registrar of companies good grounds for believing that the company is not carrying on business, and for so believing with the cause requisite for the exercise by him or her of the powers conferred by subsection (1) of that section 311 in relation to the company.

49 Amendment of section 311 of Principal Act

[...][a]

[...][b]

Amendments

a C(A)(No 2)A 1999, s 49(a) amends CA 1963, s 311(8) by the substitution for 'as if the name of the company had not been struck off.' of 'as if the name of the company had not been struck off or make such other order as seems just (and such other order is referred to in subsection (8A) as an 'alternative order').'

b C(A)(No 2)A 1999, s 49(b) inserts CA 1963, s 311(8A).

---

50 Amendment of section 311A of Principal Act

[...][a]

Amendments

a C(A)(No 2)A 1999, s 50 amends CA 1963, s 311A by the substitution for 'Without prejudice to the provisions of section 311(8) of this Act and section 12(6) of the Companies (Amendment) Act 1982' of 'Without prejudice to the provisions of section 311(8) of this Act or subsection (3) or (7) of section 12B, or subsection (1) of section 12C, of the Companies (Amendment) Act, 1982,'.

51 Amendment of section 8 of Companies (Amendment) Act, 1983

[...][a]

Amendments

a C(A)(No 2)A 1999, s 51 amends C(A)A 1983, s 8(3) by the substitution for '(7) and (8)' of '(7), (8) and (8A)'.

52 Performance of duties of registrar of companies

(1) Any act referred to in subsection (4) of section 368 of the Principal Act which, before the commencement of this section, was done to or by—

(a) an assistant registrar appointed under subsection (2) of that section, or

(b) any other person employed in the office of the registrar of companies to perform generally duties under any enactment referred to in that subsection,

shall be valid and be deemed always to have been valid as if the Minister had directed under that subsection (4) that such an act was to be done to or by such an assistant registrar or other such person (including in cases where the existing registrar of joint stock companies (or his or her successor) was not absent).

(2) On and from the commencement of this section, any act required or authorised by the Companies Acts, 1963 to 1999, the Registration of Business Names Act, 1963, or the Limited Partnerships Act, 1907, to be done to or by the registrar of companies, the registrar of joint stock companies or, as the case may be, a person referred to in the enactment concerned as 'the registrar' may be done to or by a registrar or assistant registrar appointed under section 368(2) of the Principal Act or any other person authorised in that behalf by the Minister.

(3) Subsection (4) of section 368 of the Principal Act shall cease to have effect.

53 Amendment of sections 20 and 21 of Companies Act, 1990

(1) [...][a]

(2) [...][b]

(3)

[...][c]

[...][d]

(4) The amendments effected by this section shall apply in relation to the publication or disclosure, after its commencement, of information, books or documents which have

been obtained under section 19 or 20 of the Companies Act, 1990, whether before or after that commencement.

Amendments

a C(A)(No 2)A 1999, s 53(1) amended CA 1990, s 20(3) by the substitution for 'any such criminal proceedings as are mentioned in section 21(1)(a) or (1)(b)' of 'any proceedings for an offence mentioned in section 21(1)(a).' CA 1990, s 20 (3) was repealed by IFCMPA 2005, s 68 with respect to material information seized under that section before 30 June 2005.

b C(A)(No 2)A 1999, s 53(2) substitutes CA 1990, s 21(1).

c C(A)(No 2)A 1999, s 53(3)(a) amends CA 1990, s 21(3)(g) by the deletion of 'and'.

d C(A)(No 2)A 1999, s 53(3)(b) substitutes CA 1990, s 21(3)(h) and inserts CA 1990, s 21(3)(i).

1 Brought into force by the Investment Funds, Companies and Miscellaneous Provisions Act 2005 (Commencement) Order 2005 (SI 323/2005), with effect from 30 June 2005.

---

54 Amendment of Part XIII (Investment Companies) of Companies Act, 1990

(1)

(a)

[...][a]

[...][b]

[...][c]

[...][d]

(2)

[...][e]

[...][f]

[...][g]

Amendments

a C(A)(No 2)A 1999, s 54(1)(a)(i) amends CA 1990, s 253(1)(a) by the deletion of the word 'and'.

b C(A)(No 2)A 1999, s 54(1)(a)(ii) amends CA 1990, s 253(1)(b) by the insertion after 'nominal value thereto' of 'and'.

c C(A)(No 2)A 1999, s 54(1)(a)(iii) inserts CA 1990, s 253(1)(c).

d C(A)(No 2)A 1999, s 54(1)(b) deletes CA 1990, s 253(2A)(b).

e C(A)(No 2)A 1999, s 54(2)(a) amends CA 1990, s 256(5) and (7) by the substitution for 'by promoting the sale of its shares to the public', in each place where it occurs, of 'by providing facilities for the direct or indirect participation by the public in the profits and income of the company'.

f C(A)(No 2)A 1999, s 54(2)(b) amends CA 1990, s 256(6) by the substitution for 'promote the sale of its shares to the public' of 'provide facilities for the direct or indirect participation by the public in the profits and income of the company'.

g C(A)(No 2)A 1999, s 54(3) substitutes CA 1990, s 260.

FIRST SCHEDULE

SPECIFIC PROVISIONS FROM WHICH COMPANY IS EXEMPTED UNDER PART III

Section 32

1 Sections 157 and 159 of the Principal Act in so far as they relate to an auditor's report.

2 Section 160(2) of the Principal Act.

3 Paragraphs (b), (c) and (d) of subsection (3), and subsection (4), of section 49 of the Companies (Amendment) Act, 1983.

4 Section 7 of the Companies (Amendment) Act, 1986, in so far as it relates to an auditor's report.

5 Section 15 and subsections (3), (4) and (5) of section 18 of the Companies (Amendment) Act, 1986.

6 Section 19 of the Companies (Amendment) Act, 1986, in so far as it relates to an auditor's report.

7 Sections 46 and 193 of the Companies Act, 1990.

SECOND SCHEDULE

LIST OF COMPANIES FOR PURPOSES OF SECTION 3(2)(C) OF ACT OF 1990 AND SECTIONS 32 AND 45

Sections 6, 32 and 45.

1. A company that is a member firm within the meaning of the Stock Exchange Act, 1995.
2. A company that is a stock exchange within the meaning of the Stock Exchange Act, 1995.
3. A company that is an associated undertaking or a related undertaking of a member firm or stock exchange within the meaning of the Stock Exchange Act, 1995.
4. A company that is an investment business firm within the meaning of the Investment Intermediaries Act, 1995.
5. A company that is an associated undertaking or a related undertaking of an investment business firm within the meaning of the Investment Intermediaries Act, 1995.
6. A company to which Chapter VII, VIII or IX of Part II of the Central Bank Act, 1989, applies.
7. A company that is engaged in the business of accepting deposits or other repayable funds or granting credit for its own account.
8. A company that is an associated body of a building society within the meaning of the Building Societies Act, 1989.
9. A company that is an associated enterprise of a credit institution within the meaning of the European Communities (Consolidated Supervision of Credit Institutions) Regulations, 1992 (S.I. No. 396 of 1992).
10. An investment company within the meaning of Part XIII of the Companies Act, 1990.

11. A company that is a management company or trustee within the meaning of Part XIII of the Companies Act, 1990.
12. A company that is an undertaking for collective investment in transferable securities within the meaning of the European Communities (Undertakings for Collective Investment in Transferable Securities) Regulations, 1989 (S.I. No. 78 of 1989).
13. A company that is a management company or trustee of an undertaking for collective investment in transferable securities within the meaning of the European Communities (Undertakings for Collective Investment in Transferable Securities) Regulations, 1989 (S.I. No. 78 of 1989).
14. A company that is a management company or trustee of a unit trust scheme within the meaning of the Unit Trusts Act, 1990.
15. A company that is a general partner or custodian of an investment limited partnership within the meaning of the Investment Limited Partnerships Act, 1994.
16. A company that is an undertaking with close links with a financial undertaking within the meaning of the Supervision of Credit Institutions, Stock Exchange Member Firms and Investment Business Firms Regulations, 1996 (S.I. No. 267 of 1996).
17. Any other company the carrying on of business by which is required, by virtue of any enactment or instrument thereunder, to be authorised by the Central Bank.
18. A company that is—

    (a) a holder of an authorisation within the meaning of—

        (i) Regulation 2 of the European Communities (Non-Life Insurance) Regulations, 1976 (S.I. No. 115 of 1976),

        (ii) Regulation 2 of the European Communities (Non-Life Insurance) Framework Regulations, 1994 (S.I. No. 359 of 1994),

        (iii) Regulation 2 of the European Communities (Life Assurance) Regulations, 1984 (S.I. No. 57 of 1984),

        or

        (iv) Regulation 2 of the European Communities (Life Assurance) Framework Regulations, 1994 (S.I. No. 360 of 1994),

    or

    (b) a holder of an authorisation granted under the European Communities (Non-Life Insurance) (Amendment) (No 2) Regulations, 1991 (S.I. No. 142 of 1991).
19. A company that is an insurance intermediary within the meaning of the Insurance Act, 1989.
20. A company that is an excepted body within the meaning of the Trade Union Acts, 1871 to 1990.

Company Law Enforcement Act 2001

Number 28 of 2001

PART 1

PRELIMINARY AND GENERAL

PART 6

MEASURES TO IMPROVE COMPLIANCE WITH FILING OBLIGATIONS

PART 7

COMPANY LAW REVIEW GROUP

PART 8

AUDITORS

PART 9

TRANSACTIONS INVOLVING DIRECTORS

PART 10

MISCELLANEOUS

An Act to establish a Director of Corporate Enforcement and provide for his or her appointment, terms and conditions and functions, to provide for an acting director to perform the functions of the director during exigencies, to transfer existing functions of the minister relating to the enforcement of the Companies Acts to the director, to establish a company law review group to monitor, review and advise the minister on matters relating to company law, to amend in various ways the Companies Act, 1963, the Companies Act, 1990, and various other Acts, and for related purposes. [9th July, 2001]

Be it Enacted by the Oireachtas as Follows:

PART 1
PRELIMINARY AND GENERAL

1 Short title, collective citation and construction

(1) This Act may be cited as the Company Law Enforcement Act, 2001.

(2) This Act and the Companies Acts, 1963 to 1999, may be cited together as the Companies Acts, 1963 to 2001, and shall be construed together as one Act.

2 Commencement

This Act shall come into operation on such day or days as may bc fixed by order or orders made by the Minister, either generally or with reference to any particular provision, and different days may be so fixed for different purposes and different provisions of this Act.

3 Interpretation

(1) In this Act, unless the context otherwise requires—

'Act of 1963' means the Companies Act, 1963;

'Act of 1990' means the Companies Act, 1990;

'Acting Director' means a person appointed under section 11 as the Acting Director of Corporate Enforcement;

'Companies Acts' means the Companies Act, 1963, and every enactment (including this Act) which is to be construed as one with that Act;

'Director' means the Director of Corporate Enforcement appointed under section 7(2) and includes an Acting Director while so acting and, in relation to a particular power of the Director, a delegate to whom the power is delegated under section 13;

'functions' includes powers and duties;

'Minister' means the Minister for Enterprise, Trade and Employment;

'officer of the Director' means—

(a) an officer of the Minister assigned to the Director,

(b) a member of An Garda Síochána seconded to the Director, or

(c) a person employed by the Minister or the Director under a contract for service or otherwise,

to assist the Director in carrying out functions of the Director under the Companies Acts or any other Act;

'prescribed' means prescribed by regulations made by the Minister;

'Review Group' means the Company Law Review Group established by section 67.

(2) In this Act—

(a) a reference to a Part, section or Schedule is a reference to a Part or section of, or Schedule to, this Act, unless it is indicated that reference to some other enactment is intended;

(b) a reference to a subsection, paragraph or subparagraph is to the subsection, paragraph or subparagraph of the provision in which the reference occurs, unless it is indicated that reference to some other provision is intended; and

(c) a reference to any other enactment shall, unless the context otherwise requires, be construed as a reference to that enactment as amended by or under any other enactment, including this Act.

4 Regulations

(1) The Minister may make regulations prescribing any matter or thing referred to in this Act as prescribed or to be prescribed, or in relation to any matter referred to in this Act as the subject of regulation.

(2) Regulations under this section may contain such incidental, supplementary and consequential provisions as appear to the Minister to be necessary or expedient for the purposes of the regulations or for giving full effect to this Act.

5 Laying of regulations and orders before Houses of the Oireachtas and power to revoke or amend orders

(1) Every regulation or order (other than an order made under section 2) made under this Act shall be laid before each House of the Oireachtas as soon as may be after it is made and, if a resolution annulling the regulation or order is passed by either House within the next 21 days on which that House has sat after the regulation or order is laid before it, the regulation or order shall be annulled accordingly but without prejudice to the validity of anything previously done under it.

(2) The Minister may by order revoke or amend an order (other than an order made under section 2) made under this Act (including an order under this subsection).

6 Expenses of Minister

The expenses incurred by the Minister in the administration of this Act shall, to such extent as may be sanctioned by the Minister for Finance, be paid out of moneys provided by the Oireachtas.

PART 2

DIRECTOR OF CORPORATE ENFORCEMENT

Director

7 Director of Corporate Enforcement

(1) There shall be a Director of Corporate Enforcement.

(2) The Minister shall, in writing, appoint a person to be the Director of Corporate Enforcement.

[(3) The Minister shall not appoint a person to be the Director unless the person has been duly selected following a competition under the Public Service Management (Recruitment and Appointments) Act 2004 for that position and the Minister has been advised accordingly].[a]

(4) The Director shall be a corporation sole and, notwithstanding any casual vacancy in the office from time to time, shall have perpetual succession and shall be capable in his or her corporate name of holding and disposing of real or personal property and of suing and being sued.

(5) The Director shall perform the functions conferred on him or her by or under this or any other Act and shall be assisted in the performance of those functions by the officers of the Director.

(6) All judges, courts or other persons or bodies acting judicially shall take judicial notice of the signature of the Director on or affixed to any document and it shall be presumed, unless the contrary is proved, that it has been duly signed or affixed.

Amendments

a Substituted by the Public Service Management (Recruitment and Appointments) Act 2004, s 61 and Sch 2.

---

8 Terms and conditions of appointment of Director

(1) Subject to subsection (2), a person appointed to be the Director shall hold office for such period not exceeding 5 years beginning on the date of his or her appointment, and on such terms and conditions (which shall include a scheme of superannuation under section 9), as the Minister, with the consent of the Minister for Finance, may determine, and the Minister may, if he or she thinks fit, with the consent of the Minister for Finance, continue the appointment (including an appointment previously continued under this subsection) for such further period, not exceeding 5 years at any one time, as the Minister thinks appropriate.

(2) A person appointed as the Director is, by virtue of the appointment, a civil servant within the meaning of the Civil Service Regulation Act, 1956, as amended.

(3) The Director shall not hold any other office or employment in respect of which emoluments are payable.

9 Superannuation

(1) The Minister shall, with the consent of the Minister for Finance, if he or she considers it appropriate to do so, make and carry out a scheme or schemes for the granting of superannuation benefits to or in respect of one or more of the following, namely, the Director, the Acting Director and any officer of the Director.

(2) Every such scheme shall fix the time and conditions of retirement for the person or persons to or in respect of whom superannuation benefits are payable under the scheme, and different times and conditions may be fixed in respect of different classes of such person.

(3) Every such scheme may be amended or revoked by a subsequent scheme made under this section with the consent of the Minister for Finance.

(4) No superannuation benefit shall be granted by the Minister to or in respect of the Director, the Acting Director or an officer of the Director otherwise than in accordance with a scheme under this section or, if the Minister, with the consent of the Minister for Finance, sanctions the granting of such a benefit, in accordance with that sanction.

(5) If any dispute arises as to the claim of any person to, or the amount of, any superannuation benefit payable in pursuance of a scheme or schemes under this section, such dispute shall be submitted to the Minister who shall refer it to the Minister for Finance, whose decision shall be final.

(6) A scheme under this section shall be laid before each House of the Oireachtas as soon as may be after it is made and, if a resolution annulling the scheme is passed by either such House within the next 21 days on which that House has sat after the scheme is laid before it, the scheme shall be annulled accordingly, but without prejudice to the validity of anything previously done thereunder.

(7) In this section, 'superannuation benefits' means pensions, gratuities and other allowances payable on resignation, retirement or death.

10 Removal, disqualification or cessation of Director

(1) The Minister may at any time, for stated reasons, remove the Director from office.

(2) If the Director is removed from office under this section, the Minister shall cause to be laid before each House of the Oireachtas a statement of the reasons for the removal.

(3) Where the Director is—

- (a) nominated as a member of Seanad Éireann,
- (b) nominated as a candidate for election to either House of the Oireachtas or to the European Parliament or becomes a member of a local authority, or
- (c) regarded pursuant to Part XIII of the Second Schedule to the European Parliament Elections Act, 1997, as having been elected to the European Parliament,

he or she shall thereon cease to be the Director.

(4) A person who is for the time being—

- (a) entitled under the Standing Orders of either House of the Oireachtas to sit in that House,
- (b) a member of the European Parliament, or
- (c) a member of a local authority,

is, while he or she is so entitled or is such a member, disqualified from being the Director.

Acting Director

11 Acting Director of Corporate Enforcement

(1) Subject to subsection (2), the Minister may appoint a person to be the Acting Director of Corporate Enforcement to perform the functions of the Director during—

- (a) a period, or during all periods, when the Director is absent from duty or from the State or is, for any other reason, unable to perform the functions of the Director,
- (b) any suspension from office of the Director, or
- (c) a vacancy in the office of Director.

(2) A person shall not be appointed to perform the functions of the Director for a continuous period of more than 6 months during a vacancy in the office of Director.

(3) The Minister may, at any time, terminate an appointment under this section.

Functions of Director

12 Functions of Director

(1) The functions of the Director are—

(a) to enforce the Companies Acts, including by the prosecution of offences by way of summary proceedings,

(b) to encourage compliance with the Companies Acts,

(c) to investigate instances of suspected offences under the Companies Acts,

(d) at his or her discretion, to refer cases to the Director of Public Prosecutions where the Director of Corporate Enforcement has reasonable grounds for believing that an indictable offence under the Companies Acts has been committed,

(e) to exercise, insofar as the Director feels it necessary or appropriate, a supervisory role over the activity of liquidators and receivers in the discharge of their functions under the Companies Acts,

(f) for the purpose of ensuring the effective application and enforcement of obligations, standards and procedures to which companies and their officers are subject, to perform such other functions in respect of any matters to which the Companies Acts relate as the Minister considers appropriate and may by order confer on the Director,[...][a]

(g) to perform such other functions for a purpose referred to in paragraph (f) as may be assigned to him or her by or under the Companies Acts or [any other Act, and;][b]

[(h) to act, under the Companies (Auditing and Accounting) Act 2003, as a member of the Irish Auditing and Accounting Supervisory Authority and, if appointed under section 11 of that Act, as a director of the Authority.][c]

(2) The Director may do all such acts or things as are necessary or expedient for the purpose of the performance of his or her functions under this or any other Act.

(3) Notwithstanding that he or she has been so seconded but without prejudice to subsections (5) and (6), a member of the Garda Síochána seconded to the office of the Director shall continue to be under the general direction and control of the Commissioner of the Garda Síochána.

(4) A member of the Garda Síochána so seconded shall continue to be vested with and may exercise or perform the powers or duties of a member of the Garda Síochána for purposes other than the purposes of this Act, as well as for the purposes of this Act.

(5) The Director shall be independent in the performance of his or her functions.

(6) The Director may perform such of his or her functions as he or she thinks fit through or by an officer of the Director and in the performance of those functions the officer shall be subject to the directions of the Director only.

Amendments

a C(AA)A 2003, s 51(a) deletes the word 'and' at the end of CLEA 2001, s 12(1)(f).

b C(AA)A 2003, s 51(b) amends CLEA 2001, s 12(1)(g) by substituting 'any other Act, and' for 'any other Act'.

c C(AA)A 2003, s 51(c) inserts CLEA 2001, s 12(1)(h).

---

13 Delegation

(1) Without prejudice to the generality of section 12(6), the Director may, in writing, delegate to an officer of the Director any of the Director's powers under this or any other Act, except this power of delegation.

(2) A power delegated under subsection (1) shall not be exercised by the delegate except in accordance with the instrument of delegation.

(3) A delegate shall, on request by a person affected by the exercise of a power delegated to him or her, produce the instrument of delegation under this section, or a copy of the instrument, for inspection.

(4) A delegation under this section is revocable at will and does not prevent the exercise by the Director of a power so delegated.

Transfer of Minister's Functions to Director

14 Transfer of functions

(1) Each subsection mentioned in column (3) of the sections mentioned in column (2) opposite to those subsections of the Acts mentioned in the headings to Parts 1 and 2 of the Schedule, is amended by the substitution for 'Minister', wherever occurring, of 'Director'.

(2) Where, before its relevant amendment, anything was commenced under a provision of the Companies Acts by or under the authority of the Minister, it may be carried on or completed on or after that amendment by or under the authority of the Director.

(3) A person authorised by the Minister under a relevantly amended provision shall be regarded as having been so authorised by the Director under that provision as relevantly amended.

(4) Where, before its relevant amendment, legal proceedings were pending under a provision of the Companies Acts to which the Minister is or was then the plaintiff or the prosecutor, the name of the Director shall be substituted in those proceedings for that of the Minister, or added in those proceedings as may be appropriate, and those proceedings shall not abate by reason of that substitution or addition.

(5) To avoid doubt, where, immediately before its relevant amendment, legal proceedings were pending under a provision of the Companies Acts as then in force in which the Minister was a defendant, the Director shall not be substituted for the Minister in those proceedings notwithstanding the amendment of that provision.

(6) In this section, 'relevant amendment', in relation to a provision of the Companies Acts, means an amendment by this or any other section of this Act which comprises or includes the substitution for 'Minister' of 'Director' (including the substitution of an entire provision or part of a provision which has the effect of transferring a function from the Minister to the Director), and 'relevantly amended' has a corresponding meaning.

General

15 Director or officer of Director indemnified against losses

Neither the Director nor any officer of the Director shall be liable in damages in respect of any thing done or omitted to be done in good faith by him or her in the performance or purported performance of a function under the Companies Acts or any other Act.

16 Reporting by Director

(1) The Director shall, not later than 3 months after the end of each year, present a report to the Minister about the performance of the Director's functions and other activities of the Director in that year, and the Minister shall cause a copy of the report to be laid before each House of the Oireachtas within 2 months of receipt of the report.

(2) A report under subsection (1) shall include information in such form and about such matters as the Minister may direct but nothing in that or this subsection shall be construed as requiring the Director to include in such a report information the inclusion of which therein would, in the opinion of the Director, be likely to prejudice the performance by him or her of any of his or her functions.

(3) The Director shall furnish to the Minister such information about the performance of the Director's functions as the Minister may from time to time require (other than information the provision of which under this subsection would, in the opinion of the Director, be likely to prejudice the performance by him or her of any of his or her functions).

(4) When so requested, the Director shall account to an appropriately established Committee of either House of the Oireachtas for the performance of his or her functions but in discharging his or her duties under this subsection the Director shall not be required to furnish any information or answer any questions the furnishing or answering of which would, in the opinion of the Director, be likely to prejudice the performance by him or her of any of his or her functions.

17 Disclosure of information

(1) Information obtained by virtue of the performance by the Director of any of his or her functions which has not otherwise come to the notice of the public, shall not be disclosed, except in accordance with law, by any person, including—

- (a) the Director or a former Director,
- (b) a professional or other adviser (including a former adviser) to the Director, and
- (c) an officer or former officer of the Director.

(2) Notwithstanding subsection (1), information referred to in that subsection which, in the opinion of the Director, may be required—

- (a) for a purpose or reason specified in subsection (1) of section 21 of the Act of 1990,
- (b) for the performance by a competent authority (within the meaning of that section 21) of a function or functions of the authority, or
- (c) for the performance by the Director of a function or functions of the Director,

may be disclosed by or under the authority of the Director to the extent that, in the opinion of the Director, is necessary for that purpose.

(3) Notwithstanding subsection (1), information which, in the opinion of the Director or an officer of the Director, may relate to the commission of an offence which is not an offence under the Companies Acts may be disclosed to any member of An Garda Síochána.

(4) A person who contravenes this section is guilty of an offence.

18 Information relating to offences under Companies Acts may be disclosed to Director or officer of Director.

Notwithstanding any other law, information which, in the opinion of the Competition Authority or a member of An Garda Síochána or an officer of the Revenue Commissioners, may relate to the commission of an offence under the Companies Acts may be disclosed by that Authority, member or officer to the Director or an officer of the Director.

PART 3
INVESTIGATIONS

19 Amendment of section 145 of Act of 1963

(a) [...][a]

(b) [...][b]

Amendments

a CLEA 2001, s 19(a) inserts CA 1963, s 145(3A).

b CLEA 2001, s 19(b) amends CA 1963, s 145(4) by the insertion after 'subsection (1)' of 'or (3A)'.

20 Amendment of section 7 of Act of 1990

[...][a]

Amendments

a CLEA 2001, s 20 amends CA 1990, s 7(3) by the substitution for '£500' and '£100,000' of '£5,000' and '£250,000' respectively which were converted to €6,348.69 and €317,424.51 by the Economic and Monetary Union Act 1998, s 6.

21 Amendment of section 8 of Act of 1990 — Investigation of company's affairs on application of Director

[...][a]

Amendments

a CLEA 2001, s 21 amends CA 1990, s 8(1) by the substitution for 'on the application of the Minister appoint one or more competent inspectors' of 'on the application of the Director appoint one or more competent inspectors (who may be or include an officer of officers of the Director'.

22 Amendment of section 9 of Act of 1990

[...][a]

[...][b]

Amendments

a CLEA 2001, s 22(a) amends CA 1990, s 9 by the substitution for 'If an Inspector' of '(1) If an Inspector'.

b CLEA 2001, s 22(b) inserts CA 1990, s 9(2). See the amended Act.

23 Amendment of section 10 of Act of 1990

(a) [...][a]

(b) [...][b]

(c) [...][c]

(d) [...][d]

Amendments

a CLEA 2001, s 23(a) amends CA 1990, s 10(1) by the insertion after 'reasonably able to give' of; but where any such person claims a lien on books or documents produced by the person, the production shall be without prejudice to the lien'.

b CLEA 2001, s 23(b) amends CA 1990, s 10(2) by the insertion after 'comply with the requirement' of; but where any such person claims a lien on books or documents produced by the person, the production shall be without prejudice to the lien'.

c CLEA 2001, s 23(c) substitutes CA 1990, s 10(5) and (6). See the amended Act.

d CLEA 2001, s 23(d) amends CA 1990, s 10(7) by the insertion after 'auditors' of 'accountants, book-keepers or taxation advisers,'.

24 Amendment of section 11 of Act of 1990

(a) [...][a]

(b) [...][b]

(2) [...][c]

Amendments

a CLEA 2001, s 24(1)(a) amends CA 1990, s 11(3)(b)(vi) by the deletion of 'and' from the end thereof.

b CLEA 2001, s 24(1)(b) inserts CA 1990, s 11(3)(ba).

c CLEA 2001, s 24(2) amends CA 1990, s 11(4) by the substitution for 'subsection (3)(a) or (b)' of 'subsection (3)(a), (b) or (ba)'.

25 Amendment of section 13 of Act of 1990

(a) [...][a]

(b) [...][b]

(c) [...][c]

Amendments

a CLEA 2001, s 25(a) amends CA 1990, s 13 by the substitution for 'Minister for Justice' wherever occurring of 'relevant Minister'.

b CLEA 2001, s 25(b) amends CA 1990, s 13(1) by the substitution for '£100,000' of '£250,000'.

c CLEA 2001, s 25(c) inserts CA 1990, s 13(3A). See the amended Act.

26 Amendment of section 14 of Act of 1990

[...][a]

Amendments

a CLEA 2001, s 26 inserts CA 1990, s 14(6), (7) and (8). See the amended Act.

27 Amendment of section 16 of Act of 1990

(a) [...][a]

(b) [...][b]

(c) [...][c]

(d) [...][d]

Amendments

a CLEA 2001, s 27(a) amends CA 1990, s 16(2)(d) by the deletion of 'except in a liquidation'.

b CLEA 2001, s 27(b) amends CA 1990, s 16(4) by the deletion of '(otherwise than in a liquidation)'.

c CLEA 2001, s 27(c) substitutes CA 1990, s 16(6)(a) and (b) and inserts CA 1990, s 16(6)(c).

d CLEA 2001, s 27(d) amends CA 1990, s 16(7) by the insertion after 'or the company' of 'having given notice to the Director,'.

28 Amendment of section 18 of Act of 1990

(a) [...][a]

(b) [...][b]

(c) [...][c]

Amendments

a CLEA 2001, s 28(a) amends CA 1990, s 18 by the substitution for 'An answer given by a person' of '(1) An answer given by an individual'.

b CLEA 2001, s 28(b) amends CA 1990, s 18 by the deletion of all the words from 'and a statement required' down to and including 'making it.' and the substitution of 'in any proceedings whatsoever (save proceedings for an offence (other than perjury in respect of such an answer)).'

c CLEA 2001, s 28(c) inserts CA 1990, s 18(2).

29 Repeal and substitution of section 19 of Act of 1990 — Power of Director to require production of documents

[...][a]

Amendments

a CLEA 2001, s 29 substitutes CA 1990, s 19 and inserts CA 1990, s 19A. See the amended Act.

30 Repeal and substitution of section 20 of Act of 1990

[...][a]

Amendments

a CLEA 2001, s 30 substitutes CA 1990, s 20. See the amended Act.

31 Amendment of section 21 of Act of 1990

(a) [...][a]

(b) [...][b]

(c) [...][c]

(d) [...][d]

Amendments

a CLEA 2001, s 31(a) amends CA 1990, s 21(1) by the substitution for 'Minister' where ever occurring, except in paragraph (d) of 'Director'.

b CLEA 2001, s 31(b) substitutes CA 1990, s 21(1)(a)(i)(V).

c CLEA 2001, s 31(c) inserts CA 1990, s 21(1)(fa) and (fb).

d CLEA 2001, s 31(d) substitutes CA 1990, s 21(1)(g)(ii).

32 Amendment of section 23 of Act of 1990

(a) [...][a]

(b) [...][b]

Amendments

a CLEA 2001, s 32(a) substitutes CA 1990, s 23(2).

b CLEA 2001, s 32(b) inserts CA 1990, s 23(4).

33 New section 23A of Act of 1990 — Assistance to overseas company law authorities

[...][a]

Amendments

a CLEA 2001, s 33 inserts CA 1990, s 23A. See amended Act.

34 Examination of books and documents of certain companies to be continued by Minister or authorised officer

(1) Notwithstanding subsections (2) and (3) of section 14 or any other provision of this Act, the Minister or any officer of the Minister authorised by him or her under section 19 of the Act of 1990 before the passing of this Act may, in relation to such body or bodies and to such extent as may be prescribed, continue to exercise, after such passing, the powers conferred on them respectively by sections 19 to 23 of the Act of 1990.

(2) In subsection (1), 'sections 19 to 23 of the Act of 1990' means those sections as they stand amended by this Act but with the substitution for references in them to the Director of references to the Minister or an officer of the Minister authorised by the Minister under section 19 of the Act of 1990, as appropriate.

35 Amendment of section 79 of Act of 1990

[...][a]

Amendments

a CLEA 2001, s 35 inserts CA 1990, s 79(7)(bb). See the amended Act.

36 Amendment of section 92 of Act of 1990 — Duty of relevant authority to report to Director

(a) [...][a]

(b) [...][b]

Amendments

a CLEA 2001, s 36(a) amends CA 1990, s 92 by the substitution for 'Director of Public Prosecutions' wherever occurring, except in subsection (4) of 'Director'.

b CLEA 2001, s 36(b) substitutes CA 1990, s 92(4).

37 Amendment of section 115 of Act of 1990

(a) [...][a]

(b) [...][b]

(c) [...][c]

(d) [...][d]

Amendments

a CLEA 2001, s 37(a) amends CA 1990, s 115 by the substitution for 'Director of Public Prosecutions' wherever occurring, except in subsection (4) of 'Director'.

b CLEA 2001, s 37(b) substitutes CA 1990, s 115(4).

c CLEA 2001, s 37(c) amends CA 1990, s 115(5) by the substitution for 'Minister' of 'Director'.

d CLEA 2001, s 37(d) deletes CA 1990, s 115(6).

---

38 Amendment of section 118 of Act of 1990

[...][a]

Amendments

a CLEA 2001, s 38 inserts CA 1990, s 118(2A). See the amended Act.

---

39 Amendment of section 230 of Act of 1990

(a) [...][a]

(b) [...][b]

(c) [...][c]

(d) [...][d]

Amendments

a CLEA 2001, s 39(a) amends CA 1990, s 230 by the substitution for 'Director of Public Prosecutions' wherever occurring, except in subsection (4) of 'Director'.

b CLEA 2001, s 39(b) substitutes CA 1990, s 230(4).

c CLEA 2001, s 39(c) amends CA 1990, s 230(5) by the substitution for 'Minister' of 'Director'.

d CLEA 2001, s 39(d) deletes CA 1990, s 230(6).

PART 4
RESTRICTIONS AND DISQUALIFICATIONS

40 New section 183A of Act of 1963 — Examination as to solvency status

[...][a]

Amendments

a CLEA 2001, s 40 inserts CA 1963, s 183A. See the amended Act.

---

41 Amendment of section 150 of Act of 1990

[...][a]

[...][b]

[...][c]

(2) The amendments made by paragraphs (a) and (b) of subsection (1) shall not have effect in relation to a declaration under subsection (1) of section 150 of the Act of 1990 made before the commencement of this section and, accordingly, the requirements of subsection (3) of that section 150 that shall apply in respect of a person who is the subject of such a declaration made before that commencement shall be those that applied before that commencement.

Amendments

a CLEA 2001, s 41(1)(a) amends CA 1990, s 150(3)(a)(i) by the substitution for '£100,000' of '£250,000'.

b CLEA 2001, s 41(1)(b) amends CA 1990, s 150(3)(a)(ii) by the substitution for '£20,000' of '£50,000'.

c CLEA 2001, s 41(1)(c) inserts CA 1990, s 150(4A) and (4B).

42 Amendment of section 160 of Act of 1990

[...][a]

[...][b]

[...][c]

[...][e]

[...][e]

[...][f]

Amendments

a CLEA 2001, s 42(a) inserts CA 1990, s 160(1A) and (1B).

b CLEA 2001, s 42(b)(i) amends CA 1990, s 160(2)(f) by the substitution for 'requirements' of 'requirements; or'.

c CLEA 2001, s 42(b)(ii) inserts CA 1990, s 160(2)(g), (h) and (i).

d CLEA 2001, s 42(c) inserts CA 1990, s 160(3A) and (3B). CLEA 2001, s 42(d) amends CA 1990, s 160(5) by the substitution for 'paragraph (e)' of 'paragraph (e) or (g)'.

e CLEA 2001, s 42(e) inserts CA 1990, s 160(6A).

f CLEA 2001, s 42(f) inserts CA 1990, s 160(9A) and (9B).

PART 5
WINDING-UP AND INSOLVENCY

43 Amendment of section 243 of Act of 1963 — Inspection of books by creditors, contributories and Director

[...][a]

Amendments

a CLEA 2001, s 43 inserts CA 1963, s 243(1A). See the amended Act.

44 Amendment of section 245 of Act of 1963

[...][a]

[...][b]

Amendments

a CLEA 2001, s 44(a) amends CA 1963, s 245(1) by the insertion after 'The court may' of 'of its own motion or on the application of the Director,'.

b CLEA 2001, s 44(b) substitutes CA 1963, s 245(6). See the amended Act.

45 Amendment of section 245A of Act of 1963

[...][a]

[...][b]

[...][c]

Amendments

a CLEA 2001, s 45(a) amends CA 1963, s 245A by the substitution for 'If in the course of an examination' of '(1) If in the course of an examination'.

b CLEA 2001, s 45(b) amends CA 1963, s 245A by the substitution for 'the court may order such person' of 'the court may, of its own motion or on the application of the Director, order such person'.

c CLEA 2001, s 45(c) inserts CA 1963, s 245A(2)–(6). See the amended Act.

46 Repeal and substitution of section 247 of Act of 1963 — Power to arrest absconding contributory or officer of company

[...][a]

Amendments

a CLEA 2001, s 46 substitutes CA 1963, s 247. See the amended Act.

47 Amendment of section 267 of Act of 1963

[...][a]

Amendments

a CLEA 2001, s 47 inserts CA 1963, s 267(3).

48 Amendment of section 278 of Act of 1963

[...][a]

Amendments

a CLEA 2001, s 48 amends CA 1963, s 278(1) by the insertion after 'notice of his appointment' of 'and the registrar shall forward a copy to the Director'.

49 New sections 282A to 282D of Act of 1963

[...][a]

Amendments

a CLEA 2001, s 49 inserts CA 1963, ss 282A, 282B, 282C and 282D.

50 Amendment of section 298 of Act of 1963

[...][a]

Amendments

a CLEA 2001, s 50 amends CA 1963, s 298(2) by the substitution for 'on the application of the liquidator' of 'on the application of the Director, liquidator'.

51 Amendment of section 299 of Act of 1963

[...][a]

[...][b]

[...][c]

[...][d]

[...][e]

[...][f]

Amendments

a CLEA 2001, s 51(a) inserts CA 1963, s 299(1A).

b CLEA 2001, s 51(b) amends CA 1963, s 299(2) by the substitution for 'Attorney General' wherever occurring of 'Director of Public Prosecutions'.

c CLEA 2001, s 51(c) inserts CA 1963, s 299(2A).

d CLEA 2001, s 51(d) amends CA 1963, s 299(3) by the substitution for 'the Attorney General under subsection (2)' and 'in pursuance of subsection (2)' of 'the Director of Public Prosecutions under subsection (2), or the Director under subsection (2A)' and 'in pursuance of subsection (2) or subsection (2A), as the case may be', respectively.

e CLEA 2001, s 51(e) amends CA 1963, s 299(4) by the substitution for 'Attorney General under this section, he considers' of 'Director of Public Prosecutions and the Director under this section, either the Director of Public Prosecutions or the Director considers'.

f CLEA 2001, s 51(f) amends CA 1963, s 299(5) by the substitution for 'of the Attorney General' of 'of the Director of Public Prosecutions or of the Director'.

52 Amendment of section 319 of Act of 1963

[...][a]

[...][b]

Amendments

a CLEA 2001, s 52(a) inserts CA 1963, s 319(2A).

b CLEA 2001, s 52(b) substitutes CA 1963, s 319(7) and inserts CA 1963, s 319(8).

53 New section 323A of Act of 1963 — Director may request production of receiver's books

[...][a]

Amendments

a CLEA 2001, s 53 inserts CA 1963, s 323A. See the amended Act.

54 Amendment of section 251 of Act of 1990

[...][a]

[...][b]

[...][c]

Amendments

a CLEA 2001, s 54(a) amends CA 1990, s 251(2)(a) by the insertion after '140,' of '149'.

b CLEA 2001, s 54(b) inserts CA 1990, s 251(2A).

c CLEA 2001, s 54(c) substitutes CA 1990, s 251(4).

55 Order to restrain directors and others from moving assets

The court may, on the application of a company, director, member, liquidator, receiver, creditor or the Director, order a director or other officer of a company not to remove his or her assets from the State or to reduce his or her assets within or outside the State below an amount to be specified by the court, where the court is satisfied that—

(a) the applicant has a substantive civil cause of action or right to seek a declaration of personal liability or claim for damages against the director, other officer or the company, and

(b) there are grounds for believing that the respondent may remove or dispose of his, her or the company's assets with a view to evading his, her or the company's obligations and frustrating an order of the court.

56 Liquidator to report on conduct of directors

(1) A liquidator of an insolvent company shall, within 6 months after his or her appointment or the commencement of this section, whichever is the later, and at intervals as required by the Director thereafter, provide to the Director a report in the prescribed form.

(2) A liquidator of an insolvent company shall, not earlier than 3 months nor later than 5 months (or such later time as the court may allow and advises the Director) after the date on which he or she has provided to the Director a report under subsection (1), apply to the court for the restriction under section 150 of the Act of 1990 of each of the directors of the company, unless the Director has relieved the liquidator of the obligation to make such an application.

(3) A liquidator who fails to comply with subsection (1) or (2) is guilty of an offence.

57 Director's power to examine liquidator's books

(1) The Director may on his or her own motion or where a complaint is made to the Director by a member, contributory or creditor of the company, request, specifying the reason why the request is being made, the liquidator of a company in liquidation to produce to the Director the liquidator's books for examination, either in relation to a particular liquidation process or to all liquidations undertaken by the liquidator, and the liquidator shall comply with the request.

(2) The liquidator shall answer any questions of the Director concerning the content of the books requested under subsection (1) to be produced and the conduct of a particular liquidation or all liquidations, and give to the Director such assistance in the matter as the liquidator is reasonably able to give.

(3) A request under subsection (1) may not be made in respect of books relating to a liquidation that has concluded more than 6 years prior to the request.

(4) A liquidator who fails to comply with a request or requirement under this section is guilty of an offence.

58 Reporting to Director of misconduct by liquidators or receivers

Where a disciplinary committee or tribunal (however called) of a prescribed professional body finds that a member conducting a liquidation or receivership has not maintained appropriate records, or it has reasonable grounds for believing that a member has committed an indictable offence under the Companies Acts during the course of a liquidation or receivership, the body shall report the matter, giving details of the finding or, as the case may be, of the alleged offence, to the Director forthwith and if the body fails to comply with this section it, and every officer of the body to whom the failure is attributable, is guilty of an offence.

PART 6
MEASURES TO IMPROVE COMPLIANCE WITH FILING OBLIGATIONS

59 Repeal of sections 125 and 126 of Act of 1963 and substitution of section 125 — Annual return

[...][a]

Amendments

a CLEA 2001, s 59, substitutes CA 1963, s 125 and repeals CA 1963, s 126 with effect from 1 March 2002.[1] See amended Act.

[1] Company Law Enforcement Act 2001 (Commencement) (No 2) Order 2001 (SI 438/2001).

60 Repeal and substitution of section 127 of Act of 1963 — Annual return date[a]

[...][a]

Amendments

a CLEA 2001, s 60, substitutes CA 1963, s 127 with effect from 1 March 2002.[1] See amended Act.

[1] Company Law Enforcement Act 2001 (Commencement) (No 2) Order 2001 (SI 438/2001).

61 Amendment of section 153 of Act of 1963 — Financial year and annual return date of holding company and subsidiary

[...][a]

Amendments

a CLEA 2001, s 61, substitutes CA 1963, s 153(2) with effect from 1 March 2002.[1] See amended Act.

[1] Company Law Enforcement Act 2001 (Commencement) (No 2) Order 2001 (SI 438/2001).

62 Amendment of section 370 of Act of 1963

[...][a]

Amendments

a CLEA 2001, s 62 inserts CA 1963, s 370(4) with effect from 26 October 2002.[1] See amended Act.

[1] Company Law Enforcement Act 2001 (Commencement) (No 2) Order 2001 (SI 438/2001).

63 Amendment of section 395 of Act of 1963 and repeal of Fifth Schedule

(1)

(a) [...][a]

(b) [...][b]

(2) [...][c]

Amendments

a CLEA 2001, s 63(1)(a) amends CA 1963, s 395(2)(b) with effect from 1 March 2002.[1] See amended Act.

b CLEA 2001, s 63(1)(b) inserts CA 1963, s 395(3) with effect from 26 October 2002.[2] See amended Act.

c CLEA 2001, s 63(2) repeals CA 1963, Sch 5 with effect from 1 March 2002.[3] See amended Act.

1 Company Law Enforcement Act 2001 (Commencement) (No 2) Order 2001 (SI 438/2001).
2 Company Law Enforcement Act 2001 (Commencement) (No 2) Order 2001 (SI 438/2001).
3 Company Law Enforcement Act 2001 (Commencement) (No 2) Order 2001 (SI 438/2001).

64 Amendment of section 7 of Companies (Amendment) Act, 1986

(a) [...][a]

(b) [...][b]

Amendments

a CLEA 2001, s 64(a) with effect from 26 October 2002.[1] See amended Act.

b CLEA 2001, s 64(b) inserts C(A)A 1986, s 7(1A) with effect from 26 October 2002.[2] See amended Act.

1 Company Law Enforcement Act 2001 (Commencement) (No 2) Order 2001 (SI 438/2001).
2 Company Law Enforcement Act 2001 (Commencement) (No 2) Order 2001 (SI 438/2001).

65 Amendment of section 17(1) of Companies (Amendment) Act, 1986

[...][a]

Amendments

a CLEA 2001, s 65 amends C(A)A 1986, s 17(1)(a) with effect from 1 March 2002.[1] See amended Act.

1 Company Law Enforcement Act 2001 (Commencement) (No 2) Order 2001 (SI 438/2001).

66 Special provisions applying where default in delivery of documents to registrar of companies

(1) Where the registrar of companies has reasonable grounds for believing that a person is in default in the delivery, filing or making to the registrar of a return or similar document required under the Companies Acts, the registrar may deliver to the person or, where the person believed to be in default is a company, to an officer of the company, a notice in the prescribed form stating—

(a) that the person or company has failed to deliver, file or make a specified return or similar document to the registrar under a specified section of the Companies Acts,

(b) that the person to whom the notice is delivered may, during a period of 21 days beginning on the date of the notice,

(i) remedy the default, and

(ii) make to the registrar a payment of a prescribed amount which shall be accompanied by the notice, and

(c) that a prosecution of the person to whom the notice is delivered will not be instituted during the period specified in the notice, or, if the default is remedied and the payment specified in the notice is made during that period, at all.

(2) Where a notice is delivered under subsection (1)—

(a) a person to whom it applies may, during the period specified in the notice, make to the registrar the payment specified in the notice, accompanied by the notice,

(b) the registrar may receive the payment and issue a receipt for it, and no payment so received shall in any circumstances be recoverable by the person who made it, and

(c) a prosecution in respect of the alleged default shall not be instituted in the period specified in the notice, and, if the default is remedied and the payment specified in the notice is made during that period, no prosecution in respect of the alleged default shall be instituted at all.

(3) In a prosecution for an offence to which this section applies, the onus of showing that a payment pursuant to a notice under this section has been made shall lie on the defendant or accused.

(4) All payments made to the registrar under this section shall be paid into or disposed of for the benefit of the Exchequer in such manner as the Minister for Finance may direct.

PART 7
COMPANY LAW REVIEW GROUP

67 Establishment of Company Law Review Group

There is hereby established a body to be known as the Company Law Review Group.

68 Functions of Review Group

(1) The Review Group shall monitor, review and advise the Minister on matters concerning—

(a) the implementation of the Companies Acts,

(b) the amendment of the Companies Acts,

(c) the consolidation of the Companies Acts,

(d) the introduction of new legislation relating to the operation of companies and commercial practices in Ireland,

(e) the Rules of the Superior Courts and case law judgements insofar as they relate to the Companies Acts,

(f) the approach to issues arising from the State's membership of the European Union, insofar as they affect the operation of the Companies Acts,

(g) international developments in company law, insofar as they may provide lessons for improved State practice, and

(h) other related matters or issues, including issues submitted by the Minister to the Review Group for consideration.

(2) In advising the Minister the Review Group shall seek to promote enterprise, facilitate commerce, simplify the operation of the Companies Acts, enhance corporate governance and encourage commercial probity.

69 Membership of Review Group

(1) The Review Group shall consist of such and so many persons as the Minister from time to time appoints to be members of the Review Group.

(2) The Minister shall from time to time appoint a member of the Review Group to be its chairperson.

(3) Members of the Review Group shall be paid such remuneration and allowances for expenses as the Minister, with the consent of the Minister for Finance, may from time to time determine.

(4) A member of the Review Group may at any time resign his or her membership of the Review Group by letter addressed to the Minister.

(5) The Minister may at any time, for stated reasons, terminate a person's membership of the Review Group.

70 Meetings and business of Review Group

(1) The Minister shall, at least once in every 2 years, after consultation with the Review Group, determine the programme of work to be undertaken by the Review Group over the ensuing specified period.

(2) Notwithstanding subsection (1), the Minister may, from time to time, amend the Review Group's work programme, including the period to which it relates.

(3) The Review Group shall hold such and so many meetings as may be necessary for the performance of its functions and the achievement of its work programme and may make such arrangements for the conduct of its meetings and business (including by the establishment of sub-committees and the fixing of a quorum for a meeting) as it considers appropriate.

(4) In the absence of the chairperson from a meeting of the Review Group, the members present shall elect one of their number to be chairperson for that meeting.

(5) A member of the Review Group, other than the chairperson, who is unable to attend a meeting of the Review Group, may nominate a deputy to attend in his or her place.

71 Annual Report and provision of information to Minister

(1) No later than 3 months after the end of each calendar year, the Review Group shall make a report to the Minister on its activities during that year and the Minister shall cause copies of the report to be laid before each House of the Oireachtas within a period of 2 months from the receipt of the report.

(2) A report under subsection (1) shall include information in such form and regarding such matters as the Minister may direct.

(3) The Review Group shall, if so requested by the Minister, provide a report to the Minister on any matter—

(a) concerning the functions or activities of the Review Group, or

(b) referred by the Minister to the Review Group for its advice.

PART 8
AUDITORS

72 Amendment of section 187 of Act of 1990

(a) [...][a]

(b) [...][b]

Amendments

a CLEA 2001, s 72(a) amends CA 1990, s 187(1)(a)(iii) by the insertion after 'Principal Act' of 'and holds a valid practising certificate from such a body'.

b CLEA 2001, s 72(b) inserts CA 1990, s 187(12) and (13).

---

73 Amendment of section 192 of Act of 1990

[...][a]

Amendments

a CLEA 2001, s 73 inserts CA 1990, s 192(6) and (7).

---

74 Amendment of section 194 of Act of 1990 — Duty of auditors if proper books of account not being kept or other offences suspected

(a) [...][a]

(b) [...][b]

(c) [....][c]

(d) [...][d]

(e) [...][e]

Amendments

a CLEA 2001, s 74(a) substitutes CA 1990, s 194(1)(a).

b CLEA 2001, s 74(b) amends CA 1990, s 194(1)(b) by the insertion after 'form of the notice' of 'and the registrar shall forthwith forward a copy of the notice to the Director'.

c CLEA 2001, s 74(c) inserts CA 1990, s 194(3A) and (3B).

d CLEA 2001, s 74(d) amends CA 1990, s 194(4) by the substitution for 'subsection (1)' of 'subsection (1), (3A) or (5)'.

e CLEA 2001, s 74(e) inserts CA 1990, s 194(5) and (6).

PART 9
TRANSACTIONS INVOLVING DIRECTORS

75 Amendment of section 25 of Act of 1990

[…][a]

Amendments

a CLEA 2001, s 75 inserts CA 1990, s 25(3A).

76 Amendment of section 26 of Act of 1990

[…][a]

[…][b]

[…][c]

Amendments

a CLEA 2001, s 76(a) substitutes CA 1990, s 26(1).

b CLEA 2001, s 76(b) substitutes CA 1990, s 26(3).

c CLEA 2001, s 76(c) inserts CA 1990, s 26(6).

77 Amendment of section 33 of Act of 1990

[…][a]

Amendments

a CLEA 2001, s 77 inserts CA 1990, s 33(3).

78 Repeal and substitution of section 34 of Act of 1990 — Exceptions to section 31 in certain circumstances

[…][a]

Amendments

a CLEA 2001, s 78 repeals and substitutes CA 1990, s 34.

79 Amendment of section 35 of Act of 1990 — Inter-company transactions in the same group

[...][a]

Amendments

a CLEA 2001, s 79 amends CA 1990, s 35 by the substitution for 'its holding company' wherever occurring, of 'any company which is its holding company, subsidiary or a subsidiary of its holding company'.

PART 10
MISCELLANEOUS

80 Reference Memoranda and Articles of Association

(1) The registrar of companies may accept for registration a document containing standard form text from the objects clause of a memorandum of association or from articles of association and shall assign a reference number to each document so registered.

(2) Notwithstanding anything in the Companies Acts, a document filed pursuant to subsection (1) need not relate to a particular company or contain the registered number of a company.

(3) A memorandum or articles of association may contain a statement that it is to incorporate the text of a document previously registered with the registrar pursuant to subsection (1), which document shall be identified by the reference number assigned to it by the registrar.

(4) Where a memorandum or articles of association contains a statement as referred to in subsection (3), it shall be deemed for all purposes to incorporate within it the text of the relevant document filed with the registrar pursuant to subsection (1), so that it shall form and be read as one entire document, and where such a memorandum or articles of association has been registered by the registrar and is inspected by any person, the registrar shall also make available for inspection the related document filed with him or her pursuant to subsection (1).

81 Amendment of section 7 of Act of 1963

[...][a]

Amendments

a CLEA 2001, s 81 amends CA 1963, s 7 with effect from 1 October 2001[1] by the insertion after 'The memorandum must be printed' of 'in an entire format or in a form pursuant to section 80 of the Company Law Enforcement Act, 2001'.

1 Company Law Enforcement Act 2001 (Commencement) (No 2) Order 2001 (SI 438/2001).

---

82 Amendment of section 14 of Act of 1963

[...][a]

Amendments

a CLEA 2001, s 82 amends CA 1963, s 14(a) with effect from 1 October 2001 by the insertion after 'printed' of 'in an entire format or in a form pursuant to section 80 of the Company Law Enforcement Act, 2001'

1 Company Law Enforcement Act 2001 (Commencement) (No 2) Order 2001 (SI 438/2001).

---

83 Amendment of section 17 of Act of 1963

[...][a]

Amendments

a CLEA 2001, s 83 amends CA 1963, s 17 with effect from 1 October 2001 by the insertion after 'shall be delivered to the registrar of companies' of 'in an entire format or in a form pursuant to section 80 of the Company Law Enforcement Act, 2001'.

1 Company Law Enforcement Act 2001 (Commencement) (No 2) Order 2001 (SI 438/2001).

84 Amendment of section 2 of Act of 1963

(a) [...][a]

(b) [...][b]

Amendments

a CLEA 2001, s 84(a) amends CA 1963, s 2(1) by substituting the definition of 'annual return' and by inserting the definition of 'annual return date' with effect from 1 March 2002.[1] See amended Act.

b CLEA 2001, s 84(b) amends CA 1963, s 2(1) by substituting the definition of 'undischarged bankrupt' with effect from 1 March 2002.[2] See amended Act.

1 Company Law Enforcement Act 2001 (Commencement) (No 2) Order 2001 (SI 438/2001).

2 Company Law Enforcement Act 2001 (Commencement) (No 5) Order 2001 (SI 53/2002).

85 Amendment of section 10 of Act of 1963

[...][a]

Amendments

a CLEA 2001, s 85 amends CA 1963, s 10(8) with effect from 1 October 2001[1] by the substitution for 'Minister' (second occurring) of 'registrar of companies'.

1 Company Law Enforcement Act 2001 (Commencement) (No 2) Order 2001 (SI 438/2001).

86 Amendment of section 21 of Act of 1963

[...][a]

Amendments

a CLEA 2001, s 86 amends CA 1963, s 21 with effect from 1 October 2001[1] by the substitution for 'Minister' of 'registrar of companies'.

1 Company Law Enforcement Act 2001 (Commencement) (No 2) Order 2001 (SI 438/2001).

87 Amendment of section 23 of Act of 1963

(a) [...][a]

(b) [...][b]

(c) [...][c]

Amendments

a CLEA 2001, s 87(a) amends CA 1963, s 23(1) and (2) with effect from 1 October 2001[1] by the substitution for 'Minister' (wherever occurring) of 'registrar of companies'.

b CLEA 2001, s 87(b) amends CA 1963, s 23(5) with effect from 1 October 2001[2] by the substitution for 'but if the Minister is of opinion that any other Minister' and 'that other Minister' of 'but if the registrar of companies is of opinion that any Minister' and 'that Minister', respectively.

c CLEA 2001, s 87(c) inserts CA 1963, s 23(7) with effect from 1 October 2001.[3] See amended Act.

1 Company Law Enforcement Act 2001 (Commencement) (No 2) Order 2001 (SI 438/2001).
2 Company Law Enforcement Act 2001 (Commencement) (No 2) Order 2001 (SI 438/2001).
3 Company Law Enforcement Act 2001 (Commencement) (No 2) Order 2001 (SI 438/2001).

88 Repeal and substitution of section 24 of Act of 1963

(1) [...][a]

(2) Notwithstanding the repeal effected by subsection (1) a licence granted by the Minister pursuant to section 24(1) or (2) of the Act of 1963 as in force immediately before the commencement of this section shall continue to have effect, and subsections (4) to (7) of section 24 of that Act as then in force shall continue in force in relation to the licence, as if the section had never been repealed, except that references in those subsections to the Minister, wherever occurring, shall be construed as references to the registrar of companies.

Amendments

a CLEA 2001, s 88(1) substitutes CA 1963, s 24 with effect from 1 March 2002.[1] See amended Act.

1 Company Law Enforcement Act 2001 (Commencement) (No 3) Order 2001 (SI 523/2001).

89 Amendment of section 60 of Act of 1963

(a) [...][a]

(b) [...][b]

Amendments

a CLEA 2001, s 89(a) substitutes CA 1963, s 60(2)(b) with effect from 1 October 2001.[1] See amended Act.

b CLEA 2001, s 89(b) substitutes CA 1963, s 60(6) with effect from 1 October 2001.[2] See amended Act.

1 Company Law Enforcement Act 2001 (Commencement) (No 2) Order 2001 (SI 438/2001).
2 Company Law Enforcement Act 2001 (Commencement) (No 2) Order 2001 (SI 438/2001).

90 Amendment of section 158 of Act of 1963

[...][a]

Amendments

a CLEA 2001, s 90 inserts CA 1963, s 158(6A) with effect from 1 October 2001.[1] See amended Act.

[1] Company Law Enforcement Act 2001 (Commencement) (No 2) Order 2001 (SI 438/2001).

91 Amendment of section 195 of Act of 1963

(a) [...][a]

(b) [...][b]

Amendments

a CLEA 2001, s 91(a) substitutes CA 1963, s 195(8) with effect from 1 March 2002.[1] See amended Act.

b CLEA 2001, s 91(b) inserts CA 1963, s 198(10A) with effect from 1 October 2001.[2] See amended Act.

[1] Company Law Enforcement Act 2001 (Commencement) (No 5) Order 2001 (SI 53/2005).

[2] Company Law Enforcement Act 2001 (Commencement) (No 2) Order 2001 (SI 438/2001).

92 Amendment of section 201 of Act of 1963

[...][a]

Amendments

a CLEA 2001, s 92 inserts CA 1963, s 201(6A) and (6B) with effect from 1 October 2001.[1] See amended Act.

[1] Company Law Enforcement Act 2001 (Commencement) (No 2) Order 2001 (SI 438/2001).

93 Amendment of section 213 of Act of 1963

Section 213 of the Act of 1963 is amended—

(a) [...][a]

(b) [...][b]

Amendments

a CLEA 2001, s 93(a) amends CA 1963, s 213(f) with effect from 1 October 2001[1] by the insertion after 'company' of ', other than an investment company within the meaning of Part XIII of the Companies Act, 1990, or the European Communities (Undertakings for Collective Investment in Transferable Securities) Regulations, 1989 (S.I. No. 78 of 1989),'.

b CLEA 2001, s 93(b) inserts CA 1963, s 213(fa) with effect from 1 October 2001 (except in so far as it inserts (fa)(ii) into CA 1963, s 213).[2] See amended Act.

[1] Company Law Enforcement Act 2001 (Commencement) (No 2) Order 2001 (SI 438/2001).

[2] Company Law Enforcement Act 2001 (Commencement) (No 2) Order 2001 (SI 438/2001).

94 Amendment of section 215 of Act of 1963

(a) [...][a]

(b) [...][b]

(c) [...][c]

Amendments

a CLEA 2001, s 94(a) amends CA 1963, s 215 with effect from 1 October 2001[1] by the deletion of 'and' where it occurs immediately before paragraph (f).

b CLEA 2001, s 94(b) amends CA 1963, s 215(f) with effect from 1 October 2001[2] by the substitution for 'companies.' of 'companies; and'.

c CLEA 2001, s 94(c) inserts CA 1963, s 215(g) with effect from 1 October 2001.[3] See amended Act.

1 Company Law Enforcement Act 2001 (Commencement) (No 2) Order 2001 (SI 438/2001).

2 Company Law Enforcement Act 2001 (Commencement) (No 2) Order 2001 (SI 438/2001).

3 Company Law Enforcement Act 2001 (Commencement) (No 2) Order 2001 (SI 438/2001).

95 Amendment of section 334 of Act of 1963

[...][a]

Amendments

a CLEA 2001, s 95 amends CA 1963, s 334(1) with effect from 1 October 2001[1] by the substitution for 'Minister' (twice occurring) of 'registrar of companies'.

1 Company Law Enforcement Act 2001 (Commencement) (No 2) Order 2001 (SI 438/2001).

96 Amendment of section 371 of Act of 1963

(a) [...][a]

(b) [...][b]

(c) [...][c]

Amendments

a CLEA 2001, s 96(a) amends CA 1963, s 371(1) with effect from 28 November 2001[1] by the insertion after 'by any member or creditor of the company' of ', by the Director'.

b CLEA 2001, s 96(b) amends CA 1963, s 371(3) with effect from 28 November 2001[2] by the insertion after 'penalties' of '(including restriction under section 150, or disqualification under section 160, of the Companies Act, 1990)'.

c CLEA 2001, s 96(c) inserts CA 1963, s 370(4) with effect from 28 November 2001.[3] See amended Act.

1 Company Law Enforcement Act 2001 (Commencement) (No 3) Order 2001 (SI 523/2001).

2 Company Law Enforcement Act 2001 (Commencement) (No 3) Order 2001 (SI 523/2001).

3 Company Law Enforcement Act 2001 (Commencement) (No 3) Order 2001 (SI 523/2001).

97 New section 371A of Act of 1963 — Power to compel compliance with requirement made under section 19(3)(b) of Act of 1990

[...][a]

Amendments

a CLEA 2001, s 97 inserts CA 1963, s 371A with effect from 28 November 2001.[1] See amended Act.

1 Company Law Enforcement Act 2001 (Commencement) (No 3) Order 2001 (SI 523/2001).

98 Repeal and substitution of section 381 of Act of 1963 — Improper use of 'limited' or 'teoranta'

[...][a]

Amendments

a CLEA 2001, s 98 substitutes CA 1963, s 381 with effect from 1 October 2001.[1] See amended Act.

1 Company Law Enforcement Act 2001 (Commencement) (No 2) Order 2001 (SI 438/2001).

99 Amendment of section 392 of Act of 1963

[...][a]

Amendments

a CLEA 2001, s 99 amends CA 1963, s 392 with effect from 26 October 2001[1] by the insertion after 'Houses of the Oireachtas' of 'not later than 7 months after the end of the calendar year to which the report relates'.

1 Company Law Enforcement Act 2001 (Commencement) (No 2) Order 2001 (SI 438/2001).

100 Repeal and substitution of section 383 of Act of 1963

[...][a]

Amendments

a CLEA 2001, s 100 substitutes CA 1963, s 383 with effect from 1 October 2001.[1] See amended Act.

1 Company Law Enforcement Act 2001 (Commencement) (No 2) Order 2001 (SI 438/2001).

101 New section 3A of Companies (Amendment) Act, 1982 — Additional statement to be delivered to registrar

[...][a]

Amendments

a CLEA 2001, s 101 inserts C(A)A 1982, s 3A with effect from 1 March 2002.[1] See amended Act.

[1] Company Law Enforcement Act 2001 (Commencement) (No 5) Order 2002 (SI 53/2002).

102 Amendment of section 30 of Act of 1990

Section 30 of the Act of 1990 is amended by the insertion of the following after subsection (3):[a]

[...][a]

Amendments

a CLEA 2001, s 102 inserts CA 1990, s 30(3A) with effect from 1 October 2001.[1] See amended Act.

[1] Company Law Enforcement Act 2001 (Commencement) (No 2) Order 2001 (SI 438/2001).

103 Amendment of section 110 of Act of 1990

[...][a]

Amendments

a CLEA 2001, s 103 inserts CA 1990, s 110(1)(ba) with effect from 1 October 2001.[1] See amended Act.

[1] Company Law Enforcement Act 2001 (Commencement) (No 2) Order 2001 (SI 438/2001).

104 Amendment of section 240 of Act of 1990

(a) [...][a]

(b) [...][b]

(c) [...][c]

Amendments

a CLEA 2001, s 104(a) amends CA 1990, s 240 with effect from 1 October 2001[1] by the substitution for '£1,000' (wherever occurring) of '£1,500'.

b CLEA 2001, s 104(b) amends CA 1990, s 240(1)(b) with effect from 1 October 2001[2] by the substitution for '3 years' of '5 years'

c CLEA 2001, s 104(c) inserts CA 1990, s 240(7) and (8) with effect from 1 October 2001.[3] See amended Act.

[1] Company Law Enforcement Act 2001 (Commencement) (No 2) Order 2001 (SI 438/2001).

[2] Company Law Enforcement Act 2001 (Commencement) (No 2) Order 2001 (SI 438/2001).

[3] Company Law Enforcement Act 2001 (Commencement) (No 2) Order 2001 (SI 438/2001).

105 New section 240A of Act of 1990 — Court in which proceedings for certain offences may be brought

[...][a]

Amendments

a CLEA 2001, s 105 inserts CA 1990, s 240A with effect from 1 October 2001.[1] See amended Act.

[1] Company Law Enforcement Act 2001 (Commencement) (No 2) Order 2001 (SI 438/2001).

106 Amendment of section 242 of Act of 1990

Section 242(2) of the Act of 1990 is amended—

(a) [...][a]

(b) [...][b]

Amendments

a CLEA 2001, s 106(a) amends CA 1990, s 242(2) with effect from 1 October 2001[1] by the substitution for 'Where a person is guilty' of 'Where a person is convicted on indictment'.

b CLEA 2001, s 106(b) amends CA 1990, s 242(2) with effect from 1 October 2001[2] by the deletion of 'on conviction on indictment'.

[1] Company Law Enforcement Act 2001 (Commencement) (No 2) Order 2001 (SI 438/2001).

[2] Company Law Enforcement Act 2001 (Commencement) (No 2) Order 2001 (SI 438/2001).

107 New section 249A of Act of 1990 — Power to reject documents sent for registration and amendments consequential on that section's insertion

(1) [...][a]

(2) [...][b]

Amendments

a CLEA 2001, s 107(1) inserts CA 1990, s 249A with effect from 1 March 2002.[1] See amended Act

b CLEA 2001, s 107(2) deletes CA 1990, s 248(3), (4) and (5) and s 249(5), (6) and (7) with effect from 1 March 2002.[2] See amended Act.

[1] Company Law Enforcement Act 2001 (Commencement) (No 4) Order 2002 (SI 43/2002).

[2] Company Law Enforcement Act 2001 (Commencement) (No 4) Order 2002 (SI 43/2002).

108 Amendment of section 258 of Act of 1990

Section 258 of the Act of 1990 is amended—

(a) [...][a]

(b) [...][b]

Amendments

a CLEA 2001, s 108(a) amends CA 1990, s 258 with effect from 1 October 2001[1] by the insertion after '63,' of '72(3).

b CLEA 2001, s 108(b) amends CA 1990, s 258 with effect from 1 October 2001[2] by the insertion after 'investment company' of ', or, in the case of the said Regulation 72(3), such a company other than one to which section 253(2A)(a) applies.

1 Company Law Enforcement Act 2001 (Commencement) (No 2) Order 2001 (SI 438/2001).

2 Company Law Enforcement Act 2001 (Commencement) (No 2) Order 2001 (SI 438/2001).

109 Notice by Director of intention to prosecute

(1) Where the Director has reasonable grounds for believing that a person has committed an offence under the Companies Acts which is subject to summary prosecution, the Director may deliver to the person or, where the person believed to have committed the offence is a company, to an officer of the company, a notice in the prescribed form stating—

- (a) that the person or company is alleged to have committed that offence,
- (b) that the person to whom the notice is delivered may during a period of 21 days beginning on the date of the notice—
  - (i) remedy as far as practicable to the satisfaction of the Director any default that constitutes the offence, and
  - (ii) make to the Director a payment of a prescribed amount which shall be accompanied by the notice, and
- (c) that a prosecution of the person to whom the notice is delivered in respect of the alleged offence will not be instituted during the period specified in the notice or, if the default is remedied to the satisfaction of the Director and the payment specified in the notice is made during that period, at all.

(2) Where a notice is given under subsection (1)—

- (a) a person to whom it applies may, during the period specified in the notice, make to the Director the payment specified in the notice, accompanied by the notice,
- (b) the Director may receive the payment and issue a receipt for it, and no payment so received shall in any circumstances be recoverable by the person who made it, and
- (c) a prosecution in respect of the alleged offence shall not be instituted in the period specified in the notice and, if the default is remedied to the satisfaction of the Director and the payment specified in the notice is made during that period, no prosecution in respect of the alleged offence shall be instituted at all.

(3) In a prosecution for an offence to which this section applies, the onus of showing that a payment pursuant to a notice under this section has been made shall lie on the defendant.

(4) All payments made to the Director in pursuance of this section shall be paid into or disposed of for the benefit of the Exchequer in such manner as the Minister for Finance may direct.

110 Provision of information to juries

(1) In a trial on indictment of an offence under the Companies Acts, the trial judge may order that copies of any or all of the following documents be given to the jury in any form that the judge considers appropriate:

(a) any document admitted in evidence at the trial,

(b) the transcript of the opening speeches of counsel,

(c) any charts, diagrams, graphics, schedules or summaries of evidence produced at the trial,

(d) the transcript of the whole or any part of the evidence given at the trial,

(e) the transcript of the trial judge's charge to the jury,

(f) any other document that in the opinion of the trial judge would be of assistance to the jury in its deliberations including, where appropriate, an affidavit by an accountant summarising, in a form which is likely to be comprehended by the jury, any transactions by the accused or other persons relevant to the offence.

(2) If the prosecutor proposes to apply to the trial judge for an order that a document mentioned in subsection (1)(f) shall be given to the jury, the prosecutor shall give a copy of the document to the accused in advance of the trial and, on the hearing of the application, the trial judge shall take into account any representations made by or on behalf of the accused in relation to it.

(3) Where the trial judge has made an order that an affidavit mentioned in subsection (1)(f) shall be given to the jury, he or she may in an appropriate case, with a view to further assisting the jury in its deliberations, require the accountant who prepared the affidavit to explain to the jury any relevant accounting procedures or principles.

[110A Certificate evidence and other matters

(1) In this section—

'appropriate officer' means—

(a) in respect of functions that, under the Companies Acts, are to be performed by the Minister, the Minister or an officer of the Minister,

(b) in respect of functions that, under the Companies Acts, are to be performed by the Director, the Director or an officer of the Director,

(c) in respect of functions that, under the Companies Acts, are to be performed by the inspector or inspectors appointed pursuant to Part II of the Companies Act 1990, an inspector or, where more than one inspector is appointed, any inspector, [...][a]

(d) in respect of functions that, under the Companies Acts, are to be performed by the registrar of companies, a registrar, an assistant registrar or any other person authorised in that behalf by the Minister under section 52(2) of the Companies (Amendment) (No. 2) Act [1999; and][b]

[(e) in respect of functions that, under the Companies Acts, are to be performed by the Central Bank and Financial Services Authority of Ireland—

(i) the Chief Executive of the Irish Financial Services Regulatory Authority, or

(ii) a person appointed by some other person to whom the Chief Executive of the Irish Financial Services Regulatory Authority has delegated responsibility for appointing persons for the purposes of this section;][c]

'item' includes a document and any other thing;

'notice' includes—

(a) any request, notice, letter, demand, pleading or other document, and

(b) any form of obligation that an individual may have under the Companies Acts by reason of a demand or request made by an appropriate officer, whether communicated in writing, orally or by other means.

(2) In any legal proceedings (including proceedings relating to an offence) a certificate signed by an appropriate officer in the course of performing his or her functions is, in the absence of evidence to the contrary, proof of the following:

(a) if it certifies that the officer has examined the relevant records and that it appears from them that during a stated period an item was not received from a stated person, proof that the person did not during that period furnish that item and that the item was not received;

(b) if it certifies that the officer has examined the relevant records and that it appears from them that a stated notice was not issued to a stated person, proof that the person did not receive the notice;

(c) if it certifies that the officer has examined the relevant records and that it appears from them that a stated notice was duly given to a stated person on a stated date, proof that the person received the notice on that date;

(d) if it certifies that the officer has examined the relevant records and that it appears from them that a stated notice was posted to a stated person at a stated address on a stated date, proof that the notice was received by that person at that address on a date 3 days after the date on which the document was posted;

(e) if it certifies that the officer has examined the relevant records and that it appears from them that a document was filed or registered with or delivered at a stated place, on a stated date or at a stated time is, proof that the document was filed or registered with or delivered at that place, on that date or at that time.

(3) A certificate referred to in subsection (2) that purports to be signed by an appropriate officer is admissible in evidence in any legal proceedings without proof of the officer's signature or that the officer was the proper person to sign the certificate.

(4) A document prepared pursuant to any provision of the Companies Acts and purporting to be signed by any person is deemed, in the absence of evidence to the contrary, to have been signed by that person.

(5) A document submitted under the Companies Acts on behalf of a person is deemed to have been submitted by the person unless that person proves that it was submitted without that person's consent or knowledge.

(6) A document that purports to be a copy of, or extract from, any document kept by or on behalf of the Director and that purports to be certified by—

(a) the Director,

(b) an officer of the Director, or

(c) any person authorised by the Director, to be a true copy of or extract from the document so kept is, without proof of the official position of the person purporting to so certify, admissible in evidence in all legal proceedings as of equal validity with the original document.

(7) A document that purports to be a copy of, or extract from, any document kept by the Minister and that purports to be certified by—

(a) the Minister,

(b) an officer of the Minister, or

(c) any person authorised by the Minister, to be a true copy of, or extract from, the document so kept is, without proof of the official position of the person purporting to so certify, admissible in evidence in all legal proceedings as of equal validity with the original document.

(8) A document that purports to be a copy of, or extract from, any document kept by an inspector and that is certified by—

(a) the inspector, or

(b) any person authorised by the inspector,

to be a true copy of, or extract from, the document so kept is, without proof of the official position of the person purporting to so certify, admissible in evidence in all legal proceedings as of equal validity with the original document.

[(8A) A document purporting to be a copy of, or extract from, any document kept by the Central Bank and Financial Services Authority of Ireland and that is certified by—

(a) the Chief Executive of the Irish Financial Services Regulatory Authority, or

(b) any person authorised by the Chief Executive of the Irish Financial Services Regulatory Authority,

to be a true copy of, or extract from, the document so kept is, without proof of the official position of the person purporting to so certify, admissible in evidence in all legal proceedings as of equal validity with the document so kept.][d]

(9) A document that purports to have been created by a person is presumed, in the absence of evidence to the contrary, to have been created by that person, and any statement contained in the document is presumed to have been made by the person unless the document expressly attributes its making to some other person.][e]

Amendments

a IFCMPA 2005, s 74 amends CLEA 2001, s 110A(1)(c) by deleting the word 'and' with effect from 1 July 2005.[1]

b IFCMPA 2005, s 74 amends CLEA 2001, s 110A(1)(c) by substituting '1999, and' for '1999' with effect from 1 July 2005.[2]

c IFCMPA 2005, s 74 inserts CLEA 2001, s 110A(1)(e) with effect from 1 July 2005.[3]

d IFCMPA 2005, s 74 inserts CLEA 2001, s 110A(8A) with effect from 1 July 2005.[4]

e CLEA 2001, s 110A was inserted by C(AA)A 2003, s 52 with effect from 6 April 2004.[5]

1 Investment Funds, Companies and Miscellaneous Provisions Act 2005 (Commencement) Order 2005 (SI 323/2005).

2 Investment Funds, Companies and Miscellaneous Provisions Act 2005 (Commencement) Order 2005 (SI 323/2005).

3 Investment Funds, Companies and Miscellaneous Provisions Act 2005 (Commencement) Order 2005 (SI 323/2005).

4 Investment Funds, Companies and Miscellaneous Provisions Act 2005 (Commencement) Order 2005 (SI 323/2005).

5 Companies (Auditing and Accounting) Act 2003 (Commencement) Order 2004 (SI 132/2004).

111 Non-application of certain provisions concerning acquisition by subsidiary of shares in its holding company

(1) None of the following—

(a) section 32 or 60 of the Act of 1963,

(b) Part XI of the Act of 1990, or

(c) the European Communities (Public Limited Companies Subsidiaries) Regulations, 1997 (S.I. No. 67 of 1997),

shall apply to the subscription by a subsidiary for, or the acquisition or holding by a subsidiary of, shares in its holding company if the subsidiary is a member of an approved stock exchange specified in section 17(2) of the Stock Exchange Act, 1995, acting in its capacity as a professional dealer in securities in the normal course of its business.

(2) In addition to the meaning assigned to it by section 155 of the Act of 1963, 'subsidiary' in this section means a company or other body corporate referred to in paragraph (2) of Regulation 4 of the European Communities (Public Limited Companies Subsidiaries) Regulations, 1997 (S.I. No. 67 of 1997), which, by virtue of paragraph (1) of that Regulation, is deemed to be a subsidiary of a public limited company.

112 Amendment of Freedom of Information Act, 1997

The Freedom of Information Act, 1997, is amended—

(a) [in section 46(1), by the insertion of the following after paragraph (b):

'(ba) a record held or created under the Companies Acts, 1963 to 2001, by the Director of Corporate Enforcement or an officer of the Director (other than a record concerning the general administration of the Director's office),][a]', and

(b) [in the First Schedule, by the insertion in paragraph 1(2) of 'the Office of the Director of Corporate Enforcement,'][b]

Amendments

a CLEA 2001, s 112(a) inserts Freedom of Information Act 1997, s 46(1)(ba) with effect from 28 November 2001.[1]

b CLEA 2001, s 112(b) amends Freedom of Information Act 1997, Sch 1, para 1(2) with effect from 28 November 2001.[2]

1 Company Law Enforcement Act 2001 (Commencement) (No 3) Order 2001 (SI 523/2001).

2 Company Law Enforcement Act 2001 (Commencement) (No 3) Order 2001 (SI 523/2001).

113 Amendment of section 7A of Bankers' Books Evidence Act, 1879

[Section 7A (inserted by the Central Bank Act, 1989) of the Bankers' Books Evidence Act, 1879, is amended by the insertion after 'Superintendent' and 'designated by him' of 'or the Director of Corporate Enforcement' and ', or officer of the Director of Corporate Enforcement nominated by the Director, as the case may be', respectively.][a]

Amendments

a CLEA 2001, s 113 amends the Bankers' Books Evidence Act 1879, s 7A (as inserted by the Central Bank Act 1989) with effect from 28 November 2001.[1]

[1] Company Law Enforcement Act 2001 (Commencement) (No 3) Order 2001 (SI 523/2001).

---

114 Amendment of section 9 of Consumer Information Act, 1978

[Section 9 of the Consumer Information Act, 1978, is amended by the substitution of the following for subsection (11):][a]

'(11)(a) Where the Director is through illness or any other cause absent from duty or the office of Director is vacant, the Minister may appoint a person to perform the functions of the Director during such absence or vacancy.

(b) The Minister shall not appoint a person under paragraph (a) of this subsection to perform the functions of the Director for a continuous period of more than 6 months during a vacancy in the office of Director.

(c) The Minister may at any time terminate an appointment under paragraph (a) of this subsection.

(d) A person appointed under paragraph (a) of this subsection has all the powers, rights and duties conferred on the Director by this Act and each reference in this Act to the Director shall be deemed to include a reference to such a person.'.

Amendments

a CLEA 2001, s 114, substitutes the Consumer Information Act 1978, s 11 with effect from 1 October 2001.[1]

[1] Company Law Enforcement Act 2001 (Commencement) (No 2) Order 2001 (SI 438/2001).

SCHEDULE

TRANSFER OF FUNCTIONS FROM MINISTER TO DIRECTOR
ACTS UNDER WHICH FUNCTIONS ARE TRANSFERRED

Section 14

PART 1
COMPANIES ACT, 1963
(NO. 33 OF 1963)

Item Section	*Subsection(s)*	*Section Title*	
(1)	*(2)*	*(3)*	*(4)*
1	131	(3), (4), (6)	Annual general meeting
2	384	(1)	Production and inspection of books when offence suspected

Amendments

CA 1963, ss 131 (3),(4),(6) and 384(1) are amended by the substitution for 'Minister', wherever occurring, of 'Director' with effect from 28 November 2001.[1] See amended Act.

[1] Company Law Enforcement Act 2001 (Commencement) (No 3) Order 2001 (SI 523/2001).

PART 2
COMPANIES ACT, 1990
(NO. 33 OF 1990)

Item Section	*Subsection(s)*	*Section Title*	
(1)	(2)	(3)	(4)
3	11	(3)	Inspectors' report
4	12	(2)	Proceedings on inspectors' report
5	14	(1), (2), (5)	Appointment and power of inspectors to investigate ownership of company
6	15	(1)	Power to require information as to persons interested in shares or debentures
7	16	(1), (5), (6), (7), (8), (13), (16), (18)	Power to impose restrictions on shares or debentures
8	66	(1), (4), (5), (8)	Investigation of share dealing
9	85	(6)	Penalty for failure to provide information
10	94	(2)	Obligation of professional secrecy
11	116	(3)	Cooperation with other authorities outside the State
12	117	(1)	Authorised persons Section 14.

Item Section	*Subsection(s)*	*Section Title*	
13	18	(2)	Obligation of professional secrecy
14	160	(2)	Disqualification of certain persons from acting as directors or auditors of or managing companies
15	240	(4)	Offences

Amendments

CA 1963, ss 11(3), 12(2), 14(1), (2), (5), 15(1), 16(1), (5), (6), (7), (8), (13), (16), (18), 66(1), (4), (5), (8), 85(6), 94(2), 116(3), 117(1), 118(2), 160(2), 240(4) are amended by the substitution for 'Minister', wherever occurring, of 'Director' with effect from 28 November 2001.[1] See amended Act.

[1] Company Law Enforcement Act 2001 (Commencement) (No 3) Order 2001 (SI 523/2001).

Companies (Auditing and Accounting) Act 2003

Number 44 of 2003

ARRANGEMENT OF SECTIONS

PART 1
PRELIMINARY MATTERS

PART 2
IRISH AUDITING AND ACCOUNTING SUPERVISORY AUTHORITY

PART 3

OTHER MEASURES TO STRENGTHEN THE REGULATION OF AUDITORS

PART 4

REGULATIONS AND MISCELLANEOUS MATTERS

SCHEDULE 1

TRANSFER OF FUNCTIONS TO SUPERVISORY AUTHORITY

SCHEDULE 2

An Act to provide for the establishment of a body to be known as the Irish Auditing And Accounting Supervisory Authority or, in the Irish language, Údarás Maoirseachta Iniúchta agus Cuntasaíochta na hÉireann, to give power to it to supervise the regulatory functions of the recognised accountancy bodies and other prescribed accountancy bodies, to amend company law to transfer to the supervisory authority existing functions relating to the recognition of accountancy bodies and to otherwise amend company law in relation to auditing, accounting and other matters. [23rd December, 2003]

Be It Enacted by the Oireachtas as Follows:

PART 1
PRELIMINARY MATTERS

1 Short title, collective citation and construction

(1) This Act may be cited as the Companies (Auditing and Accounting) Act 2003.

(2) This Act and the Companies Acts 1963 to 2001 may be cited together as the Companies Acts 1963 to 2003 and are to be construed together as one.

2 Commencement

(1) This Act comes into operation on the day that the Minister may, by order, appoint.

(2) Different days may be appointed under this section, by one or more orders, for different purposes or different provisions of this Act.

3 Interpretation

(1) In this Act—

'Act of 1963' means the Companies Act 1963;

'Act of 1986' means the Companies (Amendment) Act 1986;

'Act of 1990' means the Companies Act 1990;

'Companies Acts' means the Companies Act 1963 and every enactment, including this Act, that is to be construed as one with that Act.

(2) In this Act—

(a) a reference to a section, Part or Schedule is to a section or Part of, or a Schedule to, this Act, unless it is indicated that a reference to some other enactment is intended,

(b) a reference to a subsection, paragraph or subparagraph is to the subsection, paragraph or subparagraph of the provision in which the reference occurs, unless it is indicated that reference to some other provision is intended,

and

(c) a reference to any other enactment is to that enactment as amended by or under any other enactment, including this Act, unless the context otherwise requires.

PART 2
IRISH AUDITING AND ACCOUNTING SUPERVISORY AUTHORITY

4 Interpretation of this Part

(1) In this Part, except where the context otherwise requires—

'amount of turnover' and 'balance sheet total' have the same meanings as in section 8 of the Act of 1986;

'board' means the board of directors of the Supervisory Authority;

'chief executive officer' means the Chief Executive Officer of the Supervisory Authority;

'designated body' means a body that, under section 6(2), is a designated body at the relevant time;

'disciplinary committee' means any disciplinary committee or tribunal (however called) of a prescribed accountancy body;

'enactment' means a statute or an instrument made under a power conferred by a statute;

'functions' includes duties and responsibilities;

'member', in relation to a prescribed accountancy body, means—

(a) a person, or

(b) a firm,

that is, or was at the relevant time, subject to the investigation and disciplinary procedures approved under section 9(2)(c) for that body;

'Minister' means the Minister for Enterprise, Trade and Employment;

'parent undertaking' has the same meaning as in the 1992 Regulations;

'prescribed accountancy body' means—

(a) a recognised accountancy body, or

(b) any other body of accountants that is prescribed under section 48(1)(a) for the purposes of this Act;

['recognised accountancy body' means a body of accountants—

(a) recognised, or

(b) deemed, by virtue of section 191(3) or (4) of the Act of 1990, to be recognised,

by the Supervisory Authority for the purposes of—

(i) section 187 of the Act of 1990, or

(ii) the European Communities (Statutory Audits) (Directive 2006/43/EC) Regulations 2010;][a]

'reserve fund' means the fund established under section 15;

'standards', in relation to a prescribed accountancy body, means the rules, regulations and standards that body applies to its members and to which, by virtue of their membership, they are obliged to adhere;

'subsidiary undertaking' has the same meaning as in the 1992 Regulations;

'superannuation benefits' means pensions, gratuities and other allowances payable on resignation, retirement or death;

'Supervisory Authority' means the company designated by the Minister under section 5(1);

'the 1992 Regulations' means the European Communities (Companies: Group Accounts) Regulations 1992 (S.I. No. 201 of 1992);

'the 1993 Regulations' means the European Communities (Accounts) Regulations 1993 (S.I. No. 396 of 1993).

(2) In this Part 'material interest' is to be construed in accordance with section 2(3) of the Ethics in Public Office Act 1995.

Amendments

a Definition of 'recognised accountancy body' substituted by EC(SA)(Dir)R 2010, reg 14(a).

---

5 Establishment of Supervisory Authority

(1) The Minister may designate a public company to perform the functions and exercise the powers of the Supervisory Authority under this Act, if the following requirements are satisfied:

(a) the company is formed and registered under the Companies Acts after the commencement of this section;

(b) the company is a company limited by guarantee;

(c) the name of the company is the Irish Auditing and Accounting Supervisory Authority or in the Irish language Údarás Maoirseachta Iniúchta agus Cuntasaíochta na hÉireann;

(d) the memorandum of association and articles of association of the company are consistent with this Act.

(2) Section 6(1)(b) of the Act of 1963 does not apply to a company where the Minister informs the registrar of companies in writing that the Minister proposes to designate the company under subsection (1).

6 Membership

(1) The Supervisory Authority is to consist of the following members:

(a) each prescribed accountancy body that is a body corporate;

(b) if a prescribed accountancy body is not a body corporate, an individual or body corporate nominated by that prescribed accountancy body to be a member;

(c) each designated body that is a body corporate;

(d) if a designated body is not a body corporate, an individual or body corporate nominated by that designated body to be a member.

(2) Unless a regulation under section 48(1)(b) provides otherwise, each of the following is a designated body for the purposes of this section and section 11:

(a) the Irish Business and Employers Confederation;

(b) the Irish Congress of Trade Unions;

(c) the Irish Association of Investment Managers;

(d) the Irish Stock Exchange;

(e) the Pensions Board;

(f) the Irish Financial Services Regulatory Authority;

(g) the Revenue Commissioners;

(h) the Director of Corporate Enforcement;

(i) the Law Society of Ireland;

(j) any body prescribed under section 48(1)(b) as a designated body.

7 Alterations in memorandum and articles of association

Any alteration that is made in the memorandum of association or articles of association of the Supervisory Authority takes effect only if the alteration is made with the Minister's prior approval.

8 Objects

(1) The principal objects of the Supervisory Authority, which are to be included in its memorandum of association, are—

(a) to supervise how the prescribed accountancy bodies regulate and monitor their members,

(b) to promote adherence to high professional standards in the auditing and accountancy profession,

(c) to monitor whether the accounts of certain classes of companies and other undertakings comply with the Companies Acts, and, [where applicable, Article 4 of the IAS Regulation, and][a]

(d) to act as a specialist source of advice to the Minister on auditing and accounting matters.

(2) This section does not prevent or restrict the inclusion in the memorandum of association of all objects and powers, consistent with this Act, that are reasonable, necessary or proper for, or incidental or ancillary to, the due attainment of the principal objects of the Supervisory Authority.

Amendments

a Amended by Sch 1 Pt 5 of EC(IFRSMA)R 2005 (SI 116/2005).

---

9 Functions

(1) The Supervisory Authority shall do all things necessary and reasonable to further its objects.

(2) Without limiting its responsibilities under subsection (1), the functions of the Supervisory Authority are as follows:

(a) to grant recognition to bodies of accountants for the purposes of section 187 of the Act of 1990;

(b) to attach under section 192 of the Act of 1990 terms and conditions to the recognition of bodies of accountants, including terms and conditions—

(i) requiring changes to and the approval by the Supervisory Authority of their regulatory plans, and

(ii) requiring their annual reports to the Supervisory Authority on their regulatory plans to be prepared in the manner and form directed by the Supervisory Authority;

(c) to require changes to and to approve—

(i) the constitution and bye-laws of each prescribed accountancy body, including its investigation and disciplinary procedures and its standards, and

(ii) any amendments to the approved constitution or bye-laws of each prescribed accountancy body, including amendments to its investigation and disciplinary procedures and to its standards;

(d) to conduct under section 23 enquiries into whether a prescribed accountancy body has complied with the investigation and disciplinary procedures approved for that body under paragraph (c);

(e) to impose under section 23 sanctions on prescribed accountancy bodies;

(f) to undertake under section 24 investigations into possible breaches of the standards of a prescribed accountancy body;

(g) to supervise how each recognised accountancy body monitors its members and to undertake under section 25 reviews of those members;

(h) to co-operate with the recognised accountancy bodies and other interested parties in developing standards relating to the independence of auditors and to monitor the effectiveness of those standards;

(i) to monitor the effectiveness of provisions of the Companies Acts relating to the independence of auditors;

(j) to supervise the investigation and disciplinary procedures of each prescribed accountancy body, including by requiring access to its records and by requiring explanations about the performance of its regulatory and monitoring duties;

(k) to co-operate with the prescribed accountancy bodies and other interested parties in developing auditing and accounting standards and practice notes;

(l) to review under section 26 whether the accounts of companies and undertakings referred to in that section comply with the Companies Acts [and, where applicable, Article 4 of the IAS Regulation][a] and to make applications to the High Court to ensure compliance;

(m) to arrange for the regulation and supervision of individually authorised auditors by recognised accountancy bodies;

[(ma) to perform the functions conferred on it by transparency (regulated markets) law (within the meaning of Part 3 of the Investment Funds, Companies and Miscellaneous Provisions Act 2006) in respect of matters referred to in Article 24(4)(h) of the Transparency (Regulated Markets) Directive (within the meaning of that Part);][b]

[(mb) to perform the functions (and in particular the functions of public oversight) conferred on it by the European Communities (Statutory Audits) (Directive 2006/43/EC) Regulations 2010;][c]

(n) to perform any other duties or discharge any other responsibilities imposed on it by this Act or the Companies Acts.

Amendments

a Amended by Sch 1 Pt 5 of EC(IFRSMA)R 2005.

b Section 9(2)(ma) inserted by the IFCMPA 2006, s 16.

c Section 9(2)(mb) inserted by EC(SA)(Dir)R 2010, reg 14(b).

---

10 General powers

(1) The Supervisory Authority has the power to do anything that appears to it to be requisite, advantageous or incidental to, or to facilitate, the performance of its functions and that is not inconsistent with any enactment.

(2) A power conferred by subsection (1) is not to be considered to be limited merely by implication from another provision, whether of this or any other Act, that confers a power on the Supervisory Authority.

(3) The Supervisory Authority may adopt rules and issue guidelines concerning any matter that relates to its functions or powers.

(4) The Supervisory Authority may apply to the High Court for an order under section 29(7) compelling—

(a) a prescribed accountancy body to comply with a rule adopted or guideline issued under subsection (3) of this [section,][a]

(b) a recognised accountancy body to comply with a term or condition attached under section 192 of the Act of 1990 (before or after the amendment of that Act by section 32 of this Act) to the [recognition of that body, or][b]

[(c) a person [(whether an individual or otherwise)][c] on whom a relevant obligation or obligations is or are imposed to comply with that obligation or those obligations,][d]

if, in the Authority's opinion, [the body or other person concerned may fail or has failed to comply with the rule, guideline, term or condition or obligation or obligations, as the case may be.][e]

[(5) In subsection (4), the reference to a relevant obligation or obligations that is or are imposed on a person is a reference to an obligation or obligations that is or are imposed on the person by—

(a) provisions of transparency (regulated markets) law (within the meaning of Part 3 of the Investment Funds, Companies and Miscellaneous Provisions Act 2006) that implement Article 24(4)(h) of the Transparency (Regulated Markets) Directive (within the meaning of that [Part),][f]

(b) rules adopted by the Supervisory Authority under subsection (3) concerning the matters that relate to its functions under [section 9(2)(ma),][g]][h]

[(c) provisions of the European Communities (Statutory Audits) (Directive 2006/43/EC) Regulations 2010, or

(d) rules adopted by the Supervisory Authority under subsection (3) concerning the matters that relate to its functions under section 9(2)(mb).][i]

Amendments

a Amended by IFCMPA 2006, s 17(a)(i).

b Amended by IFCMPA 2006, s 17(a)(ii).

c Words '(whether an individual or otherwise)' inserted by EC(SA)(Dir)R 2010, reg 79(a).

d Amended by IFCMPA 2006, s 17(a)(iii).

e Amended by IFCMPA 2006, s 17(a)(iv).

f 'Part),' substituted for 'Part), or' by EC(SA)(Dir)R 2010, reg 79(b)(i).

g Words 'section 9(2)(ma),' substituted for 'section 9(2)(ma).' by EC(SA)(Dir)R 2010, reg 79(b)(ii).

h Inserted by IFCMPA 2006, s 17(b).

i Subparagraphs (c) and (d) inserted by EC(SA)(Dir)R 2010, reg 79(b)(iii).

11 Board of directors

(1) Subject to a regulation under section 48(1)(d), the board of directors of the Supervisory Authority is to consist of—

(a) not more than 14 directors (including the chairperson and the deputy chairperson) appointed by the Minister under subsection (2), and

(b) the person holding the office of chief executive officer who, by virtue of that [office, is a director,][a]

[and the persons appointed as such directors shall be persons who are knowledgeable in areas relevant to statutory audit.][b]

(2) Subject to a regulation under section 48(1)(d), the directors appointed by the Minister shall include—

(a) 3 persons nominated jointly by agreement among the prescribed accountancy bodies,

(b) 2 persons nominated by the Minister, one of whom—

(i) is neither an officer or employee of the Minister nor a member, officer or employee of a prescribed accountancy body, and

(ii) is appointed as chairperson by the Minister, and

(c) for each designated body, one person nominated by that body.

(3) Subject to a regulation under section 48(1)(d), the board shall not include at any one time more than 4 directors appointed under subsection (2) who are members of prescribed accountancy bodies, and of those 4 directors—

(a) 3 may be nominees of the prescribed accountancy bodies, and

(b) one may be a nominee of a designated body.

(4) If, at any time, more than one designated body proposes to nominate a member of a prescribed accountancy body for appointment to the board, the designated bodies proposing to do so shall decide among themselves which one of them is to nominate such a member.

(5) The directors may select the deputy chairperson from among those directors who are not members of a prescribed accountancy body.

(6) The term of office of a director appointed under subsection (2) shall be specified by the Minister when appointing the director and, subject to subsection (12), may not be less than 3 or more than 5 years.

(7) The members of the Supervisory Authority may not instruct the directors, at any meeting of those members or by any other means, regarding the carrying out of their duties as directors of the Supervisory Authority.

(8) Section 182 of the Act of 1963 does not apply to the Supervisory Authority.

(9) A director may resign by letter addressed to the Minister and copied to the Supervisory Authority, and the resignation takes effect on the date the Minister receives the letter.

(10) At any time, the Minister may remove for stated reasons any director appointed under subsection (2), including a director nominated under subsection (2)(b).

(11) The Minister shall fill any vacancy that arises on the board as a consequence of the resignation or removal of a director by appointing a replacement nominated in the same manner as the replaced director.

(12) A director appointed under subsection (11) to replace another holds office for the remainder of the replaced director's term of office, and the same terms and conditions apply to the new appointee.

(13) The directors may act despite one or more vacancies in their numbers.

Amendments

a Words 'office, is a director,' substituted for 'office, is a director.' by EC(SA)(Dir)R 2010, reg 81(a)(i).

b Words inserted by EC(SA)(Dir)R 2010, reg 81(a)(ii).

---

12 Chief executive officer

(1) The directors appointed under section 11(2) shall appoint a chief executive officer to—

(a) carry on, manage and control generally the administration and business of the Supervisory Authority, and

(b) perform any other functions that may be determined by the board.

(2) The chief executive officer holds office on and subject to the terms and conditions (including terms and conditions relating to remuneration and allowances) that the directors appointed under section 11(2) may, with the approval of the Minister given with the consent of the Minister for Finance, determine.

(3) The directors appointed under section 11(2) may remove the chief executive officer from office at any time.

13 Work programme

(1) The Supervisory Authority shall prepare and submit to the Minister a work programme for—

(a) in the case of the initial work programme, the period specified by the Minister, and

(b) in the case of each subsequent work programme, the period of 3 years beginning on the day after the last day of the period covered by the preceding work programme.

(2) In preparing the work programme, the Supervisory Authority shall have regard to the need to ensure the most beneficial, effective and efficient use of its resources and shall include the following information:

(a) the key strategies and activities the Supervisory Authority will pursue to further its objects and perform its functions;

(b) the outputs the Supervisory Authority aims to achieve and against which its performance will be assessed;

(c) the staff, resources and expenditures (including an annual programme of expenditure) necessary to pursue the strategies and activities mentioned in paragraph (a).

(3) In addition to capital and other expenditures, the annual programme of expenditure must include the amount of revenue to be received under section 14(1) and (2) that is to be paid into the reserve fund.

(4) With the consent of the Minister for Finance and after considering the views of the prescribed accountancy bodies, the Minister may approve, with or without amendment, the annual programme of expenditure.

(5) If the annual programme of expenditure is amended under subsection (4), the Supervisory Authority—

(a) may revise any other part of the work programme, and

(b) if it does so, shall submit to the Minister the revised work programme, including the annual programme of expenditure as amended under subsection (4).

(6) The Supervisory Authority may—

(a) if it considers it necessary to do so, undertake an interim review of a work programme, and

(b) submit to the Minister, within the period covered by that programme, an amended or supplementary work programme, including an amended or supplementary annual programme of expenditure.

(7) Subsections (4) and (5) apply with any necessary changes if an amended or a supplementary annual programme of expenditure is submitted to the Minister.

(8) Subject to subsection (9), the Minister shall ensure that a copy of each work programme (including each revised, amended or supplementary work programme) is laid before each House of the Oireachtas not later than 60 days after the date on which it was submitted to the Minister.

(9) If a revised work programme (including a revised amended or supplementary work programme) is submitted to the Minister before the unrevised work programme is laid before the Houses of the Oireachtas as required by subsection (8), only the revised work programme need be laid before the Houses.

(10) The Minister may not give directions to the Supervisory Authority concerning the discharge of a work programme, including an amended or a supplementary work programme.

14 Funding

(1) For the purposes specified in subsection (3), in each financial year, a grant not exceeding 40 per cent of the programme of expenditure approved for that year under section 13, shall, subject to the conditions, if any, that the Minister thinks proper, be paid to the Supervisory Authority out of money provided by the Oireachtas.

(2) For the purposes specified in subsection (3), the Supervisory Authority may impose, with the Minister's consent and subject to subsections (4) to (6), one or more levies in each financial year of the Supervisory Authority on each prescribed accountancy body.

(3) Money received by the Supervisory Authority under this section may be used only for the purposes of meeting expenses properly incurred by it in performing its functions and exercising its powers under—

(a) sections 24 and 26, in the case of money set aside for, or paid into, the reserve fund in accordance with section 15,

or

(b) any provision of this Act, other than sections 24 and 26, in the case of money not so set aside for, or paid into, that fund.

(4) The total amount levied in any financial year of the Supervisory Authority on all prescribed accountancy bodies—

(a) may not exceed 60 per cent of the programme of expenditure approved for that year under section 13, and

(b) requires the Minister's approval before consent is given to the imposition of any levy in that year.

(5) The Supervisory Authority shall—

(a) establish criteria for apportioning a levy among the classes of prescribed accountancy bodies,

(b) submit the criteria to the Minister for approval before imposing the levy, and

(c) specify the date on which the levy is due to be paid by those bodies.

(6) As a consequence of the apportionment of a levy under subsection (5), different classes of prescribed accountancy bodies may be required to pay different amounts of the levy.

(7) Before consenting to the imposition of a levy under this section, the Minister shall consult with the prescribed accountancy bodies and may consult with any other persons who, in the Minister's opinion, are interested in the matter.

(8) The Supervisory Authority may recover, as a simple contract debt in any court of competent jurisdiction, from a prescribed accountancy body from which the levy is due, a levy imposed under this section.

(9) For the purpose of providing for activities specified in its work programme, the Supervisory Authority may, from time to time, borrow money subject to the consent of the Minister and the Minister for Finance and to such conditions as they may specify.

15 Reserve fund and levy

(1) The Supervisory Authority shall—

(a) subject to any limit that the Minister may specify, establish and maintain a reserve fund to be used only for the purposes of performing its functions and exercising its powers under sections 24 and 26,

(b) set aside in each financial year for the reserve fund a portion of the revenue received under section 14(1) and (2),

(c) pay into the reserve fund in each financial year—

(i) the amount set aside under paragraph (b) for the fund or, if that amount is amended under section 13(4), the amended amount,

(ii) the proceeds of any levy imposed under subsection (2) of this section, and

(iii) any amounts paid to the Supervisory Authority under section 23(5)(c) or 24(7) and any costs recovered under section 26(5) or (8),

and

(d) promptly inform the Minister if, in any financial year, the total amount in the reserve fund is likely to exceed any limit specified by the Minister for the purposes of this section.

(2) With the Minister's consent and after consulting with any persons who are interested in the matter, the Supervisory Authority may, subject to subsections (3) to (7), impose in each financial year of the Supervisory Authority one or more levies on the following:

(a) each public limited company (whether listed or unlisted);

(b) each private company limited by shares that, in both the most recent financial year and the immediately preceding financial year of the company, meets the following criteria:

(i) its balance sheet total for the year exceeds—

(A) €25,000,000, or

(B) if an amount is prescribed under section 48(1)(e) for the purpose of this provision, the prescribed amount;

(ii) the amount of its turnover for the year exceeds—

(A) €50,000,000, or

(B) if an amount is prescribed under section 48(1)(e) for the purpose of this provision, the prescribed amount;

(c) each private company limited by shares that is a parent undertaking, if the parent undertaking and all of its subsidiary undertakings together, in both the most recent financial year and the immediately preceding financial year of the parent undertaking, meet the criteria in paragraph (b);

(d) each undertaking referred to in Regulation 6 of the 1993 Regulations that, in both the most recent financial year and the immediately preceding financial year of the undertaking, meets the criteria in paragraph (b);

(e) each undertaking referred to in Regulation 6 of the 1993 Regulations that is a parent undertaking, if the parent undertaking and all of its subsidiary undertakings together, in both the most recent financial year and the immediately preceding financial year of the parent undertaking, meet the criteria in paragraph (b).

(3) The total amount levied under subsection (2) in any financial year of the Supervisory Authority on all companies and undertakings—

(a) may not exceed the total amount paid into the reserve fund for that year under subsection (1)(c)(i), and

(b) requires the Minister's approval before consent is given to the imposition of any levy in that year.

(4) In determining whether to approve the total amount referred to in subsection (3), the Minister may—

(a) have regard to the Supervisory Authority's work programme,

and

(b) give due consideration to the use to which the reserve fund was put in the previous financial year.

(5) The Supervisory Authority shall—

(a) establish criteria for apportioning a levy among the classes of companies and undertakings liable to pay the levy under subsection (2),

(b) submit the criteria to the Minister for approval before imposing the levy, and

(c) specify the date on which the levy is due to be paid by those companies and undertakings.

(6) As a consequence of the apportionment of a levy under subsection (5), different classes of companies or undertakings may be required to pay different amounts of the levy.

(7) Subsection (2) does not apply in respect of a company or an undertaking of a class exempted under section 48(1)(j) from this section.

(8) Where both a parent undertaking and one or more of its subsidiary undertakings would otherwise be liable to pay a levy imposed under this section, only the parent undertaking is required to pay the levy.

(9) Subsection (8) applies whether the parent undertaking is a public limited company, a private limited company or an undertaking referred to in Regulation 6 of the 1993 Regulations.

(10) The Supervisory Authority may recover, as a simple contract debt in any court of competent jurisdiction, from a company or undertaking from which the levy is due, a levy imposed under this section.

16 Excess revenue

(1) The Supervisory Authority shall apply any excess of its revenue over its expenditure in any year to meet its programme of expenditure approved for the subsequent year under section 13, and the amounts payable under section 14(1) and (2) for the subsequent year shall be appropriately reduced.

(2) Money in, or set aside for, the reserve fund is not considered to be revenue for the purposes of this section.

17 Staff

(1) Subject to subsection (2) and to the limits of the staffing numbers specified under section 13 in its work programme, the Supervisory Authority may, from time to time, appoint persons to be members of its staff.

(2) The numbers, grades and terms or conditions of its staff shall be determined by the Supervisory Authority with the approval of the Minister given with the consent of the Minister for Finance.

(3) The Supervisory Authority may from time to time engage the services of professional and other advisers.

18 Disclosure of interests by directors

(1) In this section—

'meeting' means a meeting of the board of the Supervisory Authority or of a committee of its directors;

'specified matter' means—

(a) an arrangement to which the Supervisory Authority is a party or a proposed such arrangement, or

(b) a contract or other agreement with the Supervisory Authority or a proposed such contract or other agreement.

(2) Any director of the Supervisory Authority who is present at a meeting where a specified matter arises and who, otherwise than in his or her capacity as such a director, has a material interest in that matter shall—

(a) at the meeting disclose to the Authority the fact of the interest and its nature,

(b) absent himself or herself from the meeting or the part of the meeting during which the matter is discussed,

(c) take no part in any deliberations of the directors relating to the matter, and

(d) refrain from voting on any decision relating to the matter.

(3) Where a director discloses a material interest under this section—

(a) the disclosure shall be recorded in the minutes of the meeting concerned, and

(b) for as long as the matter to which the disclosure relates is being dealt with by the meeting, the director shall not be counted in the quorum for the meeting.

(4) Where at a meeting a question arises as to whether or not a course of conduct, if pursued by a director, would constitute a failure by him or her to comply with subsection (2)—

(a) the chairperson of the meeting may, subject to subsection (5), determine the question,

(b) the chairperson's determination is final, and

(c) the particulars of the determination shall be recorded in the minutes of the meeting.

(5) If the chairperson is the director in respect of whom the question arises, the other directors present at the meeting shall choose one of their number to be the chairperson of the meeting for the purposes of subsection (4).

(6) A director of the Supervisory Authority who, otherwise than in his or her capacity as such a director, has a material interest in a specified matter shall neither influence nor seek to influence any decision to be made by the Authority in relation to that matter.

(7) On being satisfied that a director of the Supervisory Authority has contravened subsection (2) or (6), the Minister may—

(a) if he or she thinks fit, remove that director from office, or

(b) if the director concerned is the chief executive officer, recommend to the board that he or she be removed from that office.

(8) A director removed from office under this section is disqualified for appointment under section 11 or 12.

(9) Section 194 of the Act of 1963 does not apply to a director of the Supervisory Authority.

(10) Nothing in this section prejudices the operation of any rule of law restricting directors of a company from having any interest in contracts with the company.

19 Disclosure of interests by staff

(1) A member of the staff of the Supervisory Authority who, otherwise than in his or her capacity as such a member, has a material interest in a specified matter, as defined in section 18(1), shall—

(a) disclose to the Authority the fact of the interest and its nature,

(b) take no part in the negotiation of the arrangement, contract or other agreement concerned or in any deliberation by the Authority or members of its staff relating to that matter,

(c) refrain from making any recommendation relating to the matter, and

(d) neither influence nor seek to influence a decision to be made in relation to the matter.

(2) Subsection (1) does not apply to contracts or proposed contracts of employment of members of the staff of the Supervisory Authority with the Authority.

(3) Where a person contravenes this section, the Supervisory Authority may make such alterations to the person's terms and conditions of employment as it considers appropriate or terminate the person's contract of employment.

20 Superannuation

(1) The Supervisory Authority may, if it considers it appropriate to do so, prepare and submit to the Minister a scheme or schemes for granting superannuation benefits to or in respect of one or more of the following:

(a) the chief executive officer;

(b) any staff of the Authority.

(2) Each superannuation scheme shall fix the time and conditions of retirement for all persons to or in respect of whom superannuation benefits are payable under the scheme, and different times and conditions may be fixed in respect of different classes of persons.

(3) A superannuation scheme submitted to the Minister under this section shall, if approved by the Minister with the consent of the Minister for Finance, be carried out in accordance with its terms.

(4) A superannuation scheme may be amended or revoked by a subsequent scheme prepared, submitted and approved under this section.

(5) The Supervisory Authority may not grant, or enter any arrangement for the provision of, any superannuation benefit to or in respect of a person referred to in subsection (1) except in accordance with a superannuation scheme approved under this section or approved by the Minister with the consent of the Minister for Finance.

(6) If any dispute arises as to the claim of any person to, or the amount of, a superannuation benefit payable in pursuance of a superannuation scheme approved under this section, the dispute shall be submitted to the Minister who shall refer it to the Minister for Finance whose decision shall be final.

(7) The Minister shall ensure that a superannuation scheme approved under this section is laid before each House of the Oireachtas as soon as practicable after it is approved.

(8) Either House of the Oireachtas may, by a resolution passed within 21 sitting days after the day on which the superannuation scheme is laid before it, annul the scheme.

(9) The annulment of a superannuation scheme under subsection (8) takes effect immediately on the passing of the resolution concerned, but does not affect the validity of anything done under the scheme before the passing of the resolution.

21 Accounts and audit

(1) The Supervisory Authority shall keep records of, and prepare all proper and usual accounts of—

(a) all income received by it, including the sources,

(b) all expenditure incurred by it, and

(c) its assets and liabilities.

(2) Not later than 3 months after the end of the financial year to which the accounts relate, the Supervisory Authority shall submit the accounts prepared under this section to the Comptroller and Auditor General for audit.

(3) After the audit, the Comptroller and Auditor General shall present to the Minister the audited accounts together with the Comptroller and Auditor General's report.

(4) The Minister shall ensure that, as soon as possible after the audited accounts and the report are presented to the Minister, copies of them are—

(a) laid before each House of the Oireachtas, and

(b) supplied to the prescribed accountancy bodies.

(5) The Supervisory Authority shall—

(a) at the Minister's request, permit any person appointed by the Minister to examine its accounts in respect of any financial year or other period,

(b) facilitate the examination of the accounts by the appointed person, and

(c) pay the fee that may be set by the Minister for the examination.

22 Accountability mechanisms

(1) As soon as practicable but not later than 4 months after the end of each financial year, the Supervisory Authority shall make a written report to the Minister of its activities during that year.

(2) The annual report must be prepared in such manner and form as the Minister may direct.

(3) The Minister shall ensure that a copy of the annual report is laid before each House of the Oireachtas not later than 6 months after the end of the financial year to which the report relates.

(4) Whenever required to do so by the Committee of Dáil Éireann established under the Standing Orders of Dáil Éireann to examine and report to Dáil Éireann on the appropriation accounts and reports of the Comptroller and Auditor General, the chief executive officer and the chairperson of the board shall give evidence to that Committee on the following:

(a) the regularity and propriety of the transactions recorded or to be recorded in any account subject to audit by the Comptroller and Auditor General that the Supervisory Authority is required by law to prepare;

(b) the Supervisory Authority's economy and efficiency in using its resources;

(c) systems, procedures and practices used by the Supervisory Authority for evaluating the effectiveness of its operations;

(d) any matter affecting the Supervisory Authority that is referred to in a special report under section 11(2) of the Comptroller and Auditor General (Amendment) Act 1993 or in any other report of the Comptroller and Auditor General that is laid before Dáil Éireann, in so far as the other report relates to a matter specified in any of paragraphs (a) to (c);

(5) Whenever requested by any other committee appointed by either House of the Oireachtas or appointed jointly by both Houses, the chief executive officer and the chairperson of the board shall account to the committee for the performance of the functions and the exercise of the powers of the Supervisory Authority.

(6) The Supervisory Authority shall have regard to any recommendations relating to its functions or powers that are made by a committee in response to an account given under subsection (5).

(7) In performing duties under subsection (4) or (5), neither the chief executive officer nor the chairperson of the board shall question or express an opinion on the merits of any policy of the Government or a Minister of the Government or on the merits of the objectives of such a policy.

23 Intervention in disciplinary process of prescribed accountancy bodies

(1) In this section, 'approved investigation and disciplinary procedures' means—

(a) in relation to a prescribed accountancy body that is a recognised accountancy body, the investigation and disciplinary procedures approved under section 9(2)(c) of this Act or approved under the Act of 1990 before or after the amendment of that Act by section 32 of this Act, and

(b) in relation to any other prescribed accountancy body, the investigation and disciplinary procedures approved under section 9(2)(c) of this Act.

(2) Following a complaint or on its own initiative, the Supervisory Authority may, for the purpose of determining whether a prescribed accountancy body has complied with the approved investigation and disciplinary procedures, enquire into—

(a) a decision by that body not to undertake an investigation into a possible breach of its standards by a member,

(b) the conduct of an investigation by that body into a possible breach of its standards by a member, or

(c) any other decision of that body relating to a possible breach of its standards by a member, unless the matter is or has been the subject of an investigation under section 24(2) relating to that member.

(3) For the purposes of an enquiry under this section, the Supervisory Authority may—

(a) inspect and make copies of all relevant documents in the possession or control of the prescribed accountancy body, and

(b) require the prescribed accountancy body to explain why it reached a decision referred to in subsection (2)(a) or (c) or to explain how it conducted its investigation.

(4) If, at any time before completing an enquiry under this section into a matter relating to a member of a prescribed accountancy body, the Supervisory Authority forms the opinion that it is appropriate or in the public interest that the matter be investigated under section 24, the Authority may apply to the High Court for permission to investigate the matter under that section.

(5) If not satisfied after completing the enquiry that the prescribed accountancy body complied with the approved investigation and disciplinary procedures, the Supervisory Authority may advise or admonish the prescribed accountancy body or may censure it by doing one or more of the following:

(a) annulling all or part of a decision of that body relating to the matter that was the subject of the enquiry;

(b) directing that body to conduct an investigation or a fresh investigation into the matter;

(c) requiring that body to pay to the Supervisory Authority an amount not exceeding the greater of the following:

(i) €125,000;

(ii) the amount prescribed under section 48(1)(f).

(6) Where the Supervisory Authority applies under this section to the High Court for permission to investigate under section 24 any matter relating to a member of a prescribed accountancy body or decides to direct a prescribed accountancy body to conduct an investigation or a fresh investigation under this section into any matter, the following rules apply:

(a) in the case of an application to the High Court for permission to investigate a matter, any decision of that body relating to the matter is suspended if and as soon as the body is notified by the Supervisory Authority that permission has been granted under section 29(3);

(b) in the case of a direction to conduct an investigation, any decision of that body relating to the matter is suspended as soon as the body is notified by the Supervisory Authority of the direction;

(c) in the case of a direction to conduct a fresh investigation, any decision of that body relating to the matter is suspended if and as soon as the body is notified by the Supervisory Authority that the direction has been confirmed under section 29(6).

(7) The Supervisory Authority may publish each decision made under subsection (5) and the reasons for the decision after giving the prescribed accountancy body and the member concerned not less than 3 months notice in writing of its intention to do so.

(8) The prescribed accountancy body or the member concerned may appeal to the High Court against a decision made by the Supervisory Authority under subsection (5).

(9) An appeal under subsection (8) must be brought before the expiry of the notice given under subsection (7) to the prescribed accountancy body and the member concerned.

(10) If not satisfied that a prescribed accountancy body has, when undertaking an investigation or a fresh investigation into the matter under subsection (5)(b), complied with the approved investigation and disciplinary procedures, the Supervisory Authority may appeal to the High Court against any decision of the prescribed accountancy body relating to the matter.

(11) An appeal under subsection (10) must be brought within 3 months after the Supervisory Authority was notified by the prescribed accountancy body of its decision.

(12) For the purposes of this section, any decision made or any investigation conducted by the disciplinary committee of a prescribed accountancy body is considered to have been made or conducted by the prescribed accountancy body.

[(13) For the purposes of this section 'member', in addition to the meaning assigned to that expression by section 4(1), includes, in relation to a prescribed accountancy body that is a recognised accountancy body, an individual or firm who or which, though not a member of the recognised accountancy body, is an individual or firm in relation to whom that body may exercise powers under the European Communities (Statutory Audits) (Directive 2006/43/EC) 2010.][a]

Amendments

a Subsection (13) inserted by EC(SA)(Dir)R 2010, reg 81(b).

---

24 Investigation of possible breaches of standards of prescribed accountancy bodies

(1) In this section—

'client' includes an individual, a body corporate, an unincorporated body of persons and a partnership;

'refusal' includes failure and 'refuses' includes fails;

'relevant person', in relation to an investigation of a member of a prescribed accountancy body, means—

(a) a member of the prescribed accountancy body,

(b) a client or former client of such member,

(c) if the client or former client is a body corporate, a person who is or was an officer, employee or agent of the client or former client,

(d) the prescribed accountancy body or a person who is or was an officer, employee or agent of that body, or

(e) any person whom the Supervisory Authority reasonably believes has information or documents relating to the investigation other than information or documents the disclosure of which is prohibited or restricted by law.

(2) If, in the Supervisory Authority's opinion, it is appropriate or in the public interest to undertake an investigation into a possible breach of a prescribed accountancy body's standards by a member, the Authority may do so—

(a) following a complaint, or

(b) on its own initiative,

but no investigation may be undertaken into a matter that is or has been the subject of an enquiry under section 23 relating to that member except with the permission of the High Court granted on application under section 23(4).

(3) For the purposes of an investigation under this section, the Supervisory Authority may require a relevant person to do one or more of the following:

- (a) produce to the Supervisory Authority all books or documents relating to the investigation that are in the relevant person's possession or control;
- (b) attend before the Supervisory Authority;
- (c) give the Supervisory Authority any other assistance in connection with the investigation that the relevant person is reasonably able to give.

(4) For the purposes of an investigation under this section, the Supervisory Authority may—

- (a) examine on oath, either by word of mouth or on written interrogatories, a relevant person,
- (b) administer oaths for the purposes of the examination, and
- (c) record, in writing, the answers of a person so examined and require that person to sign them.

(5) The Supervisory Authority may certify the refusal to the High Court if a relevant person refuses to do one or more of the following:

- (a) produce to the Supervisory Authority any book or document that it is the person's duty under this section to produce;
- (b) attend before the Supervisory Authority when required to do so under this section;
- (c) answer a question put to the person by the Supervisory Authority with respect to the matter under investigation.

(6) On receiving a certificate of refusal concerning a relevant person, the Court may enquire into the case and, after hearing any evidence that may be adduced, may do one or more of the following:

- (a) direct that the relevant person attend or re-attend before the Supervisory Authority or produce particular books or documents or answer particular questions put to him or her by the Supervisory Authority;
- (b) direct that the relevant person need not produce particular books or documents or answer particular questions put to him or her by the Supervisory Authority;
- (c) make any other ancillary or consequential order or give any other direction that the Court thinks fit.

(7) If the Supervisory Authority finds that the member committed a breach of the prescribed accountancy body's standards—

- (a) the Supervisory Authority may impose on the member any sanction to which the member is liable under the approved constitution and bye-laws of the prescribed accountancy body (including a monetary sanction), and
- (b) in addition, the member is liable to pay the amount specified by the Supervisory Authority towards its costs in investigating and determining the

case, excluding any costs of or incidental to an enquiry by the Court under [subsection (6),][a]

[and the fact of a sanction having been imposed on the member by the Supervisory Authority shall be disclosed by the Authority to the public and that disclosure shall include—

(i) in a case where the member is making an appeal to the High Court against the decision of the Supervisory Authority, an indication that that is so, and

(ii) if the Supervisory Authority considers it appropriate, such further particulars with respect to the matter as it thinks fit.][b]

[(7A) The manner of a disclosure under subsection (7), and the time at which it is made, shall be such as the Supervisory Authority determines to be appropriate.][c]

(8) The member who is the subject of a decision made by the Supervisory Authority under subsection (7) may appeal to the High Court against the decision.

(9) An appeal under subsection (8) must be brought within 3 months after the member concerned was notified by the Supervisory Authority of its decision.

(10) The production of any books or documents under this section by a person who claims a lien on them does not prejudice the lien.

(11) Any information produced or answer given by a member of a prescribed accountancy body in compliance with a requirement under this section may be used in evidence against the member in any proceedings whatsoever, save proceedings for an offence (other than perjury in respect of such an answer).

[(11A) For the avoidance of doubt, the following matters may, without prejudice to the generality of the preceding provisions, be the subject of an investigation by the Supervisory Authority under this section, namely matters—

(a) in relation to which a competent authority (within the meaning of the European Communities (Statutory Audits) (Directive 2006/43/EC) Regulations 2010) has decided not to withdraw a person's approval under those Regulations as a statutory auditor or audit firm; or

(b) which either—

(i) have not been considered by such a competent authority as grounds for the withdrawal of a person's approval under those Regulations as a statutory auditor or audit firm; or

(ii) having been considered by it as such grounds, are not considered by it to disclose a prima facie case for proceeding further.

(11B) Where—

(a) those matters are the subject of such an investigation by the Supervisory Authority; and

(b) a breach of standards is found by the Supervisory Authority,

subsection (7)(a) shall be read as requiring or enabling (depending on whether the breach of standards found falls within Part 4 or Chapter 3 of Part 8 of the European Communities (Statutory Audits) (Directive 2006/43/EC) Regulations 2010) the Supervisory Authority to withdraw the approval under those Regulations of the person concerned as a statutory auditor or audit firm; where such an approval is withdrawn by it, the following provisions of those Regulations shall, with any necessary modifications, apply (and not subsections (8) and (9) of this section) to that withdrawal, namely Regulation 33(11) to (14) (or, as the case may be, Regulation 34(11) to (14)) and Regulation 35.

(11C) Subsection (11B) does not prejudice the imposition, in the circumstances concerned, by the Supervisory Authority of another sanction referred to in subsection (7)(*a*) in addition to a withdrawal of approval (where withdrawal of the approval is mandatory under the foregoing Regulations) or in lieu of a withdrawal of approval (where such withdrawal is not so mandatory).][d]

(12) A finding or decision of the Supervisory Authority under this section is not a bar to any civil or criminal proceedings against the member who is the subject of the finding or decision.

[(13) For the purposes of this section 'member', in addition to the meaning assigned to that expression by section 4(1), includes, in relation to a prescribed accountancy body that is a recognised accountancy body, an individual or firm who or which, though not a member of the recognised accountancy body, is an individual or firm in relation to whom that body may exercise powers under the European Communities (Statutory Audits) (Directive 2006/43/EC) 2010.][e]

Amendments

a Words 'subsection (6),' substituted for 'subsection (6).' by EC(SA)(Dir)R 2010, reg 90(a).

b Words inserted by EC(SA)(Dir)R 2010, reg 90(b).

c Subsection (7A) inserted by EC(SA)(Dir)R 2010, reg 90(c).

d Subsections (11A)–(11C) inserted by EC(SA)(Dir)R 2010, reg 36.

e Subsection (13) inserted by EC(SA)(Dir)R 2010, reg 81(c).

25 Review of members of recognised accountancy bodies

(1) The Supervisory Authority may, if in its opinion it is appropriate to do so, undertake a review of a member of a recognised accountancy body to determine whether that body has been or is regulating its members in the manner approved under section 9(2)(b) of this Act or approved under the Act of 1990 before or after the amendment of that Act by section 32 of this Act.

(2) For the purposes of a review under this section—

(a) the Supervisory Authority may inspect and make copies of all relevant documents in the possession or control of the recognised accountancy body whose practices are under review,

(b) the member of the recognised accountancy body shall cooperate with the Supervisory Authority as if the recognised accountancy body were undertaking the review, and

(c) if the member fails to co-operate in accordance with paragraph (b) of this subsection, section 24(3) to (7) applies, with any necessary modifications, in relation to the member as if the review were an investigation under section 24.

26 Review of whether accounts comply with Companies Acts

(1) In this section—

'relevant undertaking' means—

(a) a public limited company (whether unlisted or listed),

(b) a subsidiary undertaking of a public limited company referred to in paragraph (a) (whether the subsidiary undertaking is a company or is an undertaking referred to in Regulation 6 of the 1993 Regulations),

(c) a private company limited by shares that, in both the relevant financial year and the immediately preceding financial year of the company, meets the following criteria:

(i) its balance sheet total for the year exceeds—

(A) €25,000,000, or

(B) if an amount is prescribed under section 48(1)(h) for the purpose of this provision, the prescribed amount;

(ii) the amount of its turnover for the year exceeds—

(A) €50,000,000, or

(B) if an amount is prescribed under section 48(1)(h) for the purpose of this provision, the prescribed amount,

(d) a private company limited by shares that is a parent undertaking, if the parent undertaking and all of its subsidiary undertakings together, in both the relevant financial year and the immediately preceding financial year of the parent undertaking, meet the criteria in paragraph (c),

(e) each subsidiary undertaking of a parent undertaking that comes within paragraph (d),

(f) an undertaking referred to in Regulation 6 of the 1993 Regulations that, in both the relevant financial year and the immediately preceding financial year of the undertaking, meets the criteria in paragraph (c),

(g) an undertaking referred to in Regulation 6 of the 1993 Regulations that is a parent undertaking, if the parent undertaking and all of its subsidiary undertakings together, in both the relevant financial year and the immediately preceding financial year of the parent undertaking, meet the criteria in paragraph (c), or

(h) each subsidiary undertaking of a parent undertaking that comes within paragraph (g), but does not include a company or an undertaking of a class exempted under section 48(1)(j) from this section.

(2) A reference in this section to the directors of a relevant undertaking is to be construed in the case of an undertaking that does not have a board of directors as a reference to the corresponding persons appropriate to that undertaking.

(3) Subject to subsection (12), the Supervisory Authority may give notice to the directors of a relevant undertaking concerning its annual accounts where—

(a) a copy of the annual accounts has been sent out under section 159 of the Act of 1963 or laid before the undertaking at its annual general meeting or delivered to the registrar of companies, and

(b) it appears to the Supervisory Authority that there is, or may be, a question whether the annual accounts comply with the Companies Acts [and, where applicable, Article 4 of the IAS Regulation][a].

(4) The notice to the directors of the relevant undertaking must specify—

(a) the matters in respect of which it appears to the Supervisory Authority that the question of compliance with the Companies Acts [and, where applicable, Article 4 of the IAS Regulation][a] arises or may arise, and

(b) a period of not less than 30 days within which those directors are required to give the Supervisory Authority an explanation of the annual accounts or to prepare revised annual accounts that comply with the Companies Acts [and, where applicable, Article 4 of the IAS Regulation][a].

(5) If before the end of the specified period, or such longer period as the Supervisory Authority may allow, the directors of the relevant undertaking prepare revised annual accounts, the Supervisory Authority may, taking account of the circumstances of the case and the degree of co-operation by the directors with the Supervisory Authority, require that undertaking to pay some or all of the costs the Supervisory Authority incurred under this section in relation to that undertaking.

(6) If at the end of the specified period, or such longer period as the Supervisory Authority may allow, the directors of the relevant undertaking have, in the Supervisory Authority's opinion, neither given a satisfactory explanation of the annual accounts nor revised them to comply with the Companies Acts [and, where applicable, Article 4 of the IAS Regulation][a], the Supervisory Authority may apply to the High Court for a declaration of non-compliance and an order under subsection (8).

(7) If an application is made to the Court under subsection (6), the Supervisory Authority shall give to the registrar of companies for registration—

(a) notice of the application, and

(b) a general statement of the matters at issue in the proceedings.

(8) If satisfied after hearing the application that the relevant undertaking's annual accounts referred to in subsection (3) do not comply with the Companies Acts [and, where applicable, Article 4 of the IAS Regulation][a], the Court may make a declaration to that effect and may, by order, do one or more of the following:

(a) require the directors to revise the annual accounts so that they comply with those Acts [and, where applicable, Article 4 of the IAS Regulation][a];

(b) give directions respecting one or more of the following:

(i) the auditing of the revised annual accounts;

(ii) the revision of any directors' report;

(iii) the steps to be taken by the directors to bring the court order to the notice of persons likely to rely on the annual accounts that were the subject of the declaration;

(iv) such other matters as the Court thinks fit;

(c) require the directors of the relevant undertaking to pay—

(i) the costs incurred by the Supervisory Authority under subsections (3) and (4) in relation to that undertaking, and

(ii) any reasonable expenses incurred by the relevant undertaking in connection with or in consequence of the preparation of revised annual accounts.

(9) For the purpose of subsection (8)(c), every director of the relevant undertaking at the time the annual accounts were approved is considered to have been a party to their approval unless the director shows that he or she took all reasonable steps to prevent their being approved.

(10) In making an order under subsection (8)(c), the Court—

(a) shall have regard to whether any or all of the directors who approved the annual accounts that were the subject of the declaration knew, or ought to have known, that they did not comply with the Companies Acts [and, where applicable, Article 4 of the IAS Regulation][a], and

(b) may exempt one or more directors from the order or may order the payment of different amounts by different directors.

(11) On the conclusion of the proceedings, the Supervisory Authority shall give to the registrar of companies for registration—

(a) a copy of the court order, or

(b) notice that the application has failed or been withdrawn.

(12) The Supervisory Authority shall consult with the Irish Financial Services Regulatory Authority before making any decisions under this section with respect to a company regulated by the latter Authority, including a decision to give notice under subsection (3).

(13) This section applies equally to revised annual accounts, in which case references to revised annual accounts are to be construed as references to further revised annual accounts.

(14) For the purpose of applying this section to a partnership that is referred to in Regulation 6 of the 1993 Regulations and that is a relevant undertaking—

(a) the partnership is to be treated as though it were a company formed and registered under the Companies Acts, and

(b) the section applies with any modifications necessary for that purpose.

(15) Where revised annual accounts are prepared under this section, then, subject to a direction given under subsection (8)(b), any provision of the Companies Acts respecting the preparation, auditing, circulation and disclosure of annual accounts applies with the necessary changes to the revised annual accounts.

Amendments

a Amended by Sch 1 Pt 5 of EC(IFRSMA)R 2005.

---

27 Delegation of Supervisory Authority's functions and powers

[(1) The Supervisory Authority may delegate some or all of its functions and powers under sections 23 to 26 to a committee established for that purpose and consisting of persons from one or more of the following categories of persons:

(a) persons who are, at the time the committee is established, directors of the Authority,

(b) other persons that the Authority considers appropriate.][a]

(2) Where functions or powers under a provision referred to in subsection (1) are delegated to a committee, any references in that provision to the Supervisory Authority are to be construed as references to that committee.

(3) Subject to the regulations made under section 28(4), a committee may regulate its own procedure.

(4) The Supervisory Authority may, if it reasonably considers it appropriate to do so, perform any of its other functions or exercise any of its other powers through or by any of its officers or employees or any other person duly authorised by it in that behalf[, including the determination of whether a matter should be referred to a committee established for a purpose referred to in subsection (1)].[b]

Amendments

a Subsection (1) substituted by C(MP)A 2009, s 4(1)(a).

b Words ', including the determination of whether a matter should be referred to a committee established for a purpose referred to in subsection (1)' inserted by C(MP)A 2009, s 4(1)(b).

---

28 Hearings, privileges and procedural rules

(1) The Supervisory Authority may for the purposes of exercising its functions under section 23 or 24 conduct an oral hearing in accordance with regulations made under subsection (4) of this section.

(2) A witness before the Supervisory Authority is entitled to the same immunities and privileges as a witness before the High Court.

(3) Nothing in section 23, 24 or 25 compels the disclosure by any person of any information that the person would be entitled to refuse to produce on the grounds of legal professional privilege or authorises the inspection or copying of any document containing such information that is in the person's possession.

(4) The Supervisory Authority shall make regulations respecting the procedures to be followed in conducting enquiries under section 23, investigations under section 24 and reviews under section 25.

29 Appeals to and orders of High Court, including orders confirming decisions of Supervisory Authority

(1) In an appeal under section 23(8) or (10) or 24(8), the High Court may consider any evidence adduced or argument made, whether or not adduced or made to the Supervisory Authority or other body whose decision is under appeal.

(2) On the hearing of the appeal, the Court may make any order or give any direction it thinks fit, including an order—

(a) confirming the decision under appeal, or

(b) modifying or annulling that decision.

(3) On application under section 23(4) for an order granting permission for an investigation under section 24 into a possible breach of a prescribed accountancy body's rules by a member, the Court may—

(a) grant or refuse to grant permission, and

(b) make any ancillary or consequential order it thinks fit, including, if permission is granted, an order setting aside any decision of the body relating to the member.

(4) A decision of the Supervisory Authority annulling all or part of a decision of a prescribed accountancy body under section 23(5)(a), directing a fresh investigation under section 23(5)(b) or requiring the payment of an amount under section 23(5)(c) or 24(7)(a) or (b) does not take effect until that decision is confirmed by the Court either—

(a) on appeal under section 23(8) or 24(8), or

(b) on application by the Supervisory Authority under subsection

(6) of this section.

(5) Subsection (4)(b) applies also in relation to a decision of the Supervisory Authority requiring payment of costs under section 26(5).

(6) On application by motion on notice by the Supervisory Authority for an order confirming a decision referred to in subsection (4) or (5), the Court may make an order confirming the decision or may refuse to make such an order.

[(7) On application under subsection (4) of section 10 for an order compelling compliance with—

(a) a rule adopted or guideline issued by the Supervisory Authority,

(b) a term or condition of recognition, or

(c) an obligation or obligations referred to in that subsection,

the Court may make any order or give any direction it thinks fit.][a]

Amendments

a Sub-s 7 substituted by the IFCMPA 2006, s 18.

---

30 Supervisory Authority's seal and instruments

(1) Judicial notice shall be taken of the Supervisory Authority's seal.

(2) Every document that appears to be an instrument made by the Supervisory Authority and to be sealed with its seal apparently authenticated in accordance with its articles of association shall be received in evidence and be deemed to be such instrument without proof, unless the contrary is shown.

31 Confidentiality of information

(1) No person shall disclose, except in accordance with law, information that—

(a) is obtained in performing the functions or exercising the powers of the Supervisory Authority, and

(b) has not otherwise come to the notice of members of the public.

(2) Without limiting subsection (1), the persons to whom that subsection applies include the following:

(a) a member or director or former member or director of the Supervisory Authority;

(b) an employee or former employee of the Supervisory Authority;

(c) a professional or other adviser to the Supervisory Authority, including a former adviser.

(3) Subsection (1) does not prohibit the Supervisory Authority from disclosing information referred to in that subsection—

(a) if the disclosure is, in its opinion, necessary to enable it to state the grounds on which it made a decision under section 23, 24 or 26,][a]

(b) if the information is, in its opinion, connected with the functions of, and if the disclosure is made to, any of the following:

(i) the Minister;

(ii) the Minister for Finance;

(iii) the Garda Síochána;

(iv) the Director of Public Prosecutions;

(v) the Director of Corporate Enforcement;

(vi) the Revenue Commissioners;

(vii) the Comptroller and Auditor General;

(viii) the Central Bank and Financial Services Authority of Ireland;

(ix) the Irish Takeover Panel;

(x) the Irish Stock Exchange;

(xi) the Pensions Board;

(xii) a prescribed accountancy body;

(xiii) a member of a recognised accountancy body who is qualified for appointment as an auditor;

(xiv) an inspector appointed under any other enactment;

(xv) any person prescribed under section 48(1)(i) for the purposes of this section, or][b]

[(c) if the information disclosed is to an individual or entity performing functions in another state which are similar to the functions the Authority has by virtue of the European Communities (Statutory Audits) (Directive 2006/43/EC) Regulations 2010 (including functions under this Act which the Authority has by virtue of those Regulations), provided that restrictions equivalent to those provided by this section apply in that state in relation to that individual or entity with respect to disclosure of information so given.][c]

(4) A person who contravenes subsection (1) is guilty of an offence.

Amendments

a Words 'section 23, 24 or 26,' substituted for 'section 23, 24 or 26, or' by EC(SA)(Dir)R 2010, reg 53(a).

b Words 'the purposes of this section, or' substituted for 'the purposes of this section.' by EC(SA)(Dir)R 2010, reg 53(b).

c Subparagraph (c) inserted by EC(SA)(Dir)R 2010, reg 53(c).

---

32 Transfer of certain functions to Supervisory Authority and related transitional provisions

(1) The Acts specified in Schedule 1 are amended as indicated in that Schedule.

(2) Subject to subsections (3) to (5), each body that was a recognised body of accountants immediately before the commencement of this section is a recognised accountancy body immediately after the commencement of this section.

(3) Where, on an application made by the Institute of Incorporated Public Accountants under the Act of 1990 before 15 September 2003 as though it were not a recognised body of accountants, the Minister decides, before the commencement of this section, to grant the Institute recognition (with or without terms and conditions) for the purposes of section 187 of that Act or to refuse to grant it such recognition—

(a) the decision is not invalid or ineffectual by reason only—

(i) that the recognition granted to the Institute before 29 January 2003 had not been withdrawn before the date of application, or

(ii) that the decision to grant or refuse recognition was made before the commencement of this section,

(b) if recognition is granted, the Institute is deemed to have become a recognised body of accountants on the date of the decision, subject to such terms and conditions, if any, as may be specified by the Minister at the time of granting recognition, and

(c) if recognition is refused, the Institute is deemed to have ceased to be a recognised body of accountants on the date of the decision.

(4) If for any reason a decision in relation to the application referred to in subsection (3) has not been made before the commencement of this section, the Minister shall, on the commencement of this section, refer the application to the Supervisory Authority for a decision.

(5) If, following the referral of the application, the Supervisory Authority decides to grant the Institute of Incorporated Public Accountants recognition (with or without terms and conditions) for the purposes of section 187 of that Act or to refuse to grant it such recognition, the decision is not invalid or ineffectual by reason only that the recognition granted to the Institute before 29 January 2003 had not been withdrawn before the date of application.

(6) For the removal of doubt and subject to subsection (3), section 192 of the Act of 1990 as amended by this section applies during its currency to any recognition granted to the Institute of Incorporated Public Accountants following the application referred to in subsection (3).

(7) Each person who, on the making of an application referred to in subsection (3), was a member of and held a valid practising certificate from the Institute of Incorporated Public Accountants is considered, for the purposes of section 187 of the Act of 1990, to be a member of a recognised body of accountants until the later of—

(a) the commencement of this section, and

(b) the date on which the Minister or the Supervisory Authority, as the case may be, makes a decision in relation to the application.

(8) If the Minister or the Supervisory Authority, as the case may be, decides to refuse to grant recognition to the Institute of Incorporated Public Accountants—

(a) each person referred to in subsection (7) is, from the date on which he or she ceases under that subsection to be considered to be a member of a recognised body of accountants, considered for the time being authorised to be appointed as an auditor of a company or as a public auditor, as though he or she had been granted an authorisation by the Minister under section 187(1)(a)(iv) of the Act of 1990, and

(b) section 187(14) of the Act of 1990 applies in respect of an authorisation under this subsection, except that the 3 year period referred to in that section runs from the date referred to in paragraph (a).

(9) For the removal of doubt, section 192 of the Act of 1990 as amended by this section applies during its currency to an authorisation under subsection (8).

(10) Each person who, immediately before the commencement of this section, was for the time being authorised by the Minister under section 187 of the Act of 1990 to be appointed as an auditor of a company or as a public auditor is immediately after the commencement of this section considered for the time being authorised by the Supervisory Authority to be so appointed.

(11) Any legal proceedings against the Minister that, immediately before the commencement of this section, are pending or underway and that relate to the exercise of the Minister's powers under any provision mentioned in Schedule 1 may be continued against the Minister after the commencement of this section as if that provision had not been amended by this section.

33 Liability of Supervisory Authority for acts, omissions, etc

(1) Neither the Supervisory Authority nor any person who is or was a member, director or other officer or employee of the Supervisory Authority is liable for damages for anything done, anything purported to be done or anything omitted to be done by the Supervisory Authority or that person in performing their functions or exercising their powers under this Act, unless the act or omission is shown to have been in bad faith.

(2) The matters in respect of which subsection (1) applies include, but are not limited to, the following:

(a) any advice given, or admonition or censure administered, to a prescribed accountancy body under section 23(5);

(b) any statement published under section 23(7) concerning a prescribed accountancy body;

(c) any investigation under section 24 of a possible breach of the standards of a prescribed accountancy body by a member of that body or any sanction or penalty imposed on such a member;

(d) any certificate of refusal issued by the Supervisory Authority in connection with an investigation under section 24;

(e) any review under section 25 of a member of a recognised accountancy body;

(f) any notice given or statement made by the Supervisory Authority under section 26 respecting whether an undertaking's accounts comply with the Companies Acts.

(3) Subject to any enactment or rule of law, the Supervisory Authority may indemnify any person who is or was a member, director, officer or employee of the Supervisory Authority in respect of anything done or omitted to be done by that person in good faith in carrying out duties under this Act.

(4) The power to indemnify under subsection (3) includes, but is not limited to, the power to indemnify a person referred to in that subsection for any liability to pay damages or costs because of anything done or omitted to be done by that person in carrying out duties under this Act where the liability—

(a) has been determined in proceedings before a court or tribunal in another state or arises by virtue of an agreement entered into in settlement of such proceedings, and

(b) would not have been determined had subsections (1) and (2) been applied in those proceedings or would not have been the subject of such an agreement but for that person's reliance in good faith on a legal opinion or advice that those subsections would not be applied by the court or tribunal in those proceedings.

PART 3

OTHER MEASURES TO STRENGTHEN THE REGULATION OF AUDITORS

34 Amendment of section 182 of Act of 1990 (interpretation of Part X)

Section 182 of the Act of 1990 is amended as follows:

(a) in the definition of 'public auditor' by substituting '1896 to 1993;' for ['1896 to 1993.]';[a]

(b) [...][b]

(c) by renumbering that section as section 182(1) and inserting the following: [...][c]

Amendments

a C(AA)A 2003, s 34(a) amends the definition of public auditor in CA 1990, s 182 by substituting '1896 to 1993' for '1896 to 1977'.

b C(AA)A 2003, s 34(b) inserts definitions of 'the Act of 2003', 'the 1993 Regulations' and 'the 1992 Regulations' after the definition of 'public auditor' in CA 1990, s 182. See the amended Act.

c C(AA)A 2003, s 34(c) renumbers CA 1990, s 182 as CA 1990, s 182(1) and inserts CA 1990, s 182 (2) and (3). See the amended Act.

---

35 Amendment of section 187 of Act of 1990 (qualifications for appointment as auditor)

Section 187 of the Act of 1990 is amended as follows:

(a) […][a]

(b) […][b]

(c) […][c]

Amendments

a C(AA)A 2003, s 35(a) inserts CA 1990, s 187(1A) and (1B). See the amended Act.

b C(AA)A 2003, s 35(b) inserts CA 1990, s 187(2)(h). See the amended Act.

c C(AA)A 2003, s 35(c) inserts CA 1990, s 187(14) and (15). See the amended Act.

36 Amendment of Act of 1990 — new section 192A

[…][a]

Amendments

a C(AA)A 2003, s 36 inserts CA 1990, s 192A with effect from 27 January 2009.[1] See the amended Act.

1 Companies (Auditing and Accounting) Act 2003 (Commencement) Order 2009 (SI 13/2009).

37 Amendment of section 194 of Act of 1990 (duty of auditors)

Section 194 of the Act of 1990 is amended as follows:

(a) [...][a]

(b) i[...][b]

(c) [...][c]

(d) [...][d]

(e) […][e]

Amendments

a C(AA)A 2003, s 37(a) amends CA 1990, s 194(3A)(b) by substituting 'access to books and documents' for 'access to documents'.

b C(AA)A 2003, s 37(b) amends CA 1990, s 194(3A) by substituting 'being information, books or documents' for 'being information or documents'.

c C(AA)A 2003, s 37(c) amends CA 1990, s 194(4) by substituting 'subsection (1), (3A), (5) or (5A)' for 'subsection (1), (3A) or (5)'.

d C(AA)A 2003, s 37(d) amends CA 1990, s 194(5) by inserting '(other than an indictable offence under section 125(1) or 127(12) of the Principal Act)' after 'an indictable offence under the Companies Acts'.

e C(AA)A 2003, s 37(e) inserts CA 1990, s 194(5A) and (5B). See the amended Act.

38 Amendment of section 198 of Act of 1990 (register of auditors)

[…][a]

Amendments

a C(AA)A 2003, s 38 substitutes CA 1990, s 198. See the amended Act.

39 Amendment of section 199 of Act of 1990 (provisions concerning register of auditors)

Section 199 of the Act of 1990 is amended as follows:

(a) […][a]

(b) [...][b]

(c) […][c]

(d) […][d]

(e) […][e]

(f) […][f]

Amendments

a C(AA)A 2003, s 39(a) substitutes CA 1990, s 199(1). See the amended Act.

b C(AA)A 2003, s 39(b) amends CA 1990, s 199(2) by substituting 'whose recognition is continued under section 32(2) of the Act of 2003' for 'whose recognition is renewed'.

c C(AA)A 2003, s 39(c) inserts CA 1990, s 199(2A). See the amended Act.

d C(AA)A 2003, s 39(d) inserts CA 1990, s 199(3A). See the amended Act.

e C(AA)A 2003, s 39(e) substitutes CA 1990, s 199(4). See the amended Act.

f C(AA)A 2003, s 39(f) inserts CA 1990, s 199(5). See the amended Act.

---

40 Amendment of section 200 of Act of 1990 (duty to keep registrar informed)

Section 200 of the Act of 1990 is amended as follows:

(a) […][a]

(b) […][b]

(c) […][c]

(d) […][d]

Amendments

a C(AA)A 2003, s 40(a) inserts CA 1990, s 200(2A). See the amended Act.

b C(AA)A 2003, s 40(b) inserts CA 1990, s 200(3A). See the amended Act.

c C(AA)A 2003, s 40(c) substitutes CA 1990, s 200(4). See the amended Act.

d C(AA)A 2003, s 40(d) inserts CA 1990, s 200(5). See the amended Act.

---

41 Amendment of Act of 1990 — new section 205A

[…][a]

Amendments

a C(AA)A 2003, s 41 inserts CA 1990, s 205A. See the amended Act.

---

42 Amendment of Act of 1990 — new section 205B

[...][a]

Amendments

a C(AA)A 2003, s 42 inserts CA 1990, s 205B. See the amended Act.

43 Amendment of Act of 1990 — new section 205C

[...][a]

Amendments

a C(AA)A 2003, s 43 inserts CA 1990, s 205C. See the amended Act.

44 Amendment of Act of 1990 — new section 205D

[...][a]

Amendments

a C(AA)A 2003, s 44 inserts CA 1990, s 205D. See the amended Act.

45 Amendment of Act of 1990 — new sections 205E and 205F

[...][a]

Amendments

a C(AA)A 2003, s 45 inserts CA 1990, ss 205E and 205F. See the amended Act.

46 Amendment of section 127 of Act of 1963 (annual return date)

Section 127 of the Act of 1963 (inserted by section 60 of the Company Law Enforcement Act 2001) is amended as follows:

(a) [...][a]

(b) [...][b]

(c) [...][c]

Amendments

a C(AA)A 2003, s 46(a) substitutes CA 1963, s 127(1) (as inserted by CLEA 2001, s 60). See the amended Act.

b C(AA)A 2003, s 46(b) inserting ',subject to subsection (8),' after ', the annual return date is' in CA 1963, s 127 (as inserted by CLEA 2001, s 60).

c C(AA)A 2003, s 46(c) substitutes CA 1963, s 127 (8) (as inserted by CLEA 2001, s 60). See the amended Act.

47 Amendment of section 128 of Act of 1963 (documents to be annexed to annual return)

Section 128 of the Act of 1963 is amended by substituting the following for subsection (6):

[...][a]

Amendments

a C(AA)A 2003, s 47 substitutes CA 1963, s 128(6) and inserts CA 1963, s 128(6A)–(6C). See the amended Act.

PART 4
REGULATIONS AND MISCELLANEOUS MATTERS

48 Minister's power to make regulations

(1) Subject to section 49, the Minister may make regulations respecting any matter that is referred to in this Act as prescribed or that is necessary or advisable for giving effect to this Act, including regulations—

(a) prescribing bodies of accountants for the purposes of this Act,

(b) prescribing designated bodies for the purposes of sections 6 and 11,

(c) providing that, effective on a specified date, a body referred to in section 6(2) ceases to be a designated body,

(d) varying, as a consequence of a regulation under paragraph (b) or (c), the numbers specified in section 11(1), (2) and (3) as the Minister considers necessary or expedient,

(e) prescribing for the purposes of the criteria referred to in section 15(2)(b) amounts that are higher or lower than the euro amounts specified in that section and that apply instead of the euro amounts,

(f) prescribing the amount of a penalty under section 23(5)(c),

(g) prescribing for the purpose of section 23(7) the manner in which notice is to be given,

(h) prescribing, for the purposes of the criteria referred to in paragraph (c) of the definition of 'relevant undertaking' in section 26, amounts that are higher or lower than the euro amounts specified in that definition and that apply instead of the euro amounts,

(i) prescribing for the purposes of section 31(3) persons to whom the Supervisory Authority may disclose information,

(j) exempting from all or any of sections 15 and 26 of this Act and sections 205A, 205B, 205C, 205D and 205E of the Act of 1990—

  (i) qualifying companies within the meaning of section 110 of the Taxes Consolidation Act 1997 (as inserted by section 48 of the Finance Act 2003), and

  (ii) classes of other companies and other undertakings, if the extent to which or the manner in which they are or may be regulated under any enactment makes it, in the Minister's opinion, unnecessary or inappropriate to apply those provisions to them,

(k) prescribing for the purposes of the definition of 'accounting standards' in section 205A of the Act of 1990 one or more bodies that issue statements of accounting standards,

(l) prescribing, for the purposes of the definitions of 'large private company' and 'relevant undertaking' in section 205B of the Act of 1990 or for the purposes of section 205E(9) of that Act, amounts that are higher or lower than the euro amounts specified in those definitions or in section 205E(9), as the case may be, and that apply instead of the euro amounts,

(m) prescribing for the purposes of section 205B of the Act of 1990—

(i) additional functions to be performed by audit committees,

(ii) conditions to be met under subsection (8)(c) of that section, and

(iii) supplementary rules governing the operation of those committees,

and

(n) prescribing the format in which information must be disclosed under section 205D of the Act of 1990 for audit work, audit-related work and non-audit work.

(2) On a body ceasing—

(a) to be a prescribed accountancy body because of the revocation of a regulation made under subsection (1)(a), or

(b) to be a designated body because of a regulation under subsection (1)(c),

any director who was nominated by that body under section 11 immediately ceases to hold office.

(3) Before preparing for the purposes of section 49 a draft regulation under subsection (1)(a), (e), (h) or (l) of this section, the Minister shall consider any recommendations that the Supervisory Authority may make.

(4) Subject to subsection (3), before making a regulation under this section the Minister may consult with any persons that the Minister considers should be consulted.

(5) Regulations under this section may contain any transitional and other supplementary and incidental provisions that appear to the Minister to be appropriate.

49 Prior approval by Oireachtas required for certain regulations

A regulation may not be made under section 48(1)(a), (e), (h), (j) or (l) unless—

(a) a draft of the proposed regulation has been laid before the Houses of the Oireachtas, and

(b) a resolution approving the draft has been passed by each House.

50 Laying of other regulations before Oireachtas

(1) The Minister shall ensure that a regulation made under this Act, other than one to which section 49 applies, is laid before each House of the Oireachtas as soon as practicable after it is made.

(2) Either House of the Oireachtas may, by a resolution passed within 21 sitting days after the day on which the regulation is laid before it, annul the regulation.

(3) The annulment of a regulation under subsection (2) takes effect immediately on the passing of the resolution concerned, but does not affect the validity of anything done under the regulation before the passing of the resolution.

51 Amendment of Company Law Enforcement Act 2001

Section 12(1) of the Company Law Enforcement Act 2001 is amended as follows:

(a) [...][a]

(b) [...][b]

(c) by inserting the following after paragraph (g):

[...][c]

Amendments

a C(AA)A 2003, s 51(a) deletes the word 'and' at the end of CLEA 2001, s 12(1)(f).

b C(AA)A 2003, s 51(b) amends CLEA 2001, s 12(1)(g) by substituting 'any other Act, and' for 'any other Act'.

c C(AA)A 2003, s 51(c) inserts CLEA 2001, s 12(1)(h). See the amended Act.

---

52 Amendment of Company Law Enforcement Act 2001 (certificate evidence)

The Company Law Enforcement Act 2001 is amended by inserting the following after section 110:

[...][a]

Amendments

C(AA)A 2003, s 52 inserts CLEA 2001, s 110A. See the amended Act.

---

53 Amendment of Companies (Amendment) (No. 2) Act 1999 (exemption from requirement to have accounts audited)

The Companies (Amendment) (No. 2) Act 1999 is amended as follows:

(a) [...][a]

(b) [...][b]

(c) [...][c]

(d) [...][d]

(e) [...][e]

Amendments

a C(AA)A 2003, s 53(a) amends C(A)(No2)A 1999, s 32(1) by substituting 'Subject to sections 32A and 33(1)' for 'Subject to section 33(1)'.

b C(AA)A 2003, s 53(b) amends C(A)(No2)A 1999, s 32(3)(a)(ii) by substituting '€1,500,000' for '£250,000'.

c C(AA)A 2003, s 53(c) amends C(A)(No2)A 1999, s 32(3)(a)(v)(IV) by substituting '(other than paragraph 18 thereof)' for '(other than paragraph 18 thereof),'.

d C(AA)A 2003, s 53(d) amends C(A)(No2)A 1999, s 32(3) by deleting 'and' where it occurs after paragraph (a)(v)(IV) and by repealing paragraph (b).

e C(AA)A 2003, s 53(e) inserts C(A)(No2)A 1999, s 32A. See the amended Act.

---

54 Amendment of section 43 of Companies (Amendment) (No. 2) Act 1999 (Company to have director resident in State)

Section 43 of the Companies (Amendment) (No. 2) Act 1999 is amended by inserting the following after subsection (15):

[...][a]

Amendments

a C(AA)A 2003, s 54 inserts C(A)(No 2)A 1999, s 43(16).

---

55 Amendment of section 13 of Companies (Amendment) Act 1982

Section 13 of the Companies (Amendment) Act 1982 is amended by substituting the following for subsection (2):

[...][a]

Amendments

a C(AA)A 2003, s 55 substitutes C(A)A 1982, s 13(2). See the amended Act.

---

56 Amendment of section 200 of Act of 1963 (avoidance of provisions exempting officers and auditors from liability)

Section 200 of the Act of 1963 is amended by renumbering that section as section 200(1) and by adding the following:

[...][a]

Amendments

a C(AA)A 2003, s 56 renumbers CA 1963 as CA 1963, s 200(1) and inserts CA 1963, s 201(2)–(5). See the amended Act.

---

57 Amendment of Companies Acts (default provisions)

The Companies Acts specified in Schedule 2 are amended as indicated in that Schedule.

58 Amendment of Defamation Act 1961

Paragraph II of the Second Schedule to the Defamation Act 1961 (which specifies statements that carry qualified privilege subject to explanation or contradiction) is amended by inserting the following after paragraph 6:

> '7. (1) A copy or fair and accurate report or summary of any decision, direction, report, investigation, statement or notice made, given, prepared,

published or served by the Irish Auditing and Accounting Supervisory Authority.

(2) In this paragraph, 'statement' includes the following:

(a) any advice, admonition or censure given or administered by the Irish Auditing and Accounting Supervisory Authority under section 23 of the Companies (Auditing and Accounting) Act 2003;

(b) any certificate of refusal issued by that Authority in connection with an investigation under section 24 of the Companies (Auditing and Accounting) Act 2003;

(c) any notice given or statement made by that Authority under section 26 of the Companies (Auditing and Accounting) Act 2003 respecting whether a company's accounts comply with the Companies Acts.

(3) Nothing in this paragraph or any other provision of this Act limits section 33 of the Companies (Auditing and Accounting) Act 2003.'.

59 Revocation of regulations

The Companies Act 1990 (Auditors) Regulations 1992 (SI No 259 of 1992) are revoked.

Amendments

C(AA)A 2003, s 59 revokes the Companies Act 1990 (Auditors) Regs 1992 (SI 1259/1992).

SCHEDULE 1

TRANSFER OF FUNCTIONS TO SUPERVISORY AUTHORITY

PART 1

AMENDMENT OF COMPANIES ACT 1990

Item No	*Section affected*	*Amendment*
1.	Section 187	(a) In subsection (1)(a)(i), (ii) and (vi), substitute 'Supervisory Authority' for 'Minister' wherever it appears. (b) In subsection (1)(a), substitute the following for subparagraph (iv): '(iv) he was authorised by the Minister before the 3rd day of February, 1983, and is for the time being authorised by the Supervisory Authority to be so appointed, or'.
2.	Section 189	In subsections (1), (2) and (4), substitute 'Supervisory Authority' for 'Minister' wherever it appears.
3.	Section 190	In subsections (1) and (2), substitute 'Supervisory Authority' for 'Minister' wherever it appears.
4.	Section 191	Substitute the following for section 191: 'Recognition of bodies of accountants. 191.—The Supervisory Authority may grant recognition to a body of accountants but only if satisfied— (a) that the standards relating to training, qualifications and repute required by that body for the awarding of a practising certificate to a person are not less than those specified in Articles 3 to 6, 8 and 19 of the Council Directive, and (b) as to the standards that body applies to its members in the areas of ethics, codes of conduct and practice, independence, professional integrity, auditing and accounting standards and investigation and disciplinary procedures.'.
5.	Section 192	(a) In subsections (1) and (2) substitute 'Supervisory Authority' for 'Minister' and substitute 'under or for the purposes of section 187' for 'under section 187'. (b) In subsection (3) substitute 'Supervisory Authority' for 'Minister' and substitute 'under or for the purposes of section 187' for 'under the said section 187'. (c) In subsection (4)(a) to (d) substitute 'Supervisory Authority' for 'Minister' wherever it appears. (d) In subsection (4), repeal paragraphs (e), (f) and (g).

PART 2
AMENDMENT OF THE INSTITUTE OF CHARTERED ACCOUNTANTS IN IRELAND (CHARTER AMENDMENT) ACT 1966

Item No	*Section affected*	*Amendment*
1.	Section 6	Substitute 'Supervisory Authority' for 'Government'.

SCHEDULE 2

Item No	*Acts and Provisions affected*	*Amendment*
	Companies Act 1963, sections 10(10), 12(3), 44(8), 46(2), 47(4), 57(3), 58(3), 59(5), 69(2), 70(3), 78(5), 84(2), 86(2), 91(5), 92(4), 100(3), 101(2), 107(3), 110(2), 113(5), 114(3), 114(4), 115(6), 116(9), 117(4), 128(4), 136(3), 136(5), 143(5), 143(6), 145(4), 156(3), 157(2), 179(4), 180(5), 188(2), 193(4), 194(5)(b), 194(6), 195(12), 197(3), 201(6), 202(4), 202(6), 203(3), 205(5), 224(5), 227(2), 249(3), 252(2), 256(7), 261(7), 262(2), 263(3), 263(6), 263(7), 272(2), 273(3), 273(6), 273(7), 276A(3), 278(2),	Substitute, in each of the provisions specified in column 2, 'shall be guilty of an offence and liable to a fine' for 'shall be liable to a fine'.

Item No	*Acts and Provisions affected*	*Amendment*
	280(4), 300, 301, 301A(5), 303(2), 305(2), 306(2), 310(2), 314, 317(2), 321(2), 322C(3), 358, 377(7) and 378(2)	
2.	Companies Act 1963, section 60(5)	Substitute, in the provision specified in column 2, 'shall be guilty of an offence and liable to imprisonment for a period not exceeding 6 months or to a fine not exceeding €1,904.61 or to both' for 'shall be liable to imprisonment for a period not exceeding 6 months or to a fine not exceeding £500 or to both'.
3.	Companies Act 1963, section 102(2)	Substitute for the provision specified in column 2 the following: '(2) If a judgment creditor makes default in complying with subsection (1) he shall be guilty of an offence and liable to a fine not exceeding €1,904.61, and if a company makes default in complying with that subsection, the company and every officer who is in default shall be guilty of an offence and liable to a fine not exceeding €1,904.61.'.
4.	Companies Act 1963, sections 114(2), 131(6), 159(5), 190(9), 221(2), 234(5) and 398(3)	Substitute, in each of the provisions specified in column 2, 'shall be guilty of an offence and liable to a fine' for the words 'shall be liable to a fine' in both instances in which those words occur within that provision.
5.	Companies Act 1963, section 266(6)	Substitute for the provision specified in column 2 the following: '(6) If default is made— (a) by the company in complying with subsections (1) and (2), (b) by the directors of the company in complying with subsection (3), or
		(c) by any director of the company in complying with subsection (4), the company, directors or director, as the case may be, shall be guilty of an offence and liable to a fine not exceeding €1,904.61, and in case of default by the company, every officer of the company who is in default shall be guilty of an offence and liable to a fine not exceeding €1,904.61.'.

Item No	*Acts and Provisions affected*	*Amendment*
6.	Companies (Amendment) Act 1990 section 11(7)	Substitute, in the provision specified in column 2, 'shall be guilty of an offence and liable to a fine' for 'shall be liable to a fine'.
7.	Companies Act 1990, section 50(7)	Substitute for the provision specified in column 2 the following: '(7) If default is made in complying with subsection (1) or (5) or if an inspection required under subsection (6) is refused, the company and every officer of the company who is in default shall be guilty of an offence and liable on summary conviction to a fine not exceeding €1,904.61 and, for continued contravention, to a daily default fine not exceeding €63.49 and, if default is made for 14 days in complying with subsection (4), the company and every officer of the company who is in default shall be guilty of an offence and liable to a fine not exceeding €1,904.61 and, for continued contravention, to a daily default fine not exceeding €63.49.'.
8.	Companies Act 1990, section 60(10)	Substitute, in the provision specified in column 2, 'shall be guilty of an offence and liable to a fine' for 'shall be liable to a fine' in both instances in which those words occur within that provision.
9.	Companies Act 1990, sections 80(10) and 161(6)	Substitute, in each provision specified in column 2, 'shall be guilty of an offence and liable to a fine' for the words 'shall be liable to a fine' in both instances in which those words occur within that provision.

Investment Funds, Companies and Miscellaneous Provisions Act 2005

Number 12 of 2005

PART 1
PRELIMINARY AND GENERAL

PART 2
COMMON CONTRACTUAL FUNDS

Not reproduced here

PART 3
AMENDMENTS TO PART XIII OF ACT OF 1990

PART 4
MARKET ABUSE

PART 5
PUBLIC OFFERS OF SECURITIES

42 Section 41: exceptions and exemptions
43 Restriction of liability where non-equity securities solely involved
44 Indemnification of certain persons
45 Expert's consent to issue of prospectus containing statement by him or her
46 Regulations (Part 5)
47 Penalties on conviction on indictment and defences in respect of certain offences
48 Untrue statements and omissions in prospectus: criminal liability
49 Local offers
50 Exclusion of Investment Intermediaries Act 1995
51 Power to make certain rules and issue guidelines
52 Avoidance of certain agreements
53 Amendment of section 53 of Act of 1963
54 Amendment of section 55 of Act of 1963
55 Amendment of section 57 of Act of 1963

PART 6
MISCELLANEOUS COMPANY LAW AMENDMENTS

56 Amendment of section 60 of Act of 1963
57 Electronic filing agents
58 Section 57: supplemental provisions
59 Reservation of company name
60 Section 59: supplemental provisions
61 Amendment of section 128 of Act of 1963
62 Amendment of section 195 of Act of 1963
63 Amendment of section 302(1) of Act of 1963
64 Amendment of section 371(1) of Act of 1963
65 Amendment of section 12B of Companies (Amendment) Act 1982
66 Amendment of section 22 of Companies (Amendment) Act 1986
67 Amendment of section 19 of Act of 1990
68 Amendment of section 20 of Act of 1990
69 Amendment of section 21 of Act of 1990
70 Amendment of section 166 of Act of 1990
71 Amendment of section 242 of Act of 1990
72 Replacement of references to Companies Registration Office Gazette for references to *Iris Oifigiúil*
73 Miscellaneous amendments of Companies Acts related to penalties
74 Amendment of section 110A of Company Law Enforcement Act 2001

PART 7
MISCELLANEOUS AMENDMENTS

Not reproduced here

SCHEDULE

Not reproduced here

An Act to make provision in relation to collective investment undertakings of the kind known as 'common contractual funds'; to amend Part XIII of the Companies Act 1990 and the European Communities (Undertakings For Collective Investment In Transferable Securities) Regulations 2003 (S.I. No. 211 of 2003); to make provision in relation to certain of the matters dealt with by Acts adopted by institutions of the European Communities in the fields of insider trading and manipulation and other abuses of financial markets and in the field of offers to the public of securities or the admittance of securities to trading; to effect certain miscellaneous amendments to the Companies Acts 1963 to 2003; to amend the Irish Takeover Panel Act 1997 and the Competition Act 2002; to increase the penalties for offences under the Prices Act 1958, the Restrictive Practices Act 1972 and certain enactments that relate to protection of the consumer; to amend the Industrial and Provident Societies Act 1893 and to provide for related matters. [29th June, 2005]

Be it Enacted by the Oireachtas as Follows:

PART 1
PRELIMINARY AND GENERAL

1 Short title, collective citation, and construction

(1) This Act may be cited as the Investment Funds, Companies and Miscellaneous Provisions Act 2005.

(2) Parts 3 to 6 and the Companies Acts 1963 to 2003 may be cited together as the Companies Acts 1963 to 2005 and shall be construed together as one.

2 Commencement

(1) This Act (other than sections 85 and 86) shall come into operation on such day or days as the Minister may appoint by order or orders either generally or with reference to any particular purpose or provision and different days may be so appointed for different purposes or different provisions.

(2) Without prejudice to the generality of subsection (1), an order or orders under that subsection may appoint different days for the coming into operation of section 31 so as to effect the repeal provided by that section of an enactment specified in it on different days for different purposes.

3 Interpretation generally

(1) In this Act—

'Act of 1963' means the Companies Act 1963;

'Act of 1990' means the Companies Act 1990;

'contravention' includes, in relation to any provision, a failure to comply with that provision and 'contravene' shall be construed accordingly;

'enactment' includes an instrument made under an enactment;

'Member State', where used without qualification, means Member State of the European Union;

'Minister' means the Minister for Enterprise, Trade and Employment.

(2) In this Act—

(a) a reference to a section or Part is a reference to a section or Part of this Act unless it is indicated that reference to some other enactment is intended,

(b) a reference to a subsection, paragraph or subparagraph is a reference to the subsection, paragraph or subparagraph of the provision in which the reference occurs, unless it is indicated that reference to some other provision is intended, and

(c) a reference to any other enactment shall, unless the context otherwise requires, be construed as a reference to that enactment as amended or adapted by or under any other enactment.

4 Orders and regulations

(1) Every order or regulation made under this Act (other than an order made under section 2 or 37) shall be laid before each House of the Oireachtas as soon as may be after it is made and, if a resolution annulling the order or regulation is passed by either such House within the next 21 days on which that House has sat after the order or regulation is laid before it, the order or regulation shall be annulled accordingly but without prejudice to the validity of anything previously done thereunder.

(2) The Minister may by order amend or revoke an order made under this Act (other than an order made under section 2 or 37 but including an order made under this subsection).

5 Expenses

The expenses incurred by the Minister in the administration of this Act shall, to such extent as may be sanctioned by the Minister for Finance, be paid out of moneys provided by the Oireachtas.

PART 3
AMENDMENTS TO PART XIII OF ACT OF 1990

22 Amendment of section 252 of Act of 1990

[...][a]

Amendments

a This section inserted definitions of 'management company', 'sub-fund' and 'umbrella fund' in CA 1990, s 252. See the amended Act.

---

23 Amendment of section 254 of Act of 1990

[...][a]

Amendments

a This section substituted CA 1990, s 254(2). See the amended Act.

---

24 Amendment of section 255 of Act of 1990

[...][a]

Amendments

a This section inserted CA 1990, s 255(3). See the amended Act.

25 Segregated liability of sub-funds – insertion of new sections in Part XIII of Act of 1990

[...][a]

Amendments

a This section inserted CA 1990, s 256A–256E. See the amended Act.

26 Amendment of section 257 of Act of 1990

[...][a]

Amendments

a This section inserted CA 1990, s 257(4)(e). See the amended Act.

27 Amendment of section 260 of Act of 1990

[...][a]

Amendments

a This section amended CA 1990, s 260(3) by inserting ', 43, 43A' after '41. See the amended Act.

28 Insertion of new section 260A in Act of 1990

[...][a]

Amendments

a This section inserted CA 1990, s 260A. See the amended Act.

PART 4
MARKET ABUSE

29 Interpretation (*Part 4*)

(1) In this Part—

'2003 Market Abuse Directive' means Directive 2003/6/EC of the European Parliament and of the Council of 28 January 2003 on insider dealing and market manipulation (market abuse), including that Directive as it stands amended for the time being;

'Irish market abuse law' means—

(a) the measures adopted for the time being by the State to implement the 2003 Market Abuse Directive and the supplemental Directives (whether an Act of the Oireachtas, regulations under section 3 of the European Communities Act 1972, regulations under section 30 or any other enactment (other than, save where the context otherwise admits, this Part)),

(b) any measures directly applicable in the State in consequence of the 2003 Market Abuse Directive and, without prejudice to the generality of this paragraph, includes the Market Abuse Regulation, and

(c) any supplementary and consequential measures adopted for the time being by the State in respect of the Market Abuse Regulation;

'Market Abuse Regulation' means Commission Regulation 2273/2003 of 22 December 2003;

'supplemental Directives' means—

(a) Commission Directive No. 2003/124/EC of 22 December 2003,

(b) Commission Directive No. 2003/125/EC of 22 December 2003, and

(c) Commission Directive No. 2004/72/EC of 29 April 2004.

(2) A word or expression that is used in this Part and is also used in the 2003 Market Abuse Directive or the supplemental Directives shall have in this Part the same meaning as it has in the 2003 Market Abuse Directive or the supplemental Directives, unless—

(a) the contrary intention appears, or

(b) Irish market abuse law provides otherwise.

30 Regulations (*Part 4*)

(1) The Minister may make regulations for the purposes of—

(a) giving effect to the 2003 Market Abuse Directive and the supplemental Directives, and

(b) supplementing and making consequential provision in respect of the Market Abuse Regulation.

(2) Regulations under this section may contain such incidental, supplementary and consequential provisions as appear to the Minister to be necessary or expedient for the purposes of those regulations, including provisions creating offences (but the regulations may only provide penalties in respect of a summary conviction for any such offence).

(3) Regulations under this section may also—

(a) make, for the purposes of those Regulations, provision analogous to that which was made by section 3 of the Companies (Amendment) Act 1999 (repealed by section 31) for the purposes of that Act,

(b) impose on a market operator a requirement similar to that which is imposed by Article 6(9) of the 2003 Market Abuse Directive on the person referred to in that Article 6(9).

(4) This section is without prejudice to section 3 of the European Communities Act 1972.

31 Repeal of Part V of Act of 1990 and Companies (Amendment) Act 1999

The following are repealed:

(a) Part V of the Act of 1990, and

(b) the Companies (Amendment) Act 1999.

32 Conviction on indictment of offences under Irish market abuse law: penalties

A person who is guilty of an offence created by Irish market abuse law (being an offence expressed by that law to be an offence to which this section applies) shall, without prejudice to any penalties provided by that law in respect of a summary conviction for the offence, be liable, on conviction on indictment, to a fine not exceeding €10,000,000 or imprisonment for a term not exceeding 10 years or both.

33 Civil liability for certain breaches of Irish market abuse law

(1) If a person contravenes a provision of Irish market abuse law (being a provision the purpose of which is expressed by that law to be for the implementation of Article 2, 3 or 4 of the 2003 Market Abuse Directive) the person shall be liable—

(a) to compensate any other party to the transaction concerned who was not in possession of the relevant information for any loss sustained by that party by reason of any difference between the price at which the financial instruments concerned were acquired or disposed of and the price at which they would have been likely to have been acquired or disposed of in such a transaction at the time when the first-mentioned transaction took place if that information had been generally available, and

(b) to account to the body corporate or other legal entity which issued the financial instruments concerned for any profit accruing to the first-mentioned person from acquiring or disposing of those instruments.

(2) If a person contravenes a provision of Irish market abuse law (being a provision the purpose of which is expressed by that law to be for the implementation of Article 5 of the 2003 Market Abuse Directive) the person shall be liable—

(a) to compensate any other party who acquired or disposed of financial instruments by reason of the contravention, and

(b) to account to the body corporate or other legal entity which issued the financial instruments concerned for any profit accruing to the first-mentioned person from acquiring or disposing of those instruments.

(3) Subsections (1) and (2) are without prejudice to any other cause of action which may lie against the person for contravening the provision concerned.

(4) An action under subsection (1) or (2) shall not be commenced more than 2 years after the date of the contravention concerned.

34 Supplementary rules, etc., by competent authority

(1) In this section "competent authority" means the competent authority designated under Irish market abuse law.

(2) The competent authority may make rules imposing or enabling the competent authority to impose requirements on persons on whom an obligation or obligations are imposed by Irish market abuse law, being requirements—

(a) to do or not to do specified things so as to secure that the provisions of Irish market abuse law are complied with and, in particular (without limiting the generality of this paragraph), to adopt specified procedures and use specified forms in the provision of information to the competent authority,

(b) to do or not to do specified things so as to secure the effective supervision by the competent authority of activities of the kind to which Irish market abuse law relates and, in particular (without limiting the generality of this paragraph), to make such reports or disclose such matters, at such times and in such manner, to the competent authority or other specified persons as are provided for by the rules or specified by the competent authority pursuant to the rules, being reports or a disclosure of matters that is or are required by virtue or in consequence of the operation of Irish market abuse law.

(3) Rules under this section may include rules providing for the manner in which or the matters by reference to which (or both) a determination is to be made of any issue as to whether a financial interest or interests is or are significant for the purposes of the provisions of Irish market abuse law implementing Article 5(1) of Commission Directive No 2003/125/EC of 22 December 2003.

(4) Rules under this section may contain such consequential, incidental or supplemental provisions as the competent authority considers necessary or expedient.

(5) Rules under this section shall not contain any provision that is inconsistent with Irish market abuse law or require the provision of information to any person the provision of which is not reasonably related to the purposes for which the applicable provisions of the 2003 Market Abuse Directive or the supplemental Directives have been adopted.

(6) The provisions of Irish market abuse law that are expressed by that law to be made for the purpose of enabling the imposition of administrative sanctions shall apply in relation to a contravention of rules under this section as they apply in relation to a contravention of a provision of Irish market abuse law and, accordingly, a sanction that may be imposed pursuant to the first-mentioned provisions of Irish market abuse law in respect of a contravention of a provision of that law may, in accordance with that law, be imposed in respect of a contravention of rules under this section.

(7) The competent authority may issue guidelines in writing as to the steps that may be taken to comply with Irish market abuse law.

35 Amendment of section 33AJ of Central Bank Act 1942

Section 33AJ (inserted by the Central Bank and Financial Services Authority of Ireland Act 2003) of the Central Bank Act 1942 is amended by substituting the following subsection for subsection (7):

> "(7) In this section, 'agent' includes a person appointed or authorised by the Bank, the Governor or the Chief Executive to perform any function or exercise a power under the Central Bank Acts or any other enactment.".

36 Amendment of section 33AK of Central Bank Act 1942

The definition of "Supervisory Directives" in subsection (10) of section 33AK (inserted by the Central Bank and Financial Services Authority of Ireland Act 2003) of the Central Bank Act 1942 is amended by substituting the following paragraphs for paragraph (e):

"(e) Council Directive 92/96/EEC of 10 November 1992 (OJ L360, 9.12.1992, p. 1),

(f) the 2003 Market Abuse Directive (within the meaning of Part 4 of the Investment Funds, Companies and Miscellaneous Provisions Act 2005),

(g) the supplemental Directives (within the meaning of that Part 4),

(h) the 2003 Prospectus Directive (within the meaning of Part 5 of the Investment Funds, Companies and Miscellaneous Provisions Act 2005);".

37 Application of Irish market abuse law to certain markets

(1) The Minister, after consultation with the competent authority designated under Irish market abuse law, may, by provisional order, provide that one or more provisions of Irish market abuse law that apply in relation to a market to which the 2003 Market Abuse Directive applies shall, with such modifications, if any, as are specified in the order, apply to a market specified in the order.

(2) The Minister may, by provisional order, amend or revoke a provisional order under this section (including a provisional order under this subsection).

(3) A provisional order under this section shall not have effect unless or until it is confirmed by an Act of the Oireachtas.

PART 5
PUBLIC OFFERS OF SECURITIES

38 Interpretation (*Part 5*)

(1) In this Part, unless the context otherwise requires—

"2003 Prospectus Directive" means Directive 2003/71/EC of the European Parliament and of the Council of 4 November 2003 (OJ L345, 31.12.2003, p 64.), including that Directive as it stands amended for the time being;

"body corporate" includes a company;

"EEA Agreement" means the Agreement on the European Economic Area signed at Oporto on 2 May 1992, as amended for the time being;

"EU prospectus law" means—

(a) the measures adopted for the time being by a Member State (including the State) or a Member State of the EEA to implement the 2003 Prospectus Directive,

(b) any measures directly applicable in consequence of the 2003 Prospectus Directive and, without prejudice to the generality of this paragraph, includes the Prospectus Regulation, and

(c) any supplementary and consequential measures adopted for the time being by a Member State (including the State) or a Member State of the EEA in respect of the Prospectus Regulation;

"expert", save where a different construction in respect of that expression applies for the purposes of this Part by virtue of Irish prospectus law, includes engineer, valuer, accountant and any other individual or body (whether incorporated or unincorporated) the profession of whom, or the profession of members, officers or employees of which, gives authority to a statement made by the individual or body;

"Irish prospectus law" means—

(a) the measures adopted for the time being by the State to implement the 2003 Prospectus Directive (whether an Act of the Oireachtas, regulations under section 3 of the European Communities Act 1972, regulations under section 46 or any other enactment (other than, save where the context otherwise admits, this Part)),

(b) any measures directly applicable in the State in consequence of the 2003 Prospectus Directive and, without prejudice to the generality of this paragraph, includes the Prospectus Regulation, and

(c) any supplementary and consequential measures adopted for the time being by the State in respect of the Prospectus Regulation;

"issuer" means a body corporate or other legal entity which issues or proposes to issue securities;

"local offer" means an offer of securities to the public in the State where—

(a) the offer expressly limits the amount of the total consideration for the offer to less than €2,500,000 (and the means by which that limit shall be calculated, in particular in the case of a series of such offers of securities, shall be the same as that provided for by regulations under section 46 in relation to analogous limits specified by those regulations for any purpose),

(b) the securities are other than those referred to in any of paragraphs (a) to (g) or paragraph (i) or (j) of Article 1(2) of the 2003 Prospectus Directive, and

(c) the offer is not of a kind described in Article 3(2) of the 2003 Prospectus Directive;

"Member State of the EEA" means a state that is a contracting party to the EEA Agreement;

"offer of securities to the public" has the same meaning as it has in Irish prospectus law;

"offering document" means a document prepared for a local offer which document, if prepared in connection with an offer to which the 2003 Prospectus Directive applies, would be a prospectus;

"offeror" means a body corporate or other legal entity or an individual which or who offers securities to the public;

"promoter" means, subject to subsection (5), a promoter who was a party to the preparation of a prospectus, or of the portion thereof containing an untrue statement;

"prospectus" means a document or documents in such form and containing such information as may be required by or under this Part or EU prospectus law, howsoever the document or documents are constituted, but does not include any advertisements in newspapers or journals derived from the foregoing;

"Prospectus Regulation" means Commission Regulation (EC) No. 809/2004 of 29 April 2004 implementing Directive 2003/71/EC of the European Parliament and of the Council as regards information contained in prospectuses as well as the format, incorporation by reference and publication of such prospectuses and dissemination of advertisements[2];

"securities" has the same meaning as it has in Irish prospectus law, and includes shares and debentures of a company.

(2) A word or expression that is used in this Part and is also used in the 2003 Prospectus Directive shall have in this Part the same meaning as it has in that Directive, unless—

(a) the contrary intention appears, or

(b) Irish prospectus law provides otherwise.

(3) For the purposes of this Part—

(a) a statement included in a prospectus shall be deemed to be untrue if it is misleading in the form and context in which it is included, and

(b) a statement shall be deemed to be included in a prospectus if it is contained therein or in any report or memorandum appearing on the face thereof or by reference incorporated therein.

[(3A) Without limiting the meaning of that expression in any other context in which it is used in this Part, 'statement' in section 45(2) (other than paragraph (b) thereof) and any other section of this Part that makes provision in respect of an expert includes a report and a valuation.][a]

(4) Nothing in this Part shall limit or diminish any liability which any person may incur under the general law.

(5) For the purposes of sections 41 and 43, the following persons shall be deemed not to be a promoter or a person who has authorised the issue of the prospectus—

(a) a professional adviser to any person referred to in section 41 acting as such;

(b) an underwriter or professional adviser to an underwriter acting as such.

(6) The person referred to as the "purchaser" in the following case shall be deemed to be an underwriter for the purposes of subsection (5)(b).

(7) That case is one in which—

(a) a person (the "offeror") intends to make an offer of securities to the public, and

(b) another person (the "purchaser")—

(i) agrees to purchase those securities with the intention of their immediate resale to give effect to that intention of the offeror, at a profit or subject to payment by the offeror to the purchaser of a commission, and

(ii) binds himself or herself to purchase, or procure the purchase of, any of the securities not so resold.

Amendments

a Sub-s (3A) inserted by IFCMPA 2006, s 15(a).

---

39 Construction of certain terms in Act of 1963

(1) A word or expression that is used in a provision inserted in the Act of 1963 by this Part, or in a provision of that Act amended by this Part, and which is also used in this

Part shall have in that provision, as so inserted or amended, the same meaning as it has in this Part.

(2) This section does not limit the generality of section 1(2).

40 Repeal of certain provisions of Act of 1963 and revocation

(1) The following are repealed:

(a) sections 43 to 47, 49 to 52, 54, 56 and 59, subsections (15B) and (15C) of section 60 and sections 61 and 361 to 367 of the Act of 1963, and

(b) the Third and Fourth Schedules to the Act of 1963.

(2) The Companies (Recognition of Countries) Order 1964 (S.I. No. 42 of 1964) is revoked to the extent that it is for the purposes of section 367 of the Act of 1963.

41 Civil liability for misstatements in prospectus

[(1)][a] Subject to sections 42 and 43, the following persons shall be liable to pay compensation to all persons who acquire any securities on the faith of a prospectus for the loss or damage they may have sustained by reason of—

(a) any untrue statement included therein, or

(b) any omission of information required by EU prospectus law to be contained in the prospectus, namely—

(i) the issuer who has issued the prospectus or on whose behalf the prospectus has been issued,

(ii) the offeror of securities to which the prospectus relates,

(iii) every person who has sought the admission of the securities to which the prospectus relates to trading on a regulated market,

(iv) the guarantor of the issue of securities to which the prospectus relates,

(v) every person who is a director of the issuer at the time of the issue of the prospectus,

(vi) every person who has authorised himself or herself to be named and is named in the prospectus as a director of the issuer or as having agreed to become such a director either immediately or after an interval of time,

(vii) every person being a promoter of the issuer,

(viii) every person who has authorised the issue of the prospectus (not being the competent authority designated under Irish prospectus law).

[(2) In addition to the persons specified in subsection (1) as being liable in the circumstances there set out, an expert who has given the consent required by section 45 to the inclusion in a prospectus of a statement purporting to be made by him or her shall, subject to sections 42 and 43, be liable to pay compensation to all persons who acquire any securities on the faith of the prospectus for the loss or damage they may have sustained by reason of an untrue statement in the prospectus purporting to be made by him or her as an expert.][b]

Amendments

a Existing section re-numbered as sub-s (1) by IFCMPA 2006, s 15(b)(i).

b Sub-s (2) inserted by IFCMPA 2006, s 15(b)(ii).

42 Section 41: exceptions and exemptions

(1) [...][a]

(2) A person shall not be liable under section 41 solely on the basis of a summary of a prospectus, including any translation thereof, unless it is misleading, inaccurate or inconsistent when read together with other parts of the prospectus.

(3) Subject to subsection (5), a person shall not be liable under section 41 if he or she proves—

(a) that, having consented to become a director of the issuer, he or she withdrew, in writing, his or her consent before the issue of the prospectus, and that it was issued without his or her authority or consent, or

(b) that the prospectus was issued without his or her knowledge or consent, and that on becoming aware of its issue he or she forthwith gave reasonable public notice that it was issued without his or her knowledge or consent, or

(c) that after the issue of the prospectus and before the acquisition of securities thereunder by the person referred to in section 41, he or she, on becoming aware of any untrue statement therein or omission of material information required by EU prospectus law to be contained therein, withdrew, in writing, his or her consent thereto and gave reasonable public notice of the withdrawal and of the reason therefor, or

(d) that—

(i) as regards—

(I) every untrue statement not purporting to be made on the authority of an expert or of a public official document or statement,

(II) the omission from the prospectus of any information required by EU prospectus law to be contained therein,

he or she had reasonable grounds to believe, and did up to the time of the issue of the securities, believe, that the statement was true or that the matter whose omission caused loss was properly omitted, and

(ii) as regards every untrue statement purporting to be a statement by an expert or contained in what purports to be a copy of or extract from a report or valuation of an expert, it fairly represented the statement, or was a correct and fair copy of or extract from the report or valuation, and he or she had reasonable grounds to believe and did up to the time of the issue of the prospectus believe that the person making the statement was competent to make it [and, where required by section 45, that that person had given his or her consent to the inclusion of the statement in the prospectus][b] and had not withdrawn, in writing, that consent before the publication of the prospectus or, to the defendant's knowledge, before issue of securities thereunder, and

(iii) as regards every untrue statement purporting to be a statement made by an official person or contained in what purports to be a copy of or extract from a public official document, it was a correct and fair representation of the statement or copy of or extract from the document.

(4) In subsections (5) and (6) "by reason of the relevant consent", in relation to an expert, means by reason of his or her having given the consent required of him or her by section 45 to [the inclusion in the prospectus of the statement concerned].[c]

(5) Subsection (3) shall not apply in the case of an expert, by reason of the relevant consent [...],[d] in respect of an untrue statement purporting to be made by him or her as an expert.

(6) An expert who, apart from this subsection, would under section 41 be liable, by reason of the relevant consent, [...][e] in respect of an untrue statement purporting to be made by him or her as an expert shall not be so liable if he or she proves—

(a) that, having given his or her consent to [the inclusion in the prospectus of the statement],[f] he or she withdrew it in writing before publication of the prospectus, or

(b) that, after publication of the prospectus and before the acquisition of securities thereunder by the person referred to in section 41 on becoming aware of the untrue statement, withdrew his or her consent in writing and gave reasonable public notice of the withdrawal, and of the reason therefor, or

(c) that he or she was competent to make the statement and that he or she had reasonable grounds to believe and did up to the time of such acquisition of the securities believe that the statement was true.

Amendments

a Sub-s (1) deleted by IFCMPA 2006, s 15(c)(i).

b Text substituted by IFCMPA 2006, s 15(c)(ii).

c Text substituted by IFCMPA 2006, s 15(c)(iii).

d Text deleted by IFCMPA 2006, s 15(c)(iv).

e Text deleted by IFCMPA 2006, s 15(c)(v)(I).

f Text substituted by IFCMPA 2006, s 15(c)(v)(II).

---

43 Restriction of liability where non-equity securities solely involved

[Where a prospectus is issued solely in respect of non-equity securities—

(a) only—

(i) the offeror or the person who has sought the admission of the securities to which the prospectus relates to trading on a regulated market, and

(ii) subject to, and to the extent provided in, paragraph (c), the guarantor (if any), and no other person referred to in section 41 shall be liable under that section in the circumstances in which that section applies unless—

(I) the prospectus expressly provides otherwise, or

(II) that other such person is convicted on indictment of an offence created by Irish prospectus law or an offence under section 48 in respect of the issue of that prospectus,

(b) section 383(3) of the Act of 1963 shall not apply to the directors or secretary of the issuer to the extent that such application would thereby impose a liability under section 41 on such directors or secretary, and

(c) no liability shall attach under section 41 to a guarantor of such securities save in respect of statements included in, or information omitted from, the prospectus that relate to the guarantor or the guarantee given by the guarantor.][a]

Amendment

a Section substituted by IFCMPA 2006, s 13.

44 Indemnification of certain persons

(1) This section applies where—

(a) a prospectus contains the name of a person as a director of the issuer, or as having agreed to become a director thereof, and he or she has not consented to become a director, or has withdrawn, in writing, his or her consent before the issue of the prospectus, and has not authorised or consented to the issue thereof, or

(b) the consent of an expert is required by section 45 to [the inclusion in a prospectus of a statement purporting to be made by him or her][a] and he or she either has not given that consent or has withdrawn, in writing, that consent before the issue of the prospectus.

(2) The directors of the issuer, except any without whose knowledge or consent the prospectus was issued, and any other person who authorised the issue thereof shall be liable to indemnify the person named as mentioned in subsection (1) or whose consent was required as so mentioned, as the case may be, against all damages, costs and expenses to which he or she may be made liable by reason of his or her name having been inserted in the prospectus or of the inclusion therein of a statement purporting to be made by him or her as an expert, as the case may be, or in defending himself or herself against any action or legal proceeding brought against him or her in respect thereof.

[(3)...][b]

Amendments

a Text substituted by IFCMPA 2006, s 15(d)(i).

b Subsection (3) deleted by IFCMPA 2006, s 15(d)(ii).

45 Expert's consent to issue of prospectus containing statement by him or her

[(1) The prohibition in subsection (2) only applies in relation to a prospectus if EU prospectus law requires the inclusion in the prospectus of a statement of the kind referred to in paragraph (b) of that subsection.

(2) A prospectus including a statement that is attributed to an expert shall not be issued unless—

(a) the expert has given and has not, before the publication of the prospectus, withdrawn, in writing, his or her consent to the inclusion in the prospectus of the statement in the form and context in which it is included, and

(b) a statement that the expert has given and not withdrawn, in writing, that consent appears in the prospectus.

(3) If any prospectus is issued in contravention of this section the issuer and every person who is knowingly a party to the issue thereof shall be guilty of an offence and liable to a fine.][a]

Amendments

a Section substituted by IFCMPA 2006, s 14.

46 Regulations (*Part 5*)

(1) The Minister may make regulations for the purposes of

(a) giving effect to the 2003 Prospectus Directive, and

(b) supplementing and making consequential provision in respect of the Prospectus Regulation.

(2) Regulations under this section may contain such incidental, supplementary and consequential provisions as appear to the Minister to be necessary or expedient for the purposes of those regulations, including—

(a) provisions creating offences (but the regulations may only provide penalties in respect of a summary conviction for any such offence), and

(b) provisions revoking instruments made under other enactments.

(3) This section is without prejudice to section 3 of the European Communities Act 1972.

47 Penalties on conviction on indictment and defences in respect of certain offences

(1) A person who is guilty of an offence created by Irish prospectus law (being an offence expressed by that law to be an offence to which this section applies) shall, without prejudice to any penalties provided by that law in respect of a summary conviction for the offence, be liable, on conviction on indictment, to a fine not exceeding €1,000,000 or imprisonment for a term not exceeding 5 years or both.

(2) In proceedings for an offence created by Irish prospectus law, it shall be a defence for the defendant to prove—

(a) as regards any matter not disclosed in the prospectus concerned, that he or she did not know it, or

(b) the contravention arose from an honest mistake of fact on his or her part, or

(c) the contravention was in respect of matters which, having regard to the circumstances of the case, was immaterial or as respects which, having regard to those circumstances, he or she ought otherwise reasonably to be excused.

48 Untrue statements and omissions in prospectus: criminal liability

(1) Where a prospectus is issued and—

(a) includes any untrue statement, or

(b) omits any information required by EU prospectus law to be contained in it,

any person who authorised the issue of the prospectus (not being the competent authority designated under Irish prospectus law) shall be guilty of an offence unless he or she proves—

(i) as regards an untrue statement, either that the statement was, having regard to the circumstances of the case, immaterial or that he or she honestly believed and did, up to the time of the issue of the prospectus, believe that the statement was true, or

(ii) as regards any information omitted, either that the omission was, having regard to the circumstances of the case, immaterial or that he or she did not know it, or

(iii) that the making of the statement or omission was otherwise such as, having regard to the circumstances of the case, ought reasonably to be excused.

(2) A person guilty of an offence under this section shall be liable—

(a) on summary conviction, to a [class A fine][a] or imprisonment for a term not exceeding 12 months, or

(b) on conviction on indictment, to a fine not exceeding €1,000,000 or imprisonment for a term not exceeding 5 years or both.

(3) Summary proceedings for an offence under this section may be brought and prosecuted by the competent authority designated under Irish prospectus law.

[(4)...][b]

(5) If at a trial for an offence under this section or an offence created by Irish prospectus law, the judge or jury has to consider whether the defendant honestly believed a particular thing or was honestly mistaken in relation to a particular thing, the presence or absence of reasonable grounds for such a belief or for his or her having been so mistaken is a matter to which the judge or jury is to have regard, in conjunction with any other relevant matters, in considering whether the defendant so believed or was so mistaken.

Amendments

a As implicitly substituted for "fine not exceeding €5,000" by Fines Act 2010, s 4. A class A fine currently means a fine not exceeding €5,000.

b Subsection (4) deleted by IFCMPA 2006, s 15(e).

---

49 Local offers

(1) An offering document prepared for a local offer shall contain the following statements in print in clearly legible type:

(a) on the front page or otherwise in a prominent position:

"This document,

—has not been prepared in accordance with Directive 2003/71/EC on prospectuses or any measures made under that Directive or the laws of Ireland or of any EU Member State or EEA treaty adherent state that implement that Directive or those measures,

—has not been reviewed, prior to its being issued, by any regulatory authority in Ireland or in any other EU Member State or EEA treaty adherent state, and therefore may not contain all the information required where a document is prepared pursuant to that Directive or those laws.",

(b) elsewhere in the offering document:

(i) where the offering document contains information on past performance:

"*Past performance may not be a reliable guide to future performance.*",

(ii) where the offering document contains information on simulated performance:

"*Simulated performance may not be a reliable guide to future performance.*",

(iii) "*Investments may fall as well as rise in value.*",

(iv) where securities are described as being likely to yield income or as being suitable for an investor particularly seeking income from his or her investment, and where the income from the securities can fluctuate:

"*Income may fluctuate in accordance with market conditions and taxation arrangements.*",

(v) where the primary market for the securities or the currency of the underlying business is in a currency other than euro:

"*Changes in exchange rates may have an adverse effect on the value, price or income of the securities.*",

(vi) where the securities do not constitute a readily realisable investment:

"*It may be difficult for investors to sell or realise the securities and/or obtain reliable information about their value or the extent of the risks to which they are exposed.*".

(2) Any requirement of subsection (1) as to the inclusion of a particular statement in an offering document shall be regarded as satisfied if words substantially to the effect of that statement are instead included in that document.

(3) If an offeror fails to comply with subsection (1) the offeror shall be guilty of an offence.

(4) No offering document prepared for a local offer shall be issued by or on behalf of a company or in relation to an intended company unless, on or before the date of its publication, a copy of the offering document has been delivered to the registrar of companies for registration.

(5) Summary proceedings for an offence under this section may be brought and prosecuted by the competent authority designated under Irish prospectus law or by the registrar of companies.

50 Exclusion of Investment Intermediaries Act 1995

(1) Any document issued in connection with an offer of securities by or on behalf of an issuer, offeror or person seeking admission of securities to trading on a regulated market shall not be regarded as constituting an investment advertisement within the meaning of section 23 of the Investment Intermediaries Act 1995.

(2) "Document" in subsection (1) includes, in the case of a local offer, an offering document.

51 Power to make certain rules and issue guidelines

(1) In this section "competent authority" means the competent authority designated under Irish prospectus law.

(2) The competent authority may make rules imposing or enabling the competent authority to impose requirements on persons on whom an obligation or obligations are imposed by Irish prospectus law, being requirements—

(a) to do or not to do specified things so as to secure that the provisions of Irish prospectus law are complied with and, in particular (without limiting the generality of this paragraph), to adopt specified procedures and use specified forms in the provision of information to the competent authority,

(b) to do or not to do specified things so as to secure the effective supervision by the competent authority of activities of the kind to which Irish prospectus law relates and, in particular (without limiting the generality of this paragraph), to make such reports or disclose such matters, at such times and in such manner, to the competent authority or other specified persons as are provided for by the rules or specified by the competent authority pursuant to the rules, being reports or a disclosure of matters that is or are required by virtue or in consequence of the operation of Irish prospectus law.

(3) Rules under this section may include rules providing for the manner in which or the matters by reference to which (or both) a determination is to be made of any issue as to whether a transaction or transactions is or are of a significant size for the purposes of the provisions of Irish prospectus law implementing Article 2(2)(a) of the 2003 Prospectus Directive.

(4) The reference in subsection (2) to an obligation imposed on a person by Irish prospectus law includes a reference to an obligation imposed on a person by virtue of the person's exercising a right or option provided under Irish prospectus law.

(5) Rules under this section may contain such consequential, incidental or supplemental provisions as the competent authority considers necessary or expedient.

(6) Rules under this section shall not contain any provision that is inconsistent with Irish prospectus law or require the provision of information to any person the provision of which is not reasonably related to the purposes for which the applicable provisions of the 2003 Prospectus Directive have been adopted.

(7) The provisions of Irish prospectus law that are expressed by that law to be made for the purpose of enabling the imposition of administrative sanctions shall apply in relation to a contravention of rules under this section as they apply in relation to a contravention of a provision of Irish prospectus law and, accordingly, a sanction that may be imposed pursuant to the first-mentioned provisions of Irish prospectus law in respect of a contravention of a provision of that law may, in accordance with that law, be imposed in respect of a contravention of rules under this section.

(8) The competent authority may issue guidelines in writing as to the steps that may be taken to comply with Irish prospectus law.

52 Avoidance of certain agreements

A condition—

(a) requiring or binding an applicant for securities to waive compliance with any requirement of—

(i) this Part, or

(ii) EU prospectus law, or

(b) where EU prospectus law applies, purporting to affect him or her with notice of any contract, document or matter not specifically referred to in the prospectus concerned,

shall be void.

53 Amendment of section 53 of Act of 1963

[...][a]

Amendments

a Section 53 substitutes CA 1963, s 53(1).

54 Amendment of section 55 of Act of 1963

[...][a]

Amendments

a Section 54 substitutes CA 1963, s 55(1) and (3).

55 Amendment of section 57 of Act of 1963

[...][a]

Amendments

a Section 55 substitutes CA 1963, ss 1 and adds a new sub-s 7.

PART 6
MISCELLANEOUS COMPANY LAW AMENDMENTS

56 Amendment of section 60 of Act of 1963

(1) [...][a]

(2) Section 39 applies to the construction of a word or expression used in the provisions inserted in the Act of 1963 by subsection (1) as it applies to the construction of a word or expression used in the provisions inserted in the Act of 1963 by Part 5.

Amendments

a IFCMPA 2005, s 56 substitutes CA 1963, ss 60(12) and (13).

57 Electronic filing agents

(1) A company may authorise a person (who shall be known and is in this Act referred to as an 'electronic filing agent') to do the following acts on its behalf.

(2) Those acts are—

(a) the electronic signing of documents that are required or authorised, by or under the Companies Acts or any other enactment, to be delivered by the company to the registrar of companies, and

(b) the delivery to the registrar of companies, by electronic means, of those documents so signed.

(3) Subject to the following conditions being complied with, an act of the foregoing kind done by such an agent on behalf of a company pursuant to an authorisation by the company under this section that is in force shall be as valid in law as if it had been done by the company (and the requirements of the Companies Acts or the other enactment concerned with respect to the doing of the act have otherwise been complied with (such as with regard to the period within which the act is to be done)).

(4) The conditions mentioned in subsection (3) are—

(a) that prior to the first instance of the electronic filing agent's doing of an act of the kind referred to in subsection (2), pursuant to an authorisation by the company concerned under this section, the authorisation of the agent has been notified by the company to the registrar of companies in the prescribed form, and

(b) the doing of the act complies with any requirements of the registrar of companies of the kind referred to in sections 12(2)(b) and 13(2)(a) of the Electronic Commerce Act 2000.

(5) It shall be the joint responsibility of a company and the electronic filing agent authorised by it under this section to manage the control of the documents referred to in subsection (2).

(6) An electronic filing agent shall not, by virtue of his or her authorisation under this section to act as such, be regarded as an officer or servant of the company concerned for the purposes of section 187(2)(a) of the Act of 1990.

58 Section 57: supplemental provisions

(1) A company may revoke an authorisation by it under section 57 of an electronic filing agent.

(2) Such a revocation by a company shall be notified by it, in the prescribed form, to the registrar of companies.

(3) Unless and until the revocation is so notified to the registrar of companies, the authorisation concerned shall be deemed to subsist and, accordingly, to be still in force for the purposes of section 57(3).

(4) If a revocation, in accordance with this section, of an authorisation under section 57 constitutes a breach of contract or otherwise gives rise to a liability being incurred—

(a) the fact that it constitutes such a breach or otherwise gives rise to a liability being incurred does not affect the validity of the revocation for the purposes of section 57, and

(b) the fact of the revocation being so valid does not remove or otherwise affect any cause of action in respect of that breach or the incurring of that liability.

59 Reservation of company name

(1) In this section—

'reserved' means reserved under subsection (4) for the purpose mentioned in subsection (3);

'specified period' means the period specified in the relevant notification made by the registrar of companies under subsection (5).

(2) During the specified period and any extension under section 60 of that period a company shall not be incorporated with a particular reserved name save on the application of the person in whose favour that name has been reserved.

(3) A person may apply to the registrar of companies to reserve a specified name for the following purpose, namely, the purpose of a company that is proposed to be formed by that person being incorporated with that name; such an application shall be accompanied by the prescribed fee.

(4) On the making of such an application, the registrar of companies may, subject to subsection (6), determine that the name specified in the application shall be reserved for the purpose mentioned in subsection (3).

(5) That determination shall be notified to the applicant by the registrar of companies and that notification shall specify the period (which shall not be greater than 28 days and which shall be expressed to begin on the making of the notification) for which the name is reserved.

(6) A name shall not be reserved that, in the opinion of the registrar of companies, is undesirable.

60 Section 59: supplemental provisions

(1) A person in whose favour a name has been reserved under section 59 may, before the expiry of the specified period, apply to the registrar of companies for an extension of the specified period; such an application shall be accompanied by the prescribed fee.

(2) On the making of such an application, the registrar of companies may, if he or she considers it appropriate to do so, extend the specified period for such number of days (not exceeding 28 days) as the registrar determines and specifies in a notification of the determination to the applicant.

(3) If an application for incorporation of a company with a name that has been reserved under section 59 is received by the registrar of companies during the specified period from the person in whose favour the name has been so reserved, the fee payable to the registrar in respect of that incorporation shall be reduced by an amount equal to the amount of the fee paid under section 59(3) in respect of the reservation of that name.

(4) In this section 'specified period' has the same meaning as it has in section 59.

61 Amendment of section 128 of Act of 1963

[...][a]

Amendments

a IFCMPA 2005, s 61 inserts 'of the Act of 1990' after 'section 193' in CA 1963, s 128(6B)(b).

62 Amendment of section 195 of Act of 1963

Section 195 of the Act of 1963 (inserted by the Act of 1990) is amended by inserting the following subsection after subsection (6):

[...] [a]

Amendments

a IFCMPA 2005, s 62 inserts CA 1963, s 195(6A).

63 Amendment of section 302(1) of Act of 1963

[...] [a]

Amendments

a IFCMPA 2005, s 63 inserts 'or such greater period as may be required in the notice' after 'notice requiring him to do so' in CA 1963, s 302(1).

64 Amendment of section 371(1) of Act of 1963

[...][a]

Amendments

a IFCMPA 2005, s 64 inserts 'or such greater period as may be required in the notice' after 'notice on the company or officer requiring it or him to do so' in CA 1963, s 371(1).

65 Amendment of section 12B of Companies (Amendment) Act 1982

Section 12B of the Companies (Amendment) Act 1982 (inserted by the Companies (Amendment) (No. 2) Act 1999) is amended by inserting the following subsection after subsection (8):

[...] [a]

Amendments

a IFCMPA 2005, s 65 inserts C(A)A 1982, s 12B(8A).

66 Amendment of section 22 of Companies (Amendment) Act 1986

Section 22 of the Companies (Amendment) Act 1986 is amended—

(a) in subsection (1)—

(i) [...] [a]

(ii) [...] [b]

(b) [...] [c]

Amendments

a IFCMPA 2005, s 66(a) substitutes 'shall be guilty of an offence' for 'shall be liable on summary conviction to a fine not exceeding €1,269.74' in C(A)A 1986, s 22(1), para (a).

b IFCMPA 2005, s 67(b) substitutes 'Summary proceedings' for 'Proceedings' in C(A)A 1986, s 22(1), para (b).

c IFCMPA 2005, s 67(c) substitutes 'in respect of each such failure be guilty of an offence, but—' for 'in respect of each offence be liable on summary conviction to imprisonment for a term not exceeding 6 months, or, at the discretion of the court to a fine not exceeding €1,269.74 or to both so, however, that—' in C(A)A 1986, s 22(2).

---

67 Amendment of section 19 of Act of 1990

Section 19(2) of the Act of 1990 is amended—

(a) by inserting the following after paragraph (d):

[...] [a]

(b) [...] [b]

(c) [...] [c]

Amendments

a IFCMPA 2005, s 67(a) inserts CA 1990, para 19(2)(da).

b IFCMPA 2005, s 67(b) substitutes 'have been, are or would be' for 'are or would be' in CA 1990, para 19(2)(e).

c IFCMPA 2005, s 67(c) substitutes 'have been, are or are likely' for 'are or are likely' in CA 1990, para 19(2)(e).

---

68 Amendment of section 20 of Act of 1990

(1) Subsection (3) of section 20 of the Act of 1990 is repealed.

(2) Notwithstanding the repeal by this section of subsection (3) of that section 20, that subsection (3) shall continue to apply to material information (within the meaning of that section 20) seized under that section before the commencement of this section.

Amendments

IFCMPA 2005, s 68(1) repeals CA1990, s 20(3).

---

69 Amendment of section 21 of Act of 1990

Section 21(3) of the Act of 1990 is amended by inserting the following after paragraph (e):

[...] [a]

Amendments

IFCMPA 2005, s 69 inserts CA 1990, s 21(ea) with effect from 23 August 2009.[1]

1 Investment Funds, Companies and Miscellaneous Provisions Act 2005 (Commencement) Order 2009 (SI 335/2009).

70 Amendment of section 166 of Act of 1990

Section 166 of the Act of 1990 is amended—

(a) by substituting the following subsection for subsection (1):

[...][a]

(b) by repealing subsection (3).

[...][b]

Amendments

a IFCMPA 2005, s 70(a) substitutes CA 1990, s 166(1).

b IFCMPA 2005, s 70(b) repeals CA 1990, s 166(3).

71 Amendment of section 242 of Act of 1990

Section 242 of the Act of 1990 is amended—

(a) [...][a]

(b) by inserting the following subsection after subsection (1):

[...][b]

and

(c) in subsection (2), by inserting after 'subsection (1)' 'or (1A)'.

[...][c]

Amendments

a CA 1990, s 242(1) is amended by inserting 'completes, signs' before 'produces, lodges or delivers' in each places where those words occur.

b CA 1990, s 242 is amended by inserting CA 1990, s 242(1A).

c CA 1990, s 242(2) is amended by inserting in CA 1990, s 242(2). 'or (1A)' after 'subsection (1)'.

72 Replacement of references to Companies Registration Office Gazette for references to *Iris Oifigiúil*.

Each enactment mentioned in column (2) of the Table to this section at a particular reference number is amended, in each provision of that enactment mentioned in column (3) of that Table at that reference number, by substituting for '*Iris Oifigiúil*' 'the Companies Registration Office Gazette'

TABLE		
Reference Number	*Enactment*	*Provision*
(1)	(2)	(3)
1.	Companies Act 1963	Sections 65(1)(*e*), 107(1), 227(1), 252(1) and 261(1); Subsections (1), (2), (3), (5) and (8) of section 311 (including those subsections as they have effect by virtue of section 43(15) of the Companies (Amendment) (No 2) Act 1999) and section 311A(1).
2.	Companies (Amendment) Act 1982	Subsections (1), (2) and (3) of section 12; Subsections (1), (2) and (3) of section 12A; Subsections (3) and (7) of section 12B and section 12C(1).
3.	Companies (Amendment) Act 1983	Sections 8(1), 23(7) and 55(1).
4.	Companies (Amendment) Act 1990	Subsection (2)(*a*) and (*b*) of section 12 and section 30(1).
5.	Companies Act 1990	Section 16(18).

73 Miscellaneous amendments of Companies Acts related to penalties

(1) The Act of 1963 is amended—

(a) in section 115, by substituting the following subsection for subsection (6):

[...] [a]

and

(b) [...][b]

(2) The Act of 1990 is amended—

(a) in section 60, by substituting the following subsection for subsection (10):

[...][c]

(b) [...][d]

(c) [...][e]

(d) [...][f]

(3) [...][g]

(4) Schedule 2 to the Companies (Auditing and Accounting) Act 2003 is amended—

(a) [...][h]

(b) [...][i]

Amendments

a IFCMPA 2005, s 73(1)(a) substitutes CA 1963, s 115(6).

b IFCMPA 2005, s 73(1)(b) substitutes 'shall be guilty of an offence and liable for a fine' for 'shall be liable to a fine' in CA 1963, s 128(3).

c IFCMPA 2005, s 73(2)(a) substitutes CA 1990, s 60(10).

d IFCMPA 2005, s 73(2)(b) substitutes 'shall be guilty of an offence and liable for a fine' for 'shall be liable for a fine' in CA 1990, s 80(10).

e IFCMPA 2005, s 73(2)(c) substitutes 'shall be guilty of an offence and liable to a fine' for 'shall be liable for a fine' in CA 1990, s 161(6).

f IFCMPA 2005 s 73(2)(d) inserts '(other than an indictable offence under section 125(2) or 127(12) of the Principal Act)' after 'an indictable offence under the Companies Acts' in CA 1990, s 194(5).

g IFCMPA 2005, s 73(3) repeals C(AA)A 2003, s 37, para (d).

h IFCMPA 2005, s 73(4)(a) deletes '116(6)' and '128(4)' in C(AA)A 2003, Sch 2, Item No 1, col 2.

i IFCMPA 2005, s 73(4)(b) deletes C(AA)A 2003, Sch 2, Items No 8 and 9.

74 Amendment of section 110A of Company Law Enforcement Act 2001

Section 110A of the Company Law Enforcement Act 2001 (inserted by the Companies (Auditing and Accounting) Act 2003) is amended—

(a) in subsection (1)—

(i) [...][a]

(ii) [...][b]

(iii) by inserting the following after paragraph (d):

[...][c]

(b) by inserting the following after subsection 8:

[...][d]

Amendments

a IFCMPA 2005, s 74(a)(i) deletes 'and' in CLEA 2001, s 110A(1), para (c).

b IFCMPA 2005, s 74(a)(ii) substitutes '1999, and' for '1999,' in CLEA 2001, s 110A(1), para (d).

c IFCMPA 2005, s 74(a)(iii) inserts CLEA 2001, s 110A(1), para (e).

d IFCMPA 2005, s 74(b) inserts CLEA 2001, s 110A(8A).

Investment Funds, Companies and Miscellaneous Provisions Act 2006

Number 41 of 2006

ARRANGEMENT OF SECTIONS

PART 1
PRELIMINARY AND GENERAL

PART 2
AMENDMENTS OF COMPANIES ACTS

PART 3
TRANSPARENCY REQUIREMENTS REGARDING ISSUERS OF SECURITIES ADMITTED TO TRADING ON CERTAIN MARKETS

PART 4
MISCELLANEOUS

Not reproduced here.

An Act to amend and extend the Companies Acts, the Irish Takeover Panel Act 1997, The Central Bank Act 1942, the Consumer Information Act 1978 And The Netting Of Financial Contracts Act 1995, to Provide for the Implementation of Directive 2004/109/EC of the European Parliament and of the Council of 15 December 2004 and to Provide for Related Matters.

Be It Enacted By The Oireachtas As Follows:

PART 1
PRELIMINARY AND GENERAL

1 Short title, collective citation and construction

(1) This Act may be cited as the Investment Funds, Companies and Miscellaneous Provisions Act 2006.

(2) The Companies Acts and Parts 2 and 3 shall be read together as one.

2 Commencement

(1) Subject to subsections (2) and (3), this Act shall come into operation on such day or days as the Minister may appoint by order or orders either generally or with reference to any particular purpose or provision and different days may be so appointed for different purposes or different provisions.

(2) Section 1, this section and sections 3 to 6 and 9, 10, 13, 14, 15 and 35 shall come into operation on the passing of this Act.

(3) Sections 7 and 8 shall be deemed to have come into operation on 1 July 2005.

3 Definitions

In this Act—

'Act of 1990' means the Companies Act 1990;

'Act of 1997' means the Irish Takeover Panel Act 1997;

'Act of 2005' means the Investment Funds, Companies and Miscellaneous Provisions Act 2005;

'Minister' means the Minister for Enterprise, Trade and Employment;

'Regulations of 2006' means the European Communities (Takeover Bids (Directive 2004/25/EC)) Regulations 2006 (S.I. No. 255 of 2006).

4 Orders and regulations

Every order or regulation made under this Act (other than an order made under section 2 or 24) shall be laid before each House of the Oireachtas as soon as may be after it is made and, if a resolution annulling the order or regulation is passed by either such House within the next 21 days on which that House has sat after the order or regulation is laid before it, the order or regulation shall be annulled accordingly but without prejudice to the validity of anything previously done thereunder.

5 Expenses

The expenses incurred by the Minister in the administration of this Act shall, to such extent as may be sanctioned by the Minister for Finance, be paid out of moneys provided by the Oireachtas.

Part 2
Amendments of Companies Acts

6 Statutory declarations for purposes of Companies Acts

(1) A statutory declaration made in a place outside the State (in pursuance of or for the purposes of the Companies Acts) shall be regarded as having been validly made (in pursuance of those Acts or for the purposes of them) if it is made in such a place before—

(a) a person entitled under the Solicitors Act 1954 to practise as a solicitor in the State, or

(b) a person authorised, under the law of that place, to administer oaths in that place and subsection (3), (4) or (5), as the case may be, is complied with.

(2) Subsection (1) is—

(a) without prejudice to the circumstances set out in the Statutory Declarations Act 1938 in which a statutory declaration may be made, and

(b) in addition to, and not in substitution for, the circumstances provided under the Diplomatic and Consular Officers (Provision of Services) Act 1993 or any other enactment in which a statutory declaration made by a person in a place outside the State is regarded as a statutory declaration validly made (whether for purposes generally or any specific purpose).

(3) In cases falling within subsection (1) (b) and unless subsection (4) or (5) applies, the signature of the person making the declaration (the 'declarer') and, to the extent that that law requires either or both of the following to be authenticated:

(a) the capacity in which the declarer has acted in making that declaration,

(b) the seal or stamp of the person who has administered the oath to the declarer,

shall be authenticated in accordance with the law of the place referred to in subsection (1)(b).

(4) If the place referred to in subsection (1) (b) is situate in a state that is a contracting party to the EC Convention, then (unless that Convention does not extend to that particular place) the provisions of that Convention with regard to authentication shall apply in relation to the statutory declaration concerned, including the procedures for verification of any matter in circumstances where serious doubts, with good reason, arise in respect of that matter.

(5) If the place referred to in subsection (1)(b) is situate in a state that is a contracting party to the Hague Convention but is not a contracting party to the EC Convention, then (unless the Hague Convention does not extend to that particular place) the provisions of the Hague Convention with regard to authentication shall apply in relation to the statutory declaration concerned, including the procedures for verification of any matter in circumstances where serious doubts, with good reason, arise in respect of that matter.

(6) The registrar of companies may, before receiving any statutory declaration purporting to be made in pursuance of, or for the purposes of, the Companies Acts, being a declaration—

(a) falling within subsection (1)(b), and

(b) to which neither the provisions of the EC Convention nor the Hague Convention apply as regards the authentication of it, require such proof, as he or she considers appropriate, of any particular requirements of the law referred to in subsection (3).

(7) A statutory declaration made before the passing of this Act—

(a) in a place outside the State,

(b) before—

(i) if the place is not a place in England and Wales, Northern Ireland or Scotland, a person authorised, under the law of that place, to administer oaths or a person entitled under the Solicitors Act 1954 to practise as a solicitor in the State, or

(ii) if the place is a place in England and Wales, Northern Ireland or Scotland—

(I) a person entitled under the law of England and Wales, Northern Ireland or Scotland, as the case may be, to practise as a solicitor in England and Wales, Northern Ireland or Scotland, as the case may be, or to administer oaths there, or

(II) a person entitled under the Solicitors Act 1954 to practise as a solicitor in the State,

and

(c) purporting to be made in pursuance of, or for the purposes of, the Companies Acts,

shall, if the declaration was delivered to the registrar of companies before that passing, be valid and deemed always to have been valid notwithstanding anything in the Diplomatic and Consular Officers (Provision of Services) Act 1993 or any other enactment and any-thing done on foot of that declaration's delivery to the registrar, including any subsequent registration of that declaration by the registrar, shall be valid and be deemed always to have been valid notwithstanding anything in that Act or any other enactment.

(8) Nothing in subsection (7) affects any proceedings commenced before the passing of this Act.

(9) In this section—

"EC Convention" means the Convention Abolishing the Legalisation of Documents in the Member States of the European Communities of 25 May 1987;

"Hague Convention" means the Convention Abolishing the Requirement of Legalisation for Foreign Public Documents done at the Hague on 5 October 1961;

"statutory declaration", in addition to the meaning assigned to it by the IA 2005, means a declaration that conforms with the requirements of the Statutory Declarations Act 1938, save for any requirements contained in section 1 of that Act, or any other provision of it, expressly or impliedly limiting the class of persons who may take and receive a declaration or the places in which a declaration may be received or taken.

7 Amendment of section 33 of Companies Act 1963

[...][a]

Amendments

a Substitutes the text of CA 1963, s 33.

8 Amendment of section 21 of Companies (Amendment) Act 1983

[...][a]

Amendments

a Substitutes the text of C(A)A 1983, s 21.

9 Exemption from audit requirement

(1) [...][a]

(2) Nothing in subsection (1)(b) prejudices the future exercise of the power under subsection (7) of section 32 of the Companies (Amendment) (No. 2) Act 1999 in relation to subsection (3) (as it stands amended by subsection (1)(b)) of that section 32.

Amendments

a Subsection (1) amends C(A)(No2)A 1999, ss 32(1), 32(3), 33 and 35 and inserts a new s 32B.

10 Application of section 9 and transitional provisions

(1) The amendments effected by section 9 shall apply as respects—

(a) a financial year of a company that commences not earlier than the commencement of that section, and

(b) subject to subsection (2), a financial year of a company that ends not earlier than 2 months after the commencement of that section (not being a financial year to which paragraph (a) applies).

(2) In cases falling within subsection (1)(b), section 9 shall have effect as if, instead of the subsection (2) inserted by that section in section 33 of the Companies (Amendment) (No. 2) Act 1999, there were inserted the following subsection in that section 33:

> "(2) In cases falling within section 10(1) (b) of the Investment Funds, Companies and Miscellaneous Provisions Act 2006, a notice under subsection (1) may be served on the company not later than 1 month before the end of the financial year to which the notice relates.".

11 Restrictions on, and disqualifications of, persons from acting as directors, etc

[...][a]

Amendments

a Amends CA 1990, ss 150 and 160.

12 Dematerialisation

[...][a]

Amendments

a Amends CA 1990, s 239.

13 Amendment of section 43 of Act of 2005

[...][a]

Amendments

a Substitutes IFCMPA 2005, s 43.

14 Amendment of section 45 of Act of 2005

[...][a]

Amendments

a Substitutes IFCMPA 2005, s 43.

15 Amendments of Act of 2005 consequential on amendment made by section 14

[...][a]

Amendments

a Amends IFCMPA 2005, ss 38, 41 42, 44 and 48.

16 Amendment of section 9 of Companies (Auditing and Accounting) Act 2003

[...][a]

Amendments

a Amends C(AA)A 2003, s 9(2).

17 Amendment of section 10 of Companies (Auditing and Accounting) Act 2003

[...][a]

Amendments

a Amends C(AA) 2003, s 10.

18 Amendment of section 29 of Companies (Auditing and Accounting) Act 2003

[...][a]

Amendments

a Substitutes sub-s (7) of C(AA)A 2003, s 29.

PART 3
TRANSPARENCY REQUIREMENTS REGARDING ISSUERS OF SECURITIES ADMITTED TO TRADING ON CERTAIN MARKETS

19 Interpretation (Part 3)

(1) In this Part—

"Transparency (Regulated Markets) Directive" means Directive 2004/109/EC[1] of the European Parliament and of the Council of 15 December 2004 on the harmonisation of transparency requirements in relation to information about issuers whose securities are admitted to trading on a regulated market and amending Directive 2001/34/EC, including the first-mentioned Directive as it stands amended for the time being;

"transparency (regulated markets) law" means—

(a) the measures adopted for the time being by the State to implement the Transparency (Regulated Markets) Directive and any supplemental Directive (whether an Act of the Oireachtas, regulations under section 3 of the European Communities Act 1972, regulations under section 20 or any other enactment (other than, save where the context otherwise admits, this Part)),

(b) any measures directly applicable in the State in con-sequence of the Transparency (Regulated Markets) Directive and, without prejudice to the generality of this paragraph, includes any Regulation or Decision made by the Commission pursuant to the procedure referred to in Article 27(2) of that Directive, and

(c) any supplementary and consequential measures adopted for the time being by the State in respect of any Regulation or Decision made by the Commission in consequence of the Transparency (Regulated Markets) Directive pursuant to the foregoing procedure;

"supplemental Directive" means any Directive made by the Commission in consequence of the Transparency (Regulated Markets) Directive pursuant to the procedure referred to in Article 27(2) of that Directive.

(2) A word or expression that is used in this Part and is also used in the Transparency (Regulated Markets) Directive shall have in this Part the same meaning as it has in that Directive.

20 Power to make certain regulations

(1) The Minister may make regulations for the purposes of—

(a) giving effect to the Transparency (Regulated Markets) Directive or any supplemental Directive, and

(b) supplementing and making consequential provision in respect of any Regulation or Decision made by the Commission in consequence of the first-mentioned Directive in paragraph (a) pursuant to the procedure referred to in Article 27(2) of that Directive.

(2) Regulations under this section may contain such incidental, supplementary and consequential provisions as appear to the Minister to be necessary or expedient for the purposes of those regulations, including—

(a) provisions creating offences (but the regulations may only provide penalties in respect of a summary conviction for any such offence), and

(b) provisions creating civil liability in respect of contraventions of the regulations so as to enable any person suffering loss thereby to recover compensation for that loss.

(3) Civil liability shall not be created by regulations under subsection (2) in respect of a contravention of regulations under this section save in respect of such a contravention that involves either—

(a) an untrue or misleading statement, or

(b) the omission from a statement of any matter required to be included in it,

being, in either case, a statement—

(i) that is contained in a publication made in purported compliance with a provision of transparency (regulated markets) law specified in the regulations, and

(ii) in respect of which a person suffers a loss by reason of the person's acquiring or contracting to acquire securities (or an interest in them) in reliance on that publication at a time when, and in circumstances in which, it was reason-able for the person to rely on that publication,

and the following condition is fulfilled in respect of that publication.

(4) That condition is that a person discharging responsibilities within the issuer of the securities referred to in subsection (3) in relation to that publication (being responsibilities of a kind specified in regulations under this section)—

(a) knew the statement concerned to be untrue or misleading or was reckless as to whether it was untrue or misleading, or

(b) knew the omission concerned to be dishonest concealment of a material fact.

(5) Regulations under this section may also make, for the purposes of those regulations, provision analogous to that which is made by Part IV of the Act of 1990.

(6) This section is without prejudice to section 3 of the European Communities Act 1972.

21 Conviction on indictment of offences under transparency (regulated markets) law

A person who is guilty of an offence created by transparency (regulated markets) law (being an offence expressed by that law to be an offence to which this section applies) shall, without prejudice to any penalties provided by that law in respect of a summary conviction for the offence, be liable, on conviction on indictment, to a fine not exceeding €1,000,000 or imprisonment for a term not exceeding 5 years or both.

22 Supplementary rules, etc., by competent authority

(1) In this section "competent authority" means the competent authority designated under transparency (regulated markets) law for the purposes of the provisions of the Transparency (Regulated Markets) Directive (other than Article 24(4)(h) of that Directive).

(2) The competent authority may make rules imposing or enabling the competent authority to impose requirements on persons on whom an obligation or obligations are imposed by transparency (regulated markets) law, being requirements—

(a) to do or not to do specified things so as to secure that the provisions of transparency (regulated markets) law are complied with and, in particular (without limiting the generality of this paragraph), to adopt specified procedures and use specified forms in the provision of information to the competent authority,

(b) to do or not to do specified things so as to secure the effective supervision by the competent authority of activities of the kind to which transparency (regulated markets) law relates and, in particular (without limiting

the generality of this paragraph), to make such reports or disclose such matters, at such times and in such manner, to the competent authority or other specified persons as are provided for by the rules or specified by the competent authority pursuant to the rules, being reports or a disclosure of matters that is or are required by virtue or in consequence of the operation of transparency (regulated markets) law.

(3) Rules under this section may, in particular, include rules necessary for the performance by the competent authority of the functions under Article 24 of the Transparency (Regulated Markets) Directive, other than paragraph (4)(h) of that Article.

(4) Rules under this section may contain such consequential, incidental or supplemental provisions as the competent authority considers necessary or expedient.

(5) Rules under this section shall not contain any provision that is inconsistent with transparency (regulated markets) law or require the provision of information to any person the provision of which is not reasonably related to the purposes for which the applicable provisions of the Transparency (Regulated Markets) Directive have been adopted.

(6) The provisions of transparency (regulated markets) law that are expressed by that law to be made for the purpose of enabling the imposition of administrative sanctions shall apply in relation to a contravention of—

(a) rules under this section, and

(b) rules adopted by the Irish Auditing and Accounting Supervisory Authority under section 10(3) of the Companies (Auditing and Accounting) Act 2003 concerning the matters that relate to its functions under section 9(2)(ma) of that Act,

as they apply in relation to a contravention of a provision of transparency (regulated markets) law and, accordingly, a sanction that may be imposed pursuant to the first-mentioned provisions of transparency (regulated markets) law in respect of a contravention of a provision of that law may, in accordance with that law, be imposed in respect of a contravention of rules referred to in either of the foregoing paragraphs.

(7) The competent authority may issue guidelines in writing as to the steps that may be taken to comply with transparency (regulated markets) law.

23 Amendment of section 33AK of Central Bank Act 1942

The definition of "Supervisory Directives" in subsection (10) of section 33AK (inserted by the Central Bank and Financial Services Authority of Ireland Act 2003) of the Central Bank Act 1942 is amended by substituting the following paragraphs for paragraph (h) (inserted by the Act of 2005):

> "(h) the 2003 Prospectus Directive (within the meaning of Part 5 of the Investment Funds, Companies and Miscellaneous Provisions Act 2005),
>
> (i) the Transparency (Regulated Markets) Directive (within the meaning of Part 3 of the Investment Funds, Companies and Miscellaneous Provisions Act 2006);".

24 Application of transparency (regulated markets) law to certain markets

(1) The Minister, after consultation with the competent authority referred to in section 22(1), may, by provisional order, provide that one or more provisions of transparency (regulated markets) law that apply in relation to a market to which the Transparency (Regulated Markets) Directive applies shall, with such modifications, if any, as are specified in the order, apply to a market specified in the order.

(2) A provisional order under this section shall not have effect unless or until it is confirmed by an Act of the Oireachtas.

Companies (Amendment) Act 2009

(Number 20 of 2009)

ARRANGEMENT OF SECTIONS

Section

Companies (Amendment) Act 2009

Number 20 of 2009

An Act to remove certain exceptions contained in the companies acts that apply in the cases of companies holding licences under section 9 of the Central Bank Act 1971 (or holding companies of such companies) regarding disclosure of loans to directors and transactions of an analogous nature, to otherwise amend the companies acts in respect of loans by companies (of whatever type) to directors or certain related par-ties and transactions of an analogous nature and, in particular, to amend section 40 of the Companies Act 1990 concerning criminal liability in that regard, to confer additional powers on the director of corporate enforcement with respect to access to information in the possession of companies, including information kept by them in certain registers or books, or in the possession of third parties, to amend sections 20 and 23 of the Companies Act 1990 in relation to search warrants and procedures to be followed in cases of claims of legal professional privilege, to amend sections 43 and 44 of the Companies (Amendment) (No 2) Act 1999 and to provide for related matters. [12th July, 2009]

Be it enacted by the Oireachtas as follows:

1 Definitions

In this Act—

'Act of 1990' means the Companies Act 1990;

'Act of 2001' means the Company Law Enforcement Act 2001;

'Act of 2003' means the Companies (Auditing and Accounting) Act 2003;

'Principal Act' means the Companies Act 1963.

2 Amendment of section 194 of Principal Act

Section 194 (as amended by the Act of 2003) of the Principal Act is amended—

(a) in subsection (5)(b), by substituting 'fails to comply with this subsection or subsection (5A)' for 'fails to comply with this subsection'; and

(b) […][a]

Amendments

a C(A)A 2009, s 2 inserts CA 1963, s 194(5A).

---

3 Amendment of section 371A of Principal Act

Section 371A (inserted by the Act of 2001) of the Principal Act is amended, in subsection (1), by substituting 'section 19(3)(c)' for 'section 19(3)(b)'.

4 Amendment of section 19 of Act of 1990

(1) Section 19 (inserted by the Act of 2001) of the Act of 1990 is amended—

(a) […][a]

(b) in subsection (4), by substituting 'subsection (3)(c)' for 'subsection (3)(b)' in each place where it occurs; and

(c) in subsection (9), by substituting 'a direction under subsection (1) or (3A)' for 'a direction under subsection (1)'.

(2) Nothing in subsection (1) shall be construed to mean that, but for the amendment effected by it, a direction given by the Director of Corporate Enforcement, before the passing of this Act, under section 19(3) of the Act of 1990 was limited in any way as to its effect or extent of operation or that any books or documents produced on foot of it to the Director of Corporate Enforcement were not lawfully produced to him.

Amendments

a C(A)A 2009, s 4(1)(a) substitutes CA 1990, s 19(3).

---

5 Amendment of section 20 of Act of 1990

Section 20 of the Act of 1990 is amended—

(a) in subsection (2), by substituting 'at any time or times within the period of validity of the warrant' for 'at any time or times within 1 month from the date of issue of the warrant';

(b) […][a];

and

(c) […][b].

Amendments

a C(A)A 2009, s 5(b) inserts CA 1990, s 20(2A)–(2J).

b C(A)A 2009, s 5(c) inserts CA 1990, s 20(8)–(11).

---

6 Amendment of section 23 of Act of 1990

[…][a].

Amendments

a C(A)A 2009, s 6 substitutes CA 1990, s 23(1) and inserts CA 1990, s 23(1A)–(1F).

7 Amendment of section 40 of Act of 1990

[…][a].

Amendments

a C(A)A 2009, s 7 substitutes CA 1990, s 40.

8 Disclosure of loans, etc., — amendment of exceptions applicable to directors of licensed banks and provisions as to offences and other matters

(1) Section 41 of the Act of 1990 is amended—

(a) […][a];

and

(b) […][b].

(2) […][c].

(3) Section 43 of the Act of 1990 is further amended—

(a) in subsection (7), by substituting 'subsection (2) or (5)' for 'subsection (2), (5) or (6)';

(b) in subsection (8), by substituting 'subsections (2) and (5)' for 'subsections (2), (5) and (6)';

(c) by deleting subsection (9); and

(d) […][d].

Amendments

a C(A)A 2009, s 8(1)(a) substitutes CA 1990, s 41(6).

b C(A)A 2009, s 8(1)(b) inserts CA 1990, s 41(10)–(12).

c C(A)A 2009, s 8(2) substitutes CA 1990, s 43(5) and (6) and inserts s 43(6A).

d C(A)A 2009, s 8(3)(d) inserts CA 1990, s 43(11) and (12).

9 Amendments of other provisions of Act of 1990 concerning licensed banks and disclosure of loans, etc.

Section 44 of the Act of 1990 is amended—

(a) in subsection (1), by substituting 'are required by subsection (1) or (2) of section 41 or would, but for section 41(6), be required by subsection (1) or (2) of that section' for 'would, but for section 41(6), be required by subsection (1) or (2) of that section';

(b) […][a];

(c) in subsection (8), by substituting ‘subsection (1), (3) or (4C)’ for ‘subsection (1) or (3)’; and

(d) […][b].

Amendments

a C(A)A 2009, s 9(b) inserts CA 1990, s 44(4A)–(4C).

b C(A)A 2009, s 9(d) substitutes CA 1990, s 44(9).

10 Amendment of sections 43 and 44 of Companies (Amendment) (No 2) Act 1999

(1) Section 43 of the Companies (Amendment) (No. 2) Act 1999 is amended—

(a) in subsections (1), (2), (8) and (9), by substituting ‘a Member State of the EEA’ for ‘the State’;

(b) by repealing subsection (12); and

(c) […][a].

(2) Section 44 of the Companies (Amendment) (No. 2) Act 1999 is amended—

(a) in subsection (8), by substituting ‘So far as it is the person’s residence in the State that falls to be determined for the purposes of that section, for the purposes of section 43,’ for ‘For the purposes of section 43,’; and

(b) […][b].

Amendments

a C(A)A 2009, s 10(1)(c) substitutes C(A)(No 2)A 1999, s 43(16).

b C(A)A 2009, s 10(2)(b) inserts C(A)(No 2)A 1999, s 44(12).

11 Short title and construction

(1) This Act may be cited as the Companies (Amendment) Act 2009.

(2) The Companies Acts and this Act shall be read as one.

Companies (Miscellaneous Provisions) Act 2009

(Number 45 of 2009)

ARRANGEMENT OF SECTIONS

Section

An Act to provide, in limited circumstances, for the transitional use by certain parent undertakings of internationally recognised accounting standards other than those generally accepted accounting principles and policies used in the state, to amend the Companies Act 1990, the Companies (Auditing And Accounting) Act 2003 and the European Communities (Undertakings for Collective Investment in Transferable Securities) Regulations 2003, and to provide for related matters.

Be it enacted by the Oireachtas as follows:

1 Transitional accounting standards

(1) In this section—

"accounts" means Companies Act individual accounts and Companies Act group accounts;

"relevant parent undertaking" means a parent undertaking—

(a) which does not have securities admitted to trading on a regulated market,

(b) whose securities (or whose receipts in respect of those securities) are registered with the Securities and Exchange Commission of the United States of America, or which is otherwise subject to reporting to that Commission, under the laws of the United States of America, and

[(c) which—

(i) prior to the date on which the Companies (Amendment) Act 2012 came into operation, did not make and was not required to make an annual return to the registrar of companies to which accounts were required to have been annexed, or

(ii) on or after 23 December 2009 but prior to the date on which the Companies (Amendment) Act 2012 came into operation, used, in accordance with the provisions of this Act, US generally accepted accounting principles in the preparation of its Companies Act individual accounts or its Companies Act group accounts;][a]

"US generally accepted accounting principles" means the standards and interpretations, in relation to accounting and financial statements, issued by any of the following bodies constituted under the laws of the United States of America or of a territorial unit of the United States of America:

(a) the Financial Accounting Standards Board;

(b) the American Institute of Certified Public Accountants;

(c) the Securities and Exchange Commission.

[(2) This section applies to the accounts of a relevant parent undertaking that are prepared for such of its financial years after it is incorporated in the State as end or ends not later than 31 December 2020.][b]

(3) To the extent that the use of US generally accepted accounting principles does not contravene any provision of the Companies Acts or of any regulations made thereunder—

(a) a true and fair view of the state of affairs and profit or loss of a relevant parent undertaking may be given by the use by that undertaking of those principles in the preparation of its Companies Act individual accounts, and

(b) a true and fair view of the state of affairs and profit or loss of a relevant parent undertaking and its subsidiary undertakings as a whole may be given by the use by that relevant parent undertaking of those principles in the preparation of its Companies Act group accounts.

(4) Where accounts are prepared in accordance with this section, the notes to those accounts shall contain a statement to that effect.

Amendments

a Paragraph (c) of definition of "relevant parent undertaking" substituted by C(A)A 2012, s 2(a).

b Subsection (2) substituted by C(A)A 2012, s 2(b).

---

2 Regulations

(1) In this section "accounts" means Companies Act individual accounts and Companies Act group accounts.

(2) The Minister may make regulations providing for specified categories of parent undertakings which do not have securities admitted to trading on a regulated market and providing that—

(a) a true and fair view of the state of affairs and profit or loss of a parent undertaking in such a category may be given by the preparation by it of its Companies Act individual accounts for [a specified number of its][a] financial years in accordance with specified accounting standards, and

(b) a true and fair view of the state of affairs and profit or loss of a parent undertaking in such a category and its subsidiary undertakings as a whole may be given by the preparation by that parent undertaking of its Companies Act group accounts for [a specified number of its][a] financial years in accordance with specified accounting standards.

(3) Regulations made under subsection (2) shall—

(a) specify the accounting standards, which shall be—

(i) internationally recognised, and

(ii) generally accepted accounting principles or practice of a jurisdiction—

(I) to which a majority of the subsidiaries of the parent undertaking have a substantial connection, or

(II) in which the market on which the shares of the parent undertaking are primarily admitted to trading is situated,

(b) specify the number of financial years in respect of which the regulations apply, and the date on which the latest of such financial years shall end, which shall be not later than 31 [December 2020][b], and

(c) provide that the preparation of such accounts shall not contravene any provision of the Companies Acts or of any regulations made thereunder.

(4) Every regulation under this section shall be laid before each House of the Oireachtas as soon as may be after it is made and, if a resolution annulling the regulation is passed by either such House within the next 21 days on which that House has sat after the regulation is laid before it, the regulation shall be annulled accordingly but without prejudice to the validity of anything previously done thereunder.

(5) Where accounts are prepared in accordance with regulations made under this section, the notes to those accounts shall contain a statement to that effect.

Amendments

a Words "a specified number of its" substituted for "a specified number, not to exceed 4, of its first" by C(A)A 2012, s 3(a).

b "December 2020" substituted for "December 2012" by C(A)A 2012, s 3(b).

---

3 Amendment of Companies Act 1990

The Companies Act 1990 is amended—

(a) in section 3(2), by substituting the following for paragraph (a):

[...][a]

(b) in section 7(3), by deleting ", to an amount not less than £5,000 and not exceeding £250,000,",

(c) in section 13(1), by substituting "relevant Minister." for 35 "relevant Minister, provided that no such liability on the part of the applicant or applicants shall exceed in the aggregate £250,000.",

(d) in section 212—

(i) in subsection (1)(b), by inserting "within the State" after "exchange",

(ii) by inserting the following subsection after subsection (1):

[...][b] and

(iii) in subsection (2), by deleting "subsection (1)" and substituting "subsections (1) and (1A)",

(e) in section 215(1), by inserting "or overseas market purchase" after "market purchase" in each place where it occurs,

(f) in section 226(1), by inserting "or, in the case of an overseas market purchase, within 3 working days," after "28 days",

(g) by inserting the following section after section 226:

[...][c]

(h) in section 229(1), by inserting ", other than when the purchase was an overseas market purchase," after "subsidiary",

(i) in section 256(8), by inserting ", other than a company to which section 256F applies," after "this Part applies", and

(j) by inserting the following after section 256E:

[...][d]

Amendments

a C(MP)A 2009, s 3(a) substitutes CA 1990, s 3(2)(a).

b C(MP)A 2009, s 3(d)(ii) inserts CA 1990, s 212(1A).

c C(MP)A 2009, s 3(g) inserts CA 1990, s 226A.

d C(MP)A 2009, s 3(j) inserts CA 1990, ss 256F, 256G, 256H.

4 Amendment of Companies (Auditing and Accounting) Act 2003

(1) Section 27 of the Companies (Auditing and Accounting) Act 2003 is amended—

(a) by substituting the following for subsection (1):

[...][a]

and

(b) by inserting in subsection (4) ", including the determination of whether a matter should be referred to a committee established for a purpose referred to in subsection (1)" after "behalf".

(2) For the avoidance of doubt, a committee that was established under subsection (1) of section 27 of the Companies (Auditing and Accounting) Act 2003 prior to the commencement of section 4 of the Companies (Miscellaneous Provisions) Act 2009 shall be deemed to have been properly constituted, and shall be deemed to have and to have had all the powers necessary to perform its functions notwithstanding that any of its members was a director when he or she was appointed to the committee but ceased to be such a director before the completion.

Amendments

a C(MP)A 2009, s 4(1)(a) substitutes C(AA)A 2003, s 27(1).

5 Amendment of UCITS Regulations

(1) The UCITS Regulations are amended by inserting the following after Regulation 36F (inserted by section 77 of and the Schedule to the Investment Funds, Companies and Miscellaneous Provisions Act 2005):

"Application of jurisdiction transfer provisions to investment companies established as UCITS

36G.—The provisions of sections 256F to 256H 35 of the Companies Act 1990 (inserted by section 3 of the Companies (Miscellaneous Provisions) Act 2009) shall apply to any investment company authorised pursuant to these

Regulations and for this purpose the references to authorisation shall be read as referring to authorisation pursuant to these Regulations.".

(2) In this section "UCITS Regulations" means the European Communities (Undertakings for Collective Investment in Transferable Securities) Regulations 2003 (S.I. No. 211 of 2003) as amended.

6 Short title, commencement and construction

(1) This Act may be cited as the Companies (Miscellaneous Provisions) Act 2009.

(2) This Act (other than sections 1 and 2, paragraphs (a) to (h) of section 3, and section 4) shall come into operation on such day or days as may be appointed by order or orders of the Minister for Enterprise, Trade and Employment, either generally or with reference to a particular purpose or provision, and different days may be so appointed for different purposes and different provisions.

(3) The Companies Acts and this Act are to be read together as one.

Companies (Amendment) Act 2012

ARRANGEMENT OF SECTIONS

AN ACT TO AMEND THE COMPANIES (MISCELLANEOUS PROVISIONS) ACT 2009 IN ORDER TO EXTEND THE PROVISIONS OF SECTIONS 1 AND 2 OF THAT ACT, AND TO PROVIDE FOR RELATED MATTERS. BE IT ENACTED BY THE OIREACHTAS AS FOLLOWS:

1 Interpretation

In this Act, "Act of 2009" means the Companies (Miscellaneous Provisions) Act 2009.

2 Amendment of section 1 of Act of 2009

Section 1 of the Act of 2009 is amended—

(a) [...][a]

and

(b) [...][b]

Amendments

a Subsection (a) substituted definition of "relevant parent undertaking" in C(MP)A 2009, s 1(1)(c).

b Subsection (b) substituted C(MP)A 2009, s 1(2).

---

3 Amendment of section 2 of Act of 2009

Section 2 of the Act of 2009 is amended—

(a) in paragraphs (a) and (b) of subsection (2), by substituting "a specified number of its" for "a specified number, not to exceed 4, of its first", and

(b) in subsection (3)(b), by substituting "December 2020" for "December 2015".

4 Short title and construction

(1) This Act may be cited as the Companies (Amendment) Act 2012.

(2) The Companies Acts and this Act are to be read together as one.

Division B: Secondary Legislation

European Communities (Companies) Regulations 1973

SI 163/1973

The Minister for Industry and Commerce, in exercise of the powers conferred on a Minister of State by section 3 of the European Communities Act, 1972 (No. 27 of 1972), and to give effect to the Council Directive of the European Communities of 9 March, 1968 (68/151/EEC), hereby makes the following regulations:

1 Citation and commencement

These regulations may be cited as the European Communities (Companies) Regulations, 1973, and shall come into operation on the 1st day of July, 1973.

2 Construction

These regulations shall be construed as one with the Companies Act, 1963 (No. 33 of 1963), in these regulations referred to as 'the Act'.

[**2A**(1) In these Regulations—

'certified translation' means certified to be a true and correct translation in accordance with rules drawn up by the registrar of companies and published in the Companies Registration Office Gazette;

'Directive' means First Council Directive 68/151/EEC of the Council of the European Communities of 9 March 1968 (OJ No L 65, 14.3.1963, p 8), as amended by Directive 2003/58/EC of the European Parliament and of the Council of 15 July 2003 (OJ No L 221, 4.9.2003, p 13);

'letters and order forms' means letters and order forms in paper form or in any other medium.

(2) A word or expression that is used in these Regulations and is also used in the Directive has the same meaning in these Regulations as it has in the Directive.][a]

Amendments

a Section 2A inserted by EC(C)(A)R 2007 (SI 49/2007), reg 3(a) with effect from 1 April 2007.

---

3 Application

These regulations apply to every company, being a company registered under the Act with limited liability or an unregistered company with limited liability to which certain provisions are applied by section 377(1) of the Act, and the terms 'company' and 'unregistered company' shall be construed accordingly.

4 Publication of notices

(1) A company shall [cause to be published in the Companies Registration Office Gazette][a] notice of the delivery to or the issue by the registrar of companies after the commencement of these regulations of the following documents and particulars—

(a) any certificate of incorporation of the company;

(b) the memorandum and articles of association, or the charter, statutes or other instrument constituting or defining the constitution of the company (in these regulations included in the term 'memorandum and articles of association');

(c) any document making or evidencing an alteration in its memorandum or articles of association;

(d) every amended text of its memorandum and articles of association;

(e) any return relating to its register of directors or notification of a change among its directors;

(f) any return relating to the persons, other than the board of directors, authorised to enter into transactions binding the company, or notification of a change among such persons;

(g) [its annual return and the accounting documents that are required to be published in accordance with—

(i) Fourth Council Directive 78/660/EEC of 25 July 1978 (OJ No. L222, 14.8.1978, p. 11),

(ii) Seventh Council Directive 83/349/EEC of 13 June 1983 (OJ No. L193, 18.7.1983, p. 1),

(iii) Council Directive 86/635/EEC of 8 December 1986 (OJ No. L372, 31.12.1986, p.1), and

(iv) Council Directive 91/674/EEC of 19 December 1991 (OJ No. L374, 31.12.1999, p. 7)][a];

(h) any notice of the situation of its registered office, or of any change therein;

(i) any copy of a winding up order in respect of the company;

(j) any order for the dissolution of the company on a winding up;

(k) any return by a liquidator of the final meeting of the company on a winding up.

(2) A notice shall be published within six weeks of the relevant delivery or issue.

(3) In a voluntary winding up, the liquidator shall within 14 days after his appointment [cause to be published in the Companies Registration Office Gazette][b] a notice of his appointment in addition to delivering notice to the registrar of companies as required by section 278 of the Act.

[(4) For the purposes of the provisions of Article 3(3) of the Directive the registrar of companies shall ensure that certification of electronic copies of documents or particulars guarantees both the authenticity of their origin and the integrity of their contents, by means at least of an advanced electronic signature within the meaning of Article 2(2) of Directive 1999/93/EC of the European Parliament and of the Council of 13 December 1999 (OJ No. L13, 19.1.2000, p.12).

(5) Any document or particular specified in these Regulations that is required to be delivered to the registrar of companies shall be drawn up in the Irish or English language, and may be accompanied by a certified translation of that document or particular into any other official language of the European Communities.

(6) Where a certified translation pursuant to paragraph (5) has been voluntarily disclosed and there is a discrepancy between—

(a) a document or particular required to be delivered or disclosed to the registrar of companies under paragraph (5), and

(b) the certified translation accompanying it,

the certified translation—

(i) may not be relied upon by the company as against any person dealing with the company, and

(ii) may be relied upon by a person dealing with the company as against that company, unless the company proves that the person dealing with the company had knowledge of the document or particular in the Irish or English version.][c]

Amendments

a Subparagraph (g) of reg 4(1) substituted by EC(C)(A)R 2007 (SI 49/2007), reg 3(b)(i) with effect from 1 April 2007.

b Reg 5 of the EC(C)R 2004 (SI 839/2004) substituted the words 'cause to be published in the Companies Registration Office Gazette' for 'publish in *Iris Oifigiúil*'.

c Paragraphs (4), (5) and (6) inserted by EC(C)(A)R 2007 (SI 49/2007), reg 3(b)(ii) with effect from 1 April 2007.

---

5 Text of altered memorandum and articles

Where any alteration is made in a company's memorandum or articles of association, notice of which the company is required to publish under Regulation 4, the company shall deliver to the registrar of companies, in addition to the alteration, a copy of the text of the memorandum and articles as so altered.

6 Organs authorised to bind company

(1) In favour of a person dealing with a company in good faith, any transaction entered into by any organ of the company, being its board of directors or any person registered under these regulations as a person authorised to bind the company, shall be deemed to be within the capacity of the company and any limitation of the powers of that board or person, whether imposed by the memorandum or articles of association or otherwise, may not be relied upon as against any person so dealing with the company.

(2) Any such person shall be presumed to have acted in good faith unless the contrary is proved.

(3) For the purpose of this Regulation, the registration of a person authorised to bind the company shall be effected by delivering to the registrar of companies a notice giving the name and description of the person concerned.

7 Registration of unregistered companies

(1) Every unregistered company shall, within one month after the commencement of these regulations or, if it is incorporated after such commencement, within one month of its incorporation, deliver to the registrar of companies for registration a certified copy of the memorandum and articles of association of the company as amended to date.

(2) The company shall [cause to be published in the Companies Registration Office Gazette][a] notice of the delivery of all documents required to be delivered under paragraph (1), stating in the notice the name of the company, the description of the documents and the date of delivery.

Amendments

a Reg 5 of the EC(C)R 2004 (SI 839/2004) substituted the words 'cause to be published in the Companies Registration Office Gazette' for 'publish in *Iris Oifigiúil*'.

8 Application of Act to unregistered companies

[...][a]

Amendments

a Repealed by CA 1990, s 6, effective 1 August 1991.

9 [Letters, order forms and websites

(1) Every company shall include the following particulars on its letters and order forms:

- (a) the name and legal form of the company;
- (b) the place of registration of the company and the number with which it is registered;
- (c) the address of the registered office of the company;
- (d) in the case of a company exempt from the obligation to use the word 'limited' or 'teoranta' as part of its name, the fact that it is a limited company;
- (e) in the case of a company that is being wound up, the fact that it is being wound up;
- (f) if reference is made in the letter or order form to the share capital of the company, the reference shall be to the capital that is subscribed and paid up.

(2) Where a company has a website, it shall display in a prominent and easily accessible place on that website the particulars referred to in subparagraphs (a) to (f) of paragraph (1), except that the reference in subparagraph (f) to 'in the letter or order forms' shall be construed as a reference to 'on the website'.][a]

Amendments

a Reg 9 substituted by EC(C)(A)R 2007 (SI 49/2007), reg 3(c) with effect from 1 April 2007.

10 Failure to notify documents

The documents and particulars, notice of which is required by these regulations to be [published in the Companies Registration Office Gazette],[a] may not be relied upon by the company as against any other person until after such publication unless the company proves that such person had knowledge of them. However, with regard to transactions taking place before the sixteenth day after the date of publication, they shall not be relied upon against a person who proves that it was impossible for him to have had knowledge of them.

Amendments

a Reg 5 of the EC (C) R 2004 (SI 839/2004) substituted the words 'published in the Companies Registration Office Gazette' for 'published in *Iris Oifigiúil*'.

---

11 Extension of time for delivery of documents

The court may by order at any time extend the time for delivery of documents under these regulations for such period as the court may think proper.

12 [Offences and penalties

(1) If a company fails to comply with Regulation 4, 5, 7 or 9, the company and—

(a) every officer of the company who is in default, and

(b) any person in accordance with whose directions or instructions the directors of the company are accustomed to act and to whose directions or omissions the default is attributable,

shall be guilty of an offence.

(2) A person who is convicted of an offence under these Regulations shall be liable, on summary conviction, to a [class C fine][a].

(3) Where a person has been convicted of an offence under these Regulations and there is a continuation of the offence by the person after his or her conviction, the person shall be guilty of a further offence on every day on which the contravention continues and for each such offence shall be liable, on summary conviction, to a [class E fine][b] for each day on which the offence is so continued.][c]

Amendments

a As implicitly substituted for "fine not exceeding €2,000" by Fines Act 2010, s 6. A class C fine currently means a fine not exceeding €2,500.

b As implicitly substituted for "fine not exceeding €100" by Fines Act 2010, s 8. A class E fine currently means a fine not exceeding €500.

c Reg 12 substituted by EC(C)(A)R 2007 (SI 49/2007), reg 3(d) with effect from 1 April 2007.

Given under my Official Seal, this 20th day of June, 1973.

EXPLANATORY NOTE

These Regulations give effect to Council Directive of the European Communities of 9th March, 1968 (68/151/EEC). The Regulations, which apply to companies including unregistered companies with limited liability, provide for the official notification by companies of certain registered documents and particulars by means of publication in Iris Oifigiúil [now, the Companies Registration Office Gazette] and for the publication of additional information on a company's business letters and order forms. They also modify the ultra vires rule in regard to the board of directors or any person authorised to bind a company. The Regulations extend to unregistered companies certain provisions of the Companies Act, 1963.

European Communities (Mergers and Division of Companies) Regulations 1987

SI 137/1987

ARRANGEMENT OF REGULATIONS

PART 1
PRELIMINARY

PART II
MERGERS

PART III
DIVISIONS

I, ALBERT REYNOLDS, Minister of Industry and Commerce, in exercise of the powers conferred on me by section 3 of the European Communities Act, 1972 (No. 27 of 1972) and for the purpose of giving effect to Council Directive No. 78/855/EEC of 9 October, 1978 (OJ No L295/36, 20.10.78) and No. 82/891/EEC of 17 December, 1982 (OJ L378/47, 31.12.82) hereby make the following Regulations;

PART 1
PRELIMINARY

1 Citation and commencement

(1) These Regulations may be cited as the European Communities (Mergers and Divisions of Companies) Regulations, 1987.

(2) These Regulations shall be construed as one with the Companies Acts.

(3) These Regulations shall come into operation on the 1st day of June, 1987.

2 Interpretation

(1) In these Regulations, unless the context otherwise requires—

'the Act of 1963' means the Companies Act, 1963;

'the Companies Acts' means the Act of 1963 and every enactment (including these and other Regulations made under the European Communities Act, 1972) which is to be construed as one with that Act;

'company' means a public limited company, within the meaning of the Companies (Amendment) Act, 1983, or a body corporate to which certain provisions of the Act of 1963 are applied by section 377(1) of that Act;

'director', in relation to a company which is being wound up, means liquidator;

'division' has the meaning assigned to it by Regulation 24;

'merger' has the meaning assigned to it by Regulation 4;

'Minister' means the Minister for Industry and Commerce.

['Regulations of 2007' means the Transparency (Directive 2004/109/EC) Regulations 2007 (S.I. No. 277 of 2007);][a]

(2) In these Regulations a reference to any enactment shall, unless the context otherwise requires, be construed as a reference to that enactment as amended by any other enactment including these Regulations.

Amendments

a Definition inserted by EC(MDC)(A)R 2011, reg 5(a).

---

3 Penalties

A person convicted of an offence under these Regulations shall be liable, on summary conviction, to a [class C fine][a] or, at the discretion of the court, to imprisonment for a term not exceeding 12 months or both.

Amendments

a £1,000 increased to £1,500 by CA 1990, s 240(7) as inserted by CLEA 2001, s 104. £1,500 converted to €1,904.61 by Council Regulations (EC) No 1103/97, No 974/98 and No 2866/98 and the Economic and Monetary Union Act 1988, s 6; the above being implicitly substituted, by Fines Act 2010, s 6, for a fine not exceeding the aforesaid amount. A class C fine currently means a fine not exceeding €2,500.

PART II
MERGERS

4 Interpretation of Part II

In this Part, unless the context otherwise requires—

'acquiring company', has the meaning assigned to it by Regulation 5;

'merger' means 'merger by acquisition' or 'merger by formation of a new company' within the meaning of Regulation 5(1);

'merging company' means a company which is a party to a proposed merger.

5 Mergers to which Part II applies

(1) In this Part—

(a) 'merger by acquisition' means an operation whereby an existing company ('the acquiring company') acquires all the assets and liabilities of another company or companies in exchange for the issue to the shareholders of the company or companies being acquired of shares in the acquiring company, with or without any cash payment, and with a view to the dissolution of the company or companies being acquired; and

(b) 'merger by formation of a new company' means a similar operation where the acquiring company has been formed for the purpose of such acquisition.

(2) Where a company is being wound up it may—

(a) become a party to a merger by acquisition or by formation of a new company, provided that the distribution of its assets to its shareholders has not begun at the date, under Regulation 6 (4), of the draft terms of merger, or

(b) opt to avail of the provisions of sections 201 to 204, 260 and 271 of the Act of 1963.

(3) Subject to paragraph (2), the said provisions shall not apply to merger by acquisition or by formation of a new company.

6 Draft terms of merger

(1) Where a merger is proposed to be entered into, the directors of the merging companies shall draw up draft terms of the merger in writing.

(2) The draft terms of merger shall state, at least—

(a) the name and registered office of each of the merging companies;

(b) as to each of such companies, whether it is a public company limited by shares, a public company limited by guarantee and having a share capital or a body corporate to which section 377(1) of the Act of 1963 relates;

(c) the proposed share exchange ratio and the amount of any cash payment;

(d) the proposed terms relating to allotment of shares in the acquiring company;

(e) the date from which holders of such shares will become entitled to participate in the profits of the acquiring company;

(f) the date from which the transactions of the company or companies being acquired shall be treated for accounting purposes as being those of the acquiring company;

(g) any special conditions, including special rights or restrictions, whether in regard to voting, participation in profits, share capital or otherwise, which will apply to shares or other securities issued by the acquiring company in exchange for shares or other securities in the company or companies being acquired;

(h) any payment or benefit in cash or otherwise, paid or given or intended to be paid or given to any independent person referred to in Regulation 8 and to any director of any of the merging companies insofar as it differs from the payment or benefit paid or given to other persons in respect of the merger and the consideration, if any, for any such payment or benefit.

(3) Where the merger is a merger by formation of a new company the draft terms of merger shall include or be accompanied by the memorandum or draft memorandum and the articles or draft articles of association of the new company.

(4) The draft terms of merger shall be signed and dated on behalf of each of the merging companies by two directors of each such company and that date shall, for the purposes of this Part, be the date of the draft terms of merger.

7 Directors' explanatory report

(1) [Subject to paragraph (4), a separate written report][a] ('the explanatory report') shall be drawn up in respect of each of the merging companies by the directors of each such company.

(2) The explanatory report shall at least detail and explain—

(a) the draft terms of merger;

(b) the legal and economic grounds for and implications of the draft terms of merger with particular reference to the proposed share exchange ratio, organisation and management structures, recent and future commercial activities and the financial interests of the holders of the shares and other securities in the company;

(c) the methods used to arrive at the proposed share exchange ratio and the reasons for the use of these methods;

(d) any special valuation difficulties which have arisen.

(3) The explanatory report shall be signed and dated on behalf of each of the merging companies by two directors of each such company.

[(4) This Regulation shall not apply where all of the holders of shares and other securities conferring the right to vote in general meetings of each of the merging companies have so agreed.][b]

Amendments

a Words 'Subject to paragraph (4), a separate written report' substituted for 'A separate written report' by EC(MDC)(A)R 2011, reg 5(b)(i).

b Paragraph (4) inserted by EC(MDC)(A)R 2011, reg 5(b)(ii).

---

8 Independent person's report

(1) [Subject to paragraph (11), each][a] of the merging companies shall appoint an independent person to examine the draft terms of merger and to prepare a written report on them to the shareholders of the company concerned.

(2) No person shall act as an independent person for the purposes of paragraph (1) unless he is authorised by the Minister on application by the company concerned to be such a person for the purposes of the proposed merger.

(3) One or more independent persons may be authorised by the Minister on joint application by the merging companies for all the said companies.

(4) None of the following persons shall be qualified to act as an independent person in respect of a proposed merger—

(a) a person who is or, within 12 months of the date of the draft terms of merger, has been, an officer or servant of the company;

(b) except with the leave of the Minister, a parent, spouse, brother, sister or child of an officer of the company;

(c) a person who is a partner or in the employment of an officer or servant of the company.

(5) If an independent person becomes disqualified by virtue of this regulation he shall thereupon cease to hold office and shall give notice in writing of his disqualification to the Minister within 14 days thereof, but without prejudice to the validity of any acts done by him in his capacity as independent person.

(6) Any person who acts as an independent person when disqualified from doing so under this regulation or who makes default in complying with paragraph (5) shall be guilty of an offence.

(7) The report referred to in paragraph (1) shall—

(a) state the method or methods used to arrive at the proposed share exchange ratio;

(b) give the opinion of the person making the report as to whether the proposed share exchange ratio is fair and reasonable;

(c) give the opinion of the person making the report as to whether the method or methods used are adequate in the case in question;

(d) indicate the values arrived at using each such method;

(e) give the opinion of the person making the report as to the relative importance attributed to such methods in arriving at the values decided on;

(f) any special valuation difficulties which have arisen.

(8) A person making a report under this regulation shall be entitled to require from the merging companies and their officers such information and explanation (whether orally or in writing) and to carry out such investigations as he thinks necessary to enable him to make the report.

(9) Any of the merging companies and any officer thereof who—

(a) fails to supply to an independent person any information or explanation in his power, possession or procurement which that person thinks necessary for the purposes of this report, or

(b) knowingly or recklessly makes a statement or provides a document which—

(i) is misleading, false or deceptive in a material particular, and

(ii) is a statement or document to which this paragraph applies,

shall be guilty of an offence.

(10) Paragraph (9) applies to any statement made, whether orally or in writing, or any document provided to any person making a report under this regulation being a statement or document which conveys or purports to convey any information or explanation which that person requires, or is entitled to require, under paragraph (8).

[(11) Paragraph (1) does not apply if all of the holders of shares and other securities conferring the right to vote in general meetings of each of the merging companies have so agreed.][b]

Amendments

a Words 'Subject to paragraph (11), each' substituted for 'Each' by EC(MDC)(A)R 2008, reg 2(a)(i).

b EC(MDC)R 1987, reg 8(11) inserted by EC(MDC)(A)R 2008, reg 2(a)(ii).

9 Accounting statement

(1) [Subject to paragraphs (6) and (7), where the latest annual accounts][a] of any of the merging companies relate to a financial year ended more than six months before the date of the draft terms of merger, that company shall prepare an accounting statement in accordance with the provisions of this regulation.

(2) The accounting statement shall, where required under paragraph (1), be drawn up—

(i) in the format of the last annual balance sheet and in accordance with the provisions of the Companies Acts; and

(ii) as at a date not earlier than the first day of the third month preceding the date of the draft terms of merger.

(3) Valuations shown in the last annual balance sheet shall, subject to the exceptions outlined in paragraph (4), only be altered to reflect entries in the books of account.

(4) Notwithstanding the provisions of paragraph (3), the following shall be taken into account in preparing the accounting statement—

(a) interim depreciation and provisions, and

(b) material changes in actual value not shown in the books of account.

(5) The provisions of the Companies Acts relating to the Auditor's report on the last annual accounts shall apply, with any necessary modifications, to the accounting statement required by paragraph (1).

[(6) Paragraph (1) does not apply to a merging company which makes public a half-yearly financial report covering the first 6 months of its financial year pursuant to Regulation 6 of the Regulations of 2007 if the merging company makes that report available for inspection pursuant to Regulation 12.

(7) This Regulation does not apply to a merging company if all of the holders of shares and other securities conferring the right to vote in general meetings of the company have so agreed.][b]

Amendments

a Words 'Subject to paragraphs (6) and (7), where the latest annual accounts' substituted for 'Where the latest annual accounts' by EC(MDC)(A)R 2011, reg 5(c)(i).

b Paragraphs (6) and (7) inserted by EC(MDC)(A)R 2011, reg 5(c)(ii).

---

10 Companies (Amendment) Act 1983: sections 30 and 31 restricted

[...][a]

Amendments

a Regulation 10 deleted by EC(MDC)(A)R 2011, reg 5(d).

---

11 Registration and publication of documents

(1) [Subject to paragraph (3), each of the merging companies shall][a]—

(a) deliver for registration to the registrar of companies a copy of the draft terms of merger, signed and dated as required by Regulation 6; and

(b) [cause to be published in the Companies Registration Office Gazette][b] and once at least in 2 daily newspapers circulating in the district where the registered office or principal place of business of the company is situate notice of delivery to the registrar of companies of the draft terms of merger.

(2) The requirements of paragraph (1) shall be fulfilled by each of the merging companies at least one month before the date of the general meeting of each such company which by virtue of Regulation 13 is to consider the draft terms of merger.

[(3) Paragraph (1) does not apply to a merging company if the company—

(a) publishes, free of charge on its website for a continuous period of at least 2 months, commencing at least one month before the date of the general meeting which by virtue of Regulation 13 is to consider the draft terms of merger and ending at least one month after that date, a copy of the draft terms of merger, signed and dated pursuant to Regulation 6, and

(b) causes to be published in the Companies Registration Office Gazette and once at least in 2 daily newspapers circulating in the district in which the registered office or principal place of business of the company is situate notice of publication on its website of the draft terms of merger.

(4) Where, in the period referred to in paragraph (3)(*a*), access to the company's website is disrupted for a continuous period of at least 24 hours or for separate periods totalling not less than 72 hours, the period referred to in paragraph (3)(a) shall be extended for a period corresponding to the period or periods of disruption.][c]

Amendments

a Words 'Subject to paragraph (3), each of the merging companies shall' substituted for 'Each of the merging companies shall' by EC(MDC)(A)R 2011, reg 5(e)(i).

b The Companies Registration Office Gazette was substituted for *Iris Oifigiúil* by EC(C)R 2004, (SI 839/2004), reg 6(a) with effect from 15 December 2004.

c Paragraphs (3) and (4) inserted by EC(MDC)(A)R 2011, reg 5(e)(ii).

---

12 Inspection of documents

(1) Each of the merging companies shall, [subject to paragraphs (2) and (3)][a], make available for inspection free of charge by any member of the company at its registered office during business hours (subject to such reasonable restrictions as the company in general meeting may impose so that not less than 2 hours in each day be allowed for inspection)—

(a) the draft terms of merger;

(b) the audited annual accounts for the preceding three financial years of each company or, where a company has traded for less than 3 financial years before the date of the draft terms of merger, the audited annual accounts for those financial years for which the company has traded;

(c) [where applicable, the explanatory reports][b] relating to each of the merging companies referred to in Regulation 7;

(d) [where applicable][c] the independent person's report relating to each of the merging companies referred to in Regulation 8;

(e) [where applicable, an accounting statement or half-yearly financial report in relation to any of the merging companies which is required pursuant to Regulation 9.][d]

(2) The provisions of paragraph (1) shall apply in the case of each of the merging companies for a period of one month before the general meeting which is to consider the draft of merger.

[(3) Subject to paragraph (4), paragraph (1) does not apply to a merging company if it publishes, free of charge on its website the documents listed in that paragraph for a continuous period of at least 2 months, commencing at least one month before the date of the general meeting which by virtue of Regulation 13 is to consider the draft terms of merger and ending at least one month after that date.

(4) Paragraph (3) does not apply where the entitlement referred to in paragraph (3) of Regulation 13 does not apply in consequence of the application of paragraph (3B) of that regulation.

(5) Where, in the period referred to in paragraph (3), access to the company's website is disrupted for a continuous period of at least 24 hours or for separate periods totalling not less than 72 hours, the period referred to in paragraph (3) shall be extended for a period corresponding to the period or periods of disruption.][e]

Amendments

a Words 'subject to paragraphs (2) and (3)' substituted for 'subject to paragraph (2)' by EC(MDC)(A)R 2011, reg (5)(f)(i).

b Words 'where applicable, the explanatory reports' substituted for 'the explanatory reports' by EC(MDC)(A)R 2011, reg (5)(f)(ii).

c Words 'where applicable' inserted by EC(MDC)(A)R 2008, reg 2(b).

d Subparagraph (e) substituted by EC(MDC)(A)R 2011, reg (5)(f)(iii).

e Paragraphs (3)–(5) inserted by EC(MDC)(A)R 2011, reg (5)(f)(iv).

---

13 General meetings of merging companies

(1) Subject to paragraph (4) of this regulation and to Regulation 14, the draft terms of merger shall be approved by a special resolution passed at a general meeting of each of the merging companies.

(2) Where the merger is a merger by formation of a new company, the memorandum or draft memorandum and articles or draft articles of association of the new company shall be approved by a special resolution of each of the companies being acquired.

(3) [Subject to paragraphs (3A) and (3B), the notice][a] convening the general meeting referred to in paragraph (1) shall contain a statement of every shareholder's entitlement to obtain on request, free of charge, full or, if so desired, partial copies of the documents listed in Regulation 12.

[(3A) Subject to paragraph (3B), where a shareholder has consented to the use by the company of electronic means for conveying information, the copies referred to in paragraph (3) may be provided to that shareholder by electronic mail and the notice convening the general meeting referred to in paragraph (1) shall contain a statement to that effect.

(3B) Where, for a continuous period of at least 2 months, commencing at least one month before the date of the general meeting which by virtue of this regulation is to consider the draft terms of merger and ending at least one month after that date, copies of the documents specified in paragraph (1) of Regulation 12 are available to download and print, free of charge, from the company's website by shareholders of the company, the entitlement referred to in paragraph (3) shall not apply.

(3C) Where, in the period referred to in paragraph (3B), access to the company's website is disrupted for a continuous period of at least 24 hours or for separate periods totalling not less than 72 hours, the period referred to in paragraph (3B) shall be extended for a period corresponding to the period or periods of disruption.][b]

(4) In the case of—

(a) a merger by acquisition, or

(b) [a merger by acquisition carried out by a company which holds ninety per cent or more, but not all,][c] of their shares and other securities conferring the right to vote at general meetings ('a voting right') (whether such shares and other securities are held either by the acquiring company together with or solely by other persons in their own names but on behalf of that company), or

(c) an operation to which paragraph (8) of this regulation applies,

approval of the draft terms of merger by means of a special resolution shall not be required in the case of the acquiring company provided that the following conditions are fulfilled—

(i) the provisions of Regulations 11 and 12 are complied with at least one month before the date of the general meeting of each of the companies being acquired, and

(ii) one or more members of the company holding paid up share capital amounting in total value to not less that 5% of such of the paid up share capital as confers voting right, whether or not the shares held confer a voting right, shall be entitled, under the articles of association of the company, to require the convening of a general meeting of the company to consider the draft terms of merger.

(5) The directors of each of the companies [involved in a merger][d] shall inform—

(a) the general meeting of that company, and

(b) the directors of [each of the other companies involved in the merger][e]

of any material change in the assets and liabilities of [that company][e] between the date of the draft terms of merger and the date of such general meeting.

(6) The directors of [each such other company involved in the merger][f] shall inform the general meeting of that company of the matters referred to in paragraph (5).

(7) Regulations 7, 8 and 12 shall not apply in the case of an operation under paragraph (4) (b) of this regulation provided that the conditions under Regulation 15 are fulfilled.

(8) Notwithstanding anything contained in Regulation 5, but subject to paragraph (9) of this regulation, these Regulations shall apply to an operation whereby a company ('the acquiring company') acquires all the assets and liabilities of another company or companies and the acquiring company is the holder of all of the shares and other securities conferring the right to vote at general meetings of the company or companies being acquired, whether such shares and other securities are held either by the acquiring company together with or solely by other persons in their own name but on behalf of that company.

(9) The following provisions of these Regulations shall not apply to an operation under paragraph (8), namely, Regulations 6(2)(c), 6(2)(d), 6(2)(e), 7, 8, 12(1)(c), 12 (1)(d), [19(2)(b) and 22][g].

Amendments

a Words 'Subject to paragraphs (3A) and (3B), the notice' substituted for 'The notice' by EC(MDC)(A)R 2011, reg (5)(g)(i).

b Paragraphs (3A)–(3C) inserted by EC(MDC)(A)R 2011, reg (5)(g)(ii).

c Words 'a merger by acquisition carried out by a company which holds ninety per cent or more, but not all,' substituted for 'an operation whereby one or more companies are acquired by another company which holds ninety per cent or more, but not all,' by EC(MDC)(A)R 2011, reg (5)(g)(iii).

d Words 'involved in a merger' substituted for 'being acquired' by EC(MDC)(A)R 2011, reg (5)(g)(iv).

e Words 'each of the other companies involved in the merger' substituted for 'the acquiring company' and 'that company' substituted for 'the company or companies being acquired' by EC(MDC)(A)R 2011, reg (5)(g)(v).

f Words 'each such other company involved in the merger' substituted for 'the acquiring company' by EC(MDC)(A)R 2011, reg (5)(g)(vi).

g '19(2)(b) and 22' substituted for '19(1)(b) and 21' by EC(MDC)(A)R 2011, reg (5)(g)(vii).

---

14 Meetings of classes of shareholders

Where the share capital of any of the merging companies is divided into shares of different classes, section 38 of the Companies (Amendment) Act, 1983, shall apply.

15 Purchase of minority shares

(1) Any person being—

(a) a shareholder in any of the merging companies who voted against the special resolution of the company concerned relating to the draft terms of merger, or

(b) in a case to which Regulation 13(4)(b) relates, any shareholder other than the acquiring company, may, not later than 15 days after the relevant date, request the acquiring company in writing to acquire his shares for cash.

(2) In this regulation 'the relevant date' in relation to a company means the date on which the latest general meeting of that company to consider the draft terms of merger, or of any class of the holders of shares or other securities of such company, as required by these Regulations, is held.

(3) Nothing in this regulation shall prejudice the power of the court to make any order necessary for the protection of the interests of a dissenting minority in a merging company.

16 Application for confirmation of merger by court

(1) An application to the court for an order confirming a merger shall be made jointly by all the merging companies.

(2) The application shall be accompanied by a statement of the size of the shareholding of any shareholder who has requested the purchase of his shares under Regulation 15 and of the measures which the acquiring company proposes to take to comply with such shareholder's request.

17 Protection of creditors

(1) A creditor of any of the merging companies who, at the date of publication of the notice under Regulation 11(1)(b), is entitled to any debt or claim against the company, shall be entitled to object to the confirmation by the court of the merger.

(2) If the court deems if necessary in order to secure the adequate protection of creditors of any of the merging companies it may—

(a) determine a list of creditors entitled to object and the nature and amount of their debts or claims, and may publish notices fixing a period within which creditors not entered on the list may have a claim for inclusion on that list considered;

(b) where an undischarged creditor on the list referred to in subparagraph (a) does not consent to the merger, the court may dispense with the consent of that creditor, on the company securing payment of the debt or claim by apportioning to that creditor such following amount as the court may direct—

(i) if the company concerned admits the full amount of the debt or claim, that amount;

(ii) if the company concerned does not admit the debt or claim, or if the amount is contingent or not ascertained, an amount fixed by the court after the like inquiry and adjudication as if the company were being wound up by the court.

(3) If, having regard to any special circumstances of the case it thinks proper so to do, the court may direct that paragraph (2) shall not apply as regards as regards any class of creditors.

18 Preservation of rights of holders of securities

(1) Subject to paragraph (2), holders of securities, other than shares, in any of the companies being acquired to which special rights are attached shall be given rights in

the acquiring company at least equivalent to those they possessed in the company being acquired.

(2) Paragraph (1) shall not apply—

- (a) where the alteration of the rights in the acquiring company has been approved—
  - (i) by a majority of the holders of such securities at a meeting held for that purpose, or
  - (ii) by the holders of those securities individually, or
- (b) where the holders of those securities are entitled under the terms of those securities to have their securities purchased by the acquiring company.

19 Confirmation order

(1) The court, on being satisfied that—

- (a) the requirements of these Regulations have been complied with,
- (b) proper provision has been made for—
  - (i) any dissenting shareholder of any of the merging companies who has made a request under Regulation 15, and
  - (ii) any creditor of any of the merging companies who objects to the merger in accordance with Regulation 17, and
- (c) the rights of holders of securities other than shares in any of the companies being acquired are safeguarded in accordance with Regulation 18,

may, subject to Regulation 20, make an order confirming the merger with effect from such date as the court appoints ('the appointed date').

(2) The order of the court confirming the merger shall, with effect from the appointed date, have the following effects—

- (a) all the assets and liabilities of the company or companies being acquired shall stand transferred to the acquiring company in accordance with the draft terms of merger as approved by the court;
- (b) the shareholders of the company or companies being acquired shall become shareholders in the acquiring company in accordance with the draft terms of the merger as approved by the court;
- (c) the company or companies being acquired shall, subject to paragraph (4), be dissolved;
- (d) all legal proceedings pending by or against any of the dissolved companies shall be continued with the substitution, for the dissolved company, of the acquiring company.

(3) The court may, either by the order confirming the merger or by a separate order, make provision for such matters as the court considers necessary to secure that the merger shall be fully and effectively carried out.

(4) The court may, in particular, by order—

- (a) direct that the acquiring company shall, on a date specified by the court, purchase the shares of a dissenting shareholder who has made a request under Regulation 15 and pay therefor the sum determined by the court, being not less than the market sale price of the shares on the appointed date, and

(b) provide for the reduction accordingly of the company's capital.

(5) Section 41 (1) of the Companies (Amendment) Act, 1983 (which restricts the right of a company to purchase its own shares) shall not apply to the purchase of any shares in pursuance of an order of the court under this regulation.

(6) If it is necessary for any of the companies being acquired to take any steps to ensure that its assets and liabilities are fully transferred, the court may specify a date which, save in exceptional cases, shall not be later than 6 months after the appointed date by which such steps must be taken and for that purpose may order that the dissolution of such company shall take effect on that date.

20 Limitation on power of court to make orders

An order of the court shall not be made under these Regulations in respect of a proposed merger to which the Mergers, Take-overs and Monopolies (Control) Act, 1978 applies until either—

(a) the Minister has stated in writing that he has decided not to make an order under section 9 of that Act, in relation to the proposed merger, or

(b) the Minister has stated in writing that he has made a conditional order under that section in relation to the proposed merger, or

(c) the relevant period within the meaning of section 6 of that Act (which relates to a limitation on the commencement of a merger) has elapsed without the Minister's having made an order under the said section 9 in relation to the proposed merger.

whichever first occurs.

21 Registration and publication of confirmation of merger

(1) Where the court has made an order confirming a merger an office copy thereof shall forthwith be sent to the registrar of companies for registration by such officer of the court as the court may direct.

(2) The acquiring company shall [cause to be published in the Company Registration Office Gazette][a] notice of delivery to the registrar of companies of the order of the court confirming the merger within fourteen days of such delivery and if default is made in complying with this paragraph the company and every officer of the company who is in default shall be guilty of an offence.

(3) It shall be a defence for a person charged with an offence under paragraph (2) to show that non-compliance was not due to any delay or negligence on the part of the company or person concerned.

(4) Proceedings in relation to an offence under this regulation may be brought and prosecuted by the registrar of companies.

Amendments

a The Companies Registration Office Gazette was substituted for *Iris Oifigiúil* by EC(C)R 2004, (SI 839/2004), reg 6(b) with effect from 15 December 2004.

---

22 Civil liability of directors and independent persons

(1) Any shareholder of any of the merging companies who has suffered loss or damage by reason of misconduct in the preparation or implementation of the merger by a director of any such company or by the independent person who has made a report under Regulation 8 shall be entitled to have such loss or damage made good to him by—

(a) in the case of misconduct by a person who was a director of that company at the date of the draft terms of merger – that person,

(b) in the case of misconduct by any independent person who prepared a report under Regulation 8 in respect of any of the merging companies – that person.

(2) Without prejudice to the generality of paragraph (1), any shareholder of any of the merging companies who has suffered loss or damage arising from the inclusion of any untrue statement in the draft terms of merger, the explanatory report, the independent person's report or the accounting statement provided for under Regulation 9 shall, subject to paragraphs (3) and (4), be entitled to have such loss or damage made good to him by every person who was a director of that company at the date of the draft terms of merger or, in the case of the independent person's report, by the person who made that report in relation to that company.

(3) A director of a company shall not be liable under paragraph (2) if he proves—

(a) that any of the documents referred to in paragraph (2) was issued without his knowledge or consent and that on becoming aware of their issue he forthwith informed the shareholders of that company that they were issued without his knowledge or consent, or

(b) that as regards every untrue statement he had reasonable grounds, having exercised all reasonable care and skill, for believing and did, up to the time the merger took effect, believe that the statement was true.

(4) A person who makes a report required by Regulation 8 in relation to a company shall not be liable in the case of untrue statements in his own report if he proves—

(i) that on becoming aware of the statement he forthwith informed the company concerned and its shareholders of the untruth, or

(ii) that he was competent to make the statement and that he had reasonable grounds for believing and did up to the time the merger took effect believe that the statement was true.

23 Criminal liability for untrue statements to merger documents

(1) Where any untrue statement has been included in the draft terms of merger, the explanatory report or the accounting statement, each of the directors and any person who authorised the issue of those documents shall be guilty of an offence.

(2) Where any untrue statement has been included in the independent person's report the independent person and any person who authorised the issue of the report shall be guilty of an offence.

(3) It shall be a defence for a person charged with an offence under paragraph (1) or (2) to show that, having exercised all reasonable care and skill, he had reasonable grounds for believing and did, up to the time of the issue of the documents, believe that the statement was true.

PART III
DIVISIONS

24 Interpretation of Part III

In this Part, unless the context otherwise requires—

'acquiring companies' has the meaning assigned to it by Regulation 25;

'division' means 'division by acquisition' or 'division by formation of new companies', within the meaning of Regulation 25(1).

25 Division to which Part II applies

(1) In this Part—

(a) 'division by acquisition' means an operation whereby two or more companies ('the acquiring companies') of which one or more but not all may be a new company acquire between them all the assets and liabilities of another company in exchange for the issue to the shareholders of that company of shares in one or more of the acquiring companies with or without any cash payment and with a view to the dissolution of the company being acquired, and

(b) 'division by formation of new companies' means a similar operation whereby the acquiring companies have been formed for the purposes of such acquisition.

(2) Where a company is being wound up it may—

(a) become a party to a division by acquisition or by formation of new companies, provided that the distribution of its assets to its shareholders has not begun at the date, under Regulation 26 (4), of the draft terms of a division, or

(b) opt to avail of the provisions of sections 201 to 204, 260 and 271 of the Act of 1963.

(3) Subject to paragraph (2), the said provisions shall not apply to a division by acquisition or by formation of new companies.

26 Draft terms of division

(1) Where a division is proposed to be entered into, the directors of the companies involved in the division shall draw up draft terms of the division in writing.

(2) The draft terms of division shall state, at least—

(a) the name and registered office of each of the companies involved in the division;

(b) as to each of such companies, whether it is a public company limited by shares, a public company limited by guarantee and having a share capital or a body corporate to which section 377(1) of the Act of 1963 relates;

(c) the proposed share exchange ratio and the amount of any cash payment;

(d) the proposed terms relating to allotment of shares in the acquiring companies.;

(e) the date from which holders of such shares will become entitled to participate in the profits of one or more of the acquiring companies;

(f) the date from which the transactions of the company being acquired shall be treated for accounting purposes as being those of any of the acquiring companies;

(g) any special conditions, including special rights or restrictions, whether in regard to voting, participation in profits, share capital or otherwise, which will apply to shares or other securities issued by the acquiring companies in exchange for shares or other securities in the company being acquired;

(h) any payment or benefit in cash or otherwise paid or given or intended to be paid or given to any independent person referred to in Regulation 28 and to any director of any of the companies involved in the division insofar as it differs from the payment or benefit paid or given or intended to be paid or given to other persons in respect of the division and the consideration, if any, for any such payment or benefit;

(i) the precise description and allocation of the assets and liabilities of the company being acquired to be transferred to each of the acquiring companies;

(j) the allocation of shares in the acquiring companies to the shareholders of the company being acquired and the criteria on which such allocation is based.

(3) Where the division involves the formation of one or more new companies the draft terms of division shall include or be accompanied by the memorandum or draft memorandum and the articles or draft articles of association of each of the new companies.

(4) The draft terms of division shall be signed and dated on behalf of each of the companies involved in the division by two directors of each such company and that date shall for the purposes of this Part, be the date of the draft terms of division.

(5) Where an asset of the company being acquired is not allocated by the draft terms of division and where the interpretation of those terms does not make a decision on its allocation possible, the asset or the consideration therefor shall be allocated to the acquiring companies in proportion to the share of the net assets allocated to each of those companies under the draft terms of division.

27 Directors' explanatory report

(1) [Subject to paragraphs (5) and (6), a separate written report][a] ('the explanatory report') shall be drawn up in respect of each of the companies involved in the division by the directors of each such company.

(2) The explanatory report shall at least detail and explain—

(a) the draft terms of division;

(b) The legal and economic grounds for and implications of the draft terms of division with particular reference to the proposed share exchange ratio, organisation and management structures, recent and future commercial activities and the financial interests of holders of the shares and other securities in the company;

(c) the methods used to arrive at the proposed share exchange ratio and the reasons for the use of these methods;

(d) any special valuation difficulties which have arisen.

(3) Where it is proposed that any of the acquiring companies will allot shares for a consideration other than in cash, the explanatory report shall state that the report required by section 30 of the Companies (Amendment) Act, 1983, is being or has been

prepared and that it will be delivered to the registrar of companies for registration in accordance with section 31 of that Act.

(4) The explanatory report shall be signed and dated on behalf of each of the companies involved in the division by two directors of each such company.

[(5) Regulation does not apply if all of the holders of shares and other securities conferring the right to vote in general meetings of each of the companies involved in the division have so agreed.

(6) Paragraph (1) does not apply to a company involved in a division by formation of new companies where the shares in each of the acquiring companies are allocated to the shareholders of the company being acquired in proportion to their rights in the capital of that company.][b]

Amendments

a Words 'Subject to paragraphs (5) and (6), a separate written report' substituted for 'A separate written report' by EC(MDC)(A)R 2011, reg (5)(h)(i).

b Paragraphs (5) and (6) inserted by EC(MDC)(A)R 2011, reg (5)(h)(ii).

---

28 Independent person's report

(1) [Subject to paragraph (12), each][a] of the companies involved in the division shall appoint an independent person to examine the draft terms of division and to prepare a written report on them to the shareholders of the company concerned.

(2) No person shall act as an independent person for the purposes of paragraph (1) unless he is authorised by the Minister on application by the company concerned to be such a person for the purposes of the proposed division.

(3) One or more independent persons may be authorised by the Minister on joint application by the companies involved in the division for all the said companies.

(4) None of the following persons shall be qualified to act as an independent person in respect of a proposed division—

- (a) a person who is or, within 12 months of the date of the draft terms of division, has been an officer or servant of the company;
- (b) except with the leave of the Minister, a parent, spouse, brother, sister or child or an officer of the company;
- (c) a person who is a partner or in the employment of an officer or servant of the company.

(5) If an independent person becomes disqualified by virtue of this regulation he shall thereupon cease to hold office and shall give notice in writing of his disqualification to the Minister within 14 days thereof, but without prejudice to the validity of any acts done by him in his capacity as independent person.

(6) Any person who acts as an independent person when disqualified from doing so under this regulation or who makes default in complying with paragraph (5) shall be guilty of an offence.

(7) The report referred to in paragraph (1) shall—

(a) state the method or methods used to arrive at the proposed share exchange ratio;

(b) give the opinion of the person making the report as to whether the proposed share exchange ratio is fair and reasonable;

(c) give the opinion of the person making the report as to whether such method or methods are adequate in the case in question;

(d) indicate the values arrived at using each such method;

(e) give the opinion of the person making the report as to the relative importance attributed to such methods in arriving at the values decided on;

(f) any special valuation difficulties which have arisen.

(8) [...][b]

(9) A person making a report under this regulation shall be entitled to require from the companies involved in the division and their officers such information and explanation (whether orally or in writing) and to carry out such investigations as the independent person thinks necessary to enable him to make the report.

(10) Any of the companies involved in the division and any officer thereof who—

(a) fails to supply to an independent person any information or explanation in his power, possession or procurement, and which that person thinks necessary for the purpose of his report, or

(b) knowingly or recklessly makes a statement or provides a document which—

(i) is misleading, false or deceptive in a material particular, and

(ii) is a statement or document to which this paragraph applies,

shall be guilty of an offence.

(11) Paragraph (10) applies to any statement made, whether orally or in writing, or any document provided to any person making a report under this regulation being a statement or document which conveys or purports to convey any information or explanation which that person requires, or is entitled to require, under paragraph (9).

[(12) Paragraph (1) does not apply—

(a) if all of the holders of shares and other securities conferring the right to vote in general meetings of each of the companies involved in the division have so agreed, or

(b) to a company involved in a division by formation of new companies where the shares in each of the acquiring companies are allocated to the shareholders of the company being acquired in proportion to their rights in the capital of that company,][c]

Amendments

a Words 'Subject to paragraph (12), each' substituted for 'Each' by EC(MDC)(A)R 2008, reg 2(c)(i).

b Paragraph 8 deleted by EC(MDC)(A)R 2011, reg 5(i)(i).

c EC(MDC)R 1987, reg 28(12) inserted by EC(MDC)(A)R 2008, reg 2(c)(ii) and substituted by EC(MDC)(A)R 2011, reg 5(i)(ii).

29 Accounting statement

(1) [Subject to paragraph (6), where the latest annual accounts][a] of any of the companies involved in the division relate to a financial year ended more than six months before the date of the draft terms of division, that company shall prepare an accounting statement in accordance with the provisions of this regulation.

(2) The accounting statement shall, where required under paragraph (1), be drawn up—

(i) in the format of the last annual balance sheet and in accordance with the provisions Companies Acts; and

(ii) as a date not earlier than the first day of the third month preceding the date of the draft terms of division.

(3) Valuations shown in the last annual balance sheet shall, subject to the exceptions outlined in paragraph (4), only be altered to reflect entries in the books of account.

(4) Notwithstanding the provisions of paragraph (3), the following shall be taken into account in preparing the accounting statement—

(a) interim depreciation and provisions; and

(b) material changes in actual value not shown in the books of account.

(5) The provisions of the Companies Acts relating to the auditor's report on the last annual accounts shall apply, with any necessary modifications, also to the accounting statement required by paragraph (1).

[(6) Paragraph (1) does not apply to a company involved in a division which makes public a half-yearly financial report covering the first 6 months of its financial year pursuant to Regulation 6 of the Regulations of 2007 where it makes that report available for inspection pursuant to Regulation 12.

(7) This regulation does not apply to a company involved in a division if all of the holders of shares and other securities conferring the right to vote in general meetings of the company have so agreed.][b]

Amendments

a Words 'Subject to paragraph (6), where the latest annual accounts' substituted for 'Where the latest annual accounts' by EC(MDC)(A)R 2011, reg 5(j)(i).

b Paragraphs (6) and (7) inserted by EC(MDC)(A)R 2011, reg 5(j)(ii).

---

30 Registration and publication of documents

(1) [Subject to paragraph (3), each of the companies involved in the division shall][a]—

(a) deliver for registration to the registrar of companies a copy of the draft terms of division, signed and dated as required by Regulation 26; and

(b) [cause to be published in the Companies Registration Office Gazette][b] and once at least in 2 daily newspapers circulating in the district where the registered office or principal place of business of the company is situate notice of delivery to the registrar of the draft terms of division.

(2) The requirements of paragraph (1) shall be fulfilled by each of the companies at least one month before the date of the general meeting of each such company which by virtue of Regulation 32 is to consider the draft terms of division.

[(3) Paragraph (1) does not apply to a company involved in the division if the company—

(a) publishes, free of charge on its website for a continuous period of at least 2 months, commencing at least one month before the date of the general meeting which by virtue of Regulation 32 is to consider the draft terms of division and ending at least one month after that date, a copy of the draft terms of division, signed and dated pursuant to Regulation 26, and

(b) causes to be published in the Companies Registration Office Gazette and once at least in 2 daily newspapers circulating in the district where the registered office or principal place of business of the company is situate notice of publication on its website of the draft terms of division.

(4) Where, in the period referred to in paragraph (3)(*a*), access to the company's website is disrupted for a continuous period of at least 24 hours or for separate periods totalling not less than 72 hours, the period referred to in paragraph (3)(*a*) shall be extended for a period corresponding to the period or periods of disruption.][c]

Amendments

a Words 'Subject to paragraph (3), each of the companies involved in the division shall' substituted for 'Each of the companies involved in the division shall' by EC(MDC)(A)R 2011, reg 5(k)(i).

b Words 'cause to be published in the Companies Registration Office Gazette' substituted for 'publish in *Iris Oifigiúil*' by EC(C)R 2004, (SI 839/2004), reg 6(a) with effect from 15 December 2004.

c Paragraphs (3) and (4) inserted by EC(MDC)(A)R 2011, reg 5(k)(ii).

---

31 Inspection of documents

(1) [Subject to paragraphs (3) and (4), each of the companies involved in the division shall][a], subject to paragraph (2), make available for inspection free of charge by any member of the company at its registered office during business hours (subject to such reasonable restrictions as the company in general meeting may impose so that not less than 2 hours in each day be allowed for inspection)—

(a) the draft terms of division;

(b) the audited annual accounts for the preceding three financial years of each company, or where a company has traded for less than 3 financial years before the date of the draft terms of division, the audited annual accounts for those financial years for which the company has traded;

(c) [where applicable,][b] the explanatory reports relating to each of the companies referred to in Regulation 27;

(d) [where applicable][c] the independent person's report relating to each of the companies referred to in Regulation 28;

(e) [where applicable, any accounting statement or half-yearly financial report in relation to any of the companies which is required pursuant to Regulation 29.][d]

(2) The provisions of paragraph (1) shall apply in the case of each of the companies for a period of one month before the general meeting which is to consider the draft terms of division.

[(3) Paragraph (1)(*e*) of this regulation does not apply to a company involved in a division by formation of new companies where the shares in each of the acquiring companies are allocated to the shareholders of the company being acquired in proportion to their rights in the capital of that company.

(4) Subject to paragraph (5), paragraph (1) does not apply to a company involved in the division if it publishes, free of charge on its website the documents listed in that paragraph, for a continuous period of at least 2 months, commencing at least one month before the date of the general meeting which by virtue of Regulation 32 is to consider the draft terms of division and ending at least one month after that date.

(5) Paragraph (4) does not apply where the entitlement referred to in paragraph (3) of Regulation 32 does not apply pursuant to the application of paragraph (3B) of that regulation.

(6) Where, in the period referred to in paragraph (4), access to the company's website is disrupted for a continuous period of at least 24 hours or for separate periods totalling not less than 72 hours, the period referred to in paragraph (4) shall be extended for a period corresponding to the period or periods of disruption.][e]

Amendments

a Words 'Subject to paragraphs (3) and (4), each of the companies involved in the division shall' substituted for 'Each of the companies involved in the division shall' by EC(MDC)(A)R 2011, reg 5(l)(i).

b Words 'where applicable,' inserted by 'EC(MDC)(A)R 2011, reg 5(l)(ii).

c Words 'where applicable' inserted by EC(MDC)(A)R 2008, reg 2(d).

d Subparagraph (e)(1) substituted by EC(MDC)(A)R 2011, reg 5(l)(iii).

e Paragraphs (3)–(6) inserted by EC(MDC)(A)R 2011, reg 5(l)(iv).

---

32 General meetings of the companies involved in a division

(1) Subject to paragraph (4) of this regulation and to Regulation 33, the draft terms of division shall be approved by a special resolution passed at a general meeting of each of the companies involved in the division.

(2) Where the division involves the formation of one or more new companies, the memorandum or draft memorandum and articles or draft articles of association of each of the new companies shall also be approved by a special resolution of the company being acquired.

(3) [Subject to paragraphs (3A) and (3B), the notice convening the general meeting][a] referred to in paragraph (1) shall contain a statement of every shareholder's entitlement to obtain on request, free of charge, full or, if so desired, partial copies of the documents listed in Regulation 31.

[(3A) Subject to paragraph (3B), where a shareholder has consented to the use by the company of electronic means for conveying information, the copies referred to in paragraph (3) may be provided to that shareholder by electronic mail and the notice convening the general meeting referred to in paragraph (1) shall contain a statement to that effect.

(3B) Where, for a continuous period of at least 2 months, commencing at least one month before the date of the general meeting which by virtue of this regulation is to consider the draft terms of division and ending at least one month after that date, copies of the documents specified in Regulation 31 are available to download and print, free of charge, from the company's website by shareholders of the company, the entitlement referred to in paragraph (3) shall not apply.

(3C) Where, in the period referred to in paragraph (3B), access to the company's website is disrupted for a continuous period of 24 hours or for separate periods totalling not less than 72 hours, the period referred to in paragraph (3)(*a*) shall be extended for a period corresponding to the period or periods of disruption.][b]

(4) This regulation shall not apply in the case of an acquiring company provided that the following conditions are fulfilled—

(i) the provisions of Regulations 30 and 31 are complied with at least one month before the date of the general meeting of the company being acquired, and

(ii) one or more members of the company holding paid up share capital amounting in total value to not less than 5% of such of the paid up share capital as confers the right to vote at general meetings, whether or not the shares held confer such voting right, shall be entitled, under the articles of association of the company, to require the convening of a general meeting of the company to consider the draft terms of division.

[(4A) This regulation shall not apply in the case of a company being acquired provided that the following conditions are fulfilled—

(a) the acquiring companies together hold all of the shares and other securities carrying the right to vote at general meetings of the company being acquired,

(b) the companies involved in the division comply with the requirements of Regulations 30 and 31 at least one month before the earlier of the dates specified in sub-paragraphs (e) and (f) of Regulation 26(2), and

(c) the directors of the companies involved in the division have complied with paragraph (6A).][c]

(5) [Subject to paragraph (6A), the directors of the company][d] being acquired shall inform—

(a) the general meeting of that company, and

(b) the directors of the acquiring companies,

of any material change in the assets and liabilities of the company being acquired between the date of the draft terms of division and the date of the general meeting.

(6) [Subject to paragraph (6A), the directors of the company][e] shall inform the general meeting of that company of the matters referred to in paragraph (5).

[(6A) Where paragraph (4A) applies and a general meeting of the company being acquired is not convened, the directors of the company being acquired shall inform—

(a) the members of that company, and

(b) the directors of the acquiring companies,

of any material change in the assets and liabilities of the company being acquired since the date of the draft terms of division and paragraph (6) shall be construed as referring to that information.][f]

(7) This regulation shall not apply in the case of the company being acquired where the acquiring companies together hold all the shares and other securities conferring the right to vote at general meetings of that company and where the information delivered under paragraph (4) covers any material change in the assets and liabilities after the date of the draft terms of division.

Amendments

a Words 'Subject to paragraphs (3A) and (3B), the notice convening the general meeting' substituted for 'The notice convening the general meeting' by EC(MDC)(A)R 2011, reg 5(m)(i).

b Paragraphs (3A)–(3C) inserted by EC(MDC)(A)R 2011, reg 5(m)(ii).

c Paragraph (4A) inserted by EC(MDC)(A)R 2011, reg 5(m)(iii).

d Words 'Subject to paragraph (6A), the directors of the company' substituted for 'The directors of the company' by EC(MDC)(A)R 2011, reg 5(m)(iv).

e Words 'Subject to paragraph (6A), the directors of the company' substituted for 'The directors of the company' by EC(MDC)(A)R 2011, reg 5(m)(v).

f Paragraph (6A) inserted by EC(MDC)(A)R 2011, reg 5(m)(vi).

---

33 Meetings of classes of shareholder

Where the share capital of any of the companies involved in a division is divided into shares of different classes, section 38 of the Companies (Amendment) Act 1983, shall apply.

34 Purchase of minority shares

(1) Any of the shareholders in any of the companies involved in a division who voted against the special resolution of the company concerned relating to the draft terms of division may, not later than 15 days after the relevant date request the acquiring company in writing to acquire his shares for cash.

(2) In this regulation 'the relevant date' in relation to a company means the date on which the latest general meeting of that company to consider the draft terms of division, or of any class of the holders of shares or other securities of such company, as required by these Regulations, is held.

(3) Nothing in this regulation shall prejudice the power of the court to make any order necessary for the protection of the interests of a dissenting minority in a company involved in a division.

35 Application for confirmation of division by court

(1) An application to the court for an order confirming a division shall be made by all the companies involved in a division.

(2) The application shall be accompanied by a statement of the size of the shareholding of any shareholder who has requested the purchase of his shares under Regulation 34 and of the measures which the acquiring companies propose to take to comply with such shareholder's request.

36 Protection of creditors

(1) A creditor of any of the companies involved in a division who, at the date of publication of the notice under Regulation 30(1)(b), is entitled to any debt or claim against the company, shall be entitled to object to the confirmation by the court of the division.

(2) If the court deems it necessary in order to secure the adequate protection of creditors of any of the companies involved in a division it may—

- (a) determine a list of creditors entitled to object and the nature and amount of their debts or claims, and may publish notices fixing a period within which creditors not entered on the list may have a claim for inclusion on that list considered;
- (b) where an undischarged creditor on the list referred to in subparagraph (a) does not consent to the division, the court may dispense with the consent of that creditor, on the company securing payment of the debt or claim by appropriating to that creditor such following amount as the court may direct—
    - (i) if the company concerned admits the full amount of the debt or claim, that amount;
    - (ii) if the company concerned does not admit the debt or claim, or if the amount is contingent or not ascertained, an amount fixed by the court after the like inquiry and adjudication as if the company were being wound up by the court.

(3) If, having regard to any special circumstances of the case, it thinks proper so to do, the court may direct that paragraph (2) shall not apply as regards any class of creditors.

(4) Each of the acquiring companies shall be jointly and severally liable for all the liabilities of the company being acquired.

37 Preservation of rights of holders of securities

(1) Subject to paragraph (2), holders of securities, other than shares, in any of the companies being acquired, to which special rights are attached shall be given rights in the acquiring companies at least equivalent to those they possessed in the company being acquired.

(2) Paragraph (1) shall not apply—

- (a) where the alteration of the rights in an acquiring company has been approved
    - (i) by a majority of the holders of such securities at a meeting held for that purpose, or
    - (ii) by the holders of those securities individually, or
- (b) where the holders of those securities are entitled under the terms of those securities to have their securities purchased by an acquiring company.

38 Confirmation order

(1) The court, on being satisfied that—

(a) the requirements of these Regulations have been complied with,

(b) proper provision has been made for—

(i) any dissenting shareholder of any of the companies involved in the division who has made a request under Regulation 34, and

(ii) any creditor of any of the companies who objects to the division in accordance with Regulation 36, and

(c) the rights of holders of securities other than shares in any of the companies being acquired are safeguarded in accordance with Regulation 37,

may make an order confirming the division with effect from such date as the court appoints ('the appointed date').

(2) The order of the court confirming the division shall, with effect from the appointed date, have the following effects—

(a) all the assets and liabilities of the company or companies being acquired shall stand transferred to the acquiring companies in accordance with the draft terms of division as approved by the court;

(b) the shareholders of the company being acquired shall become shareholders in the acquiring companies or any of them in accordance with the draft terms of division as approved by the court;

(c) the company or companies being acquired shall, subject to paragraph (4), be dissolved;

(d) all legal proceedings pending by or against any of the dissolved companies shall be continued with the substitution, for the dissolved company, of the acquiring companies or such of them as the court having seisin of the proceedings may order.

(3) The court may, either by the order confirming the division or by a separate order, make provision for such matters as the court considers necessary to secure that the division shall be fully and effectively carried out.

(4) The court may, in particular, by order—

(a) direct that an acquiring company shall, on a date specified by the court, purchase the shares of a dissenting shareholder who has made a request under Regulation 34 and pay therefor the sum determined by the court, being not less than the market sale price of the shares on the appointed date, and

(b) provide for the reduction accordingly of the company's capital.

(5) If it is necessary for the company being acquired to take any steps to ensure that its assets and liabilities are fully transferred, the court may specify a date which, save in exceptional cases, shall not be later than 6 months after the appointed date, by which such steps must be taken and for that purpose may order that the dissolution of such company shall take effect on that date.

(6) Section 41(1) of the Companies (Amendment) Act, 1983 (which restricts the right of a company to purchase its own shares) shall not apply to the purchase of any shares in pursuance of an order of the court under this regulation.

39 Limitation on power to make orders

An order of the court shall not be made in respect of a proposed division which involves a take-over to which the Mergers, Take-Overs and Monopolies (Control) Act, 1978 applies until either—

(a) the Minister has stated in writing that he has decided not to make an order under section 9 of that Act, in relation to the proposed take-over, or

(b) the Minister has stated in writing that he has made a conditional order under that section in relation to the proposed take-over, or

(c) the relevant period within the meaning of section 6 of that Act (which refers to a limitation on the commencement of a take-over) has elapsed without the Minister's having made an order under the said section 9 in relation to the proposed take-over,

whichever first occurs.

40 Registration and publication of confirmation of division

(1) Where the court has made an order confirming a division an office copy thereof shall forthwith be sent to the registrar of companies for registration by such officer of the court as the court may direct.

(2) Each of the acquiring companies shall [cause to be published in the Companies Registration Office Gazette][a] notice of delivery to the registrar of companies of the order of the court confirming the division within fourteen days of such delivery and if default is made in complying with this paragraph each company and every officer of the company who is in default shall be guilty of an offence.

(3) It shall be a defence for a person charged with an offence under paragraph (2) to show that non-compliance was not due to any delay or negligence on the part of the company or person concerned.

(4) Proceedings in relation to an offence under this regulation may be brought and prosecuted by the registrar of companies.

Amendments

a 'cause to be published in the Companies Registration Office Gazette' was substituted for 'publish in *Iris Oifigiúil*' by EC(C)R 2004, (SI 839/2004), reg 6(a) with effect from 15 December 2004.

---

41 Civil liability of directors and independent persons

(1) Any shareholder of any of the companies involved in a division who has suffered loss or damage by reason of misconduct in the preparation or implementation of the division by a director of any such company or by the independent person who has made a report under Regulation 28 shall be entitled to have such loss or damage made good to him by—

(a) in the case of misconduct by a person who was a director of that company at the date of the draft terms of division – that person.

(b) in the case of misconduct by any independent person who prepared a report under Regulation 28 in respect of any of the companies – that person.

(2) Without prejudice to the generality of paragraph (1), any shareholder of any of the companies who has suffered loss or damage arising from the inclusion of any untrue statement in the draft terms of division, the explanatory report, the independent person's report or the accounting statement shall, subject to paragraphs (3) and (4), be entitled to have such loss or damage made good to him by every person who was a director of that company at the date of the draft terms of division or, in the case of the independent person's report, by the person who made that report, in relation to that company.

(3) A director of a company shall not be liable under paragraph (2) if he proves—

(a) that any of the documents referred to in paragraph (2) was issued without his knowledge or consent, and that on becoming aware of their issue he forthwith informed the shareholders of that company that they were issued without his knowledge or consent, or

(b) that as regards every untrue statement he had reasonable grounds, having exercised all reasonable care and skill, for believing and did, up to the time the division took effect, believe that the statement was true.

(4) A person who made a report required by Regulation 28 in relation to a company shall not be liable in the case of untrue statements in his own report if he proves—

(i) that on becoming aware of the statement, he forthwith informed the company concerned and its shareholders of the untruth, or

(ii) that he was competent to make the statement and that he had reasonable grounds for believing and did up to the time the division took effect believe that the statement was true.

42 Criminal liability for untrue statements in division documents

(1) Where any untrue statement has been included in the draft terms of division, the explanatory report or the accounting statement, each of the directors and any person who authorised the issue of those documents shall be guilty of an offence.

(2) Where any untrue statement has been included in the independent person's report, the independent person and any person who authorised the issue of the report shall be guilty of an offence.

(3) It shall be a defence for a person charged with an offence under paragraph (1) or (2) to show that, having exercised all reasonable care and skill, he had reasonable grounds for believing and did, up to the time of the issue of the documents, believe that the statement was true.

Explanatory Note

(This note is not part of the Instrument and does not purport to be a legal interpretation.)

These Regulations implement the EEC Third and Sixth Company Law Directives concerning the mergers and divisions of public limited companies. The Regulations apply only to public limited companies, and certain unregistered companies defined in the Regulations.

Mergers

In the case of a merger, the Regulations apply to an operation whereby all the assets and liabilities of one or more companies are transferred to another company (the acquiring company), the shareholders of the company or companies being acquired become shareholders in the acquiring company and the company or companies being acquired are dissolved.

Divisions

In the case of a division, the Regulations apply to an operation whereby all the assets and liabilities of a company are transferred to more than on other company, the shareholders of the company being acquired become shareholders in the acquiring company or companies and the company being acquired is dissolved.

The provisions of the Companies Acts in relation to arrangements and reconstructions (Sections 201 to 204) are expressly disapplied in the case of the specific mergers and divisions covered in the Regulations.

The Regulations are divided into three Parts. Part 1 contains the usual preliminary provisions relating to interpretation and penalties. Part II sets out the new procedure and requirements in respect of mergers and Part III sets out the new procedure and requirements in respect of divisions.

The provisions of Parts II and III broadly cover;

(a) reporting requirements by directors of a company and by an independent person to the members of the company;

(b) approval of the merger or division by general meeting of the companies involved;

(c) inspection of relevant documents by members of the companies involved;

(d) confirmation of the merger or division by the High Court and registration and publication of the Court's decision;

(e) protection of the interests of creditors, dissenting minorities and holders of securities other than shares.

The Regulations also provide for civil liability of directors and independent person to shareholders for misconduct in relation to the merger or division and for criminal liability for false statements in any document published in connection with the merger or division.

European Communities (European Economic Interest Groupings) Regulations 1989

SI 191/1989

Arrangement of Regulations

Preliminary

Part 1
Formation and registration of groupings

Part II
Membership of groupings

Administration, activities etc

FIRST SCHEDULE
COUNCIL REGULATION (EEC) NO. 2137/85 OF 25 JULY 1985 ON THE EUROPEAN ECONOMIC INTEREST GROUPING

SECOND SCHEDULE
FORMS RELATING TO EEIGS.

I, DESMOND O'MALLEY, Minister for Industry and Commerce, in exercise of the powers conferred on me by section 3 of the European Communities Act, 1972 (No. 27 of 1972) and for the purpose of giving full effect to the provisions of Council Regulation (EEC) No. 2137/85 of the 25th day of July, 1985on the European Economic Interest Grouping (EEIG), hereby make the following Regulations.

PRELIMINARY

1 Citation and commencement

(1) These Regulations may be cited as the European Communities (European Economic Interest Groupings) Regulations, 1989.

(2) These Regulations shall come into operation on the 1st day of August, 1989.

2 Interpretation

(1) In these Regulations, unless the context otherwise requires:

'the Companies Acts' means the Companies Act, 1963, and every enactment which is to be constructed as one with that Act;

'the Council Regulation' means Council Regulation (EEC) No. 2137/85 of 25th July, 1985 on the European Economic Interest Grouping, being the Regulation set out in the First Schedule to these Regulations;

'the court' means the High Court;

'director' includes any person occupying the position of director by whichever name called;

'grouping' means a European Economic Interest Grouping, whether formed and registered in the State or elsewhere;

'the Minister' means the Minister for Industry and Commerce;

'officer' in relation to a body corporate includes a director or company secretary;

'registry' has the meaning assigned to it under Regulation 5(1) of these Regulations;

'registrar' means the registrar of groupings, within the meaning of Regulation 5(2) of these Regulations.

(2) A word or expression that is used in these Regulations and is also used in the Council Regulation shall, unless the contrary intention appears, have the same meaning in these Regulations as it has in the Council Regulation.

PART 1
FORMATION AND REGISTRATION OF GROUPINGS

3 Formation of a grouping

A grouping shall be formed upon the terms, in the matter and with the effects laid down in the Council Regulation and these Regulations.

4 Name of grouping

(1) The name of a grouping registered in the State shall include:

(a) the words 'European Economic Interest Groupings' or the initials 'EEIG', or

(b) the words 'Grupàil Eorpach um Leas Eacnamaíoch' or the initials 'GELE' unless those words or initials already form part of the name.

(2) Every invoice, order for goods or business letter issued by or on behalf of a grouping shall include the name of the grouping referred to in paragraph (1) of this Regulation.

(3) No grouping shall be registered under these Regulations by a name which, in the opinion of the Minister, is undesirable but an appeal shall lie to the court against a refusal to register on such a ground.

(4) A grouping registered under these Regulations may, subject to the approval of the Minister signified in writing, change its name.

5 Designation of registrar and registry

(1) The Companies Registration Office, being the office maintained for the purpose of the registration of companies under the Companies Acts, is hereby designated as the registry of the purpose of Articles 6, 7, 10 and 39 of the Council Regulation.

(2) For the purposes specified in paragraph (1) of this Regulation, the person for the time being holding the office of registrar of companies under the Companies Acts shall also have the function of registrar of groupings under the Council Regulation and these Regulations and is referred to in these Regulations as 'the registrar'.

6 Registration of a grouping

(1) Where the official address of a grouping is in the State, the contract for the formation of the grouping shall be delivered to the registrar.

(2) The registrar shall retain and register in a register maintained by him for that purpose any contracts for the formation of groupings delivered to him.

7 Effect of registration

(1) On the registration of a contract forming a grouping the registrar shall certify under his hand that the grouping is incorporated as a European Economic Interest Grouping.

(2) A grouping, from the date of its registration under these Regulations, shall:

(a) be a body corporate,

(b) have perpetual succession and a common seal, and

(c) have legal personality.

8 Time for filing documents and other particulars

Where a document or particular is to be filed at the registry pursuant to Article 7 of the Council Regulation, it shall be so filed within 14 days of the amendment, decision or other event giving rise to the requirement under that Article.

9 Publication of information by grouping

(1) A grouping registered in the State shall, within 21 days of its registration, cause to be published in the *Iris Oifigiúil*:

(a) the particulars referred to in Article 5 of the Council Regulation, and

(b) notice of the number, date and place of its registration.

(2) A grouping registered in the State shall, within 21 days of delivery to the registrar of the documents referred to in Article 7 (b) to (j) and 14.1 of the Council Regulation, cause to be published in the *Iris Oifigiúil* notice of such delivery.

(3) A grouping registered in the State shall, within 21 days of the termination of its registration, cause to be published in the *Iris Oifigiúil*, notice of such termination.

10 Groupings registered outside the State

(1) Any document delivered to the registrar, pursuant to Article 10 of the Council Regulation, by a grouping registered outside the State shall be certified, in the country in which the grouping is registered, as follows:

(a) certified as a true copy by an official of the registry to whose custody the original is committed, or

(b) certified as a true copy in accordance with the provisions of the Companies (Forms) Order, 1964.

(2) Any such document shall, if it is not expressed in the Irish or English language, be accompanied by a certified translation thereof.

(3) In this Regulation 'certified translation' means a translation certified to be a correct translation by:

(a) if made outside the State, an Irish diplomatic or consular officer, or any person whom any such officer certifies to be known to him as competent to translate it into the Irish or English language;

(b) if made within the State, a notary public, solicitor or barrister.

11 Notification of information by registrar

The duty of forwarding the information mentioned in Article 39.2 of the Council Regulation to the Office for Official Publications of the European Communities shall lie with the registrar.

12 Transfer of official address outside the State

(1) Where a grouping registered in the State proposes to transfer its official address to a place outside the State, the registrar may, after consultation with any Minister of the Government, the Revenue Commissioners, the Attorney General or the Director of Public Prosecutions, refuse to terminate the registration of the grouping in the State if any such person indicates that it would be in the public interest to do so.

(2) (a) Where the registrar refuses to terminate the registration of a grouping under paragraph (1) of this Regulation, the grouping may apply to the court in a summary manner to have such refusal reviewed.

(b) Where an application to review a decision by the registrar is brought pursuant to subparagraph (a) of this paragraph, the court shall confirm the decision of the registrar unless it is satisfied that the procedures laid down by, or the requirements of, these Regulations or the Council Regulation have not been compiled with in any material respect.

(c) Where the court is satisfied that the procedures laid down by, or the requirements of, these Regulations or the Council Regulation have not been compiled with in any material respect, the court may set aside the decision of the registrar and in such case shall remit the matter to the registrar who shall thereupon reconsider the matter and make a further decision in accordance with such procedures and requirements.

PART II
MEMBERSHIP OF GROUPINGS

13 Permissible number of members

[…][a]

14 Disqualification from membership

(1) The following persons shall be disqualified from membership of a grouping, namely:

(a) an undischarged bankrupt,

(b) a person convicted on indictment of any offence involving fraud or dishonesty,

(c) a person convicted on indictment of any offence in relation to a company formed and registered under the Companies Acts,

(d) a person to whom section 297 of the Companies Act, 1963, applies,

(e) a body corporate in respect of which winding-up or analogous proceedings have commenced.

(2) A person who becomes disqualified under this Regulation shall, within five days of becoming disqualified, resign from membership of a grouping and shall not act as a member of a grouping when disqualified from doing so.

15 Expulsion of member of grouping

The jurisdiction to hear and decide on applications under Article 27.2 of the Council Regulation shall lie with the court.

16 Reduction of number of members below two

If at any time the number of members of a grouping is reduced below two, and it carries on any trade, activity or business for more than one month while the number is so reduced, the following persons shall, if they know that the grouping is carrying on business with less than two members, be severally liable for the payment of the whole debts of the grouping contracted during that time, and may be severally sued thereof, namely:

(a) if the remaining member is a natural person, that person,

(b) if the remaining member is a partnership, every member of that partnership,

(c) if the remaining member is a body corporate, every person who was a director or other officer of the body corporate during the period mentioned in this Regulation.

17 Cessation of membership of a grouping

(1) Membership of grouping by a person shall cease in the event of his being adjudged bankrupt, or if he makes any arrangement or composition with his creditors generally.

(2) Membership of a grouping by a body (whether or not incorporated) shall cease on the commencement of the winding up of that body.

Administration, Activities Etc

18 Manager of a grouping

(1) The manager of a grouping may be a natural person or a body corporate.

(2) Where the manager is a body corporate:

(a) the grouping shall designate one or more natural persons as the representative of the manager,

(b) such representative shall have the same liability as if he were himself the manager, and

(c) the grouping shall deliver to the registrar particulars in relation to such representative as if he were the manager.

19 Annual Return

(1) A grouping whose official address is in the State shall, not later than 1st July in every year, make a return to the registrar in the form set out in the Second Schedule to these Regulations.

(2) Paragraph (1) shall also apply to a grouping which has a grouping establishment in the State.

(3) Nothing in this Regulation shall require a grouping to make a return before 1st July in a particular year if the date of registration in the State of such grouping or grouping establishment, as the case may be, under these Regulations was less than fifteen months before that date.

20 Prohibition on invitation of investment from the public

(1) A grouping shall not invite investment from the public.

(2) Where a grouping is convicted of an offence under this Regulation and the grouping is in the course of being wound up on the date of the conviction or commences to be wound up within 12 months after that date, the court may, on the application of the liquidator or any creditor of the grouping, declare that any of the following persons shall be personally liable, without any limitation of liability, for all or any of the debts or other liabilities of the grouping incurred in the period during which such person was acting in the capacity mentioned, namely:

(a) any member of the grouping who is a natural person,

(b) a director or member of the committee of management of any member of the grouping which is a body corporate,

(c) the manager of the grouping or, where the manager is a body corporate, the natural person who is the representative of the manager, within the meaning of Regulation 18(2).

21 Winding-up of grouping

(1) For the purposes of Articles 35 and 36 of the Council Regulation, a grouping shall be deemed to be an unregistered company, within the meaning of Part X of the Companies Act, 1963.

(2) For the purposes of that Part, the manager of a grouping shall be treated as if he were a director of a company.

(3) The Minister shall be the competent authority for the purposes of Article 32.1 of the Council Regulation.

22 Provisions of Companies Acts applied to groupings

(1) The provisions of the Companies Act set out in the Table to this Regulation shall, with any necessary modifications, apply to groupings as they apply to companies formed and registered under those Acts.

(2) A person convicted of an offence under a provision of the Companies Acts, as applied by this Regulation, shall, in lieu of the penalties therefor set out in those Acts, be liable to the penalties set out in Regulation 28.

TABLE

Act	*Provisions applied*
Companies Act, 1963	
	Sections 99 to 112.
	Section 165 to 173.
	Section 184.
	Section 205.
	Sections 293, 295 and 297.
	Section 311.
	Sections 344 to 350.
	Sections 368, 370, 379, 389, 390, and 394.
Companies (Amendment) Act, 1982	Section 12.

23 Activity contrary to public interest

(1) The Minister shall be the competent authority for the purposes of Article 38 of the Council Regulation.

(2) For the said purposes, the Minister may direct a grouping to cease or refrain from any activity which, in his opinion, is or is likely to be against the public interest, and the grouping shall comply with any such direction.

24 Furnishing false information

A person shall not, in purported compliance with any provision of the Council Regulation or these Regulations, make a statement or produce, lodge or deliver any return, report, account or other document, knowing it to be false, or recklessly make a statement or produce, lodge or deliver any such document false in a material particular.

25 Destruction, mutilation or falsification of documents

(1) A person shall not destroy, mutilate or falsify, or be privy to the destruction, mutilation or falsification of any book or document affecting or relating to the property or affairs of a grouping, or make or be privy to the making of a false entry therein.

(2) A person shall not fraudulently part with, alter or make an omission in, any such book or document.

(3) A person shall not be convicted of an offence under this Regulation if he proves that he had no intention to defeat the law.

26 Fees

In respect of the several matters mentioned in the first column of the Table to this Regulation, there shall be paid to the registrar the several fees specified in the second column of that Table.

TABLE

Matter in respect of which fee is payable.	*Amount of fee* £ (€)
For registration of a grouping to be registered in the State	[€190.46][a]
For registration of a grouping establishment in the State, where a grouping is registered in another Member State of the European Communities	[€190.46][a]
For registration of change of a grouping name.	[€190.46][a]
For registration of transfer of official address of a grouping.	[€190.46][a]
For termination of registration of a grouping.	[€31.74][b]
For registering any other document by these Regulations required to be delivered, forwarded or sent to the registrar or filed in the registry.	[€31.74][b]

Amendments

a £150 converted to €190.46 by Council Regulation (EC) No 1103/97, No 974/98 and No 2866/98 and the Economic and Monetary Union Act 1998, s 6.

b £25 converted to €31.74 by Council Regulation (EC) No 1103/97, No 974/98 and No 2866/98 and the Economic and Monetary Union Act 1998, s 6.

27 Forms

(1) The forms referred to in the Table to this Regulation and set out in the Second Schedule to these Regulations are, subject to paragraph (2), hereby prescribed as the forms to be used by groupings for the various purposes required under the Council Regulation and these Regulations.

(2) For the purpose of giving full and better effect to the Council Regulation and these Regulations, the registrar may require groupings generally to furnish him with such further information, and in such form, as he may from time to time determine, or may make such adjustments and alterations in the forms set out in the Second Schedule to these Regulations as he deems appropriate.

TABLE

Purpose	*Form*
Registration of grouping whose official address is in the State.	IG1
Registration of grouping establishment in Ireland for grouping whose official address is outside the State.	IG2
Notice of setting up of grouping establishment of grouping whose official address is in the State.	IG3
Notice of closure of grouping establishment of grouping.	IG4
Notice of manager's particulars and of termination of appointment	IG5

Notice of documents and particulars required to be filed.	IG6
Notice of proposal to transfer official address of grouping.	IG7

28 Offences and penalties

(1) A person or grouping who contravenes Article 3(2), 4(1), 7, 10, 18, 19, 25, 29, 31 or 35(4) of the Council Regulation or Regulations 4, 8, 9,14,18,19, 20(1), 24 or 25 of these Regulations, or a direction of the Minister under Regulation 23 of these Regulations shall be guilty of an offence and shall be liable on summary conviction to a [class C fine][a] or to imprisonment for a term not exceeding 12 months or to both.

(2) Where an offence which is committed by a grouping under the Council Regulation or these Regulations is proved to have been committed with the consent or connivance of or to be attributable to any neglect on the part of any member of that grouping or any person or body who was purporting to act in such capacity, that person or body shall also be guilty of an offence and shall be liable to be proceeded against accordingly as if he were guilty of the first-mentioned offence.

(3) Summary proceedings in relation to an offence under the Council Regulation or these Regulations may be brought and prosecuted by the Minister or the registrar.

(4) Notwithstanding section 10(4) of the Petty Sessions (Ireland) Act, 1851, summary proceedings under the Council Regulation or these Regulations may be instituted within three years from the date of the offence.

Amendments

a £1,000 converted to €1,269.74 by Council Regulation (EC) No 1103/97, No 974/98 and No 2866/98 and the Economic and Monetary Union Act 1998, s 6; the above being implicitly substituted, by Fines Act 2010, s 6, for a fine not exceeding the aforesaid amount. A class C fine currently means a fine not exceeding €2,500.

SCHEDULES

Regulation 2

FIRST SCHEDULE

COUNCIL REGULATION (EEC) NO 2137/85 OF 25 JULY 1985 ON THE EUROPEAN ECONOMIC INTEREST GROUPING (EEIG)

THE COUNCIL OF THE EUROPEAN COMMUNITIES

Having regard to the Treaty establishing the European Economic Community, and in particular Article 235 thereof.

Having regard to the proposal from the Commission

Having regard to the opinion of the European Parliament,

Having regard to the opinion of the Economic and Social Committee,

Where a harmonious development of economic activities and a continuous and balanced expansion throughout the Community depends on the establishment and smooth functioning of a common market offering conditions analogous to those of a national market; whereas to bring about this single market and to increase its unity a legal framework which facilities the adaptation of their activities to the economic conditions of the Community should be created for natural persons, companies, firms and other legal bodies in particular; whereas to that end it is necessary that those natural persons, companies, firms and other legal bodies should be able to co-operate effectively across frontiers;

Whereas co-operation of this nature can encounter legal, fiscal or psychological difficulties; whereas the creation of an appropriate Community legal instrument in the form of a European Economic Interest Grouping would contribute to the achievement of the above mentioned objectives and therefore proves necessary;

Whereas the Treaty does not provide the necessary powers for the creation of such a legal instrument;

Whereas a grouping's ability to adapt to economic conditions must be guaranteed by the considerable freedom for its members in their contractual relations and the internal organisation of the grouping;

Whereas a grouping differs from a firm or company principally in its purpose, which is only to facilitate or develop the economic activities of its members to enable them to improve their own results; whereas, by reason of that ancillary nature, a grouping's activities must be related to the economic activities of its members but not replace them so that, to that extent, for example, a grouping may not itself, with regard to third parties, practise a profession, the concept of economic activities being interpreted in the widest sense;

Whereas access to grouping form must be made as widely available as possible to natural persons, companies, firms and other legal bodies, in keeping with the aims of this Regulation; whereas this Regulation shall not, however, prejudice the application at national level of legal rules and/or ethical codes concerning the conditions for the pursuit of business and professional activities;

Whereas this Regulation does not itself confer on any person the right to participate in a grouping, even where the conditions it lays down are fulfilled;

Whereas the power provided by this Regulation to prohibit or restrict participation in grouping on grounds of public interest is without prejudice to the laws of member states which govern the pursuit of activities and which may provide further prohibitions or restrictions or otherwise control or supervise participation in a grouping by any natural person, company, firm or other legal body or any class of them;

Whereas, to enable a grouping to achieve its purpose, it should be endowed with legal capacity and provision should be made for it to be represented vis-a-vis third parties by an organ legally separate from its membership;

Whereas the protection of third parties requires widespread publicity; whereas the members of a grouping have unlimited joint and several liability for the grouping's debts and other liabilities, including those relating to tax or social security, without, however, that principle's affecting the freedom to exclude or restrict the liability of one or more of its members in respect of a particular debt or other liability by means of a specific contract between the grouping and a third party;

Whereas matters relating to the status or capacity of natural persons and to the capacity of legal persons are governed by national law:

Whereas the grounds for winding up which are peculiar to the grouping should be specific while referring to national law for its liquidation and the conclusion thereof;

Whereas groupings are subject to national laws relating to insolvency and cessation of payments; whereas such laws may provide other grounds for the winding up of groupings;

Whereas this Regulation provides that the profits or losses resulting from the activities of a grouping shall be taxable only in the hands of its members; whereas it is understood that otherwise national tax laws apply, particularly as regards the apportionment of profits, tax procedures and any obligations imposed by national tax law;

Whereas in matters not covered by this Regulation the laws of the member states and Community law are applicable, for example with regard to: social and labour laws, competition law, intellectual property law;

Whereas the activities of groupings are subject to the provisions of member states' laws on the pursuit and supervision of activities; whereas in the event of abuse or circumvention of the laws of a Member State by a grouping or its members that Members State may impose appropriate sanctions;

Whereas the Member States are free to apply or to adopt any laws, regulations or administrative measures which do not conflict with the scope or objective of this Regulation;

Whereas this Regulation must enter into force immediately in its entirety; whereas the implementation of some provisions must nevertheless be deferred in order to allow the Member States first to set up the necessary machinery for the registration of groupings in their territories and the disclosure of certain matters relating to groupings; whereas, with effect from the date of implementation of this Regulation, groupings set up may operate without territorial restrictions.

HAS ADOPTED THIS REGULATION:

Article 1

1. European Economic Interest Groupings shall be formed upon the terms, in the manner and with the effects laid down in this Regulation. Accordingly, parties intending to form a grouping must conclude a contract and have the registration provided for in Article 6 carried out.

2. A grouping so formed shall, from the date of its registration as provided for in Article 6, have the capacity, in its own name, to have rights and obligations of all kinds, to make contracts or accomplish other legal acts, and to sue and be sued.

3. The Member States shall determine whether or not groupings registered at their registries, pursuant to Article 6, have legal personality.

Article 2

1. Subject to the provisions of this Regulation, the law applicable, on the one hand, to the contract for the formation of a grouping, except as regards matters relating to the status or capacity of natural persons and to the capacity of legal persons and, on the other hand, to the internal organisation of a grouping shall be the internal law of the State in which the official address is situated, as laid down in the contract for the formation of the grouping.

2. Where a State comprises several territorial units, each of which has its own rules of law applicable to the matters referred to in paragraph 1, each territorial unit shall be considered as a State for the purposes of identifying the law applicable under this Article.

Article 3

1. The purpose of a grouping shall be to facilitate or develop the economic activities of its members and to improve or increase the results of those activities; its purpose is not to make profits for itself.Its activity shall be related to the economic activities of its members and must not be more than ancillary to those activities.

2. Consequently, a grouping may not:

(a) exercise, directly or indirectly, a power of management or supervision over its members' own activities or over the activities of another undertaking, in particular in the fields of personnel, finance and investment;

(b) directly or indirectly, on any basis whatsoever, hold shares of any kind in a member undertaking; the holding of shares in another undertaking shall be possible only in so far as it is necessary for the achievement of the grouping's objects and if it is done on its members' behalf;

(c) employ more than 500 persons;

(d) be used by a company to make a loan to a director of a company, or any person connected with him, when the making of such loans is restricted or controlled under the Member States' laws governing companies. Nor must a grouping be used for the transfer of any property between a company and a director, or any person connected with him, except to the extent allowed by the Member States' laws governing companies. For the purposes of this provision the making of a loan includes entering into any transaction or arrangement of similar effect, and property includes moveable and immovable property;

(e) be a member of another European Economic Interest Grouping.

Article 4

1. Only the following may be members of a grouping:

(a) companies or firms within the meaning of the second paragraph of Article 58 of the Treaty and other legal bodies governed by public or private law, which have been formed in accordance with the law of a Member State and which have their registered or statutory office and central administration in the Community; where, under the law of a Member State, a company, firm or other legal body is not obliged to have a registered or statutory office, it shall be sufficient for such a company, firm or other legal body to have its central administration in the Community;

(b) natural persons who carry on any industrial, commercial, craft or agricultural activity or who provide professional or other services in the Community.

2. A grouping must comprise at least:

(a) two companies, firms or other legal bodies, within the meaning of paragraph 1, which have their central administrations in different Member States, or

(b) two natural person, within the meaning of paragraph 1, who carry on their principal activities in different Members States, or

(c) a company, firm or other legal body within the meaning of paragraph 1 and a natural person, of which the first has its central administration in one Member State and the second carries on his principal activity in another Member State.

3. A Member State may provide that groupings registered at its registries in accordance with Article 6 may have no more than 20 members. For this purpose, that Member State may provide that, in accordance with its laws, each member of a legal body formed under its laws, other than a registered company, shall be treated as a separate member of a grouping.

4. Any Member State may, on grounds of that State's public interest, prohibit or restrict participation in groupings by certain classes of natural persons, companies, firms, or other legal bodies.

Article 5

A contract for the formation of a grouping shall include at least:

(a) the name of the grouping preceded or followed either by the words 'European Economic Interest Grouping' or by the initials 'EEIG', unless those words or initials already form part of the name;

(b) the official address of the grouping;

(c) the objects for which the grouping is formed;

(d) the name, business name, legal form, permanent address or registered office, and the number and place of registration, if any, of each member of the grouping;

(e) the duration of the grouping, except where this is indefinite.

Article 6

A grouping shall be registered in the State in which it has its official address, at the registry designated pursuant to Article 39(1).

Article 7

A contract for the formation of a grouping shall be filed at the registry referred to in Article 6. The following documents and particulars must also be filed at that registry:

(a) any amendment to the contract for the formation of a grouping, including any change in the composition of a grouping;

(b) notice of a setting up or closure of any establishment of the grouping;

(c) any judicial decision establishing or declaring the nullity of a grouping, in accordance with Article 15;

(d) notice of the appointment of the manager or managers of a grouping, their names and any other identification particulars required by the law of the Member State in which the register is kept, notification that they may act alone or must act jointly, and the termination of any manager's appointment;

(e) notice of a member's assignment of his participation in a grouping or a proportion thereof, in accordance with Article 22 (1);

(f) any decision by members ordering or establishing the winding up of a grouping, in accordance with Articles 31 or 32;

(g) notice of the appointment of the liquidator or liquidators of a grouping, as referred to in Article 35, their names and any other identification particulars required by the law of the Member State in which the register is kept, and the termination of any liquidator's appointment;

(h) notice of the conclusion of a grouping's liquidation, as referred to in Article 35 (2);

(i) any proposal to transfer the official address, as referred to in Article 14 (1);

(j) any clause exempting a new member from the payment of debts and other liabilities which originated prior to his admission in accordance with Article 26 (2).

Article 8

The following must be published, as laid down in Article 39, in the gazette referred to in paragraph 1 of that Article:

(a) the particulars which must be included in the contract for the formation of a grouping, pursuant to Article 5, and any amendments thereto;

(b) the number, date and place of registration as well as notice of the termination of that registration;

(c) the documents and particulars referred to in Article 7(b) to (j).

The particulars referred to in (a) and (b) must be published in full. The documents and particulars referred to in (c) may be published either in full or in extract form or by means of a reference to their filing at the registry, in accordance with the national legislation applicable.

Article 9

1. The documents and particulars which must be published pursuant to this Regulation may be relied on by a grouping as against third parties under the conditions laid down by the national law applicable pursuant to Article 3(5) and (7) of the Council Directive 68/151/EEC of 9 March 1968 on co-ordination of safeguards which, for the protection of the interests of members and others, are required by Member States of companies within the meaning of the second paragraph of Article 58 of the Treaty, with a view to making such safeguards equivalent throughout the Community.

2. If activities have been carried on on behalf of a grouping before its registration in accordance with Article 6 and if the grouping does not, after its registration, assume the obligations arising out of such activities, the natural persons, companies, firms or other legal bodies which carried on those activities shall bear unlimited joint and several liability for them.

Article 10

Any grouping establishment situated in a Member State other than that in which the official address is situated shall be registered in the State. For the purpose of such registration, a grouping shall file, at the appropriate registry in that Member State, copies of the documents which must be filed at the registry of the Member State in which the official address is situated together, if necessary, with a translation which conforms with the practice of the registry where the establishment is registered.

Article 11

Notice that a grouping has been formed or that the liquidation of a grouping has been concluded stating the number, date and place of registration and the date, place and title of publication, shall be given in the Official Journal of the European Communities after it has been published in the gazette referred to in Article 39(1).

Article 12

The official address referred to in the contract for the formation of a grouping must be situated in the Community. The official address must be fixed either:

(a) where the grouping has its central administration, or

(b) where one of the members of the grouping has its central administration or, in the case of a natural person, his principal activity, provided that the grouping carries on an activity there.

Article 13

The official address of a grouping may be transferred within the Community. When such a transfer does not result in a change in the law applicable pursuant to Article 2, the decision to transfer shall be taken in accordance with the conditions laid down in the contract for the formation of the grouping.

Article 14

1. When the transfer of the official address results in a change in the law applicable pursuant to Article 2, a transfer proposal must be drawn up, filed and published in accordance with the conditions laid down in Articles 7 and 8. No decision to transfer may be taken for two months after publication of the proposal. Any such decision must be taken by the members of the grouping unanimously. The transfer shall take effect on the date on which the grouping is registered, in accordance with Article 6, at the registry or the new official address. That registration may not be effected until evidence has been produced that the proposal to transfer the official address has been published.

2. The termination of a grouping's registration at the registry for its old official address may not be effected until evidence has been produced that the grouping has been registered at the registry for its new official address.

3. Upon publication of a grouping's new registration the new official address may be relied on as against third parties in accordance with the conditions referred to in Article 9 (1); however, as long as the termination of the grouping's registration at the registry for the old official address has not been published, third parties may continue to rely on the old official address unless the grouping proves that such third parties were aware of the new official address.

4. The laws of a Member State may provide that, as regards groupings registered under Article 6 in that Member State, the transfer of an official address which would result in a change of the law applicable shall not take effect if, within the two-month period referred to in paragraph 1, a competent authority in that Member State opposes it. Such opposition may be based only on grounds of public interest. Review by a judicial authority must be possible.

Article 15

1. Where the law applicable to a grouping by virtue of Article 2 provides for the nullity of that grouping, such nullity must be established or declared by judicial decision. However, the court to which the matter is referred must, where it is possible for the affairs of the grouping to be put in order, allow time to permit that to be done.

2. The nullity of a grouping shall entail its liquidation in accordance with the conditions laid down in Article 35.

3. A decision establishing or declaring the nullity of a grouping may be relied on as against third parties in accordance with the conditions laid down in Article 9 (1). Such a decision shall not of itself affect the validity of liabilities, owed by or to a grouping, which originated before it could be relied on as against third parties in accordance with the conditions laid down in the previous subparagraph.

Article 16

1. The organs of a grouping shall be the members acting collectively and the manager or managers. A contract for the formation of a grouping may provide for other organs; if it does it shall determine their powers.

2. The members of a grouping, acting as a body, may take any decision for the purpose of achieving the objects of the grouping.

Article 17

1. Each member shall have one vote. The contract for the formation of a grouping may, however, give more than one vote to certain members, provided that no one member holds a majority of the votes.

2. A unanimous decision by the members shall be required to:

(a) alter the objects of a grouping;
(b) alter the number of votes allotted to each member;
(c) alter the conditions for the taking of decision;
(d) extend the duration of a grouping beyond any period fixed in the contract for the formation of the grouping;
(e) alter the contribution by every member or by some members of the grouping's financing;
(f) alter any other obligation of a member, unless otherwise provided by the contract for the formation of the grouping;
(g) make any alteration to the contract for the formation of the grouping not covered by this paragraph, unless otherwise provided by that contract.

3. Except where this Regulation provides that decisions must be taken unanimously, the contract for the formation of a grouping may prescribe the conditions for the quorum and for a majority, in accordance with which the decisions, or some of them, shall be taken. Unless otherwise provided for by the contract, decisions shall be taken unanimously.

4. On the initiative of a manager or at the request of a member, the manager or managers must arrange for the members to be consulted so that the latter can take a decision.

Article 18

Each member shall be entitled to obtain information from the manager or managers concerning the grouping's business and to inspect the grouping's books and business records.

Article 19

1. A grouping shall be managed by one or more natural persons appointed in the contract for the formation of the grouping or by decision of the members. No person

may be a manager of a grouping if: by virtue of the law applicable to him, or by virtue of the internal law of the State in which the grouping has its official address, or following a judicial or administrative decision made or recognised in a Member State he may not belong to the administrative or management body of a company, may not manage an undertaking or may not act as manager of a European Economic Interest Grouping.

2. A Member State may, in the case of groupings registered at their registries pursuant to Article 6, provide that legal persons may be managers on condition that such legal persons designate one or more natural persons, whose particulars shall be the subject of the filing provisions of Article 7(d) to represent them. If a Member State exercises this option, it must provide that the representative or representatives shall be liable as if they were themselves managers of the groupings concerned. The restrictions imposed in paragraph 1 shall also apply to those representatives.

3. The contract for the formation of a grouping or, failing that, a unanimous decision by the members shall determine the conditions for the appointment and removal of the manager or managers and shall lay down their powers.

Article 20

1. Only the manager or, where there are two or more, each of the managers shall represent a grouping in respect of dealings with third parties. Each of the managers shall bind the grouping as regards third parties when he acts on behalf of the grouping, even where his acts do not fall within the objects of the groupings, unless the grouping proves that the third party knew or could not, under the circumstances, have been unaware that the act fell outside the objects of the grouping; publication of the particulars referred to in Article 5(c) shall not of itself be proof thereof. No limitation on the powers of the manager or managers, whether deriving from the contract for the formation of the grouping or from a decision by the members, may be relied on as against third parties even if it is published.

2. The contract for the formation of the grouping may provide that the grouping shall be validly bound only by two or more managers acting jointly. Such a clause may be relied on as against third parties in accordance with the conditions referred to in Article 9(1) only if it is published in accordance with Article 8.

Article 21

1. The profits resulting from a grouping's activities shall be deemed to be the profits of the members and shall be apportioned among them in the proportions laid down in the contract for the formation of the grouping or, in the absence of any such provision, in equal shares.

2. The members of a grouping shall contribute to the payment of the amount by which expenditure exceeds income in the proportions laid down in the contract for the formation of the grouping or, in the absence of any such provision, in equal shares.

Article 22

1. Any member of a grouping may assign his participation in the grouping, or a proportion thereof, either to another member or to a third party; the assignment shall not take effect without the unanimous authorisation of the other members.

2. A member of a grouping may use his participation in the grouping as security only after the other members have given their unanimous authorisation, unless otherwise laid

down in the contract for the formation of the grouping. The holder of the security may not at any time become a member of the grouping by virtue of that security.

Article 23

No grouping may invite investment by the public.

Article 24

1. The members of a grouping shall have unlimited joint and several liability for its debts and other liabilities of whatever nature. National law shall determine the consequences of such liability.

2. Creditors may not proceed against a member for payment in respect of debts and other liabilities, in accordance with the conditions laid down in paragraph 1, before the liquidation of a grouping is concluded, unless they have first requested the grouping to pay and payment has not been made within an appropriate period.

Article 25

Letters, order forms and similar documents must indicate legibly:

(a) the name of the grouping preceded or followed either by the words 'European Economic Interest Grouping' or by the initials 'EEIG', unless those words or initials already occur in the name;

(b) the location of the registry referred to in Article 6, in which the grouping is registered, together with the number of the grouping's entry at the registry;

(c) the grouping's official address;

(d) where applicable, that the managers must act jointly;

(e) where applicable, that the grouping is in liquidation, pursuant to Articles 15, 31, 32 or 36.

Every establishment of a grouping, when registered in accordance with Article 10, must give the above particulars, together with those relating to its own registration, on the documents referred to in the first paragraph of this Article uttered by it.

Article 26

1. A decision to admit new members shall be taken unanimously by the members of the grouping.

2. Every new member shall be liable, in accordance with the conditions laid down in Article 24, for the grouping's debts and other liabilities, including those arising out of the grouping's activities before his admission. He may, however, be exempted by a clause in the contract for the formation of the grouping or in the instrument of admission from the payment of debts and other liabilities which originated before his admission. Such a clause may be relied on as against third parties, under the conditions referred to in Article 9(1), only if it is published in accordance with Article 8.

Article 27

1. A member of a grouping may withdraw in accordance with the conditions laid down in the contract for the formation of a grouping or, in the absence of such conditions, with the unanimous agreement of the other members. Any member of a grouping may, in addition, withdraw on just and proper grounds.

2. Any member of a grouping may be expelled for the reasons listed in the contract for the formation of the grouping and, in any case, if he seriously fails in his obligations or

if he causes or threatens to cause serious disruption in the operation of the grouping. Such expulsion may occur only by the decision of a court to which joint application has been made by a majority of the other members, unless otherwise provided by the contract for the formation of a grouping.

Article 28

1. A member of a grouping shall cease to belong to it on death or when he no longer complies with the conditions laid down in Article 4(1). In addition, a Member State may provide, for the purposes of its liquidation, winding up, insolvency or cessation of payments laws, that a member shall cease to be a member of any grouping at the moment determined by those laws.

2. In the event of the death of a natural person who is a member of a grouping, no person may become a member in his place except under the conditions laid down in the contract for the formation of the grouping or, failing that, with the unanimous agreement of the remaining members.

Article 29

As soon as a member ceases to belong to a grouping, the manager or managers must inform the other members of that fact; they must also take the steps required as listed in Articles 7 and 8. In addition, any person concerned may take those steps.

Article 30

Except where the contract for the formation of a grouping provides otherwise and without prejudice to the rights acquired by a person under Articles 22(1) or 28(2), grouping shall continue to exist for the remaining members after a member has ceased to belong to it, in accordance with the conditions laid down in the contract for the formation of the grouping or determined by unanimous decision of the members in question.

Article 31

1. A grouping may be wound up by a decision of its members ordering its winding up. Such a decision shall be taken unanimously, unless otherwise laid down in the contract for the formation of the grouping.

2. A grouping must be wound up by a decision of its members:

(a) noting the expiry of the period fixed in the contract for the formation of the grouping or the existence of any other cause for winding up provided for in the contract, or

(b) noting the accomplishment of the grouping's purpose or the impossibility of pursuing it further.

Where, three months after one of the situations referred to in the first subparagraph has occurred, a members' decision establishing the winding up of the grouping has not been taken, any member may petition the court to order winding up.

3. A grouping must also be wound up by a decision of its members of the remaining member when the conditions laid down in Article (2) are no longer fulfilled.

4. After a grouping has been wound up by decision of its members, the manager or managers must take the steps required as listed in Articles 7 and 8. In addition, any person concerned may take those steps.

Article 32

1. On application by any person concerned or by a competent authority, in the event of the infringement of Articles 3, 12 or 31(3), the court must order a grouping to be wound up, unless its affairs can be and are put in order before the court has delivered a substantive ruling.

2. On applications by a member, the court may order a grouping to be wound up on just and proper grounds.

3. A Member State may provide that the court may, on application by a competent authority, order the winding up of a grouping which has its official address in the State to which that authority belongs, wherever the grouping acts in contravention of that State's public interest, if the law of that State provides for such a possibility in respect of registered companies or other legal bodies subject to it.

Article 33

When a member ceases to belong to a grouping for any reason other than the assignment of his rights in accordance with the conditions laid down in Article 22 (1), the value of his rights and obligations shall be determined taking into account the assets and liabilities of the grouping as they stand when he ceases to belong to it. The value of the rights and obligations of a departing member may not be fixed in advance.

Article 34

Without prejudice to Article 37(1), any member who ceases to belong to a grouping shall remain answerable, in accordance with the conditions laid down in Article 24, for the debts and other liabilities arising out of the grouping's activities before he ceased to be a member.

Article 35

1. The winding up of a grouping shall entail its liquidation.

2. The liquidation of a grouping and the conclusion of its liquidation shall be governed by national law.

3. A grouping shall retain its capacity, within the meaning of Article 1(2), until its liquidation is concluded.

4. The liquidator or liquidators shall take the steps required as listed in Articles 7 and 8.

Article 36

Groupings shall be subject to national laws governing insolvency and cessation of payments. The commencement of proceedings against a grouping on grounds of its solvency or cessation of payments shall not by itself cause the commencement of such proceedings against its members.

Article 37

1. A period of limitation of five years after the publication, pursuant to Article 8, of notice of a member's ceasing to belong to a grouping shall be substituted for any longer period which may be laid down by the relevant national law for actions against that member in connection with debts and other liabilities arising out of the grouping's activities before he ceased to be a member.

2. A period of limitation of five years after the publication, pursuant to Article 8, of notice of the conclusion of the liquidation of a grouping shall be substituted for any longer period which may be laid down by the relevant national law for actions against a

member of the grouping in connection with debts and other liabilities arising out of the grouping's activities.

Article 38

Where a grouping carries on any activity in a Member State in contravention of that State's public interest, a competent authority of that State may prohibit that activity. Review of that competent authority's decision by a judicial authority shall be possible.

Article 39

1. The Member States shall designate the registry or registries responsible for effecting the registration referred to in Articles 6 and 10 and shall lay down the rules governing registration. They shall prescribe the conditions under which the documents referred to in Articles 7 and 10 shall be filed. They shall ensure that the documents and particulars referred to in Article 8 are published in the appropriate official gazette of the Member State in which the grouping has its official address and may prescribe the manner of publication of the documents and particulars referred to in Article 8(c). The Member States shall also ensure that anyone may, at the appropriate registry pursuant to Article 6 or, where appropriate, Article 10, inspect the documents referred to in Article 7 and obtain, even by post, full or partial copies thereof. The Member States may provide for the payment of fees in connection with the operations referred to in the preceding subparagraphs; those fees may not, however, exceed the administrative cost thereof.

2. The Member States shall ensure that the information to be published in the Official Journal of the European Communities pursuant to Article 11 is forwarded to the Office for Official Publications of the European Communities within one month of its publication in the official gazette referred to in paragraph 1.

3. The Member States shall provide for appropriate penalties in the event of failure to comply with the provisions of Articles 7, 8 and 10 on disclosure and in the event of failure to comply with Article 25.

Article 40

The profits or losses resulting from the activities of a grouping shall be taxable only in the hands of its members.

Article 41

1. The Member States shall take the measures required by virtue of Article 39 before 1 July 1989. They shall immediately communicate them to the Commission.

2. For information purposes, the Member States shall inform the Commission of the classes of natural persons, companies, firms and other legal bodies which they prohibit from participating in groupings pursuant to Article 4(4). The Commission shall inform the other Member States.

Article 42

1. Upon the adoption of this Regulation, a Contact Committee shall be set up under the auspices of the Commission. Its function shall be:

(a) to facilitate, without prejudice to Articles 169 and 170 of the Treaty, application of this Regulation through regular consultation dealing in particular with particular problems arising in connection with its application;

(b) to advise the Commission, if necessary, on additions or amendments to this Regulation.

2. The Contact Committee shall be composed of representatives of the Member States and representatives of the Commission. The chairman shall be a representative of the Commission. The Commission shall provide the secretariat.

3. The Contact Committee shall be convened by its chairman either on his own initiative or at the request of one of its members.

Article 43

This Regulation shall enter into force on the third day following its publication in the Official Journal of the European Communities. It shall apply from 1 July 1989, with the exception of Articles 39, 41 and 42 which shall apply as from the entry force of the Regulation. This Regulation shall be binding in its entirety and directly applicable in all Member States.

Second Schedule

EUROPEAN ECONOMIC INTEREST GROUPING

Regulation of EEIG whose official address is in Ireland Registration 27 of the 1989 Regulations	Council Regulation (EEC) No 213/85 and European Communities (European Economic Interest Groupings) Regulations 1989 Grouping registration number in Ireland IR	Registration for stamp to be affixed above **IGI**

Name of grouping *in full*

____

____

Official address of grouping

____

____

Membership *Note one*

Names (including business name if different) and particulars of the members of the grouping

Name

____

____

Registered number and place of registration (if any)____________________

Legal form *Note two*______________________________

Address *Note three*______________________________

____

Name____________________________________

Registered number and place of registration (if any)____________________

Legal form *Note two*______________________________

Address *Note three*______________________________

____

Name____________________________________

Registered number and place of registration (if any)____________________

Legal form *Note two*______________________________

Address *Note three*______________________________

Presenter's Name Address

____

____

____

Telephone Number Reference

Number of continuation sheets attached ☐

Names (including business name if different) and particulars of the members of the grouping

Name

____

____

Registered number and place of registration (if any)____________________

Legal form *Note two*________________________________

Address *Note three*________________________________

____

Name

____

____

Registered number and place of registration (if any)____________________

Legal form *Note two*________________________________

Address *Note three*________________________________

____

Objects of the grouping________________________________

____

____

Duration of grouping *Note four*____________________________

____

Attachments

The contract establishing the above named grouping is herewith for registration

☐ that contract not being written in English or Irish a certified translation is herewith for registration________________________________

Declaration of Compliance

I,____

☐ A member of the above grouping

☐ A person authorised on behalf of a member of the above grouping

declare that the particulars on this form are correct and that all the requirements of the above Regulations in respect of the registration of the above grouping and of matters precedent and incidental to it have been complied with.

And I make this solemn declaration conscientiously believing the same to be true and by virtue of the provisions of the Statutory Declarations Act 1938.

Signature of Declarant________________________________

Declared before me by________________________________

who is personally known to me or who is identified to me by:

who is personally known to me

at ____

this________________day of________________19__________

Signed____________________

- ☐ Commissioner for Oaths
- ☐ Notary Public
- ☐ Peace Commissioner

Please complete using black block capitals or typewriting

Note one

Particulars of further members should be given on the prescribed continuation sheet prescribed continuation sheet

Note two

Insert ‘natural person’ if an individual, ‘legal person’ if a body corporate or ‘partnership’ as appropriate

Note three

Business address or registered office address as appropriate

Note four

If the duration is indefinite this should be stated

EUROPEAN ECONOMIC INTEREST GROUPING

Regulation of EEIG whose official address is in Ireland Registration 27 of the 1989 Regulations	Council Regulation (EEC) No 213/85 and European Communities (European Economic Interest Groupings) Regulations 1989 Grouping registration number in Ireland IR	Registration for stamp to be affixed above **IG2**

Name of grouping *in full*

____

____

Official address of grouping

____

____

County__________________________________

Establishment in Ireland__________________________________

____

Membership *Note one*

Names (including business name if different) and particulars of the members of the grouping

Name

____

____

Registered number and place of registration (if any)____________________

Legal form *Note two*__________________________________

Address *Note three*__________________________________

____

Name__________________________________

Registered number and place of registration (if any)____________________

Legal form *Note two*__________________________________

Address *Note three*__________________________________

____

Presenter's Name Address

____

____

____

Telephone Number Reference

Number of continuation sheets attached ☐

Names (including business name if different) and particulars of the members of the grouping

Name

____

____

Registered number and place of registration (if any)____________________

Legal form *Note two*________________________________

Address *Note three*________________________________

____

Name

____

____

Registered number and place of registration (if any)____________________

Legal form *Note two*________________________________

Address *Note three*________________________________

____

Attachments

A certified copy of the contract establishing the above named grouping is herewith for registration

☐ that contract not being written in English or Irish a certified translation is herewith for registration.

Declaration of Compliance

I,____

☐ A member of the above grouping

☐ A person authorised on behalf of a member of the above grouping

declare that the particulars on this form are correct and that all the requirements of the above Regulations in respect of the registration of the above grouping and of matters precedent and incidental to it have been complied with.

And I make this solemn declaration conscientiously believing the same to be true and by virtue of the provisions of the Statutory Declarations Act 1938.

Signature of Declarant____________________________

Declared before me by____________________________

who is personally known to me or who is identified to me by:

who is personally known to me

at ____________________________________

this____________day of____________19______

Signed____________

☐ Commissioner for Oaths

☐ Notary Public

☐ Peace Commissioner

Please complete using black block capitals or typewriting

Note one

Particulars of further members should be given on the prescribed continuation sheet

Note two

Insert 'natural person' if an individual, 'legal person' if a body corporate or 'partnership' as appropriate

Note three

Business address or registered office address as appropriate.

EUROPEAN ECONOMIC INTEREST GROUPING

Regulation of EEIG whose official address is in Ireland Registration 27 of the 1989 Regulations	Council Regulation (EEC) No 213/85 and European Communities (European Economic Interest Groupings) Regulations 1989 Grouping registration number in Ireland IR	Registration for stamp to be affixed above **IG3**

Name of grouping *in full*________________________________

____

Official address of grouping______________________________

____

____

Address of grouping establishment being set up______________________

____

____

____

Declaration

I,____

☐ a member of the above grouping

☐ a person authorised on behalf of a member of the above group

☐ a manager of the above grouping

declare that the particulars on this form are correct

Signature of Declarant____________________Date________________

Presenter's Name Address

Telephone Number Reference

Number of continuation sheets attached ☐

Please complete using block capitals or typewriting.

EUROPEAN ECONOMIC INTEREST GROUPING

Regulation of EEIG whose official address is in Ireland Registration 27 of the 1989 Regulations	Council Regulation (EEC) No 213/85 and European Communities (European Economic Interest Groupings) Regulations 1989 Grouping registration number in Ireland IR	Registration for stamp to be affixed above **IG4**

Name of grouping *in full*____

____

Official address of grouping______________________________________

____

____

Address of grouping establishment being set up__________________________

____

____

____

Declaration

I,____

☐ a member of the above grouping

☐ a person authorised on behalf of a member of the above group

☐ a manager of the above grouping

declare that the particulars on this form are correct

Signature of Declarant______________________Date__________________

Presenter's Name Address

Telephone Number Reference

Number of continuation sheets attached ☐

Please complete using black block capitals or typewriting

EUROPEAN ECONOMIC INTEREST GROUPING

Regulation of EEIG whose official address is in Ireland Registration 27 of the 1989 Regulations	Council Regulation (EEC) No 213/85 and European Communities (European Economic Interest Groupings) Regulations 1989 Grouping registration number in Ireland IR	Registration for stamp to be affixed above **IG5**

Section A

Name of grouping *in full*____

____

Official address of grouping_____________________________________

____

____

Section B

Name of Manager________________Date of Appointment__________________

____

Address____

____

____

Section C (i)

Attachments

A certified copy of the manager's particulars

☐ those particulars not being written in Irish or English a certified translation thereof (other than the manager's name and address is attached.

Signature of Declarant______________________Date__________________

Presenter's Name Address

Telephone Number Reference

Number of continuation sheets attached ☐

Section D

I consent to act singly/jointly* as manager of the grouping named above

Signature__________________________Date_________________________

Section E

If the grouping has more than one manager does the manager have the power to bind the grouping acting singly?

YES/NO*

If NO please specify the conditions under which managers can bind the grouping______

____

____

Section F

The appointment of the person named above as manager of the above grouping was terminated on

_________________________________19_________________

____

Declaration

I,____

☐ a member of the above grouping

☐ a person authorised on behalf of a member of the above group

☐ a manager of the above grouping

declare that the particulars on this form are correct

Signature of Declarant_______________________Date__________________

Notes on the completion of this form

1. If this form relates to the appointment of a manager(s), omit Section F.

2. If this form relates to the termination of the appointment of a manager(s), omit Section C, D and E.

Please complete using black block capitals or typewriting

To be completed only if official address of EEIG is in Ireland

To be completed only if official address of EEIG is outside Ireland

*Delete as appropriate

EUROPEAN ECONOMIC INTEREST GROUPING

Regulation of EEIG whose official address is in Ireland Registration 27 of the 1989 Regulations	Council Regulation (EEC) No 213/85 and European Communities (European Economic Interest Groupings) Regulations 1989 Grouping registration number in Ireland IR	Registration for stamp to be affixed above **IG6**

Name of grouping *in full*____

____

Official address of grouping______________________________________

____

____

Certified copy(ies) of the following document(s) is/are* attached:

Please tick appropriate box(es)

☐ an amendment to the grouping's formation contract

☐ a document evidencing a judicial decision regarding nullity

☐ an assignment of all/part* of a member's participation

☐ a document evidencing a judicial decision/members' order or decision* to wind up the grouping

☐ Liquidator's appointment/termination of appointment*

☐ a document evidencing the conclusion of liquidation

☐ an exemption clause relieving a new member from payment of debts and other liabilities which originated before his admission to membership of a grouping

Signature of Declarant____________________Date________________

Presenter's Name Address

Telephone Number Reference

Number of continuation sheets attached ☐

Declaration

I,____

☐ a member of the above grouping

☐ a person authorised on behalf of a member of the above group

☐ a manager of the above grouping

declare that the particulars on this form are correct

Signature of Declarant____________________Date________________

Please complete using black block capitals or typewriting

*Delete as appropriate

EUROPEAN ECONOMIC INTEREST GROUPING

Regulation of EEIG whose official address is in Ireland Registration 27 of the 1989 Regulations	Council Regulation (EEC) No 213/85 and European Communities (European Economic Interest Groupings) Regulations 1989 Grouping registration number in Ireland IR	Registration for stamp to be affixed above **IG7**

Section A

Name of grouping *in full*____

____

Official address of grouping____________________________________

____

____

Prosposed new official address__________________________________

____

Section B

Proposal to transfer the official address from Ireland

A copy of the Iris Oifigiúil is attached as evidence of the publication of the transfer proposal

Signed______________________Date__________________

☐ a member of the above grouping

☐ a person authorised on behalf of a member of the above group

Presenter's Name Address

Telephone Number Reference

Number of continuation sheets attached ☐

Section C

Proposal to transfer the official address into Ireland

The following documents (or certified copies thereof) are attached, together with certified translations of such of the documents as are not written in Irish or English:

☐ the contract for the formation of the grouping, together with any amendments thereto

☐ any documents filed, pursuant to the Council Regulation, at the registry in the country from which it is proposed to transfer the official address,

☐ A copy of________________________as evidence of the publication of the transfer proposal

I declare that no competent authority has opposed the transfer under Article 14(4) of the Council Regulation.

Signature of Declarant_______________________Date__________________

☐ a member of the above grouping

☐ a person authorised on behalf of a member of the above group

Please complete using black block capitals or typewriting

EUROPEAN ECONOMIC INTEREST GROUPING

Regulation of EEIG whose official address is in Ireland Registration 27 of the 1989 Regulations	Council Regulation (EEC) No 213/85 and European Communities (European Economic Interest Groupings) Regulations 1989 Grouping registration number in Ireland IR8	Registration for stamp to be affixed above **IG8**

Name of grouping *in full*____

____

Official address of grouping

____

____

____

Addresses of grouping establishments in Ireland

____

____

Membership *Note one*

Names including business name if different) and particulars of the members of the grouping

Name____

Registered number and place of registration (if any)____________________

Legal form *Note two*____

Address *Note three*____

Name____

Registered number and place of registration (if any)____________________

Legal form *Note two*____

Address *Note three*____

Name____

Registered number and place of registration (if any)____________________

Legal form NLegal form *Note two*___________________________________

Address *Note three*____

Presenter's Name	Address
Telephone Number	Reference

Number of continuation sheets attached ☐

Membership continued

Name____

Registered number and place of registration (if any)____________________

Legal form *Note two*____

Address *Note three*____

Changes in year ending 30 June 19___

Please tick appropriate box(es)

- ☐ amendment to the grouping's formation contract
- ☐ notifiable event concerning a manager
- ☐ judicial decision regarding nullity
- ☐ assignment of all/part* of a member's participation
- ☐ judicial decision/members' order or decision* to wind up the grouping
- ☐ Liquidator's appointment/termination of appointment*
- ☐ conclusion of liquidation
- ☐ proposal to transfer the official address of the grouping
- ☐ exemption clause relieving a new member from payment of debts and other liabilities which originated before his admission to membership of a grouping

Declaration

I,____

- ☐ a member of the above grouping
- ☐ a person authorised on behalf of a member of the above group

declare that the particulars on this form are correct

Signature of Declarant____________________Date_______________

Please complete using black block capitals or typewriting

Note one

Particulars of further members should be given on the prescribed continuation sheet

Note two

Insert 'natural person' if an individual, 'legal person' if a body corporate or 'partnership' as appropriate

Note three

Business address or registered office address as appropriate

* Delete as appropriate

EUROPEAN ECONOMIC INTEREST GROUPING

Continuation Sheet for Forms IG to IG8	Council Regulation (EEC) No 213/85 and European Communities (European Economic Interest Groupings) Regulations 1989	Continuation of Form
Registration 27 of the 1989 Regulations	Grouping registration number in Ireland	**IG....**
	IR8	

Name of grouping *in full*____

____

____

____

____

____

Please complete using black block capitals or typewriting

EXPLANATORY NOTE

(THIS NOTE IS NOT PART OF THE INSTRUMENT AND DOES NOT PURPORT TO BE A LEGAL INTERPRETATION.)

These Regulations give full effect to Council Regulations (EEC) No. 2137/85 on the European Economic Interest Grouping (EEIG). They provide a legal framework for groupings of natural persons, companies and other legal entities to enable them to co-operate effectively in economic activities across national frontiers within the European Community. Such groupings, if their official address is in Ireland, will be bodies corporate and have legal personality.

The Council Regulation is directly applicable in Irish Law but certain provisions within the Council Regulations need supplementary legislation. These include the designation of the registry and registrar for groupings (the Companies Registration Office and the Registrar of Companies respectively), management of groupings, qualifications and limits on membership, and winding-up. These Regulations also designate the forms to be used in relation to the registration, setting-up, closure or transfer of a grouping or in any other prescribed event.

The Regulations come into operation on 1st August, 1989.

Companies Act 1990 (Parts IV And VII) Regulations 1991

SI 209/1991

The Minister for Industry and Commerce, in exercise of the powers conferred on him by sections 3 of the Companies Act, 1990 (No. 33 of 1990), hereby makes the following Regulations:

1. (1) These Regulations may be cited as the Companies Act, 1990 (Parts IV and VII) Regulations, 1990.

(2) These Regulations shall come into operation on the 1st day of August, 1991.

2. In these Regulations, "the Act" means the Companies Act, 1990 (No. 33 of 1990).

3. (1) The Examiner and the Registrars of the High Court are hereby prescribed for the purposes of sections 103, 150 and 153 of the Act.

(2) The following officers are hereby prescribed for the purposes of section 167 of the Act, namely—

(a) in the case of proceedings in the Supreme Court, the Registrar of the Supreme Court,

(b) in the case of proceedings in the Court of Criminal Appeal, the Registrar of the Court of Criminal Appeal,

(c) in the case of proceedings or an application in the High Court, the Examiner and Registrars of the High Court,

(d) in the case of proceedings or an application in the Central Criminal Court, the Registrar of the Central Criminal Court,

(e) in the case of proceedings in the Special Criminal Court, the Registrar of the Special Criminal Court,

(f) in the case of proceedings in the Circuit Court, the County Registrar for the county in which the proceedings are heard,

(g) in the case of proceedings in the District Court, in the Dublin Metropolitan District or in the District Court Area of Cork City, the Chief Clerk for the district or area concerned, as the case may be,

(h) in the case of proceedings elsewhere in the District Court, the principal Clerk assigned to the District Court area in which the proceedings are heard.

4. (1) The particulars specified in a form set out in the Schedule to these Regulations in relation to section 150, 153 or 167 of the Act are hereby prescribed for the purposes of the relevant section.

(2) The period of 21 days is hereby prescribed for the purposes of section 167 of the Act.

Schedule

	Particulars of a court declaration of a restriction under section 150, Companies Act, 1990	Companies Acts 1963 to 1990	NO FEE **H6**

Please complete using black block capitals or typewriting	TO REGISTRAR OF COMPANIES I hereby notify you that the following person Surname________________ Forename________________
Note one Insert usual residential address	of *note one* ________________________________ ____ ____ Date of Birth________________________________ is the subject of a court declaration pursuant to section 150 (1) of the Companies Act, 1990
Note two Insert date	made on *note two*________________________________ The declaration arises from an action in respect of the following company Company Name Company Number______________ ____ ____________________________________Limited
Note three This form is to be completed by an officer of the court, prescribed for the purpose pursuant to section 150(4).	Signature *note three* Date____________ Name Block letters please OFFICIAL STAMP

Particulars of partial relief granted by a court pursuant to section 152, Companies Act, 1990

Companies Acts 1963 to 1990

NO FEE

H7

Please complete using black block capitals or typewriting

TO REGISTRAR OF COMPANIES

I hereby notify you that the following person

Note one
Insert usual residential address

of *note one* ______________________________

the court granted partial relief under section 152 of the Companies Act, 1990 to the following person

Surname________________ Forename________________

Note two
Insert usual residential address

of *note two*______________________________

____

____

Date of Birth______________________________

who is the subject of a declaration pursuant to section 150 of the Companies Act, 1990

Note three
Insert the date of the original declaration by the court

made on *note three*______________________________

The following are the details of the partial relief granted note four

Note four Include in particular the date of the expiration of the restrictions if varied by the court

____

____

____

____

____

____

The original declaration arose in respect of the following company

Company Name   Company Number________________

____

______________________________Limited

Note five
This form is to be completed by an officer of the court, prescribed for the purpose pursuant to section 153 (2).

Signature *note five*   Date__________

Name Block letters please

OFFICIAL STAMP

Particulars of a disqualification order pursuant to section 160 of the Companies Act, 1990; a conviction which has the effect of a person being deemed to be subject to a disqualification order under section 160, 161, or 164, or section 183 of the Companies Act,1963 (inserted by section 169 of the Companies Act, 1990); or a conviction under section 161(1) or 164

Companies Acts 1963 to 1990

NO FEE

H8

Please complete using black block capitals or typewriting

TO REGISTRAR OF COMPANIES

I hereby notify you that the following person

Surname__________________ Forename________________

Note one
Notification must be made within 21 days of the court decision

of *note two* ____________________________________

____

____

Note two
Insert usual residential address

Date of Birth___________________________________

note three

☐ is the subject of a disqualification order

☐ was convicted of an offence which has the effect of his being deemed to be subject to a disqualification order

Note three Tick appropriate box

☐ was convicted of an offence under section 161(1) of the Companies Act, 1990

☐ was convicted of an offence under section 164 of the Companies Act, 1990

From ____________________________________

To ______________________________________

Date of court decision__________________________

Note four
This form is to be completed by an officer of the court, prescribed for the purpose pursuant to section 167.

Signature *note four* Date__________

Name Block letters please

OFFICIAL STAMP

Particulars of relief granted or varied by a court pursuant to section 160 (8), Company Act, 1990

Companies Acts 1963 to 1990

NO FEE

H9

Please complete using black block capitals or typewriting

Note one
Notification must be made within 21 days of the court decision

Note two
Insert date on which the relief was granted or varied

Note three
Insert usual residential address

Note four
Insert the date of the original disqualification

Note five
Tick appropriate box

Note six
Include in particular the date of expiration of the disqualification if varied by the court

Note seven
This form is to be completed by an officer of the court, prescribed for the purpose pursuant to section 167

TO REGISTRAR OF COMPANIES

I hereby notify you that the following person

of *note two* ______________________________

the court granted or varied relief under section 160 (8) of the Companies Act, 1990 in respect of the following person

Surname__________________ Forename__________________

of *note three* ______________________________

____

____

Date of Birth______________________________

who was the subject of a disqualification order

dated *note four* ______________________________

The following are the details of the court decision note five

☐ Full relief granted

☐ Partial relief granted note six

☐ Relief varied note six______________________________

____

____

____

____

Company Name Company Number________________

____

______________________________Limited

Signature *note seven* Date____________

Name Block letters please

OFFICIAL STAMP

Explanatory Note

The purpose of these Regulations is to prescribe officers of the court, and the particulars, form and time within which information is to be furnished by them to the registrar of companies, for the purposes of certain sections of the Companies Act, 1990.

European Communities (Companies: Group Accounts) Regulations 1992

SI 201/1992

I, Desmond O'Malley, Minister for Industry and Commerce, in exercise of the powers conferred on me by section 3 of the European Communities Act, 1972 (No. 27 of 1972), and for the purpose of giving effect to the provisions of Council Directive No. 83/349/ EEC of 13 June, 1983 (OJ L493, 18.7.1983, pp 1–17) hereby make the following Regulations:

PRELIMINARY AND GENERAL

Citation, commencement and construction

1.(1) These Regulations may be cited as the European Communities (Companies: Group Accounts) Regulations, 1992.

(2) These Regulations shall be construed as one with the Companies Acts, 1963 to 1990.

Application

2.These Regulations shall apply to [Companies Act group accounts][a] and directors' reports for financial years beginning on or after the 1st day of September, 1992.

Amendments

a Amended by EC(IFRSMA)R 2005 (SI 116/2005), reg 6(a).

Interpretation

3.(1) In these Regulations, unless the context otherwise requires—

'associated undertaking' has the meaning assigned to it by Regulation 34;

'the Directive' means EEC Council Directive 83/349/EEC;

'directors' report' is the report referred to in Regulation 37;

['Companies Act group accounts' shall be read in accordance with Regulation 13][a];

'Member State' means a State which is a member of the European Communities;

'the Minister' means the Minister for Industry and Commerce;

'parent undertaking' means an undertaking that has one or more subsidiary undertakings;

'participating interest' has the meaning assigned to it by Regulation 35;

'the Principal Act' means the Companies Act, 1963;

'an undertaking' means a body corporate, a partnership, or an unincorporated body of persons engaged for gain in the production, supply or distribution of goods, the provision of a service or the making or holding of investments;

'undertakings dealt with in the group accounts' shall be construed as a reference to the parent undertaking drawing up the group accounts together with any subsidiary undertakings of that parent dealt with in the group accounts (excluding any undertakings dealt with in the group accounts in accordance with Regulation 32);

'the 1986 Act' means the Companies (Amendment) Act, 1986;

'the 1990 Act' means the Companies Act, 1990.

(2) In these Regulations, a reference to the directors of a company shall be construed, in the case of an undertaking which does not have a board of directors, as references to the corresponding persons appropriate to such an undertaking.

(3) In these Regulations, unless the context otherwise requires, a reference to a Regulation is to a Regulation of these Regulations, a reference to a paragraph is to the paragraph of the Regulation and a reference to a subparagraph is to the subparagraph of the paragraph, in which the reference occurs.

(4) In these Regulations, a reference to voting rights in an undertaking means the rights conferred on shareholders in respect of their shares or, in the case of an undertaking not having a share capital, on members, to vote at general meetings of the undertaking on all, or substantially all, matters.

(5) In these Regulations, in relation to an undertaking which does not have general meetings at which matters are decided by the exercise of voting rights, the references to holding a majority of the voting rights in an undertaking shall be construed as references to having the right under the constitution of the undertaking to direct the overall policy of the undertaking or to alter the terms of its constitution.

Amendments

a Amended by EC(IFRSMA)R 2005 (SI 116/2005), reg 6(b).

Subsidiary undertaking

4.(1) For the purposes of these Regulations, an undertaking shall be deemed to be a subsidiary of another, if but only if—

(a) that other—

(i) holds a majority of the shareholders' or members' voting rights in the undertaking, or

(ii) is a shareholder or member of it and controls the composition of its board of directors, or

(iii) is a shareholder or member of it and controls alone, pursuant to an agreement with other shareholders or members, a majority of the shareholders' or members' voting rights; or

(b) that other has the right to exercise a dominant influence over it—

(i) by virtue of provisions contained in its memorandum or articles, or

(ii) by virtue of a control contract; or

[(c) that other has the power to exercise, or actually exercises, dominant influence or control over it, or

(ca) that other and the subsidiary undertaking are managed on a unified basis, or][a]

(d) the undertaking is a subsidiary of any undertaking which is that other's subsidiary undertaking.

(2) In determining whether one undertaking controls the composition of the board of directors of another for the purposes of paragraph 1(a)(ii), subsection (2) of section 155 of the Principal Act shall apply to undertakings subject to these Regulations as it applies to companies subject to that section.

(3) For the purposes of paragraph (l)(a)—

(a) subject to paragraphs (c) and (d), any shares held or power exercisable—

(i) by any person as a nominee for that other; or

(ii) by, or by a nominee for, a subsidiary undertaking of that other, not being the subsidiary undertaking whose shares or board of directors are involved;

shall be treated as held or exercisable by that other,

(b) any shares held or power exercisable by that other or a subsidiary undertaking of that other, on behalf of a person or undertaking that is neither that other nor a subsidiary undertaking of that other shall be treated as not held or exercisable by that other,

(c) any shares held or power exercisable by that other or a nominee for that other or its subsidiary undertaking shall be treated as not held or exercisable by that other if they are held as aforesaid by way of security provided that such power or the rights attaching to such shares are exercised in accordance with instructions received from the person providing the security,

(d) any shares held or power exercisable by that other or a nominee for that other or its subsidiary undertaking shall be treated as not held or exercisable by that other if the ordinary business of that other or its subsidiary undertaking, as the case may be, includes the lending of money and the shares are held as aforesaid by way of security provided that such power or the rights attaching to such shares are exercised in the interests of the person providing the security.

(4) For the purposes of paragraphs (l)(a)(i) and (iii), the total of the voting rights of the shareholders or members in the subsidiary undertaking shall be reduced by the following:

(a) the voting rights attached to shares held by the subsidiary undertaking in itself, and

(b) the voting rights attached to shares held in the subsidiary undertaking by any of its subsidiary undertakings, and

(c) the voting rights attached to shares held by a person acting in his own name but on behalf of the subsidiary undertaking or one of its subsidiary undertakings.

(5) For the purposes of paragraph l(b) an undertaking shall not be regarded as having the right to exercise a dominant influence over another undertaking unless it has a right to give directions with respect to the operating and financial policies of that other undertaking which its directors are obliged to comply with.

(6) A 'control contract' as specified in paragraph l(b) means a contract in writing conferring such a right which-

(a) is of a kind authorised by the memorandum or articles of the undertaking in relation to which the right is exercisable, and

(b) is permitted by the law under which that undertaking is established.

(7) Paragraph (5) shall not be read as affecting the construction of the expression 'actually exercises a dominant influence' in paragraph 1(c).

Amendments

a Amended by EC(IFRSMA)R 2005 (SI 116/2005), reg 6(c).

Requirement to present group accounts

5.[(1) Where at the end of its financial year, the directors of a parent undertaking prepare Companies Act group accounts, those group accounts shall be prepared in accordance with these Regulations and shall be laid before the annual general meeting at the same time as the undertaking's individual accounts are so laid.][a]

(2) The group accounts referred to in (1) shall deal with the state of affairs and profit or loss of the parent undertaking and without prejudice to [Regulations 10 and 11,][b] all its subsidiary undertakings including those in liquidation and those with registered offices outside the State.

(3) Paragraph (1) shall only apply to a parent undertaking if it is established as

(a) a company limited by shares; or

(b) a company limited by guarantee.

(4) In the case of an undertaking to which these Regulations apply, references in the Companies Acts, 1963 to 1990, to [Companies Act group accounts][c] shall be construed as references to [Companies Act group accounts][c] prepared in accordance with these Regulations and the provisions of these Regulations relating to [Companies Act group accounts][c] supersede the corresponding provisions of those Acts.

(5) A parent undertaking to which this Regulation applies shall not be entitled to take advantage of section 154 of the Principal Act in relation to the preparation of group accounts or subsections (2) or (3) of section 151 of the Principal Act in relation to the form of group accounts.

Amendments

a Paragraph 1 substituted by EC(IFRSMA)R 2005 (SI 116/2005), reg 6(d)(i).

b Amended by EC(IFRSMA)R 2005, reg 6(d)(ii).

c Amended by EC(IFRSMA)R 2005, reg 6(d)(iii).

6.(1) The provisions of these Regulations concerning the layout of group accounts, the valuation methods used for determining the amounts to be included in those accounts and the information to be given in the notes on those accounts may be departed from:

(a) with regard to an undertaking to be dealt with in the group accounts to which this Regulation applies;

(b) where the undertakings to be dealt with in group accounts comprise principally undertakings to which this Regulation applies.

(2) This Regulation applies to the following undertakings:

(a) an undertaking that is the holder of a licence under the Central Bank Act, 1971,

(b) an undertaking that is a trustee savings bank certified under the Trustee Savings Banks Acts, 1863 to 1965,

(c) an undertaking engaged solely in the making of hire-purchase agreements (within the meaning of the Hire-Purchase Act, 1946) and credit-sale agreements (within the meaning of that Act), in respect of goods owned by the undertaking,

(d) an undertaking engaged in the business of accepting deposits or other repayable funds or granting credit for its own account,

[....][a],

[...][b],

(g) an undertaking that is the holder of an authorisation under the European Communities (Non-Life Insurance) Regulations, 1976 (S.I. No. 115 of 1976), or an authorisation under the European Communities (Life Assurance) Regulations, 1984 (S.I No 57 of 1984).

Amendments

a Reg 6(2)(e) was repealed by ACC Bank Act 2001, s 12(2).

b Reg 6(2)(f) was repealed by ICC Bank Act 2000, s 7(2) and Sch, Pt 2.

Exemptions related to size of group

7.(1) Subject to paragraphs (2) to (8), Regulation 5 shall not apply to a parent undertaking that is a private company in any financial year if, at the balance sheet date of the parent undertaking in that financial year and in the financial year of that undertaking immediately preceding that year, the parent undertaking and all of its subsidiary undertakings together, on the basis of their latest annual accounts satisfy two of the following three qualifying conditions:

(a) the balance sheet total of the parent undertaking and its subsidiary undertakings together does not exceed [€7,618,428],[a]

(b) the amount of the turnover of the parent undertaking and its subsidiary undertakings together does not exceed [€15,236,858],[b] and

(c) the average number of persons employed by the parent undertaking and its subsidiary undertakings together does not exceed 250.

(2) In this Regulation, 'balance sheet total' in relation to any financial year, means—

(a) where Format 1 of the balance sheet Formats set out in the Schedule to the 1986 Act is adopted in the group accounts, the aggregate of the amounts shown in the consolidated balance sheet for that year under the headings corresponding to items A and B in that Format, and

(b) where Format 2 of those formats is adopted by the company, the aggregate amounts so shown under 'Assets'.

(3) In this Regulation, 'amount of the turnover', in relation to any financial year, means the amounts of the turnover shown in the consolidated profit and loss account under headings corresponding to the relevant items in any of the Formats of profit and loss accounts set out in the Schedule to the 1986 Act.

(4) In the application of this Regulation to any period which is a financial year for the purpose of the group accounts but is not in fact a year, the amounts specified in paragraph (1)(b) shall be proportionally adjusted.

(5) An undertaking which before the commencement of these Regulations is not a parent undertaking but which becomes a parent undertaking on or after the commencement of these Regulations may avail of the exemption in paragraph (l) in respect of the financial year in which it becomes a parent if the requirements of paragraph (1) are met in that financial year.

(6) An undertaking which was a parent undertaking before such commencement may avail of the exemption in paragraph (1) in the first financial year in which accounts of the group are to be prepared in accordance with these Regulations if the requirements of paragraph (1) are met in that financial year or in the financial year immediately preceding that year.

(7) Where a parent undertaking qualifies to avail of the exemption provided for in paragraph (1) it shall continue to be so qualified, unless in the latest financial year of the undertaking and the financial year of the undertaking immediately preceding that year the requirements of paragraph (1) are not met.

(8) This Regulation shall not apply where—

[(a) any shares, debentures or other debt securities of the parent undertaking or of one of its subsidiary undertakings have been admitted to trading on a regulated market of any EEA State.][c]

(b) the parent undertaking or any of its subsidiary undertakings is an undertaking to which Regulation 6 applies.

(9) For the purposes of this Regulation, the average number of persons employed shall be that required to be disclosed in accordance with paragraph 15 of the Schedule to these Regulations.

(10) In determining for the purposes of paragraph (6) whether two of the three qualifying conditions therein mentioned have been met in respect of a financial year in a case where consolidated accounts in respect of that year are not prepared in accordance with these Regulations, paragraph (2) shall be construed as referring to the aggregate of any amounts included in the balance sheets of the parent and its subsidiary undertakings which correspond to the amounts mentioned in subparagraph (a) or (b), as may be appropriate, of that paragraph.

Amendments

a £6,000,000 converted to €7,618,428 by Council Regulations (EC) No 1103/97, No 974/98 and No 2866/98 and the Economic and Monetary Union Act 1998, s 6.

b £12,000,000 converted to €15,236,858 by Council Regulations (EC) No 1103/97, No 974/98 and No 2866/98 and the Economic and Monetary Union Act 1998, s 6.

c Paragraph 8(a) substituted by EC(IFRSMA)R 2005 (SI 116/2005), reg 6(e).

Exemptions for parent undertakings that are fully or 90 per cent owned subsidiary undertakings of EC undertakings

8.(1) Subject to paragraphs (3) and (4), Regulation 5 shall not apply to a parent undertaking if that parent undertaking ('the exempted parent') is itself a subsidiary undertaking of another undertaking established under the laws of [an EEA State][a] ('that other parent undertaking'), and

(a) that other parent undertaking holds all the shares in the exempted parent undertaking; or

(b) that other parent undertaking holds 90 per cent or more of the shares of the exempted parent undertaking and the remaining shareholders in or members of the exempted parent have approved the exemption.

(2) In determining whether paragraph (1)(a) applies shares held by directors of the exempted parent pursuant to an obligation in law or in its articles of association shall be disregarded.

(3) Paragraph (1) shall only apply if the following conditions are met:

(a) the exempted parent and, without prejudice to [Regulations 10 and 11],[b] all of its subsidiary undertakings must be dealt with in group accounts prepared by a parent undertaking which is established under the law of [a EEA State],[c] and of which the exempted parent is a subsidiary undertaking;

(b) the group accounts referred to in subparagraph (a) and the report of the directors of the parent undertaking drawing up those group accounts must be prepared and audited according to the law of the [EEA State][d] in which that parent undertaking is established and in accordance with the Directive [or in accordance with international financial reporting standards;][e]

(c) the following must be annexed to the annual return of the exempted parent next after the group accounts have been prepared in accordance with subparagraph (a):

(i) the group accounts referred to in subparagraph (a),

(ii) the directors' report referred to in subparagraph (b), and

(iii) the report of the person responsible for auditing the accounts referred to in subparagraph (a);

(d) the notes on the annual accounts of the exempted parent must disclose:

(i) the name and registered office of the parent undertaking that draws up the group accounts referred to in subparagraph (a), and

(ii) the exemption from the obligation to draw up group accounts and a directors' report;

(e) If the group accounts, directors' report or auditor's report referred to in subparagraph (c) are in a language other than the English language or the Irish language, there shall be annexed to each such document a translation in the English language or the Irish language certified in the prescribed manner to be a correct translation.

[(4) Paragraph (1) shall not apply to a parent undertaking any of whose shares, debentures or other debt securities have been admitted to trading on a regulated market of any EEA State.][f]

Amendments

a Amended by EC(IFRSMA)R 2005 (SI 116/2005), reg 6(f)(i).

b Amended by EC(IFRSMA)R 2005 (SI 116/2005), reg 6(f)(ii)(I).

c Amended by EC(IFRSMA)R 2005 (SI 116/2005), reg 6(f)(ii)(II).

d Amended by EC(IFRSMA)R 2005 (SI 116/2005), reg 6(f)(iii)(I).

e Amended by EC(IFRSMA)R 2005 (SI 116/2005), reg 6(f)(iii)(II).

f Substituted by EC(IFRSMA)R 2005 (SI 116/2005), reg 6(f)(iv).

Exemptions for other parent undertakings that are subsidiary undertakings of EC undertakings

9.(1) In cases not falling within Regulation 8(1), and subject to paragraphs (2) and (3), Regulation 5 shall not apply to a parent undertaking if that parent undertaking ('the exempted parent') is itself a subsidiary undertaking of another undertaking established under the law of [an EEA State],[a] and shareholders or members holding an aggregate of 10 per cent or more in nominal value of the total share capital of the exempted parent undertaking have not, at least six months before the end of the financial year of that undertaking, requested the preparation of group accounts in accordance with Regulation 5.

(2) Paragraph (l) shall only apply if the conditions set out in paragraph (3) of Regulation 8 are met.

[(3) Paragraph (1) shall not apply to a parent undertaking any of whose shares, debentures or other debt securities have been admitted to trading on a regulated market of any EEA State.][b]

Amendments

a Amended by EC(IFRSMA)R 2005 (SI 116/2005), reg 6(g)(i).

b Paragraph 3 substituted by EC(IFRSMA)R 2005 (SI 116/2005), reg 6(g)(ii).

[Exemption for parent undertakings included in non-EEA group accounts.

9A.(1) A parent undertaking (the 'exempted parent') is exempt from the requirement in Regulation 5 to prepare group accounts where that undertaking is itself a subsidiary undertaking and its parent undertaking ('that other parent undertaking') is not established under the law of an EEA State where—

(a) the exempted parent is a wholly-owned subsidiary of that other parent undertaking;

(b) that other parent undertaking holds more than 50 per cent of the shares in the exempted parent and notice requesting the preparation of group accounts has not been served in accordance with paragraph (2) on the exempted parent by shareholders holding in aggregate—

(i) more than half of the remaining shares in the company, or

(ii) 5 per cent of the total shares in the company.

(2) The notice referred to in paragraph (1)(b) must be served not later than 6 months after the end of the financial year before that to which it relates.

(3) Exemption under this Regulation is conditional upon compliance with all of the following conditions—

(a) that the exempted parent and all of its subsidiary undertakings are included in consolidated accounts for a larger group drawn up to the same date, or to an earlier date in the same financial year by that other parent undertaking,

(b) that those accounts and, where appropriate, the group's annual report, are drawn up in accordance with the provisions of the Seventh Council Directive 83/349/EEC of 13 June 1983 (where applicable, as modified by Council Directive 86/635/EEC of 8 December 1986 or Council Directive 91/674/EEC of 23 December 1991), or in a manner equivalent to consolidated accounts and consolidated annual reports so drawn up,

(c) that the consolidated accounts are audited by one or more persons authorised to audit accounts under the law under which that other parent undertaking which draws them up is established,

(d) that the exempted parent discloses in its individual accounts that it is exempt from the obligation to prepare and deliver group accounts,

(e) that the exempted parent states in its individual accounts the name of that other parent undertaking which draws up the group accounts referred to in subparagraph (d) and—

(i) where that other parent undertaking is incorporated outside the State, the country in which it is incorporated, or

(ii) where that other parent undertaking is unincorporated, the address of its principal place of business,

(f) that the exempted parent delivers to the registrar, within the period allowed for delivering its individual accounts, copies of that other parent's group accounts and, where appropriate, of the consolidated annual report, together with the auditors' report on them, and

(g) where any document comprised in accounts and reports delivered in accordance with paragraph (f) is in a language other than the English language or the Irish language, there is annexed to the copy of that document delivered a translation of it into the English language or the Irish language, certified in the prescribed manner to be a correct translation.

(4) The exemption under this Regulation does not apply to a parent undertaking any of whose securities are admitted to trading on a regulated market of any EEA State.

(5) Shares held by directors of a company for the purpose of complying with any share qualification requirement shall be disregarded in determining for the purposes of paragraph (1)(a) whether the company is a wholly-owned subsidiary.

(6) For the purpose of paragraph (1)(b), shares held by a wholly-owned subsidiary of that other parent undertaking, or held on behalf of that other parent undertaking or a wholly-owned subsidiary, shall be attributed to that other parent undertaking.

(7) In paragraph (4) 'securities' includes—

(a) shares and stock,

(b) debentures, including debenture stock, loan stock, bonds, certificates of deposit and other instruments creating or acknowledging indebtedness,

(c) warrants or other instruments entitling the holder to subscribe for securities falling within subparagraph (a) or (b), and

(d) certificates or other instruments which confer—

(i) property rights in respect of a security falling within subparagraph (a), (b) or (c),

(ii) any right to acquire, dispose of, underwrite or convert a security, being a right to which the holder would be entitled if the holder held any such security to which the certificate or other instrument relates, or

(iii) a contractual right (other than an option) to acquire any such security otherwise than by subscription.][a]

Amendments

a Paragraph 9A inserted by EC(IFRSMA)R 2005 (SI 116/2005), reg 6(h).

Exclusions from consolidation

10.(1) A subsidiary undertaking need not be included in group accounts where its inclusion is not material for the purposes of Regulation 14(1).

(2) Where two or more undertakings satisfy the requirements of paragraph (1) they shall, notwithstanding that paragraph, be included in group accounts if taken together they are material for the purpose of Regulation 14(1).

11. A subsidiary undertaking need not be included in group accounts where:

(a) severe long-term restrictions substantially hinder the parent undertaking in the exercise of its right over the assets or management of that subsidiary undertaking, or

(b) the information necessary for the preparation of group accounts in accordance with these Regulations cannot be obtained without disproportionate expense or undue delay, or

(c) the shares of the subsidiary undertaking are held by the parent undertaking exclusively with a view to their subsequent resale.

12.[...][a]

Amendments

a Regulation 12 deleted by EC(IFRSMA)R 2005 (SI 116/2005), reg 6(i).

General provisions in relation to group accounts

13. For the purpose of these Regulations group accounts shall comprise—

(a) a consolidated balance sheet dealing, as provided for in these Regulations, with the state of affairs of the parent undertaking and its subsidiary undertakings as a whole,

(b) a consolidated profit and loss account dealing, as provided for in these Regulations, with the profit or loss of the parent undertaking and its subsidiary undertakings as a whole, and

(c) notes on the accounts giving additional information as provided for in these Regulations.

14.(1) Group accounts shall give a true and fair view of the state of affairs as at the end of the financial year and the profit or loss for the financial year of the parent undertaking and subsidiary undertakings as a whole.

(2) Where group accounts drawn up in accordance with these Regulations would not provide sufficient information to comply with paragraph (1), any necessary additional information shall be provided in those accounts.

(3) Where, owing to special circumstances, the preparation of group accounts in accordance with Regulations 15 to 36 and the Schedule would prevent those accounts from complying with paragraph (1) (even if additional information were provided under paragraph (2) of this Regulation), the directors of the parent undertaking shall depart from the requirements of those Regulations in preparing those group accounts so far as is necessary in order to comply with that paragraph.

(4) Where, pursuant to paragraph (3), the directors of a parent undertaking depart from the requirements of these Regulations, they shall attach a note to the group accounts giving details of the particular departures made, the reasons therefor and the effect of those departures on the group accounts.

Format of accounts

15.(1) Section 4 and the Schedule to the 1986 Act shall apply to group accounts prepared in compliance with these Regulations as they apply to annual accounts prepared under that Act, with any necessary modifications to take account of differences between group accounts and annual accounts or the provisions of these Regulations.

(2) In particular, for the purposes of paragraph 45 of the Schedule to the 1986 Act, as substituted by Paragraph 4(2) of the Schedule to these Regulations, (dealings with or interests in group undertakings) as it applies to group accounts—

(a) any subsidiary undertakings of the parent undertaking not dealt with in the group accounts shall be treated as a subsidiary undertaking of the group, and

(b) if the parent undertaking is itself a subsidiary undertaking, the group shall be treated as a subsidiary undertaking of any parent undertaking of the parent undertaking, and the reference to fellow subsidiary undertakings shall be construed accordingly.

(3) Where, in the opinion of the directors, undue expense would be incurred in showing separately items B.I1 to B.I4 in Balance Sheet Formats 1 and 2, those items may be combined in the group balance sheet and shown as a single item under the heading 'Stocks'.

Group balance sheet and group profit and loss account

16. The group balance sheet and group profit and loss account shall combine in full the information contained in the separate balance sheets and profit and loss accounts of the parent undertaking and of the subsidiary undertakings included in the group accounts but with adjustments required or permitted under these Regulations.

Acquisition and merger accounting

17.(1) The provisions set out in Regulations 18 to 22 shall apply where an undertaking becomes a subsidiary undertaking of the parent undertaking.

(2) The event described in paragraph (1) is referred to in those provisions as an 'acquisition', and references to the 'undertaking acquired' shall be construed accordingly.

18. An acquisition shall be accounted for by the acquisition method of accounting unless the conditions for accounting for it as a merger are met and the merger method of accounting is adopted.

19.(1) The acquisition method of accounting is as follows.

(2) The identifiable assets and liabilities of the undertaking acquired shall be included in the consolidated balance sheet at their fair values as at the date of acquisition. In this paragraph the 'identifiable assets or liabilities' means the assets or liabilities which are capable of being disposed of or discharged separately, without disposing of a business of the undertaking.

(3) The income and expenditure of the undertaking acquired shall be brought into the group accounts only as from the date of acquisition.

(4) There shall be set off against the acquisition cost of the interest in the shares of the undertaking held by the undertakings dealt with in the group accounts, the interest of the undertakings dealt with in the group accounts in the adjusted capital and reserves of the undertaking acquired.

For this purpose—

'the acquisition cost' means the amount of any cash consideration and the fair value of any other consideration, together with such amounts (if any) in respect of fees and other expenses of the acquisition as the parent undertaking may determine, and

'the adjusted capital and reserves' of the undertaking acquired means its capital and reserves at the date of the acquisition after adjusting the identifiable assets and liabilities of the undertaking to fair values as at that date.

(5) The resulting amount if positive shall be treated as goodwill and the provisions of the Schedule to the 1986 Act in relation to goodwill shall apply.

(6) The resulting amount if negative shall be treated as a negative consolidation difference.

20.(1) Paragraph (2) shall apply where a parent undertaking acquired a subsidiary undertaking before the introduction of these Regulations but has not previously included that subsidiary undertaking in its group accounts.

(2) For the purposes of applying the acquisition method of accounting in accordance with Regulation 19, where:

- (a) there is no record of—
  - (i) the fair values as at the date of acquisition of the identifiable assets and liabilities of the undertaking acquired, or
  - (ii) the acquisition cost of the interest in the shares of the acquired undertaking held by the undertakings dealt with in the group accounts, or
- (b) where any such records cannot be obtained without unreasonable expense or delay,

the values of the identifiable assets and liabilities and the acquisition cost shall be taken to be the values and cost ascribed to them in the earliest available record made after the acquisition of that subsidiary undertaking.

21.(1) The conditions for accounting for an acquisition as a merger are—

- (a) that at least 90 per cent of the nominal value of the relevant shares in the undertaking acquired is held by or on behalf of the undertakings dealt with in the group accounts,
- (b) that the proportion referred to in paragraph (a) was attained pursuant to the arrangement providing for the issue of equity shares by the undertakings dealt with in the group accounts,
- (c) that the fair value of any consideration other than the issue of equity shares given pursuant to the arrangement by the undertakings dealt with in the group accounts did not exceed 10 per cent of the nominal value of the equity shares issued.

(2) The reference in paragraph (l)(a) to the 'relevant shares' in an undertaking acquired is to those carrying unrestricted rights to participate both in distributions and in the assets of the undertaking upon liquidation.

22.(1) The merger method of accounting is as follows.

(2) The assets and liabilities of the undertaking acquired shall be brought into the group accounts at the figures at which they stand in the undertaking's accounts, subject to any adjustment authorised or required by these Regulations.

(3) The income and expenditure of the undertaking acquired shall be included in the group accounts for the entire financial year, including the period before the acquisition.

(4) The group accounts shall show corresponding amounts relating to the previous financial year as if the undertaking had been included in the consolidation throughout that year.

(5) There shall be set off against the aggregate of—

(a) the appropriate amount in respect of shares issued by the undertakings dealt with in the group accounts as part of the arrangement referred to in Regulation 20(1)(b) in consideration for the acquisition of shares in the undertaking acquired, and

(b) the fair value of any other consideration for the acquisition of shares in the undertaking acquired, determined as at the date when those shares were acquired,

the nominal value of the issued share capital of the undertaking acquired held by the undertakings dealt with in the group accounts.

(6) The resulting amount shall be shown as an adjustment to the consolidated reserves.

23.(1) Where a group is acquired, Regulations 18 to 22 apply with the following adaptations.

(2) References to shares of the undertaking acquired shall be construed as references to shares of the parent undertaking of the group.

(3) Other references to the undertaking acquired shall be construed as references to the group; and references to the assets and liabilities, income and expenditure and capital and reserves of the undertaking acquired shall be construed as references to the assets and liabilities, income and expenditure and capital and reserves of the group after making the set offs and other adjustments required by these Regulations in the case of group accounts.

Methods of consolidation

24.(1) The methods of consolidation shall be applied consistently from one financial year to the next.

(2) If it appears to the directors of a parent undertaking that there are special reasons for departing from the principle specified in paragraph (1), they may so depart, but particulars of the departure, the reasons for it and its effect on the balance sheet and profit or loss of the parent undertaking and subsidiaries as a whole must be disclosed in the notes to the accounts.

25. Group accounts shall show the assets, liabilities, state of affairs as at the end of the financial year and profit or loss of the parent undertaking and its subsidiary undertakings dealt with in the group accounts as if they were a single undertaking. In particular:

(i) debts and claims between the undertakings dealt with in the group accounts shall be eliminated from those accounts,

(ii) income and expenditure relating to transactions between the undertakings dealt with in the group accounts shall be eliminated from those accounts,

(iii) where profits and losses resulting from transactions between the undertakings dealt with in the group accounts are included in the book values of assets, they shall be eliminated from those accounts,

(iv) paragraphs (i) to (iii) need not be complied with where the amounts involved are not material for the purpose of giving a true and fair view as required by Regulation 14.

26.(1) Group accounts must be drawn up as at the same date as the annual accounts of the parent undertaking.

(2) If the financial year of a subsidiary undertaking dealt with in the group accounts differs from that of the parent undertaking, the group accounts shall be drawn up—

(a) from the accounts of the subsidiary undertaking for its financial year last ending before the end of the parent undertaking's financial year provided that year ended no more than three months before that of the parent undertaking, or

(b) from interim accounts drawn up by the subsidiary undertaking as at the end of the parent undertaking's financial year.

Changes in composition of group

27. If the composition of the undertakings dealt with in the group accounts has changed significantly in the course of a financial year, the group accounts must include information which makes the comparison of successive sets of group accounts meaningful.

Valuation

28. In determining the amounts to be included in the group accounts, sections 5 and 6 of, and the valuation methods contained in the Schedule to, the 1986 Act shall apply and shall be applied consistently within those accounts.

29.(1) Subject to paragraph (2), a parent undertaking shall apply the same methods of valuation in drawing up group accounts as it applies in drawing up its [individual accounts].[a]

[(2) Subject to Regulation 28, paragraph (1) shall not apply where, in the opinion of the directors, a departure from the provisions of that paragraph is necessary for the purposes of Regulation 14(1) or, where in accordance with section 1 50(2)(a) or (3)(b) of the Principal Act, the parent company prepares IFRS group accounts.][b]

(3) Any application of paragraph (2) and the reasons therefor shall be disclosed in the notes to the group accounts.

30.(1) Where the assets and liabilities of an undertaking to be dealt with in the group accounts have been valued by a different method to that being used in the group accounts they shall be revalued in accordance with the method used in the group accounts and subject to paragraphs (2) and (3), shall be included in the group accounts on the basis of such revaluation.

(2) The revaluation in paragraph (l) need not be made where it is not material for the purposes of Regulation 14(1).

(3) If in the opinion of the directors of the parent undertaking there are special reasons for departing from the provisions of paragraph (l) they may do so and any such departure and the reasons therefor shall be stated in the notes to the group accounts.

31. Account shall be taken in the group accounts of any difference arising on consolidation between the tax chargeable for the financial year and for preceding financial years and the amount of tax paid or payable in respect of those years, provided that it is probable that an actual charge to tax will arise within the foreseeable future for one of the undertakings dealt with in the group accounts.

Joint ventures

32.(1) Where a parent undertaking or one of its subsidiary undertakings dealt with in the group accounts manages another undertaking jointly with one or more undertakings not dealt with in the group accounts, that other undertaking ('the joint venture') may, if it is not—

(a) a body corporate, or

(b) a subsidiary undertaking of the parent undertaking,

be proportionally consolidated in the group accounts in proportion to the rights in its capital held by the parent undertaking or the subsidiary undertakings dealt with in the group accounts as the case may be.

(2) The provisions of these Regulations relating to the preparation of group accounts shall apply, with any necessary modifications, to the inclusion of joint ventures in the consolidated accounts by proportional consolidation in accordance with paragraph (1).

Associated undertakings

33.(1) The interest of an undertaking dealt with in the group accounts in an associated undertaking, and the amount of profit or loss attributable to such an interest, shall be shown in the group accounts by way of the equity method of accounting including dealing with any goodwill arising in accordance with paragraphs 5 to 7 and 9 of the Schedule to the 1986 Act.

(2) Where the associated undertaking is itself a parent undertaking, the net assets and profits or losses to be taken into account are those of the parent and its subsidiary undertakings (after making any consolidation adjustments).

(3) The equity method of accounting need not be applied if the amounts in question are not material for the purpose of giving a true and fair view.

34.(1) For the purpose of these Regulations an 'associated undertaking' means an undertaking in which an undertaking dealt with in the group accounts has a participating interest and over whose operating and financial policy it exercises a significant influence and which is not—

(a) a subsidiary undertaking of the parent undertaking, or

(b) a joint venture proportionally consolidated in accordance with Regulation 32.

(2) Where an undertaking holds 20 per cent or more of the voting rights in another undertaking, it shall be presumed to exercise such an influence over it unless the contrary is shown.

(3) Paragraphs (3) and (4) of Regulation 4 shall apply in determining for the purposes of this Regulation whether an undertaking holds 20 per cent or more of the voting rights in another undertaking.

Participating interest

35.(1) A 'participating interest' means a qualifying capital interest held by one undertaking in another on a long-term basis for the purpose of securing a contribution to that undertaking's own activities by the exercise of control or influence arising from or related to that interest.

(2) In this Regulation 'qualifying capital interest'

(a) in relation to an undertaking with share capital means an interest in shares comprised in the allotted share capital of that undertaking,

(b) in relation to an undertaking with capital but no share capital means an interest conferring rights to share in the capital of the undertaking,

(c) in relation to an undertaking without capital means interests—

(i) conferring any right to share in the profits or liability to contribute to the losses of the undertaking, or

(ii) giving rise to an obligation to contribute to the debts or expenses of the undertaking in the event of a winding up; and

(d) includes an interest which is convertible into a qualifying capital interest as well as an option to acquire any such qualifying capital interest.

(3) Where an undertaking holds a qualifying capital interest in another undertaking and such an interest represents 20 per cent or more of all such interests in the other undertaking it shall be presumed to hold that interest on the basis and for the purpose mentioned in paragraph (1) of this Regulation unless the contrary is shown.

(4) The percentage of qualifying capital interests held in an undertaking with share capital shall be the percentage that the nominal value of the shares held represents of the nominal value of the allotted share capital of that undertaking.

(5) For the purpose of this Regulation an interest held on behalf of an undertaking shall be treated as held by it.

(6) [...][a]

(7) In the balance sheet and profit and loss formats set out in the Schedule to the 1986 Act, as amended by the Schedule to these Regulations, 'participating interest' does not include an interest in a group undertaking.

Amendments

a Paragraph 6 deleted by EC(IFRSMA) 2005 (SI 116/2005), reg 6(k).

Publication of information

36.(1) Subject to paragraph (2) the information specified in paragraphs 18 to 22 of the Schedule to these Regulations may, in lieu of being stated in the notes to the group accounts for any particular financial year, be given in a statement in writing signed by a director and the secretary of the parent undertaking and annexed to the first annual return made by the parent undertaking next after the group accounts for that year are laid before the annual general meeting of the parent undertaking if, in the opinion of the directors of the parent undertaking, compliance with paragraphs 18 to 22 would require a note to the group accounts of excessive length.

(2) Paragraph (1) of this Regulation shall not apply in relation to information concerning any particular undertaking if the financial state of that undertaking, as disclosed by its accounts, has in the opinion of the directors of the parent undertaking, a substantial effect on the profit or loss, or the amount of the assets of the parent undertaking and its subsidiaries taken as a whole.

(3) A copy of a statement annexed, pursuant to paragraph (1) of this Regulation, to the annual return referred to in that paragraph made by a parent undertaking shall be certified both by a director and the secretary of the parent undertaking to be a true copy of such statement.

37. (1) In the case of a parent undertaking preparing group accounts in accordance with these Regulations, the report of the directors of that undertaking under section 158 of the Principal Act, shall contain, in addition to the information specified in that section, the following information:

[(a) a fair review of the development and performance of the parent undertaking and of the development and performance of its subsidiary undertakings and of the position of the group as a whole, together with a description of the principal risks and uncertainties that they face, which review—

(i) shall be a balanced and comprehensive analysis of the development and performance of the business and of the position of the undertakings included in the group taken as a whole, consistent with the size and complexity of the business, and

(ii) to the extent necessary for an understanding of such development, performance or position, shall include an analysis of financial, and, where appropriate, non-financial key performance indicators relevant to the particular business, including information relevant to environmental and employee matters,

and, where appropriate, the report shall include additional explanations of amounts included in the group accounts;][a]

(b) particulars of any important events affecting the parent undertaking or any of its subsidiary undertakings which have occurred since the end of that year;

(c) an indication of likely future developments in the business of the parent undertaking and its subsidiary undertakings, taken as a group;

[(d) an indication of the activities, if any, of the parent undertaking and its subsidiary undertakings, taken as a group, in the field of research and development;

(e) the number and nominal value of shares in the parent undertaking held by that undertaking itself, by its subsidiary undertakings or by a person acting in the person's own name but on behalf of those undertakings, and

(f) in relation to the use of financial instruments by the parent undertaking and its subsidiary undertakings, taken as a group, and where material for the assessment of the assets, liabilities, financial position and profit or loss of the parent undertaking and its subsidiary undertakings, taken as a group—

(i) the financial risk management objectives and policies of the parent undertaking and its subsidiary undertakings, taken as a group, including its policies for hedging each major type of forecasted transaction for which hedge accounting is used, and

(ii) the exposure of the parent undertaking and its subsidiary undertakings, taken as a group to price risk, credit risk, liquidity risk and cash flow risk.][b]

(2) The information required by subparagraph (l)(e) may be given in the notes to the group accounts.

(3) Subsections (4) and (5) of section 158 of the Principal Act shall not apply to an undertaking to which this Regulation applies.

Amendments

a Paragraph (a) substituted by EC(IFRSMA) 2005 (SI 116/2005), reg 6(l).

b Paragraphs (d) and (e) substituted and (f) inserted by EC(FVA)R 2004 (SI 765/2004), reg 4.

---

38. It shall be the duty of the auditors of a parent undertaking, in preparing the report on group accounts required by section 193 of the Companies Act, 1990, to consider whether the information given in the report of the directors on the state of affairs of the parent undertaking and its subsidiary undertakings, as a group, relating to the financial year concerned is consistent with the group accounts for that year and they shall state in the report whether, in their opinion, such information is consistent with those accounts.

39.(1) Subject to the provisions of these Regulations, copies of the following documents shall be documents to be annexed to the annual return of the parent undertaking:

(a) group accounts drawn up by the parent undertaking in accordance with these Regulations;

(b) the report of the directors required by Regulation 37;

(c) the auditor's report referred to in Regulation 38;

and each such copy document shall be certified both by a director, and the secretary, of the parent undertaking to be a true copy of such accounts or reports, as the case may be.

(2) Where any such document is in a language other than the English language or the Irish language, there shall be annexed to each such document a translation in the English language or the Irish language certified in the prescribed manner to be a correct translation.

40.(1) Where a parent undertaking publishes its full group accounts, it shall also publish with those accounts the auditor's report in relation to those accounts referred to in Regulation 38.

(2) Where a parent undertaking publishes abbreviated group accounts relating to any financial year, it shall also publish a statement indicating—

(a) that the group accounts are not the group accounts, copies of which are required by these Regulations to be annexed to the annual return,

(b) whether the copies of the group accounts so required to be annexed have in fact been so annexed,

(c) whether the auditors of the parent undertaking have made a report under section 193 of the 1990 Act in respect of the group accounts of the parent undertaking which relate to any financial year with which the abbreviated group accounts purport to deal,

[(d) whether any matters referred to in the auditors' report were qualified or unqualified, or whether the auditors' report included a reference to any matters to which the auditors drew attention by way of emphasis without qualifying the report.][a]

(3) Where a parent undertaking publishes abbreviated group accounts, it shall not publish with those accounts the report of the auditors mentioned in subparagraph (2)(c) of this Regulation.

(4) In this Regulation—

'abbreviated group accounts', in relation to a parent undertaking, means any group balance sheet or group profit and loss account, or summary or abstract of a group balance sheet or group profit and loss account, relating to a financial year of the parent undertaking which is published by the parent undertaking otherwise than as part of the full group accounts of the parent undertaking and its subsidiary undertakings for that financial year;

'full group accounts', in relation to a parent undertaking, means group accounts and the report of the directors of the parent undertaking referred to in Regulation 37.

'publish', in relation to a document, includes issue, circulate or otherwise make it available for public inspection in a manner calculated to invite the public generally, or any class of members of the public, to read the document, and cognate words shall be construed accordingly.

Amendments

a Paragraph (d) substituted by EC(IFRSMA) 2005 (SI 116/2005), reg 6(m).

Offences

41.(1) If a parent undertaking fails to comply with a provision of Regulation 39 or 40, the parent undertaking and every officer of the undertaking who is in default shall be liable on summary conviction to a [class C fine][a].

(2) If any person, being a director of a company to which these Regulations apply, fails to take all reasonable steps to secure compliance with a requirement of Regulation 39 or 40, he shall, in respect of each offence, be liable on summary conviction to imprisonment for a term not exceeding 12 months or, at the discretion of the court, to a [class C fine],[a] or to both.

(3) In any proceedings against a person for an offence under paragraph (2) of this regulation, it shall be a defence for a director to prove that he had reasonable grounds to believe and did believe that a competent and reliable person was charged with the duty of ensuring that the provisions of these regulations were complied with and that the latter person was in a position to discharge that duty, and a person shall not be liable to

be sentenced to imprisonment for an offence under the said paragraph (2) unless, in the opinion of the court, the offence was committed wilfully.

Amendments

a £1,000 increased to £1,500 by CA 1990, s 240(7) as inserted by CLEA 2001, s 104(c), and converted to €1,904.61 by Council Regulations (EC) No 1103/97, No 974/98 and No 2866/98 and the Economic and Monetary Union Act 1998, s 6; the above being implicitly substituted, by Fines Act 2010, s 6, for a fine not exceeding the aforesaid amount. A class C fine currently means a fine not exceeding €2,500.

Amendments to the 1986 Act

42.[...][a]

Amendments

a This reg inserted CA 1986, s 1(3).

43.[...][a]

Amendments

a This reg amended C(A)A 1986, s 3(2), (3).

44.[...][a]

Amendments

a This reg amended C(A)A 1986, s 16.

45.[...][a]

Amendments

a This reg amended C(A)A 1986, s 17.

46.[...][a]

Amendments

a This reg amended C(A)A 1986, s 19(3).

SCHEDULE

PART 1

AMENDMENTS TO THE SCHEDULE TO THE 1986 ACT

1 [...][a]

Amendments

a This para substituted 'group undertakings' for 'group companies' in C(A)A 1986, Sch.

2 [...][a]

Amendments

a This para substituted 'participating interests' for 'shares in related companies' in C(A)A 1986, Sch.

3 [...][a]

Amendments

a This paragraph substituted 'undertakings in which a participating interest is held' for 'related companies' in C(A)A 1986, Sch.

4 [...][a]

Amendments

a This para substituted C(A)A 1986, Sch, Pt V.

5 [...][a]

Amendments

a This para substituted C(A)A 1986, Sch, para 63.

6 [...][a]

Amendments

a This paragraph substituted C(A)A 1986, Sch, para 64.

7 [...][a]

Amendments

a This paragraph substituted C(A)A 1986, Sch, para 73.

Application of Formats of Schedule to 1986 Act to Group Accounts

Minority Interest

8.(1) In applying Balance Sheet Formats 1 and 2 of the 1986 Act to group accounts a separate item under the heading 'Minority Interest' shall be shown—

(a) in Format 1 after item H, and

(b) in Format 2 under the general heading 'Liabilities', between items A and B.

(2) The amount to be shown under the heading 'Minority Interest' referred to in paragraph (l) shall be the amount of capital and reserves attributable to shares in subsidiary undertakings dealt with in the group accounts held by or on behalf of persons other than the parent undertaking and its subsidiary undertakings.

9.(1) In applying Profit and Loss Formats 1, 2, 3 and 4 of the 1986 Act to group accounts a separate item under the heading 'Minority Interest' shall be shown—

(a) in Format 1, between items 14 and 15,

(b) in Format 2, between items 16 and 17,

(c) in Format 3, between items 7 and 8 in both Section A and Section B, and

(d) in Format 4, between items 9 and 10 in both Section A and in Section B.

(2) The amount to be shown under the heading minority interest in accordance with paragraph (l) shall be the amount of any profit or loss on ordinary activities attributable to shares in subsidiaries dealt with in the group accounts held by or on behalf of persons other than the parent undertaking and its subsidiary undertakings.

(3) In applying Profit and Loss Formats 1, 2, 3 and 4 of the 1986 Act to group accounts a separate item under the heading 'Minority Interest' shall be shown—

(a) in Format 1, between items 18 and 19,

(b) in Format 2, between items 20 and 21,

(c) in Format 3, between items 9 and 10 in Section A and between items 8 and 9 in Section B, and

(d) in Format 4, between items 11 and 12 in Section A and between items 10 and 11 in Section B.

(4) The amount to be shown under the heading minority interest in accordance with paragraph (3) shall be the amount of any profit or loss on extraordinary activities attributable to shares in subsidiaries dealt with in the group accounts held by or on behalf of persons other than the parent undertaking and its subsidiary undertakings.

10.(1) The formats set out in the Schedule to the 1986 Act, as amended by this Schedule, shall have effect in relation to group accounts with the following modifications.

(2) In the Balance Sheet Formats the items headed 'Participating interests', that is—

(a) in Format 1, item A.III.3, and

(b) in Format 2, item A.III.3 under the heading 'ASSETS',

shall be replaced by two items, 'Interests in associated undertakings' and 'Other participating interests'.

(3) In the Profit and Loss Account Formats, the items headed 'Income from participating interests', that is—

(a) in Format 1, item 8,

(b) in Format 2, item 10,

(c) in Format 3, item B.4, and

(d) in Format 4, item B.6,

shall be replaced by two items, 'Income from interests in associated undertakings' and 'Income from other participating interests'.

PART 2
INFORMATION REQUIRED BY WAY OF NOTES TO THE GROUP ACCOUNTS

11. Without prejudice to Regulation 15, the notes to the group accounts shall also state the information required by the following provisions of this Part.

12.(1) In relation to the resulting amounts referred to in Regulation 19(5) and 19(6), there shall be stated in the notes to the group accounts the methods used in calculating those amounts and the reasons for any significant difference between such amounts for the financial year to which the group accounts refer and those for the preceding financial year.

(2) In relation to acquisitions taking place in the financial year, there shall be stated in the notes to the group accounts—

(a) the name and registered office of the undertaking acquired, or where a group was acquired, the name and registered office of the parent undertaking of that group, and

(b) whether the acquisition has been accounted for by the acquisition or the merger method of accounting.

13. Where sums originally denominated in currencies, other than the currency in which the group accounts are drawn up, have been brought into account under any items shown in the balance sheet or profit and loss account, the basis on which those sums have been translated into the currency in which the group accounts are drawn up shall be stated.

14. In respect of the aggregate of the amounts shown in the group balance sheet under the heading 'Creditors' there shall be stated—

(a) the aggregate amount of any debts included under that heading which are payable or repayable otherwise than by instalments and fall due for payment or repayment after the end of the period of five years beginning with the day next following the end of the financial year,

(b) the aggregate amount of any debts so included which are payable or repayable by instalments any of which fall due for payment after the end of that period,

(c) the aggregate amount of any debts included under that heading in respect of which any security has been given, and

(d) an indication of the nature of the securities so given.

15.(1) The following information shall be given with respect to the employees of the undertakings dealt with in the group accounts—

(a) the average number of persons employed in the financial year, by the undertakings dealt with in the group accounts, and

(b) the average number of persons employed within each category of persons employed of those undertakings.

(2) In respect of all persons employed by the undertakings dealt with in the group accounts during the financial year who are taken into account in determining the relevant annual number for the purposes of subparagraph (1)(a) of this paragraph, there shall also be stated the aggregate amount of staff costs, save insofar as this amount is stated in the group profit and loss account.

(3) The categories of persons employed by the undertakings included in the group accounts by reference to which the number required to be disclosed by subparagraph (1)(b) is to be determined shall be such as the directors of the parent undertaking may select, having regard to the manner in which the activities of the undertakings dealt with in the group accounts are organised.

(4) For the purposes of clauses (a) and (b) of subparagraph (1) of this paragraph, the average number of persons employed by the undertakings dealt with in the group accounts shall be determined by adding together the averages, for each such undertaking, calculated by the method set out in subparagraph (4) of paragraph 42 of the Schedule to the 1986 Act.

(5) The average number of persons employed during the financial year by an undertaking proportionally consolidated pursuant to Regulation 32, calculated by the manner specified in subparagraph (4), shall also be stated.

16.(1) In the case of group accounts, the pension commitments referred to in paragraph 36(4) and the emoluments and compensation referred to in paragraph 39(6) of the Schedule to the 1986 Act shall be to such commitments, emoluments and compensation relating to directors or past directors of the parent undertaking in respect of duties relating to the parent undertaking, to any of its subsidiary undertakings, to any undertakings proportionally consolidated in accordance with Regulation 32, or to associated undertakings.

(2) Section 191 of the Principal Act shall not apply to group accounts prepared in accordance with these Regulations.

[16A. (1) This paragraph applies where financial instruments have been included at fair value pursuant to Part IIIA of the Schedule to the 1986 Act.

(2) There shall be stated—

(a) the significant assumptions underlying the valuation models and techniques where fair values have been determined in accordance with paragraph 22B(4) (inserted by the European Communities (Fair Value Accounting) Regulations 2004) of the Schedule to the 1986 Act,

(b) for each category of financial instrument the fair value of the financial instruments in that category and the amounts—

(i) included in the profit and loss account, and

(ii) credited to or debited from the fair value reserve,

in respect of instruments in that category,

(c) for each class of derivative financial instrument, the extent and nature of the instruments including significant terms and conditions that may affect the amount, timing and certainty of future cash flows, and

(d) a table showing movements in the fair value reserve during the financial year.

16B. Where valuation of financial instruments at fair value has not been applied, for each class of derivative financial instrument there shall be stated—

(a) the fair value of the instruments in that class, if such a value can be determined in accordance with paragraph 22B(1) to (5) (inserted by the European Communities (Fair Value Accounting) Regulations 2004) of the Schedule to the1986 Act, and

(b) the extent and nature of the instruments.][a]

[16C. (1) Sub-paragraph (2) applies where—

(a) a parent undertaking and its subsidiary undertakings taken as a group has financial fixed assets that could be included at fair value by virtue of paragraph 22A (inserted by the European Communities (Fair Value Accounting) Regulations 2004) [or 22AA][b] of the Schedule to the Act of 1986,

(b) the amount at which those assets are included under any item in the accounts of the parent undertaking and the subsidiary undertakings taken as a group is in excess of their fair value, and

(c) the parent undertaking and its subsidiary undertakings taken as a group has not made provision for the diminution in value of those assets in accordance with paragraph 7(1) of the Schedule to the Act of 1986.

(2) There shall be stated—

(a) the amount at which either the individual assets or appropriate groupings of those assets is stated in the company's group accounts,

(b) the fair value of those assets or groupings, and

(c) the reasons for not making a provision for diminution in value of those assets, including the nature of the evidence that provides the basis for the belief that the book value will be recovered.][c]

[16D. (1) This paragraph applies where the amounts to be included in a company's group accounts in respect of investment property or living animals and plants have been determined in accordance with paragraph 22CA (inserted by the European Communities

(International Financial Reporting Standards and Miscellaneous Amendments) Regulations 2005) of the Schedule to the Act of 1986.

(2) The balance sheet items affected and the basis of valuation adopted in determining the amounts of net assets concerned in the case of each such item shall be disclosed in a note to the group accounts.

(3) In the case of investment property, for each balance sheet item affected there shall be shown, either separately in the consolidated balance sheet or in a note to the group accounts—

(a) the comparable amounts determined according to the historical cost accounting rules, or

(b) the differences between those amounts and the corresponding amounts actually shown in the consolidated balance sheet in respect of that item.

(4) In subparagraph (3), references in relation to any item to the comparable amounts determined in accordance with that subparagraph are references to—

(a) the aggregate amount which would be required to be shown in respect of that item if the amounts to be included in respect of all the assets covered by that item were determined according to the historical cost accounting rules, and

(b) the aggregate amount of the cumulative provisions for depreciation or diminution in value which would be permitted or required in determining those amounts according to those rules.][d]

Amendments

a Paragraphs 16A and 16B inserted by EC(FVA)R 2004 (SI 765/2004), reg 4.

b Words inserted by European Communities (Directive 2006/46/EC) Regulations 2009, reg 10.

c Paragraph 16C, inserted by EC(FVA)R 2004 (SI 765/2004), reg 4, was substituted by EC(IFRSMA)R 2005 (SI 116/2005), reg 6(r).

d Paragraph 16D inserted by EC(IFRSMA)R 2005 (SI 116/2005), reg 6(o).

17.(1) Subject to subparagraph (2), sections 41 to 43 of the Companies Act, 1990 shall apply to group accounts prepared under these Regulations.

(2) The particulars of any transaction, arrangement or agreement referred to in those sections, entered into with a director of the parent undertaking by an undertaking proportionally consolidated in accordance with Regulation 32, or an associated undertaking, shall be similarly stated.

18.(1)(a) The information detailed in subparagraph (2) shall be stated in relation to each undertaking dealt with in the group accounts.

(b) For the purposes of subparagraph (a), the information required by subparagraph (2)(b)(i) does not include such interests in the parent undertaking.

(2) (a) The name and registered office of the undertaking;

(b) (i) the aggregate of the qualifying capital interests held in that undertaking by the undertakings dealt with in the group accounts as a proportion of the total of such interests,

(ii) in this paragraph 'qualifying capital interest' shall have the meanings assigned to it in Regulation 35, and

(iii) for the purposes of this subparagraph, paragraph (4) of Regulation 35 shall apply in determining the percentage of qualifying capital interests held in the undertaking with share capital;

(c) by virtue of which of the provisions of Regulation 4 has the undertaking been dealt with in the group accounts;

(d) the information required by subparagraph (c) may be omitted where the undertaking has been dealt with in the group accounts by virtue of Regulation 4(1)(a), and where the proportion of capital and the proportion of voting rights held are the same.

19. The information detailed in paragraph 18(2) of this Schedule shall also be given in respect of each undertaking which has been excluded from the group accounts by virtue of the application of Regulations 10 to 12.

20.(1) The information detailed in paragraph 18(2)(a) and (b) shall be stated in relation to each associated undertaking.

(2) The information required by paragraph (l) shall also be stated in relation to associated undertakings, the interest in which has been dealt with in accordance with Regulation 33(3).

21.(1) The information detailed in paragraph 18(2)(a) and (b) shall be stated in relation to each undertaking that has been proportionally consolidated in accordance with Regulation 32.

(2) The nature of the joint management of each joint venture proportionally consolidated shall also be stated.

22.(1) The information set out in paragraph 18(2)(a) and (b) shall be stated in relation to each undertaking ('undertaking of substantial interest'), other than those referred to in paragraphs 18 to 21 in which undertakings dealt with in the group accounts and undertakings not dealt with by virtue of the application of Regulation 12, or persons acting in their own name but on behalf of such undertakings, between them hold a qualifying capital interest representing 20 per cent or more of such interests.

(2) There shall also be stated in relation to each undertaking of substantial interest, the amount of its capital and reserves and its profit or loss for its latest financial year for which accounts have been adopted.

(3) The information required by subparagraphs (1) and (2) may be omitted, where for the purposes of Regulation 14, it is of negligible importance.

(4) The information concerning capital and reserves and the profit or loss required by subparagraph (2) may also be omitted where the undertaking concerned is not required to attach its balance sheet to its annual return and where the qualifying capital interest held as described in subparagraph (1) is less than 50 per cent.

(5) For the purposes of this paragraph, paragraph (4) of Regulation 35 shall apply in determining the percentage of qualifying capital interests held in an undertaking with share capital.

23. For the avoidance of doubt, paragraphs 34, 36(5) and 42 (except subparagraph (4) as applied by paragraph 15(4) of this Schedule), of the Schedule to the 1986 Act shall not apply to group accounts prepared in accordance with these Regulations.

EXPLANATORY NOTE

(This note is not part of the Instrument and does not purport to be a legal interpretation).

The purpose of these Regulations is to give legal effect to a Council Directive (No. 83/349/EEC) on the co-ordination of national legislation on consolidated accounts.

The Regulations require Irish limited companies which have subsidiary undertakings to draw up group accounts comprising a consolidated balance sheet, a consolidated profit and loss account and notes to the accounts. The Regulations define when one undertaking is a subsidiary of another for the purposes of the preparation of the group accounts. They provide for exemptions from the requirement to prepare group accounts in particular circumstances and under specified conditions. They also allow the exclusion of some subsidiaries from the group accounts in certain specified circumstances.

The Regulations contain provisions governing the preparation of group accounts, the content of those accounts, their format and the valuation of items to be included therein. They also specify information to be included in the notes to the group accounts.

The Regulations stipulate what is to be included in the report of the directors of a parent undertaking and provide for the examination of such reports by the auditors to assess their consistency with the group accounts.

The Regulations also provide for the making available to the public of group accounts prepared in accordance with their provisions.

The Regulations contain some provisions relating to annual accounts which are consequential to the provisions of Council Directive 83/349/EEC.

Companies Act 1990 (Auditors) Regulations 1992

SI 259/1992

WHEREAS certain difficulties have arisen in regard to the implementation in Part X of the Companies Act, 1990 (No. 33 of 1990), of Council Directive No. 84/253/EEC of 10 April, 1984,[1] on the approval of persons responsible for carrying out the statutory audits of accounting documents;

AND WHEREAS it appears to me to be necessary for the purpose of implementing the said Directive to modify certain provisions of the said Part X;

NOW I, DESMOND O'MALLEY, Minister for Industry and Commerce, in exercise of the powers conferred on me by section 201 of the Companies Act, 1990, hereby make the following Regulations:

1 (1) These Regulations may be cited as the Companies Act, 1990 (Auditors) Regulations, 1992.

(2) These Regulations shall come into operation on the 21st day of September, 1992.

2 In these Regulations, "the Act" means the Companies Act, 1990 (No. 33 of 1990).

3 Subparagraph (iii) of section 187(1)(a) of the Act shall not be regarded as having been complied with by a person appointed to be the auditor of a company or a public auditor unless, both on the 31st day of December, 1990, and on the date of such appointment, he was a member of a body referred to in that subparagraph and on the later date he held a valid practising certificate from that body.

4 (1) Notwithstanding section 187 of the Act, a firm shall be qualified for appointment as auditor of a company or as a public auditor:

Provided that at least one member of the firm is entitled to hold a practising certificate from a body referred to in subparagraph (i), (ii) or (iii) of subsection (1)(a) of that section and is otherwise qualified under the said subparagraph (i), (ii) or (iii), as may be appropriate, and paragraph (b) of subsection (1) of that section for appointment as auditor of a company or as a public auditor.

(2) A practising certificate may be granted by a body referred to in paragraph (1) of this Regulation to a firm that complies with the proviso to that paragraph and, where such a certificate is so granted, it shall be deemed to be held by the member or members of the firm from time to time during the currency of the appointment who so complies or comply.

5 [...][a]

Amendments

a Regulation 5 is revoked by EC(SA)(Dir)R 2010, reg 15(2).

---

6 [...][a]

Amendments

a Regulation 6 is revoked by EC(SA)(Dir)R 2010, reg 15(2).

7 [...][a]

Amendments

a Regulation 7 is revoked by EC(SA)(Dir)R 2010, reg 15(2).

EXPLANATORY NOTE

These Regulations modify certain provisions in Part X of the Companies Act, 1990 and are designed to facilitate the proper and effective implementation of EC Council Directive No. 84/253/EEC (OJ No L126 12.5.1984 pp 20–26), provision for the implementation of which is already provided for in that Part of the Act.

European Communities (Credit Institutions: Accounts) Regulations 1992

SI 294/1992

TABLE OF CONTENTS

Regulations

I, BERTIE AHERN, Minister for Finance, in exercise of the powers conferred on me by section 3 of the European Communities Act, 1972 (No. 27 of 1972), and for the purpose of giving effect to Council Directives 86/635/EEC of 8 December 1986[1] *and 89/117/EEC of 13 February 1989*[22] *hereby make the following regulations:*

1 Citation and Construction

(1) These Regulations may be cited as the European Communities (Credit Institutions: Accounts) Regulations, 1992.

(2) These Regulations shall be construed as one with the Companies Acts, 1963 to 1990.

---

1. OJ No L372 of 31/12/1986.
2. OJ No L44 of 16/2/1989.

2 Interpretation

(1) In these Regulations, unless the context otherwise requires—

"accounts" means the balance sheet, profit and loss account and any notes on the accounts or statements forming part of the accounts whether or not required by law;

"annual return" means the annual return made to the registrar of companies under the Principal Act;

"associated undertaking" has the same meaning as in the European Communities (Companies: Group Accounts) Regulations 1992, (S.I. No. 201 of 1992);

["Bank" means the Central Bank and Financial Services Authority of Ireland][a];

"the Directive" means Council Directive 86/635/EEC of 8 December 1986;

"the Principal Act" means the Companies Act, 1963;

"the Act of 1986" means the Companies (Amendment) Act, 1986 (No. 25 of 1986);

"group accounts" means the accounts prepared in accordance with Regulation 7;

"individual accounts" means the accounts prepared in accordance with Regulation 5;

['investment property' means land or buildings (or both) held to earn rentals or for capital appreciation (or both);][b]

"parent company" means a company that has subsidiaries;

"section 2(2) company" means any company incorporated in the State and referred to in subsection (2) (other than paragraph (b)) of section 2 of the Act of 1986;

"section 2(2) parent company" has the meaning assigned to it by Regulation 7(1);

"undertaking" and "subsidiary undertaking" have the same meanings as in the European Communities (Companies: Group Accounts) Regulations, 1992.

[(1A) References in these Regulations to annual accounts giving a 'true and fair view' are references—

(a) in the case of Companies Act individual accounts, to the requirement under Regulation 5 that those accounts give a true and fair view,

(b) in the case of Companies Act group accounts, to the requirement under Regulation 7 that those accounts give a true and fair view, and

(c) in the case of IFRS accounts, to the equivalent requirement under international financial reporting standards.][c]

(2) A word or expression in these Regulations shall have the same meaning as in the Council Directive 86/635/EEC of 8 December 1986 unless the contrary is indicated.

(3) In these Regulations, unless the context otherwise requires, a reference to a regulation is to a regulation of these Regulations, a reference to a paragraph is to the paragraph of the regulation, and a reference to a subparagraph is to the subparagraph of the paragraph, in which the reference occurs.

(4) In these Regulations, unless the context otherwise requires, a reference to a balance sheet or profit and loss account shall include a reference to any notes to or documents annexed to the accounts in question giving information which is required by any provision of the Companies Acts, 1963 to 1990, [these Regulations, or international financial reporting standards][d] and required or allowed by any such provision to be given in a note to or a document annexed to a company's accounts.

(5) In these Regulations:

(i) a reference to directors shall be construed, in the case of an undertaking which does not have a board of directors, as a reference to the corresponding persons appropriate to such undertaking;

(ii) a reference to voting rights in an undertaking means the rights conferred on shareholders in respect of their shares or, in the case of an undertaking not having a share capital, on members, to vote at general meetings of the undertaking on all, or substantially all, matters;

(iii) in relation to an undertaking which does not have general meetings at which matters are decided by the exercise of voting rights, the references to holding a majority of the voting rights in an undertaking shall be construed as references to having the right under the constitution of the undertaking to direct the overall policy of the undertaking to alter the terms of its constitution.

Amendments

a "Bank" definition substituted by CBFSIA 2003, s 35 and Sch 2.

b Inserted by reg 10 and Sch 2, Item No 1(a) of EC(IFRSMA)R 2005.

c Inserted by reg 10 and Sch 2, Item No 1(b) of EC(IFRSMA)R 2005.

d Inserted by reg 10 and Sch 2, Item No 1(c) of EC(IFRSMA)R 2005.

---

3 Amendment of Act of 1986

[...][a]

Amendment

a This section inserted CA(A) 1986, s 7(1)(a)(ii). See the amended Act.

---

4 Date of Application

These Regulations shall apply to the individual and group accounts of a section 2(2) company drawn up in respect of every financial year beginning on or after the 1st day of January 1993 and the requirements of section 7(1)(a)(ii) of the Act of 1986 shall come into operation on that date.

5 Drawing up of Accounts

[(1) Subject to paragraph (2), every balance sheet and profit and loss account of a section 2 (2) company laid before the annual general meeting of the company, pursuant to section 148 of the Principal Act shall be prepared in accordance with:

(a) section 149 of the Principal Act as modified by these Regulations, or

(b) international financial reporting standards (in these Regulations referred to as "IFRS individual accounts") and section 149A of the Principal Act as modified by these Regulations,

and in either case shall comply with section 150C of the Principal Act.

(1A) Companies Act individual accounts of a section 2 (2) company prepared in accordance with section 149 of the Principal Act shall comply with the following requirements and section 149 (other than subsection (5) and, insofar as it relates to (5), subsection (7)) of that Act shall not apply to any such balance sheet or profit and loss account:

(a) every such balance sheet and profit and loss account shall comply with the Schedule to these Regulations;

(b) every such balance sheet of a company shall give a true and fair view of the state of affairs of the company as at the end of its financial year and every such profit and loss account of a company shall give a true and fair view of the profit and loss of the company for the financial year;

(c) where a balance sheet or profit and loss account drawn up in accordance with subparagraph (a) would not provide sufficient information to comply with subparagraph (b), any necessary additional information shall be provided in that balance sheet or profit and loss account or in a note to the accounts;

(d) where owing to special circumstances, the preparation of individual accounts of a company in compliance with subparagraph (a) would prevent those accounts from complying with subparagraph (b) (even if additional information were provided under subparagraph (c)) the directors of a company shall depart from the requirements of the Schedule to these Regulations in preparing those accounts insofar as is necessary in order to comply with that subparagraph;

(e) where the directors of a company depart from the requirements of this Regulation, they shall attach a note to the individual accounts of the company giving details of the particular departures made, the reasons therefor and the effect of those departures on the accounts,

and, accordingly, in the Companies Acts 1963 to 2003, in relation to a company to which these Regulations apply—

(i) references to the said section 149 shall be read as references to that section as modified by the provisions of these Regulations, and

(ii) references to the Sixth Schedule of the Principal Act shall be read as references to the corresponding provisions of these Regulations.

(1B) Where the directors of a section 2 (2) company prepare IFRS individual accounts in accordance with international financial reporting standards and section 149A of the Principal Act they shall ensure that instead of making the disclosures specified in section 149A(2) the notes to the accounts include the information required by—

(a) paragraph 74(4) of Part I of the Schedule to these Regulations (details of directors' remuneration),

(b) sections 41 to 45 of the Companies Act 1990 to be disclosed in individual accounts (transactions with directors),

(c) section 63 of the Companies Act 1990 unless it is disclosed in the directors' report (interests in shares and debentures),

(d) Regulation 10 of these Regulations (details of group undertakings),

(e) paragraph 77 of Part I of the Schedule to these Regulations (details of staff numbers and remuneration),

(f) paragraphs 51 to 54 of Part I of the Schedule to these Regulations (details of share capital and debentures),

(g) paragraph 73(4) of Part I of the Schedule to these Regulations (restriction on distributability of profits),

(h) paragraph 66 of Part I of the Schedule to these Regulations (guarantees and other financial commitments),

(i) paragraph 73(2) of Part I of the Schedule to these Regulations (financial assistance for the purchase of own shares),

(j) paragraph 6 of Part III of the Schedule to these Regulations (shares and debentures held by subsidiary undertakings), and

(k) paragraph 74(3) of Part I of the Schedule to these Regulations and section 205D (inserted by section 44 of the Companies (Auditing and Accounting) Act 2003) of the Companies Act 1990 (auditors' [remuneration), and][a]

[(l) where appropriate, paragraph 66A of Part I of the Schedule.][b]

(2) The references in paragraph (1) to the profit and loss account of a company being laid before the annual general meeting of a company shall not apply to the profit and loss account of a company if the company prepares Companies Acts individual accounts and—

(a) the company is a parent undertaking, and

(b) the company is required to prepare and does prepare Companies Acts group accounts in accordance with these Regulations, and

(c) the notes to the company's individual balance sheet show the company's profit and loss for the financial year determined in accordance with these Regulations.][c]

(3) Where, in the case of a company, advantage is taken of paragraph (2), that fact shall be disclosed in a note to the individual and group accounts of the company.

(4) Subparagraph (b) of paragraph (1) overrides the requirements of the Schedule to these Regulations and all other requirements of the Companies Acts, 1963 to 1990, as to the matters to be included in the accounts of a company or in notes to those accounts and, accordingly, where a balance sheet or profit and loss account of a company drawn up in accordance with those requirements would not provide sufficient information to comply with the said subparagraph, any necessary additional information shall be provided in that balance sheet or profit and loss account or in a note to the accounts.

Amendments

a Words substituted by European Communities (Directive 2006/46/EC) Regulations 2009, reg 14(a)(i).

b Subparagraph (l) inserted by European Communities (Directive 2006/46/EC) Regulations 2009, reg 14(a)(ii).

c Paragraphs (1) and (2) of reg 5 were substituted by reg 10 and Schedule 2, Item No 2 of Sch II Item No 2 of EC(IFRSMA)R 2005.

---

6 Publication of Accounts in Full or Abbreviated Form

(1) Where a company publishes its full accounts, it shall also publish with those accounts any report in relation to those accounts by the auditors of the company under section 193 of the Companies Act, 1990.

(2) Where a company publishes abbreviated accounts relating to any financial year, it shall also publish a statement indicating—

(a) that the accounts are not the accounts copies of which are required to be annexed to the annual return,

(b) whether the copies of the accounts so required to be so annexed have in fact been so annexed,

(c) whether the auditors of the company have made a report under section 193 of the Companies Act, 1990, in respect of the accounts of the company which relate to any financial year with which the abbreviated accounts purport to deal,

[(d) whether any matters referred to in the auditors' report were qualified or unqualified, or whether the auditors' report included a reference to any matters to which the auditors drew attention by way of emphasis without qualifying the report.][a]

(3) Where a company publishes abbreviated accounts, it shall not publish with those accounts any such report of the auditors as is mentioned in paragraph (2)(c).

(4) Where a company publishes its full individual accounts for a financial year it shall indicate if group accounts have been prepared and if so where those group accounts can be obtained.

(5) In this regulation—

"abbreviated accounts", in relation to a company, means any balance sheet or profit and loss account, or summary or abstract of a balance sheet or profit and loss account, relating to a financial year of the company which is published by the company otherwise than as part of the full accounts of the company for that financial year and, in relation to a parent company, includes an account in any form purporting to be a balance sheet or profit and loss account, or a summary or abstract of a balance sheet or profit and loss account, of the group consisting of the parent company and its subsidiaries;

"company" means a section 2(2) company;

"full accounts" means the individual or group accounts required to be annexed to the annual return;

"publish", in relation to a document, includes issue, circulate or otherwise make it available for public inspection in a manner calculated to invite the public generally, or any class of members of the public, to read the document, and cognate words shall be construed accordingly.

Amendments

a Paragraph (2)(d) of reg 6 was substituted by reg 10 and Sch 2, Item No 3 of EC(IFRSMA)R 2005.

7 Group Accounts

[(1) This Regulation applies to a parent company which is a section 2(2) company (in these Regulations referred to as a 'section 2(2) parent company') whether or not it is itself a subsidiary of another undertaking.

(2) A parent company to which this Regulation applies shall not be entitled to take advantage of section 154 of the Principal Act in relation to the preparation of group accounts or of section 151(1A), (2) and (3) of the Principal Act in relation to the form of group accounts.

(3) Every parent company to which this Regulation applies shall, in accordance with section 150 of the Principal Act, prepare group accounts at the end of its financial year dealing with the state of affairs and profit or loss of the company and its subsidiaries (including those in liquidation and those with registered offices outside the State) and those group accounts shall be laid before the next annual general meeting of the company at the same time as the individual accounts of the company are so laid and shall be annexed to the annual return of the company.

(4) The report of the auditors on the group accounts laid before the annual general meeting shall be annexed to the annual return referred to in paragraph (3).

(5) Where, in accordance with section 150(2) or (3)(b) of the Principal Act, the directors of a section 2(2) parent company prepare IFRS group accounts, they shall ensure that instead of making the disclosures specified in section 150B(2) (inserted by the European Communities (International Financial Reporting Standards and Miscellaneous Amendments) Regulations 2005) the notes to those group accounts include the information required by—

(a) paragraph 4 of Part IV of the Schedule to these Regulations (details of directors' remuneration,

(b) sections 41 to 45 of the Companies Act 1990 to be disclosed in group accounts (transactions with directors),

(c) section 63 of the Companies Act 1990 unless it is disclosed in the directors' report (interests in shares and debentures),

(d) Regulation 10 of these Regulations (details of group undertakings),

(e) paragraph 77 of Part I of the Schedule to these Regulations (details of staff numbers and remuneration),

(f) paragraphs 51 to 54 of Part I of the Schedule to these Regulations (details of share capital and debentures),

(g) paragraph 73(4) of Part I of the Schedule to these Regulations (restriction on distributability of profits),

(h) paragraph 66 of Part I of the Schedule to these Regulations (guarantees and other financial commitments),

(i) paragraph 73(2) of Part I of the Schedule to these Regulations (financial assistance for the purchase of own shares),

(j) paragraph 6 of Part III of the Schedule to these Regulations (shares and debentures held by subsidiary undertakings),

(k) paragraph 74(3) of Part I of the Schedule to these Regulations and section 205D (inserted by section 44 of the Companies (Auditing and Accounting) Act 2003) of the Companies Act 1990 (auditors' [remuneration), and][b]

[(l) where appropriate, paragraph 7A(a) of Part II of the Schedule.][c]

(6) Where in accordance with section 150(3)(a) of the Principal Act, the directors of a section 2(2) parent company prepare Companies Acts group accounts they shall, subject to paragraph (7), be prepared in accordance with Part 1 of the Schedule to these Regulations, as modified by Part II of the Schedule.

(7) (a) The Companies Act group accounts laid before the annual general meeting of a company shall give a true and fair view of the state of affairs and profit or loss of the company and subsidiaries dealt with thereby as a whole, so far as concerns members of the company.

(b) The Companies Act group accounts shall comprise the consolidated balance sheet dealing with the state of affairs of the parent and its subsidiaries as a whole, the consolidated profit and loss account dealing with the profit and loss of the parent and its subsidiaries as a whole and the notes on the accounts giving the information required by these Regulations or otherwise provided by the company.

(c) Where Companies Act group accounts drawn up in accordance with paragraph (6) would not provide sufficient information to comply with subparagraph (a), any necessary additional information shall be given in the group accounts or in a note to the accounts.

(d) Where, owing to special circumstances, the preparation of Companies Act group accounts in compliance with paragraph (6) would prevent those accounts from complying with subparagraph (a) (even if additional information were given under subparagraph (c)), the directors of the parent company shall depart from the requirements of Parts I and II (other than paragraph 2 of Part II) of the Schedule to these Regulations in preparing those accounts insofar as it is necessary to comply with that paragraph.

(e) Where the directors of a parent company depart from the requirements of these Regulations in compliance with subparagraph (d), they shall attach a note to the Companies Act group accounts of the company giving details of the particular departures made, the reasons therefor and the effect of those departures on the accounts.

(8) Where a document annexed to the annual return under this Regulation or Regulation 8, 8A, 9, 10 or 11 is in a language other than English or Irish, there shall be annexed to

any such document a translation in the English or Irish language certified in the prescribed manner to be a correct translation.

(9) The individual and group accounts, if any, of a subsidiary undertaking excluded from group accounts by virtue of the application of paragraph 2 of Part II of the Schedule to these Regulations shall be attached to the group accounts, or annexed to the annual return, of the parent company.

(10) Paragraph (9) shall not apply where the subsidiary undertaking has otherwise annexed the relevant accounts referred to in that paragraph to its annual return.][a]

Amendments

a Regulation 7 was substituted by reg 10 and Schedule 2, Item No 4 of EC(IFRSMA)R 2005 (SI 116/2005).

b Words substituted by European Communities (Directive 2006/46/EC) Regulations 2009, reg 14(b)(i).

c Subparagraph (l) inserted by European Communities (Directive 2006/46/EC) Regulations 2009, reg 14(b)(ii).

---

8 Wholly-owned Subsidiaries

(1) Paragraph (3) of regulation 7 shall not apply to a section 2(2) parent company which is itself a wholly-owned subsidiary of another undertaking [established in an EEA State][a] ("the parent undertaking") if paragraph (3) of this regulation is complied with; provided that the fact that the advantage of this regulation is being availed of shall be disclosed in a note to the accounts of the section 2(2) parent company annexed to its annual return under the Principal Act.

(2) In this regulation, a company shall be deemed to be a wholly-owned subsidiary of another if:

(a) it would be so deemed for the purposes of section 150 of the Principal Act, or

(b) that other holds 90% or more of the shares in the company and the remaining shareholders in the company have approved the treatment of the company as a wholly-owned subsidiary under this regulation.

(3) The requirements referred to in paragraph (1) are as follows:

(a) The company and its subsidiaries must be dealt with in group accounts prepared by the parent undertaking;

(b) the group accounts and the group report of the parent undertaking must be prepared and audited in accordance with the Directive or Directive 83/349/EEC of 13 June 1983 (OJ No L193 of 18/7/1983), [or prepared in accordance with international financial reporting standards and audited in accordance with either such Directive, as applicable,][b] as the case may be;

(c) the following must be annexed to the annual return of the company next after the group accounts have been prepared in accordance with subparagraph (a):

(i) the group accounts referred to in subparagraph (b),

(ii) the group annual report referred to in subparagraph (b), and

(iii) the report of the person responsible for auditing the accounts referred to in subparagraph (b);

(d) the notes on the annual accounts of the company must disclose:

(i) the name and registered office of the parent undertaking that draws up the group accounts referred to in subparagraph (b), and

(ii) the exemption from the obligation to draw up group accounts and a group annual report.

[(4) The exemption does not apply to a company any of whose securities are admitted to trading on a regulated market of any EEA State.][c]

(5) The Minister may, after consultation with the Bank, require that additional information shall be provided in the consolidated accounts of the parent undertaking or the individual accounts of the section 2(2) parent company referred to in paragraph (1) of this regulation in accordance with Article 9 of Directive 83/349 EEC.

(6) This regulation shall also apply to a section 2(2) parent company not falling under the provisions of paragraph (2) of this regulation which is itself a subsidiary of a parent undertaking [established in an EEA State][d] if the shareholders or members holding in total 10% or more of the nominal value of the shares of the parent company concerned have not at any time that is not later than six months before the end of the financial year in question requested the preparation of group accounts by that parent company in respect of that financial year.

Amendments

a Words substituted by reg 10 and Sch 2, Item No 5(a) of EC(IFRSMA)R 2005.

b Words inserted by reg 10 and Sch 2, Item No 5(b) of EC(IFRSMA)R 2005.

c Paragraph (4) substituted by reg 10 and Sch 2, Item No 5(c) of EC(IFRSMA)R 2005.

d Words substituted by reg 10 and Sch 2, Item No 5(d) of EC(IFRSMA)R 2005.

[8A Exemption for parent undertakings included in non-EEA group accounts

(1) A section 2(2) parent undertaking (the 'exempted parent') is exempt from the requirement in Regulation 7(3) to prepare group accounts where that undertaking is itself a subsidiary undertaking and its parent undertaking ('that other parent undertaking') is not established under the law of an EEA State where:

(a) the exempted parent is a wholly-owned subsidiary of that other parent undertaking;

(b) that other parent undertaking holds more than 50 per cent of the shares in the exempted parent and notice requesting the preparation of group accounts has not been served in accordance with paragraph (2) on the exempted parent by shareholders holding in aggregate –

(i) more than half of the remaining shares in the company, or

(ii) 5 per cent of the total shares in the company.

(2) The notice referred to in paragraph (1)(b) must be served not later than 6 months after the end of the financial year before that to which it relates.

(3) Exemption under this Regulation is conditional upon compliance with all of the following conditions—

(a) that the exempted parent and all of its subsidiary undertakings are included in consolidated accounts for a larger group drawn up to the same date, or to an earlier date in the same financial year by that other parent undertaking,

(b) that those accounts and, where appropriate, the group's annual report, are drawn up in accordance with the provisions of the Seventh Council Directive 83/349/EEC of 13 June 1983 (where applicable as modified by the Directive or Council Directive No.91/674/EEC of 23 December 1991), or in a manner equivalent to consolidated accounts and consolidated annual reports so drawn up,

(c) that the consolidated accounts are audited by one or more persons authorised to audit accounts under the law under which that other parent undertaking which draws them up is established,

(d) that the exempted parent discloses in its individual accounts that it is exempt from the obligation to prepare and deliver group accounts;

(e) that the exempted parent states in its individual accounts the name of that other parent undertaking which draws up the group accounts referred to in subparagraph (d) and—

(i) where that other parent undertaking is incorporated outside the State, the country in which it is incorporated, or

(ii) where that other parent undertaking is unincorporated, the address of its principal place of business,

(f) that the exempted parent delivers to the registrar, within the period allowed for delivering its individual accounts, copies of that other parent's group accounts and, where appropriate, of the consolidated annual report, together with the auditors' report on them, and

(g) where any document comprised in accounts and reports delivered in accordance with paragraph (f) is in a language other than the English language or the Irish language, there is annexed to the copy of that document delivered a translation of it into the English language or the Irish language, certified in the prescribed manner to be a correct translation.

(4) The exemption under this Regulation does not apply to a parent undertaking any of whose securities are admitted to trading on a regulated market of any EEA State.

(5) The Minister may, after consultation with the Bank, require that additional information shall be provided in the consolidated accounts of that other parent undertaking or of the individual accounts of the section 2(2) parent referred to in paragraph (1).

(6) Shares held by directors of a company for the purpose of complying with any share qualification requirement shall be disregarded in determining for the purposes of paragraph 1(a) whether the company is a wholly-owned subsidiary.

(7) For the purpose of paragraph (1)(b), shares held by a wholly-owned subsidiary of that other parent undertaking, or held on behalf of that other parent undertaking or a wholly-owned subsidiary, are attributed to that other parent undertaking.

(8) In paragraph (3) 'securities' includes:

(a) shares and stock,

(b) debentures, including debenture stock, loan stock, bonds, certificates of deposit and other instruments creating or acknowledging indebtedness,

(c) warrants or other instruments entitling the holder to subscribe for securities falling within subparagraph (a) or (b), and

(d) certificates or other instruments which confer—

(i) property rights in respect of a security falling within subparagraph (a), (b) or (c),

(ii) any right to acquire, dispose of, underwrite or convert a security, being a right to which the holder would be entitled if the holder held any such security to which the certificate or other instrument relates, or

(iii) a contractual right (other than an option) to acquire any such security otherwise than by subscription.][a]

Amendments

a Inserted by reg 10 and Sch 2, Item No 6 of EC(IFRSMA)R 2005.

---

9 Bank holding Companies

(1) The obligation to prepare group accounts in accordance with regulation 7 also applies to a parent company:

(i) which does not itself carry on any material business apart from the acquisition, management and disposal of interests in subsidiaries; and

(ii) whose principal subsidiaries are wholly or mainly credit institutions.

(2) In paragraph (1), the management of interests in subsidiaries includes the provision of services to such subsidiaries and a parent company's principal subsidiaries are those subsidiaries of the company whose results or financial position would principally affect the figures shown in the group accounts.

10 Information on Related Undertakings

(1) A company to which these Regulations apply shall give the information required by Part III of the Schedule to these Regulations by way of a note to [its individual accounts][a] or group accounts as the case may be.

(2) (a) Subject to subparagraph (b), the information specified in paragraph (1) may, in lieu of being stated in a note to the accounts of the company concerned for any particular financial year of the company, be given in a statement in writing signed by a director and the secretary, of the company and annexed to the first annual return made by the company next after its accounts for that year are laid before the annual general meeting of the company if, in the opinion of the directors of the company, compliance with paragraph (1) would require a note to the accounts of the company of excessive length.

(b) Subparagraph (a) shall not apply—

(i) in relation to information concerning a subsidiary of or an undertaking of substantial interest to a company (referred to subsequently in this subparagraph as the "second-mentioned company") if the financial state of that subsidiary or undertaking, as disclosed by its accounts, has, in the opinion of the directors of the second-mentioned company, a substantial effect on the profit or loss, or the amount of the assets, of the second-mentioned company and its subsidiaries; or

(ii) in relation to any subsidiary excluded from consolidated accounts by virtue of paragraph 2 of Part II of the Schedule to these Regulations.

(c) A copy of a statement annexed, pursuant to subparagraph (a), to the annual return referred to in that subparagraph made by a company shall be certified both by a director and the secretary of the company to be a true copy of such statement.

(3) Section 16 of the Companies (Amendment) Act, 1986, and subsections (4) and (5) of section 158 of the Principal Act shall not apply to a company to which this regulation applies.

(4) If advantage is taken of paragraph 2(a), the company shall indicate that the information required by Part III of the Schedule to these Regulations to be given in the notes to the accounts refers only to the undertakings referred to in paragraph 2(b) and that the full information required has been annexed to the annual return referred to in paragraph 2(a).

(5) In this regulation, the expression "undertaking of substantial interest" means an undertaking falling within any of paragraphs 7, 18 or 19 of Part III of the Schedule to these Regulations.

Amendments

a Words substituted by reg 10 and Sch 2, Item No 7 of EC(IFRSMA)R 2005.

---

11 Directors' Report

In the case of a section 2(2) parent company preparing group accounts in accordance with these Regulations, the report of the directors of that company under section 158 of the Principal Act, shall contain, in addition to the information specified in that section, the following information:

[(a) a fair review of the development and performance of the company's business and of its position and, in relation to its subsidiary undertakings, if any, of the development and performance of their business and of their position, during the financial year ending with the relevant balance sheet date together with a description of the principal risks and uncertainties that they face, which review—

(i) shall be a balanced and comprehensive analysis of the development and performance of the company's business and of its position and, in relation to its subsidiary undertakings, if any, of the development and performance of their business and of their position, consistent with the size and complexity of the business, and

(ii) to the extent necessary for an understanding of the company's development, performance or position, and that of its subsidiary undertakings, if any, shall include an analysis of financial, and, where appropriate, non-financial key performance indicators relevant to the particular business, including information relevant to environmental and employee matters,

and, where appropriate, the report shall include additional explanations of amounts included in the annual accounts;][a]

(b) particulars of any important events affecting the parent company or any of its subsidiary undertakings which have occurred since the end of that year;

(c) an indication of likely future developments in the business of the parent company and its subsidiary undertakings, taken as a group;

(d) an indication of the activities, if any, of the parent company and its subsidiary undertakings, taken as a group, in the field of research and development, [...][b]

(e) the number and nominal value of shares in the parent company held by the company itself, by its subsidiary undertakings or by a person acting in his own name but on behalf of the company or [subsidiary and,][c]

[(f) in relation to the company's use of financial instruments and where material for the assessment of its assets, liabilities, financial position and profit or loss—

(i) the company's financial risk management objectives and policies, including its policy for hedging each major type of forecasted transaction for which hedge accounting is used, and

(ii) the company's exposure to price risk, credit risk, liquidity risk and cash flow risk.][d]

(2) The information required by subparagraph (1)(e) may be given in the notes to the group accounts.

Amendments

a Paragraph (a) substituted by reg 10 and Sch 2, Item No 8 of EC(IFRSMA)R 2005.

b Amended by reg 3 of EC(CI) (FVA)R 2004.

c Amended by reg 3 of EC(CI) (FVA)R 2004.

d Amended by reg 3 of EC(CI) (FVA)R 2004.

[11A Corporate Governance Statement

(1) Where a section 2(2) parent company has its securities admitted to trading on a regulated market, is preparing group accounts in accordance with these Regulations, the corporate governance statement included in the report by the directors of that company under section 158 of the Principal Act, shall contain, in addition to the information specified in that section, a description of the main features of the internal control and

risk management systems of that section 2(2) parent company and its subsidiaries in relation to the process for preparing such group accounts.

(2) Where the consolidated annual report and the annual report are presented as a single report the description referred to in paragraph (1) shall be included in the section of the report by the directors referred to in paragraph (1) containing the corporate governance statement.

(3) Where a section 2(2) parent company referred to in paragraph (1), produces a corporate governance statement in the form of a separate report published in conjunction with the annual report in accordance with section 158 of the Principal Act, the description required by paragraph (1) shall form part of that separate report.

(4) In this Regulation, 'regulated market' has the meaning assigned to it by Article 4(1), point (14) of Directive 2004/39/EC.][a]

Amendments

a Regulation 11A inserted by European Communities (Directive 2006/46/EC) Regulations 2009, reg 15.

---

12 Non-Application of Principal Act

[Sections 151, 152, 158(4), (5) and (6) and 191 of the Principal Act shall not apply to a company to which Regulation 7 applies.][a]

Amendments

a Regulation 12 substituted by reg 10 and Sch 2, Item No 5(b) of EC(IFRSMA)R 2005.

---

13 Auditors' Reports

(1) The auditors of a section 2(2) company shall make a report to the members in accordance with section 193 of the Companies Act, 1990, and the company shall not be entitled to rely on the exemption referred to in [section 193(4A)(b)(inserted by the European Communities (International Financial Reporting Standards and Miscellaneous Amendments) Regulations 2005)][a] in relation to the preparation of its accounts.

(2) The report of the auditors shall also contain the information required by section 15 of the Companies (Amendment) Act, 1986, in relation to both the individual and group accounts prepared by the company to which these Regulations apply.

[(3) Where a section 2(2) parent company referred to in Regulation 11A produces a corporate governance statement in respect of a financial year in a separate report in accordance with Regulation 11A(3), the auditors of that parent company, when preparing their report under section 193 of the Companies Act 1990 (No. 33 of 1990) for that financial year, shall state in their report whether, in their opinion, the description, in the corporate governance statement, of the main features of the internal control and risk management systems referred to in Regulation 11A(1) is consistent with the group accounts for that financial year.][b]

Amendments

a Words substituted by reg 10 and Schedule 2, Item No 5(b) of EC(IFRSMA)R 2005 (SI 116/2005).

b Subsection (3) inserted by EC(Dir)R 2009, reg 16 and substituted by EC(Dir)(A)R 2010, reg 7.

14 Publication of Accounts of Credit Institutions incorporated outside the State

(1) Every credit institution incorporated outside the State which has a place of business in the State shall publish its individual accounts and its group accounts, together with the report of the directors and auditors, in such manner as may be prescribed by the Bank in accordance with Article 44 of the Directive.

(2) In implementing the provisions of this regulation, the bank shall apply the provisions of Directive 89/117/EEC of 13 February 1989 (OJ No L44 of 16/2/1989) and, in particular, Articles 2, 3 and 4 thereof.

(3) This regulation shall also apply to any financial institution incorporated outside the State with a place of business in the State which would, if it were incorporated in the State, be subject to licensing or supervision by the Bank.

(4) In paragraph (3), "financial institution" does not include an insurance company or undertaking.

15 Offences

(1) (a) If a company to which these Regulations apply fails to comply with a provision of these Regulations, the company and every officer of the company who is in default shall be liable on summary conviction to a [class B fine][a].

(b) Proceedings for an offence under this regulation may be brought and prosecuted by the Bank or, in the case of a failure by a company to annex or attach any document required by these Regulations to be annexed or attached to the annual return of that company, by the registrar of companies.

(2) If any person, being a director of a company to which these Regulations apply, fails to take all reasonable steps to secure compliance with a requirement of these Regulations, he shall, in respect of each offence, be liable on summary conviction to imprisonment for a term not exceeding [3 months][b] or, at the discretion of the court, to a [class B fine],[c] or to both.

(3).In any proceedings against a person for an offence under paragraph (2), it shall be a defence for a director to prove that he had reasonable grounds to believe and did believe that a competent and reliable person was charged with the duty of ensuring that the provisions of these Regulations were complied with and that the latter person was in a position to discharge that duty, and a person shall not be liable to be sentenced to imprisonment for an offence under the said paragraph (2) unless, in the opinion of the court, the offence was committed wilfully.

(4) If any person in any balance sheet, profit and loss account, report, note or other document required by or for the purposes of any provision of these Regulations wilfully

makes a statement false in any material particular, knowing it to be false, he shall be liable on summary conviction, to imprisonment for a term not exceeding [3 months][d] or to a [class B fine][e] or to both.

(5) In this section "director" and "officer" includes any person in accordance with whose instruction or directions the directors of the company are accustomed to act.

Amendments

a "€3,000" substituted for "£1,000" by EC(CI)(FVA)R 2004, reg 4(a); the above being implicitly substituted, by Fines Act 2010, s 5, for a fine not exceeding the aforesaid amount. A class B fine currently means a fine not exceeding €4,000.

b "3 months" substituted for "12 months" by EC(CI)(FVA)R 2004, reg 4(b)(i).

c "€3,000" substituted for "£1,000" by EC(CI)(FVA)R 2004, reg 4(b)(ii); the above being implicitly substituted, by Fines Act 2010, s 5, for a fine not exceeding the aforesaid amount. A class B fine currently means a fine not exceeding €4,000.

d "3 months" substituted for "12 months" by EC(CI)(FVA)R 2004, reg 4(c)(i).

e "€3,000" substituted for "£1,000" by EC(CI)(FVA)R 2004, reg 4(c)(ii); the above being implicitly substituted, by Fines Act 2010, s 5, for a fine not exceeding the aforesaid amount. A class B fine currently means a fine not exceeding €4,000.

SCHEDULE
FORM AND CONTENT OF ACCOUNTS OF CREDIT INSTITUTIONS AND GROUPS

Regulation 5

PART I
INDIVIDUAL ACCOUNTS

Chapter 1
General Rules And Formats

Section A
General Rules

1. (1) [Where the directors of a company prepare Companies Act individual accounts and subject to the following provisions of this Part:][a]

(a) every balance sheet of a company shall show the items listed in the balance sheet format set out below in section B of this Chapter of this Schedule; and

(b) every profit and loss account of a company shall show the items listed in either of the profit and loss account formats so set out;

in either case in the order and under the headings and sub-headings given in the format adopted.

(2) Subparagraph (1) above is not to be read as requiring the heading or sub-heading for any item to be distinguished by any number or letter assigned to that item in the format adopted.

Amendments

a Words substituted by reg 10 and Schedule 2, Item No 11(a) of EC(IFRSMA)R 2005 (SI 116/2005).

---

2. (1) Where in accordance with paragraph 1 a company's profit and loss account for any financial year has been prepared by reference to one of the formats set out in section B below, the directors of the company shall adopt the same format in preparing the profit and loss account for subsequent financial years of the company unless in their opinion there are special reasons for a change.

(2) Particulars of any change in the format adopted in preparing a company's profit and loss account in accordance with paragraph 1 shall be disclosed, and the reasons for the change shall be explained, in a note to the accounts in which the new format is first adopted.

3. (1) Any item required in accordance with paragraph 1 to be shown in a company's balance sheet or profit and loss account may be shown in greater detail than so required.

(2) A company's balance sheet or profit and loss account may include an item representing or covering the amount of any asset or liability, income or expenditure not specifically covered by any of the items listed in the balance sheet format provided or the profit and loss account format adopted, but the following shall not be treated as assets in any company's balance sheet:

(i) preliminary expenses;

(ii) expenses of and commission on any issue of shares or debentures; and

(iii) costs of research.

(3) Items to which lower case letters are assigned in any of the formats set out in section B below may be combined in a company's accounts for any financial year if either:

(a) their individual amounts are not material for the purpose of giving a true and fair view; or

(b) the combination facilitates the assessment of the state of affairs or profit or loss of the company for that year;

but in a case within paragraph (b) the individual amounts of any items so combined shall be disclosed in a note to the accounts and any notes required by this Schedule to the items so combined shall, notwithstanding the combination, be given.

(4) Subject to paragraph 4(3) below, a heading or sub-heading corresponding to an item listed in the balance sheet format or the profit and loss account format adopted in preparing a company's balance sheet or profit and loss account shall not be included if there is no amount to be shown for that item in respect of the financial year to which the balance sheet or profit and loss account relates.

4. (1) In respect of every item shown in the balance sheet or profit and loss account, there shall be shown or stated the corresponding amount for the financial year immediately preceding that to which the accounts relate.

[(2) Where the corresponding amount is not comparable with the amount to be shown for the item in question in respect of the financial year to which the balance sheet or profit and loss account relates, the former amount may be adjusted, and, if the former amount is adjusted, particulars as regards the respect or respects in which the foregoing amounts are not comparable and of the adjustment shall be given in a note to the accounts.][a]

(3) Paragraph 3(4) does not apply in any case where an amount can be shown for the item in question in respect of the financial year immediately preceding that to which the balance sheet or profit and loss account relates, and that amount shall be shown under the heading or sub-heading required by paragraph 1 for that item.

Amendments

a Subparagraph (2) substituted by SI 840/2005, reg 6.

---

5. (1) Subject to the following provisions of this paragraph and without prejudice to note (6) to the balance sheet format, amounts in respect of items representing assets or income may not be set off against amounts in respect of items representing liabilities or expenditure (as the case may be), or vice versa.

(2) Charges required to be included in profit and loss account format 1, items 11(a) and 11(b) or format 2, items A7(a) and A7(b) may however be set off against income required to be included in format 1, items 12(a) and 12(b) or format 2, items B5(a) and B5(b) and the resulting figure shown as a single item (in format 2 at position A7 if negative and at position B5 if positive).

(3) Charges required to be included in profit and loss account format 1, item 13 or format 2, item A8 may also be set off against income required to be included in format 1, item 14 or format 2, item B6 and the resulting figure shown as a single item (in format 2 at position A8 if negative and at position B6 (if positive).

6. (1) Assets shall be shown under the relevant balance sheet headings even where the company has pledged them as security for its own liabilities or for those of third parties or has otherwise assigned them as security to third parties.

(2) A company shall not include in its balance sheet assets pledged or otherwise assigned to it as security unless such assets are in the form of cash in the hands of the company.

7. Assets acquired in the name of and on behalf of third parties shall not be shown in the balance sheet.

[8. (1) The notes to the profit and loss account shall show—

- (a) dividends paid (other than dividends for which a liability existed at the immediately preceding balance sheet date) or which the company is liable to pay,
- (b) separately, any transfers between the profit and loss account and other reserves,
- (c) any increase or reduction in the balance on the profit and loss account since the immediately preceding financial year,
- (d) the profit or loss brought forward at the beginning of the financial year, and
- (e) the profit or loss carried forward at the end of the financial year.

(2) There shall be shown in the notes to the accounts the aggregate amount of any dividends proposed before the date of approval of the accounts which have not been shown in the notes to the profit and loss account in accordance with subparagraph (1).][a]

Amendments

a Paragraph (8) substituted by reg 10 and Sch 2, Item No 11(b) of EC(IFRSMA)R 2005.

Section B

The Required Formats for Accounts

Preliminary

9. (1) References in this Part of this Schedule to the balance sheet format or to profit and loss account formats are to the balance sheet format or profit and loss account formats set out below and references to the items listed in any of the formats are to those items read together with any of the notes following the formats for alternative positions for any particular item.

(2) The requirement imposed by paragraph 1 of this Part of this Schedule to show the items listed in any such format in the order adopted in the format is subject to any provision in the notes following the formats for alternative positions for any particular items.

10. A number in brackets following any item in any of the formats set out below is a reference to the note of that number in the notes following the formats.

BALANCE SHEET FORMAT

ASSETS

1. Cash and balances at central and post office banks (1)
2. Central Government bills and other bills eligible for refinancing with a central bank (20)
   (a) Exchequer bills and similar securities (2)
   (b) Other eligible bills (3)
3. Loans and advances to banks (4), (20)
   (a) Repayable on demand
   (b) Other loans and advances
4. Loans and advances to customers (5), (20)
5. Debt securities and other fixed income securities (6), (20)
   (a) Issued by public bodies
   (b) Issued by other issuers
6. Equity shares and other variable-yield securities
7. Participating interests
8. Shares in group undertakings
9. Intangible fixed assets (7)
10. Tangible fixed assets (8)
11. Called up capital not paid (9)
12. Own shares (10)
13. Other assets
14. Called up capital not paid (9)
15. Prepayments and accrued income

Total assets

LIABILITIES

1. Deposits by banks (11), (20)
   (a) Repayable on demand
   (b) With agreed maturity dates or periods of notice
2. Customer accounts (12), (20)
   (a) Repayable on demand
   (b) With agreed maturity dates or periods of notice
3. Debt securities in issue (13), (20)
   (a) Bonds and medium term notes
   (b) Others
4. Other liabilities
5. Accruals and deferred income

6. [Provisions for liabilities][a]
   (a) Provisions for pensions and similar obligations
   (b) Provisions for tax
   (c) Other provisions
7. Subordinated liabilities (14), (20)
8. Called up share capital (15)
9. Share premium account
10. Reserves
   (a) Capital redemption reserve
   (b) Reserve for own shares
   (c) Reserves provided for by the articles of association
   (d) Other reserves
11. Revaluation reserve
12. Profit and loss account

Total Liabilities

OFF-BALANCE SHEET ITEMS

1. Contingent liabilities (16)
   (1) Acceptances and endorsements
   (2) Guarantees and assets pledged as collateral security (17)
   (3) Other contingent liabilities
2. Commitments (18)
   (1) Commitments arising out of sale and option to resell transactions (19)
   (2) Other commitments

Amendments

a Words substituted by reg 10 and Sch 2, Item No 11(c) of EC(IFRSMA)R 2005.

Notes on the Balance Sheet Format and Off-Balance Sheet Items

(1) Cash and balances at central and post office banks

(ASSETS ITEM 1)

Cash shall comprise all currency including foreign notes and coins.

Only those balances which may be withdrawn without notice and which are deposited with central or post office banks of the country or countries in which the company is established shall be included in this item. All other claims on central banks must be shown under Assets items 3 or 4.

(2) Central Government bills and other eligible bills: Exchequer bills and similar securities

(ASSETS ITEM 2(A)

Central Government bills and similar securities shall comprise Exchequer bills and similar debt instruments issued by public bodies which are eligible for refinancing with central banks of the country or countries in which the company is established. Any bills or similar debt instruments not so eligible shall be included under Assets item 5, sub-item (a).

(3) Exchequer bills and other eligible bills: other eligible bills

(ASSETS ITEM 2(B)

Other eligible bills shall comprise all bills purchased to the extent that they are eligible, under national law, for refinancing with the central banks of the country or countries in which the company is established.

(4) Loans and advances to banks

(ASSETS ITEM 3)

Loans and advances to banks shall comprise all loans and advances to domestic or foreign credit institutions made by the company arising out of banking transactions. However loans and advances to credit institutions represented by debt securities or other fixed income securities shall be included under Asset item 5 and not this item.

(5) Loans and advances to customers

(ASSETS ITEM 4)

Loans and advances to customers shall comprise all types of assets in the form of claims on domestic and foreign customers other than credit institutions. However loans and advances represented by debt securities or other fixed income securities shall be included under Assets item 5 and not this item.

(6) Debt securities and other fixed income securities

(ASSETS ITEM 5)

This item shall comprise transferable debt securities and any other transferable fixed income securities issued by credit institutions, other undertakings or public bodies. Debt securities and other fixed income securities issued by public bodies shall however only be included in this item if they may not be shown under Assets item 2.

Where a company holds its own debt securities these shall not be included under this item but shall be deducted from Liabilities item 3 (a) or (b), as appropriate.

Securities bearing interest rates that vary in accordance with specific factors, for example the interest rate on the inter-bank market or on the Euromarket, shall also be regarded as fixed income securities to be included under this item.

(7) Intangible fixed assets

(ASSETS ITEM 9)

This item shall comprise:

(a) development costs;

(b) concessions, patents, licenses, trade marks and similar rights and assets;

(c) goodwill; and

(d) payments on account.

Amounts shall, however, be included in respect of (b) only if the assets were acquired for valuable consideration or the assets in question were created by the company itself.

Amounts representing goodwill shall only be included to the extent that the goodwill was acquired for valuable consideration.

There shall be disclosed, in a note to the accounts, the amount of any goodwill included in this item.

(8) Tangible fixed assets

(ASSETS ITEM 10)

This item shall comprise:

- land and buildings;
- plant and machinery;
- fixtures and fittings, tools and equipment; and
- payments on account and assets in the course of construction.

There shall be disclosed in a note to the accounts the amount included in this item with respect to land and buildings occupied by the company for its own activities.

(9) Called up capital not paid

(ASSETS ITEM 11 AND 14)

The two positions shown for this item are alternatives.

(10) Own Shares

(ASSETS ITEM 12)

The nominal value of the shares held shall be shown separately under this item.

(11) Deposits by banks

(LIABILITIES ITEM 1)

Deposits by banks shall comprise all amounts arising out of banking transactions owed to other domestic or foreign credit institutions by the company. However liabilities in the form of debt securities and any liabilities for which transferable certificates have been issued shall be included under Liabilities item 3 and not this item.

(12) Customer accounts

(LIABILITIES ITEM 2)

This item shall comprise all amounts owed to creditors that are not credit institutions. However liabilities in the form of debt securities and any liabilities for which transferable certificates have been issued shall be shown under Liabilities item 3 and not this item.

(13) Debt securities in issue

(LIABILITIES ITEM 3)

This item shall include both debt securities and debts for which transferable certificates have been issued, including liabilities arising out of own acceptances and promissory notes. (Only acceptances which a company has issued for its own refinancing and in respect of which it is the first party liable shall be treated as own acceptances).

(14) Subordinated liabilities

(LIABILITIES ITEM 7)

This item shall comprise all liabilities in respect of which there is a contractual obligation that, in the event of winding up or bankruptcy, they are to be repaid only after the claims of other creditors have been met.

This item shall include all subordinated liabilities, whether or not a ranking has been agreed between the subordinated creditors concerned.

(15) Called up share capital

(LIABILITIES ITEM 8)

The amount of allotted share capital and the amount of called up share capital which has been paid up shall be shown separately.

(16) Contingent liabilities

(OFF-BALANCE SHEET ITEM 1)

This item shall include all transactions whereby the company has underwritten the obligations of a third party.

Liabilities arising out of the endorsement of rediscontinued bills shall be included in this item. Acceptances other than own acceptance shall also be included.

(17) Contingent liabilities: Guarantees and assets pledged as collateral security

(OFF-BALANCE SHEET ITEM 1 (2)

This item shall include all guarantee obligations incurred and assets pledged as collateral security on behalf of third parties, particularly in respect of sureties and irrevocable letters of credit.

(18) Commitments

(OFF-BALANCE SHEET ITEM 2)

This item shall include every irrevocable commitment which could give rise to a credit risk.

(19) Commitments: Commitments arising out of sale and option to resell transactions

(OFF-BALANCE SHEET ITEM 2(1)

This sub-item shall comprise commitments entered into by the company in the context of sale and option to resell transactions.

(20) Claims on, and liabilities to, undertakings in which a participating interest is held or group undertakings

(ASSETS ITEMS 2 TO 5, LIABILITIES ITEMS 1 TO 3 AND 7)

The following information must be given either by way of subdivision of the relevant items or by way of notes to the accounts.

The amount of the following must be shown for each of Assets items 2 to 5:

(a) claims on group undertakings included therein; and

(b) claims on undertakings in which the company has a participating interest included therein.

The amount of the following must be shown for each of Liabilities items, 1, 2, 3 and 7:

(i) liabilities to group undertakings included therein; and

(ii) liabilities to undertakings in which the company has a participating interest included therein.

Special Rules

Subordinated assets

11. (1) The amount of any assets that are subordinated must be shown either as a subdivision of any relevant asset item or in the notes to the accounts; in the latter case disclosure shall be by reference to the relevant asset item or items in which the assets are included.

(2) In the case of Assets items 2 to 5 in the balance sheet format, the amounts required to be shown by note (20) to the format as sub-items of those items shall be further subdivided so as to show the amount of any claims included therein that are subordinated.

(3) For this purpose, assets are subordinated if there is a contractual obligation to the effect that, in the event of winding up or bankruptcy, they are to be repaid only after the claims of other creditors have been met, whether or not a ranking has been agreed between the subordinated creditors concerned.

Syndicated loans

12. (1) Where a company is a party to a syndicated loan transaction the company shall include only that part of the total loan which it itself has funded.

(2) Where a company is a party to a syndicated loan transaction and has agreed to reimburse (in whole or in part) any other party to the syndicate any funds advanced by that party or any interest thereon upon the occurrence of any event, including the default of the borrower, any additional liability by reason of such a guarantee shall be included as a contingent liability in off-balance sheet item 1, sub-item (2).

Sale and repurchase transactions

13. (1) The following rules apply where a company is a party to a sale and repurchase transaction.

(2) Where the company is the transferor of the assets under the transaction:

(a) the assets transferred shall, notwithstanding the transfer, be included in its balance sheet;

(b) the purchase price received by it shall be included in its balance sheet as an amount owed to the transferee; and

(c) the value of the assets transferred shall be disclosed in a note to its accounts.

(3) Where the company is the transferee of the assets under the transaction it shall not include the assets transferred in its balance sheet but the purchase price paid by it to the transferor shall be so included as an amount owed by the transferor.

Sale and option to resell transactions

14. (1) The following rules apply where a company is a party to a sale and option to resell transaction.

(2) Where the company is the transferor of the assets under the transaction it shall not include in its balance sheet the assets transferred but it shall enter under off-balance sheet item 2 an amount equal to the price agreed in the event of repurchase.

(3) Where the company is the transferee of the assets under the transaction it shall include those assets in its balance sheet.

Managed funds

15. (1) For the purpose of this paragraph "managed funds" are funds which the company administers in its own name but on behalf of others and to which it has legal title.

(2) The company shall, in any case where claims and obligations arising in respect of managed funds fall to be treated as claims and obligations of the company, adopt the following accounting treatment: claims and obligations representing managed funds are to be included in the company's balance sheet, with the notes to the accounts disclosing the total amount included with respect to such assets and liabilities in the balance sheet and showing the amount included under each relevant balance sheet item in respect of such assets or (as the case may be) liabilities.

PROFIT AND LOSS ACCOUNT FORMATS

FORMAT 1

Vertical Layout

1. Interest receivable and similar income (1)
   - (1) Interest receivable and similar income arising from debt securities and other fixed income securities
   - (2) Other interest receivable and similar income
2. Interest payable and similar charges (2)
3. Dividend income
   - (a) Income from equity shares and other variable-yield securities
   - (b) Income from participating interests
   - (c) Income from shares in group undertakings
4. Fees and commissions receivable (3)
5. Fees and commissions payable (4)
6. Dealing profits or losses (5)
7. Other operating income
8. Administrative expenses
   - (a) Staff costs
     - (i) Wages and salaries
     - (ii) Social security costs
     - (iii) Other pension costs
   - (b) Other administrative expenses
9. Depreciation and amortisation (6)
10. Other operating charges
11. Provisions
    - (a) Provisions for bad and doubtful debts (7)
    - (b) Provisions for contingent liabilities and commitments (8)
12. Adjustments to provisions
    - (a) Adjustments to provisions for bad and doubtful debts (9)

(b) Adjustments to provisions for contingent liabilities and commitments (10)

13. Amounts written off fixed asset investments (11)
14. Adjustments to amounts written off fixed asset investments (12)
15. Profit or loss on ordinary activities before tax
16. Tax on profit or loss on ordinary activities.
17. Profit or loss on ordinary activities after tax
18. Extraordinary income
19. Extraordinary charges
20. Extraordinary profit or loss
21. Tax on extraordinary profit or loss
22. Extraordinary profit or loss after tax
23. Other taxes not shown under the preceding items
24. Profit or loss for the financial year

FORMAT 2

Horizontal layout

A. Charges

1. Interest payable and similar charges (2)
2. Fees and commission payable (4)
3. Dealing losses (5)
4. Administrative expenses
   - (a) Staff costs
     - (i) Wages and salaries
     - (ii) Social security costs
     - (iii) Other pension costs
   - (b) Other administrative expenses
5. Depreciation and amortisation (6)
6. Other operating charges
7. Provisions
   - (a) Provisions for bad and doubtful debts (7)
   - (b) Provisions for contingent liabilities and commitments (8)
8. Amounts written off fixed asset investments (11)
9. Profit on ordinary activities before tax
10. Tax on profit or loss on ordinary activities
11. Profit on ordinary activities after tax
12. Extraordinary charges
13. Tax on extraordinary profit or loss
14. Extraordinary loss after tax
15. Other taxes not shown under the preceding items
16. Profit for the financial year.

B. Income

1. Interest receivable and similar income (1)
   - (1) Interest receivable and similar income arising from debt securities and other fixed income securities
   - (2) Other interest receivable and similar income
2. Dividend income
   - (a) Income from equity shares and other variable-yield securities
   - (b) Income from participating interests
   - (c) Income from shares in group undertakings
3. Fees and commissions receivable (3)
4. Dealing profits (5)
5. Adjustments to provisions
   - (a) Adjustments to provisions for bad and doubtful debts (9)
   - (b) Adjustments to provisions for contingent liabilities and commitments (10)
6. Adjustments to amounts written off fixed asset investments (12)
7. Other operating income
8. Loss on ordinary activities before tax
9. Loss on ordinary activities after tax
10. Extraordinary income
11. Extraordinary profit after tax
12. Loss for the financial year

Notes on the Profit and Loss Account Formats

(1) Interest receivable and similar income

(FORMAT 1, ITEM 1; FORMAT 2, ITEM B1)

This item shall include all income arising out of banking activities, including:

- (a) income from assets included in Assets items 1 to 5 in the balance sheet format, however calculated;
- (b) income resulting from covered forward contracts, spread over the actual duration of the contract and similar in nature to interest; and
- (c) fees and commissions receivable similar in nature to interest and calculated on a time basis or by reference to the amount of the claim (but not other fees and commissions receivable).

(2) Interest payable and similar charges

(FORMAT 1, ITEM 2; FORMAT 2, ITEM A1)

This item shall include all expenditure arising out of banking activities, including:

- (a) charges arising out of liabilities included in Liabilities items 1, 2, 3 and 7 in the balance sheet format, however calculated;
- (b) charges resulting from covered forward contracts, spread over the actual duration of the contract and similar in nature to interest; and

(c) fees and commissions payable similar in nature to interest and calculated on a time basis or by reference to the amount of the liability (but not other fees and commissions payable).

(3) Fees and commissions receivable

(FORMAT 1, ITEM 4; FORMAT 2, ITEM B3)

Fees and commissions receivable shall comprise income in respect of all services supplied by the company to third parties, but not fees or commissions required to be included under interest receivable.

(FORMAT 1, ITEM 1; FORMAT 2, ITEM B1)

In particular the following fees and commissions receivable must be included (unless required to be included under interest receivable):

- fees and commissions for guarantees, loan administration on behalf of other lenders and securities transactions;
- fees, commissions and other income in respect of payment transactions, account administration charges and commissions for the safe custody and administration of securities;
- fees and commissions for foreign currency transactions and for the sale and purchase of coin and precious metals; and
- fees and commissions charged for brokerage services in connection with savings and insurance contracts and loans.

(4) Fees and commissions payable

(FORMAT 1, ITEM 5; FORMAT 2, ITEM A2)

Fees and commissions payable shall comprise charges for all services rendered to the company by third parties but not fees or commissions required to be included under interest payable (Format 1, item 2; Format 2, item A1).

In particular the following fees and commissions payable must be included (unless required to be included under interest payable):

- fees and commissions for guarantees, loan administration and securities transactions;
- fees, commissions and other charges in respect of payment transactions, account administration charges and commission for the safe custody and administration of securities;
- fees and commissions for foreign currency transactions and for the sale and purchase of coin and precious metals; and
- fees and commissions for brokerage service in connection with savings and insurance contracts and loans.

(5) Dealing profits or losses

(FORMAT 1, ITEM 6, FORMAT 2, ITEMS B4 AND A3)

This item shall comprise:

(a) the net profit or net loss on transactions in securities which are not held as financial fixed assets together with amounts written off or written back with respect to such securities, including amounts written off or written back as a result of the application of paragraph 34(1) below;

(b) the net profit or loss on exchange activities, save in so far as the profit or loss is included in interest receivable or interest payable (format 1, items 1 or 2; format 2, items B1 or A1); and

(c) the net profits and losses on other dealing operations involving financial instruments, including precious metals.

(6) Depreciation and amortisation

(FORMAT 1, ITEM 9; FORMAT 2, ITEM A5)

This item shall comprise depreciation and other amounts written off in respect of balance sheet Assets items 9 and 10.

(7) Provisions: Provisions for bad and doubtful debts

(FORMAT 1, ITEM 11(A); FORMAT 2, ITEM 7(A)

Provisions for bad or doubtful debts shall comprise charges for amount written off and for provisions made in respect of loans and advances shown under balance sheet Assets items 3 and 4.

(8) Provisions: Provisions for contingent liabilities and commitments

(FORMAT 1, ITEM 11(B); FORMAT 2, ITEM A7(B)

This item shall comprise charges for provisions for contingent liabilities and commitments of a type which would, if not provided for, be shown under off-balance sheet items 1 and 2.

(9) Adjustments to provisions: Adjustments to provisions for bad and doubtful debts

(FORMAT 1, ITEM 12 (A); FORMAT 2, ITEM B5 (A)

This item shall include credits from the recovery of loans that have been written off, from other advances written back following earlier write offs and from the reduction of provisions previously made with respect to loans and advances.

(10) Adjustments to provisions: Adjustments to provisions for contingent liabilities and commitments

(FORMAT 1, ITEM 12(B); FORMAT 2, ITEM B5(B)

This item comprises credits from the reduction of provisions previously made with respect to contingent liabilities and commitments.

(11) Amounts written off fixed assets investments

(FORMAT 12, ITEM 13; FORMAT 2, ITEM A8)

Amounts written off fixed assets investments shall comprise amounts written off in respect of assets which are transferable securities held as financial fixed assets, participating interests and shares in group undertakings and which are included in Assets items 5 to 8 in the balance sheet format.

(12) Adjustments to amounts written off fixed asset investments

(FORMAT 1, ITEM 14; FORMAT 2, ITEM B6).

Adjustments to amounts written off fixed assets investments shall include amounts written back following earlier write offs and provisions in respect of assets which are transferable securities held as financial fixed assets, participating interests and group undertakings and which are included in Assets items 5 to 8 in the balance sheet format.

Chapter II
Accounting Principles and Rules

Section A
Accounting Principles

16. Subject to paragraph 22 below, the amounts to be included in respect of all items shown in [Companies Act individual accounts][a] shall be determined in accordance with the principles set out in paragraphs 17 to 21.

Amendments

a Words substituted by reg 10 and Schedule 2, Item No 11(d) of EC(IFRSMA)R 2005 (SI 116/2005).

Accounting principles

17. The company shall be presumed to be carrying on business as a going concern.

18. Accounting policies shall be applied consistently within the same accounts and from one financial year to the next.

19. The amount of any item shall be determined on a prudent basis and, in particular:

(a) only profits realised at the balance sheet date shall be included in the profit and loss account; and

(b) [all liabilities which have arisen][a] in respect of the financial year to which the accounts relate or a previous financial year shall be taken into account, including those which only become apparent between the balance sheet date and the date on which it is signed on behalf of the board of directors in pursuance of section 156 of the Principal Act.

Amendments

a Words substituted by reg 10 and Schedule 2, Item No 11(e) of EC(IFRSMA)R 2005 (SI 116/2005).

---

20. All income and charges relating to the financial year to which the accounts relate shall be taken into account, without regard to the date of receipt or payment.

[20A. The directors of a company shall, in determining how amounts are presented within items in the profit and loss account and balance sheet, have regard to the substance of the reported transaction or arrangement, in accordance with generally accepted accounting principles or practice.][a]

Amendments

a Words substituted by reg 10 and Schedule 2, Item No 11(f) of EC(IFRSMA)R 2005 (SI 116/2005).

---

21. In determining the aggregate amount of any item the amount of each individual asset or liability that falls to be taken into account shall be determined separately.

Departure from the Accounting Principles

22. If it appears to the directors of a company that there are special reasons for departing from any of the principles stated above in preparing the company's accounts in respect of any financial year they may do so, but particulars of the departure, the reasons for it and its effect on the accounts shall be given in a note to the accounts.

Section B
Valuation Rules

HISTORICAL COST ACCOUNTING RULES

Preliminary

23. Subject to paragraphs 39 to 44 of this part of this Schedule, the amounts to be included in respect of all items shown in [Companies Act individual accounts][a] shall be determined in accordance with the rules set out in paragraph 24 to 38 of this part of the Schedule.

Amendments

a Words substituted by reg 10 and Schedule 2, Item No 11(g) of EC(IFRSMA)R 2005 (SI 116/2005).

Fixed Assets

General Rules

24. Subject to any provision for depreciation or diminution in value made in accordance with paragraph 25 or 26 the amount to be included in respect of any fixed asset shall be its cost.

25. In the case of any fixed asset which has a limited useful economic life, the amount of:

(a) its cost, or

(b) where it is estimated that any such asset will have a residual value at the end of the period of its useful economic life, its cost less that estimated residual value,

shall be reduced by provisions for depreciation calculated to write off that amount systematically over the period of the asset's useful economic life.

26. (1) Where a fixed asset investment of a description falling to be included under Assets items 7 (participating interests) or 8 (shares in group undertakings) in the balance sheet format, or any other holding of securities held as a financial fixed asset, has

diminished in value, provisions for diminution in value may be made in respect of it and the amount to be included in respect of it may be reduced accordingly; and any such provisions which are not shown separately in the profit and loss account shall be disclosed (either separately or in aggregate) in a note to the accounts.

(2) Provisions for diminution in value shall be made in respect of any fixed asset which has diminished in value if the reduction of its value is expected to be permanent (whether its useful economic life is limited or not), and the amount to be included in respect of it shall be reduced accordingly; and any such provisions which are not shown separately in the profit and loss account shall be disclosed (either separately or in aggregate) in a note to the accounts.

(3) Where the reasons for which any provision was made in accordance with subparagraph (1) or (2) have ceased to apply to any extent, that provision shall be written back to the extent that it is no longer necessary; and any amounts written back in accordance with this subparagraph which are not shown separately in the profit and loss account shall be disclosed (either separately or in aggregate) in a note to the accounts.

Development Costs

27. (1) Notwithstanding that amounts representing "development costs" may be included under Assets item 9 in the balance sheet format, an amount may only be included in a company's balance sheet in respect of development costs in special circumstances.

(2) If any amount is included in a company's balance sheet in respect of development costs the following information shall be given in a note to the accounts—

(a) the period over which the amount of those costs originally capitalised is being or is to be written off; and

(b) the reasons for capitalising the development costs in question.

Goodwill

28. (1) The application of paragraphs 24 to 26 in relation to goodwill (in any case where goodwill is treated as an asset) is subject to the following provisions of this paragraph.

(2) Subject to subparagraph (3) below the amount of the consideration for any goodwill acquired by a company shall be reduced by provisions for depreciation calculated to write off that amount systematically over a period chosen by the directors of the company.

(3) The period chosen shall not exceed the useful economic life of the goodwill in question.

(4) In any case where any goodwill acquired by a company is included as an asset in the company's balance sheet the period chosen for writing off the consideration for that goodwill and the reasons for choosing that period shall be disclosed in a note to the accounts.

Intangible and tangible fixed assets

29. Assets included in Assets items 9 (Intangible fixed assets) and 10 (Tangible fixed assets) in the balance sheet format shall be valued as fixed assets.

Other fixed assets

30. Other assets falling to be included in the balance sheet shall be valued as fixed assets where they are intended for use on a continuing basis in the company's activities.

Financial fixed assets

31. (1) Debts securities, including fixed income securities, held as financial fixed assets shall be included in the balance sheet at an amount equal to their maturity value plus any premium, or less any discount, on their purchase, subject to the following provisions of this paragraph.

(2) The amount included in the balance sheet with respect to such securities purchased at a premium shall be reduced each financial year on a systematic basis, in accordance with best accounting practices, so as to write the premium off over the period to the maturity date of the security and the amounts so written off shall be charged to the profit and loss account for the relevant financial years.

(3) The amount included in the balance sheet with respect to such securities purchased at a discount shall be increased each financial year on a systematic basis, in accordance with best accounting practices, so as to extinguish the discount over the period to the maturity date of the security and the amounts by which the amount is increased shall be credited to the profit and loss account for the relevant years.

(4) The notes to the accounts shall disclose the amount of any unamortised premium or discount not extinguished which is included in the balance sheet by virtue of subparagraph (1).

(5) For the purposes of this paragraph "premium" means any excess of the amount paid for a security over its maturity value and "discount" means any deficit of the amount paid for a security over its maturity value.

Current Assets

32. The amount to be included in respect of loans and advances, debt or other fixed income securities and equity shares or other variable yield securities not held as financial fixed assets shall be their cost, subject to paragraphs 33 and 34 below.

33. (1) If the net realisable value of any asset referred to in paragraph 32 is lower than its cost the amount to be included in respect of that asset shall be the net realisable value.

(2) Where the reasons for which any provision for diminution in value was made in accordance with subparagraph (1) have ceased to apply to an extent that provision shall be written back to the extent that it is no longer necessary.

34. (1) Subject to paragraph 33 above, the amount to be included in the balance sheet in respect of transferable securities not held as financial fixed assets may be the higher of their cost or their market value at the balance sheet date.

(2) The difference between the cost of any securities included in the balance sheet at a valuation under subparagraph (1) and their market value shall be shown (in aggregate) in the notes to the accounts.

Miscellaneous and Supplementary Provisions

Excess of money owed over value received as an asset item

35. (1) Where the amount repayable on any debt owed by a company is greater than the value of the consideration received in the transaction giving rise to the debt, the amount of the difference may be treated as an asset.

(2) Where any such amount is so treated:

- (a) it shall be written off by reasonable amounts each year and must be completely written off before repayment of the debt; and
- (b) if the current amount is not shown as a separate item in the company's balance sheet it must be disclosed in a note to the accounts.

Determination of cost

36. (1) The cost of an asset that has been acquired by the company shall be determined by adding to the actual price paid any expenses incidental to its acquisition.

(2) The cost of an asset constructed by the company shall be determined by adding to the purchase price of the raw materials and consumables used the amount of the costs incurred by the company which are directly attributable to the construction of that asset.

(3) In addition, there may be included in the cost of an asset constructed by the company:

- (a) a reasonable proportion of the costs incurred by the company which are only indirectly attributable to the construction of that asset, but only to the extent that they relate to the period of construction; and
- (b) interest on capital borrowed to finance the construction of that asset, to the extent that it accrues in respect of the period of construction;

provided, however, in a case within subparagraph (b) above, that the inclusion of the interest in determining the cost of that asset and the amount of the interest so included is disclosed in a note to the accounts.

37. (1) Subject to the qualification mentioned below, the cost of any assets which are fungible assets (including investments) may be determined by the application of any of the methods mentioned in subparagraph (2) below in relation to any such assets of the same class.

The method chosen must be one which appears to the directors to be appropriate in the circumstances of the company.

(2) Those methods are:

- (a) the method known as "first in, first out" (FIFO);
- (b) a weighted average price; and
- (c) any other method similar to any of the methods mentioned above.

(3) Where in the case of any company:

- (a) the cost of assets falling to be included under any item shown in the company's balance sheet has been determined by the application of any method permitted by this paragraph; and
- (b) the amount shown in respect of that item differs materially from the relevant alternative amount given below in this paragraph;

the amount of that difference shall be disclosed in a note to the accounts.

(4) Subject to subparagraph (5) below, for the purposes of subparagraph (3)(b) above, the relevant alternative amount, in relation to any item shown in company's balance sheet, is the amount which would have been shown in respect of that item if assets of any class included under that item at an amount determined by any method permitted by this paragraph had instead been included at their replacement cost as at the balance sheet date.

(5) The relevant alternative amount may be determined by reference to the most recent actual purchase price before the balance sheet date of assets of any class included under the item in question instead of by reference to their replacement cost as at that date, but only if the former appears to the directors of the company to constitute the more appropriate standard of comparison in the case of assets of that class.

Substitution of original amount where price or cost unknown

38. Where there is no record of the purchase price of any asset acquired by a company or of any price, expenses or costs relevant for determining its cost in accordance with paragraph 36, or any such record cannot be obtained without unreasonable expense or delay, its cost shall be taken for the purposes of paragraphs 24 to 34 to be the value ascribed to it in the earliest available record on its value made on or after its acquisition by the company.

Alternative Accounting Rules

Preliminary

39. (1) The rules set out in paragraphs 24 to 38 are referred to below in this Schedule as the historical cost accounting rules.

(2) Paragraphs 24 to 27 and 31 to 35 are referred to below in this section of this Part of this Schedule as the depreciation rules; and references below in this Schedule to the historical cost accounting rules do not include the depreciation rules as they apply by virtue of paragraph 42.

40. Subject to paragraphs 42 to 44, the amounts to be included in respect of assets of any description mentioned in paragraph 41 may be determined on any basis so mentioned.

Alternative Accounting Rules

41. (1) Intangible fixed assets, other than goodwill, may be included at their current cost.

(2) Tangible fixed assets may be included at a market value determined as at the date of their last valuation or at their current cost.

[(3)Investments of any description falling to be included under Assets items 7 (Participating interests) or 8 (Shares in group undertakings) of the balance sheet format and any other securities held as financial fixed assets may be included:

- (a) at a market value determined as at the date of their last valuation,
- (b) at a value determined on any basis which appears to the directors to be appropriate in the circumstances of the company, or
- (c) at fair value determined in accordance with paragraphs 46A to 46D,

but in the case of (b) or (c) particulars of the method of valuation determined and the reasons for its determination shall be disclosed in a note to the accounts.][a]

(4) Securities of any description not held as financial fixed assets (if not valued in accordance with paragraph 34 above) may be included at their current cost.

Amendments

a Substituted by reg 5 of EC(CI) (FVA)R 2004.

Application of the depreciation rules

42. (1) Where the value of any asset of a company is determined in accordance with paragraph 41, that value shall be, or (as the case may require) be the starting point for determining, the amount to be included in respect of that asset in the company's accounts, instead of its cost or any value previously so determined for that asset; and the depreciation rules shall apply accordingly in relation to any such asset with the substitution for any reference to its cost of a reference to the value most recently determined for that asset in accordance with paragraph 41.

(2) The amount of any provision for depreciation required in the case of any fixed asset by paragraph 25 or 26 as it applies by virtue of subparagraph (1) is referred to below in this paragraph as the "adjusted amount", and the amount of any provision which would be required by that paragraph in the case of that asset according to the historical cost accounting rules is referred to as the "historical cost amount".

(3) Where subparagraph (1) applies in the case of any fixed asset the amount of any provision for depreciation in respect of that asset included in any item shown in the profit and loss account in respect of amounts written off assets of the description in question may be the historical cost amount instead of the adjusted amount, provided that the amount of any difference between the two is shown separately in the profit and loss account or in a note to the accounts.

Additional Information to be Provided in Case of Departure from Historical Cost Accounting Rules

43. (1) This paragraph applies where amounts to be included in respect of assets covered by any items shown in a company's accounts have been determined in accordance with paragraph 41.

(2) The items affected and the basis of valuation adopted in determining the amounts of the assets in question in the case of each such item shall be disclosed in a note to the accounts.

(3) In the case of each balance sheet item affected either:

- (a) the comparable amounts determined according to the historical cost accounting rules; or
- (b) the difference between those amounts and the corresponding amounts actually shown in the balance sheet in respect of that item;

shall be shown separately in the balance sheet or in a note to the accounts.

(4) In subparagraph (3) above, references in relation to any item to the comparable amounts determined as there mentioned are references to:

(a) the aggregate amount which would be required to be shown in respect of that item if the amounts to be included in respect of all the assets covered by that item were determined according to the historical cost accounting rules; and

(b) the aggregate amount of the cumulative provisions for depreciation or diminution in value which would be permitted or required in determining those amounts according to those rules.

Revaluation Reserve

44. (1) With respect to any determination of the value of an asset of a company in accordance with paragraph 41, the amount of any profit or loss arising from that determination (after allowing, where appropriate, for any provisions for depreciation or diminution in value made otherwise than by reference to the value so determined and any adjustments of any such provisions made in the light of that determination) shall be credited or (as the case may be) debited to a separate reserve ("the revaluation reserve").

(2) The amount of the revaluation reserve shall be shown in the company's balance sheet under Liabilities item 11 in the balance sheet format, but need not be shown under that name.

(3) An amount may be transferred from the revaluation reserve:

(a) to the profit and loss account, if the amount was previously charged to that account or represents realised profit, or

(b) on capitalisation;

and the revaluation reserve shall be reduced to the extent that the amounts transferred to it are no longer necessary for the purposes of the valuation method used.

(4) In subparagraph (3)(b) "capitalisation", in relation to an amount standing to the credit of the revaluation reserve, means applying it in wholly or partly paying up unissued shares in the company to be allotted to members of the company as fully or partly paid shares.

(5) The revaluation reserve shall not be reduced except as mentioned in this paragraph.

(6) The treatment for taxation purposes of amounts credited or debited to the revaluation reserve shall be disclosed in a note to the accounts.

Assets and Liabilities Denominated in Foreign Currencies

45. (1) Subject to the following subparagraphs, amounts to be included in respect of assets and liabilities denominated in foreign currencies shall be in Irish pounds (or the currency in which the accounts are drawn up) after translation at an appropriate spot rate of exchange prevailing at the balance sheet date.

(2) An appropriate rate of exchange prevailing on the date of purchase may however be used for assets held as financial fixed assets and assets to be included under Assets item 9 (Intangible fixed assets) and 10 (Tangible fixed assets) in the balance sheet format, if they are not covered or not specifically covered in either the spot or forward currency markets.

(3) An appropriate spot rate of exchange prevailing at the balance sheet date shall be used for translating uncompleted spot exchange transactions.

(4) An appropriate forward rate of exchange prevailing at the balance sheet date shall be used for translating uncompleted forward exchange transactions.

(5) This paragraph does not apply to any assets or liabilities held, or any transactions entered into, for hedging purposes or to any assets or liabilities which are themselves hedged.

46. (1) Subject to subparagraph (2), any difference between the amount to be included in respect of an asset or liability under paragraph 45 and the book value, after translation into Irish pounds (or the currency in which the accounts are drawn up) at an appropriate rate, of that asset or liability shall be credited or, as the case may be, debited to the profit and loss account.

(2) In the case, however, of assets held as financial fixed assets, of assets to be included under Assets items 9 (Intangible fixed assets) and 10 (Tangible fixed assets) in the balance sheet format and of transactions undertaken to cover such assets, any such difference may be deducted from or credited to any non-distributable reserve available for the purpose.

[Valuation at fair value

46A.(1) A company is permitted to make a valuation at fair value of financial instruments (including derivatives) at fair value.

(2) For the purposes of this Schedule commodity-based contracts that give either contracting party the right to settle in cash or some other financial instrument are considered to be derivative financial instruments, except when—

- (a) they were entered into and continue to meet the company's expected purchase, sale or usage requirements,
- (b) they were designated for such purpose at their inception, and
- (c) they are expected to be settled by delivery of the commodity.

(3) Subparagraph (1) applies only to liabilities that are—

- (a) held as part of a trading portfolio, or
- (b) derivative financial instruments.

(4) Valuation according to subparagraph (1) does not apply to—

- (a) non-derivative financial instruments held to maturity,
- (b) loans and receivables originated by the company and not held for trading purposes, and
- (c) interests in subsidiaries, associated undertakings and joint ventures, equity instruments issued by the company, contracts for contingent consideration in a business combination as well as other financial instruments with such special characteristics that the instruments, according to what is generally accepted, should be accounted for differently from other financial instruments.

[(4A) Valuation at fair value may be made by a company in respect of financial instruments which constitute liabilities other than the liabilities referred to in subparagraphs (3)(a) and (3)(b) if—

- (a) the valuation is in accordance with international accounting standards as adopted by the Commission Regulation on or before 5 September 2006, and
- (b) the associated disclosure requirements, provided for in international financial reporting standards adopted in accordance with the IAS Regulation, are made.

(4B) Valuation at fair value may be made by a company in respect of financial instruments referred to in subparagraph (4) if—

(a) the valuation is in accordance with international accounting standards as adopted by the Commission Regulation on or before 5 September 2006, and

(b) the associated disclosure requirements, provided for in international financial reporting standards adopted in accordance with the IAS Regulation, are made.

(4C) In subparagraphs (4A) and (4B)—

'Commission Regulation' means the Commission Regulation (EC) No. 1725/2003 of 29 September 2003;

'international financial reporting standards' has the meaning assigned to it by the Principal Act;

'IAS Regulation' has the meaning assigned to it by the Principal Act.][b]

(5) Assets and liabilities which qualify as hedged items under a fair value hedge accounting system, or identified portions of such assets or liabilities, may be valued at the specific amount required under that system.

46B. (1) The fair value referred to in paragraph 46A shall be determined by reference to—

(a) a market value, for those financial instruments for which a reliable market can readily be identified. Where a market value is not readily identifiable for an instrument but can be identified for its components or for a similar instrument, the market value may be derived from that of its components or of the similar instrument, or

(b) a value resulting from generally accepted valuation models and techniques, for those instruments for which a reliable market cannot be readily identified. Such valuation models and techniques shall ensure a reasonable approximation of the market value.

(2) Those financial instruments that cannot be measured reliably by any of the methods described in subparagraph (1), shall be measured in accordance with paragraphs 24 to 38.][a]

Amendments

a Amended by reg 6 of EC(CI)(FVA)R 2004.

b Subparagraphs (4A)–(4C) inserted by European Communities (Directive 2006/46/EC) Regulations 2009, reg 17.

[Other assets that may be included at fair value

46BA. (1) This paragraph applies to—

(a) investment property, and

(b) living animals and plants,

that, under relevant international financial reporting standards, may be included in accounts at fair value.

(2) Investment property and living animals and plants referred to in subparagraph (1), may be included at fair value, provided that all such investment property or, living animals and plants, as the case may be, are so included where their fair value can reliably be determined.

(3) In this paragraph, 'fair value' means fair value determined in accordance with relevant international financial reporting standards.][a]

Amendments

a Inserted by reg 10 and Sch 2, Item No 11(i) of EC(IFRSMA)R 2005.

[46C. (1) Notwithstanding paragraph 19(a), where a financial instrument is valued in accordance with paragraph 46B or an asset is valued in accordance with paragraph 46BA, a change in the value shall be included in the profit and loss account. However, such a change shall be included directly in equity, in a fair value reserve, where—

(a) the financial instrument accounted for is a hedging instrument under a system of hedge accounting that allows some or all of the change in value not to be shown in the profit and loss account, or

(b) the change in value relates to an exchange difference arising on a monetary item that form part of a company's net investment in a foreign entity.][a]

Amendments

a Substituted by reg 10 and Sch 2, Item No 11(j) of EC(IFRSMA)R 2005.

[46D. Where valuation at fair value of financial instruments has been applied, the notes on the accounts shall disclose—

(a) the significant assumptions underlying the valuation models and techniques where fair values have been determined in accordance with paragraph 46B(1)(a),

(b) per category of financial instruments, for fair value, the changes in value included directly in the profit and loss account as well as changes included in the fair value reserve,

(c) for each class of derivative financial instruments, information about the extent and the nature of the instruments, including significant terms and conditions that may affect the amount, timing and certainty of future cash flows, and

(d) a table showing movements in the fair value reserve during the financial year.][d]

Amendments

a Amended by reg 6 of EC(CI)(FVA)R 2004.

Information where investment property and living animals and plants are included at fair value

[46E.(1) This paragraph applies where the amounts to be included in a company's accounts in respect of investment property or living animals and plants have been determined in accordance with paragraph 46BA of this Schedule.

(2) The balance sheet items affected and the basis of valuation adopted in determining the amounts of the net assets concerned in the case of each such item shall be disclosed in a note to the accounts.

(3) In the case of investment property, for each balance sheet item affected there shall be shown, either separately in the balance sheet or in a note to the accounts—

- (a) the comparable amounts determined according to the historical cost accounting rules, or
- (b) the differences between those amounts and the corresponding amounts actually shown in the balance sheet in respect of that item.

(4) In subparagraph (3), references in relation to any item to the comparable amounts determined in accordance with that subparagraph are references to—

- (a) the aggregate amount which would be required to be shown in respect of that item if the amounts to be included in respect of all the assets covered by that item were determined according to the historical cost accounting rules, and
- (b) the aggregate amount of the cumulative provisions for depreciation or diminution in value which would be permitted or required in determining those amounts according to those rules.][a]

Amendments

a Inserted by reg 10 and Sch 2, Item No 11(k) of EC(IFRSMA)R 2005.

Chapter III
Notes to the Accounts

Preliminary

47. Any information required in the case of a company by the following provisions of this Part of this Schedule shall be given by way of a note to the accounts, unless otherwise provided.

General

Disclosure of accounting policies

48. The accounting policies adopted by the company in determining the amounts to be included in respect of items shown in the balance sheet and in determining the profit or loss of the company shall be stated (including such policies with respect to the depreciation and diminution in value of assets).

49. If there are changes to the accounting policies adopted by the company from one year to the next, these changes shall be stated together with the reasons for the changes and their effect on the accounts of the company.

Sums denominated in foreign currencies

50. Where any sums originally denominated in foreign currencies have been brought into accounts under any items shown in the balance sheet format or the profit and loss account formats, the basis on which those sums have been translated into Irish pounds (or the currency in which the accounts are drawn) shall be stated.

Information Supplementing the Balance Sheet

Share capital and debentures

51. (1) The following information shall be given with respect to the company's share capital:

(a) the authorised share capital, and

(b) where shares of more than one class have been allotted, the number and aggregate nominal value of shares of each class allotted.

(2) In the case of any part of the allotted share capital that consists of redeemable shares, the following information shall be given:

(a) the earliest and latest dates on which the company has power to redeem those shares,

(b) whether those shares must be redeemed in any event or are liable to be redeemed at the option of the company or of the shareholder, and

(c) whether any (and, if so, what) premium is payable on redemption.

52. If the company has allotted any shares during the financial year, the following information shall be given:

(a) the reason for making the allotment,

(b) the classes of shares allotted, and

(c) as respects each class of shares, the number allotted, their aggregate nominal value and the consideration received by the company for the allotment.

53. (1) With respect to any contingent right to the allotment of shares in the company the following particulars shall be given:

(a) the number, description and amount of the shares in relation to which the right is exercisable,

(b) the period during which it is exercisable, and

(c) the price to be paid for the shares allotted.

(2) In subparagraph (1) above "contingent right to the allotment of shares" means any option to subscribe for shares and any other right to require the allotment of shares to any person whether arising on the conversion into shares of securities of any other description or otherwise.

54. (1) If the company has issued any debentures during the financial year to which the accounts relate, the following information shall be given:

(a) the reason for making the issue,

(b) the classes of debentures issued, and

(c) as respects each class of debentures, the amount issued and the consideration received by the company for the issue.

(2) Particulars of any redeemed debentures which the company has power to reissue shall also be given.

(3) Where any of the company's debentures are held by a nominee of or trustee for the company, the nominal amount of the debentures and the amount at which they are stated in the accounting records kept by the company in accordance with section 202 of the Companies Act, 1990, shall be stated.

Fixed assets

55. (1) In respect of any fixed assets of the company included in any assets item in the company's balance sheet the following information shall be given by reference to each such item:

- (a) the appropriate amounts in respect of those assets included in the item as at the date of the beginning of the financial year and as at the balance sheet date respectively;
- (b) the effect on any amount included in the item in respect of those assets of:
  - (i) any determination during that year of the value to be ascribed to any of those assets in accordance with paragraph 41 above;
  - (ii) acquisitions during that year of any fixed assets;
  - (iii) disposals during that year of any fixed assets; and
  - (iv) any transfers of fixed assets of the company to and from the item during that year.

(2) The reference in subparagraph (1)(a) to the appropriate amounts in respect of any fixed assets (included in an assets item) as at any date there mentioned is a reference to amounts representing the aggregate amounts determined, as at that date, in respect of fixed assets falling to be included under the item on either of the following bases, that is to say:

- (a) on the basis of cost (determined in accordance with paragraphs 36 and 37), or
- (b) on any basis permitted by paragraph 41;

(leaving out of account in either case any provisions for depreciation or diminution in value).

(3) In addition, in respect of any fixed assets of the company included in any assets item in the company's balance sheet, there shall be stated (by reference to each such item):

- (a) the cumulative amount of provisions for depreciation or diminution in value of those assets included under the item as at each date mentioned in subparagraph (1)(a),
- (b) the amount of any such provisions made in respect of the financial year,
- (c) the amount of any adjustment made in respect of any such provisions during that year in consequence of the disposal of any of those assets, and
- (d) the amount of any other adjustments made in respect of any such provisions during that year.

(4) The requirements of this paragraph need not be complied with to the extent that a company takes advantage of the option of setting off charges and income afforded by paragraph 5(3) of this Part of this Schedule.

56. Where any fixed assets of the company (other than listed investments) are included under any item shown in the company's balance sheet at an amount determined in accordance with paragraph 41, the following information shall be given:

(a) the years (so far as they are known to the directors) in which the assets were severally valued and the several values; and

(b) in the case of assets that have been valued during the financial year, the names of the persons who valued them or particulars of their qualifications for doing so and (in either case) the bases of valuation used by them.

57. In relation to any amount which is included under Assets item 10 in the balance sheet format (Tangible fixed assets) with respect to land and buildings there shall be stated:

(a) how much of that amount is ascribable to land of freehold tenure and how much to land of leasehold tenure; and

(b) how much of the amount ascribable to land of leasehold tenure is ascribable to land held on long lease and how much to land held on short lease.

58. There shall be disclosed separately the amount of:

(a) any participating interests; and

(b) any shares in group undertakings

that are held in credit institutions.

Reserves and provisions

59. (1) Where any amount is transferred—

(a) to or from any reserves,

(b) to any provisions for liabilities [...][a],

(c) from any provision for liabilities [...][a] otherwise than for the purpose for which the provision was established,

and the reserves or provisions are or would but for paragraph 3(3) of this Part of this Schedule be shown as separate items in the company's balance sheet, the information mentioned in the following sub-paragraph shall be given in respect of the aggregate of reserves or provisions included in the same item.

(2) That information is:

(a) the amount of the reserves or provisions as at the date of the beginning of the financial year and as at the balance sheet date respectively,

(b) any amounts transferred to or from the reserve or provisions during that year, and

(c) the source and application respectively of any amounts so transferred.

(3) Particulars shall be given of each provision included in Liabilities item 6(c) (Other provisions) in the company's balance sheet in any case where the amount of that provision is material.

Amendments

a Words deleted by reg 10 and Sch 2, Item No 11(h) of EC(IFRSMA)R 2005.

Provision for taxation

60. The amount of any provision for deferred taxation shall be stated separately from the amount of any provision for other taxation.

Maturity analysis

61. (1) A company shall disclose separately for each of Assets items 3(b) and 4 and Liabilities items 1(b), 2(b) and 3(b) the aggregate amount of the loans and advances and liabilities included in those items broken down into the following categories:

(a) those repayable in not more than three months;

(b) those repayable in more than three months but not more than one year;

(c) those repayable in more than one year but not more than five years;

(d) those repayable in more than five years

from the balance sheet date.

(2) A company shall also disclose the aggregate amounts of all loans and advances falling within Assets item 4 (Loans and advances to customers) which are:

(a) repayable on demand; or

(b) are for an indeterminate period, being repayable upon short notice.

(3) For the purposes of sub-paragraph (1), where a loan or advance or liability is repayable by instalments, each such instalment is to be treated as a separate loan or advance or liability.

Debt and other fixed income securities

62. A company shall disclose the amount of debt and fixed income securities included in Assets item 5 (Debt securities and other fixed income securities) and the amount of such securities included in Liabilities item 3(a) (Bonds and medium term notes) that in each case will become due within one year of the balance sheet date.

Subordinated liabilities

63. (1) The following information must be disclosed in relation to any borrowing included in Liabilities item 7 (subordinated liabilities) that exceeds 10 per cent of the total for that item:

(a) its amount;

(b) the currency in which it is denominated;

(c) the rate of interest and the maturity date (or the fact that it is perpetual);

(d) the circumstances in which early repayment may be demanded;

(e) the terms of the subordination; and

(f) the existence of any provisions whereby it may be converted into capital or some other form of liability and the terms of any such provisions.

(2) The general terms of any other borrowings included in Liabilities item 7 shall also be stated.

Fixed cumulative dividends

64. If any fixed cumulative dividends on the company's shares are in arrear, there shall be stated:

(a) the amount of the arrears; and

(b) the period for which the dividends or, if there is more than one class, each class of them are in arrear.

Details of assets charged

65. (1) There shall be disclosed, in relation to each liabilities and off-balance sheet item of the balance sheet format, the aggregate amount of any assets of the company which have been charged to secure any liability or potential liability included thereunder, the aggregate amount of the liabilities or potential liabilities so secured and an indication of the nature of the security given.

(2) Particulars shall also be given of any other charge on the assets of the company to secure the liabilities of any other person, including, where practicable, the amount secured.

Guarantees and other financial commitments

66. (1) There shall be stated, where practicable:

(a) the aggregate amount or estimated amount of contracts for capital expenditure, so far as not provided for; and

(b) the aggregate amount or estimated amount of capital expenditure authorised by the directors which has not been contracted for.

(2) Particulars shall be given of:

(a) any pension commitments included under any provision shown in the company's balance sheet; and

(b) any such commitments for which no provision has been made;

and where any such commitment relates wholly or partly to pensions payable to past directors of the company separate particulars shall be given of that commitment so far as it relates to such pensions.

(3) The following information shall also be given:

(a) the nature of every pension scheme operated by or on behalf of the company including information as to whether or not each scheme is a defined benefit scheme or a defined contribution scheme,

(b) whether each such scheme is externally funded or internally financed,

(c) whether any pension costs and liabilities are assessed in accordance with the advice of a professionally qualified actuary and, if so, the date of the most recent relevant actuarial valuation,

(d) whether and, if so, where any such actuarial valuation is available for public inspection.

(4) Particulars shall also be given of any other financial commitments, including any contingent liabilities, which:

(a) have not been provided for;

(b) have not been included in the off-balance sheet items in the balance sheet format; and

(c) are relevant to assessing the company's state of affairs.

(5) Commitments within any of the preceding subparagraphs taken on behalf of or for the benefit of:

(a) any parent company or fellow subsidiary undertaking of the company; or

(b) any subsidiary undertaking of the company;

shall be stated separately from the other commitments within that sub-paragraph (and commitments within paragraph (a) shall be stated separately from those within paragraph (b)).

(6) There shall be disclosed the nature and amount of any contingent liabilities and commitments included in off-balance sheet items 1 and 2 which are material in relation to the company's activities.

[Information concerning off-balance sheet arrangements not included in balance sheet

66A. (1) The nature and business purpose of the arrangements of the company that are not included in its balance sheet and the financial impact on the company of those arrangements shall be provided in the notes to the accounts of the company if the risks or benefits arising from such arrangements are material and in so far as the disclosure of such risks or benefits is necessary for assessing the financial position of the company.

Related party transactions

66B. (1) Particulars shall be given in the notes to the accounts of the section 2(2) company of transactions which have been entered into with related parties by the company if such transactions are material and have not been concluded under normal market conditions and the particulars shall include the amount of such transactions, the nature of the related party relationship and other information about the transactions which is necessary for an understanding of the financial position of that company.

(2) [The provision of particulars][b] the provision of particulars and other information about individual transactions may be aggregated according to their nature, except where separate information is necessary for an understanding of the effects of related party transactions on the financial position of the section 2(2) company.

(3) Subparagraph (1) shall not apply to transactions which are entered into between 2 or more members of a group if any subsidiary undertaking which is a party to the transaction is wholly owned by such a member.

[...][c]

(5) A word or expression used in this paragraph has the same meaning as it has in Directive 2006/46/EC][a].

Amendments

a Paragraphs 66A–66C inserted by European Communities (Directive 2006/46/EC) Regulations 2009, reg 18.

b Words 'The provision of particulars' substituted for 'Subject to subparagraph (4), the provision of particulars' by European Communities (Directive 2006/46/EC) (Amendment) Regulations 2010, reg 8(a).

c Subparagraph (4) deleted by European Communities (Directive 2006/46/EC) (Amendment) Regulations 2010, reg 8(b).

Off-balance sheet items: group undertakings

67. (1) With respect to contingent liabilities required to be included under off-balance sheet item 1 in the balance sheet format, there shall be stated in a note to the accounts the amount of such contingent liabilities incurred on behalf of or for the benefit of:

(a) any parent undertaking or fellow subsidiary undertaking, or

(b) any subsidiary undertaking,

of the company; in addition the amount incurred in respect of the undertakings referred to in paragraph (a) shall be stated separately from the amount incurred in respect of the undertakings referred to in paragraph (b).

(2) With respect to commitments required to be included under off-balance sheet item 2 in the balance sheet format, there shall be stated in a note to the accounts the amount of such commitments undertaken on behalf of or for the benefit of:

(a) any parent undertaking or fellow subsidiary undertaking, or

(b) any subsidiary undertaking,

of the company; in addition the amount incurred in respect of the undertakings referred to in paragraph (a) shall be stated separately from the amount incurred in respect of the undertakings referred to in paragraph (b).

Transferable securities

68. (1) There shall be disclosed for each of Assets items 5 to 8 in the balance sheet format the amount of transferable securities that are listed on a recognised stock exchange and the amount of those that are unlisted.

(2) In the case of each amount shown in respect of listed securities under subparagraph (1) above, there shall also be disclosed the aggregate market value of those securities, if different from the amount shown.

(3) There shall be disclosed for each of assets items 5 and 6 the amount of transferable securities included under those items that are held as financial fixed assets and the amount of those that are not so held, together with the criterion used by the directors to distinguish those held as financial fixed assets.

Leasing transactions

69. The aggregate amount of all property (other than land) leased by the company to other persons shall be disclosed, broken down so as to show the aggregate amount included in each relevant balance sheet item.

Assets and liabilities denominated in a currency other than Irish pounds (or the currency in which the accounts are drawn up)

70. (1) The aggregate amount in Irish pounds (or the currency in which the accounts are drawn up) of all assets denominated in a currency other than Irish pounds (or the

currency used), together with the aggregate amount in Irish pounds (or the currency used) of all liabilities so denominated, shall be disclosed.

(2) For the purposes of this paragraph an appropriate rate of exchange prevailing at the balance sheet date shall be used to determine the amounts concerned.

Sundry assets and liabilities

71. Where any amount shown under either of the following items is material, particulars shall be given of each type of asset or liability included therein, including an explanation of the nature of the asset or liability and the amount included with respect to assets or liabilities of that type;

(a) Assets item 13 (Other assets),

(b) Liabilities item 4 (Other liabilities).

Unmatured forward transactions

72. (1) The following shall be disclosed with respect to unmatured forward transactions outstanding at the balance sheet date:

(a) the categories of such transactions, by reference to an appropriate system of classification;

(b) whether, in the case of each such category, they have been made, to any material extent, for the purpose of hedging the effects of fluctuations in interest rates, exchange rates and market prices or whether they have been made, to any material extent, for dealing purposes.

(2) Transactions falling within subparagraph (1) shall include all those in relation to which income or expenditure is to be included in:

(a) format 1, item 6 or format 2, items B4 or A3 (Dealing profits or losses),

(b) format 1, item 1 or format 2, item B1, by virtue of note (1)(b) to the profit and loss account formats (forward contracts, spread over the actual duration of the contract and similar in nature to interest).

[Where fair valuation has not been applied

72A. Where fair valuation has not been applied in accordance with paragraphs [46A to 46E][a]—

(a) for each class of derivative financial instruments—

(i) the fair value of the instruments, if such a value can be determined by any of the methods mentioned in paragraph 46B(1),

(ii) information about the extent and the nature of the instruments, and

(b) for financial fixed assets covered by paragraph 46A, carried at an amount in excess of their fair value and without use being made of the option to make a value adjustment in accordance with paragraph 31(2)—

(i) the book value and the fair value of either the individual assets or appropriate groupings of those individual assets,

(ii) the reasons for not reducing the book value, including the nature of the evidence that provides the basis for the belief that the book value will be recovered.][b]

Amendments

a Words substituted by reg 10 and Sch 2, Item No 11(L) of EC(IFRSMA)R 2005.

b Inserted by reg 7 of EC(CI)(FVA)R 2004.

Miscellaneous matters

73. (1) Particulars shall be given of any case where the cost of any asset is for the first time determined under paragraph 38 of this Part of this Schedule.

(2) Where any outstanding loans made under the authority of section 60 of the Principal Act, other than subsection (13)(a) of that section (various cases of financial assistance by a company for purchase of its own shares) are included under any item shown in the company's balance sheet, the aggregate amount of those loans shall be disclosed for each item in question.

(3) The aggregate amount which is recommended for distribution by way of dividend shall be stated.

Particulars of any restriction on profits available for distribution by virtue of section 224(2)(b)(1) of the Companies Act, 1990, must be stated.

Information Supplementing the Profit and Loss Account

Separate statement of certain items of income and expenditure

74. (1) The amount respectively provided for the purchase of the company's share capital, for redemption of share capital and for redemption of loans shall be stated.

(2) The amount of income from listed and unlisted investments shall be stated.

(3) [...][a]

(4) The aggregate amount of the emoluments of, and compensation in respect of loss of office to, directors and compensation paid to past directors shall be stated.

Amendments

a Subparagraph (3) is revoked by EC(SA)(Dir)R 2010, reg 15(3).

Particulars of tax

75. (1) The basis on which the charge for corporation tax, income tax and other taxation on profits (whether payable inside or outside the State) is computed shall be stated.

(2) Particulars shall be given of any special circumstances which affect liability in respect of taxation of profits, income or capital gains for the financial year concerned or liability in respect of taxation of profits, income or capital gains for succeeding financial years. [This includes the extent to which the calculation of the profit or loss is affected by the fair valuation of financial instruments and separately the extent to which it is affected by the fair valuation of other assets in accordance with paragraph 46BA.][a]

(3) The following amounts shall be stated:

(a) the amount of the charge for corporation tax;

(b) if that amount would have been greater but for relief from double taxation, the amount which it would have been but for such relief;

(c) the amount of the charge for income tax; and

(d) the amount of the charge for taxation payable outside the State of profits, income and (so far as charged to revenue) capital gains.

These amounts shall be stated separately in respect of each of the amounts which is shown under the following items in the profit and loss account, that is to say format 1 item 16, format 2 item A10 (Tax on profit or loss on ordinary activities) and format 1 item 21, format 2 item A13 (Tax on extraordinary profit or loss).

Amendments

a The sentence inserted by reg 7 of EC(CI)(FVA)R 2004 was substituted by reg 10 and Sch 2, Item No 11(m) of EC(IFRSMA)R 2005.

Particulars of income

76. (1) A company shall disclose, with respect to income included in the following items in the profit and loss account formats, the amount of that income attributable to each of the geographical markets in which the company has operated during the financial year:

(a) format 1 item 1, format 2 item B1 (Interest receivable);

(b) format 1 item 3, format 2 item B2 (Dividend income);

(c) format 1 item 4, format 2 item B3 (Fees and commissions receivable);

(d) format 1 item 6, format 2 item B4 (Dealing profits); and

(e) format 1 item 7, format 2 item B7 (Other operating income).

(2) In analysing for the purposes of this paragraph the source of any income, the directors shall have regard to the manner in which the company's activities are organised.

(3) For the purposes of this paragraph, markets which do not differ substantially from each other shall be treated as one market.

(4) Where in the opinion of the directors the disclosure of any information required by this paragraph would be seriously prejudicial to the interests of the company, that information need not be disclosed, but the fact that any such information has not been disclosed must be stated.

Particulars of staff

77. (1) The following information shall be given with respect to the employees of the company:

(a) the average number of persons employed by the company in the financial year; and

(b) the average number of persons so employed within each category of persons employed by the company.

(2) The average number required by subparagraph (1)(a) or (b) shall be determined by dividing the relevant annual number by the number of weeks in the financial year.

(3) The relevant annual number shall be determined by ascertaining for each week in the financial year:

(a) for the purposes of subparagraph (1)(a), the number of persons employed under contracts of service by the company in that week (whether throughout the week or not); and

(b) for the purposes of subparagraph (1)(b), the number of persons in the category in question of persons so employed;

and, in either case, adding together all the weekly numbers.

(4) In respect of all persons employed by the company during the financial year who are taken into account in determining the relevant annual number for the purposes of subparagraph (1)(a) there shall also be stated the aggregate amounts respectively of:

(a) wages and salaries paid or payable in respect of that year to those persons;

(b) social security costs incurred by the company on their behalf; and

(c) other pension costs so incurred.

save insofar as those amounts or any of them are stated in the profit and loss account.

(5) The categories of persons employed by the company by reference to which the number required to be disclosed by subparagraph (1)(b) is to be determined shall be such as the directors may select, having regard to the manner in which the company's activities are organised.

Management and agency services

78. A company providing any management and agency services to customers shall disclose that fact if the scale of such services provided is material in the context of its business as a whole.

Subordinated liabilities

79. Any amounts charged to the profit and loss account representing charges incurred during the year with respect to subordinated liabilities shall be disclosed.

Sundry income and charges

80. Where any amount to be included in any of the following items is material, particulars shall be given of each individual component of the figure, including an explanation of their nature and amount:

(a) in format 1:

(i) items 7 and 10 (Other operating income and charges);

(ii) items 18 and 19 (Extraordinary income and charges);

(b) in format 2:

(i) items A6 and B7 (Other operating charges and income);

(ii) items A12 and B10 (Extraordinary charges and income).

Miscellaneous matters

81. (1) Where any amount relating to any preceding financial year is included in any item in the profit and loss account, the effect shall be stated.

(2) The effect shall be stated on any transactions that are exceptional by virtue of size or incidence though they fall within the ordinary activities of the company.

(3) Particulars shall be given of any extraordinary income or charges arising in the financial year.

PART II
FORM AND CONTENT OF GROUP ACCOUNTS

Regulation 7

General rules

1. (1)[Where the directors of a company prepare Companies Act group accounts, those group accounts][a] shall comply so far as practicable with the provisions of Part I of this Schedule as if the undertakings included in the consolidation ("the group") were a single company.

(2) In particular, for the purposes of note (20) to the balance sheet format set out in Section B of Chapter 1 of Part 1 of this Schedule and paragraphs 66 (5) and 67 of Part 1 of this Schedule as it applies to group accounts—

(a) any subsidiary undertakings of the parent company not included in the consolidation shall be treated as subsidiary undertakings of the group, and

(b) if the parent company is itself a subsidiary undertaking, the group shall be treated as a subsidiary undertaking of any parent undertaking of that company, and the reference to fellow-subsidiary undertakings shall be construed accordingly.

Amendments

a Words substituted by reg 10 and Schedule 2, Item No 12(a) (what was meant to be No 12 but mistakenly called "(1)") of EC(IFRSMA)R 2005 (SI 116/2005).

---

2. (1) Subject to the exceptions authorised or required by this paragraph, all the subsidiary undertakings of the parent company shall be included in the consolidation.

(2) A subsidiary undertaking may be excluded from consolidation if its inclusion is not material for the purpose of giving a true and fair view; but two or more undertakings may be excluded only if they are not material taken together.

(3) In addition, a subsidiary undertaking may be excluded from consolidation where—

(a) severe long-term restrictions substantially hinder the exercise of the rights of the parent company over the assets or management of that undertaking, or

(b) the information necessary for the preparation of group accounts cannot be obtained without disproportionate expense or undue delay, or

(c) the interest of the parent company is held exclusively with a view to subsequent resale and the undertaking has not previously been included in consolidated group accounts prepared by the parent company.

The reference in paragraph (a) to the right of the parent company and the reference in paragraph (c) to the interest of the parent company are, respectively, references to rights and interests held by or attributed to the company in the absence of which it would not be the parent company.

[...][a]

(8) Where all the subsidiary undertakings of a parent company fall within the above exclusions, no group accounts shall be required.

Amendments

a Sub-paragraphs (4), (5), (6) and (7) deleted by reg 10 and Schedule 2, Item No 12(b) (what was meant to be No 12 but mistakenly called "(1)") of EC(IFRSMA)R 2005.

---

3. (1) The consolidated balance sheet and profit and loss account shall incorporate in full the information contained in the individual accounts of the undertakings included in the consolidation, subject to the adjustments authorised or required by the following provisions to this Schedule and to such other adjustments (if any) as may be appropriate in accordance with generally accepted accounting principles or practice.

(2) Group accounts shall be drawn up as at the same date as the individual accounts of the parent company.

(3) If the financial year of a subsidiary undertaking included in the consolidation differs from that of the parent company, the group accounts shall be made up—

(a) from the accounts of the subsidiary undertaking for its financial year last ending before the end of the parent company's financial year, provided that year ended no more than three months before that of the parent company, or

(b) from interim accounts prepared by the subsidiary undertaking as at the end of the parent company's financial year.

4. (1) Where assets and liabilities to be included in the group accounts have been valued or otherwise determined by undertakings according to accounting rules differing from those used for the group accounts, the values or amounts shall be adjusted so as to accord with the rules used for the group accounts.

(2) If it appears to the directors of the parent company that there are special reasons for departing from subparagraph (1) they may do so, but particulars of any such departure, the reasons for it and its effect shall be given in a note to the accounts.

(3) The adjustments referred to in this paragraph need not be made if they are not material for the purpose of giving a true and fair view.

5. Any differences of accounting rules as between a parent company's individual accounts for a financial year and its group accounts shall be disclosed in a note to the latter accounts and the reasons for the difference given.

6. Amounts which in the particular context of any provision of this Part of the Schedule are not material may be disregarded for the purposes of that provision.

7. (1) Debts and claims between undertakings included in the consolidation, and income and expenditure relating to transactions between such undertakings, shall be eliminated in preparing the group accounts.

(2) Where profits and losses resulting from transactions between undertakings included in the consolidation are included in the book value of assets, they shall be eliminated in preparing the group accounts.

(3) Subparagraphs (1) and (2) need not be complied with if the amounts concerned are not material for the purpose of giving a true and fair view.

[7A. The notes on the accounts shall set out information relating to—

(a) the nature and business purpose of any arrangement that is not included in the consolidated balance sheet, and the financial impact of such arrangement if the risks or benefits arising from the arrangement are material, and in so far as the disclosure of such risks or benefits is necessary for assessing the financial position, taken as a whole, of the section 2(2) parent undertaking and its subsidiaries included in the consolidated balance sheet, and

(b) subject to paragraph 7B, transactions entered into by—

  (i) the section 2(2) parent company, or

  (ii) by a subsidiary of the section 2(2) parent company included in the group accounts,

  with related parties, if the transactions are material and have not been concluded under normal market conditions and the information shall include the amounts of such transactions, the nature of the related party relationship and other information about the transactions which is necessary for an understanding of the financial position, taken as a whole, of the section 2(2) parent company and its subsidiaries included in the group accounts.

7B.A transaction referred to in paragraph 7A(b) does not include an intra-group transaction.

7C. Information provided pursuant to paragraph 7A(b) concerning individual transactions may be aggregated according to their nature except where separate information is necessary for an understanding of the effects of the related party transactions on the financial position, taken as a whole, of the section 2(2) parent company and its subsidiaries included in the group accounts.

7D. In paragraph 7A, 'consolidated balance sheet' means the balance sheet for the section 2(2) parent company and its subsidiaries.

7E. A word or expression used in paragraphs 7A to 7C has the same meaning as it has in Directive 2006/46/EC.][a]

Amendments

a Paragraphs 7A–7E inserted by European Communities (Directive 2006/46/EC) Regulations 2009, reg 19.

Acquisition and Merger Accounting

8. (1) The following provisions apply where an undertaking becomes a subsidiary undertaking of the parent company.

(2) That event is referred to in those provisions as an "acquisition", and references to the "undertaking acquired" shall be construed accordingly.

9. An acquisition shall be accounted for by the acquisition method of accounting unless the conditions for accounting for it as a merger are met and the merger method of accounting is adopted.

10. (1) The acquisition method of accounting is as follows.

(2) The identifiable assets and liabilities of the undertaking acquired shall be included in the consolidated balance sheet at their fair values as at the date of acquisition.

In this paragraph the "identifiable" assets or liabilities of the undertaking acquired means the assets or liabilities which are capable of being disposed of or discharged separately, without disposing of a business of the undertaking.

(3) The income and expenditure of the undertaking acquired shall be brought into the group accounts only as from the date of the acquisition.

(4) There shall be set off against the acquisition cost of the interest in the shares of the undertaking held by the parent company and its subsidiary undertakings the interest of the parent company and its subsidiary undertakings in the adjusted capital and reserves of the undertaking acquired.

For this purpose—

> "the acquisition cost" means the amount of any cash consideration and the fair value of any other consideration, together with such amount (if any) in respect of fees and other expenses of the acquisition as the company may determine, and
>
> "the adjusted capital and reserves" of the undertaking acquired means its capital and reserves at the date of the acquisition after adjusting the identifiable assets and liabilities of the undertaking to fair values as at that date.

(5) The resulting amount if positive shall be treated as goodwill, and if negative as a negative consolidation difference.

(6) Where in applying the acquisition method of accounting—

- (a) there is no record of—
  - (i) the fair values as at the date of acquisition of the identifiable assets and liabilities of the undertaking acquired, or
  - (ii) the acquisition cost of the interest in the shares of the acquired undertaking by the undertakings dealt with in the group accounts, or
- (b) such records cannot be obtained without unreasonable expense or delay,

the values of the identifiable assets and liabilities and the acquisition cost shall be taken to be the values and cost ascribed to them in the earliest available record made after the acquisition of that subsidiary undertaking.

11. (1) The conditions for accounting for an acquisition as a merger are—

- (a) that at least 90 per cent of the nominal value of the relevant shares in the undertaking acquired is held by or on behalf of the parent company and its subsidiary undertakings,
- (b) that the proportion referred to in paragraph (a) was attained pursuant to an arrangement providing for the issue of equity shares by the parent company or one or more of its subsidiary undertakings, and

(c) that the fair value of any consideration other than the issue of equity shares given pursuant to the arrangement by the parent company and its subsidiary undertakings did not exceed 10 per cent of the nominal value of the equity shares issued.

(2) The reference in subparagraph (1)(a) to the "relevant shares" in an undertaking acquired is to those carrying unrestricted rights to participate both in distributions and in the assets of the undertaking upon liquidation.

12. (1) The merger method of accounting is as follows:

(2) The assets and liabilities of the undertaking acquired shall be brought into the group accounts at the figures at which they stand in the undertaking's accounts, subject to any adjustment authorised or required by this Part of the Schedule.

(3) The income and expenditure of the undertaking acquired shall be included in the group accounts for the entire financial year, including the period before the acquisition.

(4) The group accounts shall show corresponding amounts relating to the previous financial year as if the undertaking acquired had been included in the consolidation throughout that year.

(5) There shall be set off against the aggregate of—

(a) the appropriate amount in respect of shares issued by the parent company or its subsidiary undertakings in consideration for the acquisition of shares in the undertaking acquired, and

(b) the fair value of any other consideration for the acquisition of shares in the undertaking acquired, determined as at the date when those shares were acquired,

the nominal value of the issued share capital of the undertaking acquired held by the parent company and its subsidiary undertakings.

(6) The resulting amount shall be shown as an adjustment to the consolidated reserves.

13. (1) Where a group of undertakings is acquired, paragraphs 10 to 12 apply with the following adaptations.

(2) References to shares of the undertaking acquired shall be construed as references to shares of the parent undertaking of the group.

(3) Other references to the undertaking acquired shall be construed as references to the group; and references to the assets and liabilities, income and expenditure and capital and reserves of the undertaking acquired shall be construed as references to the assets and liabilities, income and expenditure and capital and reserves of the group after making the set-offs and other adjustments required by this Part of the Schedule in the case of group accounts.

14. (1) The following information with respect to acquisitions taking place in the financial year shall be given in a note to the accounts.

(2) There shall be stated—

(a) the name of the undertaking acquired or, where a group was acquired, the name of the parent undertaking of that group, and

(b) whether the acquisition has been accounted for by the acquisition or the merger method of accounting.

15. In relation to the resulting amounts referred to in paragraphs 10(5) and 12(6) of this Part of the Schedule, there shall be stated in a note to the group accounts the methods used in calculating those amounts and the reasons for any significant difference between those amounts for the financial year to which the group accounts refer and the preceding financial year.

Changes in Composition of the Group

16. If the composition of the undertakings dealt with in the group accounts has changed significantly in the course of a financial year, the group accounts must include information which makes the comparison of successive sets of group accounts meaningful.

Differences in Tax Treatment

17. Account shall be taken in the group accounts of any difference arising on consolidation between the tax chargeable for the financial year and for preceding financial years and the amount of tax paid or payable in respect of those years, provided that it is probable that an actual charge to tax will arise within the foreseeable future for one of the undertakings dealt with in the group accounts.

Minority Interests

18. (1) The formats set out in Part I of this Schedule have effect in relation to group accounts with the following additions.

(2) In the Balance Sheet Format a further item headed "Minority interests" shall be added—

(a) either between "liabilities" items 7 and 8, or

(b) after "liabilities" item 12;

and under that item shall be shown the amount of capital and reserves attributable to shares in subsidiary undertakings included in the consolidation held by or on behalf of persons other than the parent company and its subsidiary undertakings.

(3) In the Profit and Loss Account Formats a further item headed "Minority interests" shall be added—

(a) in Format 1, between items 17 and 18; and

(b) in Format 2, between items A11 and A12 or between items B9 and B10;

and under that item shall be shown the amount of any profit or loss on ordinary activities attributable to shares in subsidiary undertakings included in the consolidation held by or on behalf of persons other than the parent company and its subsidiary undertakings.

(4) In the Profit and Loss Account Formats a further item headed "Minority interests" shall be added—

(a) in Format 1, between items 22 and 23, and

(b) in Format 2, between items A14 and A15 or between items B11 and B12;

and under that item shall be shown the amount of any profit or loss on extraordinary activities attributable to shares in subsidiary undertakings included in the consolidation held by or on behalf of persons other than the parent company and its subsidiary undertakings.

(5) For the purposes of paragraph 3(3) of Part I of this Schedule (power to combine items) the additional items required by the foregoing provisions of this paragraph shall be treated as items to which a letter is assigned.

Interests in Subsidiary Undertakings Excluded from Consolidation

19. (1) The interest of the group in subsidiary undertakings excluded from consolidation under paragraph 2(4) of this Part of the Schedule (undertakings with activities different from those of undertakings included in the consolidation), and the amount of profit or loss attributable to such an interest, shall be shown in the consolidated balance sheet or, as the case may be, in the consolidated profit and loss account by the equity method of accounting (including dealing with any goodwill arising in accordance with paragraphs 24, 26 and 28 of Part 1 of this Schedule).

Joint Ventures

20. (1) Where an undertaking included in the consolidation manages another undertaking jointly with one or more undertakings not included in the consolidation, that other undertaking ("the joint venture") may, if it is not—

(a) a body corporate, or

(b) a subsidiary undertaking of the parent company,

be dealt with in the group accounts by the method of proportional consolidation.

(2) The provisions of this Part relating to the preparation of consolidated accounts apply, with any necessary modifications, to proportional consolidation under this paragraph.

Associated Undertakings

21. (1) An "associated undertaking" means an undertaking in which an undertaking included in the consolidation has a participating interest and over whose operating and financial policy it exercises a significant influence, and which is not—

(a) a subsidiary undertaking of the parent company, or

(b) a joint venture dealt with in accordance with paragraph 20.

(2) Where an undertaking holds 20 per cent or more of the qualifying capital interest in another undertaking, it shall be presumed to exercise such an influence over it unless the contrary is shown.

(3) Paragraphs (3) and (4) of Regulation 4 of the European Communities (Companies: Group Accounts) Regulations, 1992, shall apply for determining whether subparagraph (2) above applies.

22. (1) The formats in Part 1 of this Schedule shall have effect in relation to group accounts with the following modifications.

(2) In the Balance Sheet format assets item 7 (Participating Interests) shall be replaced by two items headed

"Interests in associated undertakings" and

"Other participating interests".

(3) In the Profit and Loss Account formats the following items, namely:

(a) format 1, item 3(b), (Income from participating interests), and

(b) format 2, item B2(b) (Income from participating interests),

shall be replaced by the following two replacement items:

(i) "Income from participating interests other than associated undertakings", which shall be shown at position 3(b) in format 1 and position B2(b) in format 2; and

(ii) "Income from associated undertakings", which shall be shown at an appropriate position.

23. (1) The interest of an undertaking in an associated undertaking, and the amount of profit or loss attributable to such an interest, shall be shown by the equity method of accounting (including dealing with any goodwill arising in accordance with paragraphs 24, 26 and 28 of Part 1 of this Schedule).

(2) Where the associated undertaking is itself a parent undertaking, the net assets and profits or losses to be taken into account are those of the parent and its subsidiary undertaking (after making any consolidation adjustments).

(3) The equity method of accounting need not be applied if the amounts in question are not material for the purpose of giving a true and fair view.

Foreign Currency Translation

24. Any difference between:

(a) the amount included in the consolidated account for the previous financial year with respect to any undertaking included in the consolidation or the group's interest in any associated undertaking, together with the amount of any transactions undertaken to cover any such interest; and

(b) the opening amount for the financial year in respect of those undertakings and in respect of any such transactions arising as a result of the application of paragraph 45 of Part I of this Schedule may be credited to (where (a) is less than (b)), or deducted from (where (a) is greater than (b)), (as the case may be) consolidated reserves.

25. Any income and expenditure of undertakings included in the consolidation and associated undertakings in a foreign currency may be translated for the purposes of the consolidated accounts at the average rates of exchange prevailing during the financial year.

Information as to Undertaking in which Shares are Held as a Result of a Financial Assistance Operation

26. (1) The following provisions apply where the parent company of a banking group has a subsidiary undertaking which:

(a) is a credit institution of which shares are held as a result of a financial assistance operation with a view to its reorganisation or rescue; and

(b) is excluded from consolidation under paragraph 2(3)(c) (interest held with a view to resale).

(2) Information as to the nature and terms of the operations shall be given in a note to the group accounts and there shall be appended to the copy of the group accounts annexed to the annual return of the parent company a copy of the undertaking's latest individual accounts and, if it is a parent undertaking, its latest group accounts.

If the accounts appended are required by law to be audited, a copy of the auditors' report shall also be appended.

(3) If any document required to be appended is in a language other than Irish or English, the directors shall annex a translation of it into Irish or English, certified to be a correct translation.

(4) The above requirements are subject to the following qualifications:

(a) an undertaking is not required to prepare for the purposes of this paragraph accounts which would not otherwise be required to be prepared, and if no accounts satisfying the above requirements are prepared none need be appended;

(b) the accounts of an undertaking need not be appended if they would not otherwise be required to be published, or made available for public inspection, anywhere in the world, but in that case the reason for not appending the accounts shall be stated in a note to the consolidated accounts.

(5) Where a copy of an undertaking's accounts is required to be appended to the copy of the group accounts annexed to the annual return, that fact shall be stated in a note to the group accounts.

Part III

Disclosure of Information: Related Undertakings

A. Companies not Required to Prepare Group Accounts

Regulation 10

Subsidiary Undertakings

1. (1) The following information shall be given where at the end of the financial year the company has subsidiary undertakings.

(2) The name of each subsidiary undertaking shall be stated.

(3) There shall be stated with respect to each subsidiary undertaking—

(a) if it is incorporated, the country in which it is incorporated;

(b) if it is unincorporated, the address of its principal place of business.

(4) The reason why the company is not required to prepare group accounts shall be stated.

(5) If the reason is that all the subsidiary undertakings of the company fall within the exclusions provided for in paragraph (2) of Part II of this Schedule, it shall be stated with respect to each subsidiary undertaking which of those exclusions applies.

Holdings in Subsidiary Undertakings

2. There shall be stated in relation to shares of each class held by the company in a subsidiary undertaking—

(a) the identity of the class, and

(b) the proportion of the nominal value of the shares of that class represented by those shares.

Financial Information about Subsidiary Undertakings

3. (1) There shall be disclosed with respect to each subsidiary undertaking—

(a) the aggregate amount of its capital and reserves as at the end of its relevant financial year, and

(b) its profit or loss for that year.

(2) That information need not be given if the company is exempt by virtue of regulation 8 [or 8A][a] of these Regulations from the requirement to prepare group accounts (parent company included in accounts of larger group).

(3) That information need not be given if—

(a) the subsidiary undertaking is not otherwise required to publish its accounts, and

(b) the company's holding is less than 50 per cent of the nominal value of the shares in the undertaking.

(4) Information otherwise required by this paragraph need not be given if it is not material.

(5) For the purposes of this part of the Schedule the "relevant financial year" of a subsidiary undertaking is—

(a) if its financial year ends with that of the company, that year, and

(b) if not, its financial year ending last before the end of the company's financial year.

Amendments

a Words inserted by reg 10 and Schedule 2, Item No 13 of EC(IFRSMA)R 2005 (SI 116/2005).

Financial Years of Subsidiary Undertakings

4. Where the financial year of one or more subsidiary undertakings did not end with that of the company, there shall be stated in relation to each such undertaking—

(a) the reasons why the company's directors consider that its financial year should not end with that of the company, and

(b) the date on which its last financial year ended (last before the end of the company's financial year).

Instead of the date required by paragraph (b) being given for each subsidiary undertaking the earliest and latest of those dates may be given.

Further Information about Subsidiary Undertakings

5. (1) There shall be disclosed—

(a) any qualifications contained in the auditors' reports on the accounts of subsidiary undertakings for financial years ending with or during the financial year of the company, and

(b) any note or saving contained in such accounts to call attention to a matter which, apart from the note or saving, would properly have been referred to in such a qualification,

insofar as the matter which is the subject of the qualification or note is not covered by the company's own accounts and its material from the point of view of its members.

(2) The aggregated amount of the total investment of the company in the shares of subsidiary undertakings shall be stated by way of the equity method of valuation, unless—

(a) the company is exempt from the requirement to prepare group accounts by virtue of regulation 8 [or 8A][a] of these Regulations (parent company included in accounts of larger group), and

(b) the directors state their opinion that the aggregate value of the assets of the company consisting of shares in, or amounts owing (whether on account of a loan or otherwise) from, the company's subsidiary undertakings is not less than the aggregate of the amounts at which those assets are stated or included in the company's balance sheet.

(3) Insofar as information required by this paragraph is not obtainable, a statement to that effect shall be given instead.

Amendments

a Words inserted by reg 10 and Sch 2, Item No 13 of EC(IFRSMA)R 2005.

Shares and Debentures of Company Held by Subsidiary Undertakings

6. (1) The number, description and amount of the shares in and debentures of the company held by or on behalf of its subsidiary undertakings shall be disclosed.

(2) Sub-paragraph (1) does not apply in relation to shares or debentures in the case of which the subsidiary undertaking is concerned as personal representative or, subject as follows, as trustee.

(3) The exception for shares or debentures in relation to which the subsidiary undertaking is concerned as trustee does not apply if the company, or any subsidiary undertaking of the company, is beneficially interested under the trust, otherwise than by way of security only for the purposes of a transaction entered into by it in the ordinary course of a business which includes the lending of money.

Significant Holdings in Undertakings Other than Subsidiary Undertakings

7. (1) The information required by paragraphs 8 and 9 shall be given where at the end of the financial year the company has a significant holding in an undertaking which is not a subsidiary undertaking of the company.

(2) A holding is significant for this purpose if it amounts to 20 per cent or more of all interests held by the company in an undertaking.

8. (1) The name of the undertaking shall be stated.

(2) There shall be stated—

(a) if the undertaking is incorporated, the country in which it is incorporated;

(b) if it is unincorporated, the address of its principal place of business.

(3) There shall also be stated—

(a) the identity of each class of shares in the undertaking held by the company, and

(b) the proportion of the nominal value of the shares of that class represented by those shares.

9. (1)There shall also be stated—

(a) the aggregate amount of the capital and reserves of the undertaking as at the end of its relevant financial year, and

(b) its profit or loss for that year.

(2) That information need not be given if—

(a) the company is exempt by virtue of regulation 8 [or 8A][a] of these Regulations from the requirement to prepare group accounts (parent company included in accounts of larger group), and

(b) the investment of the company in all undertakings in which it has such holding as is mentioned in subparagraph (1) is shown, in aggregate, in the notes to the accounts by way of the equity method of valuation.

(3) That information need not be given in respect of an undertaking if—

(a) the undertaking is not otherwise required to publish its accounts, and

(b) the company's holding is less than 50 per cent. of the nominal value of the shares in the undertaking.

Amendments

a Words inserted by reg 10 and Sch, Item No 13 of EC(IFRSMA)R 2005.

Parent undertaking drawing up accounts for larger group

10. (1) Where the company is a subsidiary undertaking, the following information shall be given with respect to the parent undertaking of—

(a) the largest group of undertakings for which group accounts are drawn up and of which the company is a member, and

(b) the smallest such group of undertakings.

(2) The name of the parent undertaking shall be stated.

(3) There shall be stated—

(a) if the undertaking is incorporated, the country in which it is incorporated;

(b) if it is unincorporated, the address of its principal place of business.

(4) If copies of the group accounts referred to in subparagraph (1) are available to the public, there shall also be stated the addresses from which copies of the accounts can be obtained.

B. Companies Required to Prepare Group Accounts

Subsidiary undertakings

11. (1) The following information shall be given with respect to the undertakings which are subsidiary undertakings of the parent company at the end of the financial year.

(2) The name of each undertaking shall be stated.

(3) There shall be stated—

(a) if the undertaking is incorporated, the country in which it is incorporated;

(b) if it is unincorporated, the address of its principal place of business.

(4) It shall also be stated whether the subsidiary undertaking is included in the consolidation and, if it is not, the reasons for excluding it from consolidation shall be given.

(5) The relevant provisions of regulation 4, other than subparagraph 1 (a), of the European Communities (Companies: Group Accounts) Regulations 1992 which apply to each subsidiary shall be stated.

Holdings in Subsidiary Undertakings

12. (1) The following information shall be given with respect to the shares of a subsidiary undertaking held—

(a) by the parent company, and

(b) by the group;

and the information under paragraphs (a) and (b) shall (if different) be shown separately.

(2) There shall be stated—

(a) the identity of each class of shares held, and

(b) the proportion of the nominal value of the shares of that class represented by those shares.

Financial Information about Subsidiary Undertakings not Included in the Consolidation

13. (1) There shall be shown with respect to each subsidiary undertaking not included in the consolidation—

(a) the aggregate amount of its capital and reserves as at the end of its relevant financial year, and

(b) its profit or loss for that year.

(2) That information need not be given if the group's investment in the undertaking is included in the accounts by way of the equity method of valuation or if—

(a) the undertaking is not otherwise required to publish its accounts, and

(b) the holding of the group is less than 50 per cent of the nominal value of the shares in the undertaking.

(3) Information otherwise required by this paragraph need not be given if it is not material.

Further Information about Subsidiary Undertakings Excluded from Consolidation

14. (1) The following information shall be given with respect to subsidiary undertakings excluded from consolidation.

(2) There shall be disclosed—

(a) any qualifications contained in the auditors' reports on the accounts of the undertaking for financial years ending with or during the financial year of the company, and

(b) any note or saving contained in such accounts to call attention to a matter which, apart from the note or saving, would properly have been referred to in such a qualification, in so far as the matter which is the subject of the qualification or note is not covered by the consolidated accounts and is material from the point of view of the members of the parent company.

(3) In so far as information required by this paragraph is not obtainable, a statement to the effect shall be given instead.

Financial Years of Subsidiary Undertakings

15. Where the financial year of one or more subsidiary undertakings did not end with that of the company, there shall be stated in relation to each such undertaking—

(a) the reasons why the company's directors consider that its financial year should not end with that of the company, and

(b) the date on which its last financial year ended (last before the end of the company's financial year).

Instead of the dates required by paragraph (b) being given for each subsidiary undertaking the earliest and latest of those dates may be given.

Shares and Debentures of Company Held by Subsidiary Undertakings

16. (1) The number, description and amount of the shares in and debentures of the company held by or on behalf of its subsidiary undertakings shall be disclosed.

(2) Subparagraph (1) does not apply in relation to shares or debentures in the case of which the subsidiary undertaking is concerned as personal representative or, subject as follows, as trustee.

(3) The exception for shares or debentures in relation to which the subsidiary undertaking is concerned as trustee does not apply if the company, or any of its subsidiary undertakings, is beneficially interested under the trust, otherwise than by way of security only for the purposes of a transaction entered into by it in the ordinary course of a business which includes the lending of money.

Joint Ventures

17. (1) The following information shall be given where an undertaking is dealt with in the consolidated accounts by the method of proportional consolidation in the case of joint ventures—

(a) the name of the undertaking;

(b) the address of the principal place of business of the undertaking;

(c) the factors on which joint management of the undertaking is based; and

(d) the proportion of the capital of the undertaking held by undertakings included in the consolidation.

(2) Where the financial year of the undertaking did not end with that of the company, there shall be stated the date on which a financial year of the undertaking last ended before that date.

Associated Undertakings

18. (1) The following information shall be given where an undertaking included in the consolidation has an interest in an associated undertaking.

(2) The name of the associated undertaking shall be stated.

(3) There shall be stated—

(a) if the undertaking is incorporated, the country in which it is incorporated;

(b) if it is unincorporated, the address of its principal place of business.

(4) The following information shall be given with respect to the shares of the undertaking held—

(a) by the parent company, and

(b) by the group;

and the information under paragraphs (a) and (b) shall be shown separately.

(5) There shall be stated—

(a) the identity of each class of shares held, and

(b) the proportion of the nominal value of the shares of that class represented by those shares.

(6) In this paragraph "associated undertakings" has the meaning given by paragraph 21 of Part II of this Schedule and the information required by this paragraph shall be given notwithstanding that paragraph 6 of that Schedule (materiality) applies in relation to the accounts themselves.

Other Significant Holdings of Parent Company

19. (1) The information required by paragraphs 20 and 21 shall be given where at the end of the financial year the parent company has a significant holding in an undertaking which is not one of its subsidiary undertakings and does not fall within paragraph 17 (joint ventures) or paragraph 18 (associated undertakings).

(2) A holding is significant for this purpose if it amounts to 20 per cent or more of all interests in an undertaking.

20.(1) The name of the undertaking shall be stated.

(2) There shall be stated—

(a) if the undertaking is incorporated, the country in which it is incorporated;

(b) if it is unincorporated, the address of its principal place of business.

(3) The following information shall be given with respect to the shares of the undertaking held by the parent company.

(4) There shall be stated—

(a) the identity of each class of shares held, and

(b) the proportion of the nominal value of the shares of that class represented by those shares.

21.(1) There shall also be stated—

(a) the aggregate amount of the capital and reserves of the undertakings as at the end of its relevant financial year, and

(b) its profit or loss for that year.

(2) That information need not be given in respect of an undertaking if—

(a) the undertaking is not otherwise required to publish its accounts, and

(b) the company's holding is less than 50 per cent of the nominal value of the shares in the undertaking.

(3) Information otherwise required by this paragraph need not be given if it is not material.

Parent Undertaking Drawing up Accounts for Larger Group

22. (1) Where the parent company is itself a subsidiary undertaking, the following information shall be given with respect to that parent undertaking of the company which heads—

(a) the largest group of undertakings for which group accounts are drawn up and of which that company is a member, and

(b) the smallest such group of undertakings.

(2) The name of the parent undertaking shall be stated.

(3) There shall be stated—

(a) if the undertaking is incorporated, the country in which it is incorporated;

(b) if it is unincorporated, the address of its principal place of business.

(4) If copies of the group accounts referred to in subparagraph (1) are available to the public, there shall also be stated the addresses from which copy of the accounts can be obtained.

23. References in this part to shares held by a company shall be construed as being held or not being held by that company in accordance with the rules set out in regulation 4(3) of the European Communities (Companies: Group Accounts) Regulations, 1992.

PART IV
INTERPRETATION

General

1. The following definitions apply for the purposes of this Schedule and its interpretation:

"Banking activities" means activities normally undertaken by a bank or building society;

"Banking Transactions" means transactions entered into in the normal course of a deposit-taking business within the meaning of the Central Bank Act 1989;

"Fellow subsidiary": an undertaking shall be treated as a fellow subsidiary of another undertaking if both are subsidiaries of the same undertaking but neither is the other's;

"Financial fixed assets" means loans and advances and securities held as fixed assets; participating interests and shareholdings in group undertakings shall be regarded as financial fixed assets;

"Fungible assets" means assets of any description which are substantially indistinguishable one from another;

"Group" means a parent undertaking and its subsidiary undertakings;

"Group Undertakings" has the meaning assigned to it by paragraph 64 of the Schedule to the Act of 1986 as amended by the Schedule to the European Communities (Companies: Group Accounts) Regulations, 1992;

"Included in the consolidation" in relation to group accounts, or "included in consolidated group accounts", means that the undertaking is included in the accounts by the method of full (and not proportional) consolidation, and references to an undertaking excluded from consolidation shall be construed accordingly;

"Lease" includes an agreement for a lease;

"Listed security" means a security listed on a recognised stock exchange, and the expression "unlisted security" shall be construed accordingly;

"Long lease" means a lease in the case of which the portion of the term for which it was granted remaining unexpired at the end of the financial year is not less than 50 years;

"Parent" means a holding company;

"Participating interest" and "qualifying capital interest" have the meanings assigned to them by regulation 35 of the European Communities (Companies: Group Accounts) Regulations, 1992;

"Repayable on demand", in connection with deposits, loans or advances, means those amounts which can at any time be withdrawn or demanded without notice or for which a maturity or period of notice of not more than 24 hours or one working day has been agreed;

"Sale and repurchase transaction" means a transaction which involves the transfer by a credit institution or customer ("the transferor") to another credit institution or customer ("the transferee") of assets subject to an agreement that the same assets, or (in the case of fungible assets) equivalent assets, will subsequently be transferred back to the transferor at a specified price on a date specified or to be specified by the transferor; but the following shall not be regarded as sale and repurchase transactions: forward exchange transactions, options, transactions involving the issue of debt securities with a commitment to repurchase all or part of the issue before maturity or any similar transactions;

"Sale and option to resell transaction" means a transaction which involves the transfer by a credit institution or customer ("the transferor") to another credit institution or customer ("the transferee") of assets subject to an agreement that the transferee is entitled to require the subsequent transfer of the same assets, or (in the case of fungible assets) equivalent assets, back to the transferor at the purchase price or another price agreed in advance on a date specified or to be specified; and

"Short lease" means a lease which is not a long lease.

Loans

2. For the purposes of this Schedule a loan or advance (including a liability comprising a loan or advance) is treated as falling due for repayment, and an instalment of a loan or advance is treated as falling due for payment, on the earliest date on which the lender could require repayment or (as the case may be) payment, if he exercised all options and rights available to him.

Materiality

3. For the purposes of this Schedule amounts which in the particular context of any provision of this Schedule are not material may be disregarded for the purposes of that provision.

Pensions and Emoluments

4. In the case of group accounts, the pension commitments referred to in paragraph 66(2) and the emoluments and compensation referred to in paragraph 74(5) of Part I of this Schedule shall be a reference to commitments, emoluments and compensation relating to directors or past directors of the parent company in respect of duties relating to that parent or any of its subsidiary undertakings or undertakings proportionally consolidated in accordance with paragraph 20 of Part II of this Schedule.

Provisions

5. For the purposes of this Schedule and its interpretation:

(a) references to provisions for depreciation or diminution in value of assets are to any amount written off by way of providing for depreciation or diminution in value of assets;

(b) any reference in the profit and loss account formats or the notes thereto set out in Section B of Part I to the depreciation of, or amounts written off, assets of any description is to any provision for depreciation or diminution in value of assets of that description; and

(c) references to provisions for liabilities [...][a] are to any amount retained as reasonably necessary for the purpose of providing for any liability [the nature of which is clearly defined and][b] which is either likely to be incurred, or certain to be incurred but certain as to amount or as to the date on which it will arise.

Amendments

a Words deleted by reg 10 and Sch, Item No 14(a) of EC(IFRSMA)R 2005.

b Words substituted by reg 10 and Sch 2, Item No 14(b) of EC(IFRSMA)R 2005.

Staff Costs

6. In this Schedule –

(a) "Social security costs" means any contributions by the company to any state social security or pension scheme, fund or arrangement;

(b) "Pension costs" includes any other contributions by the company for the purposes of any pension scheme established for the purpose of providing pensions for persons employed by the company, any sums set aside for that purpose and any amounts paid by the company in respect of pensions without first being so set aside; and

(c) any amount stated in respect of either of the above items or in respect of the item "wages and salaries" in the company's profit and loss account shall be determined by reference to payments made or costs incurred in respect of all persons employed by the company during the financial year who are taken into account in determining the relevant annual number for the purposes of paragraph 77(1)(a).

Given under my Official Seal, this 12th day of October 1992.

Bertie Ahern,

Minister of Finance

EXPLANATORY NOTE

(*This note is not part of the Instrument and does not purport to be a legal interpretation*).

The purpose of these Regulations is to give legal effect to Council Directive 86/635/EC on the annual accounts and consolidated accounts of banks and other financial institutions, and to Council Directive 89/117/EC on the obligations of branches established in a Member State of credit institutions and financial institutions having their head offices outside the Member State regarding the publication of annual accounting documents.

The Regulations apply to licensed banks in the State and to the ACC Bank and ICC Bank. They require the banks in question to draw up and publish individual and group accounts in accordance with the Regulations and the Schedule to the Regulations. They contain provisions relating to the accounting treatment and disclosure requirements of subsidiaries, associated undertakings and joint ventures and the material to be contained in the report of the directors and the auditors. The Regulations also provide for penalties for non-compliance of up to £1,000 and 12 months' imprisonment.

The Schedule to the Regulations contains provisions governing the form and content of accounts, the format of the balance sheet and profit and loss account, the valuation of items in the accounts and the information to be given in the notes to the accounts. The Schedule also deals with the rules regarding the preparation of group accounts and sets out the nature and content of the information to be given in relation to subsidiary and other related undertakings.

The Regulations require branches of foreign banks in the State to publish the accounts of the undertaking to which they belong. The Central Bank may also require branches to publish certain information about the activities of the branches themselves in accordance with the EC Directives referred to above.

The Regulations apply in respect of all financial years of the relevant institutions beginning on or after 1 January 1993.

European Communities (Branch Disclosures) Regulations 1993

SI 395/1993

I, RUAIRÍ QUINN, Minister for Enterprise and Employment, in exercise of the powers conferred on me by section 3 of the European Communities Act, 1972 (No. 27 of 1972), and for the purpose of giving effect to Council Directive No. 89/666/EEC of 21 December 1989 [OJ No 395, 30.12.89, pp 36–39], hereby make the following regulations:

PART I
PRELIMINARY

1 Citation, commencement and construction

(1) These Regulations may be cited as the European Communities (Branch Disclosures) Regulations, 1993.

(2) These Regulations shall come into operation on the 1st day of February, 1994.

(3) These Regulations shall be construed as one with the Companies Acts, 1963 to 1990.

2 Interpretation

(1) In these Regulations, unless the context otherwise requires—

"accounting documents" means the documents referred to in Regulation 12;

"certified" means certified in the prescribed manner to be a true copy or a correct translation;

"company" in Part II or Part III, means a company to which that Part applies;

"financial year" in relation to a company, means the period for which the company draws up its accounts in accordance with the law of the country in which it is incorporated;

"memorandum of articles of association" means the documents referred to in Regulations 4(1) and 7(1);

"the Principal Act" means the Companies Act, 1963 (No. 33 of 1963);

"the 1968 Directive" means Council Directive No. 68/151/EEC of 9 March 1968 [OJ No 6, 14.3.68, pp 8–12];

"the 1989 Directive" means Council Directive No. 89/666/EEC of 21 December, 1989.

(2) A word or expression that is used in these Regulations and is also used in the 1989 Directive shall, unless the contrary intention appears, have the same meaning in these Regulations as it has in the Directive concerned.

PART II
BRANCHES OF COMPANIES FROM OTHER MEMBER STATES OF THE EUROPEAN COMMUNITIES

3 Application of this Part

This Part applies to a company—

(a) to which article 1 of the 1968 Directive applies,

(b) which is incorporated in another Member State of the European Communities, and

(c) which establishes a branch in the State,

and references in this Part to a company shall be construed accordingly.

4 Documents to be delivered to the Registrar

(1) A company shall, within one month of the date of the establishment of a branch in the State, deliver to the registrar for registration a certified copy of the memorandum and articles of association or the charter, statutes or other instrument constituting or defining the constitution of the company.

(2) A company shall notify the registrar in the prescribed form of the following matters at the same time as the delivery of the matter referred to in paragraph (1), namely—

(a) the name and legal form of the company and the name of the branch if that is different from the name of the company;

(b) a certificate of incorporation of the company;

(c) the address of the branch;

(d) the activities of the branch;

(e) the place of registration of the company and the number with which it is registered;

(f) a list of the persons who are authorised to represent the company in accordance with Article 2.1(e) of the 1989 Directive together with the following details relating to each such person:

(i) present forename and surname and any former forename and surname;

(ii) date of birth;

(iii) usual residential address;

(iv) nationality;

(v) business occupation, if any;

(vi) particulars of any other directorships of bodies corporate, whether incorporated in the State or elsewhere, held by that person, and

(vii) the extent of that person's powers in relation to the activities of the branch;

(g) without prejudice to the generality of subparagraph (f), the name and addresses of some one or more persons resident in the State authorised to accept on behalf of the company service of process and any notices required to be served on the company;

(h) without prejudice to the generality of subparagraph (f), the name and address of every person resident in the State authorised by the company to ensure compliance with the provisions of these Regulations together with a consent signed by each such person to act in this capacity;

(i) copies of the latest accounting documents prepared in relation to a financial year of the company to have been publicly disclosed in accordance with the law of the State in which it is incorporated before the end of the period allowed for compliance with a paragraph (1) in respect of the branch, or if earlier, the date on which the company complies with paragraph (1) in respect of the branch.

(3) A company shall also deliver to the registrar for registration, under cover of the prescribed form, the following documents and notices within 14 days of the occurrence of the event concerned, namely—

(a) any document making or evidencing an alteration in its memorandum or articles of association;

(b) every amended text of its memorandum or articles of association;

(c) notice of a change among the persons referred to in paragraphs (2)(f), (g), or (h) or in any of the particulars relating to such persons specifying the date of the change;

(d) notice of a change in the address referred to in paragraph (2)(c) together with the new address of the branch;

(e) notice of the winding-up of the company, the appointment of liquidators, particulars concerning them and their powers and the termination of the liquidation in accordance with disclosure by the company as provided for in Article 2 (1)(h), (i) and (j) of the 1968 Directive and particulars concerning insolvency proceedings, arrangements, compositions or any analogous proceedings to which the company is subject;

(f) the closure of the branch.

(4) Subsection (15) of section 195 of the Principal Act, as inserted by section 51 of the Companies Act, 1990, shall apply for the purposes of paragraph (2)(f).

5 Letterheads

(1) Every letter and order form used by a branch of a company shall bear the following particulars—

(a) the place of registration of the company and the number with which it is registered;

(b) the legal form of the company and the address of its registered office;

(c) in the case of a company which is being wound up, the fact that that is so;

(d) the place of registration of the branch and the number with which it is registered.

(2) If on any letters or order forms there is reference to the share capital of the company, the reference shall be to the paid-up share capital.

PART III

BRANCHES OF COMPANIES FROM STATES OTHER THAN THOSE UNDER PART II

6 Application of this Part

This Part applies to a company—

(a) which is incorporated outside the State, other than a company to which Part II applies,

(b) which is of a legal form comparable to a company to which Article 1 of the 1968 Directive applies, and

(c) which establishes a branch in the State,

and references in this Part to a company shall be construed accordingly.

7 Documents to be delivered to the registrar

(1) A company shall, within one month of the date of establishment of a branch in the State, deliver to the registrar for registration a certified copy of the memorandum and articles of association, or the charter, statutes or other instrument constituting or defining the constitution of the company.

(2) A company shall notify the registrar in the prescribed form of the following matters at the same time as the delivery of the matter referred to in paragraph (1), namely—

- (a) the name and legal form of the company, its principal place of business and its objects, where this information is not in the documents referred to in paragraph (1);
- (b) a certificate of incorporation of the company;
- (c) the address of the branch;
- (d) the activities of the branch;
- (e) the name of the branch if that is different from the name of the company;
- (f) the State in which the company is incorporated and, where the law of that State so provides, the place of registration of the company and the number with which it is registered;
- (g) a list of the persons who are authorised to represent the company in accordance with Article 8(h) of the 1989 Directive together with the following details relating to each such person:
  - (i) present forename and surname and any former forename and surname;
  - (ii) date of birth;
  - (iii) usual residential address;
  - (iv) nationality;
  - (v) business occupation, if any;
  - (vi) particulars of any other directorships of bodies corporate, whether incorporated in the State or elsewhere, held by that person, and
  - (vii) the extent of that person's powers in relation to the activities of the branch together with a statement whether that person may represent the company alone or jointly with any other person or persons;
- (h) without prejudice to the generality of subparagraph (g), the names and addresses of some one or more persons resident in the State authorised to accept on behalf of the company service of process and any notices required to be served on the company;
- (i) without prejudice to the generality of subparagraph (g), the name and address of each person resident in the State authorised by the company to ensure compliance with the provisions of these Regulations together with a consent signed by each such person to act in this capacity;
- (j) copies of the latest accounting documents prepared in relation to a financial year of the company to have been publicly disclosed in accordance with the law of the State in which it is incorporated before the end of the period allowed for compliance with paragraph (1) in respect of the branch, or if earlier, the date on which the company complies with paragraph (1) in respect of the branch.

(3) A company shall also deliver to the registrar for registration, under cover of the prescribed form, the following documents and notices within 14 days of the occurrence of the event concerned, namely—

(a) any document making or evidencing an alteration in its memorandum or articles of association;

(b) every amended text of its memorandum or articles of association:

(c) notice of a change among the persons referred to in paragraphs (2)(g), (h) or (i), or in any of the particulars relating to such persons specifying the date of the change;

(d) notice of a change in the address referred to in paragraph (2)(c) together with the new address of the branch;

(e) the winding-up of the company, the appointment of liquidators, particulars concerning them and their powers and the termination of the liquidation, insolvency proceedings, arrangements, compositions or any analogous proceedings to which the company is subject;

(f) the closure of the branch.

(4) Subsection (15) of section 195 of the Principal Act, as inserted by section 51 of the Companies Act, 1990, shall apply for the purposes of paragraph (2)(g).

8 Letterheads

(1) Every letter and order form used by a branch of a company shall bear the following particulars—

(a) the place of registration of the branch and the number with which it is registered;

(b) if the law of the State in which the company is incorporated requires entry in a register, the place of registration of the company and the number with which it is registered.

(2) If on any letters or order forms there is reference to the share capital of the company, the reference shall be to the paid-up share capital.

9 Capital

(1) Subject to paragraph (2), every company shall, at the same time as it returns to the registrar the accounts referred to in Regulation 11, return a statement, in the prescribed form, indicating the amount of the called up share capital of the company.

(2) Paragraph (1) shall not apply where the information which would be contained in the statement is contained in the documentation referred to in Regulation 7(1).

PART IV

PROVISIONS APPLICABLE TO ALL COMPANIES TO WHICH THESE REGULATIONS APPLY

10 Publication of notices

A company within the meaning of Part II or Part III of these Regulations shall [cause to be published in the Companies Registration Office Gazette][a] notice of the delivery to the registrar of the documents and particulars referred to in Regulations 4 and 7, as appropriate, within 21 days of such delivery.

Amendments

[a] Reg 5 of the EC (C) R 2004 (SI 839/2004) substituted the words "cause to be published in the Companies Registration Office Gazette" for "publish in *Iris Oifigiúil*".

11 Accounting Documents to be delivered to the registrar

(1) Subject to paragraphs (2) to (6) every company within the meaning of Part II or Part III of these Regulations shall, once in every year, deliver to the registrar the accounting documents of the company as drawn up, audited and, where so required, disclosed in accordance with the law of the State in which it is incorporated and in the case of a company to which Part II applies in accordance with Council Directives 78/660/EEC (OJ No 222, 14.08.78, pp 11–31), 83/349/EEC [OJ No 193, 18.07.83, pp 1–17] and 84/253/EEC (OJ No 126, 12.05.84, pp 20–26).

(2) A company to which Part III applies, shall, where there is no requirement in the law of the State in which it is incorporated to have accounting documents drawn up, deliver to the registrar accounting documents drawn up and audited in accordance with Council Directives 78/660/EEC and 83/349/EEC.

(3) A company to which Part III applies may, in lieu of returning accounting documents of the company drawn up and where so required disclosed, in accordance with the law of the State in which it is incorporated, return accounting documents for the company drawn up and audited in accordance with Council Directives 78/660/EEC and 83/349/EEC.

(4) The accounting documents referred to in paragraphs (1) and (3) shall be delivered under cover of the prescribed form within eleven months from the end of the company's financial year or at the same time as the accounting documents of the company are published pursuant to the law of the State in which the company is incorporated or are due to be so published, whichever is the earlier.

(5) The accounting documents referred to in paragraph (2) shall be delivered under cover of the prescribed form within eleven months of the end of the company's financial year.

(6) This Regulation shall not apply to companies that are credit institutions and financial institutions within the meaning of Council Directive 89/117/EEC (OJ No 44, 16.02.89, pp 40–42).

12 Reference to accounting documents

References in Regulations 4(2)(i), 7(2)(j) and 11 to accounting documents, in relation to a financial year of a company, are to—

(a) the accounts of the company for the period, including, if it has one or more subsidiaries, any consolidated accounts of the group,

(b) any annual report of the directors for the period,

(c) the report of the auditors on the accounts mentioned in subparagraph (a), and

(d) any report of the auditors on the report mentioned in sub-paragraph (b).

13 Translations

Every document required to be delivered or notified to the registrar under Regulations 4(1), 4(2)(i), 4(3)(a) or (b), 7(1), 7(2)(j), 7(3)(a) or (b) or 11 shall, if they are not written in the Irish or the English language, have annexed to them a certified translation thereof.

14 Miscellaneous Provisions

(1) Subject to paragraph (3), Part XI of the Principal Act shall not apply to a company as a result of that company having established a branch, where, by virtue of having established that branch, these Regulations apply.

(2) For the avoidance of doubt and subject to paragraph (4), references in these Regulations to the establishment of a branch shall include the changing of a place of business that is not a branch within the meaning of the 1989 Directive into such a branch and the date of establishment of the branch shall be construed as the date on which such change occurs.

(3) For the further avoidance of doubt, references in Part XI of the Principal Act to the establishment of a place of business shall include the changing of a branch within the meaning of the 1989 Directive into a place of business that is not a branch within the meaning of the 1989 Directive and the date of establishment of that place of business shall, for the purposes of the said Part XI, be construed as the date on which such change occurs and from that date the exemption in paragraph (1) shall not apply.

(4) (a) Subject to subparagraph (b), where a company to which these Regulations apply established a branch in the State before the commencement of the Regulations and where that branch has not closed a reference in these Regulations to the date of establishment of a branch shall in the case of that branch be construed as a reference to the date of the commencement of these Regulations.

(b) Where a company to which subparagraph (a) applies has, in respect of a branch established in the State, complied with all the requirements of Part XI of the Principal Act applicable following the establishment of that branch, the date of establishment of that branch for the purposes of applying these Regulations shall be construed as the date which is three months after the date of commencement of these Regulations.

15 Statement in prescribed form in lieu of return under regulation 4

(1) Where prior to the date referred to in Regulation 4(1) or Regulation 7(1), as appropriate, a company which has established a branch in the State, in complying with either Part XI of the Principal Act or in complying with these Regulations in respect of another branch established in the State, had returned to the registrar documents which are the same in all respects as the documents required by Regulation 4(1) or 7(1), as appropriate, and it has no outstanding obligation to make a return to the registrar so far as concerns any alterations to those documents, then the company may return, in lieu of the documents required by regulation 4(1) or 7(1), a statement in the prescribed form that this information has already been returned to the registrar.

(2) Where prior to the date referred to in Regulation 4(1) or Regulation 7(1), as appropriate, a company which has established a branch in the State, in complying with either Part XI of the Principal Act or in complying with these Regulations in respect of

another branch established in the State, had returned to the registrar particulars which are the same in all respects as the corresponding particulars required by Regulation 4(2)(f), (g) or (h) or Regulation 7(2)(g), (h) or (i), as appropriate, and it has no outstanding obligation to make a return to the registrar so far as concerns any alterations to those particulars, then the company may return, in lieu of the corresponding particulars required by Regulation 4(2)(f), (g), or (h), or Regulation 7(2)(g), (h) or (i), as appropriate, a statement in the prescribed form that this information has already been returned to the registrar.

(3) Where paragraph (1) applies, a reference to the delivery of the matter referred to in Regulation 4(1) or Regulation 7(1) shall be construed as a reference to the return of the statement referred to in paragraph (1).

16 Statement in prescribed form in lieu of return under section 352

(1) Where Part XI of the Principal Act applies to a company by virtue of its having established a place of business and where prior to the establishment of that place of business, the company has, in complying with these Regulations, returned to the registrar documents which are the same in all respects as the documents required by section 352(1)(a), and it has no outstanding obligation to make a return to the registrar under the said Regulations, so far as concerns any alterations to those documents, then the company may return, in lieu of the documents required by section 352(1)(a), a statement in the prescribed form, that this information has already been returned pursuant to the said Regulations.

(2) Where Part XI of the Principal Act applies to a company by virtue of its having established a place of business and where prior to the establishment of that place of business, the company has, in complying with these Regulations, returned to the registrar particulars which are the same in all respects as the particulars required by section 352 (1)(b) and (2), and it has no outstanding obligation to make a return to the registrar under the said Regulations, so far as concerns any alterations to those particulars, then the company may return, in lieu of the documents required by section 352 (1)(b) and (2), a statement in the prescribed form, that this information has already been returned pursuant to the said Regulations.

17 Service of process or notice

(1) Subject to paragraph (2), any process or notice required to be served on a company to which these Regulations apply shall be sufficiently served if addressed to any person whose name has been delivered to the registrar under Regulation 4(2)(g) or 7(2)(h) (or any changes notified thereto) and left at or sent by post to the address which has been so delivered.

(2) A document may be served on any such company by leaving it at or sending it by post to any branch established by the company in the State—

(a) where the company makes default it in delivering to the registrar the name and address of a person resident in the State who is authorised to accept on behalf of the company service of process; or

(b) if at any time all the persons whose names and addresses have been so delivered are dead or have ceased to so reside, or refuse to accept service on behalf of the company, or for any reason it cannot be served.

18 Duty of compliance

The duty of securing compliance by a company with the provisions of these Regulations shall, without prejudice to the duty of the company concerned, also lie upon the persons appointed by a company to ensure compliance with these Regulations.

19 Offences

(1) A person who contravenes any provision of these Regulations shall be guilty of an offence.

(2) A person guilty of an offence under paragraph (1) shall be liable on summary conviction to a [class C fine][a] or, at the discretion of the court in the case of an individual, to imprisonment for a term not exceeding 12 months or to both.

(3) A person shall not be liable to be sentenced to imprisonment for such an offence unless, in the opinion of the court, the offence was committed wilfully.

(4) Where an offence referred to in paragraph (1) committed by a body or by a person purporting to act on behalf of a body is proved to have been so committed with the consent or connivance of or to be attributable to, or to have been facilitated by, any neglect on the part of any officer or employee of that body, that person shall also be guilty of an offence.

(5) In this Regulation, a reference to a contravention includes a reference to a failure to comply.

Amendments

[a] £1,000 increased to £1,500 by CA 1990, s 240(7) as inserted by CLEA 2001, s 104 and £1,500 converted to €1,904.61 by Council Regulations (EC) No 1103/97, No 974/98 and No 2866/98 and the Economic and Monetary Union Act, 1988, s 6; the above being implicitly substituted, by Fines Act 2010, s 6, for a fine not exceeding the aforesaid amount. A class C fine currently means a fine not exceeding €2,500.

Explanatory Note

(This note is not part of the Instrument and does not purport to be a legal interpretation).

The purpose of these Regulations is to give legal effect to Council Directive (No. 89/666/EEC) concerning disclosure requirements in respect of branches opened in a Member State by certain types of company governed by the law of another State (Council Directive 89/666/EEC).

Part XI of the Companies Act, 1963 contains disclosure requirements where companies incorporated outside the State establish a place of business in the State. Where, as a result of having opened a branch, the Regulations now made apply, the requirements of Part XI will not apply in respect of that branch. The Regulations also facilitate movement between the regime now imposed and that imposed by Part XI of the 1963.

Part I of the Regulations provides for commencement, citation and interpretation of the Regulations.

Part II (Regulations 2 to 5) provides for disclosures by European Communities First Directive companies (limited companies) that establish a branch in the State.

Part III (Regulations 6 to 9) provides for disclosures by non-European Communities companies of a legal form comparable to Part II companies that establish a branch in the State.

Part IV (Regulations 10 to 19) introduce a variety of provisions applicable to both Part II and Part III companies.

European Communities (Accounts) Regulations 1993

SI 396/1993

I, RUAIRÍ QUINN, Minister for Enterprise and Employment, in exercise of the powers conferred on me by section 3 of the European Communities Act 1972 (No 27 of 1972), and for the purpose of giving effect to the provisions of Council Directives 90/604/EEC (OJ No L 317, 16.11.1990, pp 57–59) and 90/605/EEC (OJ No L 317, 16.11.1990, pp 60–62) of 8 November 1990 and Article 11 of Council Directive 89/666/EEC (OJ No L 395, 21.12.1989, pp 36–39) of 21 December 1989 hereby make the following Regulations:

PART I

PRELIMINARY AND GENERAL

Citation and construction

1.(1) These Regulations may be cited as European Communities (Accounts) Regulations, 1993.

(2) These Regulations shall be construed as one with the Companies Acts.

Application

2.(1) Parts I and II of these Regulations shall come into operation on the 1st day of January 1994.

(2) Part III of these Regulations shall apply to accounts prepared for financial years commencing on or after 1 January 1994.

(3) Part IV of these Regulations shall apply to directors' reports attached to balance sheets for financial years commencing on or after 30 June 1993.

Interpretation

3.(1) In these Regulations, unless the context otherwise requires—

"the Companies Acts" means the Companies Act, 1963, and any enactment to be construed as one with that Act;

"Member State" means a State which is a member of the European Communities;

"partnership" has the same meaning as in the Partnerships Act, 1890;

"limited partnership" means a partnership to which the Limited Partnerships Act 1907, applies;

"the 1992 Group Accounts Regulations" means the European Communities (Companies: Group Accounts), Regulations, 1992;

"the 1986 Act" means the Companies (Amendment) Act, 1986;

"undertaking" has the same meaning as in the 1992 Group Accounts Regulations.

(2) In these Regulations, unless the context otherwise requires, a reference to a Part is to a Part of these Regulations, a reference to a Regulation is to a Regulation of these Regulations, a reference to a paragraph is to the paragraph of the Regulation and a reference to a subparagraph is to the subparagraph of the paragraph in which the reference occurs.

PART II
IMPLEMENTATION OF COUNCIL DIRECTIVE 90/604/EEC

4. [...][a]

Amendments

a EC(A)R 1993, reg 4 amends C(A)A 1986, s 8(2). See amended Act.

5.(1) The documents to be delivered to the registrar of companies under section 7 or 18 of the 1986 Act or Regulation 39 of the 1992 Group Accounts Regulations or Regulation 20 of these Regulations, as the case may be, may have the money amounts referred to therein expressed in European currency units, in addition to their expression in the currency in which the documents concerned were drawn up.

(2) Where a company avails itself of the option in paragraph (1), the exchange rate used shall be that prevailing on the date of the balance sheet, and that rate shall be disclosed in a note to the accounts.

(3) In this Regulation, "European currency unit" has the meaning assigned to it by Regulation (EEC) No. 3180/78 (OJ No L379, 30.12.1978, p 1), as amended by Regulation (EEC) No. 2626/84 (OJ No L247, 16.9.1984, p 1, and by Regulation (EEC) No. 1971/89. (OJ No L189, 4.7.1989, p 1).

PART III
IMPLEMENTATION OF COUNCIL DIRECTIVE 90/605/EEC

6. This Part shall apply to the following undertakings:

(1) Unlimited companies and partnerships where all the members thereof who do not have a limit on their liability are

(a) companies limited by shares or by guarantee, or

(b) bodies not governed by the law of the State but equivalent to those in paragraph (a), or

(c) any combination of the types of bodies referred to in subparagraphs (a) and (b), and

(2) Unlimited companies and partnerships where all the members thereof who do not have a limit on their liability are

(a) (i) unlimited companies or partnerships of the type referred to in paragraph (1) that are governed by the laws of a Member State, or

(ii) bodies governed by the laws of a Member State that are of a legal form comparable to those referred to in paragraph (i), or

(b) any combination of the types of bodies referred to in subparagraph (a) and subparagraphs (a) and (b) of paragraph (1).

7.(1) Subject to these Regulations, the 1986 Act shall apply to an undertaking to which this Part applies as it applies to companies to which that Act applies.

(2) Notwithstanding section 1(1) of the 1986 Act, the term "company" in that Act shall include an unlimited company to which this Part applies and the term "private company" shall include such unlimited companies that are not public companies.

(3) Subject to these Regulations, the 1986 Act shall be applied to partnerships to which this Part applies as though those partnerships were companies formed and registered under the Companies Acts with any modifications necessary to take account of the fact that such partnerships are unincorporated.

[(4) Notwithstanding paragraphs (1), (2) and (3), an undertaking to which this Part applies shall prepare its annual individual accounts in accordance with—

(a) section 149 of the Companies Act 1963 (in these Regulations referred to as 'Companies Act individual accounts'), or

(b) international financial reporting standards (in these Regulations referred to as 'IFRS individual accounts') and section 149A of the Companies Act 1963,][a]

Amendments

a Inserted by EC(IFRS)R 2005, reg 7.

8.(1) Save as otherwise provided, in these Regulations the term "partner" shall not include a limited partner.

(2) The compliance by a limited partner with Regulations 16(2)(b) and 22 (1) shall not constitute taking part in the management of the partnership business for the purposes of section 6(1) of the Limited Partnerships Act, 1907.

9.(1) Subject to these Regulations, the 1992 Group Accounts Regulations shall apply to an undertaking to which this Part applies that is a parent undertaking as they apply to the parent undertakings referred to in Regulation 5 (3) of those Regulations.

(2) In the case of a partnership to which this Part applies the partners shall prepare the group accounts referred to in Regulation 5(1) of the 1992 Group Accounts Regulations and in the case of such partnerships any reference to group accounts prepared by the company shall be construed as a reference to group accounts prepared by the partners.

(3) Subject to these Regulations, the 1992 Group Accounts Regulations shall be applied to partnerships to which this Part applies as though those partnerships were companies formed and registered under the Companies Act with any modifications necessary to take account of the fact that such partnerships are unincorporated.

[(4) Notwithstanding paragraphs (1), (2) and (3), an undertaking to which this Part applies shall prepare its annual group accounts in accordance with—

(a) section 150A of the Companies Act 1963 (in these Regulations referred to as 'Companies Act group accounts'), or

(b) international financial reporting standards (in these Regulations referred to as 'IFRS group accounts') and section 150B of the Companies Act 1963,

and in either case shall comply with section 150C of the Companies Act 1963.][a]

Amendments

a Inserted by EC(IFRS)R 2005, reg 7(b).

10.(1) Every balance sheet and profit and loss account of a partnership to which this Part applies shall be approved by the partners and shall be signed on behalf of the partners by two of the partners authorised by the partners to do so.

(2) In the case of a partnership to which this Part applies any reference in the 1986 Act to Section 156 of the Principal Act shall be construed as a reference to paragraph (1).

11. Without prejudice to the generality of Regulation 3 (2) of the 1992 Group Accounts Regulations and save as otherwise provided in these Regulations, any reference in the 1986 Act or in the 1992 Group Accounts Regulations to directors shall, in the case of a partnership to which this Part applies, be construed as a reference to the partners of such partnerships and any duties, obligations or discretion imposed on or granted to such directors shall be deemed to be imposed on or granted to such partners.

Annual Accounts of Partnerships

12.(1) In the case of a partnership to which this Part applies, the partners shall, at some date not later than 18 months after the appropriate date and subsequently once at least in every calendar year, so however that not more than 15 months shall elapse between the preparation of the account, draw up a profit and loss account for the period, in the case of the first account, since the formation of the partnership, and in any other case, since the preceding account.

(2) The partners shall cause to be made out in every calendar year a balance sheet as at the date to which the profit and loss account is made up.

[(3) In the case of such partnerships the reference in section 3 of the 1986 Act to Companies Act individual accounts shall be read as a reference to balance sheets and profit and loss accounts drawn up pursuant to this Regulation, which, in accordance with Regulation 7(4), may be Companies Act individual accounts or IFRS individual accounts.][a]

(4) For the purposes of this Regulation the "appropriate date" shall be;

(i) in the case of the partnership formed before the commencement of these Regulations, the date referred to in Regulation 2(2), and

(ii) in the case of a partnership formed after the commencement of these Regulations, the date of the formation of the partnership.

Amendments

a Substituted by EC(IFRS)R 2005, reg 7(c).

13.(1) Subject to paragraphs (3) to (6), the provisions of sections 10, 12(1) and 18 of the 1986 Act applicable to a company qualified to be treated as a small company shall apply mutatis mutandis to a partnership to which this Part applies in respect of any financial year of the partnership if, in respect of that year and the financial year of the partnership immediately preceding that year, the partnership satisfies at least two of the conditions specified in subsection (2) of section 8 of the 1986 Act, as amended by Regulation 4.

(2) Subject to paragraphs (3) to (6), the provisions of sections 11, 12 (2) and 18 of the 1986 Act applicable to a company qualified to be treated as a medium-sized company shall apply mutatis mutandis to any partnership to which this Part applies in respect of

any financial year of the partnership if, in respect of that year and the financial year of the partnership immediately preceding that year, the partnership satisfies at least two of the conditions specified in subsection (3) of section 8 of the 1986 Act, as amended by Regulation 4.

(3) Subject to paragraph (4), in determining whether a partnership to which this Part applies is qualified to be treated in the same manner as a small company or a medium-sized company subsections (4) to (12) of section 8 and section 9 of the 1986 Act shall apply.

(4) In the case of partnerships to which this Part applies the references in subsections (7) and (8) of section 8 of the 1986 Act to incorporation shall be construed as references to the formation of such partnerships and a reference in those subsections to the commencement of the said section 7 shall be construed as a reference to the date referred to in Regulation 2 (2).

(5) In the case of partnerships to which this Part applies the statement required by section 18 (2) of the 1986 Act shall be in a position on the balance sheet immediately above the signatures required by Regulation 10.

(6) In the case of partnerships to which this Part applies the copy of the report of the auditors referred to in subsection (5) of section 18 shall be certified by two of the partners to be a true copy of such report.

14.(1) In the case of a partnership to which this Part applies, there shall be attached to every balance sheet drawn up pursuant to Regulation 12, a report of the partners containing the following information:

[(a) a fair review of the development and performance of the business of the partnership and of the development and performance of its subsidiary undertakings, if any, together with a description of the principal risks and uncertainties that they face, which review—

(i) shall be a balanced and comprehensive analysis of the development and performance of the business of the partnership and of its subsidiary undertakings, if any, consistent with the size and complexity of the business, and

(ii) to the extent necessary for an understanding of the partnership's development, performance or position, and that of its subsidiary undertakings, if any, shall include an analysis of financial, and, where appropriate, non-financial key performance indicators relevant to the particular business, including information relevant to environmental and employee matters,

and, where appropriate, the report shall include additional explanations of amounts included in the annual accounts;][a]

(b) particulars of any important events affecting the partnership or any of its subsidiary undertakings, if any, which have occurred since the end of that year;

(c) an indication of likely future developments in the business of the partnership and any of its subsidiary undertakings, if any;

(d) an indication of the activities, if any, of the partnership and any of its subsidiary undertakings, if any, in the field of research and development, and

(e) an indication of the existence of branches (within the meaning of Council Directive 89/666/EEC (OJ No L395, 21.12.1989, pp 36–39)) of the partnership outside the State and the country in which each such branch is located.

(2) The said report shall be signed on behalf of the partners by two of the partners authorised by the partners to so do.

(3) Section 13 of the 1986 Act shall not apply in the case of a partnership referred to in paragraph (1) and a reference in the 1986 Act to the report of the directors of a company shall in the case of such partnerships be construed as a reference to the report of the partners prepared pursuant to this Regulation.

Amendments

a Substituted by EC(IFRS)R 2005, reg 7(d).

---

15. Where, in the case of a partnership to which this Part applies, the partners decide to give the information specified in subsection (1) of section 16 of the 1986 Act, as amended by Regulation 44 of the 1992 Group Accounts Regulations, by way of a separate statement in accordance with subsection (3) of that section, the said statement shall be signed on behalf of the partners by two of the partners and a copy of that statement, certified by two of the partners to be a true copy of such a statement shall be returned to the registrar with the accounts for that particular financial year.

16.(1) Subject to paragraph (2), section 17 of the 1986 Act, as substituted by Regulation 45 of the 1992 Group Accounts Regulations, shall apply to a partnership to which this Part applies as it applies to a private company.

(2) In the case of a partnership to which this Part applies;

(a) the reference in section 17 to the provisions of section 7 shall be construed in accordance with Regulation 20(4), and

(b) paragraph (a) of subsection 1 of the said section 17 shall not apply but all the partners including, in the case of a limited partnership, a limited partner must declare, in writing, their consent to the exemption in respect of a financial year before the partnership can stand exempted from the requirement in respect of that year, and

(c) the notification procedure referred to in subsection (1)(b) of the said section 17 shall not apply, but a certified copy of the guarantee referred to in that subsection in respect of a financial year must be forwarded to all the partners including, in the case of a limited partnership, a limited partner before the partnership can stand exempted from the requirement in respect of that year, and

(d) paragraphs (d) and (f) of subsection (1) of the said section 17 shall not apply but the partners shall, in respect of each financial year for which it avails of the exemption, return to the registrar, in lieu of the accounts referred to in Regulation 20:

(i) a notice stating that the partnership has availed of the exemption under the said section 17,

(ii) the declarations referred to in paragraph (h) in respect of that financial year,

(iii) a certified copy of the guarantee referred to in paragraph (c) for that financial year,

[(iv) the group accounts of the parent undertaking prepared in accordance with the Seventh Council Directive or international financial reporting standards and audited in accordance with Article 37 of the Seventh Council Directive.][a]

Amendments

a Substituted by EC(IFRS)R 2005, reg 7(e).

Group Accounts of Partnerships to which this Part applies

17. Regulation 7 of the 1992 Group Accounts Regulations shall apply to a parent undertaking that is a partnership to which this Part applies as it applies to private companies under that Regulation.

18.(1) In the case of a parent undertaking that is a partnership to which this Part applies, the requirement in paragraphs (1) and (3) of Regulation 36 of the 1992 Group Accounts Regulations to have statements signed and certified by a director and the secretary shall be construed as a requirement to have such statements signed and certified by two of the partners authorised by the partners to do so.

(2) In the case of a parent undertaking that is a partnership to which this Part applies, the statements referred to in paragraph (1) shall be returned to the Registrar with the accounts for that particular financial year.

19. In the case of a parent undertaking that is a partnership to which this Part applies, the reference in Regulation 37 of the 1992 Group Accounts Regulations to the report of the directors under section 158 of the Principal Act shall be construed as a reference to the report of the partners under Regulations 14 of these Regulations.

Return by Partnership of Documents to the Register of Companies

20.(1) Subject to Regulation 13, in the case of a partnership to which this Part applies the partners shall, under cover of the prescribed form, forward to the register of companies, within six months from the end of the financial year of the partnership, a copy of the balance sheet and profit and loss account for that financial year drawn up in accordance with Regulation 12 and each such copy shall be certified, by two of the partners authorised by the partners to do so, to be a true copy of such balance sheet or profit and loss account, as the case may be.

(2) Where a partnership to which this Part applies is a parent undertaking whose partners are required to prepare group accounts in accordance with the 1992 Group Accounts Regulations, the partners shall forward a copy of the group accounts to the registrar at the same time as the documentation referred to in paragraph (1) and each such copy shall be certified, by two of the partners authorised by the partners to do so, to be a true copy.

(3) There shall be attached to the balance sheet, profit and loss accounts and group accounts referred to in paragraphs (1) and (2) a copy of the report of the auditors on and report of the partners accompanying each such balance sheet, profit and loss account or group accounts and each such copy shall be certified, by two of the partners authorised by the partners to do so, to be a true copy of each such report.

(4) Section 7 of the 1986 Act shall not apply to a partnership to which this Part applies and a reference in that Act to a provision of the said section 7 shall be construed in the case of such a partnership as a reference to the corresponding provision in this Regulation.

(5) Regulation 39 of the 1992 Group Accounts Regulations shall not apply to a partnership to which paragraph (2) applies.

(6) In the case of a partnership to which this Part applies, a reference, in the 1986 Act or in the 1992 Group Accounts Regulations to the annual return shall be construed as a reference to the return made to the registrar pursuant to this Regulation and a reference to any documents to be annexed to the annual return shall be construed as a reference to the corresponding documents to be returned pursuant to these Regulations.

21. Where a document, being a balance sheet, profit and loss account, report or statement, returned to the registrar pursuant to these Regulations, is in a language other than the English language or the Irish language, there shall be annexed to each such document a translation in the English language or the Irish language certified in the prescribed manner to be a correct translation.

Audit Provisions

22.(1) In the case of a partnership to which this Part applies, the partners, including a limited partner, if any, shall appoint auditors who shall make a report on the accounts examined by them and on every balance sheet and profit and loss account, and all group accounts drawn up pursuant to these Regulations by the partners during their tenure of office as auditors.

(2) A person shall not be qualified for appointment as an auditor under paragraph (1) unless he is qualified under the Companies Acts for appointment as auditor of a company.

(3) In the case of a partnership to which this Part applies the reference in section 15, section 18 (3)(b) and section 19 (2)(c) and (d) of the 1986 Act to an auditor's report under section 163 of the Principal Act and the reference in Regulation 38 of the 1992 Group Accounts Regulations to an auditor's report under section 193 of the 1990 Act shall be construed as references to the auditor's report referred to in paragraph (1).

Unlimited Liability

23. [...][a]

Amendments

a EC(A)R 1993, reg 23 amends C(A)A 1986, by the insertion of s 16A. See the amended Act.

Offences

24.(1) If any person, being a partner of a partnership to which this Part applies, fails to take all reasonable steps to secure compliance with a requirement of Regulations 10(1), 12(1) and (2), 13(5) and (6), 14(1) and (2), 15, 16, 20, 21 and 22, that partner and any officer of that partner who is in default, shall in respect of each offence, be liable on summary conviction to imprisonment for a term not exceeding 12 months or, at the discretion of the court, to a [class C fine][a] or to both.

(2) In any proceedings against a person for an offence under paragraph (1) of this Regulation, it shall be a defence for a partner to prove that he had reasonable grounds to believe and did believe that a competent and reliable person was charged with the duty of ensuring that the provisions of these Regulations were complied with and that the latter person was in a position to discharge that duty, and a person shall not be liable to be sentenced to imprisonment for an offence under the said paragraph (1) unless, in the opinion of the court, the offence was committed wilfully.

(3) If any person in any return, report, certificate, balance sheet or other documents required by or for the purpose of any of the provisions of these Regulations wilfully makes a statement false in any material particular, knowing it to be false, he shall be liable on summary conviction to imprisonment for a term not exceeding 12 months or, at the discretion of the court, to a [class C fine][a] or to both.

(4) A partner shall be deemed to be an officer of the partnership for the purposes of section 22 of the 1986 Act and Regulation 41 of the 1992 Group Accounts Regulations.

(5) Proceedings for an offence under this Regulation, in relation to regulations 13 (5) and (6), 15, 20, and 21 may be brought and prosecuted by the registrar of companies.

Amendments

a £1,000 increased to £1,500 by CA 1990, s 240(7) as inserted by CLEA 2001, s 104(c), and converted to €1,904.61 by Council Regulations (EC) No 1103/97, No 974/98 and No 2866/98 and the Economic and Monetary Union Act 1998, s 6; the above being implicitly substituted, by Fines Act 2010, s 6, for a fine not exceeding the aforesaid amount. A class C fine currently means a fine not exceeding €2,500.

PART IV
IMPLEMENTATION OF ARTICLE 11 OF COUNCIL DIRECTIVE 89/666/EEC

25. Section 13 of the Companies (Amendment) Act 1986, is hereby amended by the insertion of the following new subsection:

[...][a]

GIVEN under my Official Seal, this 20th day of December, 1993.

RUAIRÍ QUINN, Minister for Enterprise and Employment.

Amendments

a EC(A)R 1993, reg 25 amends C(A)A 1986, s 13 by the insertion of sub-s (e). See the amended Act.

EXPLANATORY NOTE

(This note is not part of the Instrument and does not purport to be a legal interpretation).

The purpose of these Regulations is to give legal effect to Council Directive 90/604/EEC on accounting exemptions for small and medium sized undertakings, Council Directive 90/605/EEC extending the Scope of the 4th (annual accounts) and 7th (group accounts) Company Law Directives and Article 11 of Council Directive 89/666/EEC (branch disclosures).

Part I of the Regulations contains preliminary and general provisions eg Interpretation Provisions.

Part II of the Regulations implements Council Directive 90/604/EEC. It increases the balance sheet and turnover thresholds set out in the Companies (Amendment) Act 1986 for the purpose of availing of exemptions for small and medium-sized companies. It also clarifies that a company can file accounts in ECUs as well as the currency in which they are drawn up.

Part III of the Regulations implements Council Directive 90/605/EEC. It extends the scope of the 1986 Act implementing the 4th Directive and the 1992 Group Accounts Regulations to certain types of unlimited companies and partnerships.

Part IV implements Article 11 of Council Directive 89/666/EEC (the Eleventh Directive) on disclosures by branches. Regulation 25 contains the relevant provision which requires disclosure in accounts of the existence of branches.

European Communities (Single-Member Private Limited Companies) Regulations 1994

SI 275/1994

I, RUAIRÍ QUINN, Minister for Enterprise and Employment, in exercise of the powers conferred on me by section 3 of the European Communities Act, 1972 (No. 27 of 1972), and for the purpose of giving effect to Council Directive No. 89/667/EEC of 21 December 1989 (OJ No L395, 30–12–1989, pp 40-42), hereby make the following Regulations:

1 Citation, Commencement and Construction

(1) These Regulations may be cited as the European Communities (Single-Member Private Limited Companies) Regulations, 1994.

(2) These Regulations shall come into operation on the 1st day of October, 1994.

(3) These Regulations shall be construed as one with the Companies Acts, 1963 to 1990.

2 Interpretation

(1) In these Regulations, unless the context otherwise requires—

"accounts" means the balance sheet and profit and loss account of a company referred to in section 148 of the Principal Act, together with any notes to or other documents annexed to the accounts in question giving information which is required by any provision of the Companies Acts, and required or allowed by any such provision to be given in a note to or a document annexed to a company's accounts;

"the Act of 1990" means the Companies Act, 1990 (No. 33 of 1990);

"the Companies Acts" means the Principal Act, and every enactment which is to be construed as one with that Act;

"the Directive" means Council Directive No. 89/667/EEC of 21 December 1989;

"enactment" includes an instrument made under an enactment;

"the Principal Act" means the Companies Act, 1963 (No. 33 of 1963);

"single-member company" shall be construed in accordance with Regulation 3(1);

(2) A word or expression that is used in these Regulations and is also used in the Directive has, unless the contrary intention appears, the meaning in these Regulations that it has in the Directive.

(3) In these Regulations—

(a) a reference to a regulation is a reference to a regulation of these Regulations unless it is indicated that reference to some other Regulation is intended,

(b) a reference to a paragraph or subparagraph is a reference to the paragraph or subparagraph of the provision in which the reference occurs unless it is indicated that reference to some other provision is intended.

3 Single-member private companies, limited by shares or by guarantee

(1) Notwithstanding any enactment or rule of law to the contrary, a private company limited by shares or by guarantee may be formed by one person, and may have one member (in these Regulations referred to as a single-member company), to the extent permitted by the Companies Acts and these Regulations.

(2) Any enactment or rule of law which applies in relation to a private company limited by shares or guarantee incorporated under the Companies Acts shall, in the absence of any express provision to the contrary, apply with any necessary modifications in relation to a single-member company as it applies in relation to such a company which is formed by two or more persons or which has two or more persons as members.

(3) Without prejudice to the generality of paragraphs (1) and (2), the Companies Acts shall have effect with the modifications specified in these Regulations.

4 Formation of a single-member company

Notwithstanding section 5(1) of the Principal Act, one person may, for any lawful purpose, by subscribing his or her name to a memorandum of association and otherwise complying with the requirements of the Companies Acts and these Regulations relating to registration, form an incorporated company being a private company limited by shares or by guarantee.

5 Company becoming a single-member company

(1) A private company limited by shares or by guarantee registered with two or more subscribers to its memorandum of association, in accordance with the Companies Acts, shall become a single-member company, on such date as the number of members is reduced to one and all the shares in the company are registered in the name of a sole person.

(2) Where a company becomes a single-member company pursuant to paragraph (1) it shall cause that fact and the date on which it became a single-member company and the identity of the sole member to be notified in writing in the prescribed form to the registrar of companies within 28 days after the date on which the number of members is reduced to one.

(3) If a company fails to comply with the requirements of paragraph (2), the company and every officer of the company who is in default shall be guilty of an offence.

6 Change in status of a single-member company

(1) A company which is incorporated as, or becomes, a single-member company, in accordance with the Companies Acts and these Regulations, shall cease to be a single-member company on such date as the number of members increases to more than one but shall continue to be a private company limited by shares or guarantee, as the case may be, while the number of members does not exceed 50.

(2) Where a single-member company ceases to be such pursuant to paragraph (1), it shall cause that fact and the date on which it ceased to be a single-member company to be notified in writing in the prescribed form to the registrar of companies within 28 days after the date when the number of members increased to more than one.

(3) If a company fails to comply with the requirements of paragraph (2), the company and every officer of the company who is in default shall be guilty of an offence.

7 Non-application of section 36 of Principal Act

(1) Section 36 of the Principal Act shall not apply to a private company limited by shares or by guarantee.

(2) Without prejudice to paragraph (1), a person who, before the coming into force of these Regulations, is liable by virtue of section 36 of the Principal Act (members severally liable for debts where business carried on with fewer than, in the case of private company, two members) for the payment of the debts of a private company limited by shares or by guarantee, shall not be so liable for the payment of the company's debts contracted on or after the date on which these Regulations come into force.

8 Annual General Meeting

(1) The sole member of a single-member company may decide, in the manner provided for in Regulation 9, to dispense with the holding of annual general meetings and, if he or she does so, section 131 of the Principal Act shall not apply to the company.

(2) A decision pursuant to paragraph (1) shall have effect for the year in which it is made and subsequent years, but shall not affect any liability already incurred by reason of default in holding an annual general meeting.

(3) In any year in which an annual general meeting would, but for a decision pursuant to paragraph (1) be required to be held, and in which no such meeting has been held, the sole member or the auditor of a single-member company may, by notice to the company not later than three months before the end of the year, require the holding of an annual general meeting in that year.

(4) If such a notice is given, the provisions of section 131 of the Principal Act, other than subsection (2) thereof, shall apply with respect to the calling of the meeting and the consequence of default.

(5) Where a decision to dispense with the holding of annual general meetings for a single-member company pursuant to paragraph (1) is in force, the requirements in—

- (a) section 148 of the Principal Act that the directors lay accounts before the annual general meeting,
- (b) section 158 of the Principal Act that a directors' report shall be attached to the balance sheet,
- (c) section 193 of the Act of 1990 that the auditors shall make a report on the accounts of the company at the annual general meeting, and
- (d) Regulation 5 of the European Communities (Companies: Group Accounts) Regulations, 1992 (S.I. No. 201 of 1992) that a parent undertaking lay group accounts before the annual general meeting,

shall be deemed to be satisfied where the said accounts and reports are sent to the sole member of the single-member company in accordance with section 159 of the Principal Act, with the modification that they shall be sent not less than 21 days before the appropriate date.

(6) A reference in any other provision of the Companies Acts to the accounts of a company laid before the annual general meeting of a company or the report of the auditors on or the report of the directors accompanying such accounts shall, in the case of a single-member company where a decision to dispense with the holding of annual

general meetings pursuant to paragraph (1) is in force, be construed as a reference to the accounts and reports sent to the sole member in accordance with paragraph (5).

(7) If a decision to dispense with the holding of annual general meetings under paragraph (1) ceases to have effect, sections 148 and 158 of the Principal Act, section 193 of the Act of 1990, and Regulation 5 of the European Communities (Companies: Group Accounts) Regulations, 1992 shall, with any necessary modifications, apply in relation to the accounts and reports in respect of the financial year in which the decision ceases to have effect and subsequent financial years.

(8) For the purposes of the Principal Act, the requirements—

- (a) in section 127 that the annual return must be completed within 60 days after the annual general meeting,
- (b) in section 148 that the accounts must be made up to a date not earlier than the date of the annual general meeting by more than 9 months, and
- (c) in paragraph 5 of Part I of the Fifth Schedule that the list containing specified particulars of persons who are members on the 14th day after the company's annual general meeting

shall in the case of a single-member company where a decision to dispense with the holding of annual general meetings pursuant to paragraph (1) is in force, be read as relating to a similar period relative to the appropriate date.

(9) For the purposes of this Regulation, each year the "appropriate date" shall be—

- (a) in the case of a single-member company formed as such and where a decision to dispense with the holding of annual general meetings is taken before the first such meeting is due, the last day of the month in which the anniversary of its formation falls;
- (b) in the case of a private company limited by share or by guarantee formed after the commencement of these Regulations which becomes a single-member company pursuant to Regulation 5 before holding its first annual general meeting and where a decision to dispense with the holding of annual general meetings is taken before the first such meeting is due, the last day of the month in which the anniversary of its formation falls; and
- (c) in the case of all other single-member companies, the last day of the month in which the anniversary of the last annual general meeting of the company was held falls.

9 General Meetings — powers exercisable by sole member

(1) Subject to paragraph (2), all the powers exercisable by a company in general meeting under the Companies Acts or otherwise shall be exercisable, in the case of a single-member company, by the sole member without the need to hold a general meeting for that purpose.

(2) Paragraph (1) shall not empower the sole member of a single-member company to exercise the powers in sections 160(2)(b), 160(5), and 160(6) of the Principal Act to remove an auditor from office without holding the requisite meeting provided for in the said provisions.

(3) Subject to paragraph (2), any provision of the Companies Acts which—

(a) enables or requires any matter to be done or to be decided by a company in general meeting, or

(b) requires any matter to be decided by a resolution of the company,

shall be deemed to be satisfied, in the case of a single-member company, by a decision of the member which is drawn up in writing and notified to the company in accordance with this Regulation.

(4) Where the sole member of a single-member company takes any decision which may be taken by the company in general meeting and which has effect, pursuant to paragraphs (1) and (3), as if agreed by the company in general meeting, he shall, unless the decision is taken by way of written resolution which he has already forwarded to the company, provide the company with a written record of that decision.

(5) Where the sole member notifies a decision taken by way of written resolution, or a written record of a decision taken pursuant to paragraph (4), to a single-member company of which he is the sole member, the notification shall be recorded and retained by the company in a book or by some other suitable means maintained for the purpose.

(6) The exercise by the sole member of a single-member company of any power, right or obligation under this Regulation, to which section 143 of the Principal Act, as amended, applies, shall, within 15 days, be notified by the company in writing to the registrar of companies and be recorded by him.

(7) If the sole member fails to comply with paragraph (4), or if a company fails to comply with paragraphs (5) or (6) the sole member, the company and every officer of the company who is in default shall be guilty of an offence.

(8) Failure by the sole member to comply with paragraph (4) shall not affect the validity of any decision referred to in that paragraph.

10 Quorum

Notwithstanding any provision to the contrary in the articles of a single-member company, one member present in person or by proxy shall be a quorum.

11 Non-application of other provisions of Principal Act

Sections 213(d) and 215(a)(i) of the Principal Act shall not apply to a private company limited by shares or by guarantee.

12 Connected person

[...][a]

Amendments

a Deleted by European Communities (Single Member Private Limited Companies) Regulations 1994 (Amendment) Regulations 2001 (SI 437/2001), reg 3 with effect from 1 October 2001.

---

13 Contracts with sole members

(1) Subject to paragraph (2), where a single-member company enters into a contract with the sole member of the company and the sole member also represents the company

in the transaction, whether as a director or otherwise, the company shall, unless the contract is in writing, ensure that the terms of the contract are forthwith set out in a written memorandum or are recorded in the minutes of the first meeting of the directors of the company following the making of the contract.

(2) Paragraph (1) shall not apply to contracts entered into in the ordinary course of the company's business.

(3) If a company fails to comply with paragraph (1), the company and every officer of the company who is in default shall be guilty of an offence.

(4) Subject to paragraph (5), nothing in this Regulation shall be taken to prejudice the operation of any other enactment or rule of law applying to contracts between a company and a director of that company.

(5) Failure to comply with paragraph (1) with respect to a contract shall not affect the validity of that contract.

14 Offences

A person guilty of an offence under any provision of these Regulations shall be liable, on summary conviction, to a [class C fine].[a]

Amendments

a £1,000 increased to £1500 by CA 1990, s 240(7), as inserted by CLEA 2001, s 104(c), and converted to €1904,61 by Council Regulations (EC) No 1103/97, No 974/98 and No 2866/98 and the Economic and Monetary Union Act 1998, s 6; the above being implicitly substituted, by Fines Act 2010, s 6, for a fine not exceeding the aforesaid amount. A class C fine currently means a fine not exceeding €2,500.

EXPLANATORY NOTE

These Regulations implement Council Directive No. 89/667/EEC on single-member private limited liability companies. The Directive requires Member States to provide for the formation of a company having one member and to permit a company to be a single member company, subject to certain safeguards. In relation to Ireland, it applies to private companies limited by shares or guarantee.

The Regulations provide that a sole person, whether natural or legal, will now be able to form or become a single-member limited liability company. The Regulations further provide that, subject to certain modifications, all the provisions of the Companies Acts which apply to private companies limited by shares or by guarantee will apply to single-member companies. For instance, the sole member, if he so decides, can dispense with the holding of General Meetings, including Annual General Meetings (AGM). However, certain notifications will have to be made. Also the accounts and reports that would normally be laid before the AGM of a company will still need to be prepared and forwarded to the member.

European Communities (Insurance Undertakings: Accounts) Regulations 1996

SI 23/1996

ARRANGEMENT OF REGULATIONS

I, RICHARD BRUTON, Minister for Enterprise and Employment, in exercise of the powers conferred on me by section 3 of the European Communities Act, 1972 (No. 27 of 1972), and for the purpose of giving effect to Council Directive No. 91/674/EEC of 23 December, 1991, hereby make the following Regulations:

1 Citation and Construction

(1) These Regulations may be cited as the European Communities (Insurance Undertakings: Accounts) Regulations, 1996.

(2) These Regulations shall be construed as one with the Companies Acts, 1963 to 1990.

2 Interpretation

(l) In these Regulations, unless the context otherwise requires—

"accounts" means the balance sheet, profit and loss account and any notes on the accounts or statements forming part of the accounts, whether or not required by law;

"the Act of 1986" means the Companies (Amendment) Act, 1986 (No. 25 of 1986);

"the Act of 1990" means the Companies Act, 1990 (No. 33 of 1990);

"annual return" means the annual return made to the registrar of undertakings under the Principal Act;

"associated undertaking" has the meaning assigned by paragraph 21 of Chapter 2 of Part IV of the Schedule;

["Bank" means the Central Bank and Financial Services Authority of Ireland];[a]

"company" means an undertaking as defined in Regulation 3;

"the Directive" means Council Directive 91/674/EEC of 23 December, 1991;

"group accounts" means the accounts prepared in accordance with Regulations 10 to 18;

"holding company", in relation to one or more undertakings that are subsidiaries of another undertaking, means that other undertaking;

"individual accounts" means the accounts prepared in accordance with Regulations 5 to 9;

['investment property' means land or buildings (or both) held to earn rentals or for capital appreciation (or both);][b]

[...][c];

"parent undertaking" means an undertaking that has one or more subsidiary undertakings;

"participating interest" shall be construed in accordance with paragraph 23 of Part IV of the Schedule;

"the Principal Act" means the Companies Act, 1963;

"subsidiary" shall be construed in accordance with Regulation 11;

"undertaking" means an undertaking to which these Regulations apply by virtue of Regulation 3.

[(1A) References in these Regulations to annual accounts giving a 'true and fair view' are references—

(a) in the case of Companies Act individual accounts, to the requirement under Regulation 5 that those accounts give a true and fair view,

(b) in the case of Companies Act group accounts, to the requirement under Regulation 10 that those accounts give a true and fair view, and

(c) in the case of IFRS accounts, to the equivalent requirement under international financial reporting standards.][d]

(2) In these Regulations, unless the context otherwise requires, a reference to a balance sheet or profit and loss account shall include a reference to any notes or documents annexed to the accounts in question giving information which is required by any provision of the Companies Acts, 1963 to 1990, [these Regulations or international financial reporting standards][e] and required or allowed by any such provision to be given in a note or document annexed to an undertaking's accounts.

(3) In these Regulations—

(a) a reference to directors shall be construed, in the case of an undertaking which does not have a board of directors, as a reference to the corresponding persons appropriate to such undertaking;

(b) a reference to voting rights in an undertaking means the rights conferred on shareholders in respect of their shares or, in case of an undertaking not having a share capital, on members, to vote at general meetings of the undertaking on all, or substantially all, matters;

(c) in relation to an undertaking which does not have general meetings at which matters are decided by the exercise of voting rights, the references to holding a majority of the voting rights in an undertaking shall be construed as references to having the right under the constitution of the undertaking to direct the overall policy of the undertaking to alter the terms of its constitution.

(4) A word or expression that is used in these Regulations and is also used in the Council Directive has, unless the context otherwise requires, the same meaning in these Regulations as it has in the Council Directive.

(5) In these Regulations, unless the context otherwise requires—

(a) a reference to a Regulation or a Schedule is to a Regulation of or a Schedule to these Regulations unless it is indicated that a reference to some other enactment is intended.

(b) a reference to a paragraph or a subparagraph is to a paragraph or subparagraph of the provision in which the reference occurs, unless it is indicated that reference to some other provision is intended.

Amendments

a Definition inserted by CBFSAIA 2003, s 35 and Sch 2, Item 1(a).

b Inserted by reg 11 and Sch 3, Item No 1(a) of EC(IFRSMA)R 2005.

c Definition of "Minister" deleted by CBFSAIA 2003, s 35 and Sch 2, Item 1(b).

d Inserted by reg 11 and Sch 3, Item No 1(a) of EC(IFRSMA)R 2005.

e Words substituted by reg 11 and Sch 3, Item No 1(a) of EC(IFRSMA)R 2005.

3 Application

These Regulations shall, except where otherwise provided for, only apply—

(a) to undertakings to which the European Communities (Non-Life Insurance) Regulations, 1976 (S.I. No. 115 of 1976), the European Communities (Non-Life Insurance) Framework Regulations, 1994 (S.I. No. 359 of 1994) or the European Communities (Life Assurance) Regulations, 1984 (S.I. No. 57 of 1984), the European Communities (Life Assurance) Framework Regulations, 1994 (S.I. No. 360 of 1994) apply and shall also apply to undertakings carrying on reinsurance business, and

(b) in respect of individual and group accounts of undertakings drawn up in respect of every financial year beginning on or after 1 January, 1995.

4 Modification

(1) For the purposes of enabling the Directive to have full effect, the [Bank][a] may, with the consent or on the application of any undertaking, issue a direction in writing that specified provisions of these Regulations shall apply to that undertaking with such modifications as may be specified in the direction.

(2) A direction under paragraph (1) may be subject to such conditions as the [Bank][a] considers appropriate to impose.

(3) A direction under paragraph (1) may be revoked at any time by the Minister and the Minister may at any time vary the direction on the application or with the consent of the undertaking to which it relates.

(4) A direction under paragraph (1) shall, subject to paragraph (3), apply for such period as shall be stated in the direction.

Amendments

a 'Bank' substituted for 'Minister' by CBFSAIA 2003, s 35 and Sch 2, Pt 16, Item 2.

---

5 Drawing up of accounts

[(1) Subject to paragraph (2), every balance sheet and profit and loss account of an undertaking laid before the annual general meeting of the undertaking, pursuant to section 148 of the Principal Act shall be prepared in accordance with—

(a) section 149 of the Principal Act as modified by these Regulations, or

(b) international financial reporting standards (in these Regulations referred to as 'IFRS individual accounts') and section 149A (inserted by the European Communities (International Financial Reporting Standards and Miscellaneous Amendments) Regulations 2005)) of the Principal Act as modified by these Regulations,

and in either case shall comply with section 150C (inserted by the European Communities (International Financial Reporting Standards and Miscellaneous Amendments) Regulations 2005) of the Principal Act.

(1A) Companies Act individual accounts of an undertaking prepared in accordance with section 149 of the Principal Act shall comply with the following requirements and section 149 (other than subsection (5) and, insofar as it relates to the said subsection (5), subsection (7)) of that Act shall not apply to any such balance sheet or profit and loss account:

(a) every such balance sheet and profit and loss account shall comply with the Schedule,

(b) every such balance sheet of an undertaking shall give a true and fair view of the state of affairs of the undertaking as at the end of its financial year and every such profit and loss account of an undertaking shall give a true and fair view of the profit and loss of the undertaking for the financial year,

(c) where a balance sheet or profit and loss account drawn up in accordance with subparagraph (a) would not provide sufficient information to comply with subparagraph (b), any necessary additional information shall be provided in that balance sheet or profit and loss account or in a note to the accounts,

(d) where owing to special circumstances, the preparation of individual accounts of an undertaking in compliance with subparagraph (a) would prevent those accounts from complying with subparagraph (b) (even if additional information were provided under subparagraph (c)) the directors of an undertaking shall depart from the requirements of the Schedule in preparing those accounts insofar as is necessary in order to comply with that subparagraph,

(e) where the directors of a company depart from the requirements of this Regulation, they shall attach a note to the individual accounts of the undertaking giving details of the particular departures made, the reasons therefor and the effect of those departures on the accounts,

and, accordingly, in the Companies Acts 1963 to 2003, in relation to a undertaking—

(i) references to the said section 149 shall be read as references to that section as modified by the provisions of these Regulations, and

(ii) references to the Sixth Schedule of the Principal Act shall be read as references to the corresponding provisions of these Regulations.

(1B) Where the directors of an undertaking prepare IFRS individual accounts in accordance with international financial reporting standards and section 149A of the Principal Act they shall ensure that instead of making the disclosures specified in section 149A (2) the notes to the accounts include the information required by—

(a) paragraph 21 (e) of Part III of the Schedule (details of directors' remuneration),

(b) sections 41 to 45 of the Act of 1990 to be disclosed in individual accounts and paragraph 31 (2) of Part IV of the (transactions with directors),

(c) section 63 of the Act of 1990 unless it is disclosed in the directors' report (interests in shares and debentures),

(d) paragraphs 32 to 36 of Part IV of the Schedule (details of group undertakings),

(e) paragraph 27 of Part III of the Schedule (details of staff numbers and remuneration),

(f) paragraphs 6 to 9 of Part III of the Schedule (details of share capital and debentures),

(g) paragraph 20(4) of Part III of the Schedule (restriction on distributability of profits),

(h) paragraph 18 of Part III of the Schedule (guarantees and other financial commitments),

(i) paragraph 20(2) of Part III of the Schedule (financial assistance for purchase of own shares), [...][a]

(j) paragraph 21(d) of Part III of the Schedule and by section 205D (inserted by section 44 of the Companies (Auditing and Accounting) Act 2003) of the Act of 1990 ([auditors' remuneration), and][b]

[(k) where appropriate, paragraph 19A of Part III of the Schedule.][c]

(2) The references in paragraph (1) to the profit and loss account of an undertaking being laid before the annual general meeting of an undertaking shall not apply to the profit and loss account of an undertaking if the undertaking prepares Companies Acts individual accounts and –

(a) the undertaking is a parent undertaking,

(b) the undertaking is required to prepare and does prepare Companies Acts group accounts in accordance with these Regulations, and

(c) the notes to the undertaking's individual balance sheet show the undertaking's profit and loss for the financial year determined in accordance with these Regulations.][d]

(3) Where, in the case of an undertaking, advantage is taken of paragraph (2), that fact shall be disclosed in a note to the individual and group accounts of the undertaking.

(4) The requirements of the Schedule and the Companies Acts, 1963 to 1990, as to the matters to be included in the accounts of an undertaking or in notes to those accounts shall be subject to the requirement specified in subparagraph (b) of paragraph (1) and, accordingly, where a balance sheet or profit and loss account of an undertaking drawn up in accordance with the first mentioned requirements would not provide sufficient information to comply with the said subparagraph, any necessary additional information shall be provided in such balance sheet or profit and loss account or in a note to the accounts.

Amendments

a Words deleted by European Communities (Directive 2006/46/EC) Regulations 2009, reg 20(a).

b Words substituted by European Communities (Directive 2006/46/EC) Regulations 2009, reg 20(b).

c Subparqagraph (k) inserted by European Communities (Directive 2006/46/EC) Regulations 2009, reg 20(c).

d Substituted by reg 11 and Sch 3, Item No 2 of EC(IFRSMA)R 2005 (SI 116/2005).

---

6 Format of accounts

(1) [Where the directors of an undertaking prepare Companies Act individual accounts and subject to these Regulations –][a]

(a) every balance sheet of an undertaking shall show the items listed in the balance sheet format set out in Chapter 2 of Part I of the Schedule, and

(b) every profit and loss account of an undertaking shall show the items listed in the profit and loss account format so set out,

in the order and under the headings and sub-headings given in the format concerned.

(2) Paragraph (1) shall not be construed as requiring the heading or sub-heading for any item in the balance sheet, or profit and loss account, of an undertaking to be distinguished by any letter or number assigned to that item in the formats set out in the Schedule.

(3) Where the balance sheet or profit and loss account of an undertaking has been prepared by reference to the options set out in the Schedule, the directors of the undertaking shall adopt the same options in preparing the accounts for subsequent financial years unless, in their opinion, there are special reasons for a change.

(4) Where any change is made in the format adopted in preparing a balance sheet, or profit and loss account, of an undertaking, the reasons for the change, together with full particulars of the change, shall be given in a note to the accounts in which the new format is first adopted.

(5) Any item required in accordance with the Schedule to be shown in the balance sheet or profit and loss account, of an undertaking, may be shown in greater detail than that required by the format adopted.

[(6) In respect of every item shown in the balance sheet, or profit and loss account, of an undertaking, the corresponding amount for the financial year immediately preceding that to which the balance sheet or profit and loss account refers shall also be shown and, if that corresponding amount is not comparable with the amount to be shown for the item in question in respect of the financial year to which the balance sheet or profit and loss account relates, the former amount shall be adjusted, and particulars of the adjustment and the reasons therefor shall be given in a note to the accounts.][b]

(7) Subject to paragraph (8), a heading or sub-heading corresponding to an item listed in the balance sheet format or the profit and loss account format of an undertaking, shall not be included in the balance sheet or profit and loss account, as the case may be, if there is no amount to be shown for that item in respect of the financial year to which the balance sheet or profit and loss account relates.

(8) Paragraph (7) shall not apply in any case where an amount can be shown for the item in question in respect of the financial year immediately preceding that to which the balance sheet or profit and loss account relates, and that amount shall be shown under the heading or sub-heading required by paragraph (1).

(9) Subject to the provisions of these Regulations and the provisions of the Schedule, amounts in respect of items representing assets or income may not be set off in the accounts of an undertaking against amounts in respect of items representing liabilities or expenditure, as the case may be, or vice versa.

(10) The balance sheet, or profit and loss account, of an undertaking may include an item representing or covering the amount of any asset or liability or income or expenditure not otherwise covered by any of the items listed in the format adopted but the following shall not be treated as assets in the balance sheet of an undertaking:

(a) preliminary expenses,

(b) expenses of, and commission on, any issue of shares or debentures, and

(c) costs of research.

(11) Every profit and loss account of an undertaking shall show the amount of the profit or loss of the undertaking on ordinary activities before taxation.

Amendments

a Words substituted by reg 11 and Sch 3, Item No 3 of EC(IFRSMA)R 2005.

b Subparagraph (6) substituted by SI 840/2005, reg 7.

7 Accounting Principles

Subject to Regulation 8, the amounts to be included in the [Companies Act accounts][a] of an undertaking in respect of the items shown shall be determined in accordance with the following principles:

(a) the undertaking shall be presumed to be carrying on business as a going concern,

(b) accounting policies shall be applied consistently from one financial year to the next,

(c) subject to the provisions of the Schedule, the amount of any item in the accounts shall be determined on a prudent basis and in particular—

(i) only profits which have arisen by the balance sheet date shall be included in the profit and loss account, and

(ii) [all liabilities which have arisen][b] in respect of the financial year to which the accounts relate, or a previous financial year, shall be taken into account, including those liabilities and losses which only become apparent between the balance sheet date and the date on which the accounts are signed in pursuance of section 156 of the Principal Act,

(d) all income charges relating to the financial year to which the accounts relate shall be taken into account without regard to the date of receipt or payment, [...][c]

(e) in determining the aggregate amount of any item the amount of each individual asset or liability that falls to be taken into account shall be determined [separately, and][d]

[(f) The directors of a company shall, in determining how amounts are presented within items in the profit and loss account and balance sheet, have regard to the substance of the reported transaction or arrangement, in accordance with generally accepted accounting principles or practice.][e]

Amendments

a Words substituted by reg 11 and Sch 3, Item No 4(a) of EC(IFRSMA)R 2005 .

b Words substituted by reg 11 and Sch 3, Item No 4(b) of EC(IFRSMA)R 2005.

c Word "and" deleted by reg 11 and Sch 3, Item No 4(c) of EC(IFRSMA)R 2005.

d Words substituted by reg 11 and Sch 3, Item No 4(d) of EC(IFRSMA)R 2005.

e Paragraph (f) inserted by reg 11 and Sch 3, Item No 4(e) of EC(IFRSMA)R 2005.

8 Departure from Accounting Principles

If it appears to the directors of an undertaking that there are special reasons for departing from any of the principles specified in Regulation 7 [when preparing Companies Act accounts][a], they may so depart, but particulars of the departure, the reasons for it and its effect on the balance sheet and profit and loss account of the undertaking shall be stated in a note to the accounts. for the financial year concerned, of the undertaking.

Amendments

a Words substituted by reg 11 and Sch 3, Item No 5 of EC(IFRSMA)R 2005 (SI 116/2005).

9 Publication of accounts in full or abbreviated form

(1) Where an undertaking publishes its full accounts, it shall also publish with those accounts any report in relation to those accounts by the auditors of the undertaking under section 193 of the Act of 1990.

(2) Where an undertaking publishes abbreviated accounts relating to any financial year, it shall also publish a statement indicating—

- (a) that the accounts are not the accounts copies of which are required to be annexed to the annual return,
- (b) whether the copies of the accounts so required to be so annexed have in fact been so annexed,
- (c) whether the auditors of the undertaking have made a report under section 193 of the Act of 1990, in respect of the accounts of the undertaking which relate to any financial year with which the abbreviated accounts purport to deal,
- [(d) whether any matters referred to in the auditors' report were qualified or unqualified, or whether the auditors' report included a reference to any matters to which the auditors drew attention by way of emphasis without qualifying the report.][a]

(3) Where an undertaking publishes abbreviated accounts, it shall not publish with those accounts any such report of the auditors as is mentioned in paragraph (2)(c).

(4) Where an undertaking publishes its full individual accounts for a financial year it shall indicate if group accounts have been prepared and if so where those group accounts can be obtained.

(5) Every undertaking to which these Regulations apply shall—

- (a) make available its full or abbreviated accounts in accordance with paragraphs (1) to (5) for public inspection at its head office, and
- (b) make available to the public copies of its accounts on request at a price which does not exceed the cost of making the copy.

(6) In this Regulation—

"abbreviated accounts", in relation to an undertaking, means any balance sheet or profit and loss account. or summary or abstract of a balance sheet or profit and loss account, relating to a financial year of the undertaking which is published by the undertaking otherwise than as part of the full accounts of the undertaking for that financial year and.

in relation to a parent undertaking, includes an account in any form purporting to be a balance sheet or profit and loss account, or a summary or abstract of a balance sheet or profit and loss account of the group consisting of the parent undertaking and its subsidiaries;

"full accounts" means the individual or group accounts required to be annexed to the annual return;

"publish", in relation to a document includes issue, circulate or otherwise make it available for public inspection in a manner calculated to invite the public generally, or any class of members of the public, to read the document, and cognate words shall be constructed accordingly.

Amendments

a Paragraph 2(d) substituted by reg 11 and Sch 3, Item No 6 of EC(IFRSMA)R 2005.

---

10 Group accounts

[(1) Subject to paragraph (1A), this Regulation applies to a parent undertaking whether or not it is itself a subsidiary of another undertaking.][b]

[(1A) This Regulation shall not apply to a parent undertaking whose subsidiary undertakings taken together are not material for the purpose of giving a true and fair view of the state of affairs as at the end of the financial year and the profit or loss for the financial year of that parent undertaking and those subsidiary undertakings taken as a whole.][c]

(2) A parent undertaking to which this Regulation applies shall not be entitled to take advantage of section 154 of the Principal Act in relation to the preparation of group accounts or of section 151 (2) and (3) of the Principal Act in relation to the form of group accounts.

(3) Every parent undertaking to which this Regulation applies shall, in accordance with section 150 of the Principal Act, prepare group accounts at the end of its financial year dealing with the state of affairs and profit or loss of the company and its subsidiaries (including those in liquidation and those with registered offices outside the State) and those group accounts shall be laid before the next annual general meeting of the company at the same time as the individual accounts of the company are so laid and shall be annexed to the annual return of the company.

(4) The report of the auditors on the group accounts laid before the annual general meeting shall be annexed to the annual return referred to in paragraph (3).

(5) Where, in accordance with section 150 (2) or (3)(b) of the Principal Act, the directors of an undertaking prepare IFRS group accounts, they shall ensure that instead of making the disclosures specified in section 1 50B (2) (inserted by the European Communities (International Financial Reporting Standards and Miscellaneous Amendments) Regulations 2005) the notes to those group accounts include the information required by—

(a) paragraph 30 (1) of Part IV of the Schedule (details of directors' remuneration),

(b) sections 41 to 45 of the Act of 1990 to be disclosed in individual accounts and the information required by paragraph 31 (2) of Part IV of the Schedule (transactions with directors),

(c) section 63 of the Act of 1990 unless it is disclosed in the directors' report (interests in shares and debentures),

(d) paragraphs 32 to 36 of Part IV of the Schedule (details of group undertakings),

(e) paragraph 29 of Part IV of the Schedule (details of staff numbers and remuneration),

(f) paragraphs 6 to 9 of Part III of the Schedule (details of share capital and debentures),

(g) paragraph 20 (4) of Part III of the Schedule (restriction on distributibility of profits),

(h) paragraph 18 of Part III of the Schedule (guarantees and other financial commitments),

(i) paragraph 20 (2) of Part III of the Schedule (financial assistance for purchase of own shares),

(j) paragraph 21 (d) of Part III of the Schedule and by section 205D of the Act of 1990 (auditors' remuneration),

[(k) where appropriate, paragraph 37(a) of Part IV of the Schedule.][d]

(6) Where in accordance with section 1 50(3)(a) of the Principal Act, the directors of an undertaking to which this regulation applies prepare Companies Acts group accounts they shall, subject to paragraph (7), be prepared in accordance with the provisions of Part I to Part III of the Schedule, as modified by Part IV of the Schedule.

(7) (a) The Companies Act group accounts laid before the annual general meeting of an undertaking shall give a true and fair view of the state of affairs and profit or loss of the undertaking and subsidiaries dealt with thereby as a whole, so far as concerns members of the undertaking.

(b) The Companies Act group accounts shall comprise the consolidated balance sheet dealing with the sate of affairs of the parent and its subsidiaries as a whole, the consolidated profit and loss account dealing with the profit and loss of the parent and its subsidiaries as a whole and the notes on the accounts giving the information required by these Regulations or otherwise provided by the undertaking.

(c) Where Companies Act group accounts drawn up in accordance with paragraph (6) would not provide sufficient information to comply with subparagraph (a), any necessary additional information shall be given in the group accounts or in a note to the accounts.

(d) Where, owing to special circumstances, the preparation of Companies Act group accounts in compliance with paragraph (5) would prevent those accounts from complying with subparagraph (a) (even if additional information were given under subparagraph (c)), the directors of the parent undertaking shall depart from the requirements of Parts I, II, III and IV (other than paragraph 2 of Part IV) of the Schedule in preparing those accounts insofar as it is necessary to comply with that paragraph.

(e) Where the directors of a parent undertaking depart from the requirements of these Regulations in compliance with subparagraph (d), they shall attach a note to the Companies Act group accounts of the undertaking giving details of the particular departures made, the reasons therefor and the effect of those departures on the accounts.

(8) Where a document annexed to the annual return under this Regulation or Regulation 11, 12, 12A or 13 is in a language other than English or Irish, there shall be annexed to any such document a translation in the English or Irish language certified in the prescribed manner to be a correct translation.

(9) The individual and group accounts, if any, of a subsidiary undertaking excluded from group accounts by virtue of the application of paragraph 2 of Part IV of the Schedule shall be attached to the group accounts, or annexed to the annual return, of the parent undertaking.

(10) Paragraph (9) shall not apply where the subsidiary undertaking has otherwise annexed the relevant accounts referred to in that paragraph to its annual return.][a]

Amendments

a Regulation 10 substituted by reg 11 and Sch 3, Item No 7 of EC(IFRSMA)R 2005.

b Subparagraph (1) substituted by EC(GA)R 2010, reg 5(a).

c Subparagraph (1A) inserted by EC(GA)R 2010, reg 5(b).

d Subparagraph 10(5)(k) inserted by European Communities (Directive 2006/46/EC) Regulations 2009, reg 21.

---

11 Subsidiary undertaking

(1) For the purpose of Regulations 10 to 19 and Part IV of the Schedule, an undertaking shall be deemed to be a subsidiary of another, if, but only if—

(a) that other—

(i) holds a majority of the shareholders' or members' voting rights in the undertaking, or

(ii) is a shareholder or member of it and controls the composition of its board of directors, or

(iii) is a shareholder or member of it and controls alone, pursuant to an agreement with other shareholders or members, a majority of the shareholders' or members' voting rights;

or

(b) that other has the right to exercise a dominant influence over it—

(i) by virtue of provisions contained in its memorandum or articles, or

(ii) by virtue of a control contract:

or

[(c) that other has the power to exercise, or actually exercises, dominant influence or control over it, or

(ca) that other and the subsidiary undertaking are managed on a unified basis; or][a]

(d) the undertaking is a subsidiary of any undertaking which is that other's subsidiary undertaking.

(2) In determining whether one undertaking controls the composition of the board of directors of another for the purposes of paragraph (1)(a)(ii), subsection (2) of section 155 of the Principal Act shall apply to undertakings subject to these Regulations as it applies to undertakings subject to that section.

(3) For the purpose of paragraph (1)(a)—

(a) subject to paragraphs (c) and (d), any shares held or power exercisable—

(i) by any person as a nominee for that other, or

(ii) by, or by a nominee for, a subsidiary undertaking of that other, not being the subsidiary undertaking whose shares or board of directors are involved,

shall be treated as held or exercisable by that other,

(b) any shares held or power exercisable by that other or a subsidiary undertaking of that other. on behalf of a person or undertaking that is neither that other nor a subsidiary undertaking of that other shall be treated as not held or exercisable by that other,

(c) any shares held or power exercisable by that other, or a nominee for that other or its subsidiary undertaking shall be treated as not held or exercisable by that other if they are held as aforesaid by way of security provided that such power or the rights attaching to such shares are exercised in accordance with instructions received from the person providing the security,

(d) any shares held or power exercisable by that other or a nominee for that other or its subsidiary undertaking shall be treated as not held or exercisable by that other if the ordinary business of that other or its subsidiary undertaking, as the case may be, includes the lending of money and the shares are held as aforesaid by way of security provided that such power or the rights attaching to such shares are exercised in the interests of the person providing the security.

(4) For the purposes of clauses (i) and (ii) of paragraph (1)(a), the total of the voting rights of the shareholders or members in the subsidiary undertaking shall be reduced by the following—

(a) the voting rights attached to shares held by the subsidiary undertaking in itself, and

(b) the voting rights attached to shares held by the subsidiary undertaking by any of its subsidiary undertakings, and

(c) the voting rights attached to shares held by a person acting in his own name but on behalf of the subsidiary undertaking or one of its subsidiary undertakings.

(5) For the purposes of paragraph (1)(b) an undertaking shall not be regarded as having the right to exercise a dominant influence over another undertaking unless it has a right to give directions with respect to the operating and financial policies of that other undertaking which its directors are obliged to comply with.

(6) In paragraph (1)(b) "control contract" means a contract in writing conferring such a right which—

(a) is of a kind authorised by the memorandum or articles of the undertaking in relation to which the right is exercisable, and

(b) is permitted by the law under which that undertaking is established.

(7) Paragraph (5) shall not be read as affecting the construction of the expression "actually exercises a dominant influence" in paragraph (1)(c).

Amendments

a Paragraph substituted by reg 11 and Sch 3, Item No 8 of EC(IFRSMA)R 2005.

12 Wholly-owned subsidiaries

(1) Paragraph (3) of Regulation 10 shall not apply to a parent undertaking (in this Regulation referred to as "the exempted parent undertaking") which is itself a wholly-owned subsidiary of another undertaking [established in an EEA State][a] (in this Regulation referred to as "the parent undertaking") if the requirements set out in paragraph (3) of this Regulation are complied with provided that the fact that the advantage of this Regulation is being availed of shall be disclosed in a note to the accounts of the insurance parent undertaking annexed to its annual return under the Principal Act.

(2) In this Regulation, an undertaking shall be deemed to be a wholly-owned subsidiary of another if—

(a) that other parent undertaking holds all the shares in the exempted parent undertaking, or

(b) that other holds 90 per cent or more of the shares in the undertaking and the remaining shareholders in or members of the undertaking have approved the exemption.

(3) The requirements referred to in paragraph (1) are as follows:

(a) the undertaking and its subsidiaries shall be dealt with in group accounts prepared by the parent undertaking;

(b) the group accounts and the group annual report of the parent undertaking shall be prepared and audited in accordance with the Directive or Council Directive No. 83/349/EEC of 13 June 1983, [or prepared in accordance with international financial reporting standards and audited in accordance with either such Directive, as applicable,][b] as the case may be;

(c) there shall be annexed to the annual return of the exempted parent next after the group accounts have been prepared in accordance with subparagraph (a)—

(i) the group accounts referred to in subparagraph (b);

(ii) the group annual report referred to in subparagraph (b); and

(iii) the report of the person responsible for auditing the accounts referred to in subparagraph (b).

(d) The notes on the annual accounts of the undertaking shall disclose—

(i) the name and registered office of the parent undertaking that draws up the group accounts referred to in subparagraph (b), and

(ii) the exemption from the obligation to draw up group accounts and a group annual report.

[(4) The exemption does not apply to a company any of whose securities are admitted to trading on a regulated market of any EEA State.][c]

(5) The [Bank][d] may require that additional information shall be provided in the consolidated accounts of the parent undertaking or the individual accounts of the undertaking referred to in paragraph (1) in accordance with Article 9 of Council Directive No. 83/349/EEC.

(6) This Regulation shall also apply to a parent undertaking which is not for the purposes of paragraph (2) a wholly-owned subsidiary of another undertaking where—

(a) the parent undertaking is itself a subsidiary of a parent undertaking [established in an EEA State,][e] and

(b) the shareholders or members holding in total 10 per cent or more of the nominal value of the shares of the parent undertaking concerned have not at any time that is not later than six months before the end of the financial year in question requested the preparation of group accounts by that parent undertaking in respect of that financial year.

Amendments

a Words substituted by reg 11 and Sch 3, Item No 9(a) of EC(IFRSMA)R 2005.

b Words inserted by reg 11 and Sch 3, Item No 9(b) of EC(IFRSMA)R 2005.

c Paragraph substituted by reg 11 and Sch 3, Item No 9(c) of EC(IFRSMA)R 2005.

d "Bank" substituted for "Minister" by CBFSAIA 2003, s 35 and Sch 2, Pt 16, Item 3.

e Words substituted by reg 11 and Sch 3, Item No 9(e) of EC(IFRSMA)R 2005.

[12A Exemption for parent undertakings included in non-EEA group accounts

(1) A parent undertaking (the 'exempted parent') is exempt from the requirement in Regulation 10(3) to prepare group accounts where that undertaking is itself a subsidiary undertaking and its parent undertaking ('that other parent undertaking') is not established under the law of an EEA State where—

(a) the exempted parent is a wholly-owned subsidiary of that other parent undertaking;

(b) that other parent undertaking holds more than 50 per cent of the shares in the exempted parent and notice requesting the preparation of group accounts has not been served in accordance with paragraph (2) on the exempted parent by shareholders holding in aggregate—

(i) more than half of the remaining shares in the company, or

(ii) 5 per cent of the total shares in the company.

(2) The notice referred to in paragraph (1)(b) must be served not later than 6 months after the end of the financial year before that to which it relates.

(3) Exemption under this Regulation is conditional upon compliance with all of the following conditions—

(a) that the exempted parent and all of its subsidiary undertakings are included in consolidated accounts for a larger group drawn up to the same date, or to an earlier date in the same financial year by that other parent undertaking,

(b) that those accounts and, where appropriate, the group's annual report, are drawn up in accordance with the provisions of the Seventh Council Directive 83/349/EEC of 13 June 1983 (where applicable as modified by Council Directive 86/635/EEC of 8 December 1986 or the Directive), or in a manner equivalent to consolidated accounts and consolidated annual reports so drawn up,

(c) that the consolidated accounts are audited by one or more persons authorised to audit accounts under the law under which that other parent undertaking which draws them up is established,

(d) that the exempted parent discloses in its individual accounts that it is exempt from the obligation to prepare and deliver group accounts,

(e) that the exempted parent states in its individual accounts the name of that other parent undertaking which draws up the group accounts referred to in subparagraph (d) and—

  (i) where that other undertaking is incorporated outside the State, the country in which it is incorporated, or

  (ii) where that other undertaking is unincorporated, the address of its principal place of business;

(f) that the exempted parent delivers to the registrar, within the period allowed for delivering its individual accounts, copies of that other parent's group accounts and, where appropriate, of the consolidated annual report, together with the auditors' report on them, and

(g) where any document comprised in accounts and reports delivered in accordance with paragraph (f) is in a language other than the English language or the Irish language, there is annexed to the copy of that document delivered a translation of it into the English language or the Irish language, certified in the prescribed manner to be a correct translation.

(3) The exemption under this Regulation does not apply to a parent undertaking any of whose securities are admitted to trading on a regulated market of any EEA State.

(4) The Minister may require that additional information shall be provided in the consolidated accounts of that other parent undertaking or of the individual accounts of the section 2 (3) parent referred to in paragraph (1).

(5) Shares held by directors of a company for the purpose of complying with any share qualification requirement are disregarded in determining for the purposes of paragraph 1(a) whether the company is a wholly-owned subsidiary.

(6) For the purpose of paragraph (1)(b), shares held by a wholly-owned subsidiary of that other parent undertaking, or held on behalf of that other parent undertaking or a wholly-owned subsidiary, are attributed to that other parent undertaking.

(7) In paragraph (3) 'securities' includes—

(a) shares and stock,

(b) debentures, including debenture stock, loan stock, bonds, certificates of deposit and other instruments creating or acknowledging indebtedness,

(c) warrants or other instruments entitling the holder to subscribe for securities falling within subparagraph (a) or (b), and

(d) certificates or other instruments which confer –

(i) property rights in respect of a security falling within subparagraph (a), (b) or (c),

(ii) any right to acquire, dispose of, underwrite or convert a security, being a right to which the holder would be entitled if the holder held any such security to which the certificate or other instrument relates, or

(iii) a contractual right (other than an option) to acquire any such security otherwise than by subscription.][a]

Amendments

a Reg 12A inserted by reg 11 and Sch 3, Item No 9 of EC(IFRSMA)R 2005.

13 Financial holding undertakings

(1) The obligation to prepare group accounts in accordance with Regulation 10 shall also apply to a parent undertaking, including a parent undertaking to whom Regulation 3 does not apply—

(a) which does not itself carry on any material business apart from the acquisition, management and disposal of interests in subsidiaries, and

(b) whose principal subsidiaries are wholly or mainly undertakings to which these Regulations apply.

(2) In paragraph (I), the management of interests in subsidiaries includes the provision of service to such subsidiaries and a parent undertaking's principal subsidiaries are those subsidiaries of the undertaking whose results or financial position would principally affect the figures shown in the group accounts.

14 Directors' Report

(1) In the case of a parent undertaking preparing group accounts in accordance with these Regulations, the report of the directors of that undertaking under section 158 of the Principal Act, shall contain, in addition to the information specified in that section, the following information:

[(a) a fair review of the development and performance of the undertaking's business and of its position and, in relation to its subsidiaries, if any, of the development and performance of their business and of their position, during the financial year ending with the relevant balance sheet date together with a description of the principal risks and uncertainties that they face, which review—

(i) shall be a balanced and comprehensive analysis of the development and performance of the undertaking's business and of its position and, in relation to its subsidiaries, if any, of the development and performance of their business and of their position, consistent with the size and complexity of the business;

(ii) to the extent necessary for an understanding of the undertaking's development, performance or position, and that of its subsidiaries, if any, shall include an analysis of financial, and, where appropriate, non-financial key performance indicators relevant to the particular business, including information relevant to environmental and employee matters, and, where appropriate, the report shall include additional explanations of amounts included in the annual accounts;][a]

(b) particulars of any important events affecting the parent undertaking or any of its subsidiary undertakings which have occurred since the end of that year;

(c) an indication of likely future developments in the business of the parent undertaking and its subsidiary undertakings, taken as a group;

(d) an indication of the activities, if any, of the parent undertaking and its subsidiary undertakings, taken as a group, in the field of research and development, and

(e) the number and nominal value of shares in the parent undertaking held by the undertaking itself, by its subsidiary undertakings or by a person acting in his or her own name but on behalf of the undertaking or subsidiary.

(2) The information required by subparagraph (1)(e) may be given in the notes to the group accounts.

(3) This report shall be annexed to the group's annual report.

Amendments

a Paragraph (a) of reg 14(1) substituted by reg 11 and Sch 3, Item No 10 of EC(IFRSMA)R 2005.

[14A Corporate Governance Statement

(1) Where a parent undertaking which has its securities admitted to trading on a regulated market is preparing group accounts the corporate governance statement included in the report by the directors of that undertaking under section 158 of the Principal Act, shall contain, in addition to the information specified in that section, a description of the main features of the internal control and risk management systems of that parent undertaking and its subsidiaries, taken as a whole, in relation to the process for preparing such group accounts for the parent undertaking and its subsidiaries taken as a whole.

(2) Where the consolidated annual report and the annual report are presented as a single report the description referred to in paragraph (1) shall be included in the section of the report by the directors referred to in paragraph (1) containing the corporate governance statement.

(3) Where a parent undertaking referred to in paragraph (1) produces a corporate governance statement in the form of a separate report published in conjunction with the annual report in accordance with section 158 of the Principal Act, the description required by paragraph (1) shall form part of that separate report.

(4) In paragraph (1), 'regulated market' has the meaning assigned to it by Directive 2004/39/EC.][a]

Amendments

a Regulation 14A inserted by European Communities (Directive 2006/46/EC) Regulations 2009, reg 22.

15 Non-application of Principal Act

[Sections 151, 152, 158 (4) and (5) and 191 of the Principal Act shall not apply to a company to which Regulation 10 applies.][a]

Amendments

a Words substituted by reg 11 and Sch 3, Item No 11 of EC(IFRSMA)R 2005.

16 Auditors' Report

[(1)][a] It shall be the duty of the auditors of a parent undertaking, in preparing the report on group accounts required by section 193 of the Act of 1990, to consider whether the information given in the report of the directors on the state of affairs of the parent undertaking and its subsidiary undertakings, as a group, relating to the financial year concerned is consistent with the group accounts for that year and the auditors shall state in their report whether, in their opinion, such information is consistent with those accounts.

[(2) Where a parent undertaking referred to in Regulation 14A produces a corporate governance statement in respect of a financial year in a separate report in accordance with Regulation 14A(3), the auditors of that parent undertaking, when preparing their report under section 193 of the Act of 1990 for that financial year, shall state in their report whether, in their opinion, the description, in the corporate governance statement, of the main features of the internal control and risk management systems referred to in Regulation 14A(1) is consistent with the group accounts for that financial year.][b]

Amendments

a Regulation 16 renumbered by European Communities (Directive 2006/46/EC) Regulations 2009, reg 23.

b Regulation 16(2) inserted by European Communities (Directive 2006/46/EC) Regulations 2009, reg 23 and substituted by EC(Dir)R 2010, reg 9.

17 Documents to be annexed to annual return of parent undertaking

(1) Subject to the provisions of these Regulations, copies of the following documents shall be documents to be annexed to the annual return of a parent undertaking:

(a) the group accounts, in respect of the period to which the return relates, drawn up by the parent undertaking in accordance with these Regulations;

(b) the report of the directors, in respect of the period to which the return relates, required by Regulation 14;

(c) the auditors' report, in respect of the period to which the return relates, referred to in Regulation 16;

and each such copy document shall be certified both by a director and the secretary of the parent undertaking to be a true copy of such accounts or reports, as the case may be.

(2) Where any document annexed to the annual return under this Regulation is in a language other than the English language or the Irish language, there shall be annexed to each such document a translation in the English language or the Irish language certified in the prescribed manner to be a correct translation.

18 Publication of accounts in full or abbreviated form

(1) Where a parent undertaking publishes its full group accounts, the auditors' report under Regulation 16 in respect of those accounts shall also be published by the parent undertaking.

(2) Where a parent undertaking publishes abbreviated group accounts relating to any financial year, it shall also publish a statement indicating—

(a) that the group accounts are not the group accounts, copies of which are required by these Regulations to be annexed to the annual return,

(b) whether the copies of the group accounts so required to be annexed have in fact been so annexed,

(c) whether the auditors of the parent undertaking have made a report under section 193 of the Act of 1990 in respect of the group accounts of the parent undertaking which relate to any financial year with which the abbreviated group accounts purport to deal,

[(d) whether any matters referred to in the auditors' report were qualified or unqualified, or whether the auditors' report included a reference to any matters to which the auditors drew attention by way of emphasis without qualifying the report.][a]

(3) Where a parent undertaking publishes abbreviated group accounts, it shall not publish with those accounts the report of the auditors mentioned in subparagraph (2)(c) of this Regulation.

(4) In this Regulation—

"abbreviated group accounts", in relation to a parent undertaking, means any group balance sheet or group profit and loss account, or summary or abstract of a group balance sheet or group profit and loss account, relating to a financial year of the parent undertaking which is published by the parent undertaking otherwise than as part of the full group accounts of the parent undertaking and its subsidiary undertakings for that financial year;

"full group accounts". in relation to a parent undertaking, means group accounts and the report of the directors of the parent undertaking referred to in Regulation 14:

"publish", in relation to a document, includes issue, circulate or otherwise make it available for public inspection in a manner calculated to invite the public generally, or any class of members of the public, to read the document, and cognate words shall be construed accordingly.

Amendments

a Paragraph 2(d) substituted by reg 11 and Sch 3, Item No 12 of EC(IFRSMA)R 2005.

19 Offences

(1) If an undertaking to which these Regulations apply fails after the making of these Regulations, to comply with a provision of these Regulations, the undertaking and every officer of the undertaking who is in default shall be guilty of an offence and shall be liable on summary conviction to a [class C fine][a].

(2) (a) If any person, being a director of an undertaking to which these Regulations apply, fails. after the making of these Regulations, to take all reasonable steps to secure compliance with a requirement of these Regulations. that person shall be guilty of an offence and shall be liable on summary conviction to imprisonment for a term not exceeding 12 months, or, at the discretion of the court, to a [class C fine][a] or to both.

(b) In any proceedings against a person for an offence under this paragraph, it shall be a defence for a director to prove that he or she had reasonable grounds to believe and did believe that a competent and reliable person was charged with the duty of ensuring that the provisions of these Regulations were complied with and that the latter person was in a position to discharge that duty, and a person shall not be liable to be sentenced to imprisonment for an offence under the said paragraph (2) unless, in the opinion of the court, the offence was committed wilfully.

(3) If after the making of these Regulations, any person in any balance sheet, profit and loss account, report, note or other document required by or for the purposes of any provision of these Regulations wilfully makes a statement false in any material particular, knowing it to be false, that person shall be guilty of an offence and shall be liable on summary conviction, to imprisonment for a term not exceeding 12 months or to a [class C fine][a] or to both.

(4) In this section "director" and "officer" includes any person in accordance with whose instructions or directions the directors of the undertaking are accustomed to act.

Amendments

a £1,000 increased to £1,500 by CA 1990, s 240(7) as inserted by CLEA 2001, s 104(c), and converted to €1,904.61 by Council Regulations (EC) No 1103/97, No 974/98 and No 2866/98 and the Economic and Monetary Union Act 1998, s 6; the above being implicitly substituted, by Fines Act 2010, s 6, for a fine not exceeding the aforesaid amount. A class C fine currently means a fine not exceeding €2,500.

20 Repeals and Amendments

(1) Section 7(4) of the Assurance Companies Act, 1909, (c. 49) and section 128(4)(b) of the Principal Act are hereby repealed.

(2) The Act of 1986 is hereby amended—

(a) in section (2) by the substitution of the following subsection for subsection (3):

"(3) Sections 3 to 6, 8, 12, 17, 18 and 24 of this Act do not apply in relation to undertakings to which the European Communities (Insurance Undertakings: Accounts) Regulations 1996 (No. 23 of 1996) apply by virtue of regulation 3 of those Regulations."

(b) In subsection (I) of section 7 by the insertion of the following subparagraph after subparagraph (ii) (inserted by the European Communities (Credit Institutions: Accounts) Regulations, 1992 (S.I. No. 294 of 1992)) of paragraph (a):

"(iii) in the case of an undertaking to which subsection (3) of section 2 of this Act applies, a copy of the balance sheet and profit and loss account of the undertaking drawn up in accordance with the European Communities (Insurance Undertakings: Accounts) Regulations, 1996."

SCHEDULE

FORM AND CONTENTS OF ACCOUNTS OF INSURANCE UNDERTAKINGS

PART I

THE REQUIRED FORMATS FOR ACCOUNTS

Chapters 1
General Rules

1. References in this Part of the Schedule to the items listed in the formats set out in this Part are references to those items read together with any notes following the formats which apply to any of those items.

2. (a) A number in brackets following any item in, or any heading to, the formats set out in this Part is a reference to the note of that number in the notes following the formats.

(b) In the notes following the formats the heading of each note gives the required heading or subheading for the item to which it applies and a reference to any letters and numbers assigned to that item in the formats set out in this Part.

3. (1) Items to which arabic numbers are assigned in the balance sheet format set out in Chapter 2 of this Part (except for items concerning technical provisions and the reinsurers' share of technical provisions), and items to which lower case letters are assigned in the profit and loss account format so set out (except for items I.1, I.4, II.1, II.5 and II.6) may be combined in an undertaking's accounts for any financial year in any case where—

(a) the individual amounts of such items are not material to assessing the state of affairs or profit and loss of the undertaking for the financial year concerned, or

(b) in any case where the combination of such items facilitates that assessment.

(2) Where items are combined in an undertaking's accounts pursuant to subparagraph (1), the individual amounts of any items so combined shall be disclosed in a note to the accounts.

4.(1) Funds of a group pension fund within the meaning of subparagraphs (c) and (d) of paragraph (2) of Article 1 of Council Directive 79/267/EEC of March 1979 which an insurance undertaking administers in its own name but on behalf of third parties shall be shown in the balance sheet if the undertaking acquires legal title to the assets concerned and the total amount of such assets and liabilities shall be shown separately or in the notes to the accounts, broken down according to the various assets and liabilities items.

(2) Assets acquired in the name of and on behalf of third parties shall not be shown in the balance sheet.

5. The provisions of this Schedule which relate to life assurance shall apply to health insurance written by undertakings which write only health insurance and which is transacted exclusively or principally according to the technical principles of life assurance.

6.[(1) The notes to the profit and loss account shall show—

- (a) dividends paid (other than dividends for which a liability existed at the immediately preceding balance sheet date) or which the company is liable to pay,
- (b) separately, any transfers between the profit and loss account and other reserves,
- (c) any increase or reduction in the balance on the profit and loss account since the immediately preceding financial year,
- (d) the profit or loss brought forward at the beginning of the financial year, and
- (e) the profit or loss carried forward at the end of the financial year.

(1A) There shall be shown in the notes to the accounts the aggregate amount of any dividends proposed before the date of approval of the accounts which have not been shown in the notes to the profit and loss account in accordance with subparagraph (1).][a]

(2) In the profit and loss account format set out below in Section B of Chapter 2 of this Part—

- (a) the heading "Technical account – non-life business" is for those classes of direct insurance which are within the scope of the European Communities (Non-Life Insurance) Regulations, 1976 (S.I. No. 115 of 1976), the European Communities (Non-Life Insurance) Framework Regulations, 1994 (S.I. No. 359 of 1994) and for the corresponding classes of reinsurance business. and
- (b) the heading Technical account— life assurance business is for those classes of direct insurance which are within the scope of the European Communities (Life Assurance) Regulations, 1984 (S.I. No. 57 of 1984), the European Communities (Life Assurance) Framework Regulations, 1994 (S.I. No. 360 of 1994) and for the corresponding classes of reinsurance business.

(3) Undertakings whose activities consist wholly of reinsurance or whose activities consist of direct non-life insurance and reinsurance may use the format "Technical account non life business" for all of their business.

Amendments

a Paragraph 6(1) substituted by reg 11 and Sch 3, Item No 13 of EC(IFRSMA)R 2005.

Chapter 2
Section A—The Balance Sheet

FORMAT

ASSETS

A. Called up share capital not paid (1)

B. Intangible assets (2)

I. Goodwill (3)

C. Investments

I. Land and buildings (4)

II. Investments in group undertakings and participating interests:

1. Shares in group undertakings
2. Debt securities issued by, and loans to group undertakings
3. Participating interests
4. Debt securities issued by, and loans to. undertakings in which the undertaking has a participating interest

III. Other financial investments:

1. Shares and other variable-yield securities and units in unit trusts
2. Debt securities and other fixed income securities (5)
3. Participation in investment pools (6)
4. Loans secured by mortgages (7)
5. Other loans (7)
6. Deposits with credit institutions (8)
7. Other (9)

IV. Deposits with ceding undertakings (10)

D. Investments for the benefit of life assurance policyholders who bear the investment risk (11)

Da.Reinsurers' share of technical provisions (12)

1. Provision for unearned premiums
2. Life assurance provision
3. Claims outstanding
4. Provision for bonuses and rebates (unless shown under (2).
5. Other technical provisions
6. Technical provisions for life-assurance policies where the investment risk is borne by the policyholders

E. Debtors (13)

I. Debtors arising out of direct insurance operations

1. Policyholders
2. Intermediaries

II. Debtors arising out of reinsurance operations

III. Other debtors

IV. Called up share capital not paid (1)

F. Other assets

I. Tangible assets and stocks

1. Plant and machinery
2. Fixtures, fittings, tools and equipment
3. Payments on account (other than deposits paid on land and buildings) and assets (other than buildings) in course of construction.
4. Raw materials and consumables
5. Work in progress
6. Finished goods and goods for resale

II. Cash at bank and in hand

III. Own shares (14)

IV. Other (15)

G. Prepayments and accrued income

I. Accrued interest and rent (16)

II. Deferred acquisition costs (17)

III. Other prepayments and accrued income

LIABILITIES

A. Capital and reserves

I. Called up share capital or equivalent funds (18)

II. Share premium account

III. Revaluation reserve

IV. Reserves (19)

1. The capital redemption reserve fund
2. Reserves for own shares
3. Reserves provided for by the articles of association
4. Other reserves

V. Profit or loss brought forward

VI. Profit or loss for the financial year

B. Subordinated liabilities (20)

Ba. Fund for future appropriations (21)

C. Technical provisions (22)

1. Provisions for unearned premiums: (23)

(a) gross amount ________

(b) reinsurance amount(-)(12) ________

____

2. Life assurance provision: (23) (25) (29)

(a) gross amount ________

(b) reinsurance amount(-)(12) ________

____

3. Claims outstanding: (26)

   (a) gross amount ______

   (b) reinsurance amount(-)(12) ______

   ______

4. Provision for bonuses and rebates: (27)

   (a) gross amount ______

   (b) reinsurance amount(-)(12) ______

   ______

5. Equalisation provision (28)

6. Other technical provisions: (24)

   (a) gross amount ______

   (b) reinsurance amount(-)(12) ______

   ______

D. Technical provisions for life assurance policies where the investment risk is borne by the policyholders (29)

   (a) gross amount ______

   (b) reinsurance amount(-)(12) ______

   ______

E. [Provisions for other risks][a]

1. Provisions for pensions and similar obligations
2. Provisions for taxation
3. Other provisions

F. Deposits received from reinsurers (30)

G. Creditors

I. Creditors arising out of direct insurance operations

II. Creditors arising out of reinsurance operations

III. Debenture loans

IV. Amounts owed to credit institutions

V. Other creditors including tax and social welfare

H. Accruals and deferred income

NOTES ON THE BALANCE SHEET FORMAT

(1) Called-up share capital not paid

(Assets items A and E.IV)

This item may be shown in either of the positions given in the format.

(2) Intangible assets

(Assets item B)

Amounts in respect of assets shall only be included in an undertaking's balance sheet under this item if either—

(a) the assets were acquired for valuable consideration and are not required to be shown under goodwill, or

(b) the assets in question were created by the undertaking itself.

Amendments

a Words substituted by reg 11 and Sch 3, Item No 12(b) of EC(IFRSMA)R 2005.

---

(3) Goodwill

(Assets item B.I)

Amounts representing goodwill shall only be included to the extent that the goodwill was acquired for valuable consideration.

(4) Land and buildings

(Assets item C.l)

The amount of any land and buildings occupied by the undertaking for its own activities shall be shown separately.

(5) Debt securities and other fixed income securities

(Assets item C.III.2)

This item shall comprise negotiable debt securities and other fixed income securities issued by credit institutions. other undertakings or public bodies, insofar as they are not covered by Assets item C.II.2 or C.II.4.

Securities bearing interest rates that vary in accordance with specific factors, for example the interest rate on the inter-bank market or on the Euro market, shall also be regarded as debt securities and other fixed income securities and so be included under this item.

(6) Participation in investment pools

(Assets item C.III.3)

This item shall comprise shares held by the undertaking in joint investments constituted by several undertakings or pension funds, the management of which has been entrusted to one of those undertakings or to one of those pension funds.

(7) Loans secured by mortgages and other loans

(Assets items C.III.4 and C.III.5)

Loans to policy holders for which the policy is the main security shall be included under "Other loans" and their amount shall be disclosed in the notes to the accounts. Loans guaranteed by mortgages shall be shown as such even where they are also secured by insurance policies. Where the amount of "Other loans" not secured by policies is material, an appropriate breakdown shall be given in the notes to the accounts.

(8) Deposits with credit institutions

(Assets item C.111.6)

This item shall comprise sums the withdrawal of which is subject to a time restriction. Sums deposited with no such restriction shall be shown under Assets item F.II even if they bear interest.

(9) Other

(Assets item C.III.7)

This item shall comprise those investments which are not covered by Assets items C.III.l to 6. Where the amount of such investments is significant, they shall be disclosed in the notes to the accounts.

(10) Deposits with ceding undertakings

(Assets item C.IV)

Where the undertaking accepts reinsurance this item shall comprise amounts, owed by the ceding undertakings and corresponding to guarantees, which are deposited with those ceding undertakings or with third parties or which are retained by those undertakings.

These amounts may not be combined with other amounts owed by the ceding insurer to the reinsurer or set off against amounts owed by the reinsurer to the ceding insurer.

Securities deposited with ceding undertakings or third parties which remain the property of the undertaking accepting reinsurance shall be entered in the undertaking's accounts as an investment, under the appropriate item.

(11) Investments for the benefit of life assurance policyholders who bear the investment risk

(Assets item D)

In respect of life assurance this item shall comprise, on the one hand, investments the value of which is used to determine the value of or the return on policies relating to an investment fund, and on the other hand, investments serving as cover for liabilities which are determined by reference to an index. This item shall also comprise investments which are held on behalf of the members of a tontine and are intended for distribution among them.

(12) Reinsurance amounts

(Assets item Da)

(Liabilities items C.1(b), 2(b), 3(b), 4(b) and 6(b) and D(b)).

The reinsurance amounts may be shown either under Assets item D(a) or under Liabilities items C.l(b), 2(b), 3(b), 4(b) and 6(b) and D(b).

The reinsurance amounts shall comprise the actual or estimated amounts which, under contractual reinsurance arrangements, are deducted from the gross amounts of technical provisions. Where reinsurance amounts are shown as assets under item Da, they shall be sub-divided as shown. Notwithstanding paragraph 3 of this Part, these items shall not be combined. The disclosure of reinsurance amounts shall be in the same form from one accounting year to the next. If the directors decide that a change is necessary, the reason for that change should be disclosed in the notes together with a statement of what the position would have been had the original treatment been retained.

As regards the provision for unearned premiums, the reinsurance amounts shall be calculated according to the methods referred to in paragraph 24 of Part II of this Schedule or in accordance with the terms of the reinsurance policy.

(13) Debtors

(Assets item E)

Amounts owed by group undertaking and undertakings in which the undertaking has a participating interest shall be shown separately as sub-items of Assets items E.I, E.II and E.III.

(14) Own Shares

(Assets item F.111)

The nominal value of the shares shall be shown separately under this item.

(15) Other

(Assets item F.IV)

This item shall comprise those assets which are not covered by Assets items F.I, II and III. Where such assets are material they shall be disclosed in the notes to the accounts.

(16) Accrued interest and rent

(Assets item G.I)

This item shall comprise those items that represent interest and rent that have been earned up to the balance-sheet date but have not yet become receivable.

(17) Deferred acquisition costs

(Assets item G.II)

The costs of acquiring insurance policies which are incurred during the financial year but which relate to a subsequent financial year (referred to as "deferred acquisition costs") shall be treated as follows:

(a) Costs incurred in respect of non-life shall be disclosed under this item and shall be calculated on a basis compatible with that used for unearned premiums:

(b) (i) Costs incurred in respect of life assurance business shall be deferred. Such deferral should be over such a period as is recognised to be prudent.

(ii) Costs incurred in respect of life assurance may be either disclosed under this item on the balance sheet or may be deducted by a recognised actuarial method from the mathematical reserves; where the latter method is used, the amounts deducted from the provisions shall be disclosed in the notes to the accounts.

(iii) The method of treatment of deferred acquisition costs in the accounts of a life assurance undertaking, should be the same from one financial year to the next. If, in the opinion of the directors of the undertaking, a change is necessary, the reasons for that change should be disclosed in the notes together with a statement of what the position would have been had the original method been retained.

(18) Called up capital or equivalent funds

(Liabilities item A.I)

This item shall comprise all amounts which are regarded, in accordance with the Companies Acts, 1963 to 1990, as equity capital subscribed and fully paid up or subscribed and partly paid up, to the extent paid up.

(19) Reserves

(Liabilities item A. IV)

Reserves shall be shown separately, as sub items of liabilities item A.IV in the balance sheet except for the revaluation reserve, which shall be shown as a liability under A.III.

Should it be considered necessary, the [Bank][a] may, in the future under this item, require other types of reserves for insurance undertakings not covered by Council Directive No. 78/660/EEC.

Amendments

a 'Bank' substituted for 'Minister' by CBFSAIA 2003, s 35 and Sch 2, Pt 16. Item 4.

---

(20) Subordinated liabilities

(Liabilities item B)

This item shall comprise all liabilities, whether or not represented by certificates, in respect of which there is a contractual obligation that, in the event of winding up or of bankruptcy, they are to be repaid only after the claims of all other creditors have been met.

(21) Fund for future appropriations

(Liabilities item Ba)

This item shall comprise all funds the allocation of which either to policy holders or to shareholders has not been determined by the end of the financial year.

Transfers to and from this item shall be shown in item II.12a (Transfers to or from the fund for future appropriation) in the profit and loss account.

(22) Technical provisions

(Liabilities item C)

Regulation 7(c)(ii) shall apply to the technical provisions, subject to Note (12) and Notes (23) to (28).

(23) Provision for unearned premiums

(Liabilities items C.1 and C.2)

In the case of life assurance the provision for unearned premiums may be included in Liabilities item C.2 rather than in this item.

The provision for unearned premiums shall comprise the amount representing that part of gross premiums written which is estimated to be earned in the following financial year or in subsequent financial years.

Where, in accordance with Note (24) this item also includes the amount of the provision for unexpired risks, the description of the item shall be "Provision for unearned premiums and unexpired risks".

(24) Other technical provisions

(Liabilities item C.6)

This item shall include the provision for unexpired risks. being the amount set aside in addition to unearned premiums in respect of risks to be borne by the insurance undertaking after the end of the financial year, in order to provide for all claims and expenses in connection with insurance contracts in force in excess of the related unearned premiums and any premiums receivable on those contracts. However, the provision for unexpired risks may be added to the provision for unearned premiums under item C.l. Where the amount of unexpired risks is material, it shall be disclosed separately in the notes to the accounts.

Ageing reserves should be disclosed under this item.

(25) Life assurance provision

(Liabilities item C.2)

This item shall comprise the actuarially estimated value of the undertaking's liabilities including bonuses already declared and after deducting the actuarial value of future premiums, excluding amounts covered by Note 29.

(26) Claims outstanding

(Liabilities item C.3)

This item shall comprise the total estimated ultimate cost to the undertaking of settling all claims arising from events which have occurred up to the end of the financial year, whether reported or not, less amounts already paid in respect of such claims.

(27) Provision for bonuses and rebates

(Liabilities item C.4)

This item shall comprise amounts intended for policy holders or contract beneficiaries by way of bonuses and rebates as defined in Note (5) on the profit and loss account format to the extent that such amounts have not been credited to policy holders or contract beneficiaries or included in Liabilities item Ba or in Liabilities item C.2.

(28) Equalisation provision

(Liabilities item C.5)

This item shall comprise any amounts required by law to be set aside by an undertaking to equalise fluctuations in loss ratios in future years or to provide for special risks.

An undertaking which otherwise constitutes reserves, falling to be included under liabilities item A.IV to equalise fluctuations in loss ratios in future years or to provide for special risks shall disclose that fact in the notes to the accounts.

(29) Technical provisions for life assurance policies where the investment risk is borne by the policyholders

(Liabilities items D and C.2)

This item shall comprise technical provisions constituted to cover liabilities relating to investment in the context of the assurance policies for which the policy holder bears the risk, the value of or the return on which is determined by reference to investments or by reference to an index.

Any additional technical provisions constituted to cover death risks, operating expenses or other risks (such as benefits payable at the maturity date or guaranteed surrender values) shall be included under Liabilities item C.2.

This item shall also comprise technical provisions representing the obligations of a tontine's organiser in relation to its members.

(30) Deposits received from reinsurers

(Liabilities item F)

Where the undertaking cedes reinsurance this item shall comprise amounts deposited by or withheld from other insurance undertakings under re insurance contracts. These amounts may not be merged with other amounts owed to or by those other undertakings.

Where the undertaking cedes reinsurance and has received as a deposit securities which have been transferred to its ownership, this item shall comprise the amount owed by the undertaking by virtue of the deposit.

Section B—The Profit and Loss Account

FORMAT

I. TECHNICAL ACCOUNT— NON-LIFE INSURANCE

1. Earned premiums, net of reinsurance:

(a) gross premiums written (1) ____

(b) outward reinsurance premiums (-)(2) ____ ____

(c) change in the gross provision for unearned premiums and in the gross provision for unexpired risks (+/-)(3) ____

(d) change in the provision for unearned premiums, reinsurers' share (+/-)(3) ____ ____ ____

2. Allocated investment return transferred from the non-technical account (Item III.6)(8)(9)

(a) allocated by class of business

accident and health ____

motor ____

marine, aviation and transport ____

fire and other damage to property ____

liability business ____

miscellaneous pecuniary loss ____

(b) total:

3. Other technical income, net of reinsurance

4. Claims incurred, net of reinsurance: (4)

(a) claims paid

(aa) gross amount ____

(bb) reinsurers' share(-) ______ ______

(b) change in the provision for claims

(aa) gross amount ______

(bb) reinsurers' share(-) ______ ______

5. Changes in other technical provisions, net of reinsurance, not shown under other headings (+/-).

6. Bonuses and rebates, net of reinsurance (5)

7. Net operating expenses:

(a) acquisition costs (6)

(b) change in deferred acquisition costs (+/-)

(c) administrative expenses (7)

(d) reinsurance commissions and profit participation (+/-)

7a Investment charges (8)

(a) By class of business:

accident and health ______

motor ______

marine, aviation and transport ______

fire and other damage to property ______

liability business ______

miscellaneous pecuniary loss ______

(aa) investment management expenses, including interest ______

(bb) value adjustments in investments ______

(cc) Losses on the realisation of investments ______

(b) total:

8. Other technical charges, net of reinsurance

9. Change in the equalisation provisions (+/-)

10. Sub-total (balance on the technical account for non-life insurance business (item III.1)

II. TECHNICAL ACCOUNT – LIFE ASSURANCE BUSINESS

1. Earned premiums, net of reinsurance:

(a) gross premiums written (1) ______

(b) outward reinsurance premiums (-)(2) ______ ______

(c) change in the provision for unearned premiums, net of reinsurance (+/-)(3) ______ ______

2. Investment income: (8) (9)

(a) income from participating interests, with a separate indication of that derived from group undertakings ______

(b) income from other investments, with a separate indication of that derived from group undertakings ______

(aa) income from land and buildings ______

(bb) income from other investments

(c) value readjustments on investments

(d) gains on the realisation of investments

3. Unrealised gains on investments (10)

4. Other technical income, net of reinsurance

5. Claims incurred, net of reinsurance: (4)

(a) claims paid

(aa) gross amount

(bb) reinsurers' share (-)

(b) change in the provision for claims

(aa) gross amount

(bb) reinsurers' share (-)

6. Changes in other technical provisions, net of reinsurance, not shown under other headings (+/-):

(a) Life assurance provision, net of reinsurance (3)

(aa) gross amount

(bb) reinsurers' share (-)

(b) Other technical provisions, net of reinsurance

7. Bonuses and rebates, net of reinsurance (5)

8. Net operating expenses:

(a) acquisition costs (6)

(b) change in deferred acquisition costs

(c) administrative expenses (7)

(d) reinsurance commissions and profit participation

9. Investment expenses and charges: (8)

(a) investment management expenses, including interest

(b) value adjustments on investments

(c) losses on the realisation of investments

10. Unrealised losses on investments (10)

11. Other technical charges, net of reinsurance

11a. Tax attributable to the life assurance business

12. Allocated investment return transferred to the non-technical account (-) (item III.4) (9)

12a. Transfers to or from the fund for future appropriations

13. Sub-total (balance on the technical account—life assurance business) (item III.2)

III. NON-TECHNICAL ACCOUNT

1. Balance on the technical account – non-life insurance business (item I.10)

2. Balance on the technical account – life assurance business (item II.13)

3. Investment income (8)

    (a) income from participating interests with a separate indication of that derived from group undertakings ______

    (b) income from other investments, with a separate indication of that derived from group undertakings ______

        (aa) income from land and buildings ______

        (bb) income from other investments ______

    (c) value readjustments on investments

    (d) gains on the realisation of investments

3a. Unrealised gains on investments (10)

4. Allocated investment return transferred from the life assurance technical account (item II.12) (9)

5. Investment charges: (8)

    (a) investment management expenses, including interest

    (b) value adjustments on investments

    (c) losses on the realisation of investments

5a. Unrealised losses on investments (10)

6. Allocated investment return transferred to the non-life insurance technical account (item I.2) (9).

7. Other income

8. Other charges, including value adjustments

9. Tax on profit or loss on ordinary activities

10. Profit or loss on ordinary activities after tax

11. Extraordinary income

12. Extraordinary charges

13. Extraordinary profit or loss

14. Tax on extraordinary profit or loss

15. Other taxes not shown under the preceding items

16. Profit or loss for the financial year

NOTES ON THE PROFIT AND LOSS ACCOUNT FORMAT

(1) Gross premiums written

(Non-life insurance technical account: item I.l.(a)).

(Life assurance technical account: item II.l.(a)).

This item shall comprise all amounts due during the financial year in respect of insurance contracts entered into regardless of the fact that such amounts may relate in whole or in part to a later financial year, and shall include *inter alia*:

(a) premiums yet to be written, where the premium calculation can be done only at the end of the year;

(b) single premiums including annuity premiums and, in life assurance business, single premiums resulting from bonus and rebate provisions insofar as they shall be considered as premium under the terms of the contract;

(c) additional premiums in the case of half-yearly, quarterly or monthly payments and additional payments from policyholders for expenses borne by the undertaking;

(d) in the case of co-insurance, the undertaking's portion of total premiums;

(e) reinsurance premiums due from ceding and retroceding insurance undertakings, including portfolio entries, after deduction of—

   (i) portfolio withdrawals credited to ceding and retroceding insurance undertakings, and

   (ii) cancellations.

The amounts to which this note relates shall not include the amounts of taxes or duties levied with premiums.

(2) Outward reinsurance premiums

(Non-life insurance technical account: item I.1.(b))

(Life assurance technical account: item II.1.(b))

This item shall comprise all premiums paid or payable in respect of outward reinsurance contracts entered into by the undertaking. Portfolio entries payable on the conclusion or amendment of outward reinsurance contracts shall be added; portfolio withdrawals receivable shall be deducted.

(3) Change in the provision for unearned premiums, net of reinsurance

(Non-life insurance technical account: items I.1.(c) and I.1.(d))

(Life assurance technical account: items II.l.(c) and II.6.(a))

In the case of life assurance, the change in unearned premiums may be included either in item II.l(c) or in item II.6.(a) of the life assurance technical account.

(4) Claims incurred, net of reinsurance

(Non-life insurance technical account: item I.4)

(Life assurance technical account: item II.5)

This item shall comprise all payments made in respect of the financial year including the provision for claims but excluding the provision for claims for the preceding financial year.

These amounts shall include annuities, surrenders, entries and withdrawals of loss provisions to and from ceding insurance undertakings and reinsurers, external and internal claims management costs and charges for claims incurred but not reported such as are referred to in paragraphs 27(3) and 29 of Part II (Valuation Rules) of this Schedule.

Sums recoverable on the basis of subrogation and salvage within the meaning of subparagraph (7) of the said paragraph 27 shall be deducted.

Where the difference between:

(a) the loss provision made at the beginning of the year for outstanding claims incurred in previous years, and

(b) the payments made during the year on account of claims incurred in previous years and the loss provision shown at the end of the year for such outstanding claims,

is material it shall be shown in the notes to the accounts, broken down by category and amount.

(5) Bonuses and rebates, net of reinsurance

(Non-life insurance technical account: item I.6)

(Life assurance technical account: item II.7)

Bonuses shall comprise all amounts chargeable for the financial year which are paid or payable to policyholders and other insured parties or provided for their benefit, including amounts used to increase technical provisions or applied to the reduction of future premiums, to the extent that such amounts represent an allocation of surplus or profit arising on business as a whole or a section of business, after deduction of amounts provided in previous years which are no longer required.

Rebates shall comprise such amounts to the extent that they represent a partial refund of premiums resulting from the experience of individual contracts.

Where material, the amount charged for bonuses and that charged for rebates shall be disclosed separately in the notes to the accounts.

(6) Acquisition costs

(Non-life insurance technical account: item I.7.(a))

(Life assurance technical account: item II.8.(a))

This item shall comprise the costs arising from the conclusion of insurance contracts. They shall cover both direct costs, such as acquisition commissions or the cost of drawing up the insurance document or including the insurance contract in the portfolio, and indirect costs, such as advertising costs or the administrative expenses connected with the processing of proposals and the issuing of policies.

In the case of life assurance. policy renewal commissions shall be included under item II.8.(c) in the life assurance technical account.

(7) Administrative expenses

(Non-life insurance technical account: item 1.7.(c))

(Life assurance technical account: item 11.8.(c))

This item shall include the costs arising from premium collection, portfolio administration, handling of bonuses and rebates, and inward and outward reinsurance.

They shall, in particular. include staff costs and depreciation provisions in respect of office furniture and equipment insofar as these need not be shown under acquisition costs, claims incurred or investment charges.

Item 11.8.(c) shall also include policy renewal commissions in respect of life assurance.

(8) Investment income and charges

(Non-life insurance technical account: items 1.2 and 7a)

(Life assurance technical account: items II.2 and II.9)

(Non-technical account: items III.3 and III.5)

(a) Investment income and charges relating to non-life insurance shall be disclosed in the non-technical account. Investment income and those charges attributable to the non-life technical account shall be allocated to that account by class of business, grouped as in the Revenue Account of the annual returns submitted in accordance with the European Communities (Non-life Insurance Accounts) Regulations, 1977 (S.I. No. 401 of 1977). The proportion of this and the basis on which they have been allocated as between the various classes shall be disclosed in the notes to the accounts.

(b) Investment income and charges relating to life assurance shall be disclosed in the life assurance technical account.

(c) In the case of an undertaking carrying on both life assurance and non-life insurance business, investment income and charges shall, to the extent that they are directly connected with the carrying on of the life assurance business be disclosed in the life assurance technical account.

(9) Allocated investment return

(Non-life insurance technical account: item I.2)

(Life assurance technical account: item II.2)

(Non-technical account: items III.4 and III.6)

Where part of the investment return is transferred to the non-life insurance technical account, the transfer from the non-technical account shall be deducted from item III.6 and added to item I.2.

Part of the investment return disclosed in the life assurance technical account may (to the extent that it is not attributable in the life assurance fund) be transferred to the non-technical account. The amount transferred shall be deducted from item II.12 and added to item III.4.

In the case of non-life insurance, allocated return may be transferred from one part of the profit and loss account to another in accordance with best accounting practices. The amount and reasons for such transfers and the bases on which they are made shall be disclosed in the notes to the accounts.

(10) Unrealised gains and losses on investments

(Life assurance technical account: items II.3 and II.10)

(Non-technical account: items III.3a and III.5a)

Variations between the valuation of investments at their current value or by means of one of the methods referred to in paragraph 19 of the Schedule to the Act of 1986 and their valuation at purchase price shall be treated as follows:

(a) where they relate to investments shown as assets under D of the balance sheet format they shall be fully disclosed in items II.3 and II.10 in the profit and loss account.

(b) in life assurance business those which do not fall under paragraph *(a)* of this note may be disclosed in full or in part in items II.3 and II.10 in the profit and loss account.

(c) in non-life insurance business they may be disclosed in full or in part in items III.3a and III.5a in the profit and loss account.

In the case of both paragraphs (b) and (c) of this note, where a partial disclosure is made, that shall be disclosed in the notes to the accounts, together with the full amount of the unrealised gains or losses, as the case may be, and the reasons for which the partial disclosure was made.

PART II

VALUATION RULES

Chapter 1

Historical Cost Accounting Rules

PRELIMINARY

1. Subject to paragraphs 12 to 21 of this Part, the amounts to be included in respect of all items shown in an undertaking's [Companies Act individual accounts][a] shall be determined in accordance with the rules set out in paragraphs 2 to 11 of this Part of the Schedule.

Amendments

a Words substituted by reg 11 and Sch 3, Item No 13 of EC(IFRSMA)R 2005.

General rules

2.(1) Subject to any provision for depreciation or diminution in value made in accordance with paragraph 3 the amount to be included in respect of any asset shall be its purchase price or production cost.

(2) Where investments are shown as provided in subparagraph (1), their current value shall be disclosed on the balance sheet or in the notes to the accounts.

3.(1) In the case of any asset included under Assets item B, (intangible assets), C.l (investments: land and buildings) or Fl (tangible assets and stocks) in the balance sheet format (set out in Chapter 2 of Part I of this Schedule) which has a limited useful economic life, the amount of—

(a) its purchase price or production cost, or

(b) where it is estimated that any such asset will have a residual value at the end of the period of its useful economic life, its cost less that estimated residual value,

shall be reduced by provisions for depreciation calculated to write off that amount systematically over the period of the asset's useful economic life.

(2) Where an asset falling to be included under Assets item C.II, C.III, C.IV or F.III in the balance sheet format (set out in Chapter 2 of Part I of this Schedule) has diminished in value, provisions for diminution in value may be made in respect of it and the amount to be included in respect of it may be reduced accordingly, and any such provisions which are not shown separately in the profit and loss account shall be disclosed (either separately or in aggregate) in a note to the accounts.

(3) Provisions for diminution in value shall be made in respect of any asset to which this paragraph applies which has diminished in value if the reduction of its value is expected to be permanent (whether its useful economic life is limited or not), and the amount to be included in respect of it shall be reduced accordingly; and any such provisions which are not shown separately in the profit and loss account shall be disclosed (either separately or in aggregate) in a note to the accounts.

(4) Where the reasons for which any provision was made in accordance with subparagraph (2) or (3) have ceased to apply to any extent, that provision shall be written back to the extent that it is no longer necessary, and any amounts written back in accordance with this subparagraph which are not shown separately in the profit and loss account shall be disclosed (either separately or in aggregate) in a note to the accounts.

Goodwill

4. (1) The application of paragraphs 1 to 3 in relation to goodwill (in any case where goodwill is treated as an asset) is subject to the following provisions of this paragraph.

(2) Subject to subparagraph (3), the amount of the consideration for any goodwill acquired by an undertaking shall be reduced by provisions for depreciation calculated to write off that amount systematically over a period chosen by the directors of the undertaking.

(3) The period chosen shall not exceed the useful economic life of the goodwill in question.

(4) In any case where any goodwill acquired by an undertaking is included as an asset in the undertaking's balance sheet the period chosen for writing off the consideration for that goodwill and the reasons for choosing that period shall be disclosed in a note to the accounts.

5.(1) This paragraph applies to assets included under Assets items E.I, E.II and E.III (debtors) and F.II (cash at bank and in hand) in the balance sheet.

(2) If the net realisable value of any asset referred to in subparagraph (1) is lower than its cost the amount to be included in respect of that asset shall be the net realisable value.

(3) Where the reasons for which any provision for diminution in value was made in accordance with subparagraph (2) have ceased to apply to any extent, that provision shall be written back to the extent that it is no longer necessary.

MISCELLANEOUS AND SUPPLEMENTARY PROVISIONS

Excess of money owed over value received as an asset item

6. (1) Where the amount repayable on any debt owed by an undertaking is greater than the value of the consideration received in the transaction giving rise to the debt, the amount of the difference may be treated as an asset.

(2) Where any such amount is treated as an asset, then—

- (a) it shall be written off by reasonable amounts each year and shall be completely written off before repayment of the debt, and
- (b) if the current amount is not shown as a separate item in the undertaking's balance sheet it shall be disclosed in a note to the accounts.

Determination of cost

7. The cost of an asset that has been acquired by the undertaking shall be determined by adding to the actual price paid any expenses incidental to its acquisition.

8. (1) The cost of an asset constructed by the undertaking shall be determined by adding to the purchase price of the raw materials and consumables used the amount of the costs incurred by the undertaking which are directly attributable to the construction of that asset.

(2) In addition, there may be included in the cost of an asset constructed by the undertaking—

- (a) a reasonable proportion of the costs incurred by the undertaking which are only indirectly attributable to the construction of that asset, but only to the extent that they relate to the period of construction; and
- (b) interest on capital borrowed to finance the construction of that asset, to the extent that it accrues in respect of the period of construction;

provided that, in a case to which subparagraph (h) relates, the inclusion of the interest in determining the cost of that asset and the amount of the interest so included is disclosed in a note to the accounts.

9.(1) Subject to the qualification mentioned in this subparagraph, the cost of any assets which are fungible assets as defined in paragraph 15(6) of the Schedule to the Act of 1986 may be determined by the application of any of the methods mentioned in subparagraph (2) in relation to any such assets of the same class and the method chosen shall be one which appears to the directors to be appropriate in the circumstances of the undertaking.

(2) The methods to which subparagraph (1) relates are the following:

- (a) the method known as "first in, first out" (FIFO);
- (b) a weighted average price;
- (c) any other method similar to either of the other methods mentioned in this subparagraph.

(3) Where in the case of any undertaking:

- (a) the cost of assets falling to be included under any item shown in the undertaking's balance sheet has been determined by the application of any method permitted by this paragraph, and

(b) the amount shown in respect of that item differs materially from the relevant alternative amount given below in this paragraph,

the amount of that difference shall be disclosed in a note to the accounts.

(4) Subject to subparagraph (5), for the purposes of subparagraph (3)(b), the relevant alternative amount, in relation to any item shown in an undertaking's balance sheet, is the amount which would have been shown in respect of that item if assets of any class included under that item at an amount determined by any method permitted by this paragraph had instead been included at their replacement cost as at the balance sheet date.

(5) The relevant alternative amount may be determined by reference to the most recent actual purchase price before the balance sheet date of assets of any class included under the item in question instead of by reference to their replacement cost as at that date, but only if the former appears to the directors of the undertaking to constitute the more appropriate standard of comparison in the case of assets of that class.

Substitution of original amount where price or cost unknown

10. Where there is no record of the purchase price of any asset acquired by an undertaking or of any price, expenses or costs relevant for determining its cost in accordance with paragraph 9, or any such record cannot be obtained without unreasonable expenses or delay, its cost shall be taken for the purposes of paragraphs 2 to 7 to be the value ascribed to it in the earliest available record of its value made on or after its acquisition by the undertaking.

11.(1) Subject to subparagraph (2), assets which fall to be included under Assets item FI (tangible assets and stocks) in the balance sheet format (set out in Chapter 2 of Part I of this Schedule) may be included at a fixed quantity and value.

(2) Subparagraph (1) applies to assets of a kind which are constantly being replaced, where—

(a) their overall value is not material to assessing the undertaking's state of affairs; and

(b) their quantity, value and composition are not subject to material variation.

Chapter 2
Current Value Accounting Rules

PRELIMINARY

12. (1) The rules set out in paragraphs 2 to 11 are referred to subsequently in this Schedule as "the historical cost accounting rules".

(2) Paragraphs 2, 3, 4 and 5 are referred to in this Chapter as "the depreciation rules" and references subsequently in this Schedule to the historical cost accounting rules do not include the depreciation rules as they apply by virtue of paragraph 19.

13. Subject to paragraphs 19 to 21, the amounts to be included in respect of assets of any description mentioned in paragraph 14 may be determined on any basis so mentioned.

Current value accounting rates

14. (1) Investments falling to be included under Assets item C (investments) may be included at their current value calculated in accordance with paragraphs 17 and 18.

(2) Investments falling to be included under Assets item D (unit-linked investments) shall be shown at their current value.

15. (1) Intangible assets, other than goodwill, and assets falling to be included under Assets item F.II (cash at bank and in hand), F.III (own shares) and F.IV (other) may be included at their current cost.

(2) Assets falling to be included under Assets item F.I (tangible assets and stocks) in the balance sheet format (set out in Chapter 2 of Part I of this Schedule) may be included at a market value determined as at the date of their last valuation or at their current cost.

16. The same valuation method shall be applied to all investments included in any item denoted by an arabic number or shown as assets under Assets item C.I.

Valuation of investments

17. (1) Subject to subparagraph (5) in the case of investments other than land and buildings, current value shall mean market value determined in accordance with this paragraph.

(2) Where investments are officially listed on an official stock exchange, market value shall mean the value on the balance sheet date or, when the balance sheet date is not a stock exchange trading day, on the last stock exchange trading day before that date.

(3) Where a market exists for unlisted investments, market value shall mean the average price at which such investments were traded on the balance sheet date or, when the balance sheet date is not a trading day, on the last trading day before that date.

(4) Where on the date on which the accounts are drawn up listed or unlisted investments have been sold or are to be sold within the short term, the market value shall be reduced by the actual or estimated realisation costs.

(5) Except where the equity method is applied all investments other than those referred to in subparagraphs (2) and (3) shall be valued on a basis which has prudent regard to the likely realisable value.

(6) In all cases the method of valuation shall be precisely described and the reason for adopting it disclosed in the notes to the accounts.

18.(1) In the case of land and buildings, current value shall mean the market value on the date of valuation, where relevant, reduced as provided in subparagraphs (4) and (5).

(2) Market value shall mean the price at which land and buildings could be sold under private contract between a willing seller and an arm's length buyer on the date of valuation, it being assumed that the property is publicly exposed to the market, that market conditions permit orderly disposal and that a normal period, having regard to the nature of the property, is available for the negotiation of the sale.

(3) The market value shall be determined through the separate valuation of each land and buildings item, carried out at least every five years in accordance with generally accepted methods of valuation.

(4) Where the value of any land and buildings item has diminished since the preceding valuation under subparagraph (3), an appropriate value adjustment shall be made and the lower value arrived at shall not be increased in subsequent balance sheets unless such increase results from a new determination of market value arrived at in accordance with subparagraphs (2) and (3).

(5) Where on the date on which the accounts are drawn up and buildings have been sold or are to be sold within the short term, the value arrived at in accordance with subparagraphs (2) and (4) shall be reduced by the actual or estimated realisation costs.

(6) Where it is impossible to determine the market value of a land and buildings item, the value arrived at on the basis of the principle of purchase price or production cost shall be deemed to be its current value.

(7) The method by which the current value of land and buildings has been arrived at and their breakdown by financial year of valuation shall be disclosed in the notes to the accounts.

Application of the depreciation rules

19.(1) Where the value of any asset of an undertaking is determined in accordance with paragraph 14 (in the case of assets falling to be included under assets item C.I) or paragraph 15, that value shall be, or (as the case may require) be the starting point for determining, the amount to be included in respect of that asset in the undertaking's accounts, instead of its cost or any value previously so determined for that asset; and the depreciation rules shall apply accordingly in relation to any such asset with the substitution for any reference to its cost of a reference to the value most recently determined for that asset in accordance with paragraph 14 or 15 (as the case may be).

(2) The amount of any provision for depreciation required in the case of any asset by paragraph 3 as it applies by virtue of subparagraph (1) is referred to below in this paragraph as the "adjusted amount", and the amount of any provision which would be required by that paragraph in the case of that asset according to the historical cost accounting rules is referred to as the "historical cost amount".

(3) Where subparagraph (1) applies in the case of any asset the amount of any provision for depreciation in respect of that asset included in any item shown in the profit and loss account in respect of amounts written off assets of the description in question may be the historical cost amount instead of the adjusted amount, provided that the amount of any difference between the two is shown separately in the profit and loss account or in a note to the accounts.

Additional Information to be provided

20.(1) This paragraph applies where the amounts to be included in respect of assets covered by any items shown in an undertaking's accounts have been determined in accordance with paragraph 14 or 15.

(2) The items affected and the basis of valuation adopted in determining the amounts of the assets in question in the case of each such item shall be disclosed in a note to the accounts.

(3) The purchase price of investments valued in accordance with paragraph 14 shall be disclosed in the notes to the accounts.

(4) In the case of each balance sheet item valued in accordance with paragraph 15 either—

(a) the comparable amounts determined according to the historical cost accounting rules, or

(b) the differences between those amounts and the corresponding amounts actually shown in the balance sheet in respect of that item,

shall be shown separately in the balance sheet or in a note to the accounts.

(5) In subparagraph (4) references. in relation to any item to the comparable amounts determined as there mentioned are references to—

(a) the aggregate amount which would be required to be shown in respect of that item if the amounts to be included in respect of all the assets covered by that item were determined according to the historical cost accounting rules, and

(b) the aggregate amount of the cumulative provisions for depreciation or diminution in value which would be permitted or required in determining those amounts according to those rules.

21.(1) With respect to any determination of the value of an asset of an undertaking in accordance with paragraph 14, the amount of any profit or loss arising from that determination (after allowing, where appropriate, for any provisions for depreciation or diminution in value made otherwise than by reference to the value so determined and any adjustments of any such provisions made in the light of that determination) shall be credited or (as the case may be) debited to a separate reserve (referred to in this paragraph as "the revaluation reserve"), except insofar as it has already been recognised in the life assurance technical account or the non-technical account in accordance with note 10 to the profit and loss account.

(2) The amount of the revaluation reserve shall be shown in the undertaking's balance sheet under Liabilities item A.III in the balance sheet format (set out in Chapter 2 of Part I of this Schedule).

(3) An amount may be transferred from the revaluation reserve to the profit and loss account—

(a) if the amount was previously charged to that account or represents realised profit, or

(b) on capitalisation,

and the revaluation reserve shall be reduced to the extent that the amounts transferred to it are no longer necessary for the purpose of the valuation method used.

(4) The revaluation reserve shall not be reduced except as mentioned in this paragraph.

(5) The treatment for taxation purposes of amounts credited or debited to the revaluation reserve shall be disclosed in a note to the accounts.

(6) In subparagraph (3)(b), capitalisation, in relation to an amount standing to the credit of the revaluation reserve, means applying it in wholly or partly paying up unissued shares in the undertaking to be allotted to members of the undertaking as fully or partly paid shares.

Chapter 3
General Rules

22.(1) This paragraph applies to debt securities and other fixed income securities shown as assets under C.II and C.III of the balance sheet format (set out in Chapter 2 of Part I of this Schedule) which have not been valued at market value.

(2) The amount included in the balance sheet in respect of these assets shall be their purchase price.

(3) Where the purchase price of these assets exceeds the amount repayable at maturity, the amount of the difference shall be charged to the profit and loss account or reduced each financial year on a systematic basis, in accordance with best accounting practice, so that it is completely written off when the securities are repaid. That difference shall be shown separately in the balance sheet or in the notes to the accounts.

(4) Where the purchase price of those assets is less than the amount repayable at maturity, the amount of the difference may be released to income in instalments over the period remaining until repayment. That difference shall be shown separately in the balance sheet or in the notes to the accounts.

Technical Provisions

23. The amount of technical provisions shall at all times be sufficient to cover any liabilities arising out of insurance contracts as far as can reasonably be foreseen.

Provision for unearned premiums

24.(1) Subject to subparagraph (2), the provision for unearned premiums shall be computed separately for each insurance contract.

(2) Notwithstanding subparagraph (1) statistical methods, in particular proportional and flat rate methods, may be used where they may be expected to give approximately the same results as would be obtained if individual calculations were made under subparagraph (1).

(3) In classes of insurance where the pattern of risk varies over the life of a contract, this shall be taken into account in the calculation methods.

Provision for unexpired risks

25. (1) The provision for unexpired risks shall be computed on the basis of claims and administrative expenses likely to arise after the end of the financial year from contracts concluded before that date, insofar as their estimated value exceeds the provision for unearned premiums and any premiums receivable under those contracts.

(2) In this paragraph, "unexpired risks" has the same meaning as it has in note 24 on the balance sheet format which is set out in Chapter 2 of Part I of this Schedule.

Life assurance

26.(1) Subject to subparagraph (2), the life assurance provision shall be computed separately for each life assurance contract.

(2) Notwithstanding subparagraph (1), statistical or mathematical methods may be used where they may be expected to give approximately the same results as would be obtained if individual calculations were made under subparagraph (1).

(3) A summary of the principal assumptions in making the provision under subparagraph (1) or (2) shall be given in the notes to the accounts.

(4) The computation shall be made on the basis of recognised actuarial methods annually by a Fellow Member of the Society of Actuaries in Ireland, with due regard to the actuarial principles laid down in Council Directive 92/96/EEC.

PROVISIONS FOR CLAIMS OUTSTANDING

Non-life insurance

27. (1) Subject to subparagraph (2). a provision for claims outstanding shall be computed separately for each case on the basis of the costs still expected to arise.

(2) Notwithstanding subparagraph (1), statistical methods may be used if they result in an adequate provision for claims outstanding having regard to the nature of the risks.

(3) A provision for claims outstanding shall also allow for claims incurred but not reported by the balance sheet date, the amount of the allowance being determined having regard to past experience as to the number and magnitude of claims reported after previous balance sheet dates.

(4) All claims settlement costs shall be included in the calculation of the provision for claims outstanding, irrespective of their origin.

(5) Recoverable amounts arising out of subrogation or salvage shall be estimated on a prudent basis and either deducted from the provision for claims outstanding (in which case if the amounts are material they shall be shown in the notes to the accounts) or shown as assets.

(6) Where benefits resulting from a claim are required to be paid in the form of annuity, the amounts to be set aside for that purpose shall be calculated by recognised actuarial methods.

(7) In subparagraph (5)—

"salvage" means the acquisition of the legal ownership of insured property:

"subrogation" means the acquisition of the rights of policy holders with respect to third parties.

28.(1) There shall be no implicit discounting or deductions (including by way of financial reinsurance), whether resulting from the placing of a present value on a provision for an outstanding claim which is expected to be settled later at a higher figure or otherwise effected.

(2) The [Bank][a] may, on application by the undertaking concerned. permit explicit discounting or deductions (including by way of financial reinsurance) to take account of investment income subject to compliance with the following conditions and any other conditions which the Minister may from time to time consider necessary:

- (a) the expected date for the settlement of claims shall be on average at least four years after the accounting date;
- (b) the discounting or deduction shall be effected on a recognised prudential basis; any change in that basis shall be notified, in advance, to the Minister;
- (c) when calculating the total cost of settling claims, an undertaking shall take account of all factors that could cause increases in that cost;
- (d) an undertaking shall have adequate data at its disposal to construct a reliable model of the rate of claims settlements;
- (e) the rate of interest used for the calculation of present value shall not exceed a prudent estimate of the investment income from assets invested as a provision for claims during the period necessary for the payment of such claims and that rate shall not exceed either of the following:

(i) a rate derived from the investment income from such assets over the preceding five years;

(ii) a rate derived from the investment income from such assets during the year preceding the balance sheet date.

(3) When discounting or effecting deductions, an undertaking shall, in the notes on its accounts, disclose the total amount of provisions before discounting or deduction, the categories of claims which are discounted or from which deductions have been made and, for each category of claims, the methods used, in particular the rates used for the estimates referred to in the clauses (c) and (e) of subparagraph (2), and the criteria adopted for estimating the period that will elapse before the claims are settled.

Amendments

a 'Bank' substituted for 'Minister' by CBFSAIA 2003, s 35.

Life assurance business

29. The amount of the provision for claims shall—

(a) be equal to the sums due to beneficiaries, plus the costs of settling claims,

(b) include the provision for claims incurred but not reported and

(c) be disclosed in Liabilities item C(2).

30. Any equalisation provision established under the European Communities (Non-Life Insurance) (Amendment) Regulations, 1991 (S.I. No. 5 of 1991), shall be valued in accordance with the provisions of those Regulations.

Accounting on a non-annual basis

31. (1) Where, because of the nature of the class or type of insurance in question, information relating to premiums receivable or claims payable or to both in respect of the underwriting year is, when the annual accounts are drawn up, insufficient for accurate estimates to be made, then either of the methods set out in the Table to this paragraph may be adopted and applied.

(2) The method adopted shall be disclosed in the notes together with the reasons for adopting it.

(3) The method adopted shall be applied systematically in successive years unless circumstances justify a change and where there is a change in the method applied, the effect on the assets, liabilities, financial position and profit or loss shall be disclosed in the notes to the accounts.

(4) In this paragraph and the Table hereto "underwriting year" means the financial year in which the insurance contracts in the class or type of insurance in question commenced.

TABLE

METHOD 1

(a) The excess of the premiums written over the claims and expenses paid in respect of contracts commencing in the underwriting year shall form a technical provision included in the technical provision for claims outstanding shown in the balance sheet under Liabilities item C.3.

(b) The provision may also be computed on the basis of a given percentage of the premiums written where such a method is appropriate for the type of risk insured.

(c) If necessary, the amount of this technical provision shall be increased to make it sufficient to meet present and future obligations.

(d) The technical provision constituted under this method shall be replaced by a provision for claims outstanding estimated in accordance with paragraphs 27 to 29 as soon as sufficient information has been gathered and not later than the end of the third year following the underwriting year.

(e) The length of time that elapses before a provision for claims outstanding is constituted in accordance with paragraph (d) of this method shall be disclosed in the notes to the accounts.

METHOD 2

(a) The figures shown in the technical account or in certain items within it shall relate to a year which wholly or partly precedes the financial year but by no more than 12 months.

(b) The amounts of the technical provisions shown in the accounts shall, if necessary, be increased to make them sufficient to meet present and future obligations.

(c) The length of time by which the earlier year to which the figures relate precedes the financial year and the magnitude of the transactions concerned shall be disclosed in the notes to the accounts.

PART III

NOTES TO THE ACCOUNTS

Preliminary

1. Any information required in the case of an undertaking by the following provisions of this Part of this Schedule shall be given by way of a note to the [Companies Act accounts][a], unless otherwise provided.

Amendments

a Words substituted by reg 11 and Sch 3, Item No 14(a) of EC(IFRSMA)R 2005.

General

Disclosure of accounting policies

2. The accounting policies adopted by the undertaking in determining the amounts to be included in respect of items shown in the balance sheet and in determining the profit or loss of the undertaking shall be stated, including such policies with respect to the depreciation and diminution in value of assets.

3. If there are changes to the accounting policies adopted by the undertaking from one year to the next, these changes shall be stated together with the reasons for the changes and their effect on the accounts of the undertaking.

Sums denominated in foreign currencies

4. Where any sums originally denominated in a currency other than the currency of the State have been brought into accounts under any items shown in the balance sheet format (which is set out in Chapter 2 of Part I of this Schedule) or the profit and loss account format (which is so set out), the basis on which those sums have been translated into Irish Pounds, or the currency in which the accounts are drawn, shall be stated.

5. It shall be stated whether the accounts have been prepared in accordance with applicable accounting standards and particulars of any material departure from those standards and the reason for it shall be given.

INFORMATION SUPPLEMENTING THE BALANCE SHEET

Share capital and debentures

6.(1) The following information shall be given with respect to the undertaking's share capital:

(a) the authorised share capital, and

(b) where shares of more than one class have been allotted, the number and aggregate nominal value of shares of each class allotted.

(2) In the case of any part of the allotted share capital that consists of redeemable shares, the following information shall be given:

(a) the earliest and latest dates on which the undertaking has power to redeem those shares,

(b) whether those shares have to be redeemed in any event or are liable to be redeemed at the option of the undertaking or of the shareholder, and

(c) whether any premium is payable on redemption and, if so payable, the amount of that premium.

7. If the undertaking has allotted any shares during the financial year, the following information shall be given:

(a) the reason for making the allotment,

(b) the classes of shares allotted, and

(c) as respects each class of shares, the number allotted, their aggregate nominal value and the consideration received by the undertaking for the allotment.

8. (1) With respect to any contingent right to the allotment of shares in the undertaking the following particulars shall be given:

(a) the number, description and amount of the shares in relation to which the right is exercisable,

(b) the period during which it is exercisable, and

(c) the price to be paid for the shares allotted.

(2) In subparagraph (1) "contingent right to the allotment of shares" means any option to subscribe for shares and any other right to require the allotment of shares to any person whether arising on the conversion into shares of securities of any other description or otherwise.

9.(1) If the undertaking has issued any debentures during the financial year to which the accounts relate, the following information shall be given:

(a) the reason for making the issue.

(b) the classes of debentures issued, and

(c) as respects each class of debentures, the amount issued and the consideration received by the undertaking for the issue.

(2) Particulars of any redeemed debentures which the undertaking has power to reissue shall also be given.

(3) Where any of the undertaking's debentures are held by a nominee of or trustee for the undertaking, the nominal amount of the debentures and the amount at which they are stated in the accounting records kept by the undertaking in accordance with section 202 of the Act of 1990, shall be stated.

Assets

10.(1) In respect of any assets of the undertaking included in Assets item B (intangible assets), C.I (land and buildings) and C.II (investments in group undertakings and participating interests) in the undertaking's balance sheet the following information shall be given by reference to each such item:

(a) the appropriate amounts in respect of those assets included in the item as at the date of the beginning of the financial year and as at the balance sheet date respectively;

(b) the effect on any amount included in Assets item B in respect of those assets of—

(i) any determination during that year of the value to be ascribed to any of those assets in accordance with paragraph 15;

(ii) acquisitions during that year of any assets;

(iii) disposal during that year of any assets; and

(iv) any transfers of assets of the undertaking to and from the item during that year.

(2) The reference in subparagraph (I)(a) to the appropriate amounts in respect of any assets (included in an assets item) as at any date there mentioned is a reference to amounts representing the aggregate amounts determined, as at that date, in respect of assets falling to be included under the item on either of the following bases, that is to say:

(a) on the basis of cost, determined in accordance with paragraphs 7, 8 and 9; or

(b) on any basis permitted by paragraph 14 or 15;

leaving out of account in either case any provision for depreciation or diminution in value.

(3) In addition, in respect of any assets of the undertaking included in any assets item in the undertaking's balance sheet, there shall be stated (by reference to each such item)—

(a) the cumulative amount of provisions for depreciation or diminution in value of those assets included under the item as at each date mentioned in subparagraph (1)(a);

(b) the amount of any such provision made in respect of the financial year;

(c) the amount of any adjustments made in respect of any such provisions during that year in consequence of the disposal of any of those assets; and

(d) the amount of any other adjustments made in respect of any such provisions during that year.

11. Where any assets, other than listed investments, of the undertaking are included under any item shown in the undertaking's balance sheet at an amount determined on any basis mentioned in paragraph 14 or 15 of Part II of this Schedule, the following information shall be given:

(a) the years, insofar as they are known to the directors in which the assets were severally valued and the several values; and

(b) in the case of assets that have been valued during the financial year, the names of the persons who valued them or particulars of their qualifications for doing so and, in either case, the bases of valuation used by them.

12. In relation to any amount which is included under Assets item C.I. (land and buildings) the following shall be stated:

(a) how much of that amount is ascribable to land of freehold tenure and how much to land of leasehold tenure; and

(b) how much of the amount ascribable to land of leasehold tenure is ascribable to land held on long lease and how much to land held on short lease.

Investments

13. In respect of the amount of each item which is shown in the undertaking's balance sheet under Assets item C (investments) the following shall be stated:

(a) how much of that amount is ascribable to listed investments; and

(b) how much of any amount so ascribable is ascribable to investments in respect of which there has been granted a listing on a recognised stock exchange and how much to other listed investments.

Reserves and provisions

14.(1) Where any amount is transferred—

(a) to or from any reserves, or

(b) to any [provision for other risks][a], or

(c) from any provision for [provision for other risks][a] otherwise than for the purpose for which the provision was established,

and the reserves or provisions are or would be but for paragraph 3 of Part I of this Schedule shown as separate items in the undertaking's balance sheet, the information mentioned in subparagraph (2) shall be given in respect of the aggregate of reserves or provisions included in the same item.

(2) The information to which subparagraph (1) relates is as follows:

(a) the amount of the reserves or provisions as at the date of the beginning of the financial year and as at the balance sheet date respectively.

(b) any amounts transferred to or from the reserves or provisions during that year, and

(c) the source and application respectively of any amounts so transferred.

(3) Particulars shall be given of each provision included in Liabilities item E.III (other provisions) in the undertaking's balance sheet in any case where the amount of that provision is material.

Amendments

a Words substituted by reg 11 and Sch 3, Item No 14(b) of EC(IFRSMA)R 2005.

Provision for taxation

15. The amount of any provision for deferred taxation shall be stated separately from the amount of any provision for other taxation.

Details of indebtedness

16.(1). In respect of each item shown under "creditors" in the undertaking's balance sheet there shall be stated—

- (a) the aggregate amount of any debts included under that item which are payable or repayable otherwise than by instalments and fall due for payment or repayment after the end of the period of five years beginning with the day next following the end of the financial year, and
- (b) the aggregate amount of any debts so included which are repayable or repayable by instalments any of which fall due for payment after the end of that period;

and in the case of debts to which subparagraph *(b)* relates the aggregate amount of instalments falling due after the end of that period shall also be disclosed for each such item.

(2) Subject to subparagraph *(3),* in relation to each debt falling to be taken into account under subparagraph (1), the terms of payment or repayment and the rate of any interest payable on the debt shall be stated.

(3) If the number of debts is such that, in the opinion of the directors, compliance with subparagraph (2) would result in a statement of excessive length, it shall be sufficient to give a general indication of the terms of payment or repayment and the rates of any interest payable on the debts.

(4) In respect of each item shown under "creditors" in the undertaking's balance sheet there shall be stated—

- (a) the aggregate amount of any debts included under that item in respect of which any security has been given by the undertaking; and
- (b) an indication of the nature of the securities so given.

(5) References in this paragraph to an item shown under "creditors" in the undertaking's balance sheet include references, where amounts falling due to creditors within one year and after more than one year are distinguished in the balance sheet—

- (a) in a case within subparagraph (1), to an item shown under the latter of those categories, and
- (b) in a case within subparagraph (4), to an item shown under either of those categories,

and references to items shown under "creditors" include references to items which would but for paragraph 3(1)(b) of Part I of this Schedule be shown under that heading.

17. If any fixed cumulative dividends on the undertaking's shares are in arrears, there shall be stated—

(a) the amount of the arrears, and

(b) the period for which the dividends or, if there is more than one class, each class of them are in arrears.

Guarantees and other financial commitments

18.(1) Particulars shall be given of any charge on the assets of the undertaking to secure the liabilities of any other person, including, where practicable, the amount secured.

(2) The following information shall be given with respect to any other contingent liability not provided for (other than a contingent liability arising out of an insurance contract):

(a) the amount or estimated amount of that liability;

(b) its legal nature; and

(c) whether or not any valuable security has been provided by the undertaking in connection with that liability and, if such security has been so provided, what that security is.

(3) Where practicable, there shall be stated—

(a) the aggregate amount or estimated amount of contracts for capital expenditure, so far as not provided for, and

(b) the aggregate amount or estimated amount of capital expenditure authorised by the directors which has not been contracted for.

(4) Particulars shall be given of—

(a) any pension commitments included under any provision shown in the undertaking's balance sheet, and

(b) any such commitments for which no provision has been made,

and where any such commitment relates wholly or partly to pensions payable to past directors of the undertaking separate particulars shall be given of that commitment so far as it relates to such pensions.

(5) Particulars shall also be given of any other financial commitments, other than commitments arising out of insurance contracts, which—

(a) have not been provided for, and

(b) are relevant to assessing the undertaking's state of affairs.

(6) Commitments, being commitments to which any subparagraph of this paragraph relates, which are undertaken on behalf of or for the benefit of—

(a) any parent undertaking or fellow subsidiary undertaking of the undertaking, or

(b) any subsidiary undertaking of the undertaking,

shall be stated separately from the other commitments within that subparagraph, and commitments within clause (a) of this subparagraph shall also be stated separately from those within clause (b) of this subparagraph.

Dealings with or interests in group undertakings

19. Where an undertaking is a parent undertaking or a subsidiary undertaking and any item required by Part I of this Schedule to be shown in the undertaking's balance sheet in relation to group undertakings includes—

(a) amounts attributable to dealings with or interests in any parent undertaking or fellow subsidiary undertaking, or

(b) amounts attributable to dealings with or interests in any subsidiary undertaking of the undertaking,

the aggregate amounts within subparagraphs (a) and (b) respectively. shall be shown as separate items, in the balance sheet.

[Information on arrangements not included in balance sheet

19A. (1) The following information shall be provided in the notes to the accounts for an undertaking:

(a) the nature and business purpose of the arrangements of the undertaking that are not included in its balance sheet;

(b) the financial impact on the undertaking of the arrangements referred to in clause (a) if the risks or benefits arising from such arrangements are material and in so far as the disclosure of such risks or benefits is necessary for assessing the financial position of the undertaking.

Related party transactions

19B.(1) Particulars shall be given in the notes to the accounts of an undertaking of transactions which have been entered into with related parties by the undertaking, and if such transactions are material and have not been concluded under normal market conditions and the particulars of transactions shall include the amount of such transactions, the nature of the related party relationship, and other information concerning the transactions which is necessary for an understanding of the financial position of the undertaking.

(2) [The provision of particulars][b] and other information concerning individual transactions may be aggregated according to their nature, except where separate information is necessary for an understanding of the effects of related party transactions on the financial position of the undertaking.

(3) Subparagraph (1) shall not apply to transactions which are entered into between 2 or more members of a group if any subsidiary undertaking which is a party to the transaction is wholly owned by such a member.

[...][c]

(5) A word or expression used in subparagraphs (1) to (4) has the same meaning as it has in Directive 2006/46/EC.][a]

Amendments

a Paragraphs 19A and 19B inserted by European Communities (Directive 2006/46/EC) Regulations 2009, reg 24.

b Words 'The provision of particulars' substituted for 'Subject to subparagraph (4), the provision of particulars' by European Communities (Directive 2006/46/EC) Regulations 2010, reg 10(a).

c Subparagraph (4) deleted by European Communities (Directive 2006/46/EC) Regulations 2010, reg 10(b).

Miscellaneous Matters

20.(1) Particulars shall be given of any case where the cost of any asset is for the first time determined under paragraph 11 of Part I of this Schedule.

(2) Where any outstanding loans made under the authority of section 60) of the Principal Act, other than subsection (13)(a) of that section (which relates to various cases of financial assistance by an undertaking for purchase of its own shares) are included under any item shown in the undertaking's balance sheet, the aggregate amount of those loans shall be disclosed for each item in question.

(3) The aggregate amount which is recommended for distribution by way of dividend shall be stated.

(4) Particulars of any restriction on profits available for distribution by virtue of section 224(2)(b)(i) of the Act of 1990 shall be stated.

INFORMATION SUPPLEMENTING THE PROFIT AND LOSS ACCOUNT

Separate statement of certain items of income and expenditure

21. Subject to the following provisions of this paragraph, each of the following amounts shall be stated:

(a) the amount of the interest on or any similar charges in respect of—

(i) bank loans and overdrafts, and loans made to the undertaking (other than bank loans and overdrafts) which—

(I) are repayable otherwise than by instalments and fall due for repayment before the end of the period of five years beginning with the day next following the end of the financial year, or

(II) are repayable by instalments the last of which falls due for payment before the end of that period,

and

(ii) loans of any other kind made to the undertaking:

Provided that this subparagraph shall not apply to interest or charges on loans to the undertaking from group undertakings, but shall apply to interest or charges on all loans, whether made on the security of debentures or not;

(b) the amounts respectively set aside for redemption of share capital and for redemption of loans;

(c) the amount of income from listed and unlisted investments;

(d) [...][d]

(e) the aggregate amounts of the emoluments of, and compensation in respect of loss of office to, directors and compensation paid to past directors.

Amendments

a Subparagraph (d) is revoked by EC(SA)(Dir)R 2010, reg 15(4).

Particulars of tax

22.(1) The basis on which the charge for corporation tax, income tax and other taxation on profits, whether payable in the State or outside the State, is computed shall be stated.

(2) Particulars shall be given of any special circumstances which affect liability in respect of taxation of profits, income or capital gains for the financial year concerned or liability in respect of taxation of profits, income or capital gains for succeeding financial years.

(3) The following amounts shall be stated:

- (a) the amount of the charge for corporation tax;
- (b) if the amount of the charge to corporation tax would have been greater but for relief from double taxation, the amount which it would have been but for such relief;
- (c) the amount of the charge for income tax; and
- (d) the amount of the charge for taxation payable outside the State of profits, income and (so far as charged to revenue) capital gains.

These amounts shall be stated separately in respect of each of the amounts which is shown under the following items in the profit and loss account, that is to say item III.9 (tax on profit or loss on ordinary activities) and item III.14 (tax on extraordinary profit or loss).

Particulars of business

23. (1) As regards non-life insurance, the notes to the accounts shall disclose—

- (a) gross premiums written,
- (b) gross premiums earned,
- (c) gross claims incurred,
- (d) gross operating expenses, and
- (e) the reinsurance balance.

(2) The amounts required to be disclosed by subparagraph (1) shall be broken down between direct insurance and reinsurance acceptances, if reinsurance acceptances amount to 10 per cent or more of gross premiums written.

(3) Subject to subparagraph (4), the amounts required to be disclosed by subparagraphs (1) and (2) with respect to direct insurance shall be further broken down into the following groups of classes—

- (a) accident and health,
- (b) motor third party liability,
- (c) motor other classes,
- (d) marine, aviation and transport,
- (e) fire and other damage to property,

(f) third-party liability,

(g) credit and suretyship,

(h) legal expenses,

(i) assistance, and

(j) miscellaneous,

where the amount of the gross premiums written in direct insurance for each such group exceeds ten million ECUs.

(4) The amounts relating to the three largest groups of classes in an undertaking's business shall in any event be disclosed.

24.(1) As regards life assurance, the notes to the accounts shall disclose—

(a) gross premiums written, and

(b) the reinsurance balance.

(2) The notes relating to gross premiums written shall be broken down between direct insurance and reinsurance acceptances, where reinsurance acceptances amount to 10 per cent or more of gross premiums written, and within direct insurance shall be broken down to indicate—

(a) (i) individual premiums,

(ii) premiums under group contracts,

(b) (i) periodic premiums,

(ii) single premiums,

(c) (i) premiums from non-participating contracts,

(ii) premiums from participating contracts,

(iii) premiums from contracts where the investment risk is borne by policy holders.

(3) Disclosures of any amount required by clause (a), (b) or (c) of subparagraph (2) shall not be required where that amount does not exceed 10 per cent of the gross premiums written in direct insurance.

25.(1) Subject to subparagraph (2), there shall be disclosed as regards both non-life insurance and life assurance the total gross direct insurance premiums resulting from contracts concluded by the undertaking—

(a) in the member state of the European Union where there is situated its head office,

(b) in the other member states of the European Union, and

(c) in other countries.

(2) Disclosure of any figure referred to in subparagraph (1) above shall not be required if it does not exceed 5 per cent of total gross premiums.

Commissions

26. There shall be disclosed the total amount of commissions of any kind for direct insurance business accounted for in the financial year, including acquisition, renewal, collection and portfolio management commission.

Particulars of staff

27.(1) The following information shall be given with respect to the employees of the undertaking:

(a) the average number of persons employed by the undertaking in the financial year, and

(b) the average number of persons employed within each category of persons employed by the undertaking.

(2) The average number required by clause (a) or (b) of subparagraph (1) shall be determined by dividing the relevant annual number by the number of weeks in the financial year.

(3) For the purposes of this paragraph, the relevant annual number shall be determined by ascertaining for each week in the financial year—

(a) for the purpose of subparagraph (1)(a), the number of persons employed under contracts of service by the undertaking in that week, whether throughout the week or not, and

(b) for the purpose of subparagraph (1)(b), the number of persons in the category in question of persons so employed.

and, in either case, adding together all the weekly numbers.

(4) In respect of all persons employed by the undertaking during the financial year who are taken into account in determining the relevant annual number for the purpose of subparagraph (1)(a) there shall also be stated the aggregate amounts respectively of—

(a) wages and salaries paid or payable in respect of that year to those persons,

(b) social welfare costs incurred by the undertaking on their behalf, and

(c) other pension costs so incurred.

save in so far as those amounts or any of them are stated in the profit and loss account.

(5) The categories of person employed by the undertaking by reference to which the number required to be disclosed by subparagraph (I)(b) is to be determined shall be such as the directors may select, having regard to the manner in which the undertaking's activities are organised.

Miscellaneous matters

28.(1) Where any amount relating to any preceding financial year is included in any item in the profit and loss account, the effect shall be stated.

(2) Particulars shall be given of any extraordinary income or charges arising in the financial year.

(3) The effect shall be stated of any transactions that are exceptional by virtue of size or incidence though they fall within the ordinary activities of the undertaking.

PART IV

FORM AND CONTENT OF GROUP ACCOUNTS

Chapter 1

General Rules

1.(1) [Where the directors of an undertaking prepare Companies Act group accounts, those group accounts][a] shall comply so far as practicable with the provisions of Parts I and 111 of this Schedule as if the undertakings included in the consolidation (in this Part referred to as "the group") were a single undertaking.

(2) In particular, for the purpose of note 13 to the balance sheet format (which is set out in Chapter 2 of Part I of this Schedule) and paragraphs 18(6) and 19 of Part 111 of this Schedule as it applies to group accounts—

(a) any subsidiary undertakings of the parent undertaking not included in the consolidation shall be treated as subsidiary undertakings of the group, and

(b) if the parent undertaking is itself a subsidiary undertaking, the group shall be treated as a subsidiary undertaking of any parent undertaking of that undertaking, and the reference to fellow subsidiary undertakings shall be construed accordingly.

Amendments

a Words substituted by reg 11 and Sch 3, Item No 14(a) of EC(IFRSMA)R 2005 (SI 116/2005).

2.(1) Subject to the exceptions authorised or required by this paragraph, all the subsidiary undertakings of the parent undertaking shall be included in the consolidation.

(2) A subsidiary undertaking may be excluded from consolidation if its inclusion is not material for the purpose of giving a true and fair view, but two or more undertakings may be excluded only if they are not material taken together.

(3) In addition, a subsidiary undertaking may be excluded from consolidation where—

(a) severe long-term restrictions substantially hinder the exercise of the rights of the parent undertaking over the assets or management of that undertaking, or

(b) the information necessary for the preparation of group accounts cannot be obtained without disproportionate expense or undue delay, or

(c) the interest of the parent undertaking is held exclusively with a view to subsequent resale and the undertaking has not previously been included in consolidated group accounts prepared by the parent undertaking.

[...][a]

Amendments

a Sub-paras (4), (5) and (6) of para 2 deleted by reg 11 and Sch 3, Item No 14(b) of EC(IFRSMA)R 2005 (SI 116/2005).

3.(1) The group balance sheet and group profit and loss account shall incorporate in full the information contained in the individual accounts of the parent undertaking and subsidiary undertakings included in the group accounts, subject to the adjustments authorised or required by the following provisions of this Schedule.

(2) Group accounts shall be drawn up as at the same date as the annual accounts of the parent undertaking.

(3) If the financial year of a subsidiary undertaking included in the group accounts differs from that of the parent undertaking, the group accounts shall be made up—

(a) from the accounts of the subsidiary undertaking for its financial year last ending before the end of the parent undertaking's financial year, provided that year ended no more than three months before that of the parent undertaking,

(b) where an undertaking's balance sheet date precedes the group balance sheet by more than three months, but not more than six months, that undertaking shall be included in the group accounts on the basis of interim accounts drawn up as at the group balance sheet date.

4.(1) The methods of consolidation shall be applied consistently from one financial year to the next.

(2) If it appears to the directors of a parent undertaking that there are special reasons for departing from the principle specified in subparagraph (1) they may so depart, but particulars of the departure, the reasons for it and its effect on the balance sheet and profit or loss of the parent undertaking and subsidiaries as a whole shall be disclosed in the notes to the accounts.

5. (a) Group accounts shall show the assets, liabilities, state of affairs as at the end of the financial year and profit or loss of the parent undertaking and its subsidiary undertakings dealt with in the group accounts as if they were a single undertaking and, in particular, shall show—

(i) debts and claims between the undertakings dealt with in the group accounts shall be eliminated from those accounts,

(ii) income and expenditure relating to transactions between the undertakings dealt with in the group accounts shall be eliminated from those accounts,

(iii) where profits and losses resulting from transactions between the undertakings dealt with in the group accounts are included in the book value of assets, they shall be eliminated from those accounts,

(b) clauses (i) to (iii) of subparagraph (a) need not be complied with where the amounts involved are not material for the purpose of giving a true and fair view as required by Regulation 10.

6. If the composition of the undertakings dealt with in the group accounts has changed significantly in the course of a financial year, the group accounts shall include information which makes the comparison of successive sets of group accounts meaningful.

Chapter 2
Accounting/Valuation

ACQUISITION AND MERGER ACCOUNTING

7. The following provisions of this Chapter shall apply where an undertaking becomes a subsidiary undertaking of the parent undertaking and that event is referred to in those provisions as an "acquisition", and references to the "undertaking acquired" shall be construed accordingly.

8. An acquisition shall be accounted for by the acquisition method of accounting unless the conditions for accounting for it as a merger are met and the merger method of accounting is adopted.

9.(1) The acquisition method of accounting is as set out in this paragraph.

(2) The identifiable assets and liabilities of the undertaking acquired shall be included in the consolidated balance sheet at their fair values as at the date of acquisition.

(3) The income and expenditure of the undertaking acquired shall be brought into the group accounts only as from the date of the acquisition.

(4) (a) There shall be set off against the acquisition cost of the interest in the shares of the undertaking held by the undertakings dealt with in the group accounts the interest of undertakings dealt with in the group accounts in the adjusted capital and reserves of the undertaking acquired.

(b) In clause (a) of this subparagraph "the adjusted capital and reserves of the undertaking acquired" means its capital and reserves at the date of the acquisition after adjusting the identifiable assets and liabilities of the undertaking to fair values as at that date.

(5) The resulting amount if positive shall be treated as goodwill, and if negative as a negative consolidation difference.

(6) Where in applying the acquisition method of accounting—

(a) there is no record of—

(i) the fair values as at the date of acquisition of the identifiable assets and liabilities of the undertaking acquired, or

(ii) the acquisition cost of the interest in the shares of the acquired undertaking by the undertakings dealt with in the group accounts,

or

(b) such records cannot be obtained without unreasonable expense or delay,

then the values of the identifiable assets and liabilities and the acquisition cost shall be taken to be the values and cost ascribed to them in the earliest available record made after the acquisition of that subsidiary undertaking.

(7) In this paragraph

"the acquisition cost" means the amount of any cash consideration and the fair value of any other consideration, together with such amount (if any) in respect of fees and other expenses of the acquisition as the parent undertaking may determine;

the "identifiable assets and liabilities" in relation to the undertaking acquired means the assets and liabilities which are capable of being disposed of or discharged separately, without disposing of a business of the undertaking.

10.(1) The conditions for accounting for an acquisition as a merger are as follows:

(a) that at least 90 per cent of the nominal value of the relevant shares in the undertaking acquired is held by or on behalf of the undertakings dealt with in the group accounts,

(b) that the proportion referred to in clause (a) of this subparagraph was attained pursuant to an arrangement providing for the issue of equity shares by the undertakings dealt with in the group accounts, and

(c) that the fair value of any consideration other than the issue of equity shares given pursuant to the arrangement by the undertakings dealt with in the group accounts did not exceed 10 per cent of the nominal value of the equity shares issued.

(2) In subparagraph (1)(a) "relevant shares in an undertaking acquired" means those shares carrying unrestricted rights to participate both in distributions and in the assets of the undertaking upon liquidation.

11.(1) The merger method of accounting is set out in this paragraph.

(2) The assets and liabilities of the undertaking acquired shall be brought into the group accounts at the figures at which they stand in the undertaking's accounts, subject to any adjustment authorised or required by this Part of the Schedule.

(3) The income and expenditure of the undertaking acquired shall be included in the group accounts for the entire financial year, including the period before the acquisition.

(4) The group accounts shall show corresponding amounts relating to the previous financial year as if the undertaking acquired had been included in the consolidation throughout that year.

(5) There shall be set off against the aggregate of—

(a) the appropriate amount in respect of shares issued by the undertakings dealt with in the group accounts in consideration for the acquisition of shares in the undertaking acquired, and

(b) the fair value of any other consideration for the acquisition of shares in the undertaking acquired, determined as at the date when those shares were acquired,

the nominal value of the issued share capital of the undertaking acquired held by the undertakings dealt with in the group accounts.

(6) The resulting amount by virtue of this paragraph shall be shown as an adjustment to the consolidated reserves.

12.(1) Where a group of undertakings is acquired, paragraphs 8 to 11 apply with the following adaptations.

(2) Reference to shares of the undertaking acquired shall be construed as references to shares of the parent undertaking of the group.

(3) Other references to the undertaking acquired shall be construed as references to the group, and references to the assets and liabilities, income and expenditure and capital and reserves of the undertaking acquired shall be construed as references to the assets and liabilities, income and expenditure and capital and reserves of the group after making the set-offs and other adjustments required by this Part of the Schedule in the case of group accounts.

VALUATION

13.(1) In determining the amounts to be included in the group accounts, Regulations 7 and 8 and the valuation rules contained in Part II of this Schedule shall apply and shall be applied consistently within those accounts.

(2) Subparagraph (1) shall not apply to those liabilities items the valuation of which by the insurance undertakings included in group accounts is based on the application of provisions specific to insurance undertakings nor to those assets items changes in the values of which also affect or establish policyholders' rights.

(3) Where subparagraph (2) applies, that fact shall be disclosed in the notes to the group accounts.

14. (1) Subject to subparagraph (2) a parent undertaking shall apply the same methods of valuation in drawing up group accounts as it applies in drawing up its annual accounts.

(2) Subject to paragraph 13, subparagraph (1) shall not apply where, in the opinion of the directors, a departure from the provisions of that paragraph is necessary for the purpose of Regulation 10(5)(i).

(3) Any application of subparagraph (2) and the reasons therefor shall be disclosed in the notes to the group accounts.

15.(1) Where assets and liabilities to be included in the group accounts have been valued or otherwise determined by undertakings according to accounting rules differing from those used for the group accounts, the values or amounts shall be adjusted so as to accord with the rules used for the group accounts.

(2) If it appears to the directors of the parent undertaking that there are special reasons for departing from subparagraph (1) they may do so, but particulars of any such departure, the reasons for it and its effect shall be given in a note to the accounts.

(3) The adjustments referred to in this paragraph need not be made if they are not material for the purpose of giving a true and fair view.

16. Any differences of accounting rules as between a parent undertaking's individual accounts for a financial year and its group accounts shall be disclosed in a note to the latter accounts and the reasons for the difference given.

17. Amounts which in the particular context of any provision of this Part of the Schedule are not material may be disregarded for the purposes of that provision.

DIFFERENCES IN TAX TREATMENT

18. Account shall be taken in the group accounts of any difference arising on consolidation between the tax chargeable for the financial year and for preceding financial years and the amount of tax paid or payable in respect of those years, provided that it is probable that an actual charge to tax will arise within the foreseeable future for one of the undertakings dealt with in the group accounts.

MINORITY INTERESTS

19.(1) The formats set out in Part I of this Schedule shall have effect in relation to group accounts with the modifications set out in this paragraph.

(2) In the Balance Sheet Format (which is set out in Chapter 2 of Part I of this Schedule) a further item headed "Minority interests" shall be added as Liabilities item Aa and under that item shall be shown the amount of capital and reserves attributable to shares in subsidiary undertakings included in the consolidation held by or on behalf of persons other than the parent undertaking and its subsidiary undertakings.

(3) In the profit and loss account format (which is set out in Chapter 2 of Part I of this Schedule) a further item headed "Minority interests" shall be added as item l0(a) in the non-technical account and under the said item l0(a) there shall be shown the amount of any profit or loss on ordinary activities attributable to shares in subsidiary undertakings included in the consolidation held by or on behalf of persons other than the parent undertaking and its subsidiary undertakings.

(4) In the profit and loss account format (which is set out in Chapter 2 of Part I of this Schedule) a further item headed "Minority interests" shall be added in as item 13(a) in the non-technical account and under the said item 13(a) there shall be shown the amount of any profit or loss on extraordinary activities attributable to shares in subsidiary undertakings included in the consolidation held by or on behalf of persons other than the parent undertaking and its subsidiary undertakings.

(5) For the purposes of paragraph 3 of Part I of this Schedule (power to combine items) the additional items required by the foregoing provisions of this paragraph shall be treated as items to which a letter is assigned.

(6) Investment income and charges attributable to life assurance shall be shown in the technical account. Investment income and charges attributable to non-life business may be disclosed in the non-technical account.

JOINT VENTURES

20.(1) Where a parent undertaking or one of its subsidiaries dealt with in the group accounts manages another undertaking jointly with one or more undertakings not dealt with in the group accounts, that other undertaking (in this paragraph referred to as the "joint venture") may be dealt with in the group accounts by the method of proportional consolidation if it is neither a body corporate nor a subsidiary undertaking of the parent undertaking.

(2) The provisions of this Part relating to the preparation of group accounts shall, with any necessary modifications, apply to proportional consolidation under this paragraph.

ASSOCIATED UNDERTAKINGS

21.(1) In this Part of the Schedule "associated undertaking" means an undertaking in which an undertaking dealt with in the group accounts has a participating interest and over whose operating and financial policy it exercises a significant influence, and which is not—

(a) a subsidiary undertaking of the parent undertaking, or

(b) a joint venture dealt with in accordance with paragraph 20.

(2) Where an undertaking holds 20 per cent or more of the voting rights in another undertaking, it shall be presumed to exercise such an influence over it unless the contrary is shown.

(3) Paragraphs (3) and (4) of Regulation 11 shall apply for determining whether subparagraph (2) applies.

22.(1) The interest of an undertaking dealt with in the group accounts in an associated undertaking, and the amount of profit or loss attributable to such an interest, shall be shown in the group accounts by way of the equity method of accounting including dealing with any goodwill arising in accordance with paragraphs 2 to 4 of Part 11 of this Schedule.

(2) Where the associated undertaking is itself a parent undertaking, the net assets and profits or losses to be taken into account are those of the parent and its subsidiary undertakings, after making any consolidation adjustments.

(3) The equity method of accounting need not be applied if the amounts in question are not material for the purpose of giving a true and fair view.

PARTICIPATING INTEREST

23.(1) In this paragraph—

"participating interest" means a qualifying capital interest held by one undertaking in another on a long-term basis for the purpose of securing a contribution to that undertaking's own activities by the exercise of control or influence arising from or related to that interest;

"qualifying capital interest", means—

(a) in relation to an undertaking with share capital, an interest in shares comprised in the allotted share capital of that undertaking,

(b) in relation to an undertaking with capital but no share capital, an interest conferring rights to share in the capital of the undertaking,

(c) in relation to an undertaking without capital, interests—

(i) conferring any right to share in the profits or liability to contribute to the losses of the undertaking, or

(ii) giving rise to an obligation to contribute to the debts or expenses of the undertaking in the event of a winding up,

and includes an interest which is convertible into a qualifying capital interest as well as an option to acquire any such qualifying capital interest.

(2) Where an undertaking holds a qualifying capital interest in another undertaking and such an interest represents 20 per cent or more of all such interests in the other undertaking it shall be presumed to hold that interest on the basis and for the purpose mentioned in subparagraph (1) unless the contrary is shown.

(3) The percentage of qualifying capital interests held in an undertaking with share capital shall be the percentage that the nominal value of the shares held represents of the nominal value of the allotted share capital of that undertaking.

(4) For the purpose of this paragraph an interest held on behalf of an undertaking shall be treated as held by it.

(5) For the purpose of this paragraph as it applies in relation to "participating interest" in Regulation 11(1)(c) (subsidiary undertaking)—

(a) there shall be attributed to an undertaking any interests held by any of its subsidiary undertakings, and

(b) the references in subparagraph (1) of this paragraph to the purpose and activities of an undertaking include the purpose and activities of any of its subsidiary undertakings and of the group as a whole.

(6) In the balance sheet and profit and loss formats set out in Part I of this Schedule as applied to group accounts by this Part of the Schedule "participating interest" does not include an interest in a group undertaking.

24.(1) The formats in Part I of this Schedule shall have effect in relation to group accounts with the following modifications.

(2) In the balance sheet format (which is set out in Chapter 2 of Part I of this Schedule) assets item C.II.3 (Participating Interests) shall be replaced by two items headed "Interests in associated undertakings" and "Other participating interests".

(3) In the profit and loss account format (which is set out in Chapter 2 of Part I of this Schedule) the following items, namely:

(a) item I.2(a) of the technical account – non-life insurance;

(b) item II.2(a) of the technical account – life assurance business, and

(c) item III.3(a) of the non-technical account

shall be replaced by two items, "income from interests in associated undertakings" and "income from other participating interests".

Chapter 3
Information Required

By Way of Notes to the Group Accounts

25. Without prejudice to Regulation 10, the notes to the group accounts shall also set out the information required by the following provisions of this Chapter.

26.(1) In relation to the resulting amounts referred to in paragraph 9(5) and 11(6), there shall be stated in the notes to the group accounts the methods used in calculating those amounts and the reasons for any significant difference between such amounts for the financial year to which the group accounts refer and those for the preceding financial year.

(2) In relation to acquisitions taking place in the financial year, there shall be stated in the notes to the group accounts the following:

(a) the name and registered office of the undertaking acquired, or where a group was acquired, the name and registered office of the parent undertaking of that group, and

(b) whether the acquisition has been accounted for by the acquisition or the merger method of accounting.

27. Where sums originally denominated in currencies, other than the currency in which the group accounts are drawn up, have been brought into account under any items shown in the balance sheet or profit and loss account, the basis on which those sums have, for the purposes of the accounts, been converted into the currency in which the group accounts are drawn up shall be stated.

28. In respect of the aggregate of the amounts shown in the group balance sheet under the heading "Creditors" there shall be stated the following:

(a) the aggregate amount of any debts included under that heading which are payable or repayable otherwise than by instalments and fall due for payment or repayment after the end of the period of five years beginning with the day next following the end of the financial year,

(b) the aggregate amount of any debts so included which are payable or repayable by instalments any of which fall due for payment after the end of that period,

(c) the aggregate amount of any debts included under that heading in respect of which any security has been given, and

(d) an indication of the nature of the securities so given.

29.(1) The following information shall be given with respect to the employees of the undertakings dealt with in the group accounts:

(a) the average number of persons employed in the financial year, by the undertakings dealt with in the group accounts, and

(b) the average number of persons employed within each category of persons employed by those undertakings.

(2) In respect of all persons employed by the undertakings dealt with in the group accounts during the financial year who are taken into account in determining the relevant annual number for the purposes of subparagraph (1)(a), there shall also be stated the aggregate amount of staff costs, save insofar as this amount is stated in the group profit and loss account.

(3) The categories of persons employed by the undertakings included in the group accounts by reference to which the number required to be disclosed by subparagraph (1)(b) is to be determined shall be such as the directors of the parent undertaking may select, having regard to the manner in which the activities of the undertakings dealt with in the group accounts are organised.

(4) For the purposes of clauses (a) and (b) of subparagraph (1) the average number of persons employed by the undertakings dealt with in the group accounts shall be determined by adding together the averages, for each such undertaking, calculated by the method set out in paragraph 27(3) of Part III of this Schedule.

(5) The average number of persons employed during the financial year by an undertaking proportionally consolidated pursuant to paragraph 21 of this Part, calculated by the manner specified in subparagraph (4), shall also be stated.

30.(1) In the case of group accounts, the pension commitments referred to in paragraph 18(4) of Part III of this Schedule and the emoluments and compensation referred to in paragraph 58(6) of the Schedule to the 1986 Act shall be to such commitments, emoluments and compensation relating to directors or past directors of the parent undertaking in respect of duties relating to the parent undertaking, to any of its subsidiary undertakings, to any undertakings proportionally consolidated in accordance with paragraph 21 of this Part or to associated undertakings.

(2) Section 191 of the Principal Act shall not apply to group accounts prepared in accordance with these Regulations.

31.(1) Subject to subparagraph (2), sections 41 to 43 of the Act of 1990 shall apply to group accounts prepared under these Regulations.

(2) The particulars of any transaction, arrangement or agreement referred to in those sections, entered into with a director of the parent undertaking by an undertaking proportionally consolidated in accordance with paragraph 21 of this Part of this Schedule, or an associated undertaking, shall be similarly stated.

32.(1)(a) The information set out in subparagraphs (2), (3) and (4) shall be stated in relation to each undertaking dealt with in the group accounts.

(b) For the purpose of clause (a), the information required by subparagraph (3)(a) does not include such interests in the parent undertaking.

(2) The names and registered offices of the undertakings included in the group accounts shall be set out therein.

(3) (a) The aggregate of the qualifying capital interests held in that undertaking by the undertakings dealt with in the group accounts as a proportion of the total of such interests shall be stated for the purposes of paragraph 25.

(b) In this subparagraph "qualifying capital interest" has the meanings assigned to it in paragraph 23.

(c) For the purpose of this subparagraph, paragraph 23(3) shall apply in determining the percentage of qualifying capital interests held in an undertaking with share capital.

(4) (a) There shall be set out for the purposes of paragraph 25 a note indicating by virtue of which of the provisions of Regulation 11 has the undertaking been dealt with in the group accounts.

(b) The information required by clause (c) of this subparagraph may be omitted where the undertaking has been dealt with in the group accounts by virtue of Regulation 11(1)(a), and where the proportion of capital and the proportion of voting rights held are the same.

33. The information set out in subparagraphs (2), (3) and (4) of paragraph 32 shall also be given in respect of each undertaking which has been excluded from the group accounts by virtue of the application of paragraph 2.

34.(1) The information set out in subparagraphs (2) and (3) of paragraph 32 shall be stated in relation to each associated undertaking.

(2) The information required by subparagraph (1) shall also be stated in relation to associated undertakings, the interest in which has been dealt with in accordance with paragraph 22(3).

35.(1) The information set out in subparagraphs (2) and (3) of paragraph 32 shall be stated in relation to each undertaking that has been proportionally consolidated in accordance with paragraph 20.

(2) The nature of the joint management of each joint venture, to which paragraph 20 applies, proportionally consolidated shall also be stated.

36.(1) The information set out in subparagraphs (2) and (3) of paragraph 32 shall be stated in relation to each undertaking (in this paragraph referred to as an "undertaking of substantial interest"), other than those referred to in paragraphs 32 to 35 in which undertakings dealt with in the group accounts and undertakings not dealt with by virtue of the application of subparagraphs (4) to (6) of paragraph 2, or persons acting in their own name but on behalf of such undertakings, between them hold a qualifying capital interest representing 20 per cent or more of such interests.

(2) There shall also be stated in relation to each undertaking of substantial interest, the amount of its capital and reserves and its profit or loss for its latest financial year for which accounts have been adopted.

(3) The information required by subparagraphs (1) and (2) may be omitted, where for the purposes of Regulation 10(5), it is of negligible importance.

(4) The information concerning capital and reserves and the profit or loss required by subparagraph (2) may also be omitted where the undertaking concerned is not required to attach its balance sheet to its annual return and where the qualifying capital interest held as described in subparagraph (1) is less than 50 per cent.

(5) For the purpose of this paragraph, paragraph 23(3) shall apply in determining the percentage of qualifying capital interest held in an undertaking with share capital.

[37. The notes on the group accounts shall set out information relating to—

(a) the nature and business purpose of any arrangement which is not included in the consolidated balance sheet, and the financial impact of such arrangement if the risks or benefits arising from the arrangement are material, and in so far as the disclosure of such risks or benefits is necessary for assessing the financial position, taken as a whole, of the parent undertaking and its subsidiaries included in the consolidated balance sheet, and

(b) subject to paragraph 38, transactions entered into by—

(i) the parent undertaking, or

(ii) a subsidiary of that parent undertaking included in the group accounts,

with related parties if the transactions are material and have not been concluded under normal market conditions and the information shall include the amounts of such transactions, the nature of the related party relationship and other information concerning the transactions which is necessary for an understanding of the financial position, taken as a whole, of the parent undertaking and its subsidiaries included in the group accounts.

38. A transaction referred to in paragraph 37(b) does not include an intragroup transaction.

39 Information provided pursuant to paragraph 37(b) concerning individual transactions may be aggregated according to their nature except where separate information is necessary for an understanding of the effects of the related party transactions on the financial position, taken as a whole, of the parent undertaking and its subsidiaries included in the group accounts.

40. In paragraph 37 'consolidated balance sheet' means the balance sheet prepared in respect of the group accounts.

41. A word or expression that is used in paragraphs 37 to 39 has the same meaning as it has in Directive 2006/46/EC][a].

Amendments

a Paragraphs 37–41 inserted by European Communities (Directive 2006/46/EC) Regulations 2009, reg 25.

Explanatory Note

(*This note is not part of the Instrument and does not purport to be a legal interpretation*).

These Regulations give effect to the Council Directive on the annual accounts and consolidated accounts of insurance undertakings (91/674/EEC, O.J. No. L374/7). This Directive provides for the application of the fourth and seventh company law directives to insurance companies, taking account of specific features of the accounts of insurance companies.

The fourth directive (78/60/EEC, O.J. No. L222/11) provides for co-ordinated national legislation concerning presentation of accounts and uniform valuation of assets and liabilities brought to account by all undertakings within the European Union, aimed at providing comparable sets of accounts within a range of options. It was implemented by the Companies (Amendment) Act, 1986 (No. 25 of 1986). The seventh directive (83/349/EEC, O.J. L193/1) provided for co-ordinated national legislation concerning consolidated accounts. It was implemented by the European Communities (Companies: Group Accounts) Regulations, 1992 (No. 201 of 1992).

These Regulations require insurance undertakings to prepare and to publish annually accounts (balance sheet, profit and loss account and notes), in accordance with the provisions of these Regulations. They also require (with provision for exceptions) insurance undertakings which have subsidiary undertakings or non-insurance holding companies, the most important of whose subsidiaries are insurance undertakings, to prepare and to publish group accounts in accordance with the provisions of these Regulations.

The Regulations contain provisions governing the preparation of accounts, including group accounts, the content of those accounts, their format and the valuation of items to be included. They specify information to be included in the notes to the accounts.

Companies Act, 1990 (Uncertificated Securities) Regulations 1996

SI 68/1996

ARRANGEMENT OF REGULATIONS

CHAPTER I
CITATION, COMMENCEMENT & INTERPRETATION

CHAPTER II
TRANSFERRING & RECORDING SHARES & SECURITIES

CHAPTER III
APPROVAL AND COMPLIANCE OF OPERATOR

I, PAT RABBITTE, Minister of State at the Department of Enterprise and Employment, in exercise of the powers conferred on me by section 4 of the Companies (Amendment) Act, 1977 (No. 31 of 1977) and section 239 of the Companies Act, 1990 (No. 33 of 1990) and the Enterprise and Employment (Delegation of Ministerial Functions) Order, 1995 (S.I. No. 42 of 1995), to enable title to securities to be evidenced otherwise than by a certificate and transferred without a written instrument, and make provision for certain supplemental and incidental matters, hereby make the following regulations:

CHAPTER I

CITATION, COMMENCEMENT AND INTERPRETATION

1 Citation and Construction

(1) These regulations may be cited as the Companies Act, 1990 (Uncertificated Securities) Regulations, 1996.

(2) These regulations shall be construed as one with the Companies Acts.

2 Commencement

These regulations shall come into force on the 1st April, 1996.

3 Interpretation

(1) In these regulations except where the context otherwise requires—

'the 1963 Act' means the Companies Act, 1963;

'the 1977 Act' means the Companies (Amendment) Act, 1977;

'the 1990 Act' means the Companies Act, 1990;

'the 1995 Act' means the Stock Exchange Act, 1995;

'articles of association', in the case of a company which is not a company within the meaning of section 2 (1) of the 1963 Act, shall include its charter, bye-laws or other constituent documents;

'certificate', means any certificate, instrument or other document of, or evidencing, title to, a unit or units of security;

'certificated unit of a security' means a unit of a security other than an uncertificated unit of a security as defined in this regulation;

'the Companies Acts' means the 1963 Act and any enactment which is to be construed therewith;

'company' means a company within the meaning of section 2(1) of the 1963 Act and any body corporate within the meaning of section 377(1) of the 1963 Act;

'competent authority' means any person authorised under the laws of a Member State to approve persons to operate a relevant system;

'computer' means any device or combination or succession of devices for storing and processing information, and any reference to information being derived from other information is a reference to its being derived therefrom by calculation, comparison or any other process;

'court' means a court of competent jurisdiction;

'dematerialised instruction' means an instruction sent or received by means of a relevant system;

'director', in the case of a company which is not a company within the meaning of section 2(1) of the 1963 Act, includes a member of the governing body of the company;

'enactment' includes an enactment comprised in any subordinate legislation within the meaning of the Interpretation Act, 1937;

'generate', in relation to an operator-instruction, means to initiate the procedures by which an operator-instruction comes to be sent;

'guidance', in relation to an operator, means guidance issued by the operator which is intended to have continuing effect and is issued in writing or other legible form, which if it were a rule, would come within the definition of a rule;

'instruction' includes any instruction, election, acceptance or any other message of any kind;

'interest in a security' means any legal or equitable interest or right in relation to a security, including—

(a) an absolute or contingent right to acquire a security created, allotted or issued or to be created, allotted or issued; and

(b) the interests or rights of a person for whom a security is held by a custodian or depository;

'issue', in relation to a new unit of a security, means to confer title to that unit on a person;

'issuer-instruction' means a properly authenticated dematerialised instruction attributable to a participating issuer;

'officer', in relation to a participating issuer, includes—

(a) where the participating issuer is a company, such persons as are mentioned in section 2 (1) of the 1963 Act;

(b) where the participating issuer is a partnership, a partner; or in the event that no partner is situated in the State, a person in the State who is acting on behalf of the partner; and

(c) where the participating issuer is neither a company nor a partnership, any member of its governing body; or in the event that no member of its governing body is situated in the State, a person in the State who is acting on behalf of its governing body;

'operator' means any person specified in regulation 28 or approved by the Minister under these regulations as operator of a relevant system;

'operator-instruction' means a properly authenticated dematerialised instruction attributable to an operator;

'operator-system' means those facilities and procedures which are part of the relevant system, which are maintained and operated by or for an operator, by which the operator generates operator-instructions and receives dematerialised instructions from system-participants and by which persons change the form in which units of a participating security are held;

'participating issuer' means a person who has issued a security which is a participating security;

'participating security' means a security, title to units of which is permitted by an operator to be transferred by means of a relevant system;

'practices' in relation to an operator means non-binding guidance issued by the operator;

'register of members' means a register of members maintained by a company under section 116 (1) of the 1963 Act;

'register of securities'—

(a) in relation to shares, means a register of members, and

(b) in relation to units of a security other than shares, means a register maintained by the issuer, whether by virtue of these regulations or otherwise, of persons holding the units;

'relevant system' means a computer based system and procedures which enable title to units of a security to be evidenced and transferred without a written instrument, and which facilitate supplementary and incidental matters and 'relevant system' includes an operator-system;

'rules' in relation to an operator, means rules made or conditions imposed by the operator with respect to the provision of the relevant system;

'securities' means shares, stock, debentures, debenture stock, loan stock, bonds, units in undertakings for collective investments in transferable securities within the meaning of the European Communities (Undertakings for Collective Investment in Transferable Securities) Regulations, 1989 (S.I. No. 78 of 1989), and other securities of any description;

['settlement', in relation to a transfer of uncertificated units of a security between 2 system-members by means of a relevant system, means the delivery of those units to the transferee and, where appropriate, the creation of any associated obligation to make payments, in accordance with the rules and practices of the operator, and 'settle' shall be construed accordingly;][a]

'settlement-bank' in relation to a relevant system, means a person who has contracted to make payments in connection with transfers of title to uncertificated units of a security by means of that system;

'share' means share or stock in the share capital of a company;

'system entry' means any entry or record made, supplied or stored in legible or non-legible form by any operator or any system-participant in any register of securities or in connection with the operation of a relevant system and any dematerialised instruction issued by any such persons;

'system-member', in relation to a relevant system, means a person permitted by an operator to transfer title to uncertificated units of a security by means of that system and includes, where relevant, two or more persons who are jointly so permitted;

'system-member instruction' means a properly authenticated dematerialised instruction attributable to a system-member;

'system-participant' in relation to a relevant system, means a person who is permitted by an operator to send and receive properly authenticated dematerialised instructions and 'sponsoring system-participant' means a system-participant who is permitted by an operator to send properly authenticated dematerialised instructions attributable to another person and to receive properly authenticated dematerialised instructions on another person's behalf;

'system-user', in relation to a relevant system, means a person who as regards that system is a participating issuer, system-member, system-participant or settlement-bank;

'uncertificated unit of a security' means a unit of a security title to which is recorded on the relevant register of securities as being held in uncertificated form, and title to which, by virtue of these regulations, may be transferred by means of a relevant system and corresponding expressions shall be construed accordingly;

'unit of a security' means the smallest possible transferable unit of the security (for example a single share);

and any other expression bears the meaning given to it in the 1963 Act or the 1990 Act.

(2) For the purposes of these Regulations—

(a) a dematerialised instruction is properly authenticated if it complies with the specifications in that regard contained in the rules made and practices instituted by an operator corresponding to those in paragraph 5 (b) of the Schedule to these regulations; and

(b) a dematerialised instruction is attributable to a person if it is expressed to have been sent by that person, or if it is expressed to have been sent on behalf of that person, in each case in accordance with the specifications in that regard contained in the rules made and practices instituted by an operator corresponding to those in paragraph 5 (c) of the Schedule to these regulations; and a dematerialised instruction may be attributable to more than one person.

(3) In these regulations, except where otherwise indicated—

(a) a reference to a numbered regulation is a reference to the regulation of these regulations so numbered;

(b) a reference in a regulation to a numbered paragraph is a reference to the paragraph of that regulation so numbered;

(c) a reference in the Schedule to a numbered paragraph is a reference to the paragraph of that Schedule so numbered;

(d) a reference in a paragraph to a numbered sub-paragraph is a reference to the sub-paragraph of that paragraph so numbered.

(4) References to title to securities include any legal or equitable interest in securities and references to a transfer of title include a transfer by way of security.

(5) Where, in these regulations, anything is required or allowed to be done within a number of days not exceeding six a day that is Saturday, Sunday or public holiday shall not be reckoned in computing that number.

Amendment

[a] Definition of 'settlement' inserted by the CA1990 (US)(A)R 2005, reg 2(a), with effect from 10 November 2005.

CHAPTER II
TRANSFERRING AND RECORDING SHARES AND SECURITIES

4 Formalities of Transfer of securities

(1) Notwithstanding section 79 or section 81 of the 1963 Act or section 2 (1) of the Stock Transfer Act, 1963, title to securities may be evidenced and transferred without a written instrument provided that such title is evidenced and transferred in accordance with these regulations.

(2) References in any enactment or rule of law to a proper instrument of transfer or to a transfer with respect to securities, or any expression having like meaning, shall be taken to include a reference to an operator-instruction to a participating issuer to register a transfer of title on the relevant register of securities in accordance with the operator-instruction.

(3) Paragraphs (1) and (2) of this regulation shall not have effect in relation to an operator instruction—

(a) unless the operator giving the instruction has entered into an agreement with the Revenue Commissioners in relation to the payment of any stamp duty chargeable on transfers of title to securities through the relevant system,

(b) in the event of such an agreement having been terminated prior to the performance of the instruction, unless the instruction has been performed within seven days of the termination, and for the purpose of this paragraph an agreement shall be deemed to have been terminated on the date notice of the termination is published by the Revenue Commissioners in Iris Oifigiúil and in two national newspapers, and

(c) an agreement for the purpose of this regulation shall not impose an obligation on the operator giving the instruction to pay over to the Revenue Commissioners an amount of stamp duty greater than that collected on foot of transfers of title to securities through the relevant system.

5 Transfer in writing

Section 6 of the Statute of Frauds Act (Ireland), 1695 and section 28(6) of the Supreme Court of Judicature (Ireland) Act, 1877 and any other rule of law requiring the execution under hand or seal of a document in writing for the transfer of property, shall not apply (if they would otherwise do so) to any transfer of title to uncertificated units of a security through a relevant system.

6 Participation in respect of shares

(1) Where an operator permits a class of shares in relation to which regulation 7 applies, or in relation to which a directors' resolution passed in accordance with regulation 8 is effective, to be a participating security, title to shares of that class which are recorded in a register of members as being held in uncertificated form may be transferred by means of the relevant system to which the permission relates.

(2) For the purposes of regulations 7 and 8 any shares with respect to which share warrants to bearer are issued under section 88 of the 1963 Act shall be regarded as forming a separate class of share.

7

(1) This regulation applies to a class of shares if a company's articles of association are consistent with—

- (a) the holding of shares in that class in uncertificated form,
- (b) the transfer of title to shares in that class by means of a relevant system, and
- (c) these regulations.

(2) A company may provide for the holding of shares in such a class to which this regulation applies in uncertificated form, and the transfer of title to any such shares by means of a relevant system.

8

(1) This regulation applies to a class of shares if a company's articles of association are inconsistent with—

- (a) the holding of shares in that class in uncertificated form,
- (b) the transfer of title to shares in that class by means of a relevant system, or
- (c) any provision of these regulations.

(2) A company may resolve, subject to paragraph 6 (a), by resolution of its directors (in this Chapter referred to as a 'directors' resolution') that title to shares of a class issued or to be issued by it may be transferred by means of a relevant system.

(3) Upon a directors' resolution becoming effective in accordance with its terms, and for as long as it is in force, the articles of association in relation to the class of shares which were the subject of the directors' resolution, shall not apply to any uncertificated shares of that class to the extent that they are inconsistent with—

- (a) the holding of shares of that class in uncertificated form;
- (b) the transfer of title to shares of that class by means of a relevant system; and
- (c) any provision of these regulations.

(4) Unless a company has given notice to every member of the company in accordance with its articles of association of its intention to pass a directors' resolution before the passing of such a resolution, it shall give such notice within 60 days of the passing of the resolution and a printed copy of such a directors' resolution shall be forwarded to and recorded by the registrar of companies.

(5) Notice given by the company before the coming into force of these regulations of its intention to pass a directors' resolution which, if it had been given after the coming into force of these regulations, would have satisfied the requirements of paragraph (4) shall be taken to satisfy the requirements of that paragraph.

(6) In respect of a class of shares the members of a company may by ordinary resolution—

(a) if a directors' resolution has not been passed, resolve that the directors of the company shall not pass a directors' resolution, or

(b) if a directors' resolution has been passed but not yet come into effect in accordance with its terms, resolve that it shall not come into effect; or

(c) if a directors' resolution has been passed and is effective in accordance with its terms but the class of shares has not yet been permitted by the operator to be a participating security, resolve that the directors' resolution shall cease to have effect; or

(d) if a directors' resolution has been passed and is effective in accordance with its terms and the class of shares has been permitted by the operator to be a participating security, resolve that the directors shall take the necessary steps to ensure that title to shares of the class that was the subject of the directors' resolution shall cease to be transferable by means of a relevant system and that the directors' resolution shall cease to have effect;

and the directors shall be bound by the terms of any such ordinary resolution. A printed copy of any such resolution shall be forwarded to and recorded by the registrar of companies.

(7) If default is made in complying with paragraphs (4) and (6), the participating issuer and every officer of the participating issuer who is in default shall be liable to a [class C fine].[a]

(8) A company shall not permit the holding of shares in such a class as is referred to in paragraph (1) in un-certificated form, or the transfer of title to shares in such a class by means of a relevant system, unless in relation to that class of shares a directors' resolution is effective.

(9) This regulation shall not be taken to exclude the right of the members of a company to amend the articles of association of the company, in accordance with the articles, to allow the holding of any class of its shares in uncertificated form and the transfer of title to shares in such class by means of a relevant system.

Amendments

a £250 increased to £1,500 by CA 1990, s 240(7) as inserted by CLEA 2001, s 104(c) and converted to €1,904.61 by Council Regulations (EC) No 1103/97, No 974/98 and No 2866/98 and the Economic and Monetary Union Act 1988, s 6; the above being implicitly substituted, by Fines Act 2010, s 6, for a fine not exceeding the aforesaid amount. A class C fine currently means a fine not exceeding €2,500.

---

9 Participation in respect of securities other than shares

(1) Subject to paragraph (2), where the operator permits a security other than a share to be a participating security, title to units of that security which are recorded in a register

of securities as being held in uncertificated form shall be transferred by means of a relevant system.

(2) If, in relation to any security (other than a share), the law under which it was constituted, or a current term of its issue, is consistent with—

(a) the holding of title to units of that security in uncertificated form,

(b) the transfer of title to units of that security by means of a relevant system, or

(c) these regulations,

the issuer shall not permit the holding of units of that security in uncertificated form, or the transfer of title to units of that security, by means of a relevant system.

(3) In this regulation the terms of issue of a security shall be taken to include the terms prescribed by the issuer on which units of the security are held and title to them is transferred.

10 Entries on registers

(1) A participating issuer which is a company shall enter on its register of members, in respect of any class of shares which is a participating security, the number of shares each member holds in uncertificated form and certificated form respectively.

(2) In addition to the requirements of sections 91 and 92 of the 1963 Act, a participating issuer, who, apart from this regulation, is required by or under an enactment or instrument to maintain in the State a register of persons holding securities (other than shares) issued by it, shall enter on that register in respect of any class of security which is a participating security—

(a) the names and addresses of the persons holding units of that security, and

(b) the number of units of that security each person holds in uncertificated form and certificated form respectively.

(3) A participating issuer who, apart from this regulation, is not required by or under an enactment or instrument to maintain in the State in respect of a participating security issued by it a register of persons holding units of that participating security, shall maintain in the State a register recording—

(a) the names and addresses of the persons holding units of that security in uncertificated form; and

(b) the number of such units of that security each person holds in that form.

(4) If default is made in complying with paragraphs (1), (2) or (3), the participation issuer and every officer of the participating issuer who is in default shall be liable to a [class C fine][a].

(5) For the purpose of paragraph (1) any shares with respect to which share warrants to bearer are issued under section 88 of the 1963 Act shall be regarded as a separate class of shares.

(6) No notice of any trust, expressed, implied or constructive, shall be entered on a register of securities which is maintained by virtue of paragraph (3) in relation to uncertificated units of a security, or be receivable by the registrar of such a register.

Amendments

a £500 increased to £1,500 by CA 1990, s 240(7) as inserted by CLEA 2001, s 104(c) and converted to €1,904.61 by Council Regulations (EC) No 1103/97, No 974/98 and No 2866/98 and the Economic and Monetary Union Act 1988, s 6; the above being implicitly substituted, by Fines Act 2010, s 6, for a fine not exceeding the aforesaid amount. A class C fine currently means a fine not exceeding €2,500.

11 Effect of entries on registers

(1) Subject to regulation 16 (7), an entry on a register mentioned in paragraph (1) or (2) of regulation 10 which records a person as holding units of a security in uncertificated form shall be evidence of such title to the units as would be evidenced if the entry on the register related to units of that security held in certificated form.

(2) Subject to regulation 16 (7), an entry on a register maintained by virtue of paragraph (3) of regulation 10 shall be prima facie evidence that the person to whom the entry relates has such title to the units of the security which that person is recorded as holding in uncertificated form as if the units were held in certificated form.

12 Rectification of and changes to registers of securities

(1) A participating issuer shall not rectify a register of securities in relation to uncertificated units of a security held by a system-member except—

(a) with the consent of the operator, or

(b) by order of the High Court.

(2) A participating issuer who rectifies or otherwise changes an entry on a register of securities in relation to uncertificated units of a security (except in response to an operator-instruction) shall immediately—

(a) notify the operator, and

(b) inform the system-members concerned,

of the change to the entry.

13 Closing of registers

Notwithstanding section 121 of the 1963 Act, a participating issuer shall not close a register of securities relating to a participating security without the consent of the operator.

14 Attendance and Voting at meetings

(1) For the purposes of determining which persons are entitled to attend or vote at a meeting, and how many votes such persons may cast, the participating issuer may specify in the notice of the meeting a time, not more than 48 hours before the time fixed for the meeting, by which a person must be entered on the relevant register of securities in order to have the right to attend or vote at the meeting.

(2) Changes to entries on the relevant register of securities after the time specified by virtue of paragraph (1) shall be disregarded in determining the rights of any person to attend or vote at the meeting, notwithstanding any provisions in any enactment, articles of association or other instrument to the contrary.

15 Notice of meetings

(1) For the purposes of serving notices of meetings, whether under section 134(a) of the 1963 Act, any other enactment, a provision in the Articles of Association or any other instrument, a participating issuer may determine that persons entitled to receive such notices are those persons entered on the relevant register of securities at the close of business on a day determined by the participating issuer.

(2) The day determined by a participating issuer under paragraph (1) may not be more than 7 days before the day that the notices of the meeting are sent.

16 Registration of transfers of securities

(1) A participating issuer shall register a transfer of title to uncertificated units of a security on a register of securities in accordance with an operator-instruction unless—

- (a) the transfer is prohibited—
  - (i) by order of the High Court, provided both the participating issuer and the relevant operator shall both have had actual notice of the order before the operator-instruction is sent and the fact of such actual notice on the part of both such persons shall have been established to the satisfaction of the court by the person seeking to rely on the order, or
  - (ii) by or under an enactment, or
- (b) the participating issuer it has actual notice that the transfer is—
  - (i) avoided by or under an enactment, or
  - (ii) a transfer to a deceased person, or
- (c) the circumstances described in paragraph (2) apply, or
- (d) the participating issuer is entitled by virtue of paragraph (3) to refuse to register the transfer.

(2) The circumstances referred to in paragraph (1)(c) are that the transfer is one of two or more transfers in respect of which the operator has notified the participating issuer in accordance with regulation 17(1), and that to those transfers regulation 17 (2) does not apply by virtue of regulation 17(3).

(3) A participating issuer may refuse to register a transfer of title to uncertificated units of a security in accordance with an operator-instruction if the instruction requires a transfer of units—

- (a) to an entity which is not a natural or legal person,
- (b) to a minor,
- (c) to be held jointly in the names of more persons than is permitted under the terms of issue of the security, or
- (d) where in relation to the operator-instruction the participating issuer has actual notice from the operator of any of the matters specified in regulation 35 (5) (a).

(4) A participating issuer shall notify the operator by issuer-instruction that the transfer has been registered in response to an operator-instruction to do so.

(5) A participating issuer shall not register a transfer of title to uncertificated units of a security on a register of securities unless required to do so—

- (a) by an operator-instruction,
- (b) by order of the High Court,

(c) by or under an enactment, or

(d) by regulation 36(2).

(6) Paragraph (5) shall not be taken to prevent a participating issuer from entering a person on a register of securities to whom the title to uncertificated units of a security has been transmitted by operation of law.

(7) Any purported registration of a transfer of title to an uncertificated unit of a security other than in accordance with this regulation shall be of no effect.

(8) If a participating issuer refuses to register a transfer of any shares or debentures, the participating issuer shall, within 2 months after the date on which the transfer was lodged with the participating issuer, send to the transferee notice of the refusal.

(9) If default is made in complying with paragraph (8), the participating issuer and every officer of the participating issuer who is in default shall be liable to a [class C fine].[a]

Amendments

a £250 increased to £1,500 by CA 1990, s 240(7) as inserted by CLEA 2001, s 104(c) and converted to €1,904.61 by Council Regulations (EC) No 1103/97, No 974/98 and No 2866/98 and the Economic and Monetary Union Act, 1988, s 6; the above being implicitly substituted, by Fines Act 2010, s 6, for a fine not exceeding the aforesaid amount. A class C fine currently means a fine not exceeding €2,500.

17 Registration of linked transfers

(1) Where an operator sends two or more operator-instructions requiring a participating issuer to register two or more transfers of title to uncertificated units of a security, and it appears to the operator—

(a) either—

(i) that there are fewer units of the security registered in the name of a person identified in any one of the operator-instructions as a transferor than the number of units to be transferred from that person, or

(ii) that any one of the transfers taken alone is one in relation to which it has not been established in accordance with the procedures of the relevant system that a settlement-bank has agreed to make a payment, and

(b) that registration of all of the transfers would result in each of the persons identified in the operator-instructions as a transferor having title to a number of units of a security equal to or greater than nil, and

(c) that the combined effect of all the transfers taken together would result in payment being made by the settlement-bank,

the operator may notify the participating issuer that the transfers are linked transfers.

(2) Except in the circumstances described in paragraph (3), notwithstanding that there may be fewer uncertificated units of the security registered in the name of a person identified in any one of the operator-instructions as a transferor than the number of uncertificated units to be transferred from that person, where an operator notifies a participating issuer that transfers are linked transfers, the participating issuer may either—

(a) register the combined effect of all the transfers taken together, or

(b) register all the transfers simultaneously.

(3) Paragraph (2) does not apply in a case in which—

(a) registration of the combined effect of the linked transfers, or simultaneous registration of all the transfers (as the case may be), would not result in each of the persons identified in the operator-instructions as a transferor having title to a number of uncertificated units of the security equal to or greater than nil, or

(b) one or more of the transfers constituting the linked transfers may not be registered by virtue of the circumstances specified in regulation 16(1)(a) or (b), or is to be refused registration by virtue of regulation 16(3).

18 Position of a transferee prior to entry on register

(1) At the time an operator-instruction is sent requiring a participating issuer to register on a register of securities a transfer of title to any uncertificated units of a security—

(a) the transferee shall acquire an equitable interest in the requisite number of uncertificated units of the security of the kind specified in the operator-instruction in which the transferor has an equitable interest by virtue of this regulation, or in relation to which the transferor is recorded on the relevant register of securities as having title, and

(b) the equitable interest shall subsist until the time specified in paragraph (3).

(2) For the purposes of paragraph (1)(a) it shall not be denied that the transferee has obtained the equitable interest referred to in paragraph (1)(a), solely by reason of the fact that the transferor acquired the equitable interest by virtue of paragraph (1)(a) at the same time as the transferee's equitable interest arises in that interest.

(3) Subject to any enactment or rule of law, an interest acquired under paragraph (1)—

(a) in a case other than one in which under regulation 17(2)(a) a participating issuer registers the combined effect of linked transfers, shall subsist until the time that the transferee is entered on the register of securities in respect of the transfer of the units, and

(b) in a case in which under regulation 17(2)(a) a participating issuer registers the combined effect of linked transfers, shall subsist until the time that the combined effect of all the linked transfers is registered.

(4) The requisite number for the purposes of this regulation is whichever of the following is the lower at the time that the operator-instruction is sent, namely—

(a) the number of units which are specified in the operator-instruction, and

(b) the total of the number of uncertificated units in relation to which the transferor is recorded on the register of securities as having title and the number in which the transferor has an interest by virtue of paragraph (1), less that number of units in which such interests subsist in favour of a third party by virtue of an earlier operator-instruction requiring a participating issuer to register on a register of securities a transfer of title to those units.

(5) This regulation has effect notwithstanding that the units to which the operator-instruction relates, or in which an interest arises by virtue of paragraph 1, of any of them, may be unascertained.

(6) Subject to paragraph (5), this regulation shall not be construed as conferring a proprietary interest (whether of the kind referred to in paragraph (1) or any other kind) in units of a security if the conferring of such an interest at the time specified in these regulations would otherwise be void by or under an enactment or rule of law.

(7) In this regulation—

(a) 'the transferee' means the person identified in the operator-instruction as the transferee, and

(b) 'the transferor' means the person identified in the operator-instruction as the transferor.

19 Prohibition on issue of certificates

(1) Notwithstanding any enactment, or rule of law, and in particular section 86 of the 1963 Act, but subject to regulation 20, a participating issuer shall not issue a certificate in relation to any uncertificated units of a participating security.

(2) A document issued by or on behalf of a participating issuer purportedly evidencing title to an uncertificated unit of a participating security shall not be evidence of title to the unit of the security; and in particular section 87(1) of the 1963 Act shall not apply to any document issued with respect to uncertificated shares.

20 Conversion of securities into certificated form

(1) A participating issuer shall not change a unit of a participating security from uncertificated to certificated form except—

(a) where permitted by the rules made and practices instituted by an operator, or

(b) following receipt of an operator-instruction requiring the conversion into certificated form of uncertificated units of a participating security registered in the name of a system-member, or

(c) subject to regulation 16, following receipt of an operator-instruction requiring the registration of a transfer of title to uncertificated units of a security to a person who is not a system-member, or

(d) on the registration, in accordance with regulation 36(2), of an offeror who is not a system-member as holder of the units of the security referred to in that regulation.

(2) In the circumstances specified in paragraph (1) (b), (c) and (d) a participating issuer shall—

(a) record on the register of securities that the units of the security are held in certificated form;

(b) where a certificate can be issued for the security, issue a certificate in respect of the units of the security to the relevant person; and

(c) notify the operator that the units are no longer held in uncertificated form.

(3) Every participating issuer shall, within 2 months after the date on which the issuer receives a relevant operator-instruction which can be complied with in accordance with paragraph (2), complete and have ready for delivery the certificates of all securities transferred pursuant to the operator-instruction.

(4) If default is made in complying with paragraph (3), the participating issuer and every officer of the participating issuer who is in default shall be liable to a [class C fine].[a]

(5) If any participating issuer served with a notice requiring the participating issuer to make good any default in complying with the provisions of paragraph (3) fails to make good the default within 10 days after the service of the notice, the court may on the application of the person entitled to have the certificates delivered, make an order directing the participating issuer and any officers of the participating issuer to make good the default within such time as may be specified in the order, and any such order may provide that all costs of and incidental to the application shall be borne by the participating issuer or by any officer of the participating issuer responsible for the default.

Amendments

a £250 increased to £1,500 by CA 1990, s 240(7) as inserted by CLEA 2001, s 104(c) and converted to €1,904.61 by Council Regulations (EC) No 1103/97, No 974/98 and No 2866/98 and the Economic and Monetary Union Act, 1988, s 6; the above being implicitly substituted, by Fines Act 2010, s 6, for a fine not exceeding the aforesaid amount. A class C fine currently means a fine not exceeding €2,500.

---

21 Endorsements on certificates

Any requirement in or under any enactment to endorse any statement or information on a certificate evidencing title to a unit of security (including any such requirement in section 104 of the 1963 Act)—

(a) shall not prohibit the conversion into, or issue of, units of the security in uncertificated form, and

(b) in relation to uncertificated units of the security, shall be taken to be a requirement to provide the holder of the units of security on request with the statement or information.

22 Interests in uncertificated units

The operator shall not be bound by or compelled to recognise any express, implied or constructive trust or other interest in respect of uncertificated units of a security, even if the operator has actual or constructive notice of the said trust or interest.

23 Liabilities of trustees

(1) Unless expressly prohibited from transferring units of a security by means of any computer based system, a person being a trustee or personal representative shall not be chargeable with a breach of trust or, as the case may be, with default in administering the estate by reason only of the fact that—

(a) for the purpose of acquiring units of a security which that person has the power to acquire in connection with the trust or estate, the units are paid for under arrangements which provide for them to be transferred from a system-member but not to be so transferred until after the payment of the price;

(b) for the purpose of disposing of units of security which that person has power to dispose of in connection with the trust or estate, the units are transferred to a system-member under arrangements which provide that the price is not to be paid until after the transfer is made; or

(c) for the purposes of holding units of a security belonging to the trust or estate in uncertificated form and for transferring title to them by means of a relevant system, that person has become a system-member.

(2) A trustee of a trust deed for securing an issue of debentures shall not be chargeable with a breach of trust by reason only of having consented to an amendment of the trust deed only for the purposes of—

(a) allowing the holding of the debentures in uncertificated form;

(b) allowing the exercise of rights attaching to the debentures by means of a relevant system; or

(c) allowing the transfer of title to the debentures by means of a relevant system;

provided that notice of the amendment has been given to all persons having title to the debentures at least 30 days prior to such consent becoming effective.

24 Conversion of securities into uncertificated form

(1) A participating issuer shall not change a unit of a participating security from certificated form to uncertificated form except in the circumstances specified in paragraph (2).

(2) The circumstances referred to in paragraph (1) are—

(a) where the unit of the participating-security is held by a system-member, that the participating issuer has received—

(i) a request in writing in the form required by the rules made and practices instituted by an operator to register the system-member as holding the unit in uncertificated form; and

(ii) subject to paragraph (4), the certificate relating to the certificated unit which is to be converted into uncertificated form;

(b) where the unit of the participating security is to be registered on a register of securities in the name of a system-member following a transfer of the unit to that person from a person other than a stock exchange nominee, that the participating issuer—

(i) subject to paragraph (3), has received by means of the operator-system a proper instrument of transfer in favour of the system-member relating to the unit to be transferred;

(ii) subject to paragraph (4), has received by means of the operator-system the certificate relating to the certificated unit which is to be transferred and converted into uncertificated form; and

(iii) may accept by virtue of the rules made and practices instituted by an operator that the system-member to whom the unit is to be transferred wishes to hold it in uncertificated form; and

(c) where the unit of the participating security is to be registered on a register of securities in the name of a system-member following a transfer of the unit to him from a stock exchange nominee, that the participating issuer—

(i) has received a proper instrument of transfer in favour of the system-member from the nominee relating to the unit to be transferred; and

(ii) may accept by virtue of the rules made and practices instituted by an operator that the system-member to whom the unit is to be transferred wishes to hold it in uncertificated form.

(3) The requirement in paragraph (2)(b)(i) that the participating issuer shall have received an instrument of transfer relating to the unit of the participating security shall not apply in a case where for a transfer of a unit of that security no instrument of transfer is required.

(4) The requirements in paragraph (2)(a)(ii) and (2)(b)(ii) that the participating issuer shall have received a certificate relating to the unit of the participating security shall not apply in a case where the system-member or transferor (as the case may be) does not have a certificate in respect of the unit to be converted into uncertificated form because no certificate has yet been issued to him.

(5) In the circumstances specified in paragraph (2 (a), on receipt of the request referred to in paragraph (2)(a)(i) and (except where paragraph (4) applies) the certificate referred to in paragraph (2)(a)(ii), the participating issuer shall, within two months—

(a) enter on the register of securities that the system-member holds the unit in uncertificated form; and

(b) send the operator an issuer-instruction of the entry on the relevant register of securities.

(6) In the circumstances specified in paragraph (2)(b), on receipt of the instrument of transfer referred to in paragraph (2)(b)(i) (except where paragraph (3) applies) and the certificate referred to in paragraph (2)(b)(ii) (except where paragraph (4) applies), the participating issuer shall—

(a) upon recording that the system-member holds the unit, enter on the register of securities that the unit is held in uncertificated form; and

(b) within 2 months thereafter, send the operator an issuer-instruction of the entry on the register of securities.

(7) In the circumstances specified in paragraph (2)(c), on receipt of the instrument of transfer referred to in paragraph (2)(c)(i), the participating issuer shall—

(a) upon recording that the system-member holds the unit, enter on the register of securities that the unit is held in uncertificated form; and

(b) within 2 months thereafter, send the operator an issuer-instruction of the entry on the register of securities.

(8) If default is made in complying with paragraphs (5), (6) or (7) the participating issuer and every officer of the participating issuer who is in default shall be liable to a [class C fine].[a]

(9) In this regulation, 'stock exchange nominee' has the same meaning as in the 1977 Act.

Amendments

a £250 increased to £1,500 by CA 1990, s 240(7) as inserted by CLEA 2001, s 104(c) and converted to €1,904.61 by Council Regulations (EC) No 1103/97, No 974/98 and No 2866/98 and the Economic and Monetary Union Act, 1988, s 6; the above being implicitly substituted,

by Fines Act 2010, s 6, for a fine not exceeding the aforesaid amount. A class C fine currently means a fine not exceeding €2,500.

25 New issues in uncertificated form

(1) A participating issuer may issue new units of a participating security in uncertificated form to a person if, and only if, that person is a system-member.

(2) For the purposes of calculating the number of new units to which a system-member is entitled, a participating issuer may treat a system-member's holdings of certificated and uncertificated units of a security as if they were separate holdings.

(3) On the issue in uncertificated form of new units of a participating security, the participating issuer shall by issuer-instruction notify the operator of the persons to whom the uncertificated units of a security have been issued and of the number of such units issued to each of those persons.

CHAPTER III
APPROVAL AND COMPLIANCE OF OPERATOR

26 Application for Approval

(1) A person may apply to the Minister to be approved operator of a relevant system.

(2) Any such application—

(a) shall be made in such a manner as the Minister may direct, and

(b) shall be accompanied by such information as the Minister may reasonably require for the purpose of determining the application.

(3) At any time after receiving an application and before determining it, the Minister may require the applicant to furnish additional information.

(4) The directions and requirements given or imposed under paragraphs (2) and (3) may differ as between different applications.

(5) Any information to be furnished to the Minister under this regulation shall, if the Minister so requires, be in such form or verified in such manner as the Minister may specify.

(6) Every application shall be accompanied by a copy of any rules and guidance to be issued by the applicant.

27 Grant of Approval

(1) If, on an application made under regulation 26, it appears that the requirements of the Schedule are satisfied with respect to the application, the Minister may, subject to the following paragraphs of this regulation, approve a person (in these regulations referred to as an approved operator) to operate a relevant system.

(2) Approval of an operator under this regulation shall be by written instrument and may be subject to the fulfilment of conditions specified by the Minister to ensure compliance with these regulations and shall state the date on which it takes effect and may state the date on which it terminates.

(3) Approval under this regulation shall be without prejudice to the requirements of the Competition Act, 1991.

(4) Where the Minister refuses to approve an operator on the basis of an application made under regulation 26 the Minister shall so inform the applicant in writing stating the reasons for the refusal.

28 Recognition of operator approved by competent authority

(1) A person approved by a competent authority to operate a relevant system may be granted recognition by the Minister to act as an operator for the purposes of these regulations, subject, in particular, to regulation 32.

(2) The Minister may make the recognition subject to certain conditions, either when granted or during its currency.

29 Delegation of Minister's Functions

(1) The Minister may delegate any approval and other supervisory functions under this Chapter to a designated body.

(2) The Minister may by written instrument revoke a designation under paragraph (1)—

(a) at the request of, or with the consent of, the designated body, or

(b) if at any time it appears to the Minister that the designated body is unable or unwilling to discharge all or any of the functions delegated to it.

30 Appeal to Minister

(1) Where a body designated under regulation 29(1) refuses to approve a proposed operator, it shall serve notice on the proposed operator, and on the Minister, of its refusal to grant approval and state the reason therefor.

(2) A proposed operator on whom a notice has been served under paragraph (1) of this regulation, may within 21 days of receipt of the notice, appeal to the Minister and the Minister shall consider any such appeal and may uphold or reject it.

(3) When considering an appeal under this section, the Minister shall consult with the designated body and the proposed operator concerned and any other party the Minister thinks proper, provided that the period taken for consideration does not exceed three months.

(4) If the Minister upholds an appeal made under this section, the designated body shall grant approval of the proposed operator.

(5) An appeal under this section shall be accompanied by such fee as the Minister may by regulation prescribe.

(6) The Public Offices Fees Act, 1879, shall not apply to any fees charged under this section.

31 Withdrawal of Approval

(1) The Minister may revoke approval of an operator in all or any of the following circumstances, namely, where—

(a) a request has been made in that behalf by the operator, or

(b) the operator—

(i) has failed to operate a relevant system within 12 months of the date on which the approval to be an operator was granted, or

(ii) has failed to operate as a relevant system for a period of more than 6 months, or

(iii) is being wound up.

(2) Without prejudice to the power of the Minister to revoke an approval under paragraph (1), the Minister may apply to the High Court, in a summary manner, for an order revoking the approval in any or all of the following circumstances, namely, if—

- (a) at any time it appears to the Minister that any requirement of the Schedule is not satisfied by an approved operator, or
- (b) it is expedient to do so in the interest of the proper and orderly regulation of operators, or their system users, or in order to protect investors,
- (c) the operator has, on indictment, been convicted of any offence under the Companies Acts or any offence involving fraud, dishonesty or breach of trust;
- (d) the approval was obtained by the operator knowingly or recklessly making false or misleading statements, or by knowingly or recklessly using false or misleading information;
- (e) the operator has failed to comply to a material degree with a requirement of these regulations having been first called upon to do so;
- (f) the operator no longer fulfils a condition or requirement imposed when approval was granted;
- (g) the operator becomes unable or, in the opinion of the Minister, is likely to become unable to meet its obligations to its creditors or suspends payments lawfully due.

(3) When the Minister proposes to revoke the approval of an operator or proposes to apply to the court for an order to revoke approval of an operator, the Minister shall serve notice on the operator concerned of the proposal and the reasons therefor.

(4) Where an application is made to the court under this regulation the court may make such order or orders as the circumstances may require.

(5) Where approval of an operator is revoked and where the operator concerned is not a company which is being wound up.

- (a) the former operator and its system-users shall continue to be subject to the duties and obligations imposed by these regulations until all the liabilities, duties and obligations of the said operator have been discharged to the satisfaction of the Minister, and
- (b) the former operator shall, as soon as possible, after the revocation, notify the Minister, its system users and such other persons, if any, as the Minister indicates are to be notified of the measures being taken to discharge without undue delay the liabilities, duties and obligations of the said operator.

(6) The Minister shall publish notice of any revocation of an approval of an operator in Iris Oifigiúil within 28 days of revocation.

(7) An operator whose approval has been revoked under these regulations shall cease to operate a relevant system.

(8) An application under this regulation may be heard otherwise than in public.

32 Withdrawal of Recognition

(1) The Minister may withdraw a grant of recognition in all or any of the following circumstances, namely, where—

(a) a request has been made in that behalf by the operator;

(b) if the competent authority which approved the operator has withdrawn its approval;

(c) if the operator—

(i) has failed to operate a relevant system within 12 months of the date on which recognition was granted, or

(ii) has failed to operate as a relevant system for a period of more than 6 months, or

(iii) is being wound up, or

(d) on any other grounds which seem reasonable to the Minister.

(2) The Minister shall serve on the operator notice of a proposal to withdraw a grant and shall state the reasons therefor.

(3) An operator whose grant of recognition is withdrawn pursuant to paragraph 1 (d) may appeal the Minister's decision to the Court.

(4) On hearing an application under paragraph (3), the Court may confirm or rescind the Minister's decision or make such other ancillary order as it deems fit.

(5) The operator may apply to the Court and the Court may grant an order providing for such interim or interlocutory relief as it considers appropriate.

33 Compliance order and directions

(1) If at any time it appears to the Minister that any requirement of the Schedule to these regulations is not satisfied by an approved operator, or that an approved operator has failed to comply with any obligation under these regulations, the Minister may—

(a) apply to the High Court for relief, or

(b) subject to paragraph (3), give to the operator such directions as the Minister thinks fit for securing that the relevant requirement is satisfied or obligation complied with.

(2) If on any application by the Minister under paragraph (1) (a) the court is satisfied that the requirement is not satisfied or, as the case may be, that the operator has failed to comply with the obligation in question, it may order the operator to take such steps as the court directs for securing that the requirement is satisfied or that the obligation is complied with.

(3) Before giving a direction under paragraph (1) (b) the Minister shall—

(a) if circumstances permit, consult with and afford the operator an opportunity to make representations; and

(b) so far as it is practicable to estimate it, have regard to the cost to the operator of complying with any term of any direction and to the costs to other persons resulting from the operator's compliance.

34 Requests for information from the Operator

(1) The Minister may in writing, require an approved operator to provide the Minister with specified information.

(2) The Minister, may, in writing, require an approved operator to furnish the Minister, at specified times or in respect of specified periods, with specified information, verified

in a specified manner, relating to that operator for the exercise of the Minister's functions under these regulations.

(3) An approved operator who amends, revokes or adds to any rules or guidance shall within seven days given written notice to the Minister of the amendment, revocation or addition.

CHAPTER IV
OPERATION OF AUTOMATED TRANSFER AND REGISTRATION

35 Properly authenticated dematerialised instructions

(1) This regulation has effect for the purpose of determining the rights and obligations of persons to whom properly authenticated dematerialised instructions are attributable and of persons to whom properly authenticated dematerialised instructions are addressed when such instructions relate to an uncertificated unit of a security, or relate to a right, benefit or privilege attaching to or arising from such a unit, or relating to the details of a holder of such a unit.

(2) Where a properly authenticated dematerialised instruction is expressed to have been sent on behalf of a person by a sponsoring system-participant or the operator—

(a) the person on whose behalf the instruction is expressed to have been sent shall not be able to deny to the addressee—

(i) that the properly authenticated dematerialised instruction was sent with that person's authority, or

(ii) that the information contained in the properly authenticated dematerialised instruction is correct; and

(b) the sponsoring system-participant or the operator (as the case may be) shall not be able to deny to the addressee—

(i) that he has authority to send the properly authenticated dematerialised instruction, or

(ii) that he has sent the properly authenticated dematerialised instruction.

(3) Where a properly authenticated dematerialised instruction is expressed to have been sent by a person and is not expressed to have been sent on behalf of another person, the person shall not be able to deny to the addressee—

(a) that the information contained in the properly authenticated dematerialised instruction is correct, or

(b) that the properly authenticated dematerialised instruction was sent.

(4) An addressee who receives (whether directly, or by means of the facilities of a sponsoring system-participant acting on the addressee's behalf) a properly authenticated dematerialised instruction may, subject to paragraph (5), accept that at the time at which the properly authenticated dematerialised instruction was sent—

(a) the information contained in the instruction was correct;

(b) the system-participant or the operator (as the case may be) identified in the instruction as having sent the instruction sent the instruction; and

(c) the instruction, where relevant, has been sent with the authority of the person on whose behalf it is expressed to have been sent.

(5) Subject to paragraph (6), an addressee may not accept any of the matters specified in paragraph (4) if at the time of receipt of the properly authenticated dematerialised instruction—

(a) the addressee was a person other than a participating issuer or a sponsoring system-participant receiving properly authenticated dematerialised instructions on behalf of a participating issuer, and had actual notice—

(i) that any information contained in it was incorrect;

(ii) that the system participant or the operator (as the case may be) expressed to have sent the instruction did not send the instruction; or

(iii) where relevant, that the person on whose behalf it was expressed to have been sent had not given to the operator or the sponsoring system-participant (as the case may be), identified in the properly authenticated dematerialised instruction as having sent it, authority to send the instruction on that persons behalf; or

(b) the addressee was a participating issuer or a sponsoring system-participant receiving the instruction on behalf of a participating issuer, and

(i) had actual notice from the operator of any of the matters specified in sub-paragraph (a); or

(ii) the instruction was an operator- instruction requiring the registration of title in the circumstances specified in regulation 16(1)(a), (b) or (c); or

(c) the addressee was an operator and the instruction related to a transfer of units of a security which was in excess of any limit imposed on a sponsoring system participant, by a system-member, in accordance with the rules and procedures of an operator.

(6) Notwithstanding that an addressee has received in respect of a properly authenticated dematerialised instruction actual notice of the kind referred to in paragraph (5), the addressee may accept the matters specified in paragraph (4) if at the time that the actual notice was received it was not practical for the addressee to halt processing of the instruction.

(7) A person who is permitted by this regulation to accept any matter shall not be liable in damages or otherwise to any person by reason of having relied on that matter.

(8) Subject to paragraph (7) this regulation has effect without prejudice to the liability of any person for causing or permitting a dematerialised instruction—

(a) to be sent without authority; or

(b) to contain information which is incorrect; or

(c) to be expressed to have been sent by a person who did not send it.

(9) For the purposes of this regulation—

(a) a properly authenticated dematerialised instruction is expressed to have been sent by a person or on behalf of a person if it is attributable to that person; and

(b) an addressee is the person to whom the instruction indicates it is addressed in accordance with the specifications of the operator.

CHAPTER V
MINORITY SHAREHOLDERS

36 Notices under section 204 of the 1963 Act

(1) This regulation shall apply in relation to any uncertificated units of a security to which a notice given pursuant to section 204(1) of the 1963 Act relates.

(2) On receipt of a notice transmitted pursuant to section 204(5) of the 1963 Act, a company which is a participating issuer shall on the expiration of one month from the date on which this notification was made enter the transferee company in its register of securities as the holder of the uncertificated units of the security to which the notice relates in place of the system-member who was immediately prior to such entry registered as the holder of such units as if it had received an operator-instruction requiring it to amend its register of securities in such manner.

(3) A company which amends its register of securities in accordance with paragraph (2) shall forthwith notify the operator by issuer-instruction of the amendment.

(4) In this regulation, 'the transferee company' has the same meaning as in section 204 (1) of the 1963 Act.

CHAPTER VI
SUPPLEMENTARY AND INCIDENTAL

37 Evidence of system-entries.

(1) Subject to the provisions of this regulation, a copy or reproduction of a system-entry or the relevant part of it in a legible form shall in all legal proceedings be received as prima facie evidence of such entry or record and of the matters and transactions therein entered or recorded.

(2) A copy or reproduction of a system-entry shall not be received in evidence under this regulation unless it be first proved that the system-entry was at the time of the making of the entry or record one of the ordinary entries or records of the operator or system-participant, as applicable, and that the entry or record was made, supplied or stored in the usual and ordinary course of business, and that the system-entry is in the custody or control of such person. Such proof may be given by a director, secretary or officer of such person, and may be given orally or by an affidavit sworn before any commissioner or person authorised to take affidavits.

(3) A copy or reproduction of a system-entry which was originally made in legible form shall not be received in evidence under this regulation unless it be further proved that the copy or reproduction has been examined with the original system-entry and is correct. Such proof shall be given by some person who has examined the copy or reproduction with the original entry, and may be given either orally or by an affidavit sworn before any commissioner or person authorised to take affidavit.

(4) A copy or reproduction of a system-entry which was originally made in non-legible form shall not be received in evidence under this regulation unless it be further proved that where the copy or reproduction was produced by computer, any such computer was operating properly throughout the relevant period, or if not, the circumstances were not such as to affect the reproduction of the system-entry or its contents in legible form and that the information contained in the copy or reproduction reproduces or is derived from information supplied to the computer or computers. Such proof may be given by any

person occupying a responsible position in relation to the relevant device or the management of the relevant activities (whichever is appropriate) and may be given orally or by affidavit sworn before any commissioner or person authorised to take affidavits.

(5) An operator or system-participant or any officer of such person shall not, in any legal proceedings to which such person is not a party, be compellable to produce any system-entry the contents of which can be proved under this regulation, or to appear as a witness to prove the entries, records, matters or transactions therein entered or recorded, unless by an order of a court made for special cause.

(6) On the application of any party to a legal proceeding a court may order that such party be at liberty to inspect and take copies or reproductions of any entries in a system-entry for any of the purposes of such proceeding. An order under this paragraph may be made either with or without summoning the person who has custody or control of the system-entry or any other party, and shall be served on the person who has custody or control of the system-entry three clear days before the same is to be obeyed, unless the court otherwise directs.

(7) The costs of any application to a court under or for the purposes of this regulation, and the costs of anything done or to be done under an order of a court made under or for the purposes of this regulation shall be in the discretion of the court, who may order the same or any part thereof to be paid to any party by the person who has custody or control of the system-entry, where the same have been occasioned by any default or delay on the part of such person. Any such order against such person may be enforced as if such person was a party to the proceedings.

(8) In this regulation—

> 'legal proceeding' means any civil or criminal proceeding or enquiry in which evidence is or may be given, and includes an arbitration;
>
> 'the court' means the court, judge, arbitrator, person or persons before whom a legal proceeding is held or taken;

information shall be taken to be supplied to a computer if it is supplied thereto in any appropriate form and whether it is so supplied directly or (with or without human intervention) by means of any appropriate equipment;

where in the ordinary course of business carried on by any individual or body, information is supplied with a view to its being stored or processed for the purposes of that business by a computer operated otherwise than in the ordinary course of that business, that information, if duly supplied to that computer, shall be taken to be supplied to it in the ordinary course of that business;

a document shall be taken to have been produced by a computer whether it was produced by it directly or (with or without human intervention) by means of any appropriate equipment.

Schedule

REQUIREMENTS FOR APPROVAL OF AN OPERATOR

Arrangements and Resources

1. (a) An approved operator must have adequate arrangements and resources for the effective monitoring and enforcement of compliance with the rules of the operator or, as respects monitoring, arrangements providing for that function to be performed on the operator's behalf (and without affecting the operator's responsibility) by another body or person who is able and willing to perform it.

(b) The operator's business and corporate structure must be so organised to be capable of being supervised under the regulations to the satisfaction of the Minister.

Financial Resources

2. An approved operator must have financial resources sufficient for the proper performance of the functions of an operator.

Promotion and Maintenance of Standards

3. An approved operator must be able and willing to promote and maintain high standards of integrity and fair dealing in the operation of the relevant system and to co-operate, by the sharing of information or otherwise, with the Minister and any other authority, body or person having responsibility for the supervision or regulation of investment business or other financial services.

Operation of the Relevant System

4. Where an operator causes or permits a part of the relevant system which is not the operator-system to be operated by another person (other than as his agent) the operator—

(a) shall monitor compliance by the person and that part with the requirements of this Schedule; and

(b) shall have arrangements to ensure that the person provides such information and such assistance as the operator may require in order to meet obligations under these regulations.

System Security

5. A relevant system must be constructed and operate in such a way—

(a) so as to minimise the possibility of unauthorised access to or modification of any program or data held in any computer forming part of the operator's system; and

[(b) that each dematerialised instruction is properly authenticated—

(i) in accordance with the specifications of the operator, which shall provide that each dematerialised instruction—

(I) is identifiable as being from the computers of a particular system-participant, and

(II) is designed to minimise fraud and forgery, or

(ii) if it is sent to the operator by, or by the operator to, a depository, a clearing house or a stock exchange, in accordance with specifications of that depository, clearing house or exchange to which the operator has agreed and which shall provide that each dematerialised instruction –

(I) is identifiable as being from the computers of the operator or of the depositary, clearing house or exchange which sent it, and

(II) is designed to minimise fraud and forgery;][a]

(c) that each dematerialised instruction, in accordance with the specifications of the operator, expresses by whom it has been sent and, where relevant, on whose behalf it has been sent;

(d) that each dematerialised instruction, in accordance with the specifications of the operator, indicates—

(i) where it is sent to a system-participant or the operator, that it is addressed to that system-participant or the operator; and

(ii) where it is sent to a person who is using the facilities of a sponsoring system-participant to receive dematerialised instructions, that it is addressed to that person and the sponsoring system-participant; and

(iii) where it is sent to the operator in order to send an operator-instruction to a system-participant, that it is addressed to the operator, to the system-participant and, if the system-participant is acting as a sponsoring system-participant, to the relevant person on whose behalf the sponsoring system-participant receives dematerialised instructions; and

(e) that the possibility for a system-participant to send a dematerialised instruction on behalf of a person from whom the participant has no authority is minimised.

[5A. For the purposes of paragraph 5—

'clearing house' means a body or association which provides services related to the clearing and settlement of transactions and payments and the management of risks associated with the resulting contracts and which is regulated or supervised in the provision of those services by a regulatory body, or an agency of government, of a Member State;

'depositary' means a body or association carrying on business outside the State with whom an operator has made arrangements—

(i) to enable system-members to hold (whether directly or indirectly) and transfer title to securities (other than participating securities) by means of facilities provided by that body or association; or

(ii) to enable that body or association to permit persons to whom it provides services in the course of its business to hold (whether directly or indirectly) and transfer title to participating securities by means of the operator's relevant system;

'stock exchange' means—

(i) a person who has been approved as such under section 9 of the Stock Exchange Act 1995, or

(ii) a body or association which provides services outside the State which are similar in nature to those provided by a person referred to in paragraph (i) and which is regulated or supervised in the provision of those services by a regulatory body, or an agency of government, of a Member State.][b]

Amendments

a Subparagraph 5(b) substituted by CA1990(US)(A)R 2005, reg 2(b)(i), with effect from 10 November 2005.

b Paragraph 5A inserted by CA1990(US)(A)R 2005, reg 2(b)(ii), with effect from 10 November 2005.

System Capabilities

6. A relevant system must ensure that the operator-system can send and respond to properly authenticated dematerialised instructions in sufficient volume and speed.

7. Before an operator-instruction to a participating issuer to register a transfer of uncertificated units of a security is generated, a relevant system must—

(a) be able to establish that the transferor is likely to have title to or, by virtue of regulation 18(1), an interest in, such number of units of the security as is in aggregate at least equal to the number to be transferred; or

(b) be able to notify the participating issuer, in accordance with regulation 17(1), that the transfer is one of two or more transfers which may be registered in accordance with regulation 17(2).

8. A relevant system must maintain adequate records of all dematerialised instructions.

9. A relevant system must be able—

(a) to permit each system-member to obtain a copy of any records relating to the member as are maintained by the relevant system in order to comply with paragraph 7 (a) or 8; and

(b) to make correcting entries in such records as are maintained in order to comply with paragraph 7(a) which are inaccurate.

10. A relevant system must be able to establish, where there is a transfer of uncertificated units of a security to a system-member for value, that a settlement-bank has agreed to make payment in respect of the transfer, whether alone or taken together with another transfer for value.

11. A relevant system must ensure that the operator-system is able to generate operator-instructions—

(a) requiring participating issuers to amend the appropriate registers of securities kept by them; and

(b) informing settlement-banks of their payment obligations.

12. A relevant system must—

(a) enable a system-member—

(i) to grant authority to a sponsoring system-participant to send properly authenticated dematerialised instructions on the member's behalf; and

(ii) to limit such authority by reference to the net value of the units of securities to be transferred in any one day; and

(b) prevent the transfer of units in excess of that limit.

13. A relevant system must enable system-members—

(a) to change the form in which they hold or are to hold units of a participating security; and

(b) where appropriate, to require participating issuers to issue certificates relating to units of a participating security held or to be held by them.

Operating Procedures

14. A relevant system must comprise procedures which provide that it responds only to properly authenticated dematerialised instructions which are attributable to a system-user or an operator.

15. (1) Subject to sub-paragraph (2), a relevant system must comprise procedures which provide that an operator- instruction requiring a participating issuer to register a transfer of uncertificated units of a security, or informing a settlement-bank of its payment obligations in respect of such a transfer is generated only if—

(a) it has—

(i) received a system-member instruction from the transferor; or

(ii) been required to do so by a court or by or under an enactment;

(b) it has—

(i) established that the transferor is likely to have title to, or is likely to have by virtue of regulation 18(1) an interest in, such number of units as is in aggregate at least equal to the number to be transferred; or

(ii) established that the transfer is one of two or more transfers which may be notified to the participating issuer in accordance with regulation 17(1);

(c) in the case of a transfer to a system-member for value, it has established that a settlement-bank has agreed to make payment in respect of the transfer, whether alone or taken together with another transfer for value; and

(d) the transfer is not in excess of any limit which by virtue of paragraph 12 (a) (ii) the transferor has set on an authority given to a sponsoring system-participant.

(2) A relevant system must comprise procedures which provide that an operator-instruction requiring a participating- issuer to register a transfer of uncertificated units of a security, or informing a settlement-bank of its payment obligations in respect of such a transfer may be generated if necessary to correct an error and if in accordance with the rules and practices of an operator instituted in order to comply with this Schedule.

16. (1) Subject to sub-paragraph (2), a relevant system must comprise procedures which provide that an operator- instruction to a participating issuer relating to a right, privilege or benefit attaching to or arising from an uncertificated unit of a security is generated only if it has—

(a) received a properly authenticated dematerialised instruction attributable to the system-member having the right, privilege or benefit requiring the operator to generate an operator-instruction to the participating issuer; or

(b) been required to do so by a court or by or under an enactment.

(2) A relevant-system must comprise procedures which provide that an operator-instruction to a participating issuer relating to a right, privilege or benefit attaching to or arising from an uncertificated unit of a security may be generated if necessary to correct an error and if in accordance with the rules and practices of an operator instituted in order to comply with this Schedule.

17. A relevant system must comprise procedures which ensure that, where the relevant system maintains records in order to comply with paragraph 15(b)(i), the records are regularly reconciled with the registers of securities maintained by participating issuers.

18. A relevant system must comprise procedures which—

(a) enable system-users to notify the operator of an error in or relating to a dematerialised instruction; and

(b) ensure that, where the operator becomes aware of an error in or relating to a dematerialised instruction, appropriate corrective action is taken.

Rules and Practices

19. An operator's rules and practices—

(a) must bind system-members and participating issuers—

(i) so as to ensure the efficient processing of transfers of title to uncertificated units of a security in response to operator-instructions; and

(ii) as to the action to be taken where transfer of title in response to an operator-instruction cannot be effected;

(b) must make provision for a participating issuer to cease to participate in respect of a participating security so as—

(i) to minimise so far as practicable any disruption to system-members in respect of their ability to transfer the relevant security; and

(ii) to provide the participating issuer with any relevant information held by the operator relating to uncertificated units of the relevant security held by system-members;

(c) must make provision for the orderly termination of participation by system-members and system-participation whose participating is disruptive to other system-members or system-participants or to participating issuers; and

(d) if they make provision for the designation of a subsidiary undertaking as a relevant nominee, must require that the relevant nominee maintain adequate records of—

(i) the names of the persons who have an interest in the securities it holds; and

(ii) the nature and extent of their interests,

20. An operator's rules and practices must require—

(a) that each system-participant is able to send and receive properly authenticated dematerialised instructions:

(b) that each system-member has arrangements—

(i) for properly authenticated dematerialised instructions attributable to the member to be sent;

(ii) for properly authenticated dematerialised instructions to be received by or for the member; and

(iii) with a settlement-bank for payments to be made, where appropriate, for the units of a security transferred by means of the relevant system;

(c) that each participating issuer is able to respond with sufficient speed to operator- instructions.

21. An operator must have rules which require system-users and former system-users to provide the operator with such information in their possession as the operator may require in order to meet obligations under these regulations.

EXPLANATORY NOTE

These Regulations make provision for the transfer without a written instrument, and the evidencing otherwise than by a certificate, of title to a unit of a security, in accordance with a computer-based system and procedures known as the 'relevant system'. The relevant system centres on a person known as the 'operator'. The legal framework underlying the operation of the relevant system, together with the criteria which the operator and the relevant system must meet, are enshrined in these Regulations.

Chapter I, inter alia, sets out the purpose and definitions in the Regulations. A unit of a security which may be transferred by means of the relevant system is referred to as an 'uncertificated unit'. A security, the units of which may become uncertificated, is referred to as a 'participating security'. An issuer which issues a participating security is, in relation to that security, referred to as a 'participating issuer'. Instructions sent by means of the relevant system are referred to as 'demateralised instructions'.

Chapter II mainly provides for a range of matters relating to transfers of title to securities (including transfer of uncertificated holdings, transfer from uncertificated to certificated holdings and vice-versa) through a dematerialised system, the recording and registration of such transfers and the obligations imposed on participating issuers in regard to this and certain other matters.

Chapter III provides for the approval of an operator or recognition of an operator already approved by a competent authority of a Member State of the EU, by the Minister and associated matters. Provision is also made for the Minister to delegate his approval and supervisory functions under Chapter III to a designated body, if he so wishes.

Chapter IV makes provision to prevent persons sending dematerialised instructions, and persons on whose behalf they are sent, denying particular matters relating to them. It also makes provision for persons receiving such instructions to accept with certain exceptions, that the information contained in them and matters relating to them are correct.

Chapter V makes provision for certain notices to be issued in respect of minority shareholdings resulting from a take-over situation.

Chapter VI contains certain supplementary and incidental provisions designed to overcome evidential problems which may arise in relation to system entries.

The Schedule to the Regulations sets out the requirements for approval and continuing operation of a person as an operator.

European Communities (Public Limited Companies Subsidiaries) Regulations 1997

SI 67/1997

I, RICHARD BRUTON, Minister for Enterprise and Employment, in exercise of the powers conferred on me by section 3 of the European Communities Act, 1972 (No. 27 of 1972), and for the purpose of giving effect to the provisions of Council Directive No. 92/101/EEC of 23 November, 1992 hereby make the following Regulations:

PRELIMINARY AND GENERAL

1 Citation and construction

(1) These Regulations may be cited as the European Communities (Public Limited Companies Subsidiaries) Regulations, 1997.

(2) These Regulations shall be construed as one with the Companies Acts.

2 Commencement

These Regulations shall come into operation on the 1st day of March 1997.

3 Interpretation

(1) In these Regulations, unless the context otherwise requires—

"the Companies Acts" means the Principal Act, and every enactment (including these Regulations) which is to be construed as one with that Act;

"the Principal Act" means the Companies Act, 1963 (No. 33 of 1963);

"the Act of 1986" means the Companies (Amendment) Act, 1986 (No. 25 of 1986);

"the Act of 1990" means the Companies Act, 1990 (No. 33 of 1990);

"the Directive of 1968" means Council Directive No. 68/151/EEC of 9 March 1968.

(2) In these Regulations, unless the context otherwise requires, a reference to a Regulation is to a Regulation of these Regulations, a reference to a paragraph is to a paragraph of the Regulation, and a reference to a subparagraph is to the subparagraph of the paragraph, in which the reference occurs.

4 Extension of meaning of 'subsidiary'

(1) For the purposes of Part XI of the Act of 1990, in addition to the circumstances where a company (including a body corporate) is deemed to be a subsidiary of a public limited company by virtue of section 155 of the Principal Act, a limited company (including a body corporate) within the meaning of paragraph (2) shall also be deemed to be a subsidiary of a public limited company if, but only if, the public limited company is itself a shareholder or member of the said limited company and controls alone, pursuant to an agreement with other shareholders or members, a majority of the shareholders' or members' voting rights in the company in question.

(2) For the purposes of this Regulation, a limited company (including a body corporate) is a company—

(a) to which Article 1 of the Directive of 1968 applies, or

(b) which is incorporated other than in a Member State of the European Union and is of a legal form comparable to the type of company referred to in paragraph (a).

(3) For the purposes of Part XI of the Act of 1990, a public limited company exercises its control indirectly where the control of a subsidiary is exercised through another subsidiary, pursuant to section 155(1)(b) of the Principal Act.

(4) The first reference to a company in section 224(1) of the Act of 1990 includes a body corporate.

5 Extension to section 224 of 1990 on holding of shares by subsidiaries

(1) In addition to section 224 of the Act of 1990, this Regulation shall apply where any holding company is a public limited company (in this Regulation referred to as a 'parent public company') and where its subsidiary (not being a subsidiary solely by virtue of paragraph (a)(ii) or (b) of subsection (1) of section 155 of the Principal Act) is a limited company (including a body corporate) of the type referred to in Regulation 4(2) (in this Regulation referred to as a 'public company subsidiary').

(2) A public company subsidiary shall not—

(a) subscribe for the shares of its parent public company, or

(b) purchase shares in its parent public company which are not fully paid, or

(c) provide financial assistance in accordance with subsections (2) to (11) of section 60 of the Principal Act for the purchase of or subscription for shares in its parent public company.

(3) If a public company subsidiary purports to act in contravention of paragraph (2)(a), it shall be guilty of an offence and the purported subscription shall be void.

(4) Where shares in a parent public company are subscribed for by a nominee of a public company subsidiary in contravention of paragraph (2), then for all purposes the shares shall be treated as held by the nominee on his own account and the public company subsidiary shall be regarded as having no beneficial interest in them, and the provisions of subsections (2) to (6) of section 42 of the Companies (Amendment) Act, 1983, shall, with any necessary modifications, apply.

(5) Without prejudice to any other requirements contained in or penalties imposed by the Companies Acts, where a public company subsidiary purchases, subscribes for or holds shares in its parent public company, and—

(a) the shares were not fully paid when they were purchased, or

(b) the authorisation required by section 224(3) of the Act of 1990 has not been obtained, or

(c) the shares are held as treasury shares in excess of the limit referred to in section 209(2) of that Act, or

(d) the purchase or subscription was in contravention of paragraph (2)(c),

then, unless the shares or any interest of the public company subsidiary in them are previously disposed of, the provisions of section 43(3) of the Companies (Amendment) Act, 1983, shall, with the modification that the 'relevant period' in relation to any shares shall be 12 months and with any other necessary modifications, apply to the public company subsidiary in respect of such shares.

(6) This Regulation shall not affect or prohibit—

(a) the subscription for, acquisition or holding of, shares in its parent public company by a public company subsidiary where the public company subsidiary is concerned as personal representative or where it is concerned as trustee unless the parent public company or a subsidiary thereof is beneficially interested under the trust and is not so interested only by way of security for the purposes of a transaction entered into by it in the ordinary course of a business which includes the lending of money;

(b) the allotment to, or holding by, a public company subsidiary of shares in its parent public company in the circumstances set out in section 32(5) of the Principal Act, but where the shares so allotted are held as treasury shares and the nominal value of treasury shares held by the public company subsidiary exceeds the limit referred to in section 209(2) of the Act of 1990 then, unless the shares or any interest of the public company subsidiary in them are previously disposed of, the provisions of section 43(3) of the Companies (Amendment) Act, 1983, shall with the modification that the relevant period in relation to any shares shall be 3 years and with any other necessary modifications, apply to the public company subsidiary in respect of such shares;

(c) the subscription, acquisition or holding of shares in its parent public company by a public company subsidiary where the subscription, acquisition or holding is effected on behalf of a person other than the person subscribing, acquiring or holding the shares, who is neither the parent public company itself nor a subsidiary within the meaning of Part XI of the Act of 1990 of the said parent public company;

(d) the subscription, acquisition or holding of shares in its parent public company by a public company subsidiary which is a member of an approved stock exchange specified in section 17(2) of the Stock Exchange Act, 1995 (No. 9 of 1995), acting in its capacity as a professional dealer in securities in the normal course of its business.

(7) A person guilty of an offence under this Regulation shall be liable on summary conviction to a [class C fine][a] or to imprisonment for a term not exceeding 6 months, or to both such fine and such imprisonment.

(8) (a) Where an offence under this Regulation has been committed by a public company subsidiary and is proved to have been committed with the consent or connivance of or to be attributable to any neglect on the part of a person being a director, manager, secretary or other similar officer of the public company subsidiary, or a person who was purporting to act in any such capacity, that person as well as the body corporate shall be guilty of an offence and shall be liable to be proceeded against and punished as if he or she were guilty of the first-mentioned offence.

(b) Where the affairs of a public company subsidiary are managed by its members, paragraph (a) shall apply in relation to the acts and defaults of a member in connection with his or her functions of management as if he or she were a director of the public company subsidiary.

Amendments

a £500 increased to £1,500 by CA 1990, s 240(7) (as inserted by CLEA 2001, s 104(c)), and converted to €1,904.61 by Council Regulations (EC) No 1103/97, No 974/98 and No 2866/98 and the Economic and Monetary Union Act 1998, s 6.

6 Information in directors' report regarding acquisitions by company of own shares

Section 14 of the Act of 1986 shall also apply where, in any financial year of a company, shares in the company are acquired in a public limited company by a subsidiary pursuant to section 224 of the Act of 1990, and references in paragraphs (i), (ii) and (iii) of that section to 'another person' shall be read as including a subsidiary company of a public limited company, pursuant to Part XI of that Act.

Given under my Official Seal, this 5th day of February 1997

Richard Bruton

Minister for Enterprise and Employment

EXPLANATORY NOTE

The purpose of these Regulations is to give legal effect to Council Directive 92/101/EEC which amends the Second Directive (Formation and Capital of Public Limited Companies) to apply conditions on the purchase of shares in a PLC by subsidiaries of that PLC.

Part XI of the Companies Act, 1990 already substantially implements Directive 92/101/EEC. It is proposed to complete the implementation process by extending the definition of subsidiary for the purposes of Part XI of the 1990 Act, and applying the additional requirements of the Directive to directly controlled subsidiaries.

Regulations 1–3 provide for citation, commencement and interpretation of the Regulations.

Regulation 4 extends the definition of subsidiary of a public limited company for the purposes of Part XI of the Companies Act, 1990.

Regulation 5 applies the conditions relating to the subscription, acquisition or holding of shares by a public company itself to the subscription, acquisition or holding of shares by any subsidiary of the type referred to in the Directive in its parent public limited company. It also sets out the penalty for those found guilty of an offence.

Regulation 6 extends the requirements on directors to disclose information about acquisition by a PLC of its own shares, to acquisition by a subsidiary (as defined) company of shares in its parent PLC.

Companies Act 1963 (Section 377(1)) Order 1999

SI 64/1999

I, NOEL TREACY, Minister of State at the Department of Enterprise, Trade and Employment, in exercise of the powers conferred on me by section 377(1) of the Companies Act, 1963 (No. 33 of 1963), (inserted by section 250 of the Companies Act, 1990 (No. 33 of 1990)), as adapted by the Enterprise and Employment (Alteration of Name of Department and Title of Minister) Order, 1997 (S.I. No. 305 of 1997), and the Enterprise, Trade and Employment (Delegation of Ministerial Functions) Order, 1998 (S.I. No. 265 of 1998), hereby order as follows:

1. This Order may be cited as the Companies Act, 1963 (section 377(1)) Order, 1999.

2. In this Order—

"the Act of 1990" means the Companies Act, 1990 (No. 33 of 1990);

"the Companies Acts" means the Companies Act, 1963 (No. 33 of 1963), and every enactment which is to be construed as one with that Act;

"the provisions of the Companies Acts as applied" means the provisions of the Companies Acts which, by virtue of section 377(1) of, and the Ninth Schedule to, the Companies Act, 1963 (as altered by the Companies Act, 1963 (Ninth Schedule) Regulations, 1999), apply to the bodies corporate specified in the said section 377(1);

"the provisions of the Act of 1990 as applied" means the provisions of Part XI of the Act of 1990 which, by virtue of section 377(1) of, and the Ninth Schedule to, the Companies Act, 1963 (as altered by the Companies Act, 1963 (Ninth Schedule) Regulations, 1999), apply to the bodies corporate specified in the said section 377(1).

3. There is hereby prescribed the following adaptation of the provisions of the Companies Acts as applied, namely, each of the references to articles in those provisions shall be constructed as including references to the bye-laws of the body corporate concerned.

4. There are hereby prescribed the following modifications of the provisions of the Act of 1990 as applied, namely—

(a) subsection (1) of section 210 of the Act of 1990 shall have effect as if there were inserted the following sentence at the end of that subsection—

> "For the purposes of this section the provisions of the Companies Acts governing the variation of rights attached to classes of shares shall apply to the body corporate concerned.",

(b) sections 215, 216, 222 and 226 of the Act of 1990, in so far as they apply to a public limited company, shall apply to all bodies corporate to which section 377(1) of the Companies Act, 1963, applies, other than those which, if they were registered under the Companies Acts, would be private companies.

EXPLANATORY NOTE

(*This note is not part of the Instrument and does not purport to be a legal interpretation.*)

The purpose of this Order is to facilitate the application of Part IX of the Companies Act, 1990, as altered by the Companies Act 1963 (Ninth Schedule) Regulations, 1999 to unregistered companies, by making some necessary modifications in the application of that Part to such unregistered companies.

Companies Act 1990 (Form and Content of Documents Delivered to Registrar) Regulations 2002

SI 39/2002

I, Noel Treacy, Minister of State at the Department of Enterprise, Trade and Employment, in exercise of the powers conferred on me by sections 3(3) and 248 of the Companies Act 1990 (No. 33 of 1990) as adapted by the Enterprise and Employment (Alteration of Name of Department and Title of Minister) Order 1997 (S.I. No. 305 of 1997) and the Enterprise, Trade and Employment (Delegation of Ministerial Functions) Order 1998 (S.I. No. 265 of 1998), hereby order as follows:

1. These Regulations may be cited as the Companies Act 1990 (Form and Content of Documents Delivered to Registrar) Regulations 2002.

2. These Regulations shall come into operation on 1st March 2002.

3. (1) In these Regulations—

"Acts" means the Companies Acts 1963 to 2001;

"delivered" means delivered to the registrar;

"documents" has the same meaning as in section 248 of the Companies Act 1990 (No. 33 of 1990);

"registrar" means the registrar of companies.

(2) A word or expression used in these Regulations that is also used in the Acts shall, unless the context otherwise requires, have in these Regulations the meaning that it has in those Acts.

(3) In these Regulations, unless the contrary intention appears—

(a) a reference to a paragraph is a reference to the paragraph of the provision in which the reference occurs, and

(b) a reference to a section is to a section of the Companies Act 1963 (No. 33 of 1963).

4. Documents shall be easily legible and suitable for electronic scanning and electronic copying.

5. A page of a document shall be—

(a) 297 millimetres in length and 210 millimetres in width, that is to say, A4 size, and

(b) made of white paper with a matt finish weighing not less than 80 grams per square millimetre.

6. The print in a document shall be—

(a) black in colour,

(b) not less than 1.8 millimetres in height, and

(c) suitable and adequate for electronic scanning.

7. The layout of the printed matter on a page of a document shall be such as to provide a margin of not less than one centimetre all around the printed matter, that is to say, on the top and bottom and on each side, of it.

8. A document shall not contain any colour other than the white of the paper and the black of the printed matter.

9. If an original document contains coloured print or any of its pages consist of glossy paper, a copy of the document, or a printer's proof of the document, complying with these Regulations shall be delivered.

10. Pages of a document shall be kept together by means of a clip or staple at the top left-hand corner and shall not be stitched together or otherwise bound and shall not bear any adhesive tape.

11. A document shall not consist of or contain a carbon copy or photocopy or printed matter from a dot matrix computer printer.

12. A space in a document for the insertion of information shall not be left blank but, as appropriate, "not applicable", "nil" or "none" or another similar word shall be inserted in the space.

13.(1) An amendment inserted in the contents of a document shall be initialled and dated by at least one of the signatories to the document or, if there are no signatories, by at least one of the persons who authorised its production.

(2) Subject to paragraph (3), if a document delivered by a person is returned by the registrar to the person for amendment, either, as the registrar may determine, a new document shall be prepared or the contents of the document shall be amended and initialled and dated in accordance with paragraph (1), and thereafter the document shall be delivered.

(3) If the document referred to in paragraph (2) is a statutory declaration, the person who made the declaration shall make another statutory declaration and deliver it as soon as practicable.

14.(1) Subject to paragraphs (2) and (3), the name of a company (as stated in its memorandum of association) and the address of its registered office shall be entered on the first page of a document in a prominent position.

(2) The name and address referred to in paragraph (1) shall correspond with the information previously delivered to the registrar in accordance with the Acts.

(3) If the name of the company includes one of the words or expressions "limited", "teoranta", "public limited company" or "cuideachta phoiblí theoranta", an abbreviated form of the word or expression may be used in the entry made under paragraph (1) in a document other than a document relating to the incorporation of a company, a change of name or the re-registration of a company or the memorandum or articles of association of a company.

(4) The address of the registered office of a company on a document may not be given as a post office box number.

15.(1) An individual shall be referred to in a document by his or her surname and all of his or her first names.

(2) Where the address of an individual is required to be stated in a document, his or her residential address shall be stated, unless some other address is required by law to be stated.

(3) If a document is required to be signed—

(a) the signature shall be the original, handwritten signature of the person, and

(b) the date of the signature shall be stated on the document.

16. The form and content of a document delivered under a scheme of the registrar for giving priority to the examination and registration by the registrar of the document or documents of a specified class shall be in compliance with the rules and requirements of the scheme.

17. Where any matter is included in a document under a provision of the Acts, or of an instrument made under the Acts, or such a provision is otherwise relevant to the matter, the provision shall be identified in the document.

18.(1) An application to the registrar in the form prescribed for the purposes of the Acts in relation to the registration of a company—

(a) shall correspond and be in compliance with the articles of association where the articles of association—

(i) provide for a minimum number of directors, or

(ii) contain the names of the first-appointed directors and the first-appointed secretary,

and

(b) subject to paragraph (2), may be signed by an individual acting as agent for all or any of the subscribers to the memorandum of association, but may not be completed on behalf of a company acting as such an agent.

(2) Where a subscriber referred to in paragraph (1)(b) is a company, the application to the registrar shall be signed by an officer of the company authorised in that behalf.

(3) A statutory declaration referred to in section 5(5) of the companies (Amendment) Act 1983 (No. 13 of 1983) and section 42(2) of the Companies (Amendment) (No.2) Act 1999 (No. 30 of 1999) shall be made on or after—

(a) the date of the form prescribed for the purposes of the Acts in relation to the registration of a company, or

(b) the date of the memorandum and articles of association of the company concerned,

whichever is the later.

19. If a statutory declaration of solvency for the purposes of section 256(1) (inserted by the Companies Act 1990) is made on the date of the passing of the resolution for winding up the company concerned—

(a) the time of the making of the statutory declaration shall be stated in the declaration, and

(b) the time of the passing of the resolution shall be stated in the resolution.

20. A copy of a resolution passed by a company for the purpose of a creditors' voluntary winding up of the company and delivered must bear a certificate signed by the liquidator of the company to the effect that the copy is a true copy of the resolution.

21. A document shall not refer to a person who is an officer, liquidator, receiver, or examiner, of a company or a person referred to in section 352(1)(c) unless the registrar has been notified, as required under the Acts, of the name and appointment of the person.

22.(1) Documents delivered by the liquidator of a company shall not relate to a period, or to accounts for a period, beginning at any time after its incorporation and after a period for which accounts of the company, or any other documents of the company for that period required by or under the Acts to be delivered, have not been delivered.

(2) The return in relation to a company of a liquidator—

(a) under section 263, in the case of a members' voluntary winding up,

(b) under section 273, in the case of a creditors' voluntary winding up, or

(c) under section 306 or Order 74 Rule 130 of the Rules of the Superior Courts (S.I. No. 15 of 1986) or any rules of court for the time being amending or replacing that Order, in the case of a court winding up,

shall not relate to a period that is after another period during the liquidation for which no return in relation to the company has been delivered.

23.(1) A copy of the text of a resolution passed by a company that is delivered shall be signed either by a director of the company whose appointment as a director has been notified to the registrar or, if the appointment of the secretary of the company as secretary has been so notified, by the secretary.

(2) A document shall not consist of or include a copy of the text of a resolution of a company in a voluntary winding up of the company if a statutory declaration of solvency under section 256 has not been delivered.

24. The registrar shall not accept any documents relating to the winding up of a company unless the registrar has received—

(a) a copy of the resolution for the winding up of the company, in the case of a voluntary liquidation, or

(b) an office copy of the order of the court directing the winding up of the company, in any other case.

EXPLANATORY NOTE

(This note is not part of the Instrument and does not purport to be a legal interpretation)

The purpose of these regulations is to deal with the manner of completion of documents deposited with the Companies Registration Office. They will support the Registrar on enforcement of proper quality control on documents deposited with him. The Regulations cover both the manner of delivery and return of documents. From the effective date any document sent back to the presenters if not corrected and returned within 14 days will be deemed not to have been filed.

Company Law Enforcement Act 2001 (Section 56) Regulations 2002

SI 324/2002

I, Mary Harney, Minister for Enterprise, Trade and Employment, in exercise of the powers conferred on me by section 4 of the Company Law Enforcement Act 2001 (No. 28 of 2001), hereby make the following regulations:

1. These Regulations may be cited as the Company Law Enforcement Act 2001 (Section 56) Regulations 2002.

2. The form set out in the Schedule to these regulations is hereby prescribed for the purposes of section 56(1) of the Company Law Enforcement Act 2001 (No. 28 of 2001).

Schedule

Liquidator's Report under Section 56 of the Company Law Enforcement Act 2001

Please refer to the Guidance Notes when completing this Report. These are available from the ODCE website at www.odce.ie/publications/decision.asp

Name of Company: ____

Registration Number of Company: ________________________________

Please indicate if this is the first, second, etc. or final Report filed for the above company:______

Section 1: Liquidator Details

(Question 1 to be completed in every Report. Questions 2 to 9 to be completed as part of the first Report and in every subsequent Report where a change in details arises.)

1. Name of Liquidator: ____

2. Name of Liquidator's firm *(if applicable)*: ___________________________

3. Address of Liquidator: ______________________________________

4. If you are a member of a professional body, please state which one: ____________

5. Liquidation Type *(please tick one)*:

    Creditors' Voluntary Liquidation:

    Official Liquidation:

6. If a Creditors' Voluntary Liquidation, were you the members' nominee?

Yes: No:

7. Date of your appointment as Liquidator:______________________________

8. Name of Liquidator's staff member with day-to-day responsibility for the Liquidation (*where applicable*)

____

9. Contact Details for *(please tick one):*

    the Liquidator:

    Staff Member:

Telephone Number(s): ____________________ Fax Number: ____________________

E-mail Address: ____

Section 2: Company Details

(To be completed as part of the first Report and every subsequent Report where a change in details arises)

10. Business/Trading Name(s) (please include all those used in the 12 months prior to the date of commencement of the winding up):

____

____

11. Address of Current Registered Office:

____

____

____

12. Address of any other Registered Office used in the 12 months prior to the date of commencement of the winding up:

____

____

____

13. Principal Trading Address(es) (*please include all those used in the 12 months prior to the date of commencement of the winding up, if different from the Registered Office(s) above*):

____

____

____

14. Nature of the Company's Business:

   a Please state the most relevant NACE Classification at the date of commencement of the liquidation *(see Guidance Notes)*:

   ____

   b. Please give a precise description of the Company's activities at the date of commencement of the liquidation:

   ____

   ____

   ____

15. Number of Company employees at the date of commencement of the liquidation:

____

16. Turnover for each of the last three financial years preceding the date of commencement of the liquidation:

Financial Year Ended (date): ____________ Turnover: ____________(€ amount)

Financial Year Ended (date): ____________ Turnover: ____________(€ amount)

Financial Year Ended (date): ____________ Turnover: ____________(€ amount)

17. Trading Details *(please state as a minimum month and year)*:

   a. Date of Commencement of Trading: ________________________

   b. Date of Cessation of Trading *(if applicable)*: ________________________

18. Please state, in your opinion, the reasons for the liquidation of the Company, and cite the evidence to support this opinion on a separate sheet.

19. Has there been any Scheme of Arrangement/Receivership/Examinership/ Liquidation in the Company in the 36 months prior to the date of this report?

Yes: No:

If yes, please provide relevant information, including type, name and address of any office-holder(s), date(s) of appointment/termination of appointment, copies of all notices of appointment and reports of receivers/examiners/liquidators or other office holders of the Company during that period:

____

____

____

____

____

____

20. Is there a deficiency in any tax return or payment of taxes?

Yes: No:

If so, please specify the periods, if any, for which returns are overdue and/or the amounts due:

____

____

____

____

____

____

21. Have you any information which may lead you to believe that there was a person acting as a shadow director of the Company?
(Please note that the expression 'shadow director' may include an individual or a body corporate):

Yes: No:

If yes, please provide the following details for the individual/body corporate in question:

a. Full Name:

   ____

b. Current or last known address:

   ____

   ____

   ____

   ____

c. What was the Person's role in the Company?

   ____

   ____

____

____

d. Has the Person demonstrated to you that s/he has acted honestly and responsibly in relation to the conduct of the Company's affairs?

Yes: No:

Please provide on a separate sheet details of the factors which support this answer and any other relevant information.

Section 3: Company Directors

(To be completed as part of the first Report and every subsequent Report where a change in details arises)

22. In this Section, you are required to include every person who appears to you to be, or have been, a director of the Company at the date of commencement of the winding up or at any time in the 12 months prior to the date of commencement of the winding up.

A separate copy of this Section should be used for each Person.

---

a. Full name *(including other known names)*: ____________________

b. Current or last known address: ____________________

____

c. Date of birth: ____________________

d. PPS number: ____________________

e. Period as director: ____________________

From *(date)*: ____________ To *(date)*: ____________

f. What was the Person's role in the Company? ____________________

____

____

g. Has the Person demonstrated to you that s/he has acted honestly and responsibly in relation to the conduct of the Company's affairs?

Yes: No:

Please provide on a separate sheet details of the factors which support this answer.

h. Other Directorships

(please provide full details of present/past companies of which this Person is/was a Director in the period from 12 months prior to the date of commencement of the winding up of the Company to date and include the company registration number, the date(s) of appointment/termination of the period as Director in each case and please indicate if any of these companies operated in a sector similar to the Company in liquidation):

____

____

____

Section 4: Statement of Affairs, Accounts and Report to Creditors

(To be completed as part of the first Report and every subsequent Report where a change in details arises)

23. Directors' Statement of Affairs or similar document (please attach a copy to this Report. If a copy is not attached, please state why not and attach details of the known assets and liabilities of the Company):

____

____

____

____

24. Is there a material difference between the Statement of Affairs or similar document and the expected final position?

Yes: No:

If so, please provide details of the amount and the reason for this material difference on a separate sheet.

25. Audited/Other Accounts

(please attach to this Report a copy of the last two sets of the audited accounts of the Company and the most recent draft or management accounts prepared after the last set of audited accounts. If the Company is exempted from audit, please provide a copy of the accounts laid before the AGM for the same period and the most recent draft or management accounts. If none are attached, please state why not.):

____

____

____

____

26. Report to Creditors and any other relevant material, e.g., minutes of creditors' meeting and Chairperson's statement to meeting

(please attach these documents and if they are not available, state why not):

____

____

____

____

27. Has a Committee of Inspection been appointed?

Yes: No:

If so, please provide the names and addresses of the members:

____

____

____

____

____

28. Will the winding up be completed within 18 months from the date of this report?

Yes: No:

29. Was there any material transfer of assets of the Company *(see Guidance Notes)* to any person during the period commencing 12 months prior to the date of commencement of its winding up and ending on the date of this report?

Yes: No:

If yes, please provide details, e.g., date(s) of transfer, nature of asset(s), beneficiary(ies), on a separate sheet.

30. On what date was the Company unable to trade out of its financial difficulties?

____

Section 5: Proceedings

(To be completed as part of the first Report and every subsequent Report where a change in details arises)

31. Are you asking the Director of Corporate Enforcement at this time to relieve you from the requirement to apply, pursuant to section 150 of the Companies Act 1990, for the restriction of one or more of the directors of the Company?

Yes: No:

If yes, is relief being sought for?, (please tick one)

All directors:

Certain named directors:

In either case, please name each director for which relief is sought and state the grounds upon which you consider that an application for restriction should not now be taken against each individual.

____

____

____

____

In respect of any remaining directors, please name them and indicate the grounds upon which the application for restriction will be made in each case:

____

____

____

____

32. In respect of this Company will you be applying to the High Court to disqualify any person, pursuant to section 160 of the Companies Act 1990?

Yes: No:

If yes, please name the person(s) in question and indicate the grounds upon which the application to disqualify will be taken:

____

____

____

____

33. Are any other proceedings being undertaken, or contemplated, by you against officers of the Company?

Yes: No:

If yes, please specify the nature of the proceedings, the person(s) against whom the proceedings are being or may be taken and the date/expected date of commencement of the proceedings. If proceedings have commenced please state whether they are in the High Court or Circuit Court and cite the Court record number of the case:

____

____

____

____

34. Are any other civil or criminal proceedings being undertaken, or contemplated, by any other person against the Company or any of its officers?

Yes: No:

If yes, please specify the nature of the proceedings, the person(s) against whom the proceedings are being or may be taken, the date/expected date of commencement of the proceedings and the name, address and telephone number of the person taking or contemplating the proceedings. If proceedings have commenced, please state whether they are in the High Court or Circuit Court and cite the Court record number of the case:

____

____

____

____

35. Have you made, or are you contemplating making, a report to the Director of Public Prosecutions and the Director of Corporate Enforcement under section 299 of the Companies Act 1963 (as amended by section 51 of the Company Law Enforcement Act 2001)?

Yes: No:

If yes, please specify the nature of any suspected offence(s), the person(s) to whom the report relates, the relationship of each such person to the Company and the date/expected date of submission of the report:

____

____

____

____

Section 6: Final Report

36. Outcome of restriction application(s) to the High Court (if applicable) *(please provide details for each person)*:

____

____

____

____

37. Outcome of any other court proceedings taken under the circumstances set out in questions 32, 33 and 34:

____

____

____

____

38. If the liquidation has been completed, please attach a copy of Form 14 as required to be submitted to the Companies Registration Office.

Section 7: Liquidator's Statement

(To be completed on every occasion a report is made)

I, __________________, being the liquidator of the above company, state that the details and particulars contained in this Report and all associated documentation prepared by me are true, correct and complete, to the best of my knowledge and belief.

Signed:____

Date:____

Please ensure that copies of the following are attached to this Report:

- Separate sheets (if applicable) [items 18, 22(g), 24, 29];
- Copies of notices of appointment and reports of receivers/examiners/liquidators/other office-holders (if applicable) 19;
- Statement of Affairs (or details of assets and liabilities) 23;
- Last two sets of audited accounts and draft or management accounts subsequently prepared, if any 25;
- Report to Creditors and other relevant material, including minutes of creditors' meeting, Chairperson's statement to meeting 26;
- Additional copies of Section 3: Details of Company Directors;
- Copy of CRO Form 14 (if applicable) 38;
- Any further information or documentation that you deem to be required.

EXPLANATORY NOTE

(*This note is not part of the Instrument and does not purport to be a legal interpretation*)

The purpose of these Regulations is to prescribe the form of the liquidators report for the purposes of section 56(1) of the Company Law Enforcement Act 2001.

European Communities (Corporate Insolvency) Regulations 2002

SI 333/2002

I, Mary Harney, Minister for Enterprise, Trade and Employment, in exercise of the powers conferred on me by section 3 of the European Communities Act 1972 (No. 27 of 1972) and, together with the European Communities (Personal Insolvency) Regulations 2002 (S.I. No. 334 of 2002), for the purpose of giving full effect to Council Regulation (EC) No. 1346/2000 (OJ L160 of 30.6.2000) of 29 May 2000 on insolvency proceedings, make the following regulations:

PART 1

PRELIMINARY AND GENERAL

1 Citation and construction

1. These Regulations—

(a) may be cited as the European Communities (Corporate Insolvency) Regulations 2002, and

(b) shall be construed as one with the Companies Acts, 1963 to 2001.

2 Interpretation

(1) In these Regulations—

'enforcement order' means an order under Regulation 6(5);

'insolvency proceedings' means insolvency proceedings opened in a member state of the European Communities other than the State and Denmark under Article 3 where the proceedings relate to a body corporate;

'Insolvency Regulation' means Council Regulation (EC) No 1346/2000 of 29 May 2000 on insolvency proceedings, the text of which, in the English language, is set out in the Schedule to these Regulations for convenience of reference.

(2) Unless provided otherwise, a word or expression used in these Regulations and also in the Insolvency Regulation has the same meaning in these Regulations as it has in that Regulation.

(3) References in these Regulations (other than Regulation 6) to numbered Articles without qualification are references to the Articles so numbered of the Insolvency Regulation.

3 Amendment of Companies Act 1963

The Companies Act 1963 (No. 33 of 1963) is amended—

(a) [...][a]

(b) [...][b]

(c) [...][c]

(d) [...][d]

(e) [...][e]

(f) [...][f]

and

(g) [...][g]

Amendments

a Reg 3(a) amends CA 1963, s 2(1) by the insertion of definitions of 'insolvency proceedings', 'Insolvency Regulation' and 'property'.

b Reg 3(b) inserts CA 1963, s 205A.

c Reg 3(c) inserts CA 1963, ss 227A and 227B.

d Reg 3(d) inserts CA 1963, s 250(4).

e Reg 3(e) inserts CA 1963, s 267A.

f Reg 3(f) inserts CA 1963, s 313A.

g Reg 3(g) inserts Ca 1963, s 343A.

4 Amendment of Companies (Amendment) Act 1990

[…][a]

Amendments

a Reg 4 inserts C(A)A 1990, s 1A.

5 Registration of insolvency judgments

(1) A request by a liquidator under Article 22 that the judgment opening the insolvency proceedings be registered in a public register shall be made to the person or authority responsible for keeping the register concerned.

6 Enforcement in State of insolvency judgments

(1) In this Regulation—

> 'Brussels 1 Regulation' means Council Regulation (EC) No 44/2001 of 22 December 2000 (OJ L12 of 16.1.2001) on jurisdiction and the recognition and enforcement of judgments in civil and commercial matters;
>
> 'insolvency judgment' means a judgment referred to in Article 25 of the Insolvency Regulation;

and, except where the context otherwise requires, references to numbered Articles are references to Articles so numbered of the Brussels 1 Regulation.

(2) Having regard to Article 68 of the Brussels 1 Regulation, references in Article 25 of the Insolvency Regulation to enforcement of insolvency judgments in accordance with certain Articles of the Brussels Convention are to be read as references to enforcement of those judgments in accordance with Articles 38 to 58 of the Brussels 1 Regulation.

(3) An application under the Brussels 1 Regulation for the enforcement in the State of an insolvency judgment shall be made to the Master of the High Court.

(4) The Master shall determine the application by order in accordance with the Brussels 1 Regulation.

(5) The Master shall declare the insolvency judgment enforceable immediately on completion of the formalities provided for in Article 53 without any review under Articles 34 and 35 and shall make an enforcement order in relation to the judgment.

(6) An order under paragraph (5) of this Regulation may provide for the enforcement of only part of the insolvency judgment concerned.

(7) An application to the Master under Article 39 for an enforcement order in respect of an insolvency judgment may include an application for any preservation measures the High Court has power to grant in proceedings that, apart from these Regulations, are within its jurisdiction.

(8) Where an enforcement order is made, the Master shall grant any such preservation measures so applied for.

(9) For the purposes of these Regulations references in Articles 42, 43, 45, 47, 48, 52, 53 and 57 to a declaration of enforceability are to be treated as references to an enforcement order under this Regulation.

(10) Subject to the restrictions on enforcement contained in Article 47(3), if an enforcement order has been made respecting an insolvency judgment, the judgment—

- (a) shall, to the extent to which its enforcement is authorised by the enforcement order, be of the same force and effect as a judgment of the High Court, and
- (b) may be enforced by the High Court, and proceedings taken on it, as if it were a judgment of that Court.

7 Interest on insolvency judgments and payment of costs

(1) Where, on application for an enforcement order respecting an insolvency judgment, it is shown—

- (a) that the judgment provides for the payment of a sum of money, and
- (b) that, in accordance with the law of the member state in which the judgment was given, interest on the sum is recoverable under the judgment at a particular rate or rates and from a particular date or time, the enforcement order, if made, shall provide that the person liable to pay the sum shall also be liable to pay the interest, apart from any interest on costs recoverable under paragraph (2), in accordance with the particulars noted in the order, and the interest shall be recoverable by the applicant as though it were part of the sum.

(2) An enforcement order may provide for the payment to the applicant by the respondent of the reasonable costs of or incidental to the application for the enforcement order.

(3) A person required by an enforcement order to pay costs shall be liable to pay interest on the costs as if they were the subject of an order for the payment of costs made by the High Court on the date on which the enforcement order was made.

(4) Interest shall be payable on a sum referred to in paragraph (1)(a) only as provided for in this Regulation.

8 Currency of payments under enforceable insolvency judgments

(1) An amount payable in the State under an insolvency judgment by virtue of an enforcement order shall be payable in the currency of the State.

(2) If the amount is stated in the insolvency judgment in any currency except the euro, payment shall be made on the basis of the exchange rate prevailing, on the date the enforcement order is made, between the currency of the State and any such currency.

(3) For the purposes of this Regulation a certificate purporting to be signed by an officer of an authorised institution and to state the exchange rate prevailing on a specified date between a specified currency and the currency of the State shall be admissible as evidence of the facts stated in the certificate.

(4) In this Regulation, 'authorised institution' means any of the following:

(a) a body licensed to carry on banking business under the Central Bank Acts, 1942 to 1998, or authorised to carry on such business under the ACC Bank Acts, 1978 to 2001, or regulations under the European Communities Acts, 1972 to 1998,

(b) a building society within the meaning of the Building Societies Act 1989 (No. 17 of 1989);

(c) a trustee savings bank within the meaning of the Trustee Savings Banks Acts, 1989 and 2001,

(d) An Post.

9 Preservation measures

(1) A request under Article 38 for measures to secure and preserve any of the debtor's assets in the State shall be made to the High Court.

(2) On such a request the High Court—

(a) may grant any such measures that the Court has power to grant in proceedings that, apart from these Regulations, are within its jurisdiction, and

(b) may refuse to grant the measures sought if, in its opinion, the fact that, apart from this Regulation, the Court does not have jurisdiction in relation to the subject matter of the proceedings makes it inexpedient for it to grant the measures.

10 Venue

The jurisdiction of the Circuit Court or District Court in proceedings that may be instituted in the State by a liquidator in exercise of his or her powers under Article 18 may be exercised by the judge for the time being assigned—

(a) in the case of the Circuit Court, to the circuit, and

(b) in the case of the District Court, to the district court district,

in which the defendant ordinarily resides or carries on any profession, business or occupation.

11 Language of claims

A claim lodged with a liquidator (within the meaning of the Companies Acts, 1963 to 2001) by a creditor referred to in Article 42(2) may, if not in Irish or English, be required by the liquidator to be translated, in whole or in part, into either of these languages.

12 Non-recognition or non-enforcement of judgments

It shall be for the High Court to determine whether judgments referred to in Article 25(1), or insolvency proceedings or judgments referred to in Article 26, should not be recognised or enforced on grounds mentioned in those provisions.

13 Revocation

Paragraph 2 of the Companies (Recognition of Countries) Order 1964 (S.I. No. 42 of 1964) is amended by the substitution of 'section 367' for 'sections 250 and 367'.

Schedule
Text of Insolvency Regulation

Regulation 2(1)

COUNCIL REGULATION (EC) No 1346/2000
of 29 May 2000
on insolvency proceedings

THE COUNCIL OF THE EUROPEAN UNION,

Having regard to the Treaty establishing the European Community, and in particular Articles 61 (c) and 67 (1) thereof,

Having regard to the initiative of the Federal Republic of Germany and the Republic of Finland,

Having regard to the opinion of the European Parliament[1],

Having regard to the opinion of the Economic and Social Committee [2],

1 Opinion delivered on 2 March 2000 (not yet published in the Official Journal).

2 Opinion delivered on 26 January 2000 (not yet published in the Official Journal).

Whereas:

(1) The European Union has set out the aim of establishing an area of freedom, security and justice.

(2) The proper functioning of the internal market requires that cross-border insolvency proceedings should operate efficiently and effectively and this Regulation needs to be adopted in order to achieve this objective which comes within the scope of judicial cooperation in civil matters within the meaning of Article 65 of the Treaty.

(3) The activities of undertakings have more and more cross-border effects and are therefore increasingly being regulated by Community law. While the insolvency of such undertakings also affects the proper functioning of the internal market, there is a need for a Community act requiring coordination of the measures to be taken regarding an insolvent debtor's assets.

(4) It is necessary for the proper functioning of the internal market to avoid incentives for the parties to transfer assets or judicial proceedings from one Member State to another, seeking to obtain a more favourable legal position (forum shopping).

(5) These objectives cannot be achieved to a sufficient degree at national level and action at Community level is therefore justified.

(6) In accordance with the principle of proportionality this Regulation should be confined to provisions governing jurisdiction for opening insolvency proceedings and judgments which are delivered directly on the basis of the insolvency proceedings and are closely connected with such proceedings. In addition, this Regulation should contain provisions regarding the recognition of those judgments and the applicable law which also satisfy that principle.

(7) Insolvency proceedings relating to the winding-up of insolvent companies or other legal persons, judicial arrangements, compositions and analogous proceedings are excluded from the scope of the 1968 Brussels Convention on Jurisdiction and the Enforcement of Judgments in Civil and Commercial Matters (OJ L 299, 31.12.1972, p. 32.), as amended by the Conventions on Accession to this Convention (OJ L 204,

2.8.1975, p. 28; OJ L 304, 30.10.1978; p. 1; OJ L 388, 31.12.1982, p. 1; OJ L 285, 3.10.1989, p. 1; OJ C 15, 15.1.1997, p.1).

(8) In order to achieve the aim of improving the efficiency and effectiveness of insolvency proceedings having cross-border effects, it is necessary, and appropriate, that the provisions on jurisdiction, recognition and applicable law in this area should be contained in a Community law measure which is binding and directly applicable in Member States.

(9) This Regulation should apply to insolvency proceedings, whether the debtor is a natural person or a legal person, a trader or an individual. The insolvency proceedings to which this Regulation applies are listed in the Annexes. Insolvency proceedings concerning insurance undertakings, credit institutions, investment undertakings holding funds or securities for third parties and collective investment undertakings should be excluded from the scope of this Regulation. Such undertakings should not be covered by this Regulation since they are subject to special arrangements and, to some extent, the national supervisory authorities have extremely wide-ranging powers of intervention.

(10) Insolvency proceedings do not necessarily involve the intervention of a judicial authority; the expression 'court' in this Regulation should be given a broad meaning and include a person or body empowered by national law to open insolvency proceedings. In order for this Regulation to apply, proceedings (comprising acts and formalities set down in law) should not only have to comply with the provisions of this Regulation, but they should also be officially recognised and legally effective in the Member State in which the insolvency proceedings are opened and should be collective insolvency proceedings which entail the partial or total divestment of the debtor and the appointment of a liquidator.

(11) This Regulation acknowledges the fact that as a result of widely differing substantive laws it is not practical to introduce insolvency proceedings with universal scope in the entire Community. The application without exception of the law of the State of opening of proceedings would, against this background, frequently lead to difficulties. This applies, for example, to the widely differing laws on security interests to be found in the Community. Furthermore, the preferential rights enjoyed by some creditors in the insolvency proceedings are, in some cases, completely different. This Regulation should take account of this in two different ways. On the one hand, provision should be made for special rules on applicable law in the case of particularly significant rights and legal relationships (e.g. rights in rem and contracts of employment). On the other hand, national proceedings covering only assets situated in the State of opening should also be allowed alongside main insolvency proceedings with universal scope.

(12) This Regulation enables the main insolvency proceedings to be opened in the Member State where the debtor has the centre of his main interests. These proceedings have universal scope and aim at encompassing all the debtor's assets. To protect the diversity of interests, this Regulation permits secondary proceedings to be opened to run in parallel with the main proceedings. Secondary proceedings may be opened in the Member State where the debtor has an establishment. The effects of secondary proceedings are limited to the assets located in that State. Mandatory rules of coordination with the main proceedings satisfy the need for unity in the Community.

(13) The 'centre of main interests' should correspond to the place where the debtor conducts the administration of his interests on a regular basis and is therefore ascertainable by third parties.

(14) This Regulation applies only to proceedings where the centre of the debtor's main interests is located in the Community.

(15) The rules of jurisdiction set out in this Regulation establish only international jurisdiction, that is to say, they designate the Member State the courts of which may open insolvency proceedings. Territorial jurisdiction within that Member State must be established by the national law of the Member State concerned.

(16) The court having jurisdiction to open the main insolvency proceedings should be enabled to order provisional and protective measures from the time of the request to open proceedings. Preservation measures both prior to and after the commencement of the insolvency proceedings are very important to guarantee the effectiveness of the insolvency proceedings. In that connection this Regulation should afford different possibilities. On the one hand, the court competent for the main insolvency proceedings should be able also to order provisional protective measures covering assets situated in the territory of other Member States. On the other hand, a liquidator temporarily appointed prior to the opening of the main insolvency proceedings should be able, in the Member States in which an establishment belonging to the debtor is to be found, to apply for the preservation measures which are possible under the law of those States.

(17) Prior to the opening of the main insolvency proceedings, the right to request the opening of insolvency proceedings in the Member State where the debtor has an establishment should be limited to local creditors and creditors of the local establishment or to cases where main proceedings cannot be opened under the law of the Member State where the debtor has the centre of his main interest. The reason for this restriction is that cases where territorial insolvency proceedings are requested before the main insolvency proceedings are intended to be limited to what is absolutely necessary. If the main insolvency proceedings are opened, the territorial proceedings become secondary.

(18) Following the opening of the main insolvency proceedings, the right to request the opening of insolvency proceedings in a Member State where the debtor has an establishment is not restricted by this Regulation. The liquidator in the main proceedings or any other person empowered under the national law of that Member State may request the opening of secondary insolvency proceedings.

(19) Secondary insolvency proceedings may serve different purposes, besides the protection of local interests. Cases may arise where the estate of the debtor is too complex to administer as a unit or where differences in the legal systems concerned are so great that difficulties may arise from the extension of effects deriving from the law of the State of the opening to the other States where the assets are located. For this reason the liquidator in the main proceedings may request the opening of secondary proceedings when the efficient administration of the estate so requires.

(20) Main insolvency proceedings and secondary proceedings can, however, contribute to the effective realisation of the total assets only if all the concurrent proceedings pending are coordinated. The main condition here is that the various liquidators must cooperate closely, in particular by exchanging a sufficient amount of information. In

order to ensure the dominant role of the main insolvency proceedings, the liquidator in such proceedings should be given several possibilities for intervening in secondary insolvency proceedings which are pending at the same time. For example, he should be able to propose a restructuring plan or composition or apply for realisation of the assets in the secondary insolvency proceedings to be suspended.

(21) Every creditor, who has his habitual residence, domicile or registered office in the Community, should have the right to lodge his claims in each of the insolvency proceedings pending in the Community relating to the debtor's assets. This should also apply to tax authorities and social insurance institutions. However, in order to ensure equal treatment of creditors, the distribution of proceeds must be coordinated. Every creditor should be able to keep what he has received in the course of insolvency proceedings but should be entitled only to participate in the distribution of total assets in other proceedings if creditors with the same standing have obtained the same proportion of their claims.

(22) This Regulation should provide for immediate recognition of judgments concerning the opening, conduct and closure of insolvency proceedings which come within its scope and of judgments handed down in direct connection with such insolvency proceedings. Automatic recognition should therefore mean that the effects attributed to the proceedings by the law of the State in which the proceedings were opened extend to all other Member States. Recognition of judgments delivered by the courts of the Member States should be based on the principle of mutual trust. To that end, grounds for non-recognition should be reduced to the minimum necessary. This is also the basis on which any dispute should be resolved where the courts of two Member States both claim competence to open the main insolvency proceedings. The decision of the first court to open proceedings should be recognised in the other Member States without those Member States having the power to scrutinise the court's decision.

(23) This Regulation should set out, for the matters covered by it, uniform rules on conflict of laws which replace, within their scope of application, national rules of private international law, Unless otherwise stated, the law of the Member State of the opening of the proceedings should be applicable (*lex concursus*). This rule on conflict of laws should be valid both for the main proceedings and for local proceedings; the *lex concursus* determines all the effects of the insolvency proceedings, both procedural and substantive, on the persons and legal relations concerned. It governs all the conditions for the opening, conduct and closure of the insolvency proceedings.

(24) Automatic recognition of insolvency proceedings to which the law of the opening State normally applies may interfere with the rules under which transactions are carried out in other Member States. To protect legitimate expectations and the certainty of transactions in Member States other than that in which proceedings are opened, provisions should be made for a number of exceptions to the general rule.

(25) There is a particular need for a special reference diverging from the law of the opening State in the case of rights in rem, since these are of considerable importance for the granting of credit. The basis, validity and extent of such a right in rem should therefore normally be determined according to the *lex situs* and not be affected by the opening of insolvency proceedings. The proprietor of the right in rem should therefore be able to continue to assert his right to segregation or separate settlement of the collateral security. Where assets are subject to rights in rem under the *lex situs* in one

Member State but the main proceedings are being carried out in another Member State, the liquidator in the main proceedings should be able to request the opening of secondary proceedings in the jurisdiction where the rights in rem arise if the debtor has an establishment there. If a secondary proceeding is not opened, the surplus on sale of the asset covered by rights in rem must be paid to the liquidator in the main proceedings.

(26) If a set-off is not permitted under the law of the opening State, a creditor should nevertheless be entitled to the set-off if it is possible under the law applicable to the claim of the insolvent debtor. In this way, set-off will acquire a kind of guarantee function based on legal provisions on which the creditor concerned can rely at the time when the claim arises.

(27) There is also a need for special protection in the case of payment systems and financial markets. This applies for example to the position-closing agreements and netting agreements to be found in such systems as well as to the sale of securities and to the guarantees provided for such transactions as governed in particular by Directive 98/26/EC. of the European Parliament and of the Council of 19 May 1998 on settlement finality in payment and securities settlement systems (OJ L 166, 11.6.1998, p. 45). For such transactions, the only law which is material should thus be that applicable to the system or market concerned. This provision is intended to prevent the possibility of mechanisms for the payment and settlement of transactions provided for in the payment and set-off systems or on the regulated financial markets of the Member States being altered in the case of insolvency of a business partner. Directive 98/26/EC contains special provisions which should take precedence over the general rules in this Regulation.

(28) In order to protect employees and jobs, the effects of insolvency proceedings on the continuation or termination of employment and on the rights and obligations of all parties to such employment must be determined by the law applicable to the agreement in accordance with the general rules on conflict of law. Any other insolvency-law questions, such as whether the employees' claims are protected by preferential rights and what status such preferential rights may have, should be determined by the law of the opening State.

(29) For business considerations, the main content of the decision opening the proceedings should be published in the other Member States at the request of the liquidator. If there is an establishment in the Member State concerned, there may be a requirement that publication is compulsory. In neither case, however, should publication be a prior condition for recognition of the foreign proceedings.

(30) It may be the case that some of the persons concerned are not in fact aware that proceedings have been opened and act in good faith in a way that conflicts with the new situation. In order to protect such persons who make a payment to the debtor because they are unaware that foreign proceedings have been opened when they should in fact have made the payment to the foreign liquidator, it should be provided that such a payment is to have a debt-discharging effect.

(31) This Regulation should include Annexes relating to the organisation of insolvency proceedings. As these Annexes relate exclusively to the legislation of Member States, there are specific and substantiated reasons for the Council to reserve the right to amend

these Annexes in order to take account of any amendments to the domestic law of the Member States.

(32) The United Kingdom and Ireland, in accordance with Article 3 of the Protocol on the position of the United Kingdom and Ireland annexed to the Treaty on European Union and the Treaty establishing the European Community, have given notice of their wish to take part in the adoption and application of this Regulation.

(33) Denmark, in accordance with Articles 1 and 2 of the Protocol on the position of Denmark annexed to the Treaty on European Union and the Treaty establishing the European Community, is not participating in the adoption of this Regulation, and is therefore not bound by it nor subject to its application,

HAS ADOPTED THIS REGULATION:

CHAPTER I
GENERAL PROVISIONS

Article 1

Scope

1. This Regulation shall apply to collective insolvency proceedings which entail the partial or total divestment of a debtor and the appointment of a liquidator.

2. This Regulation shall not apply to insolvency proceedings concerning insurance undertakings, credit institutions, investment undertakings which provide services involving the holding of funds or securities for third parties, or to collective investment undertakings.

Article 2

Definitions

For the purposes of this Regulation:

(a) 'insolvency proceedings' shall mean the collective proceedings referred to in Article 1(1). These proceedings are listed in Annex A;

(b) 'liquidator' shall mean any person or body whose function is to administer or liquidate assets of which the debtor has been divested or to supervise the administration of his affairs. Those persons and bodies are listed in Annex C;

(c) 'winding-up proceedings' shall mean insolvency proceedings within the meaning of point (a) involving realising the assets of the debtor, including where the proceedings have been closed by a composition or other measure terminating the insolvency, or closed by reason of the insufficiency of the assets. Those proceedings are listed in Annex B;

(d) 'court' shall mean the judicial body or any other competent body of a Member State empowered to open insolvency proceedings or to take decisions in the course of such proceedings;

(e) 'judgment' in relation to the opening of insolvency proceedings or the appointment of a liquidator shall include the decision of any court empowered to open such proceedings or to appoint a liquidator;

(f) 'the time of the opening of proceedings' shall mean the time at which the judgment opening proceedings becomes effective, whether it is a final judgment or not;

(g) 'the Member State in which assets are situated' shall mean, in the case of:
- — tangible property, the Member State within the territory of which the property is situated,
- — property and rights ownership of or entitlement to which must be entered in a public register, the Member State under the authority of which the register is kept,
- — claims, the Member State within the territory of which the third party required to meet them has the centre of his main interests, as determined in Article 3(1);

(h) 'establishment' shall mean any place of operations where the debtor carries out a non-transitory economic activity with human means and goods.

Article 3

International jurisdiction

1. The courts of the Member State within the territory of which the centre of a debtor's main interests is situated shall have jurisdiction to open insolvency proceedings. In the case of a company or legal person, the place of the registered office shall be presumed to be the centre of its main interests in the absence of proof to the contrary.

2. Where the centre of a debtor's main interests is situated within the territory of a Member State, the courts of another Member State shall have jurisdiction to open insolvency proceedings against that debtor only if he possesses an establishment within the territory of that other Member State. The effects of those proceedings shall be restricted to the assets of the debtor situated in the territory of the latter Member State.

3. Where insolvency proceedings have been opened under paragraph 1, any proceedings opened subsequently under paragraph 2 shall be secondary proceedings. These latter proceedings must be winding-up proceedings.

4. Territorial insolvency proceedings referred to in paragraph 2 may be opened prior to the opening of main insolvency proceedings in accordance with paragraph 1 only:

(a) where insolvency proceedings under paragraph 1 cannot be opened because of the conditions laid down by the law of the Member State within the territory of which the centre of the debtor's main interests is situated; or

(b) where the opening of territorial insolvency proceedings is requested by a creditor who has his domicile, habitual residence or registered office in the Member State within the territory of which the establishment is situated, or whose claim arises from the operation of that establishment.

Article 4

Law applicable

1. Save as otherwise provided in this Regulation, the law applicable to insolvency proceedings and their effects shall be that of the Member State within the territory of which such proceedings are opened, hereafter referred to as the 'State of the opening of proceedings'.

2. The law of the State of the opening of proceedings shall determine the conditions for the opening of those proceedings, their conduct and their closure. It shall determine in particular:

(a) against which debtors insolvency proceedings may be brought on account of their capacity;

(b) the assets which form part of the estate and the treatment of assets acquired by or devolving on the debtor after the opening of the insolvency proceedings;

(c) the respective powers of the debtor and the liquidator;

(d) the conditions under which set-offs may be invoked;

(e) the effects of insolvency proceedings on current contracts to which the debtor is party;

(f) the effects of the insolvency proceedings on proceedings brought by individual creditors, with the exception of lawsuits pending;

(g) the claims which are to be lodged against the debtor's estate and the treatment of claims arising after the opening of insolvency proceedings;

(h) the rules governing the lodging, verification and admission of claims;

(i) the rules governing the distribution of proceeds from the realisation of assets, the ranking of claims and the rights of creditors who have obtained partial satisfaction after the opening of insolvency proceedings by virtue of a right in rem or through a set-off;

(j) the conditions for and the effects of closure of insolvency proceedings, in particular by composition;

(k) creditors' rights after the closure of insolvency proceedings;

(l) who is to bear the costs and expenses incurred in the insolvency proceedings;

(m) the rules relating to the voidness, voidability or unenforceability of legal acts detrimental to all the creditors.

Article 5

Third parties' rights in rem

1. The opening of insolvency proceedings shall not affect the rights in rem of creditors or third parties in respect of tangible or intangible, moveable or immoveable assets — both specific assets and collections of indefinite assets as a whole which change from time to time — belonging to the debtor which are situated within the territory of another Member State at the time of the opening of proceedings.

2. The rights referred to in paragraph 1 shall in particular mean:

(a) the right to dispose of assets or have them disposed of and to obtain satisfaction from the proceeds of or income from those assets, in particular by virtue of a lien or a mortgage;

(b) the exclusive right to have a claim met, in particular a right guaranteed by a lien in respect of the claim or by assignment of the claim by way of a guarantee;

(c) the right to demand the assets from, and/or to require restitution by, anyone having possession or use of them contrary to the wishes of the party so entitled;

(d) a right in rem to the beneficial use of assets.

3. The right, recorded in a public register and enforceable against third parties, under which a right in rem within the meaning of paragraph 1 may be obtained, shall be considered a right in rem.

4. Paragraph 1 shall not preclude actions for voidness, voidability or unenforceability as referred to in Article 4(2)(m).

Article 6

Set-off

1. The opening of insolvency proceedings shall not affect the right of creditors to demand the set-off of their claims against the claims of the debtor, where such a set-off is permitted by the law applicable to the insolvent debtor's claim.

2. Paragraph 1 shall not preclude actions for voidness, voidability or unenforceability as referred to in Article 4(2)(m).

Article 7

Reservation of title

1. The opening of insolvency proceedings against the purchaser of an asset shall not affect the seller's rights based on a reservation of title where at the time of the opening of proceedings the asset is situated within the territory of a Member State other than the State of opening of proceedings.

2. The opening of insolvency proceedings against the seller of an asset, after delivery of the asset, shall not constitute grounds for rescinding or terminating the sale and shall not prevent the purchaser from acquiring title where at the time of the opening of proceedings the asset sold is situated within the territory of a Member State other than the State of the opening of proceedings.

3. Paragraphs 1 and 2 shall not preclude actions for voidness; voidability or unenforceability as referred to in Article 4(2)(m).

Article 8

Contracts relating to immoveable property

The effects of insolvency proceedings on a contract conferring the right to acquire or make use of immoveable property shall be governed solely by the law of the Member State within the territory of which the immoveable property is situated.

Article 9

Payment systems and financial markets

1. Without prejudice to Article 5, the effects of insolvency proceedings on the rights and obligations of the parties to a payment or settlement system or to a financial market shall be governed solely by the law of the Member State applicable to that system or market.

2. Paragraph 1 shall not preclude any action for voidness, voidability or unenforceability which may be taken to set aside payments or transactions under the law applicable to the relevant payment system or financial market.

Article 10

Contracts of employment

The effects of insolvency proceedings on employment contracts and relationships shall be governed solely by the law of the Member State applicable to the contract of employment.

Article 11

Effects on rights subject to registration

The effects of insolvency proceedings on the rights of the debtor in immoveable property, a ship or an aircraft subject to registration in a public register shall be determined by the law of the Member State under the authority of which the register is kept.

Article 12

Community patents and trade marks

For the purposes of this Regulation, a Community patent, a Community trade mark or any other similar right established by Community law may be included only in the proceedings referred to in Article 3(1).

Article 13

Detrimental acts

Article 4(2) (m) shall not apply where the person who benefited from an act detrimental to all the creditors provides proof that:

— the said act is subject to the law of a Member State other than that of the State of the opening of proceedings, and

— that law does not allow any means of challenging that act in the relevant case.

Article 14

Protection of third-party purchasers

Where, by an act concluded after the opening of insolvency proceedings, the debtor disposes, for consideration, of:

— an immoveable asset, or

— a ship or an aircraft subject to registration in a public register, or

— securities whose existence presupposes registration in a register laid down by law

the validity of that act shall be governed by the law of the State within the territory of which the immoveable asset is situated or under the authority of which the register is kept.

Article 15

Effects of insolvency proceedings on lawsuits pending

The effects of insolvency proceedings on a lawsuit pending concerning an asset or a right of which the debtor has been divested shall be governed solely by the law of the Member State in which that lawsuit is pending.

Chapter II
Recognition Of Insolvency Proceedings

Article 16

Principle

1. Any judgment opening insolvency proceedings handed down by a court of a Member State which has jurisdiction pursuant to Article 3 shall be recognised in all the other Member States from the time that it becomes effective in the State of the opening of proceedings.

This rule shall also apply where, on account of his capacity, insolvency proceedings cannot be brought against the debtor in other Member States.

2. Recognition of the proceedings referred to in Article 3(1) shall not preclude the opening of the proceedings referred to in Article 3(2) by a court in another Member State. The latter proceedings shall be secondary insolvency proceedings within the meaning of Chapter III.

Article 17

Effects of recognition

1. The judgment opening the proceedings referred to in Article 3(1) shall, with no further formalities, produce the same effects in any other Member State as under this law of the State of the opening of proceedings, unless this Regulation provides otherwise and as long as no proceedings referred to in Article 3(2) are opened in that other Member State.

2. The effects of the proceedings referred to in Article 3(2) may not be challenged in other Member States. Any restriction of the creditors' rights, in particular a stay or discharge, shall produce effects vis-à-vis assets situated within the territory of another Member State only in the case of those creditors who have given their consent.

Article 18

Powers of the liquidator

1. The liquidator appointed by a court which has jurisdiction pursuant to Article 3(1) may exercise all the powers conferred on him by the law of the State of the opening of proceedings in another Member State, as long as no other insolvency proceedings have been opened there nor any preservation measure to the contrary has been taken there further to a request for the opening of insolvency proceedings in that State. He may in particular remove the debtor's assets from the territory of the Member State in which they are situated, subject to Articles 5 and 7.

2. The liquidator appointed by a court which has jurisdiction pursuant to Article 3(2) may in any other Member State claim through the courts or out of court that moveable property was removed from the territory of the State of the opening of proceedings to the territory of that other Member State after the opening of the insolvency proceedings. He may also bring any action to set aside which is in the interests of the creditors.

3. In exercising his powers, the liquidator shall comply with the law of the Member State within the territory of which he intends to take action, in particular with regard to procedures for the realisation of assets. Those powers may not include coercive measures or the right to rule on legal proceedings or disputes.

Article 19

Proof of the liquidator's appointment

The liquidator's appointment shall be evidenced by a certified copy of the original decision appointing him or by any other certificate issued by the court which has jurisdiction.

A translation into the official language or one of the official languages of the Member State within the territory of which he intends to act may be required. No legalisation or other similar formality shall be required.

Article 20

Return and imputation

1. A creditor who, after the opening of the proceedings referred to in Article 3(1) obtains by any means, in particular through enforcement, total or partial satisfaction of his claim on the assets belonging to the debtor situated within the territory of another Member State, shall return what he has obtained to the liquidator, subject to Articles 5 and 7.

2. In order to ensure equal treatment of creditors a creditor who has, in the course of insolvency proceedings, obtained a dividend on his claim shall share in distributions made in other proceedings only where creditors of the same ranking or category have, in those other proceedings, obtained an equivalent dividend.

Article 21

Publication

1. The liquidator may request that notice of the judgment opening insolvency proceedings and, where appropriate, the decision appointing him, be published in any other Member State in accordance with the publication procedures provided for in that State. Such publication shall also specify the liquidator appointed and whether the jurisdiction rule applied is that pursuant to Article 3(1) or Article 3(2).

2. However, any Member State within the territory of which the debtor has an establishment may require mandatory publication. In such cases, the liquidator or any authority empowered to that effect in the Member State where the proceedings referred to in Article 3(1) are opened shall take all necessary measures to ensure such publication.

Article 22

Registration in a public register

1. The liquidator may request that the judgment opening the proceedings referred to in Article 3(1) be registered in the land register, the trade register and any other public register kept in the other Member States.

2. However, any Member State may require mandatory registration. In such cases, the liquidator or any authority empowered to that effect in the Member State where the proceedings referred to in Article 3(1) have been opened shall take all necessary measures to ensure such registration.

Article 23

Costs

The costs of the publication and registration provided for in Articles 21 and 22 shall be regarded as costs and expenses incurred in the proceedings.

Article 24

Honouring of an obligation to a debtor

1. Where an obligation has been honoured in a Member State for the benefit of a debtor who is subject to insolvency proceedings opened in another Member State, when it should have been honoured for the benefit of the liquidator in those proceedings, the person honouring the obligation shall be deemed to have discharged it if he was unaware of the opening of proceedings.

2. Where such an obligation is honoured before the publication provided for in Article 21 has been effected, the person honouring the obligation shall be presumed, in the absence of proof to the contrary, to have been unaware of the opening of insolvency proceedings; where the obligation is honoured after such publication has been effected, the person honouring the obligation shall be presumed, in the absence of proof to the contrary, to have been aware of the opening of proceedings.

Article 25

Recognition and enforceability of other judgments

1. Judgments handed down by a court whose judgment concerning the opening of proceedings is recognised in accordance with Article 16 and which concern the course and closure of insolvency proceedings, and compositions approved by that court shall also be recognised with no further formalities. Such judgments shall be enforced in accordance with Articles 31 to 51, with the exception of Article 34(2), of the Brussels Convention on Jurisdiction and the Enforcement of Judgments in Civil and Commercial Matters, as amended by the Conventions of Accession to this Convention.

The first subparagraph shall also apply to judgments deriving directly from the insolvency proceedings and which are closely linked with them, even if they were handed down by another court.

The first subparagraph shall also apply to judgments relating to preservation measures taken after the request for the opening of insolvency proceedings.

2. The recognition and enforcement of judgments other than those referred to in paragraph 1 shall be governed by the Convention referred to in paragraph 1, provided that that Convention is applicable.

3. The Member States shall not be obliged to recognise or enforce a judgment referred to in paragraph 1 which might result in a limitation of personal freedom or postal secrecy.

Article 26[1]

Public policy

Any Member State may refuse to recognise insolvency proceedings opened in another Member State or to enforce a judgment handed down in the context of such proceedings where the effects of such recognition or enforcement would be manifestly contrary to that State's public policy, in particular its fundamental principles or the constitutional rights and liberties of the individual.

[1] Note the Declaration by Portugal concerning the application of Articles 26 and 37 (OJ C 183, 30.6.2000, p. 1).

CHAPTER III
SECONDARY INSOLVENCY PROCEEDINGS

Article 27

Opening of proceedings

The opening of the proceedings referred to in Article 3(1) by a court of a Member State and which is recognised in another Member State (main proceedings) shall permit the opening in that other Member State, a court of which has jurisdiction pursuant to Article 3(2), of secondary insolvency proceedings without the debtor's insolvency being examined in that other State. These latter proceedings must be among the proceedings listed in Annex B. Their effects shall be restricted to the assets of the debtor situated within the territory of that other Member State.

Article 28

Applicable law

Save as otherwise provided in this Regulation, the law applicable to secondary proceedings shall be that of the Member State within the territory of which the secondary proceedings are opened.

Article 29

Right to request the opening of proceedings

The opening of secondary proceedings may be requested by:

(a) the liquidator in the main proceedings;

(b) any other person or authority empowered to request the opening of insolvency proceedings under the law of the Member State within the territory of which the opening of secondary proceedings is requested.

Article 30

Advance payment of costs and expenses

Where the law of the Member State in which the opening of secondary proceedings is requested requires that the debtor's assets be sufficient to cover in whole or in part the costs and expenses of the proceedings, the court may, when it receives such a request, require the applicant to make an advance payment of costs or to provide appropriate security.

Article 31

Duty to cooperate and communicate information

1. Subject to the rules restricting the communication of information, the liquidator in the main proceedings and the liquidators in the secondary proceedings shall be duty bound to communicate information to each other. They shall immediately communicate any information which may be relevant to the other proceedings, in particular the progress

made in lodging and verifying claims and all measures aimed at terminating the proceedings.

2. Subject to the rules applicable to each of the proceedings, the liquidator in the main proceedings and the liquidators in the secondary proceedings shall be duty bound to cooperate with each other.

3. The liquidator in the secondary proceedings shall give the liquidator in the main proceedings an early opportunity of submitting proposals on the liquidation or use of the assets in the secondary proceedings.

Article 32

Exercise of creditors' rights

1. Any creditor may lodge his claim in the main proceedings and in any secondary proceedings.

2. The liquidators in the main and any secondary proceedings shall lodge in other proceedings claims which have already been lodged in the proceedings for which they were appointed, provided that the interests of creditors in the latter proceedings are served thereby, subject to the right of creditors to oppose that or to withdraw the lodgement of their claims where the law applicable so provides.

3. The liquidator in the main or secondary proceedings shall be empowered to participate in other proceedings on the same basis as a creditor, in particular by attending creditors' meetings.

Article 33

Stay of liquidation

1. The court, which opened the secondary proceedings, shall stay the process of liquidation in whole or in part on receipt of a request from the liquidator in the main proceedings, provided that in that event it may require the liquidator in the main proceedings to take any suitable measure to guarantee the interests of the creditors in the secondary proceedings and of individual classes of creditors. Such a request from the liquidator may be rejected only if it is manifestly of no interest to the creditors in the main proceedings. Such a stay of the process of liquidation may be ordered for up to three months. It may be continued or renewed for similar periods.

2. The court referred to in paragraph 1 shall terminate the stay of the process of liquidation:

— at the request of the liquidator in the main proceedings,

— of its own motion, at the request of a creditor or at the request of the liquidator in the secondary proceedings if that measure no longer appears justified, in particular, by the interests of creditors in the main proceedings or in the secondary proceedings.

Article 34

Measures ending secondary insolvency proceedings

1. Where the law applicable to secondary proceedings allows for such proceedings to be closed without liquidation by a rescue plan, a composition or a comparable measure, the

liquidator in the main proceedings shall be empowered to propose such a measure himself.

Closure of the secondary proceedings by a measure referred to in the first subparagraph shall not become final without the consent of the liquidator in the main proceedings; failing his agreement, however, it may become final if the financial interests of the creditors in the main proceedings are not affected by the measure proposed.

2. Any restriction of creditors' rights arising from a measure referred to in paragraph 1 which is proposed in secondary proceedings, such as a stay of payment or discharge of debt; may not have effect in respect of the debtor's assets not covered by those proceedings without the consent of all the creditors having an interest.

3. During a stay of the process of liquidation ordered pursuant to Article 33, only the liquidator in the main proceedings or the debtor, with the former's consent, may propose measures laid down in paragraph 1 of this Article in the secondary proceedings; no other proposal for such a measure shall be put to the vote or approved.

Article 35

Assets remaining in the secondary proceedings

If by the liquidation of assets in the secondary proceedings it is possible to meet all claims allowed under those proceedings, the liquidator appointed in those proceedings shall immediately transfer any assets remaining to the liquidator in the main proceedings.

Article 36

Subsequent opening of the main proceedings

Where the proceedings referred to in Article 3(1) are opened following the opening of the proceedings referred to in Article 3(2) in another Member State, Articles 31 to 35 shall apply to those opened first, in so far as the progress of those proceedings so permits.

Article 37[1]

Conversion of earlier proceedings

The liquidator in the main proceedings may request that proceedings listed in Annex A previously opened in another Member State be converted into winding-up proceedings if this proves to be in the interests of the creditors in the main proceedings.

The court with jurisdiction under Article 3(2) shall order conversion into one of the proceedings listed in Annex B.

[1] Note the Declaration by Portugal concerning the application of Articles 26 and 37 (OJ C. 183, 30.6.2000, p. 1).

Article 38

Preservation measures

Where the court of a Member State which has jurisdiction pursuant to Article 3(1) appoints a temporary administrator in order to ensure the preservation of the debtor's assets, that temporary administrator shall be empowered to request any measures to secure and preserve any of the debtor's assets situated in another Member State, provided for under the law of that State, for the period between the request for the opening of insolvency proceedings and the judgment opening the proceedings.

CHAPTER IV

PROVISION OF INFORMATION FOR CREDITORS AND LODGEMENT OF THEIR CLAIMS

Article 39

Right to lodge claims

Any creditor who has his habitual residence, domicile or registered office in a Member State other than the State of the opening of proceedings, including the tax authorities and social security authorities of Member States, shall have the right to lodge claims in the insolvency proceedings in writing.

Article 40

Duty to inform creditors

1. As soon as insolvency proceedings are opened in a Member State, the court of that State having jurisdiction or the liquidator appointed by it shall immediately inform known creditors who have their habitual residences, domiciles or registered offices in the other Member States.

2. That information, provided by an individual notice, shall in particular include time limits, the penalties laid down in regard to those time limits, the body or authority empowered to accept the lodgement of claims and the other measures laid down. Such notice shall also indicate whether creditors whose claims are preferential or secured in rem need lodge their claims.

Article 41

Content of the lodgement of a claim

A creditor shall send copies of supporting documents, if any, and shall indicate the nature of the claim, the date on which it arose and its amount, as well as whether he alleges preference, security in rem or a reservation of title in respect of the claim and what assets are covered by the guarantee he is invoking.

Article 42

Languages

1. The information provided for in Article 40 shall be provided in the official language or one of the official languages of the State of the opening of proceedings. For that purpose a form shall be used bearing the heading 'Invitation to lodge a claim. Time limits to be observed' in all the official languages of the institutions of the European Union.

2. Any creditor who has his habitual residence, domicile or registered office in a Member State other than the State of the opening of proceedings may lodge his claim in the official language or one of the official languages of that other State. In that event, however, the lodgement of his claim shall bear the heading 'Lodgement of claim' in the official language or one of the official languages of the State of the opening of proceedings. In addition, he may be required to provide a translation into the official language or one of the official languages of the State of the opening of proceedings.

CHAPTER V
TRANSITIONAL AND FINAL PROVISIONS

Article 43

Applicability in time

The provisions of this Regulation shall apply only to insolvency proceedings opened after its entry into force. Acts done by a debtor before the entry into force of this Regulation shall continue to be governed by the law which was applicable to them at the time they were done.

Article 44

Relationship to Conventions

1. After its entry into force, this Regulation replaces, in respect of the matters referred to therein, in the relations between Member States, the Conventions concluded between two or more Member States, in particular:

(a) the Convention between Belgium and France on Jurisdiction and the Validity and Enforcement of Judgments, Arbitration Awards and Authentic Instruments, signed at Paris on 8 July 1899;

(b) the Convention between Belgium and Austria on Bankruptcy, Winding-up, Arrangements, Compositions and Suspension of Payments (with Additional Protocol of 13 June 1973), signed at Brussels on 16 July 1969;

(c) the Convention between Belgium and the Netherlands on Territorial Jurisdiction, Bankruptcy and the Validity and Enforcement of Judgments, Arbitration Awards and Authentic Instruments, signed at Brussels on 28 March 1925;

(d) the Treaty between Germany and Austria on Bankruptcy, Winding-up, Arrangements and Compositions, signed at Vienna on 25 May 1979;

(e) the Convention between France and Austria on Jurisdiction, Recognition and Enforcement of Judgments on Bankruptcy, signed at Vienna on 27 February 1979;

(f) the Convention between France and Italy on the Enforcement of Judgments in Civil and Commercial Matters, signed at Rome on 3 June 1930;

(g) the Convention between Italy and Austria on Bankruptcy, Winding-up, Arrangements and Compositions, signed at Rome on 12 July 1977;

(h) the Convention between the Kingdom of the Netherlands and the Federal Republic of Germany on the Mutual Recognition and Enforcement of Judgments and other Enforceable Instruments in Civil and Commercial Matters, signed at The Hague on 30 August 1962;

(i) the Convention between the United Kingdom and the Kingdom of Belgium providing for the Reciprocal Enforcement of Judgments in Civil and Commercial Matters, with Protocol, signed at Brussels on 2 May 1934;

(j) the Convention between Denmark, Finland, Norway, Sweden and Iceland on Bankruptcy, signed at Copenhagen on 7 November 1933;

(k) the European Convention on Certain International Aspects of Bankruptcy, signed at Istanbul on 5 June 1990.

2. The Conventions referred to in paragraph 1 shall continue to have effect with regard to proceedings opened before the entry into force of this Regulation.

3. This Regulation shall not apply:

(a) in any Member State, to the extent that it is irreconcilable with the obligations arising in relation to bankruptcy from a convention concluded by that State with one or more third countries before the entry into force of this Regulation;

(b) in the United Kingdom of Great Britain and Northern Ireland, to the extent that is irreconcilable with the obligations arising in relation to bankruptcy and the winding-up of insolvent companies from any arrangements with the Commonwealth existing at the time this Regulation enters into force.

Article 45

Amendment of the Annexes

The Council, acting by qualified majority on the initiative of one of its members or on a proposal from the Commission, may amend the Annexes.

Article 46

Reports

No later than 1 June 2012, and every five years thereafter, the Commission shall present to the European Parliament, the Council and the Economic and Social Committee a report on the application of this Regulation. The report shall be accompanied if need be by a proposal for adaptation of this Regulation.

Article 47

Entry into force

This Regulation shall enter into force on 31 May 2002.

This Regulation shall be binding in its entirety and directly applicable in the Member States in accordance with the Treaty establishing the European Community.

ANNEX A

INSOLVENCY PROCEEDINGS REFERRED TO IN ARTICLE 2(A)

BELGIË—BELGIQUE

— Het faillissement/La faillite

— Het gerechtelijk akkoord/Le concordat judiciaire

— De collectieve schuldenregeling/Le règlement collectif de dettes

DEUTSCHLAND

— Das Konkursverfahren

— Das gerichtliche Vergleichsverfahren

— Das Gesamtvollstreckungsverfahren

— Das Insolvenzverfahren

ΕΛΛΑΣ

— Πτώχευση

Η ειδική εκκαθάριση

— Η ειδική εκκαθάριση

— Η προσωρινή διαχείριση εταιρίας. Η διοίκηση και η διαχείριση των πιστωτών

— Η υπαγωγή επιχείρησης υπό επίτροπο με σκοπό τη σύναψη συμβιβασμού με τους πιστωτές

ESPAÑA

— Concurso de acreedores

— Quiebra

— Suspensión de pagos

FRANCE

— Liquidation judiciaire

— Redressement judiciaire avec nomination d'un administrateur

IRELAND

— Compulsory winding up by the court

— Bankruptcy

— The administration in bankruptcy of the estate of persons dying insolvent

— Winding-up in bankruptcy of partnerships

— Creditors' voluntary winding up (with confirmation of a Court)

— Arrangements under the control of the court which involve the vesting of all or part of the property of the debtor in the Official Assignce for realisation and distribution

— Company examinership

ITALIA

— Fallimento

— Concordato preventivo

— Liquidazione coatta amministrativa

— Amministrazione straordinaria

— Amministrazione controllata

LUXEMBOURG

— Faillite

— Gestion contrôlée

— Concordat préventif de faillite (par abandon d'acrif)

— Régime spécial de liquidation du notariat

NEDERLAND

— Het faillissement

— De surséance van betaling

— De schuldsaneringsregeling natuurlijke personen

ÖSTERREICH

— Das Konkursverfahren

— Das Ausgleichsverfahren

PORTUGAL

— O processo de falência

— Os processos especiais de recuperação de empresa, ou seja:

— A concordata

— A reconstituição empresarial

— A reestruturação financeira

— A gest ào controlada

SUOMI-FINLAND

— Konkurssi/konkurs

— Yrityssaneeraus/företagssanering

SVERIGE

— Konkurs

— Företagsrekonstruktion

UNITED KINGDOM

— Winding up by or subject to the supervision of the court

— Creditors' voluntary winding up (with confirmation by the court)

— Administration

— Voluntary arrangements under insolvency legislation

— Bankruptcy or sequestration

ANNEX B

WINDING UP PROCEEDINGS REFERRED TO IN ARTICLE 2(C)

BELGIË—BELGIQUE

— Het faillissement/La faillite

DEUTSCHLAND

— Das Konkursverfahren

— Das Gesamtvollstreckungsverfahren

— Das Insolvenzverfahren

ΕΛΛΑΣ

— Πτώχευση

— Η ειδική εκκαθάρισηε

ESPAÑA

— Concurso de acreedores

— Quiebra

— Suspensión de pagos basada en la insolvencia definitiva

FRANCE

— Liquidation judiciaire

IRELAND

— Compulsory winding up

— Bankruptcy

— The administration in bankruptcy of the estate of persons dying insolvent

— Winding-up in bankruptcy of partnerships

— Creditors' voluntary winding up (with confirmation of a court)

— Arrangements under the control of the court which involve the vesting of all or part of the property of the debtor in the Official Assignee for realisation and distribution

ITALIA

— Fallimento

— Liquidazione coatta amministrativa

LUXEMBOURG

— Faillite

— Régime spécial de liquidation du notariat

NEDERLAND

— Het faillissement

— De schuldsaneringsregeling natuurlijke personen

ÖSTERREICH

— Das Konkursverfahren

PORTUGAL

— O processo de falência

SUOMI-FINLAND

— Konkurssi/konkurs

SVERIGE

— Konkurs

UNITED KINGDOM

— Winding up by or subject to the supervision of the court

— Creditors' voluntary winding up (with confirmation by the court)

— Bankruptcy or sequestration

ANNEX C

LIQUIDATORS REFERRED TO IN ARTICLE 2(B)

BELGIË—BELGIQUE

— De curator/Le curateur

— De commissaris inzake opschorting/Le commissaire au sursis

— De schuldbemiddelaar/Le médiateur de dettes

DEUTSCHLAND

— Konkursverwalter

— Vergleichsverwalter

— Sachwalter (nach der Vergleichsordnung)

— Verwalter

— Insolvenzverwalter

— Sachwalter (nach der Insolvenzordnung)

— Treuhänder

— Vorläufiger Insolvenzverwalter

ΕΛΛΑΣ

— Ο σύνδικο

— Ο προσωρινός διαχειριστής. Η διοικούσα επιτροπή των πιστωτών

— Ο ειδικός εκκαθαριστής

— Ο επίτροπος

ESPAÑA

— Depositario-administrador

— Interventor o Interventores

— Síndicos

— Comisario

FRANCE

— Représentant des créanciers

— Mandataire liquidateur

— Administrateur judiciaire

— Commissaire à l'exécution de plan

IRELAND

— Liquidator

— Official Assignee

— Trustee in bankruptcy

— Provisional Liquidator

— Examiner

ITALIA

— Curatore

— Commissario

LUXEMBOURG

— Le curateur

— Le commissaire

— Le liquidateur

— Le conseil de gérance de la section d'assainissement du notariat

NEDERLAND

— De curator in het faillissement

— De bewindvoerder in de surséance van betaling

— De bewindvoerder in de schuldsaneringsregeling natuurlijke personen

ÖSTERREICH

— Masseverwalter

— Ausgleichsverwalter

— Sachwalter

— Treuhänder

— Besondere Verwalter

— Vorläufiger Verwalter

— Konkursgericht

PORTUGAL

— Gestor judicial

— Liquidatário judicial

— Comissão de credores

SUOMI—FINLAND

— Pesänhoitaja/boförvaltare

— Selvittäjä/utredare

SVERIGE

— Förvaltare

— God man

— Rekonstruktör

UNITED KINGDOM

— Liquidator

— Supervisor of a voluntary arrangement

— Administrator

— Official Receiver

— Trustee

— Judicial factor

EXPLANATORY NOTE

(*This note is not a part of the Instrument and does not purport to be a legal interpretation*)

These Regulations are intended to facilitate the operation of Council Regulation (EC) No. 1346/2000 of 29 May 2000 on Insolvency Proceedings, insofar as they concern corporate insolvency. The Regulations set out the necessary amendments to domestic legislation (the Companies Acts 1963 to 2001) and make necessary provisions for the good administration of the Council Regulation, which came into effect on 31 May, 2002.

The facilitation of the operation of the Council Regulation with regard to personal insolvency is set out in Statutory Instrument No. 334 of 2002.

European Communities (Credit Institutions) (Fair Value Accounting) Regulations 2004

SI 720/2004

I, Brian Cowen, Minister for Finance, in exercise of the powers conferred on me by section 3 of the European Communities Act 1972 (No. 27 of 1972), for the purpose of giving effect to Directive 2001/65/EC of the European Parliament and of the Council of 27 September 2001[1]*, hereby make the following regulations:*

1.(1) These Regulations may be cited as the European Communities (Credit Institutions) (Fair Value Accounting) Regulations 2004.

(2) These Regulations come into operation on 1 January 2005.

2.(1) In these Regulations "Principal Regulations" means the European Communities (Credit Institutions: Accounts) Regulations 1992 (S.I. No. 294 of 1992).

(2) A word or expression that is used in these Regulations (including provisions inserted into the Principal Regulations by these Regulations) and is also used in Directive 2001/65/EC of the European Parliament and of the Council of 27 September 2001 (O.J. No. L283, 27.10.01, p.28) has, unless the contrary is indicted, the same meaning in these Regulations as it has in that Directive.

3. Regulation 11 of the Principal Regulations is amended—

(a) in paragraph (d), by deleting "and" at the end of that paragraph,

(b) in paragraph (e), by substituting "subsidiary, and" for "subsidiary.", and

(c) by inserting after paragraph (e) the following:

[.....][a]

Amendments

a Reg 11(f) of EC(CIA)R 1992 inserted. See the amended Regs.

---

4. Regulation 15 of the Principal Regulations is amended by substituting—

(a) in paragraph (1)(a), "€3,000" for "£1,000",

(b) in paragraph (2)—

(i) "3 months" for "12 months", and

(ii) "€3,000" for "£1,000", and

(c) in paragraph (4)—

(i) "3 months" for "12 months", and

(ii) "€3,000" for "£1,000".

5. Paragraph 41 of Chapter II of Part I of the Schedule to the Principal Regulations is amended, by substituting for subparagraph (3) the following:

[...][a]

Amendments

a Reg 5 substitutes EC(CIA)R 1992, Sch, Pt 1, ch II para 41(3).

6. Part I of the Schedule to the Principal Regulations is amended by inserting after paragraph 46 the following:

[...][a].

Amendments

a Reg 6 inserts EC(CIA)R 1992, Sch, Pt 1, ch II para 46A–46D.

7. Chapter III of Part I of the Schedule to the Principal Act is amended—

(a) in paragraph 75(2), by inserting the following sentence:

'This includes the extent to which the calculation of the profit or loss is affected by the fair valuation of financial instruments', and

(b) after paragraph 72, by inserting the following:

[...][a]

Amendments

a Reg 7(b) inserts EC(CIA)R 1992, Sch, Pt 1, ch III para 72A.

8. Paragraphs 31(1), 32, 33, 34, 45 and 46 of Part I of the Schedule to the Principal Regulations do not apply with respect to assets and liabilities that are valued in accordance with paragraphs 46A to 46D (inserted by Regulation 6 of these Regulations) of Part I of the Schedule to the Principal Regulations.

EXPLANATORY NOTE

(*This note is not part of the instrument and does not purport to be a legal interpretation*).

The purpose of these Regulations is to give effect to Directive 2001/65/EC of 27 September 2001 which deals with the valuation rules for the annual and consolidated accounts of banks and other financial institutions.

These Regulations allow banks and other financial institutions in the EU to prepare their consolidated financial statements in accordance with generally accepted accounting principles. The impetus for this is the harmonisation of the capital markets in the EU and the desire to have a consistent set of accounting principles used in the consolidated financial statements ("group accounts") of all EU banks and financial institutions.

European Communities (Fair Value Accounting) Regulations 2004

SI 765/2004

I, Micheál Martin, Minister for Enterprise, Trade and Employment, in exercise of the powers conferred on me by section 3 of the European Communities Act 1972 (No. 27 of 1972), for the purpose of giving effect to Directive 2001/65/EC of the European Parliament and of the Council of 27 September 2001 (OJ No. L283, 27.10.01, p 28), hereby make the following regulations:

1.(1) These Regulations may be cited as the European Communities (Fair Value Accounting) Regulations 2004.

(2) These Regulations come into operation on 1 January 2005.

(3) These Regulations shall be read as one with the Companies Acts 1963 to 2003.

2. A word or expression that is used in these Regulations (including provisions inserted by these Regulations into the Companies (Amendment) Act 1986 (No. 25 of 1986) and the European Communities (Companies: Group Accounts) Regulations 1992 (S.I. No. 201 of 1992)) and is also used in Directive 2001/65/EC of the European Parliament and of the Council of 27 September 2001 has, unless the contrary is indicated, the same meaning in these Regulations as it has in that Directive.

3. The Companies (Amendment) Act 1986 is amended—

(a) in section 12(1), by inserting "31B, 31C," after "27,",

(b) in section 13 (as amended by the European Communities (Accounts) Regulations 1993 (S.I. No. 396 of 1993)), by substituting the following for paragraphs (c), (d) and (e)—

[...][a]

and

(c) in the Schedule—

(i) in Part II (HISTORICAL COST RULES IN RELATION TO THE DRAWING UP OF ACCOUNTS), in paragraph 4 (Preliminary), by substituting "Parts III and IIIA" for "Part III",

(ii) by inserting the following after paragraph 22—

[...][b]

(iii) in Part IV (INFORMATION REQUIRED BY WAY OF NOTES TO ACCOUNTS), by inserting the following after paragraph 31—

[...][c]

and

in Part VII (INTERPRETATION OF SCHEDULE), by inserting the following after paragraph 76—

[...][d]

Amendments

a Reg 3(b) substitutes C(A)A 1986, s 13(c), (d) and (e).

b Reg 3(c)(ii) inserts C(A)A 1986, ss 22A–22E.

c Reg 3(c)(iii) inserts C(A)A 1986, ss 31A–31C.

d Reg 3(c)(iv) inserts C(A)A 1986, ss 77–78.

4. The European Communities (Companies: Group Accounts) Regulations 1992 are amended—

(a) in Regulation 37(1), by substituting the following for paragraphs (d) and (e)—

[...][a]

and

(b) In Part 2 (Information required by way of notes to the group accounts) of the Schedule, by inserting the following after paragraph 16—

[...][b]

Amendments

a Reg 4(a) substitutes EC(CGA)R 1992, reg 37(1)(d) and (e).

b Reg 4(b) inserts EC(CGA)R 1992, Sch, Pt 2, paras 16A and 16B.

EXPLANATORY NOTE

(*This note is not part of the instrument and does not purport to be a legal interpretation*).

These Regulations give effect to Directive 2001/65/EC of the European Parliament and of the Council of 27 September, 2001 to allow for the fair valuation of financial instruments in accounts.

European Communities (International Financial Reporting Standards and Miscellaneous Amendments) Regulations 2005

SI 116/2005

I, Micheál Martin, Minister for Enterprise, Trade and Employment, in exercise of the powers conferred on me by section 3 of the European Communities Act 1972 (No. 27 of 1972) and for the purpose of giving full effect to Regulation (EC) No. 1606/2002 of the European Parliament and of the Council of 19 July 2002[1], for the purpose of giving further effect to the Fourth Council Directive 78/660/EEC of 25 July 1978[2], the Seventh Council Directive 83/349/EEC of 13 June 1983[3], Council Directive 86/635/EEC of 8 December 1986[4] and Council Directive 91/674/EEC[5] of 19 December 1991 and for the purpose of giving effect to Directive 2003/51 /EC of the European Parliament and of the Council of 18 June 2003[6], hereby make the following regulations:

1 OJ No. L243, 11.9.2002, p.1
2 OJ No. L222, 14.8.1978, p.11
3 OJ No. L193, 18.7.1983, p.1
4 OJ No. L372, 31.12.1986, p.1
5 OJ No. L374, 31.12.1991, p.7
6 OJ No. L178, 17.7.2003, p.16

PART I
PRELIMINARY AND GENERAL

Citation and construction

1.(1) These Regulations may be cited as the European Communities (International Financial Reporting Standards and Miscellaneous Amendments) Regulations 2005.

(2) These Regulations are to be read as one with the Companies Acts 1963 to 2003.

Application

2.(1) These Regulations apply to the preparation of annual accounts in the case of a company or undertaking the financial year of which commences on or after 1 January 2005.

(2) In the case of a company or undertaking that prepares its first annual accounts for a period ending after 1 January 2005, it may prepare IFRS accounts (within the meaning of section 2 of the Principal Act) even though its date of incorporation or formation, as the case may be, is before 1 January 2005.

Interpretation

3.(1) In these Regulations—

'Credit Institutions Regulations' means the European Communities (Credit Institutions: Accounts) Regulations 1992 (S.I. No. 294 of 1992);

'Fair Value Regulations' means the European Communities (Fair Value Accounting) Regulations 2004 (S.I. No. 765 of 2004);

'Insurance Undertakings Regulations' means the European Communities (Insurance Undertakings: Accounts) Regulations 1996 (S.I. No. 23 of 1996);

'Principal Act' means the Companies Act 1963 (No. 33 of 1963).

(2) A word or expression that is used in these Regulations (including provisions inserted by these Regulations into the Principal Act, the Companies (Amendment) Act 1983 (No. 13 of 1983), the Companies (Amendment) Act 1986 (No. 25 of 1986), the Companies Act 1990 (No. 27 of 1990), the Companies (Auditing and Accounting) Act 2003 (No. 44 of 2003), the European Communities (Companies: Group Accounts) Regulations 1992 (S.I. No. 201 of 1992), the Credit Institutions Regulations, the European Communities (Accounts) Regulations 1993 (S.I. No. 396 of 1993) or the Insurance Undertakings Regulations) and is also used in Regulation (EC) No. 1606/2002 of the European Parliament and of the Council of 19 July 2002, the Fourth Council Directive 78/660/EEC of 25 July 1978, the Seventh Council Directive 83/349/EEC of 13 June 1983, Council Directive 86/635/EEC of 8 December 1986, Council Directive 91/674/EEC of 19 December 1991 and Directive 2003/51/EC of the European Parliament and of the Council of 18 June 2003 has, unless the contrary is indicated, the same meaning in these Regulations as it has in that Regulation and those Directives.

PART 2

PREPARATION OF INDIVIDUAL AND GROUP ACCOUNTS

Preparation of individual and group accounts

4.The Principal Act is amended by substituting the following for sections 148 to 151—

[…][a]

Amendments

a EC(IFRSMA)R 2005, reg 4 substituted ss 148–151 of CA 1963.

PART 3

MISCELLANEOUS AMENDMENTS TO PROVISIONS RELATING TO ACCOUNTS

Chapter 1
Amendments to Companies (Amendment) Act 1986

5. The Companies (Amendment) Act 1986 is amended as follows-

(a) in section 3—

[…][a]

(b) in section 4—

[…][b]

(c) in section 5—

(i) in paragraph (c)(ii), by substituting ‘all liabilities which have arisen’ for ‘all liabilities and losses which have arisen or are likely to arise’,

(ii) in paragraph (d), by substituting ‘payment,’ for ‘payment, and’,

(iii) in paragraph (e), by substituting ‘separately,’ for ‘separately.’, and

(iv) by inserting the following after paragraph (e):

[...][c]

(d) in section 7—

(i) in subsection (1)(a), by substituting the following for subparagraphs (i), (ii) and (iii) and all the words from 'and a copy of the report' down to and including 'for that year, and':

[....][d]

and

(ii) by inserting the following after subsection (1) and by renumbering subsection (1A) (inserted by section 64 of the Company Law Enforcement Act 2001) as subsection (1C)—

[...][e]

(e) in section 8(4)—

(i) in paragraph (a), by deleting 'and',

(ii) in paragraph (b), by substituting 'under 'Assets', and' for 'under 'Assets'.', and

(iii) by inserting the following after paragraph (b):

[...][f]

(f) by substituting the following for sections 10, 11 and 12—

[...][g]

(g) in section 13—

(i) by substituting the following for paragraph (a):

[...][h]

and

(ii) by renumbering the existing provision as subsection (1) of that section and inserting the following:

[...][i]

(h) in section 15, by substituting 'section 193 of the Companies Act 1990' for 'section 163 of the Principal Act',

(i) in section 16(2), by substituting the following for paragraph (a):

[...][j]

(j) in section 17(1)—

(i) by substituting the following for paragraph (b):

[...][k]

and

(ii) by substituting the following for paragraph (e):

[...][l]

(k) in section 18—

(i) by substituting the following for subsection (1):

[...][m]

(ii) in subsection (2), by substituting 'An abridged balance sheet' for 'A copy of a balance sheet',

(iii) by substituting the following for subsection (3):

[...][n]

and

(iv) in subsection (4), by substituting 'abridged accounts' for 'accounts' wherever it occurs,

(l) in section 19—

(i) by substituting the following for subsection (1):

[…][o]

(ii) in subsection (2), by substituting the following for paragraph (d):

[…][p]

and

(iii) in subsection (4)–

(I) by inserting the following after the definition of 'abbreviated accounts:

[…][q]

and

(II) by substituting the following for the definition of 'full accounts':

[…][r]

and

(m) in the Schedule—

(i) in Part 1, in the Balance Sheet Formats—

(I) in Format 1, Item G, by substituting 'Provisions for liabilities' for 'provisions for liabilities and charges', and

(II) in Format 2, Item B under the heading 'LIABILITIES', by substituting 'Provisions for liabilities' for 'Provisions for liabilities and charges',

(ii) by inserting the following after paragraph 22C (inserted by Regulation 3 of the Fair Value Regulations):

[…][s],

(iii) in paragraph 22D (inserted by Regulation 3 of the Fair Value Regulations)—

(I) in subparagraph (1), by inserting 'or where the fair value at which an asset is included in accordance with paragraph 22CA of this Schedule' after 'Schedule' and

(II) in subparagraph (2), by inserting 'of the financial instrument or of the investment property or living animals or plants' after 'difference in value',

(iv) by substituting the following for paragraph 31C (inserted by the Fair Value Regulations):

[…][t],

(v) by inserting the following after paragraph 31C:

[…][u],

(vi) in paragraph 32—

(I) in subparagraph (1)(b), by substituting 'provisions for liabilities' for 'provisions for liabilities and charges', and

(II) in subparagraph (1)(c), by substituting 'provision for liabilities' for 'provision for liabilities and charges',

(vii) in paragraph 57 by renumbering the existing provision as subparagraph (1) and inserting the following:

[…][v],

(viii) by inserting the following after paragraph 65:

[…][w],

and

(ix) in paragraph 70—

(I) by deleting 'or charges', and

(II) by substituting 'the nature of which is clearly defined and' for 'or loss'.

Amendments

a Reg 5(a) amends C(A)A 1986, s 3.

b Reg 5(b) amends C(A)A 1986, s 4.

c Reg 5(c)(iv) inserts C(A)A 1986, s 5(f).

d Reg 5(d) amends C(A)A 1986, s 7(1)(a).

e Reg 5(e)(ii) inserts C(A)A 1986, ss 1A and 1B and renumbers s 1C.

f Reg 5(e)(iii) inserts C(A)A 1986, s 8(4)(c).

g Reg 5(f) substitutes C(A)A 1986, ss 10, 11 and 12.

h Reg 5(g)(i) substitutes C(A)A 1986, s 13(a).

i Reg 5(g)(ii) inserts C(A)A 1986, s 13(2).

j Reg 5(i) substitutes C(A)A 1986, s 16(2)(a).

k Reg 5(j)(i) substitutes C(A)A 1986, s 17(1)(b).

l Reg 5(j)(ii) substitutes C(A)A 1986, s 17(1)(e).

m Reg 5(k)(i) substitutes C(A)A 1986, s 18(1).

n Reg 5(k)(ii) substitutes C(A)A 1986, s 18(3).

o Reg 5(l)(i) substitutes C(A)A 1986, s 19(1).

p Reg 5(l)(ii) substitutes C(A)A 1986, s 19(2)(d).

q Reg 5(l)(iii)(I) inserts a definition of 'abridged accounts' in C(A)A 1986, s 19(4).

r Reg 5(l)(iii)(II) substitutes the definition of 'full individual accounts' in C(A)A 1986, s 19(4).

s Reg 5(m)(ii) inserts C(A)A 1986, Sch, para 22(CA).

t Reg 5(m)(iv) substitutes C(A)A 1986, Sch, para 31(C).

u Reg 5(m)(v) inserts C(A)A 1986, Sch, para 31(D).

v Reg 5(m)(vii) inserts C(A)A 1986, Sch, para 57(2).

w Reg 5(m)(viii) inserts C(A)A 1986, Sch, para 65A.

Chapter 2
Amendments to European Communities (Companies: Group Accounts) Regulations 1992

6. The European Communities (Companies: Group Accounts) Regulations 1992 are amended—

(a) in Regulation 2, by substituting 'Companies Act group accounts' for 'group accounts',

(b) in Regulation 3, by substituting the following for the definition of 'group accounts':

[…][a],

(c) in Regulation 4(1), by substituting the following for paragraph (c):

[…][b],

(d) in Regulation 5—

(i) by substituting the following for paragraph (1):

[…][c]

(ii) in paragraph (2), by substituting 'Regulations 10 and 11' for 'Regulations 10, 11 and 12', and

(iii) in paragraph (4), by substituting 'Companies Act group accounts' for 'group accounts' wherever those words occur,

(e) in Regulation 7(8), by substituting the following for paragraph (a):

[...][d]

(f) in Regulation 8—

(i) in paragraph (1), by substituting 'an EEA State' for 'a Member State,

(ii) in paragraph (3)(a)—

(I) by substituting 'Regulations 10 and 11' for 'Regulations 10, 11 and 12', and

(II) by substituting 'EEA State' for 'Member State',

(iii) in paragraph (3)(b)—

(I) by substituting 'EEA State' for 'Member State', and

(II) by inserting 'or in accordance with international financial reporting standards' after 'with the Directive',

and

(iv) by substituting the following for paragraph (4):

[…][e]

(g) in Regulation 9—

(i) in paragraph (1), by substituting 'an EEA State' for 'a Member State', and

(ii) by substituting the following for paragraph (3):

[…][f],

(h) by inserting the following after Regulation 9:

[…][g]

(i) by deleting Regulation 12,

(j) in Regulation 29—

(i) in paragraph (1), by substituting 'individual accounts' for 'annual accounts', and

(ii) by substituting the following for paragraph (2):

[…][h]

(k) in Regulation 35, by deleting paragraph (6),

(l) in Regulation 37, by substituting the following for paragraph (a):

[…][i]

(m) in Regulation 40(2), by substituting the following for paragraph (d):

[…][j]

(n) in Part 2 of the Schedule, by substituting the following for paragraph 16C (inserted by Regulation 4 of the Fair Value Regulations):

[…][k]

(o) by inserting the following after paragraph 16C:

[…][l]

Amendments

a Reg 6(b) substitutes the definition of 'group accounts' in EC(CGA)R 1992, reg 3.

b Reg 6(c) substitutes EC(CGA)R 1992, reg 4(1)(c) and inserts reg 4(1)(ca).

c Reg 6(d)(i) substitutes EC(CGA)R 1992, reg 5(1).

d Reg 6(e) substitutes EC(CGA)R 1992, reg 7(8)(a).

e Reg 6(f)(iv) substitutes EC(CGA)R 1992, reg 8(4).

f Reg 6(g) substitutes EC(CGA)R 1992, reg 9(3).

g Reg 6(h) inserts EC(CGA)R 1992, reg 9A.

h Reg 6(j) substitutes EC(CGA)R 1992, reg 29(2).

i Reg 6(l) substitutes EC(CGA)R 1992, reg 37(a).

j Reg 6(m) substitutes EC(CGA)R 1992, reg 40(2)(d).

k Reg 6(n) substitutes EC(CGA)R 1992, Sch, Pt 2, para 16C.

l Reg 6(o) inserts EC(CGA)R 1992, Sch, Pt 2, para 16D.

Chapter 3
Amendments to European Communities (Accounts) Regulations 1993

7. The European Communities (Accounts) Regulations 1993 are amended—

(a) by inserting the following after paragraph 7(3):

[…][a],

(b) by inserting the following after paragraph 9(3):

[…][b],

(c) in Regulation 12, by substituting the following for paragraph (3):

[…][c]

(d) in Regulation 14(1), by substituting the following for paragraph (a):

[…][d]

and

(e) in Regulation 16(2), by substituting the following for paragraph (d)(iv):

[…][e].

Amendments

a Reg 7(a) inserts EC(A)R 1993, para 7(4).

b Reg 7(b) inserts EC(A)R 1993, para 9(4).

c Reg 7(c) substitutes EC(A)R 1993, reg 12, para (3).

d Reg 7(d) substitutes EC(A)R 1993, reg 14(1), para (a).

e Reg 7(e) substitutes EC(A)R 1993, reg 16(2), para (d)(iv).

Chapter 4
Amendment to the Companies Act 1990

8. The Companies Act 1990 is amended in section 193 by substituting the following for subsection (4):

[…][a]

Amendments

a Reg 8 substitutes CA 1990, s 193(4).

PART 4
CONSEQUENTIAL AND MINOR AMENDMENTS

Amendments to Companies Acts 1963 to 2003

9. The Acts specified in Schedule 1 are amended as indicated in that Schedule.

Amendments to Credit Institutions Regulations

10. The Credit Institutions Regulations are amended as indicated in Schedule 2.

Amendments to Insurance Undertakings Regulations

11. The Insurance Undertakings Regulations are amended as indicated in Schedule 3.

Schedule 1

Amendments to Companies Acts 1963 To 2003

PART 1
AMENDMENTS TO PRINCIPAL ACT

Item No	*Section affected*	*Amendment*
1.	Section 2	(a) In subsection (1)— (i) substitute the following for the definition of 'accounts': […][a], (ii) insert the following after the definition of 'books and paper': […][b], (iii) insert the following after the definition of 'the Court' (inserted by section 235 of the Act of 1990): […][c], (iv) insert the following after the definition of 'document': […][d], (v) insert the following after the definition of 'group accounts': […][e], (vi) insert the following after the definition of 'Insolvency Regulation' (inserted by Regulation 3(a) of the European Communities (Corporate Insolvency) Regulations 2002 (S.I. No. 333 of 2002): […][f], (vii) insert the following after the definition of 'private company': […][g], (viii) in the definition of 'financial year' insert 'subject to subsection (1A),' after 'means,', (ix) [...][h] (x) insert the following after the definition of the 'registrar of companies': [...][i];', and (xi) insert the following after the definition of 'the time of the opening of the subscription lists': […][j]. (b) Insert the following after subsection (1): […][k].

Item No	*Section affected*	*Amendment*
2.	Section 60	Substitute the following for subsection (15C) (inserted by the Companies (Amendment) Act 1983): […][l].
3.	Section 152	(a) In subsection (1), substitute 'Companies Act group accounts prepared in accordance with sections 151 to 155 of this Act' for 'The group accounts'. (b) In subsections (2) and (3), substitute 'the group accounts referred to in subsection (1)' for 'group accounts' in each place where it occurs.
4.	Section 156	Substitute the following for subsections (1) and (2): […][m].

Amendments

a Sch 1, Pt 1, item 1(a)(i) inserts definitions of 'accounts', 'Act of 1986', 'Act of 1990' and 'Act of 2003' in CA 1963, s 2(1).

b Sch 1, Pt 1, item 1(a)(ii) inserts definitions of 'Companies Act accounts', 'Companies Act group accounts' and 'Companies Act individual accounts' in CA 1963, s 2(1).

c Sch 1, Pt 1, item 1(a)(iii) inserts definitions of '1993 Regulations' and 'Credit Institutions Regulations' in CA 1963, s 2(1).

d Sch 1, Pt 1, item 1(a)(iv) inserts definitions of 'EEA state' and 'EEA Agreement' in CA 1963, s 2(1).

e Sch 1, Pt 1, item 1(a)(v) inserts definitions of 'Group Accounts Regulations', 'IAS Regulation', 'income statement', 'individual accounts', 'IFRS accounts', 'IFRS group accounts' and 'IFRS individual accounts' in CA 1963, s 2(1).

f Sch 1, Pt 1, item 1(a)(vi) inserts definitions of 'Insurance Undertakings Regulations' and 'international financial reporting standards' in CA 1963, s 2(1).

g Sch 1, Pt 1, item 1(a)(vii) inserts a definition of 'profit and loss account' in CA 1963, s 2(1).

h Sch 1, Pt 1, item 1(a)(ix) inserts definitions of 'parent company' and 'parent undertaking' in CA 1963, s 2(1).

i Sch 1, Pt 1, item 1(a)(x) inserts a definition of 'regulated market' in CA 1963, s 2(1).

j Sch 1, Pt 1, item 1(a)(xi) inserts a definition of 'undertaking' in CA 1963, s 2(1).

k Sch 1, Pt 1, item 1(b) inserts CA 1963, s 2(1A) and (1B).

l Sch 1, Pt 1, item 2 substitutes CA 1963, s 60(15C).

m Sch 1, Pt 1, item 4 substitutes CA 1963, s 156(1) and (2).

PART 2
AMENDMENTS TO COMPANIES (AMENDMENT) ACT 1983

Item No	*Section affected*	*Amendment*
1.	Section 2	In subsection (4)— (a) in paragraph (a), insert 'or by international financial reporting standards' after 'Companies Acts', and (b) substitute the following for subsection (c) and for all the words from 'and in paragraph (c)' down to and including 'of the company': […][a].
2.	Section 9	In subsection (13), in the definition of 'unqualified report', substitute the following for paragraph (a): […][b].
3.	Section 45	Substitute the following for subsection (4)— […][c].
4.	Section 45A (inserted by section 20 of the Companies (Amendment) Act 1986)	In subsection (3), substitute the following for paragraph (b): […][d].
5.	Section 47	Substitute the following for subsection (2): […][e].
6.	Section 49	(a) In subsection (2)(a), insert '(and, where applicable, in accordance with the requirements of Article 4 of the IAS Regulation)' after 'Principal Act'. (b) In subsection (9)— (i) […][f], and (ii) […][g], (c) In subsection (10), substitute 'section 148 and either section 149 or 149A of the Principal Act, where applicable, of' for 'section 149 of'.

Amendments

a Sch 1, Pt 2, item 1(b) substitutes C(A)A 1983, s 2(c).

b Sch 1, Pt 2, item 2 substitutes C(A)A 1983, s 9(13)(a).

c Sch 1, Pt 2, item 3 substitutes C(A)A 1983, s 45(4).

d Sch 1, Pt 2, item 4 substitutes C(A)A 1983, s 45A(3)(b).

e Sch 1, Pt 2, item 5 substitutes C(A)A 1983, s 47(2).

f Sch 1, Pt 2. item 6(b)(i) substitutes C(A)A 1983, s 49(9), paras (a) and (b) in the definition of 'properly prepared'.

g Sch 1, Pt 2, item 6(b)(ii) substitutes the definition of 'relevant item' in C(A)A 1983, s 49(9).

PART 3

AMENDMENT TO THE COMPANIES (AMENDMENT) ACT 1986

Item No	*Section affected*	*Amendment*
1.	Section 1	In subsection (1), before the definition of 'company' insert the following: 'abridged accounts' has the meaning given to it by section 19 of the Principal Act;'.

PART 4

AMENDMENT TO COMPANIES ACT 1990

Item No	*Section affected*	*Amendment*
1.	Section 29	In subsection (9), substitute the following for paragraph (c): […][a].
2.	Section 41	In subsection (4), substitute 'sections 151 (2) and 154' for 'sections 150 (2) and 154'.
3.	Section 43	In subsection (8), substitute 'sections 151 (2) and 154' for 'sections 150(2) and 154'.
4.	Section 63	In subsection (2), substitute 'section 10 (1)' for 'section 10(2)'.
5.	Section 193	Substitute the following for subsection (1): […][b].
6.	Section 202	(a) In subsection (1)— (i) substitute the following for paragraph (c): […][c], and (ii) in paragraph (d), substitute 'annual accounts' for 'accounts'. (b) In subsection (6), substitute the following for 'the company's balance sheet, its profit and loss account or income and expenditure account and document annexed to any of those documents': '(and, where applicable, Article 4 of the IAS Regulation) the company's accounts and any document annexed to those accounts'.
7.	Section 205A (inserted by section 41 of the Companies (Auditing and Accounting) Act 2003)	Substitute 'individual accounts' for 'annual accounts' wherever occurring in that section.

Item No	*Section affected*	*Amendment*
8.	Section 205B (inserted by section 42 the Companies (Auditing and Accounting) Act 2003)	In subsection (2)— (a) in paragraphs (a), (b) and (d), substitute 'individual accounts' for 'annual accounts' wherever occurring, and (b) substitute the following for paragraph (b)(ii): [...][d].
9.	Section 251	In subsection (2), substitute the following for paragraph (a): '(a) sections 139, 140, 148, 149 or 149A, 203 and 204, and'.

Amendments

a Sch 1, Pt 4, item 1 substitutes CA 1990, s 29(9)(c).

b Sch 1, Pt 4, item 5 substitutes CA 1990, s 193(1).

c Sch 1, Pt 4, item 6(a)(i) substitutes CA 1990, s 202(1)(c).

d Sch 1, Pt 4, item 8(b) substitutes CA 1990, s 205B(2)(b)(ii).

PART 5

AMENDMENTS TO COMPANIES (AUDITING AND ACCOUNTING) ACT 2003

Item No	*Section affected*	*Amendment*
1.	Sections 8(1)(c), 9(2)(l), and 26(3)(b), (4)(a) and (b), (6), (8) and (10)(a).	Insert 'and, where applicable, Article 4 of the IAS Regulation' after 'Companies Acts' wherever occurring in those provisions.
2.	Section 26	In subsection (8)(a), insert 'and, where applicable, Article 4 of the IAS Regulation' after 'those Acts'.

Schedule 2

Amendments to Credit Institutions Regulations

Item No	*Provision affected*	*Amendment*
1.	Regulation 2	(a) In paragraph (1), insert the following after the definition of 'individual accounts': 'investment property' means land or buildings (or both) held to earn rentals or for capital appreciation (or both);'. (b) Insert the following after paragraph (1): […][a]. (c) In paragraph (4), substitute 'these Regulations, or international financial reporting standards' for 'or these Regulations'.
2.	Regulation 5	Substitute the following for paragraphs (1) and (2): […][b].
3.	Regulation 6	Substitute the following for paragraph (2)(d): […][c].
4.	Regulation 7	Substitute the following for Regulation 7: […][d].
5.	Regulation 8	(a) In paragraph (1), substitute 'established in an EEA State' for 'established in a Member State of the Community'. (b) In paragraph (3)(b), insert 'or prepared in accordance with international financial reporting standards and audited in accordance with either such Directive, as applicable,' after '1983,'. (c) Substitute the following for paragraph (4): […][e]. (d) In paragraph (6), substitute 'established in an EEA State' for 'established in a Member State of the Community'.
6.	Regulation 8A	Insert the following after Regulation 8: […][f]
7.	Regulation 10	In paragraph (1), substitute 'its individual accounts' for 'its accounts'.
8.	Regulation 11	Substitute the following for paragraph (a): […][g].
9.	Regulation 12	Substitute the following for Regulation 12: '12. Sections 151, 152, 158 (4), (5) and (6) and 191 of the Principal Act shall not apply to a company to which Regulation 7 applies.'.

Item No	*Provision affected*	*Amendment*
10.	Regulation 13	In paragraph (1), substitute 'section 193(4A)(b)(inserted by the European Communities (International Financial Reporting Standards and Miscellaneous Amendments) Regulations 2005)' for 'subsection (4)(f) of section 193'.
11.	Part I of Schedule	(a) In paragraph 1(1), substitute 'Where the directors of a company prepare Companies Act individual accounts and subject to the following provisions of this Part:'. See paragraph 1(1) of Part I of the Schedule to the European Communities (Credit Institutions: Accounts) Regulations 1992. (b) Substitute the following for paragraph 8: […][h]. (c) In Section B at item number 6 under the heading 'LIABILITIES', substitute 'provisions for liabilities' for 'provisions for liabilities and charges'. (d) In paragraph 16, substitute 'Companies Act individual accounts' for 'a company's accounts'. (e) In paragraph 19(b), substitute 'all liabilities which have arisen' for 'all liabilities and losses which have arisen or are likely to arise'. (f) Insert the following after paragraph 20: […][i]. (g) In paragraph 23, substitute 'Companies Act individual accounts' for 'a company's accounts'. (h) In paragraph 59(1)(b) and (c), delete 'and charges' wherever occurring. (i) Insert the following after paragraph 46B (inserted by the European Communities (Credit Institutions) (Fair Value Accounting) Regulations 2004 (S.I. No. 720 of 2004)): […][j]. (j) Substitute the following for paragraph 46C(1) (inserted by the European Communities (Credit Institution) (Fair Value Accounting) Regulations 2004). […][k]. (k) Insert the following after paragraph 46D (inserted by the European Communities (Credit Institution) (Fair Value Accounting) Regulations 2004). […][l]. (l) In paragraph 72A, (inserted by the European Communities (Credit Institution) (Fair Value Accounting) Regulations 2004 (S.I. No. 720 of 2004)) substitute '46A to 46E' for '46A to 46D'.

Item No	*Provision affected*	*Amendment*
		(m) In paragraph 75(2) (as amended by the European Communities (Credit Institution) (Fair Value Accounting) Regulations 2004) substitute— 'This includes the extent to which the calculation of the profit or loss is affected by the fair valuation of financial instruments and separately the extent to which it is affected by the fair valuation of other assets in accordance with paragraph 46BA.' for 'This includes the extent to which the calculation of the profit or loss is affected by the fair valuation of financial instruments.'.
12.	Part II of Schedule	(a) In paragraph 1 (1), substitute 'Where the directors of a company prepare Companies Act group accounts, those group accounts' for 'Accounts'. (b) In paragraph 2, delete subparagraphs (4), (5), (6) and (7).
13.	Part III of Schedule	In paragraphs 3(2), 5(2)(a) and 9(2)(a), insert 'or 8A' after 'Regulation 8', where it occurs in each of those provisions.
14.	Part IV of Schedule	In paragraph 5(c)— (a) delete 'or charges', and (b) substitute 'the nature of which is clearly defined and' for 'or loss'.

Amendments

a Sch 2, item 1(b) inserts EC(CIA)R 1992, reg 2, para (1A).

b Sch 2, item 2, substitutes EC(CIA)R 1992, reg 5, paras (1) and (2).

c Sch 2, item 3 substitutes EC(CIA)R 1992, reg 6, para (2)(d).

d Sch 2, item 4 substitutes EC(CIA)R 1992, reg 7.

e Sch 2, item 5(c) substitutes EC(CIA)R 1992, reg 8(4).

f Sch 2, item 6 inserts EC(CIA)R 1992, reg 8A.

g Sch 2, item 8 substitutes EC(CIA)R 1992, reg 11(a).

h Sch 2, item 11(b) substitutes EC(CIA)R 1992, Sch, Pt 1, para 8.

i Sch 2, item 11(f) inserts EC(CIA)R 1992, Sch, Pt 1, para 20A.

j Sch 2, item 11(i) inserts EC(CIA)R 1992, Sch, Pt 1, para 46BA.

k Sch 2, item 11(j) substitutes EC(CIA)R 1992, Sch, Pt 1, para 46C(1).

l Sch 2, item 11(k) inserts EC(CIA)R 1992, Sch, Pt 1, para 46E.

Schedule 3

Amendments to Insurance Undertakings Regulations

Item No	*Provision affected*	*Amendment*
1.	Regulation 2	(a) In paragraph (1), insert the following after the definition of 'individual accounts': 'investment property' means land or buildings (or both) held to earn rentals or for capital appreciation (or both);'. (b) Insert the following after paragraph (1): […][a]. (c) In paragraph (2), substitute 'these Regulations or international financial reporting standards' for 'or these Regulations'.
2.	Regulation 5	Substitute the following for paragraphs (1) and (2): […][b].
3.	Regulation 6	In paragraph (1), substitute 'Where the directors of an undertaking prepare Companies Act individual accounts and subject to these Regulations –' for 'Subject to the provisions of this Regulation –'.
4.	Regulation 7	(a) Substitute 'Companies Act accounts' for 'accounts' where it first occurs in that Regulation. (b) In paragraph (c)(ii), substitute 'all liabilities which have arisen' for 'all liabilities and losses which have arisen or are likely to arise'. (c) In paragraph (d), delete 'and'. (d) In paragraph (e), substitute 'separately, and' for 'separately.'. (e) Insert the following after paragraph (e): […][c].
5.	Regulation 8	Insert 'when preparing Companies Act accounts' after 'Regulation 7'.
6.	Regulation 9	Substitute the following for paragraph (2)(d): […][d].
7.	Regulation 10	Substitute the following for Regulation 10: […][e].
8.	Regulation 11	Substitute the following for paragraph (1)(c): […][f].
9.	Regulation 12	(a) In paragraph (1), substitute 'established in an EEA State' for 'established in a Member State of the European Union'.

Item No	*Provision affected*	*Amendment*
		(b) In paragraph (3)(b), insert 'or prepared in accordance with international financial reporting standards and audited in accordance with either such Directive, as applicable,' after '1983,'.
		(c) Substitute the following for paragraph (4): […][g].
		(d) In paragraph (6)(a), substitute 'established in an EEA State' for 'established in a Member State of the European Union'.
9	Regulation 12A	Insert the following after Regulation 12: […][h].
10.	Regulation 14	Substitute the following for paragraph (a): […][i].
11.	Regulation 15	Substitute the following for Regulation 15: […][j].
12.	Regulation 18	Substitute the following for paragraph 2(d): […][k].
13.	Part I of Schedule	(a) Substitute the following for paragraph 6 (1): […][l].
		(b) In Section A of Chapter 2 at item E under the heading 'LIABILITIES', substitute 'provisions for other risks' for 'provisions for other risks and charges'.
13.	Part II of Schedule	In paragraph 1, substitute 'Companies Act individual accounts' for 'accounts'.
14.	Part III of Schedule	(a) In paragraph 1, substitute 'Companies Act accounts' for 'accounts'.
		(b) In paragraph 14(1)(b) and (c), substitute 'provision for other risks' for 'provisions for liabilities and charges' in each place where it occurs.
14.	Part IV of Schedule	(a) In paragraph 1(1), substitute 'Where the directors of an undertaking prepare Companies Act group accounts, those group accounts' for 'Accounts'.
		(b) In paragraph 2, delete subparagraphs (4), (5) and (6).

Amendments

a Sch 3, item 1(b) inserts EC(IUA)R 1996, reg 2(1A).

b Sch 3, item 2 substitutes EC(IUA)R 1996, reg 5, paras (1) and (2).

c Sch 3, item 4 (e) inserts EC(IUA)R 1996, reg 7, para (f).

d Sch 3, item 6 substitutes EC(IUA)R 1996, reg 9, para 2(d).

e Sch 3, item 7 substitutes EC(IUA)R 1996, reg 10.

f Sch 3, item 8 substitutes EC(IUA)R 1996, reg 11, para (1)(c).

g Sch 3, item 9 substitutes EC(IUA)R 1996, reg 12(4).

h Sch 3, item 9 inserts EC(IUA)R 1996, reg 12A.

i Sch 3, item 10 substitutes EC(IUA)R 1996, reg 14.

j Sch 3, item 11 substitutes EC(IUA)R 1996, reg 15.

k Sch 3, item 12 substitutes EC(IUA)R 1996, reg 18, para 2(d).

l Sch 3, item 13 substitutes EC(IUA)R 1996, Sch, Pt 1, para 6(1).

EXPLANATORY NOTE

(*This note is not part of the Instrument and does not purport to be a legal interpretation*).

These Regulations give full effect to Regulation 1606/2002 of the European Parliament and of the Council of 19 July 2002 and give effect to Directive 2003/51/EC of the European Parliament and of the Council of 18 June 2003.

Prospectus (Directive 2003/71/EC) Regulations 2005

SI 324/2005

I, Micheál Martin, Minister for Enterprise, Trade and Employment, in exercise of the powers conferred on me by section 46 of the Investment Funds, Companies and Miscellaneous Provisions Act 2005 (No. 12 of 2005) and for the purpose of giving effect to Directive 2003/71/EC of the European Parliament and the Council of 4 November 2003 and for the other purposes mentioned in that section, hereby make the following regulations:

PART I
PRELIMINARY AND GENERAL

Citation

1.(1) These Regulations may be cited as the Prospectus (Directive 2003/71/EC) Regulations 2005.

These Regulations shall come into operation on 1 July 2005.

These Regulations shall be construed as one with the Companies Acts[...][a].

Amendments

a Words '1963 to 2005' deleted by P(Dir)(A)R (No 2) 2012, reg 2(a).

Interpretation

2.(1) In these Regulations, except where the context otherwise requires:

'Act of 2005' means the Investment Funds, Companies and Miscellaneous Provisions Act 2005;

'admission to trading' means admission of securities to trading on a regulated market and 'admission to trading in the State' means admission of securities to trading on a regulated market situated or operating in the State;

'approval' means the positive act at the outcome of the scrutiny of the completeness of the prospectus by the competent authority of the Home Member State including the consistency of the information given and its comprehensibility and 'approved' shall be construed accordingly;

'approved stock exchange' has the same meaning as it has in the Stock Exchange Act 1995 (No. 9 of 1995);

'Bank' means the Central Bank and Financial Services Authority of Ireland;

'base prospectus' means a prospectus containing all relevant information as specified in Regulations 19 and 20, and in case there is a supplement, Regulation 51, concerning the issuer and the securities to be offered to the public or admitted to trading, and, at the choice of the issuer, the final terms of the offering;

'collective investment undertaking other than the closed-end type' means unit trusts and investment companies:

(a) the object of which is the collective investment of capital provided by the public and which operate on the principle of risk-spreading;

(b) the units of which are, at the holder's request, repurchased or redeemed, directly or indirectly, out of the assets of the undertaking;

'Community act' means an act adopted by an institution of the European Communities;

'company' includes any body corporate;

['company with reduced market capitalisation' means a company listed on a regulated market that had an average market capitalisation of less than €100,000,000 on the basis of end-year quotes for the previous three calendar years;][a]

'competent authority of a Home Member State' means—

(a) where the State is the Home Member State, the Bank, or

(b) where the State is a Host Member State, the central competent administrative authority designated as such under the national law of the Home Member State for the purposes of the Directive;

'contravention' includes, in relation to any provision, a failure to comply with that provision and 'contravene' shall be construed accordingly;

'Court' means the High Court;

'credit institution' means an undertaking as defined by Article 1(1)(a) of Directive 2000/1 2/EC of the European Parliament and of the Council of 20 March 2000 relating to the taking up and pursuit of the business of credit institutions;

'Directive' means Directive 2003/71/EC of the European Parliament and of the Council of 4 November 2003;

['Directive' means Directive 2003/71/EC of the European Parliament and of the Council of 4 November 2003 (OJ No. L 345, 31.12.2003, p. 64) as amended by Directive 2010/78/EU and by Directive 2010/73/EU of the European Parliament and of the Council of 24 November (OJ No. L 327, 11.12.2010, p. 1);][b]

['Directive 2010/78/EU' means Directive 2010/78/EU of the European Parliament and of the Council of 24 November 2010 (OJ No. L 331, 15.12.2010, p. 120);][c]

'EEA Agreement' means the Agreement on the European Economic Area signed at Oporto on 2 May 1992, as adjusted by the Protocol signed at Brussels on 17 March 1993;

'EEA State' means a state which is a contracting party to the EEA Agreement;

'enactment' includes an instrument made under an enactment;

'equity securities' means shares and other transferable securities equivalent to shares in companies, as well as any other type of transferable securities giving the right to acquire any of the aforementioned securities as a consequence of their being converted or the rights conferred by them being exercised, provided that securities of the latter type are issued by the issuer of the underlying shares or by an entity belonging to the group of the said issuer;

'EU prospectus law' has the same meaning as it has in the Act of 2005;

['European Securities and Markets Authority' means the body established pursuant to Regulation (EU) No. 1095/2010;][d]

'functions' includes powers and duties and references to the performance of functions include, as respects the powers and duties, references to the exercise of the powers and the carrying out of the duties;

'Home Member State' means:

(a) for all issuers incorporated or formed in a Member State save in respect of securities mentioned in paragraph (c) of this definition, the Member State where the issuer has its registered office,

(b) for all issuers incorporated or formed in a state or territory which is not a Member State, save in respect of securities mentioned in paragraph (c)of this definition, the Member State where the securities are or were the subject of a public offer for the first time after 31 December 2003 or where the first application for admission to trading is or was made, at the choice of the issuer, the offeror or the person asking for admission, as the case may be, subject to a subsequent election by such an issuer if the Home Member State was not determined by its choice (but by the choice of an offeror or a person seeking admission to trading) pursuant to this paragraph,

(c) for:

(i) any issues of non-equity securities whose denomination per unit amounts to at least €1,000,

(ii) any issues of non-equity securities in a currency other than euro, whose denomination per unit amounts to at least €1,000 or the nearest practical equivalent thereto, and

(iii) any issues of non-equity securities giving the right to acquire any transferable securities or to receive a cash amount, as a consequence of their being converted or the rights conferred by them being exercised, provided that the issuer of the non-equity securities is not the issuer of the underlying securities or an entity belonging to the group of the latter issuer,

the Member State where the issuer has its registered office, or where the securities were or are to be admitted to trading or where the securities are the subject of a public offer, at the choice of the relevant person;

'Host Member State' means the state where an offer to the public is made or admission to trading is sought, when different from the Home Member State;

'implementing measures' means any measures directly applicable in consequence of the Directive and, without prejudice to the generality of the foregoing, includes the Prospectus Regulation;

'in writing' includes by facsimile;

'Irish prospectus law' has the same meaning as it has in the Act of 2005;

'issuer' means a body corporate or other legal entity which issues or proposes to issue securities;

['key information' means essential and appropriately structured information which is to be provided to investors with a view to enabling them to understand the nature and the risks of the issuer, guarantor and the securities that are being offered to them or admitted to trading on a regulated market and, without prejudice to Regulation 21(3)(b) of the Regulations of 2005, to decide which offers of securities to consider further. In light of the offer and securities concerned, the key information shall include the following elements:

(i) a short description of the risks associated with and essential characteristics of the issuer and any guarantor, including the assets, liabilities and financial position;

(ii) a short description of the risk associated with and essential characteristics of the investment in the relevant security, including any rights attaching to the securities;

(iii) general terms of the offer, including estimated expenses charged to the investor by the issuer or the offeror;

(iv) details of the admission to trading;

(v) reasons for the offer and use of proceeds;][e]

'market operator' means one or more persons who manage or operate the business of a regulated market (or who do both those things), and may be the regulated market itself;

'Member State' means a Member State of the European Union or an EEA State;

'Minister' means the Minister for Enterprise, Trade and Employment;

'non-equity securities' means all securities that are not equity securities;

'offering programme' means a plan which would permit the issuance of non-equity securities, including warrants in any form, of a similar type or class (or both), in a continuous or repeated manner during a specified issuing period;

'offer of securities to the public' or 'public offer' means a communication to persons in any form and by any means, presenting sufficient information on the terms of the offer and the securities to be offered, so as to enable an investor to decide to purchase or subscribe for those securities or apply to purchase or subscribe for those securities and this definition shall be construed as—

(a) being also applicable to the placing of securities through financial intermediaries, and

(b) as not being applicable to trading on a regulated market or any other market operated by an approved stock exchange;

'person making an offer' (or 'offeror') means a body corporate or other legal entity or an individual which or who makes an offer of securities to the public;

'prospectus' means the document or documents required to be published for the purposes of a public offer or admission to trading in accordance with EU prospectus law and includes where the context admits any supplement thereto;

'Prospectus Regulation' means Commission Regulation (EC) No. 809/2004 of 29 April 2004 implementing the Directive as regards information contained in prospectuses as well as the format, incorporation by reference and publication of such prospectuses and dissemination of advertisements;

'prospectus rules' means the rules for the time being made by the Bank under section 51 of the Act of 2005;

'publication', means publication in accordance with the applicable requirements of EU prospectus law;

['qualified investors' means persons or entities that are described in points (1) to (4) of Section I of Annex II to Directive 2004/39/EC of the European Parliament and of the Council of 21 April 2004 ('Directive 2004/39/EC') on markets in financial instruments and persons or entities who are, on request, treated as professional clients in accordance with Annex II to Directive 2004/39/EC, or recognised as eligible counterparties in accordance with Article 24 of Directive 2004/39/EC unless they have requested that they be treated as non-professional clients. Investment firms and credit institutions shall communicate their classification on request to the issuer without prejudice to the relevant legislation on data protection. Investment firms authorised to continue considering existing professional clients as such in accordance with Article 71(6) of Directive 2004/39/EC shall be authorised to treat those clients as qualified investors under this Directive;][f]

'regulated market' means a market as defined by Article 1(13) of Directive 93/22/EEC;

['Regulation (EU) No. 1095/2010' means Regulation (EU) No. 1095/2010 of the European Parliament and of the Council of 24 November 2004 (OJ No. L 331, 15.12.2010, p. 84);][g]

'relevant person' means an issuer, offeror or person seeking admission to trading as the case may be;

'securities' means transferable securities as defined by Article 1(4) of Directive 93/22/EEC with the exception of money market instruments as defined by Article 1(5) of Directive 93/22/EEC, having a maturity of less than 12 months;

'securities issued in a continuous or repeated manner' means issues on tap or at least two separate issues of securities of a similar type or class (or both) over a period of 12 months;

'small and medium-sized enterprises' means undertakings, which, according to their last annual or consolidated accounts, satisfy at least two of the following three conditions namely—

(a) an average number of employees during the financial year of less than 250;

(b) a total balance sheet not exceeding €43,000,000, and

(c) an annual net turnover not exceeding €50,000,000; 'summary' means a summary of a prospectus referred to in Regulation 21; 'supplement' means a supplement to a prospectus referred to in Regulation 51;

'units of a collective investment undertaking' means securities issued by a collective investment undertaking as representing the rights of the participants in such an undertaking over its assets;

'working day' means any day of the week (other than a Saturday or a Sunday) but does not include a public holiday (within the meaning of the Organisation of Working Time Act 1997) or a Good Friday.

(2) A word or expression that is used in these Regulations and is also used in the Directive shall have in these Regulations the same meaning as it has in the Directive unless the contrary intention appears.

(3) A reference in these Regulations—

(a) to any other enactment or to a Directive or Regulation of the Council or Commission of the European Communities shall, unless the context otherwise requires, be construed as a reference to that enactment, Directive or Regulation as amended or extended by any other enactment or, as the case may be, Directive or Regulation of the Council or Commission of the European Communities, (including, in the case of an enactment, by a Regulation of these Regulations),

(b) a reference to a Regulation or Part is a reference to a Regulation or Part of these Regulations, unless it is indicated that reference to some other provision is intended, and

(c) a reference to a paragraph, subparagraph or clause is a reference to a paragraph, subparagraph or clause of the provision in which the reference occurs, unless it is indicated that reference to some provision is intended.

(4) If the securities the subject of a public offer or admission to trading are of the type described in paragraph (c) of the definition of 'Home Member State' in paragraph (1), the Home Member State shall be determined in accordance with that paragraph (c).

(5) In any case other than that referred to in paragraph (4), the Home Member State shall be determined (by reference to the issuer whose securities are being offered to the public or admitted to trading) in accordance with paragraph (a) or (b), as the case may be, of the definition of 'Home Member State' in paragraph (1).

(6) For the purpose of the definition of 'offer of securities to the public' in this Regulation 'communication' shall include an invitation to treat.

(7) Where the total balance sheet amount of an undertaking falls to be determined for the purposes of the definition of 'small and medium enterprises' in this Regulation and the accounts of the undertaking are denominated in a currency other than the Euro, the currency in which those accounts are stated shall be converted into the Euro at the rate prevailing at the end of the financial year to which they relate.

Amendments

a Definition of 'company with reduced market capitalisation' inserted by P(Dir)(A)R 2012, reg 3(a)(i).

b Definition of 'Directive' substituted by P(Dir)(A)R (No 2) 2012, reg 2(b)(ii).

c Definition of 'Directive 2010/78/EU' inserted by P(Dir)(A)R (No 2) 2012, reg 2(b)(i).

d Definition of 'European Securities and Markets Authority' inserted by P(Dir)(A)R (No 2) 2012, reg 2(b)(i).

e Definition of 'key information' inserted by P(Dir)(A)R 2012, reg 3(a)(ii).

f Definition of 'qualified investors' substituted by P(Dir)(A)R 2012, reg 3(a)(iii).

g Definition of 'Regulation (EU) No. 1095/2010' inserted by P(Dir)(A)R (No 2) 2012, reg 2(b)(i).

Register of Natural Persons and Small and Medium-Sized Enterprises as Qualified Investors

3. [...][a]

Amendments

a Regulation 3 revoked by P(Dir)(A)R 2012, reg 3(b).

4.[...][a]

Amendments

a Regulation 4 revoked by P(Dir)(A)R 2012, reg 3(b).

5.[...][a]

Amendments

a Regulation 5 revoked by P(Dir)(A)R 2012, reg 3(b).

6. [...][a]

Amendments

a Regulation 6 revoked by P(Dir)(A)R 2012, reg 3(b).

7. [...][a]

Amendments

a Regulation 7 revoked by P(Dir)(A)R 2012, reg 3(b).

PART 2
SECURITIES OUTSIDE THE AMBIT OF THESE REGULATIONS

8.(1) These Regulations shall not apply to—

(a) units issued by collective investment undertakings other than the closed-end type,

(b) non-equity securities issued by a Member State or by one of a Member State's regional or local authorities, by public international bodies of which one or more Member States are members, by the European Central Bank or by the central banks of the Member States,

(c) shares in the capital of a central bank of a Member State,

(d) securities unconditionally and irrevocably guaranteed by a Member State or by one of a Member State's regional or local authorities,

(e) securities issued by associations with legal status or non-profit-making bodies, recognised by a Member State, with a view to their obtaining the means necessary to achieve their non-profit-making objectives,

(f) non-equity securities issued in a continuous or repeated manner by credit institutions provided that these securities—

(i) are not subordinated, convertible or exchangeable,

(ii) do not give a right to subscribe to or acquire other types of securities and that they are not linked to a derivative instrument,

(iii) materialise reception of repayable deposits,

(iv) are covered by a deposit guarantee scheme under Directive 94/19/EC of the European Parliament and of the Council on deposit-guarantee schemes,

(g) non-fungible shares of capital whose main purpose is to provide the holder with a right to occupy an apartment, or other form of immovable property or a part thereof and where the shares cannot be sold on without this right being given up;

[(h) securities included in an offer where the total consideration for the offer in the European Union is less than €5,000,000,][a]

(i) 'bostadsobligationer' issued repeatedly by credit institutions in Sweden whose main purpose is to grant mortgage loans, provided that—

(i) the 'bostadsobligationer' issued are of the same series,

(ii) the 'bostadsobligationer' are issued on tap during a specified issuing period,

(iii) the terms and conditions of the 'bostadsobligationer' are not changed during the issuing period,

(iv) the sums deriving from the issue of the said 'bostadsobligationer', in accordance with the articles of association of the issuer, are placed in assets which provide sufficient coverage for the liability deriving from securities,

[(j) non-equity securities issued in a continuous or repeated manner by credit institutions where the total consideration for the offer in the European Union is less than €75,000,000, which shall be calculated over a period of 12 months, provided that those securities:

(i) are not subordinated, convertible or exchangeable;

(ii) do not give a right to subscribe to or acquire other types of securities and that they are not linked to a derivative instrument.][b]

(2) For the purposes of paragraph (1)(e) an association or body is recognised by a Member State if it has been established by, under or pursuant to the national legislation of the Member State.

[(3) No offer of securities by an offeror or issuer shall be deemed to fall within paragraph (1)(h) unless the amount of the total consideration for the offer when aggregated with the consideration for all previous offers of securities of the same type in the issuer concerned made by the same offeror or issuer within the period of 12 months expiring on the date the offer is made is less than €5,000,000 (but excluding for the purposes of such aggregation any offer of securities made prior to the commencement of these Regulations).][c]

(4) For the purposes of any other enactment, it is declared that paragraph (3) provides the means by which the limit specified by paragraph (1)(h) is calculated.

(5) Notwithstanding subparagraph (b), (d), (h), (i) or (j) of paragraph (1), where the State is the Home Member State a relevant person may draw up a prospectus in respect of the securities mentioned in that subparagraph and submit it to the Bank for approval in accordance with these Regulations and the other provisions of Irish prospectus law.

Amendments

a Subparagraph (h) substituted by P(Dir)(A)R 2012, reg 3(c).

b Subparagraph (j) substituted by P(Dir)(A)R 2012, reg 3(c).

c Paragraph (3) substituted by P(Dir)(A)R 2012, reg 3(d).

PART 3

EXEMPTIONS FROM THE OBLIGATION TO PUBLISH A PROSPECTUS

Excluded Offers

9[(1) The obligation to publish a prospectus under Regulation 12 shall not apply to an offer of securities in the State falling within one or more of the following subparagraphs:

(a) an offer of securities addressed solely to qualified investors;

(b) an offer of securities addressed to fewer than 150 natural or legal persons, other than qualified investors;

(c) an offer of securities addressed to investors who acquire securities for a total consideration of at least €100,000 per investor, for each separate offer;

(d) an offer of securities whose denomination per unit amounts to at least €100,000;

(e) an offer of securities with a total consideration in the European Union less than €100,000, which shall be calculated over a period of 12 months.][a]

(2) Any subsequent resale of securities which were previously the subject of an offer described in paragraph (1) shall be regarded as a separate offer for the purposes of determining whether it is an offer of securities to the public within the meaning of these Regulations.

(3) The obligation to publish a prospectus pursuant to Regulation 12 shall apply to the placement of securities through financial intermediaries, if none of subparagraphs (a) to (e) of paragraph (1) apply at the final placement.

[(3A) Notwithstanding paragraphs (2) and (3), there shall be no requirement for another prospectus in any such subsequent resale of securities or final placement of securities through financial intermediaries as long as a valid prospectus is available in accordance with Regulation 30 and the issuer or the person responsible for drawing up such prospectus consents to its use by means of a written agreement.][b]

(4) No offer of securities shall be deemed to come within paragraph (1)(e) unless the amount of the total consideration for the offer when aggregated with the consideration

for all previous offers of securities of the same type in the issuer concerned made by the same offeror or issuer within the period of 12 months expiring on the date the offer is made is less than €100,000 (but excluding for the purpose of such aggregation any offer of securities made prior to the commencement of these Regulations).

Amendments

a Paragraph (1) substituted by P(Dir)(A)R 2012, reg 3(e)(i).

b Paragraph (3A) inserted by P(Dir)(A)R 2012, reg 3(e)(ii).

10.(1) The obligation to publish a prospectus pursuant to Regulation 12 shall not apply to offers of securities to the public in the State of the following types of securities—

(a) shares issued in substitution for shares of the same class already issued, if the issuing of such new shares does not involve any increase in the issued capital,

(b) securities offered in connection with a takeover by means of an exchange offer, provided that a document is available containing information which is regarded by the Bank as being equivalent to that of a prospectus, taking into account the requirements of any Community act,

[(c) securities offered, allotted or to be allotted in connection with a merger or division, provided that a document is available containing information which is regarded by the Bank as being equivalent to that of the prospectus, taking into account the requirements of European Union legislation,

(d) dividends paid out to existing shareholders in the form of shares of the same class as the shares in respect of which such dividends are paid, provided that a document is made available containing information on the number and nature of the shares and the reasons for and details of the offer,

(e) securities offered, allotted or to be allotted to existing or former directors or employees by their employer or by an affiliated undertaking provided that the company has its head office or registered office in the European Union and provided that a document is made available containing information on the number and nature of the securities and the reasons for and details of the offer; for the purpose of this subparagraph 'affiliated undertaking' includes any parent or subsidiary undertaking of the employer or another subsidiary undertaking of that parent undertaking.][a]

[(1A) subparagraph (e) of paragraph (1) shall also apply to a company established outside the European Union whose securities are admitted to trading either on a regulated market or on a third- country market. In the latter case, the exemption shall apply provided that adequate information, including the document referred to in subparagraph (e), is available at least in a language customary in the sphere of international finance and provided that the European Commission has adopted an equivalence decision regarding the third-country market concerned.][b]

(2) The reference in paragraph (1)(e) to the offering or allotment of securities by an employer or an affiliated undertaking shall, in the case of such an offer or allotment that takes place for the purpose of an employees' share scheme or an employee share

ownership trust, be construed as a reference to such offering or allotment, whether effected directly or indirectly by the employer or the affiliated undertaking.

(3) In paragraph (2)—

'employees' share scheme' means a scheme which is approved for the purposes of Chapter 1 of Part 17 of the Taxes Consolidation Act 1997 and Schedule 11 to that Act;

'employee share ownership trust' means a trust which is approved for the purposes of Chapter 2 of Part 17 of the Taxes Consolidation Act 1997 and Schedule 12 to that Act.

Amendments

a Paragraph (1)(c), (d) and (e) substituted by P(Dir)(A)R 2012, reg 3(f)(i).

b Paragraph (1A) inserted by P(Dir)(A)R 2012, reg 3(f)(i).

11.(1) The obligation to publish a prospectus under Regulation 13 shall not apply to the admission to trading in the State of the following types of securities—

(a) shares representing, over a period of 12 months, less than 10 per cent of the number of shares of the same class already admitted to trading on the same regulated market,

(b) shares issued in substitution for shares of the same class already admitted to trading on the same regulated market, if the issuing of such shares does not involve any increase in the issued capital,

(c) securities offered in connection with a takeover by means of an exchange offer, provided that a document is available containing information which is regarded by the Bank as being equivalent to that of a prospectus, taking into account the requirements of any Community act,

[(d) securities offered, allotted or to be allotted in connection with a merger or a division, provided that a document is available containing information which is regarded by the Bank as being equivalent to that of the prospectus, taking into account the requirements of European Union legislation,][a]

(e) shares offered, allotted or to be allotted free of charge to existing shareholders, and dividends paid out in the form of shares of the same class as the shares in respect of which such dividends are paid, provided that the first-mentioned shares are of the same class as the shares already admitted to trading on the same regulated market and that a document is made available containing information on the number and nature of the shares and the reasons for and details of the offer,

(f) securities offered, allotted or to be allotted to existing or former directors or employees by their employer or an affiliated undertaking, which in either case has securities already admitted to trading on the same regulated market, provided that the first-mentioned securities are of the same class as the securities already admitted to trading on that market and that a document is made available containing information on the number and nature of the securities and the reasons for and detail of the offer; for the purposes of this subparagraph 'affiliated undertaking' includes any parent undertaking or subsidiary undertaking of the employer or another subsidiary undertaking of that parent undertaking,

(g) shares resulting from the conversion or exchange of other securities or from the exercise of the rights conferred by other securities, provided that the said shares are of the same class as the shares already admitted to trading on the same regulated market,

(h) securities already admitted to trading on another regulated market, if the following conditions are satisfied—

(i) that these securities, or securities of the same class, have been admitted to trading on that other regulated market for more than 18 months,

(ii) that, for securities first admitted to trading on a regulated market after 31 December 2003, the admission to trading on that other regulated market was associated with an approved prospectus made available to the public in conformity with EU prospectus law,

(iii) that, unless subparagraph (ii) applies, for securities first admitted to listing after 30 June 1983, listing particulars were approved in accordance with the requirements of Directive 80/390/EEC or Directive 2001/34/EC,

(iv) that the ongoing obligations for trading on that other regulated market have been fulfilled,

(v) that the person seeking the admission of a security to trading under this exemption makes a summary available to the public in the manner specified in Regulation 45 and in a language accepted by the Bank,

(vi) that subject to subparagraph (vii), the contents of the summary shall comply with Regulation 21 and shall state where the most recent prospectus can be obtained (or if no prospectus in respect of the securities has been recently published shall state that fact) and where the financial information published by the issuer pursuant to its ongoing disclosure obligations is available, and

(vii) in circumstances where no prospectus has been recently published in respect of the securities, a warning similar to that referred to in Regulation 21(3) shall be required to be given and for the purpose of this clause the reference in Regulation 21(3) to a prospectus shall be construed as a reference to the most recent information disclosed to the regulated market under its ongoing disclosure obligations.

(2) The reference in paragraph (1)(f) to the offering or allotment of securities by an employer or an affiliated undertaking shall, in the case of such an offer or allotment that takes place for the purpose of an employees' share scheme or an employee share ownership trust, be construed as a reference to such offering or allotment, whether effected directly or indirectly by the employer or the affiliated undertaking.

(3) In paragraph (2) 'employees' share scheme' and 'employee share ownership trust' shall be construed in accordance with Regulation 10(3).

Amendments

a Paragraph (1)(d) substituted by P(Dir)(A)R 2012, reg 3(g).

PART 4
OBLIGATION TO PUBLISH A PROSPECTUS

12. Subject to Regulations 9 and 10, no offer of securities to the public shall be made in the State without publication of a prospectus in respect of the offer that—

(a) in a case where the State is the Home Member State, has been approved by the Bank pursuant to these Regulations and any other provisions of Irish prospectus law, or

(b) in a case where the State is a Host Member State, has been approved by the competent authority of the Home Member State pursuant to the applicable provisions of EU prospectus law.

13. Subject to Regulation 11, no securities shall be admitted to trading in the State without publication of a prospectus in respect of such admission of those securities that—

(a) in a case where the State is the Home Member State, has been approved by the Bank pursuant to these Regulations and any other provisions of Irish prospectus law, or

(b) in a case where the State is a Host Member State, has been approved by the competent authority of the Home Member State pursuant to the applicable provisions of EU prospectus law.

14. An issuer or offeror who fails to comply with Regulation 12 shall be guilty of an offence.

15. A person who has securities admitted to trading in contravention of Regulation 13 shall be guilty of an offence.

16.(1) A market operator that admits securities to trading in circumstances where it knows that that admission involves a contravention of Regulation 13 shall be guilty of an offence.

(2) A market operator in the State shall be entitled to rely on a copy of a notice of the decision of the Bank to approve a prospectus under Regulation 35, or, as the case may be, a copy of the certificate of approval from the competent authority of the Home Member State as evidence of compliance of the prospectus with EU prospectus law.

17. Without prejudice to its right to stipulate conditions for admission to trading and the production of evidence (whether in documentary form or otherwise) of compliance with those conditions following the commencement of these Regulations, a market operator in the State shall not require any person applying for admission of securities to trading on a regulated market to produce a prospectus, listing particulars or any other document equivalent thereto as a condition of admission of the securities to trading other than a prospectus drawn up and approved in compliance with the applicable provisions of EU prospectus law.

PART 5
DRAWING UP OF THE PROSPECTUS – CONTENT, FORMAT AND VALIDITY

18. The provisions of this Part shall apply to prospectuses relating to issuers or securities, as the case may be, in respect of which the State is the Home Member State.

Contents of Prospectus

19.(1) Without prejudice to Regulations 24 and 25, a prospectus shall contain all information which, according to the particular nature of the issuer and of the securities offered to the public or admitted to trading, is necessary to enable investors to make an informed assessment of—

(a) the assets and liabilities, financial position, profit and losses, and prospects of the issuer and of any guarantor, and

(b) the rights attaching to such securities.

(2) The information contained in the prospectus shall be consistent and presented in an easily analysable and comprehensible form.

(3) The prospectus shall contain information concerning the issuer and the securities to be offered to the public or to be admitted to trading.

(4) In the circumstances in which paragraph 4(b) of Schedule 2 to these Regulations applies, the prospectus shall also contain the information referred to in that paragraph.

Minimum Information

20. Without prejudice to the generality of Regulation 19 and subject to Regulation 26, the prospectus shall contain the minimum information required under the Prospectus Regulation.

Summary

21.(1) Subject to paragraph (4), a prospectus shall include a summary.

[(2) The summary shall in a concise manner and in non- technical language, provide key information in the language in which the prospectus was originally drawn up. The format and content of the summary of the prospectus shall provide, in conjunction with the prospectus, appropriate information about essential elements of the securities concerned in order to aid investors when considering whether to invest in such securities.

(2A) The summary shall be drawn up in a common format in order to facilitate comparability of the summaries of similar securities and its content should convey the key information of the securities concerned in order to aid investors when considering whether to invest in such securities.][a]

(3) The summary shall also contain a warning that—

(a) it should be read as an introduction to the prospectus,

(b) any decision to invest in the securities should be based on consideration of the prospectus as a whole by the investor,

(c) where a claim relating to the information contained in a prospectus is brought before a court, the plaintiff investor might, under the national legislation of the Member States, have to bear the costs of translating the prospectus before the legal proceedings are initiated, and [(d) no civil liability shall attach to those legally responsible for the contents of the prospectus solely on the basis of the summary unless the summary, including any translation thereof, is, when read together with the other parts of the prospectus, misleading, inaccurate or inconsistent, or does not provide, when so read, key information in order to aid investors when considering whether to invest in such securities.][b]

[(4) Where the prospectus relates to the admission to trading of non-equity securities having a denomination of at least €100,000, this Regulation shall not apply.][c]

Amendments

a Paragraph (2) substituted and para (2A) inserted by P(Dir)(A)R 2012, reg 3(h)(i).

b Paragraph (3)(d) substituted by P(Dir)(A)R 2012, reg 3(h)(ii).

c Paragraph (4) substituted by P(Dir)(A)R 2012, reg 3(h)(iii).

Single or Separate Documents

22.(1) [...][a] a prospectus may be drawn up as a single document or separate documents.

(2) A prospectus composed of separate documents shall divide the required information into—

(a) a registration document containing the required information relating to the issuer,

(b) a securities note containing the required information concerning the securities offered to the public or to be admitted to trading, and

(c) a summary.

Amendments

a Words 'Subject to Regulation 23' deleted by P(Dir)(A)R 2012, reg 3(i).

Base Prospectus

23.(1) In the following cases, at the election of a relevant person, a prospectus may consist of a base prospectus—

(a) in a case where the securities are non-equity securities, including warrants in any form, issued under an offering programme,

(b) in a case where the securities are non-equity securities issued in a continuous or repeated manner by credit institutions—

(i) if the sums deriving from the issue of those securities, under national legislation, are placed in assets which provide sufficient coverage for the liability deriving from securities until their maturity date, and

(ii) if, in the event of the insolvency of the related credit institution, the said sums are intended, as a priority, to repay the capital and interest falling due, without prejudice to the provisions of Directive 2001/24/EC of the European Parliament and of the Council of 4 April 2001 on the reorganisation and winding up of credit institutions.

(2) The information given in the base prospectus shall be supplemented, if necessary, in accordance with Regulation 51, with updated information on the issuer and on the securities to be offered to the public or to be admitted to trading.

[(3) Where the final terms of the offer are neither included in the base prospectus nor in a supplement, the final terms shall be made available to investors, filed with the Bank and communicated, by the issuer, to the competent authority of each Host Member State when each public offer is made as soon as practicable and, if possible, in advance of the beginning of the public offer or admission to trading. The final terms shall contain only information that relates to the securities note and shall not be used to supplement the base prospectus.][a]

(4) The provisions of Regulation 24(1)(a) shall be applicable in any case coming within paragraph (3).

Amendments

a Paragraph (3) substituted by P(Dir)(A)R 2012, reg 3(j).

Omission of Information

24.(1) Where pursuant to Regulation 23 the final offer price or amount of securities (or both) to be subject to a public offer cannot be included in the prospectus—

(a) the criteria or the conditions (or both) in accordance with which the above elements will be determined or, in the case of price, the maximum price, shall be disclosed in the prospectus, or

(b) it shall be a term of the offer that acceptances of or applications for the purchase or subscription of securities (whether accepted by the issuer or not) may be withdrawn or revoked during a period expiring not less

than 2 working days after a statement of the final offer price and amount of securities which will be offered to the public has been filed and published in accordance with Regulation 23(3).

25. The Bank may authorise the omission from a prospectus of information required under these Regulations or any other provision of Irish prospectus law, if it considers that—

(a) disclosure of such information would be contrary to the public interest, or

(b) disclosure of such information would be seriously detrimental to the issuer, provided that the omission would not be likely to mislead the public with regard to facts and circumstances essential for an informed assessment of the issuer, offeror or guarantor, if any, and of the rights attached to the securities to which the prospectus relates, or

(c) such information is of minor importance only for a specific offer or admission to trading and is not such as will influence the assessment of the financial position and prospects of the issuer, offeror or guarantor, if any.

26. [(1) Without prejudice to the requirement to give adequate information to investors, where, in exceptional cases, certain information required by any delegated acts to be included in a prospectus would be inappropriate to the issuers sphere of activity or to the legal form of the issuer or to the securities to which the prospectus relates, the prospectus may omit that required information but, unless there is no such equivalent information, shall contain information equivalent to that required information.

(2) Where securities are guaranteed by a Member State (including the State), a relevant person when asking for admission to trading on a regulated market, when drawing up a prospectus in accordance with Regulation 8(5), shall be entitled to omit information about such guarantor.][a]

Amendments

a Regulation 26 substituted by P(Dir)(A)R 2012, reg 3(k).

Incorporation by Reference

27.[(1) Subject to paragraph (3), information may be incorporated in a prospectus by reference to one or more previously or simultaneously published documents that have been approved by the Bank or filed with it in accordance with EU prospectus law or Directive 2004/109/EC of the European Parliament and of the Council of 15 December 2004 (OJ L 390, 31.12.2004, p 38).][a]

(2) The information incorporated by reference in accordance with paragraph (1) shall be the latest available to the issuer.

(3) The summary shall not incorporate information by reference.

Amendments

a Paragraph (1) substituted by P(Dir)(A)R 2012, reg 3(l).

28. When information is incorporated by reference pursuant to Regulation 27, a cross-reference list must be provided in order to enable investors to identify easily specific items of information.

Prospectuses Consisting of Separate Documents

29.(1) A relevant person may apply to the Bank for approval of the registration document referred to in Regulation 22.

(2) A relevant person who has a registration document approved by the Bank under paragraph (1) shall only be required to draw up a securities note and a summary when its securities are offered to the public or to be admitted to trading.

[(3) In the circumstances referred to in paragraph (2), the securities note shall, where there has been a material change or recent development which could affect investors' assessments since the latest updated registration document, provide information that would normally be provided in the registration document, unless such information is provided in a supplement in accordance with Regulation 51.][a]

(4) In the circumstances referred to in paragraph (2), the securities note and summary shall be subject to separate approval under these Regulations and any other provisions of Irish prospectus law.

(5) Where a registration document has been filed but not approved in accordance with these Regulations and any other provisions of Irish prospectus law, the entire

documentation, including updated information, shall be subject to approval in accordance with these Regulations and any other provisions of such law.

Amendments

a Paragraph (3) substituted by P(Dir)(A)R 2012, reg 3(m).

Validity of a Prospectus, Base Prospectus and Registration Document

30.(1) Provided it is updated by the issue of a supplement where required, the period of validity of a prospectus or a related document for the purposes of an offer of securities to the public or admission to trading shall be as follows—

[(a) subject to subparagraphs (b) to (d) a prospectus shall be valid for 12 months after its approval,][a]

(b) in the case of securities referred to in Regulation 23(1)(a), the base prospectus, previously filed and published, shall be valid for 12 months after its filing,

(c) in the case of non-equity securities referred to in Regulation 23(1)(b), the base prospectus as previously filed and published shall be valid until no more of the securities concerned are issued in a continuous or repeated manner,

[(d) a registration document as referred to in Regulation 22 (2)(a) previously filed and approved shall be valid for the purposes of Regulation 29 (2) for twelve months after its approval.][b]

[(2) The registration document updated, in accordance with Regulation 29(3) or Regulation 51, accompanied by the securities note and the summary note shall be considered to constitute a valid prospectus.][c]

Amendments

a Subparagraph (1)(a) substituted by P(Dir)(A)R 2012, reg 3(n)(i)(I).

b Subparagraph (1)(d) substituted by P(Dir)(A)R 2012, reg 3(n)(i)(II).

c Paragraph (2) substituted by P(Dir)(A)R 2012, reg 3(n)(ii).

PART 6
RESPONSIBILITY ATTACHING TO THE PROSPECTUS

31.(1) The provisions of this Part shall govern responsibility in respect of the contents of a prospectus relating to issuers or securities, as the case may be, in respect of which the State is the Home Member State.

(2) For the purposes of these Regulations, responsibility for the information given in a prospectus attaches, subject to the provisions of that Schedule, in each of the cases specified in Schedule 1 to these Regulations to the persons specified in the relevant case, and references in these Regulations to responsible persons shall be construed accordingly.

32.(1) The responsible persons shall be clearly identified in a prospectus by their names and functions or, in the case of legal persons, their names and registered offices.

(2) A prospectus shall contain declarations by the responsible persons that, to the best of their knowledge:

(a) the information contained in the prospectus is in accordance with the facts, and

(b) that the prospectus makes no omission likely to affect its import save information if any omitted in accordance with Regulation 25 (a).

but shall be deemed to have been made on publication of the prospectus.

(3) Neither this Regulation nor Regulation 31 prejudices section 41 of the Act of 2005.

PART 7
APPROVAL OF PROSPECTUS

Approval of the Prospectus

33. For the purposes of this Part—

'applicant' means a relevant person who applies to the Bank for approval;

'time limits' means the time limits provided for under Regulations 35 and 36.

34. The provisions of Regulations 35 to 39 shall apply in circumstances where the State is the Home Member State or where the function of approving of a prospectus has been transferred to the Bank in accordance with Regulation 41.

35.(1) An applicant shall submit a draft of the prospectus to the Bank and any other information and documents the Bank may require in accordance with the prospectus rules.

(2) Subject to paragraph (3), the Bank shall notify the applicant of its decision regarding the approval of the prospectus in writing within 10 working days after the submission of the draft prospectus in accordance with paragraph (1).

[(2A) The Bank shall notify the European Securities and Markets Authority of the approval of the prospectus and any supplement thereto at the same time as that approval is notified to the applicant. The Bank shall at the same time provide the European Securities and Markets Authority with a copy of the prospectus and any supplement thereto.][a]

(3) The reference in paragraph (2) to 10 working days shall be construed as a reference to 20 working days if the public offer involves securities issued by an issuer which does not have any securities admitted to trading and which has not previously offered securities to the public.

(4) If the Bank fails to give a decision as to whether to approve a prospectus within the time limits, such failure shall not be deemed to constitute approval by it of the application.

Amendments

a Paragraph (2A) inserted by P(Dir)(A)R (No 2) 2012, reg 2(c).

36.(1) If the Bank finds, on reasonable grounds, that the documents submitted to it are incomplete or that supplementary information is needed, the time limits referred to in Regulation 35 shall apply only from the date on which such supplementary information is provided by the applicant.

(2) If the documents submitted to it are incomplete or supplementary information is needed the Bank shall, within 10 working days of the submission of the application, notify the applicant of that fact.

37. The Bank shall not approve a prospectus unless it is satisfied that the applicable requirements imposed by or under these Regulations and any other provisions of Irish prospectus law have been complied with.

38.(1) Upon the prospectus being approved, the applicant shall file the prospectus—

(a) with the Bank forthwith, and

(b) if the issuer is a company registered under the Companies Acts 1963 to 2005, with the registrar of companies within 14 days after its publication in accordance with Part 8.

(2) An applicant who fails to comply with paragraph (1) shall be guilty of an offence.

Application to Court

39.(1) If the Bank refuses to approve a prospectus the applicant may apply to the Court in a summary manner to have such refusal reviewed.

(2) An application under paragraph (1) shall be made within 28 days after the date of notification of the Bank's decision under Regulation 35.

(3) On the hearing of an application under this Regulation, the Court shall confirm the decision of the Bank unless the applicant establishes to the Court's satisfaction that the applicant has complied with the procedures specified by these Regulations and any other provisions of Irish prospectus law in all material respects and that the prospectus meets the requirements of these Regulations and any other such provisions in all material respects.

(4) If the Court is satisfied that those procedures and requirements have been complied with in all material respects the Court may set aside the decision of the Bank and in such a case shall remit the matter to the Bank which shall thereupon reconsider the matter and make a further decision in accordance with those procedures and requirements.

Transfer to Another Competent Authority

40.(1)[The Bank may, subject to the prior notification to the European Securities and Markets Authority and][a] with the consent of the competent authority, transfer the function of approving a prospectus to the competent authority of another Member State.

(2) Any transfer under paragraph (1) shall be notified to the applicant within 3 working days after the date on which the decision by the Bank to make the transfer is made.

[(3) Article 28(4) of Regulation (EU) No. 1095/2010 shall not apply to the transfer of the approval of the prospectus in accordance with this Regulation.][b]

Amendments

a Words substituted for 'The Bank may,' by P(Dir)(A)R (No 2) 2012, reg 2(d)(i).

b Paragraph (3) inserted by P(Dir)(A)R (No 2) 2012, reg 2(d)(ii).

Transfer from Another Competent Authority

41.(1) In circumstances where the State is not the Home Member State, subject to the consent of the Bank, the competent authority of the Home Member State may transfer the function of approving a prospectus to the Bank in accordance with EU prospectus law.

(2) In the case of a transfer such as is referred to in paragraph (1) the relevant time limits shall apply from the date on which the decision by the competent authority of the Home Member State to transfer the function is made.

42. Where—

(a) the Bank has transferred the function of approving a prospectus to the competent authority of another Member State under Regulation 40, or

(b) in circumstances where the State is not the Home Member State, the competent authority of the Home Member State has transferred the function of approving a prospectus to the competent authority of another Member State under EU prospectus law,

then if the prospectus is approved by such competent authority under EU prospectus law the prospectus shall be deemed to have been approved for the purposes of these Regulations.

Liability of Bank and Other Bodies

43. Without prejudice to the generality of section 33AJ of the Central Bank Act 1942, approval of a prospectus by the Bank shall not be deemed to be or construed as a representation or warranty as to the solvency or credit – worthiness of the issuer or the truth or accuracy of the contents of the prospectus.

PART 8
PUBLICATION OF PROSPECTUS

44.(1) This Part shall apply to offers of securities to the public or admissions to trading in respect of which the State is the Home Member State.

(2) Upon a prospectus having been approved and filed in accordance with these Regulations, the relevant person shall:

(a) make the prospectus available to the public as soon as practicable and in any case, at a reasonable time in advance of, and at the latest at the beginning of, the offer to the public or the admission to trading of the securities involved,

(b) in the case of an initial public offer of a class of shares not already admitted to trading that is to be admitted to trading for the first time, make the prospectus available to the public at the earlier of the time referred to in paragraph (a) or 6 working days before the end of the offer.

(3) A relevant person who fails to comply with paragraph (2) shall be guilty of an offence.

[(4) The Bank shall make accessible to the European Securities and Markets Authority any prospectus filed in accordance with subparagraph (*a*) of paragraph (1) of Regulation 38.][a]

Amendments

a Paragraph (4) inserted by P(Dir)(A)R (No 2) 2012, reg 2(e).

45.(1) Subject to paragraph (2), a prospectus shall be deemed available to the public in accordance with Regulation 44 when published in one of the following ways—

(a) by insertion in one or more newspapers circulated throughout, or widely circulated in, the Member State or Member States in which the public offer is to be made or admission to trading is to be sought,

(b) in a printed form to be made available, free of charge, to the public at the offices of the market on which the securities are being admitted to trading, or at the registered office of the issuer and at the offices of the financial intermediaries placing or selling the securities, including paying agents,

[(c) in electronic form on the issuer's website or, if applicable, on the website of the financial intermediaries placing or selling the securities, including paying agents,][a]

(d) in an electronic form on the website of the regulated market or markets where the admission to trading is sought, or

(e) in electronic form on the website of the Bank (if the Bank decides to provide a service of publishing prospectuses on its website).

[(2) The issuer or the person responsible for drawing up a prospectus who publishes a prospectus in accordance with subparagraphs (a) or (b) of paragraph (1) shall also publish a prospectus electronically in accordance with subparagraph (c) of that paragraph.][b]

Amendments

a Subparagraph (1)(c) substituted by P(Dir)(A)R 2012, reg 3(o)(i).

b Paragraph (2) substituted by P(Dir)(A)R 2012, reg 3(o)(ii).

46.(1) In respect of a prospectus relating to equity securities (other than equity securities issued by a collective investment undertaking subject to these Regulations), the relevant person shall publish a notice stating how the prospectus has been made available pursuant to Regulation 45 and where it can be obtained by the public.

(2) A relevant person who fails to comply with paragraph (1) shall be guilty of an offence.

47.(1) In the case of a prospectus comprising several documents or incorporating information by reference (or both), the documents and information making up the prospectus may be published and circulated separately provided that the documents are made available to the public in accordance with the arrangements referred to in Regulation 45.

(2) Each such document shall indicate where the other documents constituting the full prospectus may be obtained.

48. The text and the format of the prospectus, and of any of the supplements published, shall at all times be identical to the original version approved by the Bank.

49.(1) Where the prospectus is made available by publication in electronic form pursuant to Regulation 45, a paper copy of it must nevertheless be delivered to each investor who purchases or subscribes for the securities involved (or intends to purchase or subscribes for such securities or bona fide contemplates such purchase or subscription) upon the investor's request and free of charge by the relevant person or the financial intermediaries placing or selling the securities.

(2) [A relevant person or financial intermediary][a] who fails to comply with a request under paragraph (1) shall be guilty of an offence (unless a prior request by the investor concerned in respect of the particular prospectus has already been complied with by another person referred to in that paragraph).

Amendments

a Words 'A relevant person of financial intermediary' substituted by P(Dir)(A)R 2012, reg 3(p).

---

50. The Bank shall publish on its website over a period of 12 months all the prospectuses approved (or, alternatively, at its discretion, the list of prospectuses) approved by it in accordance with Part 7, including, if applicable, a hyperlink to the prospectus published on the website of the issuer, or on the website of the regulated market.

Supplements to the Prospectus

51.[(1) A relevant person shall include in a supplement to the prospectus every significant new factor, material mistake or inaccuracy relating to the information included in the prospectus which is capable of affecting the assessment of the securities and which arises or is noted between the time when the prospectus is approved and the final closing of the offer to the public or, as the case may be, the time when trading on a regulated market begins, whichever occurs later.

(2) Such a supplement shall be the subject of the procedures under Part 7 in relation to the approval of prospectuses but these procedures shall be completed in a maximum of 7 working days and the supplement shall be published at least in the manner in which the original prospectus was published.][a]

(3) The summary, and any translations thereof, shall also be supplemented, if necessary, to take account of the new information included in the supplement.

(4) Where there are significant new factors, material mistakes or inaccuracies as referred to in paragraph (1) of which the Bank becomes aware the Bank shall require the approval and publication of a supplement.

(5) In exercising its powers under paragraph (4) the Bank shall have regard to any significant new factors, material mistakes or inaccuracies brought to its attention by [the European Securities and Markets Authority or the competent authority][b] of a Host Member State.

Amendments

a Paragraphs (1) and (2) substituted by P(Dir)(A)R 2012, reg 3(q).

b Words substituted for 'the competent authority' by P(Dir)(A)R (No 2) 2012, reg 2(f).

---

52. [(1) Where the prospectus relates to an offer of securities to the public, (to which this Part applies) persons who have already agreed to purchase or subscribe for the securities concerned before a supplement is published shall have the right, exercisable within 2 working days after the publication of the supplement, to withdraw their acceptances provided that the new factor, mistake or inaccuracy referred to in Regulation 51 (1) arose before the final closing of the offer to the public and the delivery of securities.

(2) Subject to paragraph (3), the period in paragraph (1) may be extended by the relevant person.

(3) The final date of the right of withdrawal shall be stated in the supplement.][a]

Amendments

a Regulation 52 substituted by P(Dir)(A)R 2012, reg 3(r).

PART 9

CROSS-BORDER OFFERS AND ADMISSIONS TO TRADING

53. In this Part 'third country issuer' means an issuer incorporated or having its registered office in a state or territory which is not a Member State.

Community Scope of Approvals of Prospectuses

54.(1) Where the State is a Host Member State and without prejudice to Regulations 89 and 90, a prospectus approved by the competent authority of the Home Member State (including any prospectus drawn up under Article 1(3) of the Directive or the national legislation of the Home Member State implementing the said Article 1(3)) shall be valid for a public offer or an admission to trading in the State, provided that the Bank is notified in accordance with Regulation 55.

(2) The Bank shall not undertake any approval or administrative procedures relating to prospectuses falling within paragraph (1).

(3) If there are significant new factors, material mistakes or inaccuracies, as referred to in Regulation 51, arising since the approval of a prospectus falling within paragraph (1), the Bank may draw the attention of the competent authority of the Home Member State to the need for any new information to be included in a supplement to the prospectus.

[(4) The Bank shall publish on its website a list of certificates of approval of prospectuses and any supplements thereto, which are notified to it by the competent authority of a Home Member State in accordance with Article 18(1) of the Directive or EU Prospectus Law, including, if applicable, a hyperlink to those documents published on the website of the competent authority of the Home Member State, on the website of the issuer, or on the website of the regulated market. The Bank shall keep the published list up-to-date and retain each item on the list for a period of at least 12 months.][a]

Amendments

a Paragraph (4) inserted by P(Dir)(A)R (No 2) 2012, reg 2(g).

---

55. The notification referred to in Regulation 54(1) shall consist of—

(a) the certificate referred to in Regulation 57,

(b) a copy of the prospectus, and

(c) if required by the Bank, a translation of the summary of the prospectus into English or Irish (at the election of the relevant person).

56.[(1) In circumstances where the State is the Home Member State and the Bank has approved a prospectus (including a prospectus submitted under Regulation 8(5)) the Bank shall, at the request of the relevant person or the person responsible for drawing up the prospectus, notify the competent authority of each Host Member State with a certificate of approval referred to in Regulation 57, together with a copy of the prospectus.

(2) A request to the Bank made under paragraph (1) shall be complied with by it within 3 working days after the receipt of the request or, where the request is submitted together with the draft prospectus, within one working day after the approval of the prospectus.

[(2A) In complying with a request under paragraph (1), the Bank shall also provide to the European Securities and Markets Authority a copy of the certificate referred to in Regulation 57 and a copy of the prospectus.][b]

(3) If required by the competent authority of the Host Member State under EU prospectus law, the notification under paragraph (1) shall be accompanied by the translation of the summary produced under the responsibility of the relevant person or person responsible for drawing up the prospectus.

(4) The Bank shall also notify the relevant person or the person responsible for drawing up the prospectus of the certificate of approval at the same time as it notifies the competent authority of each Host Member State.][a]

Amendments

a Regulation 56 substituted by P(Dir)(A)R 2012, reg 3(s).

b Paragraph (2A) inserted by P(Dir)(A)R (No 2) 2012, reg 2(h).

---

57. The certificate referred to in Regulations 55 and 56 is a certificate of approval attesting that the prospectus has been drawn up in accordance with the Directive and recording whether any information has been omitted from the prospectus in accordance with Article 8(2) and (3) of the Directive or the relevant provision of EU prospectus law implementing the said Article and, if so, the justification for such omission.

58. Regulations 54 to 57 shall apply to any supplement.

Issuers Incorporated in Third Countries

59.(1) This Regulation shall apply to third country issuers in respect of which the State is the Home Member State.

(2) The Bank may approve a prospectus pursuant to Part 7 for an offer of securities to the public or for admission to trading, drawn up in accordance with the legislation of the third country governing an issuer referred to in paragraph (1), provided that:

(a) the prospectus has been drawn up in accordance with international standards set by international securities commission organisations, including the IOSCO disclosure standards, and

(b) the information requirements, including information of a financial nature, are equivalent to the requirements under the Directive.

60. In the case of an offer of securities to the public or admission to trading of securities, issued by a third country issuer, in circumstances where the State is a Host Member State, the requirements of Regulations 54 and 55 and Part 10 shall apply.

Co-operation between Authorities

61.(1) The Bank shall—

(a) co-operate with the competent authorities of other Member States designated under EU prospectus law whenever necessary for the purpose of performing its functions, and

(b) render assistance to competent authorities of other Member States in the performance of their functions under EU prospectus law.

(2) In particular and without prejudice to the generality of paragraph (1), the Bank shall—

(a) exchange information and cooperate with competent authorities in other Member States when an issuer has more than one home competent authority because of its various classes of securities, or where the function of approving a prospectus has been transferred to the competent authority of another Member State pursuant to Regulation 40,

(b) closely cooperate with competent authorities in other Member State when requiring suspension or prohibition of trading for securities traded in various Member States in order to ensure (in so far as practicable) equivalent treatment between trading venues and protection of investors.

(3) Where appropriate, the competent authority of the Host Member State may request the assistance of the competent authority of the Home Member State from the stage at which a particular case is scrutinised for the purposes of approval in accordance with EU prospectus law, in particular as regards a new type or rare forms of securities.

(4) The competent authority of the Home Member State may request the competent authority of the Host Member State to furnish to it information in relation to any items specific to the relevant market.

[(5) The Bank may refer to the European Securities and Markets Authority situations where a request for cooperation under this Regulation, in particular to exchange information, has been rejected or has not been acted upon within a reasonable time.][a]

Amendments

a Paragraph (5) inserted by P(Dir)(A)R (No 2) 2012, reg 2(i).

---

62. Without prejudice to its powers under Regulations 87 and 88 and 95, the Bank may consult with market operators if, in the Bank's opinion, it is necessary to do so and, in particular, when deciding to suspend, or to request a regulated market to suspend or prohibit trading.

PART 10
USE OF LANGUAGES

Use of Languages

63. Where the State is the Home Member State the following provisions shall apply in respect of the language or languages in which the prospectus is to be drawn up and published:

(a) where an offer of securities to the public is made or admission to trading is sought only in the State, the prospectus shall be drawn up and published in a language accepted by the Bank,

(b) where an offer of securities to the public is made or admission to trading is sought in one or more Member States other than the State—

(i) the prospectus shall be drawn up and published in each Host Member State either in a language accepted by the competent authority of the Host Member State or in a language customary in the sphere of international finance, at the election of the relevant person,

(ii) the competent authority of each Host Member State may only require that the summary be translated into the official language of the Host Member State,

(iii) for the purposes of the scrutiny of the prospectus by the Bank pursuant to Part 7, the prospectus shall be drawn up either in a language accepted by the Bank or in a language customary in the sphere of international finance, at the election of the relevant person,

(c) where an offer of securities to the public is made or admission to trading is sought in more than one Member State including the State—

(i) the prospectus shall be drawn up and published in a language accepted by the Bank,

(ii) the prospectus shall also be drawn up and published in each Host Member State in a language accepted by the competent authority of the Host Member State or in a language customary in the sphere of international finance, at the election of the relevant person, and

(iii) the competent authority of each Host Member State may only require that the summary be translated into the official language of the Host Member State.

64. In circumstances where the State is the Host Member State the following provisions shall apply in relation to the language in which a prospectus is to be drawn up and published in the State—

(a) where a public offer is made or admission to trading is sought in one or more Member States other than the Home Member State then—

(i) the prospectus shall be drawn up in a language accepted by the Bank or in a language customary in the sphere of international finance, at the election of the relevant person,

(ii) the Bank may only require that the summary be translated into Irish or English, at the election of the relevant person,

(b) where the public offer is made or admission to trading is sought in more than one Member State including the Home Member State then—

(i) the prospectus shall be drawn up in a language accepted by the competent authority of the Home Member State,

(ii) the prospectus shall also be drawn up in a language accepted by the Bank or in a language customary in the sphere of international finance, at the election of the relevant person,

(iii) the Bank may only require that the summary be translated into Irish or English, at the election of the relevant person.

65. [Whether the State is the Home Member State or a Host Member State where admission to trading on a regulated market of non-equity securities whose denomination per unit amounts to at least €100,000 is sought in one or more Member States (including the State), the prospectus shall be drawn up either in a language accepted by the competent authorities of the Home Member State and the Host Member State or States or in a language customary in the sphere of international finance, at the election of the relevant person.][a]

Amendments

a Regulation 65 substituted by P(Dir)(A)R 2012, reg 3(t).

---

66. The Bank shall, from time to time, publish in such manner as it thinks fit a notice specifying—

(a) the languages accepted by it, for the time being, for the purpose of these Regulations, and

(b) any other requirements, for the time being, of it for the purposes of this Part.

67. For the purposes of this Part 'a language customary in the sphere of international finance' includes the English language.

PART 11
ANNUAL INFORMATION DOCUMENT

68. [...][a]

Amendments

a Regulation 68 revoked by P(Dir)(A)R 2012, reg 3(u).

---

69. [...][a]

Amendments

a Regulation 69 revoked by P(Dir)(A)R 2012, reg 3(u).

70.[...][a]

Amendments

a Regulation 70 revoked by P(Dir)(A)R 2012, reg 3(u).

71. [...][a]

Amendments

a Regulation 71 revoked by P(Dir)(A)R 2012, reg 3(u).

72. [...][a]

Amendments

a Regulation 72 revoked by P(Dir)(A)R 2012, reg 3(u).

PART 12
ADVERTISEMENTS

73. This Part shall apply to advertisements relating to a public offer or an admission to trading in one or more Member States—

(a) made in or from the State by or on behalf of any relevant person, or

(b) made in or from any other Member State by or on behalf of any relevant person,

in connection with a public offer or an admission to trading in respect of which the State is the Home Member State.

74.(1) Subject to paragraph (2), an advertisement to which this Part applies shall comply with the principles set out in Schedule 2 to these Regulations.

(2) Paragraph 4 of Schedule 2 to these Regulations shall not apply to cases where a relevant person is obliged to draw up a prospectus pursuant to EU prospectus law (or not being so obliged nevertheless draws up a prospectus pursuant to Regulation 8 (5) or the corresponding provisions of the national legislation of the other Member State concerned implementing the Directive).

(3) An advertisement that complies with paragraph (1) shall not be considered as a prospectus for the purpose of these Regulations.

(4) A relevant person shall be guilty of an offence if an advertisement that fails to comply with paragraph (1) is made or issued in or from the State by or on behalf of the relevant person.

75. Without prejudice to any power exercisable by the Bank under any other enactment, the Bank may monitor and supervise compliance by relevant persons with the principles set out in Schedule 2 to these Regulations.

76. For the purpose of its function under Regulation 75, the Bank may give a direction to a relevant person to do or not to do such things as are necessary to ensure compliance with the principles set out in Schedule 2 to these Regulations.

77.(1) Without prejudice to the generality of Regulation 76, a direction under that Regulation may do all or any of the following:

(a) prohibit the issue of a specified advertisement,

(b) require the relevant person to modify a specified advertisement or an advertisement of a specified description in a specified manner,

(c) prohibit the issue by the person of any advertisements which are substantial repetitions of a specified advertisement,

(d) require the relevant person to withdraw any specified advertisement or any advertisement of a specified description,

(e) require the relevant person to include specified information in any advertisement to be published by the person or on person's behalf,

(f) require the relevant person to arrange the publication of a correction of an advertisement which contravenes Regulation 74,

(g) require the relevant person to arrange the publication, in a manner specified by the Bank, of the fact that an offence under Regulation 74 has been committed by the relevant person and that a fine or term of imprisonment, if any, has been imposed on the relevant person in respect of a conviction therefor.

(2) In this Regulation 'specified' means specified in a direction under this Regulation.

(3) Where a direction has been given by the Bank under this Regulation the provisions of Regulation 88(4) to (13) shall, with any necessary modifications, apply to the direction.

(4) A direction under this Regulation may be given to any relevant person referred to in Regulation 73.

PART 13
COMPETENT AUTHORITY

Designation of Competent Authority

78.(1) The Bank is designated as the central competent administrative authority for the purposes of Article 21(1) of the Directive and shall be responsible for carrying out the obligations provided for in the Directive and for ensuring that the provisions adopted pursuant to the Directive are applied.

[(1A) The Bank shall cooperate with the European Securities and Markets Authority for the purposes of the Directive, in accordance with Regulation (EU) No. 1095/2010.

(1B) The Bank shall without delay provide the European Securities and Markets Authority with all information necessary to carry out its duties, in accordance with Article 35 of Regulation (EU) No. 1095/2010.][a]

(2) [Other than in order to meet its obligations under paragraph (1A) or (1B) above, the Bank][b] shall be independent in the performance of its functions under these Regulations.

Amendments

a Paragraphs (1A) and (1B) inserted by P(Dir)(A)R (No 2) 2012, reg 2(j)(i).

b Words substituted for 'The Bank' by P(Dir)(A)R (No 2) 2012, reg 2(j)(ii).

Delegation of functions

79.(1) The Bank may delegate to an approved stock exchange, subject to such conditions as the Bank specifies, any of the functions that it is obliged or authorised to perform under Irish prospectus law or under the Directive other than the following functions—

(a) the approval of prospectuses and supplements pursuant to Part 7 (but not any act involving the scrutiny of prospectuses or supplements),

(b) the issuing of a certificate referred to in Regulation 57,

(c) functions under Regulations 40, 41, 5 1(2), 56(1), 59(2), 79, 85, 88, 89 and 90 or this Regulation,

(d) Parts 15 and 16.

(2) Any person to whom functions are delegated under paragraph (1) shall have, by virtue of the delegation, all such powers as are necessary to perform those functions.

(3) Any delegation of functions shall be in writing and specify the functions to be performed and the conditions subject to which they are to be performed.

(4) The conditions referred to in paragraph (3) shall include a provision obliging the stock exchange to whom a function or functions concerned are delegated to act and be organised in such a manner as to avoid conflicts of interest and so that information obtained from performing the function is not used unfairly or to prevent competition.

(5) A delegation under this Regulation shall not prevent the performance by the Bank of the function delegated.

(6) Notwithstanding any delegation under this Regulation, the final responsibility for supervising compliance with the Directive and the applicable provisions of EU prospectus law and for approving prospectuses under these Regulations shall be with the Bank.

(7) The Bank shall notify the Minister of any such delegation of a function promptly and of the conditions subject to which it has been delegated.

(8) Following such notification, the Minister shall inform the Commission[, the European Securities and Markets Authority][a] and the competent authorities of other Member States designated pursuant to the Directive of any arrangements entered into with regard to the functions under this Regulation, including the conditions subject to which such functions are delegated.

(9) Where a function is delegated pursuant to this Regulation, then nothing in the Stock Exchange Act 1995 shall prevent there being specified as a condition subject to which the function is to be performed a condition requiring the rules of the stock exchange concerned or an amendment thereof to be approved by the Bank in so far as they are relevant to the function delegated.

Amendments

a Words inserted by P(Dir)(A)R (No 2) 2012, reg 2(k).

PART 14
POWERS OF COMPETENT AUTHORITY

Definitions

80. In this Part—

'authorised officer' means an authorised officer appointed under Regulation 85;

'person to whom these Regulations apply' means any relevant person or a market operator;

'records' means any book, document or any other written or printed material in any form including any information (including phone and data traffic records) stored, maintained or preserved by means of any mechanical or electronic device, whether or not stored, maintained or preserved in a legible form;

'relevant records' means records relating to the activities of persons to whom these Regulations apply;

'responsible authority' means:—

(a) the Chief Executive of the Irish Financial Services Regulatory Authority, or

(b) any person to whom the Chief Executive of that Authority has delegated responsibility for appointing authorised persons.

81.(1) The Bank shall have all the powers necessary for the performance of its functions under Irish prospectus law or the Directive.

(2) The powers provided for in this Part shall not be exercised in a manner or for a purpose inconsistent with the Directive or these Regulations.

82.(1) Following receipt of an application for approval of a prospectus the Bank (or any person to whom the Bank has delegated the function of scrutinising prospectuses under Regulation 79) shall have the power to:

(a) require the relevant person to include in the prospectus supplementary information, if necessary for investor protection,

(b) require the relevant person and the persons that control the relevant person to provide information and documents to the Bank or delegate,

(c) require auditors and managers of the relevant person as well as financial intermediaries commissioned to carry out the offer to the public or ask for admission to trading, to provide information to the Bank or delegate.

(2) The Bank shall have the following powers (by means of giving a direction under Regulation 88 in that behalf) for the purpose of regulating public offers or admissions to trading in respect of which it is the Home Member State or for the purposes specified in Regulation 90(1).

(a) to suspend a public offer or admission to trading, for a maximum of 10 consecutive working days on any single occasion, if it has reasonable grounds for suspecting that the provisions of the Directive or of EU prospectus law have not been complied with as respects the offer or admission to trading;

(b) to prohibit or suspend advertisements for a maximum of 10 consecutive working days on any single occasion if it has reasonable grounds for believing that the provisions of the Directive or of EU prospectus law have not been complied with as respects the advertisement;

(c) to prohibit a public offer if it finds that the provisions of the Directive or of EU prospectus law have not been complied with as respects the offer to trading of the securities concerned, or if it has reasonable grounds for suspecting that they will not be complied with as respects the offer;

(d) to suspend or ask the relevant regulated markets to suspend trading on a regulated market, for a maximum of 10 consecutive working days on any single occasion, if it has reasonable grounds for believing that the provisions of the Directive or of EU prospectus law have not been complied with as respects the admission to trading of the securities concerned;

(e) to prohibit trading on a regulated market if it finds that the provisions of the Directive or of EU prospectus law have not been complied with as respects the admission to trading of the securities concerned;

(f) to disclose to public the fact a relevant person is failing to comply with its obligations under EU prospectus law.

83. Once the securities have been admitted to trading the Bank may (by means of giving a direction under Regulation 88 in that behalf):

(a) require the issuer to disclose all material information which may have an effect on the assessment of the securities admitted to trading in order to ensure investor protection or the smooth operation of the market,

(b) suspend or require the relevant regulated market to suspend the securities from trading if, in its opinion, the issuer's situation is such that trading would be detrimental to investors' interests,

(c) ensure that issuers whose securities are traded on regulated markets comply with the obligations provided for in Articles 102 and 103 of Directive 2001/34/EC and that equivalent information is provided to investors and equivalent treatment is granted by the issuer to all securities holders who are in the same position, in all Member States where the offer to the public is made or the securities are admitted to trading.

84. The powers of the Bank under this Part are without prejudice to the powers of the Bank under any other Part of these Regulations or any other enactment.

Power to appoint authorised officers

85.(1) A responsible authority may, in writing—

(a) authorise such and so many persons as the authority considers necessary to be authorised officers for the purposes of these Regulations, and

(b) revoke any such authorisation.

(2) An appointment under paragraph (1)(a) may be for a specified or unspecified period.

(3) Every authorised officer shall—

(a) be furnished with a certificate of his or her appointment as an authorised officer, and

(b) when exercising a power under these Regulations of an authorised officer, produce the certificate, together with some form of personal identification, if requested to do so by a person affected by the exercise of that power.

(4) An appointment under paragraph (1) of a person as an authorised officer ceases—

(a) when the responsible authority concerned revokes the appointment,

(b) the person dies or resigns from the appointment,

(c) if the appointment is for a specified period, when the period ends,

(d) if the person appointed is an officer of the Irish Financial Services Regulatory Authority, when the person ceases to be such an officer, or

(e) if the person appointed is an officer of an approved stock exchange to which the Bank has delegated functions under Regulation 79, when the person ceases to be such an officer.

Powers of authorised officers

86.(1) An authorised officer may, for the purpose of carrying out an investigation under these Regulations, do all or any of the following—

(a) at all reasonable times enter any premises at which there are reasonable grounds to believe that there are any relevant records,

(b) search and inspect the premises referred to in subparagraph (a) and any relevant records on the premises,

(c) secure for later inspection the premises or any part of the premises in which relevant records are kept or in which the officer has reasonable grounds for believing the relevant records are kept,

(d) require any person to whom these Regulations apply to produce to the officer relevant records, and if the information is in a non-legible form, to reproduce it in a legible form or to give to the officer such information as the officer reasonably requires in relation to entries in the relevant records,

(e) inspect and take copies of relevant records inspected or produced under this Regulation (including, in the case of information in a non-legible form, a copy of all or part of the information in a permanent legible form),

(f) remove and retain any of the relevant records inspected or produced under this Regulation for such period as may be reasonable to facilitate further examination,

(g) require a person to give to the officer information (including give information by way of a written report) that the officer reasonably requires in relation to activities covered by these Regulations and to produce to the officer any relevant records that the person has or has access to,

(h) require a person by or on whose behalf data equipment is or has been used, or any person who has charge of, or is otherwise concerned with the operation of, the data equipment or any associated apparatus or material, to give the officer all reasonable assistance in relation thereto, and

(i) require a person to explain entries in any relevant records.

(2) An authorised officer shall not, except with the consent of the occupier, enter a private dwelling (other than a part of the dwelling used as a place of work) unless the officer has obtained a warrant from a judge of the District Court.

(3) Where any person from whom production of a relevant record is required claims a lien thereon, the production of it shall be without prejudice to the lien.

(4) The requirement to produce any relevant record or report or to provide information or assistance under this Regulation extends to—

(a) a liquidator or receiver of, or any person who is or has been an officer or employee or agent of, a person to whom these Regulations apply, or

(b) any other person who appears to the Bank or the authorised officer to have the relevant record or report in his or her possession or under his or her control or the ability to provide information or assistance, as the case may be.

(5) An authorised officer may, if the officer considers it necessary, be accompanied by a member of the Garda Síochána or by another authorised officer when exercising a power under this Part.

(6) A person who obstructs or impedes an authorised officer in the exercise of his or her powers under this Regulation shall be guilty of an offence.

Warrants

87.(1) When an authorised officer in the exercise of the authorised officer's powers under Regulation 86(1)—

(a) is prevented from entering any premises, or

(b) believes that there are relevant records in a private dwelling,

the authorised officer or the responsible authority by whom the authorised officer was appointed may apply to a judge of the District Court for a warrant under this Regulation authorising the entry by the authorised officer into the premises or the private dwelling, as the case may be.

(2) If on an application under paragraph (1) a judge of the District Court is satisfied, on the information of the applicant, that the authorised officer concerned—

(a) has been prevented from entering any premises, or

(b) has reasonable grounds for believing that there are relevant records in a private dwelling,

then the judge may issue a warrant under the judge's hand authorising the authorised officer, accompanied, if the judge considers it appropriate to so provide, by such number of members of the Garda Síochána as may be specified in the warrant, at any time within 4 weeks from the date of issue of the warrant, to enter, if need be by force, the premises or private dwelling and exercise any of the powers referred to in Regulation 86(1).

Directions by the Bank

88.(1) The Bank may give one or more of the directions specified in paragraph (2) if the Bank considers it necessary to do so in order to—

(a) perform its functions under these Regulations,

(b) prevent any person from contravening or continuing to contravene a provision of these Regulations or any other provision of EU prospectus law, or

(c) protect otherwise the interests of investors.

(2) Each of the following is a direction referred to in paragraph (1), namely a direction to a person—

(a) to do or not to do anything that the Bank may require to be done or not to be done in exercise of its powers under Regulation 82 or 83,

(b) not to dispose of or otherwise dissipate any assets or specified assets of the person or not to do any of those things save where specified conditions are complied with,

(c) not to dispose of or otherwise dissipate any assets or specified assets the beneficial interest in which is vested in another person or persons or not to do any of those things save where specified conditions are complied with,

(d) being a credit institution, not to make any payments from an account held with the institution by a specified person or persons save with the prior consent of the Bank,

(e) not to accept, process or execute any subscription or order on behalf of a specified person,

(f) not to carry on a business (whether on the person's behalf or another's behalf) in a specified manner or otherwise than in a specified manner,

(g) not to engage in any practice that contravenes a provision of these Regulations or any other provision of EU prospectus law,

(h) not to enter into transactions of a specified kind or not to enter into such transactions save to a specified extent or save where specified conditions are complied with,

(i) not to publish specified information,

(j) to publish or disseminate in a specified manner specified information in relation to a public offer, an admission to trading, a relevant person, securities or an advertisement to which Part 12 applies.

(3) A direction under this Regulation shall—

(a) be in writing, and

(b) specify the date from which it shall have effect and the period for which it shall have effect (which shall not exceed 12 months).

(4) A person may apply to the court for, and the court may, if it considers it appropriate to do so, grant, an order setting aside or varying a direction under this Regulation.

(5) The Bank may, as respects a direction under this Regulation which, in its opinion has not been complied with or is unlikely to be complied with, (or, in the case of a direction referred to in paragraph (2)(b) or (c), irrespective of whether it is of that opinion) apply to the court in a summary manner for such order as may be appropriate by way of enforcement of the direction and the court may, as it thinks fit, on the hearing of the application, make or refuse to make an order providing for such relief.

(6) An application for an order under paragraph (5) shall be by motion, and the court when considering the motion may make such interim or interlocutory order as it considers appropriate.

(7) An application under paragraph (4) may not be made if the direction concerned has been the subject of an order granted under paragraph (5) (but without prejudice to the right of a person, the subject of an order granted under paragraph (5), to apply subsequently to the court to have the order varied or discharged).

(8) The court may direct the hearing together of applications made under paragraphs (4) and (5) that relate to the same direction.

(9) The court may, if it thinks fit, vary or discharge an order made under paragraph (5).

(10) An application under paragraph (4) or (5) may be heard otherwise than in public.

(11) The Bank may give a direction amending or revoking a direction given by it under this Regulation but this power may not be exercised—

- (a) if an order under paragraph (5) is for the time being in force in relation to the direction, or
- (b) to extend the period specified in the direction for which it is to have effect.

(12) On the expiry of the period specified in a direction for which it is to have effect, the Bank may give another direction under this Regulation (if it considers it necessary to do so on the grounds specified in paragraph (1)), in like or different terms, to the person concerned.

(13) The powers of the Bank under this Regulation are in addition to those conferred on it by any other enactment to give directions or impose conditions or requirements.

Precautionary Measures

89. In circumstances where the State is a Host Member State and where the Bank finds or has grounds for suspecting—

- (a) a relevant person or a financial institution in charge of a public offer has contravened a provision of these Regulations or another provision of EU prospectus law, or
- (b) there has been a failure by the issuer or offeror to comply with an obligation falling on the issue or offeror by reason of the fact that the securities are admitted to trading,

it shall refer those findings or the fact of those grounds' existence to the competent authority of the Home Member State [and the European Securities and Markets Authority][a].

Amendments

a Words inserted by P(Dir)(A)R (No 2) 2012, reg 2(l).

90(1) If, despite the measures taken by the competent authority of the Home Member State in response to a referral of matters under Regulation 89 by the Bank to it (whether because those measures are inadequate or otherwise) the contravention or failure to comply referred to in that Regulation still persists, the Bank, after informing the competent authority of the Home Member State [and the European Securities and

Markets Authority][a], shall take all the appropriate measures within its power under these Regulations in order to protect investors.

(2) The Bank shall inform the Commission [and the European Securities and Markets Authority][b] of any measures taken by it under paragraph (1) at the earliest opportunity.

Amendments

a Words inserted by P(Dir)(A)R (No 2) 2012, reg 2(m)(i).

b Words inserted by P(Dir)(A)R (No 2) 2012, reg 2(m)(ii).

Privilege

91. Nothing in these Regulations shall compel the disclosure by any person of any information which he or she would, in the opinion of the Court, be entitled to refuse to produce on the grounds of legal professional privilege or authorise the taking possession of any document containing such information which is in his or her possession.

PART 15
ADMINISTRATIVE SANCTIONS

Interpretation (Part 15)

92.(1) In this Part, unless the context otherwise requires—

'adverse assessment' means an assessment in which the assessor has decided that the assessee is committing or has committed a prescribed contravention;

'assessee' means the person the subject of an assessment;

'assessment' means an assessment referred to in Regulation 93;

'assessor' means an assessor appointed under Regulation 93;

'prescribed contravention' means a contravention of—

(a) these Regulations,

(b) any obligation imposed by the Bank pursuant to a power exercised under these Regulations, or

(c) any other provision of EU prospectus law;

'qualifying holding' means—

(a) a direct or indirect holding of shares or other interest in a regulated financial service provider which represents 10% or more of the capital or the voting rights, or

(b) a direct or indirect holding of shares or other interest in a regulated financial service provider which represents less than 10% of the capital or voting rights but which, in the opinion of the Bank, makes it possible to control or exercise a significant influence over the management of the regulated financial service provider;

'regulated financial service provider' has the same meaning as it has in section 2(1) of the Central Bank Act 1942 (No. 22 of 1942) as amended by section 2(g) of the Central Bank and Financial Services Authority of Ireland Act 2004 (No. 21 of 2004);

'sanction' means any sanction referred to in any of paragraphs (a) to (f) of Regulation 99;

'specified sanctions', in relation to an adverse assessment, means the sanction or sanctions referred to in Regulation 93(8) which may be imposed on the assessee.

(2) The provisions of this Part are made for the purposes of enabling the imposition of administrative sanctions.

Bank may appoint assessor

93.(1) Where the Bank has reason to suspect that a prescribed contravention is being committed or has been committed, the Bank may appoint an assessor (or, if the Bank thinks fit to do so, more than one assessor) to conduct an assessment as to—

(a) whether or not the assessee is committing or has committed the contravention, and

(b) if the assessor finds that the assessee is committing or has committed the contravention, the sanction or sanctions, if any, which the assessor considers are appropriate to be imposed on the assessee in respect of the contravention.

(2) The Bank may appoint an assessor who is not an officer, employee or official of the Bank and any such assessor so appointed is an agent of the Bank for the purpose of performing the functions of an assessor under this Part.

(3) The Bank shall provide the assessor with such administrative services (including technical and legal advice) as the Bank considers necessary to enable the assessor to perform the assessor's functions.

(4) The assessor shall, as soon as is practicable after the assessor's appointment as an assessor, give notice of the appointment to the assessee.

(5) The notice under paragraph (4) given to the assessee by the assessor shall contain—

(a) a statement that the assessor is appointed by the Bank under this Regulation,

(b) a statement in summary form of the grounds for conducting the assessment,

(c) the notice, the assessee may—

(i) make submissions in writing to the assessor, and

(ii) request the assessor to be permitted to make oral submissions about the matters to which the notice relates, and

(d) a statement that the assessor shall conduct the assessment even if no submissions referred to in subparagraph (c) are made.

(6) The assessor shall—

(a) consider any submissions made by the assessee, and

(b) conduct such investigations relating to the assessment as the assessor considers appropriate before issuing the assessment.

(7) The assessor shall issue the assessment to the Bank when the assessment is made.

(8) Where the assessor decides that a prescribed contravention is being committed or has been committed, the assessor shall ensure that the assessment includes—

(a) a statement of the grounds upon which the assessor made the assessment that the assessee is committing or has committed the contravention,

(b) a statement in summary form of the evidence upon which the assessment is based, and

(c) a statement of the sanction or sanctions, if any, which the assessor considers are appropriate to be imposed on the assessee in respect of the contravention.

(9) The appointment of an assessor may be for a specified or unspecified period.

(10) Subject to Regulation 100(2), the assessment shall constitute the decision of the Bank, and references in this Part to an adverse assessment shall be construed accordingly.

Revocation of appointment of assessor

94.(1) Where the Bank is satisfied that the assessor has contravened paragraph (2) or is incapacitated, the Bank may revoke the appointment of the assessor at any time.

(2) The assessor (including a person proposed to be appointed as an assessor) shall—

(a) disclose to the Bank any material interest that the assessor may have in any matter that may arise during the assessment,

(b) disclose to the Bank any actual or potential conflict of interest that the assessor may have in conducting an assessment,

(c) not use any inside information (within the meaning of the Market Abuse (Directive 2003/6/EC) Regulations 2005) obtained during an assessment for any purpose other than the performance of the assessor's functions under this Part,

(d) not engage in misconduct during the assessment,

(e) perform the assessor's functions in accordance with the provisions of this Part, and

(f) issue an assessment that is not contrary to law.

Power to require witnesses to appear and give evidence

95.(1) The assessor may by notice given in or outside the State to a person require the person to do one or more of the following—

(a) appear before the assessor to give evidence (including give evidence on oath), custody or control,

(b) for the purposes of subparagraph (a) or (b), attend before the assessor from day to day unless excused from attendance or released from further attendance by the assessor.

(2) The assessor may administer oaths for the purposes of the evidence referred to in paragraph (1) (a).

(3) A witness at a hearing before the assessor has the same liabilities, privileges and immunities as a witness before the Court.

(4) Where a person ('person concerned')—

(a) fails to comply with a notice under paragraph (1),

(b) threatens or insults the assessor or any witness or person required to attend before the assessor,

(c) interrupts the proceedings of, or does not behave in an appropriate manner before, the assessor,

(d) obstructs or attempts to obstruct the assessor,

(e) discloses, or authorises the disclosure of, evidence given before the assessor or any of the contents of a document produced to the assessor that the assessor has instructed not to be published, or

(f) does anything else that, if the assessor were a court of law having power to commit for contempt, would be contempt for that court, then—

(i) the assessor may apply to the Court for an order requiring the person concerned to do one or both of the following—

(I) to comply with the notice under paragraph (1),

(II) to discontinue or not repeat the behaviour falling within any of the provisions of subparagraphs (b) to (f), or behaviour of any similar kind, and

(ii) the Court, if satisfied that there is no reasonable excuse for the failure to comply with the notice under paragraph (1) or for the behaviour concerned, as the case may be, grant the order and such other orders as it considers appropriate to ensure that the person concerned cooperates with the assessor.

Referral to Court on question of law

96.(1) The Bank or the assessor may (including at the request of the assessee) refer a question of law arising in the assessment to the Court for determination by the Court.

(2) Where a question of law is referred under paragraph (1)—

(a) the assessor shall send to the Court all documents before him or her that are relevant to the matter in question, and

(b) at the end of the proceedings in the Court in relation to the reference, the Court shall cause the documents to be returned to the assessor.

Assessee to be issued copy of any adverse assessment, etc.

97.(1) Where the assessment of the assessor is that the assessee is committing or has committed a prescribed contravention, the Bank shall—

(a) issue the assessee with a copy of the adverse assessment (or, as the Bank thinks fit, so much of the adverse assessment as constitutes the statements referred to in Regulation 93(8)), and

(b) advise the assessee that—

(i) the assessee may appeal against the adverse assessment to the Court under Regulation 98, and

(ii) the Bank may apply to the Court under Regulation 102 for an order confirming the adverse assessment (including the specified sanctions).

(2) Where the assessment of the assessor is that the assessee is neither committing nor has committed a prescribed contravention, the Bank shall issue the assessee with a statement to that effect.

Right of appeal against adverse assessment (including specified sanctions)

98.(1) The assessee may appeal to the Court against the adverse assessment (including the specified sanctions) not later than 28 days after the Bank has complied with Regulation 97(1) in relation to the assessee or within such further period as the Court allows.

(2) An appeal under paragraph (1) may be heard otherwise than in public.

(3) The Court may, pending the hearing and determination of an appeal under paragraph (1), make such interim or interlocutory orders as the Court considers necessary in the circumstances.

(4) The Court shall determine an appeal under paragraph (1) by making—

(a) an order confirming, varying or setting aside the adverse assessment (including the specified sanctions), whether in whole or in part, or

(b) an order remitting the case to be decided again by the Bank in accordance with the directions of the Court.

(5) The determination of the Court on the hearing of an appeal under paragraph (1) shall be final, except that a party to the appeal may apply to the Supreme Court to review the determination on a question of law.

(6) For the avoidance of doubt, it is declared that no variation of an adverse assessment under paragraph (4)(a) may provide for the imposition of a sanction on the assessee which is not a sanction referred to in paragraphs (a) to (f) of Regulation 99.

Sanctions that may be imposed by Bank

99. In the case of an adverse assessment, the Bank may impose on the assessee such of the following sanctions as are the specified sanctions—

(a) a private caution or reprimand,

(b) a public caution or reprimand,

(c) subject to Regulation 104(2), a direction to pay to the Bank a monetary penalty (but not exceeding €2,500,000 in any case),

(d) a direction disqualifying the assessee from being concerned in the management of, or having a qualifying holding in, any regulated financial service provider for such time as is specified in the order,

(e) if the assessee is continuing to commit a prescribed contravention, a direction ordering the assessee to cease committing the prescribed contravention,

(f) a direction to pay to the Bank all or a specified part of the costs incurred by the Bank in investigating the matter to which the assessment relates and in holding the assessment (including any costs incurred by authorised officers).

Power to correct assessments

100.(1) Where the assessor or the Bank is satisfied that there is an obvious error in the text of an assessment, the assessor or the Bank, as the case may be, may alter the text of the assessment to remove the error.

(2) Where the text of an assessment is altered under paragraph (1), the text as so altered shall be taken to be the decision of the Bank under Regulation 93(10).

(3) In paragraph (1), 'obvious error', in relation to the text of an assessment, includes—

(a) a clerical or typographical error,

(b) an error arising from an accidental slip or omission, or

(c) a defect of form.

When specified sanctions take effect

101.(1) Where—

(a) no appeal under Regulation 98 against the adverse assessment is lodged with the Court within the period for lodging the appeal, or

(b) an appeal under Regulation 98 against the adverse assessment which has been lodged with the Court within the period for lodging the appeal is withdrawn or abandoned,

then the specified sanctions, as confirmed or varied in the order, if any, obtained under Regulation 102(2)(a), shall take effect on the date of that order or such other date as the Court may specify in that order.

(2) Where an appeal under Regulation 98 against the adverse assessment is lodged with the Court within the period for lodging the appeal, then the specified sanctions, as confirmed or varied in the order, if any, obtained under Regulation 98(4)(a), shall take effect on the date of that order or such other date as the Court may specify in that order.

Enforcement of adverse assessment (including specified sanctions)

102.(1) Where—

(a) no appeal under Regulation 98 against the adverse assessment is lodged with the Court within the period for lodging the appeal, or

(b) an appeal under Regulation 98 against the adverse assessment which has been lodged with the Court within the period for lodging the appeal is withdrawn or abandoned,

then the Bank may apply to the Court for an order confirming the adverse assessment (including the specified sanctions).

(2) The Court shall determine an application under paragraph (1) by making—

(a) an order confirming, varying or setting aside the adverse assessment (including the specified sanctions), whether in whole or in part, or

(b) an order remitting the case to be decided again by the Bank in accordance with the directions of the Court.

(3) The Court shall not hear an application under paragraph (1) unless—

(a) the assessee appears at the hearing as respondent to the application, or

(b) if the assessee does not so appear, the Court is satisfied that a copy of the application has been served on the assessee.

(4) An application under paragraph (1) may be heard otherwise than in public.

(5) The Court may, on an application under paragraph (1), make such interim or interlocutory orders as the Court considers necessary in the circumstances.

(6) The determination of the Court on the hearing of an application under paragraph (1) shall be final, except that the Bank or the respondent, if any, may apply to the Supreme Court to review the determination on a question of law.

(7) For the avoidance of doubt, it is hereby declared that no variation of an adverse assessment under paragraph (2)(a) may provide for the imposition of a sanction on the assessee which is not a sanction referred to in paragraphs (a) to (f) of Regulation 99.

Publication of certain specified sanctions

103. The Bank shall publicly disclose the specified sanctions referred to in paragraphs (c) to (f) of Regulation 99, as confirmed or varied in the order concerned obtained under Regulation 98(4)(a) or 102(2)(a), that are imposed on the assessee unless the Bank considers that the disclosure would—

(a) seriously jeopardise the financial markets, or

(b) cause disproportionate damage to the parties involved.

Person not liable to be penalised twice for same contravention

104.(1) Where—

(a) a sanction referred to in Regulation 99(c) is to be imposed on the assessee by virtue of an order obtained under Regulation 98(4)(a) or 102(2)(a), and

(b) the acts which constitute the prescribed contravention to which the sanction relates also constitute an offence under a law of the State,

then the asses see is not, in respect of those acts, liable to be prosecuted or punished for that offence under that law.

(2) A sanction referred to in Regulation 99(c) in respect of a prescribed contravention shall not be imposed on the assessee where—

(a) the assessee has been found guilty or not guilty of having committed an offence under a provision of—

(i) these Regulations, or

(ii) Part 5 of the Investment Funds, Companies and Miscellaneous Pensions 2005 Act, and

(b) all or some of the acts constituting that offence also constitute the prescribed contravention.

Person not to be concerned in management of regulated financial service provider while disqualified

105.(1) A regulated financial service provider shall ensure that a person shall not be concerned in the management of, or have a qualifying holding in, the financial service provider while the person is subject to a sanction referred to in Regulation 99(d) that is in force.

(2) A regulated financial service provider who contravenes paragraph (1) shall be guilty of an offence.

Power of the Bank to resolve suspected contraventions, etc.

106.(1) Where the Bank has reason to suspect that a person ('relevant party') is committing or has committed a prescribed contravention, it may enter into an agreement in writing with the relevant party to resolve the matter (including at any time before an assessment, if any, has been issued in respect of the relevant party).

(2) An agreement entered into under paragraph (1)—

(a) is binding on the Bank and the relevant party, and

(b) may include terms under which the relevant party accepts the imposition of sanctions.

(3) An agreement entered into under paragraph (1) may be enforced by the Bank or the relevant party in a court of competent jurisdiction.

PART 16

PENALTIES, GENERAL AND OTHER MISCELLANEOUS PROVISIONS

Certain Offences and Penalties generally

107.(1) If the contravention in respect of which a person is convicted of an offence under these Regulations is continued after the conviction, the person shall be guilty of a further offence on every day on which the contravention continues.

(2) Where any offence is committed under these Regulations by a body corporate and is proved to have been committed with the consent, connivance or approval of or to have been attributable to the wilful neglect on the part of any person, being a director, manager, secretary or other officer of the body corporate or a person who was purporting to act in any such capacity, that person as well as the body corporate shall be guilty of an offence and is liable to be proceeded against and punished as if he or she was guilty of the first mentioned offence.

(3) A person who is guilty of—

(a) an offence under these Regulations other than an offence referred to in subparagraph (b), or

(b) one or more further offences under paragraph (1), for each such offence,

shall be liable on summary conviction to a [class A fine][a] or imprisonment for a term not exceeding 12 months or both.

(4) Each of the following is an offence to which section 47 (penalties on indictment) of the Investment Funds, Companies and Miscellaneous Provisions Act 2005 applies—

(a) an offence under Regulation 14,

(b) an offence under Regulation 15,

(c) an offence under paragraph (1) or (2) that relates to an offence referred to in subparagraph (a) or (b).

Amendments

a As implicitly substituted for "fine not exceeding €5,000" by Fines Act 2010, s 4. A class A fine currently means a fine not exceeding €5,000.

Annual Report of Bank

108. The Bank shall provide the Minister with a copy of the extract relating to the performance of its functions under these Regulations from its annual report to the Minster for Finance under section 300 of the Central Bank Act 1942.

Fees

109. Fees shall be payable pursuant to section 33K of the Central Bank Act 1942 in respect of the performance by the Bank of its functions under these Regulations.

Revocations and Amendments

110.(1) The following are revoked—

(a) the European Communities (Stock Exchange) (Amendment) Regulations 1991 (S.I. No. 18 of 1991),

(b) the European Communities (Transferable Securities and Stock Exchange) Regulations 1992 (S.I. No. 202 of 1992),

(c) the European Communities (Stock Exchange) (Amendment) Regulations 1994 (S.I. No. 234 of 1994).

(2) The European Communities (Stock Exchange) Regulations 1984 (S.I. No. 282 of 1984) are amended as specified in Schedule 3 to these Regulations.

Transitional Provisions

111. Issuers which are incorporated in a third country and whose securities have already been admitted to trading on a regulated market prior to 31 December 2003 and who choose the State as their competent authority in accordance with these Regulations shall notify their decision in writing to the Bank by 31 December 2005.

112. Notwithstanding Regulation 12, credit institutions or other financial institutions equivalent to credit institutions within the meaning of Article 5 of Directive 89/29 8/EEC may continue to make public offers of debt securities or other transferable securities equivalent to debt securities issued in a continuous or repeated manner within the State up to 31 December 2008 without the need to publish a prospectus under these Regulations in circumstances where but for this Regulation they would have been obliged to publish a prospectus under these Regulations.

113. Regulations 111 and 112 are in addition to the provisions of Article 35 of the Prospectus Regulation (which also contains transitional provisions).

Schedule 1

Regulation 31

1. Responsible Persons

Subject to the provisions of this Schedule, responsibility for the information given in a prospectus attaches in the following cases.

2. Equity securities

(1) This paragraph applies to a case in which the prospectus relates to equity securities (other than securities convertible into shares issued by the issuer of the underlying shares or by an entity belonging to the issuer's group).

(2) In a case to which this paragraph applies, each of the following persons is, subject to the other provisions of this Schedule, responsible for the prospectus:

- (a) the issuer of the securities;
- (b) if the issuer is a body corporate:
  - (i) each person who is a director of that body corporate when the prospectus is published; and
  - (ii) each person who has authorised himself or herself to be named, and is named, in the prospectus as a director or as having agreed

  to become a director of that body corporate either immediately or at a future time;
- (c) each person who accepts, and is stated in the prospectus as accepting, responsibility for the prospectus;
- (d) if the case involves an offer of securities to the public:
  - (i) the offeror of the securities, if this is not the issuer; and
  - (ii) if the offeror is a body corporate and is not the issuer, each person who is a director of that body corporate when the prospectus is published;
- (e) if the case involves the admission to trading of securities:
  - (i) the person seeking admission, if this is not the issuer; and
  - (ii) if the person seeking admission is a body corporate and is not the issuer, each person who is a director of that body corporate when the prospectus is published; and
- (f) each person not falling within any of the preceding provisions of this subparagraph who has authorised the contents of the prospectus.

3. All other securities

(1) This paragraph applies to a case in which the prospectus relates to securities that are not securities to which paragraph 2 applies.

(2) In a case to which this paragraph applies, each of the following persons is, subject to the other provisions of this Schedule, responsible for the prospectus:

- (a) the issuer of the securities;
- (b) each person who accepts, and is stated in the prospectus as accepting, responsibility for the prospectus;
- (c) if the case involves an offer of securities to the public, the offeror of the securities, if this is not the issuer;

(d) if the case involves the admission to trading of securities, the person seeking admission, if this is not the issuer;

(e) if there is a guarantor for the issue, the guarantor in relation to information in the prospectus that relates to the guarantor and the guarantee; and

(f) each person not falling within any of the preceding provisions of this subparagraph who has authorised the contents of the prospectus.

4. Issuer not responsible if it has not authorised offer or admission to trading

An issuer is not responsible for a prospectus under paragraph 2(2)(a) or (b) or paragraph 3(2)(a) unless the issuer has made or authorised the offer of securities to the public or the application for admission to trading in relation to which the prospectus was published.

5. Publication without directors consent

A person is not responsible for a prospectus under paragraph 2(2)(b)(i) if it is published without his or her knowledge or consent and on becoming aware of its publication he or she, as soon as practicable, gives reasonable public notice that it was published without his or her knowledge or consent.

6. Offeror not responsible in certain circumstances

A person is not responsible for a prospectus under paragraph 2(2)(d) or paragraph 3(2)(c) if:

(a) the issuer is responsible for the prospectus in accordance with this Schedule;

(b) the prospectus was drawn up primarily by the issuer, or by one or more persons acting on behalf of the issuer; and

(c) the offeror is making the offer in association with the issuer.

7. Person may accept responsibility for, or authorise, part of contents

When accepting responsibility for a prospectus under—

(a) paragraph 2(2)(c) or paragraph 3(2)(b), or

(b) authorising the contents of a prospectus under paragraph 2(2)(f) [or paragraph 3(2)(f)][a],

a person may state that her or she does so only in relation to specified parts of the prospectus, or only in specified respects, and in that case the person is responsible under those paragraphs:

(i) only to the extent specified; and

(ii) only if the material in question is included in (or substantially in) the form and context to which the person has agreed.

Amendments

a Words 'or paragraph 3(2)(f)' inserted by P(Dir)(A)R 2012, reg 3(v).

Schedule 2

Regulation 74

Advertising Principles

1. Advertisements shall state that a prospectus has been or will be published and indicate where investors are or will be able to obtain it.

2. (a) Advertisements shall be clearly recognisable as such.

   (b) The information contained in an advertisement shall not be inaccurate, or misleading.

   (c) The information shall also be consistent with the information contained in the prospectus, if already published, or with the information required to be in the prospectus, if the prospectus is published afterwards.

3. In any case, all information concerning the offer to the public or the admission to trading disclosed in an oral or written form, even if not for advertising purposes, shall be consistent with that contained in the prospectus.

4. (a) Where in connection with an offer of securities to which subparagraph (a), (b), (c) or (d) of Regulation 9(1) applies material information provided by an issuer or an offeror and addressed exclusively to some only of the investors to whom the offer is addressed, including without limitation information disclosed in the context of meetings relating to an offer of securities, shall be disclosed to all the investors to whom the offer is addressed.

   (b) In circumstances where a prospectus is required to be published under EU prospectus law, any information as referred to in subparagraph (a) provided by an issuer or offeror to an investor or group of investors and not disclosed to all the investors to whom the offer of securities is addressed shall be disclosed in the prospectus or in a supplement.

Schedule 3

Amendment of European Communities (Stock Exchange) Regulations 1984

Regulation 110.

[...][a]

Amendments

a Sch 3 effects 14 changes to EC(SE)R 1984. See amended regs.

Market Abuse (Directive 2003/6/EC) Regulations 2005

SI 342/2005

ARRANGEMENT OF REGULATIONS

PART 1

PRELIMINARY

Regulations

PART 2

INSIDER DEALING AND MARKET MANIPULATION

PART 3

FAIR PRESENTATION OF RECOMMENDATIONS

PART 4
POWERS OF THE BANK

PART 5
ENFORCEMENT PROVISIONS

PART 6
OFFENCES AND REPORTS

SCHEDULE 1
PROVISIONS APPLICABLE TO THE DEFINITION OF "ACCEPTED MARKET PRACTICES"

SCHEDULE 2
PROVISIONS APPLICABLE TO PARAGRAPH (A) OF THE DEFINITION OF "MARKET MANIPULATION"

I, Micheál Martin, Minister for Enterprise, Trade and Employment, in exercise of the powers conferred on me by section 30 of the Investment Funds, Companies and Miscellaneous Provisions Act 2005 (No. 12 of 2005) and for the purpose of giving effect to the 2003 Market Abuse Directive (being Directive 2003/6/EC of the European Parliament and of the Council of 28 January 2003 (OJ L096, 12.04.2003, p.16) on insider dealing and market manipulation (market abuse)) and for the other purposes mentioned in that section, hereby make the following regulations:

PART 1
PRELIMINARY

1 Citation, construction and commencement

(1) These Regulations may be cited as the Market Abuse (Directive 2003/6/EC) Regulations 2005.

(2) These Regulations and the Companies Acts 1963 to 2005 shall be construed together as one.

(3) Subject to paragraph (4), these Regulations shall come into operation on 6 July 2005.

(4) Regulations 11 and 12 and Part 3 shall come into operation on 1 October 2005.

2 Interpretation generally

(1) In these Regulations, unless the context otherwise requires—

'accepted market practices' means practices that are—

(a) reasonably expected in one or more financial markets, and

(b) accepted by the Bank in accordance with Schedule 1;

'act' includes an omission (and, accordingly, any reference to an act done includes an omission made);

'approved stock exchange' has the same meaning as it has in the Stock Exchange Act 1995 (No. 9 of 1995);

'Bank' means the Central Bank and Financial Services Authority of Ireland;

'contravention' includes, in relation to any provision, a failure to comply with that provision and 'contravene' shall be construed accordingly;

'Court' means the High Court;

'credit institution' means any person as defined in Article 1(1) of Directive 2000/1 2/EC of the European Parliament and of the Council of 20 March 2000 (OJ L126, 26.05.2000, p. 1) relating to the taking up and pursuit of the business of credit institutions;

'EEA Agreement' means the Agreement on the European Economic Area signed at Oporto on 2 May 1992, as amended for the time being;

'EEA State' means a state which is a contracting party to the EEA Agreement;

'enactment' includes an instrument made under an enactment;

'financial instrument' means—

(a) transferable securities as defined in Article 4 of Council Directive 93/22/EEC of 10 May 1993 (OJ L141, 11.06.1993, p. 27) on investment services in the securities field,

(b) units in collective investment undertakings,

(c) money-market instruments,

(d) financial futures contracts, including equivalent cash-settled instruments,

(e) forward interest rate agreements,

(f) interest-rate, currency and equity swaps,

(g) derivatives on commodities,

(h) any other instrument admitted to trading on a regulated market in a Member State or for which a request for admission to trading on such a market has been made, and

(i) options to acquire or dispose of any instrument falling into any of paragraphs (a) to (h) of this definition, including equivalent cash-settled instruments in particular options on currency and on interest rates;

'functions' includes powers and duties, and references to the performance of functions include, as respects powers and duties, references to the exercise of powers and the carrying out of duties;

'information of a precise nature' means information that—

(a) indicates—

(i) a set of circumstances which exists or may reasonably be expected to come into existence, or

(ii) an event which has occurred or may reasonably be expected to occur, and

(b) is specific enough to enable a conclusion to be drawn as to the possible effect of that set of circumstances or event, as the case may be, on the prices of financial instruments or related derivative financial instruments;

'information which, if it were made public, would be likely to have a significant effect on the prices of financial instruments or related derivative financial instruments' means information that a reasonable investor would be likely to use as part of the basis of the investor's investment decisions, and includes cognate expressions;

'inside information' means—

(a) information of a precise nature relating directly or indirectly to one or more issuers of financial instruments or to one or more financial instruments which has not been made public and which, if it were made public, would be likely to have a significant effect on the price of those financial instruments or on the price of related derivative financial instruments,

(b) in relation to derivatives on commodities and subject to paragraph (2), information of a precise nature which has not been made public, and relating, directly or indirectly, to one or more such derivatives and which users of markets on which such derivatives are traded would expect to receive in accordance with accepted market practices on those markets, or

(c) for persons charged with the execution of orders concerning financial instruments, information conveyed by a client and relating to the client's pending orders, which is of a precise nature, which relates directly or indirectly to one or more issuers of financial instruments or to one or more financial instruments, and which, if it were made public, would be likely to have a significant effect on the prices of those financial instruments or on the price of related derivative financial instruments;

'insider dealing' means any act which contravenes Regulation 5(1) or (2);

'investment firm' means investment firm as defined in Article 1(2) of Council Directive 93/22/EEC;

'issuer' means an issuer of any financial instrument to which these Regulations apply pursuant to Regulation 4;

'market abuse' means—

(a) insider dealing, or

(b) market manipulation;

'market manipulation' means—

(a) transactions or orders to trade—

(i) which give, or are likely to give, false or misleading signals as to the supply of, demand for or price of financial instruments, or

(ii) which secure, by a person, or persons acting in collaboration, the price of one or several financial instruments at an abnormal or artificial level,

unless the person who entered into the transactions or issued the orders to trade establishes that the person's reasons for so doing are legitimate and the transactions or orders to trade, as the case may be, conform to accepted market practices on the regulated market concerned,

(b) transactions or orders to trade which employ fictitious devices or any other form of deception or contrivance, or

(c) dissemination of information through the media, including the Internet, or by any other means, which gives, or is likely to give, false or misleading signals as to financial instruments, including the dissemination of rumours and false or misleading news, where the person who made the dissemination knew, or ought to have known, that the information was false or misleading;

'market operator'—

(a) means a person who—

(i) manages the business of a regulated market,

(ii) operates the business of a regulated market, or

(iii) manages and operates the business of a regulated market,

(b) includes a regulated market which—

(i) manages its own business as a regulated market,

(ii) operates its own business as a regulated market, or

(iii) manages and operates its own business as a regulated market;

'Member State' means a Member State of the European Communities and an EEA State;

'notify' means notify in writing;

'regulated market' means regulated market as defined in Article 1(13) of Council Directive 93/22/EEC;

'relevant community acts' means—

(a) the 2003 Market Abuse Directive,

(b) the supplemental Directives, and

(c) the Market Abuse Regulation.

(2) For the purposes of paragraph (b) of the definition of 'inside information', users of markets on which derivatives on commodities are traded shall be deemed to expect to receive information—

(a) relating, directly or indirectly, to one or more such derivatives, and

(b) which is—

(i) routinely made available to the users of those markets, or

(ii) required to be disclosed in accordance with legal or regulatory provisions, market rules, contracts or customs on the relevant underlying commodity market or commodity derivatives market.

(3) For the purposes of demonstrating the operation of the definition of 'market manipulation', the following examples are derived from that definition—

(a) conduct by a person, or persons acting in collaboration, to secure a dominant position over the supply of or demand for a financial instrument which has the effect of fixing, directly or indirectly, purchase or sale prices or creating other unfair trading conditions,

(b) the buying or selling of financial instruments at the close of the market with the effect of misleading investors acting on the basis of closing prices,

(c) taking advantage of occasional or regular access to the traditional or electronic media by voicing an opinion about a financial instrument (or indirectly about its issuer) while having previously taken positions on that instrument and profiting subsequently from the impact of opinions voiced on the price of that instrument, without having simultaneously disclosed that conflict of interest to the public in a proper and effective way.

(4) Without prejudice to the examples set out in paragraph (3) and for the purposes of applying paragraph (a) of the definition of 'market manipulation', the non-exhaustive signals set out in Schedule 2, which should not necessarily be deemed in themselves to constitute market manipulation, shall be taken into account when transactions or orders to trade are examined by market participants and competent authorities.

(5) Without prejudice to the examples set out in paragraph (3) and for the purposes of applying paragraph (b) of the definition of 'market manipulation', the non-exhaustive signals set out in Schedule 3, which should not necessarily be deemed in themselves to constitute market manipulation, shall be taken into account when transactions or orders to trade are examined by market participants and competent authorities.

(6) A word or expression that is used in these Regulations and is also used in the relevant community acts shall have in these Regulations the same meaning as it has in the relevant community acts unless the contrary intention appears.

(7) A reference in these Regulations—

(a) to any other enactment or to a Directive or Regulation of the Council or Commission of the European Communities shall, unless the context otherwise requires, be construed as a reference to that enactment, Directive or Regulation as amended or extended by any other enactment or, as the case may be, Directive or Regulation of the Council or Commission of the European Communities European Communities (including, in the case of an enactment, by a Regulation of these Regulations),

(b) a reference to a Regulation or Part is a reference to a Regulation or Part of these Regulations unless it is indicated that a reference to some other provision is intended,

(c) a reference to a Schedule is a reference to a Schedule to these Regulations unless it is indicated that a reference to some other provision is intended,

(d) a reference to a paragraph, subparagraph or clause is a reference to a paragraph, subparagraph or clause of the provision in which the reference occurs unless it is indicated that a reference to some other provision is intended.

3 Single administrative competent authority

The Bank is designated as the single administrative competent authority for the purposes of the Directive.

4 Application

(1) Subject to Regulations 5(4), 10(12) and 11(6), these Regulations shall apply to any financial instrument—

(a) admitted to trading on a regulated market in at least one Member State, or

(b) for which a request for admission to trading on a regulated market in at least one Member State has been made, whether or not any transaction in or relating to the financial instrument takes place on that market.

(2) These Regulations shall apply to—

(a) actions carried out in the State or abroad concerning financial instruments that—

(i) are admitted to trading on a regulated market situated in or operating in the State, or

(ii) for which a request for admission to trading on a regulated market situated in or operating in the State has been made, and

(b) actions carried out in the State concerning financial instruments that—

(i) are admitted to trading on a regulated market in a Member State, or

(ii) for which a request for admission to trading on a regulated market in a Member State has been made.

(3) These Regulations do not apply to transactions carried out in pursuit of monetary, exchange rate or public debt management policy by—

(a) a Member State,

(b) the European System of Central Banks,

(c) the Bank,

(d) the Minister for Finance, or

(e) the National Treasury Management Agency.

PART 2
INSIDER DEALING AND MARKET MANIPULATION

5 Insider dealing

(1) Subject to paragraphs (4) and (5) and Regulations 8(2) and (4) and 9(1), a person to whom this paragraph applies who possesses inside information shall not use that information by acquiring or disposing of, or by trying to acquire or dispose of, for the person's own account or for the account of a third party, directly or indirectly, financial instruments to which that information relates.

(2) A person to whom paragraph (1) applies shall not—

(a) disclose inside information to any other person unless such disclosure is made in the normal course of the exercise of the first-mentioned person's employment, profession or duties, or

(b) recommend or induce another person, on the basis of inside information, to acquire or dispose of financial instruments to which that information relates.

(3) Paragraph (1) shall apply to—

(a) any person who possesses the inside information concerned—

(i) by virtue of the person's membership of the administrative, management or supervisory bodies of the issuer of the financial instrument,

(ii) by virtue of the person's holding in the capital of the issuer,

(iii) by virtue of having access to the information through the exercise of the person's employment, profession or duties, or

(iv) by virtue of the person's criminal activities,

(b) if any person falling within subparagraph (a) is a legal person, and without prejudice to the generality of Regulation 52, any natural person who takes part in the decision to carry out, for the account of the legal person, any transaction in financial instruments, or

(c) subject to regulation 8(3), any other person who possesses the inside information concerned while the person knows, or ought to have known, that it is inside information.

(4) This Regulation shall also apply to a financial instrument which does not fall within Regulation 4(1) but the value of which depends on a financial instrument which falls within Regulation 4(1).

(5) Paragraph (1) does not apply to any transaction conducted in the discharge of an obligation—

(a) to acquire or dispose of any financial instrument,

(b) that has become due, and

(c) that results from an agreement concluded before the person concerned possessed the inside information concerned.

(6) Having regard to section 33(1) of the Investment Funds, Companies and Miscellaneous Provisions Act 2005, it is declared that—

(a) the purpose of paragraphs (1), (3)(a) and (b) and (5) is to implement Article 2 of the 2003 Market Abuse Directive,

(b) the purpose of paragraph (3)(c) is to implement Article 4 of the 2003 Market Abuse Directive, and

(c) the purpose of paragraph (2) is to implement Article 3 of the 2003 Market Abuse Directive.

6 Market manipulation

(1) A person shall not engage in market manipulation.

(2) Having regard to section 33(2) of the Investment Funds, Companies and Miscellaneous Provisions Act 2005, it is declared that the purpose of paragraph (1) is to implement Article 5 of the 2003 Market Abuse Directive.

7 Preventing and detecting market manipulation practices

(1) The Bank shall require that market operators—

(a) so structure their operations such that market manipulation practices are prevented and detected, and

(b) report to it on a regular basis in accordance with arrangements drawn up by the Bank.

(2) Without prejudice to the generality of paragraph (1), the Bank may impose requirements under that paragraph concerning transparency of transactions concluded, total disclosure of price- regularisation agreements, a fair system of order pairing, introduction of an effective atypical order detection scheme, sufficiently robust financial instrument reference price-fixing schemes and clarity of rules on the suspension of transactions.

8 Exemption for actions taken in conformity with takeover rules

(1) A word or expression that is used in this Regulation and is also used in the Irish Takeover Panel Act 1997 (No. 5 of 1997) shall have the same meaning in this Regulation as it has in that Act.

(2) Having access to inside information relating to another company and using it in the context of a public takeover offer for the purpose of gaining control of that company or proposing a merger with that company in conformity with rules made under section 8 of the Irish Takeover Panel Act 1997 does not of itself constitute market abuse and is not a contravention of Regulation 5 or 6.

(3) Regulation 5(3)(c) does not preclude a company ('first-mentioned company') from dealing in the financial instruments of another company ('second-mentioned company') at any time by reason only of information in the possession of an officer of the first-mentioned company that—

(a) was received by the officer in the course of the carrying out of the officer's duties, and

(b) consists only of the fact that the first-mentioned company proposes to acquire or attempt to acquire financial instruments of the second-mentioned company.

(4) Actions taken in compliance with rules made under section 8 of the Irish Takeover Panel Act 1997 (in particular rules relating to the timing, dissemination or availability, content and standard of care applicable to a disclosure, announcement, communication or release of information during the course of a public takeover offer) does not of itself constitute market abuse and is not a contravention of Regulation 5 or 6 provided that the relevant general principles set out in the Irish Takeover Panel Act 1997 are also complied with.

(5) Nothing in these Regulations affects the jurisdiction and role of the Irish Takeover Panel under the Irish Takeover Panel Act 1997.

(6) Without prejudice to the generality of paragraph (5), the Irish Takeover Panel, in performing its functions under the Irish Takeover Panel Act 1997, and the Bank, in performing its functions under these Regulations, shall have due regard to the other's performance of functions under that Act or these Regulations, as the case may be.

9 Buy-back programmes or stabilisation measures

(1) Regulations 5 and 6 do not apply—

(a) to trading in own shares in buy-back programmes, or to trading to secure the stabilisation of a financial instrument, provided that such trading is carried out in accordance with the Market Abuse Regulation (the text of which is set out, for convenience of reference, in Schedule 5), or

(b) to the purchase of own shares carried out in accordance with Part XI of the Companies Act 1990 (No. 33 of 1990).

(2) Subject to paragraph (4), the acquisition or disposal of interests in relevant share capital by a person during the stabilising period concerned, which—

(a) is done for the purpose of stabilising or maintaining the market price of securities, and

(b) is done in conformity with the Market Abuse Regulation,

shall be disregarded during the stabilising period for the purposes of sections 67 to 79 of the Companies Act 1990.

(3) Any interest in relevant share capital which—

- (a) was acquired by a person during the stabilising period for the purpose of stabilising or maintaining the market price of securities,
- (b) was so acquired in accordance with the Market Abuse Regulation, and
- (c) continues to be held by such person at the end of the stabilising period as provided in the Market Abuse Regulation,

shall be treated, for the purposes of sections 67 to 79 of the Companies Act 1990, as having been acquired by the person on the first day following the end of the stabilising period that is not a Saturday, Sunday or public holiday.

(4) Section 91(4) of the Companies Act 1990 shall operate to determine the interests which are to be notified to the Irish Stock Exchange Limited, and the manner in which they are to be so notified, under section 91(2) of that Act.

(5) For the purposes of this Regulation—

'buy-back programme' means a programme as described in, and operated in accordance with, the Market Abuse Regulation;

'relevant share capital' has the same meaning as it has in section 67(2) of the Companies Act 1990;

'stabilising period' means the limited time period provided in Article 8(2) of the Market Abuse Regulation.

10 Disclosure of inside information

(1) Subject to paragraph (7), the issuer of a financial instrument shall publicly disclose without delay inside information—

- (a) which directly concerns the issuer, and
- (b) in a manner that enables fast access and complete, correct and timely assessment of the information by the public.

(2) Without prejudice to any measures taken under paragraph (1), the issuer shall, for a period of not less than 6 months, post on the issuer's Internet site or sites any inside information that the issuer is required to publicly disclose.

(3) Subject to paragraph (7), the issuer shall not combine, in a manner likely to be misleading, the provision of inside information to the public with the marketing of the issuer's activities.

(4) The issuer shall be deemed to have complied with paragraph (1) where, upon the coming into existence of a set of circumstances or the occurrence of an event, albeit not yet formalised, the issuer has without delay informed the public of those circumstances or that event, as the case may be.

(5) Where there is any significant change concerning already publicly disclosed inside information, the issuer shall publicly and without delay disclose the change—

- (a) immediately after the change occurs, and
- (b) through the same channel as the one used for public disclosure of the original information.

(6) The issuer shall take reasonable care to ensure that the disclosure of inside information to the public is synchronised as closely as possible between all categories of investors in regulated markets in all Member States on which—

(a) the issuer's financial instruments concerned are admitted to trading, or

(b) the issuer has requested admission to trading of the financial instruments concerned.

(7) The issuer may delay the public disclosure of inside information to avoid prejudicing the issuer's legitimate interests provided that—

(a) the failure to disclose the information would not be likely to mislead the public, and

(b) the issuer is able to ensure the confidentiality of the information.

(8) For the purposes of paragraph (7), 'legitimate interests' may include any of the following circumstances—

(a) negotiations in course, or related elements, where the outcome or normal pattern of those negotiations would be likely to be affected by public disclosure (in particular, in the event that the financial viability of the issuer is in grave and imminent danger, although not within the scope of the applicable insolvency law, public disclosure of information may be delayed for a limited period where such a public disclosure would seriously jeopardise the interest of existing and potential shareholders by undermining the conclusion of specific negotiations designed to ensure the long-term financial recovery of the issuer),

(b) decisions taken or contracts made by the management body of the issuer which need the approval of another body of the issuer in order to become effective, provided that—

(i) the organisation of the issuer requires separation between those bodies, and

(ii) a public disclosure of the information before such approval together with the simultaneous announcement that this approval is still pending would jeopardise the correct assessment of the information by the public.[c]

(9) In order to ensure the confidentiality of inside information that is not disclosed to the public under paragraph (7), the issuer shall control access to the information and, in particular—

(a) take effective measures to deny access to the information to persons other than those who require it for the exercise of their functions within the issuer,

(b) take the measures necessary to ensure that a person with access to the information acknowledges the legal and regulatory duties entailed and is aware of the sanctions attaching to the misuse or improper circulation of the information, and

(c) without prejudice to paragraph (11), have in place measures which allow immediate public disclosure in case the issuer was not able to ensure the confidentiality of the information.

(10) Subject to paragraph (11), where the issuer, or a person acting on the issuer's behalf or for the issuer's account, discloses any inside information to any third party in the normal exercise of the issuer's or person's employment, profession or duties, the issuer

or person, as the case may be, shall make complete and effective public disclosure of that information, simultaneously in the case of an intentional disclosure and without delay in the case of a non-intentional disclosure.

(11) Paragraph (10) does not apply where the third party receiving the inside information is a person under an obligation of confidentiality.

(12) This Regulation does not apply to the issuer of the financial instrument concerned where the issuer neither—

(a) made a request for the financial instrument to be admitted to trading on a regulated market, nor

(b) approved the admission of the financial instrument to trading on a regulated market.

11 Disclosure of information (additional requirements)

(1) Each relevant person shall draw up a list—

(a) of those persons working for the relevant person, under a contract of employment or otherwise, who have access to inside information relating directly or indirectly to the relevant person who is the issuer, and

(b) containing the information set out in Schedule 4.

(2) Each relevant person shall regularly update the list drawn up by the relevant person pursuant to paragraph (1).

(3) The Bank may request from any relevant person any list drawn up by the relevant person pursuant to paragraph (1).

(4) A relevant person shall comply with a request under paragraph (3) made to the relevant person.

(5) Subject to paragraph (6), in this Regulation, 'relevant person' means—

(a) the issuer,

(b) a person acting on behalf of the issuer, or

(c) a person acting for the account of the issuer.

(6) This Regulation does not apply to the issuer of the financial instrument concerned (or persons acting on behalf of, or for the account of, the issuer) where the issuer neither—

(a) made a request for the financial instrument to be admitted to trading on a regulated market, nor

(b) approved the admission of the financial instrument to trading on a regulated market.

12 Managers' transactions

(1) Subject to paragraphs (3) and (4), persons discharging managerial responsibilities, within an issuer of financial instruments registered in the State, and, where applicable, persons closely associated with them, shall notify to the Bank transactions conducted on their own account relating to shares of the issuer, or to derivatives or other financial instruments linked to them.

(2) Persons discharging managerial responsibilities, within an issuer of financial instruments not registered in the State, and, where applicable, persons closely associated

with them, shall notify transactions conducted on their own account relating to shares of the issuer, or to derivatives on other instruments linked to them—

(a) if the issuer is registered in another Member State, in accordance with the rules of notification relating thereto of that Member State,

(b) if the issuer is not registered in another Member State, to the competent authority of the Member State to which the issuer is required to file the annual information in relation to shares in accordance with Article 10 of Directive 2003/71/EC of the European Parliament and of the Council of 4 November 2003 (OJ L345, 31. 12. 2003, p. 64), including the Directive as it stands amended for the time being.

(3) Notification of transactions required by paragraph (1) and, where applicable, paragraph (2)(b), shall be made to the Bank within 5 working days of the day of the transaction.

(4) Subject to paragraph (5), the Bank may provide that, where the total amount of the transactions is less than €5,000 at the end of a calendar year, no notification is required or notification may be delayed until 31 January of the following year.

(5) For the purposes of paragraph (4), the total amount of transactions shall be calculated by adding together—

(a) the transactions conducted on the own account of a person discharging managerial responsibilities within an issuer, and

(b) the transactions conducted on the own account of persons closely associated with the person referred to in subparagraph (a).

(6) A notification required by paragraph (1) shall contain the following information—

(a) the name of the person discharging managerial responsibilities within the issuer or, where applicable, the name of a person closely associated with such a person,

(b) the reason for responsibility to notify,

(c) the name of the relevant issuer,

(d) a description of the financial instrument,

(e) the nature of the transaction (for example, acquisition or disposal),

(f) the date and place of the transaction, and

(g) the price and volume of the transaction.

(7) The Bank shall ensure that public access to information concerning the transactions notified to it under this Regulation is readily available, at least on an individual basis, without delay.

(8) For the purposes of this Regulation—

'person closely associated', in relation to a person discharging managerial responsibilities within an issuer of financial instruments, means—

(a) the spouse of the person discharging managerial responsibilities,

(b) dependent children of the person discharging managerial responsibilities,

(c) other relatives of the person discharging managerial responsibilities, who have shared the same household as that person for at least one year on the date of the transaction concerned,

(d) any person—

(i) the managerial responsibilities of which are discharged by a person—

(I) discharging managerial responsibilities within the issuer, or

(II) referred to in paragraph (a), (b) or (c) of this definition,

(ii) that is directly or indirectly controlled by a person referred to in subparagraph (i) of paragraph (d) of this definition,

(iii) that is set up for the benefit of a person referred to in subparagraph (i) of paragraph (d) of this definition, or

(iv) the economic interests of which are substantially equivalent to those of a person referred to in subparagraph (i) of paragraph (d) of this definition;

'person discharging managerial responsibilities', in relation to an issuer of financial instruments, means a person who is—

(a) a member of the administrative, management or supervisory bodies of the issuer, or

(b) a senior executive—

(i) who is not a member of the bodies referred to in paragraph (a) of this definition,

(ii) having regular access to inside information relating, directly or indirectly, to the issuer, and

(iii) having the power to make managerial decisions affecting the future developments and business prospects of the issuer.

13 Suspicious transactions to be notified

(1) Any prescribed person who reasonably suspects that a transaction might constitute market abuse shall notify the Bank without delay (which notification may be a telephone call to a telephone number specified by the Bank provided that a notification in writing to the same effect is made as soon as is practicable after that call).

(2) Any prescribed person shall decide on a case-by-case basis whether there are reasonable grounds for suspecting that a transaction involves market abuse after taking into account the elements constituting market abuse.

(3) The Bank shall, on receipt of a notification under paragraph (1), transmit the notification immediately to the relevant competent authority of each regulated market on which the financial instrument concerned—

(a) is admitted to trading, or

(b) is the subject of a request to be admitted to trading of which the Bank is aware.

(4) A prescribed person required under paragraph (1) to notify the Bank shall transmit to the Bank the following information—

(a) a description of the transactions concerned, including the type of order (such as limit order, market order or other characteristics of the order) and the type of trading market (such as block trade),

(b) the reason or reasons for suspecting that the transactions might constitute market abuse,

(c) the names, or means of identification, of the persons on behalf of whom the transactions have been carried out, and of other persons involved in the transactions,

(d) the capacity in which the prescribed person operates (such as for own account or on behalf of third parties), and

(e) any other information which may be significant in reviewing the transactions.

(5) Where the information specified in paragraph (4) is not available at the time of notification—

(a) the notification shall include at least the reason or reasons why the prescribed person suspects that the transactions might constitute market abuse as specified in paragraph (4)(b), and

(b) the other information required by paragraph (4) shall be provided to the Bank as soon as it becomes available.

(6) A prescribed person shall not be liable for any act done, or purporting to be done, in good faith by the person pursuant to paragraph (1).

(7) An act referred to in paragraph (6) does not contravene any restriction on the disclosure of information.

(8) For the purposes of this Regulation, 'prescribed person' means any person (including any investment firm, credit institution or market operator) professionally arranging transactions in financial instruments who—

(a) is registered in the State, or

(b) consists of a branch operating in the State of any person (including any investment firm, credit institution or market operator)—

(i) professionally arranging transactions in financial instruments, and

(ii) registered in another Member State.

14 Restrictions on disclosure of notification under Regulation 13 and of identity of notifier

(1) A person notifying the Bank under Regulation 13 shall not inform any other person, in particular the persons on behalf of whom the transactions concerned have been carried out or parties related to those persons, of the notification, unless under an obligation to do so under an enactment or rule of law.

(2) Without prejudice to the provisions of Part 5 or the rules on the transfer of personal data laid down in Directive 95/46/EC of the European Parliament and of the Council of 24 October 1995 (OJ L281, 23.11.1995, p 31) on the protection of individuals with regard to the processing of personal data and on the free movement of such data, the Bank shall not disclose to any person the identity of the person ('notifier') having notified it under Regulation 13 of the transactions concerned if the disclosure would, or would be likely to, harm the notifier.

15 Cooperation with other competent authorities

(1) The Bank shall cooperate with and render assistance to competent authorities in other Member States whenever necessary for the purpose of performing the functions of competent authorities under the relevant community acts (in particular, the exchange of information and cooperation in investigation activities).

(2) Subject to paragraph (3), the Bank shall, on receipt of a request for information from a competent authority for the purpose referred to in paragraph (1)—

(a) immediately supply the information to that competent authority,

(b) if necessary, immediately take the measures necessary to collect the required information, or

(c) if unable to supply the requested information immediately, notify that competent authority of the reasons.

(3) The Bank may refuse to supply information requested by a competent authority for the purpose referred to in paragraph (1) where—

(a) communication may adversely affect the sovereignty, security or public policy of the State,

(b) judicial proceedings have already been initiated in the State in respect of the same actions and against the same person before the authorities of the State, or

(c) a final judgment of a court of competent jurisdiction has already been delivered in relation to such persons for the same actions in the State.

(4) The Bank shall—

(a) notify the competent authority of a refusal under paragraph (3), and

(b) if the reason for the refusal falls within paragraph (3) (b) or (c), provide as detailed information as is possible on the relevant judicial proceedings or final judgment, as the case may be.

(5) Without prejudice to the obligations of the Bank with respect to criminal proceedings in the State, the Bank shall use information received from competent authorities of other Member States pursuant to Article 16(1) of the 2003 Market Abuse Directive only—

(a) for the exercise of its function under the relevant community acts, and

(b) in the context of administrative or judicial proceedings specifically related to the exercise of those functions,

unless the Bank seeks and receives the consent of the competent authority that sent the information to use such information for other purposes or to forward the information received to competent authorities of other Member States.

(6) Without prejudice to the obligations of the competent authorities in other Member States with respect to criminal proceedings in such Member States, the Bank shall not give information to competent authorities of other Member States pursuant to Article 16(1) of the 2003 Market Abuse Directive unless such other competent authority of such other Member State agrees to use such information only—

(a) for the exercise of its functions under the relevant community acts, and

(b) in the context of administrative or judicial proceedings specifically related to the exercise of those functions,

unless the competent authority receiving information from the Bank seeks and receives the consent of the Bank to use such information for other purposes or to forward the information received to competent authorities of other Member States.

(7) The Bank shall give notice to the competent authority of another Member State, in as specific manner as possible, if it believes that—

(a) acts contrary to the relevant community acts are being, or have been, carried out within the territory of the Member State, or

(b) acts are affecting financial instruments traded on a regulated market situated in the Member State.

(8) Upon receipt by the Bank of any notice from a competent authority of another Member State that—

(a) acts contrary to the relevant community acts are being, or have been, carried out within the territory of the State, or

(b) acts are affecting financial instruments traded on a regulated market situated in the State,

then, without prejudice to the competence of that notifying competent authority, the Bank shall take appropriate action and inform the notifying competent authority of the outcome and, so far as possible, of significant interim developments.

(9) The Bank shall consult with the appropriate competent authorities on any proposed follow-up with respect to any matter which is or was the subject of any notice given or received by the Bank under paragraph (7) or (8).

(10) The Bank—

(a) may request that an investigation be carried out by a competent authority of another Member State in the territory of the Member State, and

(b) may further request that agents or employees of the Bank may accompany the personnel of the competent authority of the Member State during the course of the investigation.

(11) Subject to paragraph (13), upon receipt of a request from a competent authority of another Member State, the Bank shall conduct an investigation in the State with respect to the subject matter of the request.

(12) Subject to paragraph (13), if requested by a competent authority of another Member State, the Bank may permit personnel of the competent authority to accompany personnel of the Bank during the course of an investigation conducted under paragraph (11).

(13) The Bank may refuse to initiate an investigation upon receipt of a notice under paragraph (11), or refuse to permit the personnel of another competent authority to accompany its personnel pursuant to a request under paragraph (12), where—

(a) the investigation might adversely affect the sovereignty, security or public policy of the State,

(b) judicial proceedings have already been initiated in respect of the same actions and against the same persons before the authorities of the State, or

(c) a final judgment of a court of competent jurisdiction has already been delivered in relation to such persons for the same actions in the State.

(14) The Bank shall—

(a) notify the competent authority concerned of a refusal under paragraph (13), and

(b) if the reason for the refusal falls with paragraph (13)(b) or (c), provide as detailed information as is possible on the relevant judicial proceedings or final judgment, as the case may be.

PART 3
FAIR PRESENTATION OF RECOMMENDATIONS

16 Interpretation (Part 3)

In this Part, unless the context otherwise requires—

'distribution channels' means a channel through which information is, or is likely to become, publicly available;

'issuer' means an issuer of a financial instrument to which—

(a) these Regulations apply pursuant to Regulation 4, and

(b) a recommendation relates, directly or indirectly,

'likely to become publicly available information' means information to which a large number of persons have access;

'recommendation' means research or other information recommending or suggesting an investment strategy, explicitly or implicitly, concerning one or several financial instruments or the issuers of financial instruments, including any opinion as to the present or future value or price of such instruments, intended for distribution channels or for the public;

'related company' means a related company within the meaning of section 140 of the Companies Act 1990;

'relevant person' means a person producing or disseminating recommendations in the exercise of the person's profession or the conduct of the person's business;

'research or other information recommending or suggesting investment strategy' means—

(a) information—

(i) produced by an independent analyst, an investment firm, a credit institution, any other person whose main business is to produce recommendations or a person working for any of them under a contract of employment or otherwise, and

(ii) that, directly or indirectly, expresses a particular investment recommendation in respect of a financial instrument or an issuer of financial instruments, or

(b) information produced by persons other than the persons referred to in paragraph (a)(i) of this definition which directly recommends a particular investment decision in respect of a financial instrument.

17 Production and dissemination of recommendations

A person who produces or disseminates recommendations shall—

(a) take reasonable care to ensure that the recommendations are fairly presented, and

(b) disclose any interests in or conflicts of interest concerning the financial instruments and issuer to which the recommendation relates.

18 Identity of producer of recommendation

(1) Without prejudice to the generality of Regulation 17 but subject to Regulation 26, any person who produces a recommendation shall ensure that the recommendation discloses clearly and prominently—

(a) the name and job title of the individual who prepared the recommendation, and

(b) the name of the person responsible for its production.

(2) Subject to Regulation 26, where the relevant person responsible for the preparation or production of a recommendation is an investment firm or a credit institution, the investment firm or credit institution shall ensure that the recommendation indicates clearly and prominently the identity of the relevant competent authority of the investment firm or credit institution, as the case may be.

(3) Subject to Regulation 26, where the relevant person responsible for the preparation or production of a recommendation is neither a credit institution nor an investment firm but is subject to self-regulatory standards or codes of conduct, the relevant person shall ensure that a reference to those standards or codes, as the case may be, is disclosed clearly and prominently in the recommendation.

19 General standard for fair presentation of recommendations

(1) Subject to Regulation 26, a relevant person responsible for the preparation or production of recommendations shall take reasonable care to ensure that—

(a) facts are clearly distinguished from interpretations, estimates, opinions and other types of non-factual information,

(b) all sources are reliable or, where there is any doubt as to whether a source is reliable, this is clearly indicated, and

(c) all projections, forecasts and price targets are clearly labelled as such and that the material assumptions made in producing or using them are indicated.

(2) Subject to Regulation 26, a relevant person shall take reasonable care to ensure that any recommendation can be justified to the Bank if the Bank requests justification of the recommendation.

20 Additional obligations in relation to fair presentation of recommendations

(1) Without prejudice to the generality of Regulation 19, where a relevant person is an independent analyst, an investment firm, a credit institution, any related company, any other relevant person whose main business is to produce recommendations, or a person working for any of them under a contract of employment or otherwise, the relevant person shall take reasonable care to ensure that—

(a) subject to paragraph (2), all substantially material sources are indicated, including—

   (i) a description of the relevant issuer,

   (ii) whether or not the recommendation has been disclosed to that issuer, and

   (iii) whether or not following such a disclosure the recommendation has been amended before its dissemination,

(b) subject to paragraph (2), any basis of valuation or other methodology used to evaluate a financial instrument or an issuer of a financial instrument, or to set a price target for a financial instrument, is adequately summarised,

(c) subject to paragraph (2), the meaning of any recommendation made, such as buy, sell or hold, which may include the time horizon of the investment to which the recommendation relates, is adequately explained and any appropriate risk warning, including a sensitivity analysis of the relevant assumptions, indicated,

(d) reference is made to the planned frequency, if any, of updates of the recommendation and to any major changes in the coverage policy previously announced,

(e) the date on which the recommendation was first released for distribution is indicated clearly and prominently, as well as the relevant date and time for any financial instrument price mentioned, and

(f) where a recommendation differs from a recommendation concerning the same financial instrument or issuer, issued during the 12 months immediately preceding its release, this change and the date of the earlier recommendation are indicated clearly and prominently.

(2) Where the requirements of paragraph (1)(a), (b) or (c) would be disproportionate in relation to the length of the recommendation distributed, it is sufficient to make clear and prominent reference in the recommendation to a place where the required information can be directly and easily accessed by the public, such as a direct Internet link to that information on an appropriate Internet site of the relevant person, provided that there has been no change in the methodology or basis of valuation used.

21 General standard for disclosure of interests and conflicts of interest

(1) Subject to paragraphs (2), (3) and (4) and Regulation 26, a relevant person shall disclose in any recommendation all relationships and circumstances that may reasonably be expected to impair the objectivity of the recommendation, in particular where the relevant person has—

(a) a significant financial interest in one or more of the financial instruments which are the subject of the recommendation, or

(b) a significant conflict of interest with respect to an issuer to which the recommendation relates.

(2) Where a relevant person is a legal person, paragraph (1) also applies to any person working for, or providing a service to, the relevant person under a contract of employment or otherwise, who was involved in preparing the recommendation.

(3) Where the relevant person is a legal person, the information to be disclosed in accordance with paragraph (1) shall include the following—

(a) any interests or conflicts of interest of the relevant person or of related companies that are accessible or reasonably expected to be accessible to the persons involved in the preparation of the recommendation, and

(b) any interests or conflicts of interest of the relevant person or of related companies known to persons who, although not involved in the preparation of the recommendation, had or could reasonably be expected to have access to the recommendation prior to its dissemination to customers or the public.

(4) Where a disclosure under this Regulation would be disproportionate in relation to the length of the recommendation distributed, it is sufficient to make clear and prominent

reference in the recommendation to a place where the disclosure can be directly and easily accessed by the public, such as a direct Internet link to the disclosure on an appropriate Internet site of the relevant person.

22 Additional obligations in relation to disclosure of interests or conflicts of interest

(1) Without prejudice to the generality of Regulation 21 but subject to paragraph (4), where a relevant person is an independent analyst, an investment firm, a credit institution, any related company, or any other relevant person whose main business is to produce recommendations, the relevant person shall, in any recommendation produced by the relevant person, disclose clearly and prominently the following information on their interests and conflicts of interest—

(a) any major shareholdings that exist between the relevant person or any related company on the one hand and the issuer on the other hand,

(b) any other significant interests held by the relevant persons or any related company in relation to the issuer,

(c) where applicable, a statement that the relevant person or any related company is a market maker or liquidity provider in the financial instruments of the issuer,

(d) where applicable, a statement that the relevant person or any related company has been lead manager or co-lead manager during the previous 12 months of any publicly disclosed offer of financial instruments of the issuer,

(e) where applicable, a statement that the relevant person or any related company is party to any other agreement with the issuer relating to the provision of investment banking services, provided that this would not entail the disclosure of any confidential commercial information and that the agreement—

(i) has been in effect during the previous 12 months, or

(ii) has given rise during the same period to a payment of compensation or to a promise to pay compensation, and

(f) where applicable, a statement that the relevant person or any related company is party to an agreement with the issuer relating to the production of the recommendation.

(2) For the purposes of paragraph (1)(a), 'major shareholdings' include—

(a) a shareholding held by the relevant person or any related company that exceeds 5% of the total issued share capital in the issuer, and

(b) a shareholding held by the issuer exceeding 5% of the total issued share capital in the relevant person or any related company.

(3) Without prejudice to the generality of Regulation 21 and of paragraph (1), a relevant person which is an investment firm or a credit institution shall disclose clearly and prominently—

(a) in general terms, the organisational and administrative arrangements set up within the investment firm or the credit institution, as the case may be, for the prevention and avoidance of conflicts of interest with respect to recommendations, including information barriers,

(b) with respect to persons working for the investment firm or the credit institution, as the case may be, under a contract of employment or otherwise who are involved in preparing a recommendation, whether or not the remuneration of such persons is tied to investment banking transactions performed by the investment firm or credit institution, as the case may be, or any related company,

(c) where persons referred to in subparagraph (b) receive or purchase the shares of the issuers prior to a public offering of the shares, the price at which the shares were acquired and the date of acquisition, and

(d) on a quarterly basis, the proportion of all recommendations that fall within the categories buy, hold, sell or equivalent terms, as well as the proportion of issuers corresponding to each of those categories to which the investment firm or the credit institution, as the case may be, has supplied material investment banking services over the previous 12 months.

(4) Where a disclosure under this Regulation would be disproportionate in relation to the length of the recommendation distributed, it is sufficient to make clear and prominent reference in the recommendation to a place where the disclosure can be directly and easily accessed by the public, such as a direct Internet link to the disclosure on an appropriate Internet site of the relevant person.

23 Dissemination of recommendations produced by third parties

(1) Subject to paragraph (5), a relevant person who disseminates a recommendation produced by a third party shall ensure that the recommendation indicates clearly and prominently the identity of the relevant person.

(2) Subject to paragraph (5), where a recommendation produced by a third party is substantially altered within the disseminated information, the person disseminating the information shall clearly indicate the substantial alteration in detail.

(3) Subject to paragraph (5), where a substantial alteration referred to in paragraph (2) consists of a change of the direction of the recommendation (such as changing a buy recommendation into a hold or sell recommendation or vice versa), the person disseminating the substantial alteration shall comply with the requirements of Regulations 18 to 21 as respects the substantial alteration.

(4) Subject to paragraph (5), a relevant person who disseminates a substantially altered recommendation shall have a formal written policy so that the persons receiving the information may be directed to where they can have access to such of the following that are publicly available—

(a) the identity of the producer of the recommendation,

(b) the recommendation, and

(c) the disclosure of the producer's interests or conflicts of interest.

(5) Paragraphs (1) to (4) do not apply to news reporting on recommendations produced by a third party where the substance of the recommendation is not altered.

(6) Where there is dissemination of a summary of a recommendation produced by a third party, the relevant persons disseminating the summary shall ensure that the summary—

(a) is clear and not misleading, and

(b) mentions such of the following that are publicly available—

(i) the source document, and

(ii) where disclosures relating to the source document can be directly and easily accessed by the public.

24 Additional obligations for investment firms and credit institutions

(1) Without prejudice to the generality of Regulation 23, where the relevant person—

(a) is an investment firm or credit institution or a person working for the investment firm or credit institution, as the case may be, under a contract of employment or otherwise, and

(b) disseminates recommendations produced by a third party,

then the relevant person shall ensure that the recommendation includes a clear and prominent disclosure of the name of the competent authority of the investment firm or credit institution, as the case may be.

(2) Where the producer of a recommendation referred to in paragraph (1) has not already disseminated the recommendation through a distribution channel, the requirements of Regulation 22 shall be met by the disseminator of the recommendation.

(3) Where an investment firm or credit institution referred to in paragraph (1) has substantially altered a recommendation, Regulations 18 to 22 shall apply with all necessary modifications.

25 Non-written recommendations

The requirements of Regulations 18, 19, 20, 21(1) and 22 may be satisfied, in the case of a recommendation which is not in writing, by reference to a place where the information concerned may be directly and easily accessed by the public, such as a direct Internet link to an appropriate Internet site of the relevant person.

26 Exemption for journalists

(1) Regulations 18, 19 and 21 do not apply to recommendations produced or disseminated by journalists in the State subject to equivalent appropriate regulation.

(2) Without prejudice to paragraph (1), where a journalist acts in a journalist's professional capacity, the dissemination of information will be assessed, for the purposes of the definition of 'market manipulation', taking into account the code of conduct governing the journalist's profession, unless the journalist derives, directly or indirectly, an advantage or profit from the dissemination of the information concerned.

(3) For the purposes of this Regulation, 'equivalent appropriate regulation' means such regulation (including self-regulation) as the Bank considers equivalent to the requirements of Regulations 18, 19 and 21.

PART 4
POWERS OF THE BANK

27 Definitions (Part 4)

In this Part, unless the context otherwise requires—

'authorised officer' means an authorised officer appointed under Regulation 28(1);

'records' means any book, document or any other written or printed material in any form including any information (including phone and data traffic records) stored, maintained or preserved by means of any mechanical or electronic device, whether or not stored, maintained or preserved in a legible form;

'relevant records' means records relating to the activities of persons to whom these Regulations apply;

'responsible authority' means—

(a) the Chief Executive of the Irish Financial Services Regulatory Authority, or

(b) any person to whom the Chief Executive of that Authority has delegated responsibility for appointing authorised officers.

28 Power to appoint authorised officers

(1) A responsible authority may, in writing—

(a) authorise such and so many persons as the authority considers necessary to be authorised officers for the purposes of these Regulations, and

(b) revoke any such authorisation.

(2) An appointment under paragraph (1)(a) may be for a specified or unspecified period.

(3) Every authorised officer shall—

(a) be furnished with a certificate of his or her appointment as an authorised officer, and

(b) when exercising a power under these Regulations of an authorised officer, produce the certificate, together with some form of personal identification, if requested to do so by a person affected by the exercise of that power.

(4) An appointment under paragraph (1) of a person as an authorised officer ceases—

(a) when the responsible authority concerned revokes the appointment,

(b) the person dies or resigns from the appointment,

(c) if the appointment is for a specified period, when the period ends,

(d) if the person appointed is an officer of the Irish Financial Services Regulatory Authority, when the person ceases to be such an officer, or

(e) if the person appointed is an officer of an authority or market undertaking to which the Bank has delegated powers and functions under Regulation 33(1)(c), when the person ceases to be such an officer.

29 Powers of authorised officers

(1) An authorised officer may, for the purposes of enforcing compliance with these Regulations (including carrying out investigations in relation thereto), do all or any of the following—

(a) at all reasonable times enter any premises at which there are reasonable grounds to believe that there are any relevant records,

(b) search and inspect the premises referred to in subparagraph (a) and any relevant records on the premises,

(c) secure for later inspection the premises or any part of the premises in which relevant records are kept or in which the officer has reasonable grounds for believing the relevant records are kept,

(d) require any person to whom these Regulations apply to produce to the officer relevant records, and if the information is in a non-legible form, to reproduce it in a legible form or to give to the officer such information as the officer reasonably requires in relation to entries in the relevant records,

(e) inspect and take copies of relevant records inspected or produced under this Regulation (including, in the case of information in a non-legible form, a copy of all or part of the information in a permanent legible form),

(f) remove and retain any of the relevant records inspected or produced under this Regulation for such period as may be reasonable to facilitate further examination,

(g) require a person to give to the officer information (including give information by way of a written report) that the officer reasonably requires in relation to activities covered by these Regulations and to produce to the officer any relevant records that the person has or has access to,

(h) require a person by or on whose behalf data equipment is or has been used, or any person who has charge of, or is otherwise concerned with the operation of, the data equipment or any associated apparatus or material, to give the officer all reasonable assistance in relation thereto, and

(i) require a person to explain entries in any relevant records.

(2) An authorised officer shall not, except with the consent of the occupier, enter a private dwelling (other than a part of the dwelling used as a place of work) unless the officer has obtained a warrant from a judge of the District Court.

(3) Where any person from whom production of a relevant record is required claims a lien thereon, the production of it shall be without prejudice to the lien.

(4) The requirement to produce any relevant record or report or to provide information or assistance under this Regulation extends to—

(a) a liquidator or receiver of, or any person who is or has been an officer or employee or agent of, a person to whom these Regulations apply, or

(b) any other person who appears to the Bank or the authorised officer to have the relevant record or report in his or her possession or under his

(c) or her control or the ability to provide information or assistance, as the case may be.

(5) An authorised officer may, if the officer considers it necessary, be accompanied by a member of the Garda Síochána or by another authorised officer when exercising a power under this Part.

30 Warrants

(1) When an authorised officer in the exercise of the authorised officer's powers under Regulation 29(1)—

(a) is prevented from entering any premises, or

(b) believes that there are relevant records in a private dwelling,

(c) the authorised officer or the responsible authority by whom the authorised officer was appointed may apply to a judge of the District Court for a warrant under this Regulation authorising the entry by the authorised officer into the premises or the private dwelling, as the case may be.

(2) If on an application under paragraph (1) a judge of the District Court is satisfied, on the information of the applicant, that the authorised officer concerned—

(a) has been prevented from entering any premises, or

(b) has reasonable grounds for believing that there relevant records in a private dwelling,

then the judge may issue a warrant under the judge's hand authorising the authorised officer, accompanied, if the judge considers it appropriate to so provide, by such number of members of the Garda Síochána as may be specified in the warrant, at any time within 4 weeks from the date of issue of the warrant, to enter, if need be by force, the premises or private dwelling and exercise any of the powers referred to in Regulation 29(1).

31 Directions by Bank

(1) Without prejudice to the power of the Bank to impose directions, conditions or other requirements under any enactment, where the Bank considers it necessary to do so in order to—

(a) ensure the integrity of financial markets in Member States,

(b) enhance investor confidence in those markets, or

(c) prevent any person from contravening or continuing to contravene a provision of these Regulations or any other provision of Irish market abuse law,

the Bank may, subject to paragraphs (2) and (3), issue a direction in writing to any person.

(2) A direction under paragraph (1) shall—

(a) subject to subparagraph (b), take effect on and after such date, or the occurrence of such event, as is specified in the direction for the purpose, and

(b) shall cease to have effect—

(i) on such date, or the occurrence of such event, as is specified in the direction for the purpose, or

(ii) on the expiration of the period of 12 months immediately following the day on which the direction takes effect,

whichever is the earlier.

(3) A direction under paragraph (1) shall be a direction to do one or more of the following—

(a) suspend the trading of any financial instrument,

(b) not to dispose of or otherwise dissipate any assets or specified assets of any person or not to do any of those things save where specified conditions are complied with,

(c) not to dispose of or otherwise dissipate any assets or specified assets the beneficial interest in which is vested in another person or persons or not to do any of those things save where specified conditions are complied with,

(d) being a credit institution, not to make any payments from an account held with the institution by a specified person or persons save with the prior consent of the Bank,

(e) not to accept, process or execute any further subscription or orders on behalf of a specified person,

(f) not to carry on a business (whether on the person's behalf or another's behalf) in a specified manner or otherwise than in a specified manner,

(g) not to engage in any practice that contravenes a provision of these Regulations or any other provision of Irish market abuse law,

(h) not to enter into of transactions of a specified kind or not to enter into such transactions except to a specified extent or except where specified conditions are complied with,

(i) not to publish a specified recommendation,

(j) to publish or disseminate in a specified manner information relating to a recommendation or an issuer or a financial instrument.

(4) A person may apply to the Court for, and the Court may, if it considers it appropriate to do so, grant an order setting aside or varying a direction under paragraph (1).

(5) The Bank may, as respects a direction under this Regulation which, in its opinion has not been complied with or is unlikely to be complied with, (or, in the case of a direction referred to in paragraph (2)(b) or (c), irrespective of whether it is of that opinion) apply to the Court in a summary manner for such order as may be appropriate by way of enforcement of the direction and the Court may, as it thinks fit, on the hearing of the application, make or refuse to make an order providing for such relief.

(6) An application for an order under paragraph (5) shall be by motion, and the Court when considering the motion may make such interim or interlocutory order as it considers appropriate.

(7) An application under paragraph (4) may not be made if the direction concerned has been the subject of an order granted under paragraph (5) (but without prejudice to the right of a person, the subject of an order granted under paragraph (5), to apply subsequently to the Court to have the order varied or discharged).

(8) The Court may direct the hearing together of applications made under paragraphs (4) and (5) that relate to the same direction.

(9) The Court may, if it thinks fit, vary or discharge an order made under paragraph (5).

(10) An application under paragraph (4) or (5) may be heard otherwise than in public.

(11) The Bank may give a direction amending or revoking a direction given by it under paragraph (1) but this power may not be exercised—

(a) if an order under paragraph (5) is for the time being in force in relation to the direction, or

(b) to extend the period specified in the direction for which it is to have effect.

(12) On the expiry of the period specified in a direction for which it is to have effect, the Bank may give another direction under paragraph (1) (if it considers it necessary to do so on the grounds specified in paragraph (1)), in like or different terms, to the person concerned.

(13) The powers of the Bank under this Regulation are in addition to those conferred on it by any other enactment to give directions or impose conditions or requirements.

32 Privilege

Nothing in these Regulations shall—

(a) compel the disclosure by a person of any information which the person would, in the opinion of the Court, be entitled to refuse to produce on the grounds of legal professional privilege, or

(b) authorise the taking possession of any document containing such information which is in such person's possession.

33 Delegations, etc.

(1) The Bank may perform any of its functions under the relevant community acts—

(a) directly,

(b) in collaboration with other authorities or market undertakings,

(c) subject to paragraph (5), by delegation to other authorities or market undertakings, or

(d) by applying to the Court.

(2) Subject to paragraph (5), the Bank may delegate in writing to an approved stock exchange any one or more of its functions under these Regulations subject to such conditions as are specified in the delegation.

(3) A delegation under this Regulation does not prevent the performance by the Bank of the function delegated.

(4) Notwithstanding any delegation under this Regulation, the final responsibility for supervising compliance with the relevant community acts and the applicable provisions of Irish market abuse law shall be with the Bank.

(5) The Bank shall not delegate any of its functions under Regulation 7, 15, 28(1), 31, 53 or 54.

PART 5
ENFORCEMENT PROVISIONS

34 Interpretation (Part 5)

(1) In this Part, unless the context otherwise requires—

'adverse assessment' means an assessment in which the assessor has decided that the assessee is committing or has committed a prescribed contravention;

'assessee' means the person the subject of an assessment;

'assessment' means an assessment referred to in Regulation 35;

'assessor' means an assessor appointed under Regulation 35;

'prescribed contravention' means a contravention of—

(a) any provision of Regulation 5 or 6,

(b) any provision of Regulation 10, 11, 12 (except Regulation 12(7)), 13 (except Regulation 13(3)), 14 (except Regulation 14(2)), 17, 18, 19, 20, 21, 22, 23, 24 or 47, or

(c) a requirement under any provision of Regulation 7;

'qualifying holding' means—

(a) a direct or indirect holding of shares or other interest in a regulated financial service provider which represents 10% or more of the capital or the voting rights, or

(b) a direct or indirect holding of shares or other interest in a regulated financial service provider which represents less than 10% of the capital or voting rights but which, in the opinion of the Bank, makes it possible to control or exercise a significant influence over the management of the regulated financial service provider;

'regulated financial service provider' has the same meaning as it has in section 2(1) of the Central Bank Act 1942 (No. 22 of 1942) as amended by section 2(g) of the Central Bank and Financial Services Authority of Ireland Act 2004 (No. 21 of 2004);

'sanction' means any sanction referred to in any of paragraphs (a) to (f) of Regulation 41;

'specified sanctions', in relation to an adverse assessment, means the sanction or sanctions referred to in Regulation 35(8) which may be imposed on the assessee.

(2) The provisions of this Part are made for the purposes of enabling the imposition of administrative sanctions.

35 Bank may appoint assessor

(1) Where the Bank has reason to suspect that a prescribed contravention is being committed or has been committed, the Bank may appoint an assessor (or, if the Bank thinks fit to do so, more than one assessor) to conduct an assessment as to—

(a) whether or not the assessee is committing or has committed the contravention, and

(b) if the assessor finds that the assessee is committing or has committed the contravention, the sanction or sanctions, if any, which the assessor considers is or are appropriate to be imposed on the assessee in respect of the contravention.

(2) The Bank may appoint an assessor who is not an officer, employee or official of the Bank and any such assessor so appointed is an agent of the Bank for the purpose of performing the functions of an assessor under this Part.

(3) The Bank shall provide the assessor with such administrative services (including technical and legal advice) as the Bank considers necessary to enable the assessor to perform the assessor's functions.

(4) The assessor shall, as soon as is practicable after the assessor's appointment as an assessor, give notice of the appointment to the assessee.

(5) The notice under paragraph (4) given to the assessee by the assessor shall contain—

(a) a statement that the assessor is appointed by the Bank under this Regulation,

(b) a statement in summary form of the grounds for conducting the assessment,

(c) a statement that, within a reasonable time specified by the assessor in the notice, the assessee may—

(i) make submissions in writing to the assessor, and

(ii) request the assessor to be permitted to make oral submissions about the matters to which the notice relates, and

(d) a statement that the assessor shall conduct the assessment even if no submissions referred to in subparagraph (c) are made.

(6) The assessor shall—

(a) consider any submissions made by the assessee, and

(b) conduct such investigations relating to the assessment as the assessor considers appropriate before issuing the assessment.

(7) The assessor shall issue the assessment to the Bank when the assessment is made.

(8) Where the assessor decides that a prescribed contravention is being committed or has been committed, the assessor shall ensure that the assessment includes—

(a) a statement of the grounds upon which the assessor made the assessment that the assessee is committing or has committed the contravention,

(b) a statement in summary form of the evidence upon which the assessment is based, and

(c) a statement of the sanction or sanctions, if any, which the assessor considers is or are appropriate to be imposed on the assessee in respect of the contravention.

(9) The appointment of an assessor may be for a specified or unspecified period.

(10) Subject to Regulation 42(2), the assessment shall constitute the decision of the Bank, and references in this Part to an adverse assessment shall be construed accordingly.

36 Revocation of appointment of assessor

(1) Where the Bank is satisfied that the assessor has contravened paragraph (2) or is incapacitated, the Bank may revoke the appointment of the assessor at any time.

(2) The assessor (including a person proposed to be appointed as an assessor) shall—

(a) disclose to the Bank any material interest that the assessor may have in any matter that may arise during the assessment,

(b) disclose to the Bank any actual or potential conflict of interest that the assessor may have in conducting an assessment,

(c) not use any inside information obtained during an assessment for any purpose other than the performance of the assessor's functions under this Part,

(d) not engage in misconduct during the assessment,

(e) perform the assessor's functions in accordance with the procedures and requirements set out in this Part, and

(f) issue an assessment that is not contrary to law.

37 Power to require witnesses to appear and give evidence

(1) The assessor may by notice given in or outside the State to a person require the person to do one or more of the following—

(a) appear before the assessor to give evidence (including give evidence on oath),

(b) produce documents specified in the notice which are in the person's custody or control,

(c) for the purposes of subparagraph (a) or (b), attend before the assessor from day to day unless excused from attendance or released from further attendance by the assessor.

(2) The assessor may administer oaths for the purposes of the evidence referred to in paragraph (1)(a).

(3) A witness at a hearing before the assessor has the same liabilities, privileges and immunities as a witness before the Court.

(4) Where a person ('person concerned')—

(a) fails to comply with a notice under paragraph (1),

(b) threatens or insults the assessor or any witness or person required to attend before the assessor,

(c) interrupts the proceedings of, or does not behave in an appropriate manner before, the assessor,

(d) obstructs or attempts to obstruct the assessor,

(e) discloses, or authorises the disclosure of, evidence given before the assessor or any of the contents of a document produced to the assessor that the assessor has instructed not to be published, or

(f) does anything else that, if the assessor were a court of law having power to commit for contempt, would be contempt for that court,

then—

(i) the assessor may apply to the Court for an order requiring the person concerned to do one or both of the following—

(I) to comply with the notice under paragraph (1),

(II) to discontinue or not repeat the behaviour falling within any of the provisions of subparagraphs (b) to (f), or behaviour of any similar kind, and

(ii) the Court, if satisfied that there is no reasonable excuse for the failure to comply with the notice under paragraph (1) or for the behaviour concerned, as the case may be, grant the order and such other orders as it considers appropriate to ensure that the person concerned cooperates with the assessor.

38 Referral to Court on question of law

(1) The Bank or the assessor may (including at the request of the assessee) refer a question of law arising in the assessment to the Court for determination by the Court.

(2) Where a question of law is referred under paragraph (1)—

(a) the assessor shall send to the Court all documents before the assessor that are relevant to the matter in question, and

(b) at the end of the proceedings in the Court in relation to the reference, the Court shall cause the documents to be returned to the assessor.

39 Assessee to be issued copy of any adverse assessment, etc.

(1) Where the assessment of the assessor is that the assessee is committing or has committed a prescribed contravention, the Bank shall—

(a) issue the assessee with a copy of the adverse assessment (or, as the Bank thinks fit, so much of the adverse assessment as constitutes the statements referred to in Regulation 35(8)), and

(b) advise the assessee that—

(i) the assessee may appeal against the adverse assessment to the Court under Regulation 40, and

(ii) the Bank may apply to the Court under Regulation 44 for an order confirming the adverse assessment (including the specified sanctions).

(2) Where the assessment of the assessor is that the assessee is neither committing nor has committed a prescribed contravention, the Bank shall issue the assessee with a statement to that effect.

40 Right of appeal against adverse assessment (including specified sanctions)

(1) The assessee may appeal against the adverse assessment (including the specified sanctions) not later than 28 days after the Bank has complied with Regulation 39(1) in relation to the assessee or within such further period as the Court allows.

(2) An appeal under paragraph (1) may be heard otherwise than in public.

(3) The Court may, pending the hearing and determination of an appeal under paragraph (1), make such interim or interlocutory orders as the Court considers necessary in the circumstances.

(4) The Court shall determine an appeal under paragraph (1) by making—

(a) an order confirming, varying or setting aside the adverse assessment (including the specified sanctions), whether in whole or in part, or

(b) an order remitting the case to be decided again by the Bank in accordance with the directions of the Court.

(5) The determination of the Court on the hearing of an appeal under paragraph (1) shall be final, except that a party to the appeal may apply to the Supreme Court to review the determination on a question of law.

(6) For the avoidance of doubt, it is declared that no variation of an adverse assessment under paragraph (4) (a) may provide for the imposition of a sanction on the assessee which is not a sanction referred to in paragraphs (a) to (f) of Regulation 41.

41 Sanctions that may be imposed by Bank

In the case of an adverse assessment, the Bank may impose on the assessee such of the following sanctions as are the specified sanctions—

(a) a private caution or reprimand,

(b) a public caution or reprimand,

(c) subject to Regulation 46(2), a direction to pay to the Bank a monetary penalty (but not exceeding €2,500,000 in any case),

(d) a direction disqualifying the assessee from being concerned in the management of, or having a qualifying holding in, any regulated financial service provider for such time as is specified in the order,

(e) if the assessee is continuing to commit a prescribed contravention, a direction ordering the assessee to cease committing the prescribed contravention,

(f) a direction to pay to the Bank all or a specified part of the costs incurred by the Bank in investigating the matter to which the assessment relates and in holding the assessment (including any costs incurred by authorised officers).

42 Power to correct assessments

(1) Where the assessor or the Bank is satisfied that there is an obvious error in the text of an assessment, the assessor or the Bank, as the case may be, may alter the text of the assessment to remove the error.

(2) Where the text of an assessment is altered under paragraph (1), the text as so altered shall be taken to be the decision of the Bank under Regulation 35(10).

(3) In paragraph (1), 'obvious error', in relation to the text of an assessment, includes—

(a) a clerical or typographical error,

(b) an error arising from an accidental slip or omission, or

(c) a defect of form.

43 When specified sanctions take effect

(1) Where—

(a) no appeal under Regulation 40 against the adverse assessment is lodged with the Court within the period for lodging the appeal, or

(b) an appeal under Regulation 40 against the adverse assessment which has been lodged with the Court within the period for lodging the appeal is withdrawn or abandoned,

then the specified sanctions, as confirmed or varied in the order, if any, obtained under Regulation 44(2)(a), shall take effect on the date of that order or such other date as the Court may specify in that order.

(2) Where an appeal under Regulation 40 against the adverse assessment is lodged with the Court within the period for lodging the appeal, then the specified sanctions, as confirmed or varied in the order, if any, obtained under Regulation 40(4)(a), shall take effect of the date of that order or such other date as the Court may specify in that order.

44 Enforcement of adverse assessment (including specified sanctions)

(1) Where—

(a) no appeal under Regulation 40 against the adverse assessment is lodged with the Court within the period for lodging the appeal, or

(b) an appeal under Regulation 40 against the adverse assessment which has been lodged with the Court within the period for lodging the appeal is withdrawn or abandoned,

then the Bank may apply to the Court for an order confirming the adverse assessment (including the specified sanctions).

(2) The Court shall determine an application under paragraph (1) by making—

(a) an order confirming, varying or setting aside the adverse assessment (including the specified sanctions), whether in whole or in part, or

(b) an order remitting the case to be decided again by the Bank in accordance with the directions of the Court.

(3) The Court shall not hear an application under paragraph (1) unless—

(a) the assessee appears at the hearing as respondent to the application, or

(b) if the assessee does not so appear, the Court is satisfied that a copy of the application has been served on the assessee.

(4) An application under paragraph (1) may be heard otherwise than in public.

(5) The Court may, on an application under paragraph (1), make such interim or interlocutory orders as the Court considers necessary in the circumstances.

(6) The determination of the Court on the hearing of an application under paragraph (1) shall be final, except that the Bank or the respondent, if any, may apply to the Supreme Court to review the determination on a question of law.

(7) For the avoidance of doubt, it is declared that no variation of an adverse assessment under paragraph (2) (a) may provide for the imposition of a sanction on the assessee which is not a sanction referred to in paragraphs (a) to (f) of Regulation 41.

45 Publication of certain specified sanctions

The Bank shall publicly disclose the specified sanctions referred to in paragraphs (c) to (f) of Regulation 41, as confirmed or varied in the order concerned obtained under Regulation 40(4)(a) or 44(2)(a), that are imposed on the assessee unless the Bank considers that the disclosure would—

(a) seriously jeopardise the financial markets, or

(b) cause disproportionate damage to the parties involved.

46 Person not liable to be penalised twice for same contravention

(1) Where—

(a) a sanction referred to in Regulation 41(c) is to be imposed on the assessee by virtue of an order obtained under Regulation 40(4)(a) or 44(2)(a), and

(b) the acts which constitute the prescribed contravention to which the sanction relates also constitute an offence under a law of the State,

then the assessee is not, in respect of those acts, liable to be prosecuted or punished for that offence under that law.

(2) A sanction referred to in Regulation 41(c) in respect of a prescribed contravention shall not be imposed on the assessee where—

(a) the assessee has been found guilty or not guilty of having committed an offence under a provision of—

(i) these Regulations, or

(ii) Part 4 of the Investment Funds, Companies and Miscellaneous Provisions 2005 Act, and

(b) all or some of the acts constituting that offence also constitute the prescribed contravention.

47 Person not to be concerned in management of regulated financial service provider while disqualified

A regulated financial service provider shall ensure that a person shall not be concerned in the management of, or have a qualifying holding in, the financial service provider while the person is subject to a sanction referred to in Regulation 41(d) that is in force.

48 Power of Bank to resolve suspected contraventions, etc

(1) Where the Bank has reason to suspect that a person ('relevant party') is committing or has committed a prescribed contravention, it may enter into an agreement in writing with the relevant party to resolve the matter (including at any time before an assessment, if any, has been issued in respect of the relevant party).

(2) An agreement entered into under paragraph (1)—

- (a) is binding on the Bank and the relevant party, and
- (b) may include terms under which the relevant party accepts the imposition of sanctions.

(3) An agreement entered into under paragraph (1) may be enforced by the Bank or the relevant party in a court of competent jurisdiction.

PART 6

OFFENCES AND REPORTS

49 Offences generally and application of section 32 of Investment Funds, Companies and Miscellaneous Provisions Act 2005

(1) A person who contravenes—

- (a) any provision of Regulation 5 or 6,
- (b) any provision of Regulation 10, 11, 12 (except Regulation 12(7)), 13 (except Regulation 13(3)), 14 (except Regulation 14(2)), 17, 18, 19, 20, 21, 22, 23, 24 or 47, or
- (c) a requirement under any provision of Regulation 7,

is guilty of an offence and liable on summary conviction to a [class A fine][a] or imprisonment for a term not exceeding 12 months or both.

(2) Each offence under paragraph (1) consisting of a contravention of any provision of Regulation 5 or 6 is an offence to which section 32 of the Investment Funds, Companies and Miscellaneous Provisions Act 2005 applies.

(3) Where the contravention in respect of which a person is convicted of an offence under these Regulations is continued after the conviction, the person shall be guilty of a further offence on every day on which the contravention continues and liable on summary conviction to a [class A fine][a] or imprisonment for a term not exceeding 12 months or both for each such further offence.

Amendments

a As implicitly substituted for "fine not exceeding €5,000" by Fines Act 2010, s 4. A class A fine currently means a fine not exceeding €5,000.

---

50 Obstruction, etc. of authorised officer

A person who—

- (a) obstructs an authorised officer (within the meaning of Regulation 27) in the exercise of the powers of an authorised officer under Part 4,
- (b) without reasonable excuse, fails to comply with a request or requirement made by such an officer under Part 4, or

(c) gives such an officer information that the person knows or ought reasonably to know is false or misleading in a material particular,

is guilty of an offence and liable upon summary conviction to a [class A fine][a] or imprisonment for a term not exceeding 12 months or both.

Amendments

a As implicitly substituted for "fine not exceeding €5,000" by Fines Act 2010, s 4. A class A fine currently means a fine not exceeding €5,000.

51 False, etc. information

A person who—

(a) gives the Bank a notification under Regulation 13, or

(b) gives the assessor (within the meaning of Regulation 34) information pursuant to a requirement under Part 5,

that the person knows is false or misleading in a material particular or that the person does not believe to be true is guilty of an offence and liable upon summary conviction to a [class A fine][a] or imprisonment for a term not exceeding 12 months or both.

Amendments

a As implicitly substituted for "fine not exceeding €5,000" by Fines Act 2010, s 4. A class A fine currently means a fine not exceeding €5,000.

52 Offences by bodies corporate, etc

(1) Where an offence is committed under these Regulations by a body corporate and is proved to have been committed with the consent, connivance or approval of or to have been attributable to the wilful neglect on the part of any person, being a director, manager, secretary or other officer of the body corporate or a person who was purporting to act in any such capacity, that person as well as the body corporate is guilty of an offence and is liable to be proceeded against and punished as if that person were guilty of the first-mentioned offence.

(2) A person may be charged with having committed an offence under these Regulations even if the body corporate concerned is not charged with having committed an offence under these Regulations in relation to the same matter.

53 Summary proceedings may be brought by Bank

Summary proceedings for an offence under these Regulations may be brought and prosecuted by the Bank.

54 Annual report of Bank

The Bank shall provide the Minister with a copy extract relating to the performance of its functions under these Regulations of its annual report to the Minister for Finance pursuant to section 330 of the Central Bank Act 1942 (No. 22 of 1942) as inserted by section 26 of the Central Bank and Financial Services Authority of Ireland Act 2003 (No. 12 of 2003).

Schedule 1

Provisions Applicable to the Definition of 'accepted Market Practices'

Regulation 2(1)

Factors to be taken into account when considering market practices

1.1 For the purposes of applying the definitions of 'inside information' and 'market manipulation' in Regulation 2(1), the following non-exhaustive factors shall be taken into account by the Bank, without prejudice to collaboration with other authorities, when assessing whether they can accept a particular market practice—

(a) the level of transparency of the relevant market practice to the whole market,

(b) the need to safeguard the operation of market forces and the proper interplay of the forces of supply and demand,

(c) the degree to which the relevant market practice has an impact on market liquidity and efficiency,

(d) the degree to which the relevant practice takes into account the trading mechanism of the relevant market and enables market participants to react properly and in a timely manner to the new market situation created by that practice,

(e) the risk inherent in the relevant practice for the integrity of, directly or indirectly, related markets, whether regulated or not, in the relevant financial instrument within the whole Community,

(f) the outcome of any investigation of the relevant market practice by any competent authority or other authority mentioned in Article 12(1) of the 2003 Market Abuse Directive, in particular whether the relevant market practice breached rules or regulations designed to prevent market abuse, or codes of conduct, be it on the market in question or on directly or indirectly related markets within the Community, and

(g) the structural characteristics of the relevant market including whether it is regulated or not, the types of financial instruments traded and the type of market participants, including the extent of retail investors participation in the relevant market.

The Bank shall, when considering the need to safeguard the operation of market forces and the proper interplay of the forces of supply and demand referred to in subparagraph (b), in particular, analyse the impact of the relevant market practice against the main market parameters, such as the specific market conditions, before carrying out the relevant market practice, the weighted average price of a single session or the daily closing price.

1.2. The Bank shall not assume that practices, in particular new or emerging market practices, are unacceptable simply because they have not been previously accepted by the Bank.

1.3. The Bank shall regularly review the market practices it has accepted, in particular, taking into account significant changes to the relevant market environment, such as changes to trading rules or to market infrastructure.

European Communities (Adjustment of Non-Comparable Amounts in Accounts and Distributions by Certain Investment Companies) Regulations 2005

SI 840/2005

I, Micheál Martin, Minister for Enterprise, Trade and Employment, in exercise of the powers conferred on me by section 3 of the European Communities Act 1972 (No. 27 of 1972) and for the purpose of giving further effect to the Second Council Directive 77/91/ EEC (OJ No.L026, 31.1.1977, p.1) of 13 December 1976, the Fourth Council Directive 78/660/EEC of 25 July 1978 (OJ No.L222, 14.8.1978, p 11), the Seventh Council Directive 83/349/EEC of 13 June 1983 (OJ No.L193, 18.7.1983, p 1), Council Directive 86/635/EEC of 8 December 1986 (OJ No.L372, 31.12.1986, p 1), Council Directive 90/ 605 of 8 November 1990 (OJ No.317, 16.11.1990, p.60) and Council Directive 91/674/ EEC of 19 December 1991 (OJ No.374, 31.12.1991, p 7), hereby make the following regulations:

PART I

PRELIMINARY AND GENERAL

Citation

1. These Regulations may be cited as the European Communities (Adjustment of Non-comparable Amounts in Accounts and Distributions by Certain Investment Companies) Regulations 2005.

Application

2. These Regulations apply to the preparation of annual accounts in the case of a company or undertaking the financial year of which commences on or after 1 January 2005.

Definitions

3. In these Regulations—

'Credit Institutions Regulations' means the European Communities (Credit Institutions: Accounts) Regulations 1992 (S.I. No. 294 of 1992);

'Insurance Undertakings Regulations' means the European Communities (Insurance Undertakings: Accounts) Regulations 1996 (S.I. No. 23 of 1996).

PART 2

ADJUSTMENT OF NON-COMPARABLE AMOUNTS IN ACCOUNTS

4. Section 4 of the Companies (Amendment) Act 1986 is amended by substituting the following for subsection (8):

[...][a]

Amendments

a Substitutes C(A)A 1986, s 4(8).

---

5. Paragraph 44 of the Schedule to the Companies (Amendment) Act 1986 is amended by substituting the following for subparagraph (2):

[...][a]

Amendments

a Amends C(A)A 1986, Sch, para 44(2).

6. Paragraph 4 of the Schedule to the Credit Institutions Regulations is amended by substituting the following for subparagraph (2):

[...][a]

Amendments

a Amends EC(CI)R 1992, Sch para 4(2).

7. Regulation 6 of the Insurance Undertakings Regulations is amended by substituting the following for paragraph (6):

[...][a]

Amendments

a Substitutes EC(IU)R 1996, reg 6(6).

PART 3

DISTRIBUTIONS BY CERTAIN INVESTMENT COMPANIES

8. Section 47 of the Companies (Amendment) Act 1983, as amended by the European Communities (International Financial Reporting Standards and Miscellaneous Amendments) Regulations 2005 (S.I. No. 116 of 2005), is amended—

(a) in subsection (1)(a), by inserting, after "liabilities", "to creditors",

(b) in subsection (2)—

  (i) by substituting 'liabilities to creditors' for 'liabilities',

  (ii) by inserting after "any provision", in each place where that expression occurs, "for liabilities to creditors".

EXPLANATORY NOTE

(*This note is not part of the instrument and does not purport to be a legal interpretation*).

These regulations make amendments to the Companies Acts 1963–2005 consequential on changes in accounting practice for financial years beginning on or after 1 January 2005. Similar changes are also made for Credit Institutions and Insurance Companies.

European Communities (Takeover Bids (Directive 2004/25/EC)) Regulations 2006

SI 255/2006

I, Micheál Martin, T.D., Minister for Enterprise, Trade and Employment, in exercise of the powers conferred on me by section 3 of the European Communities Act 1972 (No. 22 of 1972), and for the purpose of giving effect to Directive 2004/25/EC of the European Parliament and of the Council of 21 April 2004 on takeover bids, hereby make the following regulations:

PART 1
PRELIMINARY AND GENERAL

1 Citation, construction and commencement

(1) These Regulations may be cited as the European Communities (Takeover Bids (Directive 2004/25/EC)) Regulations 2006.

(2) In relation to a company referred to in Regulation 4(1), the Act of 1997 and Parts 1, 2 and 3 shall be read together as one.

(3) In relation to a company referred to in Regulation 21(1), the Companies Acts and Part 4 shall be read together as one.

(4) In relation to a body corporate referred to in Regulation 22, the Companies Acts and Part 5 shall be read together as one.

(5) These Regulations come into operation on 20 May 2006.

2 Interpretation

(1) In these Regulations—

'Act of 1997' means the Irish Takeover Panel Act 1997 (No. 5 of 1997);

'collective investment undertakings other than the closed-end type' means investment companies—

(a) the object of which is the collective investment of capital provided by the public, which operates on the principle of risk-spreading, and

(b) the units of which are, at the holders' request, repurchased or redeemed, directly or indirectly, out of the assets of those companies,

and, for the purposes of this definition, action taken by such companies to ensure that the stock exchange value of their units does not vary significantly from their net asset value shall be regarded as equivalent to such repurchase or redemption;

'company' means a company within the meaning of the Companies Act 1963 (No. 33 of 1963) or any other body corporate;

'Directive' means Directive 2004/25/EC of the European Parliament and of the Council of 21 April 2004 on takeover bids;

'EEA Agreement' means the Agreement on the European Economic Area signed at Oporto on 2 May 1992, as amended for the time being;

'EEA State' means a state which is a contracting party to the EEA Agreement;

'Member State' means—

(a) a Member State of the European Communities, or

(b) an EEA State;

'offeree company' means a company, the securities of which are the subject of a bid;

'offeror' means any natural or legal person governed by public or private law making a bid;

'opted-in company' means a company in relation to which—

(a) an opting-in resolution has effect, and

(b) the conditions in Regulation 16(2) continue to be met;

'opting-in resolution' has the meaning assigned to it by Regulation 16;

'opting-out resolution' has the meaning assigned to it by Regulation 16;

'parties to the bid' means the offeror, the members of the offeror's board if the offeror is a company, the offeree company, holders of securities of the offeree company and the members of the board of the offeree company, and persons acting in concert with such parties;

'regulated market' means a market as defined by Article 1(13) of the Directive 93/22/EEC;

'security holder' means the holder of securities;

'securities' means transferable securities carrying voting rights in a company;

'takeover bid' or 'bid' means a public offer (other than by the offeree company itself) made to the holder of the securities of a company governed by the law of a Member State to acquire all or some of those securities, whether mandatory or voluntary, which follows or has as its objective the acquisition of control of the offeree company in accordance with the law of a Member State;

'Panel' means the Irish Takeover Panel;

'voluntary bid' means a bid which is a voluntary offer under the rules made by the Panel under section 8 of the Act of 1997.

(2) A word or expression that is used in these Regulations and is also used in the Directive shall have in these Regulations the same meaning as it has in the Directive.

3 Non-application of Regulations

(1) These Regulations shall not apply to—

(a) securities issued by collective investment undertakings, other than the closed-end type, or

(b) securities issued by a Central Bank of a Member State.

(2) These Regulations shall not apply to a bid made before the commencement of these Regulations.

PART 4
INFORMATION REQUIREMENTS

21 Information to be contained in directors' annual report

(1) The report, pursuant to section 158 of the Companies Act 1963, of the directors of a company which had securities admitted to trading on a regulated market in the financial year in question, shall contain, in addition to the information specified in that section, section 13 of the Companies (Amendment) Act 1986, the European Communities (International Financial Reporting Standards and Miscellaneous Amendments) Regulations 2005 (S.I. No. 116 of 2005) and any other enactment, the information specified in paragraph (2).

(2) The information mentioned in paragraph (1) is full information, by reference to the end of the financial year concerned, on the following matters—

- (a) the structure of the company's capital, including in particular—
  - (i) the rights and obligations attaching to the shares or, as the case may be, to each class of shares in the company, and
  - (ii) where there are two or more such classes, the percentage of the total share capital represented by each class,
- (b) any restrictions on the transfer of securities in the company, including in particular—
  - (i) limitations on the holding of securities, and
  - (ii) requirements to obtain the approval of the company, or of other holders of securities in the company, for a transfer of securities,
- (c) to the extent not already required to be disclosed pursuant to section 67 or 91 of the Companies Act 1990, in the case of each person with a significant direct or indirect holding of securities in the company, such details as are known to the company of—
  - (i) the identity of the person,
  - (ii) the size of the holding, and
  - (iii) the nature of the holding,
- (d) in the case of each person who holds securities carrying special rights with regard to control of the company—
  - (i) the identity of the person, and
  - (ii) the nature of the rights,
- (e) where—
  - (i) the company has an employees' share scheme, and
  - (ii) shares to which the scheme relates carry rights with regard to control of the company that are not exercisable directly by the employees,

  how those rights are exercisable,
- (f) any restrictions on voting rights, including in particular—
  - (i) limitations on voting rights of holders of a given percentage or number of votes,

(ii) deadlines for exercising voting rights, and

(iii) arrangements by which, with the company's cooperation, financial rights carried by securities are held by a person other than the holder of the securities,

(g) any agreements between shareholders that are known to the company and may result in restrictions on the transfer of securities or on voting rights,

(h) any rules which the company has in force concerning—

(i) appointment and replacement of directors of the company, or

(ii) amendment of the company's articles of association,

(i) the powers of the company's directors, including in particular any powers in relation to the issuing or buying back by the company of its shares,

(j) any significant agreements to which the company is a party that take effect, alter or terminate upon a change of control of the company following a bid, and the effects of any such agreements,

(k) any agreements between the company and its directors or employees providing for compensation for loss of office or employment (whether through resignation, purported redundancy or otherwise) that occurs because of a bid.

(3) The report of the directors referred to in paragraph (1) shall also contain any necessary explanatory material with regard to information that is required to be included in the report by that paragraph.

(4) For the purposes of paragraph (2)(a) a company's capital includes any securities in the company that are not admitted to trading on a regulated market.

(5) For the purposes of paragraph (2)(c) a person has an indirect holding of securities if—

(a) they are held on his or her behalf, or

(b) he or she is able to secure that rights carried by the securities are exercised in accordance with his or her wishes.

(6) Paragraph (2)(j) does not apply to an agreement if—

(a) disclosure of the agreement would be seriously prejudicial to the company, and

(b) the company is not under any other obligation to disclose it.

(7) The requirements of this Regulation apply in relation to reports of directors for financial years beginning on or after 20 May 2006.

PART 5

RIGHTS TO BUY OUT OR BE BOUGHT OUT IN CERTAIN CIRCUMSTANCES

22 Application of Part

(1) This Part applies in relation to a bid for a body corporate, being either—

(a) a company within the meaning of the Companies Acts 1963, or

(b) a body corporate established in the State by charter,

and which is a company a bid in respect of which the Panel has (by virtue of Regulation 6) jurisdiction to supervise.

(2) Section 204 of the Companies Act 1963 shall not apply to a bid for a company or other body corporate falling within paragraph (1) in so far as it relates to securities.

23 Right to buy out dissenting security holders

(1) This Regulation applies where an offeror, pursuant to acceptance of a bid for the beneficial ownership of all the securities (other than the securities already in the beneficial ownership of the offeror) in the capital of a company or other body corporate falling within Regulation 22(1), has acquired, or unconditionally contracted to acquire, securities which—

(a) amount to not less than nine tenths in nominal value of the securities affected, and

(b) carry not less than nine tenths of the voting rights attaching to the securities affected.

(2) Where this Regulation applies, the offeror may, not later than the relevant date, give notice to any dissenting security holder that it desires to acquire the beneficial ownership of his or her securities, and when such notice is given the offeror shall be entitled and bound to acquire the beneficial ownership of those securities on the terms on which under the bid the beneficial ownership of the securities in respect of which the bid has been accepted and is to be acquired by the offeror.

(3) For the purposes of paragraph (2), if the offeree company has issued more than one class of securities, then a notice under that paragraph may only be given by the offeror to holders of securities of the class or classes in respect of which the thresholds provided under paragraph (1)(a) and (b) have been reached.

(4) In paragraph (2) 'relevant date' means the last day of the period of 3 months beginning with the day after the last day on which the bid referred to in paragraph (1) can be accepted.

(5) For the purposes of this Regulation—

(a) securities in the offeree in the beneficial ownership of a subsidiary of the offeror shall be deemed to be in the beneficial ownership of the offeror,

(b) the acquisition of the beneficial ownership of securities in the offeree by a subsidiary of the offeror shall be deemed to be the acquisition of such beneficial ownership by the offeror, and

(c) securities shall not be treated as not being in the beneficial ownership of the offeror merely by reason of the fact that those securities are or may become the subject of a charge in favour of another person.

(6) This Regulation is subject to Regulation 27.

24 Right of certain security holders to be bought out

(1) This Regulation applies where an offeror, pursuant to acceptance of a bid for the beneficial ownership of all the securities (other than the securities already in the beneficial ownership of the offeror) in the capital of a company or other body corporate falling within Regulation 22(1), has acquired, or unconditionally contracted to acquire, some but not all of the securities to which the offer relates and the securities so acquired or unconditionally contracted to be acquired—

(a) amount to not less than nine tenths in nominal value of the securities affected, and

(b) carry not less than nine tenths of the voting rights attaching to the securities affected.

(2) Where this Regulation applies—

(a) the offeror shall, within 1 month from the circumstances referred to in paragraph (1) having arisen, give to all holders of securities in the offeree company not in the beneficial ownership of the offeror notice of the existence of those circumstances, and

(b) any such holder may, within 3 months from the giving of that notice to him or her, require, by notice given to the offeror, the offeror to acquire his or her securities,

and where a security holder gives notice under subparagraph (b) in relation to any securities, the offeror shall be bound to acquire the beneficial ownership of those securities on the terms on which under the bid the beneficial ownership of the securities of the assenting security holders was acquired by it.

(3) Regulation 25 shall apply to the steps to be taken by the offeror on foot of a notice given to the offeror under paragraph (2)(b) and matters consequential thereon as it applies to the steps to be taken by an offeror on foot of a notice given under Regulation 23(2) and matters consequential thereon with—

(a) the modification that a reference in Regulation 25 to a notice under Regulation 23(2) shall be read as a reference to a notice given under paragraph (2)(b) of this Regulation, and

(b) any other necessary modifications.

(4) This Regulation is subject to Regulation 27.

25 Steps to be taken on foot of notice under Regulation 23(2)

(1) Where a notice has been given by an offeror under Regulation 23(2), the offeror shall, before the expiration of 1 month from the date of the giving of the notice—

(a) transmit to the offeree company a copy of the notice together with, subject to paragraph (3), an instrument of transfer of the securities of the dissenting security holders executed on behalf of the dissenting security holders as transferor by any person appointed by the offeror (being either the offeror or a subsidiary of the offeror or a nominee of the offeror or of such a subsidiary), and

(b) pay to or vest in the offeree company the amount or other consideration representing the price payable by the offeror for the beneficial ownership of the securities which by virtue of Regulation 23 the offeror is entitled to acquire.

(2) Upon the foregoing things being done, the offeree company shall register as the holder of those securities the person who executed the instrument as transferee.

(3) Nothing in paragraph (1)(b) shall require an instrument of transfer for any security for which a security warrant is for the time being outstanding.

(4) Any sums received by the offeree company under this Regulation shall be paid into a separate bank account and any such sums and any other consideration so received shall

be held by the company on trust for the several persons entitled to the securities in respect of which the said sums or other consideration were respectively received.

(5) The offeree company or a nominee of the offeree company shall not be entitled to exercise any right of voting conferred by any securities in the offeror company issued to it or to its nominee as consideration or part consideration for the transfer to the offeror company of any securities of a dissenting security holder except by and in accordance with instructions given by that security holder or his or her successor in title.

(6) This Regulation is subject to Regulation 27.

26 Supplemental provisions in relation to Regulation 23 where alternative terms offered

(1) Where a bid provides that an assenting security holder may elect between two or more sets of terms for the acquisition by the offeror of the beneficial ownership of the securities affected, the notice given by the offeror under Regulation 23(2) shall be accompanied by or embody a notice stating the alternative sets of terms between which assenting security holders are entitled to elect and specifying which of those terms shall be applicable to the dissenting security holder if he or she does not before the expiration of 14 days from the date of the giving of the notice notify the offeror in writing of his or her election as between such alternative sets of terms.

(2) In the case of a bid of the kind referred to in paragraph (1), the terms upon which the offeror shall under Regulation 23(2) be entitled and bound to acquire the beneficial ownership of the securities of a dissenting security holder shall be the set of terms his or her election in respect of which the dissenting security holder has, in accordance with paragraph (1), notified to the offeror or, in default of such notification, the set of terms specified in the notice secondly mentioned in paragraph (1).

(3) This Regulation is subject to Regulation 27.

27 Applications to the Court

(1) Where a notice is given by an offeror pursuant to Regulation 23(2) a dissenting security holder may, within 21 days from the giving of the notice, apply to the High Court in a summary manner for a declaration that the conditions specified in Regulation 23 for the giving of that notice are not satisfied or that the terms on which the offeror proposes, on foot of that notice, to acquire the securities of the dissenting security holder do not comply with that Regulation (including that Regulation as it has effect by virtue of Regulation 26).

(2) On the hearing of an application under paragraph (1), the High Court shall, as it considers appropriate, grant or refuse to grant the declaration sought and—

(a) if it grants a declaration of the kind firstly mentioned in paragraph (1), it shall also declare the notice referred to in that paragraph void, and

(b) if it grants a declaration of the kind secondly mentioned in paragraph (1), it shall also declare what are the terms, by virtue of Regulation 23 or 26, upon which the securities of the dissenting security holder shall be acquired and make an order requiring the offeror to acquire those securities on those terms accordingly.

(3) A security holder who has given to an offeror a notice, pursuant to Regulation 24(2)(b), may, within 21 days from the giving of the notice, apply to the High Court in a

summary manner for a declaration that the terms on which the offeror proposes, on foot of the notice, to acquire the securities of the holder do not comply with Regulation 24(2).

(4) On the hearing of an application under paragraph (3), the High Court shall, as it considers appropriate, grant or refuse to grant the declaration sought and, if it grants the declaration, it shall also declare what are the terms, by virtue of Regulation 24, upon which the securities of the applicant shall be acquired and make an order requiring the offeror to acquire those securities on those terms accordingly.

(5) So long as an application under paragraph (1) or (3) is pending or is being determined by the High Court anything that a preceding Regulation of this Part requires to be done shall not be done until the proceedings in the High Court (including any appeal therefrom) are finally disposed of and then only if its doing would be consistent with the final order in the matter.

28 Part 5: Interpretation and Supplemental

(1) In this Part—

'assenting security holder' means a holder of any of the securities affected in respect of which the bid has been accepted;

'dissenting security holder' means a holder of any of the securities affected in respect of which the bid has not been accepted by the holder;

'securities affected' means the securities the acquisition of the beneficial ownership of which by the offeror is involved in the bid.

(2) Where a bid has been accepted by a person in respect of a part only of the securities held by him or her, he or she shall be treated, for the purposes of this Part, as an assenting security holder as regards that part of his or her holding and as a dissenting security holder as regards the remainder of his or her holding.

(3) In the application of this Part to an offeree company the capital of which consists of two or more classes of securities, references to the securities in the capital of the offeree company shall be construed as references to the securities in its capital of a particular class.

(4) Paragraph (3) is in addition to, and does not derogate from, Regulation 23(3).

(5) For the purposes of paragraph (1) of Regulation 23 and paragraph (1) of Regulation 24, when the thresholds specified in either of those paragraphs have been reached in a particular case, the offeror's receiving agent shall issue a certificate to that effect to the offeror.

GIVEN under my Official Seal, the 18th day of May 2006.

EXPLANATORY NOTE

(*This note is not part of the instrument and does not purport to be a legal interpretation*).

These Regulations give effect to Directive 2004/25/EC of the European Parliament and of the Council of 21 April 2004 on Takeover Bids.

European Communities (European Public Limited Liability Company) Regulations 2007

SI 21/2007

I, Micheál Martin, Minister for Enterprise, Trade and Employment, in exercise of the powers conferred on me by section 3 of the European Communities Act 1972 (No. 27 of 1972) and for the purpose of giving full effect to Council Regulation (EC) No. 2157/2001 of 8 October 2001 (OJ L294, 10.11.2001) on the Statute for a European company (SE), hereby make the following regulations—

PART 1
GENERAL

1 Citation and construction

(1) These Regulations may be cited as the European Communities (European Public Limited-Liability Company) Regulations 2007.

(2) The Companies Acts and these Regulations shall be construed together as one.

2 Interpretation

(1) In these Regulations—

'Act of 1963' means the Companies Act 1963 (No.33 of 1963);

'competent authority' means the authority designated by Regulation 29 (a), (b) or (c), as appropriate;

'CRO Gazette' means the electronic gazette maintained by the Registrar on the website of the Companies Registration Office pursuant to Regulation 4 of the European Communities (Companies) Regulations 2004 (S.I. No. 839 of 2004);

'Director' means the Director of Corporate Enforcement;

'EC Regulation' means Council Regulation 2157/2001/EC of 8 October 2001 (OJ L294, 10.11.2001) on the Statute for a European company (SE) (the text of which, for convenience of reference, is set out in the Schedule);

'EEA Agreement' means the Agreement on the European Economic Area signed at Oporto on 2 May 1992, as amended for the time being;

'Member State' means a state that is a contracting party to the EEA Agreement;

Notice of the making of this Statutory Instrument was published in 'Iris Oifigiúil' of 30th January, 2007.

'Registrar' means the Registrar of Companies;

'prescribed' means prescribed by regulations made under section 3 of the European Communities Act 1972 (No.27 of 1972);

'SE established by merger' means an SE established in accordance with Article 2(1);

'SE established by formation of a holding company or subsidiary company' means an SE established in accordance with Article 2(2) or 2(3), as the case may be;

'SE established by transformation' means an SE established in accordance with Article 2(4) and for the purposes of these Regulations and the European Communities (European Public Limited-Liability Company) (Forms) Regulations 2007 and any forms prescribed thereunder, it is immaterial whether the word 'transformation' or 'conversion' is used.

References in these Regulations to an 'SE' are references to a European public limited liability company within the meaning of Article 1 of the EC Regulation whose registered office is, or is to be, in the State and references to 'SEs' shall be construed accordingly;

A reference in these Regulations to a numbered Article is a reference to the Article so numbered of the EC Regulation.

A reference in these Regulations to a numbered Title is a reference to the Title so numbered of the EC Regulation.

A word or expression used in these Regulations which is also used in the EC Regulation has the same meaning as it has in that Regulation.

PART 2

REGISTRATION AUTHORITY FOR AN SE, ETC.

3 Registration authority

For the purposes of the registration of an SE in the State, the Registrar shall be subject to the duties, and shall perform the functions, specified in this Part.

4 Applications in respect of registration (Articles 2 and 3(2))

(1) Where it is proposed to register any of the following-

(a) an SE formed by merger in accordance with Article 2(1),

(b) a holding SE formed in accordance with Article 2(2),

(c) a subsidiary SE formed in accordance with Article 2(3),

(d) an SE formed in accordance with Article 2(4) by the conversion of a public limited company,

or

(e) an SE formed as the subsidiary of an SE in accordance with Article 3(2),

there shall be delivered to the Registrar an application in the prescribed form together with the documents, if any, specified in that form.

(2) In paragraph (1)(e) the reference to an SE, a subsidiary of which is to be registered under that provision, includes a reference to an SE whose registered office is in another Member State.

5 Registration of SE on transfer of its registered office to the State

Where it is proposed to transfer to the State the registered office of an SE whose registered office is situated in another member state, there shall be delivered to the Registrar an application in respect of that SE in the prescribed form together with the documents, if any, specified in that form.

6 Participation in formation of an SE by company whose head office is outside the Community

(1) A company (the 'first-mentioned company') which is registered in a Member State, but which has its head office outside any of the Member States, may participate in the formation of an SE where the Registrar is satisfied that the first-mentioned company has a real and continuous link with the State's economy.

(2) The Registrar shall not be satisfied that the first-mentioned company has such a link unless that company furnishes a statement in writing to him or her—

(a) that has been given to it by the Revenue Commissioners within the period specified in paragraph (3), and

(b) which states that the Revenue Commissioners have reasonable grounds to believe that the company has a real and continuous link with the State's economy.

(3) The period mentioned in subparagraph (a) of paragraph (2) is the period of 2 months ending on the date on which the statement referred to in that paragraph is furnished, pursuant to that paragraph, by the first-mentioned company to the Registrar.

7 Transfer of registered office from the State to another Member State

(1) Where it is proposed to transfer the registered office of an SE from the State to another Member State there shall be delivered to the Registrar, for the purposes of applying for the issue of a certificate under Article 8(8), an application in the prescribed form together with the documents, if any, specified in that form.

(2) Without prejudice to the generality of paragraph (1), a statement of solvency in the prescribed form made by—

(a) in the case of an SE falling within the one-tier system, all the members of the administrative organ, and

(b) in the case of an SE falling within the two-tier system, all the members of the management organ, together with the written authority of the supervisory organ given to the making of the statement,

shall be delivered to the Registrar, together with—

(i) accounts of the SE made up to a date falling within the period specified in paragraph (3) and

(ii) a report (the terms of which shall be unqualified) in relation to those accounts made by the auditors of the SE pursuant to section 193 of the Companies Act 1990 (No. 33 of 1990).

(3) The period mentioned in subparagraph (i) of paragraph (2) is the period of 2 months ending on the date on which the accounts referred to in that subparagraph are delivered to the Registrar.

(4) In determining whether it is proper to issue a certificate to an SE under Article 8(8) on foot of an application under paragraph (1), it shall be sufficient for the Registrar to have regard to each document (including the application and any statement, report and account) delivered to the Registrar in that behalf under this Regulation.

8 Registration of an SE

The Registrar shall register an SE formed or transformed under the provisions of Article 2 or 3, or an SE whose registered office is transferred to the State under Article 8, where he or she is satisfied that the requirements of these Regulations and the EC Regulation in respect of such formation, transformation or transfer of an SE, as the case may be, have been complied with in respect of that SE.

9 Documents sent to Registrar

(1) The Registrar shall retain any document delivered to him or her under any provision of these Regulations or the EC Regulation.

(2) For the purposes of this Regulation, documents delivered to the Registrar under Regulation 7 shall be treated as documents delivered to the Registrar on the deletion of the registration of the SE making the application under that Regulation and the provisions of Regulation 10 shall apply accordingly.

10 Application of Companies Acts with regard to registration of SEs

The provisions of the Companies Acts which apply in relation to the registration of companies and the functions and other duties of the Registrar shall also apply, with any necessary modifications, to SEs.

PART 3
DISCRETIONARY POWERS GIVEN TO MEMBER STATES BY EC REGULATION – PROVISIONS MADE IN EXERCISE THEREOF

11 Additional forms of publication of transfer proposal (Article 8(2))

(1) An SE in respect of which there is a transfer proposal referred to in Article 8(2) shall notify in writing its shareholders, and every creditor of whose claim and address it is aware, of the right to examine the transfer proposal and the report drawn up under Article 8(3), at its registered office and, on request, to obtain copies of those documents free of charge, not later than one month before the general meeting called to decide on the transfer.

(2) Every invoice, order for goods or business letter, which, at any time between the date on which the transfer proposal and report become available for inspection at the registered office of the SE and the deletion of the SE's registration on transfer, is issued by or on behalf of the SE, shall contain a statement that the SE is proposing to transfer its registered office to another Member State under Article 8 and identifying that Member State.

12 Protection of minority shareholders – right to apply to Court (Articles 8(5) and 24(2))

(1) Where it is proposed to transfer the registered office of an SE from the State to another Member State, then, notwithstanding any other provision in the Companies Acts, any member or members holding, in the aggregate, not less than 10 per cent in nominal value of the issued share capital of the SE, being persons who did not consent to or vote in favour of the resolution for the transfer, may apply to the Court—

(a) to have the decision to transfer annulled,

(b) to require the SE to acquire for cash the securities of the shareholders opposed to the transfer,

or

(c) for such other remedy as the Court considers just.

(2) On an application under paragraph (1), the Court may, as it considers appropriate, annul the decision to transfer, require the SE to acquire for cash the securities of the shareholders opposed to the transfer or grant such other remedy as it considers just.

(3) Where a company proposes to form an SE through a merger pursuant to Article 2(1), then, notwithstanding any other provision in the Companies Acts, any member or members holding, in the aggregate, not less than 10 per cent in nominal value of the issued share capital of the company, being persons who did not consent to or vote in favour of the resolution for the merger, may apply to the Court—

(a) to have the decision to merge annulled,

(b) to require the SE to acquire for cash the securities of the shareholders opposed to the merger, or

(c) for such other remedy as the Court considers just.

(4) On an application under paragraph (3), the Court may, as it considers appropriate, annul the decision to merge, require the SE to acquire for cash the securities of the shareholders opposed to the merger or grant such other remedy as it considers just.

(a) An application under paragraph (1) shall be made not later than 28 days following the day on which the resolution for the transfer is passed.

(b) An application under paragraph (3) shall be made no later than 28 days following the day on which the resolution for the merger is passed.

13 Extension of protection given by Article 8(7) to liabilities incurred prior to transfer

The first sub-paragraph of Article 8(7) shall apply to liabilities that arise (or may arise) prior to the transfer.

14 Power of competent authority in the State to oppose a transfer on public interest grounds

The Director as competent authority may exercise the power given by Article 8(14) to oppose the transfer of a registered office.

15 Management or administrative organ of SE may amend statutes where in conflict with employee involvement arrangements

Where there is a conflict between the arrangements for employee involvement made pursuant to the European Communities (European Public Limited-Liability Company) (Employee Involvement) Regulations 2006 (S.I. No. 623 of 2006) and the existing statutes of an SE, the management or administrative organ of the SE may amend those statutes in accordance with Article 12(4) without any further decision of a general meeting of shareholders.

16 Power of competent authority in the State to oppose the participation of a merging company

The Director as competent authority may exercise the power given by Article 19 to oppose the taking part, by a public company, in the formation of an SE by merger.

17 Appointment or removal of member or members of management organ by general meeting (Article 39(2))

(1) The statutes of an SE may permit the member or members of the management organ to be appointed and removed by the general meeting in accordance with Article 39(2).

(2) Paragraph (1) is without prejudice to the application (by virtue of Regulation 27) of section 182 of the Act of 1963.

18 Member of supervisory organ can request information from management organ (Article 41(3))

Each member of a supervisory organ is entitled to require the management organ to provide information of any kind which he or she needs to exercise supervision in accordance with Article 40(1).

19 Minimum number of members of an administrative organ (Article 43(2))

The minimum number of the members of the administrative organ of an SE shall be two.

20 First general meeting to be held within the 18 months following incorporation (Article 54(1))

So long as an SE holds its first annual general meeting within 18 months of its registration in the State, it need not hold such a meeting in the year of its registration or in the following year.

PART 4
PROVISIONS MADE IN FULFILMENT OF OBLIGATION TO ENACT CERTAIN MEASURES

21 Publication of terms of transfer, formation and conversion

(1) Where in respect of Article 8(2), 32(3) or 37(5), terms or draft terms of formation or conversion, or a transfer proposal are required to be publicised, there shall be delivered to the Registrar a copy of the terms, draft terms or the proposal, as the case may be, accompanied by the prescribed form specified in relation to each Article.

(2) The Registrar shall cause to be published in the CRO Gazette notice of the receipt by him or her of the copy of those terms or draft terms or such proposal, as the case may be.

22 Publication of completion of merger (Article 28)

Where an SE is formed by merger, whether its registered office is in the State or not, and a public limited company registered in this jurisdiction has taken part in that formation, the Registrar shall cause to be published in the CRO Gazette notice that the merger has been completed.

23 Publication of fulfilment of conditions for formation of a holding SE (Article 33(3))

Where, in respect of a company, the conditions for the formation of a holding SE, whether or not it is to be registered in the State, are fulfilled, the company shall deliver to the Registrar, within 14 days from such fulfilment, notice of that event in the prescribed form and the Registrar shall cause to be published in the CRO Gazette notice that those conditions have been fulfilled.

24 Publication of other documents or information

(1) Where, in respect of Article 59(3) or 65 of the EC Regulation, the occurrence of an event is required to be publicised, the Registrar shall cause to be published in the CRO Gazette notice of the receipt by him or her of the particulars of the event mentioned in that Article.

(2) Where, in respect of Article 8(12) or 15(2) of the EC Regulation, the registration of an SE, whether on formation under Title II, or on the transfer of the registered office of an SE under Article 8 or the deletion of a registration under that Article is required to be publicised, the Registrar shall cause to be published in the CRO Gazette notice of that

registration or the deletion of that registration and of the receipt of the documents and particulars related to that registration or deletion required to be delivered to the registrar by the EC Regulation or these Regulations.

25 Power to require SE to take steps to comply with requirements of Article 7

(1) If it appears to the Director that an SE no longer complies with the requirements specified in Article 7, he or she may give a direction in writing to the SE to take steps, in accordance with Article 64(1)(a) or (b), to ensure that it complies with those requirements.

(2) Such a direction shall—

(a) include a statement of the reasons upon which the direction is being given, and

(b) specify the period within which steps concerned are to be taken.

(3) Where an SE has failed to comply with a direction under paragraph (1), the Director may apply to the High Court for an order directing the SE to comply with the direction and, on the hearing of the application, the Court may make such order as it sees fit and may provide that all costs of and incidental to the application shall be borne by the SE.

(4) Section 213 of the Act of 1963 is amended by inserting the following after paragraph (e):

[...][a]

(5) Section 215 of the Act of 1963 is amended—

(a) by deleting 'and' where it occurs immediately before paragraph (g),

(b) in paragraph (g), by substituting 'paragraph; and' for 'paragraph.' where it lastly occurs, and

(c) by inserting the following after paragraph (g):

[...][b]

Amendments

a Reg 25(4) inserts CA 1963, s 213(ea).

b Reg 25(5)(c) inserts CA 1963, s 215(h).

---

26 Appeals against decisions of competent authority (Articles 8(14) and 19)

(1) This Regulation applies where—

(a) the transfer of the registered office of an SE under Article 8(14), or

(b) the taking part by a public limited company in the formation of an SE by merger under Article 19,

is opposed by the Director as competent authority under Article 8(14) or 19, as the case may be.

(2) Where this Regulation applies, the SE or the public limited company, as appropriate, may, within 21 days from being informed of the Director's decision to oppose the transfer or the taking part in the formation of an SE by merger, appeal against the Director's decision to the High Court.

(3) On the hearing of an appeal under paragraph (2), the High Court may either confirm or cancel the decision of the Director.

(4) A decision of the High Court under paragraph (3) shall be final, save that, by leave of the Court, an appeal from the decision shall lie to the Supreme Court on a specified question of law.

(5) The High Court may, on application made by the SE or the public limited company, extend the period referred to in paragraph (2) within which an appeal may be made in relation to the matter referred to in that paragraph (the 'appeal period') if, but only if, it is satisfied that—

(a) where the application for the extension is made before the end of the appeal period, there is good reason for the SE or the company being unable to make the appeal within that period, or

(b) where the application for the extension is made after the end of the appeal period, that there was a good reason for the failure of the SE or the company to make the appeal within that period and for any delay in applying for the extension.

PART 5

PROVISIONS RELATING TO THE EFFECTIVE APPLICATION OF THE EC REGULATION

27 Application of law

(1) Any enactment or rule of law which applies in relation to a public limited company incorporated under the Companies Acts shall, in the absence of any express provision to the contrary in these Regulations, apply with any necessary modifications in relation to an SE as it applies in relation to such a company.

(2) Without prejudice to the generality of paragraph (1), the Companies Acts shall, in their application to SEs, have effect with the modifications specified in these Regulations.

28 Members of organs to be treated as directors, etc.

(1) For the purposes of the application to an SE of the provisions of the Companies Acts which apply to public limited companies, the members of—

(a) the administrative organ in the case of an SE within the one-tier system, and

(b) the supervisory organ and of the management organ in the case of an SE within the two-tier system,

shall be regarded and treated as if they were directors of a public limited company and shall have and shall discharge the responsibilities of such directors accordingly.

(2) For the purposes of the application to an SE of the provisions of the Companies Acts which apply to public limited companies, the members of—

(a) the administrative organ in the case of an SE within the one-tier system, and

(b) the supervisory organ and of the management organ in the case of an SE within the two-tier system, shall designate one of their members to discharge the responsibilities that would be required to be discharged by a company secretary were the SE a public limited company and the person so designated shall have and shall discharge such responsibilities and shall be regarded and treated as if he or she were a secretary of a public limited company accordingly.

(3) For the purposes of the application to an SE of the provisions of the Companies Acts that require a document prepared by a public limited company to be signed or certified—

(a) by the secretary of the company acting alone, or

(b) jointly by that secretary and a director or, as the case may be, a specified number (which number is referred to subsequently in this Regulation as 'the requisite number') of directors of the company,

then that requirement shall be regarded as satisfied, in the case of an SE, if the document concerned is signed or certified by the member of the SE designated pursuant to paragraph (2) acting alone or, as appropriate, signed or certified jointly by that member and—

(i) in the case of an SE within the one-tier system, a member or, as the case may require, the requisite number of members of the administrative organ of the SE,

or

(ii) in the case of an SE within the two-tier system, a member or, as the case may require, the requisite number of members of the supervisory organ or the management organ of the SE.

(4) For the purposes of paragraph (3)(ii), it shall be solely at the discretion of the SE whether the requisite number is counted from amongst one alone of the organs there mentioned or partly from the one of them and partly from the other.

29 Competent authorities

The competent authorities designated under Article 68(2) are:

(a) in respect of Articles 8(7) and 8(8), the Registrar,

(b) in respect of Articles 8(14), 19, 54, 55 and 64, the Director,

(c) and in respect of Articles 25 and 26, the High Court.

30 National Gazette

For the purposes of Art 21, publication may be made in the CRO Gazette.

31 Records of an SE transferred under Article 8(11) or a public limited company ceasing to exist under Article 29(1) and (2)

(1) Where—

(a) the registration of an SE is deleted under Article 8(11) pursuant to a transfer of its registered office to another Member State; or

(b) a public limited company ceases to exist under Article 29(1)(c) or (2) (c),

the records kept by the Registrar in relation to that SE or public limited company, as the case may be, shall continue to be kept by him or her for a period of twenty years following such a deletion or cessation of existence.

(2) Where the registration of an SE is deleted, the form, and the documents, if any, accompanying it, delivered to the Registrar under Regulation 7 together with a copy of the certificate issued under Article 8(8) shall be deemed to be documents to be retained by the Registrar under Regulation 9 and the provisions of these Regulations shall apply accordingly.

32 Notification of amendments to statutes and insolvency events (Articles 59(3) and 65)

Where, under Article 59(3) or 65, publication by the Registrar in the CRO Gazette of the events mentioned in that Article is required by Article 13—

(a) in the case of Article 59(3), the amendments to the statutes shall be delivered to the Registrar by the SE accompanied by the prescribed form within 14 days from the adoption of those amendments, and

(b) in the case of Article 65, notice of the relevant event set out in the prescribed form shall be delivered to the Registrar by the SE within 14 days from the occurrence of the event.

33 Annual return date

(1) On the registration of an SE, the Registrar shall assign to the SE an annual return date for the purposes of section 127 of the Act of 1963 (inserted by the Company Law Enforcement Act 2001 (No.28 of 2001) and amended by the Companies (Auditing and Accounting) Act 2003 (No.44 of 2003)) and that date shall, subject to paragraphs (3) and (5), be the annual return date of the SE for those purposes accordingly.

(2) The secretary of the SE may serve on the Registrar, not later than 6 weeks from its date of registration, a notice in the prescribed form—

(a) requesting the Registrar to assign, as an annual return date in respect of the SE, a date specified in the notice and which is different from that assigned under paragraph (1),

and

(b) stating the reason or reasons why, in the secretary's opinion, the date so specified is more suitable than that assigned under paragraph (1).

(3) The Registrar shall consider such a notice and, if the Registrar is of the opinion that the reason or reasons (or any of them) referred to in paragraph (2)(b) and stated in the notice disclose good and substantial grounds for the secretary's opinion that the date specified in the notice is more suitable than that assigned under paragraph (1), the Registrar shall assign that date as the annual return date of the SE in place of that assigned under paragraph (1). Upon service of the notice referred to in paragraph (4) on the secretary of the SE the date so assigned shall have effect in place of the date assigned under paragraph (1) and, accordingly, shall, subject to paragraph (5), be the annual return date of the SE for the purposes of section 127 of the Act of 1963.

(4) The Registrar shall, by notice in writing served on the secretary of the SE, inform him or her whether the request made by the secretary in the notice served under paragraph (2) has been acceded to.

(5) The annual return date assigned by the Registrar under paragraph (1) or, as the case may be, paragraph (3) may be altered by the SE in accordance with the provisions of section 127 of the Act of 1963 as to the establishment of a new annual return date.

34 Offences

(1) If an SE or any of its officers fails to comply with Regulation 7, 11, 23 or 32 or Article 11 or 13, the SE and every officer who is in default shall be guilty of an offence and shall be liable on summary conviction to a [class B fine][a].

(2) Proceedings for an offence under paragraph (1) may be brought and prosecuted by the Director or the Registrar, save in the case of proceedings in respect of an offence under that paragraph consisting of a failure to comply with Article 11 or 13 which may only be brought and prosecuted by the Director.

Amendments

a As implicitly substituted for "fine not exceeding €3,000" by Fines Act 2010, s 5. A class A fine currently means a fine not exceeding €4,000.

---

35 Relationship of certain Regulations to Council Regulation

Regulations 10, 17(2) and 27 are made in consequence of, and are to be construed as being supplemental to, Article 9 and, accordingly, do not affect the direct application in the State of Article 9 or any other provision of the EC Regulation.

Schedule

COUNCIL REGULATION (EC) NO 2157/2001 OF 8 OCTOBER 2001 ON THE STATUTE FOR A EUROPEAN COMPANY (SE)

THE COUNCIL OF THE EUROPEAN UNION,

Having regard to the Treaty establishing the European Community, and in particular Article 308 thereof,

Having regard to the proposal from the Commission(1),

Having regard to the opinion of the European Parliament(2),

Having regard to the opinion of the Economic and Social Committee(3),

Whereas:

(1) The completion of the internal market and the improvement it brings about in the economic and social situation throughout the Community mean not only that barriers to trade must be removed, but also that the structures of production must be adapted to the Community dimension. For that purpose it is essential that companies the business of which is not limited to satisfying purely local needs should be able to plan and carry out the reorganisation of their business on a Community scale.

(2) Such reorganisation presupposes that existing companies from different Member States are given the option of combining their potential by means of mergers. Such operations can be carried out only with due regard to the rules of competition laid down in the Treaty.

(3) Restructuring and cooperation operations involving companies from different Member States give rise to legal and psychological difficulties and tax problems. The approximation of Member States' company law by means of Directives based on Article 44 of the Treaty can overcome some of those difficulties. Such approximation does not, however, release companies governed by different legal systems from the obligation to choose a form of company governed by a particular national law.

(4) The legal framework within which business must be carried on in the Community is still based largely on national laws and therefore no longer corresponds to the economic framework within which it must develop if the objectives set out in Article 18 of the Treaty are to be achieved. That situation forms a considerable obstacle to the creation of groups of companies from different Member States.

(5) Member States are obliged to ensure that the provisions applicable to European companies under this Regulation do not result either in discrimination arising out of unjustified different treatment of European companies compared with public limited-liability companies or in disproportionate restrictions on the formation of a European company or on the transfer of its registered office.

(6) It is essential to ensure as far as possible that the economic unit and the legal unit of business in the Community coincide. For that purpose, provision should be made for the creation, side by side with companies governed by a particular national law, of companies formed and carrying on business under the law created by a Community Regulation directly applicable in all Member States.

(7) The provisions of such a Regulation will permit the creation and management of companies with a European dimension, free from the obstacles arising from the disparity and the limited territorial application of national company law.

(8) The Statute for a European public limited-liability company (hereafter referred to as 'SE') is among the measures to be adopted by the Council before 1992 listed in the Commission's White Paper on completing the internal market, approved by the European Council that met in Milan in June 1985. The European Council that met in Brussels in 1987 expressed the wish to see such a Statute created swiftly.

(9) Since the Commission's submission in 1970 of a proposal for a Regulation on the Statute for a European public limited-liability company, amended in 1975, work on the approximation of national company law has made substantial progress, so that on those points where the functioning of an SE does not need uniform Community rules reference may be made to the law governing public limited-liability companies in the Member State where it has its registered office.

(10) Without prejudice to any economic needs that may arise in the future, if the essential objective of legal rules governing SEs is to be attained, it must be possible at least to create such a company as a means both of enabling companies from different Member States to merge or to create a holding company and of enabling companies and other legal persons carrying on economic activities and governed by the laws of different Member States to form joint subsidiaries.

(11) In the same context it should be possible for a public limited-liability company with a registered office and head office within the Community to transform itself into an SE without going into liquidation, provided it has a subsidiary in a Member State other than that of its registered office.

(12) National provisions applying to public limited-liability companies that offer their securities to the public and to securities transactions should also apply where an SE is formed by means of an offer of securities to the public and to SEs wishing to utilise such financial instruments.

(13) The SE itself must take the form of a company with share capital, that being the form most suited, in terms of both financing and management, to the needs of a company carrying on business on a European scale. In order to ensure that such companies are of reasonable size, a minimum amount of capital should be set so that they have sufficient assets without making it difficult for small and medium-sized undertakings to form SEs.

(14) An SE must be efficiently managed and properly supervised. It must be borne in mind that there are at present in the Community two different systems for the administration of public limited-liability companies. Although an SE should be allowed to choose between the two systems, the respective responsibilities of those responsible for management and those responsible for supervision should be clearly defined.

(15) Under the rules and general principles of private international law, where one undertaking controls another governed by a different legal system, its ensuing rights and obligations as regards the protection of minority shareholders and third parties are governed by the law governing the controlled undertaking, without prejudice to the obligations imposed on the controlling undertaking by its own law, for example the requirement to prepare consolidated accounts.

(16) Without prejudice to the consequences of any subsequent coordination of the laws of the Member States, specific rules for SEs are not at present required in this field. The rules and general principles of private international law should therefore be applied both where an SE exercises control and where it is the controlled company.

(17) The rule thus applicable where an SE is controlled by another undertaking should be specified, and for this purpose reference should be made to the law governing public limited-liability companies in the Member State in which the SE has its registered office.

(18) Each Member State must be required to apply the sanctions applicable to public limited-liability companies governed by its law in respect of infringements of this Regulation.

(19) The rules on the involvement of employees in the European company are laid down in Directive 2001/86/EC(4), and those provisions thus form an indissociable complement to this Regulation and must be applied concomitantly.

(20) This Regulation does not cover other areas of law such as taxation, competition, intellectual property or insolvency. The provisions of the Member States' law and of Community law are therefore applicable in the above areas and in other areas not covered by this Regulation.

(21) Directive 2001/86/EC is designed to ensure that employees have a right of involvement in issues and decisions affecting the life of their SE. Other social and labour legislation questions, in particular the right of employees to information and consultation as regulated in the Member States, are governed by the national provisions applicable, under the same conditions, to public limited-liability companies.

(22) The entry into force of this Regulation must be deferred so that each Member State may incorporate into its national law the provisions of Directive 2001/86/EC and set up in advance the necessary machinery for the formation and operation of SEs with registered offices within its territory, so that the Regulation and the Directive may be applied concomitantly.

(23) A company the head office of which is not in the Community should be allowed to participate in the formation of an SE provided that company is formed under the law of a Member State, has its registered office in that Member State and has a real and continuous link with a Member State's economy according to the principles established in the 1962 General Programme for the abolition of restrictions on freedom of establishment. Such a link exists in particular if a company has an establishment in that Member State and conducts operations therefrom.

(24) The SE should be enabled to transfer its registered office to another Member State. Adequate protection of the interests of minority shareholders who oppose the transfer, of creditors and of holders of other rights should be proportionate. Such transfer should not affect the rights originating before the transfer.

(25) This Regulation is without prejudice to any provision which may be inserted in the 1968 Brussels Convention or in any text adopted by Member States or by the Council to replace such Convention, relating to the rules of jurisdiction applicable in the case of transfer of the registered offices of a public limited-liability company from one Member State to another.

(26) Activities by financial institutions are regulated by specific directives and the national law implementing those directives and additional national rules regulating those activities apply in full to an SE.

(27) In view of the specific Community character of an SE, the 'real seat' arrangement adopted by this Regulation in respect of SEs is without prejudice to Member States' laws and does not pre-empt any choices to be made for other Community texts on company law.

(28) The Treaty does not provide, for the adoption of this Regulation, powers of action other than those of Article 308 thereof.

(29) Since the objectives of the intended action, as outlined above, cannot be adequately attained by the Member States in as much as a European public limited-liability company is being established at European level and can there-fore, because of the scale and impact of such company, be better attained at Community level, the Community may take measures in accordance with the principle of subsidiarity enshrined in Article 5 of the Treaty. In accordance with the principle of proportionality as set out in the said Article, this Regulation does not go beyond what is necessary to attain these objectives,

HAS ADOPTED THIS REGULATION:

Title I
General Provisions

Article 1

1. A company may be set up within the territory of the Community in the form of a European public limited-liability company (Societas Europaea or SE) on the conditions and in the manner laid down in this Regulation.

2. The capital of an SE shall be divided into shares. No shareholder shall be liable for more than the amount he has subscribed.

3. An SE shall have legal personality.

4. Employee involvement in an SE shall be governed by the provisions of Directive 2001/86/EC.

Article 2

1. Public limited-liability companies such as referred to in Annex I, formed under the law of a Member State, with registered offices and head offices within the Community may form an SE by means of a merger provided that at least two of them are governed by the law of different Member States.

2. Public and private limited-liability companies such as referred to in Annex II, formed under the law of a Member State, with registered offices and head offices within the Community may promote the formation of a holding SE provided that each of at least two of them:

(a) is governed by the law of a different Member State, or

(b) has for at least two years had a subsidiary company governed by the law of another Member State or a branch situated in another Member State.

3. Companies and firms within the meaning of the second paragraph of Article 48 of the Treaty and other legal bodies governed by public or private law, formed under the law of

a Member State, with registered offices and head offices within the Community may form a subsidiary SE by subscribing for its shares, provided that each of at least two of them:

(a) is governed by the law of a different Member State, or

(b) has for at least two years had a subsidiary company governed by the law of another Member State or a branch situated in another Member State.

4. A public limited-liability company, formed under the law of a Member State, which has its registered office and head office within the Community may be transformed into an SE if for at least two years it has had a subsidiary company governed by the law of another Member State.

5. A Member State may provide that a company the head office of which is not in the Community may participate in the formation of an SE provided that company is formed under the law of a Member State, has its registered office in that Member State and has a real and continuous link with a Member State's economy.

Article 3

1. For the purposes of Article 2(1), (2) and (3), an SE shall be regarded as a public limited-liability company governed by the law of the Member State in which it has its registered office.

2. An SE may itself set up one or more subsidiaries in the form of SEs. The provisions of the law of the Member State in which a subsidiary SE has its registered office that require a public limited-liability company to have more than one shareholder shall not apply in the case of the subsidiary SE. The pro-visions of national law implementing the twelfth Council Company Law Directive (89/667/EEC) of 21 December 1989 on single-member private limited-liability companies(5) shall apply to SEs mutatis mutandis.

Article 4

1. The capital of an SE shall be expressed in euro.

2. The subscribed capital shall not be less than EUR 120000.

3. The laws of a Member State requiring a greater subscribed capital for companies carrying on certain types of activity shall apply to SEs with registered offices in that Member State.

Article 5

Subject to Article 4(1) and (2), the capital of an SE, its maintenance and changes thereto, together with its shares, bonds and other similar securities shall be governed by the provisions which would apply to a public limited-liability company with a registered office in the Member State in which the SE is registered.

Article 6

For the purposes of this Regulation, 'the statutes of the SE' shall mean both the instrument of incorporation and, where they are the subject of a separate document, the statutes of the SE.

Article 7

The registered office of an SE shall be located within the Community, in the same Member State as its head office. A Member State may in addition impose on SEs registered in its territory the obligation of locating their head office and their registered office in the same place.

Article 8

1. The registered office of an SE may be transferred to another Member State in accordance with paragraphs 2 to 13. Such a transfer shall not result in the winding up of the SE or in the creation of a new legal person.

2. The management or administrative organ shall draw up a transfer proposal and publicise it in accordance with Article 13, without prejudice to any additional forms of publication provided for by the Member State of the registered office. That proposal shall state the current name, registered office and number of the SE and shall cover:

(a) the proposed registered office of the SE;

(b) the proposed statutes of the SE including, where appropriate, its new name;

(c) any implication the transfer may have on employees' involvement;

(d) the proposed transfer timetable;

(e) any rights provided for the protection of shareholders and/or creditors.

3. The management or administrative organ shall draw up a report explaining and justifying the legal and economic aspects of the transfer and explaining the implications of the transfer for shareholders, creditors and employees.

4. An SE's shareholders and creditors shall be entitled, at least one month before the general meeting called upon to decide on the transfer, to examine at the SE's registered office the transfer proposal and the report drawn up pursuant to paragraph 3 and, on request, to obtain copies of those documents free of charge.

5. A Member State may, in the case of SEs registered within its territory, adopt provisions designed to ensure appropriate protection for minority share-holders who oppose a transfer.

6. No decision to transfer may be taken for two months after publication of the proposal. Such a decision shall be taken as laid down in Article 59.

7. Before the competent authority issues the certificate mentioned in paragraph 8, the SE shall satisfy it that, in respect of any liabilities arising prior to the publication of the transfer proposal, the interests of creditors and holders of other rights in respect of the SE (including those of public bodies) have been adequately protected in accordance with requirements laid down by the Member State where the SE has its registered office prior to the transfer.

A Member State may extend the application of the first subparagraph to liabilities that arise (or may arise) prior to the transfer.

The first and second subparagraphs shall be without prejudice to the application to SEs of the national legislation of Member States concerning the satisfaction or securing of payments to public bodies.

8. In the Member State in which an SE has its registered office the court, notary or other competent authority shall issue a certificate attesting to the completion of the acts and formalities to be accomplished before the transfer.

9. The new registration may not be effected until the certificate referred to in paragraph 8 has been submitted, and evidence produced that the formalities required for registration in the country of the new registered office have been completed.

10. The transfer of an SE's registered office and the consequent amendment of its statutes shall take effect on the date on which the SE is registered, in accordance with Article 12, in the register for its new registered office.

11. When the SE's new registration has been effected, the registry for its new registration shall notify the registry for its old registration. Deletion of the old registration shall be effected on receipt of that notification, but not before.

12. The new registration and the deletion of the old registration shall be publicised in the Member States concerned in accordance with Article 13.

13. On publication of an SE's new registration, the new registered office may be relied on as against third parties. However, as long as the deletion of the SE's registration from the register for its previous registered office has not been publicised, third parties may continue to rely on the previous registered office unless the SE proves that such third parties were aware of the new registered office.

14. The laws of a Member State may provide that, as regards SEs registered in that Member State, the transfer of a registered office which would result in a change of the law applicable shall not take effect if any of that Member State's competent authorities opposes it within the two-month period referred to in paragraph 6. Such opposition may be based only on grounds of public interest.

Where an SE is supervised by a national financial supervisory authority according to Community directives the right to oppose the change of registered office applies to this authority as well.

Review by a judicial authority shall be possible.

15. An SE may not transfer its registered office if proceedings for winding up, liquidation, insolvency or suspension of payments or other similar proceedings have been brought against it.

16 An SE which has transferred its registered office to another Member State shall be considered, in respect of any cause of action arising prior to the transfer as determined in paragraph 10, as having its registered office in the Member States where the SE was registered prior to the transfer, even if the SE is sued after the transfer.

Article 9

1. An SE shall be governed:

(a) by this Regulation,

(b) where expressly authorised by this Regulation, by the provisions of its statutes or

(c) in the case of matters not regulated by this Regulation or, where matters are partly regulated by it, of those aspects not covered by it, by:

(i) the provisions of laws adopted by Member States in implementation of Community measures relating specifically to SEs;

(ii) the provisions of Member States' laws which would apply to a public limited-liability company formed in accordance with the law of the Member State in which the SE has its registered office;

(iii) the provisions of its statutes, in the same way as for a public limited-liability company formed in accordance with the law of the Member State in which the SE has its registered office.

2. The provisions of laws adopted by Member States specifically for the SE must be in accordance with Directives applicable to public limited-liability companies referred to in Annex I.

3. If the nature of the business carried out by an SE is regulated by specific provisions of national laws, those laws shall apply in full to the SE.

Article 10

Subject to this Regulation, an SE shall be treated in every Member State as if it were a public limited-liability company formed in accordance with the law of the Member State in which it has its registered office.

Article 11

1. The name of an SE shall be preceded or followed by the abbreviation SE.

2. Only SEs may include the abbreviation SE in their name.

3. Nevertheless, companies, firms and other legal entities registered in a Member State before the date of entry into force of this Regulation in the names of which the abbreviation SE appears shall not be required to alter their names.

Article 12

1. Every SE shall be registered in the Member State in which it has its registered office in a register designated by the law of that Member State in accordance with Article 3 of the first Council Directive (68/151/EEC) of 9 March 1968 on coordination of safeguards which, for the protection of the interests of members and others, are required by Member States of companies within the meaning of the second paragraph of Article 58 of the Treaty, with a view to making such safeguards equivalent throughout the Community(6).

2. An SE may not be registered unless an agreement on arrangements for employee involvement pursuant to Article 4 of Directive 2001/86/EC has been concluded, or a decision pursuant to Article 3(6) of the Directive has been taken, or the period for negotiations pursuant to Article 5 of the Directive has expired without an agreement having been concluded.

3. In order for an SE to be registered in a Member State which has made use of the option referred to in Article 7(3) of Directive 2001/86/EC, either an agreement pursuant to Article 4 of the Directive must have been concluded on the arrangements for employee involvement, including participation, or none of the participating companies must have been governed by participation rules prior to the registration of the SE.

4. The statutes of the SE must not conflict at any time with the arrangements for employee involvement which have been so determined. Where new such arrangements determined pursuant to the Directive conflict with the existing statutes, the statutes shall to the extent necessary be amended.

In this case, a Member State may provide that the management organ or the administrative organ of the SE shall be entitled to proceed to amend the statutes without any further decision from the general shareholders meeting.

Article 13

Publication of the documents and particulars concerning an SE which must be publicised under this Regulation shall be effected in the manner laid down in the laws of the Member State in which the SE has its registered office in accordance with Directive 68/151/EEC.

Article 14

1. Notice of an SE's registration and of the deletion of such a registration shall be published for information purposes in the Official Journal of the European Communities after publication in accordance with Article 13. That notice shall state the name, number, date and place of registration of the SE, the date and place of publication and the title of publication, the registered office of the SE and its sector of activity.

2. Where the registered office of an SE is transferred in accordance with Article 8, notice shall be published giving the information provided for in paragraph 1, together with that relating to the new registration.

3. The particulars referred to in paragraph 1 shall be forwarded to the Office for Official Publications of the European Communities within one month of the publication referred to in Article 13.

Title II

Formation

Section 1

General

Article 15

1. Subject to this Regulation, the formation of an SE shall be governed by the law applicable to public limited-liability companies in the Member State in which the SE establishes its registered office.

2. The registration of an SE shall be publicised in accordance with Article 13.

Article 16

1. An SE shall acquire legal personality on the date on which it is registered in the register referred to in Article 12.

2. If acts have been performed in an SE's name before its registration in accordance with Article 12 and the SE does not assume the obligations arising out of such acts after its registration, the natural persons, companies, firms or other legal entities which performed those acts shall be jointly and severally liable therefor, without limit, in the absence of agreement to the contrary.

Section 2
Formation by merger

Article 17

1. An SE may be formed by means of a merger in accordance with Article 2(1).

2. Such a merger may be carried out in accordance with:

(a) the procedure for merger by acquisition laid down in Article 3(1) of the third Council Directive (78/855/EEC) of 9 October 1978 based on Article 54(3)(g) of the Treaty concerning mergers of public limited-liability companies(7) or

(b) the procedure for merger by the formation of a new company laid down in Article 4(1) of the said Directive.

In the case of a merger by acquisition, the acquiring company shall take the form of an SE when the merger takes place. In the case of a merger by the formation of a new company, the SE shall be the newly formed company.

Article 18

For matters not covered by this section or, where a matter is partly covered by it, for aspects not covered by it, each company involved in the formation of an SE by merger shall be governed by the provisions of the law of the Member State to which it is subject that apply to mergers of public limited-liability companies in accordance with Directive 78/855/EEC.

Article 19

The laws of a Member State may provide that a company governed by the law of that Member State may not take part in the formation of an SE by merger if any of that Member State's competent authorities opposes it before the issue of the certificate referred to in Article 25(2).

Such opposition may be based only on grounds of public interest. Review by a judicial authority shall be possible.

Article 20

1. The management or administrative organs of merging companies shall draw up draft terms of merger. The draft terms of merger shall include the following particulars:

(a) the name and registered office of each of the merging companies together with those proposed for the SE;

(b) the share-exchange ratio and the amount of any compensation;

(c) the terms for the allotment of shares in the SE;

(d) the date from which the holding of shares in the SE will entitle the holders to share in profits and any special conditions affecting that entitlement;

(e) the date from which the transactions of the merging companies will be treated for accounting purposes as being those of the SE;

(f) the rights conferred by the SE on the holders of shares to which special rights are attached and on the holders of securities other than shares, or the measures proposed concerning them;

(g) any special advantage granted to the experts who examine the draft terms of merger or to members of the administrative, management, supervisory or controlling organs of the merging companies;

(h) the statutes of the SE;

(i) information on the procedures by which arrangements for employee involvement are determined pursuant to Directive 2001/86/EC.

2. The merging companies may include further items in the draft terms of merger.

Article 21

For each of the merging companies and subject to the additional requirements imposed by the Member State to which the company concerned is subject, the following particulars shall be published in the national gazette of that Member State:

(a) the type, name and registered office of every merging company;

(b) the register in which the documents referred to in Article 3(2) of Directive 68/151/EEC are filed in respect of each merging company, and the number of the entry in that register;

(c) an indication of the arrangements made in accordance with Article 24 for the exercise of the rights of the creditors of the company in question and the address at which complete information on those arrangements may be obtained free of charge;

(d) an indication of the arrangements made in accordance with Article 24 for the exercise of the rights of minority shareholders of the company in question and the address at which complete information on those arrangements may be obtained free of charge;

(e) the name and registered office proposed for the SE.

Article 22

As an alternative to experts operating on behalf of each of the merging companies, one or more independent experts as defined in Article 10 of Directive 78/855/EEC, appointed for those purposes at the joint request of the companies by a judicial or administrative authority in the Member State of one of the merging companies or of the proposed SE, may examine the draft terms of merger and draw up a single report to all the shareholders.

The experts shall have the right to request from each of the merging companies any information they consider necessary to enable them to complete their function.

Article 23

1. The general meeting of each of the merging companies shall approve the draft terms of merger.

2. Employee involvement in the SE shall be decided pursuant to Directive 2001/86/EC. The general meetings of each of the merging companies may reserve the right to make registration of the SE conditional upon its express ratification of the arrangements so decided.

Article 24

1. The law of the Member State governing each merging company shall apply as in the case of a merger of public limited-liability companies, taking into account the cross-border nature of the merger, with regard to the protection of the interests of:

(a) creditors of the merging companies;

(b) holders of bonds of the merging companies;

(c) holders of securities, other than shares, which carry special rights in the merging companies.

2. A Member State may, in the case of the merging companies governed by its law, adopt provisions designed to ensure appropriate protection for minority shareholders who have opposed the merger.

Article 25

1. The legality of a merger shall be scrutinised, as regards the part of the procedure concerning each merging company, in accordance with the law on mergers of public limited-liability companies of the Member State to which the merging company is subject.

2. In each Member State concerned the court, notary or other competent authority shall issue a certificate conclusively attesting to the completion of the pre-merger acts and formalities.

3. If the law of a Member State to which a merging company is subject provides for a procedure to scrutinise and amend the share-exchange ratio, or a procedure to compensate minority shareholders, without preventing the registration of the merger, such procedures shall only apply if the other merging companies situated in Member States which do not provide for such procedure explicitly accept, when approving the draft terms of the merger in accordance with Article 23(1), the possibility for the shareholders of that merging company to have recourse to such procedure. In such cases, the court, notary or other competent authorities may issue the certificate referred to in paragraph 2 even if such a procedure has been commenced. The certificate must, however, indicate that the procedure is pending. The decision in the procedure shall be binding on the acquiring company and all its shareholders.

Article 26

1. The legality of a merger shall be scrutinised, as regards the part of the procedure concerning the completion of the merger and the formation of the SE, by the court, notary or other authority competent in the Member State of the proposed registered office of the SE to scrutinise that aspect of the legality of mergers of public limited-liability companies.

2. To that end each merging company shall submit to the competent authority the certificate referred to in Article 25(2) within six months of its issue together with a copy of the draft terms of merger approved by that company.

3. The authority referred to in paragraph 1 shall in particular ensure that the merging companies have approved draft terms of merger in the same terms and that arrangements for employee involvement have been determined pursuant to Directive 2001/86/EC.

4. That authority shall also satisfy itself that the SE has been formed in accordance with the requirements of the law of the Member State in which it has its registered office in accordance with Article 15.

Article 27

1. A merger and the simultaneous formation of an SE shall take effect on the date on which the SE is registered in accordance with Article 12.

2. The SE may not be registered until the formalities provided for in Articles 25 and 26 have been completed.

Article 28

For each of the merging companies the completion of the merger shall be publicised as laid down by the law of each Member State in accordance with Article 3 of Directive 68/151/EEC.

Article 29

1. A merger carried out as laid down in Article 17(2)(a) shall have the following consequences ipso jure and simultaneously:

(a) all the assets and liabilities of each company being acquired are transferred to the acquiring company;

(b) the shareholders of the company being acquired become shareholders of the acquiring company;

(c) the company being acquired ceases to exist;

(d) the acquiring company adopts the form of an SE.

2. A merger carried out as laid down in Article 17(2)(b) shall have the following consequences ipso jure and simultaneously:

(a) all the assets and liabilities of the merging companies are transferred to the SE;

(b) the shareholders of the merging companies become shareholders of the SE;

(c) the merging companies cease to exist.

3. Where, in the case of a merger of public limited-liability companies, the law of a Member State requires the completion of any special formalities before the transfer of certain assets, rights and obligations by the merging companies becomes effective against third parties, those formalities shall apply and shall be carried out either by the merging companies or by the SE following its registration.

4. The rights and obligations of the participating companies on terms and conditions of employment arising from national law, practice and individual employment contracts or employment relationships and existing at the date of the registration shall, by reason of such registration be transferred to the SE upon its registration.

Article 30

A merger as provided for in Article 2(1) may not be declared null and void once the SE has been registered.

The absence of scrutiny of the legality of the merger pursuant to Articles 25 and 26 may be included among the grounds for the winding-up of the SE.

Article 31

1. Where a merger within the meaning of Article 17(2)(a) is carried out by a company which holds all the shares and other securities conferring the right to vote at general meetings of another company, neither Article 20(1)(b), (c) and (d), Article 29(1)(b) nor Article 22 shall apply. National law governing each merging company and mergers of public limited-liability companies in accordance with Article 24 of Directive 78/855/EEC shall nevertheless apply.

2. Where a merger by acquisition is carried out by a company which holds 90% or more but not all of the shares and other securities conferring the right to vote at general meetings of another company, reports by the management or administrative body, reports by an independent expert or experts and the documents necessary for scrutiny shall be required only to the extent that the national law governing either the acquiring company or the company being acquired so requires.

Member States may, however, provide that this paragraph may apply where a company holds shares conferring 90% or more but not all of the voting rights.

Section 3
Formation of a holding SE

Article 32

1. A holding SE may be formed in accordance with Article 2(2).

A company promoting the formation of a holding SE in accordance with Article 2(2) shall continue to exist.

2. The management or administrative organs of the companies which promote such an operation shall draw up, in the same terms, draft terms for the formation of the holding SE. The draft terms shall include a report explaining and justifying the legal and economic aspects of the formation and indicating the implications for the shareholders and for the employees of the adoption of the form of a holding SE. The draft terms shall also set out the particulars provided for in Article 20(1)(a), (b), (c), (f), (g), (h) and (i) and shall fix the minimum proportion of the shares in each of the companies promoting the operation which the shareholders must contribute to the formation of the holding SE. That proportion shall be shares conferring more than 50% of the permanent voting rights.

3. For each of the companies promoting the operation, the draft terms for the formation of the holding SE shall be publicised in the manner laid down in each Member State's national law in accordance with Article 3 of Directive 68/151/EEC at least one month before the date of the general meeting called to decide thereon.

4. One or more experts independent of the companies promoting the operation, appointed or approved by a judicial or administrative authority in the Member State to which each company is subject in accordance with national provisions adopted in implementation of Directive 78/855/EEC, shall examine the draft terms of formation drawn up in accordance with paragraph 2 and draw up a written report for the shareholders of each company. By agreement between the companies promoting the operation, a single written report may be drawn up for the shareholders of all the companies by one or more independent experts, appointed or approved by a judicial or administrative authority in the Member State to which one of the companies promoting

the operation or the proposed SE is subject in accordance with national provisions adopted in implementation of Directive 78/855/EEC.

5. The report shall indicate any particular difficulties of valuation and state whether the proposed share-exchange ratio is fair and reasonable, indicating the methods used to arrive at it and whether such methods are adequate in the case in question.

6. The general meeting of each company promoting the operation shall approve the draft terms of formation of the holding SE.

Employee involvement in the holding SE shall be decided pursuant to Directive 2001/86/EC. The general meetings of each company promoting the operation may reserve the right to make registration of the holding SE conditional upon its express ratification of the arrangements so decided.

7. These provisions shall apply mutatis mutandis to private limited-liability companies.

Article 33

1. The shareholders of the companies promoting such an operation shall have a period of three months in which to inform the promoting companies whether they intend to contribute their shares to the formation of the holding SE. That period shall begin on the date upon which the terms for the formation of the holding SE have been finally determined in accordance with Article 32.

2. The holding SE shall be formed only if, within the period referred to in paragraph 1, the shareholders of the companies promoting the operation have assigned the minimum proportion of shares in each company in accordance with the draft terms of formation and if all the other conditions are fulfilled.

3. If the conditions for the formation of the holding SE are all fulfilled in accordance with paragraph 2, that fact shall, in respect of each of the promoting companies, be publicised in the manner laid down in the national law governing each of those companies adopted in implementation of Article 3 of Directive 68/151/EEC.

Shareholders of the companies promoting the operation who have not indicated whether they intend to make their shares available to the promoting companies for the purpose of forming the holding SE within the period referred to in paragraph 1 shall have a further month in which to do so.

4. Shareholders who have contributed their securities to the formation of the SE shall receive shares in the holding SE.

5. The holding SE may not be registered until it is shown that the formalities referred to in Article 32 have been completed and that the conditions referred to in paragraph 2 have been fulfilled.

Article 34

A Member State may, in the case of companies promoting such an operation, adopt provisions designed to ensure protection for minority shareholders who oppose the operation, creditors and employees.

Section 4
Formation of a subsidiary SE

Article 35

An SE may be formed in accordance with Article 2(3).

Article 36

Companies, firms and other legal entities participating in such an operation shall be subject to the provisions governing their participation in the formation of a subsidiary in the form of a public limited-liability company under national law.

Section 5
Conversion of an existing public limited-liability company into an SE

Article 37

1. An SE may be formed in accordance with Article 2(4).

2. Without prejudice to Article 12 the conversion of a public limited-liability company into an SE shall not result in the winding up of the company or in the creation of a new legal person.

3. The registered office may not be transferred from one Member State to another pursuant to Article 8 at the same time as the conversion is effected.

4. The management or administrative organ of the company in question shall draw up draft terms of conversion and a report explaining and justifying the legal and economic aspects of the conversion and indicating the implications for the shareholders and for the employees of the adoption of the form of an SE.

5. The draft terms of conversion shall be publicised in the manner laid down in each Member State's law in accordance with Article 3 of Directive 68/151/EEC at least one month before the general meeting called upon to decide thereon.

6. Before the general meeting referred to in paragraph 7 one or more independent experts appointed or approved, in accordance with the national pro-visions adopted in implementation of Article 10 of Directive 78/855/EEC, by a judicial or administrative authority in the Member State to which the company being converted into an SE is subject shall certify in compliance with Directive 77/91/EEC(8) mutatis mutandis that the company has net assets at least equivalent to its capital plus those reserves which must not be distributed under the law or the Statutes.

7. The general meeting of the company in question shall approve the draft terms of conversion together with the statutes of the SE. The decision of the general meeting shall be passed as laid down in the provisions of national law adopted in implementation of Article 7 of Directive 78/855/EEC.

8. Member States may condition a conversion to a favourable vote of a qualified majority or unanimity in the organ of the company to be converted within which employee participation is organised.

9. The rights and obligations of the company to be converted on terms and conditions of employment arising from national law, practice and individual employment contracts or employment relationships and existing at the date of the registration shall, by reason of such registration be transferred to the SE.

Title III
Structure of the SE

Article 38

Under the conditions laid down by this Regulation an SE shall comprise:

(a) a general meeting of shareholders and

(b) either a supervisory organ and a management organ (two-tier system) or an administrative organ (one-tier system) depending on the form adopted in the statutes.

Section 1
Two-tier system

Article 39

1. The management organ shall be responsible for managing the SE. A Member State may provide that a managing director or managing directors shall be responsible for the current management under the same conditions as for public limited-liability companies that have registered offices within that Member State's territory.

2. The member or members of the management organ shall be appointed and removed by the supervisory organ.

A Member State may, however, require or permit the statutes to provide that the member or members of the management organ shall be appointed and removed by the general meeting under the same conditions as for public limited-liability companies that have registered offices within its territory.

3. No person may at the same time be a member of both the management organ and the supervisory organ of the same SE. The supervisory organ may, however, nominate one of its members to act as a member of the management organ in the event of a vacancy. During such a period the functions of the person concerned as a member of the supervisory organ shall be suspended. A Member State may impose a time limit on such a period.

4. The number of members of the management organ or the rules for determining it shall be laid down in the SE's statutes. A Member State may, however, fix a minimum and/or a maximum number.

5. Where no provision is made for a two-tier system in relation to public limited-liability companies with registered offices within its territory, a Member State may adopt the appropriate measures in relation to SEs.

Article 40

1. The supervisory organ shall supervise the work of the management organ. It may not itself exercise the power to manage the SE.

2. The members of the supervisory organ shall be appointed by the general meeting. The members of the first supervisory organ may, however, be appointed by the statutes. This shall apply without prejudice to Article 47(4) or to any employee participation arrangements determined pursuant to Directive 2001/86/EC.

3. The number of members of the supervisory organ or the rules for determining it shall be laid down in the statutes. A Member State may, however, stipulate the number of

members of the supervisory organ for SEs registered within its territory or a minimum and/or a maximum number.

Article 41

1. The management organ shall report to the supervisory organ at least once every three months on the progress and foreseeable development of the SE's business.

2. In addition to the regular information referred to in paragraph 1, the management organ shall promptly pass the supervisory organ any information on events likely to have an appreciable effect on the SE.

3. The supervisory organ may require the management organ to provide information of any kind which it needs to exercise supervision in accordance with Article 40(1). A Member State may provide that each member of the supervisory organ also be entitled to this facility.

4. The supervisory organ may undertake or arrange for any investigations necessary for the performance of its duties.

5. Each member of the supervisory organ shall be entitled to examine all information submitted to it.

Article 42

The supervisory organ shall elect a chairman from among its members. If half of the members are appointed by employees, only a member appointed by the general meeting of shareholders may be elected chairman.

Section 2
The one-tier system

Article 43

1. The administrative organ shall manage the SE. A Member State may provide that a managing director or managing directors shall be responsible for the day-to-day management under the same conditions as for public limited-liability companies that have registered offices within that Member State's territory.

2. The number of members of the administrative organ or the rules for determining it shall be laid down in the SE's statutes. A Member State may, however, set a minimum and, where necessary, a maximum number of members.

The administrative organ shall, however, consist of at least three members where employee participation is regulated in accordance with Directive 2001/86/EC.

3. The member or members of the administrative organ shall be appointed by the general meeting. The members of the first administrative organ may, however, be appointed by the statutes. This shall apply without prejudice to Article 47(4) or to any employee participation arrangements determined pursuant to Directive 2001/86/EC.

4. Where no provision is made for a one-tier system in relation to public limited-liability companies with registered offices within its territory, a Member State may adopt the appropriate measures in relation to SEs.

Article 44

1. The administrative organ shall meet at least once every three months at intervals laid down by the statutes to discuss the progress and foreseeable development of the SE's business.

2. Each member of the administrative organ shall be entitled to examine all information submitted to it.

Article 45

The administrative organ shall elect a chairman from among its members. If half of the members are appointed by employees, only a member appointed by the general meeting of shareholders may be elected chairman.

Section 3

Rules common to the one-tier and two-tier systems

Article 46

1. Members of company organs shall be appointed for a period laid down in the statutes not exceeding six years.

2. Subject to any restrictions laid down in the statutes, members may be reappointed once or more than once for the period determined in accordance with paragraph 1.

Article 47

1. An SE's statutes may permit a company or other legal entity to be a member of one of its organs, provided that the law applicable to public limited-liability companies in the Member State in which the SE's registered office is situated does not provide otherwise.

That company or other legal entity shall designate a natural person to exercise its functions on the organ in question.

2. No person may be a member of any SE organ or a representative of a member within the meaning of paragraph 1 who:

(a) is disqualified, under the law of the Member State in which the SE's registered office is situated, from serving on the corresponding organ of a public limited-liability company governed by the law of that Member State, or

(b) is disqualified from serving on the corresponding organ of a public limited-liability company governed by the law of a Member State owing to a judicial or administrative decision delivered in a Member State.

3. An SE's statutes may, in accordance with the law applicable to public limited-liability companies in the Member State in which the SE's registered office is situated, lay down special conditions of eligibility for members representing the shareholders.

4. This Regulation shall not affect national law permitting a minority of share-holders or other persons or authorities to appoint some of the members of a company organ.

Article 48

1. An SE's statutes shall list the categories of transactions which require authorisation of the management organ by the supervisory organ in the two-tier system or an express decision by the administrative organ in the one-tier system.

A Member State may, however, provide that in the two-tier system the supervisory organ may itself make certain categories of transactions subject to authorisation.

2. A Member State may determine the categories of transactions which must at least be indicated in the statutes of SEs registered within its territory.

Article 49

The members of an SE's organs shall be under a duty, even after they have ceased to hold office, not to divulge any information which they have concerning the SE the disclosure of which might be prejudicial to the company's interests, except where such disclosure is required or permitted under national law pro-visions applicable to public limited-liability companies or is in the public interest.

Article 50

1. Unless otherwise provided by this Regulation or the statutes, the internal rules relating to quorums and decision-taking in SE organs shall be as follows:

(a) quorum: at least half of the members must be present or represented;

(b) decision-taking: a majority of the members present or represented.

2. Where there is no relevant provision in the statutes, the chairman of each organ shall have a casting vote in the event of a tie. There shall be no provision to the contrary in the statutes, however, where half of the supervisory organ consists of employees' representatives.

3. Where employee participation is provided for in accordance with Directive 2001/86/EC, a Member State may provide that the supervisory organ's quorum and decision-making shall, by way of derogation from the provisions referred to in paragraphs 1 and 2, be subject to the rules applicable, under the same conditions, to public limited-liability companies governed by the law of the Member State concerned.

Article 51

Members of an SE's management, supervisory and administrative organs shall be liable, in accordance with the provisions applicable to public limited-liability companies in the Member State in which the SE's registered office is situated, for loss or damage sustained by the SE following any breach on their part of the legal, statutory or other obligations inherent in their duties.

Section 4
General meeting

Article 52

The general meeting shall decide on matters for which it is given sole responsibility by:

(a) this Regulation or

(b) the legislation of the Member State in which the SE's registered office is situated adopted in implementation of Directive 2001/86/EC.

Furthermore, the general meeting shall decide on matters for which responsibility is given to the general meeting of a public limited-liability company governed by the law of the Member State in which the SE's registered office is situated, either by the law of that Member State or by the SE's statutes in accordance with that law.

Article 53

Without prejudice to the rules laid down in this section, the organisation and conduct of general meetings together with voting procedures shall be governed by the law applicable to public limited-liability companies in the Member State in which the SE's registered office is situated.

Article 54

1. An SE shall hold a general meeting at least once each calendar year, within six months of the end of its financial year, unless the law of the Member State in which the SE's registered office is situated applicable to public limited-liability companies carrying on the same type of activity as the SE provides for more frequent meetings. A Member State may, however, provide that the first general meeting may be held at any time in the 18 months following an SE's incorporation.

2. General meetings may be convened at any time by the management organ, the administrative organ, the supervisory organ or any other organ or competent authority in accordance with the national law applicable to public limited-liability companies in the Member State in which the SE's registered office is situated.

Article 55

1. One or more shareholders who together hold at least 10% of an SE's subscribed capital may request the SE to convene a general meeting and draw up the agenda therefor; the SE's statutes or national legislation may provide for a smaller proportion under the same conditions as those applicable to public limited-liability companies.

2. The request that a general meeting be convened shall state the items to be put on the agenda.

3. If, following a request made under paragraph 1, a general meeting is not held in due time and, in any event, within two months, the competent judicial or administrative authority within the jurisdiction of which the SE's registered office is situated may order that a general meeting be convened within a given period or authorise either the shareholders who have requested it or their representatives to convene a general meeting. This shall be without prejudice to any national provisions which allow the shareholders themselves to convene general meetings.

Article 56

One or more shareholders who together hold at least 10% of an SE's subscribed capital may request that one or more additional items be put on the agenda of any general meeting. The procedures and time limits applicable to such requests shall be laid down by the national law of the Member State in which the SE's registered office is situated or, failing that, by the SE's statutes. The above pro-portion may be reduced by the statutes or by the law of the Member State in which the SE's registered office is situated under the same conditions as are applicable to public limited-liability companies.

Article 57

Save where this Regulation or, failing that, the law applicable to public limited-liability companies in the Member State in which an SE's registered office is situated requires a larger majority, the general meeting's decisions shall be taken by a majority of the votes validly cast.

Article 58

The votes cast shall not include votes attaching to shares in respect of which the shareholder has not taken part in the vote or has abstained or has returned a blank or spoilt ballot paper.

Article 59

1. Amendment of an SE's statutes shall require a decision by the general meeting taken by a majority which may not be less than two thirds of the votes cast, unless the law applicable to public limited-liability companies in the Member State in which an SE's registered office is situated requires or permits a larger majority.

2. A Member State may, however, provide that where at least half of an SE's subscribed capital is represented, a simple majority of the votes referred to in paragraph 1 shall suffice.

3. Amendments to an SE's statutes shall be publicised in accordance with Article 13.

Article 60

1. Where an SE has two or more classes of shares, every decision by the general meeting shall be subject to a separate vote by each class of shareholders whose class rights are affected thereby.

2. Where a decision by the general meeting requires the majority of votes specified in Article 59(1) or (2), that majority shall also be required for the separate vote by each class of shareholders whose class rights are affected by the decision.

Title IV
Annual Accounts and Consolidated Accounts

Article 61

Subject to Article 62 an SE shall be governed by the rules applicable to public limited-liability companies under the law of the Member State in which its registered office is situated as regards the preparation of its annual and, where appropriate, consolidated accounts including the accompanying annual report and the auditing and publication of those accounts.

Article 62

1. An SE which is a credit or financial institution shall be governed by the rules laid down in the national law of the Member State in which its registered office is situated in implementation of Directive 2000/12/EC of the European Parliament and of the Council of 20 March 2000 relating to the taking up and pursuit of the business of credit institutions(9) as regards the preparation of its annual and, where appropriate, consolidated accounts, including the accompanying annual report and the auditing and publication of those accounts.

2. An SE which is an insurance undertaking shall be governed by the rules laid down in the national law of the Member State in which its registered office is situated in implementation of Council Directive 91/674/EEC of 19 December 1991 on the annual

accounts and consolidated accounts of insurance undertakings(10) as regards the preparation of its annual and, where appropriate, consolidated accounts including the accompanying annual report and the auditing and publication of those accounts.

Title V
Winding Up, Liquidation, Insolvency and Cessation Of Payments

Article 63

As regards winding up, liquidation, insolvency, cessation of payments and similar procedures, an SE shall be governed by the legal provisions which would apply to a public limited-liability company formed in accordance with the law of the Member State in which its registered office is situated, including pro-visions relating to decision-making by the general meeting.

Article 64

1. When an SE no longer complies with the requirement laid down in Article 7, the Member State in which the SE's registered office is situated shall take appropriate measures to oblige the SE to regularise its position within a specified period either:

(a) by re-establishing its head office in the Member State in which its registered office is situated or

(b) by transferring the registered office by means of the procedure laid down in Article 8.

2.The Member State in which the SE's registered office is situated shall put in place the measures necessary to ensure that an SE which fails to regularise its position in accordance with paragraph 1 is liquidated.

3.The Member State in which the SE's registered office is situated shall set up a judicial remedy with regard to any established infringement of Article 7. That remedy shall have a suspensory effect on the procedures laid down in paragraphs 1 and 2.

4. Where it is established on the initiative of either the authorities or any interested party that an SE has its head office within the territory of a Member State in breach of Article 7, the authorities of that Member State shall immediately inform the Member State in which the SE's registered office is situated.

Article 65

Without prejudice to provisions of national law requiring additional publication, the initiation and termination of winding up, liquidation, insolvency or cessation of payment procedures and any decision to continue operating shall be publicised in accordance with Article 13.

Article 66

1. An SE may be converted into a public limited-liability company governed by the law of the Member State in which its registered office is situated. No decision on conversion may be taken before two years have elapsed since its registration or before the first two sets of annual accounts have been approved.

2. The conversion of an SE into a public limited-liability company shall not result in the winding up of the company or in the creation of a new legal person.

3. The management or administrative organ of the SE shall draw up draft terms of conversion and a report explaining and justifying the legal and economic aspects of the conversion and indicating the implications of the adoption of the public limited-liability company for the shareholders and for the employees.

4. The draft terms of conversion shall be publicised in the manner laid down in each Member State's law in accordance with Article 3 of Directive 68/151/EEC at least one month before the general meeting called to decide thereon.

5. Before the general meeting referred to in paragraph 6, one or more independent experts appointed or approved, in accordance with the national pro-visions adopted in implementation of Article 10 of Directive 78/855/EEC, by a judicial or administrative authority in the Member State to which the SE being converted into a public limited-liability company is subject shall certify that the company has assets at least equivalent to its capital.

6. The general meeting of the SE shall approve the draft terms of conversion together with the statutes of the public limited-liability company. The decision of the general meeting shall be passed as laid down in the provisions of national law adopted in implementation of Article 7 of Directive 78/855/EEC.

Title VI
Additional and Transitional Provisions

Article 67

1. If and so long as the third phase of economic and monetary union (EMU) does not apply to it each Member State may make SEs with registered offices within its territory subject to the same provisions as apply to public limited-liability companies covered by its legislation as regards the expression of their capital. An SE may, in any case, express its capital in euro as well. In that event the national currency/euro conversion rate shall be that for the last day of the month preceding that of the formation of the SE.

2. If and so long as the third phase of EMU does not apply to the Member State in which an SE has its registered office, the SE may, however, prepare and publish its annual and, where appropriate, consolidated accounts in euro. The Member State may require that the SE's annual and, where appropriate, consolidated accounts be prepared and published in the national currency under the same conditions as those laid down for public limited-liability companies governed by the law of that Member State. This shall not prejudge the additional possibility for an SE of publishing its annual and, where appropriate, consolidated accounts in euro in accordance with Council Directive 90/604/EEC of 8 November 1990 amending Directive 78/60/EEC on annual accounts and Directive 83/349/EEC on consolidated accounts as concerns the exemptions for small and medium-sized companies and the publication of accounts in ecu(11).

Title VII
Final Provisions

Article 68

1. The Member States shall make such provision as is appropriate to ensure the effective application of this Regulation.

2. Each Member State shall designate the competent authorities within the meaning of Articles 8, 25, 26, 54, 55 and 64. It shall inform the Commission and the other Member States accordingly.

Article 69

Five years at the latest after the entry into force of this Regulation, the Commission shall forward to the Council and the European Parliament a report on the application of the Regulation and proposals for amendments, where appropriate. The report shall, in particular, analyse the appropriateness of:

(a) allowing the location of an SE's head office and registered office in different Member States;

(b) broadening the concept of merger in Article 17(2) in order to admit also other types of merger than those defined in Articles 3(1) and 4(1) of Directive 78/855/EEC;

(c) revising the jurisdiction clause in Article 8(16) in the light of any pro-vision which may have been inserted in the 1968 Brussels Convention or in any text adopted by Member States or by the Council to replace such Convention;

(d) allowing provisions in the statutes of an SE adopted by a Member State in execution of authorisations given to the Member States by this Regulation or laws adopted to ensure the effective application of this Regulation in respect to the SE which deviate from or are complementary to these laws, even when such provisions would not be authorised in the statutes of a public limited-liability company having its registered office in the Member State.

Article 70

This Regulation shall enter into force on 8 October 2004.

This Regulation shall be binding in its entirety and directly applicable in all Member States.

(1) OJ C 263, 16.10.1989, p. 41 and OJ C 176, 8.7.1991, p. 1.

(2) Opinion of 4 September 2001 (not yet published in the Official Journal).

(3) OJ C124, 21.5.1990, p. 34.

(4) See p 22 of this Official Journal.

(5) OJ L395, 30.12.1989, p. 40. Directive as last amended by the 1994 Act of Accession.

(6) OJ L65, 14.3.1968, p. 8. Directive as last amended by the 1994 Act of Accession.

(7) OJ L295, 20.10.1978, p. 36. Directive as last amended by the 1994 Act of Accession.

(8) Second Council Directive 77/91/EEC of 13 December 1976 on coordination of safeguards which, for the protection of the interests of members and others, are required by Member States of companies within the meaning of the second paragraph of Article 58 of the Treaty, in respect of the formation of public limited liability companies and the maintenance and alteration

of their capital, with a view to making such safeguards equivalent (OJ L 26, 31.1.1977, p. 1). Directive as last amended by the 1994 Act of Accession.

(9) OJ L126, 26.5.2000, p. 1.

(10) OJ L374, 31.12.1991, p. 7.

(11) OJ L317, 16.11.1990, p. 57.

ANNEX I

PUBLIC LIMITED-LIABILITY COMPANIES REFERRED TO IN ARTICLE 2(1)

BELGIUM:

la société anonyme/de naamloze vennootschap

DENMARK:

aktieselskaber

GERMANY:

die Aktiengesellschaft

GREECE:

ανωνυμη εταιρία

SPAIN:

la sociedad anónima

FRANCE:

la société anonyme

IRELAND:

public companies limited by shares

public companies limited by guarantee having a share capital

ITALY:

società per azioni

LUXEMBOURG:

la société anonyme

NETHERLANDS:

de naamloze vennootschap

AUSTRIA:

die Aktiengesellschaft

PORTUGAL:

a sociedade anónima de responsabilidade limitada

FINLAND:

julkinen osakeyhtiö/publikt aktiebolag

SWEDEN:

publikt aktiebolag

UNITED KINGDOM:

public companies limited by shares

public companies limited by guarantee having a share capital

ANNEX II
PUBLIC AND PRIVATE LIMITED-LIABILITY COMPANIES REFERRED TO IN ARTICLE 2(2)

BELGIUM:

la société anonyme/de naamloze vennootschap,

la société privée à responsabilité limitée/besloten vennootschap met beperkte aansprakelijkheid

DENMARK:

aktieselskaber,

anpartselskaber

GERMANY:

die Aktiengesellschaft,

die Gesellschaft mit beschränkter Haftung

GREECE:

ανωνυμη εταιρία
εταιρία περιοριομένης ευνύης

SPAIN:

la sociedad anónima,

la sociedad de responsabilidad limitada

FRANCE:

la société anonyme,

la société responsabilit limite

IRELAND:

public companies limited by shares,

public companies limited by guarantee having a share capital,

private companies limited by shares,

private companies limited by guarantee having a share capital

ITALY:

società per azioni,

società a responsabilità limitata

LUXEMBOURG:

la société anonyme,

la société à responsabilité limitée

NETHERLANDS:

de naamloze vennootschap,

de besloten vennootschap met beperkte aansprakelijkheid

AUSTRIA:

die Aktiengesellschaft,

die Gesellschaft mit beschränkter Haftung

PORTUGAL:

a sociedade anónima de responsabilidade limitada,

a sociedade por quotas de responsabilidade limitada

FINLAND:

osakeyhtiö

aktiebolag

SWEDEN:

aktiebolag

UNITED KINGDOM:

public companies limited by shares,

public companies limited by guarantee having a share capital,

private companies limited by shares,

private companies limited by guarantee having a share capital

EXPLANATORY NOTE

(This note is not part of the instrument and does not purport to be a legal interpretation).

These Regulations along with the European Communities (European Public Limited-Liability Company) Forms Regulations 2006 give full effect to Council Regulation (EC) No. 2157/2001 of 8 October 2001 on the Statute for a European company (SE).

It is a new legal instrument based on European Community law that gives companies with commercial interests in more than one Member State the option of forming a European Company known formally by its Latin name of 'Societas Europaea' (SE). The European Company Statute makes it easier for companies to expand and to manage cross-border operations without the red tape of having to set up a network of subsidiaries.

European Communities (European Public Limited Liability Company) (Forms) Regulations 2007

SI 22/2007

I, MICHEAL MARTIN, Minister for Enterprise, Trade and Employment, in exercise of the powers conferred on me by section 3 of the European Communities Act 1972 (No. 27 of 1972), as amended, for the purpose of giving full effect to Council Regulation (EC) No. 2157/2001 of 8 October 2001 (OJ L294, 10/11/2001, p 1) on the Statute for a European company (SE) and the European Communities (European Public Limited-Liability Company) Regulations 2007 hereby make the following regulations:

1. (1) These Regulations may be cited as the European Communities (European Public Limited-Liability Company) (Forms) Regulations 2007.

(2) The Companies Acts and these Regulations shall be construed together as one.

2. These Regulations shall come into effect on 22nd of January 2007.

3. In these Regulations—

'Act of 1963' means the Companies Act 1963 (No. 33 of 1963);

'Act of 1982' means the Companies (Amendment) Act 1982 (No. 10 of 1982); 'Act of 1983' means the Companies (Amendment) Act 1983 (No. 13 of 1983); 'Act of 1990' means the Companies Act 1990 (No.33 of 1990);

'Act of 1999' means the Stamp Duties Consolidation Act 1999(No. 31 of 1999); 'Act of 2001' means the Company Law Enforcement Act 2001(No. 28 of 2001);

'Council Regulation' means Council Regulation 2157/2001/EC of 8 October 2001[1] on the Statute for a European Company;

'European Regulations' mean the European Communities (European Public Limited-Liability Company) Regulations 2007;

'No. 2 Act of 1999' means the Companies (Amendment) (No 2) Act 1999 (No. 30 of 1999);

'Regulations of 2002' means the Companies Act 1990 (Form and Content of Documents delivered to Registrar) Regulations 2002 (SI 39 of 2002).

4. A reference in these Regulations to a numbered Article is a reference to the Article so numbered in the Council Regulation.

5. A word or expression used in these Regulations, which is also used in the European Regulations, has the same meaning as it has in those Regulations.

6. The form set out in Part 1 of the Schedule to these Regulations (SE 1), or a form to like effect, is prescribed as the form to be used for the purposes of Articles 2(1) and 25(2) of the Council Regulation, Regulations 4(1)(a) and 28 of the European Regulations, section 3 and 3A (inserted by section 101 of the Act of 2001) of the Act of 1982, section 5 of the Act of 1983, sections 42 and 43, section 44 (other than subsection (2)) and section 45 (other than subsections (3)(b) and (5)) of the No. 2 Act of 1999, section 117 of the Act of 1999 and the Regulations of 2002.

7. The form set out in Part II of the Schedule to these Regulations (SE 2), or a form to like effect, is prescribed as the form to be used for the purposes of Article 2(2) of the

Council Regulation, Regulations 4(1)(b) and 28 of the European Regulations, section 3 and 3A (inserted by section 101 of the Act of 2001) of the Act of 1982, section 5 of the Act of 1983, sections 42 and 43, section 44 (other than subsection (2)) and section 45 (other than subsections (3)(b) and (5)) of the No. 2 Act of 1999, section 117 of the Act of 1999 and the Regulations of 2002.

8. The form set out in Part III of the Schedule to these Regulations (SE 3), or a form to like effect, is prescribed as the form to be used for the purposes of Article 2(3) of the Council Regulation, Regulations 4(1)(c) and 28 of the European Regulations, section 3 and 3A (inserted by section 101 of the Act of 2001) of the Act of 1982, section 5 of the Act of 1983, sections 42 and 43, section 44 (other than subsection (2)) and section 45 (other than subsections (3)(b) and (5)) of the No. 2 Act of 1999, section 117 of the Act of 1999 and the Regulations of 2002.

9. The form set out in part IV of the Schedule to these Regulations (SE 4), or a form to like effect, is prescribed as the form to be used for the purposes of Article 2(4) of the Council Regulation, Regulations 4(1)(d) and 28 of the European Regulations, section 3 and 3A (inserted by section 101 of the Act of 2001) of the Act of 1982, section 5 of the Act of 1983, sections 42 and 43, section 44 (other than subsection (2)) and section 45 (other than subsections (3)(b) and (5)) of the No. 2 Act of 1999, section 117 of the Act of 1999 and the Regulations of 2002.

10. The form set out in Part V of the Schedule to these Regulations (SE 5), or a form to like effect, is prescribed as the form to be used for the purposes of Article 3(2) of the Council Regulation, Regulations 4(1)(e) and 28 of the European Regulations, section 3 and 3A (inserted by section 101 of the Act of 2001) of the Act of 1982, section 5 of the Act of 1983, sections 42 and 43, section 44 (other than subsection (2)) and section 45 (other than subsections (3)(b) and (5)) of the No. 2 Act of 1999, section 117 of the Act of 1999 and the Regulations of 2002.

11. The form set out in Part VI of the Schedule to these Regulations (SE 6), or a form to like effect, is prescribed as the form to be used for the purposes of Article 8 of the Council Regulation, Regulations 5 and 28 of the European Regulations, Section 195 (8) (inserted by section 91 of the Act of 2001) of the Act of 1963, section 117 of the Act of 1999, section 43, section 44 (other than subsection (2)) and section 45 (other than subsections (3)(b) and (5)) of the No. 2 Act of 1999 and the Regulations of 2002.

12. The form set out in Part VII of the Schedule to these Regulations (SE 7), or a form to like effect, is prescribed as the form to be used for the purposes of Article 8 of the Council Regulation, Regulation 7 and 11 of the European Regulations, section 249A (inserted by section 107 of the Act of 2001) of the Act of 1990 and the Regulations of 2002.

13. The form set out in Part VIII of the Schedule to these Regulations (SE 8), or a form to like effect, is prescribed as the form to be used for the purposes of Article 8(7) of the Council Regulation, Regulation 7 of the European Regulations, section 249A (inserted by section 107 of the Act of 2001) of the Act of 1990 and the Regulations of 2002.

14. The form set out in Part IX of the Schedule to these Regulations (SE 9), or a form to like effect, is prescribed as the form to be used for the purposes of Regulation 33(2) of the European Regulations, section 249A (inserted by section 107 of the Act of 2001) of the Act of 1990 and the Regulations of 2002.

15. The form set out in Part X of the Schedule to these Regulations (SE 10), or a form to like effect, is prescribed as the form to be used for the purposes of Articles 8(2) and 13 of the Council Regulation, Regulations 7 and 21 (1) of the European Regulations, section 249A (inserted by section 107 of the Act of 2001) of the Act of 1990 and the Regulations of 2002.

16. The form set out in Part XI of the Schedule to these Regulations (SE 11), or a form to like effect, is prescribed as the form to be used for the purposes of Articles 13 and 32(3) of the Council Regulation, Regulation 21(1) of the European Regulations, section 249A (inserted by section 107 of the Act of 2001) of the Act of 1990 and the Regulations of 2002.

17. The form set out in Part XII of the Schedule to these Regulations (SE 12), or a form to like effect, is prescribed as the form to be used for the purposes of Articles 13 and 37(5) of the Council Regulation, Regulation 21(1) of the European Regulations, section 249A (inserted by section 107 of the Act of 2001) of the Act of 1990 and the Regulations of 2002.

18. The form set out in Part X III of the Schedule to these Regulations (SE 13), or a form to like effect, is prescribed as the form to be used for the purposes of Articles 13 and 33(3) of the Council Regulation, Regulation 23 of the European Regulations, section 249A (inserted by section 107 of the Act of 2001) of the Act of 1990 and the Regulations of 2002.

19. The form set out in Part XIV of the Schedule to these Regulations (SE 14), or a form to like effect, is prescribed as the form to be used for the purposes of Articles 13 and 59(3) of the Council Regulation, Regulations 24(1) and 32(a) of the European Regulations, section 249A (inserted by section 107 of the Act of 2001) of the Act of 1990 and the Regulations of 2002.

20. The form set out in Part XV of the Schedule to these Regulations (SE 15), or a form to like effect, is prescribed as the form to be used for the purposes of Articles 13 and 65 of the Council Regulation, Regulations 24(1) and 32(b) of the European Regulations, section 249A (inserted by section 107 of the Act of 2001) of the Act of 1990 and the Regulations of 2002.

Note: The forms set out in the Schedule to this Instrument are not replicated here.

EXPLANATORY NOTE

(*This note is not part of the instrument and does not purport to be a legal interpretation*).

This Regulation along with the European Communities (European Public Limited-Liability Company) Regulations 2007 give full effect to Council Regulation (EC) No. 2157/2001 of 8 October 2001 on the Statute for a European company (SE).

European Communities (Companies) (Amendment) Regulations 2007

SI 49/2007

I, MICHEÁL MARTIN, Minister for Enterprise, Trade and Employment, in exercise of the powers conferred on me by section 3 of the European Communities Act 1972 (No. 27 of 1972) and for the purpose of giving effect to Directive 2003/58/EC of the European Parliament and of the Council of 15 July 2003(OJ L221, 4.9.2–3. p 13) hereby make the following regulations:

1. (1) These Regulations may be cited as the European Communities (Companies) (Amendment) Regulations 2007.

(2) The Companies Acts and these Regulations shall be construed together as one.

(3) These Regulations shall come into operation on 1 April 2007.

2. In these Regulations 'Principal Regulations' means the European Communities (Companies) Regulations 1973 (S.I. No. 163 of 1973), as amended by the European Communities (Companies) Regulations 2004 (S.I. No. 839 of 2004).

3. The Principal Regulations are amended—

(a) [...][a]

(b) [...][b]

(c) [...][c]

(d) [...][d]

Amendments

a EC(C)R 1973 is amended by the insertion of reg 2A.

b EC(C)R 1973, reg 4 is amended by the substitution of para (1)(g) and the insertion of paras (4), (5) and (6).

c EC(C)R 1973 is amended by the substitution of reg 9.

d EC(C)R 1973 is amended by the substitution of reg 12.

EXPLANATORY NOTE

(*This note is not part of the Instrument and does not purport to be a legal interpretation*).

These Regulations give further effect to Directive 2003/58/EC amending Directive 68/151/EEC ('First Company Law Directive'). They provide for the certification of electronic copies of company documents and particulars obtainable from the Companies Registration Office. The Regulations also make provision for the voluntary filing of certified translations of company documents and particulars filed obligatorily in Irish or English. They also extend existing information disclosure requirements concerning letter and order forms to such communication in electronic form and to company websites.

Publication of company documents and particulars by electronic means in the Companies Registration Office Gazette was provided for by S.I. No. 839 of 2004.

Transparency (Directive 2004/109/EC) Regulations 2007

SI 277/2007

ARRANGEMENT OF REGULATIONS

Regulations

PART 1

PRELIMINARY AND GENERAL

PART 2

PERIODIC FINANCIAL REPORTING

PART 3

EXEMPTIONS/THIRDCOUNTRY EQUIVALENCE IN RESPECT OF PART 2

PART 4

LIABILITY FOR FALSE OR MISLEADING STATEMENTS IN CERTAIN PUBLICATIONS

PART 5

ONGOING INFORMATION ABOUT MAJOR SHAREHOLDINGS

PART 6

CONTINUING OBLIGATIONS AND ACCESS TO INFORMATION

PART 7

DISSEMINATION OF INFORMATION

PART 8

COMPETENT AUTHORITIES

PART 9

POWERS OF COMPETENT AUTHORITIES

PART 10

ADMINISTRATIVE SANCTIONS

PART 11

CO-OPERATION BETWEEN COMPETENT AUTHORITIES

PART 12

PENALTIES, GENERAL AND OTHER MISCELLANEOUS PROVISIONS

I, MICHAEL AHERN TD, Minister of State at the Department of Enterprise, Trade and Employment, in exercise of the powers conferred on me by section 20 of the Investment Funds, Companies and Miscellaneous Provisions Act 2006 (No. 41 of 2006) and the Enterprise, Trade and Employment (Delegation of Ministerial Functions) Order 2007 (S.I. No. 51 of 2007), and for the purpose of giving effect to Directive 2004/109/EC of the European Parliament and of the Council of 15 December 2004 and for the other purposes mentioned in that section, hereby make the following regulations:

PART 1

PRELIMINARY AND GENERAL

1. Citation, commencement and construction

(1) These Regulations may be cited as the Transparency (Directive 2004/109/EC) Regulations 2007.

(2) These Regulations shall come into operation on 13th June 2007.

(3) These Regulations shall be read as one with the Companies Acts.

2. Interpretation and application

(1) In these Regulations:

'Act of 2006' means the Investment Funds, Companies and Miscellaneous Pro-visions Act 2006 (No.41 of 2006);

'admitted to trading on a regulated market' means admitted to trading on a regulated market situated or operating within a Member State;

'approved stock exchange' has the same meaning as it has in the Stock Exchange Act 1995 (No. 9 of 1995);

'Bank' means the Central Bank and Financial Services Authority of Ireland;

'collective investment undertaking other than the closed-end type' means unit trusts and investment companies:

(a) the object of which is the collective investment of capital provided by the public and which operate on the principle of risk spreading; and

(b) the units of which are, at the holder's request, repurchased or redeemed, directly or indirectly, out of the assets of the undertaking;

'company' includes any body corporate;

'central competent authority of a home Member State' means—

(a) where the State is the home Member State, the Bank, or

(b) where the State is a host Member State, the central competent administrative authority designated as such under the national law of the home Member State for the purposes of the Directive;

'contravention' includes, in relation to any provision, a failure to comply with that provision;

'controlled undertaking' means any undertaking—

(a) in which a person has a majority of the voting rights, or

(b) of which a person has the right to appoint or remove a majority of the members of the administrative, management or supervisory body and is at the same time a shareholder in, or member of, the under-taking in question, or

(c) of which a person is a shareholder or member and alone controls a majority of the shareholders' or members' voting rights, respectively, pursuant to an agreement entered into with other shareholders or members of the undertaking in question, or

(d) over which a person has the power to exercise, or actually exercises, dominant influence or control;

'Court' means the High Court;

'credit institution' means an undertaking as defined by Article 4(1)(a) of Directive 2006/48/EC of the European Parliament and of the Council of 14 June 2006 relating to the taking up and pursuit of the business of credit institutions;

'debt securities' means bonds or other forms of transferable securitised debts, with the exception of securities which are equivalent to shares in companies or which, if converted or if the rights conferred by them are exercised, give rise to a right to acquire shares or securities equivalent to shares;

'Directive' means Directive 2004/109/EC of the European Parliament and of the Council of 15 December 2004;

'EEA Agreement' means the Agreement on the European Economic Area signed at Oporto on 2 May 1992, as adjusted by the Protocol signed at Brussels on 17 March 1993;

'EEA State' means a state that is a contracting party to the EEA Agreement;

'electronic means' are means of electronic equipment for the processing (including digital compression), storage and transmission of data, employing wires, radio, optical technologies, or any other electromagnetic means;

'enactment' includes an instrument made under an enactment; 'home Member State' means—

(a) in the case of an issuer of debt securities the denomination per unit of which is less than €1,000 or an issuer of shares:

(i) if the issuer is incorporated or formed in a Member State, the Member State in which it has its registered office,

(ii) if the issuer is incorporated or formed in a state or territory which is not a Member State, the Member State in which it is required to file the annual information with the competent authority in accordance with Article 10 of Directive 2003/71/EC of the European Parliament and of the Council of 4 November 2003, and

(b) in the case of an issuer of debt securities not falling within paragraph (a), the Member State chosen by the issuer from among the Member State in which the issuer has its registered office and those Member States which have admitted its securities to trading on a regulated market on their territory,

and paragraph (2) has effect for the purposes of this definition;

'host Member State' means a Member State in which securities are admitted to trading on a regulated market, if different from the home Member State;

'IAASA' means the Irish Auditing and Accounting Supervisory Authority;

'IFRS' means International Financial Reporting Standards within the meaning of Regulation (EC) No. 1606/2002;

'implementing measures' means any measures directly applicable in con-sequence of the Directive and, without prejudice to the generality of the foregoing, includes Commission Decision 2006/891/EC of 4 December 2006;

'in writing' includes by facsimile;

'issuer' means a legal entity governed by private or public law, including a State, whose securities are admitted to trading on a regulated market, the issuer being, in the case of depository receipts representing securities, the issuer of the securities represented;

'management company' means a company as defined in Article 1a(2) of Council Directive 85/611/EEC of 20 December 1985 on the coordination of laws, regulations and administrative provisions relating to undertakings for collective investment in transferable securities (UCITS);

'market maker' means a person who holds himself or herself out on the financial markets on a continuous basis as being willing to deal on own account by buying and selling financial instruments against his or her proprietary capital at prices defined by him or her;

'market operator' means one or more persons who manage or operate the business of a regulated market (or who do both those things), and may be the regulated market itself;

'Member State' means a Member State of the European Union or an EEA State;

'Minister' means the Minister for Enterprise, Trade and Employment;

'regulated information' means all information which the issuer, or any other person who has applied for the admission of securities to trading on a regulated market without the issuer's consent, is required to disclose—

(a) under the Directive,

(b) under Article 6 of Directive 2003/6/EC of the European Parliament and of the Council of 28 January 2003, or

(c) by virtue of more stringent requirements made by the Bank in exercise of the powers under Regulation 40(3) or under other laws, regulations or administrative provisions of the State adopted under Article 3(1) of the Directive;

'regulated market' means a market as defined by Article 4(1), point 14, of Directive 2004/39/EC of the European Parliament and of the Council of 21 April 2004;

'RIS' means a service of the kind commonly known as a regulatory information service;

'securities' means transferable securities as defined in Article 4(1), point 18, of Directive 2004/39/EC of the European Parliament and of the Council of 21 April 2004 with the exception of money-market instruments, as defined in Article 4(1), point 19, of that Directive having a maturity of less than 12 months;

'securities issued in a continuous or repeated manner' means debt securities of the same issuer on tap or at least two separate issues of securities of a similar type or class (or both);

'shareholder' means any person governed by private or public law, who holds, directly or indirectly:

(a) shares of the issuer in the person's own name and on the person's own account,

(b) shares of the issuer in the person's own name, but on behalf of another person,

(c) depository receipts, in which case the holder of the depository receipt shall be considered as the shareholder of the underlying shares rep-resented by the depository receipts;

'supplemental Directive' has the same meaning as it has in the Act of 2006;

'transparency (regulated markets) law' has the same meaning as it has in the Act of 2006;

'treasury shares' has the same meaning as it has in the Companies Acts;

'units of a collective investment undertaking' means securities issued by a collective investment undertaking and representing the rights of the participants in such an undertaking over its assets.

(2) (a) The definition of 'home Member State' in paragraph (1) shall be applicable to debt securities in a currency other than euro, provided that the value of such denomination per unit is, at the date of the issue, less than €1,000, unless it is nearly equivalent to €1,000.

(b) For the purposes of paragraph (b) of the definition of 'home Member State' in paragraph (1), the issuer may choose only one Member State as its home Member State. Its choice shall remain valid for at least three years unless its securities are no longer admitted to trading on any regulated market in the Community.

(3) For the purposes of the definition of 'controlled undertaking' in paragraph (1), the references to the holder's rights in relation to voting, appointment and removal include references to the rights of any other undertaking controlled by the shareholder and those of any person acting, albeit in the person's own name, on behalf of the shareholder or of any other undertaking controlled by the shareholder.

(4) A word or expression that is used in these Regulations and is also used in the Directive or a supplemental Directive, as the case may be, shall have in these Regulations the same meaning as it has in the Directive or the supplemental Directive, as the case may be.[a]

(5) A reference in these Regulations to a Directive or Regulation of the Council or Commission of the European Communities shall be construed as a reference to the Directive or Regulation as amended or extended by any other Directive or Regulation of the Council or Commission of the European Communities.

(6) These Regulations shall not apply to units issued by collective investment undertakings other than the closed-end type or units acquired or disposed of in such collective investment undertakings.

3. Application of Parts 2, 3, 5, 6 and 7 subject to Regulation 40(3)

(1) Any requirement specified in Part 2, 3, 5, 6 or 7 shall be read as being, and shall operate, subject to the Bank's not having exercised the power under Regulation 40(3) (in the circumstances where such power is exercisable) to make the person concerned subject to a more stringent requirement.

(2) Where that power is so exercised, the relevant requirement specified in any of the Parts mentioned in paragraph (1) shall, accordingly, be read and operate subject to such modifications as are necessary in consequence of the exercise of that power.

PART 2
PERIODIC FINANCIAL REPORTING

4. Annual financial report

(1) Subject to Part 3, this Regulation applies to an issuer:

(a) whose securities are admitted to trading on a regulated market, and

(b) whose home Member State is the State.

(2) An issuer shall make public its annual financial report at the latest 4 months after the end of each financial year and ensure that it remains publicly available for at least 5 years.

(3) The annual financial report shall include:

(a) the audited financial statements,

(b) a management report, and

(c) responsibility statements.

(4) (a) If an issuer is required to prepare consolidated accounts according to the Seventh Council Directive 83/349/EEC of 13 June 1983, the audited financial statements shall comprise:

(i) consolidated accounts prepared in accordance with Regulation (EC) No 1606/2002 of the European Parliament and of the Council of 19 July 2002, and

(ii) accounts of the parent company prepared in accordance with the national law of the Member State in which the parent company is incorporated.

(b) If an issuer is not required to prepare consolidated accounts, the audited financial statements shall comprise accounts prepared in accordance with the national law of the Member State in which the issuer is incorporated.

5. Supplemental provisions in relation to Regulation 4

(1) References in this Regulation to consolidated accounts, financial statements, a management report or a responsibility statement are references to consolidated accounts, financial statements, a management report or a responsibility statement referred to in Regulation 4.

(2) (a) If an issuer is required to prepare consolidated accounts, the financial statements shall be audited in accordance with Article 37 of the Seventh Council Directive 83/349/EEC of 13 June 1983 (the most recent measure adopted by the State for its implementation being the European Communities (Financial Reporting Standards and Miscellaneous Amendments) Regulations 2005 (S.I. No. 116 of 2005)).

(b) If an issuer is not required to prepare consolidated accounts, the financial statements shall be audited in accordance with Articles 51 and 51a of the Fourth Council Directive 78/660/EEC of 25 July 1978 (the most recent measure adopted by the State for their implementation being the regulations referred to in subparagraph (a)).

(c) The audit report, signed by the person or persons responsible for auditing the financial statements, shall be disclosed in full to the public together with the annual financial report.

(3) (a) If an issuer is required to prepare consolidated accounts, the management report shall be drawn up in accordance with Article 36 of the Seventh Council Directive 83/349/EEC of 13 June 1983 (the most recent measure adopted by the State for its implementation being the regulations referred to in paragraph (2)(a)).

(b) If the issuer is not required to prepare consolidated accounts, the management report shall be drawn up in accordance with Article 46 of the Fourth Council Directive 78/660/EEC of 25 July 1978 (the most recent measure adopted by the State for its implementation being the regulations referred to in paragraph (2)(a)).

(4) (a) Responsibility statements shall be made by the persons responsible within the issuer.

(b) The name and function of any person who makes a responsibility statement shall be clearly indicated in the responsibility statement.

(c) For each person making a responsibility statement, the statement shall set out that to the best of his or her knowledge:

(i) the financial statements, prepared in accordance with the applicable set of accounting standards, give a true and fair view of the assets, liabilities, financial position and profit or loss of the issuer and the undertakings included in the consolidation taken as a whole; and

(ii) the management report includes a fair review of the development and performance of the business and the position of the issuer and the undertakings included in the consolidation taken as a whole, together with a description of the principal risks and uncertainties that they face.

(5) The issuer is responsible for all information drawn up and made public in accordance with Regulation 4 and this Regulation.

6. Half-yearly financial reports

(1) Subject to Part 3, this Regulation applies to an issuer:

(a) whose shares or debt securities are admitted to trading on a regulated market, and

(b) whose home Member State is the State.

(2) (a) An issuer shall make public a half-yearly financial report covering the first 6 months of the financial year.

(b) The half-yearly financial report shall be made public as soon as possible, but no later than 2 months, after the end of the period to which the report relates.

(c) An issuer shall ensure that the half-yearly financial report remains available to the public for at least 5 years.

(3) The half-yearly financial report shall include:

(a) a condensed set of financial statements,

(b) an interim management report, and

(c) responsibility statements.

7. Supplemental provisions in relation to Regulation 6

(1) In this Regulation, 'condensed set of financial statements' means the financial statements referred to in Regulation 6(3)(a).

(2) (a) If an issuer is required to prepare consolidated accounts, the condensed set of financial statements shall be prepared in accordance with the international accounting standard applicable to the interim financial reporting adopted pursuant to the procedure provided for under Article 6 of Regulation (EC) No. 1606/2002 of the European Parliament and of the Council of 19 July 2002.

(b) If an issuer is not required to prepare consolidated accounts, the condensed set of financial statements shall contain, as a minimum, the following:

(i) a condensed balance sheet,

(ii) a condensed profit and loss account, and

(iii) explanatory notes on these accounts.

(3) (a) This paragraph applies to an issuer that is not required to prepare consolidated accounts.

(b) In preparing the condensed balance sheet and the condensed profit and loss account an issuer shall follow the same principles for recognising and measuring as when preparing annual financial reports.

(c) The condensed balance sheet and condensed profit and loss account shall show each of the headings and subtotals included in the most recent annual financial statements of the issuer. Additional line items shall be included if, as a result of their omission, the half-yearly financial statements would give a misleading view of the assets, liabilities, financial position and profit or loss of the issuer.

(d) The half-yearly financial information shall include comparative information presented as follows:

(i) balance sheet as at the end of the first 6 months of the current financial year and comparative balance sheet as at the end of the immediate preceding financial year; and

(ii) profit and loss account for the first 6 months of the current financial year with, from 2 years after 29 March 2007, comparative information for the comparable period for the preceding financial year.

(e) The explanatory notes shall include the following:

(i) sufficient information to ensure the comparability of the condensed half-yearly financial statements with the annual financial statements; and

(ii) sufficient information and explanations to ensure a user's proper understanding of any material changes in amounts and of any developments in the half-year period concerned, which are reflected in the balance sheet and the profit and loss account.

8. Further supplemental provisions in relation to Regulation 6.

(1) In this Regulation—

'condensed set of financial statements' means the financial statements referred to in Regulation 6(3)(a);

'interim management report' means the report referred to in Regulation 6(3)(b);

(2) The interim management report shall include at least:

(a) an indication of important events that have occurred during the first 6 months of the financial year, and their impact on the condensed set of financial statements, and

(b) a description of the principal risks and uncertainties for the remaining 6 months of the financial year.

(3) (a) In addition to the requirement contained in the preceding paragraph, an issuer of shares shall disclose in the interim management report the following information, as a minimum:

(i) related parties' transactions that have taken place in the first 6 months of the current financial year and that have materially affected the financial position or the performance of the enterprise during that period; and

(ii) any changes in the related parties' transactions described in the last annual report that could have a material effect on the financial position or performance of the enterprise in the first 6 months of the current financial year.

(b) If an issuer of shares is not required to prepare consolidated accounts, it shall disclose, as a minimum, any transactions which have been entered into with related parties by the issuer, including the amount of such transactions, the nature of the related party relationship and other information about the transactions necessary for an understanding of the financial position of the issuer, if such transactions are material and have not been concluded under normal market conditions.

(c) In relation to transactions referred to in subparagraph (b), information about such transactions may be aggregated according to their nature except where separate information is necessary for an understanding of the effects of related party transactions on the financial position of the issuer.

(4) (a) If the half-yearly financial report has been audited or reviewed by auditors pursuant to the Auditing Practices Board guidance on Review of Interim Financial Information, the audit report or review report shall be reproduced in full.

(b) If the half-yearly financial report has not been audited or reviewed by auditors pursuant to the Auditing Practices Board guidance on Review of Interim Financial Information, an issuer shall make a statement to this effect in its report.

(5) (a) Responsibility statements shall be made by the persons responsible within the issuer.

(b) The name and function of any person who makes a responsibility statement shall be clearly indicated in the responsibility statement.

(c) For each person making a responsibility statement, the statement shall confirm that to the best of his or her knowledge:

(i) the condensed set of financial statements, which has been pre-pared in accordance with the applicable set of accounting standards, gives a true and fair view of the assets, liabilities, financial position and profit or loss of the issuer, or the undertakings included in the consolidation as a whole as required by Regulation 7(2);

(ii) the interim management report includes a fair review of the information required by paragraph (2), and

(iii) the interim management report includes a fair review of the information required by paragraph (3), in the case of an issuer of shares.

(d) A person making a responsibility statement shall be regarded as satisfying the requirement contained in subparagraph (c) (i) by including a statement that the condensed set of financial statements have been prepared in accordance with:

(i) the international accounting standard applicable to the interim financial reporting adopted pursuant to the procedure provided for under Article 6 of Regulation (EC) No. 1606/2002 of the European Parliament and of the Council of 19 July 2002; or

(ii) for Irish issuers not using IFRS, pronouncements on half-yearly reports issued by the Accounting Standards Board; or

(iii) for all other issuers not using IFRS, a national accounting standard relating to interim reporting,

provided always that a person making such a statement has reason-able grounds to be satisfied that the condensed set of financial statements prepared in accordance with such a standard is not misleading.

(e) This application of true and fair view has no effect on the interpretation of the true and fair view for annual accounts in accordance with the Fourth Council Directive 78/660/EEC of 25 July 1978 and the Seventh Council Directive 83/349/EEC of 13 June 1983, and Regulation (EC) No 1606/2002 of the European Parliament and of the Council of 19 July 2002.

(f) In subparagraph (d)(ii) 'Irish issuers' means issuers incorporated in the State as public limited companies (within the meaning of the Companies (Amendment) Act 1983 (No. 13 of 1983)).

(6) The issuer shall be responsible for all information drawn up and made public in accordance with Regulations 6 and 7 and this Regulation.

9. Interim management statements

(1) Subject to Part 3, this Regulation applies to an issuer:

(a) whose shares are admitted to trading on a regulated market; and

(b) whose home Member State is the State.

(2) (a) An issuer, other than an issuer specified in paragraph (5), shall make public a statement by its management during the first 6 month period of the financial year and another statement by its management during the second 6 month period of the financial year, each of which is referred to in this Regulation as an 'interim management statement'.

(b) The statement required by this paragraph shall be made in a period between 10 weeks after the beginning, and 6 weeks before, the end of the relevant 6 month period.

(3) The interim management statement shall contain information that covers the period between the beginning of the relevant 6 month period and the date of publication of the statement.

(4) The interim management statement shall provide:

(a) an explanation of material events and transactions that have taken place during the relevant period and their impact on the financial position of the issuer and its controlled undertakings, and

(b) a general description of the financial position and performance of the issuer and its controlled undertakings during the relevant period.

(5) The issuer referred to in paragraph (2) (a) is an issuer that publishes quarterly financial reports:

(a) in accordance with the legislation of a Member State; or

(b) in accordance with the rules of a regulated market; or

(c) of its own initiative.

PART 3

EXEMPTIONS/THIRD COUNTRY EQUIVALENCE IN RESPECT OF PART 2

10. Exemptions not dependent on a decision of Bank

(1) Regulations 4 to 9 shall not apply to the following issuers, namely a state, a regional or local authority of a state, a public international body of which at least one Member State is a member, the European Central Bank and

Member States' national central banks, whether or not they issue shares or other securities.

(2) (a) Regulations 4 to 9 shall not apply to an issuer that issues exclusively debt securities admitted to trading on a regulated market the denomination per unit of which is at least €50,000 (or an equivalent amount).

(b) Regulations 6 to 8 shall not apply to a credit institution whose shares are not admitted to trading on a regulated market and which has, in a continuous or repeated manner, only issued debt securities provided that:

(i) the total nominal amount of all such debt securities remains below €100,000,000; and

(ii) the credit institution has not published a prospectus in accordance with Directive 2003/71/EC of the European Parliament and of the Council of 4 November 2003.

(c) Regulations 6 to 8 shall not apply to issuers already existing at the date of the entry into force of Directive 2003/71/EC of the European Parliament and of the Council of 4 November 2003 which exclusively issue debt securities unconditionally and irrevocably guaranteed by the State or by one of its regional or local authorities, on a regulated market.

11. Exemptions in respect of issuers whose registered office is in third country

(1) Where—

(a) the registered office of an issuer is in a third country, and

(b) that issuer is an issuer in respect of which the State is the home Member State, the Bank, subject to paragraphs (2) to (9), may exempt that issuer from requirements under Regulations 4 to 9 provided that the law of the third country in question lays down equivalent requirements or such an issuer complies with requirements of the law of a third country that the Bank considers as equivalent.

(2) A third country shall be deemed to lay down requirements equivalent to those of Regulation 4(3)(b) where, under the law of that country, the annual management report is required to include at least the following information:

(a) a fair review of the development and performance of the issuer's business and of its position, together with a description of the principal risks and uncertainties that it faces, such that the review presents a balanced and comprehensive analysis of the development and performance of the issuer's business and of its position, consistent with the size and complexity of the business;

(b) an indication of any important events that have occurred since the end of the financial year;

(c) indications of the issuer's likely future development.

(3) The analysis referred to in paragraph (2) (a) shall, to the extent necessary for an understanding of the issuer's development, performance or position, include both financial and, where appropriate, non-financial key performance indicators relevant to the particular business.

(4) A third country shall be deemed to lay down requirements equivalent to those of Regulation 8(2) and (3) where, under the law of that country, a condensed set of financial statements is required in addition to the interim management report, and the interim management report is required to include at least the following information:

(a) review of the period covered;

(b) indications of the issuer's likely future development for the remaining six months of the financial year;

(c) for issuers of shares and if already not disclosed on an ongoing basis, major related parties transactions.

(5) A third country shall be deemed to lay down requirements equivalent to those of Regulations [5(4)][a] and 8(5) where, under the law of that country, a person or persons within the issuer are responsible for the annual and half-yearly financial information, and in particular for the following:

(a) the compliance of the financial statements with the applicable reporting framework or set of accounting standards;

(b) the fairness of the management review included in the management report.

(6) A third country shall be deemed to lay down requirements equivalent to those of Regulation 9 where, under the law of that country, an issuer is required to publish quarterly financial reports.

(7) A third country shall be deemed to lay down requirements equivalent to those of Regulation 4(4)(a) where, under the law of that country, the provision of individual accounts by the parent company is not required but the issuer whose registered office is in that third country is required, in preparing consolidated accounts, to include the following information:

(a) for issuers of shares, dividends computation and ability to pay dividends;

(b) for all issuers, where applicable, minimum capital and equity requirements and liquidity issues.

(8) For the purposes of equivalence, the issuer must also be able to provide the Bank with additional audited disclosures giving information on the individual accounts of the issuer as a standalone, relevant to the elements of information referred to in subparagraphs (a) and (b) of paragraph (7). Those disclosures may be prepared under the accounting standards of the third country.

(9) (a) A third country shall be deemed to lay down requirements equivalent to those of Regulation 4(4)(b) in relation to individual accounts where, under the law of a third country, an issuer whose registered office is in that third country is not required to prepare consolidated accounts but is required to prepare its individual accounts in accordance with international accounting standards recognised pursuant to Article 3 of Regulation (EC) No 1606/2002 of the European Parliament and of the Council of 19 July 2002 as applicable within the Community or with third country national accounting standards equivalent to those standards.

(b) For the purposes of equivalence, if such financial information is not in line with those standards, it must be presented in the form of restated financial statements.

(c) In addition, the individual accounts must be audited independently.

(10) Notwithstanding that the Bank has, under this Regulation, exempted an issuer from requirements referred to in paragraph (1), the issuer shall comply with the requirements of Articles 19, 20 and 21 of the Directive (as implemented in the State by Parts 6 and 7) in respect of the information covered by the requirements laid down in the third country in question.

PART 4

LIABILITY FOR FALSE OR MISLEADING STATEMENTS IN CERTAIN PUBLICATIONS

12

(1) The publications to which this Regulation applies are any reports and statements published in compliance with any of Regulations 4 to 9 and 26.

(2) The securities to which this Regulation applies are—

(a) securities that are traded on a regulated market situated or operating in the State, and

(b) securities that—

(i) are traded on a regulated market situated or operating outside the State, and

(ii) are issued by an issuer for which the State is the home Member State.

(3) The issuer of securities to which this Regulation applies is liable to pay compensation to a person who has—

(a) acquired such securities issued by it, and

(b) suffered loss in respect of them as a result of—

(i) any untrue or misleading statement in a publication to which this section applies, or

(ii) the omission from any such publication of any matter required to be included in it.

(4) The issuer is so liable only if a person discharging managerial responsibilities within the issuer in relation to the publication—

(a) knew the statement to be untrue or misleading or was reckless as to whether it was untrue or misleading, or

(b) knew the omission to be dishonest concealment of a material fact.

(5) A loss is not regarded as suffered as a result of the statement or omission in the publication unless the person suffering it acquired the relevant securities—

(a) in reliance on the information in the publication, and

(b) at a time when, and in circumstances in which, it was reasonable for him to rely on that information.

(6) Except as mentioned in paragraph (8)—

(a) the issuer is not subject to any other liability than that provided for by this Regulation in respect of loss suffered as a result of reliance by any person on—

(i) an untrue or misleading statement in a publication to which this Regulation applies, or

(ii) the omission from any such publication of any matter required to be included in it, and

(b) a person other than the issuer is not subject to any liability, other than to the issuer, in respect of any such loss.

(7) Any reference in paragraph (6) to a person being subject to a liability includes a reference to another person being entitled as against him or her to be granted any civil remedy or to rescind or repudiate an agreement.

(8) This Regulation does not affect—

(a) liability to be the subject of an administrative sanction; or

(b) liability for a criminal offence.

(9) For the purposes of this Regulation—

(a) the following persons shall be regarded as persons discharging managerial responsibilities in relation to a publication—

(i) any director of the issuer (or person occupying the position of director, by whatever name called),

(ii) in the case of an issuer whose affairs are managed by its members, any member of the issuer,

(iii) in the case of an issuer that has no persons falling within clause (i) or (ii), any senior executive of the issuer having responsibilities in relation to the publication;

(b) references to the acquisition by a person of securities include references to his or her contracting to acquire them or any interest in them.

PART 5
ON-GOING INFORMATION ABOUT MAJOR SHAREHOLDINGS

13. Application of Part 5

This Part applies to an issuer:

(a) whose shares are admitted to trading on a regulated market; and

(b) whose home Member State is the State.

14. Notification of acquisition or disposal of major shareholdings

(1) A person shall notify the issuer of the percentage of voting rights he or she holds if, as a result of either or both of the events specified in paragraph (2), the percentage of voting rights which he or she holds reaches, exceeds or falls below one or more of the percentages specified in paragraph (4).

(2) The events referred to in paragraph (1) are:

(a) the acquisition or disposal by the person referred to in that paragraph of shares in the issuer, being shares to which voting rights attach;

(b) events changing the breakdown of voting rights and on the basis of information disclosed by the issuer in accordance with Regulation 20.

(3) In the case of an issuer that is not incorporated in a Member State, subparagraph (b) of paragraph (2) also applies in circumstances where events equivalent to the events specified in that subparagraph occur and on the basis of equivalent disclosed information to that mentioned in that subparagraph.

(4) The percentages referred to in paragraph (1) are: 5%, 10%, 15%, 20%, 30%, 50% and 75%, each being a percentage of the total voting rights in the issuer; each such percentage is subsequently referred to in this Part as a 'threshold'.

(5) The following shall be disregarded for the purposes of determining whether a person has an obligation to make a notification under paragraph (1), namely, voting rights attaching to:

(a) shares acquired for the sole purpose of clearing and settlement within a settlement cycle not exceeding the period beginning with the trans-action and ending at the close of the third trading day following the day of the execution of the transaction (irrespective of whether the transaction is conducted on-exchange);

(b) shares held by a custodian (or nominee) in its custodian (or nominee) capacity provided such a person can only exercise the voting rights attached to such shares under instructions given in writing or by electronic means;

(c) shares held by a market maker acting in that capacity subject to the percentage of such shares not being equal to or in excess of 10% and subject to the market maker satisfying the criteria and complying with the conditions and operating requirements specified in paragraph (4);

(d) shares held by a credit institution or investment firm provided that:

(i) the shares are held within the trading book, as defined in Article 2(6) of Council Directive 93/6/EEC of 15 March 1993, of the credit institution or investment firm;

(ii) the voting rights attached to such shares do not exceed 5%; and

(iii) the credit institution, or as the case may be investment firm, ensures that the voting rights attached to shares in the trading book are not exercised or otherwise used to intervene in the management of the issuer,

(e) shares held by a collateral taker under a collateral transaction which involves the outright transfer of securities provided the collateral taker does not declare any intention of exercising (and does not exercise) the voting rights attaching to such shares,

(f) shares acquired by a borrower under a stock lending agreement as determined by rules of the Bank from time to time.

(6) (a) References in paragraph (5) to a market maker are references to a market maker which—

(i) is authorised by its home Member State under Directive 2004/39/EC of the European Parliament and of the Council of 21 April 2004, and

(ii) does not intervene in the management of the issuer concerned, and does not exert any influence on the issuer to buy such shares or back the share price.

(b) A market maker relying upon the exemption for shares held by it in that capacity must notify the competent authority which regulates it in respect of such activities, at the latest within the time limit provided for by Regulation 21(3), that it conducts or intends to conduct market making activities on a particular issuer and shall equally make such a notification to the relevant competent authority if it ceases to conduct market making activities on the issuer concerned.

Amendments

a Subparagraph (6) substituted by T(Dir)(A)R 2010, reg 2(b).

15. Acquisition or disposal of major proportions of voting rights

(1) The notification requirements under Regulation 14(1) shall also apply to a person to the extent the person is entitled to acquire, to dispose of, or to exercise voting rights in any of the following cases or a combination of them:

(a) voting rights held by a third party with whom that person has concluded an agreement, which obliges them to adopt, by concerted exercise of the voting rights they hold, a long-term common policy towards the management of the issuer in question;

(b) voting rights held by a third party under an agreement concluded with that person providing for the temporary transfer for consideration of the voting rights in question;

(c) voting rights attaching to shares that are lodged as collateral with that person provided the person controls the voting rights and declares an intention to exercise them;

(d) voting rights attaching to shares in which that person has a life interest;

(e) voting rights that are held, or may be exercised within the meaning of subparagraphs (a) to (d), by an undertaking controlled by that person;

(f) voting rights attaching to shares deposited with that person which the person has a discretion to exercise in the absence of specific instructions from the shareholders;

(g) voting rights held by a third party in the third party's own name on behalf of that person;

(h) voting rights which that person may exercise as a proxy where the person has a discretion to exercise the voting rights in the absence of specific instructions from the shareholders.

16. Non-application of Regulations 14(1) and 15(1)(c) in certain cases

Regulations 14(1) and 15(1)(c) shall not apply in respect of voting rights attaching to shares provided to or by members of the European System of Central Banks in carrying out their functions as monetary authorities, including shares provided to or by such members under pledge or repurchase or similar agreement for liquidity granted for monetary policy purposes or within a payment system provided:

(a) the exemption under this Regulation shall apply only for a short period following the provision of the shares; and

(b) the voting rights attached to the shares during this period are not exercised.

17. Notification of voting rights arising from holding of certain financial instruments

(1) The notification requirements under Regulation 14(1) shall also apply to a person who holds, directly or indirectly, financial instruments which result in an entitlement to acquire, on such holder's own initiative alone, under a formal agreement, shares to which voting rights are attached, already issued, of an issuer.

(2) (a) Transferable securities and options, futures, swaps, forward rate agreements and any other derivative contracts, as referred to in Section C of Annex 1 of Directive 2004/39/EC of the European Parliament and of the Council of 21 April 2004, shall be considered to be financial instruments falling within paragraph (1) provided that the condition specified in subparagraph (b) is complied with and they result in an entitlement to acquire, on the holder's own initiative alone, under a formal agreement, shares to which voting rights are attached, already issued, of an issuer.

(b) The condition referred to in subparagraph (a) is that the instrument holder must enjoy, on maturity, either the unconditional right to acquire the underlying shares or the discretion as to his or her right to acquire such shares or not.

(3) In this Regulation "formal agreement" means an agreement that is binding under applicable law.

(4) For the purpose of paragraph (1) the holder of financial instruments falling within that paragraph is required to aggregate and, if necessary, notify all such instruments as relate to the same underlying issuer.

18. Aggregation of managed holdings

(1) (a) The parent undertaking of a management company shall not be required to aggregate its holdings with the holdings managed by the management company under the conditions laid down in Council Directive 85/611/EC of 20

December 1985, provided such management company exercises its voting rights independently from the parent undertaking.

(b) But the requirement for the aggregation of holdings under Regulation 17(4) applies if the parent undertaking, or another controlled under-taking of the parent undertaking, has invested in holdings managed by such management company and the management company has no discretion to exercise the voting rights attached to such holdings and may only exercise such voting rights under direct or indirect instructions from the parent or another controlled undertaking of the parent undertaking.

(2) (a) The parent undertaking of an investment firm authorised under Directive 2004/39/EC of the European Parliament and of the Council of 21 April 2004 shall not be required to aggregate its holdings under Regulations 14 and 15 with the holdings which such investment firm manages on a client-by-client basis within the meaning of Article 4(1), point 9, of that Directive, provided that:

(i) the investment firm is authorised to provide such portfolio management under point 4 of Section A of Annex 1 to that Directive;

(ii) it may only exercise the voting rights attached to such shares under instructions given in writing or by electronic means or it ensures that individual portfolio management services are con-ducted independently of any other services under conditions equivalent to those provided for under Council Directive 85/611/EEC of 20 December 1985 by putting into place appropriate mechanisms; and

(iii) the investment firm exercises its voting rights independently from the parent undertaking.

(b) But the requirement for the aggregation of holdings shall apply if the parent undertaking, or another controlled undertaking of the parent undertaking, has invested in holdings managed by such investment firm and the investment firm has no discretion to exercise the voting rights attached to such holdings and may only exercise such voting rights under direct or indirect instructions from the parent or another controlled undertaking of the parent undertaking.

(3) For the purposes of the exemption in relation to the aggregation of holdings provided by paragraph (1) or (2), a parent undertaking of a management company or of an investment firm shall comply with the following conditions:

(a) it shall not interfere by giving direct or indirect instructions or in any other way in the exercise of the voting rights held by the management company or investment firm;

(b) that management company or investment firm must be free to exercise, independently of the parent undertaking, the voting rights attached to the assets it manages.

(4) A parent undertaking which wishes to make use of either of the foregoing exemptions shall (in relation to shares which are admitted to trading on a regulated market) without delay, notify the following to the competent authority of the home Member State of issuers whose voting rights are attached to holdings managed by the management companies or investment firms:

(a) a list of the names of those management companies and investment firms, indicating the competent authorities that supervise them or that no competent authority supervises them, but with no reference to the issuers concerned;

(b) a statement that, in the case of each such management company or investment firm, the parent undertaking complies with the conditions specified in paragraph (3).

(5) The parent undertaking shall update the list referred to in paragraph (4) on an ongoing basis.

(6) Where the parent undertaking intends to benefit from either of the fore-going exemptions only in relation to the financial instruments referred to in Regulation 17, it shall (in relation to financial instruments giving an entitlement to acquire shares which are admitted to trading on a regulated market) notify to the competent authority of the home Member State of the issuer only the list referred to in paragraph (4).

(7) Without prejudice to Part 9, a parent undertaking of a management company or of an investment firm shall (in relation to shares which are admitted to trading on a regulated market) be able to demonstrate to the competent authority of the home Member State of the issuer on request that:

(a) the organisational structures of the parent undertaking and the management company or investment firm are such that the voting rights are exercised independently of the parent undertaking;

(b) the persons who decide how the voting rights are exercised are not the same for the parent undertaking and the management company or investment firm and act independently;

(c) if the parent undertaking is a client of its management company or investment firm or has a holding in the assets managed by the management company or investment firm, there is a clear written mandate for an arms-length customer relationship between the parent under-taking and the management company or investment firm.

(8) Paragraph (7) (a) shall be construed as requiring, as a minimum, that the parent undertaking and the management company or investment firm shall have established written policies and procedures reasonably designed to prevent the distribution of information between the parent undertaking and the management company or investment firm in relation to the exercise of voting rights.

(9) For the purposes of paragraph (3)—

"direct instruction" means any instruction given by the parent undertaking, or another controlled undertaking of the parent undertaking, specifying how the voting rights are to be exercised by the management company or investment firm in particular cases;

"indirect instruction" means any general or particular instruction, regardless of the form, given by the parent undertaking, or another controlled undertaking of the parent undertaking, that limits the discretion of the management company or investment firm in relation to the exercise of voting rights in order to serve specific business interests of the parent undertaking or another controlled undertaking of the parent undertaking.

(10) An undertaking whose registered office is in a third country which would have required authorisation in accordance with Article 5(1) of Council Directive 85/611/EEC

of 20 December 1985 or with regard to portfolio management under point 4 of section A of Annex 1 to Directive 2004/39/EC of the European Parliament and of the Council of 21 April 2004 if it had its registered office or, only in the case of an investment firm, its head office within the Community, shall be exempted from aggregating holdings with the holdings of its parent undertaking under paragraphs (1) and (2) provided that it complies with equivalent conditions of independence as management companies or investment firms.

(11) A third country shall be deemed to set conditions of independence equivalent to those specified in paragraphs (1) and (2) where, under the law of that country, a management company or investment firm as referred to in paragraph (10) is required to meet the following conditions:

(a) the management company or investment firm shall be free in all situations to exercise, independently of its parent undertaking, the voting rights attached to the assets it manages;

(b) the management company or investment firm shall disregard the interests of the parent undertaking or of any other controlled under-taking of the parent undertaking whenever conflicts of interest arise.

(12) A parent undertaking of a third country undertaking shall comply with the notification requirements under paragraphs (4)(a) and (6) and in addition:

(a) shall make a statement that in respect of each management company or investment firm concerned, the parent undertaking complies with the conditions of independence specified in paragraph (1);and

(b) without prejudice to Article 24 of the Directive, shall be able to demonstrate to the competent authority of the home Member State of the issuer on request that the requirements of paragraph (7) are complied with.

19. Acquisition or disposal by issuer of shares

(1) An issuer of shares shall, if it acquires or disposes of its own shares, either itself or through a person acting in his or her own name but on the issuer's behalf, make public the percentage of voting rights attributable to those shares as soon as possible, but not later than 4 trading days following such acquisition or disposal, where that percentage reaches, exceeds or falls below either or both of the following thresholds, namely, the thresholds of 5% or 10% of the voting rights.

(2) The percentage shall be calculated on the basis of the total number of shares to which voting rights are attached.

20. Disclosure by issuer

(1) An issuer shall, at the end of each calendar month during which an increase or decrease of such total number has occurred, disclose to the public—

(a) the total number of voting rights and capital in respect of each class of share that it issues,

(b) the total number of voting rights attaching to shares of the issuer that are held as treasury shares.

(2) Responsibility for all information drawn up and made public in accordance with paragraph (1) shall lie with the issuer.

21. Procedures for notification and disclosure of major holdings

(1) A notification required under Regulations 14(1) and 15 shall include the following information:

(a) the resulting situation in terms of voting rights;

(b) the chain of controlled undertakings through which voting rights are effectively held, if applicable;

(c) the date on which the threshold was reached or crossed; and

(d) the identity of the shareholder even if that shareholder is not entitled to exercise voting rights under the conditions specified in Regulation 15 and of the person entitled to exercise voting rights on behalf of that shareholder.

(2) (a) A notification required under Regulation 17(1) arising from the holding of financial instruments shall include the following information:

(i) the resulting situation in terms of voting rights;

(ii) if applicable, the chain of controlled undertakings through which financial instruments are effectively held;

(iii) the date on which the threshold was reached or crossed;

(iv) for instruments with an exercise period, an indication of the date or time period where shares will or can be acquired, if applicable;

(v) date of maturity or expiration of the instrument;

(vi) identity of the holder; and

(vii) name of the underlying issuer.

(b) The notification shall be made to the issuer of each of the underlying shares to which the financial instrument relates and, in the case of shares admitted to trading on a regulated market, to each competent authority of the home Member States of such issuers.

(c) If a financial instrument relates to more than one underlying share, a separate notification shall be made to each issuer of the underlying shares.

(3) (a) The notification to the issuer shall be effected as soon as possible, but not later than 4 trading days, the first of which shall be the day after the date on which the shareholder or the person referred to in Regulation 15—

(i) learns of the acquisition or disposal or of the possibility of exercising voting rights, or on which, having regard to the circumstances, should have learned of it, regardless of the date on which the acquisition, disposal or possibility of exercising voting rights takes effect; or

(ii) is informed about the event specified in Regulation 14(2)(b).

(b) For the purposes of subparagraph (a), the shareholder, or the person referred to in Regulation 15, shall be deemed to have knowledge of the acquisition, disposal or possibility to exercise voting rights no later than 2 trading days following the transaction.

(4) (a) For the purposes of paragraph (3), the notification obligation which arises as soon as the proportion of voting rights held reaches, exceeds or falls below the applicable thresholds following transactions of the type referred to in Regulation 15 shall be an individual obligation incumbent upon each

shareholder, or each person as referred to in Regulation 15, or both in case the proportion of voting rights held by each party reaches, exceeds or falls below the applicable threshold.

(b) In the circumstances referred to in Regulation 15(1)(a), the notification obligation shall be a collective obligation shared by all parties to the agreement.

(c) In the circumstances referred to in Regulation 15(1)(h) if a share-holder gives the proxy in relation to one shareholder meeting, notification may be made by means of a single notification when the proxy is given provided it is made clear in the notification what the resulting situation in terms of voting rights will be when the proxy may no longer exercise the voting rights discretion.

(d) If in the circumstances referred to in Regulation 15(1)(h) the proxy holder receives one or several proxies in relation to one shareholder meeting, notification may be made by means of a single notification on or after the deadline for receiving proxies provided that it is made clear in the notification what the resulting situation in terms of voting rights will be when the proxy may no longer exercise the voting rights at its discretion.

(e) When the duty to make notification lies with more than one person, notification may be made by means of a single common notification but this subparagraph does not release any of those persons from their responsibilities in relation to the notification.

(5) An undertaking is not required to make a notification in accordance with paragraph (1) if, instead, it is made by its parent undertaking or, where the parent undertaking is itself a controlled undertaking, by its own parent undertaking.

(6) Voting rights shall be calculated on the basis of all the shares to which voting rights are attached even if the exercise of such rights is suspended and shall be given in respect of all shares which are in the same class to which voting rights are attached.

(7) The number of voting rights to be considered when calculating whether a threshold is reached, exceeded or fallen below shall be the number of voting rights in existence according to the issuer's most recent disclosure made in accordance with Regulation 20(1)(a) but disregarding voting rights attached to any treasury shares held by the issuer (in accordance with the issuer's most recent disclosure of such holdings).

(8) (a) For the purposes of paragraphs (3) and (9) and Regulation 19, the calendar of trading days of the home Member State of the issuer shall apply.

(b) The Bank shall publish in its Internet site the calendar of trading days applicable in the State for purposes of subparagraph (a).

(9) On receipt of the notification under paragraph (1), but no later than 3 trading days thereafter, the issuer shall make public all the information contained in the notification.

22. Filing of information with competent authority

A person making a notification to an issuer in accordance with Regulation 14, 15, 17(1) or 21(1) shall, if the notification relates to shares admitted to trading on a regulated market, at the same time file a copy of such notification with the competent authority of the home Member State of the issuer.

23. Use of electronic means for notifications and filing

Information filed with the Bank for the purposes of this Part shall be filed using electronic means.

24. Third country issuers — equivalence

(1) Where the registered office of an issuer is in a third country, the Bank, subject to paragraphs (2) to (4), may exempt that issuer, in respect of which the State is the home Member State, from requirements under Regulations 19, 20 and 21(9) provided that the law of the third country in question lays down equivalent requirements or such an issuer complies with requirements of the law of a third country that the Bank considers as equivalent.

(2) A third country shall be deemed to set requirements equivalent to those specified in Regulation 21(9) where, under the law of that country, the period of time within which an issuer whose registered office is in that third country must be notified of major holdings and within which it must disclose to the public those major holdings is in total equal to or shorter than 7 trading days.

(3) (a) A third country shall be deemed to set requirements equivalent to those specified in Regulation 19 where, under the law of that country, an issuer whose registered office is in that third country is required to comply with the following conditions:

(i) in the case of an issuer only allowed to hold up to a maximum of 5% of its own shares to which voting rights are attached, it must make a notification whenever that threshold is reached or crossed;

(ii) in the case of an issuer allowed to hold up to a maximum of between 5% and 10% of its own shares to which voting rights are attached, it must make a notification whenever a 5% threshold or that maximum threshold is reached or crossed;

(iii) in the case of an issuer allowed to hold more than 10% of its own shares to which voting rights are attached, it must make a notification whenever that 5% threshold or that 10% threshold is reached or crossed.

(b) Notification above the 10% threshold is not required for the foregoing purpose.

(4) An issuer whose registered office is in a third country shall be deemed to meet requirements equivalent to those specified in Regulation 20 provided that the issuer is required under the law of the third country to disclose to the public the total number of voting rights and capital within 30 calendar days after an increase or decrease of such total number has occurred.

(5) Notwithstanding that the Bank has, under this Regulation, exempted an issuer from requirements referred to in paragraph (1), the issuer shall comply with the requirements of Articles 19, 20 and 21 of the Directive (as implemented in the State by Parts 6 and 7) in respect of the information covered by the requirements laid down in the third country in question.

PART 6

CONTINUING OBLIGATIONS AND ACCESS TO INFORMATION

25. Information requirements for issuers of shares and debt securities

(1) (a) Subject to Regulations 29 and 30, this Regulation applies in relation to an issuer whose home Member State is the State.

(b) References in this Regulation to securities, shares and debt securities are references to such instruments as are admitted to trading on a regulated market.

(2) (a) If an issuer of securities proposes to amend its instruments of incorporation, it must communicate the draft amendment to:

(i) the Bank, and

(ii) the regulated market on which its securities have been admitted to trading.

(b) The communication referred to in subparagraph (a) shall be effected without delay but at the latest on the date of calling the general meeting which is to vote on, or be informed of, the amendment.

(3) (a) An issuer of shares shall ensure equal treatment for all holders of shares who are in the same position.

(b) An issuer of debt securities shall ensure that all holders of debt securities ranking pari passu are given equal treatment in respect of all the rights attaching to those debt securities.

(4) An issuer of shares or debt securities shall ensure that all the facilities and information necessary to enable holders of shares or debt securities to exercise their rights are available in the home Member State and that the integrity of data is preserved.

(5) (a) Shareholders and debt securities holders shall not be prevented from exercising their rights by proxy, subject to the law of the country in which the issuer is incorporated.

(b) An issuer of shares or debt securities shall make available a proxy form, on paper or, where applicable, by electronic means to each per-son entitled to vote at a meeting of shareholders or a meeting of debt securities holders.

(c) The proxy form shall be made available either:

(i) together with the notice concerning the meeting; or

(ii) on request, after the announcement of the meeting.

(6) An issuer of shares or debt securities shall designate, as its agent, a financial institution through which shareholders or debt securities holders may exercise their financial rights.

(7) An issuer of shares or debt securities may use electronic means to convey information to shareholders or debt securities holders.

(8) To use electronic means to convey information to holders, an issuer shall comply with the following:

(a) a decision to use electronic means to convey information to share-holders or debt securities holders shall be taken in a general meeting;

(b) the use of electronic means shall not depend upon the location of the seat or residence of:

(i) the shareholder; or

(ii) persons referred to in subparagraphs (a) to (h) of Regulation 15(1); or

(iii) the debt security holder; or

(iv) a proxy representing a debt security holder;

(c) identification arrangements shall be put in place so that the share-holders, debt security holders or other persons entitled to exercise or to direct the exercise of voting rights are effectively informed;

(d) shareholders, debt security holders or persons referred to in subparagraphs (a) to (h) of Regulation 15(1) who are entitled to acquire, dispose of or exercise voting rights shall be:

(i) contacted in writing to request their consent for the use of electronic means for conveying information and, if they do not object within a reasonable period of time, their consent can be considered to have been given; and

(ii) able to request at any time in the future that information be conveyed in writing; and

(e) any apportionment of the costs entailed in the conveyance of information by electronic means shall be determined by the issuer in compliance with the principle of equal treatment referred to in paragraph (3).

26. Information about changes in rights attaching to securities

(1) An issuer of shares shall without delay disclose to the public any change in the rights attaching to its various classes of shares, including changes in the rights attaching to derivative securities issued by the issuer giving access to the shares of that issuer.

(2) An issuer of securities, other than shares admitted to trading on a regulated market, shall disclose to the public without delay any changes in the rights of holders of securities other than shares, including changes in the terms and conditions of such securities which could indirectly affect those rights, resulting in particular from a change in loan terms or in interest rates.

(3) An issuer of securities admitted to trading on a regulated market (other than an issuer which is a public international body of which at least one Member State is a member) shall disclose to the public without delay any new loan issues and in particular any guarantee or security in respect of such issues.

27. Information about meetings, issue of new shares and payment of dividends — share issuers

(1) An issuer of shares shall provide information to holders on:

(a) the place, time and agenda of meetings;

(b) the total number of shares and voting rights; and

(c) the rights of holders to participate in meetings.

(2) An issuer of shares shall publish notices or distribute circulars concerning the allocation and payment of dividends and the issue of new shares, including information on any arrangements for allotment, subscription, cancellation or conversion.

28. Information about meetings, and payment of interest — debt security issuers

(1) An issuer of debt securities shall publish notices or distribute circulars concerning:

(a) the place, time and agenda of meetings of debt securities holders;

(b) the payment of interest;

(c) the exercise of any conversion, exchange, subscription or cancellation rights and repayment; and

(d) the rights of holders to exercise their rights in relation to the matters mentioned in subparagraphs (a) to (c).

(2) If only holders of debt securities whose denomination per unit amounts to at least €50,000 (or an equivalent amount) are to be invited to a meeting, the issuer may choose as a venue any Member State, provided that all the facilities and information necessary to enable such holders to exercise their rights are made available in that Member State.

29. State, regional and local authority exemption

A State, regional or local authority with securities admitted to trading on a regulated market is not required to comply with the following:

(a) Regulations 25(4) to (7) and 26(3) in so far as those provisions relate to debt securities, and

(b) Regulation 28(1) and (2).

30. Third country equivalence

(1) Where—

(a) the registered office of an issuer is in a third country, and

(b) that issuer is an issuer in respect of which the State is the home Member State,

the Bank, subject to paragraph (2), may exempt that issuer from requirements under Regulations 25(3) to 28(2), provided that the law of the third country in question lays down equivalent requirements or such an issuer complies with requirements of the law of a third country that the Bank considers as equivalent.

(2) A third country shall be deemed to set requirements equivalent to those set out in Articles 17(2) (a) and 18(2) (a) of the Directive, as far as the content of the information about meetings is concerned, where, under the law of that country, an issuer whose registered office is in that third country is required to provide at least information on the place, time and agenda of meetings.

(3) Notwithstanding that the Bank has, under this Regulation, exempted an issuer from requirements referred to in paragraph (1), the issuer shall comply with the requirements of Articles 19, 20 and 21 of the Directive (as implemented in the State by this Part and Part 7) in respect of the information covered by the requirements laid down in the third country in question.

31. Filing of information with Bank

(1) This Regulation applies to:

(a) an issuer:

  (i) whose securities are admitted to trading on a regulated market; and

  (ii) whose home Member State is the State; and

(b) a person who has requested, without the issuer's consent, the admission of its securities to trading on a regulated market.

(2) An issuer or person referred to in paragraph (1) that discloses regulated information shall, at the same time, file that information with the Bank.

32. Use of languages

(1) Subject to paragraph (6), if securities are admitted to trading only on a regulated market in the State and the State is the home Member State, regulated information shall be disclosed in a language accepted by the Bank.

(2) Subject to paragraph (6), if securities are admitted to trading in more than one Member State including the State and the State is the home Member State regulated information shall be disclosed:

(a) in a language accepted by the Bank; and

(b) either in a language accepted by the competent authorities of each host Member State or in a language customary in the sphere of inter-national finance, at the election of the issuer.

(3) (a) Subject to paragraph (6), if securities are admitted to trading in one or more Member States excluding the State and the State is the home Member State, regulated information shall be disclosed either:

(i) in a language accepted by the competent authorities of those host Member States; or

(ii) in a language customary in the sphere of international finance, at the election of the issuer.

(b) In addition, where the State is the home Member State, regulated information shall be disclosed in a language accepted by the Bank or in another language customary in the sphere of international finance, at the election of the issuer.

(4) Subject to paragraph (6), if securities are admitted to trading on a regulated market without the issuer's consent:

(a) paragraphs (1) to (3) shall not apply to the issuer; and

(b) paragraphs (1) to (3) shall apply to the person who has requested such admission without the issuer's consent.

(5) Shareholders and a person referred to in Regulations 14, 15 and 17 shall be permitted to notify information to an issuer under these Regulations and transparency (regulated markets) law only in a language customary in the sphere of international finance. If an issuer receives such a notification, the Bank may not require the issuer to provide a translation into a language accepted by it.

(6) If securities whose denomination per unit amounts to at least €50,000 (or an equivalent amount) are admitted to trading on a regulated market in the State or in one or more Member States, regulated information shall be disclosed to the public in either a language accepted by the competent authorities of the home Member State and host Member States or in a language customary in the sphere of international finance, at the election of the issuer or of the person who, without the issuer's consent, has requested such admission.

(7) If an action concerning the content of regulated information is brought before a court or tribunal in the State, responsibility for the payment of costs incurred in the translation of that information for the purposes of the proceedings shall be in accordance with the law of the State.

(8) For the purposes of this Regulation "a language customary in the sphere of international finance" includes the English language.

PART 7
DISSEMINATION OF INFORMATION

33.

(1) This Regulation applies to:

(a) an issuer:

(i) whose securities are admitted to trading on a regulated market; and

(ii) whose home Member State is the State;

(b) a person who has applied, without the issuer's consent, for the admission of its securities to trading on a regulated market; and

(c) securities that are admitted to trading only on a regulated market in the State which is the host Member State and not in the home Member State.

(2) An issuer referred to in paragraph (1)(a), a person referred to in paragraph (1)(b) ("other person") or an issuer of securities referred to in paragraph (1)(c) shall disclose regulated information in the manner specified in paragraphs (3) to (8).

(3) When disseminating regulated information an issuer or other person shall ensure that the minimum standards specified in paragraphs (4) to (8) are complied with.

(4) Regulated information shall be disseminated in a manner ensuring that it is capable of being disseminated to as wide a public as possible, and as close to simultaneously as possible in the home Member State, and in other Member States.

(5) (a) Regulated information, other than regulated information referred to in subparagraph (b), shall be communicated to the media in unedited full text.

(b) (i) An annual financial report that is required by Regulation 4 to be made public is not required to be communicated to the media in unedited full text except for the information referred to in clause (ii).

(ii) If information is of a type that would be required to be disseminated in a half-yearly financial report then information of such a type that is contained in an annual financial report shall be communicated to the media in unedited full text.

(c) The announcement relating to the publication of the following regulated information shall include an indication of the website on which the relevant documents are available:

(i) an annual financial report that is required by Regulation 4 to be made public;

(ii) a half-yearly financial report that is required by Regulation 6 to be made public; and

(iii) an interim management statement that is required by Regulation 9 to be made public or an equivalent quarterly financial report.

(6) Regulated information shall be communicated to the media in a manner which ensures the security of the communication, minimises the risk of data corruption and unauthorised access, and provides certainty as to the source of the regulated information. Security of receipt shall be ensured by remedying as soon as possible any failure or disruption in the communication of regulated information. An issuer or other

person shall not be responsible for systemic errors or shortcomings in the media to which the regulated information has been communicated.

(7) Regulated information shall be communicated to a RIS in a way which:

(a) makes clear that the information is regulated information;

(b) identifies clearly:

(i) the issuer concerned;

(ii) the subject matter of the regulated information; and

(iii) the time and date of the communication of the regulated information by the issuer or other person.

(8) Upon request, an issuer or other person shall be able to communicate to the Bank, in relation to any disclosure of regulated information:

(a) the name of the person who communicated the regulated information to the RIS;

(b) the security validation details;

(c) the time and date on which the regulated information was communicated; and

(d) the medium in which the regulated information was communicated; and

(e) details of any embargo placed by the issuer on the regulated information, if applicable.

(9) An issuer or other person shall not charge investors any specific cost for providing regulated information.

34. Disclosure of information in third country

(1) Information that is disclosed in a third country which may be of importance to the public in the Member States shall be disclosed in accordance with the provisions of Regulations 32 and 33.

(2) In addition, paragraph (1) applies to information that is not regulated information.

35. Choice of home Member State and notifications by third country issuers

An issuer that chooses the State as its home Member State, by virtue of paragraph (b) of the definition of "home Member State" in Regulation 2(1), shall disclose that choice in accordance with this Part.

PART 8
COMPETENT AUTHORITIES

36. Designation of Competent Authorities

(1) Subject to paragraph (2), the Bank is designated as the central competent administrative authority for purposes of the Directive and shall be responsible for carrying out the obligations provided for in the Directive and for ensuring that the provisions adopted pursuant to the Directive are applied.

(2) IAASA is designated as the competent authority for purposes of subparagraph (h) of Article 24(4) of the Directive and shall be responsible for carrying out the obligations provided for in that subparagraph and for ensuring that the provisions adopted pursuant to the Directive in respect thereof are applied.

(3) The Bank and IAASA shall each be independent in the performance of its functions under these Regulations.

37. Delegation of functions

(1) The Bank may delegate to an approved stock exchange, subject to such conditions as the Bank specifies, any of the functions that it is obliged or authorised to perform under transparency (regulated markets) law or under the Directive other than the functions under Regulations 37, 39, 40, 53, 56, 57 and 58 and Parts 10 and 12.

(2) Any person to whom functions are delegated under paragraph (1) shall have, by virtue of the delegation, all such powers as are necessary to perform those functions.

(3) Any delegation of functions shall be in writing and specify the functions to be performed and the conditions subject to which they are to be performed.

(4) The conditions referred to in paragraph (3) shall include a provision obliging the stock exchange to whom a function or functions concerned are delegated to act and be organised in such a manner as to avoid conflicts of interest and so that information obtained from performing the function is not used unfairly or to prevent competition.

(5) A delegation under this Regulation shall not prevent the performance by the Bank of the function delegated.

(6) Notwithstanding any delegation under this Regulation, the final responsibility for supervising compliance with the applicable provisions of the Directive and of transparency (regulated markets) law shall be with the Bank.

(7) The Bank shall notify the Minister of any such delegation of a function promptly and of the conditions subject to which it has been delegated.

(8) Following such notification, the Minister shall inform the Commission and the competent authorities of other Member States designated pursuant to the Directive of any arrangements entered into with regard to the functions under this Regulation, including the conditions subject to which such functions are delegated.

(9) Where a function is delegated pursuant to this Regulation, then nothing in the Stock Exchange Act 1995 (No. 9 of 1995) shall prevent there being specified as a condition subject to which the function is to be performed a condition requiring the rules of the stock exchange concerned or an amendment thereof to be approved by the Bank in so far as they are relevant to the function delegated.

PART 9
POWERS OF COMPETENT AUTHORITIES

38. Definitions

In this Part—

"authorised officer" means an authorised officer appointed under Regulation 53;

"person to whom these Regulations apply" means any relevant person or a market operator;

"records" means any book, document or any other written or printed material in any form including any information (including phone and data traffic records) stored, maintained or preserved by means of any mechanical or electronic device, whether or not stored, maintained or preserved in a legible form;

"relevant person" means an issuer or any other person (other than a market operator) on whom an obligation is imposed by these Regulations;

"relevant records" means records relating to the activities of persons to whom these Regulations apply;

"responsible authority" means:—

(a) the Chief Executive of—

(i) the Irish Financial Services Regulatory Authority or

(ii) IAASA, or

(b) any person to whom the Chief Executive of either of those Authorities has delegated responsibility for appointing authorised persons.

39. Powers of Bank

(1) The Bank shall have all the powers necessary for the performance of its functions under transparency (regulated markets) law or the Directive.

(2) The powers provided for in this Part in respect of the Bank shall not be exercised in a manner or for a purpose inconsistent with the Directive or these Regulations.

40. Particular powers of Bank

(1) Without prejudice to—

(a) the generality of Regulation 39, and

(b) the subsequent provisions of this Regulation, the Bank shall, in particular, have the power to:

(i) require auditors, issuers, holders of shares or other financial instruments, or persons referred to in Regulation 14 or 17, and the persons that control them or are controlled by them, to provide information and documents to the Bank or delegate;

(ii) require the issuer to disclose the information required under sub-paragraph (i) to the public by the means and within the time limits the Bank considers necessary;

(iii) require managers of the issuers and of the holders of shares or other financial instruments, or of persons referred to in Regulation 14 or 17, to notify the information required under the Directive, or under transparency (regulated markets) law, and, if necessary, to provide further information and documents to the Bank or delegate;

(iv) monitor that the issuer discloses timely information with the objective of ensuring effective and equal access to the public in all Member States where the securities are traded and take appropriate action if that is not the case;

(v) make public the fact that an issuer, or a holder of shares or other financial instruments, or a person referred to in Regulation 14 or 17, is failing to comply with its or his or her obligations.

(2) The Bank may publish the information referred to in paragraph (1)(ii) of its own initiative in the event that the issuer or the persons that control it or are controlled by it, fail to do so and after having heard the issuer.

(3) (a) This paragraph applies where the State is the home Member State in respect of an issuer admitted to trading on a regulated market.

(b) Where this paragraph applies, the Bank may (by means of rules under section 22 of the Act of 2006) make—

(i) the issuer,

(ii) the holder of shares, or

(iii) a person referred to in Regulation 15 or 17(1),

subject to a requirement or requirements that is or are more stringent than a requirement or requirements specified in Part 2, 3, 5, 6 or 7.

(c) In exercising the power under subparagraph (b), the Bank shall have regard to the interests of investors and to the public interest.

(d) As soon as may be after it has exercised that power, the Bank shall notify, in writing, the Minister of the fact of its exercise and provide to the Minister such particulars in relation to that exercise as the Minister may request.

(4) The Bank shall arrange for the putting in place of at least one official mechanism for the central storage of regulated information in accordance with Article 21 of the Directive.

(5) The Bank shall have the following powers (by means of giving a direction under Regulation 56 in that behalf) for the purpose of regulating the disclosure of periodic and ongoing information about issuers whose securities are already admitted to trading on a regulated market and in respect of which the State is the home Member State:

(a) suspend, or request the relevant regulated market to suspend, trading in securities for a maximum of 10 days at a time if it has reasonable grounds for suspecting that the provisions of the Directive or of transparency (regulated markets) law, have been infringed by the issuer;

(b) prohibit trading on the relevant regulated market if it finds that the provisions of the Directive or of transparency(regulated markets) law have been infringed, or if it has reasonable grounds for suspecting that they would be infringed.

(6) The disclosure to the Bank by an auditor of any information, document, fact or decision on foot of a requirement made by the Bank under paragraph (1)(i) shall not be regarded as constituting a breach of any restriction on disclosure of information imposed by contract or by any law, regulation or administrative provision and shall not involve the auditor in liability of any kind.

41. Other powers of Bank not prejudiced

The powers of the Bank under this Part are without prejudice to the powers of the Bank under any other Part of these Regulations or any other enactment.

42. Functions of IAASA

(1) IAASA shall have all the powers necessary for the performance of its functions under Regulation 36(2).

(2) IAASA shall examine information drawn up pursuant to Regulations 4 to 8 by issuers whose home Member State is the State for the purpose of considering whether such information is in accordance with the relevant reporting framework.

(3) The powers provided for in this Part in respect of IAASA shall not be exercised in a manner or for a purpose inconsistent with the Directive or transparency (regulated markets) law.

43. Particular powers of IAASA — supply of information

(1) Without prejudice to the generality of Regulation 42, IAASA shall, in particular, have the power to:

(a) require any of the following persons to produce any document in his or her possession or control and to make copies of such documents, or to provide any information or explanations that it may reasonably require, for the purpose of examining and reviewing information published pursuant to Regulations 4 to 8:

(i) an issuer;

(ii) any director, manager, officer or employee of an issuer;

(iii) any persons who control or are controlled by a person referred to in clause (i) or (ii);

(iv) any person discharging managerial responsibilities of the issuer;

(v) an auditor of an issuer;

(vi) any person who fell within any of clauses (i) to (v) at a time when the document or information required by IAASA was prepared or came into existence; and

(b) certify to the Court the refusal or failure of any person referred to in any of clauses (i) to (v) of subparagraph (a) to comply with a requirement made by IAASA pursuant to that subparagraph.

(2) The disclosure to IAASA by an auditor of any information, document, fact or decision on foot of a requirement made by IAASA under paragraph (1)(a) shall not be regarded as constituting a breach of any restriction on disclosure of information imposed by contract or by any law, regulation or administrative provision and shall not involve the auditor in liability of any kind.

44. Further particular powers of IAASA — directions to issuers, etc

Where it appears to IAASA that there is, or may be, a failure by an issuer whose home Member State is the State to ensure that an annual financial report published pursuant to Regulation 4 or a half-yearly financial report published pursuant to [Regulation 6][a] complies with the relevant reporting framework, IAASA may give notice to the issuer and to the directors of such issuer specifying:

(a) the matters in respect of which it appears to IAASA that the information fails to comply with the relevant reporting framework; and

(b) a period of not less than 30 days within which the issuer shall either:

(i) provide IAASA with a written explanation of the information; or

(ii) prepare revised information;

(c) that, in the absence of a written explanation under paragraph (b)(i) or the issuance of revised information under paragraph (b)(ii), IAASA may:

(i) give a direction requiring the issuer to revise the information in accordance with instructions of IAASA specified in the direction;

(ii) seek an order of confirmation from the Court of that direction issued by IAASA; and

(iii) recover its costs from the issuer;

(d) that, in the event that IAASA seeks an order of the Court to enforce its direction, IAASA may publish notice of such application in such manner as it thinks fit.

Amendments

a "Regulation 6" substituted for "Regulation 5" by T(Dir)(A)R 2010, reg 2(c).

45. Provisions consequent on issuer's response to notice under Regulation 44

(1) If, at or before the end of the period specified in the notice under Regulation 44 in accordance with paragraph (b) thereof, or such longer period as IAASA may permit, the issuer prepares revised information as directed by IAASA in that notice, IAASA may, taking into account the circumstances of the matter, require the issuer to pay some or all of the costs IAASA incurred in examining the information published by such issuer and in performing its functions under these Regulations.

(2) If, at the end of the period specified in the notice under Regulation 44 in accordance with paragraph (b) thereof, or such longer period as IAASA may permit—

(a) the issuer has not issued revised information; and

(b) IAASA, having considered any explanations provided by the issuer or its directors or both and considered any information or documents or both provided by the issuer in response to requests from it, IAASA remains of the opinion that the information does not comply with the relevant reporting framework,

IAASA may give a direction to the issuer requiring the issuer or its directors or both to do one or more of the following:

(i) revise the annual financial report or half-yearly financial report, as applicable, in accordance with instructions of IAASA specified in the direction;

(ii) publish the revised information in the same manner as required by Regulations 4 to 8 and to make any consequential amendments to the annual or interim financial reports published in accordance with instructions of IAASA specified in the direction;

(iii) publish notice of the direction given by IAASA under this paragraph in a format and containing such information as is specified by IAASA in the direction;

(iv) pay costs specified in the direction, being costs incurred by IAASA in examining and reviewing the financial reports.

(3) A direction under paragraph (2) shall—

(a) be in writing,

and

(b) specify the date from which it shall have effect and the period for which it shall have effect (which shall not exceed 12 months).

46. Application to Court to set aside or vary direction under Regulation 45

An issuer or its directors or both may apply to the Court for, and the Court may, if it considers it appropriate to do so, grant, an order setting aside or varying a direction under Regulation 45. An application under this Regulation shall be made within 30 days after the notification of the direction or within such extended period as the Court allows.

47. Enforcement of direction under Regulation 45

(1) IAASA may, as respects a direction under Regulation 45 which, in its opinion, has not been complied with, apply to the Court in a summary manner for such order as may be appropriate by way of enforcement of the direction and the Court may, as it thinks fit, on the hearing of the application, make or refuse to make an order providing for such relief.

(2) An application for an order under this Regulation shall be by motion, and the Court when considering the motion may make such interim or interlocutory order as it considers appropriate.

48. Applications under Regulations 46 and 47: supplemental provisions

(1) An application under Regulation 46 may not be made if the direction concerned has been the subject of an order granted under Regulation 47 (but without prejudice to the right of a person to apply subsequently to the Court to have the order varied or discharged).

(2) The Court may direct the hearing together of applications made under Regulations 46 and 47 that relate to the same direction.

(3) The Court may, if it thinks fit, vary or discharge an order made under Regulation 47.

(4) An application under Regulation 46 or 47 may be heard otherwise than in public.

49. Particular powers of Court on application to it under Regulation 47

(1) If satisfied, after hearing an application of IAASA pursuant to Regulation 47, that an issuer's annual or half-yearly financial report does not comply with the relevant reporting framework in whole or in part, the Court may make a declaration to that effect and may, by order, do one or more of the following:

- (a) require the issuer or its directors or both to revise the financial report at issue so that it complies with the relevant reporting framework;
- (b) give directions respecting one or more of the following:
  - (i) the auditing of the revised annual accounts;
  - (ii) the revision of any matter contained in any annual financial report or half-yearly financial report as appropriate;
  - (iii) the steps to be taken by the issuer or directors or both to bring the order of the Court to the notice of persons likely to rely on the information that was the subject of the declaration;
  - (iv) such other matters as the Court sees fit;
- (c) require the issuer or directors or both to pay the costs incurred by IAASA in performing its functions under Regulations 44 to 46 in relation to such issuer.

(2) For the purposes of making an order under paragraph (1), the Court may:

- (a) have regard to the extent to which any or all of the directors who approved the annual or half-yearly financial report that was the subject of the direction knew, or ought to have known, that it did not comply with the relevant reporting framework; and

(b) exempt one or more directors from any order made under paragraph (1) or may order the payment of different amounts by different directors.

50. Dissemination of court order

At the conclusion of proceedings before the Court, IAASA shall disseminate in such manner as it thinks fit:

(a) a copy of the court order, or

(b) notice that the application has failed or been withdrawn.

51. Provisions in relation to revised annual and half-yearly financial reports

(1) Regulations 44, 45, 47, 48, 49 and 50 apply equally to revised annual financial reports and half-yearly financial reports, as applicable, in which case references to revised annual reports and half-yearly financial reports are to be construed as references to further revised annual financial reports and half-yearly financial reports.

(2) Where revised annual financial reports or half-yearly financial reports are prepared under any of the Regulations referred to in paragraph (1), then, subject to a direction given under Regulation 45 or any order of the Court made on foot of an application to it under Regulation 47, any provision of these Regulations or the Companies Acts respecting the preparation, auditing, circulation and disclosure of annual accounts applies with the necessary changes to the revised annual financial report or half-yearly financial report, as applicable.

52. Supplemental provisions in relation to directions of IAASA

(1) IAASA may give a direction amending or revoking a direction given by it under Regulation 45(2) but this power may not be exercised—

(a) if an order of the Court made on foot of an application to it under Regulation 47 is for the time being in force in relation to the direction, or

(b) to extend the period specified in the direction for which it is to have effect.

(2) On the expiry of the period specified in a direction for which it is to have effect, IAASA may give another direction under these Regulations if it considers it necessary to do so, in like or different terms to the person concerned.

53. Power to appoint authorised officers

(1) A responsible authority may, in writing—

(a) authorise such and so many persons as the authority considers necessary to be authorised officers for the purposes of these Regulations, and

(b) revoke any such authorisation.

(2) An appointment under paragraph (1)(a) may be for a specified or unspecified period.

(3) Every authorised officer shall—

(a) be furnished with a certificate of his or her appointment as an authorised officer, and

(b) when exercising a power under these Regulations of an authorised officer, produce the certificate, together with some form of personal identification, if requested to do so by a person affected by the exercise of that power.

(4) An appointment under paragraph (1) of a person as an authorised officer ceases—

(a) when the responsible authority concerned revokes the appointment,

(b) the person dies or resigns from the appointment,

(c) if the appointment is for a specified period, when the period ends,

(d) if the person appointed is an officer of the Bank or IAASA, when the person ceases to be such an officer, or

(e) if the person appointed is an officer of an approved stock exchange to which the Bank has delegated functions under Regulation 37, when the person ceases to be such an officer.

54. Powers of authorised officers

(1) An authorised officer may, for the purpose of carrying out an investigation under this Part, do all or any of the following—

(a) at all reasonable times enter any premises at which there are reason-able grounds to believe that there are any relevant records,

(b) search and inspect the premises referred to in subparagraph (a) and any relevant records on the premises,

(c) secure for later inspection the premises or any part of the premises in which relevant records are kept or in which the officer has reasonable grounds for believing the relevant records are kept,

(d) require any person to whom these Regulations apply to produce to the officer relevant records, and if the information is in a non-legible form, to reproduce it in a legible form or to give to the officer such information as the officer reasonably requires in relation to entries in the relevant records,

(e) inspect and take copies of relevant records inspected or produced under this Regulation (including, in the case of information in a non-legible form, a copy of all or part of the information in a permanent legible form),

(f) remove and retain any of the relevant records inspected or produced under this Regulation for such period as may be reasonable to facilitate further examination,

(g) require a person to give to the officer information (including information by way of a written report) that the officer reasonably requires in relation to activities covered by these Regulations and to produce to the officer any relevant records that the person has or has access to,

(h) require a person by whom or on whose behalf data equipment is or has been used, or any person who has charge of, or is otherwise concerned with the operation of, the data equipment or any associated apparatus or material, to give the officer all reasonable assistance in relation thereto, and

(i) require a person to explain entries in any relevant records.

(2) An authorised officer shall not, except with the consent of the occupier, enter a private dwelling (other than a part of the dwelling used as a place of work) unless the officer has obtained a warrant from a judge of the District Court.

(3) Where any person from whom production of a relevant record is required claims a lien thereon, the production of it shall be without prejudice to the lien.

(4) The requirement to produce any relevant record or report or to provide information or assistance under this Regulation extends to—

(a) a liquidator or receiver of, or any person who is or has been an officer or employee or agent of, a person to whom these Regulations apply, or

(b) any other person who appears to the Bank or IAASA, as the case may be, or the authorised officer to have the relevant record or report in his or her possession or under his or her control or the ability to provide information or assistance, as the case may be.

(5) An authorised officer may, if the officer considers it necessary, be accompanied by a member of the Garda Síochána or by another authorised officer when exercising a power under this Part.

(6) A person shall not obstruct or interfere with an authorised officer in the exercise of his or her powers under this Regulation.

55. Warrants

(1) When an authorised officer in the exercise of the authorised officer's powers under Regulation 54(1)—

(a) is prevented from entering any premises, or

(b) believes that there are relevant records in a private dwelling,

the authorised officer or the responsible authority by whom the authorised officer was appointed may apply to a judge of the District Court for a warrant under this Regulation authorising the entry by the authorised officer into the premises or the private dwelling, as the case may be.

(2) If on an application under paragraph (1) a judge of the District Court is satisfied, on the information of the applicant, that the authorised officer concerned—

(a) has been prevented from entering any premises, or

(b) has reasonable grounds for believing that there are relevant records in a private dwelling,

then the judge may issue a warrant under the judge's hand authorising the authorised officer, accompanied, if the judge considers it appropriate to so provide, by such number of members of the Garda Síochána as may be specified in the warrant, at any time within 4 weeks from the date of issue of the warrant, to enter, if need be by force, the premises or private dwelling and exercise any of the powers referred to in Regulation 54(1).

56. Directions by Bank

(1) The Bank may give one or more of the directions specified in paragraph (2) if the Bank considers it necessary to do so in order to—

(a) perform its functions under these Regulations or any other provision of transparency (regulated markets) law,

(b) prevent any person from contravening or continuing to contravene a provision of these Regulations or any other provision of transparency (regulated markets) law, or

(c) protect otherwise the interests of investors.

(2) Each of the following is a direction referred to in paragraph (1), namely a direction to a person—

(a) to do or not to do anything that the Bank may require to be done or not to be done in exercise of its powers under Regulation 40,

(b) not to dispose of or otherwise dissipate any assets or specified assets of the person or not to do any of those things save where specified conditions are complied with,

(c) not to dispose of or otherwise dissipate any assets or specified assets the beneficial interest in which is vested in another person or persons or not to do any of those things save where specified conditions are complied with,

(d) being a credit institution, not to make any payments from an account held with the institution by a specified person or persons save with the prior consent of the Bank,

(e) not to accept, process or execute any subscription or order on behalf of a specified person,

(f) not to carry on a business (whether on the person's behalf or another's behalf) in a specified manner or otherwise than in a specified manner,

(g) not to engage in any practice that contravenes a provision of these Regulations or any other provision of transparency (regulated markets) law,

(h) not to enter into transactions of a specified kind or not to enter into such transactions save to a specified extent or save where specified conditions are complied with,

(i) not to publish specified information,

(j) to publish or disseminate in a specified manner specified information in relation to disclosure requirements arising under the Directive.

(3) A direction under this Regulation shall—

(a) be in writing,

and

(b) specify the date from which it shall have effect and the period for which it shall have effect (which shall not exceed 12 months).

(4) A person may apply to the Court for, and the Court may, if it considers it appropriate to do so, grant an order setting aside or varying a direction under this Regulation.

(5) The Bank may, as respects a direction under this Regulation which, in its opinion has not been complied with or is unlikely to be complied with, (or, in the case of a direction referred to in paragraph (2)(b) or (c), irrespective of whether it is of that opinion) apply to the Court in a summary manner for such order as may be appropriate by way of enforcement of the direction and the Court may, as it thinks fit, on the hearing of the application, make or refuse to make an order providing for such relief.

(6) An application for an order under paragraph (5) shall be by motion, and the Court when considering the motion may make such interim or interlocutory order as it considers appropriate.

(7) An application under paragraph (4) may not be made if the direction concerned has been the subject of an order granted under paragraph (5) (but without prejudice to the right of a person, the subject of an order granted under paragraph (5), to apply subsequently to the Court to have the order varied or discharged).

(8) The Court may direct the hearing together of applications made under paragraphs (4) and (5) that relate to the same direction.

(9) The Court may, if it thinks fit, vary or discharge an order made under paragraph (5).

(10) An application under paragraph (4) or (5) may be heard otherwise than in public.

(11) The Bank may give a direction amending or revoking a direction given by it under this Regulation but this power may not be exercised—

(a) if an order under paragraph (5) is for the time being in force in relation to the direction,

or

(b) to extend the period specified in the direction for which it is to have effect.

(12) On the expiry of the period specified in a direction for which it is to have effect, the Bank may give another direction under this Regulation (if it considers it necessary to do so on the grounds specified in paragraph (1)), in like or different terms, to the person concerned.

(13) The powers of the Bank under this Regulation are in addition to those conferred on it by any other enactment to give directions or impose conditions or requirements.

57. Precautionary measures

In circumstances where the State is a host Member State and where the Bank or IAASA, as appropriate, finds or has grounds for suspecting that an issuer or the holder of shares or other financial instruments or the person referred to in Regulation 14 has contravened a provision of these Regulations or another provision of transparency (regulated markets) law, it shall refer those findings or the fact of those grounds' existence to the competent authority of the home Member State.

58. Supplemental provision in relation to Regulation 57

(1) If, despite the measures taken by the competent authority of the home Member State in response to a referral of matters under Regulation 57 by the Bank or IAASA to it (whether because those measures are inadequate or otherwise) the contravention referred to in that Regulation still persists, the Bank or IAASA, as the case may be, after informing the competent authority of the home Member State, shall take all the appropriate measures within its power under these Regulations in order to protect investors.

(2) The Bank or IAASA, as the case may be, shall inform the Commission of any measures taken by it under paragraph (1) at the earliest opportunity.

59. Privilege

Nothing in these Regulations shall compel the disclosure by any person of any information which he or she would, in the opinion of the Court, be entitled to refuse to produce on the grounds of legal professional privilege or authorise the taking possession of any document containing such information which is in his or her possession.

PART 10
ADMINISTRATIVE SANCTIONS

60. Interpretation (Part 10)

(1) In this Part—

"adverse assessment" means an assessment in which the assessor has decided that the assessee is committing or has committed a prescribed contravention;

"assessee" means the person the subject of an assessment; "assessment" means an assessment referred to in Regulation 61; "assessor" means an assessor appointed under Regulation 61; "prescribed contravention" means a contravention of—

(a) these Regulations,

(b) any obligation imposed by the Bank pursuant to a power exercised under these Regulations, or

(c) any other provision of transparency (regulated markets) law;

"qualifying holding" means—

(a) a direct or indirect holding of shares or other interest in a regulated financial service provider which represents 10% or more of the capital or the voting rights, or

(b) a direct or indirect holding of shares or other interest in a regulated financial service provider which represents less than 10% of the capital or voting rights but which, in the opinion of the Bank, makes it possible to control or exercise a significant influence over the management of the regulated financial service provider;

"regulated financial service provider" has the same meaning as it has in section 2(1) of the Central Bank Act 1942 (No. 22 of 1942) as amended by section 2(g) of the Central Bank and Financial Services Authority of Ireland Act 2004 (No. 21 of 2004);

"sanction" means any sanction referred to in any of subparagraphs (a) to (f) of Regulation 67(1);

"specified sanctions", in relation to an adverse assessment, means the sanction or sanctions referred to in Regulation 61(8) which may be imposed on the assessee.

(2) The provisions of this Part are made for the purposes of enabling the imposition of administrative sanctions.

61. Bank may appoint assessor

(1) Where—

(a) the Bank, in the performance of the functions assigned to it as central competent administrative authority under Regulation 36(1), has reason to suspect that a prescribed contravention is being committed or has been committed, the Bank may appoint, or

(b) IAASA, in the performance of the functions assigned to it as competent authority under Regulation 36(2), has reason to suspect that a prescribed contravention is being committed or has been committed and requests the Bank to do so, the Bank shall appoint,

an assessor (or, if the Bank thinks fit to do so, more than one assessor) to conduct an assessment as to—

(i) whether or not the assessee is committing or has committed the contravention, and

(ii) if the assessor finds that the assessee is committing or has committed the contravention, the sanction or sanctions, if any, which the assessor considers are appropriate to be imposed on the assessee in respect of the contravention.

(2) The Bank may appoint an assessor who is not an officer, employee or official of the Bank and any such assessor so appointed is an agent of the Bank for the purpose of performing the functions of an assessor under this Part.

(3) The Bank shall provide the assessor with such administrative services (including technical and legal advice) as the Bank considers necessary to enable the assessor to perform the assessor's functions.

(4) The assessor shall, as soon as is practicable after the assessor's appointment as an assessor, give notice of the appointment to the assessee.

(5) The notice under paragraph (4) given to the assessee by the assessor shall contain—

- (a) a statement that the assessor is appointed by the Bank under this Regulation and, if the appointment has been made at the request of IAASA, shall specify that to be the case,
- (b) a statement in summary form of the grounds for conducting the assessment,
- (c) a statement that, within a reasonable time specified by the assessor in the notice, the assessee may—
  - (i) make submissions in writing to the assessor, and
  - (ii) request the assessor to be permitted to make oral submissions about the matters to which the notice relates, and
- (d) a statement that the assessor shall conduct the assessment even if no submissions referred to in subparagraph (c) are made.

(6) The assessor shall—

- (a) consider any submissions made by the assessee, and
- (b) conduct such investigations relating to the assessment as the assessor considers appropriate before issuing the assessment.

(7) The assessor shall issue the assessment to the Bank when the assessment is made and, if the appointment of the assessor has been made at the request of IAASA, the Bank shall, on receipt of the assessment, immediately transmit it to IAASA.

(8) Where the assessor decides that a prescribed contravention is being committed or has been committed, the assessor shall ensure that the assessment includes—

- (a) a statement of the grounds upon which the assessor made the assessment that the assessee is committing or has committed the contravention,
- (b) a statement in summary form of the evidence upon which the assessment is based, and
- (c) a statement of the sanction or sanctions, if any, which the assessor considers are appropriate to be imposed on the assessee in respect of the contravention.

(9) The appointment of an assessor may be for a specified or unspecified period.

(10) Subject to Regulation 68(2), the assessment shall constitute the decision of the Bank, and references in this Part to an adverse assessment shall be construed accordingly.

62. Revocation of appointment of assessor

(1) (a) Where the Bank is satisfied that the assessor has contravened paragraph (2) or is incapacitated, the Bank may revoke the appointment of the assessor at any time.

(b) Where IAASA is satisfied that the assessor has contravened paragraph (2) or is incapacitated, it may request the Bank to revoke the appointment of the assessor and the Bank, on the making of such a request, if it considers it appropriate to do so, shall revoke that appointment.

(2) The assessor (including a person proposed to be appointed as an assessor) shall—

(a) disclose to the Bank, and, where appropriate, to IAASA for its information, any material interest that the assessor may have in any matter that may arise during the assessment,

(b) disclose to the Bank, and where appropriate, to IAASA for its information, any actual or potential conflict of interest that the assessor may have in conducting an assessment,

(c) not use any inside information (within the meaning of the Market Abuse (Directive 2003/6/EC) Regulations 2005 (S.I. No. 342 of 2005)) obtained during an assessment for any purpose other than the performance of the assessor's functions under this Part,

(d) not engage in misconduct during the assessment,

(e) perform the assessor's functions in accordance with the provisions of this Part, and

(f) issue an assessment that is not contrary to law.

63. Power to require witnesses to appear and give evidence

(1) The assessor may by notice given in or outside the State to a person require the person to do one or more of the following—

(a) appear before the assessor to give evidence (including give evidence on oath),

(b) produce documents specified in the notice which are in the person's custody or control,

(c) for the purposes of subparagraph (a) or (b), attend before the assessor from day to day unless excused from attendance or released from further attendance by the assessor.

(2) The assessor may administer oaths for the purposes of the evidence referred to in paragraph (1)(a).

(3) A witness at a hearing before the assessor has the same liabilities, privileges and immunities as a witness before the Court.

(4) Where a person ("person concerned")—

(a) fails to comply with a notice under paragraph (1),

(b) threatens or insults the assessor or any witness or person required to attend before the assessor,

(c) interrupts the proceedings of, or does not behave in an appropriate manner before, the assessor,

(d) obstructs or attempts to obstruct the assessor,

(e) discloses, or authorises the disclosure of, evidence given before the assessor or any of the contents of a document produced to the assessor that the assessor has instructed not to be published, or

(f) does anything else that, if the assessor were a court of law having power to commit for contempt, would be contempt for that court, then

(i) the assessor may apply to the Court for an order requiring the person concerned to do one or both of the following—

(I) to comply with the notice under paragraph (1),

(II) to discontinue or not repeat the behaviour falling within any of the provisions of subparagraphs (b) to (f), or behaviour of any similar kind, and

(ii) the Court, if satisfied that there is no reasonable excuse for the failure to comply with the notice under paragraph (1) or for the behaviour concerned, as the case may be, grant the order and such other orders as it considers appropriate to ensure that the person concerned cooperates with the assessor.

64. Referral to Court on question of law

(1) (a) The Bank or the assessor may (including at the request of the assessee) refer a question of law arising in the assessment to the Court for determination by the Court.

(b) Without prejudice to paragraph (a), where the assessor has been appointed at the request of IAASA, the Bank may, at the request of IAASA, refer a question of law arising in the assessment to the Court for determination by the Court.

(2) Where a question of law is referred under paragraph (1)—

(a) the assessor shall send to the Court all documents before him or her that are relevant to the matter in question, and

(b) at the end of the proceedings in the Court in relation to the reference, the Court shall cause the documents to be returned to the assessor.

65. Assessee to be issued copy of any adverse assessment, etc

(1) Where the assessment of the assessor is that the assessee is committing or has committed a prescribed contravention, the Bank shall—

(a) issue the assessee with a copy of the adverse assessment (or, as the Bank thinks fit, so much of the adverse assessment as constitutes the statements referred to in Regulation 61(8)) and provide a copy of the assessment to IAASA where the assessor has been appointed by the Bank at the request of IAASA, and

(b) advise the assessee that—

(i) the assessee may appeal against the adverse assessment to the Court under Regulation 66, and

(ii) the Bank may apply to the Court under Regulation 70 for an order confirming the adverse assessment (including the specified sanctions).

(2) Where the assessment of the assessor is that the assessee is neither committing nor has committed a prescribed contravention, the Bank shall issue the assessee with a statement to that effect and, where the assessor has been appointed by the Bank at the request of IAASA, shall inform IAASA accordingly.

66. Right of appeal against adverse assessment (including specified sanctions)

(1) The assessee may appeal to the Court against the adverse assessment (including the specified sanctions) not later than 28 days after the Bank has complied with Regulation 65(1) in relation to the assessee or within such further period as the Court allows.

(2) An appeal under paragraph (1) may be heard otherwise than in public.

(3) The Court may, pending the hearing and determination of an appeal under paragraph (1), make such interim or interlocutory orders as the Court considers necessary in the circumstances.

(4) The Court shall determine an appeal under paragraph (1) by making—

(a) an order confirming, varying or setting aside the adverse assessment (including the specified sanctions), whether in whole or in part, or

(b) an order remitting the case to be decided again by the Bank in accordance with the directions of the Court.

(5) The determination of the Court on the hearing of an appeal under paragraph (1) shall be final, except that a party to the appeal may apply to the Supreme Court to review the determination on a question of law.

(6) For the avoidance of doubt, it is declared that no variation of an adverse assessment under paragraph (4) (a) may provide for the imposition of a sanction on the assessee which is not a sanction referred to in subparagraphs (a) to (f) of Regulation 67(1).

67. Sanctions that may be imposed by Bank

(1) In the case of an adverse assessment, the Bank may impose on the assessee such of the following sanctions as are the specified sanctions—

(a) a private caution or reprimand,

(b) a public caution or reprimand,

(c) subject to Regulation 72(2), a direction to pay to the Bank, or, if the assessor has been appointed by the Bank at the request of IAASA, to IAASA, a monetary penalty (but not exceeding €2,500,000 in any case),

(d) a direction disqualifying the assessee from being concerned in the management of, or having a qualifying holding in, any regulated financial service provider for such time as is specified in the order,

(e) if the assessee is continuing to commit a prescribed contravention, a direction ordering the assessee to cease committing the prescribed contravention,

(f) a direction to pay to the Bank all or a specified part of the costs incurred by the Bank in investigating the matter to which the assessment relates and in holding the assessment (including any costs incurred by authorised officers).

(2) Where the assessor had been appointed by the Bank at the request of IAASA, the Bank shall consult with IAASA before exercising the powers under paragraph (1).

68. Power to correct assessments

(1) Where the assessor or the Bank is satisfied that there is an obvious error in the text of an assessment, the assessor or the Bank, as the case may be, may alter the text of the assessment to remove the error.

(2) Where the text of an assessment is altered under paragraph (1), the text as so altered shall be taken to be the decision of the Bank under Regulation 61(10).

(3) In paragraph (1), "obvious error", in relation to the text of an assessment, includes—

(a) a clerical or typographical error,

(b) an error arising from an accidental slip or omission, or

(c) a defect of form.

69. When specified sanctions take effect

(1) Where—

(a) no appeal under Regulation 66 against the adverse assessment is lodged with the Court within the period for lodging the appeal, or

(b) an appeal under Regulation 66 against the adverse assessment which has been lodged with the Court within the period for lodging the appeal is withdrawn or abandoned,

then the specified sanctions, as confirmed or varied in the order, if any, obtained under Regulation 70(3)(a), shall take effect on the date of that order or such other date as the Court may specify in that order.

(2) Where an appeal under Regulation 66 against the adverse assessment is lodged with the Court within the period for lodging the appeal, then the specified sanctions, as confirmed or varied in the order, if any, obtained under Regulation 66(4)(a), shall take effect on the date of that order or such other date as the Court may specify in that order.

70. Enforcement of adverse assessment (including specified sanctions)

(1) Where—

(a) no appeal under Regulation 66 against the adverse assessment is lodged with the Court within the period for lodging the appeal, or

(b) an appeal under Regulation 66 against the adverse assessment which has been lodged with the Court within the period for lodging the appeal is withdrawn or abandoned,

then, subject to paragraph (2), the Bank may apply to the Court for an order confirming the adverse assessment (including the specified sanctions).

(2) Where the assessor was appointed by the Bank at the request of IAASA, such an application shall not be made otherwise than at the request of IAASA but, if IAASA does make a request of the Bank to make such an application, it shall be the duty of the Bank to comply with that request.

(3) The Court shall determine an application under paragraph (1) by making—

(a) an order confirming, varying or setting aside the adverse assessment (including the specified sanctions), whether in whole or in part, or

(b) an order remitting the case to be decided again by the Bank in accordance with the directions of the Court.

(4) The Court shall not hear an application under paragraph (1) unless—

(a) the assessee appears at the hearing as respondent to the application, or

(b) if the assessee does not so appear, the Court is satisfied that a copy of the application has been served on the assessee.

(5) An application under paragraph (1) may be heard otherwise than in public.

(6) The Court may, on an application under paragraph (1), make such interim or interlocutory orders as the Court considers necessary in the circumstances.

(7) The determination of the Court on the hearing of an application under paragraph (1) shall be final, except that the Bank or the respondent, if any, may apply to the Supreme Court to review the determination on a question of law.

(8) For the avoidance of doubt, it is declared that no variation of an adverse assessment under paragraph (3)(a) may provide for the imposition of a sanction on the assessee which is not a sanction referred to in subparagraphs (a) to (f) of Regulation 67(1).

71. Publication of certain specified sanctions

The Bank shall publicly disclose the specified sanctions referred to in sub-paragraphs (c) to (f) of Regulation 67(1), as confirmed or varied in the order concerned obtained under Regulation 66(4)(a) or 70(3)(a), that are imposed on the assessee unless the Bank considers that the disclosure would—

(a) seriously jeopardise the financial markets, or

(b) cause disproportionate damage to the parties involved.

72. Person not liable to be penalised twice for same contravention

(1) Where—

(a) a sanction referred to in Regulation 67(1)(c) is to be imposed on the assessee by virtue of an order obtained under Regulation 66(4)(a) or 70(3)(a), and

(b) the acts which constitute the prescribed contravention to which the sanction relates also constitute an offence under a law of the State,

then the assessee is not, in respect of those acts, liable to be prosecuted or punished for that offence under that law.

(2) A sanction referred to in Regulation 67(1)(c) in respect of a prescribed contravention shall not be imposed on the assessee where—

(a) the assessee has been found guilty or not guilty of having committed an offence under a provision of these Regulations, and

(b) all or some of the acts constituting that offence also constitute the prescribed contravention.

73. Person not to be concerned in management of regulated financial service provider while disqualified

A regulated financial service provider shall ensure that a person shall not be concerned in the management of, or have a qualifying holding in, the financial service provider while the person is subject to a sanction referred to in Regulation 67(1)(d) that is in force.

74. Power of Bank or IAASA to resolve suspected contraventions, etc

(1) Where—

(a) the Bank, in the performance of the functions assigned to it as central competent administrative authority under Regulation 36(1), has reason to suspect, or

(b) IAASA, in the performance of the functions assigned to it as competent authority under Regulation 36(2), has reason to suspect, that a person ("relevant party") is committing or has committed a prescribed contravention, it may enter into an agreement in writing with the relevant party to resolve the matter (including at any time before an assessment, if any, has been issued in respect of the relevant party).

(2) An agreement entered into under paragraph (1)—

(a) is binding on the Bank or IAASA, as the case may be, and the relevant party, and

(b) may include terms under which the relevant party accepts the imposition of sanctions.

(3) An agreement entered into under paragraph (1) may be enforced by the Bank or IAASA, as the case may be, or the relevant party in a court of competent jurisdiction.

PART 11
CO-OPERATION BETWEEN COMPETENT AUTHORITIES

75. Co-operation between Competent Authorities

(1) The Bank and IAASA shall each—

(a) co-operate with the competent authorities of other Member States, designated under the Directive, whenever necessary, for the purpose of the performance by each of the competent authorities of the Member States (including the Bank or IAASA, as appropriate) of their functions and the making use of their powers (whether set out in the Directive, transparency (regulated markets) law or the measures for the time being adopted by another Member State to implement the Directive), and

(b) render assistance to competent authorities of other Member States in the performance of their functions (whether set out in the Directive or the measures for the time being adopted by another Member State to implement the Directive).

(2) In particular and without prejudice to its obligations under section 33AK(10) of the Central Bank Act 1942, as amended, or section 31 of the Companies (Auditing and Accounting) Act 2003, as the case may be, nothing in any law shall prevent the Bank or IAASA from exchanging confidential information. Information thus exchanged shall be covered by the obligation of professional secrecy to which the persons employed or formerly employed by the competent authorities receiving the information are subject.

(3) The Bank or IAASA may conclude, for their respective purposes, cooperation agreements with the competent authorities or bodies of third countries enabled by their respective legislation providing for the exchange of information so as to allow the carrying out of any of the tasks assigned by the Directive to the competent authorities in accordance with Article 24 of the Directive.

(4) Such an exchange of information—

(a) is subject to the authority with whom the information is exchanged guaranteeing that a level of professional secrecy at least equivalent to that referred to in Article 25 of the Directive shall apply to the information, and

(b) shall be intended for the performance of the supervisory task of the authorities or bodies mentioned in paragraph (3).

(5) Without prejudice to paragraph (4), where the information proposed to be exchanged originates in another Member State—

(a) it shall not be exchanged without the express consent of the competent authority which disclosed it in the first place, and

(b) if the purpose for which it was so disclosed was limited to any extent specified in that consent, shall be exchanged only for the purpose so specified.

PART 12
PENALTIES, GENERAL AND OTHER MISCELLANEOUS PROVISIONS

76. Offences and penalties generally

(1) If the contravention in respect of which a person is convicted of an offence under another provision of this Regulation is continued after the conviction, the person shall be guilty of a further offence on every day on which the contravention continues.

(2) Where any offence is committed under another provision of this Regulation by a body corporate and is proved to have been committed with the consent, connivance or approval of or to have been attributable to the wilful neglect on the part of any person, being a director, manager, secretary or other officer of the body corporate or a person who was purporting to act in any such capacity, that person as well as the body corporate shall be guilty of an offence and is liable to be proceeded against and punished as if he or she was guilty of the first mentioned offence.

(3) A person who contravenes Regulation 54(6) or 73 shall be guilty of an offence.

(4) A person who, knowing the information to be so false or misleading, or being reckless as to whether or not it is so false or misleading, discloses information in purported compliance with a requirement imposed on the person by or pursuant to these Regulations which is false or misleading in a material respect shall be guilty of an offence.

(5) A person who is guilty of—

(a) an offence under this Regulation other than an offence referred to in subparagraph (b),

or

(b) one or more further offences under paragraph (1), for each such offence,

shall be liable on summary conviction to a [class A fine][a] or imprisonment for a term not exceeding 12 months or both.

(6) Every offence under this Regulation is an offence to which section 21 (penalties on indictment) of the Investment Funds, Companies and Miscellaneous Provisions Act 2006 applies.

Amendments

a As implicitly substituted for "fine not exceeding €5,000" by Fines Act 2010, s 4. A class A fine currently means a fine not exceeding €5,000.

---

77. Annual report of Bank and IAASA

(1) The Bank shall provide the Minister with a copy of the extract relating to the performance of its functions under these Regulations from its annual report to the Minister for Finance under section 300 of the Central Bank Act 1942.

(2) IAASA shall give an account of the performance of its functions under these Regulations in its annual report under section 22 of the Companies (Auditing and Accounting) Act 2003.

78. Fees and charges

(1) Fees shall be payable pursuant to section 33K of the Central Bank Act 1942 in respect of the performance by the Bank of its functions under these Regulations.

(2) IAASA may, for the purpose of defraying the expenses incurred by it in performing its functions under these Regulations, impose charges on issuers admitted to trading on a regulated market at such rates as are from time to time determined by it with the consent of the Minister.

(3) The Minister shall, where he or she considers it appropriate to do so, consult with any persons who are, in the Minister's opinion, interested in the matter before he or she consents to any determination by IAASA of rates of charges under paragraph (2).

(4) Charges imposed by IAASA under paragraph (2) shall be recoverable by IAASA from the person on whom they have been imposed as a simple contract debt in any court of competent jurisdiction.

79. Transitional — provisions of a substantive nature

(1) (a) An issuer whose financial year begins on or after 20 January 2007 shall comply with Regulations 4 to 9 on and from 13th June 2007.

(b) An issuer whose financial year begins before 20 January 2007 shall comply with Regulations 4 to 9 on and from the beginning of its next financial year.

(2) (a) This paragraph applies to an issuer of debt securities which were admitted to trading on a regulated market in a Member State before 1 January 2005 if the home Member State had decided to allow such an issuer to benefit from the provisions of Article 27 of Directive 2001/34/EC of the European Parliament and of the Council of 28 May 2001 at the point of admission of those securities.

(b) For the financial years falling within the period for which this paragraph applies, such an issuer need not disclose its half-yearly financial report in accordance with Regulations 6 to 8.

(c) This paragraph applies for the period of 10 years following 1 January 2005.

(3) An issuer need not prepare its financial statements in accordance with Regulation 4(4) or 7(2) for any financial year beginning before 1 January 2007 if:

(a) the issuer's registered office is in a third country; and

(b) the issuer prepares its financial statements in accordance with inter-nationally accepted standards.

(4) (a) This paragraph applies to an issuer:

(i) whose debt securities only are admitted to trading; and

(ii) whose home Member State is the State.

(b) Such an issuer is not required to disclose financial statements in accordance with Regulation 7(2)(a) for the financial year (and that financial year only) beginning on or after 1 January 2006.

(5) (a) This paragraph applies to an issuer of debt securities:

(i) that is incorporated in a third country ("the third country");

(ii) whose home Member State is the State; and

(iii) whose debt securities were admitted to trading in a Member State prior to 1 January 2005.

(b) Such an issuer need not draw up its annual financial statements in accordance with Regulation 4(4) or its management report in accordance with Regulation 5 (3) if:

(i) the annual financial statements prepared by issuers from the third country give a true and fair view of the issuer's assets and liabilities, financial position and results;

(ii) the third country has not made mandatory the application of accounting standards referred to in Article 2 of Regulation (EC) No.1606/2002 of the European Parliament and of the Council of 19 July 2002; and

(iii) the Commission has not taken any decision, in accordance with Article 23(4)(ii) of the Directive, as to whether there is an equivalence between IAS and IFRS and:

(I) the accounting standards laid down in the law, regulations or administrative provisions of the third country; or

(II) the accounting standards of a third country (not being that referred to in subparagraph (a)(i)) with which such an issuer has elected to comply.

(6) Prior to financial years starting on or after 1 January 2009, an issuer whose registered office is in a third country may prepare its annual consolidated financial statements and half-yearly consolidated financial statements in accordance with the accounting standards of a third country provided the Bank is satisfied that one of the conditions set out in Article 1 of Commission Decision 2006/891/EC of 4 December 2006 is complied with.

(7) Notwithstanding paragraph (3) of Regulation 21, a person who holds a percentage of voting rights in respect of which there is a notification requirement under these Regulations shall notify the issuer referred to in that paragraph (3), not later than 2 months after 13th June 2007, of the percentage of voting rights he or she holds at 13th June 2007, unless he or she has already made a notification of that percentage of those voting rights in accordance with Regulation 14(1) before that date.

(8) Notwithstanding Regulation 21(9), an issuer shall disclose, in accordance with these Regulations, information the subject of a notification referred to in paragraph (7) not later than 3 months after 13th June 2007.

80. Transitional — construction of certain references

(1) References in these Regulations to a person authorised under Directive 2004/39/EC of the European Parliament and of the Council of 21 April 2004 shall be read as

including references to a person authorised under Council Directive 93/22/EEC of 10 May 1993.

(2) The reference in Regulation 18 to portfolio management under point 4 of Section A of Annex 1 to Directive 2004/39/EC of the European Parliament and of the Council of 21 April 2004 shall be read as including a reference to the service of portfolio management under point 3 of Annex A of Council Directive 93/22/EEC of 10 May 1993.

(3) References in these Regulations to a regulated market shall be read as including references to a market as defined by point 13 of Article 1 of Council Directive 93/22/EEC of 10 May 1993.

81. Relationship with Chapter 2 of Part IV of Companies Act 1990

The obligation of disclosure under Chapter 2 of Part IV of the Companies Act 1990 and the related provisions of that Chapter shall not apply to—

(a) an acquisition or disposal of shares which is required to be notified under these Regulations, or

(b) an acquisition or disposal of shares which, but for an express exemption provided by or under these Regulations (whether the word "exempted" is used or not), would be required to be notified under these Regulations.

EXPLANATORY NOTE

(*This note is not part of the instrument and does not purport to be a legal interpretation*)

These regulations along with Part 3 of the Investment Funds, Companies and Miscellaneous Provisions Act 2006 and certain rules which may be made by the competent authority (The Central Bank and Financial Services Authority of Ireland) under regulation 40(3) of the Regulations give effect to Directive 2004/109EC of the European Parliament and of the Council of 15 December 2004 on the harmonisation of transparency requirements in relation to information about issuers whose securities are admitted to trading on a regulated market and Commission Directive 2007/14/EC laying down detailed rules for the implementation of certain provisions of Directive 2004/109/EC.

European Communities (Admissions to Listing and Miscellaneous Provisions) Regulations 2007

SI 286/2007

I, MICHEÁL MARTIN, Minister for Enterprise, Trade and Employment, in exercise of the powers conferred on me by section 3 of the European Communities Act 1972 (No. 27 of 1972), and for the purpose of giving effect to Directive 2001/34/EC of the European Parliament and of the Council of 28 May 2001 (O.J. No. L 184, 6.7.2001, pp.1-66), as amended by Directive 2003/71/EC of the European Parliament and of the Council of 4 November 2003 (O.J. No. L 345, 31.12.2003, pp 64-89), and Directive 2004/109/EC of the European Parliament and of the Council of 15 December 2004 (O.J. No. L 390, 31.12.2004, pp 38-57) and giving further effect to Article 32(5) of the last-mentioned Directive, hereby make the following regulations:

1. Citation, commencement and construction

(1) These Regulations may be cited as the European Communities (Admissions to Listing and Miscellaneous Provisions) Regulations 2007.

(2) These Regulations shall come into operation on 13 June 2007.

(3) These Regulations shall be read as one with the Companies Acts.

2. Interpretation

(1) In these Regulations—

'admission to official listing' means the admission of securities to the Official List of the Irish Stock Exchange and 'official listing' shall be construed accordingly;

'Bank' means the Central Bank and Financial Services Authority of Ireland; 'Council' means the Board of the Irish Stock Exchange;

'Directive' means Directive 2001/34/EC of the European Parliament and of the Council of 28 May 2001 on the admission of securities to official stock exchange listing and on information to be published on those securities, as amended by Directive 2003/71/EC of the European Parliament and of the Council of 4 November 2003 on the prospectus to be published when securities are offered to the public or admitted to trading and amending Directive 2001/34/EC, and further amended by the Transparency (Regulated Markets) Directive;

'Irish Stock Exchange' has the meaning given to it by section 3(1) of the Stock Exchange Act 1995 (No. 9 of 1995);

'listing rules' means the rules of the Irish Stock Exchange relating to the admission to the Official List of the Irish Stock Exchange;

'Minister' means the Minister for Enterprise, Trade and Employment;

'Transparency (Regulated Markets) Directive' means Directive 2004/109/EC of the European Parliament and of the Council of 15 December 2004 on the harmonisation of transparency requirements in relation to information about issuers whose securities are admitted to trading on a regulated market and amending Directive 2001/34/EC;

'transparency (regulated markets) law' has the same meaning as it has in the Investment Funds, Companies and Miscellaneous Provisions Act 2006 (No. 41 of 2006).

(2) A reference in these Regulations to an Article or other provision of the Directive shall be construed as a reference to that Article or that provision as amended.

(3) A word or expression that is used in these Regulations and is also used in the Directive shall have in these Regulations the same meaning as it has in the Directive.

3. Application of Directive

(1) Subject to the provisions of these Regulations, the requirements of the Directive relating to the admission of securities to official listing shall have effect and be applied accordingly.

(2) The Irish Stock Exchange may make the admission of securities to official listing subject to more stringent conditions than those set out in Articles 42 to 63 of the Directive or to additional conditions:

Provided that those more stringent or additional conditions—

(i) apply generally for all such issuers or for individual classes of such issuers,

(ii) are published before application for admission of such securities is made, and

(iii) are not otherwise inconsistent with, or imposed in a manner inconsistent with, any provision of the Directive taking account of the prohibitions provided for in Article 7 and Articles 42 to 63 of the Directive. [Note]

(3) The Irish Stock Exchange may also make the issuers of securities admitted to official listing subject to additional obligations:

Provided that those additional obligations—

(i) apply generally for all such issuers or for individual classes of such issuers,

(ii) do not—

(I) relieve a person of obligations arising under, or

(II) make provision for specific matters dealt with by,

transparency (regulated markets) law (including any more stringent requirements applied on foot of the Transparency (Directive 2004/109/EC) Regulations 2007 by the Bank (being the central competent administrative authority designated for the purposes of the Transparency (Regulated Markets) Directive)), and

(iii) are not inconsistent with, or imposed in a manner inconsistent with, any provision of the Directive.

(4) For the purpose of achieving the result specified in paragraph (5), the Irish Stock Exchange shall consult with the Bank before it makes issuers generally or any individual class of issuer subject to additional obligations under paragraph (3).

(5) The result mentioned in paragraph (4) is ensuring that the requirements of—

(a) these Regulations (including any more stringent or additional conditions under paragraph (2) and any additional obligations under paragraph (3)), and

(b) transparency (regulated markets) law (including any more stringent requirements referred to paragraph (ii) of the proviso to paragraph (3)),

operate in a manner that is consistent with one another.

(6) Nothing in these Regulations shall affect or derogate from any power of the Minister for Finance under the Stock Exchange Act 1995.

4. Limited discretions conferred on Member States by Directive

The provisions of the Schedule have effect in consequence of the exercise by the State of the discretions conferred on each Member State by the Directive as to its implementation.

5. Offence

(1) The restrictions referred to in Article 107(1) of the Directive shall apply to all persons employed or formerly employed by the Irish Stock Exchange in the performance of its functions as competent authority.

(2) Any person who fails to comply with paragraph (1) or who publishes any information required to be published by the Directive which is false or misleading in a material respect knowing the information to be so false or misleading or being reckless as to whether it is so false or misleading shall be guilty of an offence.

(3) A person guilty of an offence under paragraph (2) shall be liable on summary conviction to a [class A fine][a].

(4) Where an offence under paragraph (2) is committed by a body corporate and is proved to have been committed with the consent, connivance or approval of or to have been attributable to the wilful neglect on the part of any person, being a director, manager, secretary or other officer of the body corporate or a person who was purporting to act in any such capacity, that person as well as the body corporate shall be guilty of an offence and is liable to be proceeded against and punished as if he or she was guilty of the first-mentioned offence

(5) Proceedings in relation to an offence under paragraph (2) may be brought and prosecuted by the Director of Public Prosecutions or the Director of Corporate Enforcement.

Amendments

a As implicitly substituted for "fine not exceeding €5,000" by Fines Act 2010, s 4. A class A fine currently means a fine not exceeding €5,000.

---

6. Competent authority for purposes of Directive

(1) The Irish Stock Exchange shall be the competent authority for the purposes of the Directive and shall have all the powers required to be conferred on, or which the State is permitted to confer on, the competent authority by the Directive.

(2) The Irish Stock Exchange may arrange for the discharge of its functions as competent authority by any committee, sub-committee, officer or employee of the Irish Stock Exchange and nothing in this Regulation shall prevent the Irish Stock Exchange from being assisted in, or advised on, the discharge of these functions by any committee, sub-committee, officer or employee of the Council.

7. Liability of competent authority

(1) Subject to paragraph (2), neither the Irish Stock Exchange nor any person referred to in Regulation 6(2) shall be liable in damages by reason only of non-compliance with or contravention of any obligation imposed by or by virtue of these Regulations, nor shall the Exchange or that person be so liable in respect of anything done or

omitted to be done by it or him or her in connection with the performance by the Exchange of its functions as competent authority.

(2) Paragraph (1) does not apply if the act or omission complained of was done or made in bad faith.

(3) No transaction shall be void or voidable by reason only of the fact that it was entered into in contravention of, or otherwise than in conformity with, these Regulations.

8. Office of competent authority

(1) For the purposes of the performance of its functions as competent authority pursuant to these Regulations, the Irish Stock Exchange shall maintain and administer an office in the State.

(2) The Irish Stock Exchange shall notify the Minister of the address and of any change in the address of such office.

(3) Any document may be served on the competent authority in connection with the discharge by it of its functions under these Regulations by leaving it at, or by sending it by post to, the office maintained by the Irish Stock Exchange pursuant to paragraph (1).

9. Application to High Court

(1) Where, in the performance of its functions under these Regulations, the competent authority refuses an application for admission to official listing, or where it discontinues such a listing, the issuer of the securities may apply to the High Court in a summary manner to have such refusal or discontinuation reviewed.

(2) On the hearing of an application under this Regulation, the High Court shall confirm the decision of the competent authority unless it is satisfied that the procedures specified by, or the requirements of, these Regulations or the Directive have not been complied with in any material respect.

(3) In any case where the High Court is satisfied that the procedures specified by, or the requirements of, these Regulations or the Directive have not been complied with in any material respect, the High Court may set aside the decision of the competent authority and in such a case shall remit the matter to the competent authority which shall thereupon reconsider the matter and make a further decision in accordance with such procedures and requirements.

10. Annual report of competent authority

The Irish Stock Exchange shall report annually to the Minister on the performance of its functions as competent authority in the State under the Directive and under these Regulations and, in particular, by means of such a report, shall inform the Minister of—

(a) any amendment of the listing rules or revision of its procedures pursuant to the Directive or otherwise, including—

(i) any conditions imposed for the admission of securities to official listing which are more stringent than, or additional to, the requirements for admission to official listing, and

(ii) any additional obligations imposed on the issuers of securities admitted to official listing,

(b) the nature of all securities which are admitted to official listing,

(c) the refusal of any application for admission to official listing,

(d) the suspension or discontinuation of any official listing, and

(e) any special arrangements which have been made with other Member States pursuant to Article 13 of the Directive.

11. Saving of other duties of issuers

For the avoidance of doubt, it is declared that nothing in these Regulations shall affect any obligation on issuers of securities admitted to official listing imposed by or under any other enactment.

12. Revocations

The following Regulations are revoked:

(a) the European Communities (Stock Exchange) Regulations 1984 (S.I. No. 282 of 1984); and

(b) the European Communities (Stock Exchange) (Amendment) Regulations 1995 (S.I. No. 311 of 1995).

13. Repeals

Sections 89 to 96 of the Companies Act 1990 (No. 33 of 1990) are repealed.

Schedule

Provisions consequent on exercise of certain limited discretions by State in relation to Directive's implementation

1. These Regulations shall not apply to—

(a) units issued by collective investment undertakings other than of the closed-end type, or

(b) securities issued by a Member State or by its regional or local authorities.

2. The conditions and obligations referred to in Article 10 of the Directive shall not apply to the securities issued by persons referred to in that Article.

3. Shares may be admitted to official listing where the condition referred to in Article 43 (1) of the Directive is not fulfilled, provided that the requirements of Article 43(2) of the Directive are satisfied.

4. Debt securities may be admitted to official listing where the condition referred to in Article 58 (1) of the Directive is not fulfilled, provided that the requirements of Article 58(2) of the Directive are satisfied.

5. Convertible or exchangeable debentures and debentures with warrants may be admitted to official listing if the requirement in Article 59(2) of the Directive is satisfied.

Explanatory Note

(This note is not part of the instrument and does not purport to be a legal interpretation).

These regulations replace the European Communities (Stock Exchange) Regulations 1984 (S.I. No. 282 of 1984), as amended over the years, and include amendments arising on foot of the implementation into Irish law of Directive 2004/109/EC on the harmonisation of transparency requirements in relation to information about issuers whose securities are admitted to trading on a regulated market. These Regulations also repeal Sections 89 to 96 of the Companies Act 1990 as a consequence of Article 32(5) of Directive 2004/109/EC.

European Communities (Public Limited Companies — Directive 2006/68/EC) Regulations 2008

SI 89/2008

I, MICHEÁL MARTIN, Minister for Enterprise, Trade and Employment, in exercise of the powers conferred on me by section 3 (amended by section 2 of the European Communities Act 2007 (No. 18 of 2007)) of the European Communities Act 1972 (No. 27 of 1972) and for the purpose of giving effect to Directive 2006/68/EC (OJ L264, 25.9.2006, p 64) of the European Parliament and of the Council of 6 September 2006 amending Council Directive 77/91/EEC, as regards the formation of public limited liability companies and the maintenance and alteration of their capital, hereby make the following regulations:

1. Citation, commencement and construction.

(1) These Regulations may be cited as the European Communities (Public Limited Companies — Directive 2006/68/EC) Regulations 2008.

(2) These Regulations shall come into operation on 15 April 2008.

2. Interpretation

(1) In these Regulations—

"Act of 1963" means the Companies Act 1963 (No. 33 of 1963);

"Act of 1990" means the Companies Act 1990 (No. 33 of 1990);

(2) A word or expression that is used in the amendments to the Act of 1963 or the Act of 1990, effected by these Regulations, and that is also used in the Directive has, in those amendments, the same meaning as it has in the Directive.

3. Amendment of Act of 1963

The Act of 1963 is amended—

(a) in section 73(2), by—

[...][a]

(b) in section 77 by [...][b]

Amendments

a EC(PLC)R 2008, reg 3(a) substitutes CA 1963, s 73(2).

b EC(PLC)R 2008, reg 3(b) amends CA 1963, s 77.

---

4. Amendment of Act of 1990

The Act of 1990 is amended—

(a) in section 207(2)(d), by substituting the following subparagraph for subparagraph (i):

[...][a]

(b) in section 211—

(i) [...][b]

(ii) [...][c]

Amendments

a EC(PLC)R 2008, reg 4(a) substitutes CA 1990, s 207(2)(d)(i).

b EC(PLC)R 2008, reg 4(b)(i) amends CA 1990, s 211(1).

c EC(PLC)R 2008, reg 4(b)(ii) inserts CA 1990, s 211(4).

EXPLANATORY NOTE

(*This note is not part of the Instrument and does not purport to be a legal interpretation*).

These Regulations give effect to certain provisions of Directive 2006/68/EC of the European Parliament and the Council of 6 September 2006 which amended Council Directive 77/91/EEC as regards the formation of public limited liability companies and the maintenance and alteration of their capital. The areas covered by the Regulations are matters relating to creditor protection in cases of capital reduction and purchase by a company of its own shares.

European Communities (Cross-Border Mergers) Regulations 2008

SI 157/2008

I, MARY COUGHLAN, Minister for Enterprise, Trade and Employment, in exercise of the powers conferred on me by section 3 (as amended by section 2 of the European Communities Act 2007 (No. 18 of 2007)) of the European Communities Act 1972 (No. 27 of 1972) and for the purpose of giving effect to Council Directive No. 2005/56/EC of 26 October 2005 (OJ L 310, 25.11.2005, p 1) hereby make the following regulations:

PART 1

PRELIMINARY AND GENERAL

1. Citation and construction

(1) These Regulations may be cited as the European Communities (Cross-Border Mergers) Regulations 2008.

(2) Parts 1 and 2 of these Regulations shall be construed as one with the Companies Acts 1963 to 2006.

2. Interpretation

(1) In these Regulations— 'Act of 1963' means the Companies Act 1963 (No. 33 of 1963);

'common draft terms' means the proposed terms of a cross-border merger drawn up and adopted in accordance with Regulation 5;

'company' means an Irish company or an EEA Company;

'Companies Acts' means the Companies Acts 1963 to 2006;

'Companies Register' means the register of companies maintained by the Registrar in accordance with the Companies Acts;

'cross-border merger' means a merger involving at least one Irish company and at least one EEA company, being—

- (a) a merger by acquisition,
- (b) a merger by formation of a new company, or
- (c) a merger by absorption;

'CRO Gazette' means the Companies Registration Office Gazette maintained by the Registrar pursuant to Regulation 4 of the European Communities (Companies) Regulations 2004 (S.I. No. 839 of 2004);

'Directive' means Directive 2005/56/EC on cross-border mergers of limited liability companies (OJ L 310, 25.11.2005, p 1);

'directors' explanatory report' means a report prepared and adopted in accordance with Regulation 6;

'EEA' means the European Economic Area constituted by the EEA Agreement;

'EEA Agreement' means the Agreement on the European Economic Area signed at Oporto on 2 May 1992, as adjusted by the Protocol signed at Brussels on 17 March 1993 and any subsequent amendments;

'EEA company' means a limited liability company, within the meaning of Article 2 of the Directive, that is governed by the law of an EEA State other than the State;

'EEA State' means a State that is a contracting party to the EEA Agreement;

'effective date' means—

(a) in relation to a cross-border merger in which the successor company is an Irish company, the date specified under Regulation 14(4), or

(b) in relation to a cross-border merger in which the successor company is an EEA company, the date fixed in accordance with the law of the EEA State concerned for the purposes of Article 12 of the Directive;

'expert's report' means a report prepared in accordance with Regulation 7;

'First Company Law Directive' means First Council Directive No. 68/151/EEC of 9 March 1968 (OJ L 065, 14.03.1968, p. 8) as amended by Directive 2003/58/EC of 15 July 2003 (OJ L 221, 04.09.2003, p 13);

'holding company' has the meaning assigned by section 155 of the Act of 1963;

'Irish company' means—

(a) a company within the meaning of the Act of 1963 with limited liability (other than a company limited by guarantee), or

(b) a body corporate with limited liability to which section 377(1) of the Act of 1963 applies;

'Irish merging company' means a merging company which is an Irish company;

'Irish successor company' means a successor company which is an Irish company;

'Irish transferor company' means a transferor company which is an Irish company;

'merger' includes a proposed merger;

'merger by absorption' means an operation in which, on being dissolved and without going into liquidation, a company transfers all of its assets and liabilities to a company that is the holder of all the shares or other securities representing the capital of the first-mentioned company;

'merger by acquisition' means an operation in which a company (other than a company formed for the purpose of the operation) acquires all the assets and liabilities of another company that is, or other companies that are, dissolved without going into liquidation in exchange for the issue to the members of that company, or the members of those companies, of securities or shares in the first-mentioned company, with or without any cash payment;

'merger by formation of a new company' means an operation in which 2 or more companies, on being dissolved without going into liquidation, transfer all their assets and liabilities to a company that they form, the new company, in exchange for the issue to their members of securities or shares representing the capital of that new company, with or without any cash payment;

'merging company' means—

(a) in relation to a merger by acquisition or a merger by absorption, a company that is, in relation to that merger, a transferor company or the successor company; and

(b) in relation to a merger by formation of a new company, a company that is, in relation to that merger, a transferor company;

'Merger Control Regulation' means Council Regulation (EC) No 139/2004 of 20 January 2004 on the control of concentrations between undertakings (OJ L 24, 29.01.2004, p 1.).

'Minister' means the Minister for Enterprise, Trade and Employment;

'pre-merger requirements' means the requirements of Regulations 5 to 13;

'Registrar' means the Registrar of Companies;

'Registry' in relation to an EEA State means the register maintained by that State in accordance with Article 3 of the First Company Law Directive;

'successor company', in relation to a cross-border merger, means the Irish company or EEA company to which assets and liabilities are to be, or have been, transferred from the transferor companies by way of that cross-border merger;

'transferor company', in relation to a cross-border merger, means a company, whether an Irish company or an EEA company, the assets and liabilities of which are to be, or have been, transferred by way of that cross-border merger;

'wholly-owned subsidiary', in relation to a company, means a subsidiary (within the meaning assigned to it by section 155 of the Act of 1963) the entire issued share capital of which is directly or indirectly beneficially owned by the first-mentioned company.

(2) A word or expression used but not defined in these Regulations that is also used in the Directive has the same meaning in these Regulations as it has in the Directive.

3. Penalties

A person convicted of an offence under these Regulations is liable, on summary conviction, to a [class A fine][a] or imprisonment for a term not exceeding 6 months, or to both.

Amendments

a As implicitly substituted for "fine not exceeding €5,000" by Fines Act 2010, s 4. A class A fine currently means a fine not exceeding €5,000.

PART 2
Company Law Provisions

Chapter 1
Preliminary

4. Definition

In this Part 'Court' means the High Court.

Chapter 2
Pre-merger Requirements

5. Common draft terms

(1) Where a cross-border merger is proposed to be entered into, common draft terms shall be drawn up in writing by all of the merging companies and adopted by the board of directors of each Irish merging company.

(2) The common draft terms of the merging companies shall state, at least—

(a) in relation to each of the transferor companies—

(i) its name,

(ii) its registered office,

(iii) its legal form and the law by which it is governed,

(iv) the register in which it is entered (including details of the relevant State), and

(v) its registration number in that register,

(b) in relation to the successor company—

(i) where the successor company is an existing company, the particulars specified in clauses (i) to (v) of subparagraph (a), or

(ii) where the successor company is a new company yet to be formed, what is proposed as the particulars specified in clauses (i) to (iv) of that subparagraph,

(c) except in the case of a merger by absorption—

(i) the proposed exchange ratio and amount of any cash payment,

(ii) the proposed terms relating to allotment of shares or other securities in the successor company, and

(iii) the date from which the holding of shares or other securities in the successor company will entitle the holders to participate in profits and any special conditions affecting that entitlement,

(d) the likely repercussions of the cross-border merger on employment,

(e) the date from which the transactions of the transferor companies are to be treated for accounting purposes as being those of the successor company,

(f) the rights to be conferred by the successor company on members of the transferor companies enjoying special rights or on holders of securities other than shares representing a transferor company's capital, and the measures (if any) proposed concerning them,

(g) any special advantages granted to—

(i) any director of a merging company, or

(ii) any person appointed under Regulation 7(2), or under a corresponding provision of a law of an EEA State, in relation to the merger,

(h) the successor company's articles of association or, if it does not have articles, the instrument constituting the company or defining its constitution,

(i) where appropriate, information on the procedures by which arrangements for the involvement of employees in the definition of their rights to participation in the company resulting from the cross-border merger are determined under Part 3,

(j) information on the evaluation of the assets and liabilities to be transferred to the successor company, and

(k) the dates of the accounts of every merging company which were used for the purpose of preparing the common draft terms.

(3) The common draft terms may include such additional terms as are not inconsistent with these Regulations.

(4) The common draft terms shall not provide for any shares in the successor company to be exchanged for shares in a transferor company held either—

(a) by the successor company itself or its nominee on its behalf; or

(b) by the transferor company itself or its nominee on its behalf.

6. Directors' explanatory report

(1) The board of directors of an Irish merging company shall—

(a) draw up a directors' explanatory report for the members of the company, to be made available pursuant to these Regulations, and

(b) make that report available, not less than 1 month before the date of the general meeting referred to in Regulation 10, to—

(i) the members, and

(ii) the representatives of employees or, where there are no representatives, to the employees, in accordance with these Regulations.

(2) The report shall—

(a) explain the implications of the cross-border merger for members, creditors and employees of the company,

(b) state the legal and economic grounds for the draft terms of merger.

7. Expert's report

(1) In relation to each Irish merging company, a report to the members of the company on the common draft terms shall be drawn up in accordance with this Regulation, unless—

(a) the cross-border merger is a merger by absorption,

(b) the cross-border merger is a merger in which the successor company (not being a company formed for the purpose of the merger) holds 90% or more (but not all) of the shares or other securities carrying the right to vote at general meetings of each transferor company, or

(c) every member of every merging company agrees that such report is not necessary.

(2) The report shall be prepared by a person or persons (in this Regulation referred to as the 'expert'), being—

(a) a qualified person appointed for the Irish merging company by its directors,

(b) a qualified person, or qualified persons, appointed by the Court, on the application of all of the merging companies, for all of them, or

(c) a person appointed for all the merging companies for the purposes of Article 8 of the Directive by a competent authority of another EEA State.

(3) A person is a qualified person for the purposes of subparagraphs (a) and (b) of paragraph (2), and of paragraphs (7) and (8), if that person—

(a) is eligible for appointment as an auditor in accordance with section 187 of the Companies Act 1990, and

(b) is not—

(i) a person who is or, within 12 months of the date of the common draft terms, has been an officer or employee of that company;

(ii) except with the leave of the Court, a parent, spouse, brother, sister or child of an officer of that company; or

(iii) a person who is a partner, or in the employment, of an officer or employee of that company.

(4) The report shall be made available not less than 1 month before the date of the general meeting referred to in Regulation 10 and shall be in writing and shall—

(a) state the method or methods used to arrive at the proposed exchange ratio,

(b) give the opinion of the expert whether the proposed exchange ratio is fair and reasonable,

(c) give the opinion of the expert as to the adequacy of the method or methods used in the case in question,

(d) indicate the values arrived at using each such method,

(e) give the opinion of the expert as to the relative importance attributed to such methods in arriving at the values decided on, and

(f) specify any special valuation difficulties which have arisen.

(5) The expert is entitled to require from each of the merging companies and their officers such information and explanation (whether oral or in writing), and to carry out such investigations, as the expert thinks necessary for the purposes of preparing the report.

(6) Where a company, being an Irish merging company—

(a) fails, on request, to supply to the expert any information or explanation in the power, possession or procurement of that person that the expert thinks necessary for the purposes of the report that company, being an Irish merging company and every officer in default shall be guilty of an offence, or

(b) knowingly or recklessly, makes a statement (whether orally or in writing), or provides a document, to the expert, being a statement or document which—

(i) conveys or purports to convey any information or explanation that the expert requires, or is entitled to require, under paragraph (5), and

(ii) is misleading, false or deceptive in a material particular,

that company, being an Irish merging company and every officer in default shall be guilty of an offence.

(7) If a person appointed under paragraph (a) or (b) of paragraph (2) ceases to be a qualified person, that person—

(a) shall immediately cease to hold office, and

(b) shall give notice in writing of the disqualification to the Company or to the Court (as the case requires) within 14 days of ceasing to be a qualified person,

but without prejudice to the validity of any acts done by the person under this Regulation before ceasing to be a qualified person.

(8) A person who purports to carry out the functions of an expert under this Regulation after ceasing to be a qualified person shall be guilty of an offence.

8. Registration and publication of documents

(1) [Subject to paragraphs (1A) and (1B), each][a] Irish merging company shall deliver to the Registrar for registration—

(a) a copy of the common draft terms, and

(b) a notice, in the form set out in Schedule 3, specifying in relation to each merging company—

(i) its name,

(ii) its registered office,

(iii) its legal form and the law by which it is governed,

(iv) in the case of an Irish Company, its registered number,

(v) in the case of an EEA Company, particulars of the national register in which that Company's file is kept and its registration number in that register, and

(vi) arrangements made for the exercise of the rights of creditors and of any minority members of the Merging Companies, and the address at which full information on these arrangements may be obtained free of charge.

[(1A) Paragraph (1) does not apply to an Irish merging company if it publishes, free of charge on its website for a continuous period of at least 2 months, commencing at least one month before the date of the general meeting convened in accordance with Regulation 10 and ending at least one month after that date—

(a) a copy of the common draft terms, as adopted by the board of directors of each Irish merging company as required by Regulation 5(1), and

(b) the information specified at paragraph (1)(*b*) in a form as close as practicable to the form set out in Schedule 3.

(1B) Where, in the period referred to in paragraph (1A), access to the company's website is disrupted for a continuous period of at least 24 hours or for separate periods totalling not less than 72 hours, the period referred to in paragraph (1A) shall be extended for a period corresponding to the period or periods of disruption.][b]

(2) Notice of the delivery of the common draft terms to the Registrar or, as the case may be, notice of publication on the company's website of the common draft terms, pursuant to this Regulation and the notice referred to in paragraph (1)(b) or (1A)(b) shall, at least 1 month before the general meeting referred to in Regulation 10, be caused to be published—][c]

(a) by the Registrar, in the CRO Gazette, and

(b) by the company, in two national daily newspapers.

(3) The notice published in accordance with paragraph (2) shall include—

(a) the date of delivery of the documentation,

(b) the matters specified in the notice referred to in paragraph (1)(b) [or (1A)(b)][d],

(c) a statement that copies of the common draft terms, the directors' explanatory report and the expert's report (where relevant) are available for inspection at the Irish merging company's registered office, and

(d) a statement that a copy of the common draft terms may be obtained from the Registrar [or from the company][e].

Amendments

a Words 'Subject to paragraphs (1A) and (1B), each' substituted for 'Each' by EC(MDC)(A)R 2011, reg 6(a)(i).

b Paragraphs (1A) and (1B) inserted by EC(MDC)(A)R 2011, reg 6(a)(ii).

c Words substituted for 'Notice of the delivery of the common draft terms to the Registrar pursuant to this Regulation and the notice referred to in paragraph (1)(*b*) shall, at least 1 month before the general meeting referred to in Regulation 10, be caused to be published—' by EC(MDC)(A)R 2011, reg 6(a)(iii).

d 'or (1A)(b)' inserted by EC(MDC)(A)R 2011, reg 6(a)(iv).

e Words 'or from the company' inserted by EC(MDC)(A)R 2011, reg 6(a)(v).

9. Inspection of documents

(1) [Subject to paragraph (1A), for the period][a] of 1 month immediately preceding the general meeting of an Irish merging company convened in accordance with Regulation 10, the members of that company and its employee representatives (or, if there are no representatives, the employees) shall be permitted, free of charge, to inspect at its registered office during business hours (subject to such reasonable restrictions as the company imposes but so that a period of no less than 2 hours in each day is allowed for inspection)—

(a) the common draft terms,

(b) the directors' explanatory report together with the opinion thereon, if any, received from the employee representatives, and

(c) the expert's report, if such a report is required by Regulation 7.

[(1A) Subject to paragraph (1B), paragraph (1) does not apply to an Irish merging company if, it publishes, free of charge on its website, the documents listed in paragraph (1) for a continuous period of at least 2 months commencing at least one month before the date of the general meeting convened in accordance with Regulation 10 and ending at least one month after that date.

(1B) Paragraph (1A) does not apply where the entitlement referred to in paragraph (2) does not apply as a result of the application of paragraph (2B).

(1C) Where, in the period referred to in paragraph (1A), access to the company's website is disrupted for a continuous period of at least 24 hours or separate periods totalling not less than 72 hours, the period referred to in paragraph (1A) shall be extended for a period corresponding to the period or periods of disruption.][b]

(2) [Subject to paragraph (2A), the notice][c] convening the general meeting to be held in accordance with Regulation 10 shall contain a statement of the entitlement of each member to obtain on request, free of charge, full or, if so desired, partial copies of the documents mentioned in paragraph (1).

[(2A) Subject to paragraph (2B), where a member of the company has consented to the use by the company of electronic means for conveying information, the copies referred to in paragraph (2) may be provided by electronic mail to that member and the notice convening the general meeting referred to in paragraph (2) shall contain a statement to that effect.

(2B) Where, for a continuous period of at least 2 months commencing at least one month before the date of the general meeting convened in accordance with Regulation 10 and ending at least one month after that date, full copies of the documents listed in paragraph (1) are available to download and print, free of charge, from the company's website by the members of the company and its employee representatives (or, if there are no employee representatives, the employees), the entitlement referred to in paragraph (2) shall not apply.

(2C) Where, in the period referred to in paragraph (2B), access to the company's website is disrupted for a continuous period of at least 24 hours or for separate periods totalling not less than 72 hours, the period referred to in paragraph (2B) shall be extended for a period corresponding to the period or periods of disruption.][d]

Amendments

a Words 'Subject to paragraph (1A), for the period' substituted for 'For the period' by EC(MDC)(A)R 2011, reg 6(b)(i).

b Paragraphs (1A)–(1C) inserted by EC(MDC)(A)R 2011, reg 6(b)(ii).

c Words 'Subject to paragraph (2A), the notice' substituted for 'The notice' by EC(MDC)(A)R 2011, reg 6(b)(iii).

d Paragraphs (2A)–(2C) inserted by EC(MDC)(A)R 2011, reg 6(b)(iv).

---

10. General meetings of Irish merging companies

(1) Subject to Regulation 11, the common draft terms shall be approved by a special resolution passed at a general meeting of each Irish merging company held not earlier than 1 month after the publication of the notice referred to in Regulation 8(2).

(2) The approval of the members may be made subject to—

- (a) ratification of the arrangements adopted for employee participation in the successor company in accordance with Part 3,
- (b) an order of a competent authority of another EEA State amending the exchange ratio or compensating minority members in accordance with a procedure to which Article 10.3 of the Directive applies,
- (c) receipt, where required, of—
  - (i) merger control approval from the Competition Authority under Part 3 of the Competition Act 2002 (No. 14 of 2002),
  - (ii) merger control approval from the European Commission under the Merger Control Regulation, or
  - (iii) merger control approval under the law of any other jurisdiction,
- (d) any other regulatory approval, or
- (e) such other conditions as they consider appropriate in the circumstances.

(3) [The directors of each Irish merging company shall inform—

- (a) the general meeting of that company, and
- (b) as soon as practicable, the directors of each of the other merging companies,

of any material change in the assets and liabilities of that Irish merging company between the date of the common draft terms and the date of that general meeting.][a]

(4) The directors of [each such other merging company][b] shall inform the general meeting of that company of all changes of which they have been informed pursuant to paragraph (3).

(5) The special resolution referred to in paragraph (1) may be passed in accordance with section 141(8) of the Act of 1963.

Amendments

a Paragraph (3) substituted by EC(MDC)(A)R 2011, reg 6(c)(i).

b Words 'each such other merging company' substituted for 'the successor company' by EC(MDC)(A)R 2011, reg 6(c)(ii).

11. Exemption from requirement to hold general meeting

(1) Shareholder approval of the common draft terms is not required—

(a) in the case of any transferor company in a merger by absorption, or

(b) in the case of the successor company in a merger by acquisition, if the conditions specified in paragraph (2) have been satisfied.

(2) [Subject to paragraphs (3A), (3B) and (3C), the conditions referred to in paragraph (1)(b) are the following:][a]

(a) the notice required to be published under Regulation 8(2) was published in accordance with Regulation 8(2) in respect of the successor company before the commencement of the period (in this paragraph referred to as the 'notice period') of 1 month before the date of the general meeting of the transferor company (or, where there is more than one transferor company, of the first of them to hold such a general meeting);

(b) the members of the successor company were entitled, during the notice period—

(i) [to inspect, at the registered office of the successor company, during ordinary hours of business, or to have access on the successor company's website under the conditions specified in paragraphs (1A), (1B) and (1C) of Regulation 9, to copies of—][b]

(I) the documents referred to in Regulation 9,

(II) the audited annual accounts for the preceding 3 financial years of each merging company (or, where a merging company has traded for less than 3 financial years before the date of the common draft terms, the audited annual accounts for the financial years for which the company has traded), and

(III) the accounting statement, if any, in relation to each merging company which is required to be prepared pursuant to paragraph (3),

and

(ii) to obtain copies of those documents or any part of them on request [or to download copies of them from the successor company's website pursuant to paragraphs (2A), (2B) and (2C) of Regulation 9][c];

(c) the right, conferred by paragraph (4), to requisition a general meeting has not been exercised during the notice period.

(3) [Subject to subparagraph (e), where the latest annual accounts][d] of any merging company relate to a financial year that ended more than 6 months before the date of the common draft terms, that company shall prepare an accounting statement in accordance with the following requirements:

(a) the accounting statement shall be drawn up, as at a date not earlier than the first day of the third month preceding the date of the common draft terms—

(i) in the format of the last annual balance sheet, and

(ii) in accordance with—

(I) the Companies Acts in the case of an Irish merging company, or

(II) the law of the relevant EEA State in the case of an EEA merging company,

(b) subject to subparagraph (c), valuations shown in the last annual balance sheet shall only be altered to reflect entries in the books of account,

(c) the following shall be taken into account in preparing the accounting statement—

(i) interim depreciation and provisions, and

(ii) material changes in actual value not shown in books of account, and

(d) the provisions of the Companies Acts relating to the auditor's report on the last annual accounts apply, with any necessary modifications, to the accounting statement.

[(e) this paragraph does not apply to a merging company—

(i) which makes public a half-yearly financial report covering the first 6 months of its financial year pursuant to Regulation 6 of the Transparency (Directive 2004/109/EC) Regulations 2007 (S.I. No. 277 of 2007) if it makes that report available for inspection at its registered office or on its website pursuant to subparagraph (*b*) of paragraph (2), or

(ii) if all of the holders of shares and other securities conferring the right to vote in general meetings of the company have so agreed.][e]

[(3A) Subject to paragraph (3B), where a member of the company has consented to the use by the company of electronic means for conveying information, the copies referred to in clause (i) of paragraph (2)(*b*) may be so provided.

(3B) Where, for a continuous period of at least 2 months commencing at least one month before the date of the general meeting convened in accordance with Regulation 10 and ending at least one month after that date, full copies of the documents listed in clause (i) of paragraph (2)(*b*) are available to download and print, free of charge, from the company's website by members of the company, the entitlement referred to in that clause shall not apply.

(3C) Where, in the period referred to in paragraph (3B), access to the company's website is disrupted for a continuous period of at least 24 hours or for separate periods totalling not less than 72 hours, the period referred to in paragraph (3B) shall be extended for a period corresponding to the period or periods of disruption.][f]

(4) One or more members of the successor company who together hold not less than 5% of the paid-up capital of the company which carries the right to vote at general meetings of the company (excluding any shares held as treasury shares) may require the convening of a general meeting of the company to consider the common draft terms, and section 132 of the Act of 1963 applies, with any necessary modifications, in relation to the requisition.

Amendments

a Words substituted for 'The conditions referred to in paragraph (1)(b) are the following:' by EC(MDC)(A)R 2011, reg 6(d)(i).

b Words substituted for 'to inspect, at the registered office of the successor company, during ordinary hours of business, copies of—' by EC(MDC)(A)R 2011, reg 6(d)(ii).

c Words inserted by EC(MDC)(A)R 2011, reg 6(d)(iii).

d Words substituted for 'Where the latest annual accounts' by EC(MDC)(A)R 2011, reg 6(d)(iv).

e Subparagraph (e) inserted by EC(MDC)(A)R 2011, reg 6(d)(v).

f Paragraphs (3A)–(3C) inserted by EC(MDC)(A)R 2011, reg 6(d)(vi).

---

12. Purchase of minority shares

(1) Where a majority of votes cast at the general meeting of a transferor company was in favour of the special resolution proposed pursuant to Regulation 10, a minority shareholder in that company may, not later than 15 days after the relevant date, request the successor company in writing to acquire his or her shares in the transferor company for cash.

(2) Where a request is made by a minority shareholder in accordance with paragraph (1), the successor company shall purchase the shares of the minority shareholder at a price determined in accordance with the share exchange ratio set out in the common draft terms.

(3) Nothing in this Regulation limits the power of the Court to make any order necessary for the protection of the interests of a dissenting minority in a merging company.

(4) In this Regulation—

'minority shareholder', in relation to a transferor company, means—

(a) in a case where the successor company (not being a company formed for the purpose of the merger) holds 90% or more (but not all) of the shares or other securities carrying the right to vote at general meetings of the transferor company, any other shareholder in the company, or

(b) in any other case, a shareholder in the company who voted against the special resolution;

'relevant date' means—

(a) in relation to a minority shareholder referred to in paragraph (a) of the definition of 'minority shareholder', the date of publication of the notice of delivery of the common draft terms under Regulation 8(2), or

(b) in relation to a minority shareholder referred to in paragraph (b) of the definition of 'minority shareholder', the date on which the general meeting of the transferor company was held.

13. Certificate of compliance with pre-merger requirements

On application by an Irish merging company, the Court shall, if it is satisfied that the company has completed properly the pre-merger requirements, issue a certificate to that effect, and such a certificate is conclusive evidence that the company has properly completed the pre-merger requirements.

Chapter 2
Approval in State of Cross-Border Mergers

14. Court scrutiny of cross-border merger

(1) Where the successor company in a cross-border merger is an Irish company, the Court may, on application made jointly by all the merging companies, make an order confirming scrutiny of the legality of the cross-border merger as regards that part of the procedure which concerns the completion of the cross-border merger and, where appropriate, the formation of an Irish successor company.

(2) The application shall be accompanied by a statement detailing the number and class of shares of each shareholder, if any, who has requested the purchase of his or her shares under Regulation 12 and of the measures which the successor company proposes to take to comply with each such request.

(3) Subject to Regulations 15 and 16, the Court may make an order referred to in paragraph (1) if—

(a) the successor company is an Irish company,

(b) a certificate has been issued under Regulation 13 in relation to each Irish merging company,

(c) in relation to each merging company which is an EEA company, a certificate to the same effect as a certificate issued under Regulation 13 has been issued by the competent authority of the EEA State under the law of which that company is governed,

(d) the application is made not more than 6 months after the issuing of a certificate referred to in subparagraph (b) and (c),

(e) the common draft terms to which each certificate, referred to in subparagraphs (b) and (c), relates are the same terms,

(f) any arrangements for employee participation in the successor company as are required by Part 3 have been determined,

(g) provision has been made for each creditor of any of the merging companies who establishes to the satisfaction of the Court that that creditor would otherwise be unfairly prejudiced by an order under Regulation 14, and

(h) where a request for the purchase of shares, referred to in paragraph (2), has been made, that measures have been proposed to comply with each such request.

(4) The Court shall specify, in an order, referred to in paragraph (1), the date on which the merger is to have effect.

(5) After the cross-border merger has taken effect, an order made under this Regulation is conclusive evidence that—

(a) the conditions set out in paragraph (3) have been satisfied, and

(b) the pre-merger requirements have been complied with.

15. Protection of creditors

A creditor of an Irish merging company who, at the date of publication of the notice under Regulation 8, is entitled to any debt or claim against the company, is entitled to be heard in relation to the confirmation by the Court of the cross-border merger under Regulation 14.

16. Compliance with other laws relating to mergers and take-overs

(1) The Court shall not make an order under Regulation 14 in respect of a cross-border merger that is a merger or acquisition which is referred to in section 16 of the Competition Act 2002 (No. 14 of 2002) and to which paragraph (a) or (b) of section 18(1) of that Act applies or which is referred to in section 18(3) of that Act and which has been notified to the Competition Authority in accordance with that subsection, unless—

(a) the Competition Authority has determined under section 21 or 22 of that Act that the merger may be put into effect,

(b) the Competition Authority has made a conditional determination (within the meaning of that Act) in relation to the merger,

(c) the period specified in subsection (2) of section 21 of that Act has elapsed without the Competition Authority having informed the undertakings which made the notification concerned of the determination (if any) it has made under paragraph (a) or (b) of that subsection in relation to the merger, or

(d) a period of 4 months has elapsed since the appropriate date (within the meaning of that Act) without the Competition Authority having made a determination under section 22 of that Act in relation to the merger.

(2) The Court shall not make an order under Regulation 14 in respect of a cross-border merger that is a concentration with a Community dimension (within the meaning of the Merger Control Regulation) unless—

(a) the European Commission has issued a decision under Article 8 of that Regulation declaring the concentration compatible with the common market,

(b) the concentration is deemed to have been declared compatible with the common market pursuant to Article 10(6) of that Regulation, or

(c) after a referral by the European Commission to the Competition Authority under Article 9 of that Regulation, of one of the events specified in subparagraphs (a) to (d) of paragraph (1), has occurred.

(3) The Court shall not make an order under Regulation 14 in respect of a cross-border merger while any requirement under an enactment for any other authorisation, approval, consent, waiver, licence, permission or agreement that affects the merger remains unsatisfied.

(4) Nothing in these Regulations shall be taken to imply that the satisfaction of a requirement mentioned in paragraph (3) in relation to a merging company is effective in relation to the successor company.

(5) Nothing in this Regulation shall affect any conditions to which a determination by the Competition Authority, a decision of the European Commission or an authorisation of a Regulator is subject.

(6) Nothing in these Regulations limits the jurisdiction of the Irish Takeover Panel under the Irish Takeover Panel Act 1997 (No. 5 of 1997) with respect to a cross-border merger that—

(a) involves a relevant company (within the meaning of that Act), and

(b) constitutes a takeover (within the meaning of that Act),

and, accordingly—

(i) the Irish Takeover Panel has power to make rules under section 8 of that Act in relation to cross-border mergers of that kind, to the same extent and subject to the same conditions, as it has power to make rules under that section in relation to any other kind of takeover, and

(ii) the Court, in exercising its powers under these Regulations, shall have due regard to the exercise of powers under that Act.

(7) In this Regulation 'Regulator' means any body or authority constituted by, or pursuant to, the provisions of any enactment and includes the Central Bank and Financial Services Authority of Ireland and any Minister of the Government or Minister of State.

Chapter 3

Consequences of Approval of Cross-Border Mergers

17. Copies of orders to be delivered to the Registrar

(1) The Registrar of the Court shall cause an office copy of an order under Regulation 14 to be sent to the Registrar for registration in the Companies Register.

(2) The Registrar shall cause to be published in the CRO Gazette notice of delivery to the Registrar of the order of the Court within 14 days of the delivery referred to in paragraph (1).

(3) Where an order is made by a competent authority of another EEA State in respect of a cross-border merger for the purposes of Article 11 of the Directive, every transferor company which is an Irish company shall—

(a) deliver a copy of that order to the Registrar for registration not more than 14 days after the date on which it was made, and

(b) specify in writing to the Registrar, the date on which the competent authority of that EEA State determined, pursuant to Article 12 of the Directive, the date on which the cross border merger takes effect.

(4) Where a company fails to comply with paragraph (3) the company and every officer in default shall be guilty of an offence.

18. Action to be taken by Registrar on receipt of orders

(1) Where the Registrar receives a copy of an order made under Regulation 14 the Registrar shall—

(a) in relation to each transferor company which is an EEA company, give notice of that order as soon as practicable to the authority responsible for maintaining the register in which the company file for that EEA company is kept pursuant to Article 3 of the First Company Law Directive in the EEA State concerned, and

(b) in relation to an Irish transferor company, register the copy order in respect of that company on, or as soon as practicable after, the effective date in the Companies Register.

(2) Where the Registrar receives from the authority responsible for maintaining the register of another EEA State notice, under Article 13 of the Directive, that the cross-border merger has taken effect the Registrar shall register—

(a) that notice, and

(b) the date of the receipt of that notice.

(3) The deletion of the registration of the company which is the subject of the notice referred to in paragraph (2) shall not be effected until the Registrar has received that notice.

19. Consequences of a cross-border merger

(1) Subject to paragraph (2), the consequences of a cross-border merger are that, on the effective date—

(a) all the assets and liabilities of the transferor companies are transferred to the successor company,

(b) in the case of a merger by acquisition or a merger by formation of a new company, where no application has been made by minority shareholders under Regulation 12, all remaining members of the transferor companies except the successor company (if it is a member of a transferor company) become members of the successor company,

(c) the transferor companies are dissolved,

(d) all legal proceedings pending by or against any transferor company shall be continued with the substitution, for the transferor companies, of the successor company as a party,

(e) the successor company is obliged to make to the members of the transferor companies any cash payment required by the terms of the common draft terms,

(f) the rights and obligations arising from the contracts of employment of the transferor companies are transferred to the successor company,

(g) every contract, agreement or instrument to which a transferor company is a party shall, notwithstanding anything to the contrary contained in that contract, agreement or instrument, be construed and have effect as if—

(i) the successor company had been a party thereto instead of the transferor company,

(ii) for any reference (however worded and whether express or implied) to the transferor company there were substituted a reference to the successor company, and

(iii) any reference (however worded and whether express or implied) to the directors, officers, representatives or employees of the transferor company, or any of them, were, respectively, a reference to the directors, officers, representatives or employees of the successor company or to such director, officer, representative or employee of the successor company as the successor company nominates for that purpose or, in default of nomination, to the director, officer, representative or employee of the successor company who corresponds as nearly as may be to the first-mentioned director, officer, representative or employee,

(h) every contract, agreement or instrument to which a transferor company is a party becomes a contract, agreement or instrument between the successor company and the counterparty with the same rights, and subject to the same obligations, liabilities and incidents (including rights of set-off), as would have been applicable thereto if that contract, agreement or instrument had continued in force between the transferor company and the counterparty, and any money due and owing (or payable) by or to the transferor company under or by virtue of any such contract, agreement or instrument shall become due and owing (or payable) by or to the successor company instead of the transferor company, and

(i) an offer or invitation to treat made to or by a transferor company before the effective date shall be construed and have effect, respectively, as an offer or invitation to treat made to or by the successor company.

(2) The successor company shall comply with filing requirements and any other special formalities required by law (including the law of another EEA State) for the transfer of the assets and liabilities of the transferor companies to be effective in relation to other persons.

20. Validity

A cross-border merger which has taken effect as provided for in Regulation 14(4) may not be declared null and void and the order made under Regulation 14, specifying the date on which the cross-border merger is to have effect, shall constitute conclusive evidence of the effectiveness of the cross-border merger.

21. Certain provisions of the Companies Acts not to apply

(1) [..][a].

(2) A cross-border merger does not create a subsidiary relationship to which subsection (5) of section 149 of the Act of 1963 applies, and accordingly the restrictions in that subsection have no application to the profits, losses or accounts of an Irish successor company.

(3) Section 41(1) of the Companies (Amendment) Act 1983 (which restricts the right of a Company to purchase its own shares) does not apply to the purchase of any shares in pursuance of an order of the Court under this Regulation.

Amendments

a Paragraph (1) deleted by EC(MDC)(A)R 2011, reg 6(e).

PART 3
Employee Participation

Chapter 1
Preliminary and General

22. Interpretation

In this Part—

'appointed' means, in the absence of an election, appointed by the employees and the basis on which that appointment is made may, if the employees so determine, be such as is agreed by them with the merging companies, or the successor company, as the case may be;

'consultation' means the establishment of dialogue and exchange of views between the representative body or the employees' representatives (or both) and the competent organ of the successor company at a time, in a manner and with a content which allows the employees' representatives, on the basis of the information provided, to express an opinion on measures envisaged by the competent organ which may be taken into account in the decision making process within the successor company;

'Commission' means the Labour Relations Commission;

'Court' means the Labour Court;

'employee' means a person who has entered into or works under a contract of employment and references, in relation to a merging company or a successor company, to an employee shall be read as references to an employee employed by any of them;

'employee participation' means the influence of the representative body or the employees' representatives (or both) in the affairs of a company by the way of—

(a) the right to elect or appoint some of the members of the company's supervisory or administrative organ, or

(b) the right to recommend or oppose, or both to recommend and oppose, the appointment of some or all of the members of the company's supervisory or administrative organ;

'employees' representative' means a representative elected or appointed for the purposes of these Regulations;

'establishment' means in relation to a company, a division (however described) of the undertaking physically separated from other parts of the company;

'excepted body' has the meaning assigned to it by section 6(3) of the Trade Union Act 1941 (No.22 of 1941, as amended);

'expert' means an individual, and may be the holder from time to time of a named office or position in a body corporate or other body or organisation;

'information' means the informing of the representative body or the employees' representatives (or both), by the competent organ of the successor company on questions which concern the company itself and any of its subsidiaries or establishments situated in another EEA State or which exceed the powers of the decision-making organs in a single EEA State at a time, in a manner and with a content which allows the employees' representatives to undertake an in-depth assessment of the possible impact and, where appropriate, prepare consultations with the competent organ of the company;

'involvement of employees' means any mechanism including information, consultation and employee participation, through which employees' representatives may exercise an influence on decisions to be taken within the company;

'representative body' means the body representative of the employees referred to in Schedule 1 set up for the purpose of informing and consulting the employees of a successor company situated in the EEA and, where applicable, of exercising employee participation rights in relation to the successor company;

'special negotiating body' means the body established in accordance with Regulation 25 to negotiate with the competent body of the merging companies regarding the establishment of arrangements for the involvement of employees within the successor company;

'Standard Rules' means the rules set out in Schedule 1;

'trade union' means a trade union which holds a negotiation licence under Part II of the Trade Union Act 1941 (No. 22 of 1941, as amended);

'wages' has the meaning assigned to it by the Payment of Wages Act 1991 (No. 25 of 1991, as amended).

23. Requirement for employee participation

(1) Arrangements for the participation of employees in every Irish successor company shall be established in accordance with these Regulations.

(2) Without prejudice to paragraph (3), the successor company shall be subject to the rules in force in the State concerning employee participation, if any.

(3) Notwithstanding paragraph (2), the rules in force concerning employee participation in the State, if any, shall not apply, where—

- (a) at least one of the merging companies has, in the 6 months before the publication of the common draft terms, an average number of employees that exceeds 500 and is operating under an employee participation system within the meaning of Regulation 2(1) of the European Communities (European Public Limited-Liability Company) (Employee Involvement) Regulations 2006 (S.I. No. 623 of 2006), or
- (b) there is no provision in any enactment—
  - (i) for at least the same level of employee participation as operated in the relevant merging companies, measured by reference to the proportion of employee representatives amongst the members of the administrative or supervisory organ or their committees or of the management group which covers the profit units of the company, subject to employee representation, or
  - (ii) for employees of establishments of the successor company that are situated in other EEA States of the same entitlement to exercise employee participation rights as is enjoyed by those employees employed in the State.

(4) In the cases referred to in paragraph (3), the participation of employees in the successor company and their involvement in the definition of such rights shall be regulated in accordance with Regulations 24 to 44 and in accordance with Article 12(2), (3) and (4) of Regulation (EC) No 2157/2001 (OJ L 294, 10.11.2001, p.1.) as given full

effect by the European Communities (European Public Limited Liability Company) Regulations 2007 (S.I. No. 21 of 2007).

24. Requirement to begin negotiations with employees

(1) As soon as possible after the publication of the draft terms of a cross-border merger, the management or administrative organ of each merging company shall take the necessary steps to start negotiations with the representatives of the employees of that company on arrangements for the involvement of those employees in the successor company.

(2) The steps to start negotiations shall include the provision of information about the identity of the merging companies, the number of employees in each (identified according to the EEA State in which they are located), and the number of such employees covered by an employee participation system.

(3) The information referred to in paragraph (2) shall be supplied to the employees' representative for that merging company or, where there is no such representative, to the employees themselves.

Chapter 2
Special Negotiating Body

25. Creation of special negotiating body

(1) For the purposes of the negotiations mentioned in Regulation 24, the management or administrative organs of the merging companies shall make arrangements, in accordance with this Regulation, for the establishment of a special negotiating body that is representative of the employees of the merging companies.

(2) The membership of the special negotiating body shall be determined in accordance with paragraphs (3) to (5) and the members shall be elected or appointed—

(a) in the case of members to be elected or appointed to represent employees in the State, in accordance with the procedure specified in Regulations 26 and 27, and

(b) in the case of members to be elected or appointed to represent employees in any other EEA State, in accordance with such procedures specified in laws or measures adopted by that EEA State.

(3) Subject to paragraphs (4) and (5), seats on the special negotiating body shall be distributed in proportion to the number of workers employed in each EEA State by the merging companies by allocating in respect of a relevant EEA State one seat for each portion of employees employed in that EEA State which equals 10%, or a fraction thereof, of the total number of employees employed by the merging companies in all relevant EEA States taken together.

(4) There shall be such further additional members from each EEA State as are necessary to ensure that the special negotiating body includes at least one member representing each transferor company which is registered and has employees in that EEA State, but so that—

(a) the number of additional members does not exceed 20% of the number of members provided for by paragraph (3), and

(b) the addition of members under this paragraph does not result in double representation of the employees concerned.

(5) In the application of paragraph (4), if the number of those transferor companies is greater than the number of additional seats available, those additional seats shall be allocated in relation to those companies in decreasing order of the number of employees they employ.

26. Representation of Irish employees on special negotiating body

(1) The representation on a special negotiating body of the employees in the State of the merging companies is allocated as specified in this Regulation.

(2) Where the number of seats on the special negotiating body allocated to the State is equal to the number of merging companies which have employees in the State, there shall be at least one seat for each of the merging companies, and each member elected or appointed to fill such a seat shall be considered as representing the employees of the merging company that elected or appointed them.

(3) Where the number of seats on the special negotiating body allocated to the State is greater than the number of merging companies which have employees in the State, there shall be one seat for each of the merging companies, and additional seats shall be allocated to merging companies in decreasing order of the number of employees they employ, and each member elected or appointed to fill a seat in accordance with this paragraph shall be taken to represent those employees of the companies that elected or appointed them.

(4) Where the number of seats on the special negotiating body allocated to the State is less than the number of merging companies which have employees in the State, the number of members equal to the number of available seats shall be elected or appointed according to the greatest number of votes won, and the representatives so elected or appointed shall between them represent the employees of the merging companies in the State that elected or appointed them.

(5) The references in paragraphs (2), (3) and (4) to merging companies include the concerned subsidiaries or establishments of a merging company and, where the presence of a merging company in the State is only by virtue of the presence of its concerned subsidiaries or establishments, those entities are to be taken, for the purposes of those paragraphs, to constitute that merging company.

(6) Employees of a merging company in which there are no employees' representatives shall not, by virtue of that fact alone, be prevented from exercising their right to elect or appoint members of the special negotiating body.

(7) An employee who is employed in the State by a merging company on the day the date or dates for the election of members of the special negotiating body conducted in accordance with Regulation 27 is fixed and who is, on the election day or days, an employee of such a company shall be entitled to vote in the election.

(8) Each of the following is eligible to stand as a candidate in the election of members of the special negotiating body conducted in accordance with Regulation 27, namely:

- (a) an employee who has been employed in the State by one or more of the merging companies for a continuous period of not less than one year on the nomination day,
- (b) a trade union official, whether or not he or she is an employee, and
- (c) an official of an excepted body, whether or not he or she is an employee,

provided that, in each case, he or she is nominated as such a candidate by—

(i) a trade union or an excepted body which is already recognised by the relevant merging companies located in the State for collective bargaining or information and consultation purposes, or

(ii) at least 2 employees.

27. Conduct of election

(1) Where elections of members of a special negotiating body fall to be conducted, being elections by employees in the State of merging companies, the management or administrative organs of the merging companies shall arrange for the conducting of those elections in accordance with this Regulation.

(2) The management or administrative organs of the merging companies shall, in consultation with employees or their representatives (or both), appoint one or more persons as returning officers (referred to collectively in this Regulation as the 'returning officer'), whose duties include the organisation and conduct of nominations and the election, and any person so appointed may authorise other persons to assist in the performance of those duties.

(3) Where the number of candidates on the nomination day exceeds the number of members to be elected, a poll or polls shall be taken by the returning officer and voting in the poll shall take place by a secret ballot on a day or days to be decided by the returning officer.

(4) The returning officer shall perform the duties of that office in a fair and reasonable manner and in the interests of an orderly and proper conduct of nomination and election procedures.

(5) As soon as is reasonably practicable after the result of the election is known, the returning officer shall make such arrangements as are necessary to ensure that the result is sent to the candidates, employees and employees' representatives and to the management or administrative organs of the merging companies.

(6) Once the result of the election is sent by the returning officer in accordance with paragraph (5), the candidates concerned shall be regarded as having been duly elected.

(7) All reasonable costs of the nomination and election procedure in the election shall be borne by the management or administrative organs of the merging companies.

(8) Where, for any reason, a vacancy arises amongst those of the members of the special negotiating body who have been elected in accordance with this Regulation, arrangements shall be made by the competent organs of the merging companies and the special negotiating body for that vacancy to be filled.

(9) Where a member of the special negotiating body whose nomination for election was on the basis of his or her satisfying the requirement contained in Regulation 26(8)(a) ceases to be employed by any of the merging companies, that person shall cease to be a member of the special negotiating body.

(10) Where a member of the special negotiating body whose nomination for election was on the basis of his or her satisfying the requirement contained in Regulation 26(8)(b) or (c) ceases to be an official of the trade union or excepted body concerned, that person shall cease to be a member of the special negotiation body.

28. Remit of special negotiating body

(1) The special negotiating body and the management or administrative organs of the merging companies shall negotiate and determine, by written agreement, arrangements for the involvement of employees within the successor company in accordance with the principles set out in Regulation 32.

(2) With a view to concluding that agreement, the management or administrative organs of the merging companies shall—

(a) convene a meeting with the special negotiating body and shall inform local managements accordingly, and

(b) inform the special negotiating body of the plan, the expected timetable, and the actual process of carrying out the cross-border merger, up to its registration.

(3) The management or administrative organs of the merging companies shall convene regular meetings as necessary with the special negotiating body in order to facilitate the negotiation of a written agreement referred to in paragraph (1).

(4) The agreement referred to in paragraph (1) shall be binding on the entire group of companies within the company resulting from the cross-border merger, irrespective of the EEA State in which it was signed and the location of those companies.

29. Voting procedure in the special negotiating body

(1) Subject to paragraph (2), the special negotiating body shall take its decisions (including the final decision whether to approve the entering into of an agreement under Regulation 28) by both—

(a) an absolute majority of its members, with each member having one vote, and

(b) an absolute majority of the employees represented by those members.

(2) If—

(a) at least 25% of the overall number of employees of the merging companies are covered by employee participation, and

(b) the result of negotiations would lead to a reduction of employee participation rights,

the majority required for a decision to approve the entering into of an agreement under Regulation 28 is the votes of two thirds of the members of the special negotiating body representing at least two thirds of the total number of employees, including the votes of members representing employees employed in at least two EEA States.

(3) For the purposes of paragraph (2), a reduction of employee participation rights occurs when the proportion of members of the organs of the successor company having employee participation rights is lower than the highest proportion existing within the merging companies.

(4) Any decision made in accordance with paragraph (2) shall be brought to the attention of the employees by the special negotiation body as soon as reasonably practicable and, in any event, no later than 14 days after the making of the decision.

30. Engagement of experts by special negotiating body

(1) For the purpose of the negotiations, the special negotiating body may engage experts of its choice to assist with its work.

(2) The experts may be representatives of appropriate EEA-level trade union organisations.

(3) The experts may be present at negotiation meetings in an advisory capacity at the request of the special negotiating body, where appropriate to promote coherence and consistency at EEA level.

(4) The special negotiating body may decide to inform the representatives of appropriate external organisations, including trade unions and excepted bodies, of the start of the negotiations.

31. Expenses

The reasonable expenses relating to the functioning of the special negotiating body and, in general, to negotiations under these Regulations shall be borne by the merging companies so as to enable the special negotiating body to carry out its functions in an appropriate manner.

Chapter 3
Negotiations and Agreement

32. Spirit of cooperation

(1) The parties shall negotiate or work together, as the case may be, in a spirit of cooperation with due regard for their reciprocal rights and obligations, and taking into account the interests both of the successor company and of the employees.

(2) In paragraph (1), 'parties' means—

(a) the competent organs of the merging companies and the special negotiating body, in relation to reaching an agreement in accordance with Regulation 28 on arrangements for the involvement of the employees within the successor company;

(b) the competent organ of the successor company and the representative body as set out in Schedule 1; and

(c) the supervisory or administrative organ of the successor company and the employees or their representatives (or both), with regard to a procedure for the information and consultation of employees.

33. Content of agreement

(1) Without prejudice to the autonomy of the parties, the agreement referred to in Regulation 28 shall specify—

(a) the scope of the agreement;

(b) the substance of any arrangements for employee participation that, in the course of the negotiations, the parties decide to establish, including, where applicable—

(i) the number of members of the administrative or supervisory body of the successor company whom the employees will be entitled to elect, appoint, recommend or oppose,

(ii) the procedures as to how the members referred to in clause (i) may be elected, appointed, recommended or opposed by employees, and their rights; and

(c) the date of entry into force of the agreement, its duration, the circumstances requiring renegotiation of the agreement and the procedure for its renegotiation.

(2) Unless it otherwise provides, the agreement is not subject to the Standard Rules.

34. Duration of negotiations

(1) The management or administrative organs of the merging companies and the special negotiating body shall commence negotiations as soon as the special negotiating body is established and those negotiations may continue for up to 6 months from the establishment of that body.

(2) The parties may decide, by joint agreement, to extend negotiations beyond the period referred to in paragraph (1) up to a total of one year from the establishment of the special negotiating body.

(3) The special negotiating body may decide, by a majority of two thirds of its members representing at least two thirds of the employees, including the votes of members representing employees in at least two different EEA States, not to open negotiations or to terminate negotiations already opened and to rely on the rules on employee participation in force in each of the EEA States (including the State) where the successor company has its employees.

(4) A decision under paragraph (3) shall terminate the procedure referred to in Regulation 28 for the conclusion of an agreement, and the provisions of Schedule 1 shall not apply.

35. Standard Rules

(1) In order to ensure the establishment of arrangements for the involvement of employees in the successor company, the Standard Rules apply, from the date of its registration, to the successor company if its registered office is located in the State and—

(a) the parties so agree, or

(b) no agreement has been concluded within the time limit specified in Regulation 34 and—

(i) the management or administrative organs of the merging companies decide to accept the application of the Standard Rules in relation to the successor company and, on that basis, to continue with the merger, and

(ii) the special negotiating body has not made a decision under Regulation 29(2).

(2) Part 3 of Schedule 1 applies to the successor company only if, before registration of the successor company—

(a) one or more forms of employee participation applied to one or more of the merging companies employing at least 33$^{1}/_{3}$ of the total number of employees in all merging companies in each of the EEA States concerned, or

(b) one or more forms of employee participation applied in one or more of the merging companies employing less than 33$^{1}/_{3}$ of the total number of employees in all the merging companies in the EEA States and the special negotiating body decides that the rules set out in that Part are to apply.

(3) Where there was more than one form of employee participation within the various merging companies, the special negotiating body shall choose which of those forms shall be established in the company resulting from the cross-border merger.

(4) The special negotiating body shall inform the management or administrative organs of the merging companies of any decisions taken pursuant to paragraph (3).

(5) The relevant organs of the merging companies may choose without any prior negotiation to be directly subject to the Standard Rules and to abide by them from the date of registration of the successor company.

(6) Where, following prior negotiations, the Standard Rules apply, the parties may, notwithstanding those Rules, agree to limit the proportion of employee representatives in the administrative organ of the successor company, but if in one of the merging companies employee representatives constituted at least one third of the administrative or supervisory board, the limitation may not result in a lower proportion of employee representatives in the administrative organ of the successor company than one third.

(7) Where, in accordance with paragraph (6), the parties agree to limit the proportion of employee representatives in the administrative organ, the majority required for such a decision shall be the votes of—

- (a) two-thirds of the employees including the votes of employees employed in at least two Member States, or
- (b) two-thirds of the members of the representative body representing at least two thirds of the total number of employees, including the votes of members representing employees employed in at least two Member States.

Chapter 4
Supplementary

36. Definition

In this Chapter 'relevant company' means—

- (a) a merging company, and
- (b) in relation to a merger by formation of a new company, the successor company.

37. Protection of employee participation rights

When the successor company is operating under an employee participation system, that company shall ensure that employees' participation rights are protected in the event of subsequent domestic mergers for a period of three years after the cross-border merger has taken effect, by applying, mutatis mutandis, the rules laid down in these Regulations.

38. Confidential information

(1) An individual who is or at any time was—

- (a) an employee of a relevant company,
- (b) a member of—
  - (i) the special negotiating body, or
  - (ii) the representative body,
- (c) an employees' representative for the purposes of these Regulations, or
- (d) an expert providing assistance,

shall not reveal any information which, in the legitimate interest of any relevant company, has been expressly provided in confidence to him or her or to the body by a relevant company.

(2) The duty of confidentiality imposed by paragraph (1) continues to apply after the cessation of the employment of the individual concerned or the expiry of his or her term of office.

(3) A relevant company may refuse to communicate information to a special negotiating body where the nature of that information is such that, by reference to objective criteria, it would—

- (a) seriously harm the functioning of any relevant company, or
- (b) be prejudicial to any relevant company.

(4) The Court or any member of the Court or the registrar or any officer or servant of the Court, including any person or persons appointed by the Court as an expert or mediator, shall not disclose any information obtained in confidence in the course of any proceedings before the Court under these Regulations.

39. Protection of employees' representatives

(1) A relevant company shall not penalise—

- (a) a member of the special negotiating body,
- (b) a member of the representative body,
- (c) an employees' representative performing functions under these Regulations, or
- (d) an employees' representative in the supervisory or administrative organ of a successor company who is an employee of that company or of a merging company,

for the performance of his or her functions in accordance with these Regulations.

(2) For the purposes of this Regulation, a person referred to in paragraph (1) is penalised if that person—

- (a) is dismissed or suffers any unfavourable change to his or her conditions of employment or any unfair treatment (including selection for redundancy), or
- (b) is the subject of any other action prejudicial to his or her employment.

(3) Schedule 2 has effect in relation to an alleged contravention of paragraph (1).

(4) Subject to paragraph (6), a person referred to in paragraph (1) shall be afforded any reasonable facilities, including time off, that will enable him or her to perform promptly and efficiently his or her functions as a member of the special negotiating body or representative body or as an employees' representative, as the case may be.

(5) A person referred to in paragraph (1) shall be paid his or her wages for any period of absence afforded to him or her in accordance with paragraph (4).

(6) The granting of facilities under paragraph (4) shall have regard to the needs, size and capabilities of the relevant company and shall not impair the efficient operation of that company.

(7) This Regulation applies in particular to attendance by representatives at meetings of the special negotiating body or representative body or any other meetings within the framework of an agreement referred to in Regulation 33 or Schedule 1 or any meeting of the administrative or supervisory organ.

(8) Subject to paragraph (9), this Regulation is in addition to, and not in substitution for, any rights enjoyed by an employees' representative, whether under any enactment or otherwise.

(9) If a penalisation of a person referred to in paragraph (1), in contravention of that paragraph, constitutes a dismissal of that person within the meaning of the Unfair Dismissals Acts 1977 to 2007, relief may not be granted to that person in respect of that penalisation both under Schedule 2 and under those Acts.

40. Dispute Resolution

(1) Subject to paragraph (2), a dispute between any relevant company and employees or their representatives (or both) concerning—

(a) matters provided for in Regulations 25 to 31 relating to the special negotiating body,

(b) the negotiation, interpretation or operation of an agreement in relation to Regulation 24, 33 or 34,

(c) the interpretation or operation of the Standard Rules as provided for in Regulation 35 and Schedule 1, and

(d) a matter provided for in paragraph (4), (5), (6) or (7) of Regulation 39, or

(e) a complaint by an employee or his or her representative (or both) that, in relation to Regulation 37, the company resulting from any subsequent domestic merger is being or will be misused for the purpose of depriving employees of their rights to employee involvement or of withholding those rights,

may be referred by one or more relevant company, employees employed in the State or their representatives (or both) to the Court for investigation.

(2) Such a dispute may be referred to the Court only after—

(a) recourse to the internal dispute resolution procedure (if any) in place in the relevant company concerned has failed to resolve the dispute, and

(b) the dispute has been referred to the Commission, and, having made available such of its services as are appropriate for the purpose of resolving the dispute, the Commission provides a certificate to the Court stating that the Commission is satisfied that no further efforts on its part will advance the resolution of the dispute.

(3) Having investigated a dispute under paragraph (1), the Court may make a recommendation in writing, giving its opinion in the matter.

(4) Where, in the opinion of the Court, a dispute that is the subject of a recommendation under paragraph (3) has not been resolved, the Court may, at the request of—

(a) one or more relevant company, or

(b) one or more employees or their representatives (or both),

and, following a review of all relevant matters make a determination in writing.

(5) Disputes between any relevant company and employees or their representatives (or both) concerning matters of confidential information provided for in Regulation 38 may be referred by—

(a) one or more relevant company, or

(b) any employee of the company or his or her representatives (or both), to the Court for determination.

(6) In relation to a dispute referred to it under this Regulation, the Court shall—

- (a) give the parties an opportunity to be heard by it and to present any evidence relevant to the dispute,
- (b) make a recommendation or determination, as the case requires, in writing in relation to the dispute, and
- (c) communicate the recommendation or determination to the parties.

(7) The following matters, or procedures to be followed in relation to them, shall be determined by the Court, namely:

- (a) the procedure in relation to all matters concerning the initiation and hearing by the Court of a dispute under this Regulation;
- (b) the times and places of hearings of such disputes;
- (c) the publication and notification of recommendations and determinations of the Court;
- (d) any matters consequential on, or incidental to, the matters referred to in subparagraphs (a) to (c).

(8) In deciding what constitutes confidential information, the Court may be assisted by a panel of experts.

(9) A party to a dispute under this Regulation may appeal from a determination of the Court to the High Court on a point of law and the decision of the High Court shall be final and conclusive.

(10) The Court may refer a question of law arising in proceedings before it under this Regulation to the High Court for determination and the decision of the High Court shall be final and conclusive.

41. Power of Court to administer oaths and compel witnesses

(1) The Court shall, on the hearing of a dispute referred to it for recommendation or determination under Regulation 40 or on the hearing of an appeal under Schedule 2, have power to take evidence on oath and for that purpose may cause to be administered oaths to persons attending as witnesses at that hearing.

(2) Any person who, upon examination on oath authorised by this Regulation, wilfully makes any statement which is material for that purpose and which he or she knows to be false or does not believe to be true commits an offence.

(3) The Court may, by giving notice in that behalf in writing to any person, require that person to attend at such time and place as is specified in the notice to give evidence in relation to a dispute referred to the Court for recommendation or determination under Regulation 40 or an appeal under Schedule 2, or to produce any documents in the person's possession, custody or control which relate to any such matter.

(4) A notice under paragraph (3) may be given either by delivering it to the person to whom it relates or by sending it by post in a prepaid registered letter addressed to that person at the address at which he or she ordinarily resides or, in the case of a relevant company, at the address at which the relevant company ordinarily carries on any profession, business or occupation.

(5) If a person to whom a notice under paragraph (3) has been given refuses or wilfully neglects to attend in accordance with the notice or, having so attended, refuses to give evidence or refuses or wilfully fails to produce any document to which the notice relates, that person commits an offence.

(6) A witness in a hearing of a dispute or appeal before the Court has the same privileges and immunities as a witness before the High Court.

42. Enforcement

(1) If—

(a) a party to a Court determination fails to carry out in accordance with its terms a determination of the Court in relation to a dispute under Regulation 40, or

(b) a party to a complaint under Schedule 2 fails to carry out in accordance with its terms a decision of a rights commissioner or a determination of the Court under that Schedule in relation to the complaint,

within the period specified in the determination or decision or if no such period is so specified within 6 weeks from the date on which the determination or decision is communicated to the parties, the Circuit Court shall, on application to it in that behalf by one or more of the parties to the dispute or complaint, without hearing any evidence (other than in relation to the matters aforesaid) make an order directing the party concerned to carry out the determination or decision in accordance with its terms.

(2) The reference in paragraph (1) to a determination of the Court or a decision of a rights commissioner is a reference to such a determination or decision in relation to which, at the end of the time for bringing an appeal against it, no such appeal has been brought or, if such an appeal has been brought it has been abandoned, and the references to the date on which the determination or decision is communicated to the parties shall, in a case where such an appeal is abandoned, be read as references to the date of that abandonment.

(3) In an order under this Regulation providing for the payment of compensation of the kind referred to in paragraph 2(3)(c) of Schedule 2, the Circuit Court may, if in all the circumstances it considers it appropriate to do so, direct a relevant company to pay to the employee concerned interest on the compensation at the rate referred to in section 22 of the Courts Act 1981 (No.11 of 1981), in respect of the whole or any part of the period beginning 6 weeks after the date on which the determination of the Court or the decision of the rights commissioner is communicated to the parties and ending on the date of the order.

(4) An application under this Regulation to the Circuit Court shall be made to the judge of the Circuit Court for the circuit in which the relevant company concerned has its principal place of business.

43. Workforce thresholds in other legislation

The extension of employee participation rights to employees of establishments of the successor company employed in other EEA States, referred to in Regulation 23(3)(b)(ii), shall not entail any obligation to take those employees into account when calculating the size of workforce thresholds giving rise to participation rights under national law.

44. Legal form of company

When at least one of the merging companies is operating under an employee participation system and the successor company is to be governed by such a system in accordance with the rules referred to in Regulation 23, that company shall take a legal form allowing for the exercise of employee participation rights.

Schedule 1
Standard Rules

Regulation 22

PART 1
Composition of Body Representative of Employees

1. In cases falling within Regulation 35, a representative body shall be set up in accordance with the provisions of this Part.

2. The representative body shall be composed of employees of the successor company and its subsidiaries and establishments elected or appointed from their number by the employees' representatives or, in the absence thereof, by the entire body of employees.

3. The members of the representative body shall be elected or appointed in proportion to the number of employees employed in each EEA State by the merging companies, by allocating in respect of an EEA State one seat per portion of employees employed in that EEA State which equals 10% or a fraction thereof, of the number of employees employed by the merging companies in all the EEA States taken together.

4. The election or appointment of members of the representative body shall be carried out in accordance with a procedure agreed by the special negotiating body.

5. The number of members of, and allocation of seats on, the representative body shall be adapted to take account of changes occurring within the successor company, and the representative body shall take any steps it deems necessary to ensure this.

6. Where its size so warrants, the representative body shall elect a select committee from among its members, comprising at most three members.

7. The representative body shall adopt its own rules of procedure.

8. The competent organ of the successor company shall be informed of the composition of the representative body as soon as is reasonably practicable.

9. (1) Four years after the representative body is established, it shall examine whether to open negotiations for the conclusion of an agreement referred to in Regulation 28 or to continue to apply the Standard Rules as provided for in this Schedule.

(2) If such a decision has been taken to negotiate an agreement, Regulations 29 to 31 and 33 and 34 apply with the necessary modifications and, for that purpose, references in those Regulations to 'special negotiating body' shall be construed as references to 'representative body'.

(3) Where, on the expiry of the time limit specified in Regulation 34 (as applied by this paragraph), no such agreement has been concluded, the arrangements initially adopted in accordance with the provisions of this Schedule continue to apply.

PART 2

STANDARD RULES FOR INFORMATION AND CONSULTATION

10. The competence and powers of the representative body set up in the successor company are governed by the provisions of this Part.

11. (1) The competence of the representative body shall be limited to questions which concern the successor company situated in another EEA State or which exceed the powers of the decision-making organs in a single EEA State.

(2) Without prejudice to meetings held pursuant to paragraph 13(1), the representative body has the right to be informed and consulted and, for that purpose, to meet with the competent organ of the successor company at least once a year, on the basis of regular reports drawn up by the competent organ, on the progress of the business of the successor company and its prospects, and the local management shall be informed accordingly.

(3) The competent organ of the successor company shall provide the representative body with the agenda for meetings of the administrative, or, where appropriate, the management and supervisory organ, and with copies of all documents submitted to the general meeting of its shareholders.

(4) The meeting shall relate in particular to the structure, economic and financial situation, the probable development of the business and of production and sales, the situation and probable trend of employment, investments, and substantial changes concerning organisation, introduction of new working methods or production processes, transfers of production, mergers, cut-backs or closures of undertakings, establishments or important parts thereof, and collective redundancies.

12. (1) Where there are exceptional circumstances affecting the employees' interests to a considerable extent, particularly in the event of relocations, transfers, the closure of establishments or undertakings or collective redundancies, the representative body has the right to be informed.

(2) The representative body, or where it so decides, in particular for reasons of urgency, the select committee, has the right to meet at its request the competent organ of the successor company, or any more appropriate level of management within the successor company having its own powers of decision, so as to be informed and consulted on measures significantly affecting employees' interests.

(3) Where the competent organ decides not to act in accordance with the opinion expressed by the representative body, the representative body has the right to a further meeting with the competent organ of the successor company with a view to seeking agreement.

(4) In the case of a meeting organised with a select committee, those members of the representative body who represent employees who are directly concerned by the measures in question also have the right to participate.

(5) The meetings referred to in this paragraph do not affect the prerogatives of the competent organ.

13.(1) Before any meeting with the competent organ of the successor company, the representative body or the select committee, where necessary enlarged in accordance with paragraph 12(4), is entitled to meet without the representatives of the competent organ being present.

(2) Without prejudice to Regulation 38, the members of the representative body shall inform the employees of the successor company or their representatives (or both), of the content and outcome of the information and consultation procedures.

14.(1) The representative body or the select committee may be assisted by experts of its choice.

(2) The reasonable costs of the representative body shall be borne by the successor company, which shall provide the body's members with the financial and material resources needed to enable them to perform their duties in an appropriate manner.

(3) In so far as is necessary for the fulfilment of their duties, the members of the representative body shall be entitled to time off for training without loss of wages.

PART 3

STANDARD RULES FOR EMPLOYEE PARTICIPATION

15.(1) Subject to paragraphs (6) and (7) of Regulation 35, the employees of the successor company and their representative body (or both) have the right to elect, appoint, recommend or oppose the appointment of a number of members of the administrative or supervisory body of that company equal to the highest proportion in force in the merging companies concerned before registration of the successor company.

(2) If none of the participating companies was governed by employee participation rules before registration of the successor company, the company is not required to establish provisions for employee participation.

(3) The representative body shall decide on the allocation of seats within the administrative or supervisory body among the members representing the employees from the various EEA States or on the way in which the employees of the successor company may recommend or oppose the appointment of the members of these bodies according to the proportion of the company's employees in each EEA State.

(4) If, as a consequence of a decision under subparagraph (3), the employees of one or more EEA States are not covered by the proportional criterion, the representative body shall, where possible, appoint a member from one of those EEA States, in particular the EEA State where the successor company has its registered office where that is appropriate.

(5) For the purposes of subparagraph (4) and the determination of the allocation of the seats given within the administrative or supervisory body to employees in the State, those members of the representative body representing employees in the State shall select, from amongst their number, a number of representatives equal to the number of seats available.

16. Every member of the administrative body or, where appropriate, the supervisory body of the successor company who has been elected, appointed or recommended by the representative body or, depending on the circumstances, by the employees shall be a full member with the same rights and obligations as the members representing the shareholders, including the right to vote.

Schedule 2
Redress for Contravention of Regulation 39

Regulation 39

COMPLAINTS TO RIGHTS COMMISSIONER

1. In this Schedule 'relevant companies' has the same meaning as in Regulation 36.

2. (1) A person referred to in Regulation 39(1) may present a complaint to a rights commissioner that a relevant company has contravened Regulation 39(1) in relation to him or her.

(2) Where a complaint under subparagraph (1) is made, the rights commissioner shall—

(a) give the parties an opportunity to be heard by the commissioner and to present to the commissioner any evidence relevant to the complaint,

(b) give a decision in writing in relation to it, and

(c) communicate the decision to the parties.

(3) A decision of a rights commissioner under subparagraph (2) shall do one or more of the following:

(a) declare that the complaint was or, as the case may be, was not well founded;

(b) require the relevant company to take a specified course of action;

(c) require the relevant company to pay to the person referred to in subparagraph (1) compensation of such amount (if any) as is just and equitable having regard to all the circumstances but not exceeding 2 years' remuneration in respect of the person's employment.

(4) A rights commissioner shall not entertain a complaint under this Schedule if it is presented to him or her after the expiration of the period of 6 months beginning on the date of the contravention to which the complaint relates.

(5) Notwithstanding subparagraph (4), a rights commissioner may entertain a complaint under this Schedule presented to him or her not later than 6 months after the expiration of the period referred to in subparagraph (4) if he or she is satisfied that the failure to present the complaint within that period was due to reasonable cause.

(6) A complaint shall be presented by giving notice of it in writing to a rights commissioner.

(7) A copy of a notice under subparagraph (6) shall be given to the other party concerned by the rights commissioner concerned.

(8) Proceedings under this paragraph before a rights commissioner shall be conducted otherwise than in public.

APPEALS FROM DECISIONS OF RIGHTS COMMISSIONER

3.(1) A party concerned may appeal to the Court from a decision of a rights commissioner under paragraph 2, and, if the party does so, the Court shall give the parties an opportunity to be heard by it and to present to it any evidence relevant to the appeal, shall make a determination in writing in relation to the appeal affirming, varying or setting aside the decision and shall communicate the determination to the parties.

(2) An appeal under this paragraph shall be initiated by the party concerned giving, within 6 weeks (or such greater period as the Court determines in the particular

circumstances) from the date on which the decision to which it relates was communicated to the party, a notice in writing to the Court containing such particulars as are determined by the Court under subparagraph (4) and stating the intention of the party concerned to appeal against the decision.

(3) A copy of a notice under subparagraph (2) shall be given by the Court to any other party concerned as soon as practicable after the receipt of the notice by the Court.

(4) The following matters, or the procedures to be followed in relation to them, shall be determined by the Court, namely:

(a) the procedure in relation to all matters concerning the initiation and the hearing by the Court of appeals under this paragraph,

(b) the times and places of hearings of such appeals,

(c) the representation of the parties to such appeals,

(d) the publication and notification of determinations of the Court,

(e) the particulars to be contained in a notice under subparagraph (2), and

(f) any matters consequential on, or incidental to, the foregoing matters.

(5) The Court may refer a question of law arising in proceedings before it under this paragraph to the High Court for determination, and the determination of the High Court shall be final and conclusive.

(6) A party to proceedings before the Court under this paragraph may appeal to the High Court from a determination of the Court on a point of law and the determination of the High Court shall be final and conclusive.

SUPPLEMENTAL PROVISIONS

4.(1) A rights commissioner shall provide the Court with a copy of each decision given by the commissioner under paragraph 2(2).

(2) A rights commissioner shall maintain a register of all decisions given by him or her under paragraph 2(2) and shall make the register available for inspection by members of the public during normal office hours.

(3) The Court shall publish, in a manner it considers appropriate, particulars of any determination made by it under subparagraph (4)(a), (b), (c), (e) and (f) of paragraph 3 (not being a determination as respects a particular appeal under that paragraph).

Schedule 3

Regulation 8

Form for Notice under Regulation 8

Draft terms of formation of Cross-Border Merger involving an Irish registered company
Regulation 8 (1) of the European Communities (Cross-Border Mergers) Regulations 2008
S249A Companies Act 1990 (inserted by s107 Company Law Enforcement Act 2001)
Companies Act 1990 (Form and Content of Documents Delivered to Registrar) Regulations 2002

Companies Acts 1963 to

Company number

CBM1

Please complete using black typescript or BOLD CAPITALS, referring to explanatory notes

Company name *in full*

☐ **Pursuant to Regulation 8(1) of the European Communities (Cross-Border Mergers) Regulations 2008, a copy of the Common Draft Terms is attached to this form.**

Type of merger *note one*

☐ By acquisition ☐ By formation of a new company ☐ By absorption

Company details *note two*

Copies of the Common Draft Terms , the Directors' Explanatory Report and the Expert's Report where relevant, are available for inspection at the registered office of the company, namely:

Information relating to the Company is kept by the Registrar under registered number:

Legal form and law which governs the company:

Certification *note three*

I hereby certify that the particulars contained in this form are correct and have been given in accordance with the Notes on Completion of Form CBM1.

Signature

Name *in block letters or typescript*

Date

Presenter details *note four*

Name

Address

DX number		DX exchange
Telephone number		Fax number
Email		Reference number

Particulars of the company's arrangements for exercise of the rights of creditors and members

Arrangements made for the exercise of the rights of the creditors and any minority members of the merging companies:

Full information on the arrangements made for the exercise of the rights of the creditors and any minority members of the merging companies, may be obtained free of charge, from the following address:

Particulars of other merging companies

Name of Company:

The registered office of the company:

Legal form of the company and the law by which it is governed:

Arrangements made for the exercise of the rights of the creditors and any minority members of the merging companies: *note five*

Full information on the arrangements made for the exercise of the rights of the creditors and any minority members of the merging companies, may be obtained free of charge, from the following address:

☐ If the Company is an Irish Company, Information relating to the Company is kept by the Registrar under registered number:

note one

☐ If the Company is an EEA Company, particulars of the national register in which the Company's file is kept and its registration number in that register, are as follows:

Particulars of other merging companies

Name of Company:

The registered office of the company:

Legal form of the company and the law by which it is governed:

Arrangements made for the exercise of the rights of the creditors and any minority members of the merging companies: *note five*

Full information on the arrangements made for the exercise of the rights of the creditors and any minority members of the merging companies, may be obtained free of charge, from the following address:

☐ If the Company is an Irish Company, Information relating to the Company is kept by the Registrar under registered number:

note one

☐ If the Company is an EEA Company, particulars of the national register in which the Company's file is kept and its registration number in that register, are as follows:

NOTES ON COMPLETION OF FORM CBM1
These notes should be read in conjunction with the relevant legislation.

General This form must be completed correctly, in full and in accordance with the following notes. Every section of the form must be completed.

Where "not applicable", "nil" or "none" is appropriate, please state.
Where the space provided on Form CBM1 is considered inadequate, the information should be presented on a continuation sheet in the same format as the relevant section in the form. The use of a continuation sheet must be so indicated in the relevant section.

For the purposes of this form, "EEA Company" means a company governed by the law of an EEA State other than Ireland. An EEA State is a State that is a contracting party to the Agreement on the European Economic Area, signed at Oporto on 2nd May 1992, as adjusted by the Protocol signed at Brussels on the 17th March 1993, and any subsequent amendments.

"Irish registered company" refers to a company incorporated in Ireland under the Companies Acts and does not include a company registered in Northern Ireland.

note one Please tick the relevant box.

note two Any change of registered office must be notified to the CRO.

note three This form **must** be certified by a director of the company on behalf of the Board.

note four This section must be completed by the person who is presenting Form CBM1 to the CRO. This may be either the applicant or a person on his/her behalf.

note five Where space is considered inadequate, a continuation sheet should be completed, in the same format as the relevant section.

EXPLANATORY NOTE

(*This note is not part of the Instrument and does not purport to be a legal interpretation.*)

These Regulations give effect to Directive 2005/56/EC of the European Parliament and of the Council of 26 October 2005 on cross-border mergers of limited liability companies.

European Communities (Mergers and Divisions of Companies) (Amendment) Regulations 2008

SI 572/2008

I, MARY COUGHLAN, Minister for Enterprise, Trade and Employment, in exercise of the powers conferred on me by section 3 of the European Communities Act 1972 (No. 27 of 1972) and for the purpose of giving effect to Directive No. 2007/63/EC of the European Parliament and of the Council of 13 November 2007 (

, hereby make the following regulations:

1. (1) These Regulations may be cited as the European Communities (Mergers and Divisions of Companies) (Amendment) Regulations 2008.

(2) These Regulations come into operation on 31 December 2008.

2. The European Communities (Mergers and Divisions of Companies) Regulations 1987 (S.I. No. 137 of 1987) are amended—

(a) in Regulation 8—

(i) by substituting "Subject to paragraph (11), each" for "Each" in paragraph (1), and

(ii) [...][a],

(b) in Regulation 12(1)(d) by inserting "where applicable," before "the independent person's report",

(c) in Regulation 28—

(i) by substituting "Subject to paragraph (12), each" for "Each" in paragraph (1), and

(ii) [...][b], and

(d) in Regulation 31(1)(d) by inserting "where applicable," before "the

---

Amendments

a EC(MDC)(A)R 2008, reg 2(a)(ii) inserts EC(MDC)R 1987, reg 8(11).

b EC(MDC)(A)R 2008, reg 2(c)(ii) inserts EC(MDC)R 1987, reg 28(12).

EXPLANATORY NOTE

(*This note is not part of the Instrument and does not purport to be a legal interpretation.*)

These Regulations give effect to Directive 2007/63/EC of the European Parliament and of the Council of 13 November 2007 amending Directives 78/855/EEC and 82/891/EEC concerning the requirement of an independent expert's report on the occasion of merger or division of public limited liability companies.

The change being effected to these Directives through the present Regulations is to give holders of shares and other securities with voting rights at general meetings of each of the merging companies (in the case of a merger) and each of the companies involved in a division (in the case of a division), the option, if they all so agree, to dispense with the requirement to have an examination of the draft terms of merger/written expert's report on the draft terms of a merger or division.

European Communities (Transitional Period Measures in Respect of Third Country Auditors) Regulations 2009

SI 229/2009

I, MARY COUGHLAN, Minister for Enterprise, Trade and Employment, in exercise of the powers conferred on me by section 3 of the European Communities Act 1972 (No. 27 of 1972) and for the purpose of giving effect (subject to, and in so far only as is required by, Commission Decision 2008/627/EC of 29 July 2008 (2008 (OJ No L202, 31.7.2008, p.70)) to Article 45 of Directive 2006/43/EC of the European Parliament and of the Council of 17 May 2006 (OJ No L157, 9.6.2006, p.87) and to the said Commission Decision and, in so far as is required by reason of the said giving effect, partial effect to Articles 35(1) and 36(2) of the said Directive, hereby make the following regulations:

1. (1) These Regulations may be cited as the European Communities (transitional period measures in respect of third country auditors) Regulations 2009.

(2) These Regulations shall come into operation on 26 June 2009.

(3) Section 12 of the Company Law Enforcement Act 2001 (No. 28 of 2001) shall apply in relation to these Regulations as it applies in relation to the Companies Acts, subject to the modification that references in that section to Companies Acts shall be construed as including references to these Regulations.

Interpretation

2. In these Regulations, unless otherwise indicated—

"Annex" means the Annex to the Decision;

"Article" means an Article of the Decision;

"Commission" means the Commission of the European Communities;

"competent authority" shall be construed in accordance with Regulation 3;

"Decision" means Commission Decision 2008/627/EC of 29 July 2008 (OJ No L202, 31.7.2008, p.70) concerning a transitional period for audit activities of certain third country auditors and audit entities;

"Directive" means Directive 2006/43/EC of the European Parliament and of the Council of 17 May 2006 (OJ No L157, 9.6.2006, p.87) on statutory audits of annual accounts and consolidated accounts, amending Council Directives 78/660/EEC (OJ No L 222, 14.8.1978, p.11) and 83/349/EEC (OJ No L193, 18.7.1983, p.1) and repealing Council Directive 84/253/EEC (OJ No L126, 12.5.1984, p.20);

"third country" means a country listed in the Annex;

"third country auditor" has the meaning assigned to it by Regulation 4.

Competent authority

3. For the purposes of these Regulations and the Decision the Irish Auditing and Accounting Supervisory Authority is the competent authority in the State.

Functions of competent authority

4. Where an auditor or audit entity from a third country (which auditor or audit entity is hereinafter referred to as a "third country auditor") provides to the competent authority all of the information listed at subparagraphs (a) to (e) of Article 1(1), correct and accurate in all material respects and so certified by the third country auditor concerned (and updated and recertified by him, her or it as and when necessary), and, subject to compliance with such reasonable requests for clarification or further information as the competent authority may make, pays to the authority such fee (if any) of an amount specified from time to time by the Minister sufficient to cover its administration expenses—

(a) the provisions of Article 45 of the Directive shall not apply in relation to audit reports, concerning annual accounts or consolidated accounts as referred to in Article 45(1) of the Directive for financial years starting on a date which is in the period starting on 29 June 2008 and ending on 1 July 2010, which are issued by such a third country auditor, and

(b) the competent authority shall record the said information, and shall ensure that the public is informed about—

(i) the name and address of each such third country auditor, and

(iii) the fact that the third countries concerned are not yet recognised as equivalent for the purposes of the Directive.

Confidentiality requirements

5. (1) No person shall disclose, except in accordance with law (including Regulation 4(b)), information that—

(a) is furnished pursuant to these Regulations to the competent authority, and

(b) has not otherwise come to the notice of members of the public.

(2) Without limiting paragraph (1), the persons to whom that subsection applies include the following:

(a) a member or director or former member or director of the competent authority;

(b) an employee or former employee of the competent authority;

(c) a professional or other adviser to the competent authority, including a former adviser.

(3) A person who contravenes paragraph (1) commits an offence and is liable, on summary conviction, to a fine not exceeding €2,000.

Arrangements on quality assurance reviews

6. The provisions of Regulation 4(a) shall be without prejudice to cooperative arrangements on quality assurance reviews between the competent authority and a competent authority of a third country, provided that such an arrangement meets the criteria listed at paragraphs (a) to (c) of Article 1(4).

GIVEN under my Official Seal, 23 June 2009

MARY COUGHLAN,

Minister for Enterprise, Trade and Employment.

EXPLANATORY NOTE

(This note is not part of the Instrument and does not purport to be a legal interpretation)

These Regulations give effect to Commission Decision 2008/627/EC of 29 July 2008 and provides for a transitional period in respect of the registration requirements set out at Article 45 of Directive 2006/43/EC of the European Parliament and of the Council of 17 May 2006 in respect of auditors and audit entities from the third countries listed at the Annex to the Commission Decision. The third country auditors and audit entities in question are those non-EU auditors and audit entities who audit companies incorporated outside of the European Community which have transferable securities listed to trading on a market regulated within the Community.

The Regulations which come into effect from 26 June 2009, provide for auditors and audit entities from the third countries in question, in lieu of the requirements at Article 45 of Directive 2006/43/EC of the European Parliament and of the Council of 17 May 2006, to provide stipulated information to the competent authorities in Member States who are required to record this information and ensure that the public is informed about specific aspects of the information. The Irish Auditing and Accounting Supervisory Authority (IAASA) is the competent authority in Ireland for the purposes of the Commission Decision and these Regulations.

The arrangements provided for in these Regulations apply for financial years starting on 29 June 2008 and ending on 1 July 2010.

Companies Act 1963 (Alteration of Eighth Schedule) Order 2009

SI 302/2009

I, MARY COUGHLAN, Minister for Enterprise, Trade and Employment, in exercise of the powers conferred on me by section 395 (amended by section 63(1) of the Company Law Enforcement Act 2001 (No. 28 of 2001)) of the Companies Act 1963 (No. 33 of 1963) (as adapted by the Enterprise and Employment (Alteration of Name of Department and Title of Minister) Order 1997 (S.I. No. 305 of 1997)), hereby order as follows:

1. (1) This Order may be cited as the Companies Act 1963 (Alteration of Eighth Schedule) Order 2009.

(2) This Order shall come into operation on 1st September, 2009.

2. The Eighth Schedule (inserted by the Companies (Fees) (No. 3) Order 2005 (S.I. No. 517 of 2005)) to the Companies Act 1963 (No. 33 of 1963) is altered by substituting the Part set out in the Schedule to this Order for Part 1.

3. The Companies (Fees) (No. 4) Order 2005 (S.I. No. 737 of 2005) and Companies (Fees) Order 2006 (S.I. No. 502 of 2006) are revoked.

SCHEDULE

[...][a]

Amendments

a CA 1963 (A8S) O 2009, Sch substitutes CA 1963, Sch 8, Pt 1.

EXPLANATORY NOTE

(This Note is not part of the instrument and does not purport to be a legal interpretation)

This Order alters the Eight Schedule to the Companies Act 1963 by substituting Part 1 of the Schedule.

The Order revokes the Companies (Fees) (No 4) Order 2005 (S.I. No. 737 of 2005 and the Companies (Fees) Order 2006 (S.I. No. 502 of 2006)

Companies (Fees) Order 2009

SI 304/2009

I, MARY COUGHLAN, Minister for Enterprise, Trade and Employment, in exercise of the powers conferred on me by section 103(1) of the Companies Act 1963 (No. 33 of 1963), section 311A of the Companies Act 1963 (No. 33 of 1963) (inserted by section 246 of the Companies Act 1990 (No. 33 of 1990)) and sections 59 and 60 of the Investment Funds, Companies and Miscellaneous Provisions Act 2005 (No. 12 of 2005) (as adapted by the Enterprise and Employment (Alteration of Name of Department and Title of Minister) Order 1997 (S.I. No. 305 of 1997)), hereby order as follows:

1. (1) This Order may be cited as the Companies (Fees) Order 2009.

(2) This Order shall come into operation on 1st September 2009.

2. In respect of the matters mentioned in the first column of the table set out in the Schedule, there shall be paid to the registrar the fees specified in the second column of that table.

SCHEDULE

'electronic form' means in relation to the doing of any act specified in the first column to the table the doing of that act by means of—

(a) the electronic form filing system in use by the registrar of companies, or

(b) the Companies Registration Office disk electronic filing system where the act is also effected in paper form;

'paper form' means, in relation a matter specified in the first column to the table—

(a) the filing of documents or an application in paper form, or

(b) the submission of documents in paper form.

TABLE OF FEES

Matter in respect of which Fee is payable	*Amount of Fee*
Registration of a charge to which section 99 or 101 applies or a judgment mortgage to which section 102 applies, pursuant to section 103(1) of the Companies Act 1963 (No. 33 of 1963)	Paper form — €40 Electronic form — not applicable
Application for restoration of a company pursuant to section 311A of the Companies Act 1963 (No. 33 of 1963) (inserted by section 246 of the Companies Act 1990 (No. 33 of 1990))	Paper form — €300 Electronic form — not applicable
Application to reserve a name pursuant to section 59(3) of the Investment Funds, Companies and Miscellaneous Provisions Act 2005 (No. 12 of 2005)	Paper form — not applicable Electronic form — €25

Matter in respect of which Fee is payable	*Amount of Fee*
Application, pursuant to section 60(1) of the Investment Funds, Companies and Miscellaneous Provisions Act 2005 (No. 12 of 2005), for an extension of the period for which a company name has been reserved pursuant to section 59(5) of that Act	Paper form — not applicable Electronic form — €25

EXPLANATORY NOTE

(*This Note is not part of the instrument and does not purport to be a legal interpretation*)
This Order provides for filing fees where certain documents are filed electronically or in paper form with the Registrar of Companies.

Shareholders' Rights (Directive 2007/36/EC) Regulations 2009

SI 316/2009

I, MARY COUGHLAN, Minister for Enterprise, Trade and Employment, in exercise of the powers conferred on me by section 3 (amended by section 2 of the European Communities Act 2007 (No. 18 of 2007)) of the European Communities Act 1972 (No. 27 of 1972) and for the purpose of giving effect to Directive 2007/36/EC of the European Parliament and of the Council of 11 July 2007 (OJ L 184, 14.7.2007, p 17), hereby make the following regulations:

1 Citation, commencement and construction

(1) These Regulations may be cited as the Shareholders' Rights (Directive 2007/36/EC) Regulations 2009.

(2) These Regulations shall come into operation on the date on which they are made and shall apply in relation to meetings of which notice is given, or first given, on or after that date.

(3) These Regulations shall be read as one with the Companies Acts.

2 Definition

In these Regulations, "Act of 1963" means the Companies Act 1963 (No. 33 of 1963).

3 Amendment of section 2 (General provisions as to interpretation) of Act of 1963

Section 2 of the Act of 1963 is amended—

(a) [...][a]; and

(b) [...][b].

Amendments

a Shareholders' Rights Regulations 2009, reg 3(a) inserts definitions of 'company traded on a regulated market', 'Directive 2004/25/EC' and 'electronic means' into CA 1963, s 2.

b Shareholders' Rights Regulations 2009, reg 3(b) substitutes the definition of 'regulated market' in CA 1963, s 2.

---

4 Amendment of section 132 (Convening of extraordinary general meeting on requisition) of Act of 1963

Section 132 of the Act of 1963 is amended by inserting the following subsection after subsection (1):

[...][a].

Amendments

a Shareholders' Rights Regulations 2009, reg 4 inserts CA 1963, s 132(1A).

---

5 New section 132A in Act of 1963

The Act of 1963 is amended by inserting the following section after section 132:

[…][a].

Amendments

a Shareholders' Rights Regulations 2009, reg 5 inserts CA 1963, s 132A.

6 Amendment of section 133 (Length of notice for calling meetings) of Act of 1963

Section 133 of the Act of 1963 is amended—

(a) in subsection (1)(b), by substituting "or an unlimited company, and" for "or an unlimited company.",

(b) […][a],

(c) in subsection (2)(b), by substituting "or an unlimited company, and" for "or an unlimited company.",

(d) […][b],

and

(e) in subsection (3) by inserting ", other than a company traded on a regulated market," after "A meeting of a company".

Amendments

a Shareholders' Rights Regulations 2009, reg 6(b) inserts CA 1963, s 133(1)(c).

b Shareholders' Rights Regulations 2009, reg 6(d) inserts CA 1963, s 133(2)(c).

7 New sections 133A and 133B in Act of 1963

The Act of 1963 is amended by inserting the following sections after section 133:

[…][a].

Amendments

a Shareholders' Rights Regulations 2009, reg 7 inserts CA 1963, ss 133A and 133B.

8 New sections 134A, 134B and 134C in Act of 1963

The Act of 1963 is amended by inserting the following sections after section 134:

[…][a].

Amendments

a Shareholders' Rights Regulations 2009, reg 8 inserts CA 1963, ss 134A–C.

9 Amendment of section 136 (Proxies) of Act of 1963

Section 136 of the Act of 1963 is amended by—

(a) […][a], and

(b) [...][b], and

(c) [...][c].

Amendments

a Shareholders' Rights Regulations 2009, reg 9(a) inserts CA 1963, s 136(1A) and (1B).

b Shareholders' Rights Regulations 2009, reg 9(b) inserts CA 1963, s 136(2A).

c Shareholders' Rights Regulations 2009, reg 9(c) inserts CA 1963, s 136(4A).

10 Substitution of section 138 of Act of 1963

The Act of 1963 is amended by substituting the following section for section 138:

[...][a].

Amendments

a Shareholders' Rights Regulations 2009, reg 10 substitutes CA 1963, s 138.

11 Amendment of section 139 of Act of 1963

Section 139(1) of the Act of 1963 is amended—

(a) in paragraph (a) by deleting "and",

(b) in paragraph (b) by substituting "may be, and" for "may be.", and

(c) [...][a].

Amendments

a Shareholders' Rights Regulations 2009, reg 11(c) inserts CA 1963, s 139(1)(c).

12 New section 145A of Act of 1963

The Act of 1963 is amended by inserting the following section after section 145:

[...][a].

Amendments

a Shareholders' Rights Regulations 2009, reg 12 inserts CA 1963, s 145A.

L.S. GIVEN under my Official Seal,

6 August 2009.

MARY COUGHLAN,

Minister for Enterprise, Trade and Employment.

European Communities (Directive 2006/46/EC) Regulations 2009

SI 450/2009

I, MARY COUGHLAN, Minister for Enterprise, Trade and Employment, in exercise of the powers conferred on me by section 3 of the European Communities Act 1972 (No. 27 of 1972) and for the purpose of giving effect to Directive 2006/46/EC of the European Parliament and of the Council of 14 June 20061, hereby make the following regulations:

1. (1) These Regulations may be cited as the European Communities (Directive 2006/46/EC) Regulations 2009.

(2) The Companies Acts and these Regulations shall be read together as one.

2. (1) In these Regulations—

"Act of 1986" means the Companies (Amendment) Act 1986 (No. 25 of 1986);

"Act of 1990" means the Companies Act 1990 (No. 33 of 1990);

"annual accounts" has the meaning assigned to it by the Principal Act;

"company" has the meaning assigned to it by the Principal Act;

"consolidated balance sheet" means the balance sheet dealing with the state of the affairs of a parent undertaking and its subsidiary undertakings as a whole;

"Credit Institutions Regulations" means the European Communities (Credit Institutions: Accounts) Regulations 1992 (S.I. No. 294 of 1992);

"Directive" means Directive 2006/46/EC of the European Parliament and of the Council of 14 June 2006 (OJ No L 224, 16.8.2006, p.1)1;

"Fair Value Regulations" means the European Communities (Fair Value Accounting) Regulations 2004 (SI No 765 of 2004);

"IFRS group accounts" has the meaning assigned to it by the Principal Act;

"Insurance Undertakings Regulations" means the European Communities (Insurance Undertakings: Accounts) Regulations 1996 (S.I. No. 23 of 1996);

"parent undertaking" means a body corporate, a partnership or an unincorporated body of persons engaged for gain in the production, supply or distribution of goods, the provision of a service or the making or holding of investments which has one or more subsidiary undertakings;

"Principal Act" means the Companies Act 1963 (No. 33 of 1963);

"Regulations of 1992" means the European Communities (Companies: Group Accounts) Regulations 1992 (S.I. No. 201 of 1992);

"Regulations of 2005" means the European Communities (International Financial Reporting Standards and Miscellaneous Amendments) Regulations 2005 (S.I. No. 116 of 2005);

"subsidiary undertaking" is a subsidiary of a parent undertaking; "undertaking" has the meaning assigned to it by the Principal Act.

(2) A word or expression that is used in these Regulations (including provisions inserted by these Regulations into the Principal Act, the Act of 1986, the Regulations of 1992, the Credit Institutions Regulations or the Insurance Undertakings Regulations) and is also used in the Directive, Regulation (EC) No. 1606/2002 of the European Parliament and of the Council of 19 July 2002 (OJ No. L 243, 11.9.2002, p.1)2, the Fourth Council

Directive 78/660/EEC of 25 July 1978 (OJ L 222, 14.8.1978, p.11)3 and the Seventh Council Directive 83/349/EEC of 13 June 1983 (OJ L 193, 18.7.1983, p.1)4 has, unless the contrary is indicated, the same meaning in these Regulations and those provisions as it has in the Directive, that Regulation and those Directives.

3. Part IIIA (inserted by the Fair Value Regulations) of the Schedule to the Act of 1986 is amended—

(a) in paragraph 22A(1) by inserting "and paragraph 22AA" after "of this paragraph",

(b) by inserting the following paragraph after paragraph 22A of that Part:

[...][a]

Amendments

a European Communities (Directive 2006/46/EC) Regulations 2009, reg 3(b) inserts new para 22AA into CA 1986, Sch, Pt IIIA.

4. Section 8 of the Act of 1986 is amended—

(a) in subsection (1)(a), by inserting ", subject to subsection (1A)," after "a private company",

(b) in subsection (1)(b), by inserting ", subject to subsection (1B)," after "a private company",

(c) by inserting the following subsections after subsection (1):

[...][a]

(d) by inserting the following subsection after subsection (12):

[...][b]

Amendments

a European Communities (Directive 2006/46/EC) Regulations 2009, reg 4(c) inserts new subs (1A) into CA 1986, s 8.

b European Communities (Directive 2006/46/EC) Regulations 2009, reg 4(d) inserts new subs (13) into CA 1986, s 8.

5. (1) Section 32 of the Companies (Amendment) (No. 2) Act 1999 (No. 30 of 1999) is amended—

(a) in subsection (3)(a)(v)(III) by deleting "or",

(b) in subsection (3)(a)(v)(IV) by substituting "paragraph 18 thereof, or" for "paragraph 18 thereof.",

(c) section (3)(a)(v), by inserting the following clause after clause (IV):

[...][a]

(d) by inserting the following subsection after subsection (8):

[...][b]

Amendments

a European Communities (Directive 2006/46/EC) Regulations 2009, reg 5(c) inserts new subs (V) into CA 1986, s 32(a)(v).

b European Communities (Directive 2006/46/EC) Regulations 2009, reg 5(d) inserts new subs (9) into CA 1986, s 32.

---

6. Part IV of the Schedule to the Act of 1986 is amended by inserting the following paragraphs after paragraph 36:

[...][a]

Amendments

a European Communities (Directive 2006/46/EC) Regulations 2009, reg 6 inserts new paras 36A and 36 in CA 1986, Sch, Pt IV.

---

7. (1) The notes on the consolidated accounts prepared in respect of a parent undertaking and its subsidiary undertakings shall set out information relating to—

(a) the nature and business purpose of any arrangement that is not included in the consolidated balance sheet, and the financial impact of such arrangement if the risks or benefits arising from the arrangement are material, and in so far as the disclosure of such risks or benefits is necessary for assessing the financial position, taken as a whole, of the parent undertaking and its subsidiary undertakings included in the consolidated balance sheet, and

(b) subject to paragraph (2), transactions entered into by—

(i) the parent undertaking, or

(ii) a subsidiary undertaking of that parent undertaking included in the consolidation,

with related parties, if the transactions are material and have not been concluded under normal market conditions and the information shall include the amounts of such transactions, the nature of the related party relationship and other information about the transactions which is necessary for an understanding of the financial position, taken as a whole, of the parent undertaking and its subsidiary undertakings included in the consolidation.

(2) A transaction referred to in paragraph (1)(b) does not include an intragroup transaction.

(3) Information provided pursuant to paragraph (1)(b) concerning individual transactions may be aggregated according to their nature except where separate information is necessary for an understanding of the effects of the related party transactions on the financial position, taken as a whole, of the parent undertaking and its subsidiary undertakings included in the consolidation.

8.(1) Where a parent undertaking which has its securities admitted to trading on a regulated market is preparing consolidated accounts the corporate governance statement included in the report by the directors of that undertaking under section 158 of the Principal Act shall contain, in addition to the information specified in that section, a description of the main features of the internal control and risk management systems of that parent undertaking and its subsidiary undertakings in relation to the process for preparing such consolidated accounts for the parent undertaking and its subsidiary undertakings.

(2) Where the consolidated annual report and the annual report are presented as a single report the description referred to in paragraph (1) shall be included in the section of the report by the directors referred to in paragraph (1) containing the corporate governance statement.

(3) Where a parent undertaking referred to in paragraph (1) produces a corporate governance statement in the form of a separate report published in conjunction with the annual report, in accordance with section 158 of the Principal Act, the description required by paragraph (1) shall form part of that separate report.

(4) In paragraph (4), "regulated market" has the meaning assigned to it by Directive 2004/39/EC.

[9. Where a parent undertaking referred to in Regulation 8 produces a corporate governance statement in respect of a financial year—

(a) in the report by the directors in accordance with Regulation 8(1), or

(b) in a separate report in accordance with Regulation 8(3),

the auditors of the parent undertaking, when preparing their report under section 193 of the Act of 1990 for that financial year, shall state in their report whether, in their opinion, the description, in the corporate governance statement, of the main features of the internal control and risk management systems referred to in Regulation 8(1) is consistent with the consolidated accounts for that financial year.][a]

Amendments

a Regulation 9 substituted by EC(Dir)(A)R 2010, reg 4.

10. Part 2 of the Schedule to the Regulations of 1992 is amended in paragraph 16C(a) by inserting "or 22AA" after "(inserted by the European Communities (Fair Value Accounting) Regulations 2004)".

11. Section 149A (inserted by the Regulations of 2005) of the Principal Act is amended—

(a) in subsection (1)(b)(x), by substituting "subsidiary undertakings)," for "subsidiary undertakings), and",

(b) in subsection (1)(b)(xi) by substituting "(remuneration of auditors), and" for "(remuneration of auditors).", and

(c) in subsection (1)(b), by inserting the following subparagraph after subparagraph (xi):

[...][a]

Amendments

a European Communities (Directive 2006/46/EC) Regulations 2009, reg 11(c) inserts CA 1963, s 149A(1)(b)(xii).

12. Section 150B(2) (inserted by the Regulations of 2005) of the Principal Act is amended—

(a) in paragraph (j), by substituting "subsidiary undertakings)," for "subsidiary undertakings), and",

(b) in paragraph (k) by substituting "(remuneration of auditors), and" for "(remuneration of auditors).", and

(c) by inserting the following paragraph after paragraph (k):

[...][a]

Amendments

a European Communities (Directive 2006/46/EC) Regulations 2009, reg 12(c) inserts CA 1963, s 150B(2)(l).

13. Section 158 of the Principal Act is amended by inserting the following subsections after subsection (6B) (inserted by the Central Bank and Financial Services Authority of Ireland Act 2003):

[....][a]

Amendments

a European Communities (Directive 2006/46/EC) Regulations 2009, reg 13 inserts CA 1963, s 158(6C)–(6J).

14. The Credit Institutions Regulations are amended—

(a) in Regulation 5(1B)—

(i) in subparagraph (k), by substituting "remuneration), and" for "remuneration).", and

(ii) by inserting the following subparagraph after subparagraph (k):

[...][a]

(b) in Regulation 7(5)—

(i) in subparagraph (k), by substituting "remuneration), and" for "remuneration)." and

(ii) by inserting the following subparagraph after subparagraph (k):

[...][b]

Amendments

a European Communities (Directive 2006/46/EC) Regulations 2009, reg 14(a)(ii) inserts EC(CIA)R 1992, reg 5(1B)(l).

b European Communities (Directive 2006/46/EC) Regulations 2009, reg 14(b)(ii) inserts EC(CIA)R 1992, reg 7(5)(l).

---

15. The Credit Institutions Regulations are amended by inserting the following Regulation after Regulation 11:

[...][a]

Amendments

a European Communities (Directive 2006/46/EC) Regulations 2009, reg 15 inserts EC(CIA)R 1992, reg 11A.

---

16. Regulation 13 of the Credit Institutions Regulations is amended by inserting the following paragraph after paragraph (2):

[...][a]

Amendments

a European Communities (Directive 2006/46/EC) Regulations 2009, reg 16 inserts EC(CIA)R 1992, reg 13(3).

---

17. Paragraph 46A (inserted by the Fair Value Regulations) of Part I of the Schedule to the Credit Institutions Regulations is amended by inserting the following subparagraphs after subparagraph (4):

[...][a]

Amendments

a European Communities (Directive 2006/46/EC) Regulations 2009, reg 17 inserts EC(CIA)R 1992, Sch, Pt I, paras 46A(4A)–(4C).

---

18. Part I of the Schedule to the Credit Institutions Regulations is amended by inserting the following paragraphs after paragraph 66:

[...][a]

Amendments

a European Communities (Directive 2006/46/EC) Regulations 2009, reg 18 inserts EC(CIA)R 1992, Sch, Pt I, paras 66A–66C.

---

19. Part II of the Schedule to the Credit Institutions Regulations is amended by inserting the following paragraphs after paragraph 7:

[...][a]

Amendments

a European Communities (Directive 2006/46/EC) Regulations 2009, reg 19 inserts EC(CIA)R 1992, Sch, Pt II, paras 7A–7E.

20. Regulation 5(1B) of the Insurance Undertakings Regulations is amended—

(a) in subparagraph (i), by substituting "own shares)," for "own shares), and",

(b) in subparagraph (j), by substituting "auditor's remuneration), and" for "auditors' remuneration).", and

(c) by inserting the following subparagraph after subparagraph (j):

[...][a]

Amendments

a European Communities (Directive 2006/46/EC) Regulations 2009, reg 20(c) inserts EC(IUA)R 1996, reg 5(1B)(k)).

21. Regulation 10(5) of the Insurance Undertakings Regulations is amended by inserting the following subparagraph after subparagraph (j):

[...][a]

Amendments

a European Communities (Directive 2006/46/EC) Regulations 2009, reg 21 amends EC(IUA)R 1996, reg 10(5).

22. The Insurance Undertakings Regulations are amended by inserting the following Regulation after Regulation 14:

[...][a]

Amendments

a European Communities (Directive 2006/46/EC) Regulations 2009, reg 22 inserts EC(IUA)R 1996, reg 14A.

23. Regulation 16 of the Insurance Undertakings Regulations is amended by renumbering the existing provision as paragraph (1) and inserting the following paragraph after paragraph (1):

[...][a]

Amendments

a European Communities (Directive 2006/46/EC) Regulations 2009, reg 23 inserts EC(IUA)R 1996, reg 16(2).

24. Part III of the Schedule to the Insurance Undertakings Regulations is amended by inserting the following paragraphs after paragraph 19:

[...][a]

Amendments

a European Communities (Directive 2006/46/EC) Regulations 2009, reg 24 inserts EC(IUA)R 1996, Sch, Pt III, paras 19A and 19B.

25. Chapter 3 of Part IV of the Schedule to the Insurance Undertakings Regulations is amended by inserting the following paragraphs after paragraph 36:

[...][a]

Amendments

a European Communities (Directive 2006/46/EC) Regulations 2009, reg 24 inserts EC(IUA)R 1996, Sch, Pt IV, paras 37–41.

26. (1) A person who contravenes Regulation 7, 8 or 9 is guilty of an offence and liable—

(a) on summary conviction to a [class A fine][a] or 3 months imprisonment or both, or

(b) on conviction on indictment, to a fine of €50,000 or imprisonment for a term not exceeding 3 years or both.

(2) Where an offence under these Regulations is committed by a body corporate and is proved to have been so committed with the consent or connivance of, or to be attributable to any neglect on the part of, any person, being a director, manager, secretary or other officer of the body corporate, or a person who was purporting to act in any such capacity, that person shall be guilty of an offence and shall be liable to be proceeded against and punished as if he or she were guilty of the first-mentioned offence.

(3) If the affairs of a body corporate are managed by its members, paragraph (2) shall apply in relation to the acts and defaults of a member in connection with the functions of management as if the member is a director or manager of the body corporate.

Amendments

a As implicitly substituted for "fine not exceeding €5,000" by Fines Act 2010, s 4. A class A fine currently means a fine not exceeding €5,000.

GIVEN under my Official Seal, 18 November 2009.

MARY COUGHLAN,

Minister for Enterprise, Trade and Employment.

EXPLANATORY NOTE

(*This note is not part of the Instrument and does not purport to be a legal interpretation*)

These Regulations give effect to Directive 2006/46/EC of the European Parliament and of the Council, of 14 June 2006 amending Council Directives 78/660/EEC on the annual accounts of certain types of companies, 83/349/EEC on consolidated accounts, 86/635/EEC on the annual accounts and consolidated accounts of banks and other financial institutions and 91/674/EEC on the annual accounts and consolidated accounts of insurance undertakings.

European Communities (Directive 2006/46/EC) (Amendment) Regulations 2010

SI 83/2010

I, MARY COUGHLAN, Minister for Enterprise, Trade and Employment, in exercise of the powers conferred on me by section 3 of the European Communities Act 1972 (No. 27 of 1972) and for the purpose of giving further effect to Directive 2006/46/EC of the European Parliament and of the Council of 14 June 2006 (OJ No L224, 16.8.2006, p 1), hereby make the following regulations:

1.(1) These Regulations may be cited as the European Communities (Directive 2006/46/EC) (Amendment) Regulations 2010.

(2) The Companies Acts and these Regulations shall be read together as one.

(3) These Regulations and the Principal Regulations shall be read together as one.

2.(1) In these Regulations—

"Act of 1986" has the meaning assigned to it by the Principal Regulations;

"Act of 1990" has the meaning assigned to it by the Principal Regulations;

"Credit Institutions Regulations" has the meaning assigned to it by the Principal Regulations;

"Directive" has the meaning assigned to it by Principal Regulations;

"Insurance Undertakings Regulations" has the meaning assigned to it by the Principal Regulations;

"Principal Act" has the meaning assigned to it by the Principal Regulations;

"Principal Regulations" means the European Communities (Directive 2006/46/EC) Regulations 2009 (S.I. No. 450 of 2009).

(2) A word or expression that is used in these Regulations (including provisions inserted by these Regulations into the Principal Regulations, the Principal Act, the Act of 1986, the Credit Institutions Regulations and the Insurance Undertakings Regulations) and is also used in the Directive, Regulation (EC) No 1606/2002 of the European Parliament and of the Council of 19 July 2002) (OJ No L243, 11.9.2002, p 1), the Fourth Council Directive 78/660/EEC of 25 July 1978 (OJ No L222, 14.8.1978, p 11.) and the Seventh Council Directive 83/349/EEC of 13 June 1983 (OJ No L193, 18.7.1983, p 1), has, unless the contrary is indicated, the same meaning in these Regulations and those provisions as it has in the Directive, that Regulation and those Directives.

3.(1) Regulations 3, 6, 7, 10, 11, 12, 14, 17, 18, 19, 20, 21, 24 and 25 of the Principal Regulations shall apply in respect of financial years ending on or after 18 November 2009.

(2) Regulations 6, 8 and 10 shall apply in respect of financial years ending on or after 18 November 2009.

(3) Regulations 8, 9 (amended by Regulation 4), 15, 16, 22 and 23 of the Principal Regulations shall apply in respect of financial years beginning on or after 18 November 2009.

(4) Regulations 4, 7 and 9 shall apply in respect of financial years beginning on or after 18 November 2009.

(5) Subject to paragraphs (7), (8) and (9), Regulation 13 of the Principal Regulations shall apply in respect of financial years ending on or after 18 November 2009.

(6) Subject to paragraphs (7), (8) and (9), Regulation 5 shall apply in respect of financial years ending on or after 18 November 2009.

(7) Paragraph (c) of subsection (6D) (inserted by Regulation 13 of the Principal Regulations) of section 158 of the Principal Act and paragraph (a) (amended by Regulation 5) of subsection (6H) of that section shall apply in respect of financial years beginning on or after 18 November 2009.

(8) Where a company whose securities are admitted to trading on a regulated market, referred to in subsection (6C) (inserted by Regulation 13 of the Principal Regulations) of section 158 of the Principal Act—

(a) is an investment company,

(b) the securities of that company are admitted to trading on not more than one regulated market, and

(c) the listing requirements and procedures of that regulated market do not require annual reporting, by the investment company, in relation to a corporate governance code,

Regulation 13 of the Principal Regulations and Regulation 5 shall apply in respect of financial years beginning on or after 18 November 2009.

(9) Where a company whose securities are admitted to trading on a regulated market, referred to in subsection (6C) (inserted by Regulation 13 of the Principal Regulations) of section 158 of the Principal Act—

(a) is an investment company,

(b) the securities of that company are admitted to trading on more than one regulated market, and

(c) none of the listing requirements and procedures of those regulated markets on which those securities are admitted to trading require annual reporting, by that investment company, in relation to a corporate governance code,

Regulation 13 of the Principal Regulations and Regulation 5 shall apply in respect of financial years beginning on or after 18 November 2009.

(10) In paragraphs (8) and (9) "investment company" means—

(a) an investment company authorised by the Central Bank and Financial Services Authority of Ireland pursuant to Part XIII of the Act of 1990, or

(b) an investment company authorised by the Central Bank and Financial Services Authority of Ireland pursuant to Regulation 11 (amended by Regulation 7 of the European Communities (Undertakings for Collective Investment in Transferable Securities) (Amendment No. 2) Regulations 2003 (S.I. No. 497 of 2003)) of the European Communities (Undertakings for Collective Investment in Transferable Securities) Regulations 2003 (S.I. No. 211 of 2003).

4. [...][a]

Amendments

a Regulation 4 substitutes CA 1963, s 158(6H).

5. [...][a]

Amendments

a Regulation 5 substitutes EC(Dir)R 2009, reg 9.

6. Part IV of the Schedule to the Act of 1986 is amended in the paragraph numbered 36 (inserted by Regulation 6 of the Principal Regulations) immediately following paragraph 36A (inserted by Regulation 6 of the Principal Regulations)—

(a) by substituting "36B" for "36",

(b) in subparagraph (2), by substituting "The provision of particulars" for "Subject to subparagraph (4), the provision of particulars", and

(c) by deleting subparagraph (4).

7. [...][a]

Amendments

a Regulation 7 substitutes EC(CIA)R 1992, reg 13(3).

8. Paragraph 66B (inserted by Regulation 18 of the Principal Regulations) of Part 1 of the Schedule to the Credit Institutions Regulations is amended—

(a) in subparagraph (2), by substituting "The provision of particulars" for "Subject to subparagraph (4), the provision of particulars", and

(b) by deleting subparagraph (4).

9. [...][a]

Amendments

a Regulation 9 substitutes EC(IUA)R 1996, reg 16(2).

10. Paragraph 19B (inserted by Regulation 24 of the Principal Regulations) of Part III of the Schedule to the Insurance Undertakings Regulations is amended—

(a) in subparagraph (2), by substituting "The provision of particulars" for "Subject to subparagraph (4), the provision of particulars", and

(b) by deleting subparagraph (4).

GIVEN under my Official Seal, 25 February 2010.

MARY COUGHLAN,

Minister for Enterprise, Trade and Employment.

Explanatory Note

(This note is not part of the Instrument and does not purport to be a legal interpretation)

These Regulations, along with the European Communities (Directive 2006/46/EC) Regulations 2009, S.I. No. 450 of 2009, give effect to Directive 2006/46/EC of the European Parliament and of the Council, of 14 June 2006.

Directive 2006/46/EC amends Council Directives 78/660/EEC on the annual accounts of certain types of companies, 83/349/EEC on consolidated accounts, 86/635/EEC on the annual accounts and consolidated accounts of banks and other financial institutions and 91/674/EEC on the annual accounts and consolidated accounts of insurance undertakings.

The present Regulations clarify certain aspects of S.I. No. 450 of 2009.

European Communities (Statutory Audits) (Directive 2006/43/EC) Regulations 2010

SI 220/2010

PART 1

Preliminary and General

PART 2

Miscellaneous Amendments — Amendments of Preliminary and General Nature, Amendments Adapting Certain Provisions of Companies Acts in Consequence of Directive, Etc.

PART 3

Designation of competent authorities

PART 4

Approval of Statutory Auditors and Audit Firms, Prohibition on Unapproved Persons Acting as Auditor, etc

Chapter 1

Approval of Statutory Auditors and Audit Firms

Chapter 3

Auditing Standards and Audit Reporting

Chapter 4

Transparency report

Chapter 5

Duties to notify competent authority with supervisory and other functions in event of cessation of office by statutory auditor or audit firm and restrictions on their removal

PART 6
Public Register

PART 7
Independence

PART 8
PUBLIC OVERSIGHT AND QUALITY ASSURANCE OF STATUTORY AUDITORS AND AUDIT FIRMS

CHAPTER 1
PUBLIC OVERSIGHT

CHAPTER 2
QUALITY ASSURANCE

CHAPTER 3
SYSTEMS OF INVESTIGATIONS AND PENALTIES

PART 9
AUDIT COMMITTEES

PART 10
REGULATORY ARRANGEMENTS BETWEEN MEMBER STATES

CHAPTER 1
COOPERATION WITH OTHER MEMBER STATES

I, BATT O'KEEFFE, Minister for Enterprise, Trade and Innovation, in exercise of the powers conferred on me by section 3 of the European Communities Act 1972 (No. 27 of 1972), and for the purpose of giving effect to Directive 2006/43/EC of the European Parliament and of the Council of 17 May 2006, hereby make the following regulations:

PART 1
PRELIMINARY AND GENERAL

1 Citation and construction

(1) These Regulations may be cited as the European Communities (Statutory Audits) (Directive 2006/43/EC) Regulations 2010.

(2) These Regulations shall be read as one with the Companies Acts.

2 Application

Save where otherwise provided, these Regulations apply—

(a) in so far as they relate to the conduct of statutory audits and the duties and powers of statutory auditors and audit firms in relation thereto — to the conduct of statutory audits for financial years commencing on or after the date of the making of these Regulations; and

(b) as regards each other matter provision for which is made by these Regulations — on and from the date of the making of these Regulations.

3 Interpretation

(1) In these Regulations—

"Act of 1990" means the Companies Act 1990 (No. 33 of 1990);

"Act of 2003" means the Companies (Auditing and Accounting) Act 2003 (No. 44 of 2003);

"affiliate", in relation to a statutory audit firm, means any undertaking, regardless of legal form, which is connected to the statutory audit firm by means of common ownership, control or management;

"approved", in relation to a statutory auditor or audit firm, means approved under these Regulations;

Notice of the making of this Statutory Instrument was published in "Iris Oifigiúil" of 25th May, 2010.

"audit report" means the report issued by the statutory auditor or audit firm to the members of a company in accordance with section 193 of the Act of 1990;

"audit working papers", in relation to a statutory auditor or audit firm, means material (whether in the form of data stored on paper, film, electronic media or other media or otherwise) prepared by or for, or obtained by the statutory auditor or audit firm in connection with the performance of the audit concerned, and includes—

(a) the record of audit procedures performed,

(b) relevant audit evidence obtained, and

(c) conclusions reached,

and a reference to audit working papers in relation to—

(i) a Member State auditor or audit firm, or

(ii) a third-country auditor or audit entity, shall be read accordingly;

"Commission" means Commission of the European Communities;

"competent authorities under these Regulations" has the meaning assigned to it by Regulation 16(3);

"competent authority", where used without qualification, has the meaning assigned to it by Regulation 16(2);

"competent authority with registration functions" has the meaning assigned to it by Regulation 16(2);

"competent authority with supervisory and other functions" has the meaning assigned to it by Regulation 16(2);

"Directive" means Directive No. 2006/43/EC of the European Parliament and of the Council of 17 May 2006 on statutory audits of annual accounts and consolidated accounts, amending Council Directives 78/660/EEC and 83/349/EEC and repealing Council Directive 84/253/EEC;

"EEA Agreement" means the Agreement on the European Economic Area signed at Oporto on 2 May 1992, as adjusted by the Protocol signed at Brussels on 17 March 1993;

"EEA State" means a state that is a contracting party to the EEA Agreement;
"enactment" includes an instrument made under an enactment;

"financial year", in relation to a statutory auditor or audit firm, means—

(a) subject to paragraph (b), any period in respect of which a profit and loss account or income statement is prepared by the auditor or audit firm for income tax or other business purposes, or

(b) in the case of a statutory audit firm that is a company, any period in respect of which accounts under the Companies Acts are prepared by the firm,

whether that period is of a year's duration or not;

"firm" includes a body corporate;

"group auditor" means the statutory auditor or audit firm carrying out the statutory audit of the group accounts in question;

"key audit partner" or "key audit partners" means:

(a) the one or more statutory auditors designated by a statutory audit firm for a particular audit engagement as being primarily responsible for carrying out the statutory audit on behalf of the audit firm, or

(b) in the case of a group audit, at least the one or more statutory auditors designated by a statutory audit firm as being primarily responsible for carrying out the statutory audit at the level of the group and the one or more statutory auditors designated as being primarily responsible at the level of material subsidiaries, or

(c) the one or more statutory auditors who sign the audit report;

"Member State" means a Member State of the European Union or an EEA State;

"Member State audit firm" means an audit entity approved in accordance with the Directive by a competent authority of another Member State to carry out audits of annual or group accounts as required by Community law;

"Member State auditor" means an auditor approved in accordance with the Directive by a competent authority of another Member State to carry out audits of annual or group accounts as required by Community law;

"Minister" means the Minister for Enterprise, Trade and Innovation;

"network", in relation to a statutory auditor or audit firm, means the larger structure:

(a) which is aimed at cooperation and to which the statutory auditor or audit firm belongs, and

(b) either—

(i) the clear objective of which is profit or cost-sharing, or

(ii) which shares—

(I) common ownership, control or management,

(II) common quality control policies and procedures,

(III) a common business strategy, or

(IV) the use of a common brand-name or a significant part of professional resources;

"Principal Act" means the Companies Act 1963 (No. 33 of 1963);

"public-interest entities" means—

(a) companies or other bodies corporate governed by the law of a Member State whose transferable securities are admitted to trading on a regulated market of any Member State within the meaning of point 14 of Article 4(1) of Directive 2004/39/EC,

(b) credit institutions as defined in point 1 of Article 1 of Directive 2000/12/EC of the European Parliament and of the Council of 20 March 2000 relating to the taking up and pursuit of the business of credit institutions, and

(c) insurance undertakings within the meaning of Article 2(1) of Directive 91/674/EEC;

"recognised accountancy body" means a body of accountants—

(a) recognised, or

(b) deemed, by virtue of section 191(3) or (4) of the Act of 1990, to be recognised,

by the competent authority with supervisory and other functions for the purposes of—

(i) section 187 of the Act of 1990, or

(ii) these Regulations;

"standards" means those standards of a recognised accountancy body as defined in section 4 of the Act of 2003;

"statutory audit" means an audit of individual accounts or group accounts in so far as required by Community law;

"statutory audit firm" means an audit firm which is approved in accordance with these Regulations to carry out statutory audits;

"statutory auditor" means a natural person who is approved in accordance with these Regulations to carry out statutory audits;

"third country" means a country or territory that is not a Member State or part of a Member State;

"third-country audit entity" means an entity that is entitled, under or by virtue of the laws, regulations or administrative provisions of a third country, to carry out audits of the annual or group accounts of a company incorporated in that third country;

"third-country auditor" means a natural person who is entitled, under or by virtue of the laws, regulations or administrative provisions of a third country, to carry out audits of the annual or group accounts of a company incorporated in that third country;

"third-country competent authority" means an authority in a third country with responsibilities, as respects auditors and audit entities in that country, equivalent to those of a competent authority or the competent authority with supervisory and other functions;

"transparency report" shall be read in accordance with Regulation 58.

(2) A reference in these Regulations to a registered third-country auditor or audit entity is a reference to a third-country auditor or entity registered under Chapter 2 of Part 11.

(3) A word or expression that is used in these Regulations and is also used in the Directive shall have in these Regulations the same meaning as it has in the Directive.

PART 2

MISCELLANEOUS AMENDMENTS — AMENDMENTS OF PRELIMINARY AND GENERAL NATURE, AMENDMENTS ADAPTING CERTAIN PROVISIONS OF COMPANIES ACTS IN CONSEQUENCE OF DIRECTIVE, ETC.

4 Amendment of Principal Act

(1) Section 2(1) of the Principal Act is amended—

(a) by inserting the following definition after the definition of "articles":

> "'auditor' means a statutory auditor or statutory audit firm within the meaning of the European Communities (Statutory Audits) (Directive 2006/43/EC) Regulations 2010;",

and

(b) by inserting the following definition after the definition of "subsidiary":

> "'Supervisory Authority' means the Irish Auditing and Accounting Supervisory Authority;".

(2) Section 149A(1)(b)(xi) of the Principal Act is amended by deleting "paragraph 39(5) of the Schedule to the Act of 1986 and".

(3) Section 150B(2)(fc) of the Principal Act is amended by deleting "paragraph 39(5) of the Schedule to the Act of 1986 and".

(4) Section 160 of the Principal Act is amended, in subsection (9), by inserting "(not being a body corporate)" after "firm" where it firstly occurs.

(5) The amendments effected by paragraphs (2) and (3) apply to accounts for financial years ending on or after the date falling 3 months after the date of the making of these Regulations.

5 Amendment of Companies (Amendment) Act 1986

(1) Part IV of the Schedule to the Companies (Amendment) Act 1986 (No. 25 of 1986) is amended by deleting subparagraph (5) of paragraph 39.

(2) The amendment effected by this Regulation applies to accounts for financial years ending on or after the date falling 3 months after the date of the making of these Regulations.

6 Amendment of section 187 of Act of 1990

Section 187 of the Act of 1990 is amended—

(a) in subsection (1), by deleting "either as auditor of a company or";

(b) by deleting subsection (2);

(c) [...][a];

(d) in subsection (6), by deleting "as auditor of a company or";

(e) in subsection (7), by deleting "auditor of a company or"; and

(f) in subsection (12), by deleting "as an auditor of a company or".

Amendments

a Regulation 6(c) substitutes CA 1990, s 187(3)(f).

---

7 Amendment of section 188 of Act of 1990

Section 188 of the Act of 1990 is amended, in subsection (1), by deleting "auditor of a company or".

8 Amendment of section 189 of Act of 1990

Section 189 of the Act of 1990 is amended—

(a) in subsection (1), by deleting "auditor of a company or"; and

(b) in subsection (2)(a) and (c), by deleting "auditor of a company or".

9 Amendment of section 190 of Act of 1990

[...][a].

Amendments

a Regulation 9 substitutes CA 1990, s 190.

---

10 Amendment of section 191 of Act of 1990

[...][a].

Amendments

a Regulation 10 substitutes CA 1990, s 191.

---

11 Amendment of section 192 of Act of 1990

Section 192 of the Act of 1990 is amended—

(a) in subsections (1) to (3), by inserting "or the European Communities (Statutory Audits) (Directive 2006/43/EC) Regulations 2010" after "under or for the purposes of section 187";

(b) in subsection (4)(a), by inserting "or the Regulations referred to in the preceding subsections" after "the said section 187"; and

(c) in subsection (6), by inserting "or the European Communities (Statutory Audits) (Directive 2006/43/EC) Regulations 2010" after "for the purposes of section 187".

12 Amendment of section 198 of Act of 1990

(1) Section 198 of the Act of 1990 is amended—

(a) in subsection (1)—

(i) by inserting "('the register of public auditors')" after "a register"; and

(ii) by deleting "as auditor of a company or";

(b) in subsection (2)—

(i) by deleting "as an auditor of a company or" in paragraphs (a) and (b);

(ii) by deleting "an auditor of a company or" in paragraph (c); and

(iii) by substituting "register of public auditors" for "register of auditors" in paragraph (c)(i);

and

(c) in subsection (3)—

(i) by substituting "register of public auditors" for "register of auditors" where it firstly occurs;

(ii) by substituting "a public auditor" for "an auditor" in paragraph (a); and

(iii) by substituting "register of public auditors" for "register of auditors" in paragraph (b).

13 Amendment of sections 199 and 200 of Act of 1990

(1) Section 199 of the Act of 1990 is amended—

(a) in subsection (1), by deleting "auditor of a company or";

(b) in subsection (2), by adding "as public auditors" after "in the State"; and

(c) in subsection (3), by deleting "as auditor of a company or".

(2) Section 200 of the Act of 1990 is amended—

(a) in subsection (1), by deleting "as auditor of a company or";

(b) in subsection (2), by adding "as public auditors" after "in the State"; and

(c) in subsection (3), by deleting "as auditor of a company or".

14 Amendments of Act of 2003

The Act of 2003 is amended—

(a) in section 4(1), by substituting the following definition for the definition of "recognised accountancy body":

"'recognised accountancy body' means a body of accountants—

(a) recognised, or

(b) deemed, by virtue of section 191(3) or (4) of the Act of 1990, to be recognised,

by the Supervisory Authority for the purposes of—

(i) section 187 of the Act of 1990, or

(ii) the European Communities (Statutory Audits) (Directive 2006/43/EC) Regulations 2010;"; and

(b) [...][a].

Amendments

a Regulation 14(b) inserts C(AA)A 2003, s 9(2)(mb).

---

15 Revocation of certain secondary legislation

(1) Regulations 1 to 4 of the Companies Act 1990 (Auditors) Regulations 1992 (S.I. No. 259 of 1992) are revoked save in so far as they relate to public auditors.

(2) Regulations 5 to 7 of the Companies Act 1990 (Auditors) Regulations 1992 (S.I. No. 259 of 1992) are revoked.

(3) Part I of the Schedule to the European Communities (Credit Institutions: Accounts) Regulations 1992 (S.I. No. 294 of 1992) is amending by revoking subparagraph (3) of paragraph 74.

(4) Part III of the Schedule to the European Communities (Insurance Undertakings: Accounts) Regulations 1996 (S.I. No. 23 of 1996) is amended by revoking subparagraph (d) of paragraph 21.

(5) The amendments effected by paragraphs (3) and (4) apply to accounts for financial years ending on or after the date falling 3 months after the date of the making of these Regulations.

PART 3
DESIGNATION OF COMPETENT AUTHORITIES

16 Designation of competent authorities and meaning of "competent authority" and related expressions

(1) This Regulation—

(a) designates, for the purposes of the tasks provided for in the Directive, various bodies or other persons as competent authorities in the State; and

(b) assigns a meaning to each of the following expressions used in these Regulations and which are connected with the foregoing designation, namely:

(i) "competent authority" — where that expression is used without qualification;

(ii) "competent authorities under these Regulations";

(iii) "competent authority with registration functions"; and

(iv) "competent authority with supervisory and other functions".

(2) In these Regulations, other than this paragraph—

"competent authority", where used without qualification, means a recognised accountancy body;

"competent authority with registration functions" means the Registrar of Companies;

"competent authority with supervisory and other functions" means the Irish Auditing and Accounting Supervisory Authority,

and, accordingly, each recognised accountancy body, the Registrar of Companies and the Irish Auditing and Accounting Supervisory Authority is designated as a competent authority in the State for the purposes of such of the tasks provided for in the Directive as correspond to the particular functions conferred on it or him or her by the provision concerned of these Regulations.

(3) In these Regulations "competent authorities under these Regulations" means—

(a) each of the recognised accountancy bodies;

(b) the Registrar of Companies; and

(c) the Irish Auditing and Accounting Supervisory Authority,

save that in Regulations 96 to 98, 101 and 103 to 107 the expression does not include the Registrar of Companies.

(4) Regulation 17 supplements paragraph (2) with regard to the operation of a provision of these Regulations that refers to a competent authority without qualification.

17 Operation of provisions with regard to particular recognised accountancy bodies

(1) This Regulation applies where the provision referred to in paragraph (2), (3), (4) or (5) uses the expression "competent authority" without qualification and that provision does not, by its express terms, itself indicate which recognised accountancy body is being referred to.

(2) A provision of these Regulations that confers a function on a competent authority in relation to a statutory auditor or audit firm shall be read as conferring that function—

(a) in the case of a statutory auditor who is not a member of a statutory audit firm — on the recognised accountancy body of which the statutory auditor is a member;

(b) in the case of a statutory auditor who is a member of a statutory audit firm — on the recognised accountancy body of which the statutory audit firm is a member;

(c) in the case of a statutory audit firm — on the recognised accountancy body of which the statutory audit firm is a member.

(3) With regard to the function conferred by Regulation 19 on a competent authority in relation to a natural person or firm, paragraph (2) applies as if, for each reference in that paragraph to a statutory auditor or statutory audit firm (as the case may be), there were substituted a reference to the natural person or firm, as appropriate.

(4) A provision of these Regulations requiring that an act is to be done, or enabling an act to be done, by a person (other than a person referred to in paragraph (5)(b)) in relation to a competent authority shall be read as requiring or enabling it to be done by the person in relation to—

(a) if the person is not a member of a statutory audit firm — the recognised accountancy body of which the person is a member;

(b) if the person is a member of a statutory audit firm — the recognised accountancy body of which the statutory audit firm is a member; and

(c) if the person is a statutory audit firm — the recognised accountancy body of which the statutory audit firm is a member.

(5) In the case—

(a) of a provision of the kind referred to in paragraph (2), (3) or (4);

(b) where the provision falls to be applied to a Member State auditor, a Member State audit firm, a third-country auditor or any other person who or which is not a member of a recognised accountancy body (or, as the case may be, the firm of which the person is a member is not a member of a recognised accountancy body),

the recognised accountancy body that shall perform the function concerned or, as the case may be, in relation to which the act concerned is required or enabled to be done shall be determined—

(i) by reference to arrangements, in writing, entered into by the recognised accountancy bodies amongst themselves for the purpose (which arrangements those bodies are empowered by this paragraph to enter into); or

(ii) in default of—

(I) such arrangements being entered into; or

(II) the provisions of such arrangements dealing with the particular case falling to be determined,

by the competent authority with supervisory and other functions.

(6) On a determination being made by the competent authority with supervisory and other functions for the purposes of paragraph (5)(ii), a direction in writing, reflecting the terms of the determination, shall be given by it (which direction that authority is empowered by this paragraph to give).

(7) Arrangements shall not be entered into under paragraph (5)(i) by the recognised accountancy bodies save after consultation by them with the competent authority with supervisory and other functions.

(8) If in consequence of the operation of this Regulation, the function of withdrawal of a particular approval under this Regulation falls to be discharged by a recognised accountancy body that is different from the recognised accountancy body that granted the approval:

(a) the first-mentioned accountancy body shall notify in writing the second-mentioned accountancy body of the proposal by it to withdraw the approval; and

(b) the second-mentioned accountancy body shall provide such assistance, by way of provision of information or clarification of any matter, to the first-mentioned accountancy body as the latter considers it may require so as to inform itself better on any issue bearing on the performance of the function of withdrawal,

and the procedures adopted for those purposes by the foregoing accountancy bodies shall be such as will—

(i) avoid any unnecessary delay in the performance of the function of withdrawal; and

(ii) respect the requirements of procedural fairness as concerns the auditor or audit firm in question being able to answer any part of the case made against him, her or it that is informed by those procedures being employed.

(9) In a case falling within paragraph (8), if the approval concerned is withdrawn, the first-mentioned body in that paragraph, in addition to making the notifications required by Regulation 37 and (where it applies) Regulation 38, shall notify the second-mentioned body in that paragraph of the withdrawal of approval.

18 Conflicts of interest to be avoided

The competent authorities under these Regulations shall organise themselves in such a manner so that conflicts of interests are avoided.

PART 4

APPROVAL OF STATUTORY AUDITORS AND AUDIT FIRMS, PROHIBITION ON UNAPPROVED PERSONS ACTING AS AUDITOR, ETC.

Chapter 1

Approval of Statutory Auditors and Audit Firms

19 Applications for approval, general principle as to good repute, etc.

(1) A competent authority may, on application made to it by a natural person or firm, approve, under these Regulations, the applicant as a statutory auditor or audit firm.

(2) A competent authority may, on foot of an application under paragraph (1), grant approval under these Regulations only to—

(a) natural persons; or

(b) firms,

who or which are of good repute.

(3) A competent authority may, on application to it by a third-country auditor and in accordance with Regulation 112, approve, under these Regulations, the applicant as a statutory auditor.

(4) For the purposes of this Regulation, in the case of an application under paragraph (1)—

(a) by a firm that is a Member State audit firm; or

(b) by a Member State auditor,

the fact that the applicant is a Member State audit firm or a Member State auditor, as the case may be, shall constitute conclusive evidence that the applicant is of good repute unless, arising out of the cooperation referred to in paragraph (5), a counterpart authority in the Member State where the applicant is approved as a statutory audit firm or auditor has notified the competent authority (or the competent authority with supervisory and other functions) that the counterpart authority has reasonable grounds for believing that the good repute of the audit firm or auditor has been seriously compromised.

(5) The cooperation referred to in paragraph (4) is the cooperation that the State is required to engage in by virtue of Chapter VIII (which relates to, inter alia, regulatory arrangements between Member States) of the Directive.

(6) On approving a person as a statutory auditor or audit firm, the competent authority shall assign an individual identification number to the person and a written record shall be maintained by the competent authority of all such numbers assigned by it under this paragraph.

(7) A competent authority shall, in performing its functions under this Regulation, be subject to the supervision of the competent authority with supervisory and other functions.

(8) In paragraph (4) the reference to counterpart authority shall be construed in accordance with Regulation 93.

20 Restriction as to the persons who may carry out statutory audits

Statutory audits shall be carried out only by auditors or audit firms that are approved under these Regulations.

21 Restriction on acting as statutory auditor

A person shall not—

(a) act as a statutory auditor;

(b) describe himself or herself as a statutory auditor; or

(c) so hold himself or herself out as to indicate, or be reasonably understood to indicate, that he or she is a statutory auditor,

unless he or she has been approved in accordance with the provisions of these Regulations.

22 Restriction on acting as statutory audit firm

A firm shall not—

(a) act as a statutory audit firm;

(b) describe itself as a statutory audit firm; or

(c) so hold itself out as to indicate, or be reasonably understood to indicate, that it is a statutory audit firm,

unless it has been approved in accordance with the provisions of these Regulations.

23 Offence for contravening Regulation 20, 21 or 22

(1) A person who contravenes Regulation 20, 21 or 22 is guilty of an offence and is liable—

(a) on summary conviction, to a fine not exceeding €5,000; or

(b) on conviction on indictment, to a fine not exceeding €50,000 or imprisonment for a term not exceeding 12 months or both.

(2) If the contravention in respect of which a person is convicted of an offence under paragraph (1) is continued after the conviction, the person is guilty of a further offence for each day that the contravention continues and for each such offence the person is liable—

(a) on summary conviction, to a fine not exceeding €1,000, or

(b) on conviction on indictment, to a fine not exceeding €10,000.

24 Conditions for approval as statutory auditor

A person shall not be eligible for approval as a statutory auditor unless he or she is—

(a) a member of a recognised accountancy body and holds an appropriate qualification as referred to in Regulation 26; or

(b) a Member State auditor and complies with Regulation 30; or

(c) a third-country auditor and complies with Regulations 30 and 112.

25 Transitional provision — deemed approval of persons qualified for appointment pursuant to Part X of Act of 1990

(1) Subject to Regulation 121, a person who, immediately before the commencement of this Regulation, is qualified for appointment as auditor of a company pursuant to Part X of the Act of 1990 shall, without prejudice to paragraph (3), be deemed to have been approved as a statutory auditor in accordance with these Regulations.

(2) The following paragraph has effect in the case of a person to whom paragraph (1) applies, being a person who is qualified for appointment as auditor of a company pursuant to Part X of the Act of 1990 by virtue of having been authorised by the Minister to be so appointed before 3 February 1983.

(3) The deemed approval, by virtue of paragraph (1), of a person referred to in paragraph (2) shall cease to have effect unless, as soon as may be after the commencement of this Regulation, the person becomes either—

(a) a member of; or

(b) subject to the regulation of, a competent authority.

(4) In relation to a person to whom paragraph (1) applies, Regulation 33 shall have effect as if—

(a) in paragraph (3) of that Regulation, the following subparagraph were substituted for subparagraph (b):

"(b) either—

(i) any of the conditions specified in Regulation 24(a) are not being complied with in respect of the auditor; or

(ii) in the case of a person referred to in Regulation 25(2)

who has complied with the condition specified in Regulation 25(3)(a) or (b), that condition ceases to be complied with by him or her,";

and

(b) there were substituted, in paragraph (5), for all the words beginning with "Where, having" and ending immediately before subparagraph (ii) of that paragraph, the following:

"Where, having—

(a) complied with the requirements of procedural fairness in that regard; and

(b) served any notices required for that purpose or as required by its investigation and disciplinary procedures,

the competent authority is satisfied that circumstances referred to in paragraph (3)(a) have arisen or that a statutory auditor has failed to comply with any of the conditions specified in Regulation 24(a) or, in the case of a person referred to in Regulation 25(2) who has complied with the condition specified in Regulation 25(3)(a) or (b), that that condition has ceased to be complied with by him or her, it shall, subject to paragraph (6), serve a notice in writing on the auditor stating that—

(i) it is satisfied that, as appropriate—

(I) those circumstances have arisen;

(II) such a failure has occurred; or

(III) that condition has ceased to be complied with,

in relation to the auditor;".

26 Appropriate qualification for purpose of Regulation 24(a)

(1) An individual holds an appropriate qualification, as required by Regulation 24(a), if he or she holds a qualification granted by a recognised accountancy body whose standards relating to training and qualifications for the approval of a person as a statutory auditor are not less than those specified in Schedule 2.

(2) In paragraph (1) "qualification" means a qualification to undertake an audit of individual accounts and group accounts in so far as required by Community law.

27 Conditions for approval as statutory audit firm and transitional provision

(1) In this Regulation references to a firm include references to a Member State audit firm.

(2) A firm shall not be eligible for approval as a statutory audit firm unless:

(a) the natural persons who carry out statutory audits in the State on behalf of the firm are approved as statutory auditors in accordance with these Regulations;

(b) the majority of the voting rights in the firm are held by—

(i) natural persons who are eligible for approval in the State or in any other Member State as statutory auditors; or

(ii) audit firms approved as statutory audit firms in the State or in any other Member State;

and

(c) the majority of the members of the administrative or management body of the firm are—

(i) natural persons who are eligible for approval in the State or in any other Member State as statutory auditors; or

(ii) audit firms approved as statutory audit firms in the State or in any other Member State,

and, for the avoidance of doubt, a majority, for the purposes of subparagraph (b) or (c), may be constituted by a combination of natural persons so eligible and audit firms so approved.

(3) Where the administrative or management body of the firm has no more than 2 members, then, for the purposes of subparagraph (c) of paragraph (2), one of those members shall satisfy at least the conditions in that subparagraph.

(4) Subject to Regulation 121, a firm that, immediately before the commencement of these Regulations, is qualified for appointment as auditor of a company pursuant to Part

X of the Act of 1990 shall be deemed to have been approved as a statutory audit firm in accordance with these Regulations.

(5) In relation to a firm referred to in paragraph (4), Regulation 34 shall have effect as if—

(a) in paragraph (3) of that Regulation, the following subparagraph were substituted for subparagraph (b):

"(b) the condition specified in Regulation 27(2)(a) is not being complied with in respect of the firm,"; and

(b) there were substituted, in paragraph (5), for all the words beginning with "Where, having" and ending immediately before subparagraph (ii) of that paragraph, the following:

"Where, having—

(a) complied with the requirements of procedural fairness in that regard; and

(b) served any notices required for that purpose or as required by its investigation and disciplinary procedures,

the competent authority is satisfied that circumstances referred to in paragraph (3)(a) have arisen or that a statutory audit firm has failed to comply with the condition specified in Regulation 27(2)(a), it shall, subject to paragraph (6), serve a notice in writing on the audit firm stating—

(i) it is satisfied that—

(I) those circumstances have arisen; or

(II) such a failure has occurred, in relation to the firm;".

28 Powers of Director of Corporate Enforcement

(1) The Director of Corporate Enforcement may demand of a person—

(a) acting as a statutory auditor or audit firm of a company; or

(b) purporting to have obtained approval under these Regulations to so act,

the production of evidence of the person's approval under these Regulations in respect of any period during which the person so acted or purported to have obtained such approval.

(2) If the person concerned refuses or fails to produce the evidence referred to in paragraph (1) within 30 days after the date of the demand referred to in that paragraph, or such longer period as the Director may allow, the person is guilty of an offence.

(3) A person who is guilty of an offence under this Regulation is liable—

(a) on summary conviction, to a fine not exceeding €5,000; or

(b) on conviction on indictment, to a fine not exceeding €12,500.

(4) In a prosecution for an offence under this Regulation, it shall be presumed, until the contrary is shown, that the defendant did not, within 30 days, or any longer period allowed, after the day on which the production was demanded, produce evidence in accordance with paragraph (1).

29 Evidence in prosecutions under Regulation 23

(1) Subject to paragraph (2), in proceedings for an offence under Regulation 23, the production to the court of a certificate purporting to be signed by a person on behalf of a competent authority and stating that the defendant is not approved under these Regulations by that competent authority shall be sufficient evidence, until the contrary is shown by the defendant, that the defendant is not so approved.

(2) Paragraph (1) does not apply unless a copy of the certificate concerned is served by the prosecution on the defendant, by registered post, not later than 28 days before the day the certificate is produced in court in the proceedings concerned.

(3) If the defendant in those proceedings intends to contest the statement contained in such a certificate, he or she shall give written notice of that intention to the prosecution within 21 days, or such longer period as the court may allow, after the date of receipt by him or her of a copy of the certificate from the prosecution.

Chapter 2
Aptitude Test

30 Aptitude test to be passed

(1) Subject to paragraph (2), a Member State auditor or a third-country auditor applying for approval as a statutory auditor in the State is required to sit and pass an aptitude test to demonstrate his or her knowledge of the enactments and practice that are relevant to statutory audits in the State.

(2) Paragraph (1) shall not apply to a Member State auditor or a third-country auditor if the competent authority is satisfied that he or she has otherwise demonstrated sufficient knowledge of the enactments and practice referred to in that paragraph.

(3) The competent authority with supervisory and other functions shall issue guidance to each competent authority as to the specific matters that a competent authority should have regard to in reaching a decision that it is satisfied that a person has demonstrated, in accordance with paragraph (2), the knowledge referred to in this Regulation.

(4) That guidance shall be issued by the competent authority with supervisory and other functions as soon as may be after the date of the making of these Regulations but, in any event, not later than 6 months thereafter.

(5) A competent authority may charge and impose a fee (of an amount specified from time to time by the Minister sufficient to cover the authority's administrative expenses in respect of the following) on a Member State auditor or third- country auditor in respect of the administration of an aptitude test under this Regulation in relation to him or her.

(6) A fee imposed under paragraph (5) may, in default of payment, be recovered from the Member State auditor or third-country auditor concerned as a simple contract debt in any court of competent jurisdiction.

31 Scope of aptitude test

(1) The aptitude test shall—

(a) be conducted in an official language of the State; and

(b) cover only the applicant's adequate knowledge of the enactments and practice that are relevant to statutory audits in the State.

(2) Any decision by a competent authority—

(a) as to the various matters that shall constitute the contents of the aptitude test; or

(b) that those contents shall stand altered in any manner (which decision the competent authority is empowered, by this paragraph, to make from time to time),

shall require the prior approval of the competent authority with supervisory and other functions.

32 Adequate standards to be applied in administration of aptitude test

(1) The competent authorities shall apply adequate standards in the administration of the aptitude test.

(2) No standards shall be used by a competent authority for that purpose unless those standards have (with respect to that use) first been approved by the competent authority with supervisory and other functions.

Chapter 3
Withdrawal of approval

33 Grounds for mandatory withdrawal in case of statutory auditor

(1) The procedures under this Regulation are in addition to those procedures, in the cases to which those paragraphs (8) and (9) apply, that are required by Regulation 17(8) and (9) to be employed.

(2) For the purposes of this Regulation—

(a) the cases that can constitute circumstances of an auditor's good repute being seriously compromised include cases of professional misconduct or want of professional skill on the part of the auditor; and

(b) "disciplinary committee" has the same meaning as it has in the Act of 2003.

(3) Without prejudice to Regulation 89, a competent authority shall withdraw an approval of an auditor under these Regulations if, but only if—

(a) circumstances arise (involving acts or omissions on the part of the auditor) from which the competent authority can reasonably conclude that the auditor's good repute is seriously compromised; or

(b) any of the conditions specified in Regulation 24 are no longer being complied with in respect of the auditor,

but this paragraph is subject to paragraph (5).

(4) Unless there do not exist internal appeal procedures of the competent authority as referred to in paragraph (7)(a), references in paragraphs (5) and (6) to a competent authority shall be read as references to a competent authority acting through the disciplinary committee that deals with matters at first instance.

(5) Where, having—

(a) complied with the requirements of procedural fairness in that regard; and

(b) served any notices required for that purpose or as required by its investigation and disciplinary procedures,

the competent authority is satisfied that circumstances referred to in paragraph

(3) (a) have arisen or that non-compliance, as referred to in paragraph (3)(b), with a condition has occurred, it shall, subject to paragraph (6), serve a notice in writing on the auditor stating that—

(i) it is satisfied that—

(I) those circumstances have arisen in relation to; or

(II) such non-compliance has occurred on the part of, the auditor;

(ii) as the case may be, the auditor must take specified steps to restore his or her repute to good standing, or comply with the condition concerned, within a specified period (which shall not be less than a month); and

(iii) if those steps are not taken or the condition concerned is not complied with within that specified period, it shall withdraw the approval of the auditor,

and, if but only if, as the case may be—

(I) those steps are not taken; or

(II) the condition concerned is not complied with,

within that specified period by the auditor, the competent authority shall withdraw the approval of the auditor under these Regulations.

(6) The procedure specified in paragraph (5) as concerns the service of a notice with respect to the matters specified in subparagraphs (i) to (iii) of it need not be employed if the acts or omissions concerned referred to in paragraph (3)(a) are such as, in the opinion of the competent authority, constitute professional misconduct or want of professional skill on the part of the auditor of a degree that employing that procedure would not be in the public interest but nothing in this paragraph affects the application of the requirements of procedural fairness to the withdrawal of approval.

(7) If—

(a) there exist applicable internal appeal procedures of the competent authority; and

(b) the investigation and disciplinary procedures of the competent authority provide that a decision of its disciplinary committee referred to in paragraph (4), being a decision of a nature to which this Regulation applies, shall stand suspended or shall not take effect until, as the case may be—

(i) the period for making an appeal under those procedures has expired without such an appeal having been made;

(ii) such an appeal has been made and the decision to withdraw the approval confirmed; or

(iii) such an appeal that has been made is withdrawn,

then, notwithstanding anything in the preceding provisions of this Regulation, the operation of the withdrawal of approval by that disciplinary committee shall stand suspended until the happening of an event specified in clause (i), (ii) or (iii).

(8) If—

(a) there exist applicable internal appeal procedures of the competent authority; and

(b) the investigation and disciplinary procedures of the competent authority do not provide, as mentioned in paragraph (7)(b), for the decision of the disciplinary committee referred to in that provision to stand suspended or not to take effect,

then, notwithstanding anything in those procedures, the auditor to whom that decision relates may apply to the High Court for an order suspending the operation of the withdrawal pending the determination by the relevant appellate committee of an appeal that he or she is making under those internal appeal procedures and, where such an application is made, paragraphs (11) to (14) apply to that application with—

(i) the substitution of references to an appeal under those internal appeal procedures for references to an appeal under Regulation 35; and

(ii) any other necessary modifications.

(9) If the relevant appellate committee referred to in paragraph (8) is of opinion, having regard to the particular issues that have arisen on that appeal, that, in the interests of justice, the disposal by it of an appeal referred to in that paragraph ought to include its proceeding in the manner specified in the provisions of paragraph (5) that follow subparagraphs (a) and (b) of paragraph (5), then, in disposing of that appeal, it shall proceed in the manner so specified.

(10) The competent authority shall take all reasonable steps to ensure that any appeal to the relevant appellate committee referred to in paragraph (8) is prosecuted promptly and it shall be the duty of that appellate committee to ensure that any such appeal to it is disposed of as expeditiously as may be and, for that purpose, to take all such steps as are open to it to ensure that, in so far as is practicable, there are no avoidable delays at any stage in the determination of such an appeal.

(11) Where a competent authority has made a decision to withdraw the approval of an auditor under this Regulation (that is to say a final decision of the competent authority on the matter after the internal appeal procedures (if any) of it have been employed and exhausted), the auditor may apply to the High Court for an order suspending the operation of the withdrawal pending the determination by the High Court of an appeal under Regulation 35 that he or she is making against the withdrawal.

(12) On the hearing of an application under paragraph (11), the High Court may, subject to paragraph (14), as it considers appropriate and having heard the competent authority concerned and, if it wishes to be so heard, the competent authority with supervisory and other functions (which shall have standing to appear and be heard on the application)—

(a) grant an order suspending the operation of the withdrawal; or

(b) refuse to grant such an order,

and an order under subparagraph (a) may provide that the order shall not have effect unless one or more conditions specified in the order are complied with (and such conditions may include conditions requiring the auditor not to carry out statutory audits save under the supervision of another statutory auditor or not to carry out such audits save in specified circumstances).

(13) The High Court may, on application to it by the auditor or competent authority concerned, vary or discharge an order under paragraph (12)(a) if it considers it just to do so.

(14) In considering an application under paragraph (11) or (13), the High Court shall have regard to—

(a) whether, as regards the appeal the applicant is making under Regulation 35 to the High Court, the applicant has a strong case that is likely to succeed before that Court (and, for that purpose, the High Court shall require the applicant to give an indication of the facts that will be relied upon, or of the evidence that will be adduced in the case of facts that are in controversy, by him or her on the hearing of that appeal); and

(b) the public interest and, in particular, the public interest in ensuring that there is the minimum of disruption, consistent with law, to the discharge by the competent authority concerned, as a body designated in the State for the purposes of the Directive, of the function of granting and withdrawing approval.

34 Grounds for mandatory withdrawal in case of statutory audit firm

(1) The procedures under this Regulation are in addition to those procedures, in the cases to which those paragraphs (8) and (9) apply, that are required by Regulation 17(8) and (9) to be employed.

(2) For the purposes of this Regulation—

(a) the cases that can constitute circumstances of an audit firm's good repute being seriously compromised include cases of professional misconduct or want of professional skill on the part of the audit firm or any of the one or more auditors through whom it acts; and

(b) "disciplinary committee" has the same meaning as it has in the Act of 2003.

(3) Without prejudice to Regulation 89, a competent authority shall withdraw an approval of an audit firm under these Regulations if, but only if—

(a) circumstances arise (involving acts or omissions on the part of the audit firm or auditor or auditors through whom it acts) from which the competent authority can reasonably conclude that the firm's good repute is seriously compromised; or

(b) any of the conditions specified in Regulation 27(2) are no longer being complied with in respect of the firm,

but this paragraph is subject to paragraph (5).

(4) Unless there do not exist internal appeal procedures of the competent authority as referred to in paragraph (7)(a), references in paragraphs (5) and (6) to a competent authority shall be read as references to a competent authority acting through the disciplinary committee that deals with matters at first instance.

(5) Where, having—

(a) complied with the requirements of procedural fairness in that regard; and

(b) served any notices required for that purpose or as required by its investigation and disciplinary procedures,

the competent authority is satisfied that circumstances referred to in paragraph (3(a) have arisen or that non-compliance, as referred to in paragraph (3)(b), with a condition has occurred, it shall, subject to paragraph (6), serve a notice in writing on the audit firm stating that—

(i) it is satisfied that—

(I) those circumstances have arisen in relation to; or

(II) such non-compliance has occurred on the part of, the firm;

(ii) as the case may be, the firm must take specified steps to restore its repute to good standing, or comply with the condition concerned, within a specified period (which shall not be less than a month); and

(iii) if those steps are not taken or the condition concerned is not complied with within that specified period, it shall withdraw the approval of the firm,

and, if but only if, as the case may be—

(I) those steps are not taken; or

(II) the condition concerned is not complied with,

within that specified period by the audit firm, the competent authority shall withdraw the approval of the audit firm under these Regulations.

(6) The procedure specified in paragraph (5) as concerns the service of a notice with respect to the matters specified in subparagraphs (i) to (iii) of it need not be employed if the acts or omissions concerned referred to in paragraph (3)(a) are such as, in the opinion of the competent authority, constitute professional misconduct or want of professional skill on the part of the audit firm (or the auditor or auditors through whom it acts) of a degree that employing that procedure would not be in the public interest but nothing in this paragraph affects the application of the requirements of procedural fairness to the withdrawal of approval.

(7) If—

(a) there exist applicable internal appeal procedures of the competent authority; and

(b) the investigation and disciplinary procedures of the competent authority provide that a decision of its disciplinary committee referred to in paragraph (4), being a decision of a nature to which this Regulation applies, shall stand suspended or shall not take effect until, as the case may be—

(i) the period for making an appeal under those procedures has expired without such an appeal having been made;

(ii) such an appeal has been made and the decision to withdraw the approval confirmed; or

(iii) such an appeal that has been made is withdrawn,

then, notwithstanding anything in the preceding provisions of this Regulation, the operation of the withdrawal of approval by that disciplinary committee shall stand suspended until the happening of an event specified in clause (i), (ii) or (iii).

(8) If—

(a) there exist applicable internal appeal procedures of the competent authority; and

(b) the investigation and disciplinary procedures of the competent authority do not provide, as mentioned in paragraph (7)(b), for the decision of the disciplinary committee referred to in that provision to stand suspended or not to take effect,

then, notwithstanding anything in those procedures, the audit firm to which that decision relates may apply to the High Court for an order suspending the operation of the withdrawal pending the determination by the relevant appellate committee of an appeal that it is making under those internal appeal procedures and, where such an application is made, paragraphs (10) to (14) apply to that application with—

(i) the substitution of references to an appeal under those internal appeal procedures for references to an appeal under Regulation 35; and

(ii) any other necessary modifications.

(9) If the relevant appellate committee referred to in paragraph (8) is of opinion, having regard to the particular issues that have arisen on that appeal, that, in the interests of justice, the disposal by it of an appeal referred to in that paragraph ought to include its proceeding in the manner specified in the provisions of paragraph (5) that follow subparagraphs (a) and (b) of paragraph (5), then, in disposing of that appeal, it shall proceed in the manner so specified.

(10) The competent authority shall take all reasonable steps to ensure that any appeal to the relevant appellate committee referred to in paragraph (8) is prosecuted promptly and it shall be the duty of that appellate committee to ensure that any such appeal to it is disposed of as expeditiously as may be and, for that purpose, to take all such steps as are open to it to ensure that, in so far as is practicable, there are no avoidable delays at any stage in the determination of such an appeal.

(11) Where a competent authority has made a decision to withdraw the approval of an audit firm under this Regulation (that is to say a final decision of the competent authority on the matter after the internal appeal procedures (if any) of it have been employed and exhausted), the audit firm may apply to the High Court for an order suspending the operation of the withdrawal pending the determination by the High Court of an appeal under Regulation 35 that it is making against the withdrawal.

(12) On the hearing of an application under paragraph (11), the High Court may, subject to paragraph (14), as it considers appropriate and having heard the competent authority concerned and, if it wishes to be so heard, the competent authority with supervisory and other functions (which shall have standing to appear and be heard on the application)—

(a) grant an order suspending the operation of the withdrawal; or

(b) refuse to grant such an order,

and an order under subparagraph (a) may provide that the order shall not have effect unless one or more conditions specified in the order are complied with (and such conditions may include conditions requiring the audit firm not to carry out statutory audits save under the supervision of one or more statutory auditors or one or more other statutory audit firms or not to carry out such audits save in specified circumstances).

(13) The High Court may, on application to it by the audit firm or competent authority concerned, vary or discharge an order under paragraph (12)(a) if it considers it just to do so.

(14) In considering an application under paragraph (11) or (13), the High Court shall have regard to—

(a) whether, as regards the appeal the applicant is making under Regulation 35 to the High Court, the applicant has a strong case that is likely to succeed before that Court (and, for that purpose, the High Court shall require the applicant to give an indication of the facts that will be relied upon, or of the evidence that will be adduced in the case of facts that are in controversy, by it on the hearing of that appeal); and

(b) the public interest and, in particular, the public interest in ensuring that there is the minimum of disruption, consistent with law, to the discharge by the competent authority concerned, as a body designated in the State for the purposes of the Directive, of the function of granting and withdrawing approval.

35 Appeals against withdrawal of approval

(1) A person may appeal to the High Court against the withdrawal by a competent authority of approval under these Regulations of the person as a statutory auditor or audit firm, but this is subject to paragraph (2).

(2) An appeal shall not lie under paragraph (1) unless and until any applicable internal appeal procedures of the competent authority have been employed and exhausted by the first-mentioned person in that paragraph.

(3) An appeal under paragraph (1) shall be made within one month—

(a) unless subparagraph (b) applies, after the date of the withdrawal of approval; or

(b) after the confirmation of that withdrawal on foot of the internal appeal procedures of the competent authority having been employed.

(4) On the hearing of such an appeal, the High Court—

(a) if it is satisfied that the appellant has established that there was not a reasonable basis for the decision of the competent authority concerned to withdraw the approval, shall cancel the withdrawal of the approval; or

(b) if it is not so satisfied, shall confirm the withdrawal of the approval.

(5) For the purposes of paragraph (4), there is a reasonable basis for the decision of the competent authority if, taking into account the expertise and specialist knowledge possessed by the competent authority, the decision (and the process that led to its making) was not vitiated by—

(a) any serious and significant error or a series of such errors;

(b) a mistake of law; or

(c) the evidence, taken as a whole, not supporting the decision.

(6) The High Court may, on the hearing of an appeal under paragraph (1), consider evidence not adduced or hear an argument not made to the competent authority concerned if the Court is satisfied that—

(a) there are cogent circumstances justifying the failure to adduce the evidence or make the argument to the competent authority; and

(b) it is just and equitable for the Court to consider the evidence or hear the argument, as the case may be.

(7) A notification of the outcome of an appeal under this Regulation (or of any appeal from a decision of the High Court thereunder to the Supreme Court) shall be made by the competent authority concerned to the same persons to whom a notification of a withdrawal of approval must be made by Regulation 37 and (where it applies) Regulation 38.

36 Amendment of section 24 of Act of 2003 to clarify relationship between powers thereunder and powers under these Regulations

[...][a]

Amendments

a Regulation 36 inserts C(AA)A 2003, s 24(11A)–(11C).

---

37 Certain persons to be notified of withdrawal

Without prejudice to Regulation 38, where the approval under these Regulations of a statutory auditor or audit firm is withdrawn for any reason by a competent authority, that fact and the reasons for the withdrawal shall be communicated by the competent authority to—

(a) the competent authority with supervisory and other functions; and

(b) the competent authority with registration functions,

as soon as possible, but not later than one month after the date of withdrawal of approval.

38 Other persons to be notified of withdrawal

(1) Where—

(a) the approval under these Regulations of a statutory auditor or audit firm is withdrawn for any reason by a competent authority, and

(b) the statutory auditor or audit firm is also approved in another Member State,

the competent authority shall, in addition to making the communication specified in Regulation 37, notify the relevant competent authorities of Member States where the statutory auditor or audit firm is also approved and entered in the relevant register of the fact of the withdrawal and the reasons for it.

(2) The notification under this Regulation shall be made as soon as possible, but not later than one month after the date of withdrawal of approval.

(3) If the approval under these Regulations of a statutory auditor or audit firm is withdrawn by the competent authority with supervisory and other functions under section 24 (as amended by these Regulations) of the Act of 2003, this Regulation and Regulation 37 (other than paragraph (a) of it) shall apply in relation to the withdrawal as if the references in them to the competent authority were references to the competent authority with supervisory and other functions and with any other necessary modifications.

PART 5

STANDARDS AND PROVISIONS APPLICABLE TO STATUTORY AUDITORS AND AUDIT FIRMS

Chapter 1

Standards for statutory auditors and audit firms

39 Continuing education

(1) A competent authority shall attach the following condition to an approval granted by it under these Regulations to a person as statutory auditor.

(2) That condition is one requiring the person to take part in appropriate programmes of continuing education in order to maintain his or her theoretical knowledge, professional skills and values at a sufficiently high level.

(3) In the case of a statutory auditor who is a person in relation to whom a competent authority may, by virtue of Regulation 17, perform functions under these Regulations but either—

(a) the approval of whom as a statutory auditor has not been granted by that competent authority; or

(b) the person is a person referred to in Regulation 25(1),

a like obligation to that mentioned in paragraph (2) as regards taking part in appropriate programmes of continuing education is, by virtue of this paragraph, imposed on him or her.

40 Professional ethics

The competent authorities shall subject statutory auditors and audit firms to principles of professional ethics, covering at least their public interest function, their integrity and objectivity and their professional competence and due care.

41 Independence and objectivity

Statutory auditors and audit firms are subject to the independence and objectivity requirements of Articles 22, 24 and 25 of the Directive as implemented in the State by Part 7.

42 Standards for purposes of Regulations 39 to 41

(1) The competent authorities shall, in respect of statutory auditors and audit firms—

(a) have adequate standards requiring those auditors and audit firms to comply with the obligations specified in Regulations 39 to 41, and

(b) institute adequate arrangements for the effective monitoring and enforcement of compliance with such standards.

(2) No standards shall be used by a competent authority for that purpose unless those standards have (with respect to that use) first been approved, in accordance with section 9(2)(c) of the Act of 2003, by the competent authority with supervisory and other functions.

43 Arrangements for enforcement of standards

The arrangements for enforcement referred to in Regulation 42(1)(b) shall include, in accordance with Regulations 88 and 89, provision for—

(a) sanctions which include—

(i) at the discretion of the competent authority, in accordance with the third-mentioned Regulation, the withdrawal of approval under these Regulations as a statutory auditor or audit firm;

(ii) appropriate penalties;

(iii) appropriate disciplinary measures;

(iv) appropriate regulatory sanctions, and

(b) making available to the public information relating to the measures taken and the penalties imposed in respect of statutory auditors and audit firms.

Chapter 2
Confidentiality and Professional Secrecy

44 Rules of confidentiality to apply

(1) The rules of confidentiality and secrecy of the competent authority (of which the statutory auditor or audit firm concerned is a member) shall apply with respect to information and documents to which a statutory auditor or audit firm has access when carrying out a statutory audit.

(2) The statutory auditor or audit firm, as the case may be, shall comply with those rules of confidentiality and secrecy.

(3) Where the statutory auditor or audit firm is not a member of a recognised accountancy body, then the preceding provisions of this Regulation shall apply as if the references to the rules of confidentiality and secrecy were references to the rules of confidentiality and secrecy of the competent authority that, by virtue of Regulation 17, may perform functions in relation to him, her or it.

45 Supplemental provisions in relation to Regulation 44

(1) Regulation 44 shall continue to apply with respect to an audit assignment notwithstanding—

(a) that the statutory auditor or audit firm referred to in that Regulation has ceased to be engaged in that audit assignment; or

(b) that the auditor or audit firm referred to in that Regulation ceases to be—

(i) a statutory auditor or audit firm; or

(ii) an auditor or audit firm.

(2) Accordingly, in such a case—

(a) the statutory auditor or, as the case may be, audit firm, or

(b) the former such auditor or, as the case may be, audit firm,

shall continue to comply with the rules of confidentiality and secrecy concerned.

46 Saving

Nothing in Regulation 44 or 45 shall operate to prevent a competent authority from complying with its obligations under these Regulations or the Companies Acts.

47 Incoming statutory auditor or audit firm to be afforded access to information

(1) Where a statutory auditor or audit firm is replaced by another statutory auditor or audit firm, the former statutory auditor or audit firm shall provide access to all relevant information concerning the audited entity to the incoming statutory auditor or audit firm.

(2) This Regulation applies to a replacement of a statutory auditor or audit firm that occurs on or after the date falling 3 months after the date of the making of these Regulations.

48 Access by competent authority to audit documents

(1) Where it considers it reasonably necessary to do so for the purpose of performing a particular function or particular functions under these Regulations, a competent authority may inspect and make copies of all relevant documents in the possession or control of a statutory auditor or audit firm; for that purpose it may, by notice in writing served on the statutory auditor or audit firm, require the auditor or firm either (as shall be specified) to—

- (a) furnish to it specified documents; or
- (b) permit it to have access, under specified circumstances, to all relevant documents in the possession or control of the auditor or audit firm,

within a specified period.

(2) Without prejudice to the generality of paragraph (1), the powers under that paragraph are exercisable in relation to a statutory auditor or audit firm where a complaint is made to the competent authority that the statutory auditor or audit firm has failed to comply with any requirement of these Regulations.

(3) Where the powers under paragraph (1) are exercisable, the following additional power may be exercised by the competent authority if it considers that the exercise of it is reasonably necessary to enable it to clarify any matter arising from its inspection of the documents concerned, namely a power to require the statutory auditor or a member of the statutory audit firm to—

- (a) attend before it; and
- (b) explain any entry in the documents concerned and otherwise give assistance to it in clarifying the matter concerned.

(4) In this Regulation "specified" means specified in the notice concerned.

(5) Without prejudice to paragraph (6), a person who fails, without reasonable excuse, to comply with a requirement under paragraph (1) or (3) is guilty of an offence and is liable—

- (a) on summary conviction, to a fine not exceeding €5,000, or
- (b) on conviction on indictment, to a fine not exceeding €12,500.

(6) Where a person fails to comply with a requirement under paragraph (1) or (3), the competent authority concerned may apply to the High Court for an order compelling compliance by the person with the requirement, and, on the hearing of such application, the High Court may make such an order or such other order as it thinks just.

(7) Nothing in this Regulation derogates from—

(a) the powers exercisable by a disciplinary committee in the circumstances, and under the conditions, specified in section 192A of the Act of 1990; or

(b) the bye-laws of a competent authority.

49 Access by competent authority with supervisory and other functions to documents in possession of competent authority

(1) Where it considers it reasonably necessary to do so for the purposes of performing a particular function or particular functions under these Regulations, the competent authority with supervisory and other functions may inspect and make copies of all relevant documents in the possession or control of a competent authority; for that purpose it may, by notice in writing served on the competent authority, require the authority either (as shall be specified) to—

(a) furnish to it specified documents; or

(b) permit it to have access, under specified circumstances, to all relevant documents in the possession or control of the authority,

within a specified period.

(2) Without prejudice to the generality of paragraph (1), the powers under that paragraph are exercisable in relation to a competent authority where a complaint is made to the competent authority with supervisory and other functions that the first-mentioned competent authority has failed to comply with any requirement of these Regulations.

(3) Where the powers under paragraph (1) are exercisable, the following additional power may be exercised by the competent authority with supervisory and other functions if it considers that the exercise of it is reasonably necessary to enable it to clarify any matter arising from its inspection of the documents concerned, namely a power to require an officer of the competent authority to—

(a) attend before it; and

(b) explain any entry in the documents concerned and otherwise give assistance to it in clarifying the matter concerned.

(4) In this Regulation "specified" means specified in the notice concerned.

(5) A person who fails, without reasonable excuse, to comply with a requirement under paragraph (1) or (3) is guilty of an offence and is liable—

(a) on summary conviction, to a fine not exceeding €5,000, or

(b) on conviction on indictment, to a fine not exceeding €12,500.

(6) Nothing in this Regulation derogates from the powers exercisable by the competent authority with supervisory and other functions in the circumstances, and under the conditions, specified in section 23 or 24 of the Act of 2003.

50 Professional privilege

Nothing in this Chapter compels the disclosure by any person of any information that the person would be entitled to refuse to produce on the grounds of legal professional privilege.

51 No liability for acts done in compliance with Regulations

(1) No professional or legal duty to which a statutory auditor or audit firm is subject by virtue of his or her or its appointment as a statutory auditor or audit firm shall be regarded as contravened by reason of compliance with the obligations imposed by these Regulations.

(2) No liability to the company audited or being audited, its shareholders, creditors, or other interested parties shall attach to the statutory auditor or audit firm by reason of such compliance.

(3) For the avoidance of doubt, nothing in this Regulation affects the liability of a statutory auditor or audit firm for negligence or breach of duty in the conduct of a statutory audit by him, her or it.

52 Restriction of section 31 of Act of 2003

Nothing in section 31 of the Act of 2003 shall operate to prevent a competent authority or the competent authority with supervisory and other functions from complying with its obligations under these Regulations.

53 Further amendment of section 31 of Act of 2003

Section 31(3) of the Act of 2003 is amended—

(a) in paragraph (a), by substituting "section 23, 24 or 26," for "section 23,24 or 26, or";

(b) in paragraph (b)(xv), by substituting "the purposes of this section, or" for "the purposes of this section."; and

(c) [...][a].

Amendments

a Regulation 53(c) inserts C(AA)A 2003, s 31(3)(c).

Chapter 3
Auditing Standards and Audit Reporting

54 International auditing standards to be applied

(1) On and from the adoption of international auditing standards, statutory auditors and audit firms shall carry out statutory audits in accordance with those standards.

(2) The reference in paragraph (1) to the adoption of international auditing standards is a reference to the adoption by the Commission, in accordance with the procedure referred to in Article 48(2) of the Directive, of international auditing standards.

55 Audit of group accounts — responsibility of group auditor

(1) Where a statutory audit of the group accounts of a group of undertakings is carried out—

(a) the group auditor shall bear the full responsibility for the audit report in relation to the group accounts;

(b) the group auditor shall carry out a review, and maintain documentation of such review, of the work of whoever of the following performed audit work for the purposes of the group audit, namely one or more:

(i) third-country auditors;

(ii) statutory auditors;

(iii) third-country audit entities;

(iv) statutory audit firms;

(v) Member State auditors;

(vi) Member State audit firms.

(2) The documentation referred to in paragraph (1)(b) to be retained by the group auditor shall be such as enables the competent authority to review the work of the group auditor properly.

56 Further responsibility of group auditor

(1) Where—

(a) a statutory audit of the group accounts of a group of undertakings is carried out, and

(b) a component of the group of undertakings is audited by one or more third-country auditors or audit entities that have no working arrangement as referred to in Regulation 109(1)(c) or 110(c),

the group auditor is responsible for ensuring proper delivery, when requested, to the competent authority with supervisory and other functions of the documentation of the audit work performed by those auditors or audit entities, including the working papers relevant to the group audit.

(2) To ensure such delivery, the group auditor shall retain a copy of such audit documentation, or alternatively—

(a) agree with the one or more third-country auditors or audit entities concerned arrangements for the group auditor's proper and unrestricted access, upon request, to the documentation, or

(b) take any other appropriate action.

(3) Where legal or other impediments prevent audit working papers from being passed from a third country to the group auditor, the documentation retained by the group auditor shall include—

(a) evidence that he or she has undertaken the appropriate procedures in order to gain access to the audit documentation, and

(b) in the case of an impediment other than a legal one arising from legislation of the third country or countries concerned, evidence supporting such an impediment.

57 Amendment of section 193 of Act of 1990

Section 193 of the Act of 1990 is amended—

(a) in subsection (4D), by deleting paragraph (a); and

(b) [...][a].

Amendments

a Regulation 57(b) inserts CA 1990, s 193(4G).

Chapter 4
Transparency report

58 Transparency report

(1) A statutory auditor or audit firm that carries out the statutory audit of one or more public-interest entities shall prepare and publish, within 3 months after the end of—

(a) the financial year of the statutory auditor or audit firm referred to in paragraph (2); and

(b) each subsequent financial year of the statutory auditor or audit firm,

a report in relation to that financial year (in these Regulations referred to as a "transparency report").

(2) The financial year referred to in paragraph (1)(a) is one ending on or after the date falling 3 months after the date of the making of these Regulations.

59 Contents of transparency report — general

The transparency report shall contain at least the information specified in Regulation 61 and shall be—

(a) approved by the statutory auditor or audit firm; and

(b) signed—

(i) in the case of a report prepared by a statutory auditor — by him or her; or

(ii) in the case of a report prepared by a statutory audit firm — by a partner or other member of the firm who has senior executive responsibility in relation to the affairs of the firm.

60 Publication of transparency report

The statutory auditor or audit firm shall ensure that his, her or its transparency report—

(a) is made available on a website, being a website maintained by or on behalf of the statutory auditor or audit firm, not later than 3 months after the end of the financial year of the statutory auditor or audit firm to which it relates, and

(b) remains available for a period of 3 years reckoned from the end of the period of 3 months referred to in paragraph (a).

61 Specific requirements in relation to contents of transparency report

The transparency report shall—

(a) where the subject of the report is a statutory audit firm (referred to in this Regulation as the "subject"), contain at least the information specified hereafter in this Regulation, and

(b) where the subject of the report is a statutory auditor (also referred to in this Regulation as the "subject"), contain at least so much of the information specified hereafter in this Regulation as is applicable in the case of an individual,

namely—

(i) a description of the legal structure and ownership of the subject;

(ii) where the subject belongs to a network, a description of the network and the legal and structural arrangements of the network;

(iii) a description of the governance structure of the subject;

(iv) a description of the internal quality control system of the subject and a statement by the administrative or managerial body on the effectiveness of its functioning;

(v) an indication of when the last quality assurance review referred to in Chapter 2 of Part 8 took place;

(vi) a list of public-interest entities for which the subject has carried out statutory audits during the preceding financial year;

(vii) a statement concerning the subject's independence practices which also confirms that an internal review of independence compliance has been conducted;

(viii) a statement on the policy followed by the subject concerning the continuing education of statutory auditors referred to in Regulation 39;

(ix) financial information showing the significance, from the perspective of the market, of the subject, such as the total turnover divided into fees from the statutory audit of annual and group accounts, and fees charged for other assurance services, tax advisory services and other non-audit services;

(x) information concerning the basis for the remuneration of the principals or partners.

Chapter 5

Duties to notify competent authority with supervisory and other functions in event of cessation of office by statutory auditor or audit firm and restrictions on their removal

62 Amendment of Principal Act with regard to removal of auditors

The Principal Act is further amended, with effect from the date that is 3 months after the date of the making of these Regulations—

(a) in section 160, by inserting, in subsection (5), "and subject to section 161C" after "in relation to his removal under this subsection"; and

(b) [...][a].

Amendments

a Regulation 62(b) inserts CA 1963, ss 161A–161C.

PART 6
PUBLIC REGISTER

63 Public register

(1) From the date specified in paragraph (2), the competent authority with registration functions shall maintain a register (in this Part referred to as the "public register") which shall contain the information set out in Schedule 1 in relation to—

(a) statutory auditors and audit firms; and

(b) third-country auditors and audit entities.

(2) The date referred to in paragraph (1) is the date falling 3 months after the date of making of these Regulations.

64 Notification of information to competent authority with registration functions

(1) An auditor or audit firm or a third-country auditor shall, as soon as may be after he, she or it is approved under these Regulations as a statutory auditor or audit firm, notify the relevant information to the competent authority.

(2) On receipt of that notification and its having carried out any verification of the information as seems to it to be necessary, the competent authority shall notify to the competent authority with registration functions—

(a) the relevant information contained in the first-mentioned notification; and

(b) (i) the individual identification number assigned by it to the auditor, audit firm or third-country auditor under Regulation 19(6); and

(ii) where—

(I) under Regulation 19(6) such a number exists; and

(II) by reason of the circumstances referred to in paragraph (4)(b) the relevant information notified to the competent authority does not include that number,

the number referred to in paragraph 1(c)(ii) or 2(g) of Schedule 1.

(3) The notifications under paragraphs (1) and (2) shall each be made in such form and manner as the competent authority with registration functions specifies.

(4) In this Regulation "relevant information" means the information set out in paragraph 1 or 2, as the case may be, of Schedule 1, other than that set out—

(a) in subparagraph (b) of that paragraph 1 or 2; or

(b) if, due to the simultaneous registration of a statutory audit firm and the statutory auditors that comprise that firm, the number there referred to is not available at that time, in subparagraph (c)(ii) of that paragraph 1 or subparagraph (g) of that paragraph 2.

65 Prohibition on certain acts unless registered

(1) On or after the date specified in paragraph (2), a person shall not—

(a) act as; or

(b) represent himself or herself, or hold himself or herself out, as being, a person falling within a category of person entered, or entitled to be entered, in the public register unless the person is entitled to be entered, and the name of the person is duly entered, in the public register.

(2) The date referred to in paragraph (1) is the date falling 3 months after the date of making of these Regulations.

(3) A person who contravenes paragraph (1) is guilty of an offence and is liable—

(a) on summary conviction, to a fine not exceeding €5,000, or

(b) on conviction on indictment, to a fine not exceeding €50,000.

(4) If the contravention in respect of which a person is convicted of an offence under paragraph (3) is continued after the conviction, the person is guilty of a further offence for each day that the contravention continues and for each such offence the person is liable—

(a) on summary conviction, to a fine not exceeding €1,000, or

(b) on conviction on indictment, to a fine not exceeding €10,000.

66 Obligation of statutory auditor or audit firm to notify certain information

(1) Each statutory auditor and audit firm shall, as soon as may be but not later than one month after the event, notify the competent authority of any change in the information contained in the public register relating to him, her or it.

(2) On receipt of that notification and its having carried out any verification of the information stated to have changed as seems to it to be necessary, the competent authority shall notify the change in information to the competent authority with registration functions.

(3) The competent authority with registration functions shall, as soon as may be but not later than one month after receipt of the notification referred to in paragraph (2), amend the public register to reflect the change of information so notified.

(4) A person who fails, without reasonable excuse, to comply with paragraph (1) is guilty of an offence and is liable, on summary conviction, to a fine not exceeding €5,000.

67 Information must be signed

(1) Information notified under Regulation 64(1) or 66(1) by a statutory auditor or audit firm shall be signed by the statutory auditor or, as the case may be, a person on behalf of the statutory audit firm.

(2) The signature referred to in paragraph (1) may be an electronic signature (as defined in point 1 of Article 2 of Directive 1999/93/EC of the European Parliament and of the Council of 13 December 1999 on a Community framework for electronic signatures) if the provision of a signature in that form complies with any requirements in that behalf of the competent authority with registration functions of the kind referred to in section 13(2)(a) of the Electronic Commerce Act 2000 (No. 27 of 2000).

(3) If information is notified under Regulation 64(1) or 66(1) without being signed as required by paragraph (1), the statutory auditor or audit firm concerned is guilty of an offence and is liable, on summary conviction, to a fine not exceeding €5,000.

68 Transitional provision

(1) A body of accountants referred to in subsection (3) of section 191 (inserted by Regulation 10) of the Act of 1990 shall, within one month after the commencement of these Regulations, notify to the competent authority with registration functions the relevant information (within the meaning of Regulation 64) in respect of each of its members deemed to have been approved by virtue of Regulation 25(1) or 27(4).

(2) A person referred to in Regulation 25(2) shall, within one month after the commencement of these Regulations, notify to the competent authority with registration functions the relevant information (within the meaning of Regulation 64) in respect of him or her.

(3) A person who fails, without reasonable excuse, to comply with paragraph (1) or (2) is guilty of an offence and is liable, on summary conviction, to a fine not exceeding €5,000.

69 Language of information to be entered in register

The information entered in the public register shall be drawn up in either English or Irish.

PART 7
INDEPENDENCE

70 Requirement for independence — general

When carrying out a statutory audit—

(a) the statutory auditor or audit firm, as the case may be; and

(b) in the latter case, any statutory auditor of the statutory audit firm,

shall be independent of, and not involved in the decision-taking of, the audited entity.

71 Prohibited relationships — specific provisions to secure independence

(1) A statutory auditor or audit firm shall not carry out a statutory audit if there exists a relationship of the following kind between the statutory auditor or audit firm (or a network to which he or she or it belongs) and the audited entity.

(2) That relationship is any direct or indirect financial, business, employment or other relationship (which may include the provision of additional non-audit services) from which an objective, reasonable and informed third party would conclude that the statutory auditor's or audit firm's independence is compromised.

(3) If the statutory auditor's or audit firm's independence is affected by threats, such as self-review, self-interest, advocacy, familiarity or trust or intimidation, the statutory auditor or audit firm shall apply safeguards in order to mitigate those threats. If the significance of the threats compared to the safeguards applied is such that his, her or its independence is compromised, the statutory auditor or audit firm shall not carry out the statutory audit.

(4) Without prejudice to the generality of the preceding paragraphs, a person shall not act as a statutory auditor of a company if he or she is—

(a) an officer or servant of the company,

(b) a person who has been an officer or servant of the company within a period in respect of which accounts would fall to be audited by the person if he or she were appointed auditor of the company,

(c) a parent, spouse, brother, sister or child of an officer of the company,

(d) a person who is a partner of or in the employment of an officer of the company,

(e) a person who is disqualified under this paragraph for appointment as auditor of any other body corporate that is a subsidiary or holding company of the company or a subsidiary of the company's holding company, or would be so disqualified if the body corporate were a company,

(f) a person who is disqualified under section 187(2)(f) of the Act of 1990 for appointment as a public auditor of a society that is a subsidiary or holding company of the company or a subsidiary of the company's holding company, or

(g) a person in whose name a share in the company is registered, whether or not that person is the beneficial owner of the share.

(5) Without prejudice to the generality of paragraphs (1) to (3), a statutory audit firm, regardless of its legal structure, shall not carry out a statutory audit of a company if—

(a) any principal of the audit firm is an officer or servant of the company,

(b) any principal of the audit firm has been an officer or servant of the company within a period in respect of which accounts would fall to be audited by the firm if the firm was appointed auditor of the company,

(c) the firm is disqualified under this paragraph for appointment as auditor of any other body corporate that is a subsidiary or holding company of the company or a subsidiary of the company's holding company, or would be so disqualified if the body corporate were a company, or

(d) the firm is disqualified under section 187(2)(f) of the Act of 1990 for appointment as a public auditor of a society that is a subsidiary or holding company of the company or a subsidiary of the company's holding company.

(6) Without prejudice to the generality of paragraphs (1) to (3), a person shall not carry out a statutory audit of a company on behalf of a statutory audit firm if he or she is—

(a) a person in whose name a share in the company is registered, whether or not that person is the beneficial owner of the share; or

(b) a parent, spouse, brother, sister or child of an officer of the company.

(7) In this Regulation "society" means a society registered under the Industrial and Provident Societies Acts 1893 to 1978.

72 Additional requirements in case of public-interest entities

Without prejudice to the generality of Regulation 70 or 71, a statutory auditor or audit firm shall not carry out a statutory audit of a public-interest entity—

(a) in circumstances which involve a case of self-review or self-interest, and

(b) from the circumstances of which case an objective, reasonable and informed third party would conclude that (so as to safeguard the statutory auditor's or audit firm's independence) the auditor's or firm's not carrying out that audit would be appropriate.

73 Threats to independence and other information to be recorded

A statutory auditor or audit firm shall document in the audit working papers all significant threats to his, her or its independence as well as the safeguards applied to mitigate those threats.

74 Non-intervention by certain persons in execution of audit

Neither—

(a) the owners or shareholders of a statutory audit firm or the owners or shareholders of an affiliated firm; nor

(b) the members of the administrative, management or supervisory body of such a firm or of an affiliated firm,

shall intervene in the execution of a statutory audit in any way which jeopardises the independence and objectivity of the statutory auditor who carries out the statutory audit on behalf of the statutory audit firm.

75 Restrictions with regard to fees

A competent authority shall ensure that its standards include provisions that fees for statutory audits:

(a) are not to be influenced by, or determined by, the provision of additional services to the audited entity; and

(b) are not to be based on any form of contingency.

76 Additional reporting and other requirements in case of public-interest entities

In addition to the other requirements of this Part, a statutory auditor or audit firm that carries out the statutory audit of a public-interest entity shall—

(a) confirm annually, in writing, to the audit committee of the entity his, her or its independence from the public-interest entity;

(b) disclose annually to such audit committee any additional services provided to the public-interest entity; and

(c) discuss with such audit committee the threats to the independence of the auditor or firm and the safeguards applied to mitigate those threats as documented by him, her or it under Regulation 73.

77 Rotation of key audit partner in cases of public-interest entities

(1) In this Regulation—

"7 year period" shall be read in accordance with paragraph (2);

"relevant date" means the date of appointment, being a date falling on or after 29 June 2008—

(a) of the statutory auditor or audit firm (to which the key audit partner or partners referred to in paragraph (2) belongs or belong);

(b) to the entity referred to in that paragraph.

(2) The key audit partner or partners responsible for carrying out a statutory audit of a public-interest entity shall not engage in a statutory audit of the entity at any time that,

subject to paragraph (3), is subsequent to the period of 7 years after the relevant date (in paragraphs (3) and (4) referred to as the "7 year period").

(3) The prohibition imposed by paragraph (2) on the key audit partner or partners concerned engaging in a statutory audit of the entity concerned shall cease to have effect 2 years after the 7 year period, but this is without prejudice to paragraph (4).

(4) This Regulation shall be construed and have effect so that, in the event of any period—

(a) elapsing subsequent to the 7 year period, and

(b) being a period of a duration of 7 years during which the statutory auditor or audit firm referred to in paragraph (1) continues to stand appointed to the public-interest entity concerned,

a like prohibition, and a like cessation of that prohibition, to that provided by paragraphs (2) and (3), respectively, shall apply to key audit partner or partners responsible for carrying out a statutory audit of that entity.

78 Moratorium on taking up management position in audited public-interest entity

There shall not be taken up by—

(a) a statutory auditor who carries out a statutory audit of a public- interest entity; or

(b) the key audit partner who carries out, on behalf of a statutory audit firm, a statutory audit of a public-interest entity,

a key management position in that entity before a period of at least 2 years has elapsed since the day following (should such occur) his or her resignation as a statutory auditor or key audit partner from the audit engagement.

PART 8

PUBLIC OVERSIGHT AND QUALITY ASSURANCE OF STATUTORY AUDITORS AND AUDIT FIRMS

Chapter 1

Public Oversight

79 Amendment of section 10 of Act of 2003

Section 10 of the Act of 2003 is amended—

(a) in subsection (4), by inserting "(whether an individual or otherwise)" after "person" in paragraph (c); and

(b) in subsection (5)—

(i) in paragraph (a), by substituting "Part)," for "Part), or",

(ii) in paragraph (b), by substituting "section 9(2)(ma)," for "section 9(2)(ma).", and

(iii) [...][a].

Amendment

a Regulation 79(b)(iii) inserts C(AA)A 2003, s 10(5)(c) and (d).

80 System of public oversight — responsibility of competent authority with supervisory and other functions

(1) In this Regulation "system of public oversight", in relation to statutory auditors and audit firms, means the system of oversight in the State of such persons constituted by the collective operation of—

- (a) the provisions of the Act of 2003 and the rules, regulations and guidelines made or adopted under them by the competent authority with supervisory and other functions;
- (b) the provisions of these Regulations; and
- (c) the provisions generally of the Companies Acts.

(2) The competent authority with supervisory and other functions shall be the competent authority in the State with respect to the system of public oversight of statutory auditors and audit firms.

(3) As such, and without prejudice to its functions as provided under the Act of 2003 or Regulation 83, the competent authority with supervisory and other functions shall generally superintend—

- (a) the approval and registration of statutory auditors and audit firms;
- (b) the adoption of standards on professional ethics, internal quality control of audit firms and auditing; and
- (c) continuing education, quality assurance, and investigative and disciplinary systems.

81 Further amendments of Act of 2003

The Act of 2003 is further amended—

- (a) in section 11—
  - (i) in paragraph (b) of subsection (1), by substituting "office, is a director," for "office, is a director.", and
  - (ii) by inserting at the end of subsection (1) the following:

    "and the persons appointed as such directors shall be persons who are knowledgeable in areas relevant to statutory audit.";
- (b) [...][a]; and
- (c) [...][b].

Amendments

a Regulation 81(b) inserts C(AA)A 2003, s 23(13).

b Regulation 81(c) inserts C(AA)A 2003, s 24(13).

Chapter 2
Quality Assurance

82 Competent authority with supervisory and other functions to engage in oversight of quality assurance

(1) In performing their functions under Regulations 83 and 84, the competent authorities shall be subject to public oversight by the competent authority with supervisory and other functions.

(2) The terms and conditions referred to in section 9(2)(b)(i) and (ii) of the Act of 2003 (which relate to the powers, under section 192 of the Act of 1990, of the competent authority with supervisory and other functions) may be attached to the recognition of bodies of accountants for the purpose of facilitating the performance by that competent authority of its function of public oversight of quality assurance under this Chapter as well as for any other lawful purpose.

83 System of quality assurance to be put in place

(1) Each competent authority shall ensure that it has in place a system of quality assurance of—

- (a) its members' activities as statutory auditors and audit firms; and
- (b) the activities, as statutory auditors and audit firms, of persons who, though not members of the authority, are persons in relation to whom it may perform functions under these Regulations.

(2) On and from the date specified in paragraph (3), the competent authority with supervisory and other functions shall ensure that it has in place a system of quality assurance of registered third-country auditors and audit entities to whom this Part applies by virtue of Regulation 114(1).

(3) The date referred to in paragraph (2) is the date falling 6 months after the date of the making of these Regulations.

84 Organisation of quality assurance system

(1) A competent authority shall organise its system of quality assurance in such a manner so that:

- (a) the system is independent of the reviewed statutory auditors and audit firms;
- (b) the funding for the system is secure and free from any possible undue influence by statutory auditors or audit firms;
- (c) the system has adequate resources;
- (d) the persons who carry out quality assurance reviews have appropriate professional education and relevant experience in statutory audit and financial reporting combined with specific training on quality assurance reviews;
- (e) the selection of reviewers for specific quality assurance review assignments is effected in accordance with an objective procedure designed to ensure that there are no conflicts of interest between reviewers and the statutory auditor or audit firm under review;
- (f) the scope of quality assurance reviews, supported by adequate testing of selected audit files, includes an assessment of:

(i) compliance with applicable auditing standards and independence requirements;

(ii) the quantity and quality of resources spent;

(iii) the audit fees charged; and

(iv) the internal quality control system of the audit firm;

(g) each quality assurance review is the subject of a written report which includes the main conclusions of the review;

(h) a quality assurance review of each statutory auditor or audit firm takes place:

(i) in the case of a statutory auditor or audit firm that carries out audits of one or more public-interest entities, at least, subject to paragraph (3), every 3 years;

(ii) in the case of a statutory auditor or audit firm that does not carry out audits of any public-interest entity, at least, subject to paragraph (4), every 6 years;

(i) statutory auditors and audit firms take all reasonable steps to ensure that recommendations arising from quality assurance reviews of them are implemented within a reasonable period; and

(j) there is published annually by it the overall results of quality assurance reviews carried out by it in the year in question.

(2) If a statutory auditor or audit firm fails to take all reasonable steps to ensure that recommendations arising from a quality assurance review of him, her or it are implemented within a reasonable period, the competent authority concerned shall take appropriate action, including, where applicable, subjecting the statutory auditor or audit firm, as the case may be, to the system of disciplinary actions or penalties referred to in Regulation 86 and Chapter 3.

(3) For the purpose of paragraph (1)(h)(i), the period of 3 years there mentioned that shall first apply shall be reckoned from a date beginning no earlier than the date of the making of these Regulations.

(4) For the purpose of paragraph (1)(h)(ii), the period of 6 years there mentioned that shall first apply shall be reckoned from a date beginning no earlier than the date of the making of these Regulations.

85 Quality assurance review deemed to include individual auditors in certain cases

For the purpose of Regulation 84(1)(h), a quality assurance review conducted in relation to a statutory audit firm shall be regarded as a quality assurance review of all statutory auditors carrying out audits on behalf of the firm provided that the firm has a common quality assurance policy with which each such statutory auditor is required to comply.

86 Right of competent authority as regards professional discipline

(1) Each competent authority shall have the right to take disciplinary actions or impose penalties in respect of statutory auditors and audit firms and shall have procedures in place to facilitate the taking or imposition of such action or penalties.

(2) The powers, under paragraph (c) of section 9(2) of the Act of 2003, of the competent authority with supervisory and other functions to require changes of the kind, and to

approve the matters, referred to in that paragraph (c) may be exercised for the purpose of facilitating the performance by that competent authority of its function of public oversight of quality assurance under this Chapter as well as for any other lawful purpose.

Chapter 3
Systems of investigations and penalties

87 System of investigation and penalties

Each competent authority shall, in respect of those auditors and audit firms in relation to whom, by virtue of Regulation 17, it may perform functions, institute arrangements to ensure that there are effective systems of investigations and penalties to detect, correct and prevent inadequate execution of a statutory audit by them.

88 Duty of each competent authority with regard to sanctions

(1) Each competent authority shall ensure that the contractual and other arrangements that exist between it and its members are such as enable the imposition by it of effective, proportionate and dissuasive penalties in respect of statutory auditors and audit firms in cases where statutory audits are not carried out by them in accordance with these Regulations.

(2) Those contractual and other arrangements shall comply with the requirements of procedural fairness.

(3) By virtue of this Regulation, the contractual and other arrangements referred to in paragraph (1) that subsist for the time being between a competent authority and its members shall operate and have effect so as to enable the imposition by the competent authority—

- (a) of penalties of a like character to those; and
- (b) in the cases,

referred to in that paragraph in respect of persons who, though not members of the authority, are persons in relation to whom it may, by virtue of Regulation 17, perform functions under these Regulations.

89 Scope of penalties and publicity in relation to their imposition

(1) The penalties referred to in Regulation 88, provision for which must be made by the means referred to in that Regulation, shall, where appropriate, include withdrawal of approval under these Regulations.

(2) Paragraph (1) is without prejudice to Regulations 33 and 34 (conditions for mandatory withdrawal in case of statutory auditor or audit firm).

(3) Unless there do not exist internal appeal procedures of the competent authority as referred to in Regulation 33(7)(a) or 34(7)(a), the reference in paragraph (4) to a competent authority shall be read as a reference to a competent authority acting through the disciplinary committee that deals with matters at first instance.

(4) Without prejudice to Regulation 17(8) and (9), a competent authority may, save where, in its opinion, proceeding in this manner would not be in the public interest, adopt procedures analogous to those in Regulation 33(5) or 34(5) as regards affording the statutory auditor or audit firm an opportunity to rectify the matters that have

occasioned the investigation concerned and the proposed exercise of the power of withdrawal of approval referred to in paragraph (1).

(5) If—

(a) there exist internal appeal procedures, as referred to in Regulation 33(7)(a) or 34(7)(a), of the competent authority; and

(b) the investigation and disciplinary procedures of the competent authority provide that a decision of its disciplinary committee referred to in paragraph (3), being a decision of a nature to which this Regulation applies, shall stand suspended or shall not take effect until, as the case may be—

(i) the period for making an appeal under those procedures has expired without such an appeal having been made;

(ii) such an appeal has been made and the decision to withdraw the approval confirmed; or

(iii) such an appeal that has been made is withdrawn,

then, notwithstanding anything in the preceding provisions of this Regulation, the operation of the withdrawal of approval by that disciplinary committee shall stand suspended until the happening of an event specified in clause (i), (ii) or (iii).

(6) If—

(a) there exist internal appeal procedures, as referred to in Regulation 33(7)(a) or 34(7)(a), of the competent authority; and

(b) the investigation and disciplinary procedures of the competent authority do not provide, as mentioned in paragraph (5)(b), for the decision of the disciplinary committee referred to in that provision to stand suspended or not to take effect,

then, notwithstanding anything in those procedures, the auditor or audit firm to whom that decision relates may apply to the High Court for an order suspending the operation of the withdrawal pending the determination by the relevant appellate committee of an appeal that he, she or it is making under those internal appeal procedures and, where such an application is made, paragraphs (9) to (12) apply to that application with—

(i) the substitution of references to an appeal under those internal appeal procedures for references to an appeal under Regulation 35; and

(ii) any other necessary modifications.

(7) If the relevant appellate committee referred to in paragraph (6) is of opinion, having regard to the particular issues that have arisen on that appeal, that, in the interests of justice, the disposal by it of an appeal referred to in that paragraph ought to include procedures analogous to those, as mentioned in paragraph (4), provided by Regulation 33(5) or 34(5) being adopted by it, then, in disposing of that appeal, it shall adopt procedures analogous to those in Regulation 33(5) or 34(5).

(8) The competent authority shall take all reasonable steps to ensure that any appeal to the relevant appellate committee referred to in paragraph (6) is prosecuted promptly and it shall be the duty of that appellate committee to ensure that any such appeal to it is disposed of as expeditiously as may be and, for that purpose, to take all such steps as are open to it to ensure that, in so far as is practicable, there are no avoidable delays at any stage in the determination of such an appeal.

(9) Where a competent authority has made a decision to withdraw the approval of an auditor or audit firm under this Regulation (that is to say a final decision of the competent authority on the matter after the internal appeal procedures (if any) of it have been employed and exhausted), the auditor or audit firm may apply to the High Court for an order suspending the operation of the withdrawal pending the determination by the High Court of an appeal under Regulation 35 that he, she or it is making against the withdrawal.

(10) On the hearing of an application under paragraph (9), the High Court may, subject to paragraph (12), as it considers appropriate and having heard the competent authority concerned and, if it wishes to be so heard, the competent authority with supervisory and other functions (which shall have standing to appear and be heard on the application)—

(a) grant an order suspending the operation of the withdrawal; or

(b) refuse to grant such an order,

and an order under subparagraph (a) may provide that the order shall not have effect unless one or more conditions specified in the order are complied with (and such conditions may include conditions requiring the auditor or audit firm not to carry out statutory audits save under the supervision of one or more other statutory auditors or audit firms or not to carry out such audits save in specified circumstances).

(11) The High Court may, on application to it by the auditor or audit firm or competent authority concerned, vary or discharge an order under paragraph (10)(a) if it considers it just to do so.

(12) In considering an application under paragraph (9) or (11), the High Court shall have regard to—

(a) whether, as regards the appeal the applicant is making under Regulation 35 to the High Court, the applicant has a strong case that is likely to succeed before that Court (and, for that purpose, the High Court shall require the applicant to give an indication of the facts that will be relied upon, or of the evidence that will be adduced in the case of facts that are in controversy, by him, her or it on the hearing of that appeal); and

(b) the public interest and, in particular, the public interest in ensuring that there is the minimum of disruption, consistent with law, to the discharge by the competent authority concerned, as a body designated in the State for the purposes of the Directive, of the function of granting and withdrawing approval.

(13) The fact of one or more—

(a) measures having been taken against, or

(b) one or more penalties having been imposed on,

a statutory auditor or audit firm (whether under this Part or Part 4) by a competent authority shall be disclosed by the competent authority to the public and that disclosure shall, if the competent authority considers it appropriate, include such further particulars with respect to the matter as it thinks fit.

(14) Subject to paragraph (15), the manner of such disclosure, and the time at which it is made, shall be such as the competent authority determines to be appropriate.

(15) The competent authority shall establish, and reduce to writing, criteria the purpose of which is to govern the determination by it of the matters referred to in paragraph (14); those criteria shall require the prior approval of the competent authority with supervisory and other functions.

90 Further amendment of section 24 of Act of 2003

Section 24 of the Act of 2003 is further amended—

(a) in paragraph (b) of subsection (7), by substituting "subsection (6)," for "subsection (6).";

(b) by inserting at the end of subsection (7) the following:

> "and the fact of a sanction having been imposed on the member by the Supervisory Authority shall be disclosed by the Authority to the public and that disclosure shall include—
>
> (i) in a case where the member is making an appeal to the High Court against the decision of the Supervisory Authority, an indication that that is so, and
>
> (ii) if the Supervisory Authority considers it appropriate, such further particulars with respect to the matter as it thinks fit.";

and

(c) [...][a].

Amendments

a Regulation 90(c) inserts C(AA)A 2003, s 24(7A).

PART 9
AUDIT COMMITTEES

91 Audit committees in respect of public-interest entities

(1) From the date specified in paragraph (2), the board of directors of a public-interest entity shall establish an audit committee in respect of the entity.

(2) The date referred to in paragraph (1) is the date falling 6 months after the date of the making of these Regulations.

[(3) The members of the audit committee shall include at least one independent director of the public-interest entity, that is to say, a person who—

(a) is a non-executive director of it; and

(b) otherwise possesses the requisite degree of independence (particularly with regard to his or her satisfying the condition in paragraph (4)) so as to be able to contribute effectively to the committees functions.

(4) The condition referred to in paragraph (3)(*b*) is that the director there referred to does not have, and at no time during the period of 3 years preceding his or her appointment to the committee did have—

(a) a material business relationship with the public-interest entity, either directly, or as a partner, shareholder, director (other than as a non-executive director) or senior employee of a body that has such a relationship with the entity; or

(b) a position of employment in the public-interest entity.

(5) The director referred to in paragraph (3) (or, where there is more than one director of the kind referred to in that paragraph, one of them) shall be a person who has competence in accounting or auditing.

(5A) For the purposes of paragraphs (3) and (4)(*a*) a non-executive director is a director who is not engaged in the daily management of the public-interest entity or body concerned, as the case may be.][a]

(6) Without prejudice to the responsibility of the board of directors, the responsibilities of the audit committee shall include:

(a) the monitoring of the financial reporting process;

(b) the monitoring of the effectiveness of the entity's systems of internal control, internal audit and risk management;

(c) the monitoring of the statutory audit of the annual and consolidated accounts; and

(d) the review and monitoring of the independence of the statutory auditor or audit firm, and in particular the provision of additional services to the audited entity.

(7) Any proposal of the board of directors of a public-interest entity with respect to the appointment of a statutory auditor or audit firm to the entity shall be based on a recommendation made to the board by the audit committee.

(8) The statutory auditor or audit firm shall report to the audit committee of the public-interest entity on key matters arising from the statutory audit of the entity, and, in particular, on material weaknesses in internal control in relation to the financial reporting process.

(9) Subject, in the case of subparagraph (d), to paragraph (10), this Regulation shall not apply to a public-interest entity if it is—

(a) a subsidiary undertaking within the meaning of Article 1 of Directive 83/349/EEC but only if the preceding requirements of this Regulation are complied with by a parent undertaking (within the meaning of that Article) of the first-mentioned undertaking in such a manner as ensures that any statutory audit of the first-mentioned undertaking comes within the purview of the relevant audit committee; or

(b) a collective investment undertaking as defined in Article 1(2) of Directive 85/611/EEC, or

(c) an entity that—

(i) has, as its sole object, the collective investment of capital provided by the public,

(ii) operates on the principle of risk spreading,

(iii) does not seek to take legal or management control over any of the issuers of its underlying investments, provided that it is authorised by, and subject to the supervision of, a body competent under Community law and has depositary exercising functions equivalent to those under Directive 85/611/EEC, or

(d) an entity that has, as its sole business, the issuing of asset-backed securities as defined in Article 2(5) of Commission Regulation (EC) No. 809/2004, or

(e) a credit institution within the meaning of Article 1(1) of Directive 2000/12/EC which satisfies the following conditions—

(i) its shares are not admitted to trading on a regulated market of any Member State within the meaning of point 14 of Article 4(1) of Directive 2004/39/EC,

(ii) it has, in a continuous or repeated manner, issued only debt securities, provided that the total nominal amount of all such debt securities remains below €100,000,000; and

(iii) it has not published a prospectus under Directive 2003/71/EC.

(10) An entity that avails itself of the exemption under paragraph (9)(d) shall, by means of a statement to that effect included—

(a) in any annual report published by it; or

(b) in an annual return or other periodic statement delivered by it to the competent authority with registration functions or the Irish Financial Services Regulatory Authority,

set forth the reasons for why it considers the establishment of an audit committee by it is not appropriate and, accordingly, why it has availed itself of that exemption.

(11) Paragraph (7) applies to a proposal of the board of directors (with respect to the appointment of a statutory auditor or audit firm to the public- interest entity) made at any time after the establishment of the audit committee in respect of the entity.

(12) The other provisions of this Regulation with regard to the exercise of any power or the carrying out of any duty by, or in relation to, the audit committee apply with respect to accounts of the public-interest entity for financial years beginning on or after the establishment of the audit committee in respect of the entity.

Amendments

a Subparagraphs (3)–(5) substituted and sub-para (5A) inserted by EC(SA)R 2011, reg 2.

PART 10

REGULATORY ARRANGEMENTS BETWEEN MEMBER STATES CHAPTER 1 COOPERATION WITH OTHER MEMBER STATES

92 Cooperation with other Member States

(1) With regard to the cooperation that the State is required to engage in by virtue of Article 33 (cooperation between public oversight systems at Community level) of the Directive, the competent authority with supervisory and other functions is assigned the responsibility in that behalf.

(2) For the purpose of discharging that responsibility, that competent authority shall put in place appropriate mechanisms, including arrangements with competent authorities in other Member States.

93 Specific requirements with regard to cooperation

(1) In this Regulation "counterpart authorities in other Member States" means competent authorities in other Member States with responsibilities corresponding to those of the competent authorities under these Regulations with regard to approval, registration, quality assurance, inspection and discipline.

(2) The competent authorities under these Regulations responsible for approval, registration, quality assurance, inspection and discipline shall cooperate with the counterpart authorities in other Member States whenever necessary for the purpose of those competent authorities (or, as the case may be, the counterpart authorities) carrying out their respective responsibilities under these Regulations or, as the case may be, the laws of the other Member State concerned that implement the Directive.

(3) The competent authorities under these Regulations with the foregoing responsibilities shall render assistance to the counterpart authorities in other Member States and, in particular, shall exchange information and co-operate with them in investigations related to the carrying out of statutory audits.

94 Confidentiality of information

(1) No person shall disclose, except in accordance with law, information that—

- (a) is obtained in performing the functions, under any provision of these Regulations, of any of the competent authorities under these Regulations; and
- (b) has not otherwise come to the notice of members of the public.

(2) A person who contravenes paragraph (1) is guilty of an offence and is liable—

- (a) on summary conviction, to a fine not exceeding €5,000, or
- (b) on conviction on indictment, to a fine not exceeding €12,500 or imprisonment for a term not exceeding 12 months or both.

95 Supplemental provisions in relation to Regulation 94

Without limiting Regulation 94, the persons to whom that Regulation applies include the following:

- (a) a member or director or former member or director of any board or committee, howsoever called, of any competent authority referred to in that Regulation;
- (b) an employee or former employee of any such competent authority; and
- (c) a professional or other advisor to any such competent authority, including a former advisor.

96 Obligation to supply information required for certain purposes and saving concerning confidential information

(1) Each of the competent authorities under these Regulations shall, on request and without undue delay, supply any information required for the purpose referred to in Regulation 93.

(2) Regulation 94 shall not prevent any of those competent authorities from complying with any such request or exchanging confidential information.

97 Obligation of competent authority to gather information

(1) Where necessary, each of the competent authorities under these Regulations, on receiving any request referred to in Regulation 96(1), shall, without undue delay, take the necessary measures to gather the required information.

(2) If a competent authority of whom such a request is made is not able to supply, without undue delay, the required information, it shall notify the competent authority in the other Member State that made the request of—

(a) the fact of the delay; and

(b) the reasons therefor.

98 Application of Regulation 94 to certain information

Regulation 94 shall apply to information received by each of the competent authorities under these Regulations pursuant to the cooperation or exchange of information that is required of competent authorities of Member States by Article 36 of the Directive.

99 Requesting authority to be notified if its request not complied with

(1) If—

(a) a competent authority of whom a request referred to in Regulation 96(1) is made does not comply with the request; and

(b) the case is neither—

(i) just one of a delay in complying with the request to which Regulation 97(2) relates; nor

(ii) one of a refusal to comply with the request on any of the grounds referred to in Regulation 100,

the competent authority shall notify the competent authority in the other Member State that made the request of the reasons for that failure to comply.

(2) If the competent authority referred to in subparagraph (a) of paragraph (1) is not the competent authority with supervisory and other functions, it shall also notify that competent authority of the reasons for the failure referred to in that paragraph.

100 Grounds for refusing request for information

(1) A competent authority may refuse to comply with a request referred to in Regulation 96(1) if, in its opinion—

(a) there are reasonable grounds for believing that supplying the information concerned might adversely affect—

(i) public order,

(ii) the security of the State,

(iii) the defence of the State, or

(iv) the international relations of the State, or

(b) proceedings in any court in the State have already been initiated in respect of the same actions and against the same statutory auditor or audit firm, the subject of the request; or

(c) a final determination has already been made by the competent authority in respect of the same actions and the same statutory auditor or audit firm, the subject of the request.

(2) If the competent authority referred to in paragraph (1) is not the competent authority with supervisory and other functions, it shall not exercise the power thereunder to refuse to comply with a request save after consultation with that competent authority.

(3) A competent authority that refuses, under paragraph (1), to comply with a request shall notify the competent authority in the other Member State that made the request of the reasons for the refusal.

(4) If the first-mentioned competent authority in paragraph (3) is not the competent authority with supervisory and other functions, it shall also notify that competent authority of the reasons for the refusal referred to in that paragraph.

101 Use to which information may be put

(1) In this Regulation "relevant information" means information that any of the competent authorities under these Regulations receives pursuant to the cooperation or exchange of information that is required of competent authorities of Member States by Article 36 of the Directive.

(2) Each of the competent authorities under these Regulations may use relevant information only for the performance by it of its functions under these Regulations and then only in the context of steps it takes in—

(a) investigating and detecting failures to comply with these Regulations; and

(b) initiating and employing disciplinary procedures, or maintaining proceedings in any court, in respect of any such failures.

(3) Paragraph (2) is without prejudice to any obligations, by virtue of any proceedings being maintained in any court, to which a competent authority is subject as regards the use to which it may put information referred to in that paragraph.

102 References in Regulations 103 to 105 to counterpart authority

(1) References in Regulations 103 to 105 to a counterpart authority in another Member State shall be construed in accordance with Regulation 93.

103 Counterpart authority to be notified of non-compliance with Directive

Where any of the competent authorities under these Regulations forms, on reasonable grounds, the opinion that activities contrary to the provisions of the Directive are being, or have been, carried on on the territory of another Member State, it shall, as soon as possible—

(a) notify the counterpart authority in the other Member State of that opinion; and

(b) include in that notification specific details of the matter and the grounds for its opinion.

104 Counterpart authority may be requested to carry out investigation

(1) In relation to activities that it suspects have been, or are being, carried on contrary to the provisions of the Directive, any of the competent authorities under these Regulations may request a counterpart authority in another Member State to carry out an investigation in the territory of that Member State.

(2) Such a request of a counterpart authority may be accompanied by a further request that one or more of the officers, or members of staff, of the requesting authority be allowed to accompany officers, or members of staff, of the counterpart authority in the course of the investigation.

(3) If the competent authority referred to in paragraph (1) is not the competent authority with supervisory and other functions, it shall notify that competent authority of the making of the request referred to in that paragraph and, if such be the case, the making of the further request referred to in paragraph (2).

105 Duty of competent authority to take certain action

(1) Where any of the competent authorities under these Regulations receives a notification from—

(a) the entity specifically responsible, pursuant to the laws of another Member State that implement Article 36 of the Directive, for ensuring the cooperation referred to in that Article, or

(b) the counterpart authority in another Member State,

that activities contrary to the provisions of the Directive are being, or have been, carried on in the State, it shall take appropriate action under these Regulations or the Act of 2003, as the case may be.

(2) The competent authority shall inform the notifying entity or authority of the outcome of that action, and to the extent possible, of significant developments in the period pending that outcome.

(3) If the competent authority referred to in paragraph (1) is not the competent authority with supervisory and other functions, it shall—

(a) notify that competent authority of the taking by it of the action referred to in that paragraph; and

(b) in addition to so informing, under paragraph (2), the notifying entity or authority of those matters, inform that competent authority of the outcome of that action, and to the extent possible, of significant developments in the period pending that outcome.

106 Due consideration to be given to counterparty's request for investigation

(1) Each of the competent authorities under these Regulations shall give due consideration to a request made of it, pursuant to the laws of another Member State that implement Article 36 of the Directive, to carry out an investigation in the State.

(2) If the request is acceded to by the competent authority, the investigation shall be subject to—

(a) the overall control of the competent authority; and

(b) unless the competent authority is the competent authority with supervisory and other functions, the supervision of the competent authority with supervisory and other functions.

(3) For the purpose of this Regulation—

(a) the reference in paragraph (1) to a request that is made pursuant to the laws of another Member State that implement Article 36 of the Directive is a reference to such a request, whether or not it is accompanied by a further request (made pursuant to those laws) that one or more of the officers, or members of staff, of the requesting authority be allowed to accompany officers, or members of staff, of the competent authority in the course of the investigation, and

(b) the investigation is subject to the control as mentioned in paragraph (2) even if that further request is acceded to by the competent authority.

(4) If the competent authority referred to in paragraph (1) is not the competent authority with supervisory and other functions, it shall notify that competent authority—

(a) of the making of a request of it referred to in that paragraph; and

(b) if the request is acceded to by it, of the fact of the request being so acceded to.

107 Grounds for refusing request for investigation

(1) Each of the competent authorities under these Regulations may refuse to accede to a request referred toin Regulation 106(1) made of it or a further request of the kind referred to in Regulation 106(3)(a) made of it if, in its opinion—

(a) there are reasonable grounds for believing that acceding to the request might adversely affect—

(i) public order,

(ii) the security of the State,

(iii) the defence of the State,or

(iv) the international relations of the State, or

(b) proceedings in any court in the State have already been initiated in respect of the same actions and against the same statutory auditor or audit firm, the subject of the request; or

(c) a final determination has already been made by the competent authority in respect of the same actions and the same statutory auditor or audit firm, the subject of the request.

(2) If the competent authority referred to in paragraph (1) is not the competent authority with supervisory and other functions, it shall not exercise the power thereunder to refuse to accede to a request save after consultation with that competent authority.

(3) A competent authority that refuses, under paragraph (1), to accede to a request shall notify the competent authority in the other Member State that made the request of the reasons for the refusal.

(4) If the first-mentioned competent authority in paragraph (3) is not the competent authority with supervisory and other functions, it shall also notify that competent authority of the reasons for the refusal referred to in that paragraph.

Chapter 2

Mutual recognition of regulatory arrangements between Member States

108 Article 34 of the Directive — clarification of preceding Regulations' effect

To the extent that the preceding provisions of these Regulations do not operate to achieve the following effects in the law of the State, these Regulations operate, and those preceding provisions (notwithstanding anything in them to the contrary) shall be construed as operating, in a manner so that—

(a) the principle set out in Article 34(1) of the Directive is respected, and

(b) the imposition of additional requirements of the kind referred to in Article 34(2) and (3) of the Directive is prohibited.

Chapter 3
Transfer of working papers to third-country competent authorities

109 Transfer of audit documentation to third-country competent authority

(1) Subject to Regulation 110, audit working papers or other documents held by a statutory auditor or audit firm may be transferred to a third-country competent authority only if the competent authority with supervisory and other functions, on a request being made of it in that behalf by the first-mentioned authority, determines that the following conditions are complied with (and authorises such transfer accordingly), namely—

(a) those audit working papers or other documents relate to the audit of a company which—

(i) has issued securities in the third country concerned, or

(ii) forms part of a group of companies that issue statutory consolidated accounts in the third country concerned;

(b) the third-country competent authority meets requirements which have been declared adequate in accordance with Article 47(3) of the Directive;

(c) there are working arrangements on the basis of reciprocity agreed between the competent authority with supervisory and other functions and the third-country competent authority; and

(d) the transfer of personal data to the third country concerned is in accordance with Chapter IV of Directive 95/46/EC.

(2) The working arrangements referred to in paragraph (1)(c) shall ensure that:

(a) justification as to the purpose of the request for audit working papers and other documents is provided by the third-country competent authority concerned;

(b) the audit working papers and other documents are only transferred if—

(i) an obligation similar to that provided by Regulation 94 is provided under the laws of the third country concerned in relation to persons whilst in, and in any period subsequent to their ceasing to be in, the employment of the third-country competent authority;

(ii) the relevant persons in the employment of the third-country competent authority that will deal with the matter provide an undertaking in writing to the competent authority with supervisory and other functions that they—

(I) will comply with their obligation referred to in clause (i), and

(II) deliver up possession of the audit working papers and other documents to the third-country competent authority, and do everything within their power to secure the return of them by that authority to the competent authority with supervisory and other functions, once the performance of the functions referred to in subparagraph (c) in relation to them is completed;

(c) the third-country competent authority uses audit working papers and other documents only for the performance of its functions of public oversight, quality assurance and investigations that meet requirements equivalent to those of Articles 29, 30 and 32 of the Directive;

(d) the request from a third-country competent authority for audit working papers or other documents held by a statutory auditor or audit firm can be refused by the competent authority with supervisory and other functions:

(i) where the provision of those working papers or documents would adversely affect the sovereignty of the Community or any of the following—

(I) public order (whether in the State or elsewhere in the Community),

(II) the security of the State or the Community,

(III) the defence of the State or the Community, or

(IV) the international relations of the State or the Community, or

(ii) where proceedings in any court in the State have already been initiated in respect of the same actions and against the same persons.

(3) The competent authority with supervisory and other functions has, for the purposes of the performance of its functions under the preceding paragraphs (including the taking of any steps that necessitate the perusal by it of the papers and other documents concerned so as to determine whether the transfer should be refused on any of the grounds referred to in paragraph (2)(d)), the following power.

(4) That power is to require the statutory auditor or audit firm concerned to produce to it the audit working papers and other documents; the statutory auditor or audit firm shall comply with such a requirement made of him, her or it by the competent authority with supervisory and other functions.

(5) As soon as may be after—

(a) if such a determination is made, the making by the competent authority with supervisory and other functions of a determination that the transfer of the papers and other documents be refused on any of the grounds referred to in paragraph (2)(d); or

(b) the papers and other documents are returned by the third-country competent authority to it,

the competent authority with supervisory and other functions shall secure the return to the statutory auditor or audit firm concerned of the audit working papers and other documents.

110 Derogation from Regulation 109 in exceptional cases

By way of derogation from Regulation 109, the competent authority with supervisory and other functions may, in exceptional cases, allow a statutory auditor or audit firm to transfer audit working papers and other documents directly to a third-country competent authority, provided that:

(a) an investigation has been initiated by that competent authority in the third country concerned;

(b) the transfer does not conflict with the obligations with which statutory auditors and audit firms are required to comply in relation to the transfer of audit working papers and other documents to the competent authorities;

(c) there are working arrangements with the third-country competent authority of a reciprocal nature that allow the competent authority with supervisory and other functions direct access to audit working papers and other documents of audit entities in the third country concerned;

(d) the third-country competent authority informs in advance the competent authority with supervisory and other functions of each direct request for information, indicating the reasons therefor;

and

(e) conditions similar to those specified in Regulation 109(2)(a) to (d) are satisfied.

111 Particulars of working arrangements to be notified

(1) Where the competent authority with supervisory and other functions enters into working arrangements with a third-country competent authority in accordance with Regulation 109(1)(c), particulars of those working arrangements shall be published by the first-mentioned competent authority without delay and those particulars shall include—

(a) the name of the third-country competent authority; and

(b) the jurisdiction in which it is established.

(2) Particulars of those working arrangements shall also be notified by the competent authority with supervisory and other functions to the Commission.

PART 11
THIRD-COUNTRY AUDITORS

Chapter 1
International Aspects

112 Approval of third-country auditor

(1) Without prejudice to Chapter 2 of Part 4, a competent authority may approve a third-country auditor as a statutory auditor if that person has furnished proof that he or she complies with requirements equivalent to those specified in Articles 4 and 6 to 13 of the Directive, but this is subject to paragraph (2).

(2) A third-country auditor shall not be approved under paragraph (1) unless reciprocal arrangements with the third country in question are in place, that is to say arrangements that enable—

(a) by virtue of the law of that third country, and

(b) on fulfilment by the statutory auditor concerned of requirements no more onerous than those specified by this Regulation and Chapter 2 of Part 4 for the third-country auditor's approval under paragraph (1), a statutory auditor to carry out audits in that third country.

Chapter 2
Registration and oversight of third-country auditors and audit entities

113 Registration of third-country auditors and audit entities

(1) Subject to paragraphs (5) and (6) and Regulation 119, the competent authority with supervisory and other functions shall, in accordance with the relevant provisions of Part 6 and Schedule 1, cause to be registered in the public register (within the meaning of that Part) every third-country auditor and audit entity that indicates, in writing, to that

competent authority his, her or its intention to provide an audit report concerning the annual or group accounts of a company falling within paragraph (2).

(2) The company referred to in paragraph (1) is one—

(a) incorporated outside the Community, not being a collective investment undertaking; and

(b) whose transferable securities are admitted to trading on a regulated market (within the meaning of point 14 of Article 4(1) of Directive 2004/39/EC) in the State.

(3) There shall accompany the written indication by a third-country auditor or audit entity referred to in paragraph (1) a notification, in such form and manner as that competent authority specifies, of the following information (in relation to the auditor or audit entity) to the competent authority with supervisory and other functions.

(4) That information is the information referred to in paragraph 3 of Schedule 1 but does not include the information referred to in paragraph 1(b) or 2(b) (as applied by that paragraph 3) of that Schedule.

(5) Paragraph (1) does not apply if the company referred to in that paragraph is an issuer exclusively of debt securities admitted to trading on a regulated market in a Member State within the meaning of Article 2(1)(b) of Directive 2004/109/EC, the denomination per unit of which is at least €50,000 or, in case of debt securities denominated in another currency, equivalent, at the date of issue, to at least €50,000.

(6) Paragraph (1) does not apply in respect of an audit report—

(a) for a financial year referred to in Regulation 4(a) of the European Communities (Transitional Period Measures in Respect of Third Country Auditors) Regulations 2009 (S.I. No. 229 of 2009) if the audit report is provided by a third-country auditor or audit entity that complies with Regulation 4 of those Regulations; or

(b) provided by a third-country auditor or audit entity before the date that is 3 months after the date of the making of these Regulations.

(7) Regulation 66 shall apply to third-country auditors and audit entities so registered with the substitution of references to the competent authority with supervisory and other functions for references to the competent authority and any other necessary modifications.

(8) Regulation 67 shall apply, with the necessary modifications, to a notification of information by a third-country auditor or audit entity under—

(a) paragraph (3) to the competent authority with supervisory and other functions; and

(b) Regulation 66, as applied by paragraph (7), to that competent authority.

(9) In paragraph (2) "collective investment undertaking" does not include such an undertaking of the closed-ended type.

114 Application of Part 8 to registered third-country auditors and audit entities

(1) Subject to paragraph (2), Part 8 shall apply to a third-country auditor or audit entity registered under Part 6 in pursuance of Regulation 113.

(2) A third-country auditor or audit entity registered under Part 6 in pursuance of Regulation 113 may apply to the competent authority with supervisory and other functions for an exemption from Chapter 2 of Part 8 if a quality assurance review has, under another Member State's or third country's system of quality assurance, been carried out in relation to the auditor or audit entity during the 3 years preceding the making of the application.

(3) On the making of that application if—

(a) the competent authority with supervisory and other functions is satisfied that the quality assurance review referred to in paragraph (2) has been carried out as mentioned in that paragraph; and

(b) the system of quality assurance referred to in that paragraph has been assessed as equivalent in accordance with Regulation 119,

that competent authority shall grant the exemption and the third-country auditor or audit entity shall be exempted from Chapter 2 of Part 8 accordingly.

115 Audit by non-registered auditor or audit entity — consequence

Without prejudice to Regulation 119 and unless Regulation 113(5) or (6) applies to it, an audit report provided by a third-country auditor or audit entity concerning the annual or group accounts of a company falling within Regulation 113(2) shall have no legal effect in the State if the third-country auditor or audit entity that provides it is not registered under Part 6.

116 Conditions for registration of third-country auditor or audit entity

The competent authority with supervisory and other functions may cause to be registered a third-country auditor or audit entity pursuant to Regulation 113 only if—

(a) where the applicant for registration is an audit entity (referred to in this Regulation as the "potential registrant"), the applicant satisfies so much of the conditions specified hereafter in this Regulation as are applicable to an entity, and

(b) where the applicant for registration is an auditor (also referred to in this Regulation as the "potential registrant"), the applicant satisfies so much of the conditions specified hereafter in this Regulation as are applicable to an individual,

namely—

(i) the potential registrant meets requirements equivalent to those of Articles 4 and 6 to 10 of the Directive;

(ii) the majority of the members of the administrative or management body of the potential registrant meet requirements equivalent to those of Articles 4 and 6 to 10 of the Directive;

(iii) the third-country auditor carrying out the audit on behalf of the potential registrant meets requirements equivalent to those of Articles 4 and 6 to 10 of the Directive;

(iv) the audits of the annual or group accounts referred to in Regulation 113(1) are carried out in accordance with international auditing standards as referred to in

Regulation 54, as well as the requirements referred to in Regulation 41, or with equivalent standards and requirements;

(v) the potential registrant publishes annually on a website, being a website maintained by or on behalf of the potential registrant, a report which includes the information referred to in Regulations 59 and 61 in relation to the year concerned or the potential registrant complies with equivalent disclosure requirements.

117 Competent authority with supervisory and other functions may assess matter of equivalence for purposes of Regulation 116(iv) in certain circumstances

For so long as the Commission has not taken, in accordance with the procedure referred to in Article 48(2) of the Directive, the decision under Article 45(6) thereof in relation to the matter of equivalence of standards and requirements mentioned in Regulation 116(iv), the competent authority with supervisory and other functions may, for the purposes of that provision, make an assessment of that equivalence.

118 Certain fees chargeable by competent authority with supervisory and other functions

(1) The competent authority with supervisory and other functions may charge and impose a fee (of an amount specified from time to time by the Minister sufficient to cover the authority's administrative expenses in respect of the following) on a third-country auditor or audit entity referred to in Regulation 113(1) in respect of—

(a) the registration; and

(b) the oversight, the quality assurance and the related matters of investigation, discipline and penalties,

effected or provided in relation to the auditor or audit entity under and in accordance with these Regulations.

(2) A fee imposed under paragraph (1) may, in default of payment, be recovered from the third-country auditor or audit entity concerned as a simple contract debt in any court of competent jurisdiction.

119 Exemptions in case of equivalence

(1) A third-country auditor or audit entity may apply to the competent authority with supervisory and other functions for an exemption from all or any of the provisions of Regulations 113 and 114 on the basis that the third-country auditor or audit entity is subject to systems of public oversight, quality assurance and investigations and penalties in the third country concerned that meet requirements equivalent to those of Part 8.

(2) On the making of that application if—

(a) the Commission has, in accordance with Article 46(2) of the Directive, assessed the systems referred to in paragraph (1) as meeting requirements equivalent to those in the corresponding provisions of the Directive; and

(b) the competent authority with supervisory and other functions is satisfied that the law of the third country concerned affords reciprocal rights to a statutory auditor or audit firm with regard to being granted corresponding exemptions under that law, that competent authority shall grant an exemption from all or any, as it considers appropriate, of the provisions of Regulations 113 and 114 and the third-country auditor or audit entity shall be exempted accordingly.

(3) The competent authority with supervisory and other functions shall notify the Commission of the main elements of its cooperative arrangements with systems of public oversight, quality assurance and investigations and penalties of the third country concerned, arising out of arrangements it has entered into with that third country for the purposes of the reciprocity mentioned in paragraph (2)(b).

PART 12
MISCELLANEOUS

120 Disclosure of auditors' remuneration, etc. in accounts

(1) [...][a].

(2) The amendment effected by this Regulation applies to accounts (whether individual or consolidated) for financial years ending on or after the date falling 3 months after the date of the making of these Regulations.

Amendments

a Regulation 120(1) inserts CA 1963, s 161D.

121 Saving for disciplinary proceedings in being

(1) None of the provisions of these Regulations (and, in particular, those amending the Act of 1990 or the Act of 2003) affect disciplinary proceedings in being before the commencement of these Regulations by a recognised accountancy body against any of its members and, accordingly, those proceedings may be continued on after that commencement by that body against the member or members concerned.

(2) If, as a result of such proceedings in relation to a foregoing person, the practising certificate (within the meaning of Part X of the Act of 1990) of the person is withdrawn by the body concerned or the person's membership of the body is terminated by it, then any deemed approval of the person as a statutory auditor or audit firm by virtue of Regulation 25(1) or 27(4) ceases to have effect.

(3) Where the result of the proceedings concerned is not either of those mentioned in paragraph (2), the powers of the competent authority with supervisory and other functions under section 24 of the Act of 2003 are available to that authority, and may be exercised by it, in relation to the matters, the subject of those proceedings, and the provisions of that section 24 that shall apply for that purpose are those provisions as they stand amended by these Regulations but subject to paragraph (4).

(4) The provisions of that section 24, the basis of which is that it is the law as it stands after the making of these Regulations that governs the disqualification of auditors and audit firms from being able to carry out statutory audits, shall be read subject to such modifications so that the provisions operate on the basis of the law with respect to those matters as it stood before that making and in particular that—

(a) there are no circumstances, under the law as it stands before that making, in which it is mandatory for a recognised accountancy body, by withdrawing a practising certificate (within the meaning of Part X of the Act of 1990) or terminating a person's membership of the body, to disqualify an auditor or audit firm from being able to carry out statutory audits; and

(b) the standards by reference to which it is determined whether a breach of the kind referred to in subsection (2) of that section 24 has occurred on the part of the auditor or audit firm concerned are those that would have been used for that purpose before that making,

but nothing in this paragraph prejudices the application of the provisions of these Regulations referred to in subsection (11B) of that section 24 in the event that the competent authority with supervisory and other functions withdraws, on foot of its investigation under that section, the approval of the person or firm as a statutory auditor or audit firm.

SCHEDULE 1

INFORMATION REQUIRED, BY PART 6, TO BE SUPPLIED AND ENTERED IN PUBLIC REGISTER

Statutory auditors

1. In relation to a statutory auditor, the register required to be maintained by Regulation 63 shall contain at least the following information:

(a) the name and address of the auditor;

(b) the number under which the auditor is entered in that register;

(c) if applicable—

(i) the name and address and the website address (if any) of the statutory audit firm by which the auditor is employed, or with whom he or she is associated as a partner or otherwise; and

(ii) the number under which that statutory audit firm is entered in that register;

(d) the name and address of the competent authority responsible for the regulation of the auditor;

(e) if he or she is so registered with one or more such authorities—

(i) particulars of his or her registration—

(I) as a statutory auditor, with each competent authority of another Member State and the name of the authority; and

(II) as auditor, with one or more third-country competent authorities and the name or names of it or them;

and

(ii) the number under which he or she is registered with each such authority;

(f) without prejudice to subparagraph (e), with regard to the auditor's status (if such be the case) as a Member State statutory auditor, the name and address of each competent authority responsible, in relation to him or her, for—

(i) approval as referred to in Article 3 of the Directive,

(ii) quality assurance as referred to in Article 29 of the Directive,

(iii) investigations, discipline and penalties as referred to in Article 30 of the Directive, and

(iv) public oversight as referred to in Article 32 of the Directive.

Statutory audit firms

2. In relation to a statutory audit firm, the register required to be maintained by Regulation 63 shall contain at least the following information:

(a) the name and address of the audit firm;

(b) the number under which the audit firm is entered in that register;

(c) the legal form of the audit firm;

(d) the primary contact person in the audit firm and contact details;

(e) the address of each office in the State of the audit firm and the website address (if any) of the audit firm;

(f) the name of every individual employed by or associated as partner or otherwise with the audit firm who is approved as statutory auditor under Part 3;

(g) the number under which that individual is entered in the register;

(h) the name and address of the competent authority responsible for the regulation of the audit firm;

(i) the names and addresses of the owners of, or as appropriate, shareholders in, the audit firm;

(j) the names and addresses of the directors, or other members of, as appropriate—

(i) the board of directors,

(ii) board of management, or

(iii) other administrative or management body,

of the audit firm — but where the audit firm comprises a partnership with no management structure, the provision of the address of each individual named, under subparagraph (f), as partner suffices;

(k) if applicable — the fact of the audit firm's membership of a network and either—

(i) a list of the names and addresses of member firms and affiliates of the network or,

(ii) an indication of where such information is publicly available;

(l) if the audit firm is so registered with one or more such authorities—

(i) particulars of the firm's registration—

(I) as a statutory audit firm, with each competent authority of another Member State and the name of the authority; and

(II) as an audit firm, with one or more third-country competent authorities and the name or names of it or them;

and

(ii) the number under which the firm is registered with each such authority;

(m) without prejudice to subparagraph (l), with regard to the audit firm's status (if such be the case) as a Member State statutory audit firm, the name and address of each competent authority responsible, in relation to it, for—

(i) approval as referred to in Article 3 of the Directive,

(ii) quality assurance as referred to in Article 29 of the Directive,

(iii) investigations, discipline and penalties as referred to in Article 30 of the Directive, and

(iv) public oversight as referred to in Article 32 of the Directive.

Third-country auditors and audit entities

3. (1) In relation to the case provided by Regulation 113 of the registration of a third-country auditor or audit entity, the register required to be maintained by Regulation 63 shall contain at least the information specified in the provisions of paragraph 1 or, as the case may be, 2 (as, in either case, those provisions are applied by subparagraph (2)).

(2) The provisions of paragraph 1 or 2, as the case may be, apply for the purposes of this paragraph save so much of them as are inapplicable in the case of a third-country auditor or audit entity, as appropriate.

Individual identification number and storage of information in electronic form

4. (1) There shall be assigned an individual identification number to each individual, firm and entity that is being entered in the register required to be maintained by Regulation 63, being—

(a) in a case where the information entered in respect of the individual or firm is that provided under Regulation 64, the number notified under paragraph (2)(b)(i) of that Regulation to the competent authority with registration functions;

(b) in any other case, such individual identification number as, subject to subparagraph (2), is determined and allocated by the competent authority with registration functions,

and references in paragraphs 1 and 2 to the number under which any of the foregoing persons is entered in the register shall be read as references to that identification number.

(2) Instead of its allocating a number for the purposes of subparagraph (1)(b) that has been determined by it, the competent authority with registration functions may—

(a) in specifying under any provision of these Regulations the form in which information is to be notified to it for registration (and the provision concerned of these Regulations doesn't itself provide for the notification of such a number), include in that specification a requirement that the form, as completed, include an identification number allocated to the subject of the notification by the notifier of the information; and

(b) if the number so provided in that form is satisfactory for the purpose of distinguishing the subject from other registrants, allocate, for the purposes of subparagraph (1)(b), that number so provided.

(3) The information contained in that register shall be stored in electronic form and be capable of being accessed by members of the public by electronic means.

Definition of "address"

5. In this Schedule "address", in relation to an individual, firm or entity, means the individual's or the firm's or entity's usual business address.

SCHEDULE 2

STANDARDS RELATING TO TRAINING AND QUALIFICATIONS FOR APPROVAL OF NATURAL PERSON AS STATUTORY AUDITOR

1. A natural person shall have attained university entrance or equivalent level and then—

(a) completed a course of theoretical instruction;

(b) undergone practical training; and

(c) passed an examination of professional competence of university final or equivalent examination level in the State.

2. (1) The examination of professional competence referred to in paragraph 1 shall be such as guarantees the necessary level of theoretical knowledge of subjects relevant to statutory audit and the ability to apply such knowledge in practice. Part at least of that examination shall be written.

(2) The test of theoretical knowledge included in the examination shall cover the following subjects in particular:

(a) general accounting theory and principles;

(b) legal requirements and standards relating to the preparation of annual and consolidated accounts;

(c) international accounting standards;

(d) financial analysis;

(e) cost and management accounting;

(f) risk management and internal control;

(g) auditing and professional skills;

(h) legal requirements and professional standards relating to statutory audit and statutory auditors;

(i) international auditing standards;

(j) professional ethics and independence.

(3) The examination shall also cover at least the following subjects in so far as they are relevant to auditing:

(a) company law and corporate governance;

(b) the law of insolvency and similar procedures;

(c) tax law;

(d) civil and commercial law;

(e) social security law and employment law;

(f) information technology and computer systems;

(g) business, general and financial economics;

(h) mathematics and statistics;

(i) basic principles of the financial management of undertakings.

3. (1) In order to ensure the ability to apply theoretical knowledge in practice, a test of which is included in the examination, a trainee shall complete a minimum of 3 years' practical training in, inter alia, the auditing of annual accounts, consolidated accounts or similar financial statements. At least two thirds of such practical training shall be completed with a statutory auditor or audit firm approved in any Member State.

(2) All such training shall be carried out with persons who the competent authority is satisfied possess, to an adequate standard, the ability to provide practical training.

GIVEN under my Official Seal, 20 May 2010.

BATT O'KEEFFE,

Minister for Enterprise, Trade and Innovation.

EXPLANATORY NOTE

(This note is not part of the Instrument and does not purport to be a legal interpretation.)

These Regulations give effect to Directive 2006/43/EC of the European Parliament and of the Council of 17 May 2006 on statutory audits of annual accounts and consolidated accounts, amending Council Directives 78/660/EEC on the annual accounts of certain types of companies and 83/349/EEC on consolidated accounts and repealing Council Directive 84/253/EEC on the approval of persons responsible for carrying out the statutory audits of accounting documents.

Rules of the Superior Courts (Derivative Actions) 2010

SI 503/2010

We, the Superior Courts Rules Committee, constituted pursuant to the provisions of the Courts of Justice Act 1936, section 67, by virtue of the powers conferred upon us by the Courts of Justice Act 1924, section 36, and the Courts of Justice Act 1936, section 68 (as applied by the Courts (Supplemental Provisions) Act, 1961 section 48), and the Courts (Supplemental Provisions) Act 1961, section 14, and of all other powers enabling us in this behalf, do hereby make the following Rules of Court.

Dated this 17th day of June 2010.

1. (1) These Rules, which may be cited as the Rules of the Superior Courts (Derivative Actions) 2010, shall come into operation on the 16th day of November 2010.

(2) These Rules shall be construed together with the Rules of the Superior Courts.

(3) The Rules of the Superior Courts as amended by these Rules may be cited as the Rules of the Superior Courts 1986 to 2010.

2. The Rules of the Superior Courts are amended by the insertion immediately following rule 38 of Order 15 of the following title and rule:

"**IV. Derivative Actions**

39. (1) In this rule—

"company" has the same meaning as in section 2 of the Companies Act 1963;

"derivative action" includes any action in which a claim is made on behalf of a company by a member of that company.

(2) Subject to the provisions of this rule, a derivative action may not be commenced without the leave of the Court, given in accordance with this rule.

(3) An application for leave to commence a derivative action shall be made by Originating Notice of Motion in which is sought:

(a) the leave of the Court to commence the derivative action;

(b) where relevant, an order requiring the company to indemnify the applicant in respect of the whole or part of the costs and expenses reasonably incurred by the applicant in conducting the derivative action (including any costs for which the applicant may be made liable in such action), and

(c) any interim relief of an urgent nature.

(4) The Originating Notice of Motion shall be entitled "In the matter of an intended derivative action" on the application of the applicant. The company shall be named as a respondent.

(5) The Originating Notice of Motion shall be supported by an affidavit:

(i) setting out the nature and extent of the evidence available to support the applicant's claim to be a person entitled to bring the intended derivative action;

(ii) setting out the nature and extent of the evidence available to support the applicant's assertion that the company is entitled to make the claim to which the intended derivative action relates, and where such evidence is of an expert or technical nature, the substance of that evidence shall be provided to the Court in a report of a qualified person verified by its author and exhibited to the grounding affidavit, or in other suitable form;

(iii) setting out the basis of the deponent's belief as to the existence of the facts or circumstances referred to in paragraphs (i) and (ii);

(iv) specifying the efforts, if any, made by the applicant to cause the company to prosecute the claim concerned;

(v) setting out the basis on which it is alleged that it is reasonable and prudent in the interests of the company that the applicant be given leave to commence the intended derivative action;

(vi) including evidence, where available, of the views of members other than the applicant;

(vii) to which is exhibited an opinion of counsel as to whether the applicant has a realistic prospect of success in the intended derivative action; and

(viii) to which is exhibited a draft of the summons or other originating document, and a draft of any statement of claim, in the intended derivative action.

(6) Unless the Court otherwise directs, a respondent shall be served with copies of the Originating Notice of Motion, of the grounding affidavit and any exhibits thereto at least 21 days before the date first fixed for the hearing of the Originating Notice of Motion.

(7) Where the Court is satisfied on the ex parte application of the applicant that service of the Originating Notice of Motion would be likely to frustrate some party of a relief sought, the Court may hear and determine ex parte an application for some relief sought in the Originating Notice of Motion.

(8) A respondent who has been served with the Originating Notice of Motion and who intends to oppose the application may file in the Central Office a replying affidavit setting out his grounds of opposition and verifying any facts or circumstances relied on, and shall serve a copy of any such affidavit and any exhibits thereto on the applicant and on any other respondent not later than seven days before the return date of the Originating Notice of Motion.

(9) The applicant shall be at liberty to file a further affidavit replying to any matter verified in an affidavit of a respondent, in which event a copy of that affidavit shall be served upon the respondent before the return date of the Originating Notice of Motion.

(10) An affidavit giving the names and addresses of, and the places and dates of service on, all persons who have been served with the Originating Notice of Motion, grounding affidavit and exhibits (if any) shall be filed by the applicant before the motion is heard.

(11) On the return date of the Originating Notice of Motion (or on any adjournment from such date), the Court may, in addition to any other order it may make:

(a) direct service of notice of the application on any other member or other person, including mode of service and the time allowed for such service (and the Court may for that purpose adjourn the hearing or further hearing of the application to a date specified);

(b) give directions as to the filing and delivery of any further affidavits;

(c) make such orders and give such directions (including a direction that a meeting of members take place) as it considers appropriate for the purpose of ascertaining the views of members whose interest in the subject matter of the proposed derivative action is independent of that of the applicant and the respondent;

(d) where the court has directed in accordance with the preceding paragraph that a meeting of members shall take place, give directions as to the convening and conduct of the meeting and for the reporting to the Court of the proceedings at the meeting;

(e) give a direction that the application be determined by way of plenary hearing, where it appears to the Court that the subject matter of the application is likely to involve a substantial dispute of fact or it is otherwise necessary or desirable in the interests of justice (and the Court may for that purpose make orders and give directions in relation to the exchange of pleadings or points of claim or defence between the parties);

(f) give directions as to the furnishing by the parties to the Court and delivery of written submissions;

(g) give directions as to the publication of notice of the hearing of the application and the giving of notice in advance of such hearing to any person other than a party to the proceedings who desires to be heard on the hearing of the application;

(h) hear and determine any application for relief of an interlocutory nature, whether in the nature of an injunction or otherwise.

(12) Save where the Court otherwise directs, any evidence in proceedings to which this rule relates shall be given on affidavit.

(13) An order made on an application under sub-rule (3) may:

(a) give leave to commence a derivative action on such terms or conditions as the Court sees fit to impose;

(b) give leave to continue a derivative action only until the close of pleadings, the completion of discovery, or some other specified step in the proceedings or until a specified date, and require a further application for leave to continue the derivative action beyond that step or date;

(c) require the company for the benefit of which a derivative action is allowed to be brought to indemnify the applicant in respect of the whole or part of costs and expenses reasonably incurred by the applicant in conducting the derivative action (including any costs for which the applicant may be made liable in such action);

(d) order that the derivative action may not be discontinued or compromised without the leave of the Court;

(e) give such directions and include such orders for the conduct of the proceedings on the derivative action as appear convenient for the determination of those proceedings in a manner which is just, expeditious and likely to minimise the costs of those proceedings.

(14) Where a claim which might be the subject of a derivative action arises in proceedings pending before the Court, the provisions of this rule shall, with the necessary modifications, apply to such a claim, provided that the application referred to in sub-rule (2) may, in lieu of being brought by Originating Notice of Motion, be made by motion on notice in the pending proceedings, and the Court may make any order it considers just:

(a) dispensing with any requirement of this rule, where it considers it appropriate to do so having regard to the proceedings had in the pending proceedings; or

(b) as to the hearing of the application.

(15) An application for an order that the applicant be given conduct of proceedings and continue those proceedings as a derivative action shall be made by motion on notice in the proceedings concerned. The motion shall be grounded on an affidavit sworn by or on behalf of the moving party which shall:

(a) set out the grounds on which the applicant claims that the proceedings should continue as a derivative action, and verify any facts and circumstances relied on in that regard; and

(b) set out the nature and extent of the evidence available to support the applicant's claim to be a proper person to continue the proceedings as a derivative action.

(16) An application for an order substituting another person to have conduct of a derivative action shall be made by motion on notice in the proceedings on the derivative action. The motion shall be grounded on an affidavit sworn by or on behalf of the moving party which shall:

(a) set out the grounds on which the moving party claims such substitution is necessary or desirable, and verify any facts and circumstances relied on in that regard; and

(b) set out the nature and extent of the evidence available to support the claim that the person proposed to be substituted is a proper person to continue the proceedings as a derivative action.

(17) A member referred to in sub-rule (1) may apply for leave to defend on behalf of a company a claim or a counter-claim against such company, and the provisions of this rule other than this sub-rule shall, with the necessary modifications, apply to such an application.

(18) Where, in accordance with law, an action may be authorised by leave of the Court:

(a) in which a claim is made on behalf of a body corporate (which is not a company) by a member of that body; or

(b) in which a claim is made on behalf of an unincorporated association or body by a member of that association or body, the provisions of this rule shall, unless the Court otherwise directs or permits, apply mutatis mutandis to any application for leave to commence or to have conduct of such an action, to the proceedings on any such application and to the conduct of any such action for which leave is given as if the references in this rule to a "company" (and to its members) included references to the body corporate or unincorporated association or body concerned (and to its members).

EXPLANATORY NOTE

(This does not form part of the Instrument and does not purport to be a legal interpretation.)

These rules insert a new rule 39 in Order 15 of the Rules of the Superior Courts prescribing the procedure in respect of derivative actions in the High Court.

European Communities (Group Accounts) Regulations 2010

SI 606/2010

I, BATT O'KEEFFE, Minister for Enterprise, Trade and Innovation, in exercise of the powers conferred on me by section 3 of the European Communities Act 1972 (No. 27 of 1972) and for the purpose of giving effect to Directive 2009/49/EC of the European Parliament and of the Council of 18 June 2009 (OJ No. L164, 26.6.2009, p.42), amending Council Directives 78/660/EEC and 83/349/EEC as regards certain disclosure requirements for medium-sized companies and the obligation to draw up consolidated accounts, hereby make the following regulations:

Citation and construction

1. (1) These Regulations may be cited as the European Communities (Group Accounts) Regulations 2010.

(2) The Companies Acts and these Regulations shall be construed together as one.

Application

2. These Regulations apply to the preparation of annual accounts in the case of a company or undertaking the financial year of which commences on or after 1 January 2011.

Definition

3. In these Regulations "Regulations of 2005" means the European Communities (International Financial Reporting Standards and Miscellaneous Amendments) Regulations 2005 (S.I. No. 116 of 2005).

Amendment of section 150 of Companies Act 1963

4. Section 150 (amended by Regulation 4 of the Regulations of 2005) of the Companies Act 1963 (No. 33 of 1963) is amended—

(a) [...][a],

and

(b) [...][b].

Amendments

a Subsection (a) inserts CA 1963, s 150(1A).

b Subsection (b) substitutes CA 1963, s 150(10)(a).

Amendment of the European Communities (Insurance Undertakings: Accounts) Regulations

5. Regulation 10 of the European Communities (Insurance Undertakings: Accounts) Regulations 1996 (S.I. No. 23 of 1996) (amended by Regulation 11 and paragraph 7 of Schedule 3 to the Regulations of 2005) is amended by—

(a) [...][a],

and

(b) [...][b].

Amendments

a Subsection (a) substitutes EC(IUA)R 1996, r 10(1).

b Subsection (b) inserts EC(IUA)R 1996, r 10(1A).

GIVEN under my Official Seal,

16 December 2010.

BATT O'KEEFFE,

Minister for Enterprise, Trade and Innovation.

EXPLANATORY NOTE

(This note is not part of the Instrument and does not purport to be a legal interpretation.)

These Regulations give effect to Directive 2009/49/EC of the European Parliament and of the Council of 18 June 2009 amending Council Directives 78/660/EEC and 83/349/EEC as regards certain disclosure requirements for medium-sized companies and the obligation to draw up consolidated accounts.

The Directive was adopted in the context of the EU drive to reduce administrative burdens, particularly in the accounting and auditing area, and is aimed at small and medium-sized companies.

The Regulations provide that parent undertakings which only have nonmaterial subsidiaries are to be exempted from the requirement at Article 1(1) of Directive 83/349/EEC requiring the drawing up of consolidated accounts and a consolidated annual report.

European Communities (Mergers and Divisions of Companies) (Amendment) Regulations 2011

SI 306/2011

I, RICHARD BRUTON, Minister for Jobs, Enterprise and Innovation, in exercise of the powers conferred on me by section 3 of the European Communities Act 1972 (No. 27 of 1972) and for the purpose of giving further effect to Directive No. 2007/63/EC of the European Parliament and of the Council of 13 November 2007 (O.J. No. L 300, 17.11.2007, p.47) and effect to Directive No. 2009/109/EC of the European Parliament and of the Council of 16 September 2009 (O.J. No. L 259, 2.10.2009, p.14), hereby make the following regulations:

Citation, construction and commencement

1.(1) These Regulations may be cited as the European Communities (Mergers and Divisions of Companies) (Amendment) Regulations 2011.

(2) The Companies Acts and these Regulations shall be construed together as one.

(3) Subject to paragraph (4), these Regulations come into operation on 30 June 2011.

(4) Notwithstanding Regulation 4(a) and Regulation 5(d), section 30(2)(b) of the Act of 1983 and Regulation 10 of the Regulations of 1987 continue to apply to a proposed merger in respect of which the date of the draft terms of merger or of the common draft terms as the case may be is prior to 30 June 2011.

Interpretation

2. In these Regulations—

"Act of 1983" means the Companies (Amendment) Act 1983 (No. 13 of 1983);

"Regulations of 1987" means the European Communities (Mergers and Divisions of Companies) Regulations 1987 (S.I. No. 137 of 1987).

Amendment of Section 2 of Act of 1983

3. The Act of 1983 is amended in subsection (1) of section 2 by inserting the following definitions:

"'Regulations of 1987' means the European Communities (Mergers and Divisions of Companies) Regulations 1987 (S.I. No. 137 of 1987);

'Regulations of 2008' means the European Communities (Cross-Border Mergers) Regulations 2008 (S.I. No. 157 of 2008);".

Amendment of Section 30 of Act of 1983

4 Section 30 of the Act of 1983 is amended—

(a) in subsection (2), by deleting paragraph (b),

(b) in subsection (4), by substituting "(5A)" for "(2)(b)",

(c) in subsection (5), by substituting “Subject to subsection (5A), the valuation and report required by subsection (1)” for “The valuation and report required by subsection (1)”, and

(d) [...][a].

Amendments

a Subsection (d) inserts C(A)A 1983, s 30(5A).

Amendment of European Communities (Mergers and Divisions of Companies) Regulations 1987

5. The Regulations of 1987 are amended—

(a) in Regulation 2 by inserting the following definition:

“‘Regulations of 2007’ means the Transparency (Directive 2004/109/EC) Regulations 2007 (S.I. No. 277 of 2007);”.

(b) in Regulation 7—

(i) in paragraph (1) by substituting “Subject to paragraph (4), a separate written report” for “A separate written report”, and

(ii) [...][a],

(c) in Regulation 9—

(i) in paragraph (1), by substituting “Subject to paragraphs (6) and (7), where the latest annual accounts” for “Where the latest annual accounts”, and

(ii) [...][b],

(d) by deleting Regulation 10,

(e) in Regulation 11—

(i) in paragraph (1) by substituting “Subject to paragraph (3), each of the merging companies shall” for “Each of the merging companies shall”, and

(ii) [...][c],

(f) in Regulation 12—

(i) in paragraph (1) by substituting “subject to paragraphs (2) and” for “subject to paragraph (2)”,

(iii) in subparagraph (c) of paragraph (1) by substituting “where applicable, the explanatory reports” for “the explanatory reports”,

(iii) [...][d], and

(iv) [...][e],

(g) in Regulation 13—

(i) in paragraph (3) by substituting “Subject to paragraphs (3A) and (3B), the notice” for “The notice”, and

(ii) [...][f],

(iii) in subparagraph (b) of paragraph (4) by substituting "a merger by acquisition carried out by a company which holds ninety per cent or more, but not all," for "an operation whereby one or more companies are acquired by another company which holds ninety per cent or more, but not all,",

(iv) in paragraph (5) by substituting "involved in a merger" for "being acquired",

(v) in subparagraph (b) of paragraph (5) by substituting "each of the other companies involved in the merger" for "the acquiring company", and by substituting "that company" for "the company or companies being acquired",

(vi) in paragraph (6) by substituting "each such other company involved in the merger" for "the acquiring company", and

(vii) in paragraph (9) by substituting "19(2)(b) and 22" for "19(1)(b) and 21",

(h) in Regulation 27—

(i) in paragraph (1) by substituting "Subject to paragraphs (5) and, a separate written report" for "A separate written report", and

(ii) [...][g],

(i) in Regulation 28—

(i) by deleting paragraph 8, and

(ii) [...][h],

(j) in Regulation 29—

(i) in paragraph (1) by substituting "Subject to paragraph (6), where the latest annual accounts" for "Where the latest annual accounts", and

(ii) [...][i],

(k) in Regulation 30—

(i) in paragraph (1) by substituting "Subject to paragraph (3), each of the companies involved in the division shall" for "Each of the companies involved in the division shall", and

(ii) [...][j],

(l) in Regulation 31—

(i) in paragraph (1) by substituting "Subject to paragraphs (3) and, each of the companies involved in the division" for "Each of the companies involved in the division",

(ii) in subparagraph (c) of paragraph (1) by inserting "where applicable," before "the explanatory reports",

(iii) [...][k], and

(iv) [...][l],

(m) in Regulation 32—

(i) in paragraph (3) by substituting "Subject to paragraphs (3A) and (3B), the notice convening the general meeting" for "The notice convening the general meeting",

(ii) [...][m],

(iii) [...][n],

(iv) in paragraph (5) by substituting "Subject to paragraph (6A), the directors of the company" for "The directors of the company",

(v) in paragraph (6) by substituting "Subject to paragraph (6A), the directors of the company" for "The directors of the company",

(vi) [...][o].

Amendments

a Regulation 5(b)(ii) inserts EC(MDC)R 1987, reg 7(4).

b Regulation 5(c)(ii) inserts EC(MDC)R 1987, reg 9(6) and (7).

c Regulation 5(e)(ii) inserts EC(MDC)R 1987, reg 11(3) and (4).

d Regulation 5(f)(iii) substitutes EC(MDC)R 1987, reg 12(1)(e).

e Regulation 5(f)(iv) inserts EC(MDC)R 1987, reg 12(3)–(5).

f Regulation 5(g)(ii) inserts EC(MDC)R 1987, reg 13(3A)–(3C).

g Regulation 5(h)(ii) inserts EC(MDC)R 1987, reg 27(5) and (6).

h Regulation 5(i)(ii) substitutes EC(MDC)R 1987, reg 28(12).

i Regulation 5(j)(ii) inserts EC(MDC)R 1987, reg 29(6) and (7).

j Regulation 5(k)(ii) inserts EC(MDC)R 1987, reg 30(3) and (4).

k Regulation 5(l)(iii) substitutes EC(MDC)R 1987, reg 31(1)(e).

l Regulation 5(l)(iv) inserts EC(MDC)R 1987, reg 31(3)–(6).

m Regulation 5(m)(ii) inserts EC(MDC)R 1987, reg 32(3A)–(3C).

n Regulation 5(m)(iii) inserts EC(MDC)R 1987, reg 32(4A).

o Regulation 5(m)(vi) inserts EC(MDC)R 1987, reg 32(6A).

Amendment of European Communities (Cross-Border Mergers) Regulations 2008

6 The European Communities (Cross-Border Mergers) Regulations 2008 (S.I. No. 157 of 2008) are amended—

(a) in Regulation 8—

(i) in paragraph (1) by substituting "Subject to paragraphs (1A) and (1B), each" for "Each",

(ii) [...][a],

(iii) in paragraph (2) by substituting "Notice of the delivery of the common draft terms to the Registrar or, as the case may be, notice of publication on the company's website of the common draft terms, pursuant to this Regulation and the notice referred to in paragraph (1)(b) or (1A)(b) shall, at least 1 month before the general meeting referred to in Regulation 10, be caused to be published—" for "Notice of the delivery of the common draft terms to the Registrar pursuant to this Regulation and the notice referred to in paragraph (1)(b) shall, at least 1 month before the general meeting referred to in Regulation 10, be caused to be published—".

(iv) in paragraph (3)(b) by inserting "or (1A)(b)" after "paragraph (1)(b)", and

(v) in paragraph (3)(d) by inserting "or from the company" after "from the Registrar",

(b) in Regulation 9—

(i) in paragraph (1) by substituting "Subject to paragraph (1A), for the period" for "For the period",

(ii) [...][b],

(iii) in paragraph (2) by substituting "Subject to paragraph (2A), the notice" for "The notice", and

(iv) [...][c],

(c) in Regulation 10—

(i) [...][d], and

(iii) in paragraph (4) by substituting "each such other merging company" for "the successor company",

(d) in Regulation 11—

(i) in paragraph (2) by substituting "Subject to paragraphs (3A), (3B) and (3C), the conditions referred to in paragraph (1)(b) are the following:" for "The conditions referred to in paragraph (1)(b) are the following:",

(ii) in clause (i) of paragraph (2)(b) by substituting "to inspect, at the registered office of the successor company, during ordinary hours of business, or to have access on the successor company's website under the conditions specified in paragraphs (1A), (1B) and (1C) of Regulation 9, to copies of—" for "to inspect, at the registered office of the successor company, during ordinary hours of business, copies of—",

(iii) in clause (ii) of paragraph (2)(b) by inserting "or to download copies of them from the successor company's website pursuant to paragraphs (2A), (2B) and (2C) of Regulation 9" after "on request",

(iv) in paragraph (3) by substituting "Subject to subparagraph (e), where the latest annual accounts" for "Where the latest annual accounts", and

(v) [...][e], and

(vi) [...][f], and

(e) by deleting paragraph (1) of Regulation 21.

Amendments

a Regulation 6(a)(ii) inserts EC(CBM)R 2008, reg 8(1A) and (1B).

b Regulation 6(b)(ii) inserts EC(CBM)R 2008, reg 9(1A)–(1C).

c Regulation 6(b)(iv) inserts EC(CBM)R 2008, reg 9(2A)–(2C).

d Regulation 6(c)(i) substitutes EC(CBM)R 2008, reg 10(3).

e Regulation 6(d)(v) inserts EC(CBM)R 2008, reg 11(3)(e).

f Regulation 6(d)(vi) inserts EC(CBM)R 2008, reg 11(3A)–(3C).

GIVEN under my Official Seal, 20 June 2011.

RICHARD BRUTON,

Minister for Jobs, Enterprise and Innovation.

EXPLANATORY NOTE

(This note is not part of the Instrument and does not purport to be a legal interpretation.)

These Regulations give effect to Directive 2009/109/EC of the European Parliament and of the Council of 16th September 2009 amending Council Directives 77/91/EEC, 78/855/EEC and 82/891/EeC, and Directive 2005/56/EC as regards reporting and documentation requirements in the case of mergers and divisions.

The Directive was adopted in the context of the EU drive to reduce administrative burdens, in this instance, on companies undertaking mergers or divisions.

The Regulations allow for—

- a relaxation of the reporting requirements imposed on companies under
- taking mergers or divisions, particularly where the participants in such mergers or divisions are parent companies and their subsidiaries and the shareholders resolve to dispense with certain reports.
- the avoidance of duplication where similar or equivalent reports are required by different EU instruments; and the facilitation of the use of the internet and other electronic means for the publication and dissemination of documents involved in mergers/divisions.

Division C: European Legislation

Commission Regulation (EC) No 1606/2002

of the European Parliament and of the Council of 19 July 2002 on the application of international accounting standards

THE EUROPEAN PARLIAMENT AND THE COUNCIL OF THE EUROPEAN UNION,

Having regard to the Treaty establishing the European Community, and in particular Article 95(1) thereof,

Having regard to the proposal from the Commission,[1]

Having regard to the opinion of the Economic and Social Committee,[2]

Acting in accordance with the procedure laid down in Article 251 of the Treaty,[3]

Whereas:

(1) The Lisbon European Council of 23 and 24 March 2000 emphasised the need to accelerate completion of the internal market for financial services, set the deadline of 2005 to implement the Commission's Financial Services Action Plan and urged that steps be taken to enhance the comparability of financial statements prepared by publicly traded companies.

(2) In order to contribute to a better functioning of the internal market, publicly traded companies must be required to apply a single set of high quality international accounting standards for the preparation of their consolidated financial statements. Furthermore, it is important that the financial reporting standards applied by Community companies participating in financial markets are accepted internationally and are truly global standards. This implies an increasing convergence of accounting standards currently used internationally with the ultimate objective of achieving a single set of global accounting standards.

(3) Council Directive 78/660/EEC of 25 July 1978 on the annual accounts of certain types of companies,[4] Council Directive 83/349/EEC of 13 June 1983 on consolidated accounts,[5] Council Directive 86/635/EEC of 8 December 1986 on the annual accounts and consolidated accounts of banks and other financial institutions[6] and Council Directive 91/674/EEC of 19 December 1991 on the annual accounts and consolidated accounts of insurance companies[7] are also addressed to publicly traded Community companies. The reporting requirements set out in these Directives cannot ensure the

---

1 OJ C 154 E, 29.5.2001, p. 285.

2 OJ C 260, 17.9.2001, p. 86.

3 Opinion of the European Parliament of 12 March 2002 (not yet published in the Official Journal) and Decision of the Council of 7 June 2002.

4 OJ L 222, 14.8.1978, p. 11. Directive as last amended by European Parliament and Council Directive 2001/65/EC (OJ L 283, 27.10.2001, p. 28).

5 OJ L 193, 18.7.1983, p. 1. Directive as last amended by European Parliament and Council Directive 2001/65/EC.

6 OJ L 372, 31.12.1986, p. 1. Directive as last amended by European Parliament and Council Directive 2001/65/EC.

7 OJ L 374, 31.12.1991, p. 7.

high level of transparency and comparability of financial reporting from all publicly traded Community companies which is a necessary condition for building an integrated capital market which operates effectively, smoothly and efficiently. It is therefore necessary to supplement the legal framework applicable to publicly traded companies.

(4) This Regulation aims at contributing to the efficient and cost-effective functioning of the capital market. The protection of investors and the maintenance of confidence in the financial markets is also an important aspect of the completion of the internal market in this area. This Regulation reinforces the freedom of movement of capital in the internal market and helps to enable Community companies to compete on an equal footing for financial resources available in the Community capital markets, as well as in world capital markets.

(5) It is important for the competitiveness of Community capital markets to achieve convergence of the standards used in Europe for preparing financial statements, with international accounting standards that can be used globally, for cross-border transactions or listing anywhere in the world.

(6) On 13 June 2000, the Commission published its Communication on 'EU Financial Reporting Strategy: the way forward' in which it was proposed that all publicly traded Community companies prepare their consolidated financial statements in accordance with one single set of accounting standards, namely International Accounting Standards (IAS), at the latest by 2005.

(7) International Accounting Standards (IASs) are developed by the International Accounting Standards Committee (IASC), whose purpose is to develop a single set of global accounting standards. Further to the restructuring of the IASC, the new Board on 1 April 2001, as one of its first decisions, renamed the IASC as the International Accounting Standards Board (IASB) and, as far as future international accounting standards are concerned, renamed IAS as International Financial Reporting Standards (IFRS). These standards should, wherever possible and provided that they ensure a high degree of transparency and comparability for financial reporting in the Community, be made obligatory for use by all publicly traded Community companies.

(8) The measures necessary for the implementation of this Regulation should be adopted in accordance with Council Decision 1999/468/EC of 28 June 1999 laying down the procedures for the exercise of implementing powers conferred on the Commission[8] and with due regard to the declaration made by the Commission in the European Parliament on 5 February 2002 concerning the implementation of financial services legislation.

(9) To adopt an international accounting standard for application in the Community, it is necessary firstly that it meets the basic requirement of the aforementioned Council Directives, that is to say that its application results in a true and fair view of the financial position and performance of an enterprise — this principle being considered in the light of the said Council Directives without implying a strict conformity with each and every provision of those Directives; secondly that, in accordance with the conclusions of the Council of 17 July 2000, it is conducive to the European public good and lastly that it meets basic criteria as to the quality of information required for financial statements to be useful to users.

---

[8] OJ L 184, 17.7.1999, p. 23.

(10) An accounting technical committee should provide support and expertise to the Commission in the assessment of international accounting standards.

(11) The endorsement mechanism should act expeditiously on proposed international accounting standards and also be a means to deliberate, reflect and exchange information on international accounting standards among the main parties concerned, in particular national accounting standard setters, supervisors in the fields of securities, banking and insurance, central banks including the ECB, the accounting profession and users and preparers of accounts. The mechanism should be a means to foster common understanding of adopted international accounting standards in the Community.

(12) In accordance with the principle of proportionality, the measures provided for in this Regulation, in requiring that a single set of international accounting standards be applied to publicly traded companies, are necessary to achieve the objective of contributing to the efficient and cost-effective functioning of Community capital markets and thereby to the completion of the internal market.

(13) In accordance with the same principle, it is necessary, as regards annual accounts, to leave to Member States the option to permit or require publicly traded companies to prepare them in conformity with international accounting standards adopted in accordance with the procedure laid down in this Regulation. Member States may decide as well to extend this permission or this requirement to other companies as regards the preparation of their consolidated accounts and/or their annual accounts.

(14) In order to facilitate an exchange of views and to allow Member States to coordinate their positions, the Commission should periodically inform the accounting regulatory committee about active projects, discussion papers, point outlines and exposure drafts issued by the IASB and about the consequential technical work of the accounting technical committee. It is also important that the accounting regulatory committee is informed at an early stage if the Commission intends not to propose to adopt an international accounting standard.

(15) In its deliberations on and in elaborating positions to be taken on documents and papers issued by the IASB in the process of developing international accounting standards (IFRS and SICIFRIC), the Commission should take into account the importance of avoiding competitive disadvantages for European companies operating in the global marketplace, and, to the maximum possible extent, the views expressed by the delegations in the Accounting Regulatory Committee. The Commission will be represented in constituent bodies of the IASB.

(16) A proper and rigorous enforcement regime is key to underpinning investors' confidence in financial markets. Member States, by virtue of Article 10 of the Treaty, are required to take appropriate measures to ensure compliance with international accounting standards. The Commission intends to liaise with Member States, notably through the Committee of European Securities Regulators (CESR), to develop a common approach to enforcement.

(17) Further, it is necessary to allow Member States to defer the application of certain provisions until 2007 for those companies publicly traded both in the Community and on a regulated third-country market which are already applying another set of internationally accepted standards as the primary basis for their consolidated accounts as well as for companies which have only publicly traded debt securities. It is

nonetheless crucial that by 2007 at the latest a single set of global international accounting standards, the IAS, apply to all Community companies publicly traded on a Community regulated market.

(18) In order to allow Member States and companies to carry out the necessary adaptations to make the application of international accounting standards possible, it is necessary to apply certain provisions only in 2005. Appropriate provisions should be put in place for the first-time application of IAS by companies as a result of the entry into force of the present regulation. Such provisions should be drawn up at international level in order to ensure international recognition of the solutions adopted,

HAVE ADOPTED THIS REGULATION:

Article 1
Aim

This Regulation has as its objective the adoption and use of international accounting standards in the Community with a view to harmonising the financial information presented by the companies referred to in Article 4 in order to ensure a high degree of transparency and comparability of financial statements and hence an efficient functioning of the Community capital market and of the Internal Market.

Article 2
Definitions

For the purpose of this Regulation, 'international accounting standards' shall mean International Accounting Standards (IAS), International Financial Reporting Standards (IFRS) and related Interpretations (SICIFRIC interpretations), subsequent amendments to those standards and related interpretations, future standards and related interpretations issued or adopted by the International Accounting Standards Board (IASB).

Article 3
Adoption and use of international accounting standards

1. The Commission shall decide on the applicability within the Community of international accounting standards. Those measures, designed to amend non-essential elements of this Regulation by supplementing it, shall be adopted in accordance with the regulatory procedure with scrutiny referred to in Article 6(2).

2. The international accounting standards can only be adopted if:

— they are not contrary to the principle set out in Article 2(3) of Directive 78/660/EEC and in Article 16(3) of Directive 83/349/ EEC and are conducive to the European public good and,

— they meet the criteria of understandability, relevance, reliability and comparability required of the financial information needed for making economic decisions and assessing the stewardship of management.

3 At the latest by 31 December 2002, the Commission shall, in accordance with the procedure laid down in Article 6(2), decide on the applicability within the Community of the international accounting standards in existence upon entry into force of this Regulation.

4 Adopted international accounting standards shall be published in full in each of the official languages of the Community, as a Commission Regulation, in the Official Journal of the European Communities.

Article 4

Consolidated accounts of publicly traded companies

For each financial year starting on or after 1 January 2005, companies governed by the law of a Member State shall prepare their consolidated accounts in conformity with the international accounting standards adopted in accordance with the procedure laid down in Article 6(2) if, at their balance sheet date, their securities are admitted to trading on a regulated market of any Member State within the meaning of Article 1(13) of Council Directive 93/22/EEC of 10 May 1993 on investment services in the securities field.[9]

Article 5

Options in respect of annual accounts and of non publicly-traded companies

Member States may permit or require:

(a) the companies referred to in Article 4 to prepare their annual accounts,

(b) companies other than those referred to in Article 4 to prepare their consolidated accounts and/or their annual accounts,

in conformity with the international accounting standards adopted in accordance with the procedure laid down in Article 6(2).

Article 6

Committee procedure

1. The Commission shall be assisted by an accounting regulatory committee hereinafter referred to as 'the Committee'.

2. Where reference is made to this paragraph, Article 5a(1) to (4) and Article 7 of Decision 1999/468/EC shall apply, having regard to the provisions of Article 8 thereof.

Article 7

Reporting and coordination

1. The Commission shall liaise on a regular basis with the Committee about the status of active IASB projects and any related documents issued by the IASB in order to coordinate positions and to facilitate discussions concerning the adoption of standards that might result from these projects and documents.

2. The Commission shall duly report to the Committee in a timely manner if it intends not to propose the adoption of a standard.

Article 8

Notification

Where Member States take measures by virtue of Article 5, they shall immediately communicate these to the Commission and to other Member States.

---

[9] OJ L 141, 11.6.1993, p. 27. Directive as last amended by European Parliament and Council Directive 2000/64/EC (OJ L 290, 17.11.2000, p. 27).

Article 9
Transitional provisions

By way of derogation from Article 4, Member States may provide that the requirements of Article 4 shall only apply for each financial year starting on or after January 2007 to those companies:

(a) whose debt securities only are admitted on a regulated market of any Member State within the meaning of Article 1(13) of Directive 93/22/EEC; or

(b) whose securities are admitted to public trading in a non-member State and which, for that purpose, have been using internationally accepted standards since a financial year that started prior to the publication of this Regulation in the Official Journal of the European Communities.

Article 10
Information and review

The Commission shall review the operation of this Regulation and report thereon to the European Parliament and to the Council by 1 July 2007 at the latest.

Article 11
Entry into force

This Regulation shall enter into force on the third day following that of its publication in the Official Journal of the European Communities.

This Regulation shall be binding in its entirety and directly applicable in all Member States.

Commission Regulation (EC) No 809/2004

of 29 April 2004

implementing Directive 2003/71/EC of the European Parliament and of the Council as regards information contained in prospectuses as well as the format, incorporation by reference and publication of such prospectuses and dissemination of advertisements

(Text with EEA relevance)

THE COMMISSION OF THE EUROPEAN COMMUNITIES,

Having regard to the Treaty establishing the European Community,

Having regard to Directive 2003/71/EC of the European Parliament and the Council of 4 November 2003 on the prospectus to be published when securities are offered to the public or admitted to trading and amending Directive 2001/34/EC (OJ L 345, 31.12.2003, p. 64), and in particular Article 5(5), Article 7, Article 10(4), Article 11(3), Article 14(8) and Article 15(7) thereof,

After consulting the Committee of European Securities Regulators (CESR) (CESR was established by Commission Decision 2001/527/EC (OJ L 191, 13.7.2001, p. 43) for technical advice,

Whereas:

(1) Directive 2003/71/EC lays down principles to be observed when drawing up prospectuses. These principles need to be supplemented as far as the information to be given therein, the format and aspects of publication, the information to be incorporated by reference in a prospectus and dissemination of advertisements are concerned.

(2) Depending on the type of issuer and securities involved, a typology of minimum information requirements should be established corresponding to those schedules that are in practice most frequently applied. The schedules should be based on the information items required in the IOSCO 'Disclosure Standards for cross-border offering and initial listings' (part I) and on the existing schedules of Directive 2001/34/EC of the European Parliament and of the Council of 28 May on the admission of securities to official stock exchange listing and on information to be published on those securities (OJ L 184, 6.7.2001, p. 1. Directive as last amended by Directive 2003/71/EC).

(3) Information given by the issuer, the offeror or the person asking for admission to trading on a regulated market, according to this Regulation, should be subject to European Union provisions relating to data protection.

(4) Care should be taken that, in those cases where a prospectus is composed of separate documents, duplication of information is avoided; to this end separate detailed schedules for the registration document and for the securities note, adapted to the particular type of issuer and the securities concerned, should be laid down in order to cover each type of security.

(5) The issuer, the offeror or the person asking for admission to trading on a regulated market are entitled to include in a prospectus or base prospectus additional information going beyond the information items provided for in the

schedules and building blocks. Any additional information provided should be appropriate to the type of securities or the nature of the issuer involved.

(6) In most cases, given the variety of issuers, the types of securities, the involvement or not of a third party as a guarantor, whether or not there is a listing etc, one single schedule will not give the appropriate information for an investor to make his investment decision. Therefore the combination of various schedules should be possible. A non exhaustive table of combinations, providing for different possible combinations of schedules and 'building blocks' for most of the different type of securities, should be set up in order to assist issuers when drafting their prospectus.

(7) The share registration document schedule should be applicable to shares and other transferable securities equivalent to shares but also to other securities giving access to the capital of the issuer by way of conversion or exchange. In the latter case this schedule should not be used where the underlying shares to be delivered have already been issued before the issuance of the securities giving access to the capital of the issuer; however this schedule should be used where the underlying shares to be delivered have already been issued but are not yet admitted to trading on a regulated market.

(8) Voluntary disclosure of profit forecasts in a share registration document should be presented in a consistent and comparable manner and accompanied by a statement prepared by independent accountants or auditors. This information should not be confused with the disclosure of known trends or other factual data with material impact on the issuers' prospects. Moreover, they should provide an explanation of any changes in disclosure policy relating to profit forecasts when supplementing a prospectus or drafting a new prospectus.

(9) Pro forma financial information is needed in case of significant gross change, i. e. a variation of more than 25% relative to one or more indicators of the size of the issuer's business, in the situation of an issuer due to a particular transaction, with the exception of those situations where merger accounting is required.

(10) The schedule for the share securities note should be applicable to any class of share since it considers information regarding a description of the rights attached to the securities and the procedure for the exercise of any rights attached to the securities.

(11) Some debt securities such as structured bonds incorporate certain elements of a derivative security, therefore additional disclosure requirements related to the derivative component in the interest payment should be included in the securities note schedule for debt securities.

(12) The additional 'building block' related to guarantee should apply to any obligation in relation to any kind of security.

(13) The asset backed securities registration document should not apply to mortgage bonds as provided for in Article 5(4)(b) of Directive 2003/71/EC and other covered bonds. The same should apply for the asset backed securities additional 'building block' that has to be combined with the securities note for debt securities.

(14) Wholesale investors should be able to make their investment decision on other elements than those taken into consideration by retail investors. Therefore a differentiated content of prospectus is necessary for debt and derivative securities aimed at those investors who purchase debt or derivative securities with a denomination per unit of at least EUR 50,000 or a denomination in another currency provided that the value of such minimum denomination when converted to EURO amounts to at least EURO 50,000.

(15) In the context of depository receipts, emphasis should be put on the issuer of the underlying shares and not on the issuer of the depository receipt. Where there is legal recourse to the depository over and above a breach of its fiduciary or agency duties, the risk factors section in the prospectus should contain full information on this fact and on the circumstances of such recourse. Where a prospectus is drafted as a tripartite document (i.e. registration document, securities note and summary), the registration document should be limited to the information on the depository.

(16) The banks registration document schedule should be applicable to banks from third countries which do not fall under the definition of credit institution provided for in Article 1(1)(a) of Directive 2000/12/EC of the European Parliament and of the Council of 20 March 2000 relating to the taking up and pursuit of the business of credit institutions (OJ L 126, 26.5.2000, p. 1. Directive as last amended by the 2003 Act of Accession) but have their registered office in a state which is a member of the OECD.

(17) If a special purpose vehicle issues debt and derivative securities guaranteed by a bank, it should not use the banks registration document schedule.

(18) The schedule 'securities note for derivative securities' should be applicable to securities which are not covered by the other schedules and building blocks. The scope of this schedule is determined by reference to the other two generic categories of shares and debt securities. In order to provide a clear and comprehensive explanation to help investors understand how the value of their investment is affected by the value of the underlying, issuers should be able to use appropriate examples on a voluntary basis. For instance, for some complex derivatives securities, examples might be the most effective way to explain the nature of those securities.

(19) The additional information 'building block' on the underlying share for certain equity securities should be added to the securities note for debt securities or substitute the item referring to 'information required in respect of the underlying' of the schedule securities note for derivative securities, depending on the characteristics of the securities being issued.

(20) Member States and their regional or local authorities are outside the scope of Directive 2003/71/EC. However, they may choose to produce a prospectus in accordance with this Directive. Third country sovereign issuers and their regional or local authorities are not outside the scope of Directive 2003/71/EC and are obliged to produce a prospectus if they wish to make a public offer of securities in the Community or wish their securities to be admitted to trading on a regulated market. For those cases, particular schedules should be

used for the securities issued by States, their regional and local authorities and by public international bodies.

(21) A base prospectus and its final terms should contain the same information as a prospectus. All the general principles applicable to a prospectus are applicable also to the final terms. Nevertheless, where the final terms are not included in the base prospectus they do not have to be approved by the competent authority.

(22) For some categories of issuers the competent authority should be entitled to require adapted information going beyond the information items included in the schedules and building blocks because of the particular nature of the activities carried out by those issuers. A precise and restrictive list of issuers for which adapted information may be required is necessary. The adapted information requirements for each category of issuers included in this list should be appropriate and proportionate to the type of business involved. The Committee of European Securities Regulators could actively try to reach convergence on these information requirements within the Community. Inclusion of new categories in the list should be restricted to those cases where this can be duly justified.

(23) In the case of completely new types of securities which cannot be covered by the existing schedules or any of their combinations, the issuer should still have the possibility to apply for approval for a prospectus. In those cases he should be able to discuss the content of the information to be provided with the competent authority. The prospectus approved by the competent authority under those circumstances should benefit from the single passport established in Directive 2003/71/EC. The competent authority should always try to find similarities and make use as much as possible of existing schedules. Any additional information requirements should be proportionate and appropriate to the type of securities involved.

(24) Certain information items required in the schedules and building blocks or equivalent information items are not relevant to a particular security and thus may be inapplicable in some specific cases; in those cases the issuer should have the possibility to omit this information.

(25) The enhanced flexibility in the articulation of the base prospectus with its final terms compared to a single issue prospectus should not hamper the easy access to material information for investors.

(26) With respect to base prospectuses, it should be set out in an easily identifiable manner which kind of information will have to be included as final terms. This requirement should be able to be satisfied in a number of different ways, for example, if the base prospectus contains blanks for any information to be inserted in the final terms or if the base prospectus contains a list of the missing information.

(27) Where a single document includes more than one base prospectus and each base prospectus would require approval by a different home competent authority, the respective competent authorities should act in cooperation and, where appropriate, transfer the approval of the prospectus in accordance with

Article 13(5) of Directive 2003/71/EC, so that the approval by only one competent authority is sufficient for the entire document.

(28) Historical financial information as required in the schedules should principally be presented in accordance with Regulation (EC) No 1606/2002 of the European Parliament and of the Council of 19 July 2002 on the application of international accounting standard (OJ L 243, 11.9.2002, p. 1.) or Member States' accounting standards. Specific requirements should, however, be laid down for third country issuers.

(29) For the purposes of publication of the document referred to in Article 10 of Directive 2003/71/EC, issuers should be allowed to choose the method of publication they consider adequate among those referred to in Article 14 of that Directive. In selecting the method of publication they should consider the objective of the document and that it should permit investors a fast and cost-efficient access to that information.

(30) The aim of incorporation by reference, as provided for in Article 11 of Directive 2003/71/EC, is to simplify and reduce the costs of drafting a prospectus; however this aim should not be achieved to the detriment of other interests the prospectus is meant to protect. For instance, the fact that the natural location of the information required is the prospectus, and that the information should be presented in an easily and comprehensible form, should also be considered. Particular attention should be granted to the language used for information incorporated by reference and its consistency with the prospectus itself. Information incorporated by reference may refer to historical data, however if this information is no more relevant due to material change, this should be clearly stated in the prospectus and the updated information should also be provided.

(31) Where a prospectus is published in electronic form, additional safety measures compared to traditional means of publication, using best practices available, are necessary in order to maintain the integrity of the information, to avoid manipulation or modification from unauthorised persons, to avoid altering its comprehensibility and to escape from possible adverse consequences from different approaches on offer of securities to the public in third countries.

(32) The newspaper chosen for the publication of a prospectus should have a wide area of distribution and a high circulation.

(33) A home Member State should be able to require publication of a notice stating how the prospectus has been made available and where it can be obtained by the public. Where a home Member State requires publication of notices in its legislation, the content of such a notice should be kept to the necessary items information to avoid duplication with the summary. These home Member States may also require that an additional notice in relation to the final terms of a base prospectus is to be published.

(34) In order to facilitate centralising useful information for investors a mention should be included in the list of approved prospectuses posted in the web-site of the competent authority of the home Member State, indicating how a prospectus has been published and where it can be obtained.

(35) Member States should ensure effective compliance of advertising rules concerning public offers and admission to trading on a regulated market. Proper co-ordination between competent authorities should be achieved in cross-border offerings or cross-border admission to trading.

(36) In view of the interval between the entry into force of Regulation (EC) No 1606/2002 and the production of certain of its effects, a number of transitional arrangements for historical financial information to be included in a prospectus should be provided for, in order to prevent excessive burden on issuers and enable them to adapt the way they prepare and present historical financial information within a reasonable period of time after the entry into force of Directive 2003/71/EC.

(37) The obligation to restate in a prospectus historical financial information according to Regulation (EC) N0 1606/2002 does not cover securities with a denomination per unit of at least EUR 50,000; consequently such transitional arrangements are not necessary for such securities.

(38) For reasons of coherence it is appropriate that this Regulation applies from the date of transposition of Directive 2003/71/EC.

(39) Whereas the measures provided for in this Regulation are in accordance with the opinion of the European Securities Committee,

HAS ADOPTED THIS REGULATION:

CHAPTER I
SUBJECT MATTER AND DEFINITIONS

Article 1
Subject matter

This Regulation lays down:

1. the format of prospectus referred to in Article 5 of Directive 2003/71/EC;
2. the minimum information requirements to be included in a prospectus provided for in Article 7 of Directive 2003/71/EC;
3. the method of publication referred to in Article 10 of Directive 2003/71/EC;
4. the modalities according to which information can be incorporated by reference in a prospectus provided for in Article 11 of Directive 2003/71/EC;
5. the publication methods of a prospectus in order to ensure that a prospectus is publicly available according to Article 14 of Directive 2003/71/EC;
6. the methods of dissemination of advertisements referred to in Article 15 of Directive 2003/71/EC.

Article 2
Definitions

For the purposes of this Regulation, the following definitions shall apply in addition to those laid down in Directive 2003/71/EC:

1. ‘schedule’ means a list of minimum information requirements adapted to the particular nature of the different types of issuers and/or the different securities involved;

2. 'building block' means a list of additional information requirements, not included in one of the schedules, to be added to one or more schedules, as the case may be, depending on the type of instrument and/or transaction for which a prospectus or base prospectus is drawn up;

3. 'risk factors' means a list of risks which are specific to the situation of the issuer and/or the securities and which are material for taking investment decisions;

4. 'special purpose vehicle' means an issuer whose objects and purposes are primarily the issue of securities;

5. 'asset backed securities' means securities which:

   (a) represent an interest in assets, including any rights intended to assure servicing, or the receipt or timeliness of receipts by holders of assets of amounts payable there under;

   or

   (b) are secured by assets and the terms of which provide for payments which relate to payments or reasonable projections of payments calculated by reference to identified or identifiable assets;

6. 'umbrella collective investment undertaking' means a collective investment undertaking invested in one or more collective investment undertakings, the asset of which is composed of separate class(es) or designation(s) of securities;

7. 'property collective investment undertaking' means a collective investment undertaking whose investment objective is the participation in the holding of property in the long term;

8. 'public international body' means a legal entity of public nature established by an international treaty between sovereign States and of which one or more Member States are members;

9. 'advertisement' means announcements:

   (a) relating to an specific offer to the public of securities or to an admission to trading on a regulated market; and

   (b) aiming to specifically promote the potential subscription or acquisition of securities.

10. 'profit forecast' means a form of words which expressly states or by implication indicates a figure or a minimum or maximum figure for the likely level of profits or losses for the current financial period and/or financial periods subsequent to that period, or contains data from which a calculation of such a figure for future profits or losses may be made, even if no particular figure is mentioned and the word 'profit' is not used.

11. 'profit estimate' means a profit forecast for a financial period which has expired and for which results have not yet been published.

12. 'regulated information' means all information which the issuer, or any person who has applied for the admission of securities to trading on a regulated market without the issuer's consent, is required to disclose under Directive

2001/34/EC or under Article 6 of Directive 2003/6/EC of the European Parliament and of the Council (OJ L 96, 12.4.2003, p. 16).

CHAPTER II
MINIMUM INFORMATION

Article 3
Minimum information to be included in a prospectus

A prospectus shall be drawn up by using one or a combination of the following schedules and building blocks set out in Articles 4 to 20, according to the combinations for various types of securities provided for in Article 21.

[A prospectus shall contain the information items required in Annexes I to XVII and Annexes XX to XXX depending on the type of issuer or issues and securities involved. Subject to Article 4a(1), a competent authority shall not require that a prospectus contains information items which are not included in Annexes I to XVII or Annexes XX to XXX.][a]

In order to ensure conformity with the obligation referred to in Article 5(1) of Directive 2003/71/EC, the competent authority of the home Member State, when approving a prospectus in accordance with Article 13 of that Directive, may require that the information provided by the issuer, the offeror or the person asking for admission to trading on a regulated market be completed, for each of the information items, on a case by case basis.

Amendments

a Inserted by Commission Delegated Regulation (EU) No 862/2012 of 4 June 2012.

Article 4
Share registration document schedule

1 For the share registration document information shall be given in accordance with the schedule set out in Annex I.

2 The schedule set out in paragraph 1 shall apply to the following:

1. shares and other transferable securities equivalent to shares;
2. other securities which comply with the following conditions:
   (a) they can be converted or exchanged into shares or other transferable securities equivalent to shares, at the issuer's or at the investor's discretion, or on the basis of the conditions established a the moment of the issue, or give, in any other way, the possibility to acquire shares or other transferable securities equivalent to shares;
   and
   (b) provided that these shares or other transferable securities equivalent to shares are or will be issued by the issuer of the security and are not yet traded on a regulated market or an equivalent market outside the Community at the time of the approval of the prospectus covering the securities, and that the

underlying shares or other transferable securities equivalent to shares can be delivered with physical settlement.

[Article 4a
Share registration document schedule in cases of complex financial history or significant financial commitment

1. Where the issuer of a security covered by Article 4(2) has a complex financial history, or has made a significant financial commitment, and in consequence the inclusion in the registration document of certain items of financial information relating to an entity other than the issuer is necessary in order to satisfy the obligation laid down in Article 5(1) of Directive 2003/71/EC, those items of financial information shall be deemed to relate to the issuer. The competent authority of the home Member State shall in such cases request that the issuer, the offeror or the person asking for admission to trading include those items of information in the registration document.

Those items of financial information may include pro forma information prepared in accordance with Annex II. In this context, where the issuer has made a significant financial commitment any such pro forma information shall illustrate the anticipated effects of the transaction that the issuer has agreed to undertake, and references in Annex II to 'the transaction' shall be read accordingly.

2. The competent authority shall base any request pursuant to paragraph 1 on the requirements set out in item 20.1 of Annex I as regards the content of financial information and the applicable accounting and auditing principles, subject to any modification which is appropriate in view of any of the following factors:

(a) the nature of the securities;

(b) the nature and range of information already included in the prospectus, and the existence of financial information relating to an entity other than the issuer in a form that might be included in a prospectus without modification;

(c) the facts of the case, including the economic substance of the transactions by which the issuer has acquired or disposed of its business undertaking or any part of it, and the specific nature of that undertaking;

(d) the ability of the issuer to obtain financial information relating to another entity with reasonable effort.

Where, in the individual case, the obligation laid down in Article 5(1) of Directive 2003/71/EC may be satisfied in more than one way, preference shall be given to the way that is the least costly or onerous.

3. Paragraph 1 is without prejudice to the responsibility under national law of any other person, including the persons referred to in Article 6(1) of Directive 2003/71/EC, for the information contained in the prospectus. In particular, those persons shall be responsible for the inclusion in the registration document of any items of information requested by the competent authority pursuant to paragraph 1.

4. For the purposes of paragraph 1, an issuer shall be treated as having a complex financial history if all of the following conditions apply:

(a) its entire business undertaking at the time that the prospectus is drawn up is not accurately represented in the historical financial information which it is required to provide under item 20.1 of Annex I;

(b) that inaccuracy will affect the ability of an investor to make an informed assessment as mentioned in Article 5(1) of Directive 2003/71/EC; and

(c) information relating to its business undertaking that is necessary for an investor to make such an assessment is included in financial information relating to another entity.

5. For the purposes of paragraph 1, an issuer shall be treated as having made a significant financial commitment if it has entered into a binding agreement to undertake a transaction which, on completion, is likely to give rise to a significant gross change.

In this context, the fact that an agreement makes completion of the transaction subject to conditions, including approval by a regulatory authority, shall not prevent that agreement from being treated as binding if it is reasonably certain that those conditions will be fulfilled.

In particular, an agreement shall be treated as binding where it makes the completion of the transaction conditional on the outcome of the offer of the securities that are the subject matter of the prospectus or, in the case of a proposed takeover, if the offer of securities that are the subject matter of the prospectus has the objective of funding that takeover.

6. For the purposes of paragraph 5 of this Article, and of item 20.2 of Annex I, a significant gross change means a variation of more than 25%, relative to one or more indicators of the size of the issuer's business, in the situation of an issuer.][a]

Amendments

a Inserted by Commission Regulation (EC) No 211/2007 of 27 February 2007 OJ L337 5.12.2006, p 17.

Article 5

Pro forma financial information building block

For pro forma financial information, information shall be given in accordance with the building block set out in Annex II.

Pro forma financial information should be preceded by an introductory explanatory paragraph that states in clear terms the purpose of including this information in the prospectus.

Article 6

Share securities note schedule

1 For the share securities note information is necessary to be given in accordance with the schedule set out in Annex III.

2 The schedule shall apply to shares and other transferable securities equivalent to shares.

Article 7
Debt and derivative securities registration document schedule for securities with a denomination per unit of less than EUR 50,000

For the debt and derivative securities registration document concerning securities which are not covered in Article 4 with a denomination per unit of less than EUR 50,000 or, where there is no individual denomination, securities that can only be acquired on issue for less than EUR 50,000 per security, information shall be given in accordance with the schedule set out in Annex IV.

Article 8
Securities note schedule for debt securities with a denomination per unit of less than EUR 50,000

1 For the securities note for debt securities with a denomination per unit of less than EUR 50,000 information shall be given in accordance with the schedule set out in Annex V.

2 The schedule shall apply to debt where the issuer has an obligation arising on issue to pay the investor 100% of the nominal value in addition to which there may be also an interest payment.

Article 9
Guarantees building block

For guarantees information shall be given in accordance with the building block set out in Annex VI.

Article 10
Asset backed securities registration document schedule

For the asset backed securities registration document information shall be given in accordance with the schedule set out in Annex VII.

Article 11
Asset backed securities building block

For the additional information building block to the securities note for asset backed securities information shall be given in accordance with the building block set out in Annex VIII.

Article 12
Debt and derivative securities registration document schedule for securities with a denomination per unit of at least EUR 50,000

For the debt and derivative securities registration document concerning securities which are not covered in Article 4 with a denomination per unit of at least EUR 50,000 or, where there is no individual denomination, securities that can only be acquired on issue for at least EUR 50,000 per security, information shall be given in accordance with the schedule set out in Annex IX.

Article 13

Depository receipts schedule

For depository receipts issued over shares information shall be given in accordance with the schedule set out in Annex X.

Article 14

Banks registration document schedule

1 For the banks registration document for debt and derivative securities and those securities which are not covered by Article 4 information shall be given in accordance with the schedule set out in Annex XI.

2 The schedule set out in paragraph 1 shall apply to credit institutions as defined in point (a) of Article 1(1) of Directive 2000/12/EC as well as to third country credit institutions which do not fall under that definition but have their registered office in a state which is a member of the OECD.

These entities may also use alternatively the registration document schedules provided for under in Articles 7 and 12.

Article 15

Securities note schedule for derivative securities

1 For the securities note for derivative securities information shall be given in accordance with the schedule set out in Annex XII.

2 The schedule shall apply to securities which are not in the scope of application of the other securities note schedules referred to in Articles 6, 8 and 16, including certain securities where the payment and/or delivery obligations are linked to an underlying.

Article 16

Securities note schedule for debt securities with a denomination per unit of at least EUR 50,000

1 For the securities note for debt securities with a denomination per unit of at least EUR 50,000 information shall be given in accordance with the schedule set out in Annex XIII.

2 The schedule shall apply to debt where the issuer has an obligation arising on issue to pay the investor 100% of the nominal value in addition to which there may be also an interest payment.

Article 17

Additional information building block on the underlying share

1 For the additional information on the underlying share, the description of the underlying share shall be given in accordance with the building block set out in Annex XIV.

In addition, if the issuer of the underlying share is an entity belonging to the same group, the information required by the schedule referred to in Article 4 shall be given in respect of that issuer.

2 The additional information referred to in the first subparagraph of paragraph 1 shall only apply to those securities which comply with both of the following conditions:

1. they can be converted or exchanged into shares or other transferable securities equivalent to shares, at the issuer's or at the investor's discretion, or on the basis of the conditions established a the moment of the issue or give, in any other way, the possibility to acquire shares or other transferable securities equivalent to shares;

   and

2. provided that these shares or other transferable securities equivalent to shares are or will be issued by the issuer of the security or by an entity belonging to the group of that issuer and are not yet traded on a regulated market or an equivalent market outside the Community at the time of the approval of the prospectus covering the securities, and that the underlying shares or other transferable securities equivalent to shares can be delivered with physical settlement.

Article 18
Registration document schedule for collective investment undertakings of the closed-end type

1 In addition to the information required pursuant to items 1, 2, 3, 4, 5.1, 7, 9.1, 9.2.1, 9.2.3, 10.4, 13, 14, 15, 16, 17.2, 18, 19, 20, 21, 22, 23, 24, 25 of Annex I, for the registration document for securities issued by collective investment undertakings of the closed-end type information shall be given in accordance with the schedule set out in Annex XV.

2 The schedule shall apply to collective investment undertakings of the closed-end type holding a portfolio of assets on behalf of investors that:

1. are recognised by national law in the Member State in which it is incorporated as a collective investment undertaking of the closed end type;

   or

2. do not take or seek to take legal or management control of any of the issuers of its underlying investments. In such a case, legal control and/or participation in the administrative, management or supervisory bodies of the underlying issuer(s) may be taken where such action is incidental to the primary investment objective, necessary for the protection of shareholders and only in circumstances where the collective investment undertaking will not exercise significant management control over the operations of that underlying issuer(s).

Article 19
Registration document schedule for Member States, third countries and their regional and local authorities

1 For the registration document for securities issued by Member States, third countries and their regional and local authorities information shall be given in accordance with the schedule set out in Annex XVI.

2 The schedule shall apply to all types of securities issued by Member States, third countries and their regional and local authorities.

Article 20

Registration document schedule for public international bodies and for issuers of debt securities guaranteed by a member state of the OECD

1 For the registration document for securities issued by public inter-national bodies and for securities unconditionally and irrevocably guaranteed, on the basis of national legislation, by a state which is member of the OECD information shall be given in accordance with the schedule set out in Annex XVII.

2 The schedule shall apply to:

- all types of securities issued by public international bodies,
- to debt securities unconditionally and irrevocably guaranteed, on the basis of national legislation, by a state which is member of the OECD.

[*Article 20a*

Additional information building block for consent given in accordance with Article 3(2) of Directive 2003/71/EC

1. For the purposes of the third subparagraph of Article 3(2) of Directive 2003/71/EC, the prospectus shall contain the following:

(a) the additional information set out in Sections 1 and 2A of Annex XXX where the consent is given to one or more specified financial intermediaries;

(b) the additional information set out in Sections 1 and 2B of Annex XXX where the issuer or the person responsible for drawing up the prospectus chooses to give its consent to all financial intermediaries.

2. Where a financial intermediary does not comply with the conditions attached to consent as disclosed in the prospectus, a new prospectus shall be required in accordance with the second paragraph of Article 3(2) of Directive 2003/71/EC.][a]

Amendments

a Inserted by Commission Delegated Regulation (EU) No 862/2012 of 4 June 2012.

Article 21

Combination of schedules and building blocks

1 The use of the combinations provided for in the table set out in Annex XVIII shall be mandatory when drawing up prospectuses for the types of securities to which those combinations correspond according to this table.

However, for securities not covered by those combinations further combinations may be used.

2 The most comprehensive and stringent registration document schedule, i.e. the most demanding schedule in term of number of information items and the extent of the information included in them, may always be used to issue securities for which a less

comprehensive and stringent registration document schedule is provided for, according to the following ranking of schedules:

1. share registration document schedule;
2. debt and derivative securities registration document schedule for securities with a denomination per unit of less than EUR 50,000;
3. debt and derivative securities registration document schedule for securities with a denomination per unit at least EUR 50,000.

Article 22
Minimum information to be included in a base prospectus and its related final terms

1 A base prospectus shall be drawn up by using one or a combination of schedules and building blocks provided for in Articles 4 to 20 according to the combinations for various types of securities set out in Annex XVIII.

[A base prospectus shall contain the information items required in Annexes I to XVII, Annex XX and Annexes XXIII to XXX depending on the type of issuer and securities involved. Competent authorities shall not require that a base prospectus contains information items which are not included in Annexes I to XVII, Annex XX or Annexes XXIII to XXX.][a]

In order to ensure conformity with the obligation referred to in Article 5 (1) of Directive 2003/71/EC, the competent authority of the home Member State, when approving a base prospectus in accordance with Article 13 of that Directive, may require that the information provided by the issuer, the offeror or the person asking for admission to trading on a regulated market be completed, for each of the information items, on a case by case basis.

2 The issuer, the offeror or the person asking for admission to trading on a regulated market may omit information items which are not known when the base prospectus is approved and which can only be determined at the time of the individual issue.

3 The use of the combinations provided for in the table in Annex XVIII shall be mandatory when drawing up base prospectuses for the types of securities to which those combinations correspond according to this table.

However, for securities not covered by those combinations further combinations may be used.

4 The final terms attached to a base prospectus shall only contain the information items from the various securities note schedules according to which the base prospectus is drawn up.

5 In addition to the information items set out in the schedules and building blocks referred to in Articles 4 to 20 the following information shall be included in a base prospectus:

1. indication on the information that will be included in the final terms;
2. the method of publication of the final terms; if the issuer is not in a position to determine, at the time of the approval of the prospectus, the method of publication of the final terms, an indication of how the

public will be informed about which method will be used for the publication of the final terms;

3. in the case of issues of non equity securities according to point (a) of Article 5(4) of Directive 2003/71/EC, a general description of the programme.

6 Only the following categories of securities may be contained in a base prospectus and its related final terms covering issues of various types of securities:

1. asset backed securities;
2. warrants falling under Article 17;
3. non-equity securities provided for under point (b) of Article 5(4) of Directive 2003/71/EC;
4. all other non-equity securities including warrants with the exception of those mentioned in (2).

In drawing up a base prospectus the issuer, the offeror or the person asking for admission to trading on a regulated market shall clearly segregate the specific information on each of the different securities included in these categories.

7 Where an event envisaged under Article 16(1) of Directive 2003/71/EC occurs between the time that the base prospectus has been approved and the final closing of the offer of each issue of securities under the base prospectus or, as the case may be, the time that trading on a regulated market of those securities begins, the issuer, the offeror or the person asking for admission to trading on a regulated market shall publish a supplement prior to the final closing of the offer or the admission of those securities to trading.

Amendments

a Inserted by Commission Delegated Regulation (EU) No 862/2012 of 4 June 2012.

Article 23
Adaptations to the minimum information given in prospectuses and base prospectuses

1 Notwithstanding Articles 3 second paragraph and 22(1) second subparagraph, where the issuer's activities fall under one of the categories included in Annex XIX, the competent authority of the home Member State, taking into consideration the specific nature of the activities involved, may ask for adapted information, in addition to the information items included in the schedules and building blocks set out in Articles 4 to 20, including, where appropriate, a valuation or other expert's report on the assets of the issuer, in order to comply with the obligation referred to in Article 5(1) of Directive 2003/71/EC. The competent authority shall forthwith inform the Commission thereof.

In order to obtain the inclusion of a new category in Annex XIX a Member State shall notify its request to the Commission. The Commission shall update this list following the Committee procedure provided for in Article 24 of Directive 2003/71/EC.

2 By way of derogation of Articles 3 to 22, where an issuer, an offeror or a person asking for admission to trading on a regulated market applies for approval of a prospectus or a

base prospectus for a security which is not the same but comparable to the various types of securities mentioned in the table of combinations set out in Annex XVIII, the issuer, the offeror or the person asking for admission to trading on a regulated market shall add the relevant information items from another securities note schedule provided for in Articles 4 to 20 to the main securities note schedule chosen. This addition shall be done in accordance with the main characteristics of the securities being offered to the public or admitted to trading on a regulated market.

3 By way of derogation of Articles 3 to 22, where an issuer, an offeror or a person asking for admission to trading on a regulated market applies for approval of a prospectus or a base prospectus for a new type of security, the issuer, the offeror or the person asking for admission to trading on a regulated market shall notify a draft prospectus or base prospectus to the competent authority of the home Member State.

The competent authority shall decide, in consultation with the issuer, the offeror or the person asking for admission to trading on a regulated market, what information shall be included in the prospectus or base prospectus in order to comply with the obligation referred to in Article 5(1) of Directive 2003/71/EC. The competent authority shall forthwith inform the Commission thereof.

The derogation referred to in the first subparagraph shall only apply in case of a new type of security which has features completely different from the various types of securities mentioned in Annex XVIII, if the characteristics of this new security are such that a combination of the different information items referred to in the schedules and building blocks provided for in Articles 4 to 20 is not pertinent.

4 By way of derogation of Articles 3 to 22, in the cases where one of the information items required in one of the schedules or building blocks referred to in 4 to 20 or equivalent information is not pertinent to the issuer, to the offer or to the securities to which the prospectus relates, that information may be omitted.

Article 24
Content of the summary of prospectus and base prospectus

The issuer, the offeror or the person asking for admission to trading on a regulated market shall determine on its own the detailed content of the summary to the prospectus or base prospectus referred to in Article 5(2) of Directive 2003/71/EC.

CHAPTER III
FORMAT OF THE PROSPECTUS, BASE PROSPECTUS AND SUPPLEMENTS

Article 25
Format of the prospectus

1 Where an issuer, an offeror or a person asking for the admission to trading on a regulated market chooses, according to Article 5(3) of Directive 2003/71/EC to draw up a prospectus as a single document, the prospectus shall be composed of the following parts in the following order:

1. a clear and detailed table of contents;
2. the summary provided for in Article 5 (2) of Directive 2003/71/EC;

3. the risk factors linked to the issuer and the type of security covered by the issue;
4. the other information items included in the schedules and building blocks according to which the prospectus is drawn up.

2 Where an issuer, an offeror or a person asking for the admission to trading on a regulated market chooses, according to in Article 5(3) of Directive 2003/71/EC, to draw up a prospectus composed of separate documents, the securities note and the registration document shall be each composed of the following parts in the following order:

1. a clear and detailed table of content;
2. as the case may be, the risk factors linked to the issuer and the type of security covered by the issue;
3. the other information items included in the schedules and building blocks according to which the prospectus is drawn up.

3 In the cases mentioned in paragraphs 1 and 2, the issuer, the offeror or the person asking for admission to trading on a regulated market shall be free in defining the order in the presentation of the required information items included in the schedules and building blocks according to which the prospectus is drawn up.

4 Where the order of the items does not coincide with the order of the information provided for in the schedules and building blocks according to which the prospectus is drawn up, the competent authority of the home Member State may ask the issuer, the offeror or the person asking for the admission to trading on a regulated market to provide a cross reference list for the purpose of checking the prospectus before its approval. Such list shall identify the pages where each item can be found in the prospectus.

5 Where the summary of a prospectus must be supplemented according to Article 16(1) of Directive 2003/71/EC, the issuer, the offeror or the person asking for admission to trading on a regulated market shall decide on a case-by-case basis whether to integrate the new information in the original summary by producing a new summary, or to produce a supplement to the summary.

If the new information is integrated in the original summary, the issuer, the offeror or the person asking for admission to trading on a regulated market shall ensure that investors can easily identify the changes, in particular by way of footnotes.

Article 26
Format of the base prospectus and its related final terms

1 Where an issuer, an offeror or a person asking for the admission to trading on a regulated market chooses, according to Article 5 (4) of Directive 2003/71/EC to draw up a base prospectus, the base prospectus shall be composed of the following parts in the following order:

1. a clear and detailed table of contents;
2. the summary provided for in Article 5 (2) of Directive 2003/71/EC;
3. the risk factors linked to the issuer and the type of security or securities covered by the issue(s);

4. the other information items included in the schedules and building blocks according to which the prospectus is drawn up.

2 Notwithstanding paragraph 1, the issuer, the offeror or the person asking for admission to trading on a regulated market shall be free in defining the order in the presentation of the required information items included in the schedules and building blocks according to which the prospectus is drawn up. The information on the different securities contained in the base prospectus shall be clearly segregated.

3 Where the order of the items does not coincide with the order of the information provided for by the schedules and building blocks according to which the prospectus is drawn up, the home competent authority may ask the issuer, the offeror or the person asking for admission to trading on a regulated market to provide a cross reference list for the purpose of checking the prospectus before its approval. Such list should identify the pages where each item can be found in the prospectus.

4 In case the issuer, the offeror or the person asking for admission to trading on a regulated market has previously filed a registration document for a particular type of security and, at a later stage, chooses to draw up base prospectus in conformity with the conditions provided for in points (a) and (b) of Article 5(4) of Directive 2003/71/ EC, the base prospectus shall contain:

1. the information contained in the previously or simultaneously filed and approved registration document which shall be incorporated by reference, following the conditions provided for in Article 28 of this Regulation;
2. the information which would otherwise be contained in the relevant securities note less the final terms where the final terms are not included in the base prospectus.

5 The final terms attached to a base prospectus shall be presented in the form of a separate document containing only the final terms or by inclusion of the final terms into the base prospectus.

In the case that the final terms are included in a separate document containing only the final terms, they may replicate some information which has been included in the approved base prospectus according to the relevant securities note schedule that has been used for drawing up the base prospectus. In this case the final terms have to be presented in such a way that they can be easily identified as such.

A clear and prominent statement shall be inserted in the final terms indicating that the full information on the issuer and on the offer is only available on the basis of the combination of base prospectus and final terms and where the base prospectus is available.

6 Where a base prospectus relates to different securities, the issuer, the offeror or the person asking for admission to trading on a regulated market shall include a single summary in the base prospectus for all securities. The information on the different securities contained in the summary, however, shall be clearly segregated.

7 Where the summary of a base prospectus must be supplemented according to Article 16(1) of Directive 2003/71/EC, the issuer, the offeror or the person asking for admission to trading on a regulated market shall decide on a case-by-case basis whether to

integrate the new information in the original summary by producing a new summary, or by producing a supplement to the summary.

If the new information is integrated in the original summary of the base prospectus by producing a new summary, the issuer, the offeror or the person asking for admission to trading on a regulated market shall ensure that investors can easily identify the changes, in particular by way of footnotes.

8 Issuers, offerors or persons asking for admission to trading on a regulated market may compile in one single document two or more different base prospectuses.

CHAPTER IV
INFORMATION AND INCORPORATION BY REFERENCE

Article 27
Publication of the document referred to in Article 10(1) of Directive 2003/71/EC

1 The document referred to in Article 10(1) of Directive 2003/71/EC shall be made available to the public, at the choice of the issuer, the offeror or the person asking for admission to trading on a regulated market, through one of the means permitted under Article 14 of that Directive in the home Member State of the issuer.

2 The document shall be filed with the competent authority of the home Member State and made available to the public at the latest 20 working days after the publication of the annual financial statements in the home Member State.

3 The document shall include a statement indicating that some information may be out-of-date, if such is the case.

Article 28
Arrangements for incorporation by reference

1 Information may be incorporated by reference in a prospectus or base prospectus, notably if it is contained in one the following documents:

1. annual and interim financial information;
2. documents prepared on the occasion of a specific transaction such as a merger or de-merger;
3. audit reports and financial statements;
4. memorandum and articles of association;
5. earlier approved and published prospectuses and/or base prospectuses;
6. regulated information;
7. circulars to security holders.

2 The documents containing information that may be incorporated by reference in a prospectus or base prospectus or in the documents composing it shall be drawn up following the provisions of Article 19 of Directive 2003/71/EC.

3 If a document which may be incorporated by reference contains information which has undergone material changes, the prospectus or base prospectus shall clearly state such a circumstance and shall give the updated information.

4 The issuer, the offeror or the person asking for admission to trading on a regulated market may incorporate information in a prospectus or base prospectus by making

reference only to certain parts of a document, provided that it states that the non-incorporated parts are either not relevant for the investor or covered elsewhere in the prospectus.

5 When incorporating information by reference, issuers, offerors or persons asking for admission to trading on a regulated market shall endeavour not to endanger investor protection in terms of comprehensibility and accessibility of the information.

CHAPTER V
PUBLICATION AND DISSEMINATION OF ADVERTISEMENTS

Article 29
Publication in electronic form

1 The publication of the prospectus or base prospectus in electronic form, either pursuant to points (c) (d) and (e) of Article 14(2) of Directive 2003/71/EC, or as an additional means of availability, shall be subject to the following requirements:

1. the prospectus or base prospectus shall be easily accessible when entering the web-site;
2. the file format shall be such that the prospectus or base prospectus cannot be modified;
3. the prospectus or base prospectus shall not contain hyper-links, with exception of links to the electronic addresses where information incorporated by reference is available;
4. the investors shall have the possibility of downloading and printing the prospectus or base prospectus.

The exception referred to in point 3 of the first subparagraph shall only be valid for documents incorporated by reference; those documents shall be available with easy and immediate technical arrangements.

2 If a prospectus or base prospectus for offer of securities to the public is made available on the web-sites of issuers and financial intermediaries or of regulated markets, these shall take measures, to avoid targeting residents in Members States or third countries where the offer of securities to the public does not take place, such as the insertion of a disclaimer as to who are the addressees of the offer.

Article 30
Publication in newspapers

1 In order to comply with point (a) of Article 14(2) of Directive 2003/71/EC the publication of a prospectus or a base prospectus shall be made in a general or financial information newspaper having national or supra-regional scope;

2 If the competent authority is of the opinion that the newspaper chosen for publication does not comply with the requirements set out in paragraph 1, it shall determine a newspaper whose circulation is deemed appropriate for this purpose taking into account, in particular, the geographic area, number of inhabitants and reading habits in each Member State.

Article 31
Publication of the notice

1 If a Member State makes use of the option, referred to in Article 14(3) of Directive 2003/71/EC, to require the publication of a notice stating how the prospectus or base prospectus has been made available and where it can be obtained by the public, that notice shall be published in a newspaper that fulfils the requirements for publication of prospectuses according to Article 30 of this Regulation.

If the notice relates to a prospectus or base prospectus published for the only purpose of admission of securities to trading on a regulated market where securities of the same class are already admitted, it may alternatively be inserted in the gazette of that regulated market, irrespective of whether that gazette is in paper copy or electronic form.

2 The notice shall be published no later than the next working day following the date of publication of the prospectus or base prospectus pursuant to Article 14(1) of Directive 2003/71/EC.

3 The notice shall contain the following information:

1. the identification of the issuer;
2. the type, class and amount of the securities to be offered and/or in respect of which admission to trading is sought, provided that these elements are known at the time of the publication of the notice;
3. the intended time schedule of the offer/admission to trading;
4. a statement that a prospectus or base prospectus has been published and where it can be obtained;
5. if the prospectus or base prospectus has been published in a printed form, the addresses where and the period of time during which such printed forms are available to the public;
6. if the prospectus or base prospectus has been published in electronic form, the addresses to which investors shall refer to ask for a paper copy;
7. the date of the notice.

Article 32
List of approved prospectuses

The list of the approved prospectuses and base prospectuses published on the web-site of the competent authority, in accordance with Article 14(4) of Directive 2003/71/EC, shall mention how such prospectuses have been made available and where they can be obtained.

Article 33
Publication of the final terms of base prospectuses

The publication method for final terms related to a base prospectus does not have to be the same as the one used for the base prospectus as long as the publication method used is one of the publication methods indicated in Article 14 of the Directive 2003/71/EC.

Article 34
Dissemination of advertisements

Advertisements related to an offer to the public of securities or to an admission to trading on a regulated market may be disseminated to the public by interested parties, such as issuer, offeror or person asking for admission, the financial intermediaries that participate in the placing and/or underwriting of securities, notably by one of the following means of communication:

1. addressed or unaddressed printed matter;
2. electronic message or advertisement received via a mobile telephone or pager;
3. standard letter;
4. Press advertising with or without order form;
5. catalogue;
6. telephone with or without human intervention;
7. seminars and presentations;
8. radio;
9. videophone;
10. videotext;
11. electronic mail;
12. facsimile machine (fax);
13. television;
14. notice;
15. bill;
16. poster;
17. brochure;
18. web posting including internet banners.

CHAPTER VI
TRANSITIONAL AND FINAL PROVISIONS

Article 35
Historical financial information

1 The obligation for Community issuers to restate in a prospectus historical financial information according to Regulation (EC) No 1606/2002, set out in Annex I item 20.1, Annex IV item 13.1, Annex VII items 8.2, Annex X items 20.1 and Annex XI item 11.1 shall not apply to any period earlier than 1 January 2004 or, where an issuer has securities admitted to trading on a regulated market on 1 July 2005, until the issuer has published its first consolidated annual accounts with accordance with Regulation (EC) No 1606/2002.

2 Where a Community issuer is subject to transitional national provisions adopted pursuant Article 9 of Regulation (EC) No 1606/2002, the obligation to restate in a prospectus historical financial information does not apply to any period earlier than 1 January 2006 or, where an issuer has securities admitted to trading on a regulated market on 1 July 2005, until the issuer has published its first consolidated annual accounts with accordance with Regulation (EC) No 1606/2002.

3 Until 1 January 2007 the obligation to restate in a prospectus historical financial information according to Regulation (EC) No 1606/2002, set out in Annex I item 20.1, Annex IV item 13.1, Annex VII items 8.2, Annex X items 20.1 and Annex XI item 11.1 shall not apply to issuers from third countries:

1. who have their securities admitted to trading on a regulated market on 1 January 2007;

   and

2. who have presented and prepared historical financial information according to the national accounting standards of a third country.

In this case, historical financial information shall be accompanied with more detailed and/or additional information if the financial statements included in the prospectus do not give a true and fair view of the issuer's assets and liabilities, financial position and profit and loss.

4 Third country issuers having prepared historical financial information according to internationally accepted standards as referred to in Article 9 of Regulation (EC) No 1606/2002 may use that information in any prospectus filed before 1 January 2007, without being subject to restatement obligations.

[5. From 1 January 2009, third country issuers shall present their historical financial information in accordance either with one of the following accounting standards:

(a) International Financial Reporting Standards adopted pursuant to Regulation (EC) No 1606/2002;

(b) International Financial Reporting Standards provided that the notes to the audited financial statements that form part of the historical financial information contain an explicit and unreserved statement that these financial statements comply with International Financial Reporting Standards in accordance with IAS 1 *Presentation of Financial Statements*;

(c) Generally Accepted Accounting Principles of Japan;

(d) Generally Accepted Accounting Principles of the United States of America.][a]

In addition to standards referred to in the first subparagraph, from 1 January 2012, third country issuers may present their historical financial information in accordance with the following standards:

[(a) Generally Accepted Accounting Principles of the People's Republic of China;

(b) Generally Accepted Accounting Principles of Canada;

(c) Generally Accepted Accounting Principles of the Republic of Korea.

5A. Third country issuers are not subject to a requirement, under Annex I, item 20.1; Annex IV, item 13.1; Annex VII, item 8.2; Annex X, item 20.1 or Annex XI, item 11.1, to restate historical financial information or to a requirement under Annex VII, item 8.2. bis; Annex IX, item 11.1; or Annex X, item 20.1.bis, to provide a narrative description of the differences between international accounting standards adopted under Regulation (EC) No 1606/2002 and the accounting principles in accordance with which such information is drawn up, included in a prospectus filed with a competent authority before 1 January 2009, where one of the following conditions is met:

(a) the notes to the financial statements that form part of the historical financial information contain an explicit and unreserved statement that they comply with International Financial Reporting Standards in accordance with IAS 1 Presentation of Financial Statements;

(b) the historical financial information is prepared in accordance with the Generally Accepted Accounting Principles of either Canada, Japan or the United States of America;

(c) the historical financial information is prepared in accordance with the Generally Accepted Accounting Principles of a third country other than Canada, Japan or the United States of America, and the following conditions are satisfied:

(i) the third country authority responsible for the national accounting standards in question has made a public commitment, before the start of the financial year in which the prospectus is filed, to converge those standards with Inter-national Financial Reporting Standards;

(ii) that authority has established a work programme which demonstrates the intention to progress towards convergence before 31 December 2008; and

(iii) the issuer provides evidence that satisfies the competent authority that the conditions in (i) and (ii) are met.

5a. Third country issuers are not subject to a requirement, under Annex I, item 20.1; Annex IV, item 13.1; Annex VII, item 8.2; Annex X, item 20.1 or Annex XI, item 11.1, to restate historical financial information, included in a prospectus and relevant for the financial years prior to financial years starting on or after 1 January 2015, or to a requirement under Annex VII, item 8.2.bis; Annex IX, item 11.1; or Annex X, item 20.1.bis, to provide a narrative description of the differences between International Financial Reporting Standards adopted pursuant to Regulation (EC) No 1606/2002 and the accounting principles in accordance with which such information is drawn up relating to the financial years prior to financial years starting on or after 1 January 2015, provided that the historical financial information is prepared in accordance with the Generally Accepted Accounting Principles of the Republic of India.][b]

6. The provisions of this Article shall also apply to AnnexVI, item 3.

Amendments

a Inserted by Commission Regulation (EC) No 1289/2008 of 12 December 2008.

b Inserted by Commission Regulation (EC) No 311/2012 of 21 December 2011.

Article 36
Entry into force

This Regulation shall enter into force in Member States on the twentieth day after its publication in the *Official Journal of the European Union.*

It shall apply from 1 July 2005.

This Regulation shall be binding in its entirety and directly applicable in all Member States.

ANNEXES

ANNEXES I TO XVII: SCHEDULES AND BUILDING BLOCKS

ANNEX XVIII: TABLE OF COMBINATIONS OF SCHEDULES AND BUILDING BLOCKS

ANNEX XIX: LIST OF SPECIALIST ISSUERS

ANNEX I
MINIMUM DISCLOSURE REQUIREMENTS FOR THE SHARE REGISTRATION DOCUMENT
(SCHEDULE)

1. Persons Responsible

1.1. All persons responsible for the information given in the Registration Document and, as the case may be, for certain parts of it, with, in the latter case, an indication of such parts. In the case of natural persons including members of the issuer's administrative, management or supervisory bodies indicate the name and function of the person; in case of legal persons indicate the name and registered office.

1.2. A declaration by those responsible for the registration document that, having taken all reasonable care to ensure that such is the case, the information contained in the registration document is, to the best of their knowledge, in accordance with the facts and contains no omission likely to affect its import. As the case may be, a declaration by those responsible for certain parts of the registration document that, having taken all reasonable care to ensure that such is the case, the information contained in the part of the registration document for which they are responsible is, to the best of their knowledge, in accordance with the facts and contains no omission likely to affect its import.

2. Statutory Auditors

2.1. Names and addresses of the issuer's auditors for the period covered by the historical financial information (together with their membership in a professional body).

2.2. If auditors have resigned, been removed or not been re-appointed during the period covered by the historical financial information, indicate details if material.

3. Selected Financial Information

3.1. Selected historical financial information regarding the issuer, presented for each financial year for the period covered by the historical financial information, and any subsequent interim financial period, in the same currency as the financial information.

The selected historical financial information must provide the key figures that summarise the financial condition of the issuer.

3.2. If selected financial information for interim periods is provided, comparative data from the same period in the prior financial year must also be provided, except that the requirement for comparative balance sheet information is satisfied by presenting the year end balance sheet information.

4. Risk Factors

Prominent disclosure of risk factors that are specific to the issuer or its industry in a section headed 'Risk Factors'.

5. Information about the Issuer

5.1 *History and development of the issuer*

5.1.1. The legal and commercial name of the issuer

5.1.2. The place of registration of the issuer and its registration number

5.1.3. The date of incorporation and the length of life of the issuer, except where indefinite

5.1.4. The domicile and legal form of the issuer, the legislation under which the issuer operates, its country of incorporation, and the address and telephone number of its registered office (or principal place of business if different from its registered office)

5.1.5. The important events in the development of the issuer's business.

5.2. *Investments*

5.2.1. A description, (including the amount) of the issuer's principal investments for each financial year for the period covered by the historical financial information up to the date of the registration document

5.2.2. A description of the issuer's principal investments that are in progress, including the geographic distribution of these investments (home and abroad) and the method of financing (internal or external)

5.2.3. Information concerning the issuer's principal future investments on which its management bodies have already made firm commitments.

6. Business Overview

6.1. *Principal Activities*

6.1.1. A description of, and key factors relating to, the nature of the issuer's operations and its principal activities, stating the main categories of products sold and/or services performed for each financial year for the period covered by the historical financial information; and

6.1.2. An indication of any significant new products and/or services that have been introduced and, to the extent the development of new products or services has been publicly disclosed, give the status of development.

6.2. *Principal Markets*

A description of the principal markets in which the issuer competes, including a breakdown of total revenues by category of activity and geographic market for each financial year for the period covered by the historical financial information.

6.3. Where the information given pursuant to items 6.1 and 6.2 has been influenced by exceptional factors, mention that fact.

6.4. If material to the issuer's business or profitability, a summary information regarding the extent to which the issuer is dependent, on patents or licences, industrial, commercial or financial contracts or new manufacturing processes.

6.5. The basis for any statements made by the issuer regarding its competitive position.

7. Organisational Structure

7.1. If the issuer is part of a group, a brief description of the group and the issuer's position within the group.

7.2. A list of the issuer's significant subsidiaries, including name, country of incorporation or residence, proportion of ownership interest and, if different, proportion of voting power held.

8. Property, Plants and Equipment

8.1. Information regarding any existing or planned material tangible fixed assets, including leased properties, and any major encumbrances thereon.

8.2. A description of any environmental issues that may affect the issuer's utilisation of the tangible fixed assets.

9. Operating and Financial Review

9.1. *Financial Condition*

To the extent not covered elsewhere in the registration document, provide a description of the issuer's financial condition, changes in financial condition and results of operations for each year and interim period, for which historical financial information is required, including the causes of material changes from year to year in the financial information to the extent necessary for an understanding of the issuer's business as a whole.

9.2. *Operating Results*

9.2.1. Information regarding significant factors, including unusual or infrequent events or new developments, materially affecting the issuer's income from operations, indicating the extent to which income was so affected.

9.2.2. Where the financial statements disclose material changes in net sales or revenues, provide a narrative discussion of the reasons for such changes.

9.2.3. Information regarding any governmental, economic, fiscal, monetary or political policies or factors that have materially affected, or could materially affect, directly or indirectly, the issuer's operations.

10. Capital Resources

10.1. Information concerning the issuer's capital resources (both short and long term);

10.2. An explanation of the sources and amounts of and a narrative description of the issuer's cash flows;

10.3. Information on the borrowing requirements and funding structure of the issuer;

10.4. Information regarding any restrictions on the use of capital resources that have materially affected, or could materially affect, directly or indirectly, the issuer's operations.

10.5. Information regarding the anticipated sources of funds needed to fulfil commitments referred to in items 5.2.3 and 8.1.

11. Research and Development, Patents And Licences

Where material, provide a description of the issuer's research and development policies for each financial year for the period covered by the historical financial information, including the amount spent on issuer-sponsored research and development activities.

12. Trend Information

12.1. The most significant recent trends in production, sales and inventory, and costs and selling prices since the end of the last financial year to the date of the registration document.

12.2. Information on any known trends, uncertainties, demands, commitments or events that are reasonably likely to have a material effect on the issuer's prospects for at least the current financial year.

13. Profit Forecasts or Estimates

If an issuer chooses to include a profit forecast or a profit estimate the registration document must contain the information set out in items 13.1 and 13.2:

13.1. A statement setting out the principal assumptions upon which the issuer has based its forecast, or estimate.

There must be a clear distinction between assumptions about factors which the members of the administrative, management or supervisory bodies can influence and assumptions about factors which are exclusively outside the influence of the members of the administrative, management or supervisory bodies; the assumptions must be readily understandable by investors, be specific and precise and not relate to the general accuracy of the estimates underlying the forecast.

[13.2. A report prepared by independent accountants or auditors stating that in the opinion of the independent accountants or auditors the forecast or estimate has been properly compiled on the basis stated, and that the basis of accounting used for the profit forecast or estimate is consistent with the accounting policies of the issuer.

Where financial information relates to the previous financial year and only contains non-misleading figures substantially consistent with the final figures to be published in the next annual audited financial statements for the previous financial year, and the explanatory information necessary to assess the figures, a report shall not be required provided that the prospectus includes all of the following statements:

(a) the person responsible for this financial information, if different from the one which is responsible for the prospectus in general, approves that information;

(b) independent accountants or auditors have agreed that this information is substantially consistent with the final figures to be published in the next annual audited financial statements;

(c) this financial information has not been audited.][a]

13.3. The profit forecast or estimate must be prepared on a basis comparable with the historical financial information.

13.4. If a profit forecast in a prospectus has been published which is still outstanding, then provide a statement setting out whether or not that forecast is still correct as at the time of the registration document, and an explanation of why such forecast is no longer valid if that is the case.

14. Administrative, Management, and Supervisory Bodies and Senior Management

14.1. Names, business addresses and functions in the issuer of the following persons and an indication of the principal activities performed by them outside that issuer where these are significant with respect to that issuer:

(a) members of the administrative, management or supervisory bodies;

(b) partners with unlimited liability, in the case of a limited partnership with a share capital;

(c) founders, if the issuer has been established for fewer than five years; and

(d) any senior manager who is relevant to establishing that the issuer has the appropriate expertise and experience for the management of the issuer's business.

The nature of any family relationship between any of those persons.

In the case of each member of the administrative, management or supervisory bodies of the issuer and of each person mentioned in points (b) and (d) of the first subparagraph, details of that person's relevant management expertise and experience and the following information:

(a) the names of all companies and partnerships of which such person has been a member of the administrative, management or supervisory bodies or partner at any time in the previous five years, indicating whether or not the individual is still a member of the administrative, management or supervisory bodies or partner. It is not necessary to list all the subsidiaries of an issuer of which the person is also a member of the administrative, management or supervisory bodies;

(b) any convictions in relation to fraudulent offences for at least the previous five years;

(c) details of any bankruptcies, receiverships or liquidations with which a person described in (a) and (d) of the first subparagraph who was acting in the capacity of any of the positions set out in (a) and (d) of the first subparagraph was associated for at least the previous five years;

(d) details of any official public incrimination and/or sanctions of such person by statutory or regulatory authorities (including designated professional bodies) and whether such person has ever been disqualified by a court from acting as a member of the administrative, management or supervisory bodies of an issuer or from acting in the management or conduct of the affairs of any issuer for at least the previous five years.

If there is no such information to be disclosed, a statement to that effect is to be made.

14.2. Administrative, Management, and Supervisory bodies' and Senior Management conflicts of interests

Potential conflicts of interests between any duties to the issuer, of the persons referred to in item 14.1 and their private interests and or other duties must be clearly stated. In the event that there are no such conflicts, a statement to that effect must be made.

Any arrangement or understanding with major shareholders, customers, suppliers or others, pursuant to which any person referred to in item 14.1 was selected as a member of the administrative, management or supervisory bodies or member of senior management.

Details of any restrictions agreed by the persons referred to in item 14.1 on the disposal within a certain period of time of their holdings in the issuer's securities.

15. Remuneration and Benefits

In relation to the last full financial year for those persons referred to in points (a) and (d) of the first subparagraph of item 14.1:

15.1. The amount of remuneration paid (including any contingent or deferred compensation), and benefits in kind granted to such persons by the issuer and its subsidiaries for services in all capacities to the issuer and its subsidiaries by any person.

That information must be provided on an individual basis unless individual disclosure is not required in the issuer's home country and is not otherwise publicly disclosed by the issuer.

15.2. The total amounts set aside or accrued by the issuer or its subsidiaries to provide pension, retirement or similar benefits.

16. Board Practices

In relation to the issuer's last completed financial year, and unless otherwise specified, with respect to those persons referred to in point (a) of the first subparagraph of 14.1:

16.1. Date of expiration of the current term of office, if applicable, and the period during which the person has served in that office.

16.2. Information about members of the administrative, management or supervisory bodies' service contracts with the issuer or any of its subsidiaries providing for benefits upon termination of employment, or an appropriate negative statement.

16.3. Information about the issuer's audit committee and remuneration committee, including the names of committee members and a summary of the terms of reference under which the committee operates.

16.4. A statement as to whether or not the issuer complies with its country's of incorporation corporate governance regime(s). In the event that the issuer does not comply with such a regime, a statement to that effect must be included together with an explanation regarding why the issuer does not comply with such regime.

17. Employees

17.1. Either the number of employees at the end of the period or the average for each financial year for the period covered by the historical financial information up to the date of the registration document (and changes in such numbers, if material) and, if possible and material, a breakdown of persons employed by main category of activity and geographic location. If the issuer employs a significant number of temporary employees, include disclosure of the number of temporary employees on average during the most recent financial year.

17.2. Shareholdings and stock options

With respect to each person referred to in points (a) and (d) of the first subparagraph of item 14.1. provide information as to their share ownership and any options over such shares in the issuer as of the most recent practicable date.

17.3. Description of any arrangements for involving the employees in the capital of the issuer.

18. Major Shareholders

18.1. In so far as is known to the issuer, the name of any person other than a member of the administrative, management or supervisory bodies who, directly or indirectly, has an interest in the issuer's capital or voting rights which is notifiable under the issuer's national law, together with the amount of each such person's interest or, if there are no such persons, an appropriate negative statement.

18.2. Whether the issuer's major shareholders have different voting rights, or an appropriate negative statement.

18.3. To the extent known to the issuer, state whether the issuer is directly or indirectly owned or controlled and by whom and describe the nature of such control and describe the measures in place to ensure that such control is not abused.

18.4. A description of any arrangements, known to the issuer, the operation of which may at a subsequent date result in a change in control of the issuer.

19. Related Party Transactions

Details of related party transactions (which for these purposes are those set out in the Standards adopted according to the Regulation (EC) No 1606/2002), that the issuer has entered into during the period covered by the historical financial information and up to the date of the registration document, must be disclosed in accordance with the respective standard adopted according to Regulation (EC) No 1606/2002 if applicable.

If such standards do not apply to the issuer the following information must be disclosed:

(a) the nature and extent of any transactions which are - as a single transaction or in their entirety - material to the issuer. Where such related party transactions are not concluded at arm's length provide an explanation of why these transactions were not concluded at arms length. In the case of outstanding loans including guarantees of any kind indicate the amount outstanding;

(b) the amount or the percentage to which related party transactions form part of the turnover of the issuer.

20. Financial Information Concerning the Issuer's Assets and Liabilities, Financial Position and Profits and Losses

20.1. *Historical Financial Information*

Audited historical financial information covering the latest 3 financial years (or such shorter period that the issuer has been in operation), and the audit report in respect of each year. [If the issuer has changed its accounting reference date during the period for which historical financial information is required, the audited historical information shall cover at least 36 months, or the entire period for which the issuer has been in operation, whichever is the shorter.][b] Such financial information must be prepared according to Regulation (EC) No 1606/2002, or if not applicable to a Member State national accounting standards for issuers from the Community. For third country issuers, such financial information must be prepared according to the international accounting standards adopted pursuant to the procedure of Article 3 of Regulation (EC) No 1606/2002 or to a third country's national accounting standards equivalent to these standards. If such financial information is not equivalent to these standards, it must be presented in the form of restated financial statements.

The last two years audited historical financial information must be presented and prepared in a form consistent with that which will be adopted in the issuer's next published annual financial statements having regard to accounting standards and policies and legislation applicable to such annual financial statements.

If the issuer has been operating in its current sphere of economic activity for less than one year, the audited historical financial information covering that period must be prepared in accordance with the standards applicable to annual financial statements under the Regulation (EC) No 1606/2002, or if not applicable to a Member State national accounting standards where the issuer is an issuer from the Community. For third country issuers, the historical financial information must be prepared according to the international accounting standards adopted pursuant to the procedure of Article 3 of Regulation (EC) No 1606/2002 or to a third country's national accounting standards equivalent to these standards. This historical financial information must be audited.

If the audited financial information is prepared according to national accounting standards, the financial information required under this heading must include at least:

(a) balance sheet;

(b) income statement;

(c) a statement showing either all changes in equity or changes in equity other than those arising from capital transactions with owners and distributions to owners;

(d) cash flow statement;

(e) accounting policies and explanatory notes.

The historical annual financial information must be independently audited or reported on as to whether or not, for the purposes of the registration document, it gives a true and fair view, in accordance with auditing standards applicable in a Member State or an equivalent standard.

20.2. *Pro forma financial information*

In the case of a significant gross change, a description of how the transaction might have affected the assets and liabilities and earnings of the issuer, had the transaction been undertaken at the commencement of the period being reported on or at the date reported.

This requirement will normally be satisfied by the inclusion of pro forma financial information.

This pro forma financial information is to be presented as set out in Annex II and must include the information indicated therein.

Pro forma financial information must be accompanied by a report prepared by independent accountants or auditors.

20.3. *Financial statements*

If the issuer prepares both own and consolidated annual financial statements, include at least the consolidated annual financial statements in the registration document.

20.4. *Auditing of historical annual financial information*

20.4.1. A statement that the historical financial information has been audited. If audit reports on the historical financial information have been refused by the statutory auditors or if they contain qualifications or disclaimers, such refusal or such qualifications or disclaimers must be reproduced in full and the reasons given.

20.4.2. Indication of other information in the registration document which has been audited by the auditors.

20.4.3. Where financial data in the registration document is not extracted from the issuer's audited financial statements state the source of the data and state that the data is unaudited.

20.5. *Age of latest financial information*

20.5.1. The last year of audited financial information may not be older than one of the following:

(a) 18 months from the date of the registration document if the issuer includes audited interim financial statements in the registration document;

(b) 15 months from the date of the registration document if the issuer includes unaudited interim financial statements in the registration document.

20.6. *Interim and other financial information*

20.6.1. If the issuer has published quarterly or half yearly financial information since the date of its last audited financial statements, these must be included in the registration document. If the quarterly or half yearly financial information has been reviewed or audited, the audit or review report must also be included. If the quarterly or half yearly financial information is unaudited or has not been reviewed state that fact.

20.6.2. If the registration document is dated more than nine months after the end of the last audited financial year, it must contain interim financial information, which may be unaudited (in which case that fact must be stated) covering at least the first six months of the financial year.

The interim financial information must include comparative statements for the same period in the prior financial year, except that the requirement for comparative balance sheet information may be satisfied by presenting the years end balance sheet.

20.7. *Dividend policy*

A description of the issuer's policy on dividend distributions and any restrictions thereon.

20.7.1. The amount of the dividend per share for each financial year for the period covered by the historical financial information adjusted, where the number of shares in the issuer has changed, to make it comparable.

20.8. *Legal and arbitration proceedings*

Information on any governmental, legal or arbitration proceedings (including any such proceedings which are pending or threatened of which the issuer is aware), during a period covering at least the previous 12 months which may have, or have had in the recent past significant effects on the issuer and/or group's financial position or profitability, or provide an appropriate negative statement.

20.9. Significant change in the issuer's financial or trading position

A description of any significant change in the financial or trading position of the group which has occurred since the end of the last financial period for which either audited financial information or interim financial information have been published, or provide an appropriate negative statement.

21. Additional Information

21.1. *Share Capital*

The following information as of the date of the most recent balance sheet included in the historical financial information:

21.1.1. The amount of issued capital, and for each class of share capital:

(a) the number of shares authorised;

(b) the number of shares issued and fully paid and issued but not fully paid;

(c) the par value per share, or that the shares have no par value; and

(d) a reconciliation of the number of shares outstanding at the beginning and end of the year. If more than 10% of capital has been paid for with assets other than cash within the period covered by the historical financial information, state that fact.

21.1.2. If there are shares not representing capital, state the number and main characteristics of such shares.

21.1.3. The number, book value and face value of shares in the issuer held by or on behalf of the issuer itself or by subsidiaries of the issuer.

21.1.4. The amount of any convertible securities, exchangeable securities or securities with warrants, with an indication of the conditions governing and the procedures for conversion, exchange or subscription.

21.1.5. Information about and terms of any acquisition rights and or obligations over authorised but unissued capital or an undertaking to increase the capital.

21.1.6. Information about any capital of any member of the group which is under option or agreed conditionally or unconditionally to be put under option and details of such options including those persons to whom such options relate.

21.1.7. A history of share capital, highlighting information about any changes, for the period covered by the historical financial information.

21.2. *Memorandum and Articles of Association*

21.2.1. A description of the issuer's objects and purposes and where they can be found in the memorandum and articles of association.

21.2.2. A summary of any provisions of the issuer's articles of association, statutes, charter or bylaws with respect to the members of the administrative, management and supervisory bodies.

21.2.3. A description of the rights, preferences and restrictions attaching to each class of the existing shares.

21.2.4. A description of what action is necessary to change the rights of holders of the shares, indicating where the conditions are more significant than is required by law.

21.2.5. A description of the conditions governing the manner in which annual general meetings and extraordinary general meetings of shareholders are called including the conditions of admission.

21.2.6. A brief description of any provision of the issuer's articles of association, statutes, charter or bylaws that would have an effect of delaying, deferring or preventing a change in control of the issuer.

21.2.7. An indication of the articles of association, statutes, charter or bylaw provisions, if any, governing the ownership threshold above which shareholder ownership must be disclosed.

21.2.8. A description of the conditions imposed by the memorandum and articles of association statutes, charter or bylaw governing changes in the capital, where such conditions are more stringent than is required by law.

22. Material Contracts

A summary of each material contract, other than contracts entered into in the ordinary course of business, to which the issuer or any member of the group is a party, for the two years immediately preceding publication of the registration document.

A summary of any other contract (not being a contract entered into in the ordinary course of business) entered into by any member of the group which contains any provision under which any member of the group has any obligation or entitlement which is material to the group as at the date of the registration document.

23. Third Party Information and Statement by Experts and Declarations of Any Interest

23.1. Where a statement or report attributed to a person as an expert is included in the registration document, provide such person's name, business address, qualifications and material interest if any in the issuer. If the report has been produced at the issuer's request a statement to the effect that such statement or report is included, in the form and context in which it is included, with the consent of the person who has authorised the contents of that part of the registration document.

23.2. Where information has been sourced from a third party, provide a confirmation that this information has been accurately reproduced and that as far as the issuer is aware and is able to ascertain from information published by that third party, no facts have been omitted which would render the reproduced information inaccurate or misleading. In addition, identify the source(s) of the information.

24. Documents on Display

A statement that for the life of the registration document the following documents (or copies thereof), where applicable, may be inspected:

(a) the memorandum and articles of association of the issuer;

(b) all reports, letters, and other documents, historical financial information, valuations and statements prepared by any expert at the issuer's request any part of which is included or referred to in the registration document;

(c) the historical financial information of the issuer or, in the case of a group, the historical financial information for the issuer and its subsidiary undertakings for each of the two financial years preceding the publication of the registration document.

An indication of where the documents on display may be inspected, by physical or electronic means.

25. Information on Holdings

Information relating to the undertakings in which the issuer holds a proportion of the capital likely to have a significant effect on the assessment of its own assets and liabilities, financial position or profits and losses.

Amendments

a Inserted by Commission Delegated Regulation (EU) No 862/2012 of 4 June 2012.

b Inserted by Commission Regulation (EC) No 211/2007 of 27 February 2007 OJ L337 5.12.2006, p 17.

Annex II
Pro forma financial information building block

1. The pro forma information must include a description of the trans-action, the businesses or entities involved and the period to which it refers, and must clearly state the following:

   (a) the purpose to which it has been prepared;

   (b) the fact that it has been prepared for illustrative purposes only;

   (c) the fact that because of its nature, the pro forma financial information addresses a hypothetical situation and, therefore, does not represent the company's actual financial position or results.

2. In order to present pro forma financial information, a balance sheet and profit and loss account, and accompanying explanatory notes, depending on the circumstances may be included.

3. Pro forma financial information must normally be presented in columnar format, composed of:

   (a) the historical unadjusted information;

   (b) the pro forma adjustments;

   and

   (c) the resulting pro forma financial information in the final column.

   The sources of the pro forma financial information have to be stated and, if applicable, the financial statements of the acquired businesses or entities must be included in the prospectus

4. The pro forma information must be prepared in a manner consistent with the accounting policies adopted by the issuer in its last or next financial statements and shall identify the following:

   (a) the basis upon which it is prepared;

   (b) the source of each item of information and adjustment.

5. Pro forma information may only be published in respect of:

   (a) the current financial period;

   (b) the most recently completed financial period;

   and/or

   (c) the most recent interim period for which relevant unadjusted information has been or will be published or is being published in the same document.

6. Pro forma adjustments related to the pro forma financial information must be:

   (a) clearly shown and explained;

   (b) directly attributable to the transaction;

   (c) factually supportable.

   In addition, in respect of a pro forma profit and loss or cash flow statement, they must be clearly identified as to those expected to have a continuing impact on the issuer and those which are not.

7. The report prepared by the independent accountants or auditors must state that in their opinion:

   (a) the pro forma financial information has been properly compiled on the basis stated;

   (b) that basis is consistent with the accounting policies of the issuer.

Annex III
Minimum disclosure requirements for the share securities note (schedule)

1. Persons Responsible

1.1. All persons responsible for the information given in the prospectus and, as the case may be, for certain parts of it, with, in the latter case, an indication of such parts. In the case of natural persons including members of the issuer's administrative, management or supervisory bodies indicate the name and function of the person; in case of legal persons indicate the name and registered office.

1.2. A declaration by those responsible for the prospectus that, having taken all reasonable care to ensure that such is the case the information contained in the prospectus is, to the best of their knowledge, in accordance with the facts and contains no omission likely to affect its import. As the case may be, declaration by those responsible for certain parts of the prospectus that, having taken all reasonable care to ensure that such is the case the information contained in the part of the prospectus for which they are responsible is, to the best of their knowledge, in accordance with the facts and contains no omission likely to affect its import.

2. Risk Factors

Prominent disclosure of risk factors that are material to the securities being offered and/or admitted to trading in order to assess the market risk associated with these securities in a section headed 'Risk Factors'.

[3. Essential Information][a]

3.1. *Working capital Statement*

Statement by the issuer that, in its opinion, the working capital is sufficient for the issuer's present requirements or, if not, how it proposes to provide the additional working capital needed.

3.2. *Capitalisation and indebtedness*

A statement of capitalisation and indebtedness (distinguishing between guaranteed and unguaranteed, secured and unsecured indebtedness) as of a date no earlier than 90 days prior to the date of the document. Indebtedness also includes indirect and contingent indebtedness.

3.3. *Interest of natural and legal persons involved in the issue/offer*

A description of any interest, including conflicting ones that is material to the issue/offer, detailing the persons involved and the nature of the interest.

3.4. *Reasons for the offer and use of proceeds*

Reasons for the offer and, where applicable, the estimated net amount of the proceeds broken into each principal intended use and presented by order of priority of such uses. If the issuer is aware that the anticipated proceeds will not be sufficient to fund all the proposed uses, state the amount and sources of other funds needed. Details must be given with regard to the use of the proceeds, in particular when they are being used to acquire assets, other than in the ordinary course of business, to finance announced acquisitions of other business, or to *discharge*, reduce or retire indebtedness.

4. Information Concerning the Securities to be Offered/admitted to Trading

4.1. A description of the type and the class of the securities being offered and/or admitted to trading, including the ISIN (international security identification number) or other such security identification code.

4.2. Legislation under which the securities have been created.

4.3. An indication whether the securities are in registered form or bearer form and whether the securities are in certificated form or book-entry form. In the latter case, name and address of the entity in charge of keeping the records.

4.4. Currency of the securities issue.

4.5. A description of the rights attached to the securities, including any limitations of those rights, and procedure for the exercise of those rights.

- Dividend rights:
  - fixed date(s) on which the entitlement arises,
  - time limit after which entitlement to dividend lapses and an indication of the person in whose favour the lapse operates,
  - dividend restrictions and procedures for non-resident holders,
  - rate of dividend or method of its calculation, periodicity and cumulative or non-cumulative nature of payments.
- Voting rights.
- Pre-emption rights in offers for subscription of securities of the same class.
- Right to share in the issuer's profits.
- Rights to share in any surplus in the event of liquidation.
- Redemption provisions.
- Conversion provisions.

4.6 In the case of new issues, a statement of the resolutions, authorisations and approvals by virtue of which the securities have been or will be created and/or issued.

4.7 In the case of new issues, the expected issue date of the securities.

4.8 A description of any restrictions on the free transferability of the securities.

4.9 An indication of the existence of any mandatory takeover bids and/or squeeze-out and sell-out rules in relation to the securities.

4.10 An indication of public takeover bids by third parties in respect of the issuer's equity, which have occurred during the last financial year and the current financial year. The price or exchange terms attaching to such offers and the outcome thereof must be stated.

4.11. In respect of the country of registered office of the issuer and the country(ies) where the offer is being made or admission to trading is being sought:

- information on taxes on the income from the securities withheld at source,

— indication as to whether the issuer assumes responsibility for the withholding of taxes at the source.

5. **Terms and Conditions of the Offer**

5.1. *Conditions, offer statistics, expected timetable and action required to apply for the offer*

5.1.1. Conditions to which the offer is subject.

5.1.2. Total amount of the issue/offer, distinguishing the securities offered for sale and those offered for subscription; if the amount is not fixed, description of the arrangements and time for announcing to the public the definitive amount of the offer.

5.1.3. The time period, including any possible amendments, during which the offer will be open and description of the application process.

5.1.4. An indication of when, and under which circumstances, the offer may be revoked or suspended and whether revocation can occur after dealing has begun.

5.1.5. A description of the possibility to reduce subscriptions and the manner for refunding excess amount paid by applicants.

5.1.6. Details of the minimum and/or maximum amount of application (whether in number of securities or aggregate amount to invest).

5.1.7 An indication of the period during which an application may be withdrawn, provided that investors are allowed to withdraw their subscription.

5.1.8 Method and time limits for paying up the securities and for delivery of the securities.

5.1.9 A full description of the manner and date in which results of the offer are to be made public.

5.1.10 The procedure for the exercise of any right of pre-emption, the negotiability of subscription rights and the treatment of subscription rights not exercised.

5.2. Plan of distribution and allotment

5.2.1. The various categories of potential investors to which the securities are offered. If the offer is being made simultaneously in the markets of two or more countries and if a tranche has been or is being reserved for certain of these, indicate any such tranche.

5.2.2. To the extent known to the issuer, an indication of whether major shareholders or members of the issuer's management, supervisory or administrative bodies intended to subscribe in the offer, or whether any person intends to subscribe for more than five per cent of the offer.

5.2.3. Pre-allotment disclosure:

(a) the division into tranches of the offer including the institutional, retail and issuer's employee tranches and any other tranches;

(b) the conditions under which the clawback may be used, the maximum size of such claw back and any applicable minimum percentages for individual tranches;

(c) the allotment method or methods to be used for the retail and issuer's employee tranche in the event of an over-subscription of these tranches;

(d) a description of any pre-determined preferential treatment to be accorded to certain classes of investors or certain affinity groups (including friends and family programmes) in the allotment, the percentage of the offer reserved for such preferential treatment and the criteria for inclusion in such classes or groups;

(e) whether the treatment of subscriptions or bids to subscribe in the allotment may be determined on the basis of which firm they are made through or by;

(f) a target minimum individual allotment if any within the retail tranche;

(g) the conditions for the closing of the offer as well as the date on which the offer may be closed at the earliest;

(h) whether or not multiple subscriptions are admitted, and where they are not, how any multiple subscriptions will be handled.

5.2.4. Process for notification to applicants of the amount allotted and indication whether dealing may begin before notification is made.

5.2.5. Over-allotment and 'green shoe':

(a) the existence and size of any over-allotment facility and/or 'green shoe'.

(b) the existence period of the over-allotment facility and/or 'green shoe'.

(c) any conditions for the use of the over-allotment facility or exercise of the 'green shoe'.

5.3. *Pricing*

5.3.1. An indication of the price at which the securities will be offered. If the price is not known or if there is no established and/or liquid market for the securities, indicate the method for determining the offer price, including a statement as to who has set the criteria or is formally responsible for the determination. Indication of the amount of any expenses and taxes specifically charged to the subscriber or purchaser.

5.3.2. Process for the disclosure of the offer price.

5.3.3. If the issuer's equity holders have pre-emptive purchase rights and this right is restricted or withdrawn, indication of the basis for the issue price if the issue is for cash, together with the reasons for and beneficiaries of such restriction or withdrawal.

5.3.4 Where there is or could be a material disparity between the public offer price and the effective cash cost to members of the administrative, management or supervisory bodies or senior management, or affiliated persons, of securities acquired by them in transactions during the past year, or which they have the right to acquire, include a comparison of the public contribution in the proposed public offer and the effective cash contributions of such persons.

5.4. *Placing and Underwriting*

5.4.1 Name and address of the coordinator(s) of the global offer and of single parts of the offer and, to the extend known to the issuer or to the offeror, of the placers in the various countries where the offer takes place.

5.4.2 Name and address of any paying agents and depository agents in each country.

5.4.3. Name and address of the entities agreeing to underwrite the issue on a firm commitment basis, and name and address of the entities agreeing to place the issue without a firm commitment or under 'best efforts' arrangements. Indication of the material features of the agreements, including the quotas. Where not all of the issue is underwritten, a statement of the portion not covered. Indication of the overall amount of the underwriting commission and of the placing commission.

5.4.4. When the underwriting agreement has been or will be reached.

6. Admission to Trading and Dealing Arrangements

6.1. An indication as to whether the securities offered are or will be the object of an application for admission to trading, with a view to their distribution in a regulated market or other equivalent markets with indication of the markets in question. This circumstance must be mentioned, without creating the impression that the admission to trading will necessarily be approved. If known, the earliest dates on which the securities will be admitted to trading.

6.2. All the regulated markets or equivalent markets on which, to the knowledge of the issuer, securities of the same class of the securities to be offered or admitted to trading are already admitted to trading.

6.3. If simultaneously or almost simultaneously with the creation of the securities for which admission to a regulated market is being sought securities of the same class are subscribed for or placed privately or if securities of other classes are created for public or private placing, give details of the nature of such operations and of the number and characteristics of the securities to which they relate.

6.4. Details of the entities which have a firm commitment to act as intermediaries in secondary trading, providing liquidity through bid and offer rates and description of the main terms of their commitment.

6.5. *Stabilisation: where an issuer or a selling shareholder has granted an over-allotment option or it is otherwise proposed that price stabilising activities may be entered into in connection with an offer:*

6.5.1. The fact that stabilisation may be undertaken, that there is no assurance that it will be undertaken and that it may be stopped at any time,

6.5.2. The beginning and the end of the period during which stabilisation may occur,

6.5.3. The identity of the stabilisation manager for each relevant jurisdiction unless this is not known at the time of publication,

6.5.4. The fact that stabilisation transactions may result in a market price that is higher than would otherwise prevail.

7. Selling Securities Holders

7.1. Name and business address of the person or entity offering to sell the securities, the nature of any position office or other material relationship that the selling persons has had within the past three years with the issuer or any of its predecessors or affiliates.

7.2. The number and class of securities being offered by each of the selling security holders.

7.3. Lock-up agreements

The parties involved.

Content and exceptions of the agreement. Indication of the period of the lock up.

8. Expense of the Issue/offer

8.1. The total net proceeds and an estimate of the total expenses of the issue/offer.

9. Dilution

9.1. The amount and percentage of immediate dilution resulting from the offer.

9.2. In the case of a subscription offer to existing equity holders, the amount and percentage of immediate dilution if they do not subscribe to the new offer.

10. Additional Information

10.1. If advisors connected with an issue are mentioned in the Securities Note, a statement of the capacity in which the advisors have acted.

10.2. An indication of other information in the Securities Note which has been audited or reviewed by statutory auditors and where auditors have produced a report. Reproduction of the report or, with permission of the competent authority, a summary of the report.

10.3. Where a statement or report attributed to a person as an expert is included in the Securities Note, provide such persons' name, business address, qualifications and material interest if any in the issuer. If the report has been produced at the issuer's request a statement to the effect that such statement or report is included, in the form and context in which it is included, with the consent of the person who has authorised the contents of that part of the Securities Note.

10.4. Where information has been sourced from a third party, provide a confirmation that this information has been accurately reproduced and that as far as the issuer is aware and is able to ascertain from information published by that third party, no facts have been omitted which would render the reproduced information inaccurate or misleading. In addition, identify the source(s) of the information.

Amendments

a Inserted by Commission Delegated Regulation (EU) No 862/2012 of 4 June 2012.

Annex IV
Minimum disclosure requirements for the debt and derivative securities registration document (schedule)

(Debt and derivative securities with a denomination per unit of less than EUR 50,000)

1. Persons Responsible

1.1. All persons responsible for the information given in the registration document and, as the case may be, for certain parts of it, with, in the latter case, an indication of such parts. In the case of natural persons including members of the issuer's administrative, management or supervisory bodies indicate the name and function of the person; in case of legal persons indicate the name and registered office.

1.2. A declaration by those responsible for the registration document that, having taken all reasonable care to ensure that such is the case the information contained in the registration document is, to the best of their knowledge, in accordance with the facts and contains no omission likely to affect its import. As the case may be, declaration by those responsible for certain parts of the registration document that, having taken all reasonable care to ensure that such is the case, the information contained in the part of the registration document for which they are responsible is, to the best of their knowledge, in accordance with the facts and contains no omission likely to affect its import.

2. Statutory Auditors

2.1. Names and addresses of the issuer's auditors for the period covered by the historical financial information (together with their membership in a professional body).

2.2. If auditors have resigned, been removed or not been re-appointed during the period covered by the historical financial information, details if material.

3. Selected Financial Information

3.1. Selected historical financial information regarding the issuer, presented, for each financial year for the period covered by the historical financial information, and any subsequent interim financial period, in the same currency as the financial information.

The selected historical financial information must provide key figures that summarise the financial condition of the issuer.

3.2. If selected financial information for interim periods is provided, comparative data from the same period in the prior financial year must also be provided, except that the requirement for comparative balance sheet data is satisfied by presenting the year end balance sheet information.

4. Risk Factors

Prominent disclosure of risk factors that may affect the issuer's ability to fulfil its obligations under the securities to investors in a section headed 'Risk Factors'.

5. Information about the Issuer

5.1. *History and development of the Issuer*

5.1.1. the legal and commercial name of the issuer;

5.1.2. the place of registration of the issuer and its registration number;

5.1.3. the date of incorporation and the length of life of the issuer, except where indefinite;

5.1.4. the domicile and legal form of the issuer, the legislation under which the issuer operates, its country of incorporation, and the address and telephone number of its registered office (or principal place of business if different from its registered office);

5.1.5. any recent events particular to the issuer which are to a material extent relevant to the evaluation of the issuer's solvency.

5.2. *Investments*

5.2.1. A description of the principal investments made since the date of the last published financial statements.

5.2.2. Information concerning the issuer's principal future investments, on which its management bodies have already made firm commitments.

5.2.3. Information regarding the anticipated sources of funds needed to fulfil commitments referred to in item 5.2.2.

6. Business Overview

6.1. *Principal activities*

6.1.1. A description of the issuer's principal activities stating the main categories of products sold and/or services performed;

and

6.1.2. an indication of any significant new products and/or activities.

6.2. Principal markets

A brief description of the principal markets in which the issuer competes.

6.3. The basis for any statements made by the issuer regarding its competitive position.

7. Organisational Structure

7.1. If the issuer is part of a group, a brief description of the group and of the issuer's position within it.

7.2. If the issuer is dependent upon other entities within the group, this must be clearly stated together with an explanation of this dependence.

8. Trend Information

8.1. Include a statement that there has been no material adverse change in the prospects of the issuer since the date of its last published audited financial statements.

In the event that the issuer is unable to make such a statement, provide details of this material adverse change.

8.2. Information on any known trends, uncertainties, demands, commitments or events that are reasonably likely to have a material effect on the issuer's prospects for at least the current financial year.

9. Profit Forecasts or Estimates

If an issuer chooses to include a profit forecast or a profit estimate, the registration document must contain the information items 9.1 and 9.2:

9.1. A statement setting out the principal assumptions upon which the issuer has based its forecast, or estimate.

There must be a clear distinction between assumptions about factors which the members of the administrative, management or supervisory bodies can influence and assumptions about factors which are exclusively outside the influence of the members of the administrative, management or supervisory bodies; the assumptions must be readily understandable by investors, be specific and precise and not relate to the general accuracy of the estimates underlying the forecast.

[9.2. A report prepared by independent accountants or auditors stating that in the opinion of the independent accountants or auditors the forecast or estimate has been properly compiled on the basis stated, and that the basis of accounting used for the profit forecast or estimate is consistent with the accounting policies of the issuer.

Where financial information relates to the previous financial year and only contains non-misleading figures substantially consistent with the final figures to be published in the next annual audited financial statements for the previous financial year, and the explanatory information necessary to assess the figures, a report shall not be required provided that the prospectus includes all of the following statements:

(a) the person responsible for this financial information, if different from the one which is responsible for the prospectus in general, approves that information;

(b) independent accountants or auditors have agreed that this information is substantially consistent with the final figures to be published in the next annual audited financial statements;

(c) this financial information has not been audited.][a]

9.3. The profit forecast or estimate must be prepared on a basis comparable with the historical financial information.

10. Administrative, Management, and Supervisory Bodies

10.1. Names, business addresses and functions in the issuer of the following persons, and an indication of the principal activities performed by them outside the issuer where these are significant with respect to that issuer:

(a) members of the administrative, management or supervisory bodies;

(b) partners with unlimited liability, in the case of a limited partnership with a share capital.

10.2. *Administrative, Management, and Supervisory bodies' conflicts of interests*

Potential conflicts of interests between any duties to the issuing entity of the persons referred to in item 10.1 and their private interests and or other duties must be clearly stated. In the event that there are no such conflicts, make a statement to that effect.

11. Board Practices

11.1. Details relating to the issuer's audit committee, including the names of committee members and a summary of the terms of reference under which the committee operates.

11.2. A statement as to whether or not the issuer complies with its country's of incorporation corporate governance regime(s). In the event that the issuer does not comply with such a regime a statement to that effect must be included together with an explanation regarding why the issuer does not comply with such regime.

12. Major Shareholders

12.1. To the extent known to the issuer, state whether the issuer is directly or indirectly owned or controlled and by whom and describe the nature of such control, and describe the measures in place to ensure that such control is not abused.

12.2. A description of any arrangements, known to the issuer, the operation of which may at a subsequent date result in a change in control of the issuer.

13. Financial Information Concerning the Issuer's Assets and Liabilities, Financial Position and Profits and Losses

13.1. *Historical Financial Information*

Audited historical financial information covering the latest 2 financial years (or such shorter period that the issuer has been in operation), and the audit report in respect of each year. [If the issuer has changed its accounting reference date during the period for which historical financial information is required, the audited historical information shall cover at least 24 months, or the entire period for which the issuer has been in operation, whichever is the shorter.][b] Such financial information must be prepared according to Regulation (EC) No 1606/2002, or if not applicable to a Member States national accounting standards for issuers from the Community. For third country issuers, such financial information must be prepared according to the international accounting standards adopted pursuant to the procedure of Article 3 of Regulation (EC) No 1606/2002 or to a third country's national accounting standards equivalent to these standards. If such financial information is not equivalent to these standards, it must be presented in the form of restated financial statements.

The most recent year's historical financial information must be presented and prepared in a form consistent with that which will be adopted in the issuer's next published annual financial statements having regard to accounting standards and policies and legislation applicable to such annual financial statements.

If the issuer has been operating in its current sphere of economic activity for less than one year, the audited historical financial information covering that period must be prepared in accordance with the standards applicable to annual financial statements under the Regulation (EC) No 1606/2002, or if not applicable to a Member States national accounting standards where the issuer is an issuer from the Community. For third country issuers, the historical financial information must be prepared according to the international accounting standards adopted pursuant to the procedure of Article 3 of Regulation (EC) No 1606/2002 or to a third country's national accounting standards equivalent to these standards. This historical financial information must be audited.

If the audited financial information is prepared according to national accounting standards, the financial information required under this heading must include at least:

(a) balance sheet;

(b) income statement;

(c) cash flow statement;

and

(d) accounting policies and explanatory notes

The historical annual financial information must have been independently audited or reported on as to whether or not, for the purposes of the registration document, it gives a true and fair view, in accordance with auditing standards applicable in a Member State or an equivalent standard.

13.2. *Financial statements*

If the issuer prepares both own and consolidated financial statements, include at least the consolidated financial statements in the registration document.

13.3. Auditing of historical annual financial information

13.3.1. A statement that the historical financial information has been audited. If audit reports on the historical financial information have been refused by the statutory auditors or if they contain qualifications or disclaimers, such refusal or such qualifications or disclaimers must be reproduced in full and the reasons given.

13.3.2. An indication of other information in the registration document which has been audited by the auditors.

13.3.3. Where financial data in the registration document is not extracted from the issuer's audited financial statements state the source of the data and state that the data is unaudited.

13.4. Age of latest financial information

13.4.1. The last year of audited financial information may not be older than 18 months from the date of the registration document.

13.5. *Interim and other financial information*

13.5.1. If the issuer has published quarterly or half yearly financial information since the date of its last audited financial statements, these must be included in the registration document. If the quarterly or half yearly financial information has been reviewed or audited the audit or review report must also be included. If the quarterly or half yearly financial information is unaudited or has not been reviewed state that fact.

13.5.2. If the registration document is dated more than nine months after the end of the last audited financial year, it must contain interim financial information, covering at least the first six months of the financial year. If the interim financial information is un-audited state that fact.

The interim financial information must include comparative statements for the same period in the prior financial year, except that the requirement for comparative balance sheet information may be satisfied by presenting the years end balance sheet.

13.6. *Legal and arbitration proceedings*

Information on any governmental, legal or arbitration proceedings (including any such proceedings which are pending or threatened of which the issuer is aware), during a period covering at least the previous 12 months which may have, or have had in the recent past, significant effects on the issuer and/or group's financial position or profitability, or provide an appropriate negative statement.

13.7. *Significant change in the issuer's financial or trading position*

A description of any significant change in the financial or trading position of the group which has occurred since the end of the last financial period for which either audited financial information or interim financial information have been published, or an appropriate negative statement.

14. Additional Information

14.1. *Share Capital*

14.1.1. The amount of the issued capital, the number and classes of the shares of which it is composed with details of their principal characteristics, the part of the issued capital still to be paid up, with an indication of the number, or total nominal value, and the type of the shares not yet fully paid up, broken down where applicable according to the extent to which they have been paid up.

14.2. *Memorandum and Articles of Association*

14.2.1. The register and the entry number therein, if applicable, and a description of the issuer's objects and purposes and where they can be found in the memorandum and articles of association.

15. Material Contracts

A brief summary of all material contracts that are not entered into in the ordinary course of the issuer's business, which could result in any group member being under an obligation or entitlement that is material to the issuer's ability to meet its obligation to security holders in respect of the securities being issued.

16. Third Party Information and Statement by Experts and Declarations of Any Interest

16.1. Where a statement or report attributed to a person as an expert is included in the registration document, provide such person's name, business address, qualifications and material interest if any in the issuer. If the report has been produced at the issuer's request a statement to that effect that such statement or report is included, in the form and context in which it is included, with the consent of that person who has authorised the contents of that part of the registration document.

16.2. Where information has been sourced from a third party, provide a confirmation that this information has been accurately reproduced and that as far as the issuer is aware and is able to ascertain from information published by that third party, no facts have been omitted which would render the reproduced information inaccurate or misleading. In addition, the issuer shall identify the source(s) of the information.

17. Documents on Display

A statement that for the life of the registration document the following documents (or copies thereof), where applicable, may be inspected:

(a) the memorandum and articles of association of the issuer;

(b) all reports, letters, and other documents, historical financial information, valuations and statements prepared by any expert at the issuer's request any part of which is included or referred to in the registration document;

(c) the historical financial information of the issuer or, in the case of a group, the historical financial information of the issuer and its subsidiary undertakings for each of the two financial years preceding the publication of the registration document.

An indication of where the documents on display may be inspected, by physical or electronic means.

Amendments

a Inserted by Commission Delegated Regulation (EU) No 862/2012 of 4 June 2012.

b Inserted by Commission Regulation (EC) No 211/2007 of 27 February 2007 OJ L337 5.12.2006, p 17.

Annex V
Minimum disclosure requirements for the securities note related to debt securities (schedule)

(Debt securities with a denomination per unit of less than EUR 50,000)

1. Persons Responsible

1.1. All persons responsible for the information given in the prospectus and, as the case may be, for certain parts of it, with, in the latter case, an indication of such parts. In the case of natural persons including members of the issuer's administrative, management or supervisory bodies indicate the name and function of the person; in case of legal persons indicate the name and registered office.

1.2. A declaration by those responsible for the prospectus that, having taken all reasonable care to ensure that such is the case, the information contained in the prospectus is, to the best of their knowledge, in accordance with the facts and contains no omission likely to affect its import. As the case may be, declaration by those responsible for certain parts of the prospectus that the information contained in the part of the prospectus for which they are responsible is, to the best of their knowledge, in accordance with the facts and contains no omission likely to affect its import.

2. Risk Factors

2.1. Prominent disclosure of risk factors that are material to the securities being offered and/or admitted to trading in order to assess the market risk associated with these securities in a section headed 'Risk Factors'.

[3. Essential Information][a]

3.1. *Interest of natural and legal persons involved in the issue/offer*

A description of any interest, including conflicting ones, that is material to the issue/offer, detailing the persons involved and the nature of the interest.

3.2. *Reasons for the offer and use of proceeds*

Reasons for the offer if different from making profit and/or hedging certain risks. Where applicable, disclosure of the estimated total expenses of the issue/offer and the estimated net amount of the proceeds. These expenses and proceeds shall be broken into each principal intended use and presented by order of priority of such uses. If the issuer is aware that the anticipated proceeds will not be sufficient to fund all the proposed uses, state the amount and sources of other funds needed.

4. Information Concerning the Securities to be Offered/admitted to Trading

4.1. A description of the type and the class of the securities being offered and/or admitted to trading, including the ISIN (International Security Identification Number) or other such security identification code.

4.2. Legislation under which the securities have been created.

4.3. An indication of whether the securities are in registered form or bearer form and whether the securities are in certificated form or book-entry form. In the latter case, name and address of the entity in charge of keeping the records.

4.4. Currency of the securities issue.

4.5. Ranking of the securities being offered and/or admitted to trading, including summaries of any clauses that are intended to affect ranking or subordinate the security to any present or future liabilities of the issuer.

4.6. A description of the rights attached to the securities, including any limitations of those rights, and procedure for the exercise of those rights.

4.7. The nominal interest rate and provisions relating to interest payable.

— The date from which interest becomes payable and the due dates for interest

— The time limit on the validity of claims to interest and repayment of principal.

Where the rate is not fixed, description of the underlying on which it is based and of the method used to relate the two and an indication where information about the past and the further performance of the underlying and its volatility can be obtained.

— A description of any market disruption or settlement disruption events that affect the underlying

— Adjustment rules with relation to events concerning the underlying

— Name of the calculation agent.

If the security has a derivative component in the interest payment, provide a clear and comprehensive explanation to help investors understand how the value of their investment is affected by the value of the underlying instrument(s), especially under the circumstances when the risks are most evident.

4.8. Maturity date and arrangements for the amortisation of the loan, including the repayment procedures. Where advance amortisation is contemplated, on the initiative of the issuer or of the holder, it shall be described, stipulating amortisation terms and conditions.

4.9. An indication of yield. Describe the method whereby that yield is calculated in summary form.

4.10. Representation of debt security holders including an identification of the organisation representing the investors and provisions applying to such representation. Indication of where the public may have access to the contracts relating to these forms of representation.

4.11. In the case of new issues, a statement of the resolutions, authorisations and approvals by virtue of which the securities have been or will be created and/or issued.

4.12. In the case of new issues, the expected issue date of the securities.

4.13. A description of any restrictions on the free transferability of the securities.

4.14. In respect of the country of registered office of the issuer and the country(ies) where the offer being made or admission to trading is being sought:

— information on taxes on the income from the securities withheld at source;

— indication as to whether the issuer assumes responsibility for the withholding of taxes at the source.

5. Terms and Conditions of the Offer

5.1. *Conditions, offer statistics, expected timetable and action required to apply for the offer*

5.1.1. Conditions to which the offer is subject.

5.1.2. Total amount of the issue/offer; if the amount is not fixed, description of the arrangements and time for announcing to the public the definitive amount of the offer.

5.1.3. The time period, including any possible amendments, during which the offer will be open and description of the application process.

5.1.4. A description of the possibility to reduce subscriptions and the manner for refunding excess amount paid by applicants.

5.1.5. Details of the minimum and/or maximum amount of application, (whether in number of securities or aggregate amount to invest).

5.1.6. Method and time limits for paying up the securities and for delivery of the securities.

5.1.7. A full description of the manner and date in which results of the offer are to be made public.

5.1.8. The procedure for the exercise of any right of pre-emption, the negotiability of subscription rights and the treatment of subscription rights not exercised.

5.2. *Plan of distribution and allotment*

5.2.1. The various categories of potential investors to which the securities are offered. If the offer is being made simultaneously in the markets of two or more countries and if a tranche has been or is being reserved for certain of these, indicate any such tranche.

5.2.2. Process for notification to applicants of the amount allotted and indication whether dealing may begin before notification is made.

5.3. *Pricing*

5.3.1. An indication of the expected price at which the securities will be offered or the method of determining the price and the process for its disclosure. Indicate the amount of any expenses and taxes specifically charged to the subscriber or purchaser.

5.4. *Placing and Underwriting*

5.4.1. Name and address of the co-ordinator(s) of the global offer and of single parts of the offer and, to the extend known to the issuer or to the offeror, of the placers in the various countries where the offer takes place.

5.4.2. Name and address of any paying agents and depository agents in each country.

5.4.3. Name and address of the entities agreeing to underwrite the issue on a firm commitment basis, and name and address of the entities agreeing to place the issue without a firm commitment or under 'best efforts' arrangements. Indication of the material features of the agreements, including the quotas. Where not all of the issue is underwritten, a statement of the portion not covered. Indication of the overall amount of the underwriting commission and of the placing commission.

5.4.4. When the underwriting agreement has been or will be reached.

6. Admission to Trading and Dealing Arrangements

6.1. An indication as to whether the securities offered are or will be the object of an application for admission to trading, with a view to their distribution in a regulated market or other equivalent markets with indication of the markets in question. This circumstance must be mentioned, without creating the impression that the admission to trading will necessarily be approved. If known, give the earliest dates on which the securities will be admitted to trading.

6.2. All the regulated markets or equivalent markets on which, to the knowledge of the issuer, securities of the same class of the securities to be offered or admitted to trading are already admitted to trading.

6.3. Name and address of the entities which have a firm commitment to act as intermediaries in secondary trading, providing liquidity through bid and offer rates and description of the main terms of their commitment.

7. Additional Information

7.1. If advisors connected with an issue are mentioned in the Securities Note, a statement of the capacity in which the advisors have acted.

7.2. An indication of other information in the Securities Note which has been audited or reviewed by statutory auditors and where auditors have produced a report. Reproduction of the report or, with permission of the competent authority, a summary of the report.

7.3. Where a statement or report attributed to a person as an expert is included in the Securities Note, provide such persons' name, business address, qualifications and material interest if any in the issuer. If the report has been produced at the issuer's request a statement to that effect that such statement or report is included, in the form and context in which it is included, with the consent of that person who has authorised the contents of that part of the Securities Note.

7.4. Where information has been sourced from a third party, provide a confirmation that this information has been accurately reproduced and that as far as the issuer is aware and is able to ascertain from information published by that third party, no facts have been omitted which would render the reproduced information inaccurate or misleading. In addition, identify the source(s) of the information.

7.5. Credit ratings assigned to an issuer or its debt securities at the request or with the co-operation of the issuer in the rating process. A brief explanation of the meaning of the ratings if this has previously been published by the rating provider.

Amendments

a Inserted by Commission Delegated Regulation (EU) No 862/2012 of 4 June 2012.

Annex VI
Minimum disclosure requirements for guarantees
(Additional building block)

1. Nature of the Guarantee

A description of any arrangement intended to ensure that any obligation material to the issue will be duly serviced, whether in the form of guarantee, surety, Keep well Agreement, Mono-line Insurance policy or other equivalent commitment (hereafter referred to generically as 'guarantees' and their provider as 'guarantor' for convenience).

Without prejudice to the generality of the foregoing, such arrangements encompass commitments to ensure obligations to repay debt securities and/or the payment of interest and the description shall set out how the arrangement is intended to ensure that the guaranteed payments will be duly serviced.

2. Scope of the Guarantee

Details shall be disclosed about the terms and conditions and scope of the guarantee. Without prejudice to the generality of the foregoing, these details should cover any conditionality on the application of the guarantee in the event of any default under the terms of the security and the material terms of any mono-line insurance or keep well agreement between the issuer and the guarantor. Details must also be disclosed of any guarantor's power of veto in relation to changes to the security holder's rights, such as is often found in Mono-line Insurance.

3. Information to be disclosed about the guarantor

The guarantor must disclose information about itself as if it were the issuer of that same type of security that is the subject of the guarantee.

4. Documents on display

Indication of the places where the public may have access to the material contracts and other documents relating to the guarantee.

Annex VII
Minimum disclosure requirements for asset-backed securities registration document (schedule)

1. Persons Responsible

1.1. All persons responsible for the information given in the registration document and, as the case may be, for certain parts of it, with, in the latter case, an indication of such parts. In the case of natural persons including members of the issuer's administrative, management or supervisory bodies indicate the name and function of the person; in case of legal persons indicate the name and registered office.

1.2. A declaration by those responsible for the registration document that, having taken all reasonable care to ensure that such is the case, the information given in the registration document is, to the best of their knowledge, in accordance with the facts and does not omit anything likely to affect its import. As the case may be, declaration by those responsible for certain parts of the registration document that having taken all reasonable care to ensure that such is the case, the information contained in that part of the registration document for which they are responsible is, to the best of their knowledge, in accordance with the facts and contains no omission likely to affect its import.

2. Statutory Auditors

2.1. Names and addresses of the issuer's auditors for the period covered by the historical financial information (together with any membership of any relevant professional body).

3. Risk Factors

3.1. The document must prominently disclose risk factors in a section headed 'Risk Factors' that are specific to the issuer and its industry.

4. Information about the Issuer:

4.1. A statement whether the issuer has been established as a special purpose vehicle or entity for the purpose of issuing asset backed securities;

4.2. The legal and commercial name of the issuer;

4.3. The place of registration of the issuer and its registration number;

4.4. The date of incorporation and the length of life of the issuer, except where indefinite;

4.5. The domicile and legal form of the issuer, the legislation under which the issuer operates its country of incorporation and the address and telephone number of its registered office (or principal place of business if different from its registered office).

4.6. Description of the amount of the issuer's authorised and issued capital and the amount of any capital agreed to be issued, the number and classes of the securities of which it is composed.

5. Business Overview

5.1. A brief description of the issuer's principal activities.

5.2. A global overview of the parties to the securitisation program including information on the direct or indirect ownership or control between those parties.

6. Administrative, Management and Supervisory Bodies

6.1. Names, business addresses and functions in the issuer of the following persons, and an indication of the principal activities performed by them outside the issuer where these are significant with respect to that issuer:

(a) members of the administrative, management or supervisory bodies;

(b) partners with unlimited liability, in the case of a limited partnership with a share capital.

7. Major Shareholders

7.1. To the extent known to the issuer, state whether the issuer is directly or indirectly owned or controlled and by whom, and describe the nature of such control and describe the measures in place to ensure that such control is not abused.

8. Financial Information Concerning the Issuer's Assets and Liabilities, Financial Position, and Profits And Losses

8.1. Where, since the date of incorporation or establishment, an issuer has not commenced operations and no financial statements have been made up as at the date of the registration document, a statement to that effect shall be provided in the registration document.

8.2. *Historical Financial Information*

Where, since the date of incorporation or establishment, an issuer has commenced operations and financial statements have been made up, the registration document must contain audited historical financial information covering the latest 2 financial years (or shorter period that the issuer has been in operation) and the audit report in respect of each year. [If the issuer has changed its accounting reference date during the period for which historical financial information is required, the audited historical information shall cover at least 24 months, or the entire period for which the issuer has been in operation, whichever is the shorter.][a] Such financial information must be prepared according to Regulation (EC) No 1606/2002, or if not applicable to a Member's State national accounting standards for issuers from the Community. For third country issuers, such financial information must be prepared according to the international accounting standards adopted pursuant to the procedure of Article 3 of Regulation (EC) No 1606/2002 or to a third country's national accounting standards equivalent to these standards. If such financial information is not equivalent to these standards, it must be presented in the form of restated financial statements.

The most recent year's historical financial information must be presented and prepared in a form consistent with that which will be adopted in the issuer's next annual published financial statements having regard to accounting standards and policies and legislation applicable to such annual financial statements.

If the issuer has been operating in its current sphere of economic activity for less than one year, the audited historical financial information covering that period must be prepared in accordance with the standards applicable to annual financial statements under Regulation (EC) No 1606/2002, or if not applicable to a Member States national accounting standards where the issuer is from the Community. For third country issuers, the historical financial information must be prepared according to the international accounting standards adopted pursuant to the procedure of Article 3 of Regulation (EC) No 1606/2002 or to a third country's national accounting standards equivalent to these standards. This historical financial information must be audited.

If the audited financial information is prepared according to national accounting standards, the financial information required under this heading must include at least the following:

(a) the balance sheet;

(b) the income statement;

(c) the accounting policies and explanatory notes.

The historical annual financial information must be independently audited or reported on as to whether or not, for the purposes of the registration document, it gives a true and fair view, in accordance with auditing standards applicable in a Member State or an equivalent standard.

8.2a This paragraph may be used only for issues of asset backed securities having a denomination per unit of at least EUR 50,000.

Where, since the date of incorporation or establishment, an issuer has commenced operations and financial statements have been made up, the registration document must contain audited historical financial information covering the latest 2 financial years (or shorter period that the issuer has been in operation) and the audit report in respect of each year. [If the issuer has changed its accounting reference date during the period for which historical financial information is required, the audited historical information shall cover at least 24 months, or the entire period for which the issuer has been in operation, whichever is the shorter.][b] Such financial information must be prepared according to Regulation (EC) No 1606/2002 or, if not applicable, to a Member's State national accounting standards for issuers from the Community. For third country issuers, such financial information must be prepared according to the international accounting standards adopted pursuant to the procedure of Article 3 of Regulation (EC) No 1606/2002 or to a third country's national accounting standards equivalent to these standards. Otherwise, the following information must be included in the registration document:

(a) a prominent statement that the financial information included in the registration document has not been prepared in accordance with the international accounting standards adopted pursuant to the procedure of Article 3 of Regulation (EC) No 1606/2002 and that there may be material differences in the financial information had Regulation (EC) No 1606/2002 been applied to the historical financial information;

(b) immediately following the historical financial information a narrative description of the differences between the international accounting standards adopted pursuant to the procedure of Article 3 of Regulation (EC) No 1606/2002 and the accounting principles adopted by the issuer in preparing its annual financial statements.

The most recent year's historical financial information must be presented and prepared in a form consistent with that which will be adopted in the issuer's next annual financial statements having regard to accounting standards and policies and legislation applicable to such annual financial statements.

If the audited financial information is prepared according to national accounting standards, the financial information required under this heading must include at least the following:

(a) the balance sheet;

(b) the income statement;

(c) the accounting policies and explanatory notes.

The historical annual financial information must be independently audited or reported on as to whether or not, for the purposes of the registration document, it gives a true and fair view, in accordance with auditing standards applicable in a Member State or an equivalent standard. Otherwise, the following information must be included in the registration document:

(a) a prominent statement disclosing which auditing standards have been applied;

(b) an explanation of any significant departures from International Standards on Auditing.

8.3. *Legal and arbitration proceedings*

Information on any governmental, legal or arbitration proceedings (including any such proceedings which are pending or threatened of which the company is aware), during a period covering at least the previous 12 months, which may have, or have had in the recent past, significant effects on the issuer and/or group's financial position or profitability, or provide an appropriate negative statement.

8.4. *Material adverse change in the issuer's financial position*

Where an issuer has prepared financial statements, include a statement that there has been no material adverse change in the financial position or prospects of the issuer since the date of its last published audited financial statements. Where a material adverse change has occurred, this must be disclosed in the registration document.

9. Third Party Information and Statement by Experts and Declarations of Any Interest

9.1. Where a statement or report attributed to a person as an expert is included in the registration document, provide such person's name, business address, qualifications and material interest if any in the issuer. If the report has been produced at the issuer's request a statement to that effect that such statement or report is included, in the form and context in which it is included, with the consent of that person who has authorised the contents of that part of the registration document.

9.2. Where information has been sourced from a third party, provide a confirmation that this information has been accurately reproduced and that as far as the issuer is aware and is able to ascertain from information published by that third party, no facts have been omitted which would render the reproduced information inaccurate or misleading In addition, the issuer shall identify the source(s) of the information.

10. Documents on Display

10.1. A statement that for the life of the registration document the following documents (or copies thereof), where applicable, may be inspected:

(a) the memorandum and articles of association of the issuer;

(b) all reports, letters, and other documents, historical financial information, valuations and statements prepared by any expert at the issuer's request any part of which is included or referred to in the registration document;

(c) the historical financial information of the issuer or, in the case of a group, the historical financial information of the issuer and its subsidiary undertakings for each of the two financial years preceding the publication of the registration document.

An indication of where the documents on display may be inspected, by physical or electronic means.

Amendment

a Inserted by Commission Regulation (EC) No 211/2007 of 27 February 2007 OJ L337 5.12.2006, p 17.

b Inserted by Commission Regulation (EC) No 211/2007 of 27 February 2007 OJ L337 5.12.2006, p 17.

Annex VIII
Minimum disclosure requirements for the asset-backed securities additional building block

1. The Securities

1.1. The minimum denomination of an issue.

1.2. Where information is disclosed about an undertaking/obligor which is not involved in the issue, provide a confirmation that the information relating to the undertaking/obligor has been accurately reproduced from information published by the undertaking/obligor. So far as the issuer is aware and is able to ascertain from information published by the undertaking/obligor no facts have been omitted which would render the reproduced information misleading.

In addition, identify the source(s) of information in the Securities Note that has been reproduced from information published by an undertaking/obligor.

2. The Underlying Assets

2.1. Confirmation that the securitised assets backing the issue have characteristics that demonstrate capacity to produce funds to service any payments due and payable on the securities.

2.2. *In respect of a pool of discrete assets backing the issue:*

2.2.1. The legal jurisdiction by which the pool of assets is governed

2.2.2.

(a) In the case of a small number of easily identifiable obligors, a general description of each obligor.

(b) In all other cases, a description of: the general characteristics of the obligors; and the economic environment, as well as global statistical data referred to the securitised assets.

2.2.3 the legal nature of the assets;

2.2.4 the expiry or maturity date(s) of the assets;

2.2.5 the amount of the assets;

2.2.6 loan to value ratio or level of collateralisation;

2.2.7 the method of origination or creation of the assets, and for loans and credit agreements, the principal lending criteria and an indication of any loans which do not meet these criteria and any rights or obligations to make further advances;

2.2.8 an indication of significant representations and collaterals given to the issuer relating to the assets;

2.2.9 any rights to substitute the assets and a description of the manner in which and the type of assets which may be so substituted; if there is any capacity to substitute assets with a different class or quality of assets a statement to that effect together with a description of the impact of such substitution;

2.2.10 a description of any relevant insurance policies relating to the assets. Any concentration with one insurer must be disclosed if it is material to the transaction.

2.2.11 Where the assets comprise obligations of 5 or fewer obligors which are legal persons or where an obligor accounts for 20% or more of the assets, or where an obligor accounts for a material portion of the assets, so far as the issuer is aware and/or is able to ascertain from information published by the obligor(s) indicate either of the following:

(a) information relating to each obligor as if it were an issuer drafting a registration document for debt and derivative securities with an individual denomination of at least EUR 50,000;

(b) if an obligor or guarantor has securities already admitted to trading on a regulated or equivalent market or the obligations are guaranteed by an entity admitted to trading on a regulated or equivalent market, the name, address, country of incorporation, nature of business and name of the market in which its securities are admitted.

2.2.12. If a relationship exists that is material to the issue, between the issuer, guarantor and obligor, details of the principal terms of that relationship.

2.2.13. Where the assets comprise obligations that are not traded on a regulated or equivalent market, a description of the principal terms and conditions of the obligations.

2.2.14. Where the assets comprise equity securities that are admitted to trading on a regulated or equivalent market indicate the following:

(a) a description of the securities;

(b) a description of the market on which they are traded including its date of establishment, how price information is published, an indication of daily trading volumes, information as to the standing of the market in the country and the name of the market's regulatory authority;

(c) the frequency with which prices of the relevant securities, are published.

2.2.15. Where more than ten (10) per cent of the assets comprise equity securities that are not traded on a regulated or equivalent market, a description of those equity securities and equivalent information to that contained in the schedule for share registration document in respect of each issuer of those securities.

2.2.16. Where a material portion of the assets are secured on or backed by real property, a valuation report relating to the property setting out both the valuation of the property and cash flow/income streams.

Compliance with this disclosure is not required if the issue is of securities backed by mortgage loans with property as security, where there has been no revaluation of the properties for the purpose of the issue, and it is clearly stated that the valuations quoted are as at the date of the original initial mortgage loan origination.

2.3. *In respect of an actively managed pool of assets backing the issue:*

2.3.1. equivalent information to that contained in items 2.1 and 2.2 to allow an assessment of the type, quality, sufficiency and liquidity of the asset types in the portfolio which will secure the issue;

2.3.2. the parameters within which investments can be made, the name and description of the entity responsible for such management including a description of that entity's expertise and experience, a summary of the provisions relating to the termination of the appointment of such entity and the appointment of an alternative management entity, and a description of that entity's relationship with any other parties to the issue.

2.4. Where an issuer proposes to issue further securities backed by the same assets, a prominent statement to that effect and unless those further securities are fungible with or are subordinated to those classes of existing debt, a description of how the holders of that class will be informed.

3. Structure and Cash Flow

3.1. Description of the structure of the transaction, including, if necessary, a structure diagram.

3.2. Description of the entities participating in the issue and description of the functions to be performed by them.

3.3. Description of the method and date of the sale, transfer, novation or assignment of the assets or of any rights and/or obligations in the assets to the issuer or, where applicable, the manner and time period in which the proceeds from the issue will be fully invested by the issuer.

3.4. *An explanation of the flow of funds including:*

3.4.1. how the cash flow from the assets will meet the issuer's obligations to holders of the securities, including, if necessary, a financial service table and a description of the assumptions used in developing the table;

3.4.2. information on any credit enhancements, an indication of where material potential liquidity shortfalls may occur and the availability of any liquidity supports and indication of provisions designed to cover interest/principal shortfall risks;

3.4.3. without prejudice to item 3.4.2, details of any subordinated debt finance;

3.4.4. an indication of any investment parameters for the investment of temporary liquidity surpluses and description of the parties responsible for such investment;

3.4.5. how payments are collected in respect of the assets;

3.4.6. the order of priority of payments made by the issuer to the holders of the class of securities in question;

3.4.7. details of any other arrangements upon which payments of interest and principal to investors are dependent;

3.5. the name, address and significant business activities of the originators of the securitised assets.

3.6. Where the return on, and/or repayment of the security is linked to the performance or credit of other assets which are not assets of the issuer, items 2.2 and 2.3 are necessary;

3.7. the name, address and significant business activities of the administrator, calculation agent or equivalent, together with a summary of the administrator's/calculation agents responsibilities, their relationship with the originator or the creator of the assets and a summary of the provisions relating to the termination of the appointment of the administrator/calculation agent and the appointment of an alternative administrator/calculation agent;

3.8. the names and addresses and brief description of:

(a) any swap counterparties and any providers of other material forms of credit/liquidity enhancement;

(b) the banks with which the main accounts relating to the transaction are held.

4. Post Issuance Reporting

4.1. Indication in the prospectus whether or not it intends to provide post-issuance transaction information regarding securities to be admitted to trading and the performance of the underlying collateral. Where the issuer has indicated that it intends to report such information, specify in the prospectus what information will be reported, where such information can be obtained, and the frequency with which such information will be reported.

Annex IX
Minimum disclosure requirements for the debt and derivative securities registration document (schedule)

(Debt and derivative securities with a denomination per unit of at least EUR 50,000)

1. Persons Responsible

1.1. All persons responsible for the information given in the registration document and, as the case may be, for certain parts of it, with, in the latter case, an indication of such parts. In the case of natural persons including members of the issuer's administrative, management or supervisory bodies indicate the name and function of the person; in case of legal persons indicate the name and registered office.

1.2. A declaration by those responsible for the registration document that, having taken all reasonable care to ensure that such is the case, the information contained in the registration document is, to the best of their knowledge, in accordance with the facts and contains no omission likely to affect its import. As the case may be, declaration by those responsible for certain parts of the registration document that, having taken all reasonable care to ensure that such is the case, the information contained in the part of the registration document for which they are responsible is, to the best of their knowledge, in accordance with the facts and contains no omission likely to affect its import.

2. Statutory Auditors

2.1. Names and addresses of the issuer's auditors for the period covered by the historical financial information (together with their membership in a professional body).

2.2. If auditors have resigned, been removed or not been re-appointed during the period covered by the historical financial information, details if material.

3. Risk Factors

3.1. Prominent disclosure of risk factors that may affect the issuer's ability to fulfil its obligations under the securities to investors in a section headed 'Risk Factors'.

4. Information about the Issuer

4.1 *History and development of the Issuer*

4.1.1 the legal and commercial name of the issuer;

4.1.2 the place of registration of the issuer and its registration number;

4.1.3 the date of incorporation and the length of life of the issuer, except where indefinite;

4.1.4. the domicile and legal form of the issuer, the legislation under which the issuer operates, its country of incorporation, and the address and telephone number of its registered office (or principal place of business if different from its registered office;

4.1.5. any recent events particular to the issuer and which are to a material extent relevant to the evaluation of the issuer's solvency.

5. Business Overview

5.1. *Principal activities:*

5.1.1. A brief description of the issuer's principal activities stating the main categories of products sold and/or services performed;

5.1.2. The basis for any statements in the registration document made by the issuer regarding its competitive position.

6. Organisational Structure

6.1. If the issuer is part of a group, a brief description of the group and of the issuer's position within it.

6.2. If the issuer is dependent upon other entities within the group, this must be clearly stated together with an explanation of this dependence.

7. Trend Information

7.1. Include a statement that there has been no material adverse change in the prospects of the issuer since the date of its last published audited financial statements.

In the event that the issuer is unable to make such a statement, provide details of this material adverse change.

8. Profit Forecasts or Estimates

If an issuer chooses to include a profit forecast or a profit estimate, the registration document must contain the information items 8.1 and 8.2 the following:

8.1. A statement setting out the principal assumptions upon which the issuer has based its forecast, or estimate.

There must be a clear distinction between assumptions about factors which the members of the administrative, management or supervisory bodies can influence and assumptions about factors which are exclusively outside the influence of the members of the administrative, management or supervisory bodies; be readily understandable by investors; be specific and precise; and not relate to the general accuracy of the estimates underlying the forecast.

8.2. Any profit forecast set out in the registration document must be accompanied by a statement confirming that the said forecast has been properly prepared on the basis stated and that the basis of accounting is consistent with the accounting policies of the issuer.

8.3. The profit forecast or estimate must be prepared on a basis comparable with the historical financial information.

9. Administrative, Management, and Supervisory Bodies

9.1. Names, business addresses and functions in the issuer of the following persons, and an indication of the principal activities performed by them outside the issuer where these are significant with respect to that issuer:

(a) members of the administrative, management or supervisory bodies;

(b) partners with unlimited liability, in the case of a limited partnership with a share capital.

9.2. *Administrative, Management, and Supervisory bodies' conflicts of interests*

Potential conflicts of interests between any duties to the issuing entity of the persons referred to in item 9.1 and their private interests and or other duties must be clearly stated. In the event that there are no such conflicts, a statement to that effect.

10. Major Shareholders

10.1. To the extent known to the issuer, state whether the issuer is directly or indirectly owned or controlled and by whom, and describe the nature of such control, and describe the measures in place to ensure that such control is not abused.

10.2. A description of any arrangements, known to the issuer, the operation of which may at a subsequent date result in a change in control of the issuer.

11. Financial Information Concerning the Issuer's Assets and Liabilities, Financial Position and Profits And Losses

11.1. *Historical Financial Information*

Audited historical financial information covering the latest two financial years (or such shorter period that the issuer has been in operation), and the audit report in respect of each year. [If the issuer has changed its accounting reference date during the period for which historical financial information is required, the audited historical information shall cover at least 24 months, or the entire period for which the issuer has been in operation, whichever is the shorter.][a] Such financial information must be prepared according to Regulation (EC) No 1606/2002, or if not applicable to a Member's State national accounting standards for issuers from the Community. For third country issuers, such financial information must be prepared according to the international accounting standards adopted pursuant to the procedure of Article 3 of Regulation (EC) No 1606/2002 or to a third country's national accounting standards equivalent to these standards. Otherwise, the following information must be included in the registration document:

(a) a prominent statement that the financial information included in the registration document has not been prepared in accordance with the international accounting standards adopted pursuant to the procedure of Article 3 of Regulation (EC) No 1606/2002 and that there may be material differences in the financial information had Regulation (EC) No 1606/2002 been applied to the historical financial information.

(b) immediately following the historical financial information a narrative description of the differences between the international accounting standards adopted pursuant to the procedure of Article 3 of Regulation (EC) No 1606/2002 and the accounting principles adopted by the issuer in preparing its annual financial statements.

The most recent year's historical financial information must be presented and prepared in a form consistent with that which will be adopted in the issuer's next published annual financial statements having regard to accounting standards and policies and legislation applicable to such annual financial statements.

If the audited financial information is prepared according to national accounting standards, the financial information required under this heading must include at least the following:

(a) the balance sheet;

(b) the income statement;

(c) the accounting policies and explanatory notes.

The historical annual financial information must be independently audited or reported on as to whether or not, for the purposes of the registration document, it gives a true and fair view, in accordance with auditing standards applicable in a Member State or an equivalent standard. Otherwise, the following information must be included in the registration document:

(a) a prominent statement disclosing which auditing standards have been applied;

(b) an explanation of any significant departures from international standards on auditing.

11.2. *Financial statements*

If the issuer prepares both own and consolidated financial statements, include at least the consolidated financial statements in the registration document.

11.3. *Auditing of historical annual financial information*

11.3.1 A statement that the historical financial information has been audited. If audit reports on the historical financial information have been refused by the statutory auditors or if they contain qualifications or disclaimers, such refusal or such qualifications or disclaimers must be reproduced in full and the reasons given.

11.3.2. An indication of other information in the registration document which has been audited by the auditors.

11.3.3. Where financial data in the registration document is not extracted from the issuer's audited financial statements, state the source of the data and state that the data is unaudited.

11.4. *Age of latest financial information*

11.4.1. The last year of audited financial information may not be older than 18 months from the date of the registration document.

11.5. *Legal and arbitration proceedings*

Information on any governmental, legal or arbitration proceedings (including any such proceedings which are pending or threatened of which the issuer is aware), during a period covering at least the previous 12 months which may have, or have had in the recent past, significant effects on the issuer and/or group's financial position or profitability, or provide an appropriate negative statement.

11.6. *Significant change in the issuer's financial or trading position*

A description of any significant change in the financial or trading position of the group which has occurred since the end of the last financial period for which either audited financial information or interim financial information have been published, or an appropriate negative statement.

12. Material Contracts

A brief summary of all material contracts that are not entered into in the ordinary course of the issuer's business, which could result in any group member being under an obligation or entitlement that is material to the issuer's ability to meet its obligation to security holders in respect of the securities being issued.

13. Third Party Information and Statement by Experts and Declarations of Any Interest

13.1. Where a statement or report attributed to a person as an expert is included in the registration document, provide such person's name, business address, qualifications and material interest if any in the issuer. If the report has been produced at the issuer's request a statement to that effect that such statement or report is included, in the form and context in which it is included, with the consent of that person who has authorised the contents of that part of the registration document.

13.2. *Third party information*

Where information has been sourced from a third party, provide a confirmation that this information has been accurately reproduced and that as far as the issuer is aware and is able to ascertain from information published by that third party, no facts have been omitted which would render the reproduced information inaccurate or misleading; in addition, identify the source(s) of the information.

14. Documents on Display

A statement that for the life of the registration document the following documents (or copies thereof), where applicable, may be inspected:

(a) the memorandum and articles of association of the issuer;

(b) all reports, letters, and other documents, historical financial information, valuations and statements prepared by any expert at the issuer's request any part of which is included or referred to in the registration document;

(c) the historical financial information of the issuer or, in the case of a group, the historical financial information of the issuer and its subsidiary undertakings for each of the two financial years preceding the publication of the registration document.

An indication of where the documents on display may be inspected, by physical or electronic means.

Amendments

a Inserted by Commission Regulation (EC) No 211/2007 of 27 February 2007 OJ L337 5.12.2006, p 17.

Annex X

Minimum disclosure requirements for the depository receipts issued over shares (schedule)

Information about the Issuer of the Underlying Shares

1. Persons Responsible

1.1. All persons responsible for the information given in the prospectus and, as the case may be, for certain parts of it, with, in the latter case, an indication of such parts. In the case of natural persons including members of the issuer's administrative, management or supervisory bodies indicate the name and function of the person; in case of legal persons indicate the name and registered office.

1.2. A declaration by those responsible for the prospectus that, having taken all reasonable care to ensure that such is the case, the information contained in the prospectus is, to the best of their knowledge, in accordance with the facts and contains no omission likely to affect its import. As the case may be, declaration by those responsible for certain parts of the prospectus that, having taken all reasonable care to ensure that such is the case, the information contained in the part of the prospectus for which they are responsible is, to the best of their knowledge, in accordance with the facts and contains no omission likely to affect its import.

2. Statutory Auditors

2.1. Names and addresses of the issuer's auditors for the period covered by the historical financial information (together with their membership in a professional body).

2.2. If auditors have resigned, been removed or not been re-appointed during the period covered by the historical financial information, indicate details if material.

3. Selected Financial Information

3.1. Selected historical financial information regarding the issuer, presented for each financial year for the period covered by the historical financial information, and any subsequent interim financial period, in the same currency as the financial information.

The selected historical financial information must provide the key figures that summarise the financial condition of the issuer.

3.2. If selected financial information for interim periods is provided, comparative data from the same period in the prior financial year shall also be provided, except that the requirement for comparative balance sheet information is satisfied by presenting the year end balance sheet information.

4. Risk Factors

Prominent disclosure of risk factors that are specific to the issuer or its industry in a section headed 'Risk Factors'.

5. Information about the Issuer

5.1 *History and development of the issuer*

5.1.1 the legal and commercial name of the issuer;

5.1.2 the place of registration of the issuer and its registration number;

5.1.3 the date of incorporation and the length of life of the issuer, except where indefinite;

5.1.4. the domicile and legal form of the issuer, the legislation under which the issuer operates, its country of incorporation, and the address and telephone number of its registered office (or principal place of business if different from its registered office);

5.1.5. the important events in the development of the issuer's business.

5.2. *Investments*

5.2.1. A description, (including the amount) of the issuer's principal investments for each financial year for the period covered by the historical financial information up to the date of the prospectus;

5.2.2.A description of the issuer's principal investments that are currently in progress, including the distribution of these investments geographically (home and abroad) and the method of financing (internal or external);

5.2.3.Information concerning the issuer's principal future investments on which its management bodies have already made firm commitments.

6. Business Overview

6.1. *Principal Activities*

6.1.1. A description of, and key factors relating to, the nature of the issuer's operations and its principal activities, stating the main categories of products sold and/or services performed for each financial year for the period covered by the historical financial information.

6.1.2. An indication of any significant new products and/or services that have been introduced and, to the extent the development of new products or services has been publicly disclosed, give the status of development.

6.2. *Principal Markets*

A description of the principal markets in which the issuer competes, including a breakdown of total revenues by category of activity and geographic market for each financial year for the period covered by the historical financial information.

6.3. Where the information given pursuant to items 6.1 and 6.2 has been influenced by exceptional factors, mention that fact.

6.4. If material to the issuer's business or profitability, disclose summary information regarding the extent to which the issuer is dependent, on patents or licences, industrial, commercial or financial contracts or new manufacturing processes.

6.5. The basis for any statements made by the issuer regarding its competitive position.

7. Organisational Structure

7.1. If the issuer is part of a group, a brief description of the group and the issuer's position within the group.

7.2. A list of the issuer's significant subsidiaries, including name, country of incorporation or residence, proportion of ownership interest and, if different, proportion of voting power held.

8. Property, Plants and Equipment

8.1. Information regarding any existing or planned material tangible fixed assets, including leased properties, and any major encumbrances thereon.

8.2. A description of any environmental issues that may affect the issuer's utilisation of the tangible fixed assets.

9. Operating and Financial Review

9.1. *Financial condition*

To the extent not covered elsewhere in the prospectus, provide a description of the issuer's financial condition, changes in financial condition and results of operations for each year and interim period, for which historical financial information is required, including the causes of material changes from year to year in the financial information to the extent necessary for an understanding of the issuer's business as a whole.

9.2. *Operating results*

9.2.1. Information regarding significant factors, including unusual or infrequent events or new developments, materially affecting the issuer's income from operations, indicating the extent to which income was so affected.

9.2.2. Where the financial statements disclose material changes in net sales or revenues, provide a narrative discussion of the reasons for such changes.

9.2.3. Information regarding any governmental, economic, fiscal, monetary or political policies or factors that have materially affected, or could materially affect, directly or indirectly, the issuer's operations.

10. Capital Resources

10.1. Information concerning the issuer's capital resources (both short and long term).

10.2. An explanation of the sources and amounts of and a narrative description of the issuer's cash flows.

10.3. Information on the borrowing requirements and funding structure of the issuer.

10.4. Information regarding any restrictions on the use of capital resources that have materially affected, or could materially affect, directly or indirectly, the issuer's operations.

10.5. Information regarding the anticipated sources of funds needed to fulfil commitments referred to in items 5.2.3 and 8.1.

11. Research and Development, Patents And Licences

Where material, provide a description of the issuer's research and development policies for each financial year for the period covered by the historical financial information, including the amount spent on issuer-sponsored research and development activities.

12. Trend Information

12.1. The most significant recent trends in production, sales and inventory, and costs and selling prices since the end of the last financial year to the date of the prospectus.

12.2. Information on any known trends, uncertainties, demands, commitments or events that are reasonably likely to have a material effect on the issuer's prospects for at least the current financial year.

13. Profit Forecasts or Estimates

If an issuer chooses to include a profit forecast or a profit estimate the prospectus must contain the information items 13.1 and 13.2.

13.1. A statement setting out the principal assumptions upon which the issuer has based its forecast, or estimate.

There must be a clear distinction between assumptions about factors which the members of the administrative, management or supervisory bodies can influence and assumptions about factors which are exclusively outside the influence of the members of the administrative, management or supervisory bodies; the assumptions must be readily understandable by investors, be specific and precise and not relate to the general accuracy of the estimates underlying the forecast.

[13.2. A report prepared by independent accountants or auditors stating that in the opinion of the independent accountants or auditors the forecast or estimate has been properly compiled on the basis stated, and that the basis of accounting used for the profit forecast or estimate is consistent with the accounting policies of the issuer.

Where financial information relates to the previous financial year and only contains non-misleading figures substantially consistent with the final figures to be published in the next annual audited financial statements for the previous financial year, and the explanatory information necessary to assess the figures, a report shall not be required provided that the prospectus includes all of the following statements:

(a) the person responsible for this financial information, if different from the one which is responsible for the prospectus in general, approves that information;

(b) independent accountants or auditors have agreed that this information is substantially consistent with the final figures to be published in the next annual audited financial statements;

(c) this financial information has not been audited.';

13.3. The profit forecast or estimate prepared on a basis comparable with the historical financial information.

13.4. If the issuer has published a profit forecast in a prospectus which is still outstanding, provide a statement setting out whether or not that forecast is still correct as at the time of the prospectus, and an explanation of why such forecast is no longer valid if that is the case.][a]

14. Administrative, Management, and Supervisory Bodies and Senior Management

14.1. Names, business addresses and functions in the issuer of the following persons and an indication of the principal activities performed by them outside that issuer where these are significant with respect to that issuer:

(a) members of the administrative, management or supervisory bodies;

(b) partners with unlimited liability, in the case of a limited partnership with a share capital;

(c) founders, if the issuer has been established for fewer than five years;

(d) any senior manager who is relevant to establishing that the issuer has the appropriate expertise and experience for the management of the issuer's business.

The nature of any family relationship between any of those persons.

In the case of each member of the administrative, management or supervisory bodies of the issuer and person described in points (b) and (d) of the first subparagraph, details of that person's relevant management expertise and experience and the following information:

(a) the names of all companies and partnerships of which such person has been a member of the administrative, management or supervisory bodies or partner at any time in the previous five years, indicating whether or not the individual is still a member of the administrative, management or supervisory bodies or partner. It is not necessary to list all the subsidiaries of an issuer of which the person is also a member of the administrative, management or supervisory bodies;

(b) any convictions in relation to fraudulent offences for at least the previous five years;

(c) details of any bankruptcies, receiverships or liquidations with which a person described in points (a) and (d) of the first subparagraph who was acting in the capacity of any of the positions set out in points (a) and (d) of the first subparagraph member of the administrative, management or supervisory bodies was associated for at least the previous five years;

(d) details of any official public incrimination and/or sanctions of such person by statutory or regulatory authorities (including designated professional bodies) and whether such person has ever been disqualified by a court from acting as a member of the administrative, management or supervisory bodies of an issuer or from acting in the management or conduct of the affairs of any issuer for at least the previous five years.

If there is no such information to be disclosed, a statement to that effect must be made.

14.2. *Administrative, Management, and Supervisory bodies' and Senior Management conflicts of interests*

Potential conflicts of interests between any duties to the issuer of the persons referred to in the first subparagraph of item 14.1 and their private interests and or other duties must be clearly stated. In the event that there are no such conflicts, make a statement to that effect.

Any arrangement or understanding with major shareholders, customers, suppliers or others, pursuant to which any person referred to in the first subparagraph of item 14.1 was selected as a member of the administrative, management or supervisory bodies or member of senior management.

15. Remuneration and Benefits

In relation to the last full financial year for those persons referred to in points (a) and (d) of the first subparagraph of item 14.1:

15.1. The amount of remuneration paid (including any contingent or deferred compensation), and benefits in kind granted, to such persons by the issuer and its subsidiaries for services in all capacities to the issuer and its subsidiaries by any person.

This information must be provided on an individual basis unless individual disclosure is not required in the issuer's home country and is not otherwise publicly disclosed by the issuer.

15.2. The total amounts set aside or accrued by the issuer or its subsidiaries to provide pension, retirement or similar benefits.

16. Board Practices

In relation to the issuer's last completed financial year, and unless otherwise specified, with respect to those persons referred to in point (a) of the first subparagraph of item 14.1:

16.1. Date of expiration of the current term of office, if applicable, and the period during which the person has served in that office.

16.2. Information about members of the administrative, management or supervisory bodies' service contracts with the issuer or any of its subsidiaries providing for benefits upon termination of employment, or an appropriate negative statement.

16.3. Information about the issuer's audit committee and remuneration committee, including the names of committee members and a summary of the terms of reference under which the committee operates.

16.4. A statement as to whether or not the issuer complies with its country's of incorporation corporate governance regime(s). In the event that the issuer does not comply with such a regime, a statement to that effect together with an explanation regarding why the issuer does not comply with such regime.

17. Employees

17.1. Either the number of employees at the end of the period or the average for each financial year for the period covered by the historical financial information up to the date of the prospectus (and changes in such numbers, if material) and, if possible and material, a breakdown of persons employed by main category of activity and geographic location. If the issuer employs a significant number of temporary employees, include disclosure of the number of temporary employees on average during the most recent financial year.

17.2. Shareholdings and stock options

With respect to each person referred to in points (a) and (b) of the first subparagraph of item 14.1, provide information as to their share ownership and any options over such shares in the issuer as of the most recent practicable date.

17.3. Description of any arrangements for involving the employees in the capital of the issuer.

18. Major Shareholders

18.1. In so far as is known to the issuer, the name of any person other than a member of the administrative, management or supervisory bodies who, directly or indirectly, has an interest notifiable under the issuer's national law in the issuer's capital or voting rights, together with the amount of each such person's interest or, if there are no such persons, an appropriate negative statement.

18.2. Whether the issuer's major shareholders have different voting rights, or an appropriate negative statement.

18.3. To the extent known to the issuer, state whether the issuer is directly or indirectly owned or controlled and by whom and describe the nature of such control and describe the measures in place to ensure that such control is not abused.

18.4. A description of any arrangements, known to the issuer, the operation of which may at a subsequent date result in a change in control of the issuer.

19. Related Party Transactions

Details of related party transactions (which for these purposes are those set out in the Standards adopted according to Regulation (EC) No 1606/2002), that the issuer has entered into during the period covered by the historical financial information and up to the date of the prospectus must be disclosed in accordance with the respective standard adopted according to Regulation (EC) No 1606/2002 if applicable.

If such standards do not apply to the issuer the following information must be disclosed:

(a) the nature and extent of any transactions which are - as a single transaction or in their entirety - material to the issuer. Where such related party transactions are not concluded at arm's length provide an explanation of why these transactions were not concluded at arms length. In the case of outstanding loans including guarantees of any kind indicate the amount outstanding;

(b) the amount or the percentage to which related party transactions form part of the turnover of the issuer.

20. Financial Information Concerning the Issuer's Assets and Liabilities, Financial Position and Profits and Losses

20.1. *Historical financial information*

Audited historical financial information covering the latest 3 financial years (or such shorter period that the issuer has been in operation), and the audit report in respect of each year. [If the issuer has changed its accounting reference date during the period for which historical financial information is required, the audited historical information shall cover at least 36 months, or the entire period for which the issuer has been in operation, whichever is the shorter.][b] Such financial information must be prepared according to Regulation (EC) No 1606/2002, or if not applicable to a Member States national accounting standards for issuers from the Community. For third country issuers, such financial information must be prepared according to the international accounting standards adopted pursuant to the procedure of Article 3 of Regulation (EC) No 1606/2002 or to a third country's national accounting standards equivalent to these standards. If such financial information is not equivalent to these standards, it must be presented in the form of restated financial statements.

The last two years audited historical financial information must be presented and prepared in a form consistent with that which will be adopted in the issuer's next published annual financial statements having regard to accounting standards and policies and legislation applicable to such annual financial statements.

If the issuer has been operating in its current sphere of economic activity for less than one year, the audited historical financial information covering that period must be prepared in accordance with the standards applicable to annual financial statements under Regulation (EC) No 1606/2002, or if not applicable to a Member States national accounting standards where the issuer is an issuer from the Community. For third country issuers, the historical financial information must be prepared according to the international accounting standards adopted pursuant to the procedure of Article 3 of Regulation (EC) No 1606/2002 or to a third country's national accounting standards equivalent to these standards. This historical financial information must be audited.

If the audited financial information is prepared according to national accounting standards, the financial information required under this heading must include at least the following:

(a) the balance sheet;

(b) the income statement;

(c) a statement showing either all changes in equity or changes in equity other than those arising from capital transactions with owners and distributions to owners;

(d) the cash flow statement;

(e) the accounting policies and explanatory notes.

The historical annual financial information must be independently audited or reported on as to whether or not, for the purposes of the prospectus, it gives a true and fair view, in accordance with auditing standards applicable in a Member State or an equivalent standard.

20.1a *This paragraph may be used only for issues of depository receipts having a denomination per unit of at least EUR 50,000.*

Audited historical financial information covering the latest three financial years (or such shorter period that the issuer has been in operation), and the audit report in respect of each year. [If the issuer has changed its accounting reference date during the period for which historical financial information is required, the audited historical information shall cover at least 36 months, or the entire period for which the issuer has been in operation, whichever is the shorter.][c] Such financial information must be prepared according to Regulation (EC) No 1606/2002, or if not applicable to a Member State's national accounting standards for issuers from the Community. For third country issuers, such financial information must be prepared according to the international accounting standards adopted pursuant to the procedure of Article 3 of Regulation (EC) No 1606/2002 or to a third country's national accounting standards equivalent to these standards. Otherwise, the following information must be included in the prospectus:

(a) a prominent statement that the financial information included in the registration document has not been prepared in accordance with the international accounting standards adopted pursuant to the procedure of Article 3 of Regulation (EC) No 1606/2002 and that there may be material differences in the financial information had Regulation (EC) No 1606/2002 been applied to the historical financial information;

(b) immediately following the historical financial information a narrative description of the differences between the international accounting standards adopted pursuant to the procedure of Article 3 of Regulation (EC) No 1606/2002 and the accounting principles adopted by the issuer in preparing its annual financial statements.

The last two years audited historical financial information must be presented and prepared in a form consistent with that which will be adopted in the issuer's next published annual financial statements having regard to accounting standards and policies and legislation applicable to such annual financial statements.

If the audited financial information is prepared according to national accounting standards, the financial information required under this heading must include at least the following:

(a) the balance sheet;

(b) the income statement;

(c) a statement showing either all changes in equity or changes in equity other than those arising from capital transactions with owners and distributions to owners;

(d) the cash flow statement;

(e) the accounting policies and explanatory notes.

The historical annual financial information must be independently audited or reported on as to whether or not, for the purposes of the prospectus, it gives a true and fair view, in accordance with auditing standards applicable in a Member State or an equivalent standard. Otherwise, the following information must be included in the prospectus:

(a) a prominent statement disclosing which auditing standards have been applied;

(b) an explanation of any significant departures from international standards on auditing.

20.2. *Financial statements*

If the issuer prepares both own and consolidated annual financial statements, include at least the consolidated annual financial statements in the prospectus.

20.3. *Auditing of historical annual financial information*

20.3.1. A statement that the historical financial information has been audited. If audit reports on the historical financial information have been refused by the statutory auditors or if they contain qualifications or disclaimers, such refusal or such qualifications or disclaimers must be reproduced in full and the reasons given.

20.3.2. Indication of other information in the prospectus which has been audited by the auditors.

20.3.3. Where financial data in the prospectus is not extracted from the issuer's audited financial statements state the source of the data and state that the data is unaudited.

20.4. *Age of latest financial information*

20.4.1 The last year of audited financial information may not be older than:

(a) 18 months from the date of the prospectus if the issuer includes audited interim financial statements in the prospectus;

(b) 15 months from the date of the prospectus if the issuer includes unaudited interim financial statements in the prospectus.

20.5. *Interim and other financial information*

20.5.1. If the issuer has published quarterly or half yearly financial information since the date of its last audited financial statements, these must be included in the prospectus. If the quarterly or half yearly financial information has been reviewed or audited the audit or review report must also be included. If the quarterly or half yearly financial information is unaudited or has not been reviewed, state that fact.

20.5.2. If the prospectus is dated more than nine months after the end of the last audited financial year, it must contain interim financial information, which may be unaudited (in which case that fact shall be stated) covering at least the first six months of the financial year.

The interim financial information must include comparative statements for the same period in the prior financial year, except that the requirement for comparative balance sheet information may be satisfied by presenting the years end balance sheet.

20.6. *Dividend policy*

A description of the issuer's policy on dividend distributions and any restrictions thereon.

20.6.1. The amount of the dividend per share for each financial year for the period covered by the historical financial information adjusted, where the number of shares in the issuer has changed, to make it comparable.

20.7. *Legal and arbitration proceedings*

Information on any governmental, legal or arbitration proceedings (including any such proceedings which are pending or threatened of which the issuer is aware), during a period covering at least the previous 12 months which may have, or have had in the recent past significant effects on the issuer and/or group's financial position or profitability, or provide an appropriate negative statement.

20.8. *Significant change in the issuer's financial or trading position*

A description of any significant change in the financial or trading position of the group which has occurred since the end of the last financial period for which either audited financial information or interim financial information have been published, or provide an appropriate negative statement.

21. Additional Information

21.1. *Share capital*

The following information as of the date of the most recent balance sheet included in the historical financial information:

21.1.1. The amount of issued capital, and for each class of share capital:

(a) the number of shares authorised;

(b) the number of shares issued and fully paid and issued but not fully paid;

(c) the par value per share, or that the shares have no par value;

(d) a reconciliation of the number of shares outstanding at the beginning and end of the year. If more than 10% of capital has been paid for with assets other than cash within the period covered by the historical financial information, state that fact.

21.1.2. If there are shares not representing capital, state the number and main characteristics of such shares.

21.1.3. The number, book value and face value of shares in the issuer held by or on behalf of the issuer itself or by subsidiaries of the issuer.

21.1.4. The amount of any convertible securities, exchangeable securities or securities with warrants, with an indication of the conditions governing and the procedures for conversion, exchange or subscription.

21.1.5. Information about and terms of any acquisition rights and or obligations over authorised but unissued capital or an undertaking to increase the capital.

21.1.6. Information about any capital of any member of the group which is under option or agreed conditionally or unconditionally to be put under option and details of such options including those persons to whom such options relate.

21.1.7. A history of share capital, highlighting information about any changes, for the period covered by the historical financial information.

21.2. *Memorandum and Articles of Association*

21.2.1. A description of the issuer's objects and purposes and where they can be found in the memorandum and articles of association.

21.2.2. A summary of any provisions of the issuer's articles of association, statutes or charter and bylaws with respect to the members of the administrative, management and supervisory bodies.

21.2.3. A description of the rights, preferences and restrictions attaching to each class of the existing shares.

21.2.4. A description of what action is necessary to change the rights of holders of the shares, indicating where the conditions are more significant than is required by law.

21.2.5. A description of the conditions governing the manner in which annual general meetings and extraordinary general meetings of shareholders are called including the conditions of admission.

21.2.6. A brief description of any provision of the issuer's articles of association, statutes, charter or bylaws that would have an effect of delaying, deferring or preventing a change in control of the issuer.

21.2.7. An indication of the articles of association, statutes, charter or bylaws provisions, if any, governing the ownership threshold above which shareholder ownership must be disclosed.

21.2.8. A description of the conditions imposed by the memorandum and articles of association statutes, charter or bylaws governing changes in the capital, where such conditions are more stringent than is required by law.

22. Material Contracts

A summary of each material contract, other than contracts entered into in the ordinary course of business, to which the issuer or any member of the group is a party, for the two years immediately preceding publication of the prospectus.

A summary of any other contract (not being a contract entered into in the ordinary course of business) entered into by any member of the group which contains any provision under which any member of the group has any obligation or entitlement which is material to the group as at the date of the prospectus.

23. Third Party Information, Statement by Experts and Declarations of any Interest

23.1. Where a statement or report attributed to a person as an expert is included in the prospectus provide such person's name, business address, qualifications and material interest if any in the issuer. If the report has been produced at the issuer's request a statement to that effect that such statement or report is included, in the form and context in which it is included, with the consent of that person who has authorised the contents of that part of the prospectus.

23.2. Where information has been sourced from a third party, provide a confirmation that this information has been accurately reproduced and that as far as the issuer is aware and is able to ascertain from information published by that third party, no facts have been omitted which would render the reproduced information inaccurate or misleading. In addition, the issuer shall identify the source(s) of the information.

24. Documents on Display

A statement that for the life of the prospectus the following documents (or copies thereof), where applicable, may be inspected:

(a) the memorandum and articles of association of the issuer;

(b) all reports, letters, and other documents, historical financial information, valuations and statements prepared by any expert at the issuer's request any part of which is included or referred to in the prospectus;

(c) the historical financial information of the issuer or, in the case of a group, the historical financial information for the issuer and its subsidiary undertakings for each of the two financial years preceding the publication of the prospectus.

An indication of where the documents on display may be inspected, by physical or electronic means.

25. Information on Holdings

25.1. Information relating to the undertakings in which the issuer holds a proportion of the capital likely to have a significant effect on the assessment of its own assets and liabilities, financial position or profits and losses.

26. Information about the Issuer of the Depository Receipts

26.1. Name, registered office and principal administrative establishment if different from the registered office.

26.2. Date of incorporation and length of life of the issuer, except where indefinite.

26.3. Legislation under which the issuer operates and legal form which it has adopted under that legislation.

27. Information about the Underlying Shares

27.1. A description of the type and the class of the underlying shares, including the ISIN (International Security Identification Number) or other such security identification code.

27.2. Legislation under which the underlying shares have been created.

27.3. An indication whether the underlying shares are in registered form or bearer form and whether the underlying shares are in certificated form or book-entry form. In the latter case, name and address of the entity in *charge* of keeping the records.

27.4. Currency of the underlying shares.

27.5. A description of the rights, including any limitations of these, attached to the underlying shares and procedure for the exercise of said rights.

27.6. Dividend rights:

(a) fixed date(s) on which the entitlement arises;

(b) time limit after which entitlement to dividend lapses and an indication of the person in whose favour the lapse operates;

(c) dividend restrictions and procedures for non-resident holders;

(d) rate of dividend or method of its calculation, periodicity and cumulative or non-cumulative nature of payments.

27.7. Voting rights

Pre-emption rights in offers for subscription of securities of the same class

Right to share in the issuer's profits

Rights to share in any surplus in the event of liquidation

Redemption provisions

Conversion provisions

27.8 The issue date of the underlying shares if new underlying shares are being created for the issue of the depository receipts and they are not in existence at the time of issue of the depository receipts.

27.9 If new underlying shares are being created for the issue of the depository receipts, state the resolutions, authorisations and approvals by virtue of which the new underlying shares have been or will be created and/or issued.

27.10 A description of any restrictions on the free transferability of the underlying shares.

27.11 In respect of the country of registered office of the issuer and the country(ies) where the offer is being made or admission to trading is being sought:

(a) information on taxes on the income from the underlying shares withheld at source;

(b) indication as to whether the issuer assumes responsibility for the withholding of taxes at the source.

27.12. An indication of the existence of any mandatory takeover bids and/or squeeze-out and sell-out rules in relation to the underlying shares.

27.13. An indication of public takeover bids by third parties in respect of the issuer's equity, which have occurred during the last financial year and the current financial year. The price or exchange terms attaching to such offers and the outcome thereof must be stated.

27.14. Lock up agreements:

— the parties involved,

— content and exceptions of the agreement,

— indication of the period of the lock up.

27.15. *Information about selling share holders if any*

27.15.1. Name and business address of the person or entity offering to sell the underlying shares, the nature of any position office or other material relationship that the selling persons has had within the past three years with the issuer of the underlying shares or any of its predecessors or affiliates.

27.16. *Dilution*

27.16.1. Amount and percentage of immediate dilution resulting from the offer of the depository receipts.

27.16.2. In the case of a subscription offer of the depository receipts to existing shareholders, disclose the amount and percentage of immediate dilutions if they do not subscribe to the offer of depository receipts.

27.17. *Additional information where there is a simultaneous or almost simultaneous offer or admission to trading of the same class of underlying shares as those underlying shares over which the depository receipts are being issued.*

27.17.1. If simultaneously or almost simultaneously with the creation of the depository receipts for which admission to a regulated market is being sought underlying shares of the same class as those over which the depository receipts are being issued are subscribed for or placed privately, details are to be given of the nature of such operations and of the number and characteristics of the underlying shares to which they relate.

27.17.2. Disclose all regulated markets or equivalent markets on which, to the knowledge of the issuer of the depository receipts, underlying shares of the same class of those over which the depository receipts are being issued are offered or admitted to trading.

27.17.3. To the extent known to the issuer of the depository receipts, indicate whether major shareholders, members of the administrative, management or supervisory bodies intended to subscribe in the offer, or whether any person intends to subscribe for more than five per cent of the offer.

28. Information Regarding the Depository Receipts

28.1. A description of the type and class of depository receipts being offered and/or admitted to trading.

28.2. Legislation under which the depository receipts have been created.

28.3. An indication whether the depository receipts are in registered or bearer form and whether the depository receipts are in certificated or book-entry form. In the latter case, include the name and address of the entity in charge of keeping the records.

28.4. Currency of the depository receipts.

28.5. Describe the rights attaching to the depository receipts, including any limitations of these attached to the depository receipts and the procedure if any for the exercise of these rights.

28.6. If the dividend rights attaching to depository receipts are different from the dividend rights disclosed in relation to the underlying disclose the following about the dividend rights:

(a) fixed date(s) on which the entitlement arises;

(b) time limit after which entitlement to dividend lapses and an indication of the person in whose favour the lapse operates;

(c) dividend restrictions and procedures for non-resident holders;

(d) rate of dividend or method of its calculation, periodicity and cumulative or non-cumulative nature of payments.

28.7. If the voting rights attaching to the depository receipts are different from the voting rights disclosed in relation to the underlying shares disclose the following about those rights:

— Voting rights.

— Pre-emption rights in offers for subscription of securities of the same class.

— Right to share in the issuer's profits.

— Rights to share in any surplus in the event of liquidation.

— Redemption provisions.

— Conversion provisions.

28.8. Describe the exercise of and benefit from the rights attaching to the underlying shares, in particular voting rights, the conditions on which the issuer of the depository receipts may exercise such rights, and measures envisaged to obtain the instructions of the depository receipt holders - and the right to share in profits and any liquidation surplus which are not passed on to the holder of the depository receipt.

28.9. The expected issue date of the depository receipts.

28.10. A description of any restrictions on the free transferability of the depository receipts.

28.11. In respect of the country of registered office of the issuer and the country(ies) where the offer is being made or admission to trading is being sought:

(a) information on taxes on the income from the depository receipts withheld at source;

(b) indication as to whether the issuer assumes responsibility for the withholding of taxes at the source.

28.12. Bank or other guarantees attached to the depository receipts and intended to underwrite the issuer's obligations.

28.13. Possibility of obtaining the delivery of the depository receipts into original shares and procedure for such delivery.

29. Information about the Terms and Conditions of the Offer of the Depository Receipts

29.1. *Conditions, offer statistics, expected timetable and action required to apply for the offer*

29.1.1. Total amount of the issue/offer, distinguishing the securities offered for sale and those offered for subscription; if the amount is not fixed, description of the arrangements and time for announcing to the public the definitive amount of the offer.

29.1.2. The time period, including any possible amendments, during which the offer will be open and description of the application process.

29.1.3. An indication of when, and under what circumstances, the offer may be revoked or suspended and whether revocation can occur after dealing has begun.

29.1.4. A description of the possibility to reduce subscriptions and the manner for refunding excess amount paid by applicants.

29.1.5. Details of the minimum and/or maximum amount of application (whether in number of securities or aggregate amount to invest).

29.1.6. An indication of the period during which an application may be withdrawn, provided that investors are allowed to withdraw their subscription.

29.1.7. Method and time limits for paying up the securities and for delivery of the securities.

29.1.8. A full description of the manner and date in which results of the offer are to be made public.

29.1.9. The procedure for the exercise of any right of pre-emption, the negotiability of subscription rights and the treatment of subscription rights not exercised.

29.2. *Plan of distribution and allotment*

29.2.1. The various categories of potential investors to which the securities are offered. If the offer is being made simultaneously in the markets of two or more countries and if a tranche has been or is being reserved for certain of these, indicate any such tranche.

29.2.2. To the extent known to the issuer, indicate whether major shareholders or members of the issuer's management, supervisory or administrative bodies intended to subscribe in the offer, or whether any person intends to subscribe for more than five per cent of the offer.

29.2.3. Pre-allotment Disclosure:

29.2.3.1. The division into tranches of the offer including the institutional, retail and issuer's employee tranches and any other tranches.

29.2.3.2. The conditions under which the claw-back may be used, the maximum size of such claw back and any applicable minimum percentages for individual tranches.

29.2.3.3. The allotment method or methods to be used for the retail and issuer's employee tranche in the event of an over-subscription of these tranches.

29.2.3.4. A description of any pre-determined preferential treatment to be accorded to certain classes of investors or certain affinity groups (including friends and family programmes) in the allotment, the percentage of the offer reserved for such preferential treatment and the criteria for inclusion in such classes or groups.

29.2.3.5. Whether the treatment of subscriptions or bids to subscribe in the allotment may be determined on the basis of which firm they are made through or by.

29.2.3.6. A target minimum individual allotment if any within the retail tranche.

29.2.3.7. The conditions for the closing of the offer as well as the date on which the offer may be closed at the earliest;

29.2.3.8. Whether or not multiple subscriptions are admitted, and where they are not, how any multiple subscriptions will be handled.

29.2.3.9. Process for notification to applicants of the amount allotted and indication whether dealing may begin before notification is made.

29.2.4. Over-allotment and 'green shoe':

29.2.4.1. The existence and size of any over-allotment facility and/or 'green shoe'.

29.2.4.2. The existence period of the over-allotment facility and/or 'green shoe'.

29.2.4.3. Any conditions for the use of the over-allotment facility or exercise of the 'green shoe'.

29.3. *Pricing*

29.3.1. An indication of the price at which the securities will be offered. When the price is not known or when there is not an established and/or liquid market for the securities, indicate the method for determination of the offer price, including who has set the criteria or is formally responsible for its determination. Indication of the amount of any expenses and taxes specifically *charged* to the subscriber or purchaser.

29.3.2. Process for the disclosure of the offer price.

29.3.3. Where there is or could be a material disparity between the public offer price and the effective cash cost to members of the administrative, management or supervisory bodies or senior management, or affiliated persons, of securities acquired by them in transactions during the past year, or which they have the right to acquire, include a comparison of the public contribution in the proposed public offer and the effective cash contributions of such persons.

29.4. *Placing and underwriting*

29.4.1. Name and address of the co-coordinator(s) of the global offer and of single parts of the offer and, to the extend known to the issuer, of the placers in the various countries where the offer takes place.

29.4.2. Name and address of any paying agents and depository agents in each country.

29.4.3. Name and address of the entities agreeing to underwrite the issue on a firm commitment basis, and name and address of the entities agreeing to place the issue without a firm commitment or under 'best efforts' arrangements. Indication of the material features of the agreements, including the quotas. Where not all of the issue is underwritten, a statement of the portion not covered. Indication of the overall amount of the underwriting commission and of the placing commission.

29.4.4. When the underwriting agreement has been or will be reached.

30. Admission to Trading and Dealing Arrangements in the Depository Receipts

30.1. An indication as to whether the securities offered are or will be the object of an application for admission to trading, with a view to their distribution in a regulated market or other equivalent markets with indication of the markets in question. This circumstance must be mentioned, without creating the impression that the admission to trading necessarily will be approved. If known, the earliest dates on which the securities will be admitted to trading must be given.

30.2. All the regulated markets or equivalent markets on which, to the knowledge of the issuer, securities of the same class of the securities to be offered or admitted to trading are already admitted to trading.

30.3. If simultaneously or almost simultaneously with the creation of the securities for which admission to a regulated market is being sought securities of the same class are subscribed for or placed privately or if securities of other classes are created for public or private placing, details must be given of the nature of such operations and of the number and characteristics of the securities to which they relate.

30.4. Name and address of the entities which have a firm commitment to act as intermediaries in secondary trading, providing liquidity through bid and offer rates and description of the main terms of their commitment.

30.5. Stabilisation: where an issuer or a selling shareholder has granted an over-allotment option or it is otherwise proposed that price stabilising activities may be entered into in connection with an offer:

30.6. The fact that stabilisation may be undertaken, that there is no assurance that it will be undertaken and that it may be stopped at any time.

30.7. The beginning and the end of the period during which stabilisation may occur.

30.8. The identity of the stabilisation manager for each relevant jurisdiction unless this is not known at the time of publication.

30.9. The fact that stabilisation transactions may result in a market price that is higher than would otherwise prevail.

[31. Essential Information about the Issue of the Depository Receipts][d]

31.1. *Reasons for the offer and use of proceeds*

31.1.1. Reasons for the offer and, where applicable, the estimated net amount of the proceeds broken into each principal intended use and presented by order of priority of such uses. If the issuer is aware that the anticipated proceeds will not be sufficient to fund all the proposed uses, state the amount and sources of other funds needed. Details must be given with regard to the use of the proceeds, in particular when they are being used to acquire assets, other than in the ordinary course of business, to finance announced acquisitions of other business, or to *discharge*, reduce or retire indebtedness.

31.2. *Interest of natural and legal persons involved in the issue/offer*

31.2.1. A description of any interest, including conflicting ones, that is material to the issue/offer, detailing the persons involved and the nature of the interest.

31.3. *Risk factors*

31.3.1.Prominent disclosure of risk factors that are material to the securities being offered and/or admitted to trading in order to assess the market risk associated with these securities in a section headed 'Risk factors'.

32. Expense of the Issue/offer of the Depository Receipts

32.1. The total net proceeds and an estimate of the total expenses of the issue/offer.

Amendments

a Inserted by Commission Delegated Regulation (EU) No 862/2012 of 4 June 2012.

b Inserted by Commission Regulation (EC) No 211/2007 of 27 February 2007 OJ L337 5.12.2006, p 17.

c Inserted by Commission Regulation (EC) No 211/2007 of 27 February 2007 OJ L337 5.12.2006, p 17.

d Inserted by Commission Delegated Regulation (EU) No 862/2012 of 4 June 2012.

Annex XI
Minimum Disclosure Requirements for the Banks Registration Document (schedule)

1. Persons Responsible

1.1. All persons responsible for the information given in the registration document and, as the case may be, for certain parts of it, with, in the latter case, an indication of such parts. In the case of natural persons including members of the issuer's administrative, management or supervisory bodies indicate the name and function of the person; in case of legal persons indicate the name and registered office.

1.2. A declaration by those responsible for the registration document that, having taken all reasonable care to ensure that such is the case, the information contained in the registration document is, to the best of their knowledge, in accordance with the facts and contains no omission likely to affect its import. As the case may be, declaration by those responsible for certain parts of the registration document that, having taken all reasonable care to ensure that such is the case, the information contained in the part of the registration document for which they are responsible is, to the best of their knowledge, in accordance with the facts and contains no omission likely to affect its import.

2. Statutory Auditors

2.1. Names and addresses of the issuer's auditors for the period covered by the historical financial information (together with their membership in a professional body).

2.2. If auditors have resigned, been removed or not been reappointed during the period covered by the historical financial information, details if material.

3. Risk Factors

3.1. Prominent disclosure of risk factors that may affect the issuer's ability to fulfil its obligations under the securities to investors in a section headed 'Risk factors'.

4 Information about the Issuer

4.1 *History and development of the Issuer*

4.1.1 the legal and commercial name of the issuer;

4.1.2 the place of registration of the issuer and its registration number;

4.1.3 the date of incorporation and the length of life of the issuer, except where indefinite;

4.1.4. the domicile and legal form of the issuer, the legislation under which the issuer operates, its country of incorporation, and the address and telephone number of its registered office (or principal place of business if different from its registered office);

4.1.5. any recent events particular to the issuer which are to a material extent relevant to the evaluation of the issuer's solvency.

5. Business Overview

5.1. *Principal activities:*

5.1.1. A brief description of the issuer's principal activities stating the main categories of products sold and/or services performed;

5.1.2. An indication of any significant new products and/or activities.

5.1.3. Principal markets

A brief description of the principal markets in which the issuer competes.

5.1.4. The basis for any statements in the registration document made by the issuer regarding its competitive position.

6. Organisational Structure

6.1. If the issuer is part of a group, a brief description of the group and of the issuer's position within it.

6.2. If the issuer is dependent upon other entities within the group, this must be clearly stated together with an explanation of this dependence.

7. Trend Information

7.1. Include a statement that there has been no material adverse change in the prospects of the issuer since the date of its last published audited financial statements.

In the event that the issuer is unable to make such a statement, provide details of this material adverse change.

7.2. Information on any known trends, uncertainties, demands, commitments or events that are reasonably likely to have a material effect on the issuer's prospects for at least the current financial year.

8. Profit Forecasts or Estimates

If an issuer chooses to include a profit forecast or a profit estimate the registration document must contain the information items 8.1 and 8.2.

8.1. A statement setting out the principal assumptions upon which the issuer has based its forecast, or estimate.

There must be a clear distinction between assumptions about factors which the members of the administrative, management or supervisory bodies can influence and assumptions about factors which are exclusively outside the influence of the members of the administrative, management or supervisory bodies; be readily understandable by investors; be specific and precise; and not relate to the general accuracy of the estimates underlying the forecast.

[8.2. A report prepared by independent accountants or auditors stating that in the opinion of the independent accountants or auditors the forecast or estimate has been properly compiled on the basis stated, and that the basis of accounting used for the profit forecast or estimate is consistent with the accounting policies of the issuer.

Where financial information relates to the previous financial year and only contains non-misleading figures substantially consistent with the final figures to be published in the next annual audited financial statements for the previous financial year, and the explanatory information necessary to assess the figures, a report shall not be required provided that the prospectus includes all of the following statements:

(a) the person responsible for this financial information, if different from the one which is responsible for the prospectus in general, approves that information;

(b) independent accountants or auditors have agreed that this information is substantially consistent with the final figures to be published in the next annual audited financial statements;

(c) this financial information has not been audited.][a]

8.3. The profit forecast or estimate must be prepared on a basis comparable with the historical financial information.

9. Administrative, Management, And Supervisory Bodies

9.1. Names, business addresses and functions in the issuer of the following persons, and an indication of the principal activities performed by them outside the issuer where these are significant with respect to that issuer:

(a) members of the administrative, management or supervisory bodies;

(b) partners with unlimited liability, in the case of a limited partnership with a share capital.

9.2. *Administrative, Management, and Supervisory bodies conflicts of interests*

Potential conflicts of interests between any duties to the issuing entity of the persons referred to in item 9.1 and their private interests and or other duties must be clearly stated. In the event that there are no such conflicts, make a statement to that effect.

10. Major Shareholders

10.1. To the extent known to the issuer, state whether the issuer is directly or indirectly owned or controlled and by whom, and describe the nature of such control, and describe the measures in place to ensure that such control is not abused.

10.2. A description of any arrangements, known to the issuer, the operation of which may at a subsequent date result in a change in control of the issuer.

11. Financial Information concerning the Issuer's Assets and Liabilities, Financial Position and Profits and Losses

11.1. *Historical Financial Information*

Audited historical financial information covering the latest two financial years (or such shorter period that the issuer has been in operation), and the audit report in respect of each year. [If the issuer has changed its accounting reference date during the period for which historical financial information is required, the audited historical information shall cover at least 24 months, or the entire period for which the issuer has been in operation, whichever is the shorter.][b] Such financial information must be prepared according to Regulation (EC) No 1606/2002, or if not applicable to a Member State national accounting standards for issuers from the Community. For third country issuers, such financial information must be prepared according to the international accounting standards adopted pursuant to the procedure of Article 3 of Regulation (EC) No 1606/2002 or to a third country's national accounting standards equivalent to these standards. If such financial information is not equivalent to these standards, it must be presented in the form of restated financial statements.

The most recent year's audited historical financial information must be presented and prepared in a form consistent with that which will be adopted in the issuer's next published annual financial statements having regard to accounting standards and policies and legislation applicable to such annual financial statements.

If the issuer has been operating in its current sphere of economic activity for less than one year, the audited historical financial information covering that period must be prepared in accordance with the standards applicable to annual financial statements under Regulation (EC) No 1606/2002, or if not applicable to a Member State national accounting standards where the issuer is an issuer from the Community. For third country issuers, the historical financial information must be prepared according to the international accounting standards adopted pursuant to the procedure of Article 3 of Regulation (EC) No 1606/2002 or to a third country's national accounting standards equivalent to these standards. This historical financial information must be audited.

If the audited financial information is prepared according to national accounting standards, the financial information required under this heading must include at least the following:

(a) the balance sheet;

(b) the income statement;

(c) in the case of an admission of securities to trading on a regulated market only, a cash flow statement;

(d) the accounting policies and explanatory notes.

The historical annual financial information must be independently audited or reported on as to whether or not, for the purposes of the registration document, it gives a true and fair view, in accordance with auditing standards applicable in a Member State or an equivalent standard.

11.2. *Financial statements*

If the issuer prepares both own and consolidated financial statements, include at least the consolidated financial statements in the registration document.

11.3. *Auditing of historical annual financial information*

11.3.1. A statement that the historical financial information has been audited. If audit reports on the historical financial information have been refused by the statutory auditors or if they contain qualifications or disclaimers, such refusal or such qualifications or disclaimers must be reproduced in full and the reasons given.

11.3.2. An indication of other information in the registration document which has been audited by the auditors.

11.3.3. Where financial data in the registration document is not extracted from the issuer's audited financial statements state the source of the data and state that the data is un-audited.

11.4. *Age of latest financial information*

11.4.1. The last year of audited financial information may not be older than 18 months from the date of the registration document.

11.5. *Interim and other financial information*

11.5.1 If the issuer has published quarterly or half yearly financial information since the date of its last audited financial statements, these must be included in the registration document. If the quarterly or half yearly financial information has been reviewed or audited the audit or review report must also be included. If the quarterly or half yearly financial information is unaudited or has not been reviewed state that fact.

11.5.2. If the registration document is dated more than nine months after the end of the last audited financial year, it must contain interim financial information, covering at least the first six months of the financial year. If the interim financial information is un-audited state that fact.

The interim financial information must include comparative statements for the same period in the prior financial year, except that the requirement for comparative balance sheet information may be satisfied by presenting the years end balance sheet.

11.6. *Legal and arbitration proceedings*

Information on any governmental, legal or arbitration proceedings (including any such proceedings which are pending or threatened of which the issuer is aware), during a period covering at least the previous 12 months which may have, or have had in the recent past, significant effects on the issuer and/or group's financial position or profitability, or provide an appropriate negative statement.

11.7. *Significant change in the issuer's financial position*

A description of any significant change in the financial position of the group which has occurred since the end of the last financial period for which either audited financial information or interim financial information have been published, or an appropriate negative statement.

12. Material Contracts

A brief summary of all material contracts that are not entered into in the ordinary course of the issuer's business, which could result in any group member being under an obligation or entitlement that is material to the issuer's ability to meet its obligation to security holders in respect of the securities being issued.

13. Third Party Information and Statement by Experts And Declarations of Any Interest

13.1. Where a statement or report attributed to a person as an expert is included in the registration document, provide such person's name, business address, qualifications and material interest if any in the issuer. If the report has been produced at the issuer's request a statement to that effect that such statement or report is included, in the form and context in which it is included, with the consent of that person who has authorised the contents of that part of the registration document.

13.2. Where information has been sourced from a third party, provide a confirmation that this information has been accurately reproduced and that as far as the issuer is aware and is able to ascertain from information published by that third party, no facts have been omitted which would render the reproduced information inaccurate or misleading In addition, the issuer shall identify the source(s) of the information.

14. Documents On Display

A statement that for the life of the registration document the following documents (or copies thereof), where applicable, may be inspected:

(a) the memorandum and articles of association of the issuer;

(b) all reports, letters, and other documents, historical financial information, valuations and statements prepared by any expert at the issuer's request any part of which is included or referred to in the registration document;

(c) the historical financial information of the issuer or, in the case of a group, the historical financial information of the issuer and its subsidiary undertakings for each of the two financial years preceding the publication of the registration document.

An indication of where the documents on display may be inspected, by physical or electronic means.

Amendments

a Inserted by Commission Delegated Regulation (EU) No 862/2012 of 4 June 2012.

b Inserted by Commission Regulation (EC) No 211/2007 of 27 February 2007 OJ L337 5.12.2006, p 17.

Annex XII
Minimum Disclosure Requirements for the Securities Note for derivative securities (schedule)

1. Persons Responsible

1.1. All persons responsible for the information given in the prospectus and, as the case may be, for certain parts of it, with, in the latter case, an indication of such parts. In the case of natural persons including members of the issuer's administrative, management or supervisory bodies indicate the name and function of the person; in case of legal persons indicate the name and registered office.

1.2. A declaration by those responsible for the prospectus that, having taken all reasonable care to ensure that such is the case, the information contained in the prospectus is, to the best of their knowledge, in accordance with the facts and contains no omission likely to affect its import. As the case may be, declaration by those responsible for certain parts of the prospectus that, having taken all reasonable care to ensure that such is the case, the information contained in the part of the prospectus for which they are responsible is, to the best of their knowledge, in accordance with the facts and contains no omission likely to affect its import.

2. Risk Factors

Prominent disclosure of risk factors that are material to the securities being offered and/or admitted to trading in order to assess the market risk associated with these securities in a section headed 'risk factors'. This must include a risk warning to the effect that investors may lose the value of their entire investment or part of it, as the case may be, and/or, if the investor's liability is not limited to the value of his investment, a statement of that fact, together with a description of the circumstances in which such additional liability arises and the likely financial effect.

[3. Essential Information][a]

3.1. *Interest of natural and legal persons involved in the issue/offer*

A description of any interest, including conflicting ones that is material to the issue/offer, detailing the persons involved and the nature of the interest.

3.2. *Reasons for the offer and use of proceeds when different from making profit and/or hedging certain risks*

If reasons for the offer and use of proceeds are disclosed provide the total net proceeds and an estimate of the total expenses of the issue/ offer.

4. Information Concerning the Securities to be Offered/admitted to Trading

4.1. *Information concerning the securities*

4.1.1. A description of the type and the class of the securities being offered and/or admitted to trading, including the ISIN (International Security Identification Number) or other such security identification code.

4.1.2. A clear and comprehensive explanation to help investors understand how the value of their investment is affected by the value of the underlying instrument (s), especially under the circumstances when the risks are most evident unless the securities have a denomination per unit of at least EUR 50,000 or can only be acquired for at least EUR 50,000 per security.

4.1.3. Legislation under which the securities have been created.

4.1.4. An indication whether the securities are in registered form or bearer form and whether the securities are in certificated form or book-entry form. In the latter case, name and address of the entity in charge of keeping the records.

4.1.5. Currency of the securities issue.

4.1.6. Ranking of the securities being offered and/or admitted to trading, including summaries of any clauses that are intended to affect ranking or subordinate the security to any present or future liabilities of the issuer.

4.1.7. A description of the rights, including any limitations of these, attached to the securities and procedure for the exercise of said rights.

4.1.8. In the case of new issues, a statement of the resolutions, authorisations and approvals by virtue of which the securities have been or will be created and/or issued.

4.1.9. The issue date of the securities.

4.1.10. A description of any restrictions on the free transferability of the securities.

4.1.11.

— The expiration or maturity date of the derivative securities.

— The exercise date or final reference date.

4.1.12. A description of the settlement procedure of the derivative securities.

4.1.13. A description of how any return on derivative securities takes place, the payment or delivery date, and the way it is calculated.

4.1.14. In respect of the country of registered office of the issuer and the country(ies) where the offer is being made or admission to trading is being sought:

(a) information on taxes on the income from the securities withheld at source;

(b) indication as to whether the issuer assumes responsibility for the withholding of taxes at the source.

4.2. *Information concerning the underlying*

4.2.1. The exercise price or the final reference price of the underlying.

4.2.2. A statement setting out the type of the underlying and details of where information on the underlying can be obtained:

— an indication where information about the past and the further performance of the underlying and its volatility can be obtained,

— where the underlying is a security,

— the name of the issuer of the security,

— the ISIN (international security identification number) or other such security identification code,

[— where the underlying is an index:

— the name of the index,

— a description of the index if it is composed by the issuer or by any legal entity belonging to the same group,

— a description of the index provided by a legal entity or a natural person acting in association with, or on behalf of, the issuer, unless the prospectus contains the following statements:

— the complete set of rules of the index and information on the performance of the index are freely accessible on the issuer's or on the index provider's website,

and

— the governing rules (including methodology of the index for the selection and the re-balancing of the components of the index, description of market disruption events and adjustment rules) are based on predetermined and objective criteria.

If the index is not composed by the issuer, where information about the index can be obtained.][b]

4.2.3. A description of any market disruption or settlement disruption events that affect the underlying.

5. Terms and Conditions Of The Offer

5.1. *Conditions, offer statistics, expected timetable and action required to apply for the offer*

5.1.1. Conditions to which the offer is subject.

5.1.2. Total amount of the issue/offer; if the amount is not fixed, description of the arrangements and time for announcing to the public the amount of the offer.

5.1.3. The time period, including any possible amendments, during which the offer will be open and description of the application process.

5.1.4. Details of the minimum and/or maximum amount of application, (whether in number of securities or aggregate amount to invest).

5.1.5. Method and time limits for paying up the securities and for delivery of the securities.

5.1.6. A full description of the manner and date in which results of the offer are to be made public.

5.2. *Plan of distribution and allotment*

5.2.1. The various categories of potential investors to which the securities are offered. If the offer is being made simultaneously in the markets of two or more countries and if a tranche has been or is being reserved for certain of these, indicate any such tranche.

5.2.2. Process for notification to applicants of the amount allotted and indication whether dealing may begin before notification is made.

5.3. *Pricing*

Indication of the expected price at which the securities will be offered or the method of determining the price and the process for its disclosure. Indicate the amount of any expenses and taxes specifically *charged* to the subscriber or purchaser.

5.4. *Placing and underwriting*

5.4.1. Name and address of the coordinator(s) of the global offer and of single parts of the offer and, to the extend known to the issuer or to the offeror, of the placers in the various countries where the offer takes place.

5.4.2. Name and address of any paying agents and depository agents in each country.

5.4.3. Entities agreeing to underwrite the issue on a firm commitment basis, and entities agreeing to place the issue without a firm commitment or under 'best efforts' arrangements. Where not all of the issue is under-written, a statement of the portion not covered.

5.4.4. When the underwriting agreement has been or will be reached.

5.4.5. Name and address of a calculation agent.

6. Admission to Trading and Dealing Arrangements

6.1. An indication as to whether the securities offered are or will be the object of an application for admission to trading, with a view to their distribution in a regulated market or other equivalent markets with indication of the markets in question. This circumstance shall be mentioned, without creating the impression that the admission to trading necessarily will be approved. If known, the earliest dates on which the securities will be admitted to trading shall be given.

6.2. All the regulated markets or equivalent markets on which, to the knowledge of the issuer, securities of the same class of the securities to be offered or admitted to trading are already admitted to trading.

6.3. Name and address of the entities which have a firm commitment to act as intermediaries in secondary trading, providing liquidity through bid and offer rates and description of the main terms of their commitment.

7. Additional Information

7.1. If advisors connected with an issue are mentioned in the Securities Note, a statement of the capacity in which the advisors have acted.

7.2. An indication of other information in the Securities Note which has been audited or reviewed by statutory auditors and where auditors have produced a report. Reproduction of the report or, with permission of the competent authority, a summary of the report.

7.3. Where a statement or report attributed to a person as an expert is included in the Securities Note, provide such person's name, business address, qualifications and material interest, if any, in the issuer. If the report has been produced at the issuer's request a statement to that effect that such statement or report is included, in the form and context in which it is included, with the consent of that person who has authorised the contents of that part of the Securities Note.

7.4. Where information has been sourced from a third party, provide a confirmation that this information has been accurately reproduced and that as far as the issuer is aware and is able to ascertain from information published by that third party, no facts have been omitted which would render the reproduced information inaccurate or misleading. In addition, the issuer shall identify the source(s) of the information.

7.5. An indication in the prospectus whether or not the issuer intends to provide post-issuance information. Where the issuer has indicated that it intends to report such information, the issuer shall specify in the prospectus what information will be reported and where such information can be obtained.

Amendments

a Inserted by Commission Delegated Regulation (EU) No 862/2012 of 4 June 2012.

b Inserted by Commission Delegated Regulation (EU) No 862/2012 of 4 June 2012.

Annex XIII
Minimum Disclosure Requirements for the Securities Note for debt securities with a denomination per unit of at least EUR 50,000 (Schedule)

1. Persons Responsible

1.1. All persons responsible for the information given in the prospectus and, as the case may be, for certain parts of it, with, in the latter case, an indication of such parts. In case of natural persons including members of the issuer's administrative, management or supervisory bodies indicate the name and function of the person; in case of legal persons indicate the name and registered office.

1.2. A declaration by those responsible for the prospectus that, having taken all reasonable care to ensure that such is the case, the information contained in the prospectus is, to the best of their knowledge, in accordance with the facts and contains no omission likely to affect its import. As the case may be, declaration by those responsible for certain parts of the prospectus that the information contained in the part of the prospectus for which they are responsible is, to the best of their knowledge, in accordance with the facts and contains no omission likely to affect its import.

2. Risk Factors

Prominent disclosure of risk factors that are material to the securities admitted to trading in order to assess the market risk associated with these securities in a section headed 'Risk factors'.

[3. Essential Information][a]

Interest of natural and legal persons involved in the issue

A description of any interest, including conflicting ones, that is material to the issue, detailing the persons involved and the nature of the interest.

Amendments

a Inserted by Commission Delegated Regulation (EU) No 862/2012 of 4 June 2012.

---

4. Information Concerning the Securities to be Admitted to Trading

4.1. Total amount of securities being admitted to trading.

4.2. A description of the type and the class of the securities being admitted to trading, including the ISIN (international security identification number) or other such security identification code.

4.3. Legislation under which the securities have been created.

4.4. An indication of whether the securities are in registered or bearer form and whether the securities are in certificated or book-entry form. In the latter case, name and address of the entity in charge of keeping the records.

4.5. Currency of the securities issue.

4.6. Ranking of the securities being admitted to trading, including summaries of any clauses that are intended to affect ranking or subordinate the security to any present or future liabilities of the issuer.

4.7. A description of the rights, including any limitations of these, attached to the securities and procedure for the exercise of said rights.

4.8. The nominal interest rate and provisions relating to interest payable:

— The date from which interest becomes payable and the due dates for interest.

— The time limit on the validity of claims to interest and repayment of principal.

Where the rate is not fixed, description of the underlying on which it is based and of the method used to relate the two:

— A description of any market disruption or settlement disruption events that affect the underlying.

— Adjustment rules with relation to events concerning the underlying.

— Name of the calculation agent.

4.9. Maturity date and arrangements for the amortisation of the loan, including the repayment procedures. Where advance amortisation is contemplated, on the initiative of the issuer or of the holder, it must be described, stipulating amortisation terms and conditions.

4.10. An indication of yield.

4.11. Representation of debt security holders including an identification of the organisation representing the investors and provisions applying to such representation. Indication of where investors may have access to the contracts relating to these forms of representation.

4.12. A statement of the resolutions, authorisations and approvals by virtue of which the securities have been created and/or issued.

4.13. The issue date of the securities.

4.14. A description of any restrictions on the free transferability of the securities.

5. Admission to Trading and Dealing Arrangements

5.1. Indication of the market where the securities will be traded and for which prospectus has been published. If known, give the earliest dates on which the securities will be admitted to trading.

5.2. Name and address of any paying agents and depository agents in each country.

6. Expense of the Admission to Trading

An estimate of the total expenses related to the admission to trading.

7. Additional Information

7.1. If advisors are mentioned in the Securities Note, a statement of the capacity in which the advisors have acted.

7.2. An indication of other information in the Securities Note which has been audited or reviewed by auditors and where auditors have produced a report. Reproduction of the report or, with permission of the competent authority, a summary of the report.

7.3. Where a statement or report attributed to a person as an expert is included in the Securities Note, provide such person's name, business address, qualifications and material interest if any in the issuer. If the report has been produced at the issuer's request a statement to that effect that such statement or report is included, in the form and context in which it is included, with the consent of that person who has authorised the contents of that part of the Securities Note.

7.4. Where information has been sourced from a third party, provide a confirmation that this information has been accurately reproduced and that as far as the issuer is aware and is able to ascertain from information published by that third party, no facts have been omitted which would render the reproduced information inaccurate or misleading. In addition, identify the source(s) of the information.

7.5. Credit ratings assigned to an issuer or its debt securities at the request or with the co-operation of the issuer in the rating process.

Annex XIV
Additional information building block on underlying share for some equity securities

1. Description of the underlying share

1.1. Describe the type and the class of the shares

1.2. Legislation under which the shares have been or will be created

1.3. Indication whether the securities are in registered form or bearer form and whether the securities are in certificated form or book-entry form. In the latter case, name and address of the entity in charge of keeping the records

1.4. Indication of the currency of the shares issue

1.5. A description of the rights, including any limitations of these, attached to the securities and procedure for the exercise of those rights:

- Dividend rights:
  - fixed date(s) on which the entitlement arises,
  - time limit after which entitlement to dividend lapses and an indication of the person in whose favour the lapse operates,
  - dividend restrictions and procedures for non resident holders,
  - rate of dividend or method of its calculation, periodicity and cumulative or non-cumulative nature of payments.
- Voting rights.
- Pre-emption rights in offers for subscription of securities of the same class.
- Right to share in the issuer's profits.
- Rights to share in any surplus in the event of liquidation.
- Redemption provisions.
- Conversion provisions.

1.6. In the case of new issues, a statement of the resolutions, authorisations and approvals by virtue of which the shares have been or will be created and/or issued and indication of the issue date.

1.7. Where and when the shares will be or have been admitted to trading.

1.8. Description of any restrictions on the free transferability of the shares.

1.9. Indication of the existence of any mandatory takeover bids/or squeeze-out and sell-out rules in relation to the shares.

1.10. Indication of public takeover bids by third parties in respect of the issuer's equity, which have occurred during the last financial year and the current financial year. The price or exchange terms attaching to such offers and the outcome thereof must be stated.

1.11. Impact on the issuer of the underlying share of the exercise of the right and potential dilution effect for the shareholders.

2. When the issuer of the underlying is an entity belonging to the same group, the information to provide on this issuer is the one required by the share registration document schedule.

Annex XV
Minimum disclosure requirements for the registration document for securities issued by collective investment undertakings of the closed-end type (schedule)

In addition to the information required in this schedule, the collective investment undertaking must provide the following information as required under paragraphs and items 1, 2, 3, 4, 5.1, 7, 9.1, 9.2.1, 9.2.3, 10.4, 13, 14, 15, 16, 17.2, 18, 19, 20, 21, 22, 23, 24, 25 in Annex I (minimum disclosure requirements for the share registration document schedule).

1. Investment objective and policy

1.1. A detailed description of the investment objective and policy which the collective investment undertaking will pursue and a description of how that investment objectives and policy may be varied including any circumstances in which such variation requires the approval of investors. A description of any techniques and instruments that may be used in the management of the collective investment undertaking.

1.2. The borrowing and/or leverage limits of the collective investment undertaking. If there are no such limits, include a statement to that effect.

1.3. The regulatory status of the collective investment undertaking together with the name of any regulator in its country of incorporation.

1.4. The profile of a typical investor for whom the collective investment undertaking is designed.

2. Investment Restrictions

2.1. A statement of the investment restrictions which apply to the collective investment undertaking, if any, and an indication of how the holders of securities will be informed of the actions that the investment manager will take in the event of a breach.

2.2. Where more than 20 % of the gross assets of any collective investment undertaking (except where items 2.3 or 2.5 apply) may be:

(a) invested in, either directly or indirectly, or lent to any single underlying issuer (including the underlying issuer's subsidiaries or affiliates);

or

(b) invested in one or more collective investment undertakings which may invest in excess of 20% of its gross assets in other collective investment undertakings (open-end and/or closed-end type);

or

(c) exposed to the creditworthiness or solvency of any one counterparty (including its subsidiaries or affiliates);

the following information must be disclosed:

(i) information relating to each underlying issuer/collective investment undertaking/counterparty as if it were an issuer for the purposes of the minimum disclosure requirements for the share registration document schedule (in the case of (a)) or minimum disclosure requirements for the registration document schedule for securities issued by collective investment undertaking of the closed-end type (in the case of (b)) or the minimum disclosure requirements for the debt and derivative securities with an individual denomination per unit of at least EUR 50,000 registration document schedule (in the case of (c));

or

(ii) if the securities issued by the underlying issuer/collective investment undertaking/counterparty have already been admitted to trading on a regulated or equivalent market or the obligations are guaranteed by an entity admitted to trading on a regulated or equivalent market, the name, address, country of incorporation, nature of business and name of the market in which its securities are admitted.

This requirement shall not apply where the 20% is exceeded due to appreciations or depreciations, changes in exchange rates, or by reason of the receipt of rights, bonuses, benefits in the nature of capital or by reason of any other action affecting every holder of that investment, provided the investment manager has regard to the threshold when considering changes in the investment portfolio.

2.3. Where a collective investment undertaking may invest in excess of 20% of its gross assets in other collective investment undertakings (open ended and/or closed ended), a description of if and how risk is spread in relation to those investments. In addition, item 2.2 shall apply, in aggregate, to its underlying investments as if those investments had been made directly.

2.4. With reference to point (c) of item 2.2, if collateral is advanced to cover that portion of the exposure to any one counterparty in excess of 20% of the gross assets of the collective investment undertaking, details of such collateral arrangements.

2.5. Where a collective investment undertaking may invest in excess of 40% of its gross assets in another collective investment undertaking either of the following must be disclosed:

(a) information relating to each underlying collective investment undertaking as if it were an issuer under minimum disclosure requirements for the registration document schedule for securities issued by collective investment undertaking of the closed-end type;

(b) if securities issued by an underlying collective investment under-taking have already been admitted to trading on a regulated or equivalent market or the obligations are guaranteed by an entity admitted to trading on a regulated or equivalent market, the name, address, country of incorporation, nature of business and name of the market in which its securities are admitted.

2.6. *Physical Commodities*

Where a collective investment undertaking invests directly in physical commodities a disclosure of that fact and the percentage that will be so invested.

2.7. *Property Collective investment undertakings*

Where a collective investment undertaking is a property collective investment undertaking, disclosure of that fact, the percentage of the portfolio that is to be invested in the property, as well as a description of the property and any material costs relating to the acquisition and holding of such property. In addition, a valuation report relating to the properties must be included.

Disclosure of item 4.1. applies to:

(a) the valuation entity;

(b) any other entity responsible for the administration of the property.

2.8. *Derivatives Financial instruments/Money Market Instruments/ Currencies*

Where a collective investment undertaking invests in derivatives financial instruments, money market instruments or currencies other than for the purposes of efficient portfolio management (i.e. solely for the purpose of reducing, transferring or eliminating investment risk in the underlying investments of a collective investment under-taking, including any technique or instrument used to provide protection against exchange and credit risks), a statement whether those investments are used for hedging or for investment purposes, and a description of if and how risk is spread in relation to those investments.

2.9 Item 2.2 does not apply to investment in securities issued or guaranteed by a government, government agency or instrumentality of any Member State, its regional or local authorities, or OECD Member State.

[2.10. Point (a) of item 2.2 does not apply to a collective investment undertaking whose investment objective is to track, without material modification, that of a broadly based and recognised published index. A statement setting out details of where information about the index can be obtained shall be included.][a]

3. The applicant's service providers

3.1. The actual or estimated maximum amount of all material fees payable directly or indirectly by the collective investment undertaking for any services under arrangements entered into on or prior to the date of the registration document and a description of how these fees are calculated.

A description of any fee payable directly or indirectly by the collective investment undertaking which cannot be quantified under item 3.1 and which is or may be material.

If any service provider to the collective investment undertaking is in receipt of any benefits from third parties (other than the collective investment undertaking) by virtue of providing any services to the collective investment undertaking, and those benefits may not accrue to the collective investment undertaking, a statement of that fact, the name of that third party, if available, and a description of the nature of the benefits.

The name of the service provider which is responsible for the determination and calculation of the net asset value of the collective investment undertaking.

A description of any material potential conflicts of interest which any of the service providers to the collective investment undertaking may have as between their duty to the collective investment undertaking and duties owed by them to third parties and their other interests. A description of any arrangements which are in place to address such potential conflicts.

4. **Investment Manager/Advisers**

4.1. In respect of any Investment Manager such information as is required to be disclosed under items 5.1.1 to 5.1.4 and, if material, under item 5.1.5 of Annex I together with a description of its regulatory status and experience.

4.2. In respect of any entity providing investment advice in relation to the assets of the collective investment undertaking, the name and a brief description of such entity.

5. **Custody**

5.1. A full description of how the assets of the collective investment under-taking will be held and by whom and any fiduciary or similar relationship between the collective investment undertaking and any third party in relation to custody:

Where a custodian, trustee, or other fiduciary is appointed:

(a) such information as is required to be disclosed under items 5.1.1 to 5.1.4 and, if material, under item 5.1.5 of Annex I;

(b) a description of the obligations of such party under the custody or similar agreement;

(c) any delegated custody arrangements;

(d) the regulatory status of such party and delegates.

5.2. Where any entity other than those entities mentioned in item 5.1, holds any assets of the collective investment undertaking, a description of how these assets are held together with a description of any additional risks.

6. **Valuation**

6.1. A description of how often, and the valuation principles and the method by which, the net asset value of the collective investment undertaking will be determined, distinguishing between categories of investments and a statement of how such net asset value will be communicated to investors.

6.2. Details of all circumstances in which valuations may be suspended and a statement of how such suspension will be communicated or made available to investors.

7. **Cross Liabilities**

7.1. In the case of an umbrella collective investment undertaking, a statement of any cross liability that may occur between classes or investments in other collective investment undertakings and any action taken to limit such liability.

8. **Financial Information**

8.1. Where, since the date of incorporation or establishment, a collective investment undertaking has not commenced operations and no financial statements have been made up as at the date of the registration document, a statement to that effect.

Where a collective investment undertaking has commenced operations, the provisions of item 20 of Annex I on the Minimum Disclosure Requirements for the share registration document apply.

8.2. A comprehensive and meaningful analysis of the collective investment undertaking's portfolio (if un-audited, clearly marked as such).

8.3. An indication of the most recent net asset value per security must be included in the securities note schedule (and, if un-audited, clearly marked as such).

Amendments

a Inserted by Commission Delegated Regulation (EU) No 862/2012 of 4 June 2012.

Annex XVI
Minimum disclosure requirements for the registration document for securities issued by Member States, third countries and their regional and local authorities (schedule)

1. Persons Responsible

1.1. All persons responsible for the information given in the registration document and, as the case may be, for certain parts of it, with, in the latter case, an indication of such parts. In the case of natural persons including members of the issuer's administrative, management or supervisory bodies indicate the name and function of the person; in case of legal persons indicate the name and registered office.

1.2. A declaration by those responsible for the registration document that, having taken all reasonable care to ensure that such is the case, the information contained in the registration document is, to the best of their knowledge in accordance with the facts and contains no omission likely to affect its import. As the case may be, declaration by those responsible for certain parts of the registration document that, having taken all reasonable care to ensure that such is the case the information contained in the part of the registration document for which they are responsible is, to the best of their knowledge, in accordance with the facts and contains no omission likely to affect its import.

2. Risk Factors

Prominent disclosure of risk factors that may affect the issuer's ability to fulfil its obligations under the securities to investors in a section headed 'Risk factors'.

3. Information about the Issuer

3.1. The legal name of the issuer and a brief description of the issuer's position within the national governmental framework.

3.2. The domicile or geographical location and legal form of the issuer and its contact address and telephone number.

3.3. Any recent events relevant to the evaluation of the issuer's solvency.

3.4. A description of the issuer's economy including:

(a) the structure of the economy with details of the main sectors of the economy;

(b) gross domestic product with a breakdown by the issuer's economic sectors over for the previous two fiscal years.

3.5. A general description of the issuer's political system and government including details of the governing body of the issuer.

4. Public Finance and Trade

Information on the following for the two fiscal years prior to the date of the registration document:

(a) the tax and budgetary systems;

(b) gross public debt including a summary of the debt, the maturity structure of outstanding debt (particularly noting debt with a residual maturity of less than one year) and debt payment record, and of the parts of debt denominated in the domestic currency of the issuer and in foreign currencies;

(c) foreign trade and balance of payment figures;

(d) foreign exchange reserves including any potential encumbrances to such foreign exchange reserves as forward contracts or derivatives;

(e) financial position and resources including liquid deposits available in domestic currency;

(f) income and expenditure figures.

Description of any auditing or independent review procedures on the accounts of the issuer.

5. Significant Change

5.1. Details of any significant changes to the information provided pursuant to item 4 which have occurred since the end of the last fiscal year, or an appropriate negative statement.

6. Legal and Arbitration Proceedings

6.1. Information on any governmental, legal or arbitration proceedings (including any such proceedings which are pending or threatened of which the issuer is aware), during a period covering at least the previous 12 months which may have, or have had in the recent past, significant effects on the issuer financial position, or provide an appropriate negative statement.

6.2. Information on any immunity the issuer may have from legal proceedings.

7. Statement by Experts and Declarations of Any Interest

Where a statement or report attributed to a person as an expert is included in the registration document, provide such person's name, business address and qualifications. If the report has been produced at the issuer's request a statement to that effect, that such statement or report is included, in the form and context in which it is included, with the consent of that person, who has authorised the contents of that part of the registration document.

To the extent known to the issuer, provide information in respect of any interest relating to such expert which may have an effect on the independence of the expert in the preparation of the report.

8. Documents on Display

A statement that for the life of the registration document the following documents (or copies thereof), where applicable, may be inspected:

(a) financial and audit reports for the issuer covering the last two fiscal years and the budget for the current fiscal year;

(b) all reports, letters, and other documents, valuations and statements prepared by any expert at the issuer's request any part of which is included or referred to in the registration document.

An indication of where the documents on display may be inspected, by physical or electronic means.

Annex XVII

Minimum disclosure requirements for the registration document for securities issued by public international bodies and for debt securities guaranteed by a Member State of the OECD (schedule)

1. **Persons Responsible**

1.1. All persons responsible for the information given in the registration document and, as the case may be, for certain parts of it, with, in the latter case, an indication of such parts. In the case of natural persons including members of the issuer's administrative, management or supervisory bodies indicate the name and function of the person; in case of legal persons indicate the name and registered office.

1.2. A declaration by those responsible for the registration document, that, having taken all reasonable care to ensure that such is the case, the information contained in the registration document is, to the best of their knowledge, in accordance with the facts and contains no omission likely to materially affect its import. As the case may be, declaration by those responsible for certain parts of the registration document that, having taken all reasonable care to ensure that such is the case the information contained in the part of the registration document for which they are responsible is, to the best of their knowledge, in accordance with the facts and contains no omission likely to affect its import.

2. **Risk Factors**

Prominent disclosure of risk factors that may affect the issuer's ability to fulfil its obligations under the securities to investors in a section headed 'Risk factors'.

3. **Information about the Issuer**

3.1. The legal name of the issuer and a brief description of the issuer's legal status.

3.2. The location of the principal office and the legal form of the issuer and its contact address and telephone number.

3.3. Details of the governing body of the issuer and a description of its governance arrangements, if any.

3.4. A brief description of the issuer's purpose and functions.

3.5. The sources of funding, guarantees and other obligations owed to the issuer by its members.

3.6. Any recent events relevant to the evaluation of the issuer's solvency.

3.7. A list of the issuer's members.

4. **Financial Information**

The two most recently published audited annual financial statements prepared in accordance with the accounting and auditing principles adopted by the issuer, and a brief description of those accounting and auditing principles.

Details of any significant changes to the issuer's financial position which has occurred since the end of the latest published audited annual financial statement, or an appropriate negative statement.

5. Legal and Arbitration Proceedings

5.1. Information on any governmental, legal or arbitration proceedings (including any such proceedings which are pending or threatened of which the issuer is aware), during a period covering at least the previous 12 months which are likely to have, or have had in the recent past, significant effects on the issuer's financial position, or provide an appropriate negative statement.

5.2. Information on any immunity the issuer may have from legal proceedings pursuant to its constituent document.

6. Statement by Experts and Declaration of Any Interests

Where a statement or report attributed to a person as an expert is included in the registration document, provide such person's name, business address and qualifications. If the report has been produced at the issuer's request a statement to that effect, that such statement or report is included, in the form and context in which it is included, with the consent of that person.

To the extent known to the issuer, provide information in respect of any conflict of interests relating to such expert which may have an effect on the independence of the expert in the preparation of the report.

7. Document on Display

A statement that for the life of the registration document the following documents (or copies thereof), where applicable, will be made available on request:

(a) annual and audit reports of the issuer for each of the last two financial years prepared in accordance with the accounting and auditing principles adopted by the issuer;

(b) all reports, letters, and other documents, valuations and statements prepared by any expert at the issuer's request any part of which is included or referred to in the registration document;

(c) the issuer's constituent document.

An indication of where the documents on display may be inspected, by physical or electronic means.

ANNEX XVIII
TABLE OF COMBINATIONS

	REGISTRATION DOCUMENT					
	SCHEDULES					**BUILDING BLOCK**
TYPES OF SECURITIES	Share	Debt and derivative (< EUR 50 000)	Debt and derivative (> or = EUR 50 000)	Asset -backed securities	Banks debt and derivative	**Pro forma information**
Shares (preference shares, redeemable shares, shares with preferential subscription rights; etc.)						
Bonds (vanilla bonds, income bonds, structured bonds, etc.) with a denomination of less than EUR 50 000		or			or	
Bonds (vanilla bonds, income bonds, structured bonds, etc.) with a denomination of at least EUR 50 000			or		or	
Debt securities guaranteed by a third party		or	or		or	
Derivative securities guaranteed by a third party		or	or		or	
Asset-backed securities						
Bonds exchangeable or convertible into third-party shares or issuers' or group shares which are admitted on a regulated market		or	or		or	
Bonds exchangeable or convertible into the issuer's shares not admitted on a regulated market						

	REGISTRATION DOCUMENT					
	SCHEDULES					BUILDING BLOCK
TYPES OF SECURITI ES	Share	Debt and derivative (< EUR 50 000)	Debt and derivative (> or = EUR 50 000)	Asset -backed securities	Banks debt and derivative	Pro forma information
Bonds exchangeableor convertible into group's shares not admittedon a regulatedmarket		or	or		or	
Bonds with warrants to acquire the issuer's shares not admittedto trading on a regulatedmarket						
Shares with warrants to acquire the issuer's shares not admittedto trading on a regulatedmarket						
Derivatives securities giving the right to subscribe or to acquire the issuer's shares not admittedon a regulatedmarket						
Derivatives securities giving the right to acquire group's shares not admittedon a regulatedmarket		or	or		or	
Derivatives securities giving the right to subscribe or to acquire issuer's or group shares which are admitted on a regulated market and derivatives sec. linked to any other underlying than issuer's or group shares which are not admitted on a regulated market (including any derivatives sec. entitling to cash settlement)		or	or		or	

	REGISTRATION DOCUMENT		
	SCHEDULES		
TYPES OF SECURITIES	Collective investment undertaking of the closed-end type	States and their regional and local authorities	Public international bodies/Debt Securities guaranteed by a Member State of the OECD
Shares (preference shares, redeemable shares, shares with preferential subscription rights; etc.)			
Bonds (vanilla bonds, income bonds, structured bonds, etc with a denomination of less than EUR 50 000			
Bonds (vanilla bonds, income bonds, structured bonds, etc.) with a denomination of at least EUR 50 000			
Debt securities guaranteed by a third party			
Derivative securities guaranteed by a third party			
Asset-backed securities			
Bonds exchangeable or convertible into third party shares or issuers' or group shares which are admitted on a regulated market			
Bonds exchangeable or convertible into the issuer's shares not admitted on a regulated market			
Bonds exchangeable or convertible into group's shares not admitted on a regulated market			

	REGISTRATION DOCUMENT		
	SCHEDULES		
TYPES OF SECURITIES	Collective investmentundertakingof the closed-endtype	States and their regional and local authorities	Public internationalbodies/DebtSecurities guaranteedby a Member State of the OECD
Bonds with warrants to acquire the issuer's shares not admitted to trading on a regulatedmarket			
Shares with warrants to acquire the issuer's shares not admitted to trading on a regulatedmarket			
Derivatives securities giving the right to subscribe or to acquire the issuer's shares not admittedon a regulatedmarket			
Derivatives securities giving the right to acquire group's shares not admittedon a regulatedmarket			
Derivatives securities giving the right to subscribe or to acquire issuer's or group shares which are admitted on a regulated market and derivatives sec. linked to any other underlying than issuer's or group shares which are not admittedon a regulated market (including any derivatives securities entitling to cash settlement)			

	SECURITIES NOTE						
	SCHEDULES				ADDITIONAL BUILDING BLOCKS		
TYPES OF SECURITIES	Share	Debt (<EUR 50 000)	Debt (> or = EUR 50 000)	Derivatives securities	Guarantees	Asset-backed securities	Underlying share
Shares (preference shares, redeemable shares, shares with preferential subscription rights; etc.)							
Bonds (vanilla bonds, income bonds, structured bonds, etc with a denomination of less than EUR 50 000							
Bonds (vanilla bonds, income bonds, structured bonds, etc) with a denomination of at least EUR 50 000							
Debt securities guaranteed by a third party		or	or				
Derivative securities guaranteed by a third party							
Asset-backed securities		or	or				
Bonds exchangeable or convertible into third party shares or issuers' or group shares which are admitted on a regulated market		or	or	Only point 4.2.2			
Bonds exchangeable or convertible into the issuer's shares not admitted on a regulated market		or	or				
Bonds exchangeable or convertible into group's shares not admitted on a regulated market		or	or				

	SECURITIES NOTE						
	SCHEDULES				ADDITIONAL BUILDING BLOCKS		
TYPES OF SECURITI ES	Share	Debt (<EUR 50 000)	Debt (> or = EUR 50 000)	Derivatives secu-rities	Guarantees	Asset-backed secu-rities	Underlying share
Bonds with warrants to acquire the issuer's shares not admittedto trading on a regulatedmarket		or	or	and except point 4.2.2			
Shares with warrants to acquire the issuer's shares not admittedto trading on a regulatedmarket				and except point 4.2.2			
Derivatives securities giving the right to subscribe or to acquire the issuer's shares not admittedon a regulatedmarket				except point 4.2.2			
Derivatives securities giving the right to acquire group's shares not admittedon a regulatedmarket				except point 4.2.2			
Derivatives securities giving the right to subscribe or to acquire issuer's or group shares which are admitted on a regulated market and derivatives securities linked to any other underlying than issuer's or group shares which are not admitted on a regulated market (including any derivatives securities entitling to cash settlement)							

Annex XIX
List of specialist issuers

- Property companies
- Mineral companies
- Investment companies
- Scientific research based companies
- Companies with less than three years of existence (start-up companies)
- Shipping companies.

[Annexes XX to XXIX not reproduced here.]

Commission Regulation (EC) No 1569/2007

of 21 December 2007

establishing a mechanism for the determination of equivalence of accounting standards applied by third country issuers of securities pursuant to Directives 200 3/71/EC and 2004/109/EC of the European Parliament and of the Council

THE COMMISSION OF THE EUROPEAN COMMUNITIES,

Having regard to the Treaty establishing the European Community,

Having regard to Directive 2003/71/EC of the European Parliament and of the Council of 4 November 2003 on the prospectus to be published when securities are offered to the public or admitted to trading and amending Directive 2001/34/EC (OJ L 345, 31.12.2003, p. 64), and in particular Article 7(1) thereof,

Having regard to Directive 2004/109/EC of the European Parliament and of the Council of 15 December 2004 on the harmonisation of transparency requirements in relation to information about issuers whose securities are admitted to trading on a regulated market and amending Directive 2001/34/EC (OJ L 390, 31.12.2004, p. 38), and in particular Article 23(4)(i) thereof,

Whereas:

(1) Article 23(4) of Directive 2004/109/EC requires the Commission to set up a mechanism for the determination of the equivalence of the information required under this Directive, including financial statements and the corresponding requirements under the law, regulations or administrative provisions of third countries. This Article also requires the Commission to take decisions in relation to the equivalence of accounting standards used by third country issuers, and enables the Commission to allow the use of third country accounting standards during an appropriate transitional period. Given the close interconnection of the information required under Directive 2004/109/EC with the information required under Directive 2003/71/EC, it is appropriate that the same criteria for determination of equivalence apply in the framework of both Directives.

(2) Given the objectives of Directive 2003/71/EC to ensure that investors are able to make an informed assessment of the assets and liabilities, financial position, profit and losses and prospects of an issuer, and the objectives of Directive 2004/109/EC to enable investors to make an informed assessment of the financial situation of issuers with securities admitted to trading on a regulated market, it is appropriate that equivalence should be defined by reference to the ability of investors to make a similar assessment of the issuer's financial position and prospects, irrespective of whether financial statements are drawn up in accordance with the accounting standards of a third country or with International Financial Reporting Standards (hereinafter IFRS).

(3) In order to ensure that a determination of the equivalence of third country accounting standards is made in all cases that are relevant to Community markets, the Commission should assess the equivalence of third country accounting standards either upon a request from the competent authority of a Member State or an authority responsible for accounting standards or market supervision of a third country, or on its own initiative. The Commission will first consult the Committee of the European Securities Regulators (CESR) with regard to the assessment of equivalence of the accounting standards in question. In addition, the Commission will actively monitor ongoing progress in the work by the relevant third country authorities to eliminate any requirement for Community issuers accessing the financial markets of a third country to reconcile financial statements prepared using IFRS adopted pursuant to Regulation (EC) No 1606/2002 of the European Parliament and of the Council of 19 July 2002 on the application of international accounting standards (OJ L 243, 11.9.2002, p. 1). The decision of the Commission will have to be such that Community issuers are permitted to use IFRS adopted pursuant to Regulation (EC) No 1606/2002 in the third country concerned.

(4) The President of the European Council, the President of the Commission and the President of the United States have agreed in April 2007 to promote and secure conditions for US Generally Accepted Accounting Principles (GAAP) and IFRS to be recognised in both jurisdictions without the need for reconciliation by 2009 or sooner. The Commission and the US Securities and Exchange Commission (SEC) have pursued their dialogue towards the acceptance of IFRS adopted pursuant to Regulation (EC) No 1606/2002 in the United States, which would relieve issuers using IFRS from costly reconciliation requirements. Steps should be taken to achieve similar arrangements with other countries on whose exchanges EU companies list their securities before the end of 2008. The Accounting Standards Board of Japan (ASBJ) is pursuing the implementation of its joint work programme with the International Accounting Standards Board (IASB) towards the convergence of Japanese GAAP with IFRS. The Accounting Standards Board of Canada (ACSB) published an Implementation Plan for incorporating IFRS into Canadian GAAP as from 1 January 2011.

(5) In order to promote the objectives of Regulation (EC) No 1606/2002 and to encourage the use of IFRS throughout the global financial markets, and to minimise disruption to markets in the Community, it is appropriate to take account of any convergence programme with IFRS or commitment on the part of the relevant authority of the third country to adopt IFRS. Therefore it is necessary to further specify under which conditions convergence programmes can be considered as providing a sufficient basis for allowing third country issuers to apply their national accounting standards for a transitional period. The Commission will first consult CESR on the convergence programme or the progress towards adoption of IFRS, as the case may be.

(6) The measures provided for in this Regulation are in accordance with the opinion of the European Securities Committee,

HAS ADOPTED THIS REGULATION:

Article 1
Subject matter

This Regulation lays down the conditions under which the Generally Accepted Accounting Principles of a third country may be considered equivalent to International Financial Reporting Standards (hereinafter IFRS) and introduces a mechanism for the determination of such equivalence.

Article 2
Equivalence

The Generally Accepted Accounting Principles of a third country may be considered equivalent to IFRS adopted pursuant to Regulation (EC) No 1606/2002 if the financial statements drawn up in accordance with Generally Accepted Accounting Principles of the third country concerned enable investors to make a similar assessment of the assets and liabilities, financial position, profit and losses and prospects of the issuer as financial statements drawn up in accordance with IFRS, with the result that investors are likely to make the same decisions about the acquisition, retention or disposal of securities of an issuer.

Article 3
Equivalence mechanism

The decision on the determination of the equivalence of the Generally Accepted Accounting Principles of a third country may be taken on the initiative of the Commission, upon application submitted by the competent authority of a Member State or upon application of an authority responsible for accounting standards or market supervision of a third country.

Where the Commission decides to make a determination of equivalence, whether on an application or on its own initiative, it shall make that decision public.

[*Article 4*
Conditions for the acceptance of third country accounting standards for a limited period

1. Third country issuers may be permitted to use financial statements drawn up in accordance with the accounting standards of a third country in order to comply with obligations under Directive 2004/109/EC and, by derogation from Article 35(5) of Regulation (EC) No 809/2004, to provide historical financial information under that Regulation for a period commencing any time after 31 December 2008 and expiring no later than 31 December 2014 in the following cases:

(a) the third country authority responsible for the national accounting standards concerned has made a public commitment to converge these standards with International Financial Reporting Standards at the latest by 31 December 2014 and both the following conditions are met:

(i) the third country authority responsible for the national accounting standards concerned has established a convergence programme that is comprehensive and capable of being completed before 31 December 2014;

(ii) the convergence programme is effectively implemented, without delay, and the resources necessary for its completion are allocated to its implementation;

(b) the third country authority responsible for the national accounting standards concerned has made a public commitment to adopt International Financial Reporting Standards before 31 December 2014 and effective measures are taken in the third country to secure their timely and complete implementation by that date.

2. Any decision under paragraph 1 to permit the continued acceptance of financial statements drawn up in accordance with the accounting standards of a third country shall be made in accordance with the procedure referred to in Article 24 of Directive 2003/71/EC and Article 27(2) of Directive 2004/109/EC.

3. Where the Commission permits the continued acceptance of financial statements drawn up in accordance with the accounting standards of a third country in accordance with paragraph 1, it shall review regularly whether the conditions specified in point (a) or (b) (as the case may be) continue to be met, and shall report accordingly to the European Parliament.

4. If the conditions in point (a) or (b) of paragraph 1 are no longer met, the Commission shall take a decision in accordance with the procedure referred to in Article 24 of Directive 2003/71/EC and Article 27(2) of Directive 2004/109/EC amending its decision under paragraph 1 in respect of these accounting standards.

5. When complying with this Article, the Commission shall first consult ESMA on the convergence programme or the progress towards adoption of IFRS, as the case may be.'][a]

Amendments

a Article 4 replaced by Commission Delegated Regulation (EU) No 310/2012, art 1.

Article 5

This Regulation shall enter into force on the third day following its publication in the *Official Journal of the European Union*.

This Regulation shall be binding in its entirety and directly applicable in all Member States.

Done at Brussels, 21 December 2007.

Commission Decision (2008/961/EC)
of 12 December 2008
on the use by third countries' issuers of securities of certain third country's national accounting standards and International Financial Reporting Standards to prepare their consolidated financial statements
(notified under document number C(2008) 8218)
(Text with EEA relevance)

THE COMMISSION OF THE EUROPEAN COMMUNITIES,

Having regard to the Treaty establishing the European Community,

Having regard to Directive 2004/109/EC of the European Parliament and of the Council of 15 December 2004 on the harmonisation of transparency requirements in relation to information about issuers whose securities are admitted to trading on a regulated market and amending Directive 2001/34/EC[1], and in particular Article 23(4) thereof,

Whereas:

(1) Regulation (EC) No 1606/2002 of the European Parliament and of the Council of 19 July 2002 on the application of International Accounting Standards[2] requires companies governed by the law of a Member State, whose securities are admitted to trading on a regulated market in any Member State, to prepare their consolidated accounts in accordance with International Accounting Standards, now commonly referred to as International Financial Reporting Standards, adopted pursuant to Regulation (EC) No 1606/2002 (hereinafter referred to as adopted IFRS), for each financial year starting on or after 1 January 2005.

(2) Articles 4 and 5 of Directive 2004/109/EC provide that where an issuer is required to prepare consolidated accounts, the annual and half-yearly financial statements shall comprise such consolidated accounts drawn up in accordance with adopted IFRS. Even though this requirement applies to Community and third country issuers alike, third country issuers may be exempted from this requirement provided the law of the third country in question lays down equivalent requirements.

(3) Commission Decision 2006/891/EC[3] provided that a third country issuer may also prepare its consolidated accounts, for financial years starting before 1 January 2009, in accordance with IFRS as issued by the International Accounting Standards Board (IASB), with GAAP of Canada, Japan or United States or with a GAAP of a third country which is subject to convergence with IFRS.

(4) Financial statements drawn up in accordance with IFRS as issued by the IASB provide users of these statements with a sufficient level of information to enable them to make an informed assessment of the assets and liabilities, financial position, profit and losses and prospects of an issuer. Therefore, it is appropriate to allow third country issuers to use IFRS as issued by the IASB within the Community.

(5) In order to assess the equivalence of the Generally Accepted Accounting Principles (GAAP) of a third country with adopted IFRS, Commission Regulation (EC) No 1569/

---

1. OJ L 390, 31.12.2004, p. 38.
2. OJ L 243, 11.9.2002, p. 1.
3. OJ L 343, 8.12.2006, p. 96.

2007 of 21 December 2007 establishing a mechanism for the determination of equivalence of accounting standards applied by third country issuers of securities pursuant to Directives 2003/71/EC and 2004/109/EC of the European Parliament and of the Council[4] provides for the definition of equivalence and establishes a mechanism for the determination of equivalence of GAAP of a third country. Regulation (EC) No 1569/2007 also requires that the Commission decision permit Community issuers to use IFRS adopted pursuant to Regulation (EC) No 1606/2002 in the third country concerned.

(6) In December 2007 the Commission consulted the Committee of European Securities Regulators (CESR) with regard to the technical assessment of the equivalence of the GAAP of the United States, China and Japan. In March 2008 the Commission extended the consultation with regard to the GAAP of South Korea, Canada and India.

(7) In its advice delivered in March, May and October 2008 respectively, CESR recommended finding US GAAP and Japanese GAAP equivalent to IFRS for use within the Community. Furthermore, CESR recommended the acceptance of financial statements using GAAPs of China, Canada, South Korea and India within the Community on a temporary basis, until no longer than 31 December 2011.

(8) In 2006 the United States' Financial Accounting Standards Board and the IASB concluded a Memorandum of Understanding which reaffirmed their objective of convergence between US GAAP and IFRS and outlined the work programme for this purpose. As a result of this work programme many major differences between US GAAP and IFRS have been resolved. In addition, following the dialogue between the Commission and the US Securities and Exchange Commission, reconciliation for Community issuers which prepare their financial statements according to IFRS as issued by the IASB is no longer required. Therefore, it is appropriate to consider US GAAP equivalent to adopted IFRS from 1 January 2009.

(9) In August 2007 the Accounting Standards Board of Japan and the IASB announced their agreement to accelerate the convergence by eliminating major differences between Japanese GAAP and IFRS by 2008 and the remaining differences before the end of 2011. The Japanese authorities do not require any reconciliation for Community issuers which prepare their financial statements according to IFRS. Therefore, it is appropriate to consider Japanese GAAP equivalent to adopted IFRS from 1 January 2009.

(10) According to Article 4 of Regulation (EC) No 1569/2007, third country issuers may be permitted to use other third country GAAPs which are converging or committed to adopt IFRS or which have reached a mutual recognition agreement with the Community before 31 December 2008 for a transitional period ending no later than 31 December 2011.

(11) In China, the Accounting Standards for Business Enterprises are substantially converged with IFRS and cover nearly all topics under current IFRS. However, since the Accounting Standards for Business Enterprises are applied only from 2007, there is need for further evidence of their proper application.

(12) The Accounting Standards Board of Canada made a public commitment in January 2006 to adopt IFRS by 31 December 2011 and is taking effective measures to secure timely and complete transition to IFRS by that date.

---

4. OJ L 340, 22.12.2007, p. 66.

(13) The Korean Financial Supervisory Commission and the Korean Accounting Institute made a public commitment in March 2007 to adopt IFRS by 31 December 2011 and are taking effective measures to secure timely and complete transition to IFRS by that date.

(14) The Indian Government and the Indian Institute of Chartered Accountants made a public commitment in July 2007 to adopt IFRS by 31 December 2011 and are taking effective measures to secure the timely and complete transition to IFRS by that date.

(15) Whilst no final decision on the equivalence of accounting standards converging to IFRS should be taken until an assessment of the implementation of those accounting standards by companies and auditors has been carried out, it is important to support the efforts of those countries which have undertaken to converge their accounting standards to IFRS and also of those countries which have undertaken to adopt IFRS. Accordingly, it is appropriate to allow third country issuers to prepare their annual and half-yearly financial statements in accordance with the GAAPs of China, Canada, South Korea or India in the Community for the transitional period of no more than three years.

(16) The Commission should continue to monitor, with the technical assistance of CESR, the development of those third country GAAPs in relation to adopted IFRS.

(17) Countries should be encouraged to adopt IFRS. The EU may determine that the national standards which have been determined to be equivalent may no longer be used in preparing information required under Directive 2004/109/EC or Commission Regulation (EC) No 809/2004[5] implementing Directive 2003/71/EC when those respective countries have adopted IFRS as their sole accounting standard.

(18) In the interests of clarity and transparency Decision 2006/891/EC should be replaced.

(19) The measures provided for in this Decision are in accordance with the opinion of the European Securities Committee,

HAS ADOPTED THIS DECISION:

Article 1

From 1 January 2009, in addition to IFRS adopted pursuant to Regulation (EC) No 1606/2002, with regard to annual consolidated financial statements and half-yearly consolidated financial statements, the following standards shall be considered as equivalent to IFRS adopted pursuant to Regulation (EC) No 1606/2002:

(a) International Financial Reporting Standards, provided that the notes to the audited financial statements contain an explicit and unreserved statement that these financial statements comply with international financial reporting standards in accordance with IAS 1 *Presentation of financial statements*;

(b) Generally Accepted Accounting Principles of Japan;

(c) Generally Accepted Accounting Principles of the United States of America.

Prior to financial years starting on or after 1 January 2012, a third country issuer shall be permitted to prepare its annual consolidated financial statements and half-yearly

5. OJ L 149, 30.4.2004, p. 1. Corrected by OJ L 215, 16.6.2004, p. 3.

consolidated financial statements in accordance with the Generally Accepted Accounting Principles of the People's Republic of

The Commission shall continue to monitor, with the technical assistance of the CESR, the efforts made by third countries towards a changeover to IFRS and pursue an active dialogue with authorities during the convergence process. The Commission shall submit a report on progress made in this regard to the European Parliament and the European Securities Committee (ESC) during 2009. The Commission shall also report expeditiously to Council and the European Parliament if situations arise where EU issuers in the future are required to reconcile their financial statements to the national GAAP of the foreign jurisdiction concerned.

Article 1b

The dates announced publicly by third countries in relation to a changeover to IFRS shall serve as reference dates for the abolition of equivalence recognition for those third countries.

Article 2

Decision 2006/891/EC shall be repealed with effect from 1 January 2009.

Article 3

This Decision is addressed to the Member States.

Done at Brussels, 12 December 2008.

For the Commission

Charlie McCreevy

Member of the Commission

Commission Regulation (EC) No 1126/2008

of 3 November 2008

adopting certain international accounting standards in accordance with Regulation (EC) No 1606/2002 of the European Parliament and of the Council

(Text with EEA relevance)

THE COMMISSION OF THE EUROPEAN COMMUNITIES,

Having regard to the Treaty establishing the European Community,

Having regard to Regulation (EC) No 1606/2002 of the European Parliament and of the Council of 19 July 2002 on the application of international accounting standards,[1] and in particular Article 3(1) thereof,

Whereas:

(1) Regulation (EC) No 1606/2002 requires that for each financial year starting on or after 1 January 2005, publicly traded companies governed by the law of a Member State are, under certain conditions, to prepare their consolidated accounts in conformity with international accounting standards as defined in Article 2 of that Regulation.

(2) By Commission Regulation (EC) No 1725/2003 of 29 September 2003 adopting certain international accounting standards in accordance with Regulation (EC) No 1606/2002 of the European Parliament and of the Council,[2] certain international standards and interpretations that were in existence at

September 2002 were adopted. The Commission, having considered the advice provided by the Technical Expert Group (TEG) of the European Financial Reporting Advisory Group (EFRAG), has amended that Regulation in order to include all standards presented by the International Accounting Standards Board (IASB) as well as all interpretations presented by the International Financial Reporting Interpretations Committee (IFRIC) and adopted within the Community by

October 2008 in full, except for IAS 39 (related to recognition and measurement of financial instruments), of which limited parts have been omitted.

(3) The different international standards have been adopted by a number of amending regulations. This causes legal uncertainty and difficulty in correctly applying international accounting standards in the Community. In order to simplify Community legislation on accounting standards, it is appropriate, for the sake of clarity and transparency, to incorporate in a single text the standards presently contained in Regulation (EC) No 1725/2003 and the acts amending it.

(4) Regulation (EC) No 1725/2003 should therefore be replaced by this Regulation.

(5)The measures provided for in this Regulation are in accordance with the opinion of the Accounting Regulatory Committee,

HAS ADOPTED THIS REGULATION:

---

1. OJ L 243, 11.9.2002, p. 1.
2. OJ L 261, 13.10.2003, p. 1

Article 1

The international accounting standards, as defined in Article 2 of Regulation (EC) No 1606/2002, shall be adopted as set out in the Annex hereto.

Article 2

Regulation (EC) No 1725/2003 is hereby repealed.

References to the repealed Regulation shall be construed as references to this Regulation.

Article 3

This Regulation shall enter into force on the third day following its publication in the Official Journal of the European Union.

This Regulation shall be binding in its entirety and directly applicable in all Member States.

Annex
International Accounting Standards

IAS 1	*Presentation of Financial Statements (Revised 2007)*
IAS 2	*Inventories*
IAS 7	*Statement of Cash Flows*
IAS 8	*Accounting policies, changes in accounting estimates and errors*
IAS 10	*Events after the Reporting Period*
IAS 11	*Construction contracts*
IAS 12	*Income taxes*
IAS 16	*Property, plant and equipment*
IAS 17	*Leases*
IAS 18	*Revenue*
IAS 19	*Employee benefits*
IAS 20	*Accounting for government grants and disclosure of government assistance*
IAS 21	*The effects of changes in foreign exchange rates*
IAS 23	*Borrowing costs (Revised 2007)*
IAS 24	*IAS 24 Related Party Disclosures*
IAS 26	*Accounting and reporting by retirement benefit plans*
IAS 27	*Consolidated and Separate Financial Statements*
IAS 28	*Investments in associates*
IAS 29	*Financial reporting in hyperinflationary economies*
IAS 31	*Interests in joint ventures*
IAS 32	*Financial instruments: presentation*
IAS 33	*Earnings per share*
IAS 34	*Interim financial reporting*
IAS 36	*Impairment of assets*
IAS 37	*Provisions, contingent liabilities and contingent assets*
IAS 38	*Intangible assets*
IAS 39	*Financial instruments: recognition and measurement*
IAS 40	*Investment property*
IAS 41	*Agriculture*
IFRS 1	*First-time Adoption of International Financial Reporting Standards*
IFRS 2	*Share-based payment*
IFRS 3	*Business Combinations*
IFRS 4	*Insurance contracts*
IFRS 5	*Non-current assets held for sale and discontinued operations*
IFRS 6	*Exploration for and evaluation of mineral resources*
IFRS 7	*Financial instruments: disclosures*
IFRS 8	*Operating segments*
IFRIC 1	*Changes in existing decommissioning, restoration and similar liabilities*
IFRIC 2	*Members' shares in co-operative entities and similar instruments*
IFRIC 4	*Determining whether an arrangement contains a lease*

IFRIC 5	*Rights to interests arising from decommissioning, restoration and environmental rehabilitation funds*
IFRIC 6	*Liabilities arising from participating in a specific market — waste electrical and electronic equipment*
IFRIC 7	*Applying the Restatement Approach under IAS 29 Financial reporting in hyperinflationary economies*
IFRIC 9	*Reassessment of embedded derivatives*
IFRIC 10	*Interim financial reporting and impairment*
IFRIC 12	*IFRIC Interpretation 12 Service Concessions Arrangements*
IFRIC 13	*IFRIC Interpretation 13 customer loyalty programmes*
IFRIC 14	*IFRIC Interpretation 14 IAS 19 — The Limit on a defined benefit Asset, Minimum Funding Requirements and their Interaction*
IFRIC 15	*IFRIC Interpretation 15 Agreements for the Construction of Real Estate*
IFRIC 16	*IFRIC Interpretation 16 Hedges of a Net Investment in a Foreign Operation*
IFRIC 17	*IFRIC Interpretation 17 Distributions of Non-cash Assets to Owners*
IFRIC 18	*IFRIC Interpretation 18 Transfers of Assets from Customers*
IFRIC 19	*IFRIC Interpretation 19 Extinguishing Financial Liabilities with Equity Instruments*
SIC-7	*Introduction of the euro*
SIC-10	*Government assistance no specific relation to operating activities*
SIC-12	*Consolidation — special purpose entities*
SIC-13	*Jointly controlled entities — non-monetary contributions by venturers*
SIC-15	*Operating leases — incentives*
SIC-21	*Income taxes — recovery of revalued non-depreciable assets*
SIC-25	*Income taxes — changes in the tax status of an entity or its shareholders*
SIC-27	*Evaluating the substance of transactions involving the legal form of a lease*
SIC-29	*Disclosure — service concession arrangements*
SIC-31	*Revenue — barter transactions involving advertising services*
SIC-32	*Intangible assets — website costs*

Commission Regulation (EU) No 236/2012
OF THE EUROPEAN PARLIAMENT AND OF THE COUNCIL
of 14 March 2012
on short selling and certain aspects of credit default swaps
(Text with EEA relevance)

THE EUROPEAN PARLIAMENT AND THE COUNCIL OF THE EUROPEAN UNION,

Having regard to the Treaty on the Functioning of the European Union, and in particular Article 114 thereof,

Having regard to the proposal from the European Commission,

After transmission of the draft legislative act to the national parliaments,

Having regard to the opinion of the European Central Bank,[1]

Having regard to the opinion of the European Economic and Social Committee,[2]

Acting in accordance with the ordinary legislative procedure,[3]

Whereas:

(1) At the height of the financial crisis in September 2008, competent authorities in several Member States and supervisory authorities in third countries such as the United States of America and Japan adopted emergency measures to restrict or ban short selling in some or all securities. They acted due to concerns that at a time of considerable financial instability, short selling could aggravate the downward spiral in the prices of shares, notably in financial institutions, in a way which could ultimately threaten their viability and create systemic risks. The measures adopted by Member States were divergent as the Union lacks a specific common regulatory framework for dealing with short selling issues.

(2) To ensure the proper functioning of the internal market and to improve the conditions of its functioning, in particular with regard to the financial markets, and to ensure a high level of consumer and investor protection, it is therefore appropriate to lay down a common regulatory framework with regard to the requirements and powers relating to short selling and credit default swaps and to ensure greater coordination and consistency between Member States where measures have to be taken in exceptional circumstances. It is necessary to harmonise the rules for short selling and certain aspects of credit default swaps, to prevent the creation of obstacles to the proper functioning of the internal market, as otherwise it is likely that Member States continue taking divergent measures.

(3) It is appropriate and necessary for those rules to take the legislative form of a regulation in order to ensure that provisions directly imposing obligations on private parties to notify and disclose net short positions relating to certain instruments and regarding uncovered short selling are applied in a uniform manner throughout the Union. A regulation is also necessary to confer powers on the European Supervisory

---

1. OJ C 91, 23.3.2011, p. 1.
2. OJ C 84, 17.3.2011, p. 34.
3. Position of the European Parliament of 15 November 2011 (not yet published in the Official Journal) and decision of the Council of 21 February 2012.

Authority (European Securities and Markets Authority) (ESMA) established by Regulation (EU) No 1095/2010 of the European Parliament and of the Council [4] to coordinate measures taken by competent authorities or to take measures itself.

(4) The scope of this Regulation should be as broad as possible to provide for a preventive regulatory framework to be used in exceptional circumstances. That framework should cover all financial instruments but should provide for a proportionate response to the risks that short selling of different instruments could represent. It is therefore only in the case of exceptional circumstances that competent authorities and should be entitled to take measures concerning all types of financial instruments, going beyond the permanent measures that only apply to particular types of instruments where there are clearly identified risks that need to be addressed.

(5) To end the current fragmented situation in which some Member States have taken divergent measures and to restrict the possibility that divergent measures are taken by competent authorities it is important to address the potential risks arising from short selling and credit default swaps in a harmonised manner. The requirements to be imposed should address the identified risks without unduly detracting from the benefits that short selling provides to the quality and efficiency of markets. While in certain situations it could have adverse effects, under normal market conditions, short selling plays an important role in ensuring the proper functioning of financial markets, in particular in the context of market liquidity and efficient price formation.

(6) References in this Regulation to natural and legal persons should include registered business associations without legal personality.

(7) Enhanced transparency relating to significant net short positions in specific financial instruments is likely to be of benefit to both the regulator and market participants. For shares admitted to trading on a trading venue in the Union, a two-tier model that provides for greater transparency of significant net short positions in shares at the appropriate level should be introduced. At the lower threshold, notification of a position should be made privately to the regulators concerned to enable them to monitor and, where necessary, investigate short selling that could create systemic risks, be abusive or create disorderly markets; at the higher threshold, positions should be publicly disclosed to the market in order to provide useful information to other market participants about significant individual short positions in shares.

(8) A requirement to notify regulators of significant net short positions relating to sovereign debt in the Union should be introduced as such notification would provide important information to assist regulators in monitoring whether such positions are in fact creating systemic risks or being used for abusive purposes. Such a requirement should only include private disclosure to regulators as publication of information to the market for such instruments could have a detrimental effect on sovereign debt markets where liquidity is already impaired.

(9) The notification requirements relating to sovereign debt should apply to the debt instruments issued by a Member State and by the Union, including the European Investment Bank, a Member State's government department, agency, special purpose vehicle or international financial institution established by two or more Member States

4. OJ L 331, 15.12.2010, p. 84.

that issues debt on behalf of a Member State or on behalf of several Member States, such as the European Financial Stability Facility or the prospective European Stability Mechanism. In the case of federal Member States, the notification requirements should also apply to debt instruments issued by a member of the federation. They should not, however, apply to other regional or local bodies or quasi-public bodies in a Member State that issue debt instruments. The objective of debt instruments issued by the Union is to provide balance of payments or financial stability support to Member States or macro-financial assistance to third countries.

(10) In order to ensure comprehensive and effective transparency, it is important that the notification requirements cover not only short positions created by trading shares or sovereign debt on trading venues but also short positions created by trading outside trading venues and net short positions created by the use of derivatives, such as options, futures, index-related instruments, contracts for differences and spread bets relating to shares or sovereign debt.

(11) To be useful to regulators and markets, any transparency regime should provide complete and accurate information about a natural or legal person's positions. In particular, information provided to the regulator or to the market should take into account both short and long positions so as to provide valuable information about the natural or legal person's net short position in shares, sovereign debt and credit default swaps.

(12) The calculation of short or long positions should take into account any form of economic interest which a natural or legal person has in relation to the issued share capital of a company or to the issued sovereign debt of a Member State or of the Union. In particular, it should take into account such an economic interest obtained directly or indirectly through the use of derivatives such as options, futures, contracts for differences and spread bets relating to shares or sovereign debt, and indices, baskets of securities and exchange traded funds. In the case of positions relating to sovereign debt it should also take into account credit default swaps relating to sovereign debt issuers.

(13) In addition to the transparency regime provided for in this Regulation, the Commission should consider, in the context of its revision of Directive 2004/39/EC of the European Parliament and of the Council of 21 April 2004 on markets in financial instruments,[5] whether inclusion by investment firms of information about short sales in transaction reports to competent authorities would provide useful supplementary information to enable competent authorities to monitor levels of short selling.

(14) Buying credit default swaps without having a long position in underlying sovereign debt or any assets, portfolio of assets, financial obligations or financial contracts the value of which is correlated to the value of the sovereign debt, can be, economically speaking, equivalent to taking a short position on the underlying debt instrument. The calculation of a net short position in relation to sovereign debt should therefore include credit default swaps relating to an obligation of a sovereign debt issuer. The credit default swap position should be taken into account both for the purposes of determining whether a natural or legal person has a significant net short position relating to sovereign debt that needs to be notified to a competent authority and where a competent authority suspends restrictions on uncovered credit default swap transactions for the

5. OJ L 145, 30.4.2004, p. 1.

purposes of determining the significant uncovered position in a credit default swap relating to a sovereign debt issuer that needs to be notified to the competent authority.

(15) To enable ongoing monitoring of positions, the transparency regime should also include notification or disclosure where a change in a net short position results in an increase or decrease above or below certain thresholds.

(16) In order to be effective, it is important that the transparency regime apply regardless of where the natural or legal person is located, including in a third country, where that person has a significant net short position in a company that has shares admitted to trading on a trading venue in the Union or a net short position in sovereign debt issued by a Member State or by the Union.

(17) The definition of a short sale should not include a repurchase agreement between two parties where one party sells the other a security at a specified price with a commitment to buy the security back at a later date at another specified price or a derivative contract where it is agreed to sell securities at a specified price at a future date. The definition should not include a transfer of securities under a securities lending agreement.

(18) Uncovered short selling of shares and sovereign debt is sometimes viewed as increasing the potential risk of settlement failure and volatility. To reduce such risks it is appropriate to place proportionate restrictions on uncovered short selling of such instruments. The detailed restrictions should take into account the different arrangements currently used for covered short selling. These include a separate repurchase agreement on the basis of which the person selling a security short buys back an equivalent security in due time to allow settlement of the short sale transaction and includes collateral arrangements if the collateral taker can use the security for settling the short sale transaction. Further examples include rights issues (offerings) of companies to existing shareholders, lending pools and repurchase agreement facilities provided, for instance, by trading venues, clearing systems or central banks.

(19) In relation to uncovered short selling of shares it is necessary for a natural or legal person to have an arrangement with a third party under which the third party has confirmed that the share has been located, which means that the third party confirms that it considers that it can make the share available for settlement when it is due. In order to give this confirmation it is necessary for measures to be taken vis-à-vis third parties for the natural or legal person to have a reasonable expectation that settlement can be effected when it is due. This includes measures such as a third party having allocated the shares for borrowing or purchase so that settlement can be effected when it is due. With regard to short sales to be covered by purchase of the share during the same day this includes confirmation by the third party that it considers the share to be easy to borrow or to purchase. The liquidity of the shares, in particular the level of turnover and the ease with which buying, selling and borrowing can take place with minimum market impact, should be taken into account by ESMA in determining what measures are necessary in order to have a reasonable expectation that settlement can be effected when it is due.

(20) In relation to uncovered short selling of sovereign debt, the fact that a short sale will be covered by the purchase of the sovereign debt during the same day can be considered

as an example of offering a reasonable expectation that settlement can be effected when it is due.

(21) Sovereign credit default swaps should be based on the insurable interest principle whilst recognising that there can be interests in a sovereign issuer other than bond ownership. Such interests include hedging against the risk of default of the sovereign issuer where a natural or legal person has a long position in the sovereign debt of that issuer or hedging against the risk of a decline in the value of the sovereign debt where the natural or legal person holds assets or is subject to liabilities which refer to public or private sector entities in the Member State concerned, the value of which is correlated to the value of the sovereign debt. Such assets should include financial contracts, a portfolio of assets or financial obligations, as well as interest rate or currency swap transactions with respect to which the sovereign credit default swap is used as a counterparty risk management tool for hedging exposure on financial and foreign trade contracts. No position or portfolio of positions used in the context of hedging exposures to a sovereign should be considered an uncovered position in a sovereign credit default swap. This includes any exposures to the central, regional and local administration, public sector entities or any exposure guaranteed by any referred entity. Furthermore, exposure to private sector entities established in the Member State concerned should also be included. All exposures should be considered in this context including loans, counterparty credit risk (including potential exposure when regulatory capital is required to such exposure), receivables and guarantees. This also includes indirect exposures to any of the referred entities obtained, inter alia, through exposure to indices, funds or special purpose vehicles.

(22) Since entering into a sovereign credit default swap without underlying exposure to the risk of a decline in the value of the sovereign debt could have an adverse impact on the stability of sovereign debt markets, natural or legal persons should be prohibited from entering into such uncovered credit default swap positions. However, at the very first signal that the sovereign debt market is not functioning properly, the competent authority should be able to suspend such a restriction temporarily. Such a suspension should be based on the belief of the competent authority based on objective grounds following an analysis of the indicators set out in this Regulation. Competent authorities should also be able to use additional indicators.

(23) It is also appropriate to include requirements on central counterparties relating to buy-in procedures and fines for failed settlement of transactions in shares. The buy-in procedures and late settlement requirements should set basic standards relating to settlement discipline. The buy- in and fining requirements should be sufficiently flexible to permit the central counterparty that is responsible for ensuring such procedures are in place to be able to rely on another market participant to perform operationally the buy-in or impose the fine. However, for the proper functioning of financial markets it is essential to address wider aspects of settlement discipline in a horizontal legislative proposal.

(24) Measures relating to sovereign debt and sovereign credit default swaps including increased transparency and restrictions on uncovered short selling should impose requirements which are proportionate and at the same time avoid an adverse impact on the liquidity of sovereign bond markets and sovereign bond repurchase markets.

(25) Shares are increasingly admitted to trading on different trading venues within the Union and in third countries. Many large companies based in a third country also have shares admitted to trading on a trading venue within the Union. For reasons of efficiency, it is appropriate to exempt securities from certain notification and disclosure requirements, where the principal venue for trading of that instrument is in a third country.

(26) Market making activities play a crucial role in providing liquidity to markets within the Union and market makers need to take short positions to perform that role. Imposing requirements on such activities could severely inhibit their ability to provide liquidity and have a significant adverse impact on the efficiency of the Union markets. Furthermore market makers would not be expected to take significant short positions except for very brief periods. It is therefore appropriate to exempt natural or legal persons involved in such activities from requirements which could impair their ability to perform such a function and therefore adversely affect the Union markets. In order for such requirements to capture equivalent third-country entities a procedure is necessary to assess the equivalence of third-country markets. The exemption should apply to the different types of market-making activity but not to proprietary trading. It is also appropriate to exempt certain primary market operations such as those relating to sovereign debt and stabilisation schemes as they are important activities that assist the efficient functioning of markets. Competent authorities should be notified of the use of exemptions and should have the power to prohibit a natural or legal person from using an exemption if they do not fulfil the relevant criteria in the exemption. Competent authorities should also be able to request information from the natural or legal person to monitor their use of the exemption.

(27) In the case of adverse developments which constitute a serious threat to financial stability or to market confidence in a Member State or the Union, competent authorities should have powers of intervention to require further transparency or to impose temporary restrictions on short selling, credit default swap transactions or other transactions in order to prevent a disorderly decline in the price of a financial instrument. Such measures could be necessary due to a variety of adverse events or developments including not just financial or economic events but also for example natural disasters or terrorist acts. Furthermore, some adverse events or developments requiring measures could arise in a single Member State and have no cross-border implications. Such powers need to be flexible enough to enable competent authorities to deal with a range of different exceptional circumstances. In taking such measures, competent authorities should pay due regard to the principle of proportionality.

(28) As this Regulation addresses only restrictions on short selling and credit default swaps to prevent a disorderly decline in the price of a financial instrument, the need for other types of restrictions such as position limits or restrictions on products, which may give rise to serious investor protection concerns, are more appropriately considered in the context of the Commission's revision of Directive 2004/39/EC.

(29) While competent authorities are usually best placed to monitor market conditions and to react initially to an adverse event or development by deciding if a serious threat to financial stability or to market confidence has arisen and whether it is necessary to take measures to address such a situation, powers in this regard and the conditions and procedures for their use should be harmonised as far as possible.

(30) In the case of a significant fall in the price of a financial instrument on a trading venue a competent authority should also have the ability to restrict temporarily short selling of the financial instrument on that venue within its own jurisdiction or to request that ESMA restrict such short selling in other jurisdictions in order to be able to intervene rapidly where appropriate and for a short period to prevent a disorderly decline in price of the instrument concerned. The competent authority should also be required to notify ESMA of such a decision so that ESMA can immediately inform the competent authorities of other Member States with venues which trade the same instrument, coordinate the taking of measures by those other Member States and, if necessary, assist them in reaching an agreement or take a decision itself, in accordance with Article 19 of Regulation (EU) No 1095/2010.

(31) Where an adverse event or development extends beyond a single Member State or has other cross-border implications, for example if a financial instrument is admitted to trading on different trading venues in a number of different Member States, close consultation and cooperation between competent authorities is essential. ESMA should perform a key coordination role in such a situation and should try to ensure consistency between competent authorities. The composition of ESMA, which includes representatives of competent authorities, will assist it in the performance of such a role. In addition, competent authorities should have power to take measures where they have an interest in intervening.

(32) In addition to coordinating measures by competent authorities, ESMA should ensure that measures are taken by competent authorities only where necessary and proportionate. ESMA should be able to give opinions to competent authorities on the use of powers of intervention.

(33) While competent authorities will often be best placed to monitor and to react quickly to an adverse event or development, ESMA should also have the power to take measures where short selling and other related activities threaten the orderly functioning and integrity of financial markets or the stability of the whole or part of the financial system in the Union, where there are cross-border implications and competent authorities have not taken sufficient measures to address the threat. ESMA should consult the European Systemic Risk Board (ESRB) established by Regulation (EU) No 1092/2010 of the European Parliament and of the Council of 24 November 2010 on European Union macro- prudential oversight of the financial system and establishing a European Systemic Risk Board (1)[6] where possible, and other relevant authorities where such a measure could have effects beyond the financial markets, as could be the case for commodity derivatives which are used to hedge physical positions.

(34) ESMA's powers under this Regulation to restrict short selling and other related activities in exceptional circumstances are in accordance with Article 9(5) of Regulation (EU) No 1095/2010. Those powers should be without prejudice to the powers of ESMA in an emergency situation under Article 18 of Regulation (EU) No 1095/2010. In particular, ESMA should be able to adopt individual decisions requiring competent authorities to take measures or individual decisions addressed to financial market participants under Article 18 of Regulation (EU) No 1095/2010.

6. OJ L 331, 15.12.2010, p. 1.

(35) References in this Regulation to Articles 18 and 38 of Regulation (EU) No 1095/2010 are of a declaratory nature. Those articles apply even in the absence of such references.

(36) Powers of intervention of competent authorities and ESMA to restrict short selling, credit default swaps and other transactions should be only of a temporary nature and should be exercised only for such a period and to the extent necessary to deal with the specific threat.

(37) Because of the specific risks which can arise from the use of credit default swaps, such transactions require close monitoring by competent authorities. In particular, competent authorities should, in exceptional cases, have the power to require information from natural or legal persons entering into such transactions about the purpose for which the transaction is entered into.

(38) ESMA should be given power to conduct an inquiry into an issue or practice relating to short selling or the use of credit default swaps to assess whether that issue or practice poses any potential threat to financial stability or to market confidence. ESMA should publish a report setting out its findings where it conducts such an inquiry.

(39) As some of the provisions of this Regulation apply to natural or legal persons and actions in third countries, it is necessary that competent authorities and supervisory authorities in third countries cooperate in certain situations. Competent authorities should therefore enter into arrangements with supervisory authorities in third countries. ESMA should coordinate the development of such cooperation arrangements and the exchange between competent authorities of information received from third countries.

(40) This Regulation respects the fundamental rights and observes the principles recognised in particular in the Treaty on the Functioning of the European Union (TFEU) and in the Charter of Fundamental Rights of the European Union (Charter), in particular the right to the protection of personal data provided for in Article 16 TFEU and in Article 8 of the Charter. Transparency regarding significant net short positions, including public disclosure above a certain threshold, where provided for under this Regulation, is necessary for reasons of financial market stability and investor protection. Such transparency will enable regulators to monitor the use of short selling in connection with abusive strategies and the implications of short selling on the proper functioning of the markets. In addition, such transparency could help reduce information asymmetries, ensuring that all market participants are adequately informed about the extent to which short selling is affecting prices. Any exchange or transmission of information by competent authorities should take place in accordance with the rules on the transfer of personal data as laid down in Directive 95/46/EC of the European Parliament and of the Council of 24 October 1995 on the protection of individuals with regard to the processing of personal data and on the free movement of such data.[7] Any exchange or transmission of information by ESMA should take place in accordance with the rules on the transfer of personal data as laid down in Regulation (EC) No 45/2001 of the European Parliament and of the Council of 18 December 2000 on the protection of individuals with regard to the processing of personal data by the Community institutions

7. OJ L 281, 23.11.1995, p. 31.

and bodies and on the free movement of such data,[8] which should be fully applicable to the processing of personal data for the purposes of this Regulation.

(41) Taking into consideration the principles set out in the Commission's Communication on reinforcing sanctioning regimes in the financial services sector and legal acts of the Union adopted as a follow-up to that Communication, Member States should lay down rules on penalties and administrative measures applicable to infringements of the provisions of this Regulation and should ensure that they are implemented. Those penalties and administrative measures should be effective, proportionate and dissuasive. They should be based on guidelines adopted by ESMA to promote convergence and cross-sector consistency of penalty regimes in the financial sector.

(42) In order to ensure uniform conditions for the implementation of this Regulation, implementing powers should be conferred on the Commission. Those powers should be exercised in accordance with Regulation (EU) No 182/2011 of the European Parliament and of the Council of 16 February 2011 laying down the rules and general principles concerning mechanisms for control by Member States of the Commission's exercise of implementing powers.[9] The Commission should keep the European Parliament informed of progress relating to decisions determining the equivalence of third-country legal and supervisory frameworks with requirements of this Regulation.

(43) The power to adopt acts in accordance with Article 290 TFEU should be delegated to the Commission in respect of details concerning calculating short positions, where a natural or legal person has an uncovered position in a credit default swap, notification or disclosure thresholds and further specification of criteria and factors for determining in which cases an adverse event or development creates a serious threat to financial stability or to market confidence in a Member State or the Union. It is of particular importance that the Commission carry out appropriate consultations during its preparatory work, including at the level of experts of the relevant institutions, authorities and agencies, where appropriate. The Commission, when preparing and drawing up delegated acts, should ensure a simultaneous, timely and appropriate transmission of relevant documents to the European Parliament and to the Council.

(44) The Commission should submit a report to the European Parliament and the Council assessing the appropriateness of the notification and public disclosure thresholds provided for, the operation of the restrictions and requirements relating to the transparency of net short positions, and whether any other restrictions or conditions on short selling or credit default swaps are appropriate.

(45) Since the objectives of this Regulation cannot be sufficiently achieved by the Member States, although competent authorities are better placed to monitor, and have better knowledge of, market developments, the overall impact of the problems relating to short selling and credit default swaps can be fully perceived only in a Union context, and can therefore be better achieved at Union level, the Union may adopt measures, in accordance with the principle of subsidiarity as set out in Article 5 of the Treaty on European Union. In accordance with the principle of proportionality, as set out in that

---

8. OJ L 8, 12.1.2001, p. 1.

9. OJ L 55, 28.2.2011, p. 13.

Article, this Regulation does not go beyond what is necessary in order to achieve those objectives.

(46) Since some Member States have already put in place restrictions on short selling and since this Regulation provides for delegated acts and binding technical standards which should be adopted before it can be usefully applied, it is necessary to provide for a sufficient period of time for transitional purposes. Since it is essential to specify, before 1 November 2012, key non- essential elements which will facilitate compliance by market participants with this Regulation and enforcement by competent authorities, it is also necessary to provide the Commission with the means to adopt the technical standards and delegated acts before that date,

HAVE ADOPTED THIS REGULATION:

CHAPTER I
GENERAL PROVISIONS

Article 1
Scope

1. This Regulation shall apply to the following:

(a) financial instruments within the meaning of point (a) of Article 2(1) that are admitted to trading on a trading venue in the Union, including such instruments when traded outside a trading venue;

(b) derivatives referred to in points (4) to (10) of Section C of Annex I to Directive 2004/39/EC that relate to a financial instrument referred to in point (a) or to an issuer of such a financial instrument, including such derivatives when traded outside a trading venue;

(c) debt instruments issued by a Member State or the Union and derivatives referred to in points (4) to (10) of Section C of Annex I to Directive 2004/39/EC that relate or are referenced to debt instruments issued by a Member State or the Union.

2. Articles 18, 20 and 23 to 30 shall apply to all financial instruments within the meaning of point (a) of Article 2(1).

Article 2
Definitions

1. For the purpose of this Regulation, the following definitions apply:

(a) 'financial instrument' means an instrument listed in Section C of Annex I to Directive 2004/39/EC;

(b) 'short sale' in relation to a share or debt instrument means any sale of the share or debt instrument which the seller does not own at the time of entering into the agreement to sell including such a sale where at the time of entering into the agreement to sell the seller has borrowed or agreed to borrow the share or debt instrument for delivery at settlement, not including:

(i) a sale by either party under a repurchase agreement where one party has agreed to sell the other a security at a specified price with a commitment from the other party to sell the security back at a later date at another specified price;

(ii) a transfer of securities under a securities lending agreement; or

(iii) entry into a futures contract or other derivative contract where it is agreed to sell securities at a specified price at a future date;

(c) 'credit default swap' means a derivative contract in which one party pays a fee to another party in return for a payment or other benefit in the case of a credit event relating to a reference entity and of any other default, relating to that derivative contract, which has a similar economic effect;

(d) 'sovereign issuer' means any of the following that issues debt instruments:

(i) the Union;

(ii) a Member State, including a government department, an agency, or a special purpose vehicle of the Member State;

(iii) in the case of a federal Member State, a member of the federation;

(iv) a special purpose vehicle for several Member States;

(v) an international financial institution established by two or more Member States which has the purpose of mobilising funding and provide financial assistance to the benefit of its members that are experiencing or threatened by severe financing problems; or

(vi) the European Investment Bank;

(e) 'sovereign credit default swap' means a credit default swap where a payment or other benefit will be paid in the case of a credit event or default relating to a sovereign issuer;

(f) 'sovereign debt' means a debt instrument issued by a sovereign issuer;

(g) 'issued sovereign debt' means the total of sovereign debt issued by a sovereign issuer that has not been redeemed;

(h) 'issued share capital' in relation to a company, means the total of ordinary and any preference shares issued by the company but does not include convertible debt securities;

(i) 'home Member State' means:

(i) in relation to an investment firm within the meaning of point (1) of Article 4(1) of Directive 2004/39/EC, or to a regulated market within the meaning of point (14) of Article 4(1) of Directive 2004/39/EC, the home Member State within the meaning of point (20) of Article 4(1) of Directive 2004/39/EC;

(ii) in relation to a credit institution, the home Member State within the meaning of point (7) of Article 4 of Directive 2006/48/EC of the European Parliament and of the Council of 14 June 2006 relating to the taking up and pursuit of the business of credit institutions;[10]

(iii) in relation to a legal person not referred to in point (i) or (ii), the Member State in which its registered office is situated or, if it has no registered office, the Member State in which its head office is situated;

---

10. OJ L 177, 30.6.2006, p. 1.

(iv) in relation to a natural person, the Member State in which that person's head office is situated, or, where there is no head office, the Member State in which that person is domiciled;

(j) 'relevant competent authority' means:

(i) in relation to sovereign debt of a Member State, or, in the case of a federal Member State, in relation to sovereign debt of a member of the federation, or a credit default swap relating to a Member State or a member of a federation, the competent authority of that Member State;

(ii) in relation to sovereign debt of the Union or a credit default swap relating to the Union, the competent authority of the jurisdiction in which the department issuing the debt is situated;

(iii) in relation to sovereign debt of several Member States acting through a special purpose vehicle or a credit default swap relating to such a special purpose vehicle, the competent authority of the jurisdiction in which the special purpose vehicle is established;

(iv) in relation to sovereign debt of an international financial institution established by two or more Member States, which has the purpose to mobilise funding and provide financial assistance to the benefit of its members that are experiencing or threatened by severe financing problems, the competent authority of the jurisdiction in which the international financial institution is established;

(v) in relation to a financial instrument other than an instrument referred to in points (i) to (iv), the competent authority for that financial instrument as defined in point (7) of Article 2 of Commission Regulation (EC) No 1287/2006[11] and determined in accordance with Chapter III of that Regulation;

(vi) in relation to a financial instrument that is not covered under points (i) to (v), the competent authority of the Member State in which the financial instrument was first admitted to trading on a trading venue;

(vii) in relation to a debt instrument issued by the European Investment Bank, the competent authority of the Member State in which the European Investment Bank is located;

(k) 'market making activities' means the activities of an investment firm, a credit institution, a third-country entity, or a firm as referred to in point (l) of Article 2(1) of Directive 2004/39/EC, which is a member of a trading venue or of a market in a third country, the legal and supervisory framework of which has been declared equivalent by the Commission pursuant to Article 17(2) where it deals as principal in a financial instrument, whether traded on or outside a trading venue, in any of the following capacities:

---

11. Commission Regulation (EC) No 1287/2006 of 10 August 2006 implementing Directive 2004/39/EC of the European Parliament and of the Council as regards record-keeping obligations for investment firms, transaction reporting, market transparency, admission of financial instruments to trading, and defined terms for the purposes of that Directive (OJ L 241, 2.9.2006, p. 1).

(i) by posting firm, simultaneous two-way quotes of comparable size and at competitive prices, with the result of providing liquidity on a regular and ongoing basis to the market;

(ii) as part of its usual business, by fulfilling orders initiated by clients or in response to clients' requests to trade;

(iii) by hedging positions arising from the fulfilment of tasks under points (i) and (ii);

(l) 'trading venue' means a regulated market within the meaning of point (14) of Article 4(1) of Directive 2004/39/EC, or a multilateral trading facility within the meaning of point (15) of Article 4(1) of Directive 2004/39/EC;

(m) 'principal venue' in relation to a share means the venue for the trading of that share with the highest turnover;

(n) 'authorised primary dealer' means a natural or legal person who has signed an agreement with a sovereign issuer or who has been formally recognised as a primary dealer by or on behalf of a sovereign issuer and who, in accordance with that agreement or recognition, has committed to dealing as principal in connection with primary and secondary market operations relating to debt issued by that issuer;

(o) 'central counterparty' means a legal entity which interposes itself between the counterparties to the contracts traded within one or more financial markets, becoming the buyer to every seller and the seller to every buyer and which is responsible for the operation of a clearing system;

(p) 'trading day' means a trading day as referred to in Article 4 of Regulation (EC) No 1287/2006;

(q) 'turnover' of a share means turnover within the meaning of point (9) of Article 2 of Regulation (EC) No 1287/2006.

2. The Commission shall be empowered to adopt delegated acts in accordance with Article 42 specifying the definitions laid down in paragraph 1 of this Article, in particular specifying when a natural or legal person is considered to own a financial instrument for the purposes of the definition of short sale in point (b) of paragraph 1.

Article 3
Short and long positions

1. For the purposes of this Regulation, a position resulting from either of the following shall be considered to be a short position relating to issued share capital or issued sovereign debt:

(a) a short sale of a share issued by a company or of a debt instrument issued by a sovereign issuer;

(b) entering into a transaction which creates or relates to a financial instrument other than an instrument referred to in point (a) where the effect or one of the effects of the transaction is to confer a financial advantage on the natural or legal person entering into that transaction in the event of a decrease in the price or value of the share or debt instrument.

2. For the purposes of this Regulation, a position resulting from either of the following shall be considered to be a long position relating to issued share capital or issued sovereign debt:

(a) holding a share issued by a company or a debt instrument issued by a sovereign issuer;

(b) entering into a transaction which creates or relates to a financial instrument other than an instrument referred to in point (a) where the effect or one of the effects of the transaction is to confer a financial advantage on the natural or legal person entering into that transaction in the event of an increase in the price or value of the share or debt instrument.

3. For the purposes of paragraphs 1 and 2, the calculation of a short or a long position, in respect of any position held by the relevant person indirectly, including through or by way of any index, basket of securities or any interest in any exchange traded fund or similar entity, shall be determined by the natural or legal person in question acting reasonably having regard to publicly available information as to the composition of the relevant index or basket of securities, or of the interests held by the relevant exchange traded fund or similar entity. In calculating such a short or long position, no person shall be required to obtain any real-time information as to such composition from any person.

For the purposes of paragraphs 1 and 2 the calculation of a short or long position relating to sovereign debt shall include any sovereign credit default swap that relates to the sovereign issuer.

4. For the purposes of this Regulation, the position remaining after deducting any long position that a natural or legal person holds in relation to the issued share capital from any short position that that natural or legal person holds in relation to that capital shall be considered a net short position in relation to the issued share capital of the company concerned.

5. For the purposes of this Regulation, the position remaining after deducting any long position that a natural or legal person holds in relation to issued sovereign debt and any long position in debt instruments of a sovereign issuer the pricing of which is highly correlated to the pricing of the given sovereign debt from any short position that that natural or legal person holds in relation to the same sovereign debt shall be considered a net short position in relation to the issued sovereign debt of the sovereign issuer concerned.

6. The calculation of sovereign debt under paragraphs 1 to 5 shall be for each single sovereign issuer even if separate entities issue sovereign debt on behalf of the sovereign issuer.

7. The Commission shall be empowered to adopt delegated acts in accordance with Article 42 specifying:

(a) cases in which a natural or legal person is considered to hold a share or debt instrument for the purposes of paragraph 2;

(b) cases in which a natural or legal person has a net short position for the purposes of paragraphs 4 and 5 and the method of calculation of such position;

(c) the method of calculating positions for the purposes of paragraphs 3, 4 and 5 when different entities in a group have long or short positions or for fund management activities relating to separate funds.

For the purposes of point (c) of the first subparagraph, the method of calculation shall take into account, in particular, whether different investment strategies are pursued in relation to a particular issuer through more than one separate fund managed by the same fund manager, whether the same investment strategy is pursued in relation to a particular issuer through more than one fund, and whether more than one portfolio within the same entity is managed on a discretionary basis pursuing the same investment strategy in relation to a particular issuer.

Article 4
Uncovered position in a sovereign credit default swap

1. For the purposes of this Regulation, a natural or legal person shall be considered to have an uncovered position in a sovereign credit default swap where the sovereign credit default swap does not serve to hedge against:

(a) the risk of default of the issuer where the natural or legal person has a long position in the sovereign debt of that issuer to which the sovereign credit default swap relates; or

(b) the risk of a decline of the value of the sovereign debt where the natural or legal person holds assets or is subject to liabilities, including but not limited to financial contracts, a portfolio of assets or financial obligations the value of which is correlated to the value of the sovereign debt.

2. The Commission shall be empowered to adopt delegated acts in accordance with Article 42 specifying, for the purposes of paragraph 1 of this Article:

(a) cases in which a sovereign credit default swap transaction is considered to be hedging against a default risk or the risk of a decline of the value of the sovereign debt, and the method of calculation of an uncovered position in a sovereign credit default swap;

(b) the method of calculating positions where different entities in a group have long or short positions or for fund management activities relating to separate funds.

CHAPTER II
TRANSPARENCY OF NET SHORT POSITIONS

Article 5
Notification to competent authorities of significant net short positions in shares

1. A natural or legal person who has a net short position in relation to the issued share capital of a company that has shares admitted to trading on a trading venue shall notify the relevant competent authority, in accordance with Article 9, where the position reaches or falls below a relevant notification threshold referred to in paragraph 2 of this Article.

2. A relevant notification threshold is a percentage that equals 0,2% of the issued share capital of the company concerned and each 0,1% above that.

3. The European Supervisory Authority (European Securities and Markets Authority) (ESMA) may issue an opinion to the Commission on adjusting the thresholds referred to in paragraph 2, taking into account the developments in financial markets.

4. The Commission shall be empowered to adopt delegated acts in accordance with Article 42 modifying the thresholds referred to in paragraph 2 of this Article, taking into account the developments in financial markets.

Article 6

Public disclosure of significant net short positions in shares

1. A natural or legal person who has a net short position in relation to the issued share capital of a company that has shares admitted to trading on a trading venue shall disclose details of that position to the public, in accordance with Article 9, where the position reaches or falls below a relevant publication threshold referred to in paragraph 2 of this Article.

2. A relevant publication threshold is a percentage that equals 0,5% of the issued share capital of the company concerned and each 0,1% above that.

3. ESMA may issue an opinion to the Commission on adjusting the thresholds referred to in paragraph 2, taking into account the developments in financial markets.

4. The Commission shall be empowered to adopt delegated acts in accordance with Article 42 modifying the thresholds referred to in paragraph 2 of this Article, taking into account the developments in financial markets.

5. This Article is without prejudice to laws, regulations and administrative provisions adopted in relation to takeover bids, merger transactions and other transactions affecting the ownership or control of companies regulated by the supervisory authorities appointed by Member States pursuant to Article 4 of Directive 2004/25/EC of the European Parliament and of the Council of 21 April 2004 on takeover bids[12] that require disclosure of short positions beyond the requirements of this Article.

Article 7

Notification to competent authorities of significant net short positions in sovereign debt

1. A natural or legal person who has a net short position relating to issued sovereign debt shall notify the relevant competent authority, in accordance with Article 9, where such a position reaches or falls below the relevant notification thresholds for the sovereign issuer concerned.

2. The relevant notification thresholds shall consist of an initial amount and then additional incremental levels in relation to each sovereign issuer, as specified in the measures taken by the Commission in accordance with paragraph 3. ESMA shall publish on its website the notification thresholds for each Member State.

3. The Commission shall be empowered to adopt delegated acts in accordance with Article 42 specifying the amounts and incremental levels referred to in paragraph 2 of this Article.

---

12. OJ L 142, 30.4.2004, p. 12.

The Commission shall:

(a) ensure that the thresholds are not set at such a level as to require notification of positions which are of minimal value;

(b) take into account the total amount of outstanding issued sovereign debt for each sovereign issuer, and the average size of positions held by market participants relating to the sovereign debt of that sovereign issuer; and

(c) take into account the liquidity of each sovereign bond market.

Article 8
Notification to competent authorities of uncovered positions in sovereign credit default swaps

Where a competent authority suspends restrictions in accordance with Article 14(2), a natural or legal person who has an uncovered position in a sovereign credit default swap shall notify the relevant competent authority where such a position reaches or falls below the relevant notification thresholds for the sovereign issuer, as specified in accordance with Article 7.

Article 9
Method of notification and disclosure

1. Any notification or disclosure under Article 5, 6, 7 or 8 shall set out details of the identity of the natural or legal person who holds the relevant position, the size of the relevant position, the issuer in relation to which the relevant position is held and the date on which the relevant position was created, changed or ceased to be held.

For the purposes of Articles 5, 6, 7 and 8, natural and legal persons that hold significant net short positions shall keep, for a period of 5 years, records of the gross positions which make a significant net short position.

2. The relevant time for calculation of a net short position shall be at midnight at the end of the trading day on which the natural or legal person holds the relevant position. That time shall apply to all transactions irrespective of the means of trading used, including transactions executed through manual or automated trading, and irrespective of whether the transactions have taken place during normal trading hours. The notification or disclosure shall be made not later than at 15.30 on the following trading day. The times specified in this paragraph shall be calculated according to the time in the Member State of the relevant competent authority to whom the relevant position must be notified.

3. The notification of information to a relevant competent authority shall ensure the confidentiality of the information and incorporate mechanisms for authenticating the source of the notification.

4. The public disclosure of information set out in Article 6 shall be made in a manner ensuring fast access to information on a non-discriminatory basis. That information shall be posted on a central website operated or supervised by the relevant competent authority. The competent authorities shall communicate the address of that website to ESMA, which, in turn, shall put a link to all such central websites on its own website.

5. In order to ensure consistent application of this Article, ESMA shall develop draft regulatory technical standards specifying the details of the information to be provided for the purposes of paragraph 1.

ESMA shall submit those draft regulatory technical standards to the Commission by 31 March 2012.

Power is delegated to the Commission to adopt the regulatory technical standards referred to in the first subparagraph in accordance with Articles 10 to 14 of Regulation (EU) No 1095/2010.

6. In order to ensure uniform conditions of application of paragraph 4, ESMA shall develop draft implementing technical standards specifying the means by which information may be disclosed to the public.

ESMA shall submit those draft implementing technical standards to the Commission by 31 March 2012.

Power is conferred on the Commission to adopt the implementing technical standards referred to in the first subparagraph in accordance with Article 15 of Regulation (EU) No 1095/2010.

Article 10
Application of notification and disclosure requirements

The notification and disclosure requirements under Articles 5, 6, 7 and 8 apply to natural or legal persons domiciled or established within the Union or in a third country.

Article 11
Information to be provided to ESMA

1. The competent authorities shall provide information in summary form to ESMA on a quarterly basis on net short positions relating to issued share capital and to issued sovereign debt, and on uncovered positions relating to sovereign credit default swaps, for which it is the relevant competent authority and receives notifications under Articles 5, 7 and 8.

2. ESMA may request at any time, in order to carry out its duties under this Regulation, additional information from a relevant competent authority on net short positions relating to issued share capital and to issued sovereign debt, or on uncovered positions relating to sovereign credit default swaps.

The competent authority shall provide the requested information to ESMA at the latest within 7 calendar days. Where there are adverse events or developments which constitute a serious threat to financial stability or to market confidence in the Member State concerned or in another Member State, the competent authority shall provide ESMA with any available information based on the notification requirements under Articles 5, 7 and 8 within 24 hours.

3. In order to ensure consistent application of this Article, ESMA shall develop draft regulatory technical standards specifying the details of the information to be provided in accordance with paragraphs 1 and 2.

ESMA shall submit those draft regulatory technical standards to the Commission by 31 March 2012.

Power is delegated to the Commission to adopt the regulatory technical standards referred to in the first subparagraph in accordance with Articles 10 to 14 of Regulation (EU) No 1095/2010.

4. In order to ensure uniform conditions of application of paragraph 1, ESMA shall develop draft implementing technical standards defining the format of information to be provided in accordance with paragraphs 1 and 2.

ESMA shall submit those draft implementing technical standards to the Commission by 31 March 2012.

Power is conferred on the Commission to adopt the implementing technical standards referred to in the first subparagraph in accordance with Article 15 of Regulation (EU) No 1095/2010.

CHAPTER III
UNCOVERED SHORT SALES

Article 12
Restrictions on uncovered short sales in shares

1. A natural or legal person may enter into a short sale of a share admitted to trading on a trading venue only where one of the following conditions is fulfilled:

(a) the natural or legal person has borrowed the share or has made alternative provisions resulting in a similar legal effect;

(b) the natural or legal person has entered into an agreement to borrow the share or has another absolutely enforceable claim under contract or property law to be transferred ownership of a corresponding number of securities of the same class so that settlement can be effected when it is due;

(c) the natural or legal person has an arrangement with a third party under which that third party has confirmed that the share has been located and has taken measures vis-à-vis third parties necessary for the natural or legal person to have a reasonable expectation that settlement can be effected when it is due.

2. In order to ensure uniform conditions of application of paragraph 1, ESMA shall develop draft implementing technical standards to determine the types of agreements, arrangements and measures that adequately ensure that the share will be available for settlement. In determining what measures are necessary to have a reasonable expectation that settlement can be effected when it is due, ESMA shall take into account, inter alia, the intraday trading and the liquidity of the shares.

ESMA shall submit those draft implementing technical standards to the Commission by 31 March 2012.

Power is conferred on the Commission to adopt the implementing technical standards referred to in the first subparagraph in accordance with Article 15 of Regulation (EU) No 1095/2010.

Article 13
Restrictions on uncovered short sales in sovereign debt

1. A natural or legal person may enter into a short sale of sovereign debt only where one of the following conditions is fulfilled:

(a) the natural or legal person has borrowed the sovereign debt or has made alternative provisions resulting in a similar legal effect;

(b) the natural or legal person has entered into an agreement to borrow the sovereign debt or has another absolutely enforceable claim under contract or property law to be transferred ownership of a corresponding number of securities of the same class so that settlement can be effected when it is due;

(c) the natural or legal person has an arrangement with a third party under which that third party has confirmed that the sovereign debt has been located or otherwise has a reasonable expectation that settlement can be effected when it is due.

2. The restrictions in paragraph 1 do not apply if the transaction serves to hedge a long position in debt instruments of an issuer, the pricing of which has a high correlation with the pricing of the given sovereign debt.

3. Where the liquidity of sovereign debt falls below the threshold determined in accordance with the methodology referred to in paragraph 4, the restrictions referred to in paragraph 1 may be temporarily suspended by the relevant competent authority. Before suspending those restrictions, the relevant competent authority shall notify ESMA and the other competent authorities about the proposed suspension.

A suspension shall be valid for an initial period not exceeding 6 months from the date of its publication on the website of the relevant competent authority. The suspension may be renewed for periods not exceeding 6 months if the grounds for the suspension continue to apply. If the suspension is not renewed by the end of the initial period or of any subsequent renewal period it shall automatically expire.

ESMA shall, within 24 hours of notification by the relevant competent authority, issue an opinion based on paragraph 4 on the notified suspension or renewal of suspension. The opinion shall be published on ESMA's website.

4. The Commission shall adopt delegated acts in accordance with Article 42 specifying the parameters and methods for calculating the threshold of liquidity referred to in paragraph 3 of this Article in relation to issued sovereign debt.

The parameters and methods for Member States to calculate the threshold shall be set in such a way that where it is reached, it represents a significant decline relative to the average level of liquidity for the sovereign debt concerned.

The threshold shall be defined based on objective criteria specific to the relevant sovereign debt market, including the total amount of outstanding issued sovereign debt for each sovereign issuer.

5. In order to ensure uniform conditions of application of paragraph 1, ESMA may develop draft implementing technical standards to determine the types of agreements or arrangements that adequately ensure that the sovereign debt will be available for settlement. ESMA shall, in particular, take into account the need to preserve liquidity of markets, especially sovereign bond and sovereign bond repurchase markets.

ESMA shall submit those draft implementing technical standards to the Commission by 31 March 2012.

Power is conferred on the Commission to adopt the implementing technical standards referred to in the first subparagraph in accordance with Article 15 of Regulation (EU) No 1095/2010.

Article 14
Restrictions on uncovered sovereign credit default swaps

1. A natural or legal person may enter into sovereign credit default swap transactions only where that transaction does not lead to an uncovered position in a sovereign credit default swap as referred to in Article 4.

2. A competent authority may temporarily suspend restrictions referred to in paragraph 1, where it has objective grounds for believing that its sovereign debt market is not functioning properly and that such restrictions might have a negative impact on the sovereign credit default swap market, especially by increasing the cost of borrowing for sovereign issuers or affecting the sovereign issuers' ability to issue new debt. Those grounds shall be based on the following indicators:

(a) a high or rising interest rate on the sovereign debt;

(b) a widening of interest rate spreads on the sovereign debt compared to the sovereign debt of other sovereign issuers;

(c) a widening of the sovereign credit default swap spreads compared to the own curve and compared to other sovereign issuers;

(d) the timeliness of the return of the price of the sovereign debt to its original equilibrium after a large trade;

(e) the amounts of sovereign debt that can be traded.

The competent authority may also use indicators other than those set out in points (a) to (e) of the first subparagraph.

Before suspending restrictions under this Article, the relevant competent authority shall notify ESMA and the other competent authorities of the proposed suspension and the grounds on which it is based.

A suspension shall be valid for an initial period not exceeding 12 months from the date of its publication on the website of the relevant competent authority. The suspension may be renewed for periods not exceeding 6 months if the grounds for the suspension continue to apply. If the suspension is not renewed by the end of the initial period or of any subsequent renewal period, it shall automatically expire.

ESMA shall, within 24 hours of the notification by the relevant competent authority, issue an opinion on the intended suspension or on the renewal of that suspension, irrespective of whether the competent authority has based the suspension on the indicators set out in points (a) to (e) of the first subparagraph or on other indicators. Where the intended suspension or renewal of a suspension is based on the second subparagraph, that opinion shall also include an assessment of the indicators used by the competent authority. The opinion shall be published on ESMA's website.

Article 15
Buy-in procedures

1. A central counterparty in a Member State that provides clearing services for shares shall ensure that procedures are in place which comply with all of the following requirements:

(a) where a natural or legal person who sells shares is not able to deliver the shares for settlement within four business days after the day on which settlement is due, procedures are automatically triggered for the buy-in of the shares to ensure delivery for settlement;

(b) where the buy-in of the shares for delivery is not possible, an amount is paid to the buyer based on the value of the shares to be delivered at the delivery date plus an amount for losses incurred by the buyer as a result of the settlement failure; and

(c) the natural or legal person who fails to settle reimburses all amounts paid pursuant to points (a) and (b).

2. A central counterparty in a Member State that provides clearing services for shares shall ensure that procedures are in place, which ensure that where a natural or legal person who sells shares fails to deliver the shares for settlement by the date on which settlement is due, such person must make daily payments for each day that the failure continues.

The daily payments shall be sufficiently high to act as a deterrent to natural or legal persons failing to settle.

CHAPTER IV
EXEMPTIONS

Article 16
Exemption where the principal trading venue is in a third country

1. Articles 5, 6, 12 and 15 shall not apply to shares of a company admitted to trading on a trading venue in the Union where the principal venue for the trading of the shares is located in a third country.

2. The relevant competent authority for shares of a company that are traded on a trading venue in the Union and a venue located in a third country shall determine, at least every 2 years, whether the principal venue for the trading of those shares is located in a third country.

The relevant competent authority shall notify ESMA of any such shares identified as having their principal trading venue located in a third country.

Every 2 years ESMA shall publish the list of shares for which the principal trading venue is located in a third country. The list shall be effective for a 2-year period.

3. In order to ensure consistent application of this Article, ESMA shall develop draft regulatory technical standards specifying the method for calculation of the turnover to determine the principal venue for the trading of a share.

ESMA shall submit those draft regulatory technical standards to the Commission by 31 March 2012.

Power is delegated to the Commission to adopt the regulatory technical standards referred to in the first subparagraph in accordance with Articles 10 to 14 of Regulation (EU) No 1095/2010.

4. In order to ensure uniform conditions of application of paragraphs 1 and 2 ESMA shall develop draft implementing technical standards to determine:

(a) the date on which and period in respect of which any calculation determining the principal trading venue for a share is to be made;

(b) the date by which the relevant competent authority shall notify ESMA of those shares for which the principal trading venue is in a third country;

(c) the date from which the list is to be effective following publication by ESMA.

ESMA shall submit those draft implementing technical standards to the Commission by 31 March 2012.

Power is conferred on the Commission to adopt the implementing technical standards referred to in the first subparagraph in accordance with Article 15 of Regulation (EU) No 1095/2010.

Article 17

Exemption for market making activities and primary market operations

1. Articles 5, 6, 7, 12, 13 and 14 shall not apply to transactions performed due to market making activities.

2. The Commission may, in accordance with the procedure referred to in Article 44(2), adopt decisions determining that the legal and supervisory framework of a third country ensures that a market authorised in that third country complies with legally binding requirements which are, for the purpose of the application of the exemption set out in paragraph 1, equivalent to the requirements under Title III of Directive 2004/39/EC, under Directive 2003/6/EC of the European Parliament and of the Council of 28 January 2003 on insider dealing and market manipulation (market abuse)[13] and under Directive 2004/109/EC of the European Parliament and of the Council of 15 December 2004 on the harmonisation of transparency requirements in relation to information about issuers whose securities are admitted to trading on a regulated market,[14] and which are subject to effective supervision and enforcement in that third country.

The legal and supervisory framework of a third country may be considered equivalent where that third country's:

(a) markets are subject to authorisation and to effective supervision and enforcement on an ongoing basis;

(b) markets have clear and transparent rules regarding admission of securities to trading so that such securities are capable of being traded in a fair, orderly and efficient manner, and are freely negotiable;

(c) security issuers are subject to periodic and ongoing information requirements ensuring a high level of investor protection; and

(d) market transparency and integrity are ensured by preventing market abuse in the form of insider dealing and market manipulation.

3. Articles 7, 13 and 14 shall not apply to the activities of a natural or legal person where, acting as an authorised primary dealer pursuant to an agreement with a sovereign issuer, it is dealing as principal in a financial instrument in relation to primary or secondary market operations relating to the sovereign debt.

4. Articles 5, 6, 12, 13 and 14 of this Regulation shall not apply to a natural or legal person where it enters into a short sale of a security or has a net short position in relation to the carrying out of a stabilisation under Chapter III of Commission Regulation (EC)

---

13. OJ L 96, 12.4.2003, p. 16.

14. OJ L 390, 31.12.2004, p. 38.

No 2273/2003 of 22 December 2003 implementing Directive 2003/6/EC of the European Parliament and of the Council as regards exemptions for buy-back programmes and stabilisation of financial instruments.[15]

5. The exemption referred to in paragraph 1 shall apply only where the natural or legal person concerned has notified the competent authority of its home Member State in writing that it intends to make use of the exemption. The notification shall be made not less than 30 calendar days before the natural or legal person first intends to use the exemption.

6. The exemption referred to in paragraph 3 shall apply only where the authorised primary dealer has notified the relevant competent authority in relation to the sovereign debt concerned in writing that it intends to make use of the exemption. The notification shall be made not less than 30 calendar days before the natural or legal person acting as authorised primary dealer first intends to use the exemption.

7. The competent authority referred to in paragraphs 5 and 6 may prohibit the use of the exemption if it considers that the natural or legal person does not satisfy the conditions of the exemption. Any prohibition shall be imposed within the 30 calendar day period referred to in paragraph 5 or 6 or subsequently if the competent authority becomes aware that there have been changes in the circumstances of the natural or legal person so that it no longer satisfies the conditions of the exemption.

8. A third-country entity that is not authorised in the Union shall send the notification referred to in paragraphs 5 and 6 to the competent authority of the main trading venue in the Union in which it trades.

9. A natural or legal person who has given a notification under paragraph 5 shall as soon as possible notify in writing the competent authority of its home Member State where there are any changes affecting that person's eligibility to use the exemption, or if it no longer wishes to use the exemption.

10. A natural or legal person who has given a notification under paragraph 6 shall as soon as possible notify in writing the relevant competent authority in relation to sovereign debt concerned where there are any changes affecting that person's eligibility to use the exemption, or if it no longer wishes to use the exemption.

11. The competent authority of the home Member State may request information, in writing, from a natural or legal person operating under the exemptions set out in paragraph 1, 3 or 4 about short positions held or activities conducted under the exemption. The natural or legal person shall provide the information not later than 4 calendar days after the request is made.

12. A competent authority shall notify ESMA within 2 weeks of notification in accordance with paragraph 5 or 9 of any market makers and in accordance with paragraph 6 or 10 of any authorised primary dealers who are making use of the exemption and of any market makers and authorised primary dealers who are no longer making use of the exemption.

13. ESMA shall publish and keep up to date on its website a list of market makers and authorised primary dealers who are using the exemption.

---

15. OJ L 336, 23.12.2003, p. 33.

14. A notification under this Article may be made by a person to a competent authority and by a competent authority to ESMA at any time within 60 calendar days before 1 November 2012.

Chapter V
Powers of Intervention of Competent Authorities and of ESMA

Section 1
Powers of competent authorities

Article 18
Notification and disclosure in exceptional circumstances

1. Subject to Article 22, a competent authority may require natural or legal persons who have net short positions in relation to a specific financial instrument or class of financial instruments to notify it or to disclose to the public details of the position where the position reaches or falls below a notification threshold fixed by the competent authority and where:

(a) there are adverse events or developments which constitute a serious threat to financial stability or to market confidence in the Member State concerned or in one or more other Member States; and

(b) the measure is necessary to address the threat and will not have a detrimental effect on the efficiency of financial markets which is disproportionate to its benefits.

2. Paragraph 1 of this Article shall not apply to financial instruments in respect of which transparency is already required under Articles 5 to 8. A measure under paragraph 1 may apply in circumstances or be subject to exceptions specified by the competent authority. Exceptions may in particular be specified to apply to market making activities and primary market activities.

Article 19
Notification by lenders in exceptional circumstances

1. Subject to Article 22, a competent authority may take the measure referred to in paragraph 2 of this Article where:

(a) there are adverse events or developments which constitute a serious threat to financial stability or to market confidence in the Member State concerned or in one or more other Member States; and

(b) the measure is necessary to address the threat and will not have a detrimental effect on the efficiency of financial markets which is disproportionate to its benefits.

2. A competent authority may require natural or legal persons engaged in the lending of a specific financial instrument or class of financial instruments to notify any significant change in the fees requested for such lending.

Article 20
Restrictions on short selling and similar transactions in exceptional circumstances

1. Subject to Article 22, a competent authority may take one or more of the measures referred to in paragraph 2 of this Article where:

(a) there are adverse events or developments which constitute a serious threat to financial stability or to market confidence in the Member State concerned or in one or more other Member States; and

(b) the measure is necessary to address the threat and will not have a detrimental effect on the efficiency of financial markets which is disproportionate to its benefits.

2. A competent authority may prohibit or impose conditions relating to natural or legal persons entering into:

(a) a short sale; or

(b) a transaction other than a short sale which creates, or relates to, a financial instrument and the effect or one of the effects of that transaction is to confer a financial advantage on the natural or legal person in the event of a decrease in the price or value of another financial instrument.

3. A measure taken under paragraph 2 may apply to transactions concerning all financial instruments, financial instruments of a specific class or a specific financial instrument. The measure may apply in circumstances or be subject to exceptions specified by the competent authority. Exceptions may in particular be specified to apply to market making activities and primary market activities.

Article 21

Restrictions on sovereign credit default swap transactions in exceptional circumstances

1. Subject to Article 22, a competent authority may restrict the ability of natural or legal persons to enter into sovereign credit default swap transactions or may limit the value of sovereign credit default swap positions that those persons are permitted to enter into where:

(a) there are adverse events or developments which constitute a serious threat to financial stability or to market confidence in the Member State concerned or in one or more other Member States; and

(b) the measure is necessary to address the threat and will not have a detrimental effect on the efficiency of financial markets which is disproportionate to its benefits.

2. A measure taken under paragraph 1 may apply to sovereign credit default swap transactions of a specific class or to specific sovereign credit default swap transactions. The measure may apply in circumstances or be subject to exceptions specified by the competent authority. Exceptions may in particular be specified to apply to market making activities and primary market activities.

Article 22

Measures by other competent authorities

Without prejudice to Article 26, a competent authority in relation to a financial instrument for which it is not the relevant competent authority may impose or renew a measure under Article 18, 19, 20 or 21 only with the consent of the relevant competent authority.

Article 23
Power to restrict short selling of financial instruments temporarily in the case of a significant fall in price

1. Where the price of a financial instrument on a trading venue has fallen significantly during a single trading day in relation to the closing price on that venue on the previous trading day, the competent authority of the home Member State for that venue shall consider whether it is appropriate to prohibit or restrict natural or legal persons from engaging in short selling of the financial instrument on that trading venue or otherwise limit transactions in that financial instrument on that trading venue in order to prevent a disorderly decline in the price of the financial instrument.

Where the competent authority is satisfied under the first subparagraph that it is appropriate to do so, it shall in the case of a share or a debt instrument, prohibit or restrict natural and legal persons from entering into a short sale on that trading venue or in the case of another type of financial instrument, limit transactions in that financial instrument on that trading venue in order to prevent a disorderly decline in the price of the financial instrument.

2. The measure under paragraph 1 shall apply for a period not exceeding the end of the trading day following the trading day on which the fall in price occurs. If, at the end of the trading day following the trading day on which the fall in price occurs, there is, despite the measure being imposed, a further significant fall in value of at least half of the amount specified in paragraph 5 of the financial instrument from the closing price of the first trading day, the competent authority may extend the measure for a further period not exceeding 2 trading days after the end of the second trading day.

3. The measure under paragraph 1 shall apply in circumstances or be subject to exceptions specified by the competent authority. Exceptions may in particular be specified to apply to market making activities and primary market activities.

4. A competent authority of the home Member State of a venue where a financial instrument has during a single trading day fallen by the value referred to in paragraph 5 shall notify ESMA about the decision taken under paragraph 1 at the latest 2 hours after the end of that trading day. ESMA shall immediately inform the competent authorities of the home Member States of venues which trade the same financial instrument.

If a competent authority disagrees with the action taken by another competent authority on a financial instrument traded on different venues regulated by different competent authorities, ESMA may assist those authorities in reaching an agreement in accordance with Article 19 of Regulation (EU) No 1095/2010.

The conciliation shall be completed before midnight at the end of the same trading day. If the competent authorities concerned fail to reach an agreement within the conciliation phase, ESMA may take a decision in accordance with Article 19(3) of Regulation (EU) No 1095/2010. The decision shall be taken before the opening of the next trading day.

5. The fall in value shall be 10% or more in the case of a liquid share, as defined in Article 22 of Regulation (EC) No 1287/2006, and for illiquid shares and other classes of financial instruments an amount to be specified by the Commission.

6. ESMA may issue and send to the Commission an opinion on adjusting the threshold referred to in paragraph 5, taking into account the developments in financial markets.

The Commission shall be empowered to adopt delegated acts in accordance with Article 42 modifying the thresholds referred to in paragraph 5 of this Article, taking into account the developments in financial markets.

7. The Commission shall adopt delegated acts in accordance with Article 42 specifying what constitutes a significant fall in value for financial instruments other than liquid shares, taking into account the specificities of each class of financial instrument and the differences of volatility.

8. In order to ensure consistent application of this Article, ESMA shall develop draft regulatory technical standards specifying the method of calculation of the 10% fall for liquid shares and of the fall in value specified by the Commission as referred to in paragraph 7.

ESMA shall submit those draft regulatory technical standards to the Commission by 31 March 2012.

Power is delegated to the Commission to adopt the regulatory technical standards referred to in the first subparagraph in accordance with Articles 10 to 14 of Regulation (EU) No 1095/2010.

Article 24
Period of restrictions

A measure imposed under Article 18, 19, 20 or 21 shall be valid for an initial period not exceeding 3 months from the date of publication of the notice referred to in Article 25.

The measure may be renewed for further periods not exceeding 3 months if the grounds for taking the measure continue to apply. If the measure is not renewed by the end of such a 3-month period, it shall automatically expire.

Article 25
Notice of restrictions

1. A competent authority shall publish on its website notice of any decision to impose or renew any measure referred to in Articles 18 to 23.

2. The notice shall specify at least details of:

(a) the measures imposed including the instruments and classes of transactions to which they apply and their duration;

(b) the reasons why the competent authority believes it is necessary to impose the measures including the evidence supporting those reasons.

3. A measure under Articles 18 to 23 shall take effect when the notice is published or at a time specified in the notice that is after its publication and shall only apply in relation to a transaction entered into after the measure takes effect.

Article 26
Notification to ESMA and other competent authorities

1. Before imposing or renewing any measure under Article 18, 19, 20 or 21 and before imposing any restriction under Article 23, a competent authority shall notify ESMA and the other competent authorities of the measure it proposes.

2. The notification shall include details of the proposed measures, the classes of financial instruments and transactions to which they will apply, the evidence supporting the reasons for those measures and when the measures are intended to take effect.

3. Notification of a proposal to impose or renew a measure under Article 18, 19, 20 or 21 shall be made not less than 24 hours before the measure is intended to take effect or to be renewed. In exceptional circumstances, a competent authority may make the notification less than 24 hours before the measure is intended to take effect where it is not possible to give 24 hours notice. A notification of a restriction under Article 23 shall be made before the measure is intended to take effect.

4. A competent authority that receives notification under this Article may take measures in accordance with Articles 18 to 23 in that Member State where it is satisfied that the measure is necessary to assist the competent authority making the notification. The competent authority that receives notification shall also give notice in accordance with paragraphs 1 to 3 where it proposes to take measures.

Section 2
Powers of ESMA

Article 27
Coordination by ESMA

1. ESMA shall perform a facilitation and coordination role in relation to measures taken by the competent authorities under Section 1. In particular ESMA shall ensure that a consistent approach is taken by competent authorities regarding measures taken, especially regarding where it is necessary to use powers of intervention, the nature of any measures imposed and the commencement and duration of such measures.

2. After receiving notification under Article 26 of any measure that is to be imposed or renewed under Article 18, 19, 20 or 21, ESMA shall within 24 hours issue an opinion on whether it considers the measure or proposed measure is necessary to address the exceptional circumstances. The opinion shall state whether ESMA considers that adverse events or developments have arisen which constitute a serious threat to financial stability or to market confidence in one or more Member States, whether the measure or proposed measure is appropriate and proportionate to address the threat and whether the proposed duration of any such measure is justified. If ESMA considers that the taking of any measure by the other competent authorities is necessary to address the threat, it shall also state this in its opinion. The opinion shall be published on ESMA's website.

3. Where a competent authority proposes to take or takes measures contrary to an ESMA opinion under paragraph 2 or declines to take measures contrary to an ESMA opinion under that paragraph, it shall publish on its website within 24 hours of receiving ESMA's opinion a notice fully explaining its reasons for doing so. Where such a situation arises ESMA shall consider whether the conditions are satisfied and it is an appropriate case for the use of its powers of intervention under Article 28.

4. ESMA shall review measures under this Article regularly and in any event at least every 3 months. If the measure is not renewed by the end of such a 3-month period, it shall automatically expire.

Article 28
ESMA intervention powers in exceptional circumstances

1. In accordance with Article 9(5) of Regulation (EU) No 1095/2010, ESMA shall, subject to paragraph 2 of this Article, either:

(a) require natural or legal persons who have net short positions in relation to a specific financial instrument or class of financial instruments to notify a competent authority or to disclose to the public details of any such position; or

(b) prohibit or impose conditions on, the entry by natural or legal persons into a short sale or a transaction which creates, or relates to, a financial instrument other than financial instruments referred to in point (c) of Article 1(1) where the effect or one of the effects of the transaction is to confer a financial advantage on such person in the event of a decrease in the price or value of another financial instrument.

A measure may apply in particular circumstances, or be subject to exceptions specified by ESMA. Exceptions may in particular be specified to apply to market-making activities and primary market activities.

2. ESMA shall take a decision under paragraph 1 only if:

(a) the measures listed in points (a) and (b) of paragraph 1 address a threat to the orderly functioning and integrity of financial markets or to the stability of the whole or part of the financial system in the Union and there are cross-border implications; and

(b) no competent authority has taken measures to address the threat or one or more of the competent authorities have taken measures that do not adequately address the threat.

3. Where taking measures referred to in paragraph 1 ESMA shall take into account the extent to which the measure:

(a) significantly addresses the threat to the orderly functioning and integrity of financial markets or to the stability of the whole or part of the financial system in the Union or significantly improves the ability of the competent authorities to monitor the threat;

(b) does not create a risk of regulatory arbitrage;

(c) does not have a detrimental effect on the efficiency of financial markets, including by reducing liquidity in those markets or creating uncertainty for market participants, that is disproportionate to the benefits of the measure.

Where one or more competent authorities have taken a measure under Article 18, 19, 20 or 21, ESMA may take any of the measures referred to in paragraph 1 of this Article without issuing the opinion provided for in Article 27.

4. Before deciding to impose or renew any measure referred to in paragraph 1, ESMA shall consult the ESRB and, where appropriate, other relevant authorities.

5. Before deciding to impose or renew any measure referred to in paragraph 1, ESMA shall notify the competent authorities concerned of the measure it proposes to take. The notification shall include details of the proposed measures, the class of financial instruments and transactions to which they will apply, the evidence supporting the reasons for those measures and when the measures are intended to take effect.

6. The notification shall be made not less than 24 hours before the measure is to take effect or to be renewed. In exceptional circumstances, ESMA may make the notification less than 24 hours before the measure is intended to take effect where it is not possible to give 24 hours' notice.

7. ESMA shall publish on its website notice of any decision to impose or renew any measure referred to in paragraph 1. The notice shall at least specify:

- (a) the measures imposed including the instruments and classes of transactions to which they apply, and their duration; and
- (b) the reasons why ESMA is of the opinion that it is necessary to impose the measures including the evidence supporting those reasons.

8. After deciding to impose or renew any measure referred to in paragraph 1, ESMA shall immediately notify the competent authorities of the measures taken.

9. A measure shall take effect when the notice is published on the ESMA website or at a time specified in the notice that is after its publication and shall only apply in relation to a transaction entered into after the measure takes effect.

10. ESMA shall review the measures referred to in paragraph 1 at appropriate intervals and at least every 3 months. If the measure is not renewed by the end of such a 3-month period it shall automatically expire. Paragraphs 2 to 9 shall apply to a renewal of measures.

11. A measure adopted by ESMA under this Article shall prevail over any previous measure taken by a competent authority under Section 1.

Article 29
ESMA's powers in emergency situations relating to sovereign debt

In the case of an emergency situation relating to sovereign debt or sovereign credit default swaps, Articles 18 and 38 of Regulation (EU) No 1095/2010 shall apply.

Article 30
Further specification of adverse events or developments

The Commission shall be empowered to adopt delegated acts in accordance with Article 42 specifying criteria and factors to be taken into account by the competent authorities and by ESMA in determining in which cases the adverse events or developments referred to in Articles 18 to 21 and Article 27 and the threats referred to in point (a) of Article 28(2) arise.

Article 31
Inquiries by ESMA

ESMA may, on the request of one or more of the competent authorities, the European Parliament, the Council or the Commission or on its own initiative conduct an inquiry into a particular issue or practice relating to short selling or relating to the use of credit default swaps to assess whether that issue or practice poses any potential threat to financial stability or market confidence in the Union.

ESMA shall publish a report setting out its findings and any recommendations relating to the issue or practice within 3 months as from the end of any such inquiry.

CHAPTER VI
ROLE OF COMPETENT AUTHORITIES

Article 32
Competent authorities

Each Member State shall designate one or more of the competent authorities for the purpose of this Regulation.

Where a Member State designates more than one competent authority, it shall clearly determine their respective roles and it shall designate the authority to be responsible for coordinating the cooperation and the exchange of information with the Commission, ESMA and the competent authorities of the other Member States.

Member States shall inform the Commission, ESMA and the competent authorities of the other Member States of those designations.

Article 33
Powers of competent authorities

1. In order to fulfil their duties under this Regulation, the competent authorities shall have all the supervisory and investigatory powers that are necessary for the exercise of their functions. They shall exercise their powers in any of the following ways:

(a) directly;

(b) in collaboration with other authorities;

(c) by application to the competent judicial authorities.

2. In order to fulfil their duties under this Regulation, the competent authorities shall, in accordance with national law, have the power:

(a) to gain access to any document in any form and to receive or take a copy thereof;

(b) to require information from any natural or legal person and if necessary to summon and question a natural or legal person with a view to obtaining information;

(c) to carry out on-site inspections with or without prior announcement;

(d) to require existing telephone and existing data traffic records;

(e) to require the cessation of any practice that is contrary to the provisions in this Regulation;

(f) to require the freezing and/or the sequestration of assets.

3. The competent authorities shall, without prejudice to points (a) and (b) of paragraph 2, have the power in individual cases to require a natural or legal person entering into a credit default swap transaction to provide:

(a) an explanation about the purpose of the transaction and whether it is for the purposes of hedging against a risk or otherwise; and

(b) information verifying the underlying risk where the transaction is for hedging purposes.

Article 34
Professional secrecy

1. The obligation of professional secrecy shall apply to all natural or legal persons who work or who have worked for the competent authority or for any authority or natural or legal person to whom the competent authority has delegated tasks, including auditors and experts contracted by the competent authority. Confidential information covered by professional secrecy may not be disclosed to any other natural or legal person or authority except where such disclosure is necessary for legal proceedings.

2. All the information exchanged between the competent authorities under this Regulation that concerns business or operational conditions and other economic or personal affairs shall be considered confidential and shall be subject to the requirements of professional secrecy, except where the competent authority states at the time of communication that such information may be disclosed or such disclosure is necessary for legal proceedings.

Article 35
Obligation to cooperate

The competent authorities shall cooperate where necessary or expedient for the purposes of this Regulation. In particular, the competent authorities shall, without undue delay, supply each other with information which is relevant for the purposes of carrying out their duties under this Regulation.

Article 36
Cooperation with ESMA

The competent authorities shall cooperate with ESMA for the purposes of this Regulation in accordance with Regulation (EU) No 1095/2010.

The competent authorities shall provide, without delay, ESMA with all the information necessary to carry out its duties in accordance with Regulation (EU) No 1095/2010.

Article 37
Cooperation in case of request for on-site inspections or investigations

1. The competent authority of one Member State may request assistance from the competent authority of another Member State with regard to on-site inspections or investigations.

The requesting competent authority shall inform ESMA of any request referred to in the first subparagraph. In case of an investigation or an inspection with cross-border effects, ESMA may and if requested shall coordinate the investigation or inspection.

2. Where a competent authority receives a request from a competent authority of another Member State to carry out an on-site inspection or an investigation, it may:

(a) carry out the on-site inspection or investigation itself;

(b) allow the competent authority which submitted the request to participate in an on-site inspection or investigation;

(c) allow the competent authority which submitted the request to carry out the on-site inspection or investigation itself;

(d) appoint auditors or experts to carry out the on-site inspection or investigation;

(e) share specific tasks relating to supervisory activities with the other competent authorities.

3. ESMA may request the competent authorities to carry out specific investigatory tasks and on-site inspections where information is reasonably required by ESMA to enable it to exercise a power expressly conferred on it by this Regulation.

Article 38
Cooperation with third countries

1. The competent authorities shall, where possible, conclude cooperation arrangements with supervisory authorities of third countries concerning the exchange of information with supervisory authorities of third countries, the enforcement of obligations arising under this Regulation in third countries and the taking of similar measures in third countries by their supervisory authorities to complement measures taken under Chapter V. These cooperation arrangements shall ensure at least an efficient exchange of information that allows the competent authorities to carry out their duties under this Regulation.

A competent authority shall inform ESMA and the competent authorities of the other Member States where it proposes to enter into such an arrangement.

2. The cooperation arrangement shall contain provisions on the exchange of data and information necessary for the relevant competent authority to comply with the obligation set out in Article 16(2).

3. ESMA shall coordinate the development of cooperation arrangements between the competent authorities and the relevant supervisory authorities of third countries. For that purpose, ESMA shall prepare a template document for cooperation arrangements that may be used by the competent authorities.

ESMA shall also coordinate the exchange between the competent authorities of information obtained from supervisory authorities of third countries that may be relevant to the taking of measures under Chapter V.

4. The competent authorities shall conclude cooperation arrangements on the exchange of information with the supervisory authorities of third countries only where the information disclosed is subject to guarantees of professional secrecy which are at least equivalent to those set out in Article 34. Such exchange of information shall be intended for the performance of the tasks of those competent authorities.

Article 39
Transfer and retention of personal data

With regard to transfer of personal data between Member States or between Member States and a third country, Member States shall apply Directive 95/46/EC. With regard to transfer of personal data by ESMA to Member States or to a third country, ESMA shall comply with Regulation (EC) No 45/2001.

Personal data referred to in the first paragraph shall be retained for a maximum period of 5 years.

Article 40
Disclosure of information to third countries

A competent authority may transfer to a supervisory authority of a third country data and the analysis of data where the conditions laid down in Article 25 or 26 of Directive 95/46/EC are fulfilled but such transfer shall be made only on a case-by-case basis. The competent authority shall be satisfied that the transfer is necessary for the purposes of this Regulation. Any such transfer shall be made under agreement that the third country shall not transfer the data to the supervisory authority of another third country without the express written authorisation of the competent authority.

A competent authority shall disclose information which is confidential pursuant to Article 34 and which is received from a competent authority of another Member State to a supervisory authority of a third country only where the competent authority has obtained the express agreement of the competent authority which transmitted the information and, where applicable, the information is disclosed solely for the purposes for which that competent authority gave its agreement.

Article 41
Penalties

Member States shall establish rules on penalties and administrative measures, applicable to infringements of this Regulation and shall take all measures necessary to ensure that they are implemented. Those penalties and administrative measures shall be effective, proportionate and dissuasive.

In accordance with Regulation (EU) No 1095/2010, ESMA may adopt guidelines to ensure a consistent approach is taken concerning the penalties and administrative measures to be established by Members States.

Member States shall notify the Commission and ESMA of the provisions referred to in the first and second subparagraphs by 1 July 2012 and shall notify them without delay of any subsequent amendment affecting those provisions.

ESMA shall publish on its website and update regularly a list of existing penalties and administrative measures applicable in each Member State.

Member States shall provide ESMA annually with aggregate information regarding the penalties and administrative measures imposed. If a competent authority discloses to the public the fact that a penalty or an administrative measure has been imposed, it shall, contemporaneously, notify ESMA thereof.

Chapter VII
Delegated Acts

Article 42
Exercise of the delegation

1. The power to adopt delegated acts is conferred on the Commission subject to the conditions laid down in this Article.

2. The power to adopt delegated acts referred to in Article 2(2), Article 3(7), Article 4(2), Article 5(4), Article 6(4), Article 7(3), Article 17(2), Article 23(5) and Article 30 shall be conferred on the Commission for an indeterminate period of time.

3. The delegation of power referred to in Article 2(2), Article 3(7), Article 4(2), Article 5(4), Article 6(4), Article 7(3), Article 17(2), Article 23(5) and Article 30 may be revoked at any time by the European Parliament or by the Council. A decision to revoke shall put an end to the delegation of power specified in that decision. The decision to revoke shall take effect on the day following its publication in the Official Journal of the European Union or on a later date specified therein. It shall not affect the validity of any delegated acts already in force.

4. As soon as it adopts a delegated act, the Commission shall notify it simultaneously to the European Parliament and to the Council.

5. A delegated act adopted pursuant to Article 2(2), Article 3(7), Article 4(2), Article 5(4), Article 6(4), Article 7(3), Article 17(2), Article 23(5) and Article 30 shall enter into force only if no objection has been expressed by either the European Parliament or the Council within a period of 3 months of notification of that act to the European Parliament and the Council or if, before the expiry of that period, the European Parliament and the Council have both informed the Commission that they will not object. That period shall be extended by 3 months at the initiative of the European Parliament or of the Council.

Article 43
Deadline for the adoption of delegated acts

The Commission shall adopt the delegated acts under Article 2(2), Article 3(7), Article 4(2), Article 5(4), Article 6(4), Article 7(3), Article 17(2), Article 23(5) and Article 30 by 31 March 2012.

The Commission may extend the deadline referred to in the first paragraph by 6 months.

Chapter VIII
Implementing Acts

Article 44
Committee procedure

1. The Commission shall be assisted by the European Securities Committee established by Commission Decision 2001/528/EC.[16] That committee shall be a committee within the meaning of Regulation (EU) No 182/2011.

2. Where reference is made to this paragraph, Article 5 of Regulation (EU) No 182/2011 shall apply.

Chapter IX
Transitional and Final Provisions

Article 45
Review and report

By 30 June 2013, the Commission shall, in light of discussions with the competent authorities and ESMA, report to the European Parliament and the Council on:

(a) the appropriateness of the notification and disclosure thresholds under Articles 5, 6, 7 and 8;

16. OJ L 191, 13.7.2001, p. 45.

(b) the impact of the individual disclosure requirements under Article 6, in particular with regard to the efficiency and volatility of financial markets;

(c) the appropriateness of direct, centralised reporting to ESMA;

(d) the operation of the restrictions and requirements in Chapters II and III;

(e) the appropriateness of the restrictions on the uncovered sovereign credit default swaps and the appropriateness of any other restrictions or conditions on short selling or credit default swaps.

Article 46
Transitional provision

1. Existing measures falling within the scope of this Regulation, in force before 15 September 2010, may remain applicable until 1 July 2013 provided that they are notified to the Commission by 24 April 2012.

2. Credit default swap transactions resulting in an uncovered position in a sovereign credit default swap that have been concluded before 25 March 2012 or during a suspension of restrictions on uncovered sovereign credit default swaps in accordance with Article 14(2) may be held until the maturity date of the credit default swap contract.

Article 47
Staff and resources of ESMA

By 31 December 2012, ESMA shall assess its staffing and resources needs arising from the assumption of its powers and duties under this Regulation and submit a report to the European Parliament, the Council and the Commission.

Article 48
Entry into force

This Regulation shall enter into force on the day following its publication in the Official Journal of the European Union.

It shall apply from 1 November 2012.

However, Article 2(2), Article 3(7), Article 4(2), Article 7(3), Article 9(5), Article 11(3) and (4), Article 12(2), Article 13(4) and (5), Article 16(3) and (4), Article 17(2), Article 23(5), (7) and (8), and Articles 30, 42, 43 and 44 shall apply from 25 March 2012.

This Regulation shall be binding in its entirety and directly applicable in all Member States.

Done at Strasbourg, 14 March 2012.

For the European Parliament

The President

M. SCHULZ

For the Council

The President

N. WAMMEN

Commission Delegated Regulation (EU) No 826/2012

of 29 June 2012

supplementing Regulation (EU) No 236/2012 of the European Parliament and of the Council with regard to regulatory technical standards on notification and disclosure requirements with regard to net short positions, the details of the information to be provided to the European Securities and Markets Authority in relation to net short positions and the method for calculating turnover to determine exempted shares

(Text with EEA relevance)

THE EUROPEAN COMMISSION,

Having regard to the Treaty on the Functioning of the European Union,

Having regard to Regulation (EU) No 236/2012 of the European Parliament and of the Council of 14 March 2012 on short selling and certain aspects of credit default swaps,[1] and in particular Articles 9(5), 11(3) and 16(3) thereof,

After consulting the European Data Protection Supervisor,

Whereas:

(1) This Regulation aims to establish a uniform regime for the submission of notifications and information by investors to national competent authorities or by those competent authorities to the European Securities and Markets Authority (hereinafter 'ESMA'). Since the turnover calculation to determine exempted shares is also closely linked to the giving of information concerning shares where their principal trading venue is in the Union, it should also be covered by this Regulation. To ensure coherence between such provisions, which should enter into force at the same time, and to facilitate a comprehensive view and compact access to them by persons subject to those obligations it is desirable to include all the regulatory technical standards required by Regulation (EU) No 236/2012 in a single Regulation.

(2) In relation to the notifications of net short positions on shares, sovereign debt and uncovered sovereign credit default swaps and to the public disclosure of significant net short positions on shares, uniform rules regarding the details of the information including the common standard to be used in the notification should be specified to ensure consistency in the application of the notification requirements across the Union, to foster efficiency in the reporting process and to provide comparable information to the public.

(3) To ensure the proper identification of the position holders, notification should, where available, include a code that can complement the name of the position holder. Until a single, robust and publicly recognised global legal entity identifier is available, it is necessary to rely on existing codes that some position holders may have, such as the Bank Identifier Code.

(4) For the purpose of carrying out its duties under this Regulation and under Regulation (EU) No 1095/2010 of the European Parliament and of the Council of 24 November 2010 establishing a European Supervisory Authority (European Securities and Markets Authority) (2),[2] ESMA is to be provided with information by competent authorities on a

---

1. OJ L 86, 24.3.2012, p. 1.
2. OJ L 331, 15.12.2010, p. 84.

quarterly basis in relation to notification of net short positions on shares, sovereign debt and uncovered sovereign credit default swaps, as well as with additional information on net short positions upon its request.

(5) In order to efficiently use such information, in particular with respect to the objective of ensuring the orderly functioning and integrity of the financial markets and the stability of the financial system in the Union, the quarterly information should be standardised, stable over time and of sufficient granularity, in the form of some daily aggregated data, to allow ESMA to process it and to conduct research and analyses.

(6) ESMA is not in a position to determine beforehand the specific information it may require from a competent authority, as that information may only be determined on a case-by-case basis and may include input as diverse as individual or aggregated data on the net short positions or uncovered positions in credit default swaps. Nonetheless, it is important to establish the general information to be provided in this respect.

(7) For the purposes of calculating turnover, both in the Union and in trading venues outside the Union, to determine the principal trading venue of a share, each relevant competent authority needs to determine the relevant sources of information to identify and measure the trading on a specific share. There are currently neither harmonised transaction reporting requirements in the Union for shares admitted only on multilateral trading facilities nor international standards with regard to trading statistics on individual shares on trading venues, which may show relevant variations. Thus, it is necessary to allow some flexibility to competent authorities to carry out that calculation.

(8) In order to ensure consistency, the date of application of this Regulation should be the same as that of Regulation (EU) No 236/2012. However, in order to allow sufficient time for natural and legal persons to process the list of shares exempted pursuant to Article 16 of Regulation (EU) No 236/2012, the preparation of that list and its subsequent publication on the ESMA website should take place sufficiently in advance before the application date of Regulation (EU) No 236/2012. Therefore, the method set out for turnover calculation to determine the principal venue for the trading of a share should apply from the date of entry into force of this Regulation.

(9) Since Regulation (EU) No 236/2012 recognised that binding technical standards should be adopted before that Regulation can be usefully applied, and as it is essential to specify before 1 November 2012 the required non-essential elements to facilitate compliance by market participants with that Regulation and enforcement by competent authorities, it is necessary that this Regulation should enter into force on the day following that of its publication.

(10) This Regulation is based on the draft regulatory technical standards submitted by ESMA to the Commission.

(11) ESMA has conducted open public consultations on the draft regulatory technical standards on which this Regulation is based, analysed the potential related costs and benefits and requested the opinion of the Securities and Markets Stakeholder Group established in accordance with Article 37 of Regulation (EU) No 1095/2010,

HAS ADOPTED THIS REGULATION:

CHAPTER I
GENERAL PROVISIONS

Article 1
Subject matter

This Regulation lays down regulatory technical standards specifying the following:

(a) the details of the information on net short positions to be provided to the competent authorities and disclosed to the public by a natural or legal person pursuant to Article 9(5) of Regulation (EU) No 236/2012;

(b) the details of the information to be provided to the European Securities and Markets Authority (hereinafter 'ESMA') by the competent authority pursuant to Article 11(3) of Regulation (EU) No 236/2012;

(c) the method for calculation of turnover to determine the principal venue for the trading of a share pursuant to Article 16(3) of Regulation (EU) No 236/2012.

CHAPTER II
DETAILS OF THE INFORMATION ON NET SHORT POSITIONS TO BE NOTIFIED AND DISCLOSED (ARTICLE 9 OF REGULATION (EU) NO 236/2012)

Article 2
Notification of net short positions in shares, sovereign debt and uncovered sovereign credit default swaps to competent authorities

1. A notification made under Article 5(1), Article 7(1) or Article 8 of Regulation (EU) No 236/2012 shall contain the information specified in Table 1 of Annex I to this Regulation.

The notification shall be made using a form issued by the relevant competent authority which shall take the format set out in Annex II.

2. Where the competent authority has secure systems in place that allow it to fully identify the person filing the notification and the position holder, including all the information contained in fields 1 to 7 of Table 1 of Annex I, the corresponding fields in the form may be left blank in the notification format.

3. A natural or legal person who has submitted a notification referred to in paragraph 1 which contains an error shall send, on becoming aware of the error, a cancellation to the relevant competent authority.

The cancellation shall be made using a form issued by that competent authority which shall take the format set out in Annex III.

The natural or legal person concerned shall submit a new notification in accordance with paragraphs 1 and 2 if necessary.

Article 3
Public disclosure of information on net short positions in shares

Any public disclosure of a net short position in shares that reaches, or upon having reached, subsequently falls below, a relevant publication threshold in accordance with Article 6(1) of Regulation (EU) No 236/2012 shall contain the information specified in Table 2 of Annex I to this Regulation.

Chapter III
Details of the Information to be Provided To ESMA in relation to Net Short Positions
(Article 11 of Regulation (EU) No 236/2012)

Article 4
Periodic information

Pursuant to Article 11(1) of Regulation (EU) No 236/2012, competent authorities shall provide ESMA with the following information on a quarterly basis:

(a) the daily aggregated net short position on each individual share in the main national equity index as identified by the relevant competent authority;

(b) the end of quarter aggregated net short position for each individual share which is not in the index referred to in point (a);

(c) the daily aggregated net short position on each individual sovereign issuer;

(d) where applicable, daily aggregated uncovered positions on credit default swaps of a sovereign issuer.

Article 5
Information upon request

Information to be provided by a relevant competent authority on an ad hoc basis pursuant to Article 11(2) of Regulation (EU) No 236/2012 shall include all requested information specified by ESMA that has not previously been submitted by the competent authority in accordance with Article 4 of this Regulation.

Chapter IV
Method of Calculation of Turnover to Determine the Principal Trading Venue for a Share
(Article 16 of Regulation (EU) No 236/2012)

Article 6
Turnover calculation to determine the principal venue for the trading of a share

1. When calculating turnover pursuant to Article 16 of Regulation (EU) No 236/2012, a relevant competent authority shall use the best available information, which may include:

(a) publicly available information;

(b) transaction data obtained under Article 25(3) of Directive 2004/39/EC of the European Parliament and of the Council;[3]

(c) information from trading venues where the relevant share is traded;

(d) information provided by another competent authority, including a competent authority of a third country;

(e) information provided by the issuer of the relevant share;

(f) information from other third parties, including data providers.

2. In determining what constitutes the best available information, a relevant competent authority shall ensure so far as reasonably possible that:

3. OJ L 145, 30.4.2004, p. 1.

(a) it uses publicly available information in preference to other sources of information;

(b) the information covers all trading sessions during the relevant period, irrespective of whether the share traded during all of the sessions;

(c) transactions received and included in the calculations are counted only once;

(d) transactions reported through a trading venue but executed outside it are not counted.

3. The turnover of a share on a trading venue shall be deemed to be zero where the share is no longer admitted to trading on that trading venue even if the share was admitted to trading on the trading venue during the relevant calculation period.

CHAPTER V
FINAL PROVISIONS

Article 7
Entry into force

This Regulation shall enter into force on the day following that of its publication in the Official Journal of the European Union.

It shall apply from 1 November 2012, except for Article 6 which shall apply from the date referred to in the first paragraph.

This Regulation shall be binding in its entirety and directly applicable in all Member States.

Done at Brussels, 29 June 2012.

For the Commission

The President

José Manuel BARROSO

ANNEX I

TABLE 1

List of fields for notification purpose (Article 2)

Field identifier	*Description*
1. Position holder	For natural persons: the first name and the last name For legal persons: full name including legal form as provided for in the register where it is incorporated, if applicable
2. Legal person identification code	Bank Identifier Code, if available
3. Address of the position holder	Full address (e.g. street, street number, postal code, city, state/province) and country
4. Contact details of the position holder	Telephone number, fax number (if available), e-mail address
5. Reporting person	For natural persons: the first name and the last name For legal persons: full name including legal form as provided for in the register where it is incorporated, if applicable
6. Address of the reporting person	Full address (e.g. street, street number, postal code, city, state/province) and country, when different from the position holder
7. Contact details of the reporting person	Telephone number, fax number (if available), e-mail address, when different from the position holder
8. Reporting date	Date on which the notification is submitted in accordance with ISO standard 8601:2004 (yyyy-mm-dd)
9. Issuer identification	For shares: full name of the company that has shares admitted to trading on a trading venue For sovereign debt: full name of the issuer For uncovered sovereign credit default swaps: full name of the underlying sovereign issuer
10. ISIN	For shares only: ISIN of the main class of ordinary shares of the issuer. If there are no ordinary shares admitted to trading, the ISIN of the class of preference shares (or of the main class of preference shares admitted to trading if there are several classes of such shares)
11. Country code	Two letter code for the sovereign issuer country in accordance with ISO standard 3166-1
12. Position date	Date on which the position was created, changed or ceased to be held. Format in accordance with ISO standard 8601:2004 (yyyy-mm-dd)
13. Net short position size in percentage	For shares only: percentage (rounded to 2 decimal places) of the issued share capital, expressed in absolute terms, with no '+' or '–' signs

Field identifier	*Description*
14. Net short position equivalent amount	For shares: total number of equivalent shares For sovereign debt: equivalent nominal amount in euro For uncovered sovereign credit default swaps: equivalent nominal amount in euro Figures expressed in absolute terms, with no '+' or '–' signs and the currency expressed in accordance with ISO standard 4217
15. Date of the previous notification	Date on which the last position reported by the position holder in relation to the same issuer was notified. Format in accordance with ISO standard 8601:2004 (yyyy-mm-dd)
16. Cancellation date	Date on which a cancellation form is submitted to cancel an erroneous notification previously submitted. Format in accordance with ISO standard 8601:2004 (yyyy-mm-dd)
17. Comments	Free text — optional

Table 2
List of fields for public disclosure purpose (Article 3)

Field identifier	Description
1. Position holder	For natural persons: the first name and the last name For legal persons: full name including legal form as provided for in the register where it is incorporated, if applicable
2. Name of the issuer	Full name of the company that has shares admitted to trading on a trading venue
3. ISIN	ISIN of the main class of ordinary shares of the issuer. If there are no ordinary shares admitted to trading, the ISIN of the class of preference shares (or of the main class of preference shares admitted to trading if there are several classes of such shares)
4. Net short position size in percentage	Percentage (rounded to 2 decimal places) of the issued share capital
5. Position date	Date on which position was created, changed or ceased to be held in accordance with ISO standard 8601:2004 (yyyy-mm-dd)

ANNEX II

Format of Notification Form for Net Short Positions (Article 2)

<table>
<tr><td rowspan="9">POSITION HOLDER</td><td colspan="2">First name
LAST NAME
Full company name</td><td></td></tr>
<tr><td colspan="2">BIC code
(if the holder has one)</td><td></td></tr>
<tr><td colspan="2">Country</td><td></td></tr>
<tr><td colspan="2">Address</td><td></td></tr>
<tr><td rowspan="4">Contact person</td><td>First name
Last name</td><td></td></tr>
<tr><td>Phone number</td><td></td></tr>
<tr><td>Fax number</td><td></td></tr>
<tr><td>E-mail address</td><td></td></tr>
</table>

<table>
<tr><td rowspan="7">REPORTING PERSON
(if different)</td><td colspan="2">First name
LAST NAME
Full company name</td><td></td></tr>
<tr><td colspan="2">Country</td><td></td></tr>
<tr><td colspan="2">Address</td><td></td></tr>
<tr><td rowspan="4">Contact person</td><td>First name
Last name</td><td></td></tr>
<tr><td>Phone number</td><td></td></tr>
<tr><td>Fax number</td><td></td></tr>
<tr><td>E-mail address</td><td></td></tr>
</table>

Net Short Position In Shares

1. Reporting date (yyyy-mm-dd)	
2. Name of the issuer	
2.1. ISIN code	
2.2. Full name	
3. Position date (yyyy-mm-dd)	
4. Net short position after threshold crossing Equivalent nominal amount	
4.1. Number of equivalent shares	
4.2.% of issued share capital	
5. Date of previous notification (yyyy-mm-dd)	
6. Comment	

Net Short Position in Sovereign Debt

1. Reporting date (yyyy-mm-dd)	
2. Name of the issuer	
2.1. Country code	
2.2. Full name	
3. Position date (yyyy-mm-dd)	
4. Net short position after threshold crossing Equivalent nominal amount	
5. Date of previous notification (yyyy-mm-dd)	
6. Comment	

Position in Uncovered Sovereign Credit Default Swaps

1. Reporting date (yyyy-mm-dd)	
2. Name of the issuer	
2.1. Country code	
2.2. Full name	
3. Position date (yyyy-mm-dd)	
4. Net short position after threshold crossing Equivalent nominal amount	
5. Date of previous notification (yyyy-mm-dd)	
6. Comment	

ANNEX III

FORMAT OF CANCELLATION FORM FOR ERRONEOUS NOTIFICATIONS (ARTICLE 2)

<table>
<tr><td rowspan="8">POSITION HOLDER</td><td colspan="2">First name
LAST NAME
Full company name</td><td></td></tr>
<tr><td colspan="2">BIC code
(if the holder has one)</td><td></td></tr>
<tr><td colspan="2">Country</td><td></td></tr>
<tr><td colspan="2">Address</td><td></td></tr>
<tr><td rowspan="4">Contact person</td><td>First name
Last name</td><td></td></tr>
<tr><td>Phone number</td><td></td></tr>
<tr><td>Fax number</td><td></td></tr>
<tr><td>E-mail address</td><td></td></tr>
</table>

<table>
<tr><td rowspan="7">REPORTING PERSON
(if different)</td><td colspan="2">First name
LAST NAME
Full company name</td><td></td></tr>
<tr><td colspan="2">Country</td><td></td></tr>
<tr><td colspan="2">Address</td><td></td></tr>
<tr><td rowspan="4">Contact person</td><td>First name
Last name</td><td></td></tr>
<tr><td>Phone number</td><td></td></tr>
<tr><td>Fax number</td><td></td></tr>
<tr><td>E-mail address</td><td></td></tr>
</table>

Cancelled Net Short Position in Shares

1. Cancellation date (yyyy-mm-dd)	
2. Name of the issuer	
2.1. ISIN code	
2.2. Full name	
3. Position date of the notification being cancelled (yyyy-mm-dd)	
4. Net short position after threshold crossing contained at the notification being cancelled	
4.1. Number of equivalent shares	
4.2 % of issued share capital	
5. Reporting date of the notification being cancelled (yyyy-mm-dd)	
6. Comment	

Cancelled Net Short Position in Sovereign Debt

1. Cancellation date (yyyy-mm-dd)	
2. Name of the issuer	
2.1. Country code	
2.2. Full name	
3. Position date of the notification being cancelled (yyyy-mm-dd)	
4. Net short position after threshold crossing contained at the notification being cancelled	
5. Reporting date of the notification being cancelled (yyyy-mm-dd)	
6. Comment	

Cancelled Position in Uncovered Sovereign Credit Default Swaps

1. Cancellation date (yyyy-mm-dd)	
2. Name of the issuer	
2.1. Country code	
2.2. Full name	
3. Position date of the notification being cancelled (yyyy-mm-dd)	
4. Net short position after threshold crossing contained at the notification being cancelled	
5. Reporting date of the notification being cancelled (yyyy-mm-dd)	
6. Comment	

Commission Implementing Regulation (EU) No 827/2012

of 29 June 2012

laying down implementing technical standards with regard to the means for public disclosure of net position in shares, the format of the information to be provided to the European Securities and Markets Authority in relation to net short positions, the types of agreements, arrangements and measures to adequately ensure that shares or sovereign debt instruments are available for settlement and the dates and period for the determination of the principal venue for a share according to Regulation (EU) No 236/2012 of the European Parliament and of the Council on short selling and certain aspects of credit default swaps

(Text with EEA relevance)

THE EUROPEAN COMMISSION,

Having regard to the Treaty on the Functioning of the European Union,

Having regard to Regulation (EU) No 236/2012 of 14 March 2012 of the European Parliament and of the Council on short selling and certain aspect of credit default swaps[1] and in particular Articles 9(6), 11(4), 12(2), 13(5) and 16(4) thereof,

After consulting the European Data Protection Supervisor,

Whereas:

(1) This Regulation aims to determine the list of exempted shares as a necessary step for the disclosure to the public of short positions in all non-exempted shares and the conditions under which that information should be sent to the European Securities and Markets Authority (hereinafter "ESMA"). It is therefore essential that rules also be laid down regarding arrangements and measures to be adopted with respect to those non-exempted shares. To ensure coherence between those provisions on short selling which should enter into force at the same time, and to facilitate a comprehensive view and compact access to them by persons subject to those obligations, it is appropriate to include all the implementing technical standards required by Regulation (EU) No 236/2012 in a single Regulation.

(2) To ensure the uniform application of Regulation (EU) No 236/2012 in relation to the information to be provided to ESMA by competent authorities and to achieve the efficient processing of that information, it should be exchanged electronically in a secure way using a standard template.

(3) It is important to allow easy access to and re-use of the data on net short positions that is disclosed to the market through central websites operated or supervised by a competent authority. To this end, these data should be provided in a format that allows for flexible use of data and that does not offer only the possibility of static, facsimile documents. Wherever technically possible, machine-readable formats should be used to enable users to process the information in a structured and cost-efficient way.

(4) In order to ensure the publicity of this information to the market, in addition to disclosure on the central website operated or supervised by a competent authority, it should be possible to make available the details of a net short position to the public in other ways.

---

1. OJ L 86, 24.3.2012, p. 1.

(5) It is essential for users to have two basic outputs when making public individual net short positions in shares above the relevant publication threshold. These should comprise a compact list or table of the net short positions above the publication threshold that are outstanding at the time of consultation of the central website and a list or table with historical data on all individual net short positions published.

(6) When a net short position in shares falls below a relevant disclosure threshold, the details, including the actual size of the position, should be published. In order to avoid confusion for users consulting the central websites, disclosures of positions that have fallen below 0,5% of the issued share capital of the company concerned should not remain indefinitely alongside the live positions but should be available as historical data after being displayed for 24 hours.

(7) In order to provide for a consistent and clear framework which is nevertheless flexible, it is important to specify the types of agreement to borrow and other enforceable claims having similar effect and the types of arrangement with a third party that adequately ensure that shares or sovereign debt instruments will be available for settlement, and specify the criteria such agreements and arrangements must fulfil.

(8) The use of rights to subscribe for new shares in relation to a short sale may adequately ensure availability for settlement only where the arrangement is such that settlement of the short sale is ensured when it is due. Therefore, it is essential to specify rules to ensure that the shares resulting from the subscription rights are available on or before the settlement date and in a quantity at least equivalent to the number of shares intended to be sold short.

(9) In defining time limited confirmation arrangements, it is important to specify the timeframe for covering a short sale through purchases in a way compatible with different settlement cycles in different jurisdictions.

(10) In order to adequately ensure that instruments are available for settlement where a natural or legal person entering into a short sale has an arrangement with a third party under which that third party has confirmed that the instrument has been located, it is essential that there be confidence that the third party is, when established in a third country, subject to appropriate supervision and that there are appropriate arrangements for exchange of information between supervisors. Such appropriate arrangements could include being a signatory of a memorandum of understanding established by the International Organisation of Securities Commissions (IOSCO).

(11) To ensure proper implementation of the requirement to determine whether the principal trading venue of a share is located outside the Union, transitional arrangements should be put in place for determining for the first time the list of exempted shares under Article 16 of Regulation (EU) No 236/2012. In addition, although the list of exempted shares is effective for a two year period, it is necessary to provide some flexibility as there are cases where a review of that list might be necessary during the two-year period.

(12) In order to ensure consistency, the date of application of this Regulation should be the same as that of Regulation (EU) No 236/2012. However, in order to allow sufficient time for natural and legal persons to process the list of shares exempted pursuant to Regulation (EU) No 236/2012, the preparation of that list and its subsequent publication on the ESMA website should take place sufficiently in advance before the application

date of Regulation (EU) No 236/2012. Therefore, the provisions concerning the date and period for principal trading venue calculations, the date of notification to ESMA of shares with a principal trading venue outside the Union and the effectiveness of the list of exempted shares should apply from the date of entry into force of this Regulation.

(13) Since Regulation (EU) No 236/2012 recognised that binding technical standards should be adopted before that Regulation can be usefully applied, and as it is essential to specify before 1 November 2012 the required non-essential elements to facilitate compliance by market participants with that Regulation and enforcement by competent authorities, it is necessary that this Regulation enter into force on the day following its publication.

(14) This Regulation is based on the draft implementing technical standards submitted by ESMA to the Commission.

(15) ESMA has conducted open public consultations on the draft implementing technical standards on which this Regulation is based, analysed the potential related costs and benefits and requested the opinion of the Securities Markets Stakeholder Group established in accordance with Article 37 of Regulation (EU) No 1095/2010 of the European Parliament and of the Council of 24 November 2010 establishing a European Supervisory Authority (European Securities and Markets Authority),[2]

HAS ADOPTED THIS REGULATION:

CHAPTER I
GENERAL PROVISIONS

Article 1
Subject Matter

This Regulation lays down implementing technical standards specifying the following:

(a) the means by which information on net short positions may be disclosed to the public by natural or legal persons as well as the format of information to be provided to the European Securities and Markets Authority (hereinafter "ESMA") by competent authorities pursuant to Article 9(6) and Article 11(4) of Regulation (EU) No 236/2012;

(b) the types of agreements, arrangements and measures that adequately ensure that the shares are available for settlement and the types of agreements or arrangements that adequately ensure that the sovereign debt is available for settlement pursuant to Article 12(2) and 13(5) of Regulation (EU) No 236/2012;

(c) the date and period for principal trading venue calculations, notification to ESMA and the effectiveness of the relevant list pursuant to 16(4) of Regulation (EU) No 236/2012.

2. OJ L 331, 15.12.2010, p. 84.

CHAPTER II
MEANS FOR PUBLIC DISCLOSURE OF SIGNIFICANT NET SHORT POSITIONS IN SHARES
[ARTICLE 9 OF REGULATION (EU) NO 236/2012]

Article 2
Means by which information may be disclosed to the public

Information on net short positions in shares shall be disclosed to the public by posting it on a central website operated or supervised by the relevant competent authority pursuant to Article 9(4) of Regulation (EU) No 236/2012. The information shall be disclosed to the public through means which:

(a) publish it in the format specified in Annex I in such a way as to allow the public consulting the website to access one or more tables offering all the relevant information on positions per share issuer;

(b) allow users to identify and filter on whether the net short positions in a share issuer at the time of accessing the website has reached or exceeded the relevant publication threshold;

(c) provide for historical data on the published net short positions in a share issuer;

(d) include, whenever technically possible, downloadable files with the published and historical net short positions in a machine-readable format, meaning that the files are sufficiently structured for software applications to identify reliably individual statements of fact and their internal structure;

(e) show for one day, together with the information specified in point (b), the net short positions that are published because they have fallen below the publication threshold of 0,5% of the issued share capital, before removing and transferring the information to a historical data section.

CHAPTER III
FORMAT OF THE INFORMATION TO BE PROVIDED TO ESMA BY COMPETENT AUTHORITIES IN RELATION TO NET SHORT POSITIONS
[ARTICLE 11 OF REGULATION (EU) NO 236/2012]

Article 3
Format of the periodic information

1. The information to be provided on a quarterly basis to ESMA on net short positions in shares, sovereign debt and credit default swaps pursuant to Article 11(1) of Regulation (EU) No 236/2012 shall be provided by relevant competent authorities in the format specified in Annex II to this Regulation.

2. The information referred to in paragraph 1 shall be sent to ESMA electronically through a system established by ESMA that ensures that the completeness, integrity and confidentiality of the information are maintained during its transmission.

Article 4
Format of the information to be provided upon request

1. A relevant competent authority shall provide the information on net short positions in shares and sovereign debt or on uncovered positions relating to sovereign credit default

swaps pursuant to Article 11(2) of Regulation (EU) No 236/2012 in the format specified by ESMA in its request.

2. Where information requested relates to information contained in the notification received by the competent authority pursuant to Articles 5, 7 and 8 of Regulation (EU) No 236/2012, that information shall be provided in accordance with the requirements established in Article 2 of Commission Delegated Regulation (EU) No 826/2012.[3]

3. Information requested shall be sent by the competent authority in electronic format, using a system established by ESMA for exchanging information that ensures that the completeness, integrity and confidentiality of the information are maintained during its transmission.

CHAPTER IV
AGREEMENTS, ARRANGEMENTS AND MEASURES TO ADEQUATELY ENSURE AVAILABILITY FOR SETTLEMENT [ARTICLES 12 AND 13 OF REGULATION (EU) NO 236/2012]

Article 5
Agreements to borrow and other enforceable claims having similar effect

1. An agreement to borrow or other enforceable claim referred to in Article 12(1)(b) and Article 13(1)(b) of Regulation (EU) No 236/2012 shall be made by means of the following types of agreement, contract or claim which are legally binding for the duration of the short sale:

(a) futures and swaps: futures and swap contracts leading to a physical settlement of the relevant shares or sovereign debt and covering at least the number of shares or amount of sovereign debt proposed to be sold short by the natural or legal person, entered into prior to or at the same time as the short sale and specifying a delivery or expiration date that ensures settlement of the short sale can be effected when due;

(b) options: options contracts leading to a physical settlement of the relevant shares or sovereign debt and covering at least the number of shares or amount of sovereign debt proposed to be sold short by the natural or legal person, entered into prior to or at the same time as the short sale and specifying an expiration date that ensures settlement of the short sale can be effected when due;

(c) repurchase agreements: repurchase agreements covering at least the number of shares or amount of sovereign debt proposed to be sold short by the natural or legal person, entered into prior to or at the same time as the short sale and specifying a repurchase date that ensures settlement of the short sale can be effected when due;

(d) standing agreements or rolling facilities: an agreement or facility which is entered into prior to or at the same time as the short sale, of a predefined amount of specifically identified shares or sovereign debt, which for the duration of the short sale, covers at least the number of shares or amount of sovereign debt proposed to be sold short by the natural or legal person and

[3] See page 1 of this Official Journal.

specifies a delivery or execution date that ensures settlement of the short sale can be effected when due;

(e) agreements relating to subscription rights: agreements relating to subscription rights where the natural or legal person is in possession of rights to subscribe for new shares of the same issuer and of the same class and covering at least the number of shares proposed to be sold short provided that the natural or legal person is entitled to receive the shares on or before settlement of the short sale;

(f) other claims or agreements leading to delivery of the shares or sovereign debt: agreements or claims which cover at least the number of shares or amount of sovereign debt proposed to be sold short by the natural or legal person, entered into prior to or at the same time as the short sale, and specifying a delivery or an execution date that ensures settlement can be effected when due.

2. The agreement, contract or claim shall be provided in a durable medium by the counterparty to the natural or legal person as evidence of the existence of the agreement to borrow or other enforceable claim.

Article 6

Arrangements and measures to be taken in relation to short sales of a share admitted to trading on a trading venue

[Article 12(1)(c) of Regulation (EU) No 236/2012]

1. Paragraphs 2, 3 and 4 shall determine the arrangements and measures to be taken in relation to short sales of a share admitted to trading on a trading venue pursuant to Article 12(1)(c) of Regulation (EU) No 236/2012.

2. Standard locate arrangements and measures shall mean arrangements, confirmations and measures that include each of the following elements:

(a) for locate confirmations: a confirmation provided by the third party, prior to the short sale being entered into by a natural or legal person, that it considers that it can make the shares available for settlement in due time taking into account the amount of the possible sale and market conditions and which indicates the period for which the share is located;

(b) for put on hold confirmations: a confirmation by the third party, provided prior to the short sale being entered into, that it has at least put on hold the requested number of shares for that person.

3. Standard same day locate arrangements and measures shall mean arrangements, confirmations and measures that include each of the following elements:

(a) for requests for confirmation: a request for confirmation from the natural or legal person to the third party which states that the short sale will be covered by purchases during the day on which the short sale takes place;

(b) for locate confirmations: a confirmation provided by the third party prior to the short sale being entered into that it considers that it can make the shares available for settlement in due time taking into account the amount of the possible sale and market conditions, and which indicates the period for which the shares are located;

(c) for easy to borrow or purchase confirmations: a confirmation by the third party, provided prior to the short sale being entered into, that the share is easy to borrow or purchase in the relevant quantity taking into account the market conditions and other information available to that third party on the supply of the shares or, in the absence of this confirmation by the third party, that it has at least put on hold the requested number of shares for the natural or legal person;

(d) for monitoring: an undertaking by the natural or legal person to monitor the amount of the short sale not covered by purchases;

(e) for instructions in the event of failure to cover: an undertaking from the natural or legal person that in the event that executed short sales are not covered by purchases in the same day, the natural or legal person will promptly send an instruction to the third party to procure the shares to cover the short sale to ensure settlement in due time.

4. Easy to borrow or purchase arrangements and measures shall mean arrangements, confirmations and measures when the natural or legal person enters into a short sale of shares that meet the liquidity requirements established in Article 22 of Commission Regulation (EC) No 1287/2006 (1),[4] or other shares that are included in the main national equity index as identified by the relevant competent authority of each Member State and are the underlying financial instrument for a derivative contract admitted to trading on a trading venue, that include the following elements:

(a) for locate confirmations: a confirmation provided by the third party prior to the short sale being entered into that it considers that it can make the shares available for settlement in due time taking into account the amount of the possible sale and market conditions and indicating the period for which the share is located;

(b) for easy to borrow or purchase confirmations: a confirmation by the third party, provided prior to the short sale being entered into, that the share is easy to borrow or purchase in the relevant quantity taking into account the market conditions and other information available to that third party on the supply of the shares, or in the absence of this confirmation by the third party, that it has at least put on hold the requested number of shares for the natural or legal person; and

(c) for instructions to cover: when executed short sales will not be covered by purchases or borrowing, a undertaking that a prompt instruction will be sent by the natural or legal person instructing the third party to procure the shares to cover the short sale to ensure settlement in due time.

5. The arrangements, confirmations and instructions referred to in paragraphs 2, 3 and 4 shall be provided in a durable medium by the third party to the natural or legal person as evidence of the existence of the arrangements, confirmations and instructions.

---

4. OJ L 241, 2.9.2006, p. 1.

Article 7
Arrangements with third parties to be taken in relation to sovereign debt
[Article 13(1)(c) of Regulation (EU) No 236/2012]

1. Paragraphs 2 to 5 shall determine the arrangements with third parties to be taken in relation to sovereign debt pursuant to Article 13(1)(c) of Regulation (EU) No 236/2012.

2. Standard sovereign debt locate arrangement shall mean a confirmation from the third party, prior to the short sale being entered into, that it considers that it can make the sovereign debt available for settlement in due time, in the amount requested by the natural or legal person, taking into account market conditions and indicating the period for which the sovereign debt is located.

3. Time limited confirmation arrangement shall mean an arrangement where the natural or legal person states to the third party that the short sale will be covered by purchases during the same day of the short sale and the third party confirms, prior to the short sale being entered into, that it has a reasonable expectation that the sovereign debt can be purchased in the relevant quantity taking into account the market conditions and other information available to that third party on the supply of the sovereign debt instruments on the day of entering into the short sale.

4. Unconditional repo confirmation shall mean a confirmation where the third party confirms, prior to the short sale being entered into, that it has a reasonable expectation that settlement can be effected when due as a result of its participation in a structural based arrangement, organised or operated by a central bank, a debt management office or a securities settlement system that provides unconditional access to the sovereign debt in question for a size consistent with the size of the short sale.

5. Easy to purchase sovereign debt confirmation shall mean a confirmation by the third party, provided prior to the short sale being entered into, that it has a reasonable expectation that settlement can be effected when due on the basis that the sovereign debt in question is easy to borrow or purchase in the relevant quantity taking into account the market conditions and any other information available to that third party on the supply of the sovereign debt.

6. The arrangements, confirmations and instructions referred to in paragraphs 2 to 5 shall be provided in a durable medium by the third party to the natural or legal person as evidence of the existence of the arrangements, confirmations and instructions.

Article 8
Third parties with whom arrangements are made

1. Where an arrangement referred to in Articles 6 and 7 is made with a third party, the third party shall be one of the following types:

(a) in the case of an investment firm: an investment firm which meets the requirements set out in paragraph 2;

(b) in the case of a central counterparty: a central counterparty which clears the relevant shares or sovereign debt;

(c) in the case of a securities settlement system: a securities settlement system as defined under Directive 98/26/EC of the European Parliament and of the Council[5] which settles payments in respect of the relevant shares or sovereign debt;

(d) in the case of a central bank: a central bank that accepts the relevant shares or sovereign debt as collateral or conducts open market or repo transactions in relation to the relevant shares or sovereign debt;

(e) in the case of a national debt management entity: the national debt management entity of the relevant sovereign debt issuer;

(f) any other person who is subject to authorisation or registration requirements in accordance with Union law by a member of the European System of Financial Supervision and meets the requirements set out in paragraph 2;

(g) a person established in a third country who is authorised or registered, and is subject to supervision by an authority in that third country and who meets the requirements set out in paragraph 2, provided that the third country authority is a party to an appropriate cooperation arrangement concerning exchange of information with the relevant competent authority.

2. For the purposes of points (a), (f) and (g) of paragraph 1, the third party shall meet the following requirements:

(a) participate in the management of borrowing or purchasing of relevant shares or sovereign debt;

(b) provide evidence of such participation;

(c) be able, on request, to provide evidence of its ability to deliver or process the delivery of shares or sovereign debt on the dates it commits to do so to its counterparties including statistical evidence.

Chapter V

Determination of the Principal Trading Venue for the Exemption [Article 16 of Regulation (EU) No 236/2012]

Article 9

Date and period for principal trading venue calculations

1. Relevant competent authorities shall make any calculations determining the principal trading venue for a share by at least 35 calendar days before the date of application of Regulation (EU) No 236/2012 in respect of the period between 1 January 2010 and 31 December 2011.

2. Subsequent calculations shall be made before 22 February 2014 in respect of the period between 1 January 2012 and 31 December 2013, and every two years thereafter in respect of the subsequent two year period.

3. Where the share concerned was not admitted to trading during the whole two-year period on the trading venue in the Union and the third country trading venue, the period for calculation shall be the period during which the share was admitted to trading on both venues concurrently.

Article 10

Date of notification to ESMA

Relevant competent authorities shall notify ESMA of those shares for which the principal trading venue is outside the Union at least 35 calendar days before the date of

---

5. OJ L 166, 11.6.1998, p. 45.

application of the Regulation (EU) No 236/2012 and thereafter on the day before the first trading day in March every second year commencing from March 2014.

Article 11
Effectiveness of the list of exempted shares

The list of shares for which the principal trading venue is located outside the Union shall be effective as of 1 April following its publication by ESMA, except that the first list published by ESMA shall be effective from the date of entry into application of Regulation (EU) No 236/2012.

Article 12
Specific cases of review of exempted shares

1. A relevant competent authority which determines whether the principal trading venue for a share is located outside the Union following one of the circumstances set out in paragraph 2 shall ensure that:

(a) any calculations determining the principal trading venue are made as soon as possible after the relevant circumstances arise and in respect of the two year period preceding the date of calculation;

(b) it notifies ESMA of its determination as soon as possible and, where relevant, before the date of admission to trading on a trading venue in the Union.

Any revised list shall be effective from the day following that of its publication by ESMA.

2. The provisions of paragraph 1 apply when:

(a) the shares of a company are removed from trading on a permanent basis on the principal venue located outside the Union;

(b) the shares of a company are removed from trading on a permanent basis on a trading venue in the Union;

(c) the shares of a company that was previously admitted to trading in a trading venue outside the Union are admitted to trading on a trading venue in the Union.

CHAPTER VI
FINAL PROVISIONS

Article 13
Entry into force

This Regulation shall enter into force on the day following that of its publication in the Official Journal of the European Union.

It shall apply from 1 November 2012, except for Articles 9, 10 and 11 which shall apply from the date referred to in the first paragraph.

This Regulation shall be binding in its entirety and directly applicable in all Member States.

Done at Brussels, 29 June 2012.

For the Commission

The President
José Manuel BARROSO

ANNEX I

PUBLIC DISCLOSURE OF SIGNIFICANT NET SHORT POSITIONS (ARTICLE 2)

Position holder	Name of the issuer	ISIN	Net short position (%)	Date position was created, changed or ceased to be held (yyyy-mm-dd)

ANNEX II

FORMAT OF THE INFORMATION TO BE PROVIDED TO ESMA ON QUARTERLY BASIS (ARTICLE 3)

Information	*Format*
1. Issuer identification	For shares: full name of the company that has shares admitted to trading on a trading venue For sovereign debt: full name of the issuer For uncovered sovereign credit default swaps: full name of the underlying sovereign issuer
2. ISIN	For shares only: ISIN of the main class of ordinary shares of the issuer. If there are no ordinary shares admitted to trading, the ISIN of the class of preference shares (or of the main class of preference shares admitted to trading if there are several classes of such shares)
3. Country code	Two letter code for the sovereign issuer country in accordance with ISO standard 3166-1
4. Position date	Date for which the position is reported. Format in accordance with ISO standard 8601:2004 (yyyy-mm-dd)
5. Daily aggregated net short position on main national index shares	Percentage figure rounded to 2 decimal places
6. End of quarter aggregated net short position on other shares	Percentage figure rounded to 2 decimal places
7. Daily aggregated net short positions in sovereign debt	Figure of equivalent nominal amount in Euros
8. Daily aggregated uncovered positions on credit default swaps of a sovereign issuer	Figure of equivalent nominal amount in Euros

Commission Delegated Regulation (EU) No 918/2012

of 5 July 2012

supplementing Regulation (EU) No 236/2012 of the European Parliament and of the Council on short selling and certain aspects of credit default swaps with regard to definitions, the calculation of net short positions, covered sovereign credit default swaps, notification thresholds, liquidity thresholds for suspending restrictions, significant falls in the value of financial instruments and adverse events

(Text with EEA relevance)

THE EUROPEAN COMMISSION,

Having regard to the Treaty on the Functioning of the European Union,

Having regard to Regulation (EU) No 236/2012 of the European Parliament and of the Council of 14 March 2012 on short selling and certain aspects of credit default swaps,[1] and in particular Article 2(2), Article 3(7), Article 4(2), Article 7(3), Article 13(4), Article 23(7) and Article 30 thereof,

Whereas:

(1) Regulation (EU) No 236/2012 imposes certain measures in relation to short selling and credit default swaps. Article 42 of Regulation (EU) No 236/2012 empowers the Commission to adopt delegated acts to supplement the provisions of that Regulation in accordance with Article 290 of the Treaty on the Functioning of the European Union. This delegated act supplements and amends certain non-essential elements.

(2) The provisions in this Regulation are closely linked, since the notification and publication thresholds and the determination of uncovered credit default swaps depend on the definitions and the methods of calculation of short positions while the provisions on significant falls in the value of financial instruments and falls in the liquidity of sovereign debt markets and the determination of adverse events are inextricably linked. To ensure coherence between those provisions on short selling which should enter into force at the same time, it is appropriate to include all the provisions required by Regulation (EU) No 236/2012 in a single Regulation.

(3) Regulation (EU) No 236/2012 contains certain definitions. For further clarity and legal certainty, it is appropriate to provide supplementary provisions in relation to the definitions in Article 2(1), in particular when a natural or legal person is considered to own a financial instrument for the purposes of the definition of a short sale and further specification of when a natural or legal person 'holds' a share or debt instrument for the purposes of Regulation (EU) No 236/2012 are required. The specifications are chosen to ensure that Regulation (EU) No 236/2012 has the intended effect in a consistent manner despite the divergent approach of the laws of Member States. The concepts of ownership and holding in Member States concerning securities are currently not harmonised but the provisions of Regulation (EU) No 236/2012 are only intended to apply to short selling and to be without prejudice to any future legal developments such as harmonising legislation.

(4) Regulation (EU) No 236/2012 imposes restrictions and obligations, such as notification and publication requirements, on natural or legal persons holding or

1. OJ L 86, 24.3.2012, p. 1.

entering into net short positions in shares and sovereign debt. Long and short positions in shares and sovereign debt can be held and valued in different ways. In order to ensure a consistent approach and give effect to the intention of the measures on short positions in shares and sovereign debt it is therefore necessary to further specify how net short positions should be calculated. Short sales may occur through single instruments or through baskets of sovereign debt and so it is necessary to specify how short sales through baskets are included in these calculations. In order to ensure a robust approach to the calculation of net short positions, it is necessary to apply a more restrictive approach to specifying long positions than short positions in shares. Because the value of some financial instruments depend on variations in the price of underlying instruments, it is necessary to specify how to account for this. The delta- adjusted methodology is specified since it is a commonly accepted practice.

(5) Net short positions are calculated by reference to the long and short positions held by a natural or legal person. However long and short positions may be held by different entities within a group or in different funds managed by a fund manager. Large net short positions may be concealed by distributing them amongst entities within a group or amongst different funds. To reduce avoidance and ensure that the notifications and reporting of short positions provide an accurate and representative picture, more detailed provisions specifying how the calculation of net short positions should be performed for entities within a group and for fund managers are required. To give effect to these provisions it is necessary to define the meaning of investment strategy in order to clarify which entities' short positions in a group and which funds' short positions should be aggregated. It is also necessary to define management activities to clarify which funds' short positions should be aggregated. In order to ensure that the notifications are made, it is necessary to specify which entities within a group or in different funds are required to perform the calculations and make the notifications.

(6) Regulation (EU) No 236/2012 imposes restrictions on entering into uncovered sovereign credit default swap transactions but permits sovereign covered credit default swaps entered into for legitimate hedging purposes. A wide variety of assets and liabilities may be hedged using sovereign credit default swaps but distinguishing between legitimate hedging and speculation may be difficult in many cases. Detailed and additional specification of the cases in which a sovereign credit default swap can be considered to be covered is therefore required. Where a quantitative measure of correlation needs to be specified on a consistent basis, a simple, widely accepted and understood measure such as the Pearson's correlation coefficient should be used, calculated as the covariance of two variables divided by the product of their standard deviations. Matching assets and liabilities to create a perfect hedge is in practice difficult due to the diverse characteristics of different assets and liabilities as well as volatility in their values. Regulation (EU) No 236/2012 requires a proportionate approach to measures and when defining an uncovered credit default swap, it is therefore necessary to specify how a proportionate approach should be applied to assets and liabilities hedged by a covered credit default swap. Whereas Regulation (EU) No 236/2012 does not prescribe a specific degree of correlation necessary for a covered position in a sovereign credit default swap, it is necessary to specify that correlation should be meaningful.

(7) Regulation (EU) No 236/2012 requires that a natural or legal person holding a net short position in sovereign debt in excess of a threshold should notify the relevant competent authority of these positions. An appropriate specification of this threshold is therefore required. Minimal values that would not have any significant impact on the relevant sovereign debt market should not require notification and the threshold should take into account, inter alia, the liquidity of each individual bond market and the stock of outstanding sovereign debt as well as the objectives of this measure.

(8) The data required for the calculation of notification thresholds for net short positions relating to issued sovereign debt will not be available at the date of entry into force of this Regulation. Therefore the two criteria used to set the initial notification thresholds at the date of publication should be firstly the total amount of outstanding issued sovereign debt of the sovereign issuer and secondly the existence of a liquid futures market for that sovereign debt. Revised thresholds should be adopted when the relevant data on all the criteria is available.

(9) Where the liquidity in a sovereign debt market falls below a certain threshold, the restrictions on investors entering into uncovered short sales of sovereign debt may be lifted temporarily for the purpose of stimulating liquidity in that market. Where there is a significant fall in the value of a financial instrument on a trading venue, competent authorities may prohibit, restrict short selling or otherwise limit transactions in that instrument. There are a wide variety of instruments and it is necessary to specify the threshold for each of the different classes of financial instruments taking into account, differences such as those between the instruments and the different volatilities of their respective markets.

(10) No threshold for a significant fall in the value of the unit price of a listed UCITS, except for exchange-traded funds that are UCITS, is specified in this Regulation as although the price may vary freely in the trading venue, it is subject to a rule in Directive 2009/65/EC of the European Parliament and of the Council of 13 July 2009 on the coordination of laws, regulations and administrative provisions relating to undertakings for collective investment in transferable securities (UCITS) (1)[2] which keeps the prices close to the net asset value of the UCITS. No threshold for a significant fall in the value of derivatives is specified other than those specified in this Regulation.

(11) This Regulation clarifies the intervention powers of both the relevant competent authorities and the European Securities Markets Authority (ESMA) established and exercising its powers in accordance with Regulation (EU) No 1095/2010 of the European Parliament and of the Council[3] as regards adverse events or developments. A list of these events is required to ensure a consistent approach while permitting appropriate action to be taken where unforeseen adverse events or developments occur.

(12) For reasons of legal certainty it is necessary that this Regulation enter into force on the same day as Commission Delegated Regulation (EU) No 919/2012,[4]

HAS ADOPTED THIS REGULATION:

---

2. OJ L 302, 17.11.2009, p. 32.

3. OJ L 331, 15.12.2010, p. 84.

4. See page 16 of this Official Journal.

CHAPTER I
GENERAL

Article 1
Subject matter

This Regulation lays down detailed rules supplementing the following Articles of Regulation (EU) No 236/2012 with regard to:

— Article 2(2) of Regulation (EU) No 236/2012 further specifying the definitions of ownership and short sale,

— Article 3(7) of Regulation (EU) No 236/2012 further specifying cases of and the method for calculating a net short position and the definition of holding,

— Article 4(2) of Regulation (EU) No 236/2012 further specifying uncovered positions in sovereign credit default swaps and the calculation methods for groups and fund management activities,

— Article 7(3) of Regulation (EU) No 236/2012 further specifying the notification threshold for significant short positions in sovereign debt,

— Article 13(4) of Regulation (EU) No 236/2012 further specifying the liquidity threshold for suspending restrictions on short sales of sovereign debt,

— Article 23(7) of Regulation (EU) No 236/2012 further specifying the meaning of significant falls in value of financial instruments other than liquid shares,

— Article 30 of Regulation (EU) No 236/2012 further specifying criteria and factors to be taken into account in determining in which cases the adverse events or developments referred to in Articles 18 to 21 and Article 27 and the threats referred to in point (a) of Article 28(2) of Regulation (EU) No 236/2012 arise.

Article 2
Definitions

For the purposes of this Regulation, the following definitions shall apply:

(a) 'group' means those legal entities which are controlled undertakings within the meaning of Article 2(1)(f) of Directive 2004/109/EC of the European Parliament and of the Council[5] and the single natural or legal person that controls such undertaking;

(b) 'supra-national issuer' means an issuer within the meaning of Article 2(1)(d)(i), (iv), (v) and (vi) of Regulation (EU) No 236/2012.

CHAPTER II
SUPPLEMENTARY SPECIFICATION OF DEFINITIONS PURSUANT TO ARTICLE 2(2) AND ARTICLE 3(7)(A)

Article 3
Specification of the term 'ownership' and defining a short sale

1. For the purposes of defining a short sale, the determination, where applicable, of whether a natural or legal person is considered to own a financial instrument when there

5. OJ L 390, 31.12.2004, p. 38.

are legal or beneficial ownerships thereof shall be made in accordance with the law applicable to the relevant short sale of that share or debt instrument. Where natural or legal persons are the beneficial owners of a share or debt instrument, that share or debt instrument shall be deemed to be owned by the ultimate beneficial owner, including where the share or debt instrument is held by a nominee. For the purposes of this Article, the beneficial owner shall be the investor who assumes the economic risk of acquiring a financial instrument.

2. For the purposes of points (i), (ii) and (iii) of Article 2(1)(b) of Regulation (EU) No 236/2012, and a 'short sale' within the meaning of Article 2(1)(b) of Regulation (EU) No 236/2012, does not include:

(a) the sale of financial instruments that have been transferred under a securities lending or repo agreement, provided that the securities will either be returned or the transferor recalls the securities so that settlement can be effected when it is due;

(b) the sale of a financial instrument by a natural or legal person who has purchased the financial instrument prior to the sale but has not taken delivery of that financial instrument at the time of the sale provided that the financial instrument will be delivered at such time that the settlement may be effected when due;

(c) the sale of a financial instrument by a natural or legal person who has exercised an option or a similar claim on that financial instrument, provided that the financial instrument will be delivered at such a time that the settlement may be effected when due.

Article 4
Holding

A natural or legal person is considered to hold a share or debt instrument for the purposes of Article 3(2)(a) of Regulation (EU) No 236/2012 in the following circumstances:

(a) the natural or legal person owns the share or debt instrument in accordance with Article 3(1);

(b) an enforceable claim to be transferred ownership of the share or debt instrument to the natural or legal person in accordance with the law applicable to the relevant sale.

CHAPTER III
NET SHORT POSITIONS PURSUANT TO ARTICLE 3(7)(B)

Article 5
Net short positions in shares — long positions

1. The holding of a share through a long position in a basket of shares shall, in relation to that share, also be taken into account to the extent that that share is represented in that basket.

2. Any exposure through a financial instrument other than the share which confers a financial advantage in the event of an increase in the price of the share as set out in

Article 3(2)(b) of Regulation (EU) No 236/2012 means any exposure to share capital through any one or more of the instruments listed in Annex I, Part 1.

The exposure referred to in the first subparagraph depends on the value of the share in respect of which a net short position has to be calculated, and which confers a financial advantage in the event of an increase in the price or value of the share.

Article 6
Net short positions in shares — short positions

1. A short sale of a share through the short sale of a basket of shares shall, in relation to that share, also be taken into account to the extent that that share is represented in the basket.

2. For the purposes of Article 3(1)(a) and 3(3) of Regulation (EU) No 236/2012 where a position in a financial instrument, including those listed in Annex I, Part 1, confers a financial advantage in the event of a decrease in the price or value of the share, this position shall be taken into account in calculating the short position.

Article 7
Net short positions in shares — general

The following criteria shall be taken into account for the purposes of net short positions referred to in Articles 5 and 6:

(a) it is irrelevant whether a cash settlement or physical delivery of underlying assets has been agreed;

(b) short positions on financial instruments that give rise to a claim to unissued shares, and subscription rights, convertible bonds and other comparable instruments shall not be considered as short positions when calculating a net short position.

Article 8
Net short position in sovereign debt — long positions

1. For the purposes of this Article and Annex II, pricing shall mean the yield, or where there is no yield for one of the relevant assets or liabilities or the yield is an inappropriate comparator between the relevant assets or liabilities, it shall mean the price. The holding of a sovereign debt instrument through a long position in a basket of sovereign debt instruments of different sovereign issuers shall in relation to that sovereign debt, also be taken into account to the extent that that sovereign debt is represented in that basket.

2. For the purpose of Article 3(2)(b) of Regulation (EU) No 236/2012, any exposure through an instrument other than the sovereign debt which confers a financial advantage in the event of an increase in the price of the sovereign debt means any exposure through any one or more of the instruments listed in Annex I, Part 2 provided always that their value depends on the value of the sovereign debt in respect of which a net short position has to be calculated, and which confers a financial advantage in the event of an increase in the price or value of the sovereign debt.

3. Provided always that they are highly correlated in accordance with Article 3(5) of Regulation (EU) No 236/2012 and with paragraphs 4 and 5, all net holdings of

sovereign debt of a sovereign issuer which is highly correlated with the pricing of the sovereign debt in any short position shall be included in the calculation of the long position. Sovereign debt instruments from issuers located outside the Union shall not be included.

4. For assets with a liquid market price, a high correlation between the pricing of a debt instrument of another sovereign issuer and the pricing of the debt of the given sovereign issuer shall be measured on a historical basis using daily accumulated weighted data for the 12-month period preceding the position in the sovereign debt. For assets for which there is no liquid market or where the price history is less than 12 months, an appropriate proxy of similar duration shall be used.

5. For the purposes of Article 3(5) of Regulation (EU) No 236/2012, a debt instrument and a issued sovereign debt shall be considered to be highly correlated where the Pearson's correlation coefficient is at least 80% between the pricing of the debt instrument of another sovereign issuer and the pricing of the given sovereign debt for the relevant period.

6. If the position subsequently ceases to be highly correlated based on a rolling 12-month time-frame, then the sovereign debt of the previously highly correlated sovereign issuer shall no longer be taken into account when calculating a long position. However, positions shall not be deemed to cease to be highly correlated where there is a temporary fall in the level of correlation of the sovereign debt for no more than three months below the level set out in paragraph 4, provided that the correlation coefficient is at least of 60% throughout this three-month period.

7. In calculating net short positions, it shall be irrelevant whether a cash settlement or physical delivery of underlying assets has been agreed.

Article 9
Net short positions in sovereign debt — short positions

1. A short sale of sovereign debt through the sale of a basket of sovereign debt shall in relation to that sovereign debt also be taken into account to the extent that that sovereign debt is represented in the basket.

2. For the purposes of Article 3(1)(a) and 3(3) of Regulation (EU) No 236/2012 where a position in an instrument, including those listed in Article 8(2), confers a financial advantage in the event of a decrease in the price or value of the sovereign debt, this position shall be taken into account in calculating the short position.

3. Any sovereign credit default swap referenced to a sovereign issuer shall be included in the calculation of net short positions in that sovereign debt. Sales of sovereign credit default swaps shall be considered to be long positions and purchases of sovereign credit default swaps shall be considered to be short positions.

4. If a sovereign credit default swap position is hedging a risk other than the referenced sovereign debt, the value of the hedged risk cannot be treated as a long position for the purposes of calculating whether a natural or legal person has a net short position in the issued sovereign debt of a sovereign issuer.

5. In calculating net short positions, it is irrelevant whether cash settlement or physical delivery of underlying assets has been agreed.

Article 10
Method of calculation of net short positions in relation to shares

1. For the purposes of calculating the net short position in shares pursuant to Article 3(4) of Regulation (EU) No 236/2012, the delta-adjusted model for shares set out in Annex II shall be used.

2. Any calculations by a natural or legal person of a long and short position in relation to the same shares shall use the same methods.

3. The calculation of net short positions shall take into account transactions in all financial instruments, whether on or outside a trading venue, that confer a financial advantage in the event of a change in price or value of the share.

Article 11
Calculation of net short positions for sovereign debt

1. For the purposes of Article 3(5) of Regulation (EU) No 236/2012, net short positions in sovereign debt shall be calculated by taking into account transactions in all financial instruments that confer a financial advantage in the event of a change in the price or yield of the sovereign debt. The delta- adjusted model for sovereign debt set out in Annex II shall be used.

2. In accordance with Article 3(6) of Regulation (EU) No 236/2012 positions shall be calculated for every sovereign issuer in which a natural or legal person holds a short position.

Chapter IV
Net Short Positions in Funds or Groups Pursuant to Article 3(7)(C)

Article 12
Method of calculating positions for management activities related to several funds or managed portfolios

1. The calculation of the net short position in a particular issuer shall be made in accordance with Article 3(7)(a) and (b) of Regulation (EU) No 236/2012 for each individual fund, irrespective of its legal form and for each managed portfolio.

2. For the purposes of Article 12 and Article 13, the following definitions shall apply:

(a) ‘investment strategy’ means a strategy that is pursued by a management entity, regarding a particular issuer, that aims to have either a net short or a net long position taken through transactions in various financial instruments issued by or that relate to that issuer;

(b) ‘management activities’ means management of funds irrespective of their legal form and portfolio management in accordance with mandates given by clients on a discretionary client-by-client basis where such portfolios include one or more financial instruments;

(c) ‘management entity’ means a legal person or entity, including a division, unit or department that manages, on a discretionary basis, funds or portfolios pursuant to a mandate.

3. The management entity shall aggregate the net short positions of the funds and portfolios under its management for which the same investment strategy is pursued in relation to a particular issuer.

4. When applying the method described above, the management entity shall:

(a) take into account the positions of the funds and portfolios the management of which has been delegated by a third party;

(b) exclude the positions of the funds and portfolios the management of which it has delegated to a third party.

The management entity shall report, and disclose where required, the net short position that results from paragraphs 3 and 4 when it reaches or exceeds a relevant notification or disclosure threshold in accordance with Articles 5 to 11 of Regulation (EU) No 236/2012.

5. Where a single legal entity is performing management activities together with other non-management activities, it shall apply the method described set out in paragraphs 1 to 3 to its management activities only and report, and disclose the resulting net short positions.

6. For its non-management activities that give rise to the holding of short positions by the entity for its own account, that single legal entity shall perform the calculation of the net short position in a particular issuer in accordance with Article 3(7)(a) and (b) of Regulation (EU) No 236/2012 and report, and disclose the resulting net short positions.

Article 13
Method of calculating positions for legal entities within a group that have long or short positions in relation to a particular issuer

1. The calculation of the net short position shall be made in accordance with Article 3(7)(a) and (b) of Regulation (EU) No 236/2012 for each legal entity constituting the group. The relevant legal entity, or on its behalf, the group it belongs to, shall report, and disclose, the net short position in a particular issuer when it reaches or exceeds a notification or disclosure threshold. Where one or more of the legal entities constituting the group are management entities, they shall apply the method described in Article 12(1) to 12(4) for fund and portfolio management activities.

2. The net short and long positions of all the legal entities constituting the group shall be aggregated and netted, with the exception of the positions of the management entities that perform management activities. The group shall report, and disclose where relevant, the net short position in a particular issuer when it reaches or exceeds a relevant notification or disclosure threshold.

3. When a net short position reaches or crosses the notification threshold in accordance with Article 5 or disclosure threshold in accordance with Article 6 of Regulation (EU) No 236/2012 then a legal entity within the group shall report, and disclose in accordance with Articles 5 to 11 of Regulation (EU) No 236/2012 the net short position in a particular issuer calculated according to paragraph 1 provided that no net short position at group level calculated according to paragraph 2 reaches or crosses a notification or disclosure threshold. A legal entity designated for this purpose shall report, and disclose where relevant, the net short position at group level in a particular issuer calculated according to paragraph 2 when:

(i) no notification or disclosure threshold is reached or crossed by any legal entity within the group;

(ii) a notification or disclosure threshold is reached or crossed simultaneously both by the group itself and any legal entity within that group.

CHAPTER V
COVERED SOVEREIGN CREDIT DEFAULT SWAPS PURSUANT TO ARTICLE 4(2)

Article 14
Cases which are not uncovered sovereign credit default swap positions

1. In the following cases a sovereign credit default swap position shall not be considered an uncovered position in accordance with Article 4(1) of Regulation (EU) No 236/2012.

(a) In respect of hedges for the purpose of Article 4(1)(b) of Regulation (EU) No 236/2012, the sovereign credit default swap shall not be considered an uncovered position in accordance with Article 4(1) of Regulation (EU) No 236/2012 and shall serve to hedge against the risk of decline in the value of assets or liabilities correlated with the risk of the decline of the value of the sovereign debt which the credit default swap references and where those assets or liabilities refer to public or private sector entities in the same Member State.

(b) A sovereign credit default swap position, in which assets or liabilities refer to public or private sector entities in the same Member State as the reference sovereign for the credit default swap, shall not be considered an uncovered position in accordance with Article 4(1) of Regulation (EU) No 236/2012 where it:

   (i) references a Member State, including any ministry, agency or special purpose vehicle of the Member State, or in the case of a Member State that is a federal state, one of the members making up the federation;

   (ii) is used to hedge any assets or liabilities meeting the correlation test set out in Article 18.

(c) A sovereign credit default swap position, where the assets or liabilities refer to a sovereign issuer in which the reference sovereign for the credit default swap is a guarantor or shareholder, shall not be considered an uncovered position in accordance with Article 4(1) of Regulation (EU) No 236/2012 where it:

   (i) references a Member State;

   (ii) is used to hedge any assets or liabilities meeting the correlation test set out in Article 18.

2. For the purposes of point (a) of paragraph 1, a correlation shall exist between the value of the asset or liability being hedged and the value of the referenced sovereign debt as set out in Article 18.

Article 15
Cases which are not uncovered sovereign credit default swap positions where the obligor is established or the asset or liability is located in more than one Member State

1. Where the obligor of, or counterparty to, an asset or liability is established in more than one Member State a sovereign credit default swap position shall not be considered an uncovered position in the following cases, in accordance with Article 4(1) of

Regulation (EU) No 236/2012, and provided that the correlation test in Article 18 of this Regulation is met in each case:

(a) where there is a parent company in one Member State and a subsidiary in another Member State and a loan has been made to the subsidiary. Where there is either explicit or implicit credit support to the subsidiary by the parent, it shall be permissible to purchase sovereign credit default swaps in the Member State of the parent rather than the subsidiary;

(b) where there is a parent holding company which own or controls a subsidiary operating company in a different Member States. If the parent company is the issuer of the bond but the assets and revenues that are hedged are owned by the subsidiary, it shall be permissible to buy sovereign credit default swaps referenced to the Member State of the subsidiary;

(c) to hedge an exposure to a company in one Member State which has invested in the sovereign debt of a second Member State to the extent that that company would be significantly impacted in the event of a significant fall in the value of the sovereign debt of the second Member State, provided that the company is established in both Member States. Where the correlation between this risk and the debt of the second Member State is greater than the correlation between this risk and the debt of the Member State in which the company is established it shall be permissible to buy sovereign credit default swaps referenced to the second Member State.

2. A sovereign credit default swap position shall not be considered an uncovered position in the following cases, in accordance with Article 4(1) of Regulation (EU) No 236/2012, and provided that the correlation test in Article 18 of this Regulation is met in each case:

(a) where the obligor of, or counterparty to, an asset or liability being hedged is a company which has operations across the Union or where the exposure being hedged relates to the Union or the Member States which have the euro as their currency, it shall be permissible to hedge it with an appropriate European or euro area index of sovereign bond credit default swaps;

(b) where the counterparty to an asset or liability being hedged is a supra-national issuer, it shall be permissible to hedge the counterparty risk with an appropriately chosen basket of sovereign credit default swaps referencing that entity's guarantors or shareholders.

Article 16

Justification of uncovered sovereign credit default swap positions

Any natural or legal person entering into a sovereign credit default swap position shall, on the request of the competent authority:

(a) justify to that competent authority which of the cases set out in Article 15 were fulfilled at the time the position was entered into;

(b) demonstrate to that competent authority compliance with the correlation test in Article 18 and the proportionality requirements in Article 19 in respect of that sovereign credit default swap position at any time that they hold that sovereign credit default swap.

Article 17
Hedged assets and liabilities

The following are cases where assets and liabilities may be hedged through a sovereign credit default swap position, provided the conditions set out in Articles 15 and 18 and in Regulation (EU) No 236/2012 are met:

(a) a long position in the sovereign debt of the relevant issuer;

(b) any position or portfolio used in the context of hedging exposures to the sovereign issuer referenced in the credit default swaps;

(c) any assets or liabilities which refer to public sector entities in the Member State whose sovereign debt is referenced in the credit default swap. This includes exposures to central, regional and local administration, public sector entities or any exposure guaranteed by the referred entity and may include financial contracts, a portfolio of assets or financial obligations, interest rate or currency swap transactions where the sovereign credit default swap is used as a counterparty risk management tool for hedging exposure on financial or foreign trade contracts;

(d) exposures to private sector entities established in the Member State which is referenced in the sovereign credit default swap. The exposures in question include but are not limited to loans, counterparty credit risk (including potential exposure when regulatory capital is required for such exposure), receivables and guarantees. The assets and liabilities include but are not limited to financial contracts, a portfolio of assets or financial obligations, interest rate or currency swap transactions where the sovereign credit default swap is used as a counterparty risk management tool for hedging exposure on financial contracts or trade finance exposures;

(e) any indirect exposures to any of the above entities obtained through exposure to indices, funds or special purpose vehicles.

Article 18
Correlation tests

1. The correlation test referred to in this Chapter shall be met in either of the following cases:

(a) the quantitative correlation test shall be met by showing a Pearson's correlation coefficient of at least 70% between the price of the assets or liabilities and the price of the sovereign debt calculated on a historical basis using data for at least a period of 12 months of trading days immediately preceding the date when the sovereign credit default swap position is taken out;

(b) the qualitative correlation shall be met by showing meaningful correlation, which means a correlation that is based on appropriate data and is not evidence of a merely temporary dependence. The correlation shall be calculated on a historical basis using data for the 12 months of trading days before the sovereign credit default swap position is taken out, weighted to the most recent time. A different time-frame shall be used if it is demonstrated that the conditions prevailing in that period were similar to those at the time that the sovereign credit default swap position is to be taken out or which would occur in the period of the exposure being hedged. For assets for which there is not a liquid market price or where there is not a sufficiently long price history, an appropriate proxy shall be used.

2. The correlation test in paragraph 1 shall be deemed to have been met if it can be demonstrated that:

(a) the exposure being hedged relates to an enterprise which is owned by the sovereign issuer or where the sovereign issuer owns a majority of its voting share capital or whose debts are guaranteed by the sovereign issuer;

(b) the exposure being hedged relates to a regional, local or municipal government of the Member State;

(c) the exposure being hedged relates to an enterprise whose cash flows are significantly dependent on contracts from a sovereign issuer or a project which is funded or significantly funded or underwritten by a sovereign issuer, such as an infrastructure project.

3. The relevant party shall justify that the correlation test was met at the time that the sovereign credit default swap position was entered into upon request by the relevant competent authority.

Article 19
Proportionality

1. In determining whether the size of the sovereign credit default swap position is proportionate to the size of the exposures hedged, where a perfect hedge is not possible, an exact match is not required and limited over-provision shall be permitted in accordance with paragraph 2. The relevant party shall justify upon request to the competent authority why an exact match was not possible.

2. Where justified by the nature of the assets and liabilities being hedged and their relationship to the value of the obligations of the sovereign which are within the scope of the credit default swap, a greater value of sovereign credit default swap shall be held to hedge a given value of exposures. However, this shall only be permitted where it is demonstrated that a larger value of sovereign credit default swap is necessary to match a relevant measure of risk associated with the reference portfolio, taking into account as the following factors:

(a) the size of the nominal position;

(b) the sensitivity ratio of the exposures to the obligations of the sovereign which are within the scope of the credit default swap;

(c) whether the hedging strategy involved is dynamic or static.

3. It is the responsibility of the position holder to ensure that its sovereign credit default swap position remains proportionate at all times and that the duration of the sovereign credit default swap position is aligned as closely as practicable given prevailing market conventions and liquidity with the duration of the exposures being hedged or the period during which the person intends to hold the exposure. If the exposures being hedged by the credit default swap position are liquidated or redeemed, they must either be replaced by equivalent exposures or the credit default swap position must be reduced or otherwise disposed of.

4. Provided that a sovereign credit default swap position was covered at the time it was entered into, it shall not be treated as becoming uncovered where the sole reason for the position becoming uncovered is a fluctuation in the market value of the hedged exposures or the value of the sovereign credit default swap.

5. In all circumstances, where parties accept a sovereign credit default swap position as a consequence of their obligations as members of a central counterparty which clears sovereign credit default swap transactions and as a result of the operation of the rules of that central counterparty, such a position shall be treated as involuntary and not as a position that the party has entered into and so shall not be considered uncovered pursuant to Article 4(1) of Regulation (EU) No 236/2012.

Article 20
Method of calculation of an uncovered sovereign credit default swap position

1. The calculation of a natural or legal person's sovereign credit default swap position shall be its net position.

2. When calculating the value of the eligible risks hedged or to be hedged by a sovereign credit default swap position a distinction shall be made between static and dynamic hedging strategies. For static hedging, such as direct exposures to sovereign or public sector bodies in the sovereign, the metric used shall be the jump to default measure of the loss if the entity to which the position holder is exposed defaults. The resulting value shall then be compared against the net notional value of the credit default swap position.

3. When calculating the value of market value adjusted risks for which a dynamic hedging strategy is required, the calculations must be undertaken on a risk-adjusted rather than notional basis, taking into account the extent to which an exposure might increase or decrease during its duration and the relative volatilities of the assets and liabilities being hedged and of the referenced sovereign debt. A beta adjustment shall be used if the asset or liability for which the credit default swap position is being used as a hedge is different from the reference asset of the credit default swap.

4. Indirect exposures to risks, such as through indices, funds, special purpose vehicles, and to credit default swap positions shall be taken into account in proportion to the extent the reference asset, liability or credit default swap is represented in the index, fund or other mechanism.

5. The value of the eligible portfolio of assets or liabilities to be hedged shall be deducted from the value of the net credit default swaps position held. If the resulting number is positive the position shall be considered to be an uncovered credit default swaps position in accordance with Article 4(1) of Regulation (EU) No 236/2012.

Chapter VI
Notification Thresholds for Net Short Positions in Sovereign Debt Pursuant to Article 7(3)

Article 21
Notification thresholds for net short positions relating to the issued sovereign debt

1. The relevant measure for the threshold that triggers notification to the relevant competent authority of net short positions in the issued sovereign debt of a sovereign

issuer shall be a percentage of the total amount of outstanding issued sovereign debt for each sovereign issuer.

2. The reporting threshold shall be a monetary amount. This monetary amount shall be fixed by applying the percentage threshold to the outstanding sovereign debt of the sovereign issuer and rounding up to the nearest million euro.

3. The monetary amount implied by the percentage threshold shall be revised and updated quarterly in order to reflect changes in the total amount of outstanding issued sovereign debt of each sovereign issuer.

4. The monetary amount implied by the percentage threshold and the total amount of outstanding issued sovereign debt shall be calculated in accordance with the method of calculation for net short positions in sovereign debt.

5. The initial amounts and additional incremental levels for sovereign issuers shall be determined on the basis of the following factors:

(a) the thresholds shall not require notifications of net short positions of minimal value in any sovereign issuers;

(b) the total amount of outstanding sovereign debt for a sovereign issuer and average size of positions held by market participants relating to the sovereign debt of that sovereign issuer;

(c) the liquidity of the sovereign debt market of each sovereign issuer, including, where appropriate, the liquidity of the futures market for that sovereign debt.

6. Taking into account the factors in paragraph 5, the relevant notification thresholds for the initial amount to be considered for each sovereign issuer is a percentage that equals 0,1% or 0,5% of the total amount of outstanding issued sovereign debt. The relevant percentage to be applied for each issuer shall be determined in application of the criteria described in paragraph 5, so that each sovereign issuer is assigned one of the two percentage thresholds used to calculate the monetary amounts that will be relevant for notification.

7. The two initial threshold categories at the date of entry into force of this Regulation shall be:

(a) an initial threshold of 0,1% applicable where the total amount of the outstanding issued sovereign debt is between 0 and 500 billion euro;

(b) a threshold of 0,5% applicable where the total amount of the outstanding issued sovereign debt is above 500 billion euro or where there is a liquid futures market for the particular sovereign debt.

8. The additional incremental levels shall be set at 50% of the initial thresholds and shall be:

(a) each 0,05% above the initial notification threshold of 0,1% starting at 0,15%;

(b) each 0,25% above the initial threshold of 0,5% starting at 0,75%.

9. The sovereign issuer shall move to the appropriate threshold group where there has been a change in the sovereign debt market of the sovereign issuer and, applying the factors specified in paragraph 5, that change has subsisted for at least one calendar year.

Chapter VII
Parameters and Methods for Calculating Liquidity Threshold for Suspending Restrictions on Short Sales of Sovereign Debt Pursuant to Article 13(4)

Article 22
Methods for calculating and determining the threshold of liquidity for suspending restrictions on short sales in sovereign debt

1. The measure of liquidity of the issued sovereign debt to be used by each competent authority is the turnover, defined as the total nominal value of debt instruments traded, in relation to a basket of benchmarks with different maturities.

2. The temporary suspension of restrictions on uncovered short sales in sovereign debt may be triggered when the turnover of a month falls below the fifth percentile of the monthly volume traded in the previous 12 months.

3. To perform these calculations each competent authority shall use the representative data readily available, from one or more trading venues, from over the counter (OTC) trading or from both, and inform ESMA of the data used thereafter.

4. Before the competent authorities exercise the power to lift the restrictions on short selling related to sovereign debt, they shall ensure that the significant drop in liquidity is not the result of seasonal effects on liquidity.

Chapter VIII
Significant Fall in Value for Financial Instruments Other than Liquid Shares Pursuant to Article 23

Article 23
Significant fall in value for financial instruments other than liquid shares

1. In respect of a share other than a liquid share, a significant fall in value during a single trading day compared to the closing price of the previous trading day means:

(a) a decrease in the price of the share of 10% or more where the share is included in the main national equity index and is the underlying financial instrument for a derivative contract admitted to trading on a trading venue;

(b) a decrease in the price of the share of 20% or more where the share price is EUR 0,50 or higher, or the equivalent in the local currency;

(c) a decrease in the price of the share of 40% or more in all other cases.

2. An increase of 7% or more in the yield across the yield curve during a single trading day for the relevant sovereign issuer shall be considered a significant fall in value for a sovereign bond.

3. An increase of 10% or more in the yield of a corporate bond during a single trading day shall be considered a significant fall in value for a corporate bond.

4. A decrease of 1,5% or more in the price of a money- market instrument during a single trading day shall be considered a significant fall in value for a money-market instrument.

5. A decrease of 10% or more in the price of an exchange- traded fund during a single trading day shall be considered a significant fall in value for an exchange-traded fund,

including exchange-traded funds that are UCITS. A leveraged exchange- traded fund shall be adjusted by the relevant leverage ratio to reflect a 10% fall in the price of an equivalent unleveraged direct exchange-traded fund. A reverse exchange-traded fund shall be adjusted by a factor of -1 to reflect a 10% fall in the price of an equivalent unleveraged direct exchange-traded fund.

6. Where a derivative, including financial contracts for difference, is traded on a trading venue and has as its only underlying financial instrument, a financial instrument for which a significant fall in value is specified in this Article and Article 23(5) of Regulation (EU) No 236/2012, a significant fall in value in that derivative instrument shall be considered to have occurred when there has been a significant fall in that underlying financial instrument.

CHAPTER IX
ADVERSE EVENTS OR DEVELOPMENTS PURSUANT TO ARTICLE 30

Article 24
Criteria and factors to be taken into account in determining when adverse events or developments and threats arise

1. For the purposes of Articles 18 to 21 of Regulation (EU) No 236/2012 adverse events or developments that may constitute a serious threat to the financial stability or market confidence in the Member State concerned or in one or more other Member States pursuant to Article 30 of Regulation (EU) No 236/2012 include any act, result, fact, or event that is or could reasonably be expected to lead to the following:

(a) serious financial, monetary or budgetary problems which may lead to financial instability concerning a Member State or a bank and other financial institutions deemed important to the global financial system such as insurance companies, market infrastructure providers and asset management companies operating within the Union when this may threaten the orderly functioning and integrity of financial markets or the stability of the financial system in the Union;

(b) a rating action or a default by any Member State or banks and other financial institutions deemed important to the global financial system such as insurance companies, market infrastructure providers and asset management companies operating within the Union that causes or could reasonably be expected to cause severe uncertainty about their solvency;

(c) substantial selling pressures or unusual volatility causing significant downward spirals in any financial instrument related to any banks and other financial institutions deemed important to the global financial system such as insurance companies, market infrastructure providers and asset management companies operating within the Union and sovereign issuers as the case may be;

(d) any relevant damage to the physical structures of important financial issuers, market infrastructures, clearing and settlement systems, and supervisors which may adversely affect markets in particular where such damage results from a natural disaster or terrorist attack;

(e) any relevant disruption in any payment system or settlement process, in particular when it is related to interbank operations, that causes or may cause significant payments or settlement failures or delays within the Union payment systems, especially when these may lead to the propagation of financial or economic stress in a bank and other financial institutions deemed important to the global financial system such as insurance companies, market infrastructure providers and asset management companies or in a Member State.

2. For the purposes of Article 27, ESMA shall take into account the possibility of any spillovers or contagion to other systems or issuers and, especially, the existence of any type of self-fulfilling phenomena when considering the criteria in paragraph 1.

3. For the purposes of Article 28(2)(a), a threat to the orderly functioning and integrity of financial markets or to the stability of the whole or part of the financial system in the Union shall mean:

(a) any threat of serious financial, monetary or budgetary instability concerning a Member State or the financial system within a Member State when this may seriously threaten the orderly functioning and integrity of financial markets or the stability of the whole or part of the financial system in the Union;

(b) the possibility of a default by any Member State or supra- national issuer;

(c) any serious damage to the physical structures of important financial issuers, market infrastructures, clearing and settlement systems, and supervisors which may seriously affect cross-border markets in particular where such damage results from a natural disaster or terrorist attack when this may seriously threaten the orderly functioning and integrity of financial markets or the stability of the whole or part of the financial system in the Union;

(d) any serious disruption in any payment system or settlement process, in particular when it is related to interbank operations, that causes or may cause significant payments or settlement failures or delays within the Union cross-border payment systems, especially when these may lead to the propagation of financial or economic stress in the whole or part of the financial system in the Union.

Article 25
Entry into force

This Regulation shall enter into force on the third day following that of its publication in the Official Journal of the European Union.

It shall apply from 1 November 2012.

This Regulation shall be binding in its entirety and directly applicable in all Member States.

Done at Brussels, 5 July 2012.

For the Commission

The President

José Manuel BARROSO

ANNEX I

PART 1

Article 5 and 6

- Options,
- Covered warrants,
- Futures,
- Index-related instruments,
- Contracts for difference,
- Shares/units of exchange-traded funds,
- Swaps,
- Spread bets,
- Packaged retail or professional investment products,
- Complex derivatives,
- Certificates linked to shares,
- Global depositary receipts.

PART 2

Article 7

- Options,
- Futures,
- Index-related instruments,
- Contracts for difference,
- Swaps,
- Spread bets,
- Complex derivatives,
- Certificates linked to sovereign debt.

ANNEX II

PART 1

The delta-adjusted model for shares

Article 10

1. Any derivative and cash position shall be accounted for on a delta-adjusted basis, with cash position having delta 1. In order to calculate the delta of a derivative, investors shall take into account the current implied volatility of the derivative and the closing price or last price of the underlying instrument. In order to calculate a net short position including equity or cash investments and derivatives, natural or legal persons shall calculate the individual delta-adjusted position of every derivative that is held in the portfolio, adding or subtracting all cash positions as appropriate.

2. A nominal cash short position may not be offset by an equivalent nominal long position taken in derivatives. Delta- adjusted long positions in derivatives may not compensate identical nominal short positions taken in other financial instruments due to the delta adjustment. Natural or legal persons entering into derivatives contracts giving

rise to net short positions that must be notified or published pursuant to Articles 5 to 11 of Regulation (EU) No 236/2012 shall calculate net short position changes in their portfolio arising from changes in the delta.

3. Any transaction that confers a financial advantage in the event of a change in price or value of the share held as part of a basket, index or exchange-traded fund shall be included when calculating the position in each individual share. Positions on these financial instruments shall be calculated taking into account the weight of that share in the underlying basket, index or fund. Natural or legal persons shall perform calculations in these financial instruments in accordance with Article 3(3) of Regulation (EU) No 236/2012.

4. The net short position shall be calculated by netting long and short delta-adjusted positions in a given issuer.

5. For the issued share capital, when issuers have several share classes, the total number of shares issued in each class and shall be taken into account and added up.

6. The calculation of net short positions shall take into account changes in the share capital of the issuer that may trigger or eliminate notification obligations in accordance with Article 5 of Regulation (EU) No 236/2012.

7. New shares issued from a capital increase shall be accounted for in the calculation of the total issued share capital from the day they are admitted to trading on a trading venue.

8. The net short position expressed as a percentage of the company's issued share capital shall be calculated by dividing the net short position in equivalent shares by the total issued share capital of the company.

PART 2
The delta-adjusted model for sovereign debt

Article 11

1. Any cash positions shall be taken into account using their nominal value duration adjusted. Options and other derivative instruments shall be adjusted by their delta which shall be calculated in accordance with Part 1. Calculations of net short positions containing both cash investments and derivatives shall be the individual delta-adjusted position of every derivative that is held in the portfolio, adding or subtracting all cash positions and cash positions shall have a delta equal to 1.

2. Nominal positions in bonds issued in currencies other than the euro shall be converted to euro using the last reliable updated spot currency price available. The same principle shall apply to other financial instruments.

3. Other derivatives, such as forward bonds, shall be also adjusted in accordance with paragraphs 1, 2 and 3.

4. Any economic interest or position that creates a financial advantage in sovereign debt held as part of a basket, index or exchange-traded fund shall be included when calculating the position in each individual sovereign debt. Positions on these financial instruments shall be calculated taking into account the weight of that sovereign exposure in the underlying basket, index or fund. Investors shall perform calculations in these financial instruments in accordance with Article 3(3) of Regulation (EU) No 236/2012.

5. Calculations for sovereign debt instruments with high correlation shall follow the same methods of calculation of long positions in debt instruments of a sovereign issuer. Long positions in debt instruments of a sovereign issuer the pricing of which is highly correlated to the pricing of the given sovereign debt shall be taken into account for calculation purposes. When these positions no longer meet the test of high correlation then they shall not be taken into account to offset short positions.

6. Nominal long positions of credit default swaps shall be included in the calculation as short positions. In calculating an investor sovereign credit default swaps position its net positions shall be used. Positions intended to be covered or hedged through the purchase of a credit default swap that are not sovereign bonds will not be taken into account as long positions. Credit default swaps shall be considered to have delta 1.

7. The net short position shall be calculated by netting nominal delta-adjusted equivalent long and short positions in the issued sovereign debt of a sovereign issuer.

8. The net short position shall be expressed as a monetary amount in euro.

9. Calculation of positions shall take into account changes in correlations and in the total sovereign debt of a sovereign issuer.

10. Only long positions in debt instruments of a sovereign issuer the pricing of which is highly correlated to the pricing of sovereign debt of a sovereign issuer shall be taken into account to offset short positions in the said sovereign debt. A given long position of a highly correlated debt shall only be used once to offset a short position in cases where the investor maintains several short positions of different sovereign issuers. The same long position cannot be applied several times to net off different short positions taken in highly correlated sovereign debt.

11. Natural or legal persons with multiple allocations of long positions of highly correlated debt across several different sovereign issuers shall have records that show their allocation methods.

Commission Delegated Regulation (EU) No 919/2012

of 5 July 2012

supplementing Regulation (EU) No 236/2012 of the European Parliament and of the Council on short selling and certain aspects of credit default swaps with regard to regulatory technical standards for the method of calculation of the fall in value for liquid shares and other financial instruments

(Text with EEA relevance)

THE EUROPEAN COMMISSION,

Having regard to the Treaty on the Functioning of the European Union,

Having regard to Regulation (EU) No 236/2012 of the European Parliament and of the Council of 14 March 2012 on short selling and certain aspects of credit default swaps,[1] and in particular Article 23(8) thereof,

Whereas:

(1) The method of calculation of the significant fall in value of financial instruments contained in Section C of Annex I to Directive 2004/39/EC of the European Parliament and Council of 21 April 2004 on markets in financial instruments[2] should be adapted to the various ways in which that fall is reflected depending on the type of financial instrument concerned. That method can take the form of an actual fall in price of the financial instrument, of an increase in the yield of a debt instrument issued by a corporate issuer or an increase in the yield across the yield curve for debt instruments issued by sovereign issuers.

(2) This Regulation should be read in conjunction with Commission Delegated Regulation (EU) No 918/2012,[3] which defines thresholds for the significant fall in value of illiquid shares, debt instruments issued by sovereign and corporate issuers, exchange-traded funds, money market instruments and derivatives whose sole underlying financial instrument is traded on a trading venue. This Regulation should therefore restrict itself to specifying the method of calculation of the significant fall in value of these instruments.

(3) In order to ensure consistency and legal certainty for market participants and competent authorities, the date of application of this Regulation should be the same as that of Regulation (EU) No 236/2012 and Delegated Regulation (EU) No 918/2012.

(4) Since Regulation (EU) No 236/2012 recognised that binding technical standards should be adopted before that Regulation can be usefully applied, and as it is essential to specify before 1 November 2012 the required non-essential elements to facilitate compliance by market participants with that Regulation and enforcement by competent authorities, it is necessary that this Regulation should enter into force on the day following its publication.

(5) This Regulation is based on the draft regulatory technical standards submitted by the European Securities and Markets Authority (ESMA) to the Commission.

---

1. OJ L 86, 24.3.2012, p. 1.
2. OJ L 145, 30.4.2004, p. 1.
3. See page 1 of this Official Journal.

(6) ESMA has conducted open public consultations on the draft regulatory technical standards on which this Regulation is based, analysed the potential related costs and benefits and requested the opinion of the Securities and Markets Stakeholder Group established in accordance with Article 37 of Regulation (EU) No 1095/2010 of the European Parliament and of the Council of 24 November 2010 establishing a European Supervisory Authority (European Securities and Markets Authority),[4]

HAS ADOPTED THIS REGULATION:

Article 1
Subject matter

1. This Regulation specifies the method of calculation of the 10% fall in value for liquid shares traded on a trading venue as set out in Article 23(5) of Regulation (EU) No 236/2012.

2. This Regulation also specifies the method of calculation of the fall in value for the following financial instruments traded on a trading venue as specified in Delegated Regulation (EU) No 918/2012 adopted pursuant to Article 23(7) of Regulation (EU) No 236/2012:

(a) illiquid shares;

(b) the following non-derivative financial instruments:

  (i) debt instruments issued by sovereign and corporate issuers;

  (ii) exchange-traded funds;

  (iii) money market instruments;

(c) derivatives whose sole underlying is a financial instrument traded on a trading venue.

Article 2
Method of calculation of a significant fall in value for liquid and illiquid shares

1. For a share traded on a trading venue, the fall in value shall be calculated from the official closing price of the previous trading day at that trading venue defined according to the applicable rules of that trading venue.

2. That method of calculation shall exclude any downward movement of a price resulting exclusively from a split or any corporate action or similar measures adopted by the issuer on its issued share capital which can result in an adjustment of the price by the relevant trading venue.

Article 3
Method of calculation of a significant fall in value for other non-derivative financial instruments

1. A significant fall in value for financial instruments other than shares and not falling into the categories of derivatives listed in points (4) to (10) of Section C of Annex I to Directive 2004/39/EC shall be calculated according to the method in paragraphs 2, 3 and 4.

---

4. OJ L 331, 15.12.2010, p. 84.

2. For a financial instrument for which the significant fall in value referred to in Article 23(7) of Regulation (EU) No 236/2012 is measured in relation to a price on the relevant trading venue, that fall shall be calculated from the official closing price at the relevant trading venue defined according to the applicable rules of that trading venue.

3. For a financial debt instrument issued by a sovereign issuer for which the significant fall in value referred to in Article 23(7) of Regulation (EU) No 236/2012 is measured in relation to a yield curve, that fall shall be calculated as an increase across the yield curve in comparison with the yield curve of the sovereign issuer at the close of trading of the previous trading day, as calculated based on data available for the issuer on that trading venue.

4. For a financial instrument for which the significant fall in value referred to in Article 23(7) of Regulation (EU) No 236/2012 is measured in relation to a variation of the yield, that fall shall be calculated as an increase of the current yield as compared to the yield of that instrument at the close of trading of the previous trading day, as calculated based on data available for that instrument on that trading venue.

Article 4
Method of calculation of a significant fall in value for derivatives

A significant fall in value for financial instruments falling under the categories of derivatives listed in points (4) to (10) of Section C of Annex I to Directive 2004/39/EC and which have a sole underlying financial instrument that is traded on a trading venue and for which a significant fall in value has been specified in accordance with Article 2 or Article 3, shall be calculated by reference to the significant fall in value of the underlying financial instrument.

Article 5
Entry into force

This Regulation shall enter into force on the day following that of its publication in the Official Journal of the European Union.

It shall apply from 1 November 2012.

This Regulation shall be binding in its entirety and directly applicable in all Member States.

Done at Brussels, 5 July 2012.

For the Commission

The President

José Manuel BARROSO

Index

[all references are to the provisions of the relevant legislation]

Takeovers
acting in concert, definition, SI 255/2006, r 8
company registered in State
breakthrough provisions, opting in, SI 255/2006, rr 16, 18, 19
communication of decision, SI 255/2006, r 20
further provisions, SI 255/2006, r 17
employees, notification, SI 255/2006, Sch
equal treatment, securities holders, SI 255/2006, r 7
equitable price, adjustment, SI 255/2006, r 13
interpretation, SI 255/2006, r 2
offeree
intentions, SI 255/2006, Sch
obligations, SI 255/2006, rr 7, 15
offeror's intentions, SI 255/2006, Sch
voluntary bid, SI 255/2006, r 12
Talisman Settlement System, CA 1963, s 81; C(A)A 1977, s 2
Time periods, CA 1990, s 4
Trading certificate
issue of, CA 1963, s 115; IFCMPA 2005, s 73
Transparency
administrative sanctions, SI 277/2007, rr 60–74
appointment of assessor, SI 277/2007, r 61
correcting assessments, SI 277/2007, r 68
enforcement, SI 277/2007, r 70
imposed by bank, SI 277/2007, r 67
power over witness, SI 277/2007, r 63
publication, SI 277/2007, r 71
referral to court, SI 277/2007, r 64
revocation of appointment, SI 277/2007, r 62
right of appeal, SI 277/2007, r 66
Competent Authorities, SI 277/2007, rr 37–59
co-operation between, SI 277/2007, r 75
directions by bank, SI 277/2007, r 56
functions of IAASA, SI 277/2007, r 42
powers of authorised officers, SI 277/2007, r 54
powers of bank, SI 277/2007, rr 39–41
powers of IAASA, SI 277/2007, rr 43–44
precautionary measures, SI 277/2007, r 57
privilege, SI 277/2007, r 59
warrants, SI 277/2007, r 55
dissemination of information, SI 277/2007, rr 33–35
exemptions, SI 277/2007, rr 10–11
false or misleading statements, SI 277/2007, r 12
fees and charges, SI 277/2007, r 78
financial report, SI 277/2007, rr 4–5
half-yearly, SI 277/2007, rr 6–8
interim management statements, SI 277/2007, r 9
languages, SI 277/2007, r 32
major shareholdings
acquisition or disposal, SI 277/2007, rr 14–16, 19
aggregation of managed holdings, SI 277/2007, r 18
filing, SI 277/2007, rr 22–23
notification and disclosure, SI 277/2007, rr 20–21
meetings, SI 277/2007, rr 27–28
penalties, SI 277/2007, r 76
third country equivalence, SI 277/2007, r 30
Transparency (regulated markets) law
certain markets, application to, IFCMPA 2006, s 24
conviction on indictment, offences under, IFCMPA 2006, s 21
definitions, IFCMPA 2006, ss 19, 22
power to make certain regulations, IFCMPA 2006, s 20
supplementary rules, IFCMPA 2006, s 22
Trustees
securities, acquisitions and disposals by, C(A)A 1977, s 7

Winding up (contd)
resolution, CA 1963, s 213
revenue claims, CA 1963, s 285
sick and holiday pay, CA 1963, s 285
solvency, statutory declaration of, CA 1963, s 256; SI 163/1973, rr 19, 23
statement of company's affairs, CA 1963, s 224
stay of, CA 1963, s 234
substratem, failure of, CA 1963, s 213
transfer of shares, avoidance, CA 1963, s 218
unregistered companies, CA 1963, ss 345, 350; CA 1990, s 123
    actions stayed on, CA 1963, s 348
    contributories in, CA 1963, s 346
    court power to restrain, CA 1963, s 347
wages and salaries, CA 1963, s 285
See also Contributories, Creditors, Examinations, Liquidators, Provisional liquidators; Voluntary winding up